Maclopedia

Hayden
Books

About the Contributors

Ted Alpasch is an expert on logo and font design, and has trained thousands of people in all areas of graphics and desktop publishing for the Macintosh. He is the owner of Bézier Graphic Experts, the Southwest's leading graphics training company. In his spare time, he has been known to juggle torches, bowling balls, sharp knives, and small children above his head. He is responsible for the CD interface on the *Maclopedia* CD.

David Bergsland began with a BFA cum laude in Printmaking, Etching, and Drawing & Painting from the University of Minnesota in 1971. Beginning as a freelance illustrator for many and various publishers, he finally found the beginning of his career as a graphics artist working for a printed giftware manufacturer in West Virginia. It was touristy stuff, but he loved the work.

By 1991, David had 20 years experience in printing and publishing. Most of it was as an art director for a commercial printer in New Mexico. In 1991, he was hired to completely rewrite the Commercial Printing program at the local community college, Albuquerque TVI.

Today he finds himself at the cutting edge of digital print production in New Mexico. He is focused on making new digital technology available to desktop publishers. The exciting direction of digital printing for him is the reality of completely professional printing in small shops (even a single person shop). David contributed to the Printing section of this book.

Kate Binder is a production artist and writer living on the North Shore of Massachusetts. She has written about desktop publishing for magazines, including the *National Association of Desktop Publishers Journal*. She can be reached at **UrsaDesign@aol.com**. Kate is acknowledged as the Queen of Desktop Publishing by several people, including her cats. Kate contributed to the Desktop Publishing and Printing sections of this book.

Paul Celestin started working with computers in 1976 (remember Bicentennial minutes?), saw his first Mac while working at the ASUC Computer Store at UC Berkeley in 1984, and immediately fell in love with everything Macintosh, except the price. Now things are different, and he hasn't looked back. He has worked for non-profits, Mac software companies, and freelanced as a graphic designer. He is now president of his own company, and publisher of the highly acclaimed *Apprentice CD-ROM for Mac Programmers*. He has a wife, Bernadette, and three children, Aaron, Nicholas, and Christopher. Paul compiled the goodies on the *Maclopedia* CD.

Dennis Cohen is a short, portly, old programmer at Claris Corporation who spends his work hours killing bugs, so that he may spend his free time playing bridge, reading, shooting trap, hunting, and anticipating retirement where he intends to do more of the same, with the addition of resuming his love-hate relationship with the game of golf. Dennis contributed to the Hardware section.

Don Crabb is the Associate Director of Undergraduate Studies in Computer Science at the University of Chicago and a Contributing Editor and Columnist for *MacWEEK*. Don contributed to the Mac History section of this book.

Joel Enos is the Associate Editor for Interactive Entertainment at *MacHome Journal*, the only independently published national Mac-based consumer magazine. He also has covered games and multimedia for *Electronic Entertainment* (now *PC Entertainment*) and is a contributing editor and writer for **Surface Magazine* in San Francisco. He holds a Master's Degree in Literature from San Francisco State University and a Bachelor's Degree in English from the University of the Pacific in Stockton, California.

Besides being an avid gamer, Joel is a popular culture fanatic who has yet to lose a round of *You Don't Know Jack*. Joel wrote the Entertainment section of this book.

Greg Holden is author of two other Hayden books: *Publishing on the World Wide Web* (1-56830-228-2) and *Mastering Netscape 2.0* (ISBN 1-56830-243-6). Greg is currently assistant director of publications at the University of Chicago, where he has worked since 1983. He created his first publications for the University using a Macintosh Plus and LaserWriter in 1985. He has a Master's degree in English, and when he is not surfing the Net or writing books, he likes to write poetry, listen to music, and play with his two daughters, Zosia, age 3-1/2, and Lucy, age 1-1/2.

Although Greg is a relatively recent user of the Internet (1993), he was an early enthusiast of the World Wide Web, and now explores the Web, newsgroups, and other nooks and crannies of the Internet with his PowerMac and Netscape. Greg wrote the Internet section of this book.

Scott Kelby is Editor-in-Chief and Publisher of *Mac Today*, the alternative Macintosh magazine distributed throughout the East Coast. Scott has trained thousands of Macintosh users through his work as instructor and training director for the Adobe Photoshop Seminar Tour '96 (sponsored by KW Computer Training, Inc.). Scott is one of 12 designers chosen to participate in Adobe's Design to Print project and is a Certified Adobe Instructor. Some of Scott's Photoshop work is included in the book *Adobe Photoshop: Creative Techniques* published by Hayden Books.

Scott writes a popular editorial column titled, "Life in the Mac Lane," which features a lighthearted look at Apple and Macintosh-related issues, and Scott also pens reviews and feature stories on Macintosh software/ hardware products and technologies. Scott wrote the Operating System section of this book.

Email to: **MacToday@aol.com**

Web page at **http://www.MacToday.com**

Rita Lewis has an extensive fine arts education (over 10 years) and is currently on contract as the technical illustrator for Advanced Voice Technology (a PBX manufacturer). She is the editor of *Soundviews*, the Puget Sound Chapter of the Society for Technical Communications newsletter (1990-2), and the editor of *Capital Letter*, the Washington, D.C. Chapter of the STC's newsletter (1988-9, 1993-4). Rita wrote most of the Hardware section of this book.

Brad Mohr is a Senior Computer Analyst for the Technical Japanese Program at the University of Washington, where he oversees the development of interactive Japanese language instructional software and maintains the program's Web site.

Also an independent consultant, Brad cut his teeth authoring shareware and writing reviews and commentary for his Macintosh users' group publication. He has most recently contributed to the *Programming Starter Kit for Macintosh* by Jim Trudeau (Hayden Books, 1995, 1-56830-174-X), serving as technical editor and authoring sample code. Brad wrote the Programming and Mac History sections of this book.

Email: **bmohr@tjp.washington.edu**

Web: **http://www.uwtc.washington.edu/bdm/**

Shamms Mortier lives in a one-hundred year old farmhouse in Bristol, Vermont, with his spouse and two Siamese cats. His business, Eyeful Tower Communications, is a design and production studio dedicated to graphics, and animation, and consultation. His clients have included ABC Television, The State of Vermont, Academia, and Industry, and at present he is a consultant to a major set-top box manufacturer.

He holds a Master's Degree in Instructional Media and a Doctorate in Multidisciplinary Studies, with an emphasis on Psychology and the Arts. He has written over five-hundred articles and tutorials on computer graphics and animation for national and international publications, and also writes articles on transpersonal psychology and teaching. He has taught art and animation at the college level for fifteen years. His jazz ensemble, Science Fixion, has toured Russia and the United States and has recorded two CD albums. Shamms wrote the Graphics section of this book.

Michael D. Murie is a multimedia consultant based in Boston. He is the author of the *Multimedia Starter Kit for Macintosh* (Hayden, 1-56830-113-8, $30.00) and co-author of the *QuickTime Handbook* (Hayden). He also writes for *New Media* and *MacWeek*. He was responsible for software design and development of the *Jack Kerouac ROMnibus*, a multi-platform CD-ROM published by Penguin. Michael wrote the Multimedia section of this book.

Email: **m2w@xensei.com**

Web: **http://www.xensei.com/users/m2w.**

Bill Parsons is a teacher, writer, freelance graphic designer, and electronic publishing consultant. He holds an M.F.A. from the University of Texas at Austin and a BFA from the University of North Texas. Bill contributed to the Desktop Publishing and Printing sections of this book.

Jonathan Price was a Senior Technical Writer at Apple from 1982 to 1986, where he wrote *How to Write an Apple Manual*, now incarnated as *How to Communicate Technical Information*, from Benjamin/Cummings. He left to freelance, and wrote documentation for the LaserWriter, MacWrite II, AppleLink 6, and five books about FileMaker Pro, ClarisWorks, and MacWrite. His latest is *The Trail Guide to America Online*, from Addison-Wesley. Jon wrote the interviews for this book.

John Rizzo is a San Francisco writer and consultant who bought his first Macintosh in 1984. After receiving an engineering degree and working for the Boeing Company in Seattle, Rizzo spent seven years as technical editor of *MacUser* magazine, where he is now a contributing editor. He also writes a column for *Computer Currents*, and writes about PCs and Macs for the c|net online service.

Rizzo has written for many other magazines, including *MacWeek*, *PC Magazine*, *PC Computing*, and *Web Techniques*, and has written several books on Macintosh and PC technology. He has spoken at Macworld Expo, Comdex, and other industry conferences, and now teaches at the Center for Electronic Art in San Francisco. Rizzo also has sung with the San Francisco Symphony Chorus. He has participated in several San Francisco Symphony recordings on the London label, including the Grammy Award-winning recording of Carl Orff's *Carmina Burana*, Herbert Blomstedt conducting. John contributed to the Hardware section of this book.

Jeff Roback has been using the Macintosh since its release in 1984. He is the founder of Praxis Computing, a computer consulting firm specializing in the integration of the Macintosh platform into corporate offices. Macintosh networks designed and installed by Praxis Computing can be found throughout the Los Angeles area. Praxis Computing's services are retained by both large and small corporations from diverse industries. Jeff contributed to the Networking section of this book.

Jay Rose is a sound designer consultant to high-end audio equipment manufacturers Orban, Lexicon, and EvenTide, author, audio columnist for *DV* magazine, officer in the Audio Engineering Society, and clown. You have heard his work on CNN, A&E, the Disney Channel, and elsewhere. He has a wall full of awards and a room full of digital audio gear. He also has two sons, several cats, and shares an office and a life with Carla Rose. Jay wrote the Speakers section of this book.

Carla Rose has forgotten how to sleep since becoming editor of this book. She shares an office, a house, two sons, and three or maybe four cats with her husband, Jay Rose (See also Jay Rose). This is her eleventh Macintosh book. She has also written for publications as diverse as the *Atlantic Fisherman* and the *New Yorker*, and was a senior contributing editor of *Portable Computing* magazine. Besides being an overall project editor and calming force on this project, Carla wrote the Education and Business sections of this book, as well as contributed to the Networking section in the crucial eleventh hour.

Tim Webster is still employed (to his continued surprise) as a production specialist at the University of Chicago Publications Office, where he wanders the gray area between prepress and design. He enjoys food and noise, and lives with his wife, Chris Corcoran, on the south side of Chicago—the baddest part of town. Tim contributed to the Hardware section of this book.

Tim is the co-author of *Mastering Netscape 2.0 for Macintosh*, and a contributor to *Teach Yourself Java in 21 Days for Macintosh*.

Hayden Books Team

Publisher	Lyn Blake
Publishing Manager	Laurie Petrycki
Managing Editor	Lisa Wilson
Marketing Manager	Nancy Price
Acquisitions Editor	Stacy Kaplan
Development Editor	Kezia Endsley
Project Editors	Bront Davis Carla Rose Kevin Laseau
Copy Editors	Beth Millett Becky Tapley
Technical Editors	Kate Binder Henry Bortman Shelly Brisbin Dennis Cohen Andrew Lindsay Bill Parsons Joanna Pearlstein James Staten
Publishing Coordinator	Rosemary Lewis
Cover Designer	Aren Howell
Book Designer	Gary Adair
Manufacturing Coordinator	Brook Farling
Production Team Supervisor	Laurie Casey
Indexers	Carol Sheehan Brad Herriman
Proofreaders	Heather Butler Kim Cofer Erich J. Richter Christine Tyner Pamela Volk Megan Wade Karen Walsh
Layout Technicians	Dan Caparo Terrie Deemer Joe Millay Gina Rexrode

Maclopedia

Library of Congress Catalog Number: 96-75904
ISBN: 1-56830-281-9

Warning and Disclaimer

Trademark Acknowledgments

Acknowledgments

An undertaking as big as this book owes much to many. Special thanks to…

- The authors, who put in many long days and longer nights. Thanks also to spouses, significant others, children, and pets who accepted our excuses, absences, missed meals, and fatigue with patience and understanding.

- Companies who generously provided products and information, frequently overnight. Without them, this would be a very thin book.

- The tech reviewers, who verified that things really worked the way we said they did.

- The crew at Hayden, who turned all these words into a book. Special thanks to Stacy Kaplan, Bront Davis, and Kevin Laseau, and extra-double special thanks to Kezia Endsley, who did an amazing job of keeping it all together.

- The amazing Production Team, especially Karen Walsh and Christine Tyner, who spent hours checking and rechecking alphabetization and cross references, and Joe Millay and Terrie Deemer, who spent more hours rewrapping text.

- Apple Computer, for giving us the right tool for the job.

- Personal thanks to our families (including pets) who sacrificed as much as we did for this book to materialize.

How to Reach Hayden Books

The staff of Hayden Books is committed to bringing you the best computer books. What our readers think of Hayden is important to our ability to serve our customers. If you have any comments, no matter how great or how small, we'd appreciate your taking the time to send us a note.

You can reach Hayden Books at the following:

Hayden Books
201 West 103rd Street
Indianapolis, IN 46290

Email addresses:

America Online: Hayden Bks
Internet: **hayden@hayden.com**

Visit the Hayden Books Web site at **http://www.hayden.com**

Topic Finder

Business Applications

A

At Ease
AutoCorrect

B

Backquotes
Big Business
Big:Calc Program
Budgeting, Finance Programs
Business Applications
Business Letters and Forms

C

Cell in Databases
Charting
Charting and Graphing Applications
Checking Account Software
Claris Organizer
ClarisWorks 4.0
Column in Databases
Co:Writer

D

Database
Database, Field
Database, Procedures
Database, Record
Database, Relational

E

Editions
Electronic Banking
Excel

F

FileMaker Pro
Fill, Spreadsheet
Final Draft
Finance Programs
Financial Planning Software
First Things First
Flat-File Database
Footer
Forms and Reports, Custom
Freedom
Function, Spreadsheet

G

Grammar Checker

H

Hinting
Home Repair Encyclopedia
Hyphen
Hyphen, Discretionary

I

Import/Export, Spreadsheet
In Control
Index, Creating

K

Ke:nx

L

Let's Keep It Simple Spreadsheet
LetterWorks
Lotus 1-2-3

Desktop Publishing

Education and the Macintosh

Entertainment

Graphics

Numerals

A

B

C

D

E

F

Hardware

History and Culture of the Macintosh

Scanner, Dynamic Range of

Scanner, OCR Software and

Sip and Puff Switch

Software and Hardware Errors

Upgrade Paths, PowerPC Options

Upgrade Paths, Types of

Voice Capability in Modems

History and Culture of the Macintosh

Internet

Macintosh Operating System

Multimedia

Numerals

Networking

O

Open Systems Interconnection Model

P

Packet

R

Routers

S

Serial Port

Synchronous Communication

T

Tunneling

V

V.32terbo Modem Protocol

V.34 Modem Protocol

V.FAST Modem Protocol

W

Wireless Networks

Printing

A

Additive Color

B

Background Printing

C

Chromapress

Color Gamut

Color Management

Color Matching Systems

Color, Measuring

Color Output, Buying

Color Printing

Color Resolution

Color Separations

Color Trapping

ColorBlind

ColorDrive

ColorSync

ColorSync System Profile

ColorSynergy

Constructing Efficient Files, DTP

D

Docutech

E

E-Print

F

FlipBook

H

High-Fidelity Color Printing

I

Image Manipulation for Printing

Initializing Printer Message

Ink Trapping

Programming

B

BASIC
Batch Processing
BatchIt
Benchmark Tests
Beta Testing
Beta Versions
Boolean Query
Browser (Programming)
Bug
Bug-Fix Update

C

C
C++
Code Resources
CodeWarrior
Compiled Language
CompileIt!
Compiler
Constant
Constructor
Cross-Compiler

D

Debugger, The
Debugging
Debugging Tools
Delphi
Demo Software
develop Magazine
Development Environment
Double-XX
Dynamic Language

E

EasyApp
Editor

E.T.O.
Event

F

FaceSpan
Formula
Fortran
Framework
Frontier
FutureBASIC

H

Handle
Heap

I

Infinite Loop
Inside Macintosh
Integrated Development Environment
Intellectual Property
Interface Builder
Interpreted Language

J

Java
JavaScript

L

Lingo
Linker

M

MacApp
Machine Language
Macintosh Programmer's Toolbox Assistant
MacsBug
Major Software Release
Memory Leak
Memory Mine, The
Microsoft Foundation Classes

Introduction

Welcome to *Maclopedia!*

This book contains greater depth and breadth than any other Macintosh book on the market—and gives you four ways to search for the information you need:

- Topic-based table of contents
- Fully permuted index
- Text-searchable book on the CD-ROM
- Alphabetized body text

Because *Maclopedia* is a reference tool, you can spend as little (or as much) time with it as you want. It provides you with the quick-entry answer to your questions, and enables you to go on for more (in the See Alsos) if you want.

Because the book is set up alphabetically, you will be able to find the information you need quickly and intuitively—it's all at your fingertips. In this book, you find information about every aspect of the Macintosh, including the following:

- Instructions on how to select software and hardware.
- Instructions on setting up your system and maximizing it for best performance.
- Issues and solutions for networking your Macintosh.
- Information for programming on the Macintosh.
- Information about desktop publishing and its potential application to your needs.
- Solutions for printing on the Mac and when to print professionally.
- Macintosh business applications and the latest reviews and comparison charts of word processors, spreadsheets, and databases.
- Macintosh educational applications and the latest reviews and comparison charts of "edutainment" programs, instructional games, and learning tools.
- Information on the latest games for the Mac and Internet play, including reviews and ratings of what's good and what's not.
- Bonus instructions on how to get on the Internet and how to surf the Web, as well as full coverage of Internet and Web applications and terms.
- Tips and tricks on system and application use.
- Information on the latest multimedia and graphics packages and how to use them, as well as full coverage of the terms.
- Information on the latest Mac models, their features, benefits, and drawbacks. This includes Power Macs, PowerBooks, Performas, and the like.
- Advice and comparison charts on the best hardware and software for "differently-abled" Mac users.
- Information on other hardware devices, such as pens, joysticks, mice, Zip drives, printers, modems, monitors, and keyboards.

- Information on the history of the Macintosh and the key players involved in its evolution.

- More complete coverage of all the versions of System 7.5 than any other book.

- Information on backing up data safely and performing maintenance on your machine.

- Fascinating interviews with key players in the Macintosh world, including Guy Kawasaki, Regis McKenna, Frank Casanova, Molly Tyson, Don Crabb, and many others.

Everything you need to know, or might need soon, is in this book.

Reader Assumptions

In this book, we assume that you:

- Are not an absolute beginner to a computer, but have the basic knowledge needed to get started.

- Use your Mac for your livelihood, whether it be business, pleasure, or educational purposes.

- Need time-saving tips and shortcuts to get your job done.

- Want a book that will provide you with as much or as little information as you require at the moment.

Maclopedia provides you with all the information you need to solve your own problems on your Mac, find programs that best suit your needs, make the most out of your Mac, learn time-saving shortcuts and tips, and have a little fun while you are at it! If this sounds like something you need, you have found the right book.

How to Use This Book

Maclopedia has 13 basic topic areas:

- Hardware
- Macintosh Operating System
- Business Applications
- Education and the Macintosh
- Entertainment
- Graphics
- Multimedia
- Networking
- Printing
- Programming
- History and Culture of the Macintosh

- Desktop Publishing
- Internet

Each of these topic areas has an entry filled with general information (alphabetized, of course) where you can start if you are not sure what you are looking for. Or, you can look up a specific subject and find your information pronto. To locate the Yahoo entry, for example, you would look under "Y" for Yahoo, not under Internet.

You also can search for the term on the CD, use the Index, or use the topic-based table of contents. There are many ways to find your solutions.

Book Conventions

The following typographic conventions help to clearly identify various elements in the text so you can understand what's going on:

- Bold words and phrases within the text denote entries defined in the book elsewhere.
- URLs, which are linkable on the CD, appear in a special typeface, as so **http://www.hayden.com/mac/ maclopedia**.
- Subheads within entries appear in bold and a special typeface, as so **Macintosh Models, Educational Needs**.
- Programming code appears in a special monospace typeface, as so:

```
Programming Code Appears Like Me
```

The following graphical elements also denote special text:

- The industry interviews appear in special sidebars.
- Pull quotes appear within the entries to denote particularly interesting quotes.
- Many tables appear in the text to compare and contrast products and services.

TIP These tips provide special information on the topic at hand, helping you with special tips, inside information, or secrets about the Mac.

How to Use the CD

The CD-ROM included with *Maclopedia* is an integral part of the entire package. It's packed with useful, researched, and well-organized content.

You can use it to search for any term you need to find, as well as to link to the URLs listed, provided you have an Internet connection. The entire book is included on the CD, fully searchable and hotlinked for your convenience. See the last page of the book (facing the CD) for information on how to get started.

What's on the CD

Along with the searchable text, you'll find a gaggle of commercial and shareware products on the CD for your Macintosh:

Commercial demos include:

- Black Box, Eye Candy (Alien Skin Software)
- Communigate (Stalker Software)
- F/A-18 Hornet 2.0 (Graphic Simulations)
- In Control (Attain)
- Line Share 3.3.1 (Stalker Software)
- Marathon 2 (Bungie Software)
- NewsHopper 1.2 (SW15)
- OptiMem Ram Charger (Jump Development)
- ShadowWraith and Crystal Caliburn (StarPlay Products)
- AppMaker (Bowers)
- BBEdit 3.5 (Bare Bones)
- Dark Forces (LucasArts)
- FileMaker Pro, ClarisDraw (Claris)
- Illustrator, Photoshop, PageMaker (Adobe Systems)
- Intellibots
- QC 1.2 (Onyx)
- StuffIt products (Aladdin Systems)

Shareware programs include:

- A PowerBook Suite 1.0
- AWOL Utilities (Ross Brown)
- Balloon Popper
- Chuck's Printer Driver 1.4.0
- Compact Pro (Bill Goodman)
- Data Converter 1.3
- Decor 3.0.1
- Dictionary Edit 1.3
- eDoc 1.1.1
- File Express 1.1
- Force Quit 1.0
- Gestalt Appl 2.6.6
- Godot's Faces 1.0.8
- Gopher Golf 3.0.6
- Hover Bar 1.2.8 (Guy Fullerton)
- I Ching Connexion 2.2
- Jade 1.0.2
- MacGzip 1.0
- Master FKEY 1.0
- Pandora's Box
- Phone Watcher 1.3.1
- PPPop 1.4

- Scrap It Pro 5.0.1
- Sleeper 2.0
- Style 1.4.1 (Marco Piovanelli)
- Yank 1.0 (Maui Software)
- Aaron 1.3.1
- CopyThru 2.0
- Find Text 1.3.1
- FreePPP 1.0.5
- Gelding 1.0.2
- Menu Bar Pattern 1.3
- Night Sky 2.2.1
- Pointing Device CDEV
- Spy 2.1.4
- Suntar 2.0.5
- Super Save 1.1.3
- Symbionts 2.6.2
- Talk Show 1.0
- Tech Tool 1.0.9
- TGP II 1.4.1
- Timeout CDEV
- To Scrap 1.1
- Ultima III 1.3
- UnUU 2.1
- UnZip 5.1.2
- UnShar 1.1.1
- ValueFax 2.0.8
- Word Translator 1.3
- X-Timer 1.9.1
- Xfer Pro 1.1
- Yooz 1.5.5
- ZipIt 1.3.5

Numerals

100Base-T

The most commonly used **EtherNet** standards, **ThinNet**, **ThickNet** and **10Base-T** all make use of a 10Mbps transfer rate. Originally proposed in 1992, the 100Mbps standards, including 100Base-T, are just now beginning to come into common use. Although they are still fairly expensive to implement, 100Base-T solutions are expected to drop in price just as 10Base-T solutions did previously.

You can combine an existing 10Base-T network with a new 100Base-T network by using a 10/100 bridge. The current generation of EtherNet cards include dual speeds and auto-sensing to tell the Mac whether it's on a 10Base-T or 100Base-T network.

See Also

Bridges, EtherNet; Network Topology; Networking

128-Font Limit

The number of screen **font** suitcases you can put in the Font folder is limited to 128 suitcases. Does that mean you can't have more than 128 fonts? Not at all; there are a number of ways around this limit. First, you can have more than one font in one suitcase. The Minion font family, for example, might have Minion, Minion Bold, Minion Italic, Minion Bold Italic, Minion Black, Minion Black Italic, Minion Display, and so on, all in one suitcase.

You can also create your own suitcase by **double-clicking** the font suitcase and **dragging** a screen font from one suitcase to the **icon** of the other. The selected font is copied into the new suitcase, and you can keep adding fonts to your heart's content. You might want to put serif typefaces in one suitcase and

sans serif in another, or you could separate them by vendor; ImageClub fonts in one suitcase, Adobe in another, and so on. You can also copy the entire contents of one suitcase into another by dragging one suitcase's icon on top of another.

Another way to get around the 128-font limit is by using a font utility program such as **Suitcase** or **MasterJuggler**. These enable you to store as many fonts as you want outside the System Folder's Fonts folder, bypassing the 128 font limit altogether.

To copy screen fonts from one suitcase to another, follow these steps:

1. Double-click the screen font suitcase to reveal the suitcase's contents.

2. Select the screen font(s) you want to copy to a different suitcase.

3. Drag the selected font(s) from the open suitcase to the icon of the other suitcase and release the mouse button. The selected screen fonts are copied.

4. If you want to copy an entire suitcase into another suitcase, drag the icon of the suitcase on top of the suitcase you want to copy into and release the mouse button. The contents of the suitcase are now in the new suitcase.

See Also

Double-Click; Fonts; Icons; Master Juggler; Suitcase

1394 Fire Wire

The 1394 Fire Wire is a digital transmission standard originally developed by Apple that has been proposed as an industry standard for possible industry-wide usage. This standard, which could be used in place of **SCSI**, serial lines, and other means of connecting digital devices, supports a **transfer rate** of 12.5Mbps, and can be adopted for other use in devices, such as ink jet printers, and even hard drives. Fire Wire addresses many of the limitations of SCSI by enabling hot plugging (devices being connected while other devices are on) up to 60 devices at a time, and using automatic unique addressing of devices.

See Also

Digital Video Cameras

"1984"

The year 1984 has special significance for the Macintosh. On January 24th of that year, Apple Computer introduced the Macintosh to the world for the very first time. But the real excitement started two days earlier during the Super Bowl. Early in the third quarter of the LA Raider's rout of the Washington Redskins, watchers were dazzled by a commercial unlike any they'd seen before.

Apple's "1984" commercial depicted a world straight out of George Orwell's novel of the same name: rows of bald, despondent workers sit watching "Big Brother" on a huge screen as he drones on in newspeak about the ideology of the Great State and its "Unification of Thought." Meanwhile, a woman wearing shorts and a white Macintosh T-shirt runs down a corridor as she is chased by uniformed storm troopers. She carries a sledge hammer. The runner reaches the room with the drone-like workers and hurls the hammer at the screen, smashing it to bits and letting in light and fresh air, which washes over the stunned workers. Finally, the screen displays the words, "On January 24th, Apple Computer will introduce Macintosh. And you'll see why 1984 won't be like '1984.'"

The commercial was an immediate sensation. Phone calls poured in to Apple, CBS, and Chiat/Day, the advertising agency that created the commercial for Apple. Although Apple paid to show the ad only once, it was shown on the news programs of all three national networks and many local stations. The commercial was so outrageous that it was news in itself.

To this day, "1984" remains one of the most talked about commercials of all time.

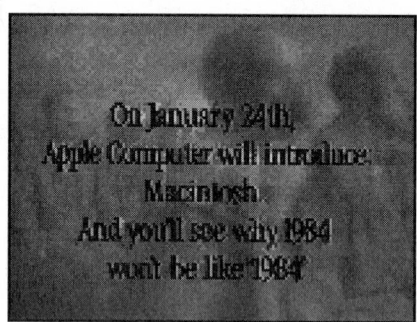

"1984" was directed by Ridley Scott, the director of such Hollywood hits as *Alien* and *Blade Runner*. It was produced at a cost of nearly one million dollars (not to mention the cost of airtime during the Super Bowl). Scott hired London skinheads to play extras as the worker drones, and paid others $125 a day to shave their heads just for the commercial.

Casting the runner was more of a challenge. After a series of models were unable to throw the hammer without getting dizzy or endangering the crew, Ridley Scott decided to look for someone a bit more athletic. Anya Major, a model and former discus thrower, fit the bill perfectly.

In hindsight it may be hard to believe, but the "1984" commercial almost didn't see the light of day. When Chiat/Day presented the finished commercial to **Steve Jobs** and **John Sculley**, they loved it. When it was shown at Apple's annual sales conference, the audience went wild. But when Apple's board of directors saw it, it was a different story. Not only did they not like it, many of them thought it was the worst commercial they had ever seen.

Based on the board's reaction, Apple sold back most of its Super Bowl airtime and planned to run a much more tame commercial, "Manuals", instead. The board hadn't outright refused to run the commercial, however, and Sculley left the final decision to Bill Campbell, the vice president of marketing, and Floyd Kvamme, executive vice president of marketing.

In the end, Campbell decided to run the commercial, and Apple managed to buy back its airtime. The rest, as they say, is history.

See Also

Jobs, Steve; Sculley, John

3D

The task of creating 3D photorealistic images or sequences occurs in three separate but interdependent tasks: **modeling**, **animation**, and **rendering**.

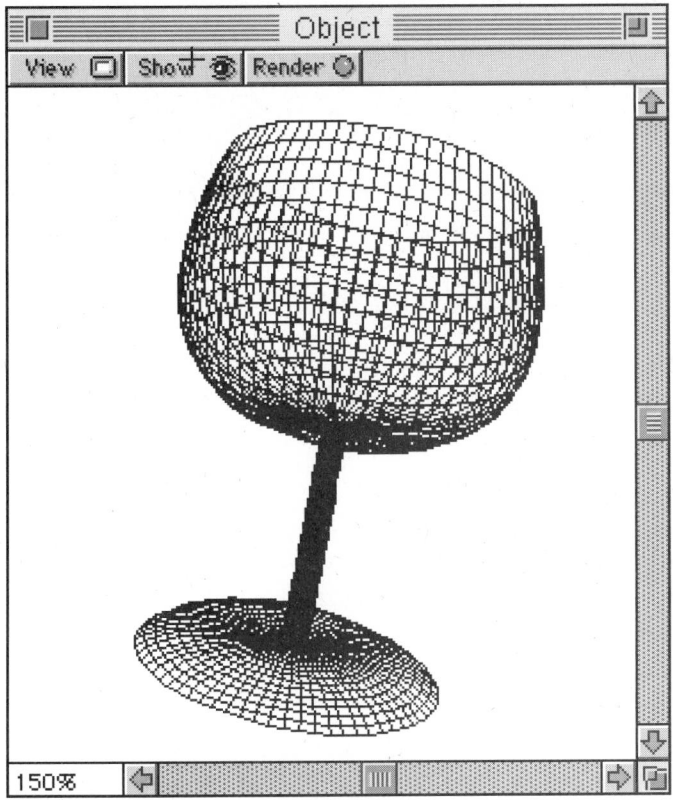

- **Modeling** is the process of creating 3D objects or scenes containing several objects. This involves tasks, such as lathing, extrusion, and free-form modeling.

- **Animation** is the process of creating a moving sequence of images. This requires that you define the motion and or changes in shape of objects, lighting, and other variables. If you only want to create 3D still images, you may not be interested in these features.

- **Rendering** is the process of creating photorealistic images. This task involves **texture mapping**—(adding surfaces to an object) as well as adding lighting.

Often the lines between these three steps are blurred; textures can be animated over time and an object can **morph** (change) its shape during animation.

Most general purpose 3D tools, such as Fractal Design's **Ray Dream Designer, Specular's Infini-D, Strata's StrataVision and StudioPro**, and Macromedia's **Extreme 3D** provide all of these functions, but not all programs do. For example, Electric Image Inc.'s **Electric Image**, a high-end animation tool, provides very limited modeling tools.

In addition to the general purpose 3D modeling and rendering packages, there are several niche products. For those who just want to create 3D logos, there are several easy-to-use packages, including Fractal Software's AddDepth, and Specular's LogoMotion. Virtus WalkThrough makes it possible to explore 3D scenes in real time, whereas KPT Bryce creates dramatic landscapes and Fractal Design's Poser models human shapes.

If you haven't used a 3D program before, be prepared to spend some time on the learning curve. 3D programs are complex because of the number of new things you'll have to learn, from how to build the basic shapes to manipulating lighting. Creating even the basic shapes (that is, anything more complex than a ball or a block) can take a lot of time.

You might want to consider buying collections of pre-built objects. Several software developers offer collections of general purpose objects specifically tailored to their application. There also are sets available from other companies. These may be useful if they have the exact objects you need, but be aware that if the objects are supplied in DXF format, you might not be able to edit them after you import them into your program.

When creating complex objects, always try to break an object down into simple parts. It's easier to work that way than to try to create a complex shape from one object. All programs provide some way to link objects together, so working in small pieces shouldn't be a problem. When creating animation, you should render in wireframe first to see whether it looks right, before spending time rendering the whole sequence. Test rendering single frames along the sequence also makes sense.

If you frequently use 3D software, you need the fastest computer you can afford—previewing scenes is time consuming. Rendering an animation sequence can take days. That's why 3D modeling programs offer **network rendering** (sometimes called a rendering farm) that use multiple computers to create the final work.

Other 3D developments that may or may not have a dramatic impact in the coming years include:

- **VRML** (Virtual Reality Modeling Language). A general purpose description for 3D models and scenes that is being used on the **World Wide Web**.

- **QuickDraw 3D.** System software developed by Apple, which could make it possible for almost any application to open and display 3D models. QuickDraw 3D uses a file format (**3DMF**) that is being adapted for use with VRML.

See Also

3DWorld; Ray Dream Designer-Studio; StrataVision

3DMF Optimizer

A freeware utility that optimizes **QuickDraw 3D** (**3DMF**) files by removing duplicate vertices and other unnecessary elements. Depending upon the efficiency of the 3D program that created the original file, 3DMF Optimizer can reduce a file's size and decrease load time and display time.

See Also

3D; QuickDraw 3D

3DWorld

3DWorld is a dedicated QuickDraw 3D application. With this application, the full potential of QuickDraw3D can be realized and explored, especially the real-time magical manipulation of textured graphics.

The interface has a gridded view plane surrounded by four palettes: Tools, Camera, Lights, and Info. The view plane may be seen from a Home View, Custom, Top, Front, Left, Right, and Back. You can also choose to "View Selected," which places the selected object in the center of the view plane. A special "Spin Around Look At" option animates the view plane, allowing you to appreciate the scene from a circular orbit. A mouse click stops the spin at the desired position. The view plane can be set for shaded rendering or wire frame. The Tools Palette contains primitive 3D Objects, Plug-ins (a separate disk of plug-ins is available from MicroSpot, and more are being written), and 3D manipulation tools. The Camera palette displays the visual icons that enable you to change views and take snapshots of a scene. The Light Palette addresses Brightness, Point Sharpness, Ambiance, Color, and Shadows on/off. All Light adjustments can be seen in real time as light plays upon the objects, including real time updating of shadows cast on the grid plane. The Info Palette enables you to adjust the Transparency, Shininess, Reflectivity, Color, Position, and Size of any selected object or group in the scene. Settings are saved with the file.

Modeling Tools The array of primitive objects is more extensive than any other 3D application in the field, and includes the standard Sphere, Cone, Cylinder, and Cube. In addition, an interactive 3D polygonal primitive can be constructed (with user-defined sides and angles), two types of user-defined 3D Multigons, multisided Lathed objects, extruded 3D Text, singular and multiple "Mountains," Pipe Extrudes, and definable Torus objects. Except for the primitive Sphere, all other 3D objects can be edited and customized, including altering the placement and size of selected faces.

Texture Mapping Because of the QuickDraw 3D functions, 3DWorld's texture mapping is displayed in real time while objects are being moved or animated. Finer texture mapping controls, such as the capability to select among various mapping types (planar, spherical, cubic, and so on) are missing. Objects are mapped by default, meaning that their shapes determine how textures are applied. Unique to this application, imported PICT files can be instantly targeted as backgrounds, foregrounds, mapped as textures to a selected object, or imported as an object themselves. The last option displays the PICT file mapped on a rectangular 3D plane that can be placed, rotated, and resized.

Lights Lights can be added as either spotlights or point lights, and can be made visible or invisible. Their various parameters are controlled from the Lights Palette.

Rendering In most cases, rendering is a moot point in 3DWorld because the main purpose of the application is to save 3DMF files. 3DMF files can be transported to any application (such as Strata StudioPro) that accepts and displays QuickDraw 3D. One of the 3DWorld plug-ins enables you to save a PICT file of the 3D display.

Included Libraries A library of plug-ins includes the following:

- Bomb—Acts as a deletion key for an object, but allows it to explode before it disappears.
- Color—Instantly applies the color to the selected object from the Tool Palette.
- CSG—An interactive Boolean operator that enables you to use one object to cut away sections of another.
- Distance—Enables you to measure the distance between any two selected points on the 3D screen.
- Gravity—Any selected object drops down to the surface of the Grid.
- Internet—Enables you to assign an URL address to any selected object.
- Mountain—Enables you to create a "Mount Fuji" with a random slope.
- Mountains—Enables you to create a range of random 3D peaks.
- Random Color—Applies a random color to a selected object.

- Save As PICT—By holding down the Option key, you can save a PICT image of the display while controlling resolution and DPI settings.
- Teleport—Instantly teleports the view camera to the center of any selected object, making this an excellent tool for moving around inside of a 3D object.
- Texture—3DWorld maps any texture once to a selected object, but this plug-in (in conjunction with the ⌘ and Option keys) enables you to map textures in a repetitive fashion on any selected object.
- VR—Enables you to interactively pan and tilt the camera.
- Walkthrough—Enables you to interactively walk through a scene, similar to moving through any virtual reality space.

Animation The 3DMF convention enables instant interactive walkthrough animations. Various 3DMF players can be downloaded from the Internet to display the full 3D environment, enabling you to navigate within it interactively with the mouse. Choosing "Walkthrough" at any time from within 3DWorld enables you to move around and among the objects in your scene in real time.

Other Special Features In keeping with the VRML (Visual Reality Modeling Language) worlds becoming more common on the Internet, you can assign a "URL" (Internet address or off-site location) to any 3D object in a 3DWorld scene. When the object is clicked while you're moving through the 3D environment on the Internet, you are instantly transported to the "address" assigned to the object. This makes 3DWorld an excellent choice for interactive Web page design. Any textured object created in StrataStudio can be saved as a 3DMF file and loaded into 3DWorld, where it can be placed in relation to other objects in an interactive 3D environment. Thus 3DWorld can be used as an animation browser for all 3DMF environments. Because StrataStudio can import DXF objects, 3DWorld can be used as an animation browser in very complex virtual reality scenes.

File Load/Save Conventions 3DMF (QuickDraw 3D) files can be loaded and saved. A special plug-in option also enables you to save PICT images of the 3D screen.

3-D Body Adventures

This CD-ROM is ideal for the child who plans a career in medicine. It's extremely detailed and contains some of the most realistic and medically accurate illustrations of any anatomy program, adult or child. The package includes two pairs of cardboard and cellophane 3D glasses, which help you see body parts in stereo format. It's more successful with some than others. The "fly through" view of the brain and ear structure are awesome, although the capillaries aren't impressive. There's a fully narrated text to accompany the 1,000 images, 3D models, and animations. The program includes the illustrations from the Visible Human Project, a production of the National Laboratory of Medicine. This set of electronically dissected drawings lets you explore the human body in a way never before possible. The result is not unlike a full-body CAT scan. You can view a cross-sectional slice at any level from head to toe.

Clicking a structure tells you its name. A separate anatomy encyclopedia describes and illustrates the muscles, skeleton, and internal organs, and features 360 degree rotation so you can see all sides of a particular spot. There's even a game, although it's basically a shoot-'em-up. You enter the patient's lungs or bloodstream and zap 10 bacteria, which are hiding out among the lung cells or brain tissue, without zapping the patient's healthy cells in the process. It's a lot harder than it sounds.

See Also
Software, Educational, Grades 7-12; Educational, K-6

3-D Rendered Graphics, Using in Games, *See 3-D Ultra Pinball; 7th Guest, The; Eastern Mind; Marathon; Rebel Assault II; Riddle of Master Lu, The; TimeLapse; Yellow Brick Road II*

3-D Speakers, *See Spatial Enhancement*

3-D Ultra Pinball

3-D Ultra Pinball from Sierra Online adds new elements to Mac pinball by using **3-D graphics** and authentic movement. You play on three separate tables, either at different times, or warping back and forth between them. Each table requires you to conquer specific challenges, which will allow you to build a space colony. Eventually, you win enough points to get a star-cruiser off the ground and win the game. Sierra Online also incorporates online help with a link to Sierra's **World Wide Web Site** directly imbedded in the game menu, a helpful trend which other game makers are also starting to follow. Other great pinball titles include Loony Labyrinth and Crystal Caliburn from **StarPlay Productions**, Tristan and Eight Ball Deluxe from Amtex Software and the forthcoming FullTilt! Pinball from Maxis.

See Also
Arcade-Style Games; Pinball Games

4D Calc

4D Calc is an add-on **spreadsheet** for **4th Dimension** database. It provides all typical **spreadsheet functions,** including analysis and forecasting of numerical data. 4D Calc can take cell formula references from database components, or can create an entire spreadsheet directly from information in the database. It will not work unless 4th Dimension is installed, although once in place, it can be used for spreadsheet functions independent of your 4D database. 4D Calc documents can be saved as Macintosh files in SYLK or text, or stored within a record as a 4th Dimension field. Because 4D Calc references information from your 4th Dimension database, changes are dynamically reflected from the database to the spreadsheet.

4D Calc's spreadsheet can hold up to 256 columns and 8,192 rows, and will hot link to other 4D modules as well. Users may build custom layouts combining the database and spreadsheet, inserting buttons, and adding menu bars and floating windows as needed. The combined system gives maximum flexibility within the 4th Dimension format.

See Also
Database; Spreadsheet

4D Server, *See Servers/Database*

7th Guest, The

The 7th Guest is as close as we have come, so far, to a horror classic on CD. The cinematic presentation of the game is simply amazing. You are the 7th Guest invited to a dinner at the creepy Stauf mansion. In the opening scene, you learn that Henry Stauf made his fortune from toys that killed the children who played with them. Seems he sold himself to the devil to get rich and the kids got the short end of the deal. You then wind up stuck in the mansion and must solve more than twenty gothic-themed puzzles, like matching skulls on pieces of cake, to get out.

©Trilobyte & Virgin Games '92
Image Modeled by Robert Stein III

The 7th Guest is a linear game, which means you must complete a certain puzzle to be able to move onto the next level. The innovative use of video, background art, and 3-D animation make playing the game similar to being in control of an interactive horror film. Most of your time in the mansion is mainly spent exploring, looking for puzzles to solve. Although not as action packed as adventure games like **Return to Zork** and **The Daedalus Encounter,** The 7th Guest succeeds on account of its originality and high production quality. The sequel, The 11th Hour, resurrects the evil events of the past as a reporter visits the scene of the crime, and vanishes while investigating the now-decaying mansion.

See Also
Adventure Games; Daedalus Encounter, The; Eastern Mind; Full Throttle; Hell; Myst; Return to Zork; Riddle of Master Lu, The; TimeLapse

8mm

8mm is a video tape format that uses small cassette tapes, containing 8mm wide tape. It provides comparatively low image quality (250 lines of resolution), which is comparable to **VHS**. Although not as popular as VHS, the small tape size makes possible camcorders of very small size. For small-sized digital video (less than 240×180 pixels) the resolution is acceptable, although because it uses a **composite** signal, the image quality (richness of color, clarity) is not as good as S-VHS and Hi-8 formats.

See Also
Hi8; QuickTime; S-VHS; VHS; Video Digitizing

11th Hour, The, *See 7th Guest, The*

24STV

A NuBus video digitize and display board manufactured by RasterOps (now owned by Truevision). The 24STV was one of the first digitizers released for the Macintosh for less than $1,500. This board is no longer manufactured. Software and a FAQ are still available at the RasterOps home page: **http:// www.rasterops.com.**

32-Bit Addressing

32-Bit addressing lets your Macintosh recognize and make use of any installed **RAM** over 8MB. The Macintosh system was originally designed to recognize only 8MB of RAM. When it became apparent that the Mac would outgrow this limit, Apple introduced an extension, called the 32-Bit Enabler, that let the system recognize additional RAM. Since **System 7** was introduced, the capability to access more than 8MB of RAM is built-in to the system and can be toggled on or off through the Memory **Control Panel** where it is now referred to as 32-Bit Addressing. In Power Mac models, 32-bit addressing cannot be turned off.

See Also

Control Panels; RAM; System 7

32-Bit Enabler Extension

The 32-Bit Enabler **extension** enables your Macintosh to recognize and make use of any installed **RAM** over 8MB. The Macintosh system was originally designed to recognize only 8MB of RAM. When it became apparent that the Mac would outgrow the 8MB limit, Apple introduced an extension, called the 32-Bit Enabler, that let the system recognize additional RAM installed besides the initial 8MB. Since **System 7** was introduced, the ability to access more than 8MB of RAM is built-in to the system and you can toggle it on or off through the Memory **control panel** where it is now referred to as 32-Bit Addressing, as shown in the following figure.

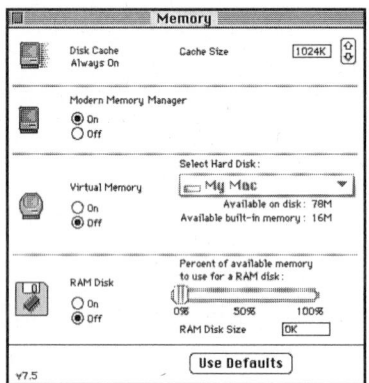

Normally, you would leave 32-bit addressing on, but there is a rare circumstance where you might need to temporarily turn it off. Today's applications are called 32-bit "clean" because they've been designed with Apple's updated specifications. But there are programs, designed before Apple introduced these updated specs, that are not 32-bit clean and might **crash** or **freeze-up** your Mac if you were to run them with 32-bit addressing turned on. To avoid this, the Memory Control Panel enables you to turn 32-bit addressing off to run an older program.

If you have installed more than 8MB of RAM, in order to have your system recognize more than 8MB of RAM, you need to turn on 32-bit addressing. To enable 32-bit addressing for Macs with over 8MB of RAM, follow these steps:

1. Choose Memory from the Control Panels folder.

2. Click the "on" radio button for 32-bit Addressing.

Note: 32-bit Addressing is on by default, but if you install additional RAM, 32-bit addressing may toggle off, and you'll have to turn it on for the system to see the newly installed RAM.

See Also

Control Panel; Memory Control Panel; Memory and Storage, Difference

601 Processor, *See Processors, PowerPC*

603 Processor, *See Processors, PowerPC*

604 Processor, *See Processors, PowerPC*

680x0 Chips, *See Processors, 680x0 Family*

A

A-10 Attack!

A-10 Attack! was designed by Eric Parker, creator of Hellcats Over the Pacific for Graphics Simulations. Hellcats is generally considered to have set the modern standard for top-of-the-line flight sims like **F/A-18 Hornet** and Flying Nightmares.

A-10 Attack! introduces the Virtual Battlefield environment. Instead of only being in charge of a single plane during battle, the Virtual Battlefield allows you to switch between vehicles, including land-based jeeps and tanks and submarines. The game adds in the elements of strategy, requiring you to control an organized fleet rather than merely participating in a computerized attack. A-10 Attack! missions take place in Germany during a communist invasion. A-10! Cuba incorporates the Virtual Battlefield environment and great scenery and graphics of A-10 Attack! and brings the action that much closer to home.

See Also

Absolute Zero; F/A-18 Hornet; Out of the Sun; Rebel Assault II; Sim Games; Wing Commander III

A-10 Cuba!, *See A-10 Attack!*

<A> Anchor Tag

<A> serves as an anchor tag that specifies a hypertext link in an HTML document on the World Wide Web. Most commonly used with the HREF attribute, (Hypertext REFerence) to denote the beginning of a link to another document, another location on the Internet, or to a particular location in the same document. The form is specified by:

```
<A HREF="URL">
```

where URL is the Universal Resource Locator of the file to which the link points.

Any text contained between the <A> and </A> tags is highlighted, either by underlining, in color, or both, as the link that, when clicked, will take the reader to the location referenced in the start tag <A HREF>.

An anchor that serves as the beginning link <HREF> to a location within the same document takes the form:

```
<A NAME="topofpage">Chapter One</A>
```

In this anchor, "topofpage" is an arbitrary name an author assigns to the link. When the author makes the origin link tag using <HREF>, this name is preceded by the pound sign (#):

```
<A HREF="#topofpage">Go to top of page</A>
```

See Also

HTML; Hyperlink; URL; Web Browser; Web Page; World Wide Web

About This Macintosh Dialog Box

In System 7 and higher, at the desktop level the About This Macintosh dialog box is found on the **Apple menu** listed as the top item. This dialog box gives you vital information on a number of important topics relating to your individual Macintosh.

The About This Macintosh dialog box shows you the model name of the Macintosh you are using and the currently installed version of the **Macintosh System Software**, as shown in the following figure.

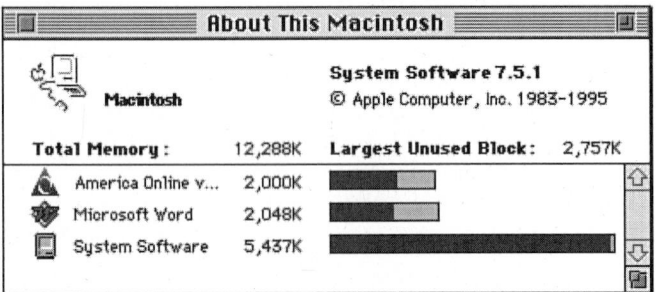

It also shows the total memory (amount of RAM) you have installed on your Macintosh, listed in **Kilobytes (K)**. Below this information, in a scrolling window, appears the listing of all open applications (if any are open) including the System (which takes up memory) and the amount of memory each of the applications is using. Beside each figure is a bar graph indicating how much of the memory allocated to that program is being used. The largest unused block of free memory still available is listed above this window.

This is a quick place to look to find the amount of total memory you have, how much is still available to you, and how much you've allocated to each program. This window is for information purposes only and you cannot make any changes to memory allocations from this dialog. The **Get Info** window (⌘-I) is used to adjust memory allocations.

Although the About This Macintosh command appears at the top of the Apple menu when you're at the desktop level, when you're working in an application, it is replaced by an "About This Application" menu command that contains information about the software application. (The name of the active program appears at the top of the Apple menu, such as About Microsoft Word.) When you select this menu command, a dialog box appears, and although they differ from program to program, they generally contain the name of the software, the version number of the installed software, the serial number, the date it was copyrighted, and often times credits listing the people who developed the product. It's also popular to have the splash screen that displays when you first launch the application appear as the About This Application dialog box.

To view the About This Macintosh information dialog box, follow these steps:

1. At the Finder, on the Apple menu, choose About This Macintosh. (It appears at the top of the Apple menu.)

2. A dialog box appears showing you information for your individual Macintosh, including memory usage, model name, and current System version.

See Also

Apple Menu; File Menu; Get Info; Memory; RAM; System Software

About This Macintosh Easter Egg

Programmers often hide a humorous message, or programmer credits, or a host of personal messages within certain applications. These personal adds-ons are called **Easter Eggs**, and one is hidden with the About This Macintosh dialog. To see the hidden Easter Egg, press and hold the Option key and select **About This Macintosh** on the **Apple menu**. (Note: When you hold the Option key, the name changes to About The Finder.)

When the dialog appears, you'll see a graphic of a mountain range and a scrolling lists of credits will soon appear with the names of the designers of all the different versions of the Macintosh Finder. Each group goes scrolling by with the date of their version, there's a pause between each group, so be patient to see them all.

To view the About This Macintosh Easter Egg, follow these steps:

1. At the Finder Level, under the Apple menu, hold the Option key and choose About This Macintosh. (It appears at the top of the Apple menu.)

2. A dialog box will appear showing you a graphic of a mountain scene, and soon a scrolling list of credits will appear naming the programmers of each version of the finder, along with the date it was created.

See Also
Apple Menu; Easter Eggs

Absolute Path

A way of describing the location of a document or object on the **Internet** so that it can be accessed by means of a **hypertext** link.

A pathname is part of the <A HREF> or **hypertext** reference in **HTML** that leads to the document or object. An absolute path, in contrast to a **relative path**, points to a destination file by starting at the top level of your directory (or folder) hierarchy and working through all the subsequent folders until the file is located.

An absolute path always begins with a backslash, for example:

```
<A HREF="/my_computer/HTTP_documents/
Web_files/company/index.html">
```

Relative path names are generally preferred to absolute path names because absolute path names are not portable. If the **Webmaster** of a **Web site** moves any of the documents linked with absolute path names to other documents, all of the hypertext references will have to be changed to reflect the new location(s).

See Also
<A> Anchor Tag; HTML; Internet; Relative Path; URL; Webmaster; Web Site; World Wide Web

Absolute versus Relative Motion

Absolute and relative motion refer to the method that the Macintosh tracks movement from an input device like a **mouse** or **graphics tablet**. Absolute-motion pointing devices have palettes or tablets on which any location correlates to a position on the screen. Relative-motion pointing devices control the cursor on the screen in less specific terms, relaying to the computer how far the cursor has moved and in which direction.

Graphics tablets are absolute-motion pointing devices. The stylus tells the Mac its physical location on the tablet, and that location is mapped to an exact location on the screen. When you move the stylus on the palette, the cursor on the screen moves to the same location on the screen. Graphics tablets are able to operate in relative motion, but their ultimate benefit is their capability to trace exact positions.

The mouse and trackball are relative-motion pointing devices. The mouse reports how far it has moved and in which direction, but does not tell the Mac where it is on the desk or mouse pad or on the screen in specific terms. Although this method is fast, it lacks the precision of absolute-motion pointing devices.

See Also
Graphics Tablets; Mouse; Touchpads; Trackballs

Absolute versus Relative Reference

Spreadsheet formulas tell the program to take a number in one **cell**, manipulate it a certain way, and put the result in another cell. To do this, you need a consistent way to specify cells. Spreadsheets assign each a unique address based on how many **columns** it is from the left margin and how many **rows** from the top of the sheet. Columns are always alphabetical and rows numerical, so the references work like the grid on a road map: if a formula refers to B5, it's talking about the specific cell in the second column (column B) and the fifth line down.

Relative Reference Spreadsheets have the ability to adapt formulas when you move them to new locations. In the figure that follows, you can put monthly sales figures in column B and then add them up in cell B14. If you want to also find a total for gross profits, you can **copy** B14 and **paste** it into C14. The program will paste the formula shown in the formula bar, but it will also do the following:

- Recognize that it's in a new column
- Assume that you want to total the new column's data
- Change itself to refer to that data

So the original formula will stay in B14, but the pasted version in C14 will be "=SUM(C2:C13)." This automatic process of changing parts of a formula to reflect a new location is called relative referencing.

Absolute Reference The relative referencing feature can create a problem if you always want to refer to a specific cell in a formula. In the figure that follows, you can add a sales incentive specified in B16 as 2.5% of gross profit. To compute January's incentive in D2, you can use the formula "=C2*B16". If you paste that formula into D3, it will correctly change the C2 row reference to C3 to compute February's incentive. But it will also change the B16 to B17, and not find the 2.5% rate. You need some way to tell the program to change one part of a formula but not another.

Almost every spreadsheet does this with a dollar sign to indicate parts of a location you don't want to change. In the figure's formula bar, you can see how to specify "B16" as an *absolute* location for figuring incentives. You can copy or move the formula anywhere, and it'll always refer to that same cell.

You could have written the original formula "=C2*1.025" and gotten the same result. But absolute addressing gives you a tremendous advantage. Imagine a large spreadsheet with individual figures for an entire sales force, and you want to try different incentive rates. Instead of typing a new rate in dozens of formulas, you simply type it into B16. Every cell with that absolute reference will update automatically.

The row, column, or both can be absolute:

- $B16 says to always use data from the B column, but move up or down as appropriate.
- B$16 says to always use row 16, but move sideways as appropriate.
- B16 will always refer to that one unique cell, no matter where the formula is moved or pasted.

	B14 ▼	=SUM(B2:B13)	
	A	**B**	**C**
1	Month	Sales	Gross Profit
2	January	$7,143	$5,209
3	February	$71,341	$44,956
4	March	$56,201	$24,102
5	April	$71,605	$57,529
6	May	$53,662	$27,517
7	June	$35,768	$24,682
8	July	$35	$21
9	August	$60,572	$32,505
10	September	$99,237	$86,722
11	October	$25,352	$14,361
12	November	$7,781	$4,855
13	December	$33,475	$19,382
14	**Total**	$522,171	
15			

	A	B	C	D
1	Month	Sales	Gross Profit	Incentive
2	January	$7,143	$5,209	$130.22
3	February	$71,341	$44,956	$1,123.90
4	March	$56,201	$24,102	$602.54
5	April	$71,605	$57,529	$1,438.23
6	May	$53,662	$27,517	$687.93
7	June	$35,768	$24,682	$617.05
8	July	$35	$21	$0.52
9	August	$60,572	$32,505	$812.62
10	September	$99,237	$86,722	$2,168.05
11	October	$25,352	$14,361	$359.02
12	November	$7,781	$4,855	$121.38
13	December	$33,475	$19,382	$484.56
14	Total	$522,171	$341,840	
15				
16	Incent. rate	2.50%		

D2   =C2*B16

See Also

Cell in Databases; Fill, Spreadsheet; Function, Spreadsheets; Spreadsheet; What-If Calculations

Absolute Zero

In Domark's space-flight simulator, Absolute Zero, the year is 2347, and Earth has managed to come into conflict with an alien colony living on Jupiter's moon Europa. The game pits you against the aliens in a series of missions that require you to maneuver various spacecraft through mines, mazes, and ice shafts. As with **Out of the Sun**, a Domark flight sim, precision timing is a necessity in Absolute Zero. Most of the challenge of the game doesn't lie in the actual mission, but in the maneuvering of the vehicle. Things can get out of control quickly, making Absolute Zero a challenge even to the experts. Absolute Zero is nicely done and offers a rollicking time for those looking for an alternative to World War II missions and military planes.

See Also

Rebel Assault II: The Hidden Empire; Sim Games

Accelerator Boards, *See CPU Upgrades*

Access Privileges

The granting of access to files contained in shared folders on computer networks. On a file sharing system like AppleShare, access can be granted either to individual users or to groups of users who work on projects together or need to share information within a department.

When a user navigates through levels of folders (or directories) held on a server connected to the Internet, the contents of some folders will be publicly available to anyone, but some folders may require access privileges that are restricted to certain users or groups.

An error message that occasionally turns up on a Web browser while searching through folders on World Wide Web servers is shown in the following figure.

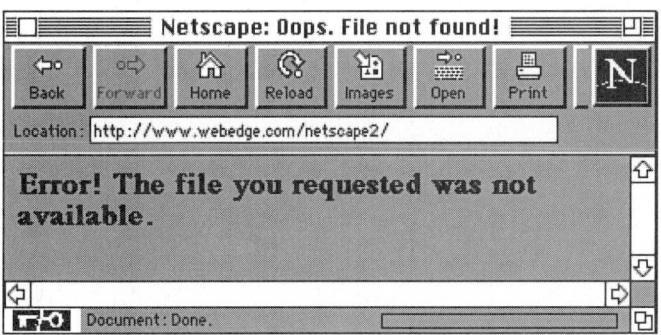

If you see a "Forbidden URL" message, it means you do not have access privileges to view the files in the folder whose URL you have accessed. (Note: This often occurs because the owner of the site has inadvertently retained restricted access to a file, or because the file is missing.)

See Also
Asynchronous Data Transfers; Bulletin Board Systems; Commercial Online Services; FTP; Internet; Networking; World Wide Web

Accidentally Jumping to the Finder, Avoiding

If you've ever been working in an application and accidentally clicked outside the document's window, you return to the **Finder**. Some users find this very annoying. In **System 7.5** and higher, there is a feature that enables you to "hide" the desktop while you're working in an application, so if you should accidentally click outside the document's window, you won't leave the application and go to the Finder. You still see the desktop background pattern, but without the mounted disks, trash can, and so on, and you won't be able to click it to make it active.

To enable this "hidden desktop" feature, open the **General Controls control panel** and uncheck "Show Desktop When In Background." This checkbox is on by default. Clicking the checkbox hides the desktop.

See Also
Finder; General Controls Control Panel; System 7.5

Accounting Methods
There are two accounting methods: Cash or Accrual basis. If you elect to keep your books on a Cash basis, transaction amounts are reported from the moment money changes hands. If you use Accrual basis, transaction amounts are reported from the moment when the transaction is entered. Most very small businesses keep cash books. Larger ones prefer the accrual method, because it gives a more accurate overall picture. MYOB (Mind Your Own Business) supports only the Cash method, whereas Peachtree Accounting gives you a choice of cash or accrual.

See Also
Financial Planning Software; MYOB; Peachtree Accounting

Accounts, Finance Programs
The most basic kind of account in your personal financial program is the checking account. Using a checking account is very simple. You put money into the account, and you write checks to tell the bank how much money to take out of the account and whom to pay it to. But there are several other kinds of accounts that your financial software can track for you, as well. Your savings account, credit cards, investments, loans, and assets can, and should, each have separate account listings within a financial program such as **Quicken**.

Quicken can hold as many as 255 related accounts in a file. Most of us don't need that many, but there's no reason not to set up a separate account for each of your assets and liabilities. In accounting terms, assets are the things you own—your checking and savings accounts, your house, your stocks, IRAs, mutual fund investments, cash on hand, and so on. Liabilities are all the things you owe—mortgages, car loans, credit cards, and other regularly occurring payments.

There are different kinds of accounts for different purposes. Bank accounts are checking, savings, and money market accounts or any cash management accounts on which you have check writing privileges. When your monthly statements arrive, it's a very simple matter to reconcile them against the account balances.

Cash accounts, as the name implies, handle cash transactions. You can enter your cash transactions in your Quicken checking account register if you have only a few and don't need to keep them separate, or you can set up a separate Quicken cash account and enter your cash transactions there. Both methods let you categorize your cash expenses so they are included in reports, graphs, and budgets, and neither method requires that you account for every penny. You should use a separate cash account if you want to keep detailed records of your cash transactions, if you prefer to use cash instead of checks or credit cards, if you need to track petty cash for your small business, or if you receive cash payments such as tips or salaries paid in cash. If you're entering cash transactions in your checking account, set up a category for them as Cash Income and Cash Expense. If you elect to open a separate register for cash transactions, you'll see that a cash account register looks much like a check register except that instead of Payment and Deposit columns, it has Spend and Receive columns.

You can record credit card transactions either by setting up a separate credit card account for each credit card, or by entering credit card transactions as bills paid in your checking account register. Credit card accounts are useful if you want detailed records of your credit card transactions or if you pay your credit card bills over time. A credit card register replaces the check register's Payment and Deposit columns with Charge and Payment. You can, of course, split out the credit card bills into categories such as dining, clothing, entertainment, auto expenses, or whatever else you use your card(s) for.

Asset and liability accounts help track such things as loan balances, the value of your car or other personal possessions, and the cost basis of your home. If you have a small business, asset and liability accounts can track capital equipment, accounts receivable, and accounts payable. If you set up accounts for all your assets and liabilities, Quicken will include them in net worth reports and graphs to give you an accurate view of your total financial picture. Consider opening asset accounts for loan notes you hold, home improvements, the contents of your home including art and antiques, prepaid medical expenses, capital equipment, and accounts receivable. Open liability accounts for loan balances, accrued liabilities, and accounts payable.

Use investment accounts (portfolio accounts and mutual fund accounts) to track what you own in stocks, bonds, mutual funds, and other types of investments that have fluctuating prices. Investment accounts help you track investment transactions, see the performance of your investments, update current market values, and create tax reports. When you use investment accounts, you can see immediately whether you are making or losing money on each investment, compare the performance of your investments, and report on income and capital gains for income tax purposes.

See Also
Finance Programs; MYOB; Quicken

Achromatic Reproduction, *See GCR (Gray Component Replacement)*

Acoustic Modems, *See Modems*

Acrobat Reader

A freeware application by Adobe Systems, Inc. that allows users to read portable documents saved in Adobe's PDF format. Many of these documents are published on the **World Wide Web**.

In order to present PostScript or other complex documents on the Web with their original layout and fonts intact they must be saved as portable documents. They can then be viewed either using Reader as a helper application to the user's Web browser, or by using the Adobe plug-in Acrobat Amber, which lets Acrobat documents appear within the window of browsers that support Amber.

Reader uses Adobe Type Manager (ATM) to simulate a document's original fonts. ATM creates rasterized images of PostScript, QuickDraw GX, or Multiple Master fonts that it keeps in memory for display on the Web as bitmaps.

Acrobat documents can be displayed with bookmarks, notes, or **hypertext** links. Acrobat also lets a user follow the flow of a story though a publication even when the story has been broken into discontinuous pieces.

See Also
Hypertext; Internet; Web Page; World Wide Web

Act!

Act! is a Personal Information Manager with integrated calendar, database, word processing, and alarms.

In the slang of the sixties, Symantec has their Act! together. Act! combines a calendar and a contact manager, allowing you to make appointments while keeping track of the people you're meeting. It can send letters and faxes at the click of a button, and will also dial the phone for you. It has an easy-to-use **icon-**driven interface and is designed to make your data accessible in the form in which you're most likely to use it. Act! records information on contacts, keeps a log of your phone calls, and reminds you to make follow-up calls. It also enables you to manage your schedule with an appointment calendar, which can be viewed by the day, week, or month. You should note, however, that the calendar is only for appointments and reminders tied to people on your list. For example, you can't make a note to get a haircut next Friday unless your barber is listed in the contact file. Even worse, the calendar doesn't indicate holidays, vacation days, or your spouse's birthday, unless you've put him or her into the contact database.

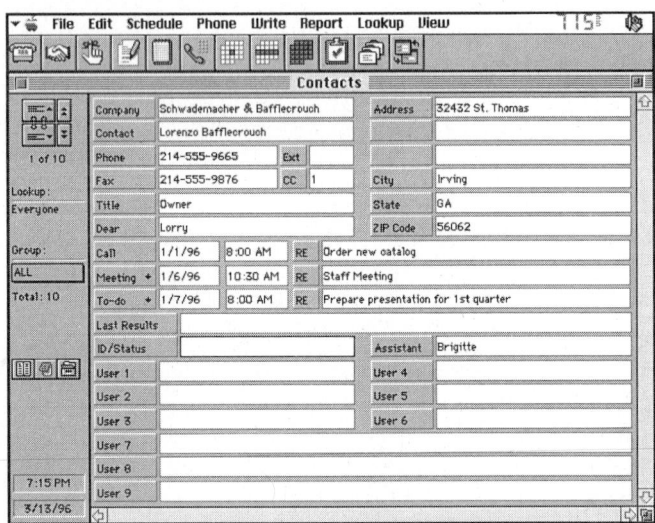

Act! has two ways for you to view and enter your information: the contact file view and calendar view. From within the contact manager (see figure), you can write business letters with an integrated word processor and print them or send them as faxes with FaxSTF. The program's drag-and-drop support makes it relatively simple to move and reschedule appointments. Much of the rest of Act!'s capabilities, however, may not be revealed until and unless you read the manual. It's not the easiest of the PIMs to master, but if you're looking for a contact manager that's strictly business, Act! will do the job.

Active Matrix Displays

The active matrix display is the highest-quality liquid crystal display (LCD) used in higher-end PowerBooks. Active matrix displays produce images that are sharp, crisper, and brighter than those created by desktop CRT monitors. The term active matrix has to do with the fact that every pixel in the display has its own transistor controlling the intensity, brightness, and color.

See Also

Passive Matrix Displays; PowerBook Displays

Active Program/Application

The active program/application is the program or application currently in front, or on top, of any other applications. If, for example, you have the applications WordPerfect, SimpleText, and PageMaker open, but the **menu bar** across the top of your screen is for WordPerfect, that means WordPerfect is the active application (you can have only one application active at a time). Therefore, if you choose the File menu and select New, a WordPerfect document opens.

If you can't tell which application is active, you can look at the mini-icon displayed in the **Applications menu** on the far right side of the menu bar. It will always display the mini-icon of the active application. If you look at the Applications menu and it shows a mini-icon of a Mac, the **Finder** is the active application. The Finder is always running, but if it's not in front, it's not the active application.

To make another launched application active, simply click the Applications menu and scroll down to choose another application. When you select one, it immediately comes to the front to become the active application. When you **Quit** an application, the application behind it becomes active.

See Also

Applications Menu; Finder; Menu; Menu Bar; Quit Command

Active Window

To make any changes to files, or to move or **launch** files, you must make the window they are located in active.

When you open a window, it immediately becomes active. If, for example, you open your hard drive, your hard drive's window is open, and it's the active window.

If you open a **folder** that's on your hard drive, a window opens to display the folder's contents, and it becomes the active window. If you open another folder that is inside the currently active window, it becomes the active window, even though the last folder's window and your hard drive's window are both still open and probably still visible. The rule here is the window that is on top (in front) is the active window. To make another window active, simply click the window or any of its contents, and it will immediately move to the front and become active. Only one window can be active at any time.

The active window always displays a gray title bar with thin lines running horizontally to let you know that it's active. A non-active window's title bar is white. Remember, even though you may be able to see other open windows, only the window in front, with the gray menu bar, is active. If, for example, you were to choose the **Edit menu** and then choose **Select All**, only items in the active window would be selected.

See Also

Edit Menu; New Folder Command; Select All Command

A.D.A.M., The Inside Story

Educational software on a CD-ROM for all ages; A.D.A.M. teaches anatomy and physiology using animation, narration, and expertly drawn medical illustrations. Adam and Eve reveal themselves layer by layer, starting with their skin (which can be set to your choice of ethnic group) and peeling down layer by layer until they reach bone. Animated sequences demonstrate such processes as the Heimlich maneuver, the action of a sunburn on your skin, and the flow of blood through the circulatory system.

In all, there are 52 animated sequences or a total of over 4 1/2 hours of animation and dialog. Parents can install the program with well-placed fig leaves and without access to the section on reproduction, if they prefer. In addition, there are a half dozen puzzles consisting of body parts to reassemble in the right order, and an on-screen medical dictionary with brief definitions of terms you'll encounter in the A.D.A.M. animated family album. Many of the animated scenes are funny, revolving around Adam's klutziness. He cuts his thumb slicing a bagel to show how blood clots, demonstrates the mechanics of a sprained ankle, and gets stung by a bee, as a working example of pain. It's a clever and well-executed way to teach anatomy.

For those who want a much more in-depth study, the A.D.A.M. company has also what it calls the Scholar series, in three levels for high school, college, and postgraduate/medical school use. With these, it becomes more evident that A.D.A.M. stands for Animated Dissection of Anatomy for Medicine. These include more complex labeling, MRI images and x-rays, and go into much greater detail.

Another CD-ROM from the A.D.A.M. company, Nine Month Miracle, takes Adam and Eve through the process of pregnancy and birth. Nine Month Miracle puts the spotlight on Eve's reproductive system, with animation and Lennart Nilsson's *in utero* photography. Throughout the programs there are also video clips of real couples going through real labor and birth, including a Cesarean birth. (There's a warning in front of this one, because it's a bit intense.) Inside the EVU (Eve's Virtual Uterus) you can watch the fetus grow and change, with occasional visits from

Eve's obstetrician to explain what's going on. A chapter for kids ages 3–9 explains the process in terms they can cope with. And there are some funny interludes with Adam dreaming about his new son. All in all, it's a light-hearted but comprehensive look at a serious subject.

See Also

Software, Educational, Adult

Adapters for Monitors, *See* Cables and Adapters for Monitors

ADB, *See Apple Desktop Bus*

ADB Port Replacements

Modems, printers, and pointing devices have historically used low-speed buses: specifically on the Mac, the **Apple desktop bus (ADB)** for keyboards and mice and serial ports for modems and printers. The ADB port has a maximum data rate of 10Kbps. This data transfer rate can no longer keep up with the requirements of graphics tablets and other more sophisticated pointing devices. Older Mac serial ports support data transfer rates of between 57 and 900 Kps. Apple began to install **GeoPort** serial ports on Power Macs and AV Macs, providing a data transfer rate of 2Mps—fast enough to handle a T1 digital-phone line. GeoPort serial connectors use the **digital signal processing** chips of AV Macs and the built-in digital signal processing power of the Power Mac to turn the Mac into a telephone answering machine, speaker phone, fax, and modem system, using the ApplePhone software that comes bundled with the **GeoPort telecom adapter**. (A GeoPort telecom adapter is illustrated in the following figure.)

Serial port and GeoPort speeds vary depending upon the Mac model, the specific devices attached to the ports, and whether the two ports are working simultaneously. GeoPort Adapters support modem speeds of up to 14.4Kbps (very slow for today's Internet communications requirements). Apple has offered the GeoPort telecom adapter for several years. Other vendors, such as Sat-Sagem USA have announced ISDN GeoPort Adapters, and IBM and AT&T have announced support for GeoPort, including devices that handle both voice and data.

The other problem is that you can only connect one device at a time to a serial or GeoPort, and no Mac has more than two such ports. There will soon be PCI cards that add additional GeoPort connections. You can also purchase automated switches, such as PortJuggler, that enable you to connect more than one device to a serial port.

According to an April 1996 *Macworld* article by Cary Lu, "Special Report: New Mac Buses on the Horizon," Apple says it may adopt a new standard for serial ports developed by Intel called the universal serial bus (USB) to replace the ADB or serial ports. USB supports data transfer rates of up to 12Mps with usable throughput rates of 6–8Mps—fast enough to support CD audio traveling with other digital information.

See Also

Apple Desktop Bus (ADB); AV Macintosh; Digital Signal Processing; GeoPort Telecom Extension; Modems

Add-On Software

In the last few years, desktop publishing software has seen huge growth in the implementation of add-on software—software that that brings additional features to the programs with which they're installed.

The page layout package QuarkXPress is widely known for the number of XTensions available that increase its functions, whereas its competitor PageMaker offers a significantly smaller selection of add-ons called plug-ins (formerly known as Additions). Illustrator and FreeHand use plug-ins and Xtras, respectively, while Photoshop and its paint-program siblings seem to have standardized on using plug-ins written for Photoshop (but are supported by the other programs).

Sun Microsystems' **Java** technology extends this concept to the **World Wide Web** (the Web browser **Netscape Navigator** now supports plug-ins), and Apple's OpenDoc technology will make it possible for applications of any kind to access "applets" that will perform individualized functions.

Features found in add-ons include extra tools (such as starburst creators for page layout packages), filters to open different file formats, modules that control scanners, special-effects filters (for draw and paint packages), and enhancements to existing features.

See Also

Java; Netscape Navigator; OpenDoc; Plug-Ins; World Wide Web; XTensions; Xtras

AddDepth

AddDepth is a product based upon a module in Ray Dream Corporation's **Ray Dream Studio**. Output from AddDepth is not targeted to animation files but to **DTP** use (output options are AddDepth, PICT, Illustrator, and EPS). It has advanced features that allow you to customize a 3D text block to fit your needs.

Styles The texture application in AddDepth is called Styles, and a list of selectable texture Styles is available on-screen as visual indicators. AddDepth Styles come in a library with the software. Each default Style may be edited so that colors and texture maps can be added or changed to a typeface's front face and bevel, side surface, and back face and bevel. Shading, Stroke and Fill, Gradation, Decal, and Invisible settings can be applied to any of the letter surfaces. In the case of "Decal," you can select from a software library of patterns and map them to the letter's front and back surfaces. To give you a better idea of the final rendered image, the AddDepth viewplane may be set to as high as 1600%.

Geometry A special geometry dialog is targeted to altering the shape and size of the beveled letter surfaces. With real-time interactive mouse movements, the front and back bevels and the depth of the bevels and the extruded surface of a type object can be altered and applied to the text object. Non-text objects can also be added to the scene. Rectangular, oval, and hexagonal surfaces can be added and adjusted as to size and depth, creating interesting backgrounds for the text. Primitive objects can also be texturized according to any of the settings in the Styles list. A LightSource dialog allows you to adjust the directional geometry of the light.

Béziers AddDepth allows full Bézier object creation with a standard pen tool and additional adjustment controls. The pen tool becomes a Bézier curve device when moved while holding down the mouse button, and a linear tool when end points of the prospective object are simply clicked. Once the shape has been made, it can be manipulated with standard Bézier control levers and reconfigured. After the face of the shape is finished, AddDepth can extrude the new object, bevel it, and texture it according to the items in the Styles list.

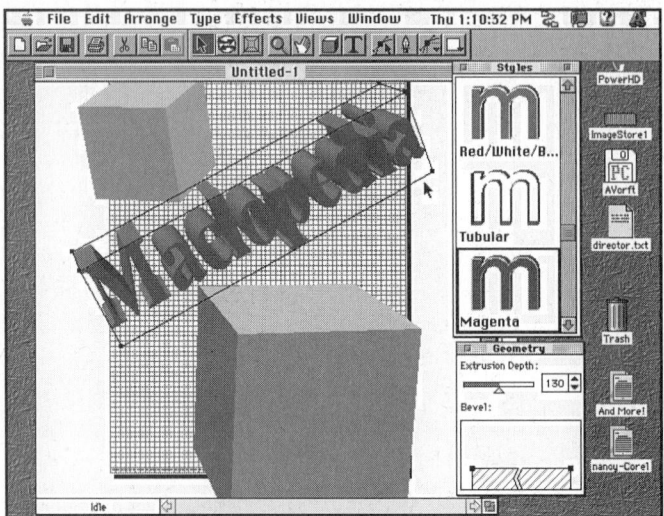

Adding to a Menu

Certain applications, such as Microsoft Word, for example, enable you to add frequently used commands to the application's **pull-down menus**. This feature is called Add to Menu. To add a command to the Microsoft Word menu, first make the command you want added visible on-screen. If, for example, the command you want to add to a menu appears within a dialog box, open that dialog box. If it appears on a ruler, display that ruler. Press ⌘-Option-+(plus sign). Use the plus sign on the keyboard to the left of the Delete key, not the plus sign on the numeric keypad.

Your arrow pointer changes to a large plus sign cursor, indicating that you're in the Add to Menu mode. With the plus sign cursor, click the command you want added to a menu (this is why the command must be visible on-screen). When you click the command, Word places the command on the menu it feels is most appropriate.

If you're not happy with Word's location for your new command, you can relocate your new command to the location of your choice using the Commands dialog box. This dialog box, found on Word's Tools menu, enables you to select a command and designate on which menu you want it to appear.

A number of other applications enable you to add frequently used commands to menus, Function keys, or AQV floating palettes for quick access.

See Also

Arrow Pointer; Click; Cursor; Dialog Box; Menu Commands; Menus; Pull-Down Menus

Additions, *See Plug-Ins*

Additive Color

Additive color refers to the RGB color system of video display in which a mixture of 100 percent red, 100 percent green, and 100 percent blue creates white. In the additive color system, each display pixel has a potential for 256 shades of one of the colors.

Address Book

An address book is a list of **email** addresses, commonly listed in a menu or floating palette, and automatically entered as the destination of an email message when an address is chosen from the address book.

The address book enables you to set up nicknames for email addresses. If, for example, you have a friend whose email address is **Bob_the_Hacker@ complicated.address.com**, you can assign the nickname "Bob" to his address. Then, when you send mail to Bob, instead of typing his whole email address in the message field, you can type "Bob," and Netscape fills in the rest.

A user sets up an address book entry in Netscape as follows:

1. Choose Address Book from the Window menu. Notice that Navigator's menus change when the new window is active.

2. Choose Add User... from the Item menu.

3. Type a shortcut into the Nickname field. In the example above, the nickname is Bob.

4. Type your friend's name in the Name field. In the example above, the name is Bob Raymond.

5. Type the address in the Email field. In the example here, it is
Bob_the_Hacker@complicated.address.com.

6. Click OK.

See Also

Email; Internet; Netscape Navigator

<ADDRESS> HTML Tag

An **HTML** tag that specifies the **email** address of a **World Wide Web** document's author. <ADDRESS> may also include other useful information such as when the document was last updated, copyright notices, or some mention of the larger organization or company to which the Web page belongs. The <ADDRESS> tag that tells a visiting **Web browser** to format any information contained within the start and end tags in the standard "address" format used by the program, usually italic. For example:

```
<ADDRESS>Copyright 1996 Hayden Books. All
rights reserved<BR>

webmaster@mcp.com</ADDRESS>
```

See Also

HTML; Web Browser; Web Page; World Wide Web

Adobe AfterEffects, *See AfterEffects*

Adobe Dimensions

Adobe Dimensions is the 3D module of Illustrator, although it can also be used as a stand-alone 3D design environment. The interface includes a ToolBox and Status Bar, and the following dialogs may also be brought to the screen: Surface Properties, Custom Color, Extrude, and Revolve. Normal, Telephoto, Wide Angle, and Custom views.

Modeling Tools The Revolve and Extrude dialogs are the central 3D modeling facilities in Dimensions. Template shapes are either drawn in the software or imported. One of the dialogs is selected, and the object is either extruded or lathed. Extrusions may be crafted with or without bevels and/or endcaps to user set depths. Lathed objects can be either hollow or filled, and can be revolved to any degree up to 360. 3D primitives include Cube, Sphere, Cone, and Cylinder. Control points can be edited on any 3D or 2D object.

Lights Dimensions has a Lighting dialog box that enables you to set global light intensity and direction.

Rendering Screen renders can be in Draft, Shaded, or Wireframe.

Animation Two kinds of animation files can be produced in Dimensions. The first, with all frames of an object on one page, is suitable for DTP work or for use as a background. The other, a sequential group of numbered frames, can be used as a true 3D animation file by such software as Adobe Premiere and other software that imports sequential files. The process is basic: "Start Sequence" targets the object or objects to include. The object(s) are moved, rotated, and/or scaled. "End Sequence" brings up an storage path dialog, allowing you to select the number of frames to be generated. The frames are generated and saved.

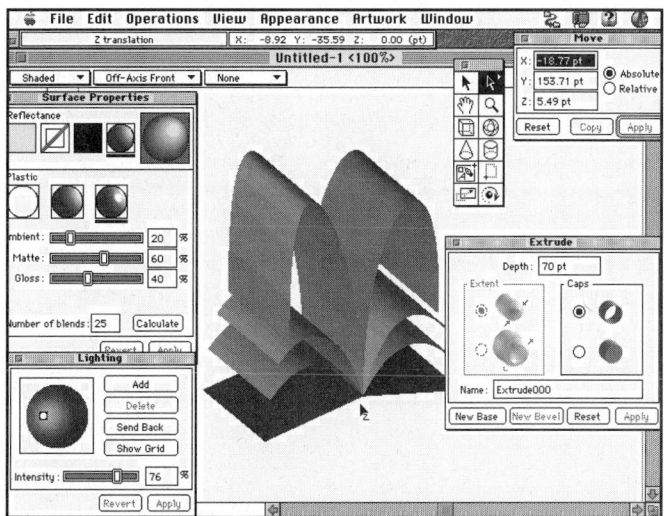

Other Special Features Undo levels, Number of Shaded Blends, and Rendering Parameters can be set in the Preferences dialog. Custom perspective views can be set with an interactive slider.

File Load/Save Conventions Dimensions exports Illustrator formats exclusively: 1.1, 88, 3, 3J, 4, 5, 5J. It saves out Dimensions 1.0 and 2.0 formats. You can open Dimensions and Swivel 3D files.

Adobe Gallery Effects/ 3 Volumes

Each volume in this three volume series contains sixteen unique image processing effects. They are grouped into two basic categories, media effects (effects that make your artwork or photograph appear as if it were rendered with a specific media) and warp effects (effects that alter and twist the picture elements in your work). All of these effects are applied with the use of a detailed dialog that gives you control over intensity and other parameters. In the descriptions that follow, we will refer to these two categories as "media" and "warp." The media effects can be intuited by their name, but we have provided a more detailed description of the Warp Effects for each volume.

Volume 1 Media Effects include Chalk and Charcoal, Charcoal, Chrome, Dark Strokes, Dry Brush, Emboss, Film Grain, Fresco, Graphic Pen, Poster Edges, Smudge Stick, Watercolor. Warp Effects include Craquelure, Mosaic, Ripple, Spatter.

Description of Volume 1 Warp Effects "Craquelure" renders visible cracks and fissures to an image selection, giving it the look of cracked plaster or stone. It is best used on portraiture to emphasize age, and on backgrounds when it is desirable to achieve a rocky look. Mosaic transforms a selection into mosaic tiles, giving you control over tile and grout size. A photograph can become a mosaic work of art or a stained glass window with this effect. Ripple breaks up the edges of images. You can control the size and magnitude. This effect is useful when you need to de-

emphasize an element in a graphic, and also acts to give water a splashing effect. Spatter is a lot like Ripple, but it creates more disturbances across the image. Uses would be the same as Ripple, but water effects would show more turbulence.

Volume 2 Media Effects include Accented Edges, Angled Strokes, Bas Relief, Colored Pencil, Grain, Note Paper, Palette Knife, Photocopy, Rough Pastels, Sprayed Strokes, Texturizer, Underpainting. Warp Effects include Diffuse Glow, Glowing Edges, Patchwork, Stamp.

Description of Volume 2 Warp Effects Diffuse Glow adds a ghostly mist in the background color to your image. It functions well when you want to add mystery or fog to a graphic. Glowing Edges transforms the graphic selection into a neon-like area of glowing primary colors, and can be used to transform a selected area into an abstracted light show. Patchwork alters the graphic selection by changing it into a collection of blocks or tiles. You can control the size and shadowing of the tiles. This effect works well for transforming a graphic into an image painted on a mosaic block wall. Stamp transforms the graphic into a two color collection of blotches. You control the smoothness and size. Use it for abstractions of a graphic.

Volume 3 Media Effects include Conte Crayon, Crosshatch, Halftone Screen, Ink Outline, Paint Daubs, Plaster, Sponge, Water Paper.

Warp Effects include Cutout, Glass, Neon Glow, Plastic Wrap, Reticulation, Stained Glass, Sumi-e, Torn Edges.

Description of Volume 3 Warp Effects Although you couldn't tell from its name, Cutout is really a media effect, transforming an image into what could be mistaken for a paint-by-the-numbers picture. Glass is a fairly complex effect. It gives you a variety of controls that allow you to select frosted glass, glass blocks, tiny lens, or even another graphic which acts as a glass filter. The intensity is also controllable.

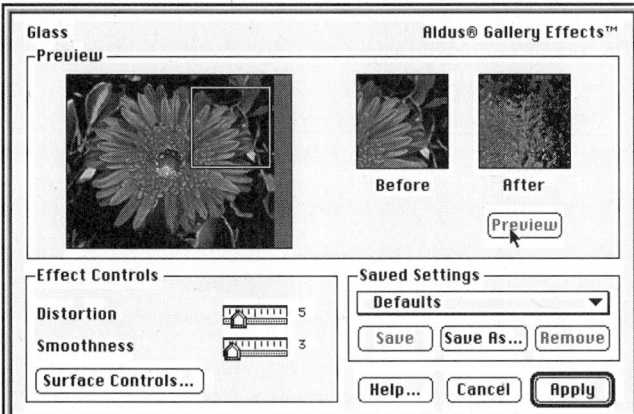

The net effect is a graphic selection that looks as if it were constructed of the same glass material as the settings chosen. This is an excellent filter for either transforming an image into a glass masterpiece or for developing glass-like graphics for 3D texture mapping. Plastic Wrap, as the name suggests, gives the impression that the graphic selection is wrapped in sheets of plastic. Reticulation uses the background/ foreground colors in Photoshop to transform a graphic selection into a two-color painting with image elements spattered. Stained Glass, as the name implies, creates a stained glass masterwork from your graphic selection. Whether it's a Tiffany lamp or a church window, this filter allows you control over the light intensity, border and cell thickness. Sumi-e treats the graphic selection as if it were constructed of filmy spider webs. It's based on Japanese brush painting. Fragile digital paintings are the end result. Torn Edges is a lot like Reticulation, but with more evidence of smearing on the overall graphic.

Adobe Illustrator 6

Adobe Illustrator has set the standard in vector graphics software for quite a while, and every upgrade brings new options. Illustrator has a wealth of accessible tools for the vector drawing artist, and many of the ways that it goes about doing things remain totally unique to this software. Understanding how to use Bézier drawing tools is a must for anyone wishing to use Illustrator to the fullest potential. Bézier drawing tools are found in most vector packages, though in some software manipulating a Bézier line is hidden beneath more common drawing options. The advantage of working with Béziers is that any shape drawn with them is always open to reconfiguration and editing, whereas other methods are less editable once the lines are placed down.

Basic Bézier Drawing Bézier line segments contain point anchors and directional levers. Each anchor has two levers extending from it. Anchors are placed at positions on a curve (most times automatically) where the line goes through a major change of direction. Because vector drawing itself is "remembered" by the computer as a series of vector or directional changes, Bézier curves are the perfect medium for vector drawing. The control levers that extend out from the anchor points are used to adjust and change the shape and convexity/concavity of the curve upon which the anchor point is centered. A shape may have any number of anchor points, depending upon its complexity. Each anchor point has only two directional levers with control points on the ends. Moving the levers adjusts the angles of the curve, moving the anchor points widens or narrows the scope or area covered by the curve. Creating shapes that do what you want them to do with fine-tuned exactness in Illustrator demands experimentation ands a good degree of familiarity with Bézier interactivity. Illustrator's Direct Selection Tool (the white arrow at the top right of the toolbox) in conjunction with the Control key on the keyboard is the way that interaction with Illustrator's Béziers occurs. That is the first editing tool to master if you hope to be an Adobe Illustrator artist.

Illustrator's Bézier drawing tool is shaped like a penpoint. Drawing with it is somewhat difficult to master for the traditional artist, and less so for the artist accustomed to working with **CAD** (Computer-Aided Drafting) software. Other Illustrator penpoint tools add anchor points to a line or remove them. An easier Illustrator tool used to draw complex shapes is the Freehand drawing tool, because it works much like one would expect. After the Freehand tool is done drawing, the line is transformed into a Bézier curve with all of the necessary anchor points in place, and open to further editing. If a **point-click** method is used with the Bézier pens, straight line segments result. Optional lines can also be created with the brush tool, which is excellent for creating calligraphic-like lines—lines that are displayed as thick and thin strokes (useful for softening the look of a vector image). Illustrator also has oval and rectangle primitive shapes. These too are transformed to Béziers on-screen. (Editable Bézier curves are the basic ingredients of all graphics in Adobe Illustrator except imported bitmaps.)

Other Drawing Tools Illustrator has a special drawing palette useful for the drawing of a spiral, vortex, star and polygon. All of these shapes are connected to dialogs that allow numeric input as far as size and number of segments. Perfect seventeen-pointed stars are just as easy to create as the standard five-pointed variety, and eleven-sided polygons present no problem. Like any other shape placed on the Illustrator screen, everything becomes an editable Bézier once it's painted down.

Tracing Images There may be times when you want to bring in a bit-mapped image and translate it to a vector graphic. Illustrator offers two ways to accomplish this. You can auto-trace a bitmapped image if it is a one-bit (two color) PICT or MacPaint file, or you can bring in an EPS image and trace over

it by hand. Auto-tracing can trace over a whole image or a part that is user determined. The EPS hand method is more tedious, but gives you more exacting control over the line segments. Both types of traced images appear as Bézier segments and can be fully edited. Illustrator comes with a sample library of Adobe Graphics Effects, image manipulation and transformation tools, that can be targeted to any bitmapped graphic included as an element of an Illustrator page (usually on a separate layer).

Typography Illustrator offers the same editing tools for typographic selections that are available for drawing shapes. Type can be edited and filled with gradients, resized and rotated. It's also possible to place type on any curved path imaginable and inside any selected shape area with a few simple mouse clicks.

Blends and Gradients One of the most complex challenges for a vector drawing program is adding color fills and gradients to vector images. Illustrator has these capabilities down cold, offering additional options as well. Blends are a separate issue which Illustrator also addresses. A blend between two objects may be what is blended, as well as their separate internal coloring. A gradient, on the other hand, refers to the multiple blending of colors in a selected object. Illustrator allows for the application of both linear and radial gradients, and comes with a default library with both types. New gradients covering all of the colors in the palette, and as many as desired at the same time, may be added. A separate gradient move tool in the toolbox allows interactive movement of the gradient inside an object as far as its placement is concerned. A single gradient, therefore, can have an infinite number of discreet looks in Illustrator. Color and pattern fills are also supported.

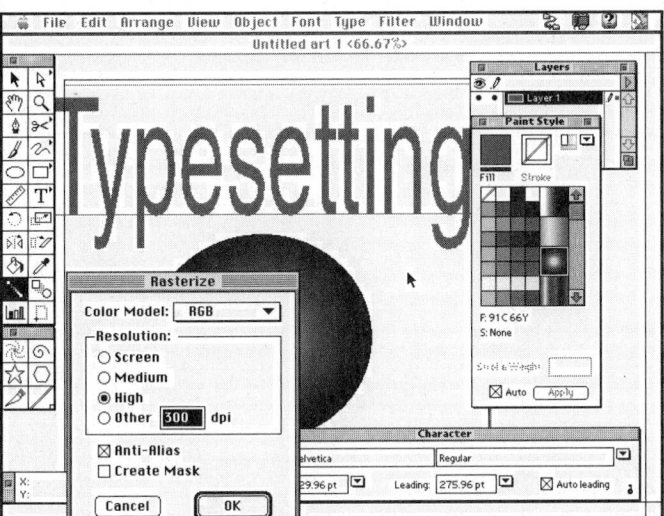

Graphs Illustrator offers a separate toolbox icon for chart and graph creation. An input box for adding numerical data is also provided, as well as a good selection of graph and chart types. If necessary, the chart or graph can be edited as any other Bézier curve can, though editing these shapes seldom makes the data clearer. Color gradients and fills can be added to the selected items.

Layers Illustrator supports the creation and use of working layers. Each layer can contain separate data that acts as a component of the final saved graphic. Using layers allows you to edit parts of a complex composited graphic that would be hard to select and separate out if you were working with only a single layer. Layers can also be transposed if needed.

File-Save Conventions Illustrator supports saved files in Adobe Acrobat, Amiga IFF, BMP, Illustrator EPS, PCX, Photoshop JPEG, Pixar and Targa, as well as most previous versions and the present version of the Illustrator specific format.

Adobe Premiere, *See Premiere*

Adobe Streamline, *See Streamline*

Adobe TextureMaker
1.0, *See TextureMaker*

Adobe Type Manager

This font utility from Adobe Systems enables you to view and resize **fonts** to any size on the screen, without having the fonts looking jagged. If you want to better understand what "the jaggies" are and why they were such a problem, you first need to know that **PostScript** fonts come in two parts: a bitmapped screen font (which draws the font on-screen) and a **printer font** (which contains smooth outlines for interpretation by PostScript-compatible printers).

Each bitmapped screen font includes several fixed point sizes of the font, like 10, 12, and 14 point. If you used the font in any of those installed point sizes, the font looked pretty good on-screen. However, if you decided you wanted to use a significantly larger size, like 72 point, these bitmapped screen fonts would look very jaggy on the screen. This happens because bitmapped screen fonts are made up of tiny pixels that look like small black squares when magnified. When you dramatically increase the size of font, you dramatically increase the size of these squares, and any curved letters would have experience a major "stair step" effect (see the following figure).

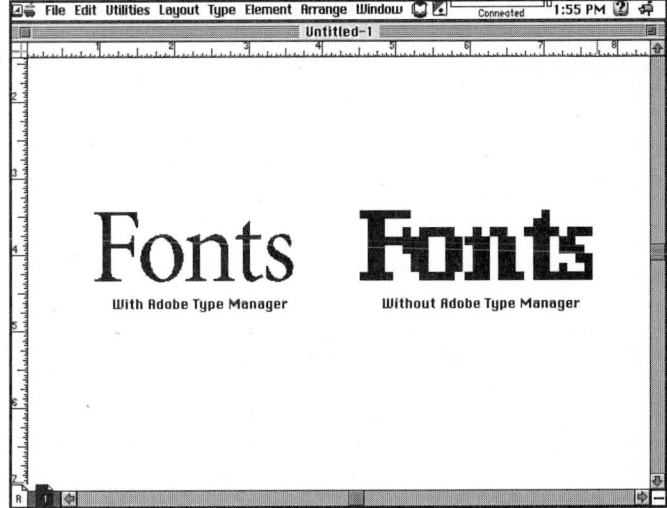

Adobe Type Manager (ATM) came to the rescue by using the PostScript printer font to interpret the font on screen, rather than just using the installed sizes in the bitmapped screen font. This way, you can use a font in any size and be able to stretch, edit, and add special effects to fonts without experiencing the jaggies. ATM takes care of rendering smooth, readable typefaces on screen for you, and if you have a **QuickDraw**-based printer (such as an Apple **StyleWriter**), ATM uses this same technology to render your fonts when they print to make them look considerably better there as well.

See Also

Font; Font Utility; PostScript Level 2; Printer Font; QuickDraw; Screen Font; StyleWriter

Adobe Type Set Value Pack, *See Fonts*

Adobe Type Twister, *See Type Twister*

Adobe Wild Type, *See Fonts*

Adult Education, *See Software, Educational, Adult*

Advent 3B2, *See Page Layout Applications*

Adventure Games

Though most computer games immerse you in outer space, an alternate universe, or at least an alternate state of mind, **Adventure Games** transport you to another world. Instead of quick-paced action and flying bullets/death rays/lasers, adventure games like **Myst** give you the chance to explore a new environment, learn its history, sometimes even interact

with the inhabitants. Adventure games are somewhat related to **Role-Playing Games** and, because they rely heavily on fantasy, they have much more plot than some other types of games like **First-Person Perspective Shooters** or **Arcade Games**.

Modern adventure games can be traced back to text-based Interactive Fiction, such as the original **Zork** series, and other games that were based on complicated plots and puzzle-solving. Puzzle-oriented adventure games like Myst, Welcome to the Future, and Majestic all feature beautiful 3D rendered graphics and soothing background music. Though some of the more advanced adventure titles are timed and require quick decisions, most allow you the opportunity to move through them at your own pace, making them a good choice for beginning gamers. Titles like **Return to Zork** and **Riddle of Master Lu** add hunting for artifacts to the puzzle solving, as well as giving the player opportunities for in-depth interaction with other characters. All adventure games give you the chance to go somewhere new and mysterious without ever leaving your desk.

Other adventure games worth trying include Angel Devoid: Face of the Enemy from Mindscape, Louis Cat Orze: The Mystery of the Queen's Necklace from IVI publishing, MTV's Club Dead from Viacom New Media and Zeddas: Servant of Sheol from Synergy Interactive.

See Also

7th Guest, The; Daedalus Encounter, The; Dark Eye, The; Eastern Mind; Full Throttle; Hell: A Cyberpunk Thriller; Myst; Non-Linear Storytelling; Residents Bad Day on the Midway; Return to Zork; Riddle of Master Lu, The; TimeLapse

AES/EBU

Audio Engineering Society/European Broadcast Union. A digital I/O connection that uses a three-conductor XLR jack, these are the same three-pin plugs as are used on professional microphones and recording equipment.

See Also

S/PDIF

AFP, *See Server*

After Dark

After Dark, by Berkeley Systems, (2095 Rose Street, Berkeley, CA 94709, (510) 540-5535, Web Site URL: **http://www.berksys.com**. Street Price of After Dark Collection: $39.95) is probably the most popular commercial **screen saver** in Macintosh history. It was an instant hit when it was introduced in 1989. Its two signature screen savers were its tropical fish tank, complete with bubbling fish tank sounds and customizable fish, and its flying toasters screen saver, which features toasters with flapping wings and slices of toast flying though space.

Berkeley Systems designed After Dark to enable the integration of additional screen saver modules to After Dark, and since 1989 Berkeley Systems has introduced literally hundreds of different screen savers, including popular themed packages such as The Simpson's TV cartoon characters, a set of Star Trek screen savers, a Disney collection, and many more. There is also a growing list of free third-party, After Dark-compatible modules available from online services or the Internet, and Berkeley Systems even hosts a competition to see who can design the best After Dark screen saver modules. You can find many of these third-party modules in the Macintosh Utilities Forum on America Online or at Berkeley Systems' Web site at **http://www.berksys.com**.

The After Dark **control panel** has a very well-designed interface that enables you to choose from a list of installed screen savers, and then control certain aspects of each "module" that you add to the collection (see the following figure).

For example, on the flying toast module, you can choose how many flying objects (toast and toasters) that you want on the screen at one time, and you can also specify how you'd like your flying toast: light, medium, or dark. There is also an icon of a speaker that enables you to individually adjust the volume for any sound effects that may accompany the modules. In the case of the original flying toasters, it was the sound of the toasters flapping their wings. In the newly updated version, the sound effect is a sound track that sings the flying toaster anthem. The people at Berkeley Systems take this stuff very seriously, but it's really all for fun.

An interesting development from Berkeley Systems is its addition of **Virex**, the **virus** checker, in the form of a screen saver. When you select the Virex screen saver, it blacks out the screen and displays green three-dimensional outlines of the icons of your hard disk, one after another, to keep the screen moving, but behind the scenes it is scanning your hard disk for any viruses. You can see the progress of the virus search in the bottom of the window listed by percentage. That way if you come back to your computer, and the search is 94 percent complete, you might want to let it go another minute and complete its search before you press any key or move the mouse to return to your normal display.

See Also

Control Panels; Screen Saver; Virex; Virus

Afterburner, *See*
Shockwave, Afterburner

AfterEffects

Originally developed by **CoSA**, which was bought by **Adobe**, After Effects is a special effects processing application for **QuickTime** movies.

It is not a direct competitor to Adobe **Premiere**, which is designed primarily for editing clips. It is certainly possible to perform cuts and transitions in After

Effects, but if that's all you need to do, buy Premiere or Avid **VideoShop** instead.

After Effects is a time-based effects program that enables you to construct effects containing multiple layers of clips. Effects are constructed in a Comp window, which acts as a preview window for the effect. It displays an area larger than just the final frame size, making it easier to arrange clips.

Clips are dragged into the Comp window and arranged. The separate Time window indicates the location of the clips at a point in time. **Key frames** are created by choosing another time and moving an element in the Comp window. The program then calculates the in-between locations of the clips. Graphical controls adjust the movement of the clip—the motion and the speed of the motion are treated as two separate editable parameters.

After Effects excels in effects processing—Adobe used some of the filtering technology in After Effects for the **CD-ROM Maker** effects in Premiere. When clips are merged together, the edges are anti-aliased. A **Bézier** drawing tool creates **masks** around clips (one clip can be feathered over another, for example). After Effects imports **Photoshop**, **filmstrip**, and **Illustrator** files. Illustrator files are anti-aliased on the fly within After Effects, making it possible to scale an Illustrator illustration to any size and see smooth edges on graphics.

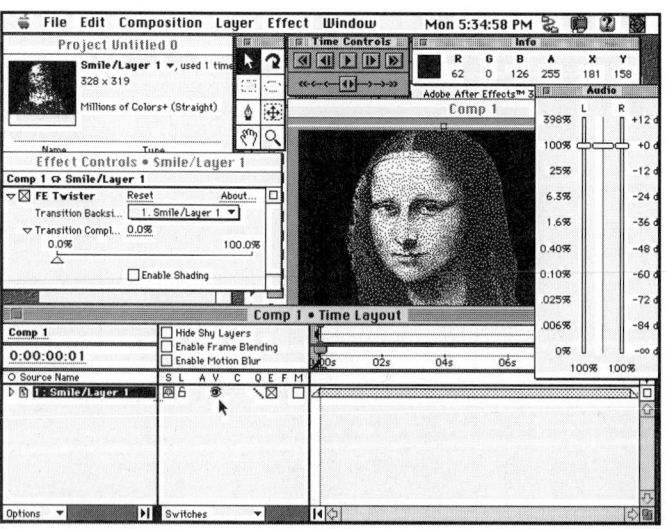

D1 video production format is supported, as well as **NTSC** and **PAL**. Unfortunately, audio editing is more limited than that found in Premiere—you can adjust only the volume.

After Effects comes in two versions: the standard and the Production Bundle. The Production Bundle adds plug-ins with greater motion controls, additional filters, and controllers for high-end recorders. These features are protected by a hardware dongle that plugs into the **ADB** port.

> Adobe Systems, Incorporated
> 1585 Charleston Road
> P.O. Box 7900
> Mountain View, California 94039-7900 USA
> Price: $995, $1995 with additional plug-ins
> Fax: 415-961-3769
> Phone: (415) 961-4400
> Web: **http://www.adobe.com/ Apps/AfterEffects.html**

See Also

Premiere; QuickTime

Afterlife

Taking a major risk with the staunchly religious set, **Afterlife** is a parody of Maxis-style **Sim games** that puts you in charge of heaven and hell. The game features the same sort of grid-like Sim interface we are all familiar from titles like **SimCity 2000** and incorporates the usual LucasArts brand of humor, graphics, and gameplay. Keep the inhabitants of the afterworld happy and you will thrive as leader of your choice of final resting place; screw up and you may find yourself being overthrown by the four surfers of the Apocalypse (complete with hip surf-twang music).

You can even set Earth to have more disasters to speed up the population of whichever side of the after-life you decide to preside over. This parody should prove to be just as popular with gamers who loves sims as the games it is parodying.

See Also

Sim Games; SimCity 2000

AIFF

Audio Interchange File Format (AIFF) is the standard audio file format for the Macintosh. AIFF files (along with .AU files) are commonly encountered on the **Internet/World Wide Web**.

AIFF allows a variety of sampling rates, sample sizes, and both mono and stereo samples. Some implementations of AIFF allow for compression of a sound file; for instance, AIFF now supports IMA, which offers 4:1 compression and is compatible with Windows machines.

Mac applications that support AIFF files include SoundApp, **SoundMachine**, and EasyAIFF. These and other sound utilities can be found at **http:// www.umich.edu/~archive/mac/sound/soundutil/**.

See Also

AU File; File Types, Internet; Helper Applications, Web; Multimedia

Airplane Games, *See Sim Games*

Alarm Clock

The Alarm Clock D/A, which appears on the **Apple menu** up through version **System 7.1**, is designed to give you an electronic reminder for important events or meetings. You can set the alarm to go off anytime you like with an audible alarm (it plays your system beep twice) or a visual alarm (it blinks your menu bar). When the alarm goes off, you'll see a flashing alarm clock appear in the **menu bar** at the top of the **applications menu**. To stop the alarm, simply reopen the alarm clock and push the alarm handle, next to the alarm time setting, to the down position.

The alarm clock actually has two views: A collapsed view and an expanded view. In the collapsed view, all you see is a thin bar with the time and a small lever. To expand the alarm clock, click the lever and the alarm functions will pop down.

To use the Alarm Clock D/A, follow these steps:

1. Choose Alarm Clock from the Apple menu.

2. If you want to set an alarm, click the level to the right of the time to expand the alarm clock to its full size. The second set of numbers from the top is the currently set alarm time.

3. Click the alarm icon, enter the desired alarm time in the middle panel, and click the alarm level to put it in the up (on) position. Close the alarm clock.

4. When the current time reaches the time you set for an alarm, the system beep will go off twice. If your sound volume is off, the menu bar will flash instead. An alarm clock icon will begin to flash on the menu bar on the application menu. To stop the alarm, choose Alarm Clock again from the Apple menu, and click the lever to the left of the time in the middle section to the down position (off).

See Also

Application Menu; Apple Menu; Menu Bar; Pop-Down Menu

Alert Box

Often, if you choose a **command**, an alert box appears that lets you know what you're about to do. If, for example, you go to empty the **trash**, you're greeted with an alert box that states, "The Trash contains 1 item. It uses 80K of disk space. Are you sure you want to permanently remove it?" The alert box gives you a second chance—a moment to stop and consider your actions—before you complete a command that cannot be undone. This is the Macintosh computer's way of looking out for you. If you open the **System Folder** and **double-click** the Finder file, for example, you'll get an alert box that tells you, "This file is used by the **System Software**. It cannot be opened." That's the Mac interacting with you.

See Also

Command; Double-Click; Empty Trash Command; System Folder; System Software; Trash

Alert Icon

When an **alert box** appears to warn you about a command or improper action you may be taking, an alert **icon** also appears. These icons change with the severity of the alert box. You may see an exclamation point inside a yield sign or you may see a Stop sign-shaped icon with an open-face hand alerting you to STOP (see the following figure). If your system experiences a **crash**, you may see an alert box with a **bomb icon** to let you know your system bombed. Pay attention!

You can alter these alert icons a number of ways. You can use third-party shareware programs to change them to full color icons or edit them using Apple's resource editor **ResEdit**. (Warning: Use ResEdit only on a copy of the **System File**, never on the original.)

See Also
Crashes, System; Icons; ResEdit; System Files

Algorithm

A **programming** term for the specific set of steps used to accomplish a task. You can think of an algorithm as a recipe. Unlike a cooking recipe, however, computer algorithms must be very specific. Programmers are always on the lookout for clearer and more efficient algorithms. It's often possible to improve a program's speed by using an improved algorithm rather than by using a faster computer!

Alias' Sketch

Alias' Sketch looks like an animation program, probably because it is the rendering and sculpting module of Alias' more expensive 3D products. Using Sketch also trains you for any animation software because modeling and rendering are integral to mastering any animation package. The most helpful attribute of Sketch is constantly updated help display, so that learning its methods and tools is made much easier as a result. Extensive attention is paid to viewing angles, which include all six cubic directions plus orthographic, bird's eye, "look at that," head on, and fit to view. Altered views can be saved and applied to other scenes. Sketch features a very high-end curve editing function that can be applied to a 3D object. Instead of functioning as a spline or Bézier editor, it allows you to point to and drag curves into new shapes in real time. It can be used to produce extremely complex raytraced renderings that can stand alone or be incorporated into other artwork. A full render list on-screen enables you to select any object (including the lights) for manipulation, making editing even a complex scene with many elements a simple task. Sketch has full text beveling and extrusion capabilities.

Drawing Tools Sketch contains both a freehand drawing pencil and a Bézier curve pen. The pencil leaves equidistant points on the drawn curve, and curves may be lathed to create 3D shapes. The Bézier pen works according to Bézier standards with attached curves and controller arms. Bézier shapes may also be lathed. A circle and rectangle shape are also included for object creation. Lathing and extruding operations are somewhat difficult compared to other 3D object creation software.

Lights Sketch has the capability to allow you to place any number of spotlights, point lights, and distant lights, in addition to ambient light settings. Spotlights can be targeted to any point on any object, and lights can be colorized.

Rendering A rendering preferences dialog enables image quality (Faceted, Hidden Line, Phong, Phong Anti-aliased, Phong and Shadows, Raytrace, Raytrace and Shadows, Raytrace and Antialiasing), DPI, Size (from a default list or user customized), Ambient Light Color and Direction, Camera Flash and Color (on or off), the creation of an Alpha Channel, Render Log, suppression of error messages, and an audible beep when rendering is complete. A very useful feature enables you to use a resizeable box to place on any area of the screen and render just that selection. This is useful for previewing textured objects and light placements. Wireframes may also be rendered in different resolutions. Backdrops, whether ramped colors or selected images from a file, are rendered right to the preview screen so that object placement is made more intuitive.

Textures Sketch has a basic list of materials and a more complete materials library. The basic list includes mostly color choices, with glass and gold added. The texture library can be viewed as a verbal list or as visual icons. The visual library shows all textures as wrapped to a sphere.

File Save/Load Conventions While still in the Edit mode, a Sketch scene can be saved as a StyleGuide, StyleGuide Export, DXF, EPSF, RIB, IGES. After a scene is rendered, it can be saved as an Alias PIX or PIX + Alpha, PICT, TIFF, or EPSF. DXF and Alias files can be imported, and Alias files can be opened.

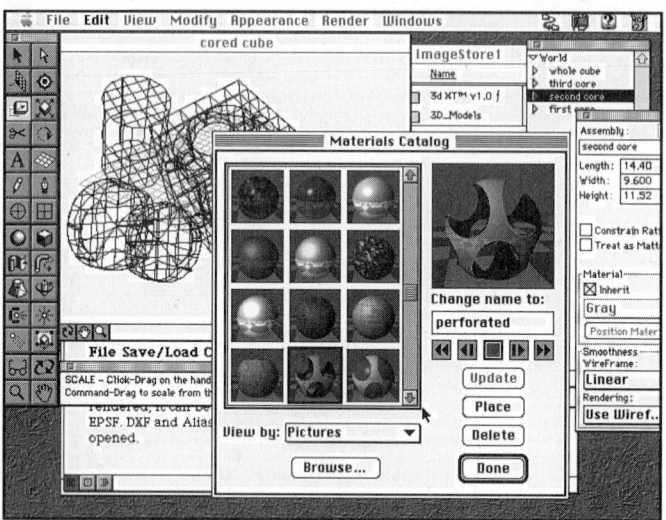

Aliases, *See Make Alias Command*

AlienSkin TextureShop

This program is an internal plug-in for Photoshop and Photoshop clones. If your interest is in creating novel organic textures, this will be a primary package for you. As if to emphasize its alien nature, textures are created by mutating chosen selections. Selected mutants are then saved out to "bins" or grouped libraries for later application. The default choices from which the mutants are created cover a wide, colorful range of possibilities, mimicking everything from cloth and stone to non-earthly flesh and mud. Though marketed by Virtus, the software was developed by AlienSkin Software, the same developers who are responsible for the Black Box Photoshop plug-in effects. This software ranks on the same high-quality level as does the KPT3 Texture Explorer from MetaTools, and compliments similar looks.

The Interface and the Creative Process TextureShop has a dual interface, one that shows the textures in a chosen library and the second that is used to size a chosen texture and render it to the selected area of the image. In the first interface level, textures are drag-dropped into a preview area. An adjustable slider is set from "none" to "oodles," giving the software directions on the degree of mutation that will take place. After the Mutate button is clicked, fifteen mutations appear in another preview area. If you like the looks of any of the mutations, they can be drag-

dropped to either an existing library of textures, or a new library group can be created for them. If dropped on the area that is titled "Light," the textures specularity and light color and direction can be altered, resulting in subtle changes in the overall texture. The next step is to drag a selected texture to an "apply" area.

Dropping the texture on the "apply" area brings you to the second level of the AlienSkin TextureShop interface. The first step here is to size the texture with the mouse or numeric indicators. This redraws the screen, showing you how the texture will tile on an image selection. Finally, you choose how to apply the texture to the image from a list of options. The texture can be applied as a texture map, height map (where the lighter areas of the texture show on the image and the darker areas just gray it out), or as a color map (without the perceived 3D roundness of the texture map). How the texture is applied is also left to the user. It can be applied as a transparent image from 0% to 100% in 10% increments, as one of a selection of blends, or on either the darks or lights of the targeted image selection. Each choice results in a very different rendered graphic.

Aligning Icons Automatically

You might already know you can have **icons** in your windows snap to an invisible grid by setting the "Snap to Grid" preference in the **Views Control Panel**. But there's a way to have a file snap to this grid without having the Snap to Grid preference turned on. Hold the ⌘ key while moving the file, and when you release the mouse button, the file snaps to the nearest point on the invisible grid, even with Snap to Grid turned off.

This trick also works in reverse: If you have Snap to Grid turned on, but you want to move a file to a location without it snapping to the grid, again hold the ⌘ key. This way you can move the item to any location you want without having it snap to the grid.

See Also
Icons; Views Control Panel

Allied General

Allied General, from Strategic Simulations, is one of the few **strategy games** that doesn't completely rely on the manual, making it a good game for beginners. You are in charge of the Allied troops while fighting Germany's blaze across Europe, Russia, and North Africa. As with most strategies, from that point on, historical accuracy is really up to you and the decisions you make.

SSI's next offering, Panzer General, is slated to be a **hybrid** Mac/DOS/Windows 95 title and should avoid the usual wait for a PC title to successfully make it over to the Mac platform.

See Also

Chaos Overlords; Pax Imperia; Sid Meier's Worlds; Spaceward Ho!; Strategy Games; V for Victory; Warcraft: Orcs and Humans

AllMIDI

Shareware available from the **Internet** that processes **MIDI** files and allows them to be played on a Macintosh.

MIDI stands for *Musical Instrument Digital Interface.* MIDI files are instructions for a computer-savvy musical instrument, usually (but not always) a synthesizer.

AllMIDI, by Paul C.H. Ho and Pink Elephant Technologies, is not strictly a **helper application** because it doesn't play the MIDI file directly; rather, it converts the MIDI file to **QuickTime**, which you can play with any QuickTime player application.

To play MIDI files that you've found on the **World Wide Web**, do the following (the following instructions refer to the **Web browser Netscape Navigator** but apply to any browser that uses helper applications):

1. Choose "Preferences" from Netscape "Options" and choose "Helper Applications" from the popup menu.

2. Click the "New" button. Enter "Audio" in the MIME type: box, "MIDI" in the subtype: box, and ".mid, .midi" in the Extensions: box.

3. Click the Browse button, and Netscape presents a File dialog box. Navigate to AllMIDI and click "OK."

4. Check the "Launch" radio button.

5. When you download a MIDI file by clicking it, Netscape converts the MIDI file to QuickTime, but it doesn't know to play the QuickTime movie. In the Finder, navigate to your Netscape downloads folder: the movie will have the same name as the MIDI file on the Net, but with a .MOV extension. Use a video player, (**Simple Player**, **Movie Player**, Sparkle, and so on) or SimpleText to play the movie.

See Also

Helper Application; Internet; MIDI; Netscape Navigator; Web Browser; World Wide Web

Alpha Editor

Alpha is an extensible text **editor** written by Pete Keleher. Unlike most applications that enable only limited customization of their basic features, almost everything about Alpha can be customized to fit your own personal style.

To customize Alpha, you use a special programming language called the Tool Command Language (Tcl). Using Tcl, you can rearrange or add to Alpha's menus, create macros that are executed at the touch of a key, or create sophisticated macro programs that interact with other applications.

Alpha is a modal editor; it behaves differently depending on the kind of file it is editing. Each mode can have entirely different menus, key bindings, and keyword colorization (syntax coloring). When you're editing a source code file written in **C**, for example, the menus, key commands, and keyword colorization are different than when editing an **HTML** document or a **Java** program. Alpha has 20 different modes, including ones for C, **C++**, **Fortran**, HTML, Java, **Pascal**, **Perl**, **PostScript**, and Tcl. Because the modes are created using Tcl, you can customize them to meet your own needs. You can also create new modes should the need arise.

```
┌─────────────────── puzzleMenu.c ───────────────────┐
  Requires: nothing
  Receives: WindowPtr, menu selection
  Changes:  nothing directly, all sorts of stuff depending on selection
  Returns:  Boolean value, true => menu selection handled
*/


Boolean PuzzleMenuDispatch (WindowPtr macWindow, long menuChoice)
{
   Boolean    handled   = false;    /* assume not handled */
   short      menuID     = HiWord(menuChoice);
   short      menuItem   = LoWord(menuChoice);
   OSErr      error      = noErr;
   WindowPtr  newWindow;

   if (menuID == kPuzzleMenuID)
   {
      handled = true;

/**********************************************************/
/* PuzzleMenuUpdate */
/**********************************************************/
/*
   Called from UpdateAppMenusHook()

   Requires: nothing
   Receives: WindowPtr
   Changes:  may change state of menu items
   Returns:  nothing
*/

void PuzzleMenuUpdate(WindowPtr macWindow)
{
   if (macWindow == nil)    /* no window */
   {
      EasyDisableMenu(puzzleG.puzzleMenu);            /* entire menu */
      EnableItem(puzzleG.puzzleMenu, kPuzzleSoundItem);  /* default sounds */
      EnableItem(puzzleG.puzzleMenu, kSetColorItem);     /* default color */
      EnableItem(puzzleG.puzzleMenu, kNewNoteItem);      /* new note window */
      return;
```

Alpha can interact with other applications and **development environments**. It can be used with the Metrowerks **CodeWarrior** and **Symantec C++** environments, as well as MacPerl and many others.

You can download Alpha from most large Mac software archives, or directly from the Alpha page at: **http://www.cs.umd.edu/~keleher/alpha.html.**

See Also

Alpha Version; C; C++; CodeWarrior; Editor; Fortran; HTML; Java; Pascal; Perl; PostScript; Symantec C++

Alpha Testing

Alpha testing is where a "rough working mockup" of the software, an **alpha version**, is tested for bugs or software glitches by the company's internal staff, rather than freelance testers or the public. Alpha testing occurs early on in the development a software or hardware product and enables developers to catch potential problems or glitches in-house before the next stage of development occurs and a beta version of the software is compiled.

See Also

Alpha Version; Beta Testing; Beta Version

Alpha Version

An alpha version of a software application is created very early in the development stage and is used internally by the company as a working model of the software. The alpha version is often the first time the software has been compiled from all the different code written to create a piece of software.

After the software has been compiled into a working alpha version, it often goes into a testing phase called **alpha testing**, where this "rough working mockup" of the software is tested for bugs or software glitches by the internal staff of the company. Alpha versions of software can be very unstable, and might not have the complete interface the public will see in the shipping version. It's not unusual to have a number of different alpha versions of the software as bugs are detected and features are added or withdrawn during this development stage. Alpha software is usually closely guarded by the company, and ideally, the public would never see the alpha version.

See Also

Alpha Testing; Beta Testing; Beta Version

Alphabetizing Filenames

You can alphabetize the **files** in any **active window** by holding down the **Option key** and choosing **Clean Up** By Name from the **Special menu.** If the window is set to View by Icon or Small Icon, all the icons snap to an invisible alignment grid and are listed in alphabetical order from left to right. If the window is set to **View by Name**, the contents already are alphabetized.

See Also

Active Window; Option Key; Special Menu; View Menu

Altair, *See Homebrew Computer Club*

Alto, *See Xerox PARC*

ALU, *See Microprocessors*

Amazon Trail

Amazon Trail is like the **Oregon Trail**, a voyage of exploration for ages 10 and up from MECC. This one takes you up the Amazon river in search of a medicinal plant to cure a strange disease that's wiping out an Inca village. Explore the rainforest and meet fascinating people from South America's past and present. Two other adventures in the same series take young explorers across Africa by bicycle, on the *Africa Trail,* and north to Alaska for the Gold Rush in *Yukon Trail.* Africa Trail traces the adventures of a world record setting bike expedition across the continent from the Sahara to Zaire.

Following the Yukon Trail to Dawson City, students fight the weather, claim jumpers, and lots more. These programs emphasize planning and decision-making skills. All these programs have the same excellent production values and well-planned student activities as the Oregon Trail. They're equally well suited for classroom and home use, and are sure to be enjoyed.

See Also
MayaQuest; Oregon Trail

Amelio, Gilbert

Dr. Gilbert F. "Gil" Amelio is the current chairman and chief executive officer of Apple Computer. He was appointed to the position in February of 1996, when Apple's board of directors asked **Michael Spindler** to step down.

Before coming to Apple, Dr. Amelio served as chairman and chief executive officer of National Semiconductor. Under his leadership, the company focused its strategy and significantly improved its financial results. During this time, Amelio also served on Apple's board of directors.

Prior to leading National Semiconductor, Amelio worked for Rockwell International, Bell Labs, and Fairchild Camera and Instrument. Amelio holds 16 patents, including a patent for the co-invention of the charge-coupled image sensor used in most consumer video cameras.

See Also
Spindler, Michael

America Online

One of the fastest-growing and largest **commercial online services**, with more than two million members who have access to a wide variety of discussion groups, news, travel, chat, and mail services. Commonly referred to as AOL.

America Online, like **CompuServe**, **Prodigy**, and the other commercial services, requires a monthly fee for membership. Members can connect for five hours per month without extra charge; beyond five hours they are billed an hourly fee for connection.

In return, members get a number of benefits, including:

- **Electronic mail** to other AOL members or, through gateways, to members of other online services or other parts of the **Internet**.

- News and reference materials online, including the Reuters and Associated Press newswires, magazines such as Time and Macworld databases, a news clipping service, stock reports.

- GNN, an Internet service.

- Travel and shopping services.

- More than 500 forums where people with similar interests can chat and share files.

- People Connection: Chat rooms and "auditoriums" where up to 2,000 people can meet celebrities online.

- Games and entertainment.

America Online offers an attractive graphical interface for browsing files and sending email (see the following figure). It also offers full access to the **Internet**, including **Gopher**, **WAIS**, **FTP**, and **Usenet**. Members can post free **home pages** on the **World Wide Web**.

You connect to AOL using its own software, which is available via FTP from **ftp://ftp.aol.com/mac/**. In early 1996, AOL announced that it had licensed Microsoft's Internet Explorer to be the standard, built-in Web browser for AOL members. Microsoft was expected to begin incorporating AOL software into Windows 95, so AOL can be accessed from the Windows 95 desktop. AOL also licensed Netscape Navigator as the standard Web browser for AOL's GNN Internet service.

When you first launch the America Online software, it will dial AOL using a toll-free number. You will be asked to select a permanent AOL phone number close to your home, as well as a secondary phone number to serve as a backup.

The AOL software will then hang up and redial using your permanent number. You will be asked to choose an AOL ID and to specify a password and a credit card that America Online will bill for your connection time. You will also have to fill in personal data.

If your phone has Call Waiting, you will need to temporarily disable it each time you connect to America Online by prefixing the America Online number with "*70" for touch-tone phones, or "1170" for pulse phones.

When you complete an America Online session, be sure to log off by choosing the "Quit" command from the "File" menu or by choosing the "Sign Off" command in the "Go To" menu. Otherwise AOL will disconnect after 30 minutes of inactivity—but you may have to pay for those 30 minutes of connection time.

See Also

AppleLink; BIX; Commercial Online Services; CompuServe; Email; eWorld; Internet; iWorld; Prodigy

AmoebArena, *See Arcade-Style Games; Crystal Crazy*

Amplifiers

An amplifier is a circuit that boosts the power of a signal. In the Macintosh world, it usually boosts the headphone-level signal at the audio output jack. The signal here is only a small fraction of a watt; depending on the **speaker** design, two to ten watts might be necessary for satisfactory levels. Amplifiers provide volume controls, and often also have tone controls, mixing inputs for the audio from a CD-ROM drive, and a headphone jack; some also have **spatial enhancement** circuits.

Although a built-in amplifier is usually supplied with computer speakers, any amplifier—from a compact stereo system to audiophile and home theater units—can handle the Mac's signal. It's your choice:

- Built-in amplifiers are easier to buy and install, don't take extra desk space (that is, they have no *footprint*), and are matched to the speaker with which they're sold. They can also be tuned to make up for deficiencies in the speaker, but this can be a danger: extreme tuning can make a bad speaker seem good on a specification sheet or in casual listening, but may add harshness or distortion that become irritating in day-to-day use.

- External amplifiers are usually higher quality, offer more control, and can provide other features including a radio receiver and inputs for tape, disc, and phonograph. Appropriate **shielded** speakers for this kind of amplifier, available at home theater and audiophile stores, are usually higher quality than those sold at computer dealers.

The relationship between the amplifier volume control and the Mac **Sound control panel** affects sound quality. For minimum noise, the Mac's volume control should be set to the top; speaker levels should then be adjusted at the amplifier. If even the lowest volume setting on an external amplifier is too loud or distorted, plug the Mac into a different amplifier input. The following figure shows the Sound control panel, properly set for multimedia speakers or an external amplifier.

Sound

Volumes ▼

This controls the external speaker or amplifer. It should be set to maximum.

This controls the internal speaker. Leave it off.

Mute ☒   ☐

Built-in   Built-in
Headphones

See Also
Speakers; Subwoofers

Analog Telephone Line

Ordinary telephone lines—those we use for voice and **modem** communications—are designed to transmit data in analog form. (The phone company refers to this as POTS, for Plain Old Telephone Service.)

Computer signals are in digital form. Although a digital signal consists of a series of pulses of two voltages that represent the ones and zeroes of digital data, an analog signal is one that continually varies in voltage (see the following figure). Telephones convert analog sound waves into analog electrical signals. Modems convert digital pulses into analog electrical signals.

Modems also transmit analog signals. The term *modem* is short for MODulator/DEModutor. The process of modulation converts the computer's digital signals to analog, and varies the electrical signal in frequency, wavelength and phase to represent information. Demodulation is when the modem takes the modulated analog signals and turns them back into pulses that represent the ones and zeros of digital data.

Analog telephone lines were designed with voice communications in mind, before the age of personal computers. As such, the quality of modem communications is limited by the quality of the analog lines, which varies. Problems that don't seriously affect voice communications, such as mild static and attenuation (a dropping of signal strength) can render modem communications at a certain speed impossible. Analog signals are fairly complex, and a small deterioration in the signal can make the data unreadable. When modems encounter a poor-quality analog line, they will automatically drop to a lower speed. Ultimately, it is the quality of analog lines that prevents modem communications from ever going much faster than today's 28.8Kbps top speed.

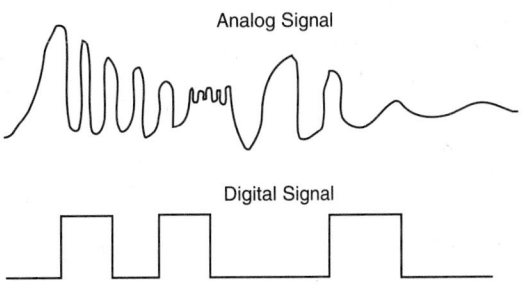

Analog Signal

Digital Signal

Most telephone companies offer an alternative communications line, the digital telephone line, also known as **ISDN**, which does not have the speed limitations of analog lines.

See Also

ISDN; Modems; Modem Cables and Connections

Anarchie

One of the two most popular **shareware FTP** clients, Peter N. Lewis's Anarchie has some advantages over Dartmouth College's **Fetch**, such as the capability to search **Archie** servers for files stored on **anonymous FTP** sites and the capability to perform multiple downloads simultaneously.

Anarchie has a number of other innovations for Macintosh users, including support for drag-and-drop, Internet Config, Apple Guide, and support for Open Transport.

You can install Anarchie anywhere on your hard disk, but its folder of bookmarks of popular sites should stay in the same folder as the Anarchie program itself. Then, follow these steps:

1. Connect to the Internet via **SLIP** or **PPP**, or by launching Anarchie itself.

2. Choose Preferences from the Edit menu.

3. Keep "Post Process Files" checked. This lets StuffIt Expander automatically debinhex and expand files that you download.

4. Click "Launch Internet Config." Anarchie uses Internet Config, another application by Peter Lewis, for most of its preferences. Internet Config enables you to specify the Archie server, Info-Mac, and Umich mirrors that are closest to you. You can also specify a destination folder for downloaded files.

After Anarchie is installed and running, you can browse one of the sites listed in its bookmarks, which include some of the popular Macintosh software archives.

Choose List Bookmarks from the File menu and double-click a site. Anarchie connects to the remote site and displays the directory listing. Double-clicking names with folders next to them takes you into that directory, and double-clicking on a file retrieves the file.

To retrieve a specific file, go to the FTP menu and choose Get. Anarchie opens the Get via FTP window, which provides fields for the name of the FTP host and the pathname of the file. You can also search for files, or have multiple listing windows open to multiple sites simultaneously.

Anarchie is scriptable and recordable via Apple's AppleScript and UserLand's Frontier, which can automate the file retrieval process.

Anarchie is an essential tool for retrieving files via **FTP** and anonymous FTP sites, and is available for $10. The latest version is available at **ftp://ftp.tidbits.com/pub/tidbits/tisk/tcp/**.

See Also

Anarchie; Anonymous FTP; Archie; Fetch; File Transfer Protocol; Internet

Andreessen, Marc

Inventor of **Mosaic**, the first graphical browser or client program for the **World Wide Web**, and currently vice-president for technology at Netscape Communications, Inc., a company he founded with Dr. James H. Clark.

Andreessen first conceived of Mosaic in 1992 when he was an undergraduate at the University of Illinois. Mosaic was developed in early 1993 by Andreessen and a team at **NCSA**, a high-performance computing and communications facility and research center at the University of Illinois. Mosaic was the first browser to make navigating the Internet fun and easy by the use of graphical icons, inline images, support for **WAIS** searches, and later, forms.

After leaving NCSA, Andreessen worked for Enterprise Integration Technologies (EIT) before he and Clark started Netscape. Andreessen and several other Mosaic team members went on to develop **Netscape Navigator**, which is currently the most popular **Web browser**.

See Also

Mosaic; WAIS; Web Browser; World Wide Web

A

Andromeda Effects Series 1 and 2

These effects come in two series. Series one is a collection of more standard filters, whereas series two allows pseudo 3D effects. Each series should be looked at separately.

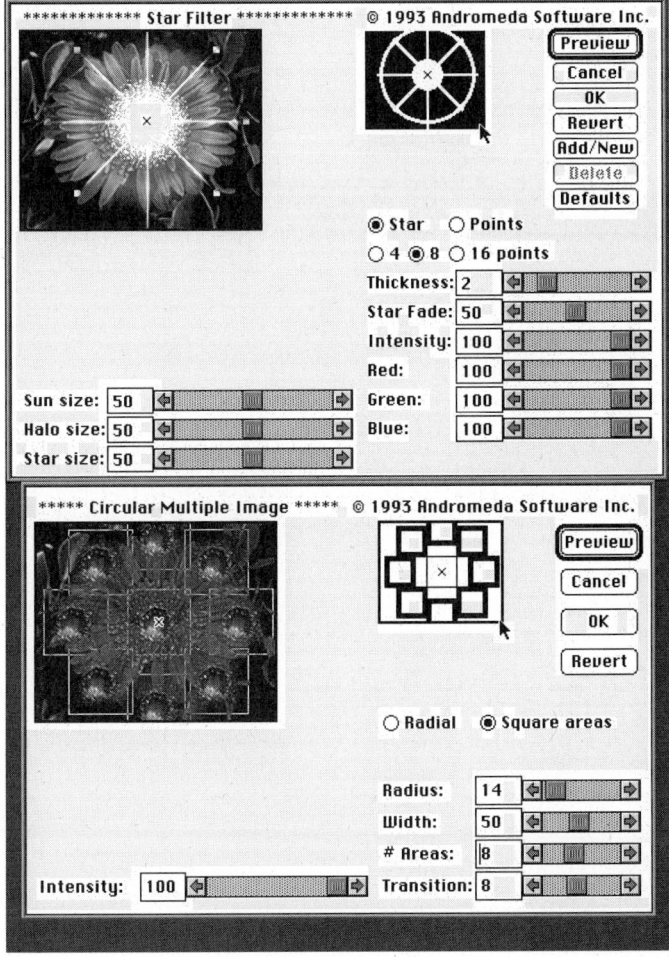

Series one contains the following filters:

1. CMulti—This filter (Circular Multiple Image) has no equal in any other package. It acts as a circular pantograph, painting a selected area in a circular pattern over the original image. A flower's center, as an example, can be painted in a ring around the flower. The user is given full control over the placement of the selected area and of the number of times the image will paint it. An option is to use a rectangular method for more rectangular effects.

2. Designs—This places a gridded design over the graphic. The grid can be sized, angled, and warped, leading to some interesting effects. A reverse grid can also be applied, making the image appear only as part of the grid.

3. Diffract—It places a diffraction lens over the selected graphic, resulting in a prism-like rainbow painted on the selection. All of the standard parameters are controllable by the user, as well as a "spokes" control which determines the number of times the diffraction will render in a circular pattern. Pushing this control all the way up creates a circular rainbow field.

4. Halo—Direction, Intensity, and Dimensions are controllable. This places a luminescent halo upon the selection.

5. Prism—This effect places a prismatic diffraction on the selection. Intensity, direction, and size are controllable.

6. Rainbow—The Rainbow effect places a rainbow spectrum on the selected graphic. The size, arc direction, width, fade amount, and intensity are user configurable. A special "Pot of Gold" checkbox allows a glowing golden aura to be rendered at the bottom of the rainbow. This is a very useful effect when applied to a photograph of a cloudy sky, and can even add a certain magic when applied carefully to an eye.

7. Reflection—This acts to place a reflected image on a user set distance in the graphic. This filter is perfect for enforcing a reflection of surrounding terrain in a still lake.

8. Star—This is the perfect filter for applying stars or star-like glows to your image. Color, fade, spokes, central core size and halo are all user determined.

9. sMulti, "Straight Multiple Image"—This effect is good for adding cloned sections to a graphic, internal tiling in a direction set by the user. The dimension and direction as well as the choice between parallel or square areas, or a combination of the two, is supported.

10. Velocity—This adds what an animator calls "speed lines" to a selected graphic. Speed lines are smears in one direction that indicate that the object was captured moving through space. This effect can be user adjusted in terms of the direction, intensity, fade, and size of the smears.

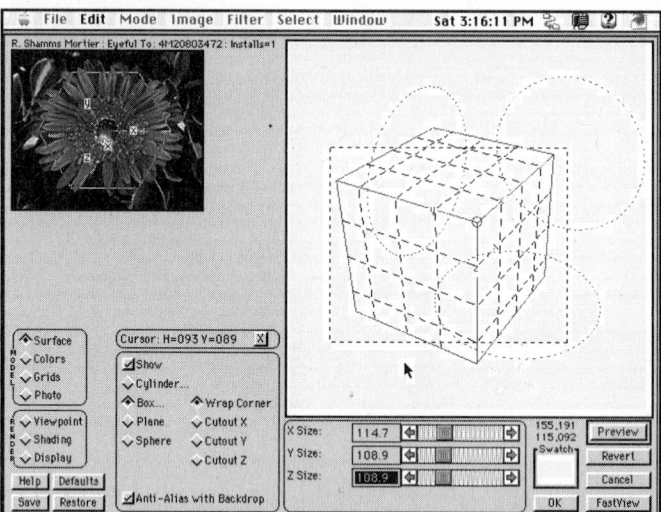

Series Two: Andromeda Effects 3D The Andromeda Effects 3D series two filters are represented by a singular interface. This effect allows you to wrap your selected image area on a sphere, box, cylinder or plane, just as if you were working in 3D space. You have control over the dimensions and placement of both the 3D shape and of the sizing and mapping of the graphic to be placed upon it. There are as many controls in this plug-in as there are in a dedicated 3D program as far as image mapping is concerned. You can adjust the lighting in 3D space, shadowing components, surface ambiance and reflectivity of the 3D object and of the image map, 3D viewpoint, visible grids, and colors. Background effects can also be added. It's a great tool for the 3D placement of logos without the expense of 3D software.

Angel Devoid: Face of the Enemy, *See Adventure Games*

Animaq

A high-end controller board used with frame-accurate tape decks. It outputs or digitizes video one a frame at a time. The software QuickPass, which comes with the board, will output any **QuickTime** movie to a video deck a frame at a time.

Although this produces very high-quality output, the video tape recorders that are required to work with this board are very expensive. If you need this quality output, you might consider using a service bureau to output your movie to tape.

See Also

Video Digitizing

Animation Compressor

This **QuickTime compressor** works best with sequences of computer-generated images. Computer images are reasonably clean compared to video images (the differences between frames is much less, because there's no camera shake, the lighting remains very constant, and there is no "noise" in the signal). Although the Animation Compressor does a very good job, it is not as efficient as the video compressors (**Cinepak**, **Apple Video**) because it is *lossless* (see Compression: Lossy versus Lossless).

Compression ranges from 1:1 to 7.5:1.

See Also

Asymmetrical Compressors; Compressor; Drop Frames; Spatial Compression; Symmetrical Compressors; Temporal Compression

Animation on the Internet

A number of ways are being developed to bring animation to the World Wide Web. Like many complex graphical elements presented over the Internet, however, their performance is limited by bandwidth, the capacity of the viewer's Internet connection to transmit data. Many users with slow dial-up modem connections have to wait agonizingly long to see a **Shockwave** animation or **Java** applet, for instance.

Shockwave is a plug-in for Netscape Navigator that allows animations created with Macromedia Director to be played within the Netscape browser window.

Netscape version 2.0 now supports the display of *Java applets,* small computer programs that use the Netscape window as a virtual computer. Some simple animation effects can also be created with **JavaScript**, Netscape's version of the Java programming language. Roaster is an application that also plays and creates Java applets.

Multipart GIF89a images, also supported by Netscape Navigator, are GIF images that consist of several separate frames or images. The series of images, when played together as a **multipart GIF**, provides simple animation on a **Web page** displayed by Netscape.

A number of virtual reality applications and plug-ins using **VRML** (Virtual Reality Markup Language) were beginning to appear as this was written, several of which were developed for the MacOS.

See Also

Audio on the Internet; Java; Multimedia; Shockwave; Video on the Internet; VRML

Animation Mapping, CD-ROM Images for

Animation mapping is a digital technique that allows you to map a sequence of still images on a 3D object, literally mapping an animation in an animation. The images have to be in a format that the animation software can read in. Color images can be wrapped on objects, and so can grayscale images. Grayscale images are often mapped to objects as bump maps, so that the lighter the surface area of the grayscale, the "higher" the perceived elevation of the bump. There are two special CD-ROMs that contain single frame image sequences that make excellent Animation Maps.

Motion Clips This is a collection of 752×480×24-bit JPEG sequences, over 8000 frames in all. Dozens of topics are represented: background gradations, clay animations, city nights, clouds, football games, Niagara Falls, toy trains and more. The average frame count is sixty, though some animations have higher numbers of frames. The size of the frames makes them perfect for background animations.

> Contact:
> Accadia Electronic Arts
> Buffalo, NY 14213-1413
> (716) 881-5215
> (716) 882-1774 FAX/BBS

Moving Textures This Precision Computer Graphics CD-ROM is dedicated to organic effects animations, and contains subjects like smoke, clouds, fire, steam and water. There are twenty-two image sequences in all, each one containing from three hundred to nine hundred frames. The caution is not to try to load these into Photoshop for translation, but to first take a sampling of them and write them to the hard disk. Photoshop does not appreciate trying to load a folder with 300 images or more. In addition to the color sequences (368×240 and 320×200 pixels), the CD contains fifteen grayscale sequences for bump mapping (192×120 pixels): boiling, burst, calm, disturb, jiggle, liquid, pour, rough, spots, swift, tide, water A and B, waves A and B. There is also one color image sequence of 300 frames of clouds in full 24-bit 736×480.

Contact:
Precision Computer Graphics
634 N. Glenoaks Blvd., Suite 367
Burbank, CA 91502-1024
(818) 842-6542

Animation Master

Animation Master is a very powerful 3D character animation tool. If you want to create animated characters, then Animation Master, or its less expensive sibling, **Martin Hash's 3-Dimensional Animation**, is probably the best choice of all tools currently available on the Macintosh.

Unfortunately, it is a very complicated program, and the documentation has tended to be poor (though there are efforts to create additional documentation; check the company's Web site.) If you already have experience using a 3D program and are interested in doing character animation, then definitely buy Animation Master. If you only want to do some 3D logos, maybe a virtual building, or have only a small need for character animation, consider another program.

Animation Master projects are called a *Choreography*. The Choreography window displays a 3D perspective of the world in which 3D models are arranged. These models are called *characters*. A character is, in essence, a model made up of different parts called *segments*. A human model might be made up of segments representing the body, neck, head, upper arm, lower arm, hand, and so on. To edit a character you select it in the Choreography window and then open the Character window, which displays just the segments that make up that model and how they are linked together. Segments are linked in a parent-child relationship. This linking is important when animating the object, so that when the arm moves, the hand and fingers move with it!

To add a segment (say a finger), you select the parent segment (the hand), and then click the Add Segment button in the toolbar, which opens the Sculpture window. In the Sculpture window you use the pen, lathe, and extrude tools to create the basic 3D objects. Animation Master provides powerful **spline** (curve) based modeling tools. You can add more control points and line segments to simple shapes, and then pull and manipulate those segments to create more complex shapes.

After there's a character in the choreography, it is animated along a path drawn in the Choreography window. The character can turn as the path turns, can face a target as it moves, or the character can actually bend along the path as it travels. The actions of the character are automated with scripts. A character can have a walking script, which stores the movement of the limbs of the character as it walks. This movement is independent of the distance the character actually travels. By applying the walking script, the character's feet and hands move as it moves along the path in the choreography. To make the movement accurate, you can define stride length for the character. This prevents the character's feet from appearing to slide as the character walks. Animation Master supports inverse kinematics.

A character's shape can be animated in three different ways: skeletal involves manipulating the position of the objects that make up the character, spine manipulates the objects themselves (bending the characters foot for example), and muscle manipulates individual surfaces of an object (use this for mouth movements.)

Animation Master offers a sophisticated set of character animation tools, but don't think it's a magic bullet. Realistic character animation is a complex business—this program just makes it easier.

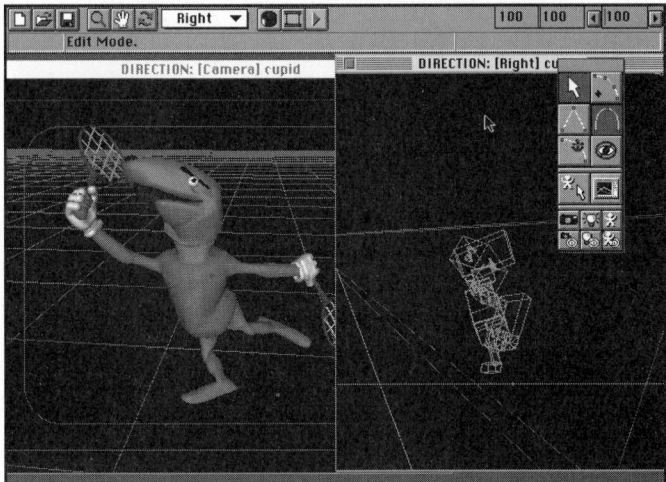

```
Right ▼        100  100  ◀ 100 ▶
Edit Mode.
DIRECTION: [Camera] cupid        DIRECTION: [Right] cu
```

See Also

3D; Animation; Extreme 3D; Infini-D; Martin Hash's 3-Dimensional Animation; Ray Dream Designer/Studio; Sketch!; StrataVision

Animation and Premiere, *See*
Premiere and Animation

Anonymous FTP

A way of accessing the contents of publicly available **FTP** (File Transfer Protocol) sites. FTP is a common way to connect to a **network**, access directories, or obtain files. FTP requires a username and a password if the user has been given access to a particular directory beforehand. Anonymous FTP allows users to use FTP as a "guest" and without a password, that is, anonymously.

See Also

File Transfer Protocol; Software Archives; TCP/IP

ANSI C, *See C*

ANTI Virus

This virus infects applications and files that resemble applications (like the Finder). ANTI does not infect the System file or document files. Applications do not have to be run to become infected. ANTI may damage applications so that they must be deleted and reinstalled.

See Also

CDEF Virus; CODE 1 Virus; CODE 352 Virus; Frankie Virus; INIT 17 Virus; INIT 1984 Virus; INIT 29 Virus; INIT 9403 Virus; INIT-M Virus; MacMag Virus; MBDF Virus; MDEF Virus; nVIR Virus; Scores Virus; T4 Virus; WDEF Virus; ZUC Virus

Anti-Virus Utility

Anti-virus utilities are designed either to stop computer **viruses** from infecting your disks, or find viruses that may be already be infecting your **hard disk** or **disks**. Computer viruses are very small programs or hidden bits of code in a program or document designed to somehow disrupt your computer. They can be as harmless as a virus that hides invisibly on your hard disk and each year on Valentine's Day displays a message that says, "Happy Valentine's Day"—or they can be as deadly as a virus that erases files or folders from your hard disk. Most viruses cause your computer to crash, **freeze up**, or engage in some sort of erratic behavior by adjusting some internal resources in your **System software**. Viruses are usually easily eradicated by using an anti-virus utility, and there are both commercial products and **shareware** products that are very effective at preventing and eradicating computer viruses.

There are a number of popular commercial anti-virus programs, including **Virex** from DataWatch and **SAM** from Symantec. There is also a very popular freeware anti-virus utility called Disinfectant that can be found on America Online in the Utilities forum or on the Internet at a variety of FTP sites. Disinfectant is both a free-standing utility and an extension that searches for viruses.

See Also

Crashes, System; SAM; System Software; Utility; Virex; Virus

AOL, *See America Online*

APDA

APDA, formerly the Apple Programmers and Developers Association, is Apple's primary distribution point for developer tools and information. APDA is the only place you can purchase many Apple developer tools and resources, such as **MPW** Pro, E.T.O., and the **Apple Developer Mailing**. The APDA catalog, known as the Apple Developer Catalog, includes all of these Apple resources, as well as an excellent selection of third-party development tools and books.

APDA carries everything from the latest hot programming environments to multimedia authoring tools to developer notes detailing the innards of Apple hardware.

APDA can be reached at:

>Apple Developer Catalog
>Apple Computer, Inc.
>P.O. Box 319
>Buffalo, NY 14207-0319
>
>US: (800) 282-2732
>Canada: (800) 637-0029
>International: (716) 871-6555
>Fax: (716) 871-6511
>Email: **apda@applelink.apple.com**
>Web: **http://devcatalog.apple.com**

API, *See Application Programming Interface (API)*

Apple III, *See Apple Computer, History*

Apple AudioVision 14 Display, *See Monitors, Common Models*

Apple Character

The Apple character (🍎) is accessed by using the keyboard shortcut Shift-Option-K. This particular character is not available in all **fonts**, but it is available in Apple's own system font, Chicago, among others.

The Apple character also appears on the Macintosh keyboard's Command key. Many people refer to the ⌘ key as the Apple key, because the Apple appears on the key. So if you hear someone say, "The keyboard shortcut is Apple-Q for Quit," they are referring to the ⌘ key.

See Also
Fonts; Option Key

Apple Computer, History

The history of Apple Computer starts long before the history of the Macintosh. In 1970, Apple Computer's two primary founders, **Steve Wozniak** and **Steve Jobs**, were introduced to each other by a mutual friend, Bill Fernandez. Fernandez was a classmate of Jobs, who was then in high school, and a neighbor of Wozniak, who was then 20 years old.

Jobs and Wozniak shared a number of common interests, including electronics and pranks. Both were loners more interested in tinkering with electronics than partying the night away.

When Wozniak was studying engineering at U.C. Berkeley, he and Jobs began building and selling a device of his own design. This "blue box" could mimic the tones used in long distance telephone switching to net the user free long distance calls. The two sold the devices door-to-door in the Berkeley dorms, and managed to make a nice profit doing so.

In 1975, Woz began attending meetings of the newly formed **Homebrew Computer Club**. He was intrigued by what he saw there: the new Altair computer, the very first personal computer. Although he would have loved to buy an Altair and start tinkering with it, he couldn't afford one, so he built his own. Wozniak's computer was based on the relatively inexpensive 6502 processor built by MOS Technology rather than the Intel 8800 in the Altair.

By that time, Steve Jobs was attending the club meetings as well. When Woz demonstrated his new computer, Jobs was impressed. He convinced Woz that they should try to sell the computers. Wozniak agreed after his employer, Hewlett Packard, decided to waive any rights they might have had to his invention.

On April 1, 1976, Apple Computer was founded as a partnership among Jobs, Wozniak, and **Ron Wayne**. Wayne worked with Jobs at Atari and had been convinced to join the partnership when Jobs offered him a 10 percent interest in Apple. The three partners set about creating the first Apple I computers, based on Wozniak's design.

Initially, these three had planned to sell the computers as bare-printed circuit boards, to which the buyers would add their own electronic components, power supply, and case. When they received their first major order from The **Byte Shop**, it was for finished computers, so they quickly changed their plan.

Conversation with Molly Tyson

As a longtime Apple employee, Molly Tyson helped shape Apple's documentation into a model for the industry; she now moves throughout the company doing management training through the Human Resources group.

Maclopedia: What was Apple like back in 1981, when you arrived?

Molly: In those days, a high percentage of users were programmers, so we had to provide technical information for them—BASIC commands, DIP switch settings, and pin numbers—while teaching novices basic computer literacy—how and why it's important to save your work on a disk. It was like a religious war when we discussed taking the technical reference out of the box, and we got lots of angry letters from hackers when we finally did.

But part of the fun of doing documentation for the Apple II and the Mac was that everyone was an avid user, so everyone always had a strong opinion about any changes to the product.

One of the challenges in documenting the Apple II and especially the Mac was that ease of use was a major selling point so there was pressure for the documentation to reflect that. One of the first commercials for the Mac showed a thin manual

floating gracefully down to the desktop while a stack of documentation from the other guy came crashing down with a thunk. When we added more features to the Mac, there was still pressure to keep the manuals small. If we'd had unlimited time to refine the interface and design the manuals, we probably could have kept the books small, but there was pressure to ship products at the earliest possible moment. This led to longer books and created friction with engineers who felt that Apple products didn't need documentation and marketers who wanted the documentation to re-enforce the ease-of-use message.

Everyone had an opinion about what users needed because we were all enthusiastic users of Apple products. One thing that helped bring some objectivity to the design process was user testing. We'd bring typical users in to use the products, and we'd sit on the other side of the glass taking notes. Inviting engineers to user testing helped resolve internal debates about the need to make features easier to use and how to document them.

Maclopedia: Did usability testing also change the way you designed the manuals?

Molly: Yes, we started using a lot more art. We had always understood graphics were important because the machine had a very visual interface. But we were struck by the way users skipped from illustration to illustration, without reading the text. Rather than trying to change the way they used manuals, we started putting more and more of the content into the illustrations. We had graphic designers as well as illustrators on staff, and a big part of their job was figuring out a book design that helped people find the information they needed. We also started hiring professional indexers because we realized how important it was to support random access to information.

Maclopedia: How did you handle electronic documentation?

Molly: At first we had separate departments doing electronic and print documentation, but that made it hard to design integrated documentation. Writers had a bias toward the medium they were most familiar with. So we encouraged them to learn to design in a variety of media so they could choose the best medium for the information they were trying to communicate. This was challenging because the tools were complicated

continues

to use. We were using QuarkXPress, a page layout program, for print documentation because we wanted writers to think visually. They needed to be comfortable using HyperCard for developing prototypes of electronic training, and they needed to learn a scripting language to develop online help. Ease of use doesn't always extend to the internal development environment!

AppleGuide, our online help system, originated in the Advanced Technology Group, but we took it over when it was time to make it practical and implementable. To make online help really helpful, you need hooks into system software. So another breakthrough was when people from the online help transferred into the engineering group.

It was hard to give up control of the help design, so we worried that it wouldn't be as effective instructionally once it moved out of the documentation group. But if we hadn't given up control, it might never have gotten into the interface. It was a tradeoff. Fortunately, instructional people like Jim Palmer— who was a major architect of the AppleGuide interface and scripting language—transferred into the engineering group along with the code, so they were in a good position to influence its development.

Maclopedia: What's stayed constant over the years at Apple?

Molly: One thing that has remained constant is people focusing on what users really want. We try not to get so enamored of any technology that we lose sight of what users are trying to do with the computer. Of course, as the company has gotten more focused on costs, it is harder to do the right thing. It doesn't feel good to make compromises to meet a price point or a marketing window of opportunity.

Maclopedia: So how have business realities like cost changed what it's like to work at Apple?

Molly: When I came there was no discussion of cost. That was an incredible luxury. And it was one of the reasons that Apple didn't feel much like a business. There were huge discussions about the best way to do things, not just best for the customer, but what would be cool, or insanely great, as Steve Jobs said. Let's try and do it that way, even if it seems impossible. At first, the new emphasis on cost felt healthy because there was something almost indulgent about not worrying about what something cost when the

customer ended up paying for it in the end. But as margins got squeezed, it went beyond fun. For instance, project managers would try to give us a cost target for documentation. It's one thing to say make it shorter, but it's different to be told the documentation can only cost x dollars.

The pressure to get products to market quickly has also increased. There was always a feeling of urgency to get products to market, but it stemmed from an excitement to get to finish. Now there is more focus on the competition and hitting a window of opportunity. This means throwing features out if necessary to meet a deadline. That goes against the original idea of building the best possible product.

Maclopedia: So on balance would you say the changes over time have been good?

Molly: I am not one of those people who spend a lot of time thinking about the good old days. There were aspects that were indulgent and manipulative, for instance, encouraging the illusion that we were all one big family and then realizing through layoffs that we're just a business after all. I think we all have to take responsibility for some of the new business realities. We have to focus more on costs because we haven't stayed far enough ahead. When our products were significantly different, we had the luxury to spend money and take time on research. With a narrower gap, we have to focus on costs and time to market.

So there is much more focus on process and being accountable for costs and schedule. There are "out of bounds" reviews when expenses exceed forecasts and schedules slip. Process wasn't part of our vocabulary in the old days. There was a freedom to that, but there were times when process would have been helpful. For example, there's no need for creative freedom when you are doing a simple revision to a product. Following a consistent process could have made us more efficient. In the ideal world, I'd like to see more of the garage mentality for cutting-edge products and consistent process for iterations.

Another big change has been the proliferation of products and the complication of the product line. It's harder for people like me to be evangelists. I still feel a lot of pride when people find out I work at Apple. But then when they say which Mac should I buy, I don't have a clue. I'm not even sure which model I have. You can't just say PowerBook, or get a Power Mac, because then they say which one. I think that's something we need to address going forward because our customers are our best salespeople, and we need to simplify the message.

The truth is there is still a lot of really exciting stuff in the works at Apple, and that makes it fun to work here despite all the emphasis on cost, total quality management, and time to market. Ideas don't always get funded ahead of time, but one way or another the good ideas get implemented. We didn't ask permission to work on AppleGuide; we found a way to do it on the side. Once we had something to show, we got the funding. I think that happens a lot at Apple. Fortunately, we have a lot of creative people at Apple and they don't always ask permission to work on projects that interest them.

Maclopedia: How have people changed?

Molly: In some ways, they haven't changed. We still have people juggling bowling pins in the lobby. You'll walk by a conference room and hear someone playing classical music on a piano. People still dress casually. We still have the loan-to-own program. It's neat to know that every single person in the company uses the technology. We don't hand out T-shirts for every project anymore, but we still have a company store full of Apple paraphernalia. But I've noticed that even the store has become more cost-conscious in the products they carry. (They used to advertise wind surfing sails with the Apple logo.)

I think that we are looking for more experience in the people we hire than we used to, and I have mixed feelings about that.

When I got hired, I had very little experience as a technical writer. I was a journalist. But I think they hired me for my writing ability, intelligence, and creativity and took it as a challenge that they could teach me the technology. I teach classes now on interviewing, and I try to encourage managers to look for the skills they need and not get too hung up on experience doing the exact job they're hiring for.

One thing that hasn't changed—and one reason I'm still here—is that Apple still values creativity. It's not a coincidence that we've had breakthroughs in desktop publishing and multimedia. People who work here are creative, so they tend to design products that help people be more creative.

Another thing I like that hasn't changed over the years is the way people treat each other. Managers don't get very far if they try to pull rank. People are more interested in the quality of your ideas than in your position or supposed expertise in a subject. As a trainer, for example, I have to know my stuff. People don't feel they have to have expertise on a subject to weigh in on it. You can't just say I'm the expert or I'm the manager and get away with it.

Maclopedia: So where does Mac go from here?

Molly: I think we have to simplify the product line. We have to do a better job of promoting the hit products that we are developing. And clearly we can't rest on our laurels. We have to keep developing products that capture people's imagination.

I am still a big fan. I get frustrated when I hear people whining or pointing fingers at other parts of the company. If things aren't working, I want to put my energy into fixing them.

To help finance the first order, Jobs sold his Volkswagen minibus and Woz sold his programmable calculator. Most of the electronic components were purchased on "Net 30" terms, so Apple did not have to make payment until 30 days after it received the parts. By working furiously, they managed to finish the computers and collect payment from The Byte Shop before the bills came due.

After this initial sale, Jobs planned to go back into debt to build more computers. Wayne was uncomfortable with the idea of being responsible for 10 percent of Apple's debt, so he resigned. Jobs began looking elsewhere for investors. He found one in **Armand C. "Mike" Markkula**. Markkula invested $92,000 of his own money for a one-third interest in Apple.

Markkula brought in **Mike Scott** to be president of the new company, and on January 2, 1977, Apple Computer was incorporated.

While Jobs was concerning himself with the business of Apple, Wozniak was busy designing the successor to the Apple I. The Apple II, which was introduced in April of 1977, was the world's first complete personal computer. It included a fully assembled computer in a case with a keyboard and expansion options.

In many ways, the Apple II was the beginning of the personal computer revolution we are still feeling today. Although primitive by today's standards, the Apple II was the first computer ordinary people could use without knowing how it worked inside. It spawned the modern software industry and made computers more accessible to non-hobbyists.

The Apple II's massive popularity quickly made Apple the largest of the new wave of personal computer companies. From its modest beginnings, Apple grew very quickly. When Apple went public on December 12, 1980, Jobs, Wozniak, and 40 other Apple employees became instant millionaires, a pattern that has since been repeated by many up-and-coming computer companies.

In the late 70s, Apple decided to pursue the business market more aggressively and designed a new computer to do so. The Apple III had an impressive set of specifications. It ran twice as fast as the Apple II, included more **RAM**, and had many of the features that most Apple II users eventually added to their machines. It could not run Apple II hardware without using a slower emulation mode, however.

From the start, the Apple III was a flop. It was Apple's first major failure. The problems were numerous, from missed specifications to components that would come loose. Sales were disappointing, and, despite several improvements, the project was finally killed in 1984, the same year the Macintosh was introduced.

Following the Apple III fiasco, Mike Scott was forced out as president and replaced by Markkula. Jobs began looking for a new CEO, eventually recruiting **John Sculley** from Pepsi in April 1983.

Meanwhile, back in 1979, two important projects were started within Apple. The first was the **Lisa**, which was to become the next generation business computer.

The other was the Macintosh, which began as a small research project headed by **Jef Raskin**.

Although technologically advanced, the Lisa was Apple's second failure. Introduced in 1983, the Lisa was overpriced and underpowered. Sales never lived up to expectations, and the Lisa and Macintosh groups were consolidated under the direction of Steve Jobs in November 1983. Two months later, Apple introduced the Macintosh.

Although the Macintosh was a better success than the Lisa, it too was overpriced and underpowered. It wasn't expandable and offered only a small monochrome display. Despite the best efforts of Apple **Evangelism**, there were very few programs that ran on the new machine.

Again, sales were disappointing. Soon after, the Macintosh was followed up by the Fat Mac, which offered much more memory. More importantly, though, was the introduction of the LaserWriter as a part of the Macintosh Office, a bold vision of networked workgroup computing. The LaserWriter, combined with PageMaker, gave the Macintosh its killer application: desktop publishing.

By 1985, Jobs had begun to be more of a liability than an asset to Apple. His tendency to meddle in projects and his confrontational style were rubbing many people the wrong way. In April, Sculley received approval from the board of directors to remove Jobs from his position as executive vice president and manager of the Macintosh division.

Less than one month later, on the eve of a business trip to China, Sculley learned from **Jean-Louis Gassée** that Jobs planned to use Sculley's absence as an opportunity to have him removed from his position. Sculley scheduled an emergency executive staff meeting, at which every member of the staff backed Sculley rather than Jobs. On May 31, Jobs was stripped of his operational responsibility and given the title of chairman, which was essentially a powerless figurehead role. Four months later, Jobs resigned from Apple Computer to start **NeXT**, a computer company designed to create computers specifically targeted at the higher education market.

Under John Sculley's leadership, Apple entered a period of massive growth. During Sculley's reign, Apple grew from $600 million in sales to almost $8 billion. The Macintosh came into its own with the introduction of the expandable SE and II series, and flourished with more powerful software and hardware.

In October 1991, Sculley led Apple into a groundbreaking alliance with its former arch rival, IBM. The IBM alliance consisted of three parts: Kaleida, Taligent, and PowerPC. The first was to develop innovative multimedia software, and the second was to carry forward Apple's "Pink" project and create an **object-oriented** operating system. But the third would be the most successful.

The *PowerPC alliance* brought together not only IBM and Apple, but Motorola as well to create a new generation of advanced microprocessors. In March 1994, Apple delivered on its part of the bargain by introducing the first Power Macintosh computers based on the PowerPC processor.

During the year leading up to the PowerPC introduction, Apple went through some tough times. The disappointing reception received by its highly touted Newton PDA didn't help matters. In June of '93, Apple's board replaced Sculley as CEO with then Chief Operations Officer **Michael Spindler**.

Spindler oversaw the successful transition to the PowerPC architecture and the beginning of Macintosh cloning. Apple's financial difficulties did not go away, however, and in 1996, the board appointed **Gilbert Amelio** to the positions of chairman and chief executive officer.

In 1996, the computer industry pundits are once again predicting the death of Apple Computer. Others say that if Apple makes it through its latest round of financial troubles, it may be reborn yet again.

See Also

Amelio, Gilbert; Byte Shop, The; Evangelism; Jean-Louis Gassée; Homebrew Computer Club; Jobs, Steve; Lisa; Macintosh, History; Markkula, A.C. "Mike"; NeXT; Raskin, Jef; Scott, Mike; Sculley, John; Spindler, Michael; Wayne, Ron; Wozniak, Steve

Apple Computer Internet Sites

Apple Computer provides a number of resources for Macintosh users on its **World Wide Web** and **FTP** sites on the **Internet**.

The main Apple Home Page on the Web (see the following figure) presents breaking news about Apple and its products, as well as links to resources for developers, support for users of hardware and software, and phone numbers to Apple offices.

Apple's **Web site** contains links to special sites for publishers, educators, multimedia developers, and people with disabilities. The following table lists various Apple resources, depending on what you want to do.

Apple Internet Resources

Purpose	*Address*
Main home page	**http://www.apple.com/**
Software and hardware info	**http://www.info.apple.com/**
Download software	**ftp.info.apple.com**
Problem or question about an Apple product	**http://til.info.apple.com/ til/til.html** (This Tech Info Library (TIL) contains a searchable index of answers to questions sent in by Macintosh users over the years.)

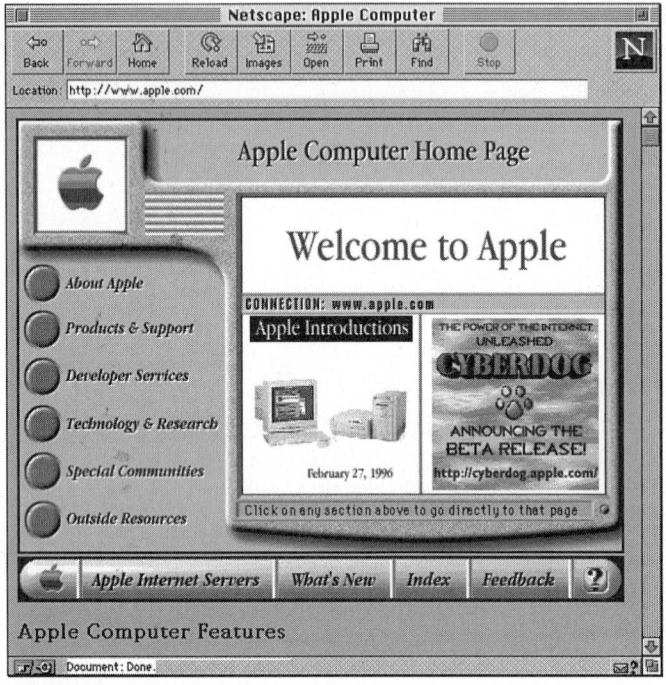

See Also

Apple Internet Router; Apple Internet Connection Kit; Apple Internet Server Solution; Apple IP Gateway; Apple Network Servers; AppleLink; AppleSearch; Cyberdog; eWorld; FTP; Internet; World Wide Web

Apple Desktop Bus (ADB)

Every method of data entry on the Macintosh, be it a **keyboard**, **mouse**, **trackball**, **touchpad**, **joystick**, **graphics tablet**, and so forth, uses the same connection and data transmission vehicle—the **Apple Desktop Bus (ADB)**.

ADB has been the port of choice since the introduction of the Mac SE in 1987. Most Macs today provide two ADB **ports** (but one **bus**). ADB ports let you chain input devices from one to another, connecting multiple peripherals to the same port. Up to 16 devices can be supported by a single ADB port, although Apple recommends that you limit connections to three for optimal performance.

All devices attached to the ADB port communicate with the Mac over a single bus. Each input device has a unique identifying address and the Mac can address more than one address at a time. The CPU controls the flow of information into the Mac. Each device requests permission to send data across the bus. The CPU cannot be interrupted while it is processing, but will only receive information when it asks for it. This is called **asynchronous serial communications**, because data does not automatically flow down the pipeline, but flows intermittently based on a signal from the CPU. Because the ADB is a serial bus and data bits flow one after another, it is not as fast as the parallel flow of information provided by **SCSI** buses. The ADB transmits data at a maximum speed of 4,500 bits per second (bps). The ADB connector is simple—four pins: one to send the ADB signals, one to supply the required power (five volts) to the input device, one to act as a ground wire, and a fourth to let you start up the Mac from your keyboard.

The Mac communicates with data input devices over the ADB via two transceiver chips: one on the logic board and the other in the input device. The **ADB Transceiver** converts bus signals from the Mac's Cuda (ADB Manager) chip into a signal that is understood by the input device. The exchange of information is further managed by one or more Versatile Interface Adapter (VIA) chips that provide RAM and storage support for the transaction.

When you press a key on your keyboard, a switch is activated that changes the flow of current from the key to the input device's microprocessor. The microprocessor sends a binary representation of the key's character to the buffer. The buffer can hold five or six characters.

The keyboard's ADB Transceiver sends a service request to the Mac's CPU. The keyboard's ADB Transceiver will respond only if the Mac is available to receive data. If the CPU is available, the Mac's ADB Transceiver sends an interrupt signal to the VIA chip, which tells the Mac operating system that there is incoming data. The Cuda chip uses the Mac's ADB Transceiver to poll all data input devices to find out which one is sending data. The keyboard's ADB Transceiver responds to the poll and the Cuda sends the ADB Transceiver a "Talk" command. The keyboard then sends the contents of the buffer to the Mac. The data is sent to the CPU as bursts of electric currents (measured in the strength and length of volts)—very low for "0" and very high for "1."

When the Mac's ADB Transceiver has received the contents of the buffer, it in turn passes the data to the VIA. The VIA sends a message to the Mac Operating System's Event Manager, which passes it to the Toolbox Event Manager; the Toolbox displays the character on the screen or carries out the key combination, and awaits the next instruction.

See Also

Bar Code and Magnetic Stripe Readers; Graphics Tablets; Joysticks; Keyboards; Logic Board Upgrade; Mouse; Pen/Handwriting Devices; Power Mac Logic Boards; SCSI Port; Serial Port; Trackballs; Touchpads; Touch Screens

Apple Developer Mailing

Apple Developer Mailing is one of the most important sources of up-to-date software and programming information for developers. Each monthly mailing includes the latest in the Developer CD Series, a set of CD-ROMs containing the latest system software, software development kits (**SDKs**), and developer documentation. There are three kinds of developer CDs that rotate throughout the year. The System Software CD concentrates on the latest in Apple System Software and Extensions, including versions of the system localized in over 30 different languages. Accompanying the System Software CD are the MacOS SDK CDs, which include complete SDKs for all current system software Extensions. The Tool Chest edition of the CD includes a wide variety of tools to help developers create great Mac programs. Finally, the Reference Library CD includes electronic versions of all of the important developer documentation, such as *Inside Macintosh*.

In addition to the Developer CDs, the mailing includes Apple Directions, a report on the current state of the Macintosh development business. Apple Directions often contains useful information about the future direction of Apple technologies. Also, the mailing frequently includes additional information on Apple technologies in the form of white papers discussing overall strategies and future directions.

The Developer Mailing is available only from **APDA**, through the Developer Catalog. A yearly subscription to the Developer Mailing costs about $150.00.

See Also

APDA; SDK

Apple Directions, *See Apple Developer Mailing*

Apple Disk Tools

The Apple Disk Tools disk is part of the Apple System Install set of **disks**, or the **CD-ROM disc** that came with your Macintosh. The Disk Tools disk contains a scaled-down version of the Macintosh operating system that enables you to **boot** your Macintosh from this disk. If for some reason you are not able to **startup** your Macintosh from the startup disk, you could then use the Disk Tools disk to start up your Mac and try to remedy or repair the situation. If, for example, you get an icon of a disk at startup with a blinking question mark rather than a **Happy Mac** icon, the computer is telling you that the Mac can't find a usable system to boot up from. You can insert the Apple Disk Tools disk and the system boots up from this disk, enabling you to look at your **System Folder**, run diagnostic utilities, and so on, to try and find out why the Macintosh is not booting from the startup system.

Besides containing a bootable version of the system, the Apple Disk Tools disk also contains Apple's free disk repair utility **Disk First Aid**, which you can use to repair some common disk errors, and **Apple's HD SC Setup** utility (its name is Apple HD Setup in System 7.5 and higher) enables you to test and initialize Apple hard disks. If you have the Apple system on **CD-ROM**, rather than on disks, a folder appears on the CD-ROM called Disk Tools, which contains approximately the same contents as the Apple Disk Tools disk.

See Also

Apple HD SC Setup; Boot; CD-ROM; Disks and Drives; Disk First Aid; Happy Mac Icon; Startup; System Folder

Apple Event

An Apple event is a message, with some data attached to it, that one application receives from another application.

Whenever two applications share data, they must use a common protocol, so that each can understand the data. An Apple event follows the Apple Event Interprocess Messaging Protocol defined by Apple Computer. The gory details (and they *are* gory) are beyond the scope of this discussion.

An Apple event tells an application to do something, or provides information an application needs to get work done. Each Apple event is a kind of message. Different messages have very different purposes.

To differentiate between various messages, each Apple event has an event class and an event ID. These are analogous to a file's creator and type. The event class and ID uniquely identify each kind of Apple event.

Apple events are organized into *suites* of related Apple events. There are suites of events devoted to text manipulation, spreadsheets, core application behavior, and so forth. One of the suites is the required suite of Apple events. These are the events that *all* applications should support.

The four required Apple events are

- Open application
- Quit application
- Open document
- Print document

The System and the Finder rely on these events to control other applications in a **multitasking** environment.

If a program does not support Apple events, the System can still work around the problem some of the

time. But Apple events are the future, and the future is now. As a programmer, you absolutely should support the four required Apple events if no others.

Most Apple events have data attached to them. Precisely what data is attached depends on the nature of the event. Apple Computer maintains an official registry of these events that specifies the class, ID, and parameters for each event. Applications can also define their own custom event types if none of the events in the registry is appropriate.

The System and Finder are not the only programs that send Apple events to other applications. Any application capable of receiving Apple events can send Apple events as well. Strictly speaking, applications cannot send events directly to one another—they must use the Apple Event Manager (see the following figure).

The Apple Event Manager relays events from one application to another, and takes care of relaying any reply back to the originator as well.

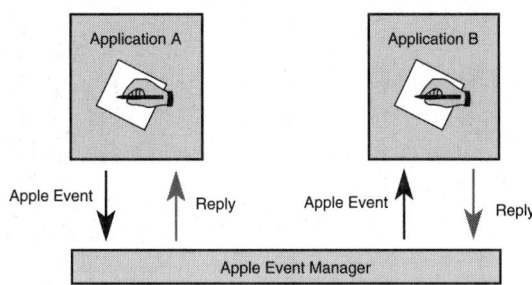

Apple events are the foundation upon which a number of important Apple technologies are built. An application must be able to respond to Apple events in order to be scriptable using **AppleScript**, **Frontier**, or any other **Open Scripting Architecture (OSA) scripting** language. In fact, the Apple events an application understands and how it responds to them define its scripting interface.

Some scriptable applications are also *recordable*. That is, the user's actions can be recorded and played back as a script. In order to be recordable, an application must not only respond to Apple events from other applications, but also use Apple events internally. In this sort of *factored* application, the human interface is separated from the core of its code. Therefore, it must send Apple events to itself to relay user input to the part of the program that acts upon that input. In this way, the Apple Event Manager can "listen in" on the Apple events to record a user's actions.

Apple events and scriptability are also at the heart of AppleGuide and OpenDoc. AppleGuide uses Apple events to manipulate applications and demonstrate how to accomplish certain tasks, and OpenDoc uses Apple events to accomplish much of the communication among running parts.

See Also

AppleGuide Extension; AppleScript; Frontier; Open Scripting Architecture (OSA); Scripting

Apple Extended Keyboard

The Apple Extended Keyboard is a versatile, ergonomically designed keyboard with 15 programmable function keys, and an adjustable keyboard angle for typing comfort.

See Also

Apple Desktop Bus; Keyboards

Apple File Exchange

Apple File Exchange is a utility program from Apple that enables you to mount, read, translate, and write files from a DOS disk onto your Macintosh. These days, in Macs using System 7.5 and higher, the capability to read and write DOS disks and files is part of the system software controlled through an **extension** called **PC Exchange**. This extension enables you to mount PC disks, and works in conjunction with **Macintosh Easy Open**, which translates the PC files into readable Mac files.

With PC Exchange, you insert a DOS-formatted disk and it mounts right on the **desktop** like a Mac disk. You can move, copy, and delete files as you would

normally. However, with Apple File Exchange, you **launch** Apple File Exchange and then insert the DOS disk. The DOS disk's contents appear in a window, and you select the items you want copied onto your hard disk. You then press the Translate button, and the selected files are translated into Macintosh files and placed on your hard disk (see the following figure).

PC Exchange has a number of other advantages over Apple File Exchange, especially after you've put the

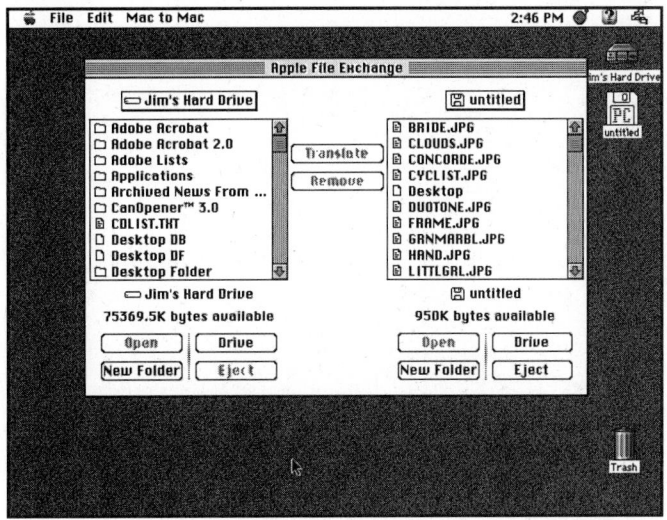

DOS files on your drive. With PC Exchange, you **double-click** the file and it opens in the Mac version of the program that created it, or you can designate a similar type of Mac program to open it instead. But with Apple File Exchange, the only file that translated well was a text file that matched the corresponding Mac file exactly. If, for example, you translate a DOS WordPerfect file with Apple File Exchange and you have the Mac version of WordPerfect, it would open right up. But if you didn't have WordPerfect, in many cases you were stuck. Macintosh Easy Open changed all that by doing the file translation for you and enabling you to open the PC file in a similar Macintosh application (similar meaning you'd open a PC word processing file in a Macintosh word processing application.)

To read and translate DOS files using Apple File Exchange, follow these steps:

1. Launch Apple File Exchange.

2. Insert a DOS disk in the disk drive.

3. Select the files you want to translate.

4. Select where on your hard disk you want the translated files to be stored.

5. Click the Translate button.

See Also

Desktop; DOS/Windows Conversions; Disks; Double-Click; Extensions; Launching a Program; PC Exchange

Apple HD SC Setup

Hard disks have to be initialized before use in a Macintosh (although most Mac hard disks are already initialized for you at the factory). Apple includes its own **utility** program for formatting Macintosh hard drives called Apple HD SC setup. (Its name has been shortened to Apple HD Setup in System 7.5 and higher.) This utility is found on Apple's Disk Tools disk and enables you to initialize a hard disk as a Macintosh hard disk and create hard disk partitions as well.

If you feel a disk may be damaged, or its driver outdated, you can use Apple HD Setup to test the disk in question. You can update the driver on a hard disk but only if it's an Apple brand hard disk. If you buy a third-party hard disk, it has its own formatting software and its own driver software built in.

See Also

Disks, Initializing; Hard Disks; Utility

Apple Internet Connection Kit

An integrated group of third-party software packages provide by Apple Computer that allows a Macintosh to connect to the Internet, download files, and navigate **Internet** and **World Wide Web** sites.

The connection kit includes:

- **Netscape Navigator** for World Wide Web browsing.

- Claris Emailer Lite for **electronic mail**.

- **Fetch** for accessing **FTP** sites.

- Apple Internet Dialer software for registering with an **Internet service provider**.

- **StuffIt Expander** for **decompressing/decoding** files.

- **NewsWatcher** for reading and posting to **Usenet** newsgroups.

- **NCSA Telnet.**

- Apple's QuickTime VR Player.

- Adobe **Acrobat Reader**.

- MacPPP.

- **RealAudio** Player.

MacTCP, however, is not included in the package, so users will have to obtain that from another source (such as the disk that accompanies the Hayden book *Internet Starter Kit for Macintosh*).

Almost all of the software in the package is freely downloadable from the Internet itself, but the package provides a starting point for an office or a local area network without an Internet connection.

The Apple Internet Dialer lets users sign on with an Internet Service Provider within a few minutes, and AppleGuide online tutorials provide information about connecting to newsgroups and other Internet related subjects.

See Also

Acrobat Reader; Decoding/Decompressing Files; Email; Fetch; FTP; Internet; Internet Service Provider; MacTCP; NCSA Telnet; Netscape Navigator; Network Communications; NewsWatcher; RealAudio; StuffIt Expander; TCP/IP

Apple Internet Router

A router is software that allows two or more local worksgroups to be connected, either to each other using industry-standard network types such as LocalTalk, Ethernet, and Token Ring, or to the **Internet**.

If a Mac running the Apple Internet Router is already connected to the Internet, the router can also provide Internet access for other users on the network. Wide

Area Extensions can be added to link AppleTalk networks using X.25 or **TCP/IP**, the protocol of the Internet.

See Also
Internet; MacTCP; Network Communications; TCP/IP

Apple Internet Server Solution
An all-in-one bundle of software and hardware designed around a Macintosh set up to function as a World Wide Web server.

Software included with the 2.0 version of the server package includes **WebSTAR** server software; the **PageMill** and BBEdit HTML editing programs; **Netscape Navigator**; **RealAudio Server**; MacDNS domain name server software; and HomeDoor 1.0, which allows a Web site administrator to serve multiple domain names from a single server.

The server software comes with **CGI** scripts to create imagemaps as well as customizable **Web page**s and **forms**.

Also included is **AppleSearch** 1.5, an application that allows a **Webmaster** to index key documents on a server so **client** software that accesses your **Web site** can search for its contents by keywords.

Two PowerPCs are offered as options for the Web server computer: the 7250/120 with 16MB of RAM, or the 8550/132 with 24MB of RAM.

See Also
AppleSearch; Apple Network Server; CGI; Imagemap; Internet; InterSLIP; Netscape Navigator; RealAudio; Server; Webmaster; Web Site, How to Organize; WebSTAR

Apple IP Gateway
An Apple IP Gateway is a gateway that lets an AppleTalk network connect to a **TCP/IP** network, such as the **Internet**.

In conjunction with **Apple Internet Router** software, the gateway provides **IP** access to any Macintosh computer on any AppleTalk network. Users on the local network can then access **Internet services** such as **FTP**, **Gopher**, and the **World Wide Web**. Apple

IP Gateway also provides **Apple Remote Access** users with remote access to IP and AppleTalk services.

The gateway assigns and maintains dynamic **IP address**es for computers on the network, allowing network administrators to use a single **MacTCP** configuration for all IP users.

TIP For more information go to **http://product.info.apple.com/productinfo/datasheets/ss/ipgateway.html**.

See Also
Apple Internet Connection Kit; Apple Internet Router; Apple Internet Server Solution; FTP; Gopher; Internet; IP; IP Address; MacTCP; Network/Communications; Internet; Web Server; WebSTAR; World Wide Web

Apple K-12 Personal Internet Solution
A bundle of software programs and hardware designed to allow an educator with a computer to connect to the **Internet**.

The package includes a modem, **Netscape Navigator**, Eudora, **InterSLIP**, and four reference CDs.

See Also
Internet; InterSLIP; Netscape Navigator; Software, Educational, K-6; Software, Educational, 7-12; Teachers, Macintosh and

Apple Key
The **modifier key**, a.k.a. the **Command key**, is also referred to as the Apple key because the Apple logo is on the Command key on Macintosh keyboards, just to the left of the Command key symbol (⌘). The Command key is the most often-used modifier key in keyboard shortcuts and is unique to the Macintosh.

You can add the Apple symbol to a document by using the keystroke combination Shift-Option-K.

See Also
Command Key; Modifier Key

Apple Logo

Apple's logo, a rainbow-colored apple with a bite missing, is one of the world's best-recognized corporate logos. It was designed by Rob Janov, then creative director at Regis McKenna, Apple's public relations firm.

The rainbow apple logo was not the first logo Apple used, however. Apple's first logo, a detailed picture of Isaac Newton sitting under an apple tree, was designed by the third and least-known Apple founder, **Ron Wayne**.

This original logo was not used for very long. **Steve Jobs** felt it wasn't bold enough for the company he was creating and hired Regis McKenna to create the logo we all know today. Because of the close multicolored stripes, reproducing the Apple logo can be quite a challenge (for printers, for example). As a result, it has been called one of the most expensive logos ever designed.

See Also

Jobs, Steve; Wayne, Ron

Apple Macintosh Color Display, *See Monitors, Common Models*

Apple Menu

This customizable pull-down menu, located on the far left side of the menu bar, is indicated by a small Apple logo icon. It enables you to put your most frequently used applications, folders, and documents on this menu for easy access or instant launching. You can also put **Desk Accessory** items there, such as the calculator or notepad, that will be available to you for instant use even when you have another application running. For example, if you're writing a business letter and need to do some math, you can go to the **Apple menu** and select the Calculator Desk Accessory (D/A), and it will appear above your open application. You can do your math, close the calculator, and you're back to your application. Many people also use the Apple menu as a convenient place from which to **launch** their applications or frequently used documents.

You add items to the Apple menu by adding items to the Apple Menu Items folder, within your System Folder. The Apple Menu Items folder has the same icon on the folder as the Apple menu does. When you add an item to this folder, it appears alphabetically in the menu. You can add applications, utilities, folders, or documents to this menu for easy access anytime you need them. **Aliases** of applications or documents are popular items to put in the Apple menu, because they instantly link to the real document or application.

A

Another feature of the Apple menu is the capability to have folders be **hierarchical** so you can click a folder in the Apple and instantly have it display a list of the folder's contents, from which you can select any item you want. A tremendous time-saver. An **alias** of the **Control Panels folder** appears in the Apple menu. You may often have to access a control panel and by clicking the alias you can see a hierarchical list of all the control panels and move to the one you want, all without ever having to open the System Folder and then the Control Panels folder within.

To remove an item from the Apple menu, all you have to do is go the Apple Menu Items folder in your system folder, and remove the item(s) you want out of the menu. Only items that appear in the Apple Menu Items folder will appear on the Apple menu.

To use an Apple menu item, follow these steps:

1. The Apple menu is found in the menu bar, its icon looks like an Apple logo. To access Apple menu items, click and hold on the Apple icon and then scroll down the item and stop at the item you desire.

2. Release the mouse to launch the item.

To add an item to the Apple menu, follow these steps:

1. You can add an item, or an alias of an item to the Apple menu by moving that item into the Apple Menu Items folder located within your System Folder.

2. After an item has been added, the next time you access the Apple menu, you'll find that the item has been added to the menu in alphabetical order.

To remove an item from the Apple menu, follow these steps:

1. Open the Apple Menu Items folder located in your System Folder.

2. Locate the item you'd like removed from the Apple menu, and drag that item out of the Apple Menu Items folder. That item is now removed from the Apple menu.

See Also

Aliases; Apple Menu; Control Panel Folder; Desk Accessories; Hierarchical File System (HSF); Launching a Program; System Folder

Apple Menu Options

This control panel device enables you to control the Apple menu options including turning on/off hierarchical submenus for the **Apple menu**, and turning on/off the Recent Items: Applications, Documents, and Servers Function, as shown in the following figure.

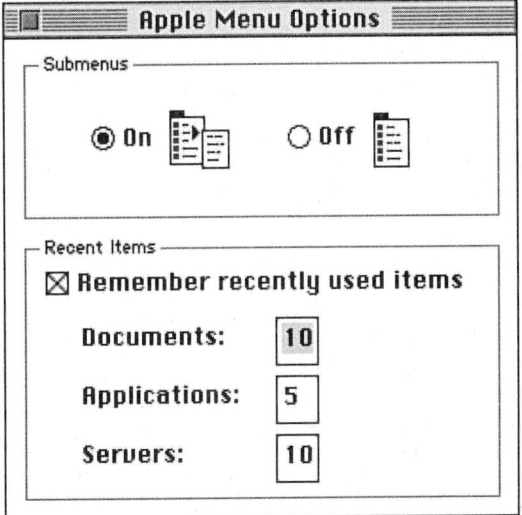

To set an Apple menu option, follow these steps

1. Choose Apple menu Options from the control panels folder under the Apple menu.

2. To enable Hierarchical **Submenus**, choose "on" from the radio buttons.

3. To enable Recent Items: Applications, Documents, and Servers, click Remember Recently Used Items; then select how many items in each category you want to have available.

See Also

Apple Menu; Control Panels; Menu; Servers

Apple Multimedia Tuner

When Apple released **QuickTime** 2.0, they made some changes to improve QuickTime playback performance. Unfortunately, some existing software could not take advantage of these new features, and sometimes performance was actually worse with QuickTime 2.0. Specifically, the pre-roll feature caused some problems. (Pre-roll is a term often used in video editing. It refers to a process in which a video deck, to ensure that it is playing video at the correct speed, starts playback at a point slightly earlier than the desired segment and pre-rolls.)

The most common side-effect was a hiccup; the QuickTime would start to play, pause or jump, and then continue playing correctly. Macromedia's **Director** suffered from this problem. To address this issue, Apple released the Apple Multimedia Tuner, which helped specific applications play movies more smoothly under QuickTime 2.0. The tuner, which is widely available on the Internet, also fixed some problems in **Sound Manager** 3.0.

The release of QuickTime 2.1 has removed the need for Apple Multimedia Tuner.

See Also

Director; QuickTime; Sound Manager

Apple Multiple Scan 14 Display, *See Monitors, Common Models*

Apple Multiple Scan 15 Display, *See Monitors, Common Models*

Apple Multiple Scan 17 Display, *See Monitors, Common Models*

Apple Multiple Scan 20 Display, *See Monitors, Common Models*

Apple Network Servers

High-end computers from Apple Computer that run AIX software, a version of UNIX, and that serve documents on the Internet.

The two servers, which were announced in early 1996, use Apple's 604 PowerPC chip and run the AIX 4.1.4 operating system licensed from IBM. Each machine can come with 32MB or 48MB of RAM. The new machines are designed to compete with the machines running UNIX that are already widespread as servers or host computers on the World Wide Web.

Servers for popular Web sites must be able to accommodate thousands or even millions of "hits" or visitors by other computers connected to the Internet. The speed of the computer directly affects the speed at which clients access Web pages or download software or other files.

Apple says that its fastest server, the NS700/150, outperforms comparable servers by Sun Microsystems, IBM, and Silicon Graphics. The Apple servers utilize a plug-and-play interface that will enable a user to easily replace any component in the machine.

See Also

HTML; Internet; Web Browser; World Wide Web

Apple Photo Access Extension

This extension enables users with CD-ROM drives to access Kodak photo CD-ROM discs. It's part of the standard install for CD-ROM drives in System 7 and higher.

See Also

CD-ROM; System 7

Apple QuickDraw 3D Accelerator, *See QuickDraw 3D Acceleration Card*

Apple Real-Time Operating System

Apple Real-Time Operating System (A/ROSE) is an **extension** containing information **EtherNet** NuBus cards and/or TokenRing NuBus cards require to work with your system. These NuBus cards have a computer chip and RAM built right into the card, and the A/ROSE extension contains the separate operating system code required by these computer chips to operate.

When you perform a system install, you select to install either EtherTalk or TokenTalk to use on your network. When you make your selection, A/ROSE is installed on your system. The A/ROSE extension is only required if you have one of these NuBus network cards installed in your machine.

See Also

EtherTalk; Extension; TokenTalk

Apple Remote Access

A huge advance in networking was provided by the introduction of Apple's Apple Remote Access, usually known as ARA. This is similar to a WAN, except instead of connecting a whole network of computers at one site to a whole network of computers at another site, ARA connects one remote computer to a distant LAN, or to a distant computer. ARA needn't work with a whole network. You can also use it to retrieve files from your home computer when you're at work, or to send reports back to the office from your PowerBook when you're on the road. ARA requires System 7, but it's not included with most Macs.

You must purchase it separately. It comes in three versions. The Personal Server is meant to be used with one host and one remote client, and includes one set of software for each. The Client Server is the Network host version. It supports multiple clients. The Remote Access Client program comes in a 10-pack, for use with ten different remote clients. PowerBooks generally come equipped with an ARA client, but you'll still need to purchase the ARA server to turn your home or office Mac into a host.

Essentially, ARA allows you to call into a network using a modem, and simulates for your computer and the remote computers a physical connection to the distant network. During an ARA connection, all network services, including email, printers, and servers are available to you exactly as they would be, just as if you were in the office. This convenience, like most, has a price, and the price you pay for "phoning home" is transfer speed. ARA is slow.

To use Apple Remote Access, you must have modems on both computers. Note that an ARA connection is nowhere near the speed of a standard network connection, so it's best to use the fastest, highest quality modem you can. You should strongly consider using a v.34 modem not only for its high speed (28,800bps and above), but also for its excellent handling of varying line conditions.

You must also choose a computer at the office to be the "Remote Access Server." This machine will answer the modem call and help your computer simulate its presence there. Apple manufactures a "MULTIPORT SERVER" card which allows one Mac to handle several phone lines, and control several remote communications simultaneously. Alternately, Shiva, Global Village, and other third parties manufacture dedicated hardware devices that support multiple dial-in users.

Remote Access Setup Setting up the Host Mac is the first step. Do this before you leave town with your PowerBook. First you must open the host Mac's Remote Access control panel and use the modem pop-up menu to find the brand and model of modem that's attached to the host. If it's not listed, call the modem manufacturer and/or check its Web site or an online service or user group BBS library. You MUST have an ARA script for your modem. Otherwise, it won't work with ARA.

After you've found the modem type and selected it, check the Answer Calls checkbox and give the host permission to answer incoming modem calls. Decide whether the incoming caller has access to everything on the network or only to the host Mac, and click the appropriate button. Next open the Users and Groups Control Panel and turn on the remote dial-in features.

For added security, you can have the host Mac call back the client to complete the remote connection. To do this, enter the call back number. When the Mac gets a call from this number, it will hang up and call back.

Setting up the client is done in much the same way. Use the Remote Access Control Panel to specify the type of modem, and then launch the Remote Access application. In the Untitled document, enter your name as it appears on the host machine. Enter your password, and the number for the host modem. It's a good idea to remind yourself that you're connected, so check the Remind me... box. This can save you many dollars in long distance charges. If you fail to acknowledge the reminder, ARA will disconnect. Finally, save the information you have entered. To connect from the remote client, click connect. The computer and modem do the rest.

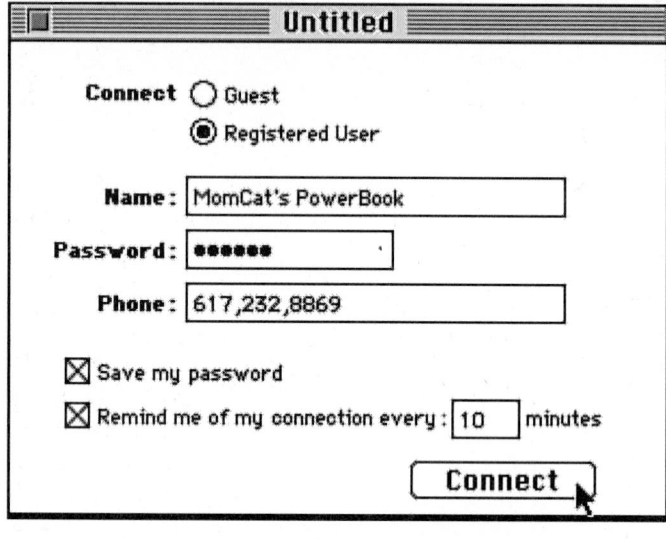

There's just one problem with ARA—the computer you call has to be ready to answer. You could leave your host Mac on all the time. Many people do, especially in business situations, when employees working at home or on trips may call in at any hour. If the host is your home Mac, and you're checking in during your Amazon canoe trip, African safari, or round the world cruise, you may not want to leave the Mac running all the time you're gone. The answer is to use PowerKey Remote, from Sophisticated Circuits. It's a little box that plugs in between the modem and the Mac. When a call comes in, it connects and then turns on the Mac. You'll have to wait while the system boots up, but once it does you're in business. It will time out and shut itself down again a few minutes after you break the connection.

A

Apple Video Compressor

Apple's video compressor, a **QuickTime compressor**, is perfect for quickly compressing video segments. The video quality is not as good as **Cinepak**, but it is good for previewing segments. This compressor is only 16-bits (this refers to the number of bits that are used to store the color information for a given pixel. A 16 bit image does not have the color fidelity of a 16-bit image). 24-bit information is reduced to 16-bits and then compressed. This compressor is **symmetrical**.

Compression ratios range from 5:1 to 12:1.

See Also

Asymmetrical Compressors; Compressor; Drop Frames; Spatial Compression; Symmetrical Compressors; Temporal Compression

AppleCD Audio Patch

An enhancement to version 2.0 of the AppleCD Audio Player that adds color and a three-dimensional look. Works only with Apple CD players and requires at least version 5.0 of the Apple CD-ROM Extension. Available from many online services.

AppleCD Audio Player

If you want to play Audio CDs in your **CD-ROM** drive, the AppleCD Audio Player enables you to operate your CD-ROM in much the same way you would a traditional audio CD player. The interface, which looks much like the front of a regular CD player from your stereo system, has the standard transport buttons for pause/play, stop, previous track, next track, and buttons to quickly scan through tracks (as shown in the figure).

Repeat button

Like a regular audio CD player, there is a display window that shows you the number of the currently selected audio track, and the elapsed time for that track. It also has a button to eject an audio CD. To the right of these buttons is a slider for controlling the volume of your audio CD. You also have buttons to choose your desired mode of play: Normal plays the tracks in order, starting with the first track, second track, and so on. The Shuffle button plays the tracks in a random order. The repeat button puts the audio CD into a loop mode that repeats the audio CD again when it reaches the end of the last track.

The AppleCD Audio Player also has a nice feature that enables you to list the songs and which track they appear on, so you can program a playlist of your favorite songs, and skip the ones you don't want to hear.

To access the playlist selection, click the green arrow below the transport controls and the playlist area will pop down. To name the CD, click in the window marked disc and type in the name of the CD. To name individual tracks, click the track number and type in the name of the track. To program your playlist, click the Prog button (Program) and the playlist window will appear. Drag and drop any track that you'd like in your playlist for this CD onto the playlist window.

Under the options menu, you can select a background color for your audio player, and the color for the indicator lights and display. You can also choose three modes of audio: Stereo, left channel only, right channel only.

To use the AppleCD Audio player, follow these steps:

1. Insert an audio CD in your CD-ROM player and choose AppleCD Audio Player from the Apple menu.

2. To hear the audio tracks in order, click the Play button. To stop the CD click Stop. To move forward, use the transport controls to move one track forward or backward, or use the scan button to rapidly skip forward or backward. To eject a CD, press the Eject button.

3. To program a playlist, click the green arrow below the normal mode button to reveal a pop-down menu where you can name the tracks by typing in their name and dragging and dropping them into a personalized playlist by clicking the Prog. (Program) button.

4. After you've named your programs, you can go directly to the track of your choice from a **pull-down menu** above the transport controls.

See Also
CD-ROM

AppleCD Speed Switch

If you own an AppleCD 300 CD-ROM drive, you can choose different speed options using the AppleCD Speed Switch Control Panel. This control panel only works with the AppleCD 300 drive.

AppleGuide Extension

The AppleGuide extension is the foundation for Apple's new built-in interactive help feature in **System 7.5** and higher. AppleGuide is accessed through the **Help menu** in the upper-right corner of the menu bar. (The Help **menu** icon is a question mark.)

The AppleGuide interface is designed to work interactively with the user, rather than just answering questions, AppleGuide walks you step-by-step through common Macintosh commands and features. One of the most unique features of AppleGuide is its use of "coach marks" that are similar to what ex-football coach/TV sports announcer John Madden uses on instant replay footage when he seemingly writes on the TV screen to show what happens next in a particular play. Apple uses a similar technology, and these "coach marks" (which appear to be hand drawn, like Maddens') appear on control panels, menus, dialog boxes, and so on instructing the user on what to do next.

If, for example, you choose the topic of **Disk Cache** and ask how to set the disk cache when you open the Memory control panel, a coach mark would appear around the area of the control panel where you adjust the size of the disk cache.

When you access AppleGuide, you're presented with a window that enables you to scroll through a list of topic areas to find the specific topic you're looking for. As you select a topic, a number of related questions a user might ask appear in the window to the right of the topics window. These questions refer to the selected topic, and you can choose questions or phrases from this specific list. Examples would be: "How do I empty the Trash?"; "How do I play an Audio CD?"; "How do I restart my computer?". Phrases include definitions of commonly used Macintosh terms. If you see a question or phrase you're interested in, select it from the list and click OK. A different dialog box now appears with your selected question, and step-by-step instructions on how to use the feature or command. These step-by-step instructions enable you to complete the tasks while you're learning and may include "coach marks" to help you. If the question is referring to menu items, these items appear in red for easy visual reference.

If the item that you need help on does not appear in the Topics listing of the AppleGuide, you can click the Index button to see a list of key words to choose from. You can also use the "Look For" button on the AppleGuide main window to search for a keyword.

Apple's goal is to have third-party commercial software take advantage of AppleGuide by offering the application's Help feature as an AppleGuide, giving the user interactive help for applications as well for general Macintosh functions.

See Also
Help Menu; Menu Bar; System 7.5

AppleLink

Apple Computer's **commercial online** information service, providing basic features such as discussion forums and **email**.

The AppleLink online service was originally available for use only by official Apple employees, dealers, and developers. Gradually Apple broadened access to the service to include consultants and other partners, and finally made limited areas of the service available to anyone who wished access and didn't mind paying the steep hourly and per-character rates and dealing with the Mac-like, but very sparse, interface.

For many years AppleLink was the only official online access channel to Apple. As software updates were released, they would often be available only on AppleLink (or available much earlier on AppleLink than on the other large services), thus forcing users anxious for the latest software to maintain AppleLink accounts and pay huge transfer fees every time a new update was released.

In 1988, Apple announced plans to release a separate online service geared toward consumers called AppleLink Personal Edition (see **America Online**),

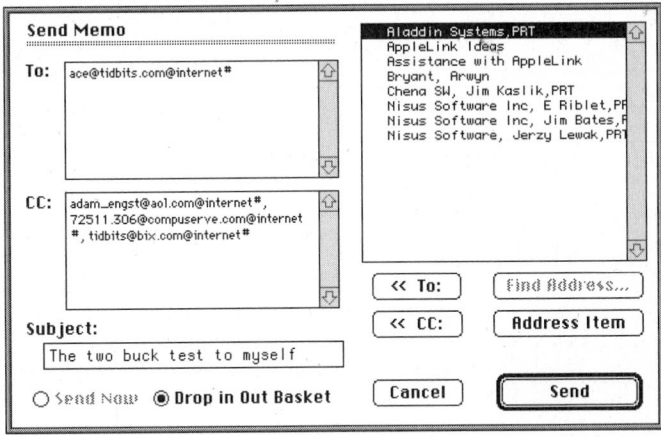

but they quickly canceled the project for political reasons. Several years later, Apple officially released the **eWorld** online service as their official channel to Apple customers. Apple had originally intended to move all of its current AppleLink users to eWorld, but as the transformation was about to take place, they changed their strategy and started providing resources and maintaining customer relations over the Internet, eventually shutting down the eWorld service altogether.

Most companies in the Macintosh market have AppleLink accounts and it's sometimes the only way to send email to companies that make Macintosh hardware and software.

AppleLink is perhaps the most expensive of the commercial online services. It also allows only messages under 32KB because that's all the text that fits in the mail software's text box. AppleLink also only accepts incoming messages under 30KB, the headers stealing 2KB or so. AppleLink's email interface is bare, although it comes with a nice address book feature as shown in the following figure.

If you want to send email to the **Internet** from AppleLink, first take your Internet address and append **@internet#** to it. (Remember that AppleLink cannot send mail to addresses longer than 35 characters.) To send email from the Internet to AppleLink, take the userid, which sometimes resembles a name or word and other times is just a letter plus some numbers, and append **@applelink.apple.com**.

To buy AppleLink's special software, visit an Apple dealer and fill out a form online that must be sent in on AppleLink by the dealer. You can also call the AppleOnline Services HelpLine at 48-974-3309, or send Internet email to **alink.mgmt@applelink.apple.com**.

As of this writing, nearly all of the resources of AppleLink are available through Apple's various Internet servers. Thus, except for Apple Dealers (who are still required to maintain accounts), AppleLink accounts are of little use and provide a very poor value for the online fees paid.

See Also

America Online; Commercial Online Services; CompuServe; Email; eWorld; Internet; URL

AppleLink Personal Edition,
See AppleLink; America Online

AppleScript

Apple's system-level **scripting** system.

For years, **DOS** and **UNIX** users jeered the Macintosh for its lack of batch files or system scripts that would enable you to control and manipulate other applications. That all changed with the release of AppleScript and **Frontier**. Using these scripting systems, you can write powerful scripts to manipulate the **Finder** or other applications in ways DOS users could only dream of.

AppleScript is included with System 7 Pro and later and works with any version of System 7. The key feature it needs in System 7 is support for **Apple events**, a special way for programs to communicate with each other and with the System and Finder.

The AppleScript language is somewhat English-like and should look familiar to anyone who has worked with **HyperCard's HyperTalk** language. A number of different *dialects* of AppleScript are also available, including several foreign language dialects. Because scripts are stored by AppleScript in a dialect-neutral format, you can view a script in whatever dialect you choose, no matter what dialect in which it was originally written.

AppleScript scripts typically are written using an **editor** designed for that purpose, rather than a plain text editor. Apple's own editor is called Script Editor and provides a basic level of functionality needed to edit scripts (see the following figure).

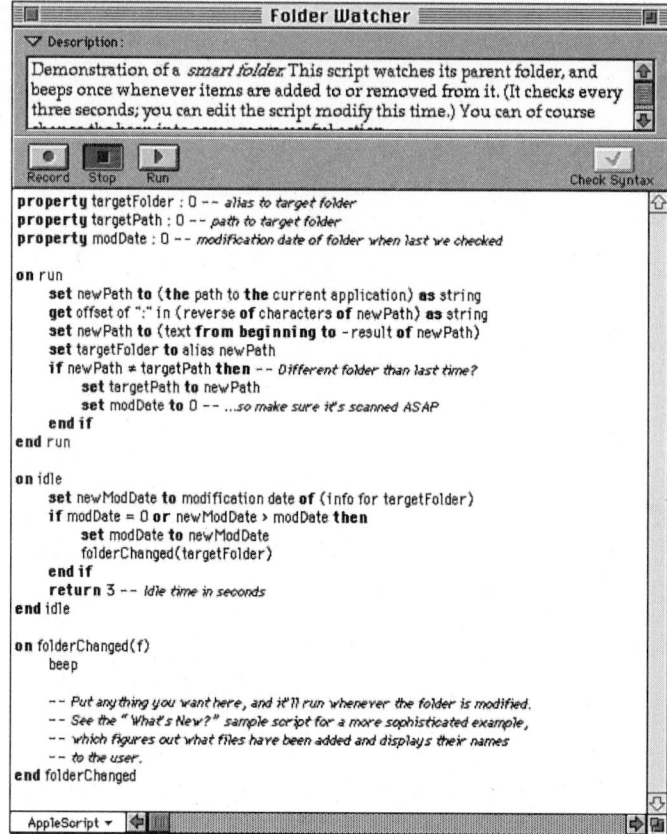

There is an area for comments about the script at the top of the script window. Below the comment area are buttons used to begin or stop recording, run the script, or check the script for proper syntax. Finally, below the buttons is the script editing area itself. Notice that each part of the script is styled according to its function. This syntax highlighting is done by the editor when you run the script or check its syntax.

Apple's Script Editor is certainly not the only script editor available. Scripter, ScriptWizard, and Script Debugger all include excellent editors with many more features than Apple's editor.

Learning AppleScript is more than a simple matter of learning the AppleScript language itself. Because each application responds to Apple events in its own way, you need to be able to determine what behavior to expect from a given application and write your scripts accordingly. Fortunately, AppleScript provides an easy way to find this information. Every scriptable application includes a dictionary of its scripting support. You can view this dictionary in the Script Editor (see figure) or other third-party editors. This example shows the dictionary for Scriptable Text Editor, a small, fully scriptable editor much like **SimpleText**.

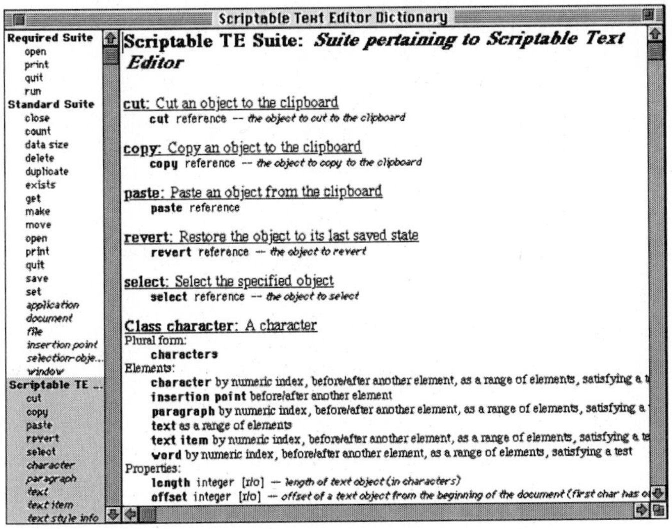

You can usually play back your recorded scripts immediately to re-create your actions, but you will probably want to edit the script to remove any unnecessary actions and add error checking.

AppleScripts generally have very limited interfaces, if any. They may display simple dialogs, but otherwise have little interaction with the user. **FaceSpan** is a user-interface tool for AppleScript that enables you to develop more complete applications based entirely on AppleScript.

From a programmer's perspective, an application can support AppleScript at any of three levels. *Scriptable* applications can be controlled partially or completely using a scripting language compatible with the **Open Scripting Architecture**. These applications respond to Apple events sent to them by other applications. *Recordable* applications send Apple events to themselves in response to user input, enabling AppleScript to record the events as they are sent. Finally, *attachable* applications are scriptable (and possibly recordable) and provide a way to run scripts from within the application (from a menu, for example). In this way, their internal capabilities are extensible using scripts.

Although AppleScript is fairly easy to learn, there is an even easier way to start scripting: by recording scripts. Not all scriptable applications are recordable, but those that are can be used with AppleScript to create scripts based on your own actions. When you start recording, AppleScript flashes a cassette tape icon over the Apple menu (see the following figure). As you work with recordable applications, all of your actions are recorded to the active script window. When you're finished recording, click the stop button.

See Also

Apple Events; FaceSpan; Open Scripting Architecture (OSA)

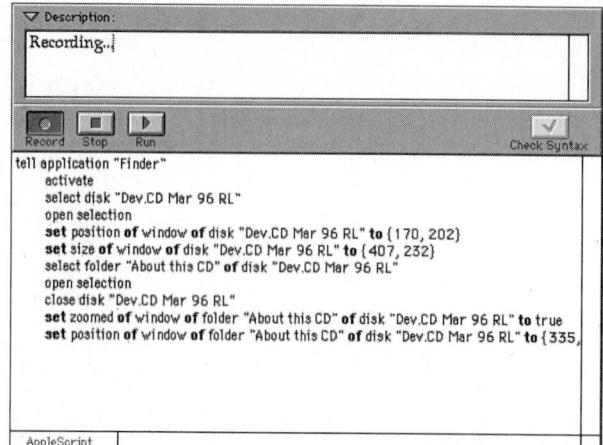

AppleScript also enables you to create mini-programs of your own and have them as icons on your desktop. This way, you can write an AppleScript for a particular task (such as removing the word alias from all aliases), drag a file onto your mini-program, and it runs its script on the dropped file.

See Also

Apple Event Manager; Keystrokes; Macros; Mouse

AppleSearch

AppleSearch is an application that indexes computer-based information organized by keywords so that users can make search queries and retrieve information they are seeking.

When used with Common Gateway Interface (CGI) scripts, AppleSearch can enable remote users to retrieve information published on the **World Wide Web** via a computer set up to function as a **Web server**.

AppleSearch includes Client and Server software. The Client software lets users make queries based on keywords and retrieve information from documents indexed with AppleSearch Server software. AppleSearch supports up to 50 connected users at a time.

AppleSearch is designed to operate on a local computer network, but can be used on a Web server with CGIs which then use AppleSearch to retrieve information.

AppleSearch indexes images and video as well as text, and also indexes any shared folder or, if the server is connected to the Internet, remote **WAIS** servers.

For more information, go to **http://product.info .apple.com/productinfo/datasheets/ss/applesearch.html**.

AppleScript Extension

The **AppleScript extension**, working with the **Apple Event Manager**, enables you to create powerful **macros** that automate routine tasks using a utility application called the **Script Editor**. In System 7.5 and higher, the Finder is scriptable, enabling you to make scripts for repetitive tasks at the Finder, but not all applications are able to use AppleScripting. (Programs that can use AppleScript are referred to as "scriptable.") However, more and more applications are now incorporating the capability to use AppleScript to automate tasks. You can, for example, have AppleScript record a series of **keystrokes** and **mouse** movements that perform a task, such as selecting Show Clipboard from the Edit menu on the desktop, and then play them back in the exact same order any time you want.

See Also

Apple Internet Router; Apple Internet Connection Kit; Apple Internet Server Solution; Internet; MacTCP; Network Communications; Web Server; WebSTAR

AppleShare

All Macs running **System 7** or higher are capable of peer-to-peer or personal file sharing. Any Mac on a network can become a file server by making one or more files, folders, applications or an entire drive available to others on the network. Although this approach is effective for one or two machines, it's not recommended for larger groups and not when several people need to use the same application at the same time. At this point, a dedicated file server is a better choice.

You dedicate one Mac to act as a file server for the others on the network. AppleShare, which can support as many as 150 users, turns a Mac into a dedicated file server. Current versions are AppleShare 3.0, which can be run on any Mac that can run System 7, and AppleShare 4.0, which can run on any 68040 Mac (except the AV series). The most powerful version, AppleShare Pro, requires a Workgroup Server 95 CPU. You can save a few dollars by not attaching a monitor to the dedicated file server. Such a configuration is known as a "headless" server.

After you install the AppleShare software on your designated server, use the AppleShare Admin program to create users and groups and to give them access to the files and applications they can work with. You can define each user's access privileges and set passwords for any items you want to limit access to. You can also specify that passwords will expire after a certain length of time, and you can copy-protect documents and programs so users can't copy them to their own hard drives or to disks.

AppleShare Extension This **extension** enables folders on selected disks to be shared with other Macs on a **network**. With AppleShare, (Apple's dedicated File-Server software) you can share files and folders on a disk, and open applications and files from other Macs on the network. AppleShare is often used in larger networks that require more control, access for more users, and additional security options.

One way to share files is to set up a file server, which is a separate hard disk (or series of disks) that everyone on the network can access. These disks can contain applications, files, documents, and any items that you want to make available to everyone on the network. (AppleShare is required if you want to share folders from a file server.) One advantage of having a file server is easy backup. All the documents that are used by network users can be stored on the file server, so backing up this one disk keeps all the documents backed up, rather than having to backup every machine on the network. Another benefit of having a dedicated file server, rather than just using Apple's built-in File Sharing feature, is speed. A dedicated machine offer significantly faster access to files and folders on the network.

You can also set up passwords to only enable certain users access to your File Server, and you can grant different levels of access to different users. Some users, for example, you may want to grant full access. Others you may only want to view files but not be able to edit them. Apple Share enables significant control over access privileges for users on the network.

See Also

File Sharing Extension; Network

Applet

Executable computer programs written in Java, a programming language developed by Sun Microsystems, Inc., and whose actions can be displayed in **World Wide Web browser**s such as HotJava and **Netscape Navigator.**

Applets written in Java turn Web clients like Netscape Navigator into virtual computers inside your computer. The Java virtual computer can interpret a variety of applets: animation programs, spreadsheet programs, and live information such as current stock quotes.

Java applets are not stored in the **HTML** that describes a **Web page**, but in a separate **URL** that is specified in <APP>, a new HTML tag. Applets present many potential benefits to Web publishers: they transfer much of the computing burden from the **server** to the client, and they bring greater security to host-client communications.

To write a Java applet, you need a Java Developer's Kit provided by Sun or another Java authoring environment provided by Roaster or other programs. For more information, go to the Java site on the Web: http://java.sun.com/.

See Also
Java; URL; Web Server; World Wide Web

AppleTalk Filing Protocol, *See Server*

AppleVision 1710AV, *See Monitors, Common Models*

Application Busy or Missing Message

If you try to open a document, but don't have the application that created the document, you will get an Application Busy or Missing message. This can mean one of a few things: You don't have the application that created the document, so your system can't find the application to launch it. (If you do indeed have the application that created it and double-clicking the document doesn't launch it, you may need to rebuild the desktop file as it may have become corrupted, which could result in the document not knowing which application created it.) If the document is a DOS/PC document, you can open a similar application and try opening it from the Open command of the application. (By similar application, I mean if it's a PC word processing document, try opening it in some sort of Macintosh word processing document.)

Lastly, it could be that the file you are trying to open cannot be opened. Many extensions, for example, add functionality to the system but cannot be opened. They are loaded into the system at startup and have no user interface for setting preferences or options. The Finder file is another example of a file that cannot be opened.

See Also
Customizing; Extensions; Extensions Manager; QuickTime; Rebuilding the Desktop; Restart; Startup; System 7

Application Heap, *See Heap*

Application Icons

Applications all have icons, and you can see them when you're in a window viewed by icon that contains applications, but when these applications are open and in use, they also have mini-icons that appear in the **Application menu** in the upper-right corner of the **menu bar**. These mini-icons enable you to see which application is the active application, and the Applications menu enables you to switch between applications.

The icon at the top of the Application menu is the icon of the **active** application. If the icon that appears at the top of the application menu is a Macintosh, the current application is the **Finder**. You can switch applications by choosing an application from the Applications menu. When you click and hold the mini-icon in the menu bar, the list of currently open applications (and their mini-icons) appear in a menu. To make one of the listed applications active, highlight your choice and release the mouse button. This application becomes the active application, and it's mini-icon appears on the menu bar.

See Also
Active Program/Application; Application Menu; Finder; Menu Bar

Application Not Found Message

If you try to open a document without the application that created it, you get an Application Not Found **message**.

This message informs you that the document cannot be opened because the application that created it is not on the **startup disk** or any mounted disk. This message also appears when you try to open a document that was created with a newer, updated version of the application. If, for example, you try to open a Word 6.0 document, and you are still using Word 5.1, you receive an Application Not Found message because the system looked for and did not find Word 6.0.

Macintosh computers running **System 7** or higher have an **extension** called **Easy Open** that tries to avoid the Application Not Found message. If you **double-click** a document and your Mac can't find the application it was created with, Easy Open displays a message box alerting you that the application can't be found. Easy Open then enables you to choose from a list of other applications on your hard disk that may **open** the document.

If, for example, you try to open a document created in WordPerfect but don't have the WordPerfect application, Easy Open gives you the option of opening that document in Microsoft Word because it can open a wide variety of text formats.

There are also third-party commercial translators such as MacLinkPlus from DataViz (55 Corporate Drive, Trumbull, CT 06611, Phone: (800) 733-0030. On the Web at **http://www.dataviz.com**) and Xtend.

These third-party translators offer some advantages over Easy Open in that they translate a wider variety of files (such as spreadsheets, databases, and graphics) and they hold the internal formatting of these documents (words that are bold, italic, and so on) and handle advanced formatting (such as tables, charts, and graphs) that may be lost when opening a file with Apple's Easy Open.

See Also

Double-Click; Easy Open; Extensions Folder; Message; Mounted; Open; Startup Disk; System 7

Application, Opening, *See*
Opening an Application

Application Programming Interface (API)

A well-defined set of function calls a program can use to interact with another piece of software, such as an **operating system**.

An Application Programming Interface, or API, is the side of an operating system seen only by programmers. Unlike the high-level view seen by users—windows, menus, icons, and so on—this interface exists entirely in one or more **programming languages**. But there is a similarity between the human interface and the API. Just as the human interface fully defines what you can and cannot do with an application, and how you go about doing it, an API fully defines what a programmer can do with an operating system or other software.

The MacOS provides an extensive API for Macintosh applications to use. This interface is known as the **Toolbox** and includes routines for every facet of a Mac program, from opening and reading files to playing QuickTime movies. Other operating systems also provide a programming interface for their applications. For example, Windows 95 and Window NT use the **Win32** API.

APIs are provided not only by operating systems. Many applications provide an API for modular extensions to the application's functionality (see the following figure). These extensions are frequently called **plug-ins**.

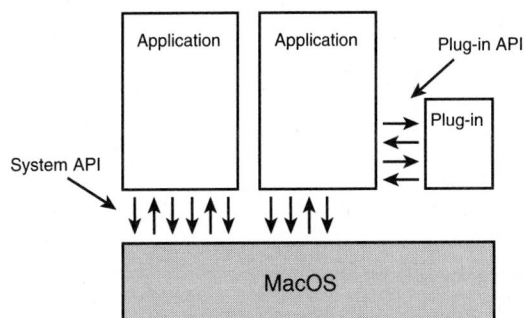

Plug-ins make use of an Application Programming Interface provided by the application. Some of the best-known examples are the Photoshop plug-in API, developed by Adobe, and the After Dark screen saver API, developed by Berkeley Systems. By writing to these APIs, any programmer can extend the functionality of these applications.

See Also

Toolbox; Win32

Applications Menu

Located on the far right of the menu bar, the Applications menu is a pull-down menu that lists open applications, with their icons to the left, as shown in the following figure. Like the Apple menu, the Applications menu isn't represented in the menu bar by a word, such as File or Edit. The icon of the application you are currently working in appears in the menu bar instead. If, for example, you are working in WordPerfect, the WordPerfect icon appears on the menu bar.

The Applications menu also enables you to switch between open applications. To access an open application, click the Applications menu and select the program you want. You also can access the Finder through the Applications menu.

The Applications menu also enables you to do the following:

- hide the active application
- **hide** the other open applications
- hide all applications
- show all applications

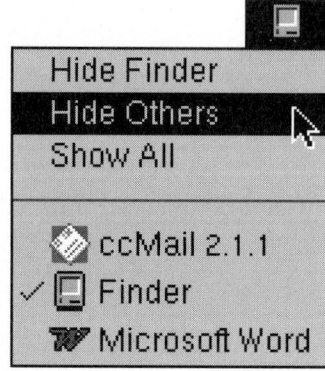

See Also
Hide Others Command

AppMaker

Most **interface builders** are designed to be used with a single programming framework: **AdLib** works with Apple's **MacApp**; **Constructor** works with Metrowerks' **PowerPlant**; and Visual Architect works with Symantec's Think Class Library. AppMaker is a different beast entirely. AppMaker can be used to create applications in a wide variety of frameworks, and can even be used with **procedural programming** projects written in **C** or **Pascal**.

Bowers Development, the creators of AppMaker, call it "Your Assistant Programmer," a fitting description. Using AppMaker, you can avoid a large part of the development time normally used for creating a program's user interface. AppMaker enables you to create the interface graphically (see the following figure) and generates the source code needed to make the interface work.

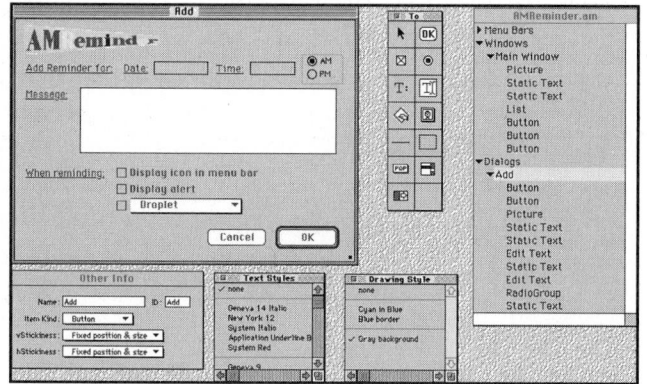

For many simple projects, AppMaker can generate a nearly complete application from a user interface standpoint, leaving only the details of your own application to be filled in. AppMaker supports procedural C and Pascal as well as the MacApp, PowerPlant, and Think Class Library (TCL) frameworks. In fact, AppMaker even supports the older Pascal versions of MacApp and TCL.

AppMaker is published by Bowers Development:

Bowers Development
97 Lowell Road
Concord, MA 01742
Email: **70731.3710@compuserve.com**
Fax: (508) 369-8224
Phone: (508) 369-8175

See Also

AdLib; Constructor; Interface Builder; MacApp; PowerPlant

Apprentice

Wonderful things can still come in small packages, as exemplified by this painting application. Delta Tao Software's Apprentice has very few bells and whistles when compared to higher-end paint programs. Its tools are few and its focus is narrow, but it does its assigned tasks very well. Its central job is two-fold: to allow you to create some interesting digital paintings in what appears to be natural media and to translate photographic images into natural media. For the second purpose, painting over photos, Apprentice allows you to load in any PICT image as a reference picture. You can toggle between the reference picture and the live painting surface by using the spacebar. Paint colors are chosen from a color wheel, or you may select to use the colors in the underlying photo by selecting "Automatic Colors" from the painting menu. You might think that Fractal Painter would be your only choice for transforming photos into paintings, but Apprentice offers some unique brushes and rendering looks that make it an excellent add-on choice, no matter what other software you are accustomed to.

Tools The Apprentice Toolbox is simple. There are no drawing or fill options, no linear or gradient possibilities, no magnifying glass (although zooming is possible with a zoom selector added to the bottom of the painting and reference picture screens). There are just six options in the Toolbox, and each one is a variant of the paintbrush: Watercolors, Chalk, Oils, Pencil, Sponge, and Custom. Above are another three associated choices: Small, Medium, and Large. That's it. These are the central operators, the painting media choices offered by Apprentice. There once was a higher-end program called "Monet" that has since had most of its features folded into Apprentice.

Brushes After selecting a brush option, you may choose one of the twenty-four brush shapes in the Brush menu. The five media selections in the Toolbox have specific brush shapes connected to them as defaults. If you select another brush shape from the list, you are automatically told that you are now operating with a Custom Brush. So it is possible to take a hard-edged brush shape normally reserved for the Pencil tool, and instead attach it to the Watercolor media tool, which instantly alters what the Watercolor media will look like when applied. Each brush shape can also be altered as to Opacity, Scatter, Color Change, Saturation, Smear and Size. All of these six options work via sliders. Taken together, the seemingly limited painting tools become an almost limitless variety of potential media looks.

Apprentice has the expanded capability to allow you to select from its own 24 default brush shapes or a replacement customized brush that fills one or more of the shape slots. To design your own custom brushes, just double-click any of the default shapes.

Other Special Menu Selections What is perceived as the direction of each brush stroke as you paint can be set by a menu command to either obey the brushing direction or not. You can save limitless brush shapes in a disk library. In addition to the documentation, a small booklet called "Making Art with Apprentice" comes with the software. In it, the user is guided through the electronic painting process in an informative and sometimes humorous way.

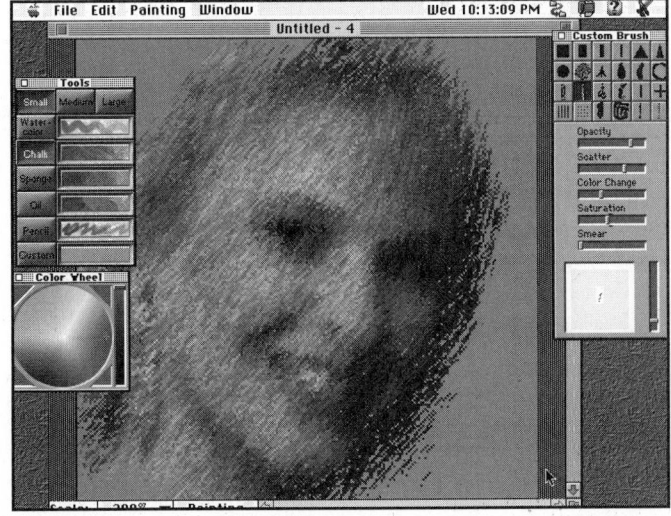

APR, *See Automatic Picture Replacement*

ARA, *See Apple Remote Access*

Arcade-Style Games

Arcade-Style Games are descendants of the arcade games most of us grew up spending hard-earned quarters on, whether we belonged to the **pinball** generation, the **Atari** Set, or cut our teeth on Mortal Kombat and Primal Rage. Arcade games (also known as twitch games) bypass a complicated storyline to bring you a quick, engrossing, often addictive experience. Simple arcade games, even the non-glorified **shareware** titles available on the Internet, hold their own because of the sheer energy of their rapid pace against the high-tech special effects of other types of computer games. This is not to say that today's arcade-style games for the Mac lack enhancements. New titles like Dust from GTE Interactive and MacPlay's **Descent** take full advantage of color, sound and the CD platform to bring you top-of-the-line bleep, shoot, and dodge action.

Arcade games can keep you playing for hours. It's also important to get a good **joystick** because of the high amount of rapid eye-hand coordination and increased risk of repetitive stress injury.

Arcade games can be broken up into a few specific categories: Pinball wanna-be's, games where you just blow things up, and games where you run around and blow things up. Just about every other form of computer game can be traced back to arcade roots.

Games in this category are mainly logical extensions of Pac-Man, Centipede and Asteroids but incorporate new technology such as **rotoscoping**, used in MacPlay's Flashback Enhanced and Prince of Persia from Brøderbund. Rotoscoping means that the game's graphics are mapped to films of actual human movement to create more lifelike action.

See Also

3-D Ultra Pinball; Crystal Crazy; First Person Perspective Shooters; Lode Runner; Shareware Games

Archie

An Archie **server** provides a single interface that allows searching through large numbers of **anonymous FTP** sites on the Internet so users can locate specific files quickly and easily.

Archie, which was developed in 1991 at McGill University in Canada, works by using normal FTP commands to obtain directory listings of hundreds of anonymous FTP sites around the world. It then puts these files listings into a database and provides a simple way of searching it.

Access to Archie servers can be made through Telnet, Gopher, the World Wide Web, special Macintosh client programs, and sometimes email. Peter Lewis' **Anarchie** is the most popular Mac Archie/FTP client.

Archie sites are located around the world. A complete list can be found in the *Internet Starter Kit.* Connecting to a site near you is usually quicker. The following table provides addresses for a few Archie sites located in the U.S.

Archie Sites in the U.S.

Site	IP Address	Location
archie.ans.net	147.225.1.10	ANS server, NY
archie.internic.net	198.49.45.10	AT&T server, NY
archie.rutgers.edu	128.6.18.15	Rutgers University
archie.sura.net	128.167.254.195	SURAnet server, MD
archie.uqam.ca	132.208.250.10	Canada
archie.wide.ad.jp	133.4.3.6	Japan
archie.kr	128.134.1.1	Korea

To log on to an Archie site you can, of course, connect via **Anarchie**. To connect via Telnet, type the site's address preceded by Telnet:

```
telnet.archie.sura.net
```

Then you log into the Archie program by entering **archie** as the userid. At the next prompt, type in the name of the file you are searching for.

See Also

Anonymous FTP; Email; Gopher; Server; Telnet; World Wide Web

Archiving, *See Backup Hardware Options*

Are You Afraid of the Dark? The Tale of Orpheo's Curse

Viacom's game tie-in to the popular Nickelodeon Television program "Are You Afraid of the Dark?" is better than some of the more technical attempts at traditional entertainment tie-ins like Blown Away and Johnny Mnemonic. In The Tale of Orpheo's Curse, two teenage siblings get locked into an abandoned theater by a mad magician. You pick one of the siblings and have to get out of the theater by midnight or you'll end up in limbo.

The non-violent theme of the game makes up for its lack of hard-core gaming qualities and awkward controls. The game is an exploration style, much like **Myst** or **Eastern Mind**. You wander through rooms, each themed with different background music and decor and try to find your way out to the next room. The puzzles are easy enough for kids to figure out and the 3D rendering makes you feel like you are playing around in a cartoon. The Tale of Orpheo's Curse has a lot going for it in terms of the success of the show, but on its own, it is still a great game that steers clear of violence and killing. For a similar sort of non-violent game, check out the Wizard of Oz based family entertainment title, **Yellow Brick Road II**.

See Also

Family Entertainment; Foul Play: Mystery at Awkward Manor; Masterpiece Mansion; Mortimer; Yellow Brick Road II

Aretha, *See Frontier*

Arithmetic and Logic Unit, *See Microprocessors*

ARM (Annotated Reference Manual), *See C++*

A/ROSE Extension, *See Apple Real-Time Operating System*

ARPANet, *See Internet*

ARQ, *See Modem Transfer Protocols*

Array

In **programming**, an array is a special kind of **variable** that contains a series of values rather than just one value.

A program, for example, that reads a text file and counts the number of occurrences of each letter of the alphabet in the file might use an array variable to hold the counts for each letter. This array would contain 26 values, each value corresponding to a letter of the alphabet. Individual elements of an array can be accessed by using an array subscript; that is, if the programmer called this alphabet counting array "X," the first value of the array (corresponding to the number of "A"s in the text) would be X_1, the second value (the number of "B"s) would be X_2, and so on, up to X_{26} (the number of "Z"s).

Array subscripts look different in different programming languages. In **C** and **Pascal**, for example, the array subscripts would be written "X[1]". Using an array is much more convenient than using separate variables for each value in a set of related data.

Arrays can also have more than one dimension. Two-dimensional arrays can be visualized like a tic-tac-toe board with varying numbers of rows and columns. The following figure demonstrates a one-dimensional array "X" as in the alphabet example, and a two dimensional array "Y" that has three rows and three columns (3| 3).

Arrays are valuable to programmers using the C programming language because C does not have a unique "string" variable type for holding strings of text characters. As a result, C strings are represented using arrays. The first character of the text string is the first element in the array, and so on.

A one-dimensional array **X**

12	3	5	6	11		2	4	0	6	1
X_1	X_2	X_3	X_4	X_5		X_{22}	X_{23}	X_{24}	X_{25}	X_{26}

A two-dimensional array **Y**

$Y_{1,1}$	$Y_{1,2}$	$Y_{1,3}$
$Y_{2,1}$	$Y_{2,2}$	$Y_{2,3}$
$Y_{3,1}$	$Y_{3,2}$	$Y_{3,3}$

See Also

Programming Tools; Structure; Variable

Arrow Keys

The Arrow keys enable you to move the **cursor** and make selections from lists without moving the **mouse**. There are four arrow keys: **Up Arrow**, **Down Arrow**, **Left Arrow**, and **Right Arrow**. They can be used at the desktop level to select items in **active windows**, and they can be used to navigate the **I-Beam cursor** in documents. Arrow keys are also popular in graphics programs where precise movements are necessary.

At the desktop level, the Arrow keys can be used to navigate through items in an active window (or even the desktop) without use of the mouse. Arrow keys can also be used with **modifier keys** to perform various commands, as shown in the following table.

Arrow Keys

Sequence	Result
⌘-Left Arrow	Collapses expanded folder
⌘-Down Arrow	Opens folder/opens next file
⌘-Right Arrow	Expands folder
⌘-Up Arrow	Goes to previous folder
⌘-Option-Up Arrow	Closes to previous window
⌘-Shift-Up Arrow	In Open/Save dialog it selects Desktop
⌘-Option-Left Arrow	Collapses all expanded folders
⌘-Option-Right Arrow	Expands all nested folders
Shift-Right Arrow	Selects character to the right of text cursor
Shift-Left Arrow	Selects character to the left of text cursor
Shift-⌘-Right Arrow	Selects word to the right of text cursor
Shift-⌘-Left Arrow	Selects word to the left of text cursor

See Also

Active Window; Cursors; Down Arrow Key; I-Beam Cursor; Left Arrow Key; Modifier Keys; Mouse; Right Arrow Key; Up Arrow Key

Arrow Pointer

The default **cursor** for your Mac is an arrow pointer. It allows you to point to objects and select them. If you're using a word processing application, such as WordPerfect, the arrow pointer converts to a text cursor (an I-Beam). But if you move your text cursor over a **scroll bar**, **pull-down menu**, or outside the text, the cursor defaults to the arrow pointer.

See Also

Cursor; Pull-Down Menu; Scroll Bar

Ascender

An ascender is that part of a character that sticks up above the rest of the character. Not all letters have ascenders. Lowercase b, d, and h are examples of letters containing ascenders.

See Also

Descender; Line Spacing; Typesetting Terms

ASCII

ASCII (American Standard Code for Information Interchange) is a set of standard numerical values for the Roman alphabet.

At the lowest level, computers can deal only with numbers. Characters, such as the alphabet, punctuation marks, and so on, must be translated into numbers before a computer can work with them. You can think of this translation as a sort of code in which each character, A, B, C, and so on, is represented by a number. Any number of codes are possible. To avoid confusion, the computer industry developed and adopted the ASCII code.

ASCII defines 128 characters. The first 32 (0-31) are control codes for tabs, carriage returns, line feeds, and the like. The 96 printable characters are shown in the following table.

The Printable ASCII Codes

32	space	48	0	64	@	80	P	96	`	112	p
33	!	49	1	65	A	81	Q	97	a	113	q
34	"	50	2	66	B	82	R	98	b	114	r
35	#	51	3	67	C	83	S	99	c	115	s
36	$	52	4	68	D	84	T	100	d	116	t
37	%	53	5	69	E	85	U	101	e	117	u
38	&	54	6	70	F	86	V	102	f	118	v
39	'	55	7	71	G	87	W	103	g	119	w
40	(	56	8	72	H	88	X	104	h	120	x
41	)	57	9	73	I	89	Y	105	i	121	y
42	*	58	:	74	J	90	Z	106	j	122	z
43	+	59	;	75	K	91	[	107	k	123	{
44	,	60	<	76	L	92	\	108	l	124		
45	-	61	=	77	M	93	]	109	m	125	}
46	.	62	>	78	N	94	^	110	n	126	~
47	/	63	?	79	O	95	_	111	o	127	

Because it only takes 7 bits of data to represent all 128 possible characters ($2^7 = 128$), every byte has an extra bit that can be used to define another 128 codes ($2^8 = 256$). Every type of computer, however, defines these additional codes differently, which is why text files containing special characters, such as curly quotes or accented characters, generally appear incorrectly when they're transferred to another kind of computer.

Although it is by far the most common, ASCII is not the only character encoding standard used on computers. For many years, IBM used an encoding standard called EBCDIC on its mainframe computers. Also, there's no way to specify non-Roman characters, such as Japanese Kanji, using ASCII. Other codes, such as JIS or shift-JIS, are used to encode these characters.

Recently, the computer industry has settled on another standard for character encoding called **Unicode**. This standard includes all of the ASCII characters, as well as characters for virtually every other written language in the world.

See Also
ASCII File

ASCII File

A standard format used to exchange data between different computer systems, programs, or computers on a network such as the **Internet** or text-only **commercial online services**. Often called a *text-only* file.

ASCII (American Standard Code for Information Exchange) is comprised of 256 codes, each code standing for a number, letter, or other character you might type in a text file.

Because ASCII is recognized by all kinds of computers, ASCII files provide a means of exchanging text and simple formatting in a document. Many commercial online providers such as **CompuServe** routinely exchange data in ASCII format.

Virtually all word processing programs, as well as other client software such as **Web browsers**, allow users to save files in text-only (ASCII) format. Often, "text-only" appears as an option when choosing "Save As..." from the File menu of the program involved.

Many documents downloaded from the Internet are in text-only format. Transporting other kinds of documents on the Net often requires **compressing** or **encoding** them in a format such as **BinHex**. Saving an **HTML** document in text-only format is a common way of creating a file to be opened and displayed on the **World Wide Web.**

If you don't save word processing files in ASCII format before sending them across the Internet, characters may not appear, or may appear as garbage.

See Also

Compressing Files; CompuServer; Encoding Files; HTML; Internet; World Wide Web

ASCII TRANSFER, *See File Transfer Protocols*

AskText XFCN

An external routine that displays modal dialogs, modeless windows, and floating palettes from within programs that support **XCMDs** and **XFCNs**. The windows' AskText displays can have multiple fonts, styles, sizes, and any number of customizable buttons.

> Heizer Software
> 300 Cedar Lane
> Largo, FL 34640
> Price: $35
> Fax: (813) 559-0614
> Phone: (800) 888-7667 or (813) 559-6422
> Web: **http://www.heizer.com**

See Also

Director; HyperCard; SuperCard; XCMD

Assembler, *See Assembly Language*

Assembly Language

A low-level **programming language** that is one step removed from **machine language**.

Assembly language is the lowest-level language used today. Each assembly language instruction corresponds directly to one line of machine code. As such, assembly language programs are inherently processor-specific, meaning that they cannot be made to run on a different family of microprocessors. For example, an assembly language program written for the Macintosh cannot be made to run on an Intel-based Windows machine without resorting to **emulation**. This is in contrast to higher-level languages, which can generally be re-**compiled** to run on another processor.

So what's the advantage of writing a program in assembly language? Well, for most programs, there is no advantage. On the other hand, an experienced assembly programmer can often write code that is more efficient and faster than equivalent code written in a high-level language. For this reason, programmers often write most of a program in a high-level language, such as **C**, and use a **profiler** to identify the most time-critical sections of code. These portions are then rewritten in assembly to give the biggest "bang for the buck."

Very low-level portions of most operating systems (like the MacOS) are also written in assembly language.

See Also

Compiled Language; Machine Language; Profiler

Assistant Toolbox Extension

This extensions enables **PowerBook** users to set preferences for a host of **system**-level functions, including: assigning **keystrokes** to put the PowerBook to **Sleep**; adjusting the movement and display options for your **arrow pointer** and **I-Beam cursor**; and selecting **screen dimming** options to conserve **battery** power.

See Also

Arrow Pointer; Batteries; Cursor; I-Beam; Keystrokes; PowerBook; Screen Dimming; Sleep; System

Asteroids, *See Arcade-Style Games; Crystal Crazy*

Astound

Gold Disk's Astound falls somewhere in between a traditional desktop **presentation program** and a full multimedia production package. Like **PowerPoint** and **Persuasion**, it supports outlining and creating overheads and speaker's notes. It also has some fairly sophisticated animation tools, such as a timeline and a sound editor. Astound has a steeper learning curve than PowerPoint, particularly for those users who have no experience with desktop presentation or graphics, but after you've figured out how to use it, Astound can do much more. The program ships on five 1.4MB disks *and* a CD-ROM that includes templates and clip media. It's accelerated for Power Mac but runs on any Macintosh using System 7.1 or higher.

Astound presentations can include any combination of text, graphics, QuickTime movies, and sounds. These can be imported from **AIFF**, **SND**, and **WAV** sound files, **JPEG**, TIFF, **PICT**, **EPS**, BMP, PCX, TGA, and **PhotoCD** graphics files, and PIC's animation. You can also add *actors*, clips of animation supplied with the program, to liven up your presentations. There are 19 animated actors in the program's file and an additional 155 on the CD-ROM. Each text block, graphic, actor, or movie can

be made to appear or disappear from the screen using any of 30 transitional effects, including reveal, dissolve, and fade. Actors also can follow a designated path across the screen. Your slides can contain interactive buttons that play sounds or movies, or allow you to jump between slides, open other presentations, or even launch other applications.

The templates supplied with Astound can be customized to suit your needs, using the tool palette and menu commands. Astound's publisher has hired some very good designers to create the backgrounds and layouts. They're much more interesting than the ones supplied with PowerPoint. There's even a texture generator, so you can create custom backgrounds and fills, and an Extrude function that automatically converts any two dimensional shape into a three dimensional one. Morphing one object into another can be effective, and Astound's Tween command does it automatically. You need only select the two (draw) objects and specify the number of intermediate steps in the transition. You can even specify a color fill for the shapes, and the background and foreground colors will adjust as one object transitions into the other.

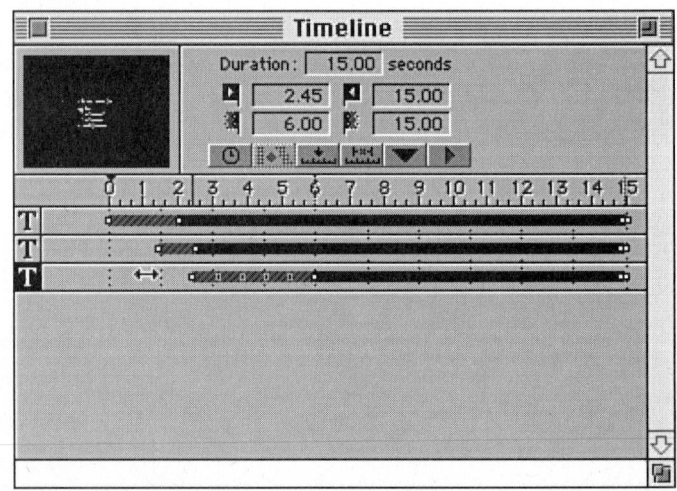

The Timeline window enables you to determine the sequence and timing of events and transitions within your presentation. It also controls the timing and duration of recorded sounds that are part of the show. Timelines are used to set the length of time each slide is on the screen, and at what point during that period animation, sounds, or morphs occur. Each object on the screen has its own timeline. Timelines are viewed and edited in the Timeline window, shown in the figure. By default, the timeline extends for the entire period that the slide is on the screen. To make something happen while the slide is on the screen, you must adjust the timeline, so that it starts and ends when the event is supposed to do so. Drag the ends of the line, or enter values in the duration boxes.

You can add sounds across multiple slides by enabling the Play in background option. It changes the timeline of the sound to an non-editable one and continues the sound from one slide to the next until you designate an end.

Astound is not the easiest program to learn and use. It lacks on-screen help, other than the most basic balloon help for commands. Its manual is confusing, and there's no documentation for the contents of the CD-ROM. The lack of help screens is a major problem for beginners. Nevertheless, if you have the patience to work with it and master its tools, Astound can produce truly astounding results.

See Also

Presentations, Adding Sound with Astound

Asymmetrical Compressors

Compressors can be divided into two broad categories of performance; symmetrical and asymmetrical.

Asymmetrical compressors take a lot longer to compress a movie than to decompress one. That means the video must be captured using some other compressor (or no compressor) and then compressed using the asymmetrical compressor. This takes quite some time, but once compressed, the video can be played in real time. **MPEG** and **Cinepak** are examples of asymmetrical compressors.

See Also

Cinepak; Compressor; MPEG; Symmetrical Compressor

Asynchronous Communication

Transmissions between computing devices can take place either synchronously or asynchronously. Asynchronous communications are very commonly used with personal computers. Nearly all Macintosh modems support asynchronous connections exclusively.

In asynchronous transmissions, the transfer of data is not as strictly moderated as with synchronous transmissions. To allow the length of time to vary between transmission of each character, asynchronous transmissions use start bits and stop bits to indicate the beginning and end of each byte transmitted. Because of the additional information needed to transmit the start and stop bits, and because of the inexact timing in this type of transfer, asynchronous transmissions are not as fast or efficient as synchronous transmissions.

See Also

Asynchronous Data Transfers; Synchronous Communications

Asynchronous Data Transfers

A common mode of communication between computers connected by low- or medium-speed modems to the **Internet**.

Asynchronous communication between computers means that the computers are not synchronized, and instead, they use start and stop bits to mark the beginning and end of each byte.

Asynchronous transfers are not as efficient as synchronous transfers which are supported by many high-speed **modems**. However, asynchronous transfers are flexible because the computers involved can send data as soon as they are ready and as long as both sending and receiving computers have been configured to use the same start and stop bits.

Whereas asynchronous transfers "start" and "stop" with every byte, synchronous transfers send data in chunks or packets, thus enabling them to exchange information faster. Synchronous communication is most commonly used between mainframe computers and on local area networks such as **LocalTalk**.

See Also

Internet; Modem; Packets

AT Commands

The Macintosh sends basic commands such as configuration and dialing numbers to a modem using a language known as the AT Command set. The words in this language are lines of commands which begin with the characters "AT" (for attention). This is also known as the "Hayes Standard" because this type of command set was originally popularized by the **Hayes** brand modems.

Although the basic commands are the same across modems (see the following table), more advanced commands such as error control, data compression, and selection of high speeds tend to be different for each manufacturer, and even for different models from the same manufacturer. The manual that comes with your modem should describe in detail each available AT command.

Basic telecommunications software such as Zterm will require these commands to configure the modem for dialing. More advanced software, such as Microphone Pro or the **America Online** client software, will simply ask for the type of modem you have and will then send all command strings for you. Other software, such as that used by Prodigy, checks the type of modem you have automatically and adjusts the command set as needed.

You may also combine multiple commands into one line, but there must be only one AT for each line (for example: ATMO DT 555-1234 turns off the speaker and then dials 555-1234).

Manufacturers usually provide a list of the commands to use for various telecommunications software. Check your modem documentation for details.

See Also

Hayes AT Command Set; Modems

Basic AT Commands

Command	Function	Comments
AT A	Answer phone	
AT DT n,	Tone dial	n=number to dial, use commas for pauses
AT DP n	Pulse dial	n=number to dial, use commas for pauses
AT H n	Hook	HO hangs up, Hl answer phone
M n	Speaker volume	MO turns off, Ml turns on
AT Z	Reset	Sets modem to power-on settings
...	Command	Returns modem to command state
0	Online	Returns to online (opposite of off-line)
SO=n	Answer rings	Sets # of rings to wait to answer phone
S7=n	Wait time	Time to wait for remote modem

At Ease

At Ease sits on top of the Finder and is designed to allow limited access to certain Macintosh applications and files without allowing access to system files or other critical areas of the **Finder**. At Ease's simple-to-use interface acts and looks like a giant folder with a large square tile representing each document or application. These tiles act as a launcher for selected documents or applications. At Ease sits on top of the Finder, so items such as the **System Folder** and the **Control Panels folder** are hidden from view. Access to the Finder is only gained through a password that is set within the At Ease Setup control panel.

When an application is launched from At Ease, all other applications are **hidden**, and when you **quit** an application, you return to the At Ease interface. From the At East Setup control panel, you can configure which applications and documents will be displayed, decide whether a password will be used to access the Finder, and assign where you'd like **saved files** to be stored.

At Ease is perfect for households with children or schools that want to offer access to the computer but want to protect files that could be removed or deleted, possibly disabling the computer.

See Also

Control Panels Folder; Finder Launcher; Hide Others Command; Quit; Save; System Folder

At Ease Setup

This **control panel** enables you to add or delete applications and set the preferences for the At Ease interface, as shown in the following figure. At Ease, which is a separate product from AppleSoft but is bundled for free with many Performa models, sits on top of your Finder, permitting access to certain applications and files without permitting access to system files items such as the **System Folder** and the **Control Panels folder** or other areas of the **Finder**. Access to the Finder is only gained through a password that is set in the At Ease Setup Control Panel. At Ease's

simple-to-use interface looks like a folder with square tiles representing each document or application. These tiles act as **launchers** for selected documents or applications.

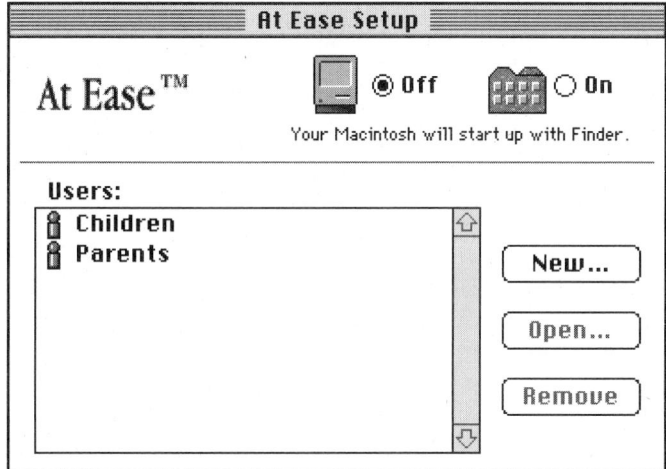

When an application is launched from At Ease, all other applications are **hidden**, and when you **quit** an application, you return to the At Ease interface. From the At East Setup Control Panel you can choose which applications and documents are displayed, decide if a password is to be used to access the Finder, and assign where you'd like **saved files** to be stored.

At Ease is perfect for households with children or schools who want to offer access to the computer but want to protect files that could be accidentally removed or deleted, possibly disabling the computer. **Network** administrators also use At Ease for Workgroups for limited access to applications over a Network.

To use the At Ease Setup Control Panel, follow these steps:

1. Choose the At Ease Setup Control Panel from the Control Panels submenu in the Apple menu (or the System Folder).

2. Use the pull-down menu in the left window to select an applications folder, and click the application you want added to the At Ease interface. Click Add to enter your selection.

3. The right side window shows a list of applications that you chose to be available in the At Ease interface.

4. When your application and document selection is complete, click OK.

See Also

Control Panel; Control Panels Folder; Finder; Hide; Launcher Control Panel; Network; Quit; System Folder

At Function, *See Function,*
Spreadsheet

AT&T/Paradyne SComsphere
3810Plus, *See Modems*

Atkinson, Bill

Bill Atkinson is a brilliant programmer whose influence is felt throughout the Macintosh community. Ironically, his professional career did not start in programming, but in chemistry.

From chemistry, Atkinson began to specialize in neuro-chemistry, the chemistry of the brain. During this time, he became fascinated by the capabilities of computer graphics and began working on programming projects in his field. One of the best known projects involved the creation of a 3D computer graphic of the human brain. The results of that project showed up on the cover of the October 1978 issue of *Scientific American.*

Shortly thereafter, Atkinson made the tough decision to pursue computers rather than chemistry and soon founded Synaptic Systems Corporation to create medical computer interfaces for use in hospital equipment.

In March of 1978, Atkinson was recruited by Apple to focus on software for the Apple II. He convinced Apple to offer UCSD **Pascal** for the Apple II, which went on to be a hit among programmers and scientists and earned Apple a great deal of respect.

One of Atkinson's greatest achievements lies at the very heart of the Macintosh. When working on the **Lisa** project, Atkinson created the software that manages arbitrary updating of regions of the screen. This software enables the Macintosh (and the Lisa) to gracefully handle overlapping windows while enabling each window to be updated independently. This task is more difficult than it seems. In fact, Atkinson believed he was re-creating a part of the Alto system he had seen at **Xerox PARC**, when in actuality, Xerox had not been able to solve the problem of arbitrary update regions.

Combined with a complete set of drawing routines, this code formed LisaDraw, the drawing package used by the Lisa. When LisaDraw moved to the Macintosh, it became QuickDraw, which remains a vital part of the **Toolbox** used by programmers today.

To showcase the capabilities of QuickDraw, Atkinson wrote MacPaint, one of the original Macintosh applications. In its day, MacPaint was as revolutionary at the Macintosh itself. Its influence is seen in today's most sophisticated graphics packages.

After the Macintosh was off the ground, Atkinson turned his talents to other projects. In 1988, Apple released his next revolutionary creation: **HyperCard**. HyperCard's graphical programming method, hypertext capabilities, and English-like programming language (HyperTalk) broke new ground once again.

In 1990, Atkinson formed **General Magic** with Andy Hertzfeld and Marc Porat. General Magic is creating software for the next generation of computing, including the Magic Cap operating system used by personal digital assistants (PDAs) from Sony and others.

See Also

General Magic; HyperCard; Lisa; Pascal; Toolbox; Xerox PARC

Atlases, *See Map and Atlas*
Programs

ATM, *See Adobe Type Manager*

A

ATM GX

ATM GX is a special version of the popular font utility Adobe Type Manager (ATM) that was introduced in System 7.5 for use with PostScript Type 1 fonts that have been converted to the GX format and with TrueType GX fonts. Like ATM, ATM GX enables a high-quality screen display and printing of fonts at any point size. ATM GX also improves the quality of output of QuickDraw-based printers (such as Apple ImageWriters and HP Deskwriters).

A-Train, *See SimCity 2000*

AU File

One of the audio file formats found on the Internet, the AU file format has a variety of aliases, including: U-Law, Mu-Law, A-Lay, u-Law, NeXT audio, and Sun audio. All are products of the UNIX operating system. AU files are fairly common as a sound format on Web pages. It's not uncommon to see AU files served side by side with AIFFs.

Shareware programs, **Sound-App** and **Sound-Machine**, can be used as a **helper app** with **browsers**, such as **Netscape**, to play AU files.

QuickTime 2.1 provides support for AU files, provided you have the appropriate applications, such as **MoviePlayer** or **SoundEdit** 16. To create a file in MoviePlayer, open the sound file and choose Export from the File menu. Choose Options before saving the new file and choose the mLaw compression format.

> Web: **http://www.mcp.com/hayden/software/Netsoftware.html**

See Also
AIFF File; Audio on the Internet; Decoding/Decompressing Files; File Types; Helper Applications; Multimedia; WAVE; World Wide Web

Audio Bit Depth

In sound digitizing, bit depth refers to the number of bits used to store a sound sample. While bit depth doesn't define the level of the sample (that's determined by the **sample rate**), it does determine the accuracy of the sample. Sound is represented by a wave form, and the bit depth of the sample is used to indicate the amplitude of the wave. The lower the bit depth, the fewer number of differences in height of the wave form that can be recorded. The higher the bit depth, the more accurate the measurement. A low bit depth produces distorted sounds.

See Also
Sampling Rate; Sound Digitizing

Audio CDs, *See AppleCD Audio Player or CD Audio (Converting to QuickTime)*

Audio Interchange File Format, *See AIFF*

Audio on the Internet

Sound on the Internet can be presented in formats such as **AIFF** (Audio Interchange File Format), **MPEG** (Motion Picture Experts Group), or **AU**. Some System 7 sounds might also be found on the Net.

The following table shows the common file formats listed with their sizes, benefits, and drawbacks.

Audio File Formats

Format	Platforms	Size	Benefits	Drawbacks
System 7 sound	Mac	Small; not able to compress	Click and Play simplicity, can be used as system sound	Mac only
AIFF	Windows/PC, Mac, UNIX, Amiga	Varies; not able to compress	Wide compatibility	High quality sound equals huge sound file
MPEG	Mac, Windows/PC, UNIX	Small size relative to sound quality; compressible	Excellent sound quality	Agonizingly slow, no good Mac player (yet)
AU	UNIX, Windows/PC, Mac	Varies; not able to compress	Wide compatibility	Many slight variations in format

To play sound files you download from the Internet, you need **helper applications** such as SoundApp, **Sound Machine**, or MPEG/CD and MPEG Audio for PowerPC. MIDI files downloaded from the Web need to be processed by an application like **AllMIDI**.

Another kind of sound file is presented by **RealAudio**. RealAudio files use **streaming**; that is, they are played by RealAudio as the file is downloaded. To play them, you can use the RealAudio Player application or a RealAudio plug-in that processes the files while you are still in the Netscape Navigator window.

See Also
AIFF; AU

Audio XCMDs

A set of external routines that provide additional sound capabilities to HyperCard stacks and other software that support **XCMDs** and **XFCNs**.

SpeakText provides support for Apple's **PlainTalk** Text-to-Speech technology. This routine to adds verbal responses to your software. PlainTalk is not required for speech but does provide the best quality.

PlayMOD plays **MOD** files and supports 8- or 16-bit sound, stereo, and sound fading.

MODToRes converts MOD files into resources (MODr) that the PlayMOD XFCN can play. This enables you to bundle the MOD files in the application, rather than to distribute them as separate files.

SndVolume XCMD is used to get and set the sound volume of the Macintosh.

No licensing fees are required to distribute applications that contain these routines.

Heizer Software
300 Cedar Lane
Largo, FL 34640
Price: $89
Fax: (813) 559-0614
Phone: (800) 888-7667 or (813) 559-6422
Web: **http://www.heizer.com**

See Also
Director; HyperCard; MOD; SuperCard; XCMD

AudioCD Access Extension

This extension adds the capability to play audio CDs in a Macintosh **CD-ROM** player. Although this extension adds the ability to play audio CD's, to hear the CD, you must use the **AppleCD Audio Player** that appears on the Apple menu.

See Also

AppleCD Audio Player; CD-ROM

AudioCD Tips

You may already know you can play audio CDs in your CD-ROM player and hear the audio through your internal Mac speaker(s) or through external multimedia speakers. What you probably didn't know is that the latest version of the **AppleCD Audio Player**, shipping with **System 7.5** and higher, has been enhanced and offers users a wide range of features and shortcuts to make enjoying audio CDs even easier.

When you insert an audio CD, you can give the CD a name by clicking the title field (or pressing the Tab key) and typing in the name of the CD. There is also a blue triangle that appears on the left side of the Audio Player. Clicking this arrow expands the interface and enables the naming of individual tracks in the same fashion you named the CD, as shown in the following figure. (You can tab from track to track.)

Naming individual tracks has three advantages:

1. You don't have to keep the CD jewel box handy to find out which tracks appear where on the CD.

2. You can go directly to the track of your choice by choosing it from a pop-up menu or by double-clicking the track's title in the list.

3. You can create a custom playlist to play only your favorite tracks on an audio CD, bypassing any tracks you don't like.

After you've entered the names of the tracks on the audio CD, you add tracks to your custom playlist by dragging the track's name from the Tracks window to the PlayList window. You can drag tracks up and down in the Play List window to put them in your desired order. To hear the tracks on your play list, press the PROG button.

You can eject a particular CD disc and reinsert it days, weeks, or months later, and the Mac will still recognize the disc's name and tracks by storing the information in the AppleCD Audio Player Preferences file.

The default color for the Audio Player is black, but you can change this color by selecting a new color from the Color menu.

A volume slider appears in the Player's interface, but you can also control the volume of the audio CDs by using the up and down arrow keys accordingly.

See Also

AppleCD Audio Player; System 7.5

Audiodeck

A utility that automatically plays **CDs** in an Apple CD-ROM drive. Options include playthrough (audio is routed to the Macintosh speaker) and shuffle or program mode playback.

The software is available on many online services.

Audiomedia II

A NuBus card that is used for digital sound recording. The single **DSP** chip is capable of simultaneously playing 4 16-bit 44.1KHz tracks. While all **Power Macs** support 16-bit sound, the Audiomedia card features professional connectors that improve the quality of the signal being recorded and played back. The Audiomedia II also includes **S/PDIF** digital connectors.

In addition to the NuBus card, the Audiomedia II card also is available as a plug-in card for the **LC** and **Performa** 400 series.

Audiomedia II comes with **Sound Designer II**, a sound editing application with an interface similar to **SoundEdit**. You can also use third-party software with the Audiomedia II, including Macromedia's **Deck II**.

> Digidesign, Inc.
> 3401-A Hillview Avenue
> Palo Alto, CA 94304-1348
> Price: $1295
> Phone: (415) 842-7900
> Web: **http://www.digidesign.com/**

See Also

Power Mac Logic Boards; Sound Designer II

Audioshop

A sound recording and editing utility that provides a very stylish interface (which can sometimes be a little confusing, because it sometimes tries too hard to act like a CD player or audio tape recorder rather than just a piece of software).

Supports most common Macintosh audio formats (**AIFF**, **SoundEdit**, and resources), as well as Windows **.WAV** and audio **CD** tracks. The program includes a play list (for playing multiple files), works on AV and Power Macs, and has simple effects, such as echo, reverb, vibrato and flange. Special tools enable you to adjust the audio waveform, editing the pitch and dynamics.

AutoCorrect

Both Microsoft Word and WordPerfect have the capability to catch most common spelling errors and correct them as you type. **Word** calls it AutoCorrect, and **WordPerfect** calls it QuickCorrect. It works the same way in both: if you make a mistake that the utility has been taught to recognize, as soon as you finish typing the word, the letters will jump into their correct position. Suppose you frequently type "hte" or "teh" instead of "the." If it's been entered into the word list, as shown here, it will change automatically.

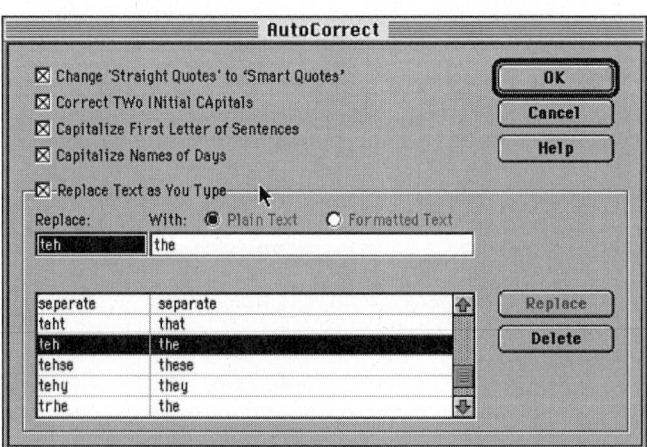

You can enter abbreviations to be spelled out, symbols to replace characters you type as placeholders, and words you forget to capitalize, like Macintosh. QuickCorrect comes with more words already installed, while AutoCorrect expects you to contribute your own mistakes.

A

Automated Mixdown

Sound mixing equipment that records changes made to volume and effects settings during a mixing, and then replays these changes during a subsequent mix. For complicated mixing jobs, this makes it possible to work on one track at a time as the mix is perfected.

See Also
Deck II; Digi Trax

Automatic Pagination

The dedicated typesetting systems of the past often contained batch paginators: software that, given proper direction at the start, would automatically (and very quickly) make up pages to a specified design.

For book and catalog producers, the advent of desktop publishing and the WYSIWYG phenomenon was in some ways a giant step backward. While modern desktop publishing software can do many things older dedicated systems couldn't, such as integration of graphics with type, there's a serious speed loss associated with having to make up each page individually.

That's why desktop publishers who work with long documents are always looking for automated pagination software. Two such options for Macintosh users are AutoPage and Pianzhang, both QuarkXTensions.

Both programs can take a pre-styled **QuarkXPress** document and automatically place graphics and footnotes, adjust facing pages so their depth matches, and create cross-references. There are some differences: For example, Pianzhang can create running headers and footers based on text in the document, such as subheads, while AutoPage can change the number of columns in mid-page, allowing more complex layouts.

AutoPage has the additional ability to work from a coded text file, using XTags, a coding language similar to but more complex than QuarkXPress's built-in **XPress Tags**.

See Also
FrameMaker; QuarkXPress; XPress Tags

Automatic Picture Replacement (APR)

Developed by **Scitex America**, a leading electronic prepress vendor, Automatic Picture Replacement (APR) is a method for automatically replacing placeholder (or proxy) images in an electronic publication file. In the APR scheme, a low-resolution placeholder image is imported into the electronic publication layout as a **for position only (FPO)** proxy. This image is then replaced by a high-resolution version when the publication file is output for printing. APR is primarily used with **Color Electronic Prepress Systems (CEPS)** located at trade shops.

See Also
Desktop Publishing and Color Electronic Prepress Systems (CEPS)

Automatically Hide Open Apps when Switching Between Programs

If you have several applications open and you want to switch to another application, you can have the current application hide (still be open and running, but hidden from view) by holding the Option key and clicking the window of another application. This is a shortcut for going to the **Applications menu** and choosing **Hide Others**.

You can use this same shortcut if you want to switch to the desktop and have the current application be hidden. Just hold the Option key and click anywhere on the desktop, and the current application becomes hidden and the desktop becomes active.

See Also
Applications Menu; Hide Others Command

Autopage, *See Automatic Pagination*

AutoPower On/Off Control Panel

This control panel, introduced in System 7.5, lets you set your Mac to turn on or off at a specified time on a daily basis or on a specified date. This feature is only available to models of Macintosh with soft power (the ability to startup from the **PowerOn key** on the keyboard).

Using the AutoPower On/Off Control Panel is a great way to protect against accidentally leaving your computer on if you've left the office for the day or for the weekend. It's also handy if you want to have the computer startup to perform a task in your absence. You can, for example, have the computer turn itself on at a specified time, and by using **AppleScript**, you can have it log on to the Internet, check to see if you have email, download your email, and then turn itself off. Another use might be to have the computer turn itself on and do a backup of your files, again using AppleScript, and then turn itself back off.

See Also

AppleScript; PowerOn Key

AutoRemounter Control Panel

This **PowerBook** control panel, first introduced in System 7.1, saves you the trouble of manually remounting a **server** or **shared disk** if your PowerBook has gone to **sleep** and lost its connections. When AutoRemounter is enabled, this **control panel** remounts the volumes to which you were last connected. There are a number of ways you can have AutoRemounter operate: remounting after your PowerBook has gone to sleep; setting the AutoRemount to remount anytime the connection goes down, or not to remount at all, as shown in the following figure.

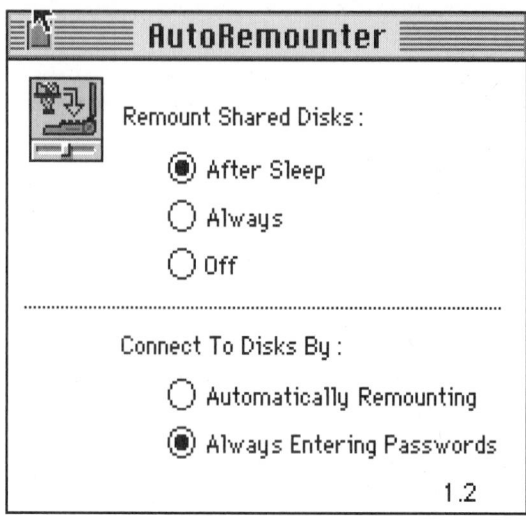

You can also specify that a password be used before a server volume is remounted. Let's say you leave your PowerBook, and it goes to sleep, terminating your connection. Someone else can wake your PowerBook and have access to the servers that AutoRemounter connects to. The password feature protects you from unauthorized server access by requiring a password each time a server is mounted.

To use the AutoRemounter Control Panel, follow these steps:

1. Choose the AutoRemounter Control Panel from the Control Panels submenu on the Apple menu (or System Folder).

2. Click the option to remount the server or shared disk.

3. Select how the connection to the server or shared disk will occur: automatically or by password only.

4. Close the control panel for the changes to take effect.

See Also

Apple Menu; Control Panel; PowerBook; Server; Shared Disk; Sleep Command

Autosync, *See Multisync Monitors*

Autotracing Applications

Anyone who deals with Macintosh graphics must also constantly deal with the dichotomy of vector graphics and **bitmapped graphics**. Sometimes you want one, sometimes the other. And sometimes the one you want isn't what you have.

That's where autotracing applications come in. These programs trace around the elements in a bitmapped graphic to create a vector graphic of the same image that can then be modified in a **drawing application**. The result is a graphic with smoother lines and curves, cleaner fills, smaller file size, and the potential to be modified quickly in a variety of ways (such as adding color).

Autotrace tools are a common feature of drawing applications, but they tend to be limited in their abilities. A dedicated application often provides better results and a greater degree of automation.

The original Mac application designed for this purpose is Streamline. It allows users to scan images or import them; retouch them with basic paint-style tools; and adjust contrast, threshold, and levels. Once the bitmapped image is to the user's liking, Streamline traces each element in one of two ways: outline or centerline.

Outline mode traces around the edges of an element, while centerline mode traces along the center of an element to make it into a line. The former is appropriate for images such as logos, while the latter is used for images with lots of lines, such as technical illustrations.

Tracer is a newer application that accomplishes the same tasks as Streamline, but it has a slightly different approach. While Streamline lets users adjust images before they're converted to obtain the best results, Tracer concentrates on more accurate tracing and editing tools to be used on the resulting vector image.

Tracer offers more accurate tracing than Streamline, with a proportionate increase in processing time. Once Tracer creates a vector image, it can be modified with a complete set of editing tools that any drawing package would envy.

Streamline can convert color images, maintaining up to 256 colors; Tracer is limited to black-and-white images, although basic color fills can be applied after the image is converted. Both applications can compensate for crooked images, straightening and smoothing lines.

Streamline can save settings for later use on similar images, and it comes with built-in settings for common image types. For those with a lot of images to convert, it can also do batch processing, converting them all in one session.

See Also

Bitmapped Graphics; Drawing Applications

A/UX

Apple's add-on A/UX software allows the Mac to run UNIX software directly. This is accomplished by replacing the standard Macintosh operating system with a hybrid of both Apple's System 7 and the UNIX operating systems. Because the resulting Macintosh has both the UNIX and System 7 operating systems, the computer can run both Macintosh and UNIX software. Once A/UX is running, the Mac speaks TCP/IP internally and it can successfully communicate with other UNIX machines.

A/UX requires fairly powerful hardware to run: at least a 68020 with PMMU, 8 MB of ram and 160 MB of free hard disk space are required. According to Apple, the following Macs support A/UX:

- Mac SE/30
- Mac II (with PMMU)
- Mac IIx
- Mac IIcx
- Mac IIci
- Mac IIfx
- Mac IIsi
- Mac Centris 610 (with third-party FPU)
- Centris 650 (With FPU)
- Quadra 610, 650, 700, 800, 900, 950
- All Power PC Macs

A/UX is installed from its CD using Apple's standard installer program. This installer program copies all necessary software to your computer and sets up a protected area (partition) of your hard disk to store the UNIX files. Upon complete installation, you'll see an A/UX icon on your desktop. When you run A/UX, the UNIX partition will mount, and finally A/UX will load and ask you for a name and password, as is standard with UNIX systems.

AV Macintosh

Apple's first AV Macintoshes, the **660AV** and **840AV**, were both based on the 68040 processor and came with an expansion board containing a **DSP** chip to handle audio and video tasks. Both Macintoshes could digitize video and record and play back 16-bit stereo audio. At that time, no other Macintosh could do this without additional hardware.

Although the AV machines offered a new approach to handling audio and video, including the new **DAV** slot, few manufacturers released hardware or software that took advantage of the AV's capabilities, perhaps because they knew the **Power Macintosh** was just around the corner. When the first AVs came out, the PowerPC chip was in its infancy.

Only eight months after the release of the AV Macs, Apple released the first Power Macintosh. These machines used a new **RISC** processor, which was much faster than the comparable 680x0 **CISC** processors found in previous Macs. With the extra speed of the processor, it was possible to perform the AV function without the DSP chip. The new Power Macintosh models all supported 16-bit stereo audio. They, however, did not support video digitizing. Apple sold AV models of the first Power Macintosh computers (the 6100, 7100, and 8100), but these were actually computers that had an added digitizing expansion board—essentially adding the V (video) functions to the Power Macintosh models.

Now Apple offers AV features in most desktop models and seems to have rejected the AV designation altogether. The latest Power Macs (7500 and 8500) come with both video and audio hardware built in, yet lack any AV designation.

See Also

Desktop Models, Macintosh Family; DSP (Digital Signal Processor)

B

Background

Programs have certain functions that can be performed in the background while another application is active. If, for example, you're downloading a file from an online service, you can send that function to the background by making another application active. The downloading of the file will continue, even though you're now working in another application. This is just one example of functions working in the background.

You also can print files in the background while you work in another application by activating the Macintosh computer's **Background Printing** feature. The drawback to having a task completed in the background is that the background task and the active application use the same resources (processing power) to complete their tasks, which can cause sluggish performance in the foreground. Often the mouse will slow down, for example, or it won't react immediately when you move it. Future versions of the **Macintosh Operating System**, however, are being redesigned to enable background tasks to be completed with no effect on foreground activities.

Background Copying, *See*
Copying Files in the Background

Background Printing

When you **print** a document from an application, that application devotes all its resources to printing, and you have to wait until the document is printed before you can move on to your next project. If you don't want to wait, you have the option of printing in the **background** while you continue to work in the

foreground. This is called Background Printing, and it is enabled by choosing Background Printing from the **Chooser**. When Background Printing is activated, your application quickly saves a temporary version of your document to your **hard drive** and then works in the background to send that file to the printer. This enables you to work in your application in the foreground while the application spools the information to the printer in the background.

The drawback to printing in the background is that both the background printing and the active application use the same resources (the same processing power) to complete their tasks. Sometimes while a process is occurring in the background, you'll get sluggish performance in the foreground. Often times, the **mouse** will slow down, or it won't react immediately when you move it. Future versions of the **Macintosh Operating System** are being redesigned to enable background tasks to be completed with no effect on the foreground activities.

See Also
Background; Chooser D/A; Hard Drive; Macintosh Operating System; Mouse; Print

Background, Web Page

Many **home pages** or other documents published on the **World Wide Web** use colors or designs that appear behind the text and images in the content window of the **Web browser** displaying the page.

Some browsers, such as **Netscape Navigator**, let the reader change the color of the background that appears on screen. (This is done in the "Colors" tab in the "General Preferences" item under the "Options" menu.)

Netscape enables users to either use the background color they have specified, or displays the background specified by the authors of the Web pages they are viewing.

The Web page author can set the background of a Web document by specifying the color in the page's source **HTML**:

```
<BODY BGCOLOR="#RRGGBB">
```

where RR, GG, and BB stand for the amount of red, green, and blue, respectively. This system of color definition, the **RGB** model, specifies the levels of these base colors as a number from 1 to 256. To squeeze 256 levels into a two-digit number, HTML specifies **hexadecimal**, or base 16, notation.

In hexadecimal notation, the numbers 10 to 15 are represented by the letters A to F. Thus, 2A in hexadecimal is ((2X16) + 12) = 44 in decimal (base 10) notation. FF is the highest two-digit number in hex notation, so to specify a pure red page, you use the sequence:

```
<BODY BGCOLOR = "#FF0000">
```

For a white page, use

```
<BODY BGCOLOR = "#000000">
```

and for a black page, use

```
<BODY BGCOLOR = "#FFFFFF">
```

You may also use a GIF image in the background of a Web page you are designing. Background image are specified with an extension to the body tag, as follows:

```
<BODY BACKGROUND = "picture.gif">
```

Some background images are shown in the following illustration.

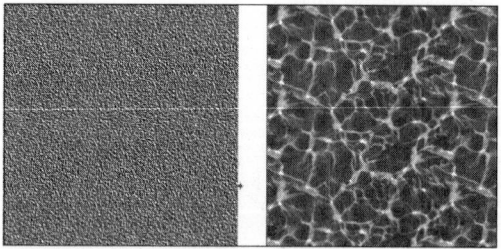

Netscape Gold's HTML editor eliminates the need for the author to use hexadecimal notation by providing a color palette. The author clicks on a color in the palette, and the background color is chosen. Numerical notation can still be used to specify a color, but base 10 rather than base 16 numbers are used. Netscape's Web Starter Site provides ready-made designs for use as background images.

See Also
Home Page; HTML; Internet; Netscape Navigator; Web Browser; World Wide Web

Backing Up

Although computers are quite reliable, there are occasions where they break down or where you experience a system crash, or worse yet, a **hard disk** crash. If any of these situations occur, it is possible that some or all of the data on your hard disk could be damaged or erased permanently. For that reason, it is essential that you make a copy of all your files and store them on an external hard disk or a series of **disks** for safekeeping. This is called backing up. This way, if you do have a serious system or hard disk crash, you can restore your important files, documents, and applications from this "backup" disk. Many people recommend that you keep a backup disk on-site, and keep a separate, identical copy off-site in case of fire, theft, or natural disaster.

It is generally recommended that you back up your files at the end of each work day. There are a number of third-party back up **utilities** that are designed to make this task easy for you.

In essence, these backup utilities store the contents of your hard drive on a disk, and when you go to back up, it updates your backup disk with any files that were created that day. This gives you an up-to-date backup of the files. Whether you need to back up to disks or to an external hard disk depends on how much data you need to back up on a regular basis.

See Also
Backing Up with CD-ROMs; Disk and Drives; Hard Disks; Utilities

B

Backing Up with CD-ROMs

There's little doubt that **CD-ROM** is the most familiar form of optical storage. (For the record, CD-ROM stands for *Compact Disk-Read Only Memory*.) CD-ROMs appear similar to audio CDs, and use the same basic technology. CD-ROMs are widely used to distribute software, especially multimedia and game software.

As the *read-only* in *read-only memory* suggests, CD-ROMs are not rewritable; they can only be used to store data once. In the early years of CD-ROM, disks were typically created by developers, and read ("played") in CD-ROM drives by end-users. In the mid-'90s, the cost of devices that could record (or "burn") CD-ROMs became more affordable to a wider range of users.

In 1996, recordable CD media can cost as little as $.015 (yes, one and a half cents) per megabyte, assuming that all 650MB of storage capacity are used when the CD is burned. (The street price of a single recordable CD is about $10.)

CD-ROM drives are relatively slow, and the process of recording a CD is substantially slower—it would take an hour (at the very least) to back up a 500MB hard disk onto a CD. Recordable CDs, or CD-Rs, as they're commonly called, are probably best used for archival storage or in conjunction with a tape backup system where the tapes are reused after a few months.

Some vendors have begun to offer to burn CD-Rs from a Mac's hard disks. If you can't justify the price of a CD recorder for yourself, but you want a nearly indestructible copy of your valuable data, this sort of service may be just for you. Check a local BBS or newsgroup (if available) for leads.

See Also

Backing Up; Backing Up with Optical Drives; Backing Up with Removable Cartridge Drives; Backup Hardware Options

Backing Up with Optical Drives

There are several variations on optical drive technology, but in general, optical drives offer substantially better data integrity than removable cartridge technology, at the cost (in some cases) of slower performance. Typically, optical drive media is cheaper per megabyte than removable drive media, but the drives themselves are substantially more expensive.

Magnetic Optical Drives Perhaps the most successful optical drive type has been the *magnetic optical*, or MO, drive. MO drives offer the ability to read and write data on fairly inexpensive media, albeit more slowly than conventional hard drives—MO disks are less than half as fast as conventional hard disks.

In mid-1996, MO media is usually available in 128MB or 230MB disks in 3.5-inch sizes, at prices from about $.07/MB to $.11/MB.

In 1996, Fujitsu introduced a relatively inexpensive MO drive that fits the expansion bays of 5300 series PowerBooks—the first such device to work with this line of PowerBook.

Other Optical Drives Research and development continues in the field of optical-based storage, and new devices using new technology seem to come out on a monthly basis. Many such devices offer hybrid CD-R/MO drives, or optical storage at hard-drive speeds, or fantastic storage size at prices approaching $.04 /MB. When considering such drives as a backup solution, be sure to examine closely the drive's speed (Some advertisements offer the meaningless statistic of the disc's RPM rate, for instance), and to weigh compatibility with other devices. A drive that uses proprietary media, no matter how cheap, is of little use if the drive is discontinued.

See Also

Backing Up; Backing Up with CD-ROMs; Backing Up with Removable Cartridge Drives; Backup Hardware Options

Backing Up with Removable Cartridge Drives

Removable cartridge drives are a popular system for backup storage. All of the drive/cartridge systems discussed here use the same basic technology as hard disks to store data, and offer comparable performance:

- **SyQuest Cartridges**—SyQuest cartridges have long been available as backup storage devices. A SyQuest cartridge (technically, a **Winchester cartridge**) is a sealed package that contains a platter like those found in conventional hard drives. The SyQuest drive itself contains the read/write heads, motor, SCSI and control circuitry, and so on. Together, the cartridge and drive act like a conventional hard drive, and are nearly as fast.

  SyQuest drives and cartridges vary in capacity: early SyQuest drives supported 44MB cartridges; the most recent models of SyQuest drives accept cartridges of varying sizes from 44MB to 270MB per cartridge. As of this writing, SyQuest storage costs vary widely depending on the size of the cartridge—from $.22/MB to $1/MB.

  SyQuest drives are very widely used, especially in the desktop publishing industry. (Very often they are used to transport large files to and from printers and service bureaus, as well as for storage.) Most, but not all, SyQuest drives come bundled with software to automate the backup process.

- **Bernoulli Drives**—These drives are very similar to SyQuest drives: the Bernoulli cartridges contain a platter in a sealed package, and the drive itself contains the read/write head, motor, and circuitry. Bernoulli drives are used in virtually the same situations as SyQuest drives, and in fact, there has always been stiff competition between the two formats, with the usual grousing by the advocates of each. (In this writer's experience, SyQuest disks are the more common format.)

Bernoulli cartridges vary in size, from 35MB to 150MB cartridges. (Early versions of the drive support cartridges up to 90MB in size.) In early 1996, storage on Bernoulli drives cost $.60/MB–$1 (or more) per megabyte.

- **Zip Drives**—In 1995, Iomega introduced the Zip drive. Zip disks use a proprietary format: They use a special platter encased in a thick, hard plastic shell that resembles a 3.5-inch disk. The disks are much sturdier than Bernoulli/SyQuest disks: Iomega claims that a Zip disk can survive an eight-foot drop without loss of data.

  Zip drives, which are also available for Windows machines, became immediately popular. Today, there is a wide base of installed Zip drives. The drives themselves are inexpensive, and the cartridges, which hold 100MB of data, are also inexpensive—about $.20/MB (or less) as of this writing. Zip drives are nearly as fast as conventional hard drives. They're small, light, and sturdy, and consequently much more portable than Bernoulli and SyQuest drives. In fact, Iomega markets a carrying case for the drive, cables, and other related Zip paraphernalia.

  There are some limitations to the Zip drive: they don't have power switches, and can't be turned off. Zip drives may only be used at location 5 or 6 of a SCSI chain—they can't be set to any other position. You must connect your Zip drive to your Mac with a special cable (included with the drive) rather than a conventional SCSI cable. (Some users on the **comp.sys.mac.hardware.storage** newsgroup have reported problems using the Zip drive and its cables with 5300-series PowerBooks.)

- **SyQuest EZ Drives**—Introduced shortly after the Iomega Zip drive, the EZ competes in the same market as the Zip drive. EZ drives are essentially tiny SyQuest drives that accept 3.5-inch cartridges and hold 135MB of data, placing EZ drives and cartridges in the same cost and storage capacity ballpark as the Iomega products. (As of this writing, EZ cartridges cost about $.15/MB.)

SyQuest claims that EZ drives are twice as fast as Zip drives. Unlike Zip drives, EZ drives feature a power switch, and may be set to any (available) location on the SCSI chain. Anecdotal evidence by some users has suggested that the EZ drive is not as sturdy as the Zip drive; neither Iomega nor anyone else has provided any evidence of this.

- **Iomega Jaz Drives**—In late 1995, Iomega released the "Jaz" drive. Jaz cartridges are a modified version of the Winchester cartridge, that is, the basis of the SyQuest drive.

    Jaz drives are moderately priced, and support 3.5-inch cartridges that can contain 540MB or 1GB (1,000MB) of data. In early 1996, Jaz storage cost about $.10 to $.15/MB.

    The Jaz drive, like the Zip, is small, light, and portable. Its speed (as published by Iomega) is faster than that of the SyQuest EZ drive. It features a power switch, and may be set at any SCSI location.

See Also

Backing Up; Backing Up with CD-ROMs; Backing Up with Optical Drives; Backing Up with Tape Drives; Backup Hardware Options

Backing Up with Tape Drives

Tape drives have traditionally been the cheapest media for the recording of data—inexpensive tapes can hold large amounts of data. They're also substantially slower than other storage media, and in some systems, less reliable.

A disk is a random-access device: the read/write head that reads the data on the disk can jump to any point on the disk quickly, just as you can put the tonearm down anywhere on a vinyl LP or skip to any track on an audio CD. To get to a particular point on a tape, the drive may need to spool through part of the tape—perhaps most of it—to get to the data you want to retrieve.

Different models of tape drive use different kinds of tape, but as a rule, tape drive media is very inexpensive. With compression, a tape drive can store large amounts of data—you can pay as little as $.01/MB. Because tape drives are slow and cheap, they are used exclusively for backups.

As a result, almost all tape drives come bundled with fairly sophisticated automated-backup software, such as Dantz's Retrospect Remote package. High-end backup software can back up all the machines on a local network, and enables the network administrator to script sophisticated backup routines: backing up servers daily and personal machines weekly, for instance, or half the machines one night, and the other half the next.

See Also

Backing Up; Backing Up with CD-ROMs; Backing Up with Optical Disks; Backing Up with Removable Cartridge Drives; Backup Hardware Options

Backing Up Your Data, *See Backup Hardware Options*

Backquotes

A backquote is a single quote mark that is printed backward. It looks like this ('). The backquote is also used to form the accent acute. On most keyboards, it shares a key with the **tilde** (~).

For example, the '90s requires the backquote before the 9. If you were to us a standard single quote, it would appear as '90s, with the quote pointed in the wrong direction. The backquote is sometimes referred to as a "curlyquote."

See Also

Smart Quotes

Backspace Key

The Backspace key on a PC keyboard is the **Delete key** on a Macintosh keyboard and appears in the same place: in the upper-right corner of the keyboard above the backslash key. Using the Delete key has the same effect as a backspace key in a text editing situation—when using the **I-beam cursor**, it deletes the next character to the left every time it is pressed. It also deletes any selected text or graphic without making a **copy** in the **Clipboard**. The Delete key performs the same functions as the **Clear command**.

See Also

Delete Key; Clear Command; Clipboard; Copy Command

Backup Hardware Options

Nearly every computer user on every platform has some kind of lost file horror story: software glitches can corrupt files into unusability, hard drives can crash, equipment can be stolen. If you have only one copy of an important file, when it's gone, you're doomed. And no matter how lovingly you treat your Mac, no matter how careful you are, sooner or later your hard drive will quit, and its data may well be unrecoverable.

For this reason, it's important to make backup copies of files on a regular basis. In a business environment, where files are of critical importance, servers and even individual machines might be backed up daily, or several times a week. An academic environment may choose to make backups on a weekly or biweekly basis. Home users can make decisions according to individual needs: anywhere from several times a week to once every several months.

Although backup is used here in the limited sense— the precautionary making of redundant copies of files on your active hard disk(s)—very often your backup storage solution will need to be used for other purposes as well. For example, you may wish to use the storage device for archiving completed jobs that you will remove from your hard disk, or transporting large files from one machine to another.

The appropriate backup hardware varies according to circumstances. The questions to consider when shopping for hardware include:

- How much data will I regularly back up?

- What is the cost per megabyte of the long-term storage?

- How accessible must the stored material be?

Naturally, you don't necessarily need to choose one solution for all of your storage needs, and you may need to improvise new solutions in special situations.

Backup Hardware Speed The speed of backup storage devices is rated in exactly the same way as conventional **hard drives**, using:

- **Transfer rate:** The rate at which the device moves data from the device to the Mac.

- **Seek time:** The average amount of time it takes for the device to move the read/write head from its current location to any arbitrary chunk of data.

Hard Disks and Floppies There's no disgrace in compulsively making extra copies of important files by hand and storing them on whatever media is at your disposal. If you're working on a *Maclopedia* entry, for example, you might want to store the MS Word file on a disk, even if you know that your hard drive is scheduled for automatic backup later.

It's of little use, however, to store all such backups in the same place as the original file. Storing the archived copy in the same folder on the same drive as the original file won't protect you from a disk crash or malfunction.

Hard Drives If you have a second hard drive, or access to a drive over a network, it's safe to store a copy of the file on the other drive. However, it's almost certainly impractical for you to back up every file you create by hand: hard disk space is too valuable (about $.30/MB to $.40/MB in 1996). Furthermore, hard drive space is limited: you can fit no more than six **SCSI devices** in a chain, and hence, no more than six hard drives.

TIP If you've got plenty of empty space available on a disk other than your main drive, the second disk is probably the most convenient device for making a temporary backup of your disk when you're installing new system software or reinitializing your startup hard drive.

Disks: Pros and Cons In the early years of the Macintosh, when 20MB hard drives were common and 80MB hard drives were considered enormous, it was common practice to back up entire hard drives onto disks with software packages such as **Norton Utilities**. Nowadays it's impractical and expensive to back up an entire hard disk to floppies.

A relatively small hard drive requires more than 150 floppies to completely archive. Backing up such a hard disk from scratch would take at least 4-5 hours of active-disk swapping by the user, during which time both the Mac and the user are unavailable for other tasks. Disks are moderately priced; in 1996, disk storage costs from $.15 to $.30 per megabyte (or even more).

Some floppy-based software packages (such as the aforementioned Norton Backup) are able to make incremental updates to backup-archives, only storing files that have changed since the last backup. This may be practical for users with an established archive who rarely create large new files; unfortunately, few users fit this description.

Floppies are fairly well-suited for the task of making backup copies of other disks—usually, original program disks. However, it's fairly simple to backup floppies on faster, cheaper media using disk-image tools such as Apple's DiskImage or the superb shareware package **ShrinkWrap**.

See Also

Backing Up with CD-ROM; Backing Up with Optical Drives; Backing Up with Removable Cartridge Drives; Backing Up with Tape Drives

Backup Utilities

There are a number of third-party utilities such as Norton Fastback (part of the Norton Utilities package) by Symantec (10201 Torre Ave, Cupertino, CA, 95104-2132, Phone (800) 441-7234. Web site at **http:// www.symantec.com**), Retrospect by Dantz Development Corporation (4 Orinda Way, Orinda, CA 94563. Phone: 510-253-3000. On the Web **http://www.dantz.com**), and Redux (by Focus Enhancements, Inc. (800 W. Cummings Park, Ste. 4500, Woburn, MA 01801) that help you back up the contents of your **hard disk**, so if you were to have a serious system or hard disk **crash**, your important files and applications would be stored on an external disk for safekeeping.

These backup utilities enable you to schedule a specific time to back up the contents of your disk and enable a wide range of customization for how you'd like your files archived onto a backup disk. You can also configure backup utilities to back up all Macs on a network.

Backup Utilities

Backup Utility	Developer	Purpose	Benefit
Norton Fastback	Symantec	Backup of files/ Archiving	Makes backing up of your files easy by backing up selected files or all files. Part of the Norton Utilities Package.
Retrospect and Retrospect Remote	Dantz Development	Backup of files/ Archiving for users on networks with large amounts of data to backup	Enables unattended automated backup. Supports wide range of devices and compresses backed up file. Ideal for tape drives.

continues

Backup Utilities (continued)

Backup Utility	Developer	Purpose	Benefit
DiskFit	Dantz Development	Backup of files/ Archiving for single computers or users with small amounts of data to backup	Does not compress files, backs up to removable disks and scheduling automatic, unattended backup to a folder on the server or another hard drive.
Redux Deluxe	Focus Enhancements	Backup of files/ Archiving	Offers quick, easy, inexpensive backup for individuals to disks, hard disks, or removable media.

See Also

Backing Up; Crashes, System; Hard Disk

Balloon Help

Apple created Balloon Help as a interactive way for new users to learn the Macintosh system. When Balloon Help is active, users can point to an item on the screen: a **folder**, **icon**, command, and so on, and a balloon, (styled after the comment balloons from comic strips), would appear with a brief description of the item the user was pointing at and how to use it. This way, if you're working in a program and you run across a feature you're not familiar with, you simply point to it with your cursor and an explanation would appear, as shown in the following figure.

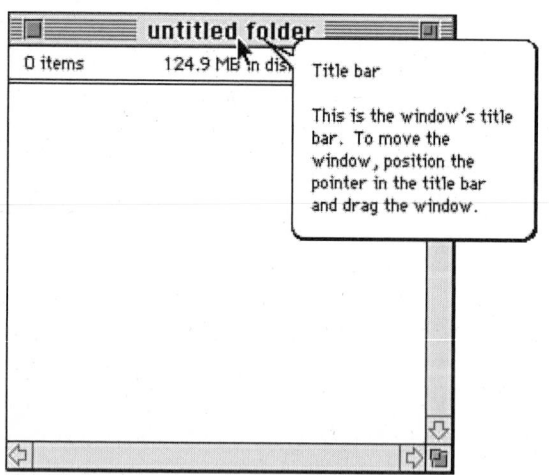

Balloon Help is available at the **desktop** and also in many applications that support Balloon Help. To activate Balloon Help, simply click and hold on the **Help** menu icon in the menu bar. (This is the second icon from the far right of the menu bar, with an icon of a question mark in a balloon.) Choose Show Balloons to activate Balloon Help and then just point to any item on your screen to see a balloon help comment. To deactivate Balloon Help, select Hide Balloons from the Help menu.

To use Balloon Help, follow these steps:

1. Choose Show Balloons from the Help menu in the menu bar. (The question mark icon, to the left of the Applications menu on the far right of the menu bar.)

2. Point to the item you'd like help with and if there is Balloon Help available for that item, a balloon will appear and will remain there until you move your cursor to another location.

To disable Balloon Help, choose Hide Balloons from the Help menu in the menu bar. (The question mark icon, to the left of the Application menu on the far right of the menu bar.)

See Also
Desktop; Help; Help Menu

Balthazar
A shareware utility that converts audio files from the .WAV sound format to System 7 sound files, and vice-versa. This software is shareware and available from online services.

See Also
Wave

Bar Code and Magnetic Stripe Readers
Bar codes solve many problems, but usually don't come to mind when discussing personal computers. Supermarket checkouts leave the impression that bar codes require big, expensive hardware. To view bar codes on your Mac, you need to install the bar code font in your font folder in the System folder. To print bar codes, you generally need the resolution of a laser printer, but dedicated mailing label printers from CoStar and Seiko can print postal bar codes successfully with thermal printing technology.

A bar code represents an identification number for an item using patterns of lines and spaces. After the bar code reader decodes the number (as illustrated in the following picture), the computer looks up the corresponding item in its database. At that point, you have access to all the information about the item. In the supermarket, the decoded product identification number triggers the computer to enter the price into the cash register. At the same time, it deducts the item from the store's inventory.

The key to bar codes' usefulness is that they trigger the release of information. Bar code readers simply automate entry of the identification number. You can do the same thing by typing numbers on a keyboard,

or even by using a voice recognition system. Many bar code formats are in use, each adapted for the needs of that particular industry. The best known is the Universal Product Code (UPC) found on virtually all retail items. The Postal Service and legal industry use their own bar codes. Various formats, including three of nine (three sets of 9-digit numbers) and two of five (two sets of 5-digit numbers, as in UPCs), are suitable for vertical application developers.

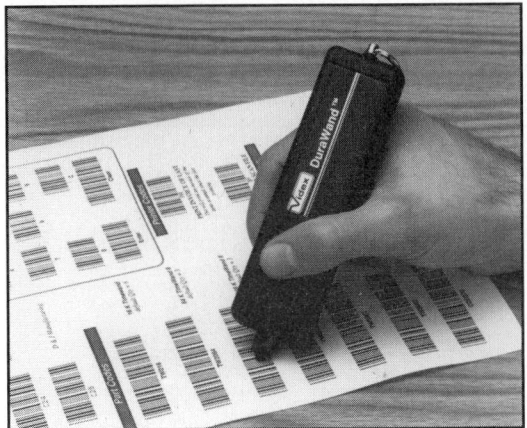

Closely related to bar codes are the magnetic stripes on credit cards and ATM cards. The advantage of magnetic stripes is that you can change and update the information stored on the cards. Bar code and magnetic stripe readers typically are **serial port** or **Apple Desktop Bus devices**.

Magnetic stripes can store a fair amount of data and you can change that data whenever necessary. They are especially useful for pseudo-money systems (such as amusement park rides, mass transit, and so forth). In these applications, the end-user "buys" a certain amount of money and "spends" it by sliding the card through a reader, which updates the data on the card. They're also used at trade shows, such as MacWorld, to scan admission badges for mailing lists.

The following table provides an overview of the bar code and magnetic stripe readers available for the Mac.

Bar Code and Magnetic Stripe Readers for the Mac

Manufacturer	Model Name	Features	Street Price
Synex	Uniscan 300 Bar Code Reader	Translates UPC, Code 39, EAN, Codabar, and 2 of 5 bar codes directly. ADB device, no driver software required	$279
DataDesigns	DD MagScan, DD Maxi-Bar, DD MaxiScan, DD MiniBar, DD ScanImage, and DD ScanPlus	Magnetic stripe and bar code readers	$395 to $3,950
Videx	DuraWand	Portable, pen-like bar code reader	$495 for pen, $100 for software, $859 for complete system
Videx	OmniWand	Portable bar code reader and palette	$1,235
Percon	Series 10 and Series 20	Bar code reader with light pen and cable. Can read magnetic stripe cards	$540 to $605
TPS Electronics	TPS Bar code and Magnetic Stripe Readers	Variety of readers. Magnetic stripe readers can record and verify data stored on cards	$369 to $2,795

See Also
Apple Desktop Bus; Keyboards; Mouse

<BASE> HTML Tag

<BASE> is a tag that goes in the head of an **HTML** document and specifies the location of the original URL of the document on the **Internet**. Useful as kind of an insurance policy; if your **Internet service provider** or the person running your Web server misplaces your document while moving around a bunch of HTML files, <BASE> indicates where it went in the first place.

See Also
HTML; Web Browser; Web Page; World Wide Web

Baseline, *See Typesetting Terms*

BASIC

A popular **programming language** developed in the early 1960s.

BASIC was developed by John Kemeny and Thomas Kurtz at Dartmouth College to help teach programming to students (the name is an acronym for Beginner's All-Purpose Symbolic Instruction Code). In the early days of personal computers, BASIC was the programming language of choice. If a new computer couldn't be programmed in BASIC, its future was in serious jeopardy, because most of the software that ran on those early computers was written by the user. Today's cornucopia of commercial software offerings didn't exist. Over time, most computer users stopped writing their own software and the importance of BASIC diminished.

But BASIC is far from dead. **Microsoft** has adopted it as the preferred macro language for its applications, and in the Windows world, Visual Basic is one of the most popular development tools. After several very quiet years, the Macintosh BASIC world is vibrant again.

Originally, BASIC required that each line of code be preceded by a line number. This was convenient in the days of punchcards, because the cards could be entered in any order—the line numbers would take care of the ordering. This simple BASIC program displays the words "Hello World!" 10 times:

```
10 FOR I = 1 TO 10
20 PRINT "Hello World!"
30 NEXT I
```

More modern versions of BASIC support a much richer feature set, including true functions and subroutines and block-style flow control statements (IF-THEN-ELSE, DO loops, and so on).

Traditionally, BASIC has been an **interpreted language**, which greatly limited the speed of programs written in it. Most of today's BASICs, however, provide **compilers** to generate native object code.

Over the years, the Macintosh has seen several versions of BASIC come and go. Today, there are three major competitors: True BASIC, Mainstay's VIP BASIC, and Staz Software's **Future Basic** II. All of these commercial environments provide a rich implementation of BASIC with full access to the **Toolbox**.

In addition to the commercial BASICs, Chipmunk BASIC (**http://www.rahul.net/rhn/cbas.page.html**) is a small freeware interpreter that is Power Mac-native. It is similar to the versions of BASIC that were included with early personal computers.

See Also

Future Basic; Interpreted Language; Toolbox

Basic Rate Interface, *See ISDN*

Basketball, *See Sports Games*

Batch Processing

Applying a series of effects or changes to multiple files. This is particularly useful when working with a large collection of graphics or QuickTime files. There are some tools that provide automated batch processing functions, and it is also possible to write AppleScripts to perform repetitive tasks.

See Also

AppleScript; CD-ROM Movie Maker; Movie Cleaner Pro

Batch Transmission, *See File Transfer Protocols*

Batchlt

BatchIt, from Gryphon Software, is the first true visual image processing system. You set it up like a chain of Tinker-Toy blocks, connecting various options together in a visual chain. The Image Processing chain links (called "tiles") can be saved, so that after a successful one is discovered and checked out, it's always available to process images in the future. Each of the Tiles assumes a task in the chain from among the choices listed here. The trick is to start out exploring and building a simple task, and then to expand to multi-processing image files. The visual blocks are much like those used to indicate steps in a programming language, which is exactly the point that BatchIt is making.

The BatchIt Tiles perform different tasks in the processing chain. They can process an entire image file (crop, change palettes and resolutions, apply a Photoshop Filter), extract specific data from an image, and also use the data from one image to apply it to another in the chain. Tiles are dragged from the Tile list and dropped in the work area. They require a minimum of 2.5 pixels between them, and they will not paste if you attempt an illegal operation. A marquee placed around a Tile group selects all of the tiles for movement or deletion. The tiles have female input ports and male output ports. Some tiles, those to be placed at the beginning of a chain, have only output ports, while those meant for the end of a chain have only an input port. As expected, data enters through an input port, and is sent on its way, after being processed, through an output port. Tiles are connected by pipeline *Links* are interactively constructed by mouse selections (as long as the connection makes logical sense). You can type notes that refer to the Link by selecting it and choosing Get Link Info from the menu. The documentation walks you through several tutorial examples.

Tiles parameters are set by accessing their associated dialogs, usually by double-clicking on an appropriate button. Each Tile has a specific task, as explained here:

- Blur—Eliminates noise in selection.
- Brightness/Contrast—Sliders on the Tile adjust these parameters.
- Calculator—A pop-up menu lists options, and the Calculator obtains the desired data from the image.
- Color—Sets a color for processing.
- Color Space—Sets the color space (RGB, HSC, CMYK, HSL).
- Convolution—Applies a convolution matrix to the graphic.
- Darken—Darkens the image by a set amount.
- Depth—Provides bit-depth data to Tiles.
- Flip—Flips the image horizontally or vertically.
- Get Color Space—Gets the color space (RGB, HSC, CMYK, HSL).
- Get Depth—Finds the most commonly used 256 (or less) colors in the images.
- Get Image Size—Gets the data for the image size and passes it on.
- Get Palette—Gets the color data of the image and passes it on.
- Invert—Turns the image into a negative.
- Lighten—Lightens the image with user-defined intensity.
- Mixer—A digital mixer with four separate input channels and one output.

- Monitor Depth—Views the images bit-depth.
- Monitor Image—Enables you to view the image at any point in the chain.
- Monitor Palette—Enables you to view the image's palette at any point in the chain.
- Monitor Value—Enables you to see the image value while it's being passed on to interested Tiles.
- Open—Enables you to select batches of images for processing.
- Palette—Your selected palette data for the image.
- Photoshop Filter Emulator—Enables you to select a Photoshop filter and its options.
- Resolution—Enables you to set a resolution, which is then passed to Tiles, such as Set Image Size and Set Canvas Size.
- Rotate—Sets the rotation value of the image.
- Save—Saves the images to a file. You can set all of the necessary parameters and data paths.
- Set Canvas Size—Adds or decreases the space around the image.
- Set Color Space—Enables you to alter the images color makeup (for example, RGB to CMYK).
- Set Image Size—Enables you to change the image's height, width, and resolution.
- Set Palette—Enables you to change image's palette type.
- Set PAL Depth—Enables you to change image's PAL depth.
- Set Resolution—Sets image resolution.
- Sharpen—Sharpens the image to a set amount.
- Sink Depth—Takes in bit-depth data.
- Sink Image—Takes in image data.
- Sink Palette—Takes in palette data.
- Sink Value—Takes in image value data.

- Splitter—Splits the image's Red, Green, Blue, and Alpha channels, and sends each on to a separate processing source.

- Value—Enables you to set a numerical value (Inches, Centimeters, Points, Picas, Pixels, Percent, None), which is passed on to other Tiles for processing.

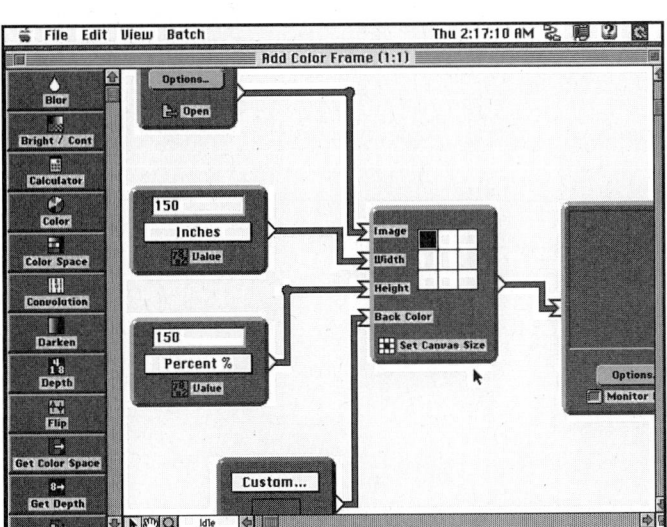

Battery DA

If you're using a **PowerBook** and running **System 7.1**, you can check how much battery life is left by accessing the Battery DA. This **Control Panel** (which has been replaced in **System 7.5** with the PowerBook control strip) displays a gauge made up of little bars reading from empty at left to full at the right. If all the bars in the gauge are highlighted, the battery is full. As the battery is used, the eight bars begin to turn white one by one until all the bars are white, indicating that no battery charge is left.

There is also a button you can use to put your PowerBook to **sleep** to conserve battery power.

To use the Battery DA, follow these steps:

1. Be sure to have a PowerBook running System 7.1 or later.

2. Choose Battery DA Clock from the Apple menu on your PowerBook.

3. The amount of battery power left is displayed in a bar gauge reading from empty at left to full on the right.

4. To put your PowerBook to sleep, click the System Sleep button.

See Also

Control Panel; PowerBook; Sleep Command; Sleep Mode; System 7.1; System 7.5

Battle Chess, *See Chess*

Baud/BPS

A system of measurement indicating the speed at which a **modem** (or printer) can send and receive data, usually called *bps* or bits per second.

One baud equals one change of signal status or one data bit per second. At low speeds a baud and a data bit are about the same. One character entered on a Macintosh keyboard consists of eight data bits or one *byte* of information. When characters are transmitted with a modem a start bit and stop bit are added to each set of eight bits. Therefore, ten bits are required to transmit one character.

At this writing, conventional modems can send and receive at rates of 14,400Bps and 28,800Bps, also expressed as 14.4Kbps and 28.8Kbps, respectively.

Other data transmission cables use *bps* to express the speed at which they handle data communications. **ISDN** lines, for instance, provide speeds of about 56Kbps to 128Kbps.

See Also

Asynchronous DataTransfer; Data Communications Standards; Modems; Internet; PPP; SLIP; World Wide Web

BBEdit

A text **editor** from Bare Bones Software.

In its early days, the "BB" in BBEdit stood for "Bare Bones." This svelte editor was stripped to the bone—doing little more than simple editing—but was fast and efficient for editing source code. BBEdit has gained a multitude of features that puts it in the upper crust of Macintosh editors. Despite the rich feature set, BBEdit remains true to its origins and is still fast and efficient.

The following figure shows some of BBEdit's features in action. The pop-up menu at the top-left of each editing window displays a context-sensitive list of locations within the file. When editing source code, this menu shows all routines within the file; when editing **HTML Web pages**, it shows all headers and links within the file. Choosing an item from the menu enables you to jump directly to that location in the file.

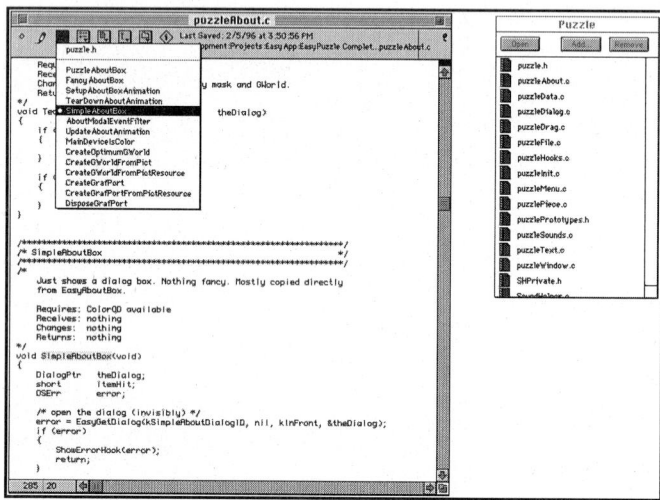

The group window at the top right enables you to gather related files and manipulate them without having to search for the files each time you need to use them.

BBEdit is fully scriptable using **AppleScript**, **Frontier**, or any other **OSA**-compatible scripting language. There is even a menu displaying any scripts present in a special scripts folder in the same folder as the BBEdit application.

In addition to scripting, BBEdit's feature set can be augmented with **plug-in** extensions. Bare Bones Software released the complete API for creating extensions, and a wide variety of freeware and shareware

extensions exist. These extensions extend BBEdit in almost unlimited ways. Extensions exist to manipulate files, send **PostScript** to a printer, and convert between character sets. There is also an extension that can use **PlainTalk** to have the computer speak the text of the current selection.

With the rise of the **World Wide Web**, BBEdit has taken on another area of text editing: creating and editing HTML text for use on the Web. Several sets of extensions have been written for BBEdit to enable it to create and manage HTML files. The most popular of these is the BBEdit HTML Extension, by Lindsay Davies (**http://www.york.ac.uk/ ~ld11/BBEditTools.html**). In BBEdit 3.5.2 and later, these extensions appear as an easily accessible floating tool palette (see the following figure).

Editing Web pages in BBEdit does not offer the near-**WYSIWYG** display of programs such as Adobe's **PageMill**, but you do completely control the HTML tags and can preview pages in your favorite Web browser directly from BBEdit.

BBEdit interacts well with other programs, such as the Symantec and Metrowerks integrated development environments (IDEs), Frontier, and Internet tools such as **Web browsers** and **FTP** clients.

BBEdit comes in two versions: BBEdit and BBEdit Lite. The lite version lacks many of the advanced features of the full version but has the advantage of being free. You can download BBEdit Lite from most online services, or directly from Bare Bones' Web site.

BBEdit is published by Bare Bones Software:

Bare Bones Software, Inc.
P.O. Box 1048
Bedford, MA 01730-1048
Email: **bbsw@netcom.com**
Fax: (508) 651-7584
Phone: (508) 651-3561
Web: **http://www.barebones.com**

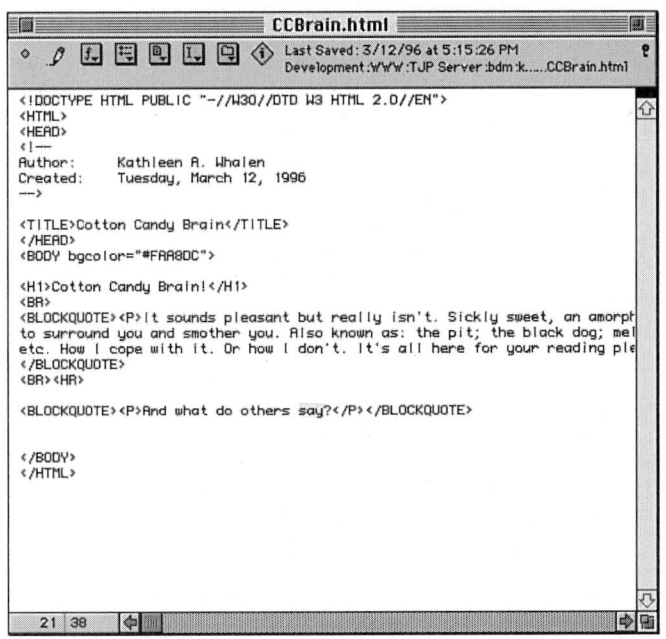

```
                    CCBrain.html
Last Saved: 3/12/96 at 5:15:26 PM
Development:WWW:TJP Server:bdm:k......CCBrain.html

<!DOCTYPE HTML PUBLIC "-//W3O//DTD W3 HTML 2.0//EN">
<HTML>
<HEAD>
<!--
Author:      Kathleen A. Whalen
Created:     Tuesday, March 12, 1996
-->

<TITLE>Cotton Candy Brain</TITLE>
</HEAD>
<BODY bgcolor="#FAA8DC">

<H1>Cotton Candy Brain!</H1>
<BR>
<BLOCKQUOTE><P>It sounds pleasant but really isn't. Sickly sweet, an amorph
to surround you and smother you. Also known as: the pit; the black dog; mel
etc. How I cope with it. Or how I don't. It's all here for your reading ple
</BLOCKQUOTE>
<BR><HR>

<BLOCKQUOTE><P>And what do others say?</P></BLOCKQUOTE>


</BODY>
</HTML>

21  38
```

See Also

AppleScript; Editor; Frontier; HTML; World Wide Web

BBS, *See Bulletin Board Systems; Online Services*

Be, *See Jean Louis Gassée*

Beach Ball/Wristwatch Cursor

If you ask your Macintosh to complete a task that takes a few moments, the **cursor** will change into an **icon** of a wristwatch, usually with the hands spinning, to let you know it's not frozen and is processing your request. A popular cursor, used by many applications to let you know that you're going to have to wait a few moments before your request is completed, is a round spinning cursor that looks like a black-and-white beach ball. More and more applications are coming out with customized "wait" cursors that feature the company logo, the product name, or a small animation. A third-party add-on called ClickChange by DublClick Software enables you to customize the wait cursor and choose from a host of wait cursors with some clever full-color animation.

See Also

Crashes, System; Cursor; Icon

BeBox, *See Jean Louis Gassée*

BeforeDark

BeforeDark is a shareware **desktop pattern** utility that enables you to use up to a full 256 x 256-pixel image size to create complex background textures. BeforeDark is a stand-alone **utility** and it enables you to create, edit, and import PICT images for use as a background texture on your desktop. BeforeDark was later transformed into a commercial desktop pattern utility called **Chameleon**, which was released as part of the Seventh Heaven Utilities for System 7 by Logical Solutions.

See Also

Chameleon; Desktop Pattern; Utility

Bell 103, *See Modem Transfer Protocols*

Bell 212a, *See Modem Transfer Protocols*

Benchmark Tests

When people compare computers and the software that runs on them, they want something quantitative—speed, size, price, or a feature list. Benchmark tests are the primary tool used to evaluate speed. For the computer itself, tests such as Speedometer are commonly run, and you can get results measured in **MIPS** (millions of instructions per second) and MegaFlOps (millions of floating point operations per second). There are also test programs that rate the efficiency of the **compilers** and other development tools for the platform, as well as being able to compare how different models relate using the same benchmark test from the same compiler. Dhrystone and Whetstone are two of the more common compiler tests. A benchmark comparing two word processors might be how quickly you can spell-check the document or change all occurrences of "IBM" to "Apple."

See Also
MIPS

Berners-Lee, Tim

One of the inventors of the **World Wide Web.** The Web was proposed by Tim Berners-Lee at CERN, the European Laboratory for Particle Physics in Switzerland. Currently Berners-Lee is director of the W3 Consortium at MIT. Home page: **http://www.w3.org/ hypertext/WWW/People/Berners-Lee-Bio.html**.

See Also
World Wide Web

Bernoulli Drive

Superficially at least, Bernoulli drives and cartridges are similar to the **SyQuest** removable hard drives familiar to many Macintosh users.

The Bernoulli drive itself is an external **SCSI** device into which the Bernoulli cartridge is placed. A special driver enables the cartridge to mount and dismount in much the same fashion as a disk.

Underneath, however, the differences are significant.

Unlike SyQuest cartridges, which use **Winchester** technology, Bernoulli cartridges are not hard disks at all. They utilize drive heads which move back and forth across a platter to read data but the platters in a Bernoulli cartridge are flexible. This flexibility is quite deliberate and enables the platters to take advantage of the **Bernoulli Effect** to keep the platters very close to the **read/write heads** with little chance of a head crash.

The platters inside a Bernoulli cartridge are spinning in a chamber filled with filtered moving air. This re-duces the air pressure between the platter and the read/write head, which induces the Bernoulli Effect, drawing the flexible platters towards the read/write heads.

See Also
Backing Up with Removable Cartridge Drives

Bernoulli Effect

Bernoulli's Law, named after its discoverer, Swiss mathematician and physicist, Daniel Bernoulli, states that the pressure exerted by a non-compressible fluid (such as air) in motion is inversely proportional to the square of its velocity. So the faster a fluid flows through a given space the lower the pressure felt by objects within or at the boundary of that space.

The Bernoulli Effect is the name given to the observed behavior of objects affected by this fluid flow.

Beta Testing

After a piece of software under development by a software manufacturer reaches the later stages of development, it is often sent into what is called beta testing. Beta testing is done after the product is **alpha tested** by the compiler's in-house staff, and the software has been recompiled to a **beta version**. There may be a number of different beta versions as bugs are fixed and features are added or deleted.

The beta version is when out-of-house users test a pre-release copy of the program for bugs, software glitches, conflicts, and generally give their thoughts on the product. Sometimes **beta testers** give important feedback on what they like about the product and what areas they feel should be improved. Beta testers are encouraged to push beta software to its limits and to use it in a variety of taxing situations to help find flaws or bugs in the program that should be caught before the final product is compiled.

Beta testers are generally not paid for their work, but they are often offered a significant discount, or even given a full-shipping version of the software product after it ships. The feedback that the company receives from beta testers is often used to make last-minute changes or bug fixes to the product before the final

B

version is compiled (referred to as the "golden master" or "going gold"). The gold master compiled at the end of the beta testing period is used to create the final shipping version sold to consumers. Theoretically, the shipping version shouldn't contain bugs and glitches. Hopefully these are caught and fixed in the alpha and beta testing stages.

See Also
Alpha Testing; Alpha Version; Beta Version

Beta Versions

Near the end of the development stage of a software or hardware product, a beta version of the product is compiled. This is compiled only after the original version of the new product, called an **alpha version**, has been thoroughly tested by the developer's in-house staff in a process called **alpha testing**. During alpha testing the software is tested and retested in-house to catch any bugs or problems with the product. After the problems are fixed and the bugs are found in the alpha version, the company recompiles the software into a near-final version called the beta version. This version is important because it is given to select members of the public to test the software or hardware product in their own environment to find any glitches or bugs in a real-world environment before the product is sold commercially. These select members of the public are called beta testers.

Beta software often goes through a number of versions as bugs are fixed and features are added or deleted. To find out which version of the beta software is being used, a beta tester can choose "About This Software" from the top of the **Apple menu**, and the application's splash screen will usually have the Beta version number listed. Also, the letter "B" is often used to denote a beta version. Example: Version 1.0b.

Beta software is often prone to crashes and other conflicts as it is solely used for testing purposes and is not a final shipping version. Beta versions also often contain "debugging" software built into the version to enable programmers at the software company to debug the software

easily. This can add to the overall size of the beta version and greatly affect performance. When the beta testing stage is over and the final version is compiled, any debugging software is removed.

See Also
Alpha Testing; Alpha Version; Beta Testing

Bézier Curves

Named after the French engineer who invented them in the early '60s for use in the body design of Renault cars, Bézier curves are defined by three points: a center point and two exterior, or control, points that control the shape of the curve but aren't on it. As seen in most **PostScript** drawing programs, these curves are defined by points with levers or "handles" coming off them. Users adjust curves by moving the handles.

Big Business

Offering more than a financial management system, Big Business bills itself as the "complete management system." It combines an accounting system with a relational database, giving you the capability to prepare and send quotes, schedule payments to vendors, and keep track of inventory and sales. It uses a series of toolbars and graphic interfaces and is designed to be networked with password protection, so that different users have access only to those functions they need or have been trained to use. The interface is occasionally confusing, as there are some icons that seem to be just for decoration.

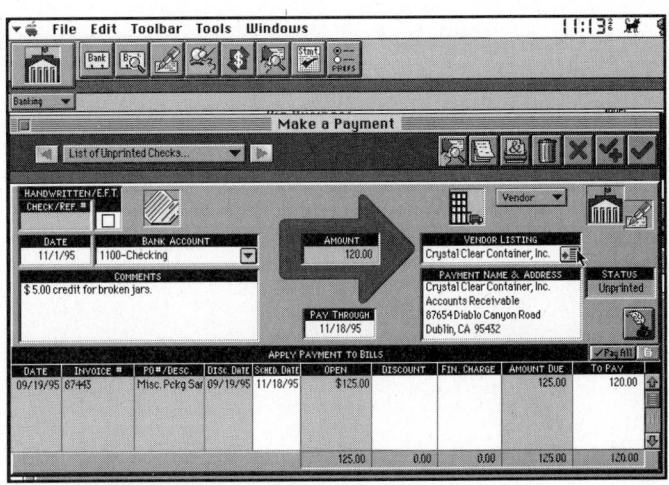

The sales staff can use Big Business' client database and product database to create quotes for customers and to reactivate dormant accounts by checking to see who hasn't bought the product in 30, 60, 90, or more days. The warehousing and shipping staff can keep a close eye on inventory and re-order items as soon as a critical level is reached. The bookkeeper can use it to post receivables and payables and to write checks to vendors. It reconciles bank balances, but it doesn't do payrolls or 1099s or any type of tax forms, including sales tax.

There's a note function that lets users pass messages, reminders, and schedules back and forth with other Big Business users on their network. Dated notes can serve as an inter-office calendar. If, for example, you plan a meeting for 9 a.m. on November 8th, a dated note will cause it to appear on the calendars of all to whom you send it.

Big Business has some very powerful features that aren't relevant to all kinds of businesses but make it an ideal program for those who are involved in sales. The major feature is the ease of recording and maintaining client contacts. Each customer has a card with contact, shipping, and billing information. A second card with the customer's sales history is linked to that card. Clicking a line entry for a previous sale brings up the invoice, so you can see exactly was what ordered. You also can see whether or not it has been paid, and if so, how long it took. The customer card is also linked to a customer folder with space to enter a call record, notes, and relevant personal information. (Many sales people use these cards to list the names of the customer's spouse and children, hobbies, or likes and dislikes.)

The customer card gives access to three kinds of customer information windows: quotes, sales orders, and invoices. The quote is a proposal to sell a product or do a job for the customer at a certain price. If the customer accepts the quote, you turn it into a sales order, which allocates the items to be shipped, specifies the shipping method, and subtracts the items from inventory. When the items are ready to be shipped, the sales order is converted into an invoice, which represents the actual sale and is posted into the accounting system. If you are preparing a quote for a customer, you can adjust the profitability of the job by simply typing in the profit margin you want to end up with. BB adjusts the selling price, based on the cost of the material(s) you use for the job, to reflect any profit margin you want.

Because Big Business can track so much data about your customers and vendors, finding exactly what you're looking for could be tricky, but, thanks to the QuickSearch function that lets the user specify exactly what information to look for, it's not. You can find all the clients in a particular city, all the bills larger than a specified amount, all the items you've purchased from a particular vendor, or all the customers who have bought a specific item. Searches are based on fields, from which you create a "sentence." For instance, combing the fields "zip code," "begins with," and "021" would find all the customers in eastern Massachusetts.

Big Business isn't for everybody. It's ideal for certain kinds of businesses, specifically those that do a lot of telemarketing, those that carry an inventory of items for sale, and those who have pricing based on volume or competitive bids. It's not the most powerful accounting program, but the sales management tools make up for many of its weaknesses. The lack of a payroll function, however, might be a problem for many users. Perhaps a future version will include this, with a tie in to salespeople's commissions.

See Also

Financial Planning Software; MYOB (Mind Your Own Business); Peachtree Accounting

Big:Calc Program

Big:Calc is the Macintosh calculator program designed especially for people with special needs. This talking calculator features big numbers and high quality speech. It works just like any other calculator program but has the advantages of really big numbers and keys, and built-in speech. Big:Calc can be used alone or with databases, spreadsheets, or number programs. At the user's option, equations can be viewed vertically or horizontally. Users can enter data by mouse, keyboard controls, or by touching the numbers on an optional TouchWindow **touch screen**.

B

Dyslexic students who frequently reverse the order of numbers receive instant acoustic feedback on the accuracy of their typing. The layout and font color and size can be changed to suit the user's age and math needs, as well as his or her preference or visual requirements. The many speech options enable users to hear numbers, functions, or entire equations depending on what best meets their needs.

Binding Margins, *See Margins and Tabs*

BinHex

A method of **encoding** Macintosh files so they can be transported across a network such as the **Internet**.

BinHex is a way of encoding files from 8-bit to 7-bit format while preserving file attributes. Macintosh files consist of both a "**resource** fork" and a "data fork." When Mac files are transferred to other operating systems, everything in the resource fork has to be moved to the data fork in order for the file to be stored in the other operating system's directory.

BinHex encoding converts a binary file to a 7-bit format while preserving attributes such as the resource fork. It can be used to encode any type of file, including word processing, graphics, spreadsheets, and software applications. BinHex'd files are signified by the extension ".hqx"—a common sight on Mac **FTP** sites such as **software archives**.

The shareware application BinHex is used to encode BinHex files, whereas BinHex or **StuffIt Expander** can be used to unencode the files.

See Also
Encoding Files; FTP; Internet; Macintosh Software Archives; StuffIt Expander; World Wide Web

Bit Depth, *See Color Resolution*

Bit-Smoothing, *See Printing Technology, PostScript Lasers, Halftoning*

Bitmap and 3D Object Formats

The development of computer graphics over the years has not always taken place in a planned manner. Software developers have introduced new products without taking the time to structure their software so that it is friendly towards similar software already on the market. When software packages can communicate with each other in some manner, we say that they can "handshake." One of the major factors that enables different computer graphics software packages to handshake is how they incorporate and address, read, and write the data that describes graphics, 3D objects, and animation. This is important to consider when purchasing a piece of computer graphics software for two main reasons. The first is that some formats are associated with a deeper representation of the data than others, so the computer graphics artist needs to have the highest data standards in mind for archiving work at the highest quality level. The second reason to dwell on the importance of file formats is that often a computer graphics artist will use several different pieces of software to accomplish a task. Each package in a group of packages may offer a needed tool or an effects capacity for the project at hand, where no one piece of software may hold all of what is needed. When that's the case, accurate handshaking has to exist between different software alternatives.

There has been an ongoing debate in the industry over whether it is best to enforce a file standard for each of the main areas of concern for computer graphics: 2D images, 3D objects, and animation. Everyone looks longingly at what was accomplished with electronic music with the implementation of the MIDI standard, even though there are some disagreements over the potentially negative outcomes of that decision. (For instance, are 16 channels of sound enough for today's production needs?) Most of us can also remember the time when there was a world-class argument going on concerning the establishment of a standard for videotape recording and playback, and the resultant demise of the Betamax format in favor of VHS. There's lots of money to be made in reinforcing a standard, especially for the company or companies that own the patent on it. So where does that leave us as far as computer graphics is concerned?

At the moment, and for the foreseeable future, it leaves us just about where we started. There will be no single standard for any of the three main areas of computer graphics at any time soon, though there are several options that professionals in the field seem to gravitate towards in all three areas.

2D Picture Formats The two groups represented here are vector graphics and bitmap graphics. Vector graphics come in several flavors, although vector drawing itself is the topic heading. Vector graphics are represented as directional data in the computer, meaning that a vector drawing can be described by notating the length and direction (curve) of each component (linear segment) of a drawing. Vector graphics can be saved in a much smaller space because the information needed to describe a very complex vector drawing comprises fairly small files. Vector graphics always print out at the highest resolution of the printer, so vector drawing is the format of choice for desktop publishing. The other 2D picture formats, called raster or bitmapped files, take much more data to describe, and hence need much larger file sizes. Bitmap graphic data has to describe not only every picture element (**pixel**) on the screen in terms of its location, but for professional 24-bit graphics the data must also describe the color and luma (light or brightness) information as well. Each pixel in a bitmap drawing must be described by from two (black and white) to 32 separate pieces of data. Pixels, the lowest denominator of a bitmap picture, are rectangular or square in shape. For that reason a close zoom in on them shows their stair-stepped or jagged edges. Bitmap graphics are used for any medium that is based on video because this stair-stepping doesn't matter in a medium that has far less resolution than printed copy demands.

There are relatively few vector file formats compared to the number of raster file formats in use. Vector formats include **PostScript**, **EPS** (Encapsulated PostScript), and a number of additional vector formats that remain particular to specific software. Bitmapped graphics however, the main vehicle for transmitting picture information in the computer

graphics realms, has at last count around 50 specific formats. Some formats are identified as Mac-specific and some as specific to other platforms, though the tendency now is to make all formats cross-platform translatable. "TIFF" ("TIF" in many Windows environments) is the highest quality format of choice for DTP work, while a format such as BMP (bit-mapped picture) is identified with Windows and MS/DOS platforms. The **GIF** format was initiated by CompuServe, IFFs are Amiga-specific, and the PICT format has long been identified as the Mac choice (some Mac software still writes and reads only PICT files). Most 2D graphics programs contain lists of file formats they can either or both read and write.

The **JPEG** format is a special case. It is what we call a "lossy" format because of the way that it saves data. In JPEG (and that includes PICT JPEGs), groups of pixels are read at one time, and the format determines if there are repetitive patterns that can be digested as a whole, with certain guesses made about how the pixels overall are grouped. Even with the highest quality JPEG (high quality = less compression), this "guessing" causes the loss of a certain number of pixels. This is not noticeable except in the case of human faces and gradients. In these two cases, there can be a visible banding in certain parts of the image. In the case of images of the human face or large gradient areas, it is not advisable to use JPEG, or if you do, always use the highest quality setting. A caution overall is to use the highest setting at all times, which often reduces the file size by at least 25 percent. The second caution is to avoid loading in a JPEG, working on it, and then saving it out as a JPEG again. All that does is to emphasize the lossiness in areas where it's likely to occur.

All of this can also be repeated when it comes to 3D object formats, except that the names of the formats are different. 3D object formats describe where a point on an object is in Cartesian XYZ space, what shape the polygons are, and where the polygon's "normal" (an imaginary line perpendicular to the plane of the polygon and usually drawn from its center) is pointing. Some 3D object formats also contain data about the objects color and other attributes, as well as what axis it sits on and its relative real-life size. The format that has come to be a near-standard for translating 3D data amongst different software and even different platforms is **DXF**, a format that started out as CAD-specific. There are, as confusing as it may sound, different flavors of DXF. Some contain more data relevant to the object than others. Most 3D software nowadays contains internal translators that enable you to import/export 3D object and scene files in a number of formats, so that a 3D scene might be modeled in one software environment and rendered in another. Although there are a number of 3D translation packages in the Windows environment, there are none on the Mac side. For this reason, a Mac-centric artist/animator has to look at the specific 3D software being purchased for its capability to read/write other 3D object formats if that is a considered need.

When it comes to 2D raster or bitmapped graphics however, the Mac is blessed with a high quality stand-alone piece of software that is known for its options in translating and processing all of the best known formats. Equilibrium's DeBabelizer is aptly named, since its mission is to bring some sense of order and handshaking to the sometimes confusing and inhospitable realm of multiple graphics format conversion. It solves most of the problems encountered by the computer graphics artist and animator who needs to translate one 2D graphics format, and even several animation formats, into other formats. DeBabelizer addresses common and uncommon 2D raster graphics formats. DeBabelizer works in one of two ways, either as a format conversion engine or as an image processor in the intermediate step between input and converted output.

File Formats DeBabelizer 1.6 has the capability to access the following file formats on the Mac: Clipboard, EPSF (grayscale and color, with or without PICT preview), **MacPaint**, **Photoshop**, PICS (animation), PICT 1 & 2, PixelPaint 1.0, **QuickTime** movies and stills, RIFF (BW, Grayscale, and **RGB**), **Scrapbook**, **Startup Screen**, **System 7** picture **icons** and previews, TGA (Truevision/Targa 8, 16, 24, 32,

compressed and uncompressed), TIFF (all formats including Thunderscan compression), and Thunderscan.

On DOS/Windows: BMP (compressed and uncompressed), Dpaint Anim, Dr. Halo, EPSF (Grayscale and color), FLI/FLC (Autodesk Animator), IMG (Ventura Publisher GEM), Lotus Pic, MSP Type 1 (Microsoft Paint), PCC, PCP (B&W PC Paint), PCX (PC PaintBrush color and B&W), Pictor, TGA (TrueVision/Targa 8, 16, 24, 32 bits, compressed and uncompressed), TIFF (Grayscale and color, also with LZW compression), and WPG (WordPerfect Graphics).

General—JPEG, Abekas digital video, BOB, GIF (interlaced and non-interlaced), **Pixar**, raw Custom, Raw RGB, RLE (CompuServe), QDV, and **PhotoCD**.

Apple Series—Apple II and IIGS (paintworks).

Commodore—Commodore 64 (Koala, crunched, packed, uncompressed).

Amiga Technologies—IFF ILBM (HAM, SHAM, DHAM), IFF (1 to 8, 16- and 24-bit, PBM).

Atari Series—Degas, NEO, Spectrum.

Silicon Graphics—Image files.

Sun Microsystems—SUN rasterfiles.

XWindows—XWD screen dump.

Cross-Platform Work There are several ways to access non-Mac system disks for translating files. You can connect DOS/Windows systems and Macs via a network cable (see your manuals for directions and needed hardware and software). You can also send files over a **modem** from one system to the other. The simplest way to get DOS/Windows files into a Mac is to use the Mac's compatibility for reading DOS/Windows disks. These can be disks or removable media (such as the new **Zip drive** cartridges).

Batch Processing DeBabelizer supports full batch processing features. You can select image processing effects or simple format conversion, target a list of files, and set the processes in motion. The batching progresses automatically.

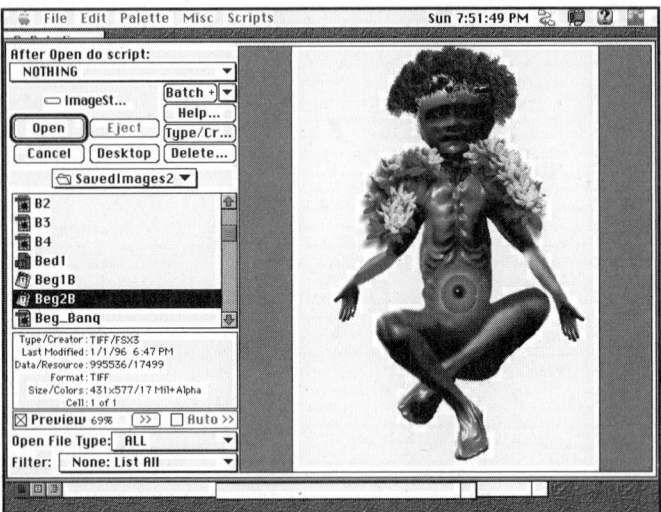

Other Features You can use any of the Photoshop filters in your Photoshop filter folder simply by telling DeBabelizer where they are in its preferences dialog. In addition to this, DeBabelizer has its own collection of image processing tools. Among these is the capability to change all of the incidences of any color in the image, finding the palette index number of any paint color, altering index numbers, painting tools, complete file info dialogs, overlaying text on the image, changing resolutions and DPI settings, scaling, dithering, generating animations, and more. This software is not meant for beginners.

Bitmap Image

Bitmap image describes a digital image created by a **scanner** or painting software that has a specified number of **pixels** per inch. Bitmap images are also called raster images and must be converted to **halftones** or **stochastic screens** to be printed.

See Also

Prepress

Bitmapped Graphics

Scanned images are probably the most common kind of bitmapped graphic. These graphics are made up of tiny dots (represented by **pixels** on the Mac's screen), each in a particular location and each a particular color.

Each dot can be modified without affecting the dots around it.

Depending on how fine the grid of dots within the image is, those dots may be visible as squares—this is what's meant by the term "pixellated." If a bitmapped image is created and then viewed or printed at a larger size than the original file, the dots again become apparent. The image looks coarse and "jaggy."

The file size of bitmapped graphics is related to the resolution and size of the image—the larger the image and the higher the resolution, the larger the file.

Vector graphics are the alternative to bitmapped graphics; these are defined in terms of lines, curves, and fills—complete objects—rather than in terms of pixels.

See Also

Pixel; Vector Images

BIX

Acronym for BYTE Information Exchange. This online commercial information service is now owned by General Videotext Corporation, but was previously the online arm of BYTE magazine.

BIX is among the oldest of the **commercial online services** and has a direct connection to the **Internet**. This makes it easier to send and receive Internet **email** than from other services. You can **FTP** files from Internet hosts, **telnet** into BIX from the Internet, and read **Usenet** news with the popular UNIX Newsreader.

The Internet discussion areas on BIX provide an excellent place to talk about exploring the Internet. Instead of storing the file on the BIX host machine and requiring an extra step to download it, BIX has set it up so that files are automatically dumped to your Mac via **ZMODEM** or whatever transfer protocol you normally use to download files from BIX. Queueing up files and then downloading them when you're done can be more efficient than sitting through each successive download, especially if the **modem** is slow.

To send email to someone on the Internet, you type the Internet email address instead of the BIX username. Sending mail to BIX is equally easy. Simply append **@bix.com** to the end of the BIX username and send it.

To get an account on BIX, have your modem dial 800-695-4882 or 617-491-5410 (use 8 data bits, no parity, 1 stop bit, full duplex). Press Return a few times until you see the **Login: (enter "bix")** prompt, and then type **bix**. At the **Name?** prompt, type **bix.net**. If you prefer, you can also telnet to BIX to sign up.

BIX has relatively high rates, but there is a special price for frequent users.

See Also

Commercial Online Services; Email; FTP; Internet; Modem; Telnet; ZMODEM

Bjarne Stroustrup, *See C++*

Black Box 2.0

This is a small collection of high quality filters. There are ten in all: Carve, Cutout, Drop Shadow, Glass, Glow, HSB Noise, Inner Bevel, Motion Trail, Outer Bevel, and Swirl. These are all warp filters in that they impose new graphics parameters and elements on the selected graphic. Each is highly user-configurable, and also contains a movable preview window.

Carve/Cutout These two filters are very similar. Carve takes the selected area of a graphic and makes it appear that the selection is carved out of the surface. Cutout takes the selection and makes it appear that the graphic has a hole cut in it. Shadow orientation and depth, color, picture density, light direction, and bevel width and shape are all addressed in Carve. Cutout enables you to change the Shadow offset blur, opacity, depth, color, and the background color. Each filter has a list of defaulted selections to get you started exploring.

Drop Shadow This is the opposite of a cutout in that the selected area seems to be raised above the surface of the image. You can set the shadow depth, opacity, and color.

Glass Unlike glass effects in other plug-ins, the Black Box glass effect appears as a much more organic overlay and can be endlessly configured to achieve whatever degree of mechanical or organic look is desired. Refraction, light source, flaw thickness and spacing, opacity, color, bevel width and highlight sharpness, and amount are all adjustable. This is a great filter to use when rendering water and can also be used to fabricate lava and other materials.

Glow This effect adds a halo glow in your choice of color, opacity, and size around any graphic selection. Use it to produce angelic halos and coronas around digital stars. Fade amounts are also configurable.

HSB Noise This effect sprinkles noise around the selection, augmented by your choice of hue, saturation, and brightness variations.

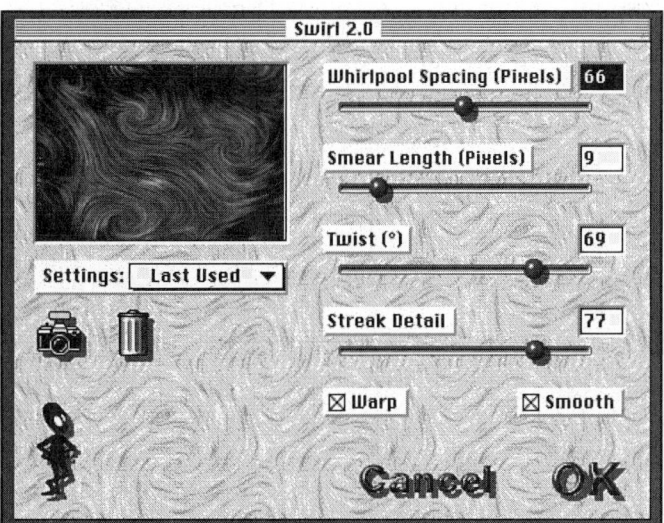

Inner Bevel / Outer Bevel Several types of bevels are supported. User configurations adjust color, shadows, and bevel sizes. An inner bevel is a carved bevel while an outer bevel pops out of the screen. Outer bevels make great multimedia buttons.

Motion Trail This is a directional smear. Pixel length, opacity, and direction can be configured.

Swirl This is the most alluring filter that Black Box offers, and no other plug-in package duplicates it. Swirls are defined disturbances in the selected graphic, and can be used to mimic hair or watery wavelets. Amounts, direction, disturbance amounts, sizes, and opacity can be configured by the user.

Black Type, *See Typesetting Terms*

Blackletter Typefaces, *See Typeface Categories*

Bleed

In the graphic arts, a bleed is any printed image that runs off the edge of the page. Photographic images, background patterns and colors, and accent graphics are the most common bleed elements in graphic design. For a bleed to occur, the image must physically extend about one-eighth of an inch beyond the trimmed edge of the page. A bleed contributes to the overall visual impact of a page design by breaking up the framing effect of margins to increase dynamic tension.

See Also

Printing

Blessing a System Folder

The folder on your **startup disk** that contains the **System** and **Finder** files is called the blessed folder. Any folder that contains these two files will have its

icon changed to a folder icon with a small Mac in the middle of the folder that looks similar to the **happy Mac** you see when you first boot your Mac. The System File and the Finder File are stored in a folder called the System Folder and it is the blessed folder. If for some reason you moved the System File and the Finder File out of your system folder and put them into a different folder, this new folder would then become the blessed folder, even though it is not named System Folder. The name System Folder is used to help you locate your Mac's System Files, but the folder that has the small Mac icon on the front of the folder is the blessed folder and it contains both your System File and your Finder File.

When you **start up** your Macintosh it will look for the blessed folder to find the necessary software to start up from.

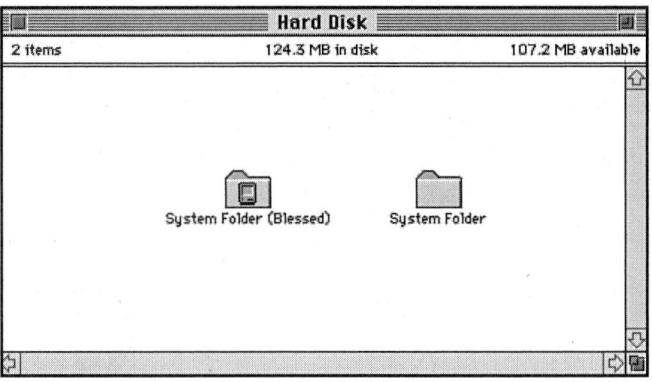

To create a blessed folder, follow these steps:

1. Create a new folder by choosing New Folder from the File menu.

2. Drag the System File and the Finder File from your system folder into this New Folder.

3. A small Finder icon will appear on the folder indicating that this is the "blessed" folder containing the System and Finder files.

See Also

Boot; Finder; Happy Mac Icon; Startup Disk; System Files

B

Blind Transfer, *See File Transfer Protocols*

Blinking Question Mark Icon

When you **start up** your Macintosh, it does a diagnostic check and looks for **system software** to load. If your Mac finds working system software, it displays a **Happy Mac** icon and loads the system. If the computer cannot find a working version of your system software, it displays a **disk icon** with a blinking question mark, alerting you that it cannot find a working system to startup from. If, for example, the system file is damaged or if one of the key system files (such as the Finder file) has been accidentally moved outside the System Folder, your Mac cannot startup from this system and will flash a blinking question mark icon instead of a Happy Mac, telling you it can't find an operable system to startup from. The Disk Tools disk (part of your system software disks from Apple) has a skinnied down version of the system on the disk, and you can insert this disk to start up your Mac. After your Mac has started up from this disk, you can look at your system to see if there is a valid System Folder on the disk you are trying to startup from.

See Also

Disk Icon; Extensions Folder; Happy Mac Icon; Startup Disk; System Files

Bliss Paint

There is some question whether this software is more of a painting or an animation program. Its painting tools are global environments (called "distributors") and brushes (called "scribblers") that produce color-cycled animated paintings in 256 colors. (The screen has to be set to a 256-color mode for you to appreciate Bliss Paint's animation output.) To capture the flavor of Bliss Paint's '60's psychedelic foundation, you only have to quit the program. A sign appears

telling you how long you have "blissed out." The blissful animations can be viewed on your monitor, or saved as **QuickTime** movies or single PICTs. In addition to its scribblers and distributors being selectable from on-screen lists, Bliss Paint lets you control the graphics with keyboard commands. Colors are assigned letter keys, while shift and option key alternatives change the waveforms and random/mouse directional choices. Number keys are used to control the oscillator speed settings, while oscillator ranges (wide/narrow and light/dark) are controlled by option-letter combinations. Other less intuitive key assignments control other color models. A full keyboard map of these input assignments comes with the program. Alternate disks packed with animations, scribblers, and distributors can be purchased separately (Geometric Bliss, Waves of Bliss, and Bliss Gallery).

Bliss distributors set the path on the rendering screen that the scribblers will be directed towards. The "corners" distributor, as an example, will place the chosen scribbler brush (such as the "sea anenome" brush) on the corners of the rendering screen. Otherwise, you can place brushes with the mouse. A brush selection area marks the spot where a chosen scribbler begins to grow. A full animation recording facility enables any Bliss animation to be written out as a QuickTime movie, and screen sizing controls are included.

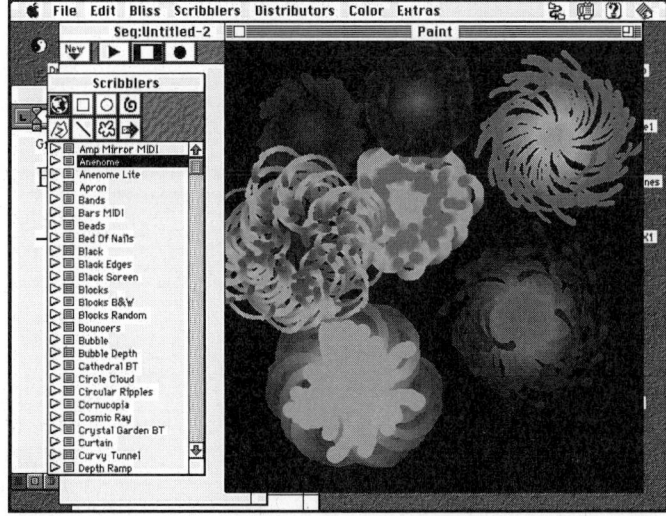

Bliss Saver is a complementary program, using Bliss Paint cycled animation paintings as screen savers. Unlike other screen saver utilities, Bliss Saver enables you to interact with the on-screen animation via keyboard hot keys, changing the colors of the cycling animations. Bliss Saver comes with its own set of animations, but you can use animations you've created in Bliss Paint as well. The only caveat is that screens must be set to 256 colors, as neither Bliss Paint nor Saver work in 16- or 24-bit modes. Normally Bliss Saver is placed in the startup file, where it works automatically when it senses screen inactivity. It may also be placed outside of the startup folder and started manually.

<BLOCKQUOTE> HTML Tag

The <BLOCKQUOTE></BLOCKQUOTE> tag in an **HTML** document on the **World Wide Web** indents or otherwise emphasizes a block of text, such as a long quotation. Typically this quote may be slightly indented or italicized. <BLOCKQUOTE> also causes a paragraph break, and includes a blank space both before and after the quotation.

See Also

HTML; Web Browser; Web Page; World Wide Web

Blood Bath, *See First Person Perspective Shooters*

Blown Away, *See Hollywood Games Connection*

Blue Meanies

Apple's **System 7** project was a huge undertaking. By the end of the development process, there were close to 1,000 people working on the project. In a project that large, with many separate pieces of software that must come together into a coherent whole, it is sometimes difficult to keep everything together.

Apple helped avoid some of the problems by forming a software integration team whose job it was to oversee the technical side of the development process and to make sure that everything worked together properly. This small group of talented programmers was known as the *Blue Meanies*.

The Blue Meanies are often erroneously given credit for writing *all* of System 7. Although their contribution was crucial to the success of the System 7 project, they were only a small fraction of the total group of people working on the project.

See Also

Macintosh Project, History

Blue Screening

Used frequently in video and film production, blue screening is a method of compositing two images. Typically, this technique places an object or person over a background image (for example, a TV weatherman appearing in front of a weather map). First the foreground object (the weatherman) is shot in front of a single color background (originally blue, many are colored green). This results in a picture of the weatherman and a single background color. Using special software (and/or hardware) this background color is made transparent, and the background image (the weather map) becomes visible where the blue area in the first image was.

The **QuickTime** video editors **Premiere** and **VideoShop** both provide blue screen effects. You choose the color in the first clip that is transparent using an ink dropper. Rather than just choose a single color, the programs enable you to specify a range of colors around the original color using a slider. Unless the original clip was created using graphics software, this is required because the color in digitized video is never completely consistent, no matter how well-lit the background. The smaller this range is, the more realistic your final image.

When producing your blue screen video, it's important to provide a clean video signal and to light the background evenly and brightly. The more pronounced the difference between the background and your foreground object, the better the effect.

See Also

Compositing; Video Digitizing

<BODY> HTML Tag

The <BODY> tag includes everything in an **HTML** document that comes after the **<HEAD>** tag. The start tag <BODY> comes after </HEAD>. The end tag </BODY> goes at the end of the document, just before </HTML>. In between <BODY> and </BODY> come the paragraphs, headings, inline images, lists, and other contents of the document that will be displayed on a **World Wide Web page**.

See Also

HTML; Web Browser; Web Page; World Wide Web

Bold, *See Boldface*

Boldface

Boldness, applied to type, designates a heavier, blacker version of a **font**. In the early days of Macintosh, the application's Style menu would enable you to apply any of six different styles to your **bitmapped** font. You could set your pages in Geneva Bold, Times Italic, Cupertino Outline, and so on. The Mac would automatically adjust the bitmap as needed, making it 20 percent wider for a bold character, applying a 12 degree right slant for italics, and so on. These styles were reasonably satisfactory on the existing **dot matrix printers** of the time.

When **laser printers** and **PostScript** outline fonts came into existence, they required a different method for specifying type. The PostScript font descriptions were written separately for each style within the font family. You'd have, for example, a font called Bookman. And with it, you'd have Bookman Bold, Bookman Italic, Bookman Light, Bookman Narrow, and even Bookman Demibold Condensed. There are also fonts that are darker than normal bold. These are designated "Black."

To make matters more confusing, you can still apply menu styles to your already styled fonts. The figure shows the results of applying the Bold style to two already dark fonts, Arrus Bold and Arrus Black.

```
Arrus Bold
Arrus Bold (styled bold)
Arrus Black
Arrus Black(styled Bold)
```

See Also

Fonts; Typesetting Terms

Bomb, *See Crashes, System*

Bomb Icon

If your system experiences a **crash** or **freezes**, an **alert box** with an icon of a bomb might appear telling you, "Sorry, a system error has occurred." This is the standard bomb alert box; it's letting you know that your system is frozen, or "bombed," as it's often called. In this alert box you have the choice of choosing Cancel or **Restart**. Unfortunately, the Cancel button never works, and, depending on how bad the system crash was, the Restart button may not work either. Usually you have to manually restart your Macintosh by pressing the Control-⌘-PowerOn key.

See Also

Alert Box; Crash; Freeze; Restart

Bookmark CD, *See develop Magazine*

Boolean Query

A Boolean query is a feature of a **Wide Area Information Server (WAIS)** that provides a search for two related keywords joined by Boolean operators such as "and," "or," or "not" that appear in a search string. Boolean queries make search engines more focused and powerful.

See Also

Internet, Searching/Navigating; Lycos; WebCrawler; World Wide Web; Yahoo

Boot

Boot is a popular computing term that means **starting up** your computer. The term boot is used as a synonym for the word start that originates from the saying "to pick oneself up from one's bootstraps." If, for example, someone tells you to boot up your computer, they're telling you to start up your computer. If they tell you you're computer won't boot, it means your computer won't start. If you're using your computer and you need to restart, you'll often hear **restarting** referred to as **rebooting**. Boot and start mean the same thing; it's just computer lingo.

See Also

Reboot; Restart

Boot Disk

Your boot disk is another term (in computer jargon) for your **startup disk**. Your startup disk is the disk that your system software is on and your Macintosh **starts up**, or boots from. Boot is basically a synonym used in the computer world for "start." So your boot disk is your startup disk. And your startup disk is the disk your Mac starts up from. That disk contains the necessary system software to startup your Mac.

See Also

Startup Disk

Boris Effects

Boris Effects is a set of plug-in effects that work with Adobe **Premiere** and Data Translation's Media 100. This set is notable for its 3D effects. The effects can be adjusted over a length of time by setting **keyframe** locations. The **plug-ins** provide a good preview of what they do, but they can take a long time to create the final movie effect.

> Artel Software
> Premiere $350
> Media 100 $695
> Email: **byamnitsky@aol.com**
> Phone: (617) 566-0870

See Also

Premiere; QuickTime

Boxing Games, *See Sports Games*

BPS, *See Baud/BPS*

Brain Games, *See Entertainment*

Breakout

Breakout was an early successor to the Pong video game. In Breakout, a ball is bounced off a paddle, controlled by the player, to smash out bricks in a wall opposite the paddle.

When **Steve Jobs** was working for Atari, he accepted an offer from Atari's head, Nolan Bushnell, to create the circuitry for this then new game. The task turned out to be beyond Jobs' skill level, so he turned to **Steve Wozniak**. Woz and Jobs worked feverishly to get the game done on a very tight deadline. Despite Woz's full time job at Hewlett Packard, he managed to get a working prototype done in four days.

Jobs paid Woz $350 for the project, which he claimed to be half of the total they were paid by Atari. Only years later did Woz learn that Jobs had actually been paid $5,000 for the project.

Ironically, Steve Wozniak's design was never used by Atari. His design was so clever that no one at Atari could figure out how it worked and therefore couldn't test it. In the end, Atari redesigned the whole game.

Breakout has shown up in interesting places since then. One of the best is an **Easter egg** in **System 7.5**. Dragging the words "secret about box" from any drag and drop-aware application (such as **SimpleText** or **Note-Pad**) onto the **desktop** reveals a simple breakout game with the names of system engineers on the blocks. Note that this Easter egg works only with the original System 7.5, not 7.5.1 or later.

See Also

Easter Egg; Jobs, Steve; Wozniak, Steve

Breakout in System 7.5

Breakout (designed originally by Steve Wozniak for Atari) has shown up in interesting places. One of the best is an **Easter egg** in System 7.5. Dragging the words "secret about box" from any drag and drop-aware application (such as SimpleText or Note Pad) onto the desktop reveals a simple breakout game with the names of system engineers on the blocks (see the following figure).

If you time it right, you can, for example, eliminate all red blocks on the screen in one click. As levels progress, spiders drop from the top of the screen. They hold blocks up and away from like colors. Also, tin cans and boulders are introduced that cannot be destroyed by the mouse. Bombs destroy anything next to them and rockets clear a straight path depending on the direction they are pointing. BreakThru is a definite time-stealer and will keep any brain teaser fan captivated for countless hours. Like other puzzle games, the simplicity of the title never really becomes monotonous, only more addictive as you try for that high score.

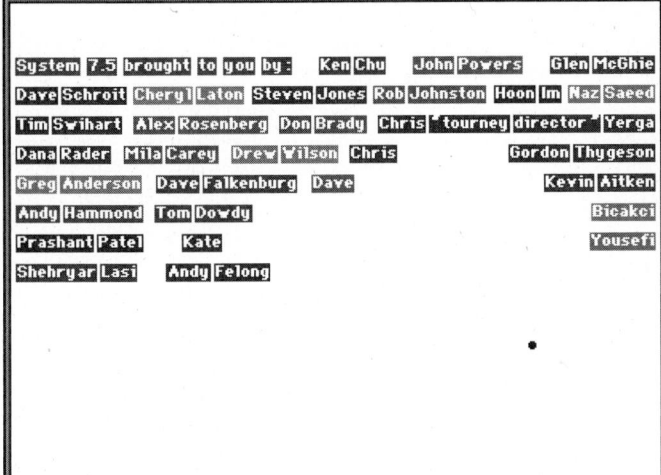

BreakThru

BreakThru resembles another Alexey Pajitnov creation, the puzzle game **Tetris**. Using the mouse, you remove colored blocks to tear down a wall. To make things more difficult, more blocks are constantly being dropped from the top of the screen, building the wall back up. Strategy is involved in eliminating all of one color at any given time; for example you can only destroy a block that is touching one of its own color, but as many are touching in a sequence are destroyed with one mouse click.

See Also

Tetris Gold; Troubled Souls; Zoop

BRI, *See ISDN*

Bridges

Bridges amplify **network** traffic in a fairly similar manner to repeaters or hubs. However, in addition to boosting the signal level, bridges are semi-intelligent devices that can look at each message they receive and decide which side of the bridge a message is addressed to. By analyzing each message, bridges only let messages cross that are intended for a computer on the opposite side. This type of device is very useful when slower connections, such as telephone lines, are used between networks. If a bridge has, for example, nodes A and B on one side, and C and D on the other, a message passing from A to B doesn't cross the bridge, and therefore doesn't slow down the functions of C and D.

Ethernet Bridging

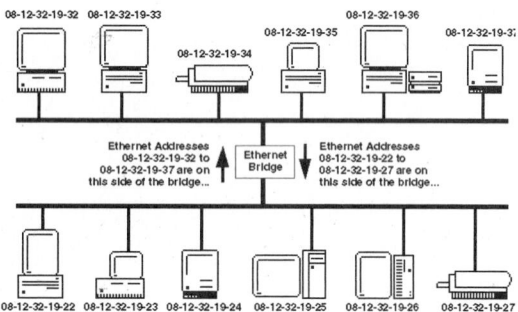

A special type of bridge, the multiport bridge or switch, is gaining increased popularity on **LANs**. The switch can separate network traffic into multiple smaller segments by quickly examining only the source and destination portions of network traffic, and keeping traffic isolated to the ports for which the traffic is destined. Because of their limited range of functions, a switch can often work more quickly and more economically than can a **router** for network segmentation.

TIP Hubs can not translate protocols between the individual ports—they cannot, for example handle EtherNet traffic on one port and LocalTalk traffic on another. Translation tasks must be performed by a router.

Brightness, *See Monitors, Image Quality*

Brightness Control Panel

This **control panel** was developed for Macintosh computers that were self-contained units with a built-in monitor (the Mac Classic and the Classic II) or had monitors that did not have external brightness dials.

The brightness control enables the user to change the brightness from maximum to minimum by **dragging** the slider until you reach the desired brightness.

See Also
Click and Drag; Control Panel

Brøderbund Software, *See KidPix Studio; Logical Journey of the Zoombinis; Myst*

Browser, *See Web Browser*

Browser (Programming)

A browser is a special kind of **editor** designed to enable you to see patterns and interrelationships in source code and easily manage large sets of code.

The browser included with **Symantec C++** (see figure) is typical of many browsers. The browser window includes a number of separate panes, each containing a certain kind of information. Browsers are best suited to managing **object-oriented programming** projects. Thus, they are often called *class browsers* after the class construct used in that programming methodology.

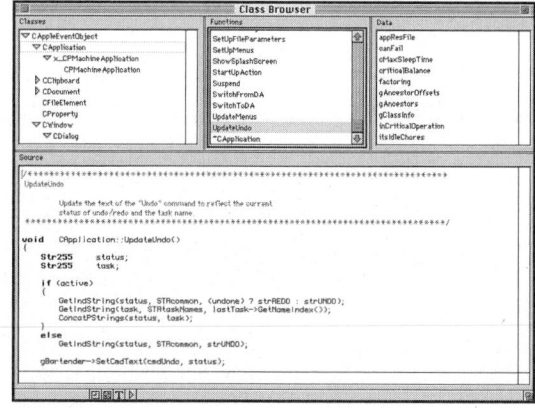

In this example, the upper left pane displays all of the C++ classes in the current project. The classes are displayed, using an outline style similar to the list views used in **Finder** windows, according to their position in the class hierarchy. The upper-middle pane shows all of the member functions of the class highlighted in the first pane (CApplication in this example). The large source pane in the bottom of the browser window displays the source code for the function highlighted in the second pane. The final pane, in the upper right, displays the data associated with the highlighted class.

Although this arrangement might seem confusing, it closely matches the way in which object-oriented programs are designed and makes viewing and editing the code much easier than it would be in an ordinary editor. In a browser, the actual *file* that contains a certain bit of code is much less important than how that code fits into the whole of the project.

Most browsers are tailored to viewing one type of code within one development environment. In fact, the Symantec C++ and **CodeWarrior** browsers are fully integrated into their host IDE. One major exception is **Object Master**, from ACIUS. Object Master works with all major development environments.

See Also

CodeWarrior; Editor; Object Master; Programming

Brush Typefaces, *See Typeface Categories*

Bryce

Need a photograph of a majestic mountain or a rocky canyon but don't have the budget to send out a photographer? Then perhaps you should consider Bryce, a 3D modeling and rendering tool designed to produce stunningly realistic images or virtual landscapes. Starting with 3D models or basic terrains, or using a terrain editor to start from scratch, the user adjusts the height and detail of surfaces, adds sky and fog effects, and can even import **DXF** models to complete the final image. The results are always amazing, although the realism depends upon how carefully you adjust the different parameters.

Other features include: rock generation capabilities, multiple light sources (such as spot lights, radial diffusion lights, and slide projection of PICT images),

and **boolean** rendering that can subtract one object from another to create very complex shapes.

Bryce features the unique interface design of Kai Krause. Always unusual, never boring, the interface may slow you down when you first start using the program—expect to spend a few hours figuring out which way is up. Also, if you don't own a Power Macintosh, expect to upgrade soon if you plan to use Bryce regularly.

Bryce produces great images, but if you want to use the images with models created in another 3D program it's probably best to either import the models into Bryce (a problem if you need animation; Bryce doesn't support it) or to export the image and **composite** the scene with the model created in the other program.

See Also

3D; Compositing

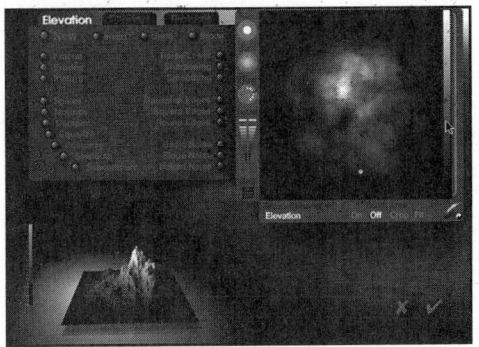

Budgeting, Finance Programs

One of the main reasons for using a financial management program is to set up and maintain a budget. Budgets are organized based on an individual's or family's income and expense categories. Typical finance programs, such as **Quicken**, enable you to enter budget amounts for some or all of the categories and subcategories you use.

You can create a budget automatically from your existing data, or you can enter amounts individually for the categories you want to budget. You can also create multiple budgets to work out different budgeting scenarios. After you've entered budget amounts, you can create reports and graphs to compare your actual income and expenses with your budget. You can also have Quicken monitor and display your budget status "as you go," so you can always see exactly how you're doing.

Before you create a budget, think about what areas you need to watch. If you typically spend money on clothes or entertainment, and then have to scramble to pay the rent, these are areas to watch very closely. If you break even every month, but can't seem to save, a budget entry for savings may be helpful. Remember to include all of your income, as well as all of your expenses, even if you choose to assign a large part of it to Miscellaneous. Quicken provides you with a list of suggested categories, from which you can choose the ones you want as budget entries. There are headings for fixed expenses such as rent and loan payments, and for flexible expenses.

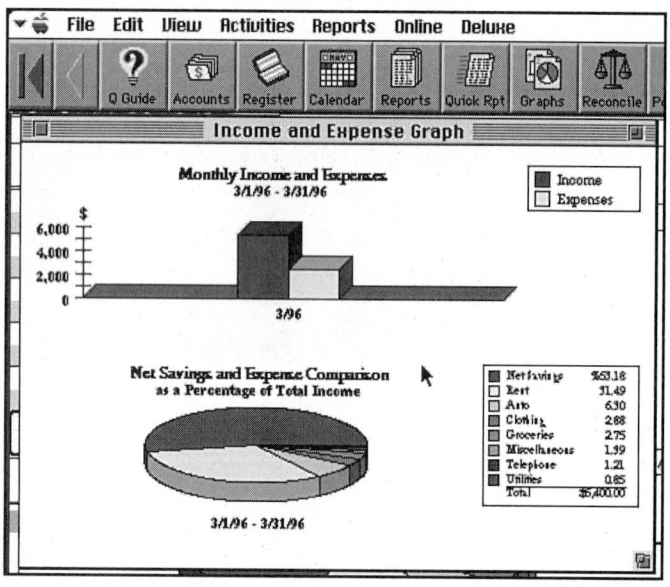

Budget reports can be viewed as lists of expenses and income, or as a chart such as the one shown here. Quicken updates the chart every time you make an entry in any of your accounts. You can also create "What-if" budgets, based on changes (plus or minus) in your income, fixed expenses, or other situations. Quicken, and most financial programs, will let you keep as many different records as you have hard disk space for. (Alas, there's no category for a new hard disk.)

See Also

Financial Planning Software; Quicken

Bug

An error in hardware or software that leads to unexpected or unwanted results.

Software errors can be classified into two types: logic bugs and coding bugs.

Logic bugs involve errors in the algorithm, which is the series of steps you use to accomplish a task. The programming code itself might be perfect; it just does the wrong thing. A good analogy is trying to make a chocolate cake from a recipe that doesn't include chocolate. No matter how well you follow the recipe (the cake-making algorithm), you won't end up with chocolate cake.

Coding bugs, on the other hand, are errors in carrying out the algorithm. Adding eggs to your cake recipe before removing the shells, for example. This type of bug runs the gamut from simple misspelled words and punctuation to memory leaks and bus errors.

Admiral Grace Hopper, the original developer of the COBOL programming language, liked to tell a story about the first *real* computer bug. A technician working on the Harvard Mark II computer tracked a problem they were having to an actual insect that had been caught between the contacts of a relay deep in the heart of the computer. The logbook of the incident (containing the bug itself) was on display for many years at the Naval Surface Warfare Center. This is often cited as the source of the term "bug" in this sense, but the word has in fact been used to mean a disruptive event as far back as Shakespeare's time.

See Also

Debugging; Debugging Tools

Bug-Fix Update

A bug-fix update is a special case of a minor upgrade that fixes just one (or a few) problem that was encountered when the software went into more widespread usage. Some companies (such as Microsoft) add a letter to the end of the version number to indicate a bug-fix update, for example, 5.1a; other companies (such as Claris) append a third digit, for example, 4.0v4. Bug-fix updates are usually available for free from the company, either via mail or from their online support areas.

See Also

Major Software Release; Minor Software Release; Registration Card

Bulging Trash Can

A bulging trash can icon indicates that items are in the **Trash**. To delete the contents of the Trash, choose Empty Trash from the **Special menu** at the top of your desktop. This will delete the contents and return the normal trash can **icon** to indicate an empty trash can.

See Also

Deleting a File; Desktop; Empty Trash Command; Special Menu; Trash

Bullet, *See Printing*

Bulletin Board Systems

A bulletin board system (BBS) is an online communication system that enables exchanging of messages and other communications.

BBSs are easy to access, the only requirements being a computer, a **modem** connected to the public telephone system, and freely available software such as ZTerm. Some require a fee for access.

Bulletin boards provide discussion, games, news, and **shareware**. Some are small and run by hobbyists, while others are extensive commercial operations. Others are run by companies to permit the exchange of information between employees.

Typically, users dial in to a BBS using the telecommunications program of their choice, although many BBSs provide their own software. When you connect for the first time you register with the systems operator (sysop) of the BBS. Then you can leave a message on the BBS addressed to "All" that introduces you to the other users, or read already posted messages.

Message areas are grouped by topic, for example, "General," "Singles," or "Television." Some BBSs only circulate messages locally, whereas others "echo" them to other BBSs.

See Also

Commercial Online Services; NCSA; Telnet

Bump Maps

Bump maps use a graphic to create the illusion of a raised surface on a 3D object, usually with just a black-and-white image. The darker or the lighter areas of the graphic represent the higher and lower portions of the surface. While not useful for creating major modeling effects, bump mapping makes it possible to add little details that otherwise would be tedious to create with the **modeler**—for example, raised rivets on a spaceship.

See Also

Alias' Sketch; Texture Mapping

Bumptz Science Carnival

This **CD-ROM** program from Theatrix is rated for kids 6-10. Maybe, if you're 6, you will instantly know what to do and how to do it. But we grown-ups have to read the instruction manual.

There's not much on-screen help in this program, only the most basic directions for most of the activities and in this parent's opinion, the puzzles are hard to solve. That said, it's a challenging, but engrossing set of puzzles for kids in the middle grades. The theme is a trip to an amusement park, generally a good place to study physics. The puzzles deal with magnetism, light, and buoyancy, and there's also an animated explanation of the physical laws that govern these qualities, along with simple experiments that can be done at home or in the classroom. The science is serious, but the program is fun.

The experiments help kids relate the scientific principles to real objects. There are three levels of difficulty, with the highest being enough to make most grown-ups stop and think. The animation is cute, and the sounds are great. **Snootz Math Trek** is similar, but deals with logic rather than physics.

See Also
Snootz Math Trek

Buried in Time, *See Daedalus Encounter, The*

Burning or Pressing a CD-ROM

It's now possible to buy a CD-R (**CD-ROM-Recorder**) for less than $1,000 that can burn a CD. This device uses a special blank, writeable CD-ROM and a high-powered laser that burns information onto the blank. This is a write-once procedure. If the process goes wrong, and it sometimes does, you have wasted a disc. Recorders start at under $1,000 (for double-speed recorders), and go up to many thousands for faster recorders. Blank discs cost about $7.00-$10.00 each. Because of the time it takes to set up and actually write the disc, most service bureaus charge between $35-$50 per disc (the charge may go down with quantity).

By comparison, pressing requires sending the data away to a pressing plant. There, a master disc is made from which the discs are injection molded—or pressed. The setup charge is very high (around $1,000), but after that the individual discs cost less than $2.00 each. Most pressing plants offer a package of mastering plus the first 100 or so discs.

The advantage to burning is that you can burn as few or as many as you need, whereas pressing is only cost-effective when you need more than 100 discs. This comparison is dependent on the cost of the CD

blanks, and the time (and labor) used to burn the individual discs. Also, using a burner you can create a **multisession** disc. This involves writing data to the disc at different times. The primary advantage of this technique is that you can add information to an existing disc. This is not possible with a pressed disc.

Writeable CDs (those created using a CD-ROM recorder) are estimated to have a shorter lifespan, from 70 to 100 years depending on the materials used in the disc, than pressed discs. Writeable discs come in several colors. In general, the gold discs are believed to have a longer shelf life than the green discs. This lifespan may be shorter if the disc is not handled correctly, exposed to high temperatures or UV light, or otherwise mishandled. The laser the computer uses to read the CD is of very low power and cannot harm the data on the disc, even after thousands of reads. CDs should last at least until it's time to replace them with a storage medium of even greater size. Already, **DVD (digital video disc)** technology promises storage capacities much higher than standard CDs.

One important point, even if you are going the pressing route, being able to burn some test discs is vital in the development process.

See Also
CD-ROMs

Bushnell, Nolan

Nolan Bushnell is the founder of Atari and **Steve Jobs'** employer during the formation of Apple Computer. Bushnell was an entrepreneur who sparked the video game craze with the game "Pong." His follow-up to Pong, **Breakout**, was designed by **Steve Wozniak**.

See Also
Apple Computer, History; Breakout; Jobs, Steve; Wozniak, Steve

Business Applications

The keyword for business and industry in the '90s is "productivity," and the main reason that even small home-based businesses can't function without a computer today is the need for increased productivity to maintain a competitive advantage in the marketplace. With the right software, your computer can handle virtually any office task from mailing a personalized letter to every client to paying the monthly bills and keeping track of appointments, tax payments, and inventories. It doesn't require coffee breaks, vacations, or a uniform allowance.

What's Out There Business software includes word processors, bookkeeping programs, databases, and spreadsheets to keep track of all kinds of information, and even desktop presentation software that delivers your sales pitch. In addition, there are specialized business applications (see **Big Business**) that combine sales, marketing, inventory, and finance into one package, swapping information between its various functions.

Project planners and flowcharting programs help keep work on track and make it easy to see who's responsible for the various parts of a project. Other specialized software helps you brainstorm concepts and organize ideas. Programs such as Inspiration help you turn ideas into action by making it easy to organize them graphically or in outline form. Of course, you don't need to be a business tycoon to use and benefit from these tools.

Conversation with Steve Ruddock

Steve Ruddock handles public relations for Claris, the spin-off company that sells Apple software such as ClarisWorks, FileMaker, ClarisImpact, and the Claris Emailer.

Maclopedia: When did you first use a Mac?

Steve: May first, 1986, I left Hewlett-Packard and began work at Regis McKenna, Inc., on the Apple account, and I used a Mac for the first time that day. Like so many, I was immediately and permanently addicted to the graphical desktop/mouse experience, even though that first machine was a 128K Mac! Shortly thereafter, I went out and bought my first Mac [of three], an SE, and immediately caused domestic strife staying up until 3 AM playing Rommel vs. Patton.

Maclopedia: How did you find your way to Claris?

Steve: As part of the Apple PR team at Regis McKenna, Inc., I actually wrote the first two press releases announcing creation of and naming of Claris in April/May 1987. In late '88, I added supervision of the Claris account to my responsibilities, working closely with Bill Campbell, John Zeisler, and other founding Claris execs. In April 1989, the original Claris PR manager, Dan Rampe, went for an extended assignment with Claris UK. On Tuesday he asked if I would be interested in the job; on Wednesday I said yes; Thursday I interviewed with Zeisler over drinks at Ming's; Friday, Zee offered me the job, and I accepted.

Maclopedia: What's it like to work at Claris, and how is the atmosphere different from Apple?

Steve: Claris is the best place to work that I know of, and I say that having worked at very good companies like HP, RMI (and sort of Apple). Claris is the most people-oriented, least bureaucratic, open-communications fostering environment I can imagine. Guys like me can walk into the CEO's office and kibitz if we want. It's also the perfect size: approaching a quarter-billion dollars in annual revenue, but we're small enough so you can be aware of and add value to lots of projects and processes going on throughout the company. It's also great to work on behalf of products that we all feel passionately about, and that we use in the same way millions of normal people do every day.

Maclopedia: So what exactly do you do to publicize a new product?

Steve: The FileMaker 3 launch is a good example. It's Claris' most important product by some measures. We sell more units of ClarisWorks than FileMaker, but FileMaker is the single most important revenue-generating product, and if you measure a product by how critical it is to the user, and how passionate they get about it, FileMaker is right up there with any application you can think of. There are hundreds of thousands of people, individuals with their own businesses, for whom FileMaker is the mission-critical application. I encounter dozens of people who have a small business, two or three people, and the automation of their business is half a dozen FileMaker databases, to track their catalog, price lists, and so on. I am biased, but I think FileMaker is the most beautiful prototypical Mac product—all these graphic views of your data.

continues

So the launch of FileMaker 3 was the most important in Claris history. We began work on that a year before the product shipped, and we held a couple of events at MacWorld in January 1995, a fun press party in the penthouse of the Fairmont hotel. This is the place where, according to legend, JFK slept with Angie Dickinson, and every Democratic president since Harry Truman has stayed there. We had 250 editors from the Mac and trade press around the world, and we pretty much put down in black and white what we were going to do in terms of building relational capabilities into FileMaker. We said, it's not coming out until late '95, but we want to be open about what we are doing. It didn't make sense to safeguard this news.

We held a briefing for the Claris Solutions Alliance members, a group of 500 independent developers of solutions. Ninety percent of them are FileMaker developers. These guys are essential to our business, building real world solutions with FileMaker, and they have to know what the future of the product is. We realized it would be difficult to keep it a secret once we told them, so we just put our cards on the table in January 1995, and in the ensuing nine months, every three months we'd go out to the top 25 publications and give them an update and beta software in progress. Along about October or November, we did a mass distribution of the beta, which was frozen at that point so all the reviewers could see that, see what it could do. We got a lot of "First Look" reviews in the November 1995 time frame, and ended up shipping on December 15, 1995. It was far and away the most successful first couple of months we have ever had.

We've done a good job of communicating to users that this was coming, and we showed the upgrade path, and we shipped it on time. Press reaction was great. In the first 30 days of calendar year 1996, FileMaker won 10 awards from Mac and Windows publications. Now January is the intense award-giving month of the year, so we can't extrapolate. Still, that's got to be impressive. And what the editors were saying was as good as we could want, if we were writing the reviews. "The easiest to use is now relational, and still easy....You could find another Mac database, but why bother?"

In 1990, we surveyed our installed base and asked what they would like to see. "We need it to be cross platform." And we did that in 1992 with FileMaker 2,

Claris is the most people-oriented, least bureaucratic, open-communications fostering environment I can imagine. Guys like me can walk into the CEO's office and kibitz if we want.

and they wanted multiple table, relational capabilities, and we have done that with FileMaker 3, making them actually easy to use. Relational databases are good for situations when you have one customer with many invoices or one invoice with many products, so you have all these one-to-many and many-to-one relationships.

Maclopedia: How well are Claris products breaking into the Windows market now?

Steve: In the past few months, FileMaker has emerged as arguably the clear #2 Windows database behind Access. Roughly half the FileMaker units sold are FileMaker Windows...which of course equates to FileMaker having about a 90 percent market share on the Mac, and 10 percent on Windows, but we are making progress in the right direction.

ClarisWorks Win is also moving in the right direction. Claris came late to the Win market, and we have found it to be expensive to get the word out, get distribution, and there is lots of inertia in that market. It takes more than great products. But we're serious about being a cross-platform leader. In fiscal year '96 we will sell more than 1 million Win units, or roughly 80/20 split Mac versus Win units.

Maclopedia: So ClarisWorks is getting more popular, too?

Steve: In fiscal year '96 we are on track to make and sell something on the order of 2 million units of ClarisWorks. The Software Publishers Association does these surveys of software sales, and they recently published the 1995 findings. One of the headlines was overall Mac software revenues declined by 13 percent. The brunt of that decline was taken by Mac spreadsheets and word processors, which is to say, almost entirely Excel and Word; they declined by 30 percent. One of the contributing factors is that ClarisWorks is, for the vast majority of people, a preferable solution for basic productivity for word processing and spreadsheets. It has made significant inroads against the bloated products, which are not really written for the mainstream user.

Maclopedia: How does ClarisWorks compare with Microsoft Works, which was also based loosely on the old AppleWorks?

Steve: The main difference is that ClarisWorks was designed from the ground up as one application using frames and Microsoft Works dates back to a series of different modules that were sort of stapled together. When you went from one application to another in Works, you were really quitting one and opening another, whereas in ClarisWorks, if you are in a word processing document, and you click the spreadsheet frame, your tools all change. Now, Microsoft Works has been getting better, thanks to the ClarisWorks challenge. The other issue Microsoft has is that Word and Excel sales are so important to them that they may not want to make Microsoft Works so great. If I am correct, and Word and Excel are losing sales to ClarisWorks, then improving Microsoft Works would only erode the Word and Excel sales even more.

Maclopedia: Some of us still like MacWrite.

Steve: MacWrite is still selling. It's not a huge seller, but there are people who like MacWrite, and it continues to sell in some quantities around the world. I think the trend for new users entering the market is to look at more robust solutions. In ClarisWorks, the word processor is more robust than MacWrite in many cases, and soon will be in many ways. There are no plans to discontinue MacWrite, but it is also true that we haven't had a major rev since the System 7 transition.

Maclopedia: Where does ClarisImpact fit in all of this?

Steve: ClarisImpact is doing well. We have the cross-platform version shipping now. It's in a touchy category of structured business graphics, pioneered by Visio on Windows. We struggle to communicate that it is more than just presentations. The real beauty of Impact is that you can create network diagrams, time lines, calendars, without ever having to run a rectangle tool or use line segments because it has all these intelligent assistants who interview you and draw all that for you. You can change the styles globally, too. And there's a cool new feature called Data Draw that sucks data out of FileMaker and puts it into an org chart, with the click of a button or a calendar.

Maclopedia: What can you tell us about Web and Net directions for Claris?

Steve: The Internet is a platform upon which our products will work in increasingly robust and creative ways. We include HTML stationery and shortcuts with ClarisWorks 4; FileMaker 4 works over the Web, it's very popular for putting up live FileMaker files. Go to the Claris home page, and you can access half a dozen FileMaker databases at www.claris.com. And we have a number of interesting Internet things coming up. ClarisWorks 5 is going to be an Open Doc container, and we may put parts of CyberDog into ClarisWorks so you could distribute ClarisWorks documents that include frames that are CyberDog parts, with either static or dynamic stuff, so I could distribute a ClarisWorks document to a bunch of people and have CyberDog go out and download a satellite picture of the current weather and put that in.

Word processing includes everything from writing letters and doing homework to preparing camera-ready newsletters and publishing books such as this one. There are also specialized word processors that do particular tasks, such as formatting a film script or screenplay, and even a program that puts your ideas on index cards. If you have a business associate or penpal in a foreign country, use a translator program such as **Power Translator** to translate your letters and other documents into French, German, or Spanish.

If you don't know what to say, use one of the **LetterWorks** customizable letters. Topics include Sales, Legal, Business, and Personal letters. Consulting and Personnel ReadyWorks supply all the necessary forms, worksheets, proposals, appraisals, and contracts to run a business. These can also be customized as needed.

Integrated "works" programs such as **ClarisWorks** combine several different kinds of applications into one. Typically, the works program will include a word processor, telecommunications software, a spreadsheet, and some kind of database. It may also have drawing and/or painting capabilities. A works package's modules usually contain fewer features than full applications. For example, Microsoft Works contains a word processor, spreadsheet, and so on, but those functions have fewer features than Microsoft's standalone applications that provide the same functionality. Often home users will find Works programs sufficient, while business users may require the features provided by a full application such as those included in **Microsoft Office.** Office is a bundle of separate applications, plus an "Office Manager" that sits on the menu bar and gives quick access to the four modules included: **Word, Excel, PowerPoint,** and **Mail**. Each is a separate program within the Microsoft package. Users have the option of installing all or some of them, and although they support each other, they don't have to be used together.

Desktop **presentation** programs such as Microsoft **PowerPoint**, Gold Disk's **Astound**, and Adobe Persuasion turn your Macintosh into a self-contained table top projector and screen, running slide show or multimedia programs you create, complete with special effects and sound. These are especially good for delivering sales presentations and for any sort of meeting in which a lot of information has to be presented in an orderly and attractive format. They also help you organize your ideas and even create the outlines and handouts for your speeches.

What Package Do You Need? Choosing the right software to run your business, or even to handle your household books, correspondence, and appointments, requires doing a bit of research. Start here, by reading the sections that relate specifically to the jobs you want to do.

■ Consider the level of complexity of the programs you need. If you're buying software for home use, you may not need all the bells and whistles of a program such as Microsoft Word. If your business requires complex accounting, but only basic word processing and a simple database, consider a combination of a works program for general use and a specialized accounting program that can be tailored to precisely suit your needs. If your business is freelance writing, you may need several different word processors to satisfy your clients' requirements, but only the easiest possible PIM and checkbook programs.

■ Before you buy, look for demonstration versions of software you're considering. Many of these are available online or in shareware collections, such as those produced on **CD-ROM** by BMUG or the Boston Computer Society. Many software dealers will let you try out programs in the store. It might even be worthwhile to rent time on a Mac at a service bureau to try working with a particular word processor, graphics, or DTP program, because these tend to be the most expensive software purchases you make.

Bibliography

For more specific information on business applications not found here, check our your local bookstore or library for these books:

Microsoft Office Macintosh Survival Guide, Charles Seiter, Tonya Joy Engst, and Barrie Sosinsky, published by Hayden Books, 1995 (1-56830-173-1).

MACWORLD ClarisWorks Companion, Steven Schwartz, published by IDG Books, 1993 (1-56884-481-6).

For More...

If you want to do this...	*Go to this entry...*
Write letters	Word Processing; Business Letters and Forms
Keep a database of clients	Database
Publish a newsletter or brochure	Desktop Publishing
Bookkeeping and accounting	Accounts, Finance Programs; Big Business
Make a slide show on your Mac	Presentation Software
Keep a calendar and phonebook	Database

Business Letters and Forms

The popularity of computers and laser printers for home and office use has made it virtually impossible to tell a small business from a large corporation by looking at the mail they send out. The only real difference between a letter from Amalgamated Soft Drink International MultiCorp and one from Aunt Betsy's Lemonade Stand is the size of the mailing list. It's not the quality of the printed matter, as long as Betsy has access to a Mac, a laser printer, and some business letter and form templates.

There are a great many sources for premade templates, and several programs that will help you make up your own. Desktop publishing programs such as **PageMaker** generally come with a set of business form templates, covering everything from basic invoice and business card layouts to annual reports. **Word processors** and **works programs** also include some sample letters and form templates. There are apt to be templates for fax covers in your fax software and templates for accounting and record keeping in your **spreadsheet** and financial management programs.

A desktop publishing program is your best choice if you must make complex forms. If a simple one is all you need, **ClarisWorks** can do the job quite nicely. So can any **drawing** program. Simple forms such as purchase orders can be created. Every time the restaurant needs to place an order, the manager opens the purchase order form, enters the vendor's name and address from a database, lists his/her order, and enters the total in his/her inventory spreadsheet. When the goods arrive, the spreadsheet entry is moved from "on order" to "on hand."

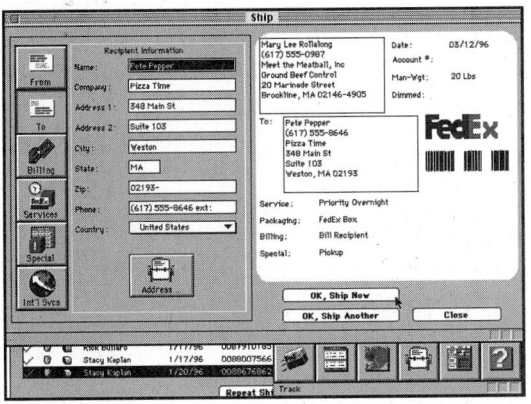

Specific forms, such as the Federal Express form and United Parcel Service shipping forms can be generated from within the computer. These companies are quite happy to provide the software to anyone who ships packages frequently. The main advantage to this is not the form's generation capability but the ability

to schedule a package pick-up via modem, and to log into a central computer to see whether your package has been delivered. You can track a missing package or find out what time one was delivered and who signed for it without ever having to listen to "music on hold." Federal Tax forms can be downloaded, too. Let your **Web browser** take you to **www.irs.ustreas.gov/prod/forms_pubs/index.html** for all the federal forms you need. At the same site you can get information on electronic filing and helpful tips on filling out your returns correctly.

Business letters, personal letters, and documents of all kinds are at your fingertips in the **LetterWorks** series. There are professionally written and designed letters, forms, and legal documents for all occasions. All of these are indexed in the accompanying handbooks, by topic, and come with suggestions for their use. There are even programs to help you generate a more effective résumé. SoftKey's Résumé Kit has several formats and a guide to help you determine what to put in, and more important, what to leave out.

Button

Many dialog boxes have features that are accessed by clicking a button. Generally a button is a rectangular, rounded-corner box with a command. Clicking a button opens a dialog box, window, or completes a command (as in the case of: "Do you want to **save** changes? Click the OK button.").

Many buttons have a **keyboard shortcut**. Anytime you see a button with a thick dark line around it, with another thin line just inside of that, it is the default button. The default button is the button you're most likely to choose, and the keyboard shortcut to choosing the default button is pressing the **Enter** or **Return** key. Either of these two keys will activate the default button in a dialog box. In many applications the **Escape key** will act as a keyboard shortcut for the **Cancel** button.

See Also

Cancel Keyboard Shortcut; Enter Key; Esc Key; Keyboard Shortcuts; Return Key

Button Disabler

This **control panel** was designed for use by educators and home Macintosh users who have children using their Mac. The idea behind this is ingenious; it enables you to disable the external **brightness** and volume knobs on certain **Performa** models of Macintosh aimed at the home and education markets. This way, children, or students, aren't able to adjust the knobs themselves.

See Also

Brightness Control Panel; Monitors, Image Quality

Bypass Internal Drive Keyboard Shortcut

If you want to **start up** your Mac from a disk other than your internal **startup disk**, hold down the ⌘-Option-Shift-Delete keys while you startup the machine. The Mac bypasses the internal disk and begins to search through the **SCSI** chain looking for a disk to start up from. When it finds a disk with the necessary startup files, it starts up. Because you've bypassed your internal drive, the new disk will not mount on the **desktop.**

To bypass the internal drive, follow these steps:

1. When you first turn on your computer, hold the ⌘-Option-Shift-Delete keys and the Mac will search the SCSI chain until it finds a startup disk to **boot** from.

2. Once it begins startup and you see the **Happy Mac**, you may release the keys.

See Also

Boot; Boot Disk; Desktop; Keyboard Shortcuts; Small Computer System Interface; Startup Disk

Bypass Virtual Memory at Startup

If you have **Virtual Memory** turned on but want to **start up** or **restart** the computer with Virtual Memory temporarily turned off, hold the **Command key** during startup, and Virtual Memory is temporarily by-

passed. The **Memory control panel** remains unchanged as this is just a temporary bypass, so if you look at the Memory control panel, you see that Virtual Memory is toggled to the "On" position. You can confirm it is off by looking at the **"About This Macintosh" dialog box** at the top of the **Apple menu** in the **Finder**. The dialog box displays only the amount of physical **RAM** you have installed and won't reflect any Virtual Memory RAM.

Virtual Memory will not be turned on again until you restart your computer.

See Also

Memory Control Panel; RAM; Virtual Memory

Byte-Code, *See Compiled Language*

Byte Shop, The

The Byte Shop was a Silicon Valley computer shop owned and run by Paul Terrell. In May 1976, The Byte Shop became Apple's first customer with an order for 50 Apple I computers at $500 each.

Terrell had seen the Apple I demonstrated by **Steve Wozniak** at a meeting of the **Homebrew Computer Club**. Although Wozniak and **Steve Jobs** had planned to sell just the bare circuit boards, Terrell expected complete computers, so they quickly managed to assemble 50 complete computers (complete circuit boards, actually) to fill the order.

See Also

Apple Computer, History; Homebrew Computer Club; Jobs, Steve; Wozniak, Steve

C

A very popular general-purpose programming language, C was developed by Brian Ritchie at Bell Labs in the 1970s. It is a successor to the nearly forgotten languages BCPL and B. It was first implemented on the UNIX operating system, and shortly thereafter, UNIX was rewritten in C. To this day, C and UNIX retain a very close association.

C is somewhat unique among high-level languages in that it's capable of performing some very low-level tasks. Using C, a programmer can directly manipulate bits, bytes, and memory addresses. Because of this position as a middle-level language, C frequently has been used to write operating systems and other low-level code that previously had to be written in assembly language.

C and its object-oriented offspring **C++** are the languages of choice for most commercial software written for the Macintosh (and most other platforms).

Compared to most other languages, C is relatively lean. The ANSI C standard defines only 32 keywords, whereas other high-level languages have 100 or more keywords. It is possible for C to be this lean because many of the functions that are a core part of other languages, such as those for input and output or advanced mathematics, are implemented as libraries in C. The primary set of libraries are gathered together in the *Standard C Library*. This simple C program uses the library routine `printf` to display the words "Hello, World!" 10 times:

```
#include <stdio.h>

main(void)
{
    for (i = 1; i < 10; i++)
    {
        printf("Hello, World!\n");
    }
}
```

It's very easy to write totally incomprehensible code in C. This has given C a somewhat bad reputation and has even spawned a contest to see who can create the most impenetrable C program—the obfuscated C contest. This, however, is really just a matter of style, and if you're careful in the way you write C code, it can be just as easy to understand as any other language. This entry, for example, in the obfuscated C contest, also prints the words "Hello, World!":

```
int i;main(){for(;i["]<i;++i){--
i;}"];read('-'-'-',i+++"Hell\
o, World!\n",'/'/'/'));}read(j,i,p){write(j/
p+p,i---j,i/i);}
```

Even a seasoned C programmer would have trouble puzzling this one out. If you keep readability and understandability in mind when you write in C, this shouldn't be a problem in your own C code.

Over the years, C has gone through several variations. The first, known as K&R C after the authors of *The C Programming Language*, Brian Kernighan and Dennis Ritchie, was similar to the initial version developed at Bell Labs. Although various implementations of K&R C were relatively compatible with one another, there were problems, so in the early 1980s, a committee was established to create a standard version of C. What emerged from the committee is now called ANSI C after the American National Standards Institute. Although the differences are relatively minor, be aware that most modern compilers get along best with the ANSI flavor of C.

C is traditionally a **compiled** language, although interpreted versions have popped up from time to time. On the Macintosh, you have more choices of C **compilers** than compilers for any other language. C compilers are available from Metrowerks, Symantec, Apple, Motorola, Language Systems, and Microsoft, among others.

See Also

C++; CodeWarrior; Library; MrC; Symantec C++; Visual C++

C++

C++ is a high-level, **object-oriented programming** language that builds upon **C**. It was developed by Bjarne Stroustrup at AT&T Bell Labs.

In addition to its object-oriented features, C++ is in many ways an improvement on C. C++, for example, improves upon C's confusing input/output library with a much more logical and easy to learn I/O system. This program prints the words "Hello, World!" on-screen.

```
int main()
{
        for (i = 1; i < 10; i++)
        {
            cout << "Hello, World!\n";
        }
        return (0);
}
```

C++ also supports function overloading: the creation of multiple functions with the same name but different arguments. A programmer, for example, can create a "print" function that prints a value to the screen. In C, the name "print" can be used for one kind of value—integer, floating point, and so on—so each additional print function needs a new name. With many different data types, the number of different functions could quickly get out of hand: PrintInteger(), PrintDouble(), PrintComplex(), PrintString(), and so on.

In C++, each function can have the same name. The compiler determines which function to use based on the kind of data passed to it. So Print(4) calls the integer version, but **Print(14.7)** calls the floating point version.

Although the advantages of C++ has over C are numerous, most programmers consider the features that support object-oriented programming to be the most reliable. These features enable programmers to write code modules that are self-contained and reusable, as well as code that easily builds upon existing code.

Many C++ compilers are available for the Macintosh. Virtually all C development environments provide support for compiling C++ code. The Metrowerks **CodeWarrior** and **Symantec C++** integrated development environments both include C++ compilers, as does Apple's **MPW**. In addition, Motorola offers a C++ compiler that is hosted by the MPW environment.

See Also

C; CodeWarrior; MPW; Object-Oriented Programming; Symantec C++; Visual C++

Cables and Adapters for Monitors

The port on the Mac into which you plug the monitor cable has several names, due to an unforeseen development in technology. These days, it is simply called the monitor port, or the display monitor port. However, for years, Apple happily referred to the port as the video port. When Mac acquired the capability to accept connections to VCRs and video cameras, Apple had to use the term video port for those connections. There is still some literature that calls the monitor port the "video port," so be careful when you are buying cables.

To connect to a monitor, most Mac models use a standard DB-15 cable, which, as the name implies, uses 15 pins on the connector. Occasionally the cable is permanently connected to the monitor.

Some Macs have a special AV port, or high-density port, which combines the monitor port with sound and the **Apple Desktop Bus (ADB)** port, also called the keyboard port. You'll need a special cable to connect a monitor to this port.

PowerBooks with display monitor ports use a VID-14 monitor output connector (which Apple still calls a video connector). The VID-14 cable has a rectangular, 14-pin connector that plugs into the PowerBook, and a standard video connector that plugs into the monitor. You can buy an adapter cable that lets you use ordinary monitor cables. The Apple part number is M3927LL/A, although it is available from other vendors.

See Also
Apple Desktop Bus; Monitors; PowerBooks; VGA Monitors, Using

Cache Switch

This control panel is designed to turn on and off the onboard memory cache on **68040-based** models of Macintosh and Performa computers. With the cache turned on, functions of some applications run faster, but some programs are incompatible with the onboard cache, and turning on this cache might cause a system crash. In this case, you can use the Cache Switch Control Panel to disable the cache, enabling you to run the program.

See Also
68040 Models; Power Mac Logic Boards

Cache, Types of, *See Power Mac, Logic Boards*

CA-Cricketdraw III, *See Charting And Graphing Applications; Drawing Applications*

CAD Mover

Kandu Software's CAD Mover is absolutely essential for Mac users who wish to port their CAD files to other platforms or file formats. It contains many more import/export options than any stand-alone CAD package.

How It Works Import a saved file that matches any of CAD Mover's import selections, and save it out as any file format that CAD Mover's export list supports (see "Export Formats"). Along the way, however, you may also have a need to utilize CAD Mover's other options. You can apply two-sided surfaces, which is very important if the object is to be rendered and viewed in many 3D programs that do not automatically apply this feature (your 3D object can suddenly disappear from view if two-sided surfaces are not present). A 2D view of the object can be displayed, with the background either gray or white. A special 3D dialog enables you to turn the preview of the object in 3D space via numeric inputs for each axis view angle. You might want to show the associated Log File, or choose the Text or PICT reader, all of which CAD Mover enables. You may choose from separate settings for Mac, MS/DOS, UNIX, and Mainframe Line Terminators, depending on which choice represents the platform that the object will be viewed and rendered on. Selected audible beeps can be set for your computer, associated with different file completion operations. Both the output units (from millimeters and inches to miles and kilometers) can be set, as well as a new sizing option for the exported object. The Fontmap can be set for imported text, and lastly, CAD Mover includes a thorough Preferences dialog that enables you to set input/output details, translation settings and display settings.

Import Formats The following import formats are supported: 3DGF, Architrion II, CGM, Claris CAD, Ddes2, Dimensions, Dreams, DXF, DXF (Binary), Envisage 3D, EPSF, Focus, Focus Text, Gerber Plotter, HPGL, IGES, MacDraft, MacDraw II, MiniCAD+ Text, MacArchitrion Text, PICT, Presenter Pro, Sculpt 3D 1 and 2, Stereo Lithography, STL (Binary), Super 3D, Super 3D Text, WaveFront, Zoom and Zoom Text.

Export Formats The following export formats are supported: 3DGF, Architrion II, Adobe Illustrator 1.1/3/5 and 88, CGM, Ddes2, Dimensions, Dreams, DXF, DXF (Binary), Envisage 3D, Focus, Focus Text, Gerber Plotter, HPGL, IGES, MacArchitrion Text, MacDraft, MiniCAD+ Text, PICT, Presenter Pro, PostScript, Sculpt 3D 1 and 2, Stereo Lithography, STL (Binary), Super 3D Text, WaveFront, Zoom, and Zoom Text.

Because the import/export options extend beyond CAD applications and cover so many standard graphics formats, this package is also of potential benefit to the general Mac artist and animator.

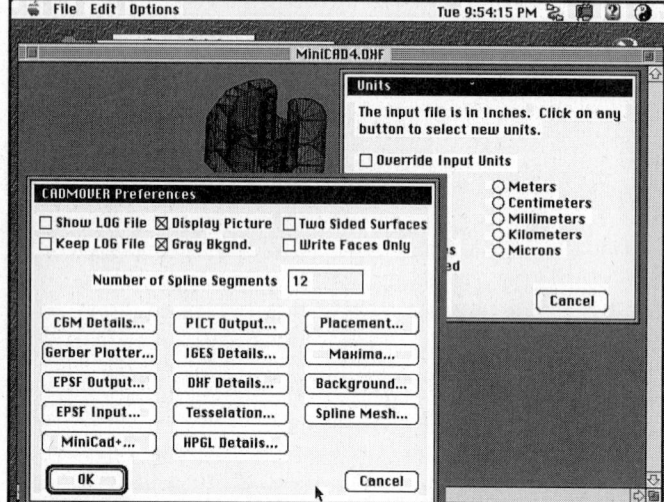

Caffeine, *See Java*

Calculator D/A

This **Apple menu** Item gives you similar features to a regular handheld or traditional desktop calculator. You can input numbers from your keyboard or **numeric keypad**, or you can click the numbers with your mouse. The layout of the calculator matches the layout of the numeric keypad, as shown in the figure.

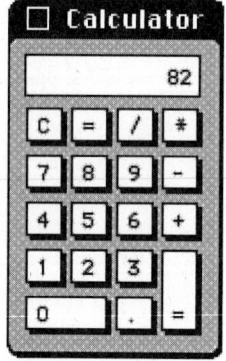

To use the Calculator D/A, follow these steps:

1. Choose Calculator from the Apple menu.

2. To clear the calculator, press the Clear key on your keypad or click the letter C on the calculator.

3. Enter the figures you want to calculate as you do on a regular calculator. The slash key is for dividing. The asterisk for multiplying. The Enter key acts as the equals key.

4. You can **copy** and **paste** any information that appears in the calculator window into any document you select by choosing Copy from the **Edit menu**, and then after you've chosen an insertion point in your document, choose Paste from the Edit menu.

See Also

Apple Menu; Copy Command; Edit Menu; Numeric Keypad; Paste Command

Calculator Keys

The **numeric keypad** on a Macintosh keyboard is set up to match the Apple **Calculator D/A** keys. The **Clear key** in the upper-left corner of the numeric keypad resets the calculator for a new calculation. To the right is the equals key (=), the slash key used for division (/), the asterisk key (*) used for multiplication, and the minus and plus signs. There is also a decimal point (a period) to the right of the zero key. The **Enter key** is used as an equals (=) key.

See Also

Calculator D/A; Clear Key; Enter Key; Numeric Keypad

Calendar Server, *See Server*

Camera-Ready, *See Printing and Binding Terminology*

Cameras, *See Digital Still Cameras; Digital Video Cameras*

Cancel Keyboard Shortcut

Pressing ⌘-. (period) is equivalent to clicking the Cancel button. If, for example, you encounter an **alert box** or dialog box with a Cancel button, you can press ⌘-. to select Cancel. If you **launch** an application or document accidentally, some applications enable you to cancel that launch by pressing the ⌘-. keys several times in succession. This cancels the launch and returns you to the **Finder**. ⌘-. is also used to cancel a **print** command after you've clicked OK and a status bar appears. You may have to press ⌘-. several times to cancel the print job.

To select Cancel in a dialog or alert box, or to stop a print job in progress, use this keyboard shortcut:

1. Press ⌘-. (period).
2. If the action is not canceled, you may have to press ⌘-. (period) several times.

See Also

Alert Box; Click; Command Key; Desktop; Finder; Keyboard Shortcuts; Launching a Program; Print Command

Cannot Be Opened...Message

If you're running an application and get an **alert box** that reads, "There is not enough **memory** to open the application," the system is telling you that you don't have enough free memory (RAM) available to open the application. If you have a number of applications already open, you may be able to free enough memory to launch the program by **quitting** one or more of the applications you have running. When you quit an application, it releases the memory it was using and makes it available for other applications to be opened.

See Also

Alert Box; Memory and Storage, Measurement Methods; Message Boxes; Quit

Canvas

The Canvas 5 upgrade was not available at the time of this writing, and will undoubtedly contain loads of revisions and add-ons. Canvas is a superlative high-end vector drawing program and has enough CAD-oriented tools to make it a program that many CAD users can use to edit their higher-end CAD output. Experienced vector drawing users will need some time to get used to Canvas tool options (many of which are unique to the software) and also where more familiar items are placed on the Canvas interface.

A Preferences dialog enables you to set up Bézier polygon options (Curve drawing choices and FreeHand tool tolerance), left-handed or right-handed coordinate systems, double-mouse click options, object dragging options, duplication offsets, and general redraw and background updating choices. The program ships with the **Pantone** colorsets, and any one of four Pantone color options can be chosen as the default (ANPA, Coated, Process, and ProSim). Other windows that can be placed on the edit screen include the Text Ruler (used to measure text blocks being placed), and the Paint, Objects, and Effects Tools icon menus. Screen zooms are handled by a special pop-out window, which lists a series of possible zooms up and down, or by a positive and negative zooming button. This is much easier to use than a series of mouse clicks with the magnifying tool, and far more exacting. An example of the Canvas approach to expanding the uses of common tools is the "Multigon manager." Here, the default polygon draw tool can be set as to polygon sides, and whether it is a spoked or outlined object, or both. Another option is the Alignment application. The standard alignment options in other programs enable you to left-right-center-top-bottom choices. Not Canvas. It greatly expands the creative possibilities by enabling you to apply different boundaries to the horizontal and vertical coordinates, and to choose among the selected objects, a drawn line, the grid, the page, or the entire document as the ordering principle. Elements can then be aligned or distributed, and a visual schematic gives you a better idea of how each choice will alter the outcome of the graphics elements and their new placements. Both the Multigon and Align functions represent how Canvas, in these and other tools, widens the potential for creating unique vector drawings. A CD-ROM with 2,000 fonts and 10,000 clip art images accompanies the software.

Basic Bézier Drawing Canvas approaches **Béziers** as intuitive drawing devices, not as creative challenges. Any object can be transformed into its Bézier components, and these can then be easily edited. Standard control arms are selectable, resizeable, and moveable. Selecting "Edit Curve" from the Objects menu turns the selected objects into a Bézier outline. When finished, a click away from the object reapplies any gradients or patterns connected to the original shape. A function that supports the Bézier editing is the Smoothing function. It applies a series of smoother Béziers automatically to the object design, turning spokes polygons into flowers as an example of its use. If you want to roughen the outlines a little, just add the Fractalize option from the Effects menu. Points on a Bézier curve can be edited, added to, or deleted by accessing any of these three choices with the pen tool. The freeform line tool makes Bézier curves, polygons, or smooth polygons (smooth enclosed freeform surfaces). All can be edited later as Béziers. All objects can be skewed, distorted, and stretched as well.

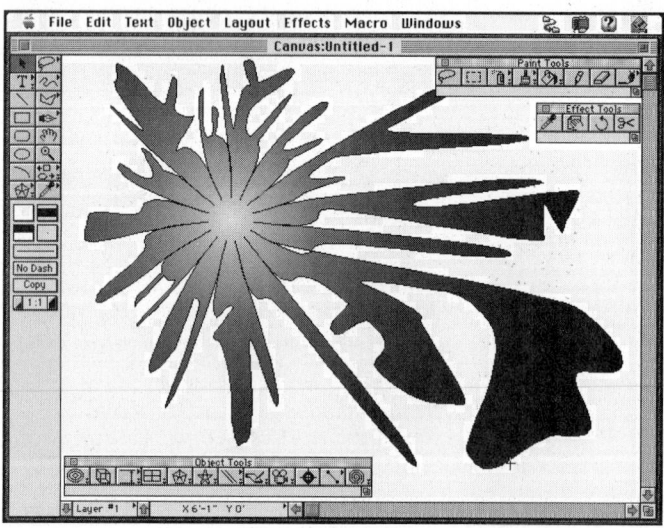

CAD Uses Canvas has dimensioning capabilities that will make many dedicated CAD programs envious. These are extremely intuitive to apply, and include options far beyond the basic necessities. A Dimensioning manager enables for linear, radial and angular types, five varieties of text placement between dimensional lines, leader and symbol options, tolerance settings, precision to ten-thousandths of a unit, measurement units (inch, pixel, centimeter, and pica), and scaling from inch equals inches and pixels to inch equals miles and kilometers. A full dimensioning standards sub-menu includes the settings for dimensioning standards options (ANSI, BS-380, DIN, ISO, and JIS). As if to emphasize its CAD uses, a 3D rectangular box can be placed in a drawing, and 2D DXF files (the CAD format of choice) can be both written and read.

Other Drawing Tools Canvas' Object Tools menu can be left open on the screen. It has drawing tool options far beyond what is expected from a vector drawing program. Among these are the following:

- **Concentric Circles**—The user can set the number of circles and how far apart they will be from each other (choosing "0" causes them to be rendered equidistant).

- **3D Rectangle**—Depth and direction are dependent on real time mouse placement.

- **Dimensioning Options**—Direction, size and measurement end points are controlled by the mouse.

- **Multigon Manager**—Sides, spokes, and outlines controlled by numeric input.

- **Star Manager**—Sides and outlines controlled in the dialog.

- **Parallel Lines Manager**—A full featured dialog is used to set the defaults, among which are dash patterns, pen pattern/size/color, number of lines, distances and spacing from one line to the next.

- **Pressure Pen Manager**—For graphics tablet users
- **QuickTime Specifications**—See the animation listing in this reference.
- **Registration Mark**—Placement
- **Line Type Selector**—Five types
- **Spiral Manager**—Spirals are placed with the mouse, but the number of spirals are set in this dialog.

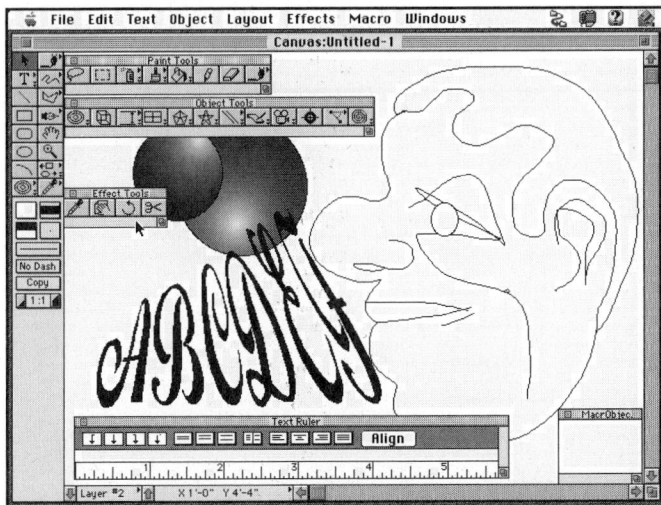

Canvas enables you to place all of the most used tools on the work screen, making it unnecessary in most cases to access them through the menu. A full list of macro keys can also be set to trigger the tools.

Tracing Images Tracing can either be handled manually by tracing over the bitmap on another layer, or automatically. If automatically, Canvas has a dedicated Trace Manager that enables you to set various tracing tolerances. The best images to auto-trace are high contrast images, with black and white being a better choice than grayscale or color. Traces may be Bézier curves, polygons, or smoothed polygons.

Typography This is another area where Canvas extends tool use. In addition to being able to write the text block in any typeface and size, Canvas also contains the following tools (usually associated with word processing and desktop publishing): justification, leading, kerning, style sets, search and replace, and spell checking. Once the type is on-screen, it can be translated to Béziers for further manipulation.

Blends and Gradients Like FreeHand, Canvas accepts only two colors in its gradient blends, and also like FreeHand, user designed blended gradients may be customized and saved to a visual library for selected applications.

Graphs Canvas has no native graphing capability, but by using the 3D rectangular shapes and color, pattern or gradient fills, bar graphs are easy to design.

Animation QuickTime movies can be placed in Canvas documents with the Movie icon. A dialog enables you to set the audio and playback rate levels. QuickTime movies can also be generated by Canvas itself, another unique feature not associated with vector drawing software. Master layers can print as backdrops to each frame of the movie, and the movie can be saved as either self contained (along with all of the elements in one file) or linked to those elements by data paths.

Layers New layers can be added in the Layer manager, and any layer can be hidden or shown as well as exchanging its place with another in the list. A layer listing is accessible at the bottom of the screen, enabling you to jump to other layers quickly.

File Load / Save Conventions Canvas addresses more than the usual number of file formats for both loading and saving. Save formats include: BMP, Canvas Prefs, Canvas drawings, CGM, DCX, DXF, EPSF, GIF, IGES, Illustrator (1.1 and 88), JPEG, MacPaint, PCX, PICT and PICT 1, QuickTime movie, Separations, StartupScreen, TIFF, WMF, WPG, and UltraPaint. Loaded files include all of the previous plus External Tool and MacDraw I and II.

Deneba ArtWorks In general, Deneba ArtWorks is a product that may be described as Canvas Jr., with the exception that it contains some tools (most notable texturing options) that its parent does not possess.

See Also

Bézier Curves; Pantone; Vector Image

Cap Height, *See Typesetting Terms*

Caps Lock Extension

This extension for **PowerBook** users was created because PowerBooks don't have a locking **Caps Lock** key. When this extension is used, an outline of an arrow appears in the far right corner of the **menu bar**, letting the user know that the Caps Lock key is engaged.

See Also

Caps Lock Key; Menu Bar; PowerBook

Caps Lock Key

The Caps Lock key, located between the Tab and Shift keys, enables you to type CAPITAL letters. The Caps Lock effects only letters, it does not effect symbols or numbers.

See Also

Keyboard; Shift Key

Card Games

The one advantage that computer card games have over a regular deck is that you can learn by yourself, without fumbling through a manual. Let's face it, who wants to join in a poker or pinochle game and be the only one who keeps saying "So, what should I do now?" The main thing to remember when checking out card games for your computer is that, with a few exceptions, they are not apt to be too elaborate in the multimedia department.

The forthcoming Perfect Partner series of games from Positronic uses 3D rendering to give background to your opponents and will be an interesting twist on the genre. Anyone For Cards? from Capstone, has annoying animated characters, and its futile attempts at humor take away from the already sluggish game play.

Although we have yet to find out if gambling on the Internet is as much of a financial gain as going to Vegas (and who knows what the inevitable legal mess will be if it is), card sharking is alive and well on CD-ROM.

Although the best thing about card games is playing them with other people, sometimes that is not necessarily an option and you just don't feel like playing solitaire (although solitaire is still a viable computer game). When money gets involved with the cards, even cybermoney, the stakes get a little higher than what you expect from a game. Therefore, most gambling titles don't fare too well under close scrutiny in comparison to the more tutorial intensive card games such as Blackjack Trainer from ConJelCo and Micro Bridge Companion from Great Game Products. Casino Game Pack from MacSoft Casino and Master Gold from Centron Software are mediocre, but still worthwhile for enthusiasts, but Virtual Vegas' Blackjack falls completely flat with its attempts at sexist humor and slow effects.

See Also

Traditional Games

Careers, *See Desktop Publishing Careers*

Carpetbag, *See Font Utility*

Cartoon-Style Animation, *See Full Throttle*

Casady & Greene, *See Crystal Crazy*

CCITT, *See Modem Standards and Speeds*

CD

The specifications for CD data have been defined primarily by the original developers of CDs, Philips and Sony. The original audio CD specification was named Red Book after the color of the specification. There have since been other formats adopted, but these products are more commonly known by other names.

Red Book: A standard audio CD.

Yellow Book: A standard **CD-ROM**. A disc written in this format usually has the "disc" logo with the words "data storage" underneath it. An extension to the Yellow Book format is **CD-ROM/XA**, a disc that can contain data as well as audio and video tracks.

Orange Book: A standard for writeable CDs developed by Philips, Sony, and Kodak. They are usually referred to as **multisession** discs. Like **Red Book audio**, this name comes from the color of the book containing the specification.

Green Book: The standard for **CD-I** (compact disc interactive).

See Also
CD-I; CD-ROM; CD-ROM/XA; Mixed-Mode CD; Multisession CD; Red Book Audio

CD Audio, Converting to QuickTime

A standard audio CD track can be imported into a **QuickTime** movie and played on the computer, provided you have QuickTime 2.0, **Foreign File Access**, and the **Audio CD Access** extension. Converting CD audio files to QuickTime or AIFF format can be useful in multimedia authoring. Most applications, such as Director and HyperCard, cannot play CD audio from the CD disc.

When the disc is inserted into the CD-ROM drive, it appears on the Macintosh desktop with an Audio Disc icon. Any application that can open a QuickTime movie, such as **Adobe Premiere** or **MoviePlayer**, can be used to perform the conversion. Simply choose File Open and select the audio disc. The File Open dialog displays the tracks on the CD and enables you to choose a track and open it. After choosing to open the file, a second dialog asks you to name and save the file. QuickTime cannot play the CD audio track directly; it must first convert it to the QuickTime file format. Depending on the speed of the computer and the length of the selection, this conversion process can take a few minutes.

Before saving the file, click the Options button in the Save File dialog. This brings up a second dialog box in which you can choose the **bit depth** and **sampling rate** for the converted file. You can also select the beginning and ending point of the sample to convert.

Click OK and then click Convert. The audio file is converted to a QuickTime movie file that can then be played in any application that supports QuickTime movies.

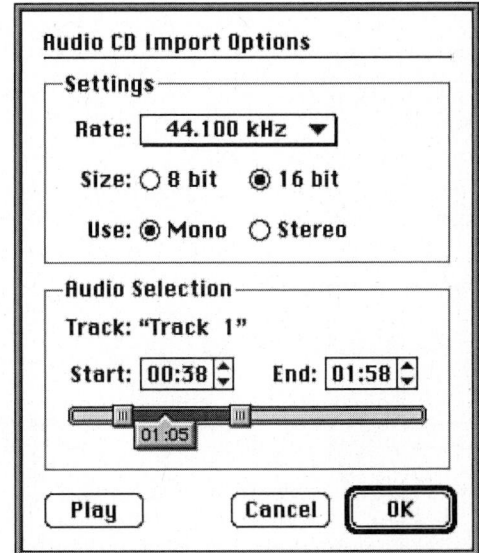

See Also
Playthrough; QuickTime

CD Plus

CD Plus was developed to overcome the problems of **Mixed-Mode CD**s, the original format for a **CD-ROM** that contains both audio and data. Mixed-mode CDs store the data as track one on the CD. Unfortunately, many audio players attempt to play track one, resulting in unexpected and unwanted results.

CD Plus takes advantage of the multisession format for CDs, and the fact that most CD-ROM players can read a multisession disc.

A CD Plus disc is actually a two-session CD. The first session contains any audio tracks written in standard **Red Book audio** format. A second session is then added that contains the data track.

Consumer audio players play the audio tracks and stop at the end of that session. They do not support multisession discs, because audio CDs are usually pressed.

When the disc is inserted into a multisession CD-ROM drive, the two sessions are recognized, and the audio and the data can be accessed by the computer.

See Also
CD-ROM; Mixed-Mode CD; Multisession CD

CD-I

Compact Disc Interactive. A **CD-ROM** disc format and a computer platform developed by **Philips** for the home entertainment market. The CDs hold CD-quality audio (as well as other levels of compressed audio that lengthen the amount of sound but degrade the sound quality), interactive programs, and **MPEG** video. The player contained a computer with RAM and operating system, as well as an MPEG decoder.

Intended primarily for entertainment, education, and games, the original players cost around $700. While they were generally regarded as capable machines, they did not offer any typical computer applications, so they were limited in use (primarily because the CD-I machine lacked a disk drive, a hard drive, or even a keyboard.) Whether it was this limitation, or their expense compared to other platforms, such as Nintendo or Sega, CD-I did not sell well in the consumer market.

CD-I hardware is no longer being sold in the U.S. consumer market, but CD-I discs are still being used to deliver some multimedia products. There is an MPEG player available that works with CD-I discs, and QuickTime may soon support CD-I playback on Power Macs.

See Also
CD-ROM

CD-ROM

CD-ROM technology is a result of the Philips and Sony corporations' research. In 1978, these companies raced to finalize development and create standards for CDs. Sony initially intended to use a 12-inch format for the discs, but when they realized that a full 12 hours of music would fit on one 12-inch disc, they considered other, smaller options (see the following figure).

Sony and Philips announced the standard 5-inch disc in 1982. Some report that this size became the standard, because it was just large enough to contain Beethoven's famous Ninth Symphony. Throughout the 1980s, Philips and Sony continued to work together to develop CD-ROM standards.

Although CD-ROMs appear almost identical to audio CDs, the distinction is that CD-ROMs can store both audio and data. An aluminum alloy is sealed within the protective plastic coating. Information is burned or pressed, in one long spiral not unlike the groove on a vinyl record album, onto this alloy, resulting in pits called data bits. The pits are read by a low-powered laser beam in the CD-ROM player. The pits absorb the laser light, resulting in little or no reflection, and areas without pits produce strong reflections. These reflective areas are referred to as lands. The patterns that develop from these reflections, and lack thereof, are transmitted to the microprocessor to be translated into sound or data.

Although CDs are a standard physical size, the amount of information that can be stored on a disc depends upon a number of factors. The most common size is 620MB, but it is possible to get up to 700MB of data on a disc. This, however, can come at the expense of error correction and readability on older drives. Also, note that multisession discs (discs that have information added to them at different times) use a significant amount of space to hold the additional indexes built when the additional data is added.

The length of time a CD-ROM will last depends on the way it was manufactured. It is possible for manufactured discs to last hundreds of years if they are manufactured correctly. Of course, it is somewhat difficult to predict given that CDs have been in existence for only a little over 10 years. Conservatively, discs manufactured at a pressing plant should last at least 100 years. If the disc is not manufactured correctly (for example, if the edge is not properly sealed), the metal surface inside can corrode, damaging or destroying the disc in only a few years.

Writeable CDs (those created using a CD-ROM recorder) are estimated to have a shorter life span: from 70 to 100 years depending upon the materials used in the disc. Writeable discs come in several colors; in general, the gold discs are believed to have a longer shelf life than the green discs. This life span may be shorter if the disc is not handled correctly, exposed to high temperatures or UV light, or otherwise mishandled. The laser used to "read" the CD is of very low power and cannot harm the data on the disc, even after thousands of reads. CDs should last at least until it's time to replace them with a storage medium of even greater size. Already, **DVD (digital video disc)** technology promises storage capacities much higher than standard CDs.

Which side is up? It's obvious which side contains the data (it's the side without the label). Actually, it's a trick question, because writeable discs are often unlabeled, making it difficult to determine which side contains the data. Usually you can tell by looking for tracks in the surface of the disc. If the top coating contains no visible circular patterns, then it's probably the non-data side. You don't have to worry too much even if you can't work it out. Insert the CD into the player or the recorder and the drive will tell you whether it likes the disc or not!

But which way up should the disc be inserted into the player? Most CD players require that you insert the CD with the label facing upwards, but there are a few that work the reverse. Again, if you can't figure it out, insert the disc and see what happens.

CDs are a surprisingly rugged medium. In a protective case (jewel cases), a CD is probably better able to survive mishandling than disks, hard disks, or removable cartridges. It is, however, wise to take reasonable precautions to ensure the long life of your discs.

CDs are resistant to minor scratches. Error correction is used to detect and hopefully fix errors that occur during reading. The most damaging scratches are those that are circular. A circular scratch can destroy a sequence of information in a track (data is written in a long spiral track on the disc), making it impossible to correct for the error. While audio CDs include algorithms to compensate for massive errors (they simply make an approximation of what the information for the audio signal should be, that is continue the current tone until it gets new data), it's impossible to guess at data and not cause problems.

Always handle a disc by the edges or by the center, and avoid touching the reflective surface of the disc. If you have to touch either side of the disc, touch the label side.

For convenience and cost savings, most CD players sold today don't use caddies (plastic trays that resemble CD jewel cases and are inserted into the drive). One advantage of caddies is that if you purchase several of them, you can leave the CD in the caddy, thus avoiding handling the CD at all.

If a disc is dirty, use a soft, dry, lint-free cloth and wipe in a radial motion either from the center out or from the side into the center of the disc. Do not wipe in a circular motion—just in case you accidentally scratch the disc during cleaning. Do not use any cleaner or solvent; many of these can damage the disc permanently. Do not use water either. Even cleaning agents sold for CDs should be used only when a disc needs serious cleaning. Try to minimize use of these chemicals. Avoid exposure to temperature extremes, humidity, and UV light.

See Also
Burning or Pressing a CD-ROM; DVD; Photo CD

CD-ROM Burning, *See Burning or Pressing a CD-ROM*

CD-ROM Movie Maker

This is a **plug-in** for Adobe **Premiere** 4.2 and is designed primarily for those who are authoring **QuickTime** movies for playback on **CD-ROM**. Because of the comparatively low transfer rate of a CD-ROM, it is important that a QuickTime movie pressed on a CD should not require a transfer rate higher than is possible on the CD-ROM player. For the largest audience, most movies are digitized to play on double-speed drives. While the **Cinepak compressor** enables the user to define the maximum transfer rate for the movie, the CD-ROM Movie Maker provides several other options that can improve the performance of the final movie.

A blur option softens edges and removes some video noise present in the original video. You can specify the data rate for the movie as well as crop and scale parameters. A noise filter removes small random changes that happen from frame to frame in digitized video, which can improve the performance of the compressor. As well as defining the frequency of **key frames** (specify a key frame every x frames), you can also force key frames by adding markers in Premiere's Construction Window. Key frames serve two purposes: they make it possible for the software to drop frames—this is necessary if the CD player cannot read the disc fast enough to play back the movie—and key frames are necessary if the user will be interacting with the movie. Specifying key frames makes it possible to improve interactivity at specific points, while improving compression (the fewer number of key frames, the smaller the resulting movie).

CD-ROM Movie Maker also enables you to specify an 8-bit palette, or create a palette, and attach it to the movie. This is useful if the movie will be played back on 8-bit monitors, because it improves both playback performance, as well as the appearance of the movie. Another nice feature is that CD-ROM Movie

Maker batch processes files (apply the same parameters to several movies automatically).

See Also
Compressor; Key Frames; Movie Cleaner Pro; Premiere; QuickTime

CD-ROMs, Object and Image, *See Object and Image CD-ROMs*

CD-ROM/XA

CD-ROM/XA is an extension to the original **Yellow Book** or **CD-ROM** standard (see **CD** for a discussion of CD formats). While the original CD-ROM format supported data only, the XA standard adds many of the features that were added to the **CD-I** format: compressed audio data and video and picture data. Many CD-ROM drives do not support CD-ROM/XA. There is currently no system software support for CD-ROM/XA, but this could change in the near future.

See Also
CD-ROM

CDEF Virus

Similar in symptoms to **WDEF**, this virus only infects the invisible Desktop file used by the Finder. System 7 cannot be infected by the CDEF virus.

See Also
Virus; WDEF Virus

Cell in Databases

A cell is an individual **field** of data arranged in a grid across a **spreadsheet**. Cells can hold numbers or text, or they can hold **formulas** telling them how to calculate the information in other cells. If a cell holds a formula, it displays the result of that calculation—and can be used as the input to a formula in another cell.

For example, if cell A1 holds the number 5 and cell B1 holds the formula "= A1 + 1," cell B1 will display the number 6. If cell C1 holds the formula "= B1 / 2," it will display the number 3.

See Also

Absolute/Relative Referencing; Circular Reference; Spreadsheet Notation

Centipede, *See Arcade-Style Games*

CEPS, *See Desktop Publishing and Color Electronic Prepress Systems (CEPS)*

Certificate, on the Web

A means of authenticating the identity of a person or organization involved in a transaction on the **World Wide Web.**

A certificate can be anything that documents the relationship between a person or organization and a **public key**. A certifying agency (for example, RSA Data Security, Inc.) creates certificates containing the owner's name and public key that attest that the owner of the key has proven to the satisfaction of the certifying agency that owner is who the owner claims to be.

A widely used standard exists for organizing certificate information into a file format that can be used by many programs on many different platforms: these files are called X.509 certificates. The X.509 standard is used by **Netscape Navigator** and many other encryption tools, such as Apple's PowerTalk technology and the public-domain encryption programs PGP and MacPGP.

X.509 certificates are signed with the "digital signature" of the certifying agency. The signature is created with the authentication features of public key technology, and is unforgeable. Both signatures and certificates operate in the background during online transactions and are unseen by users.

See Also

Electronic Commerce; Encryption; Netscape Navigator; Password Protection; Secure HTTP; Secure Sockets Layer; World Wide Web

CGI

A common gateway interface (CGI) is a standard way for applications to interact with **World Wide Web** servers on the **Internet**. The term CGI is used for both the standard interface and the applications themselves.

World Wide Web servers, such as WebSTAR, generally provide basic functionality needed by a Web site. These servers send files at the request of a **Web browser**. To add functionality to a Web site—such as forms, searching, database access, and so on—a CGI application is required. Using CGIs, Webmasters can vastly expand the services they provide to their users.

On the Macintosh, Web servers communicate with CGIs using **Apple events**. When a browser requests a URL that corresponds to a CGI application, the server bundles up all the relevant information about the request into an Apple event and sends it to the CGI. The CGI then does its magic (for example, processing and logging the input from a form) and returns information to the server that it can then pass on to the browser. This use of Apple events differs from Web servers on other platforms, such as UNIX, in which information is passed to CGIs as command line arguments.

Virtually any **programming language** can be used to create CGI applications. For many kinds of tasks, it is easiest to use a scripting language such as **AppleScript** or **Frontier**. Jon Wiederspan has written an excellent tutorial on writing CGIs in AppleScript. The tutorial is available at **http://www.comvista.com/net/www/cgilesson.html**. Jon S. Stevens revised these tutorials for learning how to create Frontier CGIs. The Frontier CGI tutorial is located at **http://www.clearink.com/fun_stuff/frontier/**. Though not as popular on Mac servers as on UNIX, **Perl** is also a frequent choice for creating CGI applications.

Although script-based CGIs offer tremendous advantages in development time and maintainability, they are not able to offer the same speed as those written in a compiled programming language such as **C** or Pascal. A number of frameworks have been written to help programmers create CGI applications. The most widely used of these is Grant Neufeld's CGI framework, written in C.

In many instances, it may not be necessary to resort to writing your own CGI at all. There are a wide variety of CGIs available that perform the most common tasks needed of CGIs. There are pre-built CGIs for handling image maps, for example, redirecting a client to another page, processing forms, and so on. Jon Wiederspan maintains a reference of available CGIs at **http://www.comvista.com/net/www/cgi.html**.

See Also

Apple Event; AppleScript; Frontier; Internet; Perl; Programming Languages; Web Browser; World Wide Web

Chameleon

This program accompanies the CorelDRAW! 6 package for the Mac. Chameleon's interface resembles that of Adobe's TextureMaker, but its operations and options are different. Like TextureMaker, it operates on a stack of planes, each of which is sandwiched together to form the final graphic. Also like TextureMaker there is a Background layer (beveled or picture frame backdrop), a Lights layer (where lights can be positioned and adjusted) and a one or a series of graphics layers (with variable opacity so you can see through them as a sandwiched graphic). Unlike TextureMaker the Light plane acts more like an Alpha channel overlay and bump map, with three movable lights, ambiance, and shading and Hilite sliders. The layering effects possible in Chameleon function much like Photoshop's layering options.

Algorithmic PreSets Oasis applies a selection of algorithmic textures to a plane between the Background and the Lights layers. These textures are represented in a list, and include: Solid Color, Clouds, Marble, Wood, Checkers, Spots, Agate, Gradient, and Picture. The last selection, Picture, enables you to add your own graphic as a layer (PICT). Except for the Picture option, the rest of the textures can be altered as to magnification and rotation, and in some cases, variance and turbulence. Each of the layers has a vari-

able opacity and combine feature. Opacities range from opaque to 25% opaque in 25% increments, and the combine features (which affect how the selected plane will be combined with its neighbors in the final rendering) include: Additive, Subtractive, Lighten, Darken, Shade, Hue Shift, and Multiply. By combining all of these variables, thousands of unique textures can be created. It's also possible to use Chameleon as a compositing platform for larger graphics backgrounds.

A preview area shows a reduced version of either one selected plane, that plane plus others below it in the stack, or all planes combined. The bottom plane acts as the final background, and it can be set to a variable beveled frame. This makes Chameleon an excellent choice for creating multimedia interactive buttons. Graphics can either be tiled or made to fill the entire area. A special "Render to Window" option enables you to see a finished rendering before saving it to disk. The Image Setup dialog enables you to set the final size for the renderings, in Pixels, Inches, or Centimeters. DPI can be set to 72 (standard for video work), 150, or 300 (the lowest setting desirable for printed output). A Render to File option writes directly to the chosen disk path. You can operate Chameleon from a new blank page, a Texture Preset mode, or in compliance with its walkthrough wizards. The Wizard mode is great for beginners.

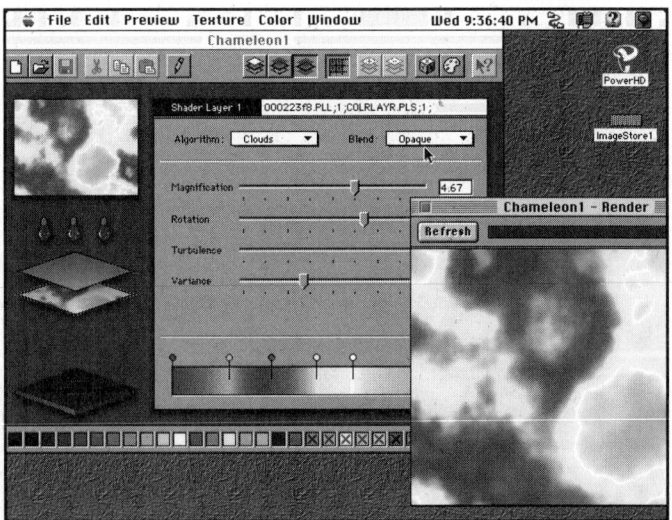

C

See Also
CorelDRAW! 6

Change Icon Name

To rename a file **icon**, **select** the icon and press **Return**. This **highlights** the file's name below the icon, enabling you to type a new name. You can also use the **arrow pointer** to highlight the icon name by **clicking** it. You can edit individual letters by clicking at the insertion point where you want to edit. The arrow pointer changes to the **I-Beam cursor**, enabling you to edit the text as you would in a text editing program.

See Also
Arrow Pointer; Click; Highlight; Icons; I-Beam Cursor; Return Key; Selecting

Changing Type and Creator

Imbedded in each Macintosh file is the file's type code and creator code. These codes tell the Mac what the file is and how it should be handled. The four-letter creator code tells the Mac which application created the file. If, for example, you created a database in ClarisWorks, the creator code is BOBO. If you **double-click** that file, the Mac looks at the creator code, sees that the document was created in ClarisWorks, launches **ClarisWorks**, and opens the document in ClarisWorks. All files created in ClarisWorks have the creator code BOBO, regardless if they were created using ClarisWorks's spreadsheet, word processor, or database.

The type code tells the Macintosh what kind of file it is (database, graphics file, text file, spreadsheet, and so on). A type code of CWDB, for example, tells the Mac that the file is a database document (created in ClarisWorks). Each type of file has a separate type code.

You can change these type and creator codes by using Apple's **ResEdit** or Norton Utilities's **Disk Editor** (part of the Norton Utilities package), plus there are dozens of freeware and shareware utilities that enable you to do the same thing quickly and easily.

Why would you want to change a type or creator code? If you have a text file that was created in WordPerfect on a PC, and you want to be able to open it in Microsoft Word on the Macintosh, you can open the WordPerfect file and change its type code to WDBN (the type code for Microsoft Word) and its creator code to MSWD (the code for a Microsoft Word text document). The next time this file is opened, Macintosh will treat the file as if it were a Macintosh Microsoft Word document, and if you double-click the file, Microsoft Word will launch and the document will open.

Some of the more popular type and creator code freeware and shareware utilities (for System 7 and higher) are

- Creator Changer
- Type Resolve (which automatically takes PC file-type codes and matches them with Mac codes)
- TC Changer

You can also change type and creator codes with the popular shareware utility DiskTop. These all are available from online services or via the Internet.

See Also
Double-Click; Internet, The; Launching a Program; Norton Utilities for Macintosh; Online Services; ResEdit

Chaos Overlords

Although **Chaos Overlords** isn't as in-depth as **Spaceward Ho!**, the unique twist on the **strategy game** theme should appeal to gamers with more urban interests. The future world of Chaos Overlords ushers us into a society ruled by corporate bigwigs and pure capitalists. A few former crime lords, dubbed the Chaos Overlords, have decided to take the power back from the leaders and get a little something out of it themselves in the bargain.

You play an overlord on a mission to kick the suits off the street and reclaim your territory. Using gangs that you conquer and then employ, you establish a hold on your 8×8 grid. Then, as you progress, you move into enemy territory and take on rival gangs. Over a modem or the Internet, you can start global warfare with other players making Chaos a welcome addition to the strategy world. To add to the strategy depth, not all gang members are fighters. Because not all grids can be taken by force alone, some are going to need to research new technology and handle the bribes of certain prominent government officials.

See Also

Allied General; Pax Imperia; Sid Meier's Worlds; Spaceward Ho! 4.0; Strategy Games; V for Victory; Warcraft: Orcs and Humans

Character Entities in HTML

An element of HyperText Markup Language (**HTML**) that allows a **World Wide Web browser** to display certain characters using predesignated codes. The characters supported by HTML correspond to the ISO-Latin 1 character set.

The characters that must be represented by character entity codes fall into two categories:

- Characters that are not recognized by HTML (accented foreign characters such as é, ü, and ç);

- Characters that perform a special function within HTML (such as the greater-than (>) and less-than (<) symbols, used to designate HTML **markup tags**.

All character entities are case-sensitive and begin with an ampersand (&) and are followed by a semicolon (;)

- < for the less-than (<) sign;

- > for the greater-than (>) sign

Some HTML editing programs enter common character entities automatically, but if you are typing an HTML document from scratch, it's best to look them up in a chart of the ISO Latin-1 characters.

See Also

HTML; Web Browser; World Wide Web

Character Spacing, *See Tracking*

Character Styles, *See Styles in Word Processors*

Charting

Any computer can crunch numbers. What made the Macintosh so popular is its capability to crunch pictures, and **spreadsheet** programmers have taken advantage of this. Every spreadsheet lets you **select** a range of **cells** and, through a menu command or palette selection, quickly turn it into an accurate chart. The result can be kept in the spreadsheet or **copied** to another program for a report or a presentation. A few of the newer programs have **assistants** or **wizards**: when you ask for a chart, they present dialog boxes that guide you through appropriate choices to see how the chart will look.

Charts also make it easier to spot trends that might be hidden in rows of numbers. In the figure from **Excel**, it's difficult to quickly tell how the regions are doing by just looking at the numbers. But the three-dimensional graph, which took only a few seconds to construct, makes it immediately obvious that South is a consistent performer and North has been having some problems.

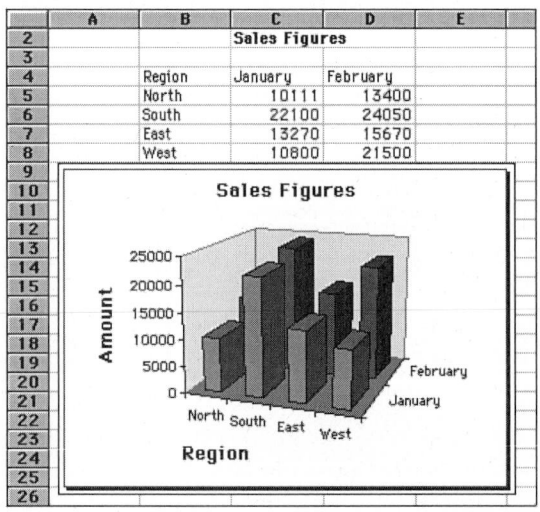

See Also

What-If Calculations

Charting and Graphing Applications

Actually drawing charts and graphs can be much more time-consuming than designing them. A number of applications exist to deal with this problem, most requiring only that the user enter the data and choose a style of chart or graph to produce a finished piece of artwork. They combine features from spreadsheet and presentation applications and throw in a few extras specifically for graphing.

DeltaGraph Pro provides more than 60 chart types, including business, financial, statistical, and scientific charts, pictographs, quality control charts, XYZ contour, and scatter plots. Graphs can be linked to existing data from Excel and other programs, and a Chart Advisor helps users determine what type of chart or graph is appropriate for the data in question. Once the graph is created, users can customize its format by changing fonts, colors, rotation, dimensions, and adding imported artwork.

A slide show feature enables users to display a series of graphs in a designated order, with artistic transitions between images. Graphs can be exported as EPS files (for importing into page layout packages) or as Illustrator files that can be edited in **Illustrator** or **FreeHand**.

For more sophisticated data analysis, KaleidaGraph offers 16 graph structures that can plot large amounts of data and mathematical functions useful to scientists, engineers, and financial analysts.

Spyglass Plot is also scientific charting software that can handle huge data sets; it supports HDF (Hierarchical Data Format) files, a standard format for supercomputers. It's part of a trio of programs that work together; the other two are Spyglass Dicer, which displays volumetric data (used in fluid dynamics, meteorology, and astrophysics) in false color, and Spyglass Transform, which generates surface and vector plots from data tables.

A third option for scientists is Igor Pro, another complex charting program that offers a large choice of data-analysis functions. Its charting capabilities are admirable (from a design standpoint) with the capability to fine-tune any element. It has a built-in Igor language that enables users to run several kinds of analyses on a data set and then save the procedure to run on other sets.

Business users, on the other hand, will find Claris Impact suited to their needs. This easy-to-learn program creates organizational, flow, and data charts; network diagrams; project time lines; and calendars. With a colorful library of styles and a large selection of clip art, Impact can produce charts and graphs with professional flair. The DataDraw feature enables charts and graphs to be linked to data from spreadsheets and databases.

In addition to charts and graphs, Impact can create multipage documents, drawings, and presentations. Claris Impact's graphs come in several simple styles and can be customized with colors, fonts, and 3D effects of the user's choice.

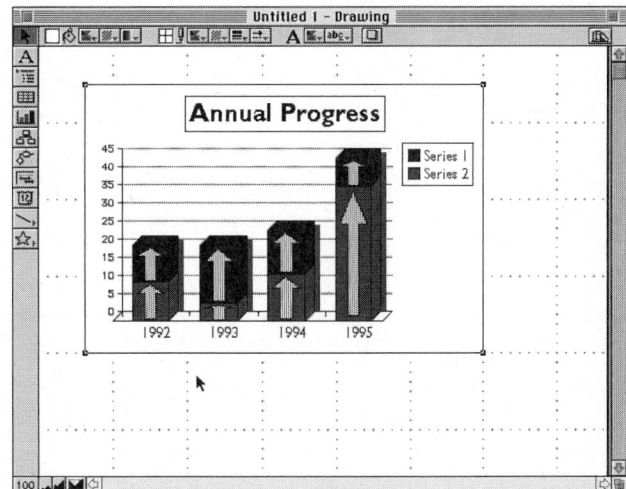

For basic graphs, CA-CricketGraph III offers 10 different types of graphs. Although it doesn't have the advanced features of other programs, it uses less RAM and it's easy to use. Charts are limited to two dimensions but can be produced in color or black and white.

See Also

FreeHand; Illustrator

Checkbox

Many dialog boxes enable you to choose from a set of options. To choose more than one option, a dialog box provides checkboxes. A checkbox is a small square box you click to select (or deselect) an option. When you select a checkbox, an "X" appears to let you know it has been selected, similar to the way you mark an "X" on a ballot.

If you were to open the **General Controls control panel**, you would see a list of options on the left with checkboxes and a list of options on the right with **radio buttons**, as shown in the figure.

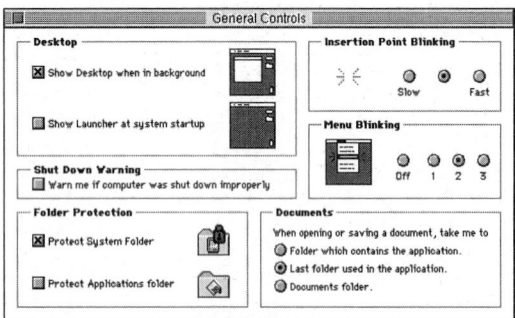

Radio buttons differ from checkboxes in that radio buttons enable only one choice. In the General Controls control panel, for example, you can have the **insertion point** blink either slow, medium, or fast, but you can only choose one. You can't have the insertion point blink medium and fast at the same time, so when you click your choice of speed with a radio button, any other choice is automatically deselected. Checkboxes, however, act independently of each other. For example, look in the General Controls Control Panel again. You can click a checkbox to protect the **System Folder**, and then click a checkbox to protect the Applications folder. Your choice to protect the System

Folder is not deselected. For this reason, checkboxes are ideal for choosing multiple items from a list of options and radio buttons are ideal when an either/or selection is required.

See Also

General Controls Control Panel; Radio Buttons; System Folder

Checking Account Software

Of the personal finance programs on the market, Intuit's **Quicken** is by far the most popular, and the easiest to use. It uses the visual metaphor of a checkbook, with a register to keep the balance and check forms to fill out. For a small fee, Intuit can supply standardized checks for your laser or pinfeed printer, which you can print from the program. You can also use CheckFree payment services with Quicken. CheckFree eliminates stamps, envelopes, checks, and paperwork because it transmits your payment advice by modem. When you enter a list of checks to be paid and log into CheckFree, the amounts will be subtracted from your bank balance and forwarded to the accounts of your creditors. Your monthly bank statement lists your CheckFree transactions, along with any paper transactions or ATM withdrawals you've made.

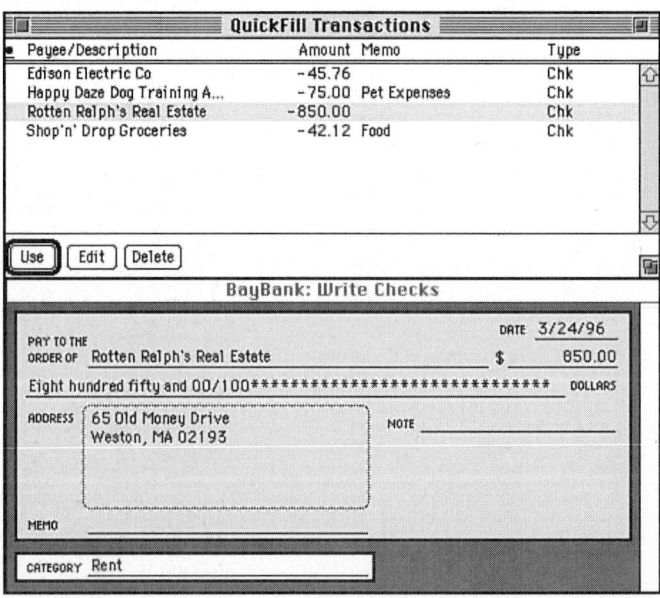

Monthly payments, such as rent or car payments, need only be entered once in Quicken. Its QuickFill feature (see figure) simplifies data entry. Checks you write can be listed in the QuickFill window. Next time you need to write a check to the same person, just click the last one and the new check is automatically filled out. If you need to change an amount, go ahead. The change will be entered in the QuickFill list, too. Even without using QuickFill, Quicken does its best to automate the check writing process. Whenever you start to enter a transaction, the program scans its records of previous ones looking for a match. If it is found, Quicken will automatically enter the address and other data for you. You can specify payment dates for monthly bills and Quicken will remind you when one is due.

See Also

Quicken

Checkmark in Menu

If a checkmark appears to the left of a command in a **menu**, it is indicating that the checked command, preferences, or option is active, as shown in the figure. If, for example, you're typing all bold text and you look on the **Font** menu, a checkmark appears beside the Bold command. If you select Bold again, the Bold setting is deactivated, your text no longer appears in bold face, and the checkmark disappears. The checkmark is the Mac's way of telling you which commands are selected.

You can also set some preferences by activating a menu option or command. If, for example, you're using a word processor and you select a word and choose the Bold option, the application will bold the word, and anytime you select that word, the Bold option will be checked in the menu. However, if you select the Bold option without any word or letters being selected, you are setting Bold as a temporary preference. The next words you type and all words thereafter will now appear in bold until you change the option in the menu bar to another setting, such as Plain Text. This change is only temporary, and if you quit or open a new document, the application's pre-set preferences will again be in place.

See Also

Fonts; Menu Commands; Menu

Chess

As far as high strategy goes, nothing created for the Mac is ever going to diminish the status of the grandmaster of all games: Chess. Although the computer Chinook has mastered checkers by beating all but one master (Marion Tinsley forfeited) in August 1994, even the IBM whiz Deep Blue still couldn't defeat world champion Kasparov during their seven day face off in February 1996. But Deep Blue came closer than Kasparov expected. In *Popular Science*, before the match, Kasparov revoked his prior boast that he would not be beaten by a computer in the 20th century saying: "I'm amazed at the amount of progress the machines have made."

On the Mac side, the leader is Mindscape's Chessmaster 3000. Although not a beginner's program (it does have an extensive tutorial, but is tough to beat) Chessmaster 3000 offers multiple options as in-depth as deciding whether the computer values pawns more than other pieces and whether its strategy will be defensive or offensive.

One thing missing from the game is network play. For this, Battle Chess from **MacPlay** is your best bet with great graphics and animation. Every time you make a move, the pieces animate accordingly, engaging in combat when they come into contact with the other side. You can turn off the options for walking and music if you want to get serious (it does slow things down), but the enhancement reminds you that you are not necessarily sitting across from your opponent at a table and that they may be on the other side of the world.

See Also
Traditional Games

Chessmaster 3000, *See Chess*

Chiat/Day, *See 1984*

Children's Software, *See Software, Educational, Grades 7-12; Software, Educational, Grades K-6*

Chimes of Death

The chimes of death, four tones the computer sounds as a warning, sound when a problem is found during the diagnostic check the Macintosh runs every time you start up the computer. These "chimes of death" are usually accompanied by a **Sad Mac icon**. Like the Sad Mac hexadecimal codes used to aid the repair technician, the chimes of death are used to tell the Apple repair technician that the problem was found during the diagnostic check.

See Also
Icons; Sad Mac Icon

Chinon ES-3000

This camera, also marketed by Kodak and Dycam, provides several features not found in other still video cameras. Most noticeably, it has a built-in 3x zoom lens, and accepts **PCMCIA** RAM cards for storing additional images. The camera is not an **SLR** camera (that is, you aren't looking through the camera lens when using the viewfinder), but the viewfinder zooms along with the zoom lens, providing a reasonably accurate indication of what you are shooting.

The camera contains 1MB of built-in memory, which is enough to hold 10 640×480 images. A 4MB PCMCIA can hold just over 40 images. Additional cards cost several hundred dollars, but provide an almost unlimited opportunity for picture taking without having to download the images to a computer.

C

The camera's shutter and zoom buttons are on the top, and an LCD panel at the back that displays the number of images available, the resolution, the flash, exposure, and auto-focus mode. Two buttons enable you to switch between features and change the selection, while a third button erases all of the images in the camera or card. The PCMCIA card is inserted into a slot on the lower edge of the back of the camera. If the card is inserted, pictures are stored on it. To use the internal memory, you must eject the card by pressing the large eject button next to the card.

The image quality is similar to that found in the other cameras, and the camera's exposure metering does a very good job in most situations. One feature that is a bit annoying is that you must hold down the shutter release for a second or two before the camera will take the picture. It also takes several seconds to save an image, making it difficult to take spontaneous pictures.

Like most other still video cameras, the ES-3000 supports 1/4 screen (320×240) and full screen (640×480) mode pictures. A third resolution, called SuperFine, produces an image of 640×480, but results in a larger file. It also reduces the number of pictures you can take. The quality of these images in some situations may be better than the standard 640×480, but often they look as though they have been over sharpened.

The control panel (above, right) can be used to control the camera remotely.

See Also

Digital Still Cameras; Still Video Cameras

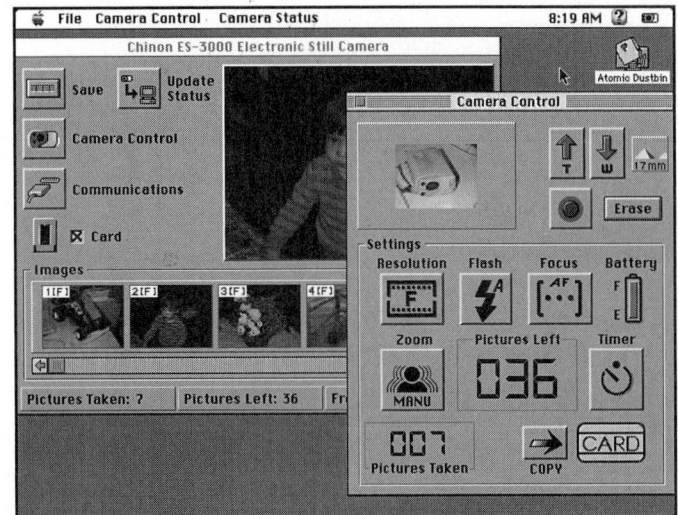

Chokes, *See Color Trapping*

Chooser D/A

This desk accessory, which appears on the **Apple menu**, lets you choose which printer you'd like to print to, or which network or server you want to connect to. The Chooser displays your choices as icons that appear in a window on the left side of the Chooser dialog, as shown in the figure. To make your selection, simply click the **icon** of your choice.

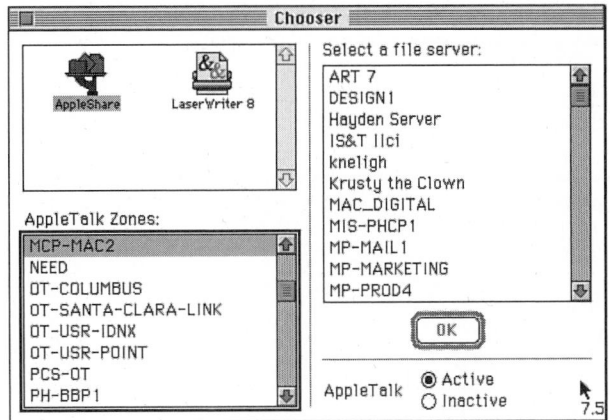

If you need to **print** a document, you'll need to choose from which printer you'd like to print. When you choose which type of printer you'd like to use (laser printers, color printers, and so on), the Chooser lists all the types of printers to which you have access. If you only have one printer, and will be printing only to that printer, you may have to access the Chooser only when you first install your printer. However, if you have multiple printers, or if you're on a network sharing one printer or a number of printers, the Chooser will need to be accessed more frequently.

The Chooser will remember the last printer you've selected, so you don't have to access the Chooser every time you want to print a document. You can just select Print and your document will print to the last printer you selected in the Chooser. However, if you want to switch printing devices, you'll need to access the Chooser to let your Mac know to which printer you want to print.

For example, if you've been printing to an Apple LaserWriter 360 for the past week, and then decide you want a color print out of a page from your Apple Color StyleWriter, you'll have to access the Chooser to switch from the LaserWriter 360 to the Color StyleWriter. After you've selected the Color StyleWriter, all subsequent print requests from your Mac will go to the Color StyleWriter until you access the Chooser again, and switch back to the LaserWriter 360.

If you are connected to a **network**, when you access the Chooser, you may see a list of **AppleTalk zones**. To access a particular zone, select it from the alphabetical listing. Also, if you're on a network and you want to connect to a server, first click the icon for your network.

To lock in the changes you've made in the Chooser, simply click the **close box** and your changes will be in effect.

The Chooser provides two other options: The capability to request **background printing** and the capability to make **AppleTalk** active or inactive.

To use the Chooser D/A, follow these steps:

1. Choose Chooser from the Apple menu.

2. Click the icon for the type of Printer you want and a list of available printers will appear in the window to the right of the icons. If you want to connect to a server, click the appropriate icon and a list of available servers will appear in the window to the right of the icons.

3. If you want your documents to print in the background, you can activate background printing here as well. You can also make AppleTalk active or inactive by choosing from radio buttons in the Chooser.

4. To lock in your choices, close the Chooser.

See Also

Apple Menu; AppleTalk; AppleTalk Zones; Background Printing; Close Box; Icons; Network; Print

Chording Keyboard, *See Keyboard*

Chromapress

Agfa's short-run digital press is actually a color printer that uses toner, just like a laser printer. It's one of several models based on the Xeikon DCP-1 engine, including IBM's 3170 and Barco's DigiPress. Like the other Xeikon models, the Chromapress can output 4,080 letter-size pages per hour (or 2,040 double-sided pages).

See Also

E-Print; Short-Run Printing

CIE

CIE is the acronym of the Commission Internationale de l'Eclairage, an international commission formed in the early 1930s for the purpose of devising a universal color standard for the graphics industry.

See Also
CIELAB; Color Gamut

CIELAB

Developed by the **Commission Internationale de l'Eclairage (CIE)** in the mid-1970s, CIELAB is a standard theoretical color space (gamut) that contains all visible color. CIELAB and a similar color space, CIELUV, were derived from, and meant to replace, an original model developed by CIE in 1931. The original model was called CIEXYZ because it defined color mathematically using the three axes—x, y, and z. In CIELAB, "L" refers to Luminance (light) and "A" and "B" refer to chrominance (color perception). The CIELAB colors are closer to human perceptions than the other models and is more widely used in color printing. In CIELUV, the letters "L," "U," and "V" have the same meaning as in CIELAB, but this model is used in color display on monitors rather than printed color. The purpose of these color standards is to establish a device-independent **color gamut** to aid in translating color accurately from one device to another.

See Also
CIE; Color Gamut

CIM, *See CompuServe*

Cinepak

Developed by SuperMac, which then merged with Radius, the Cinepak compressor is a QuickTime compressor. A movie segment compressed in Cinepak is half the size (datawise) of the same movie compressed using the **Apple Video Compressor** with similar parameters.

The compressor also has a data rate limit, which enables you to define the maximum data rate for the movie during compression. The compressor reduces the compression parameters to maintain the specified data rate. This makes Cinepak the best choice for **CD-ROM** distribution.

Cinepak is **asymmetrical**. Compressing files with Cinepak takes much longer than with the Apple Video Compressor. This is not as noticeable, however, if you are using a PowerPC, which noticeably reduces the time it takes to compress a movie with Cinepak.

See Also
Asymmetrical Compressors; Compressor; Drop Frames; Spatial Compression; Symmetrical Compressors; Temporal Compression

Circuits, Parts of the Macintosh

The Macintosh is composed of various printed circuit boards that contain integrated circuits, called chips. These chips are arranged on the boards to serve different functions.

- **CPU**—The central processing unit in Apple terminology is the total conglomeration of chips and boards that make up the intelligence of the Macintosh. But, the CPU is also the printed circuits and their associated electronics that perform the computing work for the Macintosh. The CPU printed circuit board (and other connected boards) contain the following types of semiconductors and communications connections.

- **Microprocessor**—This is the chip that executes the instructions from the Macintosh applications and operating system. You may also have a math coprocessor to speed up mathematical computations.

- **RAM**—The random-access memory or the **dynamic RAM** (DRAM) chips that temporarily hold data and instructions for use by the microprocessor. The Macintosh dynamically updates the RAM by swapping in and out information on a "least-used" or "first-in, first-out" basis. In System 7, virtual memory can be assigned the role of RAM to augment your built-in memory.

- **PRAM**—The **parameter RAM** is a small reserved portion of RAM that is protected by the batteries soldered on to the printed circuit board. PRAM is used to retain time and date information, and the name of your designated startup device, as well as other dynamic information. Because PRAM is protected by battery power, its data is not lost when the Macintosh is turned off.

- **ROM**—The **read-only memory** is "firmware" that has been permanently encoded on to the chips. ROM holds the most basic portions of the Macintosh operating system that are used in startup, as well as much of the instructions used to draw the Macintosh screens.

- **Communications Ports**—The Macintosh also uses several types of *ports* associated with the CPU and located on the back of the computer case, including a printer port, sound port (used to connect external sound devices such as MIDI processors), telephone port (used for connecting your modem to the computer), SCSI port (used for connecting SCSI devices such as external hard disks, CD-ROM units, scanners, and so on), external disk drive port, and an **Apple desktop bus** (ADB) port for attaching your keyboard, mouse, graphics tablet, and so on. (The early Macs, up through the Plus, had a non-ADB mouse.)

- **Expansion Slots**—In addition to the processor and ports, the Power Macs, Quadras, LCs, and PowerBook series contain one or more internal slots used for the installing of printed circuit boards to enhance the performance of your Macintosh. Macs currently use three types of slots: NuBus, Processor Direct Slots (PDS or LC), and PCI slots, depending on the Mac model. Such cards may include a 24-bit color card, an internal modem card, a card to connect your Macintosh to an EtherNet or Token-Ring network, a card to attach your Macintosh to a mainframe computer, and a video card.

For the Macintosh to function properly, its components need to be plugged together in a logical fashion, using the correct ports and slots to connect the correct type of peripheral device. If you do not use the proper port, the Macintosh will not recognize the plugged-in component. In addition, SCSI devices attached to the SCSI port must be linked with a termination resistor on both ends of the chain.

If your Macintosh does not turn on, be sure the components are plugged in correctly. Read the installation instructions for each peripheral to ensure that you have hooked it to the correct port, and that you have terminated any SCSI devices.

See Also

GeoPort; NuBus Slot; PCI Slot; PDS Slot; PowerPC; PRAM; Processors; RAM; ROM; SCSI Port

Circular Reference

A circular reference is a user error in a **spreadsheet**. It is the result of trying to calculate a **formula** that depends on the results of itself, sort of like the image of a mirror reflected in another mirror, reflected in itself, and on to infinity. For example, if **cell** A1 contains the formula "= B1 + 1" and cell B2 contains "= A1 + 1," the program could go back and forth between the two cells forever and never reach an answer. Rather than crash, it reports the error, usually with a dialog box or a question mark in the cell.

Most circular reference errors aren't as obvious as our example, and a dozen cells or more may be found in one huge chain. The cure is to replace one of the formulas with real data.

See Also

Cell in Databases; Formula; Spreadsheet

Civilization, *See Sid Meier's Worlds*

Claris Impact

Claris Impact is not so much a **presentation** program as it is a complete business graphics program. It can, indeed, create slide presentations, both on the Mac and as 35mm slides or overhead transparencies. It can also create reports, drawings, and outlines, and easily can incorporate timelines, tables, calendars, data charts, organization charts, and flowcharts into any of these.

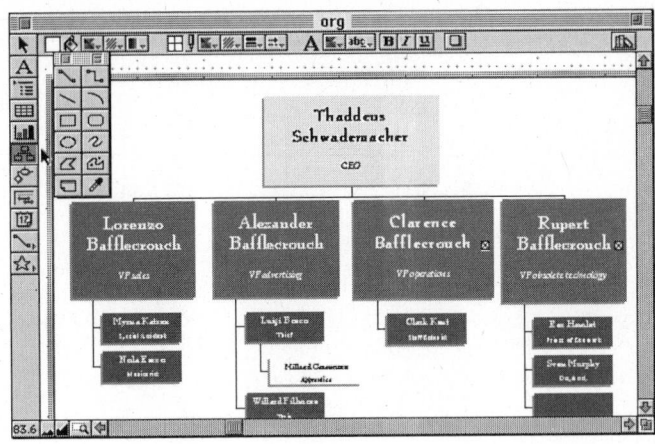

Impact can handle most, if not all, of your **desktop publishing** chores with some help from a good **word processor**. You can type directly into an Impact document, of course, and the program contains a spelling dictionary and thesaurus, but serious writers might prefer to create large blocks of text elsewhere and then import them into Impact text frames. The drawing tools are essentially the same ones provided with **Claris MacDraw Pro** or **ClarisWorks**, and are easy to use and intuitive. They enable you to use special effects, such as drop shadows, proportional resizing, and more.

Claris Impact's style selections, although limited, are an especially good feature of the application. They're shared by all of the business graphics tools, so that your presentations and other printed matter prepared with Claris Impact will have the same look. The calendar will have the same color scheme, fonts, and design elements as the brochure and desktop presentation slides. It gives your work that professional touch.

Charting is a much-used feature of Claris Impact. Organization charts are used in business to show the corporate structure, or any sort of hierarchy. If your business is more than a one- or two-person shop, you can chart the relationship of employees to each other. (You could, of course, do an organization chart for a sole proprietorship, but it would have just one square in the middle.) To create one, click the organization chart icon.

Flowcharts show relationships between processes rather than between people. Flowcharts can be done quickly using the flowchart icon.

Tables are just as easy. Click the table icon and enter the data in spreadsheet format, or import data from an existing spreadsheet.

Data charts are what you might think of as graphs. They include bar, pie, column, line, and area charts. Again, these can be created from a spreadsheet, with data either entered directly into Claris Impact or imported from ClarisWorks, Excel, or other spreadsheet programs. Click the data chart icon, and select from a variety of chart and graph formats. After you've chosen a type of graph, you can adjust the colors, shading, drop shadows, and so on.

Timelines, also called Gantt charts, show events that occur over time. Events or tasks are indicated as bars on a scale that represent seconds, hours, days, or months depending on the kind of event. Many multimedia programs use timelines to indicate how long an image stays on-screen or how long a sound should be played. Claris Impact can also create the more familiar type of calendar with a square for each day.

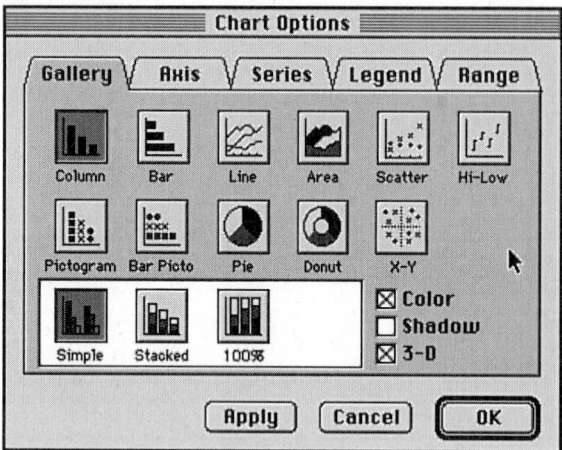

Presentations in Claris Impact can take the form of any or all of the previously mentioned documents. Use the outline format to create title slides and to outline main points in your presentation. Add graphs and charts to show allocation of resources, percentages of people involved, or whatever data is relevant. Use a master slide to maintain consistency throughout the presentation. The master slide determines the type fonts, colors, and graphics elements on each slide. Create a custom background by importing an appropriate graphic from a **photoCD** or **clip art** collection, or design your own. Keep it simple so that it doesn't interfere with the type. To rearrange your slides, go to the Slide Sorter view and drag them into the correct order. Select Run Show to view the presentation.

See Also

Charting and Graphing Applications; ClarisWorks 4.0; Desktop Publishing; Presentation Software

Claris Organizer

One of a growing number of Personal Information Managers, Claris Organizer combines calendar, address book, and to-do list functions into one easy-to-learn program with an extremely simple interface. Organizer has only four icons on its toolbar, one each for your agenda, task list, contacts, and note list. Clicking repeatedly on an icon cycles through the different ways of viewing the informa-

tion. For example, the first time you click the agenda icon, you'll see the daily schedule. The second time, you'll see a week-at-a-glance version. The third click takes you to the monthly calendar page.

A database is only as good as the information you put into it. By making it easier to put data in, Claris Organizer just may have positioned itself as the best of the PIMs. Entering data in Claris Organizer is made simple by pop-up menus, which already contain much of what you would have to type and can be customized to handle even more of it. Are there a lot of doctors or editors or CEOs in your contact file? Add a category for them. The figure shows how simple it is.

Retrieving information in Organizer is equally simple. The list mode provides quick access: start typing what you're looking for, and Organizer will scroll to the first entry that matches those letters. The Find dialog box enables searches on any one field or multiple fields. Organizer's "smart find" feature helps locate people even when you can't remember their names. Suppose that you have several clients named Steve. You're trying to call Steve who works at Custom Productions, but you don't remember his last name. In the Find box, type "Steve at C," and there he is. Or suppose that you have an appointment with your doctor, but you've forgotten when. Using the Find box, search the agenda for his name. The program will jump you ahead to the day and time. If there's more than one, Find Again will keep on taking you through all the entries with that name until you find what you're looking for.

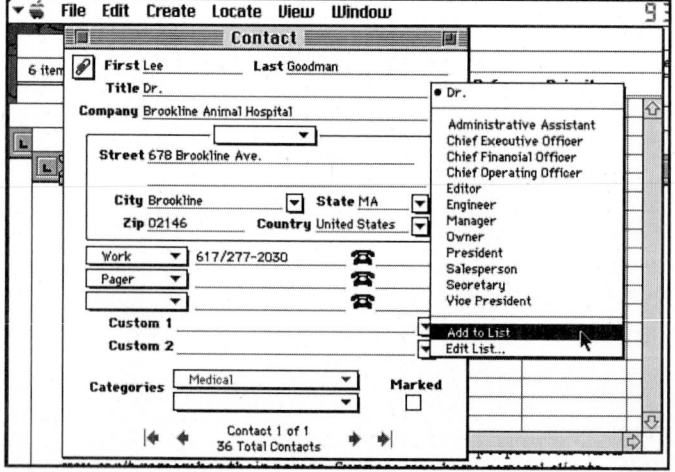

Like other good PIMs, Claris Organizer can print nicely formatted pages in your choice of styles. There are label masters, fax covers, calendar and address book pages, and even more. One especially handy feature enables you to specify a starting label on your Avery label templates. You can use up all those partial sheets of labels you've carefully set aside. Print Preview lets you see what you're getting before you print it. The only drawbacks to this program are that, unlike many of the other PIMs, it can't be opened and shared by multiple simultaneous users, and it lacks the easy menu bar access that **Now UptoDate/Now Contact** and **Expresso** provide.

See Also
Now Contact

ClarisDraw

ClarisDraw approaches the entire concept of what a drawing program should do and how it should go about doing it very differently from its competitors. Users that come to ClarisDraw from Illustrator or FreeHand will have to acclimate themselves to a very different environment in terms of tool placement, usage, and options. In many ways, ClarisDraw is a vector drawing program that masquerades as a bitmap paint program, making user interaction less daunting. The way that it enables objects to be Bézier edited is a good example. If an object in ClarisDraw is constructed from straight lines, editing a corner of the object will not produce Bézier curves, but instead just resized straight lines. The only users who will have problems with this approach are those with experience in Illustrator or FreeHand, who are used to having curve control over all line segments. New users, or those with little invested memory of other software, might find this convention more intuitive and comfortable.

Basic Bézier Drawing ClarisDraw reinvents the wheel with regard to Bézier curve editing. Polygons with straight segments cannot have those segments transformed to Bézier curves in the normal manner. Transforming a straight sided polygon will result only in the capacity to resize it interactively with the mouse. An intermediate step has to be performed first before the straight sides can be adjusted as Bézier curves. ClarisDraw expects that you first translate the polygon to a "Bézigon." After doing this and grabbing one of the poly's anchor points, the standard Bézier curve control levers appear and enable for the readjustment of the curvature of the linear segments. No other drawing software enables you to manipulate straight line segments as non-Béziers, and no other drawing software uses nomenclature such as "Bézigon." The advantage of the way that Claris addresses the Bézier modes is that it results in far more intuitive shape creation for artists not used to normative Bézier conventions. The same tool that is used to readjust a Bézier adds anchor points to any line segment by a simple mouse click. No special tool need be chosen from the toolbox for this task. In ClarisDraw, Bézier modeling becomes the domain of artists without the restrictive complications usually placed upon Bézier creations by many software engineers. ClarisDraw tries very hard to be as accessible as a standard raster paint program while offering all the features of a vector drawing program.

Other Drawing Tools Most notable in ClarisDraw is the addition of raster-based painting tools, accessed by choosing the paintbrush icon from the toolbox. This brings up another column of tools, this time related to raster painting rather than vector drawing. Paint images are handled on a special paint frame overlay. Standard bitmapped images can be modified with ClarisDraw's painting tools, unusual in a vector drawing program. Once created, a brush painting is incorporated in ClarisDraw as a standard bitmapped element.

ClarisDraw has 12 drag-and-drop symbol libraries, including trees and shrubs, computers, and flags, as well as standard universal symbolic signage (no smoking signs, and so on). These symbols come in handy for developing symbol-related posters and peripheral publications (newsletters, architectural renderings, maps, and so forth). ClarisDraw's symbol libraries hold many of the symbols needed to craft a good many of the graphics you might be faced with. All of the symbols are drag-and-drop ready.

The software also features a listing of 16 object primitives such as stars, various shaped polygons, arrows, and more. This shape library can be torn off the toolbox and placed on the editing screen. Applying a smoothing factor to these straight lined poly segments changes them to curved surfaces ready for Bézier editing. 3D effects, editable drop shadows and embosses, can also be added to objects.

Typography ClarisDraw enables you to wrap text inside or outside an object, but the non-intuitive numeric controls are difficult to understand compared to other software that accomplishes the same results. There is also no way to interact with the text (add spaces, make bolder, and so on) once the text has been attached to an object. Text, either by selected letters or whole blocks, can be translated to Bézigons. At that point, gradients, colors, and patterns can be added to the selected text objects, and Bézier manipulations can be performed. ClarisDraw enables the addition of user selected style tags for all text entries (headings, body copy, and so on). ClarisDraw's text options also lend a certain desktop publishing character to the program, adding to its versatility.

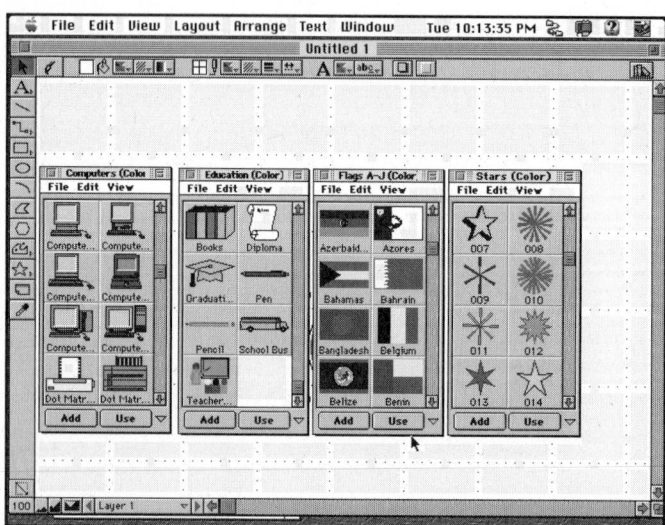

Blends and Gradients Instead of presenting the user with an on-screen dialog for creating and manipulating color gradients and blends, ClarisDraw contains three menu bar groups at the top of the screen. One is for text variants, and the other two are devoted to colorizing the internal space (paint bucket) and out-

lined borders (pen icon) of a selected object. A color palette with either 81,168 or 256 color swatches responds to user controls. Claris also has a pattern fill menu (in deference to MacPaint) and a grouping of 64 pre-designed gradient fills. Any of the patterns or gradient fills can be edited and placed in the list, but the total number of each remains the same. New edits simply replace defaulted selections. Gradient edits enable for directional, circular, or shape bursts in either 2, 3, or 4 colors. Gradients are then added between color choices. This makes ClarisDraw's gradients richer than FreeHand's, but poorer than Illustrator's. Focused light angles can also be altered in gradient edits. The figure shows how ClarisDraw's default gradient fills can be edited and saved in the pop-up library.

Graphs ClarisDraw has no internal support for developing charts or graphs directly. Instead, interested users are directed to another Claris product, **Claris Impact**.

Layers ClarisDraw supports the creation and manipulation of separate layers for separating page elements. A basic layer manager enables for layer creation and deletion, as well as locking layers in place. There are no extended layer options, nor is the layer manager visible on the edit screen (it must be accessed from the menu bar). You cannot reposition layers in the stack as is possible with other vector drawing software.

File Save Conventions The saved output from ClarisDraw is not as user editable as in Illustrator (for instance, there is no way to save a drawing in user selected dpi output). This creates less anti-aliased images when saving in the PICT format, and even the EPSF files look a bit jagged. ClarisDraw saves in Claris options, PICT, CGM (Computer Graphics Metafile), MacDraw, and MacDraw Pro, and can import/export the following formats invisibly: ASCII, DIF, EPSF, GIF, AIFF, BMP, FreeHand 3.11, JPEG, Kodak, PCX, Photoshop 2.5, PICS, Quark, QuickTime Movie, RIFF, Scitex, sfil, snd, Soundedit, Targa, TIFF (Mac and PC), MacPaint 2.0, MacWrite, Excel, MsWord, Movie, RTF, StuffIt Deluxe, SYLK, Text, and Illustrator XTND.

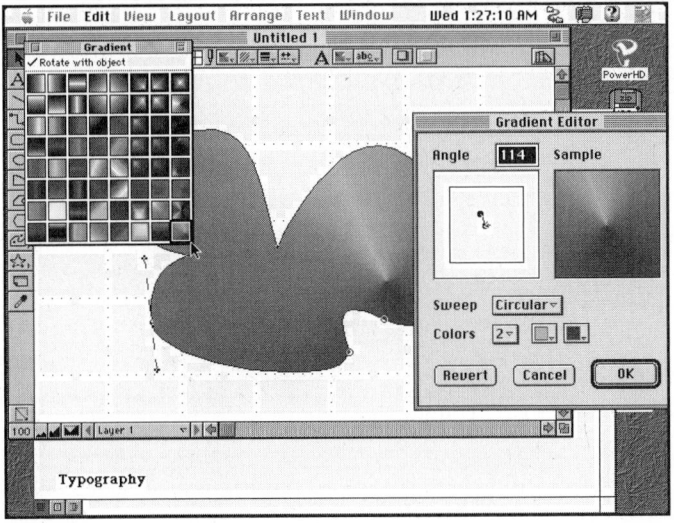

See Also

Claris Impact

ClarisWorks 4.0

ClarisWorks has come a long way since its earliest incarnation. What was originally a somewhat awkward and limited works program can now handle most of the tasks of the much beefier programs. In addition to the usual set of modules, it includes a painting module that is capable of some nifty tricks, such as gradient fills. Its word processor can handle outlines and apply style sheets to text. It also enables you to create your own styles and provides some preformatted ones to get you started. The word processor also can create Web pages using **HTML**. The spreadsheet and database functions are adequate for home or small business use, and the telecom program, while it won't get you into the Web or on **America Online,** is adequate for accessing a text-based service, such as **Delphi** or a local bulletin board.

The word processor module is probably the most critical, because it's the one people use most often. ClarisWorks comes with all kinds of goodies and gimmicks, including a library of inline graphics to brighten up your memos and newsletters. You can add your own favorite bits of art, your scanned signature, your logo, your letterhead, or whatever you like

to perk up your pages. It has a spelling checker, a dictionary, and a thesaurus. The figure below shows the Stylesheet palette, the Library palette, and the Shortcuts palette.

ClarisWorks provides a set of assistants to guide you through the creation of certain kinds of documents, including certificates, calendars, newsletters, and presentations. The certificate assistant begins by asking about the occasion for the certificate. Is it a diploma, a certificate of appreciation or membership, or something else? Then, it asks for the name of the recipient and suggests wording for the text. It also asks who, and how many people, will be signing it. Finally, you choose a border and a seal, and it's done and ready to print. The newsletter assistant is equally simple. Choose a layout, enter a title and a number of pages, and you're ready to paste the text. Working from scratch is almost as easy. The palettes can be customized to give you access to the commands you use most frequently.

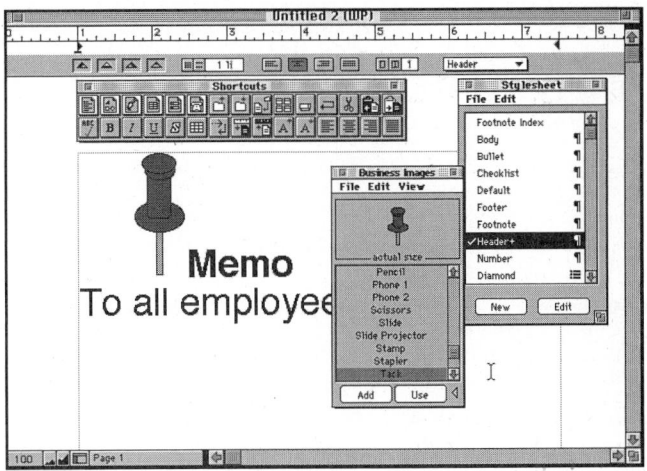

Databases and spreadsheets can be a pain in the posterior. FileMakerPro by Claris, however, is one of the less complicated ones, and ClarisWorks has retained its best features in the database module. There's stationery to maintain a checkbook and ledger, a recipe file, customer lists, and more. The spreadsheet function is equally simple to master. Auto-fill commands make data insertion easy.

Conversation with Dan Muse

As editor of *Family PC* magazine, Dan has reported on personal computers since the days of the Apple II.

Maclopedia: How did you first come in contact with a Mac?

Dan: I was working at *MicroComputing* and the publisher decided to start an Apple II publication, *InCider*, with program listings and projects articles. I helped pick some of the early programs for the Apple II+. The magazine started to evolve and began to be a business publication; when the first Macs came out, I had one of the first—the unit we were to review. I was just amazed. Most people were using WordStar and CPM at the time. I was managing editor and I did the table of contents on the Mac and played around making the fonts bigger and smaller, things you couldn't do before. I was terribly excited about it—the whole idea that you could see what you could get and play with fonts and sizes, it was a whole new world. Instead of saying to a designer, "I want it to be this size or that," I could say, "I want it to be like this" and give him an example—this was before desktop publishing.

I was with *InCider* until 1992. Most of my tenure there I was covering the Apple II, and people felt Apple was abandoning the Apple II for the Mac, which it was. We bought A+ and merged the two, and we were the best-read among educators because we covered AppleWorks and PrintShop, and we had spreadsheet and database projects you could do with AppleWorks, a huge program that never got the credit it deserved.

Maclopedia: Yes, and AppleWorks led directly to both Microsoft Works and ClarisWorks. So how did you move over to the Mac side?

Dan: I went to *Byte* in 1992 and was there for a year, and then I went to *MacWorld*. I was the senior features editor and covered a lot of Mac products. I did the PowerBook and Newton beat. I was there for the tenth anniversary of MacWorld, which was also the tenth anniversary for the Mac. Everyone there was totally committed to Macintosh, but people were beginning to realize the Windows world would not go away, and we had to deal with Mac-Windows connectivity.

Maclopedia: How did you like the trackpad?

Dan: The trackpad was typical Apple. Other companies had fooled around with it, but Apple made using the trackpad in the notebook a standard; now you get it with Gateways.

Maclopedia: How about the Newton?

Dan: I thought the Newton was a bad idea at first. You couldn't really think of anything to do with it. But I did cover the Message Pad 110 and played around with that for a few months, and I found I was using it a lot. I did my scheduling on the Newton because I commuted by train to the city, and then I'd download to the Mac. I was using Now Contact on the Mac, and you could take your address book and contact list and sync it with the Newton using the Desktop Connection Kit, connecting a cable from the Newton to the Mac.

Apple's more healthy than people think. They just need to be aggressive with pricing, and they need to make sure they are evangelizing with software developers to make sure people aren't driven away.

Maclopedia: Do you blame some of the Newton's early problems on its weakness in handwriting recognition when it first came out?

Dan: Yes, people expected handwriting recognition to be something it can't be. Most people can't even recognize their own handwriting all the time; how can you expect software to do that? But as far as taking notes, it is very effective. On the first Message Pad, you had to recognize at the time you wrote or not at all, where with the 110 you could do the handwriting first and run the recognition later.

Maclopedia: Is the Newton going anywhere now?

Dan: I don't see much growth in the marketplace. It's not a family product. I see a lot of people running around with them, but I still think it's an idea waiting for applications. People have to have a compelling reason to get one. And competition from notebooks is tougher now that they have gotten smaller and more powerful.

Maclopedia: From your perspective at *Family PC*, how is the Mac as a home machine?

Dan: It defines what families want. It is easy to set up, it is consistent, it is self-contained. You don't have to add things to it, and if you do add, it is true plug-and-play—what Windows is still trying to emulate. The top choices for games and hobbies and niche software just aren't out for the Mac, but for early learning and reference, there is everything out for the Mac.

Maclopedia: How do you envision the future of the Mac?

Dan: The Mac will be around as long as Apple keeps its pricing competitive. Among our readership, Mac users are very vocal—they watch us very closely to make sure we cover it. It doesn't matter if you are talking about engineers, business people, or home, they become zealots, part of the religion. So the Mac's place in the home and education is secure.

Also, if you look at market share, you see 90-10, Windows to Mac, but if you look at individual companies, Apple is right up there with Compaq and IBM; it has a big percentage of the marketplace.

Apple's more healthy than people think. They just need to be aggressive with pricing, and they need to make sure they are evangelizing with software developers to make sure people aren't driven away. If there is a downfall, that would be it: developers not feeling it's worth their time.

And Apple needs to continue to innovate, and make the Mac different after Windows 95, which was a step closer to the Mac in ease of use. People are watching to see what the next step for the Mac will be. Apple must distinguish itself as the premium in ease of use and consistency; that way people will continue to be religious about it.

As soon as people buy a Mac they identify with the machine. They don't do that with a PC; they may identify with what they can do with it, but not the machine. I don't know anyone who has a PC who has the connection that Mac people do. Maybe that goes back to the smiley face.

The draw and paint modules are somewhat limited, but more than adequate for drawing a diagram or cleaning up an imported graphic. ClarisWorks can import both TIFF and PICT images, but can't deal with EPS. It enables you to edit the gradient fills and to save in resolutions up through 360 dpi and in bit depth sufficient for millions of colors.

Telecommunications is generally the weak link in a Works program and ClarisWorks, unfortunately, is no exception. The program does support Z-modem file transfers and will enable you to chat via modem with a friend or transfer files back and forth. It won't get you into the **World Wide Web** or onto **Prodigy** or America Online. It *can*, as of this writing, give you text-only access to GEnie, Delphi, and **CompuServe**. How long these services are going to continue their text-based access is anybody's guess.

If you're not self-publishing the Great American Novel, running a business with more than a couple of employees, or trying to create the digital Mona Lisa, a Works program might be all you need for basic software. ClarisWorks is preferred over Microsoft Works by most users for its speed, ease of use, and word processing capability.

See Also
CompuServe; Word Processing; Works Programs; World Wide Web

Clarus, *See Dogcow*

Class, *See Object-Oriented Programming*

Class Browser, *See Web Browser*

Class Library, *See Framework*

Classic Collection: Three Classic Board Games for Your Mac

MacPlay's triple offering features three board games translated to the Mac: Risk, Scrabble, and Monopoly—which is the best of the pack. Parker Brothers has already released a networkable, 3D-enhanced version of the best-selling board game of all time for the PC but is still working on the Mac, but MacPlay's version takes less memory and should fill the space between release dates. The small board is a bit of a sacrifice, but the game is still addictive. Plus, you can option for all those crazy rules you thought you made up when you were a kid, such as putting money on free parking or having insider trading between partners. Be warned: the computer has no qualms about activity that comes suspiciously close to cheating. It will trade with itself if you have it in charge of more than one opponent. On the upside, the game is challenging and, for some reason, it is a lot easier to finish a game than on the board.

Scrabble also fares well, despite the comparatively diminutive playing area, whereas Risk works the least well of the three. MacPlay's computerized version of the popular board game is fun and is faithful to the original but is considered by some Mac lovers to be a little too DOS-like.

Another, more exotic collection of traditional games comes from Edmark. Strategy Games of the World includes Go-Moku from Japan; Mancala, an African game; and the English classic Nine Men's Morris. Play against Game Masters, with the help of your own personal strategy coach, or play against a friend. These games depend on thought, rather than random rolls of dice. As your strategy improves, so will your problem-solving skills.

See Also

Card Games; Chess; Traditional Games; You Don't Know Jack

"Clean" Reinstall

If you have a **system crash** and determine you need to reinstall the system software, you can run Apple's **installer** to reinstall a new system, but you may still be faced with the same problem that caused the crash in the first place. Apple's installer replaces only parts of the system that it deems necessary to update, so if you have a damaged **system file** or **Finder file**, a standard reinstall may install around those damaged files, leaving them damaged. For this reason, many people choose to do what is called a "clean" reinstall that installs a new copy of the Macintosh operating system for your machine in a separate folder from your old, possibly damaged, **System Folder**.

To make certain this new reinstall is a clean reinstall, you have to make sure the installer doesn't see an active system folder when it begins its installation process. If the installer sees an active folder, it updates that system. Because you don't want that (you want a clean reinstall), you need to fool the installer by **dragging** your system file into another **folder** within your system folder (such as the Preferences folder) and then renaming your old system folder (for example, Bad System Stuff). When the installer looks on your **startup disk**, it doesn't see a folder named "System Folder" and it creates a new clean copy of the system in a new folder called System Folder.

After the clean reinstall is complete, you still have access to your old system folder under its new name "Bad System Stuff." You can drag any special **control panels** or extensions that you've added to the system into your new system. It's helpful to add these extra control panels and extensions one at a time and **restart** the computer to see whether it restarts correctly. If you add them one-by-one, you can track down a conflict within your system that may have caused your problems in the first place. You should also trash your old System file and Finder file.

In System 7.5 and higher, the Installer can do a clean install for you. Just insert the Installer Disk (or the System 7.5 or higher CD-ROM disc) and launch the installer. When the installer screen appears, hold down Shift-⌘-K, and you'll have the choice of installing a brand new (clean) System Folder or updating the existing folder. Choose the clean install.

To do a clean reinstall of your system, using System 7.5 or higher, follow these steps:

1. Insert the Install Disk 1 from your set of Apple installer disks you receive when you buy your Macintosh. (If you received a CD-ROM disc instead, insert the CD-ROM disc that contains your System 7.5 software.)

2. Double-click the Installer icon to bring up the Installer window.

3. Hold down the Shift-⌘-K keys to start the clean installation.

4. You get a dialog box with two radio buttons enabling you to choose which kind of installation you want; Update Existing System Folder (the default choice), or Install New System Folder. Select "Install New System Folder" and click OK (see the following figure).

5. The Installer window appears, but this time the button that was labeled "Install" now reads "Clean Install." Click Clean Install.

This creates a new system and system folder, and your old system folder is not deleted, but is automatically renamed "Previous System Folder."

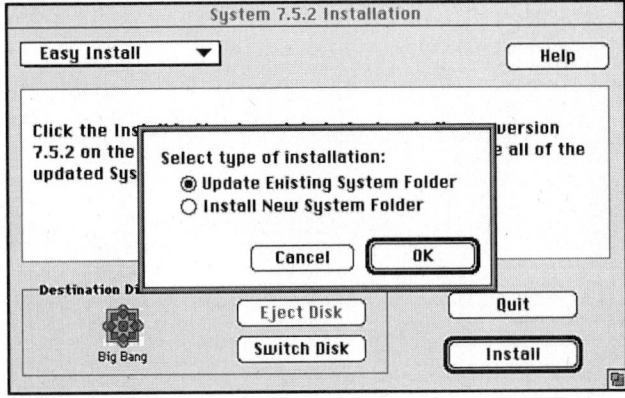

See Also

Control Panels; Crashes, System; Dragging; Finder Folder Icon; Installer Utility; Restart; Startup Disk; System Files; System Folder; Troubleshooting

Clean Up Command

Found on the **Special menu** on the **Desktop**, the Clean Up command is designed to help keep **icons** in windows organized. Each window has an invisible alignment grid. As you move files and folders around within a window, they can become disorderly looking and scattered. The Clean Up command takes these scattered icons and snaps them to the invisible grid, straightening them into orderly rows (see the following figures). This particular command is available only when the window's view option is set to View by Icon or View by Small Icon. If you want to clean up just a few items, select only those items you want cleaned up and choose Clean Up from the Special menu.

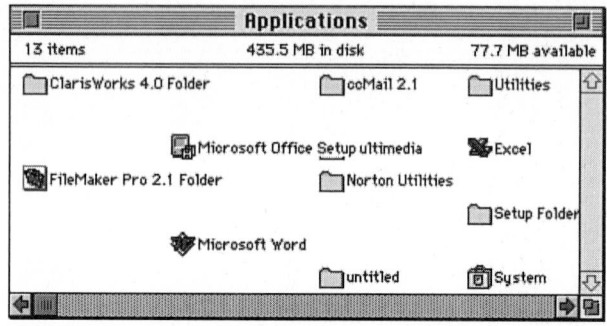

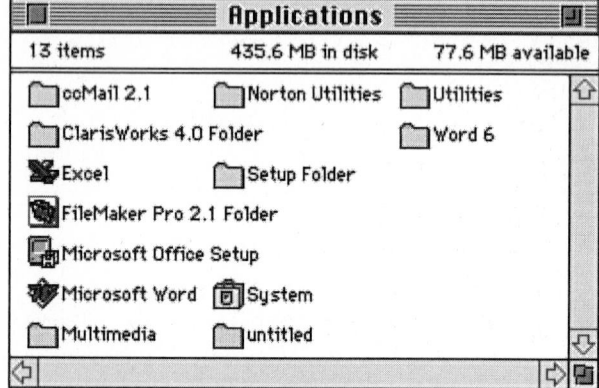

The Clean Up command also has a number of different forms it can take to help you with your housekeeping. If you select Clean Up while holding down the **Option key**, you'll notice that the Clean Up Window has changed to Clean Up by Name, which not only aligns your icons into neat columns along an invisible grid, but it also arranges them alphabetically.

You can also use the Clean Up command when no windows are open to help you straighten out your desktop. If you look under the Special menu when no windows are open, you'll see that the Clean Up command has again taken a different form and is now called Clean Up Desktop, which snaps any items on the desktop to the invisible alignment grid on the desktop. If you were to hold the Option key while choosing Clean Up Desktop, it changes to the Clean Up All form, and this time it Cleans Up by aligning all the icons on the far right edge of your desktop.

To clean up the icons in the active window, follow these steps:

1. Choose the Clean Up command from the Special menu (this works only when your windows view is set to View by Icon or View by Small Icon).

2. The icons in the windows snap to an invisible alignment grid in the window. You can choose to align them on a straight grid where the icons are side by side, or a staggered grid that staggers the icons between lines. (The staggered method works great if you have long filenames that might bump into one another on a straight grid.) You select which style of grid, straight or staggered, in the Views control panel, found under the Apple menu.

3. If you want these icons arranged alphabetically by name, hold the Option key as you choose Clean Up from the Special menu.

4. If you want to clean up the icons on your desktop, close all windows and choose Clean Up Desktop from the Special menu.

5. If you want to align all the icons on your desktop along the right edge of your desktop, hold the Option key as you choose Clean Up All from the Special menu.

See Also

Desktop; Icons; Option Key; Special Menu; View Control Panel

Clean Up All Command

The Clean Up All command helps you organize your **desktop** by automatically aligning all **icons** on your desktop along the far right edge of your screen. The Clean Up All command is only available when no windows are open. If no windows currently are open, you can press the **Option key** and choose Clean Up All from the **Special menu**, which snaps any items on the desktop to an invisible alignment grid on the far right side of your desktop. You might want to choose this function if you have icons cluttered all over your desktop and want a quick, orderly accounting of them.

See Also

Desktop; Icons; Option Key; Special Menu

Clean Up by Name, *See* *Alphabetizing Filenames*

Clean Up Desktop Command

You can use the Clean Up Desktop command when no windows are open to help you organize **icons** on your **desktop**. If you look on the **Special menu** when no windows are open, you'll see that the Clean Up Desktop command is available. By choosing the Clean Up Desktop command, items on the desktop will snap to the nearest alignment point on the invisible alignment grid on the desktop. If a window is active, you get the Clean Up Window command from the Special menu.

See Also

Desktop; Icons; Special Menu

Clear Command

This command erases an item from your document without making a copy to the **Clipboard** and basically has the same effect as the Delete key. In certain instances, you may want to delete an item without erasing the contents of the Clipboard. The Clear command is ideal for this purpose.

To clear an item, follow these steps:

1. Highlight or select the item you want to clear.
2. Select Clear from the Edit menu.
3. The selected item disappears *without* a copy being stored in memory.

See Also

Clipboard; Copy Command; Cut Command; Delete Key; Edit Menu

Clear Key

The Clear key, located in the upper-left corner of the **numeric key pad**, operates the same way the **Delete key** does, by erasing selected items without saving a copy to the **Clipboard**. Depending on your type of keyboard, it might delete from the right instead of from the left. It also acts the same way the Clear key does on a standard calculator. If you use Apple's **Calculator D/A**, use this key to clear the calculator's display for a new calculation.

See Also

Calculator D/A; Clear Command; Clipboard; Delete Key; Numeric Keypad

Clear Keyboard Shortcut

The Clear command doesn't have a keyboard shortcut assigned, but the **Delete key** performs the same function. If, for example, you want to change a filename, you can **click** the filename and select Clear from the **Edit menu**, or you can use the Delete key.

See Also

Click; Delete Key; Edit Menu; Keyboard Shortcuts

Click

To make a selection with your mouse, press the mouse button and release it. The mouse clicks to let you know that you've pressed the mouse button, or "clicked the mouse" as it's known. If you see an instruction that reads, "point and click the folder," for example, point the cursor at a folder (using the mouse), and click the mouse button. Double-click refers to pressing the mouse button quickly two times. A single click selects an item. A double-click performs a task. If you click the mouse button once on an application icon, it will select the icon, and you can drag the icon to another location. If, however, you double-click the mouse button on an application icon, it launches the application. One click tells the Mac you're selecting an item, two clicks tells the Mac to perform a task.

See Also

Double-Click; Folder; Icons; Mouse

Click and Drag

To access items on a **menu**, click and hold the mouse button with the arrow pointer on the menu title and the menu pops down, enabling you to drag the **arrow pointer** to the menu item of your choice. When you reach the menu item you want, release the **mouse button** to select it. You can also click **icons** in active windows and move them while continuing to hold the mouse button. When you've moved the icon to the desired new position, release the mouse button This is also referred to as **pressing and dragging**.

Clicking and dragging is also used in System 7.5 and above as a text editing tool in many word processing applications. You can highlight a word or phrase and drag that highlighted selection to another area in your document. This is a way to quickly edit a text document without having to use the Cut and Paste commands, which would take longer and would replace any items in the Clipboard.

Click and drag is also used to move items in and out of the Scrapbook, NotePad, Stickies, and other applications that support click and drag capabilities.

See Also
Arrow Pointer; Desktop Level; Icons; Menus; Mouse; Pop-Down Menu; Selections

Clickable Map, *See Imagemaps, Creating*

Client, *See Server*

Client-Side Imagemap, *See Imagemaps, Server-Side versus Client-Side*

Clip Art

Very few designers create all the artwork they use from scratch. For many purposes, clip art (which is sold in books and now in electronic format on disks or CDs) will work just fine, either on its own or as a starting point for a design.

Sold by a variety of companies and as **shareware**, the available styles of clip art are countless, from simple line drawings to cartoons to woodcuts to detailed perspective images in color. Formats vary as well, with black-and-white art generally available for the Mac as either TIFF or **EPS** files that can be imported into page layout or other graphics programs. Some companies remarket clip art originally sold in books by scanning it. For example, Zedcor sells a set of CDs containing tens of thousands of images, including much of the high-quality clip art created by Dover Publications.

In addition to clip art, the proliferation of multimedia and online projects has created a market for other clip media, including sounds and movies, as well as stock photography, backgrounds, and borders.

Many clip art companies are delivering "edited" or "editable" files. Many illustrations come in **Illustrator** or **FreeHand** EPS format with layers so that parts of the drawing can be used independently. Clip photography disks have images pre-silhouetted, with separate drop shadows.

In clip media, especially stock photography, it's very important to examine and understand the license agreement. Some manufacturers demand royalties or additional payments for images used for commercial distribution.

See Also
EPS; Page Layout Applications

Clipboard

The Clipboard is the Mac's temporary holding area that enables you to **Copy** or **Cut** elements from one document, and **Paste** those elements into another location or document. After you've Cut or Copied an item into the Clipboard, you can view that item by using the command Show Clipboard from the **Edit menu**. The Clipboard is designed to hold one item or one group of items at a time. If a new item enters the Clipboard (by copying or cutting an item), the previous item is deleted.

The Clipboard is often used as a way to move information between applications. If, for example, you're working on a spreadsheet, and have created a pie chart that you'd want to import into a word processing document, you can copy the pie chart graphic into the Clipboard and then switch to the word processing program. The pie chart graphic will be held in the invisible Clipboard until you select Paste from the Edit menu. Then the pie chart will be inserted into your word processing document. Holding that graphic, as you switch between programs, is a key function of the Clipboard.

See Also

Copy Command; Cut Command; Edit Menu; Paste Command

Clipping Extension

This System 7.5 and higher extension enables you to **drag and drop** text or graphics directly onto your desktop where they appear with icons as clipping files. These files can remain on your desktop and be dragged from the desktop into other documents as needed. This way you can leave frequently used items, such as logos or your address, on your **desktop** and drag them into documents as you need them.

See Also

Desktop; Drag and Drop

Clock, *See Internal Clock of the Macintosh*

Clock, Setting

To set the time for the Macintosh computer's internal clock, choose the **Date and Time control panel** from the **Control Panels** folder. You can use the Date and Time control panel to set the time by clicking the currently displayed time and entering the correct time by typing it from the keyboard or clicking the edit arrows to move the numbers in the proper direction.

To set the time for the clock using the Date and Time control panel, follow these steps:

1. Choose the Date and Time Control Panel from the Control Panels submenu of your Apple menu.

2. To set the time, click the number (hour, minutes, or seconds) and the up/down edit arrows will appear to the right. You can type the correct number or click the up arrow to move the number higher and click the down arrow to move the number lower. To make the time change complete, click the words, "Current Time." The edit arrows will disappear.

3. To turn on the menu clock , click the On button. You can set the preferences for the menu clock by clicking the Clock Options button. When your preferences are complete, click OK and close the Date & Time control panel.

See Also

Control Panels; Date & Time Control Panel

Clones, Desktop Models

Power Computing Corporation concentrates its Macintosh clone business on the middle-level desktop publishing and business users. This company offers the most variety of features and standard components. There are three levels of Power Computing clones: the Power 120, which is a first-generation clone (and has been discontinued), the PowerWave, which is a high-level Macintosh, and the PowerCurve, which serves the middle-level users.

Each model has the following features in common:

- **Use of Apple 601 or 604e PowerPC processors.** These computers use faster chip sets than Apple's comparable models with performance at 120, 132, and 150MHz. Each processor has an integrated floating-point processor and 32K internal cache.

- **CD-quality 16-bit stereo sound.** The Power Computing Macintosh clones provide the same high-level of fidelity as Apple Macs.

- **Good color display support.** The PowerCurve provides 1MB VRAM upgradable to 4MB in 3 sockets; the

PowerWave provides an accelerated 64-bit PCI video card with 2MB VRAM upgradable to 4MB. The Power 120 provides an optional video card with additional Macintosh standard and VGA monitor port along with 2MB of VRAM upgradable to 4MB.

- **Extensive expansion bays.** The Power 120 provides four expansion bays supporting either two 3.5-inch drives and one 5.25-inch drive or four 3.5-inch disk drives. The PowerWave models support three front-accessible 5.25-inch bays; one internal 3.5-inch bay for one full-size or two half-size internal disk drives.

- **Network compatibility.** The Power Computing clones come with standard EtherNet (AAUI) and ThinNet (10Base-T) ports, as well as support for Apple's LocalTalk.

- **Internal expandability.** The PowerWave and PowerCurve models provide 2 to 3 PCI and NuBus expansion slots, depending on the model. The Power 120 provides three internal NuBus slots.

- **Bundled business software.** Power Computing clones provide an extensive array of business software including: ClarisWorks 4.0, Intuit's Quicken 5.0, Insignia's SoftWindows 2.0 on a 60-day trial, Now Up-to-Date 3.5 and Now Contact 3.5, Now Utilities 5.0, Nisus Writer 4.1, Grolier Multimedia Encyclopedia, The Animals!, U.S. Atlas 5.0, World Atlas 5.0, Launch interactive media CD-ROM, FWB Hard Disk Toolkit and CD-ROM toolkit, America Online, and 250 Bitstream Type 1 and 2 Fonts.

- **CD-ROM support.** Most Power Computing models come standard with a four-speed, tray-loading CD-ROM Drive.

- **Choice of configuration.** Each Power Computing clone comes in a tower or box-chassis model.

See Also

Clones, High-End Graphics Models; Power Mac Logic Boards; Power Mac PCI Bus; Processors, PowerPC

Clones, High-End Graphics Models

Two vendors in the Macintosh clone business have decided to sell Macs in niche markets: Radius Computer and DayStar Digital. In January 1996, Umax Data Systems acquired Radius' clone business. Radius transferred its operating system license and systems designs to Umax Computer, a new division of Umax Data Systems. All of Radius' clone-engineering staff joined Umax and Radius retained 20 percent ownership in the venture. Umax Computer will sell PCI-based Macintosh clones under the Radius SuperMac brand. Radius will continue to support its NuBus-based Mac clones, but will no longer develop new clones.

Umax, like Radius has targeted its clones to digital-video and color publishing organizations. DayStar has targeted its clones to the electronic publishing market.

Umax is introducing a Macintosh clone in the Spring of 1996 featuring the 150MHz PowerPC 604e processor. This will eventually be a multiprocessor Macintosh with slots for two CPUs, but the second CPU and multiprocessing software will not be shipping until after the base model ships. According to the May 1996 issue of *MacWorld* in an article by Charles Piller "MacWorld Exclusive: Umax Clone Speeds to Top of Mac Pack, First Look at SuperMac Prototype," the SuperMac clone will be configured with 16MB of RAM (upgradable to 1G), a 512K Level-2 cache, a quad-speed, tray-loading CD-ROM drive, six PCI-slots, six expansion bays, and an optional 100-Mbps EtherNet with Ultra SCSI card. Umax is also planning to market a general-purpose business Macintosh clone to compete with the PowerCurve models by Power Computing, as well as a consumer model that would be competitive with Apple's Performas in price and performance.

Radius formerly manufactured an image-editing Macintosh called the Radius System 100 (Existing machines are still supported by Radius, but the computer has been discontinued). This is a Macintosh whose performance has been tuned for image management. It has the following qualities:

- The System 100 is based on a Power Mac 8100/110 motherboard. The "110" in the name indicates that the PowerPC 601 chip performs at 110MHz.

- A Fast-Wide Bus JackHammer SCSI accelerator card has been added to increase the performance of the Mac's input and output.

- Two hard drives: a 2G and a 500MB for extensive storage.

- The standard Apple video card is replaced by a Radius Thunder IV GX-1600 video card that increases the VRAM and increases the monitor's capability to display true 24-bit color.

- At least 40MB of RAM for added performance.

- A double-speed, tray-loading CD-ROM drive.

- Bundled image-editing software including Adobe Photoshop and Radius Color Composer.

DayStar Digital's specialization is accelerator cards. This company takes a different tactic to sell to the publishing market: multiprocessing Macintosh computers. The Genesis MP tower system began with a dual-processor Mac and has now produced a four-processor version. This means that the Genesis couples together two or four PowerPC 604 processors, each on its own daughterboard, which can be exchanged for a board with faster chips when these become available. DayStar has designed a program interface that establishes a primary processor that runs the Macintosh operating system's toolbox operations. Applications, such as Adobe **Photoshop** or **Illustrator** or **3-D graphics programs** that have been rewritten to support multiprocessing, split their computer-intensive tasks, such as vector rendering or photo-retouching, between the remaining processors. Because each processor is located on a daughterboard on the system bus, each has the same access to the motherboard's memory, and does not take up overhead competing for toolbox resources.

The DayStar Genesis MP has the following features:

- At least 32MB of RAM (the four-processor model comes equipped with 72MB of RAM) upgradable to 512MB or more.

- Three or six PCI slots compatible with Intel-standard accelerator cards and other performance add-ons.

- Eight or nine internal expansion bays that include those pre-configured with a quad-speed, tray-loading CD-ROM drive, 1G hard drive, and disk drive(s).

- Bundled image-processing software, including DayStar's Colorimeter 24 and ColorMatch software.

See Also

Clones, Desktop Models; Clones, Macintosh General; Power Mac Logic Boards; Power Mac PCI Bus; Processor's PowerPC

Clones, Macintosh General

In 1994, Apple Computer transformed its corporate culture through one small act—it licensed the Macintosh operating system and ROMs to a select number of computer manufacturers. In so doing, Apple opened its formerly proprietary hardware/software symbiosis to outside players. In the Spring of 1995, Power Computing introduced the first Macintosh-compatible machine not made by Apple. There are currently only a handful of Macintosh "clone" makers, but the list is growing.

The Macintosh computer is software and hardware. The software consists of an operating system and firmware (instructions hard-wired into the Read-Only Memory (ROM) chips. The current clone manufacturers have gained permission to use Apple Mac

ROMs and other Apple chips in their computers so as to maintain the 100 percent compatibility and "plug and play" of true Macintosh computers. Apple provides engineering assistance and compatibility certification for clone manufacturers to ensure that every clone will be Macs in everything but brand. Apple is building the same type of brand recognition for its operating system as Microsoft has built for Windows. Every Macintosh starts up by displaying the Macintosh OS logo. Clone machines also display this logo so that you know that your clone is a pure Mac.

> There are currently three active clone manufacturers: Power Computing, Umax Data Systems (who acquired Radius' clone business in January 1996 but will use Radius' SuperMac branding on their PCI-based Mac clones), and DayStar Digital. The following table outlines the computer offerings of these manufacturers.

As can be seen in the table, each vendor has approach a different segment of the Macintosh market. Power Computing is selling clones on the general market to consumers and business users who want a general-purpose computer, whereas Umax (formerly Radius) and DayStar Digital are concentrating on the high-end graphics, video, multimedia, and pre-press businesses.

IBM and Macintosh Clones

In 1994, around the same time that Apple announced the licensing of the Mac, it also formed an alliance with IBM and Motorola to create a framework of technical concepts and specifications that can be used by any hardware manufacturer to permit their machines to run a variety of operating systems, including Macintosh OS, IBM OS/2, AIX (IBM's UNIX), Sun's Solaris UNIX, and Microsoft Windows NT. This design was called the **common hardware reference platform (CHRP)**, and in 1996, Apple demonstrated the first CHRP machine, now called the **PowerPC platform**, running of the Macintosh OS. Since then, IBM has abandoned the idea of running OS/2 on the platform and there are rumors of a Macintosh license.

Each vendor also takes a different tactic in the manufacture and sales of its computers. Power Computing uses Apple Mac ROMs and chips and packages them in PC cases (either mini-tower or flat box) and sells them through mail order and some retail outlets. Radius sold its Macintosh clones directly and through some mail order catalogs. Umax is targeting high-end graphics machine users as well as the consumer and education markets, and should retain the mail order method, as well as sell through stores (although it is unknown as of the writing of this book). DayStar Digital sells only directly.

Macintosh Clones

Manufacturer	Models	Processor Type	Features
Power Computing	Power 120, PowerCurve 601/120, PowerWave 604/120, 604/132, and 604/150	PPC 601 or 604 at 120, 132 or 150MHz, 256K level-2 cache	64-bit PCI video card with 2MB VRAM, 3 or 4 expansion bays for two 3.5" drives and one 5.25" full-height drive, 2 serial ports, built-in EtherNet and 10Base-T port, 3 PCI slots or 2 PCI and 2 NuBus slots with Stargate Riser Card, 8 or 16MB RAM, 540 or 850MB, 1 or 2G hard drive, 4X speed CD-ROM drive, bundled business software

C

Manufacturer	Models	Processor Type	Features
Radius	Radius System 100	PPC 110MHz 601, 32K internal cache, 256K level-2 cache	72MB of RAM, 2G fast and wide SCSI hard drive with fast and wide controller, 24-bit color, 3 custom-designed graphics accelerator cards, 4 AT&T 32-bit digital signal processors, 2X CD-ROM, bundled Radius Dynamic Desktop, PhotoEngine software, and Radius ColorComposer software
DayStar Digital	Genesis MP	Two or 4 PPC 604 processors at 120 or 132MHz each	3- or 6-slot PCI mother-board and 9 drive bays, 16 MB of RAM, 1G hard drive, 4X CD-ROM drive
Umax	SuperMac brand	150MHz PPC 604e processor	UltraSCSI bus, 6-slot PCI, 4X CD-ROM, 6 expansion bays, multiprocessor slot (2 cpus), 16MB of RAM, 512K L-2 cache, options of 100-Mbps EtherNet and Ultra SCSI I/O card

See Also

Clones, Desktop Models; Clones, High-End Graphics Models

Close All Keyboard Shortcut

If you have a number of windows open on your **desktop** and want to close them, press the **Option key** and **click** the **active window's Close box**. This closes all windows. If you look on the **File menu**, you see the **Close Window** command. When you press the Option key, this changes to the Close All command. Option-⌘-W closes all windows, too.

To close all open windows, hold the Option key and click the active window's Close box. This will invoke the Close All command and it will close all open windows.

See Also

Active Window; Click; Close Window Command; Desktop; File Menu; Keyboard Shortcuts; Option Key

Close Command

When you are in an application and want to close the current document, you can select the Close command (⌘-W) from the File menu to close that document. You can also click the **Close box** in the upper left-hand corner of the title bar. If the document has not been saved yet, and you select the Close command, you'll get a dialog box asking you, "Save Changes Before Closing?" and shown in the figure. If you want to save your current changes, click OK, and you'll get the standard **Save dialog box** and be prompted to name your file and choose the location you'd like to save your document.

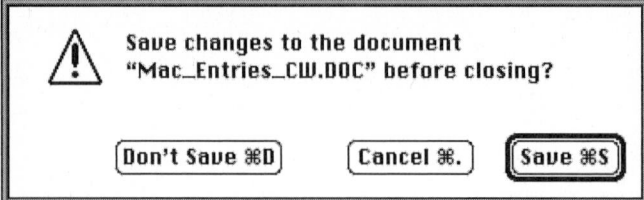

Save changes to the document "Mac_Entries_CW.DOC" before closing?

[Don't Save ⌘D]   [Cancel ⌘.]   [Save ⌘S]

If your file has already been named and you're working on an existing document, when you select the Close command, you'll get a dialog box asking you, "Save Changes Before Closing?" If you want to save the changes you made since the last time you saved, click OK, and the document is saved and then closed.

To use the Close command to close an open document, follow these steps:

1. Select Close (⌘-W) from the File menu or click the Close box in the upper left-hand corner of the title bar.

2. You'll get a dialog asking you if you want to save your changes. If you click OK, and you've previously named this document, the document closes. If you click OK and you haven't previously named this document, it takes you to the standard Save dialog, which enables you to name the document and choose the location where you would like it saved.

See Also
Save Command; Save As Command

Close to Previous Window (Keyboard Shortcut)

If you want to close the **active window**, use the keyboard shortcut Option-⌘-Up Arrow. This keyboard shortcut also works if you want to see **icons** that may be hidden by the active window. You then use Option-⌘-Down Arrow to reopen the window.

See Also
Active Window; Desktop; Icons; Keyboard Shortcuts

Close View

This **control panel** enables you to magnify the screen to a preset magnification. Perfect for users with impaired vision, this magnification tool enlarges items on your screen up to 16 times the normal size. The Close View control panel enables you to change your magnification power, toggle on or off the capability to enable Close View with a keyboard shortcut, and to invert the screen image.

To use the Close View control panel, follow these steps:

1. Choose the Close View control panel on the Control Panels submenu on the Apple menu. Note: The Close View control panel is not automatically installed with your system; you may have to drag a copy from your system disk, or in more recent versions of the system, you may have to access Close View by using the Apple Installer and choosing to custom install Close View.

2. You can now turn on or off Close View, set the magnification by clicking the up and down **edit arrows**, turn on or off **shortcuts**, and invert the screen image.

See Also
Control Panel; Keyboard Shortcuts; System Folder

Close View (Keyboard Shortcut)

If you have the **Close View control panel** installed, you can use a keyboard shortcut for Close View. Option-⌘-O turns on or off Close View and turns on or off Close View's magnification. To increase the magnification of Close View, press Option-⌘-H, and then press Option-⌘-Up Arrow. To decrease the magnification, press Option-⌘-Down Arrow. To enable the keyboard shortcuts for Close View, you must turn on the Keyboard Shortcuts feature within the Close View control panel.

See Also

Close View; Control Panels; Keyboard Shortcuts

Close Window Command

If you have a window open at the **Desktop** level, you can Select Close Window (⌘-W) from the **File menu** to close the **active window.** The Close Window command is only available when a window is active. You can also invoke the Close Window command by clicking the **Close box** of any active window, which is located in the upper-left corner of the title bar, as shown in the figure. When you close a window, the window directly behind the closed window becomes the active window. If there are no other windows open, no windows are active.

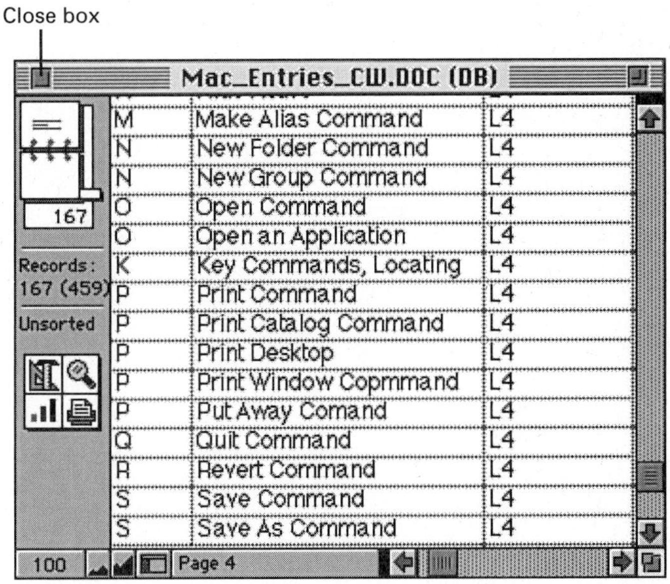

Close box

At the desktop level, if you have multiple windows open and you want to close them, you can hold down the **Option key**, which changes the Close Window command to the Close All command. By selecting the Close All command, it closes all open windows. This also works if you hold the Option key while clicking the active window's Close box.

To use the Close Window command, follow these steps:

1. Make active (by clicking it) the window you want to close.

2. Select Close Window (⌘-W) from the File menu or click the Close box in the upper left-hand corner of the title bar.

3. This closes the currently active window.

4. To close all open windows, hold the Option key before you select Close or click the Close box.

See Also

Active Window; Desktop; File Menu

CloseFlash, *See Kaidan*

CloseTake, *See Kaidan*

CMS (Color Management System), *See Color Gamut*

CMYK

Most desktop color printers use four colors—cyan (light blue), magenta, yellow, and black—in various combinations to reproduce color images. This color definition is taken from the commercial printing industry, in which color images are often reproduced on press using these four colors. Cyan, magenta, yellow, and black are known as the subtractive primary colors.

Color images stored in digital form can be defined in terms of these colors, or in other terms (such as **RGB**, which is used by video monitors). Graphics software (such as Photoshop) can convert images from one color definition to another, but there are colors in each definition that aren't achievable using other definitions.

See Also

Color Management; Process Color; RGB

Cobweb Site

Colloquial term for a **World Wide Web** site that has not been updated for a substantial length of time and whose contents are obviously out-of-date. It is considered bad form to let your site become a cobweb site.

See Also

World Wide Web

CODE 1 Virus

This virus infects applications and the System file under System 6 and System 7. CODE 1 renames your hard drive to "Trent Saburo" when an infected Mac is started on any October 31. The virus can cause system crashes.

See Also

ANTI Virus; CDEF Virus; CODE 252 Virus; Frankie Virus; INIT 17 Virus; INIT 29 Virus; INIT 1984 Virus; INIT 9403 Virus; INIT-M Virus; MacMag Virus; MBDF Virus; MDEF Virus; nVIR Virus; Scores Virus; T4 Virus; WDEF Virus; ZUC Virus

CODE 252 Virus

This virus displays the following message if triggered between June 6 and December 31 of any year:

```
You have a virus. Ha Ha Ha Ha Ha Ha Ha Now
erasing all disks.
```

However, no files are deleted. Code 252 infects the System, Finder, and applications, and may cause system crashes.

See Also

ANTI Virus; CDEF Virus; CODE 1 Virus; Frankie Virus; INIT 17 Virus; INIT 29 Virus; INIT 1984 Virus; INIT 9403 Virus; INIT-M Virus; MacMag Virus; MBDF Virus; MDEF Virus; nVIR Virus; Scores Virus; T4 Virus; WDEF Virus; ZUC Virus

Code Browser, *See Web Browser*

Code Names

Apple has a long history of using code names to refer to unreleased products. The purpose of these names varies from project to project. For some projects, the code name is a placeholder for a name that marketing hasn't invented yet. In other cases, the code names are used to help keep projects secret. Projects are generally named by the lead engineer or manager responsible for the project.

Some projects have more than one code name. The names may be used for different parts of a project (one for the software, another for the hardware, and so on), or they may be used to deliberately confuse outsiders. In fact, different names are sometimes used when talking to different people so that press leaks can be tracked back to their source.

Past and Present Code Names

Product	Code Name
At Ease	Tiny Toons
ClarisWorks	Terminator
Apple III	Sara
Macintosh 512K	FatMac
Classic	XO
Color Classic	Slice
IIvx	Brazil
LC	Pinball, Elsie, Prism
LC II	Foster Farms
Mac Plus	Mr. T
OpenDoc	Amber
Power Macintosh Project	Cognac
Power Mac 6100	PDM (Piltdown Man)
Power Mac 7100	Carl Sagan, BHA, LAW
Power Mac 8100	Cold Fusion

Product	Code Name
PowerBook 100	Derringer, Rosebud, Classic
PowerBook 140	Tim LC, Tim Lite, Leary, Replacements
PowerBook 170	Tim, RoadWarrior
Duo 210/230	BOB/W ("Best of Both Worlds")
MultiFinder	Juggler, Oggler, Twitcher
PlainTalk Speech Recognition	Casper
Color QuickDraw	Pollock
QuickTime	Warhol
QuickDraw GX	Serrano
System 7	Blue, Big Bang, Pleiades, M80
System 7.5	Mozart, Capone
QuickDraw 3D	Escher
"Copland" (System 8)	Copland

It's not unusual for Apple's code names to survive the development process and become the product's real name. "Macintosh" and "Lisa" were both code names before they became the real names of the products to which they refer.

In Apple's early days, many code names were female names; the names of the children, wives, or girlfriends of the engineers working on the project. A classic example is Lisa, rumored to be named after **Steve Jobs**' daughter. The names of Apple varieties are also frequent candidates for use as code names. Macintosh, Pippen, and Jonathan all fall into this category.

See Also

Jobs, Steve; Lisa

Code Resources

Code Resources are small, self-contained bits of executable code stored in the **resource** fork of a Macintosh file. There are actually two very different kinds of code known as code resources. The first are "CODE"-type resources. Nonnative software contains most of its program code in this type of resource. The second kind are snippets of code called by the system or another application to perform a specific task.

The Macintosh uses special code resources to draw windows, controls, and menus, and to handle events in these interface elements. These resources are often called *def procs*, short for definition procedures. The MacOS includes the standard procedures for drawing windows, menus, and controls. Programmers can create their own def procs to extend or change the default behavior.

Window definitions are stored in resources of type WDEF. To create a new window style, a programmer can create a new WDEF that draws the window in a new or different way. Similarly, menu definitions are stored in MDEF-type resources. An excellent example of each of these can be found in HyperCard's Tools menu and tools palette. The menu uses a custom MDEF to draw the menu as a set of tools; when the Tools menu is "torn off" the menu bar, it forms a floating tools palette that uses a custom WDEF (see the following figures).

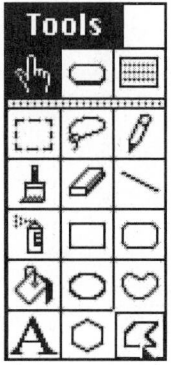
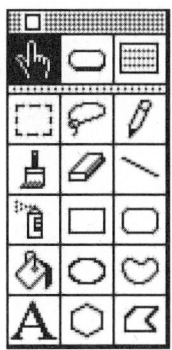

Although these definition procedures can be used to great effect, they have two disadvantages compared to the standard definitions. First, any windows, menus, or controls that use custom definition procedures do not benefit from any changes or improvements that Apple might make to the standard definitions. Second, they might not work at all under future versions of the operating system.

Definition procedures are not the only kinds of code resources. Any code that extensions or control panels execute at startup is stored in code resources of type "INIT." In fact, the main code for control panels themselves is stored in resources of type "CDEV." Other applications also make use of code resources. Many **plug-ins** (such as Photoshop plug-ins or **AfterDark** modules), for example, are implemented as code resources.

See Also

AfterDark; Plug-Ins; Programming Language; Resource

Codec, *See Compressor*

CodeWarrior

CodeWarrior is an **Integrated Development Environment** (IDE) from Metrowerks that includes a full suite of programming tools.

Many analysts have credited CodeWarrior with the smooth transition to the Power Macintosh and the quick availability of native Power Mac applications. When Metrowerks introduced CodeWarrior several months before the introduction of the first Power Macs, it was the only IDE to generate native Power Mac applications. Since then, Metrowerks has continued to update and improve CodeWarrior, and it is now a major force in the Mac development community.

As an IDE, CodeWarrior includes in one package all the tools you need to create Macintosh programs (see the following figure): a source code **editor**, **compilers**, **linkers**, a **debugger**, a programming **framework**, and an **interface builder**.

CodeWarrior uses a plug-in architecture to support multiple **programming languages** and multiple development targets from the same IDE. It currently supports **C/C++**, **Pascal**, **Java**, and can target the following platforms:

- 68K Macintosh
- PowerPC Macintosh
- x86 **Win32** (Windows 95 and Windows NT)
- PowerPC BeOS for the BeBox
- 68K Magic Cap

CodeWarrior's cross-platform support is unique among Macintosh IDEs. The Win32 tools are especially interesting. They enable you to do all your Mac and Windows development on the Mac and then transfer your finished Windows programs to a PC for debugging. CodeWarrior even includes a remote debugger that enables you to do most of the debugging from the comfort of your own Macintosh.

Along with the compilers included with CodeWarrior, Metrowerks has published the **API** for creating plug-in **compilers** and **linkers**, so third-party tools are beginning to appear for the CodeWarrior environment.

Besides the IDE, CodeWarrior includes a slew of other helpful tools. **ZoneRanger** is an excellent tool for delving into your application's memory **heap**. The **MPW** shell and MPW-hosted version of the Metrowerks compilers and linkers are also included.

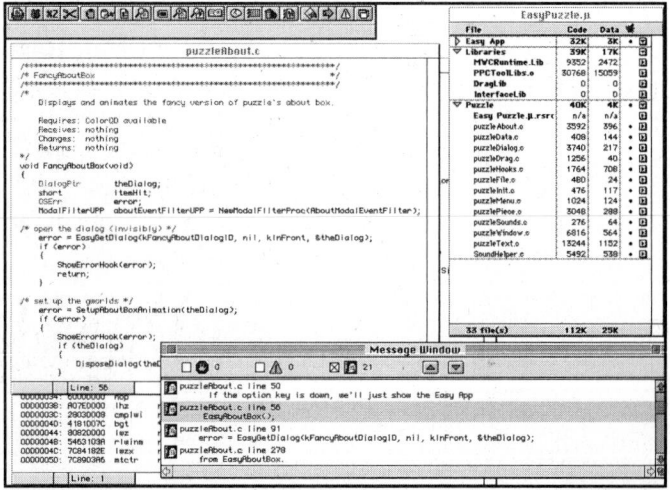

Metrowerks' **C++** application **framework** and interface builder, **PowerPlant** and **Constructor**, make producing complete applications relatively pain-free.

Metrowerks produces four versions of CodeWarrior: Gold, Academic, Bronze, and Starter Kit. The Gold and Academic versions include all the compilers previously mentioned, while the Bronze and Starter Kit versions only generate 68K code. The Academic version is available to full-time students and faculty, and all versions, other than the Starter Kit, include two free updates in addition to the initial version. CodeWarrior is available on CD-ROM only (the Gold and Academic versions nearly fill two CDs!).

Metrowerks maintains an excellent Web site (**http://www.metrowerks.com**) with product datasheets, updates, and other information, including an archive of the **comp.sys.mac.programmer.codewarrior newsgroup**.

See Also

Application Programming Interface; C; C++; Compiler; Constructor; Debugger; Editor; Framework; Heap; Integrated Development Environment; Interface Builder; Java; Linker; MPW; Pascal; PowerPlant; Win32; ZoneRanger

Collage

Marketed as a page layout program for images and a companion to **Photoshop**, Collage is designed specifically for putting multiple images together to create a composite image. To that end, it offers layering and a set of tools that are very similar to those found in **page layout applications**.

Images created in Collage can be up to 53 inches square, and they're placed on a **pasteboard** that extends off to the sides for storing elements that don't yet have a definite place in the composition. Other page layout tools include rulers, **guides**, grouping and alignment controls, and numerical controls for moving elements.

Images are imported into Collage at screen resolution—72 dots per inch. All edits are displayed on these low-resolution "screen proxies," so changes take much less time than they would if applied to the full-resolution image. Once a composition is complete, the user "renders" it to a high-resolution disk file.

A disadvantage to using Collage is that the low resolution becomes apparent when a user zooms in on an image. That is a trade-off for the speed gains and the less demanding hardware requirements of Collage.

Multiple layers enable users to treat individual elements of a composition in Collage as objects, moving, resizing, and editing them without affecting the other objects in the file. Drop shadows, feathering, transparency, and haloes can be applied to objects as easily as an italic style can be applied to text in a page layout package, and once created these additions move with the object to which they've been applied.

As **filters** are applied to an image, Collage keeps a list of each filter, so the effects of any change can be undone regardless of what has been done to the image since then. Photoshop plug-ins are supported by Collage.

While Collage supports both **CMYK** and **RGB** color definitions, the program can't convert one to the other. **PICT**, **TIFF**, and Photoshop's native format are supported, but the program can't read or write TIFF LZW (a common compression scheme used with TIFF images). If images are saved in Photoshop format, layers can be maintained and manipulated in Photoshop, furthering Collage's ambition to be the Photoshop companion.

As a proxy system, Collage works with representations of your real graphical elements, not with the actual files. Make sure that you save the mask with the graphic.

In **Photoshop**, this is done as follows.

1. After designing your image, use the Magic Wand to mask it out of the background (make sure it is masked and not the background).

2. Save the image with a unique name to a storage folder.

3. Go to the Select menu and choose Save Selection. Save it as a new channel with the same name as the present saved file.

4. Click the graphic off. When Photoshop asks if you want to save the changes first, reply Yes.

5. Open Collage and import the image that you saved. Import it again so that you can layer one on the other. You should observe that the top layered image has an opaque background. To get rid of the background (the selection channel saved with the image), go to the Element menu in Collage and down to the Mask item. Select Yes and the background will disappear. This is how you layer elements in Collage when you want their backgrounds to drop out.

If you go to Element menu/Mask option, choose Yes, and the image disappears, that means there was no mask saved as a part of the image file. At that point, you have to go back, create a mask for the image, and save it again.

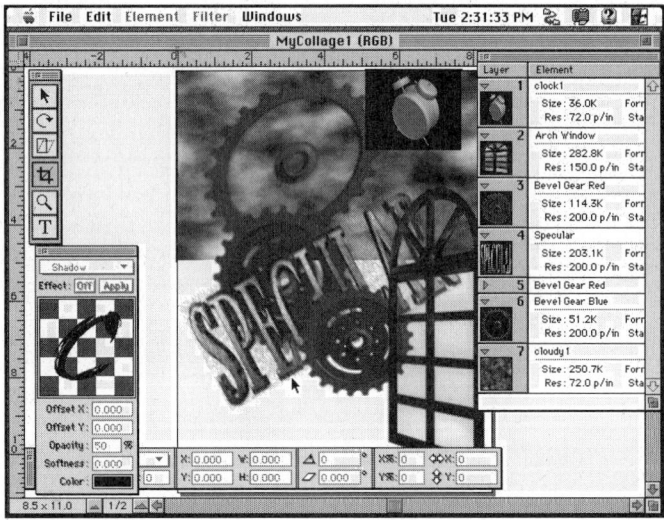

See Also
CMYK; Guides; Page Layout Applications; Pasteboard; Photoshop; RGB

Collapse Folder (Keyboard Shortcut)

To collapse an expanded folder, press ⌘-Option-Left Arrow. This keyboard shortcut works only when a

window is displayed in a **list view**. You can also use this keyboard shortcut to collapse a nested **folder**, (a folder within a folder that has been expanded). The folder will collapse leaving any other expanded nested folders still open. This keyboard shortcut is available only when a window is displayed in a list view and a folder within that window has been expanded.

To collapse a folder in a list view, follow these steps:

1. Click the icon for the expanded folder.
2. Press ⌘-Option-Left Arrow to collapse the folder.

To collapse a nested folder within a list view, follow these steps:

1. Click the **icon** of the nested folder.
2. Press ⌘-Option-Left Arrow to collapse just that folder.

See Also
Click; Copy (Keyboard Shortcut); Icon; Keyboard Shortcuts; Nested Folder

Colonization, *See Sid Meier's Worlds*

Color Control Panel

The Color control panel enables you to choose the color that indicates an item is selected and choose the accent color for window title bars. Colors are selected from a pull-down menu. After selecting a color, close the control. Your changes are now in effect, as shown in the figure.

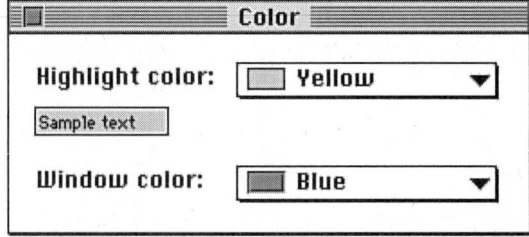

To use the Color control panel, follow these steps:

1. Choose the Color control panel from the control panels submenu on the Apple menu (or System Folder).

2. To set the highlight color, select the color of your choice from the highlight pull-down menu. To select an accent color for your window title bars, select a color from the accent pull-down menu. Close the window to make the changes take effect.

See Also
Apple Menu; Control Panels

Color Gamut

Color gamut describes the range of colors that a device can reproduce or process.

The term *color space* is also used to mean the same thing. Color gamut is an important consideration in printing, especially in desktop publishing. Because each electronic device or printing press may have different color capabilities, color is a difficult element to control. Much of the focus of the printing industry has always been on color reproduction, and the development of digital color has greatly complicated the issue. **Color printing** is more complicated now because of the device-dependency of color. Device-dependency implies that a color will not display or reproduce the same way in different devices.

In 1931 and 1978, the **Commission Internationale de l'Eclairage (CIE)** established color standards to aid in the mechanical description of color. These color standards are known as CIEXYZ, CIELAB, and CIELUV. These models define color mathematically and are considered device-independent. However, they are purely theoretical and not of much use when color must be displayed on a monitor or printed on a printing press. The CIE color models are useful when mathematical color values must be transferred from system to system.

The ostensible goal of color printing is to reproduce the colors of the natural world, but this really cannot

be done. The physical differences between the human perception of color and the capability of a mechanical device to reproduce color are impossible to overcome. Even though the differences cannot be overcome, they can be compensated for by controlling color through the use of color models, **color matching systems**, and color management systems.

Color models, such as RGB, HSB, and CMYK, represent the actual colors that an individual device can reproduce or display.

The reproduction of color can be made more predictable with a color matching system, such as Pantone, TruMatch, or FocolTone. The color space of any device can be described and controlled with a color management system (CMS), such as EFIcolor, ColorSync, or Kodak Precision. The color management systems are a relatively recent development in the effort to control and predict digital color. An organization of hardware and software companies, the International Color Consortium (ICC), has set standards for developing color profiles for electronic devices.

The essential difficulty in printing color is to satisfy human perceptual needs. The emotional context of color plays a role in this, and it is extremely difficult to satisfy everyone all the time. Because color is variable, elusive, and symbolic, much effort is made in the graphics arts to qualify it. Graphics designers and artists attempt to specify appropriate colors by considering their psychological effects or aesthetic value. The full effect of color in nature cannot be reproduced on a computer or printed on a page, but we make quality judgments nonetheless. "That sky is too blue." or "Can we cut back on the pink in the skin tones?" are phrases that might be overheard in connection with any color display or printing job.

The most important consideration in working with color gamuts, therefore, is to understand and be prepared for the inevitable differences in the way colors will look from one device to another. One of the most dramatic color shifts occurs when an image is converted from the RGB (Red, Green, Blue) color gamut of a monitor display to the CMYK (Cyan, Magenta, Yellow, Black) color gamut of the printed page. The

CMYK **process color** model simply cannot reproduce all the colors that are possible in the RGB model.

See Also
CIE; CIELAB; Color Printing; Color Separations; Desktop Publishing Color Models; High-Fidelity Color Printing; Image Manipulation for Printing; Process Color

Color Halftoning, *See PostScript Level 2*

Color Icons

You add color to an **icon** by using the **Labels menu** on the **desktop**. For example, to give a folder color, you select the folder and choose a color from the Labels menu. If the color you want doesn't appear in the Labels menu, you can create a custom label color using the **Labels control panel**.

See Also
Click; Control Panels; Desktop; Icons; Label Menu; Labels

Color Inkjet Printing, *See Printing Technology, Color*

Color Laser Printing, *See Printing Technology, Color*

Color Management

Anyone who has scanned a color photo, viewed the scan on a computer monitor, and then printed it on a color printer could explain why color management software is needed. Although it's still in an adolescent stage, color management software provides a way to make sure that those three color images (the one that is scanned, the one that is viewed on-screen, and the one that is printed) look the same.

In this scenario, it would be nice to know what you're going to get when the paper comes out of the printer. But in professional printing, where the final product is produced by a printing press that costs hundreds of dollars per hour to operate, it's not just nice, it's vital—mistakes in this field are *really* expensive.

The root of the problem lies in the fact that input, output, and display devices don't use the same methods of defining color. Monitors and some scanners use **RGB** color (with red, green, and blue combining to form a range of available colors), while printers and other scanners use **CMYK** color (cyan, magenta, yellow, and black are combined to form colors). Commercial color printing uses CMYK, as well.

But the range of colors that can be created using red, green, and blue light, as on a computer monitor, isn't the same as the range of colors that can be created using cyan, magenta, yellow, and black inks. And images that start out in one color definition (or color space)—say, in RGB on a user's monitor—often need to be converted to another color space to be used—in this case, to CMYK to be printed. The end result? The colors don't match.

Software and hardware developers have chosen to tackle this problem in a number of ways, but only lately has there been any sign of consensus.

Closed-loop color management systems only work with a specific hardware/software configuration. For example, Hewlett-Packard has produced Color Smart software that improves color reproduction in documents printed on its own color inkjet and laser printers, and QMS offers a similar product called QColor for its color laser printers.

Some graphics applications, such as **Photoshop**, have primitive but effective color-matching systems that consist of a reference image packaged with the software in both printed and digital form. The user compares the printed image with the digital image on-screen and adjusts the monitor until the two match. A scanner can be put into the loop as well.

Dedicated software to handle color management isn't perfect, by a long shot, but it's much improved from its early days. A big leap forward came in 1995, with the introduction of Apple's **ColorSync** 2.0, system-level software that enables the use and creation of "device profiles." These descriptions of individual input

C

and output devices document the particular color changes that the devices will make to images in the printing, scanning, and viewing processes and enable graphics applications to compensate for those changes.

The result, assuming the profiles are used properly and supported by all software used in the design process, will be printouts that match what is on the monitor and scans that match their originals.

But developers disagree on the best way to create and implement profiles. Some color management systems come with a library of profiles supplied by hardware manufacturers for use with their printers, scanners, and monitors. Others, claiming that this information won't be valid over the lifetime of a device, promote the use of spectrophotometers and colorimeters (**color measuring** devices) to create profiles customized to individual devices.

Another problem encountered with color management is how to define color in a neutral way that can be converted into measurements in any color space, including RGB, CMYK, HSB (hue, saturation, and brightness). The standard used by most color management software today is the CIE color space, which was developed in the 1930s by the Commission Internationale de l'Eclairage (International Commission on Illumination). CIE color definitions cover the entire visible spectrum and so can be used to define any color achievable in other color spaces.

Software to help control color has been around for a few years, but it's still in flux; as recently as early 1995 there were several competing systems with incompatible device profiles (**FotoTune**, **EfiColor**, **Kodak Precision Color Management System**, Pantone **ColorDrive**). But the release of ColorSync 2.0 spurred many software developers to base their color management systems on this new system software from Apple—and the newly revised systems can read each other's profiles, because they all use the ICC (International Color Consortium) standard for device profiles.

Profiling software that supports ColorSync 2.0 includes Linotype's **PrintOpen**, Candela's **ColorSynergy**, and Color Solutions' **ColorBlind**.

With today's technology, there are several ways to control color matching on the desktop, ranging from system-level software that users can completely ignore all the way up to dedicated application suites that enable sophisticated manipulation of color as well as adjustments to compensate for the limitations of different devices. With the advent of new printing technologies such as Pantone's Hexachrome (a six-color printing process), color management can only get more complex.

See Also

CMYK; ColorBlind; ColorDrive; ColorSync; ColorSynergy; Desktop Publishing and Color Management Systems (CMS); EfiColor; KCMS; Measuring Color; Photoshop; PrintOpen; RGB

Color Matching Systems

Color matching systems are used to standardize ink colors and aid in the specification of color for printing presses. Desktop publishing software applications provide access to several matching systems in their color dialog boxes, but the most widely used is the **PANTONE Matching System**. Commercial printers obtain licenses to use a particular matching system. To use a color matching system properly, a color swatch book for that system should be obtained. Other color matching systems are: DIC (DaiNippon), FocolTone, MUNSELL, Toyo, and TruMatch.

DIC is used for spot colors and organizes color into categories such as bright and dark. FocolTone displays colors by how they share a common percentage of each of the process colors. The MUNSELL color system organizes colors by hue, value, and chroma. Toyo is a system of spot colors organized by hue and saturation. The TruMatch system displays process colors by hue, tint, and brightness.

See Also

Color Management; Color Printing; Desktop Publishing Color Models; FocolTone; Pantone Matching System; Process Color; Toyo; TruMatch

Color, Measuring

To get accurate color results, desktop publishers need to calibrate scanners, printers, monitors, and other devices, measuring the colors these devices are generating in order to make them match. The most commonly used instruments for measuring color are spectrophotometers, colorimeters, and densitometers. These three instruments measure light to determine the color of objects or images.

Spectrophotometers measure wavelengths of light at various points along the visible spectrum to generate a curve that represents a color.

Colorimeters measure light in the same way that the human eye does, using red, green, and blue receptors. Each color component is assigned a number representing its intensity; the combination of three values are called tristimulus values.

Densitometers are similar to colorimeters, but they're designed for measuring specific materials such as printing inks. They can measure the strength of a color, but they can't accurately measure its hue.

Color measurement devices for the Mac have recently become both affordable and reasonably accurate. They include X-Rite's Digital Swatchbook, Light Source's Colortron II, and Color Savvy's ColorMouse.

See Also
Color Management

Color Model, *See Color Gamut; Color Matching Systems; Desktop Publishing Color Models*

Color Output, Buying

Although color **printers** are coming down in price faster than almost any other type of hardware in the Mac world, service bureaus and many quick print shops still make good money offering their customers color copies and color printing of supplied files. There are a couple of reasons for this.

First, it's expensive and time-consuming to print more than a few color pages at a time, so if you need quite a few copies of a color document, it may be worth it to have the output done at a service bureau. Second, most people can afford only color inkjet printers, or, at best, color laser printers, and these don't offer the most accurate color. Other technologies, such as dye sublimation and wax transfer, are better suited for use when accurate color proofing is a concern.

When buying color output, check to make sure the vendor uses a **color management** system and that color output devices are serviced and calibrated regularly. Calibration needs to be done daily to make sure color is accurate. When buying color copies, make sure vendors check each copy against the original to ensure that colors have translated accurately.

See Also
Color Management; Printers

Color Printing

If your documents contain color, you can **print** in full color using a color printer. There are different levels of color printers in every style and price range. The most popular are the inexpensive color inkjet printers that use Apple's **QuickDraw** technology. Color inkjet printers have become very affordable, and companies such as Hewlett-Packard even have black-and-white inkjet printers that can be converted to color printers by adding colored ink cartridges. Most color inkjet printers use either three or four color ink cartridges, and the quality of color inkjet printers ranges from acceptable to outstanding. Some color inkjet printers are capable of producing photographic-style quality on specially designed, coated paper. The drawback of producing this photographic quality on an inkjet printer is the printing time, which can be as long as 45 minutes for a standard 8 1/2-inch by 11-inch color page.

Among your printing options are third-party software packages that add **PostScript** compatibility to QuickDraw color inkjet printers. On the high-end, there are color **Laser Printers**, including one from Apple, and dye sublimation or thermal wax printers, which produce PostScript photographic-quality images quickly, which are popular with graphic designers for proofing their color work. PostScript dye sublimation and thermal wax printers are becoming more affordable as more and more printer companies enter this expanding market.

At one time, color printing could be achieved only on a traditional printing press, but now much color printing is done on digital presses. Therefore, a discussion of color printing in general must encompass both technologies. Color printing falls into two categories: **spot color** and **process color**.

- **Spot Color Printing.** In spot color printing, images appear as separate solid areas or tint screens of a single color usually specified from the Pantone Matching System (PMS). One, two, or three spot colors are the norm in most commercial printing jobs. Spot color printing is very common in traditional printing operations, and it is often used in business stationery and low-budget printing. Digital printing devices cannot use Pantone colors, but some copiers can apply a limited range of spot colors.

- **Process Color Printing.** Process color printing accounts for the majority of both traditional and digital printing. In process color printing, four colors (cyan, magenta, yellow, and black) are laid down by the printing device in various tint screen combinations to achieve the effect of "full" color. For this reason, process color is always used to reproduce color photographs; but, in fact, the range of colors reproduced in this way falls far short of the full spectrum of colors produced by visible light. Process color printing is also known as "four-color printing" and "full-color printing." The four colors are often referred to as CMYK.

In both spot color and process color, the colors themselves must be printed one at a time. On traditional printing presses in general, ink is applied to paper or other material from a printing plate. A separate plate is required for each color. If the press is capable of handling only one plate at a time, multicolor printing is impractical though not impossible.

In the early days of printing, additional colors were added by passing the sheet through the press more than once. Modern large presses may incorporate two, four, six, or eight color units and are able to print all the colors on both sides of the sheet in a single pass. Sometimes process colors and spot colors are used in the same printing job. This requires a six or eight color press. Varnishes may also be added instead of color. A special form of process color printing, high-fidelity printing, utilizes more than four colors with special inks and papers to achieve premium results. Even digital printing devices must apply the four process colors one at a time, and in most cases, the sheet of paper can be observed moving back and forth or up and down through the printer as each of the four colors is applied.

See Also

Color Gamut; Color Separations; High-Fidelity Color; Printing; Printing Presses, Offset; Process Color; Spot Color

Color Printers, *See Desktop Printing*

Color Resolution

Color Resolution, or bit depth, refers to the amount of color information contained in a single pixel of a digital image. All modern computers use the binary system where data is processed as either a 1 (one) or a 0 (zero). Therefore, in this binary system, the most basic color choices for a pixel are black or white (1 or 0, yes or no, on or off). This black or white pixel has a color resolution, or bit depth, of one bit (2^1). In a color computer system, the color resolution of pixels increases exponentially. In a two-bit system, each pixel may have four potential colors (2^2). In a three-bit system, each pixel may have eight potential colors (2^3) and so on. In Macintosh **desktop publishing** systems, 24-bit color is common and results in 16.7 million color choices. The following figure charts this exponential increase. The total number of possible colors increases exponentially as the number of bits in a color system increases.

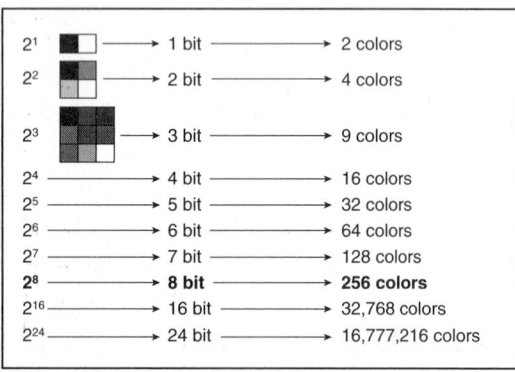

2^1	1 bit	2 colors
2^2	2 bit	4 colors
2^3	3 bit	9 colors
2^4	4 bit	16 colors
2^5	5 bit	32 colors
2^6	6 bit	64 colors
2^7	7 bit	128 colors
2^8	**8 bit**	**256 colors**
2^{16}	16 bit	32,768 colors
2^{24}	24 bit	16,777,216 colors

See Also

Desktop Publishing; Digital Halftones; Image Scanning

Color Separations

Color separations are necessary in **spot color** and **process color** printing on traditional printing presses because each color must be printed from a separate printing plate. In the traditional mechanical method, spot color separations are made either by photographing physically separated elements of a paste-up with overlays or by photographing the same paste-up once for each color and then blocking out irrelevant areas on each piece of film. The separate pieces of film are then used to make the printing plates.

This method is also used to produce process **color separations**, but in this case, a full-color image is photographed four times through special filters. Each filter enables only a specific color to be recorded on the film as a tint screen of cyan, magenta, yellow, or black. These procedures have been almost entirely sup-

planted by digital methods in the United States and many other countries.

In digital color separating, spot colors are easily output to different pieces of film from a page layout software application such as **QuarkXPress** or **Adobe PageMaker**. It is even possible to output directly to separate printing plates. Process color separations are similarly easy to create with a page layout software application or an image manipulation program such as **Adobe Photoshop**. Digital technology has greatly simplified the color separation process.

Most graphics applications enable you to create spot color and process color separations for use in offset printing. You can have these separations output for you by a service bureau or print shop that offers digital imaging.

Most graphics programs give you the option of printing the name of each spot color on the bottom of each page (or plate), so the red "plate" has the word "Red" in the bottom corner. This lets the print shop know to apply red ink when that plate runs through the press. It's a good practice to print a test spot color separation on your own laser printer to make sure the items you want in a particular color come out on the right plate. Ask your print shop what kind of artwork (film or paper) you need to supply for them to properly print your job. They may need high-resolution film negatives or RC paper output from an imagesetter, or they may be able to use regular paper from your laser printer. Always check with your printer before you output your final artwork.

Process color is used for reproducing color photographs. It uses a PostScript imagesetter to separate your color photo into four separate film negatives, each representing a color (which is why it's often referred to as four-color printing). These four process colors are: cyan, magenta, yellow, and black (CMYK). When you ask for a process color separation from a digital file, you get four film negatives back, with one representing the cyan plate, one the magenta plate, one the yellow plate, and one the black plate. Modern color printing presses use these four colors to re-create full color photographs.

When printing film negatives, you should also get a color key or Matchprint type proof (which is a color proof made from your new negatives) to see whether the file separated correctly, and to help the printer match the colors displayed in the proof to ink on the press. It's an amazing technology, but requires significant knowledge, equipment, and experience to make it work properly.

If you're thinking about creating your own color separations from a graphics application, ask your service bureau, print shop, or other pre-press professional for guidance.

See Also

Graphic Design; PageMaker; Photoshop; Prepress; Printing; Process Color; QuarkXPress; Spot Color

Color Shop, *See Service Bureaus, Trade Shops, and Desktop Publishing*

Color Space, *See Color Gamut*

Color Standards, *See Color Gamut; Desktop Publishing Color Standards*

Color Trapping

Color trapping is the process of compensating for the slight misregistration of abutting colors that sometimes occurs on a printing press. Misregistration does not always happen, but the potential causes of it are many. The type of press, the number of years it has been in service, the speed at which it runs, the skill of the operator, paper characteristics, and other factors can affect registration. In perfect registration, the press is able to place an image in exactly the same spot on the paper on every copy made. If abutting color images misregister, a sliver of the paper color may show. This is generally considered undesirable, and if even a slight chance for misregistration is present, most commercial printers will want to trap. The following figure shows an illustration of misregistered colors.

Trapping is not necessary when colors overprint one another. Usually, however, only black is overprinted. Overprinting black actually enhances its blackness. Ink colors are transparent and overprinting any color other than black results in a third color being created by the combination of the two colors. Conceivably, this can be a way to make a two-color printing job appear to have three colors, but most people would rather keep the colors pure.

To keep the colors pure, a knockout is required. In a knockout, the background color is dropped or "knocked out" in an area exactly corresponding to the size and shape of the foreground image. Therefore, if the foreground image does not exactly fit the knocked out area due to misregistration, trapping is necessary to cover the sliver of paper color that results.

The goal of trapping is to make the two images overlap very slightly at their edges. If this is done properly, the trap (the area of overlap) is not noticeable. Too much trap can create a dark line around the edges of the foreground image.

Two methods are used to create traps: choking and spreading.

- In *choking*, the knockout is made smaller.
- In *spreading*, the foreground object is made larger.

The amount of choking and spreading is very slight— 0.25 points (0.003 inch) more or less, depending on the type of paper and other factors. This is known as the trapping value. Whether to choke or spread depends on the color content of the images in question, and no trapping may be necessary if the two images contain at least 20 percent of the same color.

Trapping is a complex issue and not one to be taken lightly. The two popular page layout software applications, **Adobe PageMaker** and **QuarkXPress,** both make provisions for automatic and manual trapping of objects created in the program. Neither can trap imported graphics. The issue of trapping should be discussed with a **service bureau, trade shop,** or commercial printing firm before making any final decisions. Two dedicated trapping programs, Adobe TrapWise and Island Trapper, are often used at service bureaus and trade shops to perform automatic, and complete, trapping procedures.

See Also

PageMaker; Prepress; QuarkXPress

ColorBlind

One of a wave of **color management** systems compatible with Apple's **ColorSync** 2.0 system software, ColorBlind offers users a way to create **device profiles** for their input and output devices and use the resulting ICC-compatible profiles to adjust their color images for optimum results with their hardware.

The ColorBlind package sells for several thousand dollars as a unit, but its components can be purchased separately. The software that makes up ColorBlind includes ICC Print (the device profiler), ColorBlind Edit (for making sophisticated adjustments to the color in images), and ColorBlind Parachute (a utility that applies device profiles to previously generated color PostScript files). The package also includes an X-Rite DTP51 colorimeter (for **measuring color** output) and a set of reflective and transmissive ANSI IT8 targets (the industry standards) for scanner profiling.

Monitor profiles can be created by using the X-Rite's DTP92 Monitor Optimizer, another device (not included) that attaches to the front of a monitor and reads its color output, or by entering information provided by the monitor's manufacturer. Scanner profiles are created by scanning the supplied targets, then having ColorBlind compare the results with the supplied reference values. Creating printer profiles requires printing a supplied target file, then scanning the printout with the DTP51 colorimeter; ColorBlind compares the colors in the printout with its stored record of the colors in the original file.

See Also

Color Management; Color, Measuring; ColorSync; Device Profiles

ColorDrive

Acting as a front end to **ColorSync**, ColorDrive uses ICC profiles from any **color management** system and helps out with color management for photographic images in applications that don't support ColorSync. But its primary purpose is to ensure accurate reproduction of Pantone colors from the Pantone Matching System, Pantone Pastel Color System, Pantone Metallics Color System, Pantone Textile Color System, Pantone Plastics Color System, and Pantone Hexachrome (for six-color printing). When outputting Pantone colors, ColorDrive first looks for a Pantone-licensed printer (for which it includes **device profiles**), then passes the image to ColorSync if it can't find a profile.

See Also

Color Management; ColorSync; Device Profiles

Colorimeter, *See Color, Measuring*

ColorIt!

ColorIt!, from MicroFrontier, is extensive in its image creation and editing potential, and has a wealth of tools to do the tasks. It is the most competitive image editing and photo retouching competitor that Photoshop has on the Mac. There are some areas in which it is lacking, however, when we use Photoshop as the comparative model. It does contain vector drawing tools, more specifically a Bézier pen, but that tool has little variability compared to the Bézier operations found in Photoshop's Path routines. It also is more limited when it comes to load/save formats, and does not work as well with super large images. For 99 percent of the tasks expected of it however, it is a superlative image editing program. Some of its features far exceed those found in Photoshop. It also features multiple Undos, a capacity not found in Photoshop.

The ToolBox ColorIt! takes a very different approach to the ToolBox from any other software. Its tools are contained in a four part group that is separated into Default, Painting, Retouching, and Selection alternatives. To make matters more interesting, you can create your own set of tools at any time and save them as a custom tool set in the list of selections. Photoshop enables no customization of the ToolBox. In ColorIt!, many of the tools can be customized according to the shape and size of the drawing medium, with an interactive pop-out series of choices. A constant list of eight available tools exists in a side menu, and can be dragged and dropped in place on your toolset, exchanging places with the tool that's already there. ColorIt!'s painting options and tools make it a better choice for pure electronic painting than Photoshop, though its lack of stability for large images may be a limiting factor.

Selection Menu and Tools ColorIt! has far more selection options than Photoshop, and each is customizable from a pop-out list of interactive choices. For one, there are 11 shape choices, and an additional "custom" choice that enables you to insert your own shape. Add to this a unique lasso option that can be set to draw a freeform shape as normal, or only around either dark or light colors. This gives the user a wealth of options when drawing or surrounding a selected area. The selection menu contains all of the standard choices, with two additional features worth mentioning: Extrudes and Shadows. Each enables you to add depth to the selection, using the foreground color as the shadow or extrusion. An extrusion can either be filled with the set color, or it can be created as a path, ready for texture fills or customized painting (shading, airbrushing, and so on).

Layers ColorIt! does not support layers, and has no Layering menus. You cannot drag a selection from one page to another, although you can copy and paste it. Once positioned, it's easy to make the new selection transparent to any degree necessary, thereby fostering the creation of collages and composites.

Native Effects Filters Except for a few standard filters, ColorIt! depends mostly on plug-ins for its effects operations. Photoshop, as a comparison, has a number of its own built-in filters. The exception is the Convolution Filter, which applies a convolution matrix to the selected graphic either from a list of over thirty members or as a customizable choice. The convolution matrix has an updated preview screen so that you can explore creating your own convolutions and watch them being applied in real time. ColorIt! accepts most of the Photoshop compatible filters.

Work Modes ColorIt! can work with RGB, Grayscale (16 and 256), Black & White, CMYK, HSV and HSL images. You can also target the R, G, and B color channels separately.

Other Considerations One of the nicest features of ColorIt! is its capability to enable you to paint with textures. Textures are selectable from several included libraries, and are available at the MicroFrontier site on-line for free every once in a while. The feathering and opacity of texture brushes can be adjusted, inviting very exploratory use of the medium. Any selected image area can be grabbed from the screen and saved as a new texture in the selected library. This feature emphasizes ColorIt!'s use as a professional digital painting tool. ColorIt! is not a Power Mac native application.

File Save/Load Conventions ColorIt! can load TIFF, Mac PICT, PostScript, Paint, GIF, Photoshop 2 and 2.5, Startup Screen, Photone Prepress, and Scitex CT. It can save out all of the above (with the exception of Scitex CT) and in addition, QuickTime PICTs.

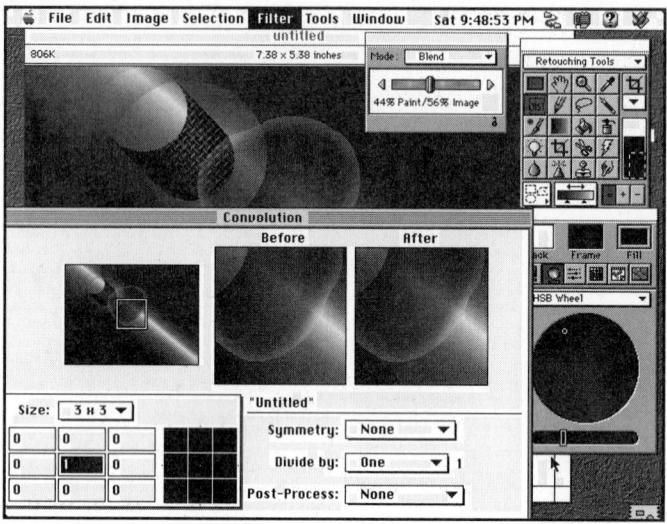

See Also

Paint Applications

Colorize 2

Colorize, from DS Design, adds color to black and white line art. This is not a simple task. The line art is often adversely effected by skips in color and other glaring results that make the art useless. Comic book artists and technical illustrators, for example, are often faced with this challenge. Colorize only accepts black and white 1-bit **TIFF** images. Images that do not fit this format must be converted before they can be imported into Colorize. Color trapping, having colors fill in to the edge of another color, is emphasized in Colorize. Colorize 2 is an extremely intelligent paint system.

The ToolBox Colorize is different than either a bitmap painting program or a vector drawing program, so its ToolBox contains tool options unique to its tasks. A brief description of the tools includes:

1. Paint and Paint To Edge—Paint To Edge is unique in that you cannot paint in any area that is not bounded by the lines that encircle the area in which you begin painting. Holding down the ⌘ key resizes the brush.

2. The Erase Tool, Erase Edge, and Erase Fragment—The Erase Tool erases only the color selected, without touching other colors. Erase to Edge erases the current color to the encircling hard edge, and Erase Fragment erases only what is under the present brush size, one step at a time.

3. Transfer/Transfer Fragment— The Transfer Tools exchange a selected color with another from the Shades dialog.

4. Line Tool—Draws a line in the current color.

5. Crop Tool—Standard tool for cropping image area. Unlike some paint programs, cropping *cannot* be undone in Colorize.

6. Outline Tool—Draws an outline around the selected area.

7. Despeckle—Used to clean up stray pixels from the image.

8. The Blend Tool—This tool paints blends and gradients of one or two colors in a selected area. It works only on a **CMYK** layer. A CMYK Layer is always at the bottom of the Shades stack.

9. Airbrush—Three variants are possible: smooth, pixelated, and a blend of the two. The airbrush also is consigned to the CMYK layer.

Selection Menu and Tools Selections are constrained automatically within the boundaries of the outlines contained in the image.

Layers Colorize treats separate colors as separate Layers. Where layers overlap, the colors blend. Color palettes are organized by choosing colors from a swatch list and dragging them to a shades list, and dropping them on a new color item. This process creates the desired palette. The color Layer at the top of the Shades palette paints over colors below it, but not above it.

Native Effects Filters The Blend and Gradient operations can be considered as effects filters in Colorize2.

Work Modes Colorize works in RGB and CMYK.

Other Considerations There is no other software on the market like this. You might find Ray Dream's JAG II software to be a perfect companion to this package as a post-production tool.

File Save/Load Conventions Colorize accepts only 1-bit black and white TIFF files as input, but can output either TIFF (LZW compression included) or EPS formats. Flat color images saved to EPS can have automatic masking, with no need for creating clipping paths.

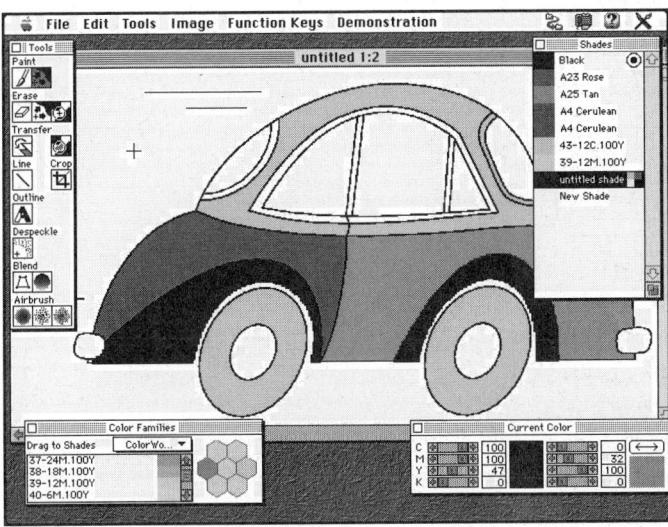

See Also
CMYK

Colormouse, *See Color, Measuring*

Colorsmart, *See Color Management*

ColorSync

Developed jointly by Apple and Linotype-Hell, a major player in the prepress industry for decades, ColorSync 2.0 is a big improvement over the original version of this **color management** technology.

Designed to compensate for the differences between the color technologies and media used by input devices (digital cameras, scanners), video monitors, and output devices (printers, printing presses), ColorSync enables the creation of "device profiles" that tell the hardware how an image should be modified when it's scanned, viewed, or printed to make sure colors always appear the same.

The original version of ColorSync, which came out with System 7.5, required profile information to be stored in separate files that had to accompany graphics files. Because of this limitation, the software was not supported by most software developers in the publishing industry. ColorSync 2.0, on the other hand, enables profiles to be stored within an image file so that the color management process is more transparent to the user. The ColorSync control panel shown here enables users to specify device profiles for their systems.

The profiles created using ColorSync are compatible with the International Color Consortium (ICC) profile specification, which is an industry standard for device profiles that are compatible across multiple platforms. Another improvement over profiles created using ColorSync 1.0 is greater detail in device profiles, leading to better color-matching results.

ColorSync 2.0 also supports devices that use more than four colors to produce an image, such as **Pantone's** Hexachrome color printing process, which uses six colors. And it runs native on Power Macs, working (Apple says) more than five times as fast as ColorSync 1.0.

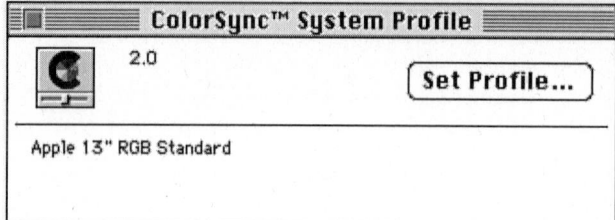

Because it's system-level software, ColorSync needs to be supported by other software to work. **Add-on software** (such as **Photoshop** plug-ins and **QuarkXTensions**) can be used to activate the features of ColorSync from within major applications; software vendors are also selling separate programs that create corrected color palettes that can be imported into graphics applications.

With its improved capabilities, ColorSync has been adopted by the major graphics software developers as a standard—which means users can stop guessing which color management system to use and start looking for better results.

See Also

Add-On Software; Color Management; Pantone Matching System; Photoshop; Plug-Ins; QuarkXPress; XTensions

ColorSync Extension

ColorSync, added as a separate extension in **System 7.1**, adds color-matching technology to your system to help you match the color you see on your monitor to a variety of color output devices (such as color printers) to help your color work be more consistent. ColorSync is part of **System 7.5** and is installed when you choose to install **QuickDraw GX**.

There's a pop-down menu in the ColorSync extension that enables you to select a profile of your current monitor (see the following figure).

```
┌─────────────────────────────────────────┐
│≡≡≡≡≡    ColorSync™ System Profile   ≡≡≡≡≡│
│ ┌──────────┐                              │
│ │▦▦▦▦│                         1.0.5      │
│ │▦▦▦▦│                                    │
│ │▭ ▪  │                                    │
│ └──────────┘                              │
│ System Profile:                           │
│ ┌───────────────────────────────────┐    │
│ │ Apple 13" RGB Standard         ▼ │    │
│ └───────────────────────────────────┘    │
└─────────────────────────────────────────┘
```

For example, if you're using an Apple 17-inch color monitor, you would choose the Apple 17-inch RGB Monitor profile from the pop-up menu. By choosing a monitor profile, you're telling ColorSync the characteristics of your particular monitor so it can help match the color your monitor displays to the profile of your output device. Apple creates ColorSync profiles for its monitors, color printers, and scanners.

After you've selected a profile for your monitor, you must select a profile for your output device. These profiles are supplied by the peripheral manufacturers themselves, but, unfortunately, not all peripheral devices have a ColorSync profile—check with your peripheral manufacturer to see whether your printer or peripheral has a ColorSync profile available. You can also create your own custom profiles by using the Set System Profile command from the pop-up menu in the ColorSync dialog box.

When ColorSync has both of these profiles, it adjusts your monitor's color to accurately show how on-screen objects appear when printed.

See Also

Monitors; PostScript Level 2; QuickDraw GX; System 7.1; System 7.5

ColorSync System Profile

The ColorSync technology was introduced in System 7.1 as a separate extension to help Macintosh users better calibrate their monitors to their output devices, so the color they see on their screen more closely matches the color that appears on the printed page. ColorSync is now part of System 7.5 as part of the QuickDraw GX installation.

Accessing the ColorSync **control panel** enables you to tell the computer what kind of monitor or input device you are using by selecting it from a pull-down menu. If you're not using an Apple-brand monitor or input device, and your output device does not appear on the list, ask the manufacturer for an Apple ColorSync profile for your device. A

C

number of manufacturers are now including these Color Sync profile files with their peripherals, including scanners and color printers.

To set a ColorSync profile for your device, follow these steps:

1. Choose the ColorSync Control Panel from the Control Panels submenu on the Apple Menu (or in the System Folder).

2. Choose the pull-down menu and select the model of monitor or other color input device from the list.

See Also
Control Panel; Monitors

ColorSynergy

Adopting Apple's **ColorSync** software as their native format, software developers are releasing **color management** software that finally promises to be effective. ColorSynergy is a package that enables users to create and use ICC-compliant **device profiles** to ensure accurate color from scanner to monitor to printer.

ColorSynergy supports a wide range of instruments for measuring color output of printers and video monitors, including the popular ColorTron II. The software comes with a reflective IT8 target image to scan for calibration, and users can order transmissive (transparency) targets.

Those who don't have a device that measures monitor output can "eyeball" a monitor profile by matching a series of gray swatches and manually entering white-point and phosphor values (information obtained from the monitor's manufacturer).

To create profiles for printers, users print a supplied file containing 504 color swatches. Then they either use a calibrated scanner to scan the image back in, or read the colors on the output with a spectrophotometer. The software compares the colors in the printed file with the original color values.

See Also
Color Management; Color, Measuring; ColorSync

Colortron II, *See Color, Measuring*

Column in Databases

A vertical stack of **cells** in a **spreadsheet**. All Macintosh spreadsheets designate columns alphabetically, starting at the left margin. If there are more than 26 columns, double or triple letters may be used. The first column is typically used for text to describe the data in each **row**.

See Also
Absolute versus Relative Reference; Database

Command Key

This is a modifier key unique to the Macintosh that is used in combination with other keys to add additional functionality to the keyboard. The Command key has two symbols on the key: the Apple logo (🍎)(which is why it's sometimes called the "Apple" key) and the unique Command key symbol (⌘). The Command key is used with other keys to create keyboard shortcuts for menu **commands** and **mouse** actions.

Command Key Actions

If you want to do this...	Use this key command...
Quit an application	⌘-Q
Find a file	⌘-F
Copy an item	⌘-C
Paste an item	⌘-V
Create new folder or document	⌘-N
Eject a disk	⌘-E
Get Info on a file	⌘-I
Undo the last action	⌘-Z
Cut an item	⌘-X
Undo the last action	⌘-Z

continues

Command Key Actions (continued)	
If you want to do this...	*Use this key command...*
Print a document	⌘-P
Cancel an action	⌘-. (period)
Open an item	⌘-O
Duplicate a file	⌘-D
Save a document	⌘-S
Close a window/document	⌘-W
Make an Alias	⌘-M
Select all items in a window	⌘-A
Put an item away/Eject a disk	⌘-Y

See Also
Commands; Mouse

Comments, in Get Info Box

You can attach a written comment to any file by entering your comments in the file's **Comments box,** located in the file's **Get Info** window. This area is for your convenience and enables you to attach a personal message or note to a particular document. These comments will not appear in your document; they will appear only in the Comments box. To access a document's Get Info window, **click** the document's icon and select Get Info (⌘-I) from the File menu. The Comment box appears at the bottom of the Get Info window, enabling you to type any message in that window. Comments that you enter in the Comments box are searchable by using the **Find File** command.

See Also
Comments Box; Find File; Get Info

Commercial Online Services

Commercial Online Services are companies that provide their own fee-based online connection services, such as **email**, computer and non-computer related discussions, file libraries, and databases of information.

You can access some of the commercial services over the **Internet** instead of over a **modem**, but this still requires you to have a connection to the Internet, whether through your employer or through an account with an Internet Service provider.

Commercial services offer two main advantages over finding a "real" Internet connection:

1. Commercial services have deals with international commercial network carriers such as SprintNet and Tymnet, so finding a local phone number is usually easier. You pay for that easier access, usually with the connect-time fee for the commercial service.

2. Commercial services find it easier to offer commercial-quality information because they can charge users to access that information and then pay the information provider. Hence, you find, for example, full-text databases of computer magazines on **CompuServe,** but you pay extra for any searches in those databases, with the revenue going to the magazine publishers.

Many commercial services have added Internet email gateways and some even offer full access to the Internet. CompuServe's WOW! service provides email accounts and unlimited Internet access for $17.95 per month, whereas **America Online** offers its own **Web browser** software. Delphi supports text-only access to the Internet, including email, gopher, FTP, and text of Web pages, but no graphics.

See Also
America Online; AppleLink; CompuServe; Internet; Web Browser; World Wide Web

Common Gateway Interface, *See CGI*

Common Hardware Reference Platform (CHRP), *See PowerPC Platform*

Communications on the Internet

The **Internet** has no central "home" location. The various **Internet services** are complex and varied, and users can choose from a growing and quickly-changing range of connection methods.

Nevertheless, the Internet does have a central "backbone," a high-speed (45Mbps) network that connects the 10 computer centers in the U.S. that comprise the National Science Foundation Network.

The basic infrastructure of Internetworking and communications is common to all users, and a number of fundamental terms and definitions can be applied to virtually all parts of the Internet.

The various parts of the Internet are connected by gateways. These gateways enable Internet users to communicate with users in **CompuServe**, for instance, or for an **America Online** user to access a **Usenet** newsgroup.

Internet, Connecting to A Macintosh user who wants to connect to the Internet for the first time has a number of options.

Email access to the Internet is supplied by:

1. Commercial online services.
2. Bulletin board services.
3. A Local Area Network-based email package with a gateway to the Internet.

All commercial online services provide email with Internet users through gateways. A number of services also provide other Internet services, such as access to Usenet, **FTP** sites, and the **World Wide Web.**

A growing number of bulletin board services (BBSs) now provide access to the Internet, especially the large nationwide BBBs such as FidoNet or MCIMail. Some local BBSs can also provide Internet connections and can be located from your local computer dealer.

Businesses that use email software such as **QuickMail** sometimes set up Internet gateways for their employees.

Shell access is a common method of Internet connection, on a public access machine, usually running a form of the UNIX operating system. Some local universities or colleges provide limited access to their machines.

UUCP access provides email and newsgroup access. UUCP stands for UNIX-to-UNIX CoPy, a protocol that copies files corresponding to email messages and news postings from a UUCP host to your machine on a periodic basis. UNIX machines in Computer Science or Engineering departments often support it.

MacTCP access is the richest and most varied way of connecting to the Internet. Apple's **MacTCP** enables a Macintosh to communicate with the Internet. A Mac with MacTCP can run a wide variety of software such as **Eudora** for email, **Anarchie** for FTP, **NCSA Telnet**, **NewsWatcher** for news, and **MacWeb** or **Mosaic** for the World Wide Web.

MacTCP connections are available from:

1. **Internet services providers**, regional: These are large national companies that provide Internet access, such as PSI (800-827-7482), Netcom (800-501-8649), or Internet Express (800-592-1240).

2. Internet service providers, local: A large number of regional or local service providers can be found around the country. Local service providers often provide services only within their own area code, and sometimes target their offerings to the needs of their community.

3. University, government, and business-based direct connections: Students and staff at universities and employees in government

offices often have Macs connected to a local network which, in turn, can be connected with MacTCP to a direct Internet connection. This is typically a very fast T1 or T3 line.

A good way to get started with an Internet connection is to purchase *Internet Starter Kit for Macintosh, Fourth Edition* (Hayden, 1995), which includes MacTCP and other essential software for connecting to the Internet, downloading files, and general navigation.

Internet, Connection Speeds Users have a number of ways to connect to the Internet. These can be divided into two basic types:

- A dial-up **modem** connection
- A direct connection

The types of connections vary in bandwidth, the amount of information a user's network line can accommodate at any given time. The higher the bandwidth, the faster the user will send and receive information.

Modems make use of **asynchronous transmissions;** they vary in the modem File Transfer Protocol they use and in their speed, as expressed in baud/bits per second (bps).

Internet Connections

Connection	Speed
Modem	Up to 28.8Kbps (depends on user's modem speed)
56Kbps	56Kbps
ISDN	64 or 128Kbps
T1	128Kbps and higher
T3	Up to 1.544Mbps
Frame Relay	56Kbps to 1.544Mbps
ATM	100Mbps and higher

Communications on the Internet make use of **host** and **client** computers. Host computers, also called **server**s, hold information and sometimes distribute or route it to individual users. Even email communications between two individuals make use of a mail server using the **SMTP** and **POP3** protocols. **Client** computers connect to hosts to view or download files, whether those files exist on a news server, a World Wide Web server, or an FTP **Mac software archive.**

Internet addressing is an essential way of locating information and finding individuals online. All computers on the Internet make use of **IP address**es. Documents, objects, and computers can be found using Uniform Resource Locator (URL) addresses. Host computers connected to the Net are assigned **domain names** using the domain name system (**DNS**).

See Also

America Online; Asynchronous Data Transfer; Commercial Online Services; CompuServe; DNS; Email; eWorld; FTP; Internet; Internet Service Provider; IP Address; MacTCP; MacWeb; Modem; Mosaic; Newswatcher; URL; Usenet; World Wide Web

Communications Standards,
See Data Communications Standards

Comp

In graphic arts, a comp (abbreviation of comprehensive) is a preliminary example of a publication. Often used in advertising design, the comp is shown to the client as a means to communicate concepts, indicate production values and overall design aesthetics, and provide a platform for discussion and revision.

Before digital color technologies were well-developed, comps were made on paper samples from the intended print run. Text, graphics, and color were laboriously applied by hand using ink pen, transfer lettering, photostats, colored markers, colored paper stock, and anything else that would approximate the finished product. Needless to say, these were not very accurate and often misled the client. Today, most comps are made on color desktop printers and are much more accurate at showing how the finished job should look.

See Also

Graphic Design

CompactPro

This popular shareware compression utility, developed by Bill Goodman (Cyclos-CP, P.O. Box 31417, San Francisco, CA, 94131-0417), offers a wide variety of compression features and preferences. CompactPro offers:

- Standard file compression.

- The capability to create archives with multiple compressed folders or files combined into one "unit."

- Encryption and password protection for safeguarding sensitive files that cannot be accessed without the proper password.

- The capability to split compressed files into multiple segments on a disk to be rejoined during decompression.

- The creation of **self-extracting archives** (.sea), which enables the recipient to expand the compacted file without having the CompactPro software.

CompactPro also offers the capability to compress files in the background while you work in the foreground. CompactPro is available in the Macintosh Utilities Forum on America Online and at various FTP sites on the Internet.

See Also

Compressing Files; .cpt Filename Extension; .sea Filename Extension

Company of Science and Art, *See CoSA*

Compiled Language

After a programmer has written a program in a high-level language, it must be converted into **machine language** before a computer can understand it. In compiled languages, a special program called a **compiler** performs this conversion all at once, translating whole blocks of source code into **object code**. This is in contrast to **interpreted** languages, which perform the conversion one line of source code at a time.

Compilation has a number of advantages. First, because the compilation process occurs separately from the actual execution of the program, execution speeds typically are significantly faster than for interpreted code. In addition, the compiler can perform various optimizations to adjacent instructions to improve speed even further.

Compiled code, however, does have its disadvantages. Because the source code is compiled into machine-specific object code, it is inherently non-portable. As a result, compiled programs cannot run on another type of computer without help from an **emulator**, a special program that converts object code from one kind of machine language to another. This isn't to say that the program can't be made to run on another machine. Frequently, this is just a matter of recompiling the same source code with a different compiler.

In addition, whenever a small change is made to the code in a compiled language, the entire module containing that code must be recompiled and linked to the rest of the program. This is one of the major advantages of **dynamic language**s over traditional statically compiled languages.

Most languages can be implemented as either interpreted or compiled, but each language is most frequently one or the other. **C**, for example, is usually compiled, whereas **BASIC** is usually interpreted, but there are interpreted versions of C and compiled versions of BASIC.

There is another method of translating source code into machine code that straddles the line between compiled and interpreted: byte-code compilation. This method uses a compiler to convert source-code into special byte-codes rather than machine language. As with other compilations, this step is done as a batch process. The byte-codes then are fed to a special interpreter and converted to machine language one at a time as they are executed. This method has a distinct speed advantage over traditional interpreted code, while maintaining its portability. **Java** is implemented as a byte-code compiled language.

See Also

Compiler; Dynamic Language; Emulator; Interpreted Language; Machine Language; Object Code

CompileIt!

CompileIt! is a compiler that turns **HyperTalk** programs into **XCMD**s, XFCNs, and other Macintosh code resources. HyperTalk, the scripting language supported by **HyperCard**, compiles (converts the script into machine readable format) each time the script is executed. This can slow down execution time. Also, anyone can open your scripts and edit them. By compiling them (turning them into machine readable format and saving them as an XCMD or XFCN) the speed of the routine improves and the script is protected.

Although a HyperTalk script can be compiled "as is" with CompileIt!, making some adjustments to the scripts (particularly in how they use variables in memory) can greatly improve performance, especially in either long complex routines or repetitive routines.

CompileIt! supports the Macintosh ROM Toolbox, **System 7.0**, the extended XCMD interface, **SuperCard** language and callback Extensions, user-defined symbols, and much more. CompileIt! can increase the speed of HyperTalk routines and protect sensitive code from prying eyes.

> Heizer Software
> 300 Cedar Lane
> Largo, FL 34640
> Price: $149
> Fax: (813) 559-0614
> Phone: (800) 888-7667 or (813) 559-6422
> Web: http://www.heizer.com

See Also

Director; HyperCard; HyperTalk; SuperCard; System 7.0; XCMD

Compiler

A special program that converts program source code from a human-readable format into machine-readable **object code**.

Most **programming languages** resemble, to some extent, a human-readable language, such as English. This can range from the almost-English of **AppleScript** to the more obscure notation of **C** or **LISP**. Unfortunately, none of these languages are directly understandable by a computer, so some program has to translate from these high-level languages to the low-level **machine language** computers understand. This program is called a compiler.

Strictly speaking, a compiler is a program that performs this translation in a batch process, typically an entire file or program at a time. This is in contrast to an interpreter, which translates code into machine language one instruction at a time.

See Also

Compiled Language; Interpreted Language; Machine Language; Object Code; Programming Languages

Component

Component is a transmission method that separates video signals into three channels, either **RGB** or **YUV**. The cables usually use large bayonet type plugs and are not supported by standard digitizing boards.

See Also

8mm; Composite; RGB; S-Video; VHS

Component Video (YUV)

A QuickTime video compressor that produces high-quality (if slightly large) files during capture.

See Also

Video Digitizing

Composite Signal

Composite signal is a transmission method for video signals that combines separate elements of the video signal—color and brightness—as one signal. The image quality is poorer than other formats such as **S-Video**. Most digitizing boards (equipment used to turn analog video into a digital video sequence) support this format.

See Also

8mm; Component; S-Video; VHS

Compositing

The process of layering multiple images to create a final composite, or complete image. To layer the images, **matte** effects (creating an image through which a second image is visible) are needed. These can be defined in a number of ways; Adobe **After Effects** enables you to draw a matte shape, while Adobe **Photoshop** uses a separate image (called an alpha mask), which defines the transparency of the layer.

A simple way to layer an image on top of another is to cut out the unwanted areas of the top layer (this is the way layers are handled in Macromedia **Director**).

Blue screening, used frequently in video and film production, is a third way of combining two images. In Blue screen a single color, or range of colors in an image are defined as the transparent color, through which a background image is visible. Adobe **Premiere**, and Avid **VideoShop** both provide Blue screening effects.

See Also

After Effects; Blue Screening; Director; Photoshop; Premiere; VideoShop

Compressing Files

Compressing a file is a way of making it smaller in order to facilitate transporting that file, storing it, or transmitting it on the Internet. Smaller files take up less disk space and require less time to transfer on a network.

In general, compression works by finding a pattern in the file and by substituting shorthand for that pattern. For example,

AAAAAAAAAAAAAA

is much longer than

25 As

Compressed files commonly contain a tiny segment of code that enables the compressed file to unstuff itself, so that the user doesn't need to find and use the appropriate decompression software. Such files are usually signified by the extension ".sea," which stands for *self-expanding archive.*

The filename extensions *.SIT* and *.CPT* denote the most common compression schemes on the Macintosh. *.SIT* signifies a file created by Aladdin Systems' StuffIt family of software, including **StuffIt Expander**. *.CPT* signifies a file created by the shareware program CompactPro. Both programs are available via **FTP** at **ftp://ftp.utexas.edu/pub/mac/compression/**.

See Also

Decoding/Decompressing Files; Encoding Files; FTP; StuffIt Expander

Compression Artifacts

With **lossy** compressors, as the compression is increased, the quality of the resulting image decreases. At some point, compression artifacts become visible to the naked eye, often as a blockiness in the image, or color bleeding (particularly where there are sharp differences between colors). With a compressor such as **JPEG**, compression artifacts become visible as blocks of color, and as halo effects around sudden changes in contrast (for example, black text on a white background).

See Also

JPEG

Compression Utilities

Compression utilities enable you to compress the size of files using software compression. Reasons for compressing files are to save hard disk space and to reduce the size of files you want to send over a phone line via **modem**. If, for example, you're uploading a file 200K in size to an online service, it can take you several minutes to upload that file, depending on the speed of your modem. However, if you compress the file, you can lower the size of that file from 30 percent to as much as 90 percent, uploading in well under one minute and saving you time. This also saves time for anyone downloading the file.

There are a number of compression utilities, including **StuffIt Deluxe** (from Aladdin), **DiskDoubler** (from Symantec), and **CompactPro** (Shareware by Bill Goodman), that are popular third-party compression utilities. All three of these utilities offer the capability to create **self-extracting archive** (.sea) files that decompress even if you don't have the original software that compressed them. If you send a colleague a file via modem, for example, and you compress the file using StuffIt to reduce the file's size, your colleague needs StuffIt to decompress the file. By creating a self-extracting archive (.sea), the software necessary to unstuff the file is included with the file. This only adds 5K to the file and is completely transparent to the recipient of the file.

Also, most compression utilities enable you to split large files into pieces when you're compressing them and rejoin them when you decompress, or unstuff the files. Let's say, for example, you have a file that is 5MB, and after you compress it, the file is reduced to 2.1MB. That is still too large to fit on a standard 1.4MB disk. To make the file fit onto disks, you can have the compression software split the 2.1MB file into a 1.3MB file and a separate 800K file. This way, you can put the 1.3MB file on one disk and the 800K file on another. When you want to unstuff the files later, you put both files on your hard disk, double-click the files, and the application will rejoin the files back into one 2.1MB file and unstuff the files.

Another common feature of compression utilities is the capability to archive multiple files into one compressed file. This is very convenient for distributing multiple files, especially over a modem.

See Also

CompactPro; DiskDoubler; Modems; .sea Filename Extension; StuffIt

Compression Utilities

Utility	Developer	Purpose	Benefit
StuffIt Deluxe	Aladdin Systems	File Compression	Reduces size of files for backup, storage, or modem transfers. Offers drag and drop "stuffing" and "unstuffing" of files
AutoDoubler	Symantec	Automatic File Compression	Automatically compresses files that are not in use
DiskDoubler Pro	Symantec	File Compression	Reduces size of files for backup, storage, or modem transfers, adds pull-down menu to menu bar for instant access
CompactPro	Bill Goodman (Shareware)	File Compression	Reduces size of files for backup, storage, or modem transfers
StuffIt Lite	Aladdin (Shareware)	File Compression	Reduces size of files for backup, storage, or modem transfers

Compressor

Software routine that compresses a digital image (reduces the size). **QuickTime** uses compression on its digital movies. Compression reduces file size, so that it can be read from disk and played in real time. Compressors are actually two routines: the routine that compresses the image, and another routine that decompresses the image. Usually, both routines are included, although this is not always the case. For example, there is a decompressor available for Kodak's **PhotoCD** format, but Kodak only licenses the compression routine to photo labs that produce the PhotoCD discs.

Compressors are often called codecs (**codecs**, short for **co**mpression/**dec**ompression). QuickTime includes these compressors: **Animation**, **Cinepak**, **Graphics**, **JPEG**, **Component Video, None,** and **Apple Video**. These compressors are suited to different tasks because of the different techniques they use to compress a movie. Compression routines can be broken down into **lossy** and **lossless** (a lossy compressor creates a much smaller image, but the quality of the image may degrade compared to the original).

A compressor designed to compress sequences of images (a video sequence) uses additional techniques that a compressor designed for still images (such as JPEG) may not use. The primary technique that a motion compressor can take advantage of is that images in a sequence are usually very similar. By saving only the differences between the current frame and the previous frame (a technique called **temporal compression**) the amount of information that needs to be saved is reduced. Some frames should still be saved in their entirety (this is called **spatial compression**) so that the user can randomly access the movie.

Note that you do not have to use a temporal compressor to compress sequences, although it is advisable. A spatial compressor would cause poor playback performance. JPEG, for example, takes several seconds to compress a single image, so it is not appropriate unless you have special hardware that performs the compression (and in fact, just to confuse the issue, some hardware compression equipment such as the Radius **VideoVision Studio** card, uses JPEG as the compressor).

Compressors are often described as being **Symmetrical** and **Asymmetrical**. A Symmetrical compressor takes approximately as much time to compress and frame as it does to decompress a file. (You can think of compression and decompression as being the equivalent of recording and playback for digital movies.) Symmetrical compressors are used for recording and rough editing of video clips. An Asymmetrical compressor takes much longer to compress than to play back, but the movies are usually much smaller than the movies created by a symmetrical compressor. This makes asymmetrical compressors ideal for distribution.

Some companies sell third-party codecs; however, if you use one of these, make sure that you can distribute a decompressor routine with the movie, so that the person to whom you send the movie can view it.

See Also

Apple Video; Asymmetrical Compressors; Component Video; Graphics; JPEG; QuickTime; Spatial Compression; Symmetrical Compressors

CompuServe

The oldest and one of the largest **commercial online services,** offering more than 2,000 discussion groups, news, travel, chat, and mail services.

CompuServe, like **America Online, Prodigy**, and the other commercial services, requires a monthly fee for membership. While many of its areas can be freely accessed by members, others require extra fees by the hour or by the minute.

In return, members get a number of benefits, including:

- CompuServe Mail: **email** to other CompuServe members or, through gateways, to members of other online services or other parts of the **Internet**.

- News and reference materials online, including the Reuters and Associated Press news wires, Ziff-Davis magazine databases, a news clipping services, stock reports.

- Travel and shopping services.

- More than 900 discussion groups called SIGs (Special Interest Groups).

- Games and entertainment.

Some of the categories listed previously fall into the "Extended Services" or "Premium Services" areas of CompuServe and carry extra charges beyond the monthly membership fee.

You can connect to CompuServe by using one of two graphical applications sold by CompuServe, Navigator or CompuServe Information Manager (CIM). The latter comes in a Macintosh version called MacCIM that is included with the book *Get on CompuServe in 5 Minutes* (Hayden, 1994).

When you first launch MacCIM you will be assigned an ID number and asked to specify a password and a credit card that CompuServe will bill for your connection time. You will also have to fill in personal data and be asked to choose mail and promotional choices.

In another screen, you will also be asked to specify a communications port. In almost all cases, the default "modem port" will work. If your phone has Call Waiting, you will need to temporarily disable it each time you connect to CompuServe by prefixing the CompuServe number with "1170."

CompuServe requires an addressing scheme in which you must prefix **>INTERNET:** to the beginning of any Internet address you use with email. Sending email from the Internet to a CompuServe member is simple as long as you realize that all CompuServe addresses are pairs of numbers such as **766.864@compuserve.com**.

Such addresses can be hard to remember and are best stored in an **address book.** (Email accounts that use recognizable names are also available as an option.)

In addition to providing a wider library of information than the other online services, CompuServe also features much more complete online messaging. Features such as 'threading' of message topics and searching for messages by sender, recipient, and topic are not available or available in a limited fashion on the other services. Therefore, when quickly looking for discussions on a particular topic, CompuServe can be a valuable resource.

Currently CompuServe is still somewhat more expensive than the other online services, but in recent months its rates have dropped dramatically so that the difference is now much less significant.

Warning: Unlike many of the other online services, CompuServe features a large number of additional databases which charge fees over and above the standard CompuServe connect charges. Be careful to look for the notices mentioning additional charges when entering new areas as some of these databases, such as the Dun & Bradstreet business reporting databases, can charge nearly $100 for a single report!

Because CompuServe was originally designed to be used by **dumb terminal** programs, it is one of the few online services to provide access from any computer without custom client software. While this terminal access is of interest from a historical perspective and in a few types of uses, Macintosh-based software is recommended to make CompuServe practical for daily use. Currently two packages are available to give CompuServe the look and feel of the Macintosh: CompuServe Information Manager and CompuServe Navigator.

- CompuServe Information Manager is the standard CompuServe package, and is relatively easy to use. This package provides a standard Mac interface to make your use of CompuServe similar to moving around the **desktop**.

■ CompuServe Navigator is designed for the more advanced user. It works using a script-style session rather than the interactive method used with CompuServe Information Manager and with other online services. To use Navigator, you set up batches of actions such as which areas you'd like to read messages in, messages you'd like to post, files you wish to download or upload, and files you wish to search for. After accepting this programming, Navigator runs an entire session unattended, then disconnects, and enables you to browse through the results while the service is off-line.

When CompuServe had higher per-minute charges and charged higher rates for faster speeds (they used to charge a premium for the 1200Bps "high speed service"), Navigator was a good method of cutting down on online bills. However, now that CompuServe has dropped its access rates, and adopted the industry standard of not charging additional fees for faster access speeds, Navigator is of limited usefulness and has become much less popular, although it does enable you to download a large number of new messages or summaries of new messages without intervention.

Although its vast library of online resources can be quite compelling, CompuServe remains more difficult to use than its primary rival, **America Online**. Therefore, for an introduction to the online world, America Online remains a better value. However, once users have gained some online skills, CompuServe may be the more satisfying service for the long term business user.

In early 1996, CompuServe announced a new service called WOW! which is aimed toward at-home computer users. WOW! provides email accounts for up to six family members, and a variety of payment options including $17.95 per month unlimited access to the Internet.

See Also

America Online; AppleLink; Commercial Online Services; Delphi; Email; eWorld; Internet; Prodigy

Computer Games, *See Entertainment*

Computer Literature, *See Hypertext Fiction*

Computer to Plate, *See Printing*

Condensed, *See Typesetting Terms*

Conflict Catcher

Conflict Catcher is a third-party commercial utility from Casady & Greene (22734 Portola Drive, Salinas, CA 93908-1119. Phone: 800-359-4920. On the Web **http://www.casadyg.com**) designed to prevent conflicts between your extensions in the **System Folder**. The key to Conflict Catcher is its capability to enable you to control how and when **extensions** and **control panels** load into your system at **startup** and how they interact with one another. Conflict Catcher also enables you to isolate groups of extensions and control panels without removing them from the system folder, which helps you track down conflicts.

If you're having a system problem, Conflict Catcher enables you to run a conflict test on your system, whereby it disables half of the extensions in your system and **restarts** the computer. If all goes well, Conflict Catcher asks you to repeat the cycle, and it loads the other half of the extensions. Conflict Catcher repeats this procedure again and again, each time using a smaller set of extensions until it isolates the culprit or culprits. If the problem is the loading sequence,

Conflict Catcher rearranges the order in which extensions are loaded to help resolve any possible conflicts. If the problem is a damaged resource, it disables the extension.

You can also reorder **startup** items by holding down the spacebar on your keyboard during startup, which makes Conflict Catcher load before any other extensions. This brings up the Conflict Catcher control panel enabling you to decide which extensions should load and in what order. You can create custom sets of extensions that will load at startup for individual users. You can also create sets of extensions that you want to have load at startup for use with a particular application.

There are other programs that enable you to manage which items are loaded at startup including Extensions Manager, which is now part of System 7.5 and higher, and Now Startup Manager (Now Software, 921 SW Washington Street, Suite 500, Portland, OR 97205-2823, Phone: 503-274-2800, Web site at **http://www.nowsoft.com**), which is a commercial extensions manager and is part of the Now Utilities package from Now Software, Inc.

See Also
Control Panel; Extensions; Restart; Startup; System; System Folder

Connecting to the Internet, *See Internet*

Constant

A constant is a special kind of programming **variable** that never changes over the course of a program's execution. It is a variable that doesn't vary. A constant always represents a single value.

Constants are useful in situations where a literal value is normally used. It is often more revealing to use a constant that has an informative name than to use the number itself. The value "42" in a program's source code, for example, has very little meaning, but if it were replaced by a constant called "kMeaningOfLife" that had the same value, its meaning would be obvious.

Constants are also helpful when a value needs to be changed by the programmer in many places throughout the program's code. If literal values were used, it would be difficult to find all occurrences and change them. On the other hand, if a constant is used, the programmer need only change the value of the constant and that change will make its way throughout the program.

See Also
Programming; Variable

Constructing Efficient Files, DTP

Desktop publishing may have made print production a lot more flexible, but there's still a right way to do some things. Following these guidelines will help you avoid problems when it comes time to print your documents or take them to a service bureau.

- Talk to your printer ahead of time about the requirements for your project—decisions you'll make as you create the project depend on this information. For example, **scanning** resolution depends on line screen, and that depends on your paper choice.

- Keep **bitmapped graphics** at the lowest possible resolution. The higher the resolution, the bigger the file and the better the chance that it or your page layout document will become corrupted or cause printing problems. For photos, never use a resolution of more than twice the line screen. If the image contains type, however, it needs a higher resolution than it would without the type to keep the letters clean.

- Blends created in **draw programs** will output better, with less "banding," than those created in page layout packages. Also, the greater the change in color value and the smaller the length of the blend, the better it will look. Blends that fade to white can be difficult for printers to work with.

C

- Illustrator blends created with custom colors are converted to **process colors**. The only way to make sure this doesn't happen is to create several blends, each of one color shading down to no color, and layer them. Make sure each object in the set is set to overprint.

- Don't "nest" **EPS** files by importing one into another. Copy and paste elements from one file to another, if necessary.

- Grouping elements in a draw application creates more complex **PostScript**. Group while you're working, but when the graphic's done ungroup.

- Keep vector-based paths as simple as possible—watch out for ones created by autotrace applications or from magic wand selections. Overly complex paths can cause the "limitcheck" PostScript error.

- Don't knock out delicate type from black or a dark color. Fine lines will fill in on press.

- Make sure the names of **spot colors** (such as **Pantone**) used in graphics files are the same as the ones named in your page layout files—otherwise, when you have color separations output you'll get separate plates for the two different spellings.

- Make the page size equal to the trim size of your document unless there's a really pressing reason not to. Any document that's going to be electronically imposed *must* be the correct trim size, and the margins must be the same on all master pages.

- You can proof **trapping** by setting the trap amount to a large value like 20 points and printing separations on a laser printer (on transparencies if you wish). Line everything up and make sure that there are traps where they should be and none where you don't want them.

- Don't scale or rotate imported graphics. Or, rather, go ahead and do it, but then go back to your image editor, scale and rotate them there, then reimport them into the page layout file.

- Don't install both **TrueType** and **PostScript** versions of the same font, and make sure you know which one you used on each document. Be aware that TrueType fonts take longer to output.

- Use the actual fonts for bold, italic, and other typeface variations.

See Also

Bitmapped Graphics; Draw Programs; EPS; Pantone Matching System; PostScript; Process Color; Scanning; Spot Color; Trapping; TrueType

Constructor

Constructor is an **interface builder** for programs developed using Metrowerks' C++ **PowerPlant** framework.

Constructor is a part of the Metrowerks **CodeWarrior** suite of development tools. It enables programmers to create and edit windows, views, text styles, and menus for use in PowerPlant programs (see following figure).

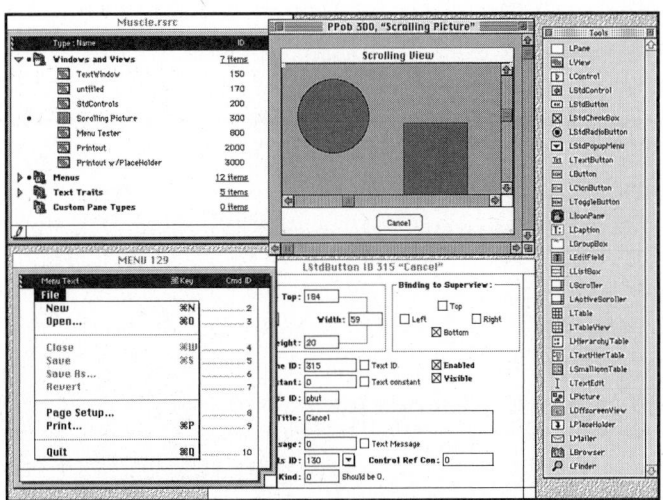

Constructor uses drag-and-drop to enable you to add controls, text, pictures, and other panes to your windows by dragging these items from the tool palette into the window you're editing. Double-clicking an item brings up its properties in a separate window. (In the figure, the properties window for the Cancel button is the partially obscured window in the lower right.)

Although Constructor gives you complete control over the visual appearance of a program's windows and dialogs, it does not automatically generate code to handle the visual aspect of a program. Fortunately, PowerPlant takes care of all of the basics for you, so you only need to add your own application-specific code.

See Also
CodeWarrior; Interface Builder; PowerPlant

Consultative Committee for International Telegraph and Telephone, *See Modem Standards and Speeds*

Consumer Models, Macintosh Family

Apple was one of the first computer manufacturers to develop a marketing strategy for the home market—the pre-packaged computer system. Apple calls these Macintoshes *Performas*. They are pure Macs packaged with bundled software, displays, faxes, modems, CD-ROM players, along with the standard memory and storage configurations found in their desktop cousins, and often auxiliary peripherals such as TV tuners and video-in cards and stereo speakers.

Performas were designed to be sold by sales personnel with little Macintosh savvy through the giant supermarket computer outlet centers, department stores, and non-traditional Apple vendors, such as office-product outlets such as Staples or Office Depot or buying clubs such as Costco/Price Club or Sam's Club.

So far, Apple has packaged only the desktop models into Performas. The individual retail outlet specifies what types of configurations and software bundles they want to market and sells only those Performa models. This is why the consumer Macs often appear confusing, they come in many flavors, one for each type of user and vendor. The following figure shows the Performa 200.

The following list describes the different types of Performas and their members:

- **Series 5xx.** The Performa 580 is the last remnant of this model that is based upon the **LC 575**. The Performa 580 is meant as a home office or college computer and comes bundled with basic business software and a variety of productivity, educational, entertainment, graphics, and utility software. The Performa 580 also includes a double-speed, tray-loading CD-ROM drive and several CD-ROM titles, including games, home and educational reference materials, and demo programs. The Performa 580 is based upon the 33 MHz 68LC040 processor.

- **Series 6xx**. The Performa 630 with and without CD, 630 DOS Compatible, 631 CD, 640 CD DOS Compatible, and 636 CD are members of this series. The 6xx series is the same as the **Quadra/Centris and LC 630** Macintosh. These computers are configured with components useful for home offices or student use. Each computer is configured slightly differently, containing different sizes of memory and hard drives. But each of these computers comes bundled with Global Village TelePort Fax (either Send or Send/Receive depending upon the model), and Apple's PC Exchange, along with various educational, business, reference, and game software; as well as clip art and fonts. If the Performa 63x comes with a CD-ROM drive, it includes several educational, reference, business, and game CD-ROM titles, along with demos of other software. The Performa 63x series also uses the 33 MHz 68LC040 processor.

- **Series 52xx**. This is a PowerPC-based Performa. It has a unique design that harkens back to the original all-in-one "Mac 128, 512K, and Plus/SE chassis," where the computer, hard disk, CD-ROM drive, and display are integrated into a single unit. It is based upon the **5200 LC** and is represented in the Performa series by the Performa 5215 CD. The 5215 includes a quadruple-speed, tray-loading CD-ROM drive and comes bundled with educational, business, games, and reference software titles and CD-ROM titles, clip art, and fonts. The Performa 52xx series uses the PowerPC 603 processor that performs at 75 MHz. In addition, the 5215CD comes with an internal 14.4K baud fax modem with full-duplex speakerphone and digital answering machine that lets you use your computer as a voice mail system and speakerphone.

- **Series 61xx.** This series introduced the PowerPC Performa line of Macintoshes and is based upon the first-generation 601 60 MHz PowerPC chip. The Performa 6116CD is the current offering in this series and is based upon the **Power Mac 6100**. These computers are configured with components useful for home offices or student use. Each of these

computers comes bundled with personal time management, reference, financial, and graphics software and CD-ROM titles, as well as clip art, fonts, and games, Global Village TelePort Fax (either Send or Send/Receive depending upon the model), At Ease, eWorld, and Apple's PC Exchange. If the Performa 63x comes with a CD-ROM drive, it includes several CD-ROM titles as well.

- **Series 62xx**. The 62xx series is a part of Apple's second-generation Power Mac line based on the 603 PowerPC processor. The 62xx Performa is a new desktop design similar to the 5300LC in performance, but built in a modular chassis rather than the 5300's all-in-one case. They use either a 75 MHz or 100 MHz 603 PowerPC processor, depending on the model. The 62xx series comes in many flavors, including the 6200 CD, 6205 CD, 6216 CD, 6218 CD, 6220 CD, 6230 CD, and 6290 CD configurations, each designed for a different market niche and sales outlet. The 62xx series of Performas include a quadruple-speed, tray-loading CD-ROM drive and comes bundled with graphics, business, educational, and reference software and CD-ROMS, as well as clip art and fonts.

- **Series 63xx.** The 63xx series is a part of Apple's second-generation Power Mac line based on the 603e PowerPC processor. The 63xx Performas are based on the same design as the 5300LC. They use a100 MHz 603e PowerPC processor. The 63xx series is currently represented by one model: the Performa 6300CD. The 63xx series of Performas include a quadruple-speed, tray-loading CD-ROM drive and comes bundled with family and home office CD and software for graphics, reference, financial, games, and assorted other educational uses, such as cooking and medical references.

A Caveat about Software Bundling

The applications included with the Performa series change constantly, depending upon what the sales outlet vendor wants to include, and what Apple decides to bundle. Thus, those software and CD-ROM categories mentioned are approximations based upon Apple's August 1995 product list. The actual bundles may be slightly different. You should also realize that the programs included with Performas sometimes are older versions, such as ClarisWorks 2.1 or Quicken 4, that must be upgraded to their current versions; or hobbled versions that provide a taste of a product which then must be upgraded to take advantage of its

full power, such as some of the games or Mangia (a recipe manager program). Another example of out-of-date inclusions is that you may receive a copy of eWorld with your Performa although Apple has announced the death of its online service as of Spring 1996. eWorld subscribers are being sent America Online memberships in lieu of eWorld.

Remember Robert Heinlein's motto "TANSTAAFL" translated as "There Ain't No Such Thing As A Free Lunch!"

The following table provides an overview of the Performa Family of Macintoshes.

The Performa Family

Series Number	Model Numbers	Processor	Memory/ Storage	Other Components
5xx Series	580	33 MHz 68LC040	5 or 8MB/250 or 500MB IDE hard disk drive, 300i + CD-ROM drive	1MB VRAM, integrated 14" color display, ADB port, 2 serial ports, 1 SCSI port, 1 LC Slot, 1 Video-In slot, 8-bit stereo sound in/16-bit stereo sound out, external fax/ modem
63x Series	630	33 MHz 68LC040	4MB/250MB	1MB VRAM, Apple Performa Plus 14" Display, Global Village TelePort Bronze 9600/2400 baud fax/send modem, ADB port, 2 serial ports, 1 SCSI port, 1 LC Slot, 1 Video-In slot, 8-bit stereo sound in/16-bit stereo sound out
	630 CD	33 MHz 68LC040	8MB/250MB, 300i+ CD-ROM drive	1MB VRAM, Apple Performa 14" Plus Display, Global Village TelePort Bronze 9600/2400 baud fax/send modem, ADB port, 2 serial ports, 1 SCSI port, 1 LC Slot, 1 Video-In slot, 8-bit stereo sound in/16-bit stereo sound out
	630 DOS Compatible	33 MHz 68LC040, 66 MHz 486DX2 DOS processor	8MB/250MB	512K VRAM, RGB 15" Display, ADB port, 2 serial ports, 1 SCSI port, 1 LC Slot, 1 Video-In slot, 8-bit stereo sound in/16-bit stereo sound out, PC game port, Sound Blaster

C

Series Number	Model Numbers	Processor	Memory/ Storage	Other Components
	631 CD	33 MHz 68LC040	8MB/500MB, 300i+ CD-ROM drive	1MB VRAM, RGB 14" Display, Global Village TelePort Gold II 14.4K baud fax/send and receive modem, ADB port, 2 serial ports, 1 SCSI port, 1 LC Slot, 1 Video-In slot, 8-bit stereo sound in/16-bit stereo sound out
	636 CD	33 MHz 68LC040 but PowerPC upgrade ready	8MB/500MB, 300i+ CD-ROM drive	1MB DRAM, monitor *not* included, ADB port, 2 serial ports, 1 SCSI port, 1 LC Slot, 1 Video-In slot, 8-bit stereo sound in/16-bit stereo sound out
	640 CD DOS Compatible	33 MHz 68LC040, 66 MHz 486DX2 DOS processor	8MB/500MB, 300i+ CD-ROM drive	1MB VRAM, RGB 15" Display, fax/send and receive modem, ADB port, 2 serial ports, 1 SCSI port, 1 LC Slot, 1 Video-In slot, 8-bit stereo sound in/16-bit stereo sound out
52xx Series	5215 CD	75 MHz 603 PowerPC, 16K internal cache, 256K level-2 cache	8MB/1G, 600i+ CD-ROM drive	1MB DRAM, RGB multiscan 15" color display, Global Village TelePort Gold IIv 14.4K baud fax/voice/modem, ADB port, 2 serial ports, 1 SCSI port, 1 LC Slot, 1 Video-In slot, 8-bit stereo sound in/16-bit stereo sound out
61xx Series	6116 CD	60 MHz 601 PowerPC , 32K cache	8MB/700MB, 600i+ CD-ROM drive	RGB 14" multiscan color display, TelePort Gold II Performa 14.4K baud fax/modem, ADB port, AAUI-15 EtherNet connector, 1 NuBus slot, 1 serial ports, 1 Video-In slot, 8-bit stereo sound in/16-bit stereo sound out
62xx Series	6200 CD	75 MHz 603 RISC w/ FPU, 16K internal cache, 256K level-2 cache	8MB/1G, 600i+ CD-ROM drive	1MB DRAM, RGB multiscan 15" color display, 14.4K baud fax/modem, ADB port, 2 serial ports, 1 SCSI port, 1 LC Slot, 1Video-In slot, 8-bit stereo sound in/16-bit stereo sound out

continues

The Performa Family (continued)

Series Number	Model Numbers	Processor	Memory/ Storage	Other Components
	6205 CD	75 MHz 603 RISC w/ FPU, 16K internal cache, 256K level-2 cache	8MB/1G, 600i+ CD-ROM drive	1MB DRAM, RGB multiscan 15" color display, 28.8K baud fax modem, ADB port, 2 serial ports, 1 SCSI port, 1 LC Slot, 1 Video-In slot, 8-bit stereo sound in/16-bit stereo sound out
	6216 CD	75 MHz 603 RISC w/ FPU, 16K internal cache, 256K level-2 cache	8MB/1G, 600i+ CD-ROM drive	1MB DRAM, RGB multiscan 15" color display, 14.4K baud fax/voice modem, ADB port, 2 serial ports, 1 SCSI port, 1 LC Slot, 1 Video-In slot, 8-bit stereo sound in/16-bit stereo sound out
	6218 CD	75 MHz 603 RISC w/ FPU, 16K internal cache, 256K level-2 cache	8MB/1G, 600i+ CD-ROM drive	1MB DRAM, RGB multiscan 15" color display, 14.4K baud fax/voice modem, ADB port, 2 serial ports, 1 SCSI port, 1 LC Slot, 1 Video-In slot, 8-bit stereo sound in/16-bit stereo sound out
	6220 CD	75 MHz 603 RISC w/ FPU, 16K internal cache, 256K level-2 cache	16MB/1.4G, 600i+ CD-ROM drive	1MB DRAM, monitor **not** included, 14.4K baud fax/voice modem, ADB port, 2 serial ports, 1 SCSI port, 1 LC Slot, TV Tuner included, 1 Video-In slot, 8-bit stereo sound in/16-bit stereo sound out
	6230 CD	75 MHz 603 RISC w/ FPU, 16K internal cache, 256K level-2 cache	8MB/1G, 600i+ CD-ROM drive	1MB DRAM, RGB multiscan 15" color display, 14.4K baud fax/voice modem, ADB port, 2 serial ports, 1 SCSI port, 1 LC Slot, TV Tuner included, MPEG Media System
	6290 CD	100 MHz 603e RISC w/ FPU, 32K internal cache, 256K level-2 cache	8MB/1.2G, 600i+ CD-ROM drive	1MB DRAM, RGB multiscan 15" color display, 28.8K baud fax/voice modem, ADB port, 2 serial ports, 1 SCSI port, 1 NuBus Slot, EtherNet port, 1 Video-In slot, 8-bit stereo sound in/16-bit stereo sound out

Series Number	Model Numbers	Processor	Memory/ Storage	Other Components
63xx Series	6300 CD	100 MHz 603e RISC w/ FPU, 32K internal cache, 256K level-2 cache	16MB/1.2G, 600i+ CD-ROM drive	1MB DRAM, RGB multiscan 15" color display, 28.8K baud fax/voice modem, ADB port, 2 serial ports, 1 SCSI port, 1 LC Slot, EtherNet port, 1 Video-In slot, 8-bit stereo sound in/16-bit stereo sound out

See Also
CD-ROM Drives; Education Models, Macintosh Family; PowerMac; PowerPC Platform

Continuous Tone
In graphics and desktop publishing, continuous tone art refers to photographs or other illustrations having a range of shades of gray or color.

See Also
Prepress; Printing

Contrast, *See Image Manipulation for Printing*

Control Key
This is a **modifier key** used with other keys to create keyboard shortcuts for **menu** commands and **mouse** actions. Although the Control key can be used by applications for keyboard shortcuts, most Macintosh applications do not have pre-set keystrokes utilizing the Control key.

A common Control key keystroke is ⌘-Control-Power Key to restart your Mac.

See Also
Command Key; Menu; Mouse

Control Panels
A convenient way to access your control panels is to place an **alias** of the Control Panels folder in the **Apple** menu. This way you can access the Control Panels folder directly from your Apple menu, without having to search through your **System Folder.** Also, if you have the **submenus** feature of **System 7.5** turned on, you get the additional benefit of being able to go directly to the control panel of your choice from the Apple menu without having to open the Control Panels folder at all. Starting with **System 7.1,** an alias of the Control Panels folder already appears in the Apple menu when the system is installed.

If you are running 7.0 or 7.01, follow these steps to add the Control Panels folder to the Apple menu:

1. Choose the Control Panels submenu on the Apple menu (or in the System Folder). Select the Control Panels folder and choose Make Alias from the File menu. This will create an alias of the Control Panels folder.

2. Place this alias in the Apple Menu Items folder in your System Folder.

3. The Control Panels folder will now appear as an item under your Apple menu.

See Also
Alias; Apple Menu; Apple Menu Items Control Panel; Submenu; System 7.1; System 7.5; System Folder

Control Panels Folder
This is a folder in your **System Folder** that enables you to customize certain aspects of your system. This folder is automatically installed when a Macintosh system is installed. (And an alias of the Control Panels folder is installed in the Apple menu in System

7.1 and higher.) Within this folder are the controls for setting your computer's **time and date** functions, **color** controls, **sound** levels, and a wide range of preferences for the Finder. You can also find many third-party control panel devices that enable further customization of your Mac's system.

See Also

Color Control Panel; Control Panels; System Folder

Control Strip

This utility, originally introduced for PowerBooks, but now part of **System 7.5.2**, is a collapsible floating palette that enables you to have one-click access to a variety of commonly used items through a series of pop-up menus.

On PowerBook models, the control strip also displays the PowerBook's battery status using a bar graph showing the estimated time left on the battery's charge. PowerBook users can access a wide range of controls from this floating palette including: your system's sound volume; the **spin-down** feature of your PowerBook to save battery life; a **file-sharing** switch to enable or disable file sharing across a network; an **AppleTalk** on/off switch (AppleTalk uses considerable battery power); an instant **sleep** feature; and a **video mirroring** switch.

For desktop users, you can configure the Control Strip to add a variety of options, such as screen depth or sound volume, from the Control Strip Control Panel. To add an item to the Control Strip, you must add a control strip module to the control strip modules folder, in the System Folder. (Shareware and freeware control strip modules are available from online services and the Internet.)

To extend the control strip, click the tab on the left and it will extend to its full length. To hide the control strip, leaving just the tab visible, click the tab again or the close box at the other end of the control strip. If you have more items on the control strip than can be displayed at its current size, click the arrows at the end of the strip to scroll through items.

To move items that are in the control strip, hold the Option key while dragging the item to its new location.

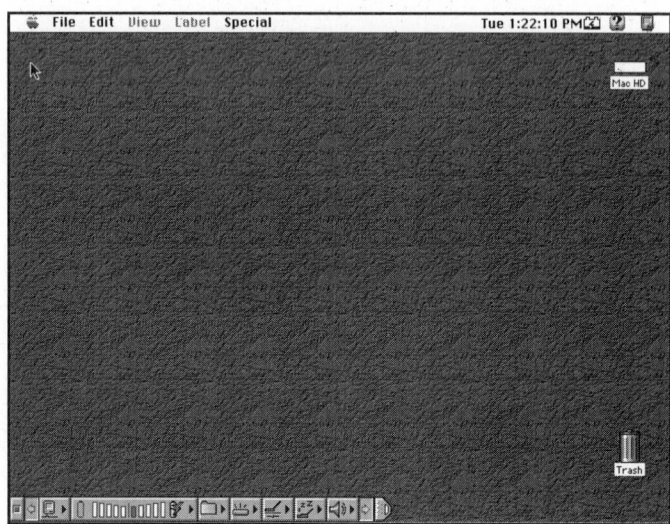

See Also

AppleTalk; File Sharing; PowerBook

Control Strip Control Panel

This **control panel** enables you to control the Control Strip feature on **PowerBook** computers or desktop Macs running **System 7.5.2** or higher.

The default for this panel is Show Control Strip, so if you don't want the floating Control Strip to appear on your Mac, simply click the button marked Hide Control Strip. You can also assign a hot key to show/hide the Control Strip.

To use the Control Strip Control Panel, follow these steps:

1. Choose the Control Strip Control Panel from the Control Panels submenu in the Apple menu (or System Folder).

2. Click show Control strip to have the floating palette display on your Mac screen, or click Hide to keep the palette hidden.

See Also

Control Panel; PowerBook; System 7.5

Control Strip Modules Folder

This enables **System 7.5 PowerBook** users to customize the features in the floating **Control Strip** palette. To remove a feature from the Control Strip, remove its module from the Control Strip Modules folder. To add a new feature, place that feature's module in the Control Strip Modules folder and **restart.**

See Also

Control Strip; PowerBook; System 7.5

Control Strip Shortcuts

There are a few shortcuts that make working with the **Control Strip** even easier than it already is. If you want to change the location of the Control Strip, hold the Option key while dragging the tab at the end of the Control Strip and relocate it to the location of your choice. To adjust the length of the Control Strip at any time, drag the tab to the desired size.

You can shrink the Control Strip down to just its tab by clicking the tab. To expand it, click the tab again. If you do not want the Control Strip visible at all, turn it off by clicking "Hide Control Strip" in the Control Strip **Control Panel**.

See Also

Control Panels; Control Strip

Controversial Themes in Games, *See Violence in Games*

Convergence, *See Monitors, Image Quality*

Converting and Translating Files

The Macintosh has the capability to read, write, and translate files from the PC platform (DOS/Windows). This capability is built in to **System 7.5** through a system extension called **PC Exchange** that enables conversion, translation, and even the capability to format PC disks. The Macintosh has the capability to read PC disks in both System 6 and 7 through third-party utilities and through Apple's own translation utility. Before PC Exchange became a part of the operating system, Apple offered a free file conversion and translation utility called **Apple File Exchange**, which enables you to mount, read, and write DOS-formatted disks. There are also third-party programs, such as **MacLinkPlus** from DataViz (55 Corporate Drive, Trumbull, CT 06611, Phone: (800) 733-0030. On the Web at **http://www.dataviz.com**) that not only translates PC documents but helps match these translated documents with Macintosh applications that can access these documents—even if the application that created the document on the PC doesn't exist on the Macintosh. MacLinkPlus also excels at translating files such as spreadsheets, databases, and graphics files, and holds formatting (such as bold and italic) as well as advanced formatting (such as tables, charts, and graphs).

See Also

Apple File Exchange; System 6; System 7; System 7.5

Cookie, *See Magic Cookie*

C

Cooperative Multitasking, *See Multitasking*

Copland, *See System 8*

Coprocessors, Types

Coprocessors are specialized processors that perform jobs, such as graphics calculations for rendering complex forms, data transfer operations, audio-visual processing, and complex mathematical calculations that the CPU can off-load. Coprocessors increase the throughput performance of the CPU by freeing up cycles for the CPU's main task—supervising the overall operations of the computer's components. The Macintosh has used four types of coprocessors over its history: math coprocessors, specialized coprocessors, graphics coprocessors, and digital signal processors.

Coprocessors, Math The introduction of a specialized chip, the 68881 math coprocessor (later succeeded by the more efficient 68882) with the 68020 and 68030 processors let these processors off-load instructions pertaining to the calculation and storage of floating-point values (number with decimal portions). Math coprocessors are also called **floating-point processors** because of their role in computing. The floating-point coprocessor-equipped Macs performed up to 200 times faster than those lacking this extra chip. The Macintosh II with its 68020 processor used the Motorola 68881 math coprocessor. Later versions of the Macintosh II family, such as the IIci, IIcx, IIfx, and so forth, that used the 68030 chip could use the more advanced 68882 math coprocessor that performed two to four times faster than the 68881. Both chips can store and process information in 10-byte chunks, accurately calculating values with up to 18 digits after the decimal point. 680x0 Macs not equipped with the coprocessor can only handle 14 digits after the decimal point. The coprocessors also contain built-in constants (values that do not change, such as the value of π) as well as transcendental and non-transcendental functions for performing trigonometric and logarithmic calculations. Because these functions and constants are hard-wired into the

coprocessor's firmware, their use does not take up precious memory and CPU cycles to recall them when they are needed.

The 68040 processor included a portion of the functions and constants of the 68882 chip built-in to its circuitry, and so could perform some of the calculations of the math coprocessor by itself. Performance was increased by the inclusion of a separate math coprocessor to perform those functions not handled by the CPU.

One of the innovations of the PowerPC processors was the inclusion of a **Floating Point Unit (FPU)** supported by pipelining and superscalar execution capabilities. The PPC 601 supports up to three instruction dispatches during a single clock cycle. This three-way pipelining easily handles integer calculations (the predominant type of instructions processed in general computing). Applications that require sophisticated graphics rendering or use a wide range of floating-point values, have these calculations off-loaded to the FPU by the CPU. Many Mac applications have now been optimized to take advantage of the presence of the FPU on the PPC chip.

The FPU supports floating-point operations on both single-precision and double-precision values (meeting the IEEE-754 floating-point standard). The IEEE standard specifies the format for single-precision, 32-bit, floating-point values and double-precision, 64-bit, floating-point values. All IEEE-754 data types are included in the 601 instruction set. This hardware support also supports the Mac operating system's SANE (Standard Apple Numeric Environment) math routines. The FPU includes 32 registers, each 64 bits in length, for performing floating-point operations. The chip can handle six pipeline stages: fetch, dispatch, decode, execute 1, execute 2, and write back, each stage taking a clock cycle; with one instruction in each stage concurrently, like peas in a pod. The FPU can also search the bottom half of the CPU's instruction queue and execute floating-point instructions that do not depend on the results of other instructions in the queue, increasing the performance of the CPU. The PPC 604 chip builds on the design

C

of the PPC 601. It contains a FPU, and *three* integer units versus the single integer unit of the 601. This design enables the PPC 604 to calculate two single-cycle integer instructions and one multiple-cycle instruction simultaneously—enabling the PPC 604 to outperform all Intel Pentium chips in both integer and floating-point performance.

Coprocessors, Specialized The Mac IIfx, Quadra AV models (660AV and 840AV), and Power Macs use several specialized coprocessors to assist in transferring data to and from the computer's modem, printer, and SCSI ports. In Power Macs, the logic board contains the Apple Memory-Mapped I/O Controller (AMIC), a Fast SCSI Driver, Ariel II, AWAC, and Curio processors to handle modem, printer, and SCSI I/O. The High-Speed Memory Controller supports data transfers between the CPU and RAM.

Coprocessors, Graphics Graphics coprocessors assist in the calculations required to render and display high-end color graphics on-screen. The American Micro Device's AMD29000 chip is included in high-speed graphics display cards. The graphics accelerator card is one type of expansion card you can add to a NuBus or PCI slot on your Power Mac.

Coprocessors, Digital Signal Processor (DSP) These chips, such as the Motorola 56001, are included in the digital audio expansion cards, such as Digidesign's Audiomedia II card, used to enhance the performance of image-editing programs such as Adobe Photoshop. Because AV cards are inserted into Processor Direct Slots (PDS), they can only be used in the NuBus-based Power Macs (the 6100, 7100, and 8100) as well as the Performa Power Macs (52xx, 62xx, and 63xx series). PCI-based Macs do not have PDS expansion capabilities, so there is currently no place to plug in the PDS-based cards. High-performance PCI AV cards should be available in late 1996. In the meantime, the Power Mac 8500 and 9500 come equipped with built in video-in and video-out and a high-speed bus architecture (essentially all of the capabilities of the AV card built into the logic board).

The Quadra AV Macs (the 660AV and 840AV) include **AT&T's 3210 DSP** chip to drive the high-speed GeoPort connector used in telephony and telecommunications. The AT&T 3210 runs its own system software (Apple Real-Time Architecture (ARTA)) that independently performs signal processing, freeing up the CPU to perform other tasks.

See Also
Power Macs, PCI Bus; Power Mac; Processors; PowerPC

Copy Command

The Copy command (⌘-C) copies the selected item into the Mac's **Clipboard.** Unlike the **Cut** command, the Copy command does not delete the selected item, it just stores a copy in the Clipboard. You can paste your copy into another location at any time by selecting **Paste** (⌘-V) from the **Edit menu**.

To copy a text item, follow these steps:

1. Select the item you want to copy.
2. Select Copy from the Edit menu or use ⌘-C.
3. Normally, the Copy command is followed by the Paste command (⌘-V), found on the Edit menu, which enables you to paste the information into another location within your document or another document.

See Also
Clipboard; Cut; Edit Menu; Paste

Copy (Keyboard Shortcut)

To **Copy** an item onto the **Clipboard**, press ⌘-C. You can paste this item as long as it remains on the Clipboard.

To copy an item, follow these steps:

1. Select an item or highlight text you want to copy.
2. Press ⌘-C to copy the item to the Clipboard.

See Also
Clipboard; Copy; Keyboard Shortcuts; Paste

Copy Protection

Making a copy of a commercial software product, other than for your own use as a backup copy, violates federal copyright law. But that doesn't stop some people from copying an application's disks and giving, or selling, the application to others. Because of this illegal practice, some software companies, including a large percentage of game manufacturers, build in a copy protection scheme to make illegally copying a disk either impossible or impractical. A popular form of copy protection appears in Macintosh-based games. When you launch the game, a dialog box appears asking you to enter a particular word from a particular page in the game's instruction manual. It might say, for example, "Please enter the 4th word in the 23rd line of page 115." If you own an illegal copy of the game, you probably don't have an instruction manual, and if you don't enter the correct word, the program will not start. This works well because even though disks are easy to copy, 100-page instruction manuals are not. Whenever you try to launch the game, an internal database of words and pages is accessed, so a different password from a different page is requested each time.

Some game manufacturers gave buyers a password sheet and asked them to provide a password from that sheet; however, people made copies of the password sheet to give to software swipers. This led software companies to print pages in a light blue ink that would not copy with a standard copier.

Another form of copy protection is to provide invisible files that include some key resources necessary to the execution of the program on the disk itself. This makes copying from your hard drive to a disk difficult because you can't see the invisible files. If someone tries to run a copy, the program won't launch because it is missing a resource from the invisible file. Gotcha!

Another form of copy protection occurs when multiple copies of the same program appear on a network. If you buy PageMaker for your machine, install it, and then try to install that same copy on a co-worker's machine, the program's built-in copy protection scheme will catch you. The first time you work in PageMaker and your co-worker launches PageMaker, a dialog box will appear stating, "Cannot launch PageMaker because a program with this same serial number is already running on another machine."

Now, a copy protection scheme works when you first install the program. When you install from a disk, a mini-program goes into your system and finds the name and serial number of your Macintosh and gives that information to the disk from which you're installing. If you take the original disk and install the program on another machine, when launched it stops and alerts you that this program already has been installed on another machine, and the application cannot be used. Gotcha again! The copy protection technology gets more advanced as software piracy (illegal copies of software) becomes more prevalent.

See Also
Find File; Get Info

Copying Files

To copy a file from one disk to another, select the file you want to copy and drag it onto the icon of the disk you want it copied onto. When you release the **mouse** button, the copying begins and a copy dialog box with a status bar appears so you can see which files are being copied and how long it takes.

Copying Files and Folders

Process	Media	Result
Click and Drag	Within hard drive	Moved
Click and Drag	To disk	Copied
Click and Drag	From disk	Moved
Option-Click and Drag	Within hard drive	Copied
Option-Click and Drag	To and from disk	Copied

C

To copy multiple files from one disk to another disk, hold the **Shift key** and select as many files as you want to copy by clicking each file. Then drag the whole group to the disk of your choice for copying. You can cancel the copying of files while the status bar is up by clicking the Cancel button or using the **keyboard shortcut** ⌘-. (period).

To copy a file from a disk to a **hard disk**, follow these steps:

1. At the **Finder**, double-click the disk to reveal the disk's contents. Select the file(s) you want to copy.

2. While the file(s) is selected, drag it from the disk's window onto your hard disk **icon** or into any open window from your hard disk, and the file is copied into the active window.

3. To cancel copying at any time, press the Cancel button on the copy dialog box or press ⌘-. (period).

To copy files from one disk to another (if you only have one disk drive), follow these steps:

1. Insert the disk containing the file you want to copy. Double-click the file to view its contents, making sure the file you want to copy is in sight.

2. Eject the disk using the Eject command (⌘-E) from the **Special menu** (Note: You must use the Eject command to copy from disk to disk). By using the Eject command, a ghosted version of the ejected disk remains on the desktop and the ejected disk's open window remains open as well. Any files in the window appear ghosted.

3. Insert the disk you want the file copied onto. (It is not necessary to open this disk's window.)

4. Click the ghosted file you want to copy in the ejected disk's open window and drag it onto the icon of the newly inserted disk. The newly inserted disk ejects and you are prompted to insert the first disk (whose icon

still appears ghosted on the desktop). After you insert the first disk, the Mac starts copying and then ejects the disk and prompts you for the disk you're copying onto. Follow the instructions with the dialog boxes.

5. Depending on the size of the file being copied, you may have to do this disk swapping a number of times before the file is copied. When you're done, a ghosted version of the disk might be on the desktop. Drag it into the **trash** to delete it.

TIP There is a simpler way to copy from one disk to another: Copy the file from the disk onto your hard disk, and then eject the disk, and insert the disk you want to copy onto. Then just drag the file from your hard disk right onto the icon of the disk and the entire file will write at one time, with no disk swapping.

See Also

Copying Files in the Background; Finder; Hard Disk; Icons; Keyboard Shortcuts; Mouse; Shift Key; Special Menu; Trash

Copying Files in the Background

In **System 7.5** and higher, you can copy files in the background while you continue to work within an application. If, for example, you have to **copy** 100 or more files to a disk, you can drag the selected files to the disk's icon to start the copying process. To continue working in your application, select the application you want to continue working with by clicking a document window or selecting the application from the Application menu in the menu bar. The files continue to copy in the background while you work.

See Also

Copying Files; System 7.5

Copying Files from Folder to Folder

To copy files from one disk to another, drag the icon of one disk to the other and it is copied. But if you want to copy a file from one **folder** into another folder, dragging it to the new folder just relocates the file; it doesn't copy it. You're moving the original. To create a copy of the file in a different folder, hold the **Option** key while dragging the file to folder. The original file stays in place while the copy is placed in the folder.

See Also

Folder; Option Key

Copying and Pasting into the Calculator

If you're working in a word processor and you're dealing with a series of mathematical calculations, you can copy these figures and paste them into the **Calculator DA** on the **Apple menu**, and it will do the math for you. If, for example, you're typing the following calculation:

124

+376

+685

+435

-16

+208

You can highlight those numbers, open the calculator, choose Paste from the Edit menu (⌘-V), and the answer is calculated by the Calculator DA. You can then copy and paste the answer back into your document.

Another calculator trick lets you enable the Apple Calculator DA to work with scientific notation! Pressing E when using the calculator switches it to this higher form of math. If you type E, then 9999, and push the "=" sign, you get infinity.

See Also

Apple Menu; Calculator D/A

Copyright, Issues on the Web

A right of intellectual property granted by the U.S. Constitution as well as by copyright laws enacted by Congress that gives authors the exclusive rights to their work for a limited time. It is an important issue in relation to material published on the **Internet** that can be copied easily with a few clicks of a mouse.

Copyrighted work cannot be distributed, sold, or used in any way inconsistent with the owner's rights. The owner can sue a copyright violator for damages and it is possible to have a court of law issue an injunction to stop the illegal use.

However, the issue of whether downloading information from the Internet or **email**ing it constitutes copyright violation is currently under debate. A task force in Washington made up of representatives from the U.S. Patent and Copyright offices, the library world, and the publishing business is discussing how and if copyright law should be changed to accommodate the new technology.

The proliferation of information being distributed electronically means that writers, graphic designers, photographers, and other artists can potentially have their work duplicated without compensation or credit.

Although work published on the Internet is already protected by copyright, you can further protect work you publish by following these steps:

1. Register your work with The Copyright Office, Information and Publication Section LM0455, Library of Congress, Washington, D.C. 20559

2. Put a copyright statement on a document such as "Copyright 1996 [Your Name]. All rights reserved."

3. Be sure to reach agreements with photographers, writers, and other artists whose work you intend to publish (or republish) online.

See Also

Encryption; HTTP; Secure HTTP; Secure Sockets Layer; Web Server; World Wide Web

Cordless Mice, *See Mouse*

CorelDraw

Corel, a name associated with only Windows applications in the past, has now moved to the Mac as well. Corel 6 for the **Power Mac**, a collection of powerful graphics programs, contains the latest version of CorelDraw. CorelDraw's feature list is impressive in both quality and variety, and contains new approaches to vector graphics not present in other vector drawing software. An associated module, CorelDream 3D, enables you to design, raytrace, and render 3D objects or text, and to quickly place the results in a CorelDraw document. No other competitive vector packages offer this capability. All applications in Corel6 are 32-bit optimized for the Power Mac, and designed to work with System 7.5 or higher. They have built-in AppleGuide, ColorSync, and QuickDraw GX support. The color models supported include Pantone, FocolTone, TruMatch, SpectraMaster, TOYO, and DIC, and Corel 6 includes a Color Manager Wizard for intuitive device calibration. Page sizes up to 150' x 150' can be incorporated with full-color bitmap patterns and a preview of PostScript texture fills. The view manager also saves custom zoom levels for later use. Corel 6 includes exacting numerical dialog input that affects Position, Rotate, Mirror, Size, and Skew, in addition to enabling mouse control over these same parameters. Whenever possible, this same convention of enabling both exacting numerical control and more intuitive visual control over all transformational operations is followed. An entire library of preset envelope controls is included as part of the Envelope dialog box, with shapes including: ovals, rectangles, stars, certificate shapes, comic book dialogue balloons, cloud shapes, teardrops, arrows, shields, object outlines, and bursts. New custom objects can also be grabbed from the screen and saved to this library. CorelDraw offers multiple UNDO features to aid in the creation of vector graphics. A Lens dialog includes Fisheye, Heat Map, Wireframe, and other effects. The most useful CorelDraw drawing effect is the PowerLine option. By selecting from a number of preset shape libraries (including your own saved customized choices) you can apply line effects to all of the shapes you draw. These shapes add a preset thickness and thinness to the lines, making them appear as more calligraphic elements. Choices include Trumpets (thin at one end and bell shaped on the other), Bullet shapes, Teardrops, Leaky Pen, and more. You can set the shape of the pen nib, the maximum width that the shaped line will include, and the pen leakiness/spread/flow. Only CorelDraw has this linear option.

Basic Bézier Drawing CorelDraw contains all of the expected Bézier drawing conventions (oval, rectangle, and freehand) and more. A standard Bézier editing function, for instance, has expanded usage when it comes to ovals. It enables you to cut away part of the oval interactively as you move the mouse, resulting in a saved arc. The arc can then be transformed into a pie section or a crescent with other CorelDraw options.

CAD Applications CorelDraw 6 fosters 2D CAD use through both its drawing and dimensioning capability. The dimensioning choices rival similar functions found in dedicated CAD software. The Dimensioning Icon is clearly accessible in the toolbox, and a pop-out menu lists all of the dimensioning types (vertical, centerline, horizontal, oblique, and more). A special Angular Dimensions dialog enables you to customize the details. It lists selections for Precision (to ten decimal points) and Units (Gradians, radians, or Degrees). Also available is a toggle for Dynamic Dimensioning and Prefix/Suffix strings.

Other Drawing Tools A Contour dialog enables you to construct what appear to be contour elevation maps from the selected shape. You control the intervening colors and the number of steps. The contours can be drawn in a centered fashion, inside or outside of the selection. A complete Extrude dialog enables you to add perceived depth with lights, colors and shading, and extrusion parameters to any selected object.

Tracing Images CorelDraw includes a separate program, CorelTrace, that automatically converts bitmap (raster) images to line art (vectors).

Typography CorelDraw includes a full-featured listing of typographic and word processing tools. On the graphic side, these include setting text to a curved path and gradient fill options. On the word processing side, this includes spell checking, thesaurus, and advanced proofreading options.

Blends and Gradients CorelDraw enables both blends and gradients. The Color Dialog is central to both operations, and it features some unique options. If the RGB palette is chosen, and a color selected, it shows both the RGB color and the **CMYK** equivalent (which is how the selected RGB will be printed, often very different from the RGB color on-screen). CorelDraw addresses CMY, CMYK, CMYK255, RGB, HSB, HLS, LAB, YIQ, Grayscale, and Registration Color. The palettes mode lists other color palette choices: Uniform Colors (default), FOCOLTone, Pantone Spot and Process, TruMatch, Spectramaster, TOYO Color Finder, and DIC Colors. Colors can be added and deleted, and customized palettes can be saved. For color blends between any two selected objects, a special Blend dialog is brought to the screen. It shows the selected number of steps targeted between the colors, and whether a linear clockwise, counter clockwise blend is desired. The "Apply" button does the rest. (Blends also morph between the two shapes.)

CorelDraw addresses linear, radial, conical, and square gradients, which it calls "Fountains." Like Illustrator, CorelDraw does not limit the user to only two colors, and in fact has more customizing gradient features than Illustrator. You can select two-color gradients and Customs. Custom gradients come in three flavors: Direct (from one color to the other across the color wheel in a linear path), Rainbow (from one color to the next in a clockwise or counterclockwise path), or Custom (where the user actually selects

all of the intermediate colors without accessing a path in the color wheel). An experiment worth trying is to create two diverse shapes at each end of a page (an oval and a rectangle for instance) and fill each with a different color gradient. Now go to the blending operation, select 15 as the number of units, select both shapes, and apply a blend. Not only will the shapes blend, but the gradients will blend in a step-by-step fashion across of the in-between shapes. Modifying this experiment to fit your needs can lead to interesting and colorful graphics applications.

Layers Corel 6 incorporates a View Manager dialog that enables you quick access to any layer in the artwork, plus the capability of adding, deleting, and zooming. The magnification features are unique in that they enable you to click-zoom on the page, area, or selected object right from the dialog.

File Load/Save Conventions CorelDraw can save out preview images in grayscale or full color with the saved files. CorelDraw opens and saves CorelDraw, Pattern, Template, and Presentation Exchange files. Import file formats include PICT and CMX, while exports include PICT, CMX, and EPS.

See Also

CMYK; ColorSync; Pantone Matching System; Power Mac; QuickDraw GX

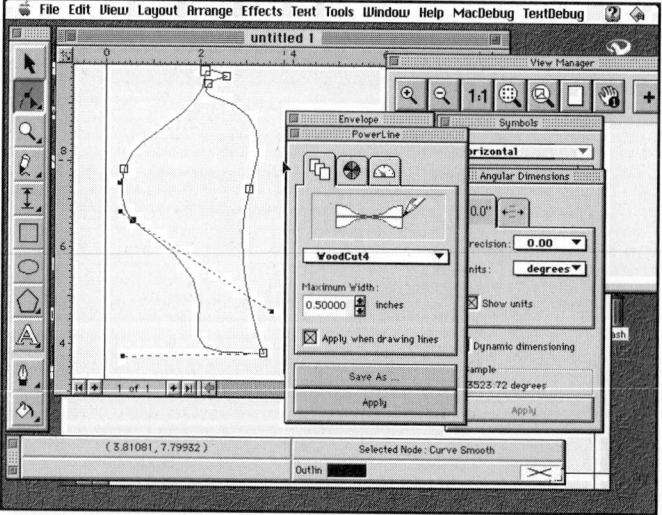

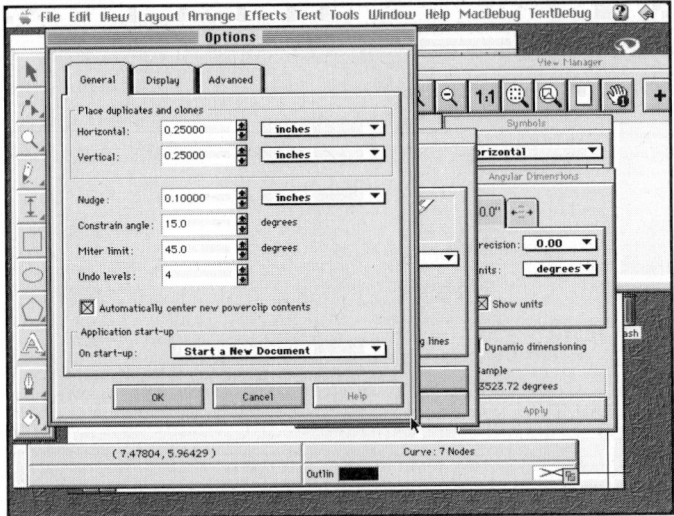

Co:Writer

Co:Writer is a word prediction program that works with your word processor. When you type a letter, it presents you with a list of words beginning with that letter. If the word you intend to use is on the list, click it. Otherwise, type the next letter—and so on, until you see the word you want. Originally intended for people with physical disabilities, the word prediction program is designed to make text entry much easier and more efficient.

If you do your typing by pressing one key at a time with a mouth stick, the implications are obvious. But as the use of these programs became a little more widespread, other advantages were discovered. Co:Writer and similar programs make text entry much easier for anyone who struggles with writing. By reading the words aloud, the word prediction program helps students who are dyslexic. It helps people who are learning disabled or have limited vocabulary to express themselves. It even helps users with low vision, because the size of the words displayed on-screen can be varied to suit their needs.

Co:Writer works easily with a keyboard and mouse or with a switch and scanning software. When the word you want to use is highlighted, click it and it becomes part of the sentence. When you finish a sentence by typing or scanning in the punctuation mark, the sentence is copied into the word processor document so you can start a new one.

Co:Writer is an "intelligent" word prediction program, which means that it makes predictions based on subject-verb agreement, grammar rules, and word relationships. It can learn which words the user prefers and make them the top choices. It can be customized for users of different ages and ability levels with a 2,000-word basic dictionary, an intermediate-level dictionary, and a 40,000-word advanced user dictionary. And all these can be edited to include personal names and phrases. Co:Writer can be taught to recognize words the user commonly misspells, and to substitute the correct spelling while saying the word

Corrupted Files

Although it doesn't happen often, a file may become damaged or corrupted. This means that the file cannot open or be used in any way. A file might become corrupt or resources might go bad for a host of reasons. If you attempt to open a file that has been damaged, most times the application with which you're trying to open the file displays a dialog box warning you that the file is corrupt and cannot be opened. The best defense against a corrupt file is to back up your files. Otherwise, you can try to open the corrupt file in a word processor that has the capability to open a host of different file formats. If, for example, Microsoft Word opens your file, you can resave it with a different name and trash the corrupt file.

CoSA

Company of Science and Art. Based in Rhode Island, CoSA is the original developer and publisher of **After Effects**, a **QuickTime** effects processor. The company and the product were purchased eventually by Adobe.

See Also

After Effects; QuickTime

aloud, training the user to learn the correct word. Co:Writer can be used by people of all ages, and is a necessity for anyone who has difficulty writing.

Couch, John, *See Lisa*

Counter, *See Typesetting Terms*

CP Anti-Virus

An antivirus application and extension are included with Central Point's general utility package, MacTools. Like **SAM**, CP **Anti-Virus** can monitor your system for virus activity.

CP Anti-Virus can detect known HyperCard viruses and known Trojan horses. It can also scan compressed archives created with CompactPro. CP Anti-Virus supports signature strings that enable it to detect (but not remove) new viruses.

See Also
SAM; Virus

CPSI, *See Printers, Color PostScript*

.cpt Filename Extension

The .cpt filename extension means the file has been compressed using Bill Goodman's **shareware CompactPro** (a shareware decompression utility found in the Utilities Forum on America Online and a various FTP sites on the Internet). This file extension enables others to know to extract (decompress) the file using CompactPro. You can have the .cpt file extension added at the end of the filename for you by choosing that option from the CompactPro Preferences **command**. The amount of compression (savings in file size) is different for each type of file. Graphics files (especially in TIFF format) seem to compress quite a bit and it's not uncommon to have a TIFF graphic to compress to 95 percent of its original size. Text files also compress well, but printer fonts (which already use an internal form of compression), application files, and sound files don't compress nearly as much.

Files compacted with CompactPro can be expanded using **StuffIt Expander** (a free decompression utility found in the Utilities Forum on America Online and a various FTP sites on the Internet) and vice versa. Files stuffed with StuffIt Deluxe or StuffIt Lite can be unstuffed by using CompactPro.

See Also
Commands; CompactPro; Compression Utilities; StuffIt Expander

CPU, *See Microprocessors*

CPU Energy Saver

This control panel enables you to limit the energy consumption of any Macintosh computer that is **energy star compliant** by turning your computer off when left idle for a specified period of time. You can set the computer to turn off after as little as 15 minutes or as much as 12 hours. You can also set a time of the day that you'd like your computer shut down. There are a host of options that enable you to automatically log off a network after a specified amount of idle time, to automatically put your monitor into **sleep mode**, and to make sure your computer won't **shut down** if there is any activity over a network.

To use the CPU Energy Saver Control Panel, follow these steps:

1. If your Macintosh model is energy star compliant, choose the CPU Energy Saver Control Panel from the Control Panels submenu on the Apple menu (or System Folder).

2. Double-click the icon to open the control panel.

3. Click the On button to make CPU Energy Saver active. To have the computer shut down during idle time, click the Idle Time checkbox and use the slider to select the amount of time, in minutes, before your computer turns itself off. For additional options, press the Option button.

See Also

Energy Star Monitor Issues

CPU Upgrades

The quest for speed, and often the need to extend the value of an existing Macintosh system, leads users to consider accelerator boards or CPU upgrades. Although not always better than a full computer replacement, they are often a more cost-effective answer. And in choosing this method, your CPU can win a major battle in the war against obsolescence and inefficiency, while staving off the inevitable for a while longer. Apple's latest Macs provide upgrade slots on the motherboard that accept special processor **daughterboards**.

See Also

Daughterboard

Crashes, System

If your system software encounters a problem while it's operating, such as not having enough memory for a particular application, you can experience a system crash. A symptom of a system crash is a **frozen mouse** (when the screen looks normal, but when you move the mouse on your desk, the cursor doesn't move on-screen), but you are more likely to get a **system error** dialog box that states, "Sorry, a system error has occurred."

Both of these point to a system software error, and you must **restart** your Mac to get things working again. System crashes (also called **freezes** or **bombs**) are a temporary situation. Restarting the Mac often takes care of the problem that caused the crash, enabling you to continue working.

In some instances, a system crash is more serious and may be caused by a conflict within your system such as conflicting **extensions**. If you restart your machine and the same system crash occurs, restart your machine while holding down the **Shift key**. This stops the system extensions from loading into your system. After this extensions off restart, see whether the system crash situation reoccurs. If it doesn't, then you may have narrowed the problem down to an extension conflict.

At this point, the process of elimination can determine which of the extensions is causing the conflict. The most widely used way to track down the culprit is to remove your system extensions, put them in a separate folder outside the System Folder, and add the extensions back to your system one at a time, restarting after you add each extension to see if the system crashes. When the crash reoccurs, you know the last extension you added is either the culprit itself or there is a conflict in the order in which the extensions are loaded into your system.

Extensions are loaded in alphabetical order, and rearranging the order in which they load can fix an extension conflict. You can add a letter or a symbol (such as ', ~, -, and so on) to the beginning of the name of the extension to change its loading order.

You can also use the **Extensions Manager** Control Panel installed with **System 7.5** to select which items are loaded into your system at startup. The Extensions Manager saves you from moving extensions in and out of your System Folder by enabling you to turn extensions on or off from the control panel. There are also commercial products, such as **Startup Manager** from Now Software (part of the **Now Utilities** package) and **Conflict Catcher** (from Casady and Greene), that control the loading of extensions and are helpful in tracking down extension conflicts.

A system bomb is another name for a **system error** or **system freeze**. The system bomb got its name because if you have a system error, the system displays a **dialog box** stating, "Sorry, a system error has occurred," with an **icon** of a bomb. A system bomb means the software is frozen or locked up, and to begin working again, you have to **restart** the Macintosh.

See Also

Errors, System; Icons; Now Utilities; Shift Key; System 7.5

Creator Code, *See Changing Type and Creator*

Crime Patrol, *See First Person Perspective Shooters*

Cropping, *See Printing and Binding Terminology*

Cross-Compiler

A special type of **compiler** that can generate programs for computer platforms different than the one on which the compiler itself runs.

The idea of a cross-compiler may seem a little unusual at first, but they are actually pretty common in the computer world. There are a number of very important reasons for using a cross-compiler.

For example, when a new computing platform is first introduced, the new machine may not be widely available to do the development on, or there may not be any development tools that run on the new platform. In the early days of the Macintosh, most development work was done on the Mac's predecessor, the **Lisa**, and cross-compiled for the Macintosh. Similarly, the first Power Mac programs were developed on IBM POWER workstations. Strictly speaking, any Power Mac program compiled on a 68K Mac (or vice versa) has been cross-compiled.

Some types of devices that we don't necessarily think of as "computers" require that their programs be written on another platform and cross-compiled. The **Newton MessagePad** is a great example. It wouldn't be practical to do development work on the Newton itself, so Newton applications are developed on the Macintosh and cross-compiled.

Another reason for cross-compiling is pure convenience. It can be much easier to do all of your development on a single kind of computer using a single development environment, rather than a different environment on a different computer for each.

Metrowerks' **CodeWarrior** Win32 cross-compiler and Microsoft's **Visual C++** Cross-Compiler for Macintosh are both examples of this class. Using Metrowerks' Win32 tools, you can develop programs for Windows 95 and Windows NT from the comfort of your own Macintosh.

See Also

CodeWarrior; Compiler; Lisa; Visual C++

Cross-Dissolve

Cross-dissolve is a video transition effect that fades the first clip into the second one. A similar audio effect is called a **cross-fade**.

See Also

Cross-Fade

Cross-Fade

A video transition effect that fades the first clip into the second one. A similar audio effect is called a **cross-dissolve.**

See Also

Cross-Dissolve

Cross-Platform Font Issues

These days most major applications are available in both Mac and Windows versions. Documents created on one platform often don't even have to be translated in a separate program to be opened in the same application on a different platform. There is another consideration, though: **fonts**.

To successfully open page layout and graphics documents created on a different platform, users must have the same fonts. They can't just have the same names—they have to be the identical fonts, from the same vendor, whether **PostScript** or **TrueType**.

Other fonts can generally be substituted when a document is opened. But if the look of the font is vital to the look of the document, it has to be the same. Also, if a different version of a font is used, line, column, and page breaks can change.

Mac users should be aware that certain Mac fonts (like Chicago, Geneva, Monaco, and New York) don't exist in Windows, just as some PC system fonts don't exist for Macs.

Characters such as curly quotation marks, ligatures, accents, and other special characters often don't translate correctly between platforms; these should always be checked after a document is translated.

See Also

Fonts; PostScript; TrueType

Crossword Wizard, *See Traditional Games*

Crystal Caliburn, *See Pinball Games*

Crystal Crazy

You can trace the origins of Crystal Crazy from Casady & Greene back to the classic arcade game Asteroids. In Asteroids, you were a spaceship in outer space who had to blast its way out of an asteroid field. Mainly, you flew around the screen and blew everything up before anything hit you.

More recently you could trace it to game author Patrick Buckland's first attempt, Crystal Quest. Originally shareware, Crystal Quest was bought by Casady & Greene as one of their first game packages. It proved highly successful, and spawned Crystal Crazy, inducing C&G to commercialize other shareware games. They've also brought us Glider Pro, Pararena, and the brand new **AmoebArena.**

In Crystal Crazy, a loose spin-off of Asteroids, your rocket ship must dodge mines and bizarre space creatures that want to shoot you or collide with you as you gather as many crystals as possible to get to the next level. You also get to smash things, pick up pool balls in order, uncover paintings, and assemble jigsaw puzzles—all while they're shooting at you.

Other Asteroid-style games include the **shareware** game Maelstrom from Ambrosia, Oids from MacSoft,

Space Madness and PegLeg from Changeling Software, and Magnet's Icebreaker. Casady & Greene's latest title, AmoebArena, has you playing an amoeba involved in an intergalactic war. Also available is Casady & Greene's original Crystal Quest, a simple version with crystals and mines but no pool balls or puzzles, which comes with a game editor that enables you to add and create your own levels and creatures.

See Also

3-D Ultra Pinball; Lode Runner: The Mad Monks' Revenge Online; Shareware Games; StarPlay Productions

Crystal Quest, *See Crystal Crazy*

CTS, *See Flow Control*

CU-SeeMe

Freeware (White Pine also has a commercial version) developed by Cornell University and several collaborators that brings videoconferencing to anyone with a Mac and a connection to the **Internet.**

CU-SeeMe brings any user with a **MacTCP**-based Internet connection, a camera, a video-capable Mac (such as a 660 AV) with a 68020 or higher processor, or a video input card the ability to do low-cost desktop videoconferencing.

The basic CU-SeeMe setup facilitates one-to-one videoconferences. By using a **reflector**, up to eight "windows," each containing live video from a separate location anywhere on the Internet, can be displayed at once, as shown in the following illustration.

Of course, the speed of a user's connection to the Internet directly affects the speed and general quality of the video display, and direct **ISDN** or T1/T3 connections make CU-SeeMe work best.

Each participant in a CU-SeeMe video conference can be a sender, a receiver, or both. CU-SeeMe is constantly being updated and improved. Recent versions support audio as well as the exchange of text and slides.

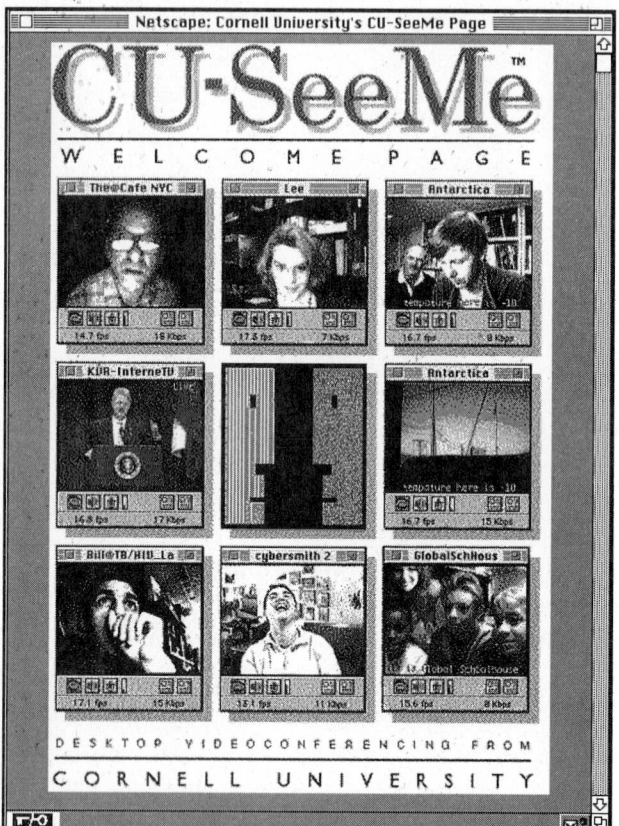

After downloading the CU-SeeMe software from the Internet (see the URL that follows), you launch the program and fill in your user preferences, as shown in the following figure.

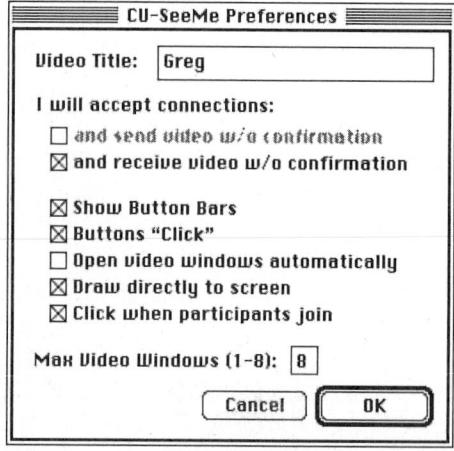

Once in CU-SeeMe, go to the "Conference" menu and choose "Connect." You must know the address to type in the Connection dialog. You can CU-SeeMe in either point-to-point mode with another person (at which point you type in their address) or broadcast mode with a CU-SeeMe reflector.

An international K-12 education project, the Global Schoolhouse Project, uses CU-SeeMe to join students around the world. Several science museums around the country have CU-SeeMe displays, including the San Francisco Exploratorium.

Home Page: **http://cu-seeme.cornell.edu/ Welcome.html**.

See Also

IP Address; ISDN; MacTCP; World Wide Web

Cupertino

Cupertino, California, is the home of Apple Computer, Inc. Located in the heart of Silicon Valley—technically Santa Clara Valley—between Palo Alto and San Jose, Cupertino is also home to many other major computer industry companies, including Symantec.

Cupertino was once a bustling agricultural community at the center of vineyards, orchards, and olive groves. The seeds of change were planted in the early part of this century when several Stanford University graduates set up a string of companies in nearby Palo Alto. These companies would go on to invent the loudspeaker and discover that vacuum tubes could be used as amplifiers, giving birth to the electronics industry.

The change continued throughout the century, with the biggest change occurring in the 50s and 60s, when the nascent semiconductor industry blossomed in Santa Clara Valley and gave it its new name: *Silicon Valley.*

See Also

Apple Computer, History; History and Culture of the Macintosh

Curly Quotes, *See Smart Quotes*

Cursor

The cursor is an on-screen tool you use to select or move objects and to enter text. The movement of the cursor is controlled through movement of the mouse, and the look and function of the cursor is controlled by the tool or task at hand. The default cursor on a Macintosh is the pointer arrow. If you open a word processor, however, the cursor immediately changes to a text cursor (which looks like an **I-Beam**). If you move the cursor to the menu bar or to the scroll bars, it immediately changes back to the pointer arrow.

Certain applications, such as graphics applications, have custom cursors that represent each tool on the tool palette. If, for example, you choose the paint brush, its cursor may look like a paint brush. If you choose an eraser tool, its cursor may look like an eraser. The three most universal cursors are the pointer arrow, the text cursor, and the wristwatch cursor. The wristwatch cursor appears whenever the computer needs a moment to process something. The hands on the wristwatch spin to let you know it will be a few moments before your command is completed.

See Also

Command; I-Beam Cursor

Curse of Dragor

The land of Xorinth has been put under the spell of the malevolent magician Dragor. Your party's mission is to infiltrate the castle and lift the curse from Xorinth. Of course, in the vein of Dungeons and Dragons, you pick your company and end up fighting all sorts of ghouls, renegade knights, and oversized arachnids.

Dragor borrows from an older style of game and interface and suffers from the PC-like commands and cursor functions, as well as the less than

comprehensive **auto-save** feature. On the other hand, if you've moved through **Might & Magic** and already mastered **Dungeon Master II**, you'll probably want to give this a try. One hopes that Strategic Simulations Incorporated's (SSI) recently released World of Aden: Entomorph and MacSoft's Odyssey will improve the standards for Mac RPG's. For now, Curse will suffice. In fact, Curse of Dragor is great for beginners just getting their feet wet and sidesteps a lot of the cumbersome game-manual reliance of similar titles.

See Also

Dungeon Master II: The Legends of Skullkeep; Might & Magic: World of Xeen

Cursive Typefaces, *See Typeface Categories*

Customizing the Macintosh

One of the benefits of the Macintosh is the ease with which you can customize your **system**. The system provides a number of built-in options for customizing your Macintosh, such as the following:

- Capability to choose a desktop pattern
- Capability to choose the default font for your file and folder names
- Capability to choose color for your window title bars

- Capability to change keyboard and mouse sensitivity
- Capability to choose from many different views for your folders and files
- Capability to choose variety of alert sounds

Besides the customization the Mac **operating system** offers, you also can choose from a host of third-party add-ons to customize your computer to fit your personal tastes.

One of the most popular add-ons for customizing your Mac is the **screen saver.** Berkeley System's AfterDark screen savers probably are the best known. From Flying Toasters to Simpsons cartoons, from Star Trek to Disney animations, AfterDark offers a wide choice for most every taste.

Another popular area for customization is your desktop pattern. Apple includes a limited selection within its **Desktop Patterns Control Panel,** but some of the more ambitious desktop patterns come from third-party tools such as WallPaper and Chameleon. In addition, growing collections of alert sounds are sold commercially (such as Kaboom) and posted as freebies on online services and the Internet.

Many of the customization tools are **utilities** that you can add to your system such as the following:

- Calendars
- Personal information managers (PIMs)
- **Font** management tools
- Third-party commercial and **shareware** utilities

See Also

Desktop Patterns Control Panel; Macintosh Operating System; System; Utilities

Cut Command

This command, found on the **Edit** menu, enables you to remove an item from your document and temporarily store that item in the **Clipboard**, so you can paste that item in a different location. You can cut text or graphics. An ideal use of the Cut command ($\mathcal{H}$-X) is moving a line of text from one paragraph to another by **highlighting** the line of text you want to move and selecting Cut from the Edit menu. The selected line of text disappears from the paragraph. You may now place your cursor at the location where you want to insert that line of text, and choose **Paste** ($\mathcal{H}$-V) from the Edit menu. The line of text you cut now appears at your insertion point. The Clipboard stores your cut item until another item is copied or cut into the Clipboard, forcing the previous item to be overridden.

To cut a text item, follow these steps:

1. Select the item you want to cut.
2. Select Cut from the Edit menu ($\mathcal{H}$-X).
3. Normally, the Cut command is followed by the Paste command ($\mathcal{H}$-V), which enables you to paste the information into another location.

To cut a graphic item, follow these steps:

1. Select the graphic you want to cut.
2. Select Cut from the Edit menu.
3. Normally, the Cut command is followed by the Paste command ($\mathcal{H}$-V), which enables you to paste the graphic into another location or into another document. If you would like to save a permanent copy of the text, or graphic, you can paste the cut item into the Scrapbook D/A.

See Also

Clipboard; Copy Command; Edit Menu

Cut (Keyboard Shortcut)

To **cut** an item and place it into the **Clipboard**, press $\mathcal{H}$-X. The Cut item will disappear, but a copy of it will remain in the Clipboard. You can paste this item for as long as it remains on the Clipboard.

To cut an item, follow these steps:

1. Select an item or highlight text you want to cut.

2. Press ⌘-X to delete the item while at the same time making a copy of the item in the Clipboard.

See Also

Clipboard; Copy; Keyboard Shortcuts; Paste

Cut (Video Editing)

In video editing, a cut is simply the point at which one clip changes to another (from original film editing terminology, where the film was actually cut).

A cut is considered a very simple editing procedure, and you can cut a movie (simply copy and paste the clips) in a program such as Apple's **MoviePlayer**.

See Also

Jump Cut; L-Cut; MoviePlayer; Transition

Cyberdog

Code name assigned to Apple Computer's suite of **client** software tools for navigating and communicating on the **Internet**.

Based on Apple's OpenDoc component software technology, Cyberdog treats **URL**s and other Internet contents as objects that can be dragged and dropped from Cyberdog's **Web browser** to another Cyberdog application or to the Finder.

Cyberdog is comprised of components that provide integrated access to **Usenet newsgroups**, **email**, the **World Wide Web**, and other **Internet services**.

One exciting feature offered by Cyberdog is the capability to embed Cyberdog viewers with live Internet connections in OpenDoc documents. When you open the document, the viewer and live data appear in it.

Cyberdog's components include:

- A notebook and a log to store URLs using drag-and-drop technology (similar to **Bookmarks** or Favorites features in other browsers).

- Email and Newsgroup clients.

- Integrated Data Viewers, which display photos, and movies in their own viewing window within the Cyberdog browser window.

- A Web browser, shown in the following figure.

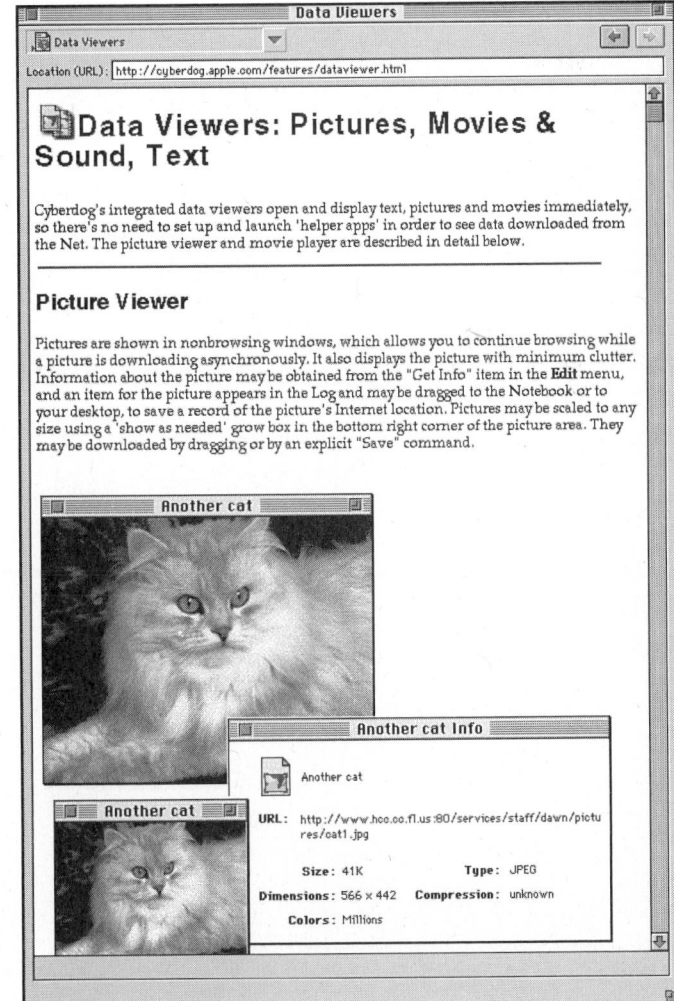

The beta version of Cyberdog's Web browser does not run as fast as other Web clients such as **Netscape Navigator**. Cyberdog also requires a good deal of memory: 8MB of RAM with virtual memory turned on, or 16MB of RAM if virtual memory is not being used.

Home Page: **http://cyberdog.apple.com/**.

See Also

Bookmarks; Internet; Internet Services; Netscape Navigator; Newsgroups; URL; Usenet; Web Browser; World Wide Web

CyberSound FX

A set of plug-in audio filters for Adobe **Premiere** that support both 8- and 16-bit audio. Premiere's audio-filtering features are currently very limited, making a package like CyberSound FX almost a necessity.

CyberSound FX is a collection of 15 audio filters. These filters fall into five broad categories: sound manipulation, tone equalization, ambiance (reverb and echo), dynamics (compression), and special effects (flange and chorus).

To apply a filter, select the audio track in the Construction window and open the Filters dialog box. Choose the CyberSound FX filter and set the parameters you want to use. Unfortunately, you can't preview the effect of the filter; the only way to hear what you have done is to make the movie and listen to it.

> InVision Interactive
> Price: $129
> Phone: (415) 812-7380
> Web: **http://www.cybersound.com**

See Also

Premiere; QuickTime

Cypher, The

EPG Multimedia's serial The Cypher runs in the CD-ROM periodical Launch Magazine, which focuses on Popular Culture, music, and fashion news. The Cypher is a continuing mystery that spans a thousand years. In the different installments, you rummage through the lives of the characters, read their journals and manuscripts, and even root through their chambers to solve puzzles that enable you to gradually piece together the solution to the mystery. Currently, EPG is working on putting together a CD with the entire run of The Cypher that will enable much more freedom of movement through the story than the segmented serial in Launch (see the following figure).

Paul Gregutt, one third of EPG, claims that The Cypher is an attempt to "put the story back in" computer entertainment. The puzzles help keep a game feel, but The Cypher is more a descendent of Interactive Fiction than puzzle or adventure games, much in the manner of The Residents' Bad Day on the Midway and The Dark Eye, both from Inscape. You can also check out the first few chapters of The Cypher at the Launch World Wide Web site at **http://www.2Launch.com/cypehr/cypher.html**.

See Also

Adventure Games; Dark Eye, The; Hypertext Fiction; Non-Linear Storytelling; Residents' Bad Day on the Midway, The

D

.dd Filename Extension

The .dd filename extension means the file has been compressed using Symantec's commercial compression utility **DiskDoubler**. This file extension lets others know to undouble (decompress) the file using DiskDoubler.

See Also

Compression Utilities; DiskDoubler

D1

A digital video production format that has rectangular rather than square pixels.

Daedalus Encounter, The

Actress Tia Carrere (*Wayne's World*) and comedian Christian Bocher star in this extravaganza from game developer Mechadeus. Daedalus Encounter has all the elements of a potential gaming flop, big budget, big names, too many discs, and so on. But surprisingly, Daedalus is fun to play and even pushes the possibilities of the CD-ROM game format to another level.

Filmed against a blue-screen background, the actors are poured into a digital environment that would cost millions in a major motion picture (actually, Hollywood could learn a thing or two from Mechadeus). You play a disembodied brain that accompanies Carrere and Bocher onto an abandoned ship overrun with metal-eating birds who aren't very friendly to humans either. The puzzles in Daedalus are tough and gameplay, although somewhat limited by the linear storyline, is engaging. The sheer ingenuity behind the design of the game, and the thrill of watching convincing actors respond to your movements, make Daedalus a breakthrough title. Although switching discs can be a pain, and non-power Macs can be a bit plodding between scenes, Daedalus is the leader of the pack when it comes to live action animated adventures. Also, if the science fiction theme suits your gaming tastes, try these titles as well: Star Trek: 25th Anniversary from MacPlay; Star Trek: The Next Generation: A Final Unity from Spectrum Holobyte; The Journeyman Project & Journeyman Project II: Buried in Time from Sanctuary Woods; and Hell from Take 2 Interactive.

See Also

Full Throttle; Myst; Return to Zork; Riddle of Master Lu, The; TimeLapse: Ancient Civilizations

Dark Eye, The

More of a game than Inscape's other non-linear storytelling venture—The Residents' Bad Day on the Midway—The Dark Eye enables you to wander through the world of Edgar Allen Poe. Based on his tales of horror, including "The Tell Tale Heart" and "The Masque of Red Death," The Dark Eye weaves a dark narrative around Poe's characters and landscapes. Dark Eye incorporates complex puzzles into the literary world and is much harder to maneuver around in than Bad Day, but is more faithful, in that respect, to its interactive fiction roots. Every choice you make in the game has a direct effect on where you end up next.

Poe fans will relish the chance to intermingle with creepy folk from their favorite works, and gamers into adventure games will most likely find The Dark Eye a worthy challenge. The bizarre mix of art-forms, including 3D rendered characters, line drawing background and 2D hallways creates a schizophrenic, disorienting mix of visual styles that probably would've made Poe proud. As with Bad Day on the Midway, hard-core gamers will be better off with non-literary based adventure games like The 7th Guest or **Myst**, but The Dark Eye is a good step in the direction of bringing a little more to gaming than simple seek and find commands. On a literary platform, The Dark Eye stands out as a unique interpretation of Poe's work.

See Also
Adventure Games; Cypher, The; Hypertext; Non-Linear Storytelling Games; Residents' Bad Day on the Midway, The

Dark Forces, *See First Person Perspective Shooters*

DAT
Originally developed as an audio tape standard, DAT (Digital Audio Tape) is now widely used as a backup medium.

The DAT format supports multiple **sampling rates** up to a maximum of 48KHz. It also supports the **CD audio** standard of 44.1KHz.

See Also
Backing Up with Tape Drives

Data Bus, Types of, *See Power Mac Logic Boards*

Data Communications Standards
Sets of standards that govern the format of data communications between computers connected by **modems** to the **Internet** or **commercial online services** such as **America Online**.

The most common standards are
- **V.22bis:** The standard governing communications at 2400 baud per second (bps).
- **V.32:** The standard for communications at 9600 bps.
- **V.32bis:** The standard governing communications at speeds of up to 14.4Kbps.
- **V. 32terbo**: An extension of V.32bis technology that allows speeds up to 19,200 bps.
- **V. FAST:** (Also called V.FAST Class) Interim modem speed that eventually led to V.34.
- **V. 34**: The standard for communications of up to 28,800 bps.
- **V.42:** The standard that provides error correction using the Microcom Networking Protocol (MNP). Checks for errors and automatically requests that data be resent if errors occur.
- **V.42.bis:** A standard that allows more data to be transmitted faster than other standards through data compression.

See Also
Asynchronous Data Transfers; Internet; Modems; Packet; Parity

Data Compression, *See Modems*

Data Fork, *See Resource*

Data Input Devices
There are many ways to get data into your Mac. Every method, be it a **keyboard**, **mouse**, **trackball**, **touchpad**, **joystick**, **graphics tablet**, and so forth, uses the same connection and data transmission vehicle—the **Apple Desktop Bus (ADB)**.

The Mac supports many different types of data input devices. The following table provides an overview of these ADB devices and their uses.

D

Data Input Devices for the Mac

Type of Device	Examples	Features	Price Range
Keyboards	Apple Extended Keyboard, Microsoft Natural Keyboard, Adesso Tru-Form keyboard, Apple Adjustable Keyboard, Health Care's Comfort Keyboard, Infogrip's BAT Personal Keyboard	Standard QWERTY with Function keys, split-angle keyboards, built-in pointing devices, height and angle adjustments, QWERTY layout of keys	$125 – $795
Mice and Trackballs	Mace Group MacAlly, Kensington's Thinking Mouse and Turbo Mouse, Itac Systems' Mouse-Trak, CH Products' Trackball Pro ADB	Single, 2-, 3-, and 4-button mice, softly rounded contours, rubberized sides	$49 – $139.95
Touchpads	Hagiwara Sys-Com's PointPad, Touche Technologies' TouchPad, Alps Electric Desktop GlidePoint, MicroQue QuePoint II	Flat, rectangular devices using weak electrical signal to sense touch.	$79 – $99
Pointers	Interlink Electronics' RemotePoint, Elo Touch Systems' TouchMonitors, FTG Data Systems' PenDirect ADB, Jabra Group's Ear Phone Streamline AV	IR receiver-based pointers, touch-sensitive monitors, cursor-control via pens	$99.95 – $199
Graphics Tablets	Wacom Technology's ArtZ II and ArtPad, CalComp Drawing Slate II	Tablet and stylus for digitizing graphics	$199 – $389.99
Joysticks	CH Products' FlightStick Pro for Mac and Jetstick, Kernel Productions' ChoiceStick 1.0.2	Game piloting devices	$74.95 – $129.95

Some input devices are eccentric because they are designed for specialized uses—to assist handicapped people to access information on computers, to assist in secretarial phone duties, or to speed up data entry. The chording keyboard, for example, solves problems for people who use the phone constantly or suffer from carpal tunnel syndrome. Voice input and control has become a rapidly growing field of interest since the introduction of the **AV Macs** and the **Power Macs.** For those working with virtual reality applications, 3D imaging, musical performance, dance, or architectural walkthroughs, a glove, headgear, or sock fitted with motion sensors allows you to manipulate objects in space. As strange and esoteric as these devices may seem, they all deserve serious consideration. Many of them are even more useful in vertical applications for the physically challenged.

- **PowerSecretary.** PowerSecretary by Articulate Systems translates spoken words into word processor-readable text using Apple's **PlainTalk** software technology. If first recognizes the spoken sounds and converts them to the most likely letters and combinations. Then, using a 120,000-word dictionary, it finds the correct words and displays them in your document at a rate up to 45 words per minute. PowerSecretary takes dictation within most applications that include text and numbers, such as spreadsheets and databases, and vertical applications in the medical and legal fields. PowerSecretary adapts itself to each user, and improves efficiency whenever users need hands-free entry. It also serves as a voice control system, similar to its other product, Voice Navigator. The street price for PowerSecretary is $2,495 plus a 16-bit sound card (such as the digital signal processor in AV Macs).

- **Voice Navigator II.** Voice Navigator II by Articulate Systems enables you to operate your Mac with voice commands. After it learns your particular vocal inflections, it executes any menu item, **Finder** function, applications command, or keyboard shortcut. It is all performed with software, but the package includes a good super-directional microphone. The street price is $699.

- **Headmaster Plus.** Headmaster Plus by Prentke Romich is a substitute for the mouse. This head-mounted pointer (see the illustration) helps those who cannot use their hands to control the Mac. A breath-activated puff switch clicks the mouse button. Headmaster Plus works with software that displays a keyboard onscreen so that users can point at letter to type them. The street price is $1,195.

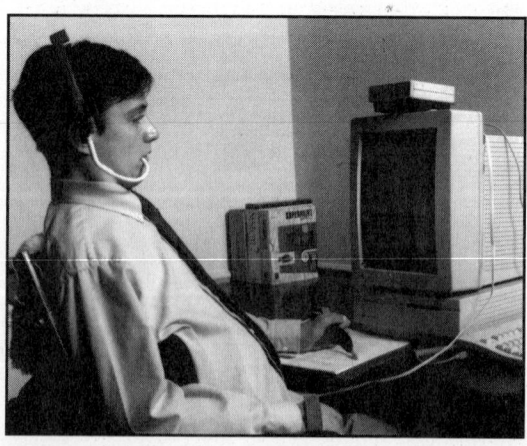

- **Ke:nx.** Ke:nx (pronounced *connects*) from Don Johnston, Inc., provides many methods of alternative computer access for the disabled with a package of hardware and software functions. You plug the input device into the Ke:nx controller box and the software opens menus, launches applications, and so forth. Over 100 products are offered in the package. The street price is $780.

See Also

Apple Desktop Bus (ADB); Apple Extended Keyboard; Bar Code and Magnetic Stripe Readers; Education and the Macintosh; Graphics Tablets; Joysticks; Ke:nx; Keyboard; Logic Boards; Mouse; Pen/Handwriting Devices; Power Mac Logic Boards; Touch Screens; Touchpads; Trackballs

Data Link

The Data Link is a subdivision of the **AppleTalk** protocol stack that provides details about how and at what speed the computers will communicate over an AppleTalk network. In some ways, this is similar to selecting the dialect of a spoken language.

The AppleTalk data links currently in use are LocalTalk, EtherNet and Token Ring.

- **LocalTalk**: LocalTalk is the data link originally defined by Apple and included in all Macintosh computers. LocalTalk is very inexpensive to setup and is easy to maintain, hence it is extremely popular for small business and home use. Despite these advantages, LocalTalk is fairly slow, transmitting data at only 230,400 bps, compared to EtherNet's 10,000,000 bps, limiting the applications in which it can be used. LocalTalk was originally designed by Apple to be used with Shielded Twisted Pair wiring as the **Transmission Media**, but is now most commonly used with unshielded twisted pair.

- **EtherNet**: EtherNet has quickly become the standard form of network data link for nearly all microcomputer network protocols. The high speeds of 10,000,000 bps coupled with the ability to support large numbers of users and diverse types of transmission media have made EtherNet a very common fixture in most business environments. A new EtherNet standard with a speed of 100,000,000 bps is gradually replacing the previous standard, and as prices for the hardware drop, you can expect to see it take over the market completely.

When first released, EtherNet was very expensive to implement on the Macintosh, often costing upwards of $1,000/workstation. Currently many Macintosh computers have support for EtherNet built in, and nearly all of the older Macs can be connected to an EtherNet network with the addition of relatively inexpensive internal or external expansion devices. Apple refers to EtherNet running under AppleTalk as EtherTalk.

- **Token Ring**: Token Ring was originally designed by IBM for use in connecting microcomputer networks to IBM mainframes. Apple refers to Token Ring running under AppleTalk as TokenTalk. While not very common in Macintosh networks on the whole, in certain large corporations, Token Ring has remained a standard for personal computer networking and thus is a requirement for Macintosh connectivity. Token Ring provides speeds comparable to EtherNet (either 4,000,00 bps or 16,000,000 bps). Token Ring's most interesting feature is its capability to incrementally handle increases in network traffic. Although activity measurement and control of LocalTalk and EtherNet networks can be difficult to predict and manage, activity on a Token Ring network scales with a predictable formula based upon the number of active users.

Despite these advantages, Token Ring is very expensive to implement on the Macintosh. Typical Token Ring cards for NuBus machines rage from $600-$1000/computer. Computers such as PowerBooks that lack PCI or NuBus slots are unable to make a direct Token Ring Connection. Thus, in spite of its advantages, few Mac-centric networks use Token Ring, opting instead for the more economical EtherNet.

See Also
EtherNet; Transmission Media

Data Table, *See What-If Calculations*

Database

A database is, quite simply, data organized in a searchable form. A telephone book is a simple form of database. The information is organized alphabetically, by name, last name first. It's useful only if you know the name of the person or business you want to call. You'd need a different kind of directory to find the name of the person whose number is 555-1234, and another differently arranged directory to find the name and number of the family at 123 Oak Street. If you were to compile these directories into one, you'd have a book three times as thick as the original.

The main advantage of a computer database is that you can organize the same information in different ways, by breaking it down into smaller, labeled segments. The information from the phone book could be divided into three categories: names, addresses, and numbers. But you'd be able to search for someone by name, by number, or by address. Each set of information (one name, address, phone number) is called a *record*. The items within it are *fields*. The computer can sift through all of the records in the **database** file to find the address and phone number to match the name you search for, or the name and address to match the number. A record can contain as many fields as necessary to handle all of the data. The file can hold as many records as necessary.

You can search for data according to any single labeled field, or by any combination of labeled fields. The more fields you identify for a search, the closer you'll come to finding your specific target. Suppose that your phone book database covered a large city, with many high-rise office and apartment buildings. If you were to search for a phone number only by address, you'd get a list of everyone at that address. Then you'd have to search those listings by name to find the number you want to call. If you searched only by name in a large city, you might find a half dozen or more "Smith, J...," but if your search was for "Smith" and "Oak St.," your chances of finding only your friend John would be much better.

To work with database files, you need a database application, also known as a database manager or DBM. (To make matters more confusing, database applications, database files, and database managers are also just called databases.) There are several kinds of database applications for specific tasks, such as **Now Contact**, **Quicken**, and In Contact. These may also be called **Personal Information Managers** or PIMs. More generalized database managers, like **FileMaker Pro**, **Phyla**, and 4th Dimension, let you design and create custom databases to handle all kinds of information. You could use one of these to design your own PIM, but it's rather like swatting a fly with a wrecking ball.

There are two major kinds of databases, **flat-file** and relational. (An object-oriented database, such as Mainstay's Phyla, is also a relational database because of the way it shares information.) Flat-file databases access just one file at a time. You might have a Christmas card list in a flat-file database like **HyperCard**. Information from a second database file, perhaps your client file, can be read and copied in, but there's no real link between the two files. If one of your clients moves, and you change the address in the client file, you won't have automatically changed the address in the Christmas card list. In a relational database, however, there's automatic access to data between files. If you changed the client's address in one record, it would appear corrected in any other file that displayed the address.

Data can be entered into a **database** in several ways. The simplest, but most time-consuming, is to scroll or tab through individual fields and type the required data into each one. In order to make the process easier,

you can use a number of different tricks and shortcuts. Pop-up menus, check boxes, and buttons are easy ways to handle yes/no fields or short lists of choices.

Suppose that one of the fields in your customer database asks for a preferred shipping method. You might have as choices US Mail, FedEx, UPS, or Airborne Express. You can format the field to show these as entries on a pop-up menu, as check boxes, or as buttons, depending on how much space there is for this field on your layout. Radio buttons are best when there are only two or three choices. The pop-up menu is best if there's one possibility that will be selected more often. Just put it at the top of the list.

In FileMaker Pro, these fields are added by typing Shift-Command-D or selecting Define Field from the File menu. Enter the name of the field and click Create. When you're done creating fields for your database, move to the Format menu and select Field Format or press Option-Command-F. This will bring up the default Field Format dialog box shown here.

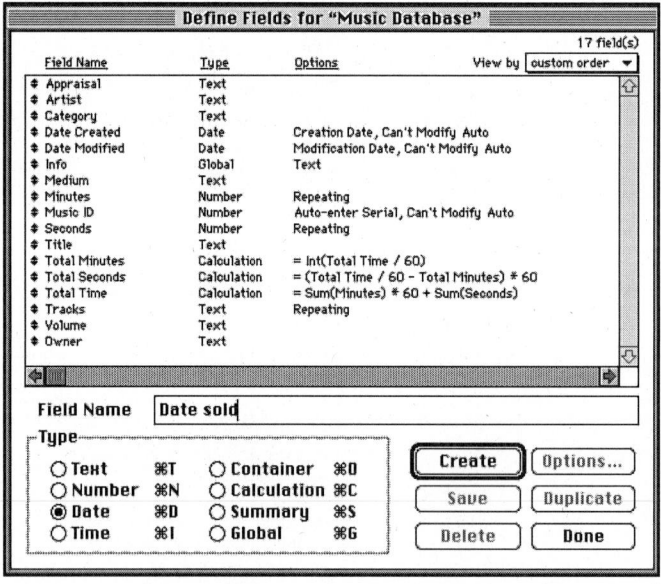

Change the style from Standard Field to whatever you need, and then enter the values for it by selecting Define Value List from the Values pop-up menu. In the example mentioned above, we'd have entered "US Mail, FedEx, UPS, Airborne Express" as the four values for our pop-up menu.

To create other kinds of fields, go back to the Define Field box and look at the list of field types in the lower left. In the figure below, we're entering a date. After you create this field, if you try to enter information in it that's *not* a date, the program will reject it.

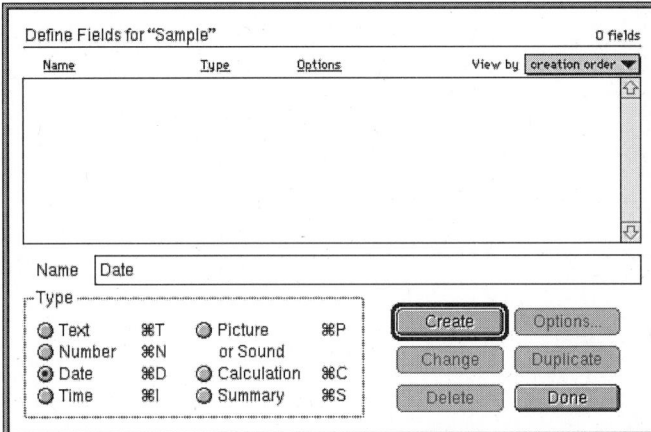

You can also create calculation fields that will give automatic totals of numbers taken from other fields. To format a calculation field, name it and click Create. You'll open a dialog box called Specify Calculation. Use it to set up the formula for the calculation, for example number*unit price.

Database Design Designing a database can be a major project or it can be quite simple, depending on your needs. The database applications available today, though extremely powerful, are generally easy to use. Most include a set of preprogrammed, customizable databases for various purposes. If all you need is a contact or personal information manager, you might not need to deal with database applications at all. There are many stand-alone applications that handle these simple database tasks very well. Among the better contact managers and PIMs, consider **Claris Organizer**, **Now Contact**, and **In Control**. One of these may solve your problems less expensively and more easily than a full-featured database.

However, if you need more information or more data handling and sorting capability, you can design a da-

tabase that will meet your needs exactly. First, decide what categories of information you need to work with, and plan a separate database file for each major category. For example, your small business might need one for customers, one for employees, and one for products. Decide what tasks you want the database to handle. Will it print mailing labels? Invoices? Will it be used to create a catalog? If, for instance, you want the database to print labels, you'll need to assign fields for name, address, city, and so on. If you want the database to do your invoices, you must plan fields for shipping and billing addresses, product code, quantity, etc., and calculated fields to turn the quantity and unit price into a net price, subtotal, shipping charge, tax, and invoice total.

Determine the relationship between the new file and any existing files. Doing so enables you to use lookups or insert fields from existing files instead of reentering the data.

Decide what layouts you will need for such activities as data entry, order entry, printing labels, printing invoices and form letters, and any other reports or **forms** you might generate with this database.

Consider whether other people will use this database, and whether you need to restrict access to any part(s) of it. If security is a factor, you can restrict access or password-protect certain files or functions.

Sketch out your forms on paper before you begin to enter them in the database. If you use window envelopes to mail your invoices, check the placement of the address block. Make sure all the information you need is included.

Keep these points in mind:

- Use separate fields for first and last name so you can search for or sort by either one.

- Use separate fields for city, state, country (if you do business abroad), and postal zone, as shown in the following figure. This will enable you to sort mailings by ZIP code or send letters to customers in a particular area.

If you combine the fields, you won't be able to sort records based on a single attribute.

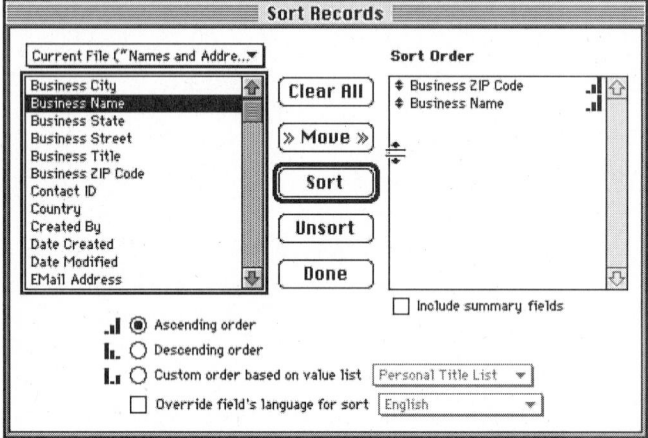

- If you're dealing with individuals as opposed to companies, be sure to include a field for titles (Dr., Mr., Ms., Rev., and so on).

See Also

Database, Relational; FileMaker Pro; Flat-File Database; HyperCard; Personal Information Manager; Phyla Database; Quicken

Database, Field

When you create a database file, you enter the data for it into fields. Fields in a pre-existing database simply look like boxes. You type or paste the information into them. If you're designing a database or adding fields to an existing one, you'll need to assign field types, attributes, and possibly formats and filters.

Field types categorize the data and control the size of the field (number of characters allowed). Field types differ with various databases, but generally they may be alphanumeric or "real numbers." Alphanumeric characters are letters and numbers treated as text. If the system will need to do arithmetic with the numbers in the field, be sure that it's a real number field and not an alphanumeric.

Field attributes place conditions on the field. A common attribute is "mandatory." The database won't accept the record if any of the fields that are tagged as mandatory have been left blank. If the field is tagged "Can't modify," database users can view the contents of the field but not change it. "Indexed" means that the data in that field can be sorted according to some rule: alphabetically, by zip codes, by numbers, or whatever you choose to apply.

Field entry formats help you structure the data that you're entering. Use them to help make sure the information you enter is consistent. For example, if you need to enter dates and assign the format MM/DD/YYYY, you will be sure that all dates entered fit that pattern. If you then need to sort by date, you can be sure that all of the dates have the same basis.

Field entry filters are another way of making sure the information you enter is correct and consistent. The filter evaluates individual characters as they're entered into the field. If an unexpected result is found, the program rejects the entry. If you're creating a field for an employee's social security number, you'd put in a filter (and a format code) so that only numbers in the XXX-XX-XXXX pattern would be accepted.

See Also

Database; Flat-File Database

Database, Procedures

Procedures are sets of instructions the database uses to perform specific tasks. A global procedure affects the whole database. An example might be adding the trademark symbol to every mention of your company's product. A file procedure is directly tied to manipulating one file. You might use a file procedure to sort your addresses by ZIP code before printing labels. A layout procedure affects only the layout with which it's associated—for instance, converting text to 10 point type before printing address labels.

Database, Record

A record is a compilation of related information. Files hold records, which are comprised of fields into which data has been entered. A single record can contain many individual pieces or fields of data. But all the data in that record pertains to it. Think of a cookbook as a kind of file, then each recipe in it is a record. The list of ingredients, directions for preparing, and number of servings are all data entered into fields on the recipe page or record.

Data can be entered into a database in several ways. The simplest, but most time-consuming, is to scroll or tab through individual fields and type the required data into each one. In order to make the process easier, you can use a number of different tricks and shortcuts. Pop-up menus, checkboxes, and buttons are easy ways to handle yes/no fields or short lists of choices.

Suppose that one of the fields in your customer database asks for preferred shipping method. You might have as choices US Mail, FedEx, UPS, or Airborne Express. You can format the field to show these as entries on a pop-up menu, as check boxes, or as buttons, depending on how much space there is for this field on your layout. Radio buttons are best when there are only two or three choices. The pop-up menu is best if there's one possibility that will be selected more often. Just put it at the top of the list.

In **FileMaker Pro**, these fields are added by typing Shift-Command-D or selecting Define Field from the File menu. Enter the name of the field and click Create. When you're done creating fields for your database, move to the Format menu and select Field Format or press Option-Command-F. This will bring up the default Field Format dialog box shown here.

Change the style from Standard Field to whatever you need, and then enter the values for it by selecting Define Value List from the Values pop-up menu. In the example mentioned above, we'd have entered "US Mail, FedEx, UPS, Airborne Express" as the four values for our pop-up menu.

To create other kinds of fields, go back to the Define Field box and look at the list of field types in the lower left.

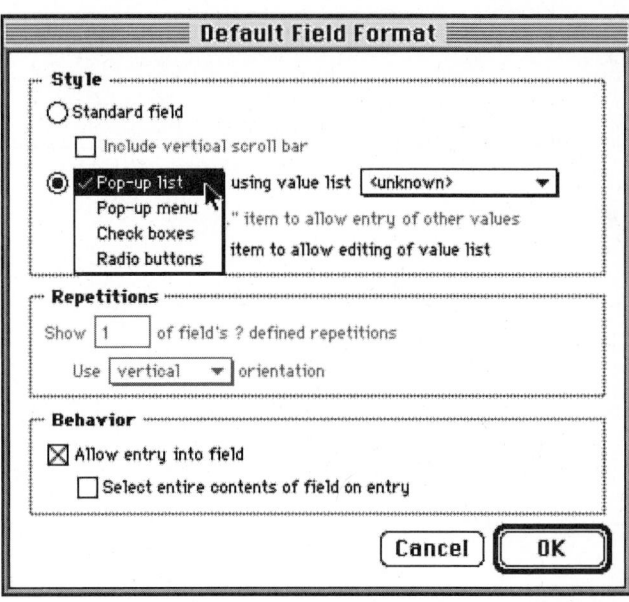

See Also
Database; Flat-File Database

Database, Relational

A relational database, such as 4th Dimension or FileMaker Pro, is one that may contain many files and can manipulate data in more than one file at a time. The files are linked together by a structure which defines their relationships. In FileMaker Pro, this is done easily in the Edit Relationships dialog box. Select the two files to link, and whenever you open the appropriate field in the first record, you'll also bring up the related one(s).

Database files can have a "one-to-many" or a "many-to-one" relationship. A "one-to-many" relationship allows one file to access and display related information from many files. Suppose that your Christmas card file contained a field you checked off if the person in that record sent you a card, and suppose you determined to send cards only to the people who'd sent them to you for the last three years. You could open a new file within the same database, asking the program to gather only the names that fit that criterion, sort by ZIP code, and print labels for this year's cards.

See Also

Database; Flat-File Database

Database Server, *See Server*

Date & Time Control Panel

The Macintosh's internal clock settings are controlled by the Date & Time control panel. There are a variety of options in this control panel that enable you to decide how the system displays time (see the following figure).

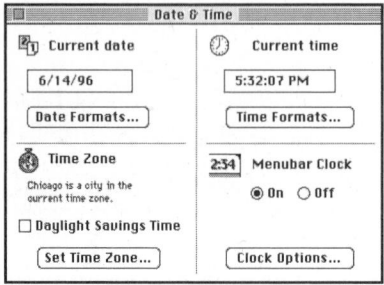

Even when the Mac is turned off, the internal clock and calendar keep running by use of an internal battery, so each time you turn your computer on, the time and date are correct. This is especially helpful if you use any programs that implement the time and date. The Macintosh also notes the time and creation date of each file on your Macintosh.

This control panel is split into four sections; The current date, the current time, the time zone, and the menu bar clock. Each has a set of options accessed by a button at the bottom of the section.

The Date section enables you to set the current date. Setting the date is only necessary when you purchase your Macintosh; the internal clock will track the date from that time forward.

The Time section enables you to set the current time and the time format including military time and time with or without seconds displayed. It also enables you to display the time in the upper right corner of the menu bar by using the Menu bar option.

The Time Zone section enables you to tell the Macintosh what time zone you're in. This is helpful if you're using the Map control panel to determine the time in different time zones around the world. There's also a daylight savings time checkbox, which when checked adds an hour to the current time. This enables you to click it on during daylight savings time without having to manually adjust the hour setting in the Time section.

The fourth section enables you to toggle the menu bar clock on or off, and you can choose from a host of preferences for the menu bar clock here as well. When turned on, this feature puts a digital clock in the upper right side of your menu bar that displays the current time in the time format of your choice. Through the clock options, you can choose the color of the menu bar clock; whether its display will includes seconds; if it will show the day of the week as well as the time; if the number separators will flash; the font that the menu clock will appear in; and you can set the clock to chime on the hour using your choice of system alert beeps.

To set the date using the Date & Time control panel, follow these steps:

1. Choose the Date & Time control panel from the Control Panels submenu on the Apple menu (or System Folder).

2. To adjust the month, day, or year, click the number representing that value. An up/down edit arrow appears to the right. You can either type the correct number or click the up arrow to move the numbers higher or click the down arrow to move the numbers lower. To confirm the date change, click the words Current Date and the edit arrows disappear.

3. To change the date format for International date formats, click the Date Formats button. You can choose from a variety of pop-up menus the prefixes used to denote the date when displayed in a long date or short date format. You can also choose the order in which the day, date, or year will be displayed. In many European countries, for example, the day is displayed first, followed by the month, then the year, rather than the way it's used in the U.S., with the month in the first position. A sample of your current date choices are displayed at the bottom of the dialog box.

To set the current time using the Date & Time control panel, follow these steps:

1. Choose the Date & Time control panel from the Control Panels submenu on the Apple menu (or System Folder).

2. To adjust the hour, minute, or seconds of the current time, click the number representing that value. An up/down edit arrow appears to the right of these numbers. You can either type the correct number or click the up arrow to move the numbers higher or click the down arrow to move the numbers lower. To confirm the time change, click the words Current Time or the clock icon, and the edit arrows disappear.

3. To turn the menu clock on, click the On button. You can set the preferences for the menu clock by clicking the clock options button. When your preferences are complete, click OK and close the Time and Date control panel.

To set the time zone where your Macintosh resides, follow this step:

1. To set the Time Zone, click on Edit Time Zones, and a scrolling list of cities appears. If your city does not appear in the list, choose a city that does appear that shares your time zone. A user in Charlotte, North Carolina, for example, could choose Miami, Florida since they're both in the Eastern Time Zone. Click OK to confirm your time zone choice, and close control panel.

To turn on the menu bar clock using the Date & Time control panel, follow these steps:

1. Choose the Date & Time control panel from the Control Panels submenu on the Apple menu (or System Folder).

2. Click the "On" radio button. Click the Clock Options button to access the preferences for the clock. Click the checkboxes on the left side to choose your menu bar display format preferences. If you want the menu bar clock to chime on the hour, click the "Chime on the hour" checkbox. You can also select, from a pop-up list, your choice of font for the display of the menu bar clock and the type size that will be used.

See Also
Control Panels

Daughterboard
A daughterboard is a special card or logic-board containing a processor, which plugs into the main logic board (motherboard) of your computer.

See Also

Logic Board Upgrade; Power Macs, PCI Models

Dead Keys

Although this a somewhat rare occurrence, it is possible that a key on your Mac's keyboard could cease to operate, or go "dead." Chances are its contacts are gummed up, and you can choose to send your keyboard in for repair or repair it yourself by carefully prying the key from the keyboard and spraying a tiny amount of lubricant (such as WD-40) on the key's stem. This should do the trick, and if it doesn't work the first time, give it another try. Remember to be stingy with the lubricant—there's no need to flood the keyboard.

Dead Mac

If your Mac is dead, you are greeted by a black screen with a **Sad Mac icon** that is frowning and has "X's" for its eyes where the **Happy Mac icon** used to be (see the following figure).

XXXXyyYY
ZZZZZZZZ

This screen is followed by a series of numbers below it designed to tell Macintosh technicians which hardware problem the Mac is encountering during **startup**. If you get a Dead, or Sad Mac, **restart** your machine. Chances are you'll be all right with the next startup, and whatever was causing this temporary Sad Mac state will be gone. It could've been a **SCSI** cable that wasn't plugged in all the way or a problem with the way a SIMM chip was making its connection inside your computer.

These problems can be the result of **RAM** not seated properly in its slot or some other RAM-related problem, or it could be a problem with an **Apple desktop bus** (ADB) port, or a host of other SCSI, printer port, or SIMM problems. If this dead Mac situation persists after you've restarted the machine several times, and you've removed all SCSI devices from the Mac, you may need to seek the help of a qualified Apple service technician.

See Also

Apple Desktop Bus; Happy Mac Icon; RAM; Restart; Sad Mac Icon; Small Computer System Interface; Startup Screen

Dead Mouse

If your **mouse** does not respond to your movements, first check to see that the mouse is firmly plugged in. If your mouse connects directly to your **keyboard**, make sure that the keyboard is firmly connected to the Macintosh.

If your mouse was working properly and suddenly froze while you were working in an application, you may have experienced a screen **freeze**, which is a software error that sometimes occurs when memory is running low. **Restarting** your computer alleviates this problem.

If your mouse appears to be acting sluggish or jumpy, you may have to clean the small rubber ball inside the mouse. You can clean this ball by turning the mouse upside down and rotating the plastic ring that holds the ball in place until it releases. Apple recommends cleaning this ball with a cotton swab moistened with alcohol, and then drying the ball with a lint-free cloth. Also, check the rollers inside the mouse, which can built up hard gummy deposits that can affect the performance of your mouse. They may need to be cleaned as well.

See Also

Crashes, System; Keyboard; Mouse; Restart

DeBabelizer, *See File*
Types, Internet

Debugger, The

Only one debugging tool has the audacity to call itself *The* Debugger. Generally called Jasik's Debugger after its author, Steve Jasik, this tool lives up to its name. Like fine wine, The Debugger is an acquired taste, but those who have managed to overcome its steep learning curve and quirky interface have been greatly rewarded by the richest feature set of any Macintosh debugger.

The Debugger is both a high- and a low-level debugger. That is, it can debug at both the source and **object code** levels. It debugs source code using standard SYM files (see **Debugging Tools**) or by interacting directly with the programming environment. An especially helpful feature, if you're just learning to debug at the object level, is The Debugger's capability to display source code interspersed with the corresponding object code.

Most low-level debuggers are stuck with very sparse interfaces, because making calls to the **Toolbox** routines normally responsible for drawing and managing the Mac interface are off-limits to low-level debuggers. The Debugger, however, sidesteps this issue by implementing its *own* interface routines that look and act much like the standard Mac interface. As a result, The Debugger is able to use windows, scrollbars, and menus.

The Debugger is capable of debugging any code that can run on the Macintosh, whether it's in a normal application, a code resource, or a Toolbox routine in ROM. It can display structured data in its own editable display window (see the following figure).

```
┌─────────────────────────────────────────────┐
│ ▢ ▤▤▤▤▤ WindowRecord_@465320 ▤▤▤▤ │
├─────────────────────────────────────────────┤
│ WindowRecord                              ⇧  │
│     0 port          : CGrafPort_@465320      │
│   108 windowKind    :        8               │
│   110 visible       : TRUE                   │
│   111 hilited       : TRUE                   │
│   112 goAwayFlag    : TRUE                   │
│   113 spareFlag     : TRUE                   │
│   114 strucRgn      : **Region_@488974       │
│   118 contRgn       : **Region_@485534       │
│   122 updateRgn     : **Region_@4859B0       │
│   126 windowDefProc : **DEFfunRsrc_@8768F0   │
│   130 dataHandle    : @485970                │
│   134 titleHandle   : @485918 = "Untitled-1" │
│   138 titleWidth    :       67               │
│   140 ControlList   : NIL                    │
│   144 nextWindow    : *WindowRecord_@465278 ⇩ │
│   148 windowPic     : NIL                    │
│   152 refCon        : $00464F28           ▢  │
└─────────────────────────────────────────────┘
```

A number of sophisticated testing tools are built into The Debugger, such as memory stress-testing tools similar to those in **QC**, and Trap Discipline, which checks the parameters passed to Toolbox routines to verify that they're valid.

The Debugger is bundled with MacNosy and CoverTest. MacNosy is a global interactive disassembler that can show any object code in assembly format. CoverTest is used in product testing to identify which program execution paths have been tested.

The Debugger and MacNosy are published by Jasik Designs.

> Jasik Designs
> 343 Trenton Way
> Menlo Park, CA 94025
> Email: **macnosy@jasik.com**
> Phone: (415) 322-1386

See Also

Debugging Tools; Object Code; QC; Toolbox

Debugging

Debugging is the process of identifying and fixing problems (**bugs**) in hardware or software.

Debugging has been called, "a pastime similar to banging one's head against a wall, but with fewer opportunities for reward." While that may be a bit of an exaggeration, few programmers relish the long hours spent tracking down obscure and sneaky bugs.

It goes without saying that the easiest way to debug a program is to avoid the problem altogether. Just as defensive driving can help avoid accidents, defensive programming can help avoid bugs. This can take many forms. The first is purely a matter of programming style. Resist the urge to be clever with special features of a language at the expense of clarity. Even if you feel you fully understand your unique programming construct at the time you write it, chances are nobody else will. And, if you're not quite as clever as you thought, debugging your code can be especially painful.

Check for errors as a routine part of your programming. If a **Toolbox** call returns an error code, for example, pay attention to it! If you're working with a **handle**, make sure it's valid before you use it. Some of the most heinous bugs can be avoided by a simple check for errors. A corollary is to expect the unexpected. If you ignore an error code because, "that call could never fail," rest assured that that call *will* fail when you least expect it. To be more general, don't assume too much, and document any assumptions you do make.

You can use *assertions* to flush out some of your incorrect assumptions. Assertions are statements added to a program during the development phase to check whether any of your assumptions are incorrect. Another method is to use a stress testing tool, such as **QC**, to force your program to run under the worst possible memory conditions. Subtle and unnoticed problems can become downright nasty when you stress your program to its limits.

So, you've programmed defensively, limited the number of assumptions you've made, and checked for errors scrupulously, but a bug still turns up in your code. What now?

Well, first you need to decide what kind of bug you have. If your program runs, but gives you the wrong results, you probably have a logic bug. You need to go back to your original algorithm and reexamine the process you've taken to get the results you want.

If your program misbehaves, you've got a coding bug of some kind. For example, if your program crashes outright or won't enable you to resize its windows, you need to track down a coding bug. These are the most common bugs and the most difficult to track down.

You can make the task of finding the source of the bug easier by being systematic.

- Fully identify and describe the bug. What is the problem? Is it worse in some situations?

- Determine whether the bug is repeatable. If possible, make it repeatable using a stress-testing tool.

- Identify which general part of your program is responsible for the bug.

- Gradually narrow the search for the bug until the offending code is found.

- Implement a fix that doesn't create other bugs.

The first step is to identify the bug and narrow, as much as possible, the scope of your search for the cause. Is the bug repeatable or apparently random? In other words, is there a set of steps you can follow that will always cause your program to misbehave in the same way? Random bugs can often be made more repeatable with a stress testing tool or **MacsBug's** heap scramble feature.

You can turn to a great many **debugging tools** to help you in your search. Stepping through some troublesome code in a debugger can often clear away the fog and make a previously hidden bug obvious. As you step, keep an eye on all of the relevant variables. Are they doing what you expect?

After you find the source of the problem, fix it! But be sure to avoid the urge to just apply a quick fix, or patch, to that one bit of code. All too often quick fixes cause problems later. Take a careful look at the code and decide whether there's a fundamental design flaw that needs to be addressed. If so, address the fundamental problem, don't just put a Band-Aid on it.

Although the drudgery of searching for a bug can be maddening, actually finding a bug (and fixing it) can be one of the most rewarding parts of programming.

See Also

Bug; Debugging Tools; Handle; MacsBug; QC; Toolbox

Debugging Tools

The process of **debugging** can be nerve-wracking. Fortunately, many tools exist to help you ferret out bugs and stomp on them. Some tools enable you to step through your code one line at a time, watching every move your code makes. Others sit silently in the background, waiting for something to go wrong, and letting you know when it does.

One of the most valuable debugging tools is often overlooked: avoiding the bug altogether. Most **compilers** provide warnings about potential errors in your code. While these errors might not be serious enough to cause the compiler to complain, they might cause trouble when your program is running. The following figure illustrates an example of a very common mistake found by the Metrowerks **CodeWarrior** C/C++ compiler.

In this case, the programmer incorrectly used the **C** assignment operator (=) rather than the equality operator (==). The result is that if an error *is* returned by the ResError function, it is effectively ignored by the program. This example seems trivial, but the same sort of error could be catastrophic if it isallowed to make its way into a finished product. Compiler error checking helps to avoid these bugs before they happen.

Other tools take this error checking a step further and can identify much more complicated problems in your source code.

In spite of the best efforts of programmers and compiler writers, some bugs do make their way into compiled code. That's when debuggers and stress testing tools come into play.

High-level or source code debuggers display the original source code (in C, **Pascal**, etcetera.) that you are debugging and enable you to step through the code one instruction at a time. In addition, you can watch variable values as your code runs (see following figure). High-level debuggers are written as applications and run like any other application. Although this makes them relatively easy to use, it also means they have certain restrictions. You cannot use them to debug code that could affect the operation of the debugger. If the bug causes a system crash, it is likely to wipe out the debugger as well. Apple's SADE, SourceBug, and Macintosh Debugger, as well as the **Symantec C++** and Metrowerks CodeWarrior debuggers are in this class.

Many high-level debuggers use special files, called SYM files, to identify the relationships between the object code being debugged and the original source code. These files are created by the **linker** when the program is created. Because the SYM format is standardized, any debugger that understands SYM files can be used to debug any program for which a SYM file has been created. This gives you some flexibility in choosing a debugger, because you don't necessarily have to use the debugger from the same company as your compiler and linker.

Calling Chain   Variable Display

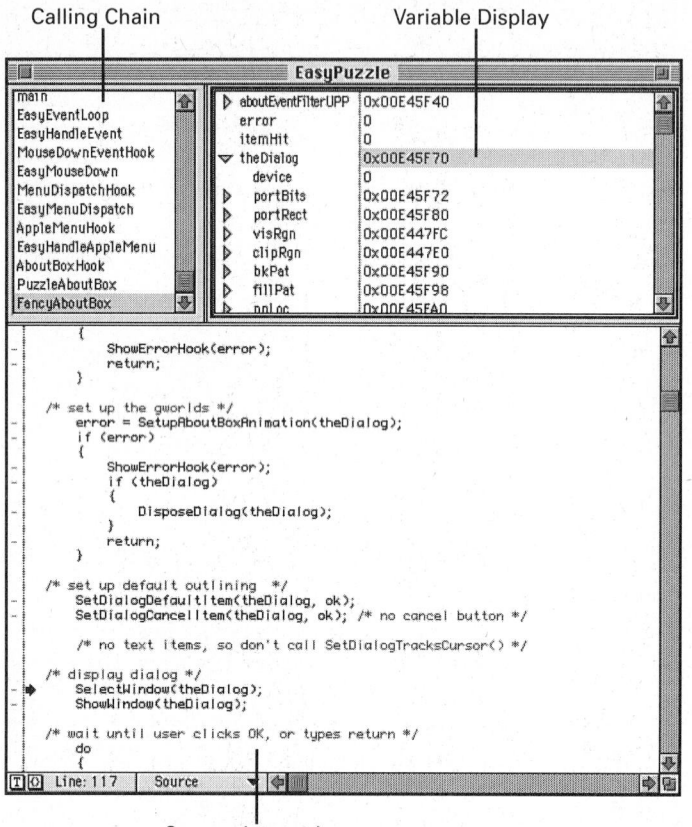

Current Instruction

Apple recently released debugging versions of parts of the operating system. So far, debug versions are available for the Modern Memory Manager, Apple Guide, and QuickDraw GX. These versions sacrifice some speed, because they double-check for errors introduced by the programs that use them.

See Also

CodeWarrior; Debugger, The; Debugging; MacsBug; Memory Mine, The; QC; Symantec C++; TMON Professional

Deck II

A sound digitizing and editing application that supports as many as 16 tracks on a **Power Macintosh**, and also supports Digidesign sound hardware.

Deck II uses an interface that resembles a four-track tape recorder, including volume sliders and playback controls. You can mix and bounce tracks, and Deck provides nondestructive editing tools (the changes don't affect the original sounds). A *scrub* feature (a tool for playing back and forth in a track at different speeds) makes it easy to locate points in a sound file, and the program also offers various automation features including automated mixdown and punch-in and punch-out points. the program also supports **QuickTime** movies and **MIDI**.

While great for recording original music and creating complicated mixes of sounds, this program might be too much for simple sound editing. A program such as **SoundEdit 16** is better suited for those tasks.

Low-level, or object-code, debuggers, such as **MacsBug** and **TMON** Professional, take almost complete control of the computer during debugging, and therefore avoid some of the difficulties that high-level debuggers frequently face. The trade-off is that these debuggers have less intuitive interfaces and generally show only the compiled object code, rather than the original source. **The Debugger** by Jasik Designs is unique in its position as both a low-level *and* a high-level debugger.

There are a number of debugging tools in addition to debuggers themselves. Memory analysis and stress-testing tools, such as **ZoneRanger**, **QC**, and The **Memory Mine**, can be invaluable. These tools force your code into a worst-case situation, where anything that can fail, will fail. They are system extensions that sit quietly in the background watching for errors in memory handling and invoke a debugger when trouble arises.

Macromedia
Price: $399
600 Townsend Street
San Francisco, CA 94103
Phone: (415) 252-2000
Web: **http://www.macromedia.com/**

See Also

Desktop Models, Macintosh Family; Digidesign; MIDI; QuickTime; SoundEdit 16

Decoding/Decompressing Files

Files downloaded from the Internet often have to be decoded or decompressed before they can be used.

One of the Internet's main benefits is the availability of software held on **host** computers such as **software archives**. Users can download this software to their own **client** computer. Usually the software is **encoded** or **compressed** to make the file smaller in size or recognizable by different types of computers.

Encoded or compressed files can be recognized by the file extension such as ".hqx," ".sit," or ".cpt." Such files can then be decoded or decompressed with a utility such as StuffIt Expander, which is itself a shareware program available on the Internet.

Other file types might also be downloaded from the Internet with compression/encoding schemes that are not common to the Macintosh. A UUCP-encoded file might be encountered on Usenet and can be decoded with the application uuUndo or uuLite. ShrinkWrap, another file decoding application, decompresses files saved in Apple's DiskImage format (Disk Image files usually carry the **filename extension** ".image."

All the aforementioned applications can be downloaded from **http://wwwhost. ots.utexas.edu/mac/pub-mac-compression. html**.

See Also

Compressing Files; Encoding Files; Filename Extensions; FTP; Host; Macintosh Software Archive; Server StuffIt Expander

Def Proc, *See Code Resource*

Default Button

The Default button enables you to override an application's **default** factory settings and replace them with settings that match your needs and personal preferences. If you're using an application that enables you to choose a new setting as a default, you will see a **button** named Default. By clicking that button, the currently chosen setting in that dialog box becomes the default setting anytime that command or feature is used.

See Also

Button; Command Key; Default Settings

Default Settings

Your Macintosh comes with preset factory settings for your convenience. These factory settings are called *default settings*. The **font** that is used to display the names of **files** and **folders**, for example, was set at the factory as Geneva. Therefore Geneva is the default font. You can change the font that displays file and folder names by choosing a different font in the **View control panel**.

Applications also have default settings for any number of items within the application. Many applications enable you to determine your own set of defaults. If you use **PageMaker**, for example, the default font is Times. Every time you open a new PageMaker document and start typing, the text is displayed in 12 point Times Roman. In PageMaker, as in many other applications, you can change the defaults to suit your needs or personal preferences.

TIP Software manufacturers often choose the user's most likely choice as the factory default.

Some applications enable you to return to the application's default settings simply by clicking a button. Other applications have a default file where current defaults are kept. If you want to permanently change the default settings, in some cases you can open a document, set the typeface, size, and other elements, and save that file as the default file.

See Also

Files; Fonts; PageMaker; Views Control Panel

DejaNews

DejaNews, which was recently added to Netscape's Internet Search page, is one of a handful of free services that enables you to search the labyrinth of Usenet newsgroups. You can find it at **http://www.dejanews.com/.**

See Also

Usenet; World Wide Web, The

Del Key

Pressing the Del key on an extended keyboard deletes the letter to the right of the cursor's insertion point, whereas the regular delete key deletes the letter to the left of the cursor's insertion point.

See Also

Cursor; Delete Key

Delete Key

The Delete key, in the same place on a Mac keyboard as the backspace key is on many PC keyboards, enables you to delete a **selected item** in an application or to delete any text character to the left of the I-Beam **cursor's** insertion point. This key treats a selected item the same as choosing **Clear** from the **Edit menu** does.

See Also

Clear Key; Cursor; Edit Menu; Selecting Items

Deleting a File

The invisible files generated when a disk is initialized are sometimes called the *housekeeping* or *record-keeping* files. These files are extremely important because they contain the information which the Finder uses to perform its functions. The Directory and Volume Bitmap files control how files are added and deleted to a disk.

When you delete a file, the file does not move. Rather, its attributes and location are removed from the Directory file(s) and the volume bitmap is updated to show that the sectors formerly taken up by the data are now free for use by another file.

You can restore the files by resurrecting the directory entry for the file. There is one problem which increases the likelihood that the file will not be totally retrievable. When the volume bitmap is told that an area of disk is free it may place a newly added file or expanded file into part of the space formerly allocated to the erased file. If this occurs, part of the file is destroyed, and the file becomes difficult to recover in its entirety.

See Also

Delete Key; Erase Disk Command; Trash

Delphi

Delphi is a **Commercial online service** first launched in1985. Delphi offers text-based Internet access including **email**, FTP, gopher, newsgroups, and text of Web sites.

Delphi also offers many special interest forums including user run "custom" forums, software libraries, news, travel, reference materials, and everything else you'd expect to find on a commercial service. It's one of the best places to go for multi-user games, offering poker, trivia, word games, and more every night of the week. Delphi requires a monthly fee for membership. Several plans are available based on the amount of time members plan to connect. One such option, the10/4 Plan, charges $10 per month for four hours of connect time, and $4 per hour thereafter.

See Also

America Online; AppleLink; BIX; Commercial Online Services; CompuServe; Email; eWorld; Internet; Prodigy

Deltagraph Pro, *See Charting and Graphing Applications*

Demo Software

To help potential customers evaluate their programs, many software publishers provide free demonstration versions.

These demo versions usually work just the same as a commercial version of the product, but important features are disabled. For example, a demo version of an equation editor might place a gray box behind each equation so that it can't be usable in a publication. Other demo versions disallow printing, place the word "DEMO" on each printed page, or stop working after a specified amount of time.

See Also

Alpha Version; Beta Versions; Beta Testing

Densitometer, *See Color Measuring*

Dependencies, QuickTime

When cutting and pasting segments of QuickTime movies in a program like Apple's MoviePlayer, the system does not actually copy the entire content of the

movie. Instead a pointer, to the segment of the movie is copied and transferred. This is done primarily for efficiency sake. Copying all that information into the Clipboard and out of the Clipboard would take a lot of time.

The edited movie is saved with the pointer to the other movies, but not with the actual movie data. The new movie is now dependent upon the other movies. This means that if you were to delete the original movie, the new movie will not play.

MoviePlayer is capable of removing these dependencies and creating a new movie with all of the clips copied into that movie. This creates a **self-contained movie**.

Not all programs create dependent movies. Adobe **Premiere**, for example, does not do this. Also, a self-contained movie is not the same as a **flattened movie**. Flattening a movie is used primarily when a movie will be played on a Windows computer, and removes the **resource** fork of the movie.

Not only are self-contained movies easier to distribute to others, they also play better, because QuickTime does not have to jump from one file, and one location on the disk, to another.

Another useful feature of MoviePlayer is the Get Movie Info option from the Movie menu. This displays information about the movie, including file size and any movies upon which the current movie is dependent.

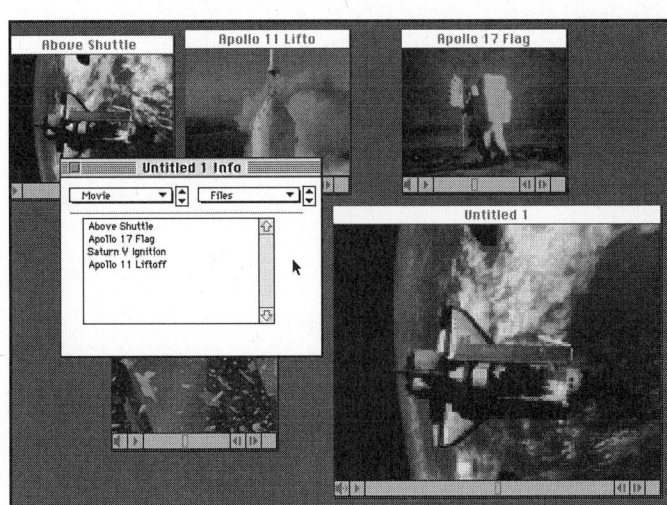

See Also

Flattened Movies; Self-Contained Movies

DeRez, *See Rez*

Descender

A descender is that part of a character that sticks down below the rest of the character. Not all letters have descenders. Lower case g, j, p, and y are examples of letters containing descenders.

See Also

Ascender; Line Spacing; Typesetting Terms

Descent

MacPlay's foray into the **First-Person Perspective Shooter** realm is something to get excited about. Mixing Shooter tactics with a Flight Sim motif, **Descent** uses a 3D rendering engine that allows for six degrees of freedom as you maneuver a spaceship through intergalactic mine shafts at breakneck speed. Descent rates as one of the most disorienting games, sending you through multiple turns, twists and loop-de-loops as you attempt to complete your missions. Because it is much less of a gore-fest than other Shooters like **DOOM II** or Hexen, Descent should appeal to those looking for the rapid pace of a shoot-em-up without the mess. Descent is arguably one of the better games in the shooter genre. The sequel, Descent II, should be available by the time this book is published.

See Also

DOOM II; Hexen: Beyond Heretic; Marathon I & Marathon II: Durandal

Deselecting a File

If you select a file and then decide you don't want to use it, you can deselect the file by clicking your cursor elsewhere in the active window. To deselect an item, it first must be selected or **highlighted** (dark gray). To deselect a file, click the **desktop** once or click just above or below the file, for example. To deselect text, simply click your cursor elsewhere within the text.

See Also

Active Window; Click; Cursor; Desktop, The; Highlight

DesignCAD 2D/3D

DesignCAD 2D/3D from DesignCAD, Inc. is one of the most widely distributed medium-end CAD programs on the world market. It offers intuitive easy to learn modeling and dimensioning tools and all of the basic CAD options most users expect. The DesignCAD environment takes the four-view approach for the layout of the editing screen (side, top, and front projection views and a perspective view all shown at once), although the user can select to work in only one of the projected views while turning the other two off. The perspective view is dedicated to rendering purposes only, although renders can also take place in any of the three selected projection views. All of the editing of the selected object takes place in one of the projection views.

Dimensioning DesignCAD has very intuitive options for adding dimensioning data to a view, so much so that you should be able to master its dimensioning routines in about two hours. Fifteen separate dimensioning options are included, including degree of arc and straight overlaps.

3D Options DesignCAD offers only two viewplane possibilities, Orthographic and Perspective. It does feature a unique capability when it comes to viewing the 3D viewplane, however, since it includes a small control box that allows you to animate the 3D view in real time in any of six directions. At any time, using this controller, you can spin the view around to preview any viewing angle in 3D space.

Text DesignCAD offers basic text commands: Font, Style, Size, and three Alignment variables. It has no capacity for translating text into extrudable data.

Symbol Library DesignCAD includes a deep symbol library for standards-oriented applications. Included are collections of symbols for Architecture, Cabinet, Electrical, Electronic, Hydraulic and Piping.

Import/Export Normal saves are as a DesignCAD database, though PICT files can be imported and PICT and RIB (MacRenderman files) can be exported. DesignCAD does include a separate program however, DesignCAD Importer/Exporter, for more extensive file imports and exports. With the aid of this module, DesignCAD can import DXF (AutoCAD release 10), IGES (International Graphics Exchange Standard), XY or XYZ coordinates, DesignCAD 2D MS/DOS and DesignCAD 3D MS/DOS. It can export a wider range of formats than it imports, including: RIB, EPSF, DXF, IGES, XY or XYZ coordinates, DC2, DC3, and two plotter language formats (HPGL and DMPL). The files targeted for MacRenderman from DesignCAD must be in the 3D isometric format.

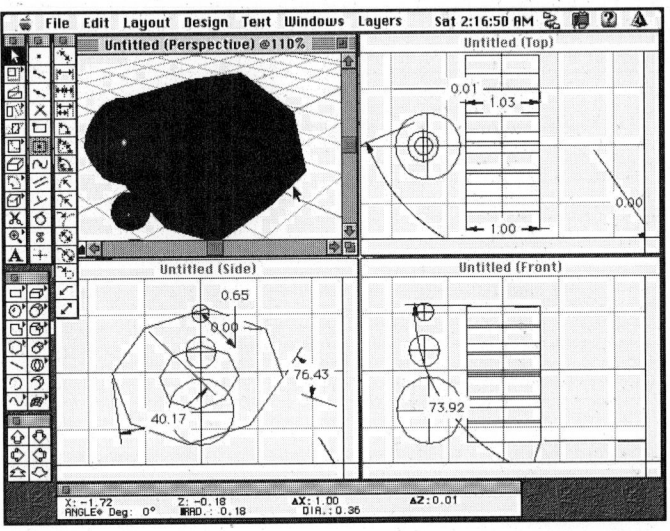

Animation Except for the controllable animation of the 3D view already mentioned, DesignCAD has no animation capacity. The only work-around might be to save a series of PICT files and then compile an animation from them in a suitable editing program.

Rendering Options DesignCAD offers basic rendering options which can be targeted to any of the XYZ views or to the 3D viewplane: Flat, Goraud or Phong shading, and the ability to alter the color and the intensity of the specularity of selected objects. There is no capacity to add additional light sources.

Special Features DesignCAD allows for the object creation "Multigons," 3D extruded polygons with any number of sides. The number of sides is set in a separate dialog. Layer addition and deletion are supported, similar to **Photoshop**. DesignCAD also includes a special smoothing algorithm that transforms angular shapes into smoother curved surfaces, a process that can be repeated as many times a necessary.

See Also

Photoshop

Designing Web Pages, *See Web Page*

Desk Accessories

Desk Accessories are designed as mini-applications that you can access while using any other application. You access them from the **Apple menu**, which always appears, regardless of which program is running, on the far left side of the menu bar. Before MultiFinder and **System 7.0**, the Macintosh did not let you open more than one application at the same time, so Apple created some mini-applications that you can access at anytime called desk accessories.

They get their name because many of the original items were based on common accessories found on an office desk, such as: a calculator, a note pad, a clock, and so on. These desk accessories were actually a part of the system and they were accessed from the Apple menu. The benefit was that you could access them in any program from the Apple menu without having to quit the program. So if you were writing a letter, and needed to do a little math, you didn't have to quit and launch a calculator—you could select it from the Apple menu and it would appear, floating above your currently running application.

DAs had to be installed directly into your system through the use of a **Font/DA mover**. This Apple utility let you choose DAs and **fonts** from a list and move them directly into the system folder. Since System 7, Apple has done away with the Font/DA mover completely and you can just drag items directly into a folder called **Apple Menu Items** within your **System Folder** to add items to the Apple menu. Besides the DAs that Apple has developed, there are dozens of Desk Accessories developed by third-party developers that do everything from act as an electronic address book to dial your phone.

See Also

Apple Menu; Apple Menu Items; Font/DA Mover; System 7.0; System Folder

Deskdraw, *See Drawing Applications*

Desktop, The

When you start your Macintosh, it goes through a **startup** procedure to load the computer's **Operating System** into memory. After a Macintosh has completed this procedure, the Macintosh desktop appears. This is where you can access **icons** for your **startup** drive, any external drives, **disks**, and the **trash can**. A **menu bar** of command menus, across the top of the desktop, enables you to access a host of computer-related tasks such as: Printing, formatting disks, restarting and shutting down the computer, launching applications, finding files, and most of the housekeeping-type functions of the computer.

The Finder is the Macintosh computer's starting place, a type of home base for beginning a session with the Mac. You'll know you're in the Finder when you see the desktop. When the computer starts, it takes you to the desktop, and when you're finished with the computer, you go back to the desktop to shut down. The Finder is a key part of the Macintosh Operating System and probably its most recognizable feature.

When Apple originally introduced the Macintosh, the desktop metaphor was designed with the same items that might appear on a real desktop in an office: A

calculator, a **notepad**, file **folders**, a **clock**, a trash can, and so on. They felt this would make learning how to operate the Macintosh much easier. Where, for example, would you throw away a file you didn't want? In the trash can, of course. Where would you store your business documents? In a file folder, of course. These metaphors proved so popular that the desktop of today looks much the same as it did when the Macintosh was introduced in 1984.

See Also

Calculator; Commands; Disk; Folders; Formatting; Hard Drive; Icons; Launching; MacOS; Menu; NotePad; Restart; Shut Down; Startup; System; Trash Can

Desktop DB

The Desktop DB is an invisible **file** that tracks which files were created by which applications. It ensures that your documents always match their respective applications. The Desktop DB also ensures that a file you created in Microsoft Word, for example, knows it's a Word file. That way, when you **double-click** a Word document, Desktop DB finds and **launches** Microsoft Word and then opens the document.

See Also

Double-Click; File; Launcher Control Panel; System

Desktop DF

As you move files on and off your **hard drive**, the Desktop DF tracks each file. It tracks those files that have been moved or deleted, and the icon for each. Over time, this file can get rather large and sometimes **corrupted**. So, occasionally, you may have to **rebuild the desktop** to get this file back down to size and operating properly. Because this file is invisible, you won't have contact with the Desktop DF, but it is working behind the scenes on every disk, tracking icons and files.

See Also

Corrupted; Hard Drive; Rebuilding the Desktop

Desktop File

The desktop file actually is two invisible system files (Desktop DB and Desktop DF) that are responsible for keeping track of the following:

- Where your files are located on your **hard disks**
- Which **icons** are associated with each file
- Any comments you've added to a file's Comments box
- Which view you've chosen for specific windows (view by name, view by icon, and so on)
- Which files are in which folders
- Other important information on your system and contents of your hard drive

Keeping track of all this is quite a complicated task. After some time the desktop file can become rather large and possibly **corrupted**. When this happens, you may see files without icons, or you may have files whose icons have switched with one another. These are the early warning signs of a corrupted desktop file that needs to be repaired through a process called **rebuilding the desktop** (which is done easily with a simple key command at startup). If this corruption continues, it can lead to a loss of files. For that reason, many users rebuild their desktops monthly as a preventative maintenance measure.

Desktop files are present in all types of disks (hard disks, disks, external drives, and so on), because they all need desktop files to keep track of their contents and organization.

See Also

Corrupted Files; Hard Disks; Icons; Rebuilding the Desktop

Desktop Level

The desktop level is the visual part of the Mac's **Finder** that is often called the Finder **Desktop**. The desktop level is where you have access to desktop items such as the **Trash** and hard drive **icon** or a mounted **disk**. After the Mac's **startup** procedure, you begin working from the desktop level. As windows and applica-

tions are opened, they stack up above one another. The desktop level is always the bottom level of all open windows and applications, with everything stacking on top of the desktop level. If you hear a reference stating, "return to the Desktop Level," it's telling you to return to the Finder and its desktop with the familiar desktop icons, such as the **Trash**, that you see when you first start your Mac.

You can select files from your hard drive or any mounted disk and drag them onto the desktop. You can even keep applications or frequently used **utilities** on the desktop for easy access. **StuffIt Expander** is a utility often left on the desktop. StuffIt Expander enables you to drag almost any **compressed file** directly onto the StuffIt Expander icon to be decompressed. Keeping it on the desktop, rather than buried within a folder on your hard drive, makes it easy to **drag-and-drop** files directly onto StuffIt Expander from any disk or folder.

See Also

Compressing Files; Disks and Drives; Drag-and-Drop; Hard Disks; Icons; Make Alias Command; Startup Sequence; StuffIt; Trash; Utility

Desktop Management Utilities, *See System and Desktop Management Utilities*

Desktop Manager Extension

This little-known Apple extension was designed for people who were making the switch from System 6 to **System 7** and were running both systems on the same computer. The way the desktop is built on these two systems is significantly different, and each time you switch from System 6 to System 7, you have to wait for the System 7 desktop to rebuild, which takes a few minutes. The Desktop Manager extension avoids this problem by adding an invisible System 7 style desktop file to System 6 that alleviates the need to **rebuild the desktop** when switching systems.

See Also

Rebuilding the Desktop; System 7.0

D

Desktop Models, Macintosh Family

In 1984, Apple made a conscious decision to design a computer that could be learned quickly and used by an ordinary person. This decision determined the look, feel, and usability features of the Macintosh in all ways. The first Macs were compact, all-in-one systems that were not expandable. Today's Macs are modular systems where you can pick and choose the type of display you want to use, your keyboard, the amount of Random Access Memory and hard disk storage you want, and the additional peripherals, such as fax/modems or CD-ROM units you want to include. Yet, all Macs retain the ease of use that is based on the deep integration of its hardware and software.

There are actually several generations of Macintoshes available based upon two types of integrated circuits: the Motorola 680x0 and the Apple/IBM/Motorola **PowerPC** 60x. 680x0 Macs are being phased out, although some consumer versions (called Performas) still use the 68040 chip and the lowest-end PowerBook, the 190, also uses this chip. If you see the term "Centris" or "Quadra," these are the last in the line of 68040 Macs. Modern Macs are based on a newer chip technology called Reduced Instruction Set Chip **(RISC)**. Most of the desktop Macs sold today are based on this PowerPC chip.

Although Apple is currently manufacturing mostly Power Macs and some specialized 68040 Performa

desktop models, and laptops, there are many existing 680x0 Macintoshes in use. Apple provides **upgrade paths** for these desktop models via three ways: Power Macintosh Upgrade Card, the Macintosh Processor Upgrade, and the **Power Mac Logic Board** Upgrade.

The following table describes how these three methods can be applied to the various existing older Macs to bring them up to Power Mac performance. DayStar Digital also offers excellent upgrade cards and logic boards for use in upgrading Quadras and Centris Macs to Power Mac 6100 or 7100 performance levels.

The Power Mac is now in its second generation of computers and offers business users an extensive array of processing power and efficiency. What you see today in the Power Mac (see the following figure) is the culmination of 20 years of research into how to make a computer both usable and affordable.

As of the writing of this book (February 1996), Apple offers five Power Mac desktop models in varying performance and configurations:

- Power Mac 6100/66 with DOS Compatibility Card
- Power Mac 7200/75
- Power Mac 7200/90
- Power Mac 7500/100
- Power Mac 8500/120
- Power Mac 9500/132

Upgrade Paths for Existing Macs

Upgrade Method	Applicable Mac Model	Description of Process
Power Mac 601 Upgrade Card	Quadra 605, 610, 630, 650, 660AV, 700, 800, 840AV, 900, and 950, Centris 610, 650, and 660AV	Owner inserts card into the 68040 Processor Direct Slot with a screwdriver.
Macintosh Processor Upgrade	Quadra 800 and 840AV, LC 475, 520, 550, 575, and 630	A complete motherboard swap performed by an authorized Apple dealer.
Power Mac 6100 Logic Board Upgrade	Quadra/Centris 610, Quadra 630, Quadra 650, Quadra 660AV	A logic board swap that must be performed by an authorized Apple dealer.

Desktop Macs come in both box and tower models. The model number denotes the type of case built. The higher the model number within the series, the more features the computer contains. Apple also designates the clock speed of each model in its name by adding a slash and a number, for example the 7500/90 and 7500/100 are two separate Power Macs within the 7xxx series containing the same feature set, but different PowerPC chip clock speeds. You will pay accordingly more for higher performance chips (measured in megahertz or MHz). The following table describes the various desktop model designs and their series numerical designations.

Desktop Macs

Series Number	Models	Characteristics
9xxx	Power Mac 9500	Tall, tower-style chassis with vertical expansion bays
8xxx	Power Mac 8500	Mini-tower chassis
7xxx	Power Mac 7100, 7200, and 7500	Square, desktop case
6xxx	Power Mac 6100	Flatter, "pizza box" case

Although Apple markets Power Mac desktop models in various configurations, all Power Macs provide the following features:

- The capability to recognize speech and to speak. This speech recognition capability is based on both the **PlainTalk** software and the processing power of the PowerPC chip.

- The **Geoport** connector. Makes Power Macs telephone-savvy, providing voice and data telephone connections via specialized chip sets. Each Power Mac contains two Geoport connectors.

- High-quality sound input and output. The fidelity of the Power Mac sound system approaches that of a compact disc.

- Support for caching. Power Macs provide a slot for a level-2 cache card that increases the performance of the processor by storing the most recently used instructions and data.

See Also

Desktop Models, Macintosh Family; Geoport; Processors, PowerPC

Desktop without Open Windows

When you restart your Macintosh, your desktop appears in the exact condition as when you shut down, meaning, it appears with any open windows and folders that were open when you shut down. To have all open windows closed when you start up, hold the Option key just before the desktop appears (after all the icons have appeared across the bottom of your screen), and your desktop appears with no windows or folders open.

Desktop Pattern

Your Macintosh computer's system enables you to customize the color and look of the background that appears on your **desktop**. You can customize the background by selecting a desktop pattern from Apple's **Desktop Patterns control panel**. This control panel provides you with a variety of designs, textures, and colors for customizing the background of your desktop.

To assign a pattern to your desktop background, scroll through the examples of patterns, and when you find one you like, **click** the Set Desktop Pattern **button**. That pattern will become your new background. The system will remember your choice, and the next time you start up, this new background choice will appear.

A number of third-party utilities are available that provide more desktop backgrounds. Some of the most popular include:

- Wallpaper
- Chameleon

Freeware desktop patterns can be **downloaded** from **online services**, and then **copied** and **pasted** directly into the Desktop Patterns control panel to add to your list of choices.

See Also

Button; Click; Control Panels; Copy Command; Desktop Pattern; Desktop, The; Online Services; Paste Command

Desktop Patterns Control Panel

The Desktop Patterns Control Panel contains a variety of desktop patterns for you to choose from. To view the various patterns, use the scroll bars to **scroll** through the patterns. If you see a pattern you'd like to have as the background of your **desktop**, click Set Desktop Pattern and the currently displayed pattern becomes your desktop's background, as shown in the figure.

You can add any PICT image to your Desktop Patterns Control Panel and it will automatically be tiled to fit your desktop, regardless of the size of your monitor. To add a PICT image to your desktop Control Panel, simply copy a PICT graphic from a graphics program (including **SimpleText**). Open the Desktop Patterns Control Panel and on the **Edit menu** choose Paste. This pastes the PICT image from the **Clipboard** into the Desktop Patterns Control Panel. This PICT image will now be a permanent part of your desktop patterns. If you want to delete a PICT, select **Clear** from the Edit menu.

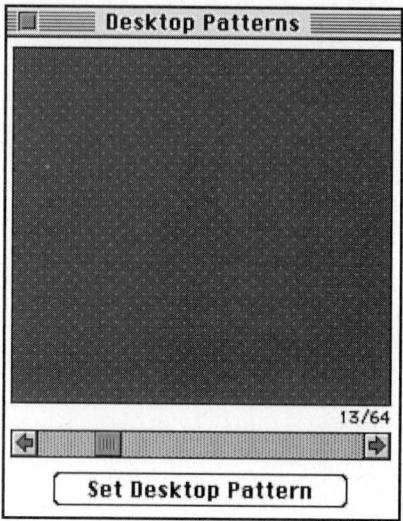

To change your desktop pattern using the Desktop Patterns control panel, follow these steps:

1. Choose the Desktop Patterns control panel from the Control Panels submenu on the Apple menu (or System Folder).

2. Scroll until you find the pattern that you'd like to use as your desktop background and click Set Desktop Pattern. That pattern is applied to your desktop.

See Also

Clear Command; Clipboard; Desktop, The; Edit Menu; SimpleText

Desktop Patterns Tricks

The **Desktop Patterns Control Panel** that comes with **System 7.5** has a hidden feature enabling you to make any desktop pattern the background for your desk accessories (such as the Find File dialog box, the **Calculator**, and so on). To add the background of your choice to your DAs, open the Desktop Patterns Control Panel. You see a button at the bottom of the window that reads, "Set Desktop Pattern." If you hold the Option key down, you'll see that the button now reads, "Set Utilities Pattern." All you need to do is choose a pattern, hold the Option key, and click "Set Utilities Pattern." The next time you open your

Calculator or Find File DA, you'll see the background pattern you've chosen as the background for these utilities.

To edit an existing desktop pattern, select the pattern you want to edit, choose Copy, and paste the pattern into a graphics program document for editing. In System 7.5 and higher, you can find the pattern you want to edit and drag it onto the desktop where it appears as a clipping file that can be opened in most graphics programs for editing. After a file has been edited, it can be copied again and pasted back into the Desktop Patterns control panel.

In System 7.5 and higher, you can drag any PICT file in your **Scrapbook** directly into the Desktop Patterns Control Panel, and vice versa.

See Also

Calculator Keys; Desktop Patterns Control Panel; Scrapbook; System 7.5

Desktop Presentation Software, *See Presentation Software*

Desktop Printing

The **desktop publishing** phenomenon has brought about a completely new way to reproduce printed matter—the desktop printer. Before desktop publishing brought professional quality printing within reach of anyone who could buy a Macintosh computer and a LaserWriter printer, printed matter was mostly generated from printing presses and various kind of duplicating machines, including the office copiers pioneered by Xerox. Office copiers still play a major role in reproducing printed matter, and some types of copiers are even used for direct output from a computer. It is the desktop printer, however, that has had the greatest impact on printing in general.

So many types of desktop printers are available, and the price ranges are so great, that many consumers find the process of choosing one very difficult. In fact, price is often the deciding factor, but this is not always the best criterion. Printing resolution, printing (imaging) technology, speed, memory, **PostScript** compatibility, and color capability are really more important factors than price. Desktop printers can be placed into the two broad categories of PostScript and non-PostScript. PostScript is the desktop publishing industry standard for printer output. It is a programming language that enables printers to produce complex high-resolution images. Further categorization is based on the printing technology itself. For example, most desktop printers are laser printers that print only in black. These use toner and an electrostatic drum technology. Other types of desktop printers use the inkjet technology (both color and black and white), thermal-wax transfer (color), or dyesublimation (color). We will discuss the difference between PostScript and non-PostScript first, and then examine each of the imaging technologies.

PostScript is fully described elsewhere in this book, but it is well to understand its benefits in regard to two basic desktop printing needs—sophisticated typography and high-resolution graphics. PostScript is the basis of the desktop publishing industry typographic standard: Adobe Type 1 fonts. These fonts are used almost universally by graphics industry professionals, and they will not print on a non-PostScript printer unless a separate processor is used. The **TrueType** font technology works with non-PostScript printers, but it is not widely accepted in professional circles. Encapsulated PostScript (EPS) graphics do not print well on non-PostScript printers. Certainly, non-PostScript printers are adequate for many types of office printing, but they are not a good choice as a primary printer in a desktop publishing operation.

Desktop printers using the electrostatic drum technology are the most ubiquitous in the desktop publishing industry and in office environments. Invented by Chester Carlson in 1937, the electrostatic printing process involves placing an electrostatic charge on the photoconductive surface of a metal drum or plate. When the charged surface is exposed to light, the charge is dissipated wherever light strikes it. This results in a charged image area, which attracts a toner composed of finely ground plastic mixed with metal particles. The toner is transferred to paper and bonded to it by heat. The process was originally marketed by Xerox and is sometimes known as Xerography. It was, of course, the technology behind the success of the first Xerox office copiers. Most brands of office copiers now use the process or a variation on it. The electrostatic charge is controlled by a laser beam in the typical laser printer. The beam itself is directed by software instructions from either the computer or the PostScript processor built into the printer. Laser printers may be either PostScript or non-PostScript with the non-PostScript printer generally being less expensive. Laser printers provide image resolutions of 300 dpi, 600 dpi, 1,200 dpi, and 1,800 dpi. Paper size ranges from 8.5×11 inches to 11.75×25 inches. The larger paper sizes allow for 11×17 inch full bleed. Laser printers do an excellent job in printing solid areas, and the higher resolution models can produce adequate **halftones** in the 65 to 100 lpi range. Considering that most newspapers use 85 lpi halftones, a high-resolution laser printer can be useful in this area of publishing. While most desktop laser printers use only black toner, highly sophisticated (and expensive) digital presses based on the same technology are now used for process color printing.

Many non-PostScript printers, such as the Apple StyleWriter, are of the inkjet type. In inkjet technology, liquid ink is sprayed or dropped on the paper through tiny nozzles. In some models the ink is already liquid, but in others, a solid ink is melted by heat. The type of paper is an important consideration for liquid ink models. Using a paper that is too absorbent can result in disappointing color and blurred images. A glossy paper especially developed for inkjet printers can actually expand the color gamut of the device. The solid ink models tend to print more brilliant color because the ink solidifies before it can soak into the paper. Paper size ranges from 8.5×11 inches to 11×17 inches. These small desktop printers are inexpensive, and some are very limited in their imaging capabilities. Inkjet resolution ranges from 360 dpi to 720 dpi, and they are very slow compared to a laser printer. Because many desktop inkjet printers are non-PostScript, they use the QuickDraw graphics language developed by Apple when they are part of a Macintosh system. Color inkjet printers can produce pleasing color images and are popular with some artists. The image quality of inkjet printers varies among the different brands, and it is wise to look at several before making a choice. A high-end inkjet printer, the Iris inkjet from Scitex America, is often used to make accurate color proofs. The Iris is, of course, much more expensive (about $100,000) than a desktop inkjet. It uses precision ink nozzles to produce high-quality calibrated color images.

Another type of desktop printer is the thermal-wax color printer. These printers produce brilliant color images by melting and bonding a wax-based pigment to the paper. The pigment is on a roll of plastic film or ribbon. Some thermal-wax printers use four colors (cyan, magenta, yellow, black) and others use only three colors (cyan, magenta, yellow). Three-color printers sometimes produce muddy-looking blacks, however. As the paper passes through the printer, colored wax is applied in dots of color. The dots build up a full-color image in much the same way as process color printing on a printing press. Paper sizes range from 8.5×11 inches to 11×17 inches. Most thermal-wax printers can utilize plain paper, but paper quality can make a big difference in image quality. Thermal-wax printers are generally more expensive than inkjet but are still moderately priced. Banding in continuous-tone gradations is sometimes a problem with thermal-wax printers, but they can be useful to graphic designers in making color comps.

The best desktop color printing comes from dye-sublimation printers. These are more expensive than inkjet and thermal-wax color printers, but the difference in image quality makes up for the extra cost. Dye-sublimation printers provide near photographic quality images by applying a dye-like pigment that is

D

absorbed into the paper in a gaseous form. This results in transparent colors that create a continuous-tone image. Otherwise, they somewhat resemble thermal-wax printers in the way they operate. Like thermal-wax printers, dye-sublimation printers use **process colors** (CMYK). Some printers are available that can switch between thermal-wax and dye-sublimation mode. A heavy paper resembling photographic paper is usually required and may range in size from 8.5×11 inches to 11×17 inches. A dye-sublimation printer is the best type to use for desktop color proofs. The 3M Rainbow, a high-end dye-sublimation printer, is often used by printing firms and prepress trade shops for color proofing on jobs to be offset printed.

In recent years, the color laser printer has become more popular due to decreasing prices. Desktop color laser printers use the same electrostatic drum and toner technology used by standard black and white laser printers. The color in toner-based images is rich-looking, with excellent density range. Output resolution for color laser printers, including color copiers with raster image processors, ranges from 300 to 600 dpi. Higher resolutions should be available soon. Most color laser printers are in the 8.5×11 inch format, but some 11×17 inch models are available. Of course, any paper suitable for a standard laser printer will work well in a color laser printer.

See Also

Color Gamut; Color Printing; Color Separations; Desktop Printers Digital Halftones; Dithering; Preflight and File Hand-Off; Prepress; Printing; Process Color

Desktop Publishing

Desktop publishing (DTP) is the process of producing any publication or document using a personal computer (PC). Personal computers are also known as desktop, or microcomputers. Most publications produced in this manner are intended to be printed on a **printing press** for mass distribution; however, many are printed using a digital printing device. Quantity and image-quality requirements usually determine whether a desktop publication will be printed on a printing press or a digital printer, such as a laser printer. The international graphics industry has been greatly affected by desktop publishing. In the United States, DTP has all but replaced traditional publishing methods. Desktop publishing has had such far-reaching effects that it is truly a technological revolution. The term, electronic publishing, is sometimes used instead of desktop publishing.

A wide range of publications can be produced using desktop computers. Desktop publications may include anything from a single-color advertising flyer to a full-color coffee table book or corporate brochure. Simple publications, such as the single-color advertising flyer, are sometimes referred to as "low-end" desktop publishing. More expensively produced desktop publications, such as the coffee-table book, are said to be "high-end." Desktop publishing on a personal computer is the first step in a process known as electronic **prepress** (EPP). Electronic prepress involves digital imaging, color adjustment, **digital halftones**, **color trapping**, page imposition, **stripping**, and high-resolution output to film or printing plates.

Conversation with Paul Brainerd

Newspaperman, computer whiz, and now environmentalist, Paul Brainerd helped Apple establish its foothold in business when he created PageMaker, the product that linked with Adobe's PostScript page description language and Apple's LaserWriter, to create a new industry—desktop publishing.

Maclopedia: How did you come to invent PageMaker?

Paul: I'd been a newspaper reporter and editor for about 10 years. In the early 1970s, I went over to Atex;

continues

they were providing DEC PDP 11s for newspapers, with VDTs—video display terminals—that were going to replace all the manual typewriters, so the writers could write at the terminal, and then go right to the typesetter without rekeying. We were right at the transition from hot metal to cold type.

In 1984, I was working for Atex, and several things came together. Atex was purchased by Eastman Kodak, and I moved out to the West Coast to manage a plant in Redmond, Washington. I got an opportunity to start my own business because they closed down the plant. You see, there were all the engineers who had just been laid off, so we started Aldus. I put in a hundred thousand dollars, and worked for a year without pay, and another year or so at half pay.

Four things came together to make it happen—along with time and good luck and hard work by several groups, and some connections. The Mac had been introduced in January 1984. John Warnock had formed Adobe, with a vision for a new printing language called PostScript. And Jonathan Seybold was being a consultant to Apple at the time, and doing work for Adobe. I had known his father, back to Volume One, Number One of the *Seybold Reports*. But Jonathan was the glue that introduced us all to one another. He said, "You should talk to Adobe. I can't tell you what they are doing because I'm under nondisclosure, but go talk to John."

Now we already had the basic concept of the microcomputer as a layout tool, but we were still defining the market, from January through June of 1984. So I went down and I introduced myself to John Warnock. He shared with me some of their ideas. And then I talked with Apple. I met Bruce Blumberg, the product manager for a product that was going to become the LaserWriter. We ended up being one of the first three companies to get a LaserWriter up here in Washington—Microsoft, Lotus, and us.

In June 1984, then, we had our vision of the software project, and Steve Jobs had the Mac with its graphic interface, and Adobe was trying to build this printer software, PostScript, so we could get output comparable to what the traditional graphics industry expected. So all these groups converged, and even then it wasn't clear how it was going to work.

Maclopedia: How did the development process go?

Paul: It was very much bottom up. People think desktop publishing came about because someone made a top-level executive decision, but it was actually driven by people at the bottom of the organization, helping each other out.

Maclopedia: How did you come up with the term "desktop publishing?"

Paul: I came up with the term in June or July 1984, at a board meeting of Aldus. One of our directors said, "Well, what are you going to call this concept?" And one of these other companies was using the term *desktop*. So I said, "Why don't we call it desktop publishing?" I worked with the press to define what desktop publishing was, and the press was really interested because every reporter is a closet book author, and a lot of people would call and ask, "What is desktop publishing," and I would go over it on the phone with them.

In early 1985, there were very few units of the Mac being sold. Apple needed to get manufacturing up. We had announced PageMaker in January of 1985, but we didn't actually start shipping PageMaker until July 1985.

> *People think desktop publishing came about because someone made a top-level executive decision, but it was actually driven by people at the bottom of the organization, helping each other out.*

And in the summer of 1985, Bruce Blumberg called, and said, "I need a marketing plan. Can you put it together in 10 weeks?" So I pulled together a marketing plan with dealer training and a video, all the components for the launch of desktop publishing, and that went to John Sculley and he approved it. Desktop publishing became a way to distinguish the Mac from the IBM PC, and gave it an entry in the door, even if it was a back door. Sculley gives credit to desktop publishing in his book, *Odyssey*, saying it was the thing that made the Mac successful because it brought more volume. Desktop publishing wasn't the only thing, but it was one thing that gave the Mac credibility.

There weren't a lot of resources. I remember sitting in a small dark room at Apple, and we wrote down on the white board what Apple would do, and Aldus, and we divided up the work. It was a real grassroots, ground-up effort. We had designers here in Seattle come in and sit down and design pages. John Rennell came over one afternoon and played around for three or four days and produced the first page of a financial newsletter. That sample page was reproduced millions of times. We supplied the content and Apple supplied the money for *Wall Street Journal* ads.

I'd come down to Cupertino, and we would talk about the projects, and then get out and walk the hallways. [Rennel] would take me over to see the education department dealing with K-12, and he'd introduce me to the people and they would say, "I need some educational examples by Monday," and that would be Thursday. So we would go back to Seattle and work all weekend and FedEx packages out, and lo' and behold, they would be in the ads a month later.

Bruce had a real problem because the Apple sales folks in the field and the marketing people were campaigning to have the LaserWriter project killed. They thought that something selling for $7,000 was a disaster, and they had just been through the Lisa, which had been a disaster at $10,000. I give credit to Steve Jobs, who really believed in the LaserWriter and kept it going. And it had Adobe PostScript. And PageMaker came up with sample pages that demonstrated the quality of what you could do with the printer.

At trade shows, people would grab the output out of their hands, it was so unbelievable.

But Apple dramatically underestimated demand, and Canon didn't have enough engines. They were in short supply. In the United States you had to wait six weeks, but in Europe you might have to wait three to six months. There just wasn't any product—for 18 months. In the UK, when we launched our promotion, we booked more orders for Apple computers in the first four weeks than they had booked in the previous year. It just took everyone by surprise.

Maclopedia: So now that you've sold Aldus and PageMaker to Adobe, what are you doing?

Paul: I'm running an environmental foundation, supporting conservation in the Northwest forest. I'm giving back some of what I've learned. We gave out almost a million dollars in 75 grants last year, mostly to small grassroots community organizations. For instance, there's a Montana group working on a watershed, which is a prime trout habitat. In Alaska, a group is working to mobilize public participation in mine licensing. Water rights are a big issue. One-third of the streams in Washington are oversubscribed in terms of sustainable water, but everyone takes it as a God-given right to have water, but it won't be there.

And I've been seeing what I can do to link technology with the schools. At the University of Oregon school of journalism, I set up a fund to set up a network for faculty and students five years ago. It became a model for the rest of the school. Almost everyone is hooked up. They have two computer classrooms, with the faculty bringing in laptops and getting access to the Web. The key to that whole thing was that I insisted they hire a full-time technical support person to provide counseling to the faculty in a nonthreatening way.

The Apple Macintosh computer has played a key role in the development of desktop publishing. The graphical user interface (GUI) developed for the Macintosh operating system (OS) provided a platform for the development of desktop publishing software. In a graphical user interface, computer processes are displayed as graphics objects. Icons, windows, menus, dialog boxes, and other objects are manipulated through a **keyboard** or **mouse** to control the computer's software functions. Desktop publishing on the Macintosh spurred the development of peripheral devices, such as **scanners** and laser printers.

Although DOS-based personal computers utilizing the Microsoft **Windows** GUI play a significant role in desktop publishing, the Macintosh computer is preferred by most graphics industry professionals. The most recent version of Microsoft Windows, Windows 95, has opened up the possibility of increased competition between the Macintosh platform and the many brands of PCs that have evolved from the original IBM PC. Windows 95 creates a GUI very similar to that of the Apple Macintosh and more effectively utilizes the computer's **CPU** to perform graphics operations. Many desktop publishing and graphics software applications are available in both Macintosh and Windows versions.

Desktop publishing has redefined the graphics industry by making graphics technology accessible to anyone who owns a personal computer. Some traditional graphics professions have been greatly affected. For example, the **typesetting** profession no longer exists as a clearly definable vocation in most of the United States. The reason for this is that people who are engaged in DTP are performing their own typesetting, and it is not necessary for them to have it done by a professional. The **graphic design** profession is another that has been affected. Prior to DTP, most printed material was designed and prepared for printing by graphics designers and graphics production personnel employed by advertising agencies, graphics design firms, trade shops, and commercial printing firms. These individuals and firms are involved in desktop publishing now; however, there are many people with no background or experience in graphics arts who are also involved in DTP. This creates a need for training and eduction that specifically addresses desktop publishing and the broader-based graphic design issues it has engendered.

Page layout software, such as Adobe **PageMaker** and **QuarkXPress**, forms the basis of most desktop publishing on the Macintosh computer. **FrameMaker**, a sophisticated publishing software application marketed by **Adobe** Systems, Inc., is popular with some book publishers. Other software with page layout and typesetting capabilities is available, but PageMaker, QuarkXPress, and FrameMaker dominate the field. These software applications provide most of the tools necessary to design and produce any kind of publication. Desktop publishing may also require other types of software applications. Vector-image drawing (Adobe Illustrator, MacroMedia FreeHand) and raster-image manipulation (Adobe Photoshop) software applications are extremely useful. The Adobe PageMaker publication window displays an electronic page on which text and graphics can be manipulated. A tool palette (upper-right) provides tools for selecting objects, and creating text and simple graphics, as shown in the figure.

The frontiers of desktop publishing and electronic prepress are being rapidly expanded by the development of faster computers and more sophisticated software, and the Internet and the World Wide Web (WWW) provide an exciting glimpse into the future of publishing. Can you imagine that future without paper publications—where all communications are electronic?

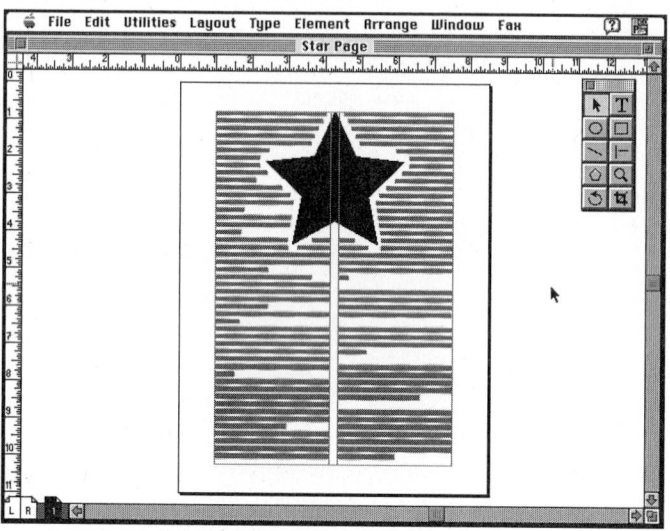

For More...

If you want to do this...

	Go to this entry...
Know more about DTP hardware	Desktop Publishing Hardware History and Culture of the Macintosh
Know more about electronic prepress	Printing
Know more about DTP software	Desktop Publishing Applications
Know more about publishing on the WWW	Internet
Know more about DTP terms	Typesetting Terms

Bibliography

For more information on desktop publishing, refer to the following books:

Desktop Publishing Success, Felix Kramer and Maggie Lovaas, published by Business One Irwin, 1991 (1-55623-424-4).

Electronic Prepress: A Hands-On Introduction, Bill Parsons, published by Delmar Publishers, 1995 (0-8273-6449-0).

Publishing on the World Wide Web, Greg Holden, published by Hayden Books, 1995 (1-56830-228-2).

Teach Yourself Web Publishing with HTML 3.0, Laura Lemay, published by Sams Net, 1996 (1-57521-064-9).

Welcome to Desktop Publishing, David Browne, published by MIS: Press, 1993 (1-55828-295-5).

Desktop Publishing Applications

Desktop publishers use many different programs to create different kinds of documents, choosing their tools just as carpenters or machinists pick the right tool for a particular job. Here's a look at the main categories of software commonly used for DTP:

- Page layout software allows you to take your ideas from words to fully-designed pages for newsletters, magazines, newspapers, or books. Programs such as Adobe **PageMaker**, **QuarkXPress**, and Adobe **FrameMaker** are designed to do many of the things modern word processors can do (such as creating running heads, automatically numbering pages, and formatting text in different styles), but they also allow for the integration of graphics, full color, and more complex formatting.

- Draw programs for the Mac include Adobe **Illustrator** and Macromedia **FreeHand**. These applications are used to create graphics based on lines, curves, and fills—**vector** graphics—from simple black and white line art to complex designs using color blends. Vector images can be scaled without any loss of resolution. Features like layers and the ability to move, skew, rotate, and otherwise alter components of a drawing make these packages very powerful.

- Adobe Photoshop is probably the best-known program for working with bitmapped graphics, like scanned photographs. Photoshop is a production workhorse for color correcting, retouching, and color separating photographs. But it's not limited to that. Photoshop and its competitors, such as HSC Live Picture, can also be used to create images from scratch, and other such applications, like Fractal Design Painter, are specifically designed as "paint" programs, used to create commercial and fine art on the Mac.

- If page layout and graphics applications are the framework of desktop publishing, fonts are like bricks. Thousands of typefaces are available, some based on designs that have been used for centuries and some as fashionable as the latest styles in shoes. A few fonts come with every Mac, but most designers end up with libraries of hundreds of fonts appropriate for any use imaginable. While the industry is dominated by PostScript fonts from Adobe, other fonts and formats (most notably TrueType, developed by Apple, and now widely distributed on Windows and Macs) are available from large "foundries" (a term left over from when type was made out of metal) and small ones, as well as from thousands of shareware authors.

- In the mid-1990s, **color management** software is just beginning to be truly useful; since the inception of desktop publishing, users have found it difficult, if not impossible, to make sure that the colors seen on a computer monitor will look the same when a piece is output from a color printer or printed on a four-color press. Now different software products can help make sure that happens—but the industry hasn't yet settled on a standard, although Apple's **ColorSync** 2.0 is being adopted by many hardware and software manufacturers.

- **Utility** programs pull all these others together. They can manage font collections (**Suitcase** and Adobe **Type Manager**), make sure all your software works together without crashing your Mac (**Conflict Catcher**), translate files back and forth from the different formats used by different applications (**MacLink**, **DeBabelizer**, Transverter Pro), compress files so they take less time to transfer over a modem (**StuffIt**), and more.

In addition to these definite categories, desktop publishers often use programs like Design Science's MathType for special purposes such as creating equations that can be imported into other documents. Other special programs create charts or tables and automate layout functions.

Whether these divisions will remain valid for long depends on two competing trends that will affect the future of desktop publishing applications. First, Apple is working on its OpenDoc technology, which allows applications to work more smoothly together on the same documents. Dozens of applets could be used to work on different parts of a document—some for creating graphics, others for setting up charts, and still others for other functions, like spellchecking. Microsoft's OLE (object linking and embedding) technology is offering the same idea on a more limited basis on both Windows and the Macintosh.

But for several years most software companies have competed to add features to their applications, rather than stripping them down to essentials. Drawing programs have built-in spellcheckers, page layout applications allow users to edit scanned photos, and word processors can act like spreadsheets. This trend has resulted in applications that tend to be large (taking up both hard-disk space and RAM) and often slow.

For the time being, users need to evaluate their needs and choose software accordingly. For many home users, a "**works**" program that incorporates many functions may be appropriate, while professional desktop publishers will probably need several different programs from the categories listed previously.

Prices vary wildly depending on a program's capabilities—a professional-level page layout application like QuarkXPress costs about $650, whereas low-end programs that claim to have the same features can costs as little as $30—so it's important to know as much about a program as possible before making a purchase. **Demo software** can help a lot—these versions of commercial applications are distributed free, but they have important features like printing disabled. Demos offer a good look at what a program does and how easy it is to use. Usually, they're available on online services, at many Internet sites, and on request from software companies, and they often come "bundled" with other software to fill up space on a disk.

See Also

Adobe Type Manager; Bitmapped Graphics; Color Management; Colorsync; Conflict Catcher; DeBabelizer; Demo Software; Drawing Applications; Fonts; FrameMaker; FreeHand; Illustrator; Live Picture; MacLink; MathType; Page Layout Applications; PageMaker; Paint Applications; Painter; Photoshop; PostScript; QuarkXPress; StuffIt; Suitcase; Utility; Vector Graphics

Desktop Publishing, Beginnings of

The first desktop publishing systems were not serious competition for **traditional publishing** methods. The **Apple Macintosh** computer with its graphical user interface (GUI) operating system provided a platform for the development of **page layout software** such as **PageMaker** and **QuarkXPress** in the mid-1980s, but there were many limitations. Early desktop publishing was performed on Macintosh computers with only 128K or 512K of **RAM**. The earliest Macs did not have **internal hard drives**, and kept all data, including operating system and software applications, on 400K **diskettes**. Since these Macs had only one built-in **diskette drive**, it was necessary to continuously switch the diskettes to operate the computer—a process humorously known as the "Macshuffle." In addition to the lack of data-storage capacity, other limitations included primitive software applications that "crashed" frequently, a poor selection of typefaces, and low-resolution output devices. Few individuals in the graphics industry were impressed with desktop publishing in its early days, and the whole process was scoffed at by many professionals.

The Macintosh rapidly grew in performance capability, however. **Hard drives**, **scanners**, and 300 dpi **laser printers** were developed, and desktop publishing began making small inroads into the traditional graphics industry. Even **DOS**-based computers joined the fray when Microsoft marketed the Windows GUI. It was not until high-resolution output capability was developed, however, that desktop publishing came into its own. By the late 1980s, electronic publication files could be output at very high resolutions on **imagesetters** such as the **Linotronic**. The **PostScript** page description language developed by **Adobe Systems, Inc**. became the DTP industry standard for high-resolution output and typography. After **Linotype-Hell**, **Scitex America**, **DuPont Crosfield**, **Screen**, and other traditional graphics industry vendors began developing high-end electronic publishing technologies in the early 1990s, desktop publishing began replacing traditional publishing.

See Also

Desktop Publishing; Desktop Publishing, History of; Desktop Publishing, Present Day; Mac History and Culture; Publishing, Traditional

Desktop Publishing Careers

The advent of desktop publishing technology opened up the graphics field to many more people. Probably the first traditional graphics industry career to be affected by desktop publishing was typesetting. In the mid-1980s, when the term "desktop publishing" was beginning to be a major buzz word, most graphic designers and other print-production specialists relied on professional typesetters for much of the typeset copy that went into a paste-up. Today, typesetting no longer exists as a clearly definable profession in most of the United States because desktop publishing enables everyone to set their own type, for better or worse. As for the typesetters themselves, many of them became desktop publishers or began providing other DTP-oriented services such as high-resolution output or training.

Of course, almost all other existing graphics and publishing industry careers have also been affected by desktop publishing. Most writers and editors have probably switched from the typewriter to the computer **wordprocessor** by now, and some authors even design and desktop publish their own books. One can hardly get a job as a graphic designer or art director with an advertising agency without some knowledge of computer graphics and **page layout software**. Trade shops and commercial printing firms have had to accommodate the new technology and even give up some traditional practices and attitudes. The **prepress** stage of print production has been greatly involved in the change to electronic technologies. Traditional prepress technicians are often faced with having to retrain, abandoning tried and true methods. Even printing industry sales personnel have had to change. Having had such a revolutionary effect on a well-established industry, it is no wonder that desktop publishing is still controversial at some levels.

Perhaps it is not the effect of desktop publishing and electronic prepress on the traditional graphics industry that is so remarkable, however. The really astonishing thing about DTP is how it has captured the imagination of so many people who were never involved in graphic design or publishing before. In the middle ages of Europe, only a privileged few members of the nobility or the clergy owned or had access to books or could even read and write. Everything was handwritten on parchment or paper that was so scarce it was used over and over again by scraping the ink off the surface. Contrast that with the newest communication revolution on the **World Wide Web**, and we must come to the conclusion that publishing is potentially in the hands of virtually everyone. The borders between the specialized areas of writing, graphic design, prepress, and print production are growing ever more blurred, and new specialties are emerging. A major difference is that the new specialties are much broader and harder to define due to the continuing tumult of change. Nevertheless, many types of jobs directly involve desktop publishing.

Two categories are useful in discussing desktop publishing careers: freelance/entrepreneurial and institutional/corporate. The freelance/entrepreneurial category is a natural for desktop publishing. For about

$10,000, one can set up a bare-bones desktop publishing business. Some may feel that number is too low for even a basic operation, but a truly frugal person can do it. The hardware and software are easy to purchase at a discount, and one really can do a decent job with a low-end Macintosh, **laser printer**, and **scanner** set up in a home office. So many options exist (as well as so many potential entry-level expenses) that many enterprising individuals make a living as independent purchasing consultants. The point is that desktop publishing is very attractive to individuals who want to be their own boss. Unfortunately, many find that it is not all that easy to make a living by setting up a desktop publishing business—a fact that freelance graphic designers have always known.

In the freelance arena, a high-level of graphic design skill and computer knowledge may be necessary to survive. Freelancers are often employed by advertising agencies, and many temporary job placement services have departments for placing graphic designers and production artists. Advertising agencies usually have high graphic design standards and expect freelancers to have a good portfolio of work to show. A temporary job service usually tests individuals seeking work in desktop publishing and business presentation graphics and then tries to match their skills with the needs of its clients. In that situation, the more adept one is in various software applications, the more work one can get. One advantage to freelancing as opposed to a full-service DTP business is that freelancers often work on-site using the employer's equipment and software. It is probably best to be prepared by having one's own desktop publishing setup, but it would be possible to be a freelancer without purchasing the hardware and software.

Lack of experience in printing production and no art and design training are major handicaps for many DTP entrepreneurs. This can be remedied to some extent by a commitment to training and education, but there is no substitute for experience. Part of the desktop publishing phenomenon is the proliferation of what professional designers consider bad design.

In fact, many traditional graphics professionals bemoan what appears to be a widespread acceptance of mediocrity throughout the desktop publishing industry. Whether this is actually true or not is beyond our purpose here. Suffice it to say that the graphics business is still changing and quality always seeks it own level. Anyone wishing to get seriously involved with graphic design and desktop publishing should be willing to make a commitment to excellence in order to succeed.

Aside from the expenses and training that may be necessary, some personal traits may affect an individual's performance as a desktop publishing freelancer or entrepreneur. These are the same traits that any self-employed person should have—self-reliance, confidence, good organizational and money-management skills, good communication and negotiation skills, and a willingness to set goals and work hard. Working in desktop publishing may require some additional qualities on top of that. The graphic design and publishing industries are notoriously deadline-driven, and the pressure of meeting deadlines (realistic or not) is more than some people can take. Patience and determination are required to operate a computer, and that often goes double in desktop publishing. Freelance work may be of a "feast or famine" nature, so there is not much job security. Attention to detail is the mark of a professional—sloppy work will not bring repeat clients. Finally, how will you react if you have worked twenty hours straight without a break to produce something you think is great, but your client rejects it out of hand and refuses to pay for the changes? And, can you wait 30, 60, or 90 days to be paid?

The institutional/corporate category may be where most desktop publishing is actually done, and it's not always done on a Macintosh computer. MS-DOS and Windows computers are very prevalent in corporate America. This is not particularly a problem for an experienced Mac user, for the Windows GUI or the Windows 95 operating system are needed to run desktop publishing software such as Adobe **PageMaker**,

QuarkXPress, and **FrameMaker**. The Windows environment is similar enough to the Mac that most people can get the hang of it rather quickly. The software applications are nearly identical on both platforms. The Macintosh has made some inroads, and loyal Mac users seeking jobs may luck out and find their favorite machine producing the company newsletter.

Regardless of which platform is in use, many different kinds of DTP situations exist in corporate or institutional environments. The types of publications produced are newsletters, technical documents, reports, sales proposals, advertising materials, catalogs, forms, books, and magazines. In most corporate settings, desktop publishing gets its start because management wants to save money and gain more creative control by bringing the design and production of publications in-house. In the early days of corporate DTP, the task of design and production often fell to barely qualified individuals who were quite overwhelmed. This situation was a boon to private training companies and consultants, and it still happens. More and more organizations are taking advantage of the growing number of people in the job market who are experienced in desktop publishing. Success in finding a DTP job in a large company may hinge on the job seeker's versatility with software and hardware. Success in the job itself will probably stem from an ability to adapt to a less than efficient operation while working to institute beneficial procedural changes. Office politics may be a hindrance. Knowing how to use more than one of the major software applications is a definite plus.

See Also

Desktop Publishing; Desktop Publishing Hardware; Desktop Publishing, Present Day; Desktop Publishing Training

Desktop Publishing and Color Electronic Prepress Systems (CEPS)

A color electronic prepress system (CEPS) is a high-end proprietary system dedicated to color image **scanning**, color correction, and **color separating**. The major vendors of CEPS are Linotype-Hell, Scitex America, DuPont Crosfield, and Screen.

See Also

Color Separations; Desktop Publishing and Digital Color; Desktop Publishing Hardware; Desktop Publishing, History of; Prepress; Scanning

Desktop Publishing and Color Management Systems (CMS)

A color management system (CMS) is a means to calibrate and control the appearance of device-dependent **digital color**. Color management systems are software applications that map the **color gamut** of an output device and use the information to control color specifications in desktop publishing software. EFIColor in **QuarkXPress**, Kodak Precision in **PageMaker**, and ColorSync from Apple are typical desktop publishing color management systems. The Kodak Precision CMS as well as other proprietary color management systems can be accessed from Adobe PageMaker's Edit Color dialog box. The CMS Source Profile dialog box allows a specific device profile to be selected.

CMS Source Profile	OK
Color Management is currently on.	Cancel

This Item Uses: **Kodak CM** ▼

Source profile: **Microtek : 600ZS** ▼

MT600ZS Ektacolor RGB input
00.05.01.02.02
Copyright (c) 1995 Eastman Kodak Company, All Rights Reserved.

See Also

Color Gamut; Color Printing; Desktop Publishing and Digital Color; PageMaker; QuarkXPress

Desktop Publishing Color Models

Color models are used in graphics software applications to specify **spot** and **process colors**. Typical color models are the process color model (CMYK), the RGB model (red, green, blue), and the HSL model (hue, saturation, lightness) or HSB model (hue, saturation, brightness). The PhotoYCC color model was developed by Eastman Kodak for photo CD systems. Although not strictly classified as color models, **color matching systems** such as PANTONE, TOYO, TRUMATCH, FOCOLTONE, and MUNSELL provide other means to specify both spot and process colors. The Edit Color dialog box in QuarkXPress provides access to color models and color matching systems. Adobe PageMaker has a similar dialog box.

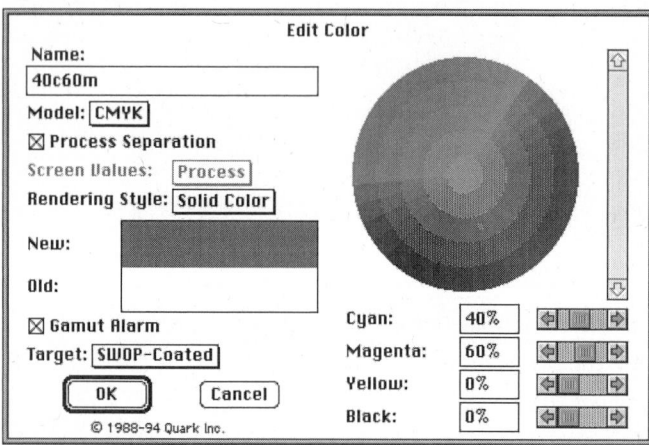

See Also

Color Matching Systems; Color Printing; Desktop Publishing and Digital Color; Process Color; Spot Color

Desktop Publishing Color Standards

A color standard is a means of standardizing color based on the science of colorimetry. Color standards, such as CIEXYZ or CIELAB, are an attempt to overcome the problems of device-dependency characteristic of **digital color**. The CIE (Commission Internationale de l'Eclairage) color standard was developed in 1931.

See Also

Color Gamut; Color Printing; Desktop Publishing; Desktop Publishing and Digital Color

Desktop Publishing CPU Requirements

Desktop publishing CPU requirements are directly related to the types of software being used and individual needs for processing speed, graphics display, data storage, and peripheral devices. Basic desktop publishing can be performed on almost any Macintosh, but faster processing speeds and plenty of RAM mean better productivity in most cases. The recent versions of many DTP software applications require 16MB of RAM or more to function well.

Processing speed has proven to be the single most important feature to determine the marketability of a computer. The Power Macintosh 9500 uses the 132MHz PowerPC 604 **RISC** microprocessor and is the fastest Mac on the market today. The Macintosh RISC (Reduced Instruction Set Computing) microprocessor was introduced in 1994 with the Power Macintosh 6100, 7100, and 8100 series after joint development by Apple, IBM, and Motorola. In addition to the 132MHz clock speed, everything about the 9500 is geared toward greater speed: a faster **internal hard** drive and disk drive, quad-speed CD-ROM, and PCI bus architecture. With the addition of an accelerated 24-bit graphics card and up to 2.0GB of internal data storage, the 9500 is a very desirable CPU for high-end desktop publishing and electronic prepress. At the low-end, good desktop publishing results may be had with almost any Macintosh that has enough RAM to run the software of choice.

The PCI (Peripheral Component Interconnect) expansion bus architecture of the Power Macintosh 9500, 8500, 7500, and 7200 series is an important development. Designed to replace the older NuBus technology, PCI bus architecture allows faster throughput for peripheral devices, graphics accelerators, and network connections. PCI cards are also less expensive than NuBus cards. Although the change to PCI may be unfortunate for owners of expensive NuBus cards, NuBus to PCI adapters are available from Second Wave, Inc.

See Also

CD-ROM; Desktop Publishing Hardware; Hardware; Power Macs, PCI Bus

Desktop Publishing and Digital Cameras

Digital cameras provide an alternative to scanners for capturing images from the real world to be included in electronic publications. Digital cameras range in cost from several hundred to thousands of dollars with the more expensive ones providing the better quality images. As is the case with scanners, image resolution and dynamic range are important characteristics. Digital cameras are similar to analog cameras in having various kinds and grades of lens assemblies. Many digital cameras also have a built-in flash. The major difference is that digital cameras store captured images as digital data rather than on film. The internal memory of the camera determines how much data can be stored. A digital camera can be connected by cable to a computer where its image date can be further processed. Digital video cameras are also available.

See Also

Desktop Publishing Input Devices

Desktop Publishing and Digital Color

Color fidelity in reproduction has always been an important concern in the graphics industry, and since the advent of desktop publishing (DTP) in the mid-1980s, digital color has become an area of rapid technological development. Digital color is important because color is device-dependent, and it is difficult to maintain an accurate rendering of a color as it is processed by each device. Color electronic prepress systems (CEPS) spurred the development of more sophisticated digital-color processing on the Macintosh and other computer platforms. It is possible for a desktop computer system to link up with a CEPS through software or hardware gateways which convert PostScript data from the DTP system into the proprietary CEPS format via a raster image processor (RIP). The problems of color fidelity are addressed by industry color standards and color management systems.

See Also

Color Gamut; Color Matching Systems; Color Printing; Desktop Publishing and Color Electronic Prepress Systems (CEPS); Desktop Publishing and Color Management Systems (CMS); Prepress

Desktop Publishing Display Monitors

The ideal desktop publishing computer monitor for the Macintosh is capable of displaying in actual size two facing 8.5-inch×11-inch pages. The 20-inch or 21-inch screen size is usually chosen for this purpose.

These numbers represent diagonal measurement. Of course, much DTP work is done on computers with smaller monitors, but the larger size contributes to productivity. With a large display, less time is spent zooming in and out, and graphic design decisions can be made with more accuracy due to the ability to view whole pages in actual size. Large display monitors are available from various manufacturers such as Apple, RasterOps, Sony, NEC, and Radius. An interesting variation on the full-page display is available from Portrait Display Labs. This manufacturer's 17-inch monitor can be rotated between landscape and portrait views. When the monitor is pivoted to portrait mode, a single 8.5-inch×11-inch electronic page easily fits the screen in actual size view with extra room for palettes and toolbars.

In addition to size, color is another important consideration for a computer display monitor being used in desktop publishing. The number of colors that can be displayed is dependent on the type of video circuitry in the computer. A 24-bit video card can enable a high-resolution monitor to display millions of colors. Special video RAM, called **VRAM**, affects the overall performance of the display.

Other needs in computer display for desktop publishing are high **resolution**, smaller **dot pitch**, and a flat screen. All the major display manufacturers strive for a flatter screen, and there are a great variety of choices in resolution and dot pitch. A top-of-the-line monitor will have a resolution (measured in **pixels**) of 1280×1024 (Sony) or 1600×1200 (Radius). A .25mm dot pitch is considered best, but some good displays have a .26mm dot pitch.

See Also

Color Resolution; Desktop Publishing Hardware; Hardware; Image Scanning, Resolution; Memory VRAM Expansion

Desktop Publishing, Future of

We are in a period of rapid technological development, and there is no reason to believe that it will slow down anytime soon. The changes brought about by new technologies today occur more rapidly and have farther-reaching effects than past technologies. The concept of the "global village" is no longer theoretical. We are in the Age of Information, and the global communication of ideas is the basic commodity. Having become standard procedure in the graphics industry (an industry based on communication), **desktop publishing** itself must change to keep up with the times. Graphics production will probably remain a hybrid of traditional and DTP for some time, but digital technology must eventually dominate. The effect of the **Internet** on global communication has started a new technological revolution that is already affecting desktop publishing. The focus of DTP and **electronic prepress** (**EPP**) is still primarily on supporting printed material. In the near future, this focus may change to the production of complex electronic images that can be presented through a variety of media that may or may not include paper.

The electronic format for the communication of ideas is already widely used. The **CD-ROM** is now integral to most computers. **Online services** are gaining popularity almost daily. Interactivity is an appealing aspect of these media and is what gives the electronic publishing format such a clear advantage over paper-based publishing. The flexibility and visual and conceptual richness of electronic media are seductive even to dedicated bibliophiles. To some, electronic publications may not be as accessible as paper publications. Surely this is a matter of education; and as new generations become acclimated to the computer screen at an early age, paper-based publishing may disappear.

See Also

Desktop Publishing; Desktop Publishing, Beginnings of; Desktop Publishing Careers; Desktop Publishing History; Desktop Publishing Online; Desktop Publishing, Present Day; Desktop Publishing Training; Internet; Publishing Traditional

Desktop Publishing Hardware

A variety of computer hardware is available for **desktop publishing** on the **Macintosh** platform, ranging from low-end to high-end. Although it is difficult to discern any clear dividing line between low-end and high-end, some hardware characteristics can be identified for each category.

A typical low-end hardware setup of today might include only relatively inexpensive equipment: a basic **CPU** such as the Macintosh Performa, Power Macintosh 6100 or 7100, or a PCI Power Macintosh 7200; a 14- or 15-inch color display monitor; and a 600 dpi **PostScript laser printer**, such as the Apple LaserWriter 4/600 PS or Select 360. Memory upgrades may be necessary to run full-featured **page layout** and **image manipulation** software, but these machines are good basic DTP platforms right out of the box.

It is true that a great deal of desktop publishing is being performed on older, slower computers and printers, but the new versions of standard software (**PageMaker**, **QuarkXPress**, **PhotoShop**, and so on.) make large demands on the hardware, and older equipment usually must be replaced or upgraded to keep up. At the low end of DTP, personal choice plays a significant role. If one is working on an older Mac and finds that it continues to adequately meet the demands placed upon it, then there is no reason to change. Fortunately (or unfortunately, depending on your point of view), the Macintosh and other computers continue to get better, faster, and relatively less expensive. The frequency of these upgrades can be disconcerting, especially when one has just purchased a system only to find that it has been superseded several months later.

High-end desktop publishing hardware includes the more powerful Macintoshes such as the PCI Power Mac 7500 and 9500. The older, but extremely fast, Power Macintosh 8500 is also a good DTP computer. Since high-end desktop publishing usually includes digital color processing, larger and higher-resolution display monitors are necessary. The Apple Multiple Scan 20-inch display is representative of this category. A **color desktop scanner** and a 600, 1200, or 1800 dpi **laser printer** are also usually found on the high-end desktop. A high-quality **color printer** might also be present in such a system.

Flatbed scanners and 35mm film and transparency scanners are common, and deskside **drum scanners** are beginning to appear in high-end DTP environments. The deskside drum scanners are related to the drum scanners found in **color electronic prepress systems (CEPS)** but are less expensive. Although the CEPS scanners provide the best color image quality and control, deskside drum scanners, such as the ICG 300i Series, yield superb results. A desktop scanner should be capable of at least 24-bit color, but 36-bit is preferable. Although scanners are more widely used, **digital cameras** are having a definite impact on DTP. The best digital images are captured with a Hasselblad or Nikon lens body mounted on a digital camera back, but good results can be obtained with a less expensive digital camera like the Apple QuickTake.

Both low-end and high-end desktop publishers often use **service bureau imagesetters** to obtain **high-resolution output** (1200 to 2540 dpi), but a 1200 to 1800 dpi laser printer can be the next best thing. Most high-resolution laser printers also allow **full-bleed** 11×17-inch printing. Examples of this type of printer are the SelectPress 1200 from GCC Technologies and the PrePress VT1200. A color printer is useful for first-level **color proofing** and **color comps**. The **dye-sublimation color printer** is often favored for its almost photographic image quality. The Fargo Pictura 310 is capable of printing in either dye-sublimation or **thermal-wax** mode and accepts sheet sizes up to 12 × 20 inches. Even an inexpensive Hewlett-Packard **color inkjet printer** can be very useful for color comps.

High-end desktop publishing systems often act as gateways to the color electronic prepress systems (CEPS) and in themselves constitute a mid-range electronic prepress category. Just as DTP hardware can be categorized as either low-end or high-end, electronic prepress can be roughly divided into mid-range and high-end. However, as noted earlier, the divisions between these categories are mutable, and they exist chiefly for the sake of discussion. Because **color reproduction** is the primary focus of high-end DTP and CEPS, CPUs and display monitors must be equal to the task of processing large and complex color files. Souped-up Macs and UNIX workstations can be found side-by-side in many trades shops and **color houses**. They are connected to large drum scanners, **raster image processors (RIPs)**, and film recorders capable of extreme precision in the various aspects of digital color imaging.

See Also

Color Printing; Desktop Printing; Desktop Publishing; Desktop Publishing CPU Requirements; Desktop Publishing and Digital Color; Desktop Publishing Display Monitors; Desktop Publishing Peripheral Devices; Desktop Publishing, Present Day; Desktop Publishing Proofing and Printing; Imagesetters; Service Bureaus, Trade Shops, and Desktop Publishing

Desktop Publishing History

Desktop publishing technology began to be developed in the mid-1980s from the collaboration of three companies: **Adobe Systems Inc.**, **Aldus Corporation**, and **Apple Computer, Inc**. Paul Brainerd, then president of Aldus Corporation, is credited with coining

the term "desktop publishing." In 1994, Aldus Corporation, the original developers of the PageMaker page layout software, merged with Adobe Systems Inc. and the Aldus name was no longer used. Adobe Systems, Inc. and Apple Computer, Inc. continue to be major players in the desktop publishing market.

In the beginning, the basic marketing premise of desktop publishing was that anyone could do it without any previous experience or education in graphics arts. Advertising by the leading vendors of desktop publishing software and hardware strongly supported this premise. Many people bought into it thinking that all one had to do to create a sophisticated brochure or newsletter was to click on a few icons with the mouse. Certainly, the Macintosh computer and software like **PageMaker** and **QuarkXPress** were marvelous innovations. They were even somewhat intuitive in their mode of operation but not to the extent hinted at in some of the advertising at that time.

As a consequence of the aggressive marketing, and due to the undeniable merits of the products, desktop publishing gained a foothold in business and industry. Because using desktop computers and software proved not so easy for everyone to learn, many forms of training began to appear. Software companies created and promoted training courses. They instituted authorization programs for outside training centers. Book publishers discovered a lucrative new market for computer books. Individual consultants began to thrive. Finally, community colleges, vocational-technical schools, and universities began offering courses and degree plans in desktop publishing and computer graphics technologies.

From the beginning, DTP was especially popular with small business entrepreneurs who saw it as a way to cut expenses and gain control over newsletters and other business publications. Early desktop publishing technology was practically ignored by many graphics professionals and held in contempt by others. The contempt was not entirely unjustified. Until the early 1990s, desktop publishing suffered from limitations in **digital imaging**, **output resolution**, **color imaging** and **separation**, **digital halftone** technology, and other areas of concern for the high-end graphics industry. Relatively slow **CPU** speeds and the lack of both standardization and a good technical support infrastructure also contributed to the slow start of DTP among professionals.

Desktop publishing would not have been possible without the graphical user interface (GUI) for operating a computer. The Apple Macintosh operating system provided such an interface. Eventually, the Microsoft Windows software provided a GUI for the DOS-based IBM PC. The Mac and the IBM PC were the first desktop computers. They are both in the category of microcomputers. Of course, the IBM PC (personal computer) was cloned by many different manufacturers, and the term "PC" was loosely applied to them all. In fact, "PC" still implies a DOS-based computer or a computer that does not use the Apple operating system.

Aldus PageMaker (now Adobe **PageMaker**) is generally considered the first desktop publishing software for the Macintosh. It was released in 1985, and was, strictly speaking, the first **page layout** software. **MacWrite**, **MacDraw**, and **MacPaint** probably qualify as the first DTP software applications if one is willing to grant a liberal interpretation of the term. They were quite unsophisticated compared to PageMaker, which was the first software to allow relatively easy manipulation of graphics elements on an electronic page.

Specifically, PageMaker created a user interface based on the traditional paste-up. Before PageMaker, it was practically impossible to create side-by-side columns on the computer. PageMaker did so with ease, and its text blocks were extremely fluid, allowing greater flexibility in graphic design. PageMaker also provided unprecedented **typographic** control and drawing tools for creating straight rule lines, rectangles, and ellipses directly on the layout. Perhaps the most important innovation found in PageMaker was the ability to import text and graphics created in other

software applications. The fact that text created in a **word-processor** and graphics created in a draw or paint program could be imported and manipulated together on the electronic page made PageMaker and, later, **QuarkXPress** and **Ready**, **Set**, **Go**, the defining software applications of the DTP movement. Aldus soon developed a Windows version of PageMaker, and it proved to be very popular in business and industry, providing a much broader-based market than the Macintosh version.

QuarkXPress was released in 1987 and began serious competition with PageMaker on the Macintosh platform. Eventually, QuarkXPress was to surpass PageMaker in popularity among graphics professionals in many parts of the U.S. This was due in part to the attention **Quark, Inc.** paid to the **prepress** aspects of its software. QuarkXPress's **color separation**, **color trapping**, and **page imposition** features quickly made it a favorite with **service bureaus**, trade shops, and printing firms. An extended version of QuarkXPress called Visionary was developed by Scitex America to link DTP systems to its proprietary high-end prepress systems. QuarkXPress differs from PageMaker in significant ways, although the two have many similarities. **Adobe Systems Inc.** has taken steps to improve PageMaker's viability as a front-end software for electronic prepress, and competition is sure to remain strong between the two.

Other page layout software applications, such as Ready, Set, Go and **FrameMaker**, have contributed to the growth and success of desktop publishing on the Mac. **PostScript** drawing programs, such as Adobe **Illustrator** and Macromedia **FreeHand** (formerly Aldus FreeHand) also play an important role. Adobe **PhotoShop** has established itself as a standard in desktop scanning and image manipulation.

Due to its strong graphics characteristics and relatively trouble-free handling of peripheral devices, the Macintosh computer has remained the DTP platform of choice for many in the graphics industry. The development of the **Power Mac** and, more recently, the **PCI Mac** would seem to assure that position for some time to come.

See Also
Desktop Publishing Applications; Desktop Publishing, Beginnings of; Desktop Publishing, Future of; Desktop Publishing Hardware; Desktop Publishing, Present Day; PageMaker; Publishing, Traditional; QuarkXPress

Desktop Publishing Industry Standards

Standards or guidelines are important in any industry but take time to develop. In the instance of the desktop publishing industry, standards are still undergoing development, although some basic guidelines have been well-established for several years. The traditional graphics industry has had well-developed standards for many years and some of those affect desktop publishing. For example, Specifications for Web Offset Publications (SWOP) are a set of professional standards for offset printing in the United States which have a particular bearing on any publication printed on web offset lithography presses. As an example of how these standards apply directly to desktop publishing, the **EFIColor CMS** (Color Management System) in **QuarkXPress** lists SWOP as a target output choice when establishing a color range (gamut) for the colors specified in a particular publication.

Standards are usually established by a leading professional or trade association, and such is the case with desktop publishing. The Graphic Communications Association (GCA) has developed one set of standards called the Electronic Mechanical Specifications (EMS), and the Scitex Graphic Arts Users Association (SGAUA) has developed another, the Computer Ready Electronic Files (CREF). Both of these standards have as their goal the elimination of problems in the process of preparing desktop publication files for high-resolution output to film or plate.

The EMS and CREF guidelines were developed by printers, separators, consultants and others who are directly involved in the processes and therefore greatly affected by problems that occur due to improper practices. When electronic publication files are prepared incorrectly, prepress technicians and printers often must troubleshoot the files, resulting in overtime, excess charges, and missed press schedules. The guidelines represent suggestions for minimizing the chance of problems. For example, the CREF document addresses issues concerning fonts, providing and marking proofs, revisions and corrections, transmittal and shipping, file naming, grids and stylesheets, text handling and special effects, trapping, frames and borders, importing graphics, defining colors, bleeds, blends and gradients, and methods of production. The EMS and CREF guideline documents can be obtained from the Graphic Communications Association and the Scitex Graphic Arts Users Association respectively.

See Also
Desktop Publishing Professional Organizations

Desktop Publishing Input Devices

The two most common computer input devices, the mouse and keyboard, are usually taken for granted because they are such key parts of any hardware system. However, on the larger Macintoshes, keyboards may have to be purchased separately from the **CPU**, and many users prefer to purchase a different mouse. Desktop publishing puts no special demands on the Mac keyboard except that an extended keyboard with "F" keys may be required if SoftWindows is used. The new ergonomic keyboards are nice and may even be necessary for individuals suffering from repetitive motion syndrome or other computer-related ailments.

Because the mouse is so important in using the Macintosh graphical user interface (GUI), it has always been a part of the Mac hardware. Graphic designers and other desktop publishers are usually intensive mouse users and may particularly suffer from one of the repetitive motion syndromes. A **trackball mouse**, **graphics tablet** with stylus, or a **trackpad** may offer some relief. The graphics tablet and stylus are almost a necessity for illustrators and others using drawing and painting software. Which mouse to use is essentially a personal choice, for they all have the same basic function. Perhaps owning one of each is not out of the question.

Scanners and **digital cameras** are important to desktop publishing operations because they allow images from the real world to be captured and digitized for processing by the computer. Scanners digitize photographs or any two-dimensional image so that they can be manipulated and included in electronic publications. Scanning three-dimensional objects can produce interesting results. The development of the digital camera has made it possible to digitize life's images on the fly. Actually, this sort of image capture was already possible with video-capture hardware and software, but the low-end digital cameras are more affordable and commonplace. Excellent image quality can be expected from the high-end digital cameras which consist of a digital camera back mounted on a traditional SLR camera body.

Desktop Publishing and the Mouse If any single piece of hardware can be said to represent desktop publishing, it would have to be the mouse. This whimsically-named device, attached to the Macintosh by its long tail, represents the power of the graphical user interface (GUI) for computers that revolutionized the graphics industry. The first Macintosh mouse was like a new bar of soap—blocky and hard to grasp. Today, it is a streamlined extension of the user's hand. The standard Macintosh mouse still has only one button; but most DOS or Windows-based computers come with a two- or three-button mouse, the extra buttons having various functions other than pointing and clicking. The basic function of the mouse is so simple and straightforward that it needs no explanation. Clean it occasionally, and it will serve you well.

Desktop Publishing and the Trackball The trackball is one of the more successful variations on the standard mouse. Although it is available in different configurations from different manufacturers, a trackball mouse is essentially a stationary platform with a ball mounted on top. Depending on the design, the ball is rolled with either the fingertips or the thumb, and clicking is done with the opposite digit. Many users feel that a trackball mouse is more precise for graphics work, and trackballs usually come with programmable features. A small trackball is commonly found on **laptop computers**.

Desktop Publishing and the Graphics Tablet A graphics tablet with cordless stylus is the perfect input accessory for an illustrator or artist working with **drawing** or **painting software**. In fact, anyone who prefers to point and click with something resembling a pen or pencil might like the graphics tablet as an input device. Many users feel that the stylus and tablet are almost a necessity for using painting software because it feels more "natural" than a standard mouse and makes it easier to create long smooth strokes. Graphics tablets come in different sizes with the larger sizes offering more precision and allowing for broader hand movements. The tablets are pressure-sensitive, and the stylus has a small button for clicking operations.

Desktop Publishing and the Trackpad A relatively recent innovation, the trackpad is a small, slightly resilient pad sensitive to the touch of a fingertip. Moving the fingertip in contact with the pad moves the mouse cursor on the computer screen. It is intended as an alternative to the standard mouse or the **trackball mouse** and has been incorporated into the newer **Apple PowerBooks**. A button is located near the edge of the pad within reach of the thumb. Many users find a trackpad easier to control than a trackball, and it may be a good alternative for individuals who need a change from the standard mouse.

See Also

Desktop Publishing Hardware; Desktop Publishing Peripheral Devices; PowerBook

Desktop Publishing and the MacOS

Desktop publishing and the Macintosh operating system go hand-in-hand. The defining aspect of the MacOS is its **graphical user interface (GUI)**, and the very nature of this interface is what made desktop publishing possible. The graphical user interface on the Mac was often bewildering to **DOS** users who had grown accustomed to the linear, text-oriented, command and response behavior of their computers; but it was a miracle for others, particularly those who had never used a computer before. At first, computers were not widely used by graphics industry professionals except in the typesetting and prepress areas, but the Macintosh proved to be an inviting tool for established, as well as would-be, graphic designers. Intuitive ease of use coupled with sophisticated graphics capability have made the Macintosh the platform of choice for many in the graphics industry.

Despite early hardware limitations (a tiny monitor screen, no **hard drive**, inadequate **RAM**, low-resolution output), developers wrote software based on the Macintosh OS that could perform amazing feats. Never before had it been so easy for a graphics production artist to draw straight rule lines or boxes. Creating rounded-corner boxes, never an easy task with ink pen or rule tape, became such a snap that most novices over-used the ability. The point, click, and drag capability of the **mouse** made it not only a symbol for the operating system's graphical interface, but also an indispensable tool for performing page layout, drawing, and painting on the Mac.

The MacOS introduced true typesetting capacity on the desktop. In spite of a limited typeface selection, early Mac users began to put the typesetting industry out of business. **Apple** developed a bitmapped font technology which was included with the operating system (the city-name fonts), but it was the development of the PostScript-based **LaserWriter** with its built-in complement of high-resolution fonts that really started the process.

The capability of the Macintosh operating system to incorporate fonts for use in all its software applications was a key factor. In fact, it was this very universality that made the MacOS so unique and successful. For the first time, software was written in such a way that all software applications had certain things in common—windows, menus, dialog boxes, and so on. Even some specific features, such as type styling conventions and drawing tools, were the same in different software applications.

Over the years, many refinements in numerous areas have contributed to the success of desktop publishing, and the Macintosh operating system remains a firm basis for development. The completely redesigned new MacOS, code-named "Copland," promises to make great improvements in memory usage and operating speed—two areas of special importance in desktop publishing.

See Also

Desktop Publishing; Desktop Publishing, Beginnings of; Desktop Publishing History; Mac History and Culture

Desktop Publishing Online

The **Internet** and the **World Wide Web** have revolutionized communication in a way that is reminiscent of the **desktop publishing** revolution of the mid 1980s. Millions of people worldwide are using the Internet to obtain and provide information. Entertainment, commerce, and social interaction are also typical online activities. The development of the World Wide Web and **HTML** (HyperText Markup Language) are part of the global online publishing phenomenon. HTML is the authoring language used to create web pages.

New software and hardware development is driven by the popularity of online information exchange just as it was driven by the early successes of desktop publishing. Web authoring and management software products such as Adobe PageMill, Allegiant Marionet, and WebSTAR from StarNine, make World Wide Web pages easier to produce by providing a simplified means to use HTML. Although paper-based publishing will no doubt be around well into the twenty-first century, online publishing is a significant force for change.

See Also

Desktop Publishing; Desktop Publishing, Future of

Desktop Publishing Peripheral Devices

In it broadest definition, a "peripheral" is any device that extends the functionality of the CPU. This includes functions such as scanning, printing, networking, telecommunications, data storage, and so on. Many of these are important in desktop publishing, particularly scanning and printing.

A peripheral device is usually connected to the Macintosh computer via a cable to the **Small Computer Systems Interface** (SCSI) port. The SCSI port is the connection outlet for scanners and external drives. Desktop scanners connected to the SCSI port may be of the flatbed type, the 35mm film or transparency type, or, more rarely, the drum type. External drives are available in many forms. They may be conventional hard drives, removable cartridge drives, optical drives, DAT (digital audio tape) drives, CD-ROM drives, WORM (write once, read many) drives, or even diskette drives. More than one SCSI device may be connected to the Macintosh SCSI port in a chain with cables connecting each device.

The NuBus card is another way to extend system functionality. On many older Macintosh computers a NuBus card is used to connect a **graphics** accelerator or **EtherNet** cable. The newer Macintoshes are designed to utilize a different kind of card, the **PCI** (Peripheral Component Interconnect) expansion bus. This card is meant to replace the older NuBus technology. Apple claims that PCI cards can perform up to three times faster than NuBus cards. PCI technology can even be used to speed up the flow of data from SCSI devices.

In a sense, printers and modems are also peripheral devices. Printers can be directly connected with a cable to the Macintosh printer port. Workgroup situations are now common where many computers are connected to each other and one or more printers via AppleTalk or EtherNet cables. This is known as a Local Area Network (LAN). The modem represents the ultimate in connectivity to other users and devices. Connected to a telephone line, a modem may be used to access online services, the Internet, or another computer at a remote location. Data transfer between computers can be useful in desktop publishing, especially when publication files need to be sent to a service bureau.

See Also

Desktop Publishing CPU Requirements; Desktop Publishing Hardware; Desktop Publishing Input Devices; Hardware

Desktop Publishing, Present Day

Today, **desktop publishing** is well-established in the graphics industry of the United States and many other countries. It is widely established as standard procedure in book and magazine publishing, and is commonly used to generate reports, newsletters, and many other documents in corporate and government offices. Authors, editors, copywriters, and others who are responsible for writing and organizing the content of a great variety of publications have provided much of the impetus by more fully utilizing desktop computers. Business owners and other entrepreneurs have continued to rely on DTP as a cost-effective way to produce advertising materials and business stationery. Advertising agencies almost universally require new hires to be proficient in **QuarkXPress** or **Adobe PageMaker**, as well as Adobe **PhotoShop**, Adobe **Illustrator**, or MacroMedia **FreeHand**, and other DTP-related software. Desktop publishing operates at many levels and takes many forms.

Advancing technology has removed many of the obstacles in the transition from traditional to desktop publishing. Some hybrid practices still exist. For example, electronic publication files can be output in a form that practically eliminates traditional **stripping** procedures. However, this may require expensive high-end proprietary hardware and software, depending on desired image quality and other factors. It is common for electronic publication files to be output on less expensive, but adequate, equipment. In this case, manual stripping or other traditional prepress activity may be necessary.

Many educational institutions have developed curricula for desktop publishing and related graphics fields. Although it originally succeeded because it incorporated formerly specialized fields such as type-setting, graphic design, reprographics, and some aspects of prepress, DTP and electronic **prepress** have become so technologically advanced that individuals are finding it increasingly necessary to specialize in one or two software applications or a single operating system. Early practitioners could easily cope with the relatively simple DTP systems of the mid-1980s, but the proliferation of new software and hardware has complicated the field.

The **Macintosh** computer is still the mainstay of high-end DTP, but the descendants of the original IBM PC are many and must be considered viable platforms for desktop publishing software. Using the **Microsoft Windows** software, these computers are used at many levels of desktop publishing in business, industry, government, and educational institutions. The ability of the Macintosh to interface smoothly with high-end prepress systems is a major factor in its success. Desktop publishing is only the first stage of the overall process of printing and publishing. Electronic documents created on a Mac or PC are primarily printed on paper or some other two-dimensional surface. The process of getting those documents from the computer to the printing press is known as electronic prepress (EPP). Electronic prepress involves image scanning (digitizing), color adjustment, high-resolution digital halftones, color trapping, electronic page imposition and stripping, and high-resolution output to film or printing plate. In some cases, electronic files are output directly to a digital printing press. Any consideration of DTP technology must include a look at EPP.

See Also

Desktop Publishing; Desktop Publishing, Beginnings of; Desktop Publishing Careers; Desktop Publishing, Future of; Desktop Publishing, History of; Desktop Publishing Process; Desktop Publishing Proofing and Printing; Desktop Publishing Training; Prepress; Publishing, Traditional

Desktop Publishing Process

The process of desktop publishing has several clearly definable stages. Although it mimics the traditional publishing process in many ways, desktop publishing has revolutionized the graphics industry by automating, combining, and simplifying many of the stages. This discussion provides an overview of the entire desktop publishing process from beginning to end.

- Stage 1 (Concept/Writing/Design)—The first stage involves the use of creativity and aesthetic principles. All publications start with ideas and the roles of authoring and graphic design are to communicate the ideas. The author, whether of an in-house company report or a major book, is responsible for expressing the ideas clearly, succinctly, and, perhaps, entertainingly. The designer uses artistic ability and creativity to devise an attractive and effective vehicle for the ideas. The author and designer may even be the same person; but, in any case, preliminary examples of the publication are prepared as rough drafts. Traditionally trained graphic designers usually prepare thumbnail sketches, full-size pencil roughs, and more finished-looking comprehensive layouts (comps) for the purpose of communicating design ideas to a client, boss, or colleague. A comp is often created on the computer using the same **page layout software** that will be used to produce the final publication files. These comps are output on a **desktop color printer** and are capable of more accurately showing color, illustrations, and actual text than were traditional comps. An electronic comp may be printed on the actual paper that will be used in final press production. Once the written word and the preliminary designs are approved, the publication is ready for the next stage.

- Stage 2 (Page Layout/Text Formatting/ Graphics)—In the second stage, text and graphics are combined in a page layout software application to create an electronic publication file. This file will be used to output the publication in some form that leads to mass reproduction. This part of the process replaces the older practice of pasting up type galleys and other elements to create a page mechanical (camera-ready copy). Incorporating text in an electronic publication file is straightforward and relatively simple. Text can be typed directly in the page layout software or imported as a word-processor file. Typographic features allow the text to be formatted and arranged on the pages according to graphic design principles and the aesthetic sensibilities of the designer. Illustrations and other graphics are incorporated by importing them into the publication file and arranging them as part of the overall design. Page layout software applications provide simple tools for creating rule lines, boxes, and frames. Boxes can be filled with patterns and tint screens directly on the electronic page. Line art graphics are often created in a drawing software application and are known as vector images or object-oriented art. Photographs and other continuous-tone images must be digitized with a scanner to be placed in the publication and are called **bitmap** or **raster image** art. Although desktop scanners can do a good job, high-end CEPS (Color Electronic Prepress Systems) scanners are often used for publications with high production values. Desktop publications can be processed and output on these high-end systems through software and hardware links, or gateways. When a CEPS is used, photographs are scanned on a high-speed drum scanner capable of very high resolutions and dynamic range. Two image files are generated: one is low resolution and the other is high resolution. The low-resolution file is provided to the designer and imported into the publication as a for-position-only (FPO) image. When the publication file is sent to the trade shop for electronic stripping and output to film or plate, the high-resolution images are automatically substituted in place

of the FPO images. Two well-known schemes for image-replacement are Open Prepress Interface (OPI) and Automatic Picture Replacement (APR).

- Stage 3 (Prepress/Printing)—At this stage the publication is ready to be printed. Many decisions must be made regarding this part of the process. The quantity desired, the printing surface (paper or other substance—often called "substrate"), the size and type of printing press, folding and binding procedures—all must be decided upon. One thing often dictates another. For example, the quantity of the reproduction run and the number of colors will probably determine many of the other factors, but quantity must be balanced with quality in an effort to obtain the best-looking results at the lowest possible price. These decisions are usually jointly made by the principals involved, such as the designer, a production manager, and a representative of the commercial printing firm. If the publication is to be printed on a traditional printing press, **prepress** activities must be performed to convert the electronic publication file into printing plates. Electronic prepress involves the substitution of high resolution images (if necessary), **color trapping**, page imposition to make a press layout, and the creation of film or plates. In some instances, film is manually assembled into press layouts in a process called **stripping**, creating flats (assemblages of film and orange masking paper) that are used in a photomechanical process to make printing plates. In desktop publishing, film or plates may be generated on an **imagesetter** at a **service bureau** or a film recorder at a CEPS trade shop. Publications printed on a digital press can be output directly from a computer, bypassing the film and/or platemaking stage.

- Stage 4 (Folding/Binding/Distribution)— The fourth and final stage in desktop publishing has scarcely changed from earlier methods, except in the area of distribution. Books, magazines, brochures, and pamphlets printed on paper are still folded and bound (and distributed) in the same manner as they have been for many years. Certainly the machines have improved and may be electronically controlled, but folding and binding have not been affected by the DTP revolution in quite the same way as stages one, two, and three. It is in the distribution of desktop published information that a new revolution is occurring. The **Internet** (information superhighway) and the **World Wide Web** have provided a new way to publish that could eliminate, or at least greatly reduce, the need for paper and all the procedures that attend printing.

See Also

Automatic Picture Replacement (APR); Color Printing; Color Separations; Color Trapping; Desktop Printing; Desktop Publishing and Color Electronic Prepress Systems (CEPS); Desktop Publishing, Future of; Desktop Publishing Online; Image Manipulation for Printing; Image Scanning; Imagesetters; Mechanical; Open Prepress Interface (OPI); PostScript; Prepress; Printing

Desktop Publishing Professional Organizations

Belonging to a professional organization has long been a way for individuals to benefit from association with others in their field. This is particularly valuable for graphic designers and others in the field of desktop publishing. Such organizations can be national, state, or local and can be categorized as professional associations, guilds, and user groups. Many groups have regular formal meetings for socializing and the presentation of educational programs. A newer category, online forums or chat groups, must be included because it fulfills many of the same needs as the more formal organizations. Trade shows such as those held by Seybold Seminars are another category of organization many in the desktop publishing and computer graphics field find valuable, especially for those who want to stay on the leading edge of technology.

The benefits of belonging to an organization are many. The members form a reliable base for networking and information exchange. Local user groups are especially good for this. All large cities and many medium to small ones have user groups. Asking around at computer stores, service bureaus, or the local community college or public library will probably reveal the names and telephone numbers of local groups. Many novices in the field find that belonging to a user group provides a resource for freelance work, new clients, and emergency aid when a hard drive suddenly won't respond at 10 p.m. on the night before an 8 a.m. deadline. User groups are usually structured around a specific platform or software application. A large umbrella group may have sub-groups called SIGs (Special Interest Groups) that deal specifically with one software application. User group meetings often feature guest speakers from local businesses, industries, or educational institutions. Larger groups may succeed in luring hardware and software developers in to give new product demonstrations. One of the most valuable aspects of a user group meeting is the open forum where anyone can ask for or give out information and advice. Larger groups may publish a newsletter with information about new products, listings of training classes, the availability of shareware, display and classified advertising, and so forth. The members of user groups are usually very helpful to each other and belonging to one can ease the isolation of computer work. Because many user groups are voluntary organizations without paid staff, members are expected to volunteer to perform the chores of keeping the organization going. Only the very large umbrella groups may have management and support staff, and members still have an opportunity to provide services. Some groups may charge small membership fees.

Associations, guilds, and other professional organizations form a somewhat broad category. These organizations may have a large national, or even international, membership. Some have local or state chapters, and all are characterized by members who belong to a specific profession or practice a particular trade. In function, they are much like user groups but less community-oriented. Members benefit from services such as newsletters, professional education programs, legal referral services, group insurance, and many other programs. Membership fees may be substantially higher than for user groups. The following is a list of well-known professional organizations associated with the desktop publishing industry:

- Association of American Publishers (AAP), 1718 Connecticut Avenue NW, Suite 700, Washington, D.C. 20009, (202) 232-3335. Internet site: **http://www.publishers.org**

- Graphic Communications Association (GCA), 100 Daingerfield Road, Alexandria, Virginia 22314-2804, (703) 519-8160. Internet site: **http://www.printing.org**

- Graphic Artists Guild (GAG), 11 West 20th Street, New York, New York 10011, (212) 463-7759. Internet site: **http://www.gag.org**

- International Prepress Association (IPA), 7200 France Avenue South, Suite 327, Edina, Minnesota 55435, (612) 896-1908

- National Association of Desktop Publishers (NADTP), 462 Old Boston Street, Topsfield, MA 01983-1232, (800) 874-4113

- Scitex Graphic Arts Users Association (SGAUA), P.O. Box 2345, 750 Old Hickory Boulevard, Suite 264, Brentwood, Tennessee 37027, (800) 858-0489

Desktop Publishing Proofing and Printing

The fact that work can be easily proofed and revised is one of the strengths of desktop publishing. Proofs for desktop graphics are of three basic types: digital proofs, off-press proofs, and press proofs.

The computer's monitor screen provides the first opportunity to proof one's publication and is the most basic kind of digital proof. The quality of black-and-white images (type and line art) can be judged to some degree on the computer screen; but color display is usually quite inaccurate, and one cannot rely on it as a final proof for color images. Desktop printers provide a more accurate way to proof black-and-white publications, and laser printer output is probably the most common form of digital proof. Thermal wax, dye sublimation, and ink-jet printers are also frequently used, especially for color proofing. Desktop color printers often do not reproduce color accurately, however. Direct digital color proofing (DDCP) systems, such as Digital MatchPrint (3M), 4Cast (DuPont), and Pressmatch (Hoechst), provide good color fidelity but require specialized equipment.

Off-press proofs are the traditional proofs made directly from the film that will be used to make printing plates. A blueline proof, such as the DuPont Dylux, is the most basic proof in this category. Bluelines are monochrome and cannot show color images. Color overlay proofs made of four pieces of film representing each of the process colors are another form of off-press proof. Color Key by 3M and Chromacheck by DuPont are typical overlay proofs. The most color-accurate off-press proof is the laminate, or integral, proof. The MatchPrint (3M) and the Cromalin (DuPont) are both popular laminate proofs. The Water Proof, a new type of laminate proof from DuPont, is becoming popular because it uses water as a solvent, doing away with the need for hazardous chemicals. It may also be laminated to the actual paper stock to be used in the printing job, providing a more accurate forecast of how the finished piece will look.

Press proofs are made on a printing press using the same plates, ink, and paper that will be used on the actual job. This provides the most accurate color proofing but is expensive and time-consuming. Such proofs are usually called "progressives" and are composed of separate sheets showing each color, various combinations of colors, and all the colors together.

Desktop publications are printed in a variety of ways, the most basic being the desktop printer. Quantity, paper size, image resolution, color fidelity, folding and binding, and distribution needs are determining factors when choosing a printing method. Desktop printers are often used to print business documents in small quantities. Larger quantities usually require commercial printing facilities. Many options exist for mass reproduction, ranging from sophisticated duplicators like the IBM DocuTech and digital presses like the Indigo E-Print to traditional offset printing.

See Also
Color Printing; Desktop Printing; Desktop Publishing Hardware

Desktop Publishing, Scanners

Scanners are a key part of desktop publishing. Photographs and other continuous-tone art must be digitized by a scanner to be incorporated into electronic publications. The best quality color scanned images come from high-end CEPS (Color Electronic Prepress Systems) scanners installed at trade shops and service bureaus. Good quality color scanning can be accomplished with flatbed or 35mm film or transparency scanners on the desktop. The quality of a scanner is determined by its resolution and dynamic range capabilities. Less expensive than CEPS scanning but better quality than desktop scanning, the Kodak Photo CD system provides a cost-effective alternative where images in several resolutions are installed on CD-ROM through the services of a professional photo lab.

See Also
Desktop Publishing and Color Electronic Prepress Systems (CEPS); Desktop Publishing Hardware; Desktop Publishing Input Devices; Service Bureaus, Trade Shops, and Desktop Publishing

Desktop Publishing Training

Typing is probably the most basic manual skill needed in desktop publishing. Next to that is the hand/eye coordination needed to operate a **mouse**. Mouse operations are intuitive and become faster and more accurate with practice so no particular training is necessary, but a typing class in the continuing education department at a community college or a typing tutorial software program will probably be required to learn touch-typing. Hunt and peck is just too slow. Even if most copy is typed by someone else, a considerable amount of keyboard input is usually involved—including those time-saving keyboard shortcuts for menu commands.

An interesting training issue was raised in the early days of desktop publishing and is still viable. It has to do with the standards for design aesthetics practiced by professional graphic designers. Before desktop publishing, most graphic designers had some kind of art background, either a college degree or certificate or a lengthy apprenticeship in the graphic design field. Desktop publishing changed that to some degree because it made graphic design tools, and the profeswht. Early advertising by Apple Computers Inc., Adobe Systems, Inc., and Aldus Corporation (the developers of the PageMaker page layout software) stressed this accessibility. Experienced graphic designers were concerned about (and offended by) the resulting proliferation of "bad" design. Naturally, many established designers felt threatened by this new technology which had not yet reached a stage of development that provided the sophistication *they* needed. At first the novelty and money-saving aspects of desktop publishing overcame the lack of aesthetically pleasing design; but, today, desktop publishing is mainstream and higher standards again apply.

In addition to the manual skills of typing and mousing and the practice of good design skills, software knowledge must be developed. Of course, basic computer literacy is a necessity. It is very difficult to master a complicated page layout or graphics software application if one has not mastered the basics of the operating system. The need for personal computer software training was recognized from the beginning, and many software developers and computer retailers provide it in various forms.

Another important area of knowledge is printing production. Although printing is rapidly moving in the direction of digital presses, traditional printing methods such as offset and gravure will no doubt be around for many more years. It is a lack of experience and training in this field that seems to be the most severe handicap for many, including experienced graphic designers. Current desktop publishing technology is encompassing the once arcane practices of **prepress** and printing production. Established graphic designers may have little knowledge of these areas because they grew accustomed to handing off finished paste-ups to the prepress technicians and waiting for a proof. Novices are simply overwhelmed by the vast body of knowledge representing the hidden part of the iceberg.

In summary, the areas of knowledge necessary to the successful practice of desktop publishing are: (1) manual skills in typing and using the mouse; (2) graphic design; (3) computer literacy and software; and, (4) printing production.

There are several options for learning the necessary skills to work in the desktop publishing field. Books are an obvious, if bewildering, choice. The sheer quantity of computer books, even those dealing specifically with DTP software, is overwhelming. The best advice is simply to take your time and look at all of them to get a sense of how different books take different approaches to the same thing. It is important that you be able to easily understand the concepts, and this is often a matter of writing style and organization. Many people find the manuals that come with software applications to be difficult, but there are plenty of alternatives at the book store. Look for a book that takes a step-by-step tutorial approach and provides pedagogical features such as exercises, lists of key terms, and a good index. Make sure the book you buy deals with the same software version that you have. Some self-tutorial training combines a workbook with audio or video tape. If being led step-by-step through a tutorial appeals to you, look for this type of publication at larger book stores and computer stores or in mail-order catalogs. Learning from a book is not for everyone, but books are a valuable reference resource in any case and are a good investment.

The electronic tutorial is another way to teach yourself a software application. Most of the major software developers provide such tutorials as part of their software packages. They are usually very professionally done and provide a quick (but shallow) experience in how the software actually works. In some cases, a printed tutorial guide is also provided.

Training classes are probably the best way to learn all four of the knowledge areas. These classes run the gamut from one short session at a self-improvement learning center to entire semesters at a college or university. The self-improvement classes are relatively inexpensive but lack depth due to time constraints. Use them mainly to get a quick introduction and possibly shorten your learning curve. The next level of training can be found at private training companies. Many of them specialize in graphics, desktop publishing, and **multimedia** software training. Regularly scheduled classes at these establishments may have a duration of one, two, or three days. This type of training is popular with corporations and institutions who do not have in-house training facilities. Private training can be expensive compared to the other types but often has the advantage of extremely knowledgeable instructors who are good communicators. When shopping for this kind of training, ask the training company for references you can check out regarding the effectiveness of the instruction. If a particular instructor seems to get the most kudos, ask for him or her when you sign up. Software companies sometimes offer training seminars with very effective instructors; however, travel may be necessary. Some computer stores offer training classes, but the training center may be a low priority item on the management agenda, resulting in indifferent training procedures and poor instructors. On the other hand, the training may be free to a purchaser of a new computer system.

Colleges and universities are the place to go for very thorough longer-term training. Regular desktop publishing and electronic prepress degree programs are offered at many community colleges and vocational-technical schools, and night classes are common. Individuals who do not wish to get a degree or certificate may enroll in computer classes in the adult education or continuing education department of a college or university. The community colleges seem to be leading the universities in setting up curricula for desktop publishing. One advantage to classes at a community college is that instructors who have practical, first-hand knowledge in their subjects are often recruited from business and industry.

See Also

Desktop Publishing; Desktop Publishing Careers; Publishing, Traditional

Desktop Publishing Utility Software

The Macintosh utility software that we discuss here falls into the broad categories of font management, file conversion, file compression, and miscellaneous useful utilities. The term "utility software" itself is rather broad but we define it as any kind of software application that focuses on a particular function, such as **virus detection** and **removal**. Utility software is packaged and sold in the same manner as large mainstream software applications, but a variety of useful freeware or shareware utilities can be found online or through users' groups.

- **Font Management**—Font data files can drastically increase the size of a Macintosh System file if they are dropped into the **System Folder**. Most desktop publishers need access to many fonts, but as power users, they want to keep the System file as small as possible in the interest of faster processing speed. The font management utility **Suitcase** (by Symantec) solves the problem by allowing the font files to be stored in a folder on a hard drive (or other storage device). Individual typefaces can then be temporarily accessed by the system through the Suitcase utility. Suitcase has many features to enhance this basic function: (1) sets of typefaces can be named and saved, (2) font (and sound) files can be compressed, (3) fonts can be viewed in their actual typeface, and (4) font conflicts can be detected and solved. These and other features make Suitcase a popular utility. Suitcase is a System Extension.

  Adobe Type Manager (ATM) is another font management utility that is so ubiquitous on the Mac it is often taken for granted. ATM is widely used because it is a necessary adjunct to Adobe Type 1 fonts, the desktop publishing and **electronic prepress** standard for font technology. The most basic function of ATM is to accurately render a font on the computer screen in any size on demand. Prior to ATM, a separate screen font file for each desired point size of type had to be installed in the

system before it could be rendered accurately on the monitor screen. When ATM is installed in the system folder, any point size of type can be rendered with only one screen font file present. ATM is a **control panel** document and **Init** file.

- **File Conversion**—In desktop publishing and other computer work, files are often transferred from one platform to another. Many desktop publishing software developers, such as Adobe Systems, Inc. and Quark, Inc. market nearly identical software versions for the Macintosh and **Windows**. The documents created in these cross-platform software applications can usually be transferred between platforms with no difficulty. File transfer can take place via local area network (LAN), **telecommunication**, the **Internet**, or diskette sharing. Problems can arise, however, in two areas: font technology and graphics file formats. As long as two computers use the same font technology there is no difficulty; but, for example, if a Macintosh **PageMaker** publication with Adobe Type 1 fonts is opened in the Windows version where **TrueType** fonts are used, font substitution must take place. Substituting a different font will probably drastically affect how text flows on the pages and create layout problems.

Graphics files can present a problem because of the many different types of formats and the software requirements for processing them. Fortunately, graphics software applications such as Adobe **Illustrator**, Adobe **Photoshop**, and Macromedia **FreeHand** can save or export graphics in various formats, including cross-platform (Mac and Windows). The native file formats of the PostScript drawing programs, Illustrator and FreeHand, are more or less fully cross-platform compatible as long as the software versions are the same. When graphics created in either one of these programs are to be imported into a **page layout application**,

D

they must be converted to the **Encapsulated PostScript (EPS)** format because native files will not import. The EPS graphics are also cross-platform compatible if they are saved or exported from the drawing program properly. An EPS graphic must have a preview image saved with it, and this image must be compatible with the particular platform. In FreeHand, for example, the Export dialog box provides many choices of file formats, and two of them are Macintosh EPS and MS-DOS EPS.

Bitmapped images saved in **Tagged Image File Format (TIFF)** are also cross-platform compatible if they are saved properly. The byte order of a Macintosh TIFF image is different from that of a PC TIFF image. Adobe PhotoShop can save a TIFF image in either format, and conversion utilities, such as DeBabelizer Toolbox, do the same job. If either EPS or TIFF images are to be transferred from a Mac to a DOS/Windows environment, only eight characters can be used for the filenames. Additionally, a three character file extension must be added: .EPS or .TIF. Another solution is the Adobe Acrobat Portable Document Format (PDF). The Adobe Acrobat software converts any document to PDF so that it can be read from virtually any computer—Mac, DOS, Windows, or UNIX. Fonts and graphics in an Acrobat document are simulations and cannot be modified. **DeBabelizer Toolbox** from Equilibrium is a popular file conversion utility for the Macintosh. DeBabelizer is actually a major software application with many different functions for processing graphics images. It provides internal scripting and batch features, editing and manipulation tools, and the ability to save in all commonly used bitmap and animation file formats. Both Acrobat and DeBabelizer can be valuable tools for Internet publishers.

Apple File Exchange is a utility developed by Apple to facilitate the exchange of diskettes and files between the Macintosh computer and computers using MS-DOS. Apple File Exchange came with the Mac system software until version 7.5. Essentially, this utility can initialize and/or read a 3.5-inch diskette in the MS-DOS/Windows format if the Mac involved has a SuperDrive disk drive. All Macintosh computers since the IIsi have been manufactured with a SuperDrive. It can also convert files created on DOS/Windows computers for use on the Macintosh and vice versa. Apple File Exchange uses two translation methods: text and binary. Text translation is used for text-only files, and binary is used for all others. Apple System 7.5 eliminated the need for Apple File Exchange, providing instead the **PC Exchange** and **Easy Open** system extensions. Beginning with System 7.5, Mac users could simply insert a DOS/Windows disk and read it directly on the desktop, using the extensions to convert files.

■ **File Compression**—Even today's multi-gigabyte hard drives can fill up pretty fast with graphics files. Some graphics file formats, such as **TIFF** and **JPEG**, can be self-compressing, but a file compression utility is often used to gain more storage capability from a hard drive. **DiskDoubler** from Symantec is popular on the Macintosh. The latest version, Norton DiskDoubler Pro, is a combination of AutoDoubler, DiskDoubler, CopyDoubler, and several other utilities. AutoDoubler compresses files automatically by about 50%, and DiskDoubler compresses files manually and can be used to create multiple-file archives. The manual DiskDoubler provides the smallest file compression. CopyDoubler is a control panel item that speeds up file copying and trash emptying.

StuffIt Deluxe is another popular file compression and archiving software for the Mac. StuffIt provides a drag-and-drop method for compressing and decompressing files. StuffIt is widely used and can be downloaded from the Internet (**www.shareware.com**).

■ **Miscellaneous Useful Utilities—**
RayDream's **JAG II** removes jagged edges from digital images. Aladdin's Desktop Tools speeds up basic file-management activities on the Mac. **RAM Doubler** and Speed Doubler from Connectix perform the functions described in their names. **Conflict Catcher 3** (Casady & Greene) helps prevent crashes and freeze-ups by pinpointing conflicts between startup files on the Mac. OneClick from WestCode Software creates customized buttons for Macintosh software.

See Also
FreeHand; Illustrator; JPEG; Photoshop; TIFF

DeskTopMovie, *See MovieTrilogy*

DeskTopText, *See MovieTrilogy*

DeskTopTV, *See MovieTrilogy*

develop Magazine

develop is Apple's technical journal for programmers and developers. It is published quarterly by **APDA**.

develop is one of the truly great things about being a Macintosh programmer. This superb journal stands up well against any technical journal on any topic. It frequently covers the latest Apple technologies in depth, sometimes before a technology is even available. The subject matter is definitely for programmers—most articles would make nonprogrammers' eyes glaze over pretty quickly. But if you are a programmer, *develop* is well worth the investment.

Each issue of *develop* is accompanied by the Bookmark CD, an excellent resource of technical documentation and source code. *develop* is also available in electronic form on Apple's developer Web site (**http://dev.info.apple.com/**) and on the CD-ROMs that accompany the Developer Mailing.

Apple Developer Catalog
Apple Computer, Inc.
P.O. Box 319

Buffalo, NY 14207-0319

US: (800) 282-2732
Canada: (800) 637-0029
International: (716) 871-6555
Fax: (716) 871-6511

Email: **apda@applelink.apple.com**
Web: **http://devcatalog.apple.com**

See Also
APDA; Apple Developer Mailing

Developer CD Series, *See Apple Developer Mailing*

Developer Mailing, *See Apple Developer Mailing*

Development Environment

Every programmer creates a suite of development tools that best serve his needs. This collection of tools is his development environment. When programmers speak of a development environment, they may mean this total collection of tools, but more likely they are referring to a single set of tools designed to work together.

Development environments fall into two major classes: integrated and non-integrated. **Integrated development environments** (IDEs) bundle a set of tools together in a closely coupled application or set of applications. IDEs typically include a source code **editor**, **compilers**, **linkers**, and **debuggers** that work together within an application or are closely coupled with a single application. Metrowerks **CodeWarrior** and **Symantec C++** are the most popular IDEs for the Macintosh.

A non-integrated environment is more like an open shell. In fact, using a non-integrated development environment is very similar to using the UNIX shell to issue individual commands or scripts to control separate compilers and other tools. The primary development shell is **MPW**, the Macintosh programmer's workshop.

An important quality in any development environment is scriptability. As the size of any development project increases, it becomes more and more important to perform routine development tasks automatically. IDEs often have this functionality built-in, but it's always helpful to be able to extend the built-in features with your own scripts. Depending on the type of environment, scripting may take a very different form. The Symantec C++ and CodeWarrior IDEs are scriptable using **AppleScript** (or **Frontier**), for example, whereas MPW supports its own rich scripting language similar to UNIX shell scripts.

See Also

AppleScript; CodeWarrior; Compiler; Debugger; Editor; Frontier; Integrated Development Environment; Linker; MPW; Programming Tools; Symantec C++

Development Tools,
See Programming Tools

Device Profiles

Making colors match between scanned images, those created on a computer, and those printed by a variety of color output devices is a tough job. Today's color management software, which attempts to do just that, relies on device profiles. These are software descriptions of how a particular input or output device (scanner, digital camera, color printer, imagesetter, video monitor) reproduces the color images it processes.

Until 1995 many color management programs produced incompatible device profiles. That spring, Apple introduced **ColorSync** 2.0, a totally new version of its own color management system software that used ICC-compliant device profiles—ones that conform to the specification laid down by the International Color Consortium. ColorSync and the ICC spec for device profiles have since been embraced by the major software developers producing color management software.

See Also

Color Management; ColorSync

Diamonds 3-D

Highly addictive combination puzzle/arcade game reminiscent of Pong at its lower levels. Diamonds 3D requires that you bounce a ball to break bricks set up in a 3D play area. Your mouse controls the paddle. Some bricks require several "hits" before they disappear. Some can be broken only by balls the same color, so you must bounce off a "color-changer" brick first. Fast action, and sometimes unpredictable vectors make this game a real challenge.

See Also

Zoop

DiaQuest, *See Animaq*

DIC, *See Color Matching Systems*

Digital Audio Tape, *See DAT*

Digital Cameras

If you're adventurous, you can skip the film stage altogether, and digitize photos right in the camera. Digital cameras range in quality from simple point-and-shoot cameras that offer experienced photographers little control to sophisticated and very expensive digital adapters for high-end photographic equipment.

As of this writing, digital cameras are a relatively new technology, and units that are adequate for professional color publishing can cost tens of thousands of dollars. It's likely that more reasonably-priced professional-quality digital cameras will begin to appear by the end of the century.

See Also

Desktop Publishing; Digital Still Cameras; Digital Video Cameras; Scanners

Digital Chisel

Digital Chisel is a multimedia authoring tool built upon Allegiant Technologies **SuperCard**. With custom programming, pre-scripted templates and a built-in database, Digital Chisel is a specialized tool that is best suited for creating quizzes and computer-based training programs. It is much easier to learn and use than SuperCard.

Digital Chisel projects are made up of a sequence of screens containing text fields and graphics. A text list window displays the order and name of the screens in a presentation. A number of multimedia tools are available for adding visual excitement to a presentation, including path- and frame-based animation, and hypertext features. Buttons can play QuickTime movies, sound, and control laser disc and CD-ROM drives, as well as provide navigation to other presentation screens. A reasonably complete 8-bit paint tool is included, along with a CD-ROM full of clip art. One problem the first-time user might have is that a lot of these elements are hidden in toolboxes, which can be difficult to find.

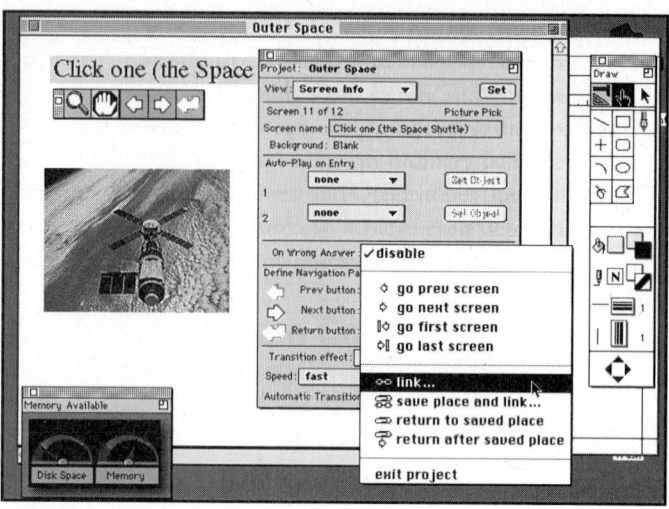

The main strength of Digital Chisel is that it can quickly and easily create interactive on-screen tests. A built-in database (which can be password-protected) enables you to track and score a user's performance, and the program can record the length of time it takes a user to complete a specific test. This makes Digital Chisel especially attractive for educational and training purposes.

When creating a presentation, you can start from scratch or use one of nine screen templates. The True/False template features fields for questions and check boxes for the two possible answers. There are also multiple choice and single field answer templates (though this type can be limiting as the user must type the answer exactly right). When a student runs the project, Digital Chisel compares the answers with those stored in the answer field during the authoring session. If a question is answered incorrectly, the program can automatically branch to a different screen.

The same amount of memory should be used when authoring as will be available when running a project, or the projector may not work correctly.

Pierian Spring Software
Portland, OR
Price: $149
Fax: (503) 222-0771
Phone: (503) 222-2044 or (800) 472-8578
Web: **http://www.pierian.com**

See Also
Astound; Director; Special Delivery

Digital Color, *See Color Gamut; Desktop Publishing and Digital Color*

Digital Gourmet

Can you really learn to cook from a computer program? Probably not, but you can certainly use a digital database to keep track of recipes, plan meals, and print grocery lists. And there are several good programs available to help you do so. One of the best is Digital Gourmet, from the Books on Disk division of TeleTypesetting, a small, friendly company in this editor's hometown. Digital Gourmet comes on a CD-ROM along with a matching **HyperCard** stack called Digital Bartender. The format is the same for each. The program comes with lots of recipes, including many Mexican and Kosher-style dishes, and some truly fabulous desserts. Drink recipes in the Digital Bartender range from the familiar to the esoteric.

There's an index which you can search alphabetically or by category. Once you've found the recipe you want, clicking a button on the recipe card adds the ingredients to your shopping list. Once you've settled on a menu, clicking the edit shopping list button will sort all the ingredients, combining the dab of butter for the chicken dish with the quarter pound for the cheese straws and so on. There are also cooking tips and nutritional information provided. It's a good idea to print out the recipes you intend to prepare. Most Macs don't react well to flour and shortening on the keyboard.

See Also

CD-ROM; HyperCard

Digital Halftones

Digital halftones are halftones created by a digital output device rather than by a camera. They are an attempt to mimic the older photomechanical halftone technology, and, if done properly, they succeed quite well. The actual quality of digital halftones versus photomechanical halftones has always been a matter of some controversy among graphics arts professionals. As is often the case with other matters in life, the older generation may sometimes regard digital halftones as an upstart technology which doesn't quite measure up to the previous one. Nevertheless, digital halftoning has all but replaced the older camera method in the United States.

Digital halftone quality has been vastly improved since the beginnings of desktop publishing in the mid-1980s. This is due primarily to the development of **imagesetters** and other output devices with a high repeatability factor. Repeatability is the ability of an imagesetter to place a laser spot in exactly the same position on the imaging area time after time. Excellent repeatability is necessary because digital halftone cells are composed of groups of the very small laser spots (or dots) produced by imagesetters. These are also called machine spots. The dpi (dots per inch) rating of an output device is an expression of how many of these tiny spots can be placed in a linear inch. These terms can be quite confusing. In fact, some imaging professionals prefer to use the term epi (elements per inch) rather than dpi when describing output resolution so as to avoid confusion with the term dot as it applies to printed halftones. This makes a lot of sense, although it is not generally accepted. Elements per inch seems a vastly more accurate way to refer to the very different kinds of dots produced by inkjet printers, toner-based laser printers, and high-resolution imagesetters. The bottom line, however, is that it takes a group of these elements, dots, or spots set closely together in a matrix to make a digital halftone cell. The halftone dot is created by a matrix of imaging elements called a halftone cell.

This cell becomes a halftone dot when it is printed. Photomechanical halftone dots are often round or elliptical, but digital halftone dots may be slightly irregular in shape. Imagesetters and film recorders make the best digital halftones because they have a higher resolution rating. They can place more of the elements per inch and the elements are more sharply defined. Laser printers can produce halftones, but the elements are fuzzy because they are created from toner. For this reason, a high-resolution laser printer (1200 or 1800 dpi) cannot produce halftones as sharp and clean as an imagesetter operating at the same resolution. High-resolution laser printer halftones are perfectly adequate for some applications though. The definition of a dot is important to the quality of the reproduction. The quality of a laser printer dot is less than the typical imagesetter dot.

IMAGESETTER(EPI)
LINE SCREEN(LPI) = Halftone dot matrix = elements/dot

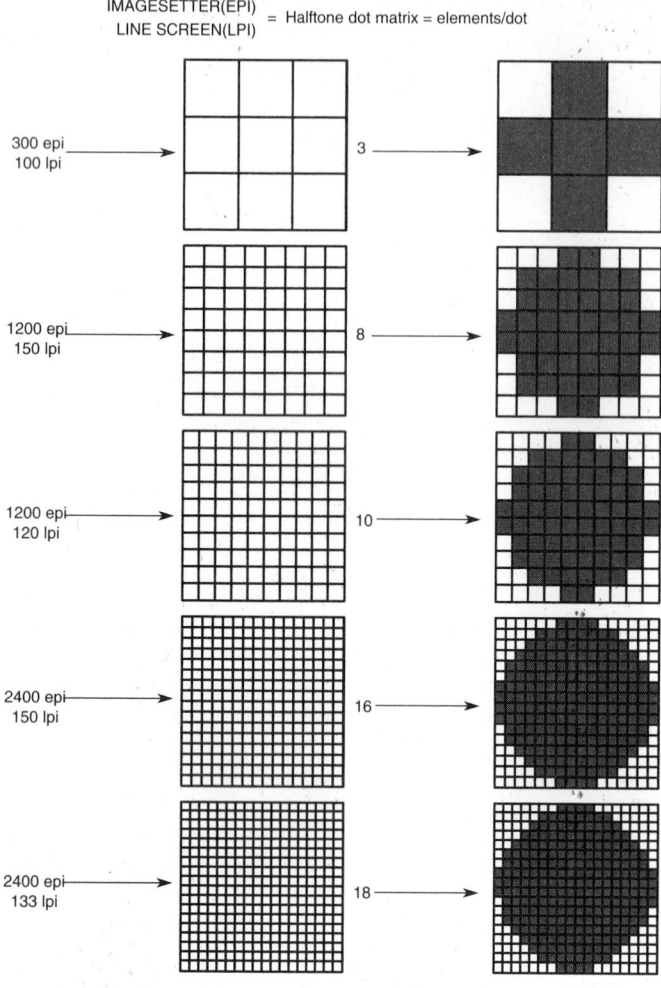

300 epi
100 lpi → [matrix] 3 →

1200 epi
150 lpi → [matrix] 8 →

1200 epi
120 lpi → [matrix] 10 →

2400 epi
150 lpi → [matrix] 16 →

2400 epi
133 lpi → [matrix] 18 →

Laser Printer Dot

Imagesetter Dot

Another confusing issue in digital terminology is the difference between dpi (dots per inch), lpi (lines per inch), and ppi (pixels per inch). It is to be hoped that dpi was clarified in the previous paragraph, so I will contrast lpi and ppi. The former is the line screen ruling, or screen frequency, of a halftone expressed in lines per inch (lpi). The latter is the linear pixel resolution of a digital image. Lines per inch (and dots per inch) should always be associated with printing output, and pixels per inch with scanning input and monitor display. It is not uncommon for dpi to be used instead of ppi in scanning terminology, but ppi seems the better term because it is more precise. To further confuse the issue, some references state linear pixel resolution as samples per inch (spi).

Because scanners are used to digitize images that will be printed as digital halftones, it is important to understand how pixels are related to the screen ruling of halftones. In scanning, a widely accepted ratio of pixels to halftone screen ruling is 2:1. This means that two pixels of a digital image are required to make one printed halftone dot. This is known as the *sampling ratio*. Actually, the pixels in a digital image are always expressed as a square unit, so two pixels are really 2×2 pixels. See the following figure; a unit of 2×2 pixels is needed to make one halftone dot using the 2:1 ratio.

The sampling ratio for converting pixels to a halftone must be determined to establish an optimum scanning resolution. This formula is expressed as follows:

screen frequency (lpi) × 2 = scanning resolution

Therefore, an image to be printed at 133 lpi has a sampling ratio of 266 ppi to 133 lpi. Some people use a multiplier of 1.5 or even 1.25 to avoid large file sizes. The digital image resolution (266 ppi in the example) is the ideal scanning resolution.

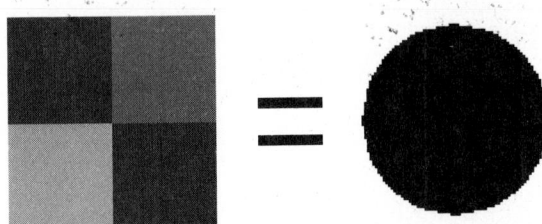

D

When a scanned image needs to be enlarged or reduced (scaled) for final output, it should be done at the time of scanning if possible. Alternatively, the digital image may be resampled in Adobe **Photoshop** or similar software. A digital image should *never* be scaled by simply enlarging or reducing it in a page layout software application unless the scaling has been compensated for at the time of scanning. If the image must be enlarged and the proper pixel content for that enlargement was not calculated when the image was scanned, Photoshop can create new pixels to maintain the original image resolution. If it is to be reduced, Photoshop can discard pixels for the same purpose. If the final size is known at the time of scanning, it is more desirable either to calculate the proper pixel content for scaling in the page layout or perform the scaling on the scanner itself. The image quality resulting from creating new pixels in Photoshop is not as good as when the image is scanned at the proper size and resolution in the first place.

If a scanned image is to be scaled in a page layout or other software application, further math is necessary to determine the proper pixel content and the optimum scanning resolution:

1. First, the total number of pixels is determined by multiplying the final image size by the digital image resolution obtained with the 2:1 formula.

   For example (using a width measurement only), a 3.5 inch wide image that will be enlarged to a final width of 6 inches multiplied by 266 ppi equals 1,596 pixels (6 inches × 266 = 1,596).

2. To determine the ideal scanning resolution for this image, divide 1,596 by the original size of the image. In this example that is 3.5 inches.

   Therefore, 1,596 divided by 3.5 equals 456 ppi, making 456 ppi the optimum scanning resolution for this image.

3. Dividing this scanning resolution (456 ppi) by the original resolution (266 ppi) will result in the percentage of enlargement for the image (170 percent). Therefore, when this image is enlarged to 170 percent of its original size, it will still have the proper number of pixels.

These formulas assume that the aspect ratio (ratio of width to height) is maintained. If the scanner allows scaling (and the process is far easier if it does), simply enter 266 as the resolution and 170 percent as the enlargement and click the Scan button.

Some desktop scanners seem to have native resolutions (suggested scanning resolutions listed in a menu), and it is probably acceptable to use one of them if it is close to the optimum number that you determined with the formula. It is also acceptable to round off the number derived from the formula. The main point to remember is not to end up with a number that is too low.

See Also

Halftones; Image Manipulation for Printing; Image Scanning; Resolution Measurement; Stochastic Screens

Digital I/O Connectors

Digital I/O connectors are used to connect digital audio gear and transmit the digital signal without having to perform a Digital/Audio and A/D conversion that is necessary if traditional cables and connectors are used. This is a concern of professional musicians and sound engineers who need to produce best-quality recordings. It's unlikely that typical computer users would need this capability, and it is only available on the most expensive plug-in audio cards for the Macintosh, such as Digidesign. The two most common connections are S/PDIF and **AES/EBU**.

See Also
AES/EBU

Digital Modems, *See ISDN*

Digital Printing, *See Printing*

Digital Scenery, Introduction

For years, organic life and the natural world were the most difficult subjects to model or emulate with any degree of believability with computer graphics media. The problem was one of sharpness and cleanliness. Nature is neither sharp nor clean, but has torn and hidden symmetry, and corners and edges where light plays unkind tricks on the eyes. Computer graphics, on the other hand, were known from the start for razor sharp visual displays and mechanistic photorealistic drama, as exemplified by the familiar animated metallic sphere flying above a checkerboard plane, reflecting every nuance of the cold virtual world below. But as the scruffy all-too-real dinosuars in Spielberg's *Jurrasic Park* demonstrated quite shockingly, computer graphics has come a long way in just a few short years. In addition to the development of larger and faster systems, more detailed texture mapping and more accurate models, the new superorganic realism now expected from computer graphics media owes its existence to two individuals and their life's work: Fibonacci and Mandelbrot.

Leonardo Fibonacci lived in the thirteenth century, and his contribution to computer graphics was the rediscovery of a mathematical formula known by the Egyptians but lost until he revived it, an arithmetic progression that now bears his name, the Fibonacci Series. The series is a simple additive process.

0, 1, 1, 2, 3, 5, 8, 13, 21, 34, 55, 89,...

You start with zero and then go to one. Add zero and one which equals one, add one and one which equals two, add two and one which equals three, add three and two which equals five, five plus three is eight, eight plus five is thirteen, and so on. As the series progresses, the last two numbers (the last divided by the second to the last as for example 89 divided by 55) gets closer and closer to 1.618. The magic is in this last number, because 1.618 seems to be present in some measure in the way nature works. Tree branches and the bones of the human body seem to evidence this magic proportion in the comparative length of their connected parts. Tree and scenery software contain Fibonaccian algorithms as based upon the proportion 1.618 as a central part of their graphics generating engines.

Mandelbrot, unlike Fibonacci, is still alive. He did his central work under the auspices of IBM in the 1960s. Mandelbrot is responsible for presenting us with the theories of fractal dimensions, the observation that the closer we magnify the natural world, the more our view of it seems to replicate the stage we just came from, an endless repeating series of like-images. With Fibonacci, the math came first. With Mandelbrot, thanks largely to the emergence of the computer as a visual tool, the graphics preceded the mathematical theories. To Fibonacci, numbers led to the appreciation of beauty, while, in Mandelbrot's thought, visual beauty led to the appreciation of beauty in numbers. Most of the software used to generate subjects in the natural world—from living things to the land, sea, and air that they live on and in—is based in good measure upon Mandelbrot's work and fractal geometry.

With the powerful and fast new computers like the Power Macs that sit in our homes and at the workplace, we can create believable virtual worlds and populate natural rolling landscapes with trees, rivers, and clouds. Thanks to the work of Fibonacci, Mandelbrot, and others, computer art is no longer the home of cold mechanistic visions alone, but a virtual environment that mirrors the beauty of nature itself.

Suggested Reading:

Ghyka, Matila, *The Geometry of Art and Life*.

Moreau, Rene, *The Computer Comes of Age*. Cambridge, Mass.: The M.I.T. Press, 1984.

Taubes, Gary, "Mathematics of Chaos." *Discover*, September 1984.

Digital Signal Processors (DSP), *See Coprocessors, Types*

Digital Still Cameras

Digital Still Cameras differ from conventional cameras in that they do not use film. Instead, a CCD (charged coupled device)—a small chip that is sensitive to light—is used to capture an image. The image is stored as digital information in RAM memory, and can then be downloaded to the computer. The primary advantage of Digital Still Cameras is the speed with which an image can be photographed and transferred to the computer. With conventional film cameras, the film must be processed before digitizing (using **PhotoCD** or a **slide** or **flatbed scanner**).

Digital Still Cameras are available in a range of prices and features, but currently there is a big step both in price and quality between the lowest priced units, which claim to offer 640×480 resolution, and the higher resolution cameras that support resolutions in the thousands of pixels. Whereas the low-end cameras cost less than $1,000, the higher resolution cameras start at around $6,000. This is in part a result of the CCDs (charged coupled devices) used to capture the image. Because the primary use of these sensors is in video cameras, which have resolutions that match standard **NTSC** images (about 640×480), those chips are the widest and cheapest.

Another problem with the low cost digital still cameras is that these cameras use a **range finder** rather than **SLR** (Single Lens Reflex). When you look through the range finder, you aren't seeing what the camera sees. This is a problem if you use lens attachments to adjust the **focal length** of the lens. Also,

these cameras compress the images, so that they fit in a reasonable amount of RAM.

Unlike video cameras and the first generation **still video cameras**, there is no need for a **digitizing board** to turn the **analog image** into a digital file. The camera does that when the picture is taken. It's just a matter of connecting the camera to the serial port of the computer and running the software that transfers the image from the camera to the computer. It can take several minutes to send all the images from the camera. To prolong battery life, it is worth purchasing a power adapter (if not supplied) to use while the camera is connected to the computer. It's not mandatory, but it will prolong the life of the batteries.

Many of these cameras offer limited options for deleting the images from the camera after you no longer need them. Most require that you delete all of the pictures, or only allow you to delete the last image taken.

All cameras use some kind of **compression** to reduce the size of the image. This can impact the quality of the image, although the biggest factor affecting quality is the CCD chips used in these cameras.

All of the lower priced digital still cameras can capture an image of at least 640×480 (see table), but when viewed on-screen, these images do not look as sharp as a comparable scanned image from a slide or flatbed scanner. The images are suitable for rough work, and quick shots, but are not suitable for final screen work except at less than full screen (640×480). The images look best when they are resized with **Photoshop**, or a comparable application, to half size, which results in a sharp image of 320×240.

Exposure is also a problem with these cameras. Exposure limitations of the sensors means that even the cheapest 35mm camera will perform better in most situations. Best results are obtained in bright, evenly illuminated conditions.

If you need images quickly, but of higher quality, it might make more sense to buy a slide or flatbed scanner, or use PhotoCD. With a slide or flatbed scanner, it is possible to have film rush developed in about an hour in most cities. Although not as quick as a digital camera, it is fast enough for many purposes (remember to add scanning time. It will probably take about two hours to capture what would take about ten minutes with the digital camera). PhotoCD usually takes at least a day.

See Also
Flatbed Scanners; NTSC; PhotoCD; Scanners; Slide Scanner; Still Video Cameras

Digital Stripping, *See Prepress*

Digital Swatchbook,
See Color, Measuring

Digital Telephone,
See Modem Cables and Connections

Digital Telephone Line,
See ISDN

Digital Video Cameras

The digital video (DV) format is a new tape format that stores a video image digitally on tape rather than as an analog signal. DV rivals the quality of Betacam SP, yet the cameras cost 1/3 that of a comparable Betacam SP camera. The image quality compares favorably to Betacam SP. DV offers 500 lines of resolution versus Betacam SPs 650, but this will be hardly noticed.

DV uses a new form of compression, similar to **MPEG**, that compresses at about 5:1, resulting in a 3.475 MB/sec data rate. It's possible to use a new digital interface—**1394 Fire Wire**—to connect the camera to a computer that is equipped with an appropriate input. The digital video signal can then be transferred directly to the computer with no need for redigitizing. If the proper translation software is provided, these files can then be opened and edited using an application such as Adobe **Premiere**.

See Also
1394 Fire Wire; Digital Still Cameras; Premiere

Digital Still Cameras

Camera	Pictures	Image Size	Price	Special Features
Chinon	10^2	640 × 480	$700	3x zoom ES-3000[1]lens PCMCIA card
Dycam 10-C[1]	10^2	640 × 480	$900	3x zoom lens PCMCIA card
Kodak DC50[1]	10^2	756 × 504	$1000	3x zoom lens PCMCIA card
Kodak DC40[3]	42	756 × 504	$700	Larger image size 48 images in memory
Logitech[3]	42	756 × 504	$700	Larger image size 48 images in memory
QuickTake 150	32	640 × 480	$700	Camera can appear as a disk drive on the desktop
Casio QV-10A	96	320 × 240	$500	Camera can connect to regular TV set and display computer graphics

1: This is essentially the same camera. The Kodak DC50 produces a picture with a larger number of pixels.

2: The camera has 1MB of on-board RAM. Additional pictures can be stored on a PCMCIA card. A 4MB card holds 43 pictures.

3: This is the same camera.

Digitizing Tablet, *See Graphics Tablets*

DigiTrax 1.2

A sound digitizing and editing application that features an interface that resembles a four-track tape recorder (that is, there are buttons for play, record, and so on, and sliders for adjusting volume).

DigiTrax can record and mix up to six tracks on a **Power Mac** or **AV** Mac. The program supports mixing and **bouncing** multiple tracks and **automated mixdown** features, can open **QuickTime** movies, and can synchronize to a **MIDI** sequencer or with **SMPTE** timecode.

While great for recording original music and creating complicated mixes of sounds, this program may be too much for simple sound editing. A program such as **SoundEdit** is better suited for those tasks.

See Also
Automated Mixdown; QuickTime; SoundEdit

> Opcode Systems
> Price: $199.95
> Phone: (415) 856-3333
> Web: **http://www.opcode.com**

DIMS, *See Memory*

Dingbat, *See Symbols*

Dingbat Fonts, *See Ornament and Dingbat Fonts*

Direct Connect Modems, *See Modems*

Director

Macromedia's Director began life as an animation package called VideoWorks. Over time, features and a **scripting** language called Lingo were added. Lingo is similar to **HyperTalk** and **SuperTalk**, the scripting languages of **HyperCard** and **SuperCard**, but just different enough to cause confusion as you switch between them.

Director is an ideal tool for creating most multimedia presentations because it's very flexible. Its primary strengths are animation and its cross-platform capabilities, which has made it one of the most popular commercial authoring tools. Director includes a built-in paint program, so editing and creating graphical elements is easy, although you may still want to use a dedicated program, such as **Photoshop**, for complex editing jobs.

The three primary parts of Director are the Cast, the Score, and the Stage. The Stage is the area in which objects are arranged and displayed during a presentation. The Cast is like a database containing the graphics, sounds, and other objects used in the presentation. The Score holds the information regarding what Cast objects appear on the Stage at what time. The Score is divided into frames, and each frame represents the Stage at a point in time.

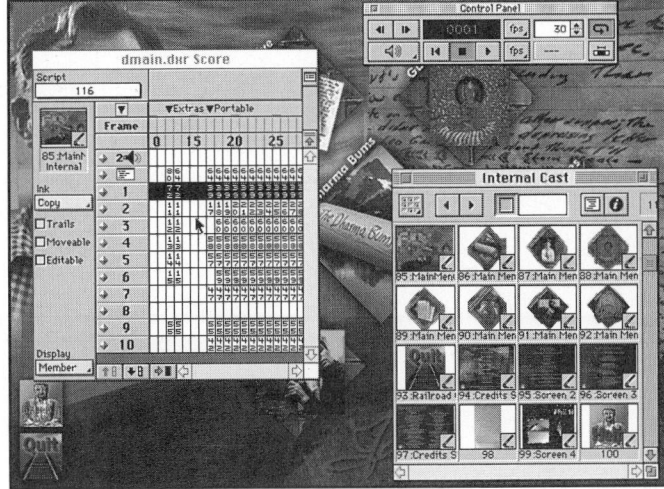

There are many tool windows in Director, including the paint tool, a text tool for creating and editing text fields, scripting and debugging windows and so forth. When you first use the program, it can be rather intimidating. Just remember that it is the Score and Cast Windows you need to become comfortable with first.

Animation is created by dragging objects from the Cast to the Stage and arranging them for each frame in the sequence. You can create each frame from scratch, or you can duplicate an existing frame, and then alter the position of the objects in the duplicated frame.

Director includes some automated positioning tools. You can place an object in position on one frame, and then in another frame several frames ahead, place the object in a different location. Director creates the in-between positions using a process called **inbetweening**, saving a lot of time when animating objects.

It is possible to create simple interactivity (stop and start an animation, for example) using timer functions in the Score without any scripting. For more complex actions you must use the Lingo **scripting** language.

Other elements, such as sounds and QuickTime movies, can be imported into the Cast and arranged on the Stage. These elements (as well as imported graphics) also can be linked to the Cast rather than imported. Linking means that they remain external files, and must be read by Director before being played. The primary advantage of this is that you can actually edit the sound files without having to re-import them. The next time Director runs the presentation it reads in the updated files.

When a movie is complete, it can be turned into a Projector, a file that runs without the user having a copy of Director. A projector adds about 300K to a movie.

Although there was a Windows Player for Director 3.0, it was only with the arrival of Director 4.0 that there was true cross-platform capability (and a Windows version of Director itself). The Director file format for both operating systems is now byte-compatible. Files created on the Macintosh can be opened in Director for Windows, edited, and then brought back to the Macintosh and changed again. All that's required is to copy the files from one machine to another. It's also possible to create a cross platform CD-ROM that has one data file, but two projectors (one for the Macintosh, the other for Windows).

You will need both copies of Director if you plan to cross-develop.

Like HyperCard, Director's functionality can be extended with special programs. These are very similar to the format of HyperCard's **XCMDs**, but Macromedia has defined its own format for Director routines called XObjects. Director also comes with an XObject called XCMDGlue. This routine serves as an interface between Director and XCMDs written for HyperCard. Many HyperCard XCMDs can be called successfully from Director using XCMDGlue. Director also supports a new plug-in format called Xtras, which a number of third party developers have released, including Xtras for MIDI playback and database handling.

See Also
HyperCard; mTropolis; Scripting; Shockwave; SuperCard 2.5

Directories and Reference Materials, *See Reference Materials and Directories*

Disable the Warning Box (Keyboard Shortcut)

When you choose **Empty Trash** to **delete** items in the **Trash**, an **alert box** warns you that you are about to permanently delete items. The alert box tells you the number of items, calculates their total file size, and asks if it's okay to empty the Trash. To disable this warning, hold the **Option key** while choosing Empty Trash from the **Special menu.** The items are deleted without the alert box appearing. You can also hold the Option key while emptying the Trash to delete locked files.

To empty the Trash without the alert box appearing, follow these steps:

1. Hold the Option key while choosing Empty Trash from the Special menu.

2. The files in the Trash are deleted without the warning box appearing.

3. If you had any locked files in the Trash, holding the Option key will also delete them as well.

See Also

Alert Box; Empty Trash; Keyboard Shortcuts; Option Key; Special Menu; Trash, Locked Files

Disabled Users, *See Big:Calc Program; Software, Special Needs*

Disc, *See CD-ROM*

Discretionary Hyphen, *See Hyphen, Discretionary*

Digital Signal Processor, *See DSP (Digital Signal Processor)*

Disinfectant

Disinfectant is a free utility written by John Norstad of Northwestern University. It includes a very detailed discussion of viruses and prevention of any known virus program. Disinfectant can install an INIT to watch over your system for known viruses and alert you when a virus is detected.

Disinfectant cannot scan compressed archives and does not detect HyperCard viruses. You cannot teach Disinfectant about new viruses; you must get an update to the program. You can obtain Disinfectant from online bulletin boards, from many Internet Web sites, or by sending a self-addressed, stamped disk mailer and disk to:

> John Norstad
> Academic Computing and Networked Services
> Northwestern University
> 2129 North Campus Drive
> Evanston, Illinois 60208

See Also

SAM; Virex; Virus

Disk Cache

You can set aside a small amount of your Mac's memory (RAM) as a separate memory section known as a disk cache. This cache contains a copy of recently or often used information from your hard disk (or other mounted disks). By setting aside this disk cache, the Mac can store these often used items in memory, rather than having to search the **hard disk** each time it needs the items. By having them handy in memory, it can add a significant boost to your Mac's speed.

For example, if you're using a program that utilizes floating palettes, the first time you open the palette the screen redraws it quickly, but did you notice that the next time you reopen that same palette, it opens much faster? That's because that palette was cached into memory. Menus are another example. Click and hold a **pull-down menu** you haven't used yet. Then release the mouse button, and click and hold it again. You'll notice that the menu now appears almost immediately. That's the disk cache in action.

You choose the amount of memory that will be set aside as a disk cache in the **Memory control panel** (see the following figure). You set the amount by using the up or down arrows to increase or decrease the amount of memory set aside as a disk cache. Although the disk cache is always turned on, changes to the disk cache take effect only after a **restart**.

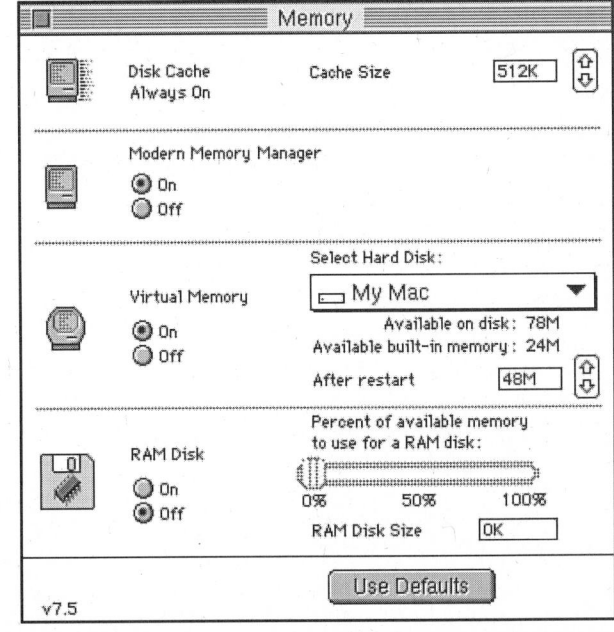

To increase or decrease the amount of disk cache, follow these steps:

1. Choose the Memory control panel from the Control Panels folder in the Apple menu.

2. In the disk cache portion of the Memory control panel (the top section) click the up arrow to increase the disk cache, or click the down arrow to decrease the cache. When you've made your selection, close the Memory control panel.

3. For your changes to take effect, you must restart your Mac.

See Also

Apple Menu; Memory Control Panel; Pull-Down Menu; Restart

Disk to Disk Copying

Copying a **file,** or a set of files, from one **disk** to another is a simple task achieved by **dragging** the files you want from one disk to the other disk. Let's say, for example, that you want to copy a text file from your **desktop** to a **disk**. Simply drag the file onto the **icon** of the disk. A copy **status bar** appears showing the progress of the copy **command**, and within a few minutes, the file is copied.

Copying Files and Folders

Process	Media	Result
Click and Drag	Within hard drive	Moved
Click and Drag	To disk	Copied
Click and Drag	From disk	Moved
Option-Click and Drag	Within hard drive	Copied
Option-Click and Drag	To and from disk	Copied

It's easy to copy from one disk to another, but it requires a few more steps (unless, of course, you happen to have two disk drives). To copy from one disk to another, follow these steps:

1. Insert the disk containing the file (or files) you wanted copied.

2. Locate the file on the disk that you want to copy.

3. Drag the file onto your hard drive icon. This copies the file to your drive.

4. **Eject** the disk.

5. Insert the disk to which you want to copy the file.

6. Locate the file you copied just moments earlier and drag it onto the icon of the disk now mounted on your desktop.

   Now you can **trash** the file you copied temporarily to your hard drive.

If you want to copy an entire disk to another disk, the process is slightly different. Insert the first disk and drag the disk icon onto the hard drive icon. Your hard drive creates a **folder** with the same name as the disk, and copies the contents of the disk to that folder. When that is complete, eject the disk and insert the second disk (the one you want to copy to). Drag the folder that you just created on your hard drive onto the icon of the second disk on your **desktop**. The folder is copied for you. Now you can trash the folder you copied temporarily to your hard drive.

See Also

Click and Drag; Command; Desktop; Disk; Eject; File; Folder; Hard Drive; Icons; Mounted; Status Bar; Trash

Disk Express II

Disk Express II is a system optimization program from Alsoft (P.O. 927, Spring, TX, 77383, 713-353-4090) designed to defragment your **hard disk** and increase your disk's access speed and overall performance. As you create new files and delete old ones, the information on your hard disk becomes fragmented into various locations. A disk optimizer utility, such as Disk Express II, defragments this information and puts the most frequently used information closest to the drive heads and puts less frequently used files further away. By making these files easily available to the drive heads, your hard disk's speed is enhanced.

Disk Express II can minimize fragmentation by keeping the files you use the most grouped together, so the access time to these files is as fast as possible. Disk Express also enables you to optimize your drive at predetermined time intervals, or you can set it up to do an optimization when your drive's level of fragmentation exceeds the level you've selected as acceptable in Disk Express' preferences.

See Also
Fragmentation; Hard Disk

Disk First Aid

Disk First Aid is a free application from Apple found on your **Disk Tools disk**, and it's used for diagnosing and repairing damaged **disks** or **hard disks**. Disk First Aid has a distinct icon that looks like an ambulance with a red cross on the side (see the following figure).

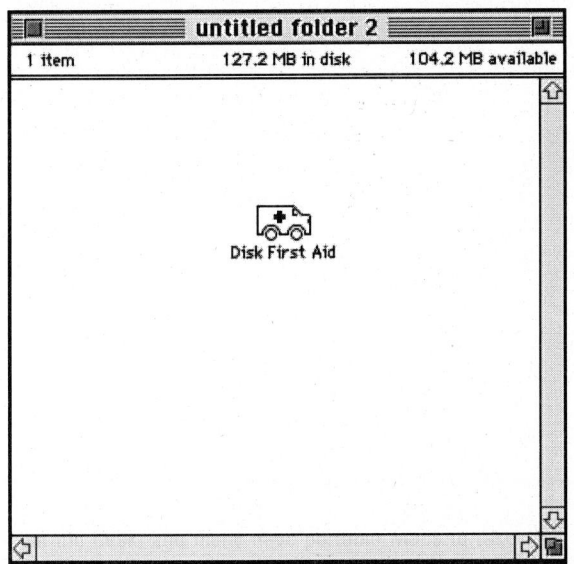

Disk First Aid doesn't offer many options; you can choose to verify a disk to see whether it's working properly, or you can choose to repair any problems it encounters during its diagnostic check. If you are running Disk First Aid from your startup disk, it can only verify the disk; it cannot make repairs on the active startup disk. If you do find a disk problem, insert the Disk Tools disk from your set of system disks and run Disk First Aid from that disk to repair your startup disk.

To verify or repair a disk using Disk First Aid, follow these steps:

1. Insert the Disk Tools disk from your set of System Disks.
2. Double-click the Disk First Aid icon to launch the utility.
3. Choose to verify or repair by clicking the appropriate button.
4. Any error message is displayed in the Disk First Aid window.

See Also
Disk; Disk Tools; Hard Disk; Startup Disk

Disk Fit

DiskFit is a commercial **backup utility** from Dantz Development Corporation (4 Orinda Way, Orinda, CA 94563. Phone: 510-253-3000. On the Web **http://www.dantz.com**) that enables you to perform a backup of your **hard disk** or disks on a network. With DiskFit, you can choose to back up your entire hard disk, request specialized backups for items such as applications and documents, or individual folders to be backed up.

This enables you to designate a folder as your backup folder, and any items you place in that folder are backed up by DiskFit when it runs its backup procedure. And, of course, DiskFit enables you to perform an **incremental backup** of your files that backs up only the files that have been changed since your last backup.

DiskFit backs up your files to disks or any removable storage medium, such as SyQuest cartridges or Zip disks, and the backups are in **Finder** format so you can open files directly from the backed up disk, rather than having to decompress or restore the requested files to your hard disk before opening the files. DiskFit also can create a report listing all the backed up files and which backup disks they appear on.

See Also

Backup Utilities; Disks; Finder; Hard Disk; Incremental Backup; Network

Disk Fragmentation

Data is written to your hard disk in blocks, one after another. These blocks are placed so the data is easily retrieved by the **hard disk's** drive heads. Over time these blocks of data on your hard disk can become fragmented into various locations. This happens as some files are deleted, new files are added, and what used to be a smooth, contiguous chunk of disk space starts to become a series of smaller fragmented spaces. When this occurs you have disk fragmentation.

This fragmentation can slow the access speed of your hard disk as it searches through your disk to find requested information. Using a disk optimizer utility defragments this information and puts the most-frequently used information nearest the drive heads and the less-frequently used files further away. With these files easily available to the drive heads, your hard disk's speed is enhanced.

The following table lists some of the most popular commercial disk optimizer utilities

See Also

Hard Disk; Norton Utilities

Disk Icon

Each disk **mounted** on your **desktop** has a corresponding **icon** that represents the type of **disk** it is. Your hard drive usually is represented by an icon shaped like a box. A disk is represented by an icon that looks like a **disk,** and a **CD-ROM** is represented by a circular disk icon that, not surprisingly, looks like a CD-ROM.

The icons that you see mounted on your desktop are either custom icons put there by the disk's manufacturer or Apple's **default** icons. You can add a different icon to your hard drive or even to a disk (if it's not **locked**) by **copying** the icon and **pasting** it in the drive's **Get Info** window. Thousands of full-color, custom icons that cover every model of Macintosh are available in a variety of styles from **online services**. Several cartoon characters also are available as icons.

See Also

CD-ROM; Copy; Default; Desktop; Disk; Get Info; Hard Drive; Icon; Locked; Mounted Disks; Online Services; Paste

Disk Images

Apple developed its own utility, Disk Copy, for making exact, reliable duplicates of any **disk**. The file Disk Copy created is called a disk image, because it is not just a copy of the disk but a mirror image of the disk and its contents.

Commercial Disk Optimizer Utilities

Optimizer Utility	Developer	Contact Info
Speed Disk	Symantec (part of Norton Utilities)	10201 Torre Ave, Cupertino, CA, 95104-2132, Phone (800) 441-7234. Web URL **http:// www.symantec.com**)
Optimizer	Symantec (part of MacTool Pro package)	10201 Torre Ave, Cupertino, CA, 95104-2132, Phone (800) 441-7234. Web URL **http:// www.symantec.com**)
DiskExpress II	AlSoft	P.O. 927, Spring, TX, 77383, (713) 353-4090

The advantages of DiskCopy are that the disk image created is an exact duplicate of what was copied from the original: all the **icons** and **folders** are in their same position with the same names and windows open; the disk image has the same name as the disk did, and any invisible files on the disk are also copied into the disk image. These disk image files are used to create duplicate disks and are ideal for making **backup copies** of software for your personal use only. Disk Copy is also popular for creating the master file to be burned onto a CD-ROM disc, as it makes an exact copy with all icons and folders in their same position.

Disk images can be used only by Apple's Disk Copy or a freeware product called ShrinkWrap that enables you to mount disk images on your hard disk's desktop where your system treats them as though they were the actual disks. You can also use ShrinkWrap to make and copy disk images without using Apple's Disk Copy.

To copy a disk image onto a disk, follow these steps:

1. Double-click the disk image file to launch Disk Copy and open the disk image in Disk Copy's copy window.

2. Click the button "Make A Copy" to make an exact duplicate of the disk image.

3. Insert the blank disk you want the disk image copied to in the disk drive.

4. The disk image is copied onto the disk you insert. When the watch icon returns to the arrow pointer, the copying is complete.

To copy a disk's disk image onto your hard disk, follow these steps:

1. Launch Disk Copy and insert into the disk drive the disk you want to copy.

2. Click the button "Read Master Floppy" to create the disk image.

3. Choose "Save Disk Image" from the File menu, which enables you to name the file (if you choose) and select where you want to save the disk image on your hard disk.

4. The disk image is copied onto your hard disk. This can later be transferred to a disk if you'd like, or you can mount the disk on your desktop using the utility program ShrinkWrap.

See Also
Backing Up; Disk; Folders; Hard Disk; Icons

Disk Is Locked Message

If you try to add a file to, or **delete** information from, a **locked** disk, a "Disk is locked" message box appears as shown in the figure. This means the disk has been manually locked with the locking tab located on the bottom side of the **disk**. Disks are locked to protect their contents from being altered or accidentally erased.

> You cannot move the selected items from the disk "Maclopedia Entertainment 7", because the disk is locked.
>
> [OK]

To unlock a disk, eject it and turn it upside down. In the lower-right corner you'll see the locking tab. When a disk is locked, you can see through the hole in the tab. To unlock, you can take your fingernail or the tip of a pen and physically push the tab to the opposite position (covering the opening) to unlock it. You can then reinsert the disk and delete or edit any files you wish on the disk.

See Also
Delete; Disk; Locking; Message Box

Disk Name (Keyboard Shortcut)

When you're viewing items in a Finder **window** and want to know what **disk** the items in the window are on, you can use a keyboard shortcut to find out. Simply press the **Command key** while clicking the window's title in the **title bar**. A **pop-up menu** will show a path to the disk, with the disk's name and icon appearing at the bottom of the list.

To find out what disk a Finder window's contents are from, follow these steps:

1. Hold the Command key and click on the window's name in the title bar.

2. A pop-up menu will display the window's path and the last name on the list will be the disk's name the files are located on.

See Also

Command Key; Disk; Icons; Keyboard Shortcuts; Pop-Up Menu; Title Bar; Window

Disk Window

If you **double-click** the icon of any **disk,** a window appears showing you the contents of that disk. When you start your Mac and double-click your **hard drive** icon, for example, a window opens to show you the contents of your hard drive. Just below the **title bar** of the disk window, the window displays how many items are in that particular window, how much storage space has been used on the hard disk (measured in **kilobytes**), and how much space is available on the disk.

> **TIP**   In 7.5, the contents depend on a setting in the Views CP. When checked, this info shows up in all Finder windows; when unchecked, it shows up in none.

See Also

Disk; Double-Click; Hard Disk; Kilobytes; Title Bar; Views Control Panel

DiskDoubler

DiskDoubler is a compression utility from Symantec (10201 Torre Ave, Cupertino, CA, 95104-2132, Phone (800) 441-7234; Web site at **http:// www.symantec.com**) that enables you to compress the size of files on your **disk** or **hard disk**. DiskDoubler comes in two parts: a free-standing utility application and a **desktop menu bar icon** enabling you to compress and expand files without having to launch

the application. The amount of file space saved depends on the type of file being compressed. Files can sometimes be compressed by 99 percent, though the average is 50-60 percent compression. The capability to compress files saves drive space and time if you're transferring files with a **modem** or over a **network**.

DiskDoubler gives you a variety of compression options, including the capability to choose from a variety of compression methods and the capability to create self-extracting archives (**.sea**). Self-extracting files can be expanded by Mac users who don't have DiskDoubler.

When a file is compressed, DiskDoubler attaches a modified version of the file's icon with a small .dd to let you know the file is compressed with DiskDoubler. To expand, or decompress the file, you can either select the file and choose Expand from the DiskDoubler **Finder** menu, or you can **launch** the program and the file will expand prior to opening.

See Also

Compression Utilities; .dd File Extension; Disk; Finder; Hard Disk; Launch; Menu Bar; Modem; Network; .sea File Extension

DiskImage Format,
See Decoding/Decompressing Files

DiskTop

DiskTop was a **shareware** product that became a commercial utility from PrairieSoft, Inc. (P.O. Box 65820, West Des Moines, Iowa 50265 U.S.A.,Phone: (515) 225-3720; email: **prairiesoft@applelink. apple.com**.) DiskTop was very popular for users running System 6 because it enabled you to open DiskTop as a **DA** (desk accessory) and perform a wide range of functions normally available only from the Mac's **Finder** (such as copying files, renaming files, deleting files, and so on) while you had an application running.

In **System 7** and beyond, you can go back to the Finder at any time without having to quit the current application, so DiskTop's use has been somewhat diminished. But before System 7, this was the only way to have access to these functions without quitting.

DiskTop also offered you functions the Finder alone did not offer, such as a multidisk search function and the ability to change type and creator codes (which require you to use Norton Disk Editor or a similar utility). A demo version (30-day working copy) of DiskTop is available in the Macintosh Utilities forum on America Online and at various FTP sites on the Internet.

See Also

Desk Accessories; Finder; Norton Utilities; Shareware; System 7

Disks and Drives

The terms disk and drive have become almost interchangeable in relation to fixed storage devices. In daily use, there is no particular reason to make much of this, but a quick examination reveals a distinction between the two terms that is worth noting.

A disk is the data storage medium itself. A drive is a device capable of reading the data on the disk. It reads this data via a pair of read/write heads that move back and forth across the disk as the disk rotates in the drive.

Disks simply hold information. They need a mechanism to use this information. That machine is called a *disk drive*. Disk drives read or write data from a disk in a several step sequence. The disk first spins to where the data is located. Then the read-write arm moves out or in to that spot and touches the disk to change the magnetic coating. The disk drive motor must spin the disk and move the arm each time a read or write is requested by the Macintosh, making data access times slower than that of the hard disk drive. When disks are being written to or read from they spin at a rate of approximately 390 to 600 revolutions per minute.

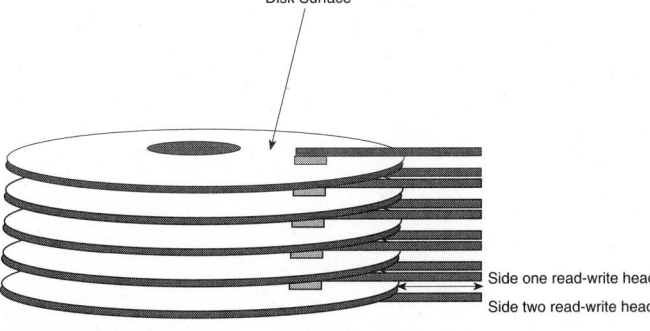

Disk Surface

Side one read-write head
Side two read-write head

Although it is not apparent from the outside, the same holds true for Winchester mechanisms. Hard disk drives (or fixed disks as they were once known) consist of both the "disk"—the hard aluminum platters or disks on which the data is stored—and the "drive"— the read/write heads and the motor which controls these heads.

The distinction between the two parts of a hard disk drive is easiest to see in removable storage devices, such as the **SyQuest** and **Zip** drives. In both cases, the cartridge, or disk, contains the data storage medium: the chassis into which the disk is placed is the drive that reads the data on the disk.

All Macintosh storage media is composed of an iron-oxide (rust) coating on some type of substrate. Disks consist of iron-oxide coated plastic (like that in a cassette tape) platter with a hole in the middle, that is surrounded by a protecting case of hard plastic (see the following figure).

There are three types of disk drives: single-sided disk drives that are capable of reading only one side of the older, single-sided 400K disks; double-sided disks drives that are capable of reading both sides of an 800K disk; and the Super Drives, which are capable of reading two sides of a high-density 1.4MB disk.

The older 400 and 800K disks have a variable rotation speed, this is because the outer tracks are longer than the inner tracks. Using a different speed to turn the disk to information stored on the outer tracks than that used to access data on the inner tracks enables the disks to hold more information. Out of a total of 80 tracks, the outer 16 tracks have 12 sectors each; the next 16 tracks contain 11 sectors each, descending in sector quantities to the inner 16 tracks that have 8 sectors each. Each sector holds 512 bytes of data. High density disks use a fixed rotation speed to enable them to be interchangeable with MS-DOS-based computers.

See Also

Hard Disks; Initialization; Storage; Winchester Disk Drive

Disks, Initializing

In order for the Macintosh's disk drives to read the magnetic iron-oxide dust on the disk it must be organized into some sort of pattern. New disks consist of randomly scattered coatings on their substrates and until they are initialized cannot be read or written to by the Macintosh because it cannot recognize any identifying markings. Initializing a disk places the Macintosh disk layout requirements on to the media making it usable to the Macintosh. These patterns lay out how the data will be stored and tracked on the disk. Norton Utilities' various modules know how these patterns should appear, as well as how data should be stored in these areas. The correct layout of the patterns is the key to repairing damaged disks and finding lost files so that they can be recovered. All disk information analysis is based on these markings.

Tracks and Sectors One type of pattern installed is the magnetic divisions used to organize the stored information. These magnetic divisions are called *tracks* and *sectors*. Each computer platform has its own unique track and sector configuration recognizable only to that system. The following figure displays an illustration of a generic disk platter's tracks and sectors.

Tracks are laid down in concentric circles around the platter's circumference. Like tree rings, they get smaller as they get nearer the center of the platter and larger at its edges. There are 160 tracks on a disk—80 on each side. Because the outer tracks are physically longer than the inner tracks, they can store more data and thus cause the drive to spin the platter more slowly when they are being accessed.

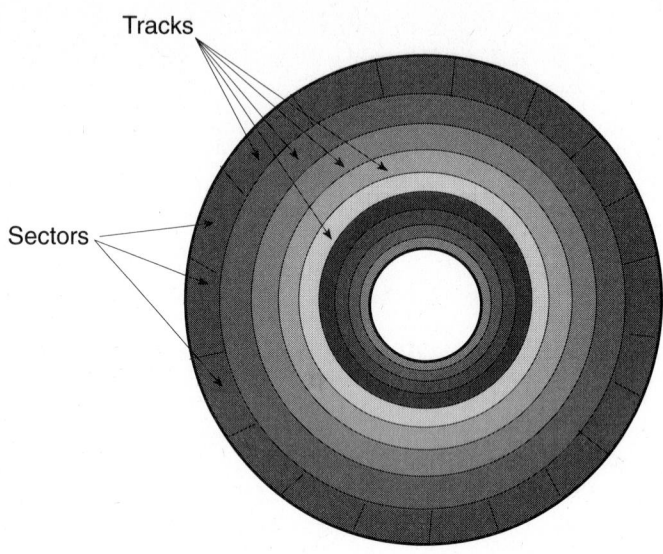

Hard Formatting When the disks are initialized as Macintosh disks, each sector's address (physical location) is electronically coded into the sector itself. This is called *address stamping*. Along with this sector preamble data special synchronization bytes are written to tell the disk controller that it is about to read a sector address. The formatting process also lays down *gap bytes*, meaningless filler bytes of data between sectors to create a timing tolerance so that the spinning platters are synchronized with the swinging of the read-write head and arm.

Another piece of data that is written into the sector directly after the address stamp is the *cyclical redundancy check* (*CRC*) bytes. These bytes of data are the result of a checksum calculation based on the value of all of the bytes written to that sector. Whenever the sector is later read from the disk, its CRC bytes are also read and the checksum recalculated. The two values are compared and if they do not match then a read error has occurred. This design is part of what Norton Utilities uses to ensure that the disks are operating correctly.

The laying down of the sector addresses, sync bytes, gap bytes, and CRC bytes is performed by the hardware with minimal instructions from the Macintosh software. This formatting process is called *low-level formatting* or *hard formatting*. The next necessary task is to format it logically.

Logical Formatting In order for the Macintosh operating system to find data out of all of the myriad megabytes of information on a disk, it is necessary to impose some order by dividing the disks up into areas reserved for specialized identification information as well as for the storage of data. The operating system builds a series of indexes and directories defining what is where, which sectors and tracks are free as opposed to which are already assigned, as well as identifying any damaged sectors that are not usable on the disk. The process of setting up this organization is called *logical formatting*. Since 1986, the Macintosh operating system has organized disks into five main areas: the boot blocks, the volume info blocks, the catalog tree, the extents tree, and the data area. Some Macintosh computers also reserve an area for partitioning information.

The result of logical formatting is the creation of a *volume*, or logical disk. Each physical hard disk can hold more than one logical disk, or volume by partitioning. Partitioning is splitting up the disk logically into separate sections. The software used to perform the partitioning writes special bookkeeping information at the front of the hard disk to tell the Macintosh how many volumes are on the disk, the location of each, as well as its size. Disks, removable disks, and most hard disks that cannot or are not partitioned do not have this information.

The volume contains the bookkeeping data in rigidly specified locations on the disk. If the information is missing, is presented in a non-specified manner, or is in the wrong location, the Macintosh cannot read the disk.

The following paragraphs describe the volume's invisible bookkeeping files and how critical they are to mapping and managing the location of your files:

- **The Boot Blocks**—The first two sectors of every disk volume is reserved for the boot blocks. Boot blocks store information needed by the Macintosh to learn how to read its internal ROM and thereby perform its startup routines. Boot blocks teach the Macintosh how to find documents and applications on the disk, the names of important system files, and Macintosh rules, such as how many files can be opened at

once, and so on. Boot blocks also contain small programs that are loaded into RAM that in turn load the critical operating system files into RAM that are needed to read the ROM information. These *bootstrap* programs are stored in the second reserved sector on the disk.

- **Volume Information Block**—The volume information block contains the definition of how the disk is structured, i.e., a "road map" to the volume. Located in this reserved area are the locations of other critical bookkeeping information areas, such as the catalog and extents trees. Other information such as the name and size of the volume, how much space is available, the location of the System folder (if this is a startup volume), and so on is also stored in this area. The volume info block also maintains the identification numbers used to label each new folder, assigning the next available ID to the next new folder you create.

- **Volume Bitmap**—The volume information block operates in conjunction with another invisible file called the *volume bitmap*. This file keeps track of the usage patterns of tracks and sectors on the disk, identifying which areas are free for new use and which are filled. Each time you save a file the File Manager checks the volume bitmap to see if there are enough free sectors to accommodate the file and annotates the map for the new inclusions to indicate that its sectors are no longer free.

- **Volume Directory**—The Macintosh stores data on a volume in the sectors in each track. Information does not remain consecutive, but is read and written into any free sectors that are available. Thus, the Macintosh needs some way to track where the bits and pieces of a document are stored on the volume. This information is kept in a *directory* that is opened during the logical formatting process. This invisible file really consists of two parts on modern *hierarchical file system (HFS)* disks—a *catalog b-tree* and an *extents b-tree* file. (All modern Macintosh operating systems use the multileveled HFS format for structuring their data. Older Macintosh operating systems use the original single-level structure called *MFS—Macintosh File System*).

- **Catalog Tree**—The Catalog tree contains an entry for every file describing its folder location (the hierarchical structure), and the size and location (starting point and ending point) of the three pieces that make up a file: the header, resource fork, and data fork. The Catalog file is used when files are stored in contiguous sectors on the disk. Resource forks store the resources used by applications, such as icons, dialog boxes, alert boxes, and other relatively static information. Data forks are used to store the highly changeable data contained in some documents. Files do not have to have all three parts—in fact most files contain only one fork, either a resource fork for applications or a data fork for data files. All files contain header information describing the file's origins and location. The first three pieces of each fork are tracked by the catalog tree. When files become *fragmented* (scattered in bits and pieces across the disk's tracks and sectors), an Extents file is opened which contains information about the location of each file fragment (the rest of the pieces or extents of the forks). HFS directories grow in size, whereas MFS formatted disks use a fixed size directory. Thus, HFS directories do not place a limit on the number of files you can create and store, because they grow as your need grows. This growth takes up room on the disk that is then not available for your work.

- **Desktop File**—Another invisible file created during the initialization of a disk is the *Desktop* file. The Desktop file maintains a catalog of icons, ensuring that the Desktop displays the correct icon for each type of document and application.

The Desktop file is not static, but changes as you add and delete files. Because the data in

the Desktop file may not always be accurate for the moment, it is a good idea to rebuild the Desktop periodically. To rebuild the Desktop, press the key combination Command-Option while you turn on the Macintosh and keep holding down the keys until the Macintosh displays a dialog box requesting whether you really want to rebuild the Desktop. A new feature of the newest System, version 7.5.3 is that when you rebuildthe Desktop file, none of the comments that you may have entered into the Get Info box are lost.

See Also

Deleting a File; Disk Drives; Finder; Saving a File; System 7.5; Trash

Disks, Interleaving

Initialization patterns affect how the Macintosh stores its data on the disk, and how it designs its databases to track the location of files on the disks. The Macintosh models differ in how the tracks and sectors are identified on the disk based upon how fast their disks can be accessed. This identification patterning is produced when the disk is initialized or formatted. The system by which the IDs are assigned is called the *interleave factor*.

When you buy a hard disk it usually comes pre-initialized (or formatted) from the factory. If it has not been formatted, each hardware vendor usually provides formatting software to use with their disk drive. If they do not supply the software, use the HD Setup program provided by Apple to format the disk.

Each of the various Macintosh model families operate at different computer speeds. Remember that the hard disk contains platters that are continually spinning at 3,600 RPM (revolutions per minute). Read-Write heads float on horizontally moving arms over the platters. The Read-Write arms move at a set speed, as do the platters. Thus, the Macintosh computer must be able to read sectors into memory at the same speed that the mechanical parts of the disk drive are moving. The time it takes to read a sector is important, because you want the computer to be able to read all of the sectors on the disk so they can all be usable. All of the current Macs read a disk as fast as it spins, except the Classic.

The Macintosh Classic and SE are slower at reading than the rest of the Macintosh family. By the time either one gets a sector, reads it into memory, and returns for another chunk of data the disk has spun far enough around that the third sector is in a position to be read. Hard drives used with Macintosh Classic and SE are formatted differently to avoid the problem of an idle computer (you don't want the computer to sit and wait while the disk spins all the way around back to the second sector). Hard drives for the Classic and SE number their sectors alternately rather than sequentially. Thus, the first sector is 1, the third sector is 2, the fifth is 3, and so on. All of the sectors are used, but the higher numbers wrap around and fill in the skipped sectors. This process of wrapping is called *interleaving*. The ratio of sectors to speed is called the *interleave factor*. The Classic and SE's interleave factor is 2 to 1. The interleave factor of all Macs based on the 68040 or PowerPC chip is 1 to 1. The Macintosh Plus uses an interleave factor of 3 to 1.

When you use Apple HD Setup or another formatting software to initialize the hard disk, it knows what Macintosh to match the formatting to, and perform the formatting accordingly. When you take a hard disk from one Macintosh model to another, reinitialize the hard disk to optimize its speed.

The Macintosh can store vast amounts of data, but this data would not be available if the Macintosh did not have a means to organize the tracking of its location on the various peripheral hard disks attached to the CPU. The Macintosh manages this task by using a protocol or set of rules by which it recognizes communications from these peripherals. This set of rules is called the *SCSI* protocol.

See Also
Disk Drives; FireWire; SCSI

Display PostScript,
See PostScript Level 2

Display Typefaces,
See Typeface Categories

Dithering
When a digital system has limited color or tonal range, dithering is used to create the illusion of more colors or grays. For example, a display monitor with only 256 colors must rely on dithering to create additional colors that might be specified by the user in a software application. Inkjet printers also use dithering to render continuous tone values of color or gray. Dithering uses a cell of pixels (display) or dots (output) that can vary in size: 3×3, 4×4, but not larger than 8×8.

Within these cells, the colors or gray tones available to the system are mixed to create the illusion of another color or tone. This is sometimes called a pattern dither. For example, red and blue dots or pixels in a cell would create the illusion of purple. Different proportions of red to blue would create different shades of purple. In this way, pattern dithering is similar to process color halftones screens, but it is always a function of inexpensive printers or monitors with limited color palettes. A diffusion dither uses the same principle of mixing pixels or dots, but it is done in a random pattern similar to a stochastic screen. For the most part, dithering is not a satisfactory substitute for higher **color resolution.**

See Also
Color Resolution; Color Separations; Desktop Printing; Printing Technology, Color; Process Color; Stochastic Screens

Dividers in the Apple Menu and Other Tricks
In **System 7** and higher, you can create dividers to keep groups of items visually separated in the **Apple menu**. This involves creating a new empty folder, pasting a new icon on the folder that is solid white,

and naming the folder with a series of dashes that create the visual divider.

To create a divider for the Apple menu, follow these steps:

1. Create a new folder (⌘-N).

2. **Double-click** the new folder to open it, then take a screen capture (Shift-⌘-3). This places a file on your startup disk called Picture 1. To view the screen capture, launch **TeachText** or **SimpleText** and open Picture 1.

3. Notice that when you open the screen capture, your cursor has changed to a crosshair. Use this crosshair to draw a small rectangular selection in an area of the screen capture that is solid white, with no type or window parts in the way. Then select Copy (⌘-C) from the Edit menu.

4. You can then close the screen capture document and return to the desktop. Select the folder you created earlier, and open the Get Info window (⌘-I). Press the Tab key to select the folder's icon in the upper-left corner. Then select Paste (⌘-V) from the Edit menu to paste the white box you copied earlier into the folder's icon. By doing so, you make the icon invisible. Close the Get Info box.

5. While the folder is still selected, press Return, which highlights the folder's name, enabling you to type a new name. Type a series of dashes (-------------------------------------) as the file's name. Now you have a dashed line with no visible icon. Drag this divider line into the Apple Menu Items folder for use as a divider. To make copies of this divider, select the divider and choose Duplicate (⌘-D) from the File menu. This appends the word Copy to the end of your divider's dashes. The system doesn't allow you to have two files in the same location with the same name, so you have to vary the number of dashes for duplicate dividers.

A popular Apple menu organization scheme is creating aliases for your applications and putting a space before the name of each application's alias. This puts all your applications at the top. Some users put a space followed by a bullet (Option-8) to make the applications stand out. When you add the divider line you created, it falls after your applications, visually separating your applications from your DAs and control panels below. Incidentally, a file whose name starts with two spaces appears before a file whose name starts with just one space. You can use multiple spaces before a file's name to let you group files together in any order you'd like.

You can control where these dividers appear in the Apple menu by adding a character as the first letter. The Apple menu sorts items in a list as follows: Numbers come before letters, so any filename starting with a number would appear before filenames with letters. The top-most item's name would start with a space, followed by items with names that start with: !, ", #, $, %, &, ', (,), *, ÷, ., and /.

After you have created an "invisible" icon (by pasting a white box into the folder's icon field), there are a number of other uses you might consider. First off, you might want to paste a copy of this white box in your Scrapbook, so you can create an invisible icon any time by copying and pasting from the Scrapbook. If, for example, you want a number of files to appear in a very small window, you can paste this white box over the current icons for these files, leaving just their names visible. This way you can push them up against each other because all that is visible is their names. You can open these documents, even though they have invisible icons, by double-clicking their name. Some people use these filenames with an invisible icon to create little reminder notes to leave on their desktop, as no icon appears, just the reminder.

Another use for the invisible icon trick is to create aliases for frequently used documents and put them all together right out on your desktop. You can put quite a few in a very small space, and have them just a double-click away.

Back to the Apple menu: Another popular Apple menu trick is to make an alias of your Apple Menu Items folder (which resides within your System Folder)

D

and put that alias on the Apple menu itself. This makes it easy to add and delete Apple menu items without having to dig through the System Folder. You just select the Apple Menu Items alias from the Apple menu and the folder opens, giving you quick easy access to its contents.

You can also add aliases of control panels to the Apple menu for quick access. If, for example, you change monitor depth often (from thousands of color down to 256 to play games), you can put an alias of the Monitors control panel on the Apple menu where you can access it without having to go into the Control Panels folder itself.

See Also

Apple Menu; Double-Click; Make Alias Command; SimpleText; System 7.0; TeachText

DNS

An acronym that stands for a number of possible terms related to *domains* on the **Internet**. Computers on the Internet are assigned names related to their domain, such as educational institutions, government, the military, commerce, and so on.

DNS can stand for:

- Domain Name System
- Domain Name Service
- Domain Name Server

Domain names on the Internet are related to the **IP addressing** system. Every computer or organization connected to the Internet is assigned an IP address. An IP address is composed of four numbers, each less than 256. Larger organizations, such as universities, may have a number of IP addresses. IP addresses can be difficult if not impossible to remember, so the domain name system was developed.

A *domain name* is a textual alias for an IP address based on the domain name system. Like an IP address, the components of a domain name are separated by a period. For example, an organization might have an IP address of **199.197.29.0**, but a domain name of

`mycompany.com`

A domain name is more than just an alias. It also serves as the name for the organization connected to the Internet. Each domain might also contain one or more subdomains that represent branches of the organization, such as:

`marketing.mycompany.com`
`admin.mycompany.com`

A domain name can exist in more than one sector of the Internet, for example:

`www.mycompany.com`
`ftp.mycompany.com`

A *domain name server* is a computer asigned to keep track of addresses in a given organization or *domain*. This **server** routes requests to specific addresses. It translates between the numeric addresses and the domain names that real people remember and use.

The *domain name system* or *service* is the system of distributing information worldwide across the Internet so that no one computer, person, or organization has to keep track of everyone in the world. Instead, computers are issued standard names with suffixes related to their domain. These suffixes, which come after the last dot or period in the domain name, are known as *top-level domains*.

The original six top-level domain names, which are still widespread on the Internet, are listed in the following table.

Top-Level Domains

Domain	Description
com	commercial
edu	educational
org	organization, usually nonprofit
mil	military
net	network
gov	government

As the Internet grows, a new solution has become necessary. The new top-level domains are based on countries, so each country is assigned its own two-letter domain. The old domains are so widespread that they still work as well.

Examples of New Top-Level Domains

Domain	Description
us	United States
uk	United Kingdom
se	Sweden
ca	Canada
jp	Japan
au	Australia

How to Obtain a DNS A domain name is a recognizable alias for the **IP address** assigned to any computer set up as a **host** or server of documents on the **World Wide Web** or other parts of the **Internet**.

As the Internet grows more popular and commercial interests with **Web site**s proliferate, it becomes more important for businesses or other organizations to obtain an easy-to-remember domain name. Customers or visitors will enter that name in a **Web browser** or other client software in order to access the group's Web site.

A group or individual wishing to set up a Web server and obtain a domain name must register with a group called Network Solutions, Inc., which maintains a WHOIS "white pages" database of domain names on the Internet in order to prevent duplication and deal with name disputes.

Network Solutions charges a registration fee and an annual fee for obtaining a domain name.

For more information go to **http://rs.internic.net/registration-services.html** or send email to **HOSTMASTER@INTERNIC.NET**.

See Also

Internet; IP Address; Server; World Wide Web, The

DocServer, *See Frontier*

Documents

Documents are files created within an application. A document can be a text file, graphic, **spreadsheet**, **database**, and so on. Each document has a name and an **icon** that visually denotes it as a document, rather than an application. A good way to remember the difference between documents and applications is: applications are created by software companies, but documents are created by users.

See Also

Database; Icons; Spreadsheet

Documents Folder

If you own a Performa brand Macintosh, you may be using the Documents folder to store documents you have created. The Documents folder (available only on System 7.0.1p or 7.1p, which was specifically designed for Performa models) is designed to help beginning Macintosh users find the files they create by automatically saving them to one folder on the desktop. The Documents folder actually is a part of Apple's launcher. It also is designed to put applications and frequently used documents in a floating launcher palette where users can launch any program or document with just one click —no digging through folders, no looking for files, and so on. The launcher's Documents folder also makes life easy for users when they want to open a file from within an application. Each application's **Open command** takes the user to the Documents folder, so they don't have to search around.

See Also

Click; Consumer Models; Macintosh Family; Desktop, The; New Folder Command

Document Icons

Each document created within an application is given an icon. This document icon has a similar look and feel of the application icon, but document icons look more like a small page or small document. A dog-eared upper-left corner is the distinguishing feature between application icons and document icons, as shown in the following figure.

See Also
Active Window; Cursor; Desktop Level

Document Names

You assign a name to a document when you **save** the document for the first time. Any document name can be changed by **clicking** the name of the file and typing a new name. If you want to change just a few letters, perhaps to fix a typo in the name, place your cursor where you want to make the edit and type a new letter or delete letters. You also can use the **arrow keys** on your keyboard to move through the letters in the document name. Document names can be up to 31 characters long and made up of letters, numbers, and simple punctuation. Another way to quickly rename a document is to click the document's icon and press the **Return key**. The name of the file is highlighted so that you can type a new name immediately.

When you create a new document in an application, it is named Untitled and will not be saved until you give it a name. Any untitled document will be erased when you **Quit** the program.

See Also
Arrow Keys; Click; Highlight; Quit Command; Return Key

Document Type Definition

Document Type Definition (DTD) is an official definition for a language, protocol, or other aspect of **Internet** operations placed on file with the Internet Engineering Task Force. The current HTML 3.0 draft

DTD, for instance, can be reviewed on the Internet so developers and users can learn about it and respond with suggestions.

See Also
HTML; Internet

Docutech

Media coverage of short-run printing tends to focus on color systems like Agfa's Chromapress. But there are plenty of short-run jobs out there in black and white, and Xerox's Docutech system has taken over 85 percent of that market.

Docutech is similar to a high-speed copier or laser printer. It uses toner to produce black-and-white pages, but unlike a typical office printer it produces as many as 135 pages per minute. It has front-loading paper trays, built-in document, scanners, and optional bindery attachments.

See Also
Chromapress; Short-Run Printing

Dogcow

The dogcow is a strange and fascinating creature often seen roaming around the Macintosh world. The surest way to spot the dogcow is by opening the LaserWriter "Page Setup" dialog box (see the following figure), where she does her best to reflect the chosen page setup options, even doing back-flips if needed.

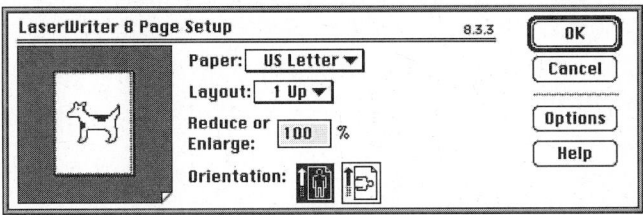

The dogcow, whose name is Clarus, has a long history on the Macintosh. She made her first appearance as a character in Susan Kare's Cairo font that shipped with the original Macintosh. Like any good Macintosh icon, the dogcow gladly volunteered her services to the LaserWriter driver.

Clarus's prominence in the Mac world didn't take off until late 1987. Two of Apple's developer Technical support (DTS) engineers, Mark Harlan and Scott "Zz" Zimmerman, were discussing exactly what sort of creature it was that lived in the page setup dialog. Was it a dog or a cow? Egged on by Harlan, Zz finally decided it was both: a dogcow. Dogcow mania was born.

At the 1988 Worldwide Developers conference, DTS gave away dogcow buttons in the debugging labs. In April 1989, a dogcow "Tech Note" was included in Apple's monthly mailing of technical information to developers. The April Fools joke was an instant hit, spreading the popularity of the dogcow even further. Before long, there were dogcow T-shirts, mousepads, sweatshirts, and a wide variety of other paraphernalia.

Naturally, the dogcow does not "moo" like a cow, nor "woof" like a dog, but rather makes a sound that combines the two: "Moof!" As for the sex of the dogcow Harlan wrote, "Of course she's a female, as are all cows; males would be referred to as dogbulls, but none exist because there are already bulldogs, and God doesn't like to have naming problems."

The definitive reference to the dogcow—"History of the Dogcow, parts 1 and 2"—was printed in *develop*, the Apple technical journal, in issues 17 and 18.

Believe it or not, the dogcow logo and "Moof!" are trademarks of Apple Computer. There is even a "Nest of Dogcattle" page on Apple's developer support Web server devoted to the Dogcow (**http:// dev.info.apple.com/dts/dogcow.html**). The Website includes the original Tech Note and the full text of the develop article, as well as a digitized "Moof!" sound.

See Also
develop Magazine; Moof!

Domain Name Server,
See DNS

Domain Name System,
See DNS

DOOM II

Although id Software recently made the original DOOM available on the Ultimate DOOM CD-ROM, **DOOM II** hasn't had any problem making it on the Mac market without a predecessor. DOOM II is a monster-killing fest in which you play a futuristic marine stranded on an abandoned space port. DOOM II is networkable—you can team up or play against friends with a variety of weapons to choose from.

Although the big guns are the most effective, DOOM II revels in violence, even offering a chain saw option where you simply run up to green spiky monsters and hack them to bits. As in all good **First Person Perspective Shooters,** the action is fast paced. DOOM II's graphics are great on a Power Mac, and the game can really rid you of built-up aggression as you glide down the myriad hallways dodging enemy fire. Like **Marathon**, DOOM II's interface is simple, showing your ammunition level, health points, and guns at your disposal. The keyboard is a little PC-oriented (DOOM II is a port after all), but this minor setback doesn't detract from the gameplay.

See Also
Descent; Violence in Games

Dorling Kindersley,
See Eyewitness

DOS Translations Utilities,
See Windows and DOS Translation Utilities

Dot Gain

Dot gain describes the phenomenon of **halftone** dots getting larger in diameter when printed on paper or another substrate. On a traditional offset printing press, dot gain is caused by the pressure of the blanket when it transfers the ink from the plate to the paper. It can be controlled through adjustments on the press. The type of paper can also affect dot gain and must be considered in the adjustments. Dot gain mostly affects middle tones in the 40 percent to 60 percent range and makes the printed image appear darker than expected. Some dot gain is inevitable, and the quality of the press has a lot to do with it. Generally, dot gain on a big six-color press will be much less than on a small duplicator. Dot gain compensation is often performed prior to film output in Color Electronic Prepress Systems (CEPS) and in Adobe Photoshop on the Macintosh.

See Also

Printing Presses, Offset; Printing and Binding Terminology

Dot-Matrix Printing,
See Printing Technology, Dot-Matrix

Dots Per Inch, *See Printing*

Dot Pitch, *See Monitors, Image Quality*

Dot Screen, *See Halftone*

Dot Sit

This is the verbal pronunciation of the filename extension that tells you the file has been compressed using the commercial or shareware versions of Raymond Lau's StuffIt compression utility by Aladdin Systems (**http://aladdinsys.com**). If, for example, you were to describe the following filename to someone, "Graphics.sit," you say "Graphics Dot Sit" to let them know the filename is Graphics and it has been stuffed (or compressed) using StuffIt.

Double-Click

You can open a document, open a window, or **launch** a program by double-clicking its **icon.** A double-click is two rapid clicks of the **mouse** in quick succession. Whereas a single click selects an icon, a double-click sets it in motion. The double-click has the same effect as **clicking** an item and then going to the **File menu** and choosing **Open.** If the icon is a window, it opens, displaying its contents. If the icon is a document, the program that created it launches and the document you selected opens. If the icon is the application, it launches.

> **TIP** You can adjust the speed at which the Macintosh recognizes a double-click in the **Mouse control panel.**

See Also

Click; File Menu; Icons; Mouse; Mouse Control Panel; Open Command

Double Prime (Keyboard Shortcut)

The double prime shortcut is shift-apostrophe while any curly quote or typographer's quotes features are disabled. There is some disagreement whether this symbol should be italicized (Command) to be a correct Prime symbol, so you may see the Double Prime symbol used both ways.

Double-XX

Double-XX is a small program (less than 80K) that contains a **HyperTalk** interpreter and **XCMD** interface. You can use it to construct programs using XCMDs and XFCNs. In a sense, it's **HyperCard** without the cards, fields, buttons, and other interface elements. Why would you want to use Double-XX instead of HyperCard? Primarily, because of its small size. HyperCard is almost 1 megabyte.

Double-XX doesn't contain any interface elements, such as windows or dialog boxes. If you need them, you have to add XCMDs that can perform that function. WindowScript, also from Hezier, is an example of an XCMD that could be used for this purpose. A license fee of $100 is required for any commercial application distributed using Double-XX.

> Heizer Software
> 300 Cedar Lane
> Largo, FL 34640
> Price: $149
> Fax: (813) 559-0614
> Phone: (800) 888-7667 or (813) 559-6422
> Web: **http://www.heizer.com**

See Also

Director; HyperCard; SuperCard 2.5; XCMDs and XFCNs

Down Arrow Key

The Down Arrow enables you to select items below a selected item in a list. If, for example, you're in an **Open dialog box**, the first item in the list is **highlighted** (selected) by default. If you want to select an item further down the list, you can use the down arrow to move to the item you're looking for. In a word processing or page layout application, the down arrow key moves your cursor down to the next line of text, enabling you to navigate downward within the document.

There are a number of modifier keys you can use with the arrow keys. Here's a table of the most common keystrokes using the arrow keys.

Arrow Keystrokes

Sequence	Result
⌘-Left Arrow	Collapses expanded folder
⌘-Down Arrow	Opens folder/Opens next file
⌘-Right Arrow	Expands folder
⌘-Up Arrow	Goes to previous folder
⌘-Option-Up Arrow	Closes to previous window
⌘-Shift-Up Arrow	In Open/Save dialog it selects desktop
⌘-Option-Left Arrow	Collapses all expanded folders
⌘-Option-Right Arrow	Expands all nested folders
Shift-Right Arrow	Selects character to the right of text cursor
Shift-Left Arrow	Selects character to the left of text cursor
Shift-⌘-Right Arrow	Selects word to the right of text cursor

Sequence	Result
Shift-⌘-Left Arrow	Selects word to the left of text cursor

See Also

Arrow Keys; Default Settings; Highlight

Downloading Software, *See* *Anonymous FTP*

Downsampling

Downsampling converts a digitized audio sample to a lower **sampling rate**. A sound, for example, can be recorded at 22Khz and then downsampled to 11KHz. The sampling rate is the number of samples (a sample refers to measuring the level of the audio signal) per second. The higher the digital sampling rate, the higher the frequency of the audio signal that can be recorded.

The sampling rate effects the size of the audio file; for simple narration it is often possible to use a lower sampling rate than is used for the music. While it is possible to simply record the audio at the lower rate rather than perform the downsampling, there are at least two reasons why you should consider recording at a higher rate and then downsampling.

First, if you need to add any effects or otherwise process the sound, the effect works best if you use the most detailed sample you have. Also, if you are sampling at 11KHz, the software measures the audio signal half as frequently as the 22KHz recording. During downsampling from 22 to 11KHz, the software takes the two adjacent samples, combines them, and averages them. Performed over the entire length of the sound, this process tends to produce a much closer approximation of the actual signal than simply digitizing at the lower rate.

Most sound editing applications, such as **SoundEdit** and **DigiTrax**, support downsampling.

See Also

Sampling Rate; Sound Digitizing

DPI, *See Resolution Measurement*

DR (Dynamic Recompilation),
See Emulator

Dracula Unleashed,
See Hollywood Games Connection

Drag-and-Drop

Drag-and-drop is a Macintosh feature that lets you drag part of a document's content from one area and drop it into a different area. It's an easier and faster way of cutting and pasting or copying. You can drag-and-drop selected text between documents, you can drag-and-drop documents onto icons of applications for immediate launching, and you can drag-and-drop between Desk Accessories such as the Scrapbook and the NotePad. Dragging-and-dropping has opened a new world of quick and easy movement of text and graphics. And now with Apple's new QuickDraw GX, you can put an icon of your printer on your desktop and drag-and-drop documents you want printed onto the printer's icon and it'll print the files.

You can use drag-and-drop within many applications for rearranging items such as text blocks. If, for example, you want to move a few lines from your opening paragraph to the last paragraph of a letter, highlight the text, drag it to the new location, and drop it. You can even see an outline of the text block as you move it through your document.

See Also

Click; Copy Command; Desk Accessories; Desktop, The; Highlight; Icons; NotePad; Paste (Keyboard Shortcut); QuickDraw GX; Scrapbook

Dragging

To drag a file means to move the file with the **mouse**. To perform this task, simply **click** the file, hold down the mouse button, and move the mouse in the direction you want to go. When you reach your destination (another folder or a **disk**), release the mouse. You'll notice that when you drag a file over a folder,

that folder **highlights** to let you know you selected it. To drop the file you're dragging into that folder, release the mouse button.

If you want to **copy** a file to a disk, click the file, drag it over the disk icon, and release the mouse button.

See Also

Click; Click and Drag; Copy Command; Highlight; Mouse; New Folder Command

Drawing Applications

Vector graphics—or object-oriented graphics—are most often created by drawing programs. These applications define images mathematically, in terms of lines, curves, and fills that make up discrete objects within a drawing.

That means that images created by drawing applications have clean lines, smooth curves, and even fills. It's easy to create drawings with lots of repetitive elements, and images can be scaled to any size, smaller or larger than the original, without any decrease in quality.

All this makes drawing programs the software of choice for creating logos, technical illustrations, and maps. But today's draw programs have new features that open up artistic possibilities and blur the lines between vector graphics and **bitmapped graphics**. Like page layout and paint packages, some drawing packages also support add-on software.

Two basic categories serve to define drawing programs: **QuickDraw** and **PostScript**. The high-end packages favored by professional illustrators use the PostScript **page description language**, while less complex programs aimed at home and business users tend to use QuickDraw. These are the languages that desktop printers speak—PostScript for most laser printers, and QuickDraw for lower-cost inkjet printers. A QuickDraw printer can't correctly output a PostScript image, while a more expensive PostScript printer can output images created using either language.

These two categories of draw program do have features in common, starting with tools for creating geometric objects (rectangles and squares, circles and ovals, straight lines and curves) and text. Users can group objects, scale them (in one direction or two, uniformly or not), rotate them, and align them with each other. Rulers, grids, and guides help in arranging drawings.

One of the hallmarks of higher-end packages is their object-management features. Layers allow users to keep groups of objects together, hiding, showing, or locking them as required; for example, a project that includes tracing a scanned image is easier if the scan is on its own layer, so it can be easily hidden to check the progress of the drawing. Grouping, on the other hand, keeps objects in the same position relative to each other, so they can be moved as a unit. Alignment and distribution tools are paramount for precision drawings.

Making curves becomes an art unto itself when using **Bézier curves**, featured in higher-end drawing packages. Although it takes awhile to master their use, these curves allow for the creation of complex shapes with a minimum of points. Fewer points means smoother curves and fewer problems outputting the final artwork.

Support for different color systems is a sure sign of a capable drawing package. Most support **process color**, named for the four-color process used in commercial printing, and Pantone **spot color**, while some support other spot color systems such as **FocolTone**. Some allow objects to be colored with a blend of two or more colors. For professional color reproduction, trapping and color separation are important features.

Other handy features include autotrace tools (which automatically trace bitmapped images to create vector objects), the ability to convert text to outlines that can then be stretched or otherwise edited, and word processing features. As the lines between application types blur, illustration packages include the capability to import text, spellcheck it, hyphenate it, kern it, and add tabs, along with paragraph **styles** that change text attributes with one click of a mouse.

Known for its plethora of features, Canvas can combine vector and bitmapped graphics in one illustration. Although it's complicated to learn and use, it leads the pack in incorporating useful (and sometimes bizarre) features, like an "envelope" tool that distorts objects.

At the top of the drawing heap are Adobe **Illustrator** and Macromedia **FreeHand**, two professional-level programs that are engaged in a perpetual features war. While each is suitable for creating everything from technical diagrams to artistic color illustrations, the differences between the two packages can spark strong partisanship among illustrators.

FreeHand is strong on precision, with numerical controls for positioning, editing, and moving objects, while Illustrator requires users to "eyeball" placement and sizes. Illustrator has a built-in chart tool (information entered into a mini-spreadsheet is automatically converted to a chart), while FreeHand supports different-sized pages within one document. Until recently, Illustrator could only import bitmapped images in **EPS** format, while FreeHand has been able to handle TIFF and **JPEG** as well. But Illustrator can create blends from several colors, while FreeHand can only blend two colors, and its layers feature is better implemented than FreeHand's.

As with most software, which package is best depends on the project at hand. Many users will find that a lower-priced program has just the right features and is easier to use, while others will want the control offered by high-end software. Compatibility is also an issue; professional desktop publishers need graphics files in formats that can be read by word-processing or page layout packages.

Lesser-Known Drawing Applications Anyone who spends time around Macintosh desktop publishers may think that **Illustrator**, **Canvas**, and **FreeHand** are the only inhabitants of the world of draw programs. But this area offers alternatives for nearly every sort of user.

If your needs are quite specific—say, a program that can produce Gantt charts—there may be a package that will work better for you than a high-end program. Similarly, if you're just at the experimental stage, not yet ready to take the plunge into the world of professional-level drawing applications, several less expensive programs are available that can give more than just a taste of what vector-based graphics are all about.

D

For business users, dedicated **charting and graphing** packages may come in handy. These applications, like Claris Impact, DeltaGraph Pro, and KaleidaGraph, will free users from worrying about lining up boxes and rules and keeping styles consistent, and they offer built-in style sheets to create professional looking charts and graphs quickly.

Those who are looking for a flexible drawing application that offers ease of use and automation should consider Claris Draw. This program is the successor to one of the first Mac programs, MacDraw, which along with MacPaint helped to popularize the Macintosh when it was first released in the mid-'80s. Today ClarisDraw combines drawing, painting, and page layout tools, and it can automatically maintain alignment, size, and connections within groups of objects. It's also known for its large library of **clip art**, which users can drag-and-drop into their documents and then alter as they wish.

Bringing "smart" tools to another level is **SmartSketch**, which—as its name implies—works like a sketch pad. The user draws with a pencil and deletes lines with an eraser, and the program does the hard work of translating the artwork into **vector images**, smoothing curves and straightening lines as it goes. As a drawing is built, SmartSketch constantly recalculates where anchor points should fall so that objects can be easily aligned with others. Users can click anywhere along the edge of an object and drag to reshape—no need to create and move anchor points manually.

The Symmetrigon and Connectigon are the trademark features of IntelliDraw, which offers Bézier curves but implements them differently than other drawing applications. Making symmetrical shapes is simplified with the Symmetrigon, and the Connectigon creates shapes that connect other objects and stretch to stay connected when the other objects are moved. Other features include a variety of ways to blend different shapes and place objects with respect to other objects.

Taking advantage of Apple's **QuickDraw GX** technology, LightningDraw GX adds sophisticated typographical and color features to its simplified interface, similar to that in SmartSketch. Surpassing the high-end programs, LightningDraw GX allows users to make colored objects "transparent" so that other colors behind them show through, modified by the color in front. Type features take full advantage of the new GX fonts, which offer many special and alternative characters and allow users to customize fonts. If these features intrigue you, GX is for you—but be warned: It eats RAM for lunch.

Expert Draw and DeskDraw are about as inexpensive as they come, yet the two offer features that just a few years ago were strictly professional-level, such as the ability to place text on a path (which can be any shape) and blend one shape into another. System 6 users can even install DeskDraw as a DA in the Apple menu, and both programs are sparing in their memory requirements.

Moving up a step on the price/features ladder, there's CA-CricketDraw III, which costs a bit more but does more, too. Users can have hours of fun extruding flat objects into simulated 3D, and tech-heads can edit PostScript code directly.

Like Canvas, SuperPaint is a hybrid program that can work with both vector and bitmapped elements in the same image.

See Also

Bézier Curves; Bitmapped Graphics; Clip Art; EPS; FocolTone; FreeHand; Illustrator; JPEG; Page Description Language; Page Layout Applications; Paint Applications; PostScript; Process Color; QuickDraw 3D; Spot Color; Style Sheets; Vector Image

Drew Virus, *See MacMag Virus*

Drivelight

Drivelight, from Symantec, (10201 Torre Ave, Cupertino, CA, 95104-2132, Phone (800) 441-7234. Web site at **http:// www.symantec.com**) is part of the **MacTools Pro** collection of diagnostic/repair, data protection, data recovery, and system enhancement modules. The Drivelight module places a small **icon** in the upper corner of the **menu bar** that blinks when any mounted disk has activity. You can set preferences on how and where you'd like this activity light to appear by selecting your options from the Drivelight control panel.

See Also

Icons; MacTools Pro; Menu Bar

DriveSavers

DriveSavers is a commercial data recovery firm (400 Bel Marin Keys Boulevard, Novato, CA 94949, Phone: 800-440-1904, on the Web at **http://www.driversavers.com**) that specializes in restoring files from severely damaged hard disks.

DriveSavers has the latest hardware and software technology for extracting data from disks that would otherwise appear to be damaged beyond repair. If you have a major drive crash and have critical information on that disk that you didn't back up, you might want to consider this type of service. Not only does DriveSavers recover the information from your damaged disk drive, but in many cases they can also repair the **hard disk**.

See Also

Backup Utilities; Hard Disks; Head Crash

Drop Frames

This term is used two ways. When coding **NTSC** video to **SMPTE**, a technique called *drop frame* maintains the correct numbering of the sequence (see the entry on SMPTE).

When digitizing or playing back digital video, sometimes the video cannot play the video back at the correct speed. This usually happens if the hardware isn't fast enough to capture or play the sequence. Digital video software, such as QuickTime, attempts to keep the sequence playing at the correct speed by dropping, or skipping, frames. While you want this to happen during playback (it means almost any hardware can play the movie in some form) you do not want to suffer dropped frames during the recording process.

See Also

Compressor; None Compressor

DropStuff, *See StuffIt Expander*

Drum Scanners

Drum scanners are the largest, most expensive, most complicated category of scanner. Drum scans are almost always of significantly higher quality than scans of the same artwork created with desktop devices—for many professionals, drum scans are the only scans of sufficient quality for print.

Typically, drum scanners are owned by service bureaus and printers' pre-press departments, and are operated by trained operators. In most small- and medium-sized production environments, designers send art to the service bureau to be drum scanned and receive the completed scan on disk, rather than doing drum scans in-house.

Drum scanners are fairly large—about the size of a filing cabinet laying on its side. The "drum" is a metal cylinder on an axle. The artwork to be scanned is wrapped around the drum, and the scanner spins the drum at high speed, bouncing light off the artwork to measure the artwork's color and tonal values.

Advantages Drum scanners use advanced optics. The human eye sees light in a non-linear fashion: a tiny change in brightness in a dark area of a photograph seems different from the same change of brightness in a light area. Drum scanners use photomultipliers, which "see" light as the eye does; desktop scanners, which use an array of charge-coupled devices (CCDs) record brightness in a more literal, flat way. As a result, drum scanners can capture subtle changes in tone. The drum scanner's high-quality optics usually provide better-focused scans than desktop devices.

Drawbacks Obviously, only flat artwork, such as photographic prints, can be wrapped around a drum. Drum scanners are expensive: basic real drum scanners cost something like $20,000 in 1996 and they require many hours of expensive training to learn to operate them.

See Also

Flatbed Scanners; Handheld Scanners; Office Scanners; Slide Scanners

Drumbeat: U-Boat II, *See Sim Games*

DSP (Digital Signal Processor)

A processor designed specifically to sample and convert digital audio and video signals. DSPs were used in the **AV Macintosh** models (660AV and 840AV) to provide video digitizing and 16-bit audio capability. With the arrival of the Power Macintosh, Apple decided to do away with the additional cost of the DSP and use the extra processing power of the Power PC chip to perform these tasks.

Before its demise in the Macintosh lineup, some manufacturers did make use of the DSP in the AV Macs. Adobe provided a patch, called AV DSP Power, for some **Photoshop** filters, enabling Photoshop 2.5 to take advantage of the processing power of the DSP in the AV Macs. The sound recording and editing application Macromedia **Deck II** also works with the AV Macs.

Several manufacturers also offered NuBus cards for Photoshop that contained DSP chips. Add-on cards, that include multiple DSPs, are available for high-quality sound recording. These are primarily of interest to sound professionals who need to record multiple 16-bit sound tracks simultaneously.

See Also

AV Macintosh; Photoshop

DTD, *See Document Type Definition*

DTP, *See Desktop Publishing*

DTR, *See Flow Control*

Dual Scan Displays

The dual scan display is a type of **passive matrix** liquid crystal display (LCD) used in some PowerBooks. Although not of the quality of **active matrix displays**, dual scan displays produce screen images that are superior to those created by ordinary passive displays. A dual-scan display draws the image on the top and bottom half of the screen at the same time, thus achieving an effective refresh rate nearly twice that of a standard passive matrix display.

See Also

Passive Matrix Displays; PowerBook Displays

Dumb Terminal Programs, *See Modems*

Dummy

In the graphical arts, a dummy is a preliminary example of a publication constructed by hand to show pagination and placement of elements on the pages. A dummy is usually quite simple and may consist only of pencil notations on folded paper stock, but it is an important communications tool that can help in estimating printing costs more accurately.

Dungeons & Dragons, *See Curse of Dragor; Might & Magic: World of Xeen; Role-Playing Games*

Dungeon Master II: The Legends of Skullkeep

Dungeon Master II: The Legends of Skullkeep from MacPlay is an example of less being more. In this case, less **multimedia** enhancement contributes to more reliable and more extensive game-play. Many companies have destroyed an otherwise perfectly good game by inserting special effects at the expense of action and story line. For example, MacPlay's own Voyeur, packed with video content, really destroys the interesting concept behind the game.

You simply don't get to do enough in-between "quick-cut" video scenes. Dungeon II proved that MacPlay learned its Voyeur lesson. They left out the video, big-name actors and fancy interfaces and swapped them for real-time action, a strategy edge, and a quick pace. Monsters move around, attack and steal things regardless of whether you are watching, making the entire experience that much more immersive. Though not a great multimedia extravaganza, Dungeon Master II is simply a good **Role-Playing game**.

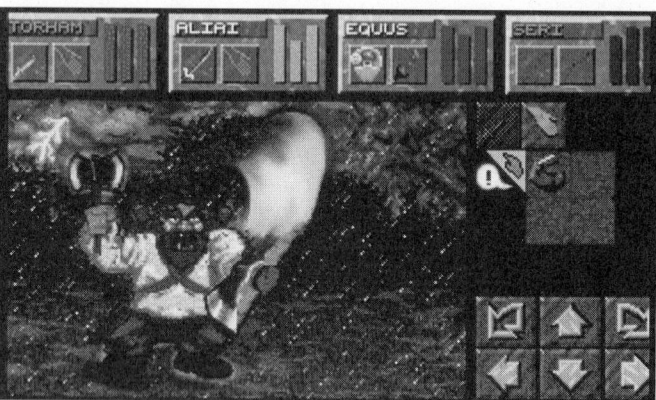

See Also

Curse of Dragor; Might & Magic: World of Xeen; Role-Playing Games

Duo, *See PowerBook Duo Series 200 and 2000 Series*

Duo Docks, *See PowerBook Duo Docks and MiniDocks*

Duotone

A duotone is a combination of two **halftones** of the same image sometimes printed in two different colors. The purpose of a duotone is to increase the density of the image or create a special color effect. Increasing the density of a printed halftone gives it a richer look with more contrast in tonal values. A duotone can more nearly capture the full tonal range of a good photograph. When two halftones are made for a duotone, one can enhance shadows while the other can enhance highlights. The two halftones may be printed in black, or in black and a color, or in two colors. Duotones can significantly increase the cost of a two-color printing job because they require more careful press work than ordinary halftones. Tritones (three halftones) and Quadritones (four halftones) are sometimes used to achieve even denser and richer-looking printed images.

Duplicate Command

This command, found on the File menu, enables you to make a duplicate of any files or folders in the **Finder**. If, for example, you have a document that you want to copy, select Duplicate (⌘-D) and the Mac makes an exact duplicate of that file and appends the word "copy" to the end of the file's name to let you know it's a copy of the original. This copy appears in the active window. You may remove the word "copy" from the name of the duplicate, but the operating system does not enable you to have two items in the same location with the same name.

The duplicate command does not copy the information to the **Clipboard** for storage and does not erase items already in the Clipboard.

To Duplicate an item at the Finder, follow these steps:

1. Select the file (or files) you want to duplicate.

2. Select Duplicate (or ⌘-D).

3. A duplicate of the selected item appears in the active window with the word "copy" added to the name of the document or item.

See Also
Clipboard; File Menu; Finder

DV, *See Digital Video Cameras*

DVD

DVD (Digital Video Disc) is a new CD format under development that will hold multiple gigabytes of information, up an entire motion picture in digital form.

See Also
CD-ROM

DXF

A generic, cross-platform **3D** file format originally developed by Autodesk, Inc., of San Rafael, CA, DXF (Drawing Interchange File) is supported by a wide variety of programs and is probably the most common method for exchanging 3D files. Unfortunately, this file format supports only basic geometric information. Textures are not supported. DXF is a somewhat inefficient way to transport files, because the files are typically much larger than a 3D program's own file format. This means that you might be unable to import complex models into your program unless you have a lot of memory.

With the introduction of Apple's **QuickDraw 3D**, more programs may adopt the **3DMF** file format. The 3DMF file format is much richer (can contain more information about a model) than the DXF format. This would make it easier to move models between programs.

> MetaTools
> 6303 Carpinteria Ave.
> Carpinteria, CA 93013
> Fax: (805) 566-6385
> Phone: (805) 566-6200
> Web: **http://www.metatools.com**

See Also
3D; 3DMF Optimizer

Dycam 10-C

This camera is the same basic body as the **Chinon ES-3000**. Refer to that camera for more details about the camera. The primary difference between the Chinon and the Dycam is the software. Dycam uses its own software, which provides similar capabilities as the Chinon software. The Dycam camera has a thread in the front of the lens that can be used to attach wide angle or zoom lenses. Because the camera is a **range finder**, if you are using such attachments, you can only see the pictures by downloading them to the computer.

See Also
Chinon ES-3000; Digital Still Cameras; SLR; Still Video Cameras

Dye Sublimation Printing,
See Printing Technology, Color

Dylan

A **dynamic language** developed by Apple.

Dylan, short for DYnamic LANguage, was designed by Apple's Cambridge Research Laboratory to be the next generation of programming languages.

Most languages force programmers to choose between the fast prototyping and development time of a dynamic language and the fast execution speed and low memory requirements of a more traditional static language. Dylan marries these two worlds. As a dynamic language, Dylan can be **compiled** *incrementally*, meaning that small changes in the source code can be compiled independently of the rest of the program and can even be linked into a running program! Also, Dylan uses a sophisticated memory handling scheme that takes care of most of the hassles of memory management.

Apple stopped work on Dylan before its Apple Dylan **Integrated Development Environment** was finished. Fortunately, Apple released the unfinished product as the Dylan Technology Release (available through **APDA**). The technology release is unsupported and is not commercial release quality, but it can give you a great taste of things to come in the world of development tools. The Technology Release is a 68K application that also runs on the Power Mac in emulation, provided the Modern Memory Manager is turned off. Applications generated by Apple Dylan run fine on 68K Macs and Power Macs alike. A PowerPC version of the Apple Dylan Technology Release is in the works from Digitool, Inc. (**http://www.digitool.com/**).

Although Apple created the Dylan language, it is not the only one working on implementing it. Several freeware implementations of Dylan are available, including Mindy (Mindy Is Not Dylan Yet) and Marlais. Neither of these environments can develop full-fledged Macintosh applications, but they're a great way to learn and explore the language. In addition, Harlequin (**http://www.harlequin.com/full/dylan.html**) is working on a commercial Dylan environment called DylanWorks. Carnegie-Mellon's Gwydion Project (**http://legend.gwydion.cs.cmu.edu/gwydion/index.html**) is also working on an implementation of Dylan for UNIX.

See Also

APDA; Dynamic Language; Integrated Development Environment

Dynamic Language

Dynamic programming languages enable you to program interactively by enabling you to quickly incorporate new or changed code into your program. LISP, **Dylan**, and SmallTalk are well-known dynamic languages.

If you make a small change to a program that was written in a traditional static language, such as **C**, **C++**, or **Pascal**, you must recompile that section of the code and link that code into the rest of the code before you can try out the change by running it. In a dynamic language, a small change requires just that bit of code be recompiled before it is inserted into the program. In fact, many dynamic languages enable you to make changes as the program runs, adding updated code to the program on the fly. This can make it much easier to iterate through the design and development process and to develop early prototypes.

This changeable nature means that dynamic languages must be able to handle a variety of tasks while the program is running ("at runtime") that are taken care of by the compiler in a static language. The speed and size overhead of this extra functionality is a major drawback to many dynamic languages, making them poorly suited to most commercial software

projects. With this extra overhead, however, comes a variety of features that can make dynamic programs much more robust than their static counterparts.

Dynamic languages provide dynamic type information and error checking at runtime. As a result, many of the errors that programmers face in static languages can be dealt with easily and won't bring a program to a screeching halt.

Similarly, dynamic languages typically hide many of the gory details of **memory management** from the programmer. Because the vast majority of all bugs in typical static language programs are caused by memory-related errors, this can make dynamic programs easier to write and debug, and less prone to errors after they're written.

Apple's Dylan language was designed to combine these advantages of a dynamic language with the execution speed and low-memory footprint of a static language.

See Also

Dylan

Dynamic Range

Dynamic range describes the capability of a scanner to distinguish a range of colors when digitizing an image. High-end scanners associated with **CEPS** (Color Electronic Prepress Systems) are much more sensitive to the range of colors in the full spectrum than are desktop scanners. Scanners with a high dynamic range can recognize the difference between two colors very close together in hue, but low dynamic range scanners might see the two colors as the same. Determining factors for dynamic range in a scanner are pixel depth, sensitivity of the CCD array, and the optical system.

See Also

Color Resolution; Image Scanning; Pixel

Dynamic Recompilation, *See Emulator*

E

E-Print

Indigo's short-run color printing system uses liquid ink, unlike its closest competitors, the Agfa Chromapress and other digital presses based on the Xeikon DCP-1 engine. The colors produced by the E-Print are closer to those produced by conventional offset printing, and the system handles elements such as fonts with fine serifs better.

See Also

Chromapress; Short-Run Printing

Earth Explorer

Earth Explorer, from Enteractive, Inc. (a division of **Apple Computer**, Inc.) is a multimedia encyclopedia of environmental topics. It gives background facts and figures as well as the history of such endeavors as whaling and power generation; it also discusses hot topics such as energy importing and exporting, ecological conservation, and possibilities of future development. Although Earth Explorer seems aimed toward kids—it is listed for ages 10 and above—the program has a large number of articles and graphics that can be useful in many adult presentations.

It's organized by category and then by topic, so the user must decide how to find a particular interest. There's a lot of worthwhile information on this CD-ROM, but finding it can be frustrating. There are "games" that have you decide whether arguments for or against a particular topic, such as building a nuclear power plant, are strong or weak. It presents both sides of these questions fairly, without seeming to get trapped in the "politically correct" point of view. The graphics are nice, and the hyperlinked definitions are extremely helpful. It's not the most in-depth presentation you could find on most of these topics, but it's a good jumping-off place for a study of environmental issues.

See Also

Software, Educational, Adult; Software, Educational, Grades 7-12; Software, Educational, K-6

Easter Egg

Programmers often add extra features or entertaining diversions to their programs that are hidden from most users. These tidbits are known as Easter eggs.

Some of the hidden "treasures," such as useful keyboard shortcuts, have a useful purpose. Other features are added as inside jokes.

A program such as the **Web browser** Netscape Navigator contains secret shortcuts to **Web sites** that are built in just for fun. Pressing Control-Option-F takes you directly to the Amazing FishCam page (a camera in the Netscape offices, pointing at a fish tank, that sends out a new **JPEG** image every few minutes) at **http://home.netscape.com/fishcam/fishcam.html**.

Some Easter eggs are undocumented features. They may be poorly tested or serve a need of a limited audience. (There is at least one program that enables certain features only if the Mac's username matches that of a particular person.) Sometimes, people find a documented feature they had overlooked and believe it to be an Easter egg. A great example is the set of command keys that can be used in the Finder. They are documented in the Help menu (and elsewhere), but because most users don't know about them, they are constantly being "rediscovered" as Easter eggs.

More often, Easter eggs serve no purpose other than to entertain or amuse. This kind of Easter egg includes hidden pictures or about boxes that can be accessed only after entering an obscure key combination, or clicking just the right place while holding down a certain set of keys. Holding down the Option key while choosing "About This Macintosh..." from the Apple menu shows the following "Silicon Valley" about box from the original Finder.

Macintosh Finder © Apple Computer, Inc. 1983-1995

Easter eggs often appear in one version of software and disappear in the next, only to reappear in another form later. The **breakout** game in System 7.5, for example, disappeared in System 7.5.1. To access this game, drag the words "secret about box" from any drag-and-drop aware application onto the desktop.

Although the game was gone in System 7.5.1, a different egg showed up on the first crop of PCI Power Macs that uses the same trigger. Some say this is one of the greatest Mac Easter eggs of all times. Instead of the breakout game, a picture of the Apple campus appears, with a flag waving in the foreground and a list of credits scrolling along the bottom of the screen. Moving the mouse changes the direction of the wind blowing the flag.

There are hundreds of other Easter eggs in various parts of the MacOS and in various applications. An excellent compendium of Macintosh eggs is located on the World Wide Web at **http://users.aol.com/ixist/easter-eggs.html**. A more general collection (including many Windows Easter eggs) is available at **http://weber.u.washington.edu/~davidnf/egg.html**.

See Also

About This Macintosh Easter Egg; Hidden Easter Eggs; History and Culture of the Macintosh, Overview; JPEG; Netscape Navigator; Web Browser; Web Site; World Wide Web

Eastern Mind: The Legends of Tong Nou

Eastern Mind is an incredible title. The combination of two- and three-dimensional graphics is virtually flawless, making it one of the best **Myst**-clones that can possibly give the original a run for its money on the shelves. Although other Myst-like titles, such as Welcome to the Future by Blue Sky Entertainment and Majestic from Piranha Interactive, are good games, only Eastern Mind forges in a new direction adding philosophy to the experience. Eastern Mind was developed by Japanese artist Osami Sato, whose gallery-level work adorns each screen. The game is based on Zen-like eastern philosophy regarding patience and life experiences.

You wake up one day to find that your soul has been stolen. From this point on you are reincarnated as nine different creatures as you go through the game looking for your soul. Each time you die, you are reincarnated with the extra wisdom that can only be attained at the moment of death by a former self. Each area is very different depending on the body you inhabit when you visit it and the order in which you get there. Only after you have died nine times and found your soul can you be whole. Although death runs through the plot of the game, Eastern Mind presents it in a non-violent, natural part of life sort of way. The innovative alternative to the Myst platform and breath-taking artwork are well worth taking a look at, especially if a game with a little spiritual substance sounds like a good change of pace.

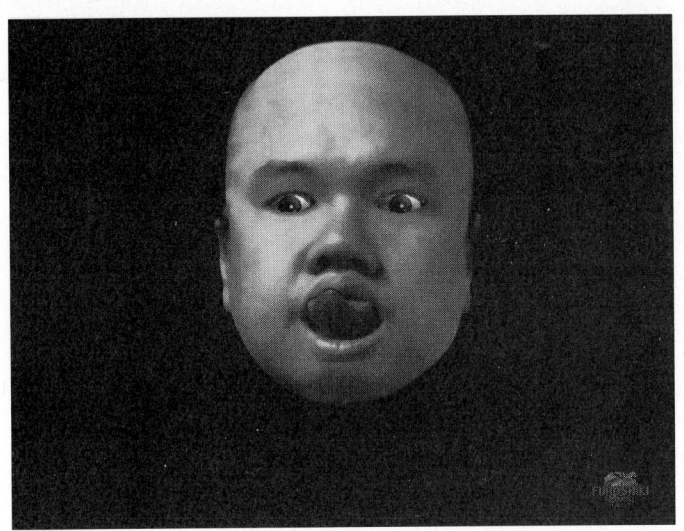

See Also

7th Guest, The; Daedalus Encounter, The; Full Throttle; Riddle of Master Lu, The; TimeLapse: Ancient Civilizations

Easy Access Control Panel

Easy Access helps people with disabilities who may have trouble using a **mouse** or the **keyboard.** Easy Access is made up of three features: Sticky Keys, Mouse Keys, and Slow Keys, as shown in the following figure. The Sticky Keys function of Easy Access enables you to perform multiple-key commands by pressing one key at a time.

```
═════════ Easy Access ═════════
⊠ Use On/Off audio feedback

Mouse Keys:      ○ On   ◉ Off
   Initial Delay :  ○ ○ ◉ ○ ○
                   long      short

   Maximum Speed :  ○ ○   ◉ ○ ○ ○   ○ ○
                   slow    medium     fast

Slow Keys:       ○ On   ◉ Off
   Acceptance Delay :  ○ ○ ◉ ○ ○
                      long      short
   ⊠ Use key click sound

Sticky Keys:     ○ On   ◉ Off
   ⊠ Beep when modifier key is set
```

The Mouse Keys function enables you to use your keyboard's built-in **numeric keypad** to emulate the actions of a mouse.

The Slow Keys function helps prevent a user from making accidental keystrokes by requiring the user to hold down a keystroke for a moment before it is registered. This way, if the user accidentally presses the wrong key, it is not registered as a valid keystroke and is ignored. To be a valid keystroke, the key must be held down for the length of time the user specified in the Slow Keys dialog.

To use the Easy Access Control Panel, follow these steps:

1. Choose the Easy Access Control Panel from the Control Panels submenu on the Apple menu (or System Folder).

2. You can enable Sticky Keys by pressing the Shift key five times. To disable Sticky Keys, press the Shift key five more times.

3. To enable Mouse Keys, press Shift-⌘-Clear (you can press them one-by-one if you have Sticky Keys enabled already). Now you can use the numeric key pad to navigate the cursor, moving one pixel at a time. To move left use the number 4; to move right, the number 6; to move the cursor up, choose 8; and to move down, choose 2. To move diagonally up, use 7 or 9; diagonally down, use 1 or 3. To click the mouse, use 5. Use 0 to hold the mouse button down and the decimal point to release it. You can also set the speed for Mouse Keys and the initial delay before movement begins in the control panel.

4. You can enable Slow Keys from the control panel, as well as request that a clicking sound be made to confirm a keystroke. You can also adjust the keystroke acceptance delay to your preference.

See Also

Keyboard; Keyboard Commands; Mouse; Numeric Keypad; Shortcuts

Easy Open Extension

If you've ever **double-clicked** a document and gotten an **alert box** stating, "Cannot open this document because the application that created it cannot be found," this extension is for you. When you try to launch a document without the application that created it, Easy Open displays a window listing the applications you do have that can open the document.

This enables you to try to open the document using an alternate application, as shown in the figure. For example, if you have a document created in WordPerfect but don't have WordPerfect installed on your **hard disk**, Easy Open enables you to open that file using another word application you have installed.

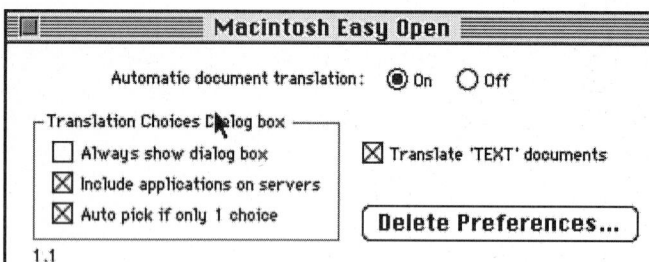

1.1

See Also

Alert Box; Double-Click; Hard Disks

EasyAIFF, *See AIFF*

EasyApp

EasyApp is an application **framework** written by Jim Trudeau. Unlike many frameworks, EasyApp is not **object-oriented**, although it does borrow some of its design from object-oriented programming techniques. EasyApp is written in **C** and was originally written for the *Programming Starter Kit for Macintosh* (Hayden Books, 1-56830-174-X).

Using EasyApp, programmers can create complex programs more quickly than they could by creating the program from scratch. Because EasyApp already includes much of the basic functionality needed in a Mac application, the programmer can concentrate on the unique functionality of his or her application.

See Also

C; Framework; Object-Oriented Programming

EBBE, *See EvenBetterBusError*

Edit Decision List, *See EDL*

Edit Menu

Located at the **desktop level**, the Edit menu is home to the **Undo**, **Cut**, **Copy**, **Paste**, **Clear**, and **Select All** commands. The Edit menu also can have additional features necessary to the application. At the desktop level, the **Show Clipboard** command appears at the bottom of the menu. Some applications also have the Show Clipboard command within the Edit menu.

> **TIP**   The Undo command appears as the top item on the Edit menu in most applications, with the **keyboard shortcut** remaining ⌘-Z.

See Also

Clear Command; Copy Command; Cut Command; Desktop Level; Finder; Keyboard Shortcuts; Menu; Paste (Keyboard Shortcut); Select All Command; Show Clipboard; Undo/Redo Command

Editions

Editions are files created using Apple's **Publish and Subscribe** feature. These editions are files that can be imported into other documents, but maintain a link to the original document that created them. This way, if the original document that created the edition (called the Publisher) is edited, the edition file is automatically updated. If you have imported (or Subscribed to) that edition file in any other documents, they are automatically updated to reflect changes in the Publisher document. This is ideal for linking graphics, tables, spreadsheets, and databases between documents for instant automatic updates.

To create an edition, follow these steps:

1. Select the item you want to publish as an edition file.

2. Choose Create Publisher from the Edit menu.

3. In the Create Publisher dialog box that appears, give your edition file a name, and choose where you want the edition file saved. Click Publish.

See Also

Publish and Subscribe

Editor

An editor is a program used to create, edit, and modify text.

Every Macintosh user is familiar with word processors—applications that enable you to create textual documents. Word processors give you a great deal of control over the appearance of the document, supporting such things as multiple styles and fonts, margins, indents, and other formatting. They also automatically wrap text from one line to the next when you reach the end of the line.

Although editors also enable you to create textual documents, that's where the similarity ends (see the following figures). Editors typically display all text in one font, size, and style. They generally do not autowrap text as you type. What editors lack in formatting tools, they more than make up for in text-handling.

Programmers use editors to edit source code. Editors often include special features to make the programmer's life easier. They might, for example, feature pop-up menus that enable you to jump quickly to any function within a file.

Some editors also are capable of *syntax highlighting*. These editors automatically identify keywords and other programming constructs by modifying their appearance to distinguish them from the rest of the code. Comments, for example, might be displayed in blue or italic.

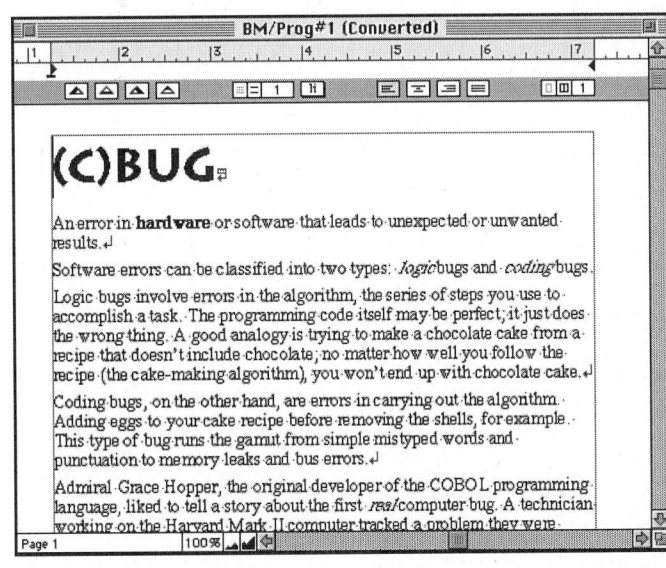

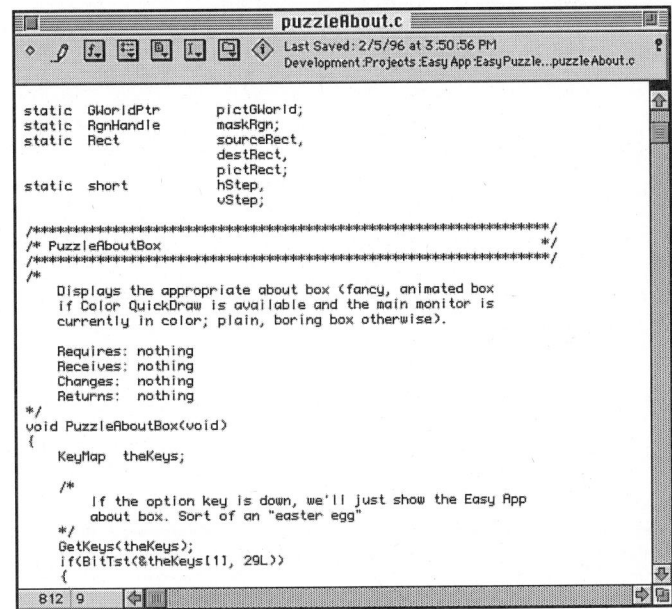

Most development environments include an editor tailored to edit source code. **Symantec C++**, **CodeWarrior**, and **MPW** all include editors well suited to programming. Stand-alone editors frequently include more features than built-in editors and sport **AppleEvent**-driven interfaces along with the development environments themselves. Editors in this class include **Alpha**, **BBEdit**, and **QUED/M**. Other editors, such as **Object Master**, are more correctly classified as **browsers**.

See Also

Alpha Editor; AppleEvent; BBEdit; CodeWarrior; MPW; Object Master; QUED/M; Symantec C++; Web Browser

EDL

Some high-end video editing equipment accepts EDLs (Edit Decision Lists). This is an electronic document (usually an **ASCII** file) that contains information about edit and transition points in video clips. By simply providing the appropriate video tape (usually **time code** in **SMPTE** format) the equipment assembles the final video using the EDL.

The advantage of EDL's is that a video can be edited using inexpensive equipment, and then the final cut is produced on the high-end equipment. This can save a great deal on money. Adobe **Premiere** outputs EDL's in several different formats.

See Also

Premiere; SMPTE; Time Code

Edmark, *See Imagination Express; Millie's Math House*

Education and the Macintosh

Education in the '90s and beyond will depend on computers as much as on teachers and books. The computer can be an instructional tool with a great deal more flexibility and potential than printed text. Given the right software, the computer can teach virtually any subject at any level from toddler to doctoral dissertation. Computer learning lets the student go at his own pace. The computer is a patient and non-judgmental teacher, enabling the student to experiment and keep trying. It doesn't punish wrong answers.

The computer as an educational tool predates Apple by several years. Seymour Papert, in his book *Mindstorms,* first proposed the benefits of computers in the classroom. Using the LOGO instruction language, students were able to program a turtle on the screen and a robotic turtle on the floor to trace patterns. The benefits of the kind of thinking needed to write instructions for the turtle carried over into other learning activities. The LOGO language is still used in many schools, although today's software is much more sophisticated. In one popular project, students combine LOGO instructions with motorized LEGO™ construction sets to create programmable, moving toys.

Since its earliest days, Apple Computer has maintained a commitment to education. In fact, the name Apple came as much out of the realization that the computer would be a natural in the classroom, as it did from Steve Jobs' year in an apple-growing commune. The Apple II was released in 1978 and soon found its way into the classrooms and hearts of teachers and students alike. Early software wasn't much better than an on-screen workbook, but the idea of using a keyboard or mouse and video display made computer learning more fun. At the same time, video games were being introduced for the home market. Game technology soon translated into more interactive, entertaining educational programs, and the computer became a necessity, rather than a luxury, in the classroom.

Apple created a separate Education division in 1992 to serve the needs of teachers, students, and school administrators, developing innovative products, services, and programs for learners of all ages. Apple's current statistics show that today, 93 percent of all students attend schools that use Apple Computers. Out of 84,000 public schools in the U.S., 98 percent now have at least one computer, and 86 percent have at least one Apple computer. Among full-time college students who own personal computers, 29 percent own Apple—a full 11 percent more than the nearest competitor. Apple has even made it easier for students and teachers to purchase their own computers with an innovative program of educational discounts.

In many cases, computers have made it possible for students with handicaps or learning disabilities to function in regular classrooms. Because the Macintosh uses the same sets of commands in all of its programs, it's easier for dyslexic students to master. The Mac's capability to speak has given many students a new way to communicate with their teachers and peers. Children with cerebral palsy affecting their speech, or those who breathe with respirators, are finally able to "talk" through the Mac. The use of devices such as switches, head pointers, and other keyboard and mouse alternatives lets people with limited movement use the computer for everything from writing letters and playing games to turning on and off lights or calling for help. Blind and visually impaired users can use outSpoken, from Berkeley Systems, to read anything on the screen. A device called the Optacon attaches to the Mac to provide a tactile representation of whatever is on-screen, by raising and lowering a block of pins that the user runs his hand over, letting blind students study maps, drawings, and scanned images along with the rest of the class.

Information on these and other products to help the differently abled is available on the World Wide Web from Apple's Worldwide Disability Solutions Group at **http://www.apple.com/disability/welcome.html**.

For More...

If you want to do this...	Go to this entry...
Know which Mac models are the best for educational purposes	Education Models, Macintosh Family
Determine the best software to teach at an adult level	Software, Educational, Adult
Determine the best software to teach at a junior-high level	Software, Educational, Grades 7-12
Determine the best software to teach at a grade-school level	Software, Educational, K-6
Learn how Macs affect the classroom	Teachers, Macintosh and
Find software that can enable disabled users to better use the Macintosh	Software, Special Needs
Determine some good sources for education on the Internet	Internet, Educational Resources on

Bibliography

For more information on the Macintosh used for educational purposes, refer to the following books:

Macs for Teachers, Michelle Robinette, published by IDG Books, 1995 (1-56884-601-0).

Mac Multimedia for Teachers, Michelle Robinette, published by IDG Books, 1995 (1-56884-603-7).

Conversation with Dale LaFrenz

Dale LaFrenz set up the Minnesota Educational Computing Consortium, which helped establish the Apple II and then the Macintosh as the computers of choice in kindergarten through 12th grade and beyond. Have you ever played Oregon Trail? You can thank MECC, and Dale, for educational experiences such as that. MECC has grown from a public institution to a private, for-profit corporation and is now being merged into Softkey International.

Maclopedia: How did your consortium get started?

Dale: This is the 25th anniversary of Oregon Trail, a fairly well known product of ours. In 1971, we got it up on a Human Factors 2000A, model 3 teletype, at ten characters per second, so the graphics were not blazing back then.

MECC was formed in 1973, to provide computing services for elementary schools through colleges, with dual Cyber 24s and teletypewriters all across the state. So we predated Apple. And the idea of using a computer in every school predated the microcomputer. We had giant time-sharing systems set up so that every school in Minnesota could have a teletypewriter linked to the Twin City area, where we put the time sharing system. That was a statewide effort. Eventually we had 3,000 teletypewriters out there, although not more than 400 coming in at a time.

Our mission was to lead the schools in the use of technology.

Along about 1977, some of our people—we call them trainers, and instructional coordinators with teachers in schools—went to a conference in California, and they came back and said, "I just saw something the size of a bread box, and it could do everything these time sharing computers do." Steve Jobs and Steve Wozniak had been showing their stuff. We went back, and they were out of the garage, in their first warehouse, and they had a vision of Apple as being significant in education, but they hadn't done anything yet.

There weren't many other schools doing much with time sharing—one at Stanford and one in Philadelphia—but here in Minnesota, this was where the big machines were being made by Control Data, Univac, Honeywell, and IBM. So we told Steve and Steve what we were doing, and we said, "We'll buy five of those and take them back to Minnesota, to see if we can sell them to the schools." And in a year we had sold 500 of them. We had a very receptive computing community, and that launched the relationship between Apple and MECC.

What we did next was take the software we had on the Cyber 74s—it was in BASIC—and converted it to BASIC on the Apple IIs. Then things started popping, and the schools started picking up on microcomputers like the Apple II, the Atari, the TRS 80, and the question was, "What do we do besides teach BASIC?" and "Where do we get software?" And the answer was, "Get it from MECC." Remember, there weren't any dealers—there weren't any evangelists—so we developed a membership program, which was a euphemism for site licensing, a fancy way of saying, "We will give you the disk, you pay the price, and you can make as many copies as you want." That helped propel Apple's machines over other machines, and got MECC into the business of making software for instruction. MECC was also the largest dealer of Apple II computers for a couple of years; then dealers started popping up, and they didn't think it was fair that a quasi-state government organization should be taking their business away from them. Of course, we said, "We started it." But that wasn't our mission, so we got out of the hardware business. Our mission was to lead the schools in the use of technology.

We kept the software program going for us full force, right up until the Mac was introduced, and the Mac didn't replace the Apple II for quite a few years—we still don't have them all replaced—so we continued to produce for the Apple II and grew that membership program for schools around the country.

About 1988 we saw that the Apple II wasn't going to be the basis for our business for long, so we got onto the Mac and DOS.

Maclopedia: Did you keep upgrading Oregon Trail?

Dale: Oregon Trail 2 is absolutely the number one program in all of education computing for the last thirteen months, either first or second on the hit list. Last week, we won the Consumer Software Award at the Software Publishers' Association meeting in San Francisco. That product won over Fantasmagoria, from Sierra Online, and In the First Degree, from Brøderbund and Lucas Arts. Pretty good competition. It's a whole new product, of course, in its 25th year. This is the

E

second version on CD-ROM, so we have live actors playing the roles in video clips, whereas in the first Apple II version we had stick figures. We were totally enamored that we were moving from the teletype-writer to the Apple II, so we could have animation and things actually moved. Can you imagine trying to type out a graphic, an image of a deer in Xs, and every X has to be put down by having the head go across the paper and make a mark?

A lot of our products today are point-to-point simula-tion, where kids travel from point X to point Y and make all the decisions along the way and then have to suf-fer the consequences. So authenticity is a big part of that. No one has done more research on the Oregon Trail than we have. So if you are crossing the river, and you decide whether to caulk the wagons and float across, or ford, we know that river will be at a certain height on that date, from Farmer's Almanac records. Now we have the Africa Trail, too, about those bicy-clers who travel from the northwest corner to the southern tip, and Amazon Trail, with a boat going down the river, and MayaTrek, exploring Central America. Those are all on CD-ROM and run on the Mac.

Gone are the days when the teacher could sit down and pound out a BASIC program and turn it over to us. Our products are developed internally now, by people with real teaching experience, and we put a lot of ef-fort into making sure that we have authentic content. For instance, for the Oregon Trail, a number of people have traveled the whole trail and done the photogra-phy, and we have spent many hours with our people in the historical archives for the Oregon Trail Society of America. Wayne Scudder, a Ph.D. in history, is our Oregon Trail expert; he can tell you anything there is to know.

Now we have 220 employees and everyone has a Mac on the desk, and many have portable Macs to take home. Half our revenue is from the school area, which is dominated by the Mac. In the other half, home rev-enues are dominated by Windows machines. If we didn't have the school market, we couldn't be so sup-portive. But our heart is with the Mac.

Education Models, Macintosh Family

Apple Computer provides the **Apple Education Se-ries**—a collection of Macintosh computers config-ured especially for grades K-12. Each Macintosh is composed of hardware and software to fit a specified educational need. These educational Macs are similar to the desktop models and consumer models, only configured with multimedia, security, networking, and compatibility features required by school systems. The following figure shows a typical Macintosh LC.

Courtesy of Apple Computer, Inc.

Educational Macs are labeled "LCs" and come in sev-eral models:

- A desktop standard workstation, called the **LC 580**. This computer is designed as an all-in-one model with a single power plug, a built-in 14-inch color monitor, as well as, **stereo speakers**, and a **microphone**. Because the computer, monitor, hard drive, and optional CD-ROM are contained in a single unit, there are no extra parts to track or cables to sort. You can also add an optional internal **double-speed, tray-loading CD-ROM drive**. The LC 580 uses the Motorola **68LC040 chip** whose performance is measured at 33MHz and that contains a built-in floating point processor.

- A Power Mac version of the standard workstation, called the **5200/75 LC**. The 5200 LC is also an all-in-one computer similar to the **Performa 5215CD**. This computer is also powered by a single plug with no external parts to track or sort. The computer is fully integrated into the stereo speakers and monitor, creating a small footprint. The monitor consists of a multiscan 15-inch color display and the computer comes with a quad-speed, tray-loading CD-ROM drive, stereo speakers, and a microphone. You can also add an external video connector card to create a real-time audio-visual authoring and development tool or a television tuner. The 5200 LC is based on the **PowerPC 603** processor running at 75MHz and comes standard with **256 kilobytes of level-2 cache** for enhanced performance.

■ A multimedia workstation based on the PowerPC chip, called **5300/100 LC**. The 5300 LC is a desktop Power Mac configured for educational use. It has the speed to support such performance-heavy tasks as 3D-modeling, Computer-Aided-Design, and other computational-based processing. The 5300 LC comes equipped with a video capture card that supports direct video input and output to an LCD projection panel or monitor; a television tuner that supports the monitoring of television on a window on the computer's

display. The workstation includes a 15-inch color monitor, quad-speed, tray-loading CD-ROM drive, stereo speakers and microphone. The computer uses a PowerPC 603e 100 MHz processor with 256K level-2 cache.

■ A **DOS-compatible** workstation, called the LC 630. The **LC 630** is based upon the Performa 630 but with the added inclusion of a 66MHz 486 DX2 DOS Compatibility Card. The DOS card lets you run MS-Windows-based software on your Mac concurrently with your Macintosh software. This configuration lets you connect your Mac to multivendor networks and share resources such as printers and file servers with other types of computers. The LC 630 is based upon a Motorola 68LC040 processor running at 33MHz. The computer comes configured with a 14-inch color display, stereo speakers, microphone, and internal double-speed, tray-loading CD-ROM drive. You can optionally add AV components to perform real-time video capture and processing as well as output the resulting program to videotape.

The following table summarizes the components and configurations included in each Macintosh model.

The Educational Macintosh Series

Macintosh Model	Processor	Memory/ Storage	Expandability	Other Options
LC 580	33MHz 68LC040	8MB/800MB	LC Slot, Serial Port, Video In, and Video Out	External Video Connector; Video-In card; Apple Presentation System
5200/75 LC	75MHz Power PC 603 RISC with 256K level-2 cache	8MB/800MB	Serial Port, Processor Direct Slot, Video-In slot, and Video-Out slot	Apple External Video Connector, Video-In card, Expansion bay for TV tuner

Macintosh Model	Processor	Memory/ Storage	Expandability	Other Options
5300/100 LC	100MHz PowerPC 603e with 256K level-2 cache	16MB/1G	LC Slot, EtherNet Port, Video-Out connector, built-in TV tuner, 16-bit stereo sound in/out	Video Capture Card
LC 630	33MHz 68LC040 and 66MHz 486 DX2 DOS Compatibility Card with 4MB DOS RAM	8MB/500MB	Serial Port; LC Slot; Video-In slot; Expansion bay for TV Tuner	Video-In card; Apple Presentation System; TV tuner

E

See Also

DOS Compatibility Card; Educational Models; Macintosh Family; Performas; Power Mac Logic Boards; PowerPC; Processors, 680x0 Family

Educational Software,

See Software, Educational, Adult; Software, Educational, Grades 7-12; Software, Educational, K-6

EfiColor

For several years, **QuarkXPress** has come with the EfiColor **XTension**, intended to handle **color management** from within XPress. Electronics for Imaging also sells EfiColor Works, which expands the XTension's capabilities and includes an interface for **Photoshop**. EfiColor Works can create **device profiles** for scanners and comes with a library of pre-created profiles for output devices and monitors.

See Also

Color Management; Device Profiles; Photoshop; QuarkXPress; XTensions

Eight Ball Deluxe, *See 3-D Ultra Pinball*

Eject Disk Command

The Eject Disk command, found on the **Special menu**, ejects a selected disk from the disk drive. After your disk has been ejected, however, a ghosted version of the disk's icon remains on your **Desktop**, as shown in the following figure.

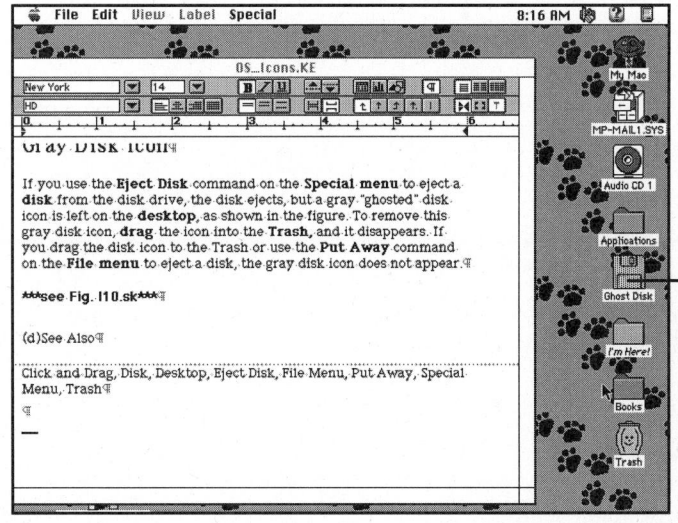

Ghosted version of disk icon

To remove the ghost version, drag the ghost disk icon into the **Trash**. It's not necessary to empty the Trash. If you drag the ghost icon into the Trash and it doesn't go away, some resources of that disk are still in use. In **System** 7 and higher, you get a dialog box stating, "The disk (the disk's name appears here) cannot be put away because it contains items that are in use." If this happens, reinsert the original disk and make certain all documents on the disk have been properly closed.

This ghosting of the disk can create additional problems. If you **double-click** the ghosted disk, the Mac brings up a dialog box asking you to reinsert the original disk. You can make this dialog box go away by pressing ⌘-. (period) on your keyboard or by inserting the original disk.

You can run into more problems if you eject a disk using the Eject Disk command and that disk has an open window when you eject it. If you try to close those windows, perhaps to reduce clutter on your desktop, you're met with a dialog box insisting that you reinsert your disk. It asks for the disk because a change to the disk has been made (a window was closed), and it needs to update that information to the original disk. Having your system demand disks that have already been ejected can be a frustrating experience.

Because of the problems that ghosting disks cause, many people prefer to use the **Put Away** command (⌘-Y) rather than Eject Disk. The Put Away command dismounts and ejects the disk but does not leave the ghosted version of the disk on the desktop.

To eject a disk from the desktop, follow these steps:

1. Click the disk's icon on your desktop to select it.

2. Choose Eject Disk (⌘-E) from the Special menu.

3. The disk ejects from the disk drive, but a ghosted version of that disk remains on your desktop.

4. To remove the ghosted disk, drag the ghosted icon of the disk into the Trash.

To eject a disk from the desktop without leaving a ghosted version of the disk, follow these steps:

1. Click the disk's icon to select it.

2. Choose Put Away from the File menu.

3. The disk ejects from the drive.

TIP   You can also eject a disk by dragging the icon of the disk into the Trash. A ghosted version of the disk does not remain on the desktop when this is done.

See Also

Desktop; Double-Click; Ejecting Stuck Disk; Finder; Put Away Command; Special Menu; System 7.0; Trash

Ejecting Stuck Disk

If you have a **disk** stuck in your **disk drive** and can't remove it by using the **Eject Disk** command from the **Special menu** or by dragging it into the **Trash**, you can eject the disk by taking an ordinary paper clip, straightening it out, and pushing the straight end into the small hole that appears just below the disk drive on the outside casing of your Macintosh. Believe it or not, that's how the disk drive was designed. When you stick in the paper clip, you'll get some resistance from a wall, but you've got to press fairly hard to get this manual override to work. Remember, it's your muscle manually popping the disk out of the drive, so don't be afraid to give it a firm push. Usually the disk comes right out. What would cause a disk to get stuck in the drive? The two most popular culprits are a bent metal door on the disk that is designed to protect the disk, or a label that is starting to peel off the disk. These two factors cause 95 percent of the stuck disk situations you run across.

To eject a stuck disk, follow these steps:

1. Straighten out an ordinary paper clip or use any thin metal wire.

2. Push the paper clip into the small paper clip-sized hole just beneath the disk drive on the front of your computer. The hole appears below and to the right of the disk drive.

3. As you push in the paper clip, you feel the paper clip hit metal. Press against that metal to manual eject the disk. It sounds crazy, but that's how it's designed to work.

See Also
Hard Disks; Online Services

Elastic Reality

Elastic Reality has been used to create more morphing sequences in major TV and Hollywood productions than any other warping or morphing software. One of the production companies that used it got an Academy Award for their efforts some years ago. A version of it exists on all major platforms, and the best electronic artists and animators have incorporated it into their study and work. It is not easy to master because of its features, but once you get control over it, morphing and warping magic will be as close as your fingertips. Elastic Reality presents the user with two screens, Project and Edit. The project screen shows the source and target image as well as an effects track, all laid out like filmstrips. An Elastic Reality "Project" contains graphics and the point-line data that addresses the graphics, and all are saved to a specified project file. If you quit the project before rendering is accomplished, the program asks if you would like to save it at that stage in order to come back later. Every option has been added to the program that addresses the needs of the professional animator, from work habits to options and tools. Elastic Reality is both a warping and morphing platform, and it operates with one image, two (source and target), or with two sequences (single frame animation files). The capacity for fine tuning morph options is Elastic Reality's main strength, and its central asset for professional use.

Interface Design The Edit window's interface was made for larger professional monitors. The Elastic Reality image area covers most of the screen, and is flanked by the non-moveable toolbox on the left and menus at the top. The toolbox is small but full-featured, and includes: Selection Arrow, Bézier Adjustment, Point Move Tool, Correspondence Point Connect Tool, Magnifying Glass (Zooms), Hand (Moves Graphic), FreeHand Curve Tool (for those who hate to work in Béziers, but need Béziers as the outcome), Bézier Curve Pen (for those who love to work in béziers), and a Rectangle and Oval Shape Tool. The top menus are used for viewing either or both source and target images, and adjusting the contrast and brightness of each. A unique slider at the top allows you to mix the percentage of each image together to view the data, or to view either source or target graphic.

How It Works Elastic Reality created many of the basic guidelines that other morphing software has incorporated since its release, so as you might expect, it too follows the basic morphing principles. Bézier curves are drawn to outline image features in the source image, and moveable clones of those points appear on the target image. Points on the curves are moved until the shaped outlines match the image features, and morphing is set in motion. Elastic Reality doesn't stop there however, but adds more fine-tuning options to the process. "Correspondence Points," the same data point on the source and target image, can be connected with correspondence lines. This allows you to make sure that no correspondence lines cross. When correspondence lines cross, the result is a morph that does unpredictable things instead of a smooth transition. Control points can slide down a curve to remove the potential for correspondence crossings. Bézier curves are handled and shaped according to customary rules, by altering the size and direction of their control arms.

A drawn curve from the source image is copied and pasted into the target image. Once there, it can be placed exactly around the desired image elements. The precision of the FreeHand tool can be set from 1 to 100. The higher the setting, the more points on the curve. A preview dialog allows you to set the preview type (Warp A, Warp B, or Morph), what percentage of the total frames or how many of the total frames will be rendered, Outer Edge handling (Fixed, Sliding, Convex Hull, Cookie Cut... all of which affect the outlines of the final rendering), edges (Soft or Hard), Precision (Fast to Best), Final Transparency (Sharp or Smooth), and Merging (Defined, Default, Linear, 50 percent or controlled by an external alpha channel source), and Blurring (from None to a percentage of the mix). Data interpolation and anti-aliasing are supported. Then the wireframe or preview is rendered, and can be played back or played in reverse with VCR-like controls. Shapes can be loaded and saved independent of the underlying graphics, to be used with other images.

Warping and Morphing Data settings like those indicated for preview options are also presented for Warping and Morphing actions. Because of the extensive care taken in fine-tuning everything in the preview mode and wireframe rendering of the shapes, there are seldom any unpleasant surprises after the sequence is rendered. This is necessary because of the extensive projects that Elastic Reality is used for, projects that often render thousands of frames at a time. Using the same settings for the morph preferences as in the previews produces the same exact results.

Animation Bringing up the output options window is the first step in the rendering process. Elastic Reality allows you to set the size of the images, aspect ratio, and whether PICT file numbers should increment or decrement (enables the animation to be recorded in reverse). The Output File Settings dialog enables you to set the output data path and whether the sequence will be a QuickTime movie, PICS, or numbered PICTs. The Output Compression dialog gives you the chance to set the compression type and image quality settings, as well as frames per second. Network users can also choose to save the data across to another platform. Rendering on a Power Mac is very fast, with single frames being rendered every few seconds. Of course, if the size settings are extremely large, they'll take longer to render.

Save/Load Conventions Projects can be saved and loaded, including all of the shapes that were drawn and correspondence point data. Sequences are rendered as QuickTime movies, PICS, or numbered PICTs.

Documentation Several animated tutorials ship with the software, and the documentation uses these to walk through each level of the warping and morphing process. In addition, a video is available that allows you to see some of the more professional uses the software has been targeted to. The software comes with two manuals, Getting Started and the User's Docs. A full explanation of creating shapes with Bézier curves is included.

Addendum Elastic Reality is a very high-end program, and it's optimized for the Power Mac. The only caution is that once learned, it becomes a very addictive pastime as well as a high-end professional tool.

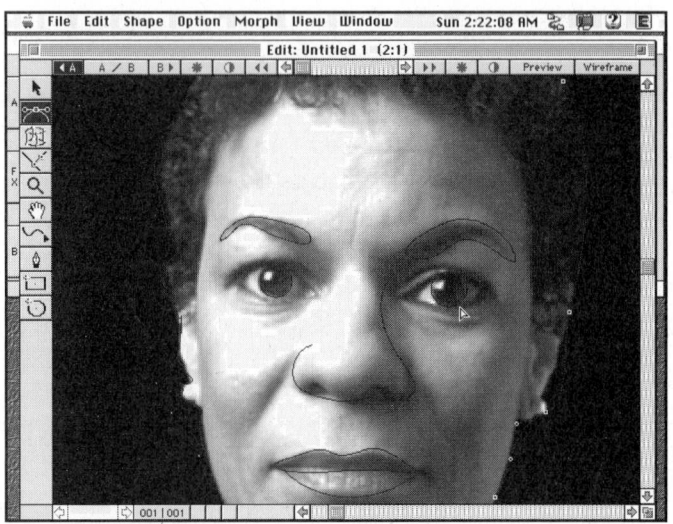

Electricimage

One of the highest end animation systems in the world.

- True 3D Inverse Kinematics—Allows models with joints to behave like their real-world equivalents.

- Renderama (55K)—Batch Processing and Network Rendering supporting slave camera render servers on Mac, Power Mac, and SGI formats.

- State-of-the-Art Anti-Aliasing—Separate controls are available for anti-aliasing levels (settings from 4×4 to 64×64) and sampling levels (settings from 1×1 to 64×64). Also includes adaptive filtering.

- Bézier Motion Path Splines—Familiar to Adobe Illustrator.
- Motion Picture and Broadcast Quality Rendering Engine.
- Sync Sound—Animate directly to sound cues. You can import and view an unlimited number of sound files (memory permitting) in any mode of the project window at frequencies from 5KHz to 64KHz.
- Smart Deformations—Add stretch, bulge, twist, and more to objects in your environment.
- Texture Mapping—With Summation or MIP filtering, which retains the quality of the original file, without jagged anti-aliasing problems. Complete control over resolution. As many as 4,000,000 textures in a scene (memory permitting).
- OMF Support—Supports image translation to and from the Open Media Framework format.
- Project Window Overview—View data in time mode, by keyframe or index. Frame rate and resolution presets include NTSC, PAL, HDTV, 35mm film, Vistavision, and IMAX.
- Vibe—Three animation tools (Randomize, Jolt, and Spring) that can add vibrations or bumps to an animation path and add random flickering values to intensity controls, with parametric control over attack, decay, hold, and frequency.
- Professional Gamma Control—Specific input and output monitors gamma control.
- Quick Render previews.
- QuickTime compatible.

Light Effects

- Five Different Types—Radial, parallel, spot, ambient, and camera point light with full color and intensity control.
- Fully Animatable—Including position, color, intensity, drop-off, inner and outer cone angles, and light factor.

- Millions of Allowable Lights—You can have 4,000,000 lights in a scene and 4,000,000 shadow casting light sources (RAM permitting).
- Lens Flares—Incorporates realistic flare transitions as an object moves to obscure the light source.
- Light Rays (88K)—Light Rays are created through 3D volumetric rendering.
- Glow Lights—Casts shadows within those glows.
- Depth Buffer Shadows—Controls how each shadow is cast.
- Fog And Smoke—Adds atmosphere to your 3D environment.
- Motion Blur.
- Motion Vector—Rendered blur, adding motion blur to a fully anti-aliased, full rendered frame.
- Frame Multi-Sample—Renders many frames and then samples them down to a final blurred image.
- Point/Line—Very effective when used with particle generation.

Internal Plug-Ins

- Mr. Nitro—Literally blow your models apart. Includes explicit motion control (gravity, air resistance, and so on).
- Mr. Blobby—For metaball style effects.
- Dicer!—Applies a user-selectable mesh to any previously made model.
- Particle Generation—Generate fountains, sparks, fireworks, and more. Every aspect is controllable and animatable.

Model/Font Import

- Imports over 30 different model formats, including formats from different platforms.
- 3D Font Models—Created instantly from PostScript Type 1 fonts with automatic bevels and fillets:

Object Deformations Arbitrary Scale, Arbitrary Shear, Twist, Taper, Bend, Bulge, Linear Wave, Circular, Wave, Bézier— including Oversample, Adaptive, Independent Sampling, Anti-Aliasing for Each Group, Sampling Levels from 1×1 to 64×64, Anti-Alias Levels from 4×4 to 64×64

Electricimage Plug-Ins: Northern Lights Productions

- Big Dipper: Used for generating star fields and asteroids. Point stars can be colored using the seven spectral star types. Model stars can be animated to tumble and roll.

- Dante: Emits particles from the surfaces of objects. Particles will follow the motions of the parent object whether it is orbiting, spinning or tumbling. Dante emits point particles and object particles.

- Zeus: Generates three-dimensional lightning effects with explicit control over turbulence, branch quantity.

- DaVinci's Chisel: Reveals hidden models one section at a time.

- LiquiFACT: A new plug-in that melts models.

Onyx Computing

- Tree: The ultimate tree modeling software. Over 100 parametric files of broadleaf and conifer trees, palms, bushes, and a collection of plants.

Develop Your Own Plug-Ins Download the Electric Socket Toolkit. The Toolkit is free of charge. It was used in the following feature films:

- *The Net*
- *Batman Forever*
- *Congo*
- *Sleepless In Seattle*
- *Drop Zone*

- *Richie Rich*
- *The Mask* by Dream Quest Images
- *Jurassic Park*
- *Species*
- *Star Trek Generations*
- *Terminator 2: Judgment Day*
- *Beverly Hills Cop III*
- *Naked Gun 33 1/3*
- *The Shadow*
- *Precious Find*

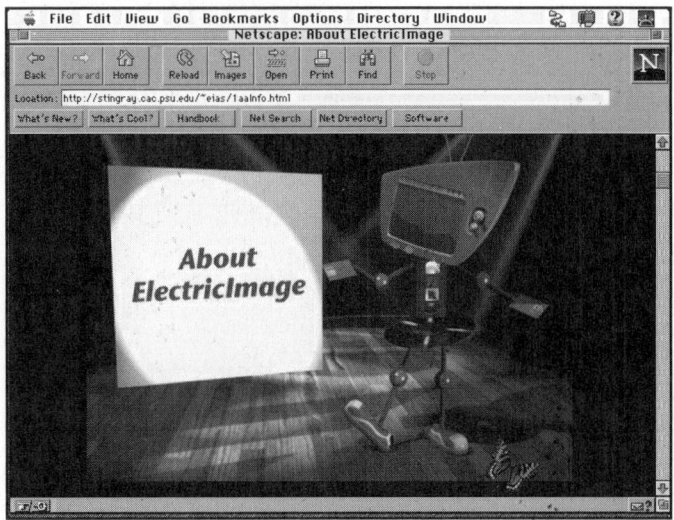

Electric Image, Inc.
Fax: (818) 577-2426
Phone: (818) 577-1627
Web: **http://stingray.cac.psu.edu/~eias/**

See Also

3D; Alias' Sketch

Electronic Banking

Electronic banking isn't as new as it might seem. Prodigy first offered it as far back as 1987. Through arrangements with a large commercial bank, Prodigy was able to offer its users checking, bill paying, and other banking services by connecting to the bank through a Prodigy gateway. The service didn't prove profitable and was later discontinued. But the notion lingered.

With the advent of the World Wide Web, there's a revival of interest in the possibility of banking by modem. Some experts believe that by the year 2000, over 13 million American households will do their banking online, rather than standing in line. Many of the nation's larger banks are already going online with Web pages giving information on their services and a password encrypted gateway to banking services. Boston's BayBank, reaching out to the thousands of college students who invade the Boston area each fall, created a virtual dormitory hallway, complete with an ATM locator, a bulletin board of events and concerts, and a daily page from a serialized mystery. As they say, "It's more fun than laundry."

Other financial services have been available online for several years. Brokerage houses have gateways on Prodigy, America Online, and CompuServe. Investors can check stock quotes and make transactions online after they're registered with the appropriate broker. For the general public, stock quotes are available at many places online, but in accordance with the rules of NASDAQ and the New York Stock Exchange, they're delayed by 15 minutes.

As of this writing, banks are moving cautiously ahead with plans to make accounts available on the Web. There are still security issues to be fully resolved, but the chances are good that by the time you read this, you'll be able to at least sign on and check your balance or transfer money between savings and checking accounts. Withdrawals are going to be a little more difficult to manage, although one suggestion is to provide users with a magnetic card scanner and a striped card. Entering the account number and running the card through the scanner would encode a credit amount, which the user could spend like cash at any place equipped to read and debit his card.

The biggest issue for potential users of an online electronic banking system isn't the security question, but rather the enforced organization it requires. According to a study commissioned by Microsoft and reported in *Money* magazine, most people still keep their bills in a shoebox or stuffed into a drawer. And most people queried wait until the last minute to pay bills. Banking by modem will demand some changes in user habits.

Electronic Banking and Security Concerns Banking online is convenient, but is it safe? Can hackers gain access to your bank account or credit card information? Despite the best efforts of some of the finest criminal minds in the world, the trillions of dollars that digitally pass back and forth each day through banks, other financial institutions, and government clearinghouses do so unmolested.

It's not that hackers and criminals can't crack the encryption codes. The government's 14-digit, supposedly uncrackable encryption scheme was "broken" in less than two weeks, by some well-meaning people who simply wanted to prove it could be done. But they couldn't do it without getting caught. It's nearly impossible to break into a system without leaving some evidence that you've done so, and the penalties are severe.

Security is less a concern in cyberspace than it is on the streets, according to government researchers at the Sandia National Labs in Albuquerque, NM. "Live" thievery is much easier. Credit card and ATM card fraud occur mainly in situations where the crook has obtained the actual card, or the number from a discarded charge slip or ATM receipt. This is not to say that such things can't happen on the Web, but it's unlikely, given the difficulty of orchestrating a large scale fraud without getting caught.

The greater risk to your personal security and privacy, many experts feel, is not the hacker cult, but rather the many government agencies with a legitimate excuse for poking through data to trace criminal activities.

Several schemes have been proposed for a digital cash system, some anonymous and untraceable and others with no privacy in the transaction system. Agencies, such as the FBI, argue that untraceable digital currency would be a boon to kidnappers and extortionists. It might be possible for a kidnapper or terrorist to demand, and get, money electronically transferred without the payer even knowing what country to which the money was being sent.

There's also the possibility of new kinds of digital crime arising, as more people begin to look for ways to get rich on the Internet. Making digital currency traceable prevents one kind of crime, but could lead to others. Imagine electronic spies following you around from a terminal somewhere, checking on the bus or trolley you take to work, the coffee and dough-nut you buy, the newspaper you get from the vend-ing box, what you have for lunch, and even who you call from the pay phone…. Could you be blackmailed for that hot fudge sundae, or the double Scotch? Does your boss want to know that you're reading the Rac-ing Form? Most of us lead entirely blameless lives, of course, but one has only to remember the McCarthy-era witch-hunts to see the fearsome possibilities.

Electronic Mail, *See Email*

Electronic Prepress,
See Prepress

Ellipsis

An ellipsis is used to indicate that something has been left out or that there has been a sudden shift from one topic to another. Even though it looks like three periods in a row (like this…), the spacing might be different. A true ellipsis is produced by pressing Op-tion and the semicolon key.

An ellipsis following a menu item means that select-ing it will open a dialog box.

Email

Email is the product of using a network to send and receive messages. Linked by high-speed data connec-tions, email enables you to compose messages and transmit them in seconds to one or more recipients anywhere around the world—as long as you know their electronic addresses. Email can be sent via the Internet as well as through the office with products like ccMail and Microsoft Mail.

Email Server, *See Server*

Emoticons

Typographical representations of things such as smil-ing faces used to annotate text with a suggestion of the author's feelings about what is being written. This set of keyboard symbols, which are sometimes called "smileys," can avoid misunderstandings with **Usenet**

audiences who can't read body language or tune into the tone of voice. Now a subculture within the cul-ture of the **World Wide Web**, emoticons can be found on T-shirts as well as in **email** messages and often are meant to be viewed by tilting your head.

For example, :-) means the author is smiling, and :-(conveys unhappiness.

See Also
Email; Thread; Usenet; World Wide Web

Empire Deluxe

In Empire Deluxe, a war **strategy game** from New World Computing, your goal is to build an empire large enough to take over that of every other player, computer or otherwise. Because the game incorpo-rates network play, even **cross platform** play between PC and Mac, you have the chance to conquer up to six possible opponents by using your weapons and manpower to plunder their empires before they burn your city to the ground. Empire Deluxe's network play is adjustable so that beginners can play against handi-capped experts, making the slaughter is a little less skewed to age and experience. You can also edit the maps, opt for random landscapes, or play a preset sce-nario. Although Empire Deluxe originally debuted on DOS, the game transports well to the Mac.

See Also
Allied General; Chaos Overlords; Pax Imperia; Sid Meier's Worlds; Spaceward Ho! 4.0; Strategy Games; V for Victory; Warcraft: Orcs and Humans

Empty Trash Command

This command, found on the **Special menu**, emp-ties the contents of the **Trash** at the **Finder** level. Items in the Trash are not erased from your disk's or hard drive's **directory** until the Empty Trash command is invoked. To view the contents of the Trash, double-click the Trash icon (a trash can). The window reveals the contents of the Trash. If there is an item in the Trash that you do not want deleted, click the item and drag it out of the Trash onto the desktop, a disk, or a hard drive window. You can also click the item you want to take out of the Trash and choose the **Put Away** command (⌘-Y), and the file goes back to the location it was in before you dragged it into the Trash.

Because the Empty Trash command permanently deletes files from your drive, the Macintosh has a number of safeguards to keep you from throwing away important files by accident. The first level of protection comes from the trash can. When you choose Empty Trash, you get a dialog box that says, "The Trash contains (the number of items in your Trash). It uses (the combined amount of disk space of all files in the Trash is calculated and displayed here) disk space. Are you sure you want to permanently remove it?," as shown in the following figure.

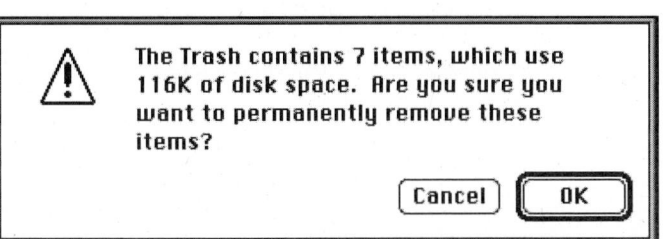

The Trash contains 7 items, which use 116K of disk space. Are you sure you want to permanently remove these items?

[Cancel] [OK]

If you're certain you want those items permanently removed, click OK; if not, press **Cancel** and the Empty Trash command is canceled, leaving your files intact inside the Trash. This safeguard gives you a chance to drag a file back out of the Trash if you put it there accidentally or change your mind.

You can turn off the Empty Trash warning by clicking the Trash can icon and selecting **Get Info** (⌘-I) from the **File menu**. When the Get Info window appears, you see a checkbox named "Warn before emptying" that is selected. Click that checkbox to deselect it. The warning dialog no longer displays and the Trash is emptied after choosing the Empty Trash command.

Another level of protection comes into play if you choose Empty Trash and the Trash contains an item that is currently in use. You get the warning dialog box, "The item (the item's name appears here) cannot be deleted because it contains items that are in use. Do you want to continue?" The dialog box gives you the choice of "Continue" or "Stop," both of which do exactly the same thing; nothing. Your item remains in the Trash, but it cannot be deleted. Only after you've closed the file that was in use can you delete the file by using the Empty Trash command.

Another situation may arise when you select the Empty Trash command and you get the warning dialog, "The Trash cannot be emptied because all of the items in it (other than folders) are locked. To delete locked items, hold down the **Option key** while you choose Empty Trash." You can take Apple's advice and hold the Option key, or you can go to the file in question, click the file, and select Get Info (⌘-I) from the File menu. In the lower-left corner, a marked checkbox called "Locked" indicates that this disk is locked and cannot be emptied from the Trash. Locking files that you don't want accidentally thrown away is a popular way to prevent the loss of important files. To unlock a file, click the locked checkbox. The file can now be deleted using the Empty Trash command.

To empty the Trash, follow these steps:

1. Select Empty Trash from the Special menu.

2. A dialog box appears telling you, "The Trash contains 1 item. It uses 2K of disk space. Are you sure you want to permanently remove it?".

3. If you want to permanently delete the items in the Trash, click OK. If not, click Cancel and the items remain in the Trash, but they are not deleted.

4. If you decide that you don't want to delete certain items in the Trash, open the Trash by double-clicking the trash can icon. This opens the Trash window, enabling you to drag items you don't want deleted back onto the desktop or your hard disk.

5. If no items are locked or currently in use, the Trash is emptied and the trash can icon, which is bulging as if it were full, changes to a regular trash can icon, indicating that the Trash has been emptied and the files within the Trash were deleted.

See Also

Cancel Keyboard Shortcut; Directory; File Menu; Finder; Get Info Command; Option Key; Put Away Command; Special Menu; Trash

Emulator

With the development of the Power Macintosh, Apple had a difficult choice to make. They could implement an entirely native operating system with a new model of program behavior (a time-consuming and compatibility-ruining proposition) or implement only the most time-critical portions of the OS in native code, and leave the rest in 68K code to be ported later. This second option has the tremendous advantages of speed and compatibility, and as a result, was the path Apple chose.

An emulator is a program that enables a program written for one kind of computer to run on another. The most widely used emulator on the Macintosh is the 68K emulator built in to every Power Macintosh. This emulator enables programs written for the Motorola 68000-series microprocessor used in earlier Macs to run flawlessly on the PowerPC chips in the Power Macs.

The 68K emulator is at such a low level in the Power Macintosh architecture that it goes completely unnoticed by most users and even programmers. In fact, the emulator lies below much of the operating system, as it is used to run parts of the MacOS that have not yet been ported to native PowerPC code.

The MacOS includes a special **Mixed Mode Manager** that enables the Macintosh to switch seamlessly from executing native PowerPC code to executing emulated 68K code without a hitch. The stability of the 68K emulator combined with the cleverness of the Mixed Mode Manager are largely responsible for the extraordinarily smooth transition to the Power Mac.

Another more obvious emulator is **SoftWindows** from Insignia (see following figure). In this case, the emulator runs as a separate application on top of the operating system. SoftWindows emulates an Intel-based personal computer running MS-DOS and Microsoft Windows.

Emulators translate individual **machine language** instructions from the instruction set of one microprocessor into the instruction set of another. For many instructions, this translation is trivial, as both instruction sets may include nearly identical instructions. Other times, there is no simple translation from one to the other. In these cases, the emulator must create a series of instructions that accomplish the same task in the end. In either case, the overhead introduced by the emulator slows down execution compared to running the code directly on a non-emulated processor. Sometimes this overhead can be dramatic, which is why SoftWindows often provides only lackluster performance, even on relatively fast Power Macs.

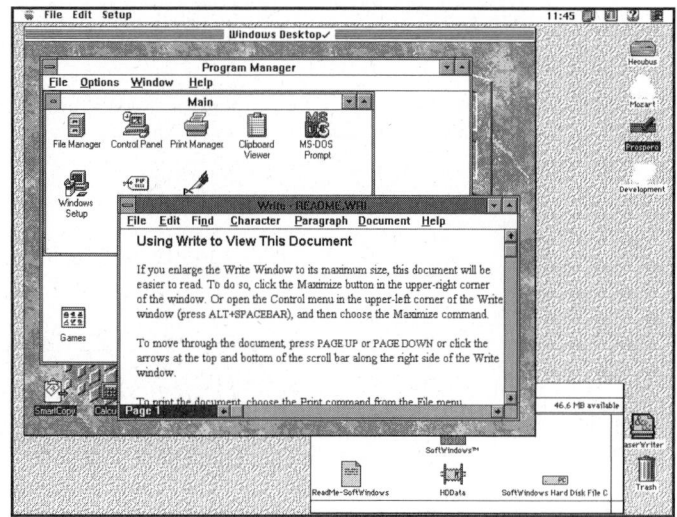

One way that emulators can improve their performance is through *dynamic recompilation* (DR). As a section of code is executed by a DR emulator, it is translated all at once (**compiled**) into the other instruction set. The emulator maintains a cache of previously translated code that can be executed again without translation.

See Also

Compiled Language; Machine Language; Mixed Mode Manager

Encapsulated PostScript File,
See EPS

Encoding Files

Encoding a file makes it transportable between different kinds of computers and different networks on the Internet. Each computer's operating system maintains a different description of what a file is and how that file is structured. Encoding is not unique to the Macintosh, but Macintosh files do have a unique structure and often require special treatment before they can be served from a non-Macintosh platform.

Macintosh files consist of both a **resource fork** and a **data fork**, either of which may be empty in particular cases. Applications, for instance, consist almost solely of resources. Word processing files consist primarily of data. Other kinds of files, such as sound files, contain both resources and data.

When you send a Mac file to a UNIX computer, for example, the contents of the resource fork must be moved over to the data fork in order for the file to be stored in the alien operating system's directory.

A standard way of storing resources in the data fork of a Macintosh file is *MacBinary II*. A MacBinary file is a special type of binary file. *A binary file* uses all eight of the bits in it; in a non-binary file, the top bit is set to zero.

Some of the networks that comprise the Internet, such as **Usenet** and **email**, do not support the transfer of binaries. The ASCII text files used on the Internet are seven-bit files, that is, they use only seven of the data bits in them.

A user who wants to transport Mac files on the Internet, must encode the file in a text-compatible format, or in other words, change the binary file to a non-binary file. The most common format for encoding Mac files as non-binary files is called **Binhex**, and Binhex files are signified by the extension ".hqx"—a common extension on **FTP** sites such as **software archives** for the Mac.

For example, if you have a Macintosh file, such as a shareware or freeware application, that you want to transmit to a site on the Internet, you need to do the following:

1. Open a freeware encoding program such as MacBinary (available at **http:// wwwhost.ots.utexas.edu/mac/pub-mac-** compression.html) or BinHex 4.0 (available at **http://web66.coled.umn.edu/Cookbook/ Utensils.html**).

2. Open the file you want to encode: on BinHex 4.0, you choose TEXT to Upload from the File menu.

3. Save the file with the correct name.

If you encounter an application saved with the file extension ".hqx," the best application for **decoding/ decompressing** that file is **StuffIt Expander**, a freeware application created by Aladdin Systems, Inc. (also available at **http://web66.coled.umn.edu/Cookbook/Utensils.html**).

See Also

Decoding/Decompressing Files; FTP; Macintosh Software Archive; StuffIt Expander

Encryption

Encryption, in general, refers to the coding or ciphering of communications so that they can only be read by the intended recipient(s). On the **Internet**, encryption refers to the coding of transmissions to and from a remote **Web server** so that sensitive information is rendered unreadable to potential intruders.

One method of encryption commonly used on the **World Wide Web** is public key cryptography, created in 1976 by Whitfield Diffie and Martin Hellman. Public key cryptography uses a set of two keys, called the **public key** and the **private key,** and both must be used for the encoding/decoding process.

A number of proposed standards have been put forth that use encryption methods to provide security on the Web, including **Secure HTTP** and **Secure Sockets Layer.**

See Also

Internet; Secure HTTP; Secure Sockets Layer; Workgroup Servers, Macintosh Family; World Wide Web

End Key

If you are at the **desktop level,** pressing the End key on an extended keyboard takes you to the bottom of the **active window**. Within an application, pressing the End key moves your **cursor** to the last space at the bottom of the document's visible window.

See Also

Active Window; Cursor; Desktop Level

Energy-Star Monitor Issues

The monitor is the single biggest consumer of power in the Mac. With dozens or hundreds of computers in a building, the energy bill for the monitors alone can be significant. Even at home, leaving a monitor on all the time can use some power.

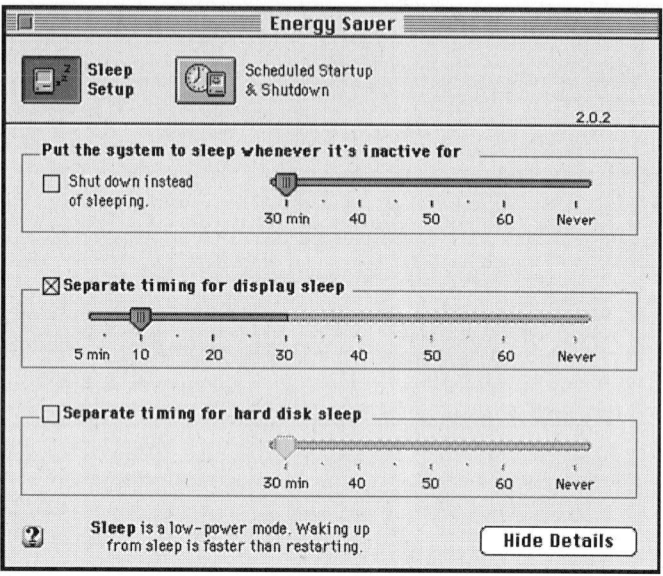

Most monitors sold today meet the EPA's Energy Star rating for equipment, which requires that less than 30 watts of power be used. Now, if you think of the light and heat a 30-watt light bulb puts out and compare it to what your monitor puts out, this may seem impossible. Monitors meet the standard by going into a sleep mode during inactive periods. A tap on a key usually brings the monitor back to life. The power savings can be substantial. For instance, the Apple 15-inch Multiple Scan monitor uses 90 watts of power in full operation, but less than 5 watts when sleeping. Even Apple's big-screen monitors use only 10 watts when asleep.

The so-called **PCI** Macs, including the Power Mac 7200, 7500, 8500, and 9500, come with an Energy Saver control panel (see the following figure) that will put the monitor to sleep, even if the monitor doesn't have its own sleep mode and is not Energy Star compliant. Energy Saver brings down power usage for the entire computer system to under 30 watts. It also spins down the hard drive, and "sleeps" the CPU, similar to the sleep state of **PowerBooks**. Only the fan stays on when the Mac is in sleep mode. Energy Saver can also schedule automatic shut downs and startups through the Energy Saver Control Panel pictured in the following figure.

Of course, the ultimate power saver for a monitor is to turn it off. You can safely turn off your monitor while leaving your Mac on.

See Also

Monitors; Monitors, Common Models; Multimedia Monitors; Multisync Monitors; Portrait and Pivoting Monitors

Enter Key

In most cases, the Enter key (on extended keyboards) is the same as the **Return key**. In a **dialog box** where you can use the Return key to choose the **default button** (any button with two dark lines around it), you can use the Enter key instead. Within applications (such as databases and spreadsheets), you can use the Enter key to move the insertion point to the next available entry point. In word processing documents or page layout documents, the Enter key functions like the Return key.

The Enter key is also used as the equals (=) key when using the Calculator D/A.

See Also

Calculator D/A; Default Button; I-Beam Cursor; Return Key

Entertainment

What good would anything be without a flashy fun side? Not everybody sits on a desk and types numbers into a spreadsheet all day. Sure, we all have to keep track of our finances and turn reports in every once in a while at the office, but the Macintosh is more than just a work horse. The Power Mac is the perfect gaming machine and more companies than ever are starting to take notice. Even companies with mainly PC games in their catalogs, such as **Sierra Online** and **7th Level**, are starting to bring their titles over to the Mac. New games for the Macintosh are coming out in record numbers and are cooler than ever, many optimized for the Power Mac.

Power Macs can handle everything from **Network**-capable software to stereo sound and top of the line high-resolution graphics to support today's influx of **3-D** and video incorporation in computer games. With the hassle-free Mac interface, without doing much more than installing a few new items into your system folder and clicking a game icon, you can be running top-selling games like **Marathon** and **Descent** in no time.

Conversation with Rochelle Garner

Rochelle Garner started writing for Regis McKenna, getting the word out about Apple, before going on to *MacWeek*. She recently has become a freelance journalist, writing for a wide spectrum of computer and business magazines. Here, she shares her perspective on Apple and the Mac.

Maclopedia: What was your first contact with the Mac?

Rochelle: In 1983, I was at Regis McKenna and our editing team got to play with the prototypes. They were so secretive—no one could see what this thing looked like. So I come to work early, it's 8 in the morning, and there it is, in the window, with the curtains all drawn like a theater. There'd been a photo shoot the night before, and they'd left it out there for anyone in the parking lot to see.

Microsoft has reached a stage where it doesn't matter if it is good or bad, and momentum carries the day.

I went through the Mac's introduction and the first 128K machine. I couldn't see it. I thought, "This is a toy." I could never really understand why my friend Paul Saffo—he's at the Institute of the Future now—was so immediately taken with the potential of the Mac... I didn't see the value until the Mac Plus.

Maclopedia: Where do you see Apple and Microsoft, today?

Rochelle: I don't talk much to developers, but I have really had to explore economies of scale and market position. Microsoft has reached a stage where it doesn't matter if it is good or bad, and momentum carries the day. Everyone hates Microsoft and every developer goes out of their way to get an alliance with Microsoft and then complains that only Microsoft makes money from the alliance.

Apple has had a series of problems over the years caused by its own hubris. Hubris got in the way, and the market did not stand still. We've reached the juncture where sheer innovation and good products will no longer compensate for what was hubris. I don't think Apple is going to go away, but it will not be a major player. It must now develop niche markets clearly—graphics, prepress, publishing, and the Web. Did you know that the single most popular platform for creating Web servers is a Mac? Unfortunately, real money is made in the mundane business applications for big business, not small, not mid-business.

I work with a Mac because I have no support. I could never do things with a Win.INI file. Everyone agrees the Mac is cheaper and easier to support. You need fewer support staff. But that doesn't matter because big business is going into client server, which is very complicated, so they are trying to get rid of Macs. I would love to be proved wrong, but Apple has really lost the big business game.

Maclopedia: What should Apple do, then?

Rochelle: Look at what is happening at the Baby Bells, particularly U.S. West, going after the residential customer with Internet access because that is where the growth is. Apple needs to figure out how to have high volumes in the home.

continues

Maclopedia: What has to change to expand the home market for computers from the current 35 to 40 percent of households?

Rochelle: The whole animal has to change. Everyone who has a PC or a Mac in the home now is attracted to the technology for one reason or another; they are drawn toward computing. But there has to be an element of fun and entertainment, like TV has, to really grab. Or a utilitarian service, like what Minitel offers in France—it isn't fun, but it serves local needs. I want to find out what events are happening in my suburb of Paris, and I can find that on Minitel. But computer manufacturers are abominable at figuring out customer needs.

The cable modem might just be the device that kickstarts a residential market, in about eighteen months (fall of 1997). It's really fast compared to 28Kbps on the fastest personal computer modems. You can have enough information flowing back and forth, and you have the cable installed in all the major markets. I can hardly wait to get rid of 28.8; I only use it because I have to; it takes forever, and that's because of the phone wiring structure, which is beyond the ken of computer manufacturers. That's where the relationships between cable and the Bells are going to be important.

You need content with immediacy; things like local services. There is no reason for the average person to really get an Internet service because the average person doesn't need to do the kind of research that I do. The average person just wants to find out what is happening locally. Where are the best schools? How are the schools doing? What is the ticket at the local convention center? I want things I can get quickly, instead of screwing around waiting to get around to the right screen. Today it is only the kids who have the stamina to keep hoofing the same thing; I just did a search, and it took 15 minutes.

I think the Mac offers some tremendous Web capabilities. I interviewed a gentleman who had put the first airline ticketing Web site up, and he said, "I used the Mac server because it is far and away the best." What he liked particularly was the operating system. Because of its nature, it's more difficult to break into the server than into a UNIX server, so with secure Web software you can transmit credit card numbers inside the country, although not outside, because we can't export the encryption software strong enough to handle it.

Maclopedia: What else would you recommend?

Rochelle: What Apple is going to have to focus on more is their internal cohesiveness. When a company has a product line with 20 custom chips, with 75 different models, that's insane. When it allows one group of research and development to create one form factor for one DuoDock, but use another for another DuoDock, that is insane. Look at the competition: Compaq has the most models with 20. It is impossible to know the difference.

What needs to be done internally is to rein in the runaway fiefdoms. They're not after power. Each is saying we know best how to do this, but there have to be constraints. They have to bring in a culture, establish a new culture, in which there are actually shared visions, shared directions. You have to have a goal, such as, "To be a billion dollar corporation," and definite strategies to get there.

At the heart, Apple is an engineering company. It happens to have been blessed with creativity, or it was. But at its soul are engineers. They do things because they are neat, like the Newton, the brain child of an egomaniac, with no utilitarian use when it first came out. Now it is quite nice to have, but who knows it because it has a bad rep. So you need a business person who does not get caught up in the neatness, the way John Sculley did, and says, "Cut bait here, trim here, go there!"

Computer games are more than just shooting your opponent or going head to head with the computer in a game of chess. The gaming industry has indeed grown so large that every consumer Mac magazine from *Wired* to *MacHome Journal* gives it generous attention.

Although spin-off versions and clones of popular **Arcade Games** are still a big part of the market, **First Person Perspective Shooters**, a modern spawn of arcade shooting games, **Adventure Games**, **Role-Playing Games**, and **Simulations** have created their own followings. In addition, **Traditional Board Games**, sports, nonviolent kids' games and the inevitable movie tie-in titles have also made a huge impact on the way we enjoy ourselves on the Mac.

E

Today's Mac games immerse you in a fanciful environment, providing an escape from daily cares. With the impending release of **Virtual Reality** software and hardware from companies such as VictorMaxx and Virtual i/o, game-related MacVirtual Reality seems just around the corner. But with production delays and constantly revised release dates, a real-life version of Star Trek: The Next Generation's Holodeck is probably still quite a ways off. The next move in gaming will most likely be toward team play, either via an Internet scavenger hunt, or a **CD-ROM** game that allows **network play**.

Titles such as Havoc from Reality Bytes and **Hexen: Beyond Heretic** from GT Interactive give cross-platform gaming a new meaning, linking PCs to Macs via a network. As gaming ultimately progresses, it will be increasingly true that there is something out there for everyone.

Game Types Table

Category Name	Description	Best Games
Arcade	Fast-paced games based on classic video arcade style games like PacMan, Asteroids, and Pitfall. This also includes pinball titles.	Looney Labyrinth, Crystal Caliburn, 3-D Ultra Pinball, Lode Runner, Power Pete, Prince of Persia, Crystal Crazy
First Person Perspective Shooters	Sometimes bloody shoot-em-ups, similar to arcade games in rapid pace, that sport a first person view of the game's landscape.	Marathon, DOOM II, Descent, Hexen

continues

Game Types Table (continued)

Category Name	Description	Best Games
Adventure	Quest and journey type games, which pit the player in another world. Often the player is required to solve a mystery, engage in battle and travel in a pack with other characters. Most adventure games have a high level of puzzles incorporated into game play. Many have a sci fi or fantasy feel. The vast majority of computer games falls into this category in one way or another.	Daedalus Encounter, The, Dark Eye, Eastern Mind, Full Throttle, Hell, Myst, Bad Day on the Midway, Return to Zork, Riddle of Master Lu, 7th Guest, TimeLapse: Ancient Civilizations
Role Playing Games (RPGs)	Similar to Dungeons & Dragons, RPGs are more complex adventure games in which the player takes on the role of a character involved in an intricate storyline. Most are based in medieval folk lore.	Might & Magic III, Curse of Dragor, Dungeon Master II: The Legends of SkullKeep
Sim Games	A large category encompassing flight simulators, games in which you control a government, and games in which you create societies from scratch. All teach you to maintain your city, plane, animal, or country as if you were in charge for real. Random elements are built in for increased similarity to real life.	Flight: F-A/18 Hornet, A-10 Attack!, Out of the Sun, Absolute Zero, Rebel Assault II, Wing Commander III Government: SimCity 2000, Afterlife
Strategy	Similar to Sim Games, strategy games put you in more specific charge of a society or government. Many strategy games have a war element and require you to maintain troops and defend yourself against or attack other players, computer or human.	Allied General, Chaos, Empire Deluxe, Pax Imperia, Civilization, Spaceward Ho!, Colonization, V for Victory, Warcraft: Orcs and Humans, Vikings
Non-Linear Storytelling	Games with a literary feel. They are similar to a book that you move through, not page by page, but by randomly picking different points of entry. You weave through a pre-designed story at your own pace.	The Resident's Bad Day on the Midway, The Dark Eye, The Cypher

Category Name	Description	Best Games
Traditional Games	Games based on non-computer entertainment such as board games, card games, and Trivia.	Classic Collection (Monopoly, Risk & Scrabble), You Don't Know Jack
Chess	Games that pit the player against the computer or an online human opponent.	Chessmaster 3000, Battle Chess
Puzzle Games	Require quick thinking and strategy to solve. Similar to non-computer games like dominoes and the Rubik's cube.	BreakThru, Tetris, Troubled Souls, Diamonds 3-D, Zoop
Sports Games	Games based on real sports. For some reason, there are no outstanding games in any field but golf for the Mac.	Golf: Links Pro CD for Macintosh, PGA Tour Golf III
Family Entertainment	Non-violent games aimed at children and families that are not considered "edutainment" or too difficult.	Are You Afraid of the Dark?, Foul Play, Masterpiece Mansion, Mortimer, Yellow Brick Road II

For More...

If you want to do this...	Go to this entry...
Find Golf	Sports Games
Find war games	Strategy Games
Find games with Live Actors	Hollywood Games Connection
Find games based on movies	Hollywood Games Connection
Find flight simulators	Sim Games
Find gambling	Traditional Games
Find games similar to Sim City	Sim Games
Find horror games	Adventure Games
Find games with political elements	Sim Games; Strategy Games
Find card games, board games, and other standard style games	Traditional Games
Find controversial games	Violence in Games

If you want to do this...	Go to this entry...
Find games with a literary element	Non-Linear Storytelling Games
Find kid's games	Family Entertainment
Find games similar to Dungeons and Dragons	Role-Playing Games
Find out about Adventure Games	Adventure Games
Find a Pinball game	Arcade-Style Games
Find out about Internet/online games	MUDs and MOOs; Network Gaming; Online Games
Find out where to find good game reviews in magazines	Magazines, Mac Gaming
Find out about games like DOOM	First Person Perspective Shooters
Find out about games like Myst	Adventure Games
Find inexpensive games online	Shareware Games

EPS

Both **vector graphics** and **bitmapped graphics** can be stored as Encapsulated PostScript, or EPS files, which are easily output by high-resolution imagesetters. Because bitmapped EPS files are larger than their TIFF counterparts, however, EPS is primarily suitable for vector graphics.

Macintosh draw programs create EPS files when graphics will need to be imported into other programs. EPS files may or may not include a low-resolution preview image, which allows users to see what the image looks like when they import it into another program, and the preview may be PICT or TIFF.

See Also

Bitmapped Graphics; Vector Graphics

EPSF, *See EPS*

Equalization

A sound processor or software that boosts or attenuates frequencies to improve sound quality. Treble and bass controls provide very simple examples of equalization.

See Also

Compressor; Limiter; Sound Digitizing

Erase Disk Command

This command permanently erases the contents of a disk or a hard disk. When you choose Erase Disk from the **Special menu**, the selected disk is **initialized**, a process that deletes the contents of the disk. To erase (or initialize) a disk, click the disk icon and select Erase Disk. A warning box appears asking you, "Completely erase disk named (the disk title and location appears here)?". It also enables you to rename the disk. Note: The Erase Disk command does not erase the contents of the startup disk. This is a built-in safety feature to keep you out of trouble.

This works the same way initializing works when you insert a brand new, unformatted disk. When you insert a disk that is not formatted for Macintosh, you get a dialog asking you whether you want to **format** that disk. If you click OK, the system erases and initializes the disk for Macintosh. Just as the Erase Disk command does. If you have the System 7.5 extension PC Exchange active, the dialog box gives you the choice of formatting the disk as a Macintosh or DOS disk. You can select the format from the pop-up list in the Erase Disk dialog box.

The Erase Disk command also performs a diagnostic check on the disk to see that it's operating properly. If for some reason there are bad sectors on your disk, or there are other problems, you'll get a dialog box telling you, "Initialization failed." This is a safeguard to keep you from writing important information to a damaged disk.

What happens if you accidentally select your startup disk and choose the Erase Disk command? Don't worry, the system is looking out for you and has already taken into account the fact that this might happen. You get a dialog box with the message, "The disk (your internal hard drive's name appears here) could not be erased because it is the startup disk which contains the active system software." This is the Mac's way of protecting your system and keeping you from initializing and erasing your **startup disk**. However, if you choose any other external or internal drives that do not contain the active system software, you get the standard dialog box asking you if you're sure you want to erase the contents of the drive. If you do, press OK, and the drive is reinitialized and the contents erased.

To erase a disk, follow these steps:

1. Click the disk you want permanently erased.

2. Select Erase Disk from the Special menu.

3. You'll get a dialog box asking you if you're sure want to initialize the disk and permanently erase the contents of the selected disk. If you're sure, click OK. If not, click Cancel.

See Also

Disks, Initializing; Special Menu; Startup Disk

Eric Virus, *See Scores Virus*

Error Correction, *See Modems, Types*

Error Messages

If you try to do something that the Mac doesn't allow (such as throwing away your startup System file) or if your Mac encounters some type of problem that needs your attention, most times you receive an error message. Some error messages are just warnings, such as when you go to initialize a disk, it displays an error message asking you if you're sure you want to permanently erase the selected disk's contents. Or if you try to name a file with more than 31 characters, it will warn you that 31 characters are the limit. There are also more serious messages that appear when the system encounters a more serious problem.

If your Mac **freezes** or **crashes**, the Mac displays an error message alerting you of the problem.

Unfortunately, by the time you see an error message, it's usually too late to avoid the crash or freeze-up, but the error message may contain an error code to help you track down the cause of the error.

These error codes, however, are too simplistic and vague to make much use of them. There are **shareware** programs that list all the Macintosh error messages by number. You can enter the number of the error code from the error message, and the shareware program displays the error code's official Apple description. The official descriptions of these error codes don't help much more than the codes themselves, unless you happen to be an Apple hardware technician.

There are other error messages that appear such as when an application suddenly quits or when you try to launch a document but don't have the application with which it was created. There are a host of messages to accompany a wide range of possible error situations.

Common Error Messages and What They Mean

Error Message	Means	What to Do Next
The Trash cannot be emptied because it contains locked items.	You have files in the Trash that are locked through the Get Info box (⌘-I) to keep them from being accidentally deleted.	Hold down the Option key while choosing Empty Trash, or click the locked file in the Trash, and Get Info (⌘-I) and uncheck the locked option.
Are you sure you want to permanently erase the contents of the selected disk?	You're about to reformat (Initialize) this disk and everything on it will be deleted forever.	If you want to erase this disk, click OK. Otherwise click cancel.
Are you sure you want to rebuild the desktop on the selected disk?	You're going to rebuild the desktop and any comments in Get Info windows will be lost (unless you're using System 7.2 or higher).	Click OK if you want to rebuild the desktop file.
This name is already taken.	You cannot have two files in the same place with the same exact name.	Pick a different name for your file.

continues

Common Error Messages and What They Mean (continued)

Error Message	Means	What to Do Next
The application is busy or missing.	You may not have the application that created the document, or the file may not be able to be opened (such as the Finder File).	If you have the application that created the document, but double-clicking it won't launch it, rebuild the desktop as it may have become corrupted. If you don't have the application that created the file, you can try to open the document from a similar-type application.
This is not a Macintosh disk. Do you want to initialize it?	The system is not recognizing this as a mountable disk.	Only click OK if you want to permanently erase the contents of the disk.
The disk could not be put away because it contains items that are in use.	A document, file, or font on the disk is open and in use, so the disk cannot be ejected.	Close all files, documents, or fonts on the disk. When all files are closed, it can be ejected.
There's not enough memory to keep windows open.	You're running very low on memory, and windows that are open at the Finder have to be closed to conserve memory.	Quit any open applications that you're not using. Close all documents that are open within applications.
Are you sure you want to shutdown your computer now?	You may have accidentally pressed the PowerOn key.	If you don't want to shutdown or restart, click the Cancel button.
The Trash contains XX items that occupy XXXK of disk space. Are you sure you want to permanently remove these items?	You are about to delete all the files in the Trash. Their combined size is shown.	You can click OK to empty the Trash, or you can click the trash can and Get Info (⌘-I) and then uncheck the checkbox marked "warn before emptying," which will disable the warning.

See Also
Crashes, System; Error, System; Quit Command; Troubleshooting the MacOS

Error Messages, Hardware and Software, *See Software and Hardware Errors*

Error Messages, Internet Connection
Error messages appear on the Macintosh screen occasionally when connecting to the **Internet** or accessing a **World Wide Web server.** Such a message does not mean the reader has done something wrong. Rather, it means the **client** software encountered an error while trying to perform the requested function.

The following figure illustrates one of the most common error messages you are likely to encounter. They occur when you unsuccessfully try to connect to a Web server or locate a file.

Netscape's network connection was refused by the server:
    www.apple.com
The server may not be accepting connections or may be busy.

Try connecting again later.

[OK]

E

The previous message means one of three things:

- The server is too busy to receive your request for a connection right now. (Too many other users may be accessing the site.)

- The server is down.

- The server never accepts connections from your site.

The most likely cause is that the server is too busy. Then again, the server may have crashed. Certain sites also limit access for security reasons.

Whatever the cause, the only course of action is to wait and try to connect again later.

The following table lists a number of other common error messages, possible causes, and possible remedies.

Common Error Messages

Message	Cause	Remedy
Server Does Not Have **DNS** Entry	Your Internet client cannot find the **URL** of the site	1) Check the address for typos or other mistakes; 2) Check your **MacTCP** control panel settings and make sure **Domain Name Server** information has been entered.
File Not Available	Client is connecting to the site, but cannot find the file you requested.	Check the filename to make sure it is correct.
Forbidden **URL**	1) Page has moved; 2) There is a typo in **anchor** pointing to the page; 3) Access to the directory is restricted.	Edit the URL to go back to the next folder up, and look for **links** that lead back to the page you want.

Error, System

A system error occurs when the system software encounters a problem that keeps it from operating. When a system error occurs you get a **dialog box** with an icon of a bomb that states, "Sorry, a system error has occurred," and your only choice is to **restart**. A restart button appears on the dialog box, but depending on how serious the system error is, it might

or might not work. If the restart button on the system error dialog box does not work, you can restart the Mac by pressing the restart button on the front of your computer, or, if your model does not have a restart button (like LCs, Quadra 605s, and so on), you can restart with the keyboard command Control-⌘-**PowerOn key**.

By restarting your Mac, the situation that caused the temporary system error usually disappears, and you can continue working. If the situation persists, you may have a system extension conflict, and you should try to isolate the extension causing the conflict (see **crashes, system** for a step-by-step method for tracking down and fixing conflicts).

See Also
Crashes, System; Error Messages; PowerOn Key; Restart

Esc Key

The Esc (Escape) key is another name for cancel, and it can be used as a keyboard shortcut for cancel in any **desktop level dialog box** that has a Cancel button. Many applications support the use of the Esc key as the Cancel button. Also, if you mistakenly **launch** an application, if you press the Esc key fast enough, the launch may be canceled. Sometimes. You have to be really quick. You can also use the keystroke ⌘-. (period) as an alternative to the Escape key.

The Escape key is also used in a keystroke combination that enables you to force quit an application or the Finder (Option-⌘-Esc key) in case an application has crashed. By using this keystroke, you can sometimes force a crashed application to quit, which gives you the opportunity to save any other open documents in other applications, and then restart the machine.

See Also
Desktop Level; Finder

EtherNet

When EtherNet was first introduced, it was an expensive way to provide networked computers with far more data-carrying capacity than they needed. But times, and computers, have changed a good deal. Today, EtherNet is acknowledged as the standard. New Macs and Power Macs intended for office use are equipped with EtherNet as well as LocalTalk connectors.

EtherNet was origtnally developed by Xerox in collaboration with Digital and Intel. Companies such as digital and Sun use EtherNet to run a variety of networking protocols for mini-computer and workstation applications, as well as for Mac and PC networking. In fact, EtherNet was developed with multiprotocol support in mind. An EtherNet network can support many different protocols at the same time. When AppleTalk protocols run over EtherNet cables, Apple calls the system EtherTalk.

Whereas LocalTalk cables have a bandwidth of 230.4Kbps, EtherNet has a bandwidth of 10Mbps or, with the new 100Base-T system, 100Mbps. So instead of being limited to a maximum of 32 nodes as LocalTalk is, EtherTalk networks can handle literally thousands of devices.

EtherNet cables are often "connected" by network bridges, microwave links, and even satellites to other EtherNet networks to create an "extended" EtherNet LAN. Many large companies have extensive worldwide EtherNet LANs with thousands of computers produced by different companies.

Because of the increased bandwidth, the throughput of an EtherNet network is higher than that of LocalTalk. Actual transmission rates will depend on many factors, such as the amount of network traffic being handled simultaneously, size of the transmitted file, and performance of the individual EtherNet controller and CPU. On average, you can expect an EtherNet network to perform three to five times better than a LocalTalk network.

Several different types of cabling can be used with EtherNet. These include ThickNet, also called Thickwire 10Base-T; ThinNet, which may be called Thinwire 10Base-2; and Twisted Pair or 10Base-T. ThickNet, as the name implies, is a thick wire, about 3/8 inch in diameter. It is actually a coaxial cable, meaning that it has one wire in the middle, surrounded by a circle of insulation, and then a second wire (which may be braided or even foil. It uses a fifteen pin D-style connector and must be terminated at both ends, much as a SCSI chain is. Because it is sturdy, and because it can accept as many as 200 devices on a 1,640 foot segment, it is frequently used as a central "backbone" for an EtherNet network. (Fiber-optic cables can also be used as backbones.) Thickwire connections are made by clamping a transceiver onto the cable. The transceiver has sharp metal pins that puncture the cable and make electrical contact with the inner and outer wires. The connector is often called a "vampire" tap.

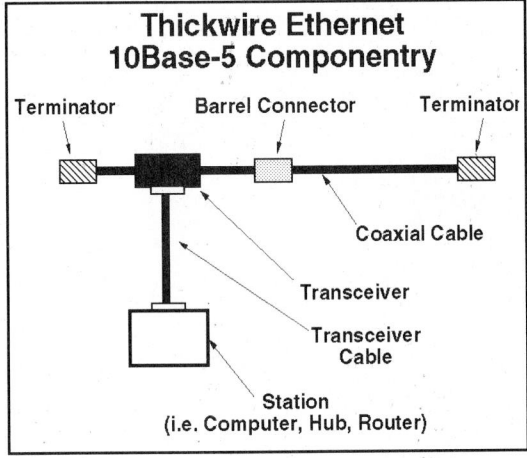

ThinNet is a thinner and more flexible type of co-axial cable, which uses BNC connectors that twist and lock into a T-shaped fitting. Although it used to be a popular choice for wiring desktop computers and workstations, it has been replaced in many facilities by twisted pair. The free ends of a ThinNet network must be terminated by resistive end caps, as shown in the following figure.

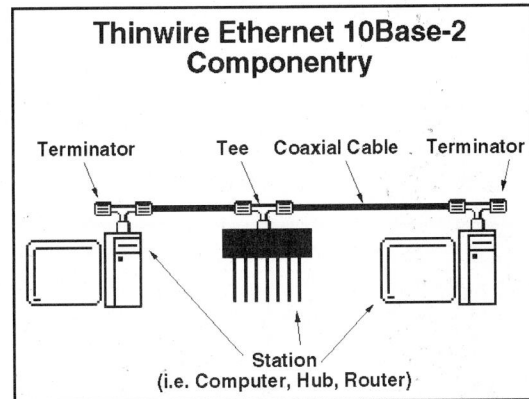

Twisted pair, or 10Base-T is the most common kind of cabling, especially for desktop computers and peripherals. It allows EtherNet to run on two pairs of standard, unshielded wires—a much lower cost type of wiring. However, 10Base-T requires that you use a hub to connect the devices on the network. Unlike the other types of cable, it cannot be used for a daisy chained network, as shown in the following figure.

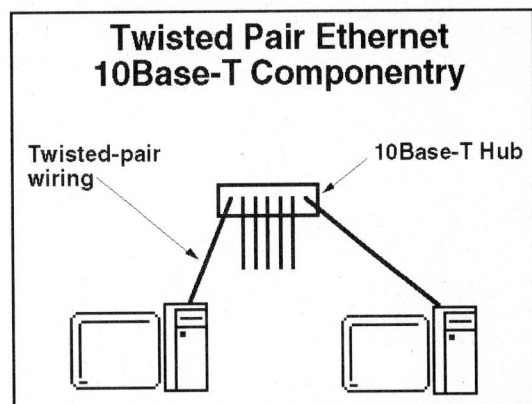

See Also

Data Link; Networking

Etiquette on the Internet,
See Netiquette

E.T.O.

E.T.O. (Essentials, Tools, Objects) is Apple's premiere development-tool CD-ROM series. It includes **MPW**, **MacApp**, **Symantec C++**, the Virtual User testing tool, Macintosh Debugger, **ResEdit**, **MacsBug**, pre-release versions of the hottest new programming toys, and lots of other stuff. E.T.O is a subscription product. Your purchase price buys three CDs—one full year of updates. Apple has recently dropped the price of E.T.O. dramatically. It is now $595.00 for new subscribers and $195.00 for renewals. E.T.O. is available only through Apple's Developer Catalog.

See Also

MacApp; MPW; MrC; ResEdit; Symantec C++

Evangelism

When Apple first introduced the Macintosh, it had a tough road ahead of it. Here was a new computer with no installed base and very little software. Unlike the early days of personal computers, when most users wrote their own software, by the time the Macintosh was introduced, most users relied upon commercial software packages to get their work done.

So, Apple needed to get software developers to write programs that would run on the Macintosh. This wasn't exactly an easy task. First, when Apple began "evangelizing" for the Mac in 1983, there were no Macintosh computers available to developers; they had to write their software on the **Lisa**. There were no Macs available to customers, either, so there was no established market for Macintosh software.

It takes a lot of time and money to create software, and developers did not want to invest a lot of time and money into a product that might not sell. Apple had to convince them that their time and money would not be wasted.

Apple sent out "evangelists" to try to convince people to develop for the Macintosh. The first Apple software evangelists were **Guy Kawasaki** and Mike Boich. Kawasaki and Boich were passionate. They pleaded with developers, told them they would be making history and changing the world! In short, they got the developers to see and believe in the Macintosh vision.

Without Apple's concerted effort to evangelize the Macintosh platform, this book might never have existed. Without the work of the software evangelists, the Mac may never have reached the "critical mass" of software any platform needs to keep going.

See Also

Kawasaki, Guy; Lisa

Even Parity, *See Parity*

EvenBetterBusError

EvenBetterBusError is a free **debugging** tool that catches memory errors caused by accessing memory location zero. It accomplishes this by periodically placing a value at location zero that causes an immediate bus or address error on every type of Macintosh. This feature, as well as many others, is included in the commercial debugging tool **QC**.

Event

The graphical interface of the Macintosh adds some interesting twists to the task of programming. Unlike older, command-line based programs that follow a

fixed path from beginning to end, Macintosh applications must be able to respond to any user action at any time. The application detects user actions by receiving *events* from the operating system.

Every kind of message an application can receive from the user, the system, or another application arrives as an event. Each application must continually ask the system for new events and respond to them appropriately. This is done in an *event loop*. The event loop repeatedly retrieves events using the **Toolbox** routine `WaitNextEvent()` and responds to them, exiting only when the user has chosen to quit the application. See the following figure.

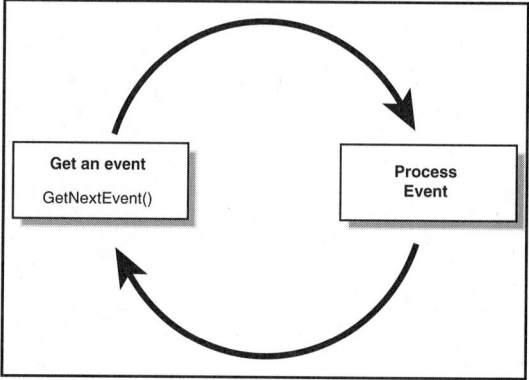

There are 11 kinds of events that an application can receive from the operating system:

- Mouse-down
- Mouse-up
- Key-down
- Key-up
- Autokey
- Disk
- Activate
- Update
- Null
- Operating system
- High-level

Each of these events can be classified as a low-level event, operating system event, or high-level event.

The first nine events are low-level events, or "original" Macintosh events defined in the very first version of the MacOS. The first four are pretty self-explanatory. Each time the user clicks the mouse button or presses a key, a mouse-down or key-down event is sent to the front application. Similarly, when the mouse button or key is released, a mouse-up or key-up event is generated. The auto-key event is generated when a single key is held down for a period of time.

Note that there is no such thing as a double-click event. Each application must determine whether a pair of clicks constitute a double-click. For each of these events, the application is informed of the location of the mouse and the exact time the event occurred, as well as details relevant to the specific event (such as which key was pressed).

If the user inserts a disk into a drive, the System generates a disk event. A good application should respond to disk events. If the disk isn't initialized, the application can initialize the disk; otherwise, this event is generally ignored.

The activate and update events apply to specific windows within an application. The activate event is actually two events masquerading as one: one that lets an application know a window is being activated, and another that lets it know a window is becoming inactive. Applications respond to these events by enabling or disabling scroll bars, showing or hiding the current selection, and making any other changes that differentiate inactive windows from active ones.

The system generates an update event for any section of a window that needs to be redrawn. When a window is revealed from behind another, for example, the application receives an update event telling it to redraw the newly revealed part of the window. Applications *must* respond to update events, or the system will continue to send them, drowning out other events.

The null event is the anti-event. When an application requests an event, and there are no other, more important events waiting, it is passed a null event. The application can use the null event as an indication that the machine is idle and then perform whatever idle-time processing it sees fit.

The operating system event—osEvt—came on the scene with **MultiFinder** and **System 6**. There is only one OS event, but it can contain any of three distinct messages. The first two are the suspend and resume events. These are sent to an application just before it is switched into the background and just after it has been returned to the foreground, respectively. The third OS event is the mouse moved event. Applications use this event to determine when the mouse has moved outside a predefined region and to respond appropriately (by changing the cursor from the arrow to the I-beam, for example).

The final class of events, high-level events, were introduced with System 7. These events are used to pass high-level messages between applications (or sometimes between different parts of the same application). Most high-level events are **Apple events**, which make all sorts of exciting stuff, such as scripting, possible.

Events are documented in the Macintosh Toolbox Essentials volume of *Inside Macintosh*. High-level events are covered in more detail in the Interapplication Communications volume.

See Also
Apple Event; Inside Macintosh; Toolbox

eWorld

Realizing that it had missed a major market opportunity in online services, Apple announced the eWorld service in January of 1994 with expectations to be operational by Spring of 1994. Because they had purchased the GUI software from **America Online**, the overall format of eWorld closely resembled that of AOL, as did its pricing structure.

Unfortunately, the timing of eWorld's release coincided with the explosive growth of the Internet. Thus, not only was the online market saturated with the third generation interfaces of **CompuServe** and America Online, but nearly all of the industry's publicity and user interest was geared toward the Internet. So, despite several interesting advances in the online interface, eWorld never gained much of a following. In early 1996, Apple made the final decision to shut down eWorld. The service was officially shut down at 12:01 AM on April 1st, 1996.

Apple had planned to move all of its existing AppleLink-based contact with its developers, sales force, and other employees and interested third parties to eWorld because of the obvious ineffectiveness of the AppleLink Interface. However, with the shut down of eWorld, Apple has revised these plans and now plans to use its many Web sites to spread information, leaving AppleLink as the only way to communicate by email with Apple Computer.

See Also

America Online; CompuServe

Excel

Excel is Microsoft's **spreadsheet** for Windows and Macintosh, and the preeminent financial and mathematical tool for the Mac. It's easily the most powerful:

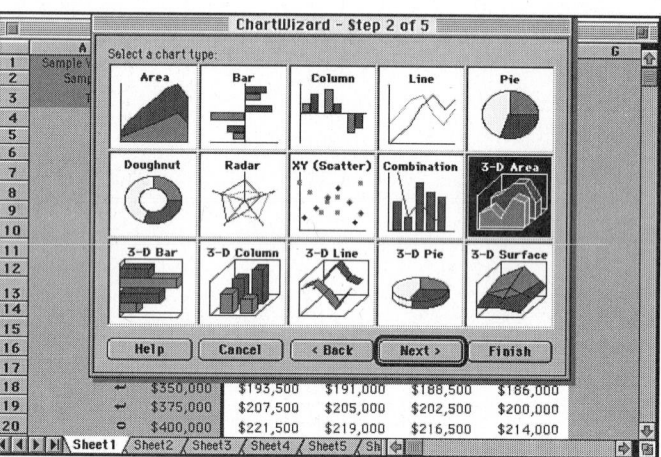

- Each page can have more than four million **cells**, and a file can have multiple pages sharing the same information.

- Data can be displayed in hundreds of different two- and three-dimensional graphs, cells can be **dragged** directly into graphs, and a single graph can display up to 32,000 data points.

- Data can also be displayed as *Pivot Tables,* which let you analyze data by dragging category names around the screen while the program generates subtotals to match.

- More than 800 prebuilt **functions** and **macros** are built-in.

- Continuous dialogs (called *Wizards*) guide you through almost every operation, using graphics where appropriate (see the following figure).

- The program even includes a **superset** of **BASIC** as its macro language.

All this power comes with a cost, as well as a $300 street price: Excel requires at least a **68040** processor to run well, and Microsoft recommends a **Power Mac** with at least 8MB of free RAM and 16 to 28MB of disk space. Because all these extra features have their own rules of operation, the learning curve can be an additional cost. The built-in help system can help if you're already spreadsheet-savvy, but isn't for beginners.

On the other hand, because it's such a popular program, there is plenty of third-party support. Dozens of books and hundreds of classes will teach you Excel, and academic computing centers often post excellent instructions on the **World Wide Web**. One of the best is **http://www.gla.ac.uk/Compserv/Doc/Mac/un606/un606.html**.

Because the Windows and Mac versions are compatible, user information as well as documents can be shared between them. You'll learn a lot about the program in the **slac.users.excel** and **comp.apps.spreadsheets newsgroups**. Downloadable macros and **templates** are available from Microsoft at **http://www.microsoft.com/msexcel/fs_xl.htm**, as well as most **shareware** sources. Commercial templates for **vertical markets** are also available, and usually advertised on the Web.

More information is available from Microsoft's Mac area at **http://www.microsoft.com/support/products/mac/office/excel.htm**.

Expanded, *See Typesetting Terms*

E

Expanded Folders

If you want the contents of a **folder** in list view, you can expand the folder by **clicking** the white arrow that appears to the left of the folder in the list. The triangle turns black, points down, and without actually opening the window for that folder, gives you a list of its contents. If there are folders within that folder, you can use the white triangle beside that folder to expand it as well. The keyboard shortcut to expand a folder in list view is ⌘-→.

See Also

Click; Folder Icon; Keyboard Shortcuts

Expansion Bus, *See Power Mac Logic Boards*

Expert Draw, *See Drawing Applications*

Export, Spreadsheet, *See Import/Export, Spreadsheet*

Express Modem

Apple's Express Modem isn't a modem at all, but is software that enables a Mac with a **GeoPort** adapter to perform the functions of a modem. The Express Modem includes modem, fax, and voice capabilities. Until now, its top speed was 14.4Kbps, but a software upgrade, expected in the summer of 1996, would increase the Express Modem's top speed to 28.8Kbps.

The Express Modem requires another piece of system software, the Apple Telecom Manager, as well as the GeoPort Telecom Adapter connected to the Modem port. The Express Modem works with any communications software that works with a hardware modem, including online service software such as America Online, terminal emulators such as ZTerm, and data software such as Apple Remote Access and Farallon Timbuktu. It also works with telephony software such as Cypress Research Megaphone. In your communication software, you simply select Express Modem, as you would any other modem, in the Modem field of the setup window.

Because the Express Modem is an application, it takes some of the Mac's memory. To save about 500K of System **RAM**, turn off the Express Modem when you aren't using it. You can do this in the Express Modem control panel.

You can still use a hardware modem even if you have the Express Modem installed. If the Express Modem control panel detects a GeoPort Telecom Adapter connected to the Modem port, the Express Modem software will process the serial communications before transmitting them through the serial port to the GeoPort Telecom Adapter. If Express Modem doesn't detect a GeoPort Adapter, it does not process serial communication, and lets it pass through the modem port so that a hardware modem can process it. If you want to use the Express Modem and the GeoPort Telecom Adapter, you should select the Modem Port in your communications software.

The Express Modem can receive voice, fax, and data calls and differentiate between them by listening to the calling tone that the calling modem sends. Although most fax machines send a calling tone and are therefore easily identified, not all modems send tones for data or voice. Use the Express Modem control panel to set a default answer mode for voice and data calls. For instance, you would set the default to voice if you were using a voice telephony application (such as MegaPhone). You would set the default to data if you were expecting to receive a data call using a program such as Apple Remote Access server.

See Also

GeoPort; ISDN; Modems

Extended Double-Click Text Selection

When you **double-click** a word, only that word is highlighted. However, it is possible to extend the selected area to include surrounding text by holding down the **mouse** button after double-clicking a word. After the second click, hold the mouse button down. Now drag the mouse to extend the highlighted area in the direction you want.

See Also

Double-Click; Mouse

Extensions (Disabled) Folder

The Extensions (Disabled) **folder** in your **System Folder** stores any **extension(s)** that you turned off (disabled) using the Extensions Manager. When you turn off an extension, the Extensions Manager puts that extension in the Extensions (Disabled) folder. To enable an extension that resides in the Extensions (Disabled) folder, **highlight** the extension's name in the Extension Manager and **restart** your Mac.

See Also

Extensions Manager Control Panel; Highlight Restart; System Folder

Extensions Folder

This **folder**, located in your **System Folder**, contains any system extensions that are loaded during **startup**. It also contains any **printer drivers** to be loaded, as well as network drivers. Extensions are used to customize and actually extend the capabilities of the Macintosh (henceforth the name: Extensions). They are designed to perform their designated task without any input from the user, whereas **control panels** enable the user to set preferences for different control panel tasks. The Extensions folder helps users better organize their System Folder by separating the control panels and extensions into separate folders.

See Also

Control Panels; Printer Drivers; Startup; System Folder

Extensions Manager Control Panel

This **control panel** enables you to decide which control panels, **extensions**, and **startup documents** load the next time your Macintosh restarts. Because many system conflicts and crashes can be traced to incompatible control panels and extensions, the ability to control, or isolate, the loading of individual extensions can be a great help.

The Extensions Manager Control Panel can also create sets of extensions for different users (see the following figure). If, for example, one user is using the Mac solely for word processing, having extensions like **QuickTime Musical Instruments** and **ColorSync** may be unnecessary and take up memory. So, that user may want to create a set of extensions for himself. However, if another user needs a lot of graphics software, they may need QuickTime, ColorSync, and other extensions to be loaded. Using the Extensions Manager, they can create a set of extensions for themselves. You have the option of displaying the Extension Manager at startup, to select the set you want to load, by holding the spacebar during startup process.

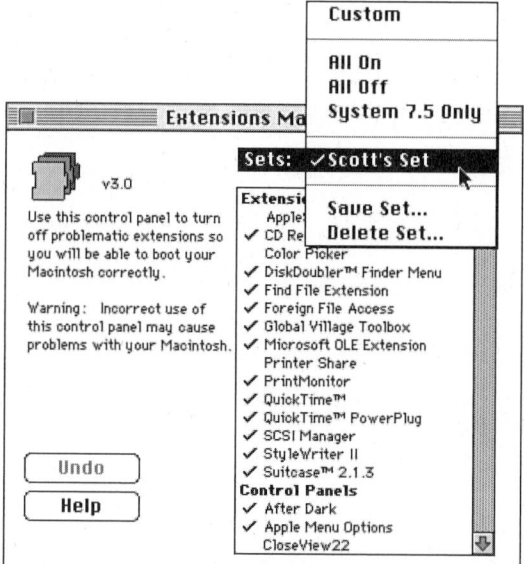

There are a number of options in the Extensions Manager, which are accessed through a pop-up menu at the top of the dialog box. You can create and save custom sets of extensions to load at **startup** and add these sets to the pop-up menu by choosing "Save Set" from this menu. You can delete sets by choosing "Delete Set." From this pop-up menu you can also choose to turn on or off all extensions, or you can choose to load just the System 7.5 extensions.

To use the Extensions Manger Control Panel, follow these steps:

1. Choose Extensions Manager from the Control Panels submenu on the Apple menu (or System Folder).

2. A list of the current set of extensions appears. Extensions, control panels, and startup items that are loading appear highlighted. To disable an extension or control, click the highlighted item. When you're done, close the Extensions manager and **restart** your computer.

3. To choose a different set of extensions than the one displayed, select a different set from the pop-up menu. From this pop-up menu you can also delete and create new sets of extensions based on the current selections in the window.

4. To create your own custom set of extensions, click the extension you want to be part of your set and choose Save Set from the pop-up menu. You'll be prompted with a dialog box asking you to name this new set. Enter a name and click OK to have your new set added to the Extension Manager's pop-up menu.

See Also

ColorSync; Control Panels; Extensions Folder; QuickTime; Restart; Startup; Startup Items Folder

Extreme 3D

Macromedia's Extreme 3D splits the working tools between an extensive toolbox and a selection of menu options and dialogs. This is done so that the interface remains uncluttered and as large as possible. One of the best features of Extreme 3D's interface is that a help line appears to explain anything the mouse passes over in the toolbox or in the menu selections. This is a great aid in learning to use and mastering the software. The toolbox itself separates the tools into three main groups: basic Tools, Object Manipulation Tools, and Object Primitives, with a few non-categorizable tools thrown in for good measure. Many of the tools also feature pop-out options, and many have associated parameter setting dialogs when double-clicked on.

Modeling Tools All of the modeling tools in the toolbox operate on the editing screen. Extrude pulls selected objects along a linear path, Cone builds simple cones by allowing you to set the base dimensions and the altitude, Sweep pulls objects along a drawn path, Lathe turns objects on an axis, Twist contorts objects on any axis, and the Skin Tool builds solids by creating volumes between and among selected planar polygons. The most professional and useful modeling tool of Extreme 3D is the ability to sculpt 3D objects by moving and twisting an object's points. This gives you the capacity to move Béziers in 3D, and the feel is like sculpting in virtual space.

Boolean Operations Extreme 3D offers no Boolean operators.

Texture Mapping Extreme 3D comes with a selection of texture Libraries on board: Chrome and Glass, Marble, Metal, Organic, Plastic, Solid, and Tiles. Given that each texture (material) can be altered or customized, the basic sets open out to many more variable choices. The textures are written to the object by an "Apply" command, and are not drag-and-drop oriented. An Objects dialog gives you a measure of control over texture mapping and other information and tile placement.

Lights Omni, Spotlight, and Distant Lights can be selected for color and shadow casting. An interactive directional control allows you to see the effects of light direction changes instantly in the scene preview rendering.

Rendering Renderings can take place on the screen or to a file. You can set adaptive or uniform smoothing and other rendering parameters in the Final Render setup dialog. Objects can be set to display double faces, so that rendering will occur no matter the angle of the objects involved (or if you fly through them). Rendering over networks is supported as well.

Included Libraries Extreme 3D is accompanied by a CD-ROM with extra texture and object libraries. Because all of the textures can edited or customized

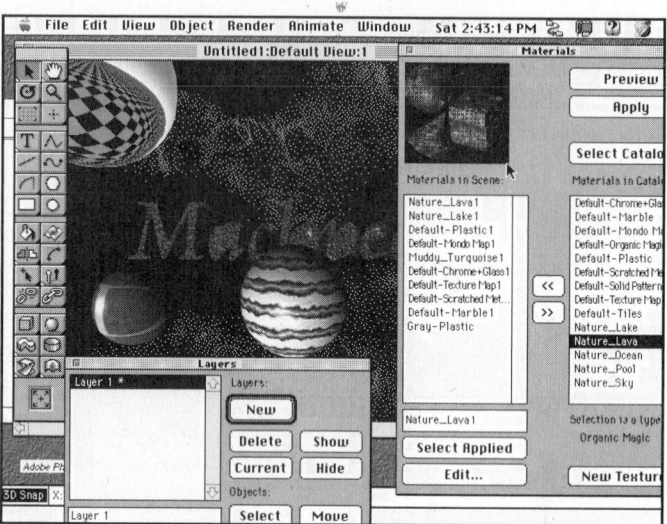

on every parameter, the amount of final items in any Extreme 3D library can be multiplied infinitely.

Animation Extreme 3D's toolbox features child-parent linking options that the animator will find quite useful for their accessibility and command sets. Child objects can be set to move only when a parent object moves or as constrained links. If your Extreme 3D animations feature things like orbiting objects around other elements or humanoid figures, object linking is extremely important. The animation script is called a "score," and the score can determine when anything—from objects to textures to surfaces—moves and what quality that movement will contain. All elements of a scene can be listed, and the scripting dialog allows you to set the total length of the animation as well as its qualities. The time of the movie can be scaled, and Eases In/Out can be applied. As the animation is being constructed, wireframe previews can be generated to check the design. Animations can be recorded to play start to finish, start to finish and then returning (ping-ponging), or start to finish in a continuing loop. A VCR-like controller is available to check the settings at each step.

Other Special Features Extreme 3D comes with a CD-ROM that shows off the animated work possible to achieve, a movie complete with movement and sound. Extreme 3D is geared to the multimedia producer/animator.

File Load/Save Conventions Aside from saving and loading its own Project Files, Extreme 3D can import Draw PICT, EPSF, DXF, 3DGF, 3D Script, Swivel 3D, Extreme 3D Tracks, and Freehand 5.x. Export formats include Draw PICT, Paint PICT, DXF, Swivel 3D, and Extreme 3D Tracks.

Extruding, *See Modeling*

Eye Candy

This AlienSkin Software packages adds some wide ranging functions to Photoshop, or to any other software that supports Photoshop plug-in filters. AlienSkin's other plug-in collection, the BlackBox Filters, focused primarily on effects that addressed areas that Photoshop's own filters didn't include. Eye Candy adds filters that are more esoteric and unusual, but computer artists will find this set as useful and full of creative potential as AlienSkin's other release.

Eye Candy includes:

- Antimatter—This filter inverts just the brightness of the image, leaving Hue and Saturation unchanged. This is somewhat similar to the photographic negative effect achieved by simply using the Invert command in Photoshop. Antimatter, however, does not alter the actual color of the image. Antimatter will change a bright red pixel to dark red rather than dark cyan, and so might be considered a specialized inversion tool.

- Polygon—Photoshop is great for creating organic airbrushed shapes, but it cannot make user-designed symmetric geometric objects. The only other way to create an equilateral triangle in Photoshop is to use

Illustrator and then import it, a rather time consuming method. Polygon generates regular polygons and stars with user definable input on number of points and radial dimensions. The Polygon filter can accomplish gradient shading in the shape (using the Fill Color menu in the lower-right of the Polygon dialog).

- Squint—This filter performs a special type of blurring that creates the characteristic halo caused by watery eyes. It can be used as an alternate effect, with different results from the blurring functions in Photoshop and other software.

- Warpo—This filter performs a variety of different types of random image warping, from shattered edge displacement to abstracted effects. A large range of image stretching results can be achieved, with renderings that emulate complex vibrations, bubbles and earthquakes.

- Fire—This filter will generate very realistic flames based upon items in a preset menu and variable sliders that address the direction and intensity of the effects.

- Smoke—This filter will generate very realistic smoke, from whispy tendrils to billowing clouds. A list of presets is included.

- Fur—This filter will be one of the most used in the set, representing an effect demanded by the majority of computer artists. It will change each pixel from the original image into a hair in a fur coat, and responds to user customization.

- Water Drops—This filter generates extremely realistic and randomly placed water drops on top of the image. It can be used to show everything from condensation on glasses to leaves after a storm.

Eyewitness

There are several titles in the *Eyewitness* CD-ROM series from DK (Dorling Kindersley). These multimedia reference guides cover Nature, Science, and World History.

We can only hope that they will produce many more in the series, because these three are marvelous. Although they're most appropriate for ages 10–15, younger and older students can benefit as well. The Science Encyclopedia features careful explanations of everything from trigonometry to the Big Bang theory, along with demonstrations of such phenomena as the physics of sound, the workings of magnetism and gravity, and much more. The universe and the periodic table have their own sections, with demonstrations and complete information.

There are biographies of scientists and mathematicians in the Who's Who section, and a Quiz Master with challenging questions on all aspects of science and math. The Nature Encyclopedia is equally comprehensive, covering animals and plants from prehistoric times up through today's endangered species and how we can help save them. Like the Science volume, the Nature Encyclopedia makes lavish use of **hypertext** references and videos. It also has "sound bites" for most animals—short clips of the sounds each one makes, and a Quiz Master game.

The History Encyclopedia is the most superficial of the three. It gives interesting facts, dates, and an overview of world history, but not much in-depth coverage. What it does exceptionally well, however, is to give a feel for the cultural and sociological context of the times. Such soundclips as Ché Guevarra's letter to his children, balalaika music, and the sounds of the Jazz Age give the student a sense of "being there," of being truly an eyewitness to history.

EZ Drives, *See Backing Up with Removable Cartridge Drives*

F

F Keys

F Keys are **keyboard shortcuts** that perform tasks by using a combination of keystrokes rather than using the **mouse**. For example, to **eject** a disk in the **disk drive**, you can use the FKey combination Shift-⌘-1. This **command** tells the disk drive to eject the disk. A popular F Key shortcut is Shift-⌘-3, which takes a screen shot (or screen capture) of whatever currently is on your screen and saves it to your **startup** disk as Picture 1 (if there isn't already a picture with that name). The screen capture can be viewed in **SimpleText**, or it can be edited in most graphics programs that can open a PICT image.

Shortcut Keys on the Mac

Key	Standard Action
F1	Undo previous action
F2	Cut highlighted item
F3	Copy highlighted item to Clipboard
F4	Paste Clipboard item where cursor is
Shift-⌘-1	Eject Disk
Shift-⌘-3	Screen shot of open screen taken
Option-⌘	Rebuild the desktop while starting
⌘-N	New Folder
⌘-.	Stop/Escape

Key	Standard Action
⌘-M	Make Alias
⌘-Y	Eject Disk
⌘-W	Close Window

Contrary to popular belief, F Keys are not the keys that appear on the top of an **extended keyboard** as F1, F2, and so on. Those are called Function keys. The first four keys have commands assigned to them: F1=**Undo**, F2=**Cut**, F3=**Copy**, and F4=**Paste**. The rest are blank and can be assigned keystrokes with a program such as QuickKeys or any application, such as Adobe Photoshop, that enables you to assign function keys to commands from within the application.

See Also

Command Key; Copy Command; Cut Command; Disk Drive; Eject Disk Command; Extended Keyboard; Keyboard Shortcuts; Mouse; Paste; Startup; SimpleText

F/A-18 Hornet

The graphics in F/A-18 Hornet are so complete in this new version, that you can actually see blades of grass as you soar through the air. This best-selling high tech military jet flight simulator offers twenty-eight missions of flight and multiple viewing options so you can set an arcade-ish or more realistic cockpit view.

A big plus for F/A-18 is that it takes into account that not everyone is already a flight sim pro and includes beginner settings so you can gradually take on more responsibility as you play. F/A-18 comes fully equipped for combat with a complex radar system, four air to air and two air to ground modes. The Korean Crisis Theatre Set adds another 28 missions with enhanced terrain detail. Network capabilities let you dog-fight other players across a **modem** or **online**. F/A-18 also incorporates features such as mission replay with multiple views, support for multiple monitors, and the capability to set the skill level of your enemy to better match your own.

See Also

A-10 Attack!; Absolute Zero; Out of the Sun; Rebel Assault II; Sim Games

FaceSpan

For all its power and flexibility, **AppleScript** has one major failing: it has no built-in support for creating scripts that have any more than a rudimentary interface. FaceSpan, originally known as Frontmost, overcomes this failing with a flourish.

FaceSpan is an **interface builder** for AppleScripts. Using FaceSpan, you can create AppleScript-based applications that feature a full Macintosh interface, including multiple windows, dialogs, menus, and more. You can create your interface by "drawing" it in FaceSpan's visual editor, and you can attach scripts to interface elements (see following figure).

Each interface element can include script handlers that are executed for user interactions such as clicking, selecting, or pointing. The handler script can manipulate other parts of the FaceSpan application, or interact directly with another scriptable application. Adding support for Macintosh drag-and-drop is a simple matter, as is adding customized Balloon Help.

Using this rich set of tools, you can create sophisticated applications that act as custom interfaces to other applications or as a client interface for database servers. FaceSpan is a great way for programmers to create quick application prototypes to test user interface ideas.

FaceSpan projects can be saved as stand-alone applications that look and act like applications written in C or Pascal. FaceSpan applications (as well as the FaceSpan extension upon which they rely) can be redistributed royalty-free.

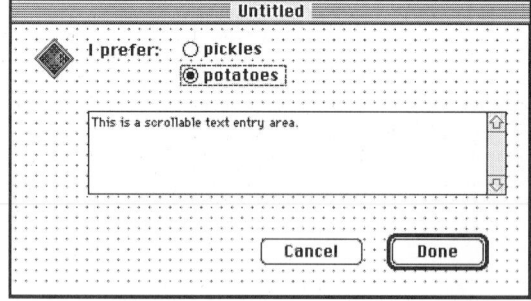

FaceSpan is published by:

> Software Designs Unlimited
> Email: **facespan.sales@sdu.com**
> Fax: (919) 968-4576
> Phone: (800) FACESPAN or
> (919) 968-7251
> Web: **http://www.sdu.com/**

See Also

AppleScript; Frontier; Interface Builder; Scripting

Fair Use

A legal doctrine by which courts can avoid rigid application of copyright law when a work is reproduced for purposes of comment, criticism, news reporting, teaching scholarship, or research. There is a lot of gray area, but to decide whether it's fair use, courts are likely to look at the purpose and character of the use, the nature of the copyrighted work, the amount and substantiality of the portion used, and the economic effect on the author. Fair use is especially relevant to material published on the **Internet**, which can be copied easily despite being protected by **copyright** law.

See Also

Copyright; Intellectual Property; Internet

Family Entertainment

For the most part, when you get away from **education/reference** software and "edutainment," there isn't much out there that appeals to kids and parents alike. Titles like Day of the Tentacle and Sam and Max Hit the Road are non-violent, but when it comes to gameplay, they're not something a younger kid can really tackle without parental help. Just recently, a flock of foreign titles including Great Britain's **Foul Play** and Japan's **Yellow Brick Road I & II** (see the following figure) have added to projects by Philips Interactive and LucasArts' attempts at non-violent, non-educational entertainment that can actually appeal to children without forcing learning down their throats.

One way to justify investing in a family computer has always been that you could learn a lot. There is no question that the extensive resources on the Internet and the multimedia reference titles available are a great reason to get into computing, but who decided that only adults were allowed to play games? The controversy over violence in games, whether or not you want your children blowing things away and wading through dead bodies in games like Blood Bath and **Marathon**, really comes from the fact that most games aren't geared for young audiences. LucasArts' Mortimer (see the following figure) and Philips' Masterpiece Mansion operate on the principle that kids learn by playing.

United States-based companies still seem to be integrating learning into their games on the whole, but in a more fun fashion. However, games like Foul Play and Yellow Brick Road II show that children's titles and family entertainment can be fun without a heavy emphasis on education.

See Also

Are You Afraid of the Dark?; Foul Play; Masterpiece Mansion; Mortimer; Yellow Brick Road II

However, there are some things that you can do with a fax modem that you can't do with a paper fax machine. For one, fax modems yield better quality than do paper fax machines in both sending and receiving. In addition, some fax modems come with optical character recognition (OCR) software, which turns the pictures of characters of a received fax into editable text (you can also buy OCR software). Because the quality of the received fax is good, you'll get fewer OCR errors by converting a fax received electronically than with a paper fax that you have to scan.

The speed at which the modem can transmit faxes varies, but is usually slower than the data speed. Fax modems that support the V.17 standard can transmit faxes at 14,400Bps.

Sending a fax is as easy as printing with most fax software. To fax a document, you usually hold down a key and pull down the File menu of an application. In place of the usual Print command you'll see a Fax command. Choosing it invokes the fax software.

FAQ

Acronym for Frequently Asked Questions, a ubiquitous feature on the **Internet**, usually in file form. Used to present basic information about virtually any topic, from software to **newsgroups** to **Web sites**.

See Also

Internet; Newsgroups; Web Page

Fax Capability in Modems

A modem's capability to fax is a useful tool for desktop users and PowerBook users staying in strange hotel rooms. Just how useful depends on the modem—some fax modems can only send faxes, while others can send and receive.

To completely replace a traditional paper fax machine, you'll need a send-and-receive fax modem and a scanner. You need the scanner to fax material that doesn't originate in electronic form, such as contracts, receipts, or maps. You first have to scan the paper to get it in an electronic format before you fax it, a two-step process. Because of this, a fax modem is not always superior to a traditional facsimile machine.

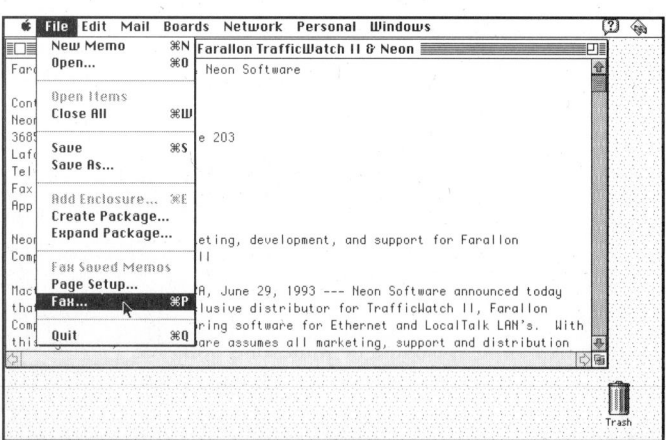

See Also

Modems

Fax Extension

This extension is part of Apple's GeoPort Express Modem Software and enables you to send and receive faxes from Power Macs and AV Macs using Apple's GeoPort feature. The GeoPort feature enables you, through a special adapter, to connect a phone line to your Power Mac or AV Mac. The Fax extension enables you to send and receive faxes through the built-in telecommunications capabilities of your computer, without the use of an external modem.

See Also

AV Macintosh; Modems

Fax Server, *See Fax Server Capabilities in Modems*

Fiber Channel, *See Ports, Future Trends*

File Assistant Extension

This extension, included with System 7.5 and higher, enables PowerBook users to update files on their desktop Mac through a process called file synchronization.. By connecting your PowerBook to your desktop Mac, or through a network connection, the File Assistant extension checks the files on the desktop Mac, and, if the corresponding files on the PowerBook have been updated, it updates the desktop Mac's files.

See Also

Networking; PowerBook

File, Determining Whether It Is Locked

To see if a file is **locked** (meaning it can't be deleted or have its contents edited) you can select the file and choose **Get Info** (Command-I) from the File menu to see if the "Locked" checkbox is checked, but there's a shortcut that saves you a trip to the Get Info box. Click the name of the file (below the icon). If the arrow pointer changes to the I-Beam cursor (enabling you to enter a new name), it's unlocked. But if the arrow pointer stays, the file is locked.

See Also

Get Info Command; Locking a File

File Formats, *See File Types, Internet*

File Is in Use Message

If you try to delete a file being used by the system or by an application by emptying the Trash, a message box alerts you that, "The file cannot be erased because the file is in use." This protects your system and important application files currently in use. If you want to delete the file, quit the application, and the file can be deleted. System files on the startup disk, such as the Finder file and System file, cannot be deleted and will display this message. Also, any file that is open, such as a document open in an application, cannot be deleted, and if you put the file in the Trash and choose Empty Trash, you'll get the alert box stating, "The file cannot be erased because the file is in use." This is to protect you from deleting important or unsaved files.

To delete a file that is in use (besides Finder or System files on a startup disk), you can close the open file and then delete the file by placing it in the Trash and choosing Empty Trash.

See Also

Customizing; Extensions Folder; Extensions Manager Control Panel; QuickTime; Restart; Startup Sequence; System 7

File Is Locked Message

If you try to delete a locked file by emptying the **Trash**, you get an **alert box** stating, "The Trash cannot be emptied because it contains items that are **locked**." Files are locked to keep them from being accidentally deleted. This alert box tells you a locked file is in the Trash.

If you want to delete a file in the Trash that is locked, you have two options: you can hold the Option key while choosing Empty Trash from the Special menu to delete the file, or you can open the Trash, select the file, and choose Get Info from the File menu (⌘-I).

In the Get Info window, uncheck the option marked "Locked" in the lower-left corner (unlocking the file) and close the Get Info window. You can then choose Empty Trash and the file will be deleted.

See Also

Alert Box; Locking a File; Trash

FileMaker Pro

Getting Started There are two ways to set up a new database in FileMaker Pro. The first, and easiest, is to use an existing template. When you select New from the File menu, you'll be given a choice of creating a new "empty" file or creating a file from a template. You'll see a scrolling list of the 44 different templates that are supplied with the application. There's also a button in this dialog box that opens up a database of information about the templates, including suggestions on how to use and customize them.

If, after reviewing the templates, you decide that none comes close to what you want to accomplish, you'll have to start from scratch. When you create a new file, you begin by defining the fields for the basic record. Each bit of information you want to enter needs a field. To simplify entry, designate the kind of field: text, date, calculation, and so forth. The figure shows an entry in a pet owner's database.

Keep all the information about your pet in one place. When you're done defining fields, click Done and you'll see a very basic layout of your new record. Select Layout from the Mode menu to customize it. You can make the text fields as big as they need to be by dragging a corner of the text box. You can reposition them on the page, add colors and patterns to the background, change the fonts and size of the label type, and paste in graphics from other programs. When you have the record form laid out the way you want it, exit the layout mode and return to browse mode to enter your data.

Using your database requires that you be able to get information out of it, too. Decide what format the output needs to be in, and use the layout mode to design the appropriate pages. The pet owner database above includes a page of information for the pet sitter or boarding kennel, with owner's name and feeding instructions as well as the immunization records. It also includes a page called "Lost Pet" which uses the photo, name, and breed from this record, plus the owner's phone number to make an instant poster when one of his animals goes AWOL. Each of these is a separate layout page. To create a different layout for your data, in layout mode, choose New Layout from the Mode menu. Discard the fields from your record that aren't needed in that layout, and add whatever else is needed. The Layout palette functions much like a Paint palette. You can draw boxes, add lines, add colored and patterned backgrounds to cards, add text, or paste in graphics from some other source.

Claris FileMaker Pro is everything a good program should be. It's powerful, versatile, easy to master, and has an excellent Help system for beginners. The current version, FileMaker Pro 3.0, has added new features that make it even more desirable. The most important of these is the capability to function as a relational database. Admittedly, it does so with less elegance than 4th Dimension, using a dialog box rather than the graphical mapping. However, it does support both one-to-one and one-to-many links.

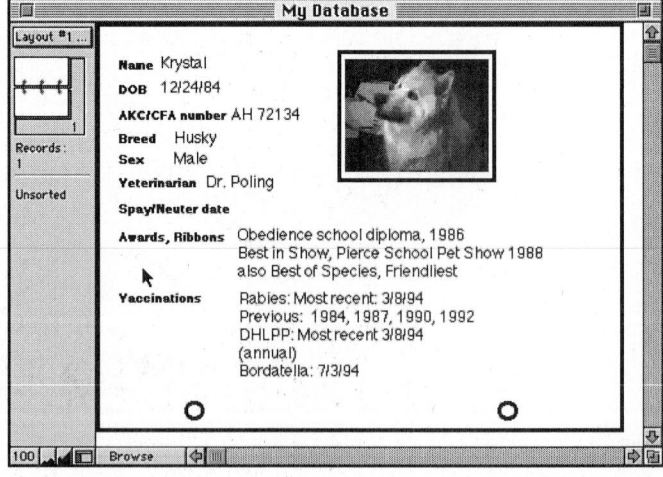

For beginners, the best news is the package of templates provided on the FileMaker Pro CD-ROM. Small business owners can adapt the 23 business templates to handle virtually all of the paperwork necessary to manage most kinds of businesses. The asset management form, for instance, accepts all the data on your office equipment, and reports on inventory and depreciation. You can look at a list to see who's due for a new desk, or how many years until your computer system's "off the books." The time card form can be tied to the personnel form, to keep track of sick days and vacation days, and can also relate to the payroll so checks issued reflect hours actually worked. And all of these forms can be pulled apart and reassembled in the layout view so that you can personalize them to suit your own business.

Teachers and school administrators can select from eight different templates for field trip forms, student records, equipment loan forms, and lots more. Around the house, FileMaker Pro can help keep track of recipes, collections, your film and video library, records and CDs, and even your family medical records, budget, and checking account. One template maintains a list of the bottles in your wine cellar. Another sets up a wedding and party planner that keeps track of the guest list, RSVPs, and gifts received, and even reminds you to send a thank you note. With a few minor modifications, you could create a report to print place cards for the dinner, envelopes for all the invitations and thank yous, and even keep the menu and guests cross-referenced so you wouldn't serve the same meal twice to the same people.

More advanced users can use AppleScript with FileMaker Pro to put their databases on the World Wide Web. Your business could serve customers via the Web by creating a catalogue of products using the Product brochure template, and posting it for browsing on your Web site. Customers would have your FileMaker Pro order form as a template, and could fill it in on-line and send orders back to you as data to be automatically entered into your FileMaker Pro merchandise handling, billing, and shipping files.

FileMaker Pro isn't the most powerful database program you can buy. That distinction probably belongs to 4th Dimension or possibly to Oracle or Helix Express. But it's the most readily useable.

Exporting Data Your FileMaker Pro files contain lots of information that could be useful to you in other applications. For instance, you might have a file that contains your company's sales figures by region, for the past several years. You can export this data into a charting program like Claris Impact or into a desktop presentation program and use it to prepare graphs and charts for your stockholders meeting. By exporting the data directly from FileMaker Pro, you guarantee its accuracy and save the time you'd otherwise have to spend typing it in and proofreading it.

Small amounts of data can most easily be transferred by simply using the Copy and Paste commands on the Edit menu, or by using the System 7 "drag-and-drop" editing. Larger amounts will be more easily transferred by exporting them in a format that another application can use. When you select Export from the file menu, you'll see a familiar Macintosh "Save as…" dialog box that lets you choose a destination for your file. There's also a pop-up menu in the box, as shown in the following figure, with a listing of possible file formats. If you're exporting data to another FileMaker Pro file, select FileMaker Pro. Most other applications can handle tab-separated text, and comma-separated text.

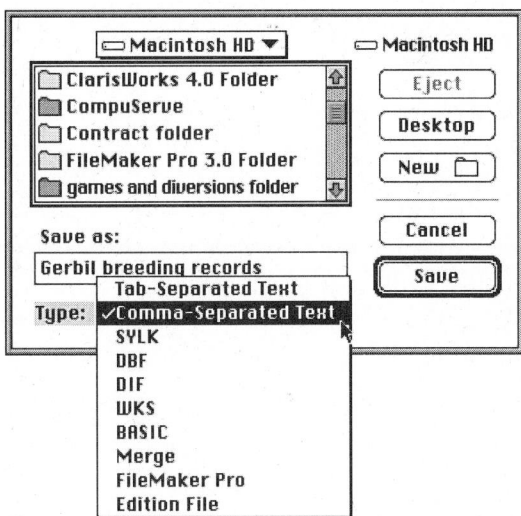

The SYLK format is used to exchange data with spreadsheet applications like Microsoft Excel. Other spreadsheet programs, notably VisiCalc for PC/Windows, use the DIF format. Lotus 1-2-3 likes the WKS format. Use Merge if you are exporting names and addresses to MacWrite Pro in order to create personalized form letters. If you're exporting the mailing list to another word processor such as Microsoft Word or WriteNow, check to see which file formats it supports. (These both accept tab-separated text.)

Importing Data If you have information in another database or in a different type of file, you can import it into FileMaker Pro and avoid having to re-enter it. Data may be imported into a new file or an existing one.

Small amounts of data can most easily be transferred by simply using the Copy and Paste commands on the Edit menu, or by using the System 7 "drag-and-drop" editing to move data from one file to another. If another application you're using, like ClarisWorks or Microsoft Word, supports "drag-and-drop" editing, you can drag data from an open FileMaker Pro file into an open Word or Works document. Drag and drop works in Browse, Layout, and Find modes, though not in Preview. In Layout mode, use "drag and drop" to transfer graphics or text. In Browse mode, use it to move text or the contents of the container field, to another field. Remember, though, that you can't put data into an application or field that doesn't support it. You can't drop a graphic into a text field or into a calculation field. If you drag the contents of a calculation field into a text field, you'll be able to read the numbers but not calculate them.

If you're importing larger amounts of data, use the Import command on the File menu. The file that you're importing from must be in one of the file formats that FileMaker Pro supports. These include tab or comma separated text, SYLK, DIF, WKS, and BASIC as well as other FileMaker Pro or ClarisWorks files. (To use ClarisWorks files, the FileMaker extensions folder must be installed in the FileMaker Pro application folder.) You also have to choose whether the data you're bringing in adds to or replaces the existing data in the file. The Add New records option will add the new data at the end of the current file.

The Replace data option removes the records in the file and substitutes the incoming data.

You can import selectively, by using the Import field Mapping dialog box shown in the figure.

The arrows indicate fields that will be imported. Dashes will be ignored. Adjust as needed by clicking the arrows to turn off fields you don't want to import.

To import data into a new file with a standard layout, select the file to import in the Open File dialog box and click Open. In the Name Converted File box, name your new file and click Save. FileMaker Pro automatically creates a text field (called fx) for each field in the new file. If you're importing from another format that contains field names, they'll be used instead of the fx designation.

See Also
Databases, Relational

File Menu

The File menu, which appears at the **desktop level** and as the first **menu** in any application, enables you to open, close, save, and print documents, as well as create new ones. The File menu also provides access to many application-specific commands.

At the Desktop level, the File menu does the following:

- Provides access to the **Get Info** window for any selected file (⌘-I)

- Enables you to invoke **Sharing** of files across a **network**

- Enables you to make **duplicates** of files (⌘-D)

- Enables you to make **aliases** of files (⌘-M)

- Provides access to the **Put Away** (⌘-Y) command for **ejecting disks** or putting recently moved files back in their original location

The File menu at the desktop also contains the built-in **Find file** (⌘-F) functions of the **System,** as well as access to the **Page Setup** and **Print dialog boxes**.

Within an application, the File menu enables you to do the following:

- Create a new document

- Open or close a document

- Save a document

- Use the Save As command on any document

- Use a variety of custom commands depending on the application

Printing dialog boxes appear under the File menu in applications. All Macintosh applications list the Quit command as the last entry at the bottom of the File menu.

See Also
Desktop; Duplicate Command; Eject Disk Command; Find File; Make Alias Command; Menu; Printing; Put Away Command; Sharing Files

Filename Extensions
A three-letter code at the end of a filename that indicates what sort of file it is. Essential in non-Macintosh environments such as the **Internet** where client software often lacks icons or other methods of identifying files. A **World Wide Web browser**, for instance, can be set up to the recognize filename extensions of files it encounters so that it can perform specific ac-

tions on them, such as opening them with a **helper application** or saving them to disk.

Some common filename extensions are listed in the following table.

Filename Extensions and File Types

Extension	File Type
Encoding Formats	
.hqx	BinHex 4.0 encoded document
.uu	uucode
Compression Formats	
.sit	StuffIt compressed document
.cpt	Compact Pro compressed document
.sea	Self-extracting archive
.Z	Compress (UNIX)
.tar	tape archive (UNIX)
.dd	DiskDoubler
.x	SuperDisk
.pit	PackIt
.zip	PKZip (Windows, DOS)
.gz	Gnu ZIP
Text Files	
.txt	ASCII text file
.html	HyperText Markup Language document
.rtf	Rich Text Format file
.etx	setext
Graphics Files	
.gif	Graphics Interchange Format
.jpeg	Joint Photographic Experts Group
.eps	Encapsulated PostScript
.tiff	Tagged Interchange File Format
.pict	PICT
.bmp	bitmap (Windows)

continues

Filename Extensions and File Types (continued)

Extension	File Type
Sound and Video Files	
.au	Ulaw (UNIX)
.aiff	Audio Interchange File Format
.ra	RealAudio
.mpeg	Motion Picture Experts Group
Other Files	
.pdf	Portable document format (Adobe)
.ps	PostScript

See Also

Helper Application; Internet; Server; World Wide Web Browser

File Server, *See Servers*

File Sharing Extension

This extension is part of Apple's file sharing technology and is loaded into the system at startup. The file sharing extension contains part of the code used by the system for file sharing. If you're going to be using file sharing, leave this extension in your System Folder.

See Also

Extensions Folder; Sharing Files; System Folder

File Sharing Icon

If **file sharing** is activated and your computer is shared on a network, the **shared folder** icon on your **desktop** will have a small darkened tab added to the top of the folder's icon with network cables attached to the folder. This tells you that File Sharing is turned on.

See Also

Desktop; File Server; Networking; Sharing Files; Sharing Folders

File Sharing Monitor

When file sharing is active, you want to see who is connected to your computer through the File Shar-ing Monitor Control panel. When you open the File Sharing Monitor, a window displays the users connected to your computer in the right window and the items that are being shared under Shared Items in the left window. A bar graph below these windows shows the amount of file sharing activity that goes from idle at the far left to busy at the far right side of the graph. You can disconnect users from your system from this **control panel** and choose how much time elapses before they are disconnected. When you type in a number, users accessing your computer receive an on-screen dialog box warning them that they will be disconnected soon. This gives them a chance to save changes to their open documents. If you want users disconnected immediately with no warning, type "0" in the Minutes Till Disconnect dialog.

To use the File Sharing Monitor control panel, follow these steps:

1. Choose the File Sharing Monitor from the Control Panels submenu on the Apple menu (or System Folder).

2. A window displays a list of connected users and a list of shared folders and disks.

3. You can disconnect users from your computer by clicking Disconnect and entering the number of minutes before users are disconnected. Users receive a disconnect warning, giving them a chance to save their documents. If you enter "0," they will be disconnected immediately.

See Also

Control Panels; Sharing Files

File Transfer Protocols

The transfer of files between computers using modems is governed by File Transfer Protocols. These protocols manage the actual transmission of the files and reassembly at the remote end. They are normally used when you upload (sending a file to a remote computer) or download (retrieve files from a remote computer). Several different transfer protocols have evolved over time. Each was designed to insure reliability and maximize transmission speed for a particular situation (see the following table).

TIP The term file transfer protocols is used in a different sense than the File Transfer Protocol (FTP) commonly referred to when speaking of the Internet. The Internet's **FTP** refers specifically to the UNIX-based File Transfer Protocol, which is part of the TCP/IP's set of network protocols.

The most basic style of transmission is called a "straight ASCII transfer" or a "Blind Transfer." Essentially this tells the computer to use no protocol at all—it sends files as straight **ASCII** characters as fast as the hardware allows. When transmitting in this fashion, the computer never stops to insure the accuracy or completeness of incoming data. Thus, although fast, this protocol isn't of much use except for the transfer of small files.

More recent protocols have added features such as error correction, but do potentially slow transmission over the theoretical maximum of a blind transmission. Many protocols now support "batch transmission" which allows you to specify multiple files to send and/or receive in advance of the transmission.

The MacBinary protocol is used when transferring Mac files to other Macintosh users. This protocol makes sure that all of the Macintosh specific information, such as Icons and resources, are kept intact. In nearly all file transfers, you'll make use of MacBinary. The only major exception is when you're sending files to DOS/Windows users. In this case, the extra information can make the file unreadable on their machines.

TIP File transfer protocols are used in addition to any error correction protocols and hardware handshaking already negotiated between the local and remote modem. More advanced protocols such as Zmodem take this into account and leave error correction solely to the hardware, speeding the overall transfer by preventing double checking of each piece of information.

If you are using an error correcting modem and the remote computer supports it, Zmodem is the protocol of choice. Zmodem's capability to resume interrupted transfers is extremely useful. In situations where Zmodem isn't available, try Ymodem-G. If you don't have an error correcting modem, use Ymodem or Xmodem-IK.

Generally the remote system will ask for your protocol preference before beginning a file transfer. After telling the remote system what you'd like to use, it will then ask you to begin the transfer. At this point, your computer will begin automatically (with Zmodem) or will issue a command to tell your computer to begin (most other protocols).

See Also
FTP; Modem Transfer Protocols

Protocol Speeds

Protocol	Speed	Error Correction	Comments
ASCII("Blind Transfer")	As fast as the hardware allows	None	Text only.
XModem	Slow	Simple Checksum	Most widely used.
XMODEM-IK	Medium	CRC	Sometimes called Ymodem.
YMODEM	Medium	CRC	Xmodem-IX with batch transfer.
Ymodem-G	Fast	none	Use only with error correcting modem.
ZMODEM	Fast	none	Use only with error correcting modem. Allows canceled download to be restarted.
MacBinary	none	none	Used for Mac-Mac transfers to insure the Mac-specific information is properly transferred.

Common File Formats

Extension	File Type	Software to Process
.aiff	Audio Interchange File Format	Sound App, SoundMachine
.au	Ulaw	UlawPlay
.cpt	Compact Pro	Compact Pro, StuffIt Expander
.dd	DiskDoubler	Disk Doubler, Expand Now
.gif	CompuServe GIF	Web browser, Giffer, JPEG View
.hqx	BinHex	BinHex, StuffIt Expander
.jpeg	Joint Photograhic Experts Group	JPEG View, Web browser
.mpeg	Motion Picture Experts Group	Sparkle
.pdf	Adobe Acrobat	Acrobat Reader
.ps	PostScript	GhostScript
.sea	Self-Extracting Archive	(Double-click to launch file)
.sit	StuffIt	StuffIt Expander
.txt	Text	
.uu	uucode (UNIX)	UULite, StuffIt Deluxe
.Z	Compress (UNIX)	MacCompress, StuffIt Expander
.z, .gz	Gzip (UNIX)	MacGzip
.zip	WinZip (Windows)	Unzip, Zipit, StuffIt Deluxe

File Types, Internet

Users who download software from the **Internet** from **FTP** or other sites will encounter a number of different file types that have been created by any number of different computers using a variety of software.

Each file type can be deduced from the three-letter extension at the end of its filename. The most common on the Internet is the extension ".hqx," which denotes a file encoded with BinHex so that it can be transported easily across the Net.

The above table lists common file type extensions, the software that was used to create that particular file type, and the software needed to process it, if necessary.

See Also

Acrobat Reader, AIFF; AU File; Decoding/Decompressing Files; Encoding Files; File Transfer Protocols; GIF; Helper Applications; JPEG

Fill, Spreadsheet

Most **spreadsheets** let you **paste** the same data or **formula** into a group of adjacent **cells** quickly, by filling. As an example, imagine an expense report with individual expenses entered in **rows** 1-10, and different categories for them in **columns** A-F. We put a formula in A11 that adds up the expenses in that category. To total the other categories, we'd **select** a horizontal line of cells starting with A11 and extending through F11 and choose the Fill Right command, usually ⌘-R. If we wanted to paste the same material into a vertical range of cells, we'd select an area with the desired information in the top cell and choose Fill Down, usually ⌘-D.

Microsoft **Excel** lets you fill by selecting a cell and dragging its boundary to cover the cells to be filled. It also can guess how you'd like a series of cells to be filled: for example, if you select a cell with "January" and extend its boundary, its neighbors will become "February," "March," and so on.

See Also

What-If Calculations

Filmstrip

A file format for editing multiframe movies, filmstrip is supported by Adobe **Premiere**, **Photoshop**, and **After Effects**. **QuickTime** movies are exported from Adobe Premiere (choose Export from the File menu) in the filmstrip format. The file can then be opened within Photoshop and edited. The file appears in Photoshop as a single document containing each image of the video in sequence. The file can be painted and edited just like any other graphics file. This makes it possible to add special effects, draw over video, or add Photoshop effects to QuickTime movie files. The Filmstrip file can then be imported back into Premiere and turned back into a QuickTime movie.

While filmstrip files make it possible to add short special effects or manually fix drop-outs, they are not the best way to create lengthy **rotoscoping** effects. Because the file is uncompressed, it quickly becomes large when exporting long movie segments. You will need a lot of RAM to edit even short segments. Consider using a program like Strata **MediaPaint** if you want to paint on long segments of video.

Final Draft

Final Draft is a **word processor** for screenwriters from MacToolkit.

Screenwriters who want to sell their scripts in Hollywood find that there are so many formatting rules and standards for margins and styles that they can easily get confused. When this happens, the script will usually be tossed aside. Final Draft, from MacToolkit, solves this problem by keeping track of formatting rules, leaving the writer free to be creative.

Final Draft has style sets that can be entered with just one or two keys on the keyboard, so that a writer can go from perfectly set action lines to character names to dialogue instantly. The style sets can also be user defined for your own standards, or can switch back and forth between film and TV formats easily.

Final Draft also has a built-in spell checker and a thesaurus for breaking writer's block. It is fully integrated with **drag-and-drop** editing, and can import and export text to and from any other word processor.

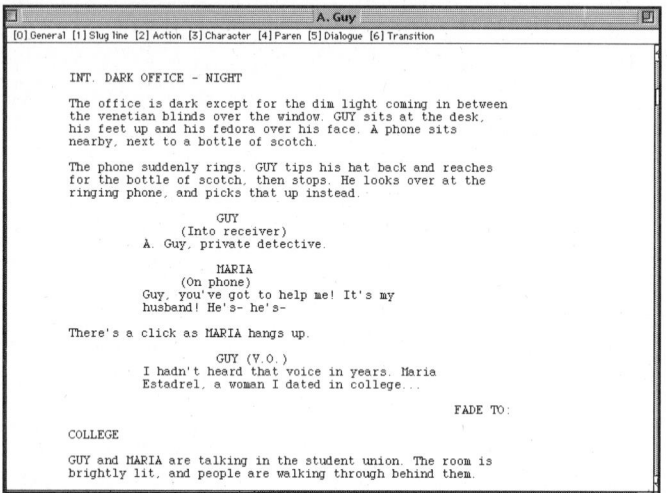

The built-in character list saves time by having Final Draft enter characters names from a user-defined list as soon as the first letters of the name are typed. ScriptNotes also save time by letting users take notes as they write in separate windows that are attached to sections of text. Final Draft then enables you to jump to each ScriptNote and shows the corresponding text, letting the user review comments quickly and easily.

For use by rich producers and starving writers, Final Draft will run on everything from a Macintosh Plus to a Power Mac, and on system 6.0.7 or higher. Final Draft is published by MacToolkit.

See Also
Drag-and-Drop; Word Processing

Finance Programs

If you asked a hundred people what chore they were happiest to have the computer do for them, chances are that at least half would answer "balancing the checkbook." Financial programs run the gamut from fairly simple check writing and checkbook reconciliation programs all the way to full-fledged accounting programs worthy of a CPA

Personal accounting programs are designed to help individuals and families manage their budgets and daily expenses. These programs are designed with a very simple check register-like interface. When you write a check, you enter the amount, the date, and the payee, and you assign it to a category. It might be food, or rent, or utilities, or medical expense, or entertainment. Set up as many categories as you want. The accounting program keeps track of the money you spend in each category, and can easily show you where your paycheck is going. You can print out reports and graphs to show how you're doing this year as compared to last year, or how well you're staying within your budget. Some programs, such as Intuit's **Quicken**, will let you tie into electronic banking facilities, too.

Small business programs are almost as simple to use. These are usually based on a double-entry system of debits and credits. Unlike the traditional bookkeeping systems with journals and ledgers and many items to keep track of, the software makes it easy to record payables and receivables as the bills come in and go out. You can use the same programs to track inventory and to keep the business checkbook up-to-date. These programs will also print invoices, purchase orders, and checks. Some programs will figure payroll deductions and taxes, too. Others will work with a payroll program or tax program, supplying the necessary input, but letting the other software do the specialized calculations. The most popular program at this level is **MYOB** accounting. The initials stand for Mind Your Own Business, and imply, quite correctly, that you don't need to hire an accountant to mind your business for you. With a program this intuitive, you can do it yourself. **Peachtree Accounting** is another modestly-priced and extremely popular package for small business use. In addition to the basic books, it can do Job Costing, Inventory, and Payroll. It also features a Custom Forms design module that will let you produce any kind of paper work your business needs. You can set up whatever kind of system you require to track the paper work, too.

Accounting software for larger businesses can get expensive and complex. The best known high-end accounting package is *Great Plains Accounting* from Great Plains Software. It uses a set of modules that work together (but can be purchased separately) to handle all kinds of transactions and produce all kinds of reports and ledger pages. By the time you've put together a functional accounting and bookkeeping system with Great Plains software, you've spent several thousand dollars and many hours. The Macintosh software is based on the PC version and has an extremely non-Mac-like interface. It's not a good choice for the beginner or for a small business, but given the cost, it's an unlikely choice, too. **Big Business**, from Automatic Software, is a better choice for a young, growing company. It combines sales, inventory, marketing, and finance into one interactive package.

In addition to financial programs, there are some specialized programs to figure your taxes. Intuit's MacInTax helps you fill out those 1040's and state forms correctly, by providing on-screen worksheets and calculating the numbers for you. You'll still have to fill out the forms yourself, but by following the steps in the program, you'll be sure they're done correctly, and that you haven't overlooked helpful deductions.

See Also

Big Business; MYOB; Peachtree Accounting; Quicken

Financial Planning Software

The hardest part of making money in the stock market isn't guessing which stocks to buy. It's keeping track of the ones you've bought and sold, and the purchase price, gain or loss, income—all those details that suddenly become relevant at tax time. You can use financial planning programs such as **Quicken** or *Managing Your Money* to maintain investment accounts (portfolio accounts and mutual fund accounts). They'll help you keep track of what you own in stocks, bonds, mutual funds, and other types of investments that fluctuate in price. Investment accounts are for investors who want to track investment transactions, see the performance of their investments, update current market values, and create tax reports. When you use investment accounts, you can see immediately whether you are making or losing money on each investment, compare the performance of your investments, and report on investment income and capital gains when you need that information to prepare your income taxes.

Investments can be entered in either an asset account or a portfolio account. To track an investment in a portfolio account, you must know the share price and dollar amount for each purchase or sale transaction. If you don't have this information, use an asset account instead. Portfolio accounts can track multiple securities. Mutual Fund accounts track just one mutual fund. If you have investments in several different mutual funds, you'll need to open separate accounts for them.

Although financial planning programs can handle most common investment needs, their investment tracking does have limitations. While programs such as Quicken can provide basic tax reports, they don't keep track of changes in tax laws. Use them to supply the numbers your accountant needs for your tax returns, but don't rely on them to tell you how much you owe.

Find Again Command

This command was used in the **System 7** and **7.1** version of Apple's Find function. When you choose the **Find** command, the first object found in its search appears in an open window. If the found file is not the file you were looking for, you can continue your search by selecting Find Again (⌘-G) from the File menu at the **desktop**. This was designed as a time saver in case you want to continue your search using the same word. Bringing up the Find File dialog box every time when you are continuing the same search is time-consuming and unnecessary.

Because of improvements to the Find File function in **System 7.5**, Find Again is used only to repeat the same entire search cycle again. Find File Again is not as necessary as it once was because the Find File function now displays all matches at once in the Find File window, rather than bringing you each match one by one.

To use Find Again to continue a search, follow these steps:

1. From the File menu, choose Find Again (⌘-G).

2. The search for the file continues using the last word entered in the Find File dialog box.

See Also

Desktop; File Menu; System 7; System 7.1; System 7.5

Find Command

To find any file on your hard drive or on a selected disk, choose Find from the **File menu** at the Desktop (⌘-F). This brings up the Find File dialog box, shown in the following figure.

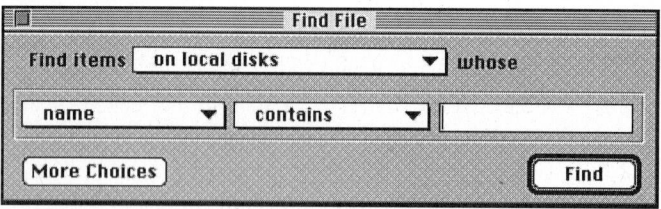

The Find File dialog box offers you a wide range of options for searching for selected files. When the Find File command finds files that match your search criteria, a separate window opens called "Items Found," which lists all the items it encountered, as shown in the following figure.

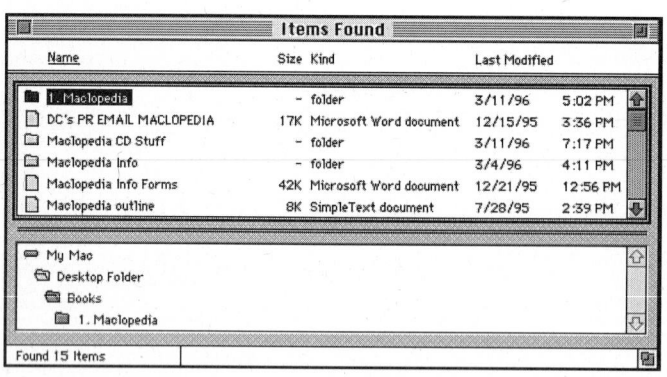

This window shows the filename, size, kind, and modification date to help you decide if it's the file you're looking for. If you click a file in the window, the path to reach that file is displayed in the lower window of the "Items Found" window. It may show, for example, that the file you selected is in your hard drive, inside your applications folder, and is inside a folder called "Utilities." You can then close the dialog box and follow that path to the file in question.

You can also double-click the item in the Find File dialog, and if that document can be open, the program that created it is launched and the file is opened. You can search by: name, size, kind, label, date created, date modified, version, comments, lock attribute, folder attribute, file type, and creator.

If you know the name of the document, a name search might bring you the fastest results. But the other search criteria are helpful as well. If you don't know the name of the file, but remember that it's over 4MB, you can use the Find File command to list all files greater than 4MB. Or you might not remember the name of your file, but if you know you created it last Thursday, you can use the date created search to list all the files created on a particular date. The date modified is excellent if you need to see which files need to be backed-up. There's a lot of flexibility to help you find misplaced files.

When you select a search criteria, such as name or size, the Find File dialog gives you a pull-down menu with options to help you narrow your search. If, for example, you know the name of the file you're looking for contained the word Red, but you don't remember the full filename, you can search for files that contain the word "Red." But if you knew for certain that the file started with the word Red, you can search only for files that start with the word Red. The More Choices button in the Find File dialog enables you to expand your searching capabilities by giving you more choices and more criteria selections with which to search.

After you've decided which search criteria you're going to use to get the fastest, most effective search, you need to decide where you want to search. The Find File dialog enables you to search a particular disk, all disks, or even over a **network** to a **server**.

To find a file, follow these steps:

1. From the File menu, choose Find (⌘-F).

2. When the Find File dialog box appears, enter the search criteria (name, size, and so on) for the file you're looking for, and indicate where you want the Find File command to look for your files.

3. Click Find to begin your search.

4. If the Find comes up with any files that match your criteria, it lists those files in a new window displaying the file's name, size, modification date, and so on. This is the "Items Found" window.

5. To see the path of an individual file, click the filename and the lower window displays the path to the file you've selected. You can also double-click to launch the file.

See Also

Backing Up; Close Command; File Menu; Filename; Hard Disks; Launcher Control Panel; Network Communications; Server

Find Dialog Box

The Find File dialog box offers you options for files. When the Find File command finds files that match your search criteria, a separate window opens called Items Found. It lists all the items it encountered, as shown in the figure. It shows the file name, size, kind, and modification date of the files to help you see if it is the file you're looking for. If you click

a file, the path to reach that file is displayed in the lower half of the Items Found window. It may show, for example, that the file you selected is in a folder called "utilities" inside your applications folder on your hard drive. You can then **close** the dialog box and follow that path to the file in question.

You can also double click the item in the Find File dialog box. This **launches** the program that created the file and opens the file. It's also handy to double-click the folder that contains the file you searched for to see what else is in that folder.

You can search by:

- Name
- Size
- Kind
- Label
- Date created
- Date modified
- Version
- Comments
- Lock attribute
- Folder attribute
- File type
- Creator

See Also

Close Command; Comments, in Get Info Box; Hard Disks; Launching a Program

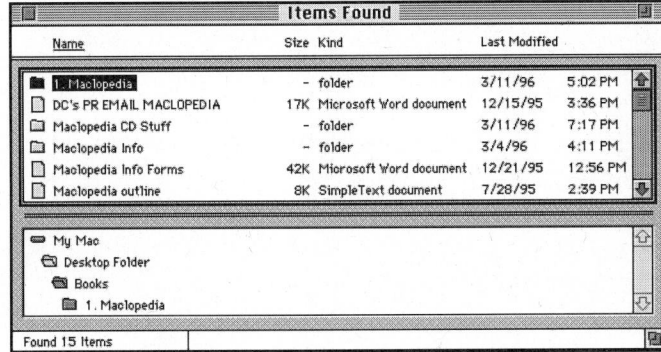

Find File

To find any file on your hard drive or on a selected disk, choose Find File from the **Apple menu**. The Find File dialog box offers you a wide range of options for searching for your selected files. When the Find File command finds files that match your search criteria, a separate window opens called "Items Found" and it lists all the items it encountered. It shows the filename, size, kind, and modification date to help you see whether the file is in fact the one you're looking for. If you click a file, you'll see the path to that file is displayed in the lower window of the "Items Found" window. It may show, for example, that the file you selected is in your hard drive, inside your applications folder, and is inside a folder called Utilities. You can then close the dialog box and follow that path to the file in question.

You can also double-click the item in the Find File dialog and if that document can be opened, it will launch the program that created it and open the file.

You can search by: name, size, kind, label, date created, date modified, version, comments, lock attribute, folder attribute, file type, and creator (see the following figure).

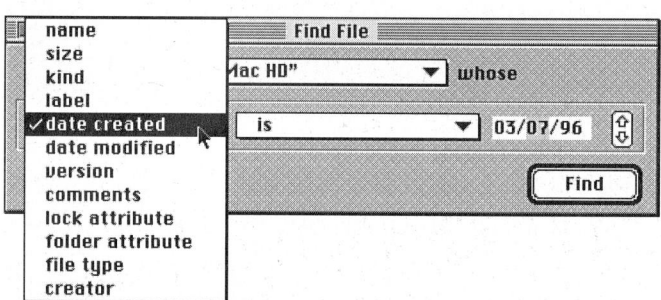

If you know the name of the document, a name search might bring you the fastest results. But the other search criteria are helpful as well. If you don't know the name of the file, but remember that it's over 4MB, you can search for all files greater than 4MB. Or you might not remember the name of your file, but if you knew you created it last Thursday, you can use the date created search to list all the files created on a particular date. The date modified is excellent if you need to see which files need to be **backed-up**. There's a lot of flexibility to help you find misplaced files.

When you select a search criteria, such as name or size, the Find File dialog gives you a pull-down menu with options to help you narrow your search. For example: If you know the name of the file you're looking for contained the word Red, but you didn't remember the full filename, you can search for files that contain the word Red. But if you knew for certain that the file started with the word Red, you can search for files that start with the word Red. You'll see the button "More Choices" in the Find File dialog. This enables you to set more specific details for your search and is helpful in narrowing your search. Each time you click the More Choices button, another layer of choices pops up (until you reach ten lines of criteria for your search). This way, rather than finding every file on your hard disk that starts with the word Red, if you know some details about the missing file, you can narrow your search to the most likely file. If, for example, you knew the file size was small, and you knew you created it on Feb. 11th, and you knew it was a font; you could set a search up that would find only the file's that are: less than 50K (you insert the size), that were created on Feb. 11th, and that are fonts.

After you've decided which search criteria you're going to use to get the fastest, most effective search, you need to decide where you want to search. The Find File dialog enables you to search a particular disk, all disks, or even over a network to a **server**.

To find a file, follow these steps:

1. On the File menu, choose Find (⌘-F).

2. When the Find File dialog box appears, enter the search criteria (name, size, and so on) for the file you're looking for, and indicate where you want the Find File command to look for your file.

3. Click Find to begin your search.

4. If the Find comes up with any files that match your criteria, it will list those files in a new window entitled "Files Found" displaying the filename, size, modification date, and so on.

F

5. To see the path of an individual file, just click the filename and the lower portion of the Files Found window will display the path to the file you've selected. You can also double-click to launch the file (if it's a launchable document).

See Also

Apple Menu; Backing Up; Find File Search Options; Server

Find File Search Options

The **Find File** D/A has **keyboard shortcuts** that enable you to increase or decrease the number of search options displayed in the Find File window. Press ⌘-M to see more options, as shown in the following figure, and ⌘-R to see fewer.

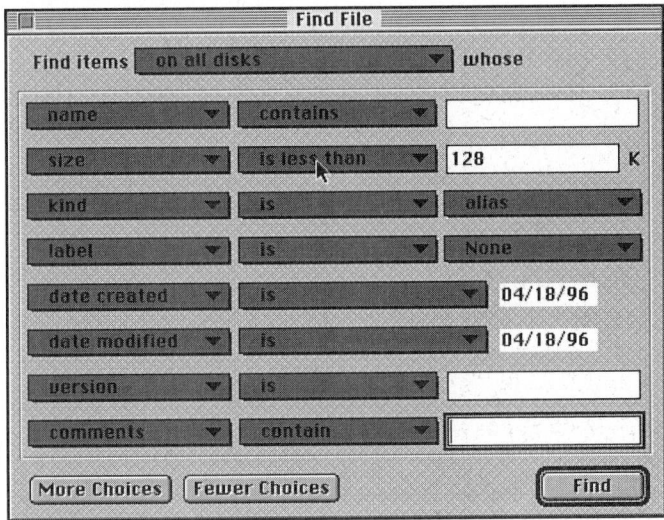

See Also

Find File; Keyboard Shortcuts

Find File Tricks

In Apple's Find File DA, there is a series of find attributes hidden beneath the surface. When you open the Find File dialog box, the first field contains a pop-up menu that lets you search by Name, Size, Kind, Label, Date Created, Date Modified, Version, Comments, Lock Attribute, Folder Attribute, File Type, and Creator. But if you hold the Option key before you select this field, you find four more attributes

have been added to the list: Contents, Name/Icon Lock, Custom Icon, and Visibility.

Probably the most important search criteria added by holding the Option key is the Contents search, which searches your hard disk for items that contain the key word you're searching for as a text item. If, for example, you were writing about Spain but didn't use the name Spain in the title of the document, by using a Contents search, you can search for documents that contain the word Spain.

Searching by Custom Icon brings you a list of files that have had their original icon replaced by a custom icon. This can help you narrow the scope of your search if you know that you either did or did not replace the original application's or document's icon with a custom icon.

The Visibility attribute lets you search for invisible items and is especially helpful for finding invisible files that some applications put in your **System Folder** when you install the program from an installer.

In **System 7.5**, you can drag a file into the third search field (right above the Find button), and the attributes of that file are entered into the find fields. If, for example, you choose a find attribute from the pop-up menu, such as Size, the file's size is already inserted. If you choose Kind, that file's kind appears in the Kind field. This is helpful when searching for a similar file based on that type and/or creator information.

When you do a search with the Find feature, the window that appears with the listing of files that match your search criteria has many of the same features as the Finder. The files in this window can be double-clicked and launched, just as in the **Finder**. You can also click an item on the list and use the **Get Info** command (⌘-I) to see the file's information. To print an item, you can press ⌘-P, and to open an item you can press ⌘-O.

Although the Find File function is greatly enhanced in System 7.5 and higher, you can still access the **System 7** Find File function (which many users are still very fond of) by pressing Command-Shift-F. This will bring up the old Find File dialog box introduced in System 7.

See Also
Find File; Finder; Get Info; System 7; System 7.5; System Folder

Finder

Also known as the desktop, the Finder is located on the Application menu in the upper-right corner of your screen. Selecting the Finder, which is represented by the little computer icon (see the following figure), brings you to the desktop. Whatever is open on your desktop—windows, folders, files, and so on—can now be selected by you.

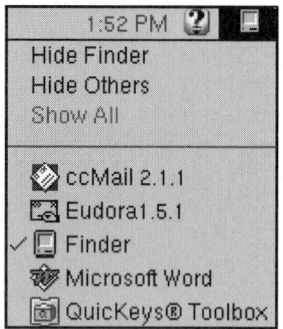

The Finder, in a sense, is your basic starting point. When you select icons or folders on your desktop, this makes the Finder active.

See Also
Finder Shortcuts; Finder Speed Tips

Finder Scripting Extension

This System 7.5 extension adds the capability to use **AppleScript** to automate repetitive tasks at the **Finder**.

See Also
AppleScript; Finder

Finder Shortcuts

There are many keyboard shortcuts available at the Finder. A list of these shortcuts appear on the **Help menu** (the question mark icon, to the left of the **Applications menu** on the far right of the menu bar). When you pull down the help menu at the Finder,

the last item is named Finder Shortcuts. If you select Finder Shortcuts, a dialog box will appear with a brief explanation of the command along with its keyboard shortcut. Many of the commands listed in Finder Shortcuts are hidden commands, meaning they can only be executed through the keyboard, and a menu with the command does not appear anywhere in the Macintosh Operating System. An example would be: **Rebuild Desktop**. There is no pull-down menu for this command, so a keyboard command is used instead, and it is listed in the Finder Shortcuts command.

See Also
Applications Menu; Dialog Box; Help Command; Keyboard Shortcuts; Rebuilding the Desktop

Finder Speed Tips

There are a number of preferences you can set at the **Finder** that can help to speed up your work. The first speed enhancement comes from understanding that everything that appears on your Mac in a window takes time to redraw on the screen, and certain items redraw faster than others. Some of these preferences are controlled from the **Views control panel**.

In the Views control panel, you can select what font you want to use for displaying filenames in the Finder. If you want to have the fastest screen redraw, leave this font at the default choice of Geneva. If you choose a font other than Geneva, it takes slightly longer to display. Another speed enhancement from the View control panel is making sure the "Calculate folder sizes" checkbox is not checked. When you have this feature on, the Mac calculates the size of each folder and displays this info in list view windows. This calculation is memory intensive and tends to slow things down. For folders with a large number of items in them, such as your fonts folder, you have to wait for the calculation to take place, and it can slow redraw down considerably. By unchecking this, the folder still appears in all list views, but the size of the folder is not calculated. Note: If you ever need to know the size of a folder, you can always select the folder and choose Get Info (⌘-I).

Another factor affecting performance is caused by the fact that color objects take longer to redraw than black and white objects. If you switch your monitor setting to black and white in the **Monitors control panel**, for example, you feel an instant jump in speed because the screen redraws more quickly if it doesn't have to use color.

See Also

Finder; Monitors Control Panel; Views Control Panel

Finding Files on the Internet,
See Archie

Finding Out a Device's SCSI ID Number

If you have an external hard disk or any other peripheral connected to your Mac through a SCSI port, you can find the SCSI ID number without looking on the hardware itself. You do this by selecting the device and choosing Get Info (⌘-I) from the File menu. In the Get Info window, beside the heading "Where:" you'll see the name of the disk and which software was used to format the disk, followed by the SCSI ID number, as shown in the following figure.

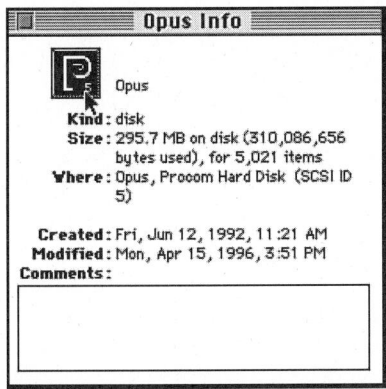

See Also

Get Info; Hard Disks; SCSI

FinePrint, See Printers, PostScript Lasers

Finger

An Internet protocol used to provide information about host computers; also, the name of a scriptable application by Peter Lewis that is used to look up individuals or other information on the **Internet**.

Finger gains access to a host computer via **port number** 79 using the Finger protocol. What finger finds depends on the information stored in a Plan file set up by the server administrator. Some servers let you see the names of users who have connected to their site, and the times they connected. Others provide a variety of personal information about the administrator.

Finger is scriptable with AppleScript, and the figure on the next page shows the results of an AppleScript that activated Finger automatically and connected to a remote **Web server** to reveal who has visited it recently.

See Also

Internet; Port Number; World Wide Web

FireWire, See 1394 FireWire; Ports, Future Trends

First Person Perspective Shooters

The first DOOM-like game, Wolfenstein 3-D showed up for the Mac in 1994. Even though it took two years to move from the PC to the Mac, it was clear that id Software was onto something and Mac gaming would never be the same again. The DOOM phenomena consists mainly of this: a guy running through corridors, shooting everything in his path. If the game is network-compatible, then you can play with a friend and shoot him, too. First Person Perspective Shooters (Shooters) are logical extensions of standard "shoot to kill" theme, but tend to incorporate a bit more of a plot. In Wolfenstein 3-D you are a soldier fighting the Nazis, while in LucasArts' Dark Forces, you seek and destroy the Empire's newest bad guy, the Dark Trooper. Especially when primed for the **Power Mac**, Shooters are a joyride of sight and sound with lots of repetitious button punching and rapid-fire. The Power Mac's faster processing and advanced video puts you in the middle of the action. However, many of the games are violent and tend to stir up a bit of controversy.

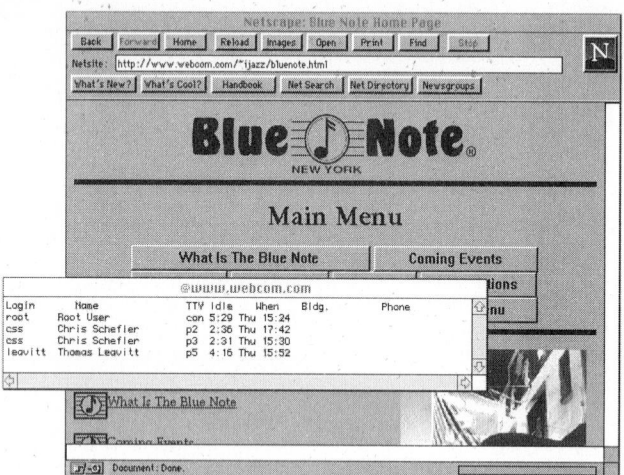

Regardless of its "gore quotient," **DOOM II**, distributed by GT Interactive, sold millions of copies on both the PC and the Mac. Shooters incorporate a first person perspective that makes you feel like you are actually tramping through corridors or through the underbrush. Instead of looking at a character that you guide across the screen, your line of vision is what it would be like to really be there. Some titles accomplish this better than others with great graphics and sound, but all tend to have the same elements including a menu bar along the bottom of the screen that lets you know how injured you are and what guns you've got.

Shooters that model themselves after arcade video games like Mad Dog McCree, where you shoot video images of actors on a large screen with a toy gun usually tend to fall flat on smaller platforms. Neither Mad

Dog, Blood Bath, or the disastrous Crime Patrol, all distributed by American Laser Games, have been able to match the sales success of the DOOM phenomena. id Software is the leader in making these titles with Wolfenstein 3-D, DOOM II and Ultimate DOOM to their credit, as well as the new **Hexen: Beyond Heretic.** Other First Person Perspective Shooters worth checking out include Sensory Overload, Marathon, and Marathon II from Bungie Software and the LucasArts Star Wars game Dark Forces. Even a level of the LucasArts game **Rebel Assault II** incorporates the first person perspective.

See Also

Descent; DOOM II; Hexen: Beyond Heretic; Marathon; Violence in Games

First Things First

Visionary Software's Organizer/Personal Information Manager isn't the easiest one to use, but it's extremely powerful and optimized for the **Power Mac**. It combines a calendar—daily, weekly, monthly, or yearly—with a very good outliner and a floating clock/calendar page that also can be anchored to the menu bar. First Things First can be networked and shared by co-workers, but you can determine whether they can change calendar items or just look at them and be reminded of group meetings and tasks you've delegated.

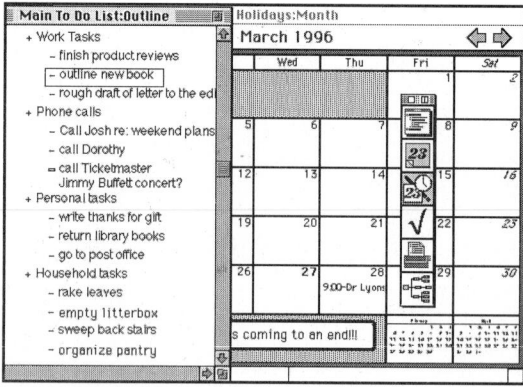

Use the outliner first to develop your goals and plans. Use the outline's hierarchy to decide what's most important, then add the sub-set of things to do to reach the goal. When you're ready to set a time to accomplish specific tasks, drag them to the calendar. Set dates and times for meetings, appointments, and reminders. FTF's calendar can do as much as any other calendar can to keep you on a schedule. It reminds you of appointments with a burst of music, unless you tell it to use one of your other system sounds. You also can use voice annotations on your calendar if you have a microphone.

The First Things First toolbar toggles back and forth between the outline and calendar views and gives you quick access to the linking and sharing features. It can print your calendar in any of the standard formats, including FiloFax, Day-Timer, Day Runner, and Franklin Planner, as well as on standard sheets of paper. It prints your outlines in any format you want, with or without hidden items, or only text you've selected.

First Things First is available as a demo program from **online services** and **bulletin boards**. The demo can be upgraded to a full working version by calling the publisher, Visionary Software, with your credit card in hand and buying a registration number. It's an ecologically sane way to distribute software. There's no wasted packaging. The program includes excellent help files, so you have no real need for a printed manual. Best of all, you can try out the software for as much as a month before you buy it—an excellent policy.

See Also
Personal Information Manager

FirstClass

BBS (**Bulletin Board System**) software by SoftArc. With FirstClass and a special add-on gateway to the **Internet**, a Macintosh BBS can include a clean graphical interface and an **email** and **Usenet** news connection.

Most of these sorts of Internet connections are handled through UUCP gateways, which means the FirstClass BBS calls an Internet host every few hours to transfer email and news.

It's also possible for a FirstClass BBS to be accessible over the Internet. You can come in by way of a standard **Telnet** session or via the graphical FirstClass software, configured to use a Telnet tool, if you have a **MacTCP**-based connection to the Internet. To find a Telnet tool you might use a telecommunications package such as MicroPhone, by Software Ventures Corp.

To configure the FirstClass client software to use Telnet:

1. Click the "Setup" button in the main screen and the "Change" button in the "Connect Via" part of the "Connection Settings" dialog.

2. In the "Communications Setup" dialog, choose "CommToolbox" from the "Connect Via" pop-up menu.

3. Click the "Configure Tool" button to choose your Telnet tool, and configure it with the Internet address of the host BBS. After you connect to a FirstClass BBS over the Internet, it looks just like any other FirstClass BBS that you'd call via modem.

FirstClass can receive Usenet newsgroups via the Internet gateway, which is an excellent way to bring more information into a fairly small BBS.

To send email on a FirstClass system, go to the "Message" menu and choose "New." FirstClass presents you with a message window. To send a message to the Internet, type the Internet address and append ,**Internet** to it.

You can get more information about the FirstClass software from SoftArc by sending email to **sales@softarc.com**. You can download the free FirstClass client software from any FirstClass BBS, or on the Internet at: **ftp://ftp.tidbits.com/pub/tidbits/tisk/bbs/first-class-client-209.hqx**.

See Also
Bulletin Board Systems; Email; Internet; Telnet; Usenet

Fixed Storage Capabilities, *See Disks and Drives*

Flagging

A way of finding a message more easily the next time a user is searching through a **Usenet** newsgroup without actually saving the message to disk. The "Flag Messages/Unflag" command on the "Message" menu in **Netscape Navigator** either adds or removes the Flag icon under the "Mark" column.

See Also

Netscape Navigator; Newsgroups, Subscribing; Thread; Usenet

Flaming

Sending a "heated" message to a fellow electronic mail correspondent, mailing list member, or **newsgroup** user in regards to a breach of "**netiquette**" on their part. Any thought, opinion, or feeling expressed is subject to a response calling into question your intelligence, common sense, and parentage. People often flame companies or large organizations, particularly the government. This often starts a "flame war" if other people don't share your opinions on a major topic. Avoid flaming other people as good **netiquette**.

See Also

Mailing List; Netiquette; Newsgroups, Subscribing; Spam; Usenet; World Wide Web

Flash-It

Flash-It is a third-party shareware program for System 6.0.3 or higher, that enables you to take **screen captures**, but adds features and functionality that Apple's Shift-⌘-3 screen-capture command doesn't offer. For example, when you activate Flash-It, your cursor turns into a cross hair cursor, and enables you to drag a selection around any item and save just that selected area as your screen capture, rather than saving the entire screen. This makes for smaller-sized captures, and requires less editing or cropping of your screen capture if all you want is a portion of the screen.

Flash-It is a **control panel,** and its preferences are set within the control panel, as shown in the following figure. In the control panel you can select a hot key that will activate Flash-It, you can select which type of file format to save the capture in, and you can set where on your **hard disk** you want the screen captures saved. Flash-It can be found in the Macintosh Utilities Forum on America Online and a variety of Mac FTP sites on the Internet.

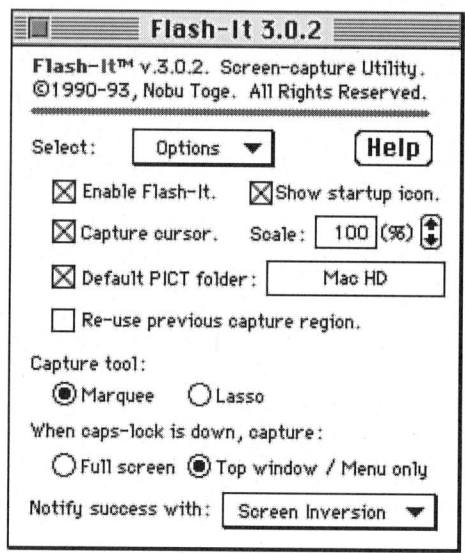

See Also

Control Panels; Hard Disks; Screen Capture

Flat Shading, *See Alias' Sketch*

Flatbed Scanners

Flatbed scanners are the most commonly-used kind of scanner in desktop publishing. In the mid-90's, high-end flatbed scanners can produce scans that are nearly as good as drum scans, and fairly inexpensive flatbed scanners are perfectly adequate for comps, artwork for Web pages, and many printing projects.

Flatbed scanners are also useful for optical character recognition (OCR) tasks. Using OCR, you can quickly enter printed documents into word-processing documents, rather than retyping the text of the documents.

Flatbed scanners can handle a wide range of materials: photographic prints, pages from books or magazines—you can even scan flat objects, like coins, directly. Many flatbed scanner handle large-format transparencies, or can be equipped with adapters to handle transparencies and even slides. Some desktop scanners also support sheet-feeder attachments for multi-page OCR jobs.

Flatbed scanners look like a small, personal copier. Artwork is placed face-down on the scanner's glass plate and the scanner moves a light bulb and sensor beneath the art. Some scanners pass a bulb *over* large-format transparencies, shining the light through the art and into the sensor.

Advantages Flatbed scanners range widely in price and quality, but good scanners are fairly inexpensive. A flatbed scanner adequate for comps, Web pages, and OCR can be purchased for a few hundred dollars. In 1996, a high-quality flatbed scanner that can be used to produce scans for print can be purchased for as little as $2,000.

Flatbed scanners are fairly easy to operate. It takes some practice to get consistently good scans from any scanner, but flatbeds are substantially easier to use, and faster, than drum scanners.

Drawbacks Flatbed scanners use CCD's to record artwork's light and dark values. (See the discussion of drum scanners.) Often, this can result in loss of detail in highlight and shadow areas of the scan.

Scans from flatbed scanners are very rarely in as sharp focus as drum scans. It's possible to compensate for this with software (such as Photoshop's "Unsharp Mask" filter), but such corrections may cause unwanted side-effects in the scan.

See Also
Drum Scanners; Handheld Scanners; Office Scanners; Slide Scanners

Flat-File Database

A flat-file database is one that contains only one file of data. There may be many individual records in the file and many fields in the record, but they're accessible only from the file, and aren't shared with any others.

A cookbook is an example of a flat-file database. Each recipe is a record, and the ingredients and instructions are fields. A HyperCard address stack like the one in this example is a flat-file database. In order to transfer the name and address to a letter, you'd have to copy it.

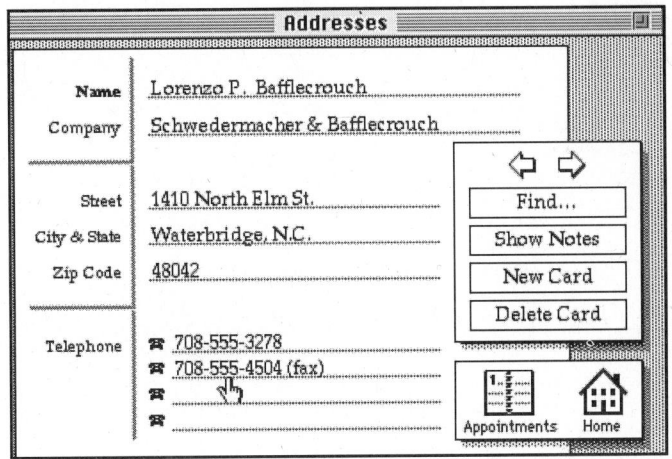

See Also
Database; HyperCard

Flattened Movies

Macintosh files contain two parts or forks: a data fork and a resource fork. The resource fork stores icons, palettes, and so on, while the data fork usually contains the major portion of data, such as the text in a word processing document. The PC operating system does not support this structure, so it is necessary to create a *flattened* **QuickTime** movie for distribution to PCs. A flattened file contains only a data fork. Utilities such as Who's **MovieShop** and Who's **MovieCleaner** provide this option, as does Adobe **Premiere**.

Flight Simulators, *See Sim Games*

FlipBook

S. H. Pierce and Company's FlipBook is dedicated printer software that allows you to create traditional paper flip books from your digital animation files. A QuickTime or PIC movie is loaded onto the screen, along with a playback controller that shows each frame in the sequence (not in frames per second rate).

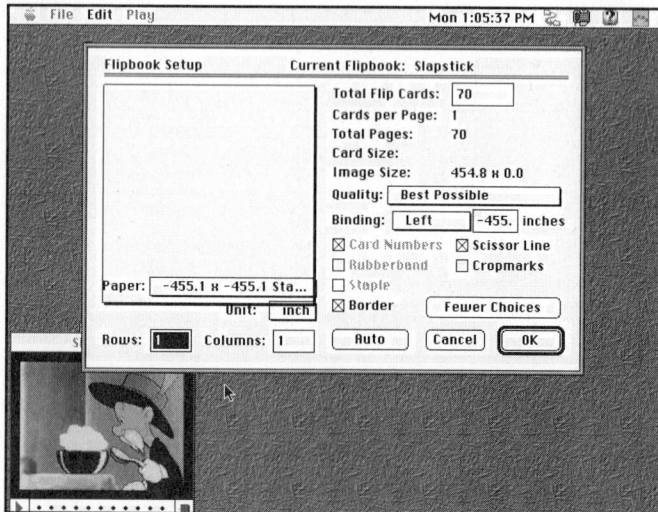

Your printers specs are indicated, and you are allowed to format the flip card printout in the Flip Setup dialog. From there, you print out the frames of the loaded movie file to the flip cards loaded in the printer. FlipBook comes with a small stack of flip cards and an order form for more.

Floating Point Coprocessors, *See Coprocessors, Types; Software FPU*

Floppy Disks, *See Disks and Drives*

Flow Control

When an **RS-232** connection is made between your Macintosh and a modem, both devices need to be ready to send and receive information simultaneously.

However, in real-world situations the Mac occasionally has data ready to send faster than the modem is able to accept. And along the same lines, there are times that the Mac is temporarily unable to receive data from the modem, possibly because it is busy performing another task, such as printing. Obviously if either side simply "loses" the information being transmitted, the communication as a whole could fail, leading to unpredictable results. To prevent data loss, the modem and the computer make use of Flow Control to keep both sides informed of each other's readiness.

Older, slower modems were able to handle flow control through software, in a process known as **XOn/XOff**. This "Software Flow Control" functioned by inserting characters into the stream of data being transmitted to indicate when to pause and resume. When the modem wanted the computer to stop transmitting (pause), it would send ASCII code 19 (Control-S, XOff). When the modem was ready to resume transmission, it would transmit the XOn character (ASCII 17, Control-Q) to inform the computer that it was ready to resume transmission.

As modem speeds grew and modem users began transmitting binary files that actually contained the XON and XOFF characters as a part of the files, this type of flow control became less practical.

Today's high speed modems perform the function of flow control by using the RTS and CTS pins in the modem cable, through a process known as Hardware Handshaking. These modems require a particular type of cable, which supports hardware handshaking. When the computer needs the modem to slow down, it drops the power on the RTS pin, signaling the modem to pause. In the opposite scenario, when the modem has fallen behind the computer, perhaps because of a temporary influx of line noise, the modem drops the CTS line to ask the computer to slow down and stop transmitting data.

One additional pin of interest for handshaking in a RS-232 serial cable is the DTR pin. This pin is used by the computer to signal the computer's overall readiness to the modem. Modems are generally configured to hang up when the computer drops the DTR pin, thus assuring the computer that a telephone line doesn't stay connected for an unexpectedly long period of time, and quickly preparing the modem for another call (after DTR is raised again).

In most computers the story stops here: the modem simply watches for the DTR and RTS pins to keep an eye on the computer, and the computer watches the CTS pin to keep an eye on the modem. A drop in RTS signals the modem to slow down, a drop in DTR signals the modem to hang up, and a drop in CTS signals the computer to slow down.

Unfortunately, the Macintosh makes use of these pins in a somewhat different way than in other systems. The DIN-8 RS-232 connector used in the Mac's serial ports has only one signal control pin, allowing it to provide the modem with either a DTR **or** a RTS signal—but not both. To accommodate this, Macintosh hardware handshaking cables tie together the DTR and the RTS lines coming from the Mac, meaning that DTR and RTS lines will always be the same from the perspective of the modem. Therefore, when connecting a Mac to an RS-232 modem, you need to configure the modem to monitor either the RTS pin (to provide full hardware handshaking) or to monitor the DTR pin (to watch for the computer's desire to hang up the modem).

Because both DTR and RTS will always be the same from the modem's perspective, it is very important to configure the modem to ignore one or the other. Generally, terminal software used to connect to online services will make use of the Hardware Handshaking feature (RTS), and therefore your modem should be configured to ignore DTR (usually done via the **AT** &D0 command). In this case, if you do not configure the modem to ignore DTR, when the computer needs the modem to slow down, it will drop its signal control pin, resulting in the modem seeing a drop RTS and DTR. The drop in the RTS pin will tell the modem to slow down as expected, but because DTR is also dropping, the modem will drop the line instantly!

Nearly all modem software today is configured to make use of the RTS pin of the modem cable. However, in some cases, software is specifically designed to make use of the DTR line instead of the RTS line. Most notably, **Apple Remote Access** 2.0 (ARA) specifically configures the Mac not to provide RTS signals, and leaves the modem set to hang-up on drop of DTR. Since ARA provides its own compression and correction, Apple's engineers feel that the computer would rarely, if ever, need the modem to slow down, and thus the capability to quickly hang up and reset the modem is more valuable. Fortunately, your ARA CCL string will take care of these settings for you, so beyond technical curiosity, you needn't be excessively concerned about what ARA is doing with DTR.

If you are installing a new high-speed modem, be sure that you use a hardware handshaking cable. Otherwise, it won't work properly and you can spend days trying to figure out what's wrong.

See Also
Networking

Flying Games, *See A-10 Attack!; Sim Games*

Flying Nightmares, *See Sim Games*

FM Screening, *See Stochastic Screens*

Focal Length
This measurement indicates how much of a scene the lens captures. Expressed in millimeters (mm), it is the distance from the optical center of the lens to the film

plane when the focus of the lens is set to infinity. The smaller the number, the wider the field of view of the lens. The wider an area is visible, the smaller objects will appear in the picture.

For a 35mm camera, a 50mm lens is considered a standard or normal lens, while a 28mm is a wide angle and a 150mm is a telephoto. However, this changes depending upon the size of the film (or CCD in the case of digital cameras) being used. For example, medium format (2 1/2") cameras use 80mm as the equivalent standard lens, while a CCD camera with a detector less than an inch in size may have a standard lens of less than 40mm.

See Also

Digital Cameras; Range Finder; SLR

FocolTone

Providing designers 763 ink spot colors, the FocolTone spot color system also allows all its colors to be converted to CMYK with reasonably accurate results (unlike the more popular Pantone color system).

See Also

CMYK; Pantone Matching System; Spot Color; Toyo; TruMatch

Folder, *See New Folder Command*

Folder Icon

The Folder icon, which by default looks like a file folder, is used to let you know that files and other folders can be placed within this folder, as shown in the following figure. Folders are used as an organizational tool for keeping files in the computer separate from each other, much the same way real file folders keep files separate in a traditional file cabinet.

The System Folder has a number of folders with special icons on them to help you distinguish these folders from other folders. The Apple Menu Items folder, for example, has a small Apple logo to help you distinguish it from the dozens of other folders in your System Folder. The fonts folder has a capital "A" on the folder to alert you, and the Control Panels folder has an icon of a slider and some buttons to help you visually locate it as well. The Extensions folder, Startup Items folder, Launcher Item folder, Preferences folder, and Print Monitor Documents folder all have this added visual cue to help you locate them in the System Folder.

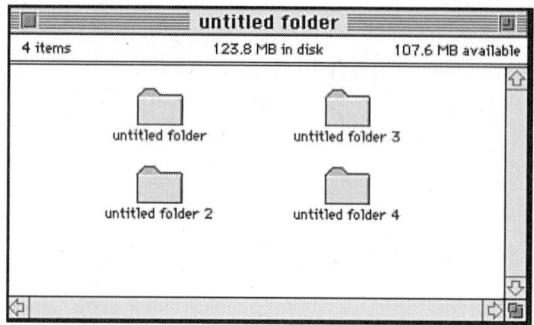

See Also

New Folder Command

Fondler, *See Font Utility*

Font Conflicts, Numbering

Each **font** has a font ID number assigned to it by its developer. If you have two fonts installed on your Macintosh that have been given the same font number by their developers, you have a font ID conflict. The conflict occurs when the Macintosh doesn't know which font you want to **print**. If, for example, you want to use a font called Tribeca, which has a font ID number of 9070, and you also have a font installed on your system called Fisheye, which also has a font ID number of 9070, the Mac doesn't know which font to print. To resolve this conflict, the Macintosh prints the first one it comes to, regardless if it's the font you wanted or not. If you selected Tribeca and Tribeca is displayed on your screen but the font FishEye prints instead, that's a font ID conflict

Font utilities such as **Suitcase** (from Symantec) and **Master Juggler** (from Alsoft) warn you if you're about to open a font that has the same ID number as a font you already have open. The new version of Suitcase (version 3.0) automatically renumbers fonts for you when necessary, but it only renumbers them temporarily (in RAM) and does not change the permanent number of the font.

Both utilities offer to automatically renumber the new font for you so it has a distinct number from any other font you have open. You can also choose to leave the numbering as is and instead close the font with the same ID number on your drive. If you're going to output your files at high resolution through a service bureau or digital imaging center, it is generally recommended that you do not renumber your fonts. That is because renumbering only works on your machine. When you take your files to a service bureau, your renumbered fonts won't match up with their fonts, and you'll again have a font ID conflict. In other words, your fonts will not correctly match up.

See Also

Font Utility; Fonts; Master Juggler; Printing; Suitcase

Font/Disk Accessories Mover

This is an Apple utility that was necessary in **System 6** for installing **fonts** or **desk accessories** (DAs) into your system. Back then, all fonts and DAs came in little suitcases, and by using the Font/DA Mover (whose icon looked like a little truck) you would move these fonts and desk accessories in and out of your system. Installed DAs appeared under what is now called the **Apple menu**.

To install a font with the Font/DA Mover, you would double-click the Font suitcase and it would launch the Font/DA Mover and open the suitcase, revealing its contents in a window on the left side of the dialog box. You would then select the fonts or desk accessories you want to install and click the Copy button, and it would copy the selected items into the System (see the following figure).

System 7 and higher have made the Font/DA Mover obsolete, as you can now install fonts by just drag-

ging them into the Fonts folder (within the System Folder) or by dragging fonts onto the System Folder icon, which places it into the Fonts folder for you. You can add DAs to the Apple menu by dragging the DA, or an **alias** of the DA, into the **Apple Menu Items folder**, also within the System Folder.

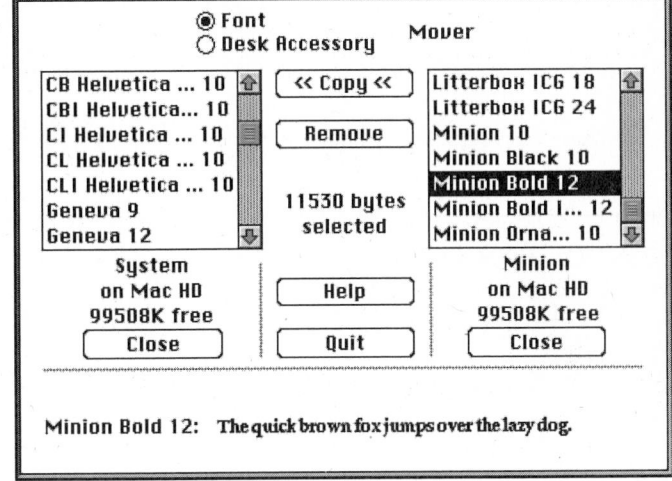

Minion Bold 12: The quick brown fox jumps over the lazy dog.

See Also

Apple Menu Items Folder; Desk Accessories; Fonts; Font Utility; System 7

Font Distributors, *See Type Foundries and Distributors*

Font Formats

The original Mac fonts were bitmapped fonts, named after cities (remember Venice and London?). There were no **outline fonts**, only bitmapped fonts, and the original Mac printers were dot-matrix, so when these were **printed** they showed the dots the letters were built from. Bitmapped fonts only look reasonably decent when they're used in the specific sizes users have screen fonts for.

Adobe's **PostScript** page description language, used in laser printers, allowed fonts to be described by their outlines, rather than in terms of a set of dots. Each font still had a bitmapped component, called a screen font and used only for screen display, but the outline font, also called a printer font, was what got sent to the printer. The printer was in charge of rendering that outline, or turning into printed dots, at the highest possible resolution. The following figure shows the icon for PostScript printer fonts.

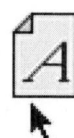

PostScript **Type 1 fonts**, as these were called, are still the standard for desktop publishing, but they've been joined by fonts in other formats.

TrueType is an outline font format created by Apple; it doesn't use PostScript to describe outlines, but the printed results are the same—high quality, smooth type printed at the printer's highest resolution. There's only one piece to a TrueType font—the suitcase file, which contains both the screen fonts and the outline fonts sent to the printer. This makes installation somewhat simpler. TrueType fonts can only be used with System 6.0.5 or later.

TrueType fonts are also available for PCs, and they've been adopted as a de facto standard in much of the business world. Home users also use TrueType fonts, particularly because they don't require a PostScript printer, as PostScript fonts do. Desktop publishers have generally rejected the TrueType format because it's not entirely compatible with PostScript output devices and because it takes longer to print. The following figure is the icon for TrueType font files.

Refinements of these two formats offer users greater type quality and the capability to create their own custom versions of fonts.

Multiple Master fonts from Adobe have built-in "design axes," created by the fonts' designers, that allow users to make custom versions of fonts that vary in weight, width, or other characteristics. **QuickDraw GX**, the print technology Apple unveiled with System 7.5, includes a **GX font** format (GX fonts can be

either PostScript or TrueType) that can include much more information than standard fonts. This will allow for more complex use of type, including making alternative characters more accessible and improving the level of **kerning** and **hinting**.

See Also

Bitmapped Fonts; Fonts; GX Fonts; Hinting; Kerning; Multiple Master Fonts; Outline Fonts; PostScript; Printing; QuickDraw GX; TrueType; Type 1 Fonts

Font ID Numbers, *See Font Utility*

Font, Installing, *See Installing Fonts*

Font Substitution

If you open a document and a **font** that is included in the document is not present in your system, a number of applications have a font substitution feature that will enable you to substitute a font of your choice to "stand in" for the font that is missing. Some applications also have automatic font substitution, which picks the closest matching font from your installed fonts to match the missing fonts.

Font substitution is also very valuable when you are working with files created on a PC. For example, if you are given a document that was created with the Windows version of **PageMaker**, you can open that file with PageMaker for Macintosh. Unfortunately, you can't be sure that you'll have the same fonts installed on your Mac that they used in their document, which was created on a PC. That's where font substitution comes in handy, because PageMaker will look in its built-in **database** and find the installed Mac font that most closely resembles the PC font, and offer to substitute it instead. If it can't find a reasonable substitution, it enables you to pick a font from a pop-up menu to substitute temporarily or permanently any time it encounters that font, by adding that font match to the application's built-in database.

See Also

Database; Fonts; PageMaker

Font Utility

There are a number of **utilities** that are designed to help you work with and better manage your **fonts**. Apple's own font utilities include the **Key Caps DA**, which helps you find special characters within any given font, and the **Font/DA Mover**, which was a necessary utility back in **System 6** that you had to use any time you wanted to install a font to your system. With **System 7** and higher, you can install fonts by just dragging them into the System folder, so this utility is no longer necessary.

There are also a number of third-party font utilities that add features to your Mac's font management capabilities, like the capability to open sets of fonts and to store and use fonts outside the Fonts folder. There is also a popular shareware font utility called **PopChar** that acts as a replacement for Apple's Key Caps DA by adding a pull-down menu to your menu bar, displaying all the special characters of the currently selected font. To choose a character to insert, you select the special character in PopChar's display window, release the mouse button, and that character will appear at the insertion point in your document. Very handy.

Font management tools enable you to create sets of fonts, and add fonts from locations other than the font folder within the System Folder. The two most popular font management tools are Suitcase (now on version 3.0) from Symantec (10201 Torre Ave., Cupertino, CA 95104-2132, Phone (800) 441-7234) and Master Juggler from Alsoft, Inc. (P.O. Box 927, Spring, TX 77383. (713) 353-4090).

One of the most popular Font Utilities is Adobe Type Manager, from Adobe System (1625 Charleston Rd., Mountain View, CA 94043. **http://www.adobe.com**) which eliminates jagged type on-screen and on the printed page at any size; and makes Type 1 fonts available to any printer.

The Type Book (from Rascal Software) enables you to view samples of your entire font collection either on-screen or by printout. It displays the font in a variety of sizes, and uses each font in a paragraph of sample text to enable you to see the font in use.

See Also

Fonts; Font/Disk Accessories Mover; Key Caps

Fonts

More than any other type of software, fonts offer users an incredible variety and quantity to choose from. The Precision Type Font Reference Guide, an extraordinarily complete type specimen book, lists more than 13,000 digital typefaces, and that's not complete by any means at all. For one thing, shareware fonts aren't included in the guide.

Mac users will find there's a font for their every mood, and they're as easy to use as choosing a name from a menu. There are some format, compatibility, and management issues to consider, but for the most part using fonts is strictly fun.

Type has come a long way since Gutenberg. Originally, printers cut their own type from metal, and in the 16th century type designers, such as Claude Garamond, began to manufacture and sell their typefaces all across Europe. Over the next few centuries, type foundries formed an industry all to themselves. The word "font" (or "fount") is derived from the word "foundry," where, originally, type was cast. Today companies that create fonts are still called foundries, but those fonts are more likely to be digital than metal.

Type foundries range from huge companies like Adobe—which along with selling thousands of fonts is also the creator of the **PostScript** page description language that's the basis of desktop publishing—to tiny one-person shops that distribute their fonts as shareware.

Over the centuries, type has mutated into many categories: oldstyle, transitional, modern, slab serif, sans serif, script, cursive, brush, graphic, display, decorative, blackletter, uncial, pi, symbol, logo, ornament—there are more, but these cover most typefaces available today. Some of these names come from the history of type (oldstyle, for example), while others describe the design of typefaces (brush) or their use (symbol). For most users, though, the categories to be concerned with are serif (like Times), sans serif (like Helvetica), and ornament fonts (like Zapf Dingbats).

The Mac's system software comes with certain fonts. Some vary from version to version (System 7.5 comes with some **GX fonts** that other systems don't have, for example). But every Mac comes with the following:

- Geneva—This is used primarily for display of file names and information within windows in the Finder. It was originally based on Helvetica (the name Helvetica comes from the Swiss name for their country, of which Geneva is the capital).

- Chicago—This is used for menu and window titles.

- Monaco—This is a sans serif font that's **monospaced**—each character takes up the same width as every other, like typewriter letters. It's also used by the Mac system software.

- Times—Originally created for the London *Times* newspaper in the 1930s, Times is widely used in all sorts of publications. It's the closest thing to a generic serif font that there is; it falls into the transitional category of typefaces, because it's similar to the transitional typefaces of the 17th century.

- Helvetica—The closest thing to a generic sans serif typeface, Helvetica is probably even more widely used than Times.

- Courier—This is a monospaced font designed to look like typewriter letters.

- Symbol—This font contains symbols used for typesetting mathematical equations, including mathematical operators and most of the Greek alphabet.

- New York—Based on Times, New York is preferred by many for screen display, because it's larger and more open, therefore easier to read onscreen.

- Palatino—An elegant but much over-used font, Palatino was designed by Herman Zapf, a famous 20th-century type designer whose name is widely known even outside the world of typography because of the next font in this list.

- Zapf Dingbats—These are ornamental characters useful for replacing bullets in bulleted lists and for other decorative applications.

Mac fonts come in more than one format: **PostScript**, **TrueType**, and GX (which can actually be PostScript or TrueType). Often, a typeface is available in more than one format, so users can choose which best meets their needs. Font formats are important under the following circumstances:

- In desktop publishing, most high-resolution output devices don't work well with TrueType fonts, even though the output quality of TrueType is essentially the same as that of PostScript. For this reason, most desktop publishing is done with Type 1 PostScript fonts.

- If you have a typeface in more than one format, you should only have one format installed at any given time. Graphics applications and output devices can be confused when they encounter two conflicting font formats.

- If you don't have a PostScript printer and your files aren't destined to be printed on one at a service bureau, you can't use PostScript fonts. TrueType fonts are a good alternative in this case.

Buying Fonts is easier today than ever. They are available at retail stores, by mail order from Mac catalog companies, from the individual foundries themselves, and from distribution companies like Precision Type. A welcome innovation in the past few years is the introduction of font libraries on compact disc, like Adobe's Type On Call, which contain entire catalogs of fonts from particular foundries. Users call or fax the CD's publisher to order fonts, and in return they receive (within a few minutes, usually) a code that allows them to copy the fonts from the CD. Before buying, users can view samples of all the fonts on a disc, as well as historical and design information.

Shareware fonts are an alternative to commercial fonts. Generally much less expensive than commercial fonts, they have the potential to be of just as high quality, and the variety available is incredible. Let the buyer beware, though: Many shareware fonts don't contain all the special characters, ligatures, and **kerning** pairs that can make commercial fonts worth the money.

See Also

Font Formats; GX Fonts; PostScript; TrueType; Type Foundries and Distributors; Typesetting Terms

Fonts, Unique Types

There are thousands of **TrueType** and **PostScript** fonts available. Typefaces of every description can be had for a few dollars, and sometimes for pennies. Not only do **fonts** appear on disks and CDs, but there are fonts available on the Web as well, sometimes for a charge and sometimes for free. Most computer font enthusiasts receive at least six mailings a year that advertise new font library collections, and newly designed typefaces. The temptation to own more than we need is always there, because fonts give emotional character to the displayed message, no matter the medium.

It's always a little dangerous telling someone else what fonts should be considered for inclusion in their library, rather like proselytizing a religious point of view. With that in mind, there are some general categories you might consider, based upon the expectations of clients and the trends of the design profession. First, it is vital to include both Helvetica (the most common sans serif face) and Times (a common serif face). Times and Helvetica come in slightly different flavors based on the type house they come from, so the specific choices are up to you. Added to this is the necessity of having some knowledge of other common faces, like Futura, Franklin, Dom Casual, Palatino, and others. Taken together, this is a good basic group of representative fonts.

Next, it is suggested that you include faces that are most common (and in fact demanded) by the soft-

ware you plan to use. A specific interface is usually designed to look its best with targeted fonts. Unless that software comes with the fonts it needs (which is becoming less and less common), you should not delete large numbers of fonts from your library. To do so risks having to load the fonts again. You may be asked to reinstall them if you do. Third, include some fonts that are outside of the common sans serif/serif category, like a script and brush font. Keep an eye on the design industry and on the trade magazines to see what fonts and font families are currently being touted. Become aware of your own tastes, your favorite fonts, and seek them out. Fonts are as much the personality of the designer as they are utilitarian ways to craft a message.

Keep an eye out for novel typefaces. They can often help you distinguish your message from that of the competition. As an example, here are a few font families and collections worthy of investigation.

The Deniart Collections Deniart (at 416-941-0919 in Toronto, Ontario, Canada) offers seven font collects in the Mac and PC formats: Castles and Shields, Egyptian Hieroglyphics (three volumes), Signals and Signs, Ancient Writing, and Meso Americans. These are not really for use as headlines or body copy, but as graphic embellishments, just as is the more common Zapf Dingbats. You can, of course, use these fonts as interpretable text if your audience is able to read the messages. Egyptian hieroglyphs, for instance, would be very useful if your task was to write a scholarly work on Egypt, and other Deniart fonts (Aztec Sun Signs, Morse Code, American Signing Alphabet for the hearing impaired, Old Persian Cuneiform, to name a few) might also serve to communicate various texts. Deniart fonts come in both **TrueType** and **PostScript Type 1** on disks.

Expresiv Fonts: Brush Script Collection World Art (One Datran Center, Suite 1500, 9100 S. Dadeland Blvd., Miami, FL 33156) markets these TrueType and PostScript fonts. The CD contains hundreds of brush script typefaces, and each is unique. If you are looking for a softer approach to type, this is a CD font collection that you should own.

Kidbag If you'd like to expand your font library with the most novel collection of fonts available, look no further than this offering from DS Design (919-319-1770). Leave the adult world behind, and write your message with children's crayons and other explorative media. KidArt, a collection of kids artwork in both black and white and color in the PICT format, is included as a bonus. KidType includes four font families that mimic the following media: crayon, marker, paint, and ruled print.

The figure shows three unique fonts you might consider for your collection (top to bottom): Hieroglyphs from Deniart, "kingsfont" from the World Art Brush Script Collection, and one of the Kids Fonts from DS Design.

See Also
Fonts

Fontmonger, *See Font Utility*

Fontographer
When the **fonts** you have just aren't quite what you need, Fontographer can help you create your own custom fonts (see the following figure).

Starting either from scratch or from an existing font, Fontographer allows you to modify font outlines, using **Bézier curve** controls similar to those found in **PostScript** drawing programs like **Illustrator** and **FreeHand**. Other drawing features include "Snap to point" and "Snap to guides," which simplify creating clean outlines. Once the outlines are complete, users can draw their own bitmapped screen fonts for any size desired, or Fontographer can create them automatically.

The program can also merge two existing fonts to come up with one that's somewhere in the middle (watch out—results are unpredictable), and it can import **EPS** files created in drawing programs as characters.

A common use for this sort of application is to add special characters (such as fractions or diacritical marks) to existing fonts, or to create logo fonts that contain all the different logos a company uses in different situations. Another handy feature is the capability to print keyboard maps.

Fontographer works with PostScript **Type 1**, Type 3, **TrueType**, and Multiple Master fonts, and it can export EPS and **PICT** files for use in draw programs.

See Also
Bézier Curves; Drawing Applications; EPS; FreeHand; Illustrator; Outline Fonts; PICT; PostScript; TrueType; Type 1 Fonts

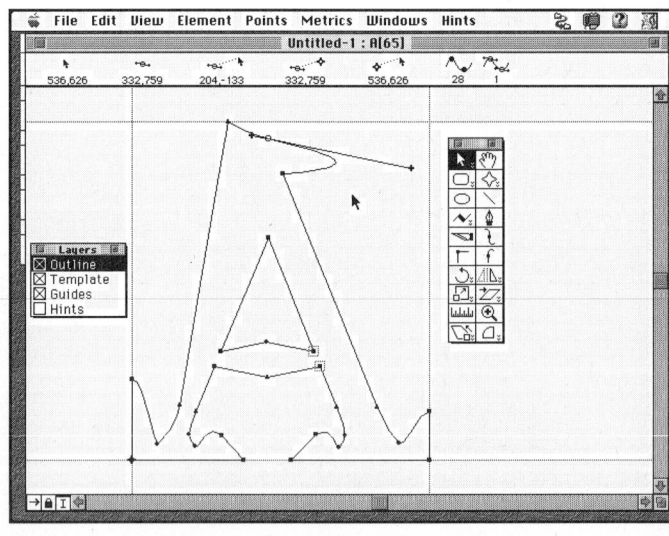

Fontstudio, *See Font Utility*

Football, *See Sports Games*

Footer

A footer is a line of information placed at the foot of consecutive pages of a document. It may contain the title, author, date, page number, and/or other information. If you wish, you can use a different first footer for the first page of a multi-page document. You may also choose to create a first footer and leave it empty, so that page numbering will begin on page two. Headers and footers are handled differently on various word processors. Microsoft Word 6 sets both from a single dialog box. Nisus has separate menu items for headers and footers, but both create them in a separate window from the main document. MacWritePro places the header or footer directly on the page so that you can see its position relative to the rest of the text.

Force Finder to Quit

When the Finder is the active application, ⌘-Option-Escape is used to force the **Finder** to quit. This is used to enable you to **rebuild your desktop** without having to restart your computer. When you use the force quit keyboard combination, a dialog box appears asking, "Force Finder to Quit? Unsaved changes will be lost."

To initiate a force quit, click Force Quit or click **Cancel** if you don't want to force quit. If you select Force Quit, click and hold the **Option** and **Command** keys, and as the Finder starts to display the desktop again (this only takes a couple of seconds) you get a dialog box asking, "Are you sure you want to rebuild the desktop on the disk '(your start up disk's name appears here)'? **Comments** in info windows will be lost." If you want to rebuild the desktop, click OK, and the desktop is rebuilt on your startup disk.

Note: Any comments that you have placed in the **Get Info** box of any files are erased. In System 7.5.3, Apple has updated the system to preserve any Get Info box comments when you rebuild the desktop.

To rebuild the desktop using Force Finder to Quit, follow these steps:

1. At the Finder, press Option-⌘-Esc.

2. A dialog box asks, "Force Finder to Quit? Unsaved changes will be lost." Click OK.

3. Hold down the Option and Command keys until you get the dialog box that reads, "Are you sure you want to rebuild the desktop on the disk '(your startup disk's name appears here)'?" Click OK and the desktop is rebuilt without having to restart your drive.

See Also

Command Key; Comments in Get Info Box; Finder; Get Info Command; Option Key; Quit Command; Rebuilding the Desktop

Force Quit Command

This keystroke combination (⌘-Option-Esc) is used to force the current application to **quit**. This can be used if you have experienced a software crash while running an application and the application no longer responds to your commands. Rather than restart the machine, oftentimes you can force quit the application and return to the **Finder**. It is recommended that you then restart the machine, because the situation that caused your application to freeze may still exist, but by force quitting, you can **restart** from the **Special menu** properly. Force quitting also gives you an opportunity to save any documents that may be open in other applications before you restart.

To force quit an application, follow these steps:

1. If the program freezes or refuses to respond to your commands, press the ⌘-Option-Escape key sequence. You get a dialog asking, "Force

(the name of the application appears here) to Quit? Unsaved changes will be lost." (They were lost anyway at the point the application got hung up.)

2. Click OK and you return to the Finder where you can Restart from the Special menu.

See Also

Finder; Quit Command; Restart; Special Menu

Forcing Items to the Top of a List

The Mac sorts items alphabetically by name as a default. If, for example, you put items into your **Apple Menu** Items folder, they appear in alphabetical order. When you're in an Open or Save dialog box, the items in the list window appear in alphabetical order. However, there are instances where you want a particular file, or group of files, to appear at the top of a list. Many people, for example, like to keep all their aliases of applications at the top of the Apple menu, with the less-used items at the bottom, so they force these application aliases to the top of the Apple menu by adding a character to the beginning of the name of each application.

If you add a space (by pressing the space bar once) in front of the name of an alias, for example, and put it in the Apple Menu Items folder, it appears at the top of the list.

Apple's code for sorting items is as follows: Numbers come before letters, so any filename starting with a number would appear before filenames with letters. The topmost item's name would start with a space, followed by items with names that start with: !, ", #, $, %, &, ', (,), *, ÷, ., and /. By using these characters at the beginning of filenames, you can group files together, or at the top of the list, by knowing how Apple sorts items alphabetically.

See Also

Apple Menu; Naming Items

Foreign File Access

Foreign File Access is a System extension used to handle non-HFS disks. **HFS (Hierarchical File System)** is the file system the Macintosh operating system uses. Foreign File Access comes with several plug-ins that enable it to recognize foreign disks. The standard plug-ins are **High Sierra**, **ISO-9660**, and **Audio CD Access**. There is also one for the **QuickTake** camera called QuickTake Access.

Foreign File Access and the ISO-9660 extension are used along with the extension **Apple Photo Access** to provide support for Kodak's **Photo CD**-format discs.

See Also

Audio CD Access; Apple Photo Access Extension; Hierarchical File System; PC Exchange; Photo CD; QuickTake

Foreign File Access Extension

This is another standard extension installed for use with Apple CD-ROM players. It enables the use of certain CD-ROMs in formats that were not designed specifically for the Macintosh. It also is an important extension for accessing audio CDs, which can also be played from Macintosh CD-ROM players.

See Also

Apple CD Audio Player; CD-ROM; Extensions Folder

Foreign Games, *See Eastern Mind; Foul Play; Yellow Brick Road II*

Foreign-Language Page Layout

Desktop publishing in languages other than English brings up some special issues: spellchecking, assuring proper hyphenation, and using alternative alphabets.

When the second language in question uses the Latin alphabet used by English, users must deal with spellchecking, assuring proper hyphenation, and using diacritical marks such as accents. These are all fairly simple issues, since most page layout packages today include foreign-language spelling and hyphenation dictionaries. As for special characters, most are accessible in common fonts; a utility such as Apple's Key Caps or Symantec's KeyFinder will come in handy when trying to locate these symbols, but they're in there.

Budget and shareware fonts, however, may *not* include special characters, so beware.

The really interesting problems come up when dealing with other alphabets: Cyrillic, Arabic, Hebrew, Japanese, Chinese. Apple's Language Kits are intended to facilitate this process.

There are two basic elements to the Language Kits:

- Foreign-language system software
- The capability to use foreign alphabets

The Apple WorldScript extension allows your Mac to use non-Latin languages, both two-byte languages such as Japanese, Chinese, and Korean, and one-byte right-to-left languages such as Arabic and Hebrew. Language Kits also include special fonts and keyboard layouts (along with keyboard overlays) for different alphabets.

Language Kits are available in the following versions: Japanese, Chinese (traditional and simplified), Arabic, Hebrew, and Cyrillic.

Not all applications are WorldScript-savvy, and some have only a degree of compatibility with WorldScript, so shop carefully. For example, Photoshop can handle traditional Chinese characters, but not simplified ones.

Desktop publishers can use non-Latin fonts with any program, although without Apple's special software the right-to-left languages need to be set left-to-right and fonts with larger character sets (primarily Asian fonts) aren't supported. There's a wide variety of foreign typefaces, ranging from those based on Latin typefaces (Minion Cyrillic, Times New Roman Greek) to those created especially for use with other languages (Rashi, a Hebrew font, and NewSeoul, a Korean one).

See Also
Fonts

Fork, *See Resource*

Formatting Disks, *See Disks, Initializing*

Formatting Text

Formatting is the term for defining the appearance of text on a page. It includes setting margins, defining the number and width of columns on the page, setting indents and tab spacing, and defining the font, size, line spacing and alignment of characters. Formatting can be accomplished in any of several ways. You can format text from the word processor's ruler or tool bar, or from dialog boxes accessible under the Format menu, or by using keyboard command shortcuts on selected text blocks.

Different word processors set margins and perform other text formatting functions in slightly different ways. Microsoft Word 6, sets margins in the Document Layout dialog box. To change the margins, put new values in the windows. Columns can be defined in the Columns dialog box or by clicking on the toolbar's columns icon and selecting the number of columns. The latter method doesn't give you a choice of column width.

Tabs and indents can be defined either by entering numbers in a dialog box, or simply by selecting the type of tab and clicking on the document ruler at the place where you want to insert a tab. By default, tab stops are set every half inch. When you define a tab, the default tabs to the left of it are automatically cleared. To set an indent, drag the indent indicator to the place where you want it. To change the indents or tabs in previously formatted text, select the block of text to be changed, and then make the change on the ruler. Text not selected will not be changed.

The Format menu (found in most word processors and DTP programs) gives you lots of options for text formatting. The Font dialog box lets you select a font, size, color, and style (plain, bold, italic, invisible, etc.)

F

and may give you additional choices regarding kerning, spacing, and position on the line. SimpleText and other basic text programs may require that you choose fonts and their attributes from a menu, rather than a dialog box or toolbar. In general, simpler programs will give you fewer options.

Forms in HTML, Creating

Forms are a feature of HyperText Markup Language (**HTML**) documents that permit two-way communication between **Web page** authors and individual readers. Forms enable Web users to make purchases on the **Internet**, fill out surveys, subscribe to publications, or submit other data to remote **Web servers**.

Forms consist of two parts, one visible on-screen, the other invisible:

1. The visible parts are the text entry fields, buttons, and checkboxes that an author creates with HTML commands.

2. The invisible part is the Common Gateway Interface (**CGI**) or **AppleScript** that processes the form data that a reader submits to a server and presents that data in a useable form to the Webmaster.

The following table lists some of the basic HTML commands used to create form input fields.

Common Form Tags in HTML

HTML Element	Attributes	Description
<FORM> </FORM>	ACTION=" "	Identifies **URL** of script to process form data.
	METHOD=" "	Possible values are GET and POST. Specifies how form input will be sent to server.
<INPUT>	TYPE=" "	Values can be CHECKBOX, TEXT, SUBMIT, RESET, IMAGE, HIDDEN.
	NAME=" "	Names the input item.
	VALUE=" "	Specifies default text or hidden value, button label, or values of check box or radio button.
	SIZE=" "	Gives size of text field.
<TEXTAREA> </TEXTAREA>	NAME=" "	Name to be submitted to gateway script.
	ROWS=" "	Number of rows.
	COLS=" "	Number of columns.
<SELECT> </SELECT>	NAME=" "	Name to be submitted to gateway script.
	SIZE=" "	Number of items to be displayed. If a value is given, the selection is a scrolling list. If no value is specified, the selection is a pop-up menu.
<OPTION>	SELECTED=" "	The SELECTED item in the pop-up or scrolling list will be selected by default.
	VALUE=" "	The value to submit if this list item is selected when the form is submitted.

The "Guest Book" form shown in the following figure provides a simple example of how HTML forms commands are displayed by a Web browser.

The preceding form is created with the following HTML:

```
<html>
<head>
<title>Guest Book</title>
</head>
<body>
<h4>Please sign my guest book.</h4>
```

Next, add the tag <FORM>...</FORM> to tell your browser that what should be displayed as a form comes between the start and end tags.

```
<FORM METHOD="POST" ACTION=". . /cgi-bin/
GuestBook">
```

The start tag of the <FORM> command includes two elements: the METHOD and the ACTION. The METHOD attribute can either be GET or POST. (The end tag </FORM> comes at the bottom of the form.) "Cgi-bin" is a folder or directory that holds the computer scripts (Common Gateway Interface (CGI)) scripts that are used to process information received from Web pages.

The ACTION attribute designates what action is to be taken when someone submits the form—in this case, put the data in a directory called "GuestBook."

Next, enter the INPUT tag. This specifies fields where data will be input:

```
<p>My name is:<INPUT NAME="guest"></p>
```

INPUT usually has two attributes: NAME and TYPE. NAME is the name of this element. By default, a box will be created where the reader can enter data.

The last form element, also an INPUT element, is a standard button that submits information to your server:

```
<p><INPUT TYPE="submit"></p>
</FORM>
</body></html>
```

Forms, CGIs to Process Once the data is submitted it would be processed on the receiving server by a CGI script written in PERL, AppleScript, or another language. Some ready-made CGIs such as Forms.acgi and Email.cgi work with the WebStar server and can be found on the Web at: **http://www.starnine.com/development/extendingwebstar.html**.

The **Frontier** scripting environment for the Macintosh also provides AppleScript CGIs, some of which parse data automatically: **http://www.webedge.com/frontier/formprocessing.html**.

See Also
AppleScript; CGI; HTML; Internet; URL; Web Page; Web Server

Forms and Reports, Custom

Most financial programs enable you to customize the look and content of such common business forms as printed checks, invoices, statements, purchase orders, and mailing labels. You can add your company logo or other art work, move fields or change their size, change the overall size of the form, or change the number of forms printed on a sheet of paper or label stock. You might decide that you need additional text fields, or fewer fields than the default format gives you. Your company may use a particular **font** or style of type. You could re-design the form to fit window envelopes you already have, or to make it more like the non-computerized ones your customers and employees were used to working with.

Some programs make the job easier than others.

If you're working with **MYOB** (Mind Your Own Business), you can customize your forms by telling the program to print a particular form, such as an invoice, then clicking the Customize button at the bottom of the Forms Selection dialog box. (For reasons known only to MYOB's programmers, you must ask to print the form before you can modify it.) Customize opens a copy of the existing format, with some (very limited) drawing tools. You can add text boxes here, choose your type, draw vertical or horizontal lines, and place graphics from the Clipboard.

Peachtree Accounting for Macintosh uses a Forms Designer module that can be reached from the Maintain menu. You may create a new form from scratch, or modify an existing one. The Peachtree manual warns users to be careful when modifying forms, lest they break the links that allow the program to place data in the fields. They advise using an existing Form Design as a template for a new form, to maintain linked operations.

In the Peachtree system, items you put on the form, such as placeholders for text, are called *objects*. There are text, data, shape, command, and paste objects. Data objects are linked to data fields in the program by command objects. Text objects print a non-changing piece of text on the form, for example "Invoice number _____." A data object would be placed next to it, along with a command object telling the program to, "read invoice number." A shape object might be a gray filled box behind the text and data objects that make up the invoice number block. Use a paste object to import a graphic, such as the company logo, from the Clipboard.

Reports also can be customized. The figure above shows how to do it in MYOB. Use the Reports menu to get an index of reports, and after selecting one, click the Customize button to get the dialog box shown in the figure. Set the text in any font and size you like and change the margins if necessary. Peachtree doesn't give you any graphic control over your reports, but you can choose whether to display items by name or by number.

See Also

Financial Planning Software; MYOB; Peachtree Accounting

Formula

A formula is a set of instructions in a **spreadsheet** cell that tell it where to find data and how to process it. The result is displayed in the cell, but the formula itself is readable in the **formula bar** whenever the cell is **selected**.

Formulas may contain text or numeric data, cell references, mathematic operators, and functions. In most programs, they must begin with an equals sign.

For example, if the formula for cell C1 is "=A1*3+B1," it will multiply the number in cell A1 by three, add the result to the number in cell B1, and then display the sum in cell C1. Because either of the referenced cells can also contain a formula, elaborate chains with one operation feeding another can be built easily.

Order of operations Our example does the multiplication first and then the addition. If A1 contained 3 and B1 contained 2, the example would yield 11. If you want to do the addition first, you can write the formula "=A1*(3+B1)" and get an answer of 15.

Spreadsheets—and most other Mac programs—always perform math operations in a specific order as follows:

1. Any operation in parentheses

2. Exponentiation

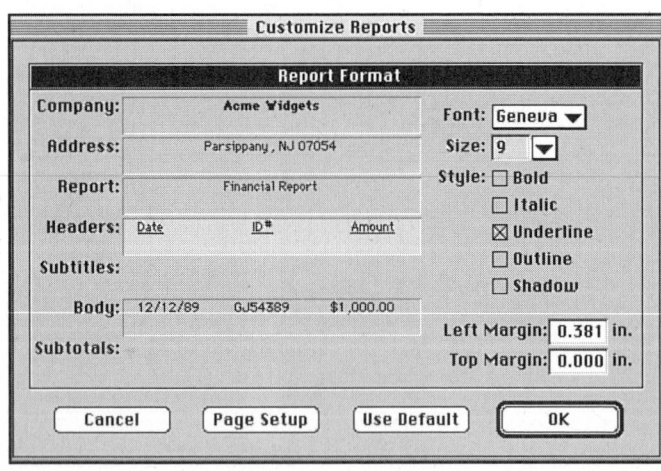

3. Identification of negative numbers (so that the − sign is interpreted correctly and not as subtraction)

4. Multiplication and division

5. Addition and subtraction

6. Equality tests (such as <, >)

If more than one operation is contained in a parenthetical set, the same rules apply within it. Parentheses can also be *nested* with multiple sets of operations to be carried out in a specific order, and the innermost set will be evaluated first. For example, "=A1^((3+B6)*B4)" will first add 3 to the contents of B6, then multiply that by the contents of B4, and finally raise A1 to that power.

If you're a non-mathematician and can't think why anyone would ever care about the above, you might find nesting handy to make sure that spreadsheet **string** operations come out the way you'd expect. You can't have too many parentheses in a formula. If you're not sure that one is required to process data in the order you want, put it in anyway: "=(A1*3)+B1" means the same thing as "=A1*3+B1."

See Also
Circular Reference; Spreadsheet

Formula Bar

A formula bar is a horizontal field across the top of a **spreadsheet**, identified by a **cell** reference, where you can enter numbers, text, or formulas for that cell. The bar always displays any formula for a cell, even though the result of that formula appears in the cell itself. You can use this feature to see whether a cell was entered as data or a formula: **select** the cell, and the original entry will appear in the formula bar.

Some spreadsheets enable you to enter data or a formula by typing directly into a cell, but most require you to select a cell and then type in the formula bar that appears. The bar always has the selected cell reference displayed on the left, and usually has buttons marked X and ✓ on it: click ✓ to put the data in the cell, or X to undo what you've typed and to restore the previous data.

To access a formula bar, click on the cell you want to change. In the figure below, you can enter a formula in cell E52 to compute ten percent of the amount in cell E51.

See Also
Circular Reference

Fortran

The very first high-level **programming language**.

Fortran, short for FORmula TRANslator, was designed to enable scientists and engineers to solve complex mathematical problems using computers without having to deal with **assembly language**. As the first high-level language, Fortran (or FORTRAN, as it was known then) rapidly became the language of choice for much programming.

Fortran has evolved over the years through three standard versions. The first, known as FORTRAN 66 (or Fortran VI), was much like the original version developed in the 1950s. It showed its roots in the days of punchcards by requiring strict column formatting (labels had to be in columns 1-5, statement bodies had to be in columns 7-72, and so on). FORTRAN 66 relied heavily on GOTO statements to control program flow rather than more sophisticated block-structuring.

Fortran 77 built upon the foundations of FORTRAN 66 and added support for block-style conditionals (IF-THEN-ELSE) and improved handling of input and output and text strings. Finally, Fortran 90 further modernized the language with the addition of powerful data structure and modular programming features, and the standardizations of many extensions to Fortran 77. Most modern Fortran **compilers** support Fortran 77, but more are adding Fortran 90 support every day.

Throughout its history, Fortran has remained true to its roots. It is still best suited to programs that are heavy in computation and calculation. As a result, very little general-purpose Macintosh software is written in Fortran, but a great deal of scientific software is.

To give you a taste of the language, this simple program displays the words "Hello, world." indefinitely:

```
C
C       Hello, world.
C

        Program Hello

        implicit none
        logical DONE

        DO while (.NOT. DONE)
            write(*,10)
        END DO
  10    format('Hello, world.')
        END
```

On the Macintosh, Fortran compilers are available from Motorola, Absoft, and Fortner Research. All three of these compilers are hosted by the **MPW** environment.

Motorola
Fortran SDK (Fortran 77)
Motorola RISC Software
6501 William Cannon Dr. West
MD: OE112
Austin, TX 78735-8598
Email: **ppcinfo@risc.sps.mot.com**
Fax: (512) 891-3798
Phone: (800) 347-8384 or (512) 891-2999
Web: **http://www.motorola.com/SPS/PowerPC/**

Absoft
Absoft F77 SDK
Absoft F90 SDK
Ab 81 Bond Street
Rochester Hills, MI 48309
Email: **sales@absoft.com**
Fax: (810) 853-0108
Phone: (810) 853-0050
Web: **http://www.absoft.com**

Fortner Research (formerly Language Systems)

LS FORTRAN
Fortner Research LLC
100 Carpenter Dr.
Sterling, VA 20164
Email: **sales@fortner.com**
Fax: (703) 689-9593
Phone: (800) 252-6479
Web: **http://www.langsys.com/langsys/**

See Also

Assembly Language; Compiler; Programming Languages

FotoTune

Agfa, a maker of high-resolution imagesetters and scanners, has its own solution to **color management**, called FotoTune. This package can produce **device profiles** for monitors and RGB scanners; it supports the use of the Colortron II spectrophotometer (a **color measuring** device) to create monitor profiles. A large selection of printer profiles is provided for desktop printers, printing presses, and film recorders.

See Also

Color Management; Device Profiles

Foul Play: Mystery at Awkward Manor

Foul Play from The Armchair Traveler Company, a British game company, is the brain child of designers William Beckett and William Donelson. The premise is much the same as that of the board game Clue. Sir John Stiffney invites six guests to dinner. In between the arrival time of 7:40 (or 7:25 if you pick a higher difficulty level) and 8:00 p.m., someone disposed of Sir Stiffney and it's your job to find out who. Up to six players take on the role of dinner guests (there's even a maid for real Clue die-hards) and take timed turns exploring the mansion.

As you wander about looking for clues, you get the chance to ask various guests you meet about common things like their whereabouts at the time of their murder and what weapons they might be more likely to use if they were going to kill someone. As in Clue, when you think you've got the killer, you can make a guess. Just click the phone to dial the police and make a guess. If you're wrong, you lose a turn. Foul Play mixes live actors against the beautifully filmed background of Holker Hall, a mansion in England's spectacular Lake District. If this game is your bag, you really don't get tired with more than four thousand possible outcomes programmed. Foul Play offers a fun family evening of whodunit with a lot of great multimedia enhancements.

See Also

Are You Afraid of the Dark?; Family Entertainment; Masterpiece Mansion; Mortimer; Yellow Brick Road II

Foundries, *See Type Foundries and Distributors*

FPO (For Position Only)

FPO refers to the use of a proxy image in a page layout to indicate the final position and size of a graphic. In paper **mechanicals** (paste-ups), an FPO image might be nothing more than a keyline with "FPO" scrawled across it in nonreproducing colored pencil, or it might be a rough sketch of the intended image or even a xerox copy. The actual image, usually a halftone, is then stripped-in during the prepress process of film assembly.

The use of FPO images is a key part of digital prepress production schemes such as **APR (Automatic Picture Replacement)** and **OPI (Open Prepress Interface).** In these output systems, high-resolution digitized images automatically replace low-resolution images embedded in an electronic publication file. The benefit of using FPO images when constructing an electronic publication is that the low-resolution images require less storage memory and speed up processing.

See Also

Automatic Picture Replacement (APR); Open Prepress Interface (OPI); Prepress

FPU, *See Coprocessors, Types*

Fractal Design's Poser

There are a number of art and animation packages that allow you to design realistic "hard" objects (reflective spheres, cars, buildings, spaceships) that can be wrapped with spectacular textures and animated across "other-worldly" backgrounds, seducing us into thinking that the world is made of only hard-edged objects. There are only a few software programs, however, that allow us to develop organic forms, at least at prices that can be afforded by the majority of computer artists and animators. Fractal Design's Poser is one such unique package.

Poser is an absolutely addicting software environment for altering and rendering variations of the human form, and doing it in a manner that is so easy and fun to learn that more experienced computer graphics artists will only need about five minutes with the documentation. Beginners may need an hour or two. Poser was designed to minimize non-visual interfacing, so that moving Poser models gives users a sense of engaging in a virtual 3D world. Clicking on any part of the human forms Poser uses as models makes the chosen elements instantly available for modification and movement.

Poser's interface has the inviting design of MetaTools' Kai's PowerTools, with 3D buttons and attenuators that have the feel of real world 3D devices. The attenuators do different things depending upon your main selections, of which there are four: Pose, Body, Camera, and Light.

- Pose—Sets the attenuators to taper, twist, side-side, and bend, and scale any selected element of the model that is chosen. The model responds instantly to assume a new pose.

- Body—A global option, sets the attenuators to adjust scale, rotation, and translation of the entire model. The model on-screen responds instantly, allowing you to set global rotations and views.

- Camera—Enables you to use the attenuators to modify camera positions and focal parameters.

- Light—Targets any of the three lights for adjustment of the parameters associated with their color and position, while a visual display shows each light's area of influence and how the model will be colorized accordingly.

Altering the Figures You can select a variety of ways that the initial Poser data sets (models) appear on-screen: Silhouette, Outline, Wireframe, and Flat Shaded. For those with PowerMacs, flat shading is the best option. It allows you to see an accurate preview of appendages and light interactions as the model is set in positions. Choosing "Depth Cued" causes elements of the Poser model closest to the camera eye to become darker and those farther away to become lighter (a great help when moving body parts in 3D space in a complicated pose). Systems with less memory can choose to work with "Bounding Box Only" figures, which change the on-screen data to a connected system of cubic objects. Poser even allows you to see how the measurement system called "seven heads" alters the models when "Head Lengths" is toggled on. Even before you alter body part shapes and sizes, Poser models can be rendered as a Man, Woman, Adolescent, Child, Toddler, Baby, Ideal Adult, or Heroic type (male or female). Models can also be textured with various default effects, such as lizard skin or leotards.

Rendering Options Poser allows Guides to be added to a scene for effect: Ground Plane, Horizon Line, and four "props" (Ball, Box, Cane, and Stairs). You can also select a backdrop picture as part of the rendering process, or choose any background color (great if you plan to do image compositing in Fractal Design painter, Photoshop, or other 2D rendering software). Dots per Inch (DPI), resolution, and image size can also be set. The rendering can be saved as a PICT file or as a Poser data file. The two main selections are "smooth" and "muscle," and each can be rendered as quick or detailed. Smooth will suffice for most needs, while muscle rendering creates anatomically correct muscle bulges on the figures. Muscle rendering is especially effective if you are going to paint clothing on the rendering in a paint package, or if the model is the Heroic type (great for comic book illustrations).

Export Poser renderings can be saved as PICT files, DXF 3D models, or RIB (Poser native) format. DXF files are saved with only the polygon data, so all Poser rendering options (like muscle maps) are lost. There are advantages, however, to exporting DXFs. You can import DXF into most 3D rendering/animation software. DXF exports can be rendered in dedicated 3D software (Strata Pro, Infini-D, Alias, RayDream Studio, ElectricImage, and so on) with all of that software's unique texture mapping capabilities, producing human figures that shine like glass or steel. When you are saving to the DXF format as an intermediate step for rendering in a 3D package, pump up the polygon number in the rendering software to get rid of polygonal faceted edges in the model (unless you want that look).

Libraries Poser has four library lists that are important to keep in mind. The first is a listing of poses. If a specific pose is chosen from this listing, it will hold for whatever figure type is assigned to it. As you explore your own model poses, perhaps by altering one of the poses in the library, you can save original posed creations. The danger here, because the software is so much fun to use, is that you will be tempted to save hundreds of new poses a week. That's OK if you have the hard drive space.

The second library is dedicated to loading and saving models whose body features have been altered. Poser allows you to choose any element of a model and resize it, leading to interesting human and non-human characters. Already in the library are obese and anorexic models, and a good selection of what appear to be alien beings. Here again, the temptation will be to alter models and save every one.

The third and fourth library deal with the camera and Lights. Default Camera positions allow you to snap to a screen view or to turn on telephoto or fish eye lenses. Light library listings have default selections like "summer," "from Below," and more. You can save your own Camera settings and Light configurations to these lists.

There are dozens of Poser paintings saved to Fractal's Web site **(http://www.fractal.com)**. You can expect animation capability and more design components in the next revisions.

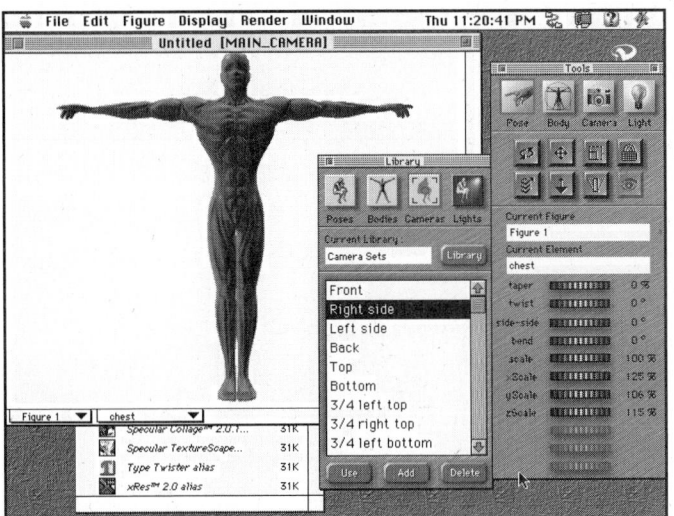

Fractal Painter 4.0

Fractal Painter is the most ambitious painting program available, and offers hundreds of unique tools and effects for digital painting. Fractal Painter is used by artists and animators throughout the world as a primary creative collection of digital tools. The documentation is clear and concise, but the program is so multifaceted that the documentation alone can only present the basic possibilities. You must experience it for yourself to appreciate it.

Painting Tools Fractal Painter utilizes all of the plug-in FX painting options Adobe's Photoshop program accesses and adds the following: Fill (allows you to fill a targeted graphic with color, with another graphic, gradation colors, or a patterned layer), Tonal Controls (Correct and Adjust Colors, Brightness/Contrast, Equalize, Negative, Posterize, imposing Printable Colors, imposing Video Legal colors, and Posterizing using the current color palette), Surface Controls (applying Lighting, Screen and Surface Textures, Color Overlay, Dye Concentration, Expressing a Surface Texture, Warping, and Quick Warping), Focus (Glass Distortion, Motion Blur (motion blurs can create an infinite array of cloud-like backgrounds), Sharpen and Soften...), Esoterica (seven different image altering options: Marbling, Auto Cloning, Instant Van Gogh, Blobs, Grid Paper, Growth, and High Pass Filter), and Objects (creates Drop Shadows and Alignments).

Make Mosaic Under the "Canvas" menu, this operator allows you to build a mosaic tiled graphic from your original art or photo in a step-by-step process. Mosaic tiles applied in Painter follow the contour of the image. This effect is also useful for making textures that map to floors and walls in a 3D scene, as well as creating backgrounds for title/credit text in video.

Painting Tools Twenty-two brush varieties, five airbrushes, nine distortion brushes, twelve special "cloner" brushes, five chalks, six masking brushes, burn, dodge, seven famous artist brushes, nine wet brushes, ten pens, five markers, two crayons, six pencils, fourteen erasers, and three charcoals. All of these can be adjusted by opacity sliders and up to nineteen separate application options.

The Image Hose This tool paints a series of images saved as "nozzle" files, which may be either user developed and saved or tapped into from the extensive Painter CD-ROM libraries. A CD-ROM of dozens of natural image nozzles is available. With the image hose nozzles, exquisite paintings of the natural world can be created. Once completed, these digital paintings can be processed through other media effects in Painter, resulting in pencil sketches, oil paintings, watercolors, mosaic tiled reproductions, charcoal drawings, and more. If none of the nozzles in Painter's library are found suitable for a task, you can take your own sequence of images or photographs and create unique image hoses. From time to time, Fractal Corporation releases separate image hose nozzle CD-ROMs packed with alternate sets of nozzles.

A large library of textures can be placed over/under any graphic to produce paper, cloth, and other looks, all variable by opacity. Textures include paper grain and 3D brush strokes, and all textures can be adjusted as to amount, shine, and reflection by sliders in a full featured dialog. Manipulation of the light source as far as direction, brightness, concentration, exposure, and color is also available.

Painter has the capability to input vector graphics, like those output by FreeHand and Illustrator, translate them into raster graphics, and open them up to all of Painter's tools and processes. **Live Picture** files can also be imported. Painter can even create pages for the **World Wide Web**, complete with "hot spot" data that can take you to other Web sites.

Painter can help you edit and overpaint video animation files. Both **QuickTime** (MAC) **and AVI** (Windows) formatted animations can be loaded into Painter. Once in, each frame can be painted with any of the tools mentioned above. So many effects are possible, Painter 4 can be called a post-production FX engine. Painter has a full-featured movie creation module that allows you to create a movie of as many frames as your memory will support. You input the frames and toggle to each as you paint moving graphics with any of the tools we've already covered. Objects loaded in can appear on all frames at once. Movies can be saved as Quicktime/AVI files or as sequential frames. Painter can help you create Clone Brush Animations. Painters "Clone" brushes allow you

to manipulate an underlying graphic in a step-by-step process. When animated, these tools produce color flows and distortions not possible by other graphic or videographic methods.

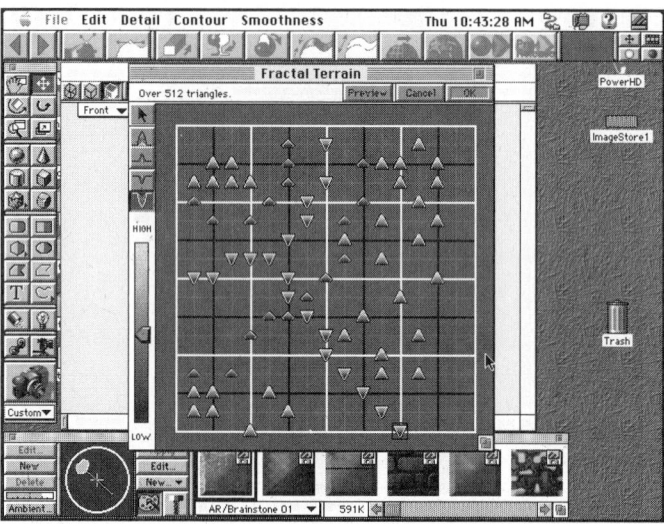

Painter can also create Image Hose Nozzle Animations. Want to create moving leaves and branches as they reveal or cover your logo? Perhaps you'd like to use natural object growth as a segue between two animated frame sequences. Painter fosters this and more with the Image Hose and the dozens of nozzles, either from the on-board library of samples or from your own saved work. Each step can be saved as a frame of an animation. Process Animation allows you to see a process unfold before your eyes. Painter has a special facility that allows you to record a script of your creative movements as they progress step-by-step, recording movements to a script file. These scripts can then be played back, so that the same tools used to create an image magically appear to duplicate the whole process in real time. Process animations are often used to tell a story, and are effective for CD-ROM multimedia as well as for broadcast.

Fractal Terrain Modeler

Fractal Terrain Modeler is a plug-in extension for Strata's StudioPro (version 1.5 and above). Once StudioPro is on-screen, Fractal Terrain Modeler is accessed by going to the Modeling menu and choosing

"Fractal Terrain." A rectangular surface representing the top view of the scene is presented, along with a selection of five tool icons, the arrow selector and four elevation placement symbols. The four elevation placement symbols represent high mountains, low mountains, medium depressions, and river channels. A global slider at the left is used to adjust the overall exaggeration of the terrain, from low rolling geography to high sharp mountain ranges. As a default, the slider is set at the midpoint.

As a part of the Fractal Terrain process, a group of associated menu items are used to fine tune the modeling. The Edit menu allows you to undo the present operation, while a clear command clears the whole terrain grid. A "Detail" menu listing includes Average, Good, High, Fine, and Excessive as options for applying the amount of detail that will be present in the finished model. Average detail in the model causes polygonal surfaces to be more apparent. On the other end, Excessive detail smoothes out the polygonal edges. Higher detail increases rendering time. Contour settings, with a default of 1.00, can be customized according to user input, and shape the terrain to less or more overall contouring. Smoothness adjustments can also be customized by the user.

The design process in Fractal Terrain is simple. Select one of the four elevation icons from the list and place it on the grid. If you want to move it to another location, use the selection arrow to relocate it. Place as many mountains, hills, depressions, and rivers as desired on the grid. When you are satisfied with the map view, use the "preview" option to see how the scene appears as an elevation model. Select OK to place the model in the main Strata editing window.

Once the model appears in the main editing window, you can apply any of the Strata StudioPro operations to it allowed for any 3D object. Textures can be dragged and dropped on the terrain, and the model can be point adjusted with Strata's bevy of point movement and alteration tools. Final rendering obeys all of the standard Strata settings.

Frame Accurate

Refers to a video tape player and recorder that can accurately display video by the frame (video is made up of a sequence of frames). These decks are usually very expensive.

See Also

Animaq; NTSC; SMPTE; Time Base Corrector

FrameMaker

While many desktop publishers have never used FrameMaker, it has a large and devoted following among those who write and publish technical materials. Designed to automate as much as possible of the page layout process, FrameMaker is not for those who are pursuing the most beautiful pages—but it can be extremely efficient.

Billed by its publisher (originally Frame Technology, now Adobe Systems) as an all-purpose document creation program,

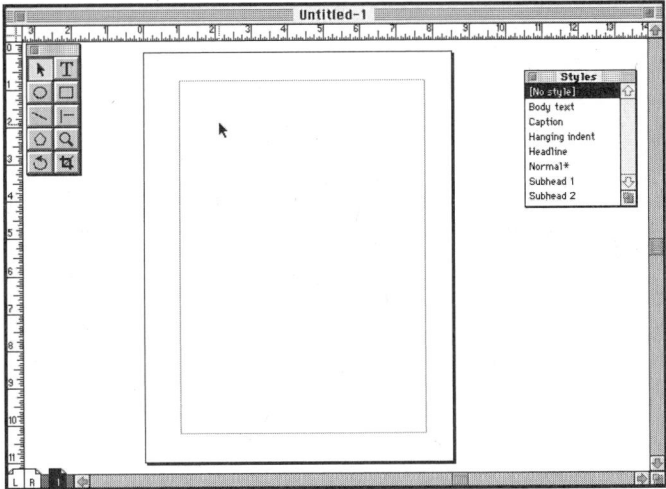

FrameMaker can be used as a word processor as well as a page layout program. Its search-and-replace capabilities are strong, and since each document opens with a text box already in place on the page and default **style sheets** already set up, it's easy to jump right in and start writing.

But FrameMaker is also used to compose math and science textbooks, mainly because of its built-in equation editor. Math equations can be created and edited right in the main document window, with a full range of symbols and operators available to users. A floating palette shows math operations such as radicals, integrals, and matrices, so users can point and click to set up an equation, but a full set of keyboard shortcuts speeds up the process for the experienced user. Typographically, FrameMaker's equations aren't perfect—they need a lot of micropositioning—but this disadvantage is outweighed for many users by the convenience of having the equation editor built in.

The program also contains a powerful table editor, which offers custom ruling and shading, straddle cells, and automatic continued lines. Automated page layout features include running heads (text can be picked up from anywhere in a document); automatic index, table of contents, cross-reference, and footnote generation; inline graphic boxes that float to the top or bottom of a page, as specified; and automatic numbering—useful for headings, lists, and equations.

Conditional text allows users to create multiple versions of a document by choosing to show or hide text marked with "condition tags." This comes in handy for projects like catalogs with European, American, and Asian versions.

Electronic publishers make use of FrameMaker's **hyperlink** feature, which allows readers of an on-screen document to click on a word to move to another document or another location in the present document. A FrameReader utility allows users to read FrameMaker documents without having the application. FrameMaker can also create **Acrobat** and **HTML** documents.

Master pages, style sheets, and tools work much the same as in other page layout applications, albeit less smoothly. Elements of other documents (master pages, style sheets, equation preferences, and so on) can be imported and applied to the present document, and styles in documents collected into a group called a book can be updated all at once. FrameMaker can also update page numbers in a book group.

Another reason for FrameMaker's popularity is that it's available not only for Mac, but also for Windows, Sun, and UNIX systems. Documents created on any of these platforms are completely compatible with the other platforms (barring font problems and incompatible graphics formats).

See Also

Acrobat Reader; HTML; Hyperlink; Page Layout Applications; Style Sheets

Frames, Creating in HTML

A feature that enables authors of **World Wide Web pages** to divide a page into separate frames within the overall "frame" of the **Web browser** window. Each frame has its own **URL** and behaves independently of adjacent frames. Frames, however, can also be linked so that a mouse click on a **hypertext** link in one frame can bring to screen a document in an adjacent frame.

Frames were created by **Netscape** for use in the Web browser Netscape Navigator. Although other browsers such as Internet Explorer have begun to recognize frames, it should be noted that many browsers will not display frames and another alternative should be provided using other **HyperText Markup Language (HTML)** commands.

Frames can be specified using HTML, and the overall commands take the place of the <BODY> </BODY> tags usually found in an HTML document, as indicated:

```
<HTML>
<HEAD>
<TITLE> </TITLE>
<FRAMESET>
</FRAMESET>
</HTML>
```

The following illustration shows a Web page that has been divided into three frames, each containing its own HTML document.

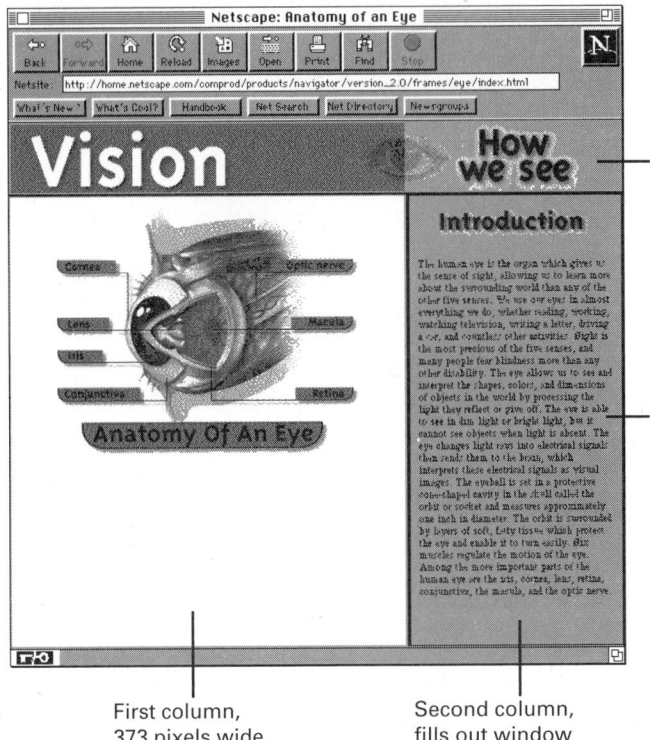

First row, 70 pixels in height

Second row, fills out window

First column, 373 pixels wide

Second column, fills out window

1. Map out your page. Make a rough pencil sketch of the frames you want to add and their approximate sizes.

2. Size rows and columns. Specify approximately how wide or how deep you want rows and columns to be (keeping in mind that they can be changed later). Remember that 72 pixels equals one inch.

3. Add <FRAMESET> and <FRAME> tags to specify how many frames your page will have, and what documents will serve as contents for each frame. Remember to accurately specify an absolute or relative path to the source documents for each frame.

4. Provide a <NOFRAMES> alternative. Using tables or other, more conventional HTML, arrange the contents of your frames within the <NOFRAMES> </NOFRAMES> tags to provide an alternative for browsers that do not display frames.

In order to create frames, an author needs to be familiar with three or four basic **HTML tags**: <FRAMESET ROWS="value">, <FRAMESET COLS="value">, <FRAME>, and <NOFRAME>.

The following table lists the tags and attributes needed to create frames.

Frames can bring several benefits to a Web page or Web site:

- They act as organizers, providing easy access to a site's contents.

- Nonscrolling frames called *ledges* remain on-screen providing advertising value.

- They add interactivity to a site and make it reduce the need to navigate back and forth between windows.

Steps involved in creating frames on a Web page include:

Web page authors might also consider specifying hypertext links to documents that open in a separate targeted window using the <TARGET> attribute. A number of predesignated values to <TARGET> can be used. For example, in the following HTML line,

```
<A HREF="info.html" TARGET="_blank">Click here</a>
```

the file named "info.html" will open in a new blank window when the user clicks the words "Click here."

Frames: The Basic HTML Tags

HTML Tag	Description
<FRAMESET> </FRAMESET>	Contains an entire set of frames or "frameset." Used in place of the <BODY> tag in an HTML document that has frames.
<FRAMESET ROWS="n, %, *">	Specifies the height of each horizontal row within a frameset. Height is expressed as n, a number of pixels; %, a percentage of the page height; or *, a variable that lets the browser determine size based on current size of browser window.
<FRAMESET COLS="n, %, *">	Specifies the width of each vertical column within a frameset. Width is expressed as n, %, or *, as above.
<FRAME> </FRAME>	Describes the size and contents of each frame within a frameset.
<FRAME SRC="URL">	Specifies the URL of the document that will be contained within the frame.
<FRAME NAME="frame_name">	Names a frame so it can be linked to another frame and respond to hyperlinks.
<FRAME MARGINWIDTH>	Determines the size of the left and right margins between frame border and contents of frame.
<FRAME MARGINHEIGHT>	Determines the size of the top and bottom margins between frame border and contents of frame.
<FRAME SCROLLING="Yes|No|auto">	Determines whether or not a frame has a scroll bar. Auto leaves it to the browser to determine if a scrollbar is needed. Default=auto.
<FRAME NORESIZE>	Prevents the frame borders from turning into "handles" that can be resized by the user. Default=NORESIZE.
<NOFRAMES> </NOFRAMES>	Specifies an alternative page layout not using frames for non-frames-friendly browsers.
<TARGET="window_name">	Enables a link in one frame to open in a new window using the TARGET attribute. The targeted window has to be named with NAME.

See Also

HTML; Hypertext; Netscape Navigator; URL; Web Browser; Web Page

Framework

In programming, a framework is a set of predefined code to "do the basics" and upon which you can build other programs.

Most programs do many of the exact same things. For example, no matter what a program's purpose is, it probably has to manage menus, respond to mouse clicks, and open and close windows. Rather than rewriting all of this functionality for every program, you can use a framework. Frameworks enable you to concentrate on those things that differentiate your program from others, so that you don't have to worry about all the things that stay the same.

Frameworks are the scaffolding upon which you can build your own programs.

Because this idea of reusable code that is easily extended meshes well with **object-oriented programming** techniques, many of the most popular application frameworks are written in object-oriented languages (typically **C++**). These include Symantec's **Think Class Library**, Metrowerks' **PowerPlant**, and the grandfather of them all, Apple's **MacApp**. These object-oriented frameworks are often called *class libraries*, because they use object classes to implement and augment the default behavior.

However, frameworks need not be object-oriented. Procedural frameworks are often called *shells*, because they are the empty shell of a program. This class includes TransSkel, Jim Trudeau's **EasyApp**, and DropShell, a framework for creating small drag-and-drop applications.

Frameworks can also be written for more specific purposes. For example, Grant Neufeld has written an excellent framework for creating **CGI** (Common Gateway Interface) applications for Macintosh Web servers, and a number of shells have been written that focus on writing Extensions, Control panels, and other smaller bits of code. Apple has even created a framework targeted exclusively at **OpenDoc** parts, the **OpenDoc Parts Framework** (OPF).

Programming using frameworks can take much of the "grunt work" out of development. **Interface builders** can make the job even easier. These programs enable you to edit visually the human interface of your program. The visual interface can then use the services of a framework to provide the expected behavior for each type of element automatically. All you need to do is write the parts of your program that do the real work!

See Also

EasyApp; Interface Builder; MacApp; Programming; PowerPlant

Frankie Virus

Not a Macintosh virus, but one that infects Macintosh emulators on Atari computers.

See Also

ANTI Virus; CDEF Virus; CODE 1 Virus; CODE 352 Virus; INIT 17 Virus; INIT 1984 Virus; INIT 29 Virus; INIT 9403 Virus; INIT-M Virus; MacMag Virus; MBDF Virus; MDEF Virus; nVIR Virus; Scores Virus; T4 Virus; WDEF Virus; ZUC Virus

Freedom

Freedom is a simple **HyperCard** stack for people who are temporarily, or permanently, unable to speak. It is particularly useful for persons with neurological disorders, such as Amyotrophic Lateral Sclerosis (Lou Gehrig's disease), and was originally developed for a young man with ALS.

Although not as sophisticated as **Talk:About**, it enables the user to convey basic wants and carry on a simple conversation by pointing and clicking the appropriate preprogrammed phrases. Freedom uses mouse clicks and minimum mouse movement to enable users to type and select phrases to be spoken. It can also be configured to work with a **sip and puff switch** or single-click switch and **scanning**, so that even the most severely motion-limited user can communicate.

Adding new phrases is simple for users who can type or who can use a mouse and scanning software with an on-screen keyboard. Because it's written in HyperCard, anyone with a copy of the HyperCard application (not the player) can resize the buttons or add icons or pictures for a user who doesn't read.

TIP Freedom is **shareware** and can be downloaded from many sites, including Apple's Disability area at **http://www2.apple.com/disability/ shareware.html**.

Shareware fees go to the S. Nathaniel Woodruff Memorial Fund (c/o The Family Center, 15 W. 5th Street, Emporium, PA 15834). Tax-deductible donations help to finance the Toy and Resource Lending Library, which provides a library of toys and books, as well as long-term loans of special needs equipment—car seats and such.

Free-Form Modeling, *See Modeling*

FreeHand

Offering professional artists the tools to create everything from complex technical illustrations to short, design-intensive multi-page documents (like brochures), FreeHand combines precision **PostScript** drawing tools with a plethora of other useful features.

The basics: FreeHand lets users create any shape—FreeHand or geometrical, with straight lines or **Bézier curves**—and apply a stroke (or border) and fill to it, in any color. The program supports **CMYK** color, as well as **Pantone spot color** and other color matching systems such as **Toyo** (common in Japan).

Objects can be moved, scaled, and skewed, while grouping allows multiple objects to be modified as a unit and layering allows objects to be easily hidden or shown, as well as moved backwards or forwards in the drawing. Precision is easily achievable, with numerical control over the positioning and movement of each object. Even **guides** can be placed and moved by typing in coordinates, as well as pulling them out from rulers. Documents can consist of one or several pages (and they can be of varying sizes).

Following in **Illustrator's** footsteps, FreeHand now supports the competition's **add-on software** as well as its own Xtras: Illustrator and **Photoshop plug-ins** add extra features to FreeHand. Its own Xtras are fairly interesting, too, including third-party add-ons that can create bar codes, import QuarkXPress documents, and estimate distances on maps created in FreeHand.

FreeHand now lets users convert a **vector** image into a **bitmapped** one by rasterizing it and saving it as a **PICT** file. These two capabilities can be combined to allow users to create shapes, rasterize them, and then apply special effects with Photoshop filters that won't work on FreeHand's original vector images.

Photoshop Acquire plug-ins work, too, allowing users to scan images directly into FreeHand.

FreeHand has strong text-handling features, including paragraph **style sheets** and floating palettes for changing text attributes. Text can be entered in FreeHand or imported from a word processing file, and its text box can be a specific size or an autoexpanding box that grows larger as text is entered. An especially nice feature brought over from **page layout applications** is the capability to paste imported images or FreeHand graphics into a line of text so that they move with the text when it's edited.

Style sheets for graphic items are a helpful feature, allowing users to keep elements consistent throughout one or many documents. Attributes affected include stroke width, stroke color, and fill color. FreeHand's interface uses several floating palettes that can be displayed, hidden, or folded up so that only their title bars show.

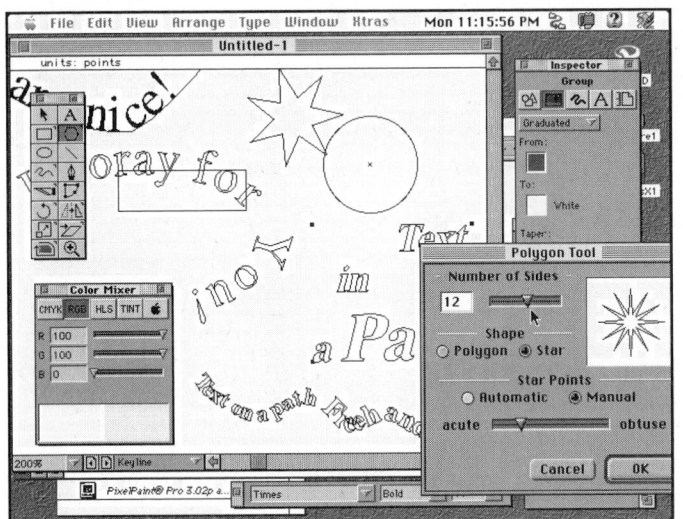

See Also

Add-On Software; Bézier Curves; Bitmapped Graphics; CMYK; Drawing Applications; Guides; Illustrator; Page Layout Applications; Photoshop; Plug-Ins; PostScript; Spot Color; Style Sheets; Toyo; Vector Image

FreeStyle

FreeStyle is a low-cost, easy-to-use music sequencer that enables you to record and edit music. You will need an external **MIDI** keyboard to work efficiently with the software.

FreeStyle includes support for musical notation, a feature not found in all sequencing software, but the program does not support lyrics, dynamics, or articulation marks. Professionals must export the music file to another program using the MIDI format, and output the music from there.

Mark of the Unicorn
Price: $200
Phone or Fax: (617) 576-2760
Web: **http://www.midifarm.com/midifarm/
motu/freestyle.htm**

Freeze, *See Crashes, System*

Frequency Modulated Screening, *See Stochastic Screens*

Frequently Asked Questions, *See FAQ*

Frontier

Frontier, a system-level scripting utility from UserLand Software, was the first **AppleEvents**-based scripting system for the Mac. In the days between the release of System 7 and the long-delayed introduction of **AppleScript**, system-level scripting on the Macintosh would have been a promise largely unfulfilled, if not for Frontier. When Apple finally did release AppleScript, it stole some of Frontier's thunder. Frontier had a tough time competing with AppleScript, especially after Apple began distributing AppleScript with the System Software. Rather than give up in the face of such adversity, Dave Winer, the creator or Frontier, decided to take a different approach. He re-christened Frontier Aretha, added a handful of **Internet**-related features, and began distributing it for free on the Internet.

Although Frontier and AppleScript are both scripting systems, they take radically different approaches to the same problem. Unlike AppleScript, Frontier runs as an application. As a result, no Extensions are needed to enable Frontier to do its magic, but the Frontier application must be running for scripts to execute. In addition, Frontier is native on the Power Macintosh and supports multiple threads, so more than one script can execute simultaneously. Combined, these give Frontier a significant speed advantage over AppleScript.

At the heart of Frontier is the *object database*, a central storage facility shared by all Frontier scripts. At its highest level, called the *root*, the object database consists of a table of objects. The objects can be scripts, variables, word processing documents, or even other tables. This table-within-a-table structure creates a hierarchy similar to folders on a Macintosh hard disk (see the following figure).

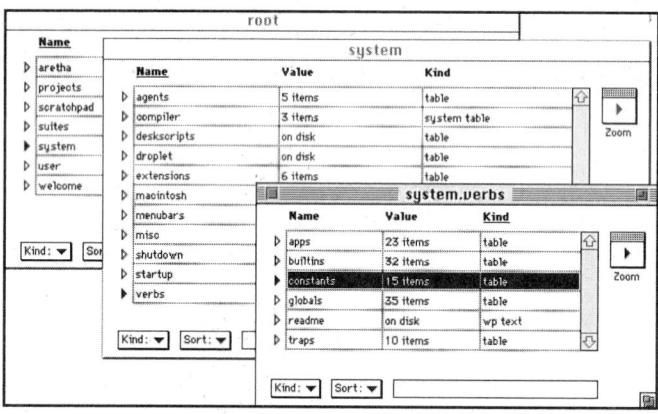

Objects below the root level are specified using a *dot notation* similar to Internet domain names. Thus, the active window in the previous figure is **system.verbs**, and the highlighted object in that window is **system.verbs.constants**.

Virtually all activity in Frontier takes place in the object database. Scripts that are currently running and their variables reside in the database, as do scripts that define much of Frontier's own functionality. This makes Frontier extremely flexible and easy to customize. In fact, you can edit Frontier's menus and attach scripts to any menu item. You can even add entirely new menus.

This capability of editing menus doesn't stop with Frontier itself. Through *menu sharing*, Frontier enables you to create custom menus

in applications written to support the menu sharing protocol, including Stuffit Deluxe, Eudora, and Netscape.

Frontier scripts are written in *UserTalk*, Frontier's own language. The following figure shows a simple script written in UserTalk. UserTalk includes a full complement of flow control constructs (if/then, loops, and so on) and a rich set of verbs to control the Finder, other applications, and the Frontier environment itself. You can use any script you've written just as you would a built-in verb.

Editing UserTalk scripts is a joy in Frontier. Script editor windows are actually outlines, so any segment of code can be collapsed as you would collapse the subtopics of an outline. For example, the highlighted line in the previous figure could be collapsed to hide the lines indented under it. This feature can make the flow of a script much clearer by hiding the details when you don't need to see them.

As the following figure shows, Frontier can also accept scripts written in AppleScript, or any other scripting language compatible with Apple's **Open Scripting Architecture** (OSA).

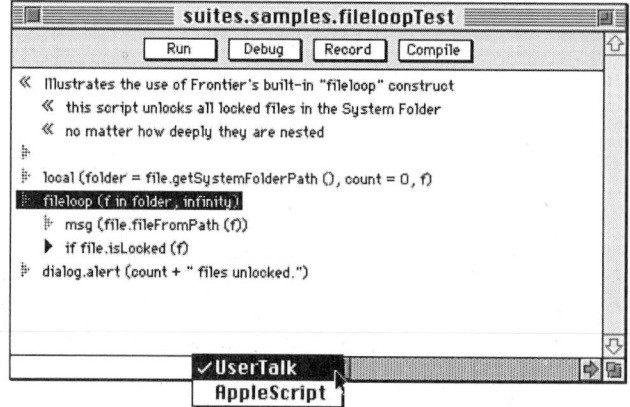

Extensive information about Frontier is available on the World Wide Web at the UserLand Web site (**http://www.hotwired.com/staff/userland/**). The Aretha release of Frontier is available for download there as well.

See Also

AppleScript; CGI; Internet; Open Scripting Architecture (OSA); Scripting

Frontmost, *See FaceSpan*

FSP (File Service Protocol)

A protocol for transferring files on the **Internet**. Performs the same function as anonymous **FTP** but costs less and provides greater security for the **Internet service provider** while presenting a friendlier interface to the **client**. Only one **server** handles all requests from clients, and only one client at a time can connect. For more information, see

```
ftp://ftp.germany.cu.net/pub/networking/
inet/fsp
```

See also

FTP; Internet Service Provider; Networking

FTP

Acronym for File Transfer Protocol, a method of transferring files to and from remote computers on the **Internet**. A *protocol* is a set of standard settings or rules recognized by different computers connected by **networks**.

More data is transferred via FTP than by any other method on the Internet. The capability to enable users to download software and transmit files is one of the Internet's biggest assets. FTP, therefore, is a protocol recognized by virtually every machine connected to the Internet.

(This entry discusses File Transfer Protocol in general. A number of specific file transfer protocols related to modems that connect to either local area networks or the Internet are discussed in **File Transfer Protocols**.)

In the Macintosh world, several FTP sites with many gigabytes of disk space store a large number of freeware and shareware programs, along with commercial demo versions of software and types of Macintosh-related information. These Macintosh **software archives** are made available to anyone connected to the Internet. Some of the best known are

```
mac.archive.umich.edu
sumex-aim.stanford.edu
```

These sites are so popular that their contents have been mirrored by other sites around the world so users in other countries can obtain files more quickly.

A user who wants to download files from a software archive needs an FTP client program such as **Anarchie** or **Fetch**. Anarchie, for instance, eliminates the need to search through long lists of files by letting the user enter a keyword to search for in an Archie database. Anarchie then returns a listing that provides full filenames and all the address information needed to retrieve the file via FTP.

A good FTP client will allow a user to create shortcuts for frequently used FTP sites. The client will also facilitate navigation between folders in a site. Some clients fail to present the user with complete information about a file's name, size, or date of creation; make sure the client you use shows the complete information as an option.

You will come across a variety of **file types** on FTP sites. Each file type can be deduced from the three-letter extension at the end of its filename. The most common is the extension ".hqx," which denotes a file encoded with BinHex so that it can be transported easily across the Net. Other common file extensions are ".txt" for an ASCII-text file, ".sit" or ".cpt" for files compressed with **StuffIt Expander** or Compact Pro, respectively, or ".sea," which is a Self-Extracting Archive that launches and expands when you double-click on it.

Keep in mind that files with suffixes such as ".zip" or ".gz" are not Mac files and you may not be able to do anything with them after you decode them.

See Also

Decoding/Decompressing Files; Encoding Files; File Transfer Protocols; Modem

Full Throttle

Designed by Tim Schafer who created both Maniac Mansion games, Full Throttle combines fluid animation with killer action. Instead of jerky cartoons and that dreaded wait between animated sequences, Full Throttle is seamless. You play Ben, a biker out to clear his name of a murder he didn't commit.

The real murderer is a corporate big shot who's trying to get rid of you and your motorcycle gang so he can have a monopoly on the biking industry. Full Throttle is full of puzzles and character interaction, in the same vein as **Return to Zork**. The animated scenes are fun to watch and the overall ambiance of the game makes you feel as if you are participating in a well-done cartoon. LucasArts-style humor adds a light touch to the generous amount of action. As you play, you become

quite fond of the characters in the game and are sad to see it end. Thank goodness (and LucasArts) for a well-produced game with a plot.

FullTilt! Pinball, *See 3-D Ultra Pinball; Pinball Games*

Function Keys

The 15 keys that appear at the top of extended keyboards are function keys that enable users and software developers, through use of a **macro** program such as QuickKeys to add certain **commands** to each key. The first four keys already have commands assigned to them: F1=**Undo**, F2=**Cut**, F3=**Copy**, F4=**Paste**, but they can be reassigned new commands. Any of these Function keys can be assigned keystrokes with a program such as QuickKeys or any application, such as Adobe Photoshop, that enables you to assign function keys to commands from within the application's preferences.

See Also

Copy Command; Cut Command; Macro; Paste Command; Undo/Redo Command

Function, Spreadsheet

A function is a set of **spreadsheet operators** to perform a complex calculation, callable by a command that can be inserted in a **formula**. It can also be non-mathematic commands to be used in formulas, including text manipulations, **lookup table** substitutions, and program-specific operations.

Functions are built into the software, and the selection varies among programs. But almost all functions include a variety of these handy shortcuts to solve financial, statistical, engineering, and text problems. Most programs have a menu or **palette** arrangement to simplify picking the proper function and adding it to a formula, but you can also type them directly into the **formula bar**.

Functions require arguments, expressed in parentheses after the command. For example, the PV function in most programs computes the present value of an investment based on periodic payments and a specified interest rate. It's expressed "PV(payment,interest,term)." To use it, substitute the three arguments with cell references or numbers: "=PV(A1,.08,20)" would use the payment amount in A1, and figure the compound value after 20 annual payments with an eight percent annual rate.

Most functions are derived from standard formulas, so you can also calculate PV with "=payment*(1-(1+interest)^-term)/interest," but having it as a function makes things a lot easier.

Text functions are similar to the string commands in **BASIC** or **HyperTalk**, and let you perform operations like substituting specific characters or deleting from the front or back of a string. Logical functions allow branching, and take the form "IF(condition,x,y)": if the condition is true the formula will execute whatever operation or function is in x; otherwise it will execute y.

Some programs require an @ sign before a function, so they are also sometimes called "at-functions."

FutureBASIC

FutureBASIC is a complete **integrated development environment** (IDE) for creating Macintosh programs using the **BASIC** programming language. Traditionally, BASIC is viewed as a beginner's language. It's name is even an acronym for *Beginner's All-purpose Symbolic Instruction Code*. Development environments like FutureBASIC could change that perception for good.

Unlike many versions of BASIC, FutureBASIC is a first-class Macintosh development environment. Not only does it create **compiled**, stand-alone applications, it can also be used to create **code resources** such as Extensions or plug-ins. Applications created with FutureBASIC are relatively small and fast—comparable to programs written in **C** or **Pascal**.

The FutureBASIC IDE includes a source code **editor** that supports automatic indenting and syntax highlighting, a source-level **debugger**, and a **compiler**

and **linker**. It also includes an excellent interface builder and code generator, "PG:PRO," that takes much of the routine drudgery out of creating an application's interface.

Because Apple does not document the Toolbox from a BASIC perspective, it can often be difficult to make full use of new system software features in BASIC. Staz Software has overcome that problem by including a conversion program that generates BASIC interfaces from the Pascal ones Apple supplies.

Although BASIC is not likely to regain the position it once had for commercial development, programmers who want to move beyond HyperCard or AppleScript might save themselves much of the learning curve of C or Pascal by starting with FutureBASIC.

FutureBASIC is published by Staz Software:

> Staz Software
> 3 Leisure Time Drive
> Diamondhead, MS 39525-3215
> Email: Staz@aol.com
> Fax: (601) 255-7086
> Phone: (601) 255-7085
> Web: **http://www.ids.net/~paumic/FutureBasic/**

See Also

BASIC; C; Code Resource; Compiled Language; Compiler; Editor; Integrated Development Environment; Linker; Pascal

FWB SCSI, *See Ports, Future Trends*

G

Gambling Games, *See Card Games*

Game Editors, *See Crystal Crazy*

Games, *See Adventure Games; Entertainment; Games; Role-Playing Games; Sim Games; Strategy Games*

Gaming, *See Entertainment*

Gaming Services on the Internet, *See Online Games*

Gamma Curve, *See Image Scanning*

Gamma Values in Scanners

Most scanning software supports the concept of gamma correction: rather than adjusting the brightness of a scan by changing all the light and dark pixels in the same way; light and dark pixels are adjusted differently to improve the balance and contrast of the image. It's almost always better to adjust tonal values with gamma controls rather than simple brightness/contrast controls.

Software controls for setting gamma value controls vary widely, but many packages allow you to enter gamma values directly. lowering a scan's gamma value from the default value of 1.0 darkens the scan; increasing the gamma value lightens the scan.

See Also
Scanners

Gantt Charts, *See Plan & Track*

Garfield Virus, *See MDEF Virus*

Gassée, Jean Louis

Jean-Louis Gassée took over as general manager of Apple France in 1981 after working for Hewlett Packard and Data General. Gassée was extremely successful there; Apple computers even outsold IBMs in France.

Gassée was brought in on the Macintosh project when **Steve Jobs** and **John Sculley** were in the midst of their falling out. He was ostensibly the Macintosh marketing director, but Sculley wanted him running the entire Mac division instead of Jobs. Gassée was extremely reluctant to get involved in the mess the Mac division had become, but was finally convinced to take the job.

When Jobs began plotting to oust Sculley, it was Jean-Louis Gassée who warned Sculley. When Jobs left Apple, Gassée became the head of product development at Apple. Though not an engineer, Gassée is a brilliant marketer and a visionary. He left Apple in 1990 and now heads Be, Inc., in San Jose, California.

Be is a new computer company that manufactures a unique multiprocessor computer targeted at technology enthusiasts. The computer, known as the BeBox, uses two (or more) PowerPC microprocessors and a new operating system (BeOS) that takes full advantage of the power of multiprocessing.

See Also

Jobs, Steve; Sculley, John

Gatekeeper

Gatekeeper is a free System **extension**/INIT developed by Chris Johnson designed to protect your system against the **WDEF** virus that infects the invisible **desktop file** on disks of all types. Gatekeeper was originally introduced back in 1990 when the WDEF virus was spreading rapidly—it would infect a hard disk and then transfer the virus to any inserted disks. Gatekeeper was designed to keep the desktop file from being altered by the WDEF virus.

Gatekeeper also stops unknown suspicious activity in the hopes of preventing virus attacks. Many genuine applications perform activities that resemble virus attacks. Gatekeeper can learn which routines should be allowed and which should be prevented. Codes can be entered into Gatekeeper to allow it to detect (but not remove) new viruses.

The proliferation of commercial virus detection software has made an appearance of the WDEF virus very rare.

See Also

Anti-Virus; Desktop File; Extensions Folder; Virus; WDEF Virus

Gateway, See Internet, Services

GCR (Gray Component Replacement)

GCR, or gray component replacement, is a technique used in **process color** printing to reduce the amount of ink needed to cover an area in the printed image. A variation of UCR (**undercolor removal**), GCR helps control ink trapping and reduces ink cost.

When three process colors (cyan, magenta, and yellow) mix and two predominate to create the hue, the third color determines the grayness of the mixture. In GCR, this gray component is replaced with black in varying percentages so that there are never more than two primary colors plus black. This is also called *achromatic reproduction*, and it affects all the colors in an image.

See Also

Color Printing; Ink Trapping; Process Color; Undercolor Removal

General Controls Control Panel

This control panel enables you to personalize preferences for your system including: The rate at which the **cursor** blinks while waiting at an insertion point; how many times a **menu** item blinks when selected; whether or not you want to see items on your **desktop** when it's in the background (such as your **hard drive**, disks, the **trash can**, and so on); whether you want to lock your **System Folder** or Applications folder to keep other users from accidentally removing items; whether you want the Mac to display a warning dialog box if the Mac was **shut down** improperly; and the default location you want when you save a file, as shown in the following figure.

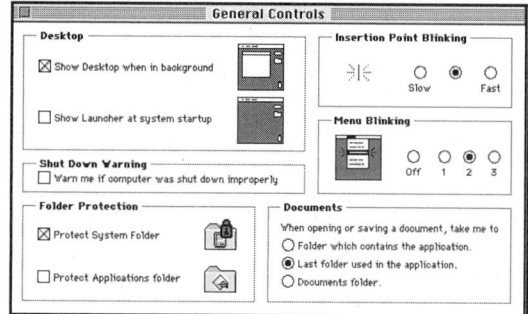

All of these preferences are available to make working on your system more convenient. To select any of these options, click the **checkbox** or **radio button** beside your selection.

To set your preferences in the General Controls Control Panel, follow these steps:

1. Open the General Controls Control Panel from the Control Panels submenu on the Apple menu (or System Folder).

2. Set your preferences by selecting the options you want.

3. Close the General Controls Panel.

See Also

Checkbox; Cursor; Desktop; Hard Disk; Menu Commands; Radio Buttons; Shut Down; System Folder; Trash

General Magic

General Magic was founded by three former Apple employees in 1990 to develop software for personal digital assistants (PDAs). Apple, Sony, and Motorola are all major investors in General Magic.

General Magic might have been just another Silicon Valley startup if not for its major investors and the names of the three founders: **Bill Atkinson**, creator of **HyperCard**, **MacPaint**, and the Mac's graphics engine, **QuickDraw**; Andy Hertzfeld, who wrote much of the original Macintosh **Toolbox**; and Marc Porat, former manager of business development for Apple's Advanced Technology Group.

There are two significant software developments created by General Magic. The first is the MagicCap operating system. This OS is used in PDAs from Sony and Motorola. The second is a technology called TeleScript, a language for creating intelligent software agents that can complete tasks without user intervention.

See Also

Atkinson, Bill; Toolbox

General MIDI

The original **MIDI** specification failed to map specific patches (sounds) to MIDI ID numbers. Different manufacturers used different numbers to identify similar sounds, resulting in unusual results when playing a MIDI file on a different keyboard to the one it was created for. General MIDI fixed that problem by assigning specific types of sounds to specific ID numbers. For example, an electric guitar is always #28, and an acoustic grand piano is #1. Drums are always on channel 10, with specific notes representing different drum parts; a kick drum is note 36 of patch 10.

See Also

MIDI

Generic Icons

The invisible **desktop file** on your Macintosh keeps track of all the file **icons** on your **hard drive**. Over time, this file becomes larger and larger as it keeps track of every icon added to and deleted from your hard drive, and occasionally it needs to be rebuilt to operate properly. If you have not **rebuilt the desktop** on your computer recently, the custom icons that normally appear on your files may start to revert to black and white generic icons. The generic icon for an application is a white diamond with a hand holding a pen. The generic icon for a document is a blank white page, as shown in the following figure.

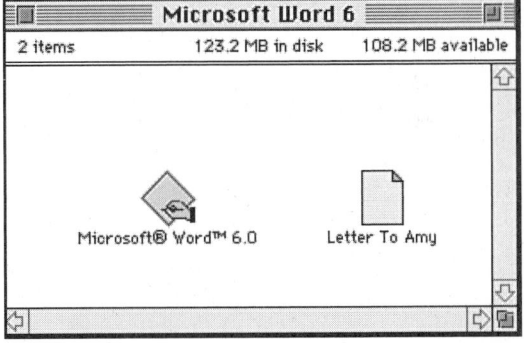

This either means that the icons have lost their bundle bits, and rebuilding your desktop may remedy the situation, or that the application that created the document is not on your hard disk, so your system treats it as a generic document and gives it a generic icon. The bundle bits are small bits of code in the file used to link a document's icon to the application that created it. When you create a document in Microsoft Word, for example, the icon looks very similar to Word's own icon. And if you double-click this icon, your system knows it's a Word document and launches Word for you. However, if the icon lost its bundle bits, or they somehow got corrupted, it would still be a Word document, but it would not know it was a Word document, and this link back to the application (and matching icon) would be temporarily lost. So when the Mac doesn't recognize this document as a Word document, it gives it a generic icon.

So if you have the application that created the document, the document may have a bundle bit problem.

You can use a repair utility program to fix this situation. Both **Norton Utilities** and **MacTools** can repair most common bundle bit problems, and you can also try Apple's free repair utility **Disk First Aid**, which is on the DiskTools disk of system install disks that you got when you first purchased your Mac. (Note: If you have a CD-ROM install disc, there is a Disk Tools folder on the CD-ROM, and Disk First Aid is in that folder.)

See Also

Desktop File; Hard Disks; Icons; Rebuilding the Desktop

GeoPort

Beginning with the AV Macs (the Quadra and Centris 660AV/840AV) Apple replaced the standard modem **Serial port** with a new connector called the GeoPort. The presence of a GeoPort-type serial port can be noted by looking for an additional ninth pin in the serial connector. The ninth pin carries power from the Mac to a device called a GeoPort Telecom Adapter or Phone Pod. This is a little box that, combined with the internal hardware in these Macs, can replace a modem.

The GeoPort technology takes advantage of the Digital Signal Processing chips in the AV Macs to let the computer itself take on many of the functions previously performed by the modem. With old style modem technology, the computer would send a modem a digital signal, which the modem converted to an analog signal and sent out to the telephone lines. (See **Modems** for additional details).

All Power Macs have GeoPort-enabled printer and modem ports, as do the older Centris 660AV, Quadra 660AV and Quadra 840AV. GeoPort-enabled serial ports have the ability to transmit data at 115,000Bps, faster than ordinary Mac serial ports, which have a limit of 56,000Bps. This is faster than ordinary modem traffic, but is useful when modems use compression and when you are connecting to **ISDN** lines. GeoPort connectors look the same as the traditional round Mac serial ports, but have 9 pins, one more than the traditional Mac serial ports.

To connect to an **analog telephone line** or a digital **ISDN line**, GeoPort requires the use of a telecommunications adapter. The most common is the Apple GeoPort Telecom Adapter (see the following figure), which connects to standard telephone lines. Like a modem, the Adapter has two connectors, one for a telephone line and one for a telephone.

The first ISDN adapter for GeoPort is the Sat-Sagem SPIGA, which has two ISDN B channels at 64Kbps each, which can be combined.

There are several advantages to using a GeoPort adapter and a software modem instead of ordinary modem, and a few disadvantages. One advantage is that there is some really innovative telephony software available that is easy to set up, use, and manage. For instance, MegaPhone from Cypress Research turns your Mac into a full-duplex speaker phone, which means that you and the party at the other end of the line can speak at the same time.

Another advantage is that you can use the same line for both fax and voice without having to turn anything on or off. The Express Modem software can recognize what type of call is received and use the appropriate software, fax or voice, to either answer the call or let you answer it.

Another bonus is that upgrades can be inexpensive software-only additions. At press time, Apple was expected to offer a 28.8Kbps software upgrade for the Apple GeoPort Telecom Adapter sometime during the summer of 1996. Previous to this upgrade, the top speed of the Express Modem and the Apple GeoPort Telecom Adapter was only 14.4Kbps, which is one of the disadvantages to using GeoPort technology.

There is also an annoying incompatibility with the Power Macintosh 7200 series, the 7500/100, the 8500/120, and the 9500 series. With these machines, you must disable LocalTalk in order to use a GeoPort Telecom Adapter by disconnecting any devices attached to the printer port. (Serial printers, which are not LocalTalk devices, can remain attached).

The GeoPort lets the Macintosh perform this translation from digital to analog and back again without the need for a modem. To use the GeoPort, you simply connect a GeoPort Telecom Adapter to your telephone line and into the GeoPort on your Mac. The Adapter is about the same size as a mouse and has, in addition to the GeoPort cable and connector, a pair of phone jacks (incoming and outgoing).

The GeoPort provides for backward compatibility with existing serial products, in addition to its new features set. You can plug an ordinary modem or fax/modem into the GeoPort or use any other device that attaches through a conventional serial port. The extra pin socket won't interfere.

The GeoPort technology makes the Mac uniquely suited to answer and process incoming telephone calls. It's bundled with AplePhone software, which lets your AV Mac turn itself into a phone-answering machine and speakerphone. By giving the computer the power to interface directly, the Mac can act as a complete voice mail system, in addition to processing standard data and fax telephone calls. AplePhone has a screen display that mimics a real phone and answering machine, right down to the blinking lights.

See Also
Express Modem; ISDN; Modems

GeoPort Telecom Extension

This extension is used when utilizing Apple's GeoPort features that enable you to connect a phone line, through a special GeoPort adapter, directly to an AV or Power Macintosh model for use in telecommunications.

See Also
Extensions Folder; Modems

Gershwin, *See System 9*

Get Info Command

The Get Info command shows you information on the item you request by pressing ⌘-I. To get information on an item, click the item and select Get Info from the **File menu**. The Get Info box is available for any item that has an icon: files, folders, documents, graphics, applications, and so on. If you Get Info on an **alias** of a file, its Get Info box tells you where the original is and there's a "Find Original" button to help you locate that original.

Get Info works only when you're in the **Finder**. When you select Get Info, a window is displayed with the item's information, including: the kind of document (a Microsoft Word document, a PageMaker document, and so on), the size of the document, where it is located, when it was created, a version number (if applicable), and so on. See the following figure.

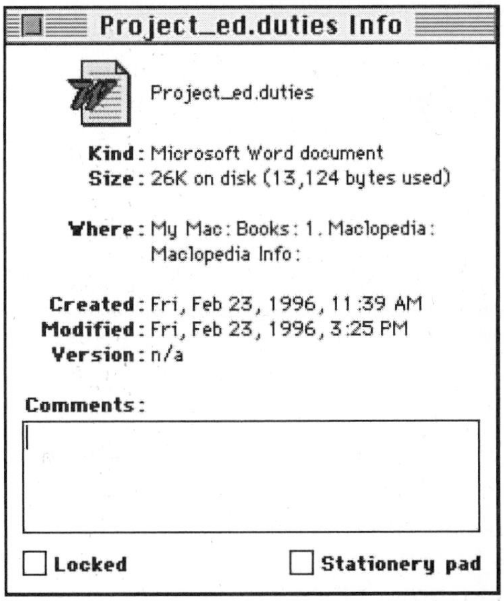

Below this information area is a **Comments box** where you can enter any comments you might have about this particular document. These comments do not appear in your document; they appear only in this box. The nice thing is that comments you put in the Comments box are searchable using the **Find File** command.

Just below the Comments box is the Locked **checkbox**. If you click the Locked checkbox, it locks that item so that it can't be altered or accidentally thrown away. If the file is already locked (an "X" appears in the checkbox), clicking the locked checkbox unlocks the file.

This is especially helpful if you have children using your Mac; you can lock any files you fear may be accidentally thrown away, such as applications and important system files.

To the right of the Locked box is the **Stationery Pad** checkbox, which enables you to turn this item into a template. If, for example, you design an elaborate form layout and think you'd want to use this form again, rather than redrawing the form from scratch each time you need a form, you can save that document as a template (stationary pad) by clicking the Stationery Pad checkbox. Any document that has been converted to a stationery pad gets a slightly different icon resembling a note pad with dog-eared corners to let you know it's a template.

The Get Info box is also where the item's **icon** is stored and where you can customize an icon. The file's current icon appears in the Get Info window to the left of the name of the file. To copy this file's icon, click the icon in the Get Info window. A square border appears around the icon to let you know it has been selected. Go to the **Edit menu** and select **Copy** (⌘-C) to make a copy of the icon. That icon is now in the **Clipboard** where you can transfer that icon to the file of your choice. To place that icon on another file, find the file that you want to have the new icon, click it, and select Get Info from the File menu. Click that file's icon in the Get Info window. Again, a box appears around the icon letting you know it's selected. Then choose **Paste** (⌘-V). This pastes the icon in the Clipboard onto the existing icon. Close the Get Info window to see the results, as shown in the figure.

If you Get Info on a program, rather than a document, the program's **memory requirements** appear in the lower-right corner. This is important

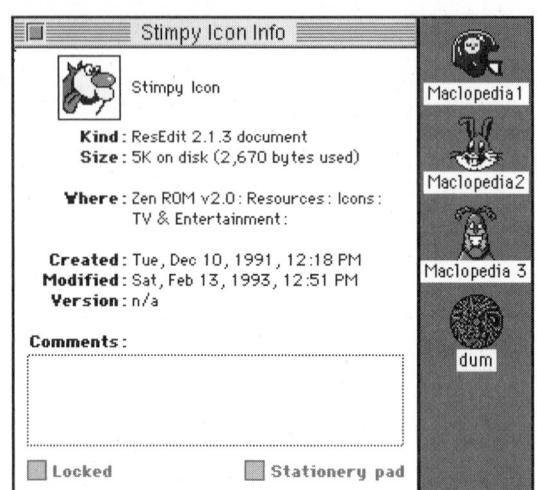

information for a number of reasons. The first number is the minimum amount of memory the manufacturer has recommended for this program to operate properly.

The second number appears in a box where you can input your own minimum memory requirements, making it higher or lower than the manufacturer's recommendations. Assume, for example, that 158K is the minimum requirement, and you decide to set it at 100K. When you try to close the Get Info window, you get a dialog box alerting you, "You have set the minimum size below 158K and this may cause the program to crash. Are you sure you want to continue?" (Having virtual memory turned on, by the way, will significantly lower the memory requirements for PowerPC-native programs.)

The last box enables you to input how much memory you'd prefer this program to use. If you have a program, for example, that is memory intensive, such as Adobe Photoshop, and you have 48MB of RAM on your computer, you may want to Get Info and assign more memory than the suggested minimum. You may want to assign 24MB just for Photoshop so that it uses the fastest memory possible: **RAM.** To do so, type the number 24,000 in that field and close the Get Info window. The next time you launch Adobe Photoshop, you have 24MB of your 48MB total set aside just for Photoshop.

To Get Info on a file, document, folder or application, follow these steps:

1. Click the item you want to Get Info on.

2. Select Get Info (⌘-I) from the File menu.

3. The Get Info window displays the item's information.

4. To lock the item to keep it from being deleted or altered, click the Locked checkbox.

5. To turn the document into a stationery pad, to use as a template, click the Stationery Pad checkbox.

6. If the item is an application, you may adjust the memory allocation for that application by entering new figures in the appropriate boxes.

7. If you want to leave a comment about this particular file, you may do so in the Comments box.

8. If the file is an Alias, the Get Info gives the location of the original file, and it has a Locate Original button to find the original file which the alias was created from.

See Also

Application Memory; Clipboard; Comments Box; Copy Command; Edit Menu; File Menu; Find File; Icon; Locked; Make Alias Command; MB; Memory Requirement; Paste; RAM; Stationery Icons

Get Info (Keyboard Shortcut)

After selecting a file, you can bring up the **Get Info** keyboard shortcut by pressing ⌘-I. You can also get info on a disk, a drive, and even the trash.

See Also

Get Info Command; Keyboard Shortcuts; Trash

Ghosting of Disk, *See Eject Disk Command*

GIF

Originally developed by the online service **CompuServe**, the Graphics Interchange Format (GIF) for **bitmapped graphics** is commonly used for graphics displayed on the World Wide Web and exchanged on the Internet. It incorporates a **compression** technique that reduces the file size with no degradation in quality.

Often pronounced "jif" (like the peanut butter), GIF is one of only three graphic file formats officially supported by HTML for inline graphics on Web pages. The other two formats are Unix-only, so GIF is the lingua franca for online and **Internet** graphics use.

Not only is it a bitmapped graphic, it's an Indexed Color bitmapped graphic, which means it uses a color table limited to a maximum of 256 colors. The idea behind indexed color is to a have a reduced color palette that can be recreated by the standard 256-color monitor. Indexed color graphics look OK onscreen but tend to print out poorly.

Photoshop has a new plug-in that allows images to be exported as GIF89a files, the newer GIF format that supports transparency (certain colors being transparent) and interlacing (the "venetian blind" effect that makes an image fill in strips on screen).

See Also

Bitmapped Graphics; CompuServe; Image Compression

GIFConverter

Shareware ($30-$45) program by Kevin A. Mitchell that converts edits graphics files in a wide variety of formats. Especially useful in preparing or converting files for presentation on the **World Wide Web,** the graphical part of the **Internet**.

Installation is simple: download GIFConverter from the Internet, and double-click the program to launch it.

To convert a file, simply choose "Open" from the "File" and navigate to the document. Choose "Save as" from the "File" menu. Choose a new graphics format from the pull-down menu in the window that opens on-screen (see the following figure).

Like other graphics conversion programs such as GraphicConverter, GIFConverter also lets an author manipulate images and select color palettes and resolution.

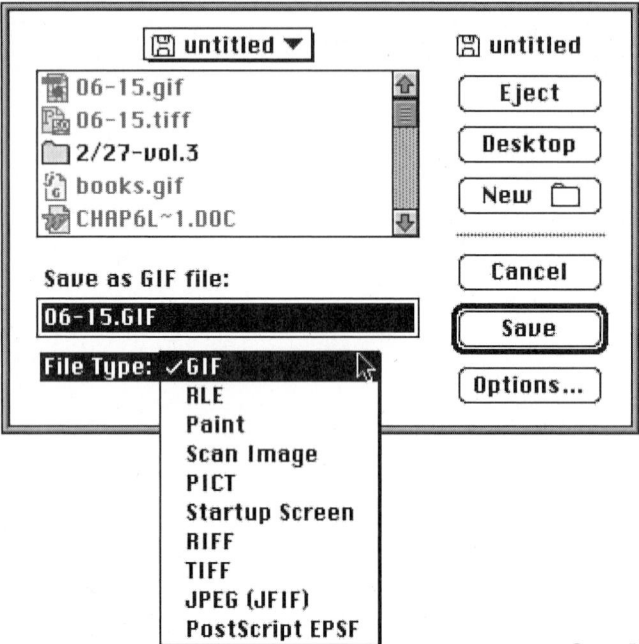

See Also

GIF; GraphicConverter; Internet; Multipart GIF Image; Transparent Images; World Wide Web

Global Village OneWorld Combo, *See Modems*

Glow

Glow defines the luminance of a **3D** object. A luminous object appears bright, as if glowing from within. A glow parameter or a glow map creates surfaces of objects, such as neon tubes. Depending on the **rendering** software, an object that glows may or may not cast light on another object.

A *glow map* is an image file that adjusts the appearance of the glow emitted by the object. Not all software supports this feature.

See Also

Rendering; Shaders

Go To Command

This command, which appears in many applications, enables you to jump from the current page to any numbered page within the document. Go To appears on the **Edit menu,** and when chosen, it displays a dialog box asking you to insert the number of the page you want to go to.

To go directly to a particular page using the Go To command, follow these steps:

1. Choose Go To (usually ⌘-G) from the Edit menu of your application.

2. Enter the page number you want to go to.

3. Click the OK button to go to that page.

See Also

Edit Menu

God Games, *See Strategy Games*

Golf Games, *PGA Tour Golf III; Sports Games*

Go-Moku, *See Classic Collection*

Gopher

Gopher, one of the most extensive **Internet services**, is distinctive for its ease of use and flexibility. Gopher originated with the Golden Gophers of the University of Minnesota. More than 1,500 sites on the Internet run the host Gopher software, which makes information available online so users can "go-fer" it.

Gopher can be likened to **File Transfer Protocol (FTP)** as a standard for information retrieval on the Internet, with one major difference: Gopher works only for retrieving rather than sending data.

Gopher can boast several major advantages over FTP, but has obvious disadvantages over graphical browsers, as shown in the following table.

Gopher: Pros and Cons

Advantages	Disadvantages
Provides a much friendlier interface than the standard command-line FTP client.	Uses character-based rather than graphical environment.
Provides access to more types of information resources than FTP—online phone books, online library catalogs, WAIS databases, email directories, Usenet news, and Archie.	Users navigate in a hierarchical, linear fashion; through levels of folders, in order to find information.
Pulls its various information sources together under a single interface and makes that information available from a basic menu system.	Gopher lacks the Web's novelty, excitement, and use of multimedia.
Uses less net bandwidth than FTP. Gopher sites are interconnected; users can move from one to another seamlessly.	

TurboGopher, the most popular Gopher client for the Macintosh, was also created at the University of Minnesota. It has the fastest perceived speed of any Gopher client, and supports the Gopher+ extensions that add new features, such as letting the server tell you the size of a file. Gopher + items can be displayed in alternate views, and may have fill-out forms associated with them.

To get connected to Gopher, download TurboGopher as follows:

1. Using Fetch, **Anarchie**, or another **FTP** client, download TurboGopher from **ftp://ftp.tidbits.com/pub/tidbits/tisk/tcp/** or **ftp://boombox.micro.umn.edu/pub/gopher/Macintosh-TurboGopher/** or from the *Internet Starter Kit* disk.

2. Double-click the TurboGopher icon to launch the program, which is configured to connect to the home Gopher server at the University of Minnesota. You will see the main menu, which appears as a line of folders (see the figure that follows). Double-click one folder to open it and begin navigating. A good place to start is "Information About Gopher."

Gopher, Searching, and Finding Information Gopherspace, the popular term for the network of Gopher servers, is huge. Navigating Gopherspace becomes possible with **Veronica**, which allows searches of either only Gopher directories or of all items in Gopherspace. **Jughead**, another search engine, allows you to conduct more focused searches. Once you find a file you want, TurboGopher can download several files at once and can obtain files while you continue to browse other Gopher sites. Helper applications work with TurboGopher to process data such as **GIF images**.

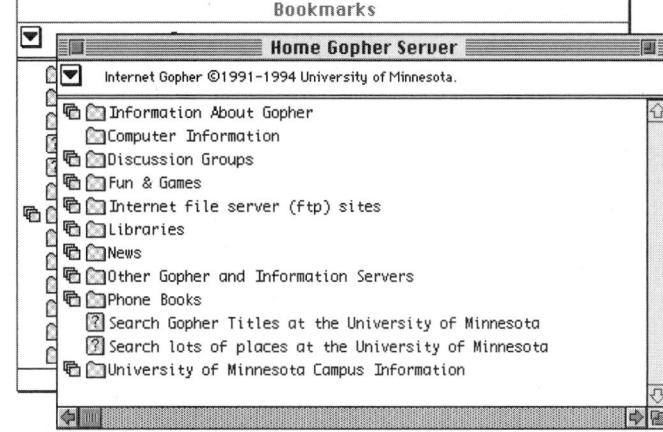

See Also

Anarchie; Archie; File Transfer Protocols; Internet Services; Jughead; GIF; TurboGopher; Veronica

Gopher Searching, *See Gopher; Jughead; Veronica*

Gopher Software, *See TurboGopher*

Gouraud Shading, *See Alias' Sketch*

Government Simulation Games, *See Sim Games*

Grammar Checker

Like the **spelling checker**, a grammar checker is built into most word processors. It works much like the spelling checker, comparing text against a set of rules. Unlike the spelling checker, however, the grammar programs often make mistakes, flagging a perfectly good sentence as incorrect and occasionally skipping mistakes that an elementary school student would catch. You can customize the grammar checker to ignore some rules and to use either the formal or casual rule set. Doing so helps avoid some of the "false" errors. Most grammar checkers also rate your writing according to a readability index, determining how many years of school you'd have to have in order to understand the material. These indices are based on the ratio of long words to short words in a sentence, and really shouldn't be taken too seriously. The readability index for this paragraph is 10.44.

Graphic Design

Graphic design is the process of applying aesthetic principles in the creation and arrangement of type, pictorial elements, and other graphic images in printed matter or in electronic displays. A graphic is usually defined as any element printed on a two-dimensional surface; however, computer-based technologies have expanded that meaning to include elements intended only for display on a computer monitor, television, or other electronic display device.

For example, multimedia displays that include both two-dimensional and three-dimensional graphics should generally follow the basic principles of graphic design. A home page on the **World Wide Web** or the display graphics of an online service or of a software application are certainly subject to graphic design precepts.

Although graphic design is thought of as an art form and follows many of the same principles as fine art, it differs to the extent that it is more commercially oriented. Communication is the basic goal of all art, but graphic design exists almost solely for that purpose. In the past, graphic designers have been called commercial artists—a category which also includes illustrators. Many graphic designers have an artistic temperament and may have been trained in the fine arts (painting, drawing, sculpture, and so on), or they may have participated in commercial art or advertising degree programs at a college or university.

Desktop publishing technology has attracted many more people to the field of graphic design, and many lack any background at all in fine art or commercial art.

Communication is such an important goal in graphic design, that creativity and self-expression can be much more restricted than in fine arts. A conservative designer follows the principle of "form follows function" and does not allow artistic expression to obscure the message. For example, using a decorative typeface that is beautiful in form but difficult to read as body copy would be considered inappropriate. This type of graphic design is necessary for most published material, and few milieus exist for designers who wish to experiment and break the rules.

The rules of graphic design involve fundamentals that govern the placement of elements on a page. Rules have also evolved for the selection and formatting of type. In fact, type may be thought of as the primary element of graphic design. The proper use of type often distinguishes an experienced professional from a novice. In fact, finesse and attention to detail are often distinguishing characteristics in a well-designed publication. For more information about the basic principles of design and typography, read *The Non-Designer's Design Book* by Robin Williams (Peachpit Press).

GraphicConverter

Shareware ($35) program by Thorsten Lemke that converts graphics files in a wide variety of formats. Especially useful in preparing or converting files for presentation on the **World Wide Web,** the graphical part of the **Internet.**

Installation is simple: downloading GraphicConverter from the Internet creates a preferences file in your System Folder. Double-click the program to launch it.

To convert a file, simply choose "Open" from the "File" and navigate to the document. Choose "Save as" from the "File" menu. Choose a new graphics format from the "Format" pull-down menu in the right half of the "Save as" window that opens on-screen (see the following figure).

After converting a file you can check a box in the "Save as" window to automatically compress that file with the shareware application **StuffIt**, if you already have StuffIt installed on your Mac.

GraphicConverter saves **GIF** files as GIF89 format, which allows **transparent** images and **Multipart GIF** animation. It also has a "Slide Show" feature, which plays all the image files in a designated folder, one after another.

Recent versions of GraphicConverter are accelerated for the PowerMac. The program requires a Mac with color **QuickDraw**, **System 7**, and at least 2MB of memory.

See Also

GIF; GIFConverter; Internet; Multipart GIF Images; Transparent Images; World Wide Web

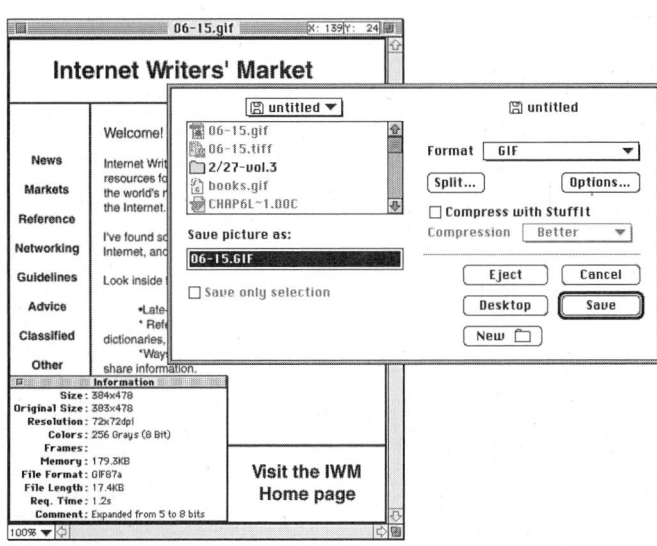

Graphics

From the day when the first Macintosh was introduced, much of the excitement it sparked was due to one function—it could draw! **MacPaint**, the program that turned the Mac into a sketch pad, was a major revolution in computer technology. It meant that the computer was no longer limited to number crunching or to being a "smart typewriter." It could also be a tool for artists and designers.

Admittedly, the first MacPaint wasn't much of a tool. It was limited to black and white, and you had to learn to draw by waving what felt like a bar of soap across your desk. But the basics were in place. It had brush, pencil, straight line, and spray can tools. It could create and fill shapes and place text characters on the page. The cut, copy, and paste functions it shared with **MacWrite** were augmented by a lasso and drag function that allowed you to move things around on the page.

People who had never considered themselves artists had lots of fun using the brick patterns, stripes, and spots, to draw houses and trees, stacks of blocks, and similar pictures. Real artists were initially less enthusiastic. How could a mouse replace a brush, or pen and ink? But soon, they began to see possibilities. Bitmapped art can convey a real sense of texture and depth. The following figure shows a drawing done entirely with the spray can.

MacPaint led to increasingly complex graphics programs. Bitmapped art paint programs were joined by object-oriented drawing programs, also called vector graphics. Color was introduced with the Mac II, and ever since the Mac has become as legitimate an art medium as any other. The Mac's digital wizardry is represented in magazine ads, product packages, on television, and even in the movies. Hollywood special effects experts rely on the Mac's capability to paint on video, and to create complex, richly detailed backgrounds for animation and titles. The following figure shows a bit of scenery rendered with KPT Bryce.

Today, there are literally dozens of graphics applications for the Mac. They still fall into the categories of paint and draw programs, and to these are added **3D** graphics and animation. These programs can do everything from creating natural-looking three-dimensional worlds and complex renderings of virtual reality scenes, to letting you do photo image manipulation and retouching that would be impossible in the most well-equipped darkroom you could imagine. The 3D programs simulate three-dimensional images on-screen.

When you reposition them or change your vantage point, they behave exactly like real-world objects. You can draw something, and then (figuratively) walk around it to see the other side.

In order to take full advantage of the Mac's graphics capabilities, you'll need a Power Mac, as well as a large color monitor and plenty of memory. A color **printer** and a **scanner** will add to your enjoyment, as will a **CD-ROM** drive. The latter item is almost a necessity because many of the high end graphics programs are only available on CD-ROM. You'll also need to spend time mastering them. As the applications become more capable, they also become harder to use. Even though these programs can do amazing things, they can't turn you into an artist overnight.

For More...

If you want to do this...	Go to this entry...
Learn how to move graphics around the screen as a movie	Premiere and Animation
Explore CAD applications	CADMover
Find out about creating scenery and natural graphics	Digital Scenery, Introduction
Find out about the different file formats for graphics	File Types, Internet
Find out what graphics shareware is and how to get it	Shareware Games
Find out about designing the human form	Fractal Design's Poser
Learn the meaning and use of graphics jargon and terms	Graphics Terms
Discover what applications are available for exploring mathematical graphics	Digital Scenery, Introduction; Koyn Fractal Studio; Theorist

If you want to do this...	Go to this entry...
Discover which applications can be used to twist and warp your graphics	Morphing

Bibliography

For more informaiton on graphics in general, try these books:

PhotoshopFX, Cathy Abes, published by Ventana Press, Chapel Hill, N.C., 1994.

Adobe After Effects, Adobe Systems Incorporated, published by Hayden Books, Indianapolis, IN, 1996.

Adobe Illustrator, Adobe Systems Incorporated, published by Hayden Books, Indianapolis, IN, 1996.

Adobe Photoshop, Adobe Systems Incorporated, published by Hayden Books, Indianapolis, IN, 1994.

Adobe Premiere, Adobe Systems Incorporated, published by Hayden Books, Indianapolis, IN, 1995.

MacWorld Complete Mac Handbook (4th Edition), Jim Heid, published by IDG Books Worldwide, Inc., Foster City, CA 1995.

Fractals for the Macintosh, Jesse Jones, published by Waite Group, Inc., Corte Madeira, CA 1993.

Computers, Chaos, Pattern, and Beauty, Clifford A. Pickover, published by St. Martin's Press, Inc., New York, NY, 1990.

Graphics, 3D

If you are looking for a general purpose tool, consider Specular's Infini-D, Strata's **StrataVision**, Strata's Studio Pro, Fractal Design's **Ray Dream Studio**, or Macromedia's **Extreme 3D**. For high-end animation, consider Electric Animation, but you'll need to buy a modeling tool as well. A Modeling and Rendering-only application to consider is **Alias' Sketch!**.

For logo animation, consider Specular **LogoMotion**, or Fractal's **AddDepth**.

Finally, here are some application's with interesting specialties. Fractal Design's **Poser** creates and poses human figures, while MetaTools **Bryce** renders landscapes from 3D models. **Virtus WalkThrough Pro** provides real time exploration capabilities or 3D models, as well as support for **VRML**.

Graphics Compressor

This QuickTime compressor only works with 8-bit graphics. If you attempt to compress a 16-bit graphic, it is converted to 8-bit during the compression routine. While this compressor can be used to compress sequences, it is not recommended. Use the **Animation Compressor** instead.

See Also

Animation Compressor; Asymmetrical Compressors; Compressor; Drop Frames; Spatial Compression; Symmetrical Compressors; Temporal Compression

Graphics Coprocessors, *See Coprocessors, Types*

Graphics File Formats

Mac graphics files come in two basic flavors—**vector** and **bitmapped**—but there are a lot of variations on those two themes. Different types of graphics and different uses demand different file formats.

Some formats are readable only by the program that creates them—for example, **FreeHand's** native format; others can be read and written by a variety of applications, as FreeHand can write **EPS** files that can be opened and imported by other programs.

The original Mac format for graphics was **MacPaint**, the native format used by a paint program of the same name that was bundled with the first Macs in 1985. It was—and still is—the most basic bitmap file format, only capable of saving black-and-white files. Then, eventually, came TIFF, a much more advanced bitmapped format that supports 24-bit color in **RGB** and **CMYK** modes. It's a very stable, cross-platform format that's the standard for scans and other photo-based art that must eventually be printed out on a high-resolution printer or imagesetter.

The vector graphics file formats developed slightly later, as there wasn't even a program that could manipulate EPS (Encapsulated Post Script) files until 1988, when Adobe's Illustrator 88 came along. But the EPS format is exceptional in that it unlocks the power of **PostScript** printers and imagesetters, allowing complex graphics made of basic points and lines to be scaled, skewed, rotated, shaded, and more. EPS files are typically a fraction of the size of their TIFF cousins, they're cross-platform compatible, and they're very stable…

PICT is a simple screen display format that's part of the Mac's basic architecture, but it's not meant for printing. It's fine for multimedia work or slide and on-screen presentations.

These days, TIFF, EPS, **GIF**, and **JPEG** are much more common names in the world of graphics formats. TIFF and GIF are used for bitmapped graphics, such as scans, while EPS is the most common format for vector graphics on the Mac. JPEG is a compression standard for color bitmapped images that can drastically reduce file size with little loss of image quality.

Macs can also read formats commonly used on other platforms, such as the BMP, CGM, and PCX formats used by PCs.

See Also

Bitmapped Graphics; EPS; FreeHand; GIF; JPEG; MacPaint; Vector Graphics

Graphics Interchange File, *See GIF*

Graphics, Morphing

Morphing takes two images and creates an effect where one image seems to reshape itself into another. This effect became widely popular a couple of years ago in music videos and movies. There are now several applications that enable you to create these sophisticated effects on a budget. They include Gryphon's **Morph** and Avid's **Elastic Reality**.

These programs enable you to take two images or clips and morph them together to create a still image or a clip of the morph. The morphing effect is defined by drawing control points and lines on the two images that indicate the parts of the image that morph together. A control point, for example, might be added to the eyes in the first image. The same control point will appear on the second image, and you must drag this point to the eyes of the character in the second image (assuming you are morphing a face to a face).

Morphing effects depend on several things: the subjects in the image (if you are morphing a face, short hair seems to morph much better than long frizzy hair), the number of control points you add (usually the more you add the better the effect), and the consistency of the background. If the background from image to image is the same then the morphing effects are more noticeable and more effective. If you morph between images with different backgrounds, the morph happens over the whole image, and looks more like a **cross-fade** or **cross-dissolve** transition effect than a morph.

See Also
Elastic Reality; Morph

Graphics Tablets

If you do serious graphics work or enjoy drawing with a pen-based object rather than a **mouse** or **trackball**, you might need a graphics tablet. True enough, you can draw and paint with a mouse, but not with the degree of control that a pen and tablet provide. For those who have highly developed skills with pen and ink or brushes and paint, a pressure-sensitive pen and tablet provide the familiar feedback of working with these real-world tools.

Tablets can be used in almost any application. For example, editing a spreadsheet or a database is easier if you can tap directly on the cell or field you want to change and not have to slide the cursor all over the screen. Complex applications, from desktop publishing to computer-aided design (CAD), often have special palettes and function keys; tapping on them saves time. Tablets can also be helpful for people entering music into a notation application via its note palette.

Graphics tablets (The MacHandwriter is shown in the illustration) are radio-frequency based devices. When you draw with the stylus, it exchanges tiny radio signals with the tablet through a grid of wires that crisscross the drawing area. The tablet determines the location of the stylus and transmits the location to the Mac. Most graphics tablets are pressure-sensitive: the harder you press the palette with the stylus, the darker or wider the pen line.

Most graphics tablets (also called digitizing tablets) are covered with a clear plastic sheet (an overlay). You can slip artwork you wish to trace under the sheet, or draw with ink-filled cartridges inserted into the stylus on tracing paper to see what you are drawing on the screen.

The biggest differences of graphics tablets from mice or trackballs are the following:

■ Working area. This factor refers to the actual size of the tablet's pressure-sensitive input area. Bigger tablets are more expensive; smaller tablets can be more comfortable if you like to hold them in your lap as you would a sketch pad.

■ Resolution. The resolution of a tablet is measured in the number of divisions per square inch. If you create finely detailed illustrations or complex CAD documents, you need more expensive models that support higher resolutions. The down side of high resolution tablets is that the amount of data throughput increases and processor performance slows down due to the large amounts of data that must be processed with each stylus movement.

Pressure-sensitive pens emulate real-world tools and, with compatible software, enable you to work on-screen just as you would on canvas. Press down on a brush, and the stroke widens. Pressing lightly on a watercolor brush creates a tiny drop of color. Nearly all major graphics applications, such as **Fractal's Painter** and Adobe **Photoshop**, support pressure-sensitive pens. Many pens do not require batteries, which usually means that all the position and pressure sensing takes place on the tablet. Most pens used with graphics tablets are cordless. Such cordless pens can be filled with ink for an intuitive, natural feeling. You can also use such a pen to actually produce an electronic signature.

Graphics tablets and styluses are **absolute-motion** pointing devices. The stylus has the ability to tell the Mac its physical location on the tablet, and that location is mapped to an exact location on the screen. When you move the stylus on the palette, the cursor on the screen moves to the same location on the screen. Graphics tablets are able to operate in relative-motion (like **mice** and **trackballs**), but their ultimate benefit is their ability to trace exact positions. The

graphics tablet and stylus also provide better pixel precision than mice or trackballs. Mice and trackballs can discern approximately 200 to 300 units of movement per inch. Graphics tablets detect 1,000 units or more per inch (known as *resolution* and measured in lines per inch (LPI)). The higher the pointing device's resolution, the better it will be for use in precise drawing.

Tablets have historically been **serial devices** because the **Apple Desktop Bus** port is not fast enough to handle the amounts of data they generate. Some manufacturers, however, have introduced products that work with the ADB port. Tablets also tend to draw more power than most ADB devices can sustain; you must be careful about the number of ADB devices on the chain.

You need a fast Mac (at least a 68040-based Quadra/ Performa) if you work in 24-bit color. A Power Mac provides the best solution to performance bottlenecks. Even though the ADB driver in **System 7.5** is not native, native applications will process the pen data throughput much more efficiently and faster on a Power Mac.

You can purchase graphics tablets in many sizes to fit your work area needs. The sizes range from 4 by 5 inches to 12 by 18 inches, and even a flexible tablet measuring 18 by 24 inches. The following table provides an overview of the types of graphics tablets available for use with the Mac.

Graphics Tablets for the Mac

Manufacturer	Model Name	Features	Street Price
Wacom Technology	ArtPad II™	Erasing UltraPen™, no batteries needed, 256 pressure levels, 2,540 lpi resolution, 4 × 5 inch tablet	$148.95
Wacom Technology	ArtZ II®	Erasing UltraPen, 6 by 8 inch, 12-by-12 inch, and 12-by-18 inch tablets; 256 pressure levels, 2,540 lpi resolution	$319.98 to $698.98

Manufacturer	Model Name	Features	Street Price
CalComp Digitizer Division	DrawingSlate II	Tablets developed for CAD applications at Lockheed, which markets them through CalComp, 6-by-9 inch, 12-by-12 inch, 12-by-18 inch tablets, 2,540 lpi with accuracy of ±0.01 inches	$395 to $595
Summagraphics	Microgrid Ultra ADB	Backlit models, ADB port compatible, 17-by-24 inches to 44-by-60 inches	$3,299 to $8,699
Hitachi Digital Graphics	StudioPad	Small tablet	$199.99

See Also

Absolute Versus Relative Motion; Apple Desktop Bus; Keyboard; Mouse; Pen/Handwriting Devices; Serial Ports; Trackballs; Touchpads; Touch Screens

Graphics Terms

Active Display Area—That part of an image visible on the display screen.

ADC (Analog to Digital Converter)—A device that changes analog real-world information into digital information that the computer can store and manipulate.

Algorithm—A formula that is used to initiate an operation.

Animation—Frames of a sequence that the eye defines as moving.

Aspect Ratio—Width to height ratio. Common ratios for computer videographics and multimedia are 3:2 and 4:3, though desktop publishing pages can be produced at any needed ratio.

Backup—A saved file that duplicates another file.

Batch Processing—An operation that targets more than one file at a time.

Bitmap—A graphic whose content is determined by its collection of picture elements or pixels.

Blue Screen—A blue background that is seen by the system as transparent so that another scene or graphic can be placed behind the foreground image.

Brightness—Luma or luminescence.

Buffer—A area of temporary memory in the computer used to store data.

Byte—A unit that represents a sequence of eight bits for computation and storage.

CAD (Computer Aided Design)—Using a computer to originate and/or modify a design.

CAM (Computer Aided Manufacturing)—Computerized process for manufacturing products direct from on-screen data.

Color Key—A special effect used to composite still or moving images in film and video. Sometimes called blue screen.

Color Picker—A Mac palette screen (Control panel device) used to select colors.

Compression—A process that squeezes data into a smaller space, for example, the JPEG file format.

Contrast—The difference between the darks and lights in an image.

Cross-platform—Referring to a file that can be accessed on more than one computer type or platform.

Data/Resource Forks—Disk files with the proper data needed to reconstruct a saved file.

Decompression—A reverse procedure used to read compressed files and reconstruct them back to their original state.

Digital—A medium that has only a binary or on/off signal.

Digitize—To grab data from the real world and translate it into digital form so that the computer can display it.

Dithering—Creating intermediate colors between any two choices by a system of dots.

Dots per Inch (DPI)—the number of discreet dots an output device can print per inch (horizontal x vertical).

Frame Grabber—A video digitizer with onboard storage capacity built in.

Grayscale—Usually refers to a spectrum of 256 gray levels.

Hard Copy—Printed or film computer output.

Histogram—A graphing of the brightness values in every pixel in a raster image.

Image Processing—Changing the elements in an image through an effect or specific algorithm.

Macintize—To place white as the first color and black as the last color in the image's palette.

Multimedia—The combining of more than one media in a presentation, as for example, sight and sound.

Palette—The range of hues in a defined spectrum.

Palette Number Index—Considering that the first color (white in a Mac palette) is number zero, the palette number of any color may be calculated by finding its numeric position.

Palette Switching—More than one palette in use in a sequence of images. This may lead to slower animation playback and can cause discomforting flickering.

Pixel (Picture Element)—The smallest element that a raster image contains whose actual size and shape is determined by the resolution of the image on-screen and the extent to which the display device can accommodate that size.

Pixel Depth—The number of bits needed to store a pixel, stated in increments that double with each succeeding level. A one bit pixel can store two colors, 2 bits four colors, 3 bits eight colors, 4 bits sixteen colors, 5 bits 32 colors, 6 bits 64 colors, 7 bits 128 colors, and 8 bits 256 colors (or shades of gray). Common pixel depth for color work is 24 bits or sixteen million plus colors, while 32 bit pixel depth includes 24 bits of color and an 8-bit "alpha channel" of grays.

Plotter—An output device that uses moving pens to create a graphic in response to computer signals.

Preferences—Settings that determine how software is configured.

RGB (Red, Green, Blue)—The three primary colors of the electron guns in a video-compatible system.

Remap—To change the colors in a palette to match another palette.

Scaling—Changing the size of an image.

Scan—To place an image in a flatbed digitizer for translating image data to digital format.

Script—A series of encoded instructions that initiate an action.

Translate—Converting one format to another.

Threshold—Setting a level at which an operation will take place.

Vector Graphics—Image elements defined by their directional heading and length.

Video Digitizer—A device that captures an image from a video source, whether a camera, VCR, or video still camera. A professional video digitizer can capture a single frame of video from a moving sequence in real time.

Graphics Programs for Children, *See KidPix Studio*

Gravure, *See Printing*

Gray Component Replacement, *See GCR*

Gray Disk Icon

If you use the **Eject Disk** command on the **Special menu** to eject a **disk** from the disk drive, the disk ejects, but a gray "ghosted" disk icon is left on the **desktop**, as shown in the figure. To remove this gray disk icon, **drag** the icon into the **Trash,** and it disappears. If you drag the disk icon to the Trash or use the

Ghost Disk

Put Away command on the **File menu** to eject a disk, the gray disk icon does not appear.

If you drag the ghost disk icon into the Trash and it doesn't go away, resources of that disk are still in use. In **System 7** and higher, you will be met with a dialog box that states, "The disk (the disk's name appears here) cannot be put away because it contains items that are in use." You have to click OK to continue. If this should happen, re-open the disk and make certain all the documents on the disk have been properly closed.

This ghosting of the disk can create additional problems. If you **double-click** the ghosted disk, the Mac brings up a dialog box asking you to reinsert the original disk. You can make this dialog box go away by hitting ⌘-. (period) on your keyboard or by inserting the original disk.

You can run into more problems if you happen to eject a disk using the Eject Disk command and that disk had an open window when you ejected it. If you try to close that window, perhaps to reduce clutter on your desktop, you are met with a dialog box insisting that you reinsert your disk. It asks for the disk because a change to the disk has been made (a window was closed) and the information needs to be updated on the original disk. Having your system demand disks that have already been ejected can be a frustrating experience.

Because of the problems that ghosting disks cause, many people prefer to use the **Put Away** command (⌘-Y) rather than using Eject Disk. The Put Away command dismounts and ejects the disk, but does not leave the ghosted version of the disk on the desktop.

See Also
Click and Drag; Disks and Drives; Desktop; Eject Disk; File Menu; Put Away; Special Menu; Trash

Gray Levels

There is a direct relationship between gray or color levels and output resolution in digital halftone production. The dots in **digital halftones** are composed of a matrix of smaller dots made by a laser imaging device. These are sometimes called laser spots or machine spots. The grouping of these smaller dots, or spots, is called a digital **halftone** cell. The number of these smaller dots within the digital halftone cell determines the potential gray or color levels of the cell. If, for example, a cell contains only four of the smaller dots, it has the potential to represent five gray levels: no dots (white), one dot, two dots, three dots, and four dots (black). In other words, a halftone image made up of these cells would be severely posterized because the cells do not contain enough laser spots to create the illusion of continuous tone. The image would have only three grays in addition to black and white.

At lower output resolutions (300 to 1200 dpi), it is difficult to achieve good halftones because there is a trade-off between the halftone screen frequency (lpi) and the device output resolution (dpi). This is because a lower screen frequency provides more gray levels at a given output resolution. The following formula can be used to determine gray levels: $(dpi/lpi)^2 + 1$ = gray levels. A 100 lpi halftone, for example, printed on a 600 dpi laser printer has some posterization because it has only 37 gray levels. (600 divided by 100 equals 6. 6 squared equals 36. 36 plus 1 equals 37.) Decreasing the lpi requirement to 65, however, yields an image with 82 gray levels—still not a great halftone but better than 37 levels. The goal is to obtain as many gray levels as possible at a given screen frequency; therefore, it becomes obvious that higher output resolutions are key.

Another factor must be considered when working with gray levels. **PostScript** Level 1 devices are limited to 256 gray levels. Level 2 PostScript supports more, but most experts agree that there is no point in striving for more than 256 levels. There is no harm in having more gray levels than are necessary, but one should avoid having too few. To determine the optimum output resolution required for a given screen frequency, a formula using the square root of 256 has been devised: lpi × 16 = dpi. Therefore, a 133 lpi halftone requires an output device with a dpi rating of at least 2,128 (133 lpi ×16 = 2128 dpi). Naturally, this is rounded off to 2,400 dpi, a common resolution for **imagesetters.** This example provides 325 gray levels—more than are needed but better than not enough!

See Also
Digital Halftones; Halftone; Resolution Measurement

Grayed Commands

If you go to a menu and the name of a command is grayed, that command is not available. A grayed-out command is also referred to as *dimmed*. Commands that are available for use appear in black type.

See Also
Fonts; Menu; Menu Commands

Grayscale, *See Image Scanning*

GrayShare, *See Printers, InkJet*

Grow Box, *See Size Box*

GUI (Graphical User Interface)

This is the interface of the Macintosh computer. It enables the use of **icons**, folders, and a **desktop**. The Macintosh uses these items, that you might find on a real desktop, as a metaphor for the interface, creating the user-friendliness for which the Mac is so well-known.

See Also
History and Culture of the Macintosh; Human Interface Guidelines

Guides

In many graphics and page layout applications, users can click on the ruler at the edge of a document window and drag to pull a positioning guide onto the page. Often, users can specify that objects moved near the guide should "snap" to the guide, facilitating alignment, and some programs also allow users to specify exactly how close an object must be to the guide to be affected by it.

See Also
Drawing Applications; Page Layout Applications

Gutter Margins, *See Margins and Tabs*

Gwydion Project, *See Dylan*

GX Fonts

Rather than the 256 characters that the Mac's system would previously allow in any font, GX fonts can contain—get ready for this—256^2, or 65,536, characters. That leaves a lot of room for things like expert and swash characters, ornaments, ligatures, and fractions. And non-Roman alphabets, such as in Asian languages, can be entirely contained in one font. GX fonts also have room for information about how an application should use a font—features like automatic ligature substitution, optical alignment (often lines that *are* centered don't *look* centered), true drawn small caps, hanging punctuation, and font-level kerning and tracking.

Adobe's Garamond Plus combines the Regular, Expert Set, Titling, and Alternate sets of Garamond. It includes accented characters, small caps, ligatures, superior and inferior numbers (drawn for that purpose, not just reduced), fractions, swashes, and ornaments. GX-aware applications allow users to enable and disable automatic use of any of these options through menu choices.

Another Adobe face, Caflisch Script, is a connecting script that uses the extra character slots for variations on each character that are chosen automatically based on which letters precede and follow it. It can also choose variations randomly, to give a more hand-drawn feel to the type.

GX could also mean an end to the screen font/printer font dichotomy of **PostScript** fonts, because GX PostScript fonts are one-piece, like **TrueType** fonts, and live in suitcases. For now, though, few page layout and graphics applications support GX.

See Also
Fontographer; Fonts; Outline Fonts; PostScript; TrueType; Typesetting Terms

Hairline Rule, *See Printing*

Halftone

Halftone is the term used to describe any use of a screen of dots or lines to print a continuous tone of gray or color. Halftone screens are necessary because of the mechanical limitations of a printing press in reproducing continuous tones.

Continuous tones imply a more or less smooth gradation of tonal values in gray or color. For example, in the most common continuous tone image, a photograph, tones of gray or color are blended smoothly throughout the image with no discernible pattern or texture. Printing devices of any kind other than photographic must print the tones of gray or color as small, discrete units of ink, toner, or dye. In a halftone, these units are represented by dots or lines. The halftone dots themselves may be round, elliptical, or square. Lines may be specified instead of dots to create a screen of evenly spaced lines that run horizontally, vertically, or at any angle. Any printed area that contains a tonal value of gray or color is considered a halftone, even if it has no variations in tone. Such solid areas of halftone are often called tint screens and are used in backgrounds. Solid (100 percent value) black or color does not require a halftone screen. The purpose of a halftone is to create an optical illusion of continuous tone. The size of the dots themselves determines the quality of this illusion. The following figure shows a blend of tonal value from black to white that is created by halftone dots small enough to create a convincing illusion of continuous tone.

Halftones may be created photographically or digitally. A halftone created with a camera is often called a *photomechanical halftone*. A halftone created by a computer is called a **digital halftone**. Some photomechanical halftones are still made, but digital halftones are increasingly common and may already account for the majority of halftones made in some areas.

A photomechanical halftone is made either by photographing the continuous-tone image through a grid pattern on glass screen with a camera or by exposing the image through a contact screen containing variable density dots. In both cases, the halftone image is recorded on film. The film is used to make contact prints or printing plates. A digital halftone is made when computer instructions are processed by a digital output device such as a **laser printer** or an **imagesetter.** The output device creates halftone dots by grouping minute laser-generated spots (also called dots) into a matrix.

Digital halftones can be rendered on a computer display monitor, but there is no point in doing so, as halftones are strictly a function of output and have no real relevance to digital display. Display images look best remaining in pixels. The pixels will be converted to halftone dots during the output process.

Photomechanical and digital halftones are similar in that they are composed of evenly spaced dots. The spacing of the dots is always constant and is measured as lines per inch (lpi). This is called the screen frequency or line screen ruling of the halftone. More halftone dots per linear inch results in a more convincing illusion of continuous tone. Paper quality and the type of printing device have the most bearing on screen frequency. For example, newspapers may use screen frequencies of 65 lpi, 85 lpi, or 100 lpi. Magazines, catalogs, and advertising materials may use 120 lpi, 133 lpi, or 150 lpi halftones. Higher screen frequencies may be used for premium and showcase printing. In halftones of photographs, wash drawings, watercolors, oil paintings, and so on, light areas contain smaller dots and dark areas contain larger dots. When halftones are enlarged, the different dot sizes are apparent, as shown in the following figure.

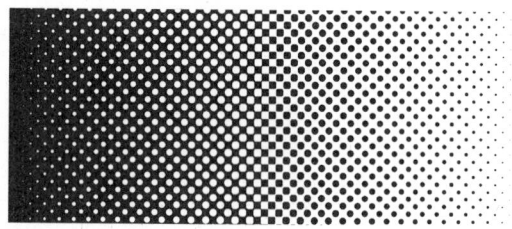

See Also
Digital Halftones; Printing Terms

Halftone Dot, *See Halftone*

Halftone Screen, *See Halftone*

Halftoning, *See Printing Technology, PostScript Lasers, Halftoning*

Handheld Scanners

Handheld scanners are small, portable scanners—usually, they look like tiny vacuum cleaners. Handheld scanners were very popular at the beginning of the desktop publishing revolution, when flatbed scanners, RAM, and disk space were expensive; in the mid-'90s, when flatbed scanners are cheap and Macs can handle large scans fairly easily, handheld scanners are not as widely used.

Handheld scanners have a scanning area that's only a few inches wide. To use them, you move the scanner slowly over the image to be scanned. It's possible to scan large areas by making several passes with the scanner and compositing the scans together. The following figure shows the ScanMan handheld scanner.

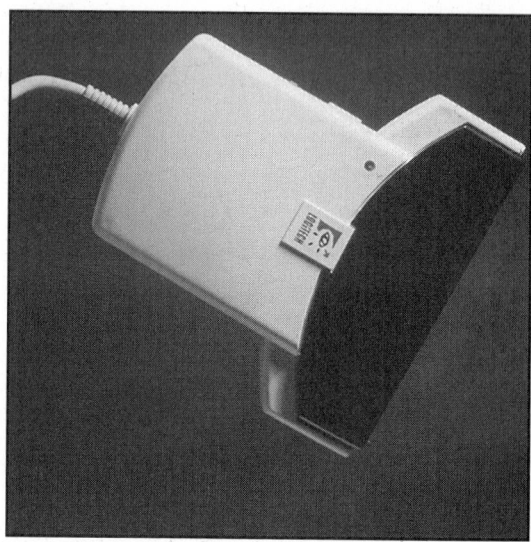

Handheld scanners are portable. In the PowerBook era, it's easy to take a scanner to the library and quickly digitize text and small pictures. They're inexpensive, but in the '90s, they're not substantially cheaper than inexpensive flatbed scanners.

It requires a steady hand to get a good scan with a handheld scanner: You must move the scanner's head across the page at a constant speed, or weird artifacts will appear in the scan. Although it's possible to composite several passes with a handheld scanner into one large image, it's usually a frustrating process.

See Also
Drum Scanners; Flatbed Scanners; Office Scanners; Slide Scanners

Handle

A handle is a variable that indirectly refers to a block of relocatable memory in an application's **heap**.

In the world of Macintosh programming, handles are one of the most important concepts to master. Handles are a strange beast and uniquely Macintosh. If you've programmed DOS or Windows and know the term handle in that context, forget it. Macintosh handles are entirely different.

In every application's heap, there is a special block of memory that contains a set of master **pointers**. Each master pointer contains the memory address of a relocatable block in the heap. A handle is a pointer to one of these special master pointers.

Why would anyone bother with all this confusion? Handles enable blocks of data to be moved in memory without confusing the application that is using them. The following figure displays an application's heap before and after the heap has been *compacted* to maximize the size of free blocks.

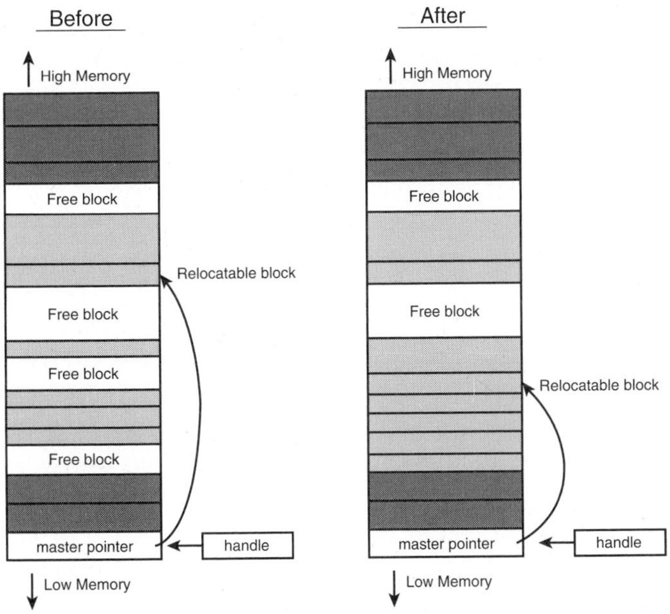

Before the relocatable blocks are moved, the handle points to a master pointer that in turn points to a specific relocatable block. During compaction, the Memory Manger moves the relocatable block and updates the value in the master pointer, so that it now points to the new location of the block. The handle never changes, but it still points indirectly to the same block of memory. This gives the Memory Manager the freedom to rearrange blocks to optimize memory usage.

Handles are used extensively in Macintosh programming. Many **Toolbox** routines that allocate memory return a handle to the calling program. When your application reads a **resource** from a file, it is given a handle to the resource, not the resource data itself.

It's important to remember that handles can only be created by the Memory Manager. Not every variable that points indirectly to a block of data is a handle, only those that point by way of a master pointer.

See Also
Heap; Pointer; Resource; Toolbox

Handwriting Recognition Systems,
See Pen/Handwriting Devices

Hanging Indent

Hanging indents extend backward into the margin of the page, rather than forward into the first line of type. They're not used in ordinary correspondence, but may be a stylistic feature of a catalogue or brochure. Using a hanging indent plus a tab is also a good quick way to format a numbered or bulleted list. To create a hanging indent, use the Paragraph dialog box as shown in the following figure, or drag the indent indicator on the document ruler backward to the place you want the line to begin.

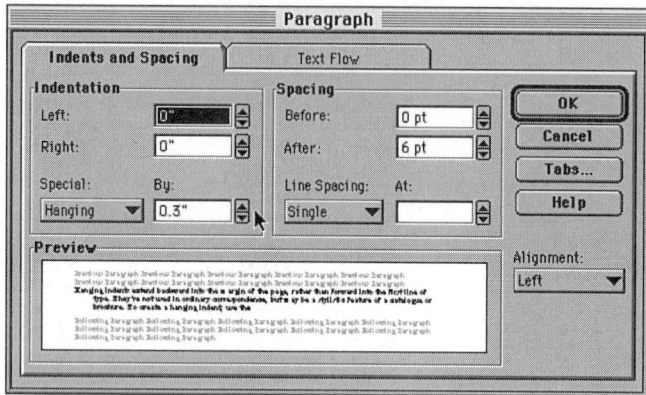

Hanging Punctuation, *See Printing*

Happy Mac Icon

Each time you **start up** your Mac, the computer runs an internal diagnostic check of the hardware and **system**. If everything checks out okay, the Mac displays the Happy Mac icon, which looks likes a small Macintosh with a smiley face, as shown in the figure.

See Also
Startup; System

Hard Copy

Hard copy is simply a printout as opposed to a file on a disk. Files can be sent by email, but hard copies must be sent by snail mail.

Hard Disk Toolkit

Hard Disk Toolkit, by FWB Inc., (1555 Adams Drive, Menlo Park, California 94025; on the Web at **http://www.FWB.com**) is a suite of disk management utilities that enables you to initialize **hard disks** using FWB's drivers, create **disk partitions**, and host of other disk-related tasks.

You can use the Hard Disk Toolkit to password protect hard disks, and it has built-in data encryption for sensitive items that need maximum protection. It also contains a benchmark testing application to measure the performance of your hard disk against industry benchmarks (a standardized performance rating for software or hardware) for speed.

See Also
Disk Partitions; Hard Disk

Hard Disk Upgrade

A hard disk upgrade can be defined as the replacement of your system's internal hard disk with a newer, faster, or more capacious hard disk.

See Also
Upgrade Paths

Hard Disks

Like all computers, the Macintosh needs a place to permanently keep the work you do, because everything you do on the computer itself disappears when you turn off the power. There are several ways to store information produced on the Macintosh. The most common vehicles are disks—both hard and floppy, although you can also store information on a remote computer that uses these media by linking to a network.

The Macintosh System and Finder perform their duties by getting and sending information back and forth between the computer and storage. The System gets information from a disk (called *reading*) and places information back on to a disk (called *writing*) by using peripheral devices called floppy and hard disk drives. Both types of drives use a pair of *read-write heads* that emit magnetism to change the charges in the iron-oxide coating representing data bits to write data to the disk.

The read-write heads re-create the magnetic fields from the platter to the head to read information from the disk. The following figure displays a simplified schematic of a disk drive mechanism.

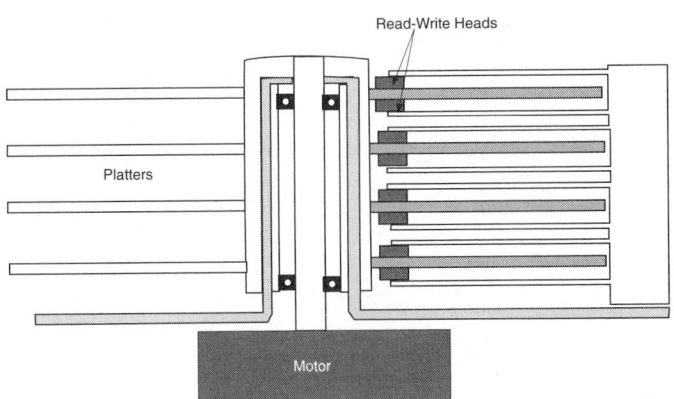

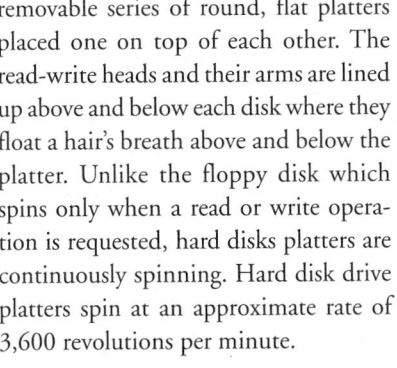

Hard disks consist of a rigid, usually non-removable series of round, flat platters placed one on top of each other. The read-write heads and their arms are lined up above and below each disk where they float a hair's breath above and below the platter. Unlike the floppy disk which spins only when a read or write operation is requested, hard disks platters are continuously spinning. Hard disk drive platters spin at an approximate rate of 3,600 revolutions per minute.

Hard disks also can hold more data in the same amount of space than a floppy because data is packed more tightly on the platter (due to the difference in the substrate—plastic in the floppy and aluminum or other flexible metal in the hard disk, and because the magnetic particles that coat this substrate are smaller). For this reason, as well as because the tightly packed data composition of the hard disk, the read-write arms do not have to travel as far along the platters to retrieve or replace the data, resulting in more efficinet performance than a floppy disk.

Disks and drives are the tools by which the Macintosh gains information. Those tools are useless if they are not instructed in how to perform work in the Macintosh environment. The Macintosh teaches the disks how to behave during a process known as *initialization*.

Floppy disks are separate from the drives that run them. This is not so with hard drives. Your hard drive is the same thing as your hard disk; the words are synonymous. Hard disks are composed of iron-oxide coated aluminum (or other flexible metal) platters encased in a hard shell. The following figure illustrates the layout of a hard disk drive.

See Also
Floppy Disks and Disk Drives; Hard Disks; Initialization

Hard Space, *See Non-Breaking Space*

Hardware

The unique aspect of the Macintosh is the deep integration of hardware with software. No other personal computer system is designed with such a symbiotic relationship. It is the capability of the processor chip, the operating system, and software to complement each other that gives the Mac its performance edge in graphics applications, and its usability edge.

We are in the midst of a Macintosh revolution as this book is being written—the Mac is moving from a hardware-codependent system to one that is hardware-independent. This transition has taken the Mac in the last three years from a computer based on a chip architecture that was complicated and expensive to manufacture and maintain, because each iteration of the **Complex Instruction Set Computer (CISC)** created numerous ripples of updates for peripheral vendors, application vendors, and Apple itself; to a **Reduced Instruction Set Computer (RISC)** chip-based computer that was simpler to manufacturer, required less upkeep by software and peripheral vendors, and was thus cheaper to sell.

What we will see shortly is a common hardware platform design using common components that can run almost any operating system. The PowerPC (as the Apple/Motorola/IBM RISC chips came to be called) Platform (PPCP) and a native **PowerPC** Macintosh operating system are coming soon (Fall 1996) and newer, faster cabling systems, networking technologies, and peripherals will most likely follow.

Conversation with Loni Hajagos

Loni Hajagos, pronounced *Hi-a-gosh*, markets FrameMaker Plus SGML software for creating large, text-intensive suites of documentation. Her product runs on the Mac, Windows, and UNIX platforms, and her users need to swap files back and forth as they move documents from one group to another, or from a parent company to a spin-off. Her engineers have to develop cross-platform code so the product works just the same way in each operating system, while allowing their idiosyncrasies.

Maclopedia: What was your first experience with a Mac?

Loni: I inherited a PowerBook from one of my coworkers. Until then I was a UNIX user. I started using it and after playing around with it for a while, the only problem I had was I couldn't figure out how to eject a floppy. Dragging the icon to the trash was not intuitive for me. But it was an epiphany! It was so friendly.

I started using the PowerBook at home whenever I had work at home, or I'd take it on the road and while away the hours in the airplane, even though in the office I was still a UNIX user.

One day I had to borrow a Windows notebook, and it was horrible. I just couldn't figure out how to use it, whereas the Mac user interface is so clean I never get lost in it. In Windows, I couldn't figure out where I was; it was thoroughly frustrating; to this day I have a prejudice against it as needlessly complicated. One of the biggest differences is that the Mac is so organic. It is thoroughly integrated from top to bottom, whereas Windows is a wrapper around DOS.

The Mac is the most pleasant computing platform I've ever dealt with. It's pretty cool when I can purchase any software and my nine-year-old can install it. A couple of weeks ago, I had the great good fortune of getting a Power Mac, and I had brought my son to work that day and he put it together, out of the box. By the time the guy from tech support came in to set it up, my son had put the system together and was exploring our internal network; he was busy downloading Mac software. Now he's not a hacker. So that's a pretty good testament!

And a few months ago we bought a CD-ROM drive for a Mac IIci and my husband—who has a lot more experience with the IBM PC—was fretting because I mail-ordered it, and how do I know it is going to work with the IIci, and how do you know it is the right cable? And I said, "Don't worry, it's a Mac; it'll work." The thing came, my son plugged it in, and it worked. On the PC, accessories are a roulette.

Maclopedia: How do your engineers feel about the Mac?

Loni: The Mac doesn't have a good reputation among developers; it's definitely a harder platform for programmers, and in our shop it gives us more trouble. We use Clear Case to manage our source code, for instance, and it doesn't work very well on the Mac. I suspect the Mac is not one of their primary markets. And the development tools are not as advanced as they are for Windows.

Maclopedia: Did the Mac architecture pose any problems when you were developing cross-platform?

Loni: In a few places. We had to change our approach to graphics importing and exporting filters because the basic structure for UNIX and Windows didn't work on the Mac. We're religious about cross-platform compatibility—we want to make everything work the same way and have the same code underneath, except for platform-specific conventions. But you have to face some re-architecting for the Mac.

Maclopedia: Was Apple helpful?

Loni: In general, the engineers have a better feeling about Apple than Microsoft as far as helping in our development. It's a more open relationship. Our engineers even helped debug some of the compilers for Apple.

Maclopedia: As a developer, what advice would you give Apple?

Loni: Play to their strength. They've been floundering not knowing where their market is. We did some stuff with Apple marketing last year, for instance; they were looking to get back their traditional focus on publishing, and they came up with a group to push on this. But it didn't go very far, which is a shame, because that is where they are the strongest.

One of the biggest differences is that the Mac is so organic. It is thoroughly integrated from top to bottom, whereas Windows is a wrapper around DOS.

And real multitasking—I mean, now they have a semblance of multitasking. They do an awfully good job of going from one thing to another seamlessly. For instance, when I have a number of documents open, it looks like they are all open simultaneously, making the users believe they can do more than one thing at a time. But if I have a big document and I want to print it, I have to wait for it to spool. If the task takes a long time, then you just have to wait, whereas with UNIX you don't think twice—you just send it and get right back to your work. In publishing and graphic arts, you want to do some things in a lights-out fashion, like color separations, and batch printing. Real multitasking, or a box with two processors in it, would buy Apple an awful lot in this market.

Licensing the operating system more, too. I would like to see Apple get back to being healthy. It's a wonderful machine. I would be very sad to lose it.

Maclopedia: How do you like the Newton?

Loni: They put a lot of stock into Newton, but it didn't pan out the way they expected it to. As a hand-held notepad it is okay, but there are lots of others that do the same thing, so it is not unique anymore. And when they first brought it out, it was going to become a full-fledged personal computer that would do general purpose things like word processing, not just manage your schedule and keep track of business cards. I have a low-tech Day Runner, and I can put an entry into that faster than my friends with Newtons can.

Maclopedia: Do you see the rest of us using the Standard General Markup Language, incorporated in your product, anytime soon? As a standard, it's a way to get free of depending on any one vendor for software, and as a language, it lets you recycle information more easily than you can when the text is full of word processing or desktop publishing codes. But will anyone other than Boeing and the Department of Defense need it?

Loni: I see SGML going down to smaller- and medium-size companies now. We are selling product to second- and third-tier companies. For instance, we sold a good-sized order to John Deere, and shortly after that we got a call from one of their outsourcing people who handle the overflow documentation—it was a small company, so they ordered ten copies of FrameMaker+SGML to keep being a supplier. We see the same thing with Boeing's suppliers. SGML is percolating down, although I don't think it is ever going to get out of the corporate world and to businesses that have to handle a lot of text-intensive documents.

Maclopedia: How are your customers handling the conversion of old documents into SGML?

Loni: It can be very expensive and time-consuming, and you have to think long and hard whether to convert old documentation and when to do it. If you don't touch a document for three years, you might just leave it on the shelf. Most customers ship their old documents off to a service bureau for conversion or hire a VAR or a systems integrator to work out the conversion for them.

continues

Maclopedia: Now that Frame has been absorbed into Adobe, what can we expect as users?

Loni: You'll see Adobe integrated with Frame products much more tightly, so you could use Illustrator as the drawing package in a seamless fashion with FrameMaker and FrameMaker+SGML. There's lots of wonderful technology lying around Adobe, and our engineers are like kids in a candy store. We'll be integrating all that stuff!

So today we are in the midst of change from the **CISC Motorola 68000** family of processors to the **RISC PowerPC 60x** family of processors, and eventually in 1997, to an operating system code-named Copland that will run on the **PowerPC Platform**—yet each will still be a Mac.

You see this change by watching the names and model numbers of Macs proliferate and change from Macintosh II to Centris to Quadra to **Power Macintosh**, and yet all of these models remain true to the Macintosh operating system. But what is a Mac?

- **A Macintosh is a hardware architecture and an operating system**. The MacOS is currently at System 7.5.3. The Mac's system is currently part "firmware," because it is hardwired on to read-only memory (**ROM**) chips, and part software based on its overlying operating system. To anthropomorphize, this makes the computer very smart. It has true **"plug and play"** capabilities. Plug a device into a Mac port, install the proper driver software, and the Mac knows and manages the device, be it a **scanner**, a **fax/modem**, a **port switch**, a **hard drive**, a **CD-ROM** drive, ad infinitum.

- **A Macintosh is software that makes the computer easy to learn and use**. The development of a sophisticated graphical user interface (GUI) enables you to control the Macintosh by pointing and clicking the button of a mouse, which in turn guides the cursor (called the *pointer*) to click buttons or icons on-screen. The action becomes very intuitive, because the icons or pictures on-screen are very representational of their purposes, be it desktop printer, trash can, document, or folder.

- **The Macintosh is a highly flexible business system**. The new **PCI**-based Power Macs use standard Intel-based expansion cards to increase the performance of graphics rendering via accelerators, increase the number of colors the monitor can display via video cards, and so forth.

- **The Macintosh is a family of computers with models to fit many marketing niches**. The **desktop models** feature flexible modular designs so that you can add exactly those components that you require to perform your job—be it electronic publisher, real-time video production, graphics designer, or number cruncher. The **consumer models**, called **Performas**, are less configurable, but more bundled to fit the home and home office uses for which they were put together. The **education models** feature components most likely to be used in schools with packaging that is easy to support and maintain. **The workgroup servers** are "souped-up" Macs with extra storage and fast communications buses for use as Web servers, network managers, or workgroup machines. The **portable Macs** come in two flavors, **PowerBooks** which are full-featured, light-weight laptop computers and the **PowerBooks Duos** which require a docking component to add ports or drives as needed.

Over the years, the Apple Macintosh has developed a set of components that together makes a Mac a "Mac." These elements are not unique to the Macintosh architecture, but as a whole create the Macintosh experience.

Hardware, Apple Desktop Bus (ADB) The **ADB** connects the keyboard and the mouse to your Mac. It can also be used to connect other input devices, such as pointing devices, joysticks, graphics tablets, or a second keyboard. Up to 27 ADB devices can coexist on an ADB port. Many higher-end Macs have two ADB ports.

Cache Macs support various ways to increase the performance of the computer. One method is to store data or instructions used often in a special area of volatile memory called *cache*. System 7 provides an adjustable **disk cache**. This cache is separate from the internal processor cache that exists on every Mac's processor. Power Macs, in addition, offer more processor cache on the MotherBoard called Level-2 Cache. These caches range in size from 256K to 1MB. Level-2 Cache is added using one of the **processor direct slots (PDS)**. Other cache cards can be added to **NuBus** and **PCI** expansion slots to further increase performance.

Hardware, CD-ROM Drives Internal **CD-ROM drives** have become a standard feature on all desktop and low-end Macs. The speed of their drive mechanisms ranges from double- to quadruple-speed (called by Apple the 300i and 600i, respectively) depending upon the Mac model (with newer Macs having the faster drive). These drives support audio CDs, Kodak PhotoCDs, Macintosh formatted CD-ROMs, and some DOS data CDs formatted for Macs.

Hardware, CPU The CPU or **central processing unit** is the engine that drives the Mac. The Mac uses one of two types of processors: Motorola 680x0 family (the 68000, 68020, 68030, and 68040 chips) or the Apple/IBM/Motorola **PowerPC chips** (the 601, 603, 603e, 604, and 604e chips). The PowerPC chips provide performance that is two to four times faster

than the same software created for 68K Mac computers. Macs can also run other operating systems concurrently with the MacOS. You can install software that emulates DOS and MS-Windows (including Windows 95 and Windows 3.1) or install an Intel processor DaughterBoard on the Mac logic board that adds a 486 SX or DX chip set that can run DOS and the different flavors of Windows.

Hardware, Ethernet Ethernet is a fast networking protocol developed by Xerox that has become a standard for most businesses and educational organizations. Ethernet supports both local and wide area networks and provides a gateway to the Internet. Apple has supported Ethernet since the Mac II with Ethernet network cards. Most modern Macs provide built-in coaxial and 10Base-T ports that support Apple's **EtherTalk** implementation of the Ethernet protocol. Macs also support their own file sharing protocol called **AppleTalk** that enables you to build small, decentralized or client/server-based networks using telephone wiring. AppleTalk runs on **LocalTalk** physical wiring to provide networking for up to 32 Mac devices (be they printers, modems, or desktop machines).

Hardware, Floppy Drives All modern Macs, except the PowerBook Duos, contain an internal 1.4MB floppy disk drive, also called a **SuperDrive**. These disk drives can read 1.4MB, 800K, and 400K formatted disks. System 7 provides PC Exchange system software that lets the drive also read DOS/Windows, OS/2, Apple II, and UNIX file formats.

Hardware, Hard Drives Without a hard drive there would be no place to store the voluminous data and instructions that comprise today's Mac operating system (System 7.5.3 is 17MB if fully installed) and application programs (MS Word is 26MB and WordPerfect is 27MB if fully installed). Gone are the days that you can fit the Mac operating system on a 400K floppy and your data on another floppy. For this reason, all Macs come with substantial storage space on an internal hard disk drive. The hard drive is actually several things: a power supply, the actual disks that store the information, **SCSI** in and out ports, and a SCSI ID counter.

H

Most hard drives have two SCSI (Small Computer System Interface) 50-pin connectors, one for connecting the drive to the Mac and the other for continuing the connection to another SCSI device. The internal hard drive is always considered by the Mac to be SCSI ID number 0. You can connect another six devices daisy chained one to another from each SCSI port. The seventh number is reserved for the Mac's **motherboard**. Each SCSI device is given a unique number from 1 to 6 which is remembered by the SCSI ID counter. The software that drives the hard drive keeps track of the devices by their SCSI ID. Modern Macs provide hard drives that range in size from 230MB to 2G.

Hardware, Infrared (IR) The desktop and PowerBook Macs contain infrared sensors and transceivers to all the transmission of data over the air waves between Macs within three feet of each other. **IR** is also used to replace the mouse as a pointing device, in the same fashion as you use a remote control device to change channels on a television. Macs with **TV tuners** also use IR to control the tuners. The Performa 630, 5200, and 6200 Macs and the PowerBook 190, 2300 Duo, and 5300 all have internal IR for **wireless communications**.

Hardware, Microphones The Macintosh is a full-scale multimedia computer. Most Macs come with a microphone or built-in microphone that can be used to send sounds into the Mac. The Mac can output the sounds to a variety of media, including disks, CD-ROMs, or the Mac's built-in 16-bit stereo speakers. Power Macs and older AV Macs also permit text-to-speech and speech-to text via an architecture called **PlainTalk** and the **Digital Signal Processor** (DSP) chip (used on 68040 AV Macs but not required on Power Macs).

Hardware, MIDI Macintosh computers support the **Musical Instrument Digital Interface (MIDI)** standard for controlling musical instruments. When you attach specialized MIDI-based hardware to the Mac's serial port and/or microphone port, you can transform your Mac into a musical workstation for creating **digital audio**.

Hardware, Connectivity Macs support most Hayes-compatible **modems** attached to the modem serial port. Modems come pre-installed on some Mac models, or can be operated externally. Some Performa Macs provide software that works with the modem to turn your Mac into a voice mail system or a facsimile system.

In 1994, with the AV Macs, Apple introduced GeoPort. **GeoPort** works with GeoPort-compatible serial ports with a hardware "pod" to provide modem, telephony, and other telecommunications features in a single package.

Hardware, Expansion Slots The Macintosh computers support three types of expansion cards, based on the bus slots used on that particular Mac model. **NuBus** slots were the earliest Macintosh architecture for upgrading the Mac with network, graphics accelerators, SCSI, data controllers, and processor accelerator cards. NuBus slots are limited by power and physical dimensions of the slot (either seven or 13-inch slots are available). Smaller footprint Macs, such as the Performa 6200, use a **processor direct slot (PDS)** that can accept a special "L-shaped" card to accommodate NuBus cards or PDS cards. The newest Power Macs have incorporated an Intel standard bus called **Peripheral Computer Interconnect (PCI)** in the place of the slower, more power-hungry NuBus architecture. PCI cards are smaller in size than NuBus slots. You can install Intel PCI upgrade cards if they supply Mac software drivers, opening up the Mac to a huge supply of upgrade options for video, networking, graphics acceleration, SCSI acceleration, and so forth.

StarGate sells a PCI to NuBus converter that allows you to install NuBus cards in PCI slots so that when you upgrade to a PCI Mac you do not lose the use of your old NuBus expansion cards.

PowerBooks include another Intel standard expansion option—the **PCMCIA** or PC card slot. This expansion slot accepts Type I or II PC cards, such as networking, modems, or hard drives.

The following table lays out a simple structure by which you can sort out which Mac fits your particular need.

The Macintosh Family

Mac Type	Model Names	Characteristics
Desktop Models	Power Mac 6100, 7200, 7500, 8500, 9500	Stand-alone computers that often include a CD-ROM drive and fax/modem. Monitor and keyboard sold separately.
Consumer Models	Performa 580, 630 family, 640 CD DOS Compatible, 5200 family, 61xx family, 62xx family, and 63xx family	Performas are the same Macs as desktop models but packaged as total systems that include color display (except the 636), keyboard, mouse, and CD-ROM drive. Some models also provide either external or internal fax/modems. All Performas come bundled with extensive software and CD-ROM titles.
Education Models	LC 580, LC 630 DOS Compatible, LC 6100/66 DOS Compatible, 5200/75 LC, and the 5300/100 LC	Similar in configurations to the Performa models but lacking the bundled software.
Portable Models	PowerBook 190s, PowerBook Duo 280c, Duo 2300, and various flavors of 5300	Light-weight laptop or dockable computers containing either a gray scale or color display and trackpad.
Workgroup Servers	Power Mac 6150, 8150, and 9150	A "souped-up" Power Mac, often bundled with a CD-ROM drive, built-in Ethernet, Apple RAID software and other client/server software bundles, DAT drives.

For More...

If you want to do this...	Go to this entry...
Find out about Macintosh models and their features	Macintosh Computer Family
Learn about Macintosh internal components	Circuits, Parts of the Macintosh
Learn about printing and printers	Printing
Learn about monitors	Monitors
Learn about mass storage devices	Storage
Learn about multimedia speakers and AV systems on the Mac	Speakers
Learn about backup hardware	Backup Hardware Options

continues

H

If you want to do this...	Go to this entry...
Find out about PowerBooks and Macintosh laptop options	Portable Computers, Macintosh Family, PowerBooks
Find out about scanners and image processing on the Mac	Scanner, Desktop
Find out about telecommunications, telephony, and communications options on the Mac	Modems; GeoPort; Online Services

Bibliography

The Macintosh Bible, 5th Edition, Darcy DiNucci, Elizabeth Castro, Aileen Abernathy, David Blatner, Connie Guglielmo, John Kadyk, Henry Knorr, and Bob Weibell, editors; published by PeachPit Press, Berkeley, CA, 1994.

MacWorld New Complete Mac Handbook, 4th Edition, Jim Heid, published by IDG Books, Worldwide, Foster City, CA, 1995.

MacWeek Upgrading and Repairing Your Mac, Lisa Lee, published by Hayden Books, Indianapolis, IN, 1995.

Insanely Great: The Life and Times of Macintosh, the Computer That Changed Everything, Steven Levy, published by Penguin Books, New York, NY, 1995.

Inside the Apple Macintosh, 2nd Edition, Peter Norton and Jim Heid, published by Brady Books of Prentice-Hall, New York, NY, 1992.

The Power Mac Book!, 2nd Edition, Ron Pronk, published by Coriolis Group Books, Scottsdale, AZ, 1996.

How Macs Work, John Rizzo and K. Daniel Clark, published by Ziff-Davis Publishing, Emeryville, CA, 1993.

Check out Apple's Home page at **http://www.apple.com**

Hardware Handshaking, *See Flow Control; Modem Cables and Connections*

Hardware and Software Errors, *See Software and Hardware Errors*

Harlan, Mark, *See Dogcow*

Hash Animation Master

This software is dedicated to character modeling and organic objects. Although you can also form colder mechanical actors to populate and move in a scene, the purpose of the software is to fill the void present as far as 3D character animation goes. Global Preferences settings include Memory (virtual memory will be accessed if this setting is too low), Polygonal Output, Perspective from a Bird's Eye (zoom factor and camera setting, also controllable with the Control and Shift keys), and the maintenance of an Error Log (keeps a list of errors that occurred when operating the software).

Modeling Tools A Character Tool panel is one of the software's main hubs for modeling and design. Here, segments can be added to and deleted from a figure, rotated and scaled, ghosted for non-rendering, "skin" added and removed, the center of gravity reoriented, and the Attributes altered. Attributes include Color, Ambiance, Roughness, Specularity, Reflectivity, Transparency, Refraction, and Specular Color. Segments can have surface attributes or material (texture maps). The other main panel is the Character Info panel, where alterations to the character can be adjusted numerically. Other modeling features include adjustable pivot points of characters, full cut/copy/paste, extrusions, lathing, and rotating and flipping control points. An Undo is included.

Boolean Operations Boolean cuts, subtracting parts of an object, are possible with the software.

Texture mapping Materials are assigned to segments by first browsing the textures list, and selecting one of the members. A Materials Editor allows you to create materials from scratch. Materials can also be stretched to accommodate different sized surfaces.

Lights In Fast Mode, the position of the light source can be chosen from nine different positions via interactive buttons.

Rendering A render button on the speed bar (shaped like a filmstrip) allows you to render a scene to a file. You can also select to render only a bounded area. If an animation file is rendered, it will play back as soon as the rendering is finished for preview. A Render Settings dialog allows you to set File Name, the Render Mode, Stereo Options (in case you want to create stereo imagery that can be appreciated with 3D stereo glasses), Output Resolution, and Render Frame Range. FPS is also set here. Ping-Pong animation loops can also be set.

Included Libraries The software comes with a CD-ROM packed with objects and pre-configured animation that can be studied, altered, and rendered. In addition, a tutorial videotape shows some of the results professionals have achieved working with the software.

Animation Hash Animation software allows you to plan and activate three types of movements in your figures: Skeletal, Muscular, and Spline based. These can be used in combination to produce both believable and (when necessary) bizarre results. Keyframe tools allow you to cut, copy, paste, delete, insert, and move to any keyframe in the list. The Skeletal Tool panel incorporates tools for Anchoring segments of the skeleton, resizing and rotating, setting the "Stride Length" (important if you don't want your walking figures to seem like they're sliding on ice as they move), and complete control over the acceleration and deceleration of skeletal parts. The Muscle Tool Panel allows you to control a selected muscle's displayed splines, adjustment of pivot points, and the acceleration and deceleration of all assigned movements. The Spline Tool Panel controls the selected spline's assignments, translations, bulging, bending, and acceleration-deceleration.

Other Special Features Setting the COG (Center Of Gravity) of an object is very important to the Hash Inverse Kinematic system incorporated into the software. This allows the animated figure to be animated

in a believable fashion. Inverse Kinematics are a primary part of the software, allowing movements that behave as their real world counterparts. The most special feature is the software's dedication to making character animation doable in the first place.

File Load/Save Conventions The Hash animation software allows you to model objects with spline patches, but exported objects are still converted to polygonal surfaces. These can be of three types: DXF, OBJ, and RIB (for Renderman). DXF produces very large files, OBJ is more efficient, and Renderman files actually include the capability of allowing for Bézier patches. Polygons per patch settings can be indicated to produce better objects, but at the expense of file size.

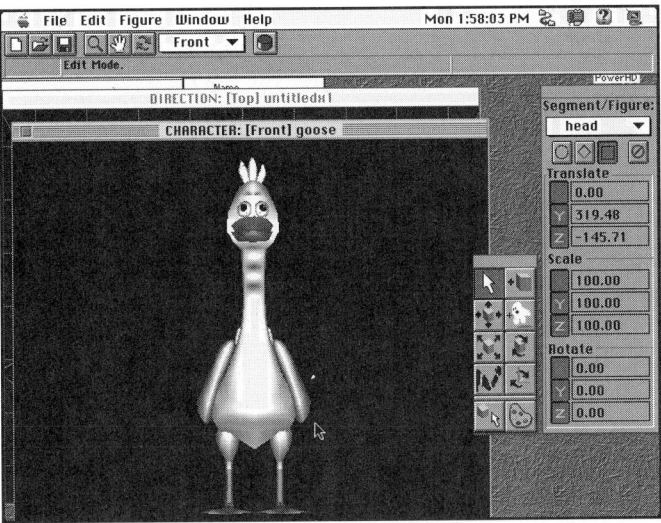

Havoc, *See Arcade-Style Games; First-Person Perspective Shooters; Network Games; Violence in Games*

Hayes-Compatible Modems

Modems which recognize and use the AT command set developed by Hayes are said to be Hayes-Compatible. Today, virtually all modems sold are Hayes-compatible.

See Also

AT Commands; Hayes AT Command Set; Modems

Hayes AT Command Set

A set of dialing and connection commands recognized by Hayes and other **modems** commonly used to connect to the **Internet** or **commercial online services** such as **America Online**.

AT commands are used by communication software to dial or hang up a phone, or establish or terminate a connection to a remote device. The squeaking and clicking sounds commonly made by modems occur as a result of AT commands.

Because your computer may be communicating with any number of computers on the Internet, each with its own modem, it is suggested that your modem recognize the AT Command Set. Most telecom packages, especially those that use Apple's Communication Toolbox, automate the entry of AT commands, so you don't have to enter manual commands such as:

```
ATDT555-1212
```

See Also

Asynchronous Data Transfers; AT Commands; Internet; Local Area Network; Modem; Packets; Parity

Head Crash

If the drive heads that read and write data on your **hard disk** ever come in contact with the spinning platter it reads from and writes to, a head crash occurs. Although this type of crash is very rare, it is also very serious. Head crashes often result in the loss of all data on the hard disk, and it's not unusual for a serious head crash to damage the hard disk to the point that it has to be replaced, which can be very costly.

Head crashes generally occur if the hard drive is jarred, hit, or dropped, especially when the disk is turned on and the drive heads are not parked. This is why you're warned to never move a computer while it's running, and to take caution when moving a hard drive from location to location. If the hard disk was severely jarred, it could cause a head crash damaging both the data and the drive. Head crashes also can be caused by a speck of dust or dirt, cat hair, and any small airborne object getting between the platter and the read/write head.

To protect your hard disk from a head crash, follow a few simple rules:

- Never move your computer when it's running.
- Always choose Shut Down from the Special menu (which will park the read/write head to protect it).
- Always use care when moving your computer when it's turned off.

See Also

Hard Disk

<HEAD> HTML Tag

The <HEAD> tag is the second tag in a "correct" **HTML** document to be posted on the World Wide Web. Anything contained within the <HEAD> and </HEAD> tags defines the properties of the entire document. Only a few tags go within the head element. The <TITLE> tag falls within the head element and must be used in any HTML document (the <HEAD> tag itself is optional, however). Text should not go between <HEAD> and </HEAD>, but <ISINDEX>, <**BASE**> and <LINK> are examples of some of the other tags that can go within the <HEAD> tag.

See Also

HTML; HTML Markup Tags; Web Browser; Web Page; World Wide Web

Headings in HTML

Highlighted words or phrases in an **HTML** document that usually appear in a larger type font than the rest of the text and act as section dividers, much like headlines in a newspaper.

Headings in HTML are numbered from H1 to H6. H1 headings appear in the largest size and are generally the most important. H6 headings are the smallest and least important ones.

Headings are formed with the heading **markup** tags, as follows:

```
<Hn>Heading Text Goes Here</Hn>
```

where n is a number from 1 to 6.

The headings on a World Wide Web home page should be a series of teasers designed to draw the reader's eye into a topic and express in a flash why the contents are important.

See Also
HTML; Web Browser; Web Page; World Wide Web

Heap

A section of an application's memory that is used for most of the application's dynamic memory allocation. Together with the **stack** and globals, this makes up an application's total memory partition.

When the system sets up your application's memory space, it creates space for global variables, allocates memory for the stack, and gives your application a tiny heap (see the following figure). In between this tiny heap and the stack is the rest of the memory assigned to your application. Your application must take over the heap using the **Toolbox** routine **MaxApplZone()**. This call causes the heap to grow until it reaches the bottom of the stack area.

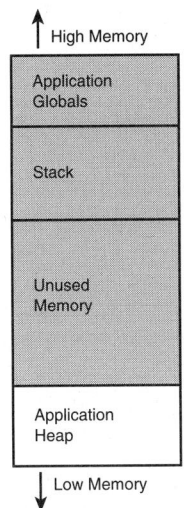

Some or all of your application code might live inside your application heap. On a 68K Mac, you can separate your code into segments that automatically load into the heap when needed. On a Power Macintosh, your code loads into the application heap as one block

and stays there. If virtual memory is on, the System keeps your application code in a separate virtual memory space, giving you more room in the application heap.

There really is no empty space inside the heap. The Memory Manager divides the heap into a series of blocks. Every byte of memory in the heap belongs to a block. There are three kinds of blocks: nonrelocatable, relocatable, and free. When your application is launched, the heap contains several small relocatable and nonrelocatable blocks and a few large free blocks. As the application runs, it creates other relocatable and nonrelocatable blocks.

Relocatable blocks are referenced using **handles**. The Memory Manager provides a routine to lock handles in memory, which keeps them from being moved. Locked handles are effectively the same as nonrelocatable blocks (until they are unlocked, that is). Nonrelocatable blocks are referenced using **pointers**.

The following figure shows the ideal placement of memory blocks. Locked relocatable blocks are at the top of the heap. Nonrelocatable blocks are low in the heap. The center of the heap consists of unlocked relocatable blocks and free blocks.

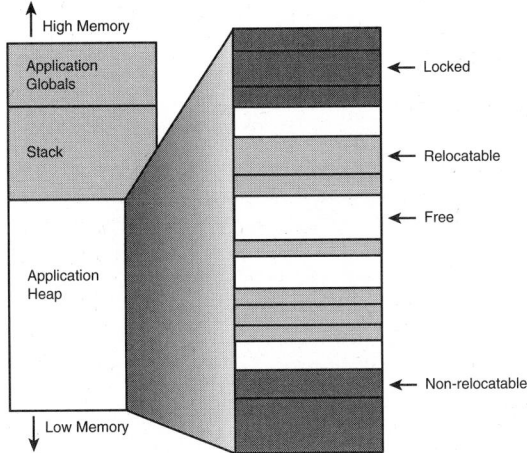

When the heap looks like this, the relocatable blocks can be moved to consolidate the free space into a single large block from which new blocks can be allocated.

The term *application heap* is used sometimes to mean an application's entire memory partition.

See Also

Handle; Pointer; Stack; System Heap

Hell: A Cyberpunk Thriller

Although **Hell** features big name actors Dennis Hopper as Mr. Beautiful and Grace Jones as Solene Solux, it doesn't utilize full-motion video to the extent of games like **Daedalus Encounter** or **Wing Commander III**. Take 2 Interactive used polygonal animation with lots of angles and bulging movements. The overall effect makes Hell look like an avant-garde animated short or an MTV music video. The plot centers around a botched attempt on your life that propels you into a convoluted and deeply layered adventure.

Grace Jones is an American dictator who has made a business deal with Hellions, the top demon of course being Dennis Hopper. Hell is an adventure game of the best sort, aside from the graphics and fanfare. The story is intricate and the character interaction, although not quite as in-depth as **Return to Zork**, is still informative and realistic. Hell is the sort of game where everything that happens is a clue and nothing is irrelevant. Mystery lovers should find it a satisfying title.

See Also

Adventure Games; Hollywood Games Connection

Hellcats Over the Pacific, *See A-10 Attack!*

Help Command

Many applications support a built-in help feature. A number of these applications enable you to access the help feature from the **Help menu** in the menu bar (the question mark icon on the far right of the menu bar). If the application you're using supports a built-in help feature, it may appear at the bottom of the Help **pull-down menu**. In other programs, Help can often be accessed by pressing the **Help key** on your keyboard, or if your application has a Window menu, Help can be accessed there as well. Still other applications put their Help menus at the top of the Apple menu. Consult your software's manual to find out if help is available and where the developer has placed it within the application.

Many applications also support Apple's **Balloon Help**, which is activated from the Help menu as well as by choosing Show Balloons. If your application supports Balloon help, you can drag your cursor over buttons or commands in your application and a small cartoon-like balloon appears with information on the item to which you're pointing.

To use an application's built-in help feature, follow these steps:

1. Choose Help from the Help menu (question mark icon) located in the far right side of the application's menu bar. If Help does not appear under this menu, try pressing the Help key on extended keyboards. If your application has a Window menu, look there as well for a Help window.

2. Each application has a slightly different Help engine, but the instructions for using Help are usually listed in the opening Help window.

3. Check at the top of the Apple menu, as some applications place their Help feature there. Many applications also support Apple Balloon Help, which is accessed through the Help menu. To access Balloon Help, choose Show Balloons under the Help menu. As you point at items in your application with your cursor, small cartoon-like balloons appear with explanations of the item you're pointing to with your cursor.

4. If you're running System 7.5 or higher, you can also look for Help in the Apple Guide, which is also accessed under the Help menu.

See Also

Balloon Help; Help Key; Help Menu; Pull-Down Menu

Help Key

Many applications have a built-in help feature that you can access by pressing the **Help** key on extended keyboards. You can also access an application's help feature by selecting Help on the application's menus, usually found on the Window menu in an application or on the Apple menu when an application is open.

Applications have built-in help features to provide answers to the most commonly asked questions by users. By including a built-in help feature, the application enables users to continue to work within their application and get instant help, rather than having to dig up the original instruction manuals.

In System 7.5 and higher, the Help feature of applications is most commonly found under the Help menu in the upper-right corner of the application's menu bar. Also found under the Help menu in System 7.5 and higher, is the Apple Guide, Apple's interactive help feature that walks you through the steps of various features and commands.

See Also
Apple Guide; Help; System 7.5

Helper Applications, Web

A *helper application* is configured with your **Web browser** to enable you to perform tasks while still running the Web browser that are independent of the browser and require another program to run. The Web browser opens the helper application, runs the program, and then closes the application without interrupting your browser.

You use helper applications to view movies, play music and other sounds, use **Acrobat** reader to read PDF files, or compress and decompress files from the Web while still in your browser application. The movie (or sound file) plays in the window of the helper application, rather than in the browser window, and the helper application icon and menu items appear at the top of the Mac's screens.

One of the most frequent activities on the Web and Internet involves downloading and then using files or applications. In this case, you need a helper application to "uncompress" or "decode" another application. The nature of the Internet requires that the files you download are:

1. Manageable in size.

2. Storable in different computer platforms.

3. Transferable by a variety of mail and other file transfer protocols.

The most common helper applications you are likely to use with your browser deal with these size and cross-platform constraints because they uncompress or unencode the files you've downloaded.

For example, when you download the helper application **RealAudio**, the file comes encoded in a format called **BinHex**. In this case you need a helper application such as BinHex 4.0 to decode RealAudio automatically after it is downloaded to your computer.

To play files that you've found on the Web, you first have to set up your preferences setting in your browser so that the browser knows what program to call. To do this, perform the following basic steps:

1. Find your Preferences or Options menu and open it.

2. Choose Helper Applications. You may have to search through the options in order to find the helper applications, as each browser labels these a little differently. The following figure shows Netscape 2.0's Preferences settings.

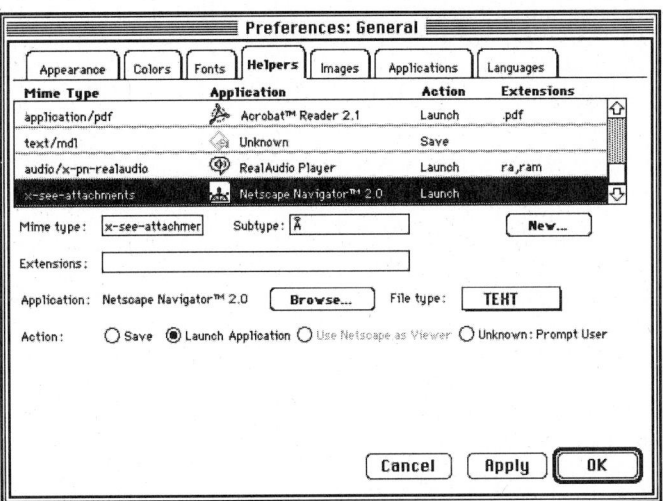

3. Choose to add a new application type. From Netscape, you click the New button. You have to enter four types of information for your browser: the **MIME type**, the subtype box, the extensions names, and the action to perform with the application. The following table lists these types and extensions for most of the common helper applications you'll use.

4. After you enter the information from the table, depending on your application, you have to browse your Mac to find the application and double-click it to associate it with these settings. Click the Browse button to do this now.

5. Pick your action; in almost all cases, it will be to Launch the application, but check the table to be sure.

Common Helper Applications' Settings

Helper Purpose	Application Names	MIME Type	Subtype	Extension(s)	Action
Read image Files	JPEGView	image	gif; jpeg	gif; jpeg	Use browser as a viewer
Listen to sounds	SoundApp; SoundMachine	audio	x-wav; x-aiff; x-snd; x-aiff	wav; snd au; aiff	Launch program
Listen to sounds	RealAudio	audio	x-pn-realaudio	rau	Launch program
Listen to sounds	MPEG Audio	audio	mpeg	mpeg	Launch program
View PostScript files	PostScript	application	postscript	.ps; .ai; and .eps	Launch program
Read cross-platform documents	Acrobat; Common Ground	reader	PDF	pdf; cmg	Launch program
Play movies	ALLMIDI; QuickTime VR	application	mid; qtm	mid; qtm	Launch program
Uncompress files	ZipIt	application	x-compressed	zip; z; gz; tgz	Launch program
Compress files	uuUndo; UULite; and ShrinkWrap	application	x-uun	uun	Launch program

Finding Helper Applications on the Web

Application	Fee	Location	Notes
Common Ground	n/a	http://bcastle.commonground.com/	Reads standard cross-platform documents
DropStuff with Expander Enhancer	n/a	http://www.aladdinsys.com	Expands compressed files
uuUndo, UULite, and ShrinkWrap		http://wwwhost.ots.utexas.edu/mac/pub-mac-compression.html	Compresses files
JPEGView	$15	http://www.med.cornell.edu/jpegview.html	Displays JPEG pictures
NIH Image	n/a	http://wwwhost.ots.utexas.edu/mac/pub-mac-graphics.html	Image editor

Application	Fee	Location	Notes
SoundApp	$20	http://wwwhost.ots.utexas.edu/mac/pub-mac-sound.html	Audio player
Sound Machine	$15	http://wwwhost.ots.utexas.edu/mac/pub-mac-sound.html	Audio player
MPEG/CD	$15	http://www.electriciti.com/~bbal/	Audio player (plays MPEGs)
MPEG Audio for PowerPC	n/a	http://www.electriciti.com/~bbal/	Audio player (plays MPEGs)
RealAudio	$25	http://www.realaudio.com/dloadintro.html	Audio player
ALLMIDI	$25	ftp://sumex-aim.stanford.edu/info-mac/snd/util/	Converts MIDI files to QuickTime
QuickTime VR	$50	http://qtvr.quicktime.apple.com/	Plays QuickTime movies and VR movies
Sparkle	n/a	ftp://sumex-aim.stanford.edu/info-mac/grf/util	Movie Player (plays MPEGs)
Acrobat reader	n/a	http://www.adobe.com/Software/Acrobat/Macintosh/ACROREAD.MAC.bin	Reads standard cross-platform documents

See Also

Internet; MIME Type; Web Browser; World Wide Web

Heretic, *See Hexen: Beyond Heretic*

Hexadecimal

Hexadecimal is a number format frequently used by programmers. Unlike decimal numbers that are expressed in base-10, hexadecimal (or hex) numbers are expressed in base-16. Because Arabic numerals only exist for the digits 0-9, hexadecimal borrows the letters A-F to represent the values 11-15. In decimal numbers, each digit position has a value 10 times greater than the one to its immediate right. Similarly, each digit in a hexadecimal number has a value 16 times greater than the one to its right.

The following figure shows the difference between the decimal and hexadecimal representations of the same number (16,290). Notice that the hexadecimal version represents the same number using fewer digits.

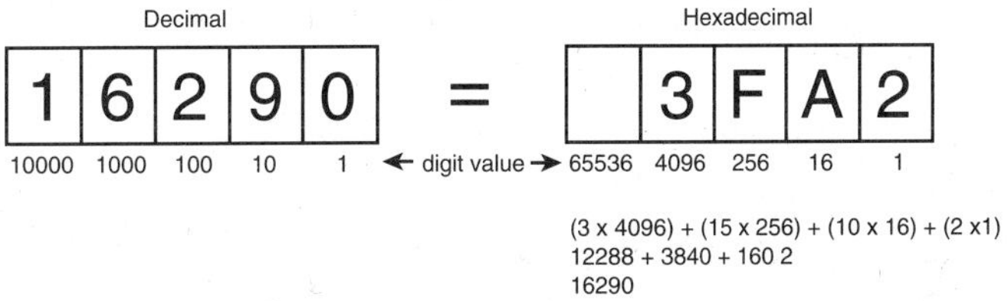

Decimal

| 1 | 6 | 2 | 9 | 0 |

10000 1000 100 10 1 ← digit value

Hexadecimal

| 3 | F | A | 2 |

→ 65536 4096 256 16 1

(3 x 4096) + (15 x 256) + (10 x 16) + (2 x1)
12288 + 3840 + 160 2
16290

Hexadecimal is well suited to dealing with digitally stored numbers. Digital numbers are stored using the values zero and one (or on and off). They are base-2. Because 16 is a power of 2 ($2^4 = 16$), digital numbers fit well into hexadecimal numbers. One byte of data, eight bits, can hold 256 possible values ($2^8 = 256$); these values can be easily represented using two hexadecimal digits ($16^2 = 256$).

Hexen: Beyond Heretic

Hexen: Beyond Heretic incorporates new heights (or lows depending on how you feel about them) into the First Person Perspective Shooter family. Developed by GT Interactive and id, the folks responsible for Wolfenstein 3-D and **DOOM II**, Hexen adds in magic spells that allow you to do everything from fly to turn your opponents into pigs.

Just be warned: Pigs bite and you will have to blow them away if you want to really be rid of them. Also, if you are playing on a **network**, you can get turned into a pig by your human opponent. You will turn back into a human eventually, but pigs aren't much of a match for the wide assortment of weapons players get to choose from. Hexen's bizarre humor spoofs the more serious violence of previous id titles like Doom II and Wolfenstein 3-D, but that doesn't diminish the amount of destruction that you are capable of invoking as you play. Hexen rates right up there with the its fellow **First Person Perspective Shooters** as a fun, but violent title.

See Also

Descent; Marathon; Violence in Games

HFS, *See Hierarchical File System*

Hickey, *See Printing*

Hidden Easter Eggs

A number of applications, utilities, and even Apple's system software often have hidden messages or hidden credits within the file placed there by the software programmers. Here's a list of some of the most popular Easter Eggs.

■ In the Finder, hold down the Option key while choosing About This Macintosh to see a graphic of a mountain range and scrolling credits of the programmers who developed various versions of the Finder. If you hold both the Option-⌘ keys while choosing "About this Macintosh" the same scene appears, but your cursor changes to a happy face with its tongue sticking out at you.

■ In the Stickies Apple menu item, open a new sticky, type "Antler!", and press Return. The background of the note displays a large moose with antlers and a credit to the software company that developed it (see the following figure).

■ In the Memory control panel, turn on Virtual Memory and hold down the Option key while selecting the pop-up menu of hard disks. The list of available disks is replaced by a list of the Virtual Memory development team, each with a submenu containing nicknames for the team members.

■ In the Monitors control panel, click the version number and you get a pop-up menu with a list of the programmers with a smiley face at the top. Hold the Option key and click again, and the smiley face sticks its tongue out at you.

■ If you turn on Balloon Help and drag your cursor over the QuickTime icon and QuickDraw 3D, the QuickTime icon's Balloon reads, "Time: N. A nonspatial continuum in which events occur in apparently irreversible succession from the past through the present to the future." Place the cursor on the QuickDraw 3D extension, and at the bottom of the help balloon you should see the message "Flatland no more. Come and follow us into the Third Dimension...."

Another Balloon Help Easter Egg is uncovered when you open the Date & Time control panel and point to the Daylight Savings Time checkbox. The Balloon tells you what it does, but at the bottom is the phrase, "Spring forward, Fall back!"

- In TeachText, hold the Option key and select About TeachText from the Apple menu. The dialog box is extended to reveal a special thanks.

- In System 7.5.2, if you type "secret about box" (without capitals or quotation marks) in Note Pad or Stickies, highlight the text, and drag the text to the desktop, you see a picture of Apple headquarters with a flag in the foreground and the logo "iguana iguana powersurgius" on the flag. By moving the mouse around, you can control the direction the flag is waving. After a while, the picture on the flag changes to something other than the iguana. If you decide you don't want to wait, hold down the letter P as you drag to the desktop and you will see a picture of the design team on the flag. If you hold down the letter Q, you'll see a pink flag with a message that says that QuickTime must be installed to see the images.

You can even make the flag break off, flutter toward the ground, and off the screen. The key is to "whip" the flag back and forth (by moving the mouse up and down on the right side of the screen) until you reach the right level of whipping action to break the flag off.

- In the Color control panel, System 7 and higher, click and hold the highlighted sample text and one of the programmer's names appears. If you click and hold again, the other programmer's name appears.

- In the Map control panel, click the version number to see the programmer's name.

See Also
Disk Cache; Easter Egg; Hard Disk; Memory Control Panel

Hidden Map Control Panel Features

The **Map control panel**, which seems simplistic and straightforward at first glance, has hidden features that add a significant amount of versatility. At its most basic, you click anywhere on the map of the world and it displays that location's current time, longitude, and latitude. You can also type the name of a city and click the Find button to have the control panel locate that exact spot on the map. The map finds most major cities and landmarks around the world, and if you type "Middle of Nowhere" it locates the exact spot.

To see all of the places in the Map's database, hold down the Option key while clicking the Find button (or pressing Return). If you continue all the way through the cycle to the beginning of the list (the letter A), it shows the name of each place it knows in that country's native language! Also, if you click and drag the arrow pointer to the edges of the map, it scrolls to reveal the rest of the planet.

The Map's black-and-white map can be replaced with a full-color map that comes with your Macintosh. To find it, open your **Scrapbook**. The first image is a full-color relief map of the world. Copy it to the **Clipboard** and paste it into the Map Control Panel's window. (It's the same map, only in color.)

There are practical applications for the Map control panel as well. If you're traveling with a PowerBook, for example, you can reset the Map's home city to your intended destination, and the Mac's internal clock is reset to that new time zone. To reset the Map's home city, click the location of the new home city on the map and then click the Set button in the bottom-right corner of the control panel window.

You can also use this Map feature to tell the time difference between your current location and your intended destination. To find out the time difference, click the place on the map you are going, and then click the words Time Zone in your control panel window. Notice that they change to the words Time

Differ to show the time difference between the two cities. An "x" in the box to the right of the hour and minute boxes means you need to add those numbers to your local time. No "x" means you subtract those hours from your local time.

See Also
Clipboard; Map Control Panel; Scrapbook

Hidden Programs
When you are working in an application, it is the active application. Any other open applications are behind the active application. You can choose to **Hide** open applications by selecting Hide Others from the **Applications menu**. This leaves the programs open, but hides them from view. If you return to the **Finder**, you can ask that all your programs be hidden from view by choosing Hide Others as well.

See Also
Applications Menu; Finder; Hide

Hide Active Application Command
To hide the active application, select Hide Application from the **Application menu** on the right side of the menu bar. The actual name of the active application appears after the word "Hide" rather than the word "Application." It may read, for example, "Hide Microsoft Word." Invoking this command hides the current application, and takes you to the **Finder** unless it has been hidden. If this is true, then you are taken to the next application listed in the Applications menu. Choosing Hide does not quit the application, it just hides the application from view, leaving it running in the background.

You can make the application active again by choosing it from the Applications menu. You can also select Show All from the Applications menu, and all windows are displayed.

To hide the active application, follow these steps:

1. Choose Hide *Application* (it reads Hide Microsoft Word, or whatever the program name is) from the Applications menu.

2. You return to the Finder, with the program still running but hidden from view.

3. To return to the application, select the Application's name from the Applications menu. If the icon for the application appears grayed, that means an application is hidden. You can activate that application by choosing it.

See Also
Applications Menu; Finder; Hide Others Command

Hide Others Command
When you are running multiple applications and want to see only the active application, you can use the Hide Others command found on the **Application menu**, as shown in the figure. Choosing Hide Others hides the other program's windows from view. Although these windows 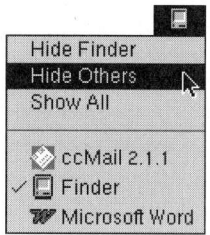 are hidden, they are still open and running and can be accessed any time by switching to another program through the Applications menu.

You can also use the Hide Others command in the **Finder** to hide all your open application windows, leaving only the desktop in view. There's a shortcut you can use that hides others when you select a program or select the Finder from the Applications menu. To use the shortcut, just hold down the **Option key** while you select your application. When the program comes to the front, all the other windows are hidden. Another option you have is the Show All command. This option reveals all open windows of active applications but does not make them active.

To Hide Others, follow these steps:

1. Click and hold the Applications menu.

2. Select Hide Others. This hides any other open applications that have documents or windows open.

To Show All, follow these steps:

1. At the Finder click and hold the Applications menu.

2. Select Show All. Any applications that have open windows become visible, but they do not become active.

See Also

Applications Menu; Finder; Hide Active; Option Key

Hierarchical File System (HFS)

The hierarchical file system (HFS) is an organizational tool that helps users keep track of their **files** using **folders** to keep files segregated. You can put a folder inside another folder without mixing the contents of the two—they remain separate, just like they do in a real file cabinet. The files that appear in your **hard drive's** main window, for example, are on one level. If you have folders on your hard drive, the items inside that folder are also on your hard drive, but for organizational purposes, they're kept separate.

To see how this works, open your main hard drive window and select **View by Name** on the **Views menu**. You'll see a hierarchical listing of the files and folders in your main window. Click the triangle beside any folder, and it expands to show you a hierarchical list of what's inside that folder. If there is a folder within that folder, you can click its triangle, and it displays the contents of that folder, which is separate from the contents of the first folder. That's HFS.

HFS helps users when they use the **Open command** from within an application. Without HFS, every file on your hard drive appears in one **scrolling** list. But because HFS was introduced by Apple in 1987, you see both files and folders when you choose the Open command from the **File menu**, but you won't see the contents of a folder until you open it because HFS keeps everything separated for you.

See Also

File Menu; Files; Folders; Hard Drive; Open Dialog; Scrolling; View By Name; Views Menu

Hierarchical View

If you're viewing a **window** in a List view (view by name, date, size, and so on), you can view the contents of any **folder** without opening it by using the hierarchical display. A triangle appears to the left of the folder's name indicating that it can be viewed hierarchically by **clicking** the triangle. The triangle then points downward, and the contents of the folder, including any **nested folders**, appear in the window as shown in the figure. This is called *expanding* the folder.

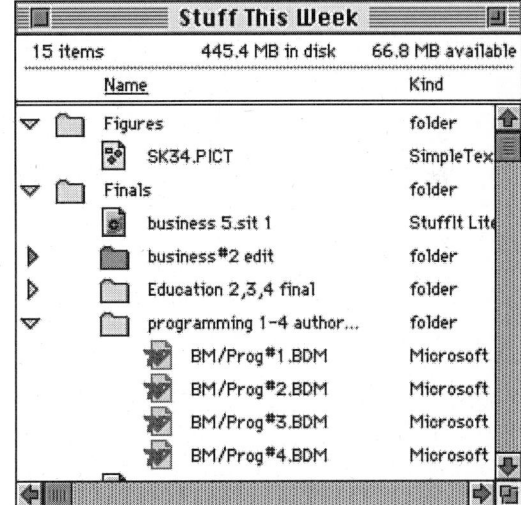

To view the contents of a folder in a list view, follow these steps:

1. Click the triangle to the left of the folder's name.

2. As the triangle points down, a list appears displaying the contents of the folder, including any nested folders.

3. To collapse the folder back to its original view, click the triangle.

See Also

Clicking; Folders; Windows

H

High-Fidelity Color Printing

High-fidelity, or Hi-Fi, color printing is a method for maximizing the fidelity of printed colors to the colors of the original image. The small color gamut of standard **process color** printing can be extended to some degree by high-fidelity color printing. Using six or seven colors (including the four standard process colors), Hi-Fi printing produces brighter color appearance; improved color modulation; and cleaner reds, greens, and blues. Pantone has developed a high-fidelity color system called Hexachrome that combines six process inks: cyan, magenta, yellow, black, orange, and green. Other systems may use cyan, magenta, yellow, black, red, green, and blue. High-fidelity color printing may include more than just extra ink colors. It may also include the use of **stochastic screens,** premium papers, varnishes, and other special effects.

See Also

Color Gamut; Color Printing; Stochastic Screens

Highlight

Highlights define the intensity of reflections caused by bright lights. A highlight produces small areas that reflect light, and adjusting the highlight parameter adjusts the brightness of the highlight area. The Highlight parameter also can adjust the size of the highlight (in some **3D** programs a separate parameter, **shininess,** adjusts the size of the highlight).

See Also

Reflections; Rendering; Shaders; Texture Mapping

Highlight Point

The highlight point in a **halftone** image is where the smallest halftone dot appears. Highlights in a halftone are the lightest areas in the image and may not even contain any dots. This is usually considered undesirable because the absence of dots can create a visual "hole" in the image. In scanning and color separating, the highlight point is one of the most important parameters. Assigning the highlight point in a scanning program involves selecting the point in the original image where halftone dots will begin to appear.

See Also

Halftones; Image Scanning

High Sierra

A format for storing information on a **CD-ROM**, High Sierra is the original name given to the **ISO-9660** standard prior to its adoption. The terms are sometimes used interchangeably, although there are some very minor differences between High Sierra and ISO-9660 as it was finally adopted.

Apple provides both a High Sierra and an ISO-9660 extension for **Foreign File Access**, the System software that recognizes non-**HFS** (HFS is Apple's file system) CDs.

See Also

CD-ROM; Foreign File Access; HFS ISO-9660

High Sierra File Access Extension

This extension enables **CD-ROMs** designed for platforms other than Macintosh (such as IBM compatibles) to be played on Macintosh CD-ROM players and vice-versa. High-Sierra refers to the name of the standard that was created to enable cross-platform use of CD-ROM discs; the High Sierra Standard.

See Also

CD-ROM

Hinting

Theoretically, **outline fonts** make it possible for type to be perfectly reproduced when it's printed. In practical use, however, outline fonts are converted to dots when they're printed, with the printer itself deciding where to place the dots to best reproduce the outline. Hinting is information contained in font files that controls that conversion back to dots from an outline format, so that the type will be reproduced faithfully no matter what the printer's resolution or the type size.

See Also

Bitmapped Fonts; Fonts; Outline Fonts

History and Culture of the Macintosh

The Macintosh is a truly unique computer. Not only did it break new ground technologically, it also inspired a fanatical following unmatched by any other computer. Many Mac users are more zealous about their choice of computer than they are about anything else.

The unique Macintosh community culture grew out of the culture of Apple Computer and its history. From Apple's start in a garage in Silicon Valley, through the development of the Macintosh, and right up to today, Apple has always walked a different path than other computer companies.

Apple's founders were a great match: **Steve Wozniak**, the brilliant technology whiz and college dropout, and **Steve Jobs**, the enlightenment-seeking visionary (and college dropout). Unlike many companies with similar beginnings, Apple had leadership in a very different form almost from the beginning. **A.C. "Mike" Markkula**, who had made his fortune at Intel and Fairchild, brought a more seasoned outlook to the fledgling company. The company's first president, **Mike Scott**, had similar experience. This match of the zealous whiz kids and the seasoned professionals set Apple apart.

Conversation with Regis McKenna

Regis McKenna shaped the country's perception of Silicon Valley, and played a major role in shaping the original idea of Apple Computer, and then the Mac.

Maclopedia: Could we ask you how you see your role in getting Apple going?

Regis: I am not...a publicist or Apple PR person. I hate the word *publicize*. It was never my intention or objective to "publicize" Apple or the Mac—I wrote the marketing plan for the Mac and helped write the marketing plan for Apple.

New technologies cannot be "publicized." There are no reference points. The more you promote a computer product without first developing the infrastructure—that is, their third-party software developers, distribution channels, early adopters (people who know what to do with a first time ever-thing called a personal computer)—the faster you go out of business. Without first educating the infrastructure of the industry, nothing would have happened. My firm did the infrastructure development. We were doing that for Apple long before the evangelists showed up.

Steve Jobs and Steve Wozniak came to my firm to ask for assistance, and they did that on the reference of Intel. So the first discussion was about putting together a business, to build a personal, well, at the time *hobby* computer, and then it became a hobby/personal computer, and that was not such a strange thing because having worked with Intel on the microprocessor, I had helped develop application notes at Intel around the whole idea of hobby computers. So in 1977, [a single board computer] wasn't such a strange idea. But they [Jobs and Wozniak] had a novel approach—providing a completely packaged computer. By that time, I had come to believe that anything was possible with technology.

The thing was that Woz had written his own version of what this next computer was going to look like, and I looked at it, and I said, "I am going to have to rewrite this in English," and he got upset, and I said, "If you want to talk to yourself and your friends, you shouldn't be here," and I ended the meeting. But Steve Jobs, who is still a very close friend, kept calling me back, and he was one of the few people who is responsible for the personal computer becoming a household item. He talked a lot about it being part of the education environment, so his vision was very strong, and he was a very relentless and driven person. So I sent them to Don Ballantine, who was a venture capitalist I had worked with before at National Semiconductor when he was VP of Marketing there, to talk about their idea and raise money. He brought in Mike Markkula to write the business plan (Mike had worked for him before), and I worked with Mike on the original business plan. We helped them set their strategies and later put together the first marketing plan and helped them manage that.

...in order to broaden the market, he had to create the automatic transmission. That was the Mac—automatic transmission.

continues

Maclopedia: Okay, with that said, what was your first contact with the Mac like?

Regis: I first saw the Mac in a little rented room down on Stevens Creek Boulevard, not near the Apple facility at all, on a Sunday morning. Steve [Jobs] came over to my house and was telling about this thing he was developing, and they were beginning to breadboard it, so we sat around and talked about what it was capable of doing.

His vision was intuitive computing You don't have to do anything; you just point and click. It was pull-down menus, real ease of use, taking the computer to the next level. He knew very well that the Apple II—although it was very far ahead because it put everything under one skin—was not enough to do serious computing, and in order to broaden the market, he had to create the automatic transmission. That was the Mac—automatic transmission.

This strange marriage has continued through much of Apple's history. While technical geniuses like **Bill Atkinson** and **Jef Raskin** were creating the products that would change the computer world forever, the seasoned marketer **John Sculley** was leading the company as a whole. At times, the rift between these groups caused serious trouble within Apple, but when things went right, these two factions could change the world.

The Macintosh has a fascinating history of its own. Started as a small project by a lone researcher, the Macintosh turned into the very heart of Apple's product line. Although the Mac borrowed from its predecessors—the Alto, developed by **Xerox PARC**, and Apple's own **Lisa**—it had a personality all its own. Ever since the incredible "**1984**" commercial that first put the Mac in the public eye, the Mac has been a computer "for the rest of us."

"The rest of us" have fun with our Macs. We search for **Easter eggs** hidden in our programs. We contemplate the mysterious **dogcow**. We gather in massive numbers at **MacWorld Expo**—a great orgy of Macintosh products and culture. And we take Macintosh **evangelism** into our own hands, "selling" the Mac at every opportunity.

More Than 10 Years After: A Personal Perspective by Don Crabb I remember where I was. I was sitting

at home watching the Super Bowl. Near the end of the first quarter, the most amazing thing happened. No, not during the game, itself (I can't even remember who played), but during a commercial break. There it was. An athletic blond woman throwing Thor's hammer at a big screen filled with the image of Big Brother. The image shattered as the voice-over intoned, "See why 1984 won't be like *1984*."

At that precise moment, I knew I'd made the right decision. You see, I was working for the University of Chicago, for The Computation Center—the University's central computing organization. For the previous 18 months, I had been part of a small group lobbying the Center's director, and many of the University's top managers, to get in on the desktop computing revolution. Because of our annoying persistence, the University signed a deal in 1983 with Apple Computer, Inc., to become a founding member of a new organization—the Apple University Consortium (AUC)—agreeing to buy at least two million dollars worth of Apple computers over the next year and succeeding years.

That agreement was risky. We and the other founding members of the AUC inked the deal while Apple's current computing line was going through terrible growing pains. The Apple III was a dog. The Lisa, although innovative and important, cost an unbelievable $10,000 per unit. And the Macintosh, although promised and impressive in its alpha and beta versions, was still just a dream. We really didn't know if the thing would fly.

And even if it did fly, we were having a tough time figuring whether there'd be software to run on the beige toaster. During our alpha and beta tests, we had exactly two applications to try—the alpha/beta MacWrite and MacPaint. Both applications stunned us with just how good and different they were than anything we were used to on Apple IIs, IBM PCs, and VT-100 terminals connected to our networked DEC system-20 mainframes.

But we were also shocked by how buggy they were. We learned to save your work every five minutes because you were guaranteed the programs would lock-up every 10 minutes. You think that today's type one errors disturb you? Those are nothing compared to the screen freezes we suffered during 1983s Mac beta testing. In the middle of something simple in MacWrite, such as highlighting selected text to change the font, the cursor would freeze. Then the application image would begin to decay, pixel-by-pixel, usually when you were showing the thing to a University gun who still thought the AUC agreement was pretty darn precipitous.

With no Shift-Option-⌘-Escape, you could forget a soft exit from these problems. You could try the programmer's switch, but that usually made things worse, so bad that you had to shut the computer off, wait a minute, then reboot, hoping that the disk containing the alpha/beta system, MacWrite, and MacPaint hadn't been fried.

Of course, we were so excited, so overwhelmed by the Mac-to-be, that while frustrating, none of these problems seemed significant. At least they didn't seem significant while we were working on the seed unit. But later, at home, when we'd reflect on what we did and did not accomplish during the day, we began to wonder if we shouldn't keep our resumes and vistas up-to-date, just in case the whole thing came crashing down around our heads.

As we moved closer to the January 1984 announcement date, we got good and bad news from Apple: The ImageWriter printer we were testing wouldn't be available at the announcement. We had to wait until March before they shipped. The external drive (so you could backup your work without disk flipping) wouldn't be ready until at least April, maybe longer. And the serial hard disk we were promised (a version of the 20MB Lisa hard drive) was going to be delayed even further. Apple had nothing to say about our 128KB RAM concerns, except that they expected software vendors to write their code tightly (they actually said this with a straight face!), and that they were going to address the limitation later in the year.

For those of us smarting under the failure of the Apple III and the Lisa, these were not hardware futures we wanted to hear about.

But good news did start to come out of Cupertino. The system and ROM Toolbox were being debugged much faster than expected, and it showed in our beta versions. MacWrite and MacPaint stopped crashing all the time. Microsoft promised a BASIC interpreter to go with Apple's promised Pascal interpreter.

The beta Mac was reasonably solid, and MacPaint and MacWrite worked. Using the Clipboard, you could cut and paste between applications (loading one and unloading the other, since they both couldn't fit into RAM at the same time). We hardly noticed the disk flipping effort such actions took, nor did we notice the real need for that promised hard disk or the additional RAM.

In January 1984, we were so mesmerized that the damn thing worked at all, that it cost much less than the Lisa, and that it was small and portable enough to lug around campus, we overlooked the first Mac's obvious shortcomings. These shortcomings became all too apparent during the following months and would have sunk Apple in 1985 if it wasn't for John Sculley, the 512KB Mac, AppleTalk, and the LaserWriter.

The Macintosh Culture: Then and Now "1984" proved that Apple Computer, Inc., and the Macintosh were very special. In fact, Apple taught us that the Mac was more than another computer—it was the embodiment of the American ethos. The Mac heralded the dawning of a new age of self empowerment and personal liberty. It implied an assault on the corporate structure promised by Big Blue, a structure that demanded strict conformity and offered limited individual potential.

Although the first version of the Macintosh was seriously underpowered and overpriced, it rapidly developed into the state-of-the-art in personal computing because of the MacOS and Finder GUI (Graphical User Interface). With hardware plug-and-play capability, instant AppleTalk networking, an intuitive graphical user interface, and much more, Apple founder Steve Jobs could rightly claim that the Mac was "insanely great." And Mac buyers knew it, even if they gritted their teeth at the high prices Apple charged for these Macs.

That arrogant attitude has gotten Apple into serious trouble in recent years. Apple can longer charge premium prices for their machines, compared to Wintel PCs, and the Apple "Not Invented Here (NIH)" syndrome caused the company to overlook hot new technology developed outside the company and to waste money trying to produce software challenging established industry standards. In addition, Apple resisted licensing its MacOS to other computer vendors (a strategy that has made Microsoft's Bill Gates a billionaire with his Windows operating system) until 1995, playing catch-up all the way.

As a result, in 1996, Apple finds itself in a pickle. It fired CEO Michael Spindler and brought in former National Semiconductor CEO Gilbert Amelio to run the show and redefine what Apple stands for and what the Mac culture ought to be about.

But all is not lost at Apple. Apple is going through many of the growing pains that a 20-year-old technology must go through. All signs point to Apple recovering and growing a new Macintosh culture—one that makes great products, but also learns to make nice with the rest of the world.

For More...

If you want to do this...	Go to this entry...
Know Apple's history	Apple Computer, History
Know how the Mac got started	Macintosh Project, History
Know about Apple's founders	Jobs, Steve; Wayne, Ron; Wozniak, Steve

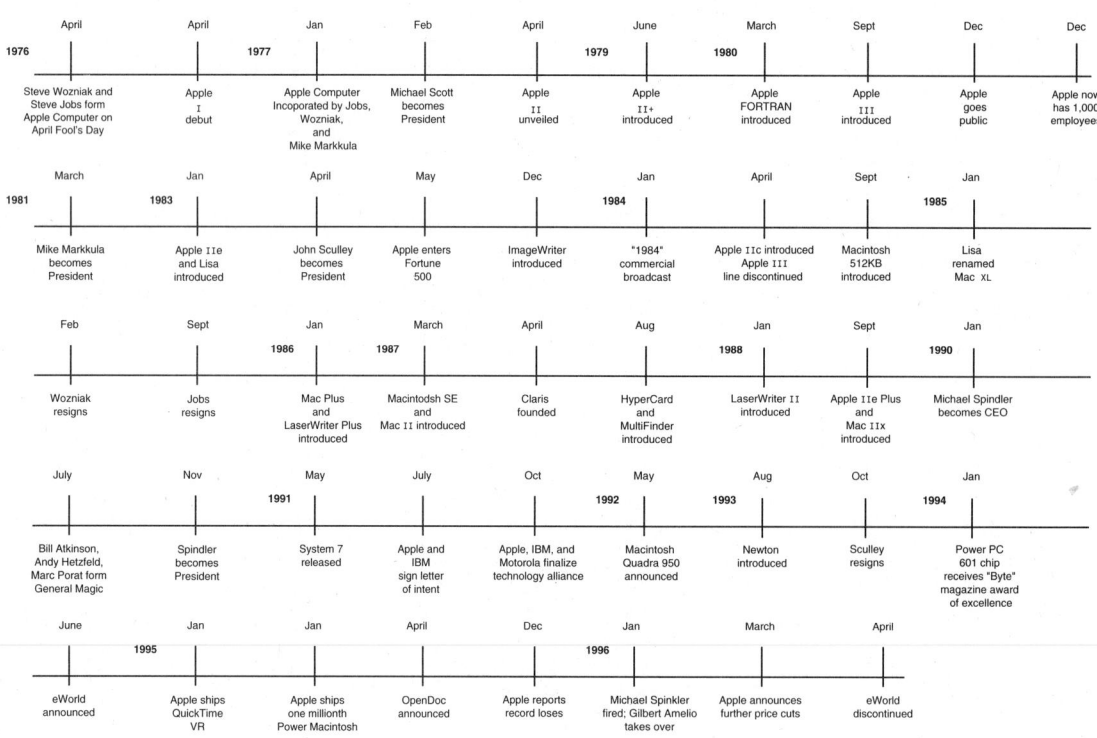

Bibliography

For more information about the history and culture of the Macintosh, refer to the following books:

Accidental Empires: How the Boys of Silicon Valley Make Their Millions, Battle Foreign Competition, And Still Can't Get a Date, Robert X. Cringely, published by Addison-Wesley, 1992 (0-8873-0621-7).

Guide to the Macintosh Underground, Bob LeVitus and Michael Fraase, published by Hayden Books, 1993 (0-672-48549-4).

Insanely Great: The Life and Times of Macintosh, the Computer That Changed Everything, Steven Levy, published by Penguin Books, 1995 (0-1402-3237-0).

The Mac Bathroom Reader, Owen W. Linzmayer, published by Sybex Books, 1994 (0-7821-1531-4).

The Macintosh Reader, Doug Clapp, editor, published by Random House Electronic Publishing, 1992 (0-6797-4242-5).

The Macintosh Way: The Art of Guerrilla Management, Guy Kawasaki, published by Harper Perennial, 1990 (0-0609-7338-2).

Odyssey: Pepsi to Apple, The Journey of a Marketing Impresario, John Sculley with John A. Byrne, published by Perennial Library, 1987 (0-0601-5780-1).

Selling the Dream: How to Promote Your Product, Company, or Ideas—And Make a Difference—Using Everyday Evangelism, Guy Kawasaki, published by Harper Collins, 1992 (0-8873-0600-4).

West of Eden, The End of Innocence at Apple Computer, Frank Rose, published by Viking, 1989 (0-6708-1278-1).

"Interview with Steve Jobs," *Playboy*, February 1985, also on WWW at **http://www.playboy.com/feb85/stevenjobs1.html.**

"The Fall of Apple," Jeff Goodell, *Rolling Stone*, April 4 and April 11, 1996.

Hit Counter

A script on a **World Wide Web server** that calculates each *hit* or visit to a **Web page** every time a connection is made, and displays the current total on the page to the current user.

See Also
World Wide Web; World Wide Web Page

Hollywood Games Connection

Any trend, sooner or later, captures the attention of Hollywood, and computer games are no exception. Although movies that are simply about computers are in no short supply (*The Net, Hackers, Virtuosity, Sneakers, Lawnmower Man 2*), many hit films aimed at kids are based on games including, Street Fighter, Mortal Kombat, and The Mario Brothers. On the flip side of the coin, almost any good action movie sooner or later has a computer game tie-in.

The current onslaught of games based on the movies include *Blown Away*, a sequel to the movie with Jeff Bridges (although he is absent from the game); an arcade game from LucasArts based on *Indiana Jones*, and the forthcoming *Die Hard* Trilogy from Fox Interactive. The best of the lot is the simple desktop diversion arcade-style game, *Indiana Jones* Desktop from LucasArts.

However, *Blown Away* holds its own against other video-heavy titles and interactive movies like *Dracula Unleashed* or *The Daedelus Encounter*. Usually due to budget and licensing reasons, games like *Blown Away* and *Johnny Mnemonic* lack the stars of the corresponding films, but big-name actors are no strangers to games.

Tia Carrere blasts her way through The **Daedelus Encounter**, which is a surprisingly good game, especially when you look at the disappointing lot of other video-intensive titles. Dennis Hopper and Grace Jones get digitized in the surreal, creepy **Hell** whereas Debbie Harry and Corey Haim get trapped in the disastrous Double Switch.

In Double Switch, you are in charge of security in a large hotel and must keep the guests safe from lurking bad-guys. In this case, the game falls flat in accuracy and action. It is difficult to tell where you need to click and when to capture the bad guys and the video scenes are hard to figure when you need to do something and when to just watch.

Voyeur from **MacPlay** starring Robert Culp is another example of multimedia enhancement actually hindering game play. The premise is interesting: you are spying on a potential presidential candidate, looking for scandalous material, but the over-abundant video takes away from the interactivity of the game. Philips Interactive is currently working on Voyeur II and hopes to add more interactivity without losing the high quality of the video.

See Also

Blown Away; Daedelus Encounter, The; Hell; Return to Zork

Home Key

If you are viewing a window in a list view, and the window has scroll bars, pressing the Home key (found only on extended keyboards) scrolls the window as far up as it can go, revealing the first items in the window.

The operation of the Home key varies from application to application, but the most common action of the Home key moves your **cursor** in front of the first visible word in a document's window.

See Also

Active Window; Cursor; Desktop Level

Home Page

The opening document of a site on the World Wide Web, part of the **Internet**. Sometimes called a welcome page.

A home page serves as the "front door" from which a reader can follow Hypertext links that lead to all of the contents of a site. Because of its introductory nature, a home page should contain a number of essential elements that will tell readers about the Web site they are visiting.

A home page can be broken into three basic divisions: a *header*, a *body*, and a *footer*.

- The page *header* includes such general information as a banner or logo, a title, an introductory **GIF** or **JPEG** image or **imagemap**, or a series of buttons or links to various locations on an individual site. It also contains a statement of purpose.

- The *body* of the home page is often set off from the header by a horizontal rule. The body contains some introductory links or a list of contents, and the basic text you want to provide.

- The *footer* can contain a surprising amount of important information and should not be overlooked. It can contain a copyright notice; an indication of when the site was last updated; an email address or name of the person who set up and maintains the site; and links to other parts of the site.

Each primary category of information contained in a Web site leads to its own path of documents. The links on the home page lead the reader through the path and, taken together, make a "tree" of information.

The better organized the middle levels of information on your site, the easier it will be to navigate, and the more useful it will be.

A personal home page often contains a photo of the subject and tells some useful information about his or her activities, as well as conveying a sense of the author's personality. One home page is shown in the following figure.

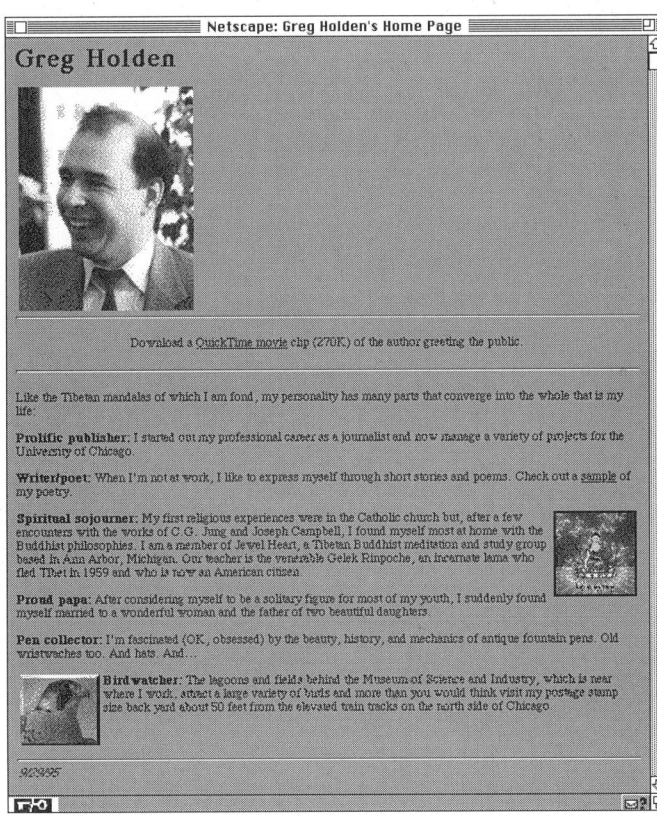

Personal home pages can easily become trivial unless the authors ask themselves some essential questions:

1. Is there a special reason people would want to read about me?

2. Do I have some service or business that people might want to utilize?

3. Do I belong to groups, companies, or large organizations that people might want to know about?

Maintaining a site's contents and checking the links to see that none are "broken" (don't lead to the correct file) are essential parts of creating both a home page and a Web site.

See Also

Internet; Web Page; World Wide Web

Home Publisher, *See Page Layout Software*

H

Home Repair Encyclopedia

This **CD-ROM** guide is a "must have" for the homeowner. It walks you, step by step, through more than 50 home projects. Minor and major emergencies, such as wine stains on the carpet, gas leaks, broken pipes, and fire, are also covered. It explains how to use common tools and tells you which ones you need in your tool box.

It even covers tools you're likely to rent rather than own: cement mixers, post hole diggers, concrete saws, floor sanders, and scaffolding as well as a dozen other heavy duty items. Animated diagrams explain how things work, and there are tips on saving money and working safely. Any page can be printed out for reference, so you needn't keep running back to the computer to see what to do next. There's a list of 800 numbers for the handyman, and a paint reference guide that explains what alkyd, latex, and similar terms really mean.

Homebrew Computer Club

In the mid-1970s, the computer world was vastly different than today. It was dominated by huge, expensive, and inaccessible mainframe computers from IBM and others, and the slightly less huge, expensive and inaccessible "minicomputers" from companies such as Digital. The idea of a "personal" computer was foreign to all but a few hobbyists.

In 1975, the first personal computer, the Altair 8800, was introduced by a small company in New Mexico. The Altair came as a kit that had to be assembled by the user. It was programmed using switches on the front panel, and even with a concerted programming effort, it couldn't really do much. But the hobbyists were hooked.

Inspired by the Altair, one group of electronics nuts began meeting as the "Homebrew Computer Club" in Menlo Park, California, near Stanford University. Within months, its membership exploded. Among the group's first members were **Steve Wozniak** and his friend **Steve Jobs**, future founders of Apple Computer.

Many of the members of the Homebrew Computer Club saw these new, affordable computers as a great liberator that would level the playing field between big corporations, that could afford mainframe computers, and everyone else, who could not. This theme would later become a major selling point of the Macintosh, "the computer for the rest of us."

In early 1976, Steve Wozniak showed his design for a new computer at a meeting of the club. Many club members were unimpressed, but Steve Jobs saw the potential of this new, cheaper design and convinced Woz to go into business producing Wozniak's new computer. Another club member, Paul Terrell, also liked the design and told Jobs to "keep in touch." Jobs showed up at Terrell's computer store, The **Byte Shop**, the next day and sealed Apple Computer's first order: 50 Apple I computers at $500 each.

See Also

Byte Shop, The; Jobs, Steve; Wozniak, Steve

Homer, *See IRC*

Hornet, *See F/A-18 Hornet*

Horror Themes in Games, *See 7th Guest, The*

Host

A computer set up to provide information and access to remote users on a network such as the **Internet**; also frequently called a **server**.

Because of the quantity of information stored on them and the number of clients that might connect to them at any one time, host computers tend to be more powerful with more storage space than client machines.

The majority of hosts on the **World Wide Web** consist of Unix workstations, but Macintoshes can perform server functions quite well by using software such as MacHTTP or **WebSTAR**.

See Also

Email; Gopher; Internet; Netscape Navigator; Workgroup Servers, Macintosh Family; World Wide Web

Hot Spot

Each **cursor** has a hot spot. This is the exact point on the cursor that invokes an action. Having a hot spot enables a cursor to be used for very precise movements and selections. The tip of the arrow is the hot spot on the **arrow pointer**, meaning you put the tip of the arrow pointer on a **file** or a folder when **selecting**. If you put only the tail of the arrow pointer on a folder and **click**, it's not selected because the tail is not the hot spot.

Knowing a cursor's hot spot is particularly important for people doing graphic design or computer-aided design (CAD) work on a Mac. Adobe Photoshop, for example, has a cursor that looks like a paint brush. However, the paint does not flow from the entire cursor; it only flows from the hot spot of that paint brush cursor.

You can set a preference to change the cursor to one that displays the exact hot spot by displaying a cursor that matches the selected brush size. This enables you to be very precise when painting.

See Also

Arrow Pointer; Click; Cursor; File; Folder; Selecting

HotJava

A **World Wide Web browser** (like **Netscape Navigator, Mosaic,** or **MacWeb**) written in Sun Microsystems' **Java** programming language.

Sun freely distributes HotJava as part of the Java Development Kit. (See **http://www.sun.com** on the Web for details.) At the time of this writing, HotJava for the Mac had not been publically released; it's expected that this package will be ported to the MacOS platform in the Spring of 1996.

Don't confuse HotJava, which is a particular program, with Java, which is a programming language.

HotJava was created as a vehicle to demonstrate the possibilities of the Java programming language—it was the first Web browser that could display Java **applets** inside the browser window, and Applet-viewing will probably remain HotJava's special niche in the browser market. HotJava works as fully functional **HTML** browser, although not as widely used as Netscape Navigator.

See Also

Applet; HTML; Java; MacWeb; Netscape Navigator; Web Browser

HSB, *See Color Gamut; Desktop Publishing Color Models*

HST, *See Modem Protocols/ Modulation Protocols*

HST Cellular, *See Modem Protocols/Modulation Protocols*

HTML

An acronym for HyperText Markup Language, a subset of Standard Generalized Markup Language (**SGML**), an internationally agreed-upon standard for representing computer documents. A language used to prepare documents for publication on the **World Wide Web**.

Information providers on the **Internet** need to make documents presentable, with elements such as headings and paragraphs preserved, across many computer platforms. HTML contains generic, easy-to-understand elements that Web browser programs running on many different kinds of computers will recognize.

HTML elements take two forms: *character entities* or *markup tags*. Character entities are codes used to present special characters that HTML cannot display otherwise, such as an accent mark. Character entities begin with an ampersand (&) and are followed by a semicolon (;).

A small *e* with an acute accent (é), is represented in HTML by the character entity

é

Markup tags allow an author to "tag" or mark text with commands that usually (not always) go on either side of the text. The beginning tag is called the start tag, for example, <HEAD>. The ending tag is called the end tag, for example, </HEAD>.

Marking up a document with HTML is the only way to get material displayed on a **Web browser**, and thus, on the Web itself. A number of utilities, such as Adobe PageMill, part of **SiteMill** and **Netscape Navigator** Gold, alleviate the need for authors to enter every HTML command by hand and, instead, allow document formatting via pull-down menus and other commands.

One of the best ways to learn practical applications of HTML is to view the source commands for a World Wide Web page using a Web browser like **Netscape Navigator**, **MacWeb**, or Mosaic.

- In Mosaic, you choose "View Source" from the "File" menu (making sure that "Enable View Source" is already checked under the "Options" menu).

- In MacWeb, choose "View Source" from the "Options" menu.

- In Netscape, choose "Document Source" from the "View" menu.

HTML has evolved through three versions, which have gradually increased Web publishers' ability to format a document. The original version, HTML 1.0, contained a number of elements that have since been discontinued or "deprecated." The most notable addition to HTML 2.0 was the capability to create forms. HTML 3.0 includes the ability to create tables, justified and text, tabs, footnotes, and style sheets.

H

Netscape and Microsoft have created a number of extensions to "official" HTML that allow their browsers to display features not covered by HTML, such as "marquee" or scrolling text, "blinking" text, inline video, or font size adjustment.

See Also

Headings in HTML; Internet; MacWeb; NCSA Mosaic; Netscape Navigator; Web Page; World Wide Web

HTML Markup Tags

Markup tags in a HyperText Markup Language (**HTML**) document allow an author to "tag" or mark text so that it can be displayed on the **World Wide Web** by a **Web browser** with the proper formatting.

Markup tags consist of commands that usually (not always) go on either side of the text. The beginning tag is called the start tag, for example, <HEAD>. The ending tag is called the end tag, for example, </HEAD>.

Marking up a document with HTML is the only way to get material displayed on a **Web browser**, and thus, on the Web itself. A number of utilities such as Adobe PageMill and **Netscape** Gold alleviate the need for authors to enter every HTML command by hand and, instead, allow document formatting via pull-down menus and other commands.

See Also

HTML; Hypertext; Web Browser; Web Page; World Wide Web

HTML Tables, *See Tables, Creating in Netscape*

HTTP, *See HyperText Transport Protocol*

Hub

As **network** cabling stretches over long distances, the signals degrade. Because of this signal degradation, unassisted network cables can not work reliably beyond certain lengths. In situations where a small number of computers must be connected over long distances, repeaters can be strategically placed at appropriate intervals to amplify the network signal, allowing extension of the network over longer distances. The most common type of repeater is the hub, which is actually a multiport repeater (examples include Farallon's StarController and Focus's TurboStar).

Hubs are used in Active Star **LocalTalk** networks and in **EtherNet** networks. In either case, the hub repeats each network signal to every node connected to the hub. There are EtherNet repeaters for all flavors of EtherNet cabling: thick, thin, and twisted-pair. In fact, with twisted-pair EtherNet (otherwise known as 10Base-T), repeaters or hubs are mandatory. All 10Base-T connections must be made through a hub.

TIP Hubs cannot translate protocols between the individual ports—they cannot, for example handle EtherNet traffic on one port and LocalTalk traffic on another. Translation tasks must be performed by a router.

See Also

EtherNet; LocalTalk

Human Interface Guidelines

The Human Interface Guidelines is a set of rules and suggestions for interface design on the Macintosh.

From its first days, the Macintosh was different. You could see what your document would look like on the screen, and you didn't need to remember strings of confusing commands to accomplish your work. Just as important, different programs behaved in the same ways. For the most part, things were *consistent* from one application to the next. If ⌘-S meant Save in MacPaint, chances are it meant the same thing in MacWrite.

Consistency is one of the most important reasons that the Mac is easy to use. Part of this consistency comes from the **Toolbox**. By using a common set of routines for things like windows and menus, programs tend to operate similarly whether they try to or not. But the single biggest contributor to consistency is Apple's Macintosh Human Interface Guidelines.

The guidelines follow 13 basic principles of interface design:

- Metaphors
- Direct Manipulation
- See-and-Point
- Consistency
- WYSIWYG (What You See Is What You Get)
- User Control
- Feedback and Dialog
- Forgiveness
- Perceived Stability
- Aesthetic Integrity
- Modelessness
- Knowledge of Your Audience
- Accessibility

You can see these principles at work throughout any good Macintosh application. ClarisWorks, for example, uses a page metaphor to tie the computer world to the real one. To edit things on the sheet of paper, you manipulate them with the mouse and keyboard. You can see and point to various commands on the menu bar or tool palette rather than having to remember arcane commands. The program is consistent within itself and with other Mac applications; for example, opening and saving a file works the same way as in other programs.

Within the limitations of screen technology, what you see in your document window is the same as what you will see when you print the document. You, the user, have control over everything; the application will not start an action on its own or arbitrarily limit your options. Similarly, the application maintains a dialog with you by providing appropriate feedback when things have gone wrong. If you make a mistake, you can generally undo it rather than living with it.

The interface remains stable as you work; if a menu item is temporarily unavailable, it is dimmed rather than disappearing completely. Aesthetically, the application is consistent and pleasing to the eye; the interface is not cluttered, nor are standard graphical elements used for non-standard purposes. Although

the application operates in several distinct modes (word processing, drawing, and so on), the modes are logical and not arbitrary; for example, you don't need to enter a special command mode before choosing from a menu. The application was designed with extensive knowledge of its target audience, as its sales will attest. Finally, the application is accessible to a wide audience, and is available in many localized versions for other languages.

Under these principles, the Human Interface Guidelines provide specific information about every aspect of Macintosh interface design. From the design of dialog boxes and alerts to the wording and arrangement of menus, the guidelines provide detailed information for creating a good Macintosh application.

Like much of Apple's programmer documentation, the Human Interface Guidelines are available in two formats: electronic and print. The electronic version is available on Apple's developer Web site (**http://dev.info.apple.com/**). In addition, Apple has created a multimedia companion to the Human Interface Guidelines. The *Making it Macintosh* CD-ROM illustrates many of the issues covered in the guidelines themselves using animated examples.

See Also
Inside Macintosh; Toolbox

HyperCard

HyperCard was, arguably, the beginning of the current multimedia wave. It was the first application that enabled users to create interactive presentations without having to write a program from scratch. Although it has mostly been superseded by its competitors (**SuperCard** does nearly everything HyperCard does and offers more features), it remains a useful tool.

Like most multimedia authoring tools, HyperCard is an interpreted environment; you need the HyperCard application to run a HyperCard presentation. HyperCard stores presentations in files called stacks. HyperCard uses a metaphor of a stack of cards. What you see on screen at any point in time is a card. That card contains text fields, graphics, and buttons. A presentation can contain any number of cards, hence the term stack.

H

Cards can be linked together by a common background. A background is like a template. Backgrounds can contain any elements that a card can contain, and any card linked to that background contains those elements. This makes it very easy to create something with many repeating records, such as an encyclopedia or an address book.

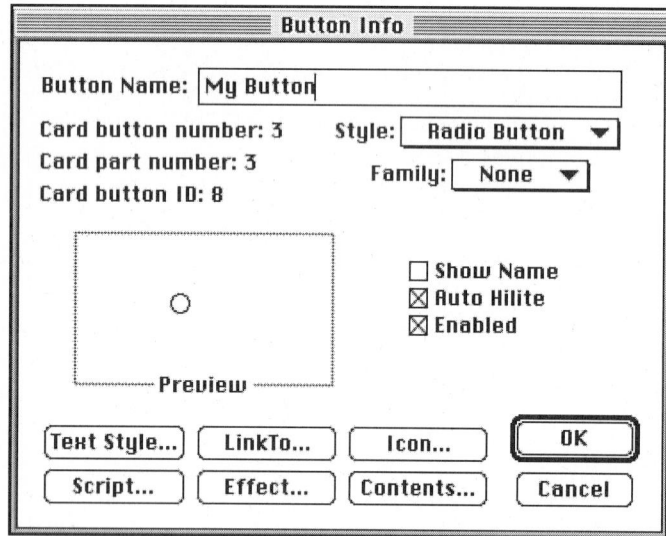

Interactivity is created using HyperCard's **scripting** language HyperTalk. A **script** is a small routine or program that performs some action, such as going to the next card in a stack. HyperCard now also supports **AppleScript**, a scripting language that can be used to control other programs (provided the developer of that program has included support for **Apple events**, the commands provided by AppleScript). Any button in HyperCard 2.3 or greater can either have a HyperTalk script or an AppleScript attached to it.

While scripting provides a tremendous amount of flexibility (it's entirely possible that you will never reach the limits of the HyperTalk language), there are nonetheless limits to what can be done with a script. The biggest limitation is that there is no direct access to the operating system. So, for example, you can't write a script that uses the serial port. **XCMDs** address this

limitation by enabling programmers to write a program using a language like C++ or Pascal, compile it as an XCMD, and place the XCMD in the HyperCard stack using a utility such as ResEdit. The XCMD can then be used by a script. There are may shareware XCMDs available, as well as some commercially available. Check online services for the latest lists of such tools.

HyperCard comes with some XCMDs that add support for color graphics and QuickTime. As part of the QuickTime VR Authoring Toolkit, there is an XCMD that supports QuickTime VR. An animation tool called ADDMotion is also included.

After a stack is completed, it can be distributed to others by adding the HyperCard Player. The stack that has the player attached to it operates like a regular HyperCard stack. The user can add new cards to the presentation and type in information, but the editing tools that enable the manipulation of graphics or repositioning of fields are not available. Make sure that if your stack makes use of color that you increase the minimum size for memory requirements of the Player application you create or the color will not display!

One of the best sources for learning HyperTalk, particularly if you have done any programming before, is the On-line HyperTalk Reference manual. This stack contains nearly all of the information you need to program in HyperTalk. It includes examples and cross-references and is also fully searchable.

HyperCard remains a very useful tool. Unfortunately, over the years Apple has been uncertain how to support and market the product. Consequently, other tools, such as **SuperCard** and **Director**, have mostly replaced it, because they offer more features and are frequently updated. Oracle has even released a new tool, Oracle Media Objects, which closely resembles HyperCard and is a **cross-platform** tool.

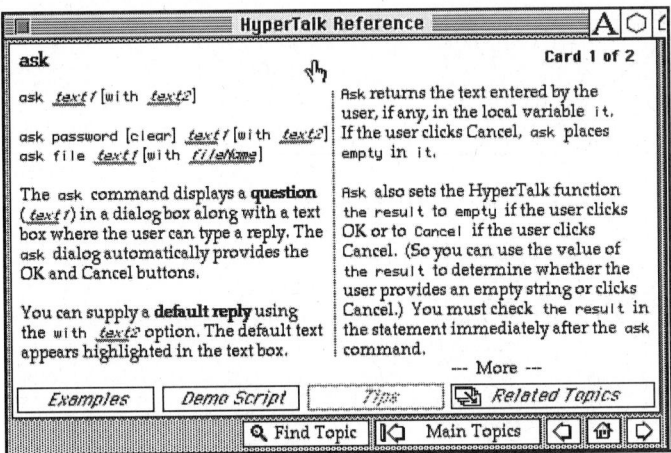

See Also

AskText XFCN; Audio XCMDs; CompileIt!; Double-XX; HyperGraph; QuickTime; QuickTime VR; Scripting; XCMDs

HyperGraph

A graphics package that can be used in any program that supports **XCMD**s (**HyperCard**, **SuperCard**, FoxPro, and so on). Use it to create line, bar, and polar graphs. HyperGraph creates a graph based on numeric information and options chosen, and places the graphic on the Clipboard.

> Heizer Software
> 300 Cedar Lane
> Largo, FL 34640
> Price: $79
> Fax: (813) 559-0614
> Phone: (800) 888-7667 or (813) 559-6422
> Web: **http://www.heizer.com**

See Also

Director; Double-XX; FoxPro; HyperCard; SuperCard; XCMD

Hyperlink

Also called an anchor or a **hypertextual** link. A link in an **HTML** document, usually distinguished by underlined or highlighted text that, when selected, takes the user to another file or **Web page**. The hypertext link is added to the document by using the HTML tag:

```
<A HREF>Clickable link text goes
here</A>.
```

See Also

HTML; HTML Markup Tags; URL, Web Browser; Web Page; World Wide Web

HyperTalk

The scripting language used in **HyperCard**.

See Also

HyperCard; Scripting; XCMDs

Hypertext

First coined by **Ted Nelson**, designer, author, and academic, the term Hypertext refers to electronic documents that contain links to other documents or other sections of the same document. These links are attached to a word or phrase (the Hypertext). Clicking the word or phrase displays the linked section.

Hypertext is used and implemented in a wide variety of authoring packages and multimedia presentations. It is particularly appropriate for reference works, such as encyclopedias and technical manuals. Many online help systems make use of Hypertext. Hypertext is the essential design philosophy of the World Wide Web.

Ted Nelson has spent many years promoting a Hypertext system called **Xanadu**. Never completely implemented, Xanadu was an electronic network that would have resembled the **World Wide Web**.

Hypertext, Tools There are few authoring systems that provide flexible tools for creating Hypertext documents, even though Hypertext is one of the classic implementations of interactivity. It's possible to create Hypertext documents using tools, such as **HyperCard**, Allegiant Technologies Inc.'s **SuperCard**, or Macromedia Inc.'s **Director**. You can manually create links, but there's no automation; they must all be created and maintained by hand. The same problem exists with tools such as Adobe **Acrobat**, which also provides capabilities for adding links to documents.

The Kerouac ROMnibus, an interactive CD-ROM produced using Director, uses colored, slightly bold text to indicate Hypertext entries that display an annotation window.

Netscape Navigator uses colored text to indicate Hypertext links; clicking a link takes you to another Web page, Web site, or might download a file.

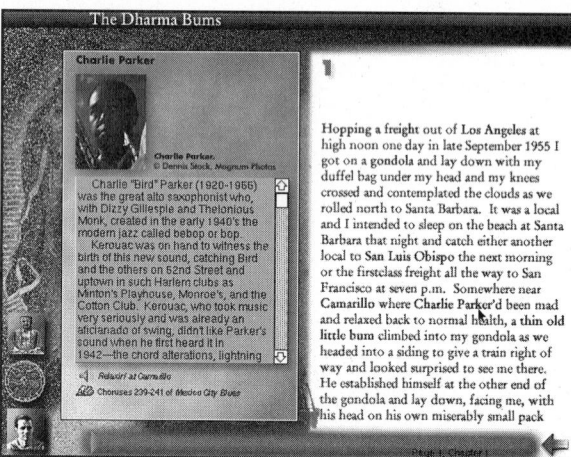

The World Wide Web provides one alternative solution for anyone considering a project requiring Hypertext. The World Wide Web depends on links, and tools are appearing that provide for the creation and maintenance of links. Adobe's **PageMill** and **SiteMill** fit this bill. Remember, HTML doesn't have to be viewed over the Internet. It can be used over local networks (**Intranet**) or from local hard drives or CD-ROMs.

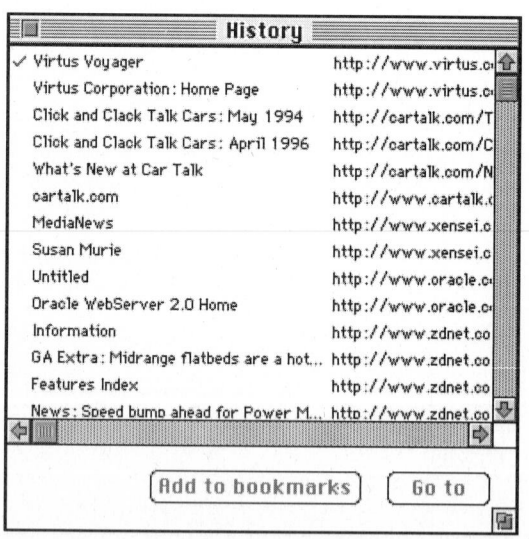

Hypertext, Design Producing a good Hypertext system is difficult, because there are so few good tools for either creating the content, or for viewing Hypertext systems. Although an HTML browser is perhaps the best solution at the moment, the Web is still a new medium and there are many limitations; for example, only some browsers support the **Shockwave** plug-in and **frames** in Web pages.

A serious limitation of most Hypertext system designs is the confusion they create for the user. Clicking links often replaces the entire content window with new content. After several following several links the user no longer has a clear idea of where they were or where they are going. World Wide Web browsers attempt to solve this problem with the Back and Forward buttons, which take the user back and forth over a chain of links that they have already accessed, and the History window.

Due to the "on-the-fly" nature of the Internet, a simple history list is perhaps the only solution for the Web. For navigation within large sites or large Hypertext documents, much better navigation techniques, such as maps and signposts indicating where the user is, should be used. Hopefully, new **HTML** features, such as **frames** (a **Netscape** addition), might eventually lead to better Hypertext systems.

Whether using HTML or some other authoring system, Hypertext document authors still have to create their content using traditional non-Hypertext tools, such as word processors or databases. This can be as difficult a process as the implementation itself. If you are about to implement a Hypertext system, your primary consideration should be the authoring and viewing environments and how easy it is to enter and maintain your information.

See Also

HTML; Intranet; PageMill; SiteMill; World Wide Web; Xanadu

Hypertext Fiction

Hypertext is closely related to interactive fiction in that it basically consists of information and content organized in a non-linear fashion. In a multimedia encyclopedia, Hypertext operates as a form of dictionary. When you read the sentence, "To get on the Internet, you will need a modem," you may want to know more about modems. By clicking on the word "modem," a hypertext link carries you to a more in-depth definition or discussion of modem, which then may be linked to an even more specific topic, such as "modem port" or "baud rate." In hypertext fiction, a story can take multiple twists and turns just following a character or line of plot that you choose. For example, in Eastgate Systems' "Victory Garden" by Stuart Moulthrop, a story about a group of college kids caught in the middle of the Persian Gulf War, you can follow certain characters to the point where someone mentioned in the first chapter may not ever be mentioned again if you don't click on that character, but if you do pick them, they become the main character. The following figure shows an excerpt from the **Cypher**.

The multiple paths through the story and the randomness of the endings make Hypertext fiction much closer than regular linear fiction to life's complex selectivity and change. Currently, Eastgate is the most prolific publisher of Hypertext fiction. Their latest titles include Patchwork Girl by Shelley Jackson, a feminist Frankenstein and Tim McLaughlin's Notes Toward Absolute Zero, a novella. Their Afternoon: a Story, is considered one of the first Hypertext works with critical literary value. Sarah Smith's King of Space, also published by Eastgate, incorporates intriguing puzzles into the Hypertext novel, but its erotic content makes it suitable only for adults.

Hypertext is somewhat similar to the gameplay involved in **MUDS** on the Internet and **non-Linear storytelling**, as well as some of the original interactive fiction and text-based **adventure games**.

See Also
Cypher, the; MUDs and MOOs; Non-Linear Storytelling Games

HyperText Transport Protocol
A simple **Internet** protocol allowing the transfer of **hypertext** information between machines on the **World Wide Web**.

Documents on the Web are linked by means of hypertext. HyperText Transport Protocol (HTTP) allows transfer of information between servers and client computers on the Web. The abbreviation HTTP appears at the beginning of **URLs** for documents contained on the Web (and is sometimes called "hot top").

See Also
HTML; Hypertext; Internet; URL; World Wide Web

Hyphen
The hyphen is, logically, what you get when you press the hyphen key. It is used to indicate that a word has been divided, as when it jumps from the end of a line to the start of the next. A hyphen is not the same as an em-dash or an en-dash. An em dash—like this one—gets its name from the fact that in a given font, it's about as wide as a capital M. An en-dash is half the length of an em-dash and is used to indicate a range of numbers, like 1–5, or as a minus sign. A hyphen is even shorter than an en-dash. Type an em-dash with the combination Option+Shift+Hyphen, and an en-dash with Option+Hyphen.

See Also
Hyphen, Discretionary

Hyphen, Discretionary
Hyphenating words makes your columns of type look less ragged, and is often necessary when the type is set justified. Word processors and desktop publishing

programs will hyphenate words automatically, according to rules supplied in the spelling dictionary. You can override these and place the hyphen where you want it, by clicking at the point where you want the word to break and pressing Option + hyphen.

You can also determine rules to follow for hyphenating words, defining the number of consecutive hyphenated lines to allow, and establishing a hyphenation zone. Words falling within the hyphenation zone would be automatically hyphenated. These discretionary hyphens are set differently, depending on the word processor, but there's usually a dialog box accessed through the Tools menu or Format menu. Because hyphenated text is often harder to read, avoid using too many consecutive hyphens.

I

I-Beam Cursor

The I-Beam cursor got its name because the **cursor** itself resembles an I-Beam used in construction. The default **arrow pointer** turns into an I-Beam cursor anytime text editing is needed. If, for example, you click a filename while using the arrow pointer, the cursor changes to an I-Beam cursor so you can enter a new name for the file. The Mac knows when you need an I-Beam cursor and changes to it whenever necessary.

The I-Beam cursor is the default cursor for any application that enables you to enter text.

For example, in Microsoft Word, when you open a new document, the cursor defaults to the I-beam for you to enter text. If you get near the **scroll bars** or **menu bar**, it changes to the arrow pointer so you can make a selection or scroll. The cursor changes back to the I-Beam cursor when your it returns to the page.

See Also

Arrow Pointer; Insertion Point; Menu Bar; Renaming Folders; Scroll Bar; Selecting Items

Icons

Icons are small pictures or drawings used to represent your **hard disk**, disks, documents, applications, shared volumes, printers, the trash can, and **folders**. If, for example, an icon appears on your **desktop** that looks like a **disk**, that icon represents a real disk in your disk drive, as shown in the figure. To view the contents of that disk, **double-click** its icon with your **mouse**, and a **window** will open showing you the disk's contents. Icons helps you recognize visually that you're viewing a disk instead of reading the name of the disk on-screen. Icons are the basis of the Macintosh interface. They make working with the Mac easier by making it a visual experience.

Apple's drag and drop technology, built-in in System 7.5 and higher, is also utilized with icons. You can take a document, for example, and drop it on top of the application's icon to launch the application and open the document. A number of utilities are designed from the ground up to use drag and drop. Expander (a utility that decompresses Stuffit files), for example, enables you to take a stuffed file, drag and drop it on its icon, causing Expander to launch, unstuff the file, and quit.

The icon that appears on a file is not permanent and can be changed at any time by **copying** another icon (or creating one of your own) and pasting this new icon into the file's **Get Info** box. The Get Info box for a file is found by clicking an icon and choosing Get Info from the File menu ($\mathcal{H}$-G). In the upper-left corner of this window, the file's icon is displayed. If you click the icon, a box appears around the icon enabling you to copy or paste over the icon. You can paste a new icon over the existing icon by choosing Paste ($\mathcal{H}$-V) from the **Edit menu**. When you close the Get Info box, the newly pasted icon appears as the icon for the file.

See Also

Desktop; Double-Click; Disks and Drives; Folders; Hard Disks; Mouse; Window

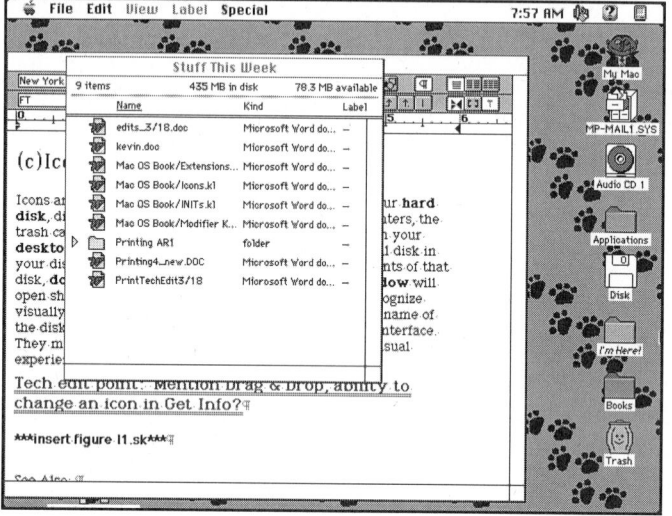

IDE, *See Integrated Development Environment*

Idea Fisher, *See Idea Generators*

Idea Generators

Before you can write the Great American Novel or even the Great American Business Presentation or Memo, you need one thing—an idea. There's software that can help you find and develop your ideas. Inspiration calls itself a "thinking environment." It helps you visually brainstorm and focus your thinking by providing the tools for you to organize and categorize your ideas. Functioning on the flowchart principle, Inspiration provides 525 different symbols that help you link ideas into relationships. Drag the idea boxes and connectors around on-screen until they make sense, and turn them into proposals, outlines, and charts. Inspiration also includes an excellent outlining program for making hierarchical outlines. You can export your outline to your pet word processor in any of five formats.

If Inspiration helps you take your ideas from point A to point B, then Idea Fisher is what you need when you reach point A with no concept whatsoever.

IdeaFisher is based on an IdeaBank of some 60,000 words, organized by categories. You might start "fishing" by looking for an animal, and then moving into the sub-categories: wild/fierce/uncivilized/tame/domesticated/large/small and so on. Entries are cross-referenced by concept and association. You can even free-associate, leap-frogging from one concept to another. The Idea Notepad keeps track of your route through the wordlists, and can export your findings as a text file. You can do a search based on any word or any two words and IdeaFisher will retrieve all of the words (by type) that are related to them in any way.

If that's not enough to get your own creativity flowing, consult IdeaFisher's Qbank. This is a list of over 5,000 questions that help you verbalize your ideas, narrow them down, or flesh them out. IdeaFisher tabulates your responses to the questions and presents you with a list of words that appear frequently in your answers. There are also special Qbank modules that ask questions to help you define and create a mission statement, grant proposal, or speech.

Three by Five, from Mac Toolkit, is a different kind of idea organizer. You make notes on virtual cards and arrange them on a virtual cork board. You also can print the cards on perforated card stock, print them as an outline, or import them into your word processor.

Finally, don't overlook your word processor as an idea generator. Both Microsoft Word and ClarisWorks have powerful outlining tools. Use the Thesaurus to fish for related words as a way of sparking ideas. When you're ready to write the final version, your outline is already in your word processor and only needs some padding to become a full-fledged presentation.

See Also

ClarisWorks; Microsoft Word; Word Processing

IEC

Founded in 1906, the IEC (International Electrical Commission) is a result of a resolution passed at the International Electrical Congress held in St. Louis in 1904.

Commission's object is to promote international co-operation on all questions of standardization and related matters in the fields of electrical and electronic engineering and thus to promote international understanding.

The IEC is composed of National Committees, of which there are presently 51, representing all the industrial countries in the world.

Ignore Internal Disk (Keyboard Shortcut)

You can ask the Mac to ignore the internal disk by holding down the ⌘-Option-Shift-Delete keys while you **boot** your computer. This makes the Mac ignore the internal disk and search through the **SCSI chain** for a disk to startup from. When it finds a disk with the startup files, it starts up from that disk. This disk does not mount on the **desktop**.

See Also

Boot; Desktop; Keyboard Shortcuts; Small Computer System Interface

Igor Pro, *See Charting and Graphing Applications*

Illustrator

Standing at the top of the draw program heap along with **FreeHand**, Illustrator is a sophisticated **PostScript** drawing application that's suitable for creating everything from simple black-and-white line drawings to complex color images.

Like most drawing packages, Illustrator offers more than one way to get shapes on the screen. There are rectangle and circle tools for drawing simple shapes, polygon tools for making polygons, stars, swirls, and spirals, and a FreeHand Sketch Tool for creating free-form shapes. A pen tool creates **Bézier curves**, the basic element of PostScript draw programs, while a pressure-sensitive brush tool (unusual for a draw program) works like a paintbrush or calligraphy pen, making broad strokes.

All Illustrator objects have a stroke (border or line) and a fill, both of which can be black, white, colored, or transparent. Objects can also be colored with gradients of multiple colors shading from one to the next, either linear (in a straight line) or radial (radiating out from a center point). Patterns, either built-in or created by the user, can also be used to fill objects.

Color-keyed layers allow objects to be hidden, stacked, and reordered easily, while masking tools allow users to show only that portion of an object that falls within the borders of the masking object.

Illustrator's graph tool simplifies the creation of graphs; it can import data from spreadsheets or text files—or use data entered directly by the user—to create one of six different types of graphs. Graphic elements can be used in graphs (stacked up to make columns in a bar graph, for example), and once the data is finalized the graph can be unlinked from its data and customized with Illustrator's drawing tools.

Bitmapped images in several formats (including TIFF, **EPS**, and **PhotoCD**) can be imported into Illustrator documents and traced or even edited using **Photoshop** plug-ins, and 1-bit (black-and-white) TIFF images can be colorized. Vector graphics can be rasterized (converted to **bitmapped images** in **RGB** or **CMYK** format) within Illustrator.

Text support is strong in Illustrator, with the single exception that the program lacks text **style sheets**. Floating palettes allow easy access to character and paragraph attributes, and plug-ins allow text to be spell checked and searched. Like most PostScript draw programs, Illustrator can convert text to editable outlines.

Implementation of the **add-on software** concept is particularly strong in Illustrator, with a wide variety of plug-ins designed for the program and the ability to use Photoshop plug-ins and FreeHand Xtras as well.

Perhaps the most powerful plug-ins Illustrator comes with are the Pathfinder filters, which allow users to perform a number of different functions on multiple paths, such as combining two paths to make one large one, creating a third path out of the intersection of two objects, and cutting an object into multiple paths defined by where another path crosses the object.

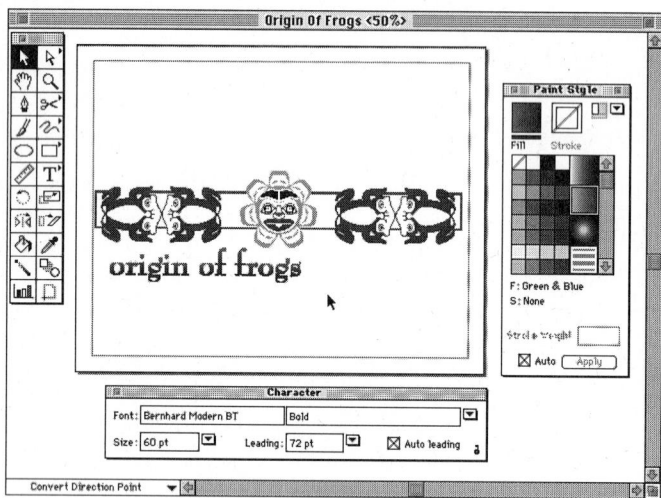

See Also

Add-On Software; Bézier Curves; Bitmapped Images; CMYK; Drawing Applications; EPS; FreeHand; PhotoCD; PostScript; Photoshop; Plug-Ins; RGB; Style Sheets

IMA

IMA (Interactive Multimedia Association) is a standard format for compressing audio. A 16-bit (stereo) sound compresses at about 4:1 with almost no detectable sound degradation. Certainly, it's much better than **downsampling** the sound, which is an alternative method of reducing the size of sounds. IMA increases the amount of sound you can store, and reduces the data rate required to play the sound, although the decompression routines themselves take up processor time and might not perform well on slower Macintosh computers.

QuickTime 2.1 and **Sound Manager** 3.1 support IMA sound compression for **AIFF** files. To create an IMA sound, open the sound in a program, such as **MoviePlayer**, and choose Export from the File menu. A dialog opens asking you to specify the name of the exported file and what you want to export to (choose AIFF file). Click the Options button and choose IMA from the Compression menu. Save the file. The resulting file is saved as an AIFF file that can be opened and played by any application that supports AIFF files, provided Sound Manager 3.1 is present on the machine being used.

An IMA-compressed AIFF file is not supported on a Windows computer. If you are creating a cross-platform sound to play under Windows, you should open the AIFF file again in MoviePlayer and save it as a QuickTime movie. This will then play on the Windows platform under QuickTime For Windows. You should test your sounds on several computers to make sure that they play satisfactorily under Windows.

Image Compression

One of the biggest problems in working with electronic graphics files, particularly **bitmapped graphics**, is their size. As the images become more and more detailed, their file size balloons—in fact, many graphic designers don't care about being rich or thin; from their point of view, you can't have too much RAM or too big a hard drive.

Compression programs like **StuffIt** or **DiskDoubler** work on any files, reducing their size to save space. But many graphics file formats have their own built-in compression schemes. These can be divided into two categories: lossy and lossless.

Lossy compression schemes cause image deterioration when used. Depending on the image and the amount of compression, the deterioration may not be noticeable, but it's there. Lossless compression schemes can't compress images as much, but they don't remove any image data, so they don't affect the quality of images.

File formats with their own compression schemes include TIFF (LZW, a lossless scheme), **GIF** (which also uses LZW), and **JPEG** (lossy). Many Mac graphics applications can also save to BMP files, a PC format that uses the lossless RLE compression.

See Also
GIF; JPEG; TIFF

Image Distortion, *See Monitors, Image Quality*

Image Manipulation for Printing

If a digitized image requires adjustments of any kind after it has been scanned, an image manipulation software application must be used. For Macintosh computer users, **Adobe Photoshop** is the only software of this type available, and it has become the desktop publishing industry standard. Many desktop scanner manufacturers provide plug-in software that enables their equipment to be operated from within Photoshop. Photoshop provides many tools for manipulating the scanned image. An image may be output directly from Photoshop or saved in a format that is compatible with page layout software applications or **PostScript** drawing programs. The following are typical and practical concerns when preparing a scanned image for printing.

File Format (File Menu/Save As)—Photoshop has the capability of saving a digitized image in many different formats. The purpose of saving an image in a file format other than Photoshop's native format is to make the image compatible with other software applications. Images to be imported into electronic page layouts should be saved in EPS (Encapsulated PostScript) or TIFF (Tagged Image File Format). TIFF seems to be favored for images imported into **Adobe PageMaker** or **QuarkXPress**. Both of these applications accept images in other formats, but TIFF is excellent for output to PostScript devices, especially if color separations are to be done. When working with a service bureau, trade shop, or printing firm, it is wise to ask them which file format is best for their equipment. TIFF images may be compressed by Photoshop to create smaller files sizes (LZW Compression). Check with your output service provider before applying any compression to TIFF images in Photoshop.

Mode Change (Mode Menu)—Continuous-tone color images appear in RGB mode in Photoshop unless they are converted to CMYK. High-end scanners can work in CMYK, but most desktop scanners use RGB. Black and white continuous-tone images normally appear in Grayscale mode. Both types of images become halftones if they are printed on a printing press, but it is not necessary to convert them to that mode in Photoshop. It is, however, desirable to convert RGB images to CMYK before performing any production work such as sharpening, contrast adjustments, ink setup, and so on because the image must be converted to CMYK to be printed. Although color display may not accurately reflect the final printed colors, it is still a good idea to perform all adjustments in the CMYK mode.

Image Size and Resolution (Image Menu/Image Size...) If an image was not scanned at the proper resolution or scale, the image's measurements can be altered in Photoshop's Image Size dialog box, as shown in the following figure. If the image needs to be resized or the resolution changed in Photoshop, the File Size constraint check box should be unchecked. This process is called resampling. Because file size, image size, and resolution are directly related to each other in a bitmapped image, removing the File Size constraint enables Photoshop to maintain the same resolution of an image when it is enlarged or reduced. Under this condition, Photoshop makes new pixels when the image is enlarged (sampling up) and discards pixels when the image is reduced (sampling down). Similarly, if the resolution number is changed with the File Size constraint removed, Photoshop can maintain the same image size. In both cases, the size of the file changes to reflect the addition or removal of pixels. Changing the image size or resolution without removing the File Size constraint results in a degraded image.

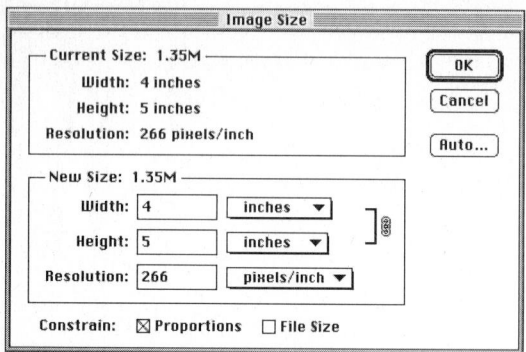

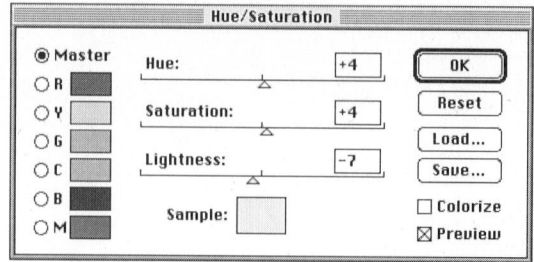

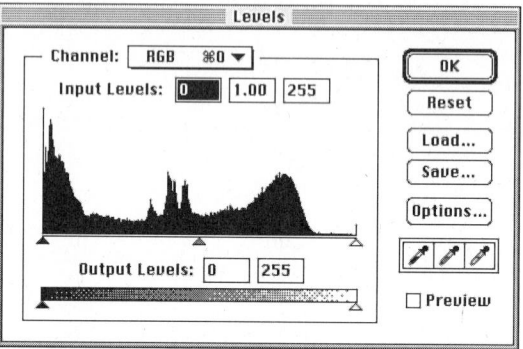

Image Adjustments (Image Menu/Adjust) The controls in Photoshop's Adjust submenu enable an image to be adjusted for tone, brightness/contrast, and color. Tone corrections are usually carried out in the Curves dialog box (as shown in the following figure) and color corrections in the Hue/Saturation dialog box (see following figure). Brightness and contrast should be adjusted in the Levels dialog box (see following figure). Most experts advise against using the Brightness/Contrast dialog box because its adjustments are too global and tend to allow highlight tones to drop out entirely and shadow tones to become too dark.

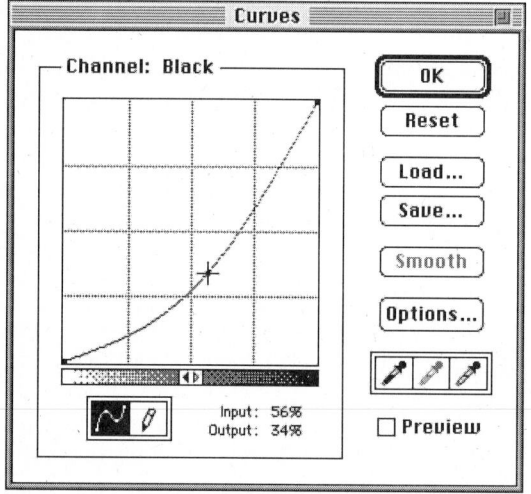

Sharpening (Filter Menu/Sharpen) The sharpening filters do what their names imply. They work by increasing contrast between adjacent dark and light pixels, particularly along clearly defined edges. The Unsharp Mask filter is recommended because it provides more control than the others. In the Unsharp Mask dialog box, shown in the following figure, the Amount setting controls the overall effect of the filter. Because every image is different, it is difficult to recommend an exact percentage for the Amount setting; however, a higher number creates a more exaggerated effect than a lower number. The Radius setting in the Unsharp Mask dialog box determines the radius of the halo of pixels that will be affected by the filter, especially along edges. If the setting is too high, the halo created around edges may be noticeable. A setting of 0.5 to 1.2 is conservative. Finally, the Threshold setting tells the filter which pixels in the image to adjust. A low number, such as 0, enables the filter to affect nearly all the pixels in the image. Higher numbers restrict change to only the most discernible edges. The default number is determined by the image itself. Try a Threshold of 5 and work up or down from that number. One of the reasons Unsharp Mask is favored by many experts is because its effects are subtle, and it takes a sharp eye and some experience to arrive at the optimum settings. You should experiment with an individual image to achieve the desired results.

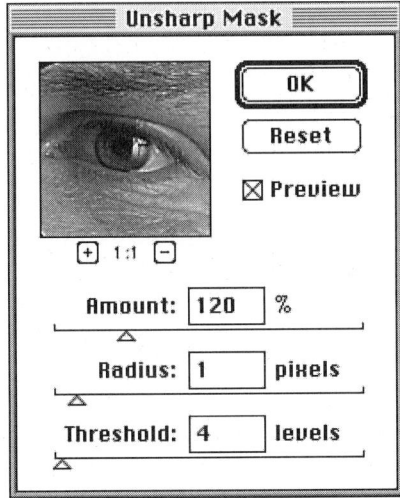

Cloning, Cropping, and so on (Tool Palette) The tools in Adobe Photoshop's Tool Palette are used to manually alter images and create new images. Images may be retouched and altered significantly with the Cloning Tool. Because it copies existing pixels and duplicates them in an adjacent area of the image, the Cloning Tool is useful in removing unwanted background objects or flaws. Cropping is an effective way to enhance the visual impact of an image or remove unwanted objects showing at the edges. Many other alterations may be performed directly on the pixels of the image, but Cloning and Cropping are the two most commonly performed actions.

Printing Ink Setup (File Menu/Preferences/Printing Inks Setup) When printing an image directly from Photoshop, this dialog box targets a specific printer, enabling the program to set an appropriate compensation for **dot gain**, as shown in the following figure. Gray balance can also be adjusted here. Gray balance

is the amount of cyan, magenta, and yellow necessary to create a neutral gray. Because process ink colors are not pure, correction must be done to produce grays that are truly neutral. A correct gray balance is necessary to produce good color separations. Changing the gray balance settings in Photoshop is seldom necessary, and a novice user should not tamper with this without consulting the prepress or printing service provider.

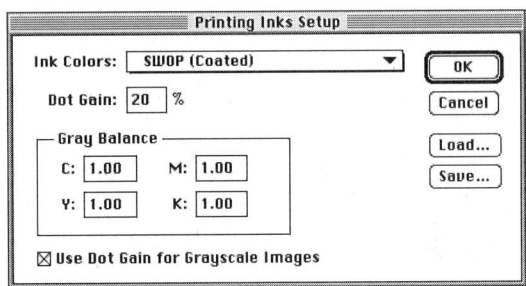

Color Separations (File Menu/Preferences/Separation Setup) An image must be converted from RGB to CMYK to be color separated for printing. The Separation Setup dialog box (shown in the following figure) controls the conversion in Photoshop and provides settings for how ink is applied to the paper. The choice between **GCR (Gray Component Replacement)** and **UCR (Undercolor Removal)** determines how black ink is applied in relation to the other three process colors (cyan, magenta, and yellow). As in the case of gray balance, these settings are not an appropriate area for experimentation, and selections should be made under the advice of an experienced printing technician.

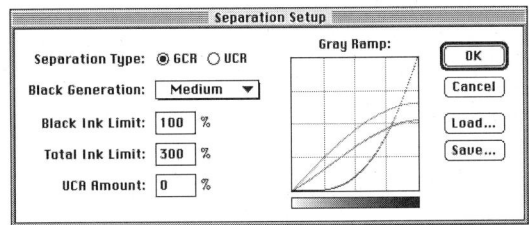

See Also

Color Printing; Color Separations; Digital Halftones; GCR (Gray Component Replacement); Halftones; Image Scanning; Ink Trapping; Process Color; Undercolor Removal

Image Registration, *See Color Trapping*

Image Scanning

Most continuous-tone images printed in publications are generated with a scanner, although digital cameras are gaining in popularity. Except in the case of expensive, high-end digital cameras, scanners still create better digital images. Photographs are the most common form of continuous-tone image, and they may be scanned as film negatives, as transparencies, or as photographic prints. When a photograph or other continuous-tone image, such as a pencil drawing or watercolor painting, is scanned, it becomes a digital image called a bitmap. Even black and white images (line art) are frequently scanned. Bitmapped images are characterized by a certain number of pixels per inch and a certain number of bits per pixel. Both of these characteristics are resolution factors and are determined when the image is digitized by the scanner. Perhaps the most important factor in scanning is the quality of the original image. Even the magic of **Adobe Photoshop** cannot compensate for poor original image quality.

Most scanners use a special computer chip called a charge-coupled device (CCD), which contains an array of light-sensitive elements . The CCD array converts photons (light energy) into electrons (electrical energy) processed in the computer as binary data. This results in pixels containing varying degrees of color or grayscale information depending on the capability of the system. The final printed form of a bitmapped image is usually a halftone, and to create the best halftone images, a scanner must store multiple bits of information in each pixel. Grayscale images must have eight bits per pixel, resulting in 256 potential levels of gray per pixel. (The **PostScript** page description language supports no more than 256 levels of gray. PostScript Level 2 supports more gray levels, but it is said that the human eye cannot perceive more.) High-quality digital color images require 24 bits per pixel to provide a potential 16.7 million colors. This number derives from multiplying the 256 shades in each of the colors of the additive system (RGB)—256 x 256 x 256 = 16,777,216. This type of color resolution is called bit depth or pixel depth.

The other type of resolution in a bitmapped image is the number of pixels per inch (ppi). This is also established when the image is digitized, but it can be altered later by resampling the image in Adobe Photoshop or some other image manipulation application. The optimum number of pixels per inch can be determined if the screen frequency of printed halftones is known. If no image enlargement or reduction is planned, multiplying the halftone screen frequency (lpi) by a factor of 2 or 1.5 provides the best scanning resolution in ppi. See the "Digital Halftones" entry for more information on scanning for halftones. As a rule, it is better for an image to have a higher than necessary resolution than one that is too low.

Although desktop flatbed and film scanners can produce high-quality images, the best scanning quality is obtained with drum scanners. Drum scanners have actually been in use since the 1970s, somewhat before the desktop publishing revolution. A drum scanner is often part of a proprietary **CEPS (Color Electronic Prepress System)**, representing the high end of desktop publishing. Generally, drum scanners are faster and have greater dynamic range than desktop scanners. They may be capable of digitizing images in CMYK mode with a pixel depth of 32 bits and linear resolutions of 2,000 ppi and more. Of course, they also are much more expensive. Lately, less expensive deskside drum scanners have been marketed, but they are not yet as ubiquitous as the desktop flatbed or film scanner.

The best desktop scanners are capable of 24-bit color and 256 levels of gray. The goal of scanning for print production is to provide images that make good

halftones and good **color separations**. The quality of the light source, the sensitivity of the CCD array, the accuracy of the optical system, and sensitivity to **highlight points** and shadow points all determine a scanner's **dynamic range** and therefore affect image quality. Density range (the range of values between the darkest and lightest points) is a primary concern when scanning. Most scanning software adjusts for density range, but it can be done manually by sampling a prescan image. Based on the highlight and shadow point information, a tone curve is established for the image. In effect, color separations must compress a fairly wide tonal range of color into a relatively narrow tonal range that can be achieved on a printing press. Mathematical algorithms in software such as Adobe Photoshop determine the proper tone compression based on the original tone curve.

See Also

Color Resolution; Color Separations; Digital Halftones; Dynamic Range; Image Manipulation for Printing; Resolution Measurement

Imagemaps, Creating

An imagemap or clickable map is an image that has been set up to act as a map; that is, every pixel is assigned coordinates. Clicking specified areas in the image sends the cursor coordinates to a **server**, which sends the user to a file in another location.

A map is a picture broken into zones. Each zone has its own **URL** or **Internet** address: a new page, a close-up of the picture, and so on. When the user clicks inside the predefined zone, a link is made to the corresponding URL.

Clickable imagemaps commonly appear on World Wide Web sites. They take advantage of the Web's ability to present information graphically by providing a visual means of accessing parts of a Web site.

A number of different software packages can be used to create an imagemap. These include WebMap, Mac-ImageMap, MapServe, or MacMapMaker.

The techniques can vary depending on what sort of software your Web site uses to serve documents on the Web: NCSA or CERN server software are among the most popular. The basic steps, though, are common to both NCSA or CERN servers:

1. Create an image that will serve as an imagemap by drawing or scanning it, or buying it from a commercial clip art package. The image should have well-defined boundaries and stand out clearly from its background. The map shown in the following figure contains clickable regions that are easy to define, such as circles and rectangles.

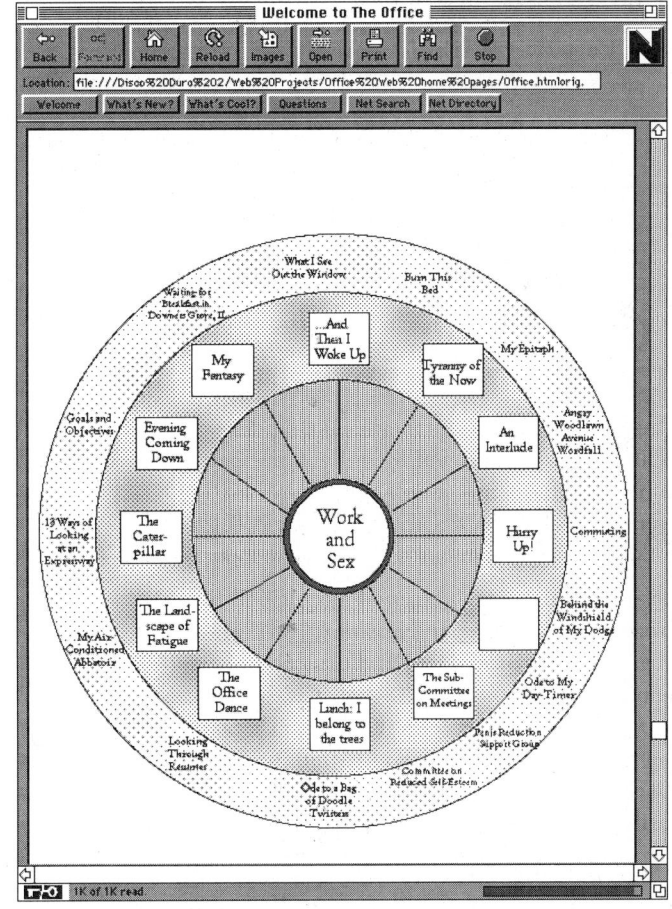

2. Define the clickable regions of the image by using a program such as WebMap. To do this, you open up your already-saved GIF image within WebMap and use WebMap's drawing tools to create a clickable region in the shape of a circle, square, or polygon by drawing them "on top" of your image.

3. Determine the x,y coordinates of the region you have created. (The 0,0 point is at the top left-hand corner of your image.) Each region you draw is assigned x,y numbers describing its boundaries. Depending on how many of these regions you draw, you will wind up with a list of these regions and coordinates. That list is called an *imagemap configuration file.* Any user who clicks within the boundaries of a particular region will be taken to a file you assign to it.

4. Set up the destination file for each of the clickable regions on your server. You may have several regions pointing to the same URL, but each region can only have one destination.

5. Enable a Common Gateway Interface (**CGI**) program to carry out the actions specified in your Configuration File. You will probably have to change a line in the CGI code to enable it to recognize both your imagemap and your configuration file.

6. Test, correct, and retest until you are sure all the links work correctly before putting your map on the Internet.

Complicated imagemap images often result in maps taking a long time to load on-screen. When the map graphics don't consume a good deal of disk space and the map itself is uncrowded, clickable maps are a useful way of hyperlinking in one place many separate documents and other elements scattered throughout a Web site.

Because imagemaps can be so complicated, though, the map creator should ensure that data is processed as quickly and efficiently as possible. The steps mentioned previously describe a server-side imagemap, where the processing of map file is done on the remote server. A relatively new kind of imagemap, the client-side imagemap, accomplishes the goals of speed and efficiency.

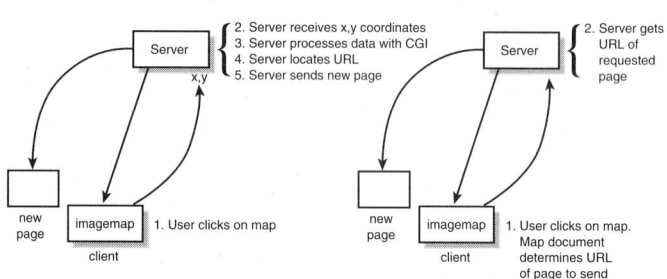

See Also

Imagemaps, Server-Side versus Client-Side; Server

Imagemaps, Server-Side versus Client-Side

The difference between client-side and server-side imagemaps is in how the link is made to the corresponding URL when the user clicks a map, as illustrated in the following figure.

A server-side imagemap is identified in Hypertext Markup Language (**HTML**) document by adding the <ISMAP> attribute to the IMG tag:

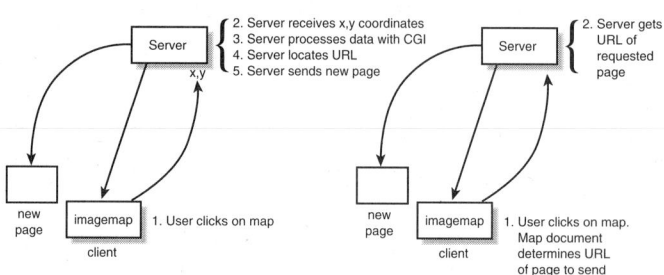

```
<IMG SRC="URL_for_map_image.gif"
ISMAP="map.html#map1">
```

In this line of HTML, <IMG SRC> identifies the graphic that represents the map the user sees on-screen. <ISMAP> identifies the map file—the document that defines clickable areas on the graphic ad associates them with separate HTML documents.

With server-side imagemap, the mouse click causes information to be sent to the remote Web server that contains the original map and all the document associated with it. The information is processed by the CGI program on the server's machine and the new document is sent to the user's **Web browser**.

With client-side imagemaps, all the important information about the map is transferred to the user's computer by the remote server, and the client computer does all the work—after all, the client machine isn't busy responding to hundreds or thousands of hits, as the server might be. The information to be transferred is embedded in the HTML document that contains the map. Client-side imagemaps respond much quicker to mouse clicks, work more efficiently, and are more secure for the map creator.

See Also

CGI; GIF; HTML; Imagemaps, Creating; Internet; Server; URL; Web Browser; Web Page; World Wide Web

Imagesetters

The imagesetter is a prime piece of equipment at a **desktop publishing service bureau**. In fact, many service bureaus evolved directly from typesetting services where imagesetters were part of the photo-typesetting equipment. In the mid 1980s, Linotype Corporation (now Linotype-Hell) began adapting their Linotronic brand of typesetting imagesetters to output desktop computer files through a **PostScript raster image processor (RIP)**. Consequently, the brand name Linotronic became as common as Kleenex or Xerox. Even now, the expression "to Lino" is associated with high-resolution output of any kind.

Imagesetters provide high-resolution output by using laser beams to expose images on photosensitive paper or film. Some imagesetters can even expose images directly on printing plates. Imagesetters are really a system of components rather than a single device. The three main components are a raster image processor (RIP), an imager, and a photo processor. Some imagesetters require typical photographic developing chemicals, but some newer devices utilize a dry thermal process that is much more environmentally friendly.

The raster image processor (RIP) is responsible for interpreting PostScript data and converting it to high-resolution bitmaps. The RIP is usually a piece of hardware, but software RIPs also exist. The imager, also called a recorder, is the largest piece of equipment. It uses laser light to expose tiny laser spots on the photosensitive imaging surface, combining the spots to create halftones and line art. The dots per inch (dpi) rating of an imagesetter actually refers to the laser spots. These are also sometimes called machine spots by technicians. These dots (or spots) are only 5 to 30 microns in diameter. Smaller dots mean higher resolutions in dots per inch. After the image has been recorded on the photosensitive paper, film, or plate, the output medium is developed in the photo processor. Of course, fresh chemicals and proper handling are crucial during the development process.

See Also

Digital Halftones; Gray Levels; Prepress; Raster Image Processor (RIP); Service Bureaus, Trade Shops, and Desktop Publishing

Imagination Express

Kids typically can invent, imagine, and create wonderful stories, but their lack of skill with illustration and text editing often slows them down or inhibits their writing efforts. Edmark has found a solution with its Imagination Express series. These programs provide the artwork, sound effects, and other tools to help kids create interactive stories and movies. There are four destinations in the series, with more to come.

Each of the four—Oceans, Rain Forest, Neighborhood, and Castle—includes a set of backgrounds, and a "cast" of characters and props to help kids tell the story. The actors and props come in the form of electronic "stickers", which the child simply drags to the background. Most have sounds attached, and many also have movement. To animate a fish, for example, the child places the fish in its starting position, clicks the camera icon, and then drags the fish where it's going.

There are sound tools that enable kids to add their own sounds and narration to the stories, as well as choosing from a pre-recorded collection of theme music and sound effects. When the creation is done, kids can print their storybooks in black and white or color, or display their movies to family and friends on-screen. The Rain Forest, Ocean, and Castle modules also include on-screen "fact books" with information that kids can use in their stories.

Immedia

Immedia is proprietary publishing format and browser from Quark, the developers of the desktop publishing program **QuarkXPress**. Immedia uses proprietary format files and a custom **World Wide Web browser** that can be used as a stand-alone program or as a plug-in for programs, such as **Netscape Navigator**. Data formats supported include text, graphics, video, and audio. The developers claim that Immedia will offer more sophisticated typography and layout than is supported by **HTML** and current browsers. At the time of writing, this product had not been released.

See Also
QuarkXPress, World Wide Web

Import/Export, Spreadsheet

Most **spreadsheets** can save or open their pages in a variety of formats to match other spreadsheet programs, and almost all are compatible with Microsoft **Excel**. Spreadsheets also let you import or export just their data without **formulas** as text files, with tab or comma characters between each **column** in a **row** and return characters at the end of each row. You'll find this handy for moving data between a spreadsheet and a **database** manager or **word processor**.

There's also a universal language, *SYLK* (for Symbolic Link), spoken by all spreadsheet programs. It creates a text file that preserves data and formulas, and any formatting you might have applied to the cells. Like its word-processor equivalent **RTF**, it's not very efficient—a small spreadsheet file becomes a very large SYLK file—but because it's completely text-based, it can be used cross-platform and sent over **email** systems.

Importing CD Audio, *See CD Audio, Converting to QuickTime*

Importing Graphics, *See Referencing*

Imposition, *See Prepress; Printing and Binding Terminology*

Improving a Performa's Picture

To fix the Trinitron Picturetube that comes with the **Performa**, open the **Monitors control panel** in the **Control Panels** folder and check Uncorrected Gamma, causing your screen to become much sharper.

See Also

Control Panels; Monitors Control Panel; Performa

IMS, *See Internet Multicasting Service*

In Control

In Control, from Attain Corp., is a planner and organizer, rather than a full-fledged PIM. It combines a calendar and outliner. The outliner, which makes and prioritizes to-do lists, can be viewed with or without the calendar page. Because it lacks the contacts file typically found in PIMs, the same company sells its own contact manager, FastPace Instant Contact. Like the **Now Up-to-Date/Now Contact** bundle, this one is well integrated so that it's easy to link information from one program to the other. The area in which In Control really shines, though, is in making to-do lists. The outliner encourages you to think of your tasks in a hierarchical order, which not only helps you set priorities for them, but also forces you to see which are dependent on other things that must happen first. Suppose, for example, that you're using In Control to plan a dinner party for a large group. When you begin listing tasks, you'll see right away that you can't send the invitations until you've set the date and confirmed the caterer and facilities.

Lists can be customized with the dates on which tasks must be accomplished and who's responsible for doing them, or with any other qualifications you choose to apply. The structure of the program lends itself to refining details.

You can add as many columns or categories of information as you want. Then you can sort the outline by priority, due dates, people assigned to the various tasks, or any order you find useful.

The calendar shows the month or a single day. The day view plans your schedule in half hour increments. The month view can be expanded to two weeks, or reduced so that you can see several months (up to twelve) at once. Date and time entries in the outliner are automatically entered on the appropriate calendar pages.

In Control can be shared across a network, while keeping some entries private. Connecting to the Public File, directly or via **Apple Remote Access**, on the workgroup server will automatically update each user's "local" files. You can choose how much of your data to share—which outline columns are to be kept private and which are available to coworkers. Further refinements are also possible. You might choose to share certain kinds of data, such as salaries or performance reviews, with some people but not with others. In Control is a flexible, powerful tool for managing your time and information, and you don't need to be a control freak to use it.

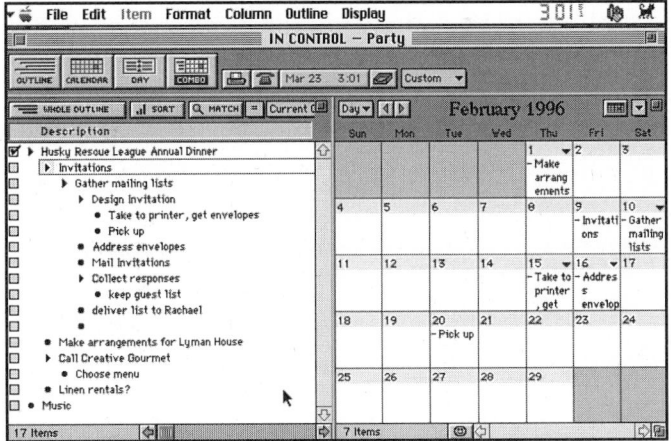

See Also

Personal Information Manager

Inbetweening

Used in animation programs, inbetweening is a process of automatic motion creation. The software enables you to define a starting and ending point for the movement of an object. These are called the **key frames**. Using the inbetweening routines, the software calculates the location of the object during the motion. This can be as simple as dividing the number of frames by the distance the object travels, and evenly spacing the motion over the sequence. Most programs (including Macromedia's **Director** and Specular's **Infini-D**) enable you to define acceleration after the first key frame, and deceleration before the next key frame, enabling more realistic movement.

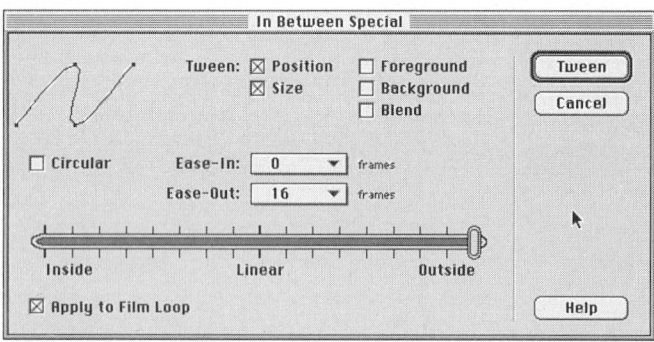

See Also

Key Frames

Incremental Backup

An incremental backup is **backing up** only the files that have been altered or edited since the last time you backed up the contents of your **hard disk**. If, for example, you backed up your hard disk on Tuesday and on Wednesday you worked on 14 different files, you don't need to back up the entire hard disk again—just the 14 files you've edited. Backing up these 14 files is an incremental backup.

There are third-party utilities that do an incremental backup for you, or you can do it manually. To manually do an incremental backup, use the **Find command** (⌘-F) at the **desktop**. When the Find dialog box appears, click the More Choices button. Then select Modified Date from the **pull-down menu**, type in today's date, and press Find. This brings you all the files that you changed today, enabling you to **copy** these files onto your backup disk(s) to complete an incremental backup for the day.

See Also

Backing Up; Copy; Desktop; Find Command; Hard Disks; Pull-Down Menu

Index, Creating

An index is an alphabetical list of topics in a document and the page numbers on which they can be found. Not all word processors or desktop publishing programs are capable of creating an index, but the more "serious" ones such as PageMaker, QuarkXPress, WordPerfect, and Microsoft Word have indexing functions built in. Each program handles indexing somewhat differently, but the general principles are similar. Indexing is done by means of an index dialog box that (unlike most dialog boxes) remains active while you enter text or scroll through existing documents, so that you can mark multiple entries. Microsoft Word's Mark Index Entry dialog box is shown in the following figure.

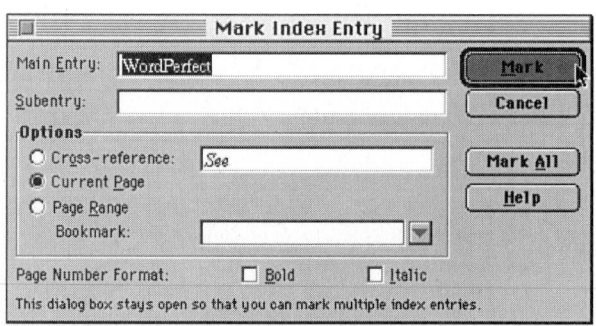

Click the button, or hit enter to mark the selected entry.

When you reach a word in the text that is to become an index entry, simply select it. It will be automatically entered in the Main entry field. To mark it, click the button. This places a non-printing tag next to the word. "Mark all" will locate every instance of that word in the document and automatically place tags next to all of them. Once you have marked all of your index entries, use the Index and Tables box as shown in the next figure to select a style for the index.

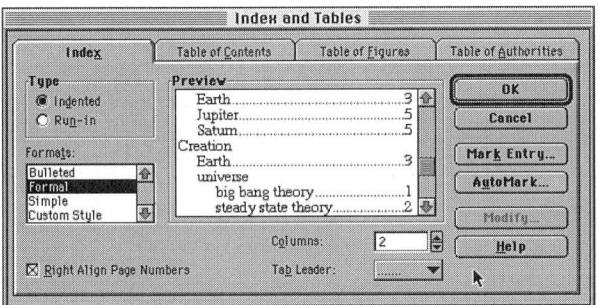

Choose an appropriate style or design your own.

The program will collate all of the marked entries, sort them, and create the index as a separate section following the document. Sub-entries and cross-references are handled from the Mark Index Entry box, too, and are collated into the index at the same time. Once the index is assembled, it can be edited, but changes will disappear if the index is then re-collated.

Indexing, *See Long-Document Management*

Indiana Jones Desktop, *See Hollywood Games Connection*

Infini-D

Infini-D sports a four view interface (top, front, side, and camera view). Other views can be added when necessary. Window sizes can be customized for size and application (NTSC, Small, Quicktime…) and number of colors. Background images are shown in the camera view. Any view selected can be instantly rendered (Wireframe, fast, better, best) with no anti-aliasing, medium, or high applied. When editing, it's best to leave rendering set to wireframe to conserve

time. Preview renders can be generated whenever necessary. Selected objects can be manipulated visually from ToolBox icons or from numerical equivalents in the floating Object Menu. Object translations in the view windows are instantly updated in the Camera window, and vice versa.

Modeling Tools Infini-D has a very full set of modeling options, and all are easily customizable to whatever degree is desired. The ToolBox features icons for the Four Primitive Groups (some members of which are very unusual):

1. Sphere, Cube, Cylinder, Cone, Plane.
2. Cup, Torus, Truncated Cylinder, partial Cylinder.
3. Extruded Triangle, Cylinder with Triangular Hole, Extruded and Twisted Pipe.
4. Twisted Object, Round Cornered Cube, Pyramid, Coiled Section, Banana (that's right! Banana!).

That's only a small hint at what Infini-D's modeling features can provide. Double clicking on any object brings up one of the best modeling utilities around. From here, you can customize any object in Infini-D's library, or design your own from scratch. Tools include a full extrusion Modeler and a symmetrical lathing process. The object that can't be designed here just can't be sculpted, period.

Boolean Operations Although objects can be designed with holes in them in Infini-D's modeling module, and combined on screen into various shapes, Infini-D has no Boolean modeling mode as such.

Texture Mapping Infini-D offers the user several modes for texture mapping an object, although drag and drop is not supported at the time of this writing. The Surface Floater window lists all of the available textures by name, and shows a view of the picture map currently selected. Double-clicking the picture stamp brings up the edit picture dialog, while selecting edit from the Surfaces Window brings up the full editing parameters dialog. All of the parameters are open for editing, including tiling, mapping, bump, and light associated (ambiance and so on) options. Consequently, any texture chosen becomes a gateway to infinite possibility. As far as applying textures to objects in the scene, full control over preview rendering quality and anti-aliasing is offered.

Lights Infini-D has a visual controller for distance, point, and spotlights that shows immediate lighting response in the camera view if higher quality rendering is on. Light intensity and shadowing are also facilitated, as is light color. A Light Info dialog is also accessible, giving you numerical control over a light's intensity and placement angles.

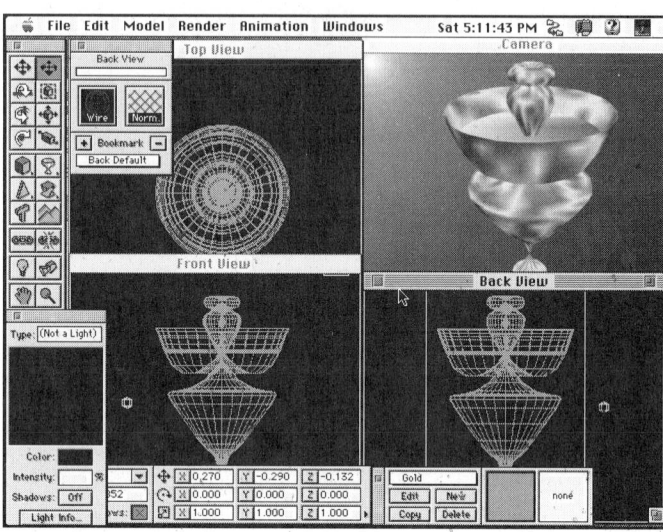

Rendering The best thing about Infini-D rendering is that you can manipulate the previews so that there are no surprises. Being able to target a high quality rendering with full anti-aliasing on in preview mode let's you know exactly what you're going to get. Coupled with the WYSIWYG lighting features, exacting rendering is made easy. Environmental Maps, Fog, and Background image settings can also be shaped with ease. Shading (Shadows) and Ray Tracing (Shadows, Reflections, Transparency) can all be switched on in the Rendering Options window. Images and animation can be rendered to disk according to view, quality, color and resolution.

Included Libraries Texture and 3D Object libraries are included with the software.

Animation Full animation features with velocity, motion paths, frame rate and number settings, and a full featured keyframe Sequencer are included.

Other Special Features Infini-D is compliant with QuickDraw 3D for viewing real textures in preview modes.

File Load/Save Conventions In addition to loading and saving files in the Infini-D format, you can import Objects (Swivel 3D and DXF), EPS files, and Images (in any resolution and color depth). Objects can be exported as DXFs.

Infinite Loop

In programming, an infinite loop is a repeating series of computer instructions that cannot exit. Many freezes are caused by the computer entering an infinite loop in which it cannot respond to user input such as mouse clicks or typing. In most cases, programmers avoid infinite loops at all cost for this very reason.

Interestingly, Infinite Loop is also the name Apple chose for a road on its main **Cupertino** campus. Apple's primary mailing address is "1 Infinite Loop." Although it might be tempting to attach some greater significance to this address, the name actually came from a contest among Apple employees.

See Also

Cupertino

InfoGenie

If your database needs are modest, and you don't want a works program because you already have a word processor and a draw program that you like, check out InfoGenie from Casady & Greene. It's not the most powerful database you can buy, but when you're using it strictly to print labels and envelopes, to keep your greeting card lists, collections, recipes, and similar kinds of information sorted and accessible, it's perfect.

InfoGenie supports both freeform and field-based datafiles. Freeform records are rather like blank index cards. You can paste any quantity of text onto one. It needn't be formatted into fields. Freeform records are ideal for storing your favorite jokes, email messages you need to keep, recipes, quotations... anything you need to be able to search, but can't break up into separate chunks. InfoGenie comes with a number of sample freeform databases, including a file of lawyer jokes, and one of quotations from former Vice-President Quayle. A row of icons above the text box guides you in scanning through the file, and also gives access to print, save, and other commands.

Field-based datafiles are the computer's version of a printed form. You fill in the blanks with the appropriate data: name, street, city, state, and so on. InfoGenie takes this information and stores it, one record per card, for as many cards as you need in your database. Field-based files are good for mailing lists of all kinds, and also for keeping track of what's in your wine cellar, record collection, or anything else that can be described in terms of its logical parts or attributes. Information such as the item name, serial number, date of purchase, and cost fit quite naturally into fields that are the same from one record to the next, and can be used to keep a list for insurance purposes as well as to tell you, in one concise form, what you've got. You may also keep the last card of a field-based database for multiple paragraphs of freeform data. This lets you add a page of notes and comments at the end of your structured data.

InfoGenie can print out reports in three different formats. It prints envelopes, labels, and lists. There are stationery documents for all of these. You can print a single envelope or label or a batch of either. You can print a single card from your database or the entire file. And you can print your files in a list view, as if they were spreadsheet entries.

You can configure InfoGenie to dial telephone numbers for you if you have a modem or Desktop Dialer. It can add the credit card string, 800 access string, or whatever additional numbers you need to dial in order to reach an outside line. (...unless you have a PBX system. Most PBX systems do not support computer dialing. You'd need to have a direct outside line installed to use this feature.)

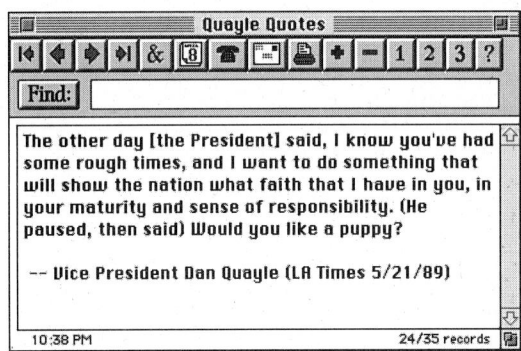

A freeform record can hold as much text as you need to put into it. InfoGenie isn't a heavy-duty relational database, like FileMaker Pro or 4D, but if your data-handling needs are light, it's quite possibly all the database you need.

See Also
Database

InfoSeek

InfoSeek is an **Internet** search engine provided by the InfoSeek Corporation of Santa Clara, California.

InfoSeek comes in two varieties: a free service and a subscription service. What you see on Netscape's "Internet Search" page lets you search Info Seek's database of **World Wide Web pages** as many times as you wish without charge. You type a word or words in the text-entry field and choose Run Query or press Return or Enter. InfoSeek then returns the first 200 Web documents related to your query. It recognizes English phrases as well as keywords, and indexes entire documents rather than just titles, headings, or keywords.

InfoSeek maintains a number of databases other than its 200,000-page/2 million article Web database, but you have to subscribe and pay fees to get access to them.

Home page for InfoSeek is **http://www2.Infoseek.com/**.

See Also
Web Page

INIT 17 Virus

This virus infects the System file and application files. The message:

```
From the depths of Cyberspace
```

is displayed only the first time an infected Macintosh is started after October 31, 1993. INIT 17 can cause system crashes.

See Also
ANTI Virus; CDEF Virus; CODE 1 Virus; CODE 252 Virus; Frankie Virus; INIT 1984 Virus; INIT 29 Virus; INIT 9403 Virus; INIT-M Virus; MacMag Virus; MBDF Virus; MDEF Virus; nVIR Virus; Scores Virus; T4 Virus; WDEF Virus; ZUC Virus

INIT 29 Virus

This rapidly spreading virus infects system, application, and document files. Infected applications do not need to be run in order for INIT 29 to spread. System crashes and printing problems are common symptoms of this virus.

See Also
ANTI Virus; CDEF Virus; CODE 1 Virus; CODE 252 Virus; Frankie Virus; INIT 17 Virus; INIT 1984 Virus; INIT 9403 Virus; INIT-M Virus; MacMag Virus; MBDF Virus; MDEF Virus; nVIR Virus; Scores Virus; T4 Virus; WDEF Virus; ZUC Virus

INIT 1984 Virus

This virus only infects System Extensions and is designed to trigger an infected system that is started on any Friday the 13th in 1991 or later. The virus changes many folder and filenames to random characters. File

creators and file types are also changed. INIT 1984 can delete some files. There are at least two Friday the 13ths each year.

See Also
ANTI Virus; CDEF Virus; CODE 1 Virus; CODE 252 Virus; Frankie Virus; INIT 17 Virus; INIT 29 Virus; INIT 9403 Virus; INIT-M Virus; MacMag Virus; MBDF Virus; MDEF Virus; nVIR Virus; Scores Virus; T4 Virus; WDEF Virus; ZUC Virus

INIT 9403

INIT 9403, also known as SysX, is very destructive. After infecting a certain number of files, INIT 9403 erases disks that are larger than 16MB mounted to your desktop.

See Also
ANTI Virus; CDEF Virus; CODE 1 Virus; CODE 252 Virus; Frankie Virus; INIT 17 Virus; INIT 1984 Virus; INIT 29 Virus; INIT 9403 Virus; INIT-M Virus; MacMag Virus; MBDF Virus; MDEF Virus; nVIR Virus; Scores Virus; T4 Virus; WDEF Virus; ZUC Virus

INIT-M Virus

This is a malicious virus that is triggered on any Friday the 13th. INIT-M damages a large number of folders and files by changing their names, file types, and creator codes. This virus only spreads under System 7.

See Also
ANTI Virus; CDEF Virus; CODE 1 Virus; CODE 252 Virus; Frankie Virus; INIT 17 Virus; INIT 1984 Virus; INIT 29 Virus; INIT 9403 Virus; MacMag Virus; MBDF Virus; MDEF Virus; nVIR Virus; Scores Virus; T4 Virus; WDEF Virus; ZUC Virus

INIT Conflicts

INITs (initialization programs) are instructions that load additional features or functionality to your **system** at **startup**. Apple now calls these additions to your system **extensions**, but they work the same way as INITs did. INIT conflicts occur as you add more INITs to your system. Sometimes a new INIT conflicts with the operation of INITs in the system and causes problems, such as freezing or crashing. This is an INIT conflict. INIT conflicts often occur during startup and **freeze** or crash your machine or display a system error before the computer completes its startup.

To resolve an INIT conflict, you have to find out which INIT is causing the conflict. If you've recently added an INIT, the solution may be **restarting** your computer while pressing the Shift key (which disables all INITs from loading into the system) and removing the culprit. But if you need the functionality that this new INIT provides, you need to remove your INITs and place them in a separate folder outside your **System Folder**. Then put the INITs back into your System Folder, one-by-one, and restart the computer after you've added each INIT. If you add an INIT and the machine suddenly freezes, you've found the conflicting INIT.

If your INIT conflict occurs during startup, renaming an INIT may resolve the conflict. INITs load alphabetically, so changing the name of an INIT will change the loading order.

Apple has included a free utility program installed with System 7.5. and higher, called **Extensions Manager** (created by an Apple employee, Ricardo Batista) that speeds up the process of elimination without having to move items in and out of your System Folder. Another popular manager of extensions is Startup Manager, which is part of the Now Utilities from Now Software. Conflict Catcher, a third-party utility from Casady and Greene, is also gaining popularity as a way to keep conflicts under control and manage the loading of your extensions.

See Also

Crashes, System; Extensions; Extensions Manager Control Panel; INITs; Restart; Shift Key

Initialization, *See Disks, Initializing*

Initializing Printer Message

The first time you startup your printer, it's initialized. This is when the Macintosh tells the printer that it is connected to a Macintosh and prepares the printer for printing. This occurs when you first turn on your printer. After it is initialized, the printer doesn't need to be initialized again, unless it is turned off or power is interrupted. When you choose the **Print** command after turning on the printer, Apple's Print Monitor displays a printing status bar. A message appears stating that the printer is being initialized.

However, if you are connected to a **network** in which Mac users and PC users share the same printer, every time you go to print your computer has to reinitialize the printer to let it know it's printing from a Mac. For that reason, you'll see the Initializing Printer **message box** before each print cycle.

See Also

Network; Message Box; Printing; Print Monitor

INITs

Initialization programs (INITs) were used to **customize** pre-System 7 Macs by adding additional functionality and features. INITs are now called **extensions** in **System 7** and higher. To use an INIT, place it in your **System Folder** (in System 6x) and **restart**. INITs load into the system during **startup**. INITs are preprogrammed to add a particular feature to your system, such as the way **QuickTime** adds movie playback capability for example. INITs don't need input from the user, and you cannot adjust the preferences or settings of an INIT.

See Also

Customizing; Extensions Folder; Extensions Manager Control Panel; INIT Conflicts; QuickTime; Restart; Startup Sequence; System 7; System Folder

Ink Trapping

Ink trapping is the term used to describe the process of printing one ink on top of another, a situation that arises in process-color printing. Ink trapping should not be confused with the **color trapping** of misregistered images. There are two types of ink trapping on a printing press: wet trapping and dry trapping. In wet trapping, wet ink is printed over wet ink. In dry trapping, wet ink is printed over dry ink. A buildup of ink in solid areas may be detrimental, so methods have been devised to prevent excessive ink trapping. The two most common are **Gray Component Replacement (GCR)** and **Undercolor Removal (UCR)**.

See Also

Color Trapping; GCR (Gray Component Replacement); Undercolor Removal

Inkjet Printing, *See Printing Technology, Inkjet*

Inserting a Disk

To insert a **disk** into your computer's **disk drive**, hold the disk with the label facing up. Turn the disk so that the arrow next to the metal shutter is pointing away from you. This arrow indicates the direction to insert the disk into the drive. Slide the disk into the disk drive opening. Make sure the arrow on the disk is face up and pointing in the direction that you're inserting the disk. The **icon** for the disk will appear on the **desktop** a few moments after the disk has been properly inserted.

If for some reason you should insert the disk incorrectly, or the disk becomes stuck in the disk drive, you can have the disk drive manually eject the disk. To do this, you must first straighten out a paper clip and insert the straight end into the small hole below the disk drive on your Mac. As you insert the paper clip into the hole, you hit a spot of resistance. At that point you should press firmly, causing the drive to do a manual eject and hopefully pop the disk out. If you're

not able to eject the disk using this paper clip method, the case may have to be opened and the disk drive taken apart to reach the trapped disk. If this is the case, refer the situation to qualified service technicians.

See Also

Desktop; Disks and Drives; Icons

Insertion Point

The insertion point is the blinking point where the next typed item is inserted into your document. If, for example, you're using a word processor, a blinking vertical line shows you where the text that you type will appear. You can move the insertion point by clicking the **I-beam** text cursor in a different location. The insertion point is now where you clicked. When you select a block of text, the insertion point disappears. It reappears at the next point you click your cursor. So if you're cutting text from one area to move to another, you can click your insertion point at the point where you want the cut text (temporarily stored in the Clipboard) to be inserted.

You can control the speed at which the insertion point blinks on the **General Controls Control Panel**. There are three speed settings: Slow, Medium, and Fast.

See Also

Click; General Controls Control Panel; I-Beam Cursor; Mouse

Inside Macintosh

Inside Macintosh is Apple's official documentation of the MacOS **Application Programming Interface** (API) **ToolBox**.

Inside Macintosh started as a three volume set that covered everything there was to know about the original Mac ToolBox. As new features were added to the System, three additional volumes were published, including the genuinely massive Volume VI, which covered the additions made in System 7. The trouble with these books was that many topics were spread over more than one book, and information in some of the early volumes was superseded by newer information in the later ones.

In 1992, Apple decided a change was in order. The entire mass of Macintosh API documentation was reorganized by topic into the *New Inside Macintosh* volumes (sometimes abbreviated as NIM). More than 24 volumes have been released, of which six full volumes are dedicated to **QuickDraw GX**.

If you're interested in getting started in Mac programming, you don't need to rush to the store and buy a copy of each *Inside Macintosh* book. In fact, you might not need to buy any! Apple has released two electronic versions of *Inside Macintosh*: the Inside Macintosh CD-ROM and the **Macintosh Programmers ToolBox Assistant** (also on CD-ROM). The first contains most of the volumes in a format that reproduces the appearance of the printed books. The second is a searchable hypertext database of all of the ToolBox routines documented in *Inside Macintosh*. Many of the *Inside Macintosh* volumes are also available in Adobe Acrobat format on Apple's Developer Web site (**http://dev.info.apple.com/**).

If you do prefer the printed versions of the books, start with the volumes that cover the basics: *Inside Macintosh: Macintosh ToolBox Essentials*, *Inside Macintosh: Imaging With QuickDraw*, *Inside Macintosh: Files*, and *Inside Macintosh: Memory*. There is also an overview volume available.

See Also
Application Programming Interface (API); Macintosh Programmers ToolBox Assistant; QuickDraw GX; ToolBox

Inside the Macintosh, *See Circuits, Parts of the Macintosh*

Inspiration, *See Idea Generators*

Installer Disk
If you want to reinstall or update your **operating system**, you need to use Apple's Installer utility program. Although it takes a number of **disks** for a complete installation, only one disk, the installer disk, called

Install or Install Me First, is needed to install a new **system**. If you are installing a new system from a **CD-ROM** version of the system software, the Installer is on the CD-ROM, but in some cases you may still need the Install Me First disk to startup the system if your CD-ROM is not bootable (meaning the CD-ROM has an installer on it and all other necessary files, but it does not have a system folder on the disc that you can startup your Mac from.)

See Also
CD-ROM

Installer Utility
When you buy a Macintosh computer, the operating system is pre-installed on the computer, but if you ever need to reinstall, or update, your **System** software, you'll use Apple's installer. The installer is a utility program that checks out which model and type of Macintosh you're using and installs into the **System Folder** only the files your particular Mac needs. You can also designate that a new System folder be created when you run the installer.

These installers are particularly useful when the installation requires that some files be added to the System Folder, and other files added to other specific folders. The installer is also helpful if the installation will require more than just one disk. It's not unusual for an installation to take 10 or more disks to install just one application, and the installer helps to provide an easy-to-use interface, which tells you which disk to insert when, and it even ejects each disk when it has completed that disk's portion of the install (see the following figure).

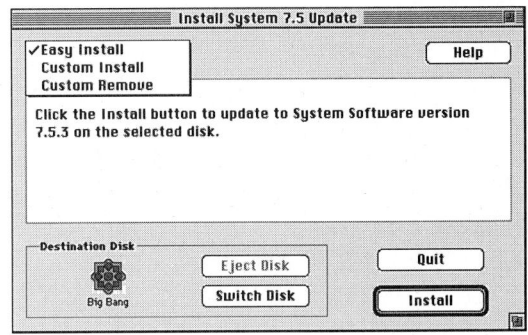

Many third-party software developers use the Apple installer with their own products, under license from Apple. So, don't be surprised if you buy a software program and the installer looks very familiar.

The installer enables you to choose between an easy install, which installs the full compliment of **fonts**, **control panels**, and virtually every Apple system feature and **extension** available, and a custom install, where you select individual items from a scrolling list of options and features you may want to install.

One of the most popular installers was designed by Apple, called the Apple Installer, and is often licensed to third-party developers. This installer works nicely because it first checks out which model and type of Macintosh you're using, and then installs only the files your particular Mac needs. The installer also offers you the choice of a one-button Easy Install, which loads the full recommended version of the application, along with any sample, tutorials, fonts, and so on that the developer has designated. If you don't want a full Easy install, you can usually choose Custom Install from the installer's **pop-up menu**.

This custom install option enables you to decide which individual files you want the installer to install. For example, when you choose Custom Install, you'll see a list of all the files an Easy install would have installed, and you can select by **checkbox** which files to install. If you see a file that you already have, such as **SimpleText**, you can choose not to check that file for installation.

If you're installing Macintosh System 7.5 or higher, there is a separate install required if want to use QuickDraw GX and PowerTalk.

See Also

Control Panels; Extensions Folder; Fonts; System Folder

Installing Fonts

In System 7 and higher, to install a **font**, make sure no applications are running. Select the font you want to install and **drag** that font into the **System Folder**. The System displays a alert box stating, "Fonts need to be stored in the Font Folder in order to be avail-

able to the Macintosh. Put the font (font name will appear here) into the Fonts folder?" If you **click** OK, the system puts the selected font into the font folder for you. The font is now installed. To remove a font, make sure no applications are running, and drag the selected font out of the fonts folder.

If you are using System 6 through System 6.7, you install fonts by using the Font/DA Mover utility to install your screen fonts directly into your System file.

See Also

Alert Box; Click and Drag; Font/DA Mover; Fonts; Icon; System Folder

Installing RAM in PowerBooks, *See PowerBook RAM*

Installing Software

Most software uses an **installer** program to install the application onto your hard drive. It used to be possible to **drag** an application off a **disk** and onto the **hard drive** to complete the installation. But with applications getting larger and larger and requiring that items be saved in the **System Folder**, installation now involves multiple disks and an installer program. One of the most popular installers is Apple's, which is licensed for use to software developers. The Apple Installer offers an Easy Install option that installs all necessary files, as well as tutorials, samples, add-ons, and so on, or you can choose a custom install that enables you to choose which items you want to install from a scrolling list.

If you're installing your system from a set of disks, after you choose an installation option, the installer determines which elements from which disks are needed to complete installation. When the installer is finished with one disk's portion of the install, it **ejects** the disk and prompts you for the disk it needs to continue.

See Also

Click and Drag; Disks and Drives; Eject Disk Command; Hard Disks; System Folder

Integrated Data Viewer

A component of Apple Computer's **Cyberdog** suite of **Internet client** applications implementing OpenDoc technology.

Along with Cyberdog's standard **World Wide Web browser** window, the Integrated Data Viewer presents images, movies, or sounds.

Whereas other browsers such as **Netscape** or **Mosaic** might display an inline image as being in-line with the text or other **Web page** content, Cyberdog's Integrated Data Viewer presents information about the size and location of the image, as well as a set of "handles" that can be used by the user to resize the image within the Cyberdog browser window. (See the following figure.)

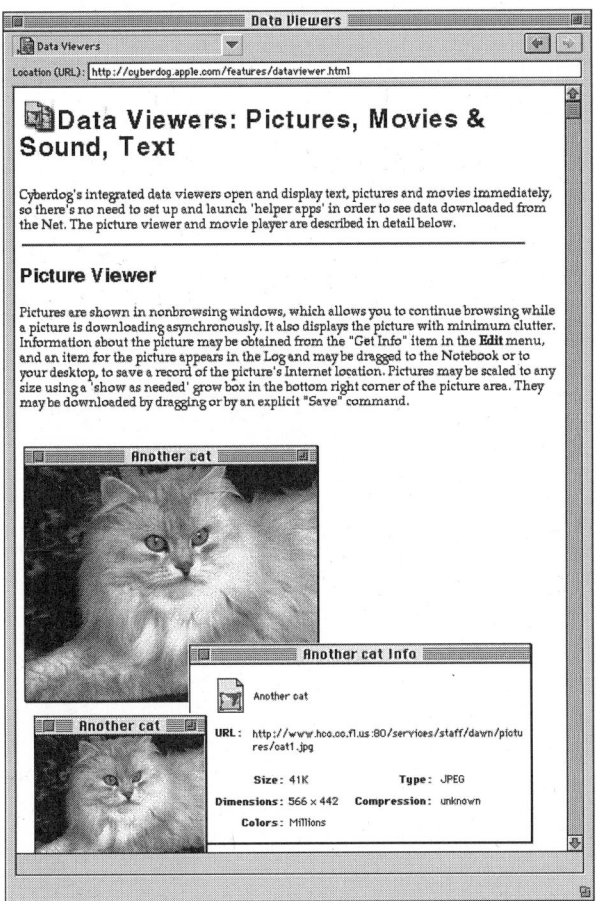

See Also

Client; Cyberdog; Internet; Web Browser; World Wide Web

Integrated Development Environment

The Integrated Development Environment (IDE) is a set of development tools designed to work together smoothly to manage all aspects of the programming process. IDEs typically include an **editor**, one or more **compilers**, and one or more **linkers** in a single application. They might also include a debugger in the same application, but it's just as likely that the debugger is a separate program closely linked to the IDE using **Apple Events**.

Unlike traditional development environments, where the burden of juggling various tools and keeping track of which source code files need to be recompiled is squarely on the programmer's shoulders, IDEs take much of that work away from the programmer.

IDEs usually organize all of the source code files and libraries into a project (see following figure). The project keeps track of which files have been changed and need to be recompiled. Relationships among source and library files are contained entirely in the project, and the makefiles required by other development environments typically are not needed.

In combination with the close integration of the editor, compiler, and linker, this gives IDEs a significant speed edge in development. It's not unusual to be able to make a change in a source code file, recompile, link, and run a program using an IDE in less time than it would take to just compile in a non-integrated environment.

Frequently, however, IDE tools are weak in their handling of very large projects. A project, for example, that includes 68K, Power Mac, and Fat versions of an application, along with an Extension or Control Panel and a custom menu definition function used in the application would be very difficult to build all at once in an IDE. Under MPW, on the other hand, it wouldn't be difficult to create a single script that takes care of the whole thing. As IDEs have become more and more scriptable, this shortcoming is gradually disappearing.

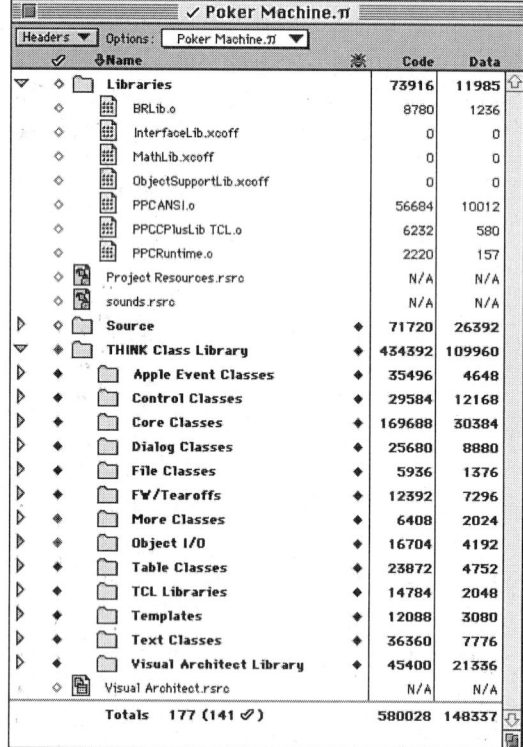

Most major development environments on the Macintosh are IDEs, with the significant exception being **MPW**. Part of the reason for this is that most non-integrated tools are designed to work in the MPW environment. In fact, many of the most popular IDE-based compilers (Symantec C++, CodeWarrior) are available in MPW versions for those programmers who would rather not use an IDE.

See Also

Apple Event; CodeWarrior; Compiler; Editor; Linker; MPW; Symantec C++

Integrated Services Digital Network, *See ISDN*

Intel Capabilities, Adding

There are two options for running Microsoft DOS and Windows 3.1 or 95 on your Mac: loading software that emulates the Intel world or installing a physical DOS-compatibility card that adds an Intel 486 chip set to your Mac.

Insignia Solutions markets SoftWindows 2.0, a PC software emulator for Macs. This is an upgrade to an original emulator that created a 286-based PC on the Mac but did not run 386-enhanced mode applications. The new software upgrade version 2.0 emulates the 486 instruction set at speeds approaching a 66MHz 486 on a 60MHz **Power Mac** with 16MB of RAM. A Windows 95 version of SoftWindows is also available, which

- Emulates an Intel 486 processor

- Provides Windows sound (.WAV format) integrated with Mac sound and microphone for Windows multimedia

- Provides simultaneous Mac and PC access to IPX and TCP/IP networks for both Ethernet and Token Ring networking with Novell Netware

- Can be controlled using AppleScript (the Mac's macro language)

- Supports Super VGA video resolution

Apple and third-party vendors offer DOS-compatibility cards for Power Macs and 68040 Macs, as well as 68040-based Macs with pre-installed PC cards that provide 50- and 66MHz 486DX2 and 100MHz DX4 chip sets. The Performa 640CD DOS Compatible and the LC 630 DOS Compatible provide built-in support for PC operating systems.

In addition, Orange Micro and Reply provide high-speed 486-based PC cards that include a Pentium OverDrive socket that lets you add a Pentium CPU (although the bus remains hobbled by the speed of the 486 processor). Orange Micro plans on offering a PCI expansion card based on the Pentium chip, as do Apple and Reply.

The following table provides an overview of the options available for adding Intel capabilities to your Mac.

See Also

Consumer Models, Macintosh Family; Power Macs, PCI Models

Running Windows on a Mac: The Available Options

Mac Model	PC Card Option	Features
Centris/Quadra 610, 650, Quadra 700, 800, 900, 950 and Power Mac 7100/66	Reply's DOS on Mac and DOS on Power Mac PDS cards	DOS on Mac comes in two speeds: 50MHz 486DX2 and 66MHz 486DX2; DOS on Power Mac Card comes in two speeds: 66MHz 486DX2 and 100MHz 486 DX4 DOS-Compatible cards in the PDS slot.
LC III, Performa 470 series, 550 series, 570 series, and Quadra 630 series SoftWindows 2.0	Apple Mac LC 630 DOS Compatible or Performa 640CD or DOS Compatible computers	Totally new computers or software emulation
Power Mac 7200, 7500, 8500, 9500	Orange Micro 400 Card or SoftWindows 2.0	PCI expansion card

Macintosh Microprocessor Technologies

Processor Model	Date Introduced	Clock Speed	Internal Cache	Bus Width	Mac Models
68000	1984	8 to 16.67 MHz	none	16-bit external bus and 32-bit internal bus	Classic, PowerBook 100, SE, Plus, 128K, 512KE
68020	1984	up to 33 MHz	256-byte instruction cache, optional 68851 PPMU	32-bit	LC and LC II, first generation Mac II
68030	1987	up to 33 MHz	built-in PPMU, 256-byte instruction	32-bit	Mac SE/30, Classic II, Color Classic, IIsi, IIci, and data caches IIcx, IIx, LCIII, IIvx, LC520, Macintosh TV

continues

Macintosh Microprocessor Technologies (continued)

Processor Model	Date Introduced	Clock Speed	Internal Cache	Bus Width	Mac Models
68040	1989	25 to 33 MHz	built-in PPMU, 4K data and instruction caches, subset of 6882 math coprocessor	6-stage pipeline, 32-bit bus width	LC/Performa 475, Performa 630 series, Centris/Quadra, 610, 650, Quadra 605, 660AV, 840AV, 700, 800, and 950, PowerBook 14x series, 16x series, 170, 180/180c, 5xx series, 190, Duo 2xx series. Workgroup Servers 60, 80, and 95
PPC 601	1994	60 to 100 MHz	32K data and instruction caches, built-in single-precision FPU	3 independently pipelined instruction units for 8-stage pipelining, 64-bit	6100, 7100, 8100, 7200. Workgroup Server 6150, 8150, and 9150
PPC 603 and 603e	1995	66 to 100 MHz	32K data and instruction caches, built-in single-precision FPU, power management features for lower power consumption	3 independently pipelined instruction units for 8-stage pipelining, 64-bit	Performa 5215, 62xx series, and 6300, PowerBook 5300, LC 5200
PPC 604	1996	100 to 150 MHz	double-precision FPU, 256K data and instruction caches	dynamic branch prediction and speculative execution, 64-bit	7500, 8500, 9500

Intellectual Property

The type of property protected by **copyright** law—original work such as plays, cartoons, television shows, personal letters, software, and so on. Intellectual properties are the children of the brain. **World Wide Web** pages, too, are intellectual property, and thus protected by copyright.

See Also

Copyright; Fair Use; World Wide Web

Intellidraw, *See Drawing Applications*

Intellihance

Intellihance works on CMYK, RGB, and Grayscale graphics. This Extensis plug-in operates either automatically or in accordance with adjusted manual input to change the selected graphic's tone, saturation, sharpness, and despeckling. Despeckling is a term used to indicate the removal of stand-alone pixels in the graphic, commonly introduced into scanned images (dust marks, and so on). In automatic mode, Intellihance adjusts the graphic according to its own intelligent assumptions based on a comprehensive investigation of the graphic. This investigation takes milliseconds, and usually goes unnoticed by the user. Passing the cursor over any selected pixel in the graphic produces a readout that describes what was changed and by how much. A comparative side-by-side view of the original graphic and a preview of the transformed graphic allows you to appreciate the changes visually, although most of the changes may be visually unnoticeable. A Preferences setting allows you to fine tune the image transformations according to Brightness (from Balanced Tones to Shadow alterations), Saturation, Sharpness (which usually adds some speckling), and Despeckle (which adds blurring).

The manual option (called "fine tuning") allows more interactive transforming with the selected graphic. Here, you can adjust the following parameters with interactive sliders: Tone (Black Point, Mid Point, White Point), Saturation (from -100 to +100), Sharpness (Amount, Radius and Threshold), and Despeckle (Amount, Lower and Upper Limits from 0 to 255). The result is an image whose every parameter is controlled by the user for printed output and visualization. The magic of Intellihance is that no matter the condition of the image addressed by it, it can intelligently and automatically apply the right stuff to bring it back from the dead.

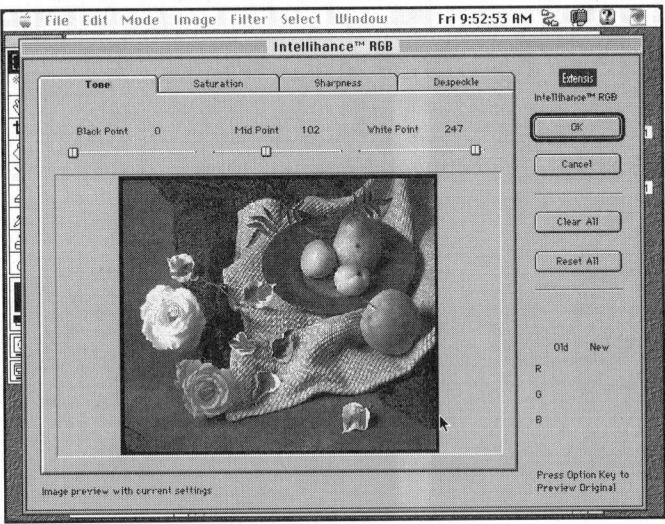

Interactive Fiction, *See Adventure Games; Hypertext; Non-Linear Storytelling Games; Return to Zork;*

Interactive Multimedia Association, *See IMA*

Interactive Presentation Programs

Interactive Presentation programs make it possible to create simple interactive presentations without **scripting**. This is usually accomplished with a library of simple actions (play a sound, mouse clicks, jump to a specified screen) that can be attached to on-screen objects. These objects act as buttons.

It's possible to create reasonably complex projects using programs such as Gold Disk Inc.'s Astound and Special Delivery. You can create kiosks, encyclopedias, and electronic brochures with these tools.

See Also

Astound

Interface Builder

Before the graphical user interface (**GUI**) of the Macintosh burst onto the scene, creating the interface of most applications was relatively simple. Because most interfaces were not graphical, they could easily be designed and laid out directly in the program's code. The Mac changed all that. With its easy-to-use interface came some programming challenges, including how to create an effective *visual* interface with non-visual tools.

This problem led to the development of today's crop of interface builders. Although interface builders exist for non-graphical computers as well, they are not as complex as those for graphical systems. Interface builders enable the programmer to "draw" the interface elements as they appear in the finished application.

The simplest interface builders are **resource** editors, such as **ResEdit** and **Resorcerer**. These enable you to visually edit simple interface elements, such as dialogs and menus. Much of the real programming work, however, is left up to you. Although Resorcerer can generate source code to handle dialog boxes, in more complicated situations, you're out of luck. The advantage of these editors as interface builders is that they work with virtually every development environment relying on standard Macintosh resources.

A significant step up from resource editors are view editors. These enable you to edit the visual view hierarchy used by a related application framework or class library. Metrowerks' **Constructor**, for example, enables you to visually edit the view resources used by Metrowerks' C++ framework, **PowerPlant**. Similarly, AdLib can be used to edit the visual hierarchy used by **MacApp** (see following figure). These interface builders do not generate code based on your interface, but they do build directly on the interface code provided by the underlying framework. In fact, in some simple cases, no additional programming is necessary.

Another step up the interface builder food chain are programs that generate much of the code needed to implement an interface. Symantec's Visual Architect and Bowers Development's AppMaker are in this category. **Visual Architect** generates code exclusively for the Think Class Library (TCL), whereas **AppMaker** generates code for PowerPlant, MacApp, TCL, or procedural programming.

Other kinds of interface builders exist for specialized programming projects. **FaceSpan**, for example, can create relatively sophisticated visual interfaces for **AppleScripts**. Many database access tools also provide visual interface builders for creating client interfaces to data stored in a database server.

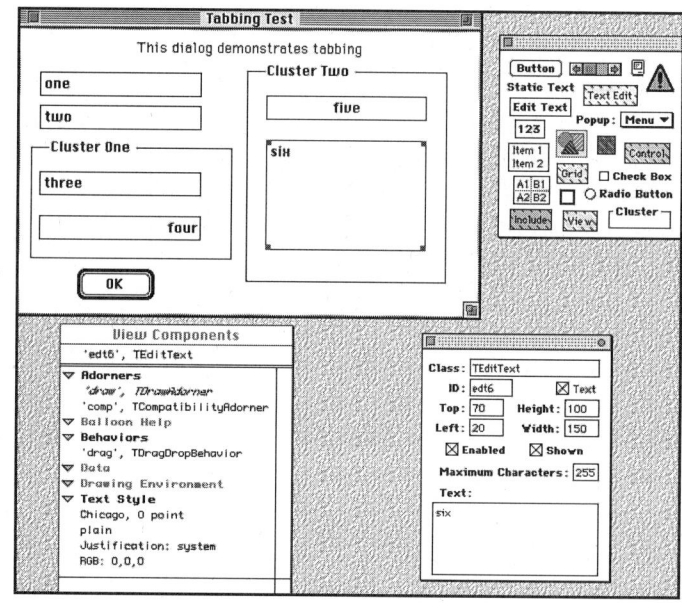

See Also

AppMaker; Constructor; FaceSpan; MacApp; PowerPlant; Resorcerer; Visual Architect

Interface Guidelines, *See Human Interface Guidelines*

Interleaving, *See Disks, Interleaving of*

Internal Cache, *See Power Macs, Logic Boards*

Internal Clock of the Macintosh

Because the Macintosh is such a symbiotic beast, it needs a coordinator to mediate between its hardware and software requirements. The coordinator or conductor for the Mac is its **internal clock**—a quartz crystal that vibrates millions of times per second when stimulated by electric current. (The vibrations are measured in megahertz (MHz), which is why we speak of "clock speeds" for microprocessors.) The internal clock's speed and its connecting circuitry controls the RAM by periodically refreshing the contents of its registers, the video display circuit's refresh rate is also governed by the clock speed, and the CPU uses the internal clock to time its access to RAM, ROM, and peripherals. The faster the clock rate, the better the performance of the computer.

Motorola produces microprocessors that resonate at different clock rates. An individual microprocessor, such as the PPC 601, can be produced and validated at several different clock rates. This is why some Power Macs with the same chips are faster than others, and why periodically Apple can give a speed boost to a Mac without renaming a model simply the exchanging a slower chip for one with a faster quartz crystal.

In November 1996, Apple is increasing the speeds of the 604 PowerPC chip to 200MHz, giving the PowerMac 7500, 8500, and 9500 a boost by replacing the 604 chip with the 604e chip.

> **TIP** Apple's plans for upgrading the second-generation Power Macs were taken from two articles in *MacWeek* by Joanna Pearlstein, 3/18/96 "Apple Plots 1996 CPU Paths" and 3/11/96 "Speed Bump Ahead for Power Macs."

See Also

Microprocessors; Processors 680x0 Family; Processors, PowerPC Family

International Electrical Commission, *See IEC*

International Keyboards (Keyboard Shortcut)

If you have a variety of international keyboard layouts in your **Keyboard control panel**, you can rotate them by using Option-⌘-Spacebar. For this keyboard shortcut to be activated, you **click** the **checkbox** entitled, "Use Option-⌘-Spacebar to rotate through keyboard layouts," on the Keyboard Control Panel.

To switch between international keyboards, use this keyboard shortcut:

1. Activate the keyboard layout toggle feature by clicking the check box in the keyboard control panel and then close the control panel.

2. Hold Option-⌘-Spacebar to toggle through layouts from the keyboard.

See Also

Checkbox; Click; Close Command; Control Panels; Keyboard Control Panel; Keyboard Shortcuts; Option Key; Spacebar

International Standards Organization, *See ISO*

International Telecommunications Union—Telecommunications Standards Sector, *See Modems*

Internet

A worldwide system of interconnected computer networks that enables data communication using services such as electronic mail (**email**), file transfer (**FTP**), the **World Wide Web**, and discussion groups (**newsgroups**).

The Internet (or, more commonly, the Net) is a way of connecting existing computer networks that greatly extends the reach of each participating computer and network. This network of networks consists of an immense number of participants, connected machines, software programs, and a massive quantity of information available almost instantly to any computer user worldwide.

Internet, Getting Connected Users wishing to connect their Mac to the Internet and access its services can use any of several different methods.

Partial Internet access can be achieved through **commercial online services** (such as **America Online**, **CompuServe**, and Apple's **Delphi**), local **bulletin board systems** (**BBSs**), **UNIX shell accounts**, and UUCP access.

Conversation with Adam Engst

Adam Engst helped launch the rest of us onto the Internet and the World Wide Web through his books (the latest being the *Internet Starter Kit for the Macintosh,* 3rd Edition, from Hayden Books) and updates (called TidBITS). You can get his latest advice by emailing info@tidbits.com, or get answers to some common questions via email at faq-adam@tidbits.com or via the Web at **http://www.tidbits.com/adam/FAQ.html.**

Maclopedia: Can you recall for us your first experience with a Mac?

Adam: In 1987 at Cornell University, I decided I wanted a job as a part-time operator in the public computer rooms. At the time, I had an Atari 1040ST and had barely ever used a Mac before. I was fairly fluent with DOS as well, and figured I could talk my way into the job. I could and I did, and figuring out how to help students on the Macs that made up half of the machines in the room I worked in was interesting, especially since many of them were taking programming courses. Amazing how much Pascal you can learn just from trying to help others. When in doubt, they forgot a semicolon...

Maclopedia: Did you have something to do with helping your parents turn to Macs? You mention that they use them in the *Internet Starter Kit.*

Adam: Yes and no. My parents had a Franklin Ace 1000 that was an Apple II clone, and it was actually the second one they'd gotten. I'd taken the first one to Cornell with me and used it until I got the Atari. Then, when the time came for them to get a new computer, I had a Mac and tried to convince them to get one, but my mother's department (Manuscripts and Archives) only had a single IBM PC. She wanted to be able to work on stuff at home, so they ended up buying some PC clone. I never liked that machine. Then, by the time that machine was nearing the end of its lifespan, the Archives had switched over to Macs, so Mom and Dad got an LCII, which they still use. I had agitated heavily for the Mac during the time of the PC, since I had to keep it running and generally help them with it. Even now, my sister and I generally help keep their Mac running, but they can do a lot more with the Mac than they ever dreamed possible with the PC.

Maclopedia: What was your experience with Macs when you were at Cornell?

Adam: As I said, I was an operator in one of the public computer rooms for a semester, and after that semester, I moved up in the ranks. The first summer I told my boss that I wanted to work full time, so I ended up taking care of another computer room for the entire day. That room had no Macs when I started, but during that summer we added 16 Macintosh SEs with a LocalTalk network and a pair of file servers. I helped design the room, and after that summer, I became a supervisor in charge [of] that room and others. A friend and I once realized we could set the shared bit on a program using ResEdit, and then multiple users could run the same program. This was useful because the only reason there were two servers in this public room was because it was the way the network people had decided on to hold 16 copies of MacDraw and the other software we had licensed for public use. Since we owned legitimate copies, my friend and I thought we could turn off an entire server and serve everything from a single one with a single copy of each program. We could, we did, and boy did we get in trouble for showing up the network people (we'd failed to ask for permission before attempting our little experiment).

Maclopedia: Do you think the Mac offers any particular advantages for people who want to use the Internet? The World Wide Web?

Adam: Yes, the Mac is by far the best Internet client machine, and that includes the Web, which is, after all, just another part of the Internet. The reason is simple. The Mac has always had the best and most consistent interface, and the more complicated the topic, the more important the interface is.

The Internet is a big, confusing place, and having a good interface on it is important. Web browsers tend to be less obviously different, since they're cross-platform to begin with, but technologies like Cyberdog show what happens when you rethink how information can and should be put together.

Maclopedia: What kind of experiences have you had with Apple employees?

Adam: I've run into two types of Apple employees. There are the sort who are just doing a job in a big company, and dealing with them is just what you'd expect. However, I've met many more people in Apple who are extremely bright, interesting folks trying to do the best job they can and still change the world. They're the people I like to hang out with when I go to trade shows, and they're the people I correspond with in email the most. I have a lot of respect for these people within Apple, since they're often fighting to produce greatness within a corporate structure, and that's not easy.

Maclopedia: What's your sense of the Apple culture?

Adam: There's a love-hate relationship people have with Apple and their Macs. Most people love their Macs and can't figure out what's in the drinking water in Cupertino. Despite that split, Mac users are the most incredibly loyal computer users I've ever run into and probably the most loyal brand customers around. The best example of this is Guy Kawasaki's EvangeList, which is a mailing list devoted to singing the praises of the Macintosh and damning the competition. The fact that you can create a mailing list of 20,000+ people who are willing to read such unabashed propaganda and contribute to it is utterly astonishing. You'd be hard

pressed to come up with a product or company that can boast such customer loyalty.

Maclopedia: What should intermediate to expert Mac users be taking advantage of, as far as tools for the Net and Web?

Adam: I think intermediate to expert Mac users should be using the best tools for the job on the Internet. Web browsers can do most things on the Internet, such as FTP, email, and Usenet news, but they're generally pretty lousy at anything other than browsing the Web. Beginners might have an excuse, but anyone who's trying to get much out of the Internet should be using tools like Anarchie, Eudora, NewsHopper, and NewsWatcher. Utilities like CyberFinder, Internet Config, and ICeTEe are essential once you get past the basics.

Maclopedia: Do you like the direction Apple seems to be headed in, combining some Net tools with Copland? If you were on the team, what advice would you give them?

Most people love their Macs and can't figure out what's in the drinking water in Cupertino.

Adam: I definitely think that building Internet tools into the operating system is a good move, but I'd caution them to remember the tenets of component software. If Apple's FTP part isn't as good as Peter Lewis's, then I want to be able to pull out Apple's easily and replace it. Apple should also seriously evangelize the best Internet developers and make sure that third-party tools can be integrated as deeply as possible. Users don't want to fuss with integration, and on the Mac they shouldn't have to.

I'd also try to get the team to think beyond the basics of what everyone does today and try to build in some technology that solves problems that really exist now. For instance, it's too hard to subscribe and unsubscribe from most mailing lists, and there's no standard way to turn one off while you go on vacation. Build in something that solves that problem—it's merely a matter of putting together the parts that exist today.

Full Internet access demands **MacTCP** and a direct (although possibly temporary) connection. Most often, these connections are accomplished via a phone line, a **modem**, and software to use the **PPP** or **SLIP** communication protocol with an Internet service provider, through whose host computer your Mac obtains Internet access. Constant, speedy connections are also possible via an **ISDN** line or a T1 or T3 dedicated line.

Internet, Hardware Two types of computers comprise the Internet: **hosts** and clients. Host computers (also called **servers**) are the machines that contain all the information and files that are consistently available online.

Client computers are the desktop computers or other machines used by people to request the information and/or files from host computers. The most common way for a client to connect to the Internet is via a modem and a phone line (see the following figure). Users can have their Macs dial into an Internet service provider, who runs a host machine directly connected to the Net, and thus be temporarily connected.

Internet, History The Internet began in 1969 as ARPANet, developed for the Advanced Research Projects Agency of the U.S. Department of Defense (ARPA).

ARPANet connected university, military, and defense contractors; its original intent was to assist researchers in sharing information. Much of that information centered on how to develop a decentralized communications network that could still operate if part of it was destroyed by nuclear attack.

Eventually, much of ARPANet's functions were taken over by the National Science Foundation Network (NSFNET), which linked researchers with five high-speed supercomputer centers. A standard protocol of choice was developed, **TCP/IP**, or Transmission Control Protocol/Internet Protocol. Because it was now possible for all sorts of computers to talk to each other, the Internet grew by leaps and bounds. In 1991 a new network was created that subsumed NSFNET: the National Research and Education Network, NREN.

These days, governmental dictates are giving way to commercial enterprise, and many companies take over maintenance of the network lines, and as businesses outpace governmental organizations in getting connected.

Internet, Size Numbers are difficult to track, because connections are often temporary and many users might connect via each machine. A CommerceNet/Nielsen survey released in October 1995 (**http://www.nielsenmedia.com/**) indicated that more than 24 million people in the U.S. and Canada use the Internet. However, another survey, by Find/SVP, reported only 9.5 million Internet users.

As of July 1995, there were 6,642,000 computers (or hosts) connected to the Internet, according to data collected by Network Wizards (**http://www.new.com/**).

Internet, Software Once users have a hardware connection to the Internet, software programs are needed to use **Internet services** such as email, newsgroups, and the **World Wide Web**. These applications (also called clients) enable the Mac to request and receive information from a remote server. MacTCP enables a Mac to speak the TCP/IP language and thus understand and be understood by other computers. Other software, such as MacPPP, is necessary for connecting via a modem

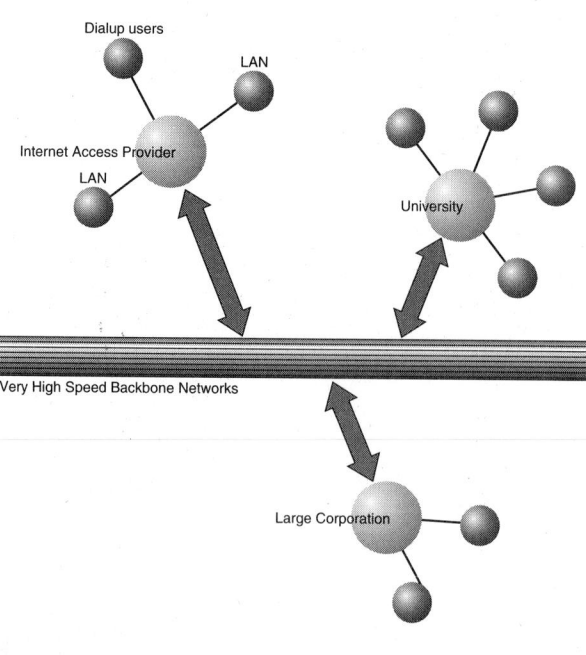

Dialup users
LAN
Internet Access Provider
LAN
University
Very High Speed Backbone Networks
Large Corporation

For More...

If you want to do this...	*Go to this entry...*
Learn about Internet services	Internet, Services
Get on the Web	World Wide Web, The
Know what HTML is	HTML
Browse the newsgroups	Newsgroups, Subscribing
Create a Web page	Web Page
Know what a server is	Macintosh Family; Web Site, How to Organize; Workgroup Servers
Know where to find Mac software	Internet; Macintosh Software Archives

Bibliography

For more information on the Internet, refer to the following references:

Internet Starter Kit for the Mac, 3rd Edition, Adam Engst, published by Hayden Books: **http://www.mcp.com/hayden/iskm/**.

Publishing on the World Wide Web, Greg Holden, published by Hayden Books.

Global Network Navigator's Internet section: **http://gnn.com/wic/wics/internet.new.html**

Internet Adapter, The, *See TIA*

Internet Address, *See IP Address*

Internet, Areas, *See Internet Services*

Internet, Educational Resources on

The **Internet** has something for everyone, and a lot of what's there is geared toward students and teachers. That's not surprising, because it originated on college campuses as a way to tie research projects to the National Science Foundation and to the other government agencies that funded them. The material on the Internet isn't only for college-level students and faculty, though. There are areas devoted to kindergarten, pre-K, Montessori, and grades 1–12. A **WebCrawler** search on "Montessori" found 88 different sites. A search on "elementary school" found 38,282 pages! And many of these have "pointers" or links to other interesting places.

There are many wonderful pages for kids and parents or teachers to explore on the **World Wide Web**. Start with a single site such as the Hands-On Children's Museum (**http://www.wln.com/~deltapac/hocm.html**) and branch out to other recommended places (see the following figure).

Their Ocean Odyssey section alone has 33 pointers to other ocean-related sites. But don't leave kids to play unsupervised. Despite the attempts to regulate what goes onto it, some of the content may be educational in ways a parent or teacher might not appreciate. Turning younger kids loose to surf the Net unattended is about as sensible as turning them loose in Times Square at midnight.

The Web can take you and your kids to places you could never go otherwise, even to places that don't exist. Boston's Museum of Science has recently placed on view on the Web a Virtual Museum with exhibits that go far beyond what's possible in a real museum. There's a dinosaur "exhibit" called Dinosauria at the

University of Berkeley (**http://ucmp1.berkeley.edu/diapsids/dinosaur.html**) that uses illustration and hypertext to take you on an detailed field trip through time, back 65 million years.

The Internet can even save you a trip to the library. Project Gutenberg (named for the inventor of moveable type) is bringing some ten thousand volumes to the computer screen. Volunteers at the Illinois Benedictine College have entered several thousand books to date (all beyond copyright or cleared, of course) as text. Such works as *Moby Dick*, *Alice in Wonderland*, and the *Scarlet Letter* can be downloaded from the Project Gutenberg FTP site, along with a catalog of all the available works. The address is (**http://www.jg.cso.uiuc.edu/pg/pg_home.html**).

Academy One is an on-line educational resource for students, educators and parents at **http://www.nptn.org/cyber.serv/AOneP**. This site presents a collection of curricula, contests, forums, and references, for K–12. It's maintained by the National Public Telecomputing Network. CollegeNET, another World Wide Web site (**http://www.unival.con/cn/collegenet.html**) includes connections to hundreds of colleges and universities, scholarship searches, discussion groups on a variety of subjects, a connection to the Princeton Review SAT prep courses, and important information on SAT, GRE, GMAT, and other entrance exams.

There are many more resources than can be listed here, and new ones are being added virtually every day. The best way to discover Web sites that will be relevant to your needs is to use a Web search utility such as **Lycos** (**http://www.lycos.com/**) or **WebCrawler** (**http://webcrawler.com/**).

See Also

Internet; Lycos; WebCrawler

Internet Explorer

A full-featured **browser** or **client** program for navigating the **World Wide Web** offered by Apple's arch rival Microsoft.

Internet Explorer, originally released for the Windows 95 platform to act as gateway to the Microsoft Network on the Internet, was released for the Macintosh in beta version in early 1996.

Internet Explorer claims to require less memory than other browsers. It does have some unique features—mainly, Microsoft's extensions to HTML, which create some exciting effects that, however, can be viewed only with Internet Explorer:

- A <MARQUEE> tag that makes text scroll across the Web browser screen, like a theater marquee.

- The capability to create "startup sounds" that play when a reader accesses a **Web page**.

- Support for in-line video.

Internet Explorer allows users to read **Usenet** news from within the browser using many **HTML** 3.0 commands and **Netscape** extensions.

Home page: **http://198.105.232.4:80/windows/ie/mac/macdl.htm**

See Also

Client; NCSA Mosaic; Netscape Navigator; PPP; SLIP; Web Browser; World Wide Web

Internet Gaming, *See Online Live Games; Shareware; MUDs and MOOs*

Internet Multicasting Service

A news and information service consisting of audio files distributed on the **Internet**, both as audio-on-demand archives and live IP multicasts.

IMS, which is supported by a number of corporations including IBM, MCI, Sun Microsystems, and O'Reilly and Associates, provides audio programs about Internet-related topics. IMS also multicasts programming from Monitor Radio, World Radio Network, CBS News, and the U.S. Congress when in session.

Internet Talk Radio files are accessible in sites around the world via **anonymous FTP**. All files are in .au format. A half-hour program is a 15MB file.

Home page: **http://town.hall.org/radio/**

See Also

AIFF Files; Anonymous FTP; .AU Files; Internet; MBONE; RealAudio; World Wide Web

Internet Protocol (IP)

Internet protocol is a protocol or set of standards designed to provide a universal method for locating and addressing **host** and client computers connected to the **Internet**.

IP was developed in 1981 for the Department of Defense Advanced Research Projects Agency (ARPA), which operated the Internet at that time. IP provides a way for interconnected computer networks to transfer "packets" of information from one computer to another. Each computer has a standard **IP address**, a series of four numbers separated by dots.

For more information see the Internet Working Group Request for Comments (RFC) 791 (**ftp://ds.internic.net/rfc/rfc791.txt**).

See Also

Host; Internet; IP Address; Servers; TCP/IP

Internet Relay Chat, *See IRC*

Internet, Searching/Navigating

A number of utilities can be used to search for specific data and navigate through the rich resources of information contained on the **Internet**.

Each of the **Internet services** organizes information differently; therefore, each has its own way of searching for information. The various search engines are described in detail elsewhere in *Maclopedia* (see entries in boldface). This following table summarizes the various search tools.

See Also

Anarchie; Archie; Anonymous FTP; FTP; HotJava; InfoSeek; Internet; Internet Services; Jughead; Lycos; Macintosh Software Archive; Mailing Lists; Mosaic; NCSA; Netscape; NewsWatcher; Telnet; Turbo Gopher; Veronica; WAIS; WebCrawler; World Wide Web

FTP (File Transfer Protocol)	Users generally employ a *client program* (such as a Fetch or **Anarchie**) to gain access to an FTP server that holds a great deal of information they can download, such as **software archives** or **mailing lists**.
Anonymous FTP	Users can log in anonymously using a program like Fetch.
Archie	A directory of anonymous FTP sites around the world, accessible via **Telnet**, or **email**, **Gopher** or **World Wide Web** clients.
Gopher	Users can run the client program **TurboGopher** to navigate Gopherspace, and conduct searches using **Veronica** or **Jughead**.
Telnet	**NCSA** Telnet is the most common Telnet application for the Macintosh.
Usenet	**NewsWatcher** is a popular client, as is **Netscape Navigator**; **DejaNews** and **InfoSeek** provide searches through newsgroup articles.
World Wide Web	Client software includes Netscape Navigator, **Mosaic**, **MacWeb**, **HotJava**; search engines include **InfoSeek**, **Lycos**, and **WebCrawler**.
WAIS	MacWAIS is a common client for WAIS servers.

Internet Servers, *See Workgroup Servers, Macintosh Family*

Internet Service Bureaus

A lot of people thought it was pretty funny when they found out you can order a pizza over the World Wide Web. But those same people probably won't laugh when they find out you can order printing services over the Internet—they'll be too busy figuring out just how much time and money they can save.

A new category of service bureaus offers customers the ability to receive near-instant turnaround on job estimates via email. Jobs can be submitted over the Internet as well, using **FTP**. These companies offer printing, copying, and binding services similar to those offered by local quick print shops, but they only work from electronic files. **Yahoo** lists a number of such businesses under Business_and_Economy: Companies: Communications and Media Services: Desktop Publishing.

See Also

FTP; Service Bureaus, Trade Shops, and Desktop Publishing; Yahoo

Internet Service Provider

An Internet Service Provider is a business or other organization that provides users with access to the **Internet**, either by letting the users dial in with **modems** to servers maintained by the provider or through providing them with faster direct connections.

Some "providers" are actually computer offices in universities or other large organizations that provide connections to employees, faculty, or students. Most are small businesses whose main customer base consists of dial-in modem users. Cable and telecommunications companies are beginning to offer Internet access along with their other services.

The criteria used to choose an Internet provider differs depending on one's needs. Those who want to dial up to the Internet for personal or family use won't have requirements as elaborate as those who need to establish a business online.

The most important thing is to find a provider that is either close to home or that offers toll-free access, so as to escape high telephone bills.

The type of Internet service you obtain from a provider depends on your level of use: whether you plan on using the Internet for personal communications and information-gathering, or whether you plan on starting a business online.

For personal use, that is, if you need to send and receive email, post and receive newsgroup messages, a **shell**, **SLIP**, or **PPP** connection is adequate. Shell accounts require you to use a command-line interface and usually to learn associated UNIX commands. SLIP and PPP accounts allow you to use MacTCP-based applications like **Web browsers**.

If you plan to go beyond simply navigating the Internet and instead want to start up an online business, you need to consider a leased line or 56Kbps link. If you might have up to a hundred visitors at once, you might have to get one or more T1 lines or a much more expensive T3 link. You also need to be prepared to create a **Web site** with a home page or pages for your business and possibly additional documents connected by hypertext links. You will be responsible for updating the contents of the site and for responding to requests or inquiries from your visitors. Discuss with your provider how many visitors you expect to have and whether you will need assistance with processing data obtained via forms or other feedback mechanisms.

The following table describes some of the typical types of connections offered by Internet service providers:

Internet Service Provider Accounts

Account	Description
Shell account	The basic bare-bones connection to the Internet. Allows users to send and receive **email**, **telnet**, **FTP**, **gopher**, and so on, but not MacTCP-based applications like Web browsers.
TIA (The Internet Adapter)	Inexpensive commercial product that allows users to run a shell account as a SLIP or PPP account.
SLIP/PPP	Basic protocols that allow users to dial up with a modem and connect to the Internet and use Mac-based graphical client software.
ISDN	High-speed network connections that provide access to the Internet via dial-up digital modems.
Leased lines	56K, T1 through T3 lines that have high speed and high **bandwidth**. Can run from $285 for the 56Kbps line to over $800 for the faster links.

A service provider can give you different types of access to the Internet, such as:

FTP   Offers users anonymous FTP space to transfer information to and from the Internet.

LAN   With a direct connection to the Internet from an ISDN service or leased lines, a user can connect a local area network to the Internet. You don't get aLAN account, but a Direct Connection or full-time connection. With proper hardware on the user's side, you can connect a LAN.

WWW   Provides space for publishing and maintaining Web pages.

Good questions to ask a potential provider include:

1. How reliable is the network connection provided by the provider? How often does the connection fail, and how often does the provider's computer equipment crash?

2. What type of connection does the provider have to the Internet? What is the **bandwidth** or capacity of that connection?

3. Does the provider have only one connection to the Internet, or several direct connections to other Internet providers to serve as backups in case of trouble?

4. How many people are on staff? Are staff people available nights, weekends, or holidays in case the system goes down?

5. Does the provider have an "Appropriate Use Policy" that users must observe? Does the provider limit access to particular information?

See Also

Anonymous FTP; Email; FTP; Internet; MacTCP; Modems; Network; PPP; Telnet; TIA; Web Page; World Wide Web

Internet, Services

There are a variety of different interfaces or protocols for locating, copying, and presenting information on the Internet.

Each Internet Service has its own **browser** or **client** software. Some services work particularly well with specific hardware configurations, such as terminals, and some specific types of data the others cannot access, such as **multimedia** files or **electronic mail**.

Most Internet Services require a connection to the Internet that uses the set of **protocols** called **TCP/IP**, or Transmission Control Protocol/Internet Protocol. Most computers, and virtually all Macintoshes, can communicate on the Internet using these protocols with **MacTCP**.

The location of a specific document, site, or object on any of the services can be located by specifying its Internet address, called a **Uniform Resource Locator (URL)**.

The following table names and describes the various Internet services, the kinds of information they can process, and some examples of typical client software.

Internet Services

Service	*Description*	*Information*	*Client Software*
Electronic Mail	Widespread system of interpersonal and business communications	Email messages, mailing lists, newsletters, multimedia (MIME) mail	Eudora, QuickMail, POPmail,
Usenet	Internet discussion groups; users subscribe to group(s) based on a topic of interest	Opinions, rumors, tips, and views posted in articles; discussion occurs in article "threads"	NewsWatcher, Nuntius, InterNews
File Transfer Protocol (FTP)	Method of retrieving and transferring software, text, and other data	Software archives, databases, libraries	Fetch, Anarchie
World Wide Web	Hypertext-based graphical information interface	Web sites and home pages published by educational, governmental, commercial, and nonprofit organizations as well as individuals	Netscape, Mosaic, MacWeb, TCP/Connect II
Gopher	Network of Gopher servers that present information in list-based, window-oriented format	News, library catalogs, FTP sites, discussion groups, phone books	TurboGopher
Wide Area Information Servers (WAIS)	Searches many online information sources and responds to complex queries	Virtually unlimited. Relates keywords and presents results using relevance feedback	MacWAIS, HyperWAIS
Telnet	Enables a computer to connect to a computer network; uses a command-line interface to access text-based information	Library catalogs, news, weather	NCSA Telnet, Comet, TN3270, MicroPhone and other telecommunications packages

Service	Description	Information	Client Software
Internet Relay Chat (IRC)	Multi-user real-time chat system	Discussion, gossip, argument, occasional celebrity interviews	ircle, Homer IRC
Multi-User Dungeon/ Multi-User Dimension (MUD)	Users assume alter egos and interact in virtual environments	Imaginative, escapist human online interactions	MacMud, MuDDweller, Meeting Space

Internet services are by no means mutually exclusive. All the services can be accessed from your Macintosh, and they often work together. You can use your World Wide Web browser to send and receive **email** and run **Telnet** as a helper application, for instance. Your choice of service depends on several factors:

1. The sort of information you want to access.

2. The way you connect to the Internet.

3. The computer equipment you use.

For instance, if you want to retrieve a large amount of information in answer to a specific question or set of keywords, you might try MacWAIS to connect a **WAIS** server. If you can't get connected to the World Wide Web due to computer memory or other constraints, try **Gopher**. To gauge other computer users' reactions to a new piece of software, or to share theories and ideas on virtually any topic, connect to a **newsgroup**, read the current articles, or join in a discussion thread. You can also subscribe to a **mailing list** to find out more about a topic of interest. To talk to others just for fun, get on an **Internet Relay Chat** line or, if you're feeling adventurous, a **MUD**.

Internet Services, Gateways A *gateway* connects two dissimilar networks, translating information so that it can pass transparently from one to the other. BITNET, FidoNet, and UUCP networks act as mail

and file gateways to the Internet. Gateways connect the various parts of the Internet, including some of the Internet services, to each other. In reality, though, the services aren't separate at all, but rather, different ways of accessing the same information, as shown in the following figures.

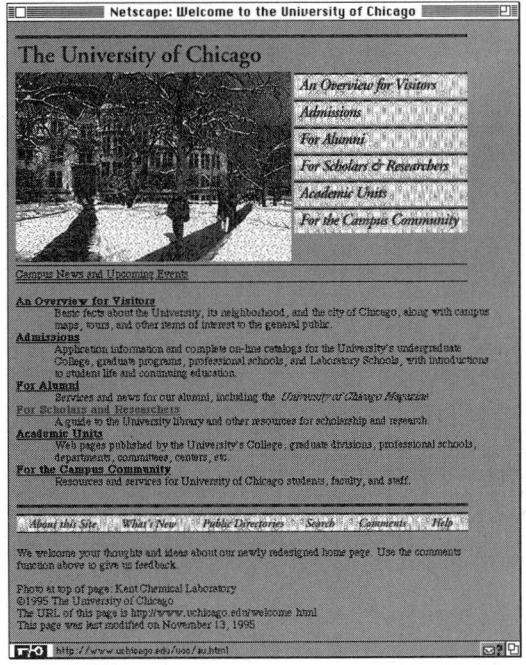

Internet Services, Obtaining Most of the client software for Internet Services can be obtained freely over the Internet itself. The first step is to obtain an Internet connection from an **Internet Service Provider (ISP)**. Most providers will give you software such as Fetch that can be used to download **shareware** Web browsers or other clients via FTP.

See Also

Anarchie; Email; FTP; Gopher; Home Page; HTML; Hypertext; Internet; IRC; MacWeb; Mailing List; Mosaic; MIME; MUDs and MOOs; Multimedia; Netscape Navigator; TCP/IP; Telnet; TurboGopher; Usenet; WAIS; Web Browser; Web Page; World Wide Web

Internet Talk Radio, *See Internet Multicasting Service*

Internetwork

An internetwork has nothing to do with "The Internet." (Technically, the Internet is actually a **WAN**.) An internetwork is composed of multiple Local Area Networks in one geographically contiguous area that have been joined together. Interconnecting these networks allows the users from each area to exchange email and files and allows for centralized management of the individual workstations. Say you have a suite of offices, and each office has two or three Macs networked together with LocalTalk and a PhoneNet daisychain. Each office has its own LAN. If you use **bridges**, **hubs**, or some other method to join the several separate LANs together, you'll create an internetwork.

Internetworks function in a similar manner to the individual local area networks (LANs), but they do require additional equipment to manage the flow of traffic between the individual LANs. Routers, bridges, repeaters, and hubs are commonly used to form the internetwork.

The interconnection of LANs spread over wide geographic areas is known as a Wide Area Network (WAN). The difference between a WAN and an internetwork is one of distance. The internetwork is still more or less local, whereas the WAN can be cross-country if necessary.

See Also

Bridges; Hub; Wide Area Network

Interpreted Language

Before any program can be executed by a computer, it must be converted from human-readable source code into **machine language** instructions that the computer can understand. Interpreted languages perform this conversion one instruction at a time as the program runs. This is in contrast to **compiled languages**, which convert source code into machine code in a single batch process before the program executes.

Interpreted languages typically incur a significant speed penalty because of the translation step that must take place before each line of code can be executed. This significant disadvantage may be outweighed by some of the advantages of interpreted languages. Because interpreted programs don't exist in machine code until they are executed, they are often much more portable than compiled programs. Provided that an interpreter exists on each type of computer, the program can be used on many different computers without change.

Interpreted languages are also capable of a much faster development time because there is no delay between making a change to some code and being able to execute that code. If the code needed to be compiled, you would have to wait for the compilation and linking to occur before you could run it. This delay may be insignificant for small programs, but for large ones it could be huge. As a result, some traditionally compiled languages are now available in special interpreted versions designed just for **debugging**.

Although most languages can be implemented as either interpreted or compiled, some are most frequently interpreted, such as **BASIC**. In addition, most macro and **scripting** languages are also implemented using an interpreter.

Another source code conversion method straddles the line between compiled and interpreted. See the **Compiled Language** entry for a discussion of these *byte-code compilers* used in languages such as Java.

See Also

BASIC; Compiled Language; Java; Machine Language

InterSLIP

Popular freeware program by InterCon that provides Serial Line Internet Protocol (SLIP) connection to the **Internet** through a dial-up **modem**. Although it is freeware, InterSLIP offers functionality equivalent to commercial programs.

To install InterSLIP, place the extension InterSLIP in your Extensions folder. A **control panel** called InterSLIP Control is available but only necessary for System 6 users. An application, InterSLIP Setup, must also be installed on your hard disk. It's a good idea to put it or an alias to it in the Apple Menu Items folder for easy access. After placing those items in the cor-

rect locations, restart your Mac. Make sure InterSLIP is selected in the main window of the MacTCP control panel, and then proceed with configuring InterSLIP.

The InterSLIP Setup application is used to configure your connection. Launch InterSLIP Setup, and from the "File" menu choose "New." InterSLIP Setup prompts you for a name with a dialog box; name your configuration and click "OK."

After creating the configuration, you must enter the correct settings for your particular modem and account. You need information from your system administrator to configure InterSLIP. (See the entry for **SLIP** for a list of questions to ask.) When you have the information, double-click the name of your configuration in InterSLIP Setup to open the configuration dialog box, as shown in the following figure.

After you have entered your modem name, password, and other settings, InterSLIP is easy to operate. Click "OK" to close the configuration window. In the InterSLIP Setup window, click "Connect." (Make sure your modem is connected and on.)

InterSLIP dials your host and signs in with a series of messages. The "Connected" message means you have connected successfully. When you are not connected, you will see the message "Idle." As soon as you connect, the "Connect" button becomes disabled and the "Disconnect" button becomes enabled. There is no automatic disconnection, so you must make sure to click the "Disconnect" button when you're finished using your SLIP account.

See Also

Asynchronous Data Transfers; Internet; MacPPP; Modems; Packet; Parity; PPP; SLIP

Intranet

An intranet is a company-wide internal network or "web" allowing file sharing and communication between offices, branches, or other companies via the **Internet** and **World Wide Web server** software.

Although all of the information contained on an intranet would be accessible to company employees, part or all of the contents could be restricted to outsiders via **password protection**, especially if the company uses a *firewall*, a security system set up to prevent outsiders from reaching a given URL or server.

The advantage to a company is that information contained on the internal network would be accessible across different computer platforms. Also, many types of information could be displayed.

See Also

Internet; World Wide Web

Inventory Control Software

Businesses that are concerned with sales, rather than services, must keep an updated inventory of the products they sell, so that they know when a particular item is running low and needs to be re-ordered. **Big Business**, from Big Software, does this quite elegantly. After you enter basic information about an item and its vendor, the program tracks the sale of that item and subtracts that order from the stock on hand. The program reminds you to order "at least" a specified number of units. It also lets you know that it's time to re-order, whenever the stock falls below a specified amount, and prints the appropriate purchase order.

Built items, items constructed from other products, are tracked as single items after they are built. A gourmet food basket, for instance, is *built* out of a basket, a box of candy, a bottle of wine, and a bag of mixed nuts. The individual box, bag, bottle, and basket are not sold separately. Prior to building the package, the components are tracked separately. When the package is assembled, the component items are removed from inventory.

Items sold as a bundle also are tracked separately. Bundled items are meant to be sold separately but are also sold together for a special price. An example might be the holiday promotion that gives you a chocolate Santa with each fruitcake you buy. The program adjusts for the bundle price and correctly removes one each of the items in the bundle from the inventory.

See Also

Big Business

Iomega Drives, *See Backing Up with Removable Cartridge Drives; Zip Drive*

IP, *See Internet Protocol (IP)*

IP Address

A four-part number that uniquely identifies a machine connected to the **Internet**. IP stands for *Internet Protocol,* the main protocol used on the Internet.

Your Internet service provider needs to assign you an IP address so it can route communications to and from your computer through its domain name server (**DNS**) and out to the Internet.

IP addresses are assigned more easily recognizable domain names, which consist of two or more words. For example:

```
IP address: 198.137.231.1
domain name: halcyon.com
IP address: 128.135.0.0
domain name: uchicago.edu
```

In some cases, your Internet provider will give you a manually addressed account that has a "static" IP address; that is, one that does not change. In many other cases, the **server** will assign you an address that is "dynamic;" that is, it differs every time you connect to the Internet, depending on what IP number is available at the time.

It becomes important to know your IP address and whether it is static or dynamic when you configure your computer software to connect to the Internet. Software such as **MacTCP**, **InterSLIP**, and **MacPPP** require that you enter your IP address information in their configuration dialog boxes.

For instance, in the MacTCP configuration dialog shown in the following figure, you choose one of the buttons in the top left section to specify whether you have a Manual, Server, or Dynamically assigned IP address. In the bottom right section, you type your Internet provider's domain name and its IP address(es).

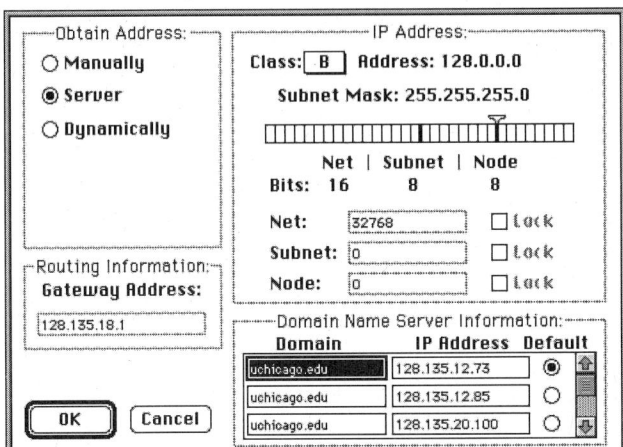

See Also
DNS; Internet; Internet Service Provider; Network; Server

IRC

Internet Relay Chat is a method of conducting real-time communications with other individuals on the **Internet**.

Internet Relay Chat (IRC) was developed by Jarkko Oikarinen of Finland in 1988 and has since spread around the world. Computer users connected to the Internet gather in groups called *channels,* usually devoted to a specific subject. Private conversations are also possible.

IRC is one of the most popular Internet services, although the communication usually amounts to little more than casual "chatting." Parents, of course, should be aware of the potential for abuse by children who either overuse "chat" or use it to discuss "adult" topics, sometimes referred to as "Hot Chat."

Two IRC client programs for the Macintosh are **ircle** and **Homer**. Users launch one of these programs and connect to one of several IRC servers, where they can either start a new chat channel or join one already in progress. Each channel is usually devoted to one topic, like a **newsgroup**, the difference being that on IRC the communication is instantaneous.

After the connection is made, whatever the user types is transmitted to other chatters around the world. The various messages and responses scroll by on the Macintosh monitor, which resembles a back-and-forth conversation.

For more information about IRC visit the IRC-Related Resources on the Internet site: **http://urth.acsu.buffalo.edu/irc/WWW/ ircdocs.html**.

See Also
CU-SeeMe; Internet

Ircle, *See IRC*

ISDN

ISDN (Integrated Services Digital Networking) is an extension to the standard public-switched telephone network that allows for telephone company customers to transmit digital data directly over the telephone wires without the use of a modem. Your Macintosh connects to an ISDN line through the use of a terminal adapter, or TA. While it's easiest to understand a TA by thinking of it as an "ISDN modem" this is technically incorrect—by definition, a modem modulates and demodulates signals from digital to analog and back to digital to allow transmissions of digital signals through the analog telephone network.

An ISDN Terminal Adapter places digital computer signals onto the phone company's digital network. (It also does some signal filtering and conditioning, but that's a relatively minor point.) The telephone companies have made ISDN service available in many areas, although it's far from universal. It requires special switching and signal handling devices at the central office although, contrary to some previously published information, it does *not* require fiber-optic cabling or anything other than ordinary telephone wire.

Standard ISDN service, known as PRI (Primary Rate Interface) consists of two lines (Bearer, or B-Channels), each capable of transfer rates of up to 64Kbps. Many ISDN TA's allow the two b-channels to be multiplexed together to form a single 128KBps transfer stream using protocols such as Bonding mode 1, or Multilink PPP.

It is important to understand that despite the theoretical 128K speed of a bonded ISDN connection, your Macintosh can only communicate with the TA as fast as the ports available to the Mac. For example, if you connect a TA to the Macintosh via the Modem port, older Macs cannot reliably reach speeds much beyond 38,400 bps. It's rather like driving a horse and buggy down an eight-lane superhighway. No matter what the speed limit of the road might be, the horse can't run more than about 20 miles an hour. PowerPC Macs can reach speeds of 115,000Kbps, but normal Mac terminal programs are require the use of Asynchronous communication, which slows down overall throughput. Even though the PowerPC "horse" runs fast, the buggy slows her down.

To make the best use of ISDN's speed, you will need a router that features a synchronous 128Kbps WAN port. This router can then transfer data to the Macintosh through a high speed Ethernet Port. It's akin to trading in the horse and buggy for a sports car.

ISDN and Digital Telephone Lines ISDN is a service provided by your local telephone company which is now available to most businesses and schools and as well as many residential locations. ISDN provides high-speed communications as an affordable price. With the basic service more than four times faster than the fastest **modem**, ISDN makes browsing the **World Wide Web** nearly instantaneous.

Communications over ISDN is faster than modem communications over **analog telephone lines** for two reasons. First, an ISDN connection device doesn't have to convert between analog and digital signals. Second, digital signals are much simpler than analog signals, and can be sent over the lines at faster rates than analog signals with better signal quality. Digital ISDN lines don't generate the kind of static you sometimes hear on standard analog telephone lines.

ISDN includes integrated voice communication, and many ISDN terminal adapters let you plug in a standard telephone handset. With ISDN, you can make a voice telephone call at the same time you send data. However, most experts recommend holding on to your analog line. Unlike analog lines, ISDN lines require power to operate. In an emergency in which your building loses power, your ISDN lines will be dead while your analog lines continue to function.

The costs of BRI ISDN service vary in different parts of the country, but can be anywhere from $20 to $50 per month. There is usually a one-time installation fee as well. The cost of ISDN is more than for standard analog telephone service, but is far less than for other high-speed options, such as dedicated **T1** lines or **Switched 56** service.

ISDN Terminal Adapters When a digital ISDN line comes into your building, you need one or two pieces of hardware to connect a Mac to it. Technically, there are two devices required—an ISDN adapter and a network terminator, called an NT1. However, you will often find the functionality of both of these devices built into one piece of hardware. You can tell if a device has a built-in NT1 if it has an ISDN "U" connector on it. Some devices connect a single Mac to the ISDN line, while others others connect to a network.

An ISDN adapter device can connect to a Mac as a plug-in card that fits into an expansion slot, or as an external device that plugs into a Mac serial port. Devices that connect to serial ports are slower than cards, because they are limited by the serial port speed, which is 56Kbps in older Macs or 115Kbps in the case of the GeoPort-enabled serial ports in Power Macs. This is slightly less than the full bandwidth of the ISDN Basic Rate Interface (BRI), which can carry 128Kbps maximum. ISDN expansion cards can transfer data at higher rates of speed, and can also offer the use of more ISDN channels than the 3 channels of BRI, However, cards often don't have built-in NT-1 functionality. Low-priced external devices such as the Motorola BitSURFR Pro and the Farallon Netopia do have a built-in NT-1.

ISDN adapters that connect to the serial port are sometimes called digital modems or ISDN modems. Some even use standard modem cables to connect the Mac. However, digital modems or ISDN modems are not actually modems at all, since there is no modulation or demodulation required for digital transmission, as there is with analog.

You can also get shared network devices, sometimes called ISDN routers, that connect to an Ethernet network and give every computer on the network access to the ISDN line. Farallon's Netopia Internet Router is a good example. These devices are the digital equivalent to shared network modems.

Most ISDN adapters come with the Mac software required to make a basic connection. There are also third-party software packages that add special functionality over ISDN, such as file transfer or video conferencing.

See Also
Analog Telephone Line; ISDN; Modems

ISO

The ISO (International Organization for Standardization) is a worldwide federation of national standards bodies from some 100 countries.

Established in 1947, the ISO is a non-governmental organization whose mission is to promote the development of standardization in the world with a view to facilitating the international exchange of goods and services, and to develop cooperation in the spheres of intellectual, scientific, technological, and economic activity.

ISO-9660

ISO-9660 is an international standard file system for **CD-ROMs** developed by the International Standards Organization. An ISO-9660 disc is readable on Macintosh, MS-DOS, and Windows systems, making it the ideal way of creating cross-platform discs. Unfortunately, because ISO-9660 does not support **resource forks** in files, it's not possible to place a Macintosh application on an ISO-9660 disc and have it play from the disc. If you need to place a Macintosh

application on a CD-ROM that is playable on both platforms, see **Mixed-Mode CD**. It is possible to transport a Macintosh application on an ISO-9660 disc, but the application is in an encoded format that must be copied from the CD and converted before it will run. One way to encode application files is to use the hqx or **BinHex** format.

Because **Adobe Acrobat** (pdf) files are byte-compatible (they can be read by different operating systems without any conversion), consider using ISO-9660 to distribute them. Other file formats that are byte compatible (and are therefore ideal for distribution on ISO-9660 discs) include **MacroMedia Director** files, and of course, **ASCII** text files.

There are two slightly different ISO-9660 formats: Level One and Level Two. Level One is almost identical to the MS-DOS file system. Files are identified by an eight-character name, followed by a period, followed by a three-character extension. Special characters are not permitted (hyphens, plus symbols, and so on), and the letters must be uppercase. A directory does not have an extension, and subdirectories can be nested up to eight levels deep.

Level Two ISO-9660 supports filenames up to 32 characters, but in most other details is the same as the Level One. Level Two discs are not usable on MS-DOS, making it questionable whether this format should be used.

Apple provides an ISO-9660 extension for **Foreign File Access**, the System software that recognizes non-**HFS** CDs.

See Also
BinHex; CD-ROM; Foreign File Access; High Sierra; Mixed-Mode CD

Italic, *See Typesetting Terms*

ITU-TSS, *See Modem Standards and Speeds*

iWorld, *See Delphi*

J

JAG II

This software, from Ray Dream Corporation, removes *jaggies* (jagged edges sometimes found in computer images) from an image by automatically anti-aliasing the edges or by increasing the resolution. It is simple and efficient, but balks at very large files (see the following figure).

- ■ The ToolBox has two selection tools: Hand Mover and Zoom.
- ■ Selection Menu and tools include Freehand and Rectangle.
- ■ File Save/Load conventions enable you to load **PICT,** TIFF, **Photoshop** 2 and 2.5, MacPaint, **QuickTime** Movie, Movie, and PICS formats. Save formats include PICT, TIFF, Photoshop 2 and 2.5, and EPS.

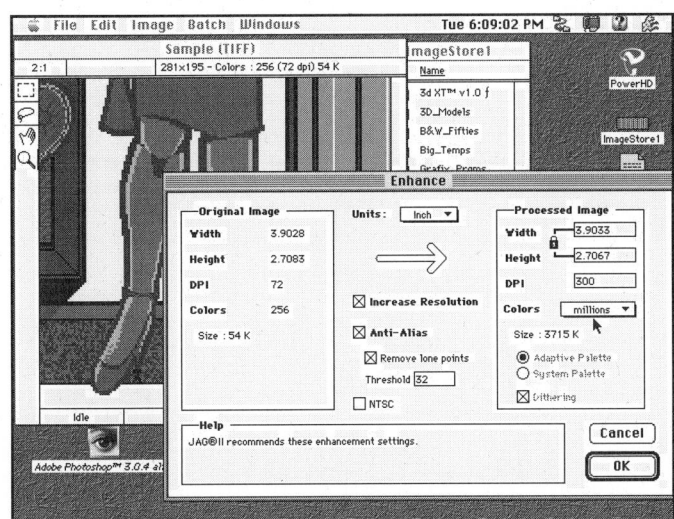

Jaggy, *See Bitmapped Graphics*

Janov, Rob, *See Apple Logo*

Japanese Games, *See Eastern Mind, Yellow Brick Road II*

Jasik's Debugger, *See Debugger, The*

Java

Java is an **object-oriented programming** language developed by **Sun Microsystems**. It addresses issues of security and cross-platform compatibility that are of special concern in the environment of the **Internet**.

(The language Java is commonly confused with the **World Wide Web** browser HotJava—see **HotJava** for more information about the browser.)

Although originally developed by Sun for programming various consumer electronic devices, such as VCRs, pagers, and TVs, Java is now being used to create programs for the **World Wide Web**. Because Java is byte-code compiled (see **Compiled Language**), programs written in Java are platform-neutral, making Java an ideal programming language for the World Wide Web, where a wide variety of platforms coexist. With a Java-compatible Web browser such as **Netscape Navigator**, a computer of any type can download a Java program (called an applet) from a Web **server** and run it.

It's important to note that, unlike **CGI** scripts, Java applets run on the client machine, not the server. This can lead to greater speed, flexibility, and interactivity on the World Wide Web;

the possibilities are only just beginning to be explored. Traditionally, bandwidth and server load have limited the extent of Web-based applications. With Java, however, there is the potential to create Web-based word processors, spreadsheets, or graphics programs.

To view Java applets, all you need is a Java-compatible Web browser, such as Netscape Navigator, that automatically displays applets when the page is loaded (see the following figure). Just like other Web content, it doesn't matter whether the applet was developed on a Macintosh.

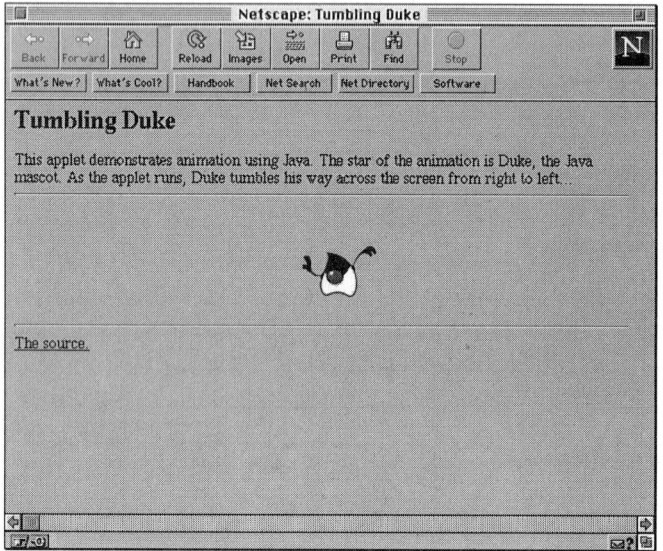

If you want to create your own Java applets, you'll need a few more tools and a lot more knowledge. First, you'll have to learn the language. Java is an object oriented language, similar to **C++** but a bit simpler. Here is a very simple Java program that displays the words "Hello World!":

```
public class HelloWorld {
    public static void main(String args[]) {
        System.out.println("Hello World!");
    }
}
```

Books on the Java language have been flooding the stores, and Sun's Java Web site (**http://java.sun.com**) also has a great deal of information to help you learn the language.

Java is clearly similar to the C++ programming language, but differs in many important particulars:

■ C++ is *machine dependent,* and C++ programmers may directly access specific physical memory locations on the **host** machine. In contrast, Java runs on the "Java virtual machine"—Java applications cannot directly access specific memory locations on the host machine, but can run on any platform that supports the virtual machine architecture. (You might think of the software that runs 68K applications on a PowerPC Mac as a "virtual 68K" machine for the PowerPC platform.)

   ■ The user of a Java application may limit the Java application's capabilities to perform security-sensitive tasks, such as reading and writing to the user's hard disk and establishing **network** connections. "**Applets**," the tiny Java applications commonly distributed over the Web, have very limited security privileges. As a result, it's (theoretically) impossible to write a virus, Trojan horse, or other malicious code in Applet format.

■ C++ and other high-level programming languages are typically translated to platform-dependent machine code; that is, *compiled,* and run at once, whereas Java applets are compiled into "pseudo-code" that is *interpreted* by the virtual machine on a line-by-line basis.

■ Java was written as a new language, and is not intended to be backwards-compatible with certain outdated features of the C language. (C++ is backwards-compatible with C.) Java implements support for features that most modern programmers find attractive, such as objects, multithreading, and automatic memory management.

Although Java is relatively easy to learn, it is by no means a beginner's language. If you choose to start your programming life with Java, be prepared to invest some time before you become proficient.

You'll also need a Java **compiler**. Several compilers are available for the Mac, including Sun's own Java Development Kit (JDK), Symantec's Caffeine compiler for the **Symantec C++** IDE, Natural Intelligence's **Roaster** IDE, and Metrowerks' **CodeWarrior** tools.

Programming for the MacOS has always been difficult, and Java makes this process only slightly less challenging for seasoned Mac developers by replacing calls to the Mac Toolbox with calls to "methods" defined in Sun's Java Developer's Toolkit. Java does facilitate porting of Java applications from other platforms to the Mac.

The Java virtual machine can exist *inside* a Web browser like **Netscape Navigator** or Microsoft **Internet Explorer**, and applets are used to deliver interactive content to Web users. Typically, applets are smaller in size (and hence quicker to load) than other multimedia formats.

Java, Pros and Cons Many programming languages exist in the world, and some of them (PERL and Python) implement similar features. Java is a well-designed language, but most important, Java marks a triumph of timing and marketing; most major players in the world of software and hardware signed some sort of licensing contract with Sun in 1995. Two of the biggest advantages of Java are that it's cross-platform and everybody's using it.

Java, Availability Java is an open standard, and The Java Development Kit is freely distributed by Sun. Users can download it from Sun's Web site (**http://java.sun.com/**). Third-party developers are free to create tools to help developers create Java applications; Natural Intelligence has already released a development tool for the Macintosh called **Roaster**, and other developers can be expected to follow suit.

Java, Future Trends Java is still a work-in-progress, and it's likely that many new features will be introduced in the first few years of Java's development. Tentative plans already underway include "just-in-time" compilation, which will allow Java to run significantly faster, and encryption-based authentication of Java programs, to add even more security.

Java is intended to be the programming lingua franca of the Internet, and if this plan is realized, Java (or its successors) will be the language in which much of the software in the world is written. Ideally, programmers (and even users) will be able to combine Java objects from different Internet sources to quickly create new, customized software packages—it's approach similar to Apple's nascent OpenDoc and Microsoft's OLE technologies.

Even if you don't want to learn the Java language, you can use Java in your own Web pages by modifying existing applets. For example, you can use the "Tumbling Duke" applet with a different set of GIF images to create your own customized "Tumbling Widget" applet. There are many sample applets available from Sun and elsewhere that can be customized in this way.

Natural Intelligence (**http://www.natural.com**) has also set up a Macintosh Java **mailing list**. To subscribe, send an email message containing just the words "subscript java-mac" to **majordomo@natural.com**. Your email address is taken automatically from the header of your message.

See Also

C; C++; CodeWarrior; HotJava; Internet; Internet Explorer; Netscape Navigator; Networking; Object-Oriented Programming; Programming; Web Browser; World Wide Web

JavaScript

A simple scripting language developed by **Netscape Communications, Inc.** that enables Web designers to embed simple executable code in their **Web pages**.

JavaScript is easier to use than Sun Microsystems' programming language **Java**, but also less powerful. JavaScript is useful for moving some simple processing tasks (for example, making sure that a form has been filled out correctly) to the **client**'s machine, thereby relieving the load on **server**-side **CGI**s, and for adding program-flow-control-like features to **Hypertext Markup Language (HTML)**.

JavaScript is easy to use—if you already program in C++ or Java. If not, it's probably not an easy first language to learn, given the scanty resources.

In order to write software that actually works, it's important to have development tools—documentation, a debugger, and a programming-friendly text editor are pretty basic requirements. These tools have not yet been released for JavaScript.

Although JavaScript is an open standard, as of this writing it's only supported by the Netscape Navigator World Wide Web browser (and is built into the 2.0 release of Navigator).

See Also

CGI; HotJava; HTML; Java; Netscape Navigator; Web Page, Designing; World Wide Web

Jaz Drives, *See Zip Drive*

Jigsaw Puzzle Application

This is a game in the **Apple menu** that takes any **PICT** image and transforms it into a jigsaw puzzle. The object of the game is to reconstruct the original image. There are a few options: When you start a new puzzle (by selecting Start New Puzzle from the Options menu) you can make the size of the jigsaw pieces Small, Medium, or Large. (Larger pieces mean a much easier puzzle.) Once you make your selection, the puzzle takes the image and scrambles it into puzzle pieces for you to reconstruct.

If you correctly reconstruct the puzzle, you'll hear a musical tune celebrating your feat. (You can turn off the sound in the **Options menu.**) If you're totally stumped, you can have the puzzle solve itself by choosing Solve Puzzle from the Options menu.

You can also set the background color of the window so it doesn't clash with your puzzle. The first time you open puzzle, it comes with a color map of the world, but you can copy and paste any PICT image directly into the puzzle and use that image as a puzzle.

To use the jigsaw puzzle, follow these steps:

1. Select Jigsaw Puzzle from the Apple menu.
2. Choose Start New Puzzle from the Options menu.
3. Select which size puzzle pieces you want to use.
4. Reconstruct the image by dragging the individual pieces into place.

See Also

Apple Menu; Copy Command; Cut Command; Paste Command

Jigsaw Puzzle Graphic, Replacing

You can replace the graphic in the **Jigsaw Puzzle DA** in the Apple menu with any **PICT** image. To change the graphic, copy a PICT image to the **Clipboard**, open the jigsaw puzzle, choose Paste from the Edit menu (⌘-V), and the new image replaces the existing puzzle image, as shown in the figure.

You also can copy any icon's image (by copying from the **Get Info** dialog box) into the jigsaw puzzle as well.

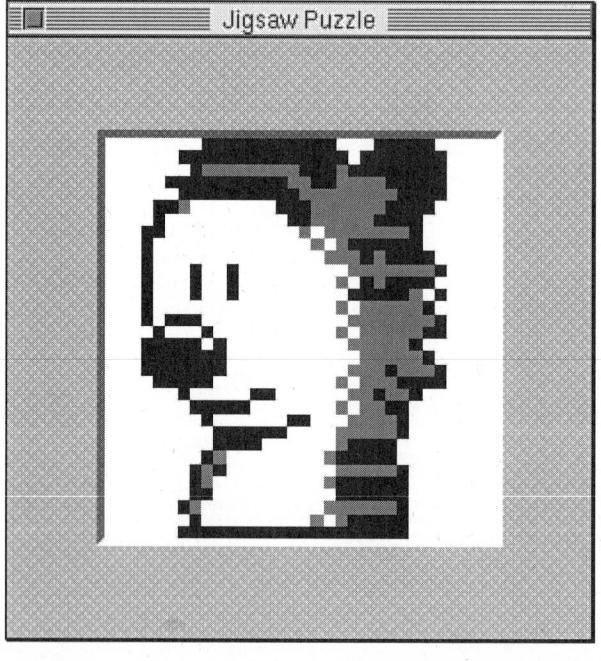

See Also
Clipboard; Jigsaw Puzzle Application

Jobs, Steve

Steve Jobs is one of the founders of Apple Computer. He grew up in Los Altos, California, a stone's throw away from **Cupertino**. Jobs was a true son of Silicon Valley; his adopted parents worked as a payroll clerk at Varian and a machinist at Spectra Physics.

Steve Jobs met **Steve "Woz" Wozniak** when he was a sophomore at Homestead High School. The two met through a mutual friend, Bill Hernandez, who was a classmate of Jobs' and a neighbor of Wozniak. As a teenager, Jobs was a loner and an electronics enthusiast, like Woz. Jobs' phone call to William Hewlett of Hewlett-Packard about some parts got him a summer job at the electronics company.

Jobs attended Reed College in Portland, Oregon. While there, he embraced the counter culture with open arms—he was on a search for enlightenment. He became a vegetarian and studied Richard Alpert's *Be Here Now*. Before long, Jobs dropped out of school.

Hoping to make a pilgrimage to India to become a follower of Alpert's guru, Jobs returned to Silicon Valley to earn some money. He managed to get a job at Atari, the video-game pioneer, where he was not well-liked and had a nasty habit of insulting the engineers. Jobs eventually managed to get his boss to send him to Germany on business. This was his ticket to India.

Steve Jobs spent several months in India, but left disillusioned. He returned to work at Atari as a technician. Between 1974 and 1976, Jobs returned frequently to Oregon, living for a time in a commune and undergoing primal scream therapy.

In 1975, Jobs began to attend meetings of the **Homebrew Computer Club** with Wozniak. When Woz built his own computer and showed it to the members of the club, Jobs had found his calling: the computer business.

Jobs convinced Wozniak to go into business selling Woz's new computer. They received an order for 50 of the new Apple Is from **The Byte Shop**, and Apple Computer was born. From the start, Jobs was driven to build Apple into something great.

While Woz focused on the technical side of the business, Jobs did everything he could to expand Apple. He convinced **A.C. "Mike" Markkula**, who had made his fortune at Fairchild and Intel, to invest in the newfound venture. Markkula managed to make the disheveled Jobs more presentable, and he helped make Jobs one of the new personal computer industry's visionary spokespeople.

In the late 70s, Jobs led the team that created Apple's first failure, the Apple III. A significant contribution to the Apple III's difficulties was Jobs himself. His specifications for the project changed almost daily. He also decided on the design of the case without regard to the parts that would have to fit inside it. When it was clear the Apple III was a failure, Jobs tried to distance himself from the fiasco by turning his sights to the **Lisa** project.

The Lisa project team was charged with designing the next generation computer to succeed the Apple II line. As the project progressed, Jobs' involvement became less and less welcome. His micro-management of every detail slowed the project down and annoyed the rest of the project team. In a 1980 reorganization,

Jobs was removed from the Lisa project by Apple president **Mike Scott**. Scott was concerned that Jobs' combative style and sometimes capricious technical decisions would lead the Lisa down the same path the Apple III had taken.

Angry, but far from defeated, Jobs turned his sights to yet another project—the small Macintosh project headed by **Jef Raskin**. Jobs gradually took control of the Macintosh project, eventually prompting Raskin to leave in 1982. Under Jobs' combative, zealous, and visionary leadership, the Macintosh project gave birth to the Macintosh product we all know and love. In the midst of it all, Jobs managed to convince **John Sculley** to leave his position at Pepsi and come to Apple as CEO.

Following the Mac's flashy debut, Jobs assumed control of the merged Lisa and Macintosh projects. As he had done before, Jobs began to meddle in parts of the business over which he had no authority. In the difficult times Apple was facing, his exploits were becoming a liability.

In May 1985, Jobs discovered that Sculley planned to have him stripped of his responsibilities, and planned a coup of his own. When Sculley was in China on business, Jobs hoped to have him removed from his position. Sculley caught wind of the plan and promptly canceled his trip. At an emergency meeting, the executive staff unanimously backed Sculley. Jobs was removed from his operational role but retained the chairmanship.

Four months later, in September 1985, Jobs resigned from Apple and announced his plans to form a new company, **NeXT**, to cater to the educational computing market. His announcement that several key Apple employees would be joining him raised the ire of Apple's board. The dispute was later settled when Jobs agreed not to hire any additional Apple employees for a period of six months and not to compete directly with Apple.

After starting up NeXT, Jobs bought the computer division of George Lucas' LucasFilm, Ltd., Pixar. In addition to creating some breakthrough animation software, Pixar is the company responsible for Disney's computer-generated movie, *Toy Story*. The hoopla surrounding *Toy Story* has put Jobs back in the spotlight.

Steve Jobs has remained a unique character in the computer industry. As John Sculley wrote in his book *Odyssey*, "He was arrogant, outrageous, intense, demanding—a perfectionist. He was also immature, fragile, sensitive, vulnerable. He was dynamic, visionary, charismatic, yet often stubborn, uncompromising, and downright impossible."

See Also

Byte Shop, The; Cupertino; Homebrew Computer Club; Markkula, A.C. "Mike;" NeXT; Raskin, Jef; Scott, Mike; Sculley, John; Wozniak, Steve

Johnny Mnemonic, See Hollywood Games Connection

Journeyman Project, See Daedelus Encounter, The

Joysticks

Joysticks enhance the fun of playing action games or sitting in a cockpit of a flight simulator. Like a mouse or trackball, they move the cursor and let you select options by pressing buttons. Most joysticks are **Apple Desktop Bus** devices.

Many companies make joysticks and the more common game pad (as shown in the illustration on the following page). However, finding a good joystick is difficult. Ruggedness is a key factor for uninhibited game play, and buttons, ergonomics, and programmability are all important. Prime factors are ease of control and rapidity of firing. Highlights of some of the better, well-known joystick models follow.

■ **MouseStick II.** MouseStick II by Advanced Gravis Computer Technology uses optical sensing to provide smooth control with up to 1,200 lines of resolution. This joystick comes with customized control settings for many popular games; you can even create your own custom settings. MouseStick II has five independent user-definable buttons, plus a full-size padded handle with adjustable tension. It is a popular joystick for flight simulation games.

- **Thunderstick-Mac.** Thunderstick by Microspeed, Inc., offers dual thumb buttons on a comfortable handle, and an x- and y-axis centering adjustment. This joystick makes aerial simulations and arcade games exciting. It has a street price of $69.95

- **QueStick II.** QueStick II by MicroQue uses a custom Motorola chip onboard to accommodate game-specific control sets. It has a special ADB address assigned by Apple to avoid conflicts with the mouse (which you can leave connected). With the QuePrefs Control Panel, you can assign specific functions to the controls (two buttons and a switch) for each game and player. Or you can select a QueSet from the library of game sets for many popular games. QueStick also provides keystroke emulation for games that work better with keystrokes than with firing buttons. The joystick handle is contoured to fit your hand comfortably, and trim pads allow you to center it precisely. The Power On LED changes color when you press any button. Cushioned feet prevent slipping and help to avoid marring tabletops. It has a street price of $49.95.

See Also
Apple Desktop Bus; Keyboard; Mouse

JPEG

JPEG (Joint Photographic Experts Group) is a **QuickTime compressor**, as well as a compression algorithm available in some graphics programs, such as Adobe **Photoshop**. JPEG is very good at compressing photographic images to very small sizes, because it is a glossy compressor designed specifically to handle photographic images. When compressing an image, you can usually choose between a range of compression values; the higher the level of compression the smaller the resulting file, but the image starts to degrade. At high compression rates the image becomes blocky. You can see blocks of color in the image rather than fine details. At medium to low compression rates, however, the difference between the image and the original is only visible by examining the image at the pixel level, and the file size is still dramatically reduced.

There are other factors to consider before using this compression algorithm. Compressing an image can take several seconds (although the faster **Power Macintosh** computers are starting to make this much less of an issue). JPEG is not suited for compressing computer graphics. The images often have high contrast areas, and **compression artifacts** are very visible around these graphics.

Although it's possible to compress a movie using the JPEG compressor, because this compression is not optimized for movies (it takes several seconds to compress a frame and doesn't use temporal compression), performance will be very poor.

Several video compression hardware boards use variations of JPEG routines to compress and decompress video. This is only possible because the hardware accelerates the compression algorithm. These movies play well only on those boards. **Compression** ratios range from 3:1 to 30:1.

Users can choose the compression ratio that will be used when saving images to JPEG format; image quality isn't usually noticeable unless ratios higher than 10:1 are chosen. JPEG graphics are common on the Internet.

See Also

Asymmetrical Compressors; Bitmapped Graphics; Compressor; Drop Frames; Spatial Compression; Symmetrical Compressors; Temporal Compression

JPEGView

A **helper application** by Aaron Giles that controls the display of **JPEG** format images.

JPEG is a popular format for images displayed on the **World Wide Web**. Although some **Web browser**s can display JPEG images inside the browser window, JPEGView lets the user control what color palette is used to display an image, the magnification of the image, and so on.

JPEGView is probably the best software for viewing JPEG images on the Mac platform. JPEGView has a very complete set of tools; the program is well documented, is System 7.5 savvy, is AppleScript scriptable and recordable, and is "postcardware"—the price of the software is a postcard to Mr. Giles.

JPEGView can only display as many colors as your video hardware allows, but it enables you to optimize the display of images on 256-color monitors.

JPEG displays images according to the monitor settings of your Mac (see the following figure). If you have the video hardware and your Monitor control panel is set to thousands or millions of colors, JPEGView displays the image by matching each pixel in the monitor to a pixel in the JPEG file and by displaying the color specified. (However, unless your monitor and the scanner that scanned the image in the first place are perfectly calibrated—it records and displays the same color in exactly the same way—the monitor only approximates the specified color.)

You have two choices for getting an image into JPEGView: You can move the images by hand, or you can configure Netscape to launch JPEGView automatically.

To open images manually, follow these steps:

1. If you are using Netscape Navigator, click and hold down the image you want to open until the pop-up menu comes up.

2. Choose "Save this Image as" from the pop-up menu. Netscape will give it a default name that you might as well use. You can save it on the desktop, or wherever is convenient.

3. In JPEGView, open the saved image file with the "Open" (⌘-O) command, or drag the file's icon onto the JPEGView icon.

To configure Netscape to open JPEGs with JPEGView, choose the "Helpers" tab from the "General Preferences" menu item. Click the "images/jpeg" line in the scrolling window, and then click the "Launch Application" radio button under Action in the bottom corner of the Preferences window. Click "OK."

See Also
GIF; Helper Applications; JPEG; Netscape Navigator; Web Browser; World Wide Web

Jughead
A service for searching that enables searching through large numbers of **Gopher** sites on the Internet so that users can locate specific files quickly and easily.

Jughead differs from **Veronica**, another Gopher search utility, because Veronica usually returns large amounts of information to search queries, whereas Jughead searches can be more focused. (Like Veronica, Jughead refers to the Archie comic strip, because Veronica servers perform Archie-like collections of information, only for Gopher rather than FTP sites.) Jughead is "officially" an acronym for *Jonzy's Universal Gopher Hierarchy Excavation and Display.*

Jughead is generally used to limit the range of a search to a certain machine, and to limit it to directory titles. Jughead, therefore, is more useful than Veronica if you know where you want to search, or if you are searching only on a Gopher server that runs Jughead.

To find a Jughead server, do a Veronica search (not case-sensitive) for "jughead -t7." Doing so will return a list of all searchable Jughead servers.

See Also
Gopher; Veronica

Juilliard Music Adventure
Juilliard is the place to go if you're serious about music. The Juilliard Music Adventure is designed to appeal to kids aged nine and up who really don't know much about music, but are starting to get interested. It's not for the kid next door who started playing violin at age three and composed her first symphony in first grade. Even though the puzzles are complex enough to require some thought and some time, for reasons known only to the people who wrote this program, they choose not to use standard musical notation. Instead there are equally complicated melody and rhythm lines in a sort of diagram format.

You select a tile and drag the dots on it up and down to raise and lower pitch. That's not quite the way Mozart did it. There's no good reason not to use "real" notes and a "real" staff. That aside, the program does teach quite a bit about rhythm and melody. Kids can compose their own music by selecting rhythm tiles and editing the melody. Then they can play back their compositions on a variety of instruments. The sound quality is good, even on the Mac's internal speaker.

There's also a game, requiring the user to visit five rooms in a castle and solve a different melody or rhythm puzzle in each. Doing so earns keys that eventually unlock the door to the throne room, where the user can compose music. Of course, users can do that without playing the game at all. Just stay outside the castle and the composition tools (such as they are) will stay outside as well. Kids who take their music lessons seriously will find this program rather limiting, but it's a good introduction for the absolute beginner.

Jump Cut
In video editing, a jump cut is a cut from one clip to another that is visually jarring to the viewer.

See Also
Cut; L-Cut; Transition Video Editing

Justification
Justification is a process that fits lines of type into a column so that both ends of the line are flush with the margins. It adds or subtracts from the amount of space between words so that the line extends all the way from the left margin to the right. If the last line of a text block is short, it may be necessary to adjust the justification so that the line ends normally. Otherwise, the words may be spread out too far, making them difficult to read. Most texthandling programs including word processors, chartmaking, and desktop publishing applications will automatically justify text. Select the block to be justified and select justify from the tool bar or dialog box.

See Also
Printing and Binding Terminology

K

Kai's Power Tools 3.0

Kai's Power Tools is a collection of plug-ins for Photoshop and Photoshop-compatible software. It is guaranteed to work with Photoshop, but some of the plug-ins have a problem outside of the strict Photoshop environment. The collection of tools addresses every need for users who want to apply image variable effects to graphics, or those who require tools that can manipulate a digital photograph with options beyond those contained in Photoshop itself.

Kai's Power Tools has always been appreciated for its collection of visually appealing user interfaces, setting a trend that most of its competition is affected by. The interfaces encourage exploration and new discoveries, giving graphics professionals and non-professionals alike the opportunity to develop limitless graphics looks for their projects. The 3.0 version of these effects tools pushes the envelope of potential creativity even further by including several new tools and revamped capacities for upgraded tools from previous versions. Kai Krause, the designer behind these effects, is recognized throughout the industry as one of the most original thinkers and developers when it comes to plug-in effects and the interfaces that let you access them.

The Tools KPT3 includes eighteen separate tools, but each has so many variables that the net result is hundreds if not thousands of distinct options. The effects are Gradient Designer, Interform, Spheroid Designer, Texture Explorer, 3D Stereo Noise, Edge F/X, Gaussian F/X, Glass Lens, Intensity F/X, Noise F/X, Page Curl, Pixel F/X, Planar Tiling, Seamless Welder, Smudge F/X, Twirl F/X, Video Feedback, and Vortex Tiling.

Gradient Designer A gradient is a smooth transition from one color to another, useful for both backdrops and for gradients addressed to targeted selections of an image. A large listing of pre-designed gradients are included, all with visual previews. The tool is easy to use at a basic level, but requires study to master. Six main controls respond to user input:

Mode: Blends, sweeps, bursts, and path shapes.

Loop: Sawtooths, triangle and pinch/punch distortions of the gradient shapes.

Repeat: Interactive mouse control over the amount of times the gradient repeats overall.

Opacity: Grayscale, detail, color and various combinations of these settings.

Glue: The way the gradient addresses the image—normally, procedurally, darken, lighten, multiply, subtract and add.

Direction: Interactive mouse control over the gradient's rotation

Options: Feathering options, real time linking, RIP toggle, and Preferences. In the Preferences menu, selections are included that enable you to load gradients defaults from the gradients library or from the graphic currently in memory. You can also enable graphic tablet interfacing if you own a graphics tablet, and change the way that Gradient Designer writes to the Mac screen. In addition, Hue, Saturation, Brightness, Contrast, Blur, Squeeze, and Cycle can be altered. All of these choices affect the spectrum of colors in the chosen gradient. The last two items, Squeeze and Cycle, move the shift of the colors according to your mouse movements.

Main uses include developing gradient backgrounds for typographic material, gradient backgrounds for slide and video presentations, and zenith to horizon blends.

Interform A "Mother" and "Father" textures are used to create an "Offspring" texture. Each of the three, Mother, Father and Offspring, are animated on the preview screen, showing you various areas of the selection each passing moment. Resultant textures can be applied to the image or selection and saved to disk. Resultant offspring can also be saved to one of ten library areas for later recall. This effect requires time to get used to and more to master. Two main controls respond to user input:

Opacity: Grayscale, detail, color, and various combinations of these settings.

Glue: The way the gradient addresses the image—normally, procedurally, darken, lighten, multiply, subtract and add.

Options: Three speed settings for the animated previews and a Preferences setting (Graphics Tablet and screen settings).

Excellent for developing textures from combinations of other textures already resident in the KPT3 texture library. This module is very game-like in design, which enhances an exploration of its features. Developed textures can be applied to 2D pages and selected areas, or used as video backdrops.

Spheroid Designer Kai describes this interface as being originally digitized from a "stale brownie," and if you look closely it's not hard to conceive of it as true. Spheroid Designer is used to wrap 3D textures around spheres, and it has so many variations and possibilities, it could act as the main topic of a dedicated graphics book. Spheres were one of the original elements of computer graphics artists, so the tool has both a historical perspective as well as a dedicated current use. This tool is simple to use at the basic level, but I doubt that it could ever be truly mastered if mastery means understanding all of its variations. It is worthy of years of study and exploration. Its controllers are numerous and varied.

KPT3 Spheroid Design Genesis Editor A separate topic unto itself, the Genesis Editor allows even more variability to the Spheroid Designer output. An interactive screen gives you control over the overall shapes that groups of spheres will take when rendered to the screen. Although a library of shapes are provided, each can be varied as to zoom, randomness of sizes, and other necessary parameters. An outline of the shapes appears for final tweaking, followed quickly by a full color preview. The Genesis Editor is especially useful when large numbers of spheres are to be rendered (either the 500 or 1,000 setting).

With this tool, you can design backgrounds that incorporate any number and variety of 3D shadowed spheres, from planets to marbles. Because of the capability to add textures from your own library of images, the rendered spheres can be personalized to your needs. One idea might be to take a graphic of a company logo and transform it into a sphere. Another might be to add realistic 3D eyes to your chosen images.

Texture Explorer This is KPT3's texture generation engine. It is accompanied by a visual library of default textures, and you can add your own saved textures to this library as well. Once a texture is chosen, its mutated cousins appear around it. These mutations can show global maximum or minimum diversity, so the final texture can be exactly what is required. If not, a close relative of the chosen texture might be a better choice. Textures can be altered as to direction, opacity, hue, and all of the other standard parameters. These KPT3 textures are "infinite" in that they vary over space, so they do not look like repeated or tiled graphics. Options include "Filling the selected area," which writes the whole texture to the area, or "Scaling to fit," which writes only a scaled version of the texture to the area.

Use these textures wherever their unique looks are called for, from backgrounds to filling in selected areas of an image. When you use the Procedural application settings (plus or minus), you'll be able to blend the textures into the painted areas of an image. Creating cloth-like effects can be accomplished in this manner.

3D Stereo Noise This renders stereograms, the current buzz in graphics that create 3D images, which can be seen without glasses when you learn how to focus your vision. The Stereo Noise effect can be applied in color or grayscale and in variable opacity over the graphic. Uses are up to the artist's needs regarding the introduction of stereo noise into an image.

Edge F/X This is one of the six F/X filters in KPT3. Once the small F/X interface is on-screen, any of the six can be called up from the interface itself. The interface appears as a magnifying glass, and can be moved interactively over an area in the image to preview the F/X settings. "Edges" are in an image that the eye sees as an outline, as for example the circular edge around a sphere. This filter allows you to adjust the contrast of an image's edges to modify the way the edges stand out from the rest of the image. Uses depend on the artist and the need to enhance or mute an image's perceived edges.

Gaussian F/X This is also known as "Gaussian Blur," but instead of verbal commands, KPT3 gives the user an interactive visual interface. Use it anytime you want to add blurring to all or part of an image.

Glass Lens This movable interface applies a spherical lens effect to any selected part of an image. It is best applied when the selection is an oval or circular shape; otherwise, the results are not predictable. There are three main choices: Soft, Normal, and Bright. Opacity and application parameters can vary. Use the Glass Lens whenever you want to transform an area of the image into a 3D sphere, complete with a perceived reflective light source.

Intensity F/X As another of the F/X group, Intensity varies the way that sharpness, fading, and other selections can be varied in their intensity when applied. Intensity F/X works in conjunction with these other effects.

Noise F/X This is different from Stereo Noise. It can be compared to the static appearing on your TV screen when there is no transmission of the video signal. Use it when you want a graphic to evidence noise, as if it were grabbed from a noisy TV station signal.

Page Curl This adds an imposed graphic that looks like the edge of a picture is curling. It works on any selected area of the image. You can vary the transparency of the curled section, and also the image "underneath" the curl. Eight different directional curls can be applied. Use it when you desire that your image evidences a curl. This application is very useful for giving images an old parchment appeal.

Pixel F/X As another of the F/X applications, Pixel F/X applies a controllable pixel based noise over the selected area of an image. This results in either dirtying up the image, or giving it a look as if it were placed behind frosted glass, depending on how the controls are adjusted. Use it when you want any of these options.

Planar Tiling If you need to see your image, or any selected part of it, tiled over an infinite plane, then this is the filter for you. The tiled look can be applied at opacity, so that you can create a composite of the tiled look and the original image. The second option in planar tiling is the Parquet mode, which tiles a surface as if seen from directly overhead with no perspective. If perspective is chosen, KPT3 allows you to interactively adjust the horizon line and vanishing points. Use it when you need to reinforce the perspective of a graphic, as for instance in the rendering of a tiled floor that seems to disappear toward the horizon.

Seamless Welder This effect creates images that are wrap-arounds, similar on the edges, so that they can be used to texture a 3D object without a visible seam. Use is for 3D artists, although there are occasions when a 2D seamless weld might be wanted.

Smudge F/X Smudge F/X is in the F/X group. It allows you to add a perceived smudge or smearing in any direction and intensity you choose on the targeted selection or the whole image. Use it when you need to enhance a felt "wind direction" in an image, or when you need to draw attention away from a background image (for instance as background to typography).

K

Twirl F/X Twirls are cyclone-like whirlpools, and this member of the F/X group allows twirls to be imposed on any selected image area in a graphic. The twirls can be adjusted as to intensity and direction, and variable opacities can be used. Twirls are useful in the creation of perceived wind and water movements, and subtle applications of them in the right photos can heighten the drama of the image.

Video Feedback This effect applies either video feedback or telescope feedback to the selected area of an image. If you've ever pointed a video camera at the monitor its transmitting signal was connected to, you have seen video feedback. It is exemplified by a series of cloned images in a spiral. Telescope feedback is just a variation on the same theme. This effect can come in handy when creating flower forms from selected areas of images, and also helps in the generation of abstracted backgrounds.

Vortex Tiling Like a black hole in deep space, vortex tiling makes it appear as if an area of an image is sucking in everything around it. KPT3 offers two different vortex possibilities: Pinch and Normal. Normal uses the whole selected area as a basis for the effect. Pinch uses only a movable section of it. The intensity and opacity of the effect can be altered to your liking, and it's all done interactively with the mouse. This effect is useful when applied to water and space graphics, adding an organic and believable look.

KPT3 System requirements: 68040 with FPU or Power Mac with System 7.x. 2MB RAM for software. (A total of 16MB of RAM is essential if you are planning to run KPT3 in Photoshop).

Kaidan

Kaidan manufactures products or accessories for the **QuickTake** camera and for use when creating QuickTime VR panoramas. Products include:

- **CloseFlash**—A flash attachment available for the QuickTake and Kodak DC40 digital still cameras. The attachment is placed in front of the camera, very close to the lens. It provides much better illumination of objects that are extremely close (a few feet) to the camera.

- **CloseTake**—Close-up lens attachments for the QuickTake camera.

- **WideTake**—A wide angle lens attachment for the QuickTake camera.

- **QuickPan**—A panoramic tripod head for use in taking multiple image QuickTime VR panoramas. The tripod head includes a detent wheel that ensures that each image is evenly spaced. There are three models currently available: one for the QuickTake camera, one for Kodak's DC40 camera, and a general purpose version for use with 35mm cameras. Note that different units are recommended for the QuickTake and DC40 because the nodal point of the cameras is different, and when taking a panorama the camera must rotate around its nodal point.

Pierian Spring Software
218 Anvil Drive—Suite 110
Feasterville, PA 19053
Fax: (215) 322-4186
Phone: (215) 364-1778
Web: **http://www.kaidan.com/**

See Also

QuickTake 100 & 150; QuickTime VR

Kaleida Labs, *See ScriptX*

Kaleidagraph, *See Charting and Graphing Applications*

Kaleidoscope

Kaleidoscope from Abbott Systems, Incorporated is the perfect software for visualizing the fractal universe connected with the mathematical graphics generated by Mandelbrot mathematics. The title bar across the top of the Kaleidoscope screen contains four buttons, from left to right:

- Close button: Quits the program.

- Icon button: Reduces the window to an icon without quitting the program.

- Zoom button: Resizes the window to its previous size.

- Menu button: Displays the Kaleidoscope menu commands.

    - Home: Displays the full Mandelbrot set.

    - Go Back: Zooms back out to previous image.

    - Open Snapshot: Opens a snapshot file.

    - Save Snapshot: Saves current image as snapshot file.

Snapshot files contain only the image parameters, not the complete image in pixels, so they take up far less space on disk than PICT files. There's no limit to the number of Snapshots you can take. You can view your Snapshots anytime, just choose Open Snapshot from the Kaleidoscope menu, or double click the Snapshot file. You can transmit Kaleidoscope images over networks, using Snapshot files for super fast transmission. The recipient must own Kaleidoscope to view them. Take a Snapshot when you have zoomed into the Mandelbrot set many levels deep and you find a particularly interesting area.

- Save as PICT: Save the current image as a PICT file.

- Page Setup: Sets printer output choices for printing.

- Print: Prints the current image.

- Draw Top to Bottom: Draws image top to bottom.

- Draw Inside Out: Draws image starting in center.

- Draw Random: Draws image in random sequence.

(The three "Draw" commands are used for aesthetic purposes only when viewing the screen changes).

The Main Display shows the current image, below which are nine other buttons:

- Redraw button (Green): Used to redraw the current image if the resolution has been changed.

- Stop button (Red): Stops image drawing. Click again to resume.

- Four Color buttons: Changes the color scheme of the image.

- Two Special Effects buttons: Causes the color scheme to cycle-animate if you have your monitor set to 256 colors. To stop the animation press ⌘-Period (.).

- Resolution button: Determines how detailed the image is drawn. Click the arrows to increase/decrease. A higher number means more resolution.

When you first start Kaleidoscope, or if you choose Home from the Kaleidoscope Menu, Kaleidoscope displays the complete image normally associated with the Mandelbrot set. To zoom in to any part of the image, point the 'cross hair' cursor to the desired part and click. A small square shows you which part of the image will be magnified to full view. If you want to magnify a larger portion, you drag the cursor to make the square bigger.

As you zoom in through many levels, you can increase the resolution parameter to get more detail. You might want to zoom in at low resolution until you reach an area that you are interested in, then recalculate the image at higher resolution (click the Stop button, change the resolution setting, and then click the Redraw button). Kaleidoscope does all image calculations in background mode, which means you can do other things while Kaleidoscope is drawing. During long calculations, you might want to reduce Kaleidoscope to an icon and leave it calculating while you continue with your other work. To stop image drawing at any time, click the Stop button. Click again to resume. To zoom back out, choose Go Back from the Kaleidoscope menu.

K

You can change the way images are colored by clicking the four Color buttons. The first two buttons are fixed color palettes, the third button is a black and white palette, and the fourth button (a question mark) assigns a palette of random colors.

Kaleidoscope can create incredible screen saver type displays. To see these, first set your monitor to 256 colors, then click the Special Effects buttons. The Mac desktop is blanked out and the current image is displayed with a moving color palette, creating an animation effect. Kaleidoscope images can be saved as PICT images for other applications.

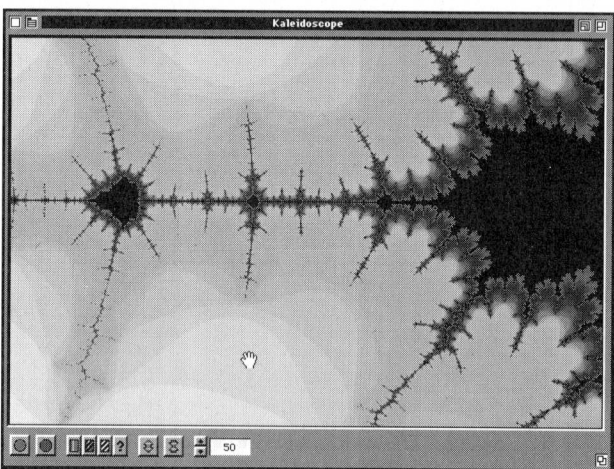

Kare, Susan

Susan Kare was creative director of the Macintosh team from 1982 to 1985. Her title during that time was Macintosh Artist. Much of Kare's work can still be seen in the Macintosh computers of today.

Kare created much of the Macintosh interface's appearance and style, including the cursors, titlebars, icons, and fonts. The MacPaint "hello" that greeted many early Macintosh users was created by Susan, as were most of the patterns and icons in MacPaint itself.

Susan designed all but one of the bitmapped fonts that shipped with the original Macintosh, including Chicago, Geneva, Cairo, New York, Toronto, Taliesin, and San Francisco. (Venice was created by **Bill**

Atkinson.) Many of these fonts were designed to be low-resolution bitmapped versions of popular copyrighted typefaces, such as Times (New York) and Helvetica (Geneva). Her Cairo font is the source of the half-dog, half-cow character that later became known as the **dogcow**.

After her time at Apple, Susan Kare worked for **NeXT** as creative director, developing NeXT's graphic identity. She left NeXT to go into business for herself as a computer interface designer and illustrator.

See Also

Atkinson, Bill; Dogcow; History and Culture of the Macintosh; NeXT

Kawasaki, Guy

Guy Kawasaki was the best known of Apple's Software evangelists, whose job it was to convince software developers to create programs that would run on the Macintosh. This **evangelism** was aptly named. Guy and his fellow evangelists were true believers in the Macintosh, zealously selling the vision of this unique new computer.

After the Mac's introduction, Kawasaki continued in his role of software evangelist for several years. In 1987, he left Apple and formed ACIUS to market the 4th Dimension (4D) database. Apple had acquired the U.S. rights to 4D from its French creator, Analyses Conseils Informations (ACI), but decided not to market it for fear of hurting Apple's relationship with Ashton-Tate.

Conversation with Guy Kawasaki
His business card used to read Software Evangelist. He inspired developers to create great software for the Mac, then went out and made some himself. He's contributed columns to *MacUser* and *MacWorld*, and has written books such as *The Macintosh Way, Selling the Dream*, and, our favorite, *How to Drive Your Competition Crazy*. Now Guy Kawasaki's back as an Apple Fellow.

Maclopedia: So how did you first get involved with the Mac?

Guy: Mike Boich showed it to me in summer 1983. When I saw it, the waters parted. They showed me the bouncing bottle caps and early MacPaint and MacWrite, and I had used an Apple II a little, but I wasn't a computer person. But it was obvious that this was it. It took thirty seconds.

Boich and I had gone to Stanford together, and he recruited me. It was purely the fact that I had gone to school with him; it had nothing to do with competence. The idea of evangelism came from Mike Murray. Basically, we used fervor and zeal but never money to convince developers to create software for a computer before it made sense to develop anything for it, hence the idea: evangelism. We would take the prototype out and show it to people, and the people who got it got it in the first thirty seconds, and the people who didn't get it right away never got it.

I worked on all the little ones, Panorama, the database (it was called Overview then), Desktop Express from Dow Jones, FileVision, just the oldest, smallest ones. The best book on Mac history back then was *The Mac Bathroom Reader*, by Owen Linzmayer.

Maclopedia: So why did you leave Apple in 1987?

Guy: I left Apple for three reasons. The first was that my job was done. Another was that, basically, I wanted to listen to my own hype about the opportunities in the Mac world, so I wanted to start my own company and make millions of dollars. And the third reason was that I was up to become a director, and I was turned down, and they said it was because while small developers loved what I did, three big ones, Lotus, Microsoft, and Ashton-Tate, weren't so in love with it, so that pissed me off so much that I left. I went to ACIUS to work with 4th Dimension until 1989, then I wrote for *MacUser* and wrote books.

Maclopedia: You came back to Apple as a Fellow, the first one in the marketing area, in 1995. How did Apple seem different?

People still come here [Apple] because they want to make the world a better place, as opposed to dominating the world.

Guy: It was a little more shell-shocked, but Apple is always shell-shocked. Someone is always predicting that we're going out of business. But after a while, you don't worry. People still come here because they want to make the world a better place, as opposed to dominating the world.

Maclopedia: Why did you come back?

Guy: I am a warrior, and a warrior needs a war. My war is to bring cool Macintosh software to fruition, create the finest developer program in the industry, and kick Microsoft's butt.

Maclopedia: How did you come up with the idea of an Internet list of pro-Mac items?

Guy: The name itself came from someone on the list— you know, I was an evangelist, so why not call it the EvangeList? But I got the idea because there was so much bad news about Apple, basically only bad news, so this was a place you could go to get good news. We have 20,000 subscribers now, with total distribution to about 100,000 people. That's one of the top 5 most popular lists today!

Maclopedia: How are Mac users different?

Guy: They're cooler, hipper, more intelligent. We use more software. Mac users have at least five pieces of software. There are six million Mac users, so that means 30 million applications. I was a software entrepreneur, and let me tell you, in a market of 30 million pieces of software you can make money. That's plenty big enough. I think it's better to be a medium-sized fish in a medium-sized, unpolluted pond than an amoeba in Microsoft's swamp.

Maclopedia: Why don't more developers port products from Windows to the Mac, then?

Guy: Three reasons. First, it takes real courage because if you're simply counting beans, it appears that the Macintosh market is 1/5th the size of the Windows market. In actuality, the Windows run rates are usually 2 to 2 1/2 times Macintosh run rates. Second, the Macintosh market intimidates many developers. Macintosh owners are very demanding and

continues

discriminating. Simply porting a Windows product to Mac without taking full advantage of Mac conventions like drag-and-drop guarantees failure. Thus the Macintosh market is smaller and tougher—definitely not for the faint-hearted. Third, we haven't tried to woo these Windows developers enough. This will be fixed.

Maclopedia: Has Apple gotten the message?

Guy: Windows 95 is the best thing to happen to Apple in a long, long time because it hit us like a 2-by-4 right between the eyes. There's a new attitude—more aggressive and forceful and competitive. And there's a realization that a huge part of Apple's success hinges on taking care of developers. We are more honest and up front with developers now. We are more open to enabling developers to lead us into areas we haven't explored. If we want to continue to lead the market with the coolest computers, we really have to take the risks that no one else would take. It's in Apple's DNA to aspire to be the most innovative company and platform in the industry—to resist the known and seize the unknown. I wouldn't be here if we were shooting for anything less.

Simple Things You Can Do to Save Apple Computer
by Guy Kawasaki

- Wear Apple/Macintosh garb to show the world that we're not crawling into holes and dying.

- Strike up a conversation with people you see using Macintosh—especially on airplanes. Reinforce that they did the right thing.

- When you stay at a hotel, go see if there are Macintoshes in the business center. If there is, thank the person. If there isn't, ask why not.

- When you see people using a PC (a dead giveaway of PC laptop is that Solitaire is running) ask them if their company forced them to use it.

- Ask store clerks why there isn't more Macintosh software on the shelves.

- Ask store clerks why there aren't more Macintosh models for sale.

- If you hear a store clerk spreading ignorance and lies, wait until the clerk has left (usually 45 seconds) and go talk to the customer about their computer needs.

- Check to see that the Macintosh floor models are running and their desktops are orderly. Do not, however, sabotage the PCs. This creates bad karma.

- Forward EvangeList postings to as many people as you can.

- Write a letter to the publications that publish stupid, insipid, inaccurate, and unfair stories. (This will keep you really busy right now). Most journalists are insecure and perceptive: after the 300th flaming message, they'll get the picture.

- Donate your old Macintosh to a school, church, or other not-for-profit. Every Macintosh out there sells more Macintoshes.

- Read *MacUser*, *MacWorld* (even though the inside back column just isn't what it used to be), *MacWEEK*, and *MacToday* on airplanes and then leave them in the seat pockets for the next passenger.

- Subscribe to the EvangeList by sending an email to: **listproc@solutions.apple.com** and include in the body of the message the text "Subscribe Macway" and your name.

Kawasaki also pursued writing, and has since written a number of excellent books on using evangelism in business and in everyday life, including *The Macintosh Way*, *Selling the Dream*, and *How to Drive Your Competition Crazy*. At various times, he has written columns for both *MacUser* and *MacWorld* magazines. He has also been involved in several start-up Macintosh software companies, including Fog City Software, the creators of Claris eMailer.

In 1995, Kawasaki returned to Apple as an Apple Fellow, charged with improving Apple's relationship with developers. In his new role, he has helped to make Apple's development tools and documentation more accessible, as well as restarted the classic zealous evangelism of the early days of the Mac.

Kawasaki has set up a mailing list for Macintosh fanatics who are personal Mac evangelists. You can subscribe to the EvangeList by sending a message to **evangelist@macway.com**.

See Also

Apple Computer, History; Evangelism; History and Culture of the Macintosh

KCMS

Used as the system-level **color management** software for Microsoft Windows 95, KCMS also works on the Mac, using supplied **device profiles** to improve the quality of color images output from Macs. Photoshop includes KCMS for importing Kodak's PhotoCD images, and DayStar Digital's ColorMatch software uses KCMS for system-wide color management. Color adjustment information is embedded in image files, so that the files can be output from any computer, whether the user has KCMS. The Input Color Characterization software enables users to create their own scanner profiles.

See Also

Color Management; Device Profiles

Keep It Simple Spreadsheet,
See Let's Keep It Simple Spreadsheet

Ke:nx

Ke:nx (pronounced "connects") is a hardware/software interface for the Macintosh that helps people with physical or cognitive challenges access computers. It comes in two parts: a box that plugs into an **ADB** port and accepts a variety of input devices, including alternate **keyboards**, switches, pointing devices, **joysticks**, and the software that enables the Mac to communicate with these devices.

PowerMouse is the Ke:nx program that turns any kind of input device into one that can work like a mouse on-screen. It also gives the user the ability to scan menus, buttons, and markers, and click a simple switch to activate them.

Ke:nx provides a way for people who cannot use the standard keyboard and mouse to successfully run any Mac software program. It enables computer users to select from a wide range of input methods, according to the kinds of physical abilities they have. In addition to accessing the computer, the Ke:nx software enables users (or their teachers or therapists) to customize, create, and print overlays for alternate keyboards to use with any program.

Ke:nx can be used with the TASH mini-keyboard as well as with KeyLargo and similar large keyboards. It's easy to remap the keys to fit popular software programs that may already be used in the classroom, or to work with common word processors and spreadsheet programs so that newly disabled adults can still manage their finances and correspondence. It will accept Morse code input and translate the radio operators' dots and dashes into standard ASCII characters for speedy text input.

By placing a keyboard on the computer screen, Ke:nx can give text access to people who can manage a mouse-type device such as a joystick or trackball, but are unable to type. When scanning is added to the on-screen keyboard, Ke:nx enables even single-switch users to write letters, play games, and make full use of all the Mac's capabilities. It literally opens a new world for many people who have been unable to use standard keyboards or pointing devices.

Ke:nx can even turn the Macintosh into a communication device with its picture-based displays, high-quality speech output, and digitized and text-to-speech capability. The included software (Ke:nx Create) helps users create their own communication keys, and it works with DynaVox, Liberator, and other standard communication devices. Ke:nx has enabled thousands of people with disabilities to make full use of the computer at home, in school, and on the job.

See Also

Co:Writer; Freedom; Talk:About

Kermit

A file transfer protocol for retrieving and sending files on the Internet. Named after the popular Kermit the Frog. Kermit is generally slower than **XMODEM**, **YMODEM**, and the top-of-the-line **ZMODEM**.

See Also

File Transfer Protocols, Modems, Modem Transfer Protocols

K

Kernighan, Brian, *See C*

Kerning

Kerning adjusts the horizontal spacing of characters in a line of type. Note that it's not the same as **tracking**, which adjusts the letter and word spacing of an entire line of type. Kerning is generally used for type larger than 14 points, because it's hard to see any noticeable difference in smaller fonts. Kerning closes the gaps between letters that, when normally spaced, appear too far apart because of the shape of the individual letters.

Letter combinations such as To, VA, and Yo, usually need to be kerned. The following figure shows an example. Most word processors apply automatic kerning when you specify a font size to kern. DTP programs such as PageMaker enable custom kerning as well, because automatic kerning might not be sufficient for all fonts.

To a Mirror, Vanity is
Priceless...

To a Mirror, Vanity is
Priceless...

See Also

Tracking

Key Caps

This is a **desk accessory** in the Apple menu that enables you to see all the characters and special symbols in any font. It gives you a visual keyboard map of all the characters that are accessed by using different modifier keys, as shown in the following figure. For example, if you need to use the trademark symbol (™) in a business letter, but don't know how to access that symbol, you'd use Keycaps. When it opens, it shows you a drawing of your keyboard and as you hold down different modifier keys (Option, Command, Shift, and so on) the keyboard graphic changes and shows you all the hidden symbols. In Key Caps, you'd instantly see that the trademark symbol is accessed by holding down the Option Key and pressing the number 2 on your keyboard.

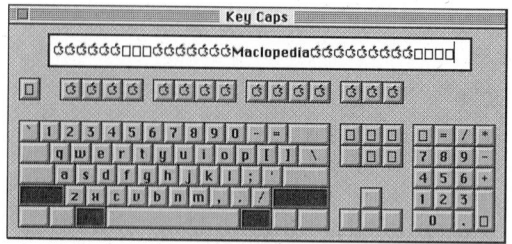

Key Caps has its own **font menu** (accessed under the Key Caps menu) that lists all the installed fonts on your system so you check as many fonts as you like for special symbols while Key Caps is open. This is helpful as not every font offers the same set of symbols. Key Caps is especially useful for finding characters in a font that is all symbols, like Zapf Dingbats or Carta. Key Caps also offers you a typing window so you can try different combinations of keys from your own keyboard, or you can point and click keys on the Key Caps keyboard.

To use Key Caps, follow these steps:

1. Choose Key Caps from the Apple menu (Key Caps comes pre-installed in the Apple menu in all Macintosh models.)

2. Choose the font you'll be working with from the pop-down list under the Key Caps menu that appears when you launch Key Caps.

3. If the character or symbol you're looking for does not appear in the window, first hold down the Shift key to see if it appears. If not, then hold down the Option key and look to see if it appears on the keyboard now. If it appears, then look down at your real keyboard and see if you can figure out which key from the screen matches the key on your keyboard. Continue to hold the Option key and type the letter that most closely matches the one on the screen. (It's okay to type with Key Caps active—the characters will only appear in the Key Caps window.

See Also
Apple Menu; Desk Accessories; Fonts

Key Commands, *See Keyboard Shortcuts*

Key Frames

This term is used in both animation and in video compression.

In animation programs, key frames are points in an animation sequence that define the bounds of a particular movement. Take, for example, a car moving from the left side of the screen to the right, over a length of 50 frames. In frame 1, the car is on the left side of the screen (key frame 1), and in frame 50, it is on the right side of the screen (key frame 2). Most animation tools will let you define these two locations, and then **inbetweens** (also called tweening) to calculate the location of the car in each frame between the first and last key frame. Most programs (such as the 2-dimensional Macromedia **Director** and Specular's **Infini-D**) enable you to adjust the motion by defining acceleration and deceleration, and create multiple key frames for a sequence.

When compressing digital video sequences, key frames provide random access capabilities for the video sequences, whereas most video **compression** algorithms produce much of their file size reductions by saving a frame as the difference between the current frame and the previous frame. For long sequences that are similar, this produces tremendous file savings, but if you want to display frame 100, then frames 1 through 99 must first be read. This is not a problem if you are sequentially playing the movie, but if you want the user to be able to jump randomly in the movie, then key frames become very important. A key frame is the whole frame compressed independent of its neighbor. When using a compressor, key frames are usually expressed as a key frame rate (that is, a key frame every x frames). It is also possible to define key frames explicitly.

See Also
Compressor; CD-ROM Movie Maker; Inbetweening; Movie Cleaner Pro; QuickTime

Keyboard

Desktop Macs do not automatically come with a keyboard. **Performa** Macs come equipped with an **Apple Extended Keyboard**, which may not be correct for your needs. So, when you purchase a Mac, you will find yourself shopping for the keyboard that best fits your requirements.

Computer keyboards resemble the typewriters from which they originated. Many other input methods are available, but the keyboard remains the most common and familiar device for inputting text and numbers into a computer. Preference for a particular keyboard design, size, ergonomics, and color are subjective to personal tastes as well as your height, plus the size and shape of your hands.

Some people are concerned with compactness because they don't want to give up desk space. Others want big keyboards bristling with lots of keys and light-emitting diodes. Touch typists have particular preferences about the mechanical resistance of the keys and the overall layout and dimensions. The little bumps on the D and K keys are there for touch typists. These bumps on the home keys are what keep your fingers in the right place. In other situations (retail and industrial users, particularly), you may need waterproof and dustproof keyboards. You should try typing on the keyboard you want to buy before making a purchasing decision.

Ergonomics are an important consideration. Take care to place your keyboard at a comfortable height. Long hours of typing can lead to carpal tunnel syndrome if your hands and wrists are at uncomfortable angles. Ideally, your hands and wrists should be flat, not bent. Most keyboards have a height adjustment, but you shouldn't use them; the back of the keyboard should be kept down, not up. Wrist rests can help level your wrists and are an essential accessory. Look for one that is soft and keeps the wrists at the least angle possible.

An alternative to the traditional keyboard that enables alphanumeric input is the *chording keyboard*. These strange-looking devices usually are curved to fit the hand with a button for each finger; you use the buttons in various combinations (like playing chords on a piano) to enter all letters of the alphabet. Court stenographers use similar devices because of their speed. Although some time must be spent learning to use it, chording keyboards can be useful for people with disabilities, as they enable them to type one handed.

If your work involves extensive numeric entry, you should have a numeric keypad. The typewriter-style row of numbers across the top of keyboards frustrates most people. Many keyboards, such as Apple's extended keyboards, have a numeric keypad built-in, but you can buy one as a separate ADB accessory. Some keyboards also offer the option of an adjustable numeric keypad to accommodate left-handed numeric entry.

The following table describes keyboards from Apple and third-party vendors and represents a cross-section of those available.

Keyboard Options for the Mac

Manufacturer	Model Name	Features	Street Price
Apple	Apple Design Keyboard	105-key extended layout, right-hand numeric keypad and 15 function keys. Works with all Macs with an ADB port. Height-adjustable, 1 ADB port and a permanent ADB cable.	$90
MicroSpeed	Mac Keyboard Deluxe	105-key extended layout that is smaller and lighter than the Apple Extended Keyboard. 4 ADB ports.	$69.95
Business Technology Manufacturing	ADB Industrial Keyboard	Waterproof and dustproof 105-key extended keyboard useful in factory or laboratory situations.	$480
Key Tronic Corp.	MacPro Plus and Trak Pro	Ergonomic and configurable extended keyboards with larger Return keys than Apple's offering along with swappable Control and Command key pads; some with attached trackballs.	$179 (MacPro Plus) and $249 (Trak Pro)
Datadesk International	TrackBoard Keyboard	Full-size (105-key) keyboard and 3-button trackball combination, programmable, color-coded key caps.	$99.95
Datadesk International	101E Keyboard	Includes **Mavis Beacon Teaches Typing** software.	$79.95
Health Care Keyboard	Comfort Keyboard	Splitable (3-way) keyboard with adjustable heights and angles for each section.	$795
Infogrip	BAT Personal Keyboard	Chording keyboard for left or right hands.	N/A
PowerUser	105 Extended Keyboard	Enlarged Enter key, "T"-shaped cursor pad, 15 function keys, second ADB port.	$59.95
Adesso	Tru-Form Keyboard	Contoured keyboard, built-in wrist support, wrist height adjustment, slit-key design.	$89.95

You can also purchase any PC-compatible keyboard and use it with your Mac by buying the $99 KeyStone adapter from Silicon Valley Bus Company.

See Also

Apple Desktop Bus; Apple Extended Keyboard; Keyboard Layouts; Keyboard Mapping

Keyboard Buffers (Keyboard Shortcut)

If you've ever chosen a **command** in an application, such as the **Print** command, and you know that you want to use the current settings in the Print dialog box, you can choose Print and then press the **Enter key** before the dialog box even appears. By pressing the Enter key, you've chosen the default button of that dialog box, which in most print dialog boxes is the command "Print." The Print dialog box will flash on the screen and disappear because the keyboard buffer stores your Enter key keystroke and places it there for you when the dialog appears. This buffer is actually a temporary memory buffer. You can see it in action anytime you type letters faster than the computer can display them. Even after you've stopped typing, the letters you've typed soon "catch-up" and display on-screen. With the keyboard buffer you can press ⌘-P (the keyboard shortcut for Print) and press the Enter key (for OK). You don't have to wait for the Print dialog box to fully draw before you can enter OK.

See Also

Command Key; Default Button; Keyboard Shortcuts; Print Command; Return Key

Keyboard Commands

There are two basic types of commands in the Macintosh environment: keyboard commands and menu commands. Keyboard commands are instructions you enter by pressing a key or combination of keys on the computer keyboard. Menu commands are commands listed in the **pull-down menus** of the **Finder** or any application. These menu commands are arranged by topic in the **menu bar** at the top of your screen. An Apple Computer logo

appears in the far left corner of the menu bar. Menu commands enable you to access certain features of an application by selecting commands using the **mouse**. Typical application menu commands are Print, New, Save, Save As, Open, and Quit, which appear under the topic heading File. Many menu commands can be accessed through **keyboard shortcuts** that activate commands without using the mouse. If a menu command has a keyboard shortcut, the keys listed to complete the shortcut are generally noted to the right of the menu command. If, for example, you click and hold the File menu, you'll notice that to the right of the Print command is the command symbol (⌘) followed by the letter P. That is telling you that the keyboard shortcut for the Print command is ⌘-P.

See Also

Command Keys; Finder Shortcuts; Keyboard Shortcuts; Menu Bar; Mouse; Pull-Down Menus

Keyboard Control Panel

The Keyboard **Control Panel** enables you to use alternate **keyboard** settings for your computer. This is helpful if you're using a keyboard layout other than U.S. English. The control panel enables you to remap the keys to the standards of foreign languages. You can also set the Key Repeat rate (the rate at which keys repeat the character if you hold down a key and how long the delay is before a character starts repeating). These options are set by using the **radio buttons** at the top of the panel.

If you have alternate keyboard layouts installed, you can select them from the list.

To use the Keyboard Control Panel, follow these steps:

1. Select Keyboard Control Panel from the Control Panels submenu on the Apple menu (or System Folder).

2. Double-click to open the control panel.

3. Select alternative keyboards from the list.

4. Select your Key Repeat Rate and Delay Until Repeat Rate by clicking the radio buttons.

See Also

Control Panels; Keyboard; Radio Buttons

Keyboard Layouts

Apple provides System files that add recognition of special symbols unique to various languages to its operating system. Each country is responsible for creating a unique version of System software to meet the specific hardware and software configuration needs. Japan, for example, has a version of System software that supports full Kanji language characters. The System software is also designed to work with the Kanji keyboard hardware to support English character input on a Kanji keyboard. Apple supports the 2-byte characters required in Kanji through its **WorldScript System Extension** in System 7.*x*. So-called 2-byte languages require twice the register space as 1-byte languages such as English to store and display the characters.

In the United States, Apple provides foreign language support with language kits, which contain custom pieces of System software and keyboard drivers and layouts to support both English and another language. Apple's Language Kit for Japanese and Chinese dialects are examples of software products containing 2-byte System software extensions and keyboard files that are accessible with English System software.

Keyboard layouts enable Mac System software to recognize custom symbols used by specific countries on any Mac keyboard. There are also dozens of Roman keyboard layouts, which include the English, French, and Spanish languages. Custom Roman keyboard layouts exist for the United States, Britain, Canada, France, Switzerland, Germany, Spain, Sweden, Norway (two styles), and Italy. If you have custom keyboard layouts installed on your System, they appear in the **Keyboard Control Panel**. You can only use one keyboard layout at any given time on your Mac, but you can change your keyboard layout without restarting your computer. Additional keyboard layouts for other languages are available from Apple and all are designed to be used with System 7.

See Also

Apple Desktop Bus; Apple Extended Keyboard; Keyboard; Keyboard Control Panel

Keyboard Mapping

The Macintosh OS recognizes the keys you press on your keyboard because it has assigned each key a unique code, or number. The Mac uses a specialized **keyboard driver** that assigns (or maps) the key code to a given character. When the keyboard driver receives a key code, it looks up the code's corresponding character in a System file called **KCHR** that contains the map to that keyboard. The driver passes the appropriate character to the active application. The **Keyboard Control Panel** (illustrated here) lets you change the KCHR resource to access other language maps.

There is also software, such as CE Software's QuickKeys and Connectix' Connectix Utilities (whose control panel window is displayed below), that lets you remap the keyboard to fit your specialized needs. For example, you can set up the Home key to Delete, or assign a key to curly quotation marks. You can also remap the keyboard from the standard **QWERTY** typewriter-style to a simpler layout, such as the **Dvorak Simplified Layout** (developed by August Dvorak in the 1940s). User groups and online services have many keyboard variations available for downloading.

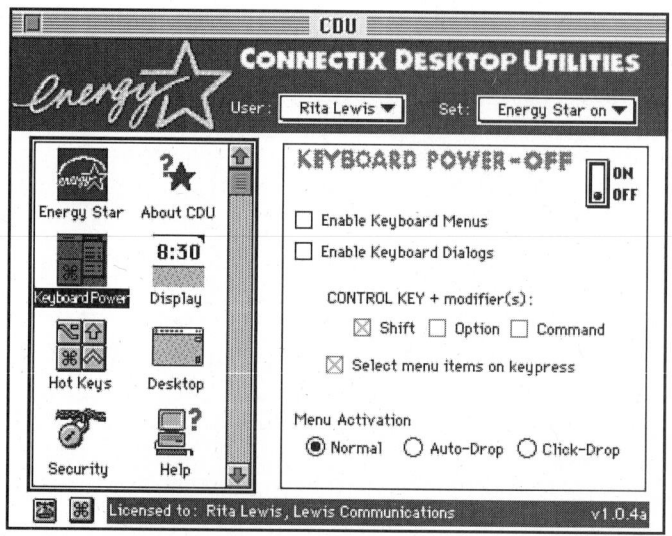

See Also

Keyboard; Keyboard Layouts; Mavis Beacon Teaches Typing

Keyboard Shortcuts

Key commands are **keyboard shortcuts** that can be much quicker than using the mouse for many tasks. If a keyboard shortcut is available for a command, the shortcut is usually listed to the right of the command in the **pull-down menus**, as shown in the figure. If, for example, you pull down the File menu at the Finder level, you see that the first listing, New Folder, has a shortcut listed to the right of it. The shortcut displayed is ⌘-N.

File	
New Folder	⌘N
Open	⌘O
Print	⌘P
Close Window	⌘W
Get Info	⌘I
Sharing...	
Duplicate	⌘D
Make Alias	⌘M
Put Away	⌘Y
Find...	⌘F
Find Again	⌘G
Page Setup...	
Print Desktop...	

The Macintosh uses a special key for most commands called the **Command key.** The Command key on your keyboard has an Apple logo imprinted on the key to the left of the Command symbol (⌘). Many of these commands use the first letter of the command to make it easy to learn these key command shortcuts, such as ⌘-N for New Folder, ⌘-O for Open, ⌘-P for Print, and ⌘-S for Save. The following table lists the most common Macintosh shortcut commands.

Key Command Shortcuts

Command	Key Sequence
Bypass Internal Drive	⌘-Option-Shift-Delete
Cancel	⌘-.
Close	⌘-W
Close All	⌘-Option-W
Close Active Window	⌘-Option-Up Arrow
Collapse an Expanded Folder	⌘-Option-Left Arrow
Copy	⌘-C
Cut	⌘-X
Duplicate	⌘-D
Delete locked files in Trash	Option-Empty Trash
Disable Trash Warning	Option-Empty Trash
Eject Disk	⌘-E
Find	⌘-F
Find Again	⌘-G
Make Alias	⌘-M
New Folder	⌘-N
Open	⌘-O
Open a Folder or Disk	⌘-Up Arrow
Paste	⌘-V
Print	⌘-P
Put Away	⌘-Y
Rebuild the Desktop (during startup)	Option-⌘
Restart	Control-⌘-PowerOn key
Save	⌘-S
Screen shot of Desktop	Shift-⌘-3
Select All	⌘-A
Toggle Keyboard layouts	⌘-Spacebar
Undo	⌘-Z
Zap Pram	⌘-Option-P-R (during startup)

K

Some applications have so many shortcuts that they run out of combinations using the Command key. Often other keys, such as the **Control key,** the **Option key,** and the **Shift key,** are added for shortcuts.

To find a key command shortcut, follow these steps:

1. Click and hold the pull-down menu of the command.

2. Visually locate the name of the command, and then look to the right of the name and see whether a keyboard shortcut exists. If it does, it is listed there, using a symbol or multiple symbols, followed by a one letter code.

3. In System 7.0 and 7.1, you can find a list of key commands in the Help menu under Finder Shortcuts. In System 7.5 and higher, these Finder shortcuts have been relocated into the Apple Guide, which is also found under the Help menu.

See Also

Control Key; Option Key; Pull-Down Menu; Shift Key

Kid Desk

If there's just one must-have program for any family with kids and a computer, it's KidPix. If there's a second, it's this one.

Kid Desk is a special desktop just for kids that gives kids access to the programs they use, but keeps them from getting into the grown-ups' files. The desktop itself is designed to be kid-friendly. It's got desk accessories, just like the grown-up ones, including a name plate, a clock, a calculator, a calendar, and a frame for a picture.

And it has others that would be helpful on any desk. There's electronic mail and voice mail (provided your Mac has a microphone). You can leave notes for your kids, and they can respond. Notes can be printed out on colorful letterhead, too. If they're not yet reading by themselves, leave a voice message. Clicking the analog clock gives you a digital clock that even speaks the time, helping the child to learn to tell time.

Kids can choose any of six different kinds of desks. There's one with a dinosaur theme, a high-tech space-age console, a Wild West desk complete with a Wanted poster, and three that are more traditional.

You can customize the desktop so that younger kids have fewer desk accessories, and older kids have the full set. Password protection keeps the kids away from the adult Finder. Because each child has his or her own desk, you can give your older child access to programs that a younger sibling isn't ready to use. You can also set up Kid Desk as the startup application, giving kids more flexibility in their computer use. And you can determine whether quitting Kid Desk exits to the Finder or shuts down the Mac. Obviously, the latter is safer if you're concerned about hard disk security. If yours is a "family" computer, shared by kids and parents or by several siblings, Kid Desk may well save your sanity as well as your irreplaceable files.

See Also

KidPix Studio

Kidmusic, A Little, *See Little Kidmusic, A*

KidPix Studio

KidPix was the first, and is still the best, graphics program for kids. Others, such as *Microsoft Artist* and *Aldus Art Explorer* have simply copied the tools and sounds that make KidPix so much fun, without making any major improvements on the original. KidPix was first developed by programmer Craig Hickman for his then three-year old son, Ben, and was originally released as shareware. Brøderbund bought the rights to it and has been distributing it, and various add-ons, since 1989. (Pretty soon, it will be putting Ben through college.)

It's a surprisingly powerful graphics program that, although geared toward kids, has most of the tools that adult graphics programs have, plus a few that grown-ups never thought of. There are all sizes and shapes of brush, including some that drip, draw with barbed wire, bubbles, or toothpaste. There are rubber stamps with funny pictures, and there are hidden pictures to uncover. The erasers don't just erase—they explode, invert, cover the page with stripes, and do a dozen other unexpected things. There's an eggbeater to re-arrange the screen, and a moving van to shift things around.

Of course, there are sounds connected to all the tools, and you can record your own sounds, too. KidPix 2 is the current disk version, and KidPix Studio is an even more expanded CD-ROM version with much more stuff… more stamps, more pictures, more sounds, animated stamps, and the capability to make QuickTime movies and slide shows from your artwork. You can narrate the movies and add sound effects, too. The program menus are bilingual English/Spanish, and there's even a "small kids mode" to protect your checkbook and other files from accidental erasure by an inquisitive three year old. The program is rated for ages 3-12, but adults have been seen spending hours at a time playing with it.

KISS, *See Let's Keep It Simple Spreadsheet*

Knockout, See Color Trapping

Knowbots

Knowbots are a species of artificial-intelligence soft-ware programs that roam the **Internet** looking for information. The data they collect resides in a num-ber of different databases that can be accessed via **Gopher, Telnet, Email,** or other interfaces.

Knowbot Information Service (KIS) on the **World Wide Web** controls a knowbot that queries databases that contain lists of server names. KIS, a free service, can search several unrelated databases based on a single query. Users may choose from several important da-tabases of users, including:

- the InterNIC white pages
- the Whois service
- the X.500 directory (more corporate-oriented)

KIS home page: **http://info.cnri.reston.va.us/kis.html.**

See Also
FTP; Internet; Internet Service Provider; Network

Kodak Color Management System, *See KCMS*

Kodak DC40

A digital still camera that can produce full screen (756 x 504 pixel resolution) and quarter screen (378 x 256) images. Note that this size equals the standard size for the **PAL** video format, and is also a standard size for PhotoCD images. The camera holds 48 full screen images, although this number is reduced if you choose the option that enables you to delete the last picture taken without deleting the other images (a feature not available on any other camera in this price range).

The camera is long and flat, with a **range finder** view system. The built-in lens cover slides open by pushing a lever at the top of the case. The shutter release button is on the top of the camera. An LCD panel at the back of the camera displays information about the number of pictures, the flash, and other modes being used. Two toggle buttons adjust the camera; press the first to jump from option to option, press the second button to change the option. Options include flash mode, self timer, and erase images.

Images are larger than the QuickTake, and the color quality in the images seems to be a little better. Expo-sure, particularly outside, tends to over exposure more than on the other cameras. While the images are slightly larger (so that the camera supports the **PAL** video format which has a larger frame size than **NTSC**) this doesn't mean that the image is noticeably better than the other cameras.

See Also
Digital Still Cameras; Still Video Cameras

K

Kodak DC50

A repackaging of the **Chinon ES-3000**, this unit comes with different software and has a slightly higher resolution image: 756 x 504 instead of 640 x 480.

See Also

Chinon ES-3000; Digital Still Camera; Dycam10-C;

Kodak PhotoCD

Perhaps the most elegant solution to scanning photos is to have someone else do the scanning for you. PhotoCD is a special file format for images developed by Kodak, and many vendors will take your undeveloped color film and return a compact disc full of high-quality digital images.

Basically, Kodak has developed a special network of new machines and technology and traditional photo lab vendors to deliver high-quality scans at a moderate price. You give your film to a vendor that offers PhotoCD services, and your film is shipped to a special service bureau that bulk-scans your film on a high-end workstation. Although the process is automated, the results are comparable in quality to drum scans.

If you're not in a hurry, PhotoCD is a great solution. Prices are about $1.50/frame for a roll of film, compared to the $25-$40 per image you'll pay for a drum scan. (You can also send individual negatives for inclusion on a PhotoCD, but the prices are slightly higher.) In larger cities, you may be able to find labs that offer a 24-hour turnaround on PhotoCDs, but in many places, you must wait as long as 7 to 10 days to get results.

See Also

Scanner, Desktop

Koyn Fractal Studio

Koyn Fractal Studio is the place to start learning about digital scenery. It will give you the terminology and a theoretical and practical understanding of how fractal geometry works. Fractal geometry is the core of digital scenery software, as well as being what has been called the greatest scientific breakthrough since particle physics. Fractals possess what is called "self similarity," an attribute that makes small parts of an object look like duplications of the entire object. This means that no matter how close you zoom in on a fractal, it always seems that you are no closer than when you started. Like realizing the creative universe in a grain of mustard seed, fractals give computer programmers the needed tools for emulating the natural world. Fractal graphics have the feel of organic objects, and take on a life of their own.

Koyn's Fractal Studio, through its documentation and on-screen tutorials, walks you through the magic of creating images with fractal tools and processes. What other scenery generators do in a hidden way, Koyn does in an articulated and expositive manner. Bushes, clouds, ferns, leaves, rock formations, and trees, can all be emulated and created with the fractal tools in Koyn. It's as if we have discovered in fractal geometry the building blocks of what we perceive as the natural world. Koyn's Fractal Studio allows us to watch as seemingly natural objects are created over time. As each calculation progresses, we get the feeling that we are watching a secret natural law unfolding.

For original creations, Koyn Fractal Studio lets the user set up a series of polygonal guides, each of which represents the way that fractal geometry will be applied to the screen. Exploration and experimentation is imperative in KFS. It takes a while to accumulate the necessary connection between what the geometric guiding polygons look like and what basic rendering can be expected.

A library of fractal shapes is included with the software, presenting an on-screen geometry of each fractal formula. Interacting at the visual level, these structures can be rotated and resized. Accessing the "render" command from the menu bar, the geometric shapes begin to develop into fractal natural objects on-screen. Clouds fill a blue background, trees grow and branch out, and leaves start their journey toward veined masterpieces. Most renders should be terminated after only a few iterations (a few seconds) if you plan to use the graphics in other designs. That's because as each iteration commences, the branching gets thicker and more detailed. Unless you are able to set the resolution very high (you have to have a lot of RAM for this), just a few renderings will produce very pleasing graphics. You can set the color of the images, or select "randomize color" for a rainbow effect. KFS allows you to save the geometric guide screens for further exploration and rendering, and the resultant graphics as PICT files.

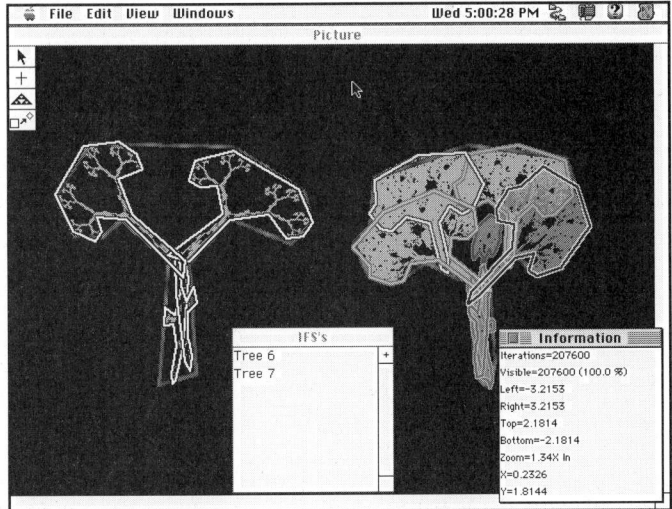

KPT Final Effects

A set of **plug-in** filters, effects, and transitions for Adobe **After Effects**, KPT Final Effects claims to produce film-quality effects that fall into eight categories: distortion, channel, image control, light, particle, perspective, stylize, and transition. The effects can be animated over time by adjusting various parameters.

> MetaTools
> Price: $695
> Email: **metasales@aol.com**
> Phone: (805) 566-6200
> Web: **http://www.metatools.com/bryce/ bryce.html**

See Also
After Effects; Plug-Ins

L

L-Cut

From video editing, an L-Cut is a more complicated variation on the simple cut. In an L-Cut, the audio is heard for a few seconds while a second clip is visible. For example, a movie shows a green pasture, you hear the sounds of cars honking and the video changes to a street scene.

The name L-Cut is used because the two pieces of film and the sound track look like an L. The following figure demonstrates an L-Cut created in Adobe **Premiere**.

To create an L-Cut, you need to use a sophisticated QuickTime editing programs, such as Premiere or Strata's **VideoShop**.

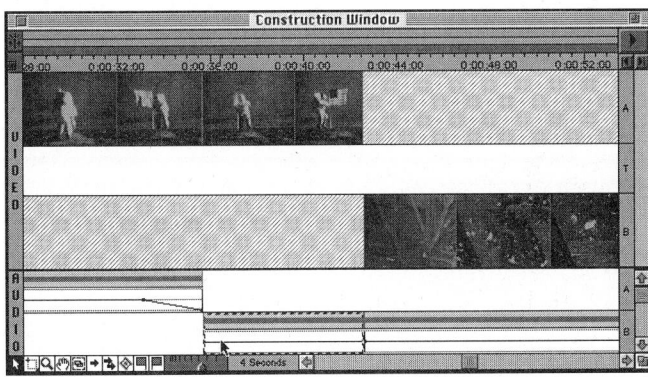

See Also

Cut; Jump Cut; Premiere; Transition; VideoShop

Label Command

On the **desktop,** you have the option of labeling a file (and color coding it if you have a color monitor) using the Label command found on the **Label menu.** You can use this labeling feature to find items in a list and to enable sorting by ever-defined categories. The individual colors or names that the label command assigns are edited through the Labels control panel in the **Control Panels** Folder.

To assign a label to an item, follow these steps:

1. Select the item you want to label by clicking it.

2. Choose the color and label you want from the Label menu.

3. The item's icon color changes to your color choice, labeling it with that color and that color's corresponding name.

4. To edit the color, or label name, choose the Labels control panel from the Control Panel folder (on the Apple menu).

See Also

Control Panels; Desktop; Labels Control Panel; Label Menu

Label Menu

The Label menu, appearing at the **desktop**, gives you the option of labeling a file (or color coding it if you have a color monitor). You can use this labeling feature to help find or sort items in a list or window. The individual colors and names the label command assigns can be edited through the **Labels control panel** in the **Control Panels** folder.

To assign a label to an item, follow these steps:

1. Select the item you want to label.

2. Choose the color and label you want from the Label menu.

3. The item's icon color changes to your color choice and is labeled with that color's corresponding name.

4. To edit the color or label name, choose the Labels Control Panel from the Control Panels folder.

See Also

Control Panels; Desktop; Label Command

Labels

The Labels control panel enables you to customize the colors and names for labels in the **Label menu** in the **Finder**. To pick a custom color for your label, click the color swatch and the **Apple Color Picker** appears giving you a wide range of color choices. Simply click the color you want and click OK. You also can edit the label names by **highlighting** the label's name and typing a name of your own.

To use the Labels control panel, follow these steps:

1. Select Labels Control Panel from the Control Panels on the Apple menu (or System Folder).

2. Double-click to open the Control Panel.

3. Click the color swatch to select a new label color. The Apple Color Picker appears, enabling you to pick the color of your choice. After you make your choice, click OK.

4. To change the name of a label, highlight the label and type your own name. Close the control panel when completed.

See Also

Apple Color Picker; Finder; Highlighting; Label Menu; Views

LAN, *See WAN*

Landscape Orientation, *See Orientation*

Language Kits, *See Foreign-Language Page Layout*

Language, Programming, *See Programming Languages*

Laptops, *See Portable Computers, Macintosh Family, PowerBooks*

Laser Printers, *See Desktop Printers*

LaserWriter, *See Desktop Printers*

LaserWriter Extension

This extension is a printer driver that enables you to use a PostScript Printer. The LaserWriter extension is accessed through the **Chooser** on the **Apple menu**. When you **click** the LaserWriter driver icon, a list of available laser printers appears in the window on the right.

See Also

Apple Menu; Chooser; Click; Icons; Printing

Lathing, *See Modeling*

Launcher Control Panel

The Launcher is a smaller version of Apple's **At Ease** that enables users to access documents and applications in a large floating palette. The Launcher operates like a floating **Apple menu**. To add an item to the Launcher, drag **aliases** or other items to the **Launcher Items folder** (in **System 7.5**, **drag** the items right onto the Launcher) where they are automatically added to the Launcher Items folder. You can add documents, **control panels**, folders, applications, and many other items to the Launcher for one-click access. To remove an item from the Launcher, remove it from the Launcher Items folder.

To have the Launcher appear at startup, select Show Launcher at System Startup in the **General Controls control panel**.

To use the Launcher control panel, follow these steps:

1. Select the Launcher control panel from the Control Panels submenu on the Apple menu (or System Folder).

2. To add an item to the Launcher, drag the item onto the Launcher Control Panel. The Launcher automatically makes an alias of the file and places it in the Launcher Items folder.

3. If your system does not support drag-and-drop, add the item, or an alias of the item, directly to the Launcher Items folder. To launch an item from the Launcher, click it.

See Also

Apple Menu; At Ease; Control Panel; Drag and Drop; General Controls Control Panel; Launcher Items Folder; System 7.5; System Folder

Launcher Items Folder

Items in the Launcher Items folder appear in the **Launcher control panel** window on the **desktop.** The Launcher enables one-click launching of documents or applications, and you can add **aliases**, applications, documents, and so on, to the Launcher by dragging their **icons** into the Launcher Items folder.

See Also

Aliases; Control Panel; Desktop; Launcher; System Folder

Launching a Program

Launch is a computer term for starting or opening an application. Launching, or opening, an application can be accomplished in a number of different ways. You can **select** the application and choose **Open** from the **File menu** to launch the application. You can double-click the **icon**, or an **alias** of the application's icon, to launch the application. You can place the application's icon, or an alias, in the **Launcher Items Folder** inside the **System Folder**, and that application can then be launched by just one click on its icon in the **Launcher** window. You also can double-click or open any document and the document opens the application that created it.

See Also

Alias; Double-Click; File Menu; Icon; Launcher Items Folder; Open; Selection; System Folder

Layout Templates, Using

PowerPoint, Microsoft's presentation program, comes with a very large collection of templates to help you design your presentation with a consistent look. Templates incorporate a type style or styles, a color scheme, and usually one or more graphics elements, such as lines, patterns, or shapes. There are approximately 150 different templates in the package, divided into three separate categories: black and white overhead transparencies, color overhead transparencies, and slides—35mm slides and on-screen presentation slides.

Formats are applied either by using the Pick a Look Wizard or by choosing Presentation Template from the Format menu. There's a Preview window that gives you a thumbnail view of the template. After you have found a style that you like that doesn't clash with your subject matter, you can modify the template as necessary. Change the color scheme from options on the Format menu. Choose Slide Background to change the underlying color, or Slide Colors to change the colors of the type and accent graphics. Slide Background also gives you the capability to change the kind or direction of the gradation used, if any, and to lighten or darken the color. As you can see in the figure, the Slide Background dialog box instantly shows the effect of the shading.

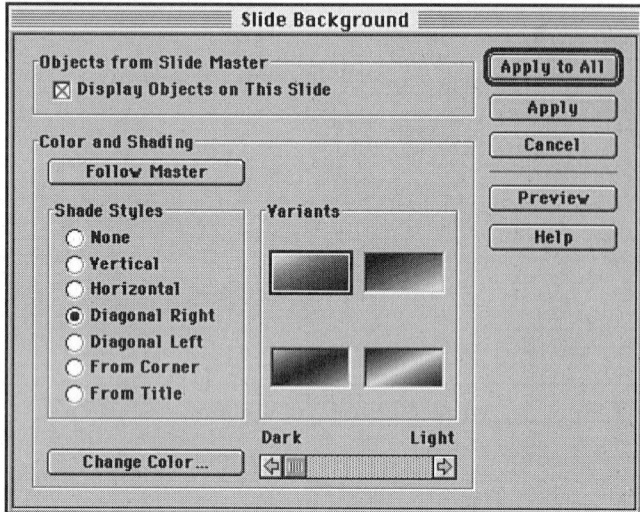

If you change the background color to one of the 88 choices, you'll see a new palette of colors for the rest of the color scheme. If none of the combinations appeal to you, click the Choose Scheme button to open the Color Scheme dialog box. After you choose a background color, you can choose a different color for text and line. Then you'll see four thumbnails of a typical slide displaying your choices, with different combinations of accent, shading, and fill colors. Choose the look you like, click Apply to All, and every slide in your program will change to the new color scheme. Click Apply if you only want to change the colors on one slide.

Slide Colors supplies a harmonizing color scheme to go with your choice of background. Each color scheme includes a set of eight carefully chosen colors to be used as the main colors of a slide presentation—the text color, the background color, fill colors, and so on. Using a color scheme helps ensure that your presentation has a professional look. The PowerPoint color schemes have been chosen by professional artists specifically for presentation use. There is a good selection of contemporary and traditional combinations.

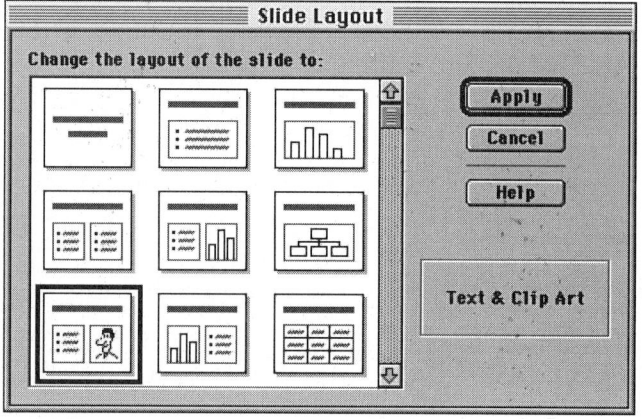

The Slide Layout dialog box lets you apply different layouts to your slides, depending on the kind of text or graphic element you are using. Again, you select from a choice of thumbnail sketches. You also can override these layouts by dragging the elements around on the slide as if you were using a draw program or use the drawing tools in the tool palette to customize your slides.

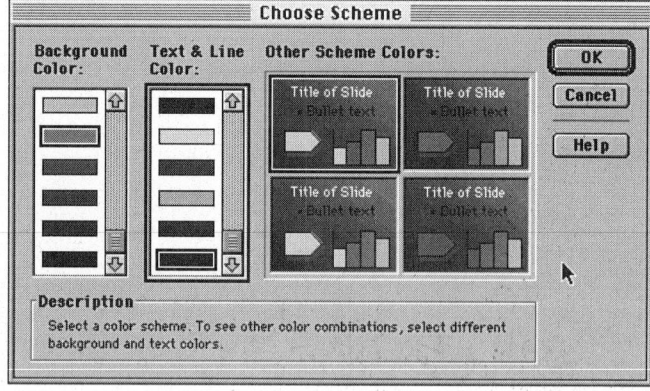

See Also

PowerPoint

LCs, *See Education Models,*
Macintosh Family

Leader Characters

Leaders, or leader characters, are the solid, dashed, or dotted lines that you see between tabs in a list. They "lead" the eye across the page. When you have tabbed text, such as an index, table of contents, or a chart, leaders make the lines easier to read, because there's an immediate visual connection between the words. Here's an example:

Chapter 1, "With all my heart" 3

Chapter 2, "We'll never part" 17

Chapter 3, "The meaning of romance" .. 39

Chapter 4, "We break up" 48

Chapter 5, "Just one more chance" 52

Leaders always run to the next tab stop, so they're self-adjusting. The program inserts and spaces the correct number of dots, hyphens, or whatever leader character you choose. In **WriteNow 4** and **MacWritePro**, you can use any character or symbol you like. **Word** restricts you to dots, dashes, or a solid line.

Left Arrow Key

Using the Left Arrow key enables you to navigate through an open document by moving the cursor to the left one character at a time. You can **select** the character to the left of the **cursor's** insertion point in a document by pressing Shift-Left Arrow key, or you can select the entire word to the left of the cursor's insertion point by pressing Shift-⌘-Left Arrow key.

In a window set to **View by Icon**, you can select the icon to the left of the selected icon by pressing the Left Arrow key.

If, for example, you're in a window displayed in **Icon view**, you can **click** a file and use the Left Arrow key to select any icons to the left of the current selection. The Left Arrow key also can be used in an application to move your insertion point to the left without using the **mouse**.

There are a number of Modifier keys you can use with the arrow keys. Here's a table of the most common keystrokes using the Arrow keys.

Arrow Keystrokes

Sequence	Result
⌘-Left Arrow	Collapses expanded folder
⌘-Down Arrow	Opens folder/opens next file
⌘-Right Arrow	Expands folder
⌘-Up Arrow	Goes to previous folder
⌘-Option-Up Arrow	Closes to previous window
⌘-Shift-Up Arrow	In Open/Save dialog it selects Desktop
⌘-Option-Left Arrow	Collapses all expanded folders
⌘-Option-Right Arrow	Expands all nested folders
Shift-Right Arrow	Selects character to the right of text cursor
Shift-Left Arrow	Selects character to the left of text cursor
Shift-⌘-Right Arrow	Selects word to the right of text cursor
Shift-⌘-Left Arrow	Selects word to the left of text cursor

See Also

Click; Cursor; File; I-Beam Cursor; Insertion Point; Mouse; Select; Views

Lemmings

Although many of Apple's early Macintosh commercials were memorable, they were not all effective. One year after its critically acclaimed and fabulously successful "**1984**" commercial, Apple had a famous dud: "Lemmings."

The Lemmings commercial drew upon many of the same themes as the "1984" commercial: freedom versus authority; creativity versus bureaucracy. But "Lemmings" committed a mortal sin in advertising: it offended its target audience.

"Lemmings" showed a line of business people wearing suits, marching along blindfolded and singing a dirge. One by one, like lemmings, they toppled off a cliff. Finally, the last in the line stopped just short of the cliff and removed his blindfold, asking, "Why am I doing this?" The ad tried to convey the mentality of business: that most executives don't think about many decisions, but rather follow what "everybody else" does. It was a plea to be creative, think for yourself, and buy a Macintosh.

Like the "1984" commercial, "Lemmings" was shown during the Super Bowl. But unlike the optimistic message of "1984," this commercial showed business people plunging off a cliff to their death (or at least into the unknown). It was downbeat and easily could be construed as offensive to the very people to whom it was trying to appeal.

The decision to run the ad was a difficult one for Apple, one it would not soon forget. Many outside observers took the commercial as an indication that Apple was out of control and out of touch.

See Also

1984; Jobs, Steve; Sculley, John

Let's Keep It Simple Spreadsheet

Casady & Greene's Let's Keep It Simple Spreadsheet (KISS) looks more like a Tinkertoy than the **spreadsheet** it really is. Instead of arranging data and **formulas** on a grid, users create data objects—simple lists of numbers for input or display—and then wire them together through mathematical operations and **functions**. This eliminates a lot of the problems beginners encounter when using traditional spread-

sheets: keeping track of whether **cells** have data or formulas, finding space for new data, and presenting a multidimensional relationship on a two-dimensional grid.

The figure shows a KISS document under construction. Objects and operators are **dragged** onto the page from **palettes** on the left, and connected by dragging a line between them. Attributes of how they'll look or process things are dragged from some 20 other palettes: the common ones are displayed along the top, and others can be invoked from menus.

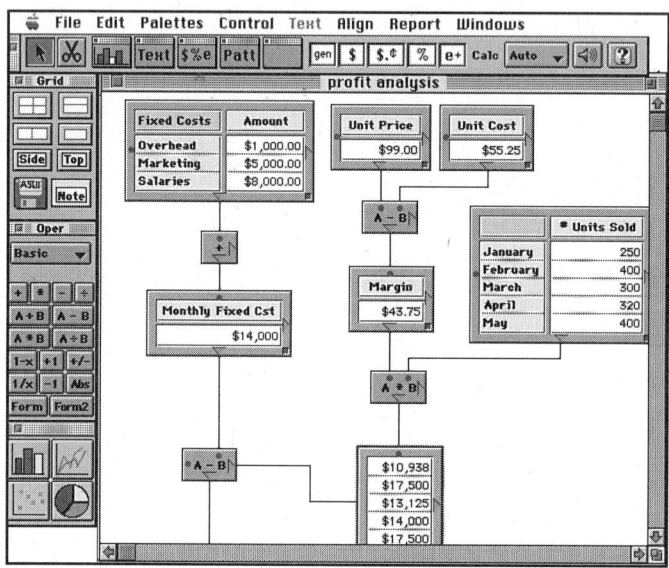

It looks simple, but can get powerful very quickly. Groups of objects can be *crunched* into a single small operator, essentially creating an editable user-defined **function**. These can be dragged onto custom palettes and re-used elsewhere. Entire spreadsheets can be crunched and linked, so a complete small business system can be built without ever having to consult a programming manual.

Spreadsheets can be displayed as multiple *reports* for different purposes, with only the relevant objects (and none of the connections) on each. Layout, text, and graphics can be different on each report, and automatically-updated graphs can be added. Data can be entered from reports, so that casual users never need to see the underlying structure.

Because the program doesn't use a traditional **row** and **column** structure, it can't import or export data in standard spreadsheet formats. It can, however, import a file into an object, which can then be connected to other objects. Although it lacks some features of a full-blown program like **Excel**, that's not surprising in something with a $130 street price.

KISS breaks a lot of conventions, but does anything you'd expect of a mid-level spreadsheet with none of the rigid structure. The program was introduced in mid-1996 and shows some of the roughness of a first-version release. Only time will tell whether users can be convinced to let go of their grids. If they do, it might prove as revolutionary as **HyperCard** was to databases, and you'll soon see active discussions on the newsgroups and libraries of user add-ons in the usual shareware sources.

See Also
Excel; Formulas; Functions; HyperCard; Spreadsheets

Letter Spacing, *See Tracking*

Letterpress, *See Printing*

LetterWorks

Letter writing is a dying art, what with phones, voice mail, and cryptic email messages. Although there's often no substitute for the written word, many people have trouble expressing themselves on paper, and that's why LetterWorks is so successful. These are collections of pre-written letters on a disk, in a text-only format that works with any word processor. There are seven volumes in the series, each consisting of a disk and a reference book. The book contains the text of all the letters on the disk.

LetterWorks topics include business, personal, and sales letters, and legal, personnel, professional, and consulting forms. These can, and should, be customized to fit your needs and situation, but serve as a basis for your own thoughts and ideas. Personal and business letters make it easier to say what you want to say, whether it's collecting an overdue bill, telling an employee that he's not meeting your expectations, or expressing sympathy for the loss of a pet or family member. There are personal letters to fit almost any

situation you can imagine, from, "Sorry I burned a hole in your sofa," to, "Explain the charges on my bill," to, "Will you marry me?" There are invitations and congratulations and thank you's and even a few, "How dare you's."

More useful, perhaps, is the Legal LetterWorks. This collection of 165 legal forms includes leases, wills, partnership agreements, power of attorney, copyright and trademark forms, and all the documents you need to start, buy, or sell a business, operate a corporation, and borrow money. Most important, there's an explanation along with the boilerplate that clarifies what you need to do to fill in the blanks. This alone could save you thousands of dollars in legal bills.

The consulting and personnel volumes are identified as ReadyWorks, because their focus is less on correspondence and more on the types of forms, reports, and other documents you need to deal with employees or provide consulting services. The employee package includes valuable tips on interviews, and the types of questions you can and can't legally ask. There are employee policy statements on everything from attendance and dress codes to employing relatives, jury duty, and sexual harassment. The consulting package includes business plans, proposals, cover letters, brochures, press releases, and requests for credit information and payment. This isn't quite all you need to start your own business, but it's a good beginning.

Ligature, *See Typesetting Terms*

Lightningdraw GX, *See Drawing Applications*

Limiter

A limiter is a sound processor that is similar to a **compressor**, but rather than reduce all signals, it reduces only loud peaks that might distort the sound.

See Also
Compressor; Equalizer; Sound Digitizing

Line Screen, *See Halftones*

Line Spacing

Line spacing refers to the amount of spacing between the lines in a paragraph. Line spacing is the distance, in points, from the top of one line to the top of the next line. It's set automatically for each font, with the distance being 120 percent of the point size of the type. Thus, a paragraph of 12 point type would have the lines set 14 points apart, automatically adding two points of leading.

Typographers express this as 12/14, or "twelve on fourteen." This is done so that the ascenders and descenders don't touch. Double spaced type doesn't double the leading, so it would be 12/26. Most word processors use single spacing as the default, but offer you a choice of 1.5 lines or double spacing as options. Many enable you to set precise spacing at increments of 1 point (1/72").

See Also

Leading

Lingo

The **scripting** language used in **Director**.

See Also

Director; Scripting; XCMDs; XObjects

Linker

A linker is a special program that combines various pieces of object code into a finished application.

Most programs are written as a set of separate source code files or modules. These modules usually refer to routines and variables in other modules. When you compile a single file of code, however, there's no way for the **compiler** to know what might be present in another module.

That's where the linker comes into play. After all of the separate modules have been compiled into **object code**, the linker puts all the pieces together by resolving any references (links) from one module to another.

Because the format of the intermediate object code is usually compiler-specific, linkers generally work with just one compiler (or one family of compilers). The Metrowerks **CodeWarrior** linker, for example, cannot link programs compiled with the **Symantec C++** compilers, and vice versa.

Along with matching links between modules, linkers perform plenty of other magic. Most modern linkers can strip out routines (or whole libraries) that are never called, helping reduce the size of the finished application. Linkers also take care of setting up any machine-specific entry or exit code needed to make an application run properly.

In traditional development environments, the linker is a separate program that you run after the compiler is done. Integrated Development Environments (IDEs), on the other hand, include the linker in the IDE. If you use an IDE to develop on the Mac, you might not even notice the linker doing its thing.

See Also

CodeWarrior; Compiler; Object Code; Symantec C++

Links Pro CD for Macintosh

Access Software is currently the leading company in regard to Mac sports games, and the only game they offer is golf. However, their Links series and add-on courses is the best game series available. The main aspect of computer golf is the same as live golf: timing the swing. The point at which you decide to let the swing go on the swing meter directly affects the amount of power that goes into the swing. Links delves into such detailed golf necessities as club selection and driving the ball. Even foot placement and wind-factor are taken into consideration when coordinating a putt.

Access does an incredible job of faithfully re-creating world-famous courses for the computer. Digitized versions of Harbour Town Links, located in Hilton Head Island, South Carolina, and Banff Springs come with the main program. Multiple add-on courses include the Firestone Country Club in Akron, Ohio; Troon North in Scottsdale, Arizona; and Mauna Kea, Island of Hawaii, with more coming every month. Links Pro and its add-ons offer many helpful options not available on a real course.

You can access animated fly-by views of the holes, as well as overhead views of the entire course to get perspective. Also, you can replay a shot, allowing you to track balls and to see what you could have done better. Access's realism is due to the amount of care that goes into digitizing the courses. Each hole is filmed from a variety of probable angles and then seamlessly digitized into the rest of the course. Links Pro even adds a voice command feature. If your Mac has Apple Speech Recognition, you don't even need to mess with the keyboard to choose clubs and so on.

See Also

PGA Tour Golf III; Sports Games

Lisa

Apple's Lisa computer was the predecessor of the Macintosh. Like the Mac, Lisa featured a built-in bitmapped display, mouse, and graphical interface.

In its closing days, it became a part of the Macintosh family, sold under the name Macintosh XL.

In the late 1970s, **Steve Jobs** began pursuing his vision of creating a totally new computer, one that would be as revolutionary and groundbreaking as the Apple II had been in its day. The Apple III project included some significant advancements, but it wasn't what Jobs had in mind.

During the same period, **Steve Wozniak** was working on creating an entirely new microprocessor for just such a new machine. When it was clear Wozniak wasn't having any success, Jobs took another approach. He hired two engineering managers from Hewlett-Packard to help realize his vision. John Couch would work on the software whereas Ken Rothmueller would lead the new Lisa project.

Initially, the Lisa was designed to be a rather conventional computer for its day. It was to be a departure from the Apple II, but not particularly groundbreaking. It was to retail for about $2000 and ship in 1981. By the end of 1979, Rothmueller's Lisa team had created a prototype of just such a machine. The computer used Motorola's hot new 68000 microprocessor, but wasn't the sort of exciting machine Jobs envisioned.

Meanwhile, Couch's software group had been doing some very interesting work with computer graphics and bitmapped displays. At the center of this work was **Bill Atkinson**. Atkinson had created a core set of drawing and graphics routines that he called LisaGraf. Eventually, these routines would grow into QuickDraw, the graphics portion of the Macintosh **Toolbox**.

During this period, Atkinson and his friend and former professor **Jef Raskin** tried to convince Steve Jobs to take a look at the work that was going on at Xerox's Palo Alto Research Center (**Xerox PARC**). By late 1979, Jobs was convinced, and in exchange for the opportunity to buy 100,000 shares of Apple stock, Xerox allowed Apple two visits to PARC.

L

Jobs and the rest of the visitors were immediately impressed—and excited—by what they saw. The Xerox Alto was unlike any computer they had ever seen. It featured a high-resolution bitmapped display and a strange new input device known as a **mouse**. Users interacted with the computer directly by pointing at objects on-screen. It was revolutionary—just what Jobs had been looking for.

Almost immediately, the direction of the Lisa project changed. It would now be a scaled-down version of the Alto, with plenty of Apple's own ingenuity added as well. By March 1980, a vision of the new Lisa had emerged. Convinced that it would be impossible to create the new machine at the target price of $2,000, Rothmueller was fired for being uncooperative.

Shortly thereafter, Jobs was removed from his role as a leader of the Lisa project by **Mike Scott**. Lisa had become Apple's most important project, and Scott felt they could not jeopardize its success by having Jobs involved. Instead, Scott put Couch in charge of the Lisa project. Angry and hurt, Jobs turned his energies to the Macintosh project that had been shaping up under the direction of Jef Raskin.

The Lisa project continued at its slow pace in part because of the major advances the team was making to the interface. Many of the concepts that are fundamental to today's graphical interfaces were created by the Lisa team, including the menu bar with pull-down menus and the **Clipboard** to move information from one application to another.

The Lisa was introduced on January 19, 1983, after Apple had spent $50 million on development. The original Lisa featured a built-in monitor, a full megabyte of RAM, two notoriously unreliably disk drives, a detachable keyboard, and a 5MB hard disk. It was bundled with a suite of seven applications that covered virtually everything a business user might need to do. What's more, Lisa could run more than one of the programs at the same time. Unfortunately, Lisa also had a very steep price tag—just under $10,000.

At $10,000, the Lisa was in many ways the first workstation rather than the next generation personal computer. As a result, Apple ended up competing less with their usual competitors—Commodore, Radio Shack,

and so on—and more with the larger computer companies who made minicomputers. It was a market in which Apple had no selling experience.

The Lisa never quite got off the ground. Initial sales were weak, and even after Apple unbundled the software and lowered the price, sales picked up only slowly. A significant part of the problem were the rumors circling the computer industry about a cheaper computer with all of Lisa's features that would be available just around the corner: the Macintosh.

Despite improvements in the second generation Lisa, the Lisa 2, sales failed to show much increase. Before it was finally discontinued in April 1985, the Lisa 2 had one last hurrah as the Macintosh XL. The XL was actually a renamed Lisa 2/10 with a software package called MacWorks that enabled it to run Macintosh software.

See Also

Apple Computer, History; Atkinson, Bill; Jobs, Steve; Macintosh, History; Raskin, Jef; Scott, Mike; Toolbox; Wozniak, Steve; Xerox PARC

List Disk (Keyboard Shortcut)

To list the available disks in an **Open** or **Save** dialog box, use the keyboard shortcut ⌘-D, which displays all of the disks available at the desktop level. The keyboard shortcut Shift-Option-' selects the disk at the top of the list.

See Also

Desktop; Dialog Box; Disks and Drives; Keyboard Shortcuts; Open; Save

List Previous Disk (Keyboard Shortcut)

In an **Open** or **Save** dialog box, you can select the previous disk by using the keyboard shortcut ⌘-Right Arrow. This chooses the previous disk (based on the order it appears on your desktop) and cycles through its contents. Pressing ⌘-Left Arrow toggles back in the opposite direction.

See Also

Keyboard Shortcuts; Open Command; Save Command

List View Date Format

When you view the contents of a **window** in a **list view** (view by name, size, kind, or date), you can choose the format in which you want the file's **modified date** displayed by using the **Date and Time control panel**. When you open the control panel, click the Date Formats button to reveal the Date dialog box. The default is the day/month/year format, but you can choose any format you want from a series of **pop-up menus** and check boxes in the dialog box. If, for example, you prefer to have the year appear first, and the day and month second and third, respectively, you can select this option from the pop-up menu. Windows displayed in the List View now show the last modified date by year, day, and month.

To change the list view date format, follow these steps:

1. Choose the Date & Time control panel from the Control Panels subfolder on the Apple menu.

2. Click the Date Formats button.

3. Choose your preference for date formats from the pop-up menus and check boxes in the dialog box, and close the control panel when your choices are complete (see the following figure).

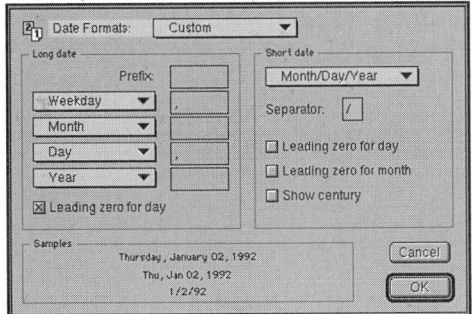

See Also

Date and Time Control Panel; List View; Modified Date; Pop-Up Menus; Window

Listing Windows with Small Icons

To list files by size, or another view option, and still view them by small icon, select a window and choose by Size from the **View menu**. Then choose by Small Icon from the View menu. Press the Option key and select Clean up by Size from the **Special menu**.

See Also

Special Menu; View Menu

Lists in HTML

Lists represent collections of items in an **HTML** document on the **World Wide Web**. HTML includes six common types of lists: ordered lists, unordered lists, definition lists, menu and directory lists, nested lists, and compact lists:

Ordered lists use numerals to designate individual list items. Ordered lists use the tags <OL> </OL>:

```
<OL>
<LI> The Coconuts (1929)
<LI> Animal Crackers (1930)
</OL>
```

The preceding HTML will be displayed as:

```
1.  The Coconuts (1929)
2.  Animal Crackers (1930)
```

Unordered lists typically use large dots called *bullets* to mark each list item. Unordered lists use the tags <UL> </UL>:

```
<UL>
<LI>Groucho
<LI>Chico
<LI>Harpo
</UL>
```

This HTML will be displayed as:

- Groucho

- Chico

- Harpo

Definition lists present a list of items, each followed by an indented paragraph under it:

```
<h3>Famous Groucho Marx Characters</h3>
<dl>
<dt>Professor Quincy Adams Wagstaff
<dd>Huxley College professor in
<em>Horsefeathers</em>
<dt>Rufus T. Firefly
<dd>President of Fredonia in <em>Duck Soup
</em>
<dt>Otis B. Driftwood
<dd>sleazy manager in <em>A Night at the
Opera</em>
</dl>
```

Note that <DD> and <DT> do not require end tags. <h3> is a heading tag, and <em> is a character style tag giving emphasis.

- *Nested lists* refer to an entire list (unordered, ordered, definition, and so on) placed within another list (unordered, ordered, definition, and so on). The nested list will be indented farther than the list that contains it.

- *Menu* and *directory lists* have been replaced by other tags in HTML that produce the same effects. A reader may still see reference to menu and directory lists on the World Wide Web, however.

- A *compact list* uses the attribute COMPACT with one of the list tags <DL COMPACT>, <OL COMPACT>, or <UL COMPACT> to compress a list and consume less space on a Web page. Because many users have small monitors, conserving space is important on the Web.

See Also
HTML; HTML Markup Tags; Web Browser; Web Page; World Wide Web

LISTSERV

LISTSERV is computer software that is used to set up and maintain mailing lists on the **Internet** and automatically add and subtract subscribers to those lists.

LISTSERV is the name of common software found on IBM mainframes (which explains the capital letters). The name has come to represent all automated

mailing lists, although other packages, such as ListSTAR by StarNine Technologies, exist for the Macintosh.

Every LISTSERV has at least two **email** addresses associated with it: the address for the LISTSERV itself and the address for the mailing list. The LISTSERV address handles subscriptions, requests to unsubscribe, and can answer questions if the user has set up an automated help file. The mailing list address receives the messages that subscribers send back and forth.

To subscribe to the TidBITS mailing list, which presents regular information about Macintosh hardware and software, send email to **listserv@ricevm1.rice.edu**. The contents of the message should assume a standard format that the LISTSERV will recognize:

SUBSCRIBE TIDBITS [your *full* name, at least two words]

The LISTSERV will return an email message confirming your subscription and providing general information about the list you have joined (it's a good idea to save this list when it comes time to unsubscribe). After you have been on a list for some time, the LISTSERV might ask you to confirm your subscription.

See Also
Email; Internet; Mailing List; Netscape; POP3 Protocol; QuickMail; SMTP; Web Server; WebSTAR; World Wide Web

Literature on CD, *See Hypertext Fiction*

Little Kidmusic, A

Many programs try to teach music with nonmusical games: learners click notes to shoot targets or battle monsters. A Little Kidmusic is more focused, organized around standard notation and solfege, and the music becomes its own reward. The computer serves as a patient accompanist as well as coach, and points are earned and immediately displayed for good musicianship.

Kidmusic uses real notation to teach musical principles for many ages:

- Preschoolers can listen to familiar songs for entertainment, and then play them with full harmonies by tapping the rhythm.

- More advanced students—up through junior high—hear spoken hints about unusual key signatures or rhythmic nuances and are asked to play (or, with additional software, sing) the music on-screen.

- Students at any level can record and then play back and see with proper notation their own songs.

In each case, the program provides rhythmic and harmonically correct background: in a sense, it plays the "left hand" while you play the melody. It even pauses and vamps when a student plays a wrong note, waiting until it hears the right one. A **MIDI** synthesizer or department-store keyboard is helpful, but not required. For kids who are serious about music, this is the way to go.

See Also
Adventure Games; Juilliard Music

Live Actors in Games, *See Daedalus Encounter, The; Foul Play; Hell; Hollywood Connection; Return to Zork; Riddle of Master Lu, The; Wing Commander III*

Live Picture

For working with large **bitmapped images** (more than 50MB), Live Picture offers many of the functions of **Photoshop**, with great increases in speed.

The Functional Interpolating Transformation System (FITS) rapidly processes edits (retouching, colorizing, distortion, compositing, lighting, feathering, and blending) and saves them in a separate file from the image data, whereas Live Picture's proprietary IVUE file format loads into RAM only the portion of the image that the user views at any given time. These innovations speed up work in Live Picture, because there's no waiting while the software applies edits to the whole image. Also, the program doesn't require

the huge amounts of RAM that Photoshop does—it will work with only 18MB.

Clone, colorize, airbrush, paint, dodge, and burn tools are available, and their size is unlimited. There are also sharpen/blur, smudge, blend, and shimmer tools. Live Picture supports **vector-based** paths for masks and clipping paths, with its own path tools, automatic silhouetting, and the capability to import paths from **FreeHand**, **Illustrator**, and Photoshop.

Colors are calculated in 48-bits, rather than 24 or 32 as with other programs, so there's no banding in blends and no color artifacts. Although Live Picture's native IVUE format is **RGB**, the program offers a Pantone color selector, as well as tools for checking and correcting **CMYK** values within an image. Adaptive separation generates and calibrates separation tables to maintain original CMYK values on output, and separation controls (including UCR, GCR, and dot gain) can be used during image editing.

Live Picture doesn't support Photoshop **plug-ins**, and it doesn't have as strong a filter set as its competitor. But it does come with a plug-in that enables you to import IVUE format files into Photoshop for tweaking. For import and export, it supports IVUE, **TIFF**, Photoshop, **PhotoCD**, **EPS/DCS** and Scitex CT.

Workflow in Live Picture is somewhat different than that of more traditional image editors; all changes are shown on-screen, but they're saved in a separate file from the image data. Changes are only applied to the entire image later, when the image is rendered to an IVUE file. Here's where the processing time comes in, but Live Picture does allow batch processing for this procedure, so users can render multiple images in one unattended session.

Each effect applied in Live Picture takes place on its own layer. This can be cumbersome, but it allows effects to be altered or undone at any time.

The program's client/server architecture enables multiple users to work on the same file, saving their changes into separate files, and swap the changes without having to swap the entire image file.

The Live Picture Process

1. A new document is opened.

2. Component graphics are loaded. These should all be FITS files (translated from other image formats).

3. The image is moved into place around its "X point," or image movement center (which can be repositioned visually or numerically). Double-clicking the X point brings up a numerical dialog for repositioning. The image's position, rotation, and scale can be altered by using numeric input areas at the top of the screen, and the image can be cropped numerically or visually.

4. The Mode tool is clicked to bring the Toolbox to the Creative Tools mode. The preset colors translate the image to whatever palettes are desired. Preview displays accompany all palette changes, and numerical controllers allow finer tuning. Updated previews of all changes are included in the Live Picture's Layer Stack.

5. Next, additional images are brought in, repositioned, and altered as needed. An interactive gradation box determines the opacity of the chosen graphic. You can manipulate the separate RGB channels of the chosen graphic, adding tints and washes, by moving interactive sliders for each channel. For instance, contrast can be altered by moving a C-Splined curve that represents the contrast of the selected image.

6. A "Build" file is created by accessing the Build menu at different points in the process. This contains DPI and sizing information. Anti-aliasing and compression can be toggled on in this file. An IVUE file is created that contains the updated image data.

7. Power Tools, including **Béziers**, are included for image creation in Live Picture. Selection tools, including masking stencils (hard and soft edged), can be applied at this point to selected images and layers. Live Picture enables you to drag-and-drop image transla-

tion elements from one layer of the composite to another layer, an appreciated feature. Live Picture's layering capabilities are far above anything comparable in Photoshop. An array of image distortion effects is also included that allows for the creation of various material-like looks (metal, glass, and so on).

8. When complete, the composited image is saved as an IVUE file, taking as little as one percent of the space on your hard drive that a decompressed standard bitmap would.

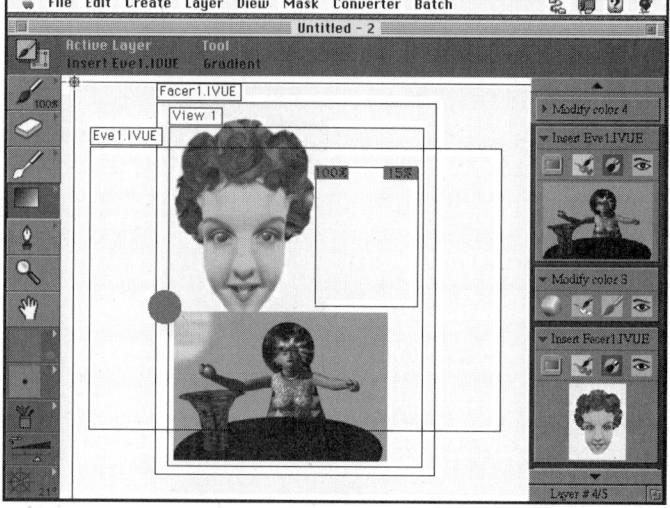

Live Picture's Secrets Layers created in Live Picture are 48-bit and resolution independent, meaning that they can be resized to any degree and still maintain their information. Gradations and other effects are usually applied in separate layers. Gradation controls are part of the selection box that surrounds an area of interest. Live Picture can also use a special "merge" function to combine different FITS files together into one composite, with each FITS file's separate layers intact. Separate merged files can be sandwiched together with each having its own level of transparency. Color correction, with full before and after previews, can be targeted to the image, including Gamma correction, contrast and other adjustments.

Live Picture has a full set of font application tools as well. Using the Type dialog, data is automatically written as a path-object to the editing screen. Bézier adjustment of letter paths is made easy by a clear view of all control points. Creations in Live Picture demand a mastery of its layering features more than anything else, because most added shapes and colors are placed on separate layers and then finalized. Live Picture's method of incorporating gradient start and end gradient percentages as a part of the selection shape is a stroke of genius, as is its use of an interactive slider to indicate layer transparency. Between the tutorial documentation and the videotape, the tools and processes of Live Picture can be mastered within hours of opening the box.

See Also

Bitmapped Images; CMYK; DCS; EPS; FreeHand; Illustrator; PhotoCD; Photoshop; Plug-Ins; RGB; TIFF; Vector Images

LocalTalk, *See*
Networking

Locked Disk, Using,
See Permanently Locked Disk, Using

Locking a Disk

Locking a **disk** protects the contents from accidental erasure or from having the disk's contents altered in any way. Locking a disk is not a software **command**; you have to lock the disk manually (using your finger or thumbnail) by setting a tab that appears on the back of the disk itself.

You cannot **delete** a file from or copy a file to a locked disk, but you can copy files from a locked disk to your **hard drive** or any other unlocked disk. Disks are locked by moving their sliding tab. The locking/unlocking tab appears on the back of the disk in the top-left corner.

When a disk is locked, you can see through the opening in the sliding tab. To unlock the disk, simply slide the tab until you cannot see through the tab's opening.

When you open any window on a locked disk, an **icon** of a lock appears in the disk's **info bar** to let you

know that the disk is locked. If you move items around on a disk, they return to their original positions the next time the disk is loaded. If you try to move a file into, or out of, a folder on a locked disk, a **dialog box** appears stating, "This command could not be completed because the disk is locked."

When you buy a new disk, it is in the unlocked position. However, when you buy software, the disks should be locked so that you don't accidentally trash important files.

See Also

Delete; Disks and Drives; Hard Disks; Icons; Info; Locked Files; Window

Locking a File

If you have an important document or file that you do not want **deleted** or edited in any way, you can lock that file to protect it. To lock a file, **click** the **icon** of the file and choose **Get Info** from the **File menu.** In the lower-left corner of the Get Info window is a **check box** to Lock the file as shown in the following figure. To lock the file, click the Locked check box and **close** the Get Info window. This protects your disk from being deleted by the **Empty Trash** command or from being edited by anyone else.

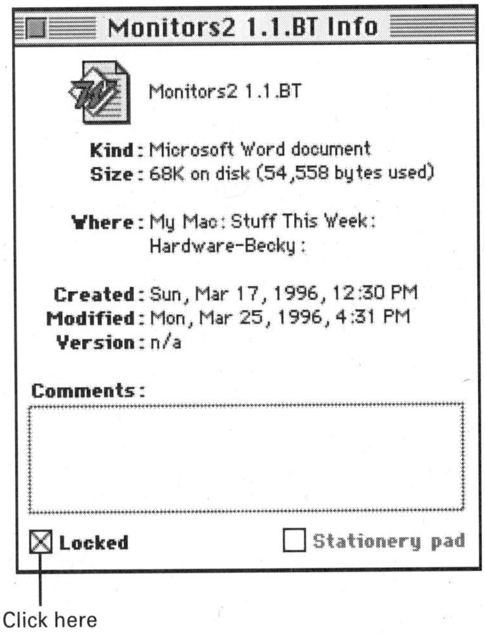

Click here

If a document you have locked is **launched**, a dialog box appears that reads, "The document is locked, so you will not be able to save any changes. Do you want to open it anyway?" If you choose to launch your locked document, you can make changes, but you have to save the changed document with a different name by choosing **Save As** from the File menu. This does not alter your original document; it is still locked. If someone tries to delete your locked file by choosing the Empty Trash command, a dialog box appears stating, "The trash cannot be emptied because it contains locked items." This is your safeguard against anyone accidentally deleting important files. There is, however, a way to empty the trash when it contains a locked document. Pressing the **Option key** while choosing Empty Trash from the **Special menu** deletes any locked files in the trash.

To lock a file, follow these steps:

1. Select the icon of the document you want to lock.

2. Choose Get Info from the File menu.

3. If it is not already checked, click the check box Locked.

4. Close the Get Info window. The file is now locked.

See Also

Checkbox; Click; Close Command; Empty Trash; File Menu; Get Info; Icons; Menu; Option Key; Save As; Special

Lode Runner: The Mad Monks' Revenge Online

The latest version of the classic Lode Runner arcade game adds an online element to one of the longest running game series this side of **Zork.**

Originally shareware, Lode Runner, a cross between an **adventure game** and **arcade** shoot 'em-up, sends you scurrying around various levels and platforms in search of color-coded keys and lost treasure. To make things more difficult, you've got to contend with hooded, red monks chasing after you. The premise is similar to that of the arcade classic Pitfall, which featured a man swinging over pits and avoiding alliga-

tors, or to more recent video games like Donkey Kong. Sierra Online has added 150 new levels in the new Lode Runner, new traps and tools, as well as the capability to play via a **modem** or **network**. You can team up with another player or compete against each other for the treasure.

Lode Runner features clear, colorful graphics that blow away the earlier versions. As repetitive arcade adventures go, Lode Runner is among the best. Other games similar to Lode Runner are Prince of Persia I & II from Brøderbund, now sold bundled together, and Power Pete from **MacPlay**.

See Also

3-D Ultra Pinball; Crystal Crazy; MUDs and MOOs; Network Games; Online Entertainment; Online Live Games; Prince of Persia; Shareware Games; StarPlay Productions

Lofting, *See Modeling*

Logic Board Upgrade

This upgrade is between models with the same case/form-factor. For example, the Mac IIx could be upgraded to a IIfx by replacing the logic board. Another, more current, Logic Board Upgrade is the Quadra 800 to PowerMac 8x00.

See Also

Upgrade Paths

Logical Address

If your network consists of only two devices, a Mac and a printer for example, you don't need to think about addressing. There's only one place for data to go. It can't easily get lost. But when you add devices, you complicate matters. You can't send data out into a network to wander. You have to tell it where to go. The way is to assign addresses. Each node has a number. The Node number is within the range of 0-255.

If you have fewer than 255 devices, or nodes, you won't run out of numbers. But large offices, schools, and other businesses may have many more nodes. So the nodes are grouped into networks. Each network can have 256 devices, and the networks can be joined by routers so that the devices on one can communicate with devices on another. Every logical connection or transaction within a network also has a socket number. The logical address combines the node number, network number, and socket number to define exactly where a data transaction is taking place. For example, Macintosh Node number 32, on network 100, is communicating over socket 164 to Laser Printer Node number 17, also on network 100, at socket 183.

Logical Journey of the Zoombinis

An innovative program from Brøderbund to teach mathematical thinking and reasoning skills by solving sets of puzzles. Students must move groups of little creatures called Zoombinis across an island to their new homeland, passing through the Allergic Cliffs, the Stone Cold Cave, past the Pizza Trolls, crossing the Bayou on Captain Cajun's swamp boat, and lots more strange scenes (twelve in all). At each stop along the way, the student must apply logic and analysis to the situation. At the Allergic Cliffs, two stone gods guard the rope bridges. Each of them is allergic to certain Zoombini features. Whenever they sneeze, one of the pegs holding up the bridge flies off. The player's task is to determine what makes one bridge guard sneeze, and send the creatures with that characteristic across the other bridge. After six sneezes, the bridge falls down. At Pizza Pass, the player must provide the troll with a pizza he likes. Then, he'll let the Zoombinis cross, but he's a very picky eater.

Each puzzle requires several different math and logic skills. All of them require the ability to match and compare attributes and combinations. Some, like the pizza problem, require organizing data and eliminating the unacceptable choices. Others, particularly the swamp ferry, demand that data be organized in sets. Each Zoombini must take a seat on the ferry next to a Zoombini with a shared characteristic. There are several levels of difficulty in each puzzle, and the program is structured so that the student must complete all the levels in order to complete the colonization of the new Zoombini homeland. The program is rated for ages 8-12, but older kids will also enjoy it, and parents might find many of the problems difficult. It's challenging and fun. What more could anyone ask of educational software?

See Also
Math Workshop

Logical Volumes

You partition your **hard disk** into two or more segments using **Apple's HD SC Setup** utility. These partitions (or logical volumes) show up on the **desktop** as separate hard drive icons, even though they are segments of the same hard drive.

You might want to create these partitions for a variety of reasons:

- Security (you can password-protect an entire partition), which is especially useful if other people use your computer.

- To keep files created by other people who use your computer separate from yours.

- For files to be **backed up.**

- For archived customer files or seldom-used letters that you don't want to retrieve from a **disk**.

One of the main reasons people partition their hard drive is for increased speed. This means they're working on one portion of their drive at any one time. The hard drive should be able to read, write, and retrieve files faster because there's less space to search and less movement of the hard drive's heads. Each time the drive's heads have to move, it takes time and slows the speed that information is processed. Less movement means quicker response time.

See Also
Apple HD SC Setup; Backing Up; Desktop; Disks and Drives; Hard Disks

Logo, *See Apple Logo*

Logo Typefaces, *See Typefaces*

LogoMotion

Specular LogoMotion takes its interface cue from Specular International's flagship animation software, **Infini-D**. If you have any experience with Infini-D, mastering the necessary learning curves in LogoMotion should be no problem. LogoMotion enables you to produce very high quality renderings and animation of text objects for **DTP**, broadcast video, and multimedia uses. A pull-down menu at the left of the screen displays LogoMotion's six design categories: Object Info, Surfaces, Bevels, Atmosphere, Stagehands, and Rendering. As each of these categories is chosen, the top menu bar changes to display sub-categories of selectable options.

Object Info Camera, Object, and Light are the three basic targets of the Object Info category. Each is associated with configurable inputs that change the way that these items behave in a scene. As new objects are added to the scene, they are listed in the Info column and can change via user numeric input. Surface properties and shadows can be targeted to objects, camera position and rotation can be altered, and Light positions can be changed.

Surfaces Surface textures in LogoMotion, selectable from a list of options, can be changed according to the following parameters: Color map, Diffusion, Hilite, Metalicity, and Reflection. In addition, graphics can be applied as a texture. Textures are targeted to objects in the display list, and once applied are rendered to the screen (as long as this is the user's choice as opposed to seeing the object in wireframe mode). The LogoMotion library of default textures can be altered endlessly until the best texture for the situation is achieved.

Bevels Every application in LogoMotion is highly real time mouse interactive, so that changing a parameter can be instantly reflected in a new rendering of the scene. The beveling function, applying a routed indentation to a text object, is the best case in point. The angle of the bevel can be altered by a pull-down menu display of the present beveled shape, and back beveling can be toggled on or off. The width and height of the bevel can be altered numerically and default bevels can be selected from a list of options.

Atmosphere This selection refers to environment mapping, the capacity of an object to reflect its surroundings. LogoMotion enables you to change both the colorization of the atmosphere and its "fog" quality.

Stagehands This category is devoted to incorporating preset animation scripts to the scene and also to reconfiguring backdrops. Each choice is reflected in a small visual display on the interface. Stagehands add animated objects to a scene without disturbing the objects placed there by the user. A camera Stagehand list also adds preset camera motions to an animation. Stagehands are invaluable for creating flying logo animation.

Rendering Rendering options include quality (wireframe to "best"), anti-aliasing, shadows on or off, and window setting sizes. File saves include PICT, compressed PICT, Pic, Tiff and QuickTime movie.

Other Features Swivel 3D or DXF 3D models can be added to a LogoMotion scene and texturized. LogoMotion has only two primitive 3D objects aside from a 3D text dialog, a cube and a sphere. This is more than adequate, because other objects in the Swivel or DXF format can always add interest to a scene.

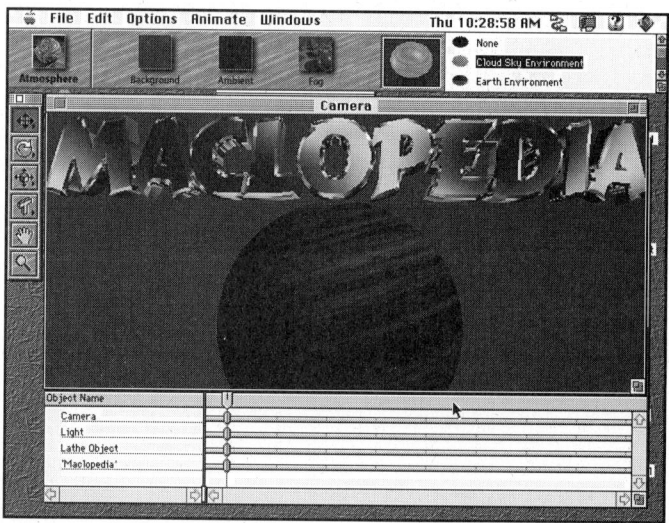

See Also
3D; Infini-D; Modeling

Long-Document Management

Desktop publishers work with all kinds of projects, ranging in size from business cards to 1,000-page textbooks. Although software publishers seem intent on making their products all things to all people, different projects call for different feature sets. The features that are most useful to those producing books and other longer documents are called long-document management tools.

This group of features includes indexing, table-of-contents creation, cross-referencing, footnoting, and the capability to group chapter files together into a book and make changes to all chapters at once. Some of these features are built into page layout packages and word processors, whereas others are available as add-on software.

Often used for its word-processor features, **FrameMaker** is a page-layout package that has many long-document management features. It allows for the insertion of several different types of invisible markers, which it later catalogs and lists as indexes and footnotes. It can also keep track of cross-references—references to text elsewhere in a book—and update page or section numbers as the pagination in a book changes.

Keeping chapter files grouped into a book is a feature that both FrameMaker and **PageMaker** offer; it allows page numbering to be updated automatically and specifies which documents to search when creating indexes and tables of contents. FrameMaker also allows paragraph styles and master pages to be applied to all documents in a book at once.

PageMaker also offers marker-driven indexing and a table-of-contents feature that, like FrameMaker's, scans documents for specific paragraph styles to be included. For example, a table of contents might include all part titles, chapter titles, and first-level headers.

In version 3, **QuarkXPress** doesn't have long-document management tools. But several of these tools are available via **XTensions**, such as Sonar Bookends (indexing, using a word list rather than markers) and Sonar TOC (table of contents generation). Version 4 of QuarkXPress, due out in 1996, is slated to incorporate these features.

See Also

FrameMaker; PageMaker; QuarkXPress; Xtensions

Loony Labyrinth, *See Pinball Games*

Lotus 1-2-3

1-2-3 is the most popular **spreadsheet** in the Windows world, so Lotus Development developed their Macintosh version both to satisfy cross-platform users and capture market share from Microsoft **Excel**. Unfortunately, the latter never happened, and Lotus saw no reason to invest in additional development. As this book went to press, the most recent version of the program was almost four years old and is no longer even listed on the Lotus **Web page**.

It's definitely showing its age. **Functions** and data-viewing options are severely limited compared to Excel, and features that are considered necessary today—like online help and automated dialogs to guide you through operations—don't even match the spreadsheet module in low-cost **ClarisWorks**.

If you regularly run spreadsheets in Windows and insist on having the same program in your Mac, you might still be able to get 1-2-3's Macintosh version from Lotus. But if you can't, don't worry. Files are compatible between it and Excel—both programs contain hints for users of the other, and the Microsoft program is a lot more powerful. For most purposes, this 1-2-3 is down for the count.

Loudspeakers, *See Speakers*

Louis Cat Orze: The Mystery of the Queen's Necklace, *See Adventure Games*

LPI, *See Halftones*

LQ ImageWriter Extension

This extension is a printer driver necessary to **print** to an Apple **ImageWriter** LQ dot-matrix printer. The LQ ImageWriter Extension is accessed through the **Chooser** on the **Apple menu**.

See Also
Apple Menu; Chooser; ImageWriter; Print

Luminance, *See Glow*

Lycos
The name of this **Internet search engine** comes from the arachnid family *Lycosidae*. Lycos was developed and is owned by Dr. Michael L. Mauldin of Carnegie-Mellon University. Lycos searches are built around full text searches. It searches **HTTP**, **FTP**, and **Gopher** sites. As of May 1, 1996, its database included 39 million link descriptions, and this number is constantly growing. Lycos also tells you when a site was last updated, and the information about file size gives you an idea of how long it will take to load on-screen.

The home page for Lycos is **http://www.lycos.com/**.

See Also
Search Engine; Searching; World Wide Web

M

μLaw Compression Format, *See*
AU

MacApp

MacApp is the grandfather of all Macintosh programming frameworks. It evolved from the Lisa Toolkit framework, written in Clascal (Pascal with classes) and was used to develop software for the Mac's predecessor, the **Lisa**. MacApp was first introduced by Apple in 1986. At that time, the **C++** programming language had not yet caught on to the extent it has today, and most of the programming for the Macintosh was done in the **Pascal** programming language. As a result, Apple developed MacApp using a special object-oriented version of Pascal known as Object Pascal.

Over the years, Mac development has moved away from Pascal, and so has MacApp. Version 3 and later are written in C++ and take advantage of many C++ language features not available in Object Pascal. Because many developers have a large investment in Pascal MacApp programs, the older version of MacApp still has a large following.

Conversation with Andy Herzfeld
Andy Herzfeld's code helped launch the Mac and keep it rolling. He's been associated with two other companies we might think of as coming out of the Apple stable, because they were started by so many Apple alumni—Radius, and General Magic. Here he reflects on the spirit of Apple.

Maclopedia: What was your first experience with the developing Mac?

Andy: I was just working at Apple, and I became friendly with Burrell Smith. He had a 6809 chip and a 256×256 7-inch screen, and he didn't have the microprocessor all set up, but he did have the video hooked up to an Apple II, so from the Apple you could poke data into the Mac frame buffer. I stayed very late the night he had just gotten it up to get a nice picture on the Apple II screen. I just found the picture lying around. It was Scrooge McDuck playing the fiddle while sitting on some money bags. I had just found some neat proportional font software for the Apple II, so I wrote, "Hi, Burrell," underneath the picture because the Apple II only had 192 scan lines. But the Mac had 256, so there was room. Burrell was shocked that this little computer could do this, and he saw this beautiful picture on the first day after the video was working. That was eight months before I actually joined the team.

The very first prototype was conceived, and the initial design was done over the Christmas of 1979 and early 1980. I did some little demos for the prototype, and I was disappointed when the little tiny Mac team moved to a separate building. In February 1981, Steve Jobs took over the project, over in Bandley One. He brought me onto the team.

Steve Jobs came over to my cubicle and said, "Well, Andy, you are on the Mac now," and I said, "Well, I want to finish up this code for the Apple II," and Steve is impatient, and said, "Oh that shit, that Apple II is shit, come over now." What he did was, he pulled the plug out of the wall socket, and started carrying the Apple II away to his car. We got into his car and drove to the new building a few blocks away. Burrell had

continues

just hooked a disk controller to the Mac, and Woz's [Steve Wozniak] design was very dependent on software—software has to provide the timing—so I made a Woz-style disk driver.

Maclopedia: What was it like to work on the first Mac team?

It was really fun, a small number of people, with a high percentage of rebels as opposed to mainstream people. They did not ask for credentials or pedigrees; it was a collection of hackers. The seed crystal was Burrell's brilliant hardware. It was an inspiring kernel of brilliance, in part because of the price performance—the absolute minimum number of chips for an incredible amount of performance for the price. In 1980, to conceive of a sub-$3,000 computer seemed miraculous, and the Mac was a $1000 computer. But the other part was the spirit of creativity, like Woz's spirit of creativity.

So I worked on the IO system, and I helped Bud Tribble get a development system so we could use a Lisa to download to a Mac.

When Bud left, my responsibility shifted to a higher level, particularly the User Interface Toolbox. That was done mainly in 1982, including the Window Manager, the Menu Manager, the control panel, and other pieces like the fonts.

In 1980, to conceive of a sub-$3,000 computer seemed miraculous, and the Mac was a $1000 computer. But the other part was the spirit of creativity, like Woz's spirit of creativity.

Maclopedia: How was the user interface developed?

Andy: I was one of three or four people who were the keepers of the interface. We had a seminal set of meetings. We started with the Lisa interface, which was already designed but evolving. We had an urge to simplify. In January 1982, Bud Tribble, Joanna Hoffman, Randy Whittington, Chris Espinosa, Steve Jobs, and I sat in a room for four days and made some basic decisions and rejected some paths, corroborated that we would take other paths. Joanna wrote that up in the first Mac interface guidelines and later Chris took over that document.

We had this notion—which was radical at the time—that we would like all applications to share a common user interface. It was an unproved concept at the time.

We thought that if we wrote all the routines and put them in ROM—though we knew developers would always rather do things their way—if we had the routines in ROM, they would see it saved them space. The Mac was very limited in memory at the time, and so then they would go along with it. Of course, we had to do a very great job at the user interface level, and at the code level.

Maclopedia: What was your special area?

Andy: I felt that the ROM was mine. Fitting all that functionality into that small space was my thing. I really worked hard on every aspect. I had done the low level IO before and Larry Kenyon took that over, and I wrote most of the original desk accessories. We committed to ROM in early September 1983, so we had another few months, and I wrote the Scrapbook and the Puzzle. I usually used assembly language to write the smallest, best programs, but I wrote the puzzle in Pascal to demonstrate that it was possible to write a desk accessory in a high-level language—but because the Pascal program had to be linked to the library, I had an overhead of 5K, which was okay because it was just a demonstration, but later the Puzzle became symbolic. More marketers were being drawn in, and one of the criticisms was that the puzzle made the Mac seem toy-like. They wanted to get rid of it as the most overtly toy-like thing, but the excuse was that it was so big, that it was 7K, total. But really, it was the spirit of the thing. So I went home that weekend and rewrote it in assembly language, and got it down to less than 800 bytes. And that dismantled the argument, so we shipped the puzzle.

Maclopedia: What was it like working with Steve Jobs?

Andy: Burrell had put in excellent sound capability, and using the fact that we could generate better sound, we wanted to amplify the analog circuit so people could hear the great sound, but we didn't have the sound driver working yet. Steve Jobs came by and said, "If you want the amplifier, I want to hear great sound coming out of the machine on Monday morning." Burrell bought me lunch and dinner and helped me design the thing to be efficient, and we wrote the four-voice engine. With the mouse you could sketch a wave form, and if you could hook it up to an oscilloscope, you could see the sound matched the drawing. I hadn't thought sound was a priority, but Steve pushed, so we did the sound driver that weekend.

Maclopedia: When did you leave Apple?

Andy: I quit in March 1984. I didn't quit because I wanted to work for myself but because they hired a manager who had an authority complex that was 180 degrees out of phase with my own authority complex. He insisted that people kowtow to him because of his organizational position. And Steve would not support me in finding a different way. Steve needed me and people like me to create the Mac, but once the essence of the Mac was created, he needed the next level objective, which was, essentially, to run Apple. Someone like me doesn't have to run Apple at all. He needed that manager for the next objective.

Maclopedia: What did you work on next?

Andy: Thunderscan. I said it was MacPaint for the rest of us because the essence of the Mac was beautiful graphics. But if you can't draw, it was very hard. Thunderscan was a low-cost way to get graphics into the machine, turning the ImageWriter into a scanner. I did the software for that. Vick Bull did the hardware.

And the Switcher. I had my switcher proof of concept done before I finished Thunderscan. Apple shipped that as mainstream software. And then Servant, which added capabilities of the MultiFinder, but it didn't work out the way I wanted. Apple really didn't use it as much as I would have liked.

I did a lot of soul searching after my problems with Servant. Servant had a lot of things that are ahead of where they are now, nine years later, even though it had weaknesses as well as strengths. What I realized was that I had to work on different stuff as a third party outside of Apple than I would have as an Apple programmer. The Mac was having a hard time. It didn't seem like the Mac would still be here. I did what I thought the Mac needed the most, and what I could do well—this multitasking program. But what I realized after Apple didn't take it up was that I should work on applications, not systems.

After having this clarity, and designing some applications I planned to work on, I fell into systems programming again, toward the end of 1987, improving the speed of the color graphics on the Mac II. The eight-bit color graphics were too slow to be usable, and I saw a possibility of improving them. But that went against my newfound wisdom. I was just drawn into it. I got onto this hot streak where I did very high quality work very fast. It wasn't what I wanted to be doing. Over two weeks, I tripled the speed of the eight-bit graphics with just a bit of software. But I was emotionally distraught. I didn't know what to do about it. I started showing it to people and it became controversial. I was at odds with my best friend Burrell. He thought Radius should own it, but I thought that was wrong because Radius had competitors and it would force everyone to patch up the graphics. It really had to come from Apple. The key, I realized, was not to charge a lot of money for Quicker Draw. That enabled the engineers to embrace it, you know, without any jealousy. I sold them non-exclusive rights, and distributed it on CompuServe, and it was incorporated into System 6. That healed the wound. I had never wanted to do system stuff again, but that worked out.

Maclopedia: When did you decide to go beyond the Mac?

Andy: At the time I was finishing Servant, I decided I had to get off the Mac. The Mac was showing its first signs of getting obsolete. It was not an object-oriented system. By then people were catching on to layering objects onto C, so you could use the objects where appropriate. I wanted to focus on more modern systems using object-oriented programming.

But Burrell was mad at me for selling Quicker Draw to Apple, so he asked me to do a proprietary thing for Radius with a hardware board using the Acorn chip and a block-transfer mode of NuBus, and I wrote a version of Quicker Draw to run on this board. That was my last real Mac project. After that I started working on an intelligent TV set.

Maclopedia: What was the intelligent TV set?

Andy: This was before the time they used the term multimedia. I did that with Hartmut Esslinger, of FROG, the German design team that did the later Macs, the NeXt box, the SPARC stations, and lots of Sony products. He had the vision of an intelligent TV set, with

continues

the schedules on the screen, and I worked on that for a year and a half, until I saw that the business underpinnings were not strong enough, so I stopped in the early '90s.

Then I got a call from my mentor, Bill Atkinson, who was very excited about Pocket Crystal at Apple, and that led to me being one of the cofounders of General Magic. The Magic Cap system software has all of my preoccupations in one.

Maclopedia: Overall, what was the effect of working with people at Apple?

Andy: I learned almost everything from a small number of people: Steve Jobs, Steve Wozniak, Burrell Smith, Bill Atkinson. The spirit of their work, each quite distinct and different, is what I call the spirit of Apple.

MacApp is a mature and feature-rich programming framework. It includes excellent core functionality, including great memory management and human interface handling. After a period of slowed development, progress on MacApp has picked up significantly. Recent releases of MacApp have added several new features. Applications created using MacApp can take direct advantage of PowerTalk, Macintosh drag-and-drop, and scripting support. MacApp is also slated to support **OpenDoc** in the near future.

Because most of MacApp is a single, large class hierarchy focused on creating applications, it is difficult to use just a part of MacApp for small projects such as control panels or **code resources**. For larger projects, however, the overhead is less of a factor.

See Also
C++; Framework; Pascal

MacBinary File, *See*
Encoding Files

MacBrowse

MacBrowse is a source code **browser** from Apple. It is distributed with the **MacApp** application **framework**, but it is not restricted to browsing only MacApp code. MacBrowse follows the familiar multi-pane window approach to browsing **object-oriented** code (see following figure).

The upper-left pane displays each class in the current project. The top center pane displays the member functions of the currently selected class, whereas the upper-right pane shows the data members. The large remaining pane is the editor, where the currently selected function is displayed.

Editing code in a browser such as MacBrowse can make it much easier to see the relationships among various parts of an object-oriented program. Rather than viewing and editing code based on its arrangement on disk (file-by-file), a browser shows code by its logical arrangement. The actual file associated with any given bit of code is of secondary importance.

See Also
Browser; Framework; MacApp

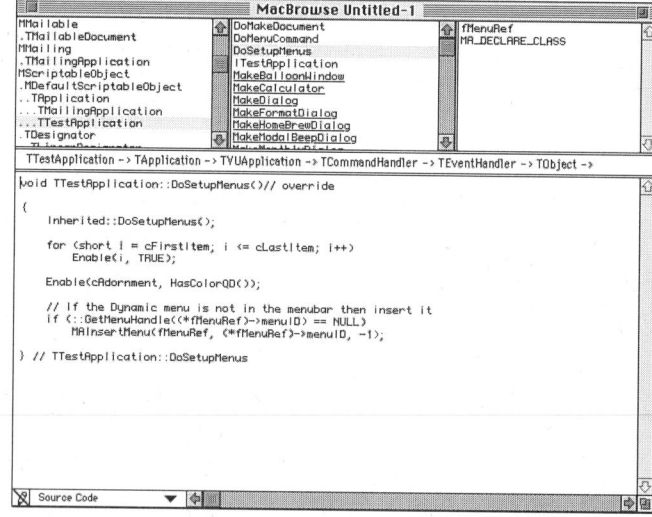

MacFrog

Educational **HyperCard** program for junior high and high school students, from Intellimation. MacFrog simulates dissecting a frog, without any of the mess, smell, or cruelty to amphibians. The program includes quizzes on the skeleton and the circulatory, digestive, and reproductive systems, as well as animated explanations of various functions. If the goal is to teach frog anatomy, this program does it as well as, or better than an actual dissection. If the goal is to teach science in a "hands on, explore and document your findings" manner, the experience of doing the dissection is as important as learning the inner workings of the frog. But there's room in the classroom for both types of learning, and MacFrog is a good alternative for those students who may not need or want to get their hands on a real frog.

Students with access to the World Wide Web can dissect a virtual frog, courtesy of Lawrence Berkeley Laboratories. It's found at **http://george.lbl.gov/ itg.hm.pg.docs/dissect/info.html** and includes MRI scans, X-rays, and scholarly discussions on various aspects of frog anatomy.

See Also

Internet, Educational Resources

Machine Language

Machine language is the set of digital instructions understood by the microprocessor. This instruction set is the only language any computer can deal with at its most basic level. In order for a computer to use a program written in any other language, such as C++ or Java, the program must first be translated into machine language using a **compiler** or interpreter.

Each type of **microprocessor** has its own unique machine language. Families of related processors, such as the PowerPC family, use nearly identical instructions in their machine languages. This way, programs created to run on one PowerPC chip can run unmodified on another. Similarly, most programs that run on one member of the 68000 series, used in earlier Macs, run just as well on another.

On the other hand, unrelated processors use entirely different instruction sets. The instruction set for a Power Mac's PowerPC processor is entirely different from the set for a Quadra's 68040. The following table demonstrates this difference. In the first column is the 68K machine language for a simple routine that handles part of the memory initialization for a Mac application. In the second column is the equivalent PowerPC machine language.

Note that these numbers are written as **hexadecimal**, in which the letters A-F are used to represent digit values of 10-15.

A Comparison of 68K and PowerPC Machine Language

68000	PowerPC
4E56 0000	7C0802A6
2F03	93E1FFFC
362E 0008	90010008
6004	9421FFC0
A036	7C7F1B78
5343	48000010
4A43	48000001
6EF8	60000000
261F	3BFFFFFF
4E5E	7FE30734
4E75	2C030000
	4181FFEC
	80010048
	38210040
	7C0803A6
	83E1FFFC
	4E800020

In order to run programs in one instruction set on another kind of processor, a special program called an **emulator** is needed to translate the instructions from one instruction set to the other.

Programs are rarely, if ever, written directly in machine language. This is because the instructions in machine language are just a series of digital numbers. Higher-level languages are designed to put a friendlier face on programming by providing a human language vocabulary. The closest thing to programming directly in machine language is **assembly language**, in which each machine language instruction is given a short mnemonic that is used in place of the actual digital instruction.

M

See Also

Assembly Language; Compiler; Emulator; Hexadecimal; Programming Languages

MacHTTP, *See WebSTAR/MacHTTP*

Macintosh Computer Family

Apple Computer introduced the first Macintosh computer in 1984 with much fanfare. This was to be a "computer for the rest of us," and as such, was designed as an all-in-one unit containing everything Apple's engineers considered important to an individual user.

The "Macintosh128K (see the following figure) was "luggable," weighing about 20 pounds in a compact footprint. Its chassis contained an **8-bit Motorola 68000** processor, nine-inch monochrome **monitor**, one floppy **disk drive**, 128 kilobytes (!) of Random Access Memory (RAM), a **mouse**, a **keyboard**, a built-in **networking** capability, and a revolutionary operating system fully integrated with the hardware. It was the resulting graphical user interface (GUI) and its intelligent connections to the computer hardware that made the Mac unique. The 128K Macintosh was concise and complete, as shown in the following figure.

You could not open the computer's chassis to add cards, although you could use its **Small Computer System Interface (SCSI)** port to hook up an external hard drive or another floppy drive to increase its storage capacity. You could also print information on a high-quality **dot-matrix printer** connected to one of its two **serial ports**. There was no other upgrade path built into the machine.

Apple has come a long way since that day. Today (as of this writing in early 1996), the Macintosh family has evolved into a multitude of models to fit the many needs of its over 20 million users. Macintoshes come in several flavors:

1. All-in-one box systems, such as the Performa 5200 or Macintosh Classic. These computers have pre-selected components giving you no choice as to size or power of your display, hard disk, or expandability, but providing exceptional price/performance.

2. Modular units that offer many choices, because the only thing that comes with the Mac is the computer processor. Apple has designed many different configurations of RAM, displays, hard drive capacities, and add-ons such as fax/modems. You choose a Mac by choosing the configuration (by model number) that fits your needs. Your Mac supplier can add additional RAM, other peripherals, and so forth, to further customize your Mac.

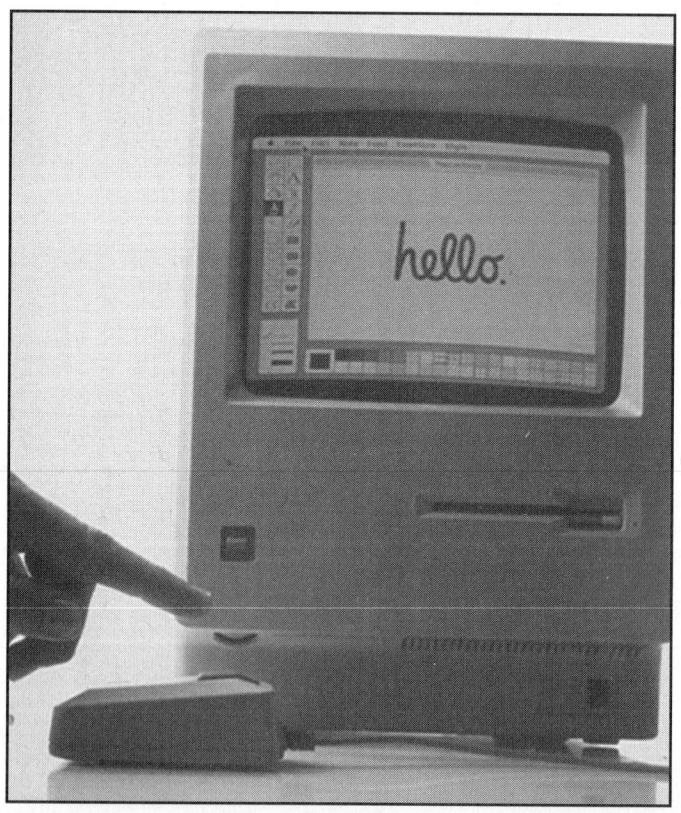

3. Portable units that are light-weight (about 6 pounds or less) and run with power from a battery pack or ac/dc plug. Mac PowerBooks and Duos, like the modular Macs, also come in many configurations of CPU type, RAM, hard disk size, screen size, and type (for example color or monochrome), and add-ons (such as a fax/modem), but all use a trackpad or trackball in the place of a mouse and include PC card slots for adding additional memory, a modem, and so on.

Within each of these Macintosh categories lie many different feature sets. Yet, all Macs provide many usability features not found in the PC world:

- Since 1984, the Mac has offered built-in networking for easy connection to Apple's **AppleTalk** local area network. More advanced Macs, including all of the **Power Macs**, provide further connection to the faster **EtherNet** network that has become a business standard.

- All Macs connect to grayscale or color displays to varying degrees of quality. Many Macs support high-grade **8- or 16-bit color** directly, letting you display millions of colors on your monitor without the use of an additional video card. With the addition of a video card, your Mac can display 24-bit color.

- All Macs provide some expandability for added processing power. Most compact and lower-cost Macs offer a **Processor Direct Slot (PDS)**, sometimes called an LC Slot. PDS slots are fast, but because of their dependence on the Mac's CPU, they do not support a standardized architecture and so are expensive to manufacture because each Mac chip requires a separate type of card. The mid-range and high-end models also provide a **NuBus Slot** that, although slower than the PDS architecture, provides a standard architecture which is not dependent on the CPU, so has more following among

third-party vendors. The most recent Macs provide a new standard slot used in the PC world, called **PCI**, that is faster than NuBus, and also provides a standard architecture. The PCI bus enables Macs to use more third-party vendor cards (with the proper software drivers).

- All Macs provide high-quality sound input and output, with most providing 16-bit stereo quality sound fidelity. Some Macs provide special features that can be used to process audio-visual input and output signals (called **AV** in earlier Mac models). These AV features also enable modern Macs to recognize speech and support extensive telephony systems.

Conversation with Frank Casanova

Frank Casanova helped Apple expand its Mac product line with screamers such as the Mac IIfx. Casanova was laid off, hired back, and now, as director of the Exploratory Products Laboratory for the Advanced Technology Group, he helps Apple figure out where it fits into the future.

Maclopedia: How did you first encounter the Mac?

Frank: I was working at Apollo Computer, a workstation manufacturer in the Boston area, in 1985. Somebody bought one at Apollo. We all took turns taking it home. It was a Mac 128KB; you were constantly swapping floppy disks. I remember bringing it home: it was unbelievably novel. My wife and I set it up on our dining room table, and it beeped and smiled, and in a few minutes, we were drawing and typing. I thought, "What an unbelievably simple machine to use, and so elegant, but hobbled from the point of view of a workstation technology." Then I realized it had the same microprocessor we had in our workstations. Apple had taken all this performance and aimed it right at the user. It did what you wanted, and put the user first. In the workstation world, we put the process first and told the user, "We'll get back to you when we are ready." It was a revelation.

continues

Maclopedia: So how did you find your way to Apple?

Frank: Through *MacWeek* magazine. At Apollo I was product manager for desktop workstations, and we added an IBM PC bus to encourage an after market. There was none at the time, absolutely zero; there were huge expensive applications but no developers. So we put this bus into the machine, and when we did that, some of the PC magazines picked up on it, saying, "Here it is, perhaps, the crossover machine from the workstation arena." Well, it turned out not to be, but *MacWeek* did an extensive interview. The folks at Apple read it, and they were thinking about starting a high performance group. Apple knew very little about high performance architecture, and how to market it. I wasn't making the decision about the microprocessor, but my job would be to rally the troops and set up a product group that would kick off with the first high performance Mac.

The first time Apple called, I said no; my family is from the East Coast, and we were going to stay there. Then they called in April. The day had started off nicely, and I parked my new sports car outside, where I could see it out my window. But the weather changed. Now my car was covered with a solid inch of ice, and Apple called.

I asked, "What's the weather like out there?" And my future boss said, "It's 70 degrees, and sunny," and I said, "FedEx me the tickets."

I went home and my wife and I went out to California. I accepted the job the same day we bought a house.

Maclopedia: Did you experience culture shock moving from Apollo to Apple?

Frank: You know, I interviewed from early in the morning to late in the day, and everyone asked me the question about culture. What they had found was that a lot of people were blown away by the lack of organization. A lot of people cannot exist in that environment, so a lot had quit. They pressed pretty hard on that point. I'm glad I didn't work here as my first job because I appreciated the unparalleled and uncontrollable growth, the passionate, intense hours—and they were long, but it was like a six billion dollar startup.

They handed you a length of rope, and you could make incredible things with it, or you could hang yourself with it, and a lot of people hung themselves with it. And there was a star system, and if you could use that to your advantage you did really well, you had great projects assigned, but if not, you were lost. I did get to take advantage of it, and have fun, and introduced a few products.

Actually, I canceled the first couple of projects because they were addressing Apple's historic problems rather than future opportunities. In the late '80s, various "skunkworks" were under way, [projects] not sanctioned by management, but we kept some activity going in the backroom that wasn't on the product platform. The skunkworks machine was fraught with risk; we were never quite sure if all the pieces would work together, but all the cards fell into place, and the Mac IIfx came out. That was my first machine. It redefined what a high end Mac was, pushed the envelope of compatibility and performance. For instance, we pushed the SCSI performance. That was part of what made the fx truly the first wicked fast Mac. The "wicked fast" expression was mine; it had been part of my normal conversation in Boston, and I was giving a presentation, and I said, "This is a wicked fast Mac," and it stuck. It took on a life of its own, and the project became big, larger than life, and dragged all of us along.

I asked, "What's the weather like out there?" And my future boss said, "It's 70 degrees, and sunny," and I said, "FedEx me the tickets."

Maclopedia: How about the 040 line?

Frank: We started the 040 project because Motorola had begun making some real progress, and we got some samples. We started off with what turned out to be the Quadra 900, but over time we realized that we could get the 040 design to support a smaller, more personal machine, so we could introduce a whole family of products—and we could bring out more than one Mac at a time.

Maclopedia: How did you come up with the name Quadra?

Frank: We were sure that the Quadras were not Mac IIs. They had new metrics, EtherNet built in, VRAM-based video, a whole new architecture—enough of a leap not to call them Mac IIs. So would it be "Mac

Insert Word Here?" such as Mac Classic? We saw how well Acura had done, so we hired a naming company and went off for a few days and hung posters of awesome technology on the walls, like Apache helicopters, and did word association games, and narrowed down to a couple that were worthwhile perusing, and Quadra was the one that evolved.

Maclopedia: And how did you move to multiple Quadras?

Frank: We decided that doing multiple machines within a product line—the 900 and 700—at the same time meant not forcing people to pay the most for a high end machine. We broke our own price performance curve.

Maclopedia: So why did you get laid off?

Frank: I joined the Power Mac team, but I didn't want to be a computer manager. I became the Futures evangelist, finding new ways to use the PowerMac. Then 1993 happened. I wasn't laid off; it was a drive-by shooting. Lots of people got laid off for no particular reason. I was not one of the most important characters adding value. My promise of added value was months away. I didn't hold the people who laid me off in bad regard. The day they handed me a check for eight months pay in one hand, I got three offers of jobs at Apple in the other. I said, "Let's talk in five months." I went out and did consulting, traveled the world, but consulting is a lot of work. I have a lot of respect for consultants now.

Maclopedia: And what are you doing at Apple now?

Frank: I came back to Apple in the Advanced Technology Group. They wanted someone who had both feet on the ground in real-life product experience, to strengthen what the lab was doing, to strengthen relations with the product divisions, and to use my presentation prowess to evangelize and get a lot of attention for our group. So I created this new group, the Advanced Technology Evangelists, looking toward the future, but not just six months or a year away, more like the next three to five years, and we brought messages back to the group, too.

Then that got old, and we repurposed me. I am a director now, and my group is called Exploratory Products. The role of my group is to smash bits of technology together and try less than traditional techniques, new interfaces, new integrations, slam an antenna on that, build twenty of them, and see what people think. My job is to break the rules of technology and supply new experiments. We tell our researchers to break the rules. We try to find out what the researchers want to do research on, and to find out what platform they want to build on, while building strategic relations with developers and leveraging the work in other labs, sharing, and trading, and leveraging those other technologies. I also manage the business plan because we can add a dose of reality to an otherwise surreal group. I do manage a group called Futurists, too, who predict social and cultural trends, and tell me where society is going to be in five years and how we can predict what we will win with.

Maclopedia: Is the Newton part of Apple's future?

Frank: Yes. The Newton was a technology that was a year or two too soon. If we brought that out today, it would be an unbelievable hit. But it is tough to change a first impression, so we have some work. But we are basing a lot of our research on Newton, because we believe in the architecture; it's small, portable, with an interesting kernel, and none of the baggage of the MacOS. The Newton is poised for a comeback.

Apple classifies Macintosh computers by processor type, consumer purpose, and market placement, which makes it very difficult for the layman to figure out which Mac is which. In addition, Mac models change based on the inclusion of cache to increase processing speeds, floating point processors for rapid mathematical computations, audio-visual processors to assist in real time AV processing, and display adapters to ease the attachment of appropriate monitors. Macs also contain faster or slower versions of the same processor chips, as well as different RAM and hard disk configurations. The variety of offerings has become bewildering.

The following table can help you sort out which Mac fits your particular need.

The Macintosh Family

Mac Type	Model Names	Characteristics
Desktop Models	Power Mac 6100, 7200, 7500, 8500, 9500	Stand-alone computers that include CPU, FPU, hard drive, 8 or 16MB RAM, CD-ROM drives, 2 serial, SCSI, ADB ports, Built-in LocalTalk and Ethernet, 16-bit stereo input/output ports, system software, and mouse. Monitor and keyboard sold separately.
Consumer Models	Performa 580, 630 630 CD, and 630 DOS Compatible, 631 CD, 636 CD, 640 CD DOS Compatible, 5200 CD, 5215 CD, 6116 CD, 6200 CD, 6216 CD, 6220 CD, 6230 CD, 6300 CD	Performas are the same Macs as desktop models, but they are packaged as total systems that include color display (except the 636), keyboard, mouse, CD-ROM drive, two serial, SCSI, ADB ports, and built-in LocalTalk. Some models also provide either external or internal fax/modems. All Performas come bundled with extensive software and CD-ROM titles.
Education Models	LC 580, LC 630 DOS Compatible, LC 6100/66 DOS Compatible, 5200/75 LC, and the 5300/100 LC	Similar in configurations to the Performa models but lacking the bundled software.
Portable Models	PowerBook 190s, PowerBook Duo 280c, Duo 2300, and various flavors of 5300	Lightweight laptop or dockable computers containing either a grayscale or color display, 8M RAM, hard drive, built-in LocalTalk, floppy drive (except Duo), 2 PC card slots, 16-bit stereo input/output ports, system software, and trackpad.
Workgroup Servers	Power Mac 6150, 8150, and 9150	PowerPC processor, DRAM, Level-2 cache, hard drive, CD-ROM drive, built-in Ethernet, Apple RAID software and other client/server software bundles, DAT drives.

Out with the Old and In with the New!

Apple has a habit of discontinuing older models without fanfare whenever they introduce new models (typically in August and January). Therefore, the model numbers mentioned in the previous table are as accurate as possible as of the printing of this book. The information for the table is taken from Apple's current (as of February 1996) product list.

According to the Apple Product List of August 28, 1995, the following Macintosh models have been

discontinued: Color Classic, LC 475, LC 520, LC 575, LC III, LC 630, Quadra 605, Quadra 610, Quadra 610 DOS Compatible, Quadra 630, Quadra 650, Quadra 950, Quadra 660AV, and Quadra 840AV.

The Performa models are especially vulnerable to change, because vendors receive configurations and associated model numbers according to their specifications. Thus, the particular models and configurations you find at one store may be significantly different from those which you find at another.

See Also

Consumer Models; Desktop Models; Duos; Education Models; Internet Servers; Laptops; LCs; Performas; PowerBooks; Power Macs; Quadras; Workgroup Servers

Macintosh Culture, *See History and Culture of the Macintosh*

Macintosh Easy Open Setup

If you don't have the application that created a document, Easy Open enables you to open that document with a different application. Let's say, for example, someone in your office gives you a document created in Word Perfect, but you don't have Word Perfect installed on your system. When you double-click the document, instead of getting a dialog box telling you that you don't have the program that created the document, you get a dialog with a list of programs you have that will open the document. If you have Microsoft Word installed, you could select it to open the document that was created in Word Perfect from the Easy Open dialog box.

In the Macintosh Easy Open control panel, you can toggle automatic document translation on and off. And you are presented with three options in the Translation Choices dialog box section of the control panel. The first checkbox asks if you always want the Easy Open dialog box displayed when translating a file. The second checkbox enables the Macintosh to easy open search for and/or launch applications over a network server (if you're connected to a network), and it enables you to choose to have Macintosh Easy Open automatically open the document if there's only one choice of application to open it with, which saves you a trip to the dialog box. You also can click a checkbox to have text documents automatically translated. There is also a button to delete all of your preferences.

To use the Macintosh Easy Open control panel, follow these steps:

1. Select the Easy Open control panel from the Control Panels submenu on the Apple menu (or System Folder).

2. Click the On button (the default).

3. Choose your translation choices from the checkboxes on the left side of the dialog box. Choose "always show dialog" box if you want to pick the application to open the document from a list of applications, rather than having Macintosh Easy Open open the application of its choice.

If you're on a network and want to enable Macintosh Easy Open to search the server for the missing application and/or launch that or a similar program, from the server, check the "include applications on servers" box. If Macintosh Easy Open only finds one application that will open the document, you can click "Auto pick if only one choice" to keep the dialog box from opening.

Macintosh Filing System (MFS)

When the Macintosh was introduced, the Macintosh filing system (MFS) kept all files on the same level, even though folders visually separated files. If, for example, you were in an application and used the **Open** command to open a document, every document on your drive appeared in the Open dialog box, not just the files in a selected folder. In 1987, Apple replaced the MFS with the improved **hierarchical filing system (HFS)**, which puts the contents of folders on different levels, enabling real separation and organization of Macintosh files by the user and by the computer.

See Also

Hierarchical Filing System

Macintosh Games, *See Entertainment*

M

Macintosh, Leaving On All the Time

There's an old theory you may have heard, that some people still subscribe to, which suggests you should always leave your Mac on because it's better to leave your hard disk running all the time than to stop it from spinning and then restart it the next day. These people are afraid of **head crashes,** which are extremely rare, especially if you use any care at all with your machine, but still (a) I don't buy it, and (b) I can't find anything official or even semi-official on it.

See Also
Head Crashes

Macintosh, Listing System Version

To see a listing of your Macintosh Operating System (MacOS), select **About This Macintosh** from the **Apple menu.** This opens a window displaying the version number of the installed System software. (The most current version, as we go to press, is System 7.5.3.)

To list the current system version, follow these steps:

1. At the desktop, select About This Macintosh from the Apple menu.

2. The version number of the installed system appears in the About This Macintosh window.

If you are in an application, and go under the Apple menu to choose "About This Macintosh," that heading is replaced by "About This Application," which usually gives you the version number of the application, the serial number, and oftentimes redisplays the application's splash screen that appears when the application is launched. Oftentimes credits for the software programmers will appear here, too.

See Also
About this Version; Apple Menu

Macintosh Office, The, *See*
Networking

Macintosh Operating System

The Macintosh OS has changed many times in the past years, evolving into a finely tuned instrument with features beyond what we might have imagined a few short years ago.

System 7.5 is an update to the Macintosh operating system that introduces a range of enhancements and new technologies, along with the usual bug fixes and performance tweaks.

Conversation with Chris Espinosa

Chris Espinosa, Apple employee #8, has been with the company since the garage. He's developed software, operating systems, documentation, hypertext, and media applications for the Apple II and Mac. Here he reflects on the changes he's seen.

Maclopedia: What was your earliest contact with Apple?

Chris: It was 1976. I was a high school student. Jobs had dropped out of college and gone to work at Hewlett-Packard, and Woz had come back to Hewlett-Packard from Reed, and they had both gone to the same high school I did. I went to the Home Brew Computing Club and met Steve Wozniak there because he lived closest to me and could give me a ride. They met on the second Wednesday of every month, up at Stanford, and it was a long ride.

I had been going around during that summer to the first half a dozen computer stores that opened in the summer of 1976, like the original Byte Shop. I spent whole days going from one to another on the buses up and down El Camino Real, playing with the machines until someone would get irritated enough to throw me out.

One machine I really enjoyed was the Apple I, because it had a keyboard and a screen instead of lights and switches, and I got to program in the advanced hex system, not binary. And one day I was writing machine language programs on an Apple I, and this guy came in with a tape, and kicked me off the machine, and loaded the tape on the machine, and that was Apple BASIC, and he offered me a job testing the Apple II that was in preparation. So I started working in December '76 in the proverbial garage, doing the final testing on the Apple II BASIC language. Then we incorporated in January 1977, and I was hired in as employee number eight.

Maclopedia: Didn't you pull together some of the original documentation?

Chris: Yes. The original documentation for the Apple II was stuff people wrote up and Mike Scott gave to his secretary, Sherry Livingston, to quick print in batches and snap into report covers. And every week or couple of weeks, the content was different. There were probably 20 or 30 versions of the mini manual, and he got tired of it, and he finally went around and rifled through everyone's desks, and found write-ups, and schematics, and had them all bound together in the Red Book, including a couple of things I had written up, like how to write games and how to make shapes. But it was really haphazard. So when I graduated from high school, Jef Raskin gave me the assignment to write a decent reference manual for the Apple II as my part-time job in college.

So I took computer science and English at Berkeley, and wrote a two hundred-page reference manual on software and hardware; everything. I got access to the university UNIX system and did all the typesetting. I didn't know that this was unusual, and I also didn't know that if you are being paid by the hour, the faster you work, the less you get paid, so at the end of that term, I came home from college with a knapsack full of dirty clothes, and camera-ready boards for the *Apple II Reference Manual.*

In the summer of 1981, I stopped college, and went to Apple full time. I wrote a lot of the books for the Apple III. Then Steve Jobs called me in and said, "I want to make you this deal. I have this great project, the Mac. Come work as the publications manager. I will pay you $40,000 a year. It will only take a year, then you can go back to college, and I will pay your tuition." This was his promise. Well, 15 years have gone by, and I still haven't gone back to college. But I took that job. I hired a group of people to do the original Macintosh documentation, some of whom were twice my age, but they put up with it.

I wrote the first couple of chapters of what turned out to be *Inside Mac* and the *Human Interface Guidelines,* and what was wonderful about working on the early Mac was that before, in the Apple II and Apple III, our

normal political boundaries between groups—that is, you are doing documentation, and we are doing software; you do your job and I will do mine—broke down. There was a tremendous sense of a group working together. Everyone had a right to be an expert on software design, user interface, how the books were written, and how the hardware was designed.

So when you did some work for the Mac project, you were obligated to run it by everyone in the division, even finance or human resources, and you had to respect the opinion of everyone in the group, even people who had no expertise in the field. That made the project appealing to a wide range of people. I have never seen that since, except there was a little of that in HyperCard. That so many really strong experts could come together and submit to the expertise of ordinary people was really wonderful. A lot of that was Andy Herzfeld and Burrell Smith and Steve Jobs wanting to make sure that everyone was respected for their input—unless they were bozos.

Maclopedia: How was it working with Steve Jobs?

Chris: He had legendary high standards. I haven't worked for him for well over 10 years, and I really have a ton of respect for what he has done with NeXt and Pixar. He has shown the stick-to-itiveness that he didn't show at Apple. At Apple everyone respected him for his vision and his drive, but his attention span was a real problem. I am really impressed that with NeXt he has taken an overblown vision and made it into a real working company.

He could be a real pain in the ass to work with because he had very high standards for visual esthetics, and things that were not good enough were sent back repeatedly to get better, until there was almost a fear bordering on paranoia about doing something that would meet his disapproval. That is why the Mac had such an impact on the visual arts community. Like we use the same icon in the manual as on the screen as is molded on the case; that kind of continuity. And the hideously arduous process of picking the graphic look for the machine, ending up with the Picasso Mac look that has lasted a very long time and was immediately captivating. The results have certainly been impressive, but being in the process was pure torture. In Steve Jobs' division, good enough wasn't. That takes a toll on people. But it worked. It was sort of self

continues

perpetuating. If Steve wouldn't let you get away with shoddy work, you wouldn't let your coworkers either. That lifted all of us.

Maclopedia: How has the Mac changed over the years?

Chris: The Mac product is a substantially different piece of technology than it was in 1984. The change has been so slow as to be imperceptible. People forget that while Steve had some of the key original visions, and pushed them, like the graphic user interface, and the Mac office idea for the Laser printer and the file server, and the overall aesthetics of the Mac, Steve and most of the Steve followers left before the Mac Plus was introduced. Steve and Andy and Burrell and Mike Murray and Bob Bellville, and most of the management team, and the key technical visionaries were all gone in mid '85. And what was left was a bunch of Apple II and Lisa people to pick up the pieces.

And while Steve Jobs had the Mac vision, it was Jean-Louis Gassée's Mac that became the product. The product was a lot more pragmatic and a lot more computer-y than Steve Jobs' Mac. Alan Kay and Jef Raskin still correctly criticize the successful Mac as way too complicated and too much like a computer. That happened when the others came in. They opened up the Mac and let it be a machine for hackers to be creative with. That allowed the Mac to live.

If we had had another two years like 1984 and 1985, with slow adoptions, slow third-party support, and an overwhelming reputation as a toy computer, the Mac would be tremendously different; we would not have multimedia or desktop publishing, for instance. It was the creativity of the programmers getting into the box that made that happen. This is what Gassée is doing with Be labs; he is creating the dream box for programmers, and it will just emerge. He is probably not wrong. But the cost is that in many ways what programmers had to put up with, originally, got foisted on Mac users—system extensions, error codes, having to manage the contents of your system file, having 294 control panels. It's just not as simple as what we wanted it to be. God bless the MacOS team. They try so hard to do the balance between simplifying enough

Sometimes the way the Finder has evolved, and drag-and-drop, are so beautiful it's poetry when it all comes together.

so it feels like a Mac and putting enough power in there so it can be a useful computer.

Sometimes the way the Finder has evolved, and drag-and-drop, are so beautiful it's poetry when it all comes together. And some things, like file sharing, never make it to the level of simplicity. You might as well put in a command line and make it hard but clear. Like what is the difference between propagating and inheriting permissions? I don't understand that.

When Steve Jobs left to form NeXt in September of 1985, the Mac program was a total disaster. It was a bunch of the B players from the Lisa team who came in and shipped the Mac Plus and the hard disk and finally got a machine that had the power to run PageMaker and pump bits to that LaserWriter. Then we had a product, but not until then.

Maclopedia: So the Mac got its start in desktop publishing. What other areas did the Mac enter early?

Chris: There are some places where Mac got in early and really stuck; they are the heart and soul of the Mac. One is higher education, the college students. Joanna Hoffman and Bud Colligan really got the Mac into the lifeblood of higher education and made it the college student thing to do to have a Mac. What you do in your rebellious youth is turn up your nose at your Dad's Lincoln and IBM PC and get a Volkswagen bug and a Mac. One of the wonderful things about college is that they are a standing wave of culture. The Mac has a lot of sustenance there.

And one thing that was really obvious, forever: kids really love the Mac. There's a program called Keywaks: any time you click the mouse or hit a key, it puts a colorful picture on the screen. It's a busy box. It takes over the whole screen. It's passed from parent to parent for eighteen-month olds. It's just wonderful. I brought home a Mac prototype in 1982, a couple of years before we shipped. One of my girlfriend's nephews, who was 5, didn't eat Christmas dinner; he learned MacPaint by himself.

Kids love the Mac. When we introduced the Mac, Apple IIs dominated K through 12. By getting developers to develop for the Mac, we managed to roll that over into all Macs. Schools are really slow to change, but elementary schools love us, and colleges love us. The publishing industry we don't have to worry about and multimedia, even though Windows is increasingly capable. People in art departments tend to prefer using the Mac, even if Windows has the same power.

People keep talking about a declining market share and no developers, but computers are different from soaps and autos, where you have to make sure you have the support. But if we keep technical parity and keep the Mac character, a lot of people just love the Mac. Some scientist at Lawrence Livermore Labs, where the government is threatening to take out the Macs, said it is like cutting off my right hand, you can do it, and I can still do my work, but I won't like it, and why the hell are you doing it?

Maclopedia: How's the Mac's relationship with big business?

Chris: The Mac has always had a tenuous relationship with big business. They like to go with the winners. Apple and the Mac have always been the underdogs. Some companies like going with the underdog, but then they complain that you are not the winner. One of the things that I have warned about is that the college strategy hurts us in business because when you graduate and get a job, you trade in the VW for an Acura, the backpack for a briefcase, blue jeans for nicer slacks, and the Mac for a PC to fit into the business world.

So there are a lot of people in business who really love us, and I think the Mac has more to bring to business because it is about doing things in a more efficient manner. The Mac makes it easier to use a computer than not to use it, and with Windows, that ain't so. But business has this love of standards and conformity and desire to embrace complexity. It's the nature of a large organization to embrace complexity, and that's why large corporations embrace Windows and reject Mac. It's standard and it's hard.

I think DOS and Windows are a conspiracy among the computer priesthood of the mini and mainframe computer age to keep job security because the Mac was threatening to reveal that computers didn't have to be hard after all.

The new features of System 7.5 included:

- A built-in hierarchical submenu for the **Apple menu** activated through the **Apple Menu Options control panel**, which enables you to toggle the submenu feature on or off. It also adds up to three folders to the Apple menu that contain **aliases** of the most recently used documents, applications, and servers, so you can relaunch a document, application, or remount a server without searching for the files themselves.

- An electronic version of post-it notes called Stickies, which enables you to have on-screen notes in your choice of size and color.

- Macintosh's **drag-and-drop** technology, enabling you to drag and drop items between applications, including the Finder.

- A new version of the NotePad DA that adds a host of new features and functionality, including drag-and-drop, the capability to create longer notes, and print notes.

- The capability to use **AppleScript** to automate certain tasks of the Finder.

- A total re-work of the online help system called **AppleGuide**, which offers interactive on-screen help and walks you through features and functions.

- A greatly improved **Find function**, with more flexibility and a new interface.

- A menu bar clock that incorporates into the new Date & Time Control Panel. The menu bar clock is a reworking of the widely popular shareware menu bar clock extension SuperClock that was a staple on many users' machines.

- A larger collection of **desktop** background **patterns** utilized through a new utility/ application called Desktop Patterns.

- A larger and updated Jigsaw Puzzle DA that enables you to copy and paste your own **PICT** graphic into the DA to use as a puzzle.

- An alias of the **Control Panels folder** that appears on the Apple menu itself and enables you to have instant access to individual control panels when the Apple menu submenus are activated.

- A new **PowerBook** feature called the **Control Strip**—a thin, floating palette that enables one-click access to a range of commonly used PowerBook features.

- An updated Scrapbook DA that accepts sound and video clips. The Scrapbook also gives you on-screen info about the items it contains (such as dimensions of the file, size of the file, format of the file, and so on).

- A **Numbers control panel** to enhance the Mac's use in foreign countries. This control panel enables you to configure the Mac to display numbers and currency in popular foreign formats. There's also a Text control panel enabling you to choose from different text formats for languages that write from right to left, top to bottom, and so on.

- The **WindowShade** feature that started life as a popular shareware utility. WindowShade enables you to roll-up a window so only its title bar is showing, much like you would roll up a traditional window shade, by double-clicking the window's title bar, even within applications. WindowShade's options are accessed through the WindowShade control panel.

- An enhanced capability to make multiple selections with a marquee (clicking and dragging with the arrow pointer cursor produces a rectangular marquee around objects in active windows). Now you can use the marquee to select items in a list view, rather than just the icon view, as in previous versions of the system.

- A freeware extension called the Extensions Manager, which was created by an Apple employee but not officially supported by Apple. This extension enables you to choose which extensions load into your system at startup and to create sets of extensions for different purposes or users.

- A new control panel called the Auto On/Off control panel that enables you to set a startup and shutdown time for your Macintosh, even if you're not there.

- The **QuickDraw GX** extension, which adds a wide array of printing, font management, typographic, and other features, including a new printing architecture that enables you to have printer drivers on your desktop where you can drag-and-drop items to be printed. QuickDraw GX incorporates a version of Adobe Type Manager (ATM) called ATM GX that is used for smooth display of fonts on-screen and for output. QuickDraw GX adds Apple's updated version of **ColorSync** (version 2.0), which is aimed at giving users a color matching system for achieving more predictable results when working in color. QuickDraw GX also opens the door for high-end typography with features such as use of ligatures, precise letter kerning, and a host of advanced typography features accessed by using specially designed GX-enhanced fonts.

- The **MacTCP** and **TCP/IP** system extensions (which were sold separately) with System 7.5 for use with the **Internet**.

- An enhanced version of the **General Controls control panel** that enables you to protect the **System Folder** from being accessed or renamed. You can also protect your application's folders. This is particular useful if children are using the machine.

- Version 8.0 of the LaserWriter Driver (besides the GX version of the LaserWriter Extension), which offers enhanced printing and a new print spooling extension.

- The **PC Exchange** extension, which enables you to read, write, and format PC disks.

- An updated **Monitors control panel** so you can change monitor resolutions on-the-fly without having to restart your machine.

■ **PowerTalk**, an electronic mail and messaging feature for use over networks.

Other enhancements in System 7.5 include faster copying of files, faster switching between applications, and faster displaying of menus. The current iteration of System 7.5 is 7.5.3.

Scheduled for release in early 1997, **System 8** (code-named Copland, after the famous composer Aaron Copland) is Apple's next major rewrite of its system software. It will be the first complete overhaul since **System 7** was introduced. Apple has noted that Copland will be aimed at addressing two major areas: user efficiency and raw speed.

Although the features that will appear in the shipping version of System 8.0 are subject to change by Apple at any time, some of the features slated for Copland are as follows:

■ A major cosmetic facelift for the Macintosh interface will be included along with the ability for different users to have different interfaces. You will also be able to have one interface for children, another interface for novices, and a separate interface for more advanced users, all on the same machine. Copland will also add themed interface looks that can be selected to suit a particular user's tastes for their working environment.

The standard interface update reportedly includes new 3D files and folders, a redesigned desktop, more built-in user control of the look of the interface, new menus, and a new typeface to replace the current system fonts of Geneva, Chicago, and Monaco.

■ Reportedly 95 percent of Copland's code is to be PowerPC native code, which will mean dramatic increases in the speed of PowerPC-based computers.

■ Apple is incorporating limited forms of protected memory to enable better overall system reliability by protecting the memory one application uses so it doesn't interfere with another open application. Copland is also going to be Apple's first step into pre-emptive **multitasking**, in which you have different applications sharing different operations more efficiently than they currently can. These long-awaited features are limited versions of what will reportedly appear in **System 9** (code-named Gershwin, also named after a famous composer, George Gershwin).

■ Much of Copland is being written as a series of modules, which enables Copland to run on nearly any Macintosh, including Macs with only 8MB of RAM. However, as more RAM is added, Copland's overall performance will increase.

■ A number of system extensions, such as **QuickDraw GX**, **QuickDraw 3D**, **PlainTalk**, **QuickTime Conferencing**, and **QuickTime VR** will be built into Copland.

■ Copland will add the capability to automate routine tasks for users.

■ Copland will have improved and enhanced windows, open/save dialog boxes, and desktop management features that will enable even greater ease in managing your files.

■ OpenDoc technology will be included in Copland, which enables software developers to create components or modules that will add functionality to applications. If, for example, you have a word processor and wish it could create Postscript graphics, you could install a module that would add this feature to your Word Processor. This will enable you to customize applications to have only the features you actually need, enabling two users to use the same application but with different features.

■ Copland will have updated **networking** capabilities enabling it to plug-and-play into most existing networks, which offers significantly greater ease in setting up and administering networks.

See Apple's Web page for more information on upcoming releases: **http://www.apple.com**.

For More...

If you want to do this... | **Go to this entry...**

If you want to do this...	Go to this entry...
Determine what is wrong with your System software	Macintosh OS Troubleshooting Repairing Your Mac
Learn more about System 7.5	System 7.5
Learn more about the available Mac models	Macintosh Computer Family
Learn how to rebuild your desktop	Rebuilding the Desktop
Learn some helpful tips and tricks	OS Tips and Tricks
Learn some System shortcuts	F Keys

Bibliography

For more information, refer to:

Guide to Macintosh System 7.5, Don Crabb, published by Hayden Books, 1995 (1-56830-109-X).

MacWorld Complete Mac Handbook, Jim Heid, published by IDG Books, 1996 (1-56884-484-0).

The Big Mac Book, Neil Salkind, published by Que Corporation, 1994 (0-88022-648-X).

The Macintosh Bible, DiNucci et al., published by Peachpit Press, 1995 (1-56609-140-3).

MacWorld Secrets, David Pogue and Joe Schorr, published by IDG Books, 1995 (1-56884-175-2).

Macintosh OS Troubleshooting

The following table can help you determine your problem more easily so you can plot a course of action to fix your Mac. See the sections **repairing** and **troubleshooting** for more information as well.

OS Symptoms and Causes

OS Problem	Possible Cause	Action
Files are losing their custom icons and reverting to generic items.	Invisible Desktop files have become corrupted.	Rebuild the Desktop by holding the Option-⌘ keys during restart.
Screen is frozen and mouse won't move.	System has crashed. Most likely it has run out of memory.	Restart the system. Generally this problem is temporary and a restart will reset the memory and enable you to continue to work.
Can't empty an item in the Trash.	File is locked.	Hold the Option key and choose Empty Trash or select the locked file, choose Get Info (⌘-I), and uncheck the "locked" option and close the Get Info window. Then choose Empty Trash again.
Having repeated system freezes or crashes.	Application may not have enough memory, or there may be an extension conflict.	If the problem occurs while using one particular program, allocate more memory to that program by selecting its icon and choosing Get Info (⌘-I). Then set the preferred size to a higher figure. You can also try turning on Virtual Memory (to use hard disk space as additional RAM) or using a third-party commercial product such as RAM Doubler from Connectix. If the problems persist, it may be an extension conflict that is causing the crashes. And lastly, it could be a corrupted system, which would require a reinstall.

OS Problem	Possible Cause	Action
You get an error message stating, "Application is busy, missing, or not found."	You may not have the application that created the document you're trying to open, or the file is not designed to be opened (such as your Finder file or a preferences file).	Launch the application first, and then use the Open command to select the document and open it. If the application is not on your disk, you may have to install it to open the document. If the link has been broken from the document to the application that created it, it could also be a sign of a corrupted desktop. You can rebuild the desktop by holding the Option-⌘ keys during restart.
Application has unexpectedly quit.	Your Mac has run out of available memory, and when the application went looking for more, it found none and quit.	Restart your Macintosh. It should be all right now. If it happens again, you may need to use **Virtual Memory** (to use hard disk space as additional RAM) accessed through the Memory Control Panel.
Mac crashes during startup.	Probably an extension conflict. Could be a corrupted System, which requires a reinstall.	Restart the Mac while holding down the Shift key. If it restarts, you probably do have an extension conflict. (See Troubleshooting on how to resolve an extension conflict.)
Alert box stating, "An error of Type 1 occurred."	An undefined error has occurred which forced the application to quit, possibly caused by an extension conflict or memory problem.	Restart the computer and chances are you'll be OK. If this continues, it may be an extension conflict, which requires troubleshooting.
Can't copy files onto a disk. Says "Disk is locked."	Disk is locked using the manual lock on the disk.	Unlock the disk by ejecting it, turning it upside down, and moving the locking tab found in the lower-right corner to the unlocked position (the small opening in the tab is covered when unlocked.)
Upon restart or startup, you get a Sad Mac icon with four musical notes.	There is some sort of hardware problem. If you just installed RAM, it's probably not seated firmly in its socket.	First try restarting the computer. Most times this will go away. If not, and you just installed more RAM, reopen the computer, remove the RAM, and then reinstall it, making sure it's firmly seated. Then close the unit and restart. If it still doesn't work, while the Mac's turned off, recheck all the SCSI cables connected to your Mac. If it's not improperly seated RAM, or a loose SCSI cable, you may have to refer your problem to an authorized Apple service technician.

continues

M

OS Symptoms and Causes (continued)

OS Problem	Possible Cause	Action
"Printer could not be found" message.	You have not selected which printer to print from in the Chooser.	Select the Chooser from the Apple men, and click the type of printer you want to use. If it's a laser printer, the laser printer's name should appear in the window on the right after you choose the LaserWriter driver. Click it and close the Chooser to make your selection complete. If this doesn't work, make sure all printer cables are snugly connected on both ends and the printer is turned on and warmed up.
You get a blinking question mark at startup.	The Mac can't find a System Folder to start up from, possibly indicating that your system has somehow become corrupted.	Try restarting the Mac. If that doesn't work, insert your Disk Tools disk (from your system software disks) or your system CD-ROM disc. Your Mac can start up from either of these disks. When it starts up, if you see your hard disk appear on the desktop, you should probably do a clean reinstall which will put a new copy of the System Folder on the disk. (See **troubleshooting** for more information.) If after installing a new system it still won't start up, unplug any attached SCSI cables; this could be the problem.

See Also

Repairing; Troubleshooting

Macintosh Programmer's Toolbox Assistant

Macintosh Programmer's Toolbox Assistant (MPTA) is a complete and up-to-date electronic hypertext version of the function reference portions of the new *Inside Macintosh* series. Each entry in MPTA includes references to the specific volume and page of *Inside Macintosh* from which it is taken.

The following figure shows the main MPTA window. From this window, you can click any underlined text to link directly to that topic. You also can select text and copy it to the Clipboard or drag it to a clipping file or any **drag-and-drop** capable program. Text typed into the Keyword field is treated as a search string. The database searches for possible matches as

you type and completes your search string with the first match it finds. In the following figure, for example, the first match found for the search string "mun" is "munger." Like THINK Reference, MPTA also supports lookups by other applications. Both **Symantec C++** and **CodeWarrior** can look up information in MPTA.

MPTA also supports page annotations. These notes appear as yellow sticky notes directly on the page and can be moved or edited to your heart's content.

Macintosh Programmer's Toolbox Assistant uses Altura's QuickView engine for search and display. You can create your own reference databases for QuickView using a special compiler from Altura, and then your own references can be searched along with the MPTA databases. In fact, Metrowerks now distributes some of the reference material for CodeWarrior in QuickView format.

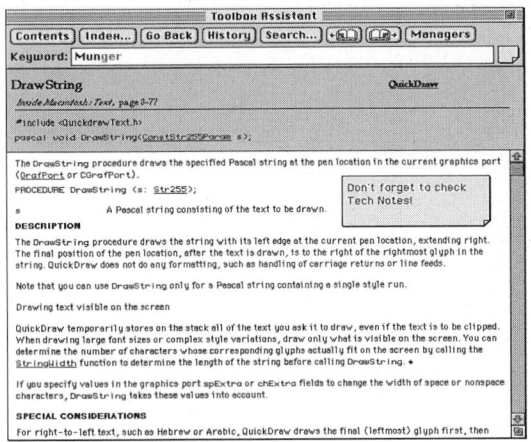

Apple posts updates and additions to the MPTA databases on the World Wide Web (**http://dev.info.apple.com/MPTA.html**). It's not unusual for new portions of the Toolbox to be documented in MPTA before they make it into *Inside Macintosh*.

See Also

C++; CodeWarrior; Inside Macintosh; Symantec C++; THINK Reference

Macintosh Programmer's Workshop, *See MPW*

Macintosh Project, History

The Macintosh project began with an idea quite different from the Macintosh we all know and love. The project was started in the spring of 1979 by Jef Raskin. Raskin had been asked to head a project to create a low-end $500 game machine. The game machine project didn't interest Raskin, but he did have another vision: to create a computer based on how people work rather than on what the technology could deliver. This *human factors* approach was original at the time.

The Macintosh started as a small research project. Raskin envisioned an "appliance" computer to be used by anybody whether they had computer experience or not. This computer would be a closed architecture, with everything built-in, including a screen, keyboard, printer, and disk drive. It would have a fixed amount of memory—64KB—so all programs could run on all Macs. It would be portable and battery

powered. The Mac would include a graphical interface that had no visible operating system, but rather a word processor-like workspace where users could edit text, perform calculations, or draw graphics.

Raskin's project to create the "Apple V," as he called it, was strongly opposed by **Steve Jobs**, who was closely involved with the **Lisa** project at the time. Apple's board gave the Macintosh project the go-ahead anyway. At first, the Macintosh project was a small *skunkworks* led by Raskin, with Burrell Smith doing much of the hardware work.

In the meantime, the Lisa project had gotten bogged down with all the changes brought on by the visit to **Xerox PARC**. The Lisa team was tired of Jobs' meddling, and when **Mike Scott** reorganized the company around product lines, Jobs was removed from the Lisa project. More than a little angered, Jobs turned his sights on the Macintosh project.

Once Jobs got involved with the Macintosh, the project grew quickly. Jobs saw the Mac as his opportunity to show up the Lisa team by creating a computer that was both cheaper and better than the Lisa.

The Macintosh project gradually took on many of the features of the Lisa, including the 68000 processor, **Bill Atkinson**'s LisaGraf (QuickDraw) graphics core, and the mouse. Raskin was strongly opposed to the mouse, favoring instead a light pen or joystick. Jobs won out, but Raskin did manage to convince the team to at least stick with a one-button mouse.

In February 1982, Raskin had had enough of Jobs and went on a leave of absence that would become permanent. The Macintosh was squarely in the hands of Steve Jobs. It became even more of a crusade under Jobs' chaotic but visionary leadership. The Macintosh team took to flying a pirate flag over its building on the Apple campus. Jobs felt, "It's more fun to be a pirate than to join the navy."

The pirates under Jobs' lead were a dedicated—perhaps fanatical—group of programmers, hardware designers, artists, and others. They routinely worked 80 or more hours per week on the Macintosh and loved it. They believed in the Macintosh vision. By the time the Mac was introduced in January 1984, Apple had incurred $78 million in development costs.

A Few of the Macintosh "Pirates"

Bill Atkinson	Wrote QuickDraw and MacPaint
Steve Capps	Co-wrote the Finder
Chris Espinosa	Documentation lead
Andy Hertzfeld	Wrote most of the Macintosh Toolbox
Bruce Horn	Co-wrote the Finder
Susan Kare	Designed the Mac's graphics and fonts
Larry Kenyon	Wrote low-level system software
Jerry Manock	Managed industrial design
Burrell Smith	Designed the digital circuit board (motherboard)
Randy Wigginton	Wrote MacWrite

What an introduction it was! In the months leading up to the Mac's introduction, Apple had carefully leaked just enough information about the new computer to get the industry excited. They used evangelism to get third-party developers to support the Mac. They gave Macs to key "luminaries" in the arts, business, and politics. And there was *the* commercial. Apple's "**1984**" commercial ran during the Super Bowl two days before the product launch. It was a sensation and put the name "Macintosh" in the minds of millions of viewers.

Sales of the original 128KB Macintosh were strong at first, but tapered off quickly. Despite the efforts of Apple's software evangelists, very little software was available for the Macintosh. It was underpowered and overpriced, but it was a great start. The Mac limped along for more than a year before things changed for the better.

In 1985, Apple rolled out the Macintosh Office: a vision of Macs networked using AppleTalk and sharing a new printer: the LaserWriter. In part because of the dismal failure of its introductory commercial—"**Lemmings**"—the Macintosh Office was not greeted

warmly by Apple's customers. One piece of Office, however, played an important role in saving the Macintosh.

Combined with Aldus PageMaker, which shipped in July 1985, and the more powerful Mac Plus introduced in January 1986, the LaserWriter started the desktop publishing revolution. Desktop publishing gave the Macintosh its "killer application," a use so compelling that users buy the computer for that use alone.

Buoyed by desktop publishing, the Macintosh survived and thrived. In 1987, the Macintosh II introduced color and expandability, ending two of the biggest complaints about earlier Macs—color and expandability. The following figure shows the Mac Classic.

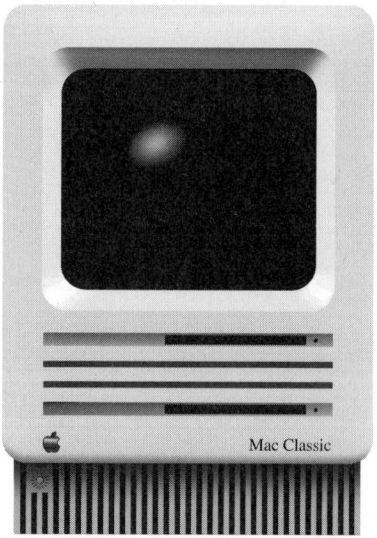

Mac Classic

Recently, the Macintosh was born again with the introduction of the **Power Macintosh**. Apple managed to perform a smooth transition to an entirely different microprocessor with little effect on the end user—except for enjoying a speedier computer.

See Also

Atkinson, Bill; Jobs, Steve; Lemmings; Lisa; Raskin, Jef; Scott, Mike; Xerox PARC

Macintosh Software Archive

The Macintosh Software Archive is a site on the **Internet** that offers a large variety of Macintosh files, freeware, and other documents archived for users who can freely download them via **anonymous FTP.**

FTP enables you to connect to a remote computer and transfer files back and forth. More data is transferred via FTP than by any other protocol on the Internet.

Millions of software files are available via FTP on sites around the world, but several sites with gigabytes of disk space are particularly well known as good sources of Mac programs.

Two of the main software archives for the Mac are

■ The Info-Mac archives at Stanford University (**ftp://sumex-aim.stanford.edu/info-mac/**).

■ The WUArchive at Washington University at St. Louis (**ftp://wuarchive.wustl.edu/**).

An estimated 20 to 50 new software titles appear on these archives every week. Because of heavy traffic, these and other software archives have a number of **mirror sites** around the world.

Anarchie, an FTP and **Archie** client program for the Mac, provides an easy way of searching the software archives. You simply enter a word contained in the file or directory name you are seeking, and Anarchie searches the Archie database of FTP sites for matches. You then receive a listing of filenames and address information so you can retrieve the data via FTP.

The following figure shows the results of a search for the keyword "penguin" using Anarchie to search the Archie database. The files are held in sites around the world, including the two mentioned previously, and others in Finland, Canada, and Australia.

Many of the files stored on the archives have been **compressed** or **encoded** so they can be transported across the network. Such files will have a **filename extension** such as ".hqx," ".sit," or ".cpt." They have to be opened with an application like **StuffIt Expander** or **BinHex.**

See Also

Anarchie; Anonymous FTP; Archie; Compressing Files; Decoding Files; Encoding Files; Filename Extension; FTP; Internet; Mirror Site

Macintosh XL, *See Lisa*

MacLink Plus

MacLink Plus is a DOS to Macintosh translation utility from Dataviz (55 Corporate Drive, Trumbull, CT 06611, Phone: (800) 733-0030. On the Web at **http://www.dataviz.com**) that enables you to convert most DOS files to a Macintosh file that can be opened and used on a Macintosh. MacLink Plus' specialty is converting those hard-to-translate files from applications that do not have a Macintosh counterpart or for other hard-to-translate items such as spreadsheets, databases, and graphics files.

MacLink Plus also excels at holding document formatting (such as bold and italic for text files) as well as advanced formatting (such as tables, charts, and graphs).

See Also

Apple File Exchange; PC Exchange

MacMag Virus

MacMag, also known as Peace, Drew, Brandow, and Aldus, infected only System files until March 2, 1988. On this date it displayed a message of peace on the screen and then deleted itself, making this virus virtually extinct.

See Also

ANTI Virus; CDEF Virus; CODE 1 Virus; CODE 352 Virus; Frankie Virus;

INIT 17 Virus; INIT 1984 Virus; INIT 29 Virus; INIT 9403 Virus; INIT-M Virus; MBDF Virus; MDEF Virus; nVIR Virus; Scores Virus; T4 Virus; WDEF Virus; ZUC Virus

Macmillan Computer Publishing Web Site

A good source for general information about the **Internet** and **World Wide Web** as well as a variety reference materials available online.

Macmillan Computer Publishing's **Web site** contains excerpts and other information about the many computer books published by its branches (including Hayden Books, publisher of *Maclopedia*).

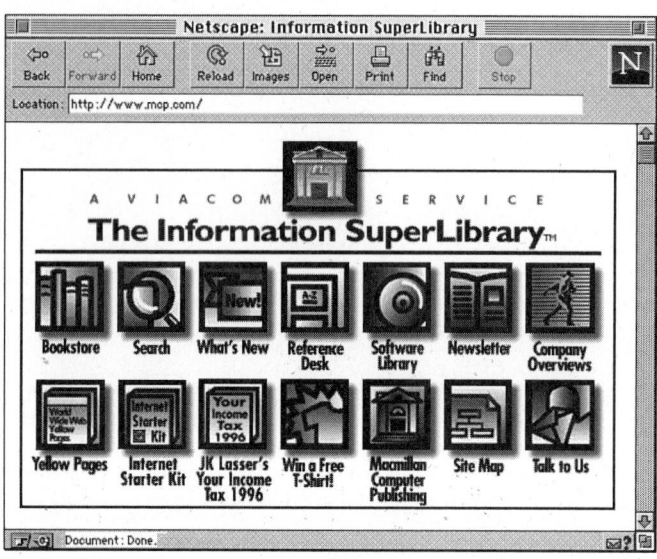

Visitors to the site at **http://www.mcp.com/** can also find useful reference guides to the Internet, including:

- The complete text of *Internet Starter Kit for Macintosh*.
- A searchable index to *New Riders' Official World Wide Web Yellow Pages*.
- Several **HTML** tutorials.
- A searchable index to J.K. Lasser's *Your Income Tax 1996*.

- Hundreds of shareware, freeware, and demo programs available for downloading from the Software Library (also available from Macmillan's **FTP** site (**ftp.mcp.com**).
- BBS forums on running a **Web site** and other topics.
- An **email** newsletter with contests and updates about the Macmillan Web site itself.

See Also
Email; FTP; HTML; Internet; Web Site; World Wide Web

MacMod Pro

An application for editing and playing **MOD** files (a music file format similar to **MIDI** and originally developed on the Amiga). Editing effects include backwards, cross-fade, and echo. A demo version is available from online services.

See Also
MIDI; MOD; Sound Trecker

MacNosy, *See Debugger, The*

MacOS Version, *See Macintosh, Listing System Version; Macintosh Operating System*

MacPaint

When the Mac first came out in the mid-'80s, it shipped with MacPaint and MacWrite. The former, although it was pretty impressive at the time, has long since been abandoned by Claris, its developer. The MacPaint format for **bitmapped graphics** is still supported by many **paint** and **draw programs**, though, because there's still a lot of artwork (including **clip art**) around in that format. MacPaint files are black and white, and they're all 7 1/2 by 10 1/2 inches, regardless of the elements they contain.

Its main, and perhaps only, strength is its capability to allow for area pattern fills. Pattern fills can be used to paint with or as fills for type.

You can also edit any pattern in the MacPaint library, using the default patterns as a basis. This is done through the Pattern dialog box. MacPaint has no capability to allow you to save the new edited pattern, unless you grab the screen and save it as a whole. MacPaint files have to be translated to bitmap format before being suitable for import into Photoshop. Once imported, they can be translated to grayscale, and from there to standard RBG. As an RGB file, color, gradients, and image effects can be applied, using MacPaint images as a basis for further creation.

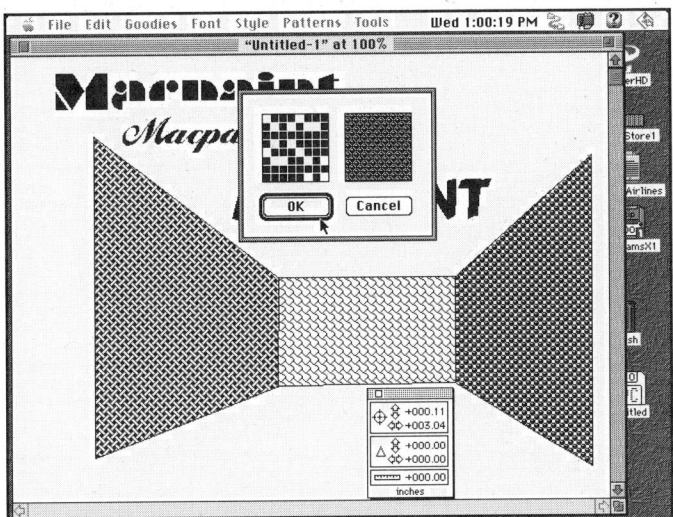

See Also

Bitmapped Graphics; Clip Art; Draw Programs; Paint Programs

MacPerl, *See Perl*

MacPPP

Popular software by Larry Blunk of Merit Network that provides a Point to Point Protocol (PPP) connection to the **Internet** through a dial-up **modem**.

To install MacPPP, place a control panel Config PPP in your Control Panels folder, and an extension called PPP in your Extensions folder. Then restart your Mac. Make sure that PPP is selected in the main **MacTCP** window. Also make sure you use Server addressing as opposed to Manually addressing with a permanent IP address.

Open the Config PPP control panel. As shown in the following figure, Config PPP is easy to set up.

The "Idle Timeout" feature in Config PPP enables you to specify a time from five to 120 minutes after which MacPPP will close the connection. If you do anything during this time, the timer resets and MacPPP starts counting again. The "Echo Interval" pop-up menu gives you the opportunity to configure MacPPP to periodically query the line to see if your connection has dropped. If MacPPP receives no response after three successive requests, MacPPP assumes that the connection has gone dead.

The "Terminal Window" checkbox brings up a built-in terminal emulator for use when you have trouble logging on, rather than having to use an external terminal emulator.

After you launch MacPPP, click the "New" button to create and name a new configuration. Click the "Config" button to bring up the "Configure Server" dialog box. This is where you set modem variables such as speed, flow control (sometimes called handshaking), tone/pulse dial, and the phone number to dial. The "Modem connect timeout" field gives you a chance to increase the amount of time MacPPP will wait for the connection to occur.

Users have two possible ways of entering their user ID and password: either a MacPPP Authentication dialog (which is not supported by all servers) or a connect script.

MacPPP has a Connect Script dialog window in which you replicate the process of logging into your host. You do this by entering the various carriage returns, ID names, and passwords you usually enter after you are connected. The Connect Script dialog provides eight data entry fields into which you enter each of these commands. By creating a connect script, MacPPP logs in for you automatically, eliminating the need to type passwords and other commands each time.

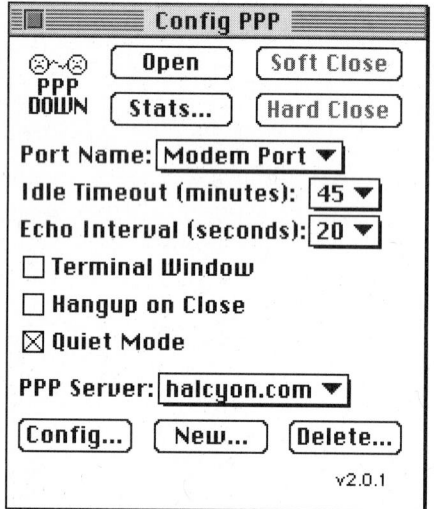

After MacPPP is configured, simply click the Open button in Config PPP or open a MacTCP-based program that opens MacTCP, which causes MacPPP to connect automatically. To close your connection, first quit all MacTCP-based applications. Then click either the Hard Close button to hang up the connection and "lock" MacPPP, or the Soft Close button to close the connection but leave open the auto-connect feature so launching a new application makes MacPPP establish a new connection.

See Also

Asynchronous Data Transfers; Internet; InterSLIP; Modem; Network; Packets; Parity; PPP; SLIP

MacRecorder

MacRecorder is a sound digitizer for the Macintosh that captures 8-bit mono sound at up to 22KHz sampling rate. It is also possible to digitize in stereo using two MacRecorders. Manufactured by Farallon but later sold to **Macromedia**, the MacRecorder came bundled with the application **SoundEdit**, and when it was released in the mid-80's, it was the cheapest

and easiest way to digitize sound on the Macintosh. The MacRecorder was attached to either the serial or printer port, and SoundEdit recorded and then edited the sound. Later, Macromedia released a system Extension, the MacRecorder Driver, that provided operating system access to the MacRecorder. This enabled you, for example, to record System beep sounds directly in the **Sound control panel** using the MacRecorder, or use the MacRecorder with other software that worked with the Macintosh internal digitizing hardware that had become available on most Macs. For example, the audio XCMD for HyperCard could use the MacRecorder only if the system extension was installed.

The small MacRecorder box contained a microphone, a line-in plug, and a volume control for adjusting the sensitivity of the microphone.

Now that all Macintosh computers come with built-in sound digitizing capabilities (even if they don't always come with a microphone!), the MacRecorder is of little use. SoundEdit, however, has been updated and is still being sold.

See Also
SoundEdit

MacRenderMan

A Macintosh application that supports RenderMan, MacRenderMan is a **rendering** language developed by Pixar. RenderMan is a language, as well as the name of products sold by Pixar that support that language.

Although capable of generating high-quality renderings, MacRenderMan is a surprisingly difficult product to use. It acts like a print driver, requiring that you select and control the renderer using the **Chooser**, which makes it difficult to set up and run. And at the time it was released it did not run well in 8 megabytes, the most common memory size.

RenderMan is a rendering language much like **PostScript** is a page description language. The scenes and models must first be written to the RenderMan file format RIB (RenderMan Interface Bytestream). These files are then turned into photographic quality images by the MacRenderMan renderer. Users can also write their own custom shaders. But because

RenderMan is a complicated language to learn, and because few third-party applications were adapted to use RenderMan, few users were able to make use of the full power of the product.

Pixar released two end-user products, Typestry and ShowPlace, but these are fairly limited tools. Certainly, neither application could be used to create the kind of animation that Pixar creates for its clients and movies. It's surprising that a company that well known for animation and rendering quality never released a powerful animation tool. Pixar no longer officially supports any of its Macintosh products.

Some third-party 3D tools, including Silicon Beach's Super 3D and Macromedia's Macromind Three-D did support MacRenderMan as an optional renderer. As an option, they had their own rendering engine, but also supported MacRenderMan.

See Also

Alias' Sketch; Pixar; ShowPlace; Typestry

Macro

A macro is any set of functions, keystrokes, or movements of the **mouse** that are recorded and assigned to one key or keystroke combination for instant playback.

You can, for example, create a Macro that launches America Online, signs on using your name and password, checks your email, saves all incoming email to your hard disk, signs back off and quits the program, with one keystroke—a macro. Any boring or repetitive task is a candidate for a macro. You can, for example, create a macro that types in your name and address anytime you type the keystroke Control-A. Or you could create a macro that backs up any file created to a back-up disk, all with one keystroke. Macros can be simple one- or two-step tasks, or they can be very complex tasks that take hours to complete.

Macros are created using a macro program (such as QuicKeys and Tempo). To create a macro, you tell the macro program to record your actions, and it will record your keystrokes and mouse movements. When you're done with the task you want recorded, you stop the recording process, and the macro application asks you to which keystroke combination you want to assign the recorded tasks. Let's say the task you recorded, as an example, was opening every file in a particular folder and resaving the files in that folder in a PC-compatible file format, and let's say the keystroke you choose was Control-F. The next time you need to convert a folder full of files from Mac to PC format, you press Control-F and the macro does the task for you, exactly as you did before. There are hundreds of uses for macros, and their aim is to automate boring repetitive tasks for you at the press of a key.

AppleScript is Apple's scripting language, for System 7 and higher, that enables you to create macros at the Finder or in any application that is scriptable. This gives applications the built-in capability to automate repetitive tasks without having to use a third-party macro application. There are also applications that are recordable, which enable you to record a series of steps from within the application. (If the application is not recordable, but it is scriptable, you can still use AppleScripts, but you have to create the scripts yourself by typing the script into the ScriptEditor, rather than having the ScriptEditor record your steps as you go.) If the program is also attachable, you can assign these scripts to menu commands or on-screen buttons for instant access.

You can have AppleScript record your actions, mouse movements, and keyboard strokes, and even save them as mini-applications (called applets). This way, you can put these applets anywhere you want and click an AppleScript icon to have it run its script. After you've created an AppleScript, you can edit these scripts in the ScriptEditor.

An example of an AppleScript might be a script to sign on to an online service, check to see if you have email, download your email into a pre-selected folder, and then log off again. System 7.5 comes with a few Finder sample scripts already written for you, and they're accessed through the Automated Tasks folder on the Apple menu.

See Also

AppleScript; Email; Mouse

Macro Language, *See Scripting*

Macro Programs

Macro utility programs such as **QuicKeys** (from CE Software) and Tempo II (from Affinity Microsystems) enable you to record keystroke or mouse movements to automate repetitive or time-consuming tasks. After a **macro** program has recorded your movements, you can assign these movements to a keyboard keystroke, or a **function key**, which "plays back" the recorded steps when pressed.

Apple had its own Macro creation program, called MacroMaker, that shipped as a part of System 6, but was discontinued with the introduction of System 7. Commercial macro programs, such as QuicKeys and Tempo, are powerful, full-featured programs that enable a wide range of customization and the capability to create and link complex macros to perform tasks very time-consuming and complex otherwise.

See Also

MacroMaker; Macros; QuicKeys; System 7

MacroMaker

MacroMaker is a macro program developed by Apple that was included with System 6. MacroMaker enables users to create **macros** to automate repetitive tasks. When MacroMaker is installed, you turn it on through an **icon** on the **menu bar** that looks like a small cassette tape. When you turn MacroMaker on, it starts recording your keystrokes and mouse movements until you select off from MacroMaker's **pull-down menu**. You can name these macros and save them to MacroMaker's pull-down menu for easy access.

MacroMaker was discontinued after System 6 and does not work with **System 7** and higher, although there are a number of full-featured third-party macro programs like **QuicKeys** and **Tempo** available for creating custom Macros.

See Also

Icon; Macros; QuicKeys; System 7

Macromedia Director, *See Director*

Macromind Three-D

A general purpose three dimensional animation and rendering package, Macromind Three-D enables you to create basic shapes (balls, rectangles, and so on) or import models. Its primary function, however, is animating and rendering objects. This program resembles, in feature set, the much more expensive, professional tool **Electric Image**. Although Macromind Three-D is quite a good tool, its performance, both while creating and previewing animation, as well as during rendering is poor.

Macromedia has discontinued Macromind Three-D and replaced it (and the companion tool **MacroModel**) with **Extreme 3D**, which offers modeling, animation, and rendering features.

See Also

3D; Extreme 3D; MacroModel

MacroModel

Released by Macromedia as a companion to their **Macromind Three-D** product, MacroModel offers sophisticated modeling tools and rendering capabilities, but for animation you have to use another product (such as Macromind Three-D). MacroModel offers spline-based editing tools for creating models, and in many ways resembles Alias' **Sketch!**

MacroModel was available for Windows, as well as the Macintosh platform. It, and Macromind Three-D, have been discontinued and replaced with a single program, Extreme 3D, which offers modeling, animation, and rendering features.

See Also

3D; Extreme 3D; Macromind Three-D

MacsBug

MacsBug was the *original* low-level **debugger** for the 68000 family of microprocessors used in the Macintosh. Motorola wrote the first versions of MacsBug before the Mac existed. In fact, the name "MacsBug" doesn't come from Macintosh at all, but rather is an acronym for Motorola Advanced Computing Systems deBUGger.

MacsBug is the low-level debugger of choice for many programmers, largely because it is available for free from Apple. But don't let that fool you into thinking it's a second-rate debugger—far from it. MacsBug is capable of doing most of the low-level chores a low-level debugger is expected to do.

Installing MacsBug is simple: Just drop it into the System Folder and restart. The System Folder doesn't have a special subfolder for debuggers. Unlike extensions and control panels, debuggers must be in the System Folder itself. When you restart with MacsBug installed, a special message is displayed in the Welcome to Macintosh dialog that lets you know it's up and running.

All properly behaved programs will run normally with MacsBug installed. It's easy to forget it's even there until a program crashes. Then, instead of the usual error dialog letting you know an application has "unexpectedly quit," you are dropped into MacsBug with a short message about the cause of the error.

For programmers accustomed to high-level debuggers, the MacsBug interface can be quite a shock.

The MacsBug screen is divided into four parts. The left side displays the contents of the processor's **registers**, as well as the name of the current application and the first few items on that application's **stack**. Along the bottom is the command line. Any commands you type will appear here. Above the command line, the next few lines of object code are displayed in disassembled form. Finally, the remainder of the screen is a scrolling region that displays the results of any commands that you enter.

Most of MacsBug's commands are beyond the scope of this book. A few of the most commonly used commands are summarized in the following table. A great place to start is the help command, which displays a

full list of all commands, as well as information on how to use some of MacsBug's more complicated features.

A Few Common MacsBug Commands

Command	Function	Comments
g	go	Continues execution after a user break
s [*n*]	step	Steps execution ahead by *n* instructions (or 1 if *n* is omitted)
es	exit application	Exit the current application
rs	restart	Unmount all disks and reboot
how	how	Shows the reason MacsBug was entered
il [addr [*n*]]	disassemble	Displays the disassembly of the next *n* lines of object code beginning at location addr
sc	stack crawl	Displays the chain of subroutine calls leading to the current instruction
hd	heap dump	Displays the contents of the current application's heap
help	help	Displays help text

A few of these commands can be useful for non-programmers as well. The most generally helpful command is *es*, which enables you to exit the current application. Using *es* after a crash can frequently give you the chance to save any open documents in other applications before you restart.

Despite its 68000 origins, recent versions of MacsBug handle **PowerPC** debugging with aplomb. Many

M

commands have been transparently extended to work properly for both 68K code and native PowerPC code. Other commands have been supplemented with PowerPC versions that act the same as their 68K counterparts.

MacsBug is freely available for Apple's World Wide Web and FTP sites (**http://www.apple.com/**, **ftp://ftp.info.apple.com/**), as well as their forums on CompuServe, and America Online.

See Also

Debugger; Heap; Register; Stack

MacTCP

Software that enables a Macintosh to communicate with other machines via **TCP/IP** (Transmission Control Protocol/Internet Protocol), a packet-based communication protocol that forms the foundation of the **Internet**.

MacTCP, along with either a direct network connection or **SLIP** or **PPP** software, enables a Macintosh to function as a machine on the Internet that can send and receive **email**, download or transmit software, or even function as a **server** for **FTP, Gopher,** or **World Wide Web** documents.

In fact, because the Internet is based on TCP/IP protocols, MacTCP is the only way for a Macintosh to have a full Internet connection.

MacTCP comes bundled with System 7.5 software. A version of MacTCP is also included on the disk that accompanies *Internet Starter Kit.*

Although MacTCP enables communication between Mac and Internet, the way a user configures MacTCP differs depending on the protocol used to connect the user's Mac to the Internet—SLIP, PPP, or direct network connection.

Another important piece of information to know before configuring MacTCP is whether your **Internet service provider** has assigned you an account that is:

- Manually addressed with a "static" **IP address**.

- Server-addressed with a "dynamic" IP address that is assigned differently each time you connect to the server.

- Dynamically, at random (which is dangerous and seldom-used).

For instance, in the MacTCP configuration dialog shown in the following figure, you choose one of the buttons in the top left section to specify whether you have a Manual, Server, or Dynamically assigned IP address. In the bottom right section, you type your Internet provider's domain name and its IP address(es).

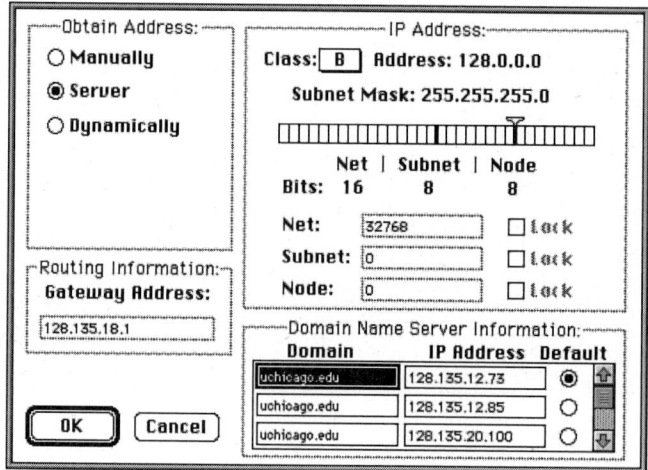

You will have to get the **domain name** and IP address information from your Internet service provider (see the entry for **SLIP** for a set of questions to ask your provider). Although you do not need them to configure MacTCP, you should at some point also get from your provider the addresses of your SMTP (Simple Mail Transport Protocol, used with email) and NNTP (Net News Transfer Protocol, used with Usenet) servers as well as your Post Office Protocol account (POP, used with email).

The following table lists examples of this account information.

MacTCP Account Information

Item	Example
Connection method	SLIP, LocalTalk, Ethernet
Addressing style	Manually, Server, Dynamically
IP address (if manually)	**192.135.191.128**
Gateway address (if necessary)	**192.135.191.253**
Network class (if manually and necessary)	A, B, or C
Subnet Mask (if manually and necessary)	Ask
Primary and secondary name servers	**198.137.231.1**
Local domain	**uchicago.edu**
SMTP mail server	**midway.uchicago.edu**
NNTP news server	**uchinews.uchicago.edu**
POP account	**gholden1@midway.uchicago.edu**
Email address	**gholden@midway.uchicago.edu**

To start working with MacTCP, copy the MacTCP control panel into the Control Panels folder in your System Folder. If you drag the program onto the closed System Folder, System 7 will move it to the right location. Also drag the Hosts file to the System Folder.

If you are upgrading from a previous version of MacTCP, open the current MacTCP control panel and write down all of the settings. Then delete the old MacTCP control panel and the MacTCP DNR file from the System Folder, as well as the MacTCP Prep file which is in the Preferences folder.

If you plan to connect to the Internet via PPP or SLIP, first install software such as InterSLIP or MacPPP (see

the entries on **InterSLIP** and **MacPPP** for specific configuration instructions).

Restart your computer and choose the MacTCP control panel to bring up the MacTCP main window, as shown here.

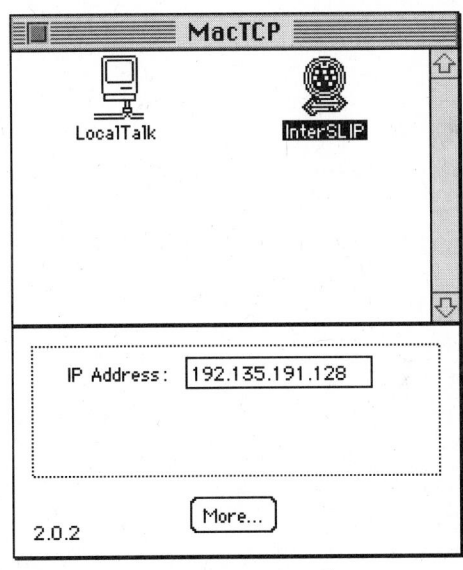

You must select one of the icons (you may have more, or fewer ones) in the upper part of the control panel to tell MacTCP how you plan to connect. If you have a LocalTalk network attached to the Internet through a router, select the LocalTalk icon. If you are on an Ethernet network, select the Ethernet icon. If you have SLIP, select the InterSLIP icon. You can set your IP address in the lower part of this window, but only if you have a manually addressed account. If you have a server-addressed account, set this box to 0.0.0.0.

Clicking the "More" button brings up the Configuration dialog illustrated earlier in this entry. See previous sections for instructions on how to fill out this dialog box.

See Also

DNS; Internet; Internet Service Provider; InterSLIP; MacPPP; Network; Router

MacTools Pro

MacTools Pro, a commercial product from Symantec, (10201 Torre Ave, Cupertino, CA, 95104-2132, Phone (800) 441-7234 Retail price: $99. Web site at **http://www.symantec.com**) is a popular suite of diagnostic/repair, data protection, data recovery, and system enhancement modules that add a host of features to your Mac's system. They include:

- Disk Fix, a full-featured repair utility similar to Norton Disk Doctor that offers a comprehensive diagnosis and repair program with complete reporting. Disk Fix also features the capability to undo a repair, if undesired results are experienced. This utility also includes AutoCheck and AutoRepair, which work in the background and during idle time to diagnose and repair problems before they become serious.

- Disk Light, a menu bar disk status indicator that blinks anytime a mounted disk is being accessed.

- TrashBack, designed to help you retrieve files that you deleted by emptying the Trash. This utility also protects files from being overwritten (which would permanently erase the file). On the other side of things, TrashBack can also wipe out files completely, leaving nary a track (to conform with Department of Defense standards), providing a layer of protection for the user by eliminating the ability of an outside individual to restore personal files from your disk that have been deleted.

- Undelete, designed as a recovery utility used as an alternative when TrashBack has not been installed.

- RAMboot, designed to build a startup disk in memory for rebooting, eliminating the need for an emergency disk and enabling you to diagnose and repair damaged disks, even on the System Startup disk, with no rebooting at all.

- SmartTips, designed to help users identify and troubleshoot hardware and other system problems and guide users, step-by-step, through repair procedures.

- Optimizer, a utility used to defragment your hard disk.

- Anti-Virus, which provides idle time scanning of your hard disk for computer viruses.

The following figure shows the opening screen of MacTools Clinic.

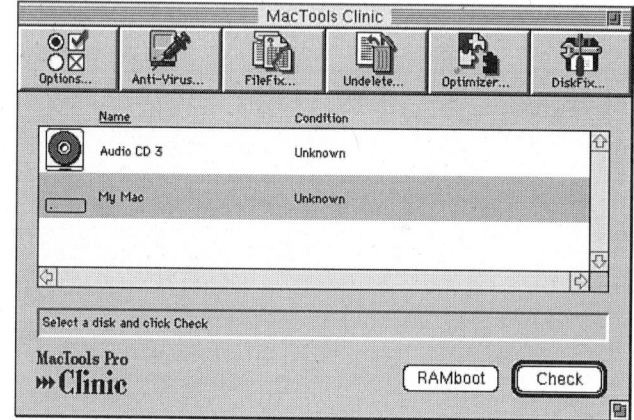

See Also

Hard Disk; Online Services

MacWAIS, *See WAIS*

MacWeb

A simple **browser** or **client** program for navigating the **World Wide Web**. Requires less memory than many other browsers, thus making it usable on a wider range of computers.

As this was being written, TradeWave was preparing to take MacWeb from shareware to commercial status. The commercial release was expected to support background images, inline **JPEG** images, and many **HTML** extensions.

The present version downloads text before graphics, stores Web pages in **cache** to speed up reloading or revisiting a page, has **bookmarks** and hotlists, and enables users to "turn off" image display to make **SLIP** or **PPP** connections easier and faster.

One innovative feature of MacWeb is a shortcut for navigating to sites you have already visited in the current session. Simply click and hold either the Forward or Back buttons. After a second or two, a pop-up menu appears, listing the history (see the following figure).

To choose Open **URL** to type or paste in a new URL, MacWeb provides a pop-up menu of your hotlist items. You can select an item from the list, which pastes its URL into the URL field.

Home page: **http://www.einet.net/EINet/MacWeb/ MacWebHome.html/**.

See Also
Bookmarks; Netscape Navigator; Web Browser; World Wide Web

MacWorks, *See Lisa*

MacWorld Expo
MacWorld Expo is a huge Macintosh-centric computer expo held several times each year. The two largest expos are in San Francisco each January and in Boston each August. Other MacWorld expos are held in Japan and Germany.

For many Macintosh aficionados, MacWorld is a required event. The expo consists of three primary parts: exhibits, or the show floor; conferences; and parties. Taken in the appropriate proportions, these make MacWorld a great time.

The exhibits are much like any trade show and include booths for virtually every major Macintosh software and hardware company. The exhibitors show their latest offerings and present demonstrations of their products. The demos are often punctuated by a door prize or two given to those patient enough to sit through the demo. Many people attend MacWorld just for these giveaways and for the excellent sale prices often offered at the show.

The conferences offer seminars on a wide variety of Mac-related topics, from education to desktop publishing to programming. Although attending the conferences adds significantly to the price, many of the sessions are excellent. The presenters are frequently the top in their field, and the keynote address is generally given by a major figure in the Macintosh world.

Last, but certainly not least, are the parties. For some, MacWorld is just a week of parties. Various hardware and software companies throw parties (or hold more sedate events, such as breakfast) for their important— and sometimes not so important—customers. These events can be quite elaborate. It's not unusual, for example, for a company to rent out Boston's Computer Museum or other similar venue to hold their MacWorld event.

Whether you go for the parties, the great information, or the free stuff, MacWorld Expo is an event not to be missed.

See Also
History and Culture of the Macintosh

M

MacWrite Pro

When the Mac first appeared on this author's desk, back in 1984, it had two programs installed. One was MacPaint, which set the standards for computer graphics. The other was MacWrite, which was just as revolutionary, in its own way. It was the first word processor that could use different **fonts**. It was also the first one that could place a graphic in a page of text. Most important, it introduced point and click word processing. Apple's MacWrite became Claris MacWrite, through some internal reorganization at Apple HQ, and kept pace with the other word processors, without raising its price through the roof, and without becoming so feature-laden that it needed a huge hard drive and outrageous amounts of RAM to make it run.

The current version, MacWritePro, has text-handling capabilities that go far beyond word processing to real desktop publishing. Like the big guys, WordPerfect and MS Word 6, it can create a Table of Contents in a long document or insert a QuickTime movie into a document. It has very convenient text, style, and tool palettes, and a function very similar to System 7.5's Stickies that enables you to place notes on your documents. If your Mac has a microphone, you also can record voice messages on your notes. MacWritePro can edit linked objects created in MathType, microExpressionist, and other programs that support EGO (Edit Graphic Object). It can create and send email via PowerTalk, and it is optimized for Power Macintosh use.

One of the best uses for MacWritePro is as a simple DTP program. It comes with a folder full of examples that includes newsletter and annual report samples, as well as fax covers, memos, and other useful business and personal documents. Each of these illustrates some of the possibilities for layout and design with MacWritePro.

This program, like many of the high end DTP programs, uses frames to hold pictures, text, tables, and notes. The preceding figure shows a page view of a newsletter, including a note frame, text frames, and graphics frames. Frames give you a great deal of flexibility in laying out pages. Text frames allow you to place a headline or a sidebar without wading through endless dialog boxes, or creating new styles. Using the graphics frame enables you to crop the graphic to fit the page. You can resize the frame by clicking and dragging it. You can also use the frame to anchor a graphic to its text. An anchored graphic is the same as an inline graphic. An invisible marker is placed in the text where the graphic should be. If you change the formatting of the text or the amount of text so that the anchor jumps to another column or page, the graphic goes with it. There are even movie frames, which display QuickTime movies. (Because QuickTime files are very large, MacWritePro saves one frame of the movie and links to its disk location.)

Of course, it also can handle ordinary writing chores. The floating palettes make formatting text a cinch. You can always see the available styles, unlike most programs that make you open and scroll down a list. Creating and editing styles is managed from the same palette. It handles mail merges quite well, with a built-in dictionary and thesaurus. It doesn't check grammar, but considering how badly other word processors do so, that's no loss. If it has a serious fault, it's that there's only one level of Undo. You can't retrace your steps if you've done something seriously stupid. But with a word processor this easy to use, you're unlikely to make stupid mistakes.

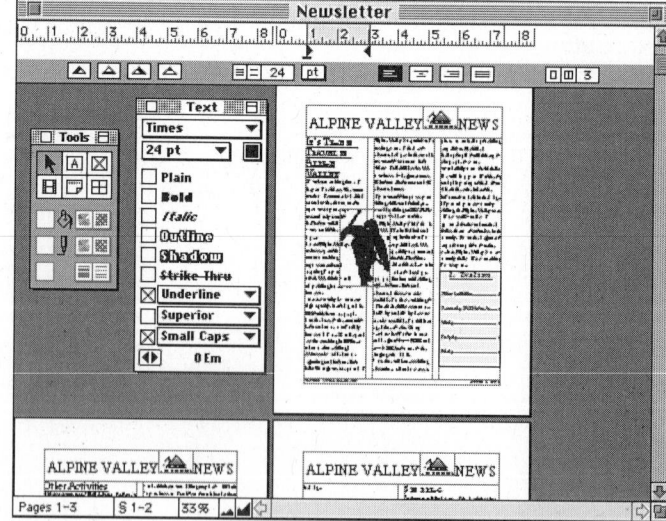

See Also

Nisus Writer; WordPerfect; Word Processors

Mad Dog McCree, *See First Person Perspective Shooters*

Maelstrom, *See Crystal Crazy*

Magazines, Mac Gaming

Just about every magazine that covers computers covers games, but Mac game coverage can be a little sparse. At this point, the best bet is the CD-ROM magazine *Inside Mac Games* (IMG). IMG offers the widest range of games and interactive entertainment coverage of any publication and comes chock full of demos and previews, as well as shareware games to download. *Inside Mac Games* is published 10 times a year and based in Canada.

On the paper publication side, *MacHome Journal* offers monthly coverage of Mac-specific games in its recently upgraded interactive entertainment section and offers up to 10 game reviews each month. PC Entertainment is a dual platform book, covering mainly the slew of PC titles before they port to the Mac, but they do a great job of keeping up with Mac games and making sure you know when a port is going to occur if the title hits the PC first. Other magazines including *ComputerLife*, *Wired*, *MacWeek*, *MacWorld*, and the online publications *MacSense* and *XYZZY News* cover Mac games more sporadically.

The best way to gauge when to pick these up is to wait for an entertainment themed issue. As time goes by and more cool games pop up for the Macintosh and more platform merging titles like **Hexen** and Havoc are released, no doubt monthly coverage will step up accordingly.

Magic Cookie

A feature of the **World Wide Web** browser **Netscape Navigator** that stores information about a user's relationship to certain **Internet** sites. Also called *HTTP Cookie*.

The "Magic Cookie" is a file that resides in your Netscape Preferences folder. You can open it with Netscape by dragging its icon onto the Netscape icon or with SimpleText. Its exact appearance varies, depending on what sites you've visited, but it should look something like the following figure.

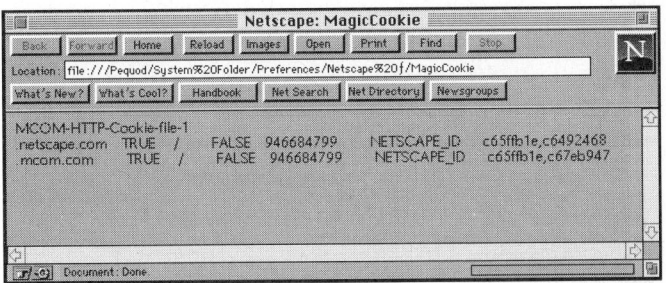

A "cookie," in this case, is a short database entry about you that a Netscape-savvy server has asked Netscape to store on your hard drive. It contains things like the name of the server's site, the parts of the server's site wherein the cookie is recognized, your user ID on the site, an expiration date for the cookie, and simple yes/no instructions on whether the cookie must be transmitted securely. (The notion that servers are maintaining a file about you obviously raises some questions about invasion-of-privacy issues.)

When you return to a site listed in the Magic Cookie file, Netscape transmits the information in the cookie to the site's server, who will know who you are. Alternatively, the server can request a cookie.

Web sites with "Shopping bag" services can make use of cookies by linking your purchase (stored on the server) with your identity (stored on your computer). There are other ways to implement shopping bag-like features without the use of cookies that many other sites use.

M

See Also

Encryption; Internet; Netscape Navigator; Secure HTTP; Secure Sockets Layer; World Wide Web

Magnetic Tape, *See Online Storage*

Magneto Optical (MO) Drives

Magneto optical drives offer the largest amount of data storage; however, they have considerably slower access times compared to hard drives and most other removable media drives. Magneto optical drives enable you to write and rewrite data to a CD-type media cartridge. These drives use 3.5 inch and 5.25 inch removable media, usually a CD-size disk in a permanent casing. The external casing is very similar to that of a floppy disk. They can store 120MB to more than 1GB of data on one disk.

One pitfall to using magneto optical drives is that the software drivers vary from drive maker to drive maker. If you plan to share magnetic optical information across different brand devices, make sure that differing drives can read each other's formatted CDs. Also, keep in mind that the magneto optical cartridges range in price form $20-40 each.

Mailbox Extension

This extension is installed if you have PowerTalk on your system. It enables support for individual mailboxes.

See Also

PowerTalk

Mailing List

A mailing list is a means of conducting **email** discussions on the **Internet** between groups of people with similar interests.

A mailing list is made up of subscribers who receive and read email messages sent by other list members. Every email message sent to the list is distributed to all of its members, any of whom can send email replies that can develop into text-based discussions.

Mailing lists are similar to **Usenet** newsgroups in that they consist of messages and replies posted to everyone in the group. The difference is that mailing list communication occurs via email. Email is more immediate than newsgroup postings that have to be collected by a news server, and mailing list subscribers do not need special client software (other than their existing email software) to read and send messages.

Mailing list discussions tend to be more focused than newsgroup postings because the number of subscribers is much smaller. Some mailing lists are used for announcements of new software or newsletters on specific topics rather than discussions.

Two kinds of mailing lists occur on the Internet:

1. Moderated lists maintained by an individual who monitors discussions and adds and subtracts subscribers to and from the list.

2. Unmoderated lists maintained by an automated server, sometimes called a **LISTSERV**.

Mailing lists can be hard to locate, but there are a few sites on the Internet that present lists of the various lists. Do a search on one of the Internet search engines, or try the DTP Internet Jumplist: **http://www.cs.purdue.edu/homes/gwp/dtp/groups.html**.

After you find a list, subscribing is easy. You either find the email address of the person who "owns" or runs the list, and send a polite message asking to be subscribed or, in the case of a LISTSERV, send a standard email message such as:

```
subscribe [your name] [your email address]
[name of mailing list]
```

You will receive an automated reply along with instructions on how to use the list and how to unsubscribe (be sure to keep this initial message in case you ever do want to know how to unsubscribe).

Traffic on mailing lists can be heavy, and it's not uncommon to receive dozens of messages a day. Mailing lists that reach a high level of traffic sometimes create digest versions that contains all the individual messages arranged in a specific way. Subscribers then receive one long message per day instead of many messages throughout the day.

See Also

Email; LISTSERV; Netscape; Internet; POP3; QuickMail; SMTP; Web Server; WebSTAR; World Wide Web

Majestic, *See Adventure Games*

Major, Anya, *See 1984*

Major Software Release

A major release is a major upgrade of the software, containing whole new groups of functionality and features. It also may include significant changes to the user interface. Frequently, it will include new file storage formats that will make files created by the new version inaccessible to users of an older version; fortunately, the new software will (almost without exception) read files created by the older versions. If the version number is two numbers, the second of which is zero separated by a decimal point (for example, 2.0), you have a major release. If the second digit is a 5 (for example, 3.5), you have a release that is probably more significant than a minor release, but that someone objected to classifying as a major release. In addition to being the highest-priced type of software upgrade, major releases will often exact additional costs in processing power enhancement, memory expansion, or storage space increases.

See Also

Software Updates

Make Alias Command

The Make Alias command is used to create an **alias** of a file. An alias is like a proxy in that it's not really a copy of the file, but rather a pointer back to the original file. It behaves much like the original file.

Here's an example of why you might want an alias and how they work. Many applications have helper files or other documents that they need to launch. These files are kept within that application's folder or in the System Folder so the program knows right where to look for them. If you were to move the application out of its original folder, it might not be able to find those auxiliary files, and might not open correctly. In short, some applications must stay inside their original folders. **Apple** created a way to give instant access to a program without having to dig through layer after layer of folders: aliases. Aliases are great for enabling access to an application in multiple places. You may want an alias of a particular application in the Apple menu, for example, plus an alias of the same application right out on your desktop. If you have a folder for your work that you access often, you may want an alias of the application there as well. Because aliases take up such little memory, you can have as many aliases in as many locations as you wish.

Making an alias is easy. Just click the program or file you want to have an alias of, and then select Make Alias from the **File menu** (⌘-M).

When you create an alias, a copy of the item's icon is created, the alias filename is italicized, and the word *alias* is appended to the filename to let you know it's an alias. Because they are not copies of the original file, just a pointer back to it, aliases are very small in size. This enables you to create an alias of any file and put it anywhere on your hard drive or on your **desktop.** When you double-click the alias, it launches the real file or program behind the scenes.

You can make aliases of files, documents, programs, folders, even the **trash** can if you want. Many people use aliases to put frequently used programs and folders in their **Apple menu.** That way, without opening their hard drive, a window, or any folders, they can launch an application or file instantly by choosing its alias. If you ever need to find the original file you used to create the alias, click the alias and choose Get Info from the File menu. The Get Info window shows you where the original file is, and the Find Original button locates the file and brings it to you.

Another excellent use of aliases is for documents that you need in two different locations on your drive. Let's say, for example, you and your partner share the same computer, and you have a folder where you keep all your standard business letters. You may also want your partner to have access to these same letters. You can make a copy of all the files and give them to your partner, or instead you can make aliases of the letters, (which take up much less space) and place the aliases in a separate folder for your partner. That way, your partner can organize the folder to his/her liking, find the business letters fast, and you both can work on the same documents without having to make any copies.

Also, if there's a document you use often, such as a template for your company letterhead, an alias comes in very handy. For easy access, put an alias of the document in the Apple menu. That way, when you need to dash off a quick letter, all you have to do is select the letterhead template directly from the Apple menu, rather than searching through folders on your hard drive to find it. Aliases are there for your convenience.

If you're on a network, you can also create an alias for the server to give you instant access. Many users put this alias on the desktop so they're never more than a click away from the server.

To make an alias, follow these steps:

1. Click the item you want to make an alias of.

2. Select Make Alias (⌘-M) from the File menu.

3. An Alias appears next to the original with the name of the alias in italics and the word *alias* appended to the end of the filename, as shown in the figure.

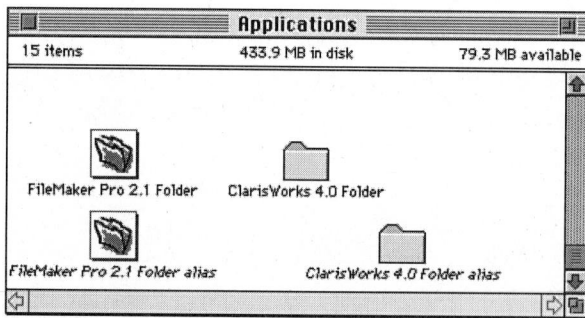

See Also
Alias; Apple Menu; File Menu; Trash

Make QTVR Object

An application that converts **QuickTime** movies into **QuickTime VR** object movies. Available from Apple's Web site (**http://www.apple.com**).

See Also
Make QTVR Panorama; QuickTime VR; QuickTime VR Authoring Tools Suite

Make QTVR Panorama

An application that converts a panoramic image into a **QuickTime VR** object movie. Available from Apple's Web site (**http://www.apple.com**).

See Also
Make QTVR Object; QuickTime VR; QuickTime VR Authoring Tools Suite

Manager, *See Toolbox*

Mancala, *See Classic Collection*

Maniac Mansion, *See Full Throttle*

Map Control Panel

This **control panel** enables you to enter the name of a major city from around the world and have the exact latitude, longitude, current time, and distance you are from the city calculated for you. The location of each city entered is highlighted on a world map that appears at the top of the Map control panel, as shown in the figure.

The Map uses the location information entered in your Date & Time control panel as a starting point to calculate your distance from various points across the globe. You can also ask the Map to show you the distance in miles between any two cities.

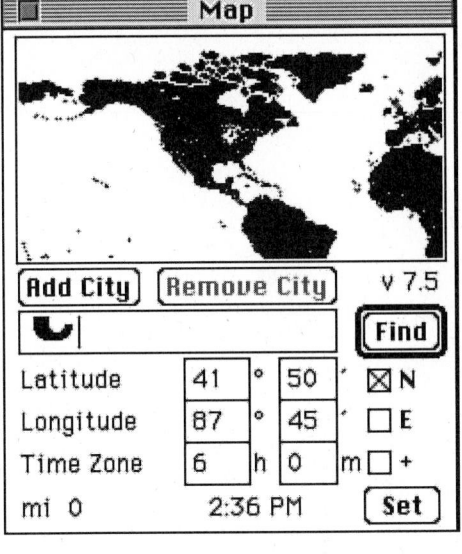

To use the Map control panel, follow these steps:

1. Choose Map from the control panels submenu on the Apple menu (or System Folder).

2. Enter the name of a major city and click Find.

3. Your location (as set by your Date & Time control panel) and the city you've entered blink on the map, and the latitude, longitude, and current time in that city and the distance between the two cities are displayed.

4. To enter a different base city (other than your own), you can enter a city name and press Set. Then enter a second city and the mileage between those two cities is calculated. You can also set a different base city to set the system clock, which is a handy when traveling with a PowerBook.

5. To see a list of the cities in the map, hold the Option key and press Return. If your city is not on the map's list of cities, you can add your city if you know the longitude and latitude of your city. Enter them in the Map control panel and click "Add City" to add your city to the map's list.

See Also
Control Panel

Map and Atlas Programs

One of the best uses for **CD-ROM** technology is the interactive map or atlas. You'll find many of these in the software catalogs and on dealer shelves. Which one to choose depends on the kind and degree of detailed information you need. A general atlas, such as DK's *Cartopedia* or Brøderbund's *Maps 'N' Facts*, gives you a comprehensive overview of the physical world, along with political boundaries and basic information about each country. Included are such details as literacy rates, exports, economic data, health statistics, and even the number of TV and radio stations and newspapers.

For a much closer look, there's DeLorme's **Street Atlas USA**, which is a massive street-level database for the entire USA on one CD-ROM. It enables you to zoom in on virtually every city, town, and rural area in the country, and shows the names of all the streets, as well as state, county, and interstate highways. The database contains more than 12 million street segments and 1.1 million geographic and man-made features, such as mountains, rivers, lakes, and prominent monuments.

Street Atlas USA is very easy to use. You type in the name of a city and state, telephone area code and exchange, or ZIP code to find any area of the country. You can then search for any street within the map you're viewing. In larger metropolitan areas, Street Atlas USA also displays block address ranges. You can even print maps directly from the program. But don't get carried away…. If you printed out all of Street Atlas USA at the highest level of detail, the finished map would cover more than 10 football fields.

See Also
Street Atlas USA

M

Marathon I & Marathon II: Durandal

Marathon, Bungie Software's answer to game players' pleas for a Mac version of **DOOM**, pits you against hostile aliens who are trying to take over the inhabitants of the spaceship Marathon. In addition, the ship's computer has gone awry and is hindering your mission to rid the ship of the unwelcome alien guests.

As in most first person shooters, the interface in Marathon shows you your stamina (how much air you have left in your space suit) as well as other necessities like weapons inventory and a motion detector for tracking aliens. **Marathon II** has twenty-nine levels and picks up seventeen years after the first game. You've been transported to the distant planet L'howan and must rid it of the evil aliens, the Phfor. The Marathon games implement more of a strategy edge than DOOM, with complex puzzles and tougher-to-kill foes. Marathon adds multilevel strategies; aliens are not always on the same level platform, lurking above and below, as well as next to you. Both Marathon I & II can be played by multiple players over a **network**; II comes with an extra serial number so you don't have to purchase a second copy.

See Also

Descent; DOOM II; Hexen: Beyond Heretic; Violence in Games

MarcoPolo

A document imaging and management system for all kinds of Macintosh documents. The paperless office is a concept whose time is coming closer. Pretty soon, we'll be storing most of our documents on our hard drive, or on removable Syquest cartridges, **CD-ROMs**, or some other high-density storage mechanism, and we could end up even worse off than we are now, with no idea where to look for anything. It's easier to flip through a file cabinet in search of a missing contract or letter than it is to look through hundreds of megabytes of miscellaneous data.

Mainstay's MarcoPolo has come to our rescue. It stores documents and files in databases called Document Centers. These contain electronic documents from all kinds of applications, compressed and tagged with keywords to help you locate the ones you need to retrieve. Related documents can be grouped together, regardless of the application that created them. Documents are displayed on the computer screen by MarcoPolo, not by their creator application. If you're looking for a particular piece of data in a spreadsheet, you don't need to install or know how to use Excel to locate it. Document centers can be password-protected for confidentiality. Use MarcoPolo to create the document center, indexing and compressing the items you put into it. Then, use MarcoPolo as needed to retrieve the document images. You can view any MarcoPolo document as a thumbnail just by clicking the name in the dialog box list. You can even run QuickTime movies and sound files within MarcoPolo (see the figure).

MarcoPolo functions with any Apple or TWAIN-compliant **scanner** to input all of your paper documents. It includes a sophisticated OCR (optical character reader) program that converts scanned text into a searchable file. It also accepts documents that are currently on your Mac in any printable format. MarcoPolo can automatically generate its document images from many common file formats, from XTND translators, or by having the file "printed" to a Chooser application, called MarcoPolo Creator, which functions like a printer driver, printing the document image into the document center files.

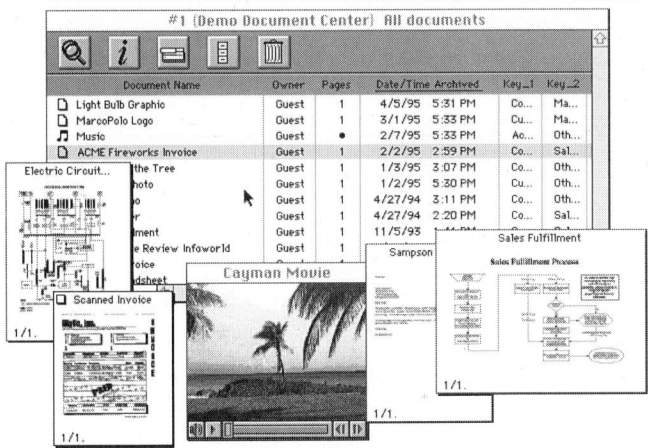

Each image is accompanied by information that helps you locate it, including its owner, archival date, and assigned keywords. If access to a document is limited, it also has attached to its file a list of users who are permitted to view it.

To locate a particular item, use the Query box. Here, we are doing a search by date and text for a document entered last month that contains the words "book" and "proposal" but not the word "Windows." The search should bring us a list of book proposals for Macintosh books. Because it's so specific, we're sure to find the exact item for which we're looking.

By combining several criteria, it's easy to construct a very detailed search. If this was a multiuser system with several people placing items into the document center, we also could search by owner. We could search multiple document centers, if we weren't sure where we'd filed it. Or we could search by a keyword, perhaps "book."

When MarcoPolo finds the document(s), it displays a list. Double-clicking an entry opens a mini-page view, which you can zoom to read at full size. Text used as a search criterion is highlighted. You cannot modify a document image in MarcoPolo. However, you can print the document, or copy it to the Clipboard and import it into another application.

See Also
OCR; Scanners

Margins and Tabs

Margins and tabs define the look of your document. Top and bottom margins define the amount of white space at the top and bottom of the document, and side margins determine the amount of white space at the sides. If a document is to be bound, you must leave extra space, called "gutter margins" or "binding margins" on the binding edge of the page. A two-sided document has the gutter margin on the left on odd-numbered pages, and on the right on even-numbered pages. Margins can be set in a dialog box, from a ruler, or by dragging them into position on the page in page view. It depends on which program you're using.

Tabs are used to line up text. There are four common types of tabs: left, center, right, and decimal. Left, center, and right refer to the position of the text relative to the tab stop. They are set differently in the various word processor and DTP programs. The figure shows tabs in WriteNow, where they're simply set on the ruler.

The left tab stop is at the left of the tabbed text. The center tab stop centers the tabbed text around it. The right tab stop is positioned at the right of the tabbed text. The decimal tab is used with a column of figures. The decimal points line up at the tab stop position, so that the number columns are always in line.

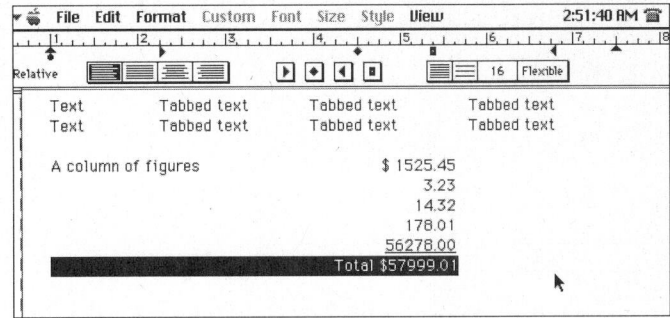

Never use the spacebar to line up columns of text. Use the tabs instead. Spaces almost always come out uneven, whereas tabs always line up.

See Also
Leaders

Mario Teaches Typing

Remember Mario? He and brother Luigi raced through strange worlds, kicking turtles and grasping stars in an attempt to rescue a princess. Well, he's back, along with Luigi and the Princess, only this time their world revolves around teaching kids to type. But they accomplish this in typical Mario style, with everything from turtles and blocks to quicksand and hungry fish who want our hero as a snack.

This program combines the fun of an arcade game with the mechanics of touch typing. The animation is cute and the music and sound effects are similar to the ones in the game. But it might have been more useful to have the letters spoken as you typed them, or at least some definite right or wrong feedback. Still, once you get into it, the rhythm of the music helps keep you moving along, and you get your score after each two minute "round" of typing. There are three levels. In the first, you practice individual letters, while you kick turtles and jump on boxes.

In the second, you're typing real words and avoiding sharks and octopuses underwater. At the third level, you must type full sentences, as you work your way through an underground tunnel full of traps. The program can handle any number of students and will print out achievement certificates as they reach each of the three levels.

See Also
Software, Educational, Adult; Software, Educational, Grades 7-12; Software, Educational, K-6

Marionet

An XCMD from Allegient Technologies, Marionet provides a scriptable interface to the Internet. The XCMD works with **SuperCard**, Apple **HyperCard**, and Macromedia **Director**, as well as programs that support **AppleScript**. Marionet supports several standard Internet protocols, including **World Wide Web** (**HTTP**), Newsgroups (**NNTP**), **Email** (SMTP/POP3 including APOP), File Transfers (**FTP**), Domain Name Services (**DNS**), and Searching (**Gopher**).

Marionet makes it possible to create an end-user interface for the Internet, such as a custom browser or mail program, or custom programs, such as online games or an electronic-directory that connects to the Internet for latest product information.

Allegient charges a license fee for commercial distribution of the XCMD: $500 per year for less than 500 users, and unlimited distribution for $1,000 per year.

Marionet requires a **TCP/IP** connection, a 68020 processor greater, System 7.1, and at least 750K for the Marionet application. A Windows version of Marionet is under development.

Markkula, A.C. "Mike"

Armand Clifford "Mike" Markkula was one of Apple's first investors. After making his fortune at Intel and Fairchild Semiconductor, he came out of retirement to help finance Apple Computer.

Following **Ron Wayne's** pullout from the original Apple partnership, **Steve Jobs** began looking for other investors. He spoke with Nolan Bushnell, his former boss at Atari, who recommended that he speak with venture capitalist Don Valentine. Although the two scruffy-looking kids in a garage didn't interest Valentine, he referred Jobs to Markkula.

Markkula apparently liked what he saw, and promptly invested $92,000 of his own money, with a commitment of up to $250,000. In return, he was given a one-third interest in Apple. When Apple went public in December 1980, Markkula got more than a 55,000 percent return on his initial investment.

Markkula helped Jobs create Apple's original business plan and has been closely involved with Apple ever since. He has generally preferred to stay out of the spotlight that is frequently on the leaders of Apple, but has always had a say in Apple business plan and strategy.

Originally, Markkula served as chairman of the board while **Mike Scott** was president. From 1981 until 1983, he served as president, during which time Jobs was chairman. When Apple recruited **John Sculley** to the positions of chairman and CEO, Markkula stepped aside. During **Michael Spindler**'s reign as president, Markkula again held the position of chairman. Most recently, Markkula stepped aside again when **Gilbert Amelio** became chairman and CEO in 1996.

See Also

Amelio, Gilbert; Jobs, Steve; Scott, Mike; Sculley, John; Spindler, Michael; Wayne, Ron

MarkUp

MarkUp is a tool for editors and anyone else who must review and make comments on documents. It's perfect for workgroups who share responsibility for reports and other files and must collaborate on their production. It enables users to edit, annotate, and review a document on transparent overlays, rather than making changes or notes directly on the page. Doing so means that the author can read the suggested changes without losing the original work. MarkUp also supports QuickTime and voice annotation, so a reviewer can add spoken comments rather than written ones, with a placeholder to indicate that there's a message to be heard.

Documents for MarkUp review can be created using any application. The user also can attach a limited version of MarkUp to a particular document, so that reviewers who do not own the program can still use it to review and edit that document. MarkUp runs on virtually any Mac from the Plus on up, and requires only System 6.0.4 or later. You can even install MarkUp as a menu option in your favorite **word processor** or other application. It works with spreadsheets, graphics programs, text files from an OCR scanner, or almost any other program from which you can open and print a document.

The procedure for creating a MarkUp file is simple. Open the document, and use the Chooser to open the MarkUp Creator, which acts like a printer driver. You'll "print" a MarkUp version of the document to your hard drive. Then, you can open it and make your edits. There's a fully editable menu of proofreader marks, and even a palette of fun marks, including a pig, thumbs up, a trash can, a light bulb to say bright idea, and many more. You can create your own palette of marks, selecting from these and the common proofreader marks. You also can modify the marks or replace them with others, using the Marks editor to redraw them at 16×16 pixels. Reviewers can leave notes in a journal attached to the MarkUp document, explaining what they have done to it. The journal stays with the MarkUp document. Click a proof mark to select it, and then click the document to place it. You can type comments directly on the document, too.

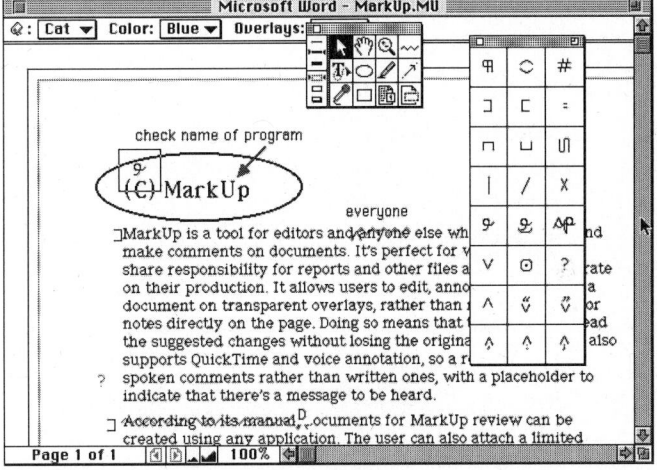

After all the reviewers have finished , you can display each marked overlay separately or merge them all together. Open the original document next to the MarkUp version and make the changes you want to make. You still have your original text, no matter what the reviewers have done to hack it up. You can copy significant changes from the MarkUp version and paste them into the original document.

The advantages to using MarkUp are many. There's no wasted paper. The document can be passed around on a network or by email. There's a record of the editing sessions, and you can tell immediately who said what. MarkUp enables reviewers to look at each other's comments, so there's a synergistic effect, resulting in a much better piece of work.

Marlais, *See Dylan*

Martin Hash's 3-Dimensional Animation

A low priced ($199!) version of Hash's 3D character animation tool **Animation Master**. This program lacks high-end compositing and imaging features, such as sub-pixel averaging and network rendering options of its more expensive sibling, but otherwise it offers the same interface and features.

If you are interested in character animation, either this program or Animation Master are probably your best choices. They support inverse kinematics, and you can create a script for a character, a set of instructions that defines how a character walks.

Unfortunately, the program is very complex, and the documentation is limited in a videotape, a couple of electronic tutorials (which only cover very specific areas and don't give a complete introduction), as well as online help which is probably only of use once you understand all the concepts.

There has been some effort to create additional documentation by users, so check out Hash's Web site for copies of these documents. For more about how this program works, read the entry for Animation Master.

See Also

3D; Animation; Extreme 3D; Infini-D; Ray Dream; Sketch!; StrataVision

Master Juggler

Master Juggler is a commercial **font**-management tool developed by Alsoft, Inc. that enables you to use and organize fonts. A key feature is its capability to store and use fonts in any location on a disk, rather than having to store all your fonts in the Fonts folder within your System folder.

Master Juggler, like its main competitor **Suitcase**, enables you to create font sets, turn these font sets on and off individually or in groups, renumber font IDs to eliminate font conflicts, and customize your fonts from outside the System Folder.

Alsoft, Inc.
P.O. Box 927
Spring, TX 77383
(713) 353-4090

See Also

Font; Font Utility; Suitcase

Master Pages

Most page layout applications allow users to set up nonprinting pages that can be used as templates to create any number of body pages with the same basic structure.

This feature is useful when composing books or other documents with a large number of similar pages. A user might design a master page for chapter openers, one for lefthand text pages, one for righthand text pages, and others for special purposes such as multiple-column indexes.

Common elements on master pages include page numbers; running headers and footers; graphics elements such as rules, logos, and blind tabs; and boxes or guides to hold text that body pages will contain.

Most page layout packages offer some degree of assistance setting up master pages. For example, most offer a way to number pages automatically.

- To make automatic page numbers in **QuarkXPress**, press ⌘-3 on a master page. This will produce the characters "<#>" on the master page and the correct page number on any body page to which that master is applied.

- In **PageMaker**, press "#" on any master page.

- In **FrameMaker**, insert the "Current Page #" variable by pressing ⌘-B, selecting "Current Page #," and clicking on "Insert."

Other master-page related features include the capability to insert other "variables" on master pages that transform to text on body pages, such as the date or time, the total page count of the document, or the filename. Some packages, such as FrameMaker, allow master page variables to insert text from the main text flow in running headers or footers—so a dictionary, for example, could automatically have the first and last entries on each page appear in that page's running header.

See Also

FrameMaker; PageMaker; QuarkXPress

Masterpiece Mansion

Philips' Masterpiece Mansion is an adeptly packaged cross between a game and an educational title. It qualifies as a game about art rather than an art CD-ROM because the basic premise lies in trying to gain access to more rooms in an art gallery. Each room presents a puzzle or trivia question related to its contents that helps you to better understand famous works of art and the people who created them (see the following figure).

The Bell Tower. Examine the art and solve puzzles to reveal your escape.

Masterpiece Mansion operates on the theory that kids will get more out of playing than they will by sifting through a boring reference title, reading entries and looking at quick video shots or cross sections (like you'd find in any old encyclopedia). Masterpiece Mansion is similar to Mortimer in that it is a sophis-

ticated, non-violent game that appeals to a wide range of ages and can realistically be called family entertainment. Philips' other title in this genre, Merlin's Apprentice, would be a logical next step. Merlin's Apprentice moves further away from educational titles, but remains true to a family format for entertainment. Merlin's Apprentice is on the next level of puzzle gaming and includes excellent cartoon style animation.

See Also

Are You Afraid of the Dark?; Family Entertainment; Foul Play; Mortimer; Yellow Brick Road II

Math Coprocessors, *See Coprocessors*

Mathematical Programs for Children, *See Logical Journey of the Zoombinis; Millie's Math House; Snootz Math Trek*

Matrox MGA Millenium, *See QuickDraw 3D Acceleration Card*

Maven

Freeware developed by Charley Kline of the University of Illinois that brings audio broadcasting to anyone with a Mac and a connection to the **Internet**.

Maven, like **CU-SeeMe**, which brings videoconferencing capability to Internet users, requires a fast connection to the Internet to work properly—an ISDN or direct connection, which is faster than dial-up modems using **SLIP** or **PPP**. An ISDN or faster connection is recommended.

M

CU-SeeMe has incorporated Maven's code into its own software to add audio capability for its users.

Mac users with versions of the MacOS earlier than 7.5 should get the current version of the **Sound Manager** before using Maven.

See Also
CU-SeeMe; Internet; ISDN; MacTCP; World Wide Web

Mavis Beacon Teaches Typing

Mavis Beacon won't rap you across the knuckles with a yardstick if you miss a key, but she *will* teach you to type—painlessly. She'll teach your kids, too, in a separate program called *Mavis Beacon Teaches Typing for Kids*. Both of these typing programs are carefully planned to advance you as soon as you're ready. Mavis analyzes your mistakes and offers suggestions in the adult version. In the kids' version, she just tells you how many stars you've earned and your speed. They're both clever programs. Mavis for adults includes an arcade game in which you drive a race car by typing quickly, and a series of interesting stories and bits of trivia to keep you involved in what you're typing. You can choose to learn either the standard QWERTY keyboard or the Dvorak keyboard, a system developed in 1936 by August Dvorak to increase typing efficiency.

Mavis for Kids uses a variety of adventures and activities to teach basic (QWERTY) keyboarding skills. To use this program at the beginner level, the child doesn't even need to know how to read. It begins with single letters, works up to short single words, and finally to real stories. The figure shows an early stage example.

Mavis for Kids has cute animation and sound effects, but (in the Power Mac version) some of the most awful music ever recorded. You can, however, turn the music off in the Preferences box. Mavis for Kids has some kid-proofing features, which are also set in the Preferences box. You can set up the program so the child can't quit, and so that he can't print from the program.

The problem with this, and with all computer typing tutors, is that it can't recognize a single mistake in a row of typed words. If you make a mistake, and don't immediately go back and correct it, everything you type from there on is wrong. This leads to, at worst, some discouragement and lousy wpm scores. It's not a serious problem, but simply one the typing student needs to be aware of.

Maxis, *See Sim Games; SimCity 2000*

Maxsurf Plus

Maxsurf Plus from Graphics Magic Software is a very high-end CAD program targeted toward the naval architect, although it has potential uses for the general Mac animator and 3D sculptor because of its control over the creation of splined surfaces. As if to suggest that possibility, a sculpted car body is included with the object files along with a dozen ship hull models.

Dimensioning Maxsurf Plus has no capability for dimensioning or dimensioning callouts. Maxsurf must be ported to other CAD software for dimensioning. Care should be taken to export the object data in a format that the targeted dimensioning software can read.

3D Options Maxsurf's perspective window features a realtime animation option that shows the selected object spinning in 3D. When stopped at a chosen perspective, the object can be seen from the direction the user desires. The perspective window is Maxsurf's only 3D option.

Text The text style and size for Maxsurf data tables can be selected and altered. There are no text options for other view data as Maxsurf has no on-board dimensioning capacity.

Import/Export Maxsurf exports data files with the Copy command in the Editing menu, a method that might be a bit confusing to experienced CAD users. Selecting "Copy" brings up a list of format choices: Clipboard, PICT, IGES (International Graphics Exchange Standard), DXF, Mac Renderman, and PostScript. The scale of the exported file can be altered at this point in the same dialog. When a selection is made, a standard Save dialog is presented (except if the choice is "Clipboard" of course). Imports are limited to getting data from the Clipboard. Maxsurf also saves and opens files in the Maxsurf format.

Rendering Options Maxsurf displays a rendering menu that allows you to choose Shading On/Off, Gaussian, Transverse or Longitudinal curvature, Convexity, and the optional display of Surface Contours and Positive/Negative values. It also allows brightness level settings (1 to 10). Rendering is displayed onscreen, and is also sent to targeted print media.

Documentation Maxsurf's 100+ pages of documentation comes in a three ring binder so that future upgraded data can be easily added. Various appendices deal with more technical topics.

Special Features Maxsurf includes special features needed by the naval architect for data manipulation and design purposes. Among these are printer and plotter setup preferences, control point control for the model, interactive curve area controls, a calculation and markers window, control points data display, smoothing and straightening controls, alignment-masking controls, precision settings, surface controls (surface types, longitudinal and transverse capability), display and grid spacing controls. A frame of reference window allows setting of Fore and Aft perpendiculars, Amidships, and DWL and Baseline for the design. Zero Point updating is also included.

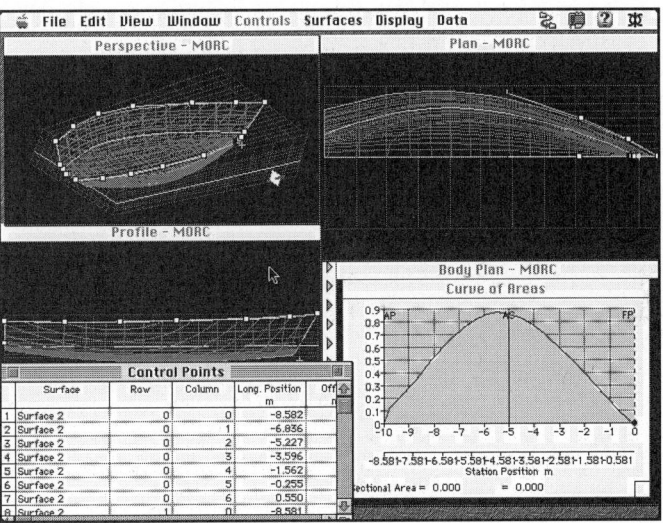

MayaQuest

This program from MECC, (the folks who produced Oregon Trail and the other Trail adventures) is an excellent introduction to the geography and culture of Mexico and Central America. It replicates the adventures of a team of EarthTrek bicycle explorers led by brothers Dan, Steve, and Nick Buettner. MayaQuest lets students become detectives and explorers in search of answers to explain the collapse of the ancient Mayan civilization. This learning adventure will take them on a virtual field trip of ancient ruins in Mexico, Guatemala, and Belize, as captured in over 1,500 photos and video clips from the actual MayaQuest expedition.

Along the way, students will have to make decisions, solve problems, and navigate rugged bike paths while keeping a sharp eye out for ruts, branches, and other hazards. They'll have assignments to complete as part of the trek, finding and reporting facts such as what color a temple was painted, what Mayan rulers wore, or how the Mayans played ball. They'll also learn about the rainforests and jungles and the many colorful birds, animals, and plants that live there.

The program's Multimedia Resource Tool enables kids to easily export any of the program's images, sounds, or text into their favorite word-processing or presentation software to create their own multimedia adventures. MayaQuest also offers a special feature for Internet users. The MayaQuest World Wide Web site (**http://www.mecc.com/mayaquest.html**) offers a wealth of additional information, photographs, and updates for the program with more adventures and additional items to search for. During the spring of 1996, the MayaQuest team will be making a second trip, sending daily reports and photos over the Internet to connected classrooms from a laptop computer and satellite transmitter. MayaQuest is a fascinating way to learn about the Mayan civilization, and because the program is bilingual English/Spanish, it's also a good addition to a language program.

See Also

Amazon Trail; Educational Software K-12; Oregon Trail

MBDF Virus

This virus infects applications, the System file, and other resource files. Applications become infected as soon as they are run on an infected system.

See Also

WDEF Virus

MBONE

A way of broadcasting or "**IP** multicasting" live audio and video over the **Internet**. Stands for Multicast Backbone on the Internet.

A virtual network of MBONE workstations send and receive real time communications and route them to other sites on the network.

Most of the software required to receive MBONE is currently designed for high-end UNIX-type workstations. In order to receive MBONE broadcasts you have to ask your Internet service provider if they receive MBONE. You also need a very fast connection to the Internet, such as a dedicated T1 or T3 line. Commercial products to make MBONE more widely available are expected to be developed in the near future. **CU-SeeMe** already provides Internet teleconferencing, however.

See Also

CU-SeeMe; Internet; World Wide Web

MDEF, *See Code Resource*

MDEF Virus

MDEF, also known as Garfield and Top Cat, infects applications, documents, the Desktop file, and the System file. Applications must be run in order to become infected. System crashes and distorted menus are both symptoms of **MDEF**.

See Also

ANTI Virus; CDEF Virus; CODE 1 Virus; CODE 352 Virus; Frankie Viru; INIT 17 Virus; INIT 1984 Virus; INIT 29 Virus; INIT 9403 Virus; INIT-M Virus; MacMag Virus; MBDF Virus; nVIR Virus; Scores Virus; T4 Virus; WDEF Virus; ZUC Virus

Mean Time Between Failures, *See MTBF*

Mean Time to Repair, *See MTTR*

Mean Time to Service Return, *See MTTSR*

Mechanical

In the graphic arts, a mechanical is the construction of poster board and overlays containing the text and other graphics elements of a publication. The mechanical is photographed with a process camera to produce film for platemaking. Such an assemblage is also known as camera-ready art or a paste-up. Mostly replaced by **desktop publishing**, mechanicals require manual skills quite different from manipulating the **mouse** and keyboard.

See Also
Graphic Design

MediaFactory 1.0

MediaFactory is designed as a simple-to-use **QuickTime** movie editor. For those who don't want to spend hundreds of dollars on Adobe **Premiere**, the alternatives are **MediaFactory** and **QuickFlix**. **VideoShop**, from Avid, is another editing application.

MediaFactory uses the project and timeline metaphor found in Premiere, and offers 26 different transitions, but no cross-dissolve. A cross-dissolve fades the first clip into the second one and is probably the most common transition used in movie editing.

Also, the audio controls are limited to adjusting the volume of the audio for the entire clip (other programs enable you to adjust the volume at different points, creating volume fades). The program's interface is difficult to use. Radius' **QuickFlix** is probably a better buy.

> Nuts Technologies
> Price: $199
> Phone: (408) 980-7800

See Also
QuickFlix

Mediagnügen

Although it is billed as a presentation program, Mediagnügen is essentially a multimedia browser. You can create catalogs containing up to 13,000 images, which might make it useful for indexing CD-ROM clip art collections, but because the program supports only **PICT** and **JPEG** files, there are serious limitations to the kinds of things you can index. Viewing and manipulating files in the catalog is not as easy as

it should be, making this program sometimes awkward to use.

> Gnügen Software
> Price: $30
> Phone: (303) 682-5380

MediaPaint

Strata's MediaPaint sets out to establish ground breaking art and animation technology. MediaPaint gives users a wide selection of painting and effects tools designed to paint on QuickTime/PICT movie frames, with no alterations done to the underlying movie until after the paintings are complete and the new movie file saved. MediaPaint allows the Mac animator to paint state-of-the-art effects on video footage, which may later be transferred to film for major theater display. MediaPaint is also a vital tool for the multimedia and game producer who needs to incorporate the quality level of effects that the public demands in both interactive edutainment and entertainment. In addition to the program and documentation (including a tutorial manual), the package comes with an excellent tutorial videotape and two CD-ROMs. The first CD features sample movies created by MediaPaint masters, and gives you a feel for the power and potential of the software. The second CD is called "Special Effects" and it contains seven new tools and eleven new filters which are described in detail in the sections that follow. MediaPaint movies can also be created from single PICT images using the "Auto Advance Point" in the software. This feature automatically inserts succeeding frames of the image, updating the painting effects as they are being used. No Mac animator, multimedia or game developer should be without this software.

MediaPaint's toolbox looks familiar at first glance because it contains many of the same standard tools found in a digital painting program (Move Hand, Zoom Magnifier, Line, Area Fill, Shape Icons, Color Selector, Eraser, Text, Area Select Tools), but a closer inspection reveals an unfamiliar set of options as well. There are three Tool Modifiers (Shrink, Layer, and Composite), an Anti-aliasing chooser, a Corner/Center tool for polygon creation, and a Line Weight

M

pop-out. Below the recognizable toolbox is where the interactive fun really begins. A scrolling area reveals a collection of named icons for a more expansive list of tools. Each of these tools is connected to a design dialog that can be accessed simply by double-clicking on the associated icon. The following data gives you a good idea of where these tools could be used. In most cases, a live animated preview allows you to paint and view the effects chosen.

Airbrush—No Preview. You may select from a standard airbrush or a pixelated flow. Sliders can be used to adjust Size, Pressure, Flow, Step, Softness, and Edge Opacity.

Arcs—You would use this anywhere that arcing electric current is needed as an effect. PreSets include Power Surge, High Tension, Tesla Coil and Jupiter's Storms. In addition to the PreSets, you can design your own arcs by altering Width, Branching, Writhe, Zagging, Tip Glow, and Heat.

Babyboom—This effect looks like fireflies or small meteorites glowing and then fading out. You can design the elements by altering Size, Noise, Opacity, Speed, Chaos, Fertility, Density, Lifespan, and Particle Trails.

Beams—You can either design your own effect or use the PreSets that include Laser, Photon Blast, Light Saber, and Pulse Cannon. The names of the PreSets should give you a good idea of where these could be used. No science fiction producer should leave home without these effects. You can alter Width, Taper, Pulses, Chaos, Amplitude, Speed, Heat, and Glow.

Blur—No Preview. The effect can be altered by Pressure and Steps sliders. Use it when you want to blur the underlying frame(s).

Bubbles—PreSets are Scuba, Soap Bubbles, and Soda. Each produces animated bubbles that cover the effect. You can customize bubbles by altering Size, Distortion, Number, Buoyancy, Lighting Direction, Growth, Shrinkage, Wobble, Turbulence, Opacity, and Hilight.

Burn—No Preview. This is a photographic darkening effect. You can adjust the Exposure and number of Steps on Shadows, Midtones, and Hilights.

Diffuse—No Preview. This effect randomizes the spread of color or pattern when applied. The effect can be altered with Spread and Step sliders.

Distort—No Preview. This is a smear effect for color or pattern painted down. Distortion and Step can be adjusted.

Dodge—No Preview. This is the opposite of the Burn effect, and the same parameters can be altered.

Fade In—No Preview. This increases the opacity of the paint when used on the Alpha level. The current brush is used. Pressure and Step can be altered.

Fade Out—No Preview. This decreases the opacity of the paint when used on the Alpha level. The current brush is used. Pressure and Step can be altered.

Fine Brush—No Preview. Allows you to fine-tune the settings of the selected brush. Pressure, Flow, and Step can be altered with sliders.

Fire—This effect can be applied to any element that needs to look like it is on fire. You can use the PreSets (Campfire, Candle, Gas Flame, Oil Fire, and Wick) or design your own customized flames. You can control Height, Direction, Speed, Turbulence, Waves, and Heat.

Fireworks—Creates fireworks explosions on the movie frames. Varieties of fireworks effects include Sky Rocket, Boomer, Patriot, and Star Halo. You can adjust the Burst for Size, Chaos, Trails, Flatness, Gravity, Parts, Radius, Flash, Wobble and Lifespan, and Rocket Size, Heat, Speed, Glow, Wobble, and Trail. The color can change over time.

Invert—No Preview. Paints the selected area in a negative of the color used. You can alter Pressure, Flow, and Step.

Lens Flare—An exploding flare object. PreSets include Simple Star, Telephoto Lens, Simple Glare, telescope, Star Ship, and Sparkle. You can customize the effect by altering Flash Size, Rays, Chaos and Glow; Glare Number, Size, Opacity, Chaos and Color. In addition, the flare can fade in and out.

Lightning—Use it to make lighting strike twice in the same place. PreSets include Rainstorm, Power Arc, High Energy, and Argon Strike. You have control over

Width, Forks, Branching, Writhe, Zagging, Taper, Heat, and Glow.

Magic Wand—No PreSets. This is a standard Wand tool whose tolerances can be set.

Pixie Dust—Use it to emulate the falling sparkles from the fairy Godmother's magic wand and like effects. Particle Attributes, Opacity, Pixie Dust Settings, Lifespan, and Particle Trails can all be customized.

Shape Painter—This feature is exactly like the Image Hose in Fractal Painter, in that it paints down a group of images saved to a file and loaded into the tool. Use it to create cel animations or effects, depending upon the brushes loaded. Shapes can be applied randomly or in order, and their Pressure, Flow, and Step can be altered.

Sharpen—No Preview. This effect is comparable to the sharpening feature in Photoshop, and adds pixelated edges to the targeted area. Pressure and Step can be altered.

Smear—No Preview. Smears the selected area. Pressure and Step can be altered.

Smudge—No Preview. Smudges the selected area. Pressure and Step can be altered.

Spin Out—Adds a group of spinning particles to the selected area. This is a great effect for producing atomic particle simulations and like effects. You can control particle Attributes, Opacity, Spinout Settings, Lifespan, and Particle Trails.

Squiggle—Like writhing electric colored worms, this effect applies animated squiggling lines to the movie painting. You can control Squiggle Settings, Fade to Film Color, Stop Squiggling Interrupts, Custom/Current Brush Settings, and Line Spacing.

The painting that is accomplished in MediaPaint never disturbs the surface of an imported movie or graphic. It sits "above" the targeted surface on its own plane. Only when the completed work is saved and loaded again is the targeted movie or graphic and the painting done on it fused. You can even save a MediaPaint project with both surfaces intact.

Stencil Painting—MediaPaint allows you to use a movie as a paintbrush to paint another movie. One use might be to create two animations, a wireframe and a fully rendered view of the same scene. Use the wireframe as a base, and apply the rendered movie in steps over the wireframe movie, slowly revealing rendered detail. The result would be a movie that displays a wireframe evolving into a fully rendered animation, an effect major studios used in both commercial and entertainment venues. All of MediaPaint's tools are available for stencil painting. Care should be taken to use two animations of the same display size and the same number of frames.

Other Uses—Movies can be constructed from scratch on blank frames. These movies can then be used as underlays for further effects. Single graphics files can also be targeted for any of the effects included.

File Load/Save Conventions—Files can be saved as MediaPaint files, QuickTime movies, or as numerated PICT files.

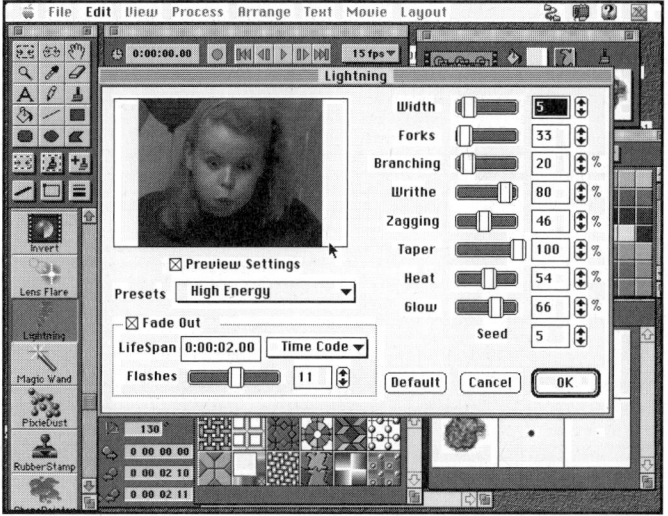

MediaTime

A NuBus video digitize and display board that includes 16-bit audio hardware based on Digidesign's AudioMedia card. This card can accept daughterboard cards, such as the **MoviePak**, which provide hardware compression and QuickTime movie playback.

The MoviePak board displays full frame, full motion video, although it actually only captures an image 1/4 the size of the full screen size, and then doubles it to provide the full screen image.

This board is no longer manufactured; software and a FAQ are still available at the RasterOps home page: **http://www.rasterops.com**.

Memory, Allocation in 680x0 Macs

The Macintosh reserves a certain amount of memory for the operating system, depending upon the version of the system you are running. This memory is used to load portions of the system, the Finder, and those system extensions required by your work. This software remains in memory while you are working. The allocation of space is dynamic, meaning that it changes as the requirements of your work session change (which applications you want open, how many documents, you are printing at the same time, and so on). RAM is allocated in 512K blocks, thus the system may reserve more memory than it needs. To check how much memory your system is reserving, pull down the Apple menu and highlight About This Macintosh (the first item in the list).

In System 7, the About This Macintosh dialog box also displays an alphabetical list of items which have been assigned a memory *partition*—blocks of memory reserved for that item. The black part of the bar shows how much memory is currently in use.

These partitions are assigned on a first-come, first-served basis. Each application requires differing amounts of RAM to operate properly. (To check to see the amount of RAM required or to change the RAM allocation to better fit your RAM availability, click the application and pull down the Get Info command from the File menu. You can type a new number in the Current Size box based on the data reported in the Suggested Size box and your requirements.

Note that the more memory available to a program, the more efficiently it will operate.

Some applications load all of their documents into RAM at one time, and other programs place only

portions of a document into RAM and swap "pages" back and forth from the disk to RAM as they are needed. The space needed to load the documents is taken from the allocated partition space for that application.

Fragmentation occurs in RAM in the same fashion as it occurs in storage. When you open and close multiple applications during a work session, the blocks of RAM are taken and freed up randomly. This causes a problem, because applications need contiguous areas of RAM to operate—they cannot use scattered blocks of memory. You defragment the memory by quitting your applications in the order they were opened, thus laying out the RAM in its proper sequence once again. You must remember this order, because the Macintosh will not provide you with guidelines. As a rule of thumb, open the programs you use most continuously first, and then open applications of lesser importance. You are less likely to create holes in the RAM with this practice.

Note that there is very little correlation between the size of the physical program stored on the disk and the amount of RAM it requires to function. You must use Get Info to learn how much memory a program requires.

See Also

Hard Disks; Memory, Allocation in Power Macs; Virtual Memory

Memory, Allocation in Power Macs

The PowerPC processor uses a new Memory Manager and a revamped way of loading applications into memory. If an application was originally written for a 68K Mac and has not been rewritten to take advantage of the PowerPC, it stores its code in the CODE resource and uses the Segment Loader to load these CODE resources into a memory partition.

If the application has been rewritten to take advantage of the new Memory Manager of the PowerPC, its executable code is stored in the data fork of an application file. The software is then divided into chunks, called fragments, which can be loaded as needed. This method of loading applications into memory also enables the PowerPC software to use virtual memory more efficiently, because it reuses the data fork of the application as a paging file to improve performance. With virtual memory on, only the needed portions of code get loaded into memory, reducing the memory requirements of that application.

See Also
Hard Disks; Virtual Memory

Memory, Capacity and Expansion

RAM resides inside the Macintosh on special circuit boards. Older Macs, such as Quadras, some LCs, and first generation Power Macs use circuitry called *single inline memory modules* or **SIMMs**. Second generation Power Macs use a more advanced type of chip called a dual inline memory module or **DIMM**.

The reason that RAM does not retain its data when the power turns off is that most memory chips are *dynamic RAM* or DRAMs which must be constantly powered by electricity to continue holding data. DIMMs and SIMMs are sized in kilobytes and megabytes which measures the density of the chip, that is, its capacity to store data.

Although chips are spoken of as being multiples of *bytes* of capacity, in actuality, chip density is measured in *kilobits* (Kbit) and *megabits* (Mbit). There are several densities of DRAMs available. Each Macintosh family can use only a certain density, with the older Macs, such as the Plus or Macintosh IIs, capable of using only the lowest density and the newest Power Mac family of processors capable of using up to the highest density. Thus, the type of Macintosh you own determines the type of DRAM density you are able to upgrade to. The most common DRAM chips come in the following densities.

(Note that the Density column measures the amount of kilobits or megabits a chip can store and the Memory Capacity column measures the total number of electronic switches this is equivalent to, each of which can be a 0 or a 1. Memory Capacity is calculated by multiplying the density by the number of bits in a kilobit (1,024) or megabit (1,048,576).)

DRAM Density

Density	*Memory Capacity*
64Kbit	65,536 bits
256Kbit	262,144 bits
1Mbit	1,048,576 bits
4Mbit	4,194,304 bits
8Mbit	8,388,608 bits
16Mbit	16,777,216 bits
32Mbit	33,554,432 bits
64Mbit	67,108,864 bits

Each SIMM has eight memory chips soldered on to its surface and each DIMM has sixteen memory chips soldered on its surface. Thus, on each SIMM or DIMM, depending upon its density, you can store: 512Kbits, 2Mbits, 8 Mbits, 32 Mbits, or 64 Mbits. Chips are tied together for a combined memory capacity so that it takes 32 256-Kbit DRAMs or eight 1-Mbit DRAMs to make 1 megabyte of RAM. Macintoshes measure their RAM capacities in these larger units. When a computer salesman speaks of the upgradability of your Macintosh as "slots," he is speaking about the number of spaces on the internal communications connection, or *bus* where these memory modules can be inserted. The Macintosh Plus and SE were the first Macintoshes to use SIMMs.

Prior to these models, Macintosh memory was soldered on to the logical board in individual chips (with capacities of 128K and 512K) and no upgradability path.

TIP The address capacity of the operating system limits the Macintosh to 8MB of RAM if you have not loaded System 7 and turned on its 32K addressing capability. With 32K addressing, the Macintosh can address up to a gigabyte of RAM.

Each Macintosh model has specific memory configuration rules. You can only install RAM modules in certain combinations on each model. The following table contains the basic rules; dealers and companies that sell DIMMs and SIMMs have complete details.

All of this abundant memory is not simply thrown open for the use of programs, but is controlled by the Finder and specifically assigned different roles.

See Also

Power Mac; Virtual Memory

Macintosh Memory Configurations

Model RAM	Soldered	Expansion Slots	SIMM Sizes (MB)	Total RAM Available (MB)
Performa 550	4	1 SIMM	1, 2, 4, 8, 16, 32MB	4, 5, 6, 8, 12, 20, 36
Quadra 605, LC 475, Performa 475, Performa 476, LC 520	4	1 SIMM	1, 2, 4, 8, 16, 32MB	4, 5, 6, 8, 12, 20, 36
Quadra 610 (Centris 610)	4	2 SIMM	4, 8, 16, 32MB	4, 8, 12, 20, 36, 40, 44, 52, 68
Quadra 650, 800	8	4 SIMM	4, 8, 16, 32MB	8, 12, 16, 20, 24, 28, 32, 36, 40, 44, 48, 52, 56, 60, 64, 68, 72, 76, 80, 84, 88, 92, 96, 104, 108, 112, 120, 136
Quadra 660AV (Centris 660AV)	8	8 SIMM	4, 8, 16, 32MB	4, 8, 12, 20, 36, 68
Quadra 840AV (Centris 840AV)	0	4 SIMM	4, 8, 16, 32MB	8, 16, 32, 64, 128
Quadra 900	4	16 SIMM	1, 4, 8, 16; 88, 96, 100, 112, 128, 132, 160, 192, 196, 208, 256MB	4, 8, 12, 16, 20, 24, 28, 32, 36, 40, 52, 64, 68, 72, 76, 80, 84, 136, 148, 256
Quadra 950	0	6 SIMM	1, 4MB	4, 8, 12, 16, 20, 24, 28, 32, 36, 40, 48, 52, 64
Power Mac 6100	8	2 SIMM	4, 8, 16, 32MB	8, 12, 16, 20, 24, 28, 32, 36, 40, 44, 48, 52, 56, 60, 64, 68, 72
Power Mac 7200	8	4 DIMM	4, 8, 16, 32MB	8, 12, 16, 20, 24, 28, 32, 36, 40, 44, 48, 52, 56, 60, 64, 68, 72

Model RAM	Soldered	Expansion Slots	SIMM Sizes (MB)	Total RAM Available (MB)
Power Mac 7500, 8500	16	8 DIMM	4, 8, 16, 32MB	8, 12, 16, 20, 24, 28, 32, 36, 40, 44, 48, 52, 56, 60, 64, 68, 72, 76, 80
Power Mac 9500	16	12 DIMM	4, 8, 16, 32, 64MB	20, 32, 48, 80, 112, 144, 208, 400, 768MB
Performa 63x series	4	4 SIMM	4, 8, 16MB	8, 12, 20MB
Performa 5215, 62300	4 or 8	4 SIMM	4, 8, 16MB	8, 12, 16, 20, 24MB
Performa 61xx series	8	2 SIMM	4, 8, 16MB	16, 24, 40MB
PowerBook 190	4 or 8	1	4, 8, 16, 32MB	8, 12, 16, 20, 24, 36, 40MB
PowerBook 5300	8	1	4, 8, 12, 16, 32, 48MB	12, 16, 20, 24, 40, 56MB
PowerBook Duo 270c	4	1	4, 8, 12MB	4, 8, 12, 16MB
PowerBook Duo 2300	8 or 20	1	8, 16, 24, 32, 40, 48MB	16, 28, 24, 36, 32, 44, 40, 52, 48, 60, 56, 68MB

M

Memory Control Panel

This control panel enables you to adjust four separate areas of the Macintosh's memory features: the disk cache, the Modern Memory Manager, Virtual Memory, and RAM disk functions, as shown in the following figure.

The **disk cache** is always on, but you can select the amount of memory that is set aside for cache memory to speed up CPU-intensive operations.

The next section enables you to toggle on and off the Modern Memory Manager on Power Macs (on non-PowerMac models, the Modern Memory Manager toggle is not present, and the 32-bit addressing toggle is in its place). The Modern Memory Manager, which is in the on position by default, is a completely re-written native version of the previous Memory Management code found in operating systems previous to System 7.1.1. The Modern Memory Manager offers better performance than the previous Memory Management code because it runs in the native PowerPC environment. If you toggle the Modern Memory Manager off, the prior version of the Memory Manager, which is burned into the RAM of the Mac, will be used instead.

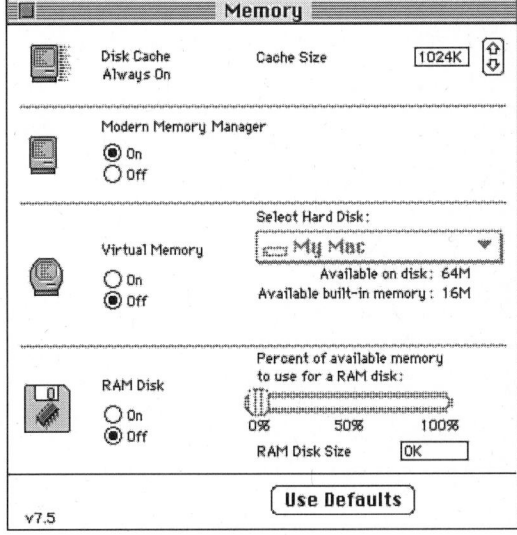

Virtual Memory can be toggled on and off from the Memory control panel, and you can select which hard disk you want to use and the amount of disk space you want to dedicate to Virtual Memory. You can also toggle the **Modern Memory Manager** on and off here and set up a RAM disk if you desire.

To use the Memory control panel, follow these steps:

1. Select Memory from the control panels submenu on the Apple menu (or System Folder).

2. To set the amount of disk cache, use the edit arrows to click the edit arrows in the direction you want the numbers to move.

3. If you want to enable virtual memory, click the On button and choose which hard drive will be used for virtual memory and how much virtual memory will be used. (A **restart** is required to activate virtual memory.)

4. To enable the Modern Memory Manager, click the On button.

5. To set up a RAM disk, click the On button and drag the slider to select the percentage of available RAM you want to designate as a RAM disk. Upon restart, your RAM disk is enabled.

See Also
32-Bit Addressing; Apple Menu; Virtual Memory

Memory Leak

A memory leak is a **programming** error in which memory is allocated but never properly released.

Suppose, for example, that an application needs an extra block of memory whenever a certain dialog box is open. When the dialog is opened, the application requests a block of memory from the System. When the dialog is closed, the application should free the memory to let the System know it's no longer using it. If it fails to do so, the System will continue to treat the memory as though it's still in use, effectively putting that block of memory out of service. Each time the dialog is opened, another bit of memory is leaked.

Memory leaks are fairly common. Minor memory leaks can easily remain unnoticed even in commercial software, but serious leaks can bring an application to its knees in a split second.

See Also
Heap

Memory Management Unit (MMU), *See Power Mac Logic Boards*

Memory Mine, The

A memory analysis and **debugging tool** from Adianta, Inc.

The process of **debugging** a Macintosh application can be especially difficult if you don't have a way to observe your application's memory usage while the program is running. The Memory Mine provides a vast array of memory usage information about any running application.

The Memory Mine is a **heap** monitoring tool similar to Metrowerks' **ZoneRanger**. Like ZoneRanger, you can use it to watch the contents of any application heap as the program runs.

When it is monitoring an application, The Memory Mine does not interfere with its operation in any way. Memory Mine's statistics display is updated constantly in the background to give you the latest information about the contents, consistency, and fragmentation of the heap. In addition, The Memory Mine can keep track of the "high water mark" of memory allocations, including the maximum number of **handle**s allocated and the maximum and minimum free memory.

The statistics collected by The Memory Mine are shown in the statistics window, and they also can be collected into a log file. This is an excellent way to keep track of an application's memory usage over time.

Finally, The Memory Mine can perform a variety of stress-testing functions, including scrambling, purging, or compacting the heap or allocating memory blocks of any size in the heap.

The Memory Mine is published by Adianta, Inc.:

Adianta, Inc.
582 Market Street #911
San Francisco, CA 95104
Email: **adianta@aol.com**
Fax: (415) 781-8053
Phone: (415) 781-8052

See Also
Bug; Debugging; Debugging Tools; Handle; Heap; ZoneRanger

Memory and Storage, Difference

Like all computers, the Macintosh separates the location where the work is performed—called *memory* or Random Access Memory (RAM) from where it resides—called *storage*. The important concept to remember about RAM is that it is *volatile* storage, meaning that it does not retain its contents when the power is turned off. *Non-volatile* storage retains data in a physical way and so does not lose its contents when the electricity is turned off. In order to retain what you have done in volatile memory, a file must be returned to its non-volatile (or permanent) storage area by *saving* it (writing it to disk).

Memory also differs from storage in that it resides in the computer as a series of memory chips on the **motherboard** (also called the logic board, where the rest of the critical components that make up the microprocessor are located, such as ROM, bus controllers, memory controllers, and so forth) and on related circuit boards in other slots. Because it physically connects to the computer, it provides a very fast access time to match the computer's exceedingly fast performance time.

Storage, on the other hand, resides outside of the computer (although some may be placed inside the physical container that also holds the *computer processing unit* (CPU)). Thus, storage is slower at sending and receiving data than is memory, because it must rely on physical connections—motors, magnetic sensors, moving arms, and spindles to connect it to the computer. Another difference between the physical storage of data and the electronic storage of data is that physical things have a greater chance of breaking than electronic things. Thus storage is more liable to damage than memory.

Another difference between memory and storage is the size differential. Before System 7's **32-bit addressing** and **virtual memory,** memory was limited by the size of the address registers of the computer. On the other hand, storage was limited only by the price you wanted to pay. Today, the size difference is blurring, because storage can be loaned to memory as virtual memory.

See Also
Hard Disks; Virtual Memory

Memory and Storage, Measurement Methods

All computers perform their functions by turning on and off electronic pulses (whether by changing their polarity or literally switching signals on and off). Data to the computer is merely a series of electromagnetic signals corresponding to electromagnetic fields that line up on positive and negative poles. These fields can be viewed as a sequence of zeroes and ones representing the positive and negative signals. The mathematics of computing is based upon this dyadic system.

The basis of computing is a mathematical system called Boolean Algebra which is designed around the *base-2,* or a *binary* way of counting. This mathematics describes how a computer physically manipulates data as well as the capacity of memory to store information, or its density. A shorthand term for *binary digit* is the word *bit,*—the smallest unit of measurement in computing, 2^1 or 01. All memory stores data in bits on computer chips and all storage media stores bits of data on magnetic materials.

M

You probably have heard the term *byte*. A byte is the next larger measurement unit, equal to eight bits (2^8—256 bits) of information. Each byte represents a single character in text. Thus, when we speak of a character of data we mean one byte of information. One thousand bytes is a *kilobyte* (actually 2^{10} or 1024 bytes) of data. Typically, the Macintosh reports its memory in both bytes and kilobytes or "K"—actually 1,024 bytes. A word is two bytes (six characters plus an extra bit) and 1K equals approximately 170 words of data.

The Macintosh requires large numbers of bytes of memory to temporarily store the application you are using, the operating system performing the work, and the document you are working on. Memory is installed in the next larger measurement unit—a *megabyte* or 2^{20} (over one million or 1,048,576) bytes or 1,024 kilobytes. To use System 7 you need at least 2 megabytes (abbreviated MB) of RAM and more RAM enables you to open more applications at one time in this *multitasking* environment (meaning the capability to run more than one operation simultaneously). Even System 6 required at least 1MB of RAM to run individual applications and the Finder and at least 2MB to use MultiFinder.

Due to the growing size of documents, applications, and operating systems, Macintosh non-volatile storage is now measured in gigabytes (abreviated as "G"), or the capability to store 2^{30} bytes—over one billion (1,073,741,824) bytes of information.

See Also
Finder; Storage

Memory Upgrade

A memory upgrade entails the addition of RAM to your computer, increasing the amount available to applications without invoking virtual memory. In most Macs, this memory is on SIMMs, but in the newer models, the memory is on DIMMs, and in a few PowerBook models, it was static RAM rather than dynamic RAM.

See Also
DIMM; DRAM; SIMM; SRAM; Virtual Memory

Menu

The **commands** and features of a particular software application, or of the Macintosh **Finder**, are found on the application's menus, as shown in the figure. These menus, called pull-down menus, appear at the top of your screen in the menu bar, which has an Apple Computer logo on the far-left side. Each menu is listed by topic on the menu bar. Commands for creating new files or saving files, for example, appear on the File menu (see the following figure).

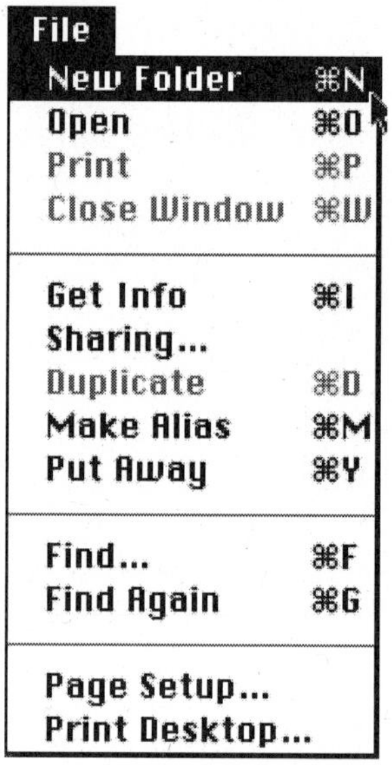

To see what's on a menu, click and hold the arrow pointer over a menu title in the menu bar. A menu of choices appears containing commands used to access the features of a program. If, for example, you're using an application and you want to print the document you're working on, click and hold the topic File in the menu bar to make the File menu appear.

On this menu you see the word Print. To select Print, continue to hold the mouse button down, drag the arrow pointer down to the Print command (a black selection bar moves with you so you can see which command you're selecting), and release the **mouse** button. Releasing the mouse button when you've selected Print tells the application that you want to print, and causes the Print dialog box to appear, enabling you to choose your printing options.

Each application has its own menu bar enabling you access to the features and commands of that program. Two menu topics are consistent throughout the Macintosh environment: the File menu and **Edit menu**. After the Apple menu, these are the first two menu topics in almost all Macintosh application menus. The Applications menu and the Help menu (both on the far right side of the menu bar) also appear in the menu bar when you're in an application.

See Also

Commands; Edit Menu; File Menu; Finder; Menu Commands

Menu Bar

The menu bar is the white horizontal bar at the top of your screen, as shown in the figure.

🍎 File Edit View Insert Format Font Tools Window Work

The menu bar gives you access to **menus** and the **commands** they contain. The names and tiny icons appearing in the menu bar designate the topics, or titles, each menu contains. To access a menu from the menu bar, click and hold a menu title or icon, and a corresponding pull-down menu appears listing the commands available on that menu. To select a command from the menu, continue to hold the **mouse** button, **drag** the **arrow pointer** to the command you want to select, and release the mouse button. The menu command, **highlighted** in black, blinks to let you know you've made a selection.

The menu bar also contains the **Apple menu**, which appears on the Apple Computer logo icon; the **Help menu**, which appears on the question mark icon; and the **Application menu**, which appears on the far right side of the menu bar and displays the mini-icon of the active application. This menu enables you to select from an application from a list of running applications. In System 7.5 and higher, a menu bar clock is built into the system and can be toggled on and off from the Date & Time control panel. Prior to System 7.5, most Mac users used a freeware control panel called SuperClock to put a clock on their menu bar.

The menu bar has different topics, or titles, in each application as software developers use the menu bar to give customized access to features of their application. However, two menu bar titles remain consistent throughout most Macintosh applications: the **File menu** and the **Edit menu**, which, after the Apple menu, are the first two menus in the menu bar.

See Also

Apple Menu; Application Menu; Desktop; File Menu; Edit Menu; Help Menu; Menus; Mouse

Menu Commands

There are two basic types of **commands** in the Macintosh environment: keyboard commands and menu commands. Keyboard commands are instructions for the computer that you enter by pressing keys on the keyboard. Menu commands are selected from either pull-down menus (which appear in the **menu bar** at the top of the screen in an application or the Finder) or pop-up menus, (which appear in dialog boxes). Many menu commands also have a keyboard shortcut which enables you to select a menu command from the keyboard without using the **mouse** to go up to the menu bar and select it manually. If a menu command has a keyboard shortcut, the shortcut is generally listed to the right of the command in the menu.

M

See Also

Commands; Dialog Box; Keyboard Shortcuts; Menu Bar; Pop-Up Menus; Pull-Down Menus

Menu Sharing, *See Frontier*

Merlin's Apprentice, *See Masterpiece Mansion*

MeshPaint

MeshPaint allows the 3D artist to paint objects in real 3D. It is the first of its kind, although it promises to set a pace and a concept that others are sure to follow. It is both Windows- and PowerMac-oriented, and supports **ElectricImage** and all 3D software that incorporates the **QuickDraw 3D** standard on the Mac (**RayDream**, StrataPro **Infini-D** and others). The process is simple. Load an acceptable object saved from one of the supported 3D programs, and use the 3D painting tools to paint on the object as you rotate it in 3D space. Although this seems simple, technologically it has taken decades to realize this potential for the desktop artist.

MeshPaint has a 3D window (used to manipulate the loaded object in 3D space) and a 2D window for each element of the object that has a separate painted or photographic texture, where the actual painting goes on. When painting is activated in the 2D painting widows, the 3D object is updated, although it may have to be re-rendered to see the results. The object at first appears as a wireframe construct in the 3D window, and responds to all manipulations performed on it in the separate 3D controls window. The wireframe may be shown as a single or multiple color. The polygonal structure of the wireframe can be set for varying detail in the Object Preferences dialog. Here you can set the color of the 2D window's background, and the color/multicolor of the wireframe. The detail level is set by a slider, and ranges from 1 to 100. The higher the slider is set, the less detail you'll see in the wireframe, with a cost of slower movement operations because of redraw time. The top number

can be set to higher values for larger objects. The way the slider is set makes a difference when painting on the object as far as the perceived detail of the polys, and can affect the way that you paint.

The 3D Object Preferences dialog also lists a shading menu. The mode may be set to flat (poly edges will be seen) or smooth (no poly edges will be visible when solid rendered). You can even select to see a shaded render all of the time on the 3D window instead of a wireframe. This is at a cost of slower rotational manipulations and successive redraws of the object.

3D Object Manipulation MeshPaint has a special rotation control window so that you can see the object in the 3D window from any angle. It has three separate control sliders: one for zooming in/out, and the other two to rotate the object in 3D space. Exacting painting can be accomplished by keeping close tabs on a zoomed-in view of the objects detail polys.

Painting Tools All of the elements in an object first must be assigned a texture, and the texture has to be told how it must be applied (planar, spherical, cylindrical and so on, and on what relative axis). Then paint is applied to 3D models by choosing a color or texture. Textures can be saved paintings or photographs, so MeshPaint makes it easy to apply facial maps to 3D humanoid models as an example. MeshPaint includes painting, straight line, fill and blur tools on-screen, and the revisions that will accompany each edition of this software are sure to include more painting tools and options.

All imported graphics are shown in their own 2D window, and the painting tools can be used to alter them on the spot. Brushes are loaded in specific libraries, and can be created externally in a paint program and saved to MeshPaint. Once a surface of the object is married to a texture, painting can be targeted to that surface, and it will map in the way that was selected. Painting on any of the targeted 2D windows is automatically applied to that 3D element of the model in the 3D window. Painting on the model in the 3D window automatically updates the respective 2D painting. This reciprocal relationship between 2D and 3D is the heart of the MeshPaint process. The selection of default brushes includes star bursts, alternate painting nubs, star wheels, whirls, and other common and uncommon shapes. Paint can be applied by stroking the 2D or 3D canvas, or by simply clicking a shape down. All brushes are resizeable.

By double-clicking any brush in the visual library, an Image Brush dialog pops up. In it, the brush image can be altered by opacity and intensity sliders. Its type can be selected from the following list: Standard, Transition, Fade, TransFade, random Opacity, Continue Fade, and Random Color (current and all). The default brushes are not editable.

Two tools that are vital to 3D painting are the Polymap and Stamper functions. Polymap generates a 2D view of the object polygon by polygon, and can be saved as a file. This map is exquisite for painting a poly-by-poly texture that will map exactly to the object later. The Stamper is another tool that 3D artists will find a myriad of uses for. It allows you to cut out a defined rectangle in a 2D map (64×64 pixels maximum) and stamp the texture down on the 3D object. It can be used, for example, to add labels to products and graffiti to walls.

Texture Mapping There has never been a way to add textures to 3D objects more intuitively than with MeshPaint. You can alter the selected 2D image during the mapping process by changing it as it is displayed on a 2D map, or by painting on it directly in 3D. Any 2D painting accomplished with MeshPaint's internal brushes on a 2D window instantly becomes a color texture map. Texture maps created in paint and photo manipulation software (Fractal **Painter** or **Photoshop** for example) become instant texture map resources for 3D objects.

Rendering A render button on the MeshPaint menu bar quickly renders the object as represented in the 3D window. Rendering has to occur each time that the object view is rotated or zoomed. The program is intelligent enough to write any changes painted on the texture in the 2D widows directly to the 3D object without re-rendering, unless you want to appreciate how it looks from another angle.

Saving the New Painted Object Painted and photorealistic textures are saved as part of the object, and can be displayed and animated in the appropriate 3D software. With MeshPaint, textures can be adjusted directly to their 3D surfaces in near real time, with no more expensive and time-consuming gaps between texture generation and 3D object renderings.

Message Boxes

Message boxes are a way for the Macintosh to communicate with the user. If there's a problem **printing** a document, if your computer freezes up, or if you try to do something you're not supposed to do, you are met with a message or alert box. These boxes contain instructions, a statement, or a question, and often have only one button you can select: the OK button, as shown in the figure.

"HaydenHP4M" is out of paper

OK

<META> HTML TAG

The <META> tag, part of HTML version 3.0, is used to embed generic information about a World Wide Web document that can be extracted for use in searching, indexing, and cataloging. Use the NAME attribute to define the type of meta-information and the CONTENT attribute for more specific information, as in:

```
META NAME="author"  CONTENT="Greg Holden
```

<META> can also be used to generate special headers to be sent by the server to the client, such as server push/client pull. <META> falls within the HEAD section of an HTML document.

See Also

<HEAD>; HTML; HTTP; Server Push/Client Pull

MFC, *See Microsoft Foundation Classes*

MFLOPS

MFLOPS, Millions of Floating Point Instructions Per Second, is a measure of CPU or FPU performance, depending upon whether the FPU is or is not integrated into the CPU.

MFS, *See Macintosh Filing System (MFS)*

Mice, *See Mouse*

Microcom Network Protocol, *See Modem Standards and Speeds*

Microprocessors

Computers process data using a specialized integrated circuit called a *central processing unit* (CPU). The CPU, also called a *microprocessor*, has four main components:

- **Registers.** Registers are special areas within a chip that are used to store data and program instructions. There are several types of registers in the CPU. Some act as scratch pads where the computer can save the

intermediate results of a computation or a series of items to be compared; other registers store the instruction or data that is currently being executed; and others keep track of where the computer is in the computation (for example which instruction is running). The Macintosh CPU has two types of registers: internal cache storage and Level-2, or external cache. The larger the cache the better the performance of the computer.

- **Arithmetic and logic unit (ALU).** The ALU performs the arithmetic and decision-making portions of computations for the CPU. The ALU operates to perform comparisons or mathematics.

- **Instruction decoder.** When a program's instruction is transferred from memory to the CPU's instruction cache, the instruction decoder translates the instruction into machine language so that the chip can process the instruction.

- **Internal address and data buses.** These are the microprocessor's interconnections to the Mac's logic board's address and data buses.

Macintosh Microprocessor Technologies

Processor Model	Date Introduced	Clock Speed	Internal Cache	Bus Width	Mac Models
68000	1984	8 to 16.67MHz	none	16-bit external bus and 32-bit internal bus	Classic, PowerBook 100, SE, Plus, 128K, 512K
68020	1984	up to 33MHz	256-byte instruction cache, optional 68851 PPMU	32-bit	LC and LC II, first generation Mac II
68030	1987	up to 33MHz	Built-in PPMU, 256-byte instruction and data caches	32-bit	Mac SE/30, Classic II, Color Classic, IIsi, IIci, IIcx, IIx, LCIII, IIvx, LC520, Macintosh TV

Processor Model	Date Introduced	Clock Speed	Internal Cache	Bus Width	Mac Models
68040	1989	25 to 33MHz	Built-in PPMU, 4K data and instruction caches, subset of 6882 math coprocessor	Six-stage pipeline, 32-bit bus width	Performa 630 series, Centris/Quadra 605, 610, 650, Quadra 660AV, 840AV, 700, and 950, PowerBook 145, 170, 500 series, 190
PPC 601	1994	60 to 100MHz	32K data and instruction caches, built-in single-precision FPU	Three independently pipelined instruction units for eight-stage pipelining, 64-bit	6100/60, 7100, 8100, 7200
PPC 603	1995	66 to 100MHz	32K data and instruction caches, built-in single-precision FPU, power management features for lower power consumption	Three independently pipelined instruction units for eight-stage pipelining, 64-bit	Performa 6200 and 6300 series, PowerBook 5300, LC 5200
PPC 604	1996	100 to 150MHz	Double-precision FPU, 256K data and instruction caches	Dynamic branch prediction and speculative execution, 64-bit	7500, 8500, 9500

The Macintosh CPU has been through a number of generations from its earliest 8MHz 68000 microprocessor to the near-future's speedy 604e PowerPC microprocessor's 200MHz. In between, Macs have moved from the Complex Instruction Set Chip (CISC) to the Reduced Instruction Set Chip (**RISC**) technology, as well as to much faster clock speeds and more complex integrated circuitry. The previous table provides an overview of the various microprocessors used in Macs.

See Also

Processors, PowerPC Chips

Microsoft Excel, *See Excel*

Microsoft Foundation Classes

Microsoft Foundation Classes (MFC) is a **C++** application **framework** for creating programs that use Microsoft's **Win32 Application Programming Interface**.

Microsoft Foundation Classes (or MFC) is an extremely popular application framework in the Microsoft Windows programming world. The framework supports most of the common Windows functionality and makes it quick and easy to implement basic Windows programs.

M

Why would a Macintosh programmer care about MFC? Because you can actually write Mac programs using MFC. Microsoft's **Visual C++** development environment includes a special Macintosh version of MFC. Programs written in MFC and compiled for the Mac use a Windows Portability Library to convert Win32 API calls to their Mac equivalents. This can result in applications that perform sluggishly and don't quite work the way a Mac program should, but for developers who want to port a Windows application (written using MFC) to the Mac, it can be a relatively painless solution.

See Also

Application Programming Interface; C++; Framework; Win32; Visual C++

Microsoft Office

Microsoft Office is not to be confused with Microsoft Works. Both are considered integrated applications, although Office is also sometimes called a *suite*. What sets Microsoft Office apart from the Works programs is that it's strictly business. There's no draw or paint module, except the very limited one that's part of Word, and there's no telecom program. What you do get with Office are full, current versions of Microsoft Word, Excel, and PowerPoint, plus a single site license for Microsoft Mail, and a mini-launcher for the three, called Office Manager. The program also includes five OLE servers, including Graph 5.0 for designing graphs, Equation 2.0 for building mathematical formulas, and an application called Organization Chart for creating common types of org charts. You also get a bargain. The Office package sells for a bit more than half the cost of purchasing the three programs separately.

Office Manager places a small icon on your menu bar, which opens a menu like the one shown in the figure. Aside from giving you access to the three programs, it also opens the help systems. You also can put other frequently used files or applications on this menu. To do so, open the Customize control panel. Select the items you want to put on the menu and click the button to add them. It's that easy.

One of the benefits of using Microsoft Office is that all three of the programs included have essentially the

same interface. The Word toolbar looks and functions just like the Excel toolbar and the PowerPoint toolbar. After you've learned your way around any one of the applications, using the others is almost automatic. All three programs include Wizards that create documents for you based on information you provide. Office also comes with some additional help features built-in. Office Cue Cards walk you through the steps in sharing information between applications. Quick Start guides you in opening and closing the applications from the menu bar, and cycling quickly through open applications. (Use ⌘-Tab.)

Microsoft Office for Macintosh easily can share files cross-platform with Microsoft Office for Windows. Office also supports drag-and-drop sharing of data between its applications, so that you can create a series of charts in Excel, add them to text you've written and formatted in Word, and turn the whole package into a PowerPoint slide show with a few mouse clicks.

The applications come either on CD-ROM or 1.4MB floppies—a *lot* of floppies. (The CD-ROM apparently contains 34 disks.) The complete installation requires 68MB of hard disk space. To run all three applications you'll need 8MB of RAM plus whatever your System 7 configuration requires. And it will not run on any of the older Macs, up through the SE, Classic, or PowerBook 100 models. The CD-ROM version includes the manuals on CD-ROM, but no printed copies. There's an order form in the box, but if you must have them, you'll pay extra for them.

About Office Manager...
Quick Start...

✓ **Microsoft Word**
Microsoft Excel
Microsoft PowerPoint

Find File...
Customize...
Setup and Uninstall...
Office Cue Cards
Office Help

See Also
Excel; PowerPoint; Word; Works Programs

Microsoft PowerPoint, *See PowerPoint*

Microsoft Windows Emulation

The Macintosh has the capability to run applications designed for the Microsoft Windows operating system for PCs, by using windows emulation software. This software enables you to open a separate window on the desktop and run an emulated version of Microsoft Windows and Windows-compatible applications. You can access a wide range of Windows software from your own Macintosh, without buying a separate computer. Another advantage is that you can **copy** and **paste** information and items between Windows applications and Macintosh applications. The drawback is that the software emulation runs the software at a slower speed than on a PC.

You can also run DOS and Windows applications from your Macintosh by using Apple's DOS Compatibility card that was designed for use in Macintosh 6100 and Performa 6100 series computers. This plug-in card contains an actual 486DX2 PC processor giving you a PC and a Macintosh computer in the same box. Apple offers this PC card already installed in the LC 640 DOS Compatible model.

There are also third-party PC plug-in cards for the Mac available from Orange Micro, which include their latest card that enables Mac users to run Microsoft Windows 95 on their Macs. Both the Apple DOS Compatible card and the Orange Micro cards offer operating speeds of Windows applications similar to that of a comparable PC computer. Another third-party PC-compatible card developer, Reply Corp., is offering PCI-based DOS cards for Apple's line of PCI-Macs.

Apple is reportedly rolling out their own series of PCI-based DOS cards, which will feature one unit with a 100MHz Cyrix 5x86 processor and a separate unit running a 100MHz Pentium chip made by Intel Corporation.

See Also
Microsoft Office; Microsoft Works

Microsoft Word, Customizing

Habits are hard to break. After you get used to a program like Microsoft Word, you can use it almost without thinking. Then, when a new version is released, which has more features than the old one, you find that they've moved all the old familiar stuff. You not only have to learn a new program, you have to unlearn the old one. The good news is that Word 6 lets you use a toolbar that has the familiar Word 5.1 buttons instead of the updated Word 6 version. You can even build your own toolbar, taking features from the existing ones, and putting the buttons where you want them. You can customize your menus and keyboard shortcuts, too.

To use the Word 5.1 toolbar, open the Toolbars dialog box from the View menu, as shown in the figure.

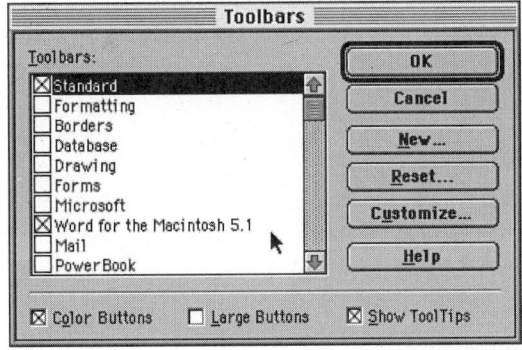

To customize toolbars, menus, or key commands, choose the Customize... command on the Tools menu. To change the toolbar, select the category of tool button to add. Click the buttons to see a description of what they do. Drag the button to the toolbar to put it there. To remove a button you don't use, click and drag it off the toolbar. To create a new toolbar, go to the toolbar box, click new, and then customize it as described previously.

To customize menus, use the Customize dialog box. Go to the menu section and use the scrolling list to add commands to the menus. To add key shortcuts, go to the keyboard section. Locate the action for which you want to create a key combination. Insert the cursor in the Press New Shortcut Key box and type the key combination you want to use. If that combination already does something else, the box will tell you so. If not, click Assign or press Return. You can also reassign the existing command to the action you've chosen by selecting it from the Current box, clicking Remove, and then assigning it as described.

Microsoft Works

Microsoft Works is one of two surviving integrated "works" programs, **ClarisWorks** being the other. It may be that the Microsoft folks aren't selling Works as enthusiastically as they might be, because the software package generates less income for the company than selling **Word**, and **Excel**, and Mail, and so on, as separate programs. Or it may be that their less than full-featured modules just don't do enough of the work. Microsoft Works would seem to suffer from this syndrome. Certainly, its word processor is a weak point. Instead of providing font, size, and style menus, it has strange little icons on a toolbar at the top of the screen, which you can turn into pop-up menus by clicking with the mouse while you press three keys. It's not intuitive, and it's slow. Speed is a problem with Works in general. It runs slowly, even on a PowerMac. A moderately good typist can get ahead of it and possibly lose text. It lacks hyphenation, so you probably wouldn't want to use it for justified text such as newsletters or brochures.

The database is awkward to use, lacking any pre-made templates or layouts. You must create your own from scratch each time, adding fields through a dialog box. Once you've created a database, you can't bring new data into it, unless you first create another new database, and use it to cut and paste into the existing one. This is impossibly inefficient. Data gets typed into a little window at the top of the page, as in a spreadsheet, not directly into the field. Pictures? Different fonts for different fields? No way.

It seems as if the company that gave us Excel ought to be able to come up with a pretty good spreadsheet module, and so they have. It has borrowed many of the good features of Excel, including everyone's favorite, the AutoSum button. But even though it enables you to use macros, drag-and-drop, and other useful tools, you can't change the font or type size within the spreadsheet, you can't wrap text within a cell, and you can't adjust row heights or column widths. You have to plan ahead.

There are some things that Microsoft Works does better than ClarisWorks, and a few that ClarisWorks can't do at all. One of these is keeping a calendar and to-do list. Microsoft Works has this function built in, and it includes day, week, and month views and will even remind you of appointments. Another is creating newsletters, certificates, and similar items. ClarisWorks has "assistants" that do these tasks, walking you through them a step at a time. Microsoft Works has "wizards" like those in Word 6. The wizards are definitely more creative at designing layouts. The art department at Microsoft must have had fun planning the paint module. It has a set of **Photoshop**-like commands (Blur, Sharpen, Grayscale, Emboss, and so on) and accepts Photoshop plug-ins. All the expected tools are there, except that it can't handle EPS files.

As for communications, both Microsoft Works and ClarisWorks have what's essentially "plain vanilla" software. It'll get you into a text-based service or let you call a friend and pass files back and forth. Both support **Z-modem** transfers. Neither, as of this writing, comes with any sort of **Internet** software or browser.

See Also
ClarisWorks

MIDI

Originally developed as a method for connecting synthesizers (keyboards), MIDI quickly was adopted for connecting computers to musical instruments. MIDI is a string of data that contains information about what key was pressed, what time it was pressed, how hard it was pressed, as well as the patch (which is a small computer program that re-creates the sound of a musical instrument). It's an excellent way to record a performance, because the MIDI file is so small, unlike digitizing a sound, which requires a lot of bandwidth. Of course, the big difference is that MIDI files do not contain any musical sounds; the synthesizer provides that information. That also means that you need a MIDI-capable keyboard or application to play back the music.

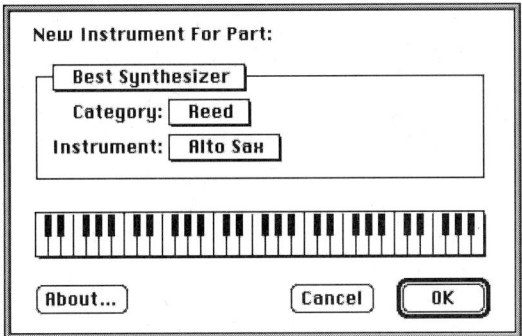

One problem of the original MIDI specification is that while it contains the patch numbers used in the song, different keyboards use the same patch number for different instruments. Patch 3 can be a piano on one synthesizer, a guitar on another. This means that unexpected results (that is, noise) could be heard if a MIDI file was played back on a different keyboard from the one on which it was created.

The development of **General MIDI** addressed this problem. General MIDI instruments assign specific sounds to specific patch ID numbers. This means that a MIDI file created using one General MIDI keyboard will play correctly on another.

Connecting a keyboard to a Macintosh requires a special MIDI cable that connects to the serial port of the Macintosh and the MIDI plug in synthesizer.

Sequencing software runs on the computer, records, and then plays back MIDI files. Sequencing software usually requires a MIDI keyboard to be attached to the computer, but that is not always the case. Some sequencing software has been released with their own patches (sound files) that play back the MIDI file through the computer sound hardware. Obviously, there are limitations to the quality of the sound—specifically the quality of the patches, the quality of the sound hardware in the computer, and the speakers through which it is played.

Apple has developed some System software to help users work with MIDI files. The MIDI Manager is System software for handling communications between MIDI instruments and the computer. The MIDI Manager comes with three parts: the Apple MIDI Driver, Patch Bay, and MIDI Manager. Although Apple intended MIDI Manager to help software developers, not all developers decided to use it; MIDI Manager was said to perform poorly compared to dedicated software.

Apple recently added new support for MIDI within QuickTime. Apple licensed a collection of patches (synthesized instruments) from Roland and included them in the **QuickTime Musical Instruments** Extension. MIDI files can be opened within any application that opens QuickTime files, and the conversion process is very similar to converting a **CD audio** file to a QuickTime movie.

To convert MIDI to a QuickTime file choose Open, from an application, such as **MoviePlayer**, and select the MIDI file. If the MIDI file came from a non-Macintosh computer, you might have to change the **file type** to "MIDI" using a program such as **ResEdit**. Then, the Open button changes to Convert. Choose Convert and the software asks you to name the new movie file. Click the Options button and you are presented with a list of the patches used in the MIDI file. You can click a patch and click the Instrument button to see a list of the synthesized sounds contained in the QuickTime Musical Instruments Extension. Note that all the General MIDI patches are listed, but not all of the patches are available (those that aren't available are italicized).

After setting up the conversion, click Close and convert the file to the QuickTime format. Note that the converted file still does not contain any actual audio information, and is only a couple of kilobytes larger than the original MIDI file. When the file is played, you must have the QuickTime Musical Instruments and QuickTime extensions installed. Also, the quality of the playback does not match that possible with a separate synthesizer.

MIDI is popular with musicians, but despite its small size and convenience, has not proved popular with multimedia producers. This is mostly because of the

M

requirements for special hardware to produce really good-quality sound. Macromedia actually removed support for playing MIDI files from **Director** when it upgraded it from 3.0 to 4.0 There is an Xtra for Director 5.0 available from Yamaha. This decision may have been prompted by the addition of MIDI support within QuickTime.

Web: **http://www.midifarm.com/**

See Also

QuickTime; Sound Digitizing

MIDI Manager, *See MIDI*

MIDI Translator II

A cable for connecting a Macintosh to multiple MIDI devices. The cable attaches to the Macintosh serial or printer port, and includes one MIDI in and three MIDI out plugs. No power supply is required.

Opcode Systems
Fax: (415) 856-3332
Phone: (415) 856-3333
Web: **http://www.opcode.com**

See Also

MIDI

Might & Magic: World of Xeen

Traditional **Role Playing Games** (RPGs) for the Mac are few and far between. Recent additions to the line-up, like **Curse of Dragor** from Domark are a welcome sight, but don't really push the technology far enough to please hard core RPG lovers. If you don't like playing in the online **MUDs**, the best game to check out is **Might & Magic**. Composed of two separate DOS titles, the port of Clouds of Xeen and Darkside of Xeen as World of Xeen is still the best Mac RPG around. In Might & Magic, you wander the land of Xeen, taking on quests and adventures depending on where you roam. Of course, along the way, you encounter more than a hundred assorted monsters that you must defeat in order to progress.

In the tradition of Dungeons & Dragons style gaming, you choose your characters and parties in various inns.

As in most advanced RPGs, reading the manual carefully is necessary for figuring out which type of character is worth creating, but if you are a true D&D fan, you're probably used to all that technical paperwork and won't be bothered. If you're a beginning gamer who wants something easier to start with, you might want to try an easier title like **Dungeon Master II** first. Although Dungeon Master may be a little too basic for advanced players, it is still a good RPG. New Might & Magic titles are released several times a year.

See Also

Adventure Games; Curse of Dragor; Dungeon Master II; Role-Playing Games

Millie's Math House

This is one of several titles from Edmark's Early Learning House series. Targeted for very young children, ages 2-5, it teaches counting skills, pattern recognition, and some very basic geometry. The animated characters are cute, but the constantly repeated instructions get annoying after the first few minutes. Some of the activities, such as the geometric game, have several levels of skill.

The object of this exercise is to learn the names of the geometric shapes. Frank Lloyd Mouse will ask for the parts he needs to build things. The child must click the appropriate shape to place it on the board. Clicking the more complicated blueprints sets up more complex patterns for the child to fill in, with more kinds and sizes of blocks. Other activities include fitting shoes to critters with big, small, or medium feet, counting and adding objects with Dorothy Duck, and decorating cookies with the number of jelly beans requested by Harley Horse. The booklets that come with the programs include suggestions for "Together Time" activities for parent and child to share.

See Also

Software, Educational, K-6

MIME Type

A standard way of identifying a file so client software can identify and process it. Often encountered on files downloaded from the **Internet** or **World Wide Web.**

MIME stands for *Multipurpose Internet Mail Extensions.* MIME is a standard on the Internet that allows the transmission of a wide variety of different kinds of files via **email**; it allows you to send not only text files, but sounds, images, and software, among other things.

When, behind the scenes, a client such as **Netscape Navigator** requests a file from a **Web server**, many servers include the file's MIME type as part of the package that contains the file. Netscape uses MIME to determine what to do with the file. If it's an **HTTP** page, text, or a **GIF** or **JPEG** file, Netscape handles the file. If not, Netscape attempts to pass the file to a **helper application.**

MIME types are divided into broad categories such as "image," "audio," "video," and "applications." There are differences between the files in a single MIME type. For example, the "application" type includes both PostScript files (essentially programs for controlling imaging equipment) and **StuffIt** files (**compressed** versions of files of any type). The only thing that **PostScript** and StuffIt files really have in common is their MIME type designation.

MIME types are further divided into *subtypes,* which categorize single, particular kinds of documents, like GIFs (a type of picture) or **AIFFs** (a type of sound). These subtypes are more practical: all GIFs are very similar in format, and a program that can read one file of a subtype can usually read all files of a subtype, although sometimes not very well. For example, **Photoshop** can open both GIF and GIF89 files, but Photoshop can't take advantage of the transparent pixels that distinguish GIF89s from garden variety GIFs.

Netscape, for instance, maintains a list of MIME types and specifications for how to process each one it encounters on the Internet. The following table lists settings a user can specify to control how Netscape uses MIME types.

Netscape MIME Types

Type	Purpose
image/GIF	Signifies a file of type "image" and subtype "GIF."
Application	Indicates the application to which a particular MIME subtype is passed.
Action	Controls the relationship between Netscape and the helper application—whether the helper application runs independently of Netscape or uses the Netscape window to display the file.
Extensions	Is a backup system for categorizing files when the Web server doesn't provide a MIME type with a file.

M

A file named on a Web server with a given subtype's extension at the end of its name is treated as a member of the subtype; for example, Netscape knows that the file Picture.gif is an Image/GIF, even if the server did not designate the MIME type when the file was transferred.

See Also

AIFF; Compressing Files; GIF;. Helper Applications, Web; HyperText Transport Protocol; Internet; JPEG; MIDI; Netscape Navigator; Server StuffIt Expander; Web Browser; World Wide Web

Mind Castle

Sub-titled "the Spell of the Word Wizard," this program plays like a game, but gives your vocabulary a pretty good workout in the process. You start on the top floor of the wizard's castle, earning clues to find the password that will let you go to the next level. Your goal, of course, is to escape before the wizard turns you into a frog. To earn the clue, you must choose the right words to complete sentences the wizard's assistant tests you with. Each correct sentence earns you a letter, which either is part of the password or eliminates one that you might guess.

There are about 600 different words in the game. They are chosen at random, but your chances of seeing the same words increase drastically if you play more than once. There's no way to add more words, unfortunately. If there were, it would be an excellent skill-building program. As it is, the game is as much a race against time as a test of word definitions. Still, it's fun, and the randomness helps give kids who might not be as proficient with words an equal chance to win.

See Also

Software, Educational, Adult; Software, Educational, K-6; Software, Educational, Grades 7-12

Mind Your Own Business, *See* *MYOB*

Mindy, *See Dylan*

MiniCAD

As one of the popular CAD options for professionals, GraphSoft's MiniCAD offers full-featured integrated industry solutions for CAD users. The Resource palette contains thousands of items in the Design and Drafting Toolkit (symbols, macros, parametric commands, database records, worksheets, and hatch patterns). New palettes and tools have replaced the commands of earlier MiniCAD versions, and extensive modifications have been made to the interface to enhance clarity and to further comply with industry standards.

Dimensioning Dimensioning is offered for constrained horizontal and vertical formats, constrained chains, constrained baseline, ordinates, centermark, diametrical/radial, angular, with the inclusion of upper/lower dimensioning limits where desired. The dimension standards are customizable as far as text positioning and alignment, tolerance sizing, and text rotation. A full Dimension Info palette is available for editing all dimension information in the drawing, with support for the following dimensioning standards: Arch, ANSI, BSI, DIN, ISO, JIS, and SIA. Customized dimensioning standards can also be added by the user.

3D Options Clearly articulated commands in the 3D menu offer a list of the following sculpting, rendering and viewing options: Creating Linked Layers (a layers option as in **Photoshop**), Extrude/Multiple Extrude/Sweep (3D object creation tools), Conversion to Mesh or Polygonal objects, Move/Rotate the working plane, Cutting 2D/3D Sections, and rotating the 3D view. All standard orthogonal 3D views are supported and selectable, and exacting perspectives can be set. In addition to orthogonal and perspective projections, MiniCAD supports Oblique Cavalier 30 and 45 degree, and Oblique Cabinet 30 and 45 degree views (familiar terms to CAD users). Rendering options include Wireframe, Quick, Solid, Shaded Solid, Shaded No-Lines, Final Shaded Solid, and Final Hidden Line.

Text MiniCAD follows all of the expected Mac standards for text insertion and font accessibility, and adds spacing and case commands. Text blocks on the page can be scaled and moved into position. MiniCAD scene files can also be exported as text files, and text scene files can be imported into MiniCAD. A special command translates any **TrueType** font into a polyline object (making the text object suitable for editing). This makes it easy to create full 3D text objects in MiniCAD. TrueType font files contain all of the necessary Bézier curve data to make this translation possible.

Symbol Library MiniCAD allows the user to select from a list of possible overlay modes: Standard, AEC, Civil, Cross Stitch, Electrical, Mechanical, Terrain Modeler, and Toolkit. Each of these modes has separate symbol libraries that provide symbol support, as for example the standard cross-hatching techniques used to represent materials in that specific overlay.

Import/Export ClarisCAD users should note that MiniCAD offers complete translation capabilities from ClarisCAD documents. The Export formats supported include PICT, EPS, DXF, Text, QuickDraw

3D, Renderman, Worksheet, Data Base, and Quicktime Movie. The Import formats supported are PICT, PICT as picture (for tracing), EPSF, DXF, Text, and Worksheet.

Animation MiniCAD has very powerful animation capabilities, allowing you to create path animations that function as virtual reality walk-throughs of any 3D model. The instructional CD guides you through each step of the process. The animations are user controlled as far as frame rate and keyframe settings, and complex camera interactions can be programmed.

Rendering Options MiniCAD has a list of preview rendering modes from wireframe and hidden line wireframes to solid, shaded, and final solid shaded options. The higher rendering modes require more **RAM**, so resetting the preferred memory size in the Info menu is highly recommended.

Special Features A complete Digital Terrain Modeler is included, allowing for the creation of DEMs (Digital Elevation maps) as either 2D contours or full 3D models from data files, 3D loci, or polygons. The 3D model can be rendered as a solid and viewed at any angle. MiniCAD has a special menu dedicated to structuring and formatting tables. MiniCAD offers a special Multiple Extrude module that can aid in the production of objects very difficult to model by standard extrusion methods.

Minidocks, *See PowerBook Duo Docks and MiniDocks*

Minor Software Release

A minor release will add a few new features and capabilities, as well as a bug-fix or two. Usually, the interface shows little change with this type of upgrade. Minor releases are generally inexpensive or free (give or take a handling charge) to registered users and are fairly safe in that they don't generally create new incompatibilities or exact new hardware costs.

You can usually tell that an upgrade is minor if the version number increments in the second digit (or in the third, although that is often the indicator of a bug-fix update).

See Also

Bug-Fix Update; Major Software Release; Registration Card

MIPS

MIPS, Millions of Instructions Per Second, is a measure of CPU speed.

Mirror Site

A location on the **Internet** that mirrors or duplicates the contents of a very popular site, such as a Mac software archive.

Mirroring a heavily visited site more evenly distributes the site's contents to locations around the world. Overseas visitors thus have a server that can be accessed more quickly, because it is closer to them. Mirror sites also provide alternatives to users who cannot gain access to a busy site either because too many visitors are connecting to it already, or because the server is "down" or offline.

See Also

Anonymous FTP; FTP; Internet; Macintosh Software Archives

Misregistration, *See Color Trapping*

Missing Application, *See Application Busy or Missing Message; Application Not Found Message*

Mister C, *See MrC*

Mixed-Mode CD

A **CD-ROM** that contains data of different formats. Usually this means combined CD-ROM data and audio tracks. Unfortunately, the data is stored in track one of the CD, and many audio CD players will read the first track and attempt to play it as "music," which results in a very loud and piercing noise. Some players detect the data track and will skip it.

CD Plus was developed as a solution to this problem. It uses the multisession format to place the audio on the first writing and then place the data in a second session.

See Also

CD Plus; CD-ROM

Mixed Mode Manager

With the development of the Power Macintosh, Apple had a difficult choice to make. They could implement an entirely **native** operating system with a new model of program behavior (a time-consuming and compatibility-ruining proposition) or implement only the most time-critical portions of the OS in native code, and leave the rest in 68K code to be ported later. This second option has the tremendous advantages of speed and compatibility, and as a result, was the path Apple chose.

But with part of the **Toolbox** in native PowerPC code and part in 68K code, there had to be a way to integrate the two; there had to be a way for PowerPC code to call a snippet of 68K code and have the **emulator** step in and run that code without any further intervention from the programmer. Apple accom-

plished this using a new part of the Toolbox called the Mixed Mode Manager.

The Mixed Mode Manager puts no burden on non-native (68K) programs. If a 68K program running on a Power Mac calls a routine written in native PowerPC code, the Mixed Mode Manager automatically adjusts. Native applications, on the other hand, have to take on a little extra burden when they call routines that could be either native or not. Native applications do this by creating *Universal Proc Pointers* (UPPs) for these routines. A UPP is a special kind of **pointer** that identifies which instruction set the routine uses (68K or PowerPC) and contains information about the routine's parameters and return value.

UPPs are only required when native code calls a routine that may or may not be native. They are not needed when PowerPC code calls another PowerPC routine, nor are they required when calling Toolbox routines. The Mixed Mode Manager is fully documented in the "Power PC System Software" volume of **Inside Macintosh**.

See Also

Emulator; Inside Macintosh; Pointer; Toolbox

MNP, *See Modem Transfer Protocols; Modem Standards and Speeds*

MOD

A musical file format originally developed for the Amiga, MOD can be thought of as a cross between a **MIDI** file and a digitized sound file. Whereas a MIDI file contains only information about how a sound is created (but requires separate MIDI synthesizer software or hardware to create the sound) and a digitized sound file is a sampling of sound every few seconds, a MOD file contains both the musical information and instrument information.

MOD files are small and provide high quality stereo playback. Special software, however, is required to play a MOD file, and with MIDI file playback now available in the Macintosh operating system (along with a large number of programs for creating and editing MIDI files), MOD will probably not gain wide acceptance.

See Also

Audio XCMDs; MIDI; Sound Digitizing

Modeling

The process of creating **3D** objects. The modeling features provided by 3D programs differ widely, but some of the most common include lathing, sweeping, extruding, and free-form modeling.

There are three common ways to create 3D objects: lathe, extrude, and free-form. In lathing, a two-dimensional shape, called a cross-section, is drawn and then the 3D shape is created by rotating that shape around an imaginary center axis.

A variation on lathing is sweeping, which is essentially lathing but with the capability to change the cross-section or the location of the cross-section during the rotation. Use sweeping to create complex objects, such as the tubing of a French horn.

Extrusion takes a two-dimensional shape and pushes it out along the third dimension to create the 3D shape. Extruding a circle creates a cylinder, extruding a square creates a cube. Lofting is a variation on extrusion in which the cross-section is varied as it is extruded.

Although extrusion and lathing are very easy and understandable methods for creating basic shapes, there are still many shapes that cannot be created using such tools. Creating a human face (perhaps one of the most difficult modeling tasks) would be impossible using either extrusion or lathing. That's why most sophisticated modeling programs offer some kind of free-form modeler. In theory, a free-form modeler enables you to create an object of almost any shape. In Marshall Hash's Animation, shapes are created by drawing control points that define

patches, which are the surfaces of the object. The shape of the surface is further defined by the shape of the lines that run between the control points. By moving the position of the control points and adjusting the shapes of the curves, you can create very complex shapes.

Unfortunately, most free-form modelers are difficult to learn and use. The problems of working with a three-dimensional shape on a two-dimensional display are most apparent when working with free-form modelers.

Another important difference between free-form modelers is how they handle curves. Polygonal modelers use straight lines between control points—to create curves, the line is divided up into even shorter segments that approximate the curve. More sophisticated modelers support curved lines called splines (also sometimes called **Bézier** curves.) These are curved lines, and not only produce better-looking models, but are easier to manipulate than polygons.

Objects rarely consist of a single 3D shape. Usually, several shapes are combined to create complex models. **Boolean** operations take two objects and use one to cut into the other, creating a negative space in the remaining object. This makes it easy to create objects that would be hard to create using other modeling tools—for example, a hole in a ball. Strata's Vision 3D is one of the few low-cost (under $1,000) tools that supports Boolean operations.

M

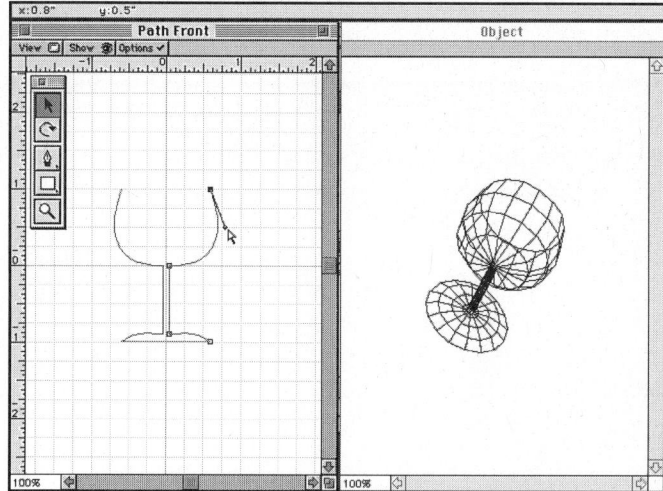

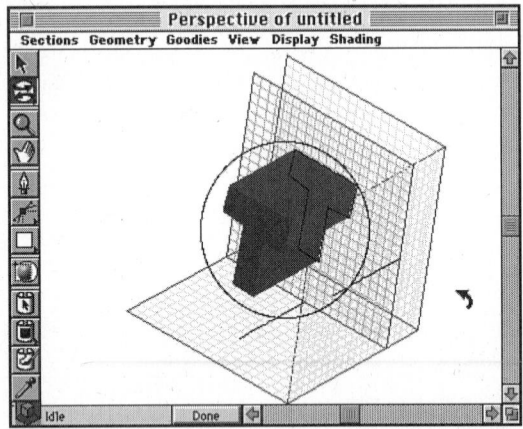

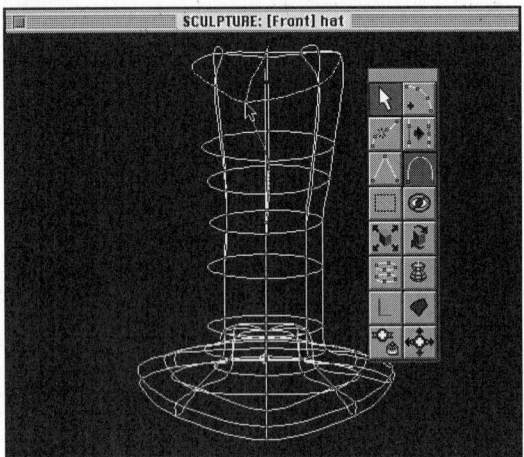

Often, the relationship between objects is defined as a parent and child relationship. The child object is connected to the parent and moves when the parent moves.

A more sophisticated relationship is called *inverse kinematics*, which is available in Fractal Design's Ray Dream Studio and Hash's **Animation Master.** Inverse kinematics causes a parent object to follow when you drag or move a child object. This is very useful for animating characters. By moving a hand, for example, the wrist and arm also move to reflect the movement of the hand.

See Also

3D; AddDepth; Animation; Animation Master; Electricimage; Extreme 3D; Infini-D; LogoMotion; Ray Dream Designer Studio; StrataVision

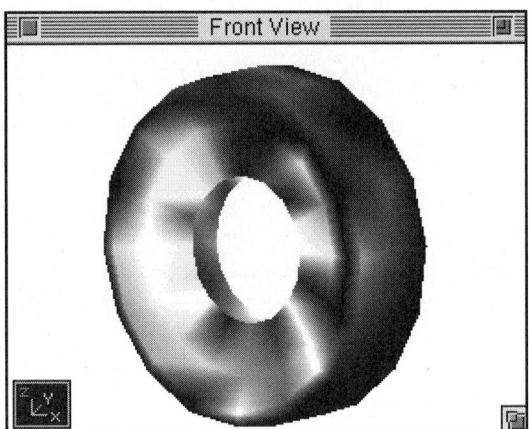

For creating non-animated scenes, you often want to connect only one object to another in relative space, so that if you move one part, the other follows. But if you are creating animated objects—a walking figure, for example—then much more complicated connections are needed. Not only do you need to define the point at which one object connects to another, but you also have to define the movement of one object relative to another—this may be along an axis of rotation (for example a knee joint) or along an axis (for example, a piston in an engine). Ideally, you should be able to define the movement as well as the limitations of the movement. Just how far can the knee joint bend?

Modem

The addition of a modem to your computer system opens the door to virtually unlimited information resources. By connecting your computer to an **online service**, such as **America Online**, or even to the **Internet**, a modem gives you access to news, airline schedules, magazines, your office **email** system, and even matchmaking databases.

The explosive growth of personal computers and of the growth of the Internet over the last several years is due in part to the high speed, yet inexpensive, communications, that modems allow.

Modems and Telecommunications Adapters Telecommunications connects people over long distances. The base of the word comes from the Greek word *tele*, meaning *far off*. Telecommunications began with the invention of the telegraph and the telephone in the 19th century, and continued with television and faxes in this century. With the advance of computer technology, modems and digital communications devices are the successors to the telegraph of the old west.

The modem is the most common telecommunications device used by computers. Modems use ordinary **analog telephone lines** to communicate with other computers anywhere in the world. Computers began to use modems several decades ago, when terminals and mainframes communicated with each other at 300 bits per second. When the personal computer came along, people continued using modems for similar purposes, to access mainframes and other personal computers with terminal emulation software.

Since then, computer telecommunications has matured into a multi-faceted technology enabler. The marriage of the telephone and the computer enables your Mac to access the Internet and online services, send faxes, and dial into **AppleTalk** networks remotely. You can set up your Mac to answer your phone and provide voice mail. Your Mac can also dial the telephone for you, and you can use your Mac as a speaker phone. The use of computers with telecommunications in these ways is called *telephony*, and is one of the fastest growing areas of personal computer technology today.

The term *modem* is short for MODulator/DEModulator. A modem converts the computer's digital signals into analog signals that are transmitted over the telephone line. You can hear some of these analog signals as squawking when a modem makes a connection. Most modems are usually hardware devices: little boxes that sit on your desk, **expansion cards** that sit inside your Mac, or credit-card-sized PC Cards for the recent **PowerBook** models. One exception is Apple's **Express Modem**, a purely software modem that uses the processing power of the Mac itself to perform the modulation and demodulation of signals. The Express Modem connects to a telephone line using Apple's **GeoPort** Telecom Adapter. The advantage of using software is that it has enabled innovative telephony software to be developed for the Mac at a lower cost than hardware solutions.

The manner in which analog signals represent data is specified by international modem standards. New standards every few years have been able to double the speed at which modems send data. The current standard, V.34, sends data at 28,800 bits per second.

However, modem technology is near the end of the line, and modem speeds will not double again. This is because V.34 has nearly reached the physical limit of analog signals being transmitted over the telephone lines. In fact, many call V.34 the final modem specification. This is at a time when data-intensive uses of modems, such as the **World Wide Web**, are increasing in popularity and in data transmission requirements. Modems can get effective throughputs that are up to four times faster than 28,800bps using compression techniques, which means a file you're downloading will get to you four times faster. However, the modem still only sends a maximum of 28,800 bits over the line every second.

The solution seems to be to abandon the modem and the telephone lines in favor of transmitting information digitally. A modem must convert signals to analog form because ordinary telephone lines and telephone company switches are not equipped to handled digital data. However, most telephone companies now offer a new type of digital telephone line called **ISDN** (short for Integrated Systems Digital Network).

M

Telephone companies have been busy for the past 10 years installing ISDN switches in their networks and now have a great deal of the United States covered. Because ISDN is digital, it is many times faster than analog modem connections could ever be. Like a telephone line, ISDN can also carry voice, but the voice signals are digitized before being sent over the wire.

Modems are not used for ISDN, but you still need one of several types of telecommunications adapters for ISDN. Some are external boxes, and some are add-in cards. Sometimes such a device is called a digital modem or an ISDN modem. Technically, both terms are oxymorons, as there is no modulation or demodulation in digital communications.

Strictly speaking, telecommunications can take place without modems by making use of non-analog telephone lines, such as ISDN. However, because by far the most common form of telecommunication is via modem, we'll use the terms interchangeably here. (See **ISDN** for an explanation of its differences from standard modem technology).

Basic Functioning The basic purpose of a modem is to serve as a translator between your computer's digital transmissions and the analog transmissions possible over standard telephone lines (also known as POTS—plain old telephone service.)

The term modem is derived from this two step process: Modulation of computer signals into analog data for transmission into the public telephone system, and Demodulation at the remote end of the analog data back into digital signals for input into a computer.

Commands for the modem such as configuration and dialing are issued by your computer in the form of AT commands. Data transmission between your modem and the remote modem are accomplished through various modem protocols.

History The first modems used a brute-force approach to connecting computers and the telephone. The modem contained "cups" into which the user would insert a standard telephone. To use this type of modem, one would configure the computer to receive data, dial a telephone number manually, wait for the screech of the answering computer, and then insert the telephone headset into the modem's cups. (Interestingly, this type is quite visual and is still shown frequently in movies and on television in otherwise "state of the art" computer centers).

Because these modems depend upon the telephone's normal headset for communications, their capability to transmit data is impaired and the likelihood of picking up background noise is quite high. Therefore, this type of modem was limited in the quality and speed of connection.

The next major step in the evolution of modems was direct connect modems. These modems plug directly into your telephone line, allowing you to be free of room noise and allowing the modem to dial for you. Direct-connect modems attach directly to telephone lines via the wall jack.

As technology improved, modems (as with most products that are technology based) were able to provide faster communication at lower prices. Although today's modems seem incredibly fast by the standards of five years ago, the same will no doubt be true in another few years.

What to Look For Like other peripherals, modems are judged by speed, features, and price. It used to be that the faster the modem speed, the more it would cost. Today, you pay more for additional features, not speed. This is because the cost of the fastest modems, the V.34 modems that operate at 28.8Kbps, has dropped to the same price as modems running at slower speeds. At this point, there is no point in getting anything slower than a V.34 modem. (In the future, it will even be hard to find anything slower than 28.8 modems.)

Among V.34 modems, however, the actual speed that the modem operates at can vary between manufactures slightly. In addition, some modems are more troublesome than others, and some handle poor line conditions better than others. Some modems have trouble communicating with other modems of certain brands.

These speed and reliability issues are difficult to get a handle on. Computer magazines that test modems in depth are a good source of information. If you've used a modem before, there's no need to limit yourself to Mac magazines—a PC magazine will work just as well, because modems are fairly cross platform devices, and many manufacturers package their modems for both Mac and PC users. Keep in mind that internal PC modems (modems on expansions cards) will not work in Macs. It is convenient if the modem comes with a Mac **modem cable** and manual geared towards Mac users, but this is not essential. You can always buy a cable separately, and most modem users never open the manual. What you do need, however, is a Mac driver for your modem. Many telecom programs such as Zterm, America Online, and **CompuServe** provide drivers for a long list of modems. If you're buying one that's meant for a PC, at least check to be sure that it has a Mac-compatible driver.

The problem is that most computer magazines, Mac and PC, don't review modems very often. Getting to the bottom of modem reliability speed issues is a tricky business, one which magazine editors are not fond of. If you already have a modem, you can find information about modems in discussion groups on the Internet and on online services such as America Online and CompuServe. Here you will find word-of-mouth information on problematic modems and those that users find trouble-free.

Features Like any piece of computer hardware, modems come with a variety of features. A feature that is essential to some people can be a waste of money to other people and can even get in the way.

The modem feature that gets the most use today is **fax** (facsimile). These days, the fax capability adds little or no additional cost to a modem. Some fax/modems can both send and receive faxes—to and from any fax source, whether it is another fax modem or a traditional paper fax machine. However some fax/modems only send faxes and can't receive them.

Fax modems are usually bundled with software for your Mac. The software can vary greatly in ease of use, and is often what differentiates one fax modem from another. If the fax modem is marketed to PC users, it will come with software for Windows but not for Mac. However, you can buy fax modem software from a variety of companies. There is even shareware fax modem software. If you don't like the fax software that came with your modem, you can run one of these other programs instead.

Some modes also have the capability to carry voice as well as faxes. These are sometimes referred to as voice/data/fax modems. With voice modems, you can set up a voice mail system on your Mac and have it answer your phone. Voice capability comes at a premium, so make sure you need it before you pay for it.

A good feature that everyone can use is a flash ROM, which provides easy upgradability. Modems with flash ROM can be upgraded with newer software, such as newer versions of the V.34 modem standard. Some modems can be upgraded to ISDN via flash ROM, a good feature if you think you might move beyond the speed limitations of an analog dial-up link.

To some, a modem is not a modem unless it has blinking status lights on the front panel. Status lights can be useful for troubleshooting problems, but few people use them on a day-to-day basis, and it does cost money for a manufacturer to add them. Some modems take status lights to the extreme and include small LCD displays on the face of the modem.

Along with the blinking lights comes the squawking of the modem as it makes a connection. Some modems are noisier than others. Although some users feel the modem dialup tones are reassuring and helpful for troubleshooting, others find the loud squawking of modems disruptive, especially in an office. Some modems squawk very quietly or not at all. Often you can set the volume of a modem using AT commands you type from a terminal emulation program such as the shareware application ZTerm, or commercial packages such as MicroPhone, SITcomm, or Smartcom.

Modems that are **Hayes compatible** use the full AT command set, a group of common modem commands used between the computer and modem for dialing, making the connection, hanging up, and other modem activities. Some manuals give you a list of these commands, so you can manually operate the modem or access special functions by typing in the commands in a terminal emulation program. However, use of AT commands falls clearly into the power user or techno-hobbiest category, and is not something many people find they need.

Notable Mac Friendly Modems Modems are relatively cross-platform devices. They use the same commands on Macs and PCs, contain the exact same hardware in the Mac and PC versions. There is no reason why you can't buy a PC fax modem and then buy third-party fax software to run on your Mac.

However, if you want everything you need in one package, you'll want a Mac-friendly modem bundle. You usually get a Mac cable and fax software that runs on a Mac. You'll also get the necessary CCL file required to work with **Apple Remote Access**, something a PC modem vendor may not have. You'll also get access to tech support people who are familiar with the Mac.

The modems listed here are all V.34 (28.8Kbps) modems, and most have fax capabilities. They vary in features and in price, but all are from companies that offer Mac-specific bundles.

AT&T/Paradyne SComsphere This industrial-strength modem has an industrial price as well, but owners of Apple Remote Access servers and bulletin boards (BBS) will appreciate the AT&T Paradyne Comsphere 3810Plus for its capability to run continuously (without attendance). It has a reputation for going and going and has received good scores for reliability and speed in several reviews. The Comsphere 3810Plus has industrial-strength features as well, including firmware that can be upgraded automatically and the ability to be managed over a network. It also includes an alphanumeric display, a row of 13 status indicators, and a watchdog timer, an internal device that detects line problems and automatically resets the modem. This latter feature prevents you from manually having to reset the modem if a connection fails, an important feature for a modem connected to a server. This is the one modem listed here that does not have fax capabilities. Be sure to ask for the Mac version. AT&T/Paradyne, 800-482-3333, 813-530-2000.

Global Village OneWorld Combo In a box no bigger than a desktop modem, the Global Village OneWorld Combo is a modem server containing one or two modems that can be shared by users on a network. It lets anyone on an **EtherNet** or **LocalTalk** network dial out via the one or two Global Village Platinum V.34 modems inside the unit. It also offers send and receive fax, and functions as an Apple Remote Access (ARA) server. With the Apple Remote Access client software installed on a remote Mac, you can dial into the OneWorld Combo server and access the network.

The OneWorld comes with the same fax software as Global Village's stand-alone modems, and is one of the best fax programs you can find. The only potential hassle is that received faxes arrive at only one Mac, or can be automatically printed to a printer. The OneWorld Combo is still a good value for a small office or work group, and gives speedy, trouble-free connections at a good price.

Global Village makes popular modems for desktop Macs, the TelePort line, and PowerBooks, the PowerPort line. The company also make modems in PC Cards for PowerBooks with PCMCIA slots. The V.34 version in each line is called the Platinum. Global Village Communications, 800-436-5591.

Practical Peripherals MacClass 288MT II V.34 The MacClass 288MT II V.34 is an inexpensive model suitable for desktops. It has been shown in reviews to make fast, clean connections, and comes from a long line of solid Mac modems. It also handles changing or deteriorating line conditions well. However, the MacClassMT II V.34 lacks a flash ROM, so it can't accept software upgrades. Still, the company has confidence in this modem, as it offers a lifetime warranty. Practical Peripherals, 805-497-4774.

Supra SupraFaxModem The SupraFaxModem is a popular and inexpensive modem that features small size and an option to upgrade to voice capability. This modem offers good performance with few problems. (Earlier Supra modems has some problems connecting to certain brands of modems, but this V.34 version seems to have been cured of the previous maladies.) However, upgrades are easy with this modem because it contains a flash ROM, which lets you install upgrades by downloading software. The SupraFaxModem also features an alphanumeric LED display, as well as four status indicator lights. Supra has been doing modems for Macs for many years and knows what Mac users expect. Supra, 800-727-8772, 360-905-1410.

U.S. Robotics Courier V.Everything with V.34 A long model name from one of the major manufacturers of modem chips. (U.S. Robotics chips are used in Supra modems, among others.) This another modem with good, trouble-free performance, and it contains both fax and voice capabilities.

The V.Everything is a business modem that is priced higher than some of the others, but also has some industrial-strength features. It can be left on all the time without attendance, as when connected to an Apple Remote Access server or a bulletin board server (BBS). This means that it doesn't have to be manually reset. It has 12 status indicator lights, and it's also available in a rack-mountable case. However, it does not have any network management features.

Although most modems enable you turn down the volume of the squawking tones with software or with primitive AT commands, the Courier V.Everything is one of the few modems with a volume control knob on the case. U.S. Robotics 800-877-2677, 708-982-5010.

Connecting to the Telephone Line Your modem connects to the phone line using a standard RJ-11 modular phone cable, much as you would connect any answering machine or fax machine. However, it's very important to note that there are actually two types of telephone systems that use the same RJ-11 Jack: analog and digital. Analog telephone systems are the types normally used in homes, or very small (one or two line) offices. Modems, fax machines, and standard telephones all require the analog system. Analog is also called (especially by phone company service people) POTS, for Plain Old Telephone Service.

Digital telephones (also referred to as keysets) require an entirely different type of signal to be transmitted through this jack. Digital telephones are the type normally used in businesses, which support multiple telephone lines (greater than two) as well as advanced features such as transfer, conference, and digital displays. ISDN phone service is also beginning to be offered in some parts of the country. It's used prima-

rily for large volume data transmission and for very high-quality broadcast transmission of voice and picture. It, too, is digital and requires a special type of digital modem for data handling. These routinely carry data at 57,000Bps, making graphics on the Web actually fun to watch.

If you're not sure which type of telephone jack you have, make sure to ask the person who is in charge of your telephones. Do NOT simply plug in your modem to see what type of jack it is—the electrical current in digital jacks can ruin both your modem and computer it is attached to.

TIP Several companies make digital to analog converters to allow you to hook up a modem to a digital phone line by a connection through the digital telephone. Results with these units vary greatly depending upon the telephone system in use and with the modem type, so ask co-workers for advice before investing.

Connecting to Your Macintosh The way the modem connects to your Macintosh is determined by the Mac model and type of modem. All Macs have serial ports (labeled Modem, Printer, or Modem/Printer depending upon the Macintosh model.) Most external modems connect to the Macintosh through a serial cable that connects to these ports. A few, notably some Global Village and SpectraCom Pocket modems, connect through the ADB port. In addition to the external port(s), the PowerBooks and certain Performa models also have a dedicated slot for an internal modem. Whether internal or external, the Macintosh communicates with the modem using Asynchronous communication.

Today's high-speed external modems require a hardware handshaking cable for connection to your Macintosh. This cable will have a standard Mac Mini-DIN 8 plug on one end, and a DB-25 connector at the other end. If your modem didn't come with a Mac cable, check with your local computer store or any of the big Mac mail-order houses to order one.

M

All modem cables are not created equal! To allow your modem and cable to function effectively, you will need what is known as a hardware handshaking modem cable. This cable provides for signals to be sent between the modem and the computer to keep everyone in synch. If the cable provided with your modem doesn't support hardware handshaking (it should specify), get one that does. This will save you lots of hours of frustration!

See Also

Analog Telephone Line; Digital Telephone Line; Express Modem; GeoPort; ISDN; Modem Cables and Connections; Modem Types

Modem Cables and Connections

The cables that connect the modem to a telephone wall jack are the same cables used to connect a telephone to a telephone wall jack. At each end of the cable is the RJ-11 connector, the same as used in telephones. Most modems have two RJ-11 connectors—one to connect to the wall jack, and another, a pass-through connector, into which you can plug a telephone for voice communications. The pass-through connector allows you to share the phone line for both voice and data transmissions, but not simultaneously.

To connect the modem to a Mac, you need a cable that plugs into the round serial ports, the Modem Port or the Printer Port. Power Macs and the old Quadra AV Macs have serial ports with 9 pins. This indicates that they are GeoPort-enabled. Apple's **GeoPort** Telecom adapter can plug into these serial ports, but non-GeoPort modem cables also work connected to these ports. The serial ports of other Macs have 8 pins.

Modems that operate at 9600Bps and faster require a hardware handshaking cable to connect to a Mac. If you are replacing an old 2400Bps modem with a modern modem, you'll need a new cable. Most new modems come with a hardware handshaking cable.

Unfortunately, you can't tell if a cable supports hardware handshaking by looking at it.

Hardware handshaking is the method that faster modems use to regulate the flow of data between the modem and the Mac to which they are connected. For instance, if the Mac is sending data to a modem faster than the modem can transmit it, the modem will tell the Mac to pause. Hardware handshaking modems use commands called Request to Send/Clear to Send (RTS/CTS), which are sometimes indicated on modems and in communications software. RTS/CTS are called *flow control* commands, used to tell the modem and the computer it is connected to when to send data and when to stop sending data. RTS/CTS is referred to as hardware handshaking because the modems contain circuitry that generate these commands, and the cable contains a special signal line. A change in voltage on this line is used indicate the RTS or CTS state.

Non-hardware handshaking cables don't have this special line. Older modems use a flow control called **Xon/Xoff**, which is sometimes called software handshaking, because there is no special hardware associated with it. Instead, a command code is sent over the data lines in the cable. Software handshaking is slower than hardware handshaking, which is why the former was replaced by the latter in higher-speed modems.

There is another type of serial cable called a null modem cable, which doesn't connect a modem at all. A null modem cable connects a Mac directly to a PC using the serial ports of both machines. It has a round eight-pin connector on the Mac side and a 15-pin (two rows of 8 and 7 pins) connector on the PC side. You can use either the Mac's printer port or modem port, but you'll have to turn AppleTalk off in the Chooser if you use the printer port. Using a null modem cable and terminal emulation software, such as the shareware ZTerm on the Mac, you can transfer files between the Mac and PC without the use of modems. The communications settings on the terminal emulation software on both machines need to be the same in order for a file transfer work.

See Also
Analog Telephone Line; Digital Telephone Line; Express Modem; GeoPort; ISDN Terminal Adapters; Modem

Modem Commands, *See Hayes AT Command Set*

Modem Port, *See Serial Port*

Modem/Printer Port, *See Serial Port*

Modem Standards and Speeds

International modem standards are set by a group known as the International Telecommunications Union—Telecommunications Standards Sector (ITU-TSS), formerly know as the CCITT (Consultative Committee for International Telegraph and Telephone). This group sets the standards that makers of modem chip sets follow, which enables modems from different manufacturers to communicate with each other.

The standards determine how many bits per second the modem will transmit, as well as methods of data compression and error checking. Each standard can communicate at all the previous slower speeds, which means they can communicate with older modems that don't support the same specification. Modems also can jump down to a slower speed if a telephone line is noisy and can't support communications at the higher speed.

The standards are named with a V and a dot, followed by a two-digit number. They are sometimes followed by "bis," which is French for "second." The table that follows starts with the most current standard and works backwards.

Table of Modem Standards

Standard	Purpose
V.34	28.8Kbps communications
V.FC, V.FastClass	28.8Kbps communications, an interim standard
V.32terbo	19.2Kbps communications
V.42bis	compression
V.42	error correction
V.32bis	14,400Bps communications
V.32	9600Bps communications
V.22bis	2400Bps communications

The V.34 standard may be the final modem specification, as it pushes data over standard telephone lines near the maximum limits that physics allows. The V.34 specification may be improved slightly, but modem connections can't get faster than 38.4Kbps, the phone system's theoretical upper limit for analog signals. Even if V.34 is improved, the changes to the specification will be so minor that the spec won't be renamed "V.34bis."

Before V.34 was finalized, several modem manufactures used an unofficial interim standard called V.FastClass, or V.FC. Most V.FC manufactures offered upgrades to V.34 when it came out. Although V.FC and V.34 are both 28.8Kbps standards, the latter has several enhancements over V.FC, including a probing tone that continually monitors and acts upon changing line conditions.

V.32terbo was used only for a short time and was never very popular. It has the spelling "terbo" instead of "turbo" because "ter" is French for "third," indicating that this was the third V.32 specification.

The V.42bis compression standard increases the actual throughput by compressing the data before sending it. The V.42bis modem on the receiving end recognizes that the data is in compressed form, and decompresses it before sending it to the computer it is plugged into. The compression in most modems can increase throughput by a factor of three or four times.

The CCITT standards incorporate server other specifications called **MNP**, for **Microcom Network Protocol**, developed by the company of the same name. For instance, V.42 incorporates MNP 2, 3, and 4 error corrections. Many modems also support MNP specifications that are not included in the CCITT standards, such as MNP 5 compression and MNP 10 error correction used in cellular communications.

See Also
Data Communications Standards; Modems

Modem Transfer Protocols

Sets of standard rules that computers use in order to accurately transfer files while connected by modem to **bulletin board services**. An important step that needs to be performed before downloading software from a network.

Modem file transfer protocols are not the same as **anonymous FTP**, a protocol used to transfer files on the **Internet**.

It is essential that you choose a file transfer protocol that matches the protocol used by the computer serving or transmitting data to you.

The following table lists some of the more common protocols.

Modem Protocols

Name of Protocol	Description
Kermit	Older file transfer format used to communicate with UNIX systems, now seldom used.
XMODEM	Widely supported but relatively slow file transport protocal that transfers files in blocks 128K in size.
XMODEM-CRC	A variety of XMODEM that uses the cyclic redundancy check error-checking method.

Name of Protocol	Description
YMODEM	Lets you send a batch of files with one command, uses CRC error-checking.
YMODEM-G	Faster variety of YMODEM that does not perform error correction, for modems already containing error-correction hardware.
ZMODEM	Very fast, reliable protocol; file transfers can be resumed following an interruption. Recommended.

See Also
Asynchronous Data Transfers; Data Communications Standards; Hayes AT Commands; Modem; Parity

Modem Types

Modems are small devices that can be located either inside or outside your computer. The word modem comes from modulate/demodulate, which succinctly describes their function. The task of the modem is to modulate the outgoing digital signal from your computer into an analog signal, which can be transmitted over a normal telephone line, and to demodulate the incoming analog signal from another computer/modem into a digital signal that your computer can understand.

Aside from their physical location (internal or external), the key differences between modems are how fast they communicate, the software which runs them, and how they connect to your computer.

External Modems An external modem is a piece of hardware that sits outside your Mac as an self-contained unit. Most are about the size of a portable CD-ROM player, although they come in literally all sizes and shapes from a plug-in PCMCIA card about the size of a single playing card to a box big enough to hold a hard drive. Most of these devices connect to your Mac through the serial port (either the modem, printer, or printer/modem port, depending upon the model in question.) PCMCIA modems, obviously plug into the appropriate slot on a PowerBook or other Mac equipped to handle them.

In an interesting repetition of history, "acoustic" external modems of are now becoming available again. Rather than plugging directly into a RJ-11 telephone jack, these types of modems connect by physically placing the modem into, or next to, the small "talk" and "listen" cups of the telephone.

Some have a pair of rubber cups that attach to the telephone handset. Others have a sort of cradle into which you place the handset. These modems are becoming popular again because of the increasing dependency people have on staying in-touch electronically. People who travel frequently can end up situations where they need to connect to the office to check for mail or transfer files, but they can't find an RJ-11 jack to connect their modem. In these situations, an acoustic modem and a payphone can be a quick fix.

Internal Modems Internal modems fit entirely inside the case of the computer. Although this type of modem is very popular in the DOS/Windows world, on the Macintosh side only PowerBooks and certain Performa Models support internal modems. The principle advantage of this type of modem is space savings.

You eliminate a piece of desktop clutter, or in the case of the PowerBook, you avoid the need to carry an extra piece of gear. The only visible indication that an internal modem is present is a telephone jack on the back of the box. The main drawback of this type of unit is that you don't see the status lights showing you when the phone is off the hook or the transmission status of data. (Certain modems, such as the Global Village PowerPort products, provide this through software indicators on the Mac's Screen). An additional drawback is that it's very difficult to share an internal modem between two or more computers. External modems can easily be unplugged from one Mac and plugged into another.

The Apple Express Modem is made for certain PowerBook and Duo models. It runs partially in soft-

ware, and so reduces the amount of RAM available for other tasks by about 300K. It supports connections up to 14.4Kbps, and handles faxing as well as modem tasks.

Although most PowerBook modems come with instructions on how to install the modem yourself, opening your PowerBook's case voids your warranty and puts your PowerBook in jeopardy. If you're at all uneasy about the process, it makes sense to let an Apple Dealer do it for you. The cost of installation pales when compared to the anxiety and repair bill caused by a broken PowerBook.

See Also
Modem

Moderated Newsgroup

A **Usenet newsgroup** moderated by an administrator who judges the appropriateness of an article before allowing it to be posted to the group at large.

Most newsgroups are unmoderated: anyone who wants to can post anything, even if it is irrelevant to the topic. Most moderators are overworked volunteers and charges of censorship can arise because the moderator may not always represent the views of the majority of the readers. Moderated groups tend to have less traffic and the messages that go through are more likely to have some worth. You can ask why a posting was rejected by a moderator so that future submissions have a better chance of reaching the rest of the group.

See Also
Newsgroups, Subscribing; Usenet

Modula-2, *See Pascal*

Moiré

Moiré is an undesirable pattern that develops when two or more **halftone** screens overlap at improper angles in the printing process. A moiré can also appear in a halftone if the image contains fabric or other finely textured surfaces. Sometimes a moiré appears on TV screens when the camera pans across a striped pattern or certain textures in clothes. Preventing a moiré pattern from appearing in printed images has always been of prime concern to **prepress** and **printing** technicians. Moiré is controlled through careful adjustment of screen angles when **process color** separations are produced and registered for printing.

See Also

Color Separations; Process Color

Monitors

Display monitors are the part of the Mac you look at the most, so it is worth getting a monitor that doesn't cause eyestrain or give you a headache. A tilt-and-swivel monitor stand can help put the monitor at a comfortable angle, but a clear, sharp, flicker-free image better prevents health problems. Monitors also differ in other ways—size, number of control knobs, and features. Knowing which of these features are important to you can aid your work on the Mac.

All display monitors create an image by shooting beams of electrons through a grill onto a screen coated with a phosphorescent material. A monitor can use one of two types of grills, an aperture grill and shadow mask, which focus the beams in slightly different ways. Aperture grill cathode ray tubes, such as the Sony Trinitron, tend to produce sharper images. The beams are aimed at thousands of tiny dots called **pixels**. The beams hit each pixel one at a time until the entire screen is drawn. They draw an entire screen full of pixels around 60 times per second.

Most display monitors sold today are color monitors, although grayscale monitors are still available. The difference in price between grayscale and color has diminished over the years, and most people find a color interface either useful or just more pleasant than grayscale. People who have color-deficient eyesight might save some money by getting a grayscale monitor.

The number of colors or grays you can display has little to do with the monitor. Most monitors today can display 16.7 million colors, which is enough for photographic-quality images. If there is a limit to the number of colors, it is in your Mac's video circuitry and the amount of **video read-only memory (VRAM)** you have. If the video circuitry supports it, the more VRAM you have, the more colors you can display. The bigger the image area, the more VRAM you need. For instance, with 2M of VRAM, the Power Mac 7500 can display 32,768 colors in an image area that measures 1024 pixels by 768 pixels. With 4M of VRAM, the 7500 can display 16.7 million colors.

The number of colors you can display is known as the *bit depth*, although it some people call it *color resolution*. A bit depth of 1 bit per pixel gives you 2 colors (black and white). A bit depth of 8 bits per pixel gives you 256 colors or grays, and 16 bits per pixel gives you 32,768 colors. You get 16.7 million colors with 24 bits per pixel.

One of great things about the Mac is that if you upgrade by buying a new monitor, you can keep your old one as well. The Mac lets you use two or more monitors by plugging the second into a video card you add to an expansion port. Having a second monitor is useful for keeping tool palettes, email, and other secondary windows while you use the other monitor for your main work documents. Because both monitors act as if they are part of a continuous work space, you can move items from one monitor to the other simply by dragging it over.

The procedure for setting up the second monitor is quite simple. You plug in the video card, plug in the second monitor, and turn on the Mac. You can use the Monitors control panel (called the Sound and Display control panel in System 7.5.2 and Monitors and Sound in System 7.5.3) to change the orientation of the monitor (see the following figure). You simply drag the icon of the second monitor to the position you'd like it relative to the first monitor. If you want the menu bar to appear on the second monitor instead of the first, in the Monitors (or Sound and Display) control panel, drag over the menu bar from one monitor icon to the next.

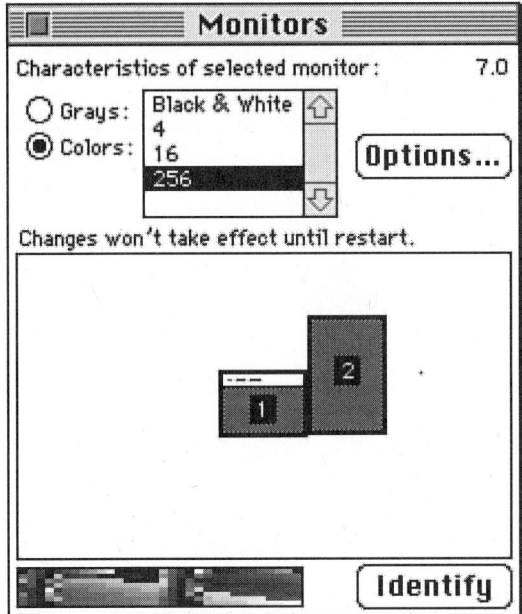

as a point of reference, and make a good starting place for comparisons. Apple's monitors are typically of good or outstanding quality, have a good set of controls, and usually get good reviews from the computer magazines. Also listed here are some of the better third-party vendors that make good alternatives to the Apple monitors in the same class or have exceptional features for specialty applications that the Apple monitors do not have.

Most of Apple's multisync monitors, and many of the third party monitors, will also work with PCs running Windows. The resolutions and refresh rate listed here apply to Macintosh operation only.

Apple Macintosh Color Display The Apple Macintosh Color Display is an entry-level monitor commonly shipped with Performas. It's low on features, but has crisp display.

Specifications:

- Size: 14 inch
- Resolutions, refresh rate: 640 by 480 pixels at 67Hz
- Tube: Sony Trinitron aperture grill
- Dot pitch: 0.26 mm

Apple AudioVision 14 Display The AudioVision 14 Display was Apple's first attempt at a multimedia monitor, with good success. Although smaller than the AudioVision 17, the sound quality is excellent for a multimedia monitor.

Specifications:

- Size: 14 inch
- Resolutions, refresh rate: 640 by 480 pixels at 67Hz
- Tube: Sony Trinitron aperture grill
- Dot pitch: 0.26 mm
- Special features: Multimedia monitor with built-in speakers and microphone

See Also

Cables and Adapters for Monitors; Energy-Star Monitor Issues; Monitors, Common Models; Monitors Control Panel; Monitors, Image Quality; Monitors, Size; Multimedia Monitors; Multisync Monitors; Portrait and Pivoting Monitors

Monitors, Common Models

There are hundreds of models of monitors that will work with most Macs, if you count the VGA monitors that work with PCs. You can choose on the basis of **monitor size**, **image quality**, and price. Reviews in computer magazines are a good source of current information about the fine points of monitors. Generally, the higher quality and more features, the more you will pay. However, the highest-quality monitor isn't always required. This is why it's best if you can see a monitor in person at least once before buying.

The following list of monitors are a cross-section of the most common quality displays and their basic specifications. Apple's line of monitors are included

Apple Multiple Scan 14 Display The Multiple Scan 14 Display is a low-end, multimedia monitor, but without the built-in microphone of the AudioVision series and with a tube of somewhat lesser quality. Its features include a headphone jack on the front panel, and it is a multisync monitor that can display multiple resolutions.

Specifications:

- Size: 14 inch
- Resolutions, refresh rate: 640 by 480 pixels at 67Hz

  800 by 600 pixels at 75Hz
- Tube: Shadow Mask
- Dot pitch: 0.28 mm
- Special features: Multimedia monitor with built-in speakers and headphone jack.

Apple Multiple Scan 15 Display An entry-level multisync monitor at the 15-inch size, often sold with lower-end Power Macs. Also includes built-in speakers, although of lower quality than the AppleVision series.

Specifications:

- Size: 15 inch
- Resolutions, refresh rate: 640 by 480 pixels at 67Hz

  832 by 624 pixels at 72Hz

- Tube: Shadow Mask
- Dot pitch: 0.28 mm
- Special features: Multimedia monitor with built-in speakers and headphone jack

Apple Multiple Scan 17 Display The Multiple Scan 17 Display is a good-quality multisync 17-inch display that produces crisp, bright colors, and sharp images.

Specifications:

- Size: 17 inch
- Resolutions, refresh rate: 640 by 480 pixels at 67Hz

  832 by 624 pixels at 72Hz

  1024 by 768 pixels at 75Hz
- Tube: Sony Trinitron aperture grill
- Dot pitch: 0.26 mm

AppleVision 1710AV The AppleVision 1710AV is one of the top multimedia monitors available, and one of Apple's best monitors. It has better sound than any other multimedia monitor, and what Apple calls a "next-generation" tube that produces crisp, sharp images. It also features a robust set of sound and video controls on the front panel.

Specifications:

- Size: 17 inch
- Resolutions, refresh rate: 640 by 480 pixels at 67Hz

  832 by 624 pixels at 72Hz

  1024 by 768 pixels at 75Hz

  1152 by 870 pixels at 75Hz

  1280 by 1024 pixels at 75Hz
- Tube: Sony Trinitron aperture grill
- Dot pitch: 0.26 mm
- Special features: Multimedia monitor with built-in speakers, microphone, and headphone jack

Apple Multiple Scan 20 Display The Multiple Scan 20 is Apple's 2-page multisync monitor, which produces a sharp display.

Specifications:

- Size: 20 inch
- Resolutions, refresh rate: 640 by 480 pixels at 67Hz

  832 by 624 pixels at 72Hz

  1024 by 768 pixels at 75Hz

  1152 by 870 pixels at 75Hz

  1280 by 1024 pixels at 75Hz

- Tube: Sony Trinitron aperture grill
- Dot pitch: 0.31 mm

NEC MultiSync 4FGe 15-Inch Color Display The 4FGe is a good alternative to the Apple 14-inch monitor line, stacking up favorably against traditional Trinitron-based monitors. The NEC 4FGe's Invar alloy shadow gives a higher contrast and brighter image than most other monitors in its class. NEC AccuColor system allows individual adjustment of the degree of color from each of the three RGB color guns. 508-264-8000.

Specifications:

- Size: 15 inch
- Resolutions, refresh rate: 640 by 480 pixels at 67Hz

  832 by 624 pixels at 72Hz

  1024 by 768 pixels at 75Hz

- Tube: Sony Trinitron aperture grill
- Dot pitch: 0.28 mm

NEC MultiSync XE17 Good all-around image quality and handy on-screen controls make the NEC MultiSync XE17 one of the better 17 inch monitors you can find for all-around quality. 508-264-8000.

Specifications:

- Size: 15 inch
- Resolutions, refresh rate: 640 by 480 pixels at 67Hz

  832 by 624 pixels at 75Hz

  1024 by 768 pixels at 75Hz

- Tube: shadow mask
- Dot pitch: 0.28 mm

NEC MultiSync XE21 The XE21 is a two-page display that features a good set of on-screen controls and bright, colorful displays. 508-264-8000.

Specifications:

- Size: 21 inch
- Resolutions, refresh rate: 640 by 480 pixels at 67Hz

  832 by 624 pixels at 75Hz

  1024 by 768 pixels at 75Hz

  1152 by 870 pixels at 75Hz

- Tube: shadow mask
- Dot pitch: 0.28 mm

Portrait Display Labs Pivot 1700 The Pivot 1700 is a different type of pivot monitor: instead of a portrait shape that pivots into a landscape mode, it is a standard 17-inch landscape monitor that pivots into a pseudo-portrait mode. 510-227-2700.

Specifications:

- Size: 17 inch
- Resolutions, refresh rate: 640 by 480 pixels at 67Hz

  832 by 624 pixels at 72Hz

  1024 by 768 pixels at 75Hz

  1152 by 870 pixels at 75Hz

  1280 by 1024 pixels at 75Hz

- Tube: shadow mask
- Dot pitch: 0.26 mm
- Special features: Pivots between portrait and landscape

M

Radius PressView 17 SR With features such as good color calibration software, small dot pitch, and very high resolutions, the PressView 17 SR is aimed at graphics professionals. The monitor also features excellent image quality and precise on-screen software controls. 408-541-6100.

Specifications:

- Size: 17 inch
- Resolutions, refresh rate: 640 by 480 pixels at 67Hz

  832 by 624 pixels at 750Hz

  1024 by 768 pixels at 75Hz

  1152 by 870 pixels at 75Hz

  1360 by 1024 pixels at 75Hz

  1600 by 1200 pixels at 69Hz
- Tube: Mitsubishi aperture grill
- Dot pitch: 0.25 mm
- Special features: High-end color calibration and color management software

Sony Multiscan 17sfII The Sony Multiscan 17 combines excellent image quality with good controls and onscreen displays that show you the settings. It sets the standard for image sharpness and has a very small dot pitch for crisp displays. Yet, the Multiscan 17sf2 is not one of the more expensive monitors and is a good value. 408-894-0555.

Specifications:

- Size: 15 inch
- Resolutions, refresh rate: 640 by 480 pixels at 67Hz

  832 by 624 pixels at 75Hz

  1024 by 768 pixels at 75Hz
- Tube: Sony Trinitron aperture grill
- Dot pitch: 0.25 mm

ViewSonic 17GA For those looking for a less expensive multimedia monitor alternative to the AppleVision 1710AV, the ViewSonic 17GA offers good colors. The sound of the built-in speakers is not as good as the AppleVision 1710AV, particularly in the bass frequencies, but it better than average. It also doesn't offer the 1280 by 1024 picture resolution that Apple's high-end multimedia monitor includes.

Specifications:

- Size: 17 inch
- Resolutions, refresh rate: 640 by 480 pixels at 67Hz

  832 by 624 pixels at 72Hz

  1024 by 768 pixels at 75Hz

  1152 by 870 pixels at 75Hz
- Tube: shadow mask
- Dot pitch: 0.26 mm
- Special features: Multimedia monitor with built-in speakers.

See Also

Cables and Adapters for Monitors; Energy-Star Monitor Issues; Monitors; Monitors, Image Quality; Monitors, Size; Multimedia Monitors; Multisync Monitors; Portrait and Pivoting Monitors

Monitors Control Panel

If your Macintosh has a grayscale or color **monitor**, you can make adjustments to the monitor or set up your system to use multiple monitors through the built-in video controls in the Monitors Control Panel, as shown in the following figure.

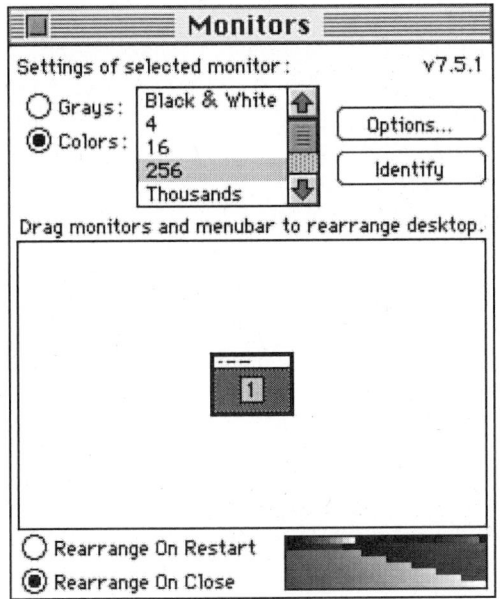

If you have a color monitor, you can choose to display the monitor in black and white, various levels of grayscale, or color. Depending on the amount of **VRAM** installed in your Macintosh, you can select:

- Black and white
- 4-bit (16 grays or colors)
- 8-bit (256 grays or colors)
- 16-bit (thousands of colors)
- 24-bit (millions of colors)

Grayscale monitors obviously cannot display color, so your choices in the Monitors Control Panel are limited to black and white, or a level of grayscale. In System 7.5.2 and higher, you can also set your screen depth (your option for how many colors or shades of gray will be displayed) from the Control Strip. (The Control Strip was introduced first on PowerBooks, and most models of PowerBooks can set their screen depth from the PowerBook version of the Control Strip.)

The Macintosh enables you to run multiple monitors (up to six at one time if you so desire), and that's accomplished through the Monitors Control Panel. When you open the Monitors Control Panel, you'll see an area with icons that represent each of the monitors connected to your Mac. You first need to determine which monitor will be the "main" monitor (which will contain the menu bar and the Apple menu). One of the icons in the Monitor window will have a miniature menu bar on it. That is the default main monitor (automatically numbered 1). To make another monitor the main monitor, click and drag that menu bar to the icon for another monitor.

These monitor icons in the Monitors Control Panel seem to float in the middle of a wide open space, but this area is used to represent the real monitor's physical location. If you connect a second monitor to your Mac, for example, and you're going to put it to the right of your main monitor on your desk, you need to have the icons in the Monitors Control Panel look the same way; the main one in the middle, and the second one to the right. You do this so your cursor knows where to go when move it from your main monitor to the second monitor. With only one monitor connected, your cursor will stop when it hits one of the four sides of your screen. But when you connect another monitor, your cursor can move over to that monitor without obstruction, as if you had one long monitor. By telling the Mac, in the Monitors Control Panel, where the second monitor is, it opens up the side and lets your cursor travel beyond the screen, over to the second screen without interruption.

You can also set the size of the screen display (measured in pixels) by clicking the Option button in the Monitors Control Panel and selecting from the list of screen sizes. The default for a 13-/14-inch monitor is 640×480 pixels.

To use the Monitors Control Panel, follow these steps:

1. Open the Monitors Control Panel from the Control Panels submenu on the Apple menu (or System Folder).

M

2. Choose a monitor setting of Colors or Grays by clicking the appropriate radio button, and then choose the bit depth you want to display.

3. To use multiple monitors, click the monitor you want to be your main monitor, and drag the icon of the menu bar onto that monitor. Click and drag the second monitor icon to match the physical setup of your monitors on your desk.

4. To switch built-in video settings to a different screen resolution, click the Options button and make your selections from the list.

See Also

Control Strip; Menu Bar; Monitors; Radio Buttons; VRAM Expansion

Monitors, Image Quality

The quality of the image that a monitor produces has to do with several factors, including screen flicker, image sharpness, and image distortion of the image and of its brightness. Each of these qualities can be governed by a number of technologies in the monitor.

Flicker and Refresh Rate You can detect a flicker in a monitor if the refresh rate is too low. The *refresh rate* is the speed at which the electron gun inside the monitor draws the screen—quickly scanning rows of pixels from top to bottom. The faster the electron gun can write, the more stable and flicker-free your screen appears, and the higher your screen refresh rate is. Lower quality monitors have lower refresh ratings and produce a noticeable flicker, like that of a fluorescent light, which makes working hard on your eyes.

Manufacturers of monitors specify the refresh rates in terms of Hertz (Hz). A monitor with a 67Hz refresh rate redraws the screen image 67 times per second. Refresh rates above 60Hz appear flicker-free to most people, although some can still detect flickering in some lighting conditions. A refresh rate of 75Hz is fast enough to prevent flicker in any lighting condition.

Sharpness The *sharpness* of an image is determined by several factors. One of these is the type of grill used to focus the beams of electrons aimed the screen. There are two types, the aperture grill used in the Sony Trinitron tube, and the shadow mask grill. Aperture grill tubes are usually, although not always, crisper than shadow mask grills.

Another design point affecting sharpness is *dot pitch*, the space between pixels, the tiny points of light in rows across the screen. A smaller dot pitch means smaller pixels, which correspond to more detailed and sharper images—if the monitor is calibrated correctly. Most quality monitors have a dot pitch of 0.28 mm or less. A small dot pitch rating is necessary for fine detail work with images and stringent CAD/CAM, where accuracy is very important. Because smaller pixels are closer together, a higher degree of detail can be achieved on-screen. Poor dot pitch ratings, in the high 30 and even 40 mm range are not recommended for exacting graphics work.

The term dot pitch most commonly refers to monitors with shadow mask grills; for "aperture grill" displays, the term is stripe pitch.

Another factor that affects the sharpness is *convergence*, the capability of the red, green, and blue beams inside the cathode ray tube to accurately hit their target pixels on-screen. When the three beams don't exactly hit the same spot, you'll see a colored corona around the edges of images. Better monitors have controls that let you adjust the convergence, but some monitors have better convergence than others. Computer magazines that review monitors often measure the misconvergence, that is, the amount the beams are not aligning. Generally, a misconvergence under 0.2 millimeters is considered good, and the closer to zero, the better.

Image Distortion *Image distortion* is when the monitor bends straight lines when displaying them. Distortion typically occurs near the corners of the screen. Bigger monitors often have more problems with image distortion than smaller monitors. Another type of distortion called pin cushioning occurs when a monitor bends the edges of the screen inward. Better monitors have controls that let you adjust for pin cushioning. These controls are a good idea, because pin cushioning can occur when you switch between resolutions on multisync monitors.

Brightness The brightness of a monitor can also be distorted, in that different areas of the screen are displayed at different brightness. To check for non-uniform brightness, you can bring up a white screen. You can easily do this by creating a new folder, opening it, and have it fill the screen. Because color is also affected by non-uniform brightness, you might want to test a monitor by filling it with a color. The easiest way to do this to go to the **Desktop Patterns control panel**, and select a pattern that is all one color. Then shut all windows and look at the Finder.

One more point about brightness: Monitors tend to dim over the years, as the phosphorescent coating on the inside of the cathode ray tube loses some of its luminance. To compensate, it's a good idea to buy a monitor that is bright enough so that you don't have to turn the brightness control all the way up, even in the brightest lighting conditions.

See Also
Monitors; Monitors, Common Models

Monitors, Size

Like television screens, the size of computer display monitors is given as a diagonal measurement from one corner of the screen to the next. However, the actual size of the display image is less than the given measurement for the cathode ray tube. For instance, the diagonal measurement of the image area of a 13-inch monitor is 11.5 inches. This is because there is an area of black around the image that acts as a buffer zone in case you need to adjust the width or height of the image area.

When purchasing a monitor, you should pay attention to both the monitor's advertised CRT size (usually 14, 15, 17 or 21 inches) and the monitor's advertised viewable image area, also called the diagonal viewing area. Monitors with the same CRT size can have substantially different viewing areas, and in some rare cases, a display advertised as 14 inches may have a larger viewing area than a display advertised as 15

inches. After of several lawsuits alleging false advertising were filed against monitor manufacturers, the manufacturers have agreed to note both the displays' CRT size and diagonal viewing area. Pay attention to both numbers.

Monitors typically come in four standard size ranges:

- Small monitors measuring from 12 to 15 inches were once the standard, but are now considered entry-level or home monitors.

- In business applications, mid-sized monitors, from 16 to 17 inches, are beginning to replace 13-inch monitors as the standard computer display. This is because prices for the mid-sized monitors have dropped considerably and offer more room for viewing tool palettes or large documents.

- A 17-inch monitor can't quite fit a full 8.5-by-11 inch page on-screen, but it does give you about 50 percent more screen space than a 14-inch monitor at 72 dots per inch.

- If you do want to display an entire page, you need a **portrait monitor**. These monitors are shaped differently than other monitors, basically following the shape of a piece of letter paper. Portrait monitors typically measure 15 inches diagonally, although they have more space than standard 15-inch monitors.

- Large monitors, measuring 19 to 21 inches, can display two full 8.5-by-11-inch pages. These monitors are standard in desktop publishing, computer graphics and design, and CAD. Of course, they are also useful for anyone who needs to keep a lot of windows open at the same time.

Beyond the standard sizes, there are extraordinarily large monitors used for giving presentations in front of a group of people. These monitors can be as large as 37 or 40 inches and cost many thousands of dollars. These monitors are good for displaying to a roomful of people; any bigger situations, such as an auditorium, require wall projection systems for proper visibility.

M

See Also

Cables and Adapters for Monitors; Energy-Star Monitor Issues; Monitors; Monitors, Common Models; Monitors, Image Quality; Multimedia Monitors; Multisync Monitors

Monopoly, *See Classic Collection*

Monospaced Fonts

The major difference between typewritten text and typeset text is that in the former each letter is the same width. Typeset text generally uses **proportional fonts**, in which some characters are narrower or wider than others. But digital monospaced fonts are available; they're often used for typesetting material like computer code and for other text that should look as though it was produced on a computer or a typewriter. Two common monospaced Mac fonts are Monaco and Courier.

See Also

Fonts; Proportional Fonts; Typeface Categories

MOO, *See MUDs and MOOs*

Moof

"Moof" is the call of the infamous **dogcow**. Because the dogcow is half dog and half cow, its call is naturally half dog and half cow also: "moo" and "woof."

The following figure shows one place you might find the dogcow; in a Page Setup dialog box.

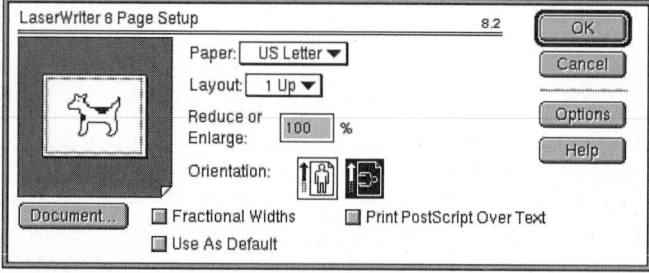

See Also

Dogcow

MooVer

MooVer can take a folder of PICT files and turn it into a **QuickTime** movie. Optionally, it can add subtitles to each frame of the movie.

This program is shareware ($10) and available from online services.

See Also

MoviePlayer; Peter's Player

Morph

Gryphon Software's Morph is named to fit its function. This software is suitable for beginners just starting to learn to manipulate the magic worlds of warping and morphing, as well as it is a challenge to experienced professionals who think they've seen it all. The advanced morphing, warping, and "caricaturing" options that this software possesses allow you to produce extremely complex still and animated graphics. Using only a few simple tools, Morph is capable of generating startling high-end results.

Morph has a small movable toolbox with seven tools: Selection Arrow, Point Tool, Connecting Line Tool, Scissors (Cut), Magnifying Glass (Zooms), Hand (Move Image), and Rotation Tool. The editing screen looks like a storyboard, which is exactly what it's called. In fact, images in a Morph sequence may be printed out as a true storyboard. A source and a target space inhabit the Storyboard, areas where you place source and target graphics. Still images can also be imported for viewing, and finished movies may be played on the Morph screens.

Morph operates in a classic morphing software fashion. Points and lines are placed around important elements of the source image, and show up over the target image. The points and lines are moved on the target image to reflect important elements. Once placed, a preview can be generated that shows how the outlined elements will move from source to target shapes. When points and connecting lines are where they should be, a movie is made that allows the source image to transform into the target. This is how all basic morphing programs work, but Morph has tools that take its possibilities far beyond the basic expectations.

In addition to being able to generate a sequence of morphing images between two graphics, Morph allows you to continue with as many internal graphics as your computer's memory will support. New source/target pairs can be added to the sequence, points and connecting lines placed around their important shapes, and the whole process repeated again. Default images of seven American presidents are included with the program to allow you to experiment with an elongated sequence, transforming one to the next in a series. All of this is accomplished without making the process any more difficult than it is in working with only two images. The final quality of the images can be selected from low, good, and better.

Warping Morph can generate quality warps. All aspects of the image can be altered by deft placement of the control points and their associated lines. Previews can be generated before you commit to the final renders. By placing control point and lines guides around the elements to be altered, background elements of the image can be prevented from moving. Any warped graphic can be exported as a PICT, TIFF, or **Photoshop** image.

Morphing As part of the previewing process, still images can be generated from any intermediate frame in a morphing sequence, and you might select to export these previews as a still image. The final quality and magic of a morphing sequence depends entirely upon how carefully the points and connecting lines are placed. The connecting lines have Bézier-like controls, so they can be shaped to follow the conforms of the selected graphic very closely. Morph also allows you to create a morphic movie or series of images from two animated sequences, the difference being that points and lines will require more movement as the animations progress. Birds in flight can become airplanes in flight, and running pigs can become bounding dogs. All it takes is a little practice and some dedicated time.

Caricatures Unique to Gryphon's Morph is the possibility of creating photo-realistic caricatures, images that have exaggerated elements that transform them into photo-cartoons. A reference image is used to apply its features to a target image, and the resulting rendering is previewed and (if you like it) saved. No other morphing package offers this direct capability.

Animation Gryphon's Morph has all of the expected controllers for generating animated morphs of any size and frame rate. Compression choices, size, key frame placement, image quality, time code options, and keytime elements are all configurable by the user. Multiple morphs can be moved around and displaced by one another as if the software were an Edit Decision List processor (EDL), an advanced function that allows maximum control over the final animation.

Save / Load Conventions Movies can be exported as QuickTime, PICS, PICT, Photoshop, and TIFF, and single images as PICT, TIFF, and Photoshop. You can also save and load the setup files for any sequence, warp or caricature.

Documentation The documentation is complete and easy to understand and is peppered with adequate tutorials and images. Better yet, the software is so intuitively designed, you probably won't need to reference the documentation at all after a few sessions of exploration. Because of its capability to generate warps, morphs and caricatures, Gryphon's Morph is recommended for beginners, intermediate learners and seasoned pros.

M

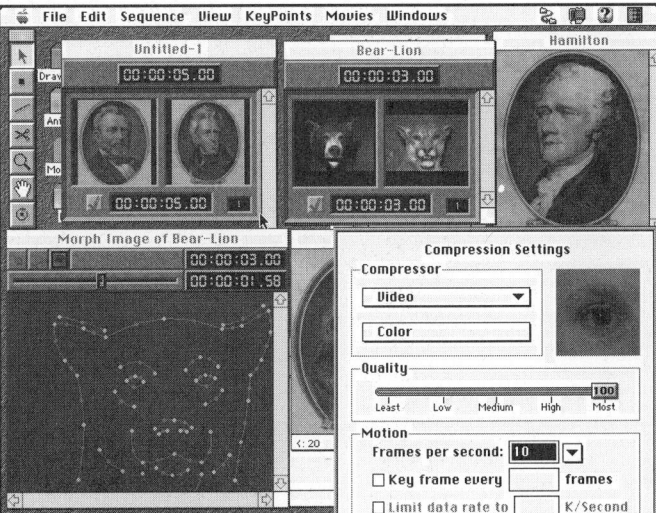

Morphing

This effect takes two images and creates an effect where one image seems to reshape itself into another. There are several applications that enable you to create these sophisticated effects on a budget, such as Gryphon's **Morph** and Avid's **Elastic Reality**.

These programs take two images or clips and morph them together to create a still image or a clip of the morph. The morphing effect is defined by drawing control points and lines on the two images that indicate the parts of the image that morph together. A control point, for example, might be added to the eyes in the first image. The same control point appears on the second image, and you must drag this point to the eyes of the character in the second image (assuming you are morphing a face to a face).

Morphing effects depend on two things.

- The subjects in the image. If you are morphing a face, short hair seems to morph much better than long frizzy hair. Also, the more control points you add, the better the effect.

- The consistency of the background. If the background from image to image is the same, the morphing effects are more noticeable and more effective. If you morph between images with different backgrounds, the morph happens over the whole image and will look more like a cross-fade or dissolve transition effect than a morph.

Gryphon Software
7220 Trade Street, Suite 120,
San Diego, CA, 92121.
Price: $149
Fax: (619) 536-8932
Phone: (619) 536-8815
Web: **http://www.gryphonsw.com/**

See Also

Elastic Reality; Morph

Mortal Kombat, *See Violence in Games*

Mortimer

The captivating scenes from the **Family Entertainment** title Mortimer from LucasArts are what you would expect from a television movie—not a CD-ROM. LucasArts' previous releases, such as Rebel Assault and **Full Throttle**, have been games targeted at adults. Mortimer uses the Rebel Assault INSANE engine (Interactive Streaming Animation Engine) so action sequences may look familiar.

However, instead of flying through vast reaches of space and shooting storm troopers, you can zoom around on the back of a flying snail, zapping frozen animals back to life. The plot of Mortimer surrounds the villain Lodius who has turned animals into statues in the process of stealing their powers and appropriating their physical characteristics. A minor education element is added by allowing you to interact with the twenty-eight animals you revive and learn more about them through short video clips, but Mortimer is mainly a lot of fun for kids, without the usual violent content.

See Also

Are You Afraid of the Dark?; Family Entertainment; Foul Play; Masterpiece Mansion; Yellow Brick Road II

Mosaic, *See NCSA Mosaic*

Motherboard, *See Power Mac Logic Boards*

MountImage

MountImage is a freeware **control panel** by Steve Christensen that enables you to mount **disk images** made with Apple's Disk Copy on your **desktop** and treat them as if they were mounted disks. MountImage also enables you to copy disk images onto disks without having to use Apple's Disk Copy. MountImage can be found in the Macintosh Utilities Forum on **America Online** or at various **FTP** sites on the **Internet**.

See Also

Control Panels; Desktop; Disk Images; Disks and Drives

Mouse

The pointing device known as a "mouse" was introduced in 1963, and since that time has become the most successful means of pointing or moving objects on a screen. Every Mac comes equipped with a mouse. These pointing devices have evolved over time, but there are basically three types: an electro-mechanical mouse, the newer opto-mechanical mouse, and optical mice.

- **Electro-Mechanical Mice.** The first Apple mouse, introduced with the Lisa in 1983, was used with the Mac 128K, 512K, and 512KE, as well as the Mac Plus, and Apple IIe and IIc. This square box housed a ball that drove two wheels whose edges were ringed with metallic encoders. The ball moves the wheels that create and break a current when the encoders spin past electrical contacts. These mice used a heavy gray ball and sliding retainer ring and were manufactured in the United States.

- **Opto-Mechanical Mice.** There have been three generations of opto-mechanical mice. The first opto-mechanical mouse used a lighter-weight black ball with a rotating retainer. This assemblage was made in Taiwan

and was not a success due to its light weight effect on the pointer's movement. The second generation mouse uses a heavier gray ball with a rotating retainer and is made in Malaysia. The newest mouse—the ADB Mouse II—has a rounded shape with the ball located closer to the front of the assemblage.

Each opto-mechanical mouse operates similarly using light-emitting diodes (LEDs) and light-sensitive transistors, called **phototransistors**, to register the movements of a rubber encased metal ball. A rubber ball touches two capstans, which in turn drive two wheels whose edges are metallically encoded. The encoded wheels are wedged between two photosensors and light sources. When the ball is rolled, the capstans turn the wheels and their ridges interrupt the light. Each break in the light is interpreted by the Mac as an increment of movement. The direction of mouse movement is defined by which photosensor picks up the interrupt first.

- **Optical Mice.** Third-party vendors are offering mice that use lasers and a sensing pad in the place of a rubber ball and wheels to track mouse movements. The light is shown from two sources and reflects off a pad covered with a fine grid of dots. The image of the grid is projected onto two separate photosensors, one senses vertical movement and the other horizontal movement. The reflection of the grid passes over the sensors, allowing circuits within the mouse to count the dots to determine the distance the mouse has moved in either direction.

All types of mice use a single button configuration (although other vendors offer 2-, 3-, and 4-button versions). The button actually is a small switch (called a *microswitch*) that completes a circuit when pressed. The Mac's OS checks the state of the mouse button each time the video circuits finish painting a complete screen image (about 60 times per second). The button is used for selecting (highlighting) and dragging objects on the screen.

M

The mouse and trackball are relative-motion pointing devices. This means that the mouse reports how far it has moved and in which direction, but does not tell the Mac where it is on the desk or mouse pad or on the screen in absolute terms. Although this method is fast, it lacks the precision of absolute-motion pointing devices like **graphics tablets**. Such pen-based devices report the exact location of the stylus relative to the tablet's surface, which is mapped to the Mac's display.

Care and Cleaning Over a period of daily use, the mouse ball picks up dirt particles, making it sticky and unreliable. To avoid this, use a mouse pad. They are inexpensive (often given away as advertising items, such as the one you get from Apple when you register your new Mac) and keep contamination out of the mouse's rolling mechanisms. Mouse pads also provide a more efficient and consistent rolling surface. Choose one with a nice photo or graphic image and it will brighten up your working environment.

But a mouse pad can't keep all dirt out of the roller. Periodically, you need to open the mouse and clean it (see your Apple manual for instructions). You can buy mouse cleaning kits with swabs and fluid at most computer stores, or less expensive Q-Tip™ swabs and alcohol at the drugstore. Cleaning usually requires using a swab or a dust-free cloth to remove dirt and dust from the mouse's internal rolling parts—the wheels, capstans, and ball.

Cordless Mice Another option for pointing and clicking is the cordless mouse. If you are using presentation software, such as Adobe Persuasion or Microsoft PowerPoint, you probably want to move around the room and not be tied to the Mac by the mouse's cable. The cordless mouse uses an infra-red link to an ADB adapter and runs on rechargeable batteries.

See Also

Absolute Versus Relative Motion; Apple Desktop Bus; Graphics Tablets; Keyboard; Pen/Handwriting Devices; Touch Screens; Touchpads; Trackballs

Mouse Control Panel

The settings for your mouse are on this control panel. You can adjust how the **cursor** reacts to the speed you move the mouse, and you can adjust the speed of a **double-click** so that when you double-click the Mac knows it's a double-click and not two single clicks. Apple created this control available because people double-click at different speeds. If you're double-clicking and not getting the desired result, you may have to slow down the Mac's recognition of your double-click, as shown in the following figure.

To use the Mouse Control Panel, follow these steps:

1. Open the Mouse Control Panel from the Control Panels submenu on the Apple menu (or System Folder).

2. Choose the setting that best suits you by clicking the radio buttons. After you make a selection, move the mouse to see if the speed feels right to you.

3. You can also set your double-click speed. Look at the little graphic of the mouse to the left. When you select a radio button, this graphic displays an animation of the double-click speed for each setting.

See Also

Apple Menu; Cursor; Double-Click; Mouse

Cordless Mice

Manufacturer	Model Name	Features	Street Price
Logitech	Cordless MouseMan	Radio-frequency controlled with 4 channels, Opto-mechanical mouse curved to fit the contours of the hand. Right and Left-hand versions	$79.95
Logitech	TrackMan Live	Cordless trackball uses radio frequencies to control the cursor up to 30 feet away from Mac. Three programmable buttons with trackball.	$129.95

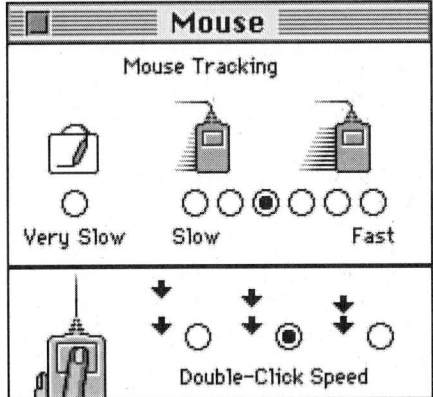

Mouse Keys (Keyboard Shortcut)

If you have the **Easy Access** Control Panel installed, you can activate the **Mouse Keys** feature of Easy Access by pressing ⌘-Shift-Clear. (Clear appears in the **numeric keypad** of your keyboard.)

To activate the Mouse keys feature of Easy Access using a keyboard shortcut, follow these steps:

1. Press the ⌘-Shift-Clear keys to activate Mouse keys.

2. Mouse keys will be activated. To disable Mouse key, press the keyboard shortcut again.

See Also

Control Panels; Easy Access; Keyboard Shortcuts; Mouse; Numeric Keypad

Movie Cleaner Pro

Movie Cleaner Pro and Movie Cleaner Lite (a shareware version of Movie Cleaner Pro) are designed for the serious **QuickTime** movie producer who has to process a lot of clips. Movie Cleaner Pro batch processes movies, and it has several features that are geared toward improving **CD-ROM** playback performance.

The blur option softens edges and reduces video noise in the image, making it possible to achieve better compression rates. Another filter removes random pixel noise, improving compression of sequences with little change in them. You also can interrupt the compression and compare before and after images.

Movie Cleaner attaches a custom color palette to a movie, and you can specify the frame rate. Unlike Adobe's **CD-ROM Movie Maker**, it can not create a color palette and you cannot specify locations for **key frames**.

Movie Cleaner is useful to anyone who has several movies to compress or is looking to get the best performance from their movies. If you already own Adobe **Premiere**, the CD-ROM Movie Maker utility offers most of the features found in Movie Cleaner. The shareware version, Movie Cleaner Lite, can be downloaded from Terran Interactive's Web site.

> Terran Interactive
> Price: $129
> Email: info@terran-int.com
> Phone: (408) 353-8859
> Web: **http://www.terran-int.com**

See Also

CD-ROM Movie Maker; Premiere; QuickTime

Movie Play

A free **QuickTime** movie player. Originally developed as part of CameraMan (a screen capture utility), it is available with Motion Works Multimedia Utilities package, or from several online sites.

It's small, simple to use, and can be used in place of Apple's **MoviePlayer** application (although MoviePlayer offers several extra features that are useful for editing).

> Motion Works International
> 524 Second Street
> San Francisco CA 94107
> Phone: (800) 800-8476 or (415) 541-9333
> Fax: (415) 541-0555

See Also

MoviePlayer; Multimedia; Peter's Player; QuickTime

MoviePak, *See MediaTime*

MoviePlayer

A viewing and editing application, MoviePlayer is available via the **Internet** and the **QuickTime CD-ROM**. MoviePlayer is a very useful utility that not only plays movies but also creates new ones using simple editing techniques.

To create or edit a movie, simply hold the Shift key and drag in the time bar of the movie (see figure). The highlighted section of the bar indicates the area of the movie that has been selected. Choose cut or copy to remove or copy that portion of the movie. Create a new movie or open an existing movie, and then paste the clip.

See Also

Movie Cleaner Pro; Premiere; QuickTime

MovieShop

A **QuickTime** utility developed by Apple, MovieShop has never officially been released (or supported), and while it has not been updated recently, it can still be obtained through Apple's developer program. This utility provides many controls and options when **recompressing** (converting from one QuickTime **compressor** to another) an existing QuickTime movie. Its capability to limit the data rate during compression is not so important now that the **Cinepak** compressor offers a data limitation parameter.

If you need a batch recompression tool, try **Movie CleanerPro** or the **CD-ROM Movie Maker** utility for Adobe **Premiere**.

See Also

Compressor; CD-ROM Movie Maker; Movie CleanerPro; Premiere; Recompression

MovieTrilogy

MovieTrilogy is a shareware collection of **QuickTime** utilities. Although they don't offer the features of commercial programs, they are inexpensive! DeskTopMovie is a movie player application that can read text-track movies if **PlainTalk** is installed. DeskTopText creates QuickTime movies containing scrolling lists of text. DeskTopTV records video on AV Macs. ScreenMovie records what is happening on the Macintosh's screen as a QuickTime movie.

These programs are available online, or send $30 to the author:

Paul Ho
P.O. Box 87042
Village Square Postal Outlet
2942 Finch Ave. East
Scarborough, Ontario, CANADA,
M1W 2T0.

Moving FX

Both Adobe **Premiere** and **After Effects** can be augmented by third party plug-in filters, greatly expanding their uses for computer artists and animators. Gryphon's Dynamic Effects is a series of plug-ins for Premiere, and Final Effects from MetaTools is a plug-in for After Effects.

Dynamic Effects Gryphon Software's Dynamic Effects is an absolute necessity for anyone who works with Adobe Premiere. It adds eighteen separate filters to Premiere's list, and replaces two of Premiere's wipes with better ones (Wipe and Iris are replaced by Smooth Wipe and Smooth Iris). The eighteen effects add image processing tricks based on Gryphon's experience gained with its flagship morphing software, Gryphon **Morph**. The documentation goes through each one, and a tutorial at the back walks users through a process that shows how to layer the filters for specific image processing results. Most of these filters are accompanied by an animated preview screen that allows you to see the effect (and any alterations you make to it) in action on your image or image sequence. Each of these effects has to be explored to be fully appreciated.

Here is the list:

- GDE Channel Delay—Allows you to delay any of the image's color channels (Red, Blue, Green and Alpha).

- GDE Channeler—Allows channel swapping and recombining in a dynamic fashion.

- GDE Color Lookup—Maps a selected palette to a range of pixels. Several sample palettes are included with the software (chrome, fire, spectrum, and zebra).

- GDE Duotone—Forces the image or sequence to become a two-color duotone.

- GDE Dust—Adds dust or speckles to the graphics, making it appear old and worn.

- GDE Dynamic B&C—Creates a smooth transition of brightness/contrast levels.

- GDE Dynamic Solarize—A smooth transition, across the entire clip, between two levels of solarization.

- GDE Dynamic Twirl—Forces an animated twirl on the clip, with user controls for start/end angles, eases, interpolation and circular types, as well as the number of bands (zero to infinity).

- GDE Dynamic ZigZag—Forces a rippling water effect on the clip, with user controls over the parameters.

- GDE Luminance Jitter—Randomly varies the luminance value of each frame, adding to a bad lighted movie effect.

- GDE Mirror—Produces extremely attractive symmetrical animations with user selectable centers of symmetry.

- GDE Offset Jitter—Produces an effect like that of a film off of the sprockets.

- GDE Roll Tiles—Clockwise and counter-clockwise tiling animations.

- GDE Room—Throws the clip into a dynamic 3D room.

- GDE Soft Focus—Animated blurring effect.

- GDE Tempus—Image delays introduced into the animation from data based upon loaded grayscale maps (a library of these come with the software, or you can create and save your own). Indescribable image alterations are the result.

- GDE Threshold—Animated posterization.

- GDE Tunnel—A zooming 3D tunnel effect.

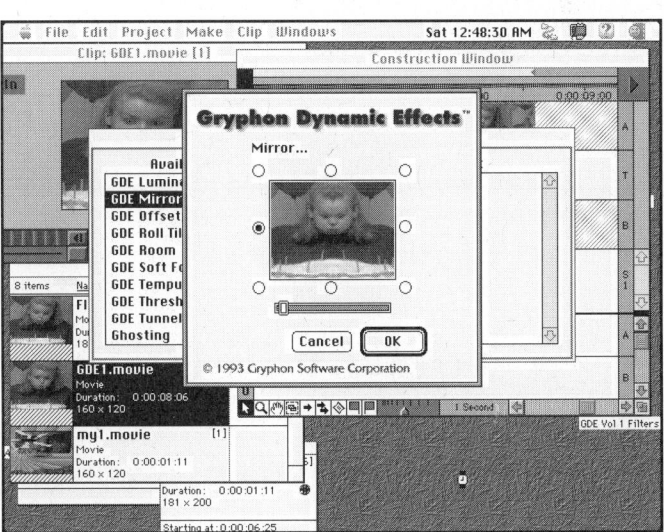

Final Effects MetaTools, known for the quality and variety of its plug-in graphics filters in the **Kai's Power Tools** set for **Photoshop** compatible programs, is also the developer of Final Effects, a set of animation oriented plug-ins for Adobe's After Effects software. These filters add functionality and variety to the already extensive filters that ship with After Effects. As is expected from MetaTools products, these **plug-ins** cover areas that the animator didn't even know existed. All of these effects are customizable according to user input.

They include:

- **Distort Menu:** FE Flow Motion—Produces strange and alluring gravitational effects that pull and funnel the image.

  FE Griddler—Cuts an image up and animates it into square sections.

  FE Lens—Creates infinite lens distortion animations.

  FE Slant—Dynamic tilts of the image horizontally.

  FE Slant Matte—Creates drop shadows for the image.

  FE Tiler—Tiles the image over the screen.

  FE Color Offset—Rotates the value of each RGB color channel.

- **Image Control Menu:** FE Threshold—Creates masked areas for non-alpha channeled images from Luminance (brightness) signals.

  FE Threshold RGB—Creates masked areas for non-alpha channeled images from RGB (color) signals.

- **Light Menu:** FE Lightburst—Places a burst of light on the image, usually targeted to its alpha channel.

- **Particle Menu:** FE Ball Action—Transforms the image into sizable balls, rather like academic molecular models.

  FE Bubble—Creates a bubbling effect in the chosen layer.

FE Particle Systems—A full blown particle system that creates evolving particles of user designed shape and density over time. Listed choices include Explosive, Sideways, Fire, Bonfire, Twirl, Fountain, Viscous, Scatterize, Sparkle, Vortexy, Rain Drops, Starlight, Smokish, Bubbly, Bally, Watery Drops, and Experimental (spheres fading towards edges). The documentation has dozens of examples and graphics. This filter is reason enough for any serious digital artist and animator to purchase both After Effects and Final Effects. Consider that any of these effects can be applied to any targeted 3D animation.

FE Particle Systems LE—A simplified version of the full blown particle systems, because the control parameters are fewer. The effects include some filters not included in the higher version however: Fractal Explosion, Jet, Jet Sides, Firefly, and 2E Experimental (like dust blowing up from the ground).

FE Pixel Poly—Breaks the targeted layer into polygons.

FE Rain—Creates a very realistic rain-like effect.

FE Snow—Creates a very realistic snow-like effect.

FE Starburst—Creates a very realistic starburst effect.

- **Perspective Menu:** FE Sphere—Wraps the intended graphic on a controllable sphere.

- **Stylize Menu:** FE Kaleida—Used to make animated kaleidoscopic graphics. Lots of fun!

  FE Page Turn—Uses one graphic to reveal another by turning its edge over.

  FE Scatterize—Scatters the pixels of the graphic over time, as if they were turning to sand and dispersing in the wind.

- **Transition Menu:** FE Image Wipe—Uses one image to wipe-reveal another.

FE Radial Scale Wipe—A radial wipe with folding edges used to reveal another image below.

FE Scale Wipe—Stretches one image to reveal another.

FE Twister—Twists and contorts the target image.

■ **Channel Menu:** FE Composite—Allows you to composite two images on a single layer, controlling the opacity of each.

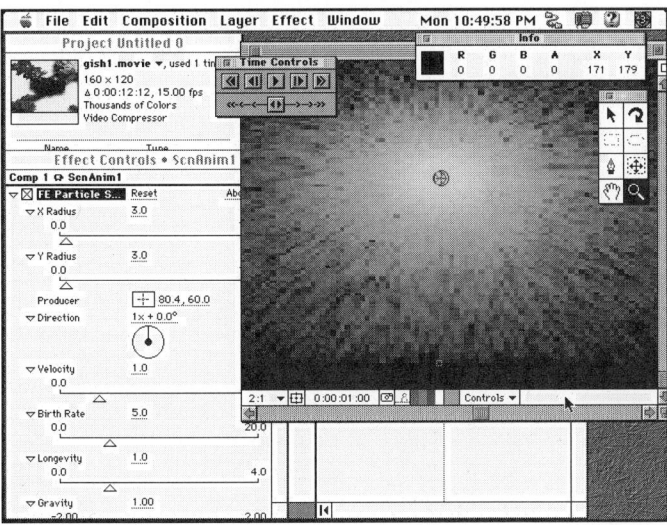

MPack

A freeware application for the Mac by John Myers and Chris Newman that encodes and decodes **MIME** attachments, files other than text documents that can be attached to **electronic mail** messages sent on the **Internet**.

MIME attachments may include graphics or other multimedia files. They must be downloaded and read by an email client that supports MIME, such as **Netscape** or Eudora.

Sometimes, however, MIME email files cannot be opened by an email reader. In that case, simply open MPack, choose Decode from the File menu, and navigate to the files you want to open. You will then be asked to specify a location for the documents.

MPack can be downloaded from the Internet at **http://wwwhost.ots.utexas.edu/mac/pub-mac-compression. html.**

See Also

Email; Internet; MIME; Netscape Navigator

MPEG

MPEG (Motion Picture Experts Group) is a compression format that is the motion video equivalent of **JPEG**. MPEG works well with video sequences and has been adopted for a wide range of hardware. Unfortunately, MPEG is highly **asymmetrical**. It takes a lot of processing horsepower to compress an MPEG sequence. For full screen playback, you need special MPEG hardware.

QuickTime supports MPEG, although it does not currently include MPEG compression routines. Software decompression for Power Macintosh models is available in QuickTime 2.5

Note that there are several MPEG standards (MPEG, MPEG2, and MPEG3). These are generally backward compatible. MPEG has not yet gained wide acceptance, because specialized hardware is required to create MPEG movies.

See Also

Asymmetrical Compressors; Compressor; Drop Frames; Spatial Compression; Symmetrical Compressors; Temporal Compression

MPTA, *See Macintosh Programmer's Toolbox Assistant*

MPW

Apple's primary **development environment** for Macintosh programming. MPW, an acronym for

Macintosh Programmer's Workshop, is a powerful command-line-based environment that hosts a vast number of **compile**rs and other tools.

The MPW environment is similar in many ways to a traditional UNIX development environment. Individual development tools, such as compilers and **linkers**, are run from a command line or by using scripts. Compilation and linking are governed by makefiles, which specify the relationships among source and object files.

Although this sort of environment has a long learning curve and is poorly suited to small projects, for larger projects with many separate parts, it's tough to beat. It's not unusual for MPW users to build all the various parts of a complex project by issuing a single command. For example, a large project may include 68K, Power Mac, and "fat" versions of an application, an Extension or Control Panel, and one or more special code resources to define custom controls or menu styles within the program. Using an **IDE**, such an undertaking would generally require several separate project files that would all have to be brought up to date, compiled, and linked. With MPW, everything can be controlled by a single makefile. This gap is closing, however, and many Mac IDEs now provide extensive **scripting** support, so that you can use **AppleScript** or **Frontier** to accomplish the same things as a makefile would in MPW.

MPW is extremely customizable. You can write complex and powerful scripts, modify or add to its menus, and attach scripts to keyboard commands.

Many third-party compilers and development tools are available for the MPW environment. Metrowerks **CodeWarrior** includes MPW versions of its **C/C++** compilers in addition to its own IDE versions. In addition, many compilers are available exclusively as MPW tools. The Motorola C/C++ and **FORTRAN** compilers fall into this category.

MPW and Apple's MPW-based tools are available from Apple in two forms: MPW Pro and E.T.O. (Essentials, Tools, Objects), both of which are distributed on CD-ROM only. MPW Pro includes the MPW environment, assemblers and C/C++ compilers for both 68K and Power Macintosh, the Macintosh Debugger, **ResEdit** and **MacsBug**, the **MacApp** framework, and the **Macintosh Programmer's Toolbox Assistant**.

E.T.O. is Apple's deluxe collection of developer tools. In addition to everything included in MPW Pro, E.T.O. includes **Symantec C++**, an electronic version of **Inside Macintosh**, and a slew of useful utilities and prerelease versions of upcoming development tools. Unlike MPW Pro, E.T.O. is sold as a subscription; your purchase price buys two updates in addition to the initial versions you receive when you buy.

Note that most third-party compilers that rely on MPW also include a copy of the MPW environment, although they generally do not include the full complement of tools supplied with MPW Pro or E.T.O.

See Also

C; C++; CodeWarrior; Compiler; Integrated Development Environment; Inside Macintosh; MacApp; Macintosh Programmer's Toolbox Assistant; MacsBug; ResEdit; Scripting; Symantec C++

MrC

MrC (pronounced "Mister C") is Apple's highly-optimized **C/C++ compiler** for the Power Macintosh. MrC is available as an **MPW** compiler, or as a plug-in compiler for the **Symantec C++** and Metrowerks **CodeWarrior IDE**s. The C++ version is sometimes called MrC++.

See Also

C; C++; CodeWarrior; Integrated Development Environment; MPW; Symantec C++

MTBF

MTBF stands for Mean Time Between Failures. It is the average time it takes for a product to fail (to cease normal operations). Commonly quoted for hard disks, it is derived from a statistical analysis of product testing commonly done in the manufacturer's facilities.

MTBF and the related measure, **MTTR** (Mean Time to Repair), are both defined officially by the **ISO** and **IEC**. A further measure, **MTTSR** (Mean Time to Service Restoral) is not. This latter measure is, however, a useful means of calculating the real running cost of any given device.

See Also
MTTR; MTTSR

mTropolis

mTropolis is a multimedia authoring program that can create cross-platform titles. Editing must be performed on a Macintosh, but players for Macintosh and Windows are provided. Like the authoring tools **HyperCard** and **SuperCard**, and unlike Macromedia's **Director**, mTropolis takes an object-oriented approach to project development. In **object-oriented programming**, objects inherit properties from other objects. For example, if highlighting is a property attached to a parent button, that property works in other buttons that are attached to the parent button; they inherit the highlighting property from the parent.

Object-oriented programming can be very powerful when creating complex interactions (it can eliminate a lot of duplication of work), but because it is also a very different way of thinking from traditional programming, it can take some time to learn.

Projects in mTropolis are broken down into sections that contain scenes. A scene is what appears on-screen. Media elements are added to a scene by drawing a frame, using the Rectangle tool, and then linking an object, such as a **QuickTime** movie, to that frame. These elements can be shared across multiple scenes.

Many actions can be added in mTropolis simply by attaching a modifier to a button. To trigger a sound when a button is clicked, for example, a sound modifier is attached to that button. Multiple modifiers can be attached to the same object. A dialog box enables you to specify the parameters for the modifier. Some of these are quite complex, including collision detection and path-based animation. mTropolis includes a proprietary cel-animation format called mToons and a utility called MovieTrax that creates and edits multiple track QuickTime movies.

For situations that require more complex behaviors, mTropolis includes a simple scripting language called MiniScript, and programmers can write external routines similar to HyperCard **XCMD**s. This, however, requires a level of programming and development sophistication even many professional developers will lack.

Unlike the competing tools (Director, SuperCard and HyperCard) completed projects are distributed as documents along with a Player. mTropolis does not create a combination document and player file.

Documentation of the first release is rather limited, but a CD containing examples is included.

With its high price compared to its primary competitor Macromedia Director, mTropolis is intended only for the professional multimedia developer. For large complex projects mTropolis could pay for itself; not only is Director complicated by its non-object oriented methodology and its animation orientation, it is almost impossible for several people to work on the same movie at the same time. But expect to spend some time becoming familiar with mTropolis, particularly if you have never worked with object-oriented programming techniques.

System requirements are: Macintosh 68020, System 7.x, at least 5MB for the application when authoring, and 2MB for the player. Under Windows: 486SX/25 or better, 8-bit color and at least 2MB of application RAM.

> mFactory Inc.
> 1440 Chapin Avenue, Suite #200
> Burlingame, CA 94010
> Price: $4,995
> Fax: (415) 548-9249
> Phone: (415) 548-0600
> Web: **http://www.mfactory.com**

See Also
Director; HyperCard; SuperCard

MTTR

MTTR stands for Mean Time to Repair. It is the sum of all time taken to repair a failed device in a given period divided by the number of times the unit fails in the same period.

MTTR does not include maintenance, fault detection and diagnosis, or down-time. It is a measure of the average time taken to bring a device back to service after repairs have begun.

MTTR and the related measure, **MTBF** (Mean Time Between Failures), are both defined officially by the ISO and IEC. A further measure, **MTTSR** (Mean Time to Service Restoral) is not. The latter measure is, however, a useful means of calculating the real running cost of a device.

See Also

MTBF; MTTSR

MTTSR

MTTSR stands for Mean Time to Service Return. It is a measure of the average time it takes to return a failed device to normal functionality. For each failure, the clock starts ticking the moment the device fails and stops only when the device is functioning normally again. It takes into account fault detection, fault diagnosis, down-time, and repair time.

The mean is established by dividing the total time the device is out of service in a given period by the number of times it is out of service in that period.

Although not an officially defined measure of the running cost of any device, it is a very useful one.

See Also

MTBF; MTTR

MTV's Club Dead, *See Adventure Games*

MUDs and MOOs

A text-based, collective forum on the **Internet** that enables groups of people to engage in virtual realities, and often rich fantasies and alter egos, all in real time. Similar to **Internet Relay Chat,** with the addition of the virtual reality element.

MUD stands for *Multi-User Dungeon* or *Multi-User Dimension.* Similar variants are MUSH (Multi-User Simultaneous Hallucination) and MOO (MUD,

Object Oriented). A MOO is a more complex form of MUD that allows an environment containing objects to be described as text.

Although communications in a MUD are text-only, their anonymity promotes creativity and fantasy. Participants can assume alter egos and describe themselves any they want. MUDs and MUSHs were originally created to provide multiplayer **role-playing adventure games**. After you reach a certain level of proficiency, you are allowed to modify the environment in real time. Each environment includes a special vocabulary used to convey gestures, emotions, and actions.

Some business applications of MUDs have been proposed, such as a virtual office space in which coworkers can meet with clients anywhere in the world.

Although MUDs generally run under UNIX, a Macintosh client exists, called MacMud. You can also connect to other UNIX MUDs with a simple MUD client program, MUDDweller. Another client, called Meeting Space, is billed as a virtual conference room.

Multi-User Dungeons for Entertainment Uses Differing from other types of online entertainment, MUDs are strongly linked to Role-Playing Games. MUDs are also similar to text-based adventures like the original Zork titles because all of your commands are typed and, most of the time, the areas are text-based. MUDS, in a nutshell, are spaces on the Internet devoted to creating an entirely immersive role-playing environment. The adventure is not scripted and the experience one has within a MUD differs from individual to individual. Basically, you create a character who suits the theme of the MUD, such as a spy in a MUD devoted to a James Bond theme or a Wizard in a fantasy/medieval area. Then you start wandering around interacting with things. The coolest part is that as you wander, there are other Internet MUD travelers, who you encounter in real time and can talk to, interact with, fight, team up with, and basically chat with, as in any other online chat room, only you need to stay in character and the talk is pure fantasy (not that most chat room conversation is not just that).

To get onto a MUD, you just figure out the **Telnet** address, make sure than you have an Internet account that supports Telnet, and dial in. One problem you might encounter is that not many major online services support Telnet because of its text-only platform, but there are smaller services dedicated to games that all have Telnet access. (**Delphi** is one of the few commercial services that provides full text-based access to the Internet.) Play starts immediately on connection. From there, you create your character and receive your quest which can range anywhere from a simple find command to a more complicated journey that will require an entire team of players to accomplish. To help out beginners, most MUDs offer a help feature, but you really learn by trial and error.

You can drop your character in some and get a few pointers on what you are doing, but many serious players in the more hard-core MUDs may be offended enough to kill you if you bring the real world into their fantasy. Many problems have arisen over gangs that take over certain MUDs and kill whoever comes unknowingly into their territory. As you travel, just make sure to bone up on the specific etiquette of the area you are in and, if you are beginner, try not to offend anybody.

If you do die, you can usually come back to life, but you'll lose all your equipment, weapons, and a healthy chunk of your experience points, which, as you know if you are familiar at all with Dungeons & Dragons and role playing, can be devastating.

MUDs tend to change addresses quickly, without notice, but there are some comprehensive lists on the net to show you where to go. Try checking out **http://www.interplay.com/mudlist** to find out if there's anything out there for you.

See Also
Internet; Internet, Services; IRC; Network Gaming; Online Games

Multifunction Drives and Jukeboxes

CD-ROM drives that do double duty as **Magneto-Optical** readers.

Multimedia

Strictly speaking, the term *multimedia* is used to define any presentation or production involving more than one media type. In practice, multimedia is usually taken to mean something that includes **animation**, **sound**, **video,** or **interactivity**—using just text and graphics is called **desktop publishing**.

What multimedia means to you depends upon what you want to do with multimedia. If it means playing games and entertainment titles, you don't have to do much at all. Most Macintosh systems today come well equipped to play back any entertainment title available. You might need to install new software, like the latest version of **QuickTime**, or a new technology like **QuickDraw 3D**, but otherwise you will not have to do too much to your hardware. If you have the money, faster **CD-ROM** drives (you can get 6x speed drives) make the playback of these titles even smoother, and consider buying external **speakers** to drastically improve the quality of audio playback.

If you are interested in multimedia authoring, there is a lot to cover. In addition to basic **graphics** skills, you need to learn about **sound** software and hardware, as well as **3D** software before you even get to Multimedia Authoring. If you need digital video, read about QuickTime and **video digitizing** as well.

M

There are a wide variety of tools available for creating multimedia presentations, from simple interactive presentation tools, such as **Special Delivery**, Apple **Media Tool**, and **Astound!**, to the more complicated and sophisticated authoring tools, such as **Director**, **HyperCard**, **SuperCard**, **mTropolis**, Media Objects, and Authorware.

Conversation with Don Norman

Don Norman brought the discoveries of cognitive psychology to computers, showing us all *The Design of Everyday Things*, as he put in the title of his book, and explaining to designers what does and does not work for an ordinary user. Norman is head of the Advanced Technology Group at Apple, in charge of polishing the interface and improving the power of new operating systems such as Copland.

Maclopedia: What were your first impressions of the Mac?

Don: My first impressions were of disappointment. I had already experienced better. I was a professor at the University of California, San Diego: I had seen, owned, or worked with superior graphic user interfaces, including Sun computers, Symbolics LISP machines, the Xerox PARC Alto, and even the Apple Lisa. The Mac was small, quaint, and impoverished compared to these other machines. Of course, it was also considerably cheaper, for it was aimed at the home marketplace, whereas the others were not, but nonetheless, to a professional, it was a letdown.

Now, this being said, it wasn't too long before my own personal machine was a Mac. I went off for a sabbatical in England carrying a Mac Plus and used the machine extensively. (That's when I wrote the book *The Design of Everyday Things* on that Mac.) DOS machines were unthinkable—they were so poorly configured and so antiquated that it never even entered my mind to consider them. Yes, I was disappointed in the Mac, but in many ways, this followed Alan Kay's pronouncement of it: "The Mac is the first machine good enough to be worth criticizing."

Maclopedia: How did you get involved with the Mac project, first, and what changes did you push for in the design?

Don: I became a consultant to Apple's Advanced Technology Group (ATG). It never occurred to me then that I might some day not only be a member of ATG, but the head. As a consultant to ATG, I worked with a number of people—all of whom still at Apple on projects such as learning. I interacted a lot with Joy Mountford's Human Interface Group—HIG is what they called themselves. And I issued pronouncements now and then about the state of the art. I didn't really get involved in design until I officially joined Apple in 1993. Since that time I have pushed for many changes. In my opinion, the machines from all manufacturers have simply become too complex. It is time for a return to the simplicity and elegance of the Mac Plus. We need systems that are easy to learn, that do the task we need and that do not require so much time and effort to learn, to configure, and to upgrade. Things like the operating system ought to be invisible to the everyday user. It is time for a change—a large change.

Maclopedia: Looking at the best of the Mac and Windows 95 products, what are some examples of the way the Mac is still in the lead, as far as interface goes?

Don: The Mac was designed for ease of use from the bottom up. This makes a difference. When one adds new equipment—a modem, or another hard drive, or a CD-ROM—it is truly "plug and play." Just plug it in and use it. My friends keep asking me about settings and drivers and I keep saying "what?" Mac users do not have to worry about them.

I have two displays on my computers, one which is mostly used for desktop management (directories and the like) and the other for my work. It is painless to move files and windows from one screen to the other: This ability is built into the OS. Not so with Windows. AppleTalk makes home and school networks effortless. Buy some cables, plug the computers into one another, and boom, you are networked. I have done it in airports, passing files to a passing friend. Try that with Windows!

It is painless to move files and windows from one screen to the other...I have done it in airports, passing files to a passing friend. Try that with Windows!

Connecting to remote networks is easy. I dial my office from my home (or while on trips across the world), and am connected to the Apple engineering network, where I have complete access to my files, to my mail systems, and even to my printers. If I want to print a document on my assistant's desk, I can do so, even if I am 3,000 miles away. It just takes a phone call.

AppleScript means that applications pass information from one to another. Again, an Apple exclusive. The list of superior aspects is actually quite large. Alas, the one point that Apple fails is marketing and advertising. Nobody seems to know about the good points.

The next operating system, code-named Copland, brings some other major advances, especially in information management. Watch for it.

Maclopedia: Do you get time to do any more writing and teaching these days?

Don: I teach classes as guest lecturer now and then. I think I will have done four lectures in classes this year. I don't have time to do a whole course; I travel too much to be available on a regular schedule.

Maclopedia: How have your former colleagues in the universities reacted to your books and your work for Apple?

Don: Quite well. In fact, after I joined Apple, I seemed to be in greater demand among my university colleagues. I get frequent requests to give talks at universities or to visit. And I am on the advisory boards of five different universities [in three countries].

Maclopedia: What new directions do you foresee under Apple's new CEO, Gilbert Amelio?

Don: Dr. Amelio has already taken charge at Apple and instituted a number of changes. He is leading us to a new, more powerful, more focused Apple. I am very optimistic about our future.

The simple interactive presentation tools enable you to create a presentation containing graphics, QuickTime, and audio by simply clicking and dragging objects into position. You can create buttons that cause the presentation to jump from screen to screen, but you are usually limited in the level of sophistication, because the programs don't have any **scripting** language. These kind of tools are great for many applications and are generally easy to learn.

The more sophisticated authoring tools add scripting or some very complex sets of options to make it possible to test user input, perform mathematical calculations, and generally add any feature you can imagine. But this flexibility often comes at the expense of ease-of-use. Expect to spend much more time learning how to use these tools.

Which program you should choose depends upon a large number of variables, including the kind of presentation you want to create, whether you need cross-platform compatibility (play on Macintosh and Windows systems), and how much money you can spend.

Although there are a lot of tools, and each has strengths and weaknesses, don't think that you have to learn everyone. this is particularly true of the authoring tools. Learn one of these tools well and you should be able to create just about any project you need.

Finally, some new software technologies (specifically, QuickDraw 3D and **OpenDoc**) are appearing first on the Power Macintosh. These new technologies make some very exciting new tools possible, although these are only just now starting to appear.

For More

Bibliography

For more information, refer to:

The Macintosh Multimedia Starter Kit, Michael D. Murie, published by Hayden Books (1-56830-113-8). Provides an introduction to multimedia and how to author multimedia productions.

Desktop Video Studio, Andrew Soderberg and Tom Hudson, published by Random House Electronic Publishing. Primer on creation and processing of digital video.

How to Digitize Video, John Wiley & Sons Guide to hardware and software for video capture and compression.

Multimedia Demystified, A Guide to the World of Multimedia and Apple Computer, Inc. Apple Computer, Inc., published by Random House Electronic Publishing. A comprehensive look at the markets, media, and organizations making up the multimedia industry.

3-D Starter Kit for Macintosh, Sean Wagstaff, published by Hayden Books. Introduction and guide to 3-D graphics.

Apple CD-ROM Handbook—A Guide to Planning, Creating and Producing a CD-ROM, Apple Computer, Inc., published by Addison-Wesley Publishing Company. Covers production of CD-ROMs step-by-step. Covers planning, production, legal, and financial considerations.

Multimedia on the Internet

Just as the Macintosh is especially well suited to presenting multimedia on the desktop or in the boardroom, the Mac also excels at presenting multimedia on the **Internet**.

The growing popularity and commercial use of the **World Wide Web**, the graphical **Internet service**, means that increasingly sophisticated applications for presenting sound, video, animation and other multimedia are appearing online.

Although some multimedia on the Internet is presented by stand-alone applications such as **SoundMachine**, others are played by plug-ins that work with **Web browser**s such as **Netscape Navigator**.

Sound on the Internet Sound on the Internet can be presented in formats such as **AIFF** (Audio Interchange File Format), **MPEG** (Motion Picture Experts Group), or **.AU**. Some System 7 sounds might also be found on the Net.

The following table shows the common file formats listed with their sizes, benefits, and drawbacks.

To play sound files you download from the Internet, you need **helper applications** like SoundApp, Sound Machine, or MPEG/CD and MPEG Audio for PowerPC. MIDI files downloaded from the Web need to be processed by an application like **AllMIDI**.

Audio File Formats

Format	Platforms	Size	Benefits	Drawbacks
System 7 sound	Mac	Small; not able to compress	Click and Play simplicity, can be used as system sound	Mac only
AIFF	Windows/PC, Mac, UNIX, Amiga	Varies; not able to compress	Wide compatibility	High quality sound equals huge sound file
MPEG	Mac, Windows/PC, UNIX	Small size relative to sound quality; compressible	Excellent sound quality	Agonizingly slow, no good Mac player (yet)
AU	UNIX, Windows/PC, Mac	Varies; not able to compress	Wide compatibility	Many slight variations in format

Another kind of sound file is presented by **RealAudio**. RealAudio files use streaming, that is, they are played by RealAudio as the file is downloaded. To play them, you can use the RealAudio Player application or a RealAudio plug-in that processes the files while you are still in the Netscape Navigator window.

Video on the Internet Many sites on the Web serve video files. Most are in **QuickTime** format, which is native to the Mac, but you might also find files in MPEG format.

QuickTime movies can be played with the QuickTime extension and **Movie Player** applications included with System 7.1 and later operating systems. (Simple Player, also by Apple and with controls identical to Movie Player's has also been widely distributed.) A QuickTime plug-in for Netscape Navigator was still being eagerly awaited as this was written.)

Apple's QuickTime VR Player is an exciting Internet application that plays both regular QuickTime movies and VR movies. VR moves are *visual representations* of scenes where in you can pan around a full 360 degrees by clicking and dragging.

MPEG videos downloaded from the Web can be played with the application Sparkle, which also plays QuickTime clips.

Multimedia, Animation A number of ways are being developed to being animation to the World Wide Web. Like many complex graphical elements presented over the Internet, however, their performance is limited by bandwidth, the capacity of the viewer's Internet connection to transmit data. Many users with slow dial-up modem connections have to wait agonizingly long to see a **Shockwave** animation or **Java applet**, for instance.

Shockwave is a plug-in for Netscape Navigator that allows animations created with Macromedia Director to be played within the Netscape browser window.

Netscape version 2.0 now supports the display of Java applets, small computer programs that use the Netscape window as a virtual computer. Some simple animation effects can also be created with **JavaScript,** Netscape's version of the Java programming language. **Roaster** is an application that also plays and creates Java applets.

Multipart GIF89a images, also supported by Netscape Navigator, are GIF images that consist of several separate frames or images. The series of images, when played together as a **multipart GIF,** provides simple animation on a **Web page** displayed by Netscape.

M

A number of virtual reality applications and plug-ins using **VRML** (Virtual Reality Markup Language) were beginning to appear as this was written, several being developed for the MacOS

As the Web grows more popular, more complex multimedia elements will appear on Web pages and continue to challenge the limitations of speed and bandwidth faced by many users without fast direct connections to the Internet.

See Also

AIFF; AllMIDI; .AU; Helper Applications; Internet; Internet Services; Java; Modem; MPEG; Multipart GIF Image; Plug-Ins; RealAudio; Shockwave; SoundMachine; VRML; Web Browser; Web Page; World Wide Web

Multimedia Monitors

The newest type of displays are multimedia monitors, which include built-in stereo speakers and often a built-in microphone. Most multimedia monitors have 17-inch screens and support multiple picture **resolutions**. You can get better sound with separate speakers, but the built-in speakers take up less space and require fewer cables. Instead of a separate cable for left and right speakers, as well as a speaker power cable, you have a single cable from the Mac's sound out port to the monitor.

Multimedia monitors are best suited for home computers, where the neatness factor of fewer cables and less space are more valuable. Multimedia monitors also cost only 5 to 10 percent more than ordinary 17-inch monitors. However, graphics professionals usually want bigger monitors, and audio professionals will probably want higher quality speakers.

The sound quality of multimedia speakers varies quite a bit from one manufacturer to the next. Speakers that face down or to the back won't sound as good as those mounted on the front of the monitor facing the user. It's also good to ask about the power rating of the speakers. The higher the power rating, the better the speakers are likely to sound.

Speakers that look like they were glued onto a monitor usually don't produce good sound. Sound caverns inside the case help create deeper, richer sounds, particularly in the bass frequencies. The AppleVision 1710AV probably has better sound than any multimedia monitor on the market because of its internal air channels. The following figure shows the Apple AudioVision.

Another feature to look for is easy-accessible monitor and volume controls. Separate bass and treble controls are desirable but not found on all monitors. Another handy feature is a front-facing headphone port and a separate headphone volume control.

See Also

Cables and Adapters for Monitors; Energy-Star Monitor Issues; Monitors; Monitors, Common Models; Monitors, Image Quality; Monitors, Size of; Multisync Monitors; Portrait and Pivoting Monitors

Multimedia Speakers, *See* *Speakers*

Multipart GIF Image

A multipart GIF image is a type of graphic image that appears to be animated when displayed on the **World Wide Web** by the **Web browser Netscape Navigator** 2.0.

GIF (Graphic Interchange Format) is a type of image compression widely used to present inline or external images on **Web pages**. One variety of GIF image, called GIF89, allows one color in its palette to be designated as "transparent," thus allowing the image to seem to "float" on the background of a Web page.

Another feature of GIF89 images is that they can consist of not just one, but multiple images or "frames." Such a series is called a multipart GIF image.

A Web browser that supports "looping" of multipart GIF images plays all of the frames over and over again. If the frames have been arranged to simulate motion, the multipart GIF image will appear to be animated.

Multipart GIFs present a number of advantages to Web page designers: they provide simple animation effects without complicated programming. No **plug-ins** or additional software are needed to create the animation effect.

At this writing (February 1996) only Netscape 2.0 supports multipart GIF images, although other browsers are likely to follow suit.

For more information see the following Web site: **http:/ /members.aol.com/royalef/gifanim.htm.**

See Also

GIF; Home Page; Internet; Web Browser; Web Page; World Wide Web

Multipurpose Internet Mail Extensions, *See MIME Type*

Multiscan, *See Multisync Monitors*

Multisession CD

The original **CD-ROM** format was a nonwriteable format. Each CD had an index containing information about the disc: location of the tracks, number of tracks, and so on. With the advent of **writeable CDs,** it became possible to record a single disc, and it also became possible to add information to an existing writeable disc, provided it wasn't already full. But because the disc directory could not be updated (the discs cannot be rewritten) a way of adding extra data to an existing disc had to be invented. This is the multisession disc format.

When new information is added to a writeable CD, a new directory, or index track, is also added. When this is done, the disc becomes a multisession disc (that is, data has been written to it at separate times). A multisession-capable player looks for the other index tracks when it detects a multisession disc. If a multisession CD is used in a CD player that does not recognize multisession discs, the player will recognize only the first session (what was written to the disk the first time). All new CD drives support the multisession format, and if you are using an older drive, it is likely that it is multisession-capable if it is at least a double-speed drive.

One of the first implementations of the multisession format was for the **PhotoCD** system developed by Kodak.

See Also

CD-I; CD-ROM; DVD; PhotoCD; Writeable CD

Multisync Monitors

Multisync monitors give you a choice of the number of **pixels** you want to display on-screen, presented as a picture resolution measured in number of pixels wide by number of pixels high. A typical Mac picture resolution is 640×480 pixels. Some Mac monitors, such as Apple's entry-level 14-inch Macintosh Color Display, have a fixed picture resolution, which means that you can't change it from 640×480. A 14-inch multisync monitor (also called multisynchronous, autosync, or multiscan) gives you a choice of several picture resolutions such as 640×480 and 800×600.

Displaying more pixels on-screen gives you a bigger desktop but shrinks the images. For instance, 640×480 pixels on a 13- or 14-inch monitor works out to display 72 dots per inch (dpi), which is known as

WYSIWYG (pronounced "Wizzy Wig") display, or "What-You-See-Is-What-You-Get." You can tell you have WYSIWYG when an inch in an application's ruler on your screen actually measures an inch long. At 800×600 pixels on a 14-inch monitor, you no longer have 72 dots per inch, and therefore no longer have WYSIWYG. An inch marked on a ruler would measure less than an inch. This has no effect on the way the file would print, but you do get the benefit of seeing more at one time on your screen. A high picture resolution with a smaller-than-WYSIWYG display comes in handy when you have a lot of tool palettes open, such as in graphics or desktop publishing, or when you need to see an entire document, such as a large spreadsheet.

For a 16-inch or 17-inch multisync monitor, the correct WYSIWYG picture resolution is 832×624 pixels. For a 21-inch monitor, 1152×870 is the WYSIWYG resolution. If you switch to 640×480 pixels on these bigger screens, objects will appear larger than WYSIWYG—an inch on a ruler will measure more than an inch. This is a handy feature if your eyesight is suffering or if you are planning to give a presentation to a room of people sitting farther away.

You change the picture resolution of a multisync monitor in a control panel. In older versions of MacOS, it's the **Monitors control panel**, and in newer version, it's the Monitors & Sound control panel (see the following figure). Most multisync monitors can switch between picture resolutions on-the-fly (without restarting). You can also buy adapters that allow you to select a picture resolution by setting dip-switches on the plug itself—handy if you have a multisync monitor, but no "switch-on-the-fly" software.

The first Mac monitors had fixed picture resolutions, but now even most of Apple's monitors are multisync. However, because multisync monitors can be bought outside the Mac-exclusive sales community, Mac owners looking to buy one can find very good prices in the larger and more competitive PC/Windows market. Often, the multisync model was meant for a PC machine, and will require an in-line or "pass-through" plug adapter to reconfigure the monitor's pinouts to fit the Mac's; check with your vendor for plug adapters that fit your particular brand of monitor. Most computer stores that carry Macintoshes have these inexpensive line adapters.

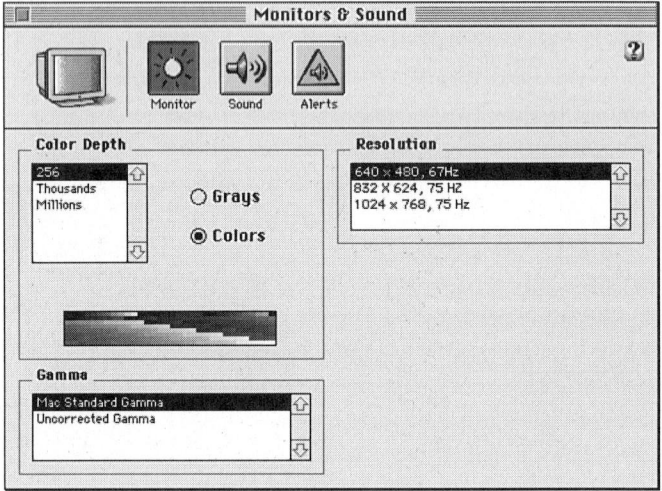

However, just because you can use multisync monitor doesn't necessarily mean you can use it to display the resolutions the monitor supports. For instance, the video circuitry in the old Mac IIci could only display at 640×480 and 640×870 (portrait mode). For these Macs, you'll need to add a video expansion card to take advantage of the multiple resolutions of a multisync monitor. Fortunately, most modern Mac models can display at multiple resolutions. All the Power Macs, as well as Quadra, and PowerBooks with monitor ports can display resolutions up to 1,152×870 pixels. The old PowerBook 100 and the Duo Dock can display at 640×480 and 832×624 pixels.

See Also

Cables and Adapters for Monitors; Energy-Star Monitor Issues; Monitors; Monitors, Common Models; Monitors Control Panel; Monitors, Image Quality; Monitors, Size of; Multimedia Monitors; Portrait and Pivoting Monitors

Multisynchronous, *See Multisync Monitors*

Multitasking

In 1984, when Apple introduced the Macintosh 128K microcomputer, multitasking was the providence of minicomputers and mainframes running such operating systems as UNIX or VM-CMS. Microcomputers performed one task at a time. You had to quit one program before proceeding to the next and there was no way to easily share data between programs. The introduction of the Macintosh changed the way people used computers by offering an operating system that allowed the integration of data from one program with another. With the MultiFinder in System 6, Apple began the process of providing an environment that support full multitasking. With **System 7**, that promise has been fulfilled.

Multitasking is the capability to run several programs simultaneously. The first small programs which could be operated alongside applications on the Macintosh were, and are, called **desk accessories**, or DAs. DAs are tiny utilities such as a **calculator**, calendar, **alarm clock**, **notepad**, or puzzle. DAs were restricted in size to a couple of kilobytes so they could fit into memory alongside the applications. You opened DAs while working in an application by pulling down the **Apple Menu** and highlighting its name with the mouse. At first, DAs would run only if their window was currently active. You switched to the DA window from your application's window when you needed to access, say, the calculator to perform simple calculations. You could exchange data between the DA and your application by using the **Clipboard**, the Macintosh's data exchange file. Thus, you could cut and paste the results of your use the DA into your application. The **Scrapbook**, **Chooser**, and **Control Panel** are all DAs.

As the Macintosh evolved, Apple took the concept of the DA and built from it the concept of working with more than one application at one time. Apple introduced the MultiFinder in System 6 as an optional way of running the Macintosh. The MultiFinder provided a multitasking environment to the Macintosh.

With System 6, DAs could continue to run in the background. New uses for DAs were found, such as Talking Moose and Menu Time, which used the **Finder** to perform background processing.

System 7 revolutionize multitasking, eliminating the memory limitation of DAs. All programs, no matter their use or size, share memory and processing time. DAs are no longer limited to access via the Apple Menu, but like any other program, can be opened and run concurrently via the Application Menu. It is the multitasking features of System 7 that put the greatest burden on the Macintosh hardware.

Like all multitasking systems, System 7 really runs only one program at a time. The illusion of several programs working at once is created by switching between applications so rapidly that it appears that everything is happening at once. The actual goal of multitasking is making use of the various applications' capability to share the systems resources. The difference between types of multitasking lies in the way in which applications pass control from one to another. There are three types of multitasking: context-switching, cooperative, and pre-emptive multitasking.

In context-switching multitasking (also called time-sharing), the resources are moved between programs on a fixed schedule. Even if an active programs doesn't currently need resources, it is provided with them. This method can be very wasteful of processing resources. In cooperative multitasking, each program can request the use of the processing resources, but other applications are not forced to respond to these requests. This method relies on the programmers developing applications that are well-behaved in this type of environment. In pre-emptive multitasking, each program is assigned a priority and can compete for resources. Windows 95 supports pre-emptive multitasking for those programs that have been rewritten to take advantage of the capability. It is also expected to be a key element in the next MacOS, code-named Copland, due later in 1996 or early 1997. Prior to these new developments, only UNIX and mainframe operating systems supported pre-emptive multitasking.

M

System 7.5 Multitasking Methods The Macintosh uses a combination of context-switching and cooperative multitasking methods. If an application requests resources, it is guaranteed a minimum share. Cooperative multitasking is used to perform background operations with programs that are designed to work in this environment. Cooperative multitasking works by giving control of computing resources to a program to use to perform one task or event and relying on that program to turn control over to the next application when the task is accomplished (or a maximum time limit has passed). If an application is not designed to cooperate within this environment, context-switching—putting one application on hold to run a second one—is used to allow you to run even poorly behaved programs. Without this feature, most older DAs would operate only when placed in the foreground and stop when moved to the background.

Neither of these multitasking methods is inherently better than the other. Both are "true" multitasking. However, most modern operating systems are moving away from cooperative multitasking and toward preemptive multitasking.

Although purists often do not accept the Macintosh operating system's claim to a multitasking capability because its multitasking is not preemptive (it does not interrupt on one application's event to perform another application's event), System 7 provides extensive performance enhancements for those programs capable of cooperative multitasking (those which follow the Macintosh System Interface Standards). Even without the added benefit of running other multitasking applications, the System 7 Finder's capabilities for printing, copying, and moving data in the background provide significant advantages without the overhead required for a pre-emptive multitasking system.

The Finder's Role The Finder is the Macintosh's file- and disk-management software. The Finder is a special application program which is initiated when you turn on your Macintosh and always runs in the background to assist you in managing disks, applications, and documents. The Finder performs several important functions which are related to multitasking. Many of these tasks related to the Finder's primary task of file management, but some are specific to enabling System 7 to provide multitasking capabilities.

MacOS 7.5 preemptively multitasks a few low-level processes such as networking, but cooperatively multitasks other processes, such as applications. As a result, if a single application refuses to give up control, either intentionally or because of a crash, no other application can proceed. The next major release of the MacOS, Copland, will provide much greater support for preemptive multitasking of application processes.

A lower level of multitasking is also possible within a single application. This is known as threading. Whenever an application has control of the computer, it executes multiple subprocesses internally. Just as with overall multitasking, threads can be cooperative or preemptive. Threads need not use the same method of multitasking as the system as a whole. For example, an operating system that uses cooperative multitasking can use pre-emptive threads within programs.

See Also
Finder; Memory; System 7.5

Multi-User Dimension, *See MUDs and MOOs*

Multi-User Dungeon, *See MUDs and MOOs*

MUNSELL, *See Color Matching Systems*

MUSHs, *See MUDs and MOOs*

Music Tools for Children, *See Juilliard Music Adventure; Little Kid Music, A; Peter and the Wolf*

Musical Instrument Digital Interface, *See MIDI*

Musicshop

A **MIDI** sequencer that works with any MIDI interface and instrument, Musicshop features a tape-deck like interface, and supports up to 16 MIDI instrument tracks per song. The MIDI information can be edited in either standard music notation or a graphic piano roll style (short and elongated dots represent the note and note duration).

A sequencer can record a performance, and then you can go back and edit the notes by simply clicking and dragging them. After a song is completed, it can be printed because Musicshop includes the Adobe Sonata music font for printing.

> Opcode Systems
> Fax: (415) 856-3332
> Phone: (415) 856-3333
> Web: **http://www.opcode.com**

See Also

MIDI

MYOB

MYOB, which stands for Mind Your Own Business, is an accounting and financial management package geared toward small businesses. It includes general ledger, checkbook, accounts receivable and accounts payable, and inventory modules. It's an ideal program for people who would rather manage their businesses than crunch numbers.

Getting started with MYOB is quite simple. There are seven "command centers:" ledger, checkbook, sales, purchases, payroll, inventory, and card file. Each one gives you access to a particular aspect of running your business. When you start, you'll need to enter information in four of these areas. The first is the General Ledger. You begin by entering your company information. MYOB walks you through the procedure with templates for different types of businesses. There are all kinds of possibilities—from sole proprietorships to retail clothing, restaurants, video stores, crafts stores, medical and law offices, and too many more to list. The figure shows a few of your choices.

After your accounts have been set up, you need to enter starting balances for them, and you'll want to use the card file module to list your clients, your employees, and your suppliers. These names can be entered directly or imported from an existing database. And that's all you have to do, until you buy or sell something. MYOB can generate invoices, purchase orders, checks, shipping labels, 1099s, and practically any kind of form you're likely to need. You can set the program up to use your own preprinted forms and fill in the blanks or to print customized invoices on plain paper.

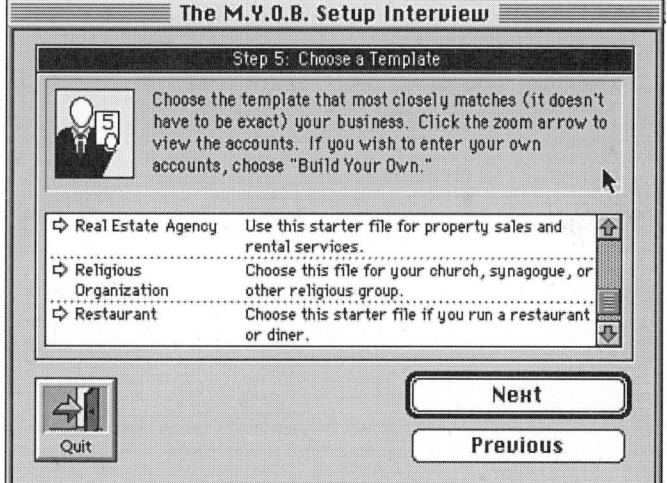

To enter a transaction, open the appropriate command center and select the kind of transaction from the chart. In the figure, it's payday, so you'll use the payroll command center to write paychecks.

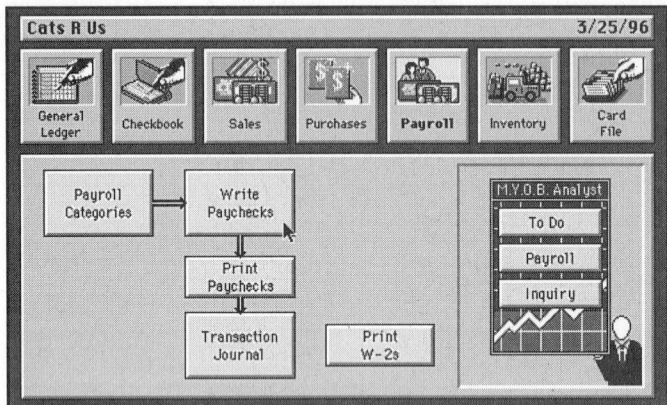

Filling in a paycheck looks much like writing any other kind of check. You've already entered each employee's information in the card file, including where they live and work, and entered their pay information—salary, other income such as tips, commissions, or bonuses, and deductions. In the Write Paycheck window, enter the date and the employee's name. That's all. MYOB looks up the pay information, calculates the salary and deductions, and writes the check, entering the employee's address from the card, and listing all the deductions on the attached voucher, as shown here. Print it, sign it, and you're done. MYOB will track the deductions and remind you when it's time to send in your payroll taxes.

Entering sales and expenses is just as easy. Choose the proper category, enter the amount, and MYOB does the rest. Inventory management is equally simple. Each item you buy, sell, or store, and each service you sell gets an inventory account. With information about each of these things stored in MYOB, you can include them on invoices and purchase orders, keep track of quantities, and analyze your sales and purchasing activity. MYOB keeps a running balance of the number of units on hand and the total dollar value of those units. It computes the average cost of a single item by dividing the total value by the number of units. Whenever you mention the item on a purchase order, it adds the quantity ordered to the existing stock, and when you list it on an invoice, MYOB deletes the number sold from the inventory quantity, and the dollar value of the goods sold from the assets. You can make adjustments to the inventory to account for loss, breakage, or other unforeseen events.

MYOB's main feature is its ease of use. If you have no experience at all with bookkeeping, you can usually manage to set up your accounts in a matter of hours. If you've used a regular ledger or "one-write" system, MYOB will be a very pleasant surprise. The flowchart and tabbed folder interface make it easy for users to intuitively do the right thing, and it's accelerated for PowerMac, so it will respond quickly to your need for information, and will leave you more time to actually run your business.

See Also

Finance Programs; Quicken

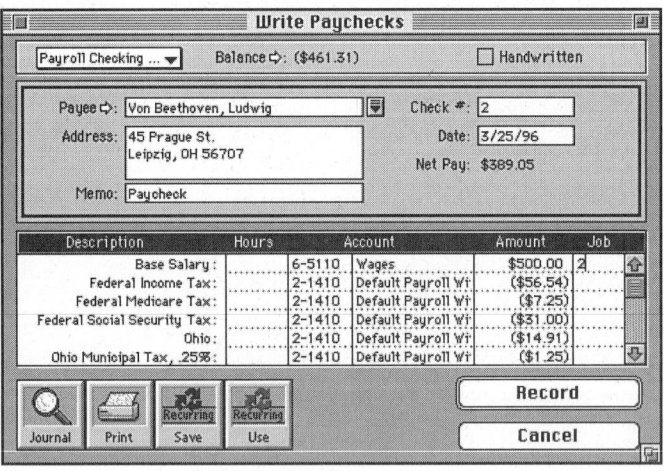

Myst

Myst revolutionized computer games by introducing a compelling, visually stunning game with a twist: there is absolutely no violent content. Myst was one of the first titles to integrate beautiful backgrounds with fluid, rather than jerky, movements through the fantasy environment.

The storyline, created by brothers Rand and Robin Miller, revolves around an abandoned world to which you're suddenly transported. You wander around the island solving brain-boggling puzzles, trying to find out what happened to the former residents and looking for a way to go home. The simple mystery premise combined with engaging tasks has made Myst one of the best-selling games of all time. In addition to spawning numerous many copycat titles, such as Sony's Eastern Mind and the forthcoming Secrets of the Luxor (based on the hotel in Las Vegas) from Mojave. Myst has also generated a hard-cover fiction novel, penned by the Miller brothers. There are even hints at an upcoming film based on the game.

See Also

Daedalus Encounter, The; Full Throttle; Return to Zork; Riddle of Master Lu, The; TimeLapse

M

N

Naming Items

In the Macintosh environment, you can name **files** and **folders** with up to 31 characters using any combination of letters or numbers, spaces, and a variety of punctuation symbols. You can name files at the **desktop** level by **selecting** the name of the file, which **highlights** the name, and typing the new name. You can also name documents when you **save** them in an application.

The advantage of the way the Macintosh enables you to name files and folders is that you can give the file and folders descriptive names that help you locate these files. If, for example, you're using your Macintosh for work-related items, you could have a folder called "customers," and inside that folder you could have a folder for each of your customers. By creating individual customer folders, you can group each customer's files into a central location, making it easy to find a particular file when a customer calls. Naming files is all about organization; there are not steadfast rules for naming files you create, but keep in mind that the easier and more descriptively you name your files, the easier it will be to find them if they are misplaced on your hard disk.

Also, be careful when renaming files that you didn't create. Many applications, for example, have support files that they require, and look for, when launching and running. If you rename files that accompany an application, the application may not be able to locate these files when needed as the application searches for the files by name.

To name a disk or a **hard disk**, **click**, or select, the current name of the disk. This highlights the disk's name, enabling you to type in a new name. You can

also select a disk you want to rename and press **Return**. This highlights the disk's name, enabling you to type a new name.

To name a disk, follow these steps:

1. Click the name of the disk, just below its icon, to highlight the name. You can also highlight the name by selecting the disk and pressing Return.

2. Type a new name for the disk and click outside the disk's icon to make your name change take effect.

Naming a File To name a file, click the name of the file below its icon. This highlights the filename, enabling you to type a new name. You can also select the file you want to rename and press the **Return**.

To name a file, follow these steps:

1. Click the name of the file below its icon to highlight the filename. Or highlight the name by selecting the disk and pressing Return.

2. Type a new name for the file and click outside the file icon to make your name change permanent.

Naming a Folder To name a folder, **click** the name of the folder. This **highlights** the folder's name, enabling you to type a new name. You can also select a folder you want to rename and press Return.

To name a folder follow these steps:

1. Click the name of the folder below the folder's icon to highlight the folder's name. You can also highlight the name by selecting the folder and pressing Return.

2. Type in a new name for the folder and click outside the folder's icon to make your name change permanent.

See Also

Click; Desktop; Hard Disks; Highlight; Return Key; Save Command; Selecting Items

NASA Virus, *See Scores Virus*

Native File Format

If you are working on a document in a word processor like ClarisWorks, you have a host of **file formats** in which to **save** a file, including ASCII, Text Only, Text with Line Breaks, MacWrite, and so on. You can choose to save the file in the application's own format: in this case ClarisWorks. This is the application's native file format. If you know you're going to open your file only in the application that created it, it's okay to save your files in a native file format. However, if you're going to import, or place, your file into another application, you may want to choose a format that is supported by the application into which you're importing the file.

If, for example, you create artwork in Adobe Illustrator and save the file in Illustrator's native file format, you will not be able to place the file into a page layout program such as PageMaker or QuarkXPress because neither of these applications can import a native Illustrator file as native files are designed to be opened by the applications that created them. However, if you saved the file as an **EPS** file, rather than a native Illustrator file, you can import the file into **PageMaker** or **QuarkXPress**, as both programs support the importing of EPS files.

More and more applications are being designed to let you open competing products' native files. Adobe Illustrator, for example, and Macromedia FreeHand are fighting neck and neck in the graphics program market, and both can save in formats that the other applications can open. But in most other cases, native files still have to opened by the applications that created them.

See Also

EPS; File Formats; Saving a File

Native Software

Software recompiled to take advantage of the PowerPC's new reduced instruction set computing (**RISC**) is referred to as native software, because it is native to the **PowerPC processor** (which Power Macs incorporate). Programs originally designed to run on 68000-series Macintosh models, for example, were native to the 68000 series of processors. Much of this software has been recompiled with a new set of reduced instructions that take advantage of the PowerPC chip to run on Power Macs. That software is now native to the Power Macs. Note that the Macintosh operating system at version 7.5.3 does not contain 100% native code.

If you have a Power Mac and run 68000-series software on your Power Mac, that software is being run in **emulation mode**. This enables the Power Mac to emulate a 68000-series computer, and although this software can operate on a Power Mac, it cannot take advantage of the PowerPC chip's speed.

See Also

Emulator; Power Mac; PowerPC Platform; RISC

Natural-Media Tools

The precise, clean nature of much of the artwork created using computers is one of the reasons for using computers in the first place. But it's not the only game in town. **Paint programs** like Fractal Design **Painter** offer digital artists tools that emulate their real-world counterparts: paintbrushes that leave brushstrokes behind, pastels that look dusty, ink that bleeds on the paper. The mathematical algorithms that make these tools work are incredibly complex, but the results are amazing—there are even digital "crayons" that leave extra chunks of "wax" on the page.

See Also

Paint Applications

Navigator, *See Netscape Navigator, CompuServe*

NCAA Championship Basketball, *See Sports Games*

NCSA

Acronym for National Center for Supercomputing Applications, a high-performance computing and communications facility and research center at the University of Illinois at Urbana-Champaign.

NCSA is the birthplace of some of the most widely used **client** software used on the Internet, including NCSA Telnet. **NCSA Mosaic,** the first graphical browser for the **World Wide Web,** was created by Marc Andreessen and fellow students working at NCSA.

NCSA's Virtual Environments Laboratory is also known for its work in advanced virtual reality research.

Home page: **http://www.ncsa.uiuc.edu/**.

See Also

Andreessen, Marc; Internet; NCSA Mosaic; Telnet; Web Browser; World Wide Web

NCSA Mosaic

The first graphical **client** or **browser** for the **World Wide Web**, developed in 1993 at the University of Illinois by **Marc Andreessen** and the team that went on to create **Netscape Navigator**.

Far from being an antique, NCSA Mosaic is still being upgraded and supported by the National Center for Supercomputing Applications at the University of Illinois. Version 2.0.1, which was current as this was being written, supports many **HTML** 3.0 tags as well as inline **JPEG** images (see the following figure).

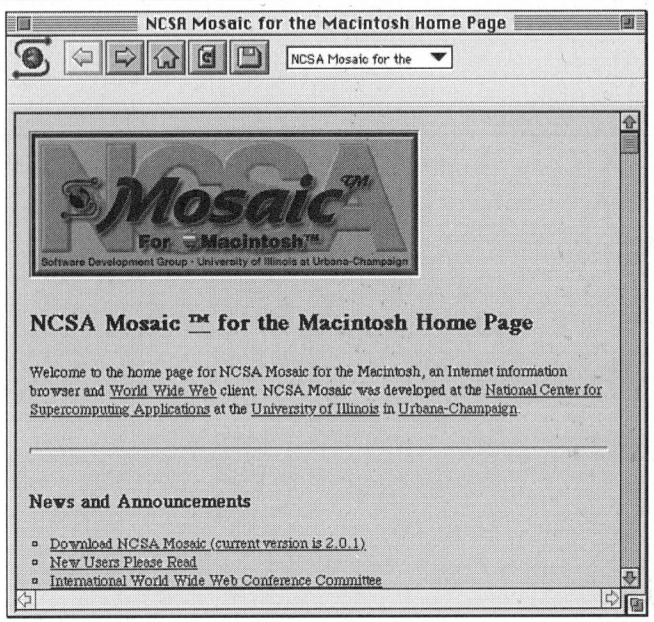

In addition, the University of Illinois granted a "master license" to Spyglass, which offers the software to be bundled with other software or hardware in volumes of 10,000 or more. Mosaic is built into several companies' browsers, including **CompuServe.**

Mosaic has a few features that its more popular rival Netscape lacks, such as the capability for users to construct custom menus with frequently visited URLs and other commands. Some menu items controlling default home pages can be configured quickly without having to scroll through Preferences windows, as in Netscape.

Mosaic's drawback is its lack of speed. Netscape's capability to perform multithreading and to work with cache files makes it run significantly faster even as the Netscape Navigator software becomes more complex.

Home page: **http://www.ncsa.uiuc.edu/SDG/Software/ MacMosaic/MacMosaicHome.html**.

See Also

Andreessen, Marc; Netscape Navigator; Server; Web Browser; World Wide Web

NEC MultiSync 4FGe 15-Inch Color Display, *See Monitors, Common Models*

NEC MultiSync XE17, *See Monitors, Common Models*

NEC MultiSync XE21, *See Monitors, Common Models*

Negotiation, Modems

Modems can only communicate with other modems when using speed, correction, and compression **protocols** that they share. At the beginning of each new communications session, modems must go through the negotiation process to find a set of matching protocols available to both modems. The process is sometimes incorrectly called handshaking. **Handshaking** more correctly refers to the flow control process that tells one computer to send, or to stop sending, data to another.

Negotiation involves the two computers, host and guest, reviewing the possible speeds each has and mutually agreeing on which to use, and making sure that they also agree on the number of bits in each byte of data exchanged, how the bytes are defined, and what parity checking, if any, they'll use. It is as if you answered your telephone and said, "Hello." The person calling replies, "God dåg."But you don't speak Swedish, so you might try, "Bon jour?" She replies, "Hola?" Ah, Spanish, you can recognize that. "Hola!" you say, and the conversation continues.

Just as two people might start with the language they're best at, modems try first to connect at the fastest speeds they have available. If they don't succeed, they try the next lower rate, and the next, until they find one that works for both. If the line is noisy, or you keep getting disconnected, set the modem to a lower starting speed. For instance, if communicating at 14.4 is unstable, reset your modem so 9600 is its top speed. Slower communications are more stable.

TIP Sometimes the process of negotiation presents so many options that the two modems get confused and fail to find any matching protocols, even though several do exist. If you have trouble getting a connecting between two particular modems, check your modem manuals for ways to disable automatic negotiation so that you can preset a particular speed, correction, and/or compression protocol.

Nested Folder

A **folder** that resides within another folder is referred to as a nested folder. If you view a folder's contents in a **list view**, you can see any nested folders by **clicking** the triangle to the left of the nested folder's name. The contents of the nested folder are displayed, including any folders nested within it, as shown in the following figure. By viewing nested folders in this fashion, you can move to any item within a folder without having to open the folder. This can be a big time-saver when you're viewing a window with many files and folders.

Although the capability to place one folder inside another folder is of great benefit once you understand how it works, it can be very confusing for new users. It might help if you try to think of it like a traditional file cabinet. In a real file cabinet, you could have a folder in the file drawer, let's name it "customers," and inside that folder you could put a file folder for each customer you have. This way, anytime you need to get to a customer file, you go to your file cabinet and look through the folder marked "customers" to find the file. You can do the exact same thing in the Macintosh environment. Putting folders inside folders helps you stay organized.

Imagine if you had 500 customers and each customer had 5 to 15 files each. If you put them in one big folder, you'd have thousands of files, and it would be really hard and time consuming, to find which files belong to which customer. To keep yourself organized, you'd need to group these files by customer, so each customer's 5 to 15 files would be in one folder with the client's name on it. And where would that folder be? In your "customers" folder.

See Also
Click

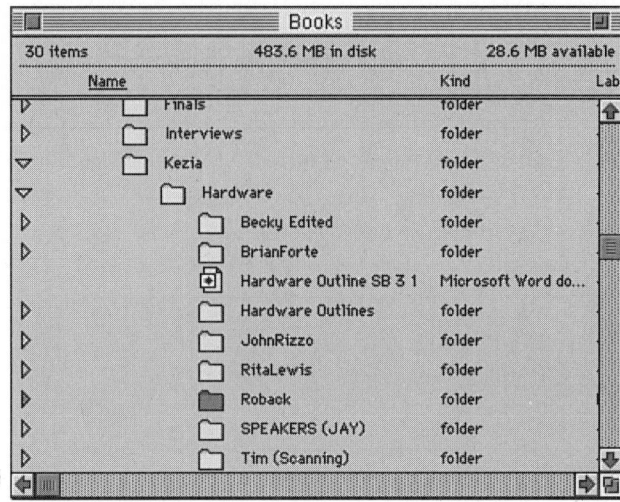

Books		
30 items	483.6 MB in disk	28.6 MB available
Name	**Kind**	**Lab**
▷ Finals	folder	
▷ Interviews	folder	
▽ Kezia	folder	
▽ Hardware	folder	
▷ Becky Edited	folder	
▷ BrianForte	folder	
Hardware Outline SB 3 1	Microsoft Word do...	
▷ Hardware Outlines	folder	
▷ JohnRizzo	folder	
▷ RitaLewis	folder	
▷ Roback	folder	
▷ SPEAKERS (JAY)	folder	
▷ Tim (Scanning)	folder	

Nesting, *See Formula*

Net, The, *See Internet*

Netfind

A simple search utility for locating email addresses on the Internet through a white pages user directory. The users enter keywords based on the name of the individuals and their locations. Netfind then returns possible individuals and their email addresses.

Netfind search page is located at **http://www.nova.edu/ Inter-Links/netfind.html.**

See Also

Email; Internet; Network; World Wide Web

Netiquette

The etiquette of **Usenet** and **Internet** communications in general. The explosive growth of Internet communications has created an entire community with its own notions of what is and is not acceptable to broadcast on the Net.

One of the best ways to get to know the culture of the Internet is to get involved in its interpersonal communication services: Usenet newsgroups, email, Internet Relay Chat, and MUDs. When you begin to participate, be sure to observe the rules of Netiquette, which try to ensure courteous and useful communication between participants.

Commonly observed rules prohibit slander, plagiarism, and **spamming** (sending unsolicited advertising to readers).

See Also

Emoticons; Flaming; Internet; Spam; Usenet; World Wide Web

Netscape HTML Tables,
See Tables, Creating in
Netscape

Netscape Navigator

Widely used and innovative **client** software that enables a user to *browse* (locate and examine) information on the **Internet's World Wide Web**. Occasionally referred to as Mozilla, the software's original code name.

Netscape was created by **Marc Andreessen** and the team from **NCSA** at the University of Illinois that created the first graphical Internet client, **Mosaic**.

A **Web browser** provides a *graphical user interface* to the Internet in general, and the World Wide Web in particular. Navigator offers the user an interface that includes a variety of buttons, menus, and toolbars, as shown in the following figure.

Here are some of the reasons why Navigator is the most popular program for browsing the World Wide Web:

- Navigator follows the Macintosh interface with menus, buttons, and drag-and-drop, and is intuitive, like the Mac.

- Navigator processes data more efficiently than other programs and in a way that lets you interact with a page before it has finished loading onscreen by using document **streaming**. Users can also stop the loading process.

N

- Navigator is fast. Its speed is due to the software's capability to make several simultaneous connections to a single Web site and load multiple documents at the same time, and the way Netscape uses disk **cache**.

- Netscape has come up with a number of extensions that extend **HTML**'s limited design capabilities**.**

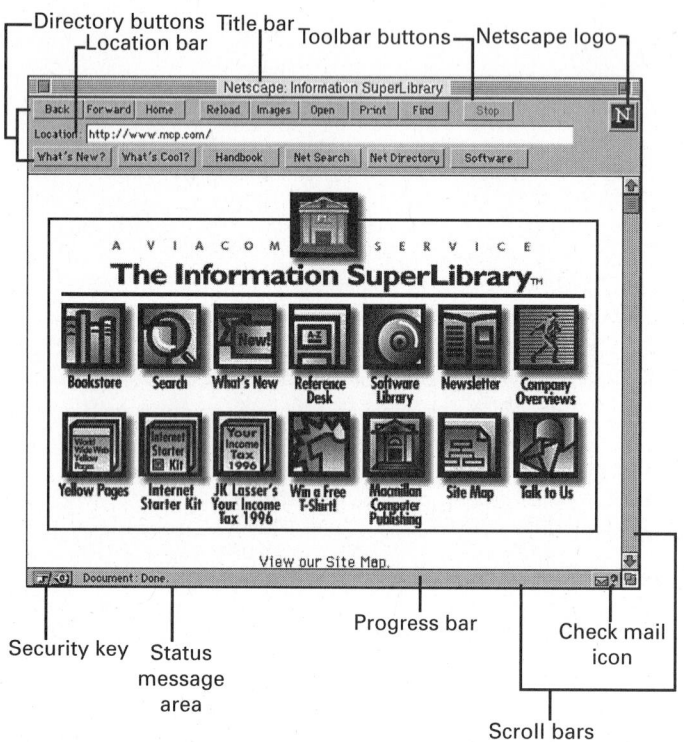

Another feature that distinguishes Netscape Navigator among Web browsers on the Mac (and among Mac programs in general) is Netscape's implementation of Apple's System 7.5 (and later) service called the Thread Manager (although you can add it by dropping the INIT into your System 7 System folder). The Thread Manager enables Navigator to *multithread*, or perform several functions simultaneously, in a way that other browsers cannot mimic.

Navigator also supports the display of images that appear on your computer screen in stages. The kinds of images that do this are called Interlaced **GIF** or Progressive **JPEG** graphics formats.

Navigator 2.0's developer, Netscape Communications Corp., has agreements with a number of other software companies, such as Sun Microsystems (which created the **Java** programming language and **HotJava** browser) and Macromedia, Inc., (which produces Macromedia **Director**, a multimedia presentation program, and **Shockwave**, a **plug-in** for Netscape).

Navigator supports secure transactions through its **Secure Sockets Layer**, the use of **encryption** to ensure that sensitive data such as financial information can only be read by the intended recipient(s).

See Also

Andreessen, Marc; Cache; Director; Email; Frames; GIF; HTML Tables; Internet; Java; JPEG; Mosaic; NCSA; Plug-Ins; Shockwave; Usenet; Web Browser; World Wide Web

NetWare, *See Servers*

Network Administration

The network administrator is the person responsible for insuring that each computer on the network can communicate properly with other network devices. In addition, the network administrator must ensure that sensitive portions of the network remain secured from unauthorized users.

Effective network administration couples the use of well thought out network policies with informed choices about the types of hardware and software that should be used. The network administrator is responsible for making policy decisions about how the network will run, and must set guidelines for the network's users to follow.

> **TIP** In a network environment, users typically assume that the administrator is responsible for *all* elements of computer maintenance. Therefore, when designing your network policies, it's very important to clearly describe which areas of maintenance you will not be performing and that you expect users to perform on their own. For example if users are responsible for backing up their own data, it is critical that you make this point clear—before they lose important files.

Passwords Passwords are involved with nearly every step of network usage. As the administrator, you should communicate guidelines to your users to help them choose their passwords. Ideally, each user's password is one that they will never forget, but one that other people wouldn't associate with them. Obvious passwords such as social security numbers, birth dates, and children's names are poor choices, as they are probably the *first* guesses an educated intruder would make. After choosing, users should be encouraged to commit their passwords to memory, *not* to write them down.

Your password policy should also specify if the users are required, asked, or even enabled to change their password. A network that requires its users to frequently change their passwords is the most secure, but also will probably be one where users will more often forget their password. While some security sys-

tems enable the network administrator access when a user has forgotten his password, others become completely inaccessible without the user's correctly entered password.

Many software packages designed for use in network environments have features to enable each user's computers to *remember* that user's password for subsequent usage of that program. These features are popular because upon startup the user's computer automatically logs into file servers and email systems, saving the user time and frustration. The drawback of these features is that they disable login security, enabling unrestricted access as long as the machine in question can be accessed.

> **TIP** Combining Auto-Login features with User station security (See next section) provides a good balance of network security and ease of use.

Backup It is important to note that each user has access to only a portion of most shared data (such as databases, file servers, or email systems) so the network administrator must take responsibility for backup of the file server as a whole. However, as mentioned in Network Policies, many network users assume by extension that the network administrator is also responsible for backing up individual workstations, so if this is not the case, the users must be made aware of this fact and be instructed on how to perform local backups.

Software Licenses One of the most difficult tasks for the network manager is ensuring compliance with software licenses. Each software package purchased has varying rules regarding where and how it may be distributed to the various users on the network. Generally, one copy of the software must be purchased for each person who will use the software.

To ensure compliance with all software licenses, the network administrator can either carefully restrict distribution of software, closely monitor each user's station, or develop guidelines for users to follow. The administration tools entry lists some of the software packages available to aid in this task.

N

Software Updates One of the most onerous tasks a network manager faces is providing users the most current version of the various software packages. To maintain consistency within an organization, the network manager must decide when, and to whom each update will be distributed. When a large number of machines much be updated, simply running install disks on each machine is not an effective means of distribution. Some programs, such as Microsoft Office have a network installer option. The administrator can sit at his or her own Mac and manage the installation on the various machines without walking around to each machine on the network with a fistful of CD-ROMs and disks.

Security In the simplest sense, network security schemes are designed to hide data and resources from users who are not authorized to access them. While it would seem one couldn't have too much security, this situation bears closer inspection. As you further protect your data, the chance of it becoming unrecoverable increases. Each form of computer security has a different compromise between security and accessibility so you must weigh your need for security with the potential for data loss.

> **TIP** The best way to maintain a high assurance of data accessibility while continuing to provide a high level of security is thorough and frequent backup of all system information.

User Station Security At the individual user's computer, your security concerns are twofold: you must protect that user's data, as well as make sure that user's computer has access to only the information and resources it is permitted to use.

Inactive User Security Inactive user security protects the system from unauthorized entry when a user temporarily leaves their computer. This type of security is most commonly a part of a screen saver package that clears the display on the monitor after a set period of inactivity. The downside of this type of security is that by restarting the computer, the password lock is reset, leaving the computer vulnerable to entry. Fortunately, this hole is easily plugged by adding the next class of software: Startup User Security.

> **TIP** Although screen savers that are application-based (such as Dark Side of the Mac) use less memory and suffer few compatibility troubles, they are less secure than applications that are installed as extensions or control panels (such as After Dark).

Startup User Security Startup user security is designed to prevent unauthorized users from starting a computer. As with idle user security, startup security depends upon the use of a password to identify the proper owner of the equipment. Startup security is generally implemented through special features of a hard disk or utility software (such as Norton DiskLock by Symantec).

Startup security protects the system at a low level of the computer's operations, the hard disk driver. Because these changes are so basic to the system's operation, if a user forgets his or her password or if the protection software itself becomes damaged, it can become impossible to recover the information stored on the computer!

Server Security The computer serving as a file, mail, database, or other type of server holds the data that all users share. While each individual's computer can only access the data that the server allows, the server itself must have access to all the data. Therefore, *all data* is accessible to anyone who can gain physical access to the server. Accordingly, it is important to make use of the previously mentioned user security types on a server, as well as using good physical security, such as locked doors or even an alarm system, on the room which contains the server.

See Also

Network Communications; Network Maintenance; Networking, Why and How; Wireless Networks

Network Communications

Computers communicate on networks by following a set of rules known as **protocols**. The protocols specify the types of communication that are allowed and provide details about exactly how this communication takes place.

The process of network communication can be most easily understood by thinking of the process in terms of a human conversation. For two computers to communicate, they must have many things in common. First, a common language (protocol) is chosen. Based upon the rules of the chosen language, a name, known as the **node number** or node **address**, is assigned to each computer participating in the conversation. Multiple computers in each location are joined into communities, which are assigned a **network number**. Finally, when communication is desired, each individual computer sends messages by breaking transmissions into units of redefined size, known as **packets**, and labeling each packet with the addresses of the sender and recipient.

Network Protocols Networked communication between computers is accomplished through a set of rules known as **network protocols**. Each individual task within these protocols is also assigned a name, making for a very large body of standards to manage. To assist in the understanding and management of these individual protocols, the Organization for Standardization (**ISO**), an international standardization body, designed a schema known as the Open Systems Interconnection Reference Model, or the **OSI**.

The OSI simplifies the sea of protocols by creating a model for the evaluation of networks. This model groups the individual processes performed by computer networks into a "stack" composed of seven "layers" of functionality. The seven layers specified by the ISO are shown in the table below. Each of the most common network protocols in use on Macintosh Networks, **AppleTalk**, **TCP/IP**, and **IPX**, have their own stack. To enable interoperability, networking vendors design their products to fit into the appropriate layer of the stacks they wish to support.

Layer 7	Application
Layer 6	Presentation
Layer 5	Session
Layer 4	Transport
Layer 3	Network
Layer 2	Data Link
Layer 1	Physical

The use of the OSI model has proved vital in the expansion of microcomputer networking. The existence of this common framework has greatly simplified the interconnection of products from various vendors and platforms. However, it is important to understand that the OSI Reference Model itself is only a framework to explain the theoretical design of network protocols.

None of the real-world protocol stacks actually follows the OSI model all the time. Instead, each vendor's protocols try to match the model as closely as possible, with certain protocols overlapping layers and not all layers behaving exactly as specified.

AppleTalk is the protocols stack designed by Apple Computer to provide network communication between Macintosh computers. Note that AppleTalk is *not* specific to any type of cabling or computer: it is simply a series of rules for network communication designed by Apple. So while AppleTalk is included in every Macintosh, it could also be spoken by other computers with the appropriate software. For example, Farallon's PhoneNET PC and Novell's Netware for Mac enable DOS compatible computers to speak AppleTalk.

Just as non-MacOS compatible computers can speak AppleTalk, it is also quite common for MacOS computers to speak protocols outside of AppleTalk. For example, Macintosh computers connected to the Internet commonly speak TCP/IP. In addition, through the use of the Mac IPX control panel, Macintosh computers can speak IPX, Novell's networking protocol stack, directly with Netware servers.

See Also

Network Administration; Network Maintenance; Networking, Why and How; Wireless Networks

Network, Connecting to UNIX and Other Operating Systems

Connections between any two computers depend upon both a physical connection and a common language to be spoken once the communication path is established. Networking a Mac to a UNIX system or a mainframe is feasible, but there are issues to consider regarding cross-platform connectivity. Connecting to these two platforms is fairly similar conceptually, but each type of connection requires a specific configuration of hardware and software.

The UNIX and mainframe environments have their own unique technical languages, and thus the terms involved with connecting to these platforms will be unfamiliar to most Macintosh users. To review briefly:

UNIX is a universal operating system designed in the early 1970s at AT&T. Because this operating system is available for nearly every computer platform, it is known as the universal computer language.

A/UX is Apple's version of UNIX. Note that A/UX has fairly powerful hardware requirements: See the A/UX entry for details about which Macs can run A/UX.

SNA, System Network Architecture, is IBM's mainframe network protocol. Conceptually, this is similar to AppleTalk, Apple's network protocol for Macintosh computers.

3270 Terminal These are the computer terminals that IBM originally designed to access its mainframe series.

Gateway A gateway is a language translator, also called a bridge. It sits between two types of computer networks, such as AppleTalk and IPX, and passes messages between two computers that speak different languages.

SNAps Gateway SNAps is Apple's IBM mainframe to Macintosh gateway. This product runs on a Macintosh that is connected to both a Macintosh network and to an IBM mainframe, translating messages between the two sides—between AppleTalk and SNA.

TCP/IP is the network protocol most commonly used by UNIX computer systems. This is similar to the AppleTalk protocol used by Macintosh computers and the SNA protocol used by IBM mainframes.

While Macs and mainframes have co-existed in corporate environments since the Mac's debut in 1984, IBM did not officially acknowledge the Mac as an appropriate method of connection to its mainframes until 1991. Mainframe communication occurs through IBM's System Network Architecture (SNA) protocol set, which is roughly analogous to Apple's AppleTalk network protocol set. As with other types of network connections, both a physical and a software connection are necessary.

Physical connection to an IBM mainframe can be done either through a direct connection to the mainframe or through a network connection. The direct connection is the original method used to connect IBM's 3270 terminals to a mainframe. This method requires modems or coaxial cable to connect the remote computer directly to one of the mainframe's cluster controller ports. While this method provides good speed and quick setup, it is quite expensive to implement. Because of the high cost, this method is useful only when a small number of Macs need to be connected to an existing network with available connections. To use the direct connection method, a card must be added to the Macintosh to support either a serial connection or a coaxial cable connection. Note that the coaxial cable connection used for mainframe connectivity is not the same as the coaxial cable connection used with thin Ethernet (ThinNet) and the serial connection is not the same as standard Macintosh modem/printer serial port connections. The Coax/Twinax Card and Apple Serial NB Card can be purchased directly from Apple.

A versatile method of connecting Macs to a mainframe is to use a LAN connection. In this scenario, a group of Macs are already connected together into a network, so only one connection between the Mac network and the mainframe is necessary to give all the Macs access to the mainframe's services. If the Macintosh network is using a data link that is supported by the mainframe, most commonly Token

Ring, then simply adding the Macintosh network to the mainframe's network connections provides the necessary physical connection. Of course, after the physical connection is made, software that speaks SNA must be added. The necessary card to join a Mac to the Token Ring LAN is also available from Apple. Ask for a Token Ring 4/16 NB Card.

If the Macs that need to be connected to the mainframe aren't running on a network data link that is supported by the mainframe, a gateway can be used. The gateway sits between the two networks, acting as a translator between the two data-links and network protocols. One such product is WallData's SNAps gateway software (previously sold by Apple). This product is installed on a Macintosh that has both a connection to the Mac network (LocalTalk or Ethernet) and a direct connection to the mainframe. This Mac then becomes the physical gateway with its software serving as a translator, intercepting messages between the two incompatible networks, and converting them to usable form.

IBM originally designed its mainframes to communicate with users via the text-based 3270 "dumb" terminals. While the Macintosh provides several methods for communicating with the mainframe, each method must essentially convince the mainframe that it is talking to one of its 3270 terminals. Therefore, each mainframe connectivity solution differs in how the mainframe's messages are displayed on the Macintosh. The most common method Macs use to communicate with mainframes is to emulate the 3270 terminals that the mainframe expects. With 3270 terminal emulation software, such as WallData's SNAps 3270, a Macintosh user is presented with a window which simulates the display of a 3270 terminal. Fortunately, emulation software enables the use of some of the typical Mac interface features such as definition of keyboard macros and reassigning of keystrokes, but gives a predominately text-based interface.

If a developer wants to maintain the standard Mac interface yet communicate with a mainframe, custom software must be written. Front end software is specifically written to present a Macintosh interface on the Mac side, while invisibly converting these actions and the mainframe's responses to and from the equivalents of 3720 terminal actions.

Connecting to UNIX UNIX is an operating system supported on nearly every computer platform from mainframes to personal computers. It was developed in the 1970s at AT&T's Bell Labs as a development environment for telecommunication systems. Since then, it has had major additions made by UC Berkeley, the Department of Defense, and most recently Sun. Today, UNIX-based workstations are commonly used in engineering and other scientific applications.

As with most Macintosh and PC computer networks, Ethernet is the most common method of physical connection between UNIX computers. If the UNIX network you need to connect to is running over Ethernet, you need only add your Mac to the network to connect to the UNIX network. But, of course, that's only half of the connection. You also need to connect the software.

The main role of the software connection is to resolve the fact that the two computers are speaking different languages. (The Mac speaks AppleTalk and the UNIX machine, TCP/IP.) This translation need not be performed at both ends of the communication as long as one computer can speak in a language the other can understand, communication can proceed. Obviously, this can be accomplished in either of two ways. By adding software to the UNIX computer so that it can speak in the Mac's native network language (AppleTalk), an unmodified Macintosh can speak to a UNIX machine (assuming the physical connection is in place). Generally, this type of setup is used to enable a UNIX file or print server to become available to the Macintosh. Because the UNIX server will be using native Macintosh protocols, the file or printer server appears in the Macintosh Chooser as would any other Macintosh file or print server. Products that perform this task are K-Ashare/K-spool by Xinet and PacerShare by Pacer Software. K-Ashare runs on a Sun or HP UNIX host, while PacerShare runs on Sun, HP, or DEC Ultrix (DEC's version of UNIX). This software is quite expensive. PacerShare, however, lists for about $5,000, and K-Ashare is only a little bit less.

A less expensive answer is to teach the Mac to speak TCP/IP. MacTCP, part of Apple's TCP/IP Connection for Macintosh, enables Macintosh programs to speak using the TCP/IP protocol language. This, used in combination with a program written specifically to make use of the MacTCP additions, enables Mac users to interact with an unmodified UNIX-TCP/IP network service. Note that to use MacTCP, you need software that was specifically written to take advantage of it: mainstream Macintosh applications completely ignore the added language capability of MacTCP.

As a third alternative, you could teach the Mac to run UNIX directly. Apple's add-on A/UX software enables the Mac to run UNIX software directly. This is accomplished by replacing the standard Macintosh operating system with a hybrid of both Apple's System 7 and the UNIX operating systems. Because the resulting Macintosh has both the UNIX and System 7 operating systems, the computer can run both Macintosh and UNIX software. Once A/UX is running, the Mac speaks TCP/IP internally and it can successfully communicate with other UNIX machines.

TIP TCP/IP is rapidly becoming part of every Mac's vocabulary, because it's included in System 7.5. Even if you're not tied into a local network with Sun workstations, IBM mainframes, and Cray supercomputers (all of which can talk to the Mac with TCP/IP); you're effectively tied into a Wide Area Network every time you sign on to your Internet Provider.

Network Control Panel

This control panel enables the user to specify a network connection and switch between different kinds of networks (such as AppleTalk or Ethernet networks). When you access this control panel, a window displays the available network connections. To select an available network to connect to, click the network's **icon**.

To select an individual zone, double-click your network icon to display a window where you can choose the AppleTalk zone you want from the list of available zones. Click OK to confirm your zone choice.

To use the Network Control Panel, follow these steps:

1. Open the Network control panel from the Control Panels submenu on the Apple Menu (or System Folder).

2. Choose the network you want to connect to by clicking its icon. Double-click the same icon to select a particular zone from the list of available zones. Select the name of the zone and click OK to make your choice complete.

3. Close the Network Control Panel.

Note: If OpenTransport is installed, this is replaced by the AppleTalk control panel, which has a different interface.

See Also
EtherTalk; Icons

Network Gaming

Network gaming essentially means that you can play a game against another person, not just a computer opponent, over a modem and phone line, a network server, or the Internet.

After you get more than three people playing a game like **Chaos Overlords** or **Hexen**, the odds are upped and a new dimension is added. The main problem many critics have with computer games is that they are antisocial. The following figure shows Marathon in action.

Some games just work better on a board or bridge table than with three or four people jammed around a single keyboard and screen. Still, games like Havoc from Reality Bytes are proving that gaming can go across a platform and across a town or continent successfully. Havoc supports network play across platforms, meaning that you can play against your friend on a PC with your Macintosh and there is nothing lost in the translation. The interface is the same on both ends.

If all games continue to bridge the gap between platforms, Mac gamers may finally see an end to the shelf space problem and the decision to go Mac may no longer be influenced by whether or not you can get a good array of games for it.

See Also

MUDs and MOOs; Online Games; Shareware Games

Network Maintenance

Network maintenance is the ongoing support of users and computers on your network. It is the task of the network administrator, either to perform all of the required tasks or to designate, and possibly to train others to do them. This task will be made much easier if you've established and discussed a thorough network policy statement with your users. While the physical wiring and configuration of the network will require occasional maintenance, much of your work will involve maintaining the network software that you install.

File Server Maintenance Because a non-functioning file server separates users from their data, it is important to keep the file servers running. The main task of file server maintenance is changing the server's internal list of users to match the changing physical and employee configurations of the company. When an employee or workstation is added, or dropped, the file server list needs to be updated accordingly. This is especially urgent if the employee did not leave voluntarily. There are too many stories told in the computer world about disgruntled employees who erased important files or planted viruses on servers after being dismissed.

In addition, you'll want to make sure that the server is continuing to operate efficiently and that it has sufficient storage resources. This means periodically defragmenting the hard drive(s) and checking to be sure that only what's needed is installed.

Email Maintenance Email maintenance is similar to file server maintenance. Your main task is to keep the email server's listing of users current. In addition, you'll probably need to perform periodic diagnostics and "cleanups" of the mail files, as required by the software you're using.

Backup Maintenance If you're using a network-wide backup scheme, you'll need to check periodically on this machine to insure that it's actually backing up the items that it thinks it is, and that it always has sufficient backup medium to perform the backups as scheduled.

If you choose not to centrally perform backup, you'll want to periodically check to insure that users are performing their own backup—because you'll be the first one they'll come screaming to when they loose their data.

Wiring Maintenance Network wiring doesn't require frequent maintenance. While wiring is often the first source of blame for network problems, if properly installed, it is rarely the actual cause of problems. It's a good idea to check the validity of the wiring periodically to spot intermittent connections, so you'll recognize any differences when things stop working properly.

The testing of network wiring is done with software that sends short messages ("pings") to different spots on the network and times the amount of time a reply takes. Periodic quick checks around the network to look for inappropriately long response times give you a good idea of the overall status of your network and can help rule out wiring conditions as the source of network troubles. Pinging won't necessarily define a wiring problem, but will tell you what area may have a problem. From there, a visual inspection, beginning with the gateway and router, and checking the indicators on the hub, will help you track down the problem. Only after you have ruled out loose connectors and problems with the gateway or router should you begin to consider a bad wire. These are easily tested with a volt meter. If there really is a wiring problem, the chances are excellent that it will be in whatever run of wiring is most difficult to reach.

> **TIP** Because network wiring can be one of the most difficult and most frustrating things to troubleshoot after it's installed, it makes a great deal of sense to plan carefully, and use high quality network wiring.

Network Maintenance Tools The task of maintaining a Macintosh network of tens or even hundreds of nodes might seem insurmountable. Fortunately, there are many tools available to the administrator to ease the tasks of network maintenance.

File Server Maintenance Several tools are available to provide file server maintenance. The most obvious ones are included with your file server package. AppleShare, for example, makes use of the "AppleShare Admin" software to perform updates to user lists and access privileges. Third party software tools, such as Santorini's Server Manager or Sonic System's Server Sentry, enable you to perform similar tasks, but add the capability to perform these tasks from any computer on the network, enabling you to configure multiple file servers from one physical location.

Network Inspection Tools Software that tests networks integrity is quite helpful when major network failures occur. Typical examples are Data Watch's NetOctopus, Sonic System's Radar, and Apple's InterPoll. These tools use test signals to show you how quickly and accurately each computer on the network can send and receive messages. In addition, these packages can give you information about the hardware in use at each network station.

Software Update Tools When many users need updates of common software packages, programs such as FileWave or NetOctopus can be immensely helpful. These packages enable the network administrator to prepare and perform updates to all stations from one central location.

Network Administration, Remote Access Apple's Remote Access (ARA) isn't a network management tool itself: it is software that uses modems to 'trick' your computer and a remote network into thinking you're physically connected and proves invaluable during network emergencies when you're off-site. Combining ARA with any of the previously mentioned tools enables you to perform your normal network administration tasks from virtually anywhere that you can attach to a phone line. Don't use Apple Remote Access connections to perform network configuration changes that could affect the network status of the machine controlling the ARA connection...or you could be rudely disconnected in the middle of your changes, and unable to reconnect!

See Also

Network Administration; Network Communications; Networking, Why and How

Network News Transfer Protocol, *See NNTP*

Network Number

The network number is a 16-bit number used to identify the AppleTalk network to which a **node** is assigned. Nodes choose their network number from an AppleTalk **router.** When no router is present on the network, they choose a number from a pre-defined range known as the startup range. The network number range is a range of network numbers that has been established within the router for use on extended network segments. Non-extended networks, such as LocalTalk, are restricted to single network numbers.

See Also

Network Administration; Network Maintenance; Networking, Why and How

Network Rendering

Using a **network** of computers to render a single **3D** scene. This is also called a rendering farm. Several software packages support network rendering, including Specular **Infini-D** (using an add-on package called **BackBurner**) and Hash's **Animation Master**.

Network rendering requires a central control program on one computer and processing programs that run on other computers on the network. The central program takes a 3D scene and delegates the scene information (including models and texture information) to the processing programs. Each program is assigned to render one part of the image—the image usually is divided into a grid of squares—and the central program receives the rendered parts and assembles them.

One advantage of this process is that the processing programs operate in the background and can be configured so that they work only during certain times. Correctly configuring them eliminates any performance degradation.

The more computers available, the faster each image is rendered. There are trade-offs, however. The network's speed and the size of the models impact performance. If the rendering process is running over a LocalTalk network, it may take so long to send the data back and forth that performance improvements are negated except for small jobs. Also, it is not worth adding significantly slower computers to the rendering farm. As an extreme example, if you had a PowerPC 604-based Power Mac and a slower 68020-based Macintosh II, it would make no sense to network them together. The rendering time contribution of the Macintosh II would be insignificant when compared to the performance of the Power Mac.

See Also

3D; Network Gaming

Network Topology

The method by which a computer network is physically laid out is known as the network topology. The various network topologies are technically independent of data links and transmission media, but each transmission medium only supports specific topologies in specific fashions.

Bus The **Bus** is the simplest type of network, and the type network Mac users are most familiar with as it is used for LocalTalk/PhoneNet networks. It consists of computers that are "chained" together, with wires starting on one computer, meeting the next, and so on until the end. (See the following figure). This configuration is also frequently called the "daisy-chain."

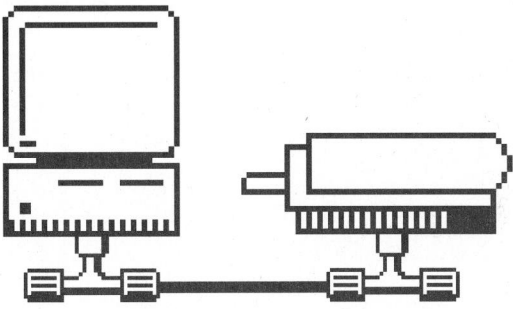

The bus topology is used with **LocalTalk**, in both Locking LocalTalk (Shielded Twisted Pair) and PhoneNet (Unshielded Twisted Pair) configurations. In addition, thin **EtherNet** (ThinNet) makes use of this topology.

The principle advantage of the bus topology is it's easy setup. Because each computer simply connects to the next, cabling is fairly straightforward, particularly in a room with multiple computers (such as a computer lab). The primary disadvantage of this type of setup is that, much like a string of Christmas lights, if the chain is broken at any point, every computer on the network becomes disconnected. In addition, it is very difficult to locate cabling faults without physically going from station to station.

Overall, bus topologies are very practical only with a small number of computers, or when most of the computers are concentrated in a single area. Beyond this, the difficulty in maintaining and troubleshooting this type of installation makes a Star topology preferable.

STAR The alternative to the BUS topology is the STAR configuration. In this type of setup, each computer is connected by a network cable to a single

N

central location. This topology can be more expensive to install, because each computer must have a wire running all the way back to the center of the network, as opposed to the bus network where each cable need only run to the next closest workstation.

The primary advantages of this topology are in the areas of manageability. Because each workstation has a dedicated cable run to a central location, problems on any single cable are isolated to that workstation.

There are two types of star networks, Passive Star and Active Star:

- The active star network uses a device known as a hub to act as a central manager of all data traffic.
- The Passive Star takes the cabling schema of the active star but works without the central hub by simply cross-connecting each workstation's cabling.

A passive star is formed when each of the star's cables are directly connected together at the center. You can do this fairly easily, using a patch panel or a telephone-style punchdown block. This creates a network that is electronically similar to the bus topology. Unfortunately, a passive star usually uses a great deal more cable than a bus because each workstation has the full cable run to the central location (see the following figure).

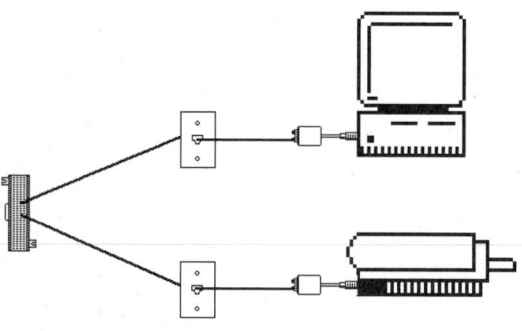

The passive star topology is only supported by a LocalTalk/PhoneNet network. The benefits of this topology are the cost savings of not using a central hub, the familiarity of cable installers with the star topology, and that cabling for a passive star prepares you to move to an Active Star network. The drawbacks of using a passive star are significant.

This type of network is notoriously unreliable when expanded beyond four "arms." Perhaps most importantly, by cross-connecting each cable run and by not using a hub, you lose the isolation advantages of the star network, as shown in the following figure.

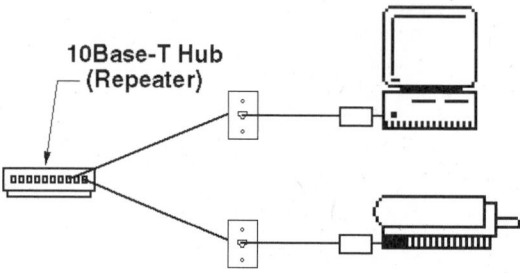

10Base-T Hub (Repeater)

An active star network makes use of a central unit known as a hub or repeater at the center of the network (see the previous figure). The hub is responsible for isolating, amplifying, retiming, and then transmitting network signals that come from each workstation, enabling for the use of many more computers over longer distances. Because it makes use of a hub, active star networks provide for very advanced monitoring and management of networks. Therefore while they are more expensive to install initially, active star networks are by far a better investment for the growing network. The active star topology can be used with 10Base-T, EtherNet, and PhoneNet.

TIP For trouble shooting purposes, keep a diagram of your network topology, including the model and serial numbers of computers and other devices on the network, and the applications (and *their* serial numbers) of software installed on the server and on its clients.

See Also

Network Administration; Network Maintenance; Networking, Why and How; Network Wiring Strategies; Wireless Networks

Network Wiring Strategies

The Macintosh supports a number of network cabling systems, from LocalTalk to FDDI (fiber-optic). Each system has its pros and cons, based on cost, reliability, and upward compatibility. There are many issues involved with the design and implementation of any wiring system. Although it's hard to generalize and cover all possible networking situations, here are a few things to keep in mind.

1. Don't get locked into a specific vendor's proprietary components or cabling scheme. Stay with the accepted industry standards.

TIP One exception to this rule is Apple's EtherNet system. It uses a special connector to link the device with the external attachment unit. Because the network side of the attachment unit (either 10Base-5, 10Base-2, or 10Base-T) still conforms to industry standards, it's less important that the device side is somewhat non-standard. To their credit, Apple has published and made this standard available for any vendor to use. The Apple EtherNet system has been adopted by virtually all of the Macintosh networking vendors, and is becoming a standard of its own.

2. Don't limit your network and wiring plans just to data. Consider integrating your networking plans with other forms of data, such as voice and video. You may be able to save money by installing these different cabling systems at the same time. In many cases, the different systems can use the same faceplate.

3. Plan for the future. You may be planning to use only LocalTalk and EtherNet, but you should seriously consider the installation of twisted-pair wiring and fiber-optic backbones that are capable of supporting current and future high-end cabling systems. Consider also the likelihood of upgrading phone service to ISDN.

One such standard for "now and later" wiring involves the installation of four pairs of UTP (Unshielded Twisted-Pair) wiring. Because 10Base-T EtherNet requires only two pairs, you have more wire than you need right away, but as 100Base-T becomes available and affordable, you're already wired for it. The most encompassing standard for UTP is published by the Electronic Industries Association and the Telecommunications Industry Association (EIA/TIA). The standard is commonly referred to EIA/TIA 568 and TSB-36, which sets a standard for Category 5 UTP media. Category 5 UTP anticipates the standards that will support bandwidths of 100 Mbps (Category 4 UTP supports the conventional EtherNet bandwidth of 10 Mbps). These standards include copper versions of the FDDI standard (CDDI) and 100 Mbps (100Base-T) implementations of EtherNet. This cabling is also sometimes referred to as "Level 5" cabling.

Another example of planning for the future is the choice of fiber-optic cabling. Fiber-optic cabling is becoming more commonplace as a medium for EtherNet backbones. In fact, an EtherNet fiber standard, IEEE 802.3—10Base-F—has been published. Fiber can be run over great distances and is immune from most forms of electromagnetic interference. (Try to avoid wrapping it around a lightning rod.) Fiber optic cabling is also the basis for the FDDI standard. Fortunately, the two standards overlap somewhat and it's desirable to implement fiber networks that conform to the FDDI standard (ANSI X3T9.5: FDDI) as well as the current and planned EtherNet fiber standards. The moral of this story is to plan for FDDI even though you're only going to use lowly EtherNet. You'll appreciate this approach in the not-so-distant future when FDDI cards sell at CompUSA for $129.

- If your LAN will need to support more than 50 users, plan on implementing a **structured wiring** approach to your network design. It's money well spent. By implementing such a system, the ongoing costs involved in support, troubleshooting, expansion, and equipment relocation are minimized.

- In accordance with your budget, plan on running multiple cable runs to each office or cubicle. The incremental cost of the additional cabling is relatively small when compared to the minor increase in labor cost.

N

Also, don't scrimp on the number of jacks provided to an office or cubicle. You can choose faceplates that have a single, double, or quadruple complement of connectors. While it's often possible to daisy-chain within a room, don't plan on this as a part of the design. Consider that you might want to add printers or other networkable peripherals to a room at any time in the future. You might also need to support devices that require multiple connections to the LAN, such as workstations, routers, and gateways. A good rule of thumb is to plan for at least twice as many connections as you actually require at present.

- Make sure that fiber and copper cable runs are within the specified length limitations, by carefully planning the location and distribution of wiring closets. Be sure to allocate additional cable length for vertical distances (not usually shown on floor plans) and the routing losses that occur when cable is snaked above ceilings and through walls.

- Speaking of wiring closets, plan the layout and design of these rooms carefully. Make sure that the room is well lighted, ventilated, and capable of being securely locked. If the room is large enough, use industry standard 19" racks to contain the network devices. Obviously, because the room may house a number of routers, gateways, and other network devices, adequate electrical service is crucial. If you have room, you may also find it convenient to install a small desk with a Mac that can be used for troubleshooting and maintenance. This Mac can also be used to maintain network configuration information, wiring diagrams, and problem logs. Quite often, this is also the room where the telephone equipment is located. Be sure that the two are kept separate as much as possible, to avoid confusion.

- Are your cables routed in such a manner as to avoid electromagnetic interference and undue mechanical stress? For example, don't drape cables around fluorescent light fixtures, and don't hang wet laundry from cables strung from the ceiling. Use common sense and consult the appropriate local codes and requirements.

- Plan to have your wiring tested before use. This is a particularly good idea for large, expensive installations that use structured wiring. The time to discover breaks or discontinuities in the cable is before network deployment. If you use a wiring contractor, be sure to include testing and validation as part of the agreement. The devices used for testing can be rather expensive, so it's likely that this task is better handled by the cable installers.

- Adopt an adequate cable marking and identification scheme. Each and every cable should be unambiguously marked—in a location that will be visible after installation. Be sure to mark both ends of the cable. Make sure the marking is permanent and won't be erased or detached. There are many adequate marking systems. Some utilize heat-shrinkable tubing, and others use labeled wiring ties.

- Document everything from the outset. Create a logical and physical diagram of your network. If you're using a cabling system that has physical hardware addresses, such as EtherNet, register these numbers along with their location and description. For this task, a spreadsheet or a simple database (such as FileMaker Pro) is ideal.

- Before you start planning, call the Black Box Corporation at (800) 552-6816. They'll send you a free catalog that's chock full of many networking products. It's like the "L.L. Bean Catalog" for networkers.

Structured Wiring Sometimes the simplest answer to wiring a network seems the most complex. The technique sometimes referred to as structured fits that definition. Every node on the network is wired to a central point, which is designated as the wiring closet. The wires meet at a punch block or patch panel, which connects them to the appropriate hub or other device.

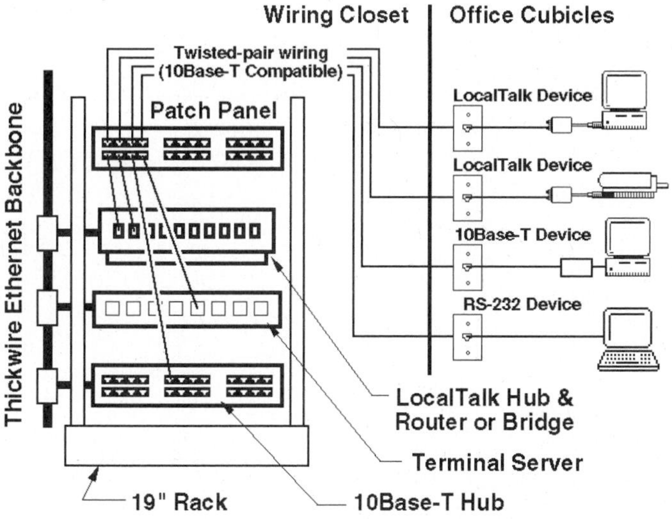

Wiring Closet | Office Cubicles

Twisted-pair wiring (10Base-T Compatible)

Patch Panel

Thickwire Ethernet Backbone

LocalTalk Device
LocalTalk Device
10Base-T Device
RS-232 Device

LocalTalk Hub & Router or Bridge
Terminal Server
19" Rack
10Base-T Hub

In this example, a star topology is used to wire all offices and cubicles with several runs of 10Base-T (or even Level 5 compliant) twisted-pair wiring. All wires converge at the master patch panel within the wiring closet. From this patch panel, connections are made to the appropriate wiring devices based on requirements of the connected device. LocalTalk devices are interconnected to a LocalTalk hub and router; EtherNet devices are connected to an EtherNet hub. While it's not shown in the figure, the 10Base-T hub could also be connected to an EtherNet-to-EtherNet router. Serially connected devices are patched to a terminal server. What's important about this scheme is that all devices use identical wiring. Changes are confined to the wiring closet. If an elderly LocalTalk Mac SE is replaced with an EtherNet Power Mac, the only required change is to move a patch cord from the LocalTalk hub to the EtherNet hub. The time saved is obvious.

Some integrated hubs merge the different hubs (such as terminal servers, 10Base-T, and even LocalTalk) into a single, unified chassis. These devices make the wiring process even easier and less cluttered by eliminating the cross-connects that are now part of the hub's backplane.

Remember that networks, like people, aren't fully grown at birth. They keep on growing and changing as the technology changes, and users are added or relocated. While it's not always necessary to upgrade immediately to the latest, fastest gimmick that comes along, growth is both healthy and inevitable. The more you can do today to anticipate and prepare for tomorrow's needs, the better off you'll be.

See Also

Network Administration; Network Communication; Network Maintenance; Networking, Why and How

Network Zones

Zones are a way to logically group network nodes. Zones are commonly defined on the basis of physical proximity. All the Macs and Laser Printers and other peripherals on the first floor of a building might be in zone 1, those on the second floor in zone 2, and so on. Zone names can be assigned to the network zones.

Zones must be no more than 32 characters long, and are case insensitive. The Zone list is a listing of available network zones, commonly displayed in the Chooser. (If there's only one zone, the Chooser doesn't display a list of zones, only a list of similar devices within the zone.)

See Also

Networking and the Chooser

N

Networking

Microcomputer networking is the interconnection of personal computers to enable pooling of resources and sharing of information. Once considered a luxury, today computer networks are commonplace, if not a requirement for today's business applications. While the large volume of new terminology specific to computer networks can be somewhat confusing, the Macintosh's ease of use certainly carries over into the area of Networking.

History In 1984 when the Mac was introduced, networking among personal computers was not very common. Apple, however, in typical industry-leading fashion, decided to include the basic software and hardware needed for networking in every Macintosh. This fundamental commitment to personal computer networking had a profound impact on the growth of network use, and the development of network applications for the Macintosh.

The first appearance of Macintosh networks in large numbers began with the introduction of the LaserWriter. Apple began to push the use of networking with the introduction of the original LaserWriter. The cost savings of having multiple computers connected to one LaserWriter (which then ran nearly $6,000) alone justified the existence of a Macintosh network. Apple dubbed this combination of multiple computers connecting to a single printer, "The Macintosh Office." The computers were connected using Apple's Locking LocalTalk connectors with shielded Twisted Pair wiring strung from computer to computer. While this was fairly straightforward to set up, the cost of the network ($150/computer) coupled with the cost of installing this shielded twisted pair cabling kept many sites from experimenting with the technology.

Conversation with Don Crabb

Don Crabb, columnist extraordinaire, helped Apple break into the university world way back with the original Apple IIs and has followed Apple's progress through the Apple III, the Lisa, and the Mac. He works in the Computer Science department at the University of Chicago.

Maclopedia: How did you first get involved with Apple?

Don: At the University of Chicago we started to get interested, that is, three or four of us working for the old computational center, in 1980, with the Apple II. We had just started getting into microcomputers on the campus then; we were the avant-garde bunch. Most of the faculty thought that microcomputers were never going to amount to much. So we started nosing around Apple and developed a relationship. We bought some equipment. We wanted to get a micro presence on campus, and Apple was the only one to go with, then. We flew out to California and met with Steve [Jobs] and Steve [Wozniak] and the relationship grew and grew. We bought some Apple IIs and bought some more, and in 1981, we bought a few PCs when they came out, but not many. We liked the way Apple did business.

In 1982, before the Apple III came out we saw the Lisa. We told them the Apple III was a piece of crap. We liked everything about the Lisa except the price. It was $10,000, the same price as a departmental computer. This was the same time Xerox was showing off the Star, which had EtherNet and distributed networks, and so we thought Apple was making a mistake on the pricing for the Lisa.

Early in 1983, Apple began showing us the Mac, and they put together the Apple University Consortium, because people were realizing that micros were not a fly-by-night thing. Of course, there were still a lot of people who thought that the fad would go away, and people would get back to time sharing and card decks.

But the prototype Mac really sealed it for us, so we signed on to the AUC and managed to convince the administration, which was a non-trivial task, to buy $2 million worth of equipment over five years—even when we were saying that the Apple III was a piece of junk, and we were basing our decision on a circuit board and a prototype steel box and a separate monitor. The first time we saw MacWrite and MacPaint, the lightbulb went off, and we said, "This is the Lisa for the rest of us."

In January 1984, when the Mac shipped, we had taken orders for over a thousand of them. For $2,499 you could get a 128KB machine, a coupon for an ImageWriter, and a coupon for the external drive. For the same money you can buy a pretty good system today. I've still got mine. I babied it. I shrink-wrapped it and put it back in the original box. Maybe somebody will start a computer museum in Chicago and buy it.

The first time we saw MacWrite and MacPaint, the lightbulb went off, and we said, "This is the Lisa for the rest of us."

The students went nuts. We could not get enough to satisfy the needs. And remember, this was a machine where we had to swap disks like mad because there was so little memory. Printers started coming in April. The first hard drive was the abominable HD20—what a piece of junk! That thing was $1,200 at AUC prices, which were the same as developer prices, but the university had no space to sell computers out of, so we commandeered space in a graduate dorm. The space was where they used to do soup preparation. You pick out your computer, you pull the cart down the loading dock and pay your money, or give your departmental order form, and wheel it out past the vegetable bins. We thought it was appropriate that a company named after a fruit was being wheeled out of the food prep area.

We sold machines like it was going out of style, because no one had ever seen a computer you could actually use yourself without having half the computer center staff sitting in your office. The computer science department, which was brand new at the time, had VT 100 terminals hooked to a DEC 20; they bought 24 128KB Macs and 4 printers and 24 external drives, and we started teaching Pascal classes. And ever since then the CS department has been all Mac. We grew the lab to 100 Power Macs today. We replace the equipment every few years. We were one of the first to do that, along with Reed, Drexel, and Carnegie Mellon. Most places stayed with time sharing on DEC 20s or VMS, but when we got the first Think Pascal, there was no turning back.

Maclopedia: How have things changed since the early years?

Don: Things were rolling pretty good for a long time. We were in the Apple University Consortium. We had a consortium meeting every year, at a site in Santa Cruz way up in the hills—but that place was completely flattened by the earthquake. Back when Bud Colligan was in charge of Apple Higher Education, we were the bunch that saved Apple's butt. If it hadn't been for higher ed, the Mac would have been a bust, because they had no solution for the installed IBM base, and their own installed base was Apple IIs, and the Mac had no way to read either one. We were treated like kings, courted, taken care of, and we produced a lot of shareware and freeware and spurred application development in a lot of places. It was an extremely cordial relationship.

But in 1990, we detected a change when Bud Colligan left and Bernie Gilford came in from Berkeley. He did not get the relationship, and Apple completely screwed up the Apple University Consortium. After the 1990 meeting in Monterey, Apple decided not to renew it. They began the cold shoulder period, where Apple Higher Ed got smaller, deals were not very good, and most people had to become developers to get prices better than AUC had, and then the AUC disappeared. If Apple had brain one, they would try to reconstitute the AUC. In the last year or so, they have put more attention on higher ed; that began with their focus on key markets.

Maclopedia: Gilbert Amelio's just taken over at Apple. What's your sense of the direction in which he'll take the company?

Don: Amelio is the right guy at the right time. At National Semiconductor, he demanded that if you have a plan, you must execute it. And at Apple everyone thinks he is equally important, so he did the right thing; he spent the first day going into every building, popping

continues

his head in the door, saying hello, and he's going to bring back the beer bashes. He's got to recreate the enthusiasm, because their best products came out of skunkworks, like the LaserWriter, and AppleTalk, that Siddhu wasn't supposed to do. The company ethos was built on hot technology. So they need to combine some of that hot product with good management. They can't overextend themselves and let people run around in a lot of different directions. They have been spending too much on too many product ideas. They ought to look at, say, 100 ideas, and narrow that down to 15, then pick five of them to be products. They've got to productize more of the technology; given a reality check, they would have killed QuickDraw GX, seeing that other industry standards would have superseded it. That way, they could have gotten Copland and Open Doc out a year sooner. Pippin is going to be a good deal; Bandai will start selling it in Japan in the spring. They could have preceded Larry Ellison's announcement of the net computer, but when you have 50 guys working on telephony, hey, come on, they have not strategized what they are doing. When Amelio was at National Semiconductor, he would only approve projects that met their corporate goals. He said, "We are not a company that can fund everyone's science project."

I think he [Amelio] should create a pure skunkworks group, 50 or 100 people, with a fixed budget, and say, "Spend it any way you want, but don't go over budget." The skunkworks group should work like a black box, not having anything to do with what Apple is currently doing. That would be one way to pull back the talent they have been losing. I read the ads, and they are looking for lots and lots of senior engineers, and those are the folks you can't afford to lose. If things got exciting again, with that adrenaline rush, they would come back. They should invent the next generation of personal computers, whatever that means, from the operating system all the way down to the hardware, forgetting about Copland, or Gershwin, or the PowerPC. They should just sit down and blue-sky, imagine what I would have sitting on my desk in 2025, if I have a desk then. They should make some new Apple Fellows, pick some people you really want to work with, and let them go off and invent.

The true revolution in Mac networking came with the introduction of Farallon's PhoneNET connector.

These connectors enabled Macintosh computers to be networked with Apple's LocalTalk protocols, but used unshielded twisted pair (UTP) cabling, the same type of writing used by telephone systems. The main advantages of UTP were its low cost to install and the fact that many buildings were already wired with this cabling. The Phone net adapters were also significantly less expensive than Apple's LocalTalk connectors ($50 versus Apple's $150). This low cost and capability to use existing wiring let to PhoneNET quickly becoming the standard for LocalTalk connections, even within Apple's corporate offices.

As network applications grew in size and in power, the speed of Apple's original LocalTalk networks became a limiting factor in the continuing growth of Macintosh networks. In response to this need, developers began delivering products to support **EtherNet**, a faster and more robust networking standard. Initially, EtherNet hardware for the Macintosh could cost over $1,000/computer, but as demand and volume grew, prices dropped accordingly. Currently, many Macintosh models include built-in support for EtherNet, requiring only a small external transceiver, similar to the one required for LocalTalk. EtherNet networks also require a hub, a central dedicated file server unless you're using EtherWave adapters.

Currently, there are several options for Mac networking. **LocalTalk** is built into every Macintosh, and is the simplest option. It is, however, not as fast as EtherNet. It uses the printer port and AppleTalk system software. Because you can connect the LocalTalk network with inexpensive connectors and ordinary phone cable, it's the lowest cost network solution. LocalTalk supports a maximum of 32 nodes, or devices (Macs, printers, other peripherals) on the network.

EtherNet is faster than LocalTalk, and supports both local and **wide area networks** (WAN). It's commonly used in business and educational applications because it's versatile and enables Internet connections. It's also more expensive and requires special cabling and special adapters. EtherNet cards have been available for Macintoshes ever since the Mac II was introduced. Many current Mac models have EtherNet capability built-in, and those that don't can add it quite easily. Farallon's EtherWave adapters enable you to connect PowerBooks, slotless Macs, printers, and other peripherals to 10Base-T EtherNet. You can also use EtherWave to create a small hub-less network.

Apple's most recent networking innovation is called **Open Transport**. It's networking software that combines the control panels and software drivers of AppleTalk, EtherNet, TCP, and LocalTalk, so you can use whichever of these networking systems is available. It has been accelerated for Power Mac. Among its helpful attributes, it enables you to change your TCP and Internet configuration without re-starting your Mac.

Today, most computers are involved in networks, either internally or through a modem providing a connection to the worldwide Internet. In addition to the basic tools incorporated into every Mac many new higher performance hardware and software networking connections are now available, enabling the Mac to perform admirably as a networked personal computer.

Advantages There are several advantages to networking your Macintosh. The most obvious advantage of a network is the capability to share expensive equipment. A single laser printer can be used by multiple people, effectively driving its cost down. Other items that only require periodic use, such as data/fax modems, can be used by everyone and centrally managed without needing to purchase and install a dedicated unit for each user.

Another major feature networking provides is the distribution of information between computers. This is accomplished through the use of **servers**. Each server on the network handles the receipt, organization, and retransmission of information between the network's users.

Finally, networking enables the computer administrator to centrally manage and monitor a company's computers. The administrator can make use of the network to distribute software updates, as well as to watch for trouble on individual computers. It is far more efficient for a technician to make a set of changes once and electronically distribute them to each computer than to walk from station to station looking for problems and making updates.

For More...

If you want to do this...	Go to this entry...
Find out about modems and how they work	Modems; Modem, Types
Learn about hooking up a modem	Modems
Learn about online services	America Online; CompuServe; Online Services; Prodigy
Learn about calling your home computer from your PowerBook	Apple Remote Access
Learn about network wiring	Network Topology; Transmission Media
Learn about EtherNet	EtherNet; Network Protocols
Learn about interconnecting networks	Bridges; Hub; Routers
Learn about managing a network	Network Administration

Bibliography

Basic Guide to Data Communications, published by Data Communications Magazine, 1991 (0-07-607026-3).

Build Your Own LAN and Save a Bundle, Aubrey Pilgrim, published by Tab/McGraw-Hill, 1992 (0-07-050108-4).

Integrating Macs with Your PC Network, Ken Maki, published by Wiley, 1994, (0-471-30505-7).

Mac Online: Making the Connection, Carla Rose, published by Windcrest, 1993, (0-8306-4254-4).

Networking the Macintosh: A Step-by-Step Guide to Using AppleTalk in Business Environments, Bill Woodcock, published by McGraw-Hill, 1993, (0-07-071684-6).

Networking and the Chooser

The Chooser is one of the least understood parts of the MacOS, but one of the coolest. With it, a user can find and select network (and local) services in an easy and consistent manner. The Chooser does many interesting things behind the scenes. It dynamically generates a list of available **network zones**. When you choose a particular service by clicking an icon, the Chooser then generates a list of those devices that meet the selection criteria. Finally, after you've selected a particular named service, the Chooser proceeds to discover the AppleTalk address of the chosen service. (You see, the names in the Chooser are for your benefit, while the network addresses are for the benefit of the Macintosh.)

Each AppleTalk device automatically generates a unique **node number**, but initially it's only known by that device. Nodes don't automatically know the node numbers of other devices. With other protocols, such as DECnet, this problem is solved manually. Someone (usually the DECnet administrator) uses a utility program to create a database of node addresses. This database is required on every DECnet node in order for that node to communicate with the other nodes.

Apple, desiring a plug-and-play environment, decided that this manual creation of node lists was not in keeping with the spirit of Macintosh. An alternative approach was developed to solve the problem of address determination. Let's consider a Mac that needs to print a document to a particular LaserWriter on the network. The Mac doesn't have any idea of the other nodes on the network. Therefore, it must go through a process of discovery to identify the available services. This is done by the AppleTalk protocol known as the Name Binding Protocol, or NBP. The process is simple.

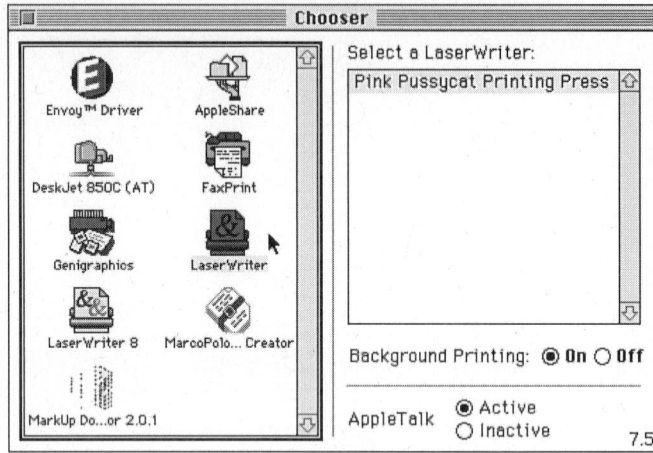

When a user opens the Chooser and clicks a service icon (such as the LaserWriter icon), the Macintosh first acquires a list of zones from the nearest routers with the Zone Information Protocol (ZIP). It then sends out an NBP Lookup Request packet. (Actually, it doesn't simply send it out, it broadcasts—or multicasts—the request to all devices on the cable. This makes sense because the Mac has no idea who to send the request to anyway.) Essentially, the NBP Lookup Request packet contains information on the requested named service. The Object name is the name of the entity that is usually assigned by a person. For a Mac, the object name is defined in the Macintosh Name field of the Sharing Setup control panel. LaserWriter object names are established by the Namer utility program. Examples of object names include: Alfie's Mac, 2nd Floor LaserWriter, and Mom's File Server.

Of course, multiple LaserWriters can respond to the NBP Lookup Request, and as they do, your Macintosh displays their names in the Chooser. Then, when you select a printer, the Macintosh simply remembers the name of the currently selected printer. This name is then stored in the memory of the Macintosh. This is why, for example, when someone moves their PowerBook from the office network to their home network, the office printer is still selected. To solve this problem, the LaserWriter must be reselected from the Chooser.

This process also offers an explanation for the rare event that occasionally happens when someone selects a printer on Friday, then the network is altered over the weekend and the printer just so happens to choose a new node number for itself. When Monday comes, the user receives a "…can't locate printer" message. Again, reselecting the printer from the Chooser solves the problem.

This NBP request/response conversation happens every time a Macintosh user selects a service from the Chooser. Because the NBP delivery mechanism involves broadcasting (or multicasting), NBP traffic can be a significant part of AppleTalk network traffic.

Networking and Education

Computer networks aren't restricted to businesses. You can also find them in classrooms and school computer labs from kindergarten on up. The only problem with networking at this level is, well… kids will be kids. There's always going to be one in the class who "accidentally," or otherwise, drags the group project to the trash, or tries to erase the shared hard drive "just to see what would happen." The solution to this, and to most other classroom computing problems is to control access to files and applications on shared systems. Several years ago, Apple introduced At Ease, a "goof-proof" desktop for the family Mac. It had a simple desktop with large buttons for accessing files and applications and two large folders to keep things organized. It also kept anyone who didn't know the password procedure from getting into the real desktop, or into any non-approved applications or folders (and especially the System Folder).

Now, there's **At Ease** for Workgroups. It can be used at the elementary level with the same child-proof desktop, or at the "experienced Mac user level" with the familiar Finder interface, with its windows, icons, and pull-down menus. Administrators can manage security in both environments, preventing users from changing system settings and controls or from deleting, accessing, or modifying files and applications that are not in their designated folders. The hard disk on each Macintosh system can also be locked to prevent users from accessing information on that disk if they start the system from another disk.

At Ease for Workgroups is designed especially for networked computers. The network administrator can configure At Ease from any Macintosh system on the network. They can also authorize teachers or other users to perform basic At Ease administrative tasks. Shared applications and documents can be stored on any file server on the AppleTalk network, and teachers can have centralized "drop-box" folders into which students can submit assignments electronically.

You can even create a list of approved CDs to prevent users from accessing unauthorized materials. And within the At Ease desktop, each CD or floppy disk conveniently appears in its own At Ease folder. At Ease for Workgroups supports up to 200 different configurations and 4,000 distinct users. It's the best way to make sure your network is child-proof.

See Also
At Ease

Networking, Why and How

While PC-based platforms require the addition of expensive and difficult-to-use hardware and software, networking on the Macintosh is actually quite easy and inexpensive. Generally, Macintosh users begin with the built-in LocalTalk networking, and expand to Ethernet as their needs (and budget) expand. Usually, one computer called the **server** is in charge of collecting and distributing information. The computers used to connect to the servers are called clients. There are several types of servers, each of which handles specific tasks.

There are several advantages to networking your Macintosh. Computer networks enable people to accomplish more with their computers than they could without the network. Networking saves both time and money. It's an investment that pays for itself very quickly.

Device Sharing The most obvious advantage of a network is the ability to share expensive equipment. This is important in the small office and even in a home situation where there might be one computer for the adults and one for the kids. A single laser printer or scanner can be used by many people, effectively driving the equipment cost down. Also, other items such as modems and fax modems can be shared by everyone, without needing to purchase one for each user.

Information Sharing Networks enable computer users to pool their information, leading to better communication. In a business setting, it's important for the secretary or office manager to know what his or her boss's schedule is. A shared calendar lets the people who need to locate someone know whether that person is in the office, in a meeting, or at an outside appointment. It lets managers plan meetings, knowing in advance that the people who must be present will be available, and it even lets users see what conference rooms will be available on a particular day and time.

It's common for several people to have input into a document or spreadsheet. These "workgroup" projects are handled much more easily when each member of the group can access the document through a central file server and make his or her additions to it without the need to deliver updated print-outs to the other members of the group, or to crowd a group of people around the screen to attempt to work together. Networking enables each member of the group to work in the comfort of his or her own office and have the same amount of control (or possibly more than) they'd have in a group meeting.

Databases are information repositories. It's only reasonable for everyone in an office to have access to the same database. Keeping a printed copy of it on each desk means reprinting every time a new customer is added, or a phone number changed. Keeping it accessible on the network saves paper, and gives everyone the same opportunity to use the most current information.

See Also
Network Administration; Network Communication; Network Maintenance; Network Wiring Strategies

New Folder Command

Folders help you organize your work. Empty new folders are created by selecting New Folder (⌘-N) from the **File menu** in the Finder. You can create as many new folders as you want, and you can place folders within other folders (just like a real file cabinet).

Folders help you stay organized by letting you group similar items together. If, for example, you're designing résumés for all your friends, you might want to create a folder called "Résumés" where you can store all of your friends' résumés.

That way, when you're looking for a particular resume, you know to look inside the resume folder. But what if one of your friends has three different lines of work and you've designed three different résumés? You can create another new folder within your "Résumés" folder and put all of this person's résumés within that folder for easy organization. Imagine how your hard drive window would look if every document you saved was saved in your startup hard drive window. Soon there would be hundreds of documents all over your main hard drive window, and finding anything would be a confusing and time-consuming task. It would be like having a real file cabinet, with no dividers.

When you select new folder, the new folder appears in the **active window.** If no window is open, the new folder appears on the desktop but can be dragged anywhere. Folders are created with the name "Untitled Folder," but the name field is already **highlighted**, ready for you to type in a new name. If you decide to create many folders at one time, each subsequent folder has a number added to the end of the folder name ("Untitled Folder 2," "Untitled Folder 3," and so on).

To create a new folder, follow these steps:

1. At the Finder level, select New Folder (⌘-N).

2. A new folder appears with the name field highlighted for you to type in a new name. You can type the new name immediately.

See Also
Active Window; File Menu; Highlight

New Group Command

If you're connected to a **network**, you can assign a number of individual **users** to one group of registered users. To create a new group, you must use the **Users & Groups** control panel and choose New Group from the **File menu**, as shown in the figure. A Group **icon** appears, and you can add user names to this group by clicking and dragging the user icons onto the Group icon. You can see the members of a given group by double-clicking the Group icon. The groups that an individual user belongs to are found by clicking the individual user's icon.

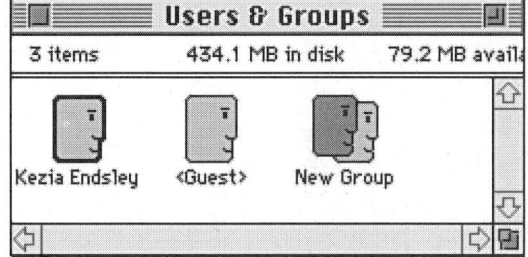

To create a new group, follow these steps:

1. Choose the Users & Groups control panel.

2. Choose New Group from the File menu.

3. Name the group, and add users to the group by clicking and dragging their user icons onto the Group icon. They are then part of that group. To see the users in a group, **double-click** the Group icon. To remove a group member, drag his or her username from the group. This group now appears in the User/Group **pull-down menu** in the **Sharing** control panel.

See Also

Control Panels; Double-Click; File Menu; Icons; Pull-Down Menu; Users and Groups

News Article

A basic unit of communication in Usenet newsgroups. Participants in a newsgroup discussion post new articles to initiate a thread or series of responses and counter-responses to articles. A typical article may include header information, quoted material from a previous message in a thread, the actual message, and sometimes the contents of a signature file.

See Also

Netscape Navigator; Netiquette; News Article, Replying to; Newsgroup, Posting to; NewsWatcher; Usenet; World Wide Web

News Article, Replying to

The way to find out more or respond in some way to a message or thread of messages on a specific topic in **Usenet.** Also called *following up* to another message.

You can respond in two ways:

■ Send **email** to the person posting the message you want to reply to.

■ Post a reply to the entire **newsgroup**.

In **NewsWatcher**, you reply to a news message as follows:

1. Use the commands in the "News" menu to bring the reply window to screen.

2. Icons at the top of the reply window let you specify if the reply should go to the newsgroup, to the poster, or to another email address that you can enter. You can also email yourself if you want to save a copy.

In **Netscape Navigator's** news reader, you reply as follows:

1. Click "Post Reply" (or "Post and Mail Reply" if you not only want to post a message but also send that message via email to the author).

N

2. Click the "Quote" button to quote the article to which you're replying. This gives your reply a context for readers who pick up the thread by reading your follow-up article. You can edit the quoted material if you like.

3. Write your response after the quoted material and click on the "Send" button. You can also click "Send Later" to queue the message to be sent in a batch.

See Also

Internet; Newsgroup; Netscape Navigator; Netiquette; NewsWatcher

Newsgroups, Posting to

A way of initiating communication on a new topic in **Usenet**, as opposed to replying to a message in an existing discussion thread.

In **NewsWatcher,** you post a message as follows:

1. Double-click on a newsgroup you want to post to in your subscription window.

2. From the "News" menu, choose "New Message." NewsWatcher brings up the New Message window, with the Newsgroups line already filled in, and the cursor on the Subject line.

3. Type your article, then click on the "Send" button to post your message to the newsgroup.

Netscape Navigator's newsgroup reader posts messages as follows:

1. Choose "Netscape News" from the "Window" menu.

2. Click "New News Message" from the "File" menu while the news window is open.

3. If you want to post copies of your articles to other groups, type a comma after the name of the current group in the "Post To:" box and enter the names of the other groups, separated by commas.

4. Type a subject in the "Subject" box.

5. Type your article. (Do not attach anything.)

6. Your signature file, if you have specified one, appears automatically in the bottom of the "Message Composition" window you are typing in.

7. Click "Send."

Users are cautioned against posting copyrighted works such as magazine articles or newspaper stories (a link to the story in question, if it can be found on the Internet, is acceptable, however). Also avoid posting scanned photos taken from TV or videotape, headline news that can be found elsewhere, or personal email.

See Also

Internet; Newsgroup; Netscape Navigator; Netiquette; NewsWatcher; Usenet

Newsgroups, Subscribing

When you first launch a client program for reading and posting to **Usenet** newsgroups, you must subscribe to the groups you want to read. This enables the client program to know what groups to present to you, rather than having to load the entire (lengthy) list of newsgroups each time you connect.

Occasionally, the newsreader software, such as **NewsWatcher** or **Netscape Navigator,** automatically subscribes you to a couple of basic groups with good information for beginners, such as **news.newusers.questions** and **news.announce.newusers.**

For the most part, however, the thousands of available newsgroups are in the "unsubscribed" category. Although most news servers do not carry a list of all newsgroups, you still have to navigate through a full group list at least once in order to subscribe to the groups you expect to visit often.

See Also

Internet; Newsgroups, Posting to; Netscape Navigator; NewsWatcher; Usenet

NewsWatcher

A well-known and popular freeware program that enables Internet users to connect to **Usenet** newsgroups and post and read messages. This news browser was developed by John Norstad and is the leading news reader for the Mac.

The first time you launch NewsWatcher, a dialog opens, asking for the addresses of your news **server** and your mail server, as shown in the figure that follows.

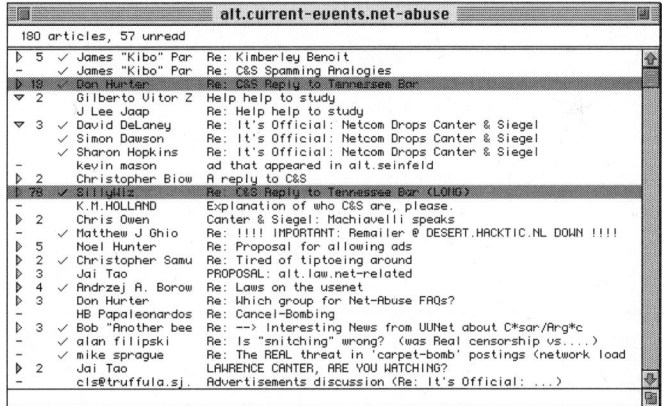

You need to ask your **Internet service provider** or system administrator for these addresses, as well as other essential information for connecting to the Internet (see the list of questions in the entry on **SLIP**, for instance).

After you enter this information, you are presented with a screen asking for your personal information and email address. After you enter this information, NewsWatcher downloads the Full Group List of newsgroups available on your news server, the computer that routes Usenet information. Downloading this list can take several minutes.

After the full list appears on-screen, choose New Group Window from the File menu. NewsWatcher then opens a small, empty window. Scroll through the Full Group List and drag groups that interest you to the small, empty window. This serves as a list of groups you expect to visit regularly, thus eliminating the need to load the full list every time you connect.

NewsWatcher's Preferences settings enable one to specify where to save files, identify a **signature file** for postings, specify font and size for viewing articles and files, and a choice of single-key navigating of messages with the keypad. A spacebar shortcut takes you to the next screen and then to the next unread message. NewsWatcher can also automatically download and decode binary files that have been posted, usually in **BinHex** or uuencoded form.

To read a newsgroup in your list, double-click it or use one of the keypad shortcuts (if you have them enabled). NewsWatcher opens another window containing the subjects of all the articles in the group. Alongside each subject is either a dash or a triangle and number, as shown in the following figure.

A dash indicates that the article is the only one in the **thread** or series of messages on a particular topic. The triangle indicates that there are more than one message, and the number indicates how many articles are in that thread. You can click the triangle to show the other articles, just as you click a triangle in the System 7 Finder to display a folder's contents.

With an article window open, you can go to the next article, next thread, or next group. You can also reply to an article via **email** or post a follow-up to the newsgroup using commands in the News window.

Because John Norstad makes the NewsWatcher source code freely available, others have enhanced the program and created "clones" such as VA.Newswatcher and YA.Newswatcher. The new programs incorporate enhanced features such as message filtering.

See Also

AppleScript; BinHex; Email; Internet; Netscape Navigator; SLIP; Usenet

NeXT

After leaving Apple in September 1985, **Steve Jobs** founded NeXT Computer, Inc., to create computers specifically targeted at the higher education market. When Jobs informed Apple's board of directors of his plan, they initially considered investing in the company until they found out that Jobs intended to take five key Apple employees with him. Apple sued but eventually dropped the suit when Jobs agreed not to hire away any other Apple employees for a period of six months.

After this inauspicious start, NeXT managed to get going. In early 1988, it received a major infusion of cash when H. Ross Perot invested $20 million.

The first NeXT computer, a sleek black cube with some impressive technical features inside, was introduced in October of 1988. The NeXT used a version of the UNIX operating system combined with a sophisticated **object-oriented development environment**, together known as NEXTSTEP.

Although NeXT aimed the machine at colleges and universities, they didn't show much interest. It was overpriced as a personal computer, but underpowered as a workstation. The computer also suffered from some of the same problems as the original Macintosh: a disk drive incompatible with everything else, no color, and poor performance.

NeXT rectified these problems in subsequent machines, but even some of these machines were plagued with problems. The one thing that managed to garner praise was the NEXTSTEP operating system. In January 1992, Steve Jobs announced that NeXT would port NEXTSTEP to run on Intel-based PCs.

In February 1993, NeXT abandoned the hardware market entirely, announcing that it would sell its hardware operations to Canon and focus its business exclusively on the NEXTSTEP operating system. Although NEXTSTEP is still a small player in the operating system wars, it has gained a significant following among developers who write custom applications for corporations. More recently, NeXT has made significant strides on the Internet with its "WebObjects" tools for building server applications for the **World Wide Web**.

See Also

Development Environment; Jobs, Steve

Next File (Keyboard Shortcut)

To move to the next file down (alphabetically) in a **window** viewed in a **list view**, use the Tab key as a keyboard shortcut. The Tab key moves you alphabetically through the contents of the active window. For example, if you're navigating through a window in the list view, rather than using the mouse to click the next item in the list, you can scroll alphabetically through the items in the list by using the **Tab key**. If you should pass an item you're looking for, you can use the keyboard shortcut Shift-Tab to move alphabetically backwards through files in the list.

See Also

Keyboard Shortcuts; Tab Key; Window

Nickel Cadmium, *See PowerBook Batteries*

Nickel Metal-Hydride, *See PowerBook Batteries*

Night Trap, *See Violence in Games*

Nine Men's Morris, *See Classic Collection*

Nine Month Miracle, *See A.D.A.M., The Inside Story*

Nisus Writer

Nisus Writer 4.0 is the current incarnation of a word processor that has been around, and largely overlooked, for quite a few years. Nisus was responsible for many of the innovations later found in other word processors, including macros, multiple undos, and the capability to zoom in and out of a page. It still has a few tricks not yet appropriated by the big names, such as noncontiguous text selection and multiple **Clipboards**. Nisus enables you to keep ten separate Clipboards. You can edit the contents, and copy and paste from all of them independently. Nisus Writer also has a powerful Find/Replace tool that can find and replace a word or phrase in any open document, not just the one in which you happen to be working. It also has the capability to search closed files, giving you the option of opening them and making changes if the search target is found. The figure below shows the Nisus Find/Replace options.

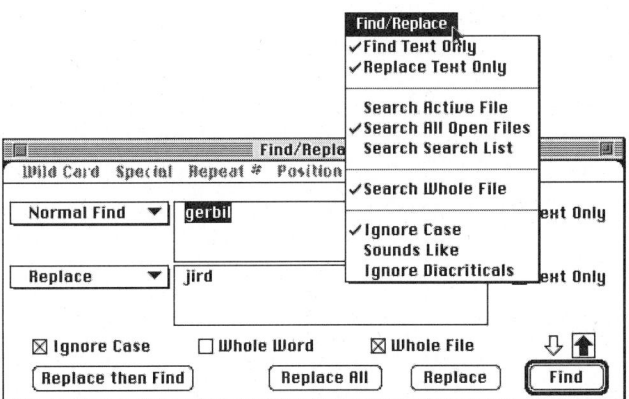

Nisus Writer 4.0 uses a new simplified interface with eight floating tool palettes. One of its strengths is its foreign language capability. If your word processing needs demand writing in several languages, Nisus Writer is your best choice. It supports over eighteen different languages, including Arabic, Hebrew, Japanese, and Russian, as well as those that use the Roman alphabet. It even has a right-to-left ruler for those languages that are written in the opposite direction as English. Some languages require system additions (for example, control panels, extensions, fonts) that can be purchased from Nisus Software or Apple Computer. Additionally, certain language capabilities require a language enabling hardware device called the Language Key. It has built-in support for text-to-speech conversion in five languages, so that you can hear the proper pronunciation of what you have written.

Nisus most definitely is *not* the best program if you need to send lots of letters. Its mail merge function is practically nonexistent. You must enter all field names, field markers, and merge commands entirely by hand. If you dread the thought of sending out mass mailings, don't even think about buying Nisus. It also is not the program of choice for creating a newsletter or setting text in any kind of creative layout. Nisus Writer restricts you to columns of equal width. You can use only one column format per document. Even worse, it's impossible to edit in the only view that displays multiple columns.

On the other hand, if your word processing consists of sending letters to your friends or business associates in other countries, or making lots of changes in plainly formatted documents, Nisus does the job quickly and easily.

See Also

MacWrite Pro; Word; WordPerfect; Word Processing; WriteNow 4.0

NNTP

A protocol or set of standards designed to enable the distribution, posting, and responses to **Usenet newsgroup** articles on the **Internet**.

NNTP (Network News Transfer Protocol) performs the essential task of enabling news articles to be stored in a central database called a news server, so that a newsgroup subscriber can view the brief title and sender information about each article and then select the ones he or she wishes to read.

Most newsgroup participants probably take NNTP for granted because it works in the background and is a well-established part of the Internet infrastructure. But enabling central storage of news on news servers via NNTP dramatically impacts network traffic.

All popular newsgroup **clients** support NNTP, including **NewsWatcher** and **Netscape Navigator**.

For more information see the Internet Working Group Request for Comments (RFC) 977 (**ftp:// ds.internic.net/rfc/rfc977.txt**).

See Also

Internet; News Article, Posting to; News Article, Replying to; Netscape Navigator; NewsWatcher; TCP/IP; Usenet; World Wide Web

Node ID, *See Node Number*

Node Identifier, *See Node Number*

Node Number

In networking, a Node number is the specific address of a computer or peripheral device that's part of a network. On an AppleTalk network, it's an 8-bit number unique to that node. It's also called the node identifier or node ID.

Non-Breaking Characters, *See Tracking*

Non-Breaking Space

Non-breaking spaces are one of several **invisible characters**. A non-breaking space keeps two words from being separated at the end of a line. If, for instance, you didn't want your client's name, Universal Buggywhip Company, to wrap around in the ad, you'd put non-breaking spaces after Universal and Buggywhip, to keep the whole name on one line. A non-breaking space is also called a hard space. Use the combination Option-Spacebar to type a non-breaking space.

Non-Linear Storytelling Games

Before the days of multimedia enhancement, 3D sound and graphics and animation, the main form of gaming was Interactive Fiction. Similar to the action of **MUDs** on the Internet, early games focused on exploring a text in much the same way that the Choose Your Own Adventure book series operated in the seventies. Using short commands like "Pick up book" and "open door," you moved to the next stage of the

story. Each scene opened with a brief description of where you were and what objects were near you. Basically, interactive fiction was an adventure game without the graphical user interface (**GUI**).

In fact, one of the most popular series of IF games was the Zork series from Infocom, which has given us the incredible multimedia game **Return to Zork** and the forthcoming Zork: Nemesis. Infocom was the leading publisher of these games, which Activision recently made available on CD packages with different themes such as The Adventure Collection and The Comedy Collection. Each CD contains one of the original Zork titles, along with other interactive games. One of the all-time greatest examples of this type of game was Douglas Adams' Hitchhiker's Guide to the Galaxy, based on the best-selling novel.

Aside from the Activision CDs and the interactive fiction and multiple MUDs on the Internet, non-linear storytelling is alive and well on CD-ROM in the form of innovative titles like **The Residents' Bad Day on the Midway** and **The Dark Eye** from Inscape and hypertext titles from Eastgate Systems. A multimedia enhanced mystery, spanning a thousand years, is available in the CD-ROM magazine *Launch*.

See Also

Cypher, The; Dark Eye, The; Residents' Bad Day on the Midway, The

None Compressor

This **compressor** saves a video sequence to disk without performing any compression. Video is simply digitized and saved to disk. This may seem an odd type of "compressor," but it is an option that makes it possible to capture video without risking **drop frames**. A fast and large hard disk is needed to accomplish this task. You won't be able to capture full frame video with this technique, because the amount of data becomes too large. After the images are captured, they should be **recompressed** in order to reduce the file size.

See Also

Asymmetrical Compressors; Compressor; Drop Frames; Spatial Compression; Symmetrical Compressors; Temporal Compression

Norton Disk Doctor

Norton Disk Doctor, part of **Norton Utilities** for the Macintosh, is a repair utility that diagnoses and repairs damaged **hard disks** or disks. This utility searches on the disks for bad areas or sectors, checks for system software damage or corruption, and searches for any problem that might cause hard disk or system crashes (see the following figure).

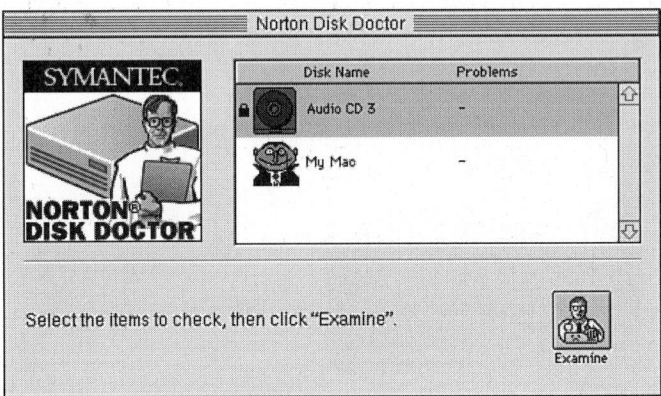

There are a number of symptoms that might cause you to call upon the Disk Doctor to give your Mac a checkup. They include frequent crashes, the inability to startup from the startup disk, missing files or files that have lost their icons, files whose names appear scrambled, and most any other unusual occurrence. It's better to be safe than sorry.

In many cases Norton Disk Doctor can repair common software problems it encounters during its search. If Norton Disk Doctor encounters a software problem, it reports the problem to you in a dialog box and gives you the option of fixing the problem (if the Disk Doctor can fix it) or ignoring the problem. To help you make your decision, this report also tells you what the nature of the problem is and how serious it is.

At the end of the diagnostic test, a complete report of the results of the Disk Doctor's tests can be viewed on-screen, saved, or printed.

Symantec
10201 Torre Ave,
Cupertino, CA, 95104-2132,
Phone: (800) 441-7234.
Web: **http:// www.symantec.com**

See Also

Crashes, System; Disks and Drives; Hard Disks

Norton Fast Find

This is a popular third-party "Find File" desk accessory that is part of the Norton Utilities suite of utility programs. Norton Fast Find offers you a very speedy Find function that is somewhat similar to Apple's own find function, except many users feel that Norton Fast Find is significantly faster than Apple's own search engine.

The list of available disks to search appears in a small window on the left of the dialog box. To select a disk, simply click it. To search all available drives, you can choose **Select All** Drives from the **Edit menu** (⌘-A). You search for files by entering a name or keyword in the "Look For:" field and then clicking the icon of a man running, as shown in the following figure.

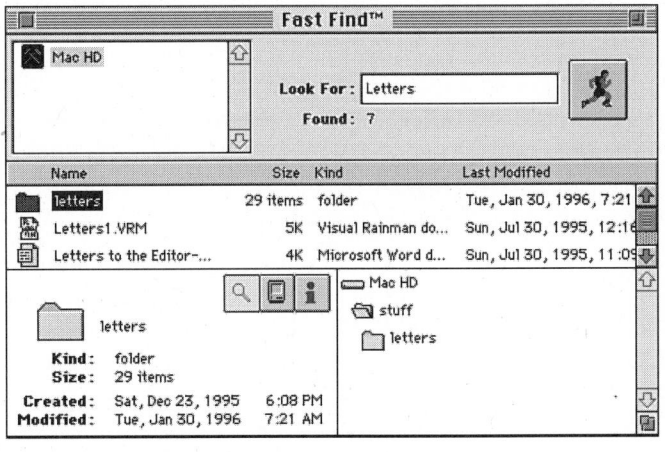

A window will display all possible matches. For more information on a particular file found in the search, click the file. The path to that file is displayed in a lower window and the file's information from the **Get Info** window is displayed, including creation date, modification date, and size. If you click the magnifying glass icon, the file's contents are displayed in a window, helping you to determine whether this is actually the file you're searching for.

If you click the icon that looks like a Mac, it returns you to the Finder and open the window where the file is located. If you click the "i" icon, it takes you to the Get Info screen for that file and you can add **comments** to the file if you wish. You can also edit other attributes in the info section as well, including editing the icon in an icon painting window.

There are a host of other options available, including moving the selected file to the desktop or into the Trash, narrowing the search by choosing specific parameters, and printing a list of the items found in the search.

To use Norton Fast Find to search for a file, follow these steps:

1. Select Norton Fast Find from the Apple menu. (The System does not automatically install Norton Fast Find; it is a third-party utility that is part of the Norton Utilities package.)

2. Enter the name, part of the name, or a keyword in the Look For field. Click the icon of the running man, or press Return, to begin your search.

3. After Norton Fast Find displays the list of matches, click any item to display the file information. For more in-depth info, use the "i" icon or the magnifying glass. If you want to access the file, click the icon that looks like a Mac and you will return to the Finder. The window that the file is located within opens and the file will be highlighted to help you find it.

Norton Speed Disk

The Norton Speed Disk utility program is part of the **Norton Utilities** package, which enables you to optimize your hard disk by defragmenting your **hard disk**. Over time, the information on your hard disk can become fragmented into various locations, as shown in the figure.

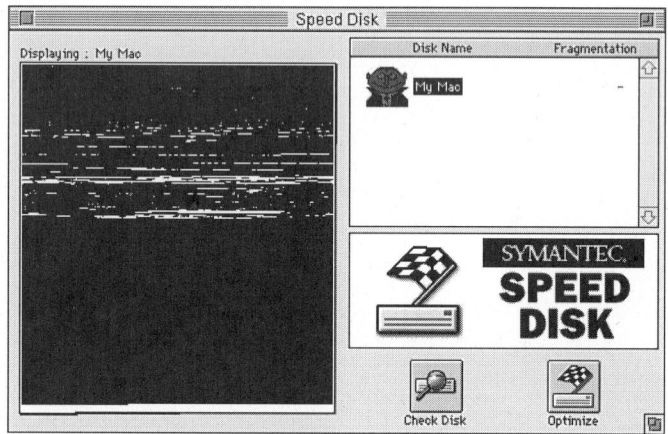

This can slow the access speed of your hard disk as it tries to find requested information. Speed Disk defragments this information and puts the most frequently used information closest to the drive heads and less frequently used further away. By making these files easily available to the hard disk, your hard disk's speed is enhanced.

Symantec
10201 Torre Ave,
Cupertino, CA, 95104-2132,
Phone: (800) 441-7234
Web: **http:// www.symantec.com**

See Also

Hard Disks; Norton Utilities for Macintosh

Norton Utilities for Macintosh

Norton Utilities is a popular suite of commercial diagnostic and system enhancement tools that add a host of features, enhancements, and repair utilities to your Mac's system. They include:

- **Norton Disk Doctor**, a repair utility designed to diagnose and repair damaged **disks** or **hard disks**. This utility searches disks for bad areas or sectors, checks for system software damage or corruption, and searches for any problem that might cause hard disk or system crashes. In many cases, Norton Disk Doctor can repair common software problems it encounters during its search. (See the following figure.)

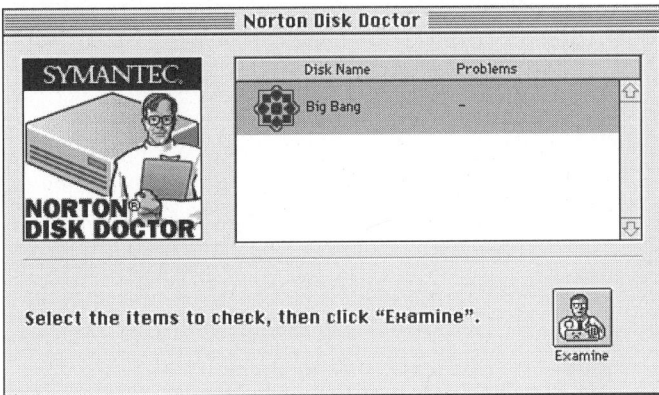

- Norton Backup offers an automated customizable backup for files on your hard disk or over a **network**.

- Norton Disk Editor enables you to view and edit a disk's resources (which in many cases contain invisible files, like the desktop file). This tool is used by professionals and technicians for repairing damaged or corrupted files.

- Norton Encrypt enables you to protect sensitive files by using an encryption algorithm to scramble the contents of a selected file and attach password protection to these files. To be able to read the files, you must enter the secret password. Encryption is popular for sending sensitive files across a **modem** or network that you don't want to be read by anyone without the proper password.

- Floppier is designed to quickly and easily copy the contents of one disk to a number of disks. An example would be a users group that offers a disk-of-the-month full with shareware titles. They can create a master disk, and Floppier copies that disk onto disks inserted into the disk drive. It even initializes unformatted disks if necessary during the copying sequence.

  - **Speed Disk** is a utility program that enables you to optimize your hard disk by defragmenting it. The information on your hard disk becomes fragmented into various locations on your hard disk. This slows the access speed of your hard disk as it searches through your disk to find requested information. Speed Disk defragments this information and puts the most frequently used information nearest the drive heads, and the less frequently used files toward the back. By making these files easily available to the hard disk, your hard disk's speed is enhanced.

- Unerase is a utility designed to recover files that you have deleted from your hard drive, often including "**trashed**" files. When you **empty the Trash**, the filename is removed from the directory as a visible file, but the file still exists on the hard disk until another file is written over it. If that file hasn't been overwritten, in most cases it can be recovered. If the file has been overwritten, it cannot be recovered. So the sooner you try to recover a trashed file, the better your chances are that it hasn't been overwritten.

N

■ Volume Recover is used when a disk is so badly damaged that you want to recover as much information as possible off the disk and store the contents of the volume on another disk before attempting to repair or reinitialize the damaged disk. If you have a severe hard disk crash, recovering the data and reinitializing the damaged disk is often your only choice.

■ Wipe Info makes certain that sensitive data deleted from a disk is in fact erased from the disk and irretrievable by using recovery software. Wipe Info deletes the file and writes over it to ensure that the file is not only erased from the disk's directory, but is erased from the disk as well. This is a necessary precaution when erasing sensitive files because when you empty the Trash, the filename is removed from the disk's directory, but the file remains on the hard disk until another file is written over it. This file can be recovered by using Unerase or another recovery utility.

■ **Disk Light** is a utility that flashes an **icon** of the active disk in the upper corner of the menu bar anytime that a disk is active. This helps you determine if your system has experienced a "freeze-up" or if it's just taking a long time to complete a request.

■ Fast Find replaces Apple's built-in Find function. The Fast Find utility is faster than Apple's Find function and offers a wide variety of added features and functions that enhance your system's find capabilities.

■ Key Finder is a replacement for Apple's **Key Caps** desk accessory that gives you a map of a selected font's special characters.

■ Norton Partition enables you to create partitions for hard disks and manage their use. You can also encrypt selected volumes and password protect their contents using this combination desk accessory and extension.

Symantec Corporation
10201 Torre Ave
Cupertino, CA, 95104-2132
Phone: (800) 441-7234
Web: **http:// www.symantec.com**

See Also

Crashes, System; Desk Accesories; Desktop File; Disks and Drives; Extensions Folder; Find Command; Hard Disks; Icons; Key Caps; Modem; Trash; Utility

Not Enough Memory Message

If you have one application running and **launch** another, you might receive an **alert box**, or message, stating, "There is not enough **memory** available to open this program." The alert message may also advise you: "To make more memory available, quit the other currently running applications," as shown in the figure.

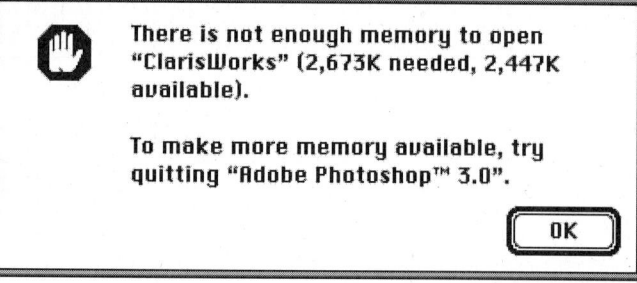

> There is not enough memory to open "ClarisWorks" (2,673K needed, 2,447K available).
>
> To make more memory available, try quitting "Adobe Photoshop™ 3.0".
>
> [OK]

This memory message deals with how the Macintosh handles **RAM**. Each program takes a certain amount of RAM to launch. If you have 16MB of RAM installed in your Macintosh, the programs you have open, combined with the **operating system**, cannot take more than 16MB of combined RAM to operate. If, for example, you have two programs open that use 5MB each, and your system is using 3M, you're using

13MB of the 16MB available. If you then try to launch an application that uses 6MB of RAM, you are exceeding the installed RAM of 16MB and get the Not Enough Memory message.

It's also possible to get the Not Enough Memory message when there isn't enough RAM available as a result of memory fragmentation. Memory fragmentation sometimes occurs when you've been running a number of different applications, and you **quit** one or more of these applications, and all of the memory used by that application is not properly released to be made available to other applications. So although it may appear that you have enough memory available to open a particular application (by checking the About This Macintosh dialog at the top of the Apple menu), the memory that is available is fragmented, and the system needs contiguous memory to open the application. Although memory fragmentation is a temporary situation, in many cases you'll need to close all your applications or even restart to free up this fragmented memory.

Sometimes the system doesn't release the memory that the application was using. When you check your memory usage by choosing **About This Macintosh** on the **Apple menu**, it looks like you have more than enough memory to launch a particular program. But when you try to launch the program, memory fragmentation causes you to get a Not Enough Memory message. You normally have to quit your applications to defragment the memory, and depending on how badly it's fragmented, you may have to **restart** your computer to make that fragmented memory available to launch programs.

Another strategy to try if you don't have enough memory available to operate a particular application (or set of applications) is to use **Virtual Memory**. This feature (available in System 7 and higher) enables you to set aside a portion of your available hard disk to use as RAM. Virtual Memory is toggled on and off through the **Memory Control Panel**, and there you can decide how much hard disk space to use for Virtual Memory and which disk to use as your "virtual

disk." A restart is required after making these choices for Virtual Memory to be initiated on your system.

The downside of Virtual Memory, when compared to actual RAM, is that it is slower than real RAM because you're accessing a hard disk and using it as RAM, and your hard disk is considerably slower than real RAM (which is your fastest source of memory). The upside is that it's free!

There is also a very popular commercial product called RAM Doubler, from Connectix Corporation (2655 Campus Drive, San Mateo, CA 94403, Phone: (800) 950-5880, Web: **http://www.connectix.com**), which works with System 6.05 or higher, and uses a Virtual Memory scheme to fool your Macintosh into thinking there's twice the available RAM than really is present. RAM Doubler works quite well, and is especially popular with PowerBook users whose units shipped with a minimum amount of RAM.

The implementation of RAM Doubler is very simple: install the application and restart your computer. If you had 8MB of RAM before you installed RAM Doubler, upon restart the system will act as though it has 16MB and lets you open applications until you've reached your new 16MB limit. To see how RAM Doubler affects your system, choose the About This Macintosh dialog box at the top of the Apple menu with RAM Doubler. You'll see two figures for memory: Built-in memory (which is the actual figure for your installed RAM) and Total Memory (which is double your installed memory, courtesy of RAM Doubler).

See Also

About This Macintosh Dialog Box; Alert Box; Apple Menu; Memory Capacity and Expansion; Memory Control Panel; Quit Command; Restart; Virtual Memory

Notebook Computers, *See* *PowerBooks*

NotePad

The NotePad, found on the **Apple menu,** acts as a replacement for a regular note pad and enables you to type brief notes. The first time you launch NotePad it gives you eight blank note pages, and you can navigate through these pages by clicking the peeled-back left corner as shown in the following figure.

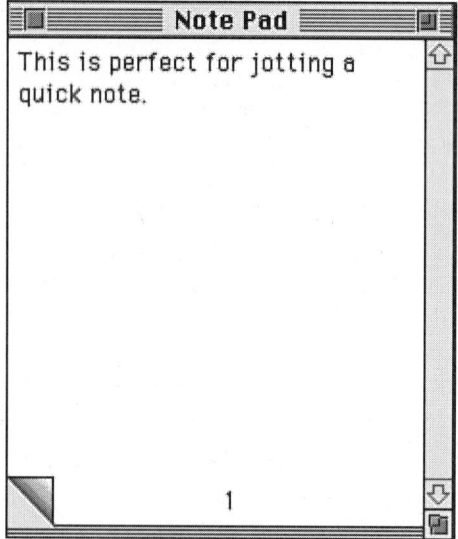

The pages make a flipping sound as your move from page to page. You can add additional note pages by choosing New Note from the File menu. You can also delete the current page by choosing Delete Note from the File menu as well. If you know which note page you want to go to, you can select **Go To** from the File menu and enter the note page number and you'll move directly there.

You can print any note by choosing **Print** from the **File menu,** which brings you the standard Apple print **dialog box.** If you want to print one copy of the note, you can bypass the Apple print dialog by choosing Print One from the File menu. The NotePad also has its own find function to help you find a particular word or phrase within your NotePad pages, by choosing Find from the Edit menu. The NotePad now enables you to set your default font for text by choosing the Preferences command in the Edit Menu.

To use the NotePad, follow these steps:

1. Choose NotePad from the Apple menu.
2. You may begin typing notes on the top page, or used the peeled-back lower-right corner to navigate to the page you want to use.
3. To add more pages, choose New Note from the File menu. To Delete a page, select Delete Note. To Find a word, use the Find function on the Edit menu and enter the word you're looking for and choose whether you want to search only the current note or all notes.

See Also

Apple Menu; File Menu; Go To Command; Stickies

Novell NetWare, *See Server*

Now Compress

This is a compression utility replaced by the built-in compression of the Now QuickFiler module that is a part of the **Now Utilities** suite of Macintosh enhancements.

See Also

Compression Utilities; Now Utilities

Now Contact

Now Contact and its fraternal twin, Now Up-to-Date, are sold bundled together, as well as separately. The chances are, if you use one, you'll use both. Now Contact has some very good features, chief among them being a Quick Contact icon on the menu bar that brings up a list of people and phone numbers. It's available anytime, even when Now Contact isn't open. Another good feature is the free-form comments area on the individual contact records, which gives you space to enter, or drag-and-drop, information from other applications. You can also view your contacts in a spreadsheet-like list view, but unlike similar programs, Now Contact lets you modify the information in individual cells while in the list view.

The single best feature of Now Contact is its easy integration with Now Up-to-Date. If you open your Now Contact record to make a note of a business call, and decide on a meeting, a couple of mouse clicks places the meeting on your calendar. If you're on an office network, a few more clicks schedules your coworkers to attend the meeting, too. The meeting appears on your calendar and as a contact item in the contact manager. The contact manager also keeps a record of notes and phone calls. The latest version of Up-to-Date includes optional ToDo lists on the calendar pages. To Do items can be assigned priority levels (None to High) and marked "in progress" or "done," as appropriate. Unlike previous versions of the software, this one supports wrap-around banners, so that your events can occur over a weekend, or for two weeks at a time. The calendar can be customized with your favorite fonts, and decorated with colorful icons.

QuickPad is a mini-application that comes with and talks to both Now Up-to-Date and Now Contact. It's a convenient way to enter appointments, notes, and other information quickly. Click the calendar icon to set a date and time for your appointment. Click the contact icon to enter the name of the person with whom you'll be meeting. The information will be transferred to the calendar and contact manager.

Now Up-to-Date, *See Now Contact*

Now Utilities

Now Utilities is a popular suite of commercial diagnostic and system enhancement tools that add a host of features, enhancements, and repair utilities to your Mac's system. The individual modules that make up Now Utilities include:

- Now Folder Menus adds the capability to make folders in the icon view hierarchical by adding a black triangle to the folder icon. You can expand the folder into a hierarchical view by clicking the folder. A hierarchical listing of the folder's contents appears.

- Now Menus enables you to arrange items in the **Apple menu** in any order you'd like, add separator bars to help you organize your Apple menu, and add additional hierarchical capabilities to the Apple menu. It also enables you to add up to two new pull-down menus to the menu bar to use as launchers for frequently used programs or documents.

- Now Profile gives you a detailed report on your Macintosh computer's hardware and software configuration, including software version numbers, installed font listings, printer drivers, **extensions**, and more.

- Now QuickFiler enables you to view all files and folders on your drive in a window and enables you to edit, rename, move, and open selected files quickly and easily. Now QuickFiler also contains a find function for locating files on your hard disk.

- Now Save enables you to set up a time interval for automatic saving of any open documents.

- Now Scrapbook is a catalog of cut/copy and pastable items that you can arrange, sort, name, and retrieve, that helps you organize and store graphics, text files, sounds, and QuickTime movies you've placed into Now Scrapbook.

- Now Startup Manager manages the loading order of extensions, startup files, **Chooser** items, and control panels to help you isolate conflicts within your system. You can also create different sets of startup items for different applications or different users.

- Now SuperBoomerang adds four **pop-up menus** to the standard **Open/Save dialog box**. The Folder menu enables you to go to any of your most recently opened folders. The File menu enables you to go to the most recent files you've used. The Drive menu enables you to have instant access to any mounted disk, and the Options menu enables you to add folders, rename files or folders, and has a find function.

N

Now SuperBoomerang also puts a recent file/folders menu on the Apple menu, but this feature is already built-in to System 7.5 and higher.

- Now WYSIWYG Menus enables you to customize the **font** menu in applications by making font names appear in their own typefaces, uniting font families, and enabling you to rearrange the sequence of fonts in the font menu for easy organization.

The latest version of Now Utilities (version 6.0) adds some new modules and updates the functionality of many of the existing modules. The new modules include:

- Now Auto Type enables you to create macros on the fly as you type commonly used phrases, such as your street address, Web URL address, signature, and so on.

- Now Shortcuts enables you to access a set of customizable Finder commands at any time by adding them to a "hot key" combination. If, for example, you've selected a folder, you can access commonly used Finder menu items without having to go up to the various menus by pressing the Now Shortcuts "hot key." A pop-up menu appears where your cursor is, and you can customize which items appear on this menu.

- Now Tabs enables you to have a small row of tabs across the bottom of the screen that give you one-click access to frequently used Finder windows. You could, for example, have your System Folder window, hard disk window, and Apple Menu Items window one click away by adding them to the Now Tabs module.

Now Software, Inc.
921 SW Washington Street, Suite 500
Portland, OR 97205-2823
Phone: 503-274-2800
Web: **http://www.nowsoft.com**

See Also

Apple Menu; Chooser DA; Clipboard; Control Panels; Extensions; Folders; Fonts; Norton Utilities; Pop-Up Menu

NREN, *See Internet*

NSFNET, *See Internet*

NTSC

NTSC (National Television System Committee of the Electronics Industries Association) is a standard for encoding and decoding an analog video signal. It is used in the United States, and several other countries (but there are other standards, such as **PAL**). The signal is made up frames of video, each frame contains 525 lines (a line is a row of phosphors on a television tube, essentially the equivalent of pixels on a computer monitor). This translates digitally to an image of 640×480 pixels, because the "lines" aren't all used for holding picture information. The top and bottom lines in the image are called the vertical banking areas. This is used as "blank time;" the time it takes the electron tube in the television set to go back up to the top of the screen to start drawing the next frame.

NTSC is an **interlaced** format. NTSC displays at 30 frames per second (actually 29.97 frames). Each frame is made up of two fields, which are the odd and even horizontal lines of the frame. The electron gun in the television set first draws one field and then the other, creating an interlaced effect. When a television camera records video, it also uses fields; first the odd horizontal lines, and then the even horizontal lines are passed to the recording device. If an object is moving rapidly while it is being photographed, feathering can sometimes be seen in the frame. Feathering is a slight offset between the position of the object in the odd lines and the even lines because the object was in a different location when the two fields were recorded. Feathering appears as jagged edges on the object.

See Also

Digital Video Cameras; PAL; QuickTime

NuBus, *See Power Mac Logic Boards*

NuBus Slots, *See Power Mac Logic Boards*

Numbers

Used for setting your preferences for numbers and currency, the Numbers **control panel** enables you to set the numbers format and how you want decimal points to be displayed. You can choose the default U.S. format or create a custom setup for an international number format and add it to the **pop-up menu**. You can choose the separators for decimals and thousands, what the currency symbol is, and whether the currency symbol appears before or after the numbers. These new settings become the custom settings in the Numbers pop-up menu. A display of the current number format appears in the bottom of the Numbers window.

Being able to choose a number format other than the default U.S. English is helpful anytime you're traveling abroad or if you're working in a foreign country. If you're working in France, for example, where the currency is French francs, you could set up your Mac to treat currency as if it were French francs, which use periods for the thousands delimiter in numbers rather than the comma used to distinguish thousands in U.S. dollars. Also, when writing out the date, many European countries list the day first, followed by the month, then the year, whereas in the U.S. we list month, day, year (9/30/96, for example).

To use the Numbers control panel, follow these steps:

1. Open the Numbers control panel from the Control Panels submenu on the Apple menu (or System Folder).

2. Choose a number format from the **pull-down menu**. This is also where you can decide whether to display the thousands separator.

4. Separators are chosen from pull-down menus or are entered from the keyboard.

5. To enter a default symbol, highlight the current symbol and type a new symbol from your keyboard.

See Also
Control Panels

Numbers, International Formatting

The Numbers **control panel** enables you to set how numbers are displayed within your system. You can choose the default U.S. format or create a custom setup for an international number format and add it to the **pop-up menu**. You can choose the separators for decimals and thousands, what the currency symbol is, and whether the currency symbol appears before or after the numbers. These new settings become the Custom settings in the Numbers pop-up menu. A display of the current number format appears in the bottom of the Numbers window.

Being able to choose a number format other than the default U.S. English is helpful anytime you're traveling abroad, or if you're working in a foreign country. If, for example, you're working in France, where the currency is French francs rather than dollars, you could set your Mac up to treat currency as if it were French francs, which use periods for the thousands delimiter in numbers rather than the comma used to distinguish thousands in U.S. dollars. Also, when writing out the date, many European countries list the day first, followed by month, then the year, where in the U.S. we list month, day, year (9/30/96 for example).

To set your Numbers preferences to an international number format, follow these steps:

1. Choose the Numbers control panel from the **Apple menu**.

2. Enter the desired foreign currency symbol, decimal symbol, and thousands symbol.

3. These settings now become the Custom setting and can be chosen from the Numbers control panel pop-up menu in the future.

See Also

Apple Menu; Control Panels; Pop-Up Menu

Numeric Keypad

The numeric keypad is styled after the keypad of a calculator and appears on the right side of some keyboards. It's designed so you can quickly enter numbers and easily use Apple's **Calculator DA**. A number of programs enable you to control the movement of the cursor with the numeric keypad.

Controlling the Pointer with Numeric Keypad You can use Apple's **Easy Access** Control Panel so that the numeric keypad controls your cursor. With Easy Access, you can control the speed and delay time of the **cursor's** movements. A number of programs use the numeric keypad to control the movement of the cursor.

The 8 key, for example, would move the cursor up, and the 2 key moves the cursor down. The 4 and 6 keys move the cursor left and right, respectively. You can move the cursor diagonally using the 7 or 9 keys to move up and the 1 and 3 keys to move down.

See Also

Calculator D/A; Cursor; Easy Access Control Panel; Keyboard

nVIR Virus

This virus is also known as nVIR-a, nVIR-b, Hpat, Jude, nFLU, MEV#, AIDS, J-nVIR, prod, nVIF-F, nCAM, MODM, and zero. When the System file is infected, a counter is set to 1,000. The counter is decreased each time the system is started or when you run an infected application. When the counter reaches zero, the virus sometimes says, "Don't panic" if MacinTalk is installed. The nVIR virus is not malicious except that it occupies memory and disk space.

See Also

ANTI Virus; CDEF Virus; CODE 1 Virus; CODE 252 Virus; Frankie Virus; INIT 17 Virus; INIT 29 Virus; INIT 1984 Virus; INIT 9403 Virus; INIT-M Virus; MacMag Virus; MBDF Virus; MDEF Virus; Scores Virus; T4 Virus; WDEF Virus; ZUC Virus

O

Oasis

Oasis is the painting program included in the Corel6 package for the Mac. Oasis accepts all Photoshop plug-ins, and searches their path out automatically when the program is installed. Plug-ins, Acquires, and Exports can be selectively turned on and off from a displayed list, a feature that can save precious time and memory. Oasis, perhaps because it comes to the Mac from another platform, does some minor things that make a Mac artist's life a lot easier. One of these is to allow you to toggle the menu bar off and on, expanding the work area just enough. In the same vein, you can also use a hot-key combination to switch the palettes off and on. The Lasso and Brushes palettes, normally accessed from the toolbox, can be torn off and placed on-screen for easier access.

Oasis has a gradient fill option that allows for the adjustment of cycles (repetitions) from 1 to 10. The result, when radial is turned on, is wave-like ripples in the gradated color selected. It's also possible to pre-determine the density of any applied effect or fill, making transparent compositions easier. The lasso selection tool can be set to choose only the static area, or it can expand or contract to include all other similar colors as those in the selected area, or all other appearances of the background. Support for HSV, RGB, CMYK, and HLS color palettes are included, and you may also add the "Video Colors" option so that only "legal" video colors are displayed with any palette choice.

Oasis offers five brushes: Artist (normal painting tool), Soften (Blurs edges), Smear (smears edges), Pull (pulls the targeted colors along with the brush), and Stretch (stretches the selection to a new area). You can also affect the graphics with brushes for Tint, Colorize, Valuate, and Saturate. An "Image Effects" window works differently than an effects application in other software. It contains a list of image operations like posterizing, brightness, and colorization. Setting the sliders causes it to apply the effects to the next selected (or present selected) area of the graphic. Experienced electronic painters will take a while to get used to this way of working. Everything considered, this is a good intermediate-level paint program.

File Save/Load Conventions Oasis loads the following formats: PICT, Apple Scrapbook, BMP, CGM, GEM IMG. GEM, IFF, JPG, PBM, PCX, PGM, Photoshop 2 and 2.5, PICT Resource, PixelPaint, PPM, RAW, RIFF, Scitex CT, TIFF, and XPM. Save formats include BMP, GIF, PCX, Photoshop 2 and 2.5, PICT Resource, Scitex CT, Targa, and TIFF. In addition, Oasis can acquire Anti-aliased PICT, Blank TIFF, EPS-DCS, Extensis Twain, Live Picture, Make Collage CMYK Table, Photo CD, Photoshop 3.0, PICT Resource, Plug-in Digitizer, QuickEdit, QuickTime (Painter and Photoshop), Scitex CT, Twain Acquire and Select Source, and Video Snapshot. It can export Amiga HAM, Cybermesh Demo and Cybermesh, EPS-DCS, Dummy Export, ImageWriter Color, Live Picture, Paths to Illustrator, Photoshop 3.0, QuickTime (Photoshop and Painter), Scitex CT, and Collage CMYK Table.

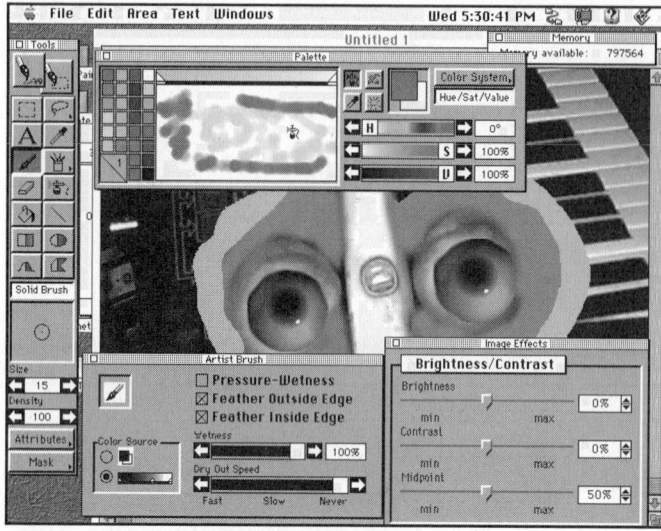

Aris Entertainment Aris Entertainment has come up with a CD-ROM that stands out as both unique and useful. The CD-ROM is called "Batiks", and the images are photos of dozens of Batik fabric designs, which make alluring backdrops for animation. Formats include large and small BMPs, PCX, TIFF (TIF), and WAV files. The CD is Windows and MAC compatible. There is a slideshow and an image browser included.

Aris Entertainment
4444 Via Marina, Suite 811
Marina Del Rey, CA 90292
(310) 821-0234
(310) 821-6463 FAX

Object, *See Programming*

Object Code

Object code is another term for **machine language** code. Any program that can be directly executed on a computer without further intervention from a **compiler** or interpreter is object code.

Object code is frequently used to describe individual parts of a program after they have been compiled but before they have been converted into a complete application by a **linker**.

See Also

Compiler; Linker; Machine Language

Object and Image CD-ROMs

No digital artist or animator can ever collect too many **3D** objects or graphics for texture mapping. There are hundreds of **CD-ROM** object and image collections available, and each contains hundreds of 3D objects and/or images. Although we don't have enough space to cover anywhere near all of these CD-ROMs, we can mention a few that you might find interesting for art and animation work. Remember that the Mac (System 7.x and later) can read PC CD-ROMs as easily as native formats, so Mac artists and animators can take advantage of most of the CD-ROMs on the market as far as 3D objects and images are concerned.

Aztech New Media Corporation Watermarks and Ghosted Backgrounds by artist David Hushion, Visual Rhythms 1 and 2, and Fashion 1 by photographer Joaquin Compta are some of the highly recommended Aztech graphics CD-ROMs. Each of these CD-ROMs gives artists and animators high quality, visually startling data to interweave with their work. The Watermarks CD is great for adding high quality backgrounds to text applications as well (multimedia text screens). The 25 backgrounds come in three TIFF sizes and formats: CMYK 32-bit for DTP, 24-bit for RGB video, and 8-bit grayscale (great for bump maps and alpha channel compositing). The second volume of the Visual Rhythms sets has 100 original photos by photographer Paul Smith, consisting of a variety of unique forms. All are suitable as backgrounds, although some might also serve for texture mapping purposes as well as DTP work. The Aztech CD-ROMs Fashion 1 and 2 consist of fashion models in various poses. For animators, these would be great tuck-in-the-corner shots, or in some cases might be composited into product-related backgrounds.

Also noteworthy from Aztech are the following:

SpaceViews 1 and 2: Each CD contains over 50 of the most awe-inspiring images of space objects and planetary phenomena. Each image comes in Lo-Res ($6 \times 8 \times 72$ DPI) and Hi-Res ($5 \times 4 \times 300$ DPI) Tiff format.

Jurassic Dinosaur: 96 royalty-free images of dinosaur fossils in two resolutions: 32-bit non-compressed color-corrected CMYK 300 DPI Tiff, and 24-bit non-compressed RGB Tiff at 72 DPI.

Gems: 99 photo images of precious gems from around the world, in two formats: 32-bit non-compressed color-corrected CMYK 300 DPI Tiff, and 24-bit non-compressed RGB Tiff at 72 DPI.

Floral Tapestry: 100 photos of flowers from around the world, in two resolutions: 32-bit non-compressed color-corrected CMYK 300 DPI Tiff, and 24-bit non-compressed RGB Tiff at 72 DPI.

Underwater Realms: 100 photos of fish, reefs, and underwater phenomena by nature photographer Joel Auerbach, in two resolutions: 32-bit non-compressed color-corrected CMYK 300 DPI Tiff, and 24-bit non-compressed RGB Tiff at 72 DPI.

Africa: African Traditional Peoples: 75 annotated images of head and body shots, groups in tribal array, villages, and the African environment, in two formats: 32-bit non-compressed color-corrected CMYK 300 DPI Tiff, and 24-bit non-compressed RGB Tiff at 72 DPI.

> Aztech New Media Corporation
> 2255 Markham Road
> Scarborough, Ontario, Canada
> M1B 2W3
> (416) 449-4787
> (416) 449-1058 FAX

Digital Wisdom "GlobeShots," produced by Mountain High Maps, is both IBM and MAC compatible, and contains over 250 colored bitmaps of global terrain shots in high relief. Included are 60 high-resolution globes on a white background and another 21 images on colored backgrounds, all in 24-bit TIFF format. The images come in a variety of subject areas, including clouds, starburst hi-lights, and saturated ocean floors. The images can be resized to fit digital art and animation needs, and are especially intended for those "pull-back" animations of the Earth. GlobeShots sells for $195.00. The Mountain High Maps full relief set of two CD-ROMs sells for $895.00.

TIP If your globe is just going to sit in a non-animated space, here's a trick you can use with the GlobeShots collection. Cut out a selected globe with a rectangular brush, getting as close to the edges of the globe picture as possible. Then select a 3D globe and use a frontal planar map for projection in your favorite 3D rendering software. The extraneous background picked up with the globe will disappear, and you'll have a nice 3D globe (as long as you don't intend to animate it). This is sometimes easier than cutting out a perfect circular brush, and it works just as well.

> Digital Wisdom, Inc.
> P.O. Box 2070
> Tappahannock, VA 22560-2070
> Tel: 1-804-758-0670
> Fax: 1-804-758-4512
> CompuServe: 72673,3360

> In Europe: Digital Wisdom Publishing, Limited

> 7 Wellington Court, Cambridge
> CB1 1HZ, United Kingdom
> Tel: +44 223-566-250
> Fax: +44 223-566-246

Image Club Image Club markets a number of CD-ROMs, "Photogear" (a collection of organic backgrounds and textures) and "Objectgear" (EPS format objects). The Objectgear graphics can be cut out with the help of the "magic wand" tool in Photoshop. The objects also come with a file of drop and cast shadows for each image, enhancing their 3D realism. 3D users might want to experiment by placing these 2D objects on 3D surfaces in a post-production painting process. The CDs are Windows/MAC compatible.

> Image Club, Inc.
> 729 Twenty Fourth Avenue Southeast
> Calgary, Alberta, Canada T2G 5K8
> Phone: 403-262-8008
> Fax: 403-261-7013
> Applelink: CDA0573
> CompuServe: 72560,2323
> America Online: **imageclub**
> Internet: **imageclub@aol.com**

Mary and Michael Question: What are the most useful backdrops that all animators lust for? Answer: Clouds. The CD-ROM is called Cloud Gallery. These are all 750 x 490 Tiffs, a collection of 32 excruciatingly beautiful images for a mere $69.00. Each of these photos is like a painting with a personality, and the emotions range from light to dark. Clouds set a mood in artwork like no other image can, making us dream and believe. There's a demo version of Fractal Design Painter for Windows included on the CD.

> Mary and Michael
> (No address available for public, use phone)
> (415) 326-9567
> **http://www.commerce.digital.com/palo-alto/
> CloudGallery/home.html**
> **http://www.commerce.digital.com/palo-alto/
> WeddingPhoto/home.html**

Accents Images You may not like to roll, but if you like to rock (textures, that is) you'll love the 115 stone images in both Windows and MAC (Photo CD format) on this CD-ROM ($49.95). These stone images are very high quality photos. Use one of the higher resolutions if you want to take advantage of extreme close-ups in your animations. These images also make excellent wrap-arounds for texture mapping, or you may want to use them in an animation to planar map a surface that emulates ground cover.

> Accents Images
> 3123 Lee Place
> Bellmore, NY 11710

BeachWare Ah, nature! This CD-ROM called the "Nature Collection" has 100 photos of the natural world ready for your next art or animation application. They come in both DOS and MAC. The DOS images are presented in both 8- and 24-bit formats. Many of the images are in a vertical or "portrait" format, so that they would have to be cropped for the standard video or "landscape" use, unless of course you want to composite several of them together as a backdrop. Included as an extra is a powerful browser utility that shows both the name of an image file as well as a thumbnail of the picture. The 24-bit files are large, resolved more for print media, and should be reduced

before using them as a background image or a texture map. All imagery is original, sharp, and highly detailed. ($49.95)

> BeachWare
> 9419 Mt. Israel Road
> Escondido, CA 92029
> (619) 735-8945
> Applelink: **BEACHWARE**
> Internet: **tomg@powergrid.electriciti.com**

Cascom, Inc. This selection is for Mac only. The name of the CD-ROM is "5000Plus", and yes, there are over 5,000 image files and more goodies on this CD-ROM. The images are separated into 30 separate folders, each with its own descriptive heading (Aerials, Foods, Mountains, and so on). All are quarter screen sized (320×200), so DTP use is limited. Video, however, is much more forgiving regarding size and resolution. Something can always be resized and still look good (especially within the NTSC framework). Although the image sizes are small, they are excellent in both variety and content, containing adequate material for both backgrounds and object texture maps. There's a browser on-board, and you can copy the database (24MB) to your hard drive if you have the room. Cascom is one of the largest suppliers of professional footage to the broadcast industry, so this CD-ROM is very high quality. There are other non-graphic files on the disk as well, and of special importance is the inclusion of a selection of multimedia effects files. Cascom also has a three volume set of multimedia effects in the QuickTime format.

> Cascom, Inc.
> 806 4th Ave. South
> Nashville, TN 37210
> (615) 256-7890

Digital Stock The subject of the Digital Stock "A la Carte" CD-ROM is food elements, and the images are good enough to eat. All of the super-sharp graphics are on a pure white background, which means that they can be cut out or "magic wanded" with Photoshop. Richard Embry, the photographer responsible for this CD-ROM collection, is a nationally known photographer in the cookbook arena, with loads of national credits. The images should find a wealth of uses by both digital artists and animators (how about morphing one food element to another, just for the effect?). The A-la-Carte CD can be purchased directly from Mr. Embry for $250.00.

> Digital Stock
> 3117 E. Northridge
> Mesa, AZ 85213
> (602) 924-0909

LightRom 3 This three CD-ROM set is from Graphic Detail. Volumes two and three contain items useful to the Mac artist and animator. Volume one contains 3D models in the NewTek LightWave format. These either have to be translated to a Mac 3D program compatible format, or the user can wait for the rumored time when a PowerPC version of LightWave will be released. Volume two contains about 1,000 objects in the 3D Studio format which a few Mac 3D programs can interpret. It also has 700 JPEG textures, applicable to Photoshop or other Mac wares. Volume three is the most useful. It has about 1,000 DEMs (Digital Elevation Models) for use with Natural Graphics Scenery Animator for the Mac.

> Graphic Detail
> 4556 S. 3rd Street
> Louisville, KY 40214
> (502) 363-2986 voice and FAX
> Internet: **michael@iglou.com**

Model Masters, L.L.C. Model Masters produces CD-ROMs of 3D object collections in a variety of file formats, predominantly DXFs. Subject matter ranges widely, from organic objects to furniture. All models are high quality. All models are well-designed and can be zoomed for detail when needed. For organic creations, they use spline-based tools and "blob" modeling.

> Model Masters, L.L.C.
> 420 Frontage Road
> Northfield, IL 60093
> (800) 306-6357

Schatztruhe "The beauty of Chaos" is the name of their CD-ROM. Created with Fractal software in Germany, this CD-ROM contains 507 Mandelbrot images in the GIF 256 color format in three resolutions (1140×890, 1024×768, and 640×480). Another 20 TIFF images are included in 24-bit format. An excellent CD-ROM for the study and use of Fractals.

> Schatztruhe
> Gesellschaft fur Software mbH
> VeronikastraB 33
> 45131 Essen, Germany

Select Effects If you enjoy viewing QuickTime movies, animated clips that you can learn from, this CD-ROM was made for you. It has 100 QuickTime movies and 50 sound effects. Studying the QuickTime animations will give you ideas on how to craft your own animations. The effects represented in these small films offer a wealth of creative suggestions to multimedia designers and digital animators. The CD is Mac and Windows compatible.

> Toucan Studios
> 19672 Stevens Creek Blvd.
> Suite 230
> Cupertino, CA 95014
> (408) 255-3291
> (408) 253-8961 FAX

Specular Replicas This CD-ROM contains over 600 3D objects and their surface maps, and is ready-made for users of Specular International's Infini-D software, as well as being portable to other 3D wares (as DXF models). Included are the following libraries: Office Furniture objects, Lamp and Chair objects, Procedural Surfaces for Infini-D, Exotic Woods image maps, packaging objects, Pattern image maps, Transportation objects, marble image maps, Dinosaur objects, Star Ship objects, Humanoid objects, and Human Character objects. The CD-ROM does not need to be unlocked.

> Specular International
> 330 Townsend Street, #208
> San Francisco, CA 94107
> (413) 253-3100
> (413) 253-0540 FAX

Strata Clips Strata Clips CD-ROM ships with many of the Strata products, but each library it contains has to be opened with a keyword that is charged for. The CD-ROM contains both 3D objects and textures, and all items are high quality and ready for animation. There is a total of 1,300 items on the CD. Many of the models are from Viewpoint Data Labs, one of the most respected 3D object developers in the country. Many of the textures were used in the famous Myst game, which was designed and animated with Strata's software.

> Strata Corporation
> 2 West St. George Blvd.
> Suite 2100
> St. George, Utah 84770
> (801) 628-5218

Valis Group The developer's of MetaFlo and other Mac software also market a high quality texture CD-ROM called Materia Prima for Mac and PC users (browsers are included). These images are organic-like paintings, and make wonderful textures wraps on 3D objects as well as backgrounds. There are 100 512×512 24-bit TIFF tileable textures, 100 512×512 8-bit tileable grayscale textures for use as bump maps, and 100 640×480 TIFF non-tileable color backgrounds.

> Valis Group
> PO Box 831
> Tiburon, CA 94920-0831
> (800) 825-4704
> (415) 435-9862 FAX

Vivid Details These CD-ROMs represent some of the highest quality imagery available. There are more than a dozen titles at this point, and all are categorized into subject areas that are applicable for both video and print. Two worthy of special attention are Flowers (Volume 9) and Old Paint (Volume 11). Each volume has three CD-ROMs in one oversized plastic case, accompanied by a full-color descriptive pamphlet. All of the images were scanned on a high-end drum scanner, and there are 12 images per CD-ROM (48 in each volume). The images come as both 9"×12"×72 DPI (2MB) and 9"×12"×300 DPI (37MB) CMYK TIFF files. The images are so large and detailed that users will find that taking sections of an image provides enough data for 3D object textures and video backdrops.

> Vivid Details
> 8228 Sulphur Mountain Road
> Ojai, CA 93023-9372
> (805) 646-0217
> (805) 646-0021 FAX

Zygote Media Group Zygote's 3D models are at the extreme high end of the quality spectrum. The digital human figures are so perfectly modeled that you have to look twice to make sure you're not looking at a photograph. Zygote's clients include top Hollywood movie makers, major TV ad agencies, and game developers. Zygote employs a sculptor on its staff to sculpt intricate elements in clay and then digitize the sculpture to import the data. They bring in templates (pictures of a finished image of the model placed behind the model) to make sure proportions are correctly sized, and use linear elements of the model to check the measurements on-screen. Zygote also uses calipers to check all dimensions of a mechanical model before it is constructed, and taking measurements from blueprints is fairly common. They also use all the best high-end software for on-screen modeling to craft highly realistic images.

> Zygote
> 1 East Center Street / Suite 215
> Provo, Utah 84601
> (800) 267-5170

3NAME3D 3Name3D is a very high-end digital custom sculpting and digitizing studio which also markets library collections of standard digital objects to the public. They promote digital "clutter" in a 3D scene, the idea that a virtual world should have a multitude of objects around to make it more believable, so their CD-ROM are full of normal "clutter" objects. They have a sculptor on the staff so that clay models can be worked up for the digitizing process. They work up storyboards and sketches before even touching the keyboard, and judge how close the camera will be to the model, so no time is wasted incorporating digital features that will never be seen. They created the 3D models used in the "500 Nations" video series, and work with very high-end industrial and film clients.

3NAME3D
1202 West Olympic Blvd. / Suite 101
Santa Monica, CA 90404

See Also
Animation Mapping, CD-ROM Images for

Object Master

Object Master, a source code **browser** and **editor** from ACI US, takes the role of browser a step further than most. Object Master can act as a complete integrated development environment by interacting with other programming tools, such as Metrowerks' **CodeWarrior**, **Symantec C++**, or Apple's **MPW**.

Unlike most editors and browsers, Object Master can scan through source code to find syntax errors before they are even compiled. Combined with its capability to control external **compilers** and other tools, this makes it possible to do virtually all development work from within Object Master.

In addition to the common split window browser style used by **MacBrowse** and others, Object Master can depict graphically object-oriented class hierarchies. Each class is displayed as a labeled box connected to its subclasses and superclasses by lines (see following figure).

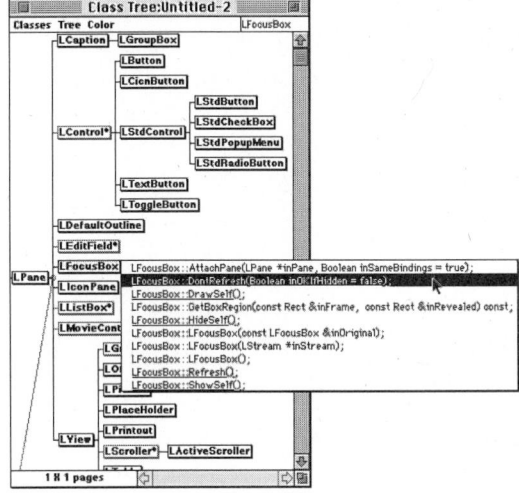

Clicking a class in the visual browser displays a menu of the member functions for that class, including (optionally) those inherited from its superclass. Selecting one of these member functions opens a window in which to edit the corresponding code. Separate "branches" of the object hierarchy can be displayed together or in separate windows, and the graphical browser window can also display data members for each class directly.

Object Master provides extensive language-specific support, including syntax checking and keyword highlighting. It is also scriptable using AppleScript or Frontier.

There are two versions of Object Master: Object Master and Object Master Universal. Both versions support **C** and **C++** and integrate with CodeWarrior, Symantec C++, and MPW environments. The Universal version adds support for **Pascal** and Modula-2 programming.

Object Master is published by ACI US:

ACI US, Inc.
20883 Stevens Creek Blvd.
Cupertino, CA 95014
Phone: (800) 384-0010
Web: **http://www.acius.com/Pages/GUI/**
ACI_US/English/Products/
ProductGroups/ObjectMaster.html

See Also
Browser; C; C++; CodeWarrior; Editor; Integrated Development Environment; MacBrowse; MPW; Pascal; Symantec C++

Object Oriented Programming, *See Programming*

Oblique, *See Typesetting Terms*

OCR, *See Scanners, OCR Software and*

Odd Parity, *See Parity*

Office Scanners

A new breed of scanners has begun to emerge in the mid-90's. These scanners are small, even portable, inexpensive scanners intended for OCR and FAX work, rather than for desktop publishing. Visioneer's Paperport is one of the first such devices: it's a little wider than a piece of paper, and fits easily between a monitor and keyboard. You can simply insert pages to be scanned in the slot of the device, and it quickly scans the page and spits it back out. (Other office scanners may handle paper in different ways, and some small scanners are optimized for scanning business cards.)

Office scanners aren't meant for desktop publishing applications, and they won't produce scans of sufficient quality for layouts. However, they are easy to use and ideally suited for OCR applications.

See Also
Drum Scanners; Flatbed Scanners; Handheld Scanners; Slide Scanners

Offset Printing, *See Printing*

On-Demand Printing

On-demand printing describes quick-turnaround printing procedures that require very few preliminary steps, eliminating the time-consuming and expensive makeready of traditional printing presses. This is an entirely new classification of printing. There is an entirely new concept to be dealt with—the run-length of only one copy. Before digital presses, one of the major cost factors in printing was the set up, or press makeready. In traditional printing this is still true.

In traditional **prepress**, many things have to be done after the artwork is completed. First of all, a photographic negative is made of the artwork. **Halftones** have to be shot. All of the pieces have to be assembled on orange masking sheets (called *flats*). Halftones have to be precisely positioned on a separate flat to line up with the negatives on the master sheet. This is just a brief summary. Often, for complicated color jobs, there are dozens of flats. Each one takes five to fifteen minutes and costs $5–15 dollars. Each piece of film costs about the same. When everything is assembled, a plate is made at a cost of $25 to $150 (depending on the size of the press). Then it takes about 15 minutes to hang the plate and get it into proper alignment at a cost per color of $25 to $50. Then, from 50 to 300 sheets of paper are run through the press to get the colors printing at the proper density. These setup charges could total from a minimum of $25 (one color with plastic printing plates) to a maximum of several thousand dollars (complicated process color with metal plates) before a single sheet prints acceptably. Even when traditional prepress is bypassed with digital methods, **traditional printing presses** require the expensive makeready process.

As a result of these time-consuming and expensive procedures, traditional printing often charges the same price for anything under 1,000 sheets. If you want one copy or 1,000, it costs the same. If you print many thousands of copies, the setup charges are amortized, and the cost per copy ends up being very cheap. These price benefits do not occur until at least 2,000 copies are printed. As a result, buyers of traditional printing try to order large quantities. When ordering 20,000 copies, the cost per thousand drops to only a small percentage of the cost for the first thousand.

Digital presses enable jobs to be printed with virtually no setup costs. The only cost is the time it takes to open the file and print it from the computer. There is no film to be shot, no film assembly, no separate plate making. This is the basis for on-demand printing. This simple process prompts a radical re-thinking of the entire printing process.

Take for example those 20,000 copies mentioned earlier. There have been various studies on the use of printed materials such as brochures, catalogs, and other corporate promotional materials indicating that a large percentage of waste is normal. The following scenario is all too familiar. A company needs 5,000 brochures, but they get such a good price break on higher quantities that they order 20,000. They distribute the 5,000 and warehouse the rest. Several months later they might use another 5,000 copies. However, after another six months or even a year, they often discover that the material is no longer viable due to changes in personnel, telephone numbers, addresses, and so on. As a consequence, they have to discard the other 10,000. This example is representative of the average situation. Almost half of warehoused printed materials get tossed. When you add the cost of printing to the cost of warehousing, these printed pieces get pretty expensive.

It is in situations such as these that on-demand printing has its real value. In on-demand printing, the cost per thousand is quite a bit more expensive compared to the cost per thousand of traditionally printed materials. However, since there are no setup charges, the cost per thousand is the same whether you print 5,000 or 50. Eliminating warehousing costs can make on-demand printing of 3,000 or less competitive with traditional printing. Factoring in the reduced waste (0), makes on-demand competitive up to 5,000 copies per run.

Some sources indicate that most printing consists of more than 5,000 copies per run. However, this may not be true. Other sources such as *On-Demand Printing*, by Fenton and Romano (Graphic Arts Technical Foundation, 1995) state otherwise. They make the statement, "Almost 56 percent of commercial, book, and office printing, including duplicating and copying, falls in the category of run lengths from 500 to 5,000 impressions." Another 16.6 percent of printing has run lengths of under 500. This indicates that almost three quarters of all printing has a run length of under 5,000 impressions. We must realize that an impression (one sheet of paper printed

once) can have several copies of a publication on it. A 5.5×8.5-inch flyer, for example, can be printed four up on an 11×17-inch sheet. This means that 20,000 copies of that flyer still require only 5,000 impressions.

These issues lead to several conclusions. First, digital presses can have a huge impact on short-run printing. Second, digital presses win out, bottom line, for any printing runs less than 2,000 copies. Three, as the benefits of on-demand printing become more apparent, the percentage of short-run printing will greatly increase.

See Also

Prepress; Printing

On-Demand Printing, DocuTech System

The Xerox DocuTech system originated the on-demand printing concept. It has evolved to a publishing system that can print 600×600 dpi at a rate of 135 simplex (single-sided) 8.5×11-inch sheets a minute. This translates to 67.5 duplex sheets per minute. Although these are not phenomenal printing speeds, the DocuTech's primary focus is business and government, where a typical print run might be only 200 copies of a 2,000 page manual. In these cases, what is needed is complete document handling with strong inline finishing capabilities. This is where DocuTech shines.

DocuTech uses a network server based on Novell Netware that supports PCs, Macs, and Sun workstations. It has five major components: scanner, controller, console, printer, and finisher.

Everything is integrated to enable the DocuTech to work as a complete printshop. All document management takes place on the console. This is where the Job Tickets are created. They are required before a job can be printed. In other words, it is very difficult to print something on the DocuTech without proper documentation. This greatly benefits billing procedures in most offices. The scanner can digitize images at 600 dpi, but it is better to transfer digital images from a supported workstation. The controller can be used to do minor image manipulation.

One of DocuTech's weak points is its **RIP (Raster Image Processor)**. It is a co-processor board on the network server and is quite slow when processing most graphics. Text can be processed much faster. A second bottleneck is the network itself. EtherNet communications within the machine are limited to 10MB per minute. Obviously, DocuTech has problems with large **Photoshop** graphics.

The DocuTech excels in finishing capabilities. The controller can do simple **page imposition** up to the 11×17-inch page size limit. The DocuTech can impose 8.5×11 inch, 8.5×5.5 inch, and 8.5×7 inch booklets. With all of DocuTech's inline and off-line finishing capabilities, even complex jobs can be done easily. With inline finishing, the machine outputs completed books or booklets. The standard DocuTech has built-in staplers and stackers that can staple a group of pages on the corner or on the side. One optional device can collate, saddle stitch, and three-knife trim—outputting finished, saddle-stitched booklets. Another option is an inline perfect binder that produces booklets with squared-off folding edges. The DocuTech can produce finished books up to 1.6 inches thick. There is also an off-line perfect binder that mills the binding edges and folds the cover around the glued edge. This produces a very professional-looking book up to 1.6 inches thick with a maximum size of 13.75×15 inches. The DocuTech system also provides spine printers for perfect bound books, case binders that produce hardcover books, and adhesive binders that produce books that open flat. The DocuTech is designed to produce completed books economically in small quantities.

See Also

On-Demand Printing; Printing Terminology, Traditional

On-Demand Printing, Types of

An interesting new capability related to on-demand printing is the so-called targeted catalog. It is now possible to call the 800 number of a mail-order company, give the operator some personal data, and then receive a customized catalog containing only the pages that interest you. This suggests other possibilities: custom brochures, individualized price lists, and so on. In some cases, a top quality fax machine can become the **on-demand printing** device.

This type of capability is being used by college professors to create custom textbooks. There has been controversy about copyright infringement and royalties, but those details are being worked out. Basically, a teacher can choose chapters, illustrations, pages, articles, and other items from a list that the school printshop has licensed. After those choices are made, a student simply brings in a card with the choices listed and a custom book is printed (at very competitive rates). This way, there is no storage problem with unpurchased books. If a book is needed, a book is printed!

A variation of the on-demand concept reverses the normal paradigm. In the U.S., large printing firms are centrally located together near distribution centers. In the print and distribute model, tons of materials are printed and then shipped where needed. Shipping costs are on the increase, though. Remember that paper is wood without any of the open fill of the wood-fiber cells. Paper is very heavy stuff. Even trucks have a hard time with the size of many of the shipments. A hundred thousand books can easily weigh tons.

On-demand printing reverses this scenario to distribute and print. An electronic file can be distributed (globally, if necessary) in digital form, often through the **Internet**. It is received by individual on-demand digital printers that print the required numbers locally. Although not completely digital, distribute and print has been performed for years by giants such as *USA Today*. This widely distributed newspaper transmits electronic publication files via satellite to printing plants all over the country, such as Boston Offset in the Boston area. This enables the paper to be printed and distributed locally. Now it can be done by anyone. A couple of global printing networks have started and fizzled. However, this type of printing is getting more common and will probably become commonplace due to increasing shipping costs for printed materials.

One of the most common forms of distribute and print is broadcast fax. In this method, a document is automatically faxed to a phone list. Many newsletters are distributed in this manner. This system has not become quite as obnoxious as the phone call during dinner, but it has that potential. Unless discretion is used, this type of technology becomes self-defeating. People may be so offended by the unsolicited material that the image of the broadcasting company is damaged. A second problem is the actual quality of the printing. Most fax machines are crude at best. Even the good ones are usually only 200 dpi. In addition, most of them cannot do grayscale images. All in all, broadcast fax is an inferior method for on-demand printing.

One of the most promising solutions to the problem of fax quality is the **PostScript** fax. Although they are not widely used, some 600 dpi PostScript printers can receive a faxed PostScript document and print it out. This enables almost professional quality printing to be sent over the phone lines. If this becomes commonplace, the broadcast fax may take on new credibility.

See Also
On-Demand Printing

OneWorld, *See Server/Fax, Server/ Modem, Server/Remote Access*

Online

Online means that your computer is directly connected with a host computer in a client/server network, be it interoffice, to a printer, or to the Internet.

Online Entertainment, *See MUDs and MOOs; Network Gaming; Online Games*

Online Etiquette

As with any other society, the online world has developed its own etiquette. Some of its aspects are practical, while others are more traditional than functional. However, to maximize your enjoyment of online services, as well as to avoid unintentionally offending other online users, it's best that you follow this society's rules, just as you would at any other social gathering.

Abbreviations When you're communicating through an electronic medium, the standard non-verbal cues to meaning, such as facial gestures and laughter are not available. You frequently have no clue whether the person you're "talking" to understands that you meant to make a joke. You can't tell whether her or his response was meant in fun or as an insult to your appearance, ethnic origin, and typing skills. It is often hard to fully understand what someone means, particularly in casual conversation, based upon the words alone.

To make up for this, a set of abbreviations and **emoticons** is used to make up for these inadequacies. Here are some of the more common abbreviations, and examples of their uses.

Common Online Abbreviations

Symbol	Meaning	Example
<G>	Grin	"I'm joking." "Windows 95 is so easy to install!"<g>
:)	Smile (smile) General happiness	"I got my new PowerBook today!":)
: (	Frown(frown) General unhappiness	"My PowerBook doesn't work!":(
IMHO	In my (humble) opinion...	"The Mac is simply superior, IMHO"
BTW	By the way...	"Btw, have you seen cybergrrl on the net?"
FWIW	For what it's worth	"FWIW, you might try backing up your hard drive BEFORE the crash next time. <G>"
LOL	Laughing Out Loud	"Your cat ate your mouse?" LOL!

Emphasis One of the oldest and most strictly enforced rules of online etiquette is the use of upper- and lowercase in messages. The use of uppercase is generally reserved to indicate emphasis on a particular word or phrase. Because uppercase is used to indicate emphasis on a word, A MESSAGE IN ALL UPPERCASE OFTEN IMPLIES THAT THE SENDER IS SCREAMING! Although sometimes its appropriate to scream, a multi-paragraph message in all caps will either go unread or lead to a ration of replies detailing this rule of etiquette. On the other hand, many people use *only* lowercase, making their writing resemble the work of poet e. e. cummings. This is entirely acceptable, as is the use of asterisks or underscores to set off words being emphasized. *This* is an _example_. Spelling and typing mistakes are common, in forum postings, email, and especially in live conferences. It's customary to ignore mistakes, unless you absolutely can't decipher the words.

Replies Most online systems and newsgroups keep messages for some time after the original interchange, so that other callers can benefit from what was discussed. However, you never know how long each message will last, or where future callers will jump into the trail of messages (usually called a "thread" of messages), so its considered polite to quote the relevant part of the original message in a reply. For example:

From: John Doe

To: ALL

How the heck can I get my monitor to show something on the display? I turn the computer on, and nothing appears on the monitor. I've got a Mac II cx and an Apple 13" display. I'd really appreciate any help!

Thanks,

John

From Freddy Smith

To: John Doe

<<How the heck can I get my monitor to show something on the display?>>

Try turning on the monitor... Fred<g>

When you quote a previous message, use some sort of symbol, such as the <<>> ones shown previously,

or an introduction like "On 4/1/96, REEBOK asked "How can I get a replacement manual for my IIsi?" Quote enough of the message so others can tell what you're responding to, but don't quote the whole thing if it's long. And, if you're replying to a reply, don't quote the entire thread, as some newsgroup members seem compelled to do. It just wastes time.

Flames Sometimes people use the electronic message boards to say things they wouldn't have the nerve or decency to say in person. Such messages, generally called flames, are most often seen in Internet newsgroups, but may also appear on forums or bulletin boards in the online services. When one person posts a flame, inevitably several more respond with flames of their own. Brutal "flamewars" scare others away, and eventually become boring for everyone else who uses the message center. A moderated forum is likely to have a "no flame" rule, and may bar access to anyone who refuses to respect it. Keep the tone of your messages friendly. Try not to type anything that you wouldn't say in person to a casual friend. Overall, the online community is a friendly bunch, and are always willing to help newcomers. Stay within the rules, jump in, and ask for help as you go. You won't be sorry you did.

See Also

Netiquette

Online Games

Online entertainment is almost as vast as the range of game types on CD-ROM. Each of the commercial online services offers something in the way of online gaming that differs from games like MUDs and shareware. CompuServe offers game forums that are mainly discussion groups about different types of Mac games. Typing "Go Macfun" will get you to the Macintosh Entertainment Forum.

GEnie, the underdog of online services, has the largest array of multi-player gaming options and, being text-based, is cross-platform. On Genie, type "Games." Delphi, also a text-based service, offers nightly live trivia games, word games, and multi-player poker, as well as several other multi-player games.

Most of the big online services including Prodigy and AOL periodically offer games such as Fantasy Sports Leagues, trivia games, and Internet scavenger hunts as well as traditional arcade and text-based games.

The best bet besides a MUD for online gaming are the smaller, game-dedicated networks like Sim-Net and GameNet. Sim-Net and GameNet work by using a combination of **Apple Remote Access (ARA)**, the Internet and an email service called First Class Client. The services offer the same type of benefits of the larger services such as chat-rooms, **email** and message-boards, but they are completely devoted to games and gaming. Price-wise, they cost a lot less than CompuServe or America Online and, if you are really into online games, you can't go wrong with them as they offer a lot more than either larger service. An all-Mac based service, Outland, is probably the most beneficial of the bunch. Backgammon lovers will rejoice over MacF.I.B.S. (First Internet Backgammon Server) which runs with **Mac TCP/PPP** software and Internet access. There is no additional fee for hooking up, other than the Internet connection and you can play against real people as opposed to playing the computer. (For those without Internet access, Backgammon from MacSoft should more than fulfill your curiosity).

If you have Internet access with a fast connection and love puzzles and trivia, check out **www.riddler.com**. Riddler is a sponsored game network that gives you the chance to earn real money and real prizes. There's no cost to join, beyond the cost of your Internet connection.

See Also

MUDs and MOOs; Network Gaming; Shareware Games

Online Services

Although the purpose of a **modem** is to connect your computer to another computer, the simple connection between two computers generally isn't that interesting. What makes telecommunications exciting is the ability to dial up computers that are connected to many other computers and to large databases, either through a private online service such as **America Online**, **Prodigy**, **CompuServe**, or directly to the worldwide **Internet**. (See each topic separately for a detailed discussion.)

The commercial online services are nationwide computer networks which allow you to exchange messages and files with other computer users around the world by simply calling the closest branch of their network. They have dial-in numbers local to most major cities, and charge you one-time sign-up fees plus an hourly fee for the amount of time spent online. Commercial services provide many features in addition to email and forum messages and libraries of downloadable files.

All the major services offer news and weather that's updated frequently, research facilities including online encyclopedias, searchable databases of magazines and other reference material, travel services including access to the same SABRE reservations system that travel agencies use, convenient online catalog shopping, and a great deal more. Most have some kind of interactive games that you can play by yourself or with others. All have an area for live conversation, called "chat" or "conference".

What makes the services worthwhile to most users, though, is the opportunity to share information in forums. A forum is a sort of public **bulletin board** within the service, on which a user can read what other people have written about a particular topic and add in his or her comments. Forums are generally built around a particular topic, such as a hobby or sport, an occupation, a particular computer or software product worthy of discussion, or any kind of affinity group you could name.

There are forums for fans of Jimmy Buffett; fans of B-movie director Ed Wood, Jr.; fans of (and those who as ardently dislike) Rush Limbaugh, Howard Stern, and virtually any other public figure. There are forums for readers and writers of mysteries, romances, and cookbooks. There are support groups online for every possible medical problem and most psychological disorders. There are health and wellness forums to balance things out. There are forums for kids, parents, and even cats, bunnies, and dogs. (Their owners do the typing, of course.)

Private online services, often known as a BBS (Bulletin Board System) are set up by individuals, user groups, or companies either for recreation or profit. They consist of a single computer system, with telephone numbers located in one area. Although these types of services have a smaller number of callers and available files, they are often free, and are good meeting places for people of similar interests. As with many things in the computer world, the progression of the Internet is rapidly diminishing interest in private BBSs. In many cases today's **Web pages** and **FTP** sites are replacing what was once the realm of the local BBS.

Overview of Commercial Online Services*

America Online	Low cost, easy to use. More limited than Internet.
CompuServe	Vast resources, more difficult to use.
Prodigy	Non-Mac standard interface.
eWorld	Has been discontinued.
AppleLink	Very pricey. Of interest mainly to Apple dealers and employees.
GEnie	No graphical interface.
Internet	Worldwide resources, growing exponentially. Can be very inexpensive in some areas. More difficult to set up and use. Most broad in usage.

*See each topic individually for additional discussion.

See Also
America Online; AppleLink; Bulletin Board Systems; CompuServe; eWorld; Internet

Onslaught, *See V for Victory*

Open Command

This command enables you to open a document, folder, disk, or program. To open an item, select the item and select Open from the **File menu** (⌘-O) in the **Finder**, and that item opens. **Double-clicking** an item also invokes the Open command.

Folders and disks open by displaying a window where you can see their contents. Files open when the program that created them is **launched** and then the user opens a particular document. Programs open by launching. After an item has opened, if you look at the item's icon, you'll see that it's now filled with a series of dots, indicating that the file is open. You can also open more than one item at a time with the Open command by selecting multiple files while holding the Shift key and then choosing Open. This opens all selected items, one after another.

To open an item, follow these steps:

1. In the Finder level, select Open (⌘-O) on the File menu or double-click the item.

2. If the item is a disk or a folder, the item opens a window showing you its contents. If the item is a document, it launches the program and displays the document. If the item is a program, it launches the program.

See Also
Double-Click; File Menu; Launching a Program

Open Command (Keyboard Shortcut)

When opening a **document**, **disk,** or **folder**, you can use the keyboard shortcut ⌘-O. This works at both the **desktop** level and within applications.

See Also
Desktop; Folders; Keyboard Shortcuts; Open Dialog Box

Open Dialog Box

The Open dialog box appears when you are in an application and want to open a document, as shown in the following figure. Most Macintosh programs use the same shortcut to open a file within a program as they do to open a file in the **Finder** (⌘-O).

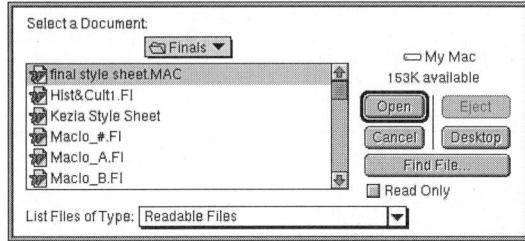

When the Open dialog box appears, select the document you want to open from a scrolling list within the dialog box. If the document you want does not appear in the list, you can use the **pull-down menu** above the scrolling list to go back to your hard drive and select another folder.

If the document is on an external drive or on a **disk**, you can click the **Desktop** button, which enables you to look on any of the devices mounted on your **desktop**. If you're in a folder and want a quick way to get back to hard drive level, click the icon of your hard drive in the upper-right corner of the Open dialog box. That takes you to, and lists, the contents of that drive.

When you locate the folder that contains the document you're looking for, double-click it to show the contents of the folder. When you locate the exact file you want to open, you can either double-click it to open the file, select it, and then click the Open button, or select a file or folder and press the Return key.

See Also

Desktop; External Drive; Open Command; Pull-Down Menus

Open Folder/Disk (Keyboard Shortcut)

You can open any **folder** or **disk** by selecting the folder or disk and using the keyboard shortcut ⌘-Down Arrow. You can also open a selected file or disk by pressing ⌘-O as a keyboard shortcut for the Open command.

To open a folder/disk using a keyboard shortcut, follow these steps:

1. Select the folder/disk by navigating from folder to folder using the **arrow keys**.

2. When you've selected the folder/disk you want to open, press ⌘-Down Arrow to open the selected folder/disk.

See Also

Arrow Keys; Folder; Keyboard Shortcuts

Open Media Framework Standard

A cross-platform standard developed by Avid and adopted by the IMA (Interactive Multimedia Association) as a recommended format for data exchange. Providing you have software that understands it, audio and video can be transferred between a Macintosh and other operating systems, including Windows and Silicon Graphics.

See Also

VideoFusion

Open Next (Keyboard Shortcut)

In an **Open dialog box** of an application, you are presented with a list of files and folders that you can open. The first file in the list is already highlighted by default. If you don't want to open that file, you can select and open the next file, or folder, down the list (they appear alphabetically) by pressing ⌘-Down Arrow. This keyboard shortcut saves you a step by not only selecting the next available file or folder down the list, but it also opens the file or folder for you.

See Also

Keyboard Shortcuts; Open Command

Open Prepress Interface (OPI)

Open Prepress Interface is an extension of the **PostScript** page-description language that enables automatic image replacement during film output. Specifically, OPI substitutes high-resolution images for low-resolution placeholder (proxy) images incorporated into an electronic publication file by its originator. The OPI scheme is most frequently used at color trade shops and service bureaus. The service provider uses a high-end scanner to produce very high-resolution (2,000 ppi and above) digitized images, but because these images are difficult to process on a desktop computer due to their large file sizes, a low-resolution proxy image is supplied to the client. The proxy image is usually a TIFF and can be placed into any page layout or graphics software application that supports OPI.

When a PostScript publication file is output for **color separations**, OPI PostScript comments specify the page location, layout position, size, and cropping for the placeholder images. At the service bureau or trade shop, a prepress software application, such as Adobe Color Central, reads the OPI comments and substitutes the high-resolution versions before imaging the separations.

See Also

Automatic Picture Replacement (APR); Color Separations; Image Scanning

Open Scripting Architecture (OSA)

When Apple's engineers were designing the foundations of **scripting** on the Mac, they realized that same scripting language would not be best suited for everyone. Rather than facing the chaotic possibility that many separate language vendors would each create their own completely separate scripting system, they designed the Open Scripting Architecture.

This architecture enables users to write scripts in a variety of languages, all of which use the same basic mechanism (**Apple events**) to communicate with the individual applications that the scripts control.

Each OSA-compatible scripting system implements a scripting *component* that translates commands written in its own language into a string of Apple events that the Apple Event Manager then passes on to the scripted application. The OSA component can also translate the other direction (from Apple events to its own language) when recording.

Both **AppleScript** and **Frontier**'s UserTalk are OSA-compatible scripting systems. As a result, the AppleScript Script Editor can execute UserTalk scripts and Frontier can execute scripts written in AppleScript. Neither program has any special support for the other's language, but because they each use the Open Scripting Architecture, they work fine with the other's language.

See Also

Apple Events; AppleScript; Frontier; Scripting

Open Systems Interconnection Model

The Open Systems Interconnection model, or OSI for short, is a network model designed by the International Standards Organization (ISO) that divides network communications into seven functional layers. The layers provide a communications relay from one system to another, with each layer responsible for a particular type of network service. The OSI design has become the standard for LAN product design. The layers are

- Physical
- Data Link
- Network
- Transport
- Session
- Presentation
- Application

The first two layers deal with data transmission. The physical layer is where the actual physical cabling exists. Three different kinds of EtherNet and two kinds of Token Ring cable are defined in this layer. The Data Link refers to the specific kind of cabling employed.

It places a frame, a sort of network delivery vehicle, around the data being sent. Frames are specific to the kind of cable being used. When you choose a network driver on the Mac's Network control panel, you're defining the Data Link frame to use. It's as if you had several roads, all going to the same place, but only blue cars can drive on one road, red cars on another, and green cars on the third. You can put your data package into any colored car and send it to its destination. The color of the car (or the data link frame) determines the route, whether it's LocalTalk, EtherNet, TokenTalk, or some other network driver.

The next three layers are concerned with protocols. The network layer addresses the message for delivery. It turns the data into a datagram—a packet with destination and return addresses specific to a particular networking protocol. The Transport layer insures reliable delivery of the message packet. If a portion of the message is garbled, it's the task of this layer to retransmit the garbled bits until they're received correctly. The Session layer deals with establishing and maintaining a connection between the computers so that messages may be sent and received. It also manages the communications to assure a logical sequence to them. The final two layers are concerned with the format and the message itself. The Presentation layer manages file formats such as PostScript, ASCII text, and Microsoft Word. It also manages access formats such as AFP (Apple Filing Protocol) and TCP/IP. Finally, the Application layer is the place where network services and applications reside. It uses the formats established in the previous layer.

OpenDoc, *See Cyberdog*

Opening an Application

To open an application you have four choices. You can select the application by clicking the icon for the application and choosing Open from the **File menu**. You can also simply **double-click** the application's icon to launch the application. The third way to launch an application is to double-click a document created by the application you want to launch. This launches the application and opens the document you selected by double-clicking. The fourth way is to select a document created by the application and choose Open from the File menu. This launches the application and opens the selected document.

To open an application, follow these steps:

1. Click the application you want to open and choose Open from the File menu.

2. Double-click the application.

   You can also double-click any document created by the application and it launches the application and opens the document you double-clicked.

3. You can also select a document created by the application and choose Open from the File menu. This also launches the application, and then opens the selected document.

See Also
Application Icons; Double-Click; File Menu

Opening and Closing Files

There's a host of little tips and tricks that can make opening and closing files more efficient. In System 7 and higher, there's another way to open documents besides choosing Open (⌘-O) or **double-clicking**. You can drag a document onto the icon of the application that created it and the application will launch, opening the document.

To open a number of documents at once, select them all (by Shift-clicking or dragging a marquee selection over them) and choose Open from the **File menu**. The documents launch the applications that created them and open, one after another, in the application. The document that you selected last appears as the active document. Keep this in mind when you make your selections, and you can have the document you want to work on first open and waiting for you, with the others behind, by selecting it last.

If you choose to open a document, and then change your mind before the document is open, in most cases you can press ⌘-. (period) to cancel the opening of the document.

Another shortcut to opening a file is to select the file (by typing the first few letters of its name) and press ⌘-Down arrow. This opens the document and closes the window that the document was in.

To close an open window at the **Finder**, you have three choices:

- Click the Close box (in the upper-left corner of the window's title bar).

- Choose Close from the File menu.

- The quickest way is to choose ⌘-W (the keyboard shortcut for Close).

TIP   If you hold the Option key while choosing any of the three methods for closing a window, all open windows are closed.

See Also
Double-Click; File Menu; Finder

Operations, How the Macintosh Works

The Macintosh runs using a complex interaction between the applications you load, the operating system that manages both files and how they appear on-screen, and the hardware that performs the work. The **Finder** is the System's interface between your programs and the hardware. When the Macintosh is operating properly, each part does its job transparently. The figure that follows provides an illustration of the types of functions performed by the System software in maintaining the look and feel of the Macintosh.

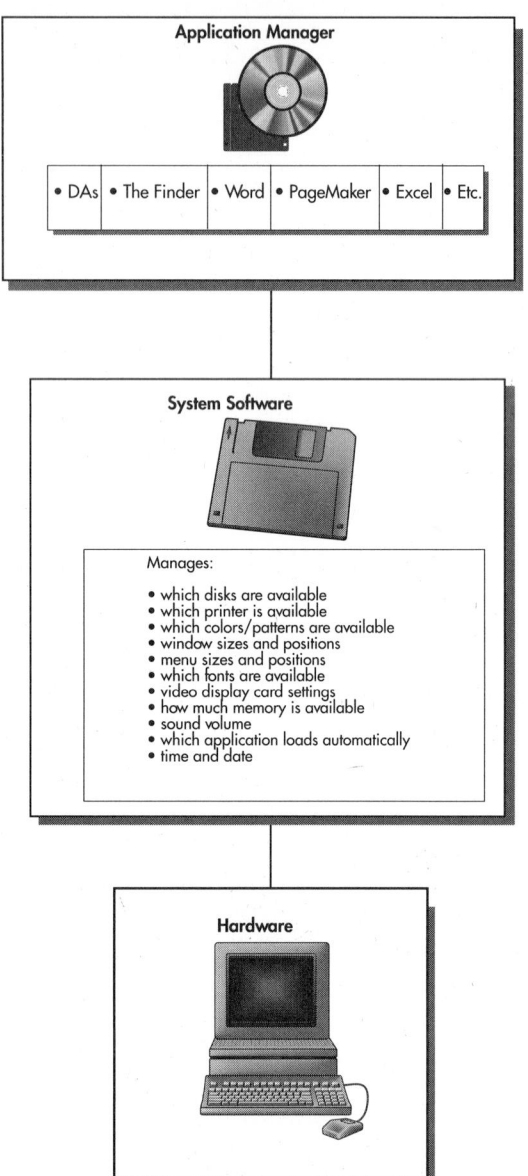

PowerPC-based Macs use an emulator program hard-wired into their ROM to translate 680x0 instructions into PowerPC instructions line-by-line (also called an interpreter). The emulator does not translate memory management unit (MMU) or floating-point instruction (FPU) instructions, which may cause problems in those 680x0 applications that require a floating point processor (such as Photoshop or Microsoft Excel). Early versions of these programs that are not re-written to be PowerPC-native will crash or not launch on a Power Macintosh. Power Macs also make use of new system software available in System 7.1.2, (although the current system version is 7.5.3 that offers more Power Mac native enhancements), that supports shared libraries (such as spell checkers, graphics modules, Photoshop filters, and so forth). The Shared Library Manager opens up these semi-private and shared resources to all applications that support shared libraries. This way, any word processing program or graphics program that has this capability can use, for example, a public thesaurus by linking to it using the Shared Library Manager.

See Also

Coprocessors, Types; Macintosh Operating Systems; PowerPC

Operators, *See Spreadsheet Notation*

OPF, *See OpenDoc Part Framework*

OPI, *See Open Prepress Interface*

Optical Character Recognition, *See Scanners, OCR Software and*

Optical Drives, *See Backing Up with Optical Drives*

Option Key

This **modifier key** is designed to be used with other keys to add additional functionality to the keyboard and is used with other keys to access certain symbols in fonts. It's also used with the **Command key** and **Shift key** in keyboard shortcuts for **menu** commands and **mouse** actions.

Option Keys

Sequence	Result
Option-1	¡
Option-2	™
Option-3	£
Option-4	¢
Option-5	
Option-6	§
Option-7	¶
Option-8	•
Option-9	ª
Option-—	–
Option-=	
Option-q	œ
Option-w	
Option-e	´
Option-r	®
Option-t	†
Option-y	¥
Option-u	¨
Option-i	^
Option-o	ø
Option-p	
Option-a	å
Option-s	ß
Option-d	
Option-f	ƒ
Option-g	©
Option-h	·
Option-j	
Option-k	°
Option-l	¬
Option-;	… (ellipsis)
Option-'	æ

continues

Option Keys (continued)

Sequence	Result
Option-z	
Option-x	
Option-c	ç
Option-v	
Option-b	
Option-n	˜
Option-m	µ
Option-,	
Option-.	
Option-/	÷
Option-\	«
Option-Shift-Q	Œ
Option-Shift-U	¨
Option-Shift-O	Ø
Option-Shift-P	
Option-Shift-A	Å
Option-Shift-'	Æ
Option-Shift-C	Ç
Option-Shift-V	
Option-Shift-?	¿
Option-Shift-+	±
Option-Shift— (dash)	—
Option-Shift-8	°

See Also

Commands; Command Key; Menu Bar; Mouse; Shift Key

Order of Operations, *See Formula*

Orientation

This word evokes images of freshpersons in beanies looking bewildered on the first day of college, but it actually refers to the position of text or an image on a piece of paper. There are two orientations: *portrait* and *landscape*. In portrait orientation, the page is taller than it is wide. In landscape orientation, it is just the opposite; the page setup is wider than it is tall. The icons that indicate them in a typical word processor page set up box are shown in the figure, along with a pair of suggested improvements.

Orientation:

Orientation:

Ornament and Dingbat Fonts

Probably the best-known ornament **font** is Zapf Dingbats, which almost everyone with a Mac has. Designed by Hermann Zapf in 1978, this font contains a collection of ornamental, essentially meaningless, symbols that can be used to spice up a design. These range from abstract starbursts and hearts to checkmarks and arrows. And believe it or not, "dingbat" is a traditional printer's term for an ornamental element.

Some ornamental fonts contain reproductions of historical printer's ornaments, while others are completely modern. Some are made to form borders when whole strings of characters are typed together. Common character types are abstract curliques and stylized leaves and flowers.

A related category of typefaces is picture fonts, in which each character is a drawing of some sort; these images tend to be more complex than dingbats, and they can be a substitute for **clip art**.

See Also

Clip Art; Fonts; Picture Fonts; Typeface Categories

Orphans, *See Widows and Orphans*

Orwell, George, *See "1984"*

OS Tips and Tricks

For tips and tricks on the MacOS, use this table to find the entries you want:

Tips and Tricks Guide

Description	Entry
How to select text better	Extended Double-Click Text Selection
Get more Find File options	Find File Search Options
Need to determine SCSI ID	Finding Out a Device's SCSI ID Number
Fix the screen on your Performa	Improving a Performa's Picture
Reuse a disk that seems permanently locked	Permanently Locked Disk, Using
Fix a bad floppy disk	Rebuilding the Desktop on a Disk
Quick access to files Dialog Boxes	Saving Time in Open and Save Dialog Boxes
Align icons automatically	Aligning Icons Automatically
Save time with windows	Time-Saving Window Tips
Copy files to folders	Copying Files from Folder to Folder
Create screen shots	Screen Capture, Opening and Editing
Best use calculator	Copying and Pasting into the Calculator
Desktop Pattern Tricks	Desktop Patterns Tricks
Find File Tricks	Find File Tricks
Map control panel secrets	Hidden Map Control Panel Features
Using the Jigsaw Graphic	Jigsaw Puzzle Graphic, Replacing

Description	Entry
Starting up with other disks	Bypass Internal Drive Keyboard Shortcut
Is a file locked?	File, Determining whether It Is Locked
Control order of folders and files	Forcing Items to the Top of a List
Using Stickies	Stickies Tips and Tricks
Temporarily disabling virtual memory	Bypass Virtual Memory at Startup
Using the Control Strip	Control Strip Shortcuts
Hide desktop	Accidentally Jumping to the Finder, Avoiding
Background Copying	Copying Files in the Background
Using the Audio CD	AudioCD Tips
Getting back lost items after a crash	Restoring Unsaved Items After a Crash
Quick rename	Renaming Files Without Using the Mouse
Apple menu tricks	Dividers in the Apple Menu and Other Tricks
Trash tips	Trash Tips
Quick Finder usage	Finder Speed Tips

OSA, *See Open Scripting Architecture*

Osamu Sato, *See Eastern Mind*

OSI Model, *See Open Systems Interconnection Model*

Out of Memory Message

This is a warning message the Mac displays when you're nearly out of **memory** (RAM). This is the Mac's way of warning you that you're close to a memory error, and if you don't make some memory available, by **quitting** open applications or closing open windows, the program you're working in may quit without warning.

You may see this message when you have a number of applications open and you're just about out of memory. This message warns you and enables you to take action: close open applications, close open windows, and so on to free up some more memory.

If you get this message often, it may be time to buy additional RAM for your machine, but you can also look at other methods of making more RAM available to your Mac, such as turning on **Virtual Memory** in the Memory control panel (System 7 and higher), which enables you to use a portion of your available hard disk space as RAM. There is also a commercial product called RAM Doubler from Connectix Corporation that uses a Virtual Memory scheme to make your Mac think there's twice as much memory available than is installed on your machine. It works quite well, and if you have, for example, 8MB on your machine, after installing RAM Doubler, the system will think it has 16MB and will let you open applications until you reach the 16MB limit.

See Also

Memory; Quit; Virtual Memory

Out of the Sun

Flying Nightmares, the first game optimized for the **Power Mac,** was Domark's first attempt at a Mac **flight sim**. Domark's follow-up, **Out of the Sun,** sported a much improved version of Nightmares and offered one of the more technically realistic flight sims available. Although not up to the degree of finesse of later titles **F/A-18 Hornet** and **A-10 Attack!,** Out of the Sun is a great game and requires no small amounts of skill to master.

World War II buffs will enjoy the historically accurate setting of the missions: Midway, D-Day, and the battle of Kursk. You can even play as an ally or a Nazi, depending on your mood. The only real drawbacks of the game are the low resolution graphics and the absence of **network** play. Beginners may want to try out the easier levels of F/A-18, but for experts, the realism and high level difficulty of Out of the Sun should be right up your alley.

See Also

A-10 Attack!; Absolute Zero; F/A-18 Hornet; Rebel Assault II; Sim Games; Wing Commander III

Outline Fonts

Also known as printer fonts, outline fonts contain character descriptions that are sent to the output device when a document containing those fonts is printed. Each character is described by its outline, so it can be printed accurately at any size. **PostScript fonts** contain bitmapped fonts as well, which are used for screen display, while **TrueType fonts** contain only outline fonts.

See Also

Fonts; PostScript; TrueType

Output Devices, *See Desktop Printing; Printing*

Output, High Resolution, *See Resolution Measurement*

Output, Preparing Files for

When you're ready to take your files to a **service bureau** or **printer** for output, there are a few steps to follow that will help make sure things work out as planned.

- Delete unused items from the **pasteboard**, delete unused colors, and do a Save As.

- Organize your disk so that the service bureau staff can easily find everything they'll need.

- Include all graphics referenced, including those embedded in other graphics. List them and indicate their formats. Don't forget ones placed on **master pages**.

- List all fonts, including those used in **EPS** files, indicating their full name (Helvetica isn't the same as Helvetica Neue), format (**TrueType** or **PostScript**), and vendor (different companies offer different versions of many classic fonts).

- List and include preference files and required **add-on software**.

- Supply a laser printout, color if possible, otherwise with colors printed as grays.

- List the following: the application the files were created in; how many files and which ones are to be output; media you want output (film, RC, laser proofs, Iris prints, and so on); and how you want the files output (positive/negative, right- or wrong-reading, size percentage, with or without crops, spreads or individual pages, imposed flats, resolution, line screen, and composite or separated); and any other relevant information, such as paper stock, ink colors, whether there are bleeds, whether there are folds or perforations required, and how many copies you need.

- Indicate whether work needs to be done on the files before they can be output, such as trapping, and how many plates there are, if you're having **color separations** output.

- Last thing before you send off your disk, open your documents on a computer not networked to the one you created them on. Install the fonts you've listed, check graphics links, and print the document to make sure you've included all the necessary files.

See Also

Add-On Software; Color Separations; EPS; Master Pages; Pasteboard; PostScript; Printers and Service Bureaus; Trapping; TrueType

Overprinting, *See Color Trapping*

P

Packet

A packet is a sequence of binary data. It has a defined format, with some additional bits of information forming a "head" preceding the data, and a "tail" following it. These carry information that the network router needs to know about the packet, including its destination and source. The packets are formed by the controller in the source computer and the data is extracted and reassembled by the controller in the destination computer.

Packets are used in two forms of packet communication:

- Packet broadcasting sends the packet data simultaneously to several remote stations. Each one examines the packet address. Only the recipient downloads the entire packet. The rest ignore it.

- Packet switching networks use routers that direct packets to their destinations.

Pacman, *See Arcade-Style Games*

Page Control Keys

These keys, which appear only on extended keyboards, give you one-button control over your document for such actions as **scrolling** up or down, moving your **cursor** to the beginning or end of a document, deleting, and invoking the **Help** feature contained in many programs. Page Control keys are not supported by all applications.

See Also
Cursor; End Key; Help Key; Home Key; PageDown Key; PageUp Key; Scroll Bars

Page Description Language

Macs use special programming languages to communicate with output devices, mainly **QuickDraw** and **PostScript**. The latter is the standard for laser printers and high-resolution imagesetters, while the former is the Macintosh's native graphics language and is usually used to communicate with less-expensive inkjet printers. QuickDraw also creates the on-screen image that users see, even if they're working in a PostScript-based drawing or page layout program. PostScript has more functions and can thus produce more complex graphics with greater precision than QuickDraw.

See Also
PostScript; QuickDraw 3D

Page Down Key

The Page Down key, which appears on extended keyboards, **scrolls** down one screen in the **active window** or open document

See Also
Active Window; Scroll Bars

Page Imposition, *See Prepress*

Page Layout, *See Graphic Design*

Page Layout Applications

The basic tool of the desktop publisher is the page layout application, which replaces the pasteboard and X-acto knife of old. Using these programs, users create documents that range in size from one to hundreds of pages, incorporating both text and graphics.

One of the most hotly debated questions in desktop publishing is—and has been for years—which page layout package is the best?

The answer is simple: It depends. All professional page layout packages include certain features, but each implements them differently, so each program is particularly appropriate for some kinds of design and production work. Every designer has a preference, too, and that's what leads to so many friendly arguments. While applications are often marketed by their laundry lists of features, the *way* they work is often more important than how many different things they can do.

The three most popular page layout applications, as well as their less expensive cousins, all start with a basic metaphor of pages. Each lets users determine the size of the pages in a document, and each allows for customized margins and text areas. **PageMaker** and **QuarkXPress** have virtual pasteboards next to their pages for placing items that aren't needed right away (see the following figure), while **FrameMaker** instead offers extra reference pages where users can store graphics that will be used throughout a document.

Master pages in each application hold elements that will be applied to all the pages in a document. For example, a chapter of a book might have master pages for the first page, the right and left pages, and maybe special pages such as those holding full-page graphics. In PageMaker and FrameMaker, when a master page is applied to one of a document's body pages, the items from the master page can't be deleted or changed on the body page—the only way to change them is to apply a different master page. QuarkXPress allows users to change or remove master page items on body pages.

Rulers in each program help users position items on the page, and PageMaker and QuarkXPress have movable guides (non-printing colored lines) that can be pulled onto pages. For more precision, all three programs let users type in the exact desired position of any element using a dialog box, while QuarkXPress and PageMaker also have floating palettes where this information can be entered.

All three programs support **style sheets**, which can change the attributes—font, leading, spacing, and indents—of text paragraphs with one click. FrameMaker also offers character-level style sheets, which allow users to change the style of individual words or characters. These are useful, for example, in math texts with lots of characters in a symbol font.

Each program has tools for making rules, different-shaped graphic boxes, and text boxes. QuarkXPress requires that each graphic be located inside a box, while FrameMaker and PageMaker don't. Text, on the other hand, must be inside a box in FrameMaker and QuarkXPress, but PageMaker uses a "window-shade" analogy for text that allows it to be placed directly on the page without drawing a text box first.

Importing graphics files created in other programs is a fundamental part of working with a page layout application. FrameMaker and PageMaker give users the choice of copying the contents of such a file into page layout files or just **referencing** the file, so that both files

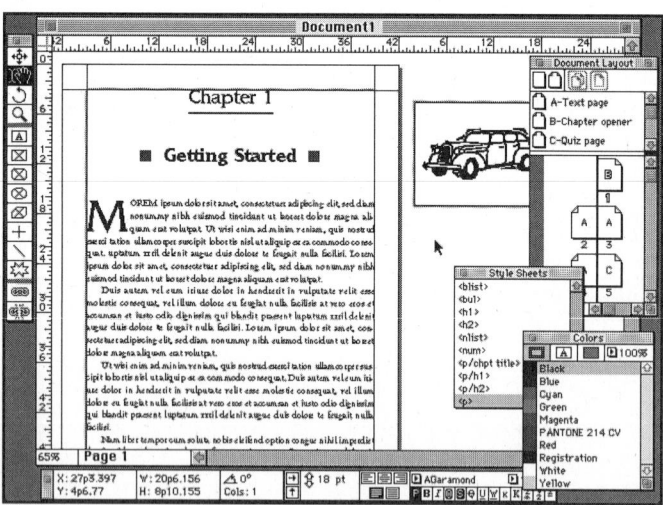

have to be present to print the document. QuarkXPress only allows referencing.

If users don't find the features they need in these programs, PageMaker and QuarkXPress both support **add-on software** that supplies more features. Adobe calls them **Plug-Ins**, and Quark calls them **XTensions**. One thing to keep in mind, however, is that there are many more of these for QuarkXPress than for PageMaker, and FrameMaker doesn't support this concept at all.

In the end, users have to decide which features are most important to them personally and for the projects they'll be working on. For example, PageMaker is popular because it's easy to learn—its user interface appeals to novices. It's also been around the longest of the three, and publisher Adobe has a portfolio of other applications that work well with it, such as Photoshop and Illustrator.

QuarkXPress, on the other hand, is commonly thought of as harder to learn, but its users tend to be devoted. Because it was the first page layout package to incorporate solid support for **process** and **spot color**, it's favored among designers of color pieces like magazines and brochures. Book designers like it because it allows many master pages.

FrameMaker, with its built-in equation and table **editors**, appeals to publishers of technical, scientific, and mathematical documents. Also, features such as automatic running heads and footers, floating anchored boxes, indexing, and cross-referencing make FrameMaker popular with anyone creating long documents that change constantly, because the program repositions graphics and updates heads, tables of contents, indexes, and cross-references automatically.

See Also
Add-On Software; FrameMaker; Master Pages; PageMaker; Plug-Ins; Process Color; QuarkXPress; Referencing; Spot Color; Style Sheets; Table Editors; XTensions

Page Proofs, *See Desktop Publishing Proofing and Printing*

Page Setup Command

If you're using a printer with your computer, the Page Setup command on the **Desktop** gives you access to your printer's options for paper sizes, scaling, page orientation, and more, as shown in the figure (but depending on your particular printer's features). If you have access to multiple printers, each printer may display a different dialog window from the Page Setup command. The Page Setup command shows the options for the printer currently selected in the **Chooser**.

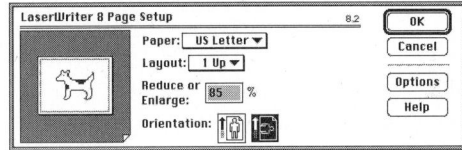

Many programs also enable you to access the Page Setup dialog from within the **File menu.** The **keyboard shortcut** to reach to Page Setup dialog from within a number of programs is Shift-F8.

To use the Page Setup command to set your printing options in the Finder, follow these steps:

1. Select Page Setup from the File menu at the Finder level.
2. The Page Setup dialog appears for the currently selected printer in the Chooser.
3. Select the options you require in the dialog box and click OK when complete. The Page Setup dialog box closes and updates the current Page Setup options to your new settings.

See Also
Chooser DA; File Menu; Keyboard Shortcuts

Page Up Key

The Page Up key, which appears on extended keyboards, **scrolls** up one screen in the **active window** or open document.

See Also
Active Window; Scroll Bars

PageMaker

When most people think of desktop publishing, they think of PageMaker. It has dominated the DTP world almost since its release, and although it wasn't the first Macintosh **page layout application**, it has been the most influential and certainly the most popular.

Designers have long argued over which is better: **QuarkXPress**'s precision-planning approach to page layout, or PageMaker's on-the-fly approach. Those who favor the latter use PageMaker to create everything from business cards to full-length books. The competition between it and competitors, notably QuarkXPress, over the last several years has resulted in an extremely powerful program that's as easy to use as ever.

Documents in PageMaker start with a blank page. Users arrange margin and column **guides** as they wish, import text, then place it wherever they want by clicking a "loaded" cursor on the page. Unlike QuarkXPress or **FrameMaker**, there's no need to draw a text box before importing text, and graphics work the same way—just import and click the page to position the graphic.

Earlier versions of PageMaker had only one set of **master pages**, left and right, which meant users had to recreate the layout of many special pages every time they occurred. With that problem remedied in PageMaker 6.0 and later versions, users can create multiple master page spreads in each document. Master pages can be laid out from scratch or based on existing body or master pages in a document. When applied, they don't affect items already on a page, and users have the option to hide master page items on individual pages.

Style sheets work the same as in other page layout packages: Users can define styles from scratch, base them on existing styles, import them from other documents, and apply them with a single click on a floating palette.

Like other applications, PageMaker supports add-on software, called **plug-ins**, that supplies additional features. For example, a plug-in called Galley Oops looks for typesetting errors such as multiple spaces, multiple punctuation marks, and mismatched quotes and brackets. Photoshop image-editing plug-ins are also available from within PageMaker, allowing users to modify imported images.

With PageMaker's long-document management features, users can automate some parts of the book composition process.

Automatic indexing is accomplished by placing invisible markers in the text of a publication; when the Index command is invoked, PageMaker scours the publication for markers and compiles an alphabetical list with page numbers. It supports up to three entry levels and can add cross-references automatically.

Tables of contents are generated by listing the style tags that should be included. For example, if chapter titles and first-level headings in each chapter were to be included in a table of contents, style sheets for those elements would contain the "Include in TOC" attribute. When a

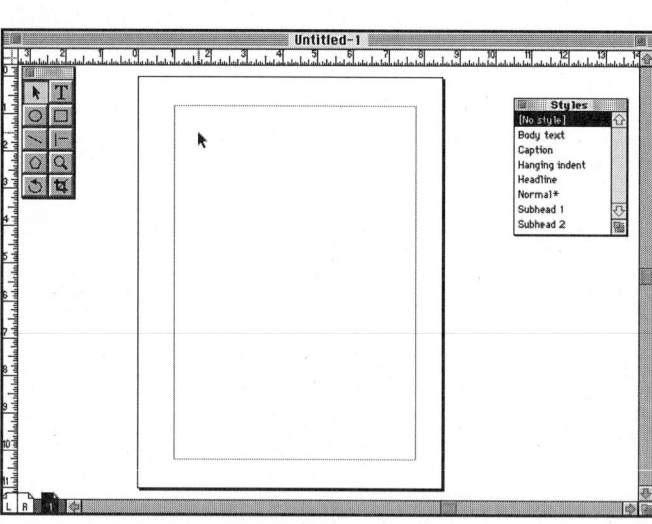

publication is complete, the "Create TOC" command lists all text tagged with that attribute, along with page numbers.

See Also

Add-On Software; FrameMaker; Guides; Master Pages; Page Layout Applications; Plug-Ins; QuarkXPress; Style Sheets

PageMill, *See SiteMill*

Paint Applications

Applications designed for working with **bitmapped graphics** are generally referred to as "paint programs," although the name may be misleading. The majority of work done with this class of software consists of **scanning** and retouching photos and other existing artwork—but it's also possible to create fine art on the computer using these programs.

Images created in paint programs are made up of thousands of tiny dots. If the images are scanned, each dot shows what the scanner "saw" when it looked at the corresponding location on the original. In the case of artwork created from within the paint program, each dot is colored when the user either "paints" over it or uses a filter that alters the artwork overall (such as lightening it or blurring it).

Images can be scanned by using software that comes with the scanner or in many cases by "acquiring" the scan—operating the scanner—from within a paint program through an **add-on software**.

Once the image is opened in the paint program, it can be retouched using tools similar to those found in a traditional darkroom—burning and dodging—and many more. For great precision, users can edit images one **pixel** at a time, removing or altering features of the image at will. Paint programs usually offer several methods of adjusting the brightness and contrast of images, as well as adjusting individual colors or gray levels throughout an image or in only one section.

In general, paint programs offer many tools that let users change existing images into new ones through processes as simple as colorizing or as complicated as

completely rearranging the objects in an image. This capability has brought out two legal issues relating to copyrights (how much do you have to change an image before it belongs to you and not the original artist?) and credibility (when it's so easy to make undetectable changes to a photo, how can anyone trust "photographic evidence"?).

Although paint programs are often used as "digital darkrooms," artists have taken to the Mac like ducks to water, using this class of software to create everything from collages to "paintings" that can't be distinguished from their natural-media counterparts. Often used in conjunction with tools such as **graphics tablets** and scanners, paint programs offer the ability to paint, draw, airbrush, and more—and undo a mistake instantly. Artists can easily save work to go back to later (no brushes to clean and no drying time), add pieces of one work to another, and make dozens of changes to an image very quickly, with the ability to change their minds at any time and go back to a previous stage of a work.

High-resolution color printers, such as the Iris, enable artists to produce prints of their work on demand, and new frontiers (such as the **World Wide Web**) offer digital artists new venues for their work that traditional artists will never be able to penetrate.

For the sake of convenience, paint programs can be placed in three broad groups, although there's a lot of overlap within these. While they can be and often are used to create original artwork, programs such as **Photoshop** and **Live Picture** are excellent choices for cleaning up or editing existing images. Painter can replace an entire artist's workshop with its faux **natural-media tools**, so it's great for creating original artwork. **Collage** is a good example of a program that doesn't try to do it all and therefore does one thing very well—it's designed specifically for creating composite images.

Image-editing applications are heavy on selection tools that let users indicate what part of an image they want to change, as well as color-correction controls, sharpening and blurring filters, and other special-effects filters, such as Emboss and Posterize. They typically

P

open and save to a variety of file formats; in fact, Photoshop has often been treated as a fancy file-conversion utility.

Artistic painting applications, on the other hand, are filled with features that emulate the artists' tools they replace. Chalk, oil paints, watercolors, scratchboard, charcoal—all are available to users of Painter and PixelPaint Pro, along with infinite variations in brush size, shape, and texture. Pressure-sensitive graphics tablets let artists draw as they ordinarily would, only with the advantages of working in a digital format.

Although some of its features are available in other programs, Collage defines a category all by itself: compositing applications. Collage includes powerful masking tools, and it allows users to treat parts of an artwork as individual objects. It speeds work up by displaying only 72-dpi (screen-resolution) images, so the software doesn't have to redraw high-resolution images every time an object is moved, while the high-resolution images are maintained and saved into the file behind the scenes.

Add-on software for paint programs, like Photoshop **plug-ins**, is what provides much of the power of this class of software. Filters modify an image in countless ways, from sharpening its outlines to turning it into a stereogram by hiding it behind a seemingly random pattern of dots. Some add-ons come with paint programs; others, like the Kai's Power Tools series, are from third-party developers. Some of these add-ons can even be used in **draw programs**.

Lesser-Known Paint Applications The range of paint programs is truly comprehensive, running all the way from $20 packages that offer basic paint tools up to $1,000 programs used to produce the sophisticated graphics we see in national magazines, on TV, and on the World Wide Web.

At the low end of the price range, there's UltraPaint. This $20 package offers basic color and black and white painting tools with blended fills, a magic wand tool, masking, editable brushes, and an auto-trace tool. It also incorporates some image manipulation features, like contrast and brightness adjustment and sharpening, and some features only the high-end programs had until recently, like vector drawing tools and layers.

As its name implies, PhotoFix is designed for photo retouching and manipulation. It supports PICT, TIFF, EPS, GIF, and PhotoCD formats, allowing users to sharpen images and adjust their brightness, contrast, and color or gray levels. **Photoshop** plug-ins are supported, but PhotoFix doesn't come with any; other features include a clone tool similar to Photoshop's rubber stamp and the ability to create masks. Its High Quality Printing (HQP) feature optimizes results with low-end inkjet and laser printers by allowing users to calibrate the printers and by dithering color images ahead of time if they're to be printed on black and white printers. An included PhotoFix Browser can scan a disk and create a catalog of all PhotoFix-readable graphics files.

PhotoFlash offers similar features, including the ability to catalog images, but the image-editing tools are less comprehensive—no masking capability, and it doesn't support some of the more powerful Photoshop plug-ins. "DeDust" and "DeScratch" tools are particularly useful for cleaning up scanned images. When searching PhotoFix image catalogs, users can draw a quick sketch of the image they want and the program will attempt to find images similar to the sketch.

Designed primarily for manipulating photos, PhotoDeluxe is intended for home and small-office users with scanners. Its filters can distort, sharpen, and scale existing images, and it supports Photoshop plug-ins. Graphics formats supported include Photoshop, GIF, JPEG, TIFF, PICT, EPS, BMP, and PCX. To help out novices, PhotoDeluxe offers templates (like calendars and greeting cards) and step-by-step instructions on how to use its functions.

PixelPaint Pro combines features of Painter and Photoshop, with some of the natural media tools Painter offers (realistic-looking paints, pastels, and so on), brightness and contrast controls, and an innovative "Wet Paint" mode that lets users arrange shapes as they would in a draw program before applying paint effects.

Offering many of the functions of Photoshop for one-sixth the price is ColorIt!, which supports pressure-sensitive graphics tablets and offers less powerful but simpler controls for functions similar to Photoshop's, such as sharpening and adjusting color and gray levels. A convolution editor allows users to design their own filters for applying edge-detection and embossing-style effects.

Canvas and SuperPaint are hybrid programs that offer both paint and draw tools, with SuperPaint concentrating more on the paint side and Canvas more on the draw side.

See Also

Add-On Software; Bitmap Image; Collage; Graphics Tablets; Live Picture; Natural-Media Tools; Photoshop; Pixel; Plug-Ins; Image Scanning; World Wide Web

PAL

PAL (Phase Alternation by Line) is a transmission standard made up of 625 lines— at 25 frames per second. On a computer screen, this translates into an image of 576 x 768 pixels. Note: this is why the **PhotoCD** format is based on images of this size.

PAL is used in Great Britain, Germany, and several other countries. Developed after NTSC, it is similar to that system; the primary difference being the way color information is encoded. This difference results in better quality color from PAL.

The systems are not interchangeable, but it is possible to convert between them. Although **VHS** and other recording and playback formats are available for both NTSC and PAL, you cannot play a PAL VHS tape on an NTSC VHS recorder unless the machine has been designed for that purpose.

See Also

Digital Video Camera; NTSC; QuickTime

Palo Alto Research Center, *See Xerox PARC*

Pantone Matching System

The most popular **spot color** system in use in the United States, the Pantone system offers several selections of colors: Pantone Matching System, Pantone

Pastel Color System, Pantone Metallics Color System, Pantone Textile Color System, Pantone Plastics Color System, and Pantone Hexachrome (for six-color printing). Similar in principle to the FocolTone and Toyo color systems, Pantone offers both printed swatchbooks and digital ones accessible through major graphics applications. The system allows designers to choose colors that can be reproduced by single inks (for best results) or converted to CMYK equivalents (usually imperfectly).

See Also

CMYK; Color Matching Systems; FocolTone; Spot Color; Toyo; TruMatch

Panzer General, *See Allied General*

Paper, *See Printing Papers, Types of*

Paragraph Return, *See Soft Return*

Paragraph Styles, *See Styles in Word Processors*

Parameter RAM (PRAM), *See Circuits, Parts of the Macintosh*

PARC, *See Xerox PARC*

Parity

A simple, but relatively old-fashioned method of error checking used in data communications between computers connected via **modems** to the **Internet**.

A parity bit is used by a computer or other device to verify that it has accurately received a byte of information from a remote device. The transmitting computer processes the data bits in a byte of information according to a standard formula, and then sets the parity bit to even, odd, or none, depending on the result of the processing.

The receiving computer processes each byte it receives according to the same formula as the transmitting computer. Then it checks the parity bit to verify that it came up with the same result. If the result is in error, the receiving computer asks the transmitting device to resend.

Parity bits are set using the communications software you use with your modem. There are three possible settings:

1. Odd, which means that an odd number of data bits is always transmitted. If an even number of 1 bit is sent within a byte, the transmitting device adds an additional bit to maintain odd parity. The device on the receiving end then verifies that an odd number has been received.

2. Even, which means that the transmitting computer always sends an even number of bits. If an odd number of 1 bit is sent within a byte, an additional bit is added to maintain even parity. The device on the receiving end then verifies that an even number has been received.

3. None (the most common setting), which means no parity bit is sent or received.

Parity checking is a very basic method of error correction, and is no longer widely used for modem communications. Most modem connections now ask you to set the parity to None so that the parity bit is ignored, leaving error identification and correction to higher level protocols within the modem or within the terminal software. Parity is part of the modem protocol settings most often expressed simply as "N-8-1". This stands for "No parity, 8-bit bytes, one stop bit."

See Also

Asynchronous Data Transfers; Internet; Modems; Packet

Parsing, *See Saving a File*

Partioning, *See Logical Volumes*

Pascal

Pascal is a highly-structured programming language designed by Dr. Niklaus Wirth at ETH (Eidgenössische Technische Hochschule) in Zürich, Switzerland.

In the early days of the Macintosh, virtually all high-level programming was done in Pascal. Much of the original **Toolbox** was written in Pascal, and the interfaces to most Toolbox routines use Pascal conventions to this day. In fact, all but the most recent volumes of *Inside Macintosh* include code samples in Pascal only. Apple even added some **object-oriented** additions to Pascal to create Object Pascal, in which the first two major versions of **MacApp** were written. However, the reign of Pascal has gradually given way to **C** and **C++**.

Pascal was designed to be a teaching language, one that would encourage (and enforce) a systematic discipline in programming style. Pascal is a strongly typed language; a variable of one type cannot be used as another type without an explicit conversion. An integer, for example, cannot be used directly as a **pointer**. As a result, many problems often associated with type conversions are avoided. Pascal also offers *range-checking* on arrays.

This Pascal program prints the words "Hello, World!" ten times:

```
PROGRAM HelloWorld(Input, Output);
BEGIN
      FOR index := 1 to 10 DO
          BEGIN
              Writeln('Hello, World!');
          END
END
```

Pascal is traditionally a **compiled language**, although several interpreted and byte-code versions have been used in the past. Over the years, Pascal has spawned a number of other languages, including Object Pascal, Clascal, and Modula-2.

A fair amount of Macintosh development still takes place using Pascal. Metrowerks includes a Pascal compiler in its **CodeWarrior** integrated development environment (IDE). Other Pascal compilers are available from Language Systems and Symantec, although the Symantec compiler (Think Pascal) does not support Power Macintosh development, and no updates are planned.

See Also
C; C++; Compiled Language; Inside Macintosh; Interpreted Language; MacApp; Pointer; Programming; Toolbox

Passive Matrix Displays
The passive matrix display is an economical type of liquid crystal display (LCD) used in lower-end PowerBooks. Passive matrix LCDs create images that are not as sharp as **active matrix displays** and redraw screen images at a slower rate.

See Also
Active Matrix Displays; PowerBook Displays

Password
The password is the key that admits you to an online service, BBS, shared or networked file, or to any other semi-secure computer function. Some hard drive partitioning programs let you set passwords for some or all of the partitions on a drive. Passwords are only as secure as you let them be. If you write your passwords on little yellow stickies next to the computer screen, don't be surprised if your co-workers or family read your email. The temptation to snoop, although rude and/or illegal, is nearly universal.

It's far safer to choose passwords you can remember, and to not keep them written down. When you choose a password, try to avoid the most obvious ones. It's easy for anyone who wants to get into your files to find out your birthdate, your social security number, the name of your spouse or child. It's much less likely they'd remember the name of your favorite teacher, childhood pet, or grandfather. The safest passwords of all are those which are random combinations of numbers and letters or even non-alphanumeric characters like %&*#. These are, of course, also the hardest ones to remember. To help protect your password, change it often. Don't use the same password for all your accounts, and never use the one you use for your bank card or phone card. That's asking for trouble.

Password Protection
The requirement that a user enter a password for gaining access to a computer, **network,** or folder. Usually encountered in an environment where others might have access to your computer, such as in an office or school, or when connecting to the **Internet** or **commercial online services**.

The danger is that others might send information out across the Internet using your certificates (electronic documents that can be used to identify to others on the Internet that you are really who you say you are).

When you are using a password to get into a site, there are three things to remember:

1. Passwords do not provide security. They protect the site from unauthorized users, but they don't necessarily encrypt transmissions. Just because you've submitted a password to get to a page doesn't mean that the page is secure.

2. Do not use the same password at more than one site. If your password to a particular site on the Internet is somehow compromised, or if you submit a password to an untrustworthy person, your account at all other sites that use the same password are potentially compromised as well. It is especially important not to use the password to an account on a commercial service like **America Online** or **CompuServe** as a password for an Internet site.

3. Do not use passwords that are in the dictionary. Most passwords are stored on a host machine in encrypted form. If an intruder gains access to stored passwords, the simple encryption that protects the password is hard for a non-cryptographer to break. It's relatively easy to encrypt an online dictionary using common coding schemes and compare the words in the encrypted dictionary to the stolen encrypted passwords. If the hacker finds a match, your password is known.

See Also

Anonymous FTP; File Transfer Protocols; Internet; Secure Sockets Layer; Secure HTTP

Password Security

This **control panel** was introduced with the **PowerBook** 5300 series to add password protection security to control access to the PowerBook's **hard disk** and contents.

See Also

Control Panels; Hard Disks; PowerBook

Paste Command

The Paste command inserts the contents of the **Clipboard** into your document. If you're pasting text, the text appears at the location of your text cursor. This is ideal for rearranging blocks of text or copying and pasting a graphic from one location to another. The Paste command is usually preceded by either the **Copy** or **Cut** command, which places a selected item into the Clipboard to be pasted.

To paste an item from the Clipboard, follow these steps:

1. Place your cursor where you want the previously copied or cut item to appear in your document.

2. Select Paste from the Edit menu or use ⌘-V.

3. The contents of the Clipboard are inserted into your document at the location of your cursor.

See Also

Clipboard; Copy Command; Cut Command; Edit Menu

Paste (Keyboard Shortcut)

To **Paste** an item stored in the **Clipboard**, press ⌘-V. You can paste this item for as long as it remains on the Clipboard.

To paste an item, follow these steps:

1. Select an insertion point in your document where you'd like the item pasted. If the item in your clipboard is a file or a folder, the copy will paste in the active window.

2. Press ⌘-V to paste the item currently residing in Clipboard.

See Also

Clipboard; Copy (Keyboard Shortcut); Keyboard Shortcuts; Paste Command

Paste Special Command

This command appears in the Edit menu of a number of applications (such as Microsoft Word and Excel). Many of the applications that use a Paste Special command implement it in a slightly different way. In Microsoft Word, for example, you can use Paste Special after you've copied an item from one document, such as a table of numbers, and you want to paste that information into a different document. By using Paste Special you can keep that pasted information linked back to the original document where it was created. If you go back to the original document and change the numbers in the table, they are updated in the new document because the pasted data has been linked back to the original through Paste Special. Microsoft Excel uses Paste Special to paste information between cells and enables you to choose whether to paste the value, formula, formatting, or all of these into the receiving cell. Check your software's manual to see if Paste Special is supported and what its particular features are for your application.

To used Paste Special, follow these steps:

1. Select the item you want to copy.

2. Select Copy from the Edit menu (⌘-C).

3. Switch to the document where you want the copied information to appear and choose Paste Special from the Edit menu. The Paste Special dialog box appears where you choose, from the pop-up list, the document you want the copied information linked to. You then choose to paste the information from another document, or you choose Paste Link to

update the current document when any change is made to the original.

See Also

Clipboard; Cut Command; Edit Menu; Paste Command

Pasteboard

Page layout and draw programs for the Mac generally use the metaphor of a page on which graphic elements and text can be placed. To further extend the parallel with traditional paste-up, these programs often also allow items to be placed on the area around the page, called the pasteboard. Items on the pasteboard don't print, but do contribute to the size of the file; it's a handy place to store elements not used in the current incarnation of a document that may be needed later.

Patch, *See MIDI*

Pathologically Eclectic Rubbish Lister, *See Perl*

Pax Imperia

Pax Imperia originally from Changeling Software (now distributed by Blizzard), is a **strategy game** set in outer space in which your goal is to conquer the galaxy. Because the game is so complex, it a necessity to read through the excessive manual, but the end result will be worth it. Pax Imperia is a great game.

You are in charge of colonizing the galaxy, and conquering those areas that aren't complacent about your arrival. In addition to the strategic government decisions of a game like **SimCity 2000**, you've now also got to take into account the air quality and other standards of living that various forms of alien life need to survive on other worlds. This gets more and more complicated as you realize that, this being a science fiction game, your "people" may not necessarily be human (this is where knowing the intricate descriptions of different life forms in the manual comes in handy). As with other strategy games, you operate on a budget and are constantly under the threat of potential attack or natural disaster. Pax Imperia is a great

diversion and should provide many hours of distraction from earthly life. Pax Imperia II upgrades the graphics and gameplay and broadens the amount of universe available to settle.

See Also

Allied General; Chaos Overlords; Sid Meier's Worlds; Spaceward Ho! 4.0; Strategy Games; V for Victory; Warcraft: Orcs and Humans

PC Cards and Slots

PC Card slots are small external expansion ports in some Macintosh PowerBook models, PC-compatible laptops, Apple's Newton, and other devices. The slots hold PC Cards, credit card-sized expansion devices that can contain such functionality as system memory, modems, networking interfaces, and other hardware. You can even buy tiny hard disk drives mounted on PC Cards capable of holding several hundred megabytes of data.

Both cards and slots are also referred to by the term *PCMCIA*, short for Personal Computer Memory Card International Association, the name of the standards group responsible for the PC Card standards. In Macintosh PowerBooks, PC Cards inserted into a slot show up in the Finder in the form of an icon. You eject a PC Card by dragging its icon to the trash, as you do with a floppy disk.

PC Card slots first appeared in Macs in the series 500 PowerBooks as an add-on device, the 3.8-ounce PowerBook PCMCIA Expansion Module (the term "PCMCIA" has since been dropped from the name). The PC Card module replaces the left battery and plugs into the PowerBook with a processor-direct slot connector.

PC Card slots are standard on 5000 series models and in the PowerBook 190 and 190cs. All PowerBooks with PC Card slots can hold up to two cards. The PCMCIA standards groups define three types of PC Cards that can fit these slots. Type I PC cards are the oldest group, and are used mostly for memory (although they aren't used much today). The most common PC cards are Type II, which are 5 millimeters thick. Type II PC Cards can provide memory, modems, network interface, data acquisition, and other functions. It is quite common to find Type II cards that function as both a modem and an Ethernet interface. These dual-purpose cards have two connectors on the slim edge of the card, which stick out of the PowerBook when the card is inserted.

PowerBooks with PC Card slots can hold one or two Type I or Type II cards. They can also accommodate a single Type III card in the two slots. Type III cards are about twice as thick as Type II cards, and are mostly used for miniature hard disks.

See Also

PowerBook 100 Series; PowerBook 500 Series; PowerBook 5000 Series

PC Exchange

This control panel, which now ships with **System 7.5** and higher, enables you to mount and format DOS-compatible disks and drives. PC Exchange also enables you to choose how PC files are accessed on your Macintosh when you **open** them. If, for example, you are given a PC file, you can designate which Macintosh application opens that file based on the three-letter DOS suffix it contains.

If you insert a DOS-formatted disk into your disk drive, PC Exchange **mounts** the disk as if it were a Macintosh disk, except that the **icon** for the disk has the letters PC on it (sporting a typeface very similar to the one used for IBM's own logo). If you drag a Macintosh file onto a mounted PC disk, PC Exchange changes the file's name to match PC naming conventions and adds the necessary three-letter DOS suffix.

To use PC Exchange to open PC documents, follow these steps:

1. Select PC Exchange from the Control Panels submenu on the Apple menu (or System Folder) as shown in the following figure.

2. Click the On radio button to activate PC exchange.

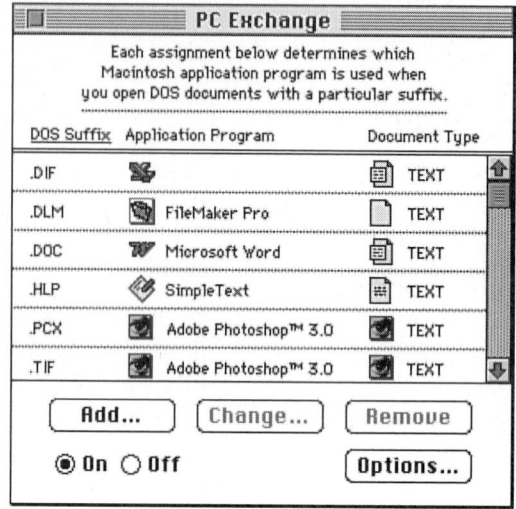

3. The default conversion is displayed. Any PC file with the DOS .txt suffix is opened in Apple's **SimpleText**. To change or remove that preference, click the application in the list and select Change to enter a new application, or click Delete to remove it from the application entirely. To add a new entry, click Add.

4. A new window appears, as shown in the following figure, where you assign the Macintosh application the DOS suffix of the DOS files it opens. To do this, type the three-letter DOS suffix in the first field, choose the Macintosh application you want to open the files with in the selection box. Finally, indicate the PC document types that will be recognized by your application. When done, click OK and you're returned to the main PC Exchange window where you see your new selection in the list.

5. Close the PC Exchange Control Panel to activate your selections.

To use PC Exchange to format PC disks, follow these steps:

1. Insert a Macintosh, PC, or unformatted disk into the disk drive.

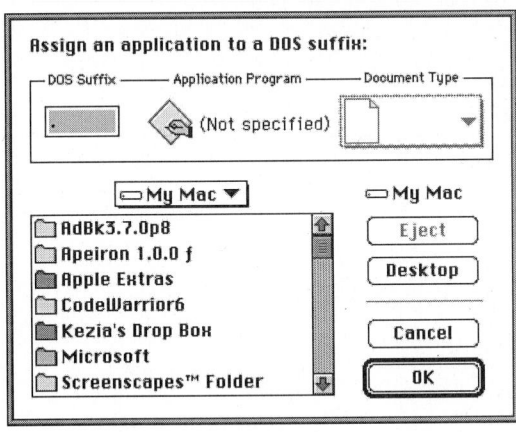

2. Select **Erase Disk** from the **Special menu** in the **Finder**.

3. A dialog box displays asking you if you're sure you want to erase the selected disk. There's also a pop-up menu where you can choose to format the disk in either the Macintosh format or the DOS format, as shown in the figure. To format the disk as a PC disk, select DOS 1.4 and click Erase to erase the disk and reinitialize it.

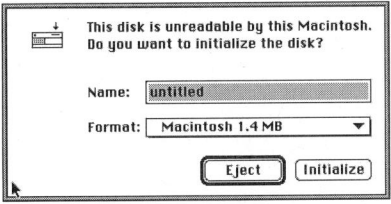

See Also

Erase Disk Command; Finder; Icons; SimpleText; Special Menu; System 7.5; Windows and DOS Translation Utilities

PC Setup Control Panel

This control panel is used by Macintosh models that have Apple's DOS Compatibility Card installed. Options for using the PC card are accessed through this control panel.

See Also

Windows and DOS Translation Utilities

PCI Bus, *See Power Macs, PCI Bus*

PCI Slots, *See Power Macs, PCI Bus*

PCM

PCM (Pulse Code Modulation) is a method for digitally recording sound on magnetic tape. This format is used with some tape formats, most notably Hi-8.

PCMCIA, *See PC Cards and Slots*

PDF Document, *See Portable Document*

PDS Bus, *See Power Mac Logic Boards*

Peace Virus, *See MacMag Virus*

Peachtree Accounting

A business that has more than a few employees and someone other than the boss keeping the books is ready for a more sophisticated accounting program. Peachtree Accounting fills the bill admirably, both for small businesses that intend to remain small and those that hope to grow.

Like **MYOB** (Mind Your Own Business), Peachtree Accounting for Macintosh (PAM, for short) walks you through the steps of starting up your business accounts. Begin by entering the company information—name, address, tax numbers, type of business (corporation, sole-proprietorship, sub s corporation, and so on), whether you'll use batch posting or real-time posting, and whether your books should be set up on an accrual or cash basis. If you don't know the answer to these questions, the Help button gives you additional information about your options, and there are also message boxes called SmartGuides that appear when you're about to begin a new step. These give you quick explanations of what the program does and how to put the right data into it at that point. Context-sensitive help is available on any of PAM's screens.

PAM includes a set of templates for various businesses. Choose the one for the business that's most like yours. PAM copies its chart of accounts, and then helps you determine your accounting periods, quarterly or monthly, and the proper dates for the fiscal year. Having done all this, you must now enter beginning balances for all of your accounts. If you're not familiar with standard accounting procedures, this can be tricky. PAM isn't intended for the beginner or the family checking account. A setup checklist helps you make sure you've completed all of the steps, 15 in all.

After completing all the steps, you can finally begin to use the program. File folder tabs and miniature flowcharts give you access to most of the accounting functions. The rest can be opened from menus. Peachtree's payroll system can handle up to 100 employees and can distribute their wages over multiple jobs and multiple expense accounts. As you'd expect, it handles all kinds of payroll taxes and deductions and prints the necessary forms to file for federal, state, and local taxes. Updated tax information can be obtained from Peachtree, and you're only entitled to one free tax update. After that, there's a charge for the disk. Peachtree also charges for telephone support. New users get 30 days for free, but after that, there's a $3.00 per minute charge for phone support.

PAM also provides fully customizable forms and reports, although the customization process is far from intuitive. The Form Designer is meant to be used by an object-oriented programmer rather than a graphic artist. You build an image of your form on-screen using text objects, data objects, shape objects, picture objects, and command objects. It's not a task for a novice, and probably beyond the capability of the average bookkeeper/receptionist/office jack-of-all-trades. If your business requires many custom forms, consider hiring a consultant to do the programming and to set up your systems.

See Also
Financial Planning Software; MYOB

PegLeg, *See Crystal Crazy*

Pen/Handwriting Devices
Pen input has become a popular solution for specialized needs, but still has many mainstream analysts and users confused about its future. Some people enjoy the convenience; others can't imagine why anyone would want pen input. These devices will never replace the keyboard, but they have an application, along with voice input and bar code readers. If you don't think so, check out what the UPS and Federal Express drivers carry with them (or at least watch the ads on TV.) These pen-input notebooks capture and transmit information for the package tracking system so that the company can tell you precisely where your package is at any given moment. Some systems even digitize your signature with time and date stamping.

In conditions such as these, pen input is far better than paper and pencil, but it is impractical for keyboard-based devices. So far, the Windows market has more pen input hardware and software than the Mac market. All Windows systems use single-character recognition software rather than word recognition software. Single character recognition is slower to input and recognize but is ideal for numerical entry purposes.

What can you do with pen input for the Mac? Consider a nurse checking on patients. He or she can write down the vital signs by filling out a series of electronic forms on a tablet. When finished, the nurse plugs the tablet into a docking station, which downloads all the data. Doctors can access each patient's information at their convenience from a computer connected to the system, or via modem. In the business world, a salesman making field calls can fill out an electronic order form and send it back to the office via modem. The form does all the calculations, and with no errors resulting from data re-entry. Shipping can take place within minutes of the form's reception, if necessary.

Pen-based input systems use a graphics tablet or touch screen (as illustrated below) to let you enter data by writing it or drawing it. Generally, they go one step further with software that converts your input into word processor-readable text and neater drawings (re-drawing your squiggles into real circles, boxes, and straight lines).

There are currently two popular pen-based systems available to the general public (others are developed by vertical markets or specific companies, such as those used by UPS and Federal Express).

- **MacHandwriter.** MacHandwriter is a package that includes a cordless pen, an ADB tablet, and recognition software. This device uses a block printing system to recognize individual characters on a grid. MacHandwriter does not recognize cursive handwriting or entire words, only individual letters. For tasks such as filling out forms, taking sales orders, entering data into medical records, or taking inventory, MacHandwriter often is a better choice than a keyboard. You can also use it as a standard graphics tablet. The MacHandwriter has a street price of $399.

- **Apple Newton MessagePad 130.** The Apple Newton Message Pad with the Newton Version 2.0 operating system can be used as an alternative input device for the Mac with the use of the Connection Kit. The Connection Kit gives you a direct route into your desktop Mac or PowerBook. The Personal Digital Assistant (PDA) provides a built-in notepad, to-do list, datebook, telephone log, address file, and Pocket Quicken software for financial information storage. The MessagePad 130 provides user-controllable backlighting and increased system memory from earlier versions. You can also receive faxes, pages, and email and connect to the Internet. The Newton Message Pad 130 has a street price of $799.95.

See Also

Apple Desktop Bus; Graphics Tablets; Keyboard; Mouse; Trackballs; Touchpads; Touch Screens

PEP, *See Modem Transfer Protocols*

Pepsi Generation, *See Sculley, John*

Peregrine, *See Prograph*

PerfectPartner Card Games, *See Card Games; Traditional Games*

Performas, *See Consumer Models, Macintosh Family*

Perl

Perl is an **interpreted** programming language that is well-suited for manipulating text and files. It was developed on the UNIX operating system by Larry Wall at NASA's Jet Propulsion Laboratory. The Macintosh version, MacPerl, was developed by Matthias Neeracher and Tim Endres.

As with many UNIX-based tools, the meaning of the name "Perl" is at the center of a lighthearted dispute. Some claim it is the "Practical Extraction and Report Language." Others believe it stands for "Pathologically Eclectic Rubbish Lister." Either way, Perl is a powerful and relatively friendly language that has a tremendous following in the UNIX world, as well as a small but growing following on the Macintosh.

Perl combines the best features of **C** with the best features of the most commonly used UNIX shells and shell scripting languages. Because it is interpreted, it is generally considered a macro or **scripting** language, rather than a full-fledged programming language, but Perl can handle many tasks much more easily than C and doesn't suffer from the long development cycle of a **compiled language**.

The Perl syntax should look somewhat familiar to anyone who has programmed in C. Perl is very flexible in the syntax that it accepts, which makes it very forgiving to the kinds of mistakes that can drive C programmers crazy.

The simple listing prints the phrase "Hello, World!" 10 times:

```
$i = 1;
while ($1 < 10) {
        print "Hello, World!\n";
} continue {
        $i++;
}
```

Perl has excellent string and text-handling capabilities. It is well-suited for search-and-replace operations, as well as data processing applications in which large amounts of textual data need to be boiled down into a few short summaries. Perl includes excellent pattern-matching capabilities as well, so you can search for *patterns* rather than concrete strings (for example, all lines longer than 3 characters and ending in .html).

Because of its strength in handling text and file input and output, Perl is the favored language among many

Internet **CGI** programmers. Perl CGIs are especially common on UNIX Web servers, but even Macintosh Webmasters turn to Perl occasionally.

MacPerl adds some Macintosh-specific features to the standard Perl distribution, including support for dialogs and Apple events. MacPerl is available on most major online services and Internet archive sites, as well as directly from the distribution directory at **ftp:// nic.switch.ch/software/mac/perl** or **ftp://ftp.eunet.ch/ software/mac/perl**. The MacPerl Web page is at **http:/ /err.ethz.ch/members/neeri/macintosh/perl.html**.

See Also
C; CGI; Compiled Language; Interpreted Language; Scripting

Permanently Locked Disk, Using

If you have a disk with the **write protect tab** released and the disk drive still won't let you alter the disk's contents, put a small piece of tape over the write protect tab. This should solve the problem. If not, bite the bullet and buy a new disk.

See Also
Locking a Disk

Personal File Sharing, *See Sharing Files*

Personal Information Manager

Nobody's ever really defined what Personal Information Managers are supposed to manage. That's why there are so many different ones on the shelves. Some are basically calendars. Others combine calendar, to-do list, and a simple database for phone numbers and addresses. Those that have more than one feature typically have hot links between them so that you can enter a meeting in the calendar and link it to the address and phone number of the person with whom you're meeting. PIMs come in all flavors, from serious (In Control, Act!) to silly (StarTrek: The Next Generation's StarDate and the Peanuts Family Organizer).

A good information manager should be able to handle the kinds of information you need to keep track of, and it shouldn't make you jump through hoops to put data in or get it out again. After all, the PIM is supposed to make your life easier. Ideally, the PIM will take the place of all those random scraps of paper that held lists and phone numbers and notes and reminders. And it will replace your pocket calendar, or at least will work with it. Most PIMs can print out calendar pages in formats you're already familiar with, like DayTimer, Day Runner, or Filofax (see the following figure).

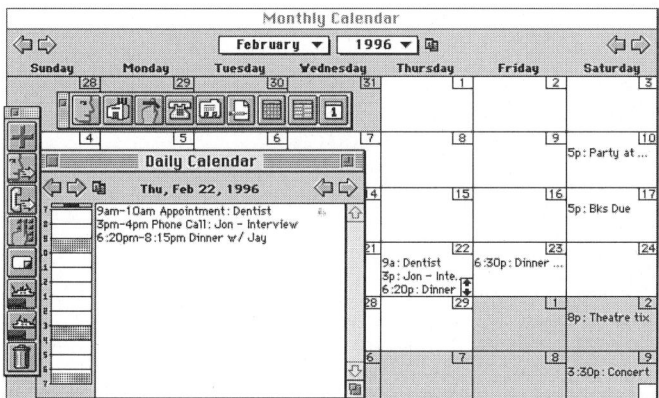

When you're at your computer, the PIM should be able to remind you of upcoming appointments with a discreet message and a beep. It should be able to open up contact information, and possibly even dial the phone for you. It should be able to generate a fax to anyone on your contact list and, assuming you have a fax/modem installed, it should be able to send the fax for you, without your needing to go into some other program to write the message or create the document.

Not all PIMs can manage all of these tasks. Some have other features as well as those described here. Before you invest in PIM software, think about the kinds of jobs you want it to do. If all of your contacts are already in a database, you may not need the address book feature. In this case, In Control may be your best choice. It works with common database programs like FileMaker Pro, and includes a calendar and an "action outliner," which is a prioritized to-do list. If you're starting from scratch in information management, look for a program that is easy to use and can do everything. You might be happy with the Now UptoDate and Now Contact package. These are two separate programs that are designed to work together. Or, you might like Berkeley Systems Expresso, an all-in-one program with easy data entry features. StarDate is Expresso with some added gimmicks.

Peter and the Wolf

Sergei Prokofiev's classic orchestral fairy tale for children comes to the Mac screen by way of an Oracion CD-ROM, part of the Claris Family Entertainment collection. The artwork is lovely, although the music really needs to be heard through external speakers. This program does a fine job of introducing the story and the instruments in the symphony orchestra. The instruments, and the musical phrases they play, can be studied in depth, with a line of the actual score.

The familiar themes can be played over and over by solo piano or the full orchestra, and the story can be read separately.

Of course, the whole production is the centerpiece of the program, from introducing the instruments on stage through the telling of the story against a backdrop of animated characters and scenes. For kids used to Disney-style animation, the very limited movement in the story scenes may be a disappointment. Equally disappointing is the quiz section, which ought to be, but isn't necessarily, about the music or the story. Still, it's worthwhile and kids who like music will adore it.

See Also

Juilliard Music Adventure; KidMusic

Peter's Player

A **QuickTime** player application that is optimized for smooth movie playback. It can load and play a movie from RAM (if there is enough available), and it can adjust the monitor bit-depth for best playback.

Amongst other options, Peter's Player displays movies on a black background without a menu bar.

The software is free for personal use and available from many online services.

See Also

Movie Play; MoviePlayer; QuickTime

Peter Rabbit's Math Garden

The art and music are lovely in this educational game from Mindscape. Beatrix Potter's classic characters, Peter Rabbit, mean old Mr. McGregor, Mrs. Tiggywinkle, and all the rest lead youngsters through various counting and arithmetic activities. The program is rated for ages 4-8, but will appeal most to kids on the younger end of the scale. The activities are scaled at three levels. The most difficult problems are at a second grade level. This figure shows Jeremy Fisher catching fish.

You must help by clicking the fish that match his baskets while they're nibbling the bait. After he catches a fish, you click the basket to show Jeremy where to put the fish. When the baskets are full, you must solve an equation related to the numbers, such as $5 + 3 > 6$, by putting the correct signs in it.

The trickiest part of the game is to catch the falling radishes that are your reward for solving a set of problems. The radishes can be swapped with Peter for plants to put in your on-screen garden. However, they fall very fast, and it's extremely difficult to click them before they disappear. Kids may find this frustrating. This adult did. Without the right number of radishes, you can't plant your garden, but you can always cheat. Pressing Control-R adds radishes to your basket while you're in the garden. This may, however, teach your children a lesson you'd rather they didn't learn.

PG:PRO, *See FutureBASIC*

PGA Tour Golf

People who are serious about golf probably wouldn't be satisfied with any version of the game that involves a mouse instead of a mashie niblick. However, PGA Tour Golf is a fine way to spend a rainy day, and enables you to play against some of the big names in pro golf on courses you've more likely read about than set spiked foot on. You can watch the big-leaguers play, or choose your partner and play a round yourself. But first visit the driving range and the practice tee. After you've mastered the art of clicking the mouse at the split-second to send the ball in a straight line rather than off into the rough, the bunker, or the pond, you're well on your way to the leader board. It's more edutainment than education.

If you're looking for golf tips, check out Sportware's *Golf.* It puts less emphasis on play and more on learning the terms, etiquette, and demonstrating the proper stance, grip, swing, and follow through. It also gives information about many well known US golf resorts and suggests tours for the golfer, with play at several interesting courses.

PGA Tour Golf III

PGA Tour Golf III from Electronic Arts is right up there with its main competitor **Links Pro CD for**

Macintosh, but lacks the add-on capability of Links. Regardless, if you don't get sick of the three courses offered with PGA, this will keep any golf enthusiast occupied.

Unlike Links, PGA offers you the chance to go head-to-head with pro golfers like Tom Kite and Fuzzy Zoeller. Like Links Pro CD from Access, the key to PGA is timing your swing to the meter. Instead of being at the bottom of the screen as it is in Links, PGA's meter follows the actual arm of the animated golfer. PGA III's graphics are fully detailed and look as great as those in Links Pro, but the game falls short in the group play aspect. PGA Tour Golf III is not networkable and you have fewer options, and fewer courses, than Links.

See Also

Links Pro CD for Macintosh; Sports Games

ph Server

A served database of **email** addresses and other personal information about users on a particular **network**, often maintained by educational institutions. "ph" is the name of the software often used to access a ph server. Designed to provide fast access to information held in a database, especially information that changes often, such as names of personnel or students.

See Also

Web Browser; World Wide Web

PhoneNet

A device by Farallon Computing that allows Macs to connect to each other and to printers on LocalTalk networks using telephone-style wire and jacks. Each PhoneNet connector uses standard modular accessories such as extension cables, RJ-11 snap-in plugs, and telephone wall jacks.

See Also

LocalTalk; Network

Phong Shading, *See Rendering*

PhotoBubble

A competitor to **QuickTime VR**, PhotoBubble produces navigable panoramic movies containing hotspots that the user can click. Unlike QuickTime VR, which builds parameters from multiple single images taken with a regular wide-angle lens, PhotoBubble stitches together two images taken with a 180-degree fish-eye lens. This has two advantages: it creates a view that covers the entire field (QuickTime VR is limited to about 95 degrees depending upon the lens used to take the images), and it also reduces the number of pictures you have to take. Taking only two pictures, however, might not be a blessing; lighting interior spaces becomes much more difficult with such a wide area to photograph (requiring more lights than you need when using QuickTime VR) and the lens is much more expensive. Also, you have to use a paint program to remove the legs of the tripod from the image (although you also might have to do some of this in QuickTime VR).

Another limitation is that PhotoBubble does not support 3D object movies (movies of objects you can examine from any angle) and the files are generally larger than **QuickTime** movies.

PhotoBubble is scheduled to ship both Macintosh and Windows versions starting at $500, and will include plug-ins for **Director**. Demos are available from the company Web site.

PhotoBubble
Price: $500 and up
Phone: (423) 690-5600
Web: **http://www.usit.net/omniview**

See Also
QuickTime VR; 3D

PhotoCD

Marketed to both desktop publishers and consumers, PhotoCD is an easy and inexpensive way to transfer photographs to compact discs in the form of high-quality color scans.

For consumers, PhotoCD has two advantages over printed photographs: PhotoCD images can be displayed like slide shows on a television, and compact discs don't deteriorate the way printed photos do. For desktop publishers, who use scanned photos anyway, PhotoCD scans are much cheaper than scans done by a service bureau—just a couple dollars apiece—although the jury's still out on whether the quality is the same.

Images stored on PhotoCDs are scanned at five different resolutions, from a tiny preview image to an 18MB file that can be used for magazine work. Each disc holds about 100 images, scanned either from a roll of film or existing photo prints, and images don't have to be added all at the same time. Processors range from service bureaus to traditional photo processors—like the corner drugstore.

When PhotoCDs first came out, not all CD-ROM drives supported their proprietary format. That's changed since then; all drives sold in the last few years read PhotoCDs just fine, and most graphics applications can work directly with PhotoCD files.

See Also
Kodak PhotoCD

PhotoEnhancer

If you have a Kodak DC 40 camera, this software is for you. PhotoEnhancer was designed to address the output of the Kodak Digital 40 camera, but this product from PictureWorks also can be used to treat your images on file. In fact, for smaller tasks that don't require a lot of adjustment, PhotoEnhancer is a good choice.

If no Kodak camera is plugged into a serial input on the capture board, the specific items that address the camera are dimmed, leaving you to explore the other commands and processes. The software has one dedicated Camera menu for Kodak Digital 40 interactions. Here you can view all of the slides in the camera as a series of thumbnails, or move them to the disk. They are in the **TIFF** format. The camera controls are accessible via the computer. You can use them to snap pictures using the computer as a remote controller and change the setting of the camera (erasing slides, for example, and setting other parameters). You also can open the slide table or separate slides from the File menu.

The toolbox The toolbox features eight choices: Move Page, Zoom, four selection drawing marquees tools

(Rectangular, Polygonal, Lasso, and Magic Wand), Sharpen and Blur, and a Lighten and Darken brush. PhotoEnhancer does not apply color. A small floating palette of four brush sizes accompanies the tools.

Selection Menu and Tools Outside of the four selection tools in the toolbox, there is no separate selection menu.

Layers PhotoEnhancer has no capacity to incorporate layers.

Native Effects Filters Surprisingly, the software has quite a few native filters, and although they are basic and not adjustable, they can be used in normal image manipulation as well as with a camera connected. The filters are listed under the Enhance and Smart Pix menus. Enhance lists Adjust (Negate, Lighten, Darken, and Equalize), Soften, Sharpen, Intensify, and Lighten Shadows. SmartPix, geared towards adjusting light anomalies that affect color in photos, applies the following filters as either Faster or Better: Daylight (Bright or Cloudy), Shadow (Light or Heavy), Inside, Inside Flash, and Fluorescent. These tools also can be used with non-DC 40 images.

PhotoEnhancer's best feature is a By Example photo editing dialog that enables you to control the color palettes of the image, as indicated by a visual display of twelve adjustable possibilities. The visual displays can be set for Focus, Exposure, Brightness/Contrast, and Color, and can display a spectrum of options, from Fine to Coarse.

Work Modes The software enables you to work in Millions of Colors, Thousands of Colors, 256 Colors or Grays, 16 Grays, or Black and White.

File Save/Load Conventions JPEG, TIFF, PICT (with compression choices of None, Least, Average, and Most), and EPSF, as well as the DC 40 native format are addressed.

See Also
Chinon ES-3000; Digital Still Cameras

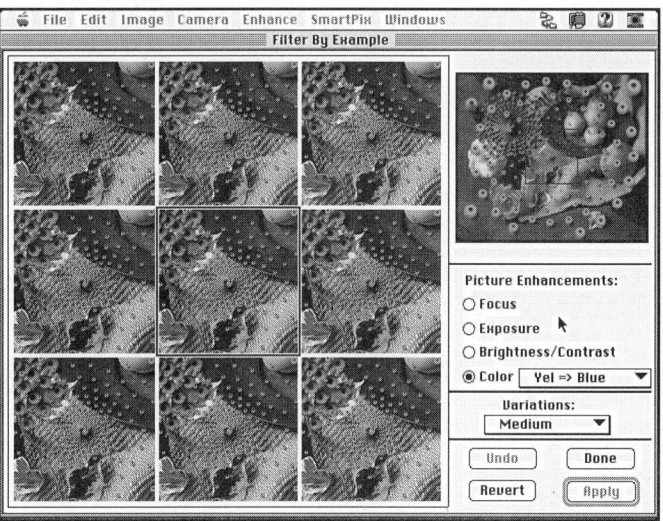

PhotoFix

Microspot's PhotoFix is an image processing program dedicated to photo retouching and print output. It features an Image Corrections dialog with a before and after preview of the selected image. You can adjust the RGB mix and the brightness/contrast of the image with sliders. A special Auto setting allows the machine to apply some intelligence on its own. PhotoFix has a Feather/Transparency tool that seamlessly pastes images on images, performing an invisible transition from the border of the pasted graphic to the background. The same dialog has an opaque setting.

The toolbox The toolbox is designed with all of the standard Tools, with the exception of a selection arrow. Most of the Tools have associated settings dialogs that appear in response to a double-click of the mouse. The Magic Wand can be set to alternate parameters, Light or Color. This is very useful, and adds to PhotoFix's mission as a professional retouching tool.

Selection Menu and Tools The rectangular selector has an interesting list of options in its dialog. Besides custom and Clipboard choices, you can choose Passport Photo, Postcard, or US Letter for constrained sizes.

Layers PhotoFix does not support layers. Selected items are moved with the arrow keys instead of a

P

selection arrow. PhotoFix enables you to separate images into individual RGB layers that can be edited separately and combined back into RGB for archiving.

Native Effects Filters Although PhotoFix doesn't ship with any of its own filters, it accepts **Photoshop**-compatible **plug-ins** without a hitch. It also enables you to change plug-in directories without quitting the program, unlike all other software. This is very useful if you need to group your plug-ins in separate folders.

Work Modes PhotoFix addresses RGB, Indexed Color, Grayscale, and Bitmaps.

Other Considerations PhotoFix provides up to 32 levels of undo. The software also contains an extensive browser/cataloging utility to help you find and group your images. The color palette is easier to adjust than in most other software, enabling you to change foreground and background colors with an included picker and slider. PhotoFix ships with a PhotoCD titled "Scenes of France," which is loaded with images you can use and explore. PhotoFix also boasts a special Floating Color palette that can save up to 16 colors for easy access. PhotoFix conveniently locates the zoom and DPI settings on a pop-out menu connected to the viewframe.

HQP is a PhotoFix term that means High Quality Printing, and it is unique to this software. HQP can dither an image to look like 256 grays even though your printer doesn't support grayscale output. Also, it is capable of adjusting the image to fit the requirements of your printer as far as color hue and density. The printers it supports include: StyleWriter, StyleWriter II, ImageWriter, DeskWriter 550c, DeskWriter C, DeskWriter, LaserJet 4ML, and StyleWriter 2400.

File Save/Load Conventions PhotoFix saves images as TIFF (LZW compressed or uncompressed) and PICT (**JPEG** compressed or uncompressed). When it comes to loading images however, the choices include: PICT PhotoFix, PICT, TIFF, Photoshop, **AIFF**, **Freehand** 3.11 Preview, EPSF, **GIF**, GIF 87 and 89,

JPEG, PhotoCD, MacPaint, TIFF PC, PIC, PCX, Quark 3.2, **QuickTime** Movie(s), RIFF, Scitex CT, Sound Edit, Targa, and BMP.

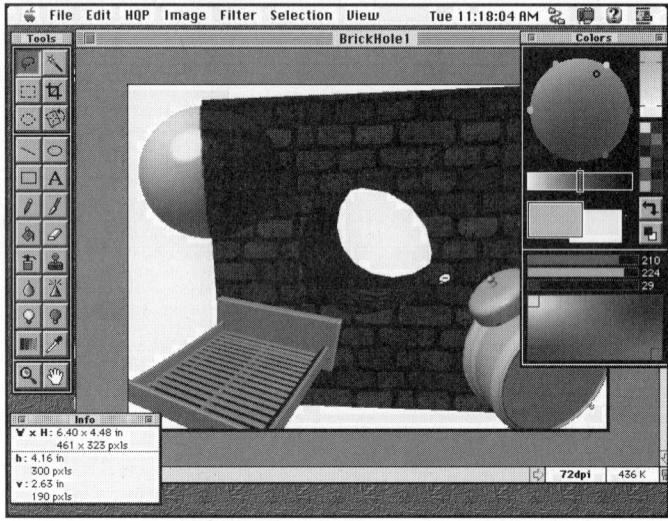

PhotoFusion

PhotoFusion is a product normally targeted at videographic producers, but because the software can be used for quality image compositing, it has uses for the artist/photographer and animator as well. PhotoFusion works with the technology called *blue/green screen compositing*, the same technology that Hollywood has used for years to make Superman and spaceships fly across impossible background scenes, along with many other special effects uses.

PhotoFusion is an Adobe **Photoshop** Acquire module, and its hardware key must be plugged in for it to operate. PhotoFusion is a resolution independent module that takes over after it is accessed in Photoshop, and then sends its results back to Photoshop for image saving. Images are loaded into PhotoFusion, and then saved to Photoshop.

The Process

■ First, selected images are photographed against a greenscreen or bluescreen background, scanned into your system, and saved to disk. You also can cut imagery out of paper and, using either the green or blue colorcards provided, scan the desired images.

- Next, open PhotoFusion and add a foreground and background image. Backgrounds must be equal to or greater than the size of the foreground imagery. A sample is then taken of the background color. Multiple samples can be taken in any order desired. PhotoFusion then creates a grayscale linear mask (an alpha channel) of the data, with areas darker than whiter ones in the composite.

- Preview the composited image. Save it to Photoshop for final saving or other image processing. There are several options for saving the picture and the newly created mask back to Photoshop.

Complete control over the density of both the foreground and background masks is offered in PhotoFusion, leading to explorations of multiple transparencies and fog effects. Animators can use this process to composite image sequences behind the foreground plane. Digital photographers especially will like the quality of the composites that are generated without having to use the Magic Wand tool. Animators who have a video capture card in their systems can use a video camera to shoot against a PhotoFusion legal color greenscreen or bluescreen. This footage, saved as numbered PICT frames, then enables animated foregrounds over animated or still backgrounds.

Other Considerations You are advised to use the PhotoFusion suggested blue or green colors as the drop out colors. To this end, the software includes a card listing three companies that manufacture the required blue and green color paint or cloth that PhotoFusion users can employ in the chroma keying process.

File Save/Load Conventions PhotoFusion saves images as RGB files to Photoshop. If you want to bring them into PhotoFusion again, they must be saved as Photoshop 2.0 or 2.5 images from within Photoshop. You can view the four associated PhotoFusion image layers at anytime (foreground, background, Alpha mask, and Composited Result).

Photomechanical Process, *See* *Prepress*

Photoshop

Adobe's Photoshop is the image editing software that everyone else tries to emulate. Although it may lack some of the tools and tricks that other competitive packages have and allow, it remains the most widely used image editing software in the world. Photoshop has set the standard for image editing interface design, the standardization of the tool set, and the way that it can be depended on to produce files that are ready for professional printing applications. It is also the central application that plug-in developers write for most, so that other software that uses plug-ins usually has to be Photoshop-compatible. Although Photoshop prefers to leave the vector image creation and manipulation to its sister software, Illustrator, it does have a full complement of vector (path) creation and editing tools.

For the professional, it's not a question of whether or not you should own Photoshop or another package, but what other software you may want in addition to Photoshop. Adobe's Photoshop remains the standard against which competing software, in fact all image dedicated software, is judged.

The Toolbox Photoshop's Toolbox contains both selection and painting options. Headed by three selection tools and a move operator, plus the ubiquitous "hand" for moving the page, the balance of the tools are used for image retouching and creation. A zooming feature is accessed by the standard magnifying glass option. Next comes Flood Fill, Line, Gradient Fill, the Color Picker Eyedropper, Eraser, pencil, Airbrush, Brush, Stamper, Cloning, Smudge, Focus, and Toning. The bottom of the Toolbox features the Foreground/background color swatches, standard screen mode, and the masking screen mode. At the very bottom are the toggles for zooming the work area. You may think that there's nothing too special about these tools because Adobe has made them the standard expectation over the years, but all of them are able to interact with the image to produce quality transformations. Double-clicking the icons in the Toolbox brings up the options and brushes dialog where finer control over the tools parameters can be set.

Selection Menu and Tools Work on an imported graphic can be accomplished in two ways: globally or on a selected area. Selection options therefore become very important for image editing. Photoshop has limited area selection brushes: an oval/rectangle selector and a freehand selector. The freehand selection tool may be constrained to draw a straight-edged polygon if the Option key is held down while it is being used.

The selection menu contains items that interact with the area of the graphic outlined by the selection tools. You can select All (the whole picture), None (turns off all selections), or Inverse (inverts the selected area with the rest of the picture). The inverse option is important when retouching a graphic because it's often easier to outline the inverse selection and then to use this menu option than to operate in the opposite fashion. "Float Controls" brings up the dialog that allows you to control the opacity and blending of the floating selection or the composited layer; it's vital when creating collages and composites. "Color Range" is another unique Photoshop selection feature, allowing you to select areas of the image by color and tone for selection and masking. Feath-

ering and other modification choices allow for the incremental adjustment of the selected image area. The marquee that surrounds an area can also be toggled on or off, and the selection can be saved and loaded later as a separate graphic.

Layers A separate dialog is dedicated to Layers, Channels, and Paths. Layers are separate graphic elements, and they may be composited and combined in a myriad of ways to attain a new graphic using the Float Controls dialog. Channels refer to the color separation of the graphic. In RGB mode, the Channels represent RGB and then R, G, and B separately. Any channel or group of channels can be toggled on and off for specific image manipulation operations, and then switched back on. DTP users will want to work in the CMYK channel mode. Paths are the most important connection selection process in Photoshop, greatly expanding the potential variety of the selection tools, and adding the capacity to incorporate vector graphics inside Photoshop. The paths section of the layers-Channels-Paths dialog is where these operations are centered. Here, an area selection on-screen can be transformed into a Path and adjusted to fit any desired shape, something not possible with the selection tools alone. This is all done with Bézier curve pen tools that create, add to, delete, and move points on the selection. The Photoshop manual contains excellent tutorials that walk you through the process. Selections can be interchanged with paths, edited, and turned back into selections.

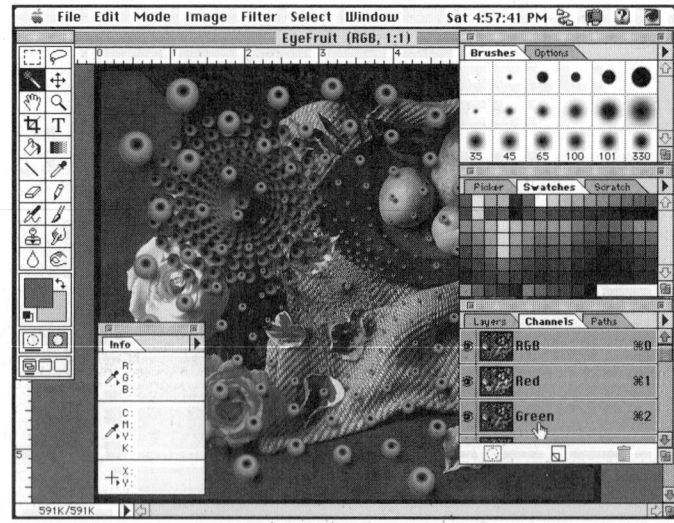

Native Effects Filters Photoshop features a good number of its own special effects and other filters, even without considering the hundreds of filters that may be purchased from other developers. Photoshop native filters include: Blurs, Color (Change Color, Colorize, remove Color), Distortions (Pinch, Polar Coordinates, Ripple, Shear, Spherize, Twirl, Ripple, ZigZag), Noise modes, Pixelations (Color Halftone, Crystallize, Facet, Fragment, Mezzotint, Mosaic, Pointillize), Sharpen, Stylizations (Diffuse, Emboss, Extrude, Solarize, and more), and Video (De-Interlace and NTSC "legal" colors). A very important set of imaging filters is listed under "Render." The five items here are Clouds, Difference Clouds, Lens Flare, Lighting, and Texture Fill. Clouds/Difference Clouds adds fractalized clouds to the selected area, and Lens Flares can be sized and customized before painting down in accordance with a visual preview. The Lighting Effects filter is one of the most extensive in both options and customizing controls. Texture Fill applies a previously saved grayscale graphic as an alpha channel layer over the picture. Photoshop also lists a number of image altering choices to fill its internal filter list.

Work Modes Photoshop enables users to incorporate and work in the following graphics modes: Bitmap, Grayscale, Duotone, Indexed Color, RGB, CMYK, LAB, and Multichannel. It also includes a Color table and CMYK previewing. It is always possible to switch modes back and forth.

Other Considerations Photoshop contains a Print Preview screen that is much more full-featured than much of its competition. Its Image sizing and Canvas sizing capabilities are first-rate and very fast. Images that have been altered can be instantly reverted to their original features.

File Save/Load Conventions Photoshop loads Photoshop, Illustrator, Amiga, BMP, CompuServe, EPS, Filmstrip, JPEG, CMS, MacPaint, PCX, PICT, Pixar, PixelPaint, RAW, Scitex CT, Targa, and TIFF files. It saves all but Illustrator files, but it does export paths

to Illustrator. It also exports Amiga HAM. A number of other import/export converters for Photoshop are available from Internet sources as freeware or shareware.

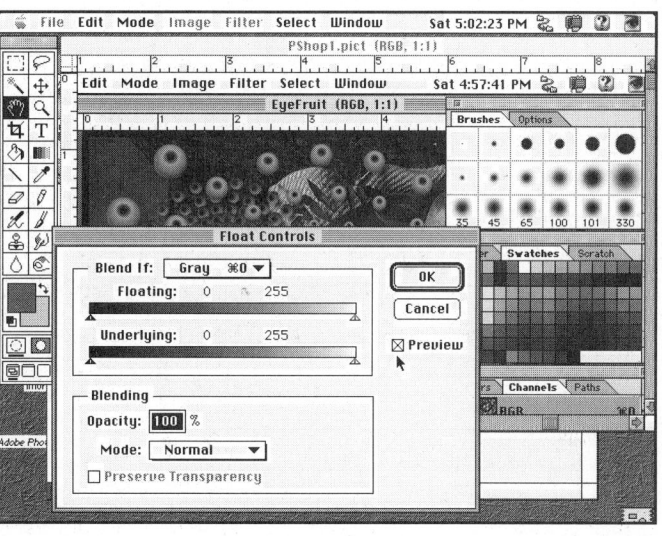

Phyla Database

Just when you think you have databases figured out, along comes Phyla. If you've never worked with a database before, you're an ideal candidate to learn Phyla. On the other hand, if you already know even a little about database terminology and how they handle information, you'd have to unlearn it. Phyla is different.

Phyla is an object-oriented database, and uses the language of object-oriented systems such as biological or linguistic classifications. A class is like a file. An object is like a record. An attribute is like a field. But in order to support the paradigm of objects and their hierarchical structure, the people who designed Phyla determined that it was more effective to use the appropriate terms. It is, after all, a more natural way of looking at the world. Objects fit into classes, have relations, constraints, and inheritance. Once you accept this as the basis for a database structure, it begins to make sense. Let's take a concrete example.

You have a company. You have a staff of twelve people and a bunch of office equipment. Your staff is a class.

P

So is the equipment. The individual people are objects, in Phyla terminology. So are the desks, chairs, computers, and coffee pot. The people are members of the staff class. The coffeepot is a member of the equipment class. Each of these objects has attributes, characteristics which describe it. Employee attributes include their names, phone numbers, addresses, social security numbers, and so on. Equipment attributes include model, serial number, perhaps year purchased (for depreciation), and location. Relations tie specific objects from one class to specific objects from another. Fred, from the staff class, "uses" a walnut desk and black posture chair from the "equipment class." The desk and chair are "used by" Fred. Relations can also be established within a class. Fred "manages" Suzy. Suzy "is managed by" Fred. Objects in a class can be classified into subclasses. The sales department consists of Fred and Suzy. They're the sales subclass. Suzy's Macintosh is part of the equipment class, computer subclass. All these relationships make it fairly easy to model real-life situations, without a lot of complex programming.

Phyla databases use two windows: a definition window, which defines the classes and subclasses, with their attributes and relations; and a content window, which holds object stacks for each class created in the definition window. The object stacks are where you keep track of objects within the class, and list their attributes. Objects may be entered into the database and viewed using forms you create with the form editor, or in an outline showing their relationships to other objects in their class.

The same object may be viewed in several contexts at once, and since the database is fully relational, if you change the data in an attribute, it changes everywhere at once. To establish a relation between two classes, you simply connect them with a line.

See Also
Database

PictShow

This freeware application displays **QuickTime** movies and sound, as well as **PICT** and **GIF** images in a presentation format. Simply place the files in a folder and PictShow does the rest. There aren't a lot of features. You can specify whether the program automatically advances to the next item or waits for a mouse click, but the price is right!

Picture Fonts

They're not really typefaces, but they're definitely **fonts**. Picture fonts, with drawings instead of letters, are handy to use for icons and spot illustrations as an alternative to **clip art**, and there's an incredible variety to choose from.

Some have specific purposes. Logo fonts contain common corporate logos, credit card logos, and TV network logos, while other pictorial fonts show hands spelling out the American Sign Language alphabet (Mini Pics ASL Alphabet), symbols used on maps (Carta), or playing cards and dice (Linotype Game Pi).

Other picture fonts are strictly for fun. The style of these varies from cartoons to woodcuts to human outlines similar to those shown on restroom doors. A good example is Giddyup Thangs, a collection of Western-style images (cacti, horses, cowboy hats, and a six-shooter) intended to be used with Adobe's Giddyup font, in which the letters appear to be formed from ropes.

The convenience of using picture fonts comes from the fact that they're available simply by choosing the font name from a menu, and they can be sized simply by typing in a point size—no importing, no scaling. Apply color just as you would to text. Individual elements in the pictures can't be colored, unless you convert the letters to outlines using a draw program like **Illustrator** or **FreeHand**.

See Also
Clip Art; Fonts; FreeHand; Illustrator; Ornament and Dingbat Fonts; Typeface Categories

Pilot Simulators, *See Sim Games*

PIM, *See Personal Information Manager*

Pinball Games

If you think it's a lost cause to try and recreate pinball on the computer, Loony Labyrinth and Crystal Caliburn (distributed by StarPlay) should change your mind. The realism is as close as you can get on-screen and the themes are as hokey as the ones you'd find on any real life pinball table. In Loony Labyrinth, you play inside the Minotaur of Crete's maze. Crystal Caliburn is loosely based on Arthurian Legend, sending you in search of the Holy Grail. The best thing about these two titles, aside from the detail that went into such standard pinball elements as strategy shot accuracy, are the lush graphics and realistic flipper and bumper action.

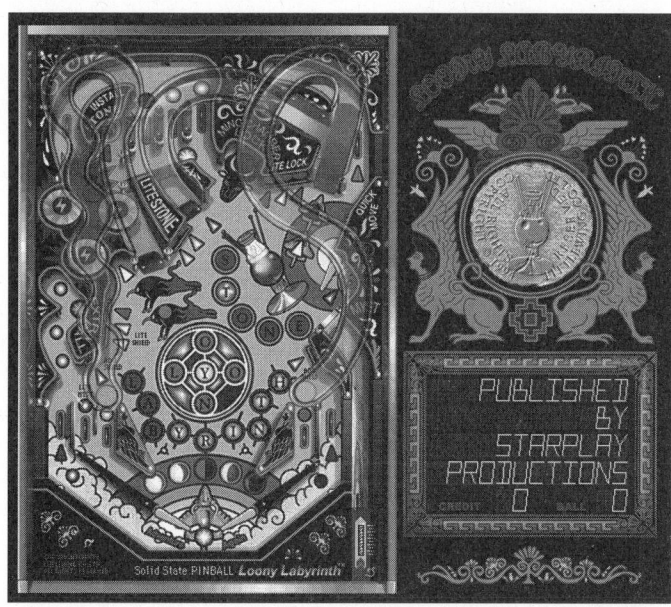

Loony Labyrinth is a bit less of a challenge, but great for less experienced players. If you are a real aficionado of the original pinball machines, nothing is really going to compare to the real thing, but both Loony Labyrinth and Crystal Caliburn should be able to capture your attention if you give them a chance. Maxis, creators of **SimCity 2000** and other bestselling **Sim Games** like **SimTower** are also currently working on FullTilt! Pinball.

See Also

3D Ultra Pinball; Arcade-Style Games

Pirates!Gold, *See Sid Meier's Worlds*

Pitfall, *See Lode Runner: The Mad Monks Revenge Online*

Pivoting Monitors, *See Portrait and Pivoting Monitors*

Pixar

Best known for its motion picture success *Toy Story*, a fully computer-animated motion picture, Pixar, based in Richmond, CA, has long been known in the 3D computer modeling world for the quality of its **rendering** software, called RenderMan. Pixar has released a version of RenderMan for the Macintosh called **MacRenderMan**, as well as two end-user tools: Typestry and ShowPlace. Unfortunately, Pixar has since abandoned the Macintosh market.

Pixar
1001 W. Cutting Blvd.
Richmond, CA 94804
Fax: (501) 236-0388
Phone: (510) 236-4000
Web: **http://www.pixar.com**

See Also

MacRenderMan; ShowPlace; Typestry

Pixar Typestry

Pixar is known more as a high-end animation house than as a developer of marketable computer graphics products, the only exception being their proprietary "RenderMan" software (used by many Hollywood studios to produce state-of-the-art computer rendered animation). Typestry doesn't pretend to be an all-around 3D program, but centers instead upon one narrow targeted aspect of 3D graphics, 3D text graphics and animation.

Features Drawing from their RenderMan technology and experience, Typestry exhibits more professional options than many programs that claim to be full featured 3D art and animation programs. We will look at its features under four separate headings: importation of text objects, addition of backdrops and lights, rendering options, and animation capacity.

Text Objects Importing a text object into Typestry couldn't be more straightforward. Just select any typeface you have, write your message (any number of lines that will fit on the screen), and render. This will give you a front faced 3D text rendering. A digital object has no personality without a texture, and Pixar calls Typestry textures "looks." Typestry comes with a special Looks CD whose libraries are "unlocked" as you purchase them. There are dozens of textures in each separate library. A default Looks Library comes with the software. Included are metals, marbles, woods, and other more esoteric algorithmic textures that take on the personality of organic textures, skin, glass, and non-earthly looks. Any objects stored as a font file can be translated into a Typestry element. Adobe Illustrator saves can be imported into Typestry as text objects, rendered with any chosen Look, and animated.

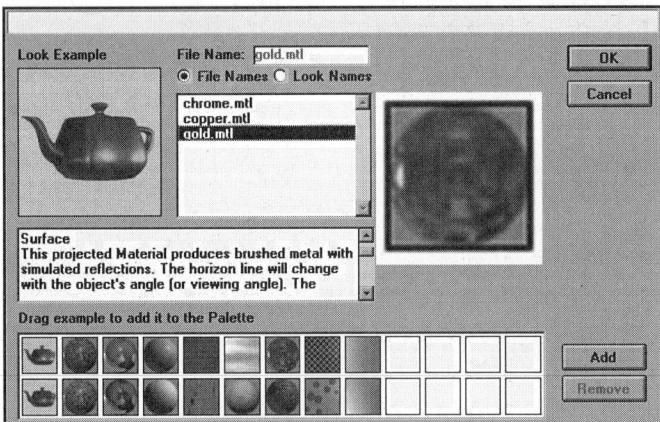

3D text can be built as a normal extrusion, as a tubular arrangement, or as a 3D "Flag." Extrusions come with their own bevel editor, so one need not be chained to default extrusion samples. Tubular text has the look of outline-only text. The tubular outline's cross section may be circular, square, or scooped out. "Flags" in Typestry are special 3D surfaces (wavy flags, banners, disk, sphere, cylinder) upon which the text is placed. You can choose to see only the text, the text as a cutout on the surface, or just the surface. A "PixarPerfs" font is installed with the program that allows you to create all sorts of interesting objects for use as props or for integrating with the text. Animation can be targeted to Typestry flags so that they move over time.

Typestry renderings can be set to "quick and dirty" modes or very high quality renderings. Typestry eats up a lot of RAM in its rendering process, so the more RAM you are able to have on your system when using Typestry, the better. It's not a good idea to multitask while Typestry is running unless you have more than 30MB of RAM available.

Backgrounds and Lights You can select backgrounds from Typestry's background effects or use one of your own saved graphics as a Typestry background. Typestry's internal backgrounds are specialized graphics designed to highlight foreground text. You can select from "Wall," "Floor," or both "Wall and Floor." Selecting both gives you the appearance of a 3D perspective environment. Walls and/or Floors may be texturized just like any 3D text object, and either may be placed at different distances from the eye or "camera". Your original graphics can be painted to a background as a planar surface or as seen through a fish-eye lens.

Typestry's Lights is represented by a graphic matrix with paired sliders that address nine separate lighting positions plus ambient lighting and environment mapping. The lights can act as slide projectors for images in addition to other more esoteric options, an effect that causes subtle light changes in an animated sequence. Shadows can be toggled on or off, and the intensity and color of all lights can be set. Full front lighting and back lighting are also supported.

Animation As with most other 3D computer animation software, you deal with keyframe events and timelines to produce animation in Pixar's Typestry. The whole process is called "composing a score." Numbered single frames are saved out to a file, then composited into an animation by a utility called "Movie Maker." This process is used to create both QuickTime or Video for Windows animation.

Particle Effects Typestry has a fully implemented particle system on board that allows you to add animated particles, from sparks to marbles, to finished renderings. The particle generator is accessed by a specific series of commands, all of which are given high visibility in the documentation.

Pixar's Typestry is a complex high end package. Don't expect to master it quickly. Getting walls and floors to render logically by understanding their placement is a difficult task, as is understanding how to apply pictures to backdrops or objects (reflection settings). You will not be able to produce the fancy graphics shown in the manual without some long effort and dedicated study.

Pixel

This word is derived from the term Picture Element. It refers to the individual dots that make up the image on a computer screen or in a bit-mapped image.

PlainTalk Speech Recognition

This technology, for AV Macs or Power Macs, enables the user to activate certain **commands** on the Macintosh by speaking into a microphone connected to the Mac. With PlainTalk enabled, your Mac can respond to your verbal commands using the PlainTalk Speech Editor and Speech Setup control panels.

To use verbal commands, turn on PlainTalk in the Speech Setup Control Panel. This control panel enables you to toggle speech recognition on or off, and has a slider to let you adjust how tolerant or strict you want speech recognition to be. (If you work in an environment with a lot of background noise, you may want to move the slider closer to the Strict setting, so the computer doesn't accidentally pick up commands from co-workers.)

You can also designate verbal confirmation (or feedback) from your Mac and choose from a pop-up menu of male or female voices to use for this feedback.

When PlainTalk is activated, a speech recognition feedback window appears that shows you the status of PlainTalk and the name of the command being carried out. If PlainTalk doesn't recognize a spoken command, it displays the phrase, "Pardon me?"

Because PlainTalk uses AppleScript to execute your commands, setting up a verbal command is very much like setting up an AppleScript macro, and PlainTalk's speech editor looks like a close cousin of the AppleScript Script Editor used for creating or editing AppleScript scripts. For an application to accept speech commands, it must be AppleScriptable. If not, PlainTalk enables you to use QuicKeys (the commercial product from CE Software) macros to carry out the spoken commands.

After you've created a script to carry out a command, these scripts are stored in the Speakable Items folder, and the scripts are named by the verbal command you'll use to activate the scripts. If, for example, you created a script that will launch ClarisWorks, you might name the script "Open ClarisWorks." And when you have PlainTalk active and speak the sentence "Computer, Open ClarisWorks" into the Power Mac's or AV Mac's microphone, the Open ClarisWorks runs and opens ClarisWorks for you. Incidentally, the term "Computer" is the default word that snaps the PlainTalk recognition to attention, so verbal commands should be preceded by the word "Computer." You can change this default name in the Speech Setup control panel.

See Also

AV Macintosh

PlainTalk Speech Recognition Extension

This extension, for **AV Macs** or Power Macs, is designed to incorporate speech recognition into the Macintosh system. It is used in conjunction with the Speech Editor and Speech Setup control panels to enable the user to activate certain **commands** through spoken voice commands via a microphone connected to the Mac.

See Also

AV Macintosh; PlainTalk Speech Recognition

Plan & Track

A project planning and management program from Mainstay, Plan & Track makes Gantt charts for project planning. A Gantt chart is a timeline, with bars representing aspects of a project set on a calendar scale to show how long each is expected to take from start to completion. Plan & Track, however, goes beyond the Gantt chart to add other powerful management tools, including spreadsheet and cost estimate integration.

It's fully compatible with the Windows version and supports drag-and-drop editing. Plan & Track has been accelerated for Power Mac, but will run on any Mac with a hard drive, System 6.0.7 or later, and at least 4MB RAM. It's easily installed, because there's only one 800K floppy disk.

Use Plan & Track whenever you need to relate tasks and events over a period of time. The graphics, usually depicting task bars and milestones, show how long a planned activity is expected to last, and when particular events occur during the timeframe shown. You can add art to your charts to make them more attractive, and use colored bars to help differentiate one person or group's task from another.

Plan & Track can incorporate spreadsheets and graphs into the plan, enabling you to relate numerical data, such as costs over time or predicted earnings from a program. It also adds an earned value system, which is based on a plan, and shows how value is earned or expended throughout a project. The planned value summary serves as a cost estimate calendar that shows the result of each task within the overall plan and its associated costs. This enables management to adjust timing of certain project aspects to allow for anticipated income, or to delay if cash flow problems occur. The earned value variances are computed automatically, based on no adjustments and show how cost over-runs and schedule deviation can result in a project coming in late and over-budget. The information helps managers plan and track projects of all kinds and all sizes, from an hourly roofing job to a multi-year agricultural project, or virtually anything that takes time and costs money.

See Also

Business Applications; Charting and Graphing Applications; Claris Impact; Personal Information Managers

Plates, *See Printing Methods, Traditional*

Playthrough

Playthrough is a parameter in the **Sound control panel** that can be set when choosing between microphone and **CD-ROM** player as the input device when recording audio. This is also a parameter available in some sound digitizing applications programs such as SoundEdit.

If playthrough is set, the sound can be played through the Macintosh speaker, whether or not it is being recorded. With this parameter set, you play a CD and perform other tasks while listening to the audio.

In most cases, only Macintosh models with internal CD-ROM drives can play CD audio through the internal speaker and the stereo headphone jack on the back panel of the computer. This is because the sound from the CD drive is fed through a sound-input connector on the logic board.

Alternatively, if the Macintosh has an external microphone jack, you can feed the sound from an external CD player into the jack, or you can purchase speakers with dual inputs, such as Apple's AppleDesign Speakers. You then can listen to both CD audio and the sound coming from the computer.

For other Macintosh computers that don't support internal CD-ROM drives but do have a sound-in jack, the freeware **PlayThrough** (by Andreas Pardeike) may help. Connect a cable from the headphone output of the CD player to the input jack on the back of the Macintosh. Note that you may have to use an attenuating cable to adjust the volume of the output.

See Also

CD-ROM; Sound Control Panel

PlayThrough (Application)

A shareware application that provides playthrough capabilities to many Macintosh models with an external CD-ROM player. Available from online services.

See Also

Playthrough

Plug-In Effects

Just as plug-ins can expand the uses of painting programs, so vector drawing possibilities can be widened by plug-in use. There are not quite as many plug-in libraries available for vector drawing software as there are for raster (bitmap) painting programs, but the plug-ins that are available create hundreds of new variations for targeted vector selections. Three vendors stand out as major developers of vector graphics plug-ins: BeInfinite Software, Letraset Corporation, and MetaTools. Each of the three vector plug-in suites that these companies market is unique in its own respect, helping the vector artist to create truly original designs. If you are planning to use these effects in programs other than Adobe **Illustrator** or Macromedia **FreeHand**, check with the developer first to ascertain compatibility.

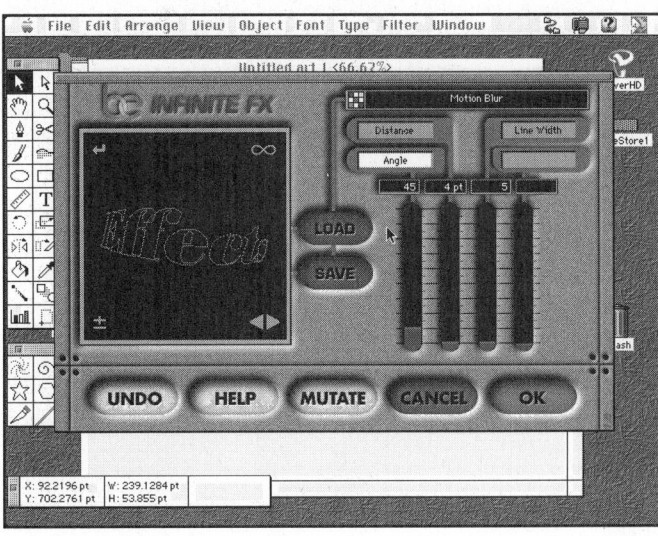

InfiniteFX BeInfinite Software's InfiniteFX (version 1.5) lists 55 separate and unique vector effects. At any time during the manipulation of an effect, you can trade that effect for another in the list. The visual interface allows you to preview all the alterations and adjustments as they are being made, so there are no unpleasant surprises afterwards. The InfiniteFX interface features a visual preview screen and four sliders. Depending on the effect chosen, one to four of the sliders are active and are associated with altering one of the dimensions addressed by the selected effect. As the sliders are moved, the changes in the parameter of the effect can be seen on the visual preview screen. InfiniteFX filters are envelope filters that apply a range of Bézier curves to the selected graphic's outlines. The interface allows for zooming in on the preview, and customized effects can be saved and loaded again. A help button brings up text that explains what an effect does.

Infinite FX are associated with subgroups, so we will list them within the groups they appear in:

1. Pure Transformation.

2. Cornerize (and inward/outward), continuous one way and other way, exaggerate, Flip-Flop, Perp, Rocker, TCB.

3. Wiggle (Everything, Corners, Rockers, Inbound, Outbound, Horizontal, Vertical, Horizontal/Vertical Corner, Horizontal/Vertical Inbound).

4. Balloon (Up & Down, Sideways, Everywhichway), bend Up/Sideways, Shear Vertical/Horizontal, taper (Up/Down/Left/Right).

5. Twist (Horizontal/Vertical), Waves (Atmospheric/Oceanic), Rippling (Vertical/Horizontal).

6. Antispin, Blast, Fisheye, Motion Blur, Pinch, Pond Ripples, SpinIt, Zig Around, Zoom.

7. Smart Addpoints, Cylinder Wrap, Metabloat, Metacalligraphy, Metapunk, Polar to Rectangular, Rectangular to Polar.

Most of the effect names give you some idea of the visual shapes, while others have no logical connection. Experimentation is the key. InfiniteFX runs in both Illustrator and FreeHand.

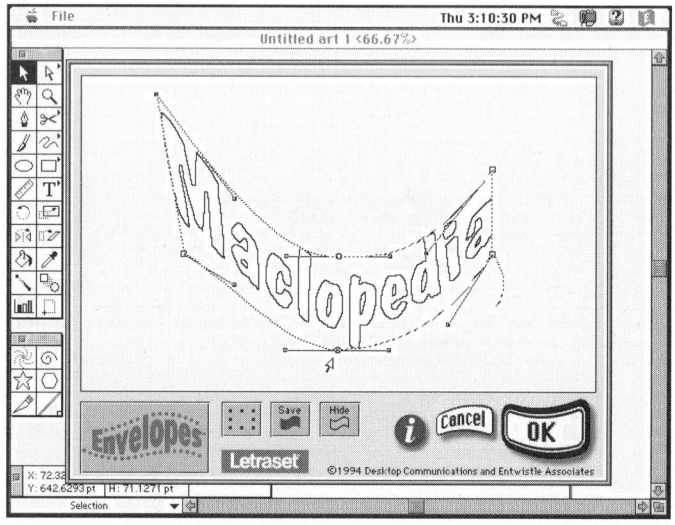

Envelopes Letraset's Envelopes plug-ins give you the capability to edit the Bézier curves until you get the exact shape you're looking for. The plug-in filters are grouped in separate libraries that define their general similarity. The libraries are named: Envelope Library, Curved Perspectives, Straight Perspectives, Super Perspectives, and Twists and Spirals. Having the capacity to tweak the assigned shapes instead of just accepting them as applied increases the possibility of getting never-before-seen results. Any new shape you discover can also be saved as an archetype for further experimentation. Because the default shapes are identified by code numbers, it's wise to keep the documentation handy to find the initial shape. After a numerically indicated shape is chosen, however, the full visual library associated with it comes to the screen, so selecting the exact shape to explore is simple. The Envelopes interface enables you to turn the object off so that the Bézier manipulations are made clearer. New Bézier nodes can be added to the outline simply by clicking the line with the Option key held down. The Illustrator and Freehand Envelopes plug-ins are not interchangeable, so you will have to purchase separate versions of these plug-in libraries if you want to run both Illustrator and Freehand. The Freehand Envelopes also include shapes not found in the Illustrator version.

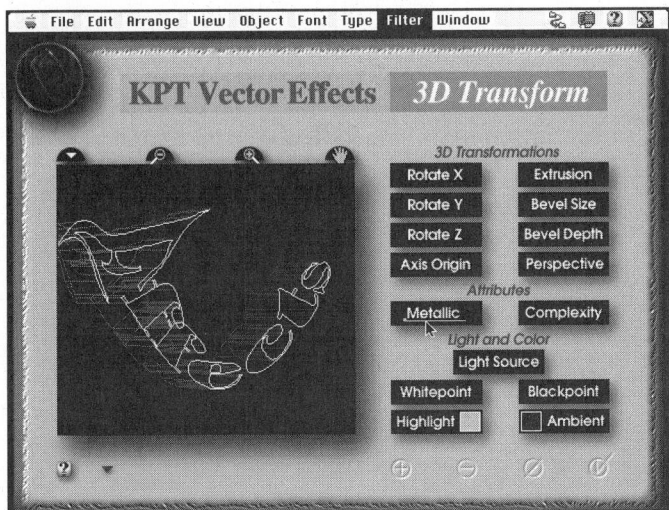

VectorFX VectorFX from MetaTools gives the vector artist a clear way of achieving effects normally associated with bitmap graphics. This program takes a very different approach than the other plug-ins take, preferring to add elements to a shape rather than sculpt them into a new form. VectorFX will work with both Illustrator and Freehand. Thirteen plug-ins are included, and it should be noted that all effects include a large library of preset parameters:

1. 3D Transform: This effect adds 3D depth to the selected graphic. Rotation on any plane, "metalicity" (reflective property), color variations, degree of depth and beveling, and perspective alignment can be adjusted. This effect is probably the most desired one that vector artists need and ask for. A full-featured help screen is available.

2. Colortweak: This effect allows you to adjust and apply color to the selected graphic or to its "shadow." A full panel of color parameter controls is included. The effect can be applied

through the VectorFX interface or "live" via a small on-screen menu. A full-featured help screen is available.

3. Emboss: Embossing adds the feel of chiseling to a graphic, as if it were cut out of stone. VectorFX Embossing allows you to adjust the contrast, angle, and amount of the effect. Soft Embossing is also possible, giving a grainy airbrushed feel to the selected graphic. A full-featured help screen is available.

4. Flare: Flares are seldom associated with vector graphics, being a more common application in bitmap art. VectorFX applies flares determined by your adjustment of Radius, Halo, and Amount of spokes in the flare. Flares may be moved around on the preview screen. A full-featured help screen is available. The flare is written over the selected graphic area.

5. Neon: Neon adds a gradient glow around the selected graphic, a smoothing effect that adds both depth and texture. Brightness and Amount can be adjusted. A full-featured help screen is available.

6. Inset: This effect bloats out the selected graphic, ballooning it and smoothing the edges. The Amount is adjustable and can be previewed. A full-featured help screen is available.

7. Point Editor: This effect allows discrete control over all of the Bézier control points on the selected object. They can be selectively targeted and moved by numeric input without disturbing those points that you desire to remain in place. A full-featured help screen is available.

8. Resize and Reposition: This effect does just what it says, resizes and repositions the selected graphic. A full-featured help screen is available.

P

9. Shadowland: This is another much-requested effect. Both cast and dimensional shadows can be added to the selected object. Multiples of the shadow can be cloned, and a spiral angle can be added to them. A full two-color gradient can be targeted to the shadow, and the halosity, size, and brightness adjusted. Hundreds of shadow effects can be created with this single plug-in. A full-featured help screen is available.

10. ShatterBox: (Not available for Freehand) This effect shatters the selected image in response to your input parameters, causing explosions and the breaking of symmetries. The degree and extent of the effect is user controlled. A full-featured help screen is available.

11. Sketch: This effect applies a randomness to the selected graphic, so that the result can be compared to a child's crayon drawing. If the effect is applied too generously, the result is tangled chaos. A full-featured help screen is available.

12. Vector Distort: This effect applies adjustments to the vector graphic normally associated with Photoshop bitmap effects: Swirl, Spherize, Rotate, Magnify, Zig, Zag, Zig Zag, and Warp Frame. A full visual preview constantly updates the view, and any or all of these effects can be applied at once. A full-featured help screen is available.

13. Warp Frame: Full control over the selection's Bézier control arms is possible here, with the ability to warp the selection in any direction. A full-featured help screen is available.

Extensis' DrawTools Extensis' Draw Tools enables you to warp the selected graphic on either a splined or a Bézier controlled plane in addition to other effects. Draw Tools gives you three groups of effects

that can be applied to either or both Adobe Illustrator and Macromedia Freehand: Draw Tools Color, Draw Tools Move, and Draw Tools Shape.

DrawTools Color is a collection of five filters that allow you to edit color ramps; mix and replace colors; convert objects to grayscale; and create duotones, tritones, and multitones in the selected graphic. Draw Tools Colors supports RGB, CMY, and IHS color models in addition to CMYK and K (black and white, grayscale). When addressing color models not supported by Illustrator or Freehand, Draw Tools Colors converts the results to CMYK before applying them to the illustration. Certain caveats and restrictions apply when working with color gradients. The color mixer filter provides quick and easy color mixing tools, and the filters color graph transformation files can be loaded and saved. Selected full-color graphics or the entire page may be converted to grayscale in one easy step. There is also a randomizing feature that replaces all selected colors in an illustration, or just those in the selected object. Layers can also be exchanged with one another.

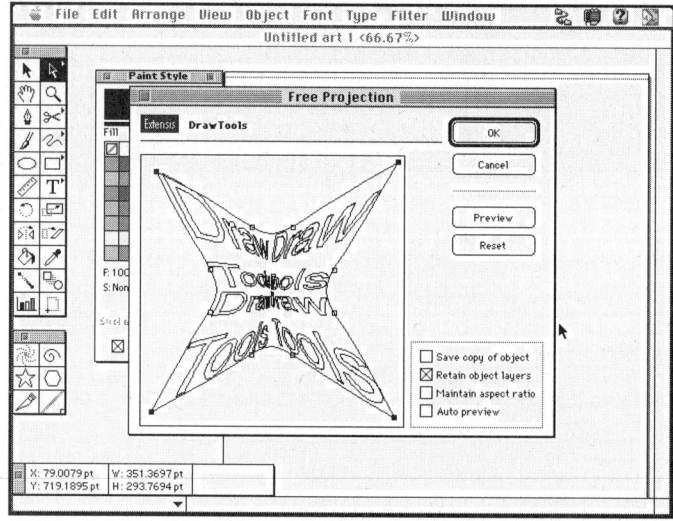

DrawTools Move saves you time when the task is to move the order and position of any number of selected graphics in the illustration. By clicking the backward or forward buttons as many times as need, the selected object, group, or multiselection is moved to the appropriate layer in accordance with the number of mouse clicks. Objects can also be repositioned any-where on the page by altering their coordinates as displayed in a DrawTools Move dialog, which also displays the selected measurement system being applied (inches, centimeters, and so on). Selected objects may be resized according to either their di-mensions or to mathematical operators (add to, subtract from, multiply by, and divide by).

DrawTools Shape filter works on single, grouped, and multiple object selections. When multiple objects are transformed, their hierarchical structure is retained. Smooth and precise alterations are assured because Shapes translates all linear components to splines and then to Béziers. In Illustrator, Shape options are brought to the screen with separate menu selections, while in Freehand a global dialog appears with all options visually displayed. The following Shape trans-formation options are included:

- Globe—Makes it appear as if the selected graphic has been wrapped on a 3D globe, the height, width, and angle of which are user controlled.

- Cylinder—Causes the selected object to be wrapped on a 3D-like cylinder with user controls for height, diameter, interpolation (extent of view from top or bottom), and angle.

- Cone—Wraps the selected object into a 3D-like cone shape with user controls over height, base diameter, top diameter, interpo-lation (extent of view from top or bottom), and angle.

- Water/Amplified Waves—Allows the selected object to be affected by wavelike transforms, where the user controls the frequency and amplitude of the wave.

- Diamond—Transforms the selected object into a diamond-like shape with user controls over height, width, and angle.

- Free Projection—Enables the user to transform the selected object by using spline and Bézier controls to reshape a grid that controls the objects shape.

Plug-Ins

Often used as a generic term for **add-on software**, "plug-ins" originally referred to add-ons specifically used by **Photoshop**. Now the term is used for add-ons used by all Adobe programs, including **PageMaker**.

Plug-ins for Photoshop allow the program to import and export additional image formats (such as PCX and JPEG), control scanners, and apply special ef-fects to images. The third category offers the splashi-est products, like Kai's Power Tools (and other assorted KPT packages), Gallery Effects (which can turn an ordinary photo into a fresco or a pen-and-ink draw-ing), and Paint Alchemy, which applies natural-looking brushstrokes to an image.

PageMaker plug-ins (formerly called Additions) offer functions like automatic drop caps, expert kerning, grouping, and automatic running headers and footers.

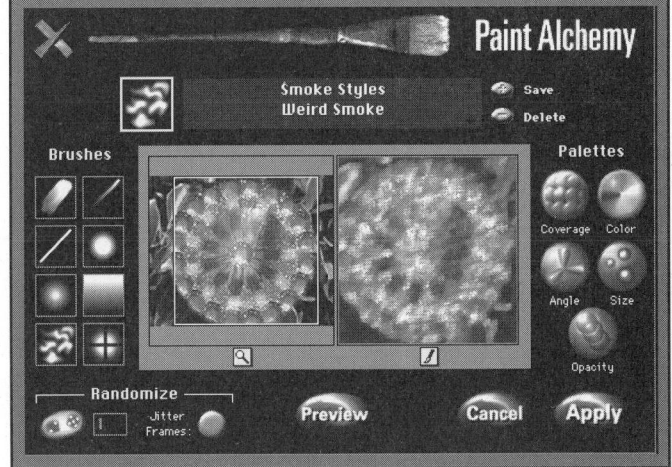

P

See Also
Add-On Software

PlugInfinite

PlugInfinite is a plug-in utility that should be owned by everyone who is overwhelmed by the number of plug-ins that reside in their library. Often, when called upon to do a specific image manipulation task, it's necessary to use only a few plug-in effects, if any. At those times, the digital artist may wish that the plug-in list could be customized for specific projects. PlugInfinite from BeInfinite Software does just that. Most importantly, all of PlugInfinite's effects can be removed if you find that your plug-ins aren't acting right. Smaller plug-in groups also require less memory from your system.

The process is straightforward. First, use the Add button on PlugInfinite's window to search and add selected plug-ins from your plug-ins folder. Selecting Save or Save As from the window brings up a save dialog. Select a new name to save the plug-ins group to, and you now have a selection that will appear in your effects menu that will list only the plug-ins you grouped under that heading. You can configure as many new groups as you'd like, customizing selected plug-ins for specific tasks.

Plug-ins and plug-in menus can also be renamed, so that their function more correctly matches your understanding of what they do when applied. If you have plug-ins that you never use, and that you think you never will, they can be disabled by PlugInfinite. You can also use this software to get more information about the plug-in. PlugInfinite can display the following plug-in data:

- Label—Descriptive information.

- Original Name—The name before you changed it. You can use Restore to change it back.

- Original Menu—The original menu before you changed it. You can use Restore to change it back.

- Type—Type categories are Acquire, Export, File Format, Accelerator, Parser, General, and Filter. Your plug-in will probably be listed as a Filter type.

- Requires Host—Shows if the plug-in requires a specific host program to run.

- PowerPC—States if PowerPC code is resident.

- Animatable—States if plug-in has animation capabilities.

- Filename—Complete file and path names of plug-in location.

- Size/version—Size/version of the plug-in.

- Modes—States if the plug-in addresses any or all of the following modes: Bitmap, Grayscale, Indexed color, RGB, CMYK, HSL, HSB, Multichannel, Duotone, and LAB.

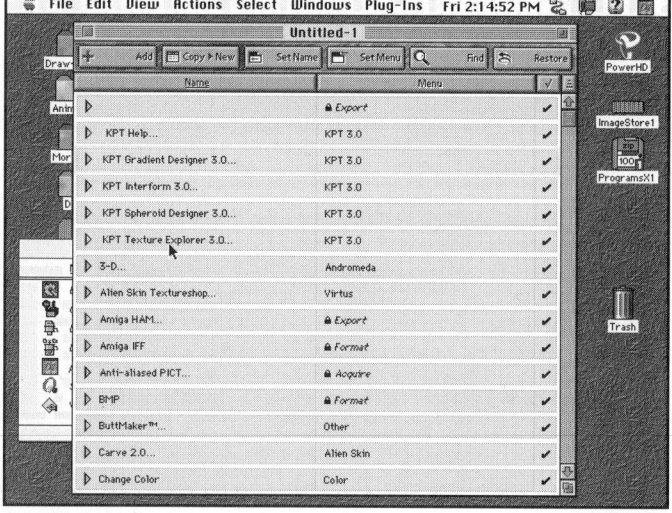

PMS, *See Color Matching Systems*

Point, *See Typesetting Terms*

Point Size

Type size is specified in points: 10-point type, 18-point type, 72-point type, and so on. When points are used to measure other things, there are 12 points to the pica and six picas to the inch, and therefore 72 points to an inch, but one of the mysteries of type is that 12-point type isn't 12 points tall, and 72-point type isn't one inch tall.

At one time, 12-point type was likely to be 12 points tall—if measured from the bottom of the descenders up to the top of the ascenders. However, this is no longer true for most typefaces.

See Also

Fonts

Point to Point Protocol, *See MacPPP*

Pointer

A pointer is simply a variable that contains the location of a block of memory. It is often more convenient to work with a pointer than with the original block of memory itself. For one thing, pointers are typically quite a bit smaller than most blocks of memory. (On the Macintosh, pointers are 32-bits long—4 bytes.) Rather than passing around the entire block of memory, programs just pass around the pointer.

Because the data pointed to by a pointer cannot be moved in memory without making the pointer invalid (the pointer would continue to point where the data used to be), this data must be fixed in memory. The fixed data is called nonrelocatable and it can cause havoc with the **heap**. If you allocate many pointers without paying attention to where they are in the heap,

the Memory Manager might have a hard time moving relocatable blocks to consolidate the free memory in the heap. The nonrelocatable blocks get in the way.

See Also

Handle; Heap; Toolbox

Pointer Mode

The Pointer Mode Control Panel was designed for use with the Power Mac 7200 model, and it enables the **cursor** to remain visible on screen when taking a **screen capture** (Shift-⌘-3). It may also reduce the flickering that occurs when the cursor is over a graphic.

See Also

Cursor; Screen Capture

POP3 Protocol

A protocol or set of standards designed to allow the retrieval of electronic mail messages from a central mail server.

POP3 (Post Office Protocol, Version 3) allows mail messages to be retrieved from a machine that holds such messages. POP3 is designed to operate in environments where an electronic mail system operating with **SMTP** (Simple Mail Transfer Protocol) is impractical due to cost constraints or the lack of a computer with an **IP address** connected to the Internet.

All popular email **client**s support POP3, including **Eudora** and **Netscape Navigator**.

For more information see the Internet Working Group Request for Comments (RFC) 1460 (**ftp:// ds.internic.net/rfc/rfc1460.txt**).

See Also

Email; Internet; IP Address; Netscape Navigator; SMTP; TCP/IP; World Wide Web

Pop-Up Menu

Menus in a dialog box or window are pop-up menus. Pop-up menus have a downward-pointing black triangle right after the menu's title that tells you it's a pop-up menu. When you **click and hold** a pop-up **menu**, a menu appears offering a list of selections from which to choose.

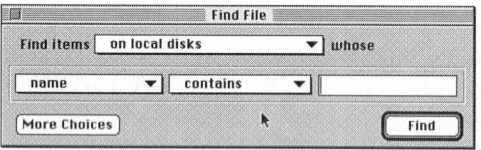

Pop-up menus, for example, are the menus in the **Find File** dialog box that enable you to select what criteria you want to use for your file search. The first pop-up menu defaults to a "name" search, but because you can see a black triangle pointing downward, you know that "name" is an item on a pop-up menu. Clicking and holding the name title causes a menu to appear where you can choose to search by: size, kind, label, date created, date modified, version, comments, and lock. You select items from a pop-up menu the same way you select items from a **pull-down menu** in the menu bar; by holding the mouse button and dragging the **arrow pointer** until the selection you want is highlighted and then releasing the mouse button.

See Also

Arrow Pointer; Find File; Menu; Menu Bar; Mouse; Pull-Down Menu

Port Number

An **Internet** server or **host** computer uses port numbers to designate specific channels for accessing particular kinds of information.

Port numbers sometimes appear in Universal Resource Locators (**URL**s) when a user accesses a server on the Internet. In order to get **World Wide Web** information from that server, the user's computer needs to access port number 80 on the server. To get **Gopher** information, port 70 is used, and so on.

Port numbers are not physical SCSI ports or serial ports, but virtual channels leading to information on a computer. A few of the common port numbers used on the Internet are given in the following table.

Common Internet Port Numbers

Port Number	Description
20, 21	File Transfer Protocol (data on 20, control on 21)
23	Telnet
25	Simple Mail Transfer Protocol
53	Domain Name Server
70	Gopher
79	Finger
80	World Wide Web
110	Post Office Protocol, Version 3
119	Network News Transfer Protocol
123	Network Time Protocol
194	Internet Relay Chat Protocol

Port number access happens behind the scenes during Internet communications, so users do not have to configure ports themselves.

See Also

DNS; FTP; Internet; IP; IP Address; IRC; NNTP; POP3 Protocol; Server; SMTP; Telnet; World Wide Web

Portable Computers, Macintosh Family

Apple Computer is the leading supplier of laptop computers with its PowerBook series. The PowerBook family of Macintosh computers comes in two types: a portable all-in-one computer and a dockable system that combines the portability of the laptop with the connectability and flexibility of a desktop system. Apple also is moving its laptops to the PowerPC RISC chip and is using the IBM/Motorola/Apple-designed PowerPC 603e, a special chip designed to use less power and produce less heat. The following figure shows the PowerBook 160.

Both the laptop and dockable models have several common features:

■ Apple PowerBooks use a liquid-crystal display (LCD) screen. There are several types of LCD displays: backlit supertwist, active-matrix, and **passive matrix displays.** All have been used in PowerBooks, depending upon the model, and whether it has a color version. PowerBooks are moving to an **active matrix display** because the passive-matrix displays are prone to a problem called ghosting or shadowing where objects that are moved around the screen leave a trail of images in their wakes. Only the PowerBook 190 and 5300 still use a passive-matrix LCD; all of the rest of the PowerBook models use an active-matrix color or dual-scan color LCD system.

■ PowerBooks use a different type of pointing device than the mouse that is standard on a desktop system. All current models of the PowerBook use a unique pointing system called a **trackpad** that senses your finger's movements on the pad and repeats that movement on the screen using coupling capacitance.

■ PowerBooks contain a built-in microphone and support 16-bit stereo sound input and output.

■ PowerBooks support PC Cards via a **PCMCIA port** that provide enhancements, such as telecommunications, Ethernet connections, faxes, and modems, as well as additional RAM or removable storage.

■ PowerBooks are powered on the road by a rechargeable battery or AC adapter. Battery power life depends upon many factors, such as the brightness of the screen and how much input/output activity to hard and floppy drives occurs, but you can expect two to four hours of power from a Nickel-metal-hydride battery.

See Also

PC Cards and Slots; PowerBook; PowerBook DuoDocks and Minidocks; PowerPC Platform (PPCP)

The following table provides an overview of the PowerBook family.

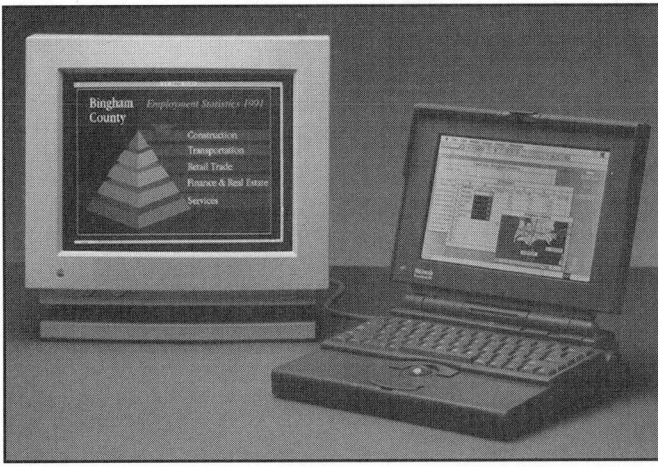

The PowerBook Series of Macintoshes

Model Number	Processor	Memory/Storage	Display	Options	Battery
PB 190	33 MHz 68LC040	4 or 8M/500M, SuperDrive 1.4M floppy	9.5" Passive-matrix grayscale	PC Card slot for 2 type I or Type II PC cards or 1 Type III PC Card; IDE connector for third-party solutions, ADB Port, SCSI Port	3-5 hr. NiMH
PB 190cs	33 MHz 68LC040	8M/500M, SuperDrive 1.4M floppy	10.4" dual-scan passive-matrix color display	PC Card slot for 2 type I or Type II PC cards or 1 Type III PC Card; IDE connector for third-party solutions, ADB Port, SCSI Port	3-5 hr. NiMH
PB Duo 2300	100 MHz PowerPC 603e	8 or 20M/750M or 1G	9.5" active-matrix color display	Docking connector, 2 serial ports, PC Card slot for 2 type I or Type II PC cards or 1 Type III PC Card; IDE connector for third-party solutions, ADB Port, SCSI port	2-4 hr. NiMH
PB 5300	100 MHz PowerPC 603e, 16K data cache, 16K level-2 cache	8M/500M, SuperDrive 1.4M floppy	9.5" passive-matrix grayscale display	PC Card slot for 2 type I or Type II PC cards or 1 Type III PC Card; IDE connector for third-party solutions, ADB Port, SCSI Port	3-5 hr. NiMH
PB 5300cs	100 MHz PowerPC 603e, 16K data cache, 16K level-2 cache	8 or 16M/500 or 750M, SuperDrive 1.4M floppy	10.4" dual-scan passive-matrix color display	PC Card slot for 2 type I or Type II PC cards or 1 Type III PC Card; IDE connector for third-party solutions, ADB Port, SCSI Port	3-5 hr. NiMH
PB 5300c	100 MHz PowerPC 603e, 16K data cache, 16K level-2 cache	8 or 16M/500 or 750M, SuperDrive 1.4M floppy	10.4" active-matrix color display	PC Card slot for 2 type I or Type II PC cards or 1 Type III PC Card; IDE connector for third-party solutions, ADB Port, SCSI Port	3-5 hr. NiMH
PB 5300ce	117 MHz PowerPC 603e, 16K data cache, 16K level-2 cache	32M/1.1G, SuperDrive 1.4M floppy	10.4" active-matrix color display	PC Card slot for 2 type I or Type II PC cards or 1 Type III PC Card; IDE connector for third-party add-ons, ADB Port, SCSI Port	3-5 hr. NiMH

Portable Document

A way of "preserving" or fixing a document so that it can be viewed with its original layout, type fonts, and graphics intact whether or not the reader has the software that was used to create the document.

Portable documents can be used wherever documents need to be shared by users who have different hardware or software configurations. They are particularly useful on the **Internet** because:

1. Internet publishers need to make their work accessible to readers who use virtually every computer and software combination imaginable;

2. Most ways of publishing material on the Internet, such as HyperText Markup Language **(HTML)**, provide only limited formatting options. To put a printed booklet or brochure online its text and graphics must be converted to simple layouts that do not allow a choice of typefaces, for instance.

Some publishers on the World Wide Web make publications available in conventional HTML format as well as in portable document formats, to give readers an option of viewing them with their original formatting intact. To view the portable documents, however, readers are required to download or otherwise obtain freely available "reader" software.

Several software packages give publishers the option of converting an electronic publication to a "portable" format. The packages and their owners include:

1. Acrobat (Adobe Systems)

2. Common Ground (Common Ground Software, Inc.)

3. Envoy (The Novell Applications Group)

4. Replica (Farallon Computing, Inc.)

Besides duplicating, as closely as possible, a document's type fonts and graphics, some of the programs go a step or two further to provide other benefits. These include such navigational features as **hypertextual links**, thumbnails (very small reproductions) of each page, a table of contents, and so on. Acrobat, also provides a security (read-only) option.

All of the programs mentioned above create portable documents. You should choose the product whose software you are already familiar with. Acrobat and Common Ground are the most popular formats seen on the Internet.

See Also

HTML; Hypertext; Internet; World Wide Web

Portrait Orientation, *See* *Orientation*

Portrait and Pivoting Monitors

Portrait monitors are the oddballs of computer display monitors, in that they are designed to display a letter-sized page in its entirety. Most display monitors, regardless of size or picture resolution, have the same aspect ratio, the ratio of the width to the length. The standard aspect ratio most monitors use is about 4-to-3. Because the width is longer than the length, ordinary monitors are often called *landscape monitors*. Portrait monitors, on the other hand, are taller than they are wide, with an aspect ratio of 4-to-5.4375. The standard WYSIWYG picture resolution for a portrait monitor is 640 x 870 pixels.

Pivoting monitors, invented by Radius, work as both a portrait and a landscape monitor. When oriented vertically, the monitor displays in portrait mode. You can grab the display and rotate it 90 degrees, and the monitor automatically changes to landscape mode.

The pixel resolution is slightly different from either portrait or landscape monitor, but is closer to the former. The monitor in the figure is the Portrait Pivot 1700, based on Radius's PrecisionColor Pivot.

Portrait monitors are useful for people dealing with text, such as writers and editors. However, many of the people who needed portrait monitors have been moving to two-page monitors, which have been dropping in cost over the past few years. As such, portrait monitors have been losing popularity.

See Also

Cables and Adapters for Monitors; Energy-Star Monitor Issues; Monitors; Monitors, Common Models; Monitors, Image Quality; Monitors, Size; Multimedia Monitors; Multisync Monitors; VGA Monitors, Using

Ports, Future Trends

With the advent of the fast PCI bus as well as storage that requires high-performance input and output, the Mac's **small computer system interface (SCSI)—** the so-called **SCSI-1** architecture—and **Apple desktop bus** (ADB) protocols are beginning to show their age. There are various ways to increase the throughput of peripherals to keep up with the new storage system drives and meet the data transfer demands of color imaging, multimedia, and networking. SCSI supports a throughput rate of 5 Mbps on 50-pin connectors supporting 25 wires, including eight each for data and grounding. Newer technologies have doubled and quadrupled the data transfer rates. The following technologies are competing to replace SCSI-1.

- **SCSI-3.** A new specification for SCSI that supports existing SCSI protocols as well as new implementations of cabling, connector, and data transfer schemes.

- **Universal Serial Bus (USB)**. Intel's new PC standard for serial ports may replace the Mac's ADB or GeoPort.

Poser

One of the most difficult tasks in drawing is creating realistic human forms. Making realistic **3D** models of human forms can be even harder. Artists tradition-

ally used small wooden models as guides for the human form. Enter Poser from Fractal Design; it's the 3D equivalent of the artist's model.

Poser provides a collection of body shapes than can be adjusted and posed as desired. From the Figure Type menu you choose between a variety of body styles: from Male and Female to Skeleton and Stick. You then adjust the height and proportions of the figure to customize the shape. You can choose between different body parts, but while the major parts of the body (arms and legs) can be manipulated, individual parts of the hands and feet cannot be adjusted.

After the figure is selected, it can be easily twisted and adjusted to the desired pose. Poser uses inverse kinematics to make adjusting the figure into realistic poses very easy.

Lights can be added, and the camera can be moved to view the figure from different angles. There are also some simple static objects that can be added to the scene. A completed body shape and pose can be saved to be used again later, and a saved pose can be applied to another figure.

The program supports **Phong** shading to render the final image, and adds an alpha mask for use in another program, such as Fractals' **Painter** or Adobe **Photoshop**.

While Poser is used primarily to create 2D artwork for use in other illustration programs, it can also export models in **RIB** (Renderman Interface Bytestream) and **DXF** format. Unfortunately, when imported into a 3D program, you can't manipulate the figure; it's exported as a single shape.

For those who need realistic looking human figures, whether for 2D or in 3D illustration, Poser could be the answer to your biggest nightmares.

Fractal Design Corp.
P.O. Box 2380
Aptos, CA
Price: $99
Fax: (408) 688-8836
Phone: (408) 688-5300
Web: **http://www.fractal.com**

See Also

3D; Photoshop

PosterWorks

S.H.Pierce and Company has developed the solution for artists who need proof prints and final copy large enough for billboards or gallery displays. PosterWorks is a printing program that manipulates your output to target both high-end commercial printing services as well as desktop printers. PosterWorks output can be printed to a series of smaller pages, which can then be pasted together for a view of the final enlargement. The main edit screen shows a display grid and a preview of the imported graphics, both of which can be toggled off or on. Graphics files can be placed on top of each other for composite printouts. The view of the finished work can be altered by percentage or measurement equivalents, and a straight line drawn anywhere on the screen returns its measurement.

Files can be saved as PosterWorks native or as Bureau files for transference to professional printing facilities. The art can be calibrated for Cyan, Magenta, Yellow, Press Curves, Gray Balance, UCR, GCR, Black, and Color Check. The output saturation and scanner matrix can be enhanced and Halftone Corrections set. After the art is set, it can be targeted to your on-site printer, or saved as a Bureau file and sent off-site.

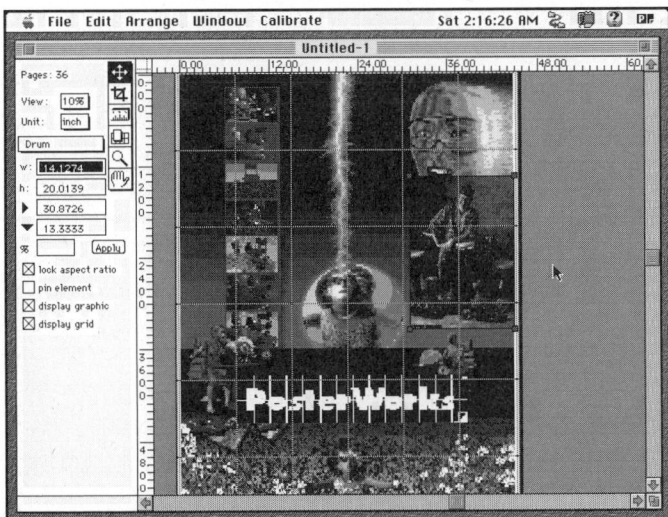

Posting to a Newsgroup, See
Newsgroup, Posting to

PostScript

PostScript is **Adobe Systems'** page description language. PostScript printers use controllers which reside in the printer's body. The controller is a computer, usually based upon a RISC chip or Motorola CISC chips and using two or more megabytes of Random Access Memory (RAM), as well as Read Only Memory (ROM) chips containing the printer fonts stored in outline form.

When you send a document to the printer by selecting the **Print** command in your application, the Macintosh **Printer Manager** checks to see if there is a communications link to the printer. (Under System 7.5.1 and higher, you can see this happen by double-clicking the desktop printer icon—the resulting Printer window displays the status of the printing process, commencing with a message saying "Looking for LaserWriter." Earlier System 7 versions required you to open the PrintMonitor under the Apple menu to view similar information.)

Under System 7, the Macintosh has deleted the LaserPrep utility required under System 6 to download the custom PostScript Dictionary to the printer before the first use of the printer each time you turn it on. The PostScript Dictionary contains translations for QuickDraw's shorthand commands which speed up the printing process over AppleTalk networks. During the process of downloading, the PrintMonitor shows the message "Initializing Printer." Under System 7, only those portions of the PostScript Dictionary required to perform a specific print job are downloaded as needed. This also enables you to mix System 6 and System 7 versions of printer drivers on a network connected to the same printer.

When initialization is complete, the Printer Manager sends the application's QuickDraw routines translating the page layout specifications to the printer driver, which in turn translates QuickDraw into PostScript commands. The PrintMonitor or Desktop Printer displays the alternating messages "Processing Job" and "Preparing data" during this process. During the transmission of the PostScript program, the printer's controller receives the code and it is read by the PostScript interpreter and scan converts the image into a bitmapped page which is stored in the controller's page buffer. The interpreter uses the font outlines stored in ROM to create the required fonts specified in the code. The controller then uses the bitmap to govern the engine's imaging mechanism, and flushes the image and the PostScript code after the page is printed.

PostScript Printers provide extensive benefits in terms of performance, cost savings, and flexibility. Because PostScript scan converts the QuickDraw code, the application program does not have to know the resolution of the printer you are using. You can therefore print on many different PostScript printers using the same file and application program. The difference will be the quality of the output. In addition, each bitmapped page takes up at least one megabyte of memory.

Because the controller performs the scan, the page is stored in the printer's page buffer and not on the Macintosh, requiring less storage on the Macintosh to be dedicated to printing. Multiple Macintoshes and personal computers can share one printer, because the PostScript and page buffer resides in the printer. Each PostScript printer contains print server software in its ROM allowing up to 32 machines to share the printer. The print server software acts as the interface between the Macintosh and the controller during the printing process. PostScript is a programming language, and as such can be upgraded and improved to provide extended features, such as shading, gradients, special effects, and other modifications to fonts and graphics.

Hewlett-Packard, Apple, QMS, DataProducts, and NEC specialize in manufacturing PostScript laser printers for many market niches. The popular HP LaserJet 4MP Printer is illustrated here.

PostScript is the industry standard because it enables text and graphics created in a computer software application to be printed at very high resolutions through a PostScript interpreter and **raster image processor (RIP)**. PostScript is essentially a coded output lan-

guage consisting of commands that instruct a device to draw lines, fill shapes, render type, and so on. The following are lines of PostScript code randomly chosen from the instructions to create an Adobe **Illustrator** pattern called Art Deco:

```
%!PS-Adobe-3.0
%%Creator: Adobe Illustrator(TM) 5.5
%%Title: (Art Deco)
%%BeginSetup
%%IncludeFont: Helvetica
/egrave/ecircumflex/edieresis/iacute/igrave
/icircumflex/idieresis/ntilde
```

Of course, this code would not produce any results when processed by a printing device. A large amount of code must be processed to provide even simple shapes, patterns, and text. Occasionally, the PostScript processors attached to laser printers and imagesetters encounter errors and cannot finish the output. A PostScript error can be caused by any number of things, and even an experienced programmer may not be able to find the cause. Difficulty in PostScript output can be mostly avoided by proper software usage and by following certain guidelines.

System 7 has enhanced the performance of PostScript Laser Printers by providing new Toolbox managers for printing and positioning text. These managers increase the fidelity of a document's page description between different types of printers.

Creating PostScript Files The process of printing to a **PostScript** printer goes something like this: The user issues a Print command, the application creates a temporary PostScript spool file, PrintMonitor sends the PostScript file to the printer, and the printer turns the PostScript code into dots of toner on paper.

Sometimes, though, there are good reasons for splitting that process into two parts—creating the PostScript file, but not sending it to the printer until a later time. For example, a lot of high-end prepress software (for **trapping**, color correction, and imposition) needs to be fed PostScript files to work on, rather than native application files. Service bureaus can output PostScript files without having the graphics placed in the documents, and there's no chance that an element will be accidentally moved or changed when the file is opened to be output. And if you know what you're doing, you can even "hack" the PostScript code to make changes in the document.

Making a PostScript file is a pretty simple task.

1. After choosing the Print command, change the destination in the Print dialog box from "Printer" to "PostScript file." This changes the Print button to a Save button.

2. Click Save.

3. The dialog box that comes up next will vary depending on the printer drive you're using. If you're using LaserWriter 7, it looks like a standard Save dialog box, as shown in the figure. Type a name for the file, choose a folder to save it in, and click on Save again.

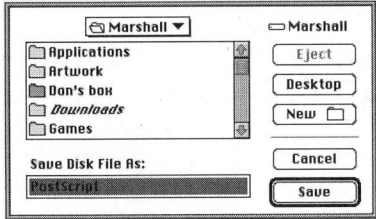

4. Under LaserWriter 8, other options will be presented at this point. You can choose to generate a plain PostScript job, or you can create an **EPS** file that can be imported into other files as a graphic. EPS files can have standard, enhanced, or no previews. If you

generate a PostScript file, you can use ASCII or binary encoding (ASCII is the default). Finally, you must choose whether you want to include font information in the PostScript file. If the fonts are included, they don't need to be present in order to print the file later. PostScript files can include no fonts, all the fonts, all fonts except the standard 13 (like Times), or all fonts except those mentioned in the printer description file.

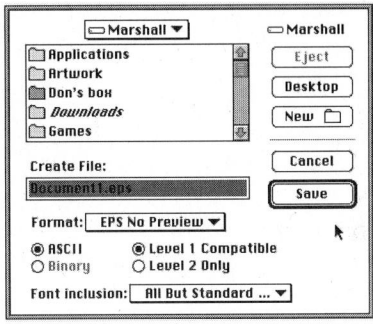

5. After assigning a name, choosing your options, and clicking on Save, you'll see the document spool to disk, just as though it were printing.

Be aware that PostScript files can be pretty large, especially if they include a lot of graphics and fonts.

See Also

Adobe Type Manager; Desktop Publishing Industry Standards; Fonts; PostScript Level 2; Preflight and File Hand-Off; Printer Drivers; Printing; Service Bureau Dos and Don'ts for Desktop Publishers

PostScript Fax, *See PostScript Level 2*

PostScript Interpreters, *See Printers, Color PostScript*

PostScript Level 2

In 1993, Adobe updated PostScript to PostScript Level 2 to add support for color printing and other new printer features, as well as to enhance existing features. PostScript Level 2 drivers (either LaserWriter

8.3 from Apple or PSPrinter 8.3.1 from Adobe) support the following features:

- **The addition of color extensions to the base language.** This gives PostScript the ability to describe and print colors as they are seen on the screen. Display PostScript (the screen-description language version of PostScript) is also included in the base language.

- **Compresses and decompresses documents.** Also, printers that support Level 2 can fax PostScript documents, cache patterns and forms between multiple printings of the same document, and generate accurate screen angles for smoother halftone printing.

- **Device-independent color support.** This feature provides a way to view documents on any monitor, print them on any printer, and have the colors appear the same from machine to machine. Apple's **ColorSync** technology in System 7.5.1 and higher manages color by providing support for the translation of RGB screen color schemes to CMYK data used by printers to define colors. Full color translation is not yet available except where applications provide the exact matches between color profiles used by the printer and the Macintosh. ColorSync and PostScript Level 2 are not 100 percent compatible in this regard, because they do not use the same device profiles to describe RGB colors. Each version of ColorSync (now at version 2.0) and the printer driver (now at version 8.3) comes closer to using the same profiles or substituting correct versions if profiles are not available.

- **Enhanced halftoning algorithm.** PostScript Level 2 describes more lines per inch and smaller angles on screen, and can thus generate a higher-resolution image. Because there is more color and halftone information available, color separations are smoother. You can also create a low-resolution version of a document for fast draft printing.

- **The inclusion of printer-specific features within printer drivers.** Each printer now provides a printer page description (PPD) document, a portable ASCII file that tells the printer driver about the printer's specific features, such as what type of paper is in which tray, or how long the printer stays awake before shutting down to save energy. Printer vendors can more easily upgrade their printers and not worry about a new driver by simply adding new features to the PPD for the driver to read. Any information located on the PPD is reflected in the Print and Page Setup windows in your applications.

- **Support for PostScript faxing.** PostScript Fax supports a base resolution for a fax of 200 dots per inch by 100 dots per inch (the CCITT Group III fax protocol) and includes the Error Correction Mechanism used by Group III faxes. If you purchase the PostScript Fax card, you can turn your PostScript printer into a fax machine.

- **Increases the speed and efficiency of printing.** PostScript Level 2 rewrote the way that memory is allocated by the printer so that all printer memory is allocated to all printer tasks and not partitioned to separate tasks in a linear fashion as was the case in Level 1 PostScript. The addition of pattern and form caching, the ability to render and download forms and patterns that are used repeatedly (such as logos) to an area of printer memory lets them be used multiple times when printing multiple versions of the same document.

- **Faster rasterizing.** Adobe incorporated a revamped **Adobe Type Manager (ATM)** rasterizer into Level 2. ATM is a set of PostScript subroutines that generates scaleable font outlines on the fly for display on the screen, speeding up font rendering for non-PostScript output devices. Level 2 also supports TrueType font rendering.

See Also

Desktop Printing; Fonts; PostScript; Printer Drivers

PostScript Print Servers, *See*
Printers, Color PostScript

PostScript Printers, *See Desktop*
Printing; Printing

Power Key

The Power key starts up (or boots) certain Macintosh computers. Although this Power key appears on most Apple keyboards, only those computers that support the soft boot feature can use the Power key to start up.

The Power key can be used with other modifier keys to restart any model of Macintosh by pressing the ⌘-Control-Power key regardless of whether it can start up with the Power key. This performs the same action as choosing Restart from the **Special menu**. In **System 7.5**, you can use the Power key to shutdown or restart by pressing the Power key while the computer is running. When you press the Power key, you get a dialog box asking, "Are you sure you want to shut down your computer now?" The dialog box offers three buttons: Shut Down (which confirms your intention to shut down), Restart (which restarts your machine as if you selected Restart from the Special menu at the Finder), and Cancel, if you press the PowerOn key accidentally or if you just changed your mind.

See Also
Cancel Keyboard Shortcut; Restart; Shut Down Command; Special Menu; Startup Sequence; System 7.5

Power Mac, *See Desktop Models,*
Macintosh Family

Power Mac, Compatibility with

The Power Macs have had a remarkably smooth introduction history, considering the amount of 680x0-based software that exists. Application software incompatibility rarely occurs with the PowerPC chips

in Power Macs. In fact, more compatibility problems occurred when the first 040 Macs were launched than with Power Macs.

The incompatibilities that do occur with Power Macs are usually older System extension files or control panels. If you do have problems with an older piece of software or hardware, call the manufacturer to see if an update or patch has been written to address the problem.

Another workaround for addressing error messages accompanying 68K software on a Power Mac is to turn off the Modern Memory mode in the Memory control panel and restart the Mac. Applications that say they are "Accelerated for PowerPC" or programs that are written specifically for the PowerPC perform better with the Modern Memory Manager selected.

When the Power Macs were first introduced, the following incompatibilities occurred, and may still occur on first-generation Power Macs (for example 6100, 7100, and 8100s).

- PDS expansion cards designed for 68K Macs will not fit or work on Power Macs.

- If your 68K program uses a floating-point processor (FPU), such as Microsoft Excel or Adobe Photoshop, they will not operate because the older System 7.5.1 emulator does not include an FPU. You can add a piece of shareware called **SoftwareFPU** or upgrade to a PowerPC version of the program that does take advantage of the PowerPC's built-in FPU.

- Audio-visual software that takes advantage of the AT&T DSP chip in the 68K AV Macs will not work, because the Power Mac handles digital signal processing without using a specialized chip.

- Some older hard drives do not support the SCSI Manager Version 4.3 used in System 7.5.1 and later Power Mac operating systems. If you are using an older Apple hard drive, use the HD SC Setup version 7.3 or later (that comes with your Power Mac) to update the hard drive.

The following programs do not work on a Power Mac:

- Claris MacDraw 1.0.

- Berkeley's After Dark Screen Savers, versions 1.0 and 2.0.

- PageMaker 4.2 will not work, upgrade to versions 5.0 or 6.0.

- Symantec's Think C before version 6.0.1.

- AppleTalk Remote Access version 1.0.

- AppleSearch 1.0.

- AppleShare 4.0.

- Apple A/UX (Apple's version of UNIX). Apple's PowerOpen based on IBM's AIX UNIX will operate on a Power Mac.

- Connectix RAM Doubler version 1.0 doesn't work because it makes direct calls to the 68030/40's Memory Management Unit. Versions 1.5 and later have fixed this problem. Use the PCI patch, version 1.6 on PCI-based Power Macs.

There is a difference between being "compatible" with PPC and being "PPC Software" in terms of performance. Almost all programs will operate with the 680x0 emulator built-in to the Power Macs, but those programs that are written in native PPC code take advantage of the special instructions and properties of the PowerPC chips and run many times faster than emulated programs. Those native PPC programs will not run on older 680x0-based Macs.

Certain applications provide two versions of their code on the installation disks—one for 68K Macs and one for PPC Macs—along with an installer program that recognizes what type of Mac you are using. These applications install a Fat Binary version of their programs that will run faster on a Power Mac or will run on a 68K Mac. Other applications sell separate versions of their applications. Look for the "Accelerated for Power Macintosh" red label for optimized versions of the programs.

See Also

Desktop Models, Macintosh Family; Emulator; Processors, PowerPC

Power Mac Card

Macintosh computers with a 68040 processor direct slot (such as Quadras) can be upgraded to a PowerPC processor through a PowerPC upgrade card. The upgrade card comes with a Power Macintosh Card Control Panel that enables the user to choose which processor to use, the 68040 or the PowerPC processor, by toggling on or off the upgrade card. If you turn the card on or off, the switch of processors won't take effect until the Mac is restarted.

Power Mac Logic Boards

There are two different logic boards, also called motherboards, used on Power Macs: a NuBus Power Macintosh Logic Board and a PCI Power Macintosh Logic Board. All 6100, 7100, 7200, 8100 non-AV, and PowerPC Performa models use the NuBus motherboard. In fact, all Macs that use either the 601 or 603e chips use NuBus motherboards. All newer PCI-based Power Macs that run on the 604 chip, namely the 8500 and 9500 models, use the PCI-based motherboard.

NuBus is a standard that was developed at MIT and refined in 1985 by a committee composed of representatives from MIT, AT&T, Texas Instruments, Apple, and other companies. The NuBus standard specifies how expansion boards access the internal bus to the physical qualities of the NuBus slots. Motherboards for NuBus-based Power Macs contain the same chips as PCI-based motherboards, only the expansion bus structure is radically different. The expansion bus is a path that an add-on expansion card's data travels from the card to the computer and back. The fastest expansion cards use local bus designs because the cards have direct access to the CPU. PDS and PCI bus designs use this method. NuBus requires a controller to grant permission before its data gains access to the CPU.

Power Mac Logic Boards, NuBus-Based MotherBoard Components The basic mother or logic board consists of several functional parts: Read-Only Memory (ROM), Memory Arrays, Internal Cache, Processor Direct Slots (PDS) for expansion, NuBus controller and card slots, Squidlet, High-Speed Memory Controller (HMC), Input/Output Controller (Apple Memory-Mapped I/O Controller or AMIC), Internal Floppy Disk Connector (SWIM III),

Fast SCSI Driver and internal SCSI bus, Cuda, Ariel
II, and AWAC (the last three components being the
controllers of the multimedia and AV portions of the
Power Mac). The following graphic illustrates the layout of a NuBus-based logic board.

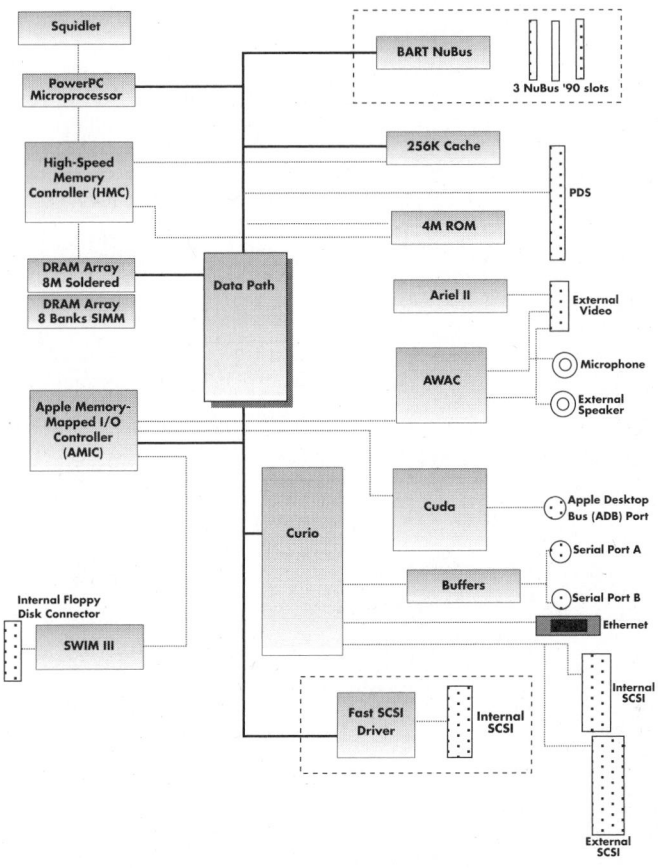

The NuBus logic board contains the following components.

■ **Read Only Memory (ROM).** A 4MB Read-
Only Memory chip contains hard-wired
instructions that perform such functions as
startup tests and partitioning memory for the
use of the system. ROM contains those
portions of the operating system that are
basic to the Mac, such as reading, writing,
understanding peripheral locations, and so
forth. The rest of the operating system is
software and consists of such components as
resource files, control panels, extensions, and
the Finder. ROM-based firmware is sometimes called the Macintosh toolbox.

■ **Random Access Memory (RAM).** Dynamic
Random Access Memory (DRAM) is special
volatile memory that is refreshed frequently.
NuBus-based Power Macs ship with 8MB of
RAM soldered on to the logic board. Other
slots are available to upgrade the amount
of RAM. RAM is installed into NuBus
Macs via 72-pin single in-line memory
modules (SIMMs). These SIMMs must
have an access time of at least 80
nanoseconds (ns). All Power Macs do not
have the same number of expansion slots
for RAM upgrades. SIMMs are installed
in pairs. You need to ensure that the
SIMMs are called "non-composite, fast-
paged RAM" so that they will fit in the
Power Mac's slots.

■ **Level-2 Cache.** You can add another
256K of volatile memory to store
frequently used instructions or data by
inserting a 160-pin SIMM cache card
in the Level-2 cache slot. The Power
Mac 8100 came with a 256K Level-2
cache card already installed. The 6100
and 7100 made installing this cache
optional.

■ **Processor Direct Slots (PDS).** The
PDS card you place in the PDS slot
has direct access to the CPU's control,
address, and data buses. This fast,
local-bus design makes PDS an
efficient method for adding accelerator
or video upgrade cards, because it is
faster than NuBus. There is only one PDS
expansion card option available on any Mac
and the PDS has no design standards, because
the card has direct access to many different
microprocessors, each PDS card is designed
for a separate PowerPC microprocessor. All
Power Macs use the PDS to insert AV
capabilities (the Digital Signal Processor) into
the 6100, 7100, and 8100 AV Macs. Other
7100 and 8100s that are not AV-capable, use
the PDS to upgrade the video RAM (VRAM).
Macs use up to 640K of system RAM to store
video frames, limiting 14 and 15 inch
monitors to the display of 32,768 colors and

16 and 17 inch displays to 256 colors. Larger monitors are not supported. By adding a VRAM expansion card containing 1, 2, or 4MB of VRAM, you can gain access to up to 16.7 million colors on a 20 or 21 inch monitor.

- **NuBus Slots.** The 7100 and 8100 Power Macs contain three NuBus slots for system expansion. NuBus cards do not directly access the CPU, but instead use a special NuBus bus that connects to a Versatile Interface Adapter (VIA) chip. Because NuBus cards can add many different capabilities to the Mac, it needs a controller to play traffic cop and limit access to the CPU to requested instructions. The NuBus cards are controlled by a bus master called the BART Controller. The Bus Master works with the High-Speed Memory Controller to regulate access to the CPU and avoid bottlenecks and other priority problems. NuBus cards are self-configuring. Information stored on ROM on the card is read by the System 7.5 Slot Manager to identify itself and to manage its data flow. NuBus cards contain 96 pins in three rows of 32 pins. All Macintosh II NuBus cards fit the Power Mac NuBus slots. The self-configuring nature of the card means that you do not have to set dip switches or add jumper cables to ensure that the expansion card operates correctly.

- **Squidlet.** The Squidlet is a chip that synchronizes the operations of the six clocks used in the Power Mac to control the CPU and subsystems on the logic board. There are two other clocks on every Power Mac: a system clock that controls the rate of execution of instructions within the CPU (this is the clock that sets the speed of the computer) and a CPU bus clock that controls the rate of data transfer across the system bus. The Squidlet chip controls the operations of six other clocks: Cuda that provides timing for the real-time clock; a pixel clock that controls the rate of redraws on 16 inch monitors; an Ethernet and SCSI clock; an I/O clock that controls the timing of data transfers across input and output components, serial

communications, and the 12 inch monitor of all-in-one Macs; a Sound clock that controls sound sampling; and a VGA clock that provides controls for VGA monitors.

- **High-Speed Memory Controller (HMC).** The HMC chip controls all memory operations that are not directly handled by the PowerPC 601 or 603e **memory-management unit (MMU).** For example, the HMC arbitrates requests for control of the CPU bus between NuBus expansion cards. The HMC also manages transfers between RAM and the CPU, L-2 cache and the CPU, and ROM and the CPU; as well as providing support for the built-in memory input/output features of the 601 chip.

- **Apple Memory-Mapped I/O Controller (AMIC).** Power Macs support high-level direct memory access (DMA) services for most peripheral devices that lets these I/O devices transfer data to and from memory without requiring access to the computer. The AMIC chip works in conjunction with the HMC chip to manage this data transfer. The peripheral device must be DMA-compliant (and most modern SCSI, Ethernet, floppy disk drives, monitors, and serial devices are compliant) for the direct memory transfer to operate.

- **SWIM III.** This is the controller that operates the floppy disk drive. The SWIM III controller supports DMA and can read the format used by DOS disks automatically if PC Exchange software is running in the System Folder.

- **Curio.** This chip controls the operations of input/output between Ethernet, serial, and SCSI ports and the Mac. Each port has its own controller that works with the Curio I/O chip to transfer data between the port and the AMIC chip. Ethernet communications are handled by the Media Access Controller for Ethernet (MACE) chip on either an Ethernet network interface card or via built-in

Ethernet hardware support. Most Power Macs provide built-in support for two types of Ethernet (coaxial and 10Base-T) ports, along with a LocalTalk port. The Serial Communications Controller (SCC) on the Curio chip manages I/O for the two GeoPort serial ports of every Power Mac. Both ports support fax/modem or printing (LocalTalk) connections. The Curio chip also controls the **small computer system interface (SCSI)** device access to the computer for both internal and external SCSI devices. All floppy, CD-ROM, and hard disk drives are SCSI drives.

- **Cuda.** This chip manages the 4-pin **Apple Desktop Bus (ADB)** serial port, as well as manages other functions such as powering the Mac on and off and managing reset commands.

- **AWAC.** The Audio Waveform Amplifier and Convert (AWAC) chip manages the stereo sound input and output on all Power Macs. Power Macs support 16-bit sound sampling. This gives the Power Mac the sound fidelity of a good CD-player.

- **Ariel II.** This chip provides the built-in video capabilities for the high-density, 45-pin AudioVision monitor port on all Power Macs. This port supports Apple's AudioVision 14-inch monitor that integrates video input and sound input and output via built-in stereo speakers and a built-in Apple PlainTalk microphone for sound output.

See Also

Desktop Models, Macintosh Family; Power Mac, PCI Bus; Processors, Power PC;

Power Mac Logic Boards, ROM System Enablers

Every Macintosh, since its advent in 1984, has placed a portion of its operating system into Read-Only Memory (ROM). These hard-wired instructions are common to all Power Macs. Prior to System 7, every time that Apple introduced a new Macintosh model, it had to redesign its ROM chips to support that unique hardware configuration. System 7 liberated the Mac hardware slightly from its ROM by incorporating a machine-specific startup code, called an Enabler. Machines released prior to System 7 are powered by a single enabler, and those that were introduced after System 7 (a plethora), each have their own enabler file stored in the System Folder that provides hardware information about that specific model to the Start Manager. The following table tells you what enabler to use with what Mac.

System Enablers for Macintosh Computers

Macintosh	System Enabler Used	Current Version	Note
IIvi, IIvx	001	1.0.1	Improved support for high speed serial communications and improved accuracy of the system clock. Also addressed a rare problem where floppies may not be ejected properly at shutdown.

continues

System Enablers for Macintosh Computers (continued)

Macintosh	System Enabler Used	Current Version	Note
LC III	003	1.0	
Centris 610, 650, Quadra 610, 650, 800	040	1.1	Added support for Quadra 610 and Quadra 650.
LC 475, LC 575, Quadra 605	065	1.0	
Centris 660AV, Quadra 660AV and 840AV	088	1.1	Added support for Quadra 660AV.
PowerBook 160, 165c, 180, 180c	131	1.0.3	System Enabler 131 replaces System Enabler 111 and System Enabler 121. Corrected a problem involving the serial driver. If a user has the serial driver open, but is not transmitting, and then puts the PowerBook to sleep, any attempt to transmit upon waking, would cause the system to hang. Added support for the PowerBook 165.
Performa 450, 460, 466/7	308	1.0	No enabler is required under System 7.5.
Performa 550, 560	332	1.1	No enabler is required under System 7.5.
Performa 475, 476, 575, 577/8	364	1.1	No enabler is required under System 7.5.
Color Classic	401	1.0.5	Fixed a problem involving erratic mouse movement with Apple II mouse-based applications running on the Apple IIe card installed in the PDS slot.
LC 520, LC 550	403	1.0.1	
Macintosh TV	404	1.0	
Performa 630, 635CD, Quadra 630, LC 630	405	1.0	No enabler is required under System 7.5.
Performa 5200CD, Power Mac 5200/75 LC, Performa 6205CD	406	1.0	No enabler is required under System 7.5.
Power Mac 9500/120/132, 7200/75/90	701	1.1	
Power Mac 7500/100, 8500/120	701	1.2	

Macintosh	System Enabler Used	Current Version	Note
PowerBook 150	PB 150 Enabler	1.1	No enabler is required under System 7.5.
PowerBook 520, 520c, 540, 540c	PB 500 Series Enabler	1.0.2	No enabler is required under System 7.5.
PowerBook 190, 5300	PB 5300/2300/190 enabler	1.2.1	
PowerBook Duo 210, 230, 250, 270C	PowerBook Duo Enabler	1.0	
Power Mac 6100/60, 7100/66, 8100/80	PPC Enabler	1.0.2	No enabler is required under System 7.5.
Power Mac 6100/66, 7100/80, 8100/110/110,	PPC Enabler	1.1.1	Requires System 7.5 and Finder 7.1.5.

See Also

Power Mac Logic Boards; System 7.5

Power Mac, PCI Bus

The second generation of Power Macs arrive with a new expansion bus design called Peripheral Component Interconnect (PCI). The PCI standard provides a faster, wider bus architecture than NuBus, but also brings with it Intel standards that could be incompatible with Macintosh systems. The following graphic illustrates the PCI bus design. Notice that the bus is more flexible than the NuBus bus design illustrated in the section on Power Mac Logic Boards.

Like the NuBus architecture, the PCI bus architecture uses an auto-configuration model, so that dip switches and jumper cables are not required. The bus architecture depends on a cache-based bridge chip that manages the transfer of data from multiple PCI devices. The PCI card has direct access to the CPU, like the PDS card, but the bridge chip caches the card's data if the CPU is busy. In some ways, the PCI bus is a cross between NuBus and PDS, only more expandable.

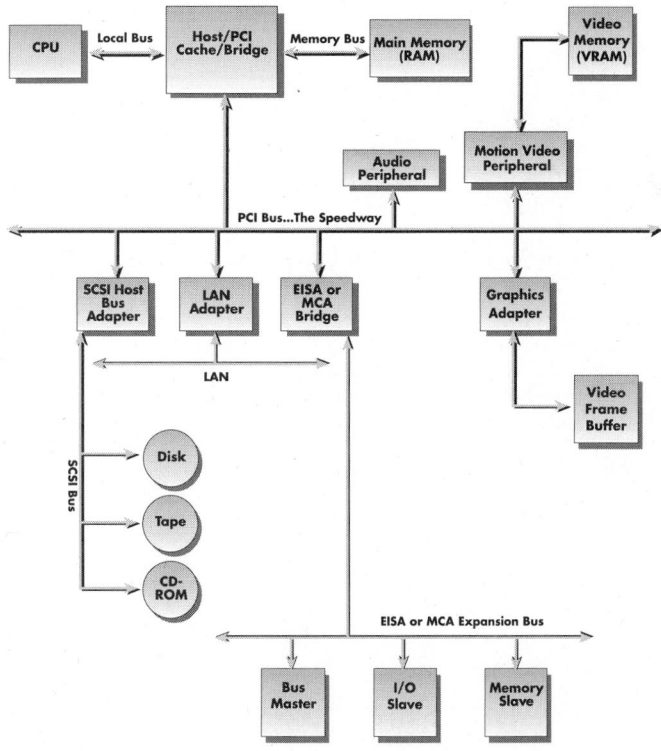

Unlike the NuBus's use of arbitration cycles via the VIA chip and BART controller, PCI directly accesses the CPU, setting up one data transfer while the previous is still running. PCI is rapidly becoming the standard bus architecture in personal computers. This provides inter-compatibility between DOS-based PCs and Macs, because the same PCI card can be used in either machine, as long as the PCI card comes with a Macintosh software driver.

See Also
NuBus Slots; Power Mac Logic Boards

Power Macs, PCI Models
In the Summer of 1995, Apple introduced the second generation of Power Macintoshes. These Power Macs incorporate the PCI expansion slots, as well as other innovations that increased the flexibility and performance of the computers. There are currently four PCI-based Macintoshes: the 9500, 8500, 7500, and 7200; each with varying PowerPC performance rates and other configuration differences. Each PCI-based Mac has the following features in common.

- The use of the Peripheral Component Interconnect (PCI) architecture in these Macs provides significant performance over the slower, but more downwardly compatible NuBus architecture of the first generation of Power Macs (the discontinued 6100, 7100, and 8100 models). Because PCI is a stable standard architecture used by many vendors for PC expansion cards, there will be more willingness to manufacture expansion cards meeting the same standards for Macs, thus increasing the availability and lowering the price of the cards.

- A shift from **SIMMs** to **DIMMs (dual in-line memory modules)** for memory expansion cards. SIMMs contain 72 pins and transfer data in 32-bit chunks. Because the Power Mac had a 64-bit memory architecture, you needed to install SIMMs in pairs. DIMMs contain 168 pins to support 64-bit data transfers, so they provide a more flexible and efficient memory expansion design.

- The PCI-based Power Macs included two Ethernet ports, retaining the AAUI port, but adding a port for 10Base-T Ethernet that does not require an adapter.

- The SCSI bus of the 9500 and 8500 Power Macs is faster than that used in the first generation Power Macs. In addition, true direct-memory access (DMA) schemes are used to bypass the CPU when transferring data over SCSI and PCI buses, as well as through the serial and Ethernet ports.

- The ROM included in the second generation Power Macs includes a new 680x0 emulator that uses dynamic recompilation emulation (DME) rather than linear recompilation, to speed up the performance of 680x0 programs running on the Power Mac.

- System 7.5.2 that was included on these PCI-based Macs contained more PowerPC-native code than earlier versions, and so performed better with the new hardware.

- Apple has defined a structure for graphics acceleration. The new standard provides a basis for third-party developers to design accelerators without having to reinvent acceleration schemes for each new card. Prices for video cards should reflect the lower research and development costs.

- The PCI-based Macs, as well as the Performas based on the PowerPC 603e chip, include power-saving features similar to those found on PowerBooks.

- The PCI-based Power Macs also were redesigned to provide easier upgrade paths to the next level of processor. These Macs place the CPU on a four by seven-inch card that can be unplugged and replaced by a faster one (for example, the next iteration of 604e chips can be placed in the 7500, 8500, or 9500 chassis by slipping out the old daughterboard and installing a new one containing the faster chip). Each processor upgrade slot is identical, allowing a 7500 to be upgraded to an 8500 by replacing its daughterboard with that of the 8500, and so forth. Multiprocessing is available by adding a second CPU on to the daughterboard. When a faster chip is added, the internal buses run faster as well, boosting video and memory-accessing performance, as well as SCSI performance. This is because the buses are only operating at a third of the speed of the processor. Each time you up the processor speed, the buses can go faster (up to their limit of 50MHz).

The following table provides an overview of the various configurations available for PCI-based Power Macs.

The following graphics show several of the PCI Power Macs, the 8500/120; the 7500/100; and the 7200/90.

See Also
Desktop Models, Macintosh Family; Power Macs, PCI Bus

The PCI-Based Power Mac Family

Model/ Clock Rate	CPU	RAM (Max RAM) / DIMM Slots	Hard Drive	PCI Slots	L-2 Cache	VRAM (Max VRAM)
7200/75	601	8MB (256MB)/4	500MB	3	none	1MB (4MB)
7200/90	601	8MB (256MB)/4	500MB	3	none	1MB (4MB)
7500/100	601	16MB (512MB)/8	500MB	3	none	2MB (4MB)
8500/120	604	16MB (1.5G)/8	1G	3	256K	2MB (4MB)
9500/120	604	16MB (1.5G)/12	1G	6	512K	2MB (4MB)
9500/32	604	16MB (1.5G)/12	2G	6	512K	none (none) requires a separate video card

Power Mac, Upgrading from 680x0, *See Upgrade Paths, Types of*

Power Pete

Billed as a children's game, Power Pete, from StarPlay, is an action figure come to (animated) life in a little toy shop of horrors. Killer clowns, crazed robots, maddened monkeys, and an army of evil toys are out to destroy the innocent fuzzy bunnies. Armed only with an arsenal of toothpaste guns, foam ball shooters, exploding birthday cakes, and other toy shop weapons, you—as fearless Power Pete—must rescue the bunnies, through 15 levels of mayhem. Fast scrolling action and digitized speech, along with a full musical soundtrack, add to the fun. It may be a bit much for younger kids.

See Also

Adventure Games

Power Translator

Teachers of foreign languages will be upset, if not unemployed, when the word gets out about this program. In less than a minute, Globalink's Power Translator can do a better translation than a high school student after three years of studying German, French, or Spanish. Power Translator can translate over 20,000 words per hour, at up to 90 percent accuracy. It has a vocabulary of about 250,000 words and phrases in its online dictionary, and can be customized to speak your occupational jargon, favorite slang, or pet phrases. It can work with virtually any **word processor** that can save a file as text and with all popular **OCR scanning programs** and Macintosh-compatible **scanners**. And it translates in both directions—English to Spanish, French, or German and Spanish, French, or German into English. (You do need a separate program for each foreign language you intend to translate.)

Using Power Translator is simple. After you start the program, open any text file. It will appear in an editable window. Flag proper names and any words you don't want the program to try and translate. Select the text and choose translate from the menu, or use the command key shortcut. A progress bar appears in a dialog box. Depending on how much text you're working with, in a few seconds to a minute or two, your translation will be complete. It will show up in a second window alongside the original. At this point, you can touch up any awkward or incorrect phrases. Because word order in English is often different from word order in another language, some phrases get turned inside out, but these are easily untangled. You can make any corrections you deem necessary before saving the translated file. Words the program doesn't recognize will be marked with @@ signs. If the program can't produce the correct form of a verb, it will provide the infinitive marked @+. The figure shows a sample translation in Spanish.

The manual is bilingual, which enables French, German, or Spanish speakers to translate their words into English. Menus can also be translated into the language you've installed.

Inexplicably, the program *will* read back the text it has translated, but only in English. It will not attempt to pronounce the French, German, or Spanish equivalent. You may choose to ignore this "feature" by doing a custom installation of the program rather than a full installation. In doing so, you can avoid cluttering your System Folder with Macintalk Pro and all the voices that come with it.

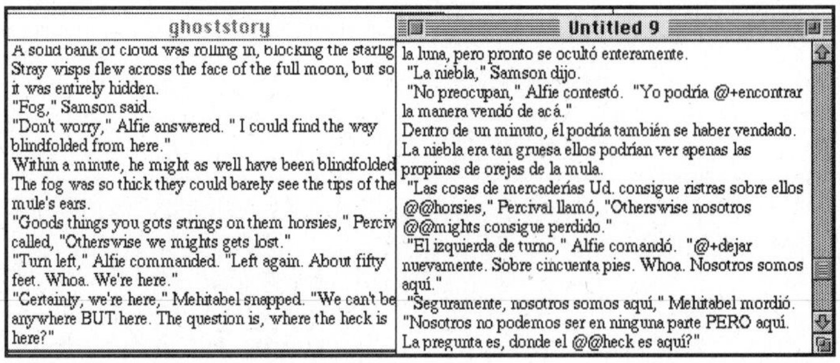

PowerBook

Macintosh PowerBook is the name Apple gives to its line of laptop computers. Designed for portability, the various models of PowerBooks have all weighed under eight pounds including battery, built-in display, and built-in keyboard. PowerBooks contain all of the basic components of desktop Macs: processor, **RAM**, **hard disk**, ROM, and ports, and they can run either on batteries or on AC power. PowerBooks are fully-functional Macintoshes, and can run the same software as desktop models. The following figure shows the PowerBook Duo 230.

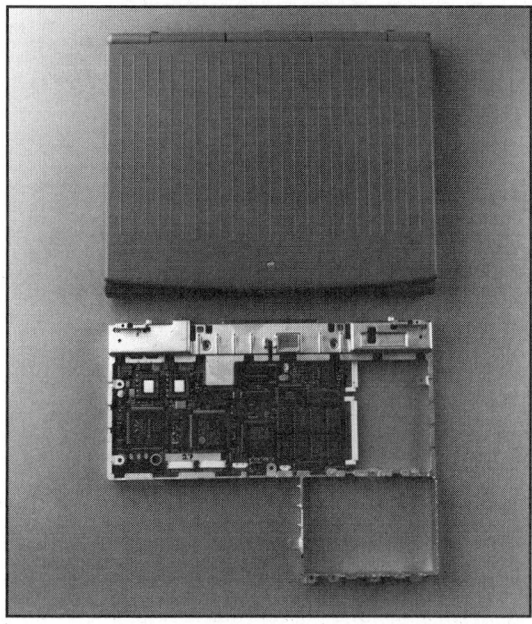

PowerBooks are typically not top-of-the line Macintoshes, mostly because they need to run on a low-power version of a Mac microprocessor that is not as fast as the full-power versions used in desktops. Any new PowerBook model is as powerful as the contemporary mid-to-lower-end desktop Macs designed for home and school. In addition, faster new processors usually show up in desktop Macs several years before the low-power versions become available for PowerBooks. Power limitations also mean that PowerBooks don't hold as much RAM as desktop models.

When the PowerBook was first introduced in 1991, it was an innovative and influential development in the PC laptop market. Features that PowerBooks pioneered have now became standard on most PC laptop models. These features include a keyboard that has an area for wrist placement and an integrated pointing device. The first PowerBooks included trackballs, although most current models have a trackpad.

Conversation with Perry Fox

As Manager of PowerBook Quality and Reliability, Perry Fox has put his computers through more torture tests than most of us can imagine. Much of what he does would violate the warranty, so he cautions the rest of us to leave these stunts to professionals.

Maclopedia: How did you get involved with Apple?

Perry: Back in 1984-85 when the Mac first came out, my wife was working at Apple, and she had an employee discount program, and I started using it for work I was doing for another company. People deemed it a toy, and I thought, "If this is a toy, it is a pretty cool toy." I'm able to do presentations, word processing, put some spreadsheets together. It was making my life a lot easier. Then my wife met someone in the service organization at Apple, and they were looking for a product manager. And I thought, "There is one company I would go to because of the really cool things they were doing." And there was a match. I started ten years ago working in the service area, for five years, and then made the transition to research and development (R&D). PowerBooks are under R&D, along with desktop and imaging.

Maclopedia: When do you get involved testing the PowerBooks?

Perry: We work early on with the products when they are coming up to speed, taking a shape that begins to look like a user's type of model, where there is actually some functionality built in, and it's fairly stable. We look at design margin testing, where we take the product and accelerate the lifecycle by increasing the temperature in a small chamber, and inducing vibration as well, to find out where in the product does it break? Where is the weakest link? This is real true reliability testing.

Then, when we get to the point where the design is stable, we look at oddball testing. These things are not warranted. They fall under the category of abuse. But we want to find out what will happen if we do violate the warranty. For instance, a lot of people use PowerBooks on an airplane; they are eating peanuts and having a Coke, and you have to play out that scenario. We oil up our fingers to find out what happens

continues

P

to the trackpad. We'll pour a Coke over the keyboard and see what happens; can we just wash it off, or dry it off, and have it still function? Turns out, yes, it does. But not in all cases. Don't try this at home. Then we take mayonnaise and hand lotion and rub it over the trackball and trackpad, and find out how they respond.

Whenever we come out with a new box, we do something we started early on as a benchmark. We'll get a car and drive over it. We've evolved the PowerBook line, and throughout those iterations, we have driven over a PowerBook 140, and PowerBook 180, and then the Duo line. We haven't done the 5300 yet. Or we rely on our customers to do this test, and send us anecdotes. "I was driving fifty miles an hour and I forgot that my PowerBook was on top of the car." Or one woman was in the big earthquake in Northridge, California and her apartment was completely destroyed. She was madly looking for her PowerBook because it had so much important data on it, and the cops were urging her to get out, and she found it crushed under a bunch of stuff, and it started functioning. She used the backlight as a flashlight to pick out some other things before they herded her out.

We had a letter come in recently. This person was dropping off her fiancé in Massachusetts. He's a grad student at Harvard, has written eight books, and all of them are on the PowerBook. "So I proceeded to back up onto Massachusetts Avenue, and I ran over something on the road that went bump bump. It was George's PowerBook." Amazingly, it booted up. There was no damage, except for tire tracks on the screen. We've had PowerBooks submerged in water, dried out with hairdryers, work fine. In one Jacques Cousteau project, it fell overboard. Somebody dove over and got it out. They dried it out and it continued to work.

Up in space, they use PowerBooks on the shuttle to tell where they are. Looking down you wonder, where am I in relation to that? So somebody developed a program that runs on a PowerBook and tracks their shuttle and where they are in relation to the earth. Now we don't *position* the PowerBook this way. It violates the warranty. We test them, typically, at an altitude spec of about 8,000 feet, which is what you would see inside a pressurized airplane at 35,000 feet, but we have had people take PowerBooks up to the top of Mount Everest, at 22,000 feet. That definitely violates the spec.

Maclopedia: Do you go out and see how customers are treating their PowerBooks?

Perry: Yes, we try to spend time with our customers. What we did one time was send an engineer off with one of our customers, for a day in the life of sales force automation, a fly on the wall. We watched how this person took the PowerBook, threw it in a bag, threw the bag in a van, and went off to their next account. So the engineer could report, "Here is how they are really using it." And that affects how we test, to make sure we are testing it the way people use it.

Maclopedia: But you don't have time to test it for years, right?

Perry: No, so we accelerate the product life. If its life cycle is 5-8 years, we have to test it in six weeks. So we put it in a walk-in oven at elevated temperatures and find out what temperatures it can withstand. Humidity and vibration. The machines are stacked up, and shaken. In the past, the standard was you put it on the shelf and let it run. But you can't assume a customer will put a PowerBook on a shelf, unless you give them SuperGlue and glue it to the desk. (Then that usage pattern would be valid!) It could go up to 140 degrees, it could go down to zero degrees, and people still expect certain things—that even if I am in Minnesota in the middle of winter, and I have the PowerBook in the trunk of my car, I can pull it out, go into a conference room at seventy degrees, and it better work!

We have had people take PowerBooks up to the top of Mount Everest, at 22,000 feet. That definitely violates the spec.

We found out that the extendible feet were breaking off. For the latest PowerBook, we spent a lot of time designing feet that don't break, and, if they do break, it is a 25 cent part. You just pop it off, and pop it back in. So there was extensive testing of feet. "Let's make it robust, and let's make a backup plan, just in case someone does damage it."

Maclopedia: Do you have to invent your own torture test equipment?

Perry: Yes, we come up with fixtures to test out products. With the 5300 we came out with the PCMCIA slot, and the thinking there was that we don't know if people are going to do this but they can plug in the cards multiple times, so we came up with a fixture that pushes the card in, runs some software, accesses the card, ejects the card, and then pushes it back in, to make sure we can do this thousands of times.

Our biggest challenges are with the new technologies coming out and the new computing paradigms. You look at the notebook market. The first breakthrough was we can take a desktop and shrink it down, and make it portable. Then the PowerBook 140 and 170 came out, running on batteries, so you can use them on an airplane, and everywhere you want, so that was a new way for users to use the product, and we had to meet their expectations. There's probably going to be another paradigm to address from the reliability perspective. We are involved during the development of the products, when the new paradigm is evolving, so we hear all the early scoping, product marketing, and design engineering, and we are looking at our piece of the pie asking ourselves, "How are we going to test it? How are they going to use this thing?" So we have to really understand how customers are going to use the machine, and what their expectations will be, and design new test methodologies to stay ahead of the customer.

Another innovation was the **PowerBook Duo**, a smaller, lighter version of the PowerBook meant to function as both a portable and a desktop computer. As a portable Mac, the Duos weigh several pounds less than standard PowerBooks. The reason for this weight difference lies in the fact that they don't include a floppy drive or many of the ports found in standard PowerBooks. As a desktop Mac, PowerBook Duos can plug into one of several types of **Duo docks**, which include ports such as video and EtherNet. A full-sized Duo Dock from Apple contains all the ports of a desktop Mac, as well a floppy disk drive and NuBus slots that can accept expansion cards.

Most standard PowerBook models contain many of the same ports as desktop Macs. You can connect Mac keyboards and mouses to a PowerBook's **Apple Desktop Bus (ADB)** port and external hard disk, or CD-ROM drives to the **SCSI** port. You can plug a PowerBook into a **LocalTalk** network or printer, and some models contain an **EtherNet** port as well. All except the earliest PowerBook models can connect to external monitor displays. All of the ports are the same as desktop Macs, except for the SCSI port and monitor ports, which are square on the PowerBook.

In addition to the ports, more recent PowerBook models have expansion slots made for laptop computers. While earlier PowerBooks contained internal expansion slots, more recent models use externally accessible **PC card slots**, which accept credit card-sized modems, networking cards, and other expansion cards.

PowerBook Series The model numbers of PowerBooks may seem mysterious at first, but Apple has always followed a standard naming convention that identifies the type of PowerBook. This naming convention is similar to that used for desktop Macs. PowerBook models with three digits (such as the 520) have 680x0 processors. PowerBooks with four digits (such as the 5300) have PowerPC processors. PowerBook Duos begin with a "2" (as in 2xx and 2xxx). The designation "c" (as in 2300c) means that the model has a color display screen.

The lowest-powered model was the PowerBook 100. Increasingly higher model numbers are indicative of the relative power and feature set of the unit, not necessarily the chronological order of the introduction of the models. For example, the PowerBook 150 came out several years after the PowerBook 170.

So far, Apple has produced five lines of PowerBook models: the **PowerBook 100 series**, the **PowerBook Duo 200 series**, the **PowerBook 500 series**, the **PowerBook Duo 2000 series**, and the **PowerBook 5000 series** (see Table below). Models in the 100 series, the 2300 series, and the 5000 series are currently in production. The original three PowerBooks introduced in 1991 were the 100, 140, and 170. The 200 series introduced the PowerBook Duos. The 500 series were the first PowerBooks with 68040 processors, and the 2000 and 5000 series were the first PowerPC processors. PowerBooks use batteries that are made of the nickel cadmium (NiCad) type or one of several types of Nickel metal hydride (NiMH).

P

The PowerBook Families

Series	Processor	Weight	Battery	Max RAM	Pointing
100	68030*	5.5-7 lbs	NiCad**	8, 14, or 40MB	trackball***
Duo 200	68030/040	4-5 lbs	NiMH	24 or 40MB	trackball
500	68LC040	6.5-7.5 lbs	NiMH	36MB	trackpad
Duo 2000	PPC 603e	4.8 lbs	NiMH	64MB	trackpad
5000	PPC 603e	5.5-6.2 lbs	NiMH	56MB	trackpad

*except the PowerBook 100, which had a 68HC000, and the 190, which has a 68LC040

**except the 100, which had a lead-acid, and the 190, which has a NiMH

***except the 190, which has a trackpad

The future direction of PowerBooks depends both on the technology of desktop computers and laptop computers. Like desktop Macs, the speed of PowerBooks will continue to increase as processors and RAM get faster, providing more power for each dollar.

On the laptop front, display technology will continue to provide better displays and decreasing costs. While the first PowerBooks had black-and-white screens, today's models have either grayscale or color screens. In addition, battery life improves as battery weight shrinks. The next battery type will probably be lithium ion, which will add several hours of battery life. However, the biggest change in the short term may be the introduction of Mac-compatible laptop clones produced by companies other than Apple. The additional competition should produce innovation and drive costs down.

See Also

PowerBook 100 Series; PowerBook 500 Series; PowerBook 5000 Series; PowerBook Duo 200 Series; PowerBook Duo 2000 Series; PowerBook Batteries; PowerBook Display; PowerBook Disk Drive; PowerBook Hard Drives; PowerBook Internal Modems; PowerBook RAM; PowerBook Trackballs and Trackpads; Small Computer System Interface

PowerBook 100 Series

As Apple's longest running line of PowerBooks, the PowerBook 100 series is Apple's most diverse line. The first PowerBooks belonged in the 100 series, and Apple continued to add new technology in additional 100 series current models. Today, the 100 series represents the low end of the PowerBook choices available.

Most of the 100s share a similar set of basic specifications (see table that follows). Most models use 68030 processors and nickel cadmium (NiCad) batteries. Some models also have a 68882 floating point math coprocessor. All models come with either 2 or 4MB of RAM on the logic board, with a single RAM slot to add a RAM expansion card. The type of RAM expansion card varies between models. Most PowerBook 100 models have a standard set of Mac ports, as well as a floppy drive. The displays vary widely in type, size, number of colors, and resolution.

All 100s have the standard Mac ports, including LocalTalk (printer) SCSI and Apple Desktop Bus (for keyboards and mice). The PowerBooks 160, 165, 165c, 180, 180c, 190, and 190cs have an external video outport to which you can connect an external display monitor. (The video outport is optional on the 190 and 190cs.) (See figure.)

The two oddballs of the 100 series are the PowerBook 100 itself, the least powerful model, and the PowerBook 190, the most recent and the most powerful in the series. The PowerBook 100 was one of the first three PowerBooks, along with the 140 and 170. It is unique, however, in that it is the only PowerBook with a 68HC000 processor, the low-power version of the 68000. The 100 was also the only PowerBook that could run versions of Mac OS earlier than System 7.x. It was the only PowerBook with a lead-acid battery, and was the only non-Duo PowerBook not to have a built-in disk drive. Instead, it had a special port connector that allowed you to plug in an external disk drive. At 5.1 pounds, the PowerBook 100 was the lightest non-Duo model made.

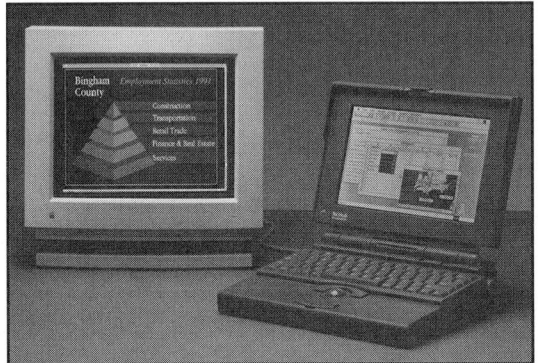

The recent PowerBook 190 and 190cs also have different processors and batteries than the rest of the line. They are the only PowerBooks of the 100 series run by a 68LC040, the low-power version of the 68040 processor. The 190s are also the only PowerBook 100s that are upgradable to a PowerPC 603e processor. (Even the higher-end 500 series PowerBooks are not upgradable to PowerPC processor.) The 190 models are the first in the series to use nickel metal hydride batteries, which hold a charge longer than NiCad batteries. They were also the first of the series to use a **trackpad** cursor control device.

The 190s include some of the features of the PowerBook 5000 series. They include two PC Card slots (also known as PCMCIA slots) for use with the credit card-sized PC Card expansion cards. The slots can accommodate two Type I or Type II cards, or a single Type III card. A 16-bit, CD-quality sound output port is another feature of the two 190 models. The 190cs is the only series 100 model to use a dual-scan display, a type of screen that produces images of better quality than does passive matrix, but not as good as those produced on active matrix displays.

Specifications, PowerBook 100 Series

Model	CPU Speed	Display Type	Colors/Resolution	RAM: Min/Max
100	16MHz	9" passive matrix	black & white@640×400	2/8MB
140	16MHz	10" passive matrix	black & white@640×400	2/8MB
145	25MHz	10" passive matrix	black & white@640×400	2/8MB
145B	25MHz	10" passive matrix	black & white@640×400	4/8MB
150	33MHz	9.5" passive matrix	4 grays@640×480	4/40MB
160	33MHz	10" passive matrix	16 grays@640×400	4/14MB
165	33MHz	10" passive matrix	16 grays@640×400	4/14MB
165c*	33MHz*	9" passive matrix	256 colors@640×400	4/14MB
170*	25MHz	10" active matrix	black & white@640×400	2/8MB
180*	33MHz	10" active matrix	16 grays@640×400	4/14MB
180c*	33MHz	8.5" active matrix	256 colors@640×480	4/14MB
190	66MHz	9.5" passive matrix	16 grays@640×480	4/40MB
190cs	66MHz	10.4" dual scan	256 colors@640×480	4/40MB

*Also include 68882 floating point math coprocessor

P

Another recent model, the 150, also has some unique features. The 150 plays the role that the 100 did in the early days, in that it is the lowest cost and lightest PowerBook (5.5 pounds) now available. Like the earlier PowerBooks, it uses a trackball for its cursor control device and a NiCad type battery.

See Also
PowerBooks

PowerBook 500 Series

The PowerBook 500 series (see figure) offers bigger screens, faster processors, and lighter-weight plastic than the previous 100 and 200 series models (see table). The 500 series PowerBooks increase battery life over previous models with the ability to hold two nickel metal hydride batteries and by using batteries that contain their own microprocessors and built-in power management circuitry.

The 500-series PowerBooks has some other firsts as well. They added function keys to the keyboard for the first time, and are the only models to include built-in Ethernet ports. **Trackpads** first appeared in 500-series models. PowerBook 500 models were the first Mac that enabled users to change their own RAM and hard disk drives. You can obtain access to the 500's interior by removing a few screws and lifting up the keyboard. In previous models, only Apple-licensed technicians could make changes in RAM and hard disk configurations, or the warranty would be voided.

PowerBook 500 models were also the first Macs that could use PC Cards, the credit card-sized expansion cards you insert without opening the computer. PC Card functionality is an option installed as a 3.8-ounce adapter, called the PowerBook PCMCIA Expansion Module. (PCMCIA, which stands for the Personal Computer Memory Card International Association, is an older name for PC Card hardware.) The adapter installs into the left battery bay and plugs into the 500s' processor-direct slot (PDS). The PC Card adapter can hold two Type II cards, or one thicker Type III card. You also need to install software that comes with the adapter.

The PowerBook 500 models sound better than earlier PowerBooks, with built-in stereo speakers and CD-quality audio. PowerBook 500s can also record in stereo through the use of an external microphone (the built-in microphone is mono only) and stereo recording software, such as Farallon's SoundEdit Pro or Opcode Systems' AudioShop.

Table of Specifications

Model	CPU	Display Type	Colors/Resolutions	RAM: Min/Max
520	25MHz	9.5"passive matrix	16 grays@640×480	/36
520c	25MHz	9.5"dual scan	256 colors@640×480	/36
540	33MHz	9.5"active matrix	64 grays@640×480	/36
540c	33/66MHz	9.5"active matrix	256 colors@640×480	/36
			32,768 colors @640×400	/36

In one way, the 500 is inferior to some of the 100 series models. For example, none of the PowerBook 500s contain a floating point math unit, as do several of the 100 series. This means that the 500 series PowerBooks can't run software that requires floating point math, such as certain CAD and graphics programs. Although the 68040 processors used in some desktop Macs have built-in floating point, the low-power 680LC40 processors don't. The PowerPC-based PowerBooks (the series 2000 and 5000) do have floating point units built into their processors.

The PowerBook 500s are upgradeable to PowerPC processors via Apple's Macintosh PowerBook Processor Card Upgrade Kit with PowerPC 603e for PowerBook 500. The card contains a 100MHz processor, and replaces the CPU card that plugs into the logic board.

See Also

PC Cards and Slots; PowerBook; PowerBook 100 Series; PowerBook 5000 Series; PowerBook Duo 2000 Series

PowerBook 5000 Series

The PowerBook 5000 series are PowerPC-based laptops with a modular design. The 5000-series PowerBooks use PowerPC 603e processors. Running PowerPC native software, the low-power 603e models run two to four times faster than the 68030 and 040-based PowerBook 100 and 500 models can. The 603e in the 5300 runs at 100MHz, and is slightly slower than the 100MHz **PowerPC 601** found in desktop models such as the Power Mac 7500. There is also a model with a 117MHz processor (see table).

Series 5000 PowerBooks give you a choice of passive matrix, dual-scan, and active matrix flat panel displays. The dual scan screens produce images of better quality than passive matrix, but not as good as those produced on active matrix displays.

The 5000 series also contain two PC Card slots (also known as PCMCIA slots) for use with the credit card-sized PC Card expansion cards. The slots can accommodate two Type II cards, or a single Type III card. Unlike most other PowerBooks, the 5000 models don't have an internal modem slot, so a PC Card modem is your only option.

Another important feature of the 5000 series is the modular design, which enables the units to be reconfigured by the user. If you remove three torx screws on the bottom of the unit, the keyboard lifts for easy access to RAM and hard disk.

The floppy disk drive sits in an expansion bay and also can be easily removed. You can pop out the floppy drive by pushing a latch on the bottom of the unit. You can replace the floppy drive with other storage devices, for example, additional hard drives or removable cartridge drives such as the Fujitsu PowerBook DynaMO 230, a 3.5" magneto optical drive that uses 230MB cartridges. The floppy slot uses a standard IDE connector. You can even plug in Apple's PC Card Storage Tray, which holds four Type II PC Cards or two Type III PC Cards. The PowerBooks weigh 0.4 pounds less with the storage tray installed than with the floppy drive installed.

Other features include the capability to put the PowerBook to sleep by closing the lid. A blinking LED lets you know the unit is in sleep mode. You'll find a

Table of Specifications

Model	CPU Speed	Display Type	Grays/Colors	RAM: Min/Max
5300	100MHz	9.5"passive matrix	16 grays@640×480	8/64MB
5300cs	100MHz	10.4"dual scan	256 colors@640×480	8/64MB
5300c	100MHz	10.4"active matrix	256 colors@640×480	8/64MB
			32,768*colors@640×480	
5300ce	117 MHz	10.4"active matrix	32,768colors@800×600	32/64MB

*with 1MB VRAM installed

useful assortment of ports, including SCSI, LocalTalk, sound-out and built-in microphone, and optional video out port. The built-in Ethernet port of the 500 series is missing here. Apple expects you to use an Ethernet interface on a PC Card if you need it. There are many such cards that also contain a modem, as well.

One interesting port is an infrared window for moving files between PowerBooks through the air. The infrared window uses **AppleTalk** network protocols running at **LocalTalk** speeds, 230.4Kbps. The infrared window can also connect the PowerBook to a wired AppleTalk network through the use of Farallon's AirDock. This gives the PowerBook user access to printers and file servers.

The keyboard includes 12 half-sized F keys, an Escape key, and a Power-On key. Hold the Power key down a second or so, and you'll bring up the Restart dialog box, which gives you an option to Restart, Sleep Cancel, or Shutdown.

See Also

PowerBook, PowerBook 100 Series, PowerBook Duo 2000 Series

PowerBook Batteries

PowerBooks have used three basic technologies: lead acid, nickel cadmium (NiCad), and nickel metal-hydride (NiMH), with some variations of the NiMH. Certain types of NiMH batteries types are interchangeable in different models. All types of PowerBook batteries can be recharged in a PowerBook plugged into an AC outlet or in an external battery recharger.

With each new generation of PowerBooks, Apple uses a new type of battery to support more powerful and power-consuming features in PowerBooks. Battery life depends on how much power the PowerBook draws (see table on the following page) as much as it has to do with the type of battery. Color screens draw more power than grayscale or black-and-white, and the PowerPC 603e processor uses more power than 680x0. How a user operates the PowerBook also affects battery life. These factors include the brightness of the screen, how much the user accesses the hard drive

and floppy drive, and whether the user runs a RAM disk, which can save a considerable amount of power.

The original PowerBook 100 is the only PowerBook that uses a lead acid battery, the same type of battery technology used in automobiles. Like the no-maintenance automobile batteries, PowerBook 100 batteries were sealed. Lead-acid batteries can hold a charge longer than NiCad batteries, and can last through a large number of recharges, but contain more hazardous materials than other types and therefore represent more of a disposal problem.

NiCad batteries were used in most of the PowerBook 100 line, except for the PowerBook 100 itself and the 190 and 190cs. NiCad batteries hold a charge for a shorter amount of time than any other type of batteries. In addition, they have a shorter total life than other types of batteries because the amount of usable power stored in the battery reduces with each recharge. At the end of a NiCad battery's life span, a charged battery can only run the PowerBook for a half hour or less. You can lengthen the overall life span of a NiCad battery by letting it discharge completely before recharging it.

Nickel Metal-Hydride (NiMH) batteries are the most commonly used batteries in PowerBooks today. They recharge more quickly than NiCad batteries do, and have longer life spans. They hold a greater voltage, and hold more power per unit volume than NiCad batteries.

Apple has used several types of NiMH in PowerBooks over the years. The Original NiMH, called Type 1, was first used in the PowerBook Duo 210 and 230. A Type II was used in the PowerBook Duo 270c, 280, and 250. Eventually, Type II NiMH replaced the Type I battery in the 210 and 230 as well.

Type III NiMH was introduced in the 280c, and used in the Duo 2300. It holds about 15 percent more power than Type II. You can use Type III batteries with the other Duos with the addition of a System Enabler file that comes with the battery.

PowerBook 500 series introduced another version of the NiMH battery, the PowerBook Intelligent Battery. These batteries contain their own processors to actively manage the power flow to the PowerBook and to give the PowerBook an accurate indication of how much power is left.

Apple PowerBook Battery Specifications

PowerBook	Battery	Hours	Charged Voltage	Part/Model Number
100	lead-acid	2-to-4	6.0 V	661-0782/M3053
140, 145, 170	NiCad	2-to-3	6.75 V	661-0754/M5417
145B	NiCad	2-to-3	6.75 V	661-0789/M5653
140, 145, 170	NiCad	2-to-3	6.75 V	661-0013/M5654
165c, 180c	NiCad	1-to-2	6.75 V	661-0013/M5654
190, 190cs	NiMH	2.5-to-4.5	16.1 V	661-1028/M3254
Duo 210,230	NiMH Type I	2.5-to-4	13.5 V	661-1656/M7782
Duo250,270c	NiMHTypeII	2-to-4	13.5 V	661-1735/M1499
Duo 280	NiMHTypeII	2-to-4	13.5 V	661-1735/M1499
Duo 280c	NiMHTypeIII	2-to-4	13.5 V	661-0053/M1499
520, 520c	NiMH PBIB*	2-to-3.5	10.8 V	661-0055/M1906
540, 540c	NiMH PBIB*	2-to-3.5	10.8 V	661-0055/M1906
Duo 2300c	NiMHTypeIII	2-to-4	13.5 V	661-0053/M1499
5300	NiMH	2.5-to-4.5	16.1 V	661-1028/M3254

PBIB=PowerBook Intelligent Battery

The most advanced type of battery used in a PowerBook, the lithium ion battery, was never seen by the general public. Lithium ion battery technology received a setback when Apple pulled them out of PowerBook 5300s in the summer of 1995, several months before the introduction of the 5300 series. Several of the lithium ion batteries caught fire at Apple, so the company quickly replaced them with nickel metal hydride batteries. Lithium ion batteries are the most advanced type of battery, and were supposed to provide 3–5 hours of use in the PowerPC-based PowerBooks. It is possible we will see new versions of the lithium ion battery in the future.

See Also
PowerBook

PowerBook Control Panel
The PowerBook control panel is designed to help the PowerBook user manage and conserve battery power. The control panel itself has two modes; Easy (which collapses the control panel down to a small window with only a slider visible for setting your choice between better conservation or better performance; and Custom, which expands the control panel to its full size and enables access to additional conservation features set by using sliders, such as:

- How many minutes of inactivity until the PowerBook goes into a state of sleep.

- How many minutes of inactivity until the screen dims.

- How many minutes of inactivity until the hard disk spins down.

On certain models of PowerBook, this control panel also gives you the option, through a checkbox, to reduce the processor speed to conserve battery power.

PowerBook Displays
PowerBook displays are flat-panel screens that use variations of liquid crystal display (LCD) technology.

The displays in PowerBooks create better pictures than desktop CRT display monitors, with brighter, sharper images and more vivid colors. However, flat panel displays are quite a bit more expensive to produce than CRT monitors, which is why you don't see many flat-panel LCD displays on desktop computers.

If you're using your **PowerBook** in a presentation and you want to have the image on the presentation screen to appear on your PowerBook screen as well, you can select video mirroring in the PowerBook Display control panel and toggle video mirroring on. You can also use video mirroring with an external monitor. On some newer models of PowerBook, there's a screen-dimming control in this control panel.

Like desktop monitors, PowerBook displays are made up of tiny dots called pixels, about 72 of them per inch. Unlike desktop monitors, the pixels in LCD screens are square and sharply defined.

The screens used in the first PowerBooks, the 100, 140, and 170, were black-and-white screens, which display one-bit of color information, or two colors (black and white) per pixel. Black-and-white screens have not been used in PowerBook models for many years, but grayscale screens are still available. Grayscale adds values of gray that are in between black and white. A 2-bit grayscale screen can display 4 grays and a 4-bit screen can display 16 grays.

When you add color, you drive up the cost and use more power, but you enhance the user experience. Color displays start at 8-bits per pixel, or 256 colors. The highest-resolution LCD screens can display up to 32,768 colors (16-bit).

Regardless of how many colors or grays a screen can display, all PowerBook displays are one of two basic types: active matrix screens or passive matrix screens. Active matrix produces the highest quality images, and are the best computer display devices. Each pixel in an active matrix display has its own transistor to determine the level of intensity. Active matrix colors are bright with good contrast, and the objects are sharp and well-defined. These displays can react quickly to rapidly changing graphics, and can be seen clearly from wide viewing angles, which makes them the best displays to use for presentations.

Passive matrix, which used to be called supertwist, is a more economical LCD technology. Images on passive matrix screens are usually difficult to view at wide angles. Passive matrix screens don't draw as fast as active matrix screens, so quickly moving objects can blur. Small objects, such as the arrow cursor, can disappear from view when you move them.

Some PowerBooks come with an enhanced type of passive matrix screen called a dual-scan display. A dual-scan display draws (or *scans*) the top and bottom half of the screen at the same time, thus achieving an effective refresh rate nearly twice that of a standard passive-matrix display. It draws images on the screen faster, reducing the blurring or disappearing effects of fast-moving objects. It also makes colors appear brighter than ordinary passive matrix displays.

TIP All PowerBook displays are lit from behind, or backlit. If you are using a PowerBook in bright light, you can save battery power by turning the backlighting partially or all the way down.

See Also

Monitors; PowerBook 100 Series; PowerBook 500 Series; PowerBook 5000 Series; PowerBook Duo 200 Series; PowerBook Duo 2000 Series

PowerBook Duo 200 Series

The PowerBook Duos are designed to function as two computers—a laptop Mac when away from your desk, and a desktop Mac when at your desk. As laptops, the Duos are lighter, thinner, and easier to carry than standard PowerBooks because they don't contain floppy drives and many of the ports of standard PowerBook. Instead, the Duos contain one serial port (LocalTalk-enabled) and a special 152-pin connector for connecting to a Dock. The Duos all contain a slot for an optional internal modem.

A Duo functions as a desktop Mac when you plug it into Apple's **Duo Dock** (see figure on following page).

A Duo Dock provides the standard ports of a desktop Mac, including video circuitry and **VRAM** to support an external monitor. The Duo Dock also contains a floppy disk drive, an internal hard drive, and several NuBus Expansion ports. Smaller, portable docks that plug into the 152-pin connector are also available. Sometimes called minidocks, these portable connectors can add various combinations of ports and a connector for an external floppy disk drive.

PowerBook Duo 210 and Dock The 200 series of Duos make up most of the Duo models. At press time there was one other Duo model, the 2300, which has a PowerPC processor. The Duo 200 series models use either a 68030 or 68LC040 processor (see table), the lower power version of the 68040 used in desktop models, such as the Quadra line. Software that

requires floating point math (such as some drawing and CAD programs) only runs on the Duo 270c because it is the only series 200 Duo that contains a 68882 floating point math coprocessor. While the 68040 processor in some desktop Macs includes a built-in floating point math processing unit, the 68LC040 used in the Duo 280 and 280c does not have a floating point math unit.

You can upgrade any of the models in the Duo 200 series to a PowerPC processor by replacing the logic board with Apple's Logic Board Upgrade Kit, which includes a 100MHz PowerPC 603 chip and 8MB of built-in RAM (expandable to 56MB). This upgrade gives an old Duo the functionality of a Duo 2300.

The Duo 200 PowerBooks all come with a 19-mm trackball that is smaller than the trackballs in the PowerBook 100 series and use several types of nickel-metal-hydride batteries. The Duo 210 and 230 use a Type I nickel-metal-hydride battery for 2 to 4.5 hours of power and a recharging time of 2 hours. The Duo 250, 270c, and 280 use a Type II nickel-metal-hydride battery, which provides 2.5 to 6 hours (4 hours on the color 270c) of power. The 280c uses a Type III battery, which provides 2-to-4 hours of use on this color machine.

See Also

PowerBook; PowerBook 100 Series; PowerBook Duo 2000 Series

P

Table of Specifications

Model	CPU	Display Type	Colors/Resolution	RAM: Min/Max
210	25MHz 030	9.1"passive matrix	16 grays@640×400	4/24MB
230	33MHz 030	9.1"passive matrix	16 grays@640×400	4/24MB
250	25MHz 030	9"active matrix	16 grays@640×400	4/24MB
270c	33MHz 030*	8.4"active matrix	256 colors@640×480	4/32MB
			32,768 colors @640×400	
280	66MHz 040	9"active matrix	16 grays@640×400	4/40MB
280c	66MHz 040	8.4"active matrix	256 colors@640×480	4/40MB
			32,768 colors @640×400	

*Also includes 68882 floating point math coprocessor

PowerBook Duo 2000 Series

At press time, there was only one 2000 series PowerBook Duo model, the 2300c. It has most of the same features (see the following table) of the **PowerBook Duo 200 series**, such as light weight (4.8 pounds), and a slim profile for easy portability, and a 152-pin processor-direct slot connector for connecting to a PowerBook Duo Dock Plus. This connects the Duo 2300c to desktop peripherals, such as monitor, keyboard, floppy and hard disks, and full-sized expansion cards, or smaller minidocks.

The main difference between the 2300c and the series 200 Duos is the former's PowerPC processor, the 603e, which runs PowerPC native software two to four times faster than the 68030 and 040-based PowerBook Duo 200 models can. (In effect, the 2300c is the Duo version of the PowerBook 5300.) The 603e in the 2300 runs at 100MHz, and is slightly faster than the 100MHz **PowerPC 601** found in desktop models, such as the Power Mac 7500.

The Duo 2300c uses a Type III nickel-metal-hydride battery with an estimated battery life of 2–4 hours. It includes a **trackpad** that is more advanced than the trackpad in the PowerBook 500 and 5000 series. The 2300c's trackpad is clickable, so you can use it for click-and-drag actions, as well as for opening files and folders. The Duo 2300c includes the LocalTalk (printer) port found in most Mac models, and has an internal slot for an optional fax modem card. The 2300c comes with a 750MB or 1.1GB hard disk.

See Also

PowerBook; PowerBook 5000 Series; PowerBook Duo 200 Series

PowerBook Duo Docks and MiniDocks

Duo Docks are desktop docking bays for PowerBook Duos that connect a Duo with all the ports, peripherals, expansion capabilities, and networking and communication facilities of a desktop Mac. The docks connect to the Duo via a 152-pin processor-direct slot connector. You install a PowerBook Duo in a Duo Dock by closing the lid and inserting it into the slot in the Dock. A key lock prevents anyone but you from removing the Duo from the Duo Dock. There are also smaller docks called minidocks, which are connectors that provide the Duo with more ports.

There are two Duo Docks, the original PowerBook Duo Dock created for the PowerBook Duo 200 series, and the PowerBook Duo Dock Plus used with the Duo 2000 series. The original Duo Dock can hold a floppy disk drive, an optional 3.5" SCSI hard drive, and an optional 68882 math coprocessor. It includes built-in video circuitry and 512K of VRAM for connecting external Apple RGB, VGA, and SVGA display monitors and displaying up to 256 colors (8-bit). If you expand the RAM to 1MB, the Duo Dock can display 32,000 colors (16-bit). Users usually place the monitor on top of the Duo Dock, which is designed to support up to 85 pounds.

The Duo Dock contains ports, including an HDI-30 SCSI port, sound-in and -out ports, and an Apple Desktop Bus (ADB) port for a keyboard, mouse, and other input devices. There are two standard Mac serial ports (a LocalTalk-enable printer port and a modem port), and a pass-through port for the optional modem in the PowerBook Duo 200 models. Inside, there are two internal NuBus expansion slots that can hold standard Mac expansion cards.

Table of Specifications

Model	CPU Speed	Display Type	Colors/Resolutions	RAM: Min/Max
2300c	100MHz	9.5"active matrix	256 colors@640×480 32,768 colors @640×400	8/56MB

The PowerBook Duo Dock Plus contains the same ports and slots but with expanded capacity. For example, 1MB of VRAM is standard, supporting thousands of colors on monitors up to 17 inches and 256 colors on 20- and 21-inch monitors. The Duo Dock Plus also supports multiscan monitors. In addition to the ports on the original Duo Dock, the Plus has an Ethernet port.

Apple's Duo MiniDock is a bar that measures about 10.6" long by 3.2" and plugs into the back of the Duo. Unlike the Duo Dock, the MiniDock is designed to be carried around with the PowerBook Duo, weighing only 1.24 lb. It contains the circuitry and 512K VRAM for a video out port, an ADB port, two serial ports, an HDI-30 SCSI port, and an HDI-20 port for the external 1.4MB floppy disk drive. It also has a modem pass-through port to support a modem in the PowerBook Duo notebook computer, and sound in and out ports.

PowerBook Floppy Disk Drive

PowerBooks use **floppy disk drives** with similar capabilities to those used in desktop Macs, but they are usually lighter and slimmer. Like those in the desktop Macs, PowerBooks floppy drives can read Mac 1.44MB, 800K, and 400K disks, as well as 1.44MB DOS-formatted disks.

The floppy disk drive in most PowerBook models is permanent; however, the PowerBook 5300s have a removable floppy drive that sits in an expansion bay. You can pop out the floppy drive by pushing a latch on the bottom of the unit. You can then replace the floppy drive with other storage devices, such as additional hard drives or removable cartridge drives.

The PowerBook 100 and the PowerBook Duos don't have a built-in floppy drive. The PowerBook 100 has an HDI-20 connector to which you can connect an external floppy drive. For Duos, you can add an HDI connector by plugging in a minidock.

See Also

PowerBook 100 Series; PowerBook 5000 Series; PowerBook Duo 200 Series; PowerBook Duo 2000 Series; PowerBook Duo Docks and MiniDocks

PowerBook Hard Disk Drives

Hard disks inside PowerBooks have ranged in capacity from 20MB in the first PowerBook 100 to over a gigabyte in some current models. All PowerBook models, except the Power Duos, have a SCSI port for connecting external hard drives, CD-ROM drives, and other removable storage devices.

The internal hard disk drive of the PowerBook 150 uses the IDE interface instead of the more standard SCSI bus. (Internal IDE drives are also used on some desktop models, such as the Performa 630.) IDE is less expensive and faster than SCSI. However, you can't daisy-chain IDE drives together the way you can SCSI devices. This is why the PowerBook 100 also has an external SCSI port, as do all PowerBooks except the Duo models.

The PowerBook SCSI port does not use the standard 25-pin connector of the desktop Macs, but instead uses a small, square HDI-30 connector. To connect external hard drives to this port, you need a PowerBook SCSI cable, which has an HDI-30 on one end and a standard 50-pin SCSI connector at the other end. You can also get PowerBook SCSI cables that have a 25-pin connector instead of the 50-pin for devices that require the former connector.

SCSI Mode All PowerBook and PowerBook Duo models except the 140, 145, 145B, and 170 have a feature called SCSI mode, sometimes called SCSI direct, which allows the PowerBook to act as an external disk drive to a desktop Mac. In SCSI mode, you connect the SCSI ports of a desktop Mac and a PowerBook together, and the PowerBook appears as a hard disk icon in the desktop Mac's Finder. You can then transfer files between the two machines simply by dragging the file icons. SCSI is much faster than a network connection, making SCSI mode a good method for backing up or transferring large amounts of data between the desktop Mac and the PowerBook.

To connect the two machines together, go to the laptop's PowerBook control panel, turn SCSI mode on, and shut the PowerBook down. You must also shut down the desktop Mac. You'll need a cable with an HDI-30 connector at one end and a 25-pin SCSI connector at the other end. You can also use two SCSI cables that don't have a common connector, joined by an adapter. Once connected, you can start up both Macs, and the PowerBook's hard disk will mount in the desktop Mac's Finder.

See Also
Hard Disks; PowerBook; Small Computer Systems Interface

PowerBook Infrared Beaming

The PowerBook 500 and 5000 series have the capability to beam data through the air using infrared (IR) signals. Infrared beaming is optional on the 190 and 190cs. The infrared window can move files between PowerBooks using **AppleTalk** network protocols running at **LocalTalk** speeds, 230.4Kbps. The PowerBooks must be within a 30 degree angle of the IR window. The PowerBooks that are within range automatically recognize each other by using a piece of software called IRTalk. Each PowerBook then creates a new folder for any other PowerBook it sees within IR range. To transfer a file to the other user, you drag the file to the other user's folder.

The infrared window can also connect the PowerBook to a wired AppleTalk network through the use of Farallon's AirDock. This gives the PowerBook user access to printers and file servers.

PowerBook Internal Modems

Many PowerBook models contain an internal expansion slot that holds a modem card (see figure). Functionally, these modems are nearly identical to the external modems used with desktop Macs, minus the blinking LEDs. Internal modems contain a single RJ-ll connector for plugging in a standard telephone line cable. Although most modem cards come with instructions on how to install the modem, a user can void the warranty by opening a PowerBook's case on all models except the 500 series, the 5000 series, and the Duo 2000 series.

Later models with PCMCIA slots did away with the modem slot, because it is easier to insert a PC Card modem than to install an internal expansion card. The types of connectors for interfacing with the telephone cable vary with the manufacturer. Some PC Card modems use a thin connector called an X-Jack that directly accepts the cable's RJ-11 plug. X-Jacks are retractable and disappear into the PC Card when not in use. Other PC Card modems use a special adapter cable that plugs into the edge of the card on one end and accepts the RJ-11 plug on the other end.

See Also
Modems; PC Cards and Slots

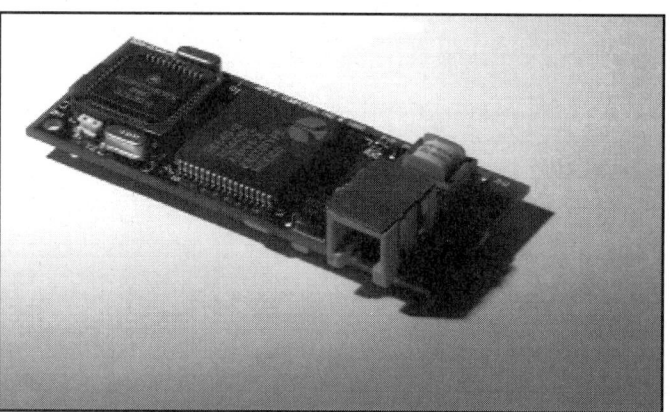

PowerBook RAM

PowerBooks come with some RAM soldered to the logic board, and some on a RAM card. PowerBooks don't use SIMM modules, as do desktop Macs, but instead use special RAM expansion cards. As might be expected, these expansion cards cost more than standard SIMM modules. In addition, PowerBooks have a single RAM connector for this card. This means that adding RAM in a PowerBook requires that you replace one RAM card with a bigger-capacity RAM card, rendering the existing card useless.

RAM cards come in three basic styles that vary in thickness. PowerBook 500 series models require the thinnest type of RAM cards, the so-called thin small-outline package (TSOP) cards. These cards can also fit into any other type of PowerBook. The 1.2 mm thick RAM chips on TSOP cards sit on both sides of the card. The next thickest RAM cards are small-out-line J-lead (SOJ) RAM cards, which use chips that are 2.5 mm thick, but the chips only sit on one side of the card. The thickest RAM cards are the flat-pack cards, which use chips on both sides of the card that vary in thickness between 1.2 and 2.7 mm. SOJ and flat-pack RAM cards can fit in certain PowerBook models. RAM card shapes also vary with different models.

Installing RAM PowerBook RAM first became user-upgradeable with the PowerBook 500 series. The RAM in PowerBook 5000 and 2000 series models can also be installed by the user. In these models, you can access the RAM by removing three torx screws on the bottom of the PowerBook. This enables you to remove the keyboard, which exposes the RAM. In other PowerBook models, opening the case voids the warranty unless it's done by an Apple-certified technician. However, if the warranty has already expired, you can do it yourself.

To access the RAM card in the PowerBook 100, first remove the battery. Close the PowerBook (screen down) and lay it top down on a table. Remove the screws and rubber tabs from the bottom of the case. Some screws can be removed with a Phillips screwdriver. Flip the unit over and release the monitor fasteners before opening the case. The monitor should now be free and the keyboard can be lifted out.

To open a PowerBook 140, 145, 150, 160, 165, 165c, 180, 180c, 190, and 190cs, remove the battery and close the unit. Lay it top down. Using T-8 and T-10 torx drivers, remove the screws on the bottom and the one under the rear flap near the internal modem port. Separate the two pieces of the case carefully. There are very delicate cables inside the case that have to be disconnected gently. The case comes apart as a clam-shell fitting. Flip the unit over so that the screen is up and open the case. Expert RAM installers do not have to completely remove the top of the PowerBook's case or disconnect the ribbon cables to install the RAM cards. If you separate the case about two inches, you should have enough room to install the RAM card.

Disassembly of the Duo 200s is similar, except that after the screws are removed from the bottom of the case, flip the unit over and open the screen. The keyboard should be loose. Lift the keyboard up and fold it over gently. The RAM card installs in the upper right corner of the interior of the case.

See Also
Memory PowerBook; PowerBook 100 Series; PowerBook 5000 Series; PowerBook Duo 200 Series; PowerBook Duo 2000 Series

PowerBook Setup

This control panel enables you to configure the **internal modem** for your **PowerBook** and select a SCSI ID number for the PowerBook's hard disk. This enables you to connect it to another Macintosh computer as an external hard-disk drive, as you would an- other SCSI peripheral. You can set a time for an automatic wake-up as well.

To use the PowerBook Setup control panel, follow these steps:

1. Select PowerBook Setup control panel from the Control Panels submenu on the Apple menu (or System Folder).

2. Choose between a Compatible or Normal modem setting by clicking the appropriate radio button. (Apple describes the difference between normal mode and compatible mode this way: "In the Normal mode, the modem is addressed via the System 7 Communication Toolbox, and this leaves your external serial port available for use. If your communication program is NOT compatible with the Communication Toolbox, set the PowerBook Setup control panel to Compatible. This mode prevents the external serial port from being addressed by other programs, as well as preventing communication with a serial printer.")

3. To set a SCSI ID, click the radio button by the ID number to which you want the PowerBook's internal hard-disk drive assigned.

4. To set an automatic wake-up, click the Wake-Up check box. To enter a new time and date for the wake-up, click the value you want to change to select it and up and down arrows will appear enabling you to click the up arrow to increase the value, or the down arrow to decrease it. After you've selected the value you want to change, you may find it easier to just enter the numbers by typing them in from the keyboard.

See Also
PowerBook; Small Computer System Interface

PowerBook Trackballs and Trackpads

PowerBooks all include either a built-in trackball or trackpad centered in front of the keyboard. Both are cursor control devices that can be used instead of a mouse. A mouse button is located surrounding or adjacent to trackballs and trackpads to enable you to click.

Older PowerBooks come with the trackball, which is basically an upside-down mouse; instead of dragging the mouse's ball around a desk, you drag your hand across the ball. The ball turns two roller bearings, which measure how much the ball was moved and its acceleration. The ball in the PowerBook 100 series measures 31 millimeters, and is easier to handle than the 19 millimeter trackballs in series PowerBook Duo 200 models.

Trackballs occasionally require cleaning, as dust can jam the trackball's roller bearings. You can remove a PowerBook trackball by turning the collar around the trackball in a counter-clockwise direction. The ball will then lift out, exposing the roller bearings.

Apple no longer ships PowerBooks with trackballs. The PowerBook 190, the PowerBook 500 series, the Duo 2300, and the PowerBook 5000 series all use trackpads. You control the cursor by dragging a finger over the trackpad. As with a mouse or a trackball, dragging your finger faster moves the cursor a farther distance on the screen. The most advanced trackpads are on the Duo 2300. These trackpads are clickable, so you can use them for click-and-drag actions, as well as for opening files and folders, without the need to hit a separate button.

Trackpads contain two sets of wires at 90 degrees to each other with current flowing through both sets. This creates an electromagnetic field above the trackpad. When your finger touches the trackpad, it disturbs the field, which in turn changes the current in the wires nearest your finger through an effect called coupling capacitance. The PowerBook trackpad circuitry uses the altered currents to detect where the cursor should be at any given moment. You must use your finger, rather than fingernail, pencil end, or other object. Otherwise, the trackpad won't register your input.

See Also
Mouse; Trackballs

PowerBook Video Out Port

Many PowerBook models have the capability to connect to an external monitor through a monitor port. These models are the PowerBooks 160, 165, 165c, 180, 180c, 190, 190cs, the 500 series, and the 5000 series, as well as on many Duo docks. (The video out port is optional on the 190 and 190cs.) The video out port on PowerBooks doesn't use the same 15-pin connector as the monitor port on desktop Macs, but it requires the use of a converter cable.

Some PowerBooks have two modes for external display. The first is called dual display, which allows the external monitor and the built-in screen to display different images or different applications at the same time. This is the same type of display you get when you connect two monitors to a desktop Mac.

The other type of external PowerBook display is called video mirroring, which simultaneously displays the same image on both screens. Video mirroring is useful for giving a presentation to an audience. In this case, the external display might not be a monitor, but a video projection system.

PowerFPU, *See SoftwareFPU*

PowerPC Chips, *See Processors, PowerPC*

PowerPC Platform (PPCP)

In the Fall of 1996, new Macintosh Operating System (OS)-compatible machines based on a new hardware architecture will be available. The new architecture, called the **PowerPC Platform (PPCP)**, is a universal standard developed by Apple, IBM, and Motorola that if followed, will enable the compliant computer to run PowerPC-native versions of Windows NT, Solaris (Sun Microsystems' version of UNIX), AIX (IBM's flavor of UNIX), OS/2, Novell Netware, and Macintosh OS without recompiling the software. The computers will be manufactured not just by Apple or its licensed clone-makers, but by many more vendors, including IBM, Motorola, Canon, DayStar Digital, Pioneer, IPC Technologies (parent company of Austin Direct), Zenith Data Systems, and Umax, along with smaller computer vendors and international consortiums such as TNPC (Taiwan New PC Consortium). This should provide consumers with a wider range of price, performance, and configurations, and open the Macintosh to the total world of PC peripherals, keyboards, mice, printers, and so

forth. The secret of PPCP is that it will be based on industry-standard components available from numerous suppliers.

The PPCP's goal is to bring down the price of PowerPC-based systems to compete with Intel-based hardware by increasing the availability of components and flexibility of hardware. Chip sets and their supporting architecture will be available from well-known suppliers, such as National Semiconductor, Motorola, Texas Instruments, and VLSI Technology. Apple demonstrated the first PPCP system running the Mac OS in late January 1996 and plans to ship the first system in November 1996. Other vendors are expected to also deliver their first versions in the same time frame. Umax, Power Computing, and DayStar Digital plan to offer PPCP machines.

A consortium of hardware manufacturers will certify systems as PPCP-compliant. PPCP-compliant systems should be able to run the Mac OS. There will be three types of PPCP boxes: server, desktop, and laptop machines; designs for the latter two are required to run the Mac OS, but servers are not. Apple plans to offer its OS for retail sale, and Mac ROMs will be available for users whose PPCP systems did not come with a ROM in the Mac slot. With the advent of Copland, the Mac's next operating system, the Mac ROM will no longer be required, because the goal of the operating system is to be hardware-independent.

As the following diagram shows, the PPCP (formerly called Common Hardware Reference Platform or CHRP) 1.0 describes a hybrid system with a PowerPC processor, PCI slots, and interchangeable Mac and Intel I/O options. Minimum memory requirements for desktop and laptop systems is 8MB, expandable to at least 32MB; an Apple desktop bus (ADB) or PS/2 connector (or both) for keyboard and a two-button mouse; 16-bit stereo, full-duplex audio; and a SCSI, IDE, or PC Card hard drive. To be PPCP-compliant, the computer requires a Centronics port (the latest version of the PC parallel printer port).

Desktop and portable units should have either the Mac 4MB ROM or at least a socket where it can be added. Many vendors will go beyond the minimum requirements listed in the table and include ISA slots (a low-cost expansion card option for cards that do not require a high-speed bus).

Apple has pledged to modify the Mac OS to support the alien drivers. You should be able to plug and play PC peripherals if those vendors supply Macintosh drivers for their devices.

The beauty of the PPCP specification is Apple's capability to configure machines to fit specific market niches more cheaply and with more availability of components. There are still questions about licensing the Mac OS to PPCP vendors and the actual shipping dates of systems, but the price of Mac-compatible systems should come down as more vendors offer this versatile computer.

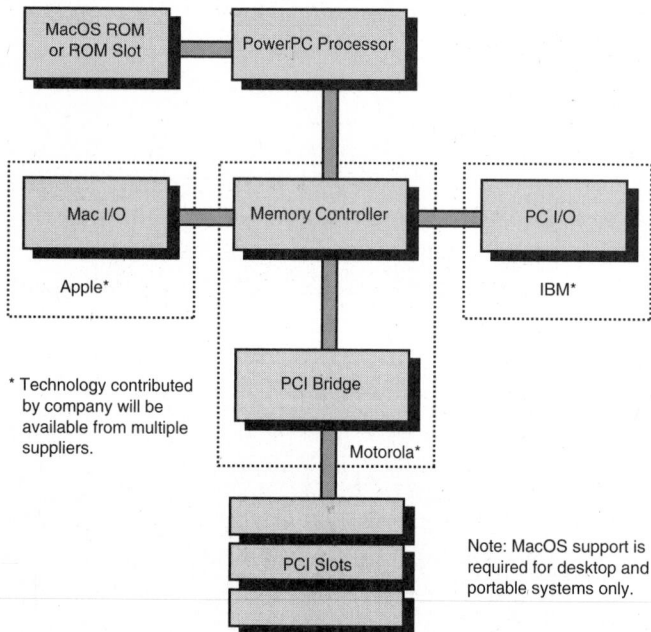

Note: MacOS support is required for desktop and portable systems only.

See Also

Power Macs, PCI Bus; System 7.5

PowerPlant

PowerPlant is a **C++** programming **framework** included with **CodeWarrior** by Metrowerks. Compared to the other major players in the Macintosh framework world—**MacApp** and the **Think Class Library**—PowerPlant is a newcomer. As a result, it is less mature than the others. On the other hand, because it was developed recently, it includes many new Apple technologies at its core.

PowerPlant, for example, has had support for Macintosh drag-and-drop, **scripting**, and the Power Macintosh from the start. It also supports Apple's **PowerTalk** software, **QuickTime**, and multiple threads of execution.

PowerPlant, an **object-oriented** framework, makes excellent use of multiple-inheritance in its object hierarchy. Utility functions needed by several classes are implemented as "mix-in" classes that can be inherited in order to add that functionality to any class. As a result, code written with PowerPlant is not burdened with functions it does not need. Combined with the overall design of the framework, this makes it possible to use just a part of the framework—just the part that handles menu management, for example—without the overhead of the whole framework. It also makes it possible to use PowerPlant to create non-application code, such as **plug-ins** or **control panels**.

PowerPlant is complemented by Metrowerks' **Constructor**, an interface builder that works with PowerPlant's visual aspects. Other tools can also be used to create the interface for PowerPlant applications, such as Bowers Development's **AppMaker**.

See Also

C++; CodeWarrior; Constructor; Control Panels; Framework; MacApp; Object-Oriented Programming; Plug-Ins; Think Class Library; Threads

PowerPoint

Microsoft PowerPoint is a powerful desktop presentation program, available as a stand-alone or as part of the Microsoft Office suite. It takes you from an outline of your presentation through making the slides, speaker's notes, and audience handouts. PowerPoint can display your presentation on the Mac screen, or output it as 35mm slides, overhead transparencies, as well as on paper.

Working with PowerPoint is made easier by its collection of automated features. Like its office mates, Word and Excel, PowerPoint comes with a collection of pre-formatted templates. It also uses Wizards, Microsoft's quick start helpers that ask you a series of questions about your project and then give you the appropriate templates to get you started. PowerPoint even has an Auto-Content Wizard to help you outline your program, based on the kind of message you're trying to convey. There's one for sales, one for training, one for recommending strategies, and even one for delivering bad news—six in all. Choose the one that's closest to your purpose, and it will open in outline view, with the suggested outline topics already in place. Add your own topics and ideas.

After your outline is fleshed out, consider the format of the slides. You can see what text appears on a slide by clicking the small slide icon to the left of the outline topic. Choose a look for your presentation either by using the Pick a Look Wizard or by selecting and applying one of the templates provided in the PowerPoint folder. After you've looked at your slides, you might move some of the text around, edit the text, or add more slides and more points to your speech. All of this is done easily in the outline view. At this point,

it's also a good idea to run the spelling checker. It's right there on the toolbar, just as it is in Word. It can use the same custom dictionaries you may have already created for Word, saving you the time otherwise spent re-entering them. The program ships with five OLE servers, including Graph 5.0 for designing graphs, Equation 2.0 for building mathematical formulas, and an application called Organization Chart for creating common types of org charts.

As you look through your slides, decide whether any of them would benefit from additional graphics. You can use art from any available source; import it on the Clipboard, use the Picture command on the Import menu, or select from PowerPoint's clip art collection. Drawing tools within the program enable you to add shapes, colors, and lines to your slides without importing them. There is no freehand drawing tool, however, so your options are somewhat limited.

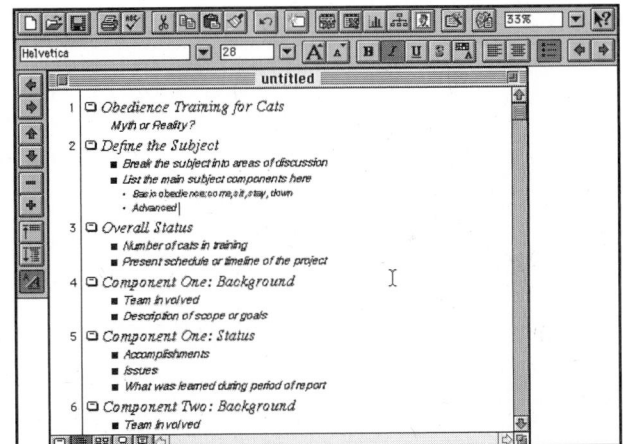

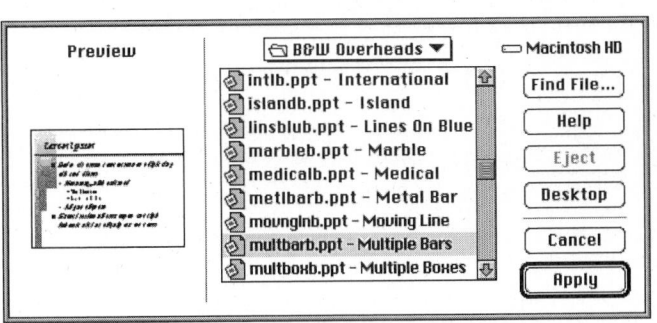

When you're satisfied with the appearance and content of the slides, think about how to get from one to the next. In the Slide Sorter view, you can add special effects, including builds in which you pop on a bullet list one item at a time, and transitions of various kinds. Transitions are selected from a pop-up list, which has too many to count. You'll see a preview of the effect in the Transitions box, as shown in the figure. You can set times for the slides to remain on-screen, so that the show runs automatically, or you can change slides manually with a mouse.

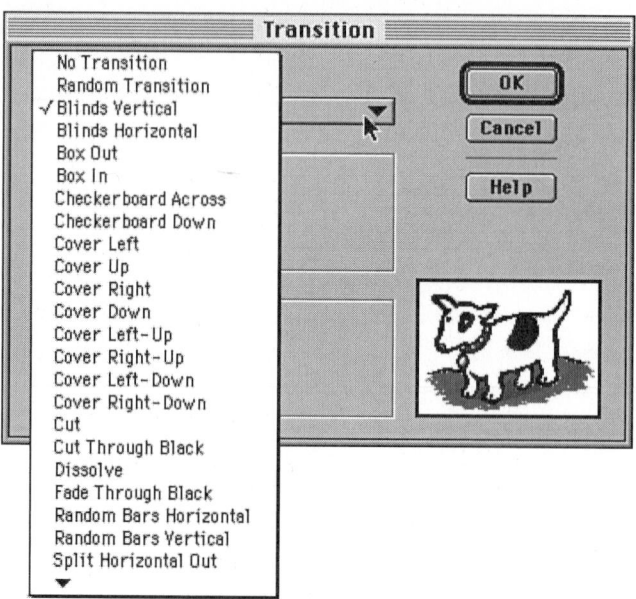

Review your show to make sure it's the way you want it. If you're going to run it from the computer, make sure you've saved your work. Putting a backup copy on a floppy disk is a good idea. If you'll be turning your visuals into multicolored overhead projection slides or 35mm slides, you'll need to print them to a Postscript file to take to a service bureau. Black line overhead slides can be printed on a laser printer. Some color inkjet printers can handle colored overhead transparencies, but the colors are rarely satisfactory. Print the handouts and speaker's notes. Finally, rehearse your show several times to be sure you've got the timing right and that you've covered all the points you intended to cover.

PowerPoint includes a run-time viewer that can be distributed with your program, so that others may view it without installing the whole application. Although it lacks many of the animation features found in Adobe Persuasion, it's easier to learn and has the major advantage of seamless integration with both Macintosh and Windows versions of the other Office suite components.

See Also

Astound; Director; Multimedia; Presentations, Adding Sound with Astound

PowerTalk Extension

This extension enables the integration of Apple's PowerTalk technology into your system. PowerTalk, introduced in **System 7 Pro**, and now part of **System 7.5** and higher, enables users on a **network** to send **email** to network users and brings a range of messaging and telecommunications features to the Mac.

When PowerTalk is installed, it adds three new **icons** to the Mac **desktop**: a mailbox, for receiving incoming email messages from the network or via modem; a catalog containing the names of the services you're connected to and the info for signing on to each, which keeps you from accessing the **Chooser** each time you want to sign on to a network; and the PowerTalk Keychain, which contains your personal passwords for signing on networks and services. (The last icon, PowerTalk Keychain, doesn't appear on the desktop until you've made your first connection to a service. It appears after that point.)

See Also

Chooser DA; Desktop, The; Email; Icons; Networking; System 7 Pro; System 7.5

PowerTalk Setup

This control panel, which works on any Mac that supports **PowerTalk**, enables you to toggle PowerTalk collaboration services on or off using a **radio button** (changes take effect upon restart). There is also a check box that enables you to lock your keychain after a specified number of minutes of inactivity. There's a box for you to type how many minutes of activity until the keychain is locked.

The keychain automatically locks when you shut down your Mac, and asks you for your keychain access code at startup.

Lastly, you can access your PowerTalk Keychain through a button in the control panel where you can add services to your keychain or change your password, among other options.

See Also

Radio Buttons

PPD, *See Printer Drivers*

PPP

PPP stands for Point-to-Point Protocol, a way of establishing a temporary, low-speed connection to the **Internet** through a dial-up **modem**.

Both **PPP** and **SLIP** (Serial Line Internet Protocol) accounts are designed to work with much slower connection methods than the dedicated network connections to the Internet enjoyed by government, educational, and nonprofit organizations. But because they work with low-cost modems, PPP and SLIP provide decent performance in normal situations to large numbers of people.

PPP is generally considered a preferable protocol over SLIP, because PPP is more carefully designed and more flexible than SLIP. Both, however, support popular and widely used **MacTCP**-based programs such as **Anarchie**, **Fetch**, and **TurboGopher.**

Two different programs provide PPP connections for the Macintosh: **MacPPP** from Merit Network, Inc., and InterPPP from InterCon Systems. InterPPP supports AppleTalk over PPP, which is not true of MacPPP. If you do not have an Internet connection, you can obtain the software when you establish an account with an **Internet service provider**. You can also get MacPPP from the disk that accompanies the Internet Starter Kit.

When establishing an account with an Internet service provider certain information is necessary in order to configure PPP or SLIP, as shown in the table included with the entry for **SLIP.**

Some PPP hosts cause a computer "timeout" to occur if your computer has been idle for a certain amount of time while connected to the Internet. This might be considered a courtesy, especially if you are paying for connection time and forget to disconnect before leaving your workstation.

If your connection hangs up before you are finished (and if you use manual addressing, where you specify an **IP address** when you dial in), simply switch back to the ConfigPPP or other PPP setup control, disconnect, and then reconnect. If, however, you use server addressing (in which the server assigns an IP address to you each time you log in), you must quit all active MacTCP programs before you reconnect via PPP. Otherwise, your MacTCP program (such as a Web browser) will get confused when you reconnect with a different IP address than you had before.

See Also

Asynchronous Data Transfers; Internet; InterSLIP; Modem; Networking; Packets; Parity; MacPPP; SLIP

Practical Extraction and Report Language, *See Perl*

Practical Peripherals MacClass 288MT II V.34, *See Modems*

PRAM, *See Circuits, Parts of the Macintosh*

Precision Bitmap Alignment, *See Printing Technology, PostScript Lasers, Halftoning*

Preemptive Multitasking, *See Multitasking*

Preferences

The Finder has its own set of preferences (as do most applications) that are accessed in a number of different ways. Control panels enable users to choose options, or preferences, for how they want certain features of the Finder set up. The Views control panel, for example, enables users to set their preferences for how much information is displayed in windows when they are in a list view, as well as what size the icons will be in list views. Users also get to choose what font they'd like for their system font (used for folder and filenames). These are all preferences for the Finder, even though they don't appear under a section or menu called preferences.

The following table contains a list of some of the most common Finder preferences and explains how to set them.

Most applications enable you to choose your favorite settings, or preferences, for certain features or tools in the application. These preferences enable you to configure the program to suit your personal tastes. When you open an application the first time, the default preferences are activated. You can set your own preferences by selecting Preferences, which usually appears under the **File** or **Edit menus**.

The preference settings for an application are stored as a file in the Preferences folder **nested** in the **System Folder**. Having preferences stored as a file is advantageous for a number of reasons. If you set preferences for an application and then decide you want to return to the default preferences, remove the application's preference file from the Preferences folder, and the next time you **launch** the application, it automatically builds a new preferences file using the default preferences. Having a preference file is also advantageous when multiple people work on the same Mac. Each person can put their own preferences file into the Preferences folder before they launch, giving them their own customized settings while they work. When they quit the application, they can remove their preferences file, and the next user can add theirs.

See Also

Edit Menu; File Menu; Launching a Program; Nested Folder; System Folder

Preferences Settings

Preference	Control Panel	Action
Set sound volume	Sound	Use slider to raise or lower overall speaker volume.
Set the Date	Date & Time	The current date is displayed. Click the day, month, or year and change by typing in new info or using the Up/Down Arrows in the dialog box to scroll higher or lower.
Set the Time	Date & Time	The current time is displayed. Click the hour or minutes to make a change by typing in new info, or use the Up/Down Arrows in the dialog box to scroll higher or lower.

Preference	Control Panel	Action
Choose color mode for your monitor	Monitors	You can choose to set your monitor to Black and White or Color, and choose to display 4-bit, 8-bit, 16-bit (thousands of colors), or 24-bit (millions of colors), depending on how much VRAM you have installed.
Change the desktop background pattern	Desktop Patterns	Scroll through the list of installed patterns and click "Set Desktop Pattern" to confirm your selection.
Add submenus to the Apple menu	Apple Menu Options	Toggle submenus on or off by clicking the appropriate radio button.
Select the color for highlighting text	Color	Choose a color from the pop-up menu or create a custom color by choosing Other.
Choose which extensions will load during startup	Extensions Manager	A scrolling list of extensions will appear. Click to toggle on/off any extension. The check mark means the extension will load at startup.
Protect the System Folder or Applications folder from access	General Controls	Click the check box beside your choice of security.
To choose how long the delay is before a key repeats itself	Keyboard	Click radio buttons ranging from slow to fast. You can choose the key repeat rate here as well.
Change the colors or names in the Labels menu	Labels	To change the name, just highlight the name and type over it with a new name. To choose a color, click a color in the list, and the Apple color picker will appear where you can click to choose the color of your choice.
To turn on Virtual Memory	Memory	Toggle Virtual Memory on and choose the disk you want to use as a virtual disk from the pop-up menu. Then choose how much memory you want to have upon restart using Virtual Memory.
To set how fast the mouse will track	Mouse	Click radio buttons ranging from slow to fast, and you can also choose which speed the Mac will interpret as a double-click.
To change the number format to support a foreign currency	Numbers	Use the pop-up menus to select separators and currency symbols.
To choose which folders will be shared across a network, and the access privileges of network users	Network	Use the pop-up menus to choose the users and use the check boxes to determine each user's level of access.

P

continues

Preferences Settings (continued)

Preference	Control Panel	Action
To roll up an active window to just its title bar	WindowShade	Click radio buttons to choose how many clicks necessary to "roll up" a window. Also you can choose to use Modifier Keys if you don't want to double-click, and you can toggle on/off the WindowShade sound.
To choose which disk will be the startup disk	Startup Disk	Click the icon of the mounted disk you want to use as the startup disk.
To have icons snap to an invisible grid for alignment	Views	Click Snap to Grid and choose whether you want a straight grid or a staggered grid.
To adjust how fast the insertion point blinks	General Controls	Click radio buttons ranging from slow to fast, and you can also choose how fast the selection bar will blink in menus when you make a selection.
To increase or decrease the size of the disk cache	Memory	Click the arrows in the dialog box to move the disk cache size higher or lower.
To put a folder with aliases of recently used items in the Apple menu	Apple Menu Options	Toggle Recent Items on and choose how many items you want to be available by typing in the number in the available boxes.

Preferences File

Most applications create a preferences file that contains the default settings for the program. These files are stored in the **Preferences folder** within the **System Folder**. Many applications enable users to adjust an application to suit their own personal tastes. In Microsoft Word, for example, you can choose which commands appear under which menus, and you can choose certain commands to appear as buttons on a ribbon at the top of your window for one-click access. Once these choices, or preferences, have been made, they are written and stored in the preferences file. You do not need to open the Preferences folder again to make these changes. They are saved for you. The average user doesn't really use the Preferences folder; it's really for use by the applications themselves.

If you have selected your own preferences for an application, and then decide that you want to return to old default preferences, find the application's preference file in the Preferences folder, and **delete** it. The next time you **launch** the application, it will build a new preferences file using the application's default preferences. The following figure shows an example of what you might find in the Preferences folder in your System Folder.

See Also

Delete Key; Preferences Folder; System Folder

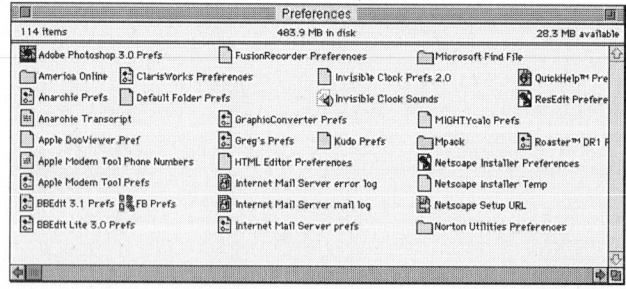

Preferences Folder

The Preferences folder, located in the **System Folder**, is where the preference files created by applications and utilities are stored. These preference files contain the settings for any user-definable controls of the application.

Each application has its own set of preferences and they are usually accessed in the applications File or Edit menu.

See Also
Preferences File; System Folder

Preflight and File Hand-Off

Preflight is the process of checking an electronic publication for possible output problems before it is handed to a service provider. In some instances, preflight may be part of the service provided by a service bureau or trade shop; however, it makes more sense (and is more economical) if one performs a preflight check on electronic publication files before they are sent to the service provider. Preflight is a term borrowed from aeronautics where a pilot performs a preflight check for airworthiness. A digital preflight check insures that your document will print and that you have done everything required by the service provider to output your document correctly.

Although proofing a publication is important, it constitutes a separate activity and is covered in the **proofs** entry under desktop publishing. We will concentrate here on preflight and hand-off and discuss the steps necessary for a smoother transition from your computer to the printed page. Adequate communication with the service provider is a critical part of the preflight process. You should always seek their advice and recommendations if you are not absolutely sure of the correct procedures. The final disposition of a publication project should always be in mind from the beginning. That means understanding the requirements of final output and reproduction and how they affect the design and prepress stages of a publication. As a rule, the later a problem must be corrected in the publication process, the more costly it is. Recognizing and fixing problems early is the goal of preflight.

The following steps are recommended in preparing a document for imaging (preflight):

- Printing your publication on your own desktop printer (preferably a PostScript-compatible one) is the first step. If the document will not print on your own printer, it probably will not print at the service bureau. Besides, you should always include a laser proof when you hand the files off to the service provider.

- Prepare a report for the service provider that contains information about your document. The report should be a summary of all the aspects of your publication. Describe the publication in ordinary terms, such as: "Pamphlet, $8^1/_2 \times 11$ inches, printed 2 sides, no bleeds, accordion fold, 2-colors (PMS 186 & black)." Mention technical aspects of output you may have discussed with the service provider. These may include output resolution, halftone screen frequency, trapping amounts, **PPD** (PostScript printer description) used, UCR or GCR settings, and the use of any image replacement scheme such as APR or OPI. List all fonts used in the publication, including those used in imported **vector images**. List all the pages of a multiple page publication by page number and indicate general page contents and any special graphics treatments such as **bleeds**. You should also indicate the presence of imported graphics and whether an individual graphic is "live" or "FPO" (for position only). List all filenames used in a multiple-file document. Identify the locations of all files and what software created them. In **process color** and **spot color** jobs, list the number of **color separations** that will be needed for each page, including varnishes. Mention any special printing effects, such as blind embossing and foil stamping, or the use of special paper stock. Any information you can think of should be in the report. It is better to have too much than not enough.

P

- Delete all unnecessary pages from the publication file.

- Check all linked graphics to make sure they are still linked and updated.

- Make sure that all print and page setup dialog box settings are appropriate for the final output device. This means you must know exactly what device will be used at the service bureau and have its PPD installed on your computer.

- Check all colors and make sure they are named correctly. Delete any unused colors. In spot colors, each color must have only one name.

- Make sure all bleed elements actually extend off the edge of the page about one pica or the amount specified by your service provider.

- Check **trap** specifications.

- Find out whether the service provider wants the publication file in **PostScript** format or native format. Giving them the file in native format allows them to open the file and make changes or adjustments. If you give them a PostScript file, the service provider cannot make any corrections. Converting the publication file to PostScript converts all page layout information, embedded and linked graphics, and fonts into a single PostScript language file ready to be downloaded directly to a **raster image processor** (RIP). This is a good thing to do if your service provider does not have the page layout software you used or does not have the same fonts you used. Do not try it unless you are absolutely sure you know what you are doing. Get detailed instructions from the service provider.

Handing off your publication files to a service provider can occur through telecommunications or an online service, but most people copy them to disks, SyQuest, **Bernoulli**, or **Zip** cartridges, or a portable hard drive. Be sure to copy all linked graphics files along with the publication files. If a linked graphic is not present when the publication is output, a low-resolution screen image will be substituted. Use a data-compression program to reduce file sizes if necessary. Make sure your service provider will have no difficulty expanding the files.

See Also

Desktop Publishing Proofing and Printing; Service Bureau Do's and Don'ts for Desktop Publishers

Premiere

The most popular QuickTime editor for the Macintosh, Premiere provides many features, including hundreds of transitions and filters and support for time code and batch processing. Primary competitor is Strata's **VideoShop**.

If you need to do simple editing (**cuts** rather than **transitions**, no sound editing), you can edit movies using Apple's **MoviePlayer** application.

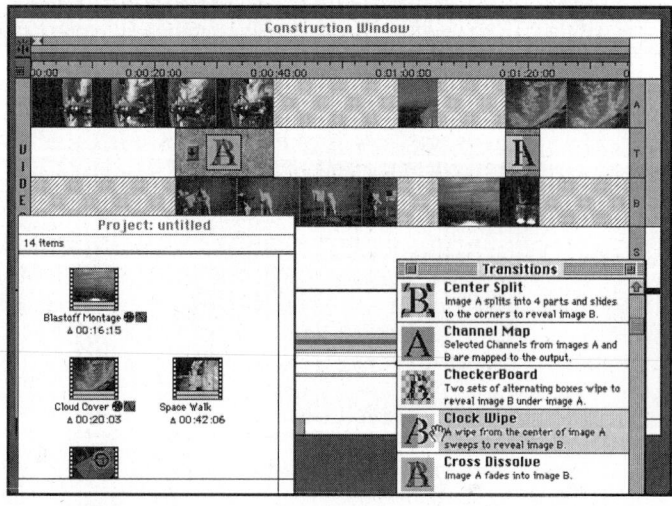

The primary working window in Premiere is the Construction window, where clips are arranged and transitions and filter effects added. Premiere displays a visual segment representing the length of each video clip in the Construction window. Clips are arranged in either the A or the B channel in the Construction window. **Transitions** are added by dragging them from the Transition window into the Transition channel of the Construction window. A Transition occurs over the length of the overlap between two clips that are in channels A and B. If you have ever worked with traditional video editing equipment you will quickly grasp how to use Premiere; if you haven't, you may have to spend a bit of time getting comfortable with how the software works.

Premiere includes a large selection of Transitions, from wipes and dissolves to unusual effects, such as a paint splatter.

Filters Whereas a transition is an effect that takes place between two clips, most filters work on a single clip. These effects are much like the image filters found in Photoshop, although they can be different in that an effect can change over the length of the clip (perhaps becoming more pronounced further along the clip).

Premiere provides basic sound editing tools, including some filters. The most important capability, apart from cutting the audio, is adjusting the sound volume of a clip, fading the sound in or out. There are also some third party sound effects available, which greatly expand Premiere's capabilities.

While it sounds like a simple program (all you do is drag a few clips into the Construction window and have Premiere build your movie), Premiere is actually a very complex program. This is obvious in the large selection of filters and transitions provided. Premiere also includes such features as support for automatically digitizing clips, generating **EDLs** (Edit Decision Lists), and a utility designed specifically for creating movies that play from CD-ROM.

See Also
CD-ROM Movie Maker; QuickTime; VideoShop

Premiere and Animation

There are three ways to engage in "painting on movies." The first is to be able to use actual digital painting tools to do the trick, such as those found in Strata's **MediaPaint**. The second is to paint with animated visual effects, which MediaPaint also allows you to do, in addition to Adobe's **After Effects** software. The third method that can be defined as "painting on a movie" is when you use another movie as the tool, in essence, painting on a movie with a movie. MediaPaint is also good at this method, as is Adobe's Premiere. Premiere is usually thought of as video editing software, but the digital artist and computer animator must not be chained to software categories at the expense of taking some creative risks.

In addition to stitching image sequences together, as any editing software is built to accomplish, Premiere also offers the computer animator a way to paint with video on video. It can accomplish this in several ways. The first is to simply use its editing capabilities to make an animation stronger by presenting the same scene over again from a different vantage point. This saves time and adds interest—two seemingly opposing forces. The computer animator saves time by recording the same scene from two or more vantage points. Nothing in the scene is moved. You have seen this effect when Hollywood movies show you expensive scene setups, like a building blowing up, several times in a row but from different angles. In the same way, a computer animator can record the action in the same scene through two or more cameras. In Premiere, the scenes can be sewn together. Even if you plan to add effects to the scene in MediaPaint or AfterEffects, all that's needed is to add the effects from different vantage points; you don't have to set the scene up all over again.

Premiere has a very deep list of filters, which are effects that can be applied to images and image sequences in either or both the A and B channels. The selected image clip is highlighted in the Premiere Construction window, and the Filters list can be found in the Clips menu. A Filter is chosen and applied to the clip. Filters can be stacked, and their order in the apply list affects the visual outcome of the effects process. Many items in the list of filters that ship with

P

Premiere look a lot like the list of filters that ship with Photoshop, except that Premiere applies these filters to moving as well as still images. The filters are the following: Antialias, Backwards Video, Bend, Black and White, Blur, Blur More, Brightness and Contrast, Camera Blur, Color Balance, Color Offset/Pass/Replace, Convolution Kernel, Crop, Crystallize, Emboss, Extract, Field Interpolate, Find Edges, Gamma Correction, Gaussian Blur, Gaussian Sharpen, Ghosting, Horizontal Flip, Hue and Saturation, Image Pan, Invert, Levels, Mesh Warp, Mosaic, Pinch, Pointillize, Posterize, Posterize Time, Radial Blur, Replicate, Resize, Ripple, Roll, Sharpen Edges, Sharpen More, Solarize, Spherize, Tiles, Tint, Twirl, Vertical Flip, Video Noise, Wave, and Zig-Zag. From this list, you can see the image processing applications, and should think of Premiere as an artist's tool, comparable to Photoshop for animated sequences.

In addition to sewing animations together in a linear fashion, you can have one scene "disclose" another. The first scene can wash off the screen and reveal the second, and the second animation can fall away like leaves and reveal the third, and so on. These segues are called "wipes" in video terms, but to the animator, they are known as transition effects. They add immediate interest, even if the same subject matter is being repeated before and after the transition. Premiere comes loaded for action with its list of ready-made transitional wipes, and each can be customized further to fit the animators' needs. They are as follows (when we use the word "image" in the following descriptions, it is used to mean either static pictures or animations):

- Additive Dissolve—Image A fades into B.
- Band Slide—Image A slides over B in horizontal/vertical bars.
- Band Wipe—Image B is revealed under A from the center out.
- Barn Doors—B is revealed under A from the center out.
- Center Merge—Image A splits into four parts and slides to the center to reveal B.
- Center Peel—Image A curls from the center with a shaded back and reveals B.
- Center Split—Image A splits into four parts and slides to the corners to reveal B.
- Checkerboard—Alternating boxes wipe to reveal B under A.
- Clock Wipe—Center wipe from A reveals B.
- Cross Dissolve—Image A fades into B.
- Cross Stretch—Image B stretches as A shrinks.
- Cross Zoom—Image A zooms in, B zooms out.
- Cube Spin—A spins to reveal B, as mapped on two faces of a cube.
- Curtain—Image A is drawn back to reveal B.
- Direct —Image B is passed through.
- Displace—Red and Green channels of A displace pixels of B.
- Dither Dissolve—Image A dissolves into B.
- Doors—Image B swings in over A on horizontal or vertical doors.
- Fold Up—Image A repeats folds to reveal B.
- Funnel—Image A is pulled through a funnel to reveal B.
- Inset—Corner wipe reveals A under B.
- IrisCross/Diamond/Points/Round/Square/Star—Shaped wipe reveals B under A.
- Luminance Map—Luminance of A is wrapped onto B.
- Multi-Spin—Image B spins in from rectangles.
- Non-Additive Dissolve—Luminance of A is wrapped onto B*.
- Page Peel—Image A curls back to reveal B.
- Page Turn—Image A turns back to reveal B.
- Paint Spatter—Image B revealed under A by paint spatters.
- Peel Back—Image A curls in four parts to reveal B.
- PICT Mask—A user-selected PICT is used to mask B onto A.

- Pinwheel—Multiple wipes sweep to reveal B under A.

- Push—Image B pushes A to one side.

- Radial Wipe—Image B revealed under A by radial sweep.

- Random Blocks—Random boxes reveal B under A.

- Random Wipe—Random wipe reveals B under A.

- Roll Away—Roll reveals B under A.

- Slash Slide—B slides over A in sections.

- Slide—B slides over A.

- Sliding Bands—B is revealed under A by sliding bars.

- Sliding Boxes—Sliding boxes reveal B under A.

- Spin—B spins over A.

- Spin Away—B spins in to reveal A.

- Spiral Boxes—Spiral wipe reveals B under A.

- Split—Image A splits to reveal A.

- Stretch—B stretches over A.

- Swap—Images swap places.

- Swing In/Out—B swings over A.

- Swirl—B spins in swirling.

- Take—Image B is passed through.

- Texturize—A is mapped onto B*.

- Three-D—Source images are mapped onto red and blue channels (creates art for 3D glasses!).

- Venetian Blinds—Horizontal wipes reveal B under A.

- Wedge Wipe—Wedge wipe from A reveals B.

- Wipe—A wipes to reveal B.

- Zig-Zag Blocks—Blocks wipe to reveal B under A.

- Zoom—B zooms to cover A.

The asterisked items indicate how a composited image may be built from animated files, giving the Premiere user another method for creating a collage.

Premiere also features a special channel reserved for image and animation compositing, complete with drop out screening that reveals one image or animation under another. The artist can use this capacity to build a composited graphic or animation. Adobe Premiere has a long list of special video options as well, which will be discussed under the Premiere heading. It is absolutely vital that the computer animator keep in mind the fact that animations (after they are broken up into single frame sequences, which Premiere can do) can be mapped to any 3D surface or object in most Mac 3D animation software. This is what makes Premiere as much the animator's tool as the videographer's.

See Also

After Effects; MediaPaint

Prep File (Keyboard Shortcut)

When you choose to **print** a document, the Mac sends a prep file to the printer to initialize the printer. In **System 6**, if you needed to create a **PostScript** file for printing, you had to use the key command ⌘-K after you chose the Print command. Choosing ⌘-K meant a prep file was with the PostScript file for printing that would initialize the printer for you. With **System 7** and higher, you don't need to use a key command to create PostScript files because PostScript files are a **check box** in the application's Print **dialog box**.

If you wanted to create a PostScript file *without* the prep file, you used the keyboard shortcut ⌘-F after you chose the Print command to create a PostScript file. This keyboard shortcut should only be used after the printer has been initialized, as it will not include the prep File within the PostScript file.

See Also

Checkbox; Keyboard Shortcuts; PostScript; Print Command; System 7

Prepress

Prepress is a broad term covering many technologies, old and new, but it specifically applies to activities performed for the purpose of preparing things to be printed. At one time, this included many skillful manual activities for which individuals were specifically trained, usually through apprenticeship. Today, the term must include electronic activities, and many of the individuals performing them have no training at all and may, unfortunately, have only a dim understanding of the process. Sometimes, understanding how a thing used to be done is helpful in understanding the new way. With that in mind we will look first at the traditional prepress procedures and then contrast the new electronic prepress techniques.

Traditional It should be noted that traditional prepress is by no means a thing of the remote past. In many places all over the United States and the world it is still practiced as a routine part of the printing process. Electronic methods are steadily replacing traditional methods, but the transition is not complete. This is another good reason for desktop publishers to gain a better understanding of the processes involved. Traditional prepress picks up where the graphic designer or paste-up artist leaves off. That is, the paper **mechanical** created by these individuals is handed-off to a prepress trade shop or, more likely, to a commercial printing firm with in-house prepress facilities. (A mechanical is a construction of paper-based text and **line art** graphic elements "pasted-up" on a piece of poster board. Overlays are used for **color separations**, type reverses, and windows for **halftones**.)

The paper mechanical is then photographed with a special graphic arts camera called a process camera. This results in loose pieces of negative (and sometimes positive) film. Photographs or other **continuous-tone** art to be included in the publication are photographically recorded on film also, but with a difference. Unlike the black-and-white line art on the mechanical, continuous-tone images must be converted to **halftones**. This is done either through the process camera or with a contact exposure device. Any background tints of color must also be created with halftone screens. Full color continuous-tone images must also be converted to halftones by separating them into the process color components of cyan, magenta, yellow, and black. A separate piece of halftone film is required for each color because a separate printing plate will be created for each color. A piece of film used to make a printing plate for a specific color is called a "**printer**," that is, cyan printer, magenta printer, and so on. Film for color halftones can be obtained from a process camera, but color scanners were used even before the advent of desktop publishing.

All the loose pieces of film containing line and halftone images must be assembled and attached to each other before plates can be made to print the images on paper. In fact, the actual pages of the publication must be laid out to print in a specific orientation to the paper stock. These procedures are known as image assembly, **stripping**, and page imposition, respectively. Image assembly and stripping involve much precise hand work. The pieces of film are brought together on a light table, and using special knives, scissors, various kinds of tape, and a special orange mounting paper, the stripper carefully assembles everything into a complete unit called a flat. At this stage, proofs are made to show the client how the elements have been assembled, and time is allowed for adjustments or corrections.

Each color in a multicolor printing job dictates a separate flat, and extreme care must be taken to ensure that the colors will register properly with one another when printed. Even after highly accurate stripping, colors may not register properly on the press. Any misregistration must be anticipated and compensated for by making slight reductions and/or enlargements of graphic elements during the camera process. This is called **trapping**, and it results in slight overlapping of colors on the press, preventing any show-through of paper.

Page imposition is the process of arranging the pages of a publication to print in a certain way on a sheet of paper. Economics, color requirements, press availability, paper stock size, printing quantity, and binding method, are all factors that help determine page imposition. There may be from two to 64 pages on each side of a sheet of paper. This is called a press form. Various kinds of page arrangements are used in a press form, depending on the size and type of press. Pages are arranged to minimize paper waste and take advantage of press capabilities. The figure shows an eight-page form where the same printing plate produces two copies of the publication on the same sheet. After the first pass through the press, the sheet must be turned over from left to right to print the other side. With the making of printing plates, the traditional prepress process is ended, and the printing stage begins.

Electronic The electronic prepress process is much simpler because computers do most of the work. Nearly all page layout and other graphics work is now done on a computer so the traditional mechanical is out of the picture. The publication files created on a computer are electronic mechanicals, which require no camera processing; they are output directly to devices that provide film negatives on which all the page elements are fully assembled with trapping allowances automatically included. Some manual stripping may be required for the page imposition of very large printed sheet sizes, but electronic stripping is increasingly the norm. Color separation is controlled by software, as are halftones of every kind. Even film may become unnecessary as direct-to-plate techniques become more common. Totally digital presses even eliminate the need for printing plates. Some electronic prepress activities, such as high-resolution scanning, color correction, color separating, trapping, and page imposition, are performed at **service bureaus**, trade shops, or in-house facilities at printing firms. Expensive proprietary systems known as CEPS (Color Electronic Prepress Systems) developed by traditional prepress vendors such as Linotype-Hell, Scitex America, DuPont Crosfield, and Screen are, to some extent, replacing traditional prepress equipment. These same companies have developed less expensive electronic prepress systems that utilize off-the-shelf software and hardware. However, the originators of electronic publication files, whether experienced or not, are frequently responsible for prepress activities, such as halftone production and trapping. The separate procedures of prepress are being absorbed in automatic software functions as desktop publishing and electronic prepress technologies become ever more sophisticated with each passing year.

See Also

Color Separations; Desktop Publishing and Color Electronic Prepress Systems (CEPS); Desktop Publishing Proofing and Printing; Digital Halftones; Mechanical; Printing; Printing Presses

Presentation Software

Whether you're speaking to a room full of people or making a one-to-one sales pitch, having some kind of visual reinforcement helps get the message across. For many years, public speakers relied on slides or overhead transparencies. They were awkward, but they did the job as long as they didn't get out of order, were inserted right side up, and were colorful and legible enough to hold the viewer's interest. Good slides or overhead transparencies were generally produced by artists or graphic arts companies at a cost of anywhere from $10–100 per slide.

Laser printers and **word processor**s or outlining programs opened up the world of presentation graphics to non-artists. Anybody could set type on the screen and run a sheet of transparency film through the printer. But options were limited. The sheets came in only a few colors as well as clear. To add a line to the text already shown, you could flop a second piece of film over the first, but in the age of MTV and video effects, that just wasn't exciting. Soon, software designers realized that the same tricks they used to create graphics for titles and video games could be applied by ordinary people to create slide shows and presentations right on the computer screen. And very soon the Mac was making **multimedia**.

There are two kinds of presentation software for business use. The traditional method for displaying business graphics is still essentially a slide show, although it may incorporate **QuickTime** movie clips and sounds. Adobe Persuasion, **Claris Impact,** and Microsoft **PowerPoint** are traditional presentation programs, designed to produce programs of slides full of charts, bulleted lists, and clip art graphics. Of course, quite a few other programs also can handle at least a limited form of slide show, including DeltaGraph Pro, **Excel**, and even **KidPix**. The non-traditional way is to use a multimedia program, such as Passport Producer, Macromedia **Director,** or Gold Disk **Astound.**

The differences between the traditional and non-traditional are significant. Traditionally, you would plan your speech by starting with an outline. Persuasion and PowerPoint both include outliners with robust text-handling features. PowerPoint's outliner is shown in this figure.

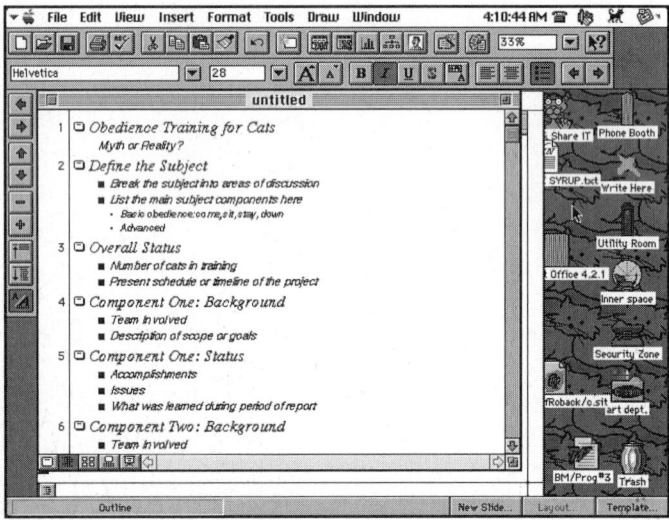

Begin by entering the main topics of your speech, and below them enter the sub-topics and points you want to make. Each topic becomes a slide. Formatting the slides is simple, especially if you're willing to accept one of the template "looks." Select one and then view your slides in that format. If it's not quite what you had in mind, try a different one. Typical presentation programs give you a variety of traditional, modern, and casual looks. If you can't find one that suits your message, use the tools provided to create your own. Start with a colored background and a readable font. Add a graphic, perhaps a company logo or a symbol.

A bar in a contrasting color helps direct the reader's eye to the type. Keep the same master layout for all of your slides. Switching colors or layouts from one slide to the next distracts the viewer from your message. Stick to 8-bit color, if possible, because it processes faster, and there won't be a delay between slides. If you'll be running the presentation on someone else's Mac, stick to common fonts like Helvetica.

Otherwise, you run the risk of having the slides appear in some illegible font that's been substituted for your own favorite custom typeface. Avoid using too many special effects, animated transitions, and so on. Aside from distracting the audience, they'll slow down the Mac to the point where your show becomes jerky and might even crash.

Presentation programs can do a good deal more for you than just putting slides on a screen. They also can convert the outline into speaker's notes for you and make the slides into audience handouts containing thumbnails of the visuals and selected explanatory text.

Although traditional presentation programs expect you to do the talking, even though they might add some sound effects or music, multimedia programs generally can stand on their own. They use more sound, more animation, more QuickTime clips, and inevitably more memory. Many are interactive, making them good choices for kiosk displays, as well as training materials or overviews of new products or services. The viewer can choose what to look at next or can follow a branching path through the information. Still, the typical multimedia program doesn't require a degree from film school to operate. Some are based on the familiar outline model. Others use a simple timeline, letting you control the duration of events on the screen.

You might make the company logo bounce in and jump around for five seconds while some bouncy music plays to grab the audience's attention, and then dissolve to a title slide, followed by a graph that grows as the narrator talks about the expanding market for your new product, which pops in... and so on.

More complicated or seriously interactive multimedia shows might require an authoring program, such as Macromedia **Director** or even HyperCard. They're more difficult, but allow you to insert many interactive options for the viewer.

See Also

Astound; Claris Impact; Director; HyperCard; Multimedia; PowerPoint

Presentations, Adding Sound with Astound

A well-executed sound track makes your presentation appear much more professional and makes it more effective for stand-alone use. It's not difficult to add music, sound effects, and narration with Astound. Adding sound to your presentations is also a good way to add emphasis to key points, even when you're doing the narration in person.

If your system has the capability to record sound (a built-in or external microphone), you can record your own sound effects and narration. You can also import sounds from other sources in any of the following formats: the Mac's own **SND** resources, **SoundEdit** or SoundEdit Pro files, Audio IFF or compressed IFF (**AIFF** or AIFFc), Amiga IFF, and Waveform Audio (PC/Windows .WAV) sound file formats.

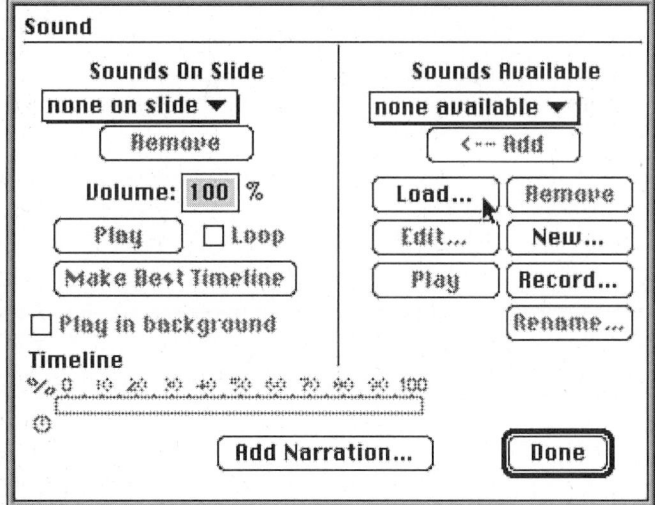

You must load a sound into memory before you can work with it. After it's loaded, you can use it anywhere in your presentation, as many times as necessary. Astound's sound tool can be opened from the

toolbar. (The sound tool is represented by the speaker icon.) The left side of the Sound dialog box (see preceding figure) holds the options for the current slide, and the right side lists any sounds currently available in Astound's memory, and gives you options for loading and working with them. To load a sound, click the Load... button to open the Load Sound dialog box.

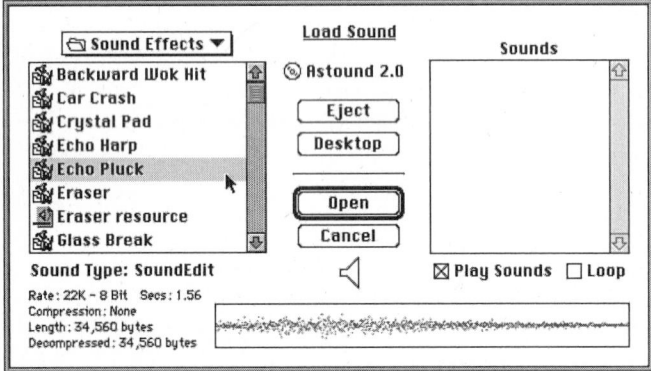

Select the sound you want to use. The Sound's information is displayed at the bottom of the dialog box, and you can hear it by clicking the Play Sounds check box, or the Loop box to hear it repeated continuously. To change the volume, click the speaker icon. The number of sound waves shown indicates the relative volume level (1–3). Clicking the Open button adds it to the list of sounds available on the right side of the dialog box.

To add a sound to a slide, return to the Sound dialog box. Select a sound and click the Add button. Enter the percentage of volume for playback, and adjust the timeline for the length of time the sound should last. Click Done. The sound will play when the slide comes on.

To add sound across multiple slides, select the slides while you're looking at the presentation in Slide Sorter view and then open the Sound dialog box. Select the sound and click the Add button. The sound is added to the slide(s) selected. To make it play uninterrupted, be sure the Play in background check box is enabled. If the sound file isn't long enough, enable the Loop

check box. Click Done. The sound will play during the selected slides.

The Sound Editor function enables you to edit existing sounds and record new ones. To open it, select Edit or New from the Sound dialog box. The sound is represented by its wave shape. You can select a piece of it by dragging a marquee around the desired section with the mouse, and can use the Cut, Copy, and Paste commands to shorten or lengthen it.

To insert silence in the middle of a sound, click the Command button. It is located on the bottom right side of the sound edit window, and marked with the cloverleaf command symbol (⌘). Clicking it opens a pop-up menu of sound editing commands. Select the place where you want the silence, and select Silence... from the pop-up menu. The selected piece of sound is replaced with silence. As an alternative, you can add blank space, which is silent, without cutting any of the sound. Select the insertion point, and choose Insert Blank Space from the pop-up menu. Enter the length of time for the silence in the window that appears.

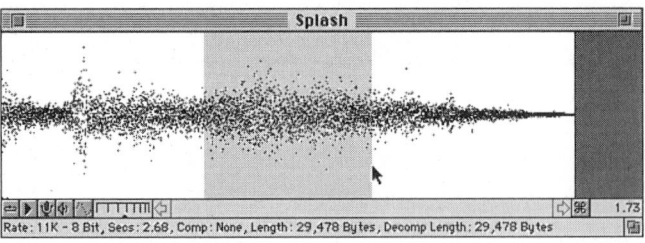

To record new sounds, return to the Sound dialog box and click the Record button to open the Sound Recording options and Record boxes. The Options box selects the input device and the format. Higher sample rates and sizes sound better but use more memory. The Record box has tape recorder style buttons. Click Record, Stop, and Play as needed.

To record narration over your slides, click the Add Narration button in the Sound dialog box. Choose whether to add it to the current slide only or to the whole presentation. When ready, click the Begin button. A record level indicator appears on the screen. Start talking. Use the spacebar to toggle the recording on and off. When you're done, if the presentation is still playing, press the Esc key to bail out.

See Also
Astound; Claris Impact; Multimedia; Presentation Software; Sound Control Panel

Press

You can press an item on-screen by using the **mouse** to place the arrow pointer over the item, and pressing the **mouse** button. When you need to access a **menu**, you press and hold the mouse button until the menu pops down for you to make a selection. You can use the mouse to press buttons in dialog boxes by moving the **arrow pointer** over a button and pressing the mouse button.

See Also
Arrow Pointer; Menu; Mouse; Selecting Items

Press Any Key

If you have a **PowerBook** and it is in **sleep mode**, you can awaken the PowerBook for use by pressing any key. Any key is not an individual key on your keyboard, it is an actual reference to pressing any key on the keyboard. For example, if your PowerBook is in sleep mode you can wake it by pressing the L key, or the R key, a number, a letter, return, delete, it doesn't matter, literally pressing any key will wake the computer. Don't worry, the key you press will only act to wake the PowerBook, it will not perform an action, so if you press the letter M to wake the PowerBook, and you had a word processor open, rest assured that it will not type a letter M in your document.

If you are using a **desktop Mac model** and you use a **screen saver** to protect your screen from burn-in, you can also press any key to deactivate the screen saver and return your screen to normal operation.

See Also
Desktop Models, Macintosh Family; PowerBook; Screen Saver; Sleep Mode

Press Form, *See Prepress*

Previous File (Keyboard Shortcut)

If you're viewing the contents of an active **window** in a **list view**, you can move backwards alphabetically through the files and folders in the list by using the keyboard shortcut Shift-Tab. For example, if you're using the **tab key** to move alphabetically through a window's list of contents, and you pass an item you're looking for, you can use the keyboard shortcut Shift-Tab to move backwards alphabetically to previous file in the list. Each time you press Shift-Tab it moves backward alphabetically one file at a time.

See Also
Keyboard Shortcuts; Tab Key; Window

Primes (Keyboard Shortcut)

The keyboard shortcut for the Prime symbol is found by pressing the apostrophe key while disabling any type of curly quote or typographer's quotes feature. The double Prime symbol is found by using Shift-Apostrophe key, also while any curly quote or typographer's quotes feature are disabled. There is some disagreement whether these symbols should be italicized (Command) to be correct Prime symbols, so you may see Prime symbols used both ways.

See Also
Desktop, The; Keyboard Shortcuts; Open Command

P

Prince of Persia

From Brøderbund, Prince of Persia I, II, and soon III, are fairly typical "fight your way through the maze and rescue the princess" games. The art and animation places them a cut above average. Cut is a good word, too, when the prince lands on a trap full of sharp knives or gets run through by a scimitar. Death is frequent and graphic in these arcade-style games. Parental attention is advised, especially for younger players.

See Also

Arcade-Style Games; Entertainment

Print Catalog Command

This command, available only in System 6.x, enables you to print the contents of all open windows on the **Desktop**, even if the window is not the **active window.**

To use Print Catalog, select Print Catalog from the File menu at the desktop.

See Also

Active Window; Desktop

Print Command

When you want to print a document, use the Print command found on the **File menu** (⌘-P) to tell the program how many copies you want, which pages to print, and other necessary printing information. When you select Print, a print **dialog box** is displayed, as shown in the figure. Each program's print dialog box may look somewhat different, depending on the program and which printer you're using, but they all share similar characteristics.

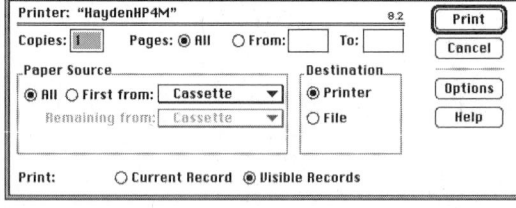

Most Print dialog boxes ask you how many copies you want and if you want to print all of the pages in your document or just print a range, such as pages five through eight. Often there is a **radio button** or check box asking you to select the quality of print output from draft to best quality. The dialog box often asks if your paper source is a paper cartridge or you are going to manually feed the paper into the printer. These and many more choices are often available in the Print dialog box. One thing is consistent; after you've made your selections for number of copies, page range, and so on, you click the button "Print" to start the print cycle in motion.

As you're printing, often a status bar appears to show the progress of your printing, moving from left to right as your document nears completion. You can cancel your print job at any time during this period by pressing ⌘-. on your keyboard or clicking a **Cancel** button on the status bar, if one is available.

To print a document, follow these steps:

1. While the document is in the active window, select Print from the File menu (⌘-P).

2. When the print dialog box appears, enter the number of copies of your document you want and which pages are to be printed. There may be other questions to be answered; read the entire dialog box.

3. When you've entered the information, click Print.

4. A number of applications now have a Print One Copy command that's a real time-saver. This command lets you print one copy of the current document without having to go into a Print dialog box. Print One Copy is found under the File menu of certain applications. Apple's SimpleText is an example of an application that has the Print One Copy command.

See Also

Cancel Keyboard Shortcut; File Menu; Radio Buttons

Print Desktop Command

If you're at the **desktop** and have no windows active, you can print a screen capture of your desktop using the Print Desktop command. To find the Print Desktop command, click the desktop (making the desktop active), or close all open windows, and look on the **File menu.** The command that used to say **Print Window** has now changed to Print Desktop. Select Print Desktop and the standard Print dialog box appears. To print the desktop, click Print.

To Print your desktop, follow these steps:

1. At the Finder level, click the desktop or close all open windows, either of which makes the desktop active.

2. Select Print Desktop from the File menu.

3. Enter the desired number of copies in the Print dialog box and click Print.

See Also

Desktop, The; File Menu; Print Window Command

Print Dialog Box

When you select Print on the **File Menu** (⌘-P), a print dialog box appears, as shown in the figure. Different program's might have different print dialog boxes depending on the program and printer you're using, but they all share similar characteristics.

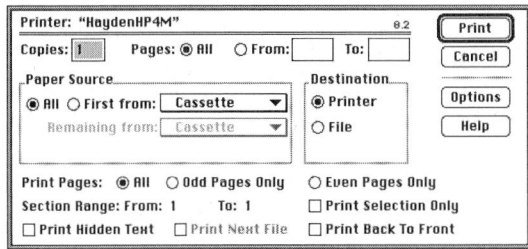

Most print dialog boxes ask you how many copies you want, and whether you want to print all the pages in your document or just a range, such as pages five to eight. Often there is a **radio button** or check box asking you to select the quality of print output from draft to best quality. Often you are asked if your paper source is a paper cartridge or paper you're going to manually feed the printer. These and many more choices are available in a print dialog box. One thing is consistent; after you've made your selections for number of copies, page range, and so on, you click the button "Print" to start printing.

If you have a fax/modem, which can send faxes directly from your computer, these are often partially controlled from the Print dialog box. Some popular fax/modem software, for example, enables you to access a fax command by holding down the Option key, which changes the Print command change to the Fax command. You still will use the Print dialog box, but instead of printing the page out to paper, it now prints it to an electronic file sent by modem as if it were faxed from a traditional fax machine.

See Also

File Menu; Radio Buttons

Print Monitor Extension

This extension enables the user to print documents in the background while working on a different application in the foreground. The Print Monitor works in the background unless there is a problem that needs attention or you select Print Monitor from the **Application menu** while a document is being printed in the background. **Background printing** is enabled from within the **Chooser** on the **Apple menu**.

See Also

Apple Menu; Application Menu; Background Printing; Chooser

Print Options Box

The Options button in the **print dialog box** (⌘-P) brings up a dialog box enabling you to specify certain options for printing, page orientation, and so on. The particular set of options you see, and the layout of the print Options dialog box itself, vary depending on the printer you are using. The print Options dialog box is usually accessed by clicking the Options button in the Print dialog box.

Each printer has it's own set of options. If, for example, you're printing to an Apple StyleWriter II and you click the Print Options box, it opens a dialog enabling you to choose to clean the ink cartridge before it prints the job.

If you're using a LaserWriter, you'll be greeted with a wider range of options. You might, for example, have the choice of adding a cover page (before or after the document), of choosing between a black-and-white, color/grayscale, or calibrated color/grayscale. And you may be able to request special reporting for PostScript errors.

Some applications have their own customized print dialog boxes that add a wide array of choices. Applications such as QuarkXPress and Adobe PageMaker have added their own print dialog boxes, and their print options include things such as tiling large documents, printing non-consecutive pages, adding copy marks and registration marks for use by a print shop, printing negatives, choosing which colors will print, and a wide array of specific options that would not be available in a standard Print dialog box.

When your desired options are set, click the OK button, which returns you to the Print dialog box. From there you can click OK to start printing.

See Also

Print Dialog Box; Printing

Print Server

If you're on a network with users who all use the same printer, or a number of different printers, a print server acts as a storage device for spooled files and as a printing traffic manager for sending jobs to the selected printers in the background for you. A print server works something like Apple's **background printing**, but instead of spooling the print files to your own computer, the files are spooled to a print server that holds and directs the files to the proper printer for you.

To use background printing, you don't have to be connected to a network. The spooled file is stored on your computer until it is printed. However, network users can take advantage of a Print Server and have the spooled files stored on the print server until they are printed.

See Also

Background Printing; Printing; Spooler

Print Spooler

A print spooler enables you to **print** documents in the background by making a temporary copy of your document and sending the copy to the printer. Your document prints in the background while you continue to work in the foreground. This copy is referred to as being spooled. Print spooling is used with Apple's **background printing** and with a **print server** that spools files over a **network**. There are a number of third-party spoolers available that enable background printing and management of spooled documents to be printed.

See Also

Background Printing; Chooser DA; Networking; Print Command; Spool File

Print Window Command

This command enables you to print the active window in the **Finder.** The Print Window command is found on the **File menu.** To print a window, open the window you want to have printed, select Print Window from the File menu, enter the number of copies you want to print, and click Print. This command prints the entire contents of the selected window, even if you cannot see the entire contents on your screen without scrolling. The Print Window command prints the window in the **view** format you have selected. If, for example, you have your window view set to icon view, your window prints the icon view. If you have the view set to **view by name,** that view prints.

To print a window, follow these steps:

1. On the Finder level, open the window you want to print.

2. Select Print Window from the File menu. (This command appears only when a window is active.)

3. Enter the desired number of copies in the Print dialog box and click Print.

See Also
File Menu; Finder; Print Desktop Command

Printer Descriptions (PPDs)

A number of applications, especially graphics-related applications, ship with an installed list of printer descriptions designed to be used with that particular application. Many of these printer description files (called PPDs) can be accessed through the Chooser (Apple includes printer drivers for most of its printers with the operating system); others are built into the Print dialog box of the application.

By having printer descriptions built into the application, the software developer can have the printer take advantage of special printing features included in the application, such as the capability to print non-consecutive pages, or to tile large images onto multiple sheets of paper to be pasted together to make a full-sized image. If, for example, you're using Adobe PageMaker and select the **Print command**, the Print dialog box offers a **pop-up menu** of printer descriptions for you to choose from. **Click** and hold to find the name of your printer and select it as your printer description. By making this selection, the application now knows which printer you'll be using and can take advantage of any special printing features PageMaker offers.

See Also
Pop-Up Menu; PostScript; Print Command

Printer Drivers

A printer driver is the intermediary program that translates the QuickDraw commands used by the application to specify how a document should look into commands that can be used by a specific printer to print the document. Each printer has its own printer page description file (PPD) that tells the printer driver about specific features of that printer. These features, in turn, are displayed on the **Page Setup** and **Print** dialog boxes in all programs.

The application program does not speak directly to the printer driver, but uses the resources of the System's **Printer Manager** to pass the QuickDraw-based document appearance specifications to the printer driver you selected via a system utility called the **Chooser**. By dividing the responsibilities for printing between the application program and the System, the application program does not have to have its own printing routines for each printer. The application uses QuickDraw and the printer drivers translate QuickDraw into the specific language used by its printer. By using printer drivers, the Macintosh maintains its important consistent interface between programs.

The Printer Driver also provides the Page Setup and Print dialogs used in the application program to initiate the printing process.

System 7 upgraded the LaserWriter printer driver, changing the **Page Setup** and **Print** dialog boxes to include an increased variety of paper sizes and types, including envelopes. The Version 8.3 driver also creates a desktop printer (as displayed in the illustration below) that you can use to drag and drop files from the desktop to the printer without having to actually open the application. The desktop printer also manages the print job in the same fashion as the Print Monitor did in older versions of the LaserWriter driver.

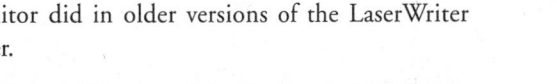

The introduction of QuickDraw GX in 1994, further enhanced the Macintosh printing experience by allowing the printing of individual page sizes and formats, partial pages, unique page sizes, and an easy way to specify different printers for different portions of a project (for example an inkjet for proofing and an imagesetter for final output). In 1995, Apple introduced new printer drivers, **LaserWriter 8.3, StyleWriter 1200, 2200, 2400,** and **2500,** that incorporated many of the printer features of QuickDraw GX.

See Also

Desktop Printing; Portable Document; Print Command; QuickDraw GX

Printer Fonts

If you're using Type 1 PostScript fonts, there are two files necessary for viewing and **printing** the **font**: A screen font and a printer font.

The screen font, whose **icon** appears to be a small suitcase with the letter "A" on its side as shown in the figure, contains bit-mapped versions of the font that are used by the Macintosh to display the typeface on the screen, henceforth the name screen fonts. These bit-mapped fonts are designed for viewing on-screen (where the resolution of your monitor is 72 dots per inch), but if you tried to print screen fonts on a 300-dots-per-inch laser printer, the fonts would seem jaggy and be unacceptable as they're resolution (dpi) is too low. That's where printer fonts come in.

The printer font, shown in the figure, contains the mathematical PostScript instructions that any PostScript printer needs to create clean, smooth outlines for printing the font. If you have a PostScript-compatible printer, this

printer font is actually downloaded from your computer to your printer during the print cycle.

Both the screen font and the printer font should be together in the Fonts folder (within the System Folder), or together in a separate folder outside the System Folder if you're using a font management utility such as Suitcase (from Symantec) or Master Juggler (from Alsoft). The printer font is also used by Adobe Type Manager, a very popular font utility from Adobe Systems, which enables users to view and resize **fonts** to any size on-screen, or print to non-PostScript printers without having the fonts print jagged.

Apple invented their own font technology called TrueType, which is designed to use just one part (a printer font and screen font in just one suitcase) that can be resized, viewed on-screen, and printed without any jaggies. The capability to use TrueType fonts is built into System 7 and higher, but you can also use TrueType fonts with System 6.07 or 6.08 by adding Apple's TrueType extension to the system. Although TrueType didn't unseed PostScript Type 1 fonts as the standard on the Mac, Apple did license the TrueType technology to Microsoft for use on the PC platform with Windows 3.1, and TrueType is now the font standard on the PC platform.

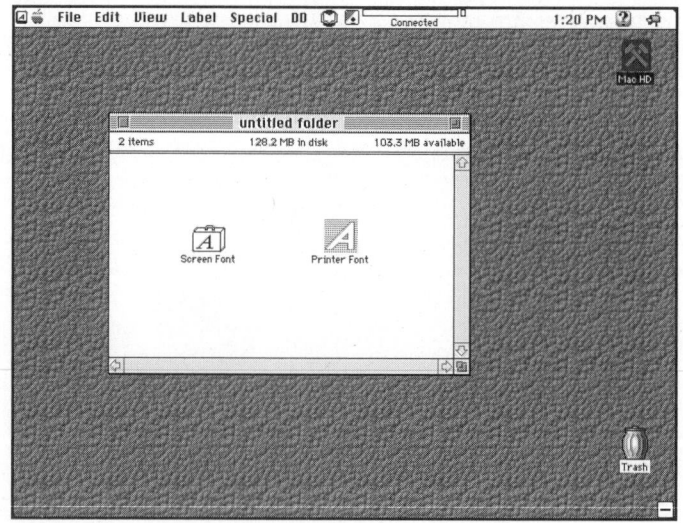

QuickDraw GX, an enhanced printing and font technology from Apple released in System 7.5 and higher, introduces a new font format called GX fonts. These GX fonts enable users to employ advanced typographic features such as ligatures and precise kerning. Like TrueType, GX fonts use only one part (not a separate screen and printer font), and they have a special version of Adobe Type Manager called ATM GX designed to enhanced display and printing features. QuickDraw GX is a part of System 7.5 but requires a separate installation and is not installed during a standard installation.

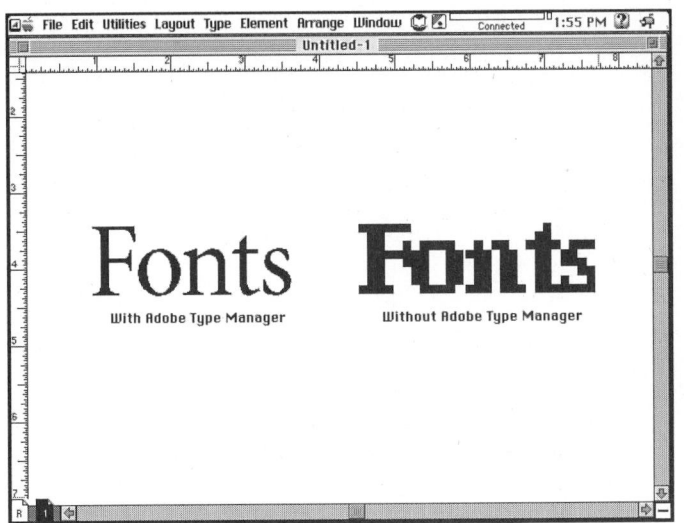

See Also
Fonts; Icons; Printing; QuickDraw GX

Printer Page Description Document (PPD), *See PostScript Level 2*

Printer Port, *See Serial Port*

Printers, Color

There are many color printers on the market. They range in price from "personal printers" under $500 to high-end publishing tools that can cost over $10,000. The cost per page for color output also is higher than that for monochrome output. Laser and inkjet printers based their resource usage (the amount

of toner required per page) on a budget of five percent of a page. Thermal Wax output costs more because each page uses a new ink ribbon, regardless of its contents. Pages can cost up to $25 to $50 with these high-end printers, although they cost less if you are printing onto transparencies that use more wax pigments to cover the page, and so produce less waste.

In the table that follows, notice that there is a significant difference in the speed with which a printer can print black-and-white pages (often 4 to 16 pages per minute) versus colored pages (which can take several minutes per page). Producing colored images takes more processing time for the RIP, because it must calculate how much cyan, yellow, magenta, and black to apply to create the colors on your screen. The printer takes longer as well, since even single-pass systems take longer to apply four colors than to apply one color.

PostScript Options for Color Printers
Some use the Macintosh as the controller, such as the color inkjets, others are more expensive because they contain a PostScript RIP. You can also add a software PostScript RIP to your Mac by installing TeleTypesetting Company's T-Script. This is a software-based PostScript interpreter that runs on your Mac. Another option available for Apple's inkjets is a true Adobe PostScript Level 2 interpreter that runs on the Mac. Hewlett-Packard sells a PostScript RIP driver kit for the DeskWriter 560c. Each of these interpreters lets you print encapsulated PostScript illustrations, such as those from Adobe Illustrator or Macromedia FreeHand, on your color printer even if it does not contain a PostScript RIP. Another option is to use software that turns your Mac into a print server, such as GDT Softworks StyleScript. High-end color printers rely on Adobe's Configurable PostScript Interpreter (CPSI) to process color PostScript print jobs and send them to printers.

The following table provides an overview of the kinds of color printers available at different price ranges. Note that this list is not exhaustive and that the technology is changing constantly.

Color Printers for the Macintosh

Type of Printer	Manufacturer	Model Name	Features	Street Price
Color Inkjet	Apple	Color StyleWriter 2200	Portable 720 by 360 dpi monochrome, 360 dpi color printer	$419
Color Inkjet	Apple	Color StyleWriter 2400	Color and Black cartridges, 360 dpi	$525
Color Inkjet	Epson America	Stylus Pro	720 dpi, 1 ppm, Ethernet option	$849 w/ software RIP for Mac
Color Inkjet	Hewlett-Packard	DeskJet 340cm	600 by 300 dpi, 3 ppm, 30 sheet feeder, HP ColorSmart and RET technologies	$299
Color Inkjet	Hewlett-Packard	DeskJet 850c	300 dpi, 1 ppm, Ethernet optional	$499
Color Inkjet	Hewlett-Packard	DeskJet 1600CM	300 dpi, 6M RAM, 2 ppm, Ethernet standard, PostScript standard	$1,999
Color Inkjet	Hewlett-Packard	DeskJet 855c	600 dpi, 3 ppm color, 7 ppm black, ColorSmart and Color RET technologies	$498
Color Inkjet	Hewlett-Packard	DeskWriter 660c	600 dpi, 1.5 ppm, 27 Scaleable fonts, 512K RAM	$379
Color Inkjet	Lexmark	Color Jetprinter 4079 Plus	360 dpi, 4M RAM, 1 ppm, Ethernet optional, PostScript standard	$2,699
Color PostScript Laser	Lexmark	Optra C	600 dpi, 8M RAM, 3 ppm, Ethernet optional	$6,400

Type of Printer	Manufacturer	Model Name	Features	Street Price
Color PostScript Laser	QMS	Magicolor CX/32	600 dpi, 32M RAM, 6 ppm, Ethernet standard	$7,999
Color PostScript Laser	Tektronix	Phaser 550	600 dpi, 8M RAM, 4 ppm, Ethernet optional	$6,995
Color PostScript Laser	Xerox	XPrint 4925	600 dpi, 24M RAM, 3 ppm, Ethernet optional	$8,546
Color Thermal Wax	Fargo	Pictura 310e	300 dpi, 4 ppm, Ethernet standard	$5,995 w/ software RIP for Mac
Color Thermal Wax	Fargo	Primera Pro	600 by 300 dpi, 1.5 ppm, Ethernet optional	$1,895 w/ software RIP for Mac
Color Thermal Wax	General Parametrics	Spectra*Star 240	300 dpi, 6M RAM, 2ppm, Ethernet optional, PostScript standard	$2,795
Color Thermal Wax	General Parametrics	Spectra*Star 280	600 by 300 dpi, 10M RAM, 2 ppm, Ethernet optional, PostScript standard	$3,650
Color Workgroup Printers	Apple	Color LaserWriter 12/600 PS	600 dpi, 12M RAM, 3 ppm, Ethernet standard	$6989
Dye sublimation	Fargo Electronics	Pictura 310	300 dpi, Adobe Configurable PostScript Interpreter (CPSI) server program optional	$4,995
Dye sublimation	General Parametrics	SpectraStar DSx	600 by 300 dpi, color image setter, PostScript standard	$7,695
Dye Sublimation	Nikon Electronic Imaging	Nikon Coolprint	300 dpi, Adobe Configurable PostScript Interpreter (CPSI) server program optional	$2,350
Dye sublimation	Seiko Instruments	Professional Colorprint	300 dpi, combination dye-sub and thermal-wax technologies	under $10,000

See Also
Printers, Color PostScript; Printers, InkJet; Printing Technology, Color

Printers, Color PostScript

Most color printers contain RISC processors, ROM-based fonts, and PostScript interpreters and many megabytes of RAM, some printers depend on a print server system where software—typically Adobe's **Configurable PostScript Interpreter (CPSI)** resides. CPSI turns the Mac it resides on into a PostScript controller that converts the PostScript commands that describes the print job, generates a bitmapped image of the document, and transmits it via SCSI or parallel cable to the printer.

CPSI can run on a Mac Quadra 950, but performance is greatly enhanced if you run the software on a PowerMac, such as a 7200 or 7500 with at least 40MB of RAM. CPSI requires a minimum of 6MB of RAM, but its performance is extra slow until you add at least 24MB of RAM. Many service bureaus run CPSI on Macs configured with 96MB of RAM. Some printers require that you print your documents to disk at PostScript files and then process these files through CPSI. In this case it is important to indicate on the original document which type of printer it will run on, or CPSI will not recognize it as a PostScript file.

See Also
PostScript Level 2; Print Server

Printers, Connecting to Non-Macintosh Laser

The Macintosh can run on non-Macintosh compatible laser printers, especially the popular HP LaserJets. The LaserJet uses the Macintosh's QuickDraw routines to convert bitmap graphics and text to images that can be printed by the laser. The HP uses its standard font cartridges, which are interpreted by special Macintosh software.

The easiest way to connect a Macintosh to an HP LaserJet is to add LocalTalk and PostScript to the printer. LocalTalk is the Macintosh's implementation of AppleTalk network protocol, which is built into every Macintosh. HP markets a LocalTalk port called an Interface Kit for AppleTalk/HP LaserJet. You can also run the printer off of an external bridging device. You can install PostScript by using a PostScript font cartridge or use a PostScript emulator software on your Macintosh.

Pacific Data Product markets PacificTalk and Extended Systems markets BridgePort, two good external LocalTalk bridging devices, which appear on the **Chooser** in the Macintosh, enabling you to select the LaserJet as the printer.

Freedom of the Press from Custom Applications is a PostScript emulator software package that runs on your Macintosh to simulate the behavior of PostScript. Custom also markets a less expensive, slimmed down version of Freedom of the Press, called Freedom of the Press Light. This lighter version, when operating with Adobe Type Manager or TrueType, provides extensive font support.

If you are not running on a network, you use a Macintosh printer driver to connect to the LaserJet. Insight Development markets MacPrint bundled with the required serial port cable you need to hook into the HP printer. MacPrint uses QuickDraw to convert fonts to bitmapped images for the printer and supports dozens of HP cartridges, as well as the built-in fonts that come with the laser. You cannot use a PostScript font cartridge when using MacPrint. The package also includes a utility called Font Mapper that creates bitmapped screen fonts corresponding to the HP's cartridge fonts. It supports 63 cartridges and internal LaserJet fonts. With TrueType you do not need to use this utility.

JetLink Express from GDT Softworks is a similar product to MacPrint, but supports Type 1 and 3 fonts and automatic font substitutions. Its printer driver supports Apple's Communications Toolbox, which is part of System 7. Grappler from Orange Micro is another printer driver software package.

These non-Macintosh options are not as fast as PostScript or QuickDraw laser printer performance, but enable you to run Macintoshes in personal computer environments.

See Also

PostScript; Printers, InkJet

Printers, Dot-Matrix

The basic dot-matrix for the Macintosh is manufactured by Apple and is called the ImageWriter II (the ImageWriter is now obsolete).

The ImageWriter II contains a slot for an AppleTalk card to hook up the printer for sharing on a network, and has a better paper feed mechanism than the original ImageWriter. The ImageWriter II provides high-quality dot-matrix printing because it uses nine very small pins in its print head.

Apple also manufactured a 27-pin print head printer it called the ImageWriter LQ, which was not successful because of its awkward use of fonts three-times larger than the specified font to generate its bitmap images, and other printing problems. The printer has been discontinued.

Other vendors also manufacture dot-matrix printers, which will operate with QuickDraw on the Macintosh. Seikosha markets the SP-1000AP made by Epson and Seiko. This is a highly reliable, inexpensive printer that uses Tandy ribbons and parts. The printer is quiet, but relatively slow (15 characters per second) versus the ImageWriter's 45 characters per second. The upside of this lack of speed is the precision of its printing quality. Olympia markets the NP30APL, which is more expensive than the Seikosha, but cheaper than the Apple printer. The performance of the Olympia is close to that of the ImageWriter I. The NP30APL also runs off of personal computers.

The Macintosh is compatible with the Epson LQ family of impact printers. All that you need is a serial port on the printer (this may be optional), an Epson printer driver software, and the proper cable (the same cable used to connect the ImageWriter I to the Macintosh). Toshiba America Information Systems, Inc. markets MacMatrix, a Macintosh printer driver that can be used with any of its four 24-pin dot-matrix impact printers, which also run off of personal computers.

PrintLink Collection from GDT Softworks is a collection of Macintosh printer drivers that enable you to interconnect your Macintosh to hundreds of 24-pin and 9-pin printers, including those made by Okidata, NEC, Epson, Diconix, and Panasonic. The package also includes the cable you need to complete the hook up.

Compatibility of Macs with Non-Apple Dot-Matrix Printers: A Warning

The top margin of non-Apple dot-matrix printers is not compatible with the ImageWriter printer driver's code. A solution is to reset the margins in your documents to .67 inches (four lines from the top) and 1.33 inches on the bottom (eight lines) so that you do not have to waste the first page of paper and manually wind the second page to the top of the print head each time you print (a standard personal computer activity).

See Also

Printing, Technology, Dot-Matrix; Printers, Connecting to Non-Macintosh Laser

Printers, Hardware Issues

Before the advent of the Macintosh with its **WYSIWYG** environment and graphical user interface, displaying a document and printing it were two separate operations. Because the WYSIWYG screen display uses similar technologies to that used in printing a document, this is no longer true. **QuickDraw** guides both processes, ensuring that both text and graphics are drawn as specified.

Before the advent of desktop publishing and electronic typesetting, computer users used the term *letter-quality* to define their printing requirements. Letter quality meant output that looked typewritten. Printers that produced this output were called formed-letter printers and used actual metal or plastic type brushed with ink, which was pressed into the paper. Some of the type cartridges were removable, which allowed you to slightly vary your type characters, but they all looked typewritten versus typeset. Today, because users have seen examples of computer output that looks like it was typeset, letter-quality has come to refer to high-quality dot-matrix printing. The Macintosh has changed users' perceptions of what is acceptable output.

The Macintosh was sold originally with a dot-matrix printer called the ImageWriter. In 1986, Apple replaced the first ImageWriter with an updated one called the ImageWriter II, which included a connection for sharing the printer over a network. As time progressed, users required a higher quality, faster, quieter printing process for the Macintosh's graphics and text. Vendors introduced laser printers, which increased the quality of the output. These lasers used either Adobe's **PostScript** page description language to rasterize fonts, or more recently, use the Macintosh's QuickDraw to rasterize their images. Vendors have also developed bridges to enable Macintosh to print on non-PostScript

laser printers, thermal printers, and ink jet printers. Color QuickDraw and PostScript Level 2 has been used to enable Macintoshes to print out in color, as well. Lastly, the Macintosh also supports high-end electronic typesetters, such as Linotronics, to produce extremely high-quality but expensive print-outs.

Today, printers are proliferating so fast and the technology for electronic typesetting is developing at such a rapid rate that truly paperless publishing is becoming more of a reality rather than hyperbole. The following table provides an overview of the types of printers and their features available to Macintosh users.

Macintosh Printer Features

Printer Type	Features	Price Range	Suggested Usefulness
Dot-matrix	144 dpi, print wires and ribbon-based	under $200	printing mailing labels or any other print job that requires continuous-feed paper stock. Does not support individual paper sheets or envelopes.
InkJet	360 to 720 dpi, microscopic nozzles spray solid or liquid ink, uses Mac to control print job; can support a software-based PostScript RIP	$200 to $500	Home computing, draft printing, mailing labels or low-quality printing jobs, limited paper-stock weights supported.
QuickDraw Laser printers	300 to 600 dpi, photocopier technology that uses the Mac to control the printing process	under $700	Good for printing text-heavy documents that do not rely on encapsulated PostScript for graphics and lack emulators for other printers so can only be used with Macs.
PostScript Laser printers	300 to 1,200 dpi, photocopier technology uses on-board computer to control printing	under $1,000 and up	Desktop publishing and proofing output due to high resolution and accuracy of font and image reproduction.
Color printers; Color Laser, Thermal-Wax, Dye-Sublimation, Color InkJet, and Hybrid Color Imagesetters	300 dpi on up to 1200 dpi	$500 on up	Color presentations using transparencies or film or business graphics, proofing color publications, scanned images and illustrations before submitting to four-color printing processes.

See Also

PostScript; Printing, Color; Printers, InkJet; Printers, QuickDraw; Printers, Workgroup

Printers, InkJet

In 1990, Apple introduced the StyleWriter inkjet printer which is based upon the Canon BJ-10e Bubble-Jet. The lightweight StyleWriter provides a 360-dpi resolution for the same price as the ImageWriter II. The printer performs slightly slower than the dot-matrix printer, (half a page per minute in best mode) but is much quieter. Ink cartridges cost about $22.99 and last for up to 500 pages of letter-size paper. The printer requires high-grade cotton bond paper to perform at its highest levels.

Today, there are many inkjet printers priced under $300. Inkjets use the Mac's QuickDraw routines to perform the calculations needed to print a document, and therefore contain relatively simple mechanisms for printing. Inkjets use a disposable print head that contains a supply of water-based ink connected to an array of microscopic nozzles. The print head moves right to left across a page spraying dots through the nozzles. Today's technology is such that inkjet printers can print to a precision of 720 by 600 dots per inch (dpi). The downside of this precision is that on plain paper, the ink spreads causing fuzzy output. The best quality output requires that you use special coated papers that do not absorb the ink.

Hewlett-Packard manufactures the DeskWriter 520 inkjet printer which produces output at a resolution of 600 by 300 dpi on plain paper by using a print head consisting of 50 jet heads (the horizontal resolution is achieved by finely controlling the left to right position of the print head via HP's **Resolution Enhancement Technology (RET)** that smoothes character edges by adjusting the position of the dots (dithering). The HP DeskWriter uses its own set of outline fonts (Helvetica, Courier, Times, and Symbol) and you can upgrade the fonts to include the rest of the 35 Apple fonts. The HP printer has a very economical footprint and contains a recessed cable well enabling you to place it against a wall. The HP is slower than most laser printers, but very quiet. The ink is water-soluble, which makes it prone to smearing if the paper gets wet. The HP DeskWriter also comes with an AppleTalk connection enabling you to share it among several Macintoshes on a network. The DeskWriter automatically senses envelopes and adjusts its print head to accommodate the extra thickness, making it a superior office machine.

The Apple StyleWriter series is slightly cheaper than HP's DeskWriter series price tag, but it produces a similar quality output with 360 dpi and a smaller weight and footprint for the printer mechanism. There are currently four StyleWriters: 1200, 2200, 2400, and 2500, each associated with a different market niche. The StyleWriter 1200 is the printer for low-end use. It is a monochrome printer that provides good quality output at 720 dpi. The StyleWriter 2200 can be run on batteries and is color-capable (meaning that you can add a color cartridge to allow this printer to produce spot color output). The StyleWriter 2400 is a color inkjet that produces 720 by 380 dpi output via two cartridges—a black and a three-color cartridge. You can also replace both cartridges with Apple's high-performance Ink Cartridge that increases the speed and quality of the output considerably for monochrome printing.

Brother International manufactures the HJ-400. This printer is not the best option, because it does not handle grayscale printing.

Another cheaper alternative to inkjet printing is purchasing the standard HP DeskJet Plus along with GDT Softwork's JetLink Express software. The JetLink software enables you to run all of HP's laser and inkjet printers off of your Macintosh. The package also comes with the cables required to connect your Macintosh and the same outline fonts as come with the DeskWriter. The DeskJet is the generic HP inkjet printer, and therefore is much cheaper than the DeskWriter which has been modified for use with the Macintosh.

Kodak markets the Diconix M150 portable inkjet printer which runs on nickel-cadmium batteries and is the size of a thick novel. GCC markets the Diconix M150 as the WriteMove and bundles it with BitStream TrueType fonts. The Kodak Diconix printer has been upgraded to the M150 Plus and bundled with Adobe Type Manager and 13 Type 1 fonts in residence. Both Diconix printers print at resolutions of 192 dpi and weigh 3 3/4 pounds, including batteries.

The following table provides an overview of monochrome inkjet printers available for the Macintosh. The list is by no means exhaustive.

See Also
Printing Technology, InkJet

Printers, PostScript Lasers

In 1985, Apple introduced the first laser printer to incorporate PostScript. It was called the LaserWriter and was based upon the Canon CX engine. Apple upgraded the LaserWriter's engine to a higher-level Canon engine and added PostScript version 47, naming the upgrade the LaserWriter Plus. Both the LaserWriter and LaserWriter Plus were configured with 1.5MB of RAM which limited their capability to use downloaded fonts.

Apple next introduced the LaserWriter II family, based upon Canon's second generation of printer engines, the SX. The LaserWriter IINT was the lowest level of PostScript laser in this family. It was built around the Motorola 68000 chip running at 12 MHz. It came

with 11 resident Type 1 fonts. The next level of performance was provided by the LaserWriter IINTX which is based upon the 68020 chip and was configured with 2MB of RAM, expandable up to 12MB. The NTX also came with 11 resident fonts, but you could connect a hard disk to the printer's SCSI port to store additional fonts. These printers are discontinued.

Today, Apple manufactures a range of PostScript Laser printers to fit every marketing niche. The LaserWriter 4/600 PS is the grandson of Apple's original PostScript laser printers. This printer is marketed for home office users and provides PostScript Level 2 laser printing with 64 resident PostScript and TrueType fonts and can be upgraded from 2 to 4MB of RAM.

Today's PostScript laser printers are based on RISC processors that provide enhanced performance at lower costs. Adobe is not the only producer of PostScript, since third-party vendors have created clones that interpret PostScript commands for their printers.

PostScript printers have proliferated on the market. The table on the following page lists "personal lasers"—those which can be connected to up to 32 Macs in small network situations. Note that the list is representative but not exhaustive.

Monochrome InkJet Printers

Manufacturer	Model Name	Features	Street Price
Apple	StyleWriter 1200	Monochrome 720 dpi	$269
Apple	StyleWriter II	Monochrome 360 dpi	$289
Hewlett-Packard	DeskWriter 520	Monochrome 600 by 300 dpi	$365
Hewlett-Packard	DeskWriter 600	600 dpi, optional color print cartridge	$239
Hewlett-Packard	DeskWriter 560c	600 by 300 dpi, color print cartridge, PostScript optional	$259

Personal PostScript Laser Printers

Manufacturer	Model Name	Features	Street Price
Apple	Personal LaserWriter 320	RISC engine, 300 dpi, FinePrint and PhotoGrade (w/memory upgrade)	$949
Apple	LaserWriter Select 360	10 ppm RISC engine, 600 dpi, PostScript Fax option	$1,400
Apple	LaserWriter 4/600 PS	4ppm, 600 dpi, PostScript Fax option	$780
Digital Equipment Corp.	DEClaser 1152	17 fonts, 70 sheet feeder, 300 dpi	$699
Hewlett-Packard	LaserJet 5MP	600 dpi, 3M RAM, 6 ppm, RISC processor	$1,049
Hewlett-Packard	LaserJet 4ML	300 dpi, RISC engine, Printer Control Language	$1,279
NEC	SilentWriter 640	300 dpi, 6 ppm RISC engine, 250 sheet feeder	$799
NEC	SilentWriter 1097	600 dpi, 10 ppm RISC engine, 250 sheet feeder	$1,399
QMS	420 Print System	600 dpi, 70 sheet feeder, 68020 engine	$1,195
Texas Instruments	MicroWriter	23 fonts, 250 sheet feeder, 300 dpi	$799
Texas Instruments	MicroWriter PS65	65 fonts, 250 sheet feeder, 300 dpi	$1,099
Texas Instruments	MicroLaser Pro 600	8 ppm RISC engine, 600 dpi, 2 250 sheet feeders, optional EtherNet	$1,599

See Also

Printers, Color PostScript; Printers, Workgroup

Printers, QuickDraw Lasers

Laser printers that rely on the Macintosh for their processing are called "Personal" or "QuickDraw" printers. With the advent of **Adobe Type Manager** and **TrueType** fonts, this type of printer has become a viable option for work that does not require the printing of extensive graphics. Laser printers print faster than inkjets because their photocopier engines print an entire page at one pass. Most QuickDraw laser printers print four to six pages per minute (the actual performance is based on the complexity of the job, of course). Laser printers give sharper output than inkjet printers because their technology does not depend on spraying ink onto the paper and they often come with software that smoothes character edges and produces sharper halftone images.

Apple manufactures the series of LaserWriter Select QuickDraw Laser printers, each for under $1,000. The $719 LaserWriter Select 360 provides resolution enhancement for both text and graphics (with the addition of 4MB of memory for graphics rendering). Apple PhotoGrade image-enhancement technology sharpens scanned images and fonts. The LaserWriter Select 360 uses a Fuji-built print engine that processes five pages per minute on the average.

See Also

Adobe Type Manager (ATM); Printing Technology, Lasers; TrueType

Printers, Workgroup Lasers

Workgroup printers are the workhorses of organizations. These are printers that must be fast (process at least eight pages per minute), dependable, networkable, and high quality (at least 600 dpi output). These printers also must be able to handle large print jobs, and therefore have a large sheet feed capacity (at least 250 sheets per tray). All of these printers run PostScript Level 2 and come with a LocalTalk connection and at least an option of an EtherNet connection. The following figure displays the QMS 860 Plus, which is a graphics workhorse.

The following table provides an overview of the prices and features available for workgroup printers. Note that this list is not exhaustive as this is a very competitive printer market.

See Also

PostScript Level 2; Printers, PostScript Laser

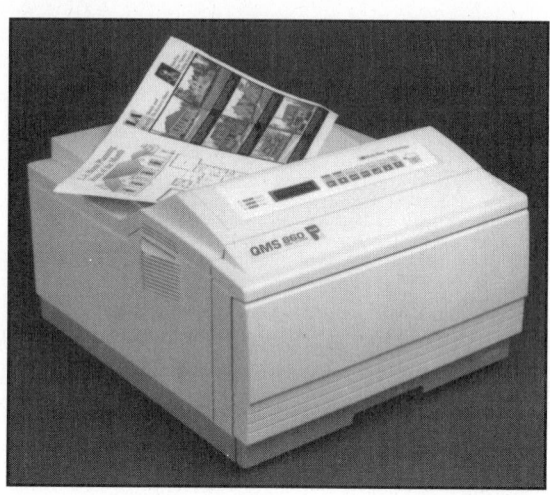

Workgroup PostScript Laser Printers

Manufacturer	*Model Name*	*Features*	*Street Price*
Apple	LaserWriter 16/600 PS	600 dpi, PostScript Fax option, 16 ppm	$2,299
Apple	LaserWriter Pro 810	400 dpi default, capable of 800 dpi; tabloid and legal size printing, 8MB RAM, 20 ppm, EtherNet and PostScript fax standard	$4,899
GCC Technologies	Elite XL 1208 Super Size	1200 dpi, legal size page, RISC engine, 32MB RAM, PostScript standard	$5,999
GCC Technologies	Elite XL 608	600 dpi, 8 ppm, legal size page, RISC engine, 6MB RAM, PostScript standard	$2,399
GCC Technologies	Elite XL 808	800 dpi, 8 ppm, AccuGray technology, RISC engine, 12MB RAM, PostScript standard	$2,999
GCC Technologies	Elite XL 1208	1200 dpi, 8 ppm, AccuGray technology, RISC engine, 24MB RAM, PostScript standard	$4,299
GCC Technologies	Elite XL 616	600 by 300 dpi, 16 ppm, Ethernet standard, RISC engine, PostScript standard	$2,599
Hewlett-Packard	LaserJet 4MV	600 dpi, tabloid-size paper	$3,549
Lexmark	Optra Lx	1200 dpi, legal-size paper	$3,298
DataProducts	Typhoon 20	800 dpi, tabloid-size paper full bleed, optional PostScript fax modem	$4,495
Xante	Accel-a-Writer 8200	1200 dpi (additional RAM upgrade is required), full tabloid-size bleed	$5,299

Printing

Printing is essentially the process of transferring an image to a two-dimensional surface. The operative word is "transferring" because that is how printing differs most markedly from original two-dimensional art. Printing also implies multiple copies, but in digital printing, one copy may be sufficient. Printing is a blend of art and technology. This is true even of older printing techniques such as lithography—practiced now only in fine arts printmaking—but which, not so long ago, was the height of technology. If traditional processes are used, manual skill is necessary to create a paper **mechanical**, operate a process camera, perform prepress procedures, generate **proofs**, make plates, and run the press—not to mention folding and binding. Even the new digital techniques require some manual skill, although not nearly to the extent that older techniques do. There is only slight comparison between operating a mouse and cutting and pasting.

The printing industry is doing very well. In spite of predictions of a paperless society in the future, we are printing things at an unprecedented rate today. The proliferation of books and magazines (and bookstores) is remarkable. In addition, millions of laser, inkjet, and other desktop printers are thrusting out sheet after sheet of printed matter all over the world. There is no longer any doubt that the desktop publishing phenomenon is a vital force driving the printing industry today. Many futurists agree that it is only a matter of time until traditional printing presses, with their noise and harmful chemicals, go the way of linotype machines and other recently viable technologies that people under fifty associate with the remote past. In fact, change is so rapid in the field of electronic publishing that one is hard-pressed to keep up. Newer, better, and (sometimes) cheaper hardware and software appear yearly or even bi-annually. Desktop publishing and printing is hugely popular and is routine in many business and institutional environments. Ironically, graphics industry professionals were slow to embrace the new technology, but one cannot get a job as a graphic designer in the United States today without some level of expertise in graphics and page layout software applications. The Internet is responsible for a new direction in mass communications, but old-fashioned paper printing will no doubt be around for a good while longer.

Conversation with Sandy Benett

Wondering whether the Newton operating system and Apple's Message Pads are succeeding? Sandy Benett, who worked at Go when they were creating a pen-based operating system, is acting Vice President of Apple's Newton Systems Group.

Maclopedia: So you've recently rolled out a new version of the Newton operating system. How is it better than the earlier ones?

Sandy: In the past, we definitely had a problem. The way we first marketed the message pads, we put a lot of emphasis on handwriting recognition, and people were disappointed, so we got a lot of negative feedback. We have moved away from marketing the Message Pad as a handwriting recognition device; it is much more than that.

We have learned that 95 percent of the people who buy Message Pads have desktop computers, so what we are trying to do now is to deliver and market products that allow you to take information from your desktop with you in a mobile fashion. We don't believe they want to take their desktop with them; if they did, they would take a laptop. But they want the information, so we have been working with Now, Act, Meeting Maker, and others to provide applications that run on the Message Pad and the Mac or PC, and the data can be shared with each other.

We've also been targeting specific markets where there are, or will be, specific off-the-shelf solutions. Take, for example, forms for the insurance industry. We work with a third party so that you can create a form in Newton, fill in the forms on the Message Pad, and upload to an application that runs on the desktop. This takes out the whole problem of transcription for claims adjusters, meter readers, census bureau people—anyone out of the office filling out forms.

continues

P

Maclopedia: Where are you testing this idea?

We have about 200 pilot programs from service people to delivery people to medical records. We have installations at Johns Hopkins Hospital in Baltimore and Brigham and Women's Hospital in Boston. Residents carry Message Pads with PCMCIA cards with the Physician's Desk Reference, so instead of having to lug around the big medical books they just plug in the appropriate card—and because it is all electronic, you can search on it and follow hyperlinks from one subject to the next. I can do research right at the bedside.

Maclopedia: How do you prepare electronic versions of books for the Newton?

Sandy: Two ways. Using a product we have just put on the market called Newton Press, you can take any word processing or graphic file on your desktop, drop it on top of this icon, and it creates a Newton book. You can do more formatting there, modifying it for the Newton screen. The second way is part of the Newton toolkit, BookMaker, which allows you to create professional-quality books that are formatted for the Newton and load them into the cards.

Maclopedia: What other applications are being developed?

Sandy: Harris has developed an application for telephone repair people. They have ruggedized a device based on the Message Pad 120 with a geographical positioning satellite device and an RF radio. The repair guy gets the form over the radio, climbs up the pole, does the repair, fills out the forms up there, and radios the information back to the home office.

Digital Ocean, another licensee, is working with American Airlines looking at giving out Message Pads to platinum and gold travelers. [The travelers] can make online reservations, query their Advantage account, check their itinerary—over the phone or wirelessly—while they are on the road. That's in a pilot stage. The software will call directly into the SABRE system, so the first option is always American flights.

Maclopedia: So you are licensing the Newton operating system to other vendors?

Sandy: Yes, we're aggressively licensing the Newton technology. We have seven or eight active licensees right now, and we have different kinds of relations—people who are developing products from scratch, people who are licensing actual boards and modifying existing designs to cover markets in which we are not adept or don't have the resources to attack, or don't have expertise, like the ruggedization Harris and Digital Ocean are doing. We are trying to create a platform for these devices, and we don't have the expertise in all the areas, but we want this to be the standard. We've been very active in licensing it, so it will be more pervasive. We are still on the hook to create the [Newton] market because it is our technology, and our licensees are watching the market reaction.

> *We have moved away from marketing the Message Pad as a handwriting recognition device; it is much more than that.*

Maclopedia: Are you still suffering from people's disappointment with the original Newton?

Sandy: Yes, we went out too early and hyped the device too much, and got some negative reactions. That has put doubts in a lot of people's minds. I think 2.0 answers a lot of those questions. Reviews have been uniformly positive—Best OS at Comdex, Mobility Award for Best OS. A lot of people who gave us negative reviews have now published positive reviews and say, "The Newton has finally arrived."

Maclopedia: So, what about the handwriting recognition? Has that been improved?

Sandy: It's significantly better and fitter. We have two different handwriting recognition engines. One is the paragraph engine; it's not as dictionary dependent, and the dictionary has gone from 10KB to well over 30KB in the current operating system. Word segmentation and printed characters also work better. In addition, we have added some work done here by our Advanced Technology Group on a printed character recognizer; it works very well on printed handwriting—as long as you don't connect your characters—above 90 percent.

So the user has the option now to write connected characters with the paragraph engine, or to print and use the character recognizer.

And then Palm Computing has developed an application called Graffiti, which recognizes a restricted character set. You learn to write each character in one stroke. You have to learn a slightly different alphabet, but you can write in the little window, or on the main one, and people who use it find it to be one hundred percent accurate. The other engines are more like handwriting. With Graffiti, you write a character, and then you write another, so you don't get the spatial relationship. Some people say it is like typing with one finger. But the Palm guys say everyone in their office writes memos with it because it becomes that fluid after a while.

Maclopedia: So I'm on the road and I've written a note. How do I send it?

Sandy: That depends on what service you want. You can have a modem PCMCIA card and plug the phone into it and do email over it as you would from a PC. You can attach to a cellular phone and do your email from your car. Motorola has created an integrated product based on our Message Pad 110, using the Motorola wireless modem card, the ARDIS wireless network, and RadioMail's gateway services. A lot of companies already use that network to communicate with their sales force and do email. With so many standards, we are still evaluating the market, staying flexible. We may come out with an integrated product when one of these emerging technologies comes out ahead. In Europe, GSM is ahead, a digital cellular standard that works throughout the European Economic Union. I can have a GSM phone in France and while I am in Sweden, someone dials my French number but reaches me in Sweden. GSM is a clean, digital cellular network, and handles data well, and short messages; it's a world standard except in the U.S. and even in the U.S. a similar system, called PCS, a subset of GSM, is gaining acceptance. We're hoping that one standard will emerge in the U.S.

Maclopedia: Where does the Newton technology stand in relation to the Internet and the Web?

Sandy: We have the potential to make a big impact. We are working on including a TCP/IP stack in the Newton; that should be shipping in June, and when that ships, All Pen Software will have a net browser that runs on the Newton. We also have Eudora for Internet mail, and they will have a client, so you can do remote Internet access and do browsing. But browsing will be limited. You cannot download pictures of Jupiter; they're too big and in color. But for text browsing and research, these devices will be used very well, particularly with our new attachable keyboard. You go to your meeting with the Message Pad and a pen and take notes, then back in the hotel you have to do email, so you attach the keyboard—it's 90 percent normal size, very light—and take care of your email. You don't have to lug a laptop around. I just put it in my carry-on luggage and it just goes through the scanners because it is all solid state. Once or twice people ask me to turn it on, and I just turn it on. It isn't like asking you to turn on a PowerBook, where you have to wait three minutes, or the battery is low so you have to find the cord and find an outlet.

Printing Methods, Digital Digital printing eliminates many of the labor-intensive aspects of traditional printing. In digital printing, **prepress** and makeready are compressed into software functions. At its simplest level, digital printing means no more than pressing Command-P-Return on the Mac keyboard. (Command-P-Return is the universal keyboard shortcut for printing a single copy with the default settings of the Printing dialog box in most Macintosh software.) The Adobe **PostScript** page description language is behind most digital printing today. PostScript is an output code which is processed by computers to convert digital images to printed images. The PostScript-compatible Apple LaserWriter was the first digital printer to make graphics industry professionals sit up and take notice. The first PostScript LaserWriter was not much of a machine compared even to today's low-end laser printers, which are less expensive, faster, and print at higher resolutions, but it contributed to the ultimate success of desktop publishing. Now, digital printing has moved into the realm of process color with digital presses that can actually compete with traditional printing presses. One of the benefits of digital printing is that it is more feasible to print small quantities (short-run printing). It is still more economical to use traditional printing methods for large quantities. The economics are changing, however, as digital printing technologies mature. For the foreseeable future, traditional printing presses will probably always be used for huge printing jobs and premium color printing—national magazines, mass-marketing materials, catalogs, and so on—but digital printers will no doubt come into their own and be utilized for much of the "small-time" printing.

Desktop Printers The majority of digital printing still takes place on black and white desktop printers, although color printers are appearing on more and more desktops. Desktop printers are no doubt often used for small-quantity reproduction, but they have limitations. They are very slow compared to printing presses, duplicators, and high-speed copiers. Only a few models have the ability to automatically print on both sides of a sheet (duplexing). Most are limited to automatic paper feed of U.S. letter and legal size sheets only, although tabloid and full-bleed tabloid-size laser printers are increasingly common. Envelopes and smaller pieces of paper usually have to be hand-fed to the printer. On the plus side, nearly all desktop printers—whether laser, inkjet, thermal-wax, or dye-sublimation—provide good image quality. Black and white laser printers with 1200 dpi and 1800 dpi output resolution can even reproduce good quality halftone images. All color desktop printers are getting better and less expensive, but the color laser printer is seen by some as the paragon of color desktop publishing. Working on the same principle as regular laser printers, these printers may represent the largest area of growth in desktop digital color printing in the next few years.

Copiers Next to desktop printers, copiers are the most common type of digital printers. To qualify as a digital printer, a copier must have a direct interface with a computer and **raster image processor** (RIP). Probably the most common RIP found on color copiers is the Fiery from EFI (Electronics for Imaging). The RIP enables a color copier to process PostScript files in a manner similar to other digital printers. Color copiers with the Fiery RIP can produce good-looking color images at 400 dpi due to 8-bit color resolution and special **halftone** algorithms. New technology color copiers from Canon and other manufacturers print at much higher speeds than older models, making them more competitive with printing presses for short-run color printing. A new color model developed by Xerox and Scitex America called the Spontane can print up to 40 pages per minute with excellent image quality. High-speed black and white copiers can definitely compete with offset duplicators and other small printing presses and have replaced them in some instances. Taking data directly from a network server or computer workstation, these copiers produce good quality printing in the 300 to 600 dpi range. Some systems, manufactured by companies such as IBM and Seimans, print 8 $1/2$ ×11-inch duplex pages in the 300 to 450 pages per minute range. High-speed copier systems can provide a turnkey solution to **on-demand printing** by combining all necessary functions into one unit.

Digital Presses The terms "digital press" and "digital printer" are somewhat interchangeable, and we make a distinction here mainly for the sake of discussion. For the lack of any major differences between the two, we will specify that a digital press is larger, more sophisticated, much more expensive, and more likely to be found only at commercial printing firms and trade shops. Two early entries in this field have the trade names Xeikon and Indigo. Both can utilize a Macintosh workstation. The Xeikon DCP-1 uses dry toners to simultaneously print 600 dpi full-bleed 6-bit color on both sides of an 11 by 17-inch sheet of paper. Much like an ordinary laser printer, it uses the electrostatic process and heat fusing but has ten imaging cylinders. Paper is fed into the printer from a roll (web). The DCP-1 has optional binding features for folding, stacking, inserting, stitching, and trimming. Xeikon is based in Belgium, and the DCP-1 is distributed in North America by AM Multigraphics. The Agfa Chromapress is a similar device that uses the Xeikon technology. Another electrostatic digital press called the Indigo E-Print uses a unique liquid toner called ElectroInk. This is a special polymeric ink that hardens on the paper quickly without heat. The Indigo's printing process differs slightly from other electrostatic devices in that the image is transferred from the drum to an offset blanket which transfers the image to paper. The E-Print 1000 is sheet-fed and has only one imaging cylinder, requiring a separate pass through the press for each color. Another model, the E-Print 4000 has four imaging cylinders and can print four colors at once but only on one side of the sheet. Both models print up to 11×17 inches at 800 dpi resolution and can be interfaced to a Macintosh workstation. Another digital press which appeals more to the traditional segment of the printing industry is made by Heidelberg, a well-known manufacturer of high-quality printing presses. The Heidelberg GTO-DI is a modified offset lithography press which allows printing plates to be imaged directly on the press cylinders. This is accomplished with a plate-imaging technology called Presstek Pearl which uses laser diodes to "burn" the plate. These plates use silicon instead of water to repel ink, making the GTO-DI a "waterless" printing press. Being an actual offset press, the Heidelberg GTO-DI lives up to its name by producing superior image quality at very high speeds.

Printing Methods, Traditional The early stages of traditional printing are described in the Prepress entry, but we will briefly review them here before discussing printing methods. Before desktop publishing made it possible to set type, create and scan graphics, and combine the two in electronic page layouts, paper mechanicals, or paste-ups, were required. The mechanicals were converted to many pieces of film (negatives and positives) which included both line and halftone images. This was usually done with a special graphics camera. These pieces of film were then combined in a process called image assembly and stripping. The complete assembly of film is called a flat. The combined film was then used to create proofs and, after any corrections or adjustments, used to make printing plates. In some cases, plates were made directly from the paste-up, bypassing the film stage, but this was done primarily on low-budget "quick-print" jobs. The traditional prepress process is by no means totally in the past. It is certainly being rapidly replaced by digital methods but is still used in some areas.

The majority of printing is done by the offset lithography process, but significant publications, such as *National Geographic*, are printed on a gravure press. Other printing methods, such as letterpress, flexography, and screen printing also exist, and we will describe each of them here.

Offset Lithography is something of a misnomer because "lithography" literally means "writing with stone." Both parts of the word have their roots in Greek—*lithos* (stone) and *graphia* (writing). In fact, smooth limestone blocks were first used as printing plates in the lithography process, but today plates are made from metal (or paper and plastic in some cases). The word "offset" comes from the fact that the plates do not directly contact the paper. The image on the plate is transferred to a rubber blanket and then transferred to the paper from the blanket. In the original lithography using limestone blocks, paper was pressed directly onto the inked stone, then pulled away to reveal the printed image. This ancient method is still used in fine art printmaking. The offset process is preferred for modern printing presses because the rubber blanket conforms better to tiny surface variations in the paper, and it is easier on the paper at high speeds. Another reason for using an offset blanket is that the images to be printed can be "right reading" on the plate itself. This simply means that one can read text and other images on the plate in the same manner that they will be read on the paper. Applying the plate directly to the paper would result in a mirror image. Right reading plates are easier to work with because the image is exactly the same as on the paper.

The lithography process is based on the fact that oil and water do not mix. A thin film of water coating the non-image areas of the plate prevents oil-based ink from adhering to that area. Ink can only adhere to the image area of the plate because it has an ink-receptive coating. Waterless printing plates that use silicone to repel ink have been developed. An offset printing plate has a photosensitive surface, and images are created on it by exposing it to light through an assembled film flat. The exposure is performed in a special platemaking device, and technicians refer to the process as burning the plate. A flat is aligned to the plate with a pin register system. The exposed areas fuse to the plate material and become ink-receptive. The plate is developed with a chemical that removes the non-fused areas. Even when digital methods have been used to generate the film, offset printing plates are still made in this manner. Of course, direct-to-plate imaging is becoming more common, but a digitally-imaged offset printing plate still behaves the same on the press.

The printing unit of an offset press is a series of rollers that carries the ink and water from trays called fountains and applies them to the plate, which is mounted on a cylinder. The plate transfers the ink to the blanket cylinder which in turn makes an impression on the paper. The paper is pressed against the blanket by an impression cylinder to ensure complete ink transfer. Paper is sometimes referred to as substrate—a more generic term which could include any printable material. Other units built into the press load paper and register it in the correct position for each impression. Delivery units remove and stack the printed material. See the bibliography following the Printing entry for sources of more information.

Gravure printing differs from offset printing mainly in the type of plate used. Also called rotogravure, gravure printing uses cylindrical plates bearing images composed of microscopic ink-filled cells. The cells vary in size and depth and create impressions that are essentially halftone images—even solid areas. One of the benefits of gravure printing is high-quality color on even relatively low-grade papers, as long as they are smoothly finished. Because gravure plates are more expensive than offset plates, it is used primarily for large print runs (over 100,000 copies), but it can be very economical in that milieu. Gravure printing is not as common as offset and is usually available only in large metropolitan areas or industrial centers.

Letterpress printing is very much like using a rubber stamp. Images are printed by inking a raised image area and applying this to paper. The most famous printer in western culture, Johannes Gutenberg, used a letterpress made from a wine press. In 1440, Gutenberg created a sensation by mounting movable type in his press and printing with ink on paper. Printing with movable type actually appeared much earlier (11th century) in China and Korea. The oldest printed text preserved for us to see was printed by the letterpress method in Korea in 1397. Before Gutenberg, all books in Europe were manuscripts, laboriously handwritten by scribes. Gutenberg may not have been first to invent the printing press, but he must be given credit for recognizing and developing its commercial aspects.

Three methods are used in letterpress: platen, rotary, and flatbed. A platen press opens and closes like a clamshell and can print only one sheet at a time. The rotary press prints by rolling paper between two cylinders where one cylinder holds the plate and the other provides pressure. A flatbed press rotates a cylinder holding the paper over a moving flat plate. The platen press is still sometimes used to print very short run jobs such as invitations or personal stationery. It is also used for embossing, die-cutting, and scoring. The market for letterpress is very small, and it has declined almost to obsolescence.

Screen Printing is a simple method requiring only a fabric screen (silk is often used), ink, and a device called a squeegee. Screen printing is often done manually and is a favorite technique for fine arts printmaking. Whether manual or mechanized, the process is basically the same. The screen is mounted in a frame and carries an image which is formed by blocking some parts of the fabric and leaving others open. This is accomplished with hand- or machine-made stencils or by spreading a light-sensitive emulsion over the screen and exposing it through a negative. Ink is forced through the screen with the squeegee, a flexible rubber blade wiped with moderate pressure across the image, carrying ink along with it. Even coarse halftones can be printed, and screen printing is widely used for small quantities of signs, posters, bumper stickers, T-shirts, caps, and many other surfaces that cannot be printed any other way. In fact, just about any surface can be screen printed. Large automated screen printing operations can be found even in small or medium-sized cities.

Flexography is a way to print on nonporous substances such as plastic or foil. It is done on a special press that uses flexible rubber or polymer plates, and the image is applied directly to the substrate. Flexography inks are more liquid than offset inks, and they dry very quickly. Flexography is used to print packaging materials in large quantities. Plastic bags are printed with flexography, but it is also used to print labels, decals, and even porous substances like corrugated cardboard and wallpaper.

Embossing and Debossing are ways to add a third dimension in printing. By pressing paper between two dies, an image is molded from the paper fibers. An image raised above the paper surface is embossed; a depressed image is debossed. Embossing an image with no ink or foil present is called blind embossing.

Die Cutting creates shapes such as holes or irregular edges in the paper. This is usually done in a letter press with thin metal strips embedded in wood. The metal strips are bent to the desired shape and pressed into the paper to cut the shape.

Foil Stamping uses a die with a raised image to press a thin film of pigment-bearing plastic against the paper. The pigment is bonded to the substrate with heat resulting in a very opaque image that can cover any underlying color. Most foils are shiny and metallic in appearance but are available in matte finishes, pastels, and even wood grain. Any material that will not be damaged by heat and pressure can be foil stamped.

Engraving is a very old printing process but is still used all over the world to print currency. It is sometimes used for prestige stationery or wedding invitations. Engraving requires a metal plate with the image cut (engraved) into the surface. Ink is applied to the plate and wiped away leaving some in the engraved areas. The press forces paper against the plate, picking up the ink. Because engraving ink is very viscous, the resulting image is slightly raised above the surface of the paper. Halftones cannot be printed with engraving, but engraved art using a crosshatch technique was developed to a high level in past centuries. Take a close look at your paper money.

Thermography is a form of raised printing intended as an inexpensive substitute for engraving. In thermography, an offset press is used to apply slow-drying ink which is sprayed with a special resin powder that will blend with the ink and swell under heat.

For More...

If you want to do this...	*Go to this entry...*
Know more about traditional printing	Color Printing; Prepress
Know more about digital printing	Desktop Printing
Know more about desktop publishing	Desktop Publishing
Learn printing terms	Printing and Bindery Terms

Bibliography

For more information on printing and the graphic arts, refer to the following books:

Design for Desktop Publishing, John Miles, published by Chronicle Books, 1987 (0-87701-479-5).

Electronic Prepress: A Hands-On Introduction, Bill Parsons, published by Delmar Publishers, 1995 (0-8273-6449-0).

Getting It Printed, Mark Beach, Steve Shepro, Ken Russon, published by Coast to Coast Books, 1986 (0-9602664-7-X).

Graphic Design with PageMaker 6.0, Bill Parsons, published by Delmar Publishers, 1996 (0-8273-7814-9).

Pocket Guide to Digital Prepress, Frank J. Romano, published by Delmar Publishers, 1996 (0-8273-7198-5).

Pocket Pal, A Graphic Arts Production Handbook, Michael H. Bruno, Editor, published by International Paper, 1992.

The Color Mac, Second Edition, Marc D. Miller and Randy Zaucha, published by Hayden Books, 1995 (1-56830-126-X).

The Non-Designer's Design Book, Robin Williams, published by Peachpit Press, Inc., 1994 (1-56609-159-4).

P

Printing and Binding Terminology

Basis Weight is the weight in pounds of a ream of paper in the basic size for its grade.

Binding is the process of fastening together sheets or **signatures** of paper with glue, wire, or thread.

Blanket refers to the thick rubber sheet used to transfer ink from the plate to the paper in an **offset press**.

Bleed is the appearance of a printed element seeming to run off the edge of the page.

Blind Embossing is **embossing** that does not involve any ink or foil.

Blueline is a type of proof where all colors show as blue images on white paper.

Bulk is an expression of the thickness of paper in thousandths of an inch.

Burn is a term describing the exposure of a photosensitive surface, such as an offset printing plate, to light.

Case Binding is the process of gluing signatures to a hard cover to create books.

Cast Coated is coated paper stock with a very shiny surface similar to that of a glossy photograph.

Coated Paper, also called coated stock, is paper coated with clay to improve ink holdout.

Collating is assembling sheets of paper into proper sequence.

Color Bar refers to the strip of colors printed near the edge of a press sheet to help evaluate ink density.

Color Correction is the process of adjusting and enhancing color prior to printing.

Color Swatch is a sample of an ink color.

Comb Binding is a book binding process that uses a plastic comb inserted through holes in the paper.

Comp is the abbreviation of *comprehensive dummy*, a simulation of a printed piece.

Contrast (in graphic design) refers to a noticeable difference between two elements, such as large and small, dark and light, smooth and textured. In image manipulation and printing, contrast is the difference between the lightest lights and darkest darks of an image.

Corner Marks are lines printed to show the corners of a page.

Cromalin is the DuPont trade name for an integral color proof.

Crop marks, also called tick marks, indicate the part of an image to be cropped.

Cropping is eliminating portions of an image around its edges.

Cyan is one of the process colors (blue).

Density Range is the range of tones between the darkest and lightest areas of an image.

Dot Gain is the phenomenon of halftone dots printing larger on paper than they are on negatives or plates.

Dummy refers to a preliminary drawing or layout roughly showing pagination and the approximate placement of visual elements.

Embossing is the process of pressing an image into the paper so that it is raised above the surrounding surface.

Emulsion is the coating of chemicals on paper, film, or printing plate that is sensitive to light.

Finish is the surface characteristic of a paper.

Flat refers to an assembly of film taped to masking material ready for making a printing plate.

French Fold refers to folding a printed piece with two folds at right angles to each other.

Ghosting is the phenomenon of a faint image appearing in the wrong place on a printed sheet.

Gripper Edge is the edge of a sheet of paper that a press grips as the sheet is fed into it. The gripper edge must contain no images.

Halftone is a term for converting a grayscale or color image into a pattern of dots for printing. Digital halftone dots are composed of a cell of smaller spots made by the output device.

Highlights are the lightest areas in a halftone.

House Sheet is the general purpose paper always kept in stock by a printing firm. It is economical to use because they order it in large quantities.

Image Assembly is the prepress process of **stripping** together separate pieces of film prior to platemaking.

Imposition is the arrangement of pages on a press sheet.

Ink Holdout is a characteristic of paper that allows ink to dry on its surface rather than be absorbed.

Line Art is any image to be printed that is not a halftone.

Live Image refers to any graphic in an electronic publication file that should print as is or is linked to a source file stored with the publication.

Magenta is one of the process colors (pinkish red).

Matchprint is the 3M trade name for an integral color **proof**.

Mechanical refers to a paste-up of camera-ready copy composed of type, graphics, and other line copy elements. Instructions to the printer are often included on overlays.

Moiré is an undesirable pattern in halftones resulting from improperly aligned screens.

Overprinting is printing over a previously printed image.

Paper Grain is the direction in which fibers are aligned when the paper is made.

Paste-up refers to the process of adhering type and other elements to a mounting board to make up a mechanical.

Perfect Binding uses glue to bind signatures together with a cover.

Point is a unit of measure. In paper, it refers to one thousandth of an inch. In typography and graphic design, it refers to one seventy-second of an inch. In graphic design and production, points are the basic units of picas. One pica contains 12 points.

Press Check refers to looking at the first sheets to come off the press for the purpose of final authorization for the print run.

Press Proof refers to a proof made on the printing press using the same plates, ink, and paper to be used in the actual print run.

Progressive Proof is a proof showing each color of a job separately and in combination with other colors.

Register is the position of printed elements in relation to the edges of the sheet and other printed elements. Properly printed elements are said to be "in registration."

Register Marks are cross-hair lines that aid strippers and printers in registering **color separations**—sometimes called printer's marks.

Reverse is the act of printing type or other images reversed out of a background color so that paper color shows through.

Rough, also called "pencil rough" is the term applied to a simple sketch showing approximate placement of text and graphics in a publication.

Saddle Stitch is a binding method that uses staples to hold the folded pages of a publication together at the **spine**—often used for magazines.

Scoring is a finishing process in printing that helps heavy paper fold cleanly along a straight line.

Screen Ruling is the number of rows of dots per inch in a **halftone**—also called *screen frequency* and measured in lines per inch (lpi).

Screen Tint refers to a printed area of halftone dots that are all the same size, resulting in a shade or tint of color less than 100 percent.

Self-mailer is a printed piece designed to be mailed without an envelope.

Shadow is the other end of the tonal range from the **highlight** of a halftone, also called the shadow point and the highlight point. The complete tonal range established by these two points determines the contrast of a reproduction and should match the contrast of the original image.

P

Side Stitching is a binding method that uses staples through one edge of the pages.

Signature is the term used for a sheet of printed pages that is folded and combined with other signatures to make up a publication. Signatures may have from 2 to 64 pages on each side of the sheet.

Slurring is an undesirable effect in printing halftones where the dots become slightly elongated.

Spine refers to the binding edge of a signature or publication.

Spiral Binding is the use of wire or plastic spirals looped through holes in the paper.

Stochastic dots are halftone dots in a random arrangement rather than a pattern.

Stripping is the process of assembling film into flats prior to making plates. A person who performs this prepress activity is called a *stripper*.

Substrate is a generic term for anything that is printed upon.

Thumbnail is often used to describe a small rough sketch.

Transfer Key is a type of integral color proof developed by 3M.

Trim Size is the size of a printed piece after excess paper has been cut away.

Watermark describes an image created in paper during its manufacture. Watermarks can usually only be seen if the paper is held up to a light. Some DTP and word processing applications can add a printed watermark to the page, by printing an image in a very light screen tint.

Printing Papers, Types of

In both traditional and digital printing, paper has obvious importance. Its effects are often subtle, sometimes flashy, and, when used incorrectly, can be disastrous. Different papers print differently whether on an offset press or a laser printer. Therefore, several factors may compete with one another in the choice of papers—aesthetics, practicality, and economics.

Fortunately all printing paper is designed to be both reasonably beautiful and practical at the same time, so the choice may often fall along economic lines. In any event, beware of the grossly inappropriate, such as a soft absorbent sheet fed to the inkjet printer or a glossy coated stock that repels the glue on Cheshire mailing labels.

There are many different categories, or grades, of printing paper, and the grading can be confusing. Papers are graded according to their use and each comes in a basic size. The widely respected *Pocket Pal Graphics Arts Production Handbook* published since 1934 by International Paper names 11 different categories. Other sources name some of the same grades, leave some out, add others, or use different names. We will attempt a consensus by identifying eight different categories: bond, text, book, offset, cover, board, newsprint, and specialty. Alternative names for the same grade will be noted. An excellent account of how paper is made and finished can be found in the book, *Getting It Printed* by Beach, Shepro, and Russon. This book also provides many more details about paper characteristics in easy to understand language. See the bibliography following the Printing entry.

Many sources, including the venerable *Pocket Pal,* list "coated" along with the others as a separate grade of paper, but some of the other clearly defined grades, such as book and cover, come either coated or uncoated, so we will consider them generic categories rather than specific grades of paper. Coated paper is so named because it is actually coated with a layer of clay. The amount of clay and a process called calendering that compresses the paper's surface has a great effect on the appearance of coated stock. The basic characteristic of coated paper is that ink does not soak in very much, staying on the surface to dry. This makes images look sharper and have better detail. Ink also looks more glossy on coated paper. Coated papers are classified according to how they look and feel, as are most other papers. Gloss coat is shiny. Dull coat is, well, dull. It is sometimes referred to as suede or velvet. Matte coat is somewhere between gloss and dull. Coated paper usually comes only in white or shades thereof. It is designed to show off color printing and needs no strong color of its own. On the other side of the coin is uncoated paper. Its surface is all paper, and it absorbs ink much more than coated stock. Printed images tend to be a little fuzzier-looking on uncoated paper, but ink dries quickly on it, and this is a definite advantage in many cases. Uncoated paper also comes in several shades of white, but, unlike coated paper, it can easily be obtained in colors. Now, we will briefly discuss each of the specific paper categories. The basic size of each grade in inches is shown in parenthesis.

Bond (17×22) This is the category with which we are all most familiar. Inexpensive bond papers are commonly used in copiers, fax machines, and laser printers. There are many different types and finishes of bond papers. They are often distinguished by their cotton fiber content, and expensive stationery bond is usually made from 100 percent cotton fiber. Today, many bonds contain varying amounts of recycled fiber. Stationery bond papers often have either a laid or linen finish.

Text (25×38) Text refers to the textured surface of paper in this category. Text papers also come in many attractive colors, and with their interesting textures, they are among the most beautiful papers. Most text papers are treated with **sizing** to make them more suitable for offset printing. (Sizing is a chemical added to the paper to protect it from the water present in offset printing.)

Book (25×38) Book papers are the workhorses of the printing industry. They are available either coated or uncoated and are certainly found in most books. Book papers are considered general purpose papers and are less expensive than text papers. They come in a wider range of weights and bulk than other papers. They usually have either a smooth finish or a slightly textured surface called antique. Uncoated book papers are available in six to eight standard colors.

Offset (25×38) Offset is another name for book paper, but technically, there is a difference between the two. Offset paper is book paper that has been treated with sizing to make it resistant to the moisture present in offset printing. Unsized book paper can be used for letterpress and gravure printing and any other process that does not involve high moisture levels, but most of the book paper used every day can be classified as offset.

Cover (20×26) Cover paper is really just heavy-weight book or text paper. It is made to complement these papers and is used for covers on booklets, brochures, and so on. It is also frequently used for many special jobs such as pocket folders and cards of various kinds.

Board Board stock is very heavy and rigid paper. Several subcategories of board stock are common. Index ($22^1/_2$ ×35 and $25^1/_2$ × $30^1/_2$) is inexpensive, very stiff paper that is good for writing on with an ink pen. Tag (24×36) is an inexpensive paper especially manufactured for tags. It is not a glamorous paper but very good at what it does. Bristol ($22^1/_2$ × $28^1/_2$) is softer and more attractive than either index or tag and even comes in semi-attractive colors. It is inexpensive and makes a good low-budget substitute for book and text cover stocks.

Newsprint (24×36) You guessed it! Newsprint is used in printing newspapers (and by budding artists in drawing classes). It is characterized by a soft absorbent finish and not-quite-white color.

Specialty Carbonless paper, onionskin paper, Bible paper, Kraft paper (used for grocery bags), dry-gum labels, pressure-sensitive labels, and synthetic paper all qualify as specialty papers because they don't fit neatly anywhere else.

See Also
Desktop Printing; Printing

Printing Plates, *See Printing*

Printing Presses, Offset

Offset lithography presses are either sheetfed or webfed. This refers to the manner in which paper is fed to the press, and it is the only real difference between the two. On a sheetfed press, paper is inserted and printed one sheet at a time, but the web press gets its paper from a large roll mounted on the press. The paper from the roll is printed as a continuous piece (the "web") and not cut into separate sheets until just before it comes off the press. Offset presses are further distinguished by the largest size of paper they can print. The smallest sheetfed offset presses are called duplicators and can print sheets of paper up to 12 by 18 inches. Duplicators are often used to print only one color of ink on uncoated paper and are most frequently found at quick-print and in-house shops. Some are capable of multicolor printing, but duplicators were designed to print small jobs quickly and cannot be expected to attain the same quality as larger presses. Large sheetfed presses are manufactured in a variety of sizes. The 25 × 38-inch press size is very common, but sheetfed presses are available in sizes ranging from 12 × 18 inches to 55 × 78 inches.

Web presses also come in a variety of sizes relative to the paper size they can handle. The forms web press is the smallest and is designed to print business forms using a 17-inch wide roll of paper. The half web press uses paper rolls up to 26 inches wide. Full-size web presses use 38-inch rolls. Web presses can be operated at very high speeds, and the sight and sound of the web of paper flying through the press rollers and cylinders is an impressive one. Web presses are generally used to print larger quantities than sheetfed presses because they are more economical at a certain point. Any print job needing over 20,000 press sheets might be a candidate for the web press. A quantity of 100,000 sheets would certainly call for a web press. In many cases, a press sheet carries more than one copy of the publication. The appropriate size and type of press is part of the economic equation that is usually worked out by a printing cost estimator.

Many sheetfed and web presses can print more than one color in one pass through the press. Some large presses have as many as eight ink units. Each unit is capable of applying a separate color or varnish as the paper runs through. A multicolor press that can print both sides of the sheet in one pass is called a perfecting press.

See Also
Color Printing; Printing

Printing Problems

Why is it that the times you can't get your document to print are also the times you most need it to print—*now*? That's a mystery, but there are a few things you can try when your printer refuses to budge and you can't fathom the error messages PrintMonitor is giving you. Note that these tips are for those of us who haven't yet made the switch to QuickDraw GX, which is a whole different story in some ways.

- If the printer is running out of memory (you might get a message about this, or it might just refuse to print), try unchecking "Larger print area" in Page Setup. Imaging that extra area around the edges of the page can be just enough to send a printer over the edge.

- The higher the number of fonts, the greater the chances that you'll run into printing problems. Try reducing the number of fonts in a single document. Also, checking "Unlimited downloadable fonts" in Page Setup will force the Mac to download each font every time it's used on a page, and the printer will flush that font from its memory at the end of each use.

- Printing one page at a time can help in two ways. First, if there's a problem graphic or font in a document, this can help you find it. Second, it can keep the printer's memory from getting overloaded.

- Watch out for PICT files, which can cause mysterious output problems on PostScript printers, and stick with TIFF and EPS graphics as much as possible.

- Vector graphics with too many points (this is a problem with autotraced graphics and with some clip art) can really tax a printer.

- If you suspect the problem lies with the graphics in your file, try suppressing printout of them when you print. Deleting and reimporting graphics can sometimes flush out problems.

- Try different printer drivers: LaserWriter 7, LaserWriter 8, Adobe's PSPrinter (almost but not quite identical to LaserWriter 8), and maybe the proprietary one that came with your printer. And if your application uses PDF files (like QuarkXPress—you select one in Page Setup) make sure you're using the right one.

Printing Technology, Color

All color printers mix three pigments—cyan, yellow, and magenta—to produce all other colors. These colors are called the primary colors and serve as the basis for all color printing. When all three colors are mixed equally, the result is a type of black. Many color printers add a real black for a richer mix. The resulting system is called **CMYK** or **process color**.

Color printers can take several forms: they can use liquid or solid ink sprayed on the page (inkjet and phase change inkjet), solid wax that is melted on a page (thermal wax), and pigments that are burned at different temperatures to produce the colors (dye sublimation). Lastly, some laser printers mix powdered toner in the four process colors. Printers are categorized by how they apply their pigments, so we speak of dye sublimation printers, thermal wax printers, color laser, and inkjet printers.

Halftoning and Dithering to Generate Color Output

Like monochrome inkjet and laser printers, these color printers apply pigments by overlaying dots of their primary colors. Thus, a red dot is composed of a yellow dot overlaid by a magenta dot. Eight-colors are relatively easily produced by overlaying two primary colors together for a resulting palette of cyan, yellow, magenta, black, red, green, blue, and white (the application of no pigment). Other colors are created by a process called **dithering**.

Color dithering is the application of the primary color dots in complex patterns that create an optical illusion that one is seeing other colors. It is very difficult to hide the dot patterns, since all of the dots are the same size and different pattern arrangements cause different qualities of results. Only high-end printers can apply color to continuous areas of paper and avoid the dotting affect.

The other way that color printers gain the effect of various color hues is through color halftoning. This is mostly used to print scanned images. First the image is separated into its cyan, yellow, black, and magenta components (called color separations). Halftoning is the use of dots of different sizes to represent the different amounts of gray in a picture. Color halftoning varies the amounts of cyan, yellow, magenta, and black in each separation to gain the illusion of various hues. Each separation screen is rotated to a different angle, causing their dots to overlap and form small circles called rosettes. Because the rosettes and dithering are noticeable to the naked eye at 300 dpi (the standard output quality of a color printer), these outputs are not usable to proof a color balance or the details of a color picture.

Color Printing, InkJet Technology InkJet printers are the cousins of dot-matrix printers. Rather than use wires tapping a ribbon, inkjet printers spray ink out of microscopic nozzles in the print head. Bubble-jet printers use a heating element to create bubbles that expand to force drops of ink to fall from the print head. The Hewlett-Packard DeskWriter series and Apple StyleWriter series use this technology. Other inkjet printers send an electronic signal to a piezo-electric diaphragm within the print head that forces a drop of ink to be ejected from the nozzles. The colors of ink (cyan, magenta, yellow, and black) are all laid down on a single pass, causing fewer registration problems than printers that make four passes and lay each color down separately. Because the ink is a liquid, plain paper absorbs the ink, making clear images difficult to produce.

A second type of color inkjet printer uses a slightly different technology to lay down its colored dots. The Phase Change Ink Jet melts blocks of cyan, magenta,

P

yellow, and black wax in ink reservoirs. The melted ink is sprayed onto the page through microscopic nozzles in the print head. Phase change ink jet printers also lay down the colored inks in a single pass. Because the inks are wax-based they solidify much more rapidly than liquid inks dry, allowing these printers to print more easily on plain papers. The downside is that less ink is absorbed by the paper and the use of a high-pressure roller to flatten the solidified ink causes the printing of images that are not as sharp as other technologies.

Color Printing, Color Laser Technology Color lasers apply color by using a four-chamber toner developer unit containing cyan, magenta, yellow, and black toner powder. The image exposed by light on to the photosensitive drum take on an electrical charge. Those charged areas attract toner as the drum rotates past the developing unit. Because only one type of toner can be released at a time, the drum must make four passes past the developer to apply four colors. After each exposure, the paper is passed across the toner-coated drum. After the four passes, the resulting colored image's toner is fused to the paper using a heated roller. The problem with this technology is registration errors. If the paper is not aligned perfectly on to the photosensitive drum the colors will not be applied accurately, leaving fuzzy borders between colored areas.

Color laser printers can print color at higher resolutions than thermal wax or dye sublimation systems. The Apple Color LaserWriter series prints true 600 dpi resolution output. Many printers also use resolution-enhancement technologies, such as Color PhotoGrade from Apple or Hewlett-Packard's Resolution Enhancement Technology to sharpen the text or images by fine-tuning the dot sizes used to create the output.

Color Printing, Thermal Wax Technology Thermal wax transfer printers use a system where wax-based pigments of each process color (cyan, yellow, magenta, and black) are positioned on a roll of transfer ribbon, one after another. The transfer ribbon is placed between the print head's thousands of heating elements

and the paper. The heating elements in the print head are turned on and off, causing the different colors to melt on to the paper as dots. One color is applied for each of four passes of the paper over the print heads and transfer ribbon. The same problem of registration as occurs in the color laser process occurs here, since if the paper is not aligned perfectly with the ribbon, colors will have fuzzy edges or areas of no color where the match was not made.

A newer technology used by Seiko's Professional ColorPoint PSF and Fargo's Primera Pro and Pictura 310 printers mix thermal wax transfer technology with dye sublimation technology. These hybrid thermal wax/dye-sublimation machines remove the thermal wax ribbon and paper and replace them with the dye sublimation's plastic film. These printers produce more realistic colors, since the plastic film coated with process colors can produce continuous color, whereas the thermal wax system cannot. The system is cheaper than dye sublimation, since less-expensive thermal-wax paper can be used for rough proofs and dye-sublimation paper can be used for final prints.

Color Printing, Dye Sublimation Technology Dye sublimation and film recorders on the upper end of the color printing world do not have these drawbacks. Dye sublimation printing is performed by passing a plastic film coated with cyan, yellow, magenta, and black dye across a print head containing approximately 2,400 heating elements. Each heating element can produce 255 different temperatures, with more dye being transferred the hotter the element gets. The special polyester-resin coated paper is passed over the heating elements four times for the four dyes; and the dyes are sublimated into gases and diffused on to the coatings, producing dots of color. The variation in the density of the dyes that are transferred to the paper create continuous tones. Film recorders use red, green, and blue lights to produce images on 35mm slide film. A filter wheel controlled by Mac produces the correct amounts of primary colors which are then placed on the 4-by-5-inch Polaroid print or transparency film.

See Also
Dithering; Imagesetters; Printing, PostScript Lasers; Process Color

Printing Technology, Dot-Matrix

Dot-matrix printers produce images by hitting an inked ribbon with very small, moveable pins (called *print wires)*. Each pin in the printer's print head produces a single dot. The pins are arranged in a matrix. The printer controls which pin strikes the ribbon and which ones remain stationary to direct the pattern on the paper. The resolution (clarity and crispness of the output) depends upon the number of pins and their size.

Apple used to sell several dot-matrix printers under the name *ImageWriter*. The ImageWriter II is the most popular product, and the only one still available. The ImageWriter II has a nine-pin printer head and produces a resolution in Best Quality mode of 144 horizontal dpi by 160 vertical dpi.

Dot Matrix printers can print in three modes: draft, faster-print, and best. In draft mode the Macintosh sends the printer straight ASCII code and its spacing requirements only. The printer supplies the font by which it prints the document. Draft mode was designed to show you where each word would begin on the page if the actual bitmapped characters and graphics were used, making the spacing of the printer's internal font characters very disproportional. When you use the faster-print mode, the Macintosh does send the printer bitmapped images of fonts and graphics, but as a page image. Because the page image is too large to send in one piece, the Macintosh System's Print Manager generates the bitmap in stages in a process called *banding*. It flushes each section out of its memory after it sends it to the printer. In best quality the Macintosh also uses banding to transmit the bitmapped image to the printer. The quality is in-

creased because the Macintosh generates a bitmap image that is twice the size of the page and then scales the image down to size before sending it to the printer. Because the larger image takes more memory, banding this image takes 47 passes to the printer.

Fonts and Dot-Matrix Printing
The scaling process impacts how the Macintosh uses fonts to print on a dot-matrix printer in best mode. When you select best mode, the Macintosh selects a font twice the size of the one specified and then shrinks its bitmap 50 percent. If you have not installed a font twice the size of the specified font, the Macintosh uses one four-times the required size, and if that font is not available, the Font Manager scales the next appropriate size. ImageWriter fonts typically provide fixed fonts for 9, 10, 12, 14, 18, 20, and 24 point sizes. Other sizes require the system to approximate the scaling using an available font size. This causes the output to look distorted.

Best mode increases the quality of the printout an additional measure by causing the print head to make twice the number of passes over the paper. Before the second pass the printer rolls the paper up one-half a dot, thus causing the second pass to slightly overlap the first, filling in images and increasing the intensity of the print.

TrueType fonts increase the number of high-quality fonts which can be printed on the dot-matrix printer because QuickDraw scales the font to whatever size you specify using the outline font files as a template. Using TrueType you can print any point size font. In best mode QuickDraw rasterizes the bitmap image creating a font twice as large as required so that less hinting is required to build an accurate representation of the character. Larger fonts carry more information than their smaller counterparts. The font is reduced 50 percent in the scanning process to produce a denser, sharper print image.

Hints to Make Your Printing Easier

One way of making your images clearer when printing bitmapped graphics on a dot-matrix printer is to select the Tall Adjusted option in the Page Setup message dialog box. This option adjusts the Macintosh output from 72 dpi to the 80 dpi vertical resolution of the printer, thus generating a proportional image.

To avoid the irregular word spacing which occurs in draft mode, change your document's font to a monospaced font, such as Monaco, for printing out a draft. The fixed-spaced font on the screen will then match the spacing of the printer's internal font, making the draft easier to read. Change your document to a more professional bitmapped font when you are ready to print your final copy.

To increase the quality of your printout in Best mode, select fonts with uniform stroke widths, such as Geneva, Monaco, and Courier. These fonts scale more clearly than variable-stroke fonts, such as New York.

Always install fonts in groups of two—9 point with 18 point, 10 point with 20 point, etc. so that the Font Manager has the larger font available for scaling in best mode.

The clearest text font for use with the ImageWriter family is Boston II which is a shareware font available from Apple Macintosh users' groups. Use fonts with city names for best results, since these fonts were designed to be printed and displayed at 72 to 80 dpi.

The highest quality output in best mode is produced by using an older printer ribbon, since there is less smudging of characters from the double-pass process due to high levels of ink on the ribbon. Dot-matrix printers use inked ribbons which dry out over time. Do not stock-pile your ribbons, but buy them one at a time.

See Also

TrueType; Type 1 Fonts

Printing Technology, InkJet

InkJet printers operate on the same principles as dot-matrix printers, only they use tiny squirts of ink instead of pins to print their dots on the page. InkJet resolutions are better than dot matrix printers, but most are not as good as laser printing resolutions. InkJet resolution averages 360 dpi on best mode, but Apple manufactures a color inkjet that averages 720 dpi in best mode for black and white text.

Most inkjet printers come bundled with **Adobe Type Manager** to rasterize **Type 1 fonts** on the Macintosh. They also come with their own set of outline fonts (Helvetica, Courier, Times, and Symbol) and can be upgraded to 35 or more resident fonts. Inkjets, like dot-matrix printers, receive rasterized images of **TrueType fonts**, which they use in conjunction with, or in the place of, their resident fonts. InkJet printers are therefore not limited in their ability to print Adobe and TrueType fonts, since all of the hinting and scan conversion processes occur on the Macintosh. Their only limitation is that they do not support PostScript-based graphic formats, such as Encapsulated PostScript, Adobe Illustrator, or Macromedia FreeHand graphics. You need a PostScript add-on card or interpreter to print PostScript graphics.

Inkjets use special inks which tend to bleed on regular printer paper, although the technology is better today than when inkjets were first introduced in the late 1980s. Most vendors recommend printing on special coated papers made for inkjet printers when printing in best mode.

InkJet printers are very compact, since their printing mechanism is very simple. There are several portable inkjet printers.

Apple's StyleWriter family and Hewlett-Packard's DeskWriter family (displayed in the illustration that follows) are popular desktop inkjet printers that offer both color and monochrome machines.

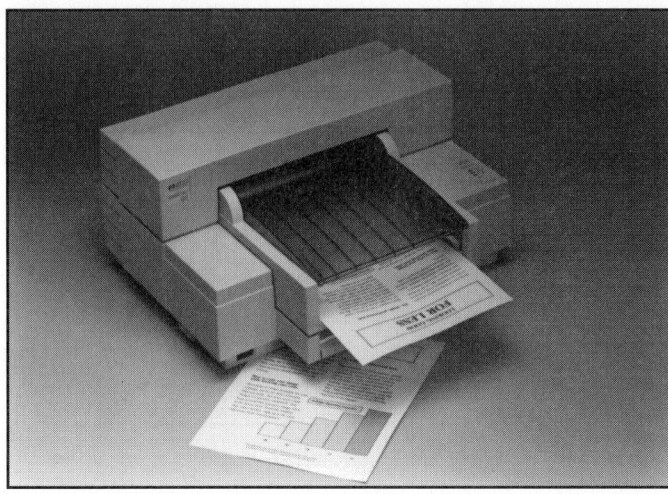

details of a graphic drawing, because it prints at a resolution of 1,200, 800, 600, or 300 dpi versus the 144 dpi of high-quality dot-matrix printers or 720× 360 dpi of inkjets. Laser printing is also faster than dot-matrix printing and quieter.

Laser printers are more complex than dot-matrix printers because they use a laser to shine a light creating the dots on the page. The laser printer consists of an engine (a type of photocopier which manages the paper feeding and prints the image) and a controller (which accepts printing instructions from page description languages and governs the engine following those routines). The difference between PostScript printers and other printers is that the controller is housed in the printer in PostScript laser printers versus using the Macintosh's QuickDraw to control the printing process.

The printer engine consists of the following components:

- A light-sensitive rotating drum or belt.

- A laser assembly which is aimed at the drum through a series of mirrors and lenses.

- A toner reservoir. Toner is a fine plastic powder coated with a polymer causing it to retain a negative electric charge. Some laser printers separate the toner from a developer (a second powder).

- Wires carrying high voltages called charging coronas. Charging coronas electrically charge the drum as it rotates the paper through the engine, allowing the toner to be transferred to the paper.

- A fusing assembly to melt the toner particles so that they adhere to the paper.

Older StyleWriters, such as the StyleWriter II or the StyleWriter 2400, connect via a serial cable to the Mac's modem or printer ports. StyleWriters use drivers that incorporate GrayShare or ColorShare technologies that allow you to share the printer over a network. The StyleWriter is connected to the modem port and the network is attached to the LocalTalk printer port. You will need a port splitter box, such as Port Juggler, if you also use a modem. Use the Chooser's Setup screen to turn on printer sharing. The GrayShare or ColorShare option (turned on by clicking the Share This Printer check box in the StyleWriter Sharing Setup dialog box) turns your Mac into a print server. Note that performance slows way down, since it is your Mac that is processing any other user's print job.

The Hewlett-Packard DeskWriters connect to the LocalTalk port and can be shared on a network like any other printer via the Chooser.

See Also

Fonts; Networking; PostScript; Print Server; Printers, Color; Printers, InkJet; TrueType Fonts; Type 1 Fonts

Printing Technology, Laser

Laser printers produce output which is better able to render the subtleties of electronic type as well as the

Raster Image Processors (RIPs) Laser printers which contain controllers use them to manage the rasterizing of images. Laser printers, like Macintosh video screens, are raster devices. A 300 dpi resolution laser inscribes over 3,300 scan lines per page on the photo-conductive surface of the drum. Because the controller manages this process, it is sometimes called a *raster-image processor* (RIP).

There are two types of RIPs, depending upon the language they use to communicate an application program's page specifications—PostScript printers and QuickDraw printers.

Laser printers that do not have resident controllers to control the print engine are called *QuickDraw* laser printers. They do not use PostScript as their page description language, but rather use the power of QuickDraw to rasterize TrueType outline fonts or Type 1 fonts with Adobe Type Manager before sending the bitmap image to the printer. These printers are becoming the most popular printers in the Macintosh market.

The problem with some of the QuickDraw printers is that they cannot connect to the Apple LocalTalk networks, thus cannot be shared among Macintoshes. They are also slower than PostScript printers and require more overhead storage on the Macintoshes because they perform their rasterizing, hinting, and scan converting on the Macintosh. It is quite possible to run out of memory during a print job when using a non-PostScript printer.

The benefit of using a non-PostScript printer is that it is cheaper, since it does not have the expensive microprocessor and software components required of a PostScript printer. It is usually smaller and lighter for the same reason, so takes up less desk space.

See Also
PostScript; PostScript Level 2; QuickDraw

Printing Technology, PostScript and Fonts

Many PostScript printers use outline fonts burned into ROM to support the scan conversion process. These fonts are called *resident fonts*. The printers can contain from 17 to 35 or more resident fonts and these fonts are then organized into font families, such as Helvetica, Times, Garamond, and so forth.

These resident fonts can be supplemented by downloading outline fonts from your Macintosh. System 7 includes a utility called the LaserWriter Font Utility for use in downloading, memory checking, and font listing on your laser printer. These downloaded fonts are stored in a reserved area of printer memory called *virtual memory*. There is a limited supply of VM on the printers (approximately 400 to 500 kilobytes on a 2MB RAM printer), enough to store approximately eight fonts (depending upon their sizes). You can also attach a hard disk to many PostScript printers via its SCSI port to store downloaded fonts. The printer takes the fonts it needs automatically during the printing process. Many Macintoshes can share these fonts, reducing the required storage space dedicated to font storage on individual Macintoshes.

The use of a SCSI hard disk on the printer provides a larger font cache, because the overflow from the RAM cache is automatically sent to the hard disk. The printer uses half of the hard disk for downloadable font storage and the other half for font caching. Many font vendors also market fonts on compact disks (CDs) and will release the locks on fonts selectively via telephone after charging a fee for each font it unlocks. You can then download the font from the CD to the Macintosh or printer's hard disk.

The PostScript interpreter in the printer's controller creates a bitmapped image of the outline font using a process called hinting. The resulting bitmap is stored in a reserved area of printer memory called the *font cache*. The controller uses the font's bitmap as needed during the scan conversion process. Using a font stored in the font cache speeds up the conversion process immeasurably. The controller manages the font cache by flushing font bitmaps on a "least recently used" basis. The larger the font cache, the more storage space is available for storing font images. In addition, added performance is provided to the printing process through the use of pre-built bitmaps of commonly used fonts and sizes which are stored on the ROM chips of most printers.

This image collection includes the full ASCII character set in Courier 10 point, as well as letters, numbers, and common punctuation in 12 point Helvetica and Times. Many printers also build font images when they are not performing an actual print job. This is called *idle-time font-scan conversion*. Fonts created during this process are stored in the font cache. The number of pre-built fonts depends upon the size of the font cache.

When you try to print a document which contains TrueType fonts on a PostScript printer, these pre-built Type 1 fonts take precedence over your TrueType raster images. The output from the printer will not contain TrueType images, but rather these pre-built images. TrueType scan conversion works best on non-PostScript laser printers where no conflict with built-in fonts can arise.

See Also
Adobe Type Manager; Fonts; PostScript Level 2; TrueType; Type 1 Fonts

Printing Technology, PostScript Lasers, Halftoning

A laser printer can't automatically produce shades of gray. This is a problem with the prevalence of scanned images and gray-scale monitors which can produce millions of shades of gray. The printer uses a process called halftoning which converts the image into dot patterns, with gradations of dots representing the gradations of gray. Halftoning is also called screening, since the shades of gray are reproduced through the illusion of patterns of dots of black ink on white paper. Halftone screens are defined in the number of lines per inch (lpi), the more lines per inch available, the more precise the image reproduced. The laser printer combines printer dots into cells to produce its halftones. The higher the printer resolution, the better the quality of its halftones (since each cell can be smaller—more dots per inch). The practical limit of a 300 dpi laser printer is 53 lpi (a magazine's halftones are measured at 120 lpi, and a newspaper's at 65 lpi, so these halftone images from the laser are not as legible). When you print halftones on a 600 dpi printer, you can create 71 lpi halftones, like those a newspaper produces. Typesetters which operate at resolutions of 2450 dpi and higher can produce magazine-quality 120 lpi halftone images. When you scan an image you need to know the line screen used by the printer that will output your job.

The halftones are variations in the size of the dots produced by the laser. Depending on the arrangement of the dots and their variability, you are able to get different grayscale qualities.

Bit-Smoothing on PostScript Laser Printers

Some applications, notably Adobe PageMaker, smooth the jagged edges of bitmapped images. When you print a paint application's output which has been drawn at 72 dpi, the laser printer scales the output to 300 dpi, or higher. Because the 300 dpi is not a multiple of 72 dpi, the image will be distorted. To repair this problem, always select the precision bitmap alignment option in the Page Setup dialog box. The precision bitmap alignment option rescales the image to 288 dpi, which is a multiple of 72 dpi, thus avoiding the distortion.

See Also
PostScript Level 2; Printers, Color

Printing Text

All word processors print, and all do so in pretty much the same way. When you've entered and formatted your text, and are ready to print, select Print from the File menu, press ⌘-P, or click the printer icon on your word processor's toolbar, if it's available. This opens the Print dialog box, or if you have just changed printers, you'll see a reminder to check your page setup. Checking page setup before you print is always a good idea, especially if you have more than one printer, or use fax software and a modem. The Page Set up dialog box is used to change document-specific and/or printer-specific settings, like paper size and **orientation**.

The Page Setup settings are stored in the Mac's memory with the pages to which they relate. The Page Setup dialog box looks different, and may contain different options, depending on which word processor you happen to be using. The Print dialog box also varies with the printer you use, as well as with the word processor and your system software. (If

QuickDraw GX is installed, you'll see an additional menu item called Print One Copy. It should be self-explanatory.)

Another good idea, and one which most of the current word processors support, is Print Preview. This File menu item lets you see on-screen what your printed page will look like before you commit to printing it.

All print dialog boxes ask you how many copies you want, whether you want to print the entire document or only selected pages, and any special instructions such as collating the pages of multiple copies or printing to a PostScript file instead of to a printer.

When you select the print command, the print dialog box appears, as shown in the following figure, enabling you to choose from a variety of printing options based on the printer you have selected in the Chooser and the application you're in.

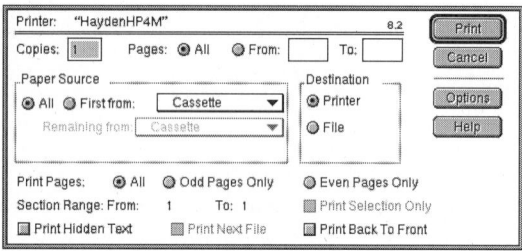

The **Chooser**, appearing on the **Apple menu**, enables you to tell your Macintosh which printer you want to print your document. If, for example, you have a laser printer and a color inkjet printer, icons for both of these printers appear in the Chooser, and you can select the printer you want to use, as shown in the figure.

For users using QuickDraw GX, Apple's new advanced architecture for printing available as a separate install in System 7.5 and higher, you can put printer icons on the desktop, which enables you to drag documents onto the desired printer icon to print the document.

The Print dialog box enables you to choose how many copies of the document you would like, which pages you would like to print, and other options such as print quality and paper tray selection. Some applications, particularly graphics programs, have their own print dialog boxes that replace the Apple print dialog

box, adding special features and options specific to that application. Also, some applications (including Apple's own Stickies and NotePad) now have an additional command in the File menu called Print One, or Print One Copy, which enables you to print one copy of the current document without having to access the Print dialog box.

The Macintosh uses two basic types of technology to print a page: **PostScript**, an advanced page description language developed by Adobe; and **QuickDraw**, Apple's proprietary technology that the Mac uses to draw text and graphics on-screen. A QuickDraw printer essentially draws what appears on-screen on a piece of paper. Because QuickDraw technology is built into the Mac, rather than the printer, like PostScript, the speed that a document prints at on a QuickDraw printer has a lot to do with the speed of the Mac that is printing the document.

PostScript printers work in an entirely different way. The PostScript technology is built into the printer. PostScript is a computing language developed by Adobe Systems as a way to display and print text or graphic images that are resolution-independent (meaning the same file that shows up on your screen at 72 dpi can be printed to a PostScript laser printer at 300 or 600 dpi, and then output to a PostScript laser printer at 1200 or 2540 dpi, enabling the page to be printed at the maximum resolution of the printer that is printing the page). Graphics applications such as Adobe Illustrator and Macromedia FreeHand rely on this technology to render high-resolution, object-oriented images, rather than bitmapped images. Images are interpreted by the Postscript RIP (raster image processor) in the printer to give you a high-resolution printout of your page, which can be made up of either text or graphics. **Fonts** designed to take advantage of Postscript printing are called Postscript or Type 1 fonts.

In System 7.5, Apple also introduced a new page description language, printing, and font technology called QuickDraw GX that improves upon QuickDraw by adding the capability to have advanced typographic features implemented automatically, the capability to have desktop printer icons for drag-and-drop printing, and many other advanced printing and typographic features.

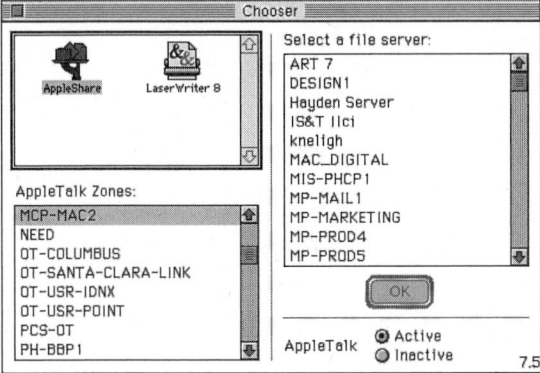

See Also

Apple Menu; Desktop; File Menu; Fonts; Orientation; Page Setup; PostScript; Print Command; QuickDraw GX

PrintOpen ICC

Linotype-Hell, long a manufacturer of high-end prepress equipment including imagesetters and scanners, has its own entry in the **color management** field: PrintOpen ICC, designed to generate ICC-compliant **device profiles** that can help make color output more accurate.

Linotype's color technology is the basis for Apple's **ColorSync** 2.0 system software, which has become the standard for color management applications. Running on top of ColorSync, PrintOpen ICC comes in two versions, regular and PrintOpen Lite. The latter eliminates a couple of the more obscure features of PrintOpen ICC, offering most of the same functionality with much simpler controls.

Profiles are created through a standard process: Print a supplied file, and then measure the results with a spectrophotometer so the software can quantify the difference between what the color's supposed to be and what a particular printer actually produces.

See Also

Color Management; ColorSync; Device Profiles

Printout, *See Hard Copy*

Private Key

A Web user's personal key, which is never distributed on the **Internet**, used in public/private key transactions on the Internet. A key is a very complicated encrypted series of numbers that would take so long to decode that it's essentially unbreakable. Allows users to read encrypted messages while others cannot.

Private and **public keys** are generated by the individual computer user. The freeware program Pretty Good Privacy (PGP), which is available for the Mac and other platforms, enables a user to generate both private and public keys at a user-specified level of encryption complexity.

See Also

Internet; Public Key; Secure Sockets Layer; World Wide Web

Problem Analysis

Problem analysis is the first phase of any programming project. Unfortunately, this phase is often overlooked to the peril of the programming team working on the project.

The purpose of problem analysis is to get a complete understanding of the programming project to be undertaken. This phase is primarily a time to ask questions about the project as a whole and answer them before continuing.

The most basic question to answer is, "What will the program do?" Not *how* will the program go about doing it, but *what* it will do. Will it be a killer spreadsheet application or a niche utility? A totally new concept in personal productivity or a plug-in for an existing product? This seems like common sense—and it is—but many programming projects are doomed to failure because different members of the development team have very different ideas about the need the program will fill.

Just as important is whether the need is already filled by another solution. Unless you are specifically setting out to challenge another application, you should question whether or not you should even pursue a new programming project if a solution is already available.

After you've identified the overall purpose of the project, it's time to work on some of the details. If you're creating a new widgetmaker application, decide what it takes to make a widget. What kind of widgets? How fast does the program have to run? Who is the target audience? Keep asking questions until you've fully defined the problem. Then you can begin to break the problem down further and ask the same questions about each separate part of the problem. But remember, you should do all of this before you've written a single line of code or even begun to think about which **algorithms** to use to accomplish the program's purpose.

There are a number of more formal methods of problem analysis, especially in the area of object-oriented programming. These methods use a rigorous series of steps to create an analytical overview of the problem to be solved then break down the problem further into its constituent parts. Object-oriented analysis uses the techniques of object-oriented programming to define a problem in object terms.

By spending time completing a thorough problem analysis, you can save yourself a lot of time and agony later in the development process.

See Also
Programming; Program Design

Process Color

Process color refers to the use of four standard ink colors to print the spectrum of colors represented in original full-color, **continuous-tone** images. The original images are usually photographic transparencies, prints, or negative film, but they may also be paintings or other original works of art. These four standard ink colors are cyan, magenta, yellow, and black. They are often represented by their first letters: CMYK. Original continuous-tone images must be converted to this CMYK model to be printed on a printing press or digital printing device. If the images are to be printed on a traditional printing press, they must be color-separated because each color requires a separate printing plate.

In process-color printing, **halftone** screens of these four colors are printed in different combinations. The colored dots of the halftone images combine visually to give the impression of a full spectrum of colors. The position of each halftone screen relative to the others is critical in process color printing. Actually, black and white halftone screens are also printed at some angle deviating from absolute horizontal and vertical—usually 45 degrees—but in process color printing the angles are crucial. The overlapping process color screens can create an undesirable secondary pattern called a **moiré**. The best screen angles have been worked out over the years for both photomechanical and digital halftones. A one-tenth degree error in screen angle can cause serious moiré effects.

See Also
Color Printing; Color Separations; Halftones

Processor Direct Slots (LC Slots), *See Power Mac Logic Boards*

Processors, 680x0s Family

In the past twelve years of Macintosh development, Apple has worked with Motorola to develop ever more powerful processors. The performance of a microprocessor is measured in the number of electronic pulses the processor's clock emits per second. This speed is spoken of as million cycles per second, or megahertz (MHz). The first Macintoshes, the 128K, 512K, 512KE, Plus, SE, Classic, and PowerBook 100, used the MC68000 that was rated at 8 to 16.67 MHz. The last chip used from the 680x0 family, the 68040, was rated at 33 MHz—a four-fold increase in performance.

The dance of chip and computer manufacturers to make faster chips and then to makes computers that can make use of these increases in efficiencies has been the driving force of the so-called Information Age.

History of the 680x0 Family In 1979, Motorola introduced the MC68000 microprocessor. Although the

Mac was not the first computer to use the chip (computers such as the Apple Lisa and Xerox Star also ran on this graphically-oriented chip), the Macintosh's future was firmly tied to it when it was selected as the brains for the Macintosh.

In 1984, Motorola introduced the successor chip to the 68000, the 68020. This processor offered faster performance while remaining downwardly compatible with software written for the 68000. This chip was used in the first modular Macs: the Macintosh II and LC.

In 1987, Motorola introduced the 68030. This chip was not much faster than the 68020, but offered design innovations, such as a built-in Paged-Memory Management Unit (PMMU) that provided support for System 7's **virtual memory**. Apple incorporated the 68030 into its second generation Macintosh II line of computers: The Macintosh IIx, IIcx, IIci, IIvi, IIvx, Performa 400 and 600, and SE/30, as well as most of the first generation PowerBooks (the 145, 170, 180, and so forth).

In 1990, Motorola introduced what would be the last Complex Instruction Set Computer (CISC) chip used in Macs: the 68040. This chip was considerably faster than the 68030 and included further design innovations, such as a built-in math coprocessor. The Centris and Quadra 605, 610, 630, 650, 660AV, 840AV, and 950 all were based on the 68040 processor. Today, the 63x line of Performas, the PowerBook 190, and the 640 DOS-compatible all use the 68040 chip. In addition, each 68040 Mac can be upgraded to a specialized 68040, the 68LC040, that includes a built-in floating-point processor for enhanced computational performance.

The 68000 Chip The 68000 processor seems very antiquated today with its 68,000 transistors and its hybrid 16- and 32-bit buses, but at the time of its development it was leading-edge. The processor could handle information internally in 32-bit chunks, although it transferred its data back to RAM or I/O in 16-bit chunks. The 68000 did not have room for cache memory, and ran at 16.67 MHz.

The 68020 Chip The 68020 provided several innovative features over the 68000, producing a clock rate of 33 MHz (or twice the performance of its predecessor.

- The 68020 provides both internal and external 32-bit data and instruction buses, or twice as much data in the same amount of time as the 68000.

- The 68020 contains a 256-byte instruction cache. This is a small area of the chip reserved for storing the most recently used instructions so that they can be used by the CPU again without calling out to memory for their retrieval. Motorola claimed that performance was boosted 40 percent by the inclusion of the instruction cache.

The 68030 Chip Although the 68030 did not show an improvement in performance, this chip took a leap in design that formed the backbone for the System 7 operating system.

- The 68030 included a built-in paged memory-management unit (PMMU), mentioned previously. The PMMU enables 68030-based Macs to swap chunks of information (called pages) between the hard disk and RAM, thus artificially increasing the amount of volatile memory available to programs. This "virtual memory" scheme allowed these Macs to run larger programs and background programs.

- The 68030 added a 256-byte data cache to the existing instruction cache to hold the most recently used data which can be sent to the CPU without calling on RAM or disk.

- The 68030 introduced a parallel bus design, called the Harvard-style bus architecture, that consisted of two 32-bit address and data buses. The address and data buses operate in parallel, letting the CPU perform multiple

P

tasks simultaneously. Using this bus design, the CPU can simultaneously access its data and instruction caches, as well as external memory simultaneously.

The 68040 Chip The 68040 chip consisted of 1.2 million transistors, four times the number used in the 68030 and six times the number used in the 68020 chip. In addition, the 68040 retained the PMMU of its predecessor and added a subset of the 68882 math coprocessor that was an optional add-on in earlier Macs (chips with this feature are called 68LC040s). The built-in math coprocessor lets the 68040 handle some of the mathematical computations that would ordinarily be off-loaded to the math coprocessor.

- The 68040 used two built-in 4K caches: one for data and one for instructions. In addition to their much larger capacity, these caches operate in a fast mode called copy-back.

- The 68040 retained the Harvard-style bus architecture of the 68030.

- The 68040 included a six-stage pipeline design, enabling the CPU to decode and execute several program instructions at the same time (during a single CPU clock cycle).

See Also

Coprocessors, Types; Macintosh Computer Family; PowerPC

Processors, Future Prospects

Apple recently announced a speed boost for its second generation Power Macs, as well as the introduction of a new model. According to the March 11, 1996, edition of *MacWeek*, as shown in the table that follows, the new Power Macs will run on up to 150 MHz 604 chips.

Even with the previously stated speed boosts, the future belongs to the **PowerPC Platform (PPCP)**-based Macs along with multiprocessing Macs and faster 604 chips, as well as future chip designs such as the 64-bit 620 and the universal 615. According to *MacWeek's* March 18, 1996 edition, in November 1996, Apple will introduce its first PPCP Mac.

This Mac, currently code-named Orient Express, will use a 166 MHz 604e processor with a possible configuration of 16MB RAM, 1.2G hard drive, CD-ROM drive, and Level-2 cache. *MacWeek* says that Apple plans to move its mid-range and high-end Power Macs to the PowerPC Platform by mid-1997. Apple also is entering the multiprocessing arena currently supported by the DayStar Digital Genesis clones. Apple will release a Power Mac 8500 and a 9500 with two 200-MHz PowerPC 604e chips at a price of $6,500 to compete against the Genesis MP that uses four 100 MHz 601 chips for its multiprocessing, priced at $24,000.

The following table presents other developments for Macintoshes in 1996.

Power Mac Speed Boost Models*

Model Name	Processor	Old Clock Time	New Clock Time	Configuration
7200	601	90 and 100MHz	120MHz	8 or 16MB/1.2G/CD/Level 2 cache
7500	601	100MHz	none	discontinued
7600	new model	none	604 at 120MHz	16MB/1.2G/CD/Level 2 cache
8500	604	120MHz	132MHz	16MB/1.2G/CD/Level 2 cache
8500	604	132MHz	150MHz	16MB/2G/CD/Level 2 cache
9500	604	120 and 132MHz	150MHz	16MB/2G/CD/Level 2 cache

*Chart taken from "Speed bump ahead for Power Macs," by Joanna Pearlstein, page 1, MacWeek (March 11, 1996, Volume 10, Number 10).

Future Power Mac Speed Boost Models*

Model Name	Processor	Old Clock Time	New Clock Time	Configuration
7200	604e	120MHz	166MHz	16MB/1.2G/CD/Level 2 cache
7600	604e	120MHz	180MHz	16MB/2G/CD/Level 2 cache
8500	604e	150MHz	200MHz	16MB/4G/CD/Level 2 cache
9500	604e	150MHz	200MHz	16MB/4G/CD/Level 2 cache

Chart taken from "Apple Plots 1996 CPU paths: PPC 604e engine to drive Macs," by Joanna Pearlstein, page 1, MacWeek (March 18, 1996, Volume 10, Number 11).

Processors, PowerPC

The **PowerPC** is an architecture, a design for a computer system, and not strictly a particular chip set. The architecture tells computer manufacturers what standards to follow when designing all of the computer systems that comprise the CPU: processor, memory, registers, and so forth. The PowerPC architecture began as an IBM research project to design a Reduced Instruction Set Computer (**RISC**) for its RS/6000 workstations. IBM was seeking to design a computer that would fit on a single chip, a uniprocessor.

The result was the first PowerPC chip: the 601. All 601 chips are manufactured by IBM, although they are purchased by Apple and Motorola. This made the 601 more expensive than later PowerPC chips (because they are made by a single vendor) and was considered a bridge chip to newer technologies. This is why there has been a rapid jump to faster, cheaper 603 and 604 chips that are not only manufactured by IBM, but by Motorola and other companies. The more competition for Apple's business (because Apple is the main user of PowerPC chips and one of the largest individual manufacturers of personal computers), the cheaper and more available the product.

Back in the 1970s, when the RISC technology was being studied by IBM, computer scientists analyzed which instructions were most used by programs. The scientists also realized that the more space there is near the processor to store instructions and data that is being used, the higher the performance of the computer. To make room for the added registers and cache, they jettisoned all but 39 instructions. RISC chips imitate complex instructions by connecting simple instructions together into modules. These "emulated" complex instructions could run rapidly because of the increased cache and registers. By the time that the chips were ready for manufacturing in the early 1980s, the manufacturing technology had improved so much, that rather than not having enough space for instructions on a chip that could hold ten thousand transistors, chip makers could build chips that could hold three or four million transistors in the same or smaller space. Because of this increase, the manufacturers put all of the instructions back on the chips, and even added some additional instructions.

They also had room to keep the increased registers, at least 32, and cache. RISC is thus a misnomer, because the chips have as many or more instructions as older CISC chips. The difference is in how the instructions are stored and loaded, as well as in redesigns of other components because there was less concern with backward compatibility than was the case with each iteration of CISC chip.

The PowerPC consists of six parts: Branch Processor (BPU), Instruction Cache, Fixed point (integer) Processor (IU), Floating Point Processor (FPU), Data Cache, and Main Memory.

One example of the flexibility of the design of the PowerPC is that fact that it can store its data streams arranged in series of eight characters (called a byte) either like a Macintosh or like an Intel PC, making it easier to run different existing system software, such as DOS, Windows 3.1, OS/2, Windows NT, AIX, and Macintosh OS without having to recompile the operating systems. (In computer parlance, the storage of data in registers in a particular order is a technical operation termed *byte ordering*.)

There are currently three PowerPC processors: the 601, the 603 (and its child the 603e), and the 604.

Processors, PowerPC, The 601 Chip As stated previously, the 601 is a bridge chip between the CISC processors and more innovative later RISC processors. It is 132 square millimeters, or 40 percent larger than the Intel 486 chip, but it contains approximately 2.8 million transistors on four layers of metal—nearly twice the number of transistors as the 486. Yet, the 601 also contains a 32K cache, whereas the Intel 486 chip only has room for an 8K on-chip cache. In order to manufacture such a tightly packed chip, IBM used an advanced technology that was able to etch one-half micron (0.5-millionth of a meter) electrical-current pathway (called a trace width) into the silicon wafer. With such small trace widths, IBM was able to pack many more transistors on to a single chip. In addition, because the chips could be small, IBM could cut many more 601 chips without flaws from its 8-inch wafers, thus lowering the price of the chip.

The 601 processor supports 69 new instructions, mostly to improve the management of cache, single-precision, floating-point operations, and bit-shifting operations. In addition, the 601 increases its performance because it includes fully interlocking hardware between its execution units and all its pipelines (the number of instructions that can be processed during a clock cycle, in this case, three). The processor also provides a 64-bit wide data bus (although it only supports 32-bit wide instructions). The 601, like all later PowerPC processors, contains an on-board floating point processor. FPUs are used by graphically-intense programs, such as Adobe Photoshop, many games, and mathematically-intense applications such as computer-aided-design (CAD). Many Macintosh applications have been optimized to take advantage of the built-in FPU, thus further increasing the performance of the Power Macintosh.

The 601 processor contains a 32K on-chip cache. Instructions and data are stored on the same cache,

called a unified cache scheme. Later RISC processors use a split-cache scheme that increases the CPU performance by splitting the data from the instructions into two separate 16K cache.

IBM released the 601 chips at five clock speeds: 60, 66, 80, 100, and 110 MHz. These speeds are achieved with a very low power consumption of 7 watts, further lowering the price of the chip. The 601 chip is currently used in Power Macintosh models 6100, 7100, 8100, and 7200.

Processors, PowerPC, The 603 Chip The 603 chip was designed by IBM and Motorola to be used as a low-cost, low-power consuming PowerPC chip. These chips were to be used in laptop computers and other computers that require low power consumption. The 603 as originally designed could not support 68K emulation, which is necessary to run the Macintosh operating system. IBM and Motorola went back to the drawing board and came up with the 603e processor. At 75 MHz base speed, the 603e is slightly faster than the base speed of the 601 and 603 (which was clocked at 66 MHz). The benefit of the 603e is that it operates as a computer with 3.3 volts (as compared to most chip sets on desktop computers that require 5 volts). The 603e processor integrates 1.6 million transistors on an 85 square-millimeter wafer. It also uses the .5-micron fabrication technology used by the 601, so is smaller and thinner than the 601. It further lowers its power requirements by adding more functional units over and above the three-instruction pipeline of the 601. As shown in the logical data and instruction flow diagram that follows, the 603e adds a Load/Store Unit (LSU) and a system-register unit (SRU) to manage power consumption. The LSU and SRU can be separately disabled if not in use, further saving power. There are three built-in power saving modes: doze, nap, and sleep. All of these features provide the 603e chip with a power consumption of 3 watts, less than half the dissipation of the 601.

The 603 was meant for use in PowerBooks, but has also been used in new Power Macintosh Performa models, specifically the Performa, 6300, and 5300 families, as well as the PowerBook 5300. Note that the Performa and LC 5200 and 6200 Macs still use the 603 chip.

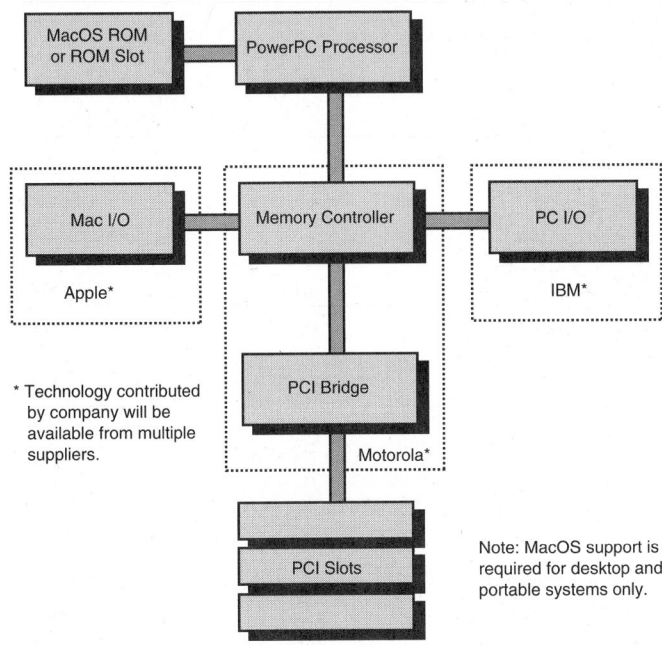

* Technology contributed by company will be available from multiple suppliers.

Note: MacOS support is required for desktop and portable systems only.

Processors, PowerPC, The 604 Chip The PowerPC 604 processor is the backbone of the Power Mac and PowerPC Platform. It is designed for use in everything from low-end workstations to Web servers. The 604 chips are the successor chips to the 601, and are used in the newest PCI-based Power Macintoshes: the 7500, 8500, and 9500 systems.

The 604 processor is the first chip that is able to issue four instructions in parallel (as compared to the three-way pipeline of the 601 and 603 chips)—a very high level of superscalar performance. In fact, the 604 actually has a six-way pipeline that can execute and retire up to six instructions simultaneously: a floating-point unit (FPU), a branch-processing unit (BPU), a load/store unit (LSU), and three integer units (IUs). The three IUs are set up so that two can process single-cycle instructions and the third handles multiple-cycle instructions. This design makes the 604 the fastest integer and float-point processing computer on the market.

The 604 has redesigned the unified cache of the 601 to create a separate 16K data cache and a 16K instruction cache for better CPU throughput. The in-struction cache can issue four instructions per clock cycle while the data cache supplies two words (each word being eight bytes) per cycle. The 604 also uses functional units to manage the flow of instructions through the processor and execution units to further increase its efficiency.

The 604 processor contains 3.6 million transistors on a 196 square-millimeter wafer and can operate at 3.3 volts. It also contains a nap mode like the 603 for power savings. Because of the number of transistors available, the 604 chip contains all of the 32-bit instructions defined by IBM's PowerPC architecture.

The 604 processor has been rated to run at 120, and 132 MHz and currently is implemented on the 8500 and 9500 Power Macs.

In 1995, Motorola and IBM announced an extended version of the 604 chip, called the 604e processor. This processor is for use in high-performance power Macs and for upgrades to existing 601 Power Macs. The 604e achieves 150 MHz speeds, yet is smaller and operates cooler than the 604. The new .35-micron fabrication technology allows IBM and Motorola to pack more transistors into a smaller space. The 604e returns to the concept of a unified cache, only double the size of the 601's cache at 64K. This 64K data and instruction cache improves the performance of 68K Mac emulation.

See Also
Power Macs; PowerPC

Prodigy
One of the three largest **commercial online services** in the U.S. Like **CompuServe** and **America Online**, Prodigy provides news, bulletin boards, interest groups, and **email**—but not much support for Mac users.

Prodigy gives its customers full access to the **World Wide Web** and the **Internet**. Its Web software, simply called Web Browser, has been available for Windows and a Mac version has been promised.

Prodigy.net offers Internet-only access to subscribers, and offers **Netscape Navigator** 2.0 software.

Prodigy home page: **http://www.prodigy.com/**.

Prodigy.net: **http://home.prodigy.net/**.

See Also

America Online; Commercial Online Services; CompuServe; Email; Internet; Netscape Navigator; World Wide Web

Professional Organizations,
See Desktop Publishing Professional Organizations

Profiler

An application used to monitor and record the performance characteristics of an application or other software.

It is often difficult or impossible for programmers to determine the performance of a certain section of code without running it. But even if you do run it, it can be tough to determine just how much time is spent in each routine and how often each routine is called without adding significant amounts of extra code to your program. Profilers make this job much easier by "watching" your program and reporting on its behavior.

Metrowerks **CodeWarrior** includes an excellent profiler. This profiler keeps track of your program using small stubs of code that are automatically added to your pro-

gram by the **compiler**. The only changes you need to make to your source code are a couple of lines at the beginning and end of your application to initialize the profiler and dump the results to a file. This approach adds some overhead to the program, but this overhead typically is evenly distributed over the entire program and very small compared to the time spent in your own code.

After you've exercised your program in whatever way you want, you can view the results of the profiling. This figure shows the profile results of a very simple application.

This simple application includes four functions: test, test2, test3, and test4. The profiler displays the functions in a hierarchy much like list views in the **Finder**. According to the display, test called test2, which in turn called both test3 and test4. The function test4 was also called by test3. The profiler lists test4 twice, so that you can tell whether it behaves differently depending on which function calls it.

For each function, the profiler displays the total number of times it is executed and the total and average time spent in each function (both alone and with all its subfunctions, or children). In this example, it's easy to see that most of the program's time is spent in functions test2 and test3. Armed with this information, you can focus your optimization efforts on these functions and avoid wasting time optimizing other, less time-consuming functions.

See Also

CodeWarrior; Compiler

Function Name	Count	Only	%	+Children	%	Average	Maximum
▽ test	1	0.069	0.0	2490.434	100.0	0.069	0.069
▽ test2	15	1239.997	49.8	2490.365	100.0	82.666	84.087
▽ test3	15	1249.753	50.2	1250.045	50.2	83.317	83.675
test4	15	0.292	0.0	0.292	0.0	0.019	0.021
test4	15	0.323	0.0	0.323	0.0	0.022	0.022

ExamplePPC.prof
Method: Detailed Timebase: PowerPC Saved at: 1:08:33 AM 2/26/96 Overhead: 0.820

Program Design

Program design is the second major phase of a programming project. After the problem has been defined in the **problem analysis** phase, you can move on to program design. As with problem analysis, many programmers skimp on program design and pay the consequences later in the development process.

A thorough problem analysis should give you an excellent picture of the features, needs, and overall purpose of a project. In program design, you take that picture and use it to create a blueprint for building the actual program. Many times, the program design flows naturally from the problem analysis.

This is the part of a programming project in which you determine how to go about accomplishing the purpose of a new program. What **algorithms** will be used? What limits will the program have? What development environment, programming language, and other development tools will you use?

The program design should be completed before any actual coding begins. If you jump into writing code before the program design is complete, you are likely to implement things in non-optimal ways, or in ways that compromise the design of other parts of the program. It's easy to fall into the trap of "just trying something out" before the design is finished. In some cases—such as in the design of an application's human interface—this may be appropriate, but in most cases, you run the risk of creating something that will be difficult to change later should the overall design require it.

Problem analysis and program design are the foundations of a successful programming project. Like a building's foundation, skimping on this part of the project can bring the whole project crumbling to the ground later.

See Also

Algorithm; Problem Analysis; Programming

Programming

Programming is the act of making a computer do what you want it to. It includes everything from creating a simple macro in a word processor to writing the word processor program itself. It can be a lifetime career, a weekend pastime, or something that goes unnoticed in your day-to-day computer use. It can be one of the most rewarding aspects of computing (as you watch the computer do exactly what *you* told it to do) and one of the most frustrating (as you stare in amazement as the computer does something you *know* you didn't tell it to do).

There are two major kinds of programming: **scripting**, and everything else. Scripting generally involves creating programs—or scripts—that control other applications. Some scripts do not control other applications, but are little programs in themselves. The other kind of programming involves creating those other applications.

Conversation with Dave Mark

Dave Mark has introduced thousands of folks to Macintosh programming through a series of books starting with *The Macintosh C Programming Primer,* affectionately known as "The Primer." In his latest, *Learn HTML on the Macintosh,* he reflects on his early experiences programming for the Mac and gives tips on how to get started.

Maclopedia: How did you first get involved with the Mac?

Dave: I bought my first Mac during the Mac's "first 100 days." I fell in love with it right off the bat. It has been my personal computer of choice since then. In the beginning, I was just fascinated by MacWrite and MacPaint. I loved the fact that I could write a letter with all these different fonts and then go into MacPaint, draw a picture, and paste it into the letter. Unbelievable! The first thing I did with my Mac was

continues

this great picture of my dog, a great pyrenees. I copied the picture, pasted it into a letter, printed it, and sent it to my mom. MacWrite and MacPaint blew me away—the consistency across applications, the crisp, clean, high-contrast graphics; I loved Chicago 12 point, the squareness of the pixels...

As soon as I started using the Mac, I knew that I had to figure out how to program it. I already had a relationship with Apple because I had done a series of educational games for the Apple II. I got in touch with them, and they promised to send me their technical documentation. What they sent was a loose-leaf binder filled with all these Xeroxed pages. This binder was the first incarnation of Inside Macintosh (at least the first version of IM that I ever saw). The first thing I learned was that programming the Mac was hard. Very hard.

I started to develop friendships with other people, and a community of wannabe developers started forming. We would call each other and ask, "Well, how did you do this, and how do you bring up a dialog box at boot time, and how do you write an extension?" UCSD Pascal was the first environment I used, then I moved on to Aztec C. Aztec C was a miniature UNIX-like environment that ran on the Mac. Incredibly, it ran on a 128K Mac. One thing I remember about those early days is this sense of pioneering spirit that everyone had. Folks were taking apart their Macs and attaching things to it, like hard drives and color monitors. Back then, floppy disks were like gold. Back in 1984, floppies were expensive (or maybe I was just a lot poorer!) and not that plentiful.

Eventually, I made my way to Think C, and then finally to what I use now, Metrowerks CodeWarrior. CodeWarrior has become the development environment of choice, the darling of Mac programmers. CodeWarrior supports C, C++, Pascal, Java—all the major programming languages. It allows you to produce applications that run on the Mac, Windows 95, Windows NT, Magic Cap (the hand-held device), the Be box, and some other platforms as well. CodeWarrior was the first development environment to generate native PowerPC code (code that runs native on a Power Macintosh).

When the Power Macs were first being built, Apple didn't even have their own compilers finished. Developers had this cool new machine, but no way to take advantage of its speed. So along comes this upstart company, Metrowerks, and they save the day. Cool!

I've worked on a lot of different applications over the years. One application I really enjoyed was this front end for a natural language processing engine. Basically, you'd feed messages into this engine and it would analyze the messages using rules of English grammar. It would turn the message contents into entries in a database. We'd then turn this expert system loose on the database and it would make sense of all the data pulled from the messages. Pretty crazy stuff.

Since the Mac came out, I've pretty much spent most of my waking hours learning how to program it. From 1984 to about 1987, I filled up these notebooks with notes on Mac programming. From the basics to the arcane tricks that were guaranteed to be incompatible with the next system release, I wrote it all down. My friend Cartwright and I got the idea to try to write a book that would take people through the process of writing a Mac application. We hooked up with Addison-Wesley, and that was when the first Macintosh C Programming Primer ("The Primer") came out. We discovered that programming the Mac was not really hard (as I originally thought), but there were just a lot of details you had to be aware of. Cartwright and I gathered up all those details and put them in one place.

Eventually, writing Mac programming books became my full-time job. Teaching people to program is incredibly gratifying.

There was clearly a need for books like that. When it came out, it definitely found its readership. It was a popular book, so I got the chance to write more of them. Eventually, writing Mac programming books became my full-time job. Teaching people to program is incredibly gratifying.

Maclopedia: Is it getting easier for people from the Windows side to program for the Mac?

Dave: It is getting easier for Windows programmers to understand the Macintosh way (to borrow a phrase from Guy Kawasaki) because Windows 95 has come such a long way; it's such an improvement over Windows 3.1. When Windows first came out (I think it was in 1986), I spent some time learning how to program in it. At the time, the PC was still a pretty primitive beast. A lot of the Windows design seemed to parallel the Macintosh programming model. For example, Windows had adopted the event loop model of programming, something that was revolutionary back when the Mac started using it. So from the beginning there were some similarities, but Windows and Macs were still so different, it was like pairing apples and oranges. In the beginning, Windows was a pane-based system, not a true windows system; as it matured, it became more and more a true windows system. Finally, Windows 95 seems to have brought real layered windowing sophistication to the masses. To be fair to Apple, they've had this level of sophistication pretty much from the very beginning. I think they just never got their marketing right.

The point is, now Windows programmers are dealing with an operating system that is much closer to the MacOS than they've ever had before. It is no longer such a heavy change to move from Windows to the Mac. In addition, we have seen languages like C++ come of age, and programming frameworks like PowerPlant become generally available. A framework like PowerPlant does most of the dirty work of running and administering your application, so you can concentrate on the plugging in of the code that implements the behavior of objects like windows, menus, buttons, and icons.

A framework is like a generic application. Your job is to customize this generic application, to shape it so it fits your vision. The generic application knows how to put a window up on the screen, for example. It doesn't know how to draw in the window, but it probably knows how to resize and relocate the window. So you need to provide the code that draws inside the window. By taking advantage of the framework, you don't have to rewrite the code that creates, resizes, or relocates the window. So one thing a framework gives you is reusable code. More importantly, an object framework makes it really easy to attach your code to the framework. For example, it is relatively easy to add code that draws the contents of a window. So both Windows programmers and Mac programmers are learning how to do things the same way: how to build applications using frameworks.

Maclopedia: What would you recommend to a new programmer or a Windows programmer coming to the Mac?

Dave: There are basically four steps to becoming a Mac programmer: Learn C, learn the Mac Toolbox, learn C++, and learn a framework like PowerPlant. What you do first depends on where you fit on this curve. If you are brand new to programming or to the C programming language, check out *Learn C on the Macintosh* published by Addison-Wesley. Once you get beyond the basics, go to your bookstore and check out the Mac programming section. There are a lot of really good Mac programming books out there. Find one you like and stick with it.

Metrowerks has a product called Discover Programming for the Macintosh, which is a nice way to get started with CodeWarrior, even if you don't have any programming experience at all. It sells for about $79, and it comes with a whole series of electronic books, including *Learn C on the Macintosh*. I'm part of the team that put the Discover products together, and I'm pretty proud of them.

Maclopedia: What do you think about Java?

Dave: Java is really cool! Java is a very C++-like programming language used to develop applications that you can download from the Internet, typically from someone's Web page. The language is designed to be completely platform-independent, so if you develop your Java applet on a Mac, it will run on a UNIX box or under Windows; and if you develop on a Windows machine, it will run on a UNIX box or under MacOS.

Basically, the way this works is that the Java source code is compiled into Java byte code. To run Java byte code, you run it on top of the Java Virtual Machine, or VM—a byte code interpreter. There is a Java VM written for the Mac, for Windows, and UNIX. As long as you have the Java VM running on your machine, you just throw the Java applet at the Java VM, and it interprets the applets differently, depending on what machine you are on. The byte code that says "Create a new window" will create a Mac-like window on a Mac, or a Windows-like window on a Windows machine. The beauty of Java is that it is completely cross-platform. If you are interested in Java, you might check

continues

P

out Discover Programming with Java, another Metrowerks product.

Maclopedia: So what are you working on these days?

Dave: I'm keeping myself busy. Besides working on creating new Discover products, I'm part of a team that has opened an Internet cafe at 322 Montezuma St. in Santa Fe, New Mexico. The cafe is called Zuma's. The phone number is (505) 820-2729. The Web address is **http://www.nets.com/zumacafe/**.

Zuma's is actually a restaurant with a bunch of Internet-connected computers and a lot of really friendly people. We are trying to create an environment where people can come and have a good time, but we are also trying to create an environment that fosters learning, community involvement, and community awareness. I hope that everyone who reads this will stop by and say hello the next time they are in Santa Fe.

There are many computer users who program by scripting more than by any other way. Macintosh users can use **AppleScript**, which is included with the MacOS, to script many everyday tasks. Using the script recording feature, it is possible to create scripts without knowing a thing about the **programming language** used to create the scripts. More advanced scripters may turn to UserLand **Frontier**, which offers a different approach to scripting.

Although scripting can be used to solve many of the programming problems that arise, it is often impractical (or impossible) to create much of the software used everyday by scripting. Large applications like Photoshop or Microsoft Office cannot be created without more sophisticated programming methods.

Any programming project goes through a series of steps from the conception of the idea to the final release of the software. Programmers first do a **problem analysis** to identify exactly what the software will do. This is followed by the **program design**, when the design details of the program are completed. Only then do programmers begin **writing code**, **compiling** that code, and **debugging** it. If performance is an issue, they may then **profile** the code to identify slow sections that need optimization.

The Macintosh hosts a tremendous selection of **programming tools** from which to choose. From self-contained **integrated development environments (IDE)**, such as Metrowerks' **CodeWarrior** and **Symantec C++**, to the massive **MPW** environment, there is a tool to suit every style.

Programmers turn to a wide variety of **programming language**s to create applications, system software, Extensions, and other software. Every language limits the programmer's code to a well-defined vocabulary with which to write a program. This enables a special kind of program, a **compiler**, to convert the code into the **machine language** that the computer can understand. A large percentage of all Macintosh development is done in three languages: **C**, **C++**, and **Pascal**.

The Macintosh is the first successful mainstream computer built from the ground up with a graphical interface, making programming on the Macintosh unique. The MacOS includes a vast toolbox of routines that programmers call upon to do things such as create windows and menus, draw into the window, manipulate files, or even play a QuickTime movie. The toolbox is documented in Inside Macintosh, an every-growing set of hefty books that includes the details of virtually every routine in the toolbox.

Macintosh programs must repeatedly check for user actions such as mouse clicks and key presses by asking the operating system for them. Responding to this stream of **events** is at the core of every Macintosh application. Another feature that makes the Mac unique is the way the Mac extensively uses **handles** for dynamically allocated memory.

Part of the Mac's ease of use comes from the consistency of applications. Although a few bad programs inevitably make their way into the world, most programs follow Apple's Macintosh **human interface guidelines**, a set of specific do's and don'ts for programmers. The guidelines are responsible for virtually every Macintosh program starting its menu bar with the Apple, File, and Edit menus; command keys for actions such as saving and opening being consistent; and why it's unusual to see a Macintosh program that is visually disturbing.

For More...

Bibliography

For more information on Programming the Macintosh, refer to the following books:

Applied Mac Scripting, Tom Trinko, published by MIS Press.

Code Complete, Steve McConnell, published by Microsoft Press.

Danny Goodman's AppleScript Handbook, 2nd Edition, Danny Goodman, published by Random House

Foundations of Mac Programming, Dan Parks Sydow, published by IDG Books.

A Fragment of Your Imagination: Code Fragments and Code Resources for PowerMacintosh and Macintosh Programmers, Joseph Zobkiw, published by Addison-Wesley.

How to Write Macintosh Software, 3rd Edition, Knaster, published by Addison-Wesley.

Inside Macintosh (multiple volumes), Apple Computer, published by Addison-Wesley.

Learn C on the Macintosh, Dave Mark, published by Addison-Wesley.

Learn C++ on the Macintosh, Dave Mark, published by Addison-Wesley.

Mac Programming for Dummies, Dan Parks Sydow, published by IDG Books.

Macintosh Human Interface Guidelines, Apple Computer, published by Addison-Wesley.

Macintosh Programming Secrets, 2nd Edition, Knaster & Rollin, published by Addison-Wesley.

Macintosh Programming Techniques, Dan Parks Sydow, published by M&T Books.

More Macintosh Programming Techniques, Dan Parsk Sydown, published by M&T Books.

Power Macintosh Programming Starter Kit, Thom Thompson, published by Hayden Books.

Programming Starter Kit for Macintosh, Jim Trudeau, published by Hayden Books.

The Tao of AppleScript: BMUG's Guide to Macintosh Scripting, Derrick Schneider & Hans Hansen, published by Hayden Books.

Tricks of the Mac Game Programming Gurus, McCormack, Ragnemalm, Celestin, et. al., published by Hayden Books.

Ultimate Mac Programming, Dave Mark, published by IDG Books.

Zen and the Art of Resource Editing: The BMUG Guide to ResEdit, 4th Edition, Derrick Schneider & Hans Hansen, published by Hayden Books.

The following magazines are also useful:

develop, The Apple Technical Journal

MacTech Magazine

Programming Languages

In this day of intelligent agents and voice recognition, you might think it is easy to get a computer to do what you want: just tell it in plain English (or any other human language). Sadly, that day is a long way off. Computers don't really understand any human languages yet. A programmer has to tell a computer what to do in the *computer's* language, and the best computer languages are still quite different than human languages.

At the most basic level, computers only understand one language: **machine language**. This is the set of instructions the computer's microprocessor is designed to understand. On the Macintosh, this instruction set can be either the PowerPC instruction set for Power Macs, or the 68000 instruction set for older Macs. Within each processor family, the instruction sets are nearly identical. For example, the MC68000 micro-processor used in the original Mac understands virtually the same instruction set used by the MC68040 processor in the Quadra models. Similarly, the PowerPC 601 understands the same instruction set as the PowerPC 620.

Despite the fact that computers only understand machine language, programs written in machine language are extremely rare. This is because no one wants to memorize all of the individual numerical codes for each instruction and keep track of where each variable is stored in memory. The closest thing to programming in machine language is using **assembly language**. In assembly, each machine language instruction is given a mnemonic name so that, for example, addition uses the add instruction and subtraction uses the sub instruction. Assembly also enables the use of abstract, named variables in place of concrete memory locations. After the programmer has completed the assembly program, a special program, called an assembler, converts the mnemonics and variables into **object code**, the machine language version of the program.

For example, here's a little routine called EasyGetMoreMasters:

```
EasyGetMoreMasters:    link      a6,#$0000
➡4E560000
       +$04    move.l    d3,-(sp)      2F03
       +$06    move.w    $0008(a6),d
➡362E0008
       +$0A    bra.s     EasyGetMoreMasters+$10
➡6004
       +$0C    _MoreMasters          A036
       +$0E    subq.w    #$1,d3        5343
       +$10    tst.w     d3            4A43
       +$12    bgt.s     EasyGetMoreMasters+$0C
➡6EF8
       +$14    move.l    (sp)+,d3      261F
       +$16    unlk      a6            4E5E
       +$18    rts                     4E75
```

The right column is the machine code for the routine (in **hexadecimal** notation). It has no real meaning to most programmers. On the left, however, is an assembly version of the same code. Although it still

might not seem very intelligible, it is clear that with a little training, it could be understood.

Assembly language is a low-level language, one in which much of the programming burden is put on the programmer and the vocabulary of the language is relatively similar to machine language. Further up the programming food chain are high-level languages such as **C**, **Pascal**, and **Dylan**. These languages provide the programmer with a much richer vocabulary with which to write programs. They also tend to be much closer to human language than machine language.

Programs written in a high-level language must be converted into machine language before they can be run on a computer. If the high-level instructions are converted one at a time as they are executed, it is an **interpreted** language. If, on the other hand, the program is converted all at once before execution, it is a **compiled** language. The programs that perform the translation are known as interpreters and **compiler**s respectively.

With very few exceptions, there is nothing inherent in a language that determines whether it is interpreted or compiled. **BASIC,** for example, is available most commonly as an interpreted language, but the original BASIC, as well as several recent implementations, are compiled.

High-level languages are processor independent. The compiler is designed to translate the language into object code specific to a particular processor. Before the advent of high-level languages, programmers had to learn a new language for each kind of computer they wanted to program; now they just need to use a different compiler for each kind of computer.

The rich vocabulary of high-level languages enables them to communicate the same instructions much more quickly and concisely. A single line of C code might expand into a full page or more of machine language instructions.

The EasyGetMoreMasters routine looks like this in C:

```
void EasyGetMoreMasters (short
numberMasterBlocks)
```

```
{
        while (numberMasterBlocks > 0)
        {
            MoreMasters();
            numberMasterBlocks--;
        }
}
```

This version contains only four functional lines of code compared to the 11 lines in the assembly version. In addition, if the subroutine `MoreMasters()` (which is actually a Macintosh **Toolbox** routine) was implemented on another type of computer, this same code could be compiled for that computer. The same thing can't be said for the assembly version.

High-level languages are as diverse as human languages. Many of these are considered *general-purpose* languages designed to solve a wide variety of problems. C, Pascal, and BASIC are all in this category. Others are tailored to certain types of problems. Fortran, for example, is designed to be used for numerical calculations. Conversely, **LISP** isn't designed to work with numbers at all; it is designed to work with *lists* of things.

Other languages are even more specialized. **SQL**, for example, is designed exclusively to query and manipulate relational databases.

See Also

Assembly Language; BASIC; C; Compiled Language; Compiler; Dylan; Fortran; Hexadecimal; Interpreted Language; Machine Language; Object Code; Pascal

Programming Tools

Programmers rely on a wide variety of applications and other tools to help create the world-class programs that make the Macintosh what it is today. Each phase of the programming process has its own set of tools to make the programmer's job easier.

During the design phase of most projects, program-

mers rely primarily on the tools in their head: their brain and reasoning powers. And perhaps more importantly, programmer's use the thoughts and opinions of their program's target audience to complete the problem analysis and program design.

Prototyping tools can also come in handy in the early phase of a programming project. These tools enable the programmer to quickly mock-up the look, feel, and basic functionality of a program without much effort. Using these tools, the programmer can eliminate many potential design flaws before the real development work begins.

There are several kinds of prototyping tools available. The first are separate from a programmer's primary development environment. They provide quick prototypes, but these prototypes generally cannot be carried forward into later phases of the development process. **HyperCard** and **FaceSpan** are excellent examples of this kind of prototyping tool.

Other types of prototyping tools integrate with other development tools to create prototypes that can be built upon to create finished programs. Visual **interface builders** are often used in conjunction with a **framework** to create this type of prototype.

Following the design and prototyping phase of a project is the real meat of the development cycle. At this point, programmers rely on a full-fledged development environment. These tools provide a centralized application from which other tools can be run. In the Macintosh development world, most development tools use the Macintosh Programmer's Workshop (**MPW**) environment or their own integrated environment. **Integrated Development Environment**s (IDEs) pull many development tools into a single application (see following figure).

Whether the development environment is integrated or not, it includes many of the same parts. First, an **editor** is included to enter and modify source code.

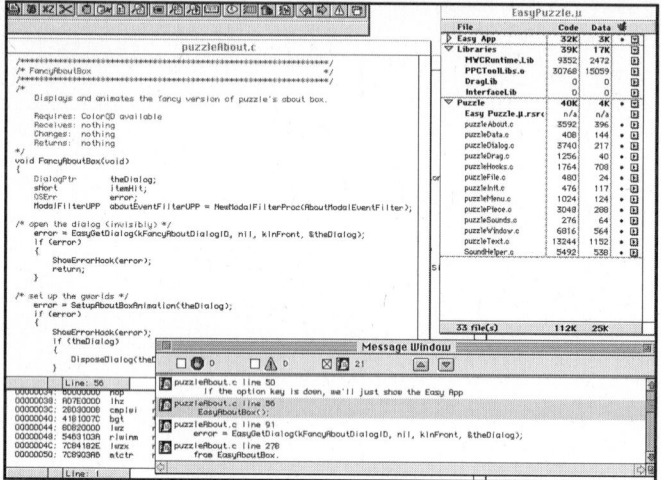

Most IDEs include a built-in editor, but external editors that run as a separate application are also popular. Many programmers use a **browser** to view code in a more structured and organized way.

Browsers are especially useful for programs written using a **framework**. These code collections are like scaffolding upon which you build your application. By using a framework, you can side-step much of the routine drudgery involved in programming basic functionality for each application you write.

One set of tools unique to the Macintosh are **resource editors**. These tools enable you to edit the menus, dialog boxes, test strings, and other user-interface tidbits in your application independent of the source code.

Next are **compilers** and **linkers**. These are the tools that convert source code into **object code** that can be run as an application or other type of program. Each kind of compiler recognizes a single programming language and generates code for a single kind of computer (for example, a **C** compiler for the Power Macintosh, or a **Pascal** compiler for 68K Macs). Many development environments include several compilers.

After you've written and compiled a program, you must make sure it works properly and flush out any **bug**s that made their way into your code. At this point,

you would turn to the wide array of **debugging tools**, including **debuggers** and stress-testing tools (which put extra stress on your program to help make subtle problems more obvious).

After a programming project is stable and usable, you may want to use a **profiler** to identify slow parts of the program. It's important to rely on a profiler rather than trying to optimize every part of the program from the start because many parts of a program have little effect on the overall speed of the finished product.

There are a wide variety of other specialized development tools beyond the scope of this discussion. The best way to learn the intricacies of development and the interactions among various development tools is to start programming!

See Also

Browser; Bug; C; Compiler; Debugger; Debugging Tools; Development Environment; Editor; FaceSpan; Framework; HyperCard; Integrated Development Environment; Interface Builder; Linker; MPW; Object Code; Pascal; Profiler; Resource Editor

Prograph

A uniquely graphical **programming language** and IDE from Pictorius, Prograph is unlike any other programming language. Rather than programming by editing text files that are compiled into machine code, you program in Prograph by editing graphical flow diagrams. These diagrams aren't just a representation of the program, like a flow chart, they *are* the program (see following figure). This avoids many of the trivialities of text-based programming.

This simple function uses a dialog box to ask the user to enter a number, and then it calculates the sum of all numbers between zero and the number entered. Finally, it displays the result in another dialog.

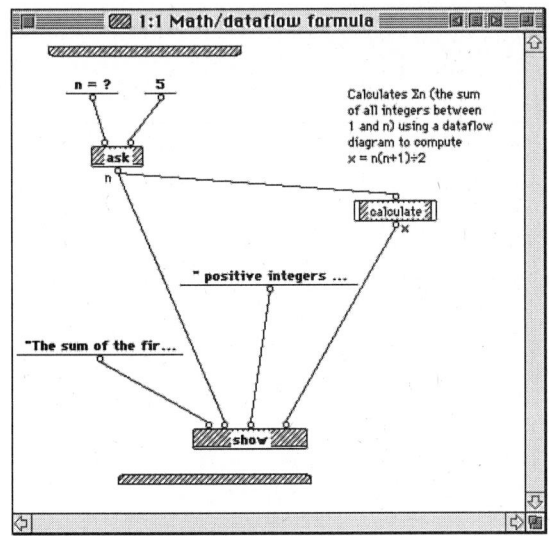

Prograph isn't limited to this sort of simple stuff, either. You have full access to the Macintosh **Toolbox** from within Prograph, so it is as powerful as any text-based programming language.

Prograph is a dynamic object-oriented language, and includes an extensive application **framework**. Because it is dynamic, you can edit programs while they're running. The commercial versions include compilers for both 68K and Power Macintosh applications.

The Prograph IDE includes an integrated **compiler**, **interpreter**, and **debugger**. When you're in the process of creating an application, you can run the application (or any part of it) in the IDE using the interpreter. After you've got all the kinks worked out, you can compile it to a stand-alone application just as you would in any other development environment.

There are three "flavors" of Prograph available. Prograph Classic is freeware. It is the predecessor of the current commercial versions. Prograph CPX is a full-strength professional development environment, and Prograph Peregrine is specially tailored to developing client-server applications and databases. All three versions use the same graphical language.

Prograph is published by Pictorius.

Pictorius Incorporated
Email: **sales@pictorius.com**
Fax: (902) 455-2246
Phone: (800) 927-4847 or (902) 455-4446
Web: **http://www.pictorius.com/**

See Also

Compiler; Framework; IDE; Interpreter; Object-Oriented; Toolbox

PROmotion

PROmotion, from Motion Works International, is a 2D paint, sound editing, and animation program. It is designed especially for multimedia producers, but may be used for any task that requires animated output. It has a three module interface: Paint, Sound, and Action.

Paint The Paint module has a selection of media brushes for painting and drawing operations, and a Patterns application. Props can be loaded and edited with the paint tools and saved out to the library for later use. The painting tools are basic, so it might be a better idea to use another paint program to create the graphics, and import them into PROmotion.

The Paint palette appears whenever a new Actor or Prop is added or needs to be edited. The tools contained include the Pencil (draws thin freeform lines), Brush (paints with a selected brush shape), Paint Bucket (area fills), Spray Can (pixelated air-brush), Text (adds text blocks), Eraser (removes data), Color Pick-up (selects a color from art), Line (draws straight lines), and Shapes (draws oval, rounded rectangle, enclosed curves, rectangle, and polygonal shapes).

Sounds PROmotion has a built-in sound module that records, edits, and adds a wealth of special effects to sounds. It requires a Mac Recorder sound digitizer on board with a mic attached for sampling real world audio. The PROmotion software can help you play back up to 16 sounds simultaneously, as long as your system hardware is up to it.

P

Animations PROmotion includes an Animation Options Setup window. Here, you may select the FPS and total number of frames, Hide or Show Cursor, Menu Bar and Palettes, and choose other settings. Two types of graphics can be imported, Actors and Props. An actor can be an animated multi-framed sequence, but a Prop is always a single-frame graphic. Animated transitions can be attached to Props so that they enter and/or exit in a step-by-step (Stamp, Scroll, Dissolve, Zoom Rectangles, Angular Wipe, Checker Board, Iris, Circle and Rectangular Wipe, fade, Pixelize).

The Actors in a PROmotion animation can be either single images or multiple image sequences (called ANIMbrushes in the industry). Either way, they can be animated by setting them on a path that moves them around and in and out of the frame. Everything in a PROmotion animation is controlled by the Media Controller palette. It allows you to create, edit, and manipulate the Actors, Props, Sounds, Cues, and Events that make the animation what it is. From the media Controller, you gain access to the libraries where all of the components of the animation are stored.

Timelines PROmotion's Timeline Editor allows you to see all of the tracks in the animation at a glance, so that you can edit exactly where specific events are to occur and how long they are to last. All of this is accomplished interactively with click-and-drag features that make editing a snap. If you need to modify any elements data, just double-click on its icon in the Timeline Editor.

Included Libraries PROmotion includes dozens of animated Actors and Props that can be placed instantly in the animation environment.

File Load/Save Conventions PROmotion imports previously saved Actors, Props, Sounds, and paths. In addition, you can bring in new actors from PICS files, Props from PICT files, and sounds from SND files. You can export Actors as PICS, Props as PICTs, and edited sounds as SND files. Animations can be exported as PICS, QuickTime Movies, After Dark Screen Saver modules, and Stand Alone Player movies (that you can distribute). You can also save out PROmotion project files and numbered PICTs.

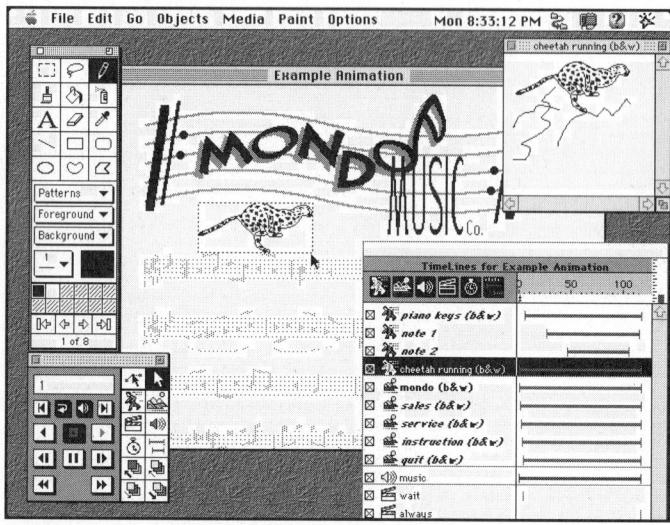

Proofs, *See Desktop Publishing Proofing and Printing*

ProPhone

ProPhone is a phone number **database** for the Macintosh **CD-ROM** by Pro CD, Inc. When you need to find a phone number in a hurry, ProPhone can help. After you type in a name, the database will give you a list of all phone numbers and addresses for that name.

ProPhone can be quite useful for small business owners to help them find new customers. Searches can be run by name, address, state, zip code, phone number, and type of business. You can also search by proximity—for example, to find all the newspapers within a 100 mile radius or the 50 closest doctors. Data is geo-coded to six decimal places, following the GPS mapping system, for extreme accuracy. Locations are pinpointed as closely as 10 feet. Lists of names, addresses, and phone numbers can be exported to any word processor, or put into a database (see the following figure).

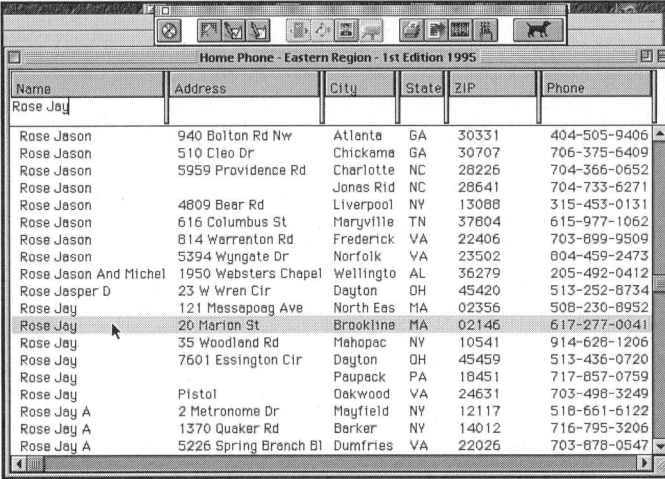

Pro CD, Inc. comes out with update phone CDs quarterly, containing updated phone book listings, on everything from the white pages, yellow pages, business listings, and Canadian phone books. The current version, as of this writing, includes 38 million updated listings and a total of 100 million listings.

In addition, ProPhone can print mailing labels in a variety of formats with a click of the mouse and connect to your modem to dial numbers at the touch of a button. It will even sort your mailing labels by zip code (or ZIP + 4) before printing them, so that you can save money on bulk mailings. ProPhone is published by Pro CD, Inc.

Proportional Fonts

On most typewriters, each character is the same width. Most digital fonts are proportional. Each character is drawn to look its best, which means that some are narrower or wider than others. Digital fonts in which the characters are the same width are called **monospaced fonts.**

See Also

Fonts; Monospaced Fonts

Protected Memory

The most common application **bugs** are memory-related errors. These bugs result from simple mistakes

with **pointers** or **handles** and can be very difficult to track down. Part of the problem is that there is nothing to keep an errant application from reading or writing to memory that doesn't belong to it. Memory that is a part of the system or another application, for example, is not protected. This sort of mistake can cause an innocent application to crash because of something another application did, often making these bugs very difficult to track down. This also makes it risky to continue using the computer without restarting following a crash.

There are two ways to avoid this sort of trouble: force programmers to write perfect code, or keep applications from touching memory that doesn't belong to them. The first, although a noble concept, is impossible. The second is at the heart of protected memory. A system with protected memory can prevent one process from accessing the memory of another process without specifically requesting such access.

Because of these restrictions, no application can cause another to crash because of an improper memory access. That is not to say that one application cannot cause another to crash, but because many such situations are the result of memory bugs, the likelihood is much lower. It's important to realize that protected memory is not a silver bullet that stops all bugs dead in their tracks. Applications that misbehave under a protected memory system still won't work. In fact, bugs that had previously gone undetected could become showstoppers.

System 7.5 (and all earlier versions of the MacOS) lack memory protection. Some degree of memory protection is expected in the Copland release of the MacOS, with complete memory protection in a future release.

See Also

Bug; Handle; Pointer; System 8

Protocol Encapsulation, *See*
Tunneling

ProView

ProView is a simple tool for creating slide show presentations. The program imports only PICT and **JPEG** files, and there are no paint tools for editing images or draw tools for creating simple objects, such as lines and rectangles. Text must be pasted via the **Clipboard** or created in the program. A button tool adds buttons that link between screens, but there are no transition effects, which is probably the biggest weakness of this product. The program also plays **QuickTime** movies.

> E-magine
> 345 West 58th St, Suite 10T
> New York, NY 10019
> Price: $70
> Email: **magazine@panix.com**
> Phone: (212) 262-0223
> Web: **http://www.e-magine.com/**

See Also

Presentation Software

Public Key

Widely distributed key used in public/**private key** transactions on the **Internet**. A key is a very complicated encrypted series of numbers that would take so long to decode that it's essentially unbreakable. The benefit of a public key is that it is widely available. The fact that a public key is widely available does not lessen security because the public key works only with a private key.

See Also

Private Key; Secure Sockets Layer

Public News Server

Most **Internet service provider**s offer their users an **NNTP** server that provides access to **Usenet** newsgroup postings.

However, so many newsgroups exist that most news servers do not offer them all. If your Internet provider either doesn't offer access to Usenet, or does not include a newsgroup you want to connect to, you may still be able to gain access via a public news server.

Public news servers offer a free NNTP connection to a limited number of users on a first-come, first-served basis. Many of these servers are read-only; that is, they do not allow posting of messages.

A list of public news servers can be found at **http:// www.phoenix.net/pdn/datanet/news.html**.

See Also

Internet; Newsgroups, Posting to; News Article; News Article, Posting to; News Article, Replying To; Newswatcher; Usenet; World Wide Web

Publish and Subscribe

Publish and subscribe is an Apple technology introduced in System 7 that enables you to have automatic updating in a document by linking documents together. This way, when you update an item in the first document, publish and subscribe updates the same item in the linked document. It's somewhat similar to copying and pasting an item between two documents, with the exception that a link exists between the two documents.

If, for example, you create a pie chart using a spreadsheet application, you could import that pie chart into a word processing document using Publish and Subscribe. Then the next day, if you went back into the spreadsheet application and modified the pie chart, the word processing document would automatically be updated with the new pie chart. That's the beauty of Publish and Subscribe. Unfortunately, even though the Publish and Subscribe technology is now built into the system, not all applications support it, and those that do all seem to implement it in a slightly different way with different commands appearing in different places from application to application. Maybe that's why Publish and Subscribe hasn't become a very popular feature on the Mac.

The way Publish and Subscribe works is first you select which items in your document you want to publish (make available for linking). If, for example, you have a table in your word processing document, you would select the table and choose Create Publisher, which makes your document the publishing document and creates a separate file of the table called an edition file. You can name this edition file and save it anywhere you want. This edition file is linked to the original document that created it, the publishing document. This way, if you make any changes to the table within your document, the edition file is updated when you save your document.

This edition file of the table can now be used in other documents (which will be called the Subscribing document). You import the edition file into your document by using the Subscribe To command from within an application. If you are working on a different document, for example, and decide you want to use the table you created earlier, you can select Subscribe To from within your application and choose the edition file of the table to import the table into your new document. If the next day you go back to your original document (the publishing document) and change some of the figures in the table, they are updated in your new document automatically because you imported the edition file in your new document. You could use that same table (the edition file) in as many documents as you'd like, and when you update the publisher documentation, any document that imported that table is updated.

Publish and Subscribe is also ideal for **network** users, where multiple people are working on the same document. If one network user updates a particular graphic on a page, it is updated on everyone's copy on the network as well.

To publish an item, follow these steps:

1. Select the item you want to publish and choose the Create Publisher command from the **Edit menu**.

2. This brings up the Create Publisher dialog box enabling you to name and **save** the selected item. This saved item becomes the edition file, and your document is now referred to as the publisher.

3. To use the edition file in another document, choose Subscribe To from the Edit menu. The Open dialog box appears, enabling you to choose the edition file and import it into your document. Highlight the edition file you want and click the Subscribe button.

4. This imports the Edition file into your document. If any changes are made in the original publisher document, the edition file is updated in your document.

See Also
Edit Menu; Network

Publishing, Traditional

Traditional publishing began in the fifteenth century when a German artisan named Johann Gutenberg invented movable type which could be inked and pressed onto paper. There is some evidence that this process actually dates back to ancient China, but Gutenberg and others developed it to the extent that it revolutionized the way information was disseminated. After the invention of movable type, printed material could be widely distributed for the first time in Western history. The most famous publication from this period is the Bible that Gutenberg printed on his printing press. Other types of early publications included scholarly and popular books, periodicals, newspapers, and the broadside—a kind of early advertising flyer.

P

Prior to the development of the printing press by Gutenberg and other European artisans, written communication was extremely limited. Books and other documents had to be laboriously hand-written and copied, a task often performed by monks and other members of religious orders. Such documents were often highly embellished with art and were greatly treasured. These handmade documents are called manuscripts, and many are preserved today in museums.

Printing presses and the publishing process have continued to evolve over the centuries, but **desktop publishing** is the first major revolutionary development since Gutenberg. Desktop publishing is rapidly replacing traditional publishing throughout the world but is especially predominant in the United States.

The traditional publishing process involves many separate procedures. These procedures are usually carried out by specialists, such as writers, editors, graphic designers, typesetters, reprographics camera operators, paste-up artists, prepress technicians, printing press operators, bindery workers, and others. In contrast, desktop publishing requires fewer separate stages; and, consequently, fewer individuals are involved.

In the traditional publishing process, a publication begins with a rough draft which shows pagination and preliminary content. A comprehensive, or **comp,** layout is then developed to approximate how the publication will look when it has been printed. At this stage, the production of page **mechanicals** begins with typesetting and reprographics camera work for artwork, illustrations, logos, and other graphic elements. Page mechanicals, also called camera-ready art or paste-ups, are the final stage of **page layout.** In a mechanical, all the type and graphic elements are mounted on a layout board. Type and camera-ready line art are pasted down with adhesive, and film overlays are used to incorporate windows for **halftones** or to provide **color separation.** The page mechanicals are then used to begin the process of making printing plates.

The platemaking process begins with the mechanicals being photographed by a reprographics camera using very sensitive film that can capture the smallest detail. The film is assembled into pages in a process known as **stripping.** Metal or plastic printing plates with a photosensitive surface are prepared by exposing them to light through the assembled film. The publication is then printed and folded or bound into a book.

See Also
Color Printing; Color Separations; Desktop Publishing; Prepress; Printing

Pull-Down Menu

Most of the commands to operate your Macintosh and software applications are accessed through pull-down menus. Pull-down menus appear in the **menu bar,** the white horizontal bar at the top of your screen. To access a pull-down menu, you click and hold the title of your choice in the menu bar and a corresponding pull-down menu appears with a listing of commands that are available to you. You can choose a command from the pull-down menu by holding the **mouse** button and dragging the **arrow pointer** down until the command you want is highlighted, and then releasing the **mouse** button.

See Also
Arrow Pointer; Menu Bar; Mouse

Punchdown Block

A punchdown block is a connection system that enables you to easily connect twisted pair wiring, the kind that is used for LocalTalk and similar network cabling. Wires for up to 12 devices can be punched down to each of the two 50 pin Telco connectors wired on the sides of the block. The punchdown block uses a special punch tool, which strips and inserts the wire into its connector in one easy motion. The tools are available wherever electronic supplies are sold. Blocks can also be purchased through telephone supply stores and electronics stores. The punchdown block is frequently used as a connector for passive star networks.

Put Away Command

If you need to eject a disk or move an item back to its original location, Put Away is the best method. When you click a disk on your **desktop** and choose Put Away from the **File menu** (⌘-Y), the disk is ejected and its icon removed from your desktop. If you use Eject Disk from the **Special menu,** the disk is ejected, but a ghosted version of the disk remains on your desktop. This can cause a number of problems. So Put Away is the preferred way to eject a disk.

Put Away is also an excellent housekeeper. If you drag a file out of a folder and on to your desktop for easy access, when you're through you can use Put Away to put that file back exactly where you brought it from. Also, if you put a file in the **Trash**, and later decide that you *don't* want to delete that file, you can click the file in the Trash and choose Put Away. It removes the selected item from the Trash and puts it back where it was before you dragged it into the Trash.

If you're on a **network,** Put Away is also good for disconnecting you from a shared disk. Just select the shared disk and choose Put Away and you're disconnected.

To use the Put Away command to eject a disk, follow these steps:

1. Click the disk on your desktop.

2. Select Put Away from the File menu (⌘-Y).

3. The disk ejects without leaving a ghosted disk icon on your desktop.

To use the Put Away command to put a file back to its original location, follow these steps:

1. Click the file, even if it's in the Trash.

2. Select Put Away from the File menu (⌘-Y).

3. The file returns to the last place it was before its current location.

See Also
Desktop; File Menu; Special Menu; Trash

P

Q

QC

QC is a System extension/control panel developed by Onyx Technologies that provides programmers with a suite of stress-testing and memory-**debugging** tools.

The most common errors Macintosh programmers make are memory related. These frequently involve misusing **handle**s and **pointer**s, or failing to check whether or not a **Toolbox** call returned an error code. Memory errors are often difficult to catch, because symptoms appear long after the error has occurred, at points seemingly unrelated to the real cause of the problem. Also, memory errors occur sporadically, as a result of a number of other factors, or they may cause the machine to freeze, making traditional debugging techniques useless.

QC makes the debugging job much easier by catching most memory errors as soon as they happen. At the very least, it can make sporadic errors reproducible, which is often all it takes to find the cause.

One of the most helpful features of QC is that it can be turned on and off on an application-by-application basis. That way, only errors in the program you're debugging are captured; other applications run normally. Using the QC Control Panel (see following figure), you also can specify which test you would like to perform for each application. Any changes you make in the Control Panel take effect immediately.

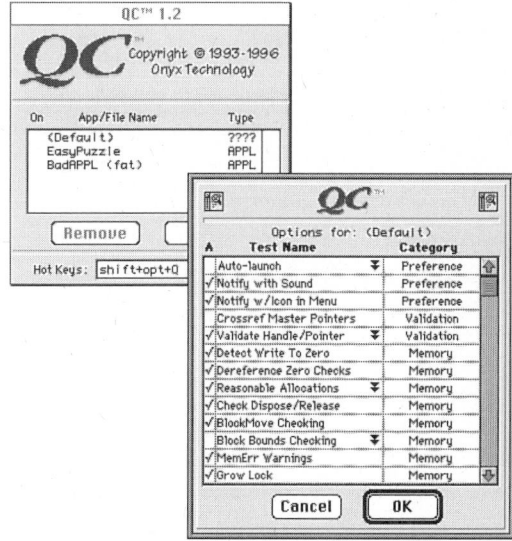

The suite of tests QC performs is exhaustive. It checks for attempts to store information at memory location zero, reasonable memory allocations, use of invalid handles and pointers, block bounds checking (writing beyond the end of a block of memory), and many others. QC tests applications in a worst-case position by scrambling and purging the application's heap at every memory allocation.

When QC does find an error, it reports the error by breaking into a low-level debugger or making a sound. When debugging with the Metrowerks **CodeWarrior** debugger, QC notifies the debugger of the error, so that it can flag the offending source code instruction.

QC supports all Macs running System 7 or higher. A demonstration version is included on the CD-ROM accompanying this book.

QC is available from Onyx Technologies:

> Onyx Technologies
> 7811 27th Ave W
> Bradenton, FL 34209
> Email: **onyxtech@aol.com**
> Fax: (941) 795-5901
> Phone: (941) 795-7801
> Web: **http://www.std.com/onyxtech/**

QTVR Player

An application that plays **QuickTime VR** movies. It is available from Apple's Web site (**http://www.apple.com**) in both Macintosh and Windows versions. It can be used as a **helper application** with a **World Wide Web browser**.

See Also

Make QTVR Object; Make QTVR Panorama; QuickTime VR

Quadra Monitors Extension

This extension is used by the **Monitors control panel** on Quadra and Centris models of Macintosh (with the exception of Quadra and Centris AV models) to describe the Quadra and Centris built-in video capabilities.

See Also

Monitors Control Panel; QuarkXpress

QuarkXPress

Competing with other page layout applications such as **PageMaker** and **FrameMaker**, QuarkXPress (created by Colorado-based Quark, Inc.) has made a name for itself with its precise type controls, multiple **master pages**, and **XTension** technology, which allows users to customize XPress with add-on features sold by Quark and by third-party vendors.

XPress (also commonly called Quark) is used to format documents ranging from business cards and brochures all the way up to highly technical math and science textbooks. It's extremely popular in the maga-zine publishing world because of its well-designed color handling features—it was the first page layout application to be able to output color separations complete with automatic trapping. Book publishers who work on the desktop (many book composition houses still use high-end dedicated systems) like QuarkXPress because its elegant implementation of master pages and **style sheets** allows users to quickly produce large numbers of pages based on a common design.

QuarkXPress allows you to have as many as 127 master pages or master page spreads (if you're using facing pages). Items placed on a master page are also placed on any body page to which that master page is applied, and once those items are on the body page they can be removed or altered as needed.

Each QuarkXPress document can have up to 127 paragraph style sheets per document. When applied to a paragraph (by choosing from a list of style sheets while your cursor is in that paragraph), a style sheet changes the font, size, leading, color, and other attributes of the text in that paragraph, all at once. In its next release, version 4.0, QuarkXPress will also support character-based style sheets, which only affect the characters that are selected when the style sheet is applied. This feature, previously available only through XTensions, such as FaceIt! and XStyle, is useful for bullets that need to be changed to a **dingbat** font, or when working with mathematical texts that require characters to be set in math fonts like Symbol.

Although QuarkXPress currently lacks the native capability to create indexes and tables of contents and link multiple documents into a book, version 4.0, due out in 1996, is slated to contain these features.

XTensions are separate programs that only work as part of QuarkXPress. They can range from freeware XTensions that make silly sounds at every Quark function to the $7,500 book pagination XTension Autopage Pro from KyTek, Inc. The Sonar Bookends and Sonar TOC XTensions from Virginia Systems can, respectively, make indexes and tables of contents. They're installed in the same folder that holds the XPress application, and they show up as extra dialog boxes, menu items, or floating palettes. Hundreds of these add-ons are available, many of them from an

XTension retailer called XChange (303-229-0620; **http://www.xpsi.com/**). Shareware and freeware XTensions can be found on most online services and at many ftp sites, particularly **ftp://ftp.telalink.net/pub/quark** and **ftp.quark.com**. One of the most impressive XTensions is Quark's own Immedia, set to ship this June, which will allow Quark documents to be enhanced with multimedia capabilities like video and CD-quality sound playback, as well as built-in World Wide Web Internet links.

QUED/M

QUED/M (QUality EDitor with Macros) is a programmer's **editor** from Nisus Software. QUED/M is an old-timer among Macintosh editors. Its predecessor, QUED, was one of the first editors available for the Mac. The current version is anything but out-of-date and sports a number of very nice features.

One of QUED/M's best features is its capability to *fold* text out of view. Folding is akin to viewing source code as an outline rather than all at one level. Like folders in the Finder's list views, you can open or close (fold or unfold) sections of code to hide or show more detail. Folding is especially handy for hiding the details of loops and if-then-else constructs to get a better view of the overall flow of a section of code.

In the following figure, the section of code marked with a black bar along the margin has been marked for folding. Double-clicking the bar hides all but the first line of this code from view. QUED/M also supports window splitting, which enables two sections of a file to be viewed and edited at the same time.

QUED/M can display a view of a set of files using its Catalog window. This window works much like a standard Open File dialog box, except that it can be left open at all times.

As its name implies, QUED/M provides a comprehensive macro language for manipulating files, although it has only limited support for **AppleScript**. It provides syntax coloring of **C/C++** keywords and has excellent search-and-replace capability. QUED/M also has a feature that can save a lot of time and anguish: multiple undos.

QUED/M is published by Nisus Software:

Nisus Software, Inc.
P.O. Box 1300
107 S. Cedros Ave.
Solana Beach, CA 92075
Email: **quedm@nisus-soft.com**
Fax: (619) 481-6154
Phone: (800) 890-3030
Web: **http://www.nisus-soft.com**

See Also
C; C++; Editor

Quest Games, *See Adventure Games; Non-Linear Storytelling Games; Role-Playing Games*

QuickCorrect, *See AutoCorrect*

QuickDraw 3D

System software that applications use to display 3D models. QuickDraw 3D is an **extension** that must be installed in the System Folder, and currently only runs on the Power Macintosh.

Displaying a 3D object in a non-3D modeling and rendering package has previously required that the image be copied and pasted into that application (for example, a word processing document). The idea behind QuickDraw 3D is that the user can copy and paste the information describing the 3D model, and QuickDraw 3D displays the model in the word processing document. Not only would it render the object in the window, but the user can click and drag the model to view it from different angles. QuickDraw 3D provides the rendering engine, the user interface, and the file format (**3DMF**) used to transport the information, so that the developer doesn't have to do much to add this capability to their application.

Some 3D applications have already added support for QuickDraw 3D, primarily because it's a fast rendering engine. QuickDraw 3D produces reasonable quality images, but they don't match the quality of **ray tracing**. Hardware developers are already offering QuickDraw 3D acceleration cards that improve the performance of QuickDraw 3D.

See Also
3D

QuickDraw 3D Acceleration Card

A **QuickDraw 3D** accelerator takes over the rasterization process, freeing the CPU of this task. There currently are a few boards available that are designed to help improve QuickDraw performance, but in most cases their performance is less than impressive, particularly given their prices. Also, a QuickDraw 3D accelerator might not even improve the performance of the work that you are doing. If you want to view QuickDraw 3D models or use a **VRML** browser that supports QuickDraw 3D, then an accelerator probably will be useful. If you are working with 3D modeling programs, however, remember that QuickDraw 3D does not replace **Phong** or **ray tracing**, and a QuickDraw 3D accelerator does not accelerate these tasks. An accelerator provides faster, fairly realistic previews, but you still have to revert to wireframe for the fastest response.

- **Apple's QuickDraw 3D Accelerator** ($400; (408) 996-1010) This card is priced competitively and offers very good performance. It produces good-looking images and supports

transparency, constructive solid geometry (CSG), and alpha channels. It does not connect to an external monitor, unlike other boards, but can accelerate QuickDraw 3D renderings to multiple monitors on the same machine.

- **Matrox MGA Millenium** ($649; (514) 685-2630) An accelerator and graphics board in one (hence the higher price compared to the Apple), this board provides moderate speed improvements. Image quality is not as good as nonaccelerated images, and the board does not support texture mapping. Buy this board primarily for the graphics support.

See Also
QuickDraw 3D

QuickDraw GX

Debuting as part of System 7.5, QuickDraw GX is an extension to the Mac's printing and display software. It includes a new **font format** and changes in printing, color matching, and document portability.

Desktop printing is a handy feature of QuickDraw GX; rather than using the Chooser and PrintMonitor, users can print by dragging-and-dropping documents onto printer icons, and they can manage print jobs by double-clicking on the icons to see what's being printed on each printer.

Users can create portable digital documents that can be viewed and printed on any other Mac with QuickDraw GX, even without the original fonts and application.

GX fonts contain more information than the previous standard font formats, **PostScript** and **TrueType**, so that they can have many more special and alternative characters; they can contain much more **kerning** and **hinting** information; and they can be printed right to left, as is customary for some foreign languages.

GX doesn't make PostScript and TrueType fonts obsolete, but they have to be "enabled" using an included utility program. After they are enabled, they can be used like GX fonts, but they don't contain the special features of the latter.

See Also

Font Formats; Fonts; GX Fonts; PostScript; QuickDraw 3D; TrueType

QuickDraw GX Extension

This extension adds enhanced graphics and type capabilities to the Mac and includes:

- The capability to use specially designed GX format fonts that enable automatic kerning and enhanced typographic control.

- The **ColorSync** color matching profiles to provide consistent color between the monitor's display and color output device.

- The capability to incorporate foreign language type and foreign type layout conventions.

- A greatly enhanced printing architecture.

See Also

ColorSync; GX Fonts; QuickDraw GX

QuickDraw Laser Printing Technology,
See Printers, QuickDraw Lasers; Printing Technology, Laser

Quicken

Quicken is a personal financial management software from Intuit. The current releases, Quicken 6 (on disk) and Quicken Deluxe 6 (on CD-ROM), are PowerMac native, and run on any Mac with System 7 and a 68020 or better processor.

To those of us who find most financial matters incomprehensible, Quicken is a breath of fresh air. It's easy to use, and it makes sense. When you first open the program, you'll see something that looks like a check register. Quicken uses the register to keep track of your balance and the money that comes and goes

from your account. Payments, deposits, ATM transactions, interest, and fees are entered here, either by you, or automatically if your bank supports online banking. You'll begin by entering your starting balance in the register. Then, when you start writing checks, the program automatically transfers the information from the check into the register, does the necessary arithmetic, and shows you your new balance. Because computers don't generally make mistakes in math, you can be sure that your balance reflects the numbers you've entered.

Most of us have to live within a budget these days, and Quicken helps make it easier—not by adding extra money in the "fun" categories, although that would be nice, but by showing you where the money goes each month, and helping you monitor your expenses. You can decide how much money you're willing to spend in each category, or in the case of fixed expenses, how much you must spend. Then, tell Quicken what time period the expense covers. Enter it by using the pop-up menu shown in the following figure. Quicken calculates the portion of the expense that's covered in the monthly budget and inserts the appropriate budget figures.

When you need to see whether you can afford to rent a movie, buy a new shirt, or take a vacation, all you need to do is to look at the budget monitor. If your inflow is greater than your outflow, you've got a green light to go ahead. Otherwise, you know you need to cut back. For more detailed answers, use the reports function to ask Quicken to give you exactly the data you want. If yours is a common question like, "How much did I spend last month on groceries?" you can use the EasyAnswers function. Click on the question and the category and time period you're inquiring about. Quicken will instantly create a report with the answers.

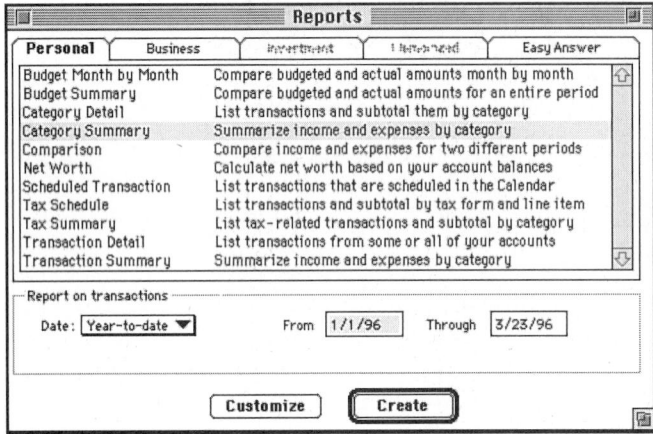

Quicken can track your investments, too. If you have a modem attached to your Mac, it will download current stock quotes. Quicken Deluxe includes a database of 4,400 mutual fund rankings from Morningstar, the leading source of mutual fund information and performance rankings. Search the database according to your goals: look for low-risk funds, high-yield funds, funds with five stars, funds with a better than average five year or ten year performance record, or any combination of characteristics.

Online banking lets you use your modem to download current information from your checking, savings, and credit-card accounts at any participating bank directly into your Quicken file. Banks and credit card companies that are currently online include American Express, Bank of Boston, Chase Manhattan, CitiBank, First Chicago, First Interstate, Sanwa Bank California, Union Bank, and Wells Fargo, along with about fifty others as of this writing. If you've already recorded checks in your Quicken register, online banking compares your data with the bank's, warns you about any discrepancies, and marks checks as having cleared; otherwise, the bank will fill out your register for you over the modem.

Quicken Deluxe also includes a convenient Home Inventory database, in which you can keep a list of

your furniture, art, appliances, and other possessions, for insurance purposes and as part of your net worth. The CD-ROM includes tips from Quicken users and personalized financial advice from financial experts Marshall Loeb and Jane Bryant Quinn. The only drawback to this program is that it doesn't include a printed manual. You can either read the CD-ROM version on-screen, or pay an extra $15 for a printed one.

Reconciling bank statements against their accounts is a necessary chore, but it's seldom fun. **Quicken** users may find the task a pleasure after doing it the old fashioned way. (Other financial management programs use a very similar method.) Simply enter the new balance or ending balance from your statement in the reconciliation window and check to make sure that the previous balance or beginning balance that Quicken has entered matches the amount on the statement. Add any interest payments or charges, as shown in the dialog box in the figure.

Click OK and then check off the transactions that are shown on the statement from those on the list Quicken displays. Don't mark checks that haven't cleared the bank yet. As you check off the items that have cleared, Quicken subtracts them. The "Difference This Statement" amount shown in the figure will diminish as you check off the cleared checks. When it reaches zero, the account is balanced.

If the account doesn't balance, you need to compare the check amounts actually debited against those you entered. Banks can make coding mistakes, and they may have taken more, or less, of your money than you intended them to do. Quicken will offer to make an adjusting entry to compensate for an unbalanced account. If you accept it, the Quicken balance is correctly synchronized with the bank's balance. Be sure you can identify the mistake before you let Quicken fix it. Otherwise, it will compound over several months and become harder to locate.

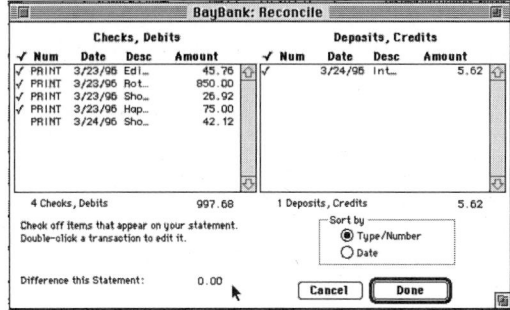

See Also

Finance Programs

QuicKeys

QuicKeys is a commercial macro **scripting** utility from CE Software. It enables you to create a macro for any keystroke, mouse movement, or combination of both to carry out long, boring, or repetitive tasks with a keystroke.

To create a macro, activate QuicKeys and it records your keystrokes and mouse movement. When you've done the task, you stop the recording process, and the macro application asks you to which keystroke combination do you want to assign the recorded tasks. There are hundreds of uses for macros, and their aim is to automate boring, tedious, or repetitive tasks for you at the press of a key. Besides the advantage of not having to enter each step for a repetitive task, QuicKeys macros complete tasks faster than you could manually.

QuicKeys enables you to set up a specific set of macros for each application, including the Finder and a separate set of macros that are global (such as a

QuicKeys macro that types in the date anytime it's invoked, regardless of which program you're using). QuicKeys enables you to create simple point and click-type macros, real-time macros (where it records every movement, including pauses and mistakes), or sequences which can be very complex. After you have created a macro in QuicKeys, you can go back and edit the macro to update it or fix any mistakes you may have made while creating the original macro.

Unlike system-level scripting systems, such as **AppleScript** and **Frontier**, QuicKeys is less centered on integrating applications and creating complex scripts than it is with simplifying everyday tasks. Using QuicKeys, you can create a simple macro that perfoms a task and assign that macro to a keystroke. This functionality is great for standardizing command keys across all applications. Rather than living with the command keys written into an application, QuicKeys enables you to expand or modify that functionality to suit your own needs.

As its name implies, QuicKeys is best at assigning functions to keystrokes. This includes the ability to launch an application (or several), choose a printer, switch applications, or type a long block of text, all with a single key press. This last feature is especially helpful for commonly used words and phrases. If you find yourself typing your address several times a day, you can create a QuicKey macro to do it for you at the press of a key.

QuicKeys can record a sequence of user events and play them back as a macro. Unlike AppleScript, QuicKeys records the exact string of events, including pauses, mouse movement and clicks, and keystrokes. If, for example, you close a window by clicking its close box while recording, AppleScript records that you closed the window, whereas QuicKeys records that you clicked the mouse at a certain location.

Because of its different focus, QuicKeys is not in direct competition with AppleScript or Frontier. In fact, one of QuicKey's best features is its ability to trigger a script written in AppleScript or Frontier at the press of a key. QuicKeys works with all applications, not just those written with special support for scripting.

QuicKeys is published by CE Software:

> CE Software, Inc.
> P.O. Box 65580
> West Des Moines, IA
> Email: **feedback@cesoft.com**
> Fax: (515) 221-1806
> Phone: (800) 523-7638
> Web: **http://www.cesoft.com/**

See Also

AppleScript; Finder Shortcuts; Frontier; Macro; Scripting

QuickFLIX!

This low-end QuickTime video editing tool is based on **VideoFusion**, an editing and special effects package that is available from Radius. QuickFLIX! features the same interface and similar features as VideoFusion, but with fewer transitions and filter effects. The software digitizes video, providing you have hardware capable of digitizing (if you don't have an AV Macintosh you will need a video digitizing board).

Clips are assembled and transitions applied in the Storyboard window. Clips can be edited in the Time View, while the Player Window plays back the final movie (see following figure). For the home and occasional user it is all that is needed.

See Also

QuickTime; VideoFusion

QuickMail

Electronic mail system by CE Software used on many Macintosh-based Local Area Networks. The version 3.5 release provides access to commercial online services and the Internet.

QuickMail's button bar and menu interface (see the following figure) complements the Mac's own interface.

Other QuickMail 3.5 features include:

- Drag-and-drop message handling.

- A "mail log" feature that indicates whether sent messages have been read, filed, forwarded, or deleted by the recipients.

- A built-in spell checker.

- QuickConference, which enables users to have real-time conversations on their desktops.

  - The capability to add emphasis to messages with stylized (bold, italic) text.

CE Software claims that almost one-third of all Mac email users choose QuickMail.

Web:

http://www.cesoft.com/info/
productlist.html

See Also

Commercial Online Services; Electronic Mail; Internet; POP3 Protocol; SMTP; World Wide Web

QuickMovie, *See MovieTrilogy*

QuickPan, *See Kaidan*

QuickPass, *See Animaq*

QuickTake 100 & 150

The QuickTake video camera was one of the first digital still cameras available for less than $1,000. The QuickTake 100 was the first release. Apple later increased the memory size and quality of the images and released it as the 150.

The QuickTake is a **range finder** camera, with fixed focus and a built-in flash. The camera is long and flat. In the front of the camera is a sliding lens cover. Be careful when you open the cover. Your natural inclination is to put a finger in the hole through which the lens appears. At the back of the camera is an LCD panel that displays how many pictures have been taken and how much memory is left. The flash can be programmed to fire automatically, always fire, or be turned off. The resolution of the pictures (640 x 480 or 320 x 240) can be chosen by pressing buttons next to the LCD display. A third button erases all images in the camera.

The shutter release is on the top of the camera, and the standard tripod mount is on the bottom. The camera is powered by four AA batteries. There is also a slot that slides back to reveal connections for an AC power supply (recommended for use while the camera is connected to the computer) and a serial port for connecting the camera to a computer.

The QuickTake is easy to use—just point and shoot. After taking a picture, you must wait for several seconds while the camera stores the image. This makes it impossible to take a quick sequence of images even if you don't need to use the flash.

Like most Apple products, the QuickTake is very well designed. The software is perhaps the best part of this camera, and is better than any of the software available with the other digital still cameras currently available. As well as an application for downloading and performing simple editing to images, there is a **control panel** that enables you to mount the camera as though it is a disk drive.

The QuickTake saves files in its own custom format, which although efficient, takes noticeably longer to decompress than other formats, such as **JPEG**. Also, if someone doesn't have the camera, they won't be able to view the image. You could give them **QuickTake extension**, but it is better to open the image and save it in another format.

Apple received assistance in developing this camera from Kodak, who then released their own low resolution digital camera, the **DC40**.

For those interested in creating low resolution QuickTime panoramic movies, **Kaidan** has released a tripod mount that works with the QuickTake.

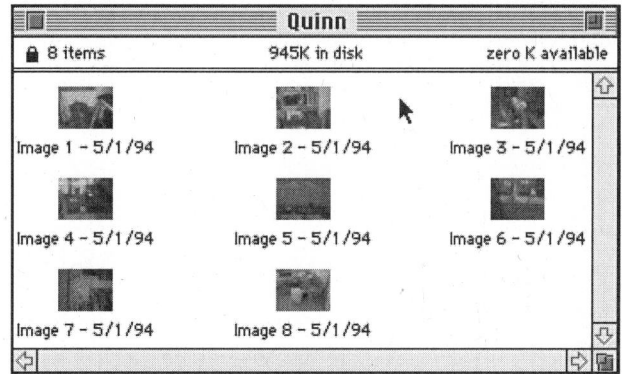

The QuickTake camera, with the help of a special control panel, can appear as a disk drive on the Macintosh desktop. Simply drag the images from the QuickTake folder to the hard drive to download them from the camera.

See Also

Chinon ES-3000; Digital Still Cameras; Digital Video Cameras; Kodak DC40; Still Video Cameras

QuickTime

QuickTime is a system **extension** developed by Apple that adds the capability of capturing and playing **digital video** sequences on a Macintosh. Depending upon your computer, you will need the QuickTime extension, the QuickTime PowerPlug extension (for Power

Macintosh users), and the QuickTime Musical Instruments extension. As with all extensions, if you plan to install QuickTime, first check to see that it is not already installed in your System Folder. Also, the QuickTime extension is usually labeled QuickTime™ with the trademark symbol, but some version have been distributed without it, resulting in multiple copies of the extension in the System Folder.

After it is installed, you still need an application to play a QuickTime movie. Apple has a utility called **MoviePlayer** that does just this and is probably the best program to use. There are some shareware and freeware utilities available as well. Check online services for these.

QuickTime makes it possible to record and play back video sequences on the computer. Playing video on a computer requires synchronizing audio and video information so that they appear to be playing together, as well as a method for dealing with the tremendous amount of information used to represent the frames in the video. A single frame of video at 24 bit depth is 640 × 480 is almost 1 megabyte. At 30 fps (frames per second), that is about 30 megabytes a minute.

Compression reduces the size of the images; however, current compression algorithms require a lot of computing power to decompress an image. That's why, even with compression, it is usually necessary to reduce the frame size and frame rate of the video.

QuickTime movies can be created in a number of ways. Video can be digitized using a **video digitizer**. Most of the new Power Macintosh models and AV Mac's include built-in digitizing hardware capable of capturing

at low frame rates and sizes (15 frames per second at 1/4 screen 320×240 is about the maximum).

Looking to edit QuickTime movies? If you don't want to spend any money at all, get a copy of Apple's **MoviePlayer** utility. You can cut and paste video segments together, but you can't create transitions or other dazzling effects. It's available on-line at Apple's Web site (**http://www.apple.com**).

For a very little money, you can get a copy of Radius's **QuickFLIX** (it's also bundled with some software and computers). QuickFLIX provides a larger collection of effects and transitions.

If you're serious about QuickTime editing you need Adobe's **Premiere**, or Strata's **VideoShop**. They provide just about all the editing tools most users need. You also can edit using Adobe's **After Effects**, but its real strength is in post processing special effects, so it's better suited as a tool to use along with an editing program. Radius's **VideoFusion** also is capable of being used as an editor. It offers some unique effects and costs less than After Effects. Strata's **MediaPaint** is an effects program also, but it actually enables you to paint on the movie!

Many applications can output QuickTime sequences, including most **3D** rendering software. For special effects, morphing software, such as Gryphon's **Morph** and Avid's **Elastic Reality**, take two images or sequences and create a dynamic blend of the two as a QuickTime movie.

To capture screen activity (what's happening on the Macintosh screen) to a QuickTime movie, a utility called **CameraMan** is available from Motion Works. The shareware utility **ScreenMovie** also can accomplish this. Animation programs, such as Macromedia's **Director** and Motion Works **ProMotion**, output animation in QuickTime format.

You might also want to look at sound editing applications, such as Sound Edit and Deck (both from Macromedia), that can edit the audio in QuickTime movies with much greater control than that provided in the editing applications previously mentioned.

QuickTime has uses outside just Digital Video. QuickTime incorporates support for **MIDI** (a sound format), and a MIDI file can be opened and played using QuickTime. **CD audio** discs can be opened and played from within QuickTime. The QuickTime compressors, also called **codecs** (**Animation, Apple Video, Cinepak, Graphics, JPEG, Component Video and None**), can be used to compress single PICT images. QuickTime includes support for the **PhotoCD** image format. **QuickTime VR** makes it possible to create a virtual reality environment, and QuickTime **video conferencing** provides a means to conference over phone lines.

See Also

Codec; Digital Video Cameras; JPEG; Key Frames; MIDI; PhotoCD

QuickTime Extension

This extension activates Apple's **QuickTime** technology, which enables you to play and create video movies. You still need a host application to use the technology, such as Apple's **MoviePlayer** to view a QuickTime movie, or Adobe's Premiere to create your own QuickTime movies.

See Also

MoviePlayer; QuickTime

QuickTime Musical Instruments

This extension to the QuickTime architecture contains a library of digital musical instrument sounds Apple has licensed for use on the Mac from Roland, a leading manufacturer of electronic musical instruments.

See Also

MIDI; QuickTime

QuickTime Power Plug Extension

This **extension** contains the Power Mac native code required to use Apple's **QuickTime** 2.0 video extension on Power Macintosh models. This extension comes pre-installed on Power Macs.

See Also

Extensions Folder; QuickTime

QuickTime VR

QuickTime VR technology makes possible a virtual reality environment using photographic quality images.

Most virtual reality environments (for example, Virtus's **WalkThrough Pro** and **VRML** viewers) use 3D models, or mathematical descriptions, to create a world that the user explores in real time. **3D** modeling is seriously limited by the speed of the computer. To avoid this problem, QuickTime VR uses images that have already been produced (either photographically or generated by a 3D modeling program) and stored on disk. This way the software has only to read the files and display the scene as needed, rather than calculate the scene from the mathematical models.

QuickTime VR provides very realistic simulations that require very little processing speed. Navigating in the 3D world of QuickTime VR, however, is more limited than exploring a mathematical 3D world. In a mathematically represented world, you can move to almost any position. In a QuickTime VR world, you can only go to the places where a picture was taken.

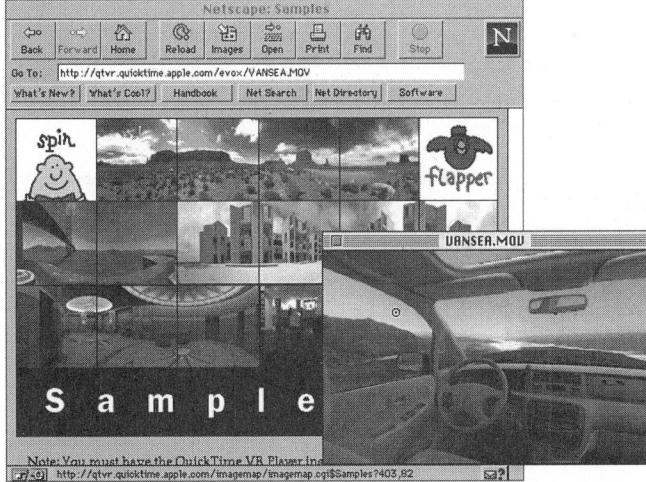

Q

QuickTime VR uses QuickTime's **compression** routines and file format to store the photographs. You must have QuickTime installed on your machine, and you must use the **QTVRPlayer** (available from Apple's World Wide Web site **http://www.apple.com**) to play these movies.

QuickTime VR movies are of two types—**panoramic** and **object**—and are used for very different purposes.

A **panoramic** QuickTime VR movie is created from a panoramic image of up to 360 degrees. The image is displayed in a window that shows a portion of the image stretched to appear optically correct. The user can zoom in and out of the scene and rotate the view to look in any direction. Hotspots in the image can be clicked to jump to other movies.

A panoramic movie can be created from a single panoramic image photographed using a panoramic camera. But these cameras are expensive. **QuickTime VR Authoring Tools Suite**, the authoring environment used to create QuickTime VR movies, includes a program that will take a sequence of images shot with a regular 35mm camera and join them together into a single panoramic image.

Object movies are very different from panoramas. These represent an object that the user can examine from any angle. These movies are made up of many images of the object. You will need some kind of rig that can hold the camera in position as the images are taken if you want to create an object movie.

If you want to make QuickTime VR movies, you should purchase the QuickTime VR Authoring Tools Suite, because it provides several different tools. It's available from **APDA** for $499. Apple has made available two tools for free that will take a single panoramic image or a sequence of image and turn them into QTVR movie. They provide fewer options, but the price is right! **Make QTVR Object** makes an object movie, while **Make QTVR Panorama** creates panoramic movies. They are available on Apple's Web site **http://www.apple.com**.

See Also

PhotoBubble; QuickTime; VRML

QuickTime VR Authoring Tools Suite

Authoring tools for creating QuickTime VR panoramic and object movies. While you can use the free applications **Make QTVR Object** and **Make QTVR Panorama** to create these movies, only the Authoring Tool Suite includes tools for joining together multiple images into a single panoramic photograph, and for linking multiple movies together.

See Also

Make QTVR Object; Make QTVR Panorama; QuickTime VR

Quit Command

When you want to quit an application, go to the **File menu** and select Quit (⌘-Q). If the open document has not been **saved,** the application asks you whether you want to save any changes to the document before quitting.

You have the option of saving the document or **canceling** the Quit command. It should be noted that quitting an application shuts the application, whereas closing a document leaves the program up and running, but closes that document.

To quit an application, follow these steps:

1. Save any open documents.

2. Select Quit from the File menu (⌘-Q).

3. The program quits and returns you to the Finder or any other open applications.

See Also

Cancel Keyboard Shortcut; File Menu; Save Command

Q

R

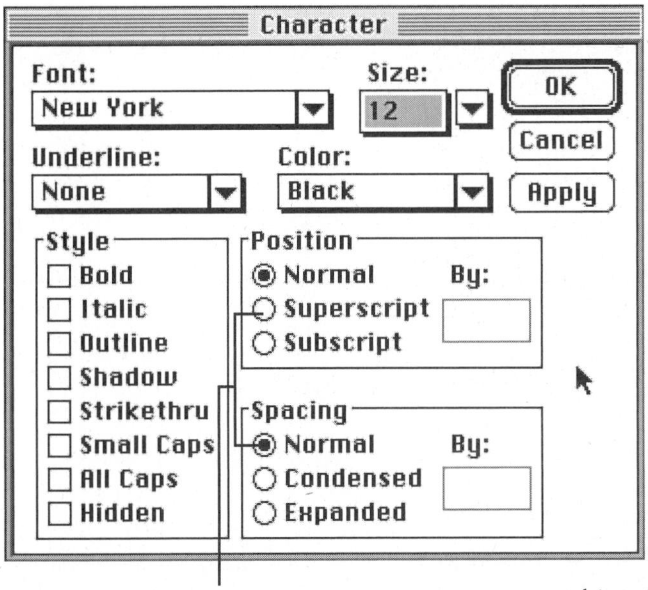

Radio Buttons

Radio buttons are round buttons in **dialog boxes** that enable you to choose from a list of options by clicking the button of your choice, as shown in the figure. If, for example, you choose the **Print** command from the **File menu** in an application, the dialog box might enable you to choose from three different print quality levels: Best, Normal, or Draft. Each of these choices has a corresponding radio button. To select an option, click the radio button beside your choice. When you click a radio button, a smaller black circle appears within the radio button to confirm that it's selected.

Radio buttons are mutually exclusive, meaning they're designed for situations where only one option from a list can be selected. In the previous example, you can only choose one print quality: Best, Normal, or Draft. You can't choose Best and Draft; you have to choose one or the other. Radio buttons are linked behind the scenes, so if you click one radio button, any others for that particular selection are automatically deselected.

See Also

File Menu; Print

Radius PressView 17 SR,
See Monitors, Common Models

RAID Arrays

RAID stands for *Redundant Array of Inexpensive Disks*, although it is also sometimes written as *Independent* rather than *Inexpensive*. Perhaps the drive manufacturers don't want to give you the wrong idea.

The RAID concept originally appeared when small **disk drives** were slow and large drives were fast and expensive. Several inexpensive drives, linked together to create a RAID drive, appear to the Macintosh as a large virtual drive that has a much faster transfer rate than the individual small drives. This is achieved by splitting the data across the drives as it is being written. Alternatively, data can be duplicated between multiple drives to create an on-the-fly backup.

Radio buttons

Several manufacturers now offer RAID drives. These are sold as a single case containing multiple mechanisms, along with the special software needed to format and use the drive. A RAID drive appears on the Macintosh desktop as a normal single disk drive.

There is also software available that can be used to create a RAID using existing separate drive mechanisms. This is an inexpensive way of creating a faster and larger drive, but it might not be the best thing to do. For best performance, the drives should have the same capacity. Also, it's best to work with relatively new drives; a failure of either drive makes all data useless. For these reasons, it's probably best to buy a dedicated RAID drive if you need the performance.

With the dramatic reduction of disk drive prices in the past few years, some of the reasons for RAID no longer exist; but a RAID drive is still generally faster than a single-drive mechanism, making it particularly useful for demanding video digitizing tasks. Before buying, check the throughput required by your **digitizer** and the specifications for the RAID and single-drive mechanisms before spending the extra money for a RAID.

See Also

Backing Up; Disks and Drives

RAM, *See Memory*

RAM Cache and RAM Disks

By using a RAM cache and/or setting up a RAM disk, you are manually setting aside a part of your system's memory where it can store frequently used items from your **hard disk**. By keeping these items in this separate memory, your computer can quickly access this information rather than searching on the hard disk each time it needs that data.

Both the amount of memory set aside for a RAM cache (also called disk cache) and the creation of a RAM Disk are accessed through the **Memory Control Panel.**

See Also

Disk Cache; Hard Disks; Memory Control Panel

RAM Doubler

RAM Doubler, from Connectix Corporation (2655 Campus Drive, San Mateo, CA 94403, Phone: 800-950-5880, Web site **http://www.connectix.com**), works with System 6.05 or higher and uses a **Virtual Memory** scheme to fool your Macintosh into thinking there's twice the available RAM than there really is. RAM Doubler works quite well and is popular with PowerBook users whose units shipped with a minimum amount of RAM.

The implementation of RAM Doubler is very simple: Install the application and restart your computer. If you had 8MB of RAM before you installed RAM Doubler, upon restart the system will act as though it has 16MB and will enable you to open applications until you've reached your new 16MB limit. To see how RAM Doubler affects your system, choose the "**About This Macintosh**" dialog box at the top of the Apple menu with RAM Doubler on. You'll see two figures for memory: Built-in memory (which is the actual figure for your installed RAM) and Total Memory (which is double your installed memory, courtesy of RAM Doubler).

See Also

About This Macintosh; Not Enough Memory Message

Random Access Memory, *See Memory*

Random Data Access

This random data access is made possible because a disk drive's read/write heads can move back and forth across the face of a disk while the disk is spinning. Data stored close to the center of a disk is, in practical terms, no further away from the read/write heads than data stored at the very edges of the platter.

Range Finder

A range finder camera uses a separate lens to provide the preview of the image you are taking with the camera. When you look through the camera's view finder, you aren't seeing what the lens is seeing, because you are looking through the separate lens.

Range Finder cameras are a problem when taking a picture very close to an object (differences between the actual camera's lens and the view finder lens are greatest as objects move closer to the camera). Range Finder cameras are also a problem if you use a lens attachment to adjust the focal length of the lens.

Compared to **SLR** cameras, Range Finder cameras are cheaper and easier to make, they also tend to be lighter, and quieter (they don't have to flip up the mirror while the picture is being taken).

See Also

Digital Cameras; Focal Length; SLR

Raskin, Jef

Jef Raskin, a former professor turned computer consultant, joined Apple in 1978 as manager of the Publications department. Raskin went on to start the New Product Review and Application Software divisions.

More importantly to this book, Raskin was the driving force behind the original Macintosh project at Apple. Long before it looked anything like today's Mac, Raskin envisioned a machine that could be used as an appliance. It would be cheap, easy to use, and self-contained.

Raskin began the Macintosh research project in September 1979. The Macintosh he envisioned would cost less than $500 and be so easy to use that manuals would truly be irrelevant. It would also be portable and run for up to two hours on battery power.

By the time Raskin resigned from Apple in 1982 over differences with **Steve Jobs**, the Macintosh project looked much more like a scaled-down **Lisa**, and much more like the Macintosh that was eventually released.

After leaving Apple, Raskin became a writer and consultant. In March 1987, he was presented with a Mac Plus designated as the one millionth Macintosh.

See Also

History and Culture of the Macintosh; Jobs, Steve; Lisa

Raster Image Processor (RIP)

The RIP interprets **PostScript** data into very high-resolution bitmapped images (raster images). Because it must process huge amounts of complex data very quickly, it is a source of potential problems. All sorts of things can "choke up" a RIP, but improper and overly complicated graphics techniques are a common source of difficulty. For example, embedding an **EPS** (**Encapsulated PostScript**) graphic in another EPS graphic is definitely frowned upon by service bureaus (where RIPs most often reside). Many service bureaus and other service providers have electronic publication file guidelines they are happy to share with you. Raster image processor problems are usually addressed in these guidelines.

Raster image processors are either hardware or software, but hardware RIPs are favored because they are faster. Speed is a major concern in the economics of a service bureau because it affects how much data can be processed in a workday and therefore how many clients can be served.

See Also

Imagesetters; PostScript; Prepress; Printing

Ray Dream Designer/Studio

Ray Dream Designer/Studio is an easy-to-use, low-cost **3D modeling** program that has been marketed primarily to illustrators and other users with a non-3D background.

The original product, Ray Dream Designer, featured only modeling and **rendering** features. Ray Dream Designer 4.0 added a plug-in architecture that makes it possible to add features and effects. The first plug-in from Ray Dream Designer was an animation tool; the tool and Ray Dream Designer are sold as the Ray Dream Studio package.

The modeler in Ray Dream supports lathing and extrusion, and you can create multiple cross-sections of an extrusion, as well as adjust the shape along which the extrusion is made (it's effectively a sweep tool). 2D surfaces are drawn using a **Bézier** pen tool, but after the shape has been created, you cannot edit the individual surfaces—you can only go back and edit the basic cross sections and paths in the models.

Surfaces and libraries of models are accessed from separate windows. Surfaces are dragged from the surface window onto the surface of models. Ray Dream also supports rotoscoping (applying **QuickTime** movies as a texture to an object).

Designer also has Wizard tools that help you quickly create basic shapes and scenes.

The new animation tool is surprisingly powerful, supporting such features as inverse kinematics and *point at* (which causes an object to always face another object as it is animated). Ray Dream offers some additional plug-in modules that include layered fog and additional camera lenses (including a panoramic lens).

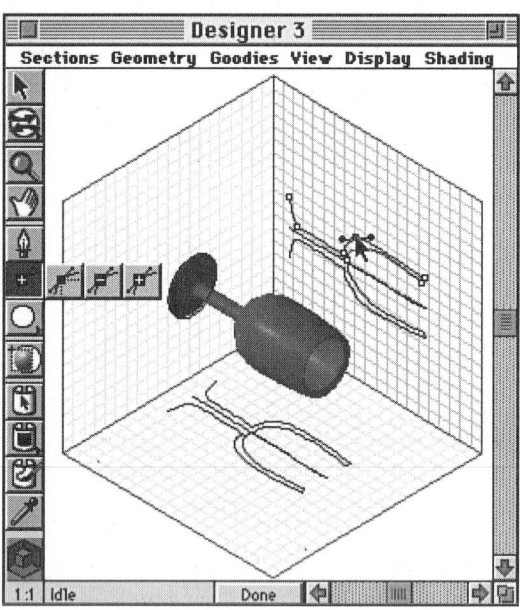

Fractal Design
Price: $499
Phone: (408) 688-5300
Web: **http://www.fractal.com**

See Also

3D; Modeling

Ray Dream's AddDepth, *See AddDepth*

Ray Tracing, *See Alias' Sketch*

Read Me Files

Read Me **files** are documents included with applications to give last minute information about the application, additional instructions, or a personal note from the developer. These files are usually in **TeachText** or **SimpleText** format, and it's not unusual for software developers to include either the TeachText or SimpleText application on the same disk in case the user doesn't have it.

Read Me files are very popular for **shareware** and **freeware** authors who distribute their products through **online services** or the **Internet**.

Because these files are transferred via phone lines, rather than by disk, they include Read Me files for their application instructions, credits, and if it's shareware, where to send the check. TeachText has been around since the Mac was introduced, it's automatically installed with your **System**, and it's included with most every application you buy. Shareware and freeware authors feel pretty confident you'll have a copy of TeachText or SimpleText on your **hard drive** and be able to read their Read Me files.

See Also

Files; Hard Disks; Internet; Online Services; SimpleText; TeachText

Read-Only Memory (ROM), *See Power Mac Logic Boards*

Read/Write Heads

Read/write heads are responsible for transferring data (writing) to the computer's hard drive as well as retrieving (reading) the information that has been stored there. Read/write heads also make random data access possible, because they can move back and forth across the face of a disk while the disk is spinning. Data stored close to the center of a disk is, in practical terms, no further away from the read/write heads than data stored at the very edges of the platter.

See Also

Disks and Drives; Online Storage

RealAudio

RealAudio is a system with several parts:

- A "file format" used to transfer sound files over the **Internet** in real time.
- Commercial software to create and serve RealAudio content.
- Free client software that receives and plays RealAudio content.

As CPUs and **network** connections increase in speed and **bandwidth**, it becomes more feasible to transfer video and audio files over networks such as the **Internet**. RealAudio (the company) has advanced this technology to the point that users of RealAudio 1.0 could receive low-quality audio over 14,400-baud **modem** connections.

RealAudio files don't contain the actual sounds—rather, the audio data is "streamed" from the server machine to the client machine. The streamed data is compressed by the server and decompressed by a RealAudio player or **plug-in** application on the user's computer. This approach avoids time-consuming writes to the client's disk and massive sound files, albeit with an unmistakable effect on sound quality.

RealAudio enables users to receive content that it just isn't practical to deliver in **AIFF**/Mu-law/**MPEG** format—large files such as the complete soundtrack to *Plan 9 from Outer Space* ,which would take days to download and dozens or hundreds of megabytes to store.

RealAudio's sound quality suffers as a result. It's often compared to AM radio.

In 1995, when RealAudio was released, the format was used primarily in conjunction with the World Wide Web. It's possible that RealAudio might develop a usefulness outside the context of the Web, as a sort of Internet radio. Given the popular success of the Web, however, it's likely that RealAudio will continue to be used as a soundtrack.

If you have a 28.8 modem or better, be sure to download the RealAudio 2.0 **client** package, which includes a Netscape Navigator plug-in. If you've got a 14.4 modem or slower, you can use the RealAudio 1.0 client. Both versions of the software install all of the necessary components automatically. Version 1.0 even configures Netscape to use RealAudio as a helper application.

You can download the RealAudio client software, and get more information about the "studio" and **server** software at **http://www.RealAudio.com**.

See Also

AIFF; Bandwidth; Internet; Modems; MPEG; Netscape Navigator; Networking; Plug-Ins; Server

Rebel Assault II: The Hidden Empire

Rebel Assault II, a Star Wars-based game, gives you the chance to man the helm of such famed vessels as the Millennium Falcon and an Imperial Tie-Fighter. Rebel II is visually astounding, employing 3D graphics, animation, and live actors.

R

As in other LucasArts products, the images are flaw-lessly mixed into an action-packed scenario. Each mode gives you the chance to play an entirely differ-ent sort of game, including one reminiscent of Dark Forces, sticking you into on-the-ground combat, mi-nus a protective vehicle, in the tradition of a **First Person Perspective Shooter**. Rebel Assault II, with its special effects, many-tiered plots, and varied missions, is a breathtaking experience that should prove challenging enough for flight sim pros, while still appealing to a more general, less flight-sim expe-rienced audience.

See Also

Absolute Zero; Sim Games

Reboot

Reboot is a computer jargon synonym for the word **restart**. To reboot your computer is to restart your computer. If, for example, you're using your computer and need to restart, you'll often see **restarting** referred to as **rebooting**. Reboot and restart mean the same thing.

See Also

Boot; Restart

Rebuild Desktop (Key-board Shortcut)

To **rebuild the desktop** file on your Macintosh, press the Option-⌘ keys just before the **desktop** appears when start-ing up your Mac. The desktop appears after the last extension or control panel loads into your system (you can watch their icons load at the bottom of your screen during startup), and just before the desktop appears the startup screen disappears. Holding down Option-⌘ just before the desktop appears brings up an alert box asking if you want to rebuild the desktop on your startup disk. If you want to rebuild the desktop of the disk, click OK in the dialog box. After rebuilding your **startup disk**, it then asks if you want to rebuild the desktop(s) of other mounted volume(s). To rebuild the desktop on other mounted volumes, **click** OK in the dialog box, and the desktop on the named disk is rebuilt.

See Also

Desktop; Keyboard Shortcuts; Rebuilding the Desk-top; Startup Disk

Rebuilding the Desktop

Each disk has invisible files called the desktop files (the desktop DB and desktop DF) that keep track of which files are on the disk, which files have been de-leted, which **icon** belongs with which file, and a host of other important file-tracking duties.

As hundreds of files are moved on and off your hard drive, the desktop file can get pretty large and be-come corrupt. If you let it go on long enough, you may start to have problems with icons disappearing, and, eventually, the files disappearing. To prevent this, you should rebuild the desktop every so often, which replaces the old desktop file with a new one. How often you should rebuild this desktop file is a subject of debate, but many users rebuild theirs once a month just to be on the safe side. Of course, if you're experiencing problems with icons disappearing or other symptoms (listed previously), you should rebuild your desktop immediately.

To rebuild the desktop, **restart** your Mac and hold down the Option and Command keys just before the **Desktop** is displayed. You get a dialog box, as shown in the following figure, asking "Are you sure you want to rebuild the desktop file on the disk (your hard drive's name appears here)? Comments in info windows will be lost." (The loss of comments in the Get Info Windows was fixed in System 7.5.3.)

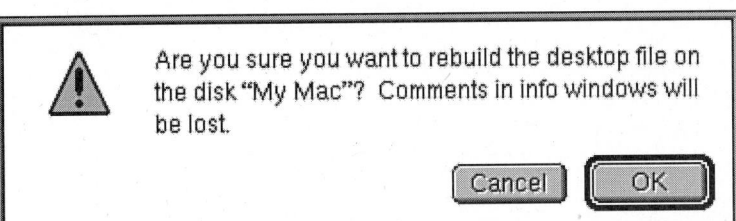

To rebuild your desktop, click OK. The comments are the personal comments, if any, you added to the **Get Info** window of a file. If you haven't left any comments, this is irrelevant to you. Click OK. A status bar appears, as shown in the following figure, with a gray bar progressing from left to right to show you that the rebuild is in progress. When complete, you are returned to the Finder.

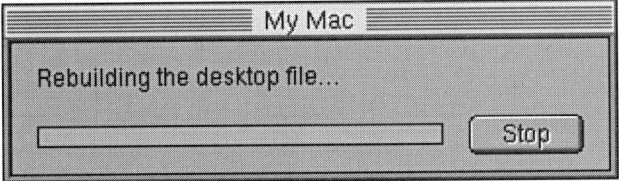

How do you know when it's time to rebuild the desktop? One warning sign is when your icons start to change to the generic icons. If you look at your Microsoft Word application icon, for example, the custom, full-color icon is replaced by a black-and-white icon of a diamond-shaped box with a hand holding a pen on it. This is a classic warning sign of a corrupt desktop file—time to rebuild. Rebuilding takes only a few minutes (the bigger your drive, the longer it takes) and many people do it once a month whether it needs it or not. It's good practice to get in the habit of doing it monthly. This helps ensure that your desktop file is always in good repair. Also, some experts recommend that you rebuild your desktop after a crash just to be safe.

To rebuild the desktop, follow these steps:

1. Restart your Macintosh.

2. Hold down the Option-⌘ keys just before you see the desktop.

3. A dialog box asks you if you're sure you want to rebuild the desktop.

4. Click OK.

5. After the desktop has been rebuilt, you'll be prompted to see if you want to rebuild the desktop on any other mounted disks (including disks.)

See Also

Command Key; Desktop; Finder; Get Info Command; Hard Disks; Icons; Option Key; Restart

Rebuilding the Desktop on a Disk

Just as your hard disk's desktop can grow, so can the invisible desktop file on a disk. In fact, it's not unusual to see a **disk** showing it has "zero" items on the disk, but it has 200-300K on the disk. That is the desktop file. To get this desktop file back down to its original size (just 1K), you rebuild the disk's desktop. There are a number of ways to accomplish this.

1. Hold down the ⌘-Option keys while inserting a disk into the disk drive. This brings up the standard "Do you want to rebuild the desktop on the selected disk?" dialog box. Click OK to **rebuild the desktop** on the disk.

2. You can also rebuild the desktop on a disk already mounted on the desktop by doing a force quit (Option-⌘-Esc) at the Finder. When the Finder starts its force quit, hold the Option-⌘ keys before the desktop appears and you'll get the standard "Do you want to rebuild the desktop on the selected disk?" dialog box. The drawback here is this dialog box appears for all mounted disks, so you have to click Cancel for any disks that you don't want rebuilt.

3. Probably the quickest and easiest way to rebuild the desktop of a disk comes via the shareware utility DiskSweeper by Jim Speth. Drag the icon of a disk onto DiskSweeper's icon, and in a few seconds the desktop is rebuilt and back down to 1K. You can find DiskSweeper on most online services and on the Internet.

If you want to erase disks as soon as you insert them, hold down the ⌘-Option-Tab keys as you insert the disk. You immediately see the dialog box asking whether you want to erase the disk.

See Also
Disks; Rebuilding the Desktop

Recent Applications Folder

This is an option for the **Apple menu** that creates a folder in the Apple menu and keeps track of the last applications you've used, which enables you to choose those applications from the Apple menu. You might use this time-saver in a situation where you used an application earlier in the day and need to use it again. Rather than searching around your drive, and digging through folders to find the application, you can just pull down the Apple menu, look in the Recent Applications folder, and just relaunch it from there.

It appears there because you used it recently. You can set the number of applications you would like remembered in this dialog box. If you only want it to remember the last three you used, you can set the preference to three in the **Apple Menu Options control panel**.

To enable the Recent Applications folder, follow these steps

1. Choose Apple Menu Options from your Control Panel folder.

2. Click: Remember Recently Used Items, then under the area marked Recent Items: Applications, simply enter the number for how many recently used applications you want to have available to you in the Recent Applications folder.

3. When you've entered the number, close the Options control panel, and the Recent Applications folder will now appear in the Apple menu tracking, making your recent applications available.

See Also
Apple Menu; Control Panels Folder

Recent Documents Folder

This is an option for the **Apple menu** that creates a folder in the Apple menu and keeps track of the most recent documents you've opened, which enables you to choose those documents from the Apple menu. You might use this time-saver in a situation where you worked on a document earlier in the day and need to use it again. Rather than searching around your drive, and digging through folders to find the document, you can just pull down the Apple menu, look in the Recent Documents folder, and just relaunch it from there. It appears there because you used it recently. You can set the number of documents you would like remembered in this dialog. If you only want it to remember the last six documents you used, you can set the preference to six in the **Apple Menu Options control panel**.

To enable the Recent Documents folder, follow these steps:

1. Double-click the Apple Menu Options control panel, located within the Control Panels folder within your System Folder.

2. Click: Remember Recently Used Items, and then under the area marked Recent Items: Documents, simply enter the number for how many recent documents you want to have available to you in the Recent Documents folder.

3. When you've entered the number, close the Options control panel, and the recent documents folder will now appear in the Apple menu tracking, making your recent documents available.

See Also

Apple Menu; Apple Menu Options; Control Panel Folder

Recent Servers Folder

This is an option for the **Apple menu** that creates a folder in the Apple menu and keeps track of the most recent servers you've been connected to, which enables you to choose those servers again from the Apple menu. You might use this time-saver in a situation where you worked on a server earlier in the day and need to access it again. Rather than finding the server and signing on again, now you can just pull down the Apple menu, look in the Recent Servers folder, and access that server directly from there. It appears there because you used it recently. You can set the number of servers you would like remembered in this dialog. If you only want it to remember the last three servers you used, you can set the preference to three in the **Apple Menu Options control panel**.

To enable the Recent Servers folder, follow these steps

1. Double-click the Apple Menu Options control panel, located within the Control Panels folder within your System Folder.

2. Click Remember Recently Used Items, and then under the area marked Recent Items: Servers, simply enter the number of recently used servers you want to have available to you in the Recent Servers folder.

3. When you've entered the number, close the Options control panel and the Recent Servers folder will now appear in the Apple menu tracking, making a list of servers you used most recently available to you.

See Also

Apple Menu; Apple Menu Options; Control Panels

Recompression

Applying a new compressor to a **QuickTime** clip that has already been compressed. Often, video is captured using either no **compression**, or using the Component Video compressor. Neither of these are appropriate for distributing the movie to others because of the size of the files. During the editing phase the movie is recompressed using Cinepak or some other compressor.

Sometimes, clips are compressed using one compressor, and then have to be recompressed either with a different setting, or with a different compressor. If at all possible, this should be done with the original clips, rather than recompressing the movie that has already been compressed. Using compression routines on a clip multiple times results in much poorer image quality due to the combined effects of the compression algorithm.

See Also

Compression; Digitizing Video; QuickTime

Record, *See Structure*

Red Book Audio

Red Book Audio refers to standard CD audio files. Most audio CDs conform to this standard. A disc that uses this standard usually has the disc logo with "digital audio" written below it. CD audio is stereo 16-bits, sampled at 44.1KHz sampling rate.

The term *Red Book* refers to the color of the book containing the specification for the CD audio discs.

The AppleCD Audio Player desk accessory can be used to play a CD audio disc, although it does not access the files directly. If you have an internal CD player, you can listen to the CD through the Macintosh sound hardware, if you have an external CD player, you must use headphones to hear the audio or use a cable to connect the output of the CD to external speakers.

The Macintosh file system recognizes CD audio thanks to a Foreign File Access Extension plug-in called **Audio CD Access**. This enables the Macintosh to read CD audio files and convert them to a format that other applications can use. The CD files are converted to a **QuickTime** movie, and can be played from any application that supports QuickTime. Or, after they are converted to QuickTime, using a QuickTime editor such as Adobe Premiere, the movie can be converted to AIFF format. Converting CD Audio files to QuickTime or AIFF format can be useful in multimedia authoring. Most applications, such as Director and HyperCard, cannot play CD audio from the CD disc. Remember that most CD audio discs are protected by copyright law.

See Also
CD-ROM; QuickTime

Redo Command, *See Undo/Redo Command*

Reference Materials and Directories

The CD-ROM is ideal for all kinds of reference materials, including directories and other searchable databases. A single CD-ROM can hold a lot of data, up to 650MB, which is quite a mouthful.

Publishers eager to put all that space to good use have brought out reference discs of everything from the *Star Trek Interactive Technical Manual* to the ultimate phone book, *70 Million US Households*. Naturally, the

quality and validity of the information varies. Users report that some of the 70 million families have moved or changed their phone numbers, and a companion volume, *11 Million US Businesses*, has similar inaccuracies. On the other hand, the *Phone Disc PowerFinder 96* series has gotten excellent reviews from many sources, as has the **ProPhone** series.

If you need to find out where the people or businesses you're looking up are located, try **StreetAtlas, USA** from DeLorme Mapping. There are twelve million streets on this disc, giving you a detailed map of all fifty states that also includes lakes, ponds, rivers, railroads, and other landmarks. You may never get lost again.

You can find just about any topic you can name on a CD-ROM. There are reference guides to cooking, sex, history, science, the arts, and so on. *Digital Beethoven* introduces you to 44 classical composers and a CyberOrchestra. *Everything Weather*, produced by the Weather Channel, has a database of typical weather around the world. Use it to decide what to pack for your next vacation. You can also check out the QuickTime clips on the century's wildest storms. *4 Paws of Crab* is a delightfully quirky look at the culture and cooking of Thailand.

Stephen Hawking's *Brief History of Time* is a classic "must have," whether or not you understand astrophysics. Along with the text of the book, it includes a biography of the amazing Dr. Hawking and a clip of his appearance on *Star Trek: The Next Generation. Cinemania* is an interactive movie guide, with reviews by such luminaries as Roger Ebert and Leonard Maltin.

Health care professionals and medical students will be delighted with the series of anatomy guides from Gold Standard Multimedia. They include *Human Anatomy*, with 6000 photographic images of cadaver specimens, plus the fundamentals of gross anatomy and dissection techniques. *Radiologic Anatomy* includes X ray, MRI, CT, angiography, fluoroscopy, and contrast studies. *Microscopic Anatomy* offers a logical organization of 1200 histologic slides and electron microphotographs.

You also can zoom to a full screen enlargement of any slide. Gold Standard Multimedia also produced *Clinical Pharmacology*, the equivalent of a 7,000+ page guide to prescription and non-prescription drugs, including patient-specific reports and much more.

To find out what's available in your field, check your newsstand for a copy of the *Macintosh Multimedia & Product Registry*, published quarterly by Redgate. It lists over 8,000 pieces of hardware and software specifically for Mac and Power Mac, including approximately 2,000 CD-ROM titles.

Referencing

Most desktop publishing projects involve combining more than one kind of document into one file: Word processing documents and graphics files are brought together in a page layout package to create a final design.

There are two ways to combine such files. First, as almost always happens with text, information from one file can be copied into another. This can also be done with graphics. Under this system, all information is contained in the final file, which can end up being very large. The original graphics files are no longer needed to view or print the final combined document.

The other method is referencing, by which the original graphic or text file is "referred to" when the combined document is viewed or printed. All the referenced files must remain together with the final document.

See Also
Publish and Subscribe

Reflection and Reflection Maps

Related to **texture mapping** and **shaders**, reflection defines the surface reflectivity of a **3D** object.

Reflection maps can be used to specify what is reflected in an object (for example, an image file could be reflected in the surface of a mirrored ball), saving you the trouble of actually creating the objects that you want reflected in the ball. Most programs support reflectivity, and some support reflection maps.

See Also
Alias' Sketch

Reflectivity, *See Reflection and Reflection Maps*

Reflector

A machine with a **TCP/IP** connection to the **Internet** that has been set up to multicast, or distribute, video and audio signals to one or more sites using software such as **CU-SeeMe**. Without a reflector, only two participants can have a conference using CU-SeeMe software. A CU-SeeMe user can connect to a reflector site and distribute video over the **World Wide Web**. Users are asked to notify the contact person for each reflector before multicasting, and to minimize connection time.

See Also
CU-SeeMe; World Wide Web

Refresh Rate, *See Monitors, Image Quality*

Registration Card

Keeping up with new versions of software starts with filling out the registration card, usually a little piece of cardboard resembling those in most other consumer products such as TVs, radios, vacuum cleaners, and toasters. Increasingly, however, software companies are including interactive registration options with their software, invoked either when you install the software or when you launch it. (The software continues to ask you to register until you either register or configure it to no longer ask you that question.)

Registered owners have several advantages. For example, many companies will automatically send free copies of upgrades to registered owners. They will also mail discount offers for newer versions to registered owners.

The major drawback to registering your software is that you will now receive extra, possibly unwanted, mail concerning the company's other products.

See Also
Software Upgrades

Relative Motion, *See Absolute Versus Relative Motion*

Relative Path, Internet

A relative path is a way of describing the location of a document or object on the **Internet** so that it can be accessed by means of a **hypertext link**.

A pathname is part of the A HREF or **hypertext** reference in **HTML** that leads to the document or object. A relative path, in contrast to an **absolute path**, points to a destination file by describing its relation to the originating document.

The directories that a **Web browser** has to go through to reach the destination document are separated by **slashes**. Two dots ("..") indicate the folder above the current one. For example, if the document is in the same folder as the originating document, you need to enter only the following HTML:

```
<A HREF="document.html">
```

If the document is located in a folder called "files," which is located in the current folder:

```
<A HREF="book/document.html">
```

If the document is one folder up from the current directory:

```
<A HREF="../document.html">
```

The following figure gives examples of various relative path names.

Relative path names are generally preferred to absolute path names because absolute path names are not portable. If the Webmaster of a Web site moves any of the documents linked with absolute path names to other documents, all of the hypertext references will have to be changed to reflect the new location(s).

See Also

<A> Anchor Tag; Absolute Path; HTML; Internet; Webmaster; World Wide Web

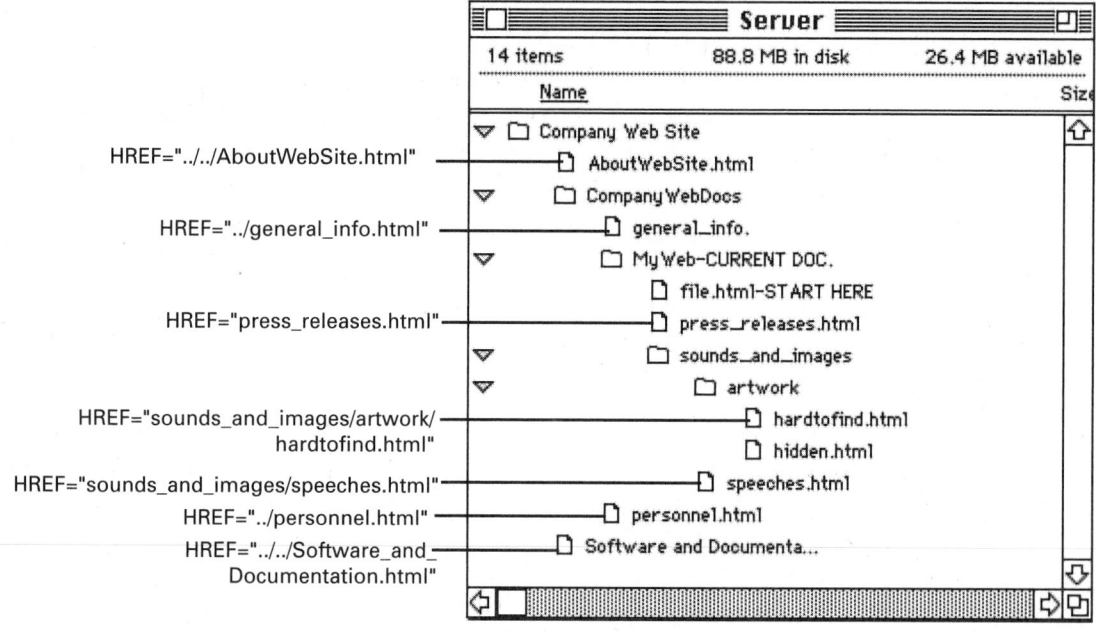

Remote Access, *See Apple Remote Access*

Remote Shutdown Utility

Using Remote Shutdown, a shareware utility, you can shut down or restart any Mac on a network from another Mac on the same network. This capability for one Mac to control the actions or commands of another is called program linking. Program linking is only available in System 7 and higher and is activated through the **Sharing Setup** control panel by clicking the Start button under Program Linking. You also need to activate Program Linking in the Users and Groups control panel in the User Options dialog box by clicking the checkbox for Program Linking.

See Also

Networking; Program Linking; Restart; Sharing Setup; Shutdown

Removing Items from the Hard Drive

If you installed a software program, **extension**, or **control panel** by dragging it from a **disk** to your **hard disk**, you can permanently remove the item by dragging it into the **trash** can at the **desktop** and choosing Empty Trash from the **Special menu**. However, if you used an installer utility to install the application or extension, these installers often install invisible files or alter system resources that cannot be seen. In this case, you need to use the original installer utility and perform an uninstall, which removes the selected program or extension and removes any invisible files or other actions performed during the original install. This uninstall feature is not available for all applications.

To perform an uninstall, insert the disk with the Install program on it and launch the installer. Click the "Custom Install" button. Hold the Option key and this will change the Install button to the Remove button, which enables you to uninstall, or remove, an installed program and any accompanying files that were installed.

To uninstall, or remove, an installed application, follow these steps:

1. Launch the installer program for the application.

2. Click the Custom Install button.

3. Hold the Option key and the Install button changes to the Remove button.

4. Click Remove to uninstall the application and any accompanying files that were installed.

See Also

Control Panels; Copying Files; Desktop; Hard Disk; Special Menu; Trash

Renaming Files Without Using the Mouse

You can find a specific file and rename it without ever touching the **mouse**, provided you are in the right folder:

1. To locate the file you want to rename, type the first few letters of the filename to jump right to it.

2. If you have a number of files whose first few letters are the same, use the arrow keys on the keyboard to move quickly to the file you're looking for.

R

3. When you find it, rename the file by pressing Return or the Enter key to highlight the **filename**. Enter the new name for the file and press Return or Enter again.

4. If you make a mistake while typing or change your mind before you're finished, before you press Return or Enter, press ⌘-Z, which undoes your changes.

See Also

Mouse; Naming Items

Rendering Farm, *See Network Rendering*

RenderMan, *See MacRenderMan*

Repairing Your Mac

Troubleshooting is the process of discovering what's wrong, why it's wrong, and how to fix it. It is important to think logically and clearly about the problem, eliminate what variables you can, and systematically work to a solution. Some of the things to check for hardware problems include: are cables fully seated in their connectors; are there sharp bends (indicating a possible broken wire) in cords and cables; and do you hear the hard disk spin up when you start your Mac?

You will begin the hunt by narrowing the search to the three main components of any computer system: the hardware, the software, and the user. Some problems can be caused by a combination of hardware and software, as is the case when faulty hardware causes the software to malfunction. But before you dig into the technicalities of hardware and software, it's best to start with the user because user-caused problems are the easiest to discover and fix.

There is an old story about a user who complained to his company's computer department that the new Mac installed on his desk wasn't working. When asked what exactly the problem was, the user replied that the machine wouldn't turn on, even when he pressed the foot pedal. It soon became apparent to the problem solver that the user had no idea what the Mac's mouse was used for.

While few users are as computer-naive as this one, there is a moral to this story that can be applied to everyday problem solving: don't assume the user knows what he is talking about. This applies even if the user is you—you could be staring the problem right in the face and not realize it, so be careful about your assumptions. Ask yourself if there is a real problem. For example, what seems like a frozen or crashed screen may simply be a task that is taking a long time to complete, as may be the case during network access.

Whether you are the user or the problem solver, it's important to be very clear about terminology when communicating with another person. If you are working by yourself, verify terminology with a manual or reference book.

There are a few places the user could have gone wrong. This includes using software incorrectly, forgetting to turn hardware or software features on, and accidentally deleting related files, such as extensions and preference files. A good place to start to look for a user problem is with settings in a control panel or the preference command in application software. A user may not be aware of all the settings on the Mac hardware or software, or even that there are areas that enable you to change the setting. Also, consider the possibility that someone else could have used the Mac and changed a setting while the user was away.

Software is the most common location of Mac problems; there are many ways for things to go wrong with software. Brand new software can come with problems built right in. Bugs, or errors, in the code, are not uncommon, and are usually fixed with a minor upgrade. Software installed on your hard drive can become damaged due to random fluctuations in magnetic fields near your hard drive, or due to a computer virus. A sector on a hard drive can go bad, taking a vital piece of your application or system software with it. Software can also be incompatible with other programs on your Mac, so that problems show up only when two or more specific pieces of software are running at the same time.

You can look for specific indications that your problem is based in software rather than hardware. Problems such as applications unexpectedly quitting or crashing are usually based in software. If you are getting error messages while in an application, your problem is most likely software-based. Other problems, such as those related to networks or peripherals, could be either hardware or software.

One of the most common sources of problems is System software, particularly extension files (called **INITs** in System 6) and control panels. Extension files are small programs that load into memory during startup, and are always running in the background. Control panels are similar to extensions, except that they enable you to change settings that control hardware and software. Incompatibilities can occur when two or more extensions or control panels claim the same areas in memory. This can cause repeatable or random problems, including frozen screens and system crashes. There are usually no incompatibilities with Apple System software; the problems occur with extensions and control panels from other companies or individuals.

Application-based problems are also possible. An application may not function properly if it doesn't have enough memory allocated to it, particularly if you are working with large files. Some applications will let you know that they need more memory, whereas others will perform slowly, quit, or even crash. You can increase the memory allotted to an application by selecting the application icon in the Finder and selecting Get Info in the Finder's File menu (⌘+I).

Reinstalling System and application software using the original installation floppies can often clear up problems. Other times, you may just have to remove the problem software if it contains bugs or conflicts with other software.

Hardware problems tend to be easier to locate than software problems, but are often more costly to fix. Typical hardware problems include Macs and peripherals that have malfunctioning subsystems as well as cables that are damaged or just slightly disconnected. The offending subsystems can include a RAM SIMM, a power supply, a nonfunctioning keyboard, and hard drives. Disk drive problems are particularly worrisome because they can cause you to lose your data. Unfortunately, drive problems are not uncommon, which is why you should make frequent backups of your data. This is particularly true for PowerBooks that are carried around a lot—they are prone to disk drive problems.

A totally dead Mac almost always has hardware at the root of the problem. If the Mac does turn on, hardware problems can prevent your Mac from booting. If you don't see the Happy Mac icon at the beginning of the startup procedure, you will get one of several other icons. A Sad Mac icon and the Sad Mac musical chord often indicate a hardware problem, including RAM or startup disk problems. A disk icon with a question mark means the Mac could not find a boot disk, indicating a problem with the disk hardware or cables, or System software. A disk icon with an X means that the Mac found a startup disk, but the disk or System software is damaged.

One way to uncover the exact cause of a problem is to find out what is *not* causing the problem by removing or disabling the item, or otherwise proving that it is functioning correctly. Other suspects can be eliminated from consideration because they have an alibi—they were turned off, not in use, or busy doing something else. It's a good idea to take a survey of control panel settings and the state of hardware (on or off) before beginning a lengthy program of elimination.

R

Process of Elimination The process of elimination often starts with extension files and control panels. First, you will want to turn all of these files off at the same time to see if the problem disappears. You can do this while holding the Shift key down after you restart. If the problem is still there, you've eliminated all extensions and control panels from consideration. If the problem has disappeared, you've narrowed your search to this class of files.

To eliminate individual extension files and control panels from the suspect list, remove them one at a time from the System folder, or turn them off one by one with an extensions manager utility such as Apple Extensions Manager. After disabling a file, restart the Mac and try to reproduce the problem. If the problem is still there, the file is probably not guilty. (We say *probably* because sometimes a combination of three extension files will cause a problem when any two will work fine.) Repeat this until the problem disappears, and you've found your incompatible file.

If you have several dozen control extensions loading at startup, you may be able to speed up this process of elimination by removing half of the extensions and control panels and restarting. If the problem is still there, remove the remaining one-half of the files and restart. When the problem disappears, you've discovered the culprit file is in the last batch you removed. Replace half of the last batch you removed and restart. Keep doing this until you find your bad file. With this method, you'll need to keep close track of which files you've eliminated, but it can be faster than removing one file at a time.

If you determine that the extensions and control panels are not causing the problems, you may want to consider other files in the System folder, such as the Finder and System files. Unlike extensions, these files can't be removed because the Mac requires them for normal operation. However, you can replace them with fresh copies. Always make a backup of your System file before replacing it, because you may want to reinstall it if something goes wrong. Although the Finder can be replaced by a simple drag-and-drop, you should use an Apple System disk and Installer program to replace your System file; otherwise, sounds or fonts stored inside the file can be lost (this is not a concern under System 7).

If reinstalling the System software doesn't clear up the problem, you may need to re-create your System file from scratch. In this case, remove the System and Finder files to a safe location, such as another disk and reinstall using the Installer application. *Never* put your System file in the Trash "for safe keeping," as you can lose it for good in the event of a crash. Keep your old System file on a separate disk until you have all your software reinstalled and working correctly.

If you suspect an application, you can use the process of elimination to make sure that the malfunction doesn't occur in other applications. After you've determined that it is indeed a single application that has a problem, you can try reinstalling it to correct for corrupted code. You can also try turning features off one at a time in a preferences box to isolate the problem to a specific task and identify a bug.

The process of elimination also works with hardware. You can prove that major components (such as hard drives, monitors, RAM SIMMs, expansion cards, and cables) are working by replacing them with parts that you know are working, or by trying them in another Macintosh. You may be able to narrow down the problem to one of the Mac's ports, all of which reside on the logic board. For problems on the logic board, the best you can usually do is to narrow down the search to a functional group. For example, if you've determined that your ADB cable and keyboard are working by trying them on another Mac, you can conclude that the ADB circuitry on the logic board is malfunctioning. However, it is impractical to determine which chips on the board are causing the problem.

After you have isolated a candidate culprit, either hardware or software, try to reproduce the problem by returning the suspect to its original configuration. If the problem reoccurs, you have been successful. However, some problems act randomly. In this case, you will have to use your Mac for a longer period of time with and without the suspect software or hardware to see if the problem reoccurs.

Isolation by Positive Symptoms Positive symptoms make it easy to identify the problem but often indicate a severe or fatal problem. A positive symptom includes smoke from a piece of hardware, or a loud noise from systems with moving parts, such as disk drives and printers. Bent, broken, or corroded components on the logic board, expansion cards, and connectors are other symptoms to look for. Excessive heat is another. (Be sure to shut off and unplug the Mac before touching internal parts.) Many parts are normally warm when operating—85 degrees Centigrade is not unusual for electronic components—but you should be able to touch them for a few seconds without getting burned. If a hard drive is very hot, there is a good chance it is dead.

Software can also exhibit positive symptoms. An example of this would be a problem (such as crashing or freezing of the screen) that regularly occurs when you activate a certain feature or press a certain key combination.

Totally Dead One of the most frustrating problems you can encounter occurs when you press the start button on your Mac and nothing happens. Sometimes everything isn't dead, just a major component. Sometimes everything is dead. In either case, you have a hardware problem. "That's nice," you may say, "but how can I eliminate suspects if nothing works and there isn't any smoke or flames?" The answer is to look at each of the few systems that could be preventing your Mac from working. Start with the indicator lights.

No Power LED LED indicator lights are found on your Mac, on external hard drives, modems, printers, and other peripherals. If the indicator is not lighting, it is possible that the LED itself is the problem, but it is not very likely. LEDs use very little power and are almost immortal. You can open up the case to see if the wire connecting the LED to the logic board is still plugged in. This is easy to do with most Macs, but not so easy with an external hard drive. Unless you've been messing around inside the box, a loose LED wire is not likely to be the problem, either. You should check the following items:

■ Is the device turned on?

This sounds like a dumb question, and actually, it is a dumb question, but the only thing checking can hurt is your pride. Check

the power switch of the Mac and all hard drives or other devices on the SCSI chain. If the Mac is plugged into a power strip, make sure that the strip is turned on as well.

Some Quadras and Apple Workgroup Servers have power keys. Make sure that the key is inserted and turned to the on ("1") position.

Occasionally, the keyboard power-on switch may not be functioning. Try unplugging the keyboard and restarting with the power-on switch on the back of the Mac.

■ Is your Mac receiving external power?

Make sure that your Mac is getting power from the AC outlet it is plugged into by plugging something into it. A radio is good because you hear when it's on and don't have to be looking at it while you fiddle with circuit breakers. If the AC outlet checks out okay, plug your test device into any power strips your Mac may be plugged into.

If your radio remains silent, check the fuses and circuit breakers in the power chain. If you're at home, you may have blown a house fuse or tripped a circuit breaker, or an office circuit may have become overloaded. (Your room's lights may be on a separate circuit.) Power strips sometimes have fuses of their own to protect against power surges, so check those as well. Also check peripherals for built-in fuses or circuit breakers.

■ Is your Mac's power supply okay?

If the external power checks out okay, the problem may be with internal power, the power supply. A power supply in a Mac or peripheral takes high-voltage (100 to 250 volts) AC power and turns it into several lower DC voltages that the various circuits can use. Power supplies are analog devices, full of big capacitors and resistors, rather than digital chips, which can burn out with age.

Older Mac models (before the SE) are notoriously prone to power supply problems due to lack of cooling fans and to capacitors that have low heat tolerances. However,

R

power supplies can go south in any Mac or peripheral. You can damage a power supply by plugging your Mac into an AC outlet that is not properly grounded. Plugging your three-pronged plug into a two-pronged outlet by using a converter plug can also damage the Mac's power supply, unless you ground the converter plug to a pipe or other true ground source. A power surge in the AC line can also damage your Mac's power supply, which is why a surge protector is a good idea.

If you have a bad power supply, you may have experienced a shrinking screen in the days or weeks before your Mac went dead. A shrinking screen is a sign that the monitor isn't getting the power it needs. CD-ROM drives with faltering power supplies may not read CD-ROM discs properly, and may not read audio discs at all.

If your Mac isn't working, try replacing the power supply with one you know works from another Mac of the same model. Although it is difficult to remove the power supply in older Macs (such as the Plus, SE, and SE/30), it is a snap in other models, such as the IIci and some Quadra models.

Nothing on the Screen If the LED indicators do light up and you hear startup sounds but nothing appears on the screen, the Mac is probably on, and its power supply is okay. Once again, it's good to start with a dumb question.

- Is the monitor on?

  The monitor isn't something most of us are used to turning off, so it's often overlooked. However, some users, to conserve energy, will turn the monitor off while leaving the Mac on for network access. The power switch on most monitors is usually at the back.

  Is the monitor plugged in? Remember, there are two cables that need to be plugged in: the power and the video. The power cable is usually plugged into the back of the Mac, but it doesn't have to be. It could be plugged into another power source such as a power strip or the back of an external hard drive, which may not be turned on.

Are the contrast and brightness turned all the way down? Check these knobs by turning them all the way through from one extreme position to the opposite position.

- Are the cables OK?

  Check to see that the cables are fully seated on both the monitor and the Mac. However, like all cables, monitor cables can go bad. With frequent bending, a wire can break on the inside of the cable, or come loose from the connector. The best way to identify a bad cable is to switch it with another cable on another Mac. If the cable is bad, throw it away. Troubleshooting and fixing a cable can be done, but it is not worth the time and will result in a cable of questionable reliability.

  Check for bent pins on the cable. Pins can bend if someone has forced the cable into the Mac's port. You can straighten bent pins with needle-nose pliers, but be careful not to break the pins.

No Sounds A Mac is not a full Mac without sound. If you get your Mac to start up and display successfully, but the Mac falls silent, check for these areas:

- Startup Sounds

  If there are no startup sounds, check to see if you have headphones or other cables plugged into the sound out port. A cable in this port will disable all sounds. If you have an AV Mac, check to see if the cards are seated, or if cables are plugged into the sound out ports on the AV card.

  If the sound port and AV cards are okay, open the Mac and check to see if the wire connecting the internal speaker to the logic board is plugged in on both ends.

- Volume Setting

  If you do get startup sounds, but nothing after that, the volume setting in the Sound control panel is probably set to zero. If this is so, the menu bar will blink whenever a system beep is supposed to occur. This is a convenient setting for PowerBook users, who may be working on an airplane or in a library.

Repair Utility	Developer	Contact Info
Norton Disk Doctor	Symantec (part of Norton Utilities)	10201 Torre Ave, Cupertino, CA, 95104-2132, Phone (800) 441-7234. Web URL **http:// www.symantec.com**)
DiskFix	Symantec (part of Mac Tool Pro package)	10201 Torre Ave, Cupertino, CA, 95104-2132, Phone (800) 441-7234. Web URL **http:// www.symantec.com**)
Disk First Aid	Apple	Free, found on Disk Tools disk

However, even with the Sound volume set to zero, you may hear some sounds faintly, such as a dialing modem.

If all else fails, try the above third-party utilities.

See Also
Troubleshooting the MacOS

Repeater, *See Hub*

Reports, Custom, *See Forms and Reports, Custom*

Request to Send/ Clear to Send (RTS/ CTS), *See Modem Cables and Connections*

ResEdit
Depending on your perspective, ResEdit has a number of very different faces. If you're a programmer, ResEdit enables you to create resources, such as dialog boxes, **icons**, and **menus** for your own applications. If you're a power user, it's a nifty tool that enables you to customize your Mac in ways you can barely imagine. And if you're a beginning Macintosh user, it's a mysterious program you've heard mentioned in the same breath as grim warnings of potential catastrophe.

Of course, ResEdit is all of these things. Used carelessly, ResEdit can make applications completely unusable. But used with care, it can enable you to do some amazing things. Simply put, ResEdit enables you to create and edit **resources**, bits of structured data stored in the resource forks of Macintosh files.

Why would a nonprogrammer want to edit resources? Because properly written Macintosh applications rely on resources for much of their human interface. For example, this figure shows ResEdit's view of a menu stored in a MENU resource.

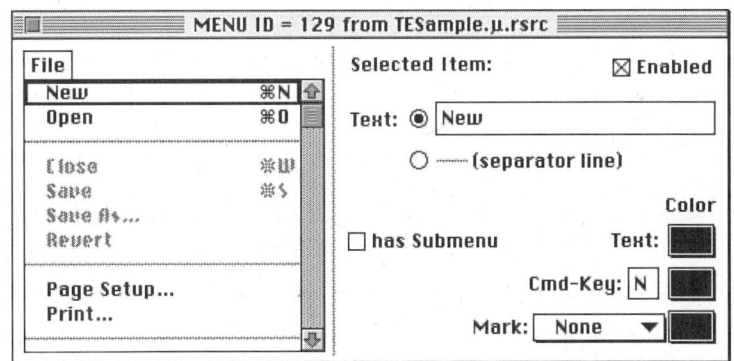

Using ResEdit, you can modify the text of any menu item (including its color and style), add or change command keys, or even add new menu items. This last case, however, could be disastrous.

R

Applications normally know which menu item has been picked by that item's menu number. The menu number is a special identification number assigned to the menu as a whole, and the item number is the number of the item within the menu. So, for example, the New item in the previous figure would be identified as item 1 in menu 129. If you modify the resource by removing the New item, Open would now be item 1 in menu 129. As a result, choosing Open in the running application would create a new document window.

This leads to an important warning about ResEdit. Always work on a *copy*, not the original. If you somehow do irreparable damage to the file you're ResEditing, you can always revert to the original. Similarly, never edit a running application, including the System and Finder. This is one of the surest ways to confuse an application.

ResEdit is a great way to create or edit icons (see the following figure) and other visual resources, such as dialogs. The icon editor in ResEdit is not as full featured as a full-fledged paint program, but it does a great job of the basics.

the Mac. This utility enables you to change the name of menu items, add commands to menus, or create **keyboard shortcuts** for **commands** that don't exist in the current application. You can edit the words in dialog boxes or message boxes, and you can choose from a host of resources to change to your liking. Each file's icon is stored within its resources, and you can use ResEdit to alter, or create your own new icons as ResEdit has its own icon editor and creation paint program built right in.

To use ResEdit, drag a copy of the file (remember: a *copy* of a file) whose resources you want to edit onto the ResEdit icon. (If you're using **System 6**, you'll have to launch ResEdit and choose the file manually.) When ResEdit opens a file, it displays icons that represent the various resources in that particular file, with a four-character code used by programmers to help identify which resource is which.

There are icons, for example, for menus, alert boxes, dialog boxes, windows, and so on. **Double-clicking** one of these icons takes you to another window listing all the editable resources for this item. Find the item you want to edit and double-click it. This brings

Icon Family ID = 129 from Easy Puzzle.µ.rsrc

up an edit window. These windows look slightly different from resource to resource as in one edit window you might be editing a menu, the next window might be editing an icon or a sound. After you've completed your edits, you can save the changes to the file, and those changes become permanent. If you decide you don't want to make these changes permanent, you can always choose Revert from the File menu, and the file will revert to the unaltered version you started from.

With ResEdit you can edit either an application's resources or the resources of the Mac's system and **Finder**. By editing these resources, you can customize the appearance of your applications or the look of

To edit a file's resources with ResEdit, follow these steps:

1. Make a copy of the file whose resources you want to edit.

2. Drag the icon of the copied file onto the ResEdit icon.

3. The file's editable resources open in a window displaying icons and Apple's four-character code for each resource. Double-click the resource type you want to edit. This brings up another window listing the available resources under that type. Double-click an item in the list to enter the edit window for that particular resource.

4. Each edit window is slightly different depending on the resource you're editing. After you've made your changes, select Save from the File menu to make these changes.

From a programmer's perspective, ResEdit is a capable resource editor, but is not the best in its class. That honor is reserved for **Resorcerer**, from Mathemaesthetics. In particular, ResEdit's capability to edit complex resources, using templates, is limited; some resources are especially difficult to edit using ResEdit, but a snap in Resorcerer. On the other hand, for many programmers, ResEdit is all they ever need.

ResEdit is available for free from Apple via its Web site (**http://www.apple.com/**) or its areas on America Online and CompuServe.

See Also

Commands; File Menu; Finder; Icons; Keyboard Shortcuts; Menus; Resorcerer; Resource; Resource Editing; System

Reset (Keyboard Shortcut)

On Macintosh LC models there is a keyboard shortcut for resetting (or restarting) the computer. You can use ⌘-Shift-Power key. The standard keyboard that Apple shipped with the LC models has a PowerOn key on the keyboard , but unfortunately you can't use this key to startup LC models. However, If you're using System 7.5 or higher, you can shutdown by pressing the PowerOn key. You are greeted with a dialog box asking if you're sure you want to shut down your computer, and you also have the option of restarting by clicking a restart button. You can also cancel if you press the PowerOn key by mistake while working.

See Also

Keyboard Shortcuts; Restart

Residents' Bad Day on the Midway, The

Inscape's latest collaboration with graphic artist Jim Ludtke and the elusive musical group The Residents brings a whole new style of gaming to the interactive arena. Bad Day on the Midway is a non-linear story focusing on a series of bizarre murders taking place among carnival freaks.

Instead of answering questions and giving commands, Bad Day requires you to inhabit different characters' minds as you wander the ground, piecing together the events and clues that lead up to solving the mystery. The trick is that certain characters have access to certain places and other people react differently to each of the different folk they meet. For example, if you are inhabiting the mind of the Dog Lady, you will learn different clues than if you are in the IRS man. The mix of 3D and 2D graphics in Bad Day on the Midway is the perfect complement to Ludtke's artistry and animation, also seen in The Residents' Gingerbread Man and The Residents' Freak Show. The homes and trailers of the carnival residents are full of multimedia treats and clues to the curious affliction that seems to be killing carnies off at an alarming rate.

Bad Day offers you the chance that no book can, a random point of entry to a story and the chance to wander through it. You learn the narrative as you go, in no particular order. Consequently, your experience can vary from play to play, making it a bit longer lasting than a book as well. Much like hypertext fiction, you can go through the story multiple times and experience a different series of events and encounters. The eerie feel, strange humor, and incredible artwork weave well with this enticing and disturbing tale.

See Also

Adventure Games; Dark Eye, The; Non-Linear Storytelling Games

Resize Box, *See Size Box*

Resolution, Image, *See Image Scanning; Resolution Measurement*

Resolution Measurement

Two forms of resolution must be considered in digital graphics—image resolution and device resolution. Image resolution is measured in **pixels** (picture elements) per inch (ppi). High resolution in an image means that it appears more like a continuous-tone image. A continuous-tone image, such as a photograph, does not appear to have individual picture elements. However, whether an image appears continuous or not depends on the viewing distance. Even photographic film has a grain, which is somewhat analogous to pixels.

Device resolution reflects the ability of an imaging device to transfer the image resolution. This simply means that when an image is printed, its resolution in pixels must be translated into device resolution. Device resolution is measured in dots per inch (dpi). A certain number of pixels are needed to make a certain number of dots when the image is printed. This is known as the sampling ratio. Two types of dots are used in printing—**halftone** dots and **stochastic** dots. Digital halftone dots are composed of a cell of smaller spots made by the output device, and stochastic dots are a random arrangement of these same smaller spots.

See Also

Color Resolution; Digital Halftones; Dithering; Stochastic Screens

Resorcerer

Resorcerer, from Mathemaesthetics, is the undisputed king of **resource** editors.

It takes a great program to compete with a free competitor, as Resorcerer does with Apple's **ResEdit**, but to many programmers, Resorcerer is worth every penny in saved time.

At its heart, Resorcerer provides many of the same features as ResEdit. It's capable of editing a wide variety of resources graphically or using templates. That's where the similarity ends. Where ResEdit stops, Resorcerer keeps going.

Resorcerer has an excellent graphical editor for color icons, patterns, cursors, and so on that includes features, such as anti-aliasing that are normally found in stand-alone graphics programs.

Balloon help resources are frequently overlooked by many programmers because of the difficulty involved in adding them to a program using ResEdit. Resorcerer, on the other hand, edits all types of balloon help resources handily.

Resorcerer's template editor can handle extremely complex resources that cause ResEdit to choke. Two examples of resources that Resorcerer can handle that ResEdit can't are: **Apple event** terminology resources, which are used to tell **AppleScript** how to interact with an application, and PPob resources, which are used to define views in Metrowerks' **PowerPlant** (see the following figure).

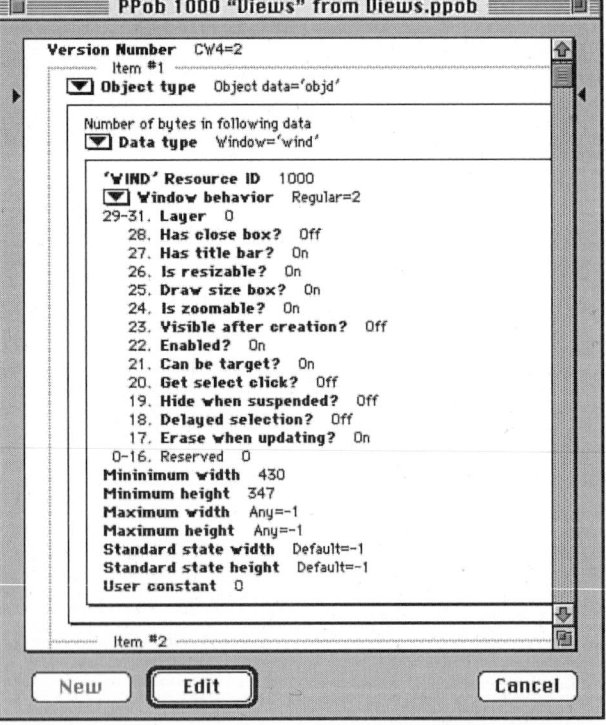

Resorcerer also includes a template-based PICT editor that's capable of viewing and editing the individual instructions that make up a PICT image. Careful use of this editor can help pare down significantly the size of some PICTs without affecting their appearance.

One of Resorcerer's most useful features is its capability to search all resources in a file for any text or **hexadecimal** string. This makes it very easy to find text hidden in a resource. It also can compare two resource files and flag non-matching resources.

Finally, Resorcerer effectively bridges the gap between resource *editors* and resource *compilers* with its support for **Rez** scripts. Most resources can be converted to Rez format, *DeRezzed*, as easily as copying to the Clipboard. Similarly, Resorcerer can convert most Rez files directly into resources.

Resorcerer is published by Mathemaesthetics.

Mathemaesthetics, Inc.
P.O. Box 298
Boulder, CO 80306
Email: **resorcerer@aol.com**
Fax: (303) 440-0504
Phone: (303) 440-0707

See Also

AppleEvent; AppleScript; Hexadecimal; ResEdit; Resource; Rez

Resource

A resource is data of any kind stored in a structured format. That's pretty general—let's get a little more specific.

The designers of the MacOS realized that much of what a computer program uses are definable tidbits of data that can be stored in standard formats. The information required to draw a window, create a menu, or display a dialog box has constant elements. The data in those elements might vary depending upon what the window looks like, how the menu operates, or the contents of the dialog box; however, each of these items has certain features that can be defined and stored in a set format. Any data orga-

nized and stored in such a structured format can be a resource.

Each kind of resource has a particular assigned type. A resource type is a unique sequence of four characters. Apple Computer has defined many common resource types for Mac interface features, such as windows and menus. Examples of some common Macintosh resource types include:

- WIND—data that describes a window
- MENU—data that describes a menu
- CODE—executable 68K code
- DLOG—dialogwindow data
- DITL—dialog item list
- ICON—a 32×32 pixel bitmap
- PICT—data that defines a picture
- snd—data that defines a sound (ends with a space)

Because a file can contain more than one of each type of resource, resources are also identified by an ID number in the range −32768 to 32767. Therefore, to fully identify a single resource, you must specify both a resource *type* and a resource *ID*.

One of the most important advantages of resources is that they can be accessed independently of a program's compiled code. In fact, 68K code is stored in resources of type "CODE."

Each file on the Macintosh consists of two parts, or *forks*: a data fork and a resource fork. The contents of each fork vary depending on the type of file. The following table summarizes how various kinds of files use the data and resource forks.

Along with resource data, the resource fork contains a resource map that catalogs the resource type, ID number, name, attributes, and location of each resource in the resource fork. The map lets the resource manager know where each resource is located, so that each request for a resource does not involve a sequential search of the whole fork. When loaded into memory, the resource map also identifies which resources have been read into memory and where in memory they are located.

Fork Contents

File Type	Data Fork	Resource Fork
Document	document data	document-related resources
68K Application	empty	resources and 68K code
Power Mac Application	code	resources
Fat Application	Power Mac code	resources and 68K code

The resource manager provides a full set of routines to create, read, manipulate, delete, open, and close the resource fork of a file. The GetResource() routine, for example, takes a resource type and ID as input parameters and returns a **handle** to the resource data.

Resource Editor

Resources would provide little advantage if they had to be compiled into a program from the start and could not be edited separately. Thanks to the Mac's use of separate data and resource forks for each file, however, resources can be modified using a resource editor without affecting data or other resources in the file.

Two types of programs are available for creating resources: resource *editors*, which provide a friendly visual interface to edit resources, and resource *compilers*, which work much like any other compiler, converting a text description into actual resources. **ResEdit** and **Resorcerer** are in the first category, whereas **Rez** is in the second.

Although either type of program can be used to create any type of resource (with a few exceptions), many programmers use a resource editor to create visual resources, such as menus, windows, dialogs, and icons, and use a resource compiler for more textual resources, such as lists of strings, or balloon help text.

See Also
Compiler; Handle; ResEdit; Resorcerer; Rez; Toolbox

Resource Fork, *See Resource*

Restart

When you first turn on your Macintosh computer, you are starting up; the act of turning on the computer and having it load the system software. If while working you have a system error or software problem, you may have to restart your computer. By choosing to restart, you turn the computer off and then turn it right back on, flushing the computer of anything you were doing and starting from scratch, as if you had just turned it on for the first time.

A restart can be done through a command, a **keyboard shortcut**, through a button on the front of some models of Macintosh, or by turning off the power switch on the back of the Macintosh and then turning it back on (although the last way is the least recommended). If you need to restart, you can return to the **Finder** and choose the Restart command from the **Special menu**.

This capability restarts the computer and reloads the system software as if you just turned it on for the first time. A keyboard shortcut, Control-⌘-PowerOn key, does the same thing: a restart. Also, in System 7.5 and higher, if you press the PowerOn key on the keyboard, a dialog box appears asking you, "Are you sure you want to Shut Down your computer now?" You have the choice of shutting down or restarting by clicking the appropriate button. You can also cancel this command if you press the PowerOn key by mistake.

Certain models of Macintosh have a reset or a restart button on the front or side of the Macintosh. It's usually a small round button near the bottom of the computer. Pressing that button restarts the computer. If all else fails, you can turn the power off on the back of your computer and turn it back on, but it is recommended that you use one of the previous methods first and only turn the computer off manually if none of the other methods work. Also, if you have a system error, the dialog box that lets you know you are experiencing a system error might include a Restart button right on the dialog box, and if your mouse is not frozen from the system error, you may be able to click the Restart button to invoke a restart.

Restarts are sometimes required after a new application or **extension** is installed, or even if you've made changes in control panels. The changes don't take effect until you restart. Restarting enables these new items to properly load into your system. Also, if you need to rebuild your desktop file (in case it has become corrupted), you can hold down the Option-⌘ keys during the restart and you'll be prompted with a dialog asking if you want the desktop rebuilt.

The act of restarting is also often referred to as **rebooting**.

To restart your Macintosh, follow these steps:

1. In the Finder, choose Restart from the Special menu. Or you can press the keyboard shortcut: Control-⌘-PowerOn key.

2. If your model of Macintosh has a restart button on the bottom front of your computer case, you can press the restart button to restart.

3. You can also press the PowerOn key and then press the restart button that appears in the Shut Down dialog box.

4. If none of these methods works, turn the power button on the back of the computer to the Off position, wait a second or two, then turn it back on. This is the least recommended way and should be used only if the other methods fail to restart your Mac.

See Also

Extensions Folder; Finder; Keyboard Shortcut; Mouse; Special Menu; Startup

Restoring Unsaved Items After a Crash

In **System 7** and higher, there are certain instances where you can restore an unsaved file after a **crash**. If you're working in an application and the machine freezes up without giving you the opportunity to save an open document, you may not be out of luck. Upon restart, look in the trash can on the desktop (by double-clicking the trash can icon). If it contains a folder titled, "Rescued Items," you may be in luck. Look in the folder to see if any files appear with the name of the application you were using followed by the word "Temp." This is the invisible temporary file that was held in **RAM** while you were working. When you restart, the Mac looks for these files to put in this folder. If you find a rescued file you think might be the temp file for the document you were working on, drag it out of the **Trash**. Then try to open the rescued file from within the application it was created in. In many cases it opens, and you may be able to retrieve some or possibly even all of the information from the document you were working with before the crash.

However, don't count on there always being a Rescued Items folder. This function doesn't work with all applications or all situations and cannot be relied upon; always do saves as you're working on your documents in case you should have a crash. That's your only real protection; the Rescued Items folder is a worst case scenario, last ditch effort to retrieve your work.

See Also
System 7; Trash

RET, *See Printers, Inkjet*

Retrospect Remote, *See Backing Up with Tape Drives*

Return Key

The Return key is used for a host of actions on the Macintosh. It moves the **I-Beam** text cursor to the beginning of the next line for paragraph breaks. It also serves as a keyboard shortcut for changing the name of a file. Clicking the file and pressing the Return key highlights the name, enabling you to change it. The Return key is also used to choose the default button in dialog boxes. (The default button has two dark outlines around it.)

The Return key and Enter key (appearing on extended keyboards) share many of the same functions.

See Also

Cursors; Enter Key; Highlighting

Return to Zork

Return to Zork is an amazing accomplishment on many levels. Unlike many CD-ROM games, the incorporation of live actors is actually well done and the characters effectively draw you into the mythical land. From the old drunk at the windmill station to the giggly witch in the swamp, you interact with believable characters as you explore a wonderful and sometimes terrifying world. For older gamers, Zork is a text adventure come to life. In the days before multimedia enhancement, one of the most popular forms of gaming was interactive fiction. Reading lines of text, you entered a few simple commands at the end of each scenario and were taken to the next level of the story. Depending on the choice you made, the story would take multiple twists and turns. Infocom's original Zork was based on Adventure, a very early computer game created on a mainframe at Stanford.

In Return to Zork, live characters are seamlessly integrated into the **3D rendered** landscape. Like **Myst**, much of the Zork world has been turned into a barren wasteland, but there are still enough people to talk to, so that you can find out where everyone went. To get to the bottom of things, you need to gather as many off-the-wall artifacts as you can, solving puzzles long the way. Some aspects of Return to Zork are so complicated that even veteran gamers will end up frustrated (you really need a Strategy Guide to get you through this one) but overall, the game is a perfect example of how multimedia can and should spice up the **adventure game** format. Activision's latest installment, Zork: the Nemesis, will be available soon.

See Also

Adventure Games

Revert Command

The Revert command, found on the **File menu** in many applications, reverts your document to its last saved version. For example, if you open a document that you've been working on for days, and you make a few changes and then decide the changes weren't necessary, rather than retracing all your steps, you can choose Revert and the document reopens in the form it was last saved in.

When you initially open a document, revert does not appear. The Revert command appears only when changes have been made to a document, giving you the option of returning to the previously saved version. Not all applications support the Revert command. To see whether yours does, look on the File menu after you've made changes to a document that had been previously saved. If Revert does not appear on the File menu, then the revert function is not supported.

To use the Revert command, follow these steps:

1. Pull down the File menu in your application and look for the Revert Command (if it's not there, your program does not support Revert).

2. Select Revert and you'll get a dialog box asking you whether it's OK to revert to the previously saved version.

3. If you want to Revert that document, click OK.

4. Your document reappears in its previous form.

See Also

File Menu; Save Command

Rez

Rez is a compiler used to generate **resources** from a text description or the format of the text description (the Rez *language*).

Unlike more visual resource editors, such as **ResEdit** and **Resorcerer**, Rez uses a text-based approach to creating resources. Originally an MPW tool, Rez has spawned a family of resource compilers capable of understanding the same resource description language. Both **Symantec C++** and **CodeWarrior** include their own resource compilers that function similarly to Rez.

The Rez language is fairly straightforward and should look familiar to anyone who has programmed in **C** or **C++**. The following figure shows a short example of the Rez language.

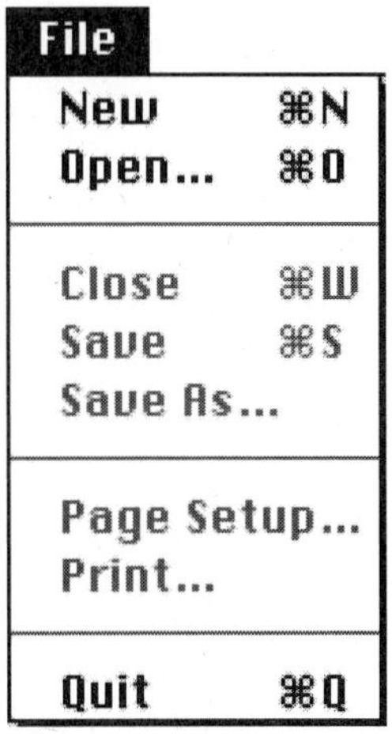

The following code shows the Rez language from the figure:

```
resource 'MENU' (mFile, "File menu", preload) {
        mFile, textMenuProc,
        MenuItem11,
        enabled, "File",
        {
            "New",
                noicon, "N", nomark, plain;
            "Open…",
                noicon, "O", nomark, plain;
            "-",
                noicon, nokey, nomark, plain;
            "Close",
                noicon, "W", nomark, plain;
            "Save",
                noicon, "S", nomark, plain;
            "Save As…",
                noicon, nokey, nomark, plain;
            "-",
                noicon, nokey, nomark, plain;
            "Page Setup…",
                noicon, nokey, nomark, plain;
            "Print…",
                noicon, nokey, nomark, plain;
            "-",
                noicon, nokey, nomark, plain;
            "Quit",
                noicon, "Q", nomark, plain;
        }
};
```

R

The whole idea of describing resources in a textual format might seem a little backward. After all, why would you want to describe a resource in Rez when you can just *draw* it in ResEdit? Well, there are some very good reasons.

Although some resources, such as icons, would be difficult to create in Rez, others, such as lists of text strings or balloon help resources, are well suited to a text representation. And some very complex resources, such as **PowerPlant** "ppob" resources, can't be created in ResEdit at all (Resorcerer and **Constructor** can handle them).

Because the Rez language supports C-style include files, it's easy to keep resource ID numbers consistent between a set of C or C++ source files and the resources themselves. Also, text descriptions of resources are frequently easier to include in books or to transfer to other computers whose files aren't blessed with resource forks.

No discussion of Rez would be complete without a mention of its sister, DeRez. DeRez, reversing the process of Rez, creates a text description of compiled resources. Combined with a resource editor, Rez and DeRez make a powerful combination.

See Also
C; C++; CodeWarrior; Constructor; MPW; PowerPlant; ResEdit; Resorcerer; Resource

RGB

The colors of light used to display images on video monitors (including televisions and computer monitors) are red, green, and blue. These are considered the additive primary colors, and they're used by many scanners as well.

Color images stored in digital form can be defined in terms of these colors, or in other terms (such as **CMYK**, which is used in the printing industry). Graphics software (such as Photoshop) can convert images from one color definition to another, but there are colors in each definition that aren't achievable using other definitions.

See Also
Color Gamut; Color Management; CMYK; Desktop Publishing Color Models

RIB (RenderMan Interface Bytestream)

The file format used by **RenderMan**, the high-quality rendering software from **Pixar**.

See Also
MacRenderMan

Rich Text Format (RTF)

Rich Text Format (RTF) is a file format developed by Microsoft to make it easier to transfer files between different programs or across platforms to DOS, Windows, or UNIX computers. RTF retains all of the formatting by converting it to instructions that other applications can interpret. All Microsoft applications can read and interpret these files, as can most other word processors and desktop publishing programs. When you copy formatted text into the Mac scrapbook, it's saved as RTF, so that it will appear in the same font and style when you later paste it somewhere else.

Riddle of Master Lu, The

This title from Sanctuary Woods puts you in the shoes of Ripley of "Ripley's Believe It or Not" fame. You and your assistant Mei Chi return from the "speaking" statue of Memnon to find that your office has been trashed and your business partner Feng Li has been left tied to a chair with a vicious cobra on the loose. From there, you enter the world of 1936 Peiping, China in an attempt to solve the mystery of who ransacked your place.

In addition, you are constantly on the lookout for strange articles to send back to New York to the Ripley museum in an attempt to raise public interest and generate revenue. The development team at Sanctuary Woods has done a great job integrating video with two- and three-dimensional artwork. Some hard-core gamers may find waiting for the characters to move a little slow, but the puzzles are tough and the game interesting enough to hold your attention. The re-creation of 1930s China and New York is quite authentic looking and draws you into the time and the story. Sanctuary Woods has recently released a new version of Master Lu that is optimized for the Power Mac and should do away with some of the wait time.

See Also

7th Guest, The; Daedalus Encounter, The; Eastern Mind; Full Throttle; Hell; Myst; Return to Zork; TimeLapse

Right Alignment

Text that is right aligned has a straight margin on the right, and a ragged margin on the left. It's also called "flush right" or "right justified." The easiest way to do it, in virtually any word processor more sophisticated than **SimpleText**, is to click the right alignment text icon on the toolbar (**Microsoft Word**, **WordPerfect**) or on the ruler (**MacWritePro**, **WriteNow**).

See Also

MacWritePro; Microsoft Word; SimpleText; WordPerfect

Right Arrow Key

The Right Arrow key enables you to navigate through an open document by moving the cursor to the right one character at a time. You can **select** the character to the right of the **cursor's** insertion point in a document by pressing Shift-Right Arrow key, or you can select the entire word to the right of the cursor's insertion point by pressing Shift-⌘-Right Arrow key.

In a window set to **View by Icon**, you can select the icon to the right of the selected icon by pressing the Right Arrow key.

If you're in a window displayed in an **Icon view**, for example, you can **click** a **file** and then use the Right Arrow key to select any icons to the right of the current selection.

There are a number of modifier keys you can use with the arrow keys. This table includes the most common keystrokes using the arrow keys.

See Also

I-Beam Cursor; Insertion Point; Mouse

Arrow Keystrokes

Sequence	Result
⌘-Left Arrow	Collapses Expanded Folder
⌘-Down Arrow	Open Folder/Open Next File
⌘-Right Arrow	Expand Folder
⌘-Up Arrow	Go to Previous Folder
⌘-Option-Up Arrow	Close to Previous Window
⌘-Shift-Up Arrow	In Open/Save Dialog, Selects Desktop
⌘-Option-Left Arrow	Collapses All Expanded Folders
⌘-Option-Right Arrow	Expands All Nested Folders
Shift-Right Arrow	Selects Character to the Right of Text Cursor
Shift-Left Arrow	Selects Character to the Left of Text Cursor
Shift-⌘-Right Arrow	Selects Word to the Right of Text Cursor
Shift-⌘-Left Arrow	Selects Word to the Left of Text Cursor

RIP, *See Printing Technology, Laser; Raster Image Processor*

RISC

RISC is the acronym for Reduced Instruction Set Computing. This **PowerPC** processor design achieves its high processing speed by implementing many simple instructions. These instructions usually are of a fixed length and execute very rapidly, usually one instruction for every tick of the system clock. This speed is accomplished by limiting what each instruction can do. A handful of instructions, for example, load data from memory to a register, or store data from a register to memory. All other instructions perform fast operations on the contents of the processor's many registers.

These instructions are carefully tailored to minimize overlap between the operations of other instructions. This lets processor designers add execution units—subsections of the processor dedicated to a specific function, such as an integer math unit and a floating-point math unit—that can run in parallel and boost performance by executing two or more instructions simultaneously. As you might expect, simpler instructions require you to use more of them to implement a specific task, so RISC programs typically are larger than Complex Instruction Set Computing (CISC) programs.

See Also
Power Mac; PowerPC Platform (PPCP)

Risk, *See Classic Collection*

Ritchie, Brian, *See C*

RJ-11, *See Modem*

Roaster, *See Java*

Rock, Rap, 'n' Roll

This interactive CD-ROM, officially called Mega Rock, Rap, 'n' Roll, enables you to play with melody and rhythm to create songs in a variety of styles. Rock Rap 'n' Roll is a digital music machine designed to let kids and adults have fun with music. It uses pre-composed music attached to a colorful interface to let a user "doodle" with music. The end result can be loose and unstructured or can be a rich, mixed down song. The name is a little misleading, because there are actually ten different musical styles represented, all the way from Big Band and Reggae to TechnoPop and Africa. After you select a style, you're presented with a palette of melody segments. You click the melodies to hear them.

Select the ones you think might sound good in sequence, and line them up. Then add extra instruments and singers. You can play along, using the keyboard to change pitch. When you've rehearsed your composition, you can record it and save it. This program doesn't pretend to teach music. But it demonstrates styles, and is a lot of fun to play with. Because the segments have been pre-composed to relate to each other, you're practically guaranteed to end up with a song that's worth keeping.

See Also
Juilliard Music; KidMusic; Peter and the Wolf

Role-Playing Games

Role-Playing Games (RPGs), closely related to **Adventure games**, are similar to the Dungeons & Dragons craze of the early eighties. In Dungeons & Dragons, people played according to a series of class levels, hit points, talent and skill levels that were determined by rolling multi-sided dice. Each player would create several characters as his or her party and then engage in battle with other players' characters by rolling the dice. Depending on the roll, your characters gained experience or hit points, or would be injured or even killed by your opponent.

Many players banded together in groups and played as teams. As far as interactive RPGs go, they draw on the main aspects of D&D and use them to immerse you in a computerized fantasy world. The plots of RPGs are generally much more in-depth than adventure games and provide detailed world histories, species profiles, and sketches of specific characters and class levels. Titles such as **Might & Magic III: Worlds of Xeen** from New World Computing get into the technical aspects of the role-playing genre, incorporating dice rolls into character selection and hit and skill points into game play.

See Also
MUDs and MOOs

ROM, *See Power Mac Logic Boards*

Root Directory

A disk's root directory is the first level you access when you open a hard disk, and the contents of this directory are presented in a window; it is the base level, the root, of all your other areas. If, for example, you're at the Finder and want to look at the contents of your hard disk, you double-click the hard disk's icon. A window appears showing you the contents of the Root Directory of this hard disk.

If you're working in an application and someone tells you that a particular file is stored at the root directory, they're telling you that the file is located in your hard drive's main level. Although this term is very popular on the PC platform, it is rarely used in the Macintosh environment.

See Also
Hard Disks

Root Level, *See Root Directory*

ROT 13

A crude system of encoding **email** or **newsgroup** messages to be transmitted on the Internet.

ROT-13 unscrambling is accessible via **Netscape Navigator** 2.0's mail or news windows. ROT-13 allows possibly offensive communications to be encoded so they cannot be accidentally read by someone who is likely to be offended. Each letter is converted to a number (a=1, b=2, and so forth), adding 13 to the number, and then converting back into letters.

See Also
Email; Internet; Netscape Navigator; Usenet

Rothmueller, Ken, *See Lisa*

Rotoscoping

This term describes the process of drawing or painting on top of film or video. Rotoscoping is sometimes used in traditional animation.

Rotoscoping also is used in some 3D programs to describe a process that maps a sequence of images onto an object's surface. This process is sometimes referred to as animated **texture mapping** and can be used to create effects, such as an animated picture of the screen of a 3D model of a television screen. Most 3D programs that offer this feature use a **QuickTime** movie as the source for the sequence of images. Programs that offer this feature include Specular International Inc.'s **Infini-D** and Fractal Design Corp.'s **Ray Dream Designer**.

See Also
QuickTime; Texture Mapping

Routers

Routers are the network devices that act as controllers, directing and forwarding network **packets** as they deem appropriate. Although many network devices such as **hubs** and even **bridges** simply repeat and pass on all information they see, routers are responsible for dissecting and reading each packet they receive to determine the appropriate destination.

If you have a network that has grown so large that you want to split it into smaller, more manageable networks that are connected to each other, or if you want to connect a small network to other networks, perhaps in the same building but on different floors, you can use a router to link these networks.

In a sense, bridges, switches, and repeaters are similar to the traffic police who wave cars through intersections when their turn has arrived. Routers, on the other hand, act like security guards at the front gate of a building who stop each car and check for identification, to ensure that the driver is in the appropriate place, and then provide more detailed directions on the best route to your final destination.

Beyond routing traffic, routers also possess the capability to translate between network protocols. For example, a router is used to connect Macs on **EtherNet** and Macs on **LocalTalk**. This enables you to gradually upgrade an office by purchasing new computers with EtherNet, but enable full connectivity to older Macs and printers that are using LocalTalk. Routers are also used to connect Mac networks to the Internet or to larger networks where protocols such as IPX are used.

See Also
Bridges; EtherNet; Hub; LocalTalk; Packets

Row in Databases
A row is a horizontal line of **cells** in a **spreadsheet**. All Macintosh spreadsheets designate rows numerically, starting at the top. The first few rows are typically used for identifying text, showing the title of the spreadsheet and a description of each **column**.

See Also
Absolute/Relative Referencing; Circular Reference; Spreadsheet Notation

RS-232
The most widely standard used for the connection of personal computers to asychrononous peripherals is known as RS-232. Most personal computers (and early Macintosh computers) implement this type of connection using industry standard DB-9 or DB-25 ports. Recent Macintosh computers use a slight

variation of this standard, the RS-422 serial port with a circular DIN-8 connector. (The **GeoPort** is a further variation of this connector.)

See Also
GeoPort

RTF, *See Rich Text Format*

RTS, *See Flow Control*

S

S-Video

S-Video is a transmission method for video signals that separates the color and brightness information into separate channels (and separate cables) and results in better image quality compared to **composite**. The plug for this format resembles, but is not the same as, a Macintosh serial plug. Most digitizing boards support this format, and it is the preferred format to use if your camera and digitizer support it.

See Also

8mm; Composite Signal; Component Video (YUV); NTSC; PAL; VHS

Sad Mac Icon

Every time you **start up**, the computer runs an internal diagnostic check of your hardware and the **system**, and if the computer cannot start up due to a problem encountered during this check, the Mac displays a black **monitor** screen with a Sad Mac icon. The Sad Mac icon is a Macintosh icon with a frown and two Xs for eyes, as shown here.

You could say it is exactly the opposite of the **Happy Mac** icon that appears when everything checks out okay. Below the Sad Mac icon is a **hexadecimal** code designed to let an Apple repair technician know what problem was encountered during startup.

Generally when you get the Sad Mac icon, you will also hear four musical tones which are known as "the chimes of death." These "chimes of death," like the Sad Mac hexadecimal code, are used to aid the Apple repair technician as to which type of problem was found during the diagnostic check.

Seeing the Sad Mac icon is not unusual if you've recently installed additional **RAM** because if RAM chips are not seated correctly, they can cause the Sad Mac to display. If the Sad Mac appears after installing RAM, make sure the RAM chips are seated properly. Other Sad Mac codes may indicate problems with an **ADB** port, **NuBus** slots, **SCSI**, and more. It's also a good idea to **shut down** and check the connection of all your cables, including the cables of any SCSI devices, mouse and keyboard cables, power cables, modem cables, and so on to make sure they're all securely in place.

If you get a Sad Mac and you've checked to see that your RAM is properly seated, restart the Macintosh. The Sad Mac situation may have rectified itself. Occasionally, when a Sad Mac icon appears at startup, restarting makes the Sad Mac go away without explanation.

See Also

Apple Desktop Bus (ADB); Disks and Drives; Happy Mac Icon; Memory, Capacity and Expansion; Monitors; Restart; Serial Port (SCSI); Small Computer Systems Interface; Shut Down Command; Startup Screen

SAM

SAM is a popular commercial **virus** detection and eradication program from Symantec designed to detect viruses and repair any infected files on your hard disk or any external disks. One of SAM's key features is its capability to scan mounted disks for viruses during periods of inactivity. The current version of SAM (version 4.0) also scans files that have been compressed with **DiskDoubler**, AutoDoubler, **CompactPro**, **StuffIt**, and **Now Compress**.

The current version is also now native for the Power Macintosh, and has an increased scan speed that is reportedly five times faster than the previous version.

A nice feature of SAM is its capability to be updated on-the-fly as new viruses are detected, which enables enhanced protection without having to upgrade the entire program every time a new virus is discovered. SAM also provides automatic virus updating of virus definition files through a modem.

> Symantec
> 10201 Torre Ave.
> Cupertino, CA 95104-2132
> Phone: (800) 441-7234
> Web: http:// www.symantec.com

See Also
Anti-Virus; Hard Disks; Virex; Virus

Sample Editor
A freeware sound editor that includes such features as cross-fades, reverb, and speed and pitch adjustment. The program also displays the sound's waveform. Available from **online services**.

See Also
Audioshop; Sound Sculptor; SoundEdit 16; SoundEffects; SoundStudio Lite; Ultra Recorder

Sampling Rate
In **sound digitizing**, sampling rate (or frequency) refers to the number of times that the change in amplitude of the analog audio sound is measured. The sampling rate is measured in Hz (spelled Hertz,

pronounced "hurts," and sometimes referred to as *cycles per second*). The higher the sample rate, the higher the frequency of sound that can be recorded. The highest frequency that is digitized is exactly half the frequency of the sampling rate: a 44KHz sampling rate reproduces sounds with a frequency of up to 22KHz. Why? Sound is represented by a wave that represents amplitude against time. Over time the wave cycles up and down; the lower the tone of the sound, the longer the wave. The cycling of the wave is also measured in Hz. If a sample is taken at 44KHz and the sound wave is at 22KHz, the wave appears to be at the same point every time the sample is taken. This results in no change, or silence.

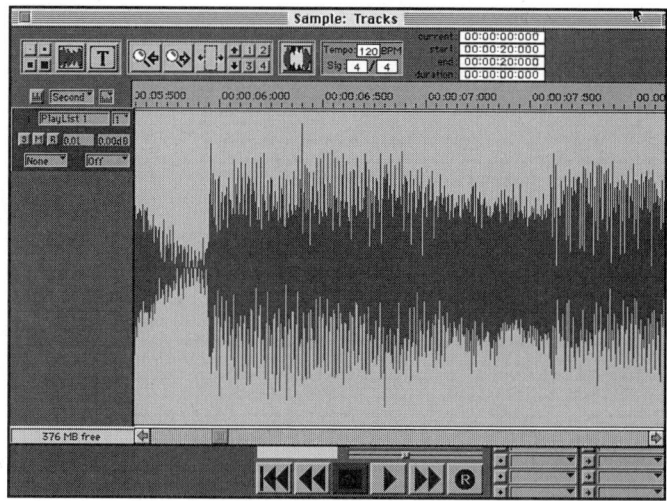

The quality of the digitized sound is also determined by the **audio bit depth** of the sample.

See Also
Color Resolution; Sound Digitizing

San Jose Flu, *See Scores Virus*

Sans Serif, *See Typesetting Terms*

Save As Command
Use this command when you want to create a new document with the changes you have made, but leave

the original document intact. You'll find Save As in the **File menu** of your application.

For example, let's say you've been working on a graphics project for several days, and the file is named "Artwork." You open the document and make some wild changes. You're not sure if you want to make these changes permanent, so you use the Save As command under the File menu and give this document a different name. You might now call it Artwork2. This way, it leaves the original document, named Artwork, untouched and creates a new document called Artwork2. You'll see that the name of the document (found up in the title bar of the active window) has now changed to Artwork2. This is your way of knowing that you're now working on a new file, and not the original file named Artwork.

To use the Save As command, follow these steps:

1. Under the File menu of your application, select Save As.

2. The Save As dialog box appears prompting you to name your file.

3. Name your file and choose the location you'd like your file saved.

4. Click Save or hit Return to save the new document.

See Also
File Menu

Save Command

To save a document you're working on, use the Save command, found on the **File menu** (⌘-S). This brings up a dialog box asking you to name the document and it enables you to choose the location you'd like the document saved to, as shown in the figure. After you've made this initial save, you can use the Save command anytime you've completed a part of your document that you want to save. Many people press the Save command shortcut (⌘-S) every few minutes, so if there is a power surge or other problem and their computer should turn off or crash, they "saved" their work and are able to reopen the document that has their latest changes already saved.

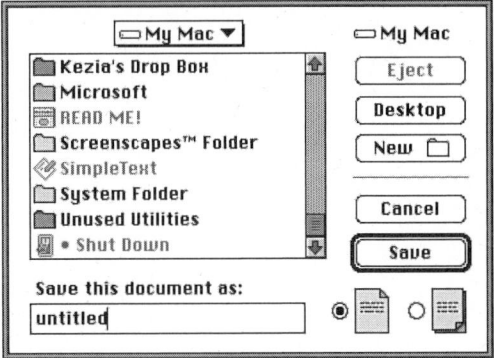

TIP Some applications also now offer you the option of an "AutoSave," which basically invokes the Save command for you by use of a timer, as shown in the figure. You can decide how many minutes you would like to go by between saves and it does the saves for you. Consult the instruction manual for your software to see whether it offers an autosave feature.

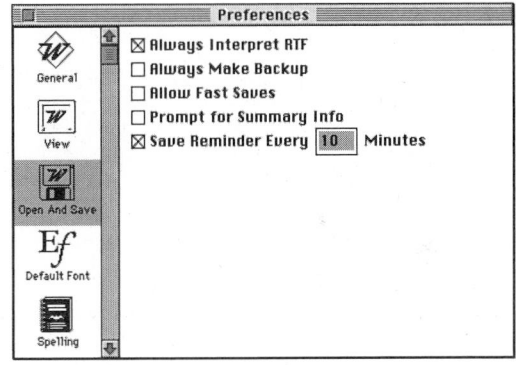

When you choose Save, the save dialog box appears prompting you to name the document. The default name for any new document is "Untitled" and the name "Untitled" is already **highlighted** for you in the save box, so all you have to do when it comes up is begin typing the new name.

Then choose the location you want to save the file by using the **scrolling** window to navigate to a selected folder. If you need to select a folder that is not on the selected drive, you can click the **Desktop button** that gives you access to all disks mounted on your desktop. If you'd like a new folder to save your document in, you can click the **New Folder** button in the Save dialog box and it prompts you to name your new folder. After you've named it, it moves the scrolling dialog to that folder for you to save your document. When you're ready to save, click Save.

There are a number of shortcuts you can use in the Save dialog box. To jump directly to a particular folder in the currently displayed list, type the first letter of the name of that folder and it jumps there. For example, if at the bottom of your list you have a folder called Zapf Dingbats, you can either scroll all the way down there, or just type a "Z" to jump there. You can also use the arrow keys on your keyboard to move up and down the list. The **Return key** selects Save and the **Escape key** selects **Cancel** in this dialog box.

To save a new document, follow these steps:

1. From the File menu of your application, select Save (⌘-S).

2. The Save dialog box appears, prompting you to name your file.

3. Name your file and choose the location where you'd like your file saved.

4. Click Save or press Return to save the document.

To save a document that is already named, follow these steps:

1. From the File menu of the application, select Save (⌘-S).

2. Your changes are saved from the point you selected Save.

To save a document that is already named with a different name, see **Save As Command**.

See Also

Cancel Keyboard Shortcut; Desktop; Esc Key; File Menu; Highlight; New Folder Command; Return Key; Save As Command; Scroll Bars

Saving a File

When you select Save As... from the **File menu** of a document, you set up a series of activities performed by the **Finder** to correctly identify and store your information so it can be accurately retrieved the next time you need it. Every application on a Macintosh should behave the same way, because the operating system and not the program performs the work of saving a file. What happens is as follows:

1. In the Directory dialog box, type a name for the file in the highlighted box and select a folder where you want to store the file.

2. The Finder passes control of the process to the File Manager by informing the File Manager of the new file's name and directory ID. In addition, the application tells the File Manager the location of the new document in RAM.

   The Macintosh operating system already knows the ID of the folder where the file is to be placed. (If you are working in System 7 and assign a new folder the System goes through a series of additional steps to assign the next consecutive ID number from those maintained by the Volume Info Block.)

3. The File Manager checks in the Volume Info Block area for the amount of free space available. The File Manager compares this quantity to the size of the new document, adds an additional amount of space for growth and reserves enough space to accommodate the file. The File Manager then looks up in the Volume Info Block the sector number of the next available block of space on the disk. When the space is located on the disk, the File Manager marks the sectors as "in use" in the volume bitmap and copies the document into this area from RAM.

4. The File Manager then records the location of the document in the volume directory. In this case, because the document is stored in consecutive sectors, only the catalog b-tree list is required.

   Data is recorded in the catalog b-tree in *nodes*. There are two types of nodes: index nodes and leaf nodes. Index nodes identify where information is stored within the tree and leaf nodes identify the information itself. Nodes are stored in different levels, from the root outward. Within a level, nodes are interlinked. Using a nodal structure enables the System to locate files more quickly because the data is broken into pieces.

The "b" in b-tree stands for "balanced." The node structure serves as a visible map of the location of leaves on the tree. As stated previously, each file has a name and folder ID number. The index nodes are structured so that nodes on the left of a node are lower ID numbers and those on the right of a node refer to higher numbers. The lowest level index node is called the *root node*. The root node's location is referenced in the volume info block, and therefore is known to the File Manager. Each node level refers to a range of IDs, called a *record*, pointing to another higher level node on the tree. The top-most level of the tree contains the leaf nodes that store the information pointing to the actual file's location.

The system operates like trying to find a specific apartment when you only know the name of its owners. First you have to find the location of the apartment building by locating the intersection of a street with another street. When you locate the apartment building, you must look up the owner's name in the apartment directory to correlate it with an apartment number. You do not want to check each floor for the specific apartment number, and the directory tells you that your apartment (say 601) is on the sixth floor. You go up the elevator to the sixth floor. Signs on the walls say turn right for 625 to 650 and left for apartments 600 to 624. You turn left and count each apartment number until you reach the one you want. The street address of the apartment building is like the index nodes taking you close to the location of your quarry. The apartment directory is

another level of index node, taking you even closer. The floor signs are like the leaf nodes, telling you specifically where your apartment will be. The apartment is like the file, located in its specified site.

5. When saving a new document, the File Manager searches the catalog b-tree for the leaf node associated with the folder in which the new document is to be stored. This is performed by comparing the folder's directory ID with the numbers stored in each index node record, searching each index node level until it locates the leaf. The act of locating the leaf node is called *parsing*. The following figure displays an illustration of parsing the catalog b-tree for file number 220, "My File."

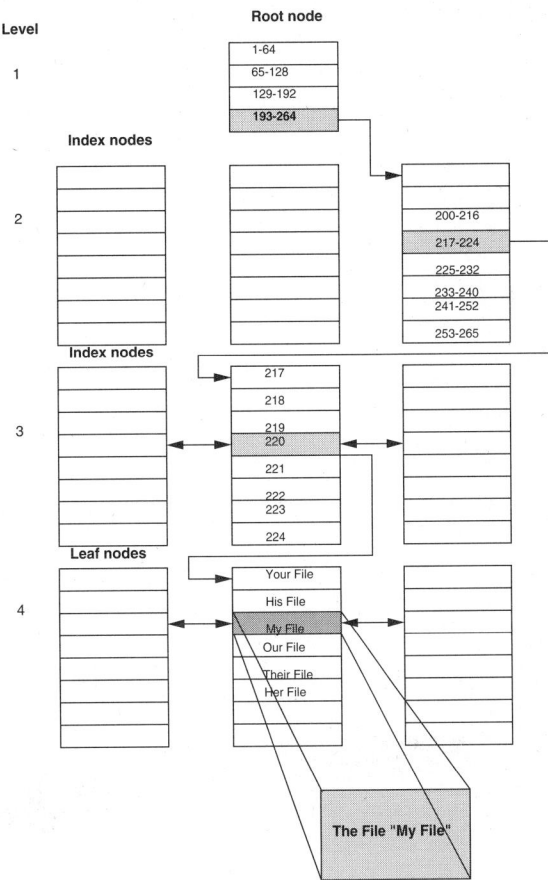

6. When the leaf node is located, the Hierarchical File System checks to ensure that the document name is unique for that leaf. When the check affirms that the name has not been previously taken, all of the information about the document, such as its size, the location of three pieces of its resource forks and three pieces of its data forks, and so on, is stored in a leaf record in that leaf node.

7. You see a document within a folder on the Desktop, all of the rest of the activities performed to place it there are invisible.

What Happens When You Update a Document?

Each time you save an existing document, the File Manager performs the following steps (the same sequence as when you save a file).

1. In the Directory dialog box, type a name for the file in the highlighted box and select a folder where you want to store the file.

2. The Finder passes control of the process to the File Manager by informing the File Manager of the new file's name and directory ID. In addition, the application tells the File Manager the location of the new document in RAM.

3. The File Manager checks in the volume info block area for the amount of free space available. The File Manager compares this quantity to the size of the new document, adds an additional amount of space for growth and reserves enough space to accommodate the file. The File Manager then looks up in the Volume Info Block the sector number of the next available block of space on the disk. When the space is located on the disk, the File Manager marks the sectors as "in use" in the volume bitmap and copies the document into this area from RAM.

4. The File Manager then records the location of the document in the volume directory. In this case, because the document is stored in

consecutive sectors, only the catalog b-tree list is required.

5. When saving a new document, the File Manager searches the catalog b-tree for the leaf node associated with the folder in which the new document is to stored. This is performed by comparing the folder's directory ID with the numbers stored in each index node record, searching each index node level until it locates the leaf. The act of locating the leaf node is called *parsing*.

6. When the leaf node is located, the Hierarchical File System checks to ensure that the document name is unique for that leaf. When the check affirms that the name has not been previously taken, all of the information about the document, such as its size, the location of three pieces of its resource forks and three pieces of its data forks, and so on, is stored in a leaf record in that leaf node.

Most likely your file has outgrown the blocks originally assigned to it. The File Manager locates the next available free space on the disk. The File Manager records the fragmented piece of the document in the catalog b-tree at the leaf node of the fragment under the same name as the original file. Information about up to six pieces can be recorded in the catalog b-tree for each file before the extents b-tree must be used.

See Also

Disks and Drives; Finder; Save As Command

Saving Time in Open and Save Dialog Boxes

You can save a considerable amount of scrolling in Open and Save dialog boxes by using some of the shortcuts Apple has included in the system. When you're in an Open dialog box, for example, you can use keyboard shortcuts to rapidly move through the list of available files. If you know the name of the file you want, for example, just type the first letter of the filename and the list jumps to the first file containing that letter. You can even type the first two letters in quick succession to get even closer to the file you want. If, for example, the file you want is called Asteroids, you can type the letters A-S, one right after the other, to jump to the first file that starts with those two letters. You can navigate up and down the list, file by file, by using the up and down arrow keys on the keyboard.

In a Save dialog box, you have a field for naming the file, and a scrolling window where you select where the file will be saved. If you click the scrolling window itself, it will highlight (as if it was selected), and then you can use the same keyboard shortcuts (for the open dialog) to navigate quickly through the list. You can also use the Tab key in the Save dialog box to switch between the name field and the scrolling window.

Other shortcuts:

- To jump to the top of the list, press the spacebar.

- To jump to the file closest to the letter Z (presumably near the end), type the letter Z.

- If you want to jump to the last item in the list, press the Tilde key (~) without holding the Shift key.

- If you want to cancel the Open/Save function and close the dialog box, press ⌘-. (period) or the Esc key.

- In a Save or Save As dialog box, you can create a new folder by pressing ⌘-N.

- You can jump directly to the **desktop** by pressing ⌘-D or ⌘-Shift-Up arrow.

After you have selected the file you're looking for or where you want to save the file (in a Save or Save As dialog box) you can press the Return or Enter key to confirm your selection.

Anytime you're in a dialog box that contains a **checkbox** or **radio button**, you can toggle that button on or off by clicking anywhere on the name of the checkbox instead of trying to click the checkbox or radio button, which makes toggling these items much easier. If, for example, you're in a Print dialog box, you can choose one of three quality modes (Best, Normal, or Draft) by clicking any of the three words instead of trying to click the radio button.

Scan Bits

Scan bits refers to the number of levels of gray (or colors) that a scanner can "perceive." Almost all scanners available in the mid-'90s can record 256 levels of gray or 256 levels each in the image's red, green, and blue channels. Two hundred fifty six levels can be stored in 8 bits of information ($2^8 = 256$) so you'll often see color scanners described as 24-bit scanners.

Some new, high-end scanners record more than 8 bits in each channel—usually, these scanners sample 10 bits in each channel, that is, they are 30-bit scanners. Even if your eye can perceive 1,024 (2^{10}) levels of gray, your screen can't display more than 8 bits, and your image-editing software isn't built to handle this information. Rather, the extra information is used to "round off" each sample to a more accurate 8-bit value than an 8-bit scanner can produce.

See Also

Scanner, Buying

Scanner, Buying

There are many issues to consider when choosing a scanner. The most significant measurements of a scanner's power are its resolution and dynamic range. However, there are practical issues to consider as well. The importance of these issues depends on your particular needs.

Resolution A scanner's resolution is measured in *dots per inch* or **dpi**. The higher the scanner's resolution, the more fine detail the scanner can capture. In most cases, you will be scanning at a resolution of 300 dpi, but if you plan to enlarge the scanned image, scanning at a higher resolution may be necessary. Resolutions of 300, 600, and even 1,200 dpi are common on flatbed scanners; slide scanners commonly provide even higher resolutions: 2,700 or 3,000 dpi slide scanners are not uncommon.

You'll often see the phrase *interpolated resolution* in scanner advertisements. Interpolation is a mathematical procedure for guessing what color (or level of gray) the dots between the dots that have actually been scanned should be. A scanner with true resolution of 600 dpi will produce scans of better quality than a scanner with an interpolated resolution of 600 dpi *when scanning at 600 dpi.* The two scanners will usually produce comparable results scanning at the true resolution of the lower-resolution scanner.

Scan Bits *Scan bits* refers to the number of levels of gray (or colors) that a scanner can "perceive." Almost all scanners available in the mid-'90s can record 256 levels of gray or 256 levels each in the image's red, green, and blue channels. Two hundred fifty six levels can be stored in 8 bits of information ($2^8 = 256$) so you'll often see color scanners described as 24-bit scanners.

Some new, high-end scanners record more than 8-bits in each channel—usually, these scanners sample 10 bits in each channel; that is, they are 30-bit scanners. Even if your eye can perceive 1,024 (2^{10}) levels of gray, your screen can't display more than 8- bits, and your image-editing software isn't built to handle this information. Rather, the extra information is used to "round off" each sample to a more accurate 8-bit value than an 8-bit scanner can produce.

Dynamic Range Even among scanners with the same number of scan bits, some scanners are better than others at picking out subtle differences in color, such as fine details in an image's highlight or shadow areas.

Dynamic range is measured in many different ways. Most often, you'll see it measured on a 0–4 scale, where 4 is the ideal—the quality produced by drum scanners. Even a scanner with limited dynamic range can usually produce an acceptable scan of a good photograph that does not contain extensive light and dark areas. However, such scanners have trouble with poorly-balanced photographs, or good photographs containing dramatic tonal effects.

This dynamic range scale doesn't tell you anything about where the scanner's particular weaknesses are. Some scanners have special trouble with highlight areas, and some have trouble with shadow areas. There isn't a good way to quantify the scanner's weaknesses, but most reviews of scanners in Mac magazines identify the scanner's problem areas.

Single-Pass versus 3-Pass Scanners Some scanners can scan color artwork in a single pass; some scanners must make 3 passes—one each for the scan's red, green, and blue channels. In a real-world production environment, single pass scanners are definitely more desirable. Three-pass scanners are slow, and 3-pass slide scanners are terribly slow. Furthermore, artwork can sometimes shift slightly during the scanning process, and if this happens with a 3-pass scanner, the image's channels will be out of alignment.

Sheet Feeder Users who will routinely use scanners to input multi-page documents for processing by OCR software will want to investigate the availability of sheet feeder attachments for the model of scanner they are considering.

Transparency Adapter Most advertising agencies and design studios that do color work will need to scan slides and large-format transparencies from time to time. Some scanners can handle transparencies without special attachments, and some require transparency adapters. In most cases, these solutions handle medium- and large-format transparencies, and may not provide for mounted slides.

Scanning Area It's very frustrating to try to scan an image that's larger than your scanner can accommodate. It's possible to scan the image in more than one pass and composite the image together in an image-editing program, but this approach is time-consuming and requires that the artwork is perfectly straight on the scanning bed each time. If you expect that you will routinely scan large art, you should consider the scanner's maximum scanning area as part of your decision.

An excellent resource for information about scanners, with extensive tables that detail the features of many models of currently available scanners can be found at **http://www.hsdesign.com/scanning/tablescanner_table2.html.**

See Also

Desktop Publishing; Drum Scanners; Flatbed Scanners; Handheld Scanners; Office Scanners; Slide Scanners

Scanner, Desktop

There are many different kinds of desktop scanners, and many different software applications and **plug-ins** you may use to control a scanner. Almost all hardware/software packages address the basic issues of resolution and tonal balance and there are basic procedures to follow, no matter how the specific features are organized on your particular system.

Choosing a Scanning Mode Most scanning software packages offer several different modes of scanning: bitmap, grayscale, color, and in many cases, "halftone."

Bitmap mode is sometimes called "line art," and it's best suited for scanning one-color line art illustrations. Bitmaps are significantly smaller in file size and memory requirements than grayscale and color scans of the same physical size. However, they don't resize very well. If you're not sure how large your image will be, scan it in grayscale and convert it to bitmap format in your image-editing application when the layout is finalized.

The grayscale and color modes are most commonly used for day-to-day scanning. You can certainly scan black-and-white prints using color mode, with excellent results, but color images are three times as large as grayscale images of the same size.

The halftone mode of most scanning software converts grayscale photographs to black-and-white halftones—patterns of tiny dots that simulate levels of gray—on-the-fly, as the image is scanned. There isn't a good reason to do this nowadays. Halftones don't resize well at all, and can't be corrected or sharpened in your image-editing software. It's most appropriate to scan in grayscale and let your service bureau (or your laser printer) create the halftone when you output your job.

Calculating Correct Resolution It's very important to scan images for print at the correct resolution. If the resolution is too low, the image will look pixelated (that is, bad); if the resolution is too high, it will be difficult to work with in your image-editing program, difficult or impossible to print, slow to load over the **Web**, and wasteful of hard disk space. Fortunately, it's easy to calculate the correct resolution for a scan.

If you're scanning line art, you should scan at the resolution of the output device, if possible. For a 600 dpi laser printer, for instance, you should scan at 600 dpi. If your image will be sent to a 1,200–1,600 dpi imagesetter for output, scan your image in grayscale at half the imagesetter's resolution and, when you convert the grayscale image to bitmap mode, increase the image's resolution to that of the imagesetter.

The resolutions for grayscale images recommended in the table that follows are based on final sizes of the image: if the image must be resized, you may need to adjust the scan resolution so that the resized image will be of the correct resolution. Most scanning software handles scaling automatically. If yours doesn't, consult your image-editing software's manual for information about how the software handles resolution when images are resized.

Typical Resolutions

Medium	Resolution
Web page	72 dpi
Ink on coated paper	225–300 dpi
Ink on newsprint	150–200 dpi
Laser printer or Docutech	150 dpi

S

In general, the resolution of the scan should be twice the line screen that the press or laser printer uses. However, the previous table is not a substitute for discussing a job with a commercial printer; if you haven't talked to your printer about a particular job, put down *Maclopedia* and give them a call right now.

> **TIP** If you're scanning a big stack of things for comps (rough layouts) and you don't know the size the images will be in the final piece, you can scan the pictures at low resolution and rescan them later—it will make the scanning and design process go much more quickly.

Making Tonal Adjustments If you're scanning art for a **Web page**, what you see on-screen is pretty much what readers will see with a **Web browser**, and you can adjust everything by eye. If you intend to print what you're scanning, *do not* trust your monitor. Your monitor's screen is not made out of paper, and it doesn't represent what the printed piece will look like. The following is an introduction to the basic issues, but you must consult your printer about the specifics of your project and the printer's press.

The monitor is backlit, and images appear brighter on-screen than they will on paper. When you adjust the brightness of the scan with your scanning or image-editing software, you should make the image a little brighter than what looks good on-screen.

A monitor's pixels can display any level of gray; on paper, grays are simulated with patterns of tiny black dots. If you're printing with ink (rather than with toner, as on a laser printer) some dots will spread out on press, making the grays darker. (This is called **dot gain**.) You may need to compensate for dot gain in your scans: you should ask what sort of dot gain you can expect from your printer's press and how you should compensate for it. Your printer may wish to have the pre-press department deal with this issue—unless you know *exactly* what you're doing, let your printer handle it.

Even if your monitor is perfectly calibrated—and it's probably not—it displays a wider range of colors than can be printed with **CMYK** (a.k.a. process, 4-color) printing. For best results, you should calibrate your scanner using the software provided by the manufacturer, calibrate your monitor, and use a software color-management tool such as Apple's ColorSync or Pantone ColorDrive to maintain consistent use of color across applications.

See Also

ColorSync; Docutech; Gamma Values in Scanners; Monitors, Scanners, OCR Software and

Scanner, Dynamic Range of

Dynamic range is measured in many different ways. Most often, you'll see it measured on a 0–4 scale, where 4 is the ideal—the quality produced by drum scanners. Even a scanner with limited dynamic range can usually produce an acceptable scan of a good photograph that does not contain extensive light and dark areas. However, such scanners have trouble with poorly-balanced photographs, or good photographs containing dramatic tonal effects.

This dynamic range scale doesn't tell you anything about where the scanner's particular weaknesses are. Some scanners have special trouble with highlight areas, and some have trouble with shadow areas. There isn't a good way to quantify the scanner's weaknesses, but most reviews of scanners in Mac magazines identify the scanner's problem areas.

Scanner, OCR Software and

Optical Character Recognition (OCR) software analyzes a scanned page of text and produces a word processor document that contains the same text. OCR is a developing science and still produces some bizarre results, but high-end OCR packages running on Power Macs can now process documents at nearly 100 percent accuracy.

Each OCR software package uses different techniques to accomplish the conversion from image to text, but from the user's perspective, most packages behave in the same way: the user specifies a file or files to be converted, the machine attempts to convert the file, and prompts the user about any words that it cannot recognize.

OCR packages vary in price and sophistication. High-end packages incorporate a variety of tools for deciphering image files, and can accurately process text in any roman or italic typeface, even if the text is in multiple columns, with little input from the user. Some less sophisticated packages may be optimized for particular fonts or page layouts and may require more input from the user, including "training" the software to recognize new typefaces.

See Also

Scanners, Buying; Scanners, Desktop

Scanner Types, *See Flatbed Scanners; Handheld Scanners; Office Scanners; Slide Scanners*

Scanning, *See Image Scanning*

Scanning Software

Software for use by motion-disabled persons that places a keyboard on-screen, with a cursor moving over it. The user activates a switch to stop the cursor and select the letter it's on. Then the cursor moves again until another letter is selected. Although it's slow, it enables many people to use a computer who otherwise would be unable to do so.

See Also

Co:Writer; Freedom

Scenery Animator

Natural Graphics' Scenery Animator is a scenery creator and animation tool. There are three types of scenes that can be manipulated in this software. First, Scenery Animator can import DEM (Digital Elevation Model) files. DEMs are available from the USGS (United States Geographical Survey) as data sets, and are often posted free on-line. DEMs are available for just about every location on the Earth, and there are several planetary DEMs available for lunar, Martian,

and Venusian terrain. Scenery Animator comes with a collection of six DEMs (Mount St. Helens, Grand Canyon, a moon view, and others), and additional DEM sets (32 in all) can be purchased directly from Natural Graphics. The second method for creating a scenery model in Scenery Animator is to use the random number generator on-board to construct an original geography. You can determine the height, and even set trees (oaks or redwoods) to cover a percentage of the terrain. Scenery Animator geography is fractal-based, and you can set the "edge" of the terrain to a discrete distance or make it infinite. The last method for loading in a scene is to choose a scene already saved out from a previous work session. You can alter any scene that is loaded in.

The Camera View Not only does the Camera View act as a preview of the overall scene, but it can be used to move the camera until just the right position is found for a keyframe. You can take advantage of panning left and right or up and down, moving forward or back, banking on any angle, and adjusting the pitch. All of these controls are vital when determining the drama of an animated fly-through of a scene. An adjustable rectangle on the Camera View screen enables you to change the focal length of the "lens."

The Map View This is a top/side toggle-able view elevation map of the loaded scene, complete with a colorization of the different elevations (lighter equals higher terrain). Along the left side of this Viewport are eight icons: path Modification Arrow, Move-View Hand, Camera Angle/Focus Tool, camera Position Crosshair, a "lake" tool, two Path Construct Tools (linear and curved), and a positionable magnification rectangle. The tools are straightforward to use and intuitively designed. Fine tuning controls with numerical inputs for camera, sun, and path alterations exist in a separate dialog box. The "lake" tool places water at whatever level in the top view you select and everywhere below that level on the same contour lines. This makes it easy to place a watery surface at the base of mountain cliffs.

S

Landscape Controls Land, sky, water, and trees are controllable in Scenery Animator. Each has a separate dialog that alters needed parameters. In land, you can alter the snow, rock, vegetation, and soil min/max elevation levels and the distribution of each. Sky has a toggle for both clouds and gradient, a cloud height setting, and cloud position and density. In water, you can turn ocean and waves on or off and also set the altitude for the ocean. With the tree setting, you can select between oaks and redwoods and set their min/max altitude and coverage percentage. A separate "smooth" setting smoothes out the sharpness of a landscape.

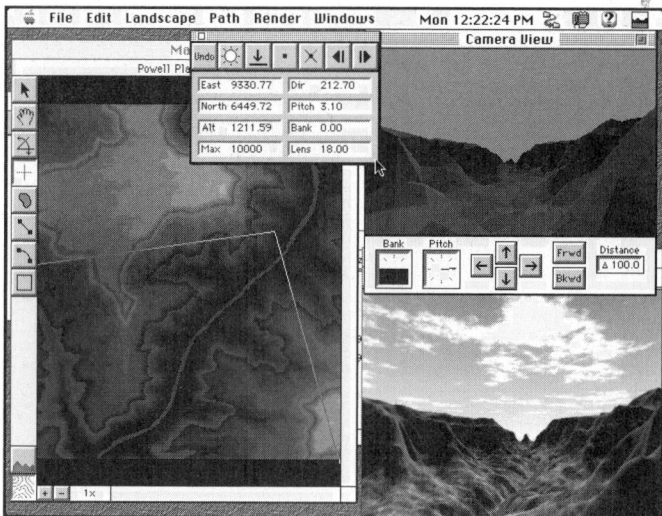

Rendering Rendering a graphic based upon the settings is a snap. Simply go to the Render menu, set the size of the render (custom sizes are supported along with custom DPI settings), and choose a storage path. You can also select an area of a scene and save it out as a **DXF** file so it can be rendered in any 3D software that supports DXF imports.

Animation Scenery Animator has a simple keyframe setting system for animated sequences that beats 90 percent of the animating software available. Settings are easy to configure, simple to alter, and quick to preview. Everything can be tweaked until it's just right.

Science Fiction Themes in Games, *See Absolute Zero; Adventure Games; Daedalus Encounter, The; Descent; First Person Perspective Shooters; Rebel Assault II; Spaceward Ho!; TimeLapse: Ancient Civilzations*

Science Programs for Children, *See A.D.A.M. The Inside Story; Bumptz Science Carnival; MacFrog; Undersea Adventure; What's the Secret; Widget Workshop*

Scores Virus

Scores, also known as Eric, Vult, NASA, and San Jose Flu, infects **System**, **NotePad**, and **Scrapbook** files and creates two invisible files in your System folder named Scores and Desktop (not the same as the normal Desktop file). After your system becomes infected, Scores tries to spread to each application you run. This virus spreads only itself, but that occupies memory and disk space.

See Also

ANTI Virus; CDEF Virus; CODE 1 Virus; CODE 252 Virus; Frankie Virus; INIT 17 Virus; INIT 1984 Virus; INIT 29 Virus; INIT 9403 Virus; INIT-M Virus; MacMag Virus; MBDF Virus; MDEF Virus; nVIR Virus; T4 Virus; Virus; WDEF Virus; ZUC Virus

Scott, Mike

Mike Scott was the first president of Apple Computer. He was brought in by **Mike Markkula** shortly after Apple was incorporated. Scott served as president until 1981. Following the dismal failure of the Apple III, Scott fired many people, creating an uproar that led to his demotion from president to vice-chairman. Shortly thereafter, he left Apple.

See Also
Apple Computer, History; Markkula, A.C. "Mike"

Scott, Ridley, *See 1984*

Scrabble, *See Classic Collection*

Scrapbook

The Scrapbook is used as a permanent holding place for items that you want to have access to after the computer is **shut down**. The Scrapbook enables you to store text, graphics, sounds, **QuickTime** movies, and any item that you can **copy** and **paste**.

You can see the contents of the Scrapbook by using the **scroll bar** below the display window, and the type of object and size are listed in the lower window. The item's dimensions (if it's a graphic) or duration (if it's a sound or video clip) are listed in the lower window on the far right.

You add items to the Scrapbook by cutting and pasting them, and you can remove the currently displayed item by choosing **Clear** from the **Edit menu**. The difference between the Scrapbook and the **Clipboard** is the Scrapbook is a permanent storage place and Scrapbook items are written to a file that resides in the **System Folder**, whereas Clipboard items are temporary and are erased when another item enters the Clipboard or the computer is shut down.

To use the Scrapbook DA, follow these steps:

1. Choose Scrapbook from the Apple menu.

2. If you have an item that you've copied, you may enter that item into the Scrapbook by selecting Paste from the Edit menu.

3. The item will appear in the Scrapbook window as the current item and will be retained in the Scrapbook's memory for use at another time.

4. To use an item from the Scrapbook, find the item you want and choose Copy from the Edit menu. You may then close the Scrapbook and go to the document you want to use the copied item from and select Paste from the Edit menu to insert the Scrapbook item.

See Also
Clear Command; Clipboard; Copy Command; Edit Menu; Paste Command; QuickTime; Scroll Bars; Shut Down Command; System Folder

Screen Capture

A screen capture enables you to take a picture of the image on your screen and save it to your **hard disk** in PICT format. The first screen capture appears in your hard drive window as Picture 1. Subsequent screen captures are numbered as Picture 2, Picture 3, and so on. To capture a screen image (also referred to as a screen shot, screen grab, or print screen) press Shift-⌘-3. The sound of a camera shutter tells you that a screen capture has been made. You can open screen captures in any program that supports PICT format, including **SimpleText**.

To create a Screen Capture, follow these steps:

1. Press Shift-⌘-3.

2. Look in the main window of your hard drive for a document entitled Picture 1 (or Picture 2, 3, and so on, if this is not your first screen capture).

3. You can view your screen capture by opening it in SimpleText or any program that enables you to view and edit PICT images.

See Also
Hard Disks; SimpleText

Screen Capture (Keyboard Shortcut)

The keyboard shortcut to take a screen picture (also called **screen capture**, screen grab, or screen shot) is Shift-⌘-3. When you press these keys, you hear the sound of a camera shutter, and the screen momentarily freezes as the screen picture is taken. The picture is saved to your **startup disk** as a PICT file titled Picture 1 (if this is your first screen picture). If not, the pictures are numbered Picture 2, Picture 3, and so on.

To create a screen picture, follow these steps:

1. Press Shift-⌘-3.

2. You'll hear a camera shutter sound to signify the screen picture has been made.

3. The screen picture will appear as a PICT document on your startup drive, named Picture 1.

See Also

Keyboard Shortcuts; Screen Capture; Startup Disk

Screen Capture, Opening and Editing

You can create a screen capture (a photo of your screen) by pressing the keyboard shortcut Shift-⌘-3. You hear the clicking sound of a camera shutter, and the capture is taken and placed on your startup disk. Your first screen capture is named Picture 1. Subsequent captures are named Picture 2, Picture 3, and so on. You can open a screen capture in a graphics program that supports PICT format, but you can also open screen captures in either **TeachText** (Apple's bare-bones text editor) or in **SimpleText** (the updated version of TeachText).

To open the screen capture, use the Open command found on the File menu of SimpleText and TeachText.

When you have the screen capture open, notice that your text cursor has changed to a crosshair cursor. This enables you to make a rectangular selection of your screen capture and copy it to the **Clipboard**. From there you can paste this selection into the **Scrapbook** or any program that enables you to cut and paste from the Clipboard.

See Also

Clipboard; Scrapbook; Screen Capture; SimpleText; TeachText

Screen Capture Utility

If at any time you want to create a picture of what's on your computer screen, you can create what's called a screen capture. This screen capture is like taking a photograph of your screen and saving it to a file on your hard disk. The keyboard command to take a screen capture (also referred to as a screen print, screen grab, or screen shot) is Shift-⌘-3.

When you press this combination, you will hear the sound of a camera shutter, and the screen will momentarily freeze as the screen picture is taken. The screen capture is saved to your **startup disk** as a PICT file titled Picture 1 (if this is your first screen picture; if not, the pictures will be numbered Picture 2, Picture 3, and so on). The main advantage of taking a screen capture is that you get a full color representation of the screen, which you can resize, edit in a graphics program, and print out. A screen capture differs from Printing the Desktop in that it gives you a full-color file that you can manipulate in a graphics application, or cut and paste sections from within TeachText or SimpleText. If you Print the Desktop, it does just that; it prints a copy of what it sees to a printer.

> **TIP** If all you need is a printout of the desktop, and don't need a file that you can edit or save, then you can skip the screen capture process altogether and choose Print Desktop from the File menu at the desktop with all windows closed.

There are also a number of third-party shareware utilities that add more precise control and additional features for taking screen captures, such as **Flash-It** and Capture, both of which offer a wide variety of options. You can find both in the Utilities section of **America Online** or at a variety of Mac **FTP** sites on the **Internet**.

To create a screen picture, follow these steps:

1. Press Shift-⌘-3.

2. You'll hear a camera shutter sound to signify the screen capture has been made.

3. The screen capture will appear as a PICT document on your hard drive entitled "Picture 1."

See Also

Screen Capture; Startup Disk

Screen Control Panel

Some of the newer Macs (such as the Performa LC 580s or the Performa 5200 series) that have the computer and monitor all in once piece have the Screen **control panel** to adjust the brightness of the screen because some models don't have external controls. The old Mac Classic and Classic II had a similar control panel called **Brightness** that did the same thing for those all-in-one units.

See Also

Brightness Control Panel; Control Panels

Screen Saver

Screen savers are **utility** programs that usually take the form of **control panels.** When screen savers were originally introduced, the idea behind a screen saver was that if you were to leave your computer unattended for a long period of time—for example, if you went out on an appointment, left your computer on, and didn't come back for two or three hours—then the fear would be that the image on-screen would "burn" into the phosphors of your monitor, forever damaging your screen. If you've ever used an Automatic Teller Machine at the bank, often you'll see the bank's "welcome" screen has burned in to the ATM's monitor screen and you can see a ghosted image of it even while you're viewing other sections on the ATM's monitor. However, most experts today will tell you that the phosphors now used in monitors don't allow screen burn-in to take place, so screen savers are more for entertainment purposes than providing an important screen protection task.

What a screen saver essentially does is keep things moving on your screen so that nothing stays still long enough to burn in. You can set a time interval for when you want the screen saver to kick in, like after a 10- or 20-minute period of inactivity. Some of the first screen savers were utilities that you had to launch, and they would black out the screen and display crude animation—of fireworks or outlines of geometric objects moving across your screen—to protect your screen.

To bring your computer screen back to normal, you just press any key or move the mouse. An added feature of many screen savers is password protection to keep other people from accessing your computer after a screen saver comes on. If, for example, you were to walk away from your computer, after a specified time the screen saver would come on. Normally, someone else could sit down at your computer and move the mouse or press a key to return the regular computer screen. But if you have your screen saver password protected, the person trying to access your computer is prompted to enter a password before the screen saver turns off and enables access to the computer. If the person doesn't have your password, your machine is protected.

Today's screen savers are mostly control panels, which enables them to start after a period of inactivity, rather than you having to remember to launch a screen saver utility before you walk away from your computer. Also, today's screen savers have become very popular, as they now offer quite extravagant visual entertainment, with full-color customizable screen savers, screen saver interactive games, sound tracks to accompany the screen savers, and theme-oriented screen savers such as Star Trek; The Simpsons; Disney; and many more.

S

Probably the most popular screen savers come from Berkeley Systems (2095 Rose Street, Berkeley, CA 94709, (510) 540-5535, Web Site URL: **http://www.berksys.com**. Street Price of After Dark Collection: $39.95) with its **After Dark** Screen Saver collection.

The kicker here is that with today's more sophisticated monitors, many experts believe that screen savers are totally unnecessary and the worry over screen burn-in is a thing of the past. Besides, many new monitors have a built-in sleep mode that powers down the monitor and blanks the screen, and in **System 7.5** and higher, you can use the Energy Saver Control Panel to do the same thing. That notwithstanding, the entertainment value screen savers provide has made them a very popular, in fact almost a "must-have," utility for every new Mac owner.

See Also
After Dark; Control Panels; Monitors; Utility

Screen Shot, *See Screen Capture Utility*

ScreenMovie, *See MovieTrilogy*

Screenscape
Screenscape is a commercial **desktop pattern utility** from KiwiSoft that enables you to choose from a variety of background patterns. There are also a number of third-party background patterns that you can use with Screenscape that are available from the Macintosh Utilities Forum on **America Online** and at various **FTP** sites on the **Internet**.

See Also
Desktop Pattern

Script Editor, *See AppleScript*

Scripting
The term scripting was introduced with **HyperCard**, and referred to programs written using the HyperCard programming language **HyperTalk**. The term scripting was probably used so that people didn't think they had to learn programming.

HyperTalk is an English-like programming language that is reasonably easy to learn. It is, however, still a computer programming language. If you already know a computer language like **BASIC**, you should have no trouble learning HyperTalk, but if you have never written a program before, it will take a while to learn how to do that.

Scripting languages add flexibility to multimedia authoring tools. They enable you to add calculation routines and complex interactions to projects.

HyperTalk spawned several other scripting languages. Allegient's **SuperCard** has a scripting language called **SuperTalk**, which is a superset of the HyperTalk language. **Lingo** is the scripting language for Macromedia's **Director**. It is still classified as a scripting language, but it is very different from HyperTalk. Other multimedia authoring tools, including **mTropolis** and Oracle Media Objects, also contain scripting languages.

Apple went on to produce **AppleScript**, a scripting language that is similar to HyperTalk but designed for use across the operating system and with different applications. AppleScript can automate complicated processes, such as updating databases.

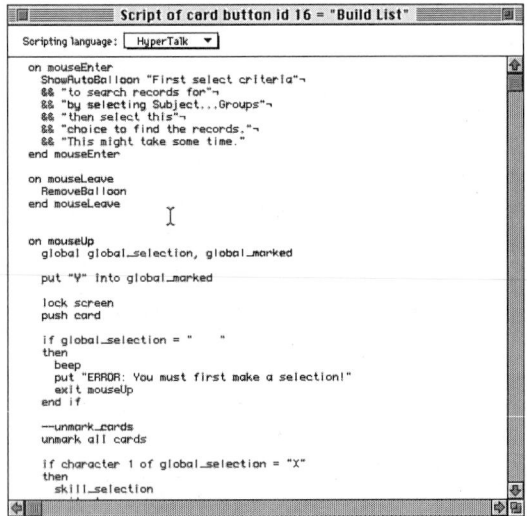

Scripting creates programs that control other programs. The programs you create, scripts, can manipulate applications in sophisticated ways. By creating scripts, you can simplify complex tasks and integrate complex interactions among applications. You can generally execute a script with a simple double-click of the mouse.

In the past, scripting was one of the weak points on the Macintosh. Its graphical interface made it especially difficult to create scripts. Today, there are two major types of scripting on the Macintosh. In the first, you create scripts, or macros, that manipulate the user interface of an application just as if you were using the application directly. Your scripts move the mouse, click buttons, and enter text just as if you were using a mouse and keyboard. The biggest disadvantage of this scripting system is that they rely on the visual layout of an application to be consistent. If they expect a window to be in the upper-right corner of the screen, they direct their actions there even if the window is actually in the lower-left corner.

The most popular of these macro scripting systems is **QuicKeys**, from CE Software; Tempo, from Affinity Microsystems; and Keyquencer, a shareware program by Alessandro Levi Montalcini. Each of these programs enables you to record a series of user interface events as a macro and play the macro back at the touch of a key.

Because these programs mimic user input, they do not rely on any support from the application. Virtually any application, **control panel**, or **desk accessory** can be controlled using macros. As a result, this kind of scripting is especially useful for scripting programs (or parts of programs) that do not support the second kind of scripting, OSA scripting.

OSA stands for **Open Scripting Architecture**, a system-level scripting framework that supports multiple scripting systems. These systems take advantage of the MacOS's built-in support for scripting in the form of **Apple events**. Apple events are messages you can send to an application to get it to do something you want (or to ask it to send you some information). Most major applications respond to a wide variety of Apple events. Apple events are like a puppet's strings:

If you pull them in the right ways, you can make an application dance.

Because Apple events interact directly with a program's core, they avoid the issue of user interface interaction completely. Scripts relying on Apple events generally are unconcerned about the physical layout of windows, menus, and controls, but rather deal directly with the actions that these controls initiate.

Fortunately, you don't usually have to deal with the gory details of Apple events directly when you create scripts. All the low-level details are taken care of by the scripting system you decide to use. The two major scripting systems for the Macintosh are Apple's AppleScript and UserLand **Frontier** (also known as Aretha).

Each of these scripting environments provides a rich language you can use to control the system or other applications. By writing scripts in these languages, you can create a series of AppleEvents that pull the strings in the right way to get applications to do whatever you want them to.

Both AppleScript and Frontier have strong followings. AppleScript has the advantages of being supplied by Apple with the operating system. It also has a language that somewhat resembles normal human language. In fact, separate "dialects" of AppleScript exist for a number of languages, including English, French, and Japanese. In addition, many third-party tools exist for working with AppleScript, including Main Event's Scripter, Late Night Software's Script Debugger, and Full Moon Software's ScriptWizard. On the other hand, AppleScript can be slow at some tasks (especially handling strings of text), and it is not native on the Power Macintosh.

Frontier is native on the Power Mac, supports simultaneous threads of execution, and provides a centralized object database for storing scripts and data. Frontier also has excellent debugging capabilities built-in. On the down side, its language, UserTalk, is generally more difficult for non-programmers to grasp than AppleScript, and its current status as a free product means that support is handled by a group of volunteers (which may or may not be a disadvantage).

S

Before you can script an application using either AppleScript or Frontier, the application must be *scriptable*. This means it supports a sufficiently complete set of AppleEvents to enable scripts to access much of its functionality. For non-scriptable applications, you can side-step this problem to some extent using PreFab Software's Player, which provides user interface manipulation functionality much like a macro language from within AppleScript or Frontier.

Among the applications that *are* scriptable, some enable you to record your actions and play them back as a script. These recordable applications make script creation much easier by eliminating much of the difficult programming work.

Besides these system-level scripting systems, many individual applications support their own internal scripting language. Microsoft's applications, for example, use a dialect of BASIC for scripting. Many applications that used their own scripting language in previous versions have moved toward enabling scripting using AppleScript. Some applications provide a "scripts" menu that enables you to execute scripts directly within the application without having to resort to launching a separate script from the Finder. These applications are classified as attachable because they enable scripts to be attached to their basic functionality.

See Also

Apple Event; AppleScript; Frontier; Open Scripting Architecture; Thread

ScriptX

ScriptX is a multimedia language developed by Kaleida Labs, a joint venture of Apple and IBM. ScriptX is both a development environment (a tool for creating **multimedia** productions) and a delivery platform (software to playback the production). Applications are developed in ScriptX, and *players* that support the ScriptX language were to be developed for standard platforms (Mac, Windows, and so on), as well as set top boxes for interactive television. ScriptX incorporated features that catered to different standards. Graphics, for example, could be stored in multiple formats and then displayed according to the quality

of the platform—a television set has a much lower screen resolution than a computer monitor.

Unfortunately, although ScriptX showed tremendous promise, and Kaleida Labs shipped a development platform for ScriptX, there were no end-user tools; programs that had the ease of use of something like Macromedia **Director** or **Oracle Media Objects**. Developing in ScriptX presented the same challenges as developing in a programming language. In a sense, that's all it really is: a programming language with features that are designed to cater to the development of multimedia presentation. Apple and IBM failed to agree on how to solve this problem, whether to develop their own end-user tools or wait for other companies to supply them, and eventually decided to disband the company and each take parts of the language for possible use in future products.

Scroll Bars

Anytime a **window** has more items or information than can fit on-screen, scroll bars appear, as shown in the figure. If the information in the window extends beyond the left or right side of the window, the bottom scroll bar appears enabling you to scroll to the left or right to find the additional files or information. If the information extends beyond the top or bottom of the window, a scroll bar appears on the right side of the window enabling you to scroll up and down to reveal the additional items or information.

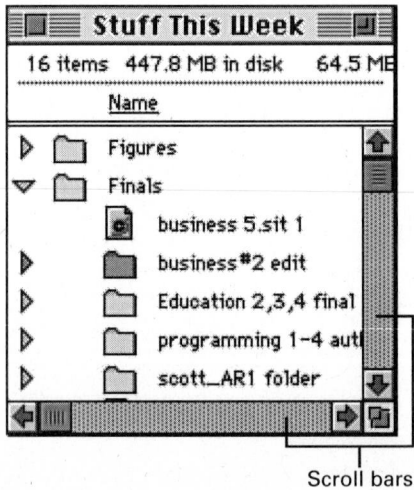

Scroll bars

You can scroll around a window three different ways:

- Grab the scroll box and drag it in the direction you want to go. When you release the scroll box, the window jumps to that location.

- Use the scroll arrows at each end of the scroll bar. To scroll up, click and hold the up arrow that appears at the top of the window. To scroll down, click and hold the down arrow that appears at the bottom of the window. The same goes for the left and right scroll arrows, click and hold on the arrow that points in the direction you want to scroll.

- Click in the path of the scroll bar and the window jumps in that direction one screenful at a time.

See Also
Window

Sculley, John

John Sculley was CEO of Apple Computer from 1983 until 1993. He was recruited to Apple from PepsiCo, where he served as president of Pepsi-Cola USA. During his time at Pepsi, Sculley was best known as the marketer who masterminded the "Pepsi Generation" advertising campaign that ushered in the era of "lifestyle" ads that sell a product by creating a feeling rather than directly selling the product's features.

After **Mike Scott** was forced out of his position as president of Apple in 1981, **Mike Markkula** reluctantly took an operational role in the leadership of Apple. Markkula preferred a less involved role, so the search for a new leader for Apple began. After a lengthy search and subsequent negotiation, John Sculley assumed the role of president and CEO of Apple on April 8, 1983.

Sculley was Apple founder **Steve Jobs'** choice for CEO, and initially the two got along well. The two led the company jointly through the final development and introduction of the Macintosh.

After the Mac's initial sales spurt tapered off, Apple was in tough financial times. The company needed to focus on the bottom line to make it through the difficult period. Unfortunately, Jobs had a habit of meddling in the smallest details of many projects, and was gradually seen as a liability to the company.

In a major power struggle, Sculley forced Jobs out of his operational role in May 1985. In September of that year, Jobs left Apple for good, angry that the man he brought in to lead Apple had forced him out.

Following Jobs' departure, Sculley managed to lead Apple through its difficult times and into a huge era of growth and innovation. By the early '90s, however, Apple was facing stiff price competition from other personal computer manufacturers. Sculley failed to properly manage the increasingly meager margins on Apple's products, and in June 1993, he stepped down as CEO, retaining the position of chairman.

In October 1993, Sculley left Apple to take the job of president and CEO of Spectrum Information Technologies, a small East coast start-up that made products that integrate computers with cellular phone and paging technologies. His stay with Spectrum didn't last long. When he learned of a number of ongoing investigations and lawsuits targeting Spectrum, he resigned and sued the company. They counter-sued, citing breach of contract, among other charges. In the end, Sculley and Spectrum dropped their lawsuits against one another, and Sculley moved out of the public eye.

Sculley is now president of Live Picture, a small company that develops and markets an innovative image editing application of the same name.

See Also
Jobs, Steve; Markkula, A.C. "Mike"; Scott, Mike

Sculpt 3D

As **MacPaint** represents 2D drawing in a historical place of honor as the first software of its kind, Byte by Byte's Sculpt represents **3D** rendering and animation on the Mac. But there is a difference: whereas

S

users of MacPaint still own it because of a reverence for its place in computer graphics history, owners of Sculpt 3D use it because of what it can still do, even after all these years and the advances in technology. It may not have all of the bells and whistles touted by the competition, but it remains a good choice for learning computer graphics processes, as well as still possessing tools that can help you craft some beautiful basic animation.

The Interface Sculpt has the classic 3D interface, a design which it was instrumental in turning into the accepted standard that lasted a long time. A TriView that represents the volume of 3D space from three look points and a Perspective rendered view dominate the screen.

Modeling Tools A vertex Pointer in the toolbox allows you to select any vertex on an object for modification. It can be interactively pulled away from the object or treated with the modifications in the Scene/Actions menu. Modifications include Resize, Extrude, Offset Surface, Subdivide, Trim, Intersect, Weld, Reduce, Fill, Reflect, Lathe, Twist, Loft, Bevel, Randomize, Hide, and Reveal. Sculpt includes a list of primitive shapes that can be used as building blocks to sculpt more complex shapes: Sphere, Hemisphere, Block, Prism, Disk, Circle, Cylinder, Tube, Cone, Terrain, and Text.

The Terrain Tool is one of the most complex and option-filled you will find anywhere. It allows you to reference a TIFF or PICT image as an elevation map channel, and has user input controls for Texture, Dimensions, Elevation, and Terrain Type (Parallel or Planar, Cylindrical, and three Spherical object receptors). You could take a logo and have it appear as a 3D surface on a sphere quite easily with this tool. Nothing like it exists in other software.

Boolean Operations Sculpt allows for true **Boolean** adding, subtracting, and intersecting of selected shapes. Surfaces are divided into two groups, the Tool and the Object, and Boolean interactions are applied.

Texture Mapping Sculpt has a built-in attributes list (Dull, Shiny, Metallic, Mirror, Glass, Solid Glass, Luminous, and Background). An extremely intricate Texture machine allows you to add new textures based on highly interactive designs that reference dozens of user set parameters, including graphics input.

Lights Lights in Sculpt can be adjusted by altering their Color, Brightness, Beam Shape, and Projected Image components. A special "Sun Time" feature allows you to set the light to mimic dates of the year, down to the hour, minute, and seconds. A Fall-Off expert control allows you to design the lights' fall-off parameters.

Rendering Once all of the parameters are set in the Rendering Preferences, rendering can commence. Single files or a batch of files can be targeted for rendering.

Animation Sculpt 3D remains an image sculpting and rendering engine, with no features for keyframe animating. The only way to achieve animation from Sculpt 3D is to render files one at a time from different camera/target parameters. We have included it in the animation section of the book because it was instrumental in the development of most of the rendering and animation engines that have been introduced since it was born.

Other Special Features Sculpt includes measurement items called "Scrulers" that indicate the units of measurement set, and allow you to measure distances and objects in 3D space. A rotation arrow in the corner of the Perspective view animates the scene and allows you to see it from all perspectives as you orbit the virtual space.

File Load/Save Conventions Scenes can be loaded and saved as Sculpt 3D version 1, 2, and 4 (version 3 was skipped over), **DXFs**. Sculpt can open and render images in the PRIM (Photo Realistic Image Manager, Sculpt's priority format), TIFF, and PICT formats. Sculpt has dialog called the DXF Scene File Machine that allows DXF files to be imported and exported. The unit of measurement and scale are set here.

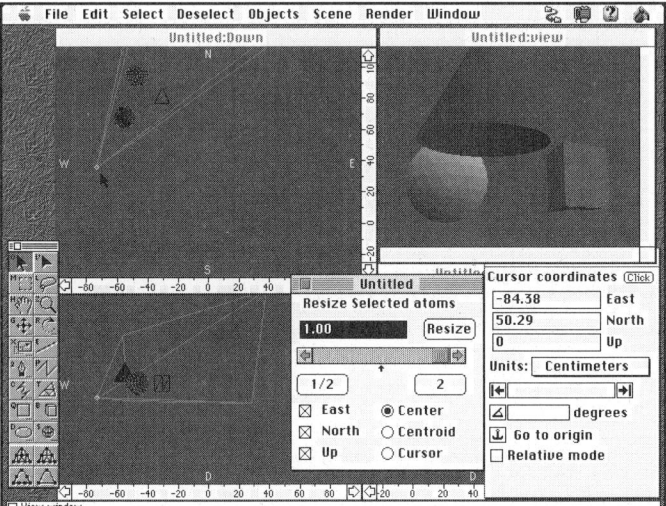

SCSI, *See Small Computer System Interface*

SCSI-3

A new SCSI specification called **SCSI-3** provides a speed boost to input and output via new SCSI-3-compliant expansion cards that plug into the PCI slot on the **Power Mac**. SCSI-3 is still being discussed by standards committees, but a general outline of its contents is available. SCSI-3 would be backwards-compatible with today's SCSI protocols (meaning that you would be able to plug in older devices into the new ports) as well as forwards-compatible with the several new interface designs and data transfer schemes in development (meaning that devices that support new connection schemes would also fit). SCSI-3 would break the seven-device limit of connectivity to support up to 127 devices on a single bus. In addition, you can attach new peripherals while your Mac is turned on (called hot plugging).

One of the biggest transitions within SCSI-3 is the switch from parallel buses to serial buses for data transfer. Three of the four SCSI-3 protocols in development rely on serial data transfer systems where data streams follow single file down a single wire, rather than concurrently down several wires as they do on

parallel buses. New wiring systems resistant to interference plus new signaling schemes enable serial buses to perform at higher-clock speeds over longer cables than parallel buses.

Because the new serial design requires storage drive manufacturers to completely redesign their data transfer schemes, the first SCSI-3-compliant protocol being offered is based on a parallel bus. The new specification is called **Ultra SCSI**. Ultra SCSI has doubled the SCSI clock rate from 10MHz to 20MHz. This increased throughput doubles the speed of Ultra SCSI to 40 megabytes per second (Mbps). The previous winner in the throughput race was SCSI Fast and Wide (also called SCSI-2), which could transfer data at 20Mbps. Power Macs currently support SCSI-2. SCSI Fast and Wide supports 32 data lines (although most implementations use only 16 lines).

Ultra SCSI is supported on Quantum and Seagate large hard drives (4.3GB drives), and Hewlett-Packard also endorses Ultra SCSI. The problem with Ultra SCSI is that it does not address the cabling sensitivity issues of the current SCSI protocol. Because of its very fast data transfer rate, Ultra SCSI requires single-ended 68- or 80-pin connectors (current SCSI requires 50-pin connectors), supports only one ground line for all data lines, and has a maximum length of 1.5 meters.

Another SCSI-3 protocol that is getting much attention is **Fibre Channel**. Fibre Channel is a serial system that uses fiber optic cabling as well as copper wires (such as telephone twisted pairs or coaxial cables). Fibre Channel would support copper cables up to 100 meters long and fiber optic cables up to 10 kilometers long. There would be no address switches or terminators because Fibre Channel would be self-configuring and hot-pluggable. Up to 127 devices could be attached with data-transfer rates of up to 100Mbps. Fibre Channel supports several connectivity designs, but the one supported by most PC

S

manufacturers is called Fibre Channel-Arbitrated Loop (FC-AL). In this cabling topology, devices on the bus are connected in a circle and "talk to each other" to determine the timing of data transfers. Quantum, Seagate, and Hewlett-Packard support Fibre Channel and plan to manufacture drives based on this protocol. You can also use Fibre Channel's protocol for network cabling, because it supports proprietary protocols, such as **AppleTalk**, as well as more standard networking protocols, such as **EtherNet**.

IBM is competing against Fibre Channel with its serial data transfer protocol entry, Serial Storage Architecture (SSA). SSA provides the same benefits as Fibre Channel at a slower data transfer speed (80Mbps) by using 9-pin connectors and 6-wire cables connected to two ports in pairs. Although SSA is supported by Windows and mainframe vendors, no Macintosh vendor has announced support for SSA for the Mac.

Apple is developing a new data transfer protocol code-named **FireWire** (also known as P1394, the preliminary IEEE specification number). FireWire enables data transfer rates of up to 12.5Mbps running at one of three speeds: 100Mbps, 200Mbps, or 400Mbps, over 9-pin cables similar to those used on home video games. The protocol would support up to 63 devices on a single bus (a branching chain topology from multiple computers), be hot-pluggable, self-configuring, and cables between devices can be up to 4.5 meters long. In addition, P1394 cables can supply up to 60 watts of power, letting you operate devices without a separate power cord. FireWire is evolving into an interface for multimedia devices, such as video cameras, digital still cameras, and video cassette recorders, because FireWire emphasizes the collection of real-time data. Sony is building FireWire connectors into its digital video cameras. The Sony camera uses a new compression format, called DVC, with 100Mbps 1394 controllers to send digital images to the Mac. The P1394 specification is also replacing **MIDI**, because FireWire supports multiple streams of full digital audio along with MIDI-style control codes.

FireWire may be slower than Fibre Channel, but it is less expensive and its controllers are simpler to implement than other SCSI-3 designs. PCI expansion cards are available with FireWire for Power Macs from SCSI-adapter companies such as Adaptec. By late 1996 or early 1997, Macs will include a P1394 port with an internal and external connector or multiple FireWire ports, negating the need for PCI expansion cards.

See Also

Multimedia; Networking; Ports, Future Trends; Small Computer System Interface

SCSI ID, *See Finding Out a Device's SCSI ID Number*

SCSI Manager 4.3 Extension

This extension works with SCSI devices connected to your Mac. This latest update to the SCSI manager extension speeds up data transfers between **SCSI** devices by making them more efficient.

This extension is now built into the system on Power Mac models, so it is only necessary in non-**Power Mac** models.

See Also

Power Macs; SCSI-3; Small Computer System Interface

SCSI Probe

SCSI Probe is a freeware **utility** (**control panel**) for System 6.0 and higher (by Robert Pollack and found in the Macintosh Utilities Forum on **America Online** and at various **FTP** sites on the **Internet**) that is used for identifying and mounting devices connected to your SCSI port. SCSI also identifies the device type, vendor name, and the current version number of the SCSI driver for each peripheral, as shown in the following figure.

A nice feature of SCSI Probe is the ability to assign a "hot key" that mounts SCSI disks. If, for example, you have an external removable tape drive (such as a

SyQuest drive) and you insert the disk and it doesn't mount on the desktop, you can press the SCSI Probe "hot key" combination and it will send a mount instruction to the disk that will mount the disk and have it appear on the desktop.

When you open the SCSI Probe Control Panel, it shows you a list of all SCSI ID numbers and the device connected at each number (if any), the type of peripheral (**disk**, **CD-ROM**, **CPU**, and so on), the name of vendor for the product, the product's name, and the current version.

SCSI Probe also has three buttons: Update, which refreshes the SCSI Probe display by checking the SCSI chain to see which peripherals are connected; Mount, which mounts any disks that are not mounted, but are mountable; and Options, which enables you to set your "hot key" for mounting disks and other preferences for SCSI Probe.

See Also

Desktop; Small Computer System Interface; Troubleshooting

SDK

An SDK, or Software Development Kit, is a set of tools and information that helps programmers develop software for a technology. Apple, for example, releases a new SDK for most new parts of the MacOS as they

are released. These kits contain sample code, APIs, and documentation to get a programmer started with the new technology. Other companies also release SDKs for their products. An SDK is available from Adobe for developing **Photoshop plug-ins**. Similarly, Berkeley Systems has an **After Dark** SDK that gives programmers everything they need to know to develop modules for the After Dark screen saver.

See Also

Application Programming Interface; Plug-Ins

.sea Filename Extension

The .sea (self-extracting archive) filename extension means the file has been compressed but has a built-in decompression engine that enables it to be decompressed even if you don't have the application that compressed it. This is a popular compression format supported by most **compression utilities** such as **StuffIt**, **DiskDoubler**, and **CompactPro**, and .sea files appear quite often on **online services** or the **Internet**. You use a self-extracting archive when you're sending a file to someone and you're not sure if they have the software to decompress, or expand, the compressed file. By creating an .sea file, the decompression routine is built into the file. This is transparent to the user and adds only 5K to the file. The programs mentioned here have a **checkbox** or menu option to make your file a self-extracting one by clicking the box on the lower-left side.

See Also

CompactPro; Compressing Files; DiskDoubler; Internet; Online Services; StuffIt

Search Engines, *See Lycos; WAIS*

Secrets of the Luxor, *See Myst*

Sections in Word Processing

Sections can be thought of as subdocuments within a master word processor document. Each section has its own **formatting** attributes. To create separate sections in a document, insert a section break where you want the new section to start. You can divide a document into as many sections as you want, using different formatting for each section. Section properties include headers and **footers**, **margins**, page size and **orientation**, and page numbers. If you want a section property, such as a header or page numbering, to carry through the entire document, create it as part of the master document rather than as part of a single section.

See Also
Word Processing

Secure HTTP

Security system developed by EIT/Terisa Systems to provide security for transactions on the **World Wide Web**.

Secure HTTP, or S-HTTP, is a security standard, or a set of instructions for encrypting files to be used by software developers when creating applications and other tools for the Web.

S-HTTP is a security-enhanced version of **HyperText Transport Protocol** (HTTP), the protocol that governs communications on the World Wide Web. S-HTTP is considered a "higher level" protocol than **Secure Sockets Layer**, which concentrates on the link between **servers** and clients.

Terisa and a number of other software developers, including **Netscape**, have agreed that S-HTTP and Netscape's security standard SSL be integrated into Terisa's SecureWeb client and Server development toolkits.

See Also
Encryption; HyperText Transport Protocol; Secure Sockets Layer; Workgroup Servers, Macintosh Family; World Wide Web, The

Secure Sockets Layer

Security system developed by **Netscape** Communications to provide security for transactions on the **World Wide Web**. An open standard that all Web developers may use when creating applications and other tools for use with Netscape.

The term "layer" in "Secure Sockets Layer" (SSL) is used because SSL is implemented at an intermediate stage between **TCP/IP** (the protocol for Internet communications) and application protocols such as HTTP (the protocol for the transmission of Web documents).

Netscape and the SSL use a technology called *public key cryptography,* with software licensed from RSA Data Security, Inc. Public key cryptography uses a set of two keys, called the **public key** and the **private key**, and both must be used for encoding and decoding secure messages.

When you read a Web page that has been secured with SSL, the page has been encrypted with the private key of the Web site that is serving that page. The public key is sent along with the page, and Netscape uses the public key to decode the page. When you send data to the server, it is encrypted with the public key that the server provided.

Netscape's domestic implementation of SSL uses high-grade, 128-bit encryption, whereas the overseas version uses 40-bit encryption.

See Also
Encryption; HyperText Transport Protocol; Secure HTTP; Workgroup Servers, Macintosh Family; World Wide Web, The

Select All Command

If you want to simultaneously select every item in the **active window** use Select All, under the **Edit menu,** and all items in that window, visible or not, are selected at once. If, for example, you have a folder and you want to delete all the items in the folder, but don't want to delete the folder, you can open the folder and use the Select All Command. It selects all the files within that folder simultaneously and you can drag them, as a group, into the **Trash**.

Select All is also available in most applications, where it usually appears under the application's Edit menu. You might use Select All if, for example, you're working on a letter in a word processor and you've decided you want to change the typeface you're using for the entire letter. You can click your cursor anywhere within your letter and choose Select All from the application's Edit menu. This selects the entire text, even if it appears on multiple pages, so you can change the typeface and be sure that the typeface for the entire letter changes at once.

To use the Select All command, follow these steps:

1. Open the window where you want to simultaneously move, or open, everything within that window.

2. Under the Edit menu choose Select All (⌘-A).

3. You can now move, or open, all the selected items at once as a group.

4. When your move, or other change, is complete, simply click outside the selected area to remove your selection so you may return to other tasks.

See Also
Active Window; Edit Menu

Selecting Items

To select an item, **click** the **icon** for that item. You know it is selected because the icon turns black. This darkening is called **highlighting**. Once you've selected an item, the next action you take affects it.

You can select multiple items by clicking the first item you want and then clicking any other item while pressing the **Shift key**. You can select as many items as you like as long as the Shift key is pressed. You can also select multiple items by dragging a marquee around the items. A marquee appears when you take the **arrow pointer** and **drag** a marquee around the objects you want to select. Any objects that fall within the area of the marquee are selected. You can select multiple objects with the marquee in an **icon** or list view of a window.

To select an option from a **menu**, click the menu and drag your **cursor** down the menu. A black highlight

bar appears on the menu at the location of your cursor. When you highlight the **command** you're looking for, release the cursor and the black selection bar blinks to let you know you've made a selection.

If you're in an **Open** dialog box and you need to select a file from a scrolling list, click the name of the file you want to select. The file's name becomes highlighted using the color you've selected as your highlight color in the **Color control panel**.

You select text using the **I-Beam cursor**, which appears anytime you need to enter text. To select text, click at the beginning of the text and drag your cursor over the words, or letters, you want to select.

To select a file, folder, or disk in a Finder window, follow these steps:

1. Click the file's icon.

2. The icon becomes darkened, or highlighted, to let you know it's selected.

To select a file in an Open dialog or an application, follow these steps:

1. Click the filename in the list.

2. The file becomes highlighted in the list using the color you've chosen as your highlight color in the Colors control panel.

To select multiple files, follow these steps:

1. Click the first file you want to select.

2. Hold the Shift key and click the second file you want to select. You may add as many files as you like while still holding the Shift key.

To select multiple files using the selection marquee, follow these steps:

1. Click and hold the arrow pointer.

2. Drag the arrow pointer, which now produces a marquee, over the items you wish to select. Any items that fall within the marquee become selected. To deselect the items, click where there's no icon.

S

To select an item from a menu, follow these steps:

1. Click the menu and drag the cursor to the command you want to select.

2. Release the mouse at the desired command. A black highlight bar flashes to let you know you have selected the command.

To select text, follow these steps:

1. Click your I-Beam cursor at the beginning of the text you want to select and press the mouse button.

2. Drag your cursor over the text, or letters, you want to select.

3. The text becomes highlighted to indicate it is selected.

See Also

Arrow Pointer; Click; Color Control Panel; Cursor; Highlight; I-Beam Cursor; Icons; Menu; Mouse; Open Command; Shift Key; View Menu

Self-Contained Movies

QuickTime supports dependencies. A QuickTime movie can contain pointers to clips in other movies. This makes the process of cutting and pasting movie clips much faster and easier (the operating system doesn't have to copy the actual information, only information about where the movie is located). Although dependencies make sense for ease of use, playback can suffer, because the system has to read information from a different location on the disk. It is also useless to send someone a movie that uses dependencies.

To solve this problem, you must make the movie self-contained. To do this in Apple's **MoviePlayer** program, first open the movie. Then choose **Save As** from the **File Menu**. The Save As dialog box (following figure) contains the following options: Save normally (allowing dependencies), which creates another file that still contains pointers to the other movies; and Make movie self-contained, which makes a new movie that contains all of the movie data and is not dependent upon the other files. The dialog also displays the

difference in file size—a movie with dependencies is considerably smaller than a self-contained movie.

Note that QuickTime editing programs Adobe **Premiere** and Strata's **VideoShop** create movies that are self-contained.

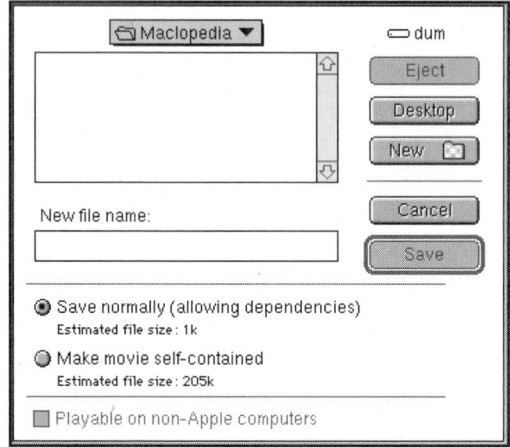

See Also

Dependencies; Flattened Movies; QuickTime

Self-Expanding Archive, *See Compressing Files; .sea Filename Extension*

Separations, *See Color Separations*

Sequencing, *See MIDI*

Serial Line Internet Protocol, *See SLIP*

Serial Port

The serial port of a Macintosh allows the computer to communicate **asynchronously** with devices such as **modems**, **printers**, and **LocalTalk** networks. Each Macintosh model has different configurations of serial ports. Many desktop models have two serial ports, one labeled as Modem, the other as Printer. (Performa models with internal modems only have one port, labeled printer). Newer PowerBook models have one serial port labeled printer/modem. More recent models have replaced the serial port with a **GeoPort**, which accepts serial devices but also lets the Mac use a GeoPort telecom adapter instead of an actual modem.

See Also

Asynchronous Communication; GeoPort

Serial Switch Control Panel

This control panel, found in Macintosh IIfxs and Quadra 950 models provides compatibility for some applications that use the printer or modem port. The only option in this control panel is to make the serial port faster or more compatible.

Serif, *See Typesetting Terms*

Server

In networks where multiple Macintosh computers are joined together, certain pieces of software and/or hardware may be dedicated to the task of managing the distribution of information between individual computers. These computers, called servers, are ideally dedicated to each task at hand. Each computer on the network that logs into the server is referred to as a "client."

Technically speaking it is the software that "makes" the central computer a server. So, when not enough equipment is available to dedicate one computer for each server task, a single CPU can "serve" more than one piece of software, being both a file server and a calendar server, for example. It's customary to refer to the hardware as the "server," and the applications it's handling as the "server software."

File Servers A file server allows computer users to share disk files among networked computers. In practice, the file server functions as a single hard drive that is attached to every computer on the network. Thus, other users can access files you save to the server.

Because you may not want to share everything you save, file servers usually have carefully controlled access, letting certain users and groups access certain folders and files within the server and blocking access to other restricted areas. Servers that are able to provide this service to Macintosh clients are referred to as AFP (**AppleTalk** Filing Protocol) servers. The actual server can be a Mac, PC, or UNIX system, so long as the software supports the AFP protocol. Users may not even know that their server isn't a Mac, because the server's disk drive mounts on the **desktop** as if it were a Mac.

The most basic way to share files with another Mac user is to use the "personal file sharing" built into Macintosh system software since version 7.0. This combination of control panel and system extension allows you to share your hard drive with other users on your network. Although very convenient, personal file sharing slows down the computer it is running on, does not provide very fast file transfers, and can only handle a small number of connected users at one time.

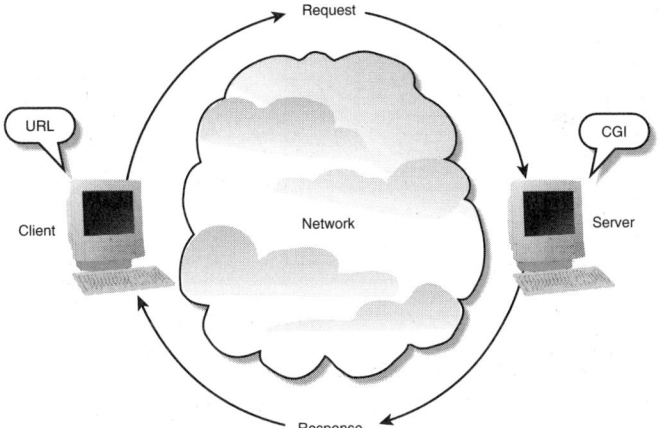

When sharing files with many people, and when speed is important, it makes sense to dedicate a computer to be a file server, and provide it with AppleShare Server software (not to be confused with the **Chooser Extension** "AppleShare" which provides the ability to connect to any AFP server.). AppleShare server turns the Macintosh using it into a dedicated file server. Those computers and users being served are clients.

For better or worse, the computer providing the file server services does not necessarily need to be a Macintosh. Most file servers popular on the Wintel platform, such as Novell NetWare and Windows NT also support Macintosh clients. If you're a dedicated Mac user, you may want to consider using an Apple Workgroup Server. The current models are essentially **PowerPC** models with large hard drives (1-2GB), **CD-ROM**, and **DAT** drives. Many also include the Apple Internet Server Solution package for the **World Wide Web**. Most include **RAID** software for disk mirroring although the RAID hardware must be purchased separately. The Workgroup Server 95 can also run **A/UX** system software. Upgrades are available to turn existing Quadra 900s or 950s to Workgroup Server 95 status. These kits must be installed by an Authorized Apple Service Provider and include PDS cards, appropriate software, and in some cases logic board upgrades.

Novell NetWare servers are a frequent choice for Mac/PC connectivity. They allow a PC to be configured as an AFP server, so that Macs can access it via AppleTalk. PC users can access the same server via Novell's IPX protocols, letting users share files between the two platforms. NetWare requires an Intel-based PC to run (386, 486, Pentium, and so on), but provides outstanding performance. When a limited number of users are connected to the server at one time, the AppleShare line compares favorably with Novell servers. As the amount of usage goes up, however, the Novell servers show dramatically better performance. Unfortunately, most of the setup and maintenance of NetWare servers must be done from a DOS-based machine.

Email Servers An electronic mail server is a specialized type of server designed to handle electronic messages sent between users. Many email servers can handle both interoffice mail and mail sent to outside people through the **Internet**. CE Software's QuickMail, Claris Emailer, and Microsoft Mail are some of the more common applications for inter-office and intra-office mail. They provide both client and server components that work on an AppleTalk network and can also send email through a gateway into the Internet. These email packages let you send files as enclosures to accompany messages you type, and even let you request a return receipt, so you'll know when your mail has been read. The recipient can save the enclosed file on his or her own disk. Each of these mail applications has its own method of use, but the general setup is the same for all. One Mac must be designated as the email server. It becomes a sort of electronic post office, storing messages and relaying them to their destinations. The email server can also be used to run other applications, but having to play mailman may cause it to slow down periodically as the mail is handled. If you have a choice of several machines, designate the fastest and most reliable one as the email server. Don't choose the one that is used for processor-intensive CAD, graphics, or database handling, or one that is used for games (which also monopolize the processor).

Calendar Servers A calendar server is an application consisting of a calendar and data file of appointments and other events entered by individual users for distribution to others within a company. **Now Up-To-Date** and **First Things First** are typical examples of network-able calendars. They allow executives to share calendars with their assistants, and administrators to plan department-wide events from a central location. Some systems have more advanced abilities to perform scheduling of meetings based upon the events stored in each person's calendar.

Print Servers In normal operations, a printer can only handle one print "job" at a time. Thus, when several people try to print to the same networked printer, each one has to wait for the previous person's print session to end before theirs can begin. A print server provides a more intelligent method of capturing each print job. As each user attempts to print, the print server collects the print job that would otherwise be sent to the printer and holds it in memory. As the jobs come in, it queues them, sending them to the printer one after another. It is similar to the Mac's built-in print spooler, **PrintMonitor**, except that being an external device, it doesn't interfere with the individual computers operations at all. It doesn't tie up their RAM and doesn't slow down other processing, as an internal print spooler can.

Database Servers The increase in networked computers has led to an increase in attempts to intelligently manage large volumes of data by using databases which allow many people access to the same data. These services are provided by database servers. Some database programs, such as Microsoft's FoxPro, use file servers to store common data and share the information between users. This type of scenario forces each database client to do all of the data processing work. Other database software, such as ACI's 4th Dimension, act as a true database server. 4D's database server intelligently communicates with the database clients using a client-server motif in which processing of data is distributed between the two machines. It also functions cross-platform, running on Windows 95 and Windows NT as well as Mac.

Remote Access Server Remote access servers provide the ability to connect to the network from remote locations through the use of modems or other wide-area communications hardware. Generally these units consist of a specialized piece of hardware dedicated to the task. These devices are not computers, or even servers, but boxes to which you can connect modems and networks. One can also set up a Macintosh to be a remote access server with Apple's Apple Remote Access software or Apple's Multiport Remote Access Server hardware. The client computer makes use of Apple's Apple Remote Access (ARA) client software to connect to the remote access server. The Multiport server is a card that you put into a Mac, and then attach modems. It allows the Mac to communicate with several remote clients at once, each over a separate modem and phone line.

Fax Server Fax servers provide the ability for each person on a network to send and/or receive faxes by computer without dedicating hardware to this purpose on each machine. These provide a tremendous savings to a large office, because the server requires only one or two telephone lines and fax modems that are then shared by the entire office, much as one fax machine is set up for an office, instead of placing one on each person's desk.

In addition to sending and receiving conveniences, fax servers provide for easy tracking of outgoing and incoming faxes without the need to check each individual computer. As with other server types, a Fax server can be composed of a specialized piece of hardware (Such as the Global Village OneWorld Fax Server) or can be composed of software running on a Macintosh (such as 4Site's Fax server).

Modem Server Much in the way that a fax server shares a fax modem between people a network, a modem server shares the data transfer functions of a modem with each user. Each time a user needs to make an outgoing data call, the modem server forms a "virtual" connection to that computer, simulating a directly attached modem. This can result in large cost savings, because only a few modems and telephone lines can be effectively shared within a large offices.

Server Push/Client Pull

An extension (or, unofficial addition) to HyperText Markup Language (**HTML**) created by Netscape that allows a server on the **World Wide Web** to refresh the data displayed on-screen by a **client** at regular intervals.

Server push and client pull are two ways in which a Web reader can get information from a server. Along with the traditional **hypertextual** method—the user clicks on a link and gets information—this give the server the capability to "push" data to the browser.

In server push, the server sends down a bundle of data, and sends more data at predetermined intervals.

In client pull, the server sends data, along with a directive to reload the data in a specified amount of time, such as every five seconds.

Both methods are used as a crude way of adding animation to Web document, by refrehing inline images on a regular basis. Server push/client pull only work with the Web browser **Netscape Navigator.**

See Also

Hypertext; HTML; Netscape Navigator; Web Browser; World Wide Web

S

Server-Side Imagemap, *See*
Imagemaps, Creating

Service Bureau Dos and Don'ts for Desktop Publishers

When working with a service bureau is it important to maintain a high level of professionalism by being well-informed and performing certain essential steps. The following is a list of "dos and don'ts" that will expedite prepress services.

- Fill out the service bureau worksheet or job order completely. These forms are available at the service bureau.

- Make sure that you and the service bureau are using the same software applications and that you have the same versions.

- Prior to taking electronic publication files to the service bureau, discuss with them issues such as **trapping, overprinting, halftone screen ruling** (lpi), and **color separating.** It is important to clarify who has the responsibility for setting up the software to perform these functions.

- Find out whether the service bureau prefers to work with native file formats or **PostScript** files. This can have a bearing on who performs trapping, sets screen rulings, and so on.

- Be sure to include all the computer files that are necessary to output your job. Do not include unnecessary files or duplicate files.

- Use the same font technology as that used by the service bureau. **Adobe Type 1** fonts are standard. Don't give your printer-font files to the service bureau. It is illegal.

- Make sure that you have a backup copy of all files.

- Don't be afraid to ask questions and clarify misunderstandings.

- Clearly label and number all disks or cartridges that you send to the service bureau.

- Provide a directory of files and their disk locations.

See Also

Desktop Publishing; Service Bureaus, Trade Shops, and Desktop Publishing

Service Bureaus, Trade Shops, and Desktop Publishing

Service bureaus and trade shops provide output and other **prepress** services for **desktop publishing.** Service bureaus for DTP often developed from typesetting and reprographic camera houses which served the traditional graphics industry. The **imagesetter** is a primary piece of equipment for a service bureau. Imagesetters evolved from phototypesetting systems and are capable of very high output resolutions and good-quality **color separation.** The Linotronic is a well-known brand of imagesetter manufactured by Linotype-Hell. Imagesetters are also manufactured by Agfa, Tegra Varityper, Scitex America, and Optronics.

Trade shops, sometimes called color houses, are usually dedicated to high-end color reproduction. They often utilize expensive proprietary hardware and software dedicated to color scanning, color separation, electronic page imposition, and high-resolution output to film recorders capable of large formats. These high-end systems are known as **color electronic prepress systems (CEPS)**. Many trade shops are turning to less expensive mid-range systems based on off-the-shelf hardware and software.

See Also

Color Separations; Desktop Publishing and Color Electronic Prepress Systems (CEPS); Desktop Publishing Hardware; Image Scanning; Imagesetters; Prepress

SGML

An acronym for Standard Generalized Markup Language, an interationally agreed-upon standard for representing computer documents. A language used to markup documents for publication on the **Internet**. HyperText Markup Language (**HTML**), commonly used on the **World Wide Web**), is a subset of SGML.

SGML was created for IBM in the late 1960s as GML (General Markup Language). SGML is a computer language that describes document types rather than specific documents, thus allowing a document to be defined by a computer and establishing a logical relationship between its parts. It allows a document to be marked up so that it can be translated from computer to computer but doesn't provide for how it will appear on an individual screen.

Every SGML document has three parts: a *declaration*, a *prologue*, and *references*:

- The declaration means that when HTML is declared to be an SGML document, it will conform to the rules for SGML documents, such as "Document names can be no longer than 72 characters" or "End tags must begin with (</)."

- The prologue means that at the beginning of an SGML or HTML document there is a Document Type Definition specifying what its attributes are. At the beginning of an HTML document, the first tag is <HTML>.

- The references are the tags and other instructions that make up the body of the document.

See Also

HTML; Internet; Web Page; World Wide Web, The

Shaders

Shaders are mathematical algorithms used to apply colors and textures to **3D** models. Shaders usually are limited in their output (a wood shader can produce only wood textures), but they usually produce high-quality results. Objects appear to have been carved out of the texture—the grain matches throughout the object, for example. Shaders and texture maps create surfaces on 3D objects. Which you should use depends upon the effect you want to create. It also depends on the library of shaders and textures you have available. One advantage texture mapping has over shaders is that you can simply create a new surface by drawing or digitizing the surface you need.

There are basic types of shaders (for example, "wood"), and each has parameters that you can adjust (the color of the wood, the size of the grain in the wood). 3D programs usually include a collection of shaders, and you might be able to purchase more, although very few software developers have released additional shaders for their products.

Why use shaders instead of texture mapping? First, shaders usually come with the program and are easy to apply and adjust. Second, they produce very high-quality results; you would have to spend a lot of time scanning and adjusting parameters to produce a texture map wood that looks as good as that produced by a shader. Finally, and perhaps most important, because shaders are programs and not pre-scanned images, they can be more sophisticated in the way they cover a surface. Take, for example, a wooden bowl. A shader applies wood grain so that it appears to actually go through the surface of the bowl (from the outside to the inside surface). With texture mapping, the surface is applied to the object, and the grain outside the bowl will probably not match the grain inside.

A shader enables you to adjust predefined parameters, such as color or detail (for example, the size and waviness of the wood grain), **reflectivity**, **luminance**, **highlights**, **shininess**, **transparency**, and refraction of light through an object

See Also

Texture Mapping

S

Shared Devices

Any device, such as a workgroup printer or a **network** modem, that can be shared is called a shared device. If, for example, you have four Macintosh computers connected to the same **printer**, this printer would be a shared printer, or a shared device. Your Mac can also be a shared device if you have a number of people on a network who can access files or folders on your machine.

See Also

Networks; Sharing Files; Sharing Setup Control Panel

Shareware Games

The concept behind shareware games is simple and strange. Basically, there are non-commercial games on the **Internet** that you can download to your computer and play for free... sort of.

The hitch is that you are expected, on your honor, to pay for the game by sending a check to the creator if you decide to keep it. Because the Internet is so vast, there is no real way to check if you paid for your copy or not, but the developers of these often amazing games rely on your checks to keep them making more. Many games that started out as shareware have ended up being huge commercial hits later in life. Wolfenstein 3D, the precursor to the **DOOM** phenomena, started out as shareware, and two of the best arcade games available, Maelstrom and Apieron are shareware games created by Ambrosia Software.

Unlike demo versions of commercial games that give you only a taste of the action, most of the time, you get to play the entire shareware game before you decide if you want it. No teasers and tricks.

Because they must be downloaded, most of the best shareware games are arcade style and don't take up a lot of memory. Consequently, you can buy

compilation CDs like CD Funhouse 10.1 from Wayzata and All the Best Mac Games '96 from Lazerworks with more than 500 games apiece on one CD. Often, the CDs cost less than the download time of getting them off the Net. Of course, you are still obligated to pay the shareware fee for any game you actually use more than once or twice.

If you really want to check out the latest and hottest game before the masses get it and the big guys start making a lot of money off of it, try out the shareware areas like the Mac Games section of **America Online** (Keyword: MGM) and various Mac game areas on **CompuServe**. The following figure shows all the best Mac games of 1996 CD.

Also, a good way to start is to use an Internet search tool such as **Netscape** to find lists of the best shareware games. In addition to full games, a lot of cool stuff called patches, which can change the inner make-up of an existing game exist in Cyberspace including patches that insert Barney the purple dinosaur and Beavis and Butthead into Wolfenstein 3-D instead of Nazis.

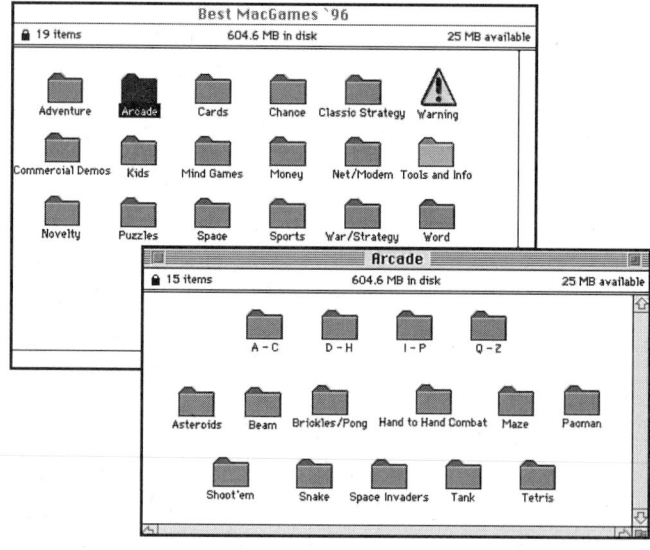

See Also

MUDs and MOOs; Network Gaming; Online Games

Sharing Command

If your Macintosh is being shared over a **network** and you are sharing your computer with other users, the Sharing command offers you control over access privileges to your folders, and it also gives you control of folders that you own on other shared drives.

The Sharing command is found under the **File menu** at the **Desktop** level and this brings up the **Sharing Window** where you can choose, by using a **pop-down menu** of users on the network and a series of **checkboxes**, which users have access to which files and folders on your shared Macintosh.

To use the Sharing command to limit access to your files and folders, follow these steps:

1. Choose Sharing from the File menu.

2. The Sharing Window appears and you can choose a username on your network from the pop-up menu, and then choose their access privileges with the corresponding checkboxes.

3. When your choices are complete, close the Sharing Window.

See Also

Checkboxes; Disks and Drives; File Menu; Network; Pop-Up Menu; Sharing Setup Control Panel

Sharing Files

If you have files on your Macintosh that other people in your office can access, you can share these files using **file sharing**. This enables you to let users on a **network** have access to files you have designated as shared files. The capability to share files is built right into the Macintosh operating system. With file sharing you can designate that users have access to all your files or just individual folders.

This sharing of files is controlled through the **Sharing Setup control panel,** as shown in the figure. This control panel enables you to initiate/disconnect file sharing, and it provides a level of security by password-protecting access to your machine. You will also need to name your Macintosh and assign your-

self a username. This is done in the Sharing Setup control panel as well. This name will be used by other users on the network to access folders you've selected on your computer for sharing.

You can turn off file sharing at any time by clicking the Stop button on the Sharing Setup control panel. A dialog box appears asking you to enter how many minutes should elapse before you want file sharing disconnected. If you want file sharing disconnected, enter the number 0 at this dialog box.

TIP If your computer has File Sharing turned on, but you're not sharing any files, you should turn File Sharing off. File sharing can slow your computer down and slow down the entire network because the more users on the network, the more strain and traffic on the network.

If you want to enable access only to certain network users, you can decide which users have access in the **Users and Groups** control panel. Within this control panel, you can create a list of users who will have access to your files, and you can create groups of users with access as well. You may want, for example, to set up one group of users that will have full access to all your files, while you may want another group to just have limited access.

Each user with access is represented by an **icon** of a person's face. To create a group, open the Users and Groups control panel, and under the File menu choose New Group. This creates a group icon, and you can name this group. To add users to this group, drag the user's icon onto the group icon, release the mouse button, and that user is added to the group. You can also **double-click** the group icon, which will open its window, and you can drag a user into the group. You delete users from a group the same way—double-click to open the group's window, select the user you want to delete, and drag the icon into the trash can.

You can set each person's access privileges by double-clicking this icon, which presents the Users and Groups options dialog box. In this dialog, you determine how much access they'll have to your shared volumes and folders when they log on to your Mac over a network.

To add a new user to a group, choose New User from the File menu and a new icon for that user is created. Each user can be named (you can use their real names to help you keep track) and you can determine how much access each new user will have to your shared files and folders by double-clicking on the user's icon. This will bring up the File Sharing Options window where you can assign a user password and if the user will have access to your shared folders.

You can also enable a guest (another user on the network that's not part of your regular users or groups) to sign on and have access to shared files. This is controlled through the "Guest" icon that appears in the Users and Group control panel. You can double-click this Guest icon to bring up the Guest Preferences dialog box that enables you to choose whether guests will be allowed to connect and have access to only the folders or volumes you have allowed everyone on the network access to.

After you've set up who connects and what their access privileges are, you can determine which file, folders, and disk you make available to them by choosing **Sharing** from the **File menu**. This brings up the **Sharing window** where you can choose, by using **pop-up menus** of users and groups and a series of **checkboxes**, which users and groups have access to which folders on your Macintosh.

To use the Sharing Setup control panel to name your Mac, follow these steps:

1. Select the Sharing Setup from your Control Panels folder in the Apple menu.

2. Under Owner name, type your name.

3. Type a password that will give you the ability to make changes to your setup if necessary.

4. Give your Macintosh a name. (Keep in mind that this name will be visible to other network users.)

To turn File Sharing on, follow these steps:

1. Choose Sharing Setup from your Control Panels folder.

2. Click Start to enable file sharing to begin.

3. Close the control panel.

4. In System 7.5 and higher, you can turn File Sharing on from the Control Strip.

To turn File Sharing off, follow these steps:

1. Choose Sharing Setup from your Control Panels folder.

2. Choose Stop, and when the dialog box appears, enter how many minutes until File Sharing disconnects. To disconnect immediately, enter 0 and click OK.

3. Close the control panel.

4. In System 7.5 and higher, you can also turn File Sharing off from the Control Strip.

See Also

Checkboxes; Double-Click; File Menu; File Sharing Icon; Network; Pop-Up Menu; Sharing Command; Sharing Setup Control Panel; Sharing Window; Users and Groups

Sharing Folders

If you are connected to a **network**, you can designate certain folders on your Macintosh as being available to other users on the network. After you have selected which folder, or folders, is to be available to network users, you can then set up a different level of access privileges for each group of users on the network.

There are, for example, some groups that you may want to have full access to this shared folder and the ability to create files, edit existing files, delete files, and so on, but there are other groups that you may want to grant the ability to view the folder, but not make changes or add to it. And there may be yet other groups that you don't want to have any access or even see this folder at all. You can make these determinations in the **Sharing Window** dialog box, which appears when you choose **Sharing** from the **File menu**. This dialog box lists each group and enables you to choose the level of access privileges through a series of checkboxes.

In the Sharing Window dialog box, you can toggle on or off the capability for a folder to be shared by clicking the checkbox marked, "Share this item and its contents." After you've made this folder available for sharing, you can choose who the owner (person in charge) of this folder will be. Normally, you would name yourself, but you can also designate a different network user to be the owner of this shared folder by choosing their name from the pop-up menu in the dialog box. If you choose a different user (other than yourself), this user will then have the ability to set access privileges for this shared folder.

You determine which users, or groups of users, will have access to your shared folder through this dialog box. The user or group's names will appear in a pop-up menu, and you can choose from three different levels of access for each user or group: the ability to see folders, the ability to see files, and the ability to make changes to these files. There is also a checkbox below this pop-up menu called "Everyone," where turning this on enables access to your shared folder by guests on the network. You can then designate the access privileges of guests the same way you did for users and groups.

See Also
File Menu; File Sharing; Network; Sharing Window

Sharing Setup Control Panel
The ability to share files with others is controlled from the Sharing Setup control panel. This control panel is divided into three sections: Network Identity (where you name your Mac, enter your name as owner, and assign a password); the File Sharing section where you toggle file sharing on/off; and the Program Linking section, where you toggle program linking on/off.

After you've entered your Network identity information, you can enable file sharing by clicking the Start button. If file sharing is already on, you can turn off file sharing at any time by clicking the Stop button under the file sharing section. A dialog box appears asking you to enter how many minutes before you want file sharing disconnected. If you want file sharing disconnected immediately, enter zero at this dialog.

To turn off File Sharing on the Sharing Setup control panel, follow these steps:

1. Choose Sharing Setup from the Control Panels submenu on the Apple menu (or System Folder).

2. Select Stop in the dialog box that appears and enter how many minutes before file sharing is disconnected. To disconnect immediately, enter 0 and click OK.

3. Close the control panel.

See Also
Sharing Files; Sharing Folders

Sharing Window
The Sharing Window is the dialog box where you determine how much control users or groups of users **sharing files** and folders on your Macintosh have. Through the Sharing Window you can determine different access privileges for users or groups of users on the **network**, and you can designate that guests on the network have the same access.

S

You can, for example, enable a particular user to have the ability to see a folder's contents, edit these contents, **trash** files, and add files of their own. You can then designate that a different user only be able to view the contents but not edit or add files to that folder. And for another user, you can deny access to the folder entirely by locking them out.

In the Sharing Window dialog box, you can toggle on or off the capability for a folder to be shared by clicking the checkbox marked, "Share this item and its contents." After you've made this folder available for sharing, you can choose who the owner (person in charge) of this folder will be. Normally, you would name yourself, but you can also designate a different network user to be the owner of this shared folder by choosing their name from the pop-up menu in the dialog box. If you choose a different user (other than yourself), this user will then have the ability to set access privileges for this shared folder.

You determine which users, or groups of users, will have access to your shared folder through this dialog box. The user or group's names appear in a pop-up menu, and you can choose from three different levels of access for each user or group: the ability to see folders, the ability to see files, and the ability to make changes to these files. There is also a checkbox below this pop-up menu called "Everyone," where turning this on enables access to your shared folder by guests on the network. You can then designate the access privileges of guests the same way you did for users and groups.

There are two more checkboxes in this dialog box. The first, marked "Make all currently enclosed folders like this one," enables you to easily assign the same access privileges to folders that are enclosed within your shared folder. The last checkbox, marked "Can't be moved, renamed, or deleted," should be checked if you don't want other users on the network to have the ability to move, rename, or delete your shared folder. Most users leave this option turned on as a preventative measure.

To access the Sharing Window, follow these steps:

1. Select the hard disk or folder on your Macintosh that you want to make available to users on your network.

2. Choose Sharing from the **File menu**.

3. The Sharing Window dialog box will appear. The name of the shared disk or folder will appear along with a pop-up menu listing the users/groups and checkboxes for each level of privilege. By clicking a checkbox, you're enabling that privilege for the user whose name appears on the pop-up menu.

See Also
File Menu; Network; Sharing Files

Sharpening, *See Image Manipulation for Printing*

Sharpening Controls in Scanners

Most image-editing programs offer some sort of sharpening controls, and most scans from the desktop need sharpening.

Some software applications, like Adobe **Photoshop**, offer more than one sharpening tool. The most subtle and controllable tool is "Unsharp Mask," which allows you to adjust the amount of sharpening effect by moving a slider back and forth. It's important to remember that your monitor is low-resolution, and an image that looks just right on-screen will probably be over-sharp and grainy when it's output. Learning to apply the right amount of sharpening takes some practice, but the general rule of thumb is that sharpening should be subtle—the results should be visible, but just barely visible, on-screen. The figure shows an image being sharpened in Photoshop—notice that the image is slightly grainy as a result of oversharpening.

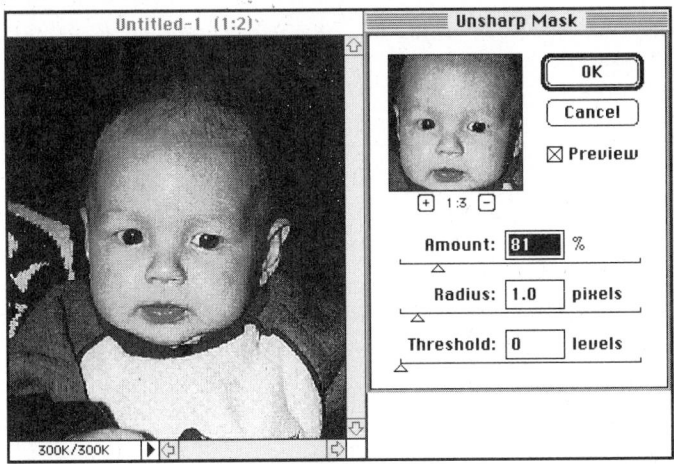

Many common image-editing operations—resizing pictures, making tonal adjustments—can blur the image. For this reason, it's best to save sharpening as the last step of the scanning/editing procedure.

See Also
Desktop Publishing; Photoshop; Scanner, Desktop

Shell, *See Framework*

Shell Account

This is the basic bare-bones connection to the **Internet**, running on top of a host's operating system, usually UNIX. It enables a user to access **Usenet**, send and receive email, access FTP, access Telnet, and access **Gopher**. Shell users use a terminal emulator like MicroPhone or Zterm to connect to the Internet. Shell account users, however, cannot use applications such as **Netscape**, which require a MacTCP-based connection unless they run an application like The Internet Adapter (**TIA**). If you have a shell account and want to access the **Web**, you need Lynx, a UNIX-based Web client.

See Also
Email; File Transfer Protocols; Gopher; Internet; Netscape Navigator; Networking; Usenet

Shift Key

The Shift key on a Macintosh keyboard has two functions: It acts as the key that enables you to type capital letters and access punctuation marks, as you would on a typewriter, and it's also used as a modifier key in conjunction with other keys or actions in keyboard shortcuts or commands.

To type a capital letter, hold the Shift key and type the letter of your choice. To use the Shift key as a modifier key, you use it in conjunction with an action or other keys. If, for example, you've selected a file and want to select additional files, you can hold the Shift key and add additional files to your selection by clicking them. The Shift key is enabling you to add more items to your selection. An example of using the Shift key with other keys would be when you want to take a **screen capture** (a picture of the computer screen), you use the keyboard command Shift-⌘-3.

See Also
Command Key; Screen Capture

Shininess

Shininess defines the size of reflections caused by bright lights on **3D** objects. Although a highlight parameter adjusts the intensity of a reflection, shininess adjusts the size of the reflections.

Shockwave

Shockwave is a **World Wide Web browser** plug-in that enables browsers to play **Director** movies over the Web. The plug-in is installed into a browser that supports **plug-ins** (such as **Netscape**).

A special EMBED tag is added to the **HTML** file. When the HTML file is opened, the animation is first downloaded, and then played by the Shockwave plug-in. The animation appears within the browser window.

```
<EMBED HEIGHT=64 WIDTH=64
SRC="minislid.dcr">
```

An example of the EMBED tag used for Shockwave movies. The Height and Width are recommended and define the size of the movie; you should use this as it enables the browser to display the rest of the page before the animation completes loading. The SRC parameter is the name of the movie.

If a browser doesn't support Shockwave, you might want to display a graphic in place of the movie. The <NOEMBED> tag can be used around such instructions; anything within the <NOEMBED> tags will be ignored by a Shockwave capable browser.

Shockwave is dependent upon an additional product from Macromedia called **Afterburner**. Afterburner compresses Director files into the Shockwave format for quick transfer over the Web. Even so, the current transmission speeds of **Internet** connections impose a serious limitation on the scope of productions that can currently be viewed (you probably don't want to download a movie larger than 200K).

Shockwave supports most Director features, but not all. A serious consideration for applications running over the Internet is security. To minimize the chance of someone creating an unfriendly, **virus**-like application using Shockwave, the first version does not support any functions, such as system access and file I/O, that could be used to do anything devious. Hopefully, future versions will add such support along with security features similar to those found in **Java**.

Movies created for Shockwave should be small—no more than a few hundred kilobytes. The movie is turned into a Shockwave-compatible movie by running it through the Afterburner utility, which compresses the graphics and strips out all of the unneeded information in the file (including the uncompiled scripts).

Note: You cannot decompress an Afterburner movie into a movie that Director can open.

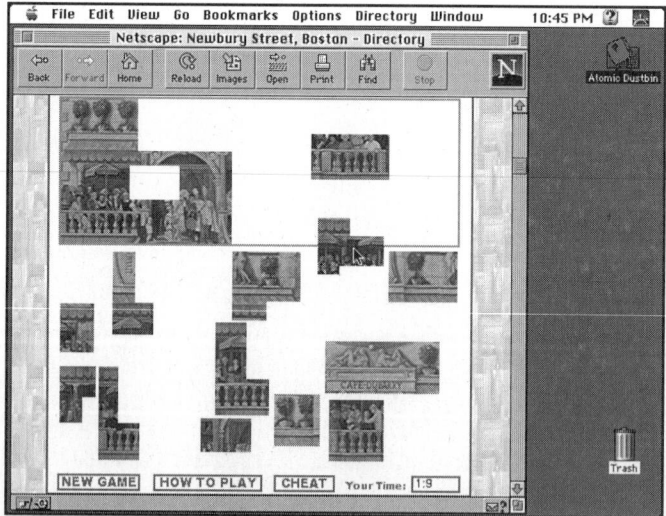

See Also

Afterburner; Director; Netscape; World Wide Web

Shockwave, Afterburner

Macromedia's Shockwave is a **plug-in** for the **Netscape Navigator World Wide Web browser**. With Shockwave installed, Navigator is able to play Macromedia **Director** "movies" *inside* the Navigator window. Afterburner is the tool that developers use to put Director files on Web pages.

Macromedia's commercial application Director is arguably the standard for creating multimedia presentations. With the easy-to-use, animation-friendly scripting language called **Lingo**, developers without extensive programming experience can create stand-alone interactive packages.

Afterburner is a freely distributed software package that allows developers to prepare Director files for distribution on the **Internet**. (Basically, this preparation consists of squeezing the files to as small a size as possible, to reduce load-time and conserve bandwidth.)

It's probably easier for programming novices to create "interactive content" using the Director environment than by using **Java** or other high-level programming languages. In fact, it's possible to create arresting animation with Director without doing any programming at all. Although Director is commercial software, Shockwave and Afterburner are free.

Unlike Java, Lingo and Director are proprietary formats. Until Macromedia decides otherwise, Shockwave will be able to display content created by Director and Lingo rather than by other languages or applications.

You can find more information and download Shockwave and Afterburner for Macromedia's Web site at **http://www. macromedia.com**.

For end users, there's not much point in *not* installing Shockwave…after all, it's free. Keep in mind that it will add about a one megabyte to Netscape's RAM requirement after it loads.

Director is already firmly established as a tool for creating multimedia content, and it's likely that Director movies will quickly be used extensively on Web pages—more so on slick, commercial sites than on home-brewed home pages.

To install the Shockwave plug-in, simply put it in the Plug-ins folder in your Netscape folder, and restart Navigator…that's it. To use Afterburner to prepare your files for the Web, refer to the documentation that's distributed with Afterburner.

See Also

Afterburner; Internet; Java; Macromedia Director; Multimedia; Multipart GIF Image; Netscape Navigator; Plug-In; World Wide Web, The

Shoot-Em-Ups, *See First Person Perspective Shooters*

Shooting Games, *See First Person Perspective Shooters*

Shortcuts, *See Keyboard Shortcuts*

Short-Run Printing

Now that we're all thinking in color these days, more and more business documents are printed in color. Documents like limited-run promotional fliers, brochures, and presentation materials are prime candidates for short-run color printing.

The new digital color presses—actually high-speed color printers and color copiers with Mac front ends—are capable of producing thousands of color pages per hour, at a cost ranging from 20 cents to $2.00 per page. They can print single- or double-sided documents. Combined with new binding techniques, they can supply a dozen or a thousand reasonably high-quality color documents overnight.

Offset printing is still more affordable for longer print runs, offset print quality is higher, and the newer machines can't handle as many types of paper and card stock as offset presses. But print shops are finding their customers are generally happy with the results from machines like Agfa's **Chromapress**, Indigo's **E-Print**, and, for black and white work, Xerox's **Docutech** system.

See Also

Chromapress; Docutech; E-Print

Show All Command, *See Hide Others Command*

Show Clipboard Command

This command, found under the **Edit menu,** opens a window that shows you the current contents of the Mac's **Clipboard** (the temporary holding space for items that you are copying or cutting to paste elsewhere). The contents of the Clipboard are the last items you **cut** or **copied** into the Clipboard. If, for example you cut three folders from a window, when you ask to Show Clipboard, you'll see the name of those three folders. If you cut or copied text, you'll see the text, or if you copied a graphic you'll see that graphic residing in the keyboard.

The Clipboard shows the contents as none, if there are no items in the Clipboard. When you **shut down**, any items in the Clipboard are deleted. You may use the Show Clipboard command while at the **Finder**, and also in any application that enables you to choose Show Clipboard from the application's Edit menu.

To use the Show Clipboard command, follow these steps:

1. At the Finder level, select Show Clipboard.

2. A window opens showing you the current contents of the Clipboard. If there are no item currently in the Clipboard, it displays the contents as none.

See Also

Clipboard; Copy Command; Cut Command; Edit Menu; Finder; Shut Down Command

ShowPlace

A simple 3D scene **modeler** developed by **Pixar,** ShowPlace uses **MacRenderMan** (which was bundled with ShowPlace) to render still scenes. The tool

S

provides basic 3D primitives, such as a ball, a cone, and a small library of 3D objects. It is a very limited product. Also, the MacRenderMan software requires a lot of memory to produce even comparatively simple scenes.

Pixar no longer supports any of its Macintosh products.

See Also

MacRenderMan; Pixar; Reflection Maps; Shaders; Texture Mapping; Typestry Highlight

ShrinkWrap, *See Decoding/Decompressing*

Shut Down Command

When you are finished using your Macintosh and want to turn the computer off, it is recommended that you select Shut Down from the **Special menu.** By selecting Shut Down, some models of Macintosh, including all PowerBook models, turn themselves off. Other models (like the LC models, Quadra and Centris 610s, Quadra 605s) change the monitor screen to black and display the message, "It is now safe to turn off your Macintosh." If you get this message, to turn off your Macintosh you'll have to switch the on/off button on the back of your Macintosh to the off position (down). You may also have to switch off your monitor, depending on your model of Macintosh.

Apple recommends that you always turn off your Macintosh by first selecting Shut Down, as this gives the Macintosh time to write any information it has been storing in **RAM** to your **hard drive** before the power is turned off. This protects your information and also resets the hard drive for your next start up.

Starting in **System 7.5**, Macintosh models that have a PowerOn key can now also Shut Down by hitting the PowerOn key while the Macintosh is operating. While using your Macintosh, if you hit the Power-On key, you'll get a message asking: "Are You Sure You Want To Shut Down Your Computer Now?" and

offers you three choices: **Cancel**, **Restart,** or Shut Down. If you click Shut Down, it performs the Shut Down command of your particular Macintosh model. Clicking the Restart button performs the Restart Command. Cancel exits this dialog box with no command initiated. This warning dialog is a safety feature in case you accidentally were to hit the Start-up key on your keyboard.

Also in System 7.5 and higher is an Apple menu item called Shut Down, that lets you choose Shut Down from the Apple menu. By having Shut Down as an Apple menu item, you also enables you to make an Alias of the Shut Down Apple menu item and place it on the desktop, or anywhere on your hard disk for easy access.

To use the Shut Down command to turn your computer off, follow these steps:

1. At the Finder level, close all open programs and documents.

2. Select Shut Down from the Special menu

3. Depending on your model of Macintosh, your computer either shuts down and turns off, or it displays a message telling you it's OK to turn off your computer, and in that case, you'll have to switch the On/Off switch in the back of your Macintosh to the Off position (down).

4. You can also choose Shut Down from the Apple menu in System 7.5 and higher.

To use the Shut Down command to turn off your computer from your keyboard (using System 7.5 or higher), follow these steps:

1. Close all documents and programs and hit the Power On key on your keyboard, located on the top right or top center of your keyboard (depending on which keyboard model you're using).

2. A dialog box appears asking you if you want to shut down your Macintosh.

3. Click Shut Down. Depending on your model of Macintosh, your computer either shuts down and turns off, or it displays a message telling you it's OK to turn off your computer, and in that case, you'll have to switch the On/Off switch in the back of your Macintosh to the Off position (down).

4. You can also choose Shut Down from the Apple menu in System 7.5 and higher.

See Also

Memory; Restart; Special Menu

Shut Down Message

There are models of Macintosh computers (Classics and LCs, for example) that do not completely shut themselves off when you choose **Shut Down** from the **Special menu**. On these models, choosing Shut Down prepares the Mac to be turned off by parking the heads of the hard disk (this protects the hard disk's read/write heads from touching the disk—which would destroy data—by moving the disk's head to a safe location. You should never move your computer while it's running; shut down first so the read/write heads are parked), saving any information in the Mac's internal memory, and resetting the Mac for the next startup. If your Mac is one of these models, you receive a message when you select the Shut Down command that reads, "It is now safe to switch off your Macintosh." After that message appears, you can switch the Mac's On/Off switch to the Off position.

See Also

Shut Down Command; Special Menu

Sid Meier's Worlds

Sid Meier is generally considered by critics to be the guru of all **strategy games.** His Civilization stands out as a milestone accomplishment in computer gaming. The first three titles to bear his moniker, Colonization, Pirates!Gold, and Civilizations from MicroProse, focus on specific points in history with amazing attention to historic detail. Meier definitely had his history books open when he programmed Civilization, which brings you from the prehistoric era to today; Colonization, featuring the settlements of early America; and Pirates!Gold.

As time goes by, in Civilization and Colonization you move from rock weapons to the A-bomb as you attempt to keep neighborly relations with the inevitable other societies that crop up here and there. Pirates!Gold adds more of an adventure feel, putting you into battle on the high seas. Likewise, Vikings, a Meier endorsed strategy game from GTE Interactive, concentrates on the initial discoveries of the nomadic colonies and also incorporates war and adventure tactics.

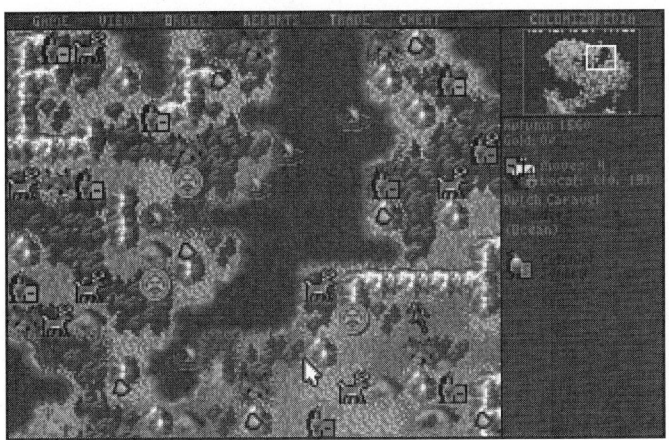

See Also

Allied General; Chaos Overlords; Pax Imperia; Spaceward Ho!; Strategy Games; V for Victory

S

Silicon Valley, *See Cupertino*

Sim Games

Sim (short for simulation) games cover just about everything from piloting a U-Boat submarine during World War II to fighting off Darth Vader's Imperial Tie Fighters in **Rebel Assault II**, a Star Wars adaptation. The most popular simulation games (sims) are flight simulators that allow you to engage in intense battle simulations against weather conditions that would fell even the Wright brothers. The following figure shows SimCity 2000.

The graphic detail on flight simulators like **F/A-18 Hornet** will leave you breathless. However, flight sims are not an easy shoot 'em up experience. They usually require that you master the massive flight manual that invariably comes with each game. However, after you learn to fly your Mac, it's generally pretty easy to switch from one flight sim to another. Space Sims like **Absolute Zero** from Domark, creator of the flight sims Flying Nightmares and **Out of the Sun**, are a spin-off genre that put you in navigational control of a starship.

Maxis-style Sim games give you the opportunity to play overlord in a variety of situations. One day you might be the owner of a high-rise tower, the next day

you're the ruler of the world (in SimLife). SimCity (now released as SimCity Classic), debuted in 1989 and gave gamers the tools to create an entire city and oversee it as it progresses. SimCity appealed to a wide audience for a lot of the same reasons that **Myst** did, it was virtually non-violent and you could actually learn something during the gaming process. Since 1989, Maxis has released SimEarth, SimTower, SimAnt, SimIsland, SimFarm, and the much improved **SimCity 2000** as well as a scaled down children's version entitled SimTown.

See Also

A-10 Attack!; Absolute Zero; F/A-18 Hornet; Out of the Sun; Rebel Assault II; SimCity 2000; Wing Commander III

SimCity Classic, *See* *SimCity 2000*

SimCity 2000

Maxis' **Sim games** create a virtual environment that responds to your every decision. In 1989, SimCity introduced us to the Maxis universe. Starting with nothing more than a terrain broken up into a grid, you build your city from the ground up. As you zone each individual square for industrial, residential, or commercial buildings, artificial life (sims) move in and build factories or shopping malls accordingly. Soon, you are worrying about schools, water pipes, roads, highways, pollution, and the like. SimCity 2000, released in 1993, pumped up the graphics to 3D, added a terrain editor so you could create your own landscape before you even start out, and an urban renewal kit with other styles of architecture including futuristic space-style homes and buildings.

If your people are really unhappy, they will riot and start fires, destroying property. And you always need to be on the lookout for natural disasters. If you want a real challenge, check out the included preset scenarios in SimCity 2000: clean up after the San Francisco Earthquake or the put out the infamous Oakland Hills fire. If you finish them in time, you get to add the cities to those you have unlimited access to play around with. Maxis' other titles build on the SimCity premise, allowing you to build everything from a high rise tower to new life forms. When you start to grow weary of city life, check out SimTower, SimEarth, SimFarm, SimAnt, SimLife, A-Train, and a children's title, SimTown. SimCity Enhanced was a failed attempt to jazz up the format with multimedia and merely proved that what's not broken doesn't need to be fixed.

See Also

Afterlife; Sim Games

SimEarth, *See Sim Games; SimCity 2000*

SimLife, *See Sim Games; SimCity 2000*

Simple Mail Transfer Protocol, *See SMTP*

SimplePlayer

SimplePlayer is an application that enables you to view and make simple **cut**- and **paste**-type edits to **QuickTime** movies. SimplePlayer has been replaced by **MoviePlayer** in current system software.

See Also

Cut Command; MoviePlayer; Paste Command; QuickTime; System Software

SIMS, *See Memory*

SimpleText

SimpleText is a "no-frills" text editor that enables you to create and edit simple text documents. SimpleText

is a replacement for Apple's **TeachText**, which was introduced with the original Macintosh. Although TeachText did little more than enable you to type some text and **save** the document, SimpleText adds some features that make use of some of Apple's latest technology while still being a small, simple application. SimpleText is installed with a **System** install and is often used for viewing **Read Me files** that accompany software programs and shareware and freeware applications (see the following figure).

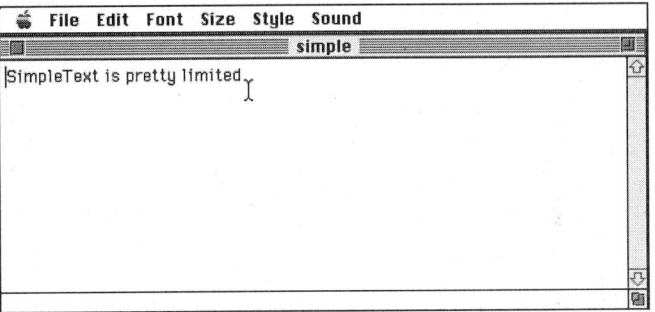

When you launch SimpleText, it opens a blank text document with a blinking **cursor**. After you've typed some text, you can choose a **font**, size, and style (bold, italic, and so on) from SimpleText's **menus**. SimpleText also enables you to imbed a recorded message into a SimpleText document using the Apple Microphone (for Macs that have audio input capabilities). If you have Apple's **PlainTalk** enabled on your Mac, you can also ask SimpleText to speak aloud any selected text within a SimpleText document.

SimpleText enables you to open any PICT document (such as **screen captures**) and supports Apple's **drag and drop** feature.

See Also

Cursor; Drag and Drop; Font; Menus; PlainTalk; Read Me Files; Save Command; Screen Capture; System Software; TeachText

SimTower, *See Sim Games; SimCity 2000*

SimTown, *See Sim Games; SimCity 2000*

Sip and Puff Switch

A breath-activated switch which can be triggered by sipping or puffing on a straw. Used by motion-disabled people to access a computer or other device. Often used with scanning software and an on-screen keyboard as a replacement for a regular keyboard.

See Also

Co:Writer; Freedom

.sit Filename Extension

The .sit filename extension means the file has been compressed using either Aladdin System's **StuffIt** or the shareware version of StuffIt. This file extension tells others to unstuff (decompress) the file using StuffIt or StuffIt Expander.

See Also

Compression Utilities; .sea Filename Extension; StuffIt

SiteMill

SiteMill is an application by Adobe Systems Inc. that helps manage the contents of a **World Wide Web** site on a computer that has been set up to function as a **Web server**.

SiteMill also includes software for authoring **Web pages** that eliminates the need to enter many **HTML markup tags,** an activity that can be time-consuming and repetitious (this software is also sold separately by Adobe under the name PageMill). After creating a Web document, you can preview it easily using SiteMill software and then **upload** the document to either your or your **Internet service provider's** Web server.

SiteMill is especially helpful in facilitating the process of checking for and correcting broken **hypertext links** that join Web documents to one another. A link is created by making a hypertext reference to the destination file and specifying the **URL** (Internet address) of that file using either an **absolute** or **relative path** name.

If the documents contained on a Web server are moved from one folder to another, some (or all) of the links pointing to those documents will become incorrect. Rather than having to alter all the links one by one, SiteMill summarizes errors in a list and allows a **Webmaster** to correct any link errors quickly using the Mac's drag-and-drop technology.

Both SiteMill and PageMill have the advantage of being particularly well integrated with the Macintosh interface, in contrast to other HTML editing programs, which are based on the UNIX or Windows operating systems. PageMill is a little limited in its scope of HTML that it can create but is good for beginners or simple projects.

See Also

Absolute Path; HTML Markup Tags; Internet; Internet Service Provider; Relative Path; Uploading Files; Web Browser; Web Page; Web Site; Webmaster; World Wide Web

Size Box

This box enables you to **drag** a window to resize it. The size box is in the lower-right corner of every **active window** and is marked by an **icon** of a small box on top of a larger one (see the following figure).

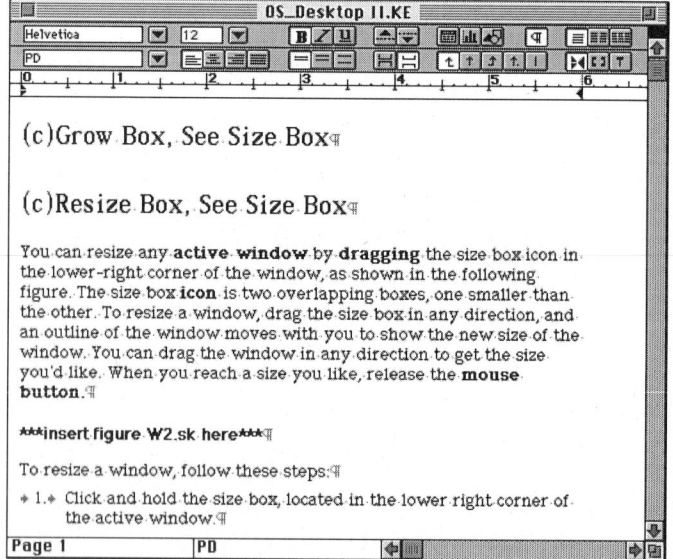

As you drag the size box, an outline of the window moves with you to give you an idea of how big, or little, your resized window will be.

To use the size box to resize a window, follow these steps:

1. Click the size box in the lower-right corner of the active window, and drag in the direction to which you want the window resized.

2. When you reach a desired size, release the mouse.

See Also
Active Window; Click and Drag; Icons; Window

Sketch!

Sketch! is a modeling and rendering tool. It does not support animation, but its modeler is powerful and complements tools such as **Electricimage**.

Models are created and arranged in a scene window. You can switch between a 3D perspective and views from above, beneath, and at the sides of your scene, but you can't have multiple windows on the scene. A pen tool (which draws **Bézier curves**, also called **splines**) creates basic two-dimensional shapes, which are extruded or lathed. A pencil tool, for drawing freehand shapes is also available, but the pen tool provides much greater control. Because the work area is presented as a three-dimensional space (see figure), Sketch! provides drawing planes—a two-dimensional grid—on which you draw the basic shapes. This plane can be moved in any dimension to create multiple cross sections that are then *skinned* (covered with a surface). Sketch! does not support **Boolean** operations, but a curve can be treated as a hole on the face of another curve, effectively cutting a hole in that surface.

After a 3D object has been created you can edit individual splines that make up the 3D object. Using the Putty Tool, any

spline can be moved in 3D space. For new users this is the most fascinating feature, but new users would be best served to avoid this feature and concentrate on getting their 2D cross sections right instead. It is very difficult to create accurate 3D shapes by simply clicking and dragging.

Perhaps one of the most unique features of Sketch! is the Match Backdrop feature. This feature enables you to use a scanned photograph for the background of your 3D model. Using Match Backdrop, you can have your model cast shadows on the image, and objects in the image appear to cast shadows on the model. This is done by aligning the model on the background, and then adding extra objects that represent the objects in the scanned image, but which aren't rendered in the final scene. These new objects cast and receive shadows, but aren't visible in the image!

Sketch! also includes Sketch!Net, a method for accelerating rendering time by distributing rendering across several machines on a network. You can use up to 16 machines, and there's no extra charge for using the rendering engines (unlike some packages which offer this feature at an extra cost).

See Also
3D; Animation Master; Extreme 3D; Infini-D; Modeling; Network Rendering; Ray Dream; StrataVision

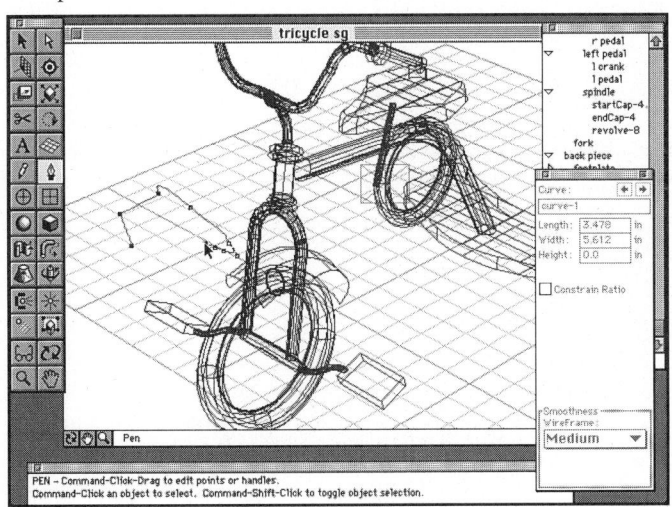

Sleep Command

This command, used on Macintosh PowerBook computers and PCI-based Power Macintosh models running **System 7.5.2** and higher, is designed to put your computer into a **sleep mode** to preserve battery consumption or energy, in the case of desktop models, without turning off the computer. When a PowerBook is in sleep mode, found under the **Special menu** in PowerBooks, the hard drive spins down (which saves battery consumption) and the monitor is turned off, and the PowerBook goes into a mode where battery consumption is at its lowest, without turning the PowerBook off. You can wake a PowerBook from its sleep mode by pressing any key and the monitor redisplays and the drive spins up, enabling you to work again almost instantly.

To put a PowerBook into sleep mode, follow these steps:

1. Choose Sleep from the Special menu. You can also select the Sleep Mode from the **Battery DA,** or you can use the Sleep keyboard shortcut: ⌘-Shift-Zero. You can also set a timer to put your PowerBook to sleep after a specified time of inactivity. This timer is set in the **PowerBook Control Panel.**

2. To Wake the PowerBook from sleep, press any key.

See Also

Battery DA; Control Panels; PowerBook; PowerBook Control Panel; Sleep Mode; Special Menu

Sleep Mode

To conserve battery power, **PowerBooks** and PCI Power Mac models of Macintosh computers can go into a sleep mode, which essentially spins down the hard drive, dims the screen, and places the Mac into a sleep state. Enough power is used to keep whatever was last in memory still in memory. Sleep mode does not turn the Mac off, it just winds it down so the absolute minimum of battery power is being exerted.

To "wake" a Mac from its sleep mode, all you have to do is press any key, and it springs back to life, or "awakes."

The reason the drive spins down and the screen dims is that these are two areas that put a considerable drain on the battery, and by putting these features into sleep mode, you save battery power for when you are using the computer and don't waste it while it sits idle. You can program a PowerBook to go into sleep mode after a predetermined length of inactivity, or you can put the PowerBook into sleep mode at any time by choosing Sleep from the **Special menu**. You can also put the PowerBook into sleep mode from the PowerBook's **control strip**.

To put a PowerBook into sleep mode, select Sleep from the Special menu.

To wake the PowerBook from its sleep mode, press any key and it "wakes up."

> **TIP** For System 7.1 users, you can enter the sleep mode from the **Battery DA** found in the **Apple menu**. To enter sleep mode, click the System Sleep button.

To set the time interval for automatic sleep mode for a PowerBook, follow these steps:

1. Choose the PowerBook control panel from the Control Panels folder.

2. Switch the button to Custom mode and the dialog box will expand with additional features.

3. Use the slider, by clicking and dragging the slider, to set how many minutes until the system sleeps. There is a separate setting for determining how long until the drive spins down, and how long until the screen dims.

See Also

Apple Menu; Battery DA; Control Panels; Control Strip; PowerBook Control Panel, Press Any Key; Special Menu

Slide Scanners

Slide scanners are desktop scanners designed to handle photographic slides and (in some cases) medium-format transparencies. Most of the color photography used for color printing is delivered and stored in transparency—rather than print—format, and slide scanners offer a convenient way to deal with slides.

Because a slide's image area is small, slide scanners scan at high resolution, to allow you to substantially enlarge the scanned image. Slide scanners also allow you to scan slides without removing them from their mountings—rarely possible with a transparency-adapted flatbed scanner.

However, slide scanners can be excruciatingly slow. Although this may not be the case with every model on the market, it would be best to try and test the particular model you want to purchase before you put down your money.

See Also

Drum Scanners; Flatbed Scanners; Handheld Scanners; Office Scanners; Scanner, Desktop

Slide Shows, Running

Your Mac can display your presentation as a slide show, using your computer as a screen or using it to drive an LCD projection panel, external monitor, or video projector. When you run the show, the slides, with their text, art, and graphics, occupy the whole screen. All the tools, menus, and other screen elements are hidden, so that they don't distract the audience from watching your show. The computer effectively turns into a slide projector for the duration of the presentation…unless you have some other program running in the background that could interfere. Be sure to disable calendar programs that might flash a reminder of a later appointment in the middle of your show, or automated email retrieval programs that might dial your modem.

Using your computer to display the program has many advantages. You save the time and expense of creating slides. You can play movies and sounds during a slide show, and use special effects, such as transitions and builds for variety. You have more flexibility, as you can change your presentation right up to the last minute or keep certain slides hidden unless you have extra time to fill and decide to use them. You can rehearse your presentation and save the timings, so that the slides automatically advance as you speak.

If you are running the show from a **PowerBook**, you might want to load just a run-time version, such as **PowerPoint** Viewer, rather than the full program. It comes on a separate floppy or in a separate folder on the **CD-ROM** version of **Microsoft Office**. If your PowerBook has a black and white screen, be sure you've checked your presentation on it for readability. Some templates are better than others for black and white or grayscale display. Also, if you're running from a PowerBook, keep the transitions simple and avoid QuickTime clips or complicated effects that could slow down the show.

See Also

PowerPoint; Presentation Software

S/Link

S/Link is a **batch** audio conversion utility that converts sound to the following audio formats: **SND**, **AIFF**, **.WAV**, VOC, **MOD**, IFF, OMF, Sound Designer I, **Sound Designer II**, **SoundEdit**, and **QuickTime** movies.

It can open just about any audio file. You can then specify the desired conversion settings, or select a portion of the file to convert. Additionally, S/Link can open any file containing a sound. Specify the desired conversion settings and it will convert an entire folder. You can also select a portion of a file for conversion.

> Synclavier
> Price: $249
> Phone: (603) 448-8887

See Also

AIFF; Batch Processing; MOD; SND; Wave

S

SLIP

SLIP stands for Serial Line Internet Protocol, a way of establishing a temporary, low-speed connection to the **Internet** through a dial-up **modem**.

Both SLIP and **PPP** (Point to Point Protocol) accounts are designed to work with much slower connection methods than the dedicated network connections to the Internet enjoyed by government, educational, and nonprofit organizations. But because they work with low-cost modems, SLIP and PPP provide decent performance in normal situations to large numbers of people.

SLIP is simpler than PPP and thus more prevalent; however, PPP is more carefully designed and more flexible. Both, however, support popular and widely used **MacTCP**-based programs such as **Anarchie**, **Fetch**, and **TurboGopher**.

Three different programs provide SLIP connections for the Macintosh: MacSLIP from Hyde Park software, VersaTerm SLIP from Synergy Software, and **InterSLIP** from InterCon Systems. InterSLIP is available as freeware on the Internet. If you do not have an Internet connection, you can obtain the software when you establish an account with an **Internet service provider,** or from the disk that accompanies *Internet Starter Kit* by Adam Engst (ISBN 1-56830-197-9).

When establishing an account with an Internet service provider, you will need certain information in order to configure SLIP or PPP, as shown in the following table.

SLIP/PPP Information

Subject	Question
Phone number	What number do you call to connect to your server?
Login name	What is the SLIP or PPP account login name?
Password	What password should you provide when logging in?
MTU/MRU	What is the maximum transmission/receive unit size?

Subject	Question
Header Compression	Should you use RFC 1144 TCP Header Compression?
Login Procedure	What should you expect to receive from your host machine and how should your machine respond when logging in?
IP address	What is your IP number (if a manually addressed account)?
Gateway Address	What is your gateway IP number?
Domain Name Server	What is the IP number of your primary domain name server?

Some SLIP hosts cause a computer "timeout" to occur if your computer has been idle for a certain amount of time while connected to the Internet. This might be considered a courtesy, especially if you are paying for connection time and forget to disconnect before leaving your workstation.

If your connection hangs up before you are finished (and if you use manual addressing, where you specify an **IP address** when you dial in), simply switch back to the InterSLIP Setup or other SLIP setup control, disconnect, and then reconnect. If, however, you use server addressing (in which the server assigns an IP address to you each time you log in), you must quit all active MacTCP programs before you reconnect via SLIP. Otherwise, your MacTCP program (such as a **Web browser**) will get confused when you reconnect with a different IP address than you had before.

See Also

Asynchronous Data Transfers; Internet; InterSLIP; MacPPP; Modems; Networking; Packet; Parity; PPP

Slow Keys

The Slow Keys function, found in the **Easy Access control panel**, helps prevent handicapped users from making accidental keystrokes by letting the user hold down a keystroke for a moment before it is registered. This way, if the user accidentally presses the wrong key, it doesn't register as a valid keystroke and is ignored. To be a valid keystroke, the key must be held down for the length of time the user specifies in the Slow Keys dialog box within the Easy Access control panel.

To enable slow keys, follow these steps:

1. Choose Easy Access from the Control Panels folder (from the Apple menu).

2. Click to enable Slow Keys. You can also request that a clicking sound be made to confirm a keystroke.

3. You can adjust the keystroke acceptance delay to your personal preference. Close the control panel to activate Slow Keys.

See Also
Control Panels; Easy Access Control Panel

SLR

SLR (Single Lens Reflex) refers to the way the camera provides a preview of the picture. With a single lens reflex camera, you are actually looking through the lens—a mirror diverts the light to the view finder. SLR camera design makes it possible to change the **focal length** of the camera lens and still accurately frame your picture.

See Also
Digital Still Cameras; Focal Length; Range Finder

Small Caps, *See Typesetting Terms*

Small Computer System Interface (SCSI)

The Macintosh can have up to seven peripheral devices attached to its processor. Macintosh manages the physical placement of storage devices through its SCSI bus.

What Is SCSI and How Does It Work? Macintosh uses the *small computer serial interface (SCSI)*

protocol to link hard disks and other peripherals to the computer. The SCSI bus provides high-speed parallel data transmission. All internal and most external **hard drives** are called *SCSI devices* because they connect to the Macintosh through the SCSI port. Each Macintosh has one SCSI port and one internal 50-pin ribbon connector to connect any internal hard drive. Thus, if you are using more than one peripheral device, such as scanners, CD-ROM, external and internal hard disks, and so on, you must loop them one to the other in a *daisy chain* configuration. Up to seven peripheral devices can be chained together, including the internal hard disk.

You must terminate the SCSI devices to keep the signal traveling between the devices from echoing back after reaching the end of the chain. This is done by using a *terminating resistor*. Most SCSI devices have built-in terminators, and are thus called *self-terminating*. Both the first and last device on the chain must be terminated.

Every SCSI device has an ID number by which it is known to the Macintosh. Each device in the chain has a unique number from 1 to 6 (the computer is automatically 7 and the internal hard drive is automatically 0). This SCSI address specifies its priority on the SCSI bus. The higher the number, the greater the priority when two devices vie for computer attention at the same time. All software on the Macintosh uses the SCSI IDs to locate volumes and files. **Norton Utilities** knows the rules for SCSI identification and connections and checks that they are correct as part of its analysis.

To keep your Macintosh operating correctly, turn on every device in the SCSI chain each time you turn on the Macintosh. If your Macintosh does not recognize a peripheral on the chain, check the SCSI ID to ensure that each device has a unique ID. Most peripherals have a dial on their back panels where their SCSI identification is set. Look at this dial to verify that the SCSI ID is a number from 0 to 7, but not 0 or 7. You can also run software utilities, such as Show SCSI, which display the Macintosh's records of how the SCSIs are connected. Most of these types of utilities are available as shareware from user's groups or bulletin boards such as Prodigy or **CompuServe**.

S

How the SCSI Bus Works The SCSI bus accommodates many different peripherals. The Macintosh needs to know which peripheral it is addressing. The solution to this problem is a protocol whereby the device that begins the communication is called the *initiator*—typically the Macintosh, and the device the communication is being sent to is termed the *target*—usually a hard disk. The SCSI bus uses seven different operating modes, called *phases*. by which information is passed back and forth between initiator and target.

- **Bus-free phase:** When no peripheral device is using the bus, the bus-free phase indicates that the bus is available for use.

- **Arbitration phase:** The initiator gains control of the bus, thus shutting off any other use of the bus for the duration of the communication.

- **Selection phase:** The initiator calls the address of the target device. The target device acknowledges the call.

- **Command phase:** The initiator sends the commands it wants accomplished to the target. The target device acknowledges the receipt of the command.

- **Data phase:** The target device sends the requested data to the initiator.

- **Status and message phases:** The target device sends two types of status and message information completing the data transfer and exiting from the bus.

The SCSI bus is controlled by a SCSI chip which operates in two modes—*normal* mode which uses the computer to manage the communications operation and *pseudo–DMA* (*direct-memory access*) mode in which data can be transferred between peripherals bypassing the computer. During normal mode operations the SCSI driver software manages the communications process between the computer and the SCSI device. This mode of operation places a burden on the computer which has to manage this operation (run the software). The overhead slows down the performance of the Macintosh. Thus, the Macintosh also uses pseudo–DMA mode after the software initiates the data transfer to actually perform the data transmission. Pseudo–DMA mode uses the embedded codes in the SCSI chip to manage the operation, leaving the computer free. The SCSI chip uses one of its internal registers (called the *Bus and Status* register) to control the reception and passing of data between peripherals.

The Macintosh does continue to monitor the performance of the SCSI operation, checking the SCSI chip's Bus and Status register for the status of the operation.

See Also
SCSI-3; SCSI Probe

Smart Quotes

Typographer's quotation marks, like the "66 & 99" ones we all learned in grade school, curve around the quotation they enclose. These are also called "curly" quotes. The typewriter was designed with only one all-purpose quotation mark, sometimes called "straight" quotes. Because the computer keyboard is designed to be as much like the typewriter keyboard as possible, it has the straight quote key (").

Because computer type fonts include typographer's quotes, but the key combination required to use them is awkward, most **word processors** and other programs let you choose to use "smart quotes." This is a function that automatically replaces the straight quotes with the appropriate curly quotes. It also replaces the straight apostrophe with a single curly quote.

One caveat about using curly quotes: when you're exchanging documents with PC or UNIX users, sometimes curly quotes will get translated to strange characters. This also happens when using curly quotes in **email** messages.

See Also
Backquotes; Word Processors

SmartKeys

There are significant differences between typing on a typewriter and typesetting on a Macintosh.

SmartKeys, a freeware **control panel** developed by Maurice Valaski, helps typewriter users make the jump to Macintosh by changing common typewriter keystrokes into typesetting keystrokes. On a typewriter, for example, it is proper to put two spaces between sentences. But on a computer only one space is required. When you have SmartKeys installed, it removes the second space. In all, SmartKeys fixes six common areas where typewriter conventions need to be replaced with typesetting or computer conventions. This way, a typist can type in the format they're accustomed to while the document they're typing is converted to typesetting conventions.

The six SmartKey functions are as follows:

- **Quotes:** Converts straight "dumb" quotes and apostrophes into curly quotes and curly quotation marks used in typesetting.

- **Space:** Removes the second space between sentences.

- **Dash:** Converts two dashes to an "em dash" used in typography.

- **Ligatures:** Converts common letters pairs, like Fl and Fi, into more elegant ligatures that combine the two letters to keep the dot on the small "i" and the serif on the small "l" from interfering with the capital "F."

- **Kill Doubled Caps:** If you type two capital letters next to each other followed by a lowercase letter, SmartKeys interprets this as a mistake and lowers the second capital letter for you.

- **Shifted Punctuation:** When using the **Shift key** for capitalization, it's easy to accidentally type a greater than (<) or less than (>) mathematical symbol instead of a period or comma. SmartKeys shifted punctuation replaces the mathematical symbols greater than and less than with the appropriate punctuation.

See Also

Control Panel; Shift Key; Smart Quotes

SmartSketch

Because of its wealth of basic figure libraries and **drag-and-drop** capabilities, SmartSketch is an excellent vector drawing program with a selection of very unique, high-end features. The single-most applauded feature in SmartSketch is its ability to show you a full anti-aliased view of a vector drawing. This is a feature not found in any other vector drawing package. This double feature, smoothing (for the graphics) and text smoothing (for text), can be left on if your system has enough **RAM** and is fast enough so that you will never see a jagged edge in a graphic or text block. SmartSketch has 17 EasyArt libraries, collections of topical **clip art** in vector format that can be drag-dropped in place on the editing page. All the EasyArt subjects are editable, so any part of an object can be resized, rotated, or reshaped. SmartSketch offers no gradient tools and has no function for automatically translating bitmaps to vectors. Its smooth drawing tools, however, add ease and functionality when hand tracing bitmap art.

Included with SmartSketch are EasyArt Libraries, groups of images in a cartoon style. Libraries can also be created from your own selection of created work. The figure shows a sample.

S

Without making a big deal about it, SmartSketch offers one of the most intuitive **Bézier** editing functions of any vector drawing program available. While on-screen line segments are being moved with the cursor, sliding down their length and then moving them allows them to become curved Bézier sections. No control levers are provided, but none are needed to intuitively get the curve to behave as needed. In addition, SmartSketch has a smooth freehand function that acts to translate all freehand graphics into smoothed curves when smoothing is turned on.

Each of the selections in the toolbox has an associated submenu list of options. The Pencil tool, as an example, has color, line type (dashed, and so on), line option (straight, freehand, oval, rectangle), and line width settings. The Paint Bucket Fill tool has options not found in competitive packages, allowing you to fill non-closed areas with color. Almost everything that is needed as far as drawing/painting options is provided in the toolbox without asking the user to access commands from the menu bar.

SmartSketch supports export saves in PICT, Illustrator 88, **EPS** with preview, and AutoCAD **DXF**, and SmartSketch format saves of the page (preserving all of the SmartSketch data).

SMPTE

SMPTE (Society of Motion Picture Television Engineers) is a **time code** format that indexes frame based sequences of images (whether on film or video). It uses a format of HH:MM:SS:FF where HH=hours, MM=minutes, SS=seconds, and FF=frame number. SMPTE works well with film where there are exactly 24 frames per second. **NTSC** video is more of a problem, because NTSC is not really 30 frames per second; it's 29.97 frames per second. Because SMPTE has no provision for fractions smaller than a frame, errors start to appear (that is differences between the actual frame number and the number assigned using SMPTE). To solve this problem, a system called **drop frames** is often used. The video is numbered as if it is 30 frames per second, but when the error becomes large enough, a frame number is dropped. In this way,

although the frame numbering may be slightly off the exact frame time, the hours, minutes, and seconds figures remain correct.

See Also
NTSC; Striped; Time Code

SMTP

A protocol or set of standards designed to allow the transfer of **electronic mail** reliably and efficiently on the **Internet**.

SMTP (Simple Mail Transfer Protocol) performs the essential task of sending mail across various parts of the Internet.

To transport mail from sender to recipient, the message has to go through a number of intermediate machines called mail servers. Each one of the mail servers has to OK the transmission until the final destination is reached. If one of the machines cannot send the message along for some reason it will be "bounced" back to the sender, usually with detailed information about where the problem occurred.

All popular email **clients** support SMTP, including Eudora, **QuickMail**, and **Netscape Navigator**. To support SMTP in QuickMail, you need to buy and install a gateway as well.

For more information, see the Internet Working Group Request for Comments (RFC) 821 (**ftp:// ds.internic.net/rfc/rfc821.txt**).

See Also
Email; Gopher; Netscape Navigator; QuickMail; World Wide Web

SND

SND is the **Resource ID** for a sound file. The file contains digitized sound, and was the first sound file format for the Macintosh. Storing sounds as resources has its advantages: the sounds can be stored inside the file in the **resource fork**, and it's very easy to use a program, such as **ResEdit,** to add or remove sound resources from the file. This is a great way, for example, to add sounds to a **HyperCard** stack.

Sound resources must be loaded entirely into memory before they are played. That's no problem for a small sound, but if you have a 1MB sound, there is the possibility that there may not be enough memory available to load and play the sound. If there isn't enough memory, nothing happens; the sound is simply not played.

For long sounds, consider using the **AIFF** file format to save sounds. It's possible to **stream** an AIFF file, and AIFF is also cross-platform.

See Also
AIFF; Digitizing Sound; Wave (.WAV)

Snootz Math Trek

This program, for ages 6-10, should probably be named Logic Trek, or Sequencing Trek, for those are the skills it teaches. Nothing in these games uses numbers. Instead, kids are introduced to doing things in sequence, as when they help Foozle get dressed. His outfits must be assembled in a particular order. Sequences are acoustic in the Street Music game, which requires that kids listen and repeat (by clicking the sources of) a series of sounds. Other games include fitting geometric shapes into frames, hide and go seek, using a grid and compass points, and a jazzed-up version of the very old game Nine Men's Morris.

The colorful animation and funny sounds make these games appealing, and most of them have two or three levels of difficulty, so kids will be able to play with them a bit longer than otherwise. The geometry puzzles do repeat, but other activities are more random so the program can be enjoyed more than once or twice.

See Also
Bumptz Science Carnival

Society of Motion Picture Television Engineers, *See* *SMPTE*

Socket Number

A socket number is an 8-bit number that uniquely identifies a socket. A socket is an addressable entity within an **AppleTalk** node. With AppleTalk, there are 256 potential sockets. Numbers 0 and 255 aren't used, so there are actually 254 possible socket numbers. Numbers 1–127 are reserved for special Apple system use, and 128–254 are pooled resources, available for use by applications. Socket numbers are assigned for transactions and returned to the pool when the transaction is finished.

See Also
Logical Address

Soft Return

A soft return is a line break that the word processing program inserts when the end of the line reaches the right hand margin. It's indicated by an invisible character. The location of soft returns changes automatically if you change the width of the margins or insert or delete text. On a Macintosh, text wraps automatically onto the next line, inserting a soft return. A hard return ends the paragraph. Non-Macintosh word processors use a combination of a carriage return and linefeed (CR/LF) at the end of each line. When you import text into a Macintosh word processor, you might need to remove these characters so that the text will wrap correctly.

See Also
Word Processors

SoftPC

SoftPC, from Insignia Solutions, is a software utility that gives your Mac the capability to run applications originally designed for **Microsoft** DOS for PCs by opening a separate window on the desktop where you can launch DOS-compatible applications in a software emulation mode. SoftPC comes with a version of MS/DOS already installed. SoftPC operates in two modes: real mode and protected mode, which enables you to run applications that are designed to take advantage of extended DOS memory. Both of these are designed to emulate an Intel processor within the Macintosh environment. Operating in the protected mode enables you to utilize extended DOS memory. Other features include support for VGA graphics, MS-DOS 5.0, and CD-ROM Extensions, and Novell NetWare.

The advantage of SoftPC is you can access DOS-based software from your Macintosh without buying a separate computer. The drawback is the software emulation runs DOS software at a slower speed than it would on a PC.

> Insignia Solutions
> 2200 Lawson Lane
> Santa Clara, CA 95054
> Phone: (408) 327-6000
> Web site: **http://www.Insignia.com**

See Also
SoftWindows

Software Archives, *See Macintosh Software Archive*

Software, Business Applications, *See Business Applications*

Software Development Kit, *See SDK*

Software, Educational, Adult

You're never too old to learn, and there's plenty of software to interest the adult with a thirst for knowledge. **CD-ROMs** cover the full range of subjects from astronomy (Scientific American Library: The Planets) to zoology. Other programs teach you art, golf, photography, cooking, crafts, and even (a must for "mouse-potatoes") physical fitness. Better Homes and Gardens Guides to Gardening, Home Planning, and Great American Cooking let you lead a more elegant life. Digital Gourmet and Digital Bartender cover the basics of food and drink preparation.

Hobbies are well-represented on the software shelves. Whether your passion is baseball cards, comic books, or dogs, there's a program to help. The ComicBase not only has an encyclopedia of information and prices of over 50,000 comics, it tracks the value of your collection. The Wizard of Dogs is an interactive guide to dog care and training, with comprehensive information on health, grooming, socializing, training, and much more. Ever wondered what goes on behind the curtain? Check out An Insider's View of Magic, from HarperCollins with TV's Harry Anderson.

As for sports, there's golf, skiing, martial arts, and Active Trainer, which comes with a tape measure and fat caliper to assess your body mass, and over 85 minutes of video footage that teaches you what exercises you need and how to do them. Get golf tips from Breaking 100, or advanced tips from Breaking 90. Get the lowdown on golf courses all over the country in Sportware's Golf, along with golf etiquette, instruction, and course architecture. The sound effects on this CD will transport you right into a summer day. If you dream of turning pro, try PGA Tour Golf. Or how about mountain biking with SingleTrak Mind, or for something really wild, Maniac Sports! Bungee jumping, kayaking, surfing, sky diving, and more.... Learn the history, the equipment, and the techniques, and then go for broke. **QuickTime** movies pause so you can decide what to do next. One more cartwheel, or is it time to...oops. It *was* time to land.

Health topics are a natural for interactive programs. There's Body Works; Nine Month Miracle; ADAM, The Inside Story; half a dozen different health and medical encyclopedias, even some programs to help you relax. Wilson Learning's Keep Your Cool teaches you to do just that, with a carefully plotted series of lessons and exercises in relieving stress.

Lawrence Productions Job Success and Job Readiness series teach you how to put together a résumé, how to handle job interviews, and how to get ahead once you've gotten the job.

And finally, there are programs to teach you to use other programs. Personal Training Systems has software to explain **System 7.5**, to teach you the ropes of **ClarisWorks**, or Intuit, or **Microsoft Office**. MacAcademy offers videotapes to watch while you sit at the Mac, to train you in any of several dozen programs.

See Also

ADAM; ClarisWorks; Microsoft Office; System 7.5

Software, Educational, K-6

Software for the K-6 set is, unfortunately, more geared toward "skill drills" emphasizing speed in solving arithmetic problems, and phonics exercises. One of the better ones is MECC's Math Munchers Deluxe. Animation and funny sounds keep children interested while they work on math problems from simple addition through fractions and decimals.

History and science explorations are popular topics for this age group, and there are many programs available. EcoAdventures teaches students about endangered plants and animals in the rainforests and the oceans. The Oregon Trail is a historical simulation of a trip across the country by wagon train. Other programs introduce astronomy, dinosaurs and fossils, geography, and music.

Beginning readers will benefit from the many children's books available as interactive **CD-ROMs**. The stories are narrated, with words highlighted on the screen as they're spoken. Most of these stories are bi-lingual, commonly Japanese/English or Spanish/English. All have colorful illustrations with hidden "buttons." When the child clicks on the picture and hits one of the buttons, something happens. Each page of the story may have anywhere from six to a dozen or more different buttons, each with sounds and animation. They're not marked in any way, so it's necessary to explore. Several companies publish these interactive books, among them Brøderbund "Living Books" and the Learning Company's Reader Rabbit Interactive Reading Journey.

Conversation with Gene Longo

Gene Longo's title is Home Learning Manager at Apple, and his job is to use Apple's traditional lead in school computing as a way to get people to buy Macs for the home.

Maclopedia: What did you first use a Mac for?

Gene: Oh gosh, back in '84, when I was working for a dealership—and this is pretty embarrassing—it was to use the desktop publishing to create a resume to send to Apple.

Maclopedia: So did you get the job?

Gene: Yes! I worked in education in the field, with kindergarten through 12. I started as an MSR and supported Virginia, Maryland, and D.C., and then I became an account exec. I came to Apple headquarters in 1993, to sort of marry working in the dealership and working in the field, to build a bridge between the education and the home markets.

We show parents the new tools, and the light bulb goes off.

Maclopedia: How are you helping folks learn at home with the Mac?

Gene: We're working closely with the K-12 organizations, and we've formed the Home Learning Advisory Council. We brought in 12 learning experts from around the country, and we meet semiannually to establish those bridges. They have really driven the things we've brought to market, such as the family computing workshops. They were getting a lot of questions like, "Should I buy a computer for the home, and if so, what kind?" This tool was to help parents.

Because there might be some real credibility issues if Apple presented the workshop directly, they said, "Give us the tools, and we can control the message." So we put together a Just-Add-Water kit with a presentation, parent materials, invitation templates, flyers, and interactive CD-ROM, for the schools to put

continues

S

on the workshops. The school calls an 800 number and the school itself hosts the event. We give them a script. We made it a solutions message, not a sales message, very thematic, like, how to do research with multimedia tools and the Internet, and here is how kids would write reports. We show parents the new tools, and the light bulb goes off. You'll see the presenter showing an electronic encyclopedia, and you can see they are amazed. We have on average 80 parents a night, but we've had up to 300 parents, and grandparents, at 1,250 workshops so far, and we've just launched Phase II for 5,000 more schools. It's a good time for the schools to talk about their technology plans, or bond referendums, or budget.

Maclopedia: Is Apple making any strategic alliances in this area?

Gene: Yes, we have a strategic alliance with the Public Broadcasting System called Bring Learning Home, and around that we have alliances with Scholastic, National Geographic, and the Computer Learning Foundation, a clearinghouse for schools and parents, to foster technology—they have a newsletter and an annual computer learning contest every October. We're setting up a Web site for all the partners. We're underwriting PBS where they take their educational programming from Sesame Street to Where in the World is Carmen Sandiego? and they wrap a service around it for community centers, daycare centers, and parents—a form of TV outreach. We're going to 100 markets this fall.

Maclopedia: What trends do you see in learning products for the home?

Gene: We're seeing a flood of companies developing stuff around the Internet for kids. Every day we come across something new. Ensuring that schools have access is a problem, but homes are easier because the new computers come with modems built-in these days. One neat new product is a kid's Web creation tool from Vividus, the folks who made Cinemation; like KidPix, it's easy to use, and lets you create your own home page. Surfwatch and Yahoo are creating a kids' site called YaHooligans; that'll be really hot. And we are working on putting together a kids' Internet kit, a software bundle to be marketed at retail.

Maclopedia: Do you think these Internet terminals are going to catch on in the home market?

Gene: I don't know if you are going to see these Internet appliances come in. Our advisory council had really mixed feeling about those. In the home computer market, some industry experts say the pace is slowing down, but we see people ramping up the price points, buying higher price tags, more memory, faster CD-ROM, a lot more life and extendibility.

Beginning artists and writers can make good use of the computer, just as professionals do. KidPix and similar graphics programs help young Picassos turn their ideas into art. Brøderbund's Amazing Writing Machine and Davidson's KidWorks turn out books, stories, essays, poems, and journals, complete with artwork.

Reference materials for the early grades tend to be topic-specific. There are Encyclopedias of Science and Nature, Animals, Mammals, Plants, the Solar System, and so on. A few more general works include a CD-ROM version of David Macaulay's excellent The Way Things Work, Macmillan's Dictionary for Children, and several good atlas programs.

See Also

Juilliard Music Adventure; Mavis Beacon Teaches Typing; MayaQuest; Student Essentials

Software, Educational, Grades 7-12

Education is serious business for students in junior high and high school. At this age, kids are learning foreign languages, doing research papers, and studying for the achievement tests they need to score well on in order to get into college. Of course, there are all kinds of programs to help them in these endeavors. Language programs such as Rosetta Stone or Zingo Lingo will teach basic vocabulary and help with pronunciation. **MayaQuest** teaches Spanish as well as the geography of Central America and archaeology of the Mayan Empire. Junior high and high school students don't necessarily need their math or language arts programs sugar-coated into game formats as younger kids might, but that's not to say that a program can't be interesting and fun. The excellent MECC "trail" programs (Oregon Trail, Yukon Trail, and so on) are examples of educational software for older students that are fun and keep them motivated to learn, without unnecessary fooling around.

Teens with an interest in theater will probably find a lot to like about MECC's Opening Night. They can direct plays using the scenery, props, and cast of characters provided on this two-CD set. Hollywood is a similar, but simpler program, with a cartoon format. Young musicians may enjoy the **Juilliard Music Adventure**, or might prefer to Rock, Rap 'n' Roll. Interactive Physics programs will intrigue the science-minded teen, whereas the Cartoon Guide to Physics may help de-mystify the subject for the rest of us.

The tools a high school student needs to succeed haven't really changed all that much. Among the basics are a good dictionary and a good encyclopedia, a thesaurus, and some way to organize and write neat term papers. Novell has put all of these into one package, along with **WordPerfect 3.5**, and other goodies. **Student Essentials** is a truly useful package. If you prefer a different word processor, the other components of the package are also available separately. Both Compton and Grolier publish CD-ROM encyclopedias, updated annually. Most word processors include a spell checker and Thesaurus, but for definitions and pronunciation, Webster's is still the standard. Random House Webster's Dictionary is a good choice. And for those last minute book reports, Monarch Notes covers the classics, including works by 226 different authors.

With the computer becoming more and more part of everything we do, one of the most important skills anyone can have these days is typing. Programs such as **Mavis Beacon Teaches Typing** will have your kids up to 50 words per minute in a few weeks. It's a skill that will come in handy in college, too. Speaking of college, choosing one and getting accepted is the fo-

cus of the last two years of high school. This is the time when kids prepare for and take the SAT, ACT, and achievement tests that determine their future. Kaplan and Princeton Review are two of the biggest names in test coaching. Both have released software to help students score higher on the SATs and similar tests. Princeton's College Advisor is another popular tool, with details on over 1,200 colleges, plus information on the admissions process from the essay and recommendations to securing financial aid.

See Also

Juilliard Music Adventure; Mavis Beacon Teaches Typing; MayaQuest; Student Essentials

Software FPU

Software FPU is a freeware utility that fools certain software applications that require a built-in FPU (Floating Point Unit) into thinking a real FPU is installed in your computer. This enables you to run software that would normally require an FPU without having one installed.

It works this way; when you launch a program that needs an FPU, the software takes a look at the system's configuration, and if it doesn't see an FPU, it displays an alert box stating that the program requires an FPU, and then the program **quits**. With Software FPU loaded, when you launch an application, Software FPU tells the application that the computer has an FPU installed, and the software, thinking an FPU is installed, launches. FPU-intensive tasks are much slower than they would have been with an FPU installed.

Software FPU does not increase the speed or emulate the function of an FPU. It's job is to fool applications that need an FPU into thinking there is one. Pretty clever.

See Also

Coprocessors, Types; Quit Command

S

Software Handshaking, *See*
Modem Cables and Connections

Software and Hardware Errors

A user error generally results in the machine doing something different than you wanted. By contrast, if your error involves a system crash, such as a bomb, "Unexpected Quit," or any other crash your problem is not a user error—you've run into a software or hardware error.

Although the information in these error messages (for example, ID=1, or "out of memory") appears to be a good clue toward your problem, it usually isn't. When the system software sees something it doesn't like, it takes over and sends you one of these messages. Because the computer can only tell you the last thing that went wrong, it's nearly impossible to tell where the things *first* went wrong just by looking at what finally got the system software's attention.

The presence of these boxes should serve as a notice to you to start looking for a software or hardware error.

When you get this type of error, make a note of which number comes up on-screen and what the error message says. Although a Type-39 may not mean anything to you, it may mean something to a technical support person.

The one exception to this rule is the "**Sad Mac**" error codes that occur immediately upon startup. This error is usually caused by a bad memory SIMM, and the code will tell you which board is bad. See the chapter on hardware troubleshooting for details

Software Errors Although the most obvious component of your computer system is the hardware, virtually everything your computer does is controlled by software. Most pieces of hardware, including external hard drives, CD ROM drives, printers, scanners, and network connectors use their own software to tell your computer how to communicate with them.

Software errors result from intrinsic bugs in one piece of software or from normal commands in multiple

programs giving your computer conflicting instructions. Chances are that the authors of each of your software packages didn't have the opportunity to test their software with every type of computer setup, so no piece of software can work for everybody without minor adjustments.

Also, bugs frequently appear only in combinations of several pieces of hardware or software, making problems even harder to track down.

Software errors frequently occur when you use an older pieces of software with a newer piece of software or hardware. Virtually every piece of commercial software undergoes numerous updates after it is first released. Sometimes the updates fix bugs users discovered, other times the updates allow older software to work with newer computers or pieces of hardware.

After you discover a bug or incompatibility, check with your software company to see if an update is available. Often times, they won't send out notices of the update, and the only way to receive the update is to call and report the problem. **Online services** are a particularly good way to keep informed of these updates.

The best clue that you have found a software conflict is a completely reproducible problem. If the exact same sequence of actions always causes a crash, you almost certainly are experiencing a software problem.

Hardware Errors Hardware errors occur when something is physically wrong with your computer: a faulty chip on the logic board, blown capacitors, dust on a read/write head, a torn cable, and so on. Because hardware failures affect components used throughout your computer, they'll cause problems in various unrelated functions of your computer.

Hardware failures usually occur in the components subject to lots of wear, such as floppy drives, printers, and mice. Although consistent, reproducible failures are the hallmarks of software trouble, intermittent failures should point you toward hardware failure. Because most of the computer's hardware is tested or used during startup, if you can successfully get to the desktop, most of your hardware is fine.

All the major hardware components are automatically tested on startup, so the best clue of a hardware problem is getting the "Sad Mac" bomb and error tones (**"Chimes of Death"**) immediately upon turning on your computer. Pressing the Interrupt and Restart buttons simultaneously, or pressing the interrupt button during power on, will always cause a Sad Mac. It's no cause for alarm.

If a problem appears suddenly and seems to affect ALL aspects of your computer's operation, you very likely have a hardware problem. Sometimes if you have a problem with an external storage drive, the computer will boot but that drive won't be mounted.

Network Errors Network errors are a fairly new phenomenon for Mac users. This type of error involves a problem with the cabling or other network hardware between two computers. You'll run into these problems when using applications such as email, networked file servers, or anything else that depends upon interaction between computers.

Network cabling is subject to the same principles that govern all hardware—unless you've been putting stress on it, chances are it won't fail spontaneously. Check the obvious—that the cables are still plugged in—then check the software.

The first thing to do is determine if the problem is with the computers, or with the network itself. True network troubles usually show up as similar problems occurring randomly on nearly several of the computers on a network. They should also follow the logistics of the physical wires of the network. A problem that suddenly appears on just one computer, even if it involves network services, usually is a problem with that computer, not the network.

Of course, a problem with the computer acting as the server will appear to be a network problem, because everyone's computer will be affected—but it's actually a software or hardware problem with that computer.

Solving the Problem Hardware problems can be tricky to solve and are the least common, so it's usually best to start by looking for user and software errors unless you have a *very* strong suspicion that the

hardware is at fault. Aside from requiring more electronics knowledge, hardware troubleshooting also carries several liabilities. Both software and hardware problems can cause you to lose your data. Back up your files onto some other storage medium before you begin troubleshooting.

Safety Computer equipment is designed to be safe for normal use, but when you open the case, you put both yourself and the equipment at danger unless you take the necessary safety precautions. The high voltages and currents present in computers are the major danger to you. Power supplies and monitors are the most dangerous components. Don't disassemble these unless you're a qualified technician. The high voltage potentials in you, caused by static electricity, are the major danger to your equipment. If you don't know how to use a wrist grounding strap and follow other static avoidance techniques, don't take your Mac apart.

Because of the danger to both you and your computer, opening and altering the hardware of your computer system usually voids the manufacturer's warranty.

Where to Go From Here Once you've identified which area your problem is in, read the appropriate entry here for advice on how to identify and solve your problem. If this doesn't seem to help, next check into online services for advice from users with similar setups. Chances are someone has seen, or heard, of a problem like yours before and can point you in the right direction toward solving it.

If you still can't find the answer, or you're running out of time, it may be time to use a consultant. Computer consultants deal with computer conflicts daily and are often in touch with major software and hardware vendors, keeping abreast of potential problems. Although hiring a consultant is not inexpensive, if your business is losing money quickly because of computer errors, it may be well worth the expense. Ask other computer users or contact the manufacturers of your software and hardware for referrals to a good consultant. Most consultants belong to a local Macintosh User's Group. By attending the meetings you can often get free advice from these experienced professionals.

S

Software, Installing, *See*
Installing Software

Software, Special Needs

From its beginning, the Macintosh was designed with the needs of disabled users in mind. One of the features designed into the first Mac 128 was the capability to speak written text. In 1987, Berkeley Systems obtained a small Federal grant to develop the Mac's built-in MacinTalk into a utility that would let blind, visually impaired, and dyslexic people use the computer. The result was outSPOKEN, an easy to use screen reader that works with nearly all Mac software. Users can listen as they write, have text spoken back to them, and even use the Mac's menus and icons by steering the cursor over them. This is accomplished by pressing the keys on the numeric keypad. (On the **PowerBook**, a key re-mapping program enables the user to substitute a corner of the regular keyboard, toggling back and forth between typing and cursor control.) People with partial vision may be helped with **Close View**, a utility that's part of the Mac's **Easy Access** utility. It magnifies the screen to make the type easier to see.

Of course, people are "differently abled" in many different ways. Many Mac users can read the screen with no difficulty, but moving a mouse or typing on a regular keyboard is out of the question. For these people, there are high-tech and low-tech solutions ranging from a simple mouth stick to an optical sensor that tracks the movement of a dot on the user's forehead. The mouthstick is a device with a mouthpiece and a sturdy stick. The users simply bite down on the mouthpiece and move their heads to press keys with the stick. A plastic guide over the keyboard helps guard against typing mistakes. Word prediction software such as Don Johnston Company's **Co:Writer** also helps make the writing process easier.

Both Head Mouse and Madenta Tracker use optical sensors to track movement. They require no wires or headgear, just an adhesive dot that's placed on the user's forehead, chin, eyeglasses, or even a finger or foot, whatever the user has best control of. These devices will enable you to draw, play games, or use the computer in any way that anyone else can. There are extra large keyboards and also extra small keyboards for people with limited movement but good fine motor control. There are switches that send Morse code, and switches that have a simple "yes/no" function. And there's software to work with all of these devices. The most common program puts a keyboard on the screen so the switch user or mouse-alternative user can type by pointing to the letters on-screen. Discover:Screen works with most word processing software, as well as with the **Internet** and commercial **online services**, opening a new world for people who might not otherwise be able to get online.

People who can't use a keyboard for typing may soon be able to dictate their words directly into the Mac. MacinTalk Pro, System 7's speech recognition extension makes voice input a reality. Articulate Systems is the leader in this field. Their Voice Navigator, which only handled menu commands, has been replaced by Power Secretary, which takes dictation as well as carrying out your commands. (Now, if it could only make coffee…)

Making coffee isn't an impossibility either. The X-10 environmental control modules and switches let your Mac turn on the coffee maker, the TV, a lamp, or other electrical device with a single click, a very useful tool for those who can't get out of bed. This system can accept up to 256 different switches, keyed to a map on the Mac. Selecting any one and clicking will turn the associated device on or off.

The Mac's capability to speak has lead to still another use—as a replacement for one's own voice. Perhaps the best-known user of this feature is physicist Stephen Hawking, who uses a PowerBook attached to his electric wheel chair to give lectures all over the world. Dr. Hawking writes his speeches ahead of time, of course, but the Mac can also be used for spontaneous conversation with the help of programs such as **Talk:About** and Co:Writer. Talk:About lets the user have real conversations instead of simply pointing to a menu of canned phrases of wants and needs. With the addition of the Co:Writer word prediction software, users can create new sentences quickly enough to make the conversation flow smoothly. There are also simpler speech programs to get started. **Freedom** is a **HyperCard** stack that contains pre-programmed phrases, and allows you to add your own by simply typing them in. With MacinTalk Pro installed, you can select from a menu of voices to find the one that's most appropriate.

The bottom line is that there's a special solution to any special needs access problem. The best place to find out what's available is at **http://www2.apple.com/disability/disability.html**. The following table is a helpful reference to the entries in this book to special needs software and hardware.

If you have difficulty with...	*Try using...*
Reading the screen	outSpoken, CloseView
Typing	Large keyboard, Tash mini-keyboard, head pointer and on-screen keyboard
Using the mouse	Joysticks, switches, head pointer
Speaking	Freedom, MacinTalk Pro, Talk:About
Hearing	Flashing menu bar (set sound level to zero to make menu flash for alerts)
Writing	Co:Writer

See Also
Co:Writer; Freedom; Talk:About

Software, System
Your computer, **mouse**, **keyboard**, **CD-ROM** drive, and **monitor** are all hardware. What you see operating on-screen is software. Software is a set of instructions for performing tasks on your computer. The software that loads into your computer when you **start up** your Macintosh is the Macintosh **system software** from Apple, along with any third-party extensions or

applications/documents in your Startup folder. This system software is designed to run on Macintosh brand computers and provides the interface you see when working on a Macintosh. The **desktop**, the **trash** can, files, folders, and icons are all part of the system software.

When you want to type a letter or design a graphic, you open software applications. Applications are also often referred to as programs. Smaller applications that perform particular tasks, such as repair or compression, are called **utilities**. Applications, programs, and utilities are all terms to describe software.

See Also
Desktop; Icons; System Software; Trash

Software for Teachers, *See Teachers, Macintosh and*

Software Upgrades
Macintosh computers require system software in order to access Mac hardware and run software applications. In 1994, with the introduction of **System 7.5**, Apple gave their Macintosh operating system a name: MacOS.

Upgrading to a completely new version of system software can involve many changes, including upgrading hardware and versions of software applications. If you are happy with your current system software features and performance, consider what features are available in a new version of system software or in a system update release before purchasing or installing the upgrade. In general, new system software releases offer consistent backward compatibility with most software applications and work on Macintosh computers with at least 4MB of memory, although 8MB is preferred (and is required on a **Power Mac**). If you are considering adding more system software to your Mac, make sure that you have enough memory and hard drive space available for all system software and any applications you intend to use with the new technologies.

See Also

Bug-Fix Update; Major Release; Minor Release; Registration Card

SoftWindows

SoftWindows, from Insignia Solutions, (2200 Lawson Lane, Santa Clara, CA 95054, Phone: (408) 327-6000. On the Web **http://www.Insignia.com**) is a software utility that gives your Mac the capability to run applications originally designed to be used with the Microsoft Windows 3.1 operating system for PCs by opening a separate window on the desktop where you can launch Windows-compatible applications in a software emulation mode. The advantage is you can access a wide range of Windows software from your Macintosh without buying a separate computer. SoftWindows comes with Microsoft Windows 3.11/MS DOS 6.22 Operating System already installed.

Another advantage is that you can **copy** and **paste** information and items between these Windows applications and Macintosh applications. The drawback is that the software emulation runs the software at a slower speed than it would on a PC.

Insignia Solutions recently announced a new version of SoftWindows, called SoftWindows 95 that enables Mac users to run Windows 95 software on their Macs. SoftWindows also comes with a new TurboStart™ feature that enables Power Mac users to launch Windows 95 in a fraction of the time it takes a regular PC. SoftWindows also comes with the Microsoft Windows 95 pre-installed.

See Also

SoftPC

Sony Multiscan 17sfII, *See Monitors, Common Models*

Sound, Adding, *See Presentations, Adding Sound with Astound*

Sound App

Sound App is a shareware program by Norman Frankes that plays **AU** and **.WAV** sound files. Sound App can be used as a **helper app** to play AU files, which are used widely on the **World Wide Web**.

> Web: **http://www.mcp.com/hayden/software/Netsoftware.html**

See Also

MoviePlayer; QuickTime; SoundMachine; .WAV

Sound Control Panel

This control panel enables you to control the overall volume of your Macintosh and your system alert sounds by using a slider to move from softer (at the bottom) to louder (at the top).

The Sound control panel is also where you select what sound will be your system's alert sound (to "beep" at you anytime the Mac needs your attention). You can choose alert sounds from the window to the right of the alert sound volume slider.

To choose an alert sound, follow these steps:

1. Choose Sound from the control panels submenu in the Apple menu (or System Folder).

2. Click the name of the sound on the right side of the window. The alert sound will play once to let you hear how it sounds.

3. Close the Sound control panel to confirm your choice.

You can click the Add button to add sounds of your own. When you click the Add button, the recording dialog box comes up, which enables you to record your own alert sounds and name them, by using Apple's built-in, or external microphone (depending on which model you have).

To record your own alert sound, follow these steps:

1. Make sure a microphone is connected to your Mac. Some Macs have built-in microphones, as do some Apple monitors. If not, you can connect a microphone via the input jack on the back of your Mac marked with the icon of a broadcast microphone.

2. Choose Sound from the Control Panels submenu on the Apple menu (or System Folder).

3. Click the Add button to bring up the Recording dialog box. This dialog box has similar controls to a standard tape player; record, stop, pause, and play. Plus you have a meter to show you how much input you're getting from the microphone.

4. When you're happy with the alert sound you've recorded, save the sound by clicking the Save button. You'll be prompted to name the sound, and after naming it and clicking OK, this new sound will appear in the window listing all available alert sounds. Click the name of any sound to hear it.

You can also choose, from the pop-up menu Sound In, what source to record from (you could record from a CD-ROM audio disk or microphone), and you can choose Sound Out to choose a device to playback recorded sounds and choose the playback quality of recorded sounds.

See Also
Apple Menu; Control Panels

Sound Designer II

A sound digitizing and editing application developed for editing 16-bit sound, and bundled with any of Digidesign's sound-digitizing hardware products. Sound Designer uses an interface that resembles **SoundEdit**; the digitized sound is displayed as a wave form, which can be edited by selecting segments and cutting and pasting. You can add effects to the selected portion of the audio, and plug-in modules are supported.

Sound Designer II includes a pen tool for editing the wave form—you draw over the wave form to remove pops or other defects in the sound.

Digidesign, Inc.
3401-A Hillview Avenue
Palo Alto, CA 94304-1348
Price: $1295
Phone: (415) 688-0600
Web: **http://www.digidesign.com/**

See Also
Audiomedia II

Sound Digitizing

The Macintosh model will determine the quality you get when digitizing sound. If you own an older Macintosh (such as a Macintosh IIci), you have no built-in sound recording hardware and will need something like the **MacRecorder**. Several models with built-in sound digitizing hardware (such as the Quadras) support only 8-bit sound recording. All **AV Macs**, Power Macs, and some 68040 Macs (the PowerBook 500s for example) can record and playback sound in 16-bit. This is referred to as CD quality because **CD Audio** disks are 16-bit.

When converting an analog sound wave into digital data, the quality of the sound is determined by bit depth and **sample rate**. The higher the bit depth and sample rate, the higher the quality of the sound. That also means that the size of the audio files grows much larger too.

Considering that many sounds are only played back through the small internal Macintosh speaker, often it makes sense to record sounds at 8-bits, 22KHz (an acceptable average quality) rather than at 16-bits, 44.1KHz. Sampling at very low rates (8-bits, 8KHz) is not recommended because of the poor quality, but you should experiment to determine what works with the sound you are recording.

Prior to the AV Macintosh, Macs accepted mic-level signals. All models now support line-level audio. Although this is an advantage in many respects, it does mean that most microphones cannot be used without a microphone pre-amplifier. The Apple **PlainTalk** microphone has a built-in preamp.

To record audio, you need an audio recording and editing application. There are several shareware applications, such as **Ultra Recorder, SoundStudio Lite, SoundEffects, Sound Sculptor**, and **Sample Editor**. Commercial sound applications include **Audioshop, Deck II, DigiTrax**, and SoundEdit Pro. The application you use depends upon your requirements. If you only want to record a sound effect, your requirements will be different than if you want to record a band (where applications like Deck II or DigiTrax would be best).

S

If you want to import an audio CD song into your Macintosh you can open it using almost any **QuickTime** application, provided that you have QuickTime and **Sound Manager** 3.0.

One thing to remember is that even if you only need a 22kHz sound, recording at the highest quality possible, editing and then **downsampling** (converting to the lower rate) results in the best sound.

See Also
Downsampling; Sampling Rate

Sound on the Internet, *See Audio on the Internet*

Sound Manager

The Sound Manager is a free **extension** from Apple that enables applications to record digital audio from your Mac using the Mac's microphone. The latest version of **Sound Manager** (Version 3.1) adds support for 16-bit digital CD-quality audio; native code for increased performance on Power Mac models, which enhances performance as much as seven-fold; redirection of sound to third-party hardware cards; the capability to continue to work while alert sounds are playing; and support for plug-in audio compression and decompression software. The Sound Manager is an extension, but it also includes a special version of the **Sound Control panel** as well.

Sound in PowerBooks

Most PowerBooks, except the 100, 140, 145, 145B, and 170, have built-in monaural microphones. The 100 and the 150 don't have sound input capability. The 140, 145, and 170 originally shipped with external microphones that plugged into the sound-in port in the back. The 145B has a sound port, but did not come with a microphone.

Most PowerBooks also have sound out ports. This port is stereo in most models, although it is mono in the original PowerBook 100, the Duo 200 series, and the Duo 2300c. The Duo Docks also have a mono sound-out port. All PowerBooks have at least one speaker, and the PowerBook 500s have built-in stereo speakers.

The 500 and 5000 series PowerBooks support CD-quality sound at 16-bit, 44KHz sampling with the use of an external microphone, provided the microphone supports it. You can use the **Sound control panel** to switch to 44KHz on that microphone. However, because the Sound control panel can't record in stereo, you have to use a multimedia authoring application such as Farallon's SoundEdit Pro or Opcode Systems **Audioshop**.

Sound Sculptor

A shareware sound editing application that offers a surprising number of tools and features, including pitch bending and a wave drawing tool. The program creates synthesized sound using oscillators, filters, and other synthesizer processes. Available from online services.

See Also
Audioshop; Sample Editor; SoundEdit 16; SoundEffects; SoundStudio Lite; Ultra Recorder

Sound Siphon

A utility that extracts any **snd** sound resources from a file and saves them as System 7 sound files.

See Also
ResEdit

Sound Trecker

A player application for MOD files, a music file format similar to MIDI that was originally developed for the Amiga.

See Also
MacMod Pro; MIDI; MOD

SoundEdit 16

Originally developed by Farallon as a digitizing and sound editing application for 8-bit, 22KHz audio, over the years SoundEdit 16 has been upgraded so that now it supports **CD** quality (16-bit, 44.1KHz), and you can even open and edit **QuickTime** movie sound tracks. SoundEdit 16 cannot control an audio CD, but it is possible to open a CD audio track and convert it to a QuickTime movie.

Sound is digitized and edited in a waveform window. You select, cut, copy, and paste sections of the audio track. The number of tracks that can be opened at once are limited only by disk space and available RAM. SoundEdit 16 provides basic mixing capabilities—you can choose multiple tracks and mix them together, adjusting their relationship and the volume of each track. This is acceptable for mixing sound effects, but if you want to perform complex mixing, either **Deck II** or **DigiTrax** would probably be a better choice.

SoundEdit 16 offers 3D frequency displays, which look amazing on-screen (and may be useful for scientific research comparing different sounds), but they're of limited use to most digitizing and editing applications. SoundEdit 16 also comes with a CD containing sound effects and music clips.

> Macromedia
> 600 Townsend Street
> San Francisco, CA 94103
> Price: $379
> Phone: (415) 252-2000
> Web: **http://www.macromedia.com/**

See Also

MacRecorder

SoundEffects

A sound recording and editing program that supports multiple channels and special effects, such as echo, fade, and filter. This program is shareware ($15) and is available from online services.

See Also

Audioshop; Sample Editor; Sound Sculptor; SoundEdit 16; SoundStudio Lite; Ultra Recorder

SoundMachine

SoundMachine is a shareware ($10) sound player application by Rod Kennedy that processes audio files downloaded from the **World Wide Web**.

SoundMachine supports both **.AU**-variants and **AIFF** files. It can record sounds, and offers great control over playback: You can pause, play sounds backward

and forward at different speeds, and so on. SoundMachine also supports the queueing of multiple sound files to be played in sequence.

All of SoundMachine's player controls are very neatly organized into a small control dialog box, as shown in the following figure.

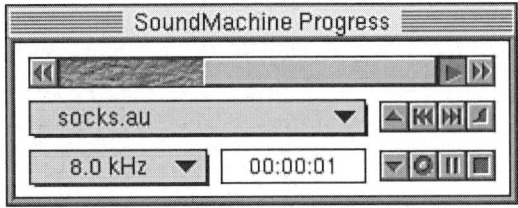

SoundMachine supports Balloon Help/Apple Guide, and the balloons provide a detailed description of the function of each of the buttons on the control panel. Some of the more interesting buttons include:

- The "Format" button (on the right end of the middle row), which allows you to change playback format (for example, from AIFF to .AU) *during* playback.

- The "Loop" button, which enables you to play selections in a repeating loop.

- The "Sampling Rate" pop-up menu, which enables you to change the playback speed on-the-fly.

See Also

AIFF; .AU File; Helper Applications, Web; Multimedia; Netscape Navigator; Web Browser; World Wide Web

SoundMaster

A utility that can be programmed to play different sounds when different system actions occur, such as ejecting a disk or restarting the computer.

SoundScape

A control panel that plays bird calls at random intervals. Use it to unnerve your cat. It is a shareware title available on the **Internet**.

SoundStudio Lite

A shareware sound recording and editing application. Can record to disk and save in standard sound formats, including **AIFF**. The shareware fee is $10 and the software is available from online services.

See Also

Audioshop; SoundEdit 16; SoundEffects; Sound Sculptor; Ultra Recorder

Spacebar

The spacebar inserts a space between words, just like the spacebar on a typewriter. It is occasionally used with the **Option** or **Command key** in a **keyboard shortcut** in an application. If, for example, you're working in a word processing application and you press Option-Shift-Spacebar, a non-breaking space is inserted.

A popular application keyboard shortcut is to press the ⌘ key and the spacebar to turn your **cursor** into a magnifying glass in order to zoom the magnification of a page.

See Also

Command Key; Option Key

Spaceward Ho! 4.0

Spaceward Ho! goes beyond giving you the chance to simply create a town or manage a feudal village (as in Warcraft) and lets you form an entire galaxy of up to 150 planets. Spaceward Ho! is a great improvement on the space **strategy game** format (also see **Pax Imperia**).

You start out with an initial civilization which generates income that enables you to make starships. As in other strategy games, every management decision you make directly affects your chances at interplanetary domination. For example, if you aren't letting your people advance as much as those of the other players, you may be in for some serious trouble. Make sure you keep track of how much money you will need for such things as weapons and various high level technical advancements. Spaceward Ho! also includes a network play mode so you can play against others over the **Internet** or a **modem**.

See Also

Allied General; Chaos Overlords; Pax Imperia; Sid Meier's Worlds; Strategy Games; V for Victory

Spam

Spam is 1) A tinned pork product whose letters are an acronym for Spiced Pork and Ham. Spam was immortalized in a routine by the British comedy troupe Monty Python in which the word "Spam" was repeated over and over by a waitress reading off a menu. On the **Internet,** Spam has come to mean a particular repetitious or bandwidth-consuming act of absolutely no redeeming value. 2) To send an unsolicited advertising message or other inappropriate listings across the Internet to huge numbers of **newsgroups** and **mailing lists**.

See Also

Flaming; Internet; Mailing Lists; Netiquette; Newsgroups

Spatial Compression

Compression technique used to compress the original image to as small a size as possible. This is often used in combination with **temporal compression**, where a frame is compressed based on the difference between it and the previous frame in the sequence.

See Also

Asymmetrical Compressors; Compressor; Symmetrical Compressors; Temporal Compression

Spatial Enhancement

The human ear and brain evolved to hear in three dimensions. Motion picture and home theater systems use multiple channels, with speakers behind as well as in front of the viewer, to stimulate it. Concert halls are designed so the music echoes off the rear and side walls, and surrounds the listener. But, although we hear the world in a 360-degree panorama, multimedia **speaker** systems are flat. The sound source is arranged on a single plane, and the speakers are so close that room echoes disappear.

Your brain can "hear" behind you by paying attention to minute timing differences between sounds that enter the ear directly, and those that have to flow around the head and outer ear shell. (That, by the way, is why ears have such a convoluted shape.) It's possible to predict these timing differences, and apply them electronically. When done properly the effect is astonishing: sounds come from the screen, but also from the sides and even behind you. Music sounds like you're in a concert hall, and not just listening to speakers. Professional recording studios have joysticks so they can position individual tracks anywhere around the listener.

Labtec Spatializer and NuReality Vivid 3D equipment contains circuits to simulate this effect in multimedia systems, available either as speaker systems or add-on **amplifiers**.

Because multimedia soundtracks are premixed, the circuits can't place individual instruments around the listener. All they can do is apply a generalized widening effect. Sounds that never had an acoustic reality—electronic music and fantasy environments—profit the most from this processing. Real-world

instruments and symphonic music can sound good or bad, depending on how you set the processor's controls. Narrations and dramatic voices sound artificially reverberant.

In short, these enhancement technologies don't do anything to help you hear the soundtrack better, and are of little use in training or business applications. But they're a heck of a lot of fun when you're playing games.

NuReality, 2907 Daimler Street, Santa Ana, CA 92705, 714-442-1080, fax 714-852-1059, **http://www.nureality.com**

Labtec Enterprises, 3801 Northeast 109th Ave, Vancouver, WA 98682, 360-896-2000, fax 360-896-2020

See Also

Speakers

S/PDIF

Sony/Philips Digital Interface Format. A digital **I/O** connection that uses standard RCS phono jacks. Low-end **DAT** recorders and audio cards, such as Digidesign's **Audiomedia II,** use this interface.

See Also

AES/EBU

Special Menu

The Special menu, which appears at the **desktop** level, enables you to:

- Organize your **icons** with the **Clean Up** command.
- Delete files from a disk with the **Empty Trash** command.
- Initialize a disk by using the **Erase Disk** (⌘-E) command.
- Eject a mounted disk by using the **Eject Disk** command.
- **Shut Down** and **Restart** your computer.

S

Note: On PowerBooks and PCI Power Macs, Sleep is also on this menu.

See Also

Clean Up Command; Desktop; Eject Disk Command; Erase Disk Command; Empty Trash Command; Icons; Restart; Shutdown

Specular Collage, *See Collage*

Specular Highlight, *See Highlight*

Speech Recognition

A number of models of Power Macintosh computers, as well as non-Power Mac models denoted with an AV (for AudioVisual), are capable of recognizing spoken commands. These commands are sent to the Macintosh through the Mac's built-in or external microphone (depending on which model and monitor you have, as some monitors have the microphone built-in).

Apple's voice recognition technology is called **PlainTalk**, and it is enabled through a series of system **extensions**. Through PlainTalk, your Mac responds to your spoken word to carry out a variety of Finder level commands and other commands that are common among applications on the Macintosh platform, such as Print, Quit, Copy, and so on. PlainTalk works by using AppleScript technology to carry out simple **macros**. These macros are stored in the Speakable Items folder within your **System Folder**.

Items in the Speakable Items folder are simple macros created with Apple's Speech Editor that enable you to assign a spoken word to a command within the Mac's interface. You can, for example, assign the spoken words "open find" to have your Mac launch the **Find File** dialog box. Any macro can be performed from a spoken word using this PlainTalk technology.

See Also

AppleScript; AV Macintosh; Extensions Folder; Find File; Macro; PlainTalk

Speak All Command

Used in AV Macintosh Computers, the Speak All command uses the AV Mac's PlainTalk technology to have the Macintosh verbally speak selected words or paragraphs.

Speakable Items Folder

Macros for **commands** you want to activate using the voice recognition capabilities of **Power** and **AV Macs** are placed in the Speakable Items folder. When Apple's **PlainTalk extension** is enabled you can use the Mac's microphone to enter spoken words to control certain commands of your computer.

Speech Editor creates the macros you assign to a spoken word command. For example, you can assign the spoken words "Open Find" to launch the **Find File** command.

See Also

AV Macintosh; Extensions Folder; Find File; PlainTalk

Speakers

The original Macintosh and **Mac Plus** had built-in speakers that were entirely appropriate for their use. They were close to the user, faced the right direction, didn't overpower the small black-and-white picture, and had sufficient range to handle the system beeps and occasional talking moose with no trouble. But as the Mac gained multimedia power, its speakers haven't kept up.

The speaker system in modern Macs has about the same quality as a cheap motel alarm clock. It's squeezed in with no attention to acoustics, and frequently points away from the user. This isn't necessarily bad design on Apple's part. With modular Macs, the **CPU** might be placed under the desk, or even in another room—it doesn't make sense to waste resources on good speakers in that box.

Third-party add-on speakers can help you get more out of your Mac. By putting the source close to your ears, they create what recording engineers call a "nearfield sound": this cancels out acoustic problems in the room, and enables you to hear more of what the original soundtrack or software designer had in mind.

Because the sound is localized near the **monitor** screen, the speakers help you focus your attention and block out external noises. And because the speakers are close to your ears, they don't have to be very loud to create a full impression. Because a lower volume is radiated in the room, office colleagues get *less* out of your Mac so they can concentrate on their own work.

The typical configuration consists of two identical-looking plastic or wooden boxes, somewhat shorter than the monitor and about a third as wide. One box contains just a loudspeaker; the other also has an **amplifier** and some controls. The amplifier unit plugs into your Mac's headphone jack and a power source, and both units are placed next to the monitor. To avoid interference with the monitor, speakers must have shielding.

Because a primary goal is just to put the sound source in the right place, even a low-cost solution can help. Radio Shack's #40-1359 system ($30/pair) doesn't have much better components than the Mac built-ins, but is easy to mount next to a monitor. The nearfield positioning enables you to hear more of what the little speaker can produce.

Better speakers can be had for $100/pair, and will genuinely improve your Mac's sound. High-quality ones start around $300/pair, and—although they're not as loud or rugged—can approach the sonic quality of professional broadcast systems. If you already have a good stereo system in the room and your monitor sits on the CPU, you might not need an additional system for multimedia: connect one of the stereo's inputs to the Mac's headphone jack, and adjust the relative levels through the **Sound control panel** and the stereo's volume control (see the following figure).

When they're properly balanced, you'll get directional cues from the computer's speaker mixed with extra high and low notes from the stereo.

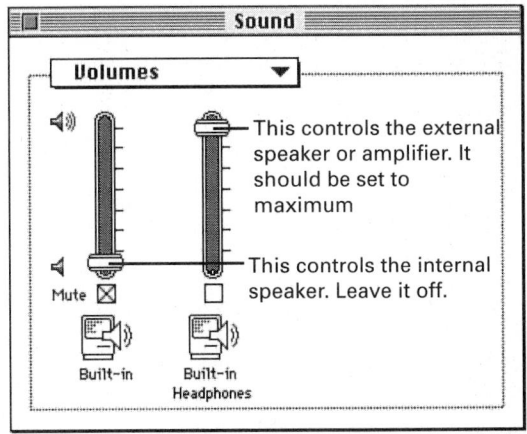

See Also

Spatial Enhancements; Speaker, Shielding; Speaker, Wireless

Speakers, Buying

Very few decisions in audio are as subjective as "what speaker sounds the best?" Even the highest-quality studio systems add their own artifacts, so choosing the right speaker often is a question of which artifacts you like. Specifications—particularly those on consumer products—don't help. Frequency response means nothing without corresponding descriptions of linearity and distortion, and the pretty response curves in some systems' advertising have little to do with real-world acoustic devices.

Phrases like "digital-ready" are an insult: speakers are inherently analog, and the cheapest clock radio speaker is as digital as the fanciest studio monitor. Even meaningful terms like porting (which allows stronger bass) won't tell you much, because so much depends on the actual speaker design.

The best way to choose a speaker is by listening. If you can, bring the system to your computer and audition your favorite programs and multimedia discs. Set the speakers to a normal volume, and listen for naturalness, a clear rather than muffled sound, intelligible voices, and distinct (as opposed to boomy) bass. These specific characteristics are part of any good speaker. Turn the volume down and make sure you still hear these things. Then turn it up and check for harshness and rattles.

If you have to evaluate speakers in a store, control as much of the process as possible. Play a CD you know well and have heard recently on a good system. Stand close to the speakers and set them to a normal volume. Never try to compare more than two systems at once. Don't be pressured to a particular brand or price range, unless you personally hear a distinct improvement. If you're considering **subwoofer** systems, be sure you also bring vocal or spoken-word CDs: these designs sometimes sacrifice the critical midrange, and human voices can get lost or sound artificial. Incidentally, the best multimedia speaker systems don't necessarily come from computer stores. Home theater has very high standards, and a store specializing in that technology may be able to sell you appropriately shielded speakers from a surround-sound system.

Make sure the controls are located where you'll be able to use them; and if you share your office with someone else, a headphone jack can help ease tensions. If you're going to be using the speakers with an external **CD-ROM drive**, look for a second set of inputs: external CD audio doesn't appear on the Mac's output connector, and requires additional cables.

If a speaker is otherwise ideal but lacks those inputs, you can use a small mixer or switch box from an electronics store. (Don't use a Y-connector for this purpose, because wiring the Mac and CD-ROM outputs directly together can add distortion.)

See Also

Spatial Enhancement; Speaker, Wireless

Speakers Connecting

Every Macintosh has an audio output jack, with an icon that resembles a loudspeaker. Early models had monaural outputs, but since mid-1993, all desktop systems and most PowerBooks have been equipped with stereo sound even if they have only one front-panel speaker. A standard eighth-inch miniature phone plug, the kind found on portable stereo headphones, fits the jack perfectly.

You can plug headphones directly into the back of your Mac for private listening (you might have to turn off the internal speaker in the **Sound control panel**). Speakers require more signal strength, so multimedia systems have an **amplifier** mounted in one of the speaker boxes. A cable runs from the back of the Mac to the amplifier/speaker, another cable runs from it to the other speaker, and a third from the amplifier to the power source—usually a wall-mounted transformer, similar to those supplied with cordless phones. The speaker system's instructions should tell you whether the amplifier unit goes on the left or the right side of the video monitor, but the choice isn't critical unless a program has left-right directional cues. Proper cables for Mac built-in audio are almost always supplied with the speakers, even if there's no mention of Macintosh on the box. If you have a third-party **AudioMedia** or **NuMedia** sound card, you'll need different connectors. The icon in the figure identifies the proper jack to use during a typical speaker hookup.

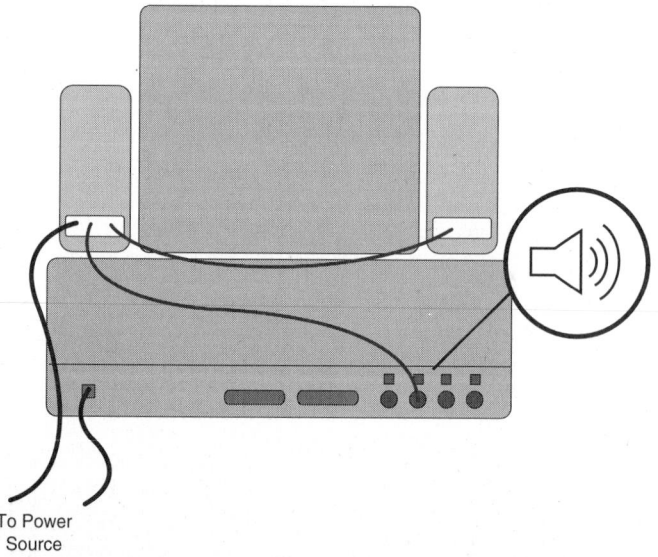

To Power
Source

Three-piece speaker systems usually put the amplifier in the **subwoofer** box. In this case, run a cable from the Mac to the subwoofer, and then a wire from the subwoofer to each of the monitor-mounted speakers. A similar arrangement applies to four-piece systems with a separate amplifier unit: cable goes from the Mac to the amplifier, and from there to each of the speakers.

You can also connect a Mac to a standard stereo amplifier to play through larger audiophile speakers, a home theater unit, or a meeting-room PA system. Use the *line*, *tuner*, or *tape* input of the amplifier. In most cases this will be a pair of phono jacks. Appropriate cables are available from any electronics store; two choices are Radio Shack #42-2475 and #42-2481. So-called Audiophile, premium, or oxygen-free cables won't add anything to the sound quality.

Some amplifier or home theater connections can experience an annoying hum, usually caused by conflicts between various electrical grounds. If the hum is coming from a cable-TV system, the best solution is to isolate the TV cable. The Web page **http://www.tiac.net/users/jcrose/cablehum.html** details various cures. If the hum is between two audio-only components, an audio transformer (such as Radio Shack #270-054) can help.

See Also
Amplifiers; Speaker, Wireless; Subwoofers

Speakers, Sources

Many so-called multimedia speakers are merely re-labeled generic designs, often from offshore sources, with no thought given to how they'll be used. On the other hand, the following manufacturers have actually tried to create a product that's appropriate for Mac multimedia. Quality varies greatly between individual models within a brand, and manufacturers not listed may also create good products, so a careful selection process is very important.

Advent, 25 Tri-State Office Ctr., Lincolnshire, IL 60069, 800-477-3257, fax 708-317-3836

Altec Lansing Multimedia, P.O. Box 277, Milford, PA 18337, 800-648-6663, fax 717-296-1222

Apple Computer, One Infinite Loop, Cupertino, CA 95014, 800-776-2333

Audiophile, 7416 Washington Ave South, Eden Prairie, MN 55344, 800-727-6863, fax 612-944-8335

Audix Corporation, 24981 Calle Arenal, Lake Forest, CA 92630, 714-588-8072, fax 714-588-8172

Bose Corporation, The Mountain, Framingham, MA 01701, 800-444-2673, fax 508-879-3965

Cambridge SoundWorks, 311 Needham St., Newton, MA 01468, 800-367-4434, fax 617-527-3194

Koss Corporation, 4129 N. Port Washington Rd., Milwaukee, WI 53212, 800-872-5677, fax 414-964-8615

Labtec Enterprises, 3801 Northeast 109th Ave., Vancouver, WA 98682, 360-896-2000, fax 360-896-2020

NEC Technologies Inc., 1414 Massachusetts Ave., Boxborough, MA 01719; 800-632-4636, 508-264-8000

Radio Shack, 1500 One Tandy Center, Fort Worth, TX 76102; 800-843-7422

Roland U.S., 7200 Dominion Circle, Los Angeles, CA 90040-3696. 213-685-5141, fax 213-722-0911

Sony Electronics Inc., One Sony Dr., Park Ridge, NJ 07656; 1-800-222-7669

Yamaha America, 6600 Orangethorpe Ave., Buena Park, CA 90620; 800-301-7076, fax 714-228-3913

See Also
Spatial Enhancements; Speaker, Buying; Speaker, Wireless

Speakers, Shielding

A loudspeaker is essentially an electric motor: it works by passing current through a coil in a magnetic field. Instead of turning a shaft, the coil vibrates a diaphragm. (There are a few non-magnetic speakers, but good ones are too big to be practical for multimedia.) The coil must have very little mass so it can respond to changing sounds, which means the magnet has to be correspondingly bigger. And that's the problem.

The image on your computer monitor is also controlled by magnets, which sweep the electron beam across the screen. A nearby speaker magnet can interfere with this sweeping and distort the picture with rainbow-hued bulges. (In extreme cases, it magnetizes part of the monitor so the distortions stay even after you've moved the speakers. If this happens, degauss the monitor.)

Multimedia speakers are shielded to protect the picture. Stray magnetism is kept away so the image stays pristine. Actually, "shielding" is a misnomer: instead of a bulky ferric shield, speaker manufacturers use extra magnets, strategically placed, to focus the field in the right place. Generally, any speaker system intended for multimedia has sufficient shielding to be placed near a monitor.

The exception is **subwoofers**. These need immense magnets—often weighing a few pounds—to do a good job, and most are too big to live on your desktop. Although it's unlikely that an unshielded subwoofer will interfere with your picture, its large flat top is a tempting storage space. It's safe to keep papers and CDs there, but not floppy disks or backup tapes.

Picture monitors also radiate magnetic fields. Although these are too weak to interfere with a speaker, they may cause noise in other audio equipment. Nearby microphones and radios can be affected, often with a high-pitched whine. Changing the position of the components a few inches can help this kind of interference.

See Also

Speakers; Subwoofers

Speakers, Wireless

If you need to hear your Mac from across the room—or even down the hall—consider a wireless **speaker** system. These consist of three units:

- A high-frequency transmitter that plugs into the Mac's **audio output**.
- Two combination receiver-**amplifier**-speaker units that can be placed up to 150 feet away.

Unlike wireless television remote controls, the speakers don't have to be able to "see" the transmitter: the signal is broadcast through the air, and can pass through walls or floors. These systems may be impractical with a PowerBook: because most transmitters use the electrical wires in the walls as an antenna, they must be plugged in.

Wireless systems from Recoton and Radio Shack are convenient and flexible, but are expensive ($180 to $250) and don't offer the same audio quality as similarly priced wired systems. They can be handy for presentations, training, and temporary setups.

Recoton Corporation, 2950 Lake Emma Rd., Lake Mary, FL 32746, 407-333-8900

Radio Shack, 1500 One Tandy Center, Fort Worth, TX 76102, 800-843-7422

Special Characters, *See Special Symbols*

Special Delivery

Special Delivery is a scriptless multimedia authoring tool that can create presentations, kiosks, or other multimedia projects. Projects in Special Delivery are made up of slides that are navigable via buttons that can jump to any other slide in the project. In many respects, Special Delivery is more like a presentation program, such as Adobe Persuasion, than a multimedia authoring tool, such as Macromedia **Director**, that is oriented toward interactive presentations.

To create slides, you arrange objects, such as **QuickTime** movies and graphics, in the Layout View window. These objects must be placed in frames, which are called *portals*. Any object can be treated as a button; a button is something that triggers an event. An event might be the playback of a QuickTime movie or a transition to another slide. More than one event can be triggered by a button. All events are attached to objects in the Button View mode.

There are four categories of events that can be triggered in Special Delivery: Navigation, which takes you to a slide; Data, which controls movies; Portal, which hides or shows an object; and Presentation, which provides overall control, such as sound adjustment. To add an event to an object, choose an event from the Button menu and draw a line from the button to the object. If, for example, you want to start a QuickTime movie, the action is drawn from the button to the QuickTime movie. For navigation, a line is drawn from the button to anywhere in the slide. By default, the Button View only displays a rectangle representing each object, which can make it difficult to see what you are doing. You can, however, choose to see a preview of the objects, which helps in designing projects.

The whole presentation can be viewed in a thumbnail view, which displays small images that represent the individual slides. The order of these can be changed by clicking and dragging them, although this only affects the presentation if you are viewing the slides sequentially.

Buttons in Special Delivery can flash when they are clicked or light up when the cursor is over them. You also can set up delayed links, so that there is a pause before an action is triggered. Special Delivery also includes a Note View for creating speaker notes.

Special Delivery's strength lies in producing multimedia kiosks and presentations. You can't create your own art or animation, but you'll have no problem producing interactive presentations. The program is easy to use, small, and fairly efficient. All graphics are

stored outside of the presentation file, so they must be included if you send your presentation to someone else. Special Delivery also includes a Player that can be distributed with presentations.

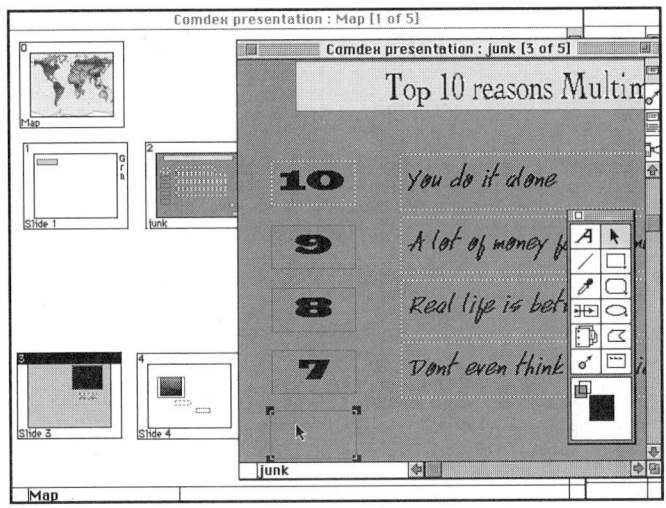

Currently, Special Delivery is not PowerPC native.

A presentation is Special Delivery. The presentation window (left) previews the slides that make up the presentation while the Button View (right) is used to add events to buttons.

Interactive Media Corp.
Los Altos, CA
Price: $399
Fax: (415) 324-4590
Phone: (415) 948-0745
Web: **http://www.imcinfo.com**

See Also
Astound; Digital Chisel; Director

Special Symbols

Many **fonts** have built-in special symbols and characters, such as the ™ symbol, the accents in the word résumé, or the ¢ symbol, that are accessed using modifier keys (a combination of the Option key and another key). Special currency symbols such as the British pound symbol (£) or the Japanese yen symbol

(¥) are considered special symbols. To find the key-stroke combinations for these special symbols, use the **Key Caps** D/A and hold different modifier keys to reveal the location of special symbols in the Key Caps keyboard display window.

To use the Key Caps D/A to add special symbols, follow these steps:

1. Choose Key Caps from the Apple menu.

2. Select the font you're using from the Key Caps menu.

3. Press the Option key, Command key, Shift key, or Control key to have the Key Caps keyboard reveal the location of special symbols.

4. You can then press the keys on your keyboard that correspond with the keys on the Key Caps keyboard to access special symbols, or you can click the keys in the Key Caps keyboard with your arrow pointer.

5. After you have determined the keystroke combination for a special symbol, you can return to your document and press that keystroke combination to insert the symbol of your choice.

The following table lists the special symbols you can enter into a document.

Special Symbols

Sequence	Result
Option-1	¡
Option-2	™
Option-3	£
Option-4	¢
Option-5	
Option-6	§
Option-7	¶
Option-8	•
Option-9	ª
Option --	–

Sequence	Result
Option-=	≠
Option-q	œ
Option-w	
Option-e	´
Option-r	®
Option-t	†
Option-y	¥
Option-u	¨
Option-i	^
Option-o	ø
Option-p	
Option-a	å
Option-s	ß
Option-d	
Option-f	ƒ
Option-g	©
Option-h	˙
Option-j	
Option-k	°
Option-l	¬
Option-;	… (ellipsis)
Option-'	æ
Option-z	
Option-x	
Option-c	ç
Option-v	
Option-b	
Option-n	˜
Option-m	µ
Option-,	
Option-.	
Option-/	÷
Option-\	«
Option-Shift-Q	Œ

Sequence	Result
Option-Shift-U	¨
Option-Shift-O	Ø
Option-Shift-P	
Option-Shift-A	Å
Option-Shift-'	Æ
Option-Shift-C	Ç
Option-Shift-V	
Option-Shift-?	¿
Option-Shift-+	±
Option-Shift— (dash)	—
Option-Shift-8	°

See Also

Fonts; Key Caps DA; Modifier Keys

Spell Check

Word processors, **desktop publishing programs**, and some other text-centered applications include spelling checkers as part of the program. These work by comparing the words in the document against a dictionary of as many as 100,000 correctly spelled words. If there's no match, the word is assumed wrong and the closest correct word is suggested. You can replace the misspelled word with a click, or ignore it. If the word is correct but not in the dictionary, you can add it to your own custom dictionary, keeping different custom dictionaries for different jobs.

This figure shows the spelling dialog box from **Microsoft Word**. Note that you can choose to change just the word selected or change every occurrence of the misspelled word.

Spindler, Michael

Michael Spindler was CEO of Apple Computer from 1993 until early 1996. Before that, Spindler served as COO.

Spindler, who the press often called "Diesel" because of his no-nonsense approach to management, oversaw the successful transition of the Macintosh from the original 68000 architecture to the Power Macintosh. He also led Apple in its move to license the Macintosh operating system to clone makers.

In February of 1996, Apple's board of directors asked Spindler to step down after several quarters of poor performance and management difficulties. He was replaced as CEO in February 1996 by **Gilbert Amelio**.

See Also

Amelio, Gilbert; Sculley, John

Spool File

A temporary spool file is created when **background printing** is enabled and you choose to **print** a document. When you choose to print a document with background printing on, a spool file is created inside the **Print Monitor** Documents folder in your **System Folder**. That file is sent to the printer to be printed in the background while you continue to work on another task in the foreground. After the file prints, this temporary file is deleted.

Besides the ability to print in the background, you also have the ability to change the printing order of spooled files in the Print Monitor dialog box. If, for example, you're printing a number of files and you want the file you last sent to the printer to move to the head of the line and be printed next, you can rearrange the printing order of the spooled files in the Print Monitor window. The Print Monitor window, accessed through the **Applications menu** while documents are being printed in the background, enables you to edit the printing order or to cancel any spooled file waiting to be printed, as shown in the figure.

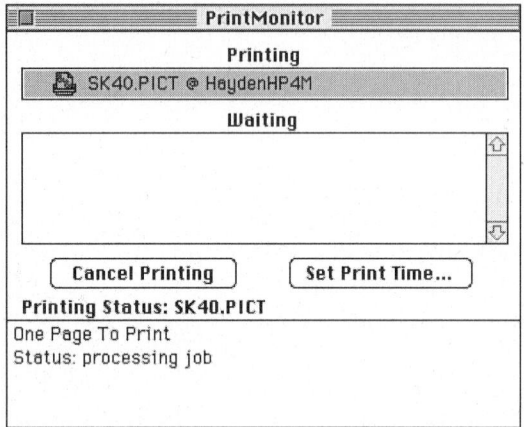

See Also

Applications Menu; Background Printing; Chooser; Print; Print Monitor; System Folder

Spooler

Spooler is a term used to describe any program that enables you to **print** documents in the background. Apple's built-in spooler is enabled by **background printing** in the **Chooser**. Spooling takes place when you have background printing enabled and choose to print a document. A temporary copy of your document is created, or spooled, and sent to the printer so your document can print in the background while you continue to work in the foreground. There are also a number of third-party spoolers available that enable background printing and management of spooled documents to be printed.

See Also

Background Printing; Chooser; Print Command; Spool File

Sports Games

You might get the impression, looking at the sports games that are available for the Macintosh, that statistically people who buy Macs only play golf. There are already great golf games currently available for the

Mac: **Links Pro CD for Macintosh** and **PGA Tour Golf III**. In addition, Blue Sky Entertainment is currently working on a game of full-motion enhanced street golf more akin to miniature golfing. The following figure shows a scene from the Links Pro CD.

Slowly, companies seem to be noticing that there is a hole in the marketplace and adding to the numbers. But, the one good thing about not having an over-abundance of titles is not having to guess which title is best. With sports games, there is really no more than one choice for any given category. GTE's NCAA Championship Basketball will possibly prove that sports games, when done well, are as profitable as coming up with the next **DOOM** or **Myst**.

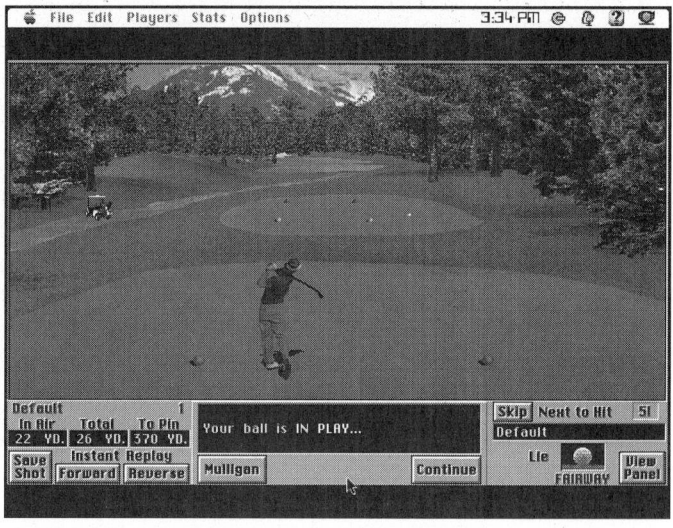

In addition to PGA Tour Golf III (see the following figure) and Links Pro CD for Macintosh, 4D Boxing from Electronic Arts offers blocky but accurate animated ringside action for those into the sport. Also, two football titles give you the chance to coach, PlayMaker's PlayMaker Football and Merit's Tom Landry Strategy Football are not quite an action fan's dream, but they will suit someone interested in the strategy behind the game.

On the whole, if you want real action, you'll want to write some letters to bug Electronic Arts into creating a Mac version of the awesome PC title FIFA Soccer.

See Also

Links Pro CD for Macintosh; PGA Tour Golf III

Sportware's Golf, *See PGA Tour Golf III*

Spot Color

Spot colors are usually **PANTONE** Matching System inks printed as solids or tints, but the term can be used to describe any color printing that is not **process color**. Sometimes spot colors are added to process color printing, resulting in six or even eight-color print runs.

See Also

Color Printing; Process Color

Spreads, *See Color Trapping*

Spreadsheet

If it weren't for spreadsheets, the Macintosh might not exist at all. In the late 1970s, Apple's main product—the Apple II—was considered a hobbyist's curiosity, appropriate only for nerds. Dan Bricklin's *VisiCalc*, one of the first commercial software packages for microcomputers, changed that. It looked like an accountant's reconciliation pad on the Apple screen, but could automatically change sums and percentages each time you entered a new number. It was revolutionary, and so handy that business executives started buying Apple II computers for high-level corporate planning and **what-if** projections. The influx of cash let Apple develop the first Mac, and VisiCalc became the model for every spreadsheet that followed.

Ironically, the original Mac's small screen and limited memory weren't suited for business-class spreadsheets. *Lotus 1-2-3*, running on IBM PC clones, quickly became the standard. It drove the sale of many early MS-DOS computers, and contributed to Microsoft's tremendous market-share advantage over Apple.

As more powerful systems with larger screens came along, the Mac's built-in graphics enabled programmers to add powerful charting and other graphic functions to their spreadsheets. Once again, the advantage tipped to Macintosh, and a bevy of Mac programs appeared (including Ashton-Tate Full Impact, Informix Wings, Microsoft MultiPlan, Lotus Jazz, and *Lotus 1-2-3*. Of those, 1-2-3 is the only spreadsheet still on the market, but Lotus has halted further development of the program. Yet another irony: 1-2-3 now dominates MS-DOS and Windows, and Microsoft's **Excel** has become the leading spreadsheet for the Mac!

Spreadsheet history might be convoluted, but the software exists to simplify the management of numeric data. If you've ever prepared an expense report or set a family budget, you've already mastered the basic concepts (see figure). Items are entered in horizontal **rows**, and assigned to vertical **columns** for different categories. Individual **cells** can hold text or a number, or they can be told to display the sum of all the numbers in a row or column. It's like a page of accounting paper with a built-in calculator.

S

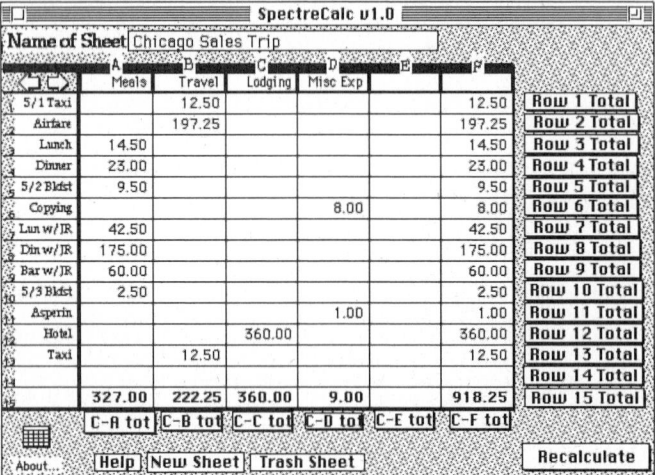

The figure shows SpectreCalc, an incredibly low-cost Hypercard Stack by Justin Higgins (the $5 shareware fee includes a complete mini-works program). It's filled out as an expense report, entering data in the first four columns. The program calculated the horizontal totals in column F, and the vertical ones in row 15. Cell F15—spreadsheets always identify their cells by column and row—contains the grand total. A salesperson could quickly prepare this card without doing any math, submit a printout, and—assuming JR's business is worth the expense—expect to get $918.25 reimbursed. (SpectreCalc is shareware from SpectralDesign and can be downloaded at **http://www.digitalnation.com/sd.**)

Along with sums and other calculator operations (including exponentiation and logarithms), most spreadsheets also include prebuilt **functions** for the following:

- Statistics (such as deviation, trend lines, Fisher transformations, and kurtosis).

- Finance (such as future value, various depreciation schemes, and internal rate of return).

- Date and Time (letting you do things like "add 28 hours to 4:00 PM, April 2, 1997").

- Math (such as geometric functions, factorials, and matrix algebra).

- Boolean algebra.

Built-in graphing routines let you turn straightforward columns of business numbers into persuasive charts. All current programs allow easy **import** and **export** of data to **word processors** and **databases,** as well as other spreadsheets, and all have extensive online help.

The choice of Macintosh spreadsheets has remained stable for a while, split between the small-business sized integrated module in **ClarisWorks**, and the monstrous (up to one billion elements in a project) Excel. Despite the differences in power, both programs use a similar philosophy for entering and manipulating data: essentially they follow a model that hasn't changed since VisiCalc. A mid-1996 entry from **Casady & Greene**, **KISS**, automates and hides many spreadsheet functions to simplify the interface and make it more Mac-like.

Most spreadsheets have elaborate text functions, so you can tell a cell to automatically include words from other cells, change its case, or replace one word with another based on specified criteria. Because they also can sort by multiple **keys** and criteria, they can manage databases. The figure that follows shows a multipage spreadsheet in Excel, combining financial analysis and inventory control. It could be extended to include point-of-sale, accounts payable, and anything else the business needed.

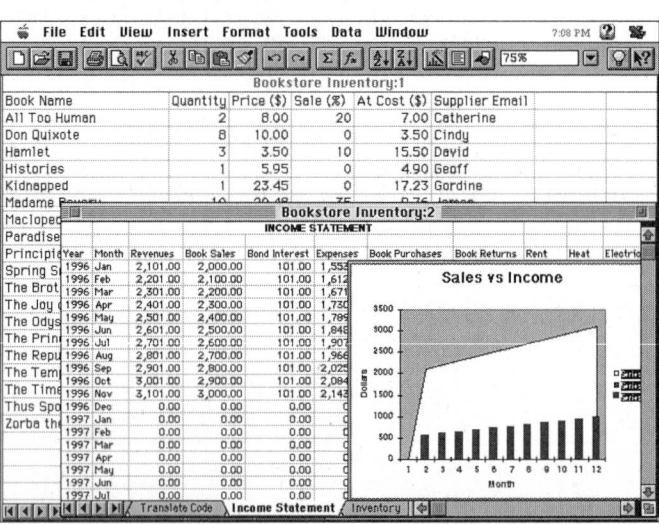

There's a constant and lively discussion of spreadsheets and their functions on the **comp.apps.spreadsheets** newsgroup.

Spreadsheet Notation Spreadsheets—and almost every other Macintosh mathematical tool—use a standard way to specify operations. Although + and – obviously mean "add" and "subtract," other symbols may be hard to find or differ from the math you learned in school. The following *operators* are used by spreadsheets to speed data entry and accommodate a limited keyboard.

Operators in Spreadsheets

Character Displayed	You Type	Mathematical Meaning
*	*	multiply ("3*4" means *three times four*)
/	/	divide
^	shift 6	exponent ("2^3" means *two to the third power*)
	option +	not equal to
<	shift comma	less than
>	shift period	greater than

Templates Templates are like stationery pads for **spreadsheets**. They contain pre-built **formulas**, tables, and charts to solve common problems ranging from lease/buy decisions to typesetting in a book. You can type in data that makes sense for your situation, see the result immediately, and save that version of the spreadsheet as a file; the template remains unchanged so you can use it again.

Templates usually come with a program and additional ones are sold by third-party suppliers to solve specific programs, but there are also thousands of them available as freeware. An Internet search with the name of your program and "template" can yield pages of solutions, ready for you to open in your spreadsheet.

See Also

Absolute versus Relative Referencing; Formula; Formula Bar; Function, Spreadsheet

Spreadsheet Fill, *See Fill, Spreadsheet*

Squizz of Power

Human Software's Squizz of Power is a splashy image warping plug-in for Photoshop. It requires about 4MB of RAM over and above what it takes to run Photoshop, and it should probably be reserved for Power Mac owners because of its complexity and speed requirements. It works in two modes, grid and brush. In the Grid mode, Squizz overlays a grid on the entire image or a selected area of an image. The brush mode allows for more organic warping controlled by mouse movements. Forget about multitasking with any other software while Squizz is on-screen. It won't allow it. Squizz is also a plug-in for Photoshop only, and won't show up as a filter in other software.

Grid Mode In Grid mode the actual grid can be toggled on or off. When off, it works the same, so you'll have to remember what points are being moved. The advantage of this toggle is to see a better preview. In grid mode, a variable sized grid is placed over the image selection. Points on the grid are selected with a special Squizz pointer (multiple points can be selected while holding down the Shift key while clicking with the mouse). Symmetry can be turned on with a mouse click, forcing horizontally or vertically symmetrically spaced grid points (or both horizontal and vertical points) to react at the same time. This is effective when you want to expand or contract a large area of the selection in a symmetrical manner (like an expanding or contracting balloon). As points on the grid are moved, corresponding areas of the underlying image selection are stretched to match the direction and placement of the altered points. Grid warping is a standard option for most warping/morphing programs. When the warped preview matches the desired warping look, the effect is applied.

S

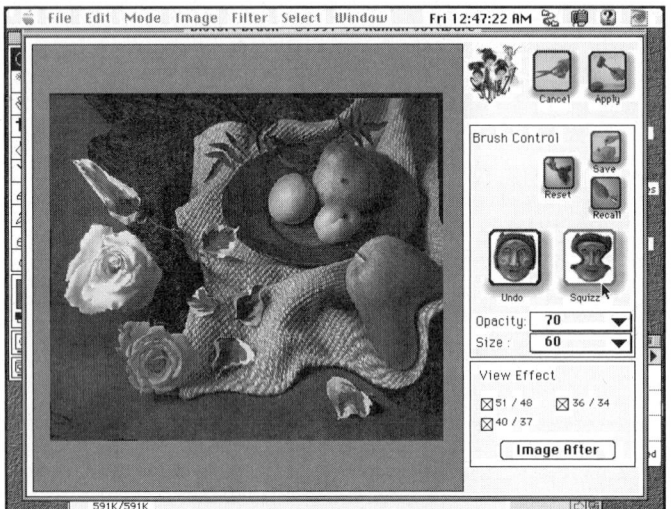

Brush Warping This is a new method for warping not offered by other software, and the feel is much less mechanical. Imagine having a paint brush that warps an image in the direction you paint in, and you get the idea of this Squizz choice. The only difference is that the brush has an icon that looks like a spraying paint canister. Setting the size and opacity of the effect gives you control over the way the surrounding pixels respond to the Squizz mouse movements. A special undo option causes the brush to work in reverse as you paint, undoing movements in a flowing fashion. A recall button snaps the image back to its original form before warping was applied. Previewing can show the altered image or the original image so you can compare the two. Squizz is an excellent choice for plug-in warp effects in Photoshop.

Stack

The stack is a section of an application's memory that stores local variables and function parameters. Together with the **heap** and globals, this makes up an application's total memory partition.

The contents of a stack are stored in stack *frames*. You create a stack frame, which is simply a series of values pushed onto the stack, every time you make a function call. The stack frame includes the function parameters and any local variables created by the function, as well as the return memory address, so that the code can jump back to correct place in the calling routine. The frame stays in existence while that routine is executing. The frame is discarded by removing all of its values from the stack when the routine ends.

As a result, the stack is a dynamic data space. Every time you make a function call, a new stack frame appears. Every time a function returns, a frame disappears. Curiously, the part of the stack that is lowest in memory is called the top of the stack, because that's where a new stack frame appears. The stack is a last-in, first-out (LIFO) pile. It is like a stalactite hanging from the ceiling of a cave—you add new stack frames at the tip (low in memory), making the stack a little longer, and you take them off the tip, making the stack a little shorter (see the following figure).

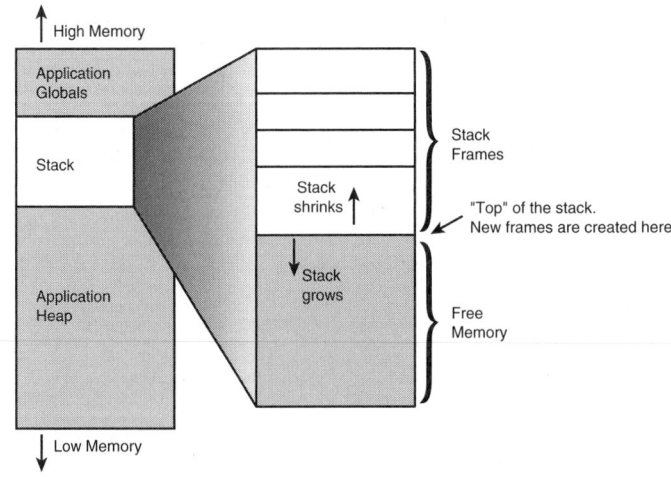

For the most part, stack management is transparent. When you compile your application's code, the **compiler** creates the necessary machine-level commands to create and destroy stack frames.

Unless you specify otherwise, the System sets the size of the stack for you when your application is started. Most of the time, the default size is fine. If your application makes unusual demands on the stack, the stack can grow down in memory to collide with the heap. This can cause disaster as the stack frames stomp all over your application's heap.

See Also

Compiler; Heap

Stand-Alone Modelers

Stand-alone modelers concentrate on one thing, creating 3D models. They are not meant to be final rendering platforms nor are they designed to handle animation tasks. Normally, they leave everything but modeling to the software that they export to. Amapi, from Yonowat, is an excellent case in point, although the modeling software from Pixar, marketed by the Valis Group, is a bit more extensive. Each has its differences in term of tools and interfaces, but each is dedicated to the same primary task, 3D modeling.

Amapi from Yonowat The first thing that you notice about Amapi is that its interface is nothing like any other 3D software that you own. Sliding your mouse to the right toggles among three separate tool sets, any member of which is activated by a mouse click. Everything in Amapi attempts to follow the modality of a 3D virtual reality environment. Objects are "placed" upon a workbench in the center of the screen, where they are worked on. You don't have to place them there, but you are somehow convinced that that's where they ought to be. The global environment can be rotated by using the arrow keys to spin around the workspace. Test rendering takes place when you hit the Return key.

Amapi has three toolboxes, and you select them by sliding the mouse to the right of the screen. They are: Construction, modeling, and Assembly. The first toolbox allows you to select Amapi primitives and place them on the Worktable. The second toolbox has tools that allow you to interact with your objects to shape them further, and the third toolbox has tools for grouping and welding objects together (or separating them apart). Every tool in Amapi works interactively with the object on-screen, from moving and rotating to pushing and pulling control points.

Lights You can place lights in Amapi to visualize preview renders, but this is just a test, because you would normally save light placement for the final rendering software.

Other Special Features Although Amapi comes with a manual, the real way to master it is to work through the five interactive on-screen tutorials: Getting Started, Self Training, Lasso, Smoothing, and Shell.

File Load/Save Conventions Amapi imports include Amapi, DXF, PICT, Text, IGES, QuickDraw 3D, and Illustrator files. Exports include Amapi, DXF, CADrender, Atlantis, Text, RayDream, 3DGF, Caliray, KPT Bryce, IGES, FACT, Explore, Amapi-1, STL, QuickDraw 3D, Illustrator, and RIB.

S

Pixar's Showplace Pixar's Showplace, marketed by the Valis Group, is one of the most exquisite and option loaded modelers around. It has enough modeling options to keep you exploring for a long time. each of the modelers comes with its own option laden dialog. They include:

1. Blinds—3D Venetian blinds in various types, customized by height and width adjustments.

2. Simple Shapes—Box, Cone, Cylinder, Disk, Hyperboloid, Paraboloid, Rectangle, Sphere, and Torus.

3. Curtains—Can be adjusted by Number of Folds, Depth of Folds, and a Closed to Open slider.

4. Fireworks—Can be adjusted by Flecks, Tri-Flecks, Blobs, Time since Explosion, Number of Sparks, Gravity.

5. Lissajous Explorer—A full 3D modeler in itself, dedicated to sculpting Lissajous curved surfaces with adjustable parameters.

6. Terrain—A full digital terrain modeler, with over a dozen adjustable parameters.

7. RoomMaker—A room modeler with toggles for floor and ceiling. This four walled room, seen from above, accepts your placement of doors and windows. A 3D model is then created from your interactions.

8. Stair Generator—A straight or spiraling staircase. You control height, width, depth, number of stairs, Step up to Next Stair, and Percentage Overhang.

9. Type Gizmo—A full featured 3D type engine, that gives you control over Font, Sizing, beveling, and depth of Bevel.

In addition, Showplace can import DXF and Illustrator files for modeling. Controls are also present for creating objects from scratch with extrusions and lathing. Showplace can also function as a full scene and model renderer, as it has its own libraries of textures and includes light generation and placement.

Lights You can place three types of lights: Distant, Point, or Spot. Lights can be adjusted as to Color, Angle, Intensity, and Penumbra (depending on the kind of light). Shadows are rendered by quality: Low, Medium, High, Extra, Gonzo.

Other Special Features The lathing operator is one of the fastest around, giving you Bezier tools to produce an outline and then lathing it on an axis. A shaded view pops up almost instantaneously on a Power Mac. Showplace is still considered a stand-alone modeler because it has no animation features of its own.

File Load/Save Conventions Showplace saves only Showplace and Stationary file formats, but imports DXF and Illustrator formats, in addition to Showplace files.

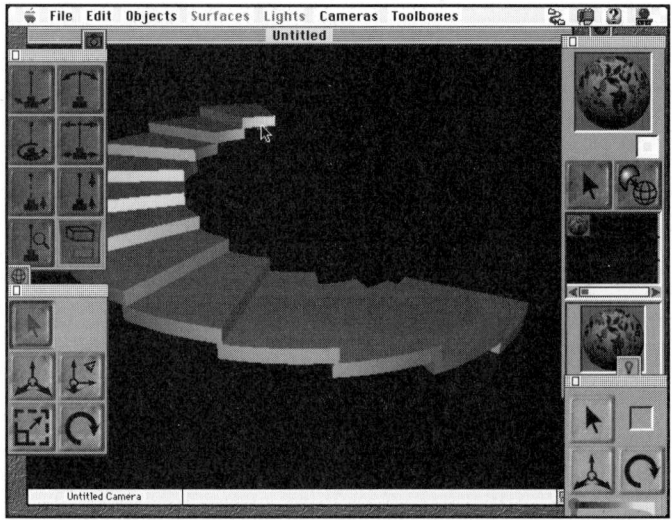

Standards, *See Desktop Publishing Color Standards; Desktop Publishing Industry Standards*

Star, *See Xerox PARC*

Star Trek, *See Daedalus Encounter, The*

Star Trek: 25th Anniversary, *See Daedalus Encounter, The*

Star Trek: The Next Generation: A Final Unity, *See The Daedalus Encounter*

Star Wars, *See First Person Perspective Shooters; Rebel Assault II*

StarDate/Expresso

StarDate is the PIM for Trekkies. It's a combination calendar, address book, and to-do list with a StarTrek: the Next Generation motif. The calendar pages feature designs identified as Deep Space, Romulan, Klingon, and the like. There's even one with the Enterprise console. Expresso is a similar PIM, also from Berkeley Systems, but a little less weird. It has twenty different calendar backgrounds, which range from pale pastel designs to a cowhide motif featuring a hilarious animated cow. The cow pops up in various disguises with appropriate sounds. In the figure that follows, you can hear the surf.

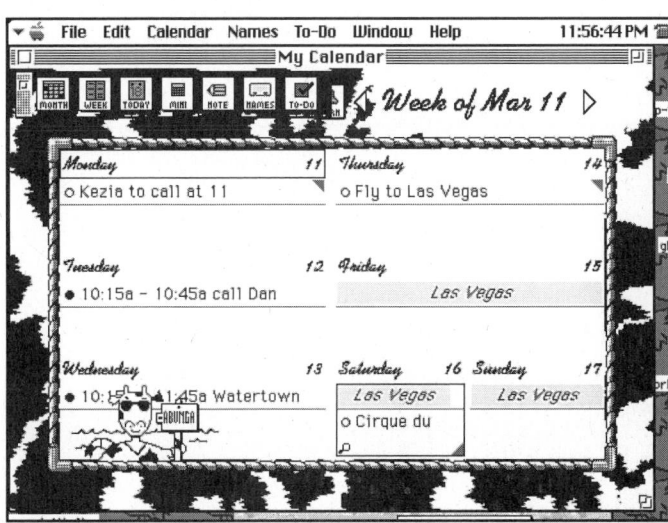

Both programs use the same basic "engine," which gives you a to-do list, phone list, and a notepad with post-'em notes that you can attach to your calendar. System 7.5's Stickies make this last feature sort of redundant, but Expresso's notes are available at the click of a button. The to-do list lets you set priorities for your items, and you can enjoy the satisfaction of clicking them off when they're done. The address list is quickly searchable by clicking on the initial of the last name, or by typing even a couple of letters from the name in the "Find" box.

These are all fairly standard features for a calendar program. What sets Expresso and StarDate apart is their ability to turn your calendar into a Screen Poster and display it constantly as the desktop. When you want to know what the date is, or when your next appointment is, or what you're doing Saturday night, just click on the Flashback button and the screen will pop to the front. When it's not active, it sits there behind any open windows and behind your icons, and you can still read whatever's written on it. You don't have to put your clients, or your life, on hold while your calendar program opens.

See Also

Personal Information Managers

Startup Disk

The disk that your Macintosh starts up from is called the startup disk. This is the disk that contains the Macintosh **system software** on it. Generally, your internal **hard disk** is your **startup** disk, but you can request that another disk be the startup disk by choosing Startup Disk from the **Control Panels folder** and designating that a different disk become the startup disk (see the following figure). The disk that you designate must have a copy of the system software on it that works with your model of Macintosh. More than one disk can be a startup disk, and it's not unusual to have different

S

startup disks with different versions of the system. Many users do this to test a new system before making a full commitment to it, as the new system might have certain incompatibility problems or bugs at first. This "dual-startup disk" was very popular when Apple introduced System 7 and some System 6 software was not yet "System 7 Savvy."

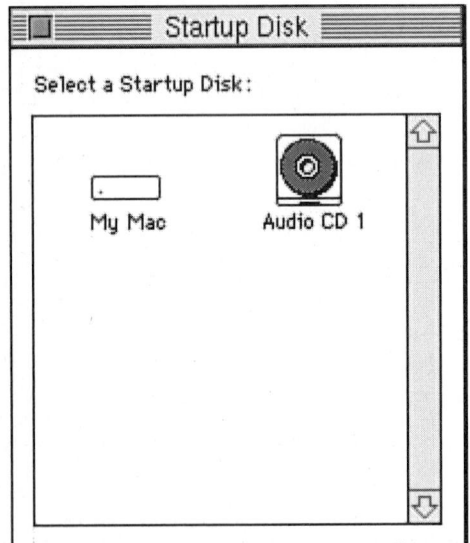

To assign which disk is your startup disk, follow these steps:

1. Choose Startup Disk from the Control Panels menu.

2. The dialog box lists any mounted disks. To select a disk as a startup disk, click the icon of the disk you want to designate as the startup disk, and choose the Startup Disk control panel.

3. Upon **restart**, the computer looks at the disk you designated as the startup disk for the system software to startup from. If that disk does not have the proper system software, the Mac then looks at other mounted disks in search of system software from which to start up.

See Also

Hard Disk; Icons; Restart; Startup; Startup Control Panel; System Software

Startup Items Folder

The Startup folder is a folder in the **System Folder** where you can place items you want to launch, or execute their particular task, each time you **start up**. If, for example, you have a particular application that you use every day, such as FileMaker Pro, you can place an **alias** (⌘-M) of the FileMaker Pro application in the Startup Items folder. The next time you start your Macintosh, FileMaker Pro is launched and ready for use. You can also put documents or aliases of documents in the startup folder and it will both launch the document and open the application that created the document at startup. Basically, anything you put in this folder is opened at startup, as if you have **double-clicked** it yourself. The following figure shows a startup items folder.

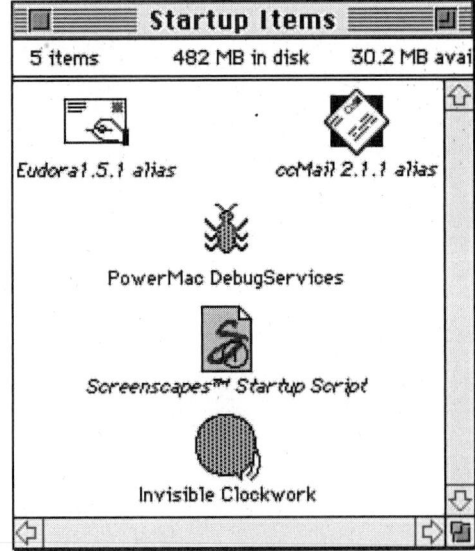

You can place a variety of items in the Startup folder, such as sounds that you want to play each time you start your Mac, or you can even have it play a

QuickTime movie at startup. If for some reason you don't want the items in your Startup folder to open, hold down the Shift key just before the **desktop** appears during startup and the items in the Startup Items folder will be bypassed. The desktop appears after all the **extensions** and **control panels** have loaded. The startup screen disappears, and in a few moments the desktop starts to appear. It's during this pause between the startup screen disappearing and the desktop appearing that you should hold down the Shift key to bypass any startup items from launching.

See Also

Control Panels; Desktop; Double-Click; Extensions; Make Alias Command; QuickTime; Startup; System Folder

Startup Manager

Startup Manager is a commercial third-party utility from Now Software that enables you to control which **extensions** load into your system during **startup** and the order in which they load. Startup Manager, which is part of the **Now Utilities** suite of system enhancements, also offers a host of other features for customizing the display and loading of extensions into your system.

See Also

Extensions Folder; Extensions Manager; Now Utilities

Startup Movie

When your Macintosh starts up, you are greeted with the standard, "Welcome to Macintosh" **startup screen**, but you can choose to startup with a **QuickTime** movie instead by placing the QuickTime movie in your System Folder and **restarting** your Mac. To have a startup movie play, you must have the QuickTime extension installed in your extensions folder.

To have a QuickTime movie play during startup, follow these steps:

1. Rename the QuickTime movie, "Startup Movie."

2. Drag this newly renamed QuickTime movie into your System Folder.

3. Restart your Mac and the movie plays during startup. If the movie runs out before startup is completed, the movie displays the last frame of the movie on your screen until the desktop appears.

See Also

Extensions Folder; QuickTime; Restart; Startup Screen

Startup Screen

When you **start up** your Macintosh, you are greeted with a startup screen. The default startup screen reads "Welcome To Macintosh" and has a small artist's rendition of the original Macintosh.

This startup screen is displayed while your **extensions** and **control panels** are loading into the system. If you are using System 7.5.1 or higher, this startup screen appears only momentarily and then disappears to be replaced by the new MacOS startup screen. This new startup screen is displayed during the loading of extensions and control panels.

Although the default startup screen displays each time you start up your Mac, you can create your own startup screen in any graphics program that supports PICT resource file formats and have it displayed at startup rather than the "Welcome to Macintosh" or "MacOS" startup screens. If you do not have a graphics program that supports the PICT resource file format, you can use Apple's resource editing utility **ResEdit** to manually replace the default startup screen with any regular PICT format graphic.

To create your own startup screen, follow these steps:

1. Open a graphics application that supports the PICT resource format. A program such as Adobe Photoshop is ideal for designing your custom startup screen because it supports the PICT resource file format, and you can create your document size in pixels, although any

S

program that supports these functions can be used. Create a new document sized at 640×480 pixels (which is the standard display size for a 13- or 14-inch monitor).

2. Design your startup screen in the program, and when finished choose **Save As** from the **File menu**.

3. To work as a startup screen, it is absolutely critical that you name your file StartupScreen (Just one word with no spaces, and the "S" in Screen must be capitalized).

4. After you've named the file, you must save the file as a PICT resource file, not a PICT file.

5. After you've properly named the file StartupScreen and you've saved it in a PICT resource format, drag this file into the System Folder and restart your Mac. If you've followed the steps outlined here, your new startup screen will appear at startup, just after the **Happy Mac**.

If for some reason your startup screen does not appear, and the standard default screen appears, re-check to make sure you named your file StartupScreen (no spaces and the S in Screen is uppercase) and that you saved the file as a PICT resource and not as a standard PICT file.

See Also

Default Settings; File Menu; Happy Mac Icon; ResEdit; Save As Command; Startup Sequence

Startup Sequence

When you start up or **restart** your Macintosh, the computer has an order or sequence it goes through to find a system to start up from. The computer looks for a system in the **disk drive** first. If your Mac has an additional internal disk drive (like many Mac SE models did), it searches there second, and then it searches for an external disk drive. If it doesn't find a system at any disk drives, the computer looks to the **Startup Disk control panel** to see if a startup disk has been selected by the user. If one has been selected,

it starts up from that drive; if not, the Mac continues its search for a startup disk by looking at the internal drive for a system, and then at the **SCSI chain** for the highest numbered SCSI device, and if it still doesn't find a system, it returns back to the internal drive for another search there. If the Mac still doesn't find anything, it continues to search up and down the SCSI chain. While the computer is searching desperately for a disk to start up from, the monitor displays an icon of a disk with a flashing question mark to alert you to the situation that the computer cannot find the system software to start up from.

See Also

Disk Drive; Blinking Question Mark Icon; Restart; Startup Manager

Stationary Icons

To protect a file from being permanently edited, you can request that the file become a Stationary Pad (a template). When you select this option, a stationary icon appears, as shown in the figure. The stationary icon looks like a note pad with a dog-eared lower right corner. You create a Stationary Pad by selecting a file and choosing **Get Info** (⌘-I) from the **File menu**. Within the Get Info window there is a **checkbox** for the Stationary Pad feature. The stationary pad icon appears in the Get Info window when the Stationary Pad feature is checked. This is the Mac's way of alerting you that this document is set up as a template. When you launch a stationery pad document, you are actually opening an untitled copy of the document. When you save the document, give it a different name than the original stationary pad, so the original is left intact.

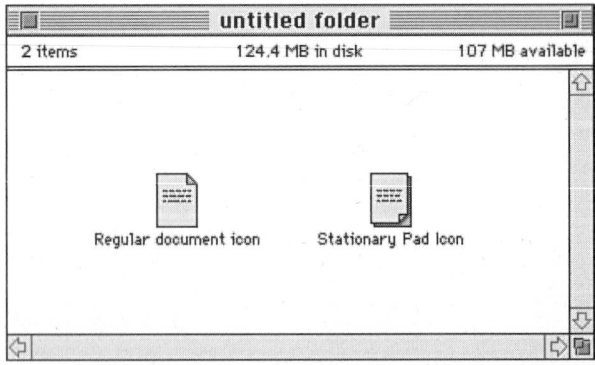

See Also
Checkbox; File Menu; Get Info; Save; Stationary Pad

Stickies

Stickies is a **System 7.5** and higher utility that appears as an **Apple menu** item. Stickies enables you to create on-screen "Post-it" type notes in a variety of sizes and colors and "stick" them anywhere you want on your **desktop**. Although this may seem to be a one-trick pony, Stickies has a lot of features. You can, for instance, select any **font**, size, and style for a sticky note and print it. In fact, you can choose to print the active note, or you can choose to print all notes. Stickies keeps track of when the note was created and when it was last modified (just like the system does for regular files), and you can access this information from within the Stickies application.

Another nice feature of Stickies is that you can **drag-and-drop** selected information between Stickies and other applications that support Apple's drag-and-drop technology. You can also drag text from a note right onto the desktop where it is assigned an **icon** as a text clipping. You can import this text clipping as text into other applications. You can also import text into Stickies or export text from a Sticky Note to be imported into another application. If you import text into Stickies and the text takes more room than the Sticky can display, the Sticky Note adds scroll bars for you.

You can customize the size of any sticky note by dragging the lower-right corner of the note (the note's size box) to your desired size, and you can choose a color for any Sticky Note by choosing the color from the Stickies' color menu.

Stickies is a popular item to have an alias of in your **Startup Items folder**, so when you start up your Mac, Stickies launch and open on your desktop.

To create a Sticky Note, follow these steps:

1. Choose Stickies from the Apple menu.
2. Choose New Note from the File menu.
3. A blank Sticky Note appears with a blinking cursor, ready for you to enter text. You can change the color of the note by choosing a color from the Stickies Color menu, and you can resize the note by dragging the **size box** in the lower right-hand corner.
4. Stickies remain running as an application until you choose Quit from the Stickies **File menu.**

See Also
Apple Menu; Desktop; Drag and Drop; File Menu; Fonts; Icons; Size Box; Startup Items Folder; System 7.5

Stickies Tips and Tricks

Stickies has much more flexibility than may appear at first glance, including incorporating some word processing features. It enables you, for example, to import any plain text file directly into a sticky note using the Import Text command. The text file open in a new note window, in the font and style you've defined as your default.

Stickies also has a set of navigation keyboard shortcuts. You can use ⌘-left arrow or ⌘-right arrow to go to the beginning or end of a line of text. (Even **SimpleText** doesn't support that.) The Home and End keys on extended keyboards move you to the beginning and end of a note. ⌘-down arrow sends you to the end of a note and places your cursor there as well. This is a quick way to add material to the end of an already lengthy note: Press ⌘-down arrow and start typing.

To keep desktop clutter to a minimum, Option-click a note's zoom box and the note collapses to a single line (select this as the default in the Preferences setting to skip the Option key). You can also choose a collapsed note as your default note style. When a new note is created, the note window appears collapsed but opens as soon as you start typing and expands to the length of your text.

If you want to constrain the resizing of a note to one direction, hold down the Shift key as you drag. You can do this with text in the note, and the text will reflow to fit in the box.

When you close a note, a standard dialog box appears asking if you want to save the note or close it without saving it. Instead of clicking the Don't Save button, press ⌘-D to close without saving.

You can also set a Sticky note as a stationery document (a sort of a template). Make a new note, go to the Note menu, and choose Text Style. There you can assign font, style, and size. Then go to the Color menu and choose the color of your note. You can even include text that you need every day, such as "To-Do List" across the top of the note.

When you're done, choose Export Text from the File menu and select the Save As Stationery checkbox. Give the note a name, click the Save button, and watch as a separate note file is created. Now, whenever you want to use that note style, double-clicking the stationery document launches Stickies and creates a blank sticky note with the attributes you specified.

See Also
SimpleText; Stickies

Sticky Note, *See Stickies*

Still Video Cameras

In the late 1980s, several companies sold still video cameras. The Canon Xapshot is probably the best known, but Sony also sold such cameras. These cameras stored their photographs on a small, internal disk, and had composite video-out plugs for connecting to a television set. The companies marketed these cameras as replacements for slides and slide projectors.

By connecting these cameras to a **video digitizing** board, it was possible to capture these images and use them on the computer.

Unfortunately, the image quality of these cameras was much lower than the quality of the current digital cameras (mostly due to the compression limitations caused by the disk recording technology). Canon offered a non-consumer camera that captured and stored double the amount of information captured by the Xapshot, resulting in an image similar to that of the current low-end digital cameras, but this camera cost over $2,000 and required an additional piece of hardware to capture the images (the camera didn't offer video out).

The current digital still cameras offer much better quality at a price competitive with the video cameras.

See Also
Digital Still Cameras; PhotoCD

STiP Professional

STiP Professional (*S*creens, *T*rees and scr*i*ptable *P*layer) is a multimedia authoring tool that creates cross-platform (Macintosh and Windows) interactive titles. STiP uses the same flow chart metaphor for creating presentations as found in Authorware (perhaps its closest competitor) and other products, but it is unique among tools that use this metaphor in that it also includes a powerful programming language.

Presentation elements, including graphics, video, and audio, are imported into the program, and there are also simple drawing tools within the program. Surprisingly, the programming language STiP provides is unlike the scripting languages found in **Director** and **HyperCard**, so it may take you longer to learn than other programs.

Despite a slightly unusual interface, this program is useful for those developing cross-platform titles. A demo version is available from MacVonk's Web site.

MacVonk Canada Inc.
940, 6th Ave. S.W.
Suite 850
Calgary, AB Canada
Price: $1295
Email: **mvc@eworld.com**
Fax: (403) 232-6425
Phone: (403) 232-6545
Web: **http://www.ccinet.ab.ca/macvonk**

See Also
Multimedia

Stitcher

The Stitcher is a utility that is part of the **QuickTime VR** Authoring Tool. It merges several sequential images of a scene to create a single panoramic image.

See Also
QuickTime VR

Stochastic Screens

Sometimes called FM (Frequency Modulated) screens, stochastic screens are a way to print **continuous-tone** images that differs markedly from the **halftone** method. Unlike regular halftone dots that are spaced evenly, stochastic dots are randomly placed in the image area and are quite small in comparison. In stochastic screens, the screen angles and screen frequency are not relevant, and **moiré** patterns are eliminated. Stochastic screening is often used in high-fidelity **color printing** because it is easier to print more than four colors. Stochastic screens require very precise production techniques and expensive high-resolution plates.

See Also
Digital Halftones; Halftones

Stop Bit, *See Asynchronous Communication*

Storage

Early electronic data storage media were not particularly robust. The stern warning on those *punch cards*—do not fold, bend, mutilate, or spindle under penalty of law—was deadly serious. An extra hole in such a card could render all the data on the card useless.

Magnetic tape was considerably more robust. Early personal computers, including the Apple II, often came with a distinct port into which you could plug a standard audio-cassette recorder for use as a data storage device.

Tape drives, however, have one significant design flaw—they are not a random access medium. To get two pieces of information, one of which is at the beginning of the tape spool and the other at the end, required the tape to wind the entire tape spool past the stationary read/write heads.

The disk drive, a combination of a spinning platter and moving read/write heads, was the breakthrough that changed data storage forever. Although being able to access information on a disk very quickly was a great advantage, the capability of randomly accessing information stored on a disk made the idea of online, immediately available data realistic.

This random data access is possible because a disk drive's read/write heads can move back and forth across the face of a disk while the disk is spinning. Data stored close to the center of a disk is, in practical terms, no further away from the read/write heads than data stored at the very edges of the platter.

The first disk drives used giant floppy disks 8 1/2 inches to 14 1/2 inches. The first hard disk drives were developed by IBM in 1973 under the code name **Winchester**. Despite advances in speed and capacity, the modern hard disk is still a recognizable descendant of that original Winchester technology.

See Also
Backing Up; DAT; Disks and Drives; Hard Disks

Storyboard: Artist and Quick

Animation design begins with the storyboard process. Keyframes are illustrated and notated, and a global view of the production is laid out. Traditionally, this has been hand work, accomplished with pen and ink and a constant referencing of the script. Power Production Software is attempting to change all of that with its two storyboarding packages: Storyboard Artist and Storyboard Quick. Of the two, Storyboard Artist is the more full-featured software, although Quick may serve as both an introduction to Artist and a satisfactory alternative for lower end productions and needs. We will concentrate on Storyboard Artist.

The Interface Storyboard Artist allows you to design frames of a storyboard that can be printed out or saved as digital files. The interface is designed to allow you instant access to tools without cramping the picture area.

The Placement Methods There are three ways to place images in a Storyboard Artist frame: By using the presets from the included libraries, by drawing on the frame with a pen tool, and by importing graphics from your own image database. Each of these methods, or a mix of all three, allows you the maximum creative tools with which to design a professional storyboard of any planned animation or digital slide sequence. All object types can be moved forward or backward in the display stack.

1. Preset Method

    Storyboard Artist comes with its own image libraries of characters, backgrounds, and 2D objects, all ready for placement on a storyboard frame. All of these graphics are accessed through a pop-up menu with visual icons. Storyboard graphics are open to rotation by clicking on any one of four rotation icons on the interface, one of the software's most unique and useful time-saving features. If you import a character that fits your need, but does not appear in the perspective desired, you can select different perspectives of the same object by clicking on the rotation icons. Running figures turn in space, objects in a room are seen from different angles, and background scenes are altered. Text blocks can also be added to the frame.

2. Hand Drawn Method

    The software has a pencil tool that allows you to draw in a storyboard frame. Once drawn, the new 2D object can be colorized and filled with a pattern, and saved to the library. This is useful for altering characters and filling in details needed in a specific project.

3. Import Graphics Method

    PICT files (including numbered sequences) and QuickTime movie files can be imported into a Storyboard Artist frame. Once imported, they can be resized like any other graphic element. This means that you could just as well import frames from grabbed video as you could graphics, and layer everything in one composition.

Frame Controls Frames can be added to or duplicated on the storyboard at any time, and selected members can be deleted when necessary. Frames appear in the Sequence window for access and previewing. A "TV Safe" dimensioning box can be overlayed on any selected frame to allow you to see where to place characters. navigating to a specific frame is aided by the visual stamps of the sequence members.

Captions Captioning is a standard need when creating a storyboard, whether to delineate the narration or to reference other things that should be paid attention to. Storyboard Artist includes targeted captioning for each frame in a sequence.

Sounds Clicking in the Sound Channel on the timeline allows you to import sound that will begin at that point. Sound files can also be recorded directly, as long as you have the right hardware on your system. There are two sound channels on the timeline that can be interactively mixed.

File Load/Save Conventions Storyboard Artist can export EDLs (Edit Decision Lists). PICT files, and numbered PICT files, can be imported, as well as QuickTime movies. Objects, Frames (in either vector or bitmap formats), and Projects can be exported. Project exports can be as PICT File series, QuickTime, or PowerPlayer (an on-board player).

Frame slide shows can be run while within the software. Current Frames can be saved to File and Clipboard, and selected Objects can be saved to PICT or Clipboard. QuickTime movies can also be linked to specific frames for playback and display.

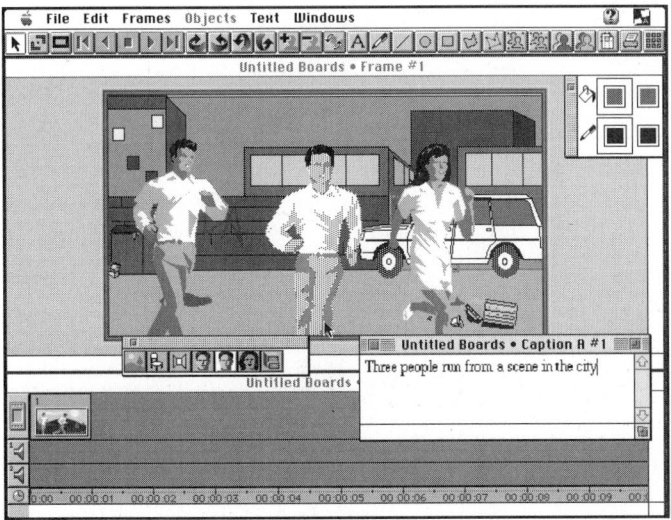

Strata Studio Blitz

Strata Blitz's interface design allows the maximum room for crafting and editing a scene, at the same time giving you access to all of the tools. Strata has mastered the drag-drop texture technique, and to that end includes all of the textures in a visual display as well as in a verbal list along side of it. Blitz has been designed so that all of the commands are accompanied by visual icons, and naming conventions follow the logical expectation of common language rather than the jargon common only to engineers. All of this creates a more gentle and faster learning curve for new and experienced users.

Modeling Tools Blitz has a full set of modeling tools (including Metaballs, Surfacing, Skinning, and four Swept Surfaces: Extrude, Path Extrude, Lathe, and Sweep), and includes the capability to allow for spline based modeling.

Boolean Operations Blitz has one of the easiest to understand Boolean modeling modes around. After the Boolean modular is brought up, you choose a target object and the "drill" object from a list of all of the objects in the scene. Three alternatives are listed: Union, Intersection, and Subtraction. Selecting "OK" performs the task.

Texture Mapping This is another area where Blitz sparkles. In addition to having the capacity to design any of your own textures, Blitz allows you to adjust the way that they map onto the object (Planar, Decal, Cubic, Cylindrical I and II, and Spherical). The drag-drop feature is also tied to Apple's QuickDraw 3D, allowing you to see a representation of the texture mapping while still in the edit mode.

Lights Spotlights and point lights can be placed in the scene. Both have associated dialogs that allow you to set intensity, Color, Seven Default Gels (Horizontal Blinds, Jungle Canopy, Magenta Wash, Sunrise/Sunset Wash, Vertical Blinds, and Windows). Custom gels can also be incorporated. A gel makes it appear as if the light is being strained through the gels shapes. Full Mapping procedures can be targeted to a gel (Planar, Decal, Cubic, Cylindrical I and II, and Spherical), with horizontal and vertical size controllers. Tiling and light textures can also be applied for customizing the gel sets, and more expert features are offered to control the lights down to the most basic projection and mapping levels.

Rendering A full rendering module is included, with adjustable user sizes and resolutions, quality controls, and special effects renderers that apply rendered "media looks" to the scene (Art Deco, Chalk, Crackled, Dry Brush, Fur, pencil, Seurat, Soft Oils, Van Gogh, and Watercolor). When animated, the media effects filters produce startling painterly effects.

Included Libraries A CD-ROM packed with 3D objects and extra textures ships with the software. Also included is a large library of drag-and-drop textures and other graphics.

Animation Strata Blitz utilizes a keyframe animation system with easy to master visual controls. The timelines between keyframes can be manipulated as well as components of the keyframes themselves.

S

Other Special Features Blitz has one of the most exquisite particle animation modules around. With it, you can Atomize (with adjustable sliders for Detail, Instability, Energy, and Life), Explode (with adjustable sliders for Force, Gravity, and Life), and Shatter (with adjustable sliders for Tumble, Gravity, and Life) any selected object. It's always best when targeting objects for particle dispersion that you first break them up into smaller polys, or else you'll have large shards floating around (unless that's your desire). Blitz includes a Morphing module that does not demand that source and target items in a morph have the same number of polygons. Two alternate morphing possibilities are included: morph into particles and then recombine to form the target shape, and straight polygonal morphing. StrataVision 3D is Strata's medium end rendering software, sold separately from Blitz.

File Load/Save Conventions Files can be opened as Strata Pro, 3DMF, DXF, EPSF Preview, IGES, Illustrator, MiniCAD+, PICS, Strata Image, Strata Clip, Super3D, Suspended Rendering, and Swivel 3D. Saved formats include Strata Pro, 3DMF, DXF, EPSF, PICT, Strata Image, Strata Clip, TIFF, and VRML. In addition, DXF 3D objects can be imported and placed in a scene.

StrataVision

StrataVision is an all purpose **3D** tool that offers modeling, animation, and rendering features. It is a sister product to Strata's more expensive **StudioPro**, which has a similar interface, but offers many more features.

Strata launches with a single window view of the 3D world you are working in, but you can open other windows and change their orientation to your preference. Strata can be a little awkward to navigate. Positioning windows the way you want them can often be difficult. When using the window rotation tool, for example, there's no visual feedback, as you drag, of how far you have rotated the model inside the window.

Strata supports basic primitive objects: sphere, cube, cylinder, and cone. These can be edited in the 3D Sculptor, shaping and forming an object by clicking and dragging individual splines (the curves that define the shape of the object). Strata imports **EPS** files, and it also enables you to draw and edit spline curves (although you must do this in the 2D editor, because there's no pen tool available in the main tool box). In addition to **lathing** and extrusion, StrataVision also can sweep objects.

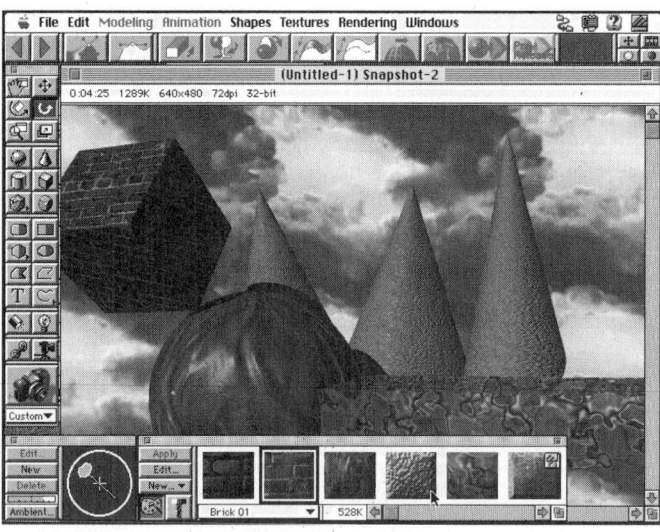

StrataVision includes a **Boolean** editor (one of the few under $1,000 modeling tools that does). The Boolean editor adds or subtracts one object from another to create new, more complex shapes. Unfortunately, it can be difficult to use, because you have to choose objects from a text list of the objects, and it's easy to choose the wrong one! Strata also lacks a palette with numeric and positioning information.

StrataVision's animation controls are implemented through a Sequencer window, which displays the **key frames** for the movement of the selected object. The

Sequencer window only displays the selected object. Strata also displays the path of the object on the other windows, so that you can actually see where the object is going to move relative to the current position of other objects in the model. StrataVision supports plug-in extensions that alter the animation effects.

See Also

3D; Animation Master; Extreme 3D; Infini-D; Modeling; Network Rendering; Ray Dream; Sketch!

StrataType 3D

Those users with any **StrataVision** or Strata 3D Pro experience are going to be immediately attracted to this software because its interface is so similar to the Strata flagship 3D products. This is a very high end font rendering package, although version 1.0 has no animation capabilities (Strata would prefer that you port the output from this package to its more full featured 3D packages for animation purposes). StrataType 3D produces 2D renderings for video and DTP applications, and also creates 3D objects for the Strata Studio Pro and StrataVision artist and animator.

The StrataType 3D toolbox contains four basic tools: the selection arrow (used to select and move targeted objects), rotation tool, text icon, and the camera icon, which triggers rendering mode selections.

The rotation tool allows you to grab a text object and rotate it in any of the XYZ planes. Visible handles around the selected object are grabbed and moved. The rotation tool can also be used to move the entire object from the center point.

Clicking on the text icon and then on the view screen triggers the StrataType 3D text dialog. Any **TrueType** or **PostScript** font in regular, bold, or italic settings can be used as the text object's building font. An input area allows for the spelling out of your text block. A separate letter spacing input box allows you to adjust the distance from one letter to the next. A visual library of 3D extrusion options can be viewed via a slider, and a 3D extrusion format selected. A 3D effects library is also viewable by slider. It contains selections that display the typography in different 3D positions, around the varied axis in an arc, on vertical and horizontal planes, as a wave, and other choices. Selecting one of these options places your text data in that shape on the view screen. You can also edit the extrusion choices by altering both the extruded depth and the degree and shape of the 3D beveling to customize the text object. When the dialog is closed, your chosen text line with the applied shape and extruded bevels is written to the view screen in a preview mode.

The camera icon triggers the rendering options dialog. Rendering options range from draft, to good, better and best, in either full color or grayscale. Anti-aliasing can be checked on or off, and super sampling (how many times the data is read for finer anti-aliased rendering) can be selected as either medium or high (slowest setting but best quality). Texture detail can be set to low, medium, or high from a separate list. Complete sizing and DPI settings are included.

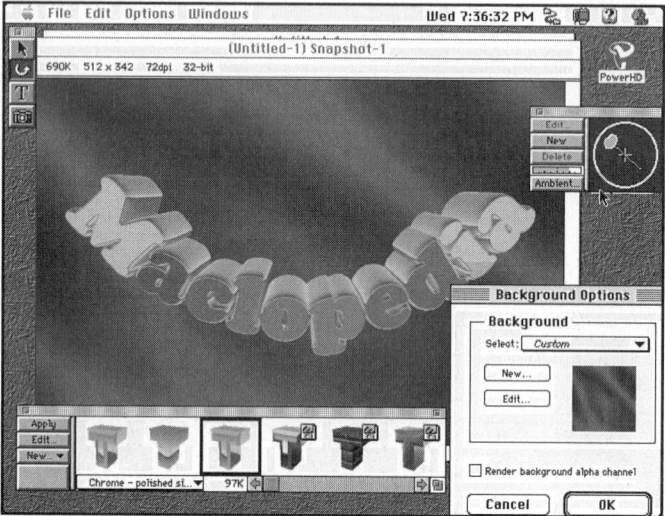

Imports StrataType 3D can open StrataType 3D, StrataClip 3D, PICT, and Illustrator 3.0+ file formats. A list of exceptions to the Illustrator option are listed in the manual.

Exports Finished renderings can be exported as EPSF, Strata Image, PICT, and TIFF. Objects can be saved as DXF, StrataType, EPSF, PICT, StrataImage File, StrataClip 3D file, or a TIFF. StrataClip 3D is a file format used by Strata on its StrataClips CD-ROM, the files of which can be opened by calling Strata and paying the suggested fees. A few StrataClip objects are included as samples with StrataType 3D.

Textures Taking advantage of Apple's **QuickDraw 3D** technology, all textures in StrataType 3D can be drag-dropped on the object. The same texture menu Strata Studio and StrataVision users have become familiar with is included in StrataType 3D. A visual display of the textures enables you to select the desired texture from the library of options. Displayed textures can be edited and customized, and new textures added to the library when needed. New textures can be created from your own graphic images, or from a list of procedural algorithms (Polka Dot, Marble, Mixer, Stone, and Wood). A special texture Options menu allows you to alter the way that the selected texture is mapped to the object.

Lighting A lighting dialog controls the direction of any chosen light, its color, gel setting (which may include projected pictures), gel color, light type, and shadowing intensity. New lights can be added and edited whenever desired.

Backgrounds New backgrounds can be selected from a list or constructed from your own saved graphics. The listed backgrounds can be edited and altered as to color and bit depth, and any background may be targeted as an alpha channel (a grayscale overlay whose intensity of lights and darks affects the color image's visibility).

Strategy Games

Political **strategy games** like **Warcraft: Orcs and Humans** place you in charge of feudal towns and work on much the same cause and effect premise as **SimCity**. In Warcraft, from Blizzard Software, you are in charge of building a town, which is then populated with peasants who work, fight, and play within the confines of the town. As in the Maxis games, your townspeople interact with each other while you are not watching. In Warcraft, they can even be killed, so you need to pay close attention.

Sid Meier, generally heralded as the greatest of all strategy game makers, has been responsible for great strategy games such as Civilization, Colonization, and Pirates! Gold, all published by MicroProse.

Although simulation games often incorporate aspects of political and battle tactics, strategy games put you in charge of entire societies that must be controlled and protected.

War strategy games, such as Allied General and the V for Victory series from Three Sixty, recreate famous battles from World War II. If you make the right or wrong moves, you can change history and have the Nazi's win World War II or cause the North to lose the civil war. U-Boat and the new sequel U-Boat II:

Drumbeat, which put you in command of a World War II submarine, incorporate a sim aspect, allowing you to navigate the sub and learn about underwater battle tactics and strategy. U-Boat puts you in charge of various missions in Europe, whereas Drumbeat has you offshore from Key West up the East coast of the United States, monitoring merchant ships.

Strategy games are by no means limited to simply controlling and watching the results of your decisions being carried out by computer generated characters. These games make you think on your toes and engage in fierce battles. When played over a network, the feeling of outsmarting an opponent gives you the type of thrill you get from a good game of chess.

See Also

Allied General; Chaos Overlords; Empire Deluxe; Pax Imperia; Sid Meier's Worlds; Spaceward Ho!; V for Victory; Warcraft: Orcs and Humans

Strategy Games of the World,
See Classic Collection: Three Classic Board Games for Your Mac

Streaming

A method of transmitting data gradually from a host to a client computer on the **Internet**, enabling a user to interact with the data before transmission has been completed.

Streaming is a fundamental component of navigating or "surfing" the **World Wide Web**. **Web browsers** like **Netscape Navigator** enable a user to see information and to interact with a **Web site** while Netscape is still gathering data from that site. Instead of waiting for a document to be assembled in its entirety before it is displayed, the data is sent to the user's screen much more quickly and appears in stages.

This streaming of data allows a user to scroll down or even stop loading a Web page after only a portion of it has appeared on the browser screen. Streaming is integral to some of the relatively new multimedia applications that provide content on the Web, such as

RealAudio, which streams audio data to the Web browser, so that sounds can be played as soon as they are downloaded.

See Also

Internet; Netscape Navigator; RealAudio; Web Browser; Web Page; World Wide Web

Streamline

When you need to use your favorite bitmap illustration in a vector environment, you need to translate it to a vector format. That's where Adobe Streamline comes in handy. High contrast bitmap images translate very well as two and four color vector graphics, while bitmap images with a lot of detail in separate color areas must be translated to higher level vectors, perhaps with as many as 256 colors. It is with the more complex bitmaps that you run into potential problems, as each small area of color has to be translated to a vector shape. It's always wise to translate the graphic in a bitmap program first, repainting it to a lower number of colors when possible. Streamline has controls that address every situation, from simple to complex.

Settings and Conversion Setups The first step in the process is to tell Streamline what you want the vector graphic to look like in terms of shape and color. A Settings dialog enables you to select a number of preset possibilities or to customize and name your own set. If a preset is chosen, its complete data breakdown, in terms of each setting, is listed. You can customize the setup in the Conversion Setup dialog, so that when you return to the Settings dialog, the complete transformed data is listed as well. The Conversion Setup dialog sets the exact number of colors the vector graphic will have, the conversion method, accuracy, and line options. A preview button shows you these settings applied to the on-screen bitmapped graphic.

Conversion The Convert command starts the translation process. A counter keeps track of the number of polygons generated. Each color must be converted separately, so if you have chosen a sixteen color vector rendering, the program has to separate the bitmap into sixteen colors and render each set in turn. When it is finished, the rendered vector art appears on-screen in place of the bitmap. An Undo command returns the graphic to its bitmap data if you're not satisfied.

Post Editing Shape and Color After the rendering meets your approval, you can use other tools in Streamline to finalize the new artwork. Selecting any one or a group of vector areas from the artwork displays their control points. Selected graphic elements can be cut, copied, pasted, or smoothed (which rounds off the shapes). In addition, by selecting an area and accessing the Custom Color or Paint Style dialogs, any element of the vector can be re-colored. When everything is complete, the new vector art is saved to disk.

File Load/Save Conventions Streamline can open TIFF, TIFF compressed, PICT, MacPaint, and Photoshop (2 and 2.5) images. Finished vector art can be saved as Adobe Illustrator, PICT, or DXF formats for either the Mac or IBM platforms.

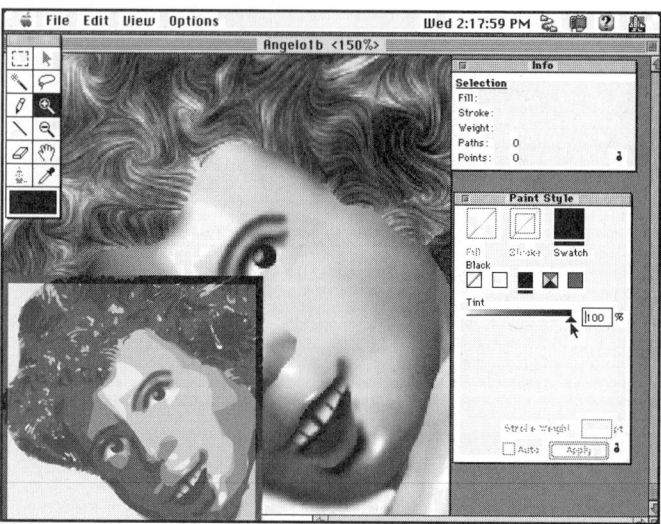

See Also
Illustrator; Photoshop

Street Atlas USA

Street Atlas USA is a street atlas of the United States from DeLorme on **CD-ROM**. Street Atlas USA has loaded in the names of every street in the US, including Hawaii and Alaska. With multiple levels of zoom on the map, you can plot a route to the corner store, or the corner of the state, or anywhere else you'd like to go.

Street Atlas USA provides a highly detailed, seamless map database of the entire country. Users can zoom in on every city, town, and rural area in the United States. The database contains more than 12 million street segments and 1.1 million geographic and man-made features, such as mountains, rivers, lakes, and prominent monuments.

The atlas has 16 levels of zoom, going from the top one showing the whole United States at once, to level 16, showing an area about 4000 by 2000 feet. In addition to street names, Street Atlas USA also shows attractions, airports, major hills, rivers, and so on.

Also, Street Atlas USA has a built-in search engine that can scan for street names, major features, such as rivers, or attractions, zip codes, and phone number exchanges. With a built-in labeler, you can take notes directly on the map as you plot out a route, or simply mark down where important things are.

Street Atlas USA will run on a Macintosh PowerBook with a CD-ROM drive, so it can go along on drives to Grandma's and bail you out when you're lost from going over the river and through the woods. If you don't own a portable computer, Street Atlas USA can also print out its maps at any level of detail. Street Atlas USA is published by DeLorme Mapping.

See Also
CD-ROM

Street Fighter, *See Hollywood Games Connection*

Striped

Video tape that has **time code** displayed in a section of the image. This is used to preview the video and note clips and edit points (pieces of video that are to be digitized or edited).

See Also

SMPTE; Time Code

Stripping

Although it's the subject of a lot of jokes in the publishing trade, stripping is actually a fine craft. Printing plates are made by exposing chemically treated plate material (metal or special plastics) to light through film negatives. Today much of that film comes out of the **imagesetter** all in one piece, but that wasn't always the case. Strippers are the people who line up and attach smaller pieces of film to create composite films that can be used to make printing plates.

See Also

Imagesetters

Stroustrup, Bjarne, *See C++*

Structure

In **programming**, a structure is a **variable** that can hold a collection of different kinds of information together in a single variable. The name structure varies in different **programming languages**; in **Pascal**, structures are called records. Structures are useful when gathering related information. A programmer of a payroll application, for example, might create a structure to hold each employee's information: name, address, social security number, salary, and so on. Each of these individual parts of the structure is different (some are text strings, some are numbers, and so on), but they can all be grouped into a single structure.

See Also

Pascal; Programming; Programming Language; Variable

Student Essentials

Novell knows what students need. Within two CD-ROMs, they've put together a package that includes practically all the software a high school or college student needs to be successful in the academic arena. It may even help with social life, because it contains a set of Internet tools to let you surf the **Web** and put up your own **home page** (Internet access not included).

First, there's a word processor. Because Novell did the choosing, it's WordPerfect 3.5. This word processor is as full-featured as anyone could want. It even does **HTML** conversion for Web publishing. Among the features that make it especially convenient for students, are language modules for writing in French, German, and Spanish. Each language module has both a spelling dictionary and thesaurus, so you can do

S

homework in four languages. (Other modules are also available, even for such uncommon languages as Swedish, Turkish, Flemish, and Icelandic.)

Next, there's an encyclopedia. Compton's Interactive, to be specific.... This is one of the most popular interactive reference tools ever, with over 35,000 articles, 7,000 pictures, 100 full-motion videos, 3D animation and presentations, music and sound clips, an atlas, US and world timelines, and an idea generator to help you get started on your research.

Can't find the right word? Use the Thesaurus, part of Random House Webster's Electronic Dictionary and Thesaurus. Sure, there's a spelling checker built into the word processor. But this one, accessible on the Apple menu from any program, gives you the meaning, the spelling, the etymology, and the pronunciation of the word.

The next piece of the package is Bookends, a bibliographic tool, to help with term paper references. And to print the term paper as beautifully as possible, choose from one of 100 Bitstream/TrueType fonts. Next, there's Student Assist, a personal information manager that's geared to student needs. It keeps your class schedule, assignments, appointments, calendar, to-do lists, addresses and phone numbers, and even more information, cross-referenced and accessible at a click. It's a great way to get, and stay, organized.

Finally, the Internet toolkit includes **Netscape Navigator**, the leading Web browser, and Envoy, an electronic document publisher that preserves the look and feel of your WordPerfect documents, no matter where you send them.

If you're a liberal arts major, this package is all you need. If your future lies more in the math and science area, consider adding a scientific calculator (or using the one that comes with **System 7.5**) and possibly some special purpose software like Interactive Physics, or maybe **Myst** or **Descent**. After all, you can't study *all* the time.

See Also
HTML; Netscape Navigator; WordPerfect

StuffIt

StuffIt is the original Macintosh **compression** program written by a high school student named Raymond Lau. StuffIt was originally distributed as a shareware program, but now it is a commercial software program called StuffIt Deluxe distributed by Aladdin Systems (**http://www.aladdinsys.com**). (There is still a shareware version of StuffIt, StuffIt Lite, that has a stripped down set of features and is available from most online services.)

StuffIt Deluxe enables you to compress selected files, combine multiple files into one compressed archive, password protect compressed files so they cannot be "unstuffed" without the proper password, and create **self-extracting archives** (.sea). The amount of compression (savings in file size) is different for each type of file. Graphics files (especially in TIFF format) seem to compress quite a bit, and it's not uncommon to have a TIFF graphic to compress to 95% of its original size. Text files also compress well, but printer fonts (which already use an internal form of compression), application files, and sound files don't compress nearly as much.

Conversation with Raymond Lau
Ray Lau invented StuffIt, the most popular compression software in the Mac world, when he was a teenager. He's now a grad student at MIT.

Maclopedia: What was your first experience with a Mac, or, from your early experiences, what stands out?

Ray: My first exposure to a Mac was the original Mac 128K back in the April of 1984. What impressed me the most at the time was the ease with which a printer, the original ImageWriter, can be set up. You just plug it in and pick Print and it worked! My prior experiences with computers were with a wide assortment of home computers (for example, the Apple II, the Commodore 64, and so on) and in no case was one able to just plug in a new peripheral and have it work immediately. Of course, other early positives included the WYSIWYG nature of MacWrite (the only word processor at the time), the sharp monitor (albeit in black and white), and the mouse-based interface. A big negative at the time was the constant floppy swapping. This was before there were hard drives, so you had to keep your system files, applications, and data files on floppies.

Of course, things would never fit on just one 400K floppy, hence the need to constantly swap each time you did anything.

Maclopedia: How did you get the idea for StuffIt and what were your experiences as you developed it?

Ray: The Macintosh was still a new platform in '87 and many enthusiasts, myself included, had an insatiable appetite for trying new software. We would frequent CompuServe, GEnie, the local BBS, and so on. The dominant compression utility for the Mac back then was PackIt III. PackIt was somewhat slow, but it was missing one feature which I, and many others, longed for. Namely, to get to, say, the fifth file, you had to wait for it to decompress the first four files. There was no way to skip around. An acquaintance with whom I frequently exchanged files by modem showed me several compression utilities on the DOS platform which did allow the user to skip around and to also to list an archive's contents. The seed for a new application was thus firmly planted. During the summer of '87, the first version of StuffIt was created. As an added bonus, the algorithm I had decided to implement also compressed files better than PackIt III. By fall, .sit had become a dominant Macintosh standard.

I would say that there were two particularly memorable experiences during my subsequent work on StuffIt. The major one was, of course, the initial effort to establish the product as a standard. The other memorable experience, or rather series of experiences, was the transition from a shareware to a commercial product. The lessons learned here are too numerous to list. I've learned several lessons about creating a decent piece of software. Perhaps the most important is: If it isn't easy to use, people will not use it. StuffIt was born in a power-user environment, and quite a few interface enhancements and feature set simplifications were needed along the way. How many jokes have been made about the difficulty of programming a VCR? Along the same lines, there is something to be said about polish. By this I mean that a good piece of software should be pleasant and smooth to use. I am a self-professed utilitarian, but I've now come to believe that the extra effort needed for the final 10 percent is a must for a good product. Putting the finishing touches on a piece of software has also taught

I've learned several lessons about creating a decent piece of software. Perhaps the most important is: If it isn't easy to use, people will not use it.

me some of my own limitations. I am not that good of an artist, but fortunately, in an advanced society like ours, specialization is the norm and not the exception.

Maclopedia: How did you get the word out about your creations?

Ray: To this date, I am surprised that word got out at all. Certainly, I wasn't a major marketing and distribution powerhouse. All I did was post the early versions on CompuServe, GEnie, Delphi, and several local BBSs. At some point, several New York based BBSs started accepting uploads in .sit, and shortly thereafter, one of the commercial services and then the others followed. Why things worked out is a question to which I will probably never learn the definitive answer. Some of the favorable factors included: 1) The dominant driving forces behind the online community at the time were what might be considered the Macintosh power users, who were more receptive to adopting new standards if technological merits warranted, and 2) The previous standard, PackIt III, did not appear to be actively supported, whereas I exhibited a clear willingness to continue supporting StuffIt.

Maclopedia: Can you tell us about some of the engineers you've met or worked with, to give us a glimpse behind the scenes of the culture that spawned the Mac?

Ray: My personal experiences with people who worked for Apple itself were far and few in between, so I am going to take some liberty and instead mention a fellow programmer who is a true hacker in the Macintosh tradition. This person is Leonard Rosenthal, who Aladdin, my publisher, was fortunate enough to have hired. This was a person who would never tire of playing with the latest system software enhancements Apple has to offer, who would come up with trick after trick, and who knows almost everyone in the Macintosh software engineering community. We met via email, exchanging ideas and comments about each others' products. Because we lived in different cities, it wasn't until years later that we met in person. But Leonard would have an answer—be it the correct answer, a decent guess, or a referral to someone else in the know—to every Mac-related programming question I had ever sent his way. And best of all, he

continues

S

would respond very promptly to email. Leonard is also one of the truly best prototypers I've seen. You give him a new API from Apple and within short order, he will have some neat demo employing the new technology.

Maclopedia: Where do you see the Mac's strengths now, and where would you advise the company to go in the future?

Ray: Despite the arrival of Windows 95, I still believe that the Mac remains a smoother, easier, and more pleasant to use platform. Sure, there are some features in Windows which the Mac lacks, but consider doing something as mundane as simple file sharing between two computers on anything but a Mac. The few features which the MacOS lacks can be easily implemented by Apple. I would say that the Mac's greatest strength is probably the loyal support of its users. It is hard to put a finger on exactly why there is an almost cult-like following among many. Perhaps this is so because of its elegance or maybe even because of its status as the alternative OS. Nevertheless, the following needs to be maintained. I guess I am admittedly a power user, so I may not be in the best position to judge how Apple can maintain this loyalty.

As far as my loyalty is concerned, I would say that Apple needs to maintain favorable price/performance profiles, particularly at the high performance end of the scale (Pentium Pros are pretty damn impressive in performance at a reasonable cost), maintain a competitive position in terms of software availability (this unfortunately seems to be a particularly vulnerable area), and aggressively roll out improvements in the MacOS, especially in terms of reliability and performance in multitasking environments (I reboot my Mac several times a day due to crashes. I reboot my Sun UNIX-based workstation once every few weeks).

unstuff it, even if she doesn't own StuffIt. Self-extracting archives are very popular on **online services** and on the **Internet**, and **America Online** has adopted StuffIt as its compression utility of choice.

If you upload multiple files, AOL's software stuffs (compresses) these files, and if you download a stuffed file, AOL's software unstuffs it for you.

You can tell a file is stuffed if the filename extension .sit follows the filename. If, for example, you compressed a graphic file named "fish" with StuffIt, it would then be named "fish.sit" to alert you, or anyone else, that the file was compressed using StuffIt. If the file was compressed as a self-extracting archive, the filename would be either "fish.sea" or "fish.sit.sea".

The following figure shows how you can set up StuffIt to unstuff with a password only.

A freeware utility called "StuffIt Expander" was introduced a few years back by Aladdin Systems that enables you to unstuff any StuffIt file by dragging the **icon** of the stuffed file and dropping it on the icon of the StuffIt Expander. The nice thing is, this expander decompresses most any compressed file you drop on it, not just StuffIt files, so it's not uncommon to see this utility out on a user's **desktop** for instant decompression. Or, as I'm sure Aladdin Systems would prefer, Unstuffing.

See Also

America Online; Compression Utilities; Desktop; Drag-and-Drop; Internet; .sea Filename Extension

When you create an .sea, a small decompression utility is embedded within the stuffed file, adding 5K to the file. This utility enables the recipient of the file to

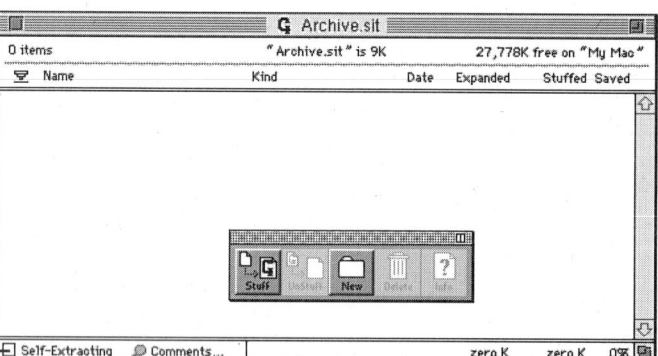

Self-Extracting Archive button

StuffIt Expander

Freeware program by Aladdin Systems, Inc. that expands **compressed** or **encoded files** downloaded from the **Internet**.

One of the Internet's main benefits is the availability of software held on host computers such as **software archives**. Users can download this software to their own **client** computer. Usually the software is encoded or compressed to facilitate transportation. Such files can then be decoded or decompressed with StuffIt Expander, which is a freeware program available on the Internet.

StuffIt Expander will expand files encoded with BinHex 4.0, which have the file extension ".hqx," as well as the compression formats used by StuffIt (.sit) and CompactPro (.cpt).

A related application, DropStuff with Expander Enhancer, provides StuffIt Expander with native PowerPC decompression code and allows it to expand a wider range of files than it could otherwise.

Both DropStuff and StuffIt Expander can be downloaded from **ftp://ftp.aladdinsys.com/pub/**.

See Also

Compressing Files; Encoding Files; Internet; Server

Style Sheets

If you do anything with a word processor beyond writing the most basic letters or term papers, learning to use style sheets will save you many hours otherwise spent in formatting text. Style sheets let you maintain consistent formatting through long documents, or through multi-document projects. Aside from being easier to read and follow, a consistently formatted document looks more professional. Whether you're working on a newsletter, a report to stockholders, or a lost cat poster, appearance matters. It tells your reader, "Hey, I know what I'm doing here."

A style sheet lets you apply character and paragraph formats all at once by selecting the text and then selecting the appropriate style to apply to it. With just a mouse click, you can turn a random page of text into 12 point Palatino Bold italic in magenta, set flush left, single spaced, with the first line indented .2", space before 12 pt, space after 6 pt. Isn't that easier than applying all of those attributes one at a time, and remembering them all so that you can assign them to the next similar block of text? Obviously, it is. All of the current versions of stand-alone word processors and DTP programs use style sheets. Works programs, unfortunately, do not.

A style sheet is a collection of style definitions. Each style definition, which is usually just called a style, refers to one very specific set of attributes. Typically a style sheet will include one or more styles for headlines, one for text, and as many as are needed for table heads, tables, and captions. Reformatting the document is simple after styles are assigned. Suppose you're working on a book like this one, and you decide that subheads, rather than being set in bold face, will be set in italics. Going through the manuscript and changing each one could take days. But, assuming that you have properly assigned the definition to all of the subheads, if you change the style definition, every one of the subheads will update to reflect the change. If you have created styles that are based on other styles, changing the original will change every style based on it, as well.

When you open a new document, unless you've already specified a style sheet to apply to it, your page will be set in the style called Normal, or possibly Untitled or Default, depending on the program. This style applies your word processor's default font, size, and other characteristics when nothing else is specified. If your new pages always start out with 12 point Geneva, set flush left, and single spaced, those are your default settings. Each word processor sets its defaults differently. In Microsoft Word 6, they're defined in the Font dialog box shown in the figure. In Word Perfect, you choose a font and size from the Font menu in Preferences.

S

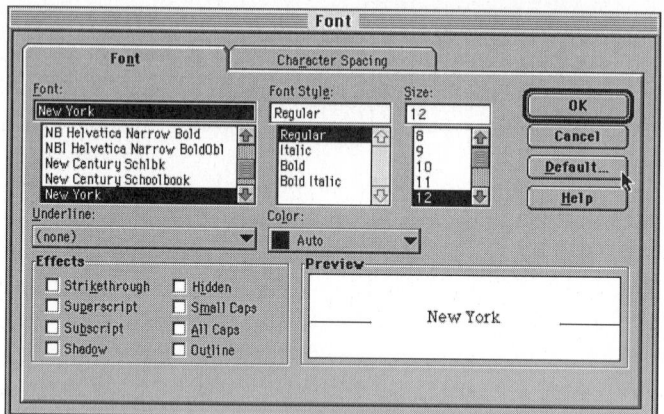

There are two kinds of styles that you'll be concerned with: character styles and paragraph styles. Character styles define *only* the character itself—its font, size, color, and so on. In the preceding sentence, for example, we applied a character style to the word "only." Paragraph styles define these things and also the position of the words on the page, including alignment, indents, whether to hyphenate words, whether to apply widow and orphan controls, and how much space to place between paragraphs. Paragraph styles always apply to the entire paragraph. Styled text (text that has styles applied to it) carries the style information as an invisible part of the document. If you copy styled text into a new document, the styles will be copied along with the text and added to that document's style sheet.

See Also

Styles in Word Processors

Styles in Word Processors

Styles, Applying to Text Styles can be applied in several ways. The most obvious is to select the name of the style from the list of available styles, and then, when you enter text, it will appear in the chosen style. Some word processors, notably Microsoft Word, place a style list on the toolbar for quick access. You also can find the style list in a dialog box. An easier way is to let the first style you apply set the styles for the rest of the document. Often, a paragraph formatted with

a particular style is routinely followed by another paragraph that also has a particular style. In a newspaper story, for example, the headline is followed by a byline and then the text of the story. After you create the style for the headline, using the "next style" option lets you define the byline style as the one that always follows the headline. Then, assign the text style as "next" after the byline style. When you press Return after typing the headline, the word processor will automatically apply the next style, which is the byline style, and so on. Text is most often followed by more text, so the style you'd specify there would be "next" style, "same" style.

Styles, Creating When you create styles for a style sheet, you'll more often be concerned with paragraph styles than with character styles. Paragraph styles apply to the entire paragraph, while character styles only apply to an individual character or word. There are also "override" styles, which are changes you make to a document by adjusting the ruler settings, or by choosing a new font, or type size or style from the menu. These take precedence over the styles you have previously applied.

Each word processor creates styles in a slightly different way, and all of them give you at least two ways to do it. One way, which is generally available in all word processors, is to open the Style dialog box. It may be located on a Style menu, as in Nisus Writer, or under the Format menu as in Microsoft Word 6, or the Custom menu in WriteNow 4.0. Create a style from scratch by selecting its attributes from the Style dialog box. The figure that follows shows how this looks in Microsoft Word 6.

The "next" style or "style for following paragraph" is a handy feature. If you're going to be working with a document that uses several levels of headings and subheads within the text, you can save time by letting the heading style include the information that the next style to apply is the text style.

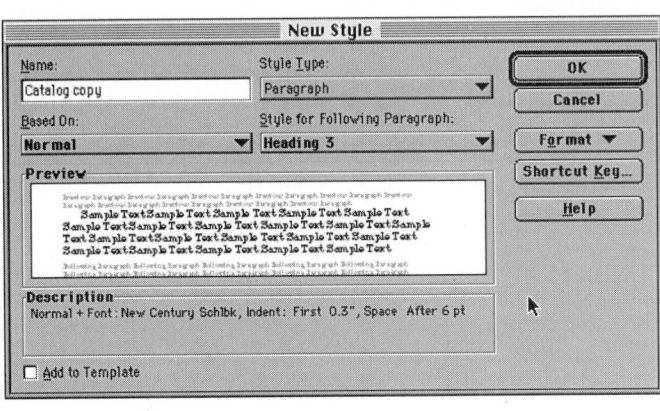

By doing so, you don't have to stop and change your style after you've entered the heading. You can go right on typing. Similarly, the text style generally uses the "same" style as the style for the following paragraph, so you can keep writing without going back to the style sheet. You can even format a table, without returning to the style list, by starting with the table heading style, making the next style the table style, and the next from that the table caption style.

The other way to create a style is by example. First, create your document by using the basic text formatting techniques to change the default text style, including its font, alignment, spacing, and so on. When you have achieved a style you want to preserve for future use, select a piece of the text as an example. Open the paragraph styles dialog box and select New. You'll see the attributes of your new style displayed. Name it and click OK to save it.

Styles, Modifying After you've assigned a style to a piece of text, that doesn't mean you're stuck with it forever. You can modify the paragraph style you've assigned by changing its attributes. You can modify a piece of text within the paragraph, without changing the rest of the paragraph, by applying a character style, or you can make a one time change, without disturbing any of the rest of the formatting, by using an override style.

You can think of these three different kinds of styles as being three levels of priority.

Paragraph styles have the lowest priority. They are the basic margin, indent, font, size, and style settings that are saved and used to format the paragraph. They can be saved, copied from one document into another, and redefined. When a paragraph style is redefined, every instance in which that style appears in the document will be updated automatically.

Character styles have the next higher level of priority. They let you define a font, style, color, or size for a key word or phrase. Use a character style to preserve the original format of any piece of text that you don't want to change when you redefine the underlying style. Like paragraph styles, character styles can be saved, redefined, and copied into other documents. They also update automatically when they are redefined.

Override styles have the highest level of priority. As the name implies, an override style overrides both paragraph and character styles that have already been applied. Override styles are used for a one time, one place change. They can't be saved as styles, and they don't apply to any text except that which has been selected to be overridden.

To modify an existing paragraph style, open the Style dialog box and look for a button labeled Edit or Modify. Make the changes you want and click OK to confirm them. Every paragraph to which the style was applied will change automatically to reflect the modification. Microsoft Word gives you a shortcut to accomplish this. Modify a piece of text. With the text selected, click the style listing on the toolbar.

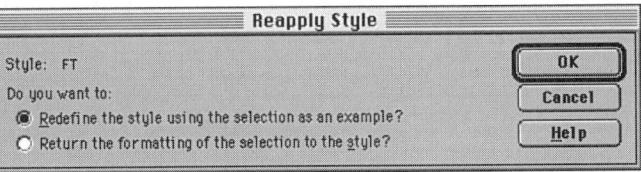

S

You'll see a dialog box, like the one in the figure, titled Reapply Style asking you whether you want to change the style to match the selection or reapply the existing style to the selected text.

See Also

Style Sheets

StyleWriter Extension

This is a printer driver necessary for **printing** to an Apple StyleWriter. The StyleWriter printer driver is accessed through the **Chooser** on the **Apple menu**. To select a StyleWriter as your printer, simply **click** the StyleWriter **icon** in the Chooser window.

See Also

Apple Menu; Chooser; Click; Icon; Printing

Stylus, *See Graphics Tablet*

Submenus

Some **menus** items have a black triangle pointing right. This tells you that the menu has a submenu. When you drag the **cursor** over a **menu item** with a black triangle and pause, a submenu menu appears, enabling you to choose an item from a list. If, for example, you're working in a word processor and want to change the point size of your type, you look on the Text menu. You may see menu items named Font, Size, Type, and so on, and beside each one is a black right-pointing triangle. If you select Size, a listing of available sizes pops up, and you can **drag** your cursor directly to the size you want. Releasing the **mouse button** carries out your size change.

To use a submenu, follow these steps:

1. Click and hold a menu item that has a right-pointing triangle.

2. A submenu pops up. Drag your cursor directly to the item in the pop-down menu you want to select.

3. Release the mouse button to make your selection.

See Also

Cursor; Drag-and-Drop; Menu; Mouse

Sub-Pixel Averaging

Any program that creates bit-mapped images generates **pixels** (the smallest elements that make up the picture). When generating these images—whether creating them from models in a 3D program, resizing a graphic in a graphic imaging program, or applying an effect in a QuickTime editing program—the software has to choose the color for each pixel; however, the color is only an approximation of the what the color should be. Sub-pixel averaging creates a more accurate color by calculating the colors of different areas that the pixel covers in the image and averaging them.

If, for example, a 3D program generates the same image at 72 dpi and 144 dpi, one pixel in the first image would be represented by four pixels in the second image. By averaging the color values of the four pixels at 144 dpi, a more accurate color is calculated for the single pixel in the 72 dpi image.

Sub-pixel averaging improves the appearance of images, but takes longer to create.

See Also

Pixel

Subscribing to a Newsgroup, *See Newsgroups, Subscribing*

Subscript, *See Typesetting Terms*

Subtractive Color

Subtractive color refers to the **process color** model (CMYK) in which 100 percent cyan, magenta, and yellow combine to make black. Due to impurities in printing inks, this black is not a true black but more of a very dark brown. For this reason, true black ink is added to process colors for printing and is represented by the "K," which stands for **key color**.

See Also
Color Printing; Color Separations; Process Color

Subwoofers

It takes a large speaker to make a low note. As frequencies go down, bigger masses of air have to be moved for the same loudness. The laws of physics insist that a speaker small enough to mount next to a monitor isn't capable of full bass. Fortunately, those same laws make it harder to tell where the low notes are coming from.

Multimedia manufacturers take advantage of both these facts with three-piece systems. Two small **speakers** are placed near the monitor to handle midrange and treble, while a third bass speaker is hidden out of the way. You get a directional, stereo signal centered around the video screen with all the oomph of a large bass cabinet.

Subwoofers can be added to any speakers, and make a satisfying upgrade for serious multimedia users. A few three-piece systems use very tiny satellite speakers near the monitor, and a tuned subwoofer that attempts to carry some of the midrange signal as well. These can be impressive in demos with carefully-chosen music, but be unsatisfactory when playing midrange-heavy, voice-oriented multimedia.

The high and low signals are separated electrically at the subwoofer. This complicates wiring slightly, because you have to run cables from the **CPU** to the subwoofer, and then from the subwoofer to the speakers. In most cases the **amplifier** is also located at the subwoofer, which puts the controls in an awkward place—often, under a desk or in a corner of the workspace. A more sophisticated bi-amplification system, used in high-end auto sound and a few multimedia systems, has separate amplifier-and-control unit you can place on your desk. Wires go from the CPU to the control unit, and then to each of the three speakers.

Physical location can make a big difference in subwoofer efficiency. The best place is the corner of a room, where large wall surfaces reflect and reinforce the bass signal. This might not be practical in a computer setting, and most subwoofers come with suggestions for alternate placement.

It's best to test many locations to see which will sound best. If you're reluctant to move a heavy loudspeaker around the room for testing, put the speaker near the computer keyboard (close to where your ears would be), play some music, and move your head to each potential speaker location. See which provides the fullest bass. It may seem silly to crawl around, sticking your head into corners of the workspace, but a similar strategy is often used by professionals.

See Also
Speaker, Buying; Speaker, Connecting; Speaker, Shielding

Suitcase

Suitcase is a font-management **utility**, from Symantec (10201 Torre Ave, Cupertino, CA, 95104-2132, Phone (800) 441-7234 Web site at **http://www.symantec.com**) that enables you to use and organize fonts outside the Fonts folder within your System Folder. One of the main benefits of Suitcase is that it enables you to create font sets. You can create a set of fonts for a particular task or for particular client job if you're a designer, and you can open and close these sets on demand through Suitcase.

If, for example, you are working on a design job for a client, and her logo uses the fonts Frutiger, Commercial Script, and Helvetica Inserat Roman, you can create a set containing just those three fonts, and when you're working on her jobs, you can have her font set temporarily open. This way, if you don't use those three fonts on a regular basis, you don't have to have them open all the time, but when you need them, they're easily accessible.

Suitcase offers a host of other font management utilities, including viewing and renumbering **font ID numbers** (in the latest version, 3.0, this renumbering is temporary and is done automatically), creating and renaming font sets, viewing the contents of a particular suitcase, and creating empty suitcases. Suitcase also enables you to set a preference that puts Suitcase in the Apple menu, and you can request that it be the top item on the menu.

In the latest version of Suitcase (version 3.0) you can now designate specific fonts to be open when a particular application is launched. You could, for example, designate that only Helvetica and Times be opened anytime you launch Stickies.

See Also

Font; Font Utility; Master Juggler; Utility

Suite Programs, *See Works Programs*

SuperCard 2.5

Allegient's SuperCard is very similar to **HyperCard** (read HyperCard, Metaphor), with several powerful additions. SuperCard supports color graphics within the application and has its own color paint tools. Although a HyperCard stack can only be displayed in one window, a SuperCard project can contain several windows, each containing a different collection of cards. This makes it possible to create much more complicated and interesting projects.

SuperCard suffered a period of poor support after its original publisher (Silicon Beach Software) was purchased by Aldus, and Aldus didn't really know what to do with SuperCard. The product was then sold to Allegient Technologies, which has done a lot of work to support and improve it. They recently shipped a Windows Player and **Marionet**, an Internet scripting collection of routines.

SuperCard's language, SuperTalk, is a superset of **HyperTalk**. Most HyperTalk instructions work directly in SuperCard, but SuperTalk adds several new language instructions that are unique to SuperCard's special features. For an introduction to scripting, read **Scripting**.

SuperCard also supports most HyperCard **XCMDs** and **XFCNs**, making it possible to add functionality to SuperCard.

Definitely consider SuperCard if you have a complicated project that requires color or multiple windows.

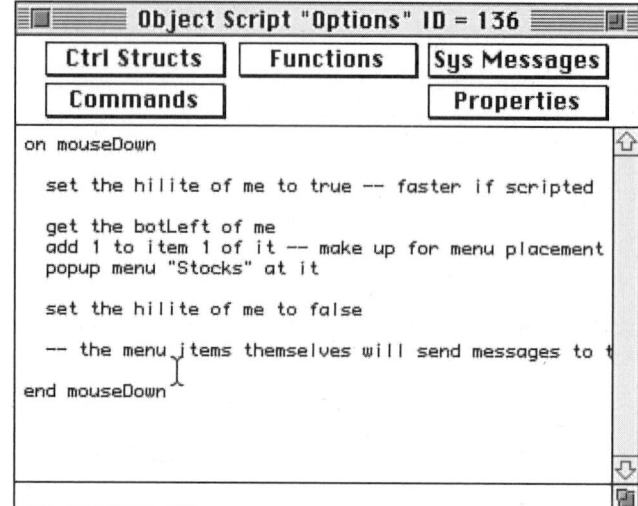

See Also

HyperCard; XCMDs

Superscript, *See Typesetting Terms*

SuperTalk

The scripting language used in **SuperCard**. It is a superset of the scripting language **HyperTalk** (the language used in HyperCard).

See Also

Scripting; SuperCard 2.5; XCMDs

Supra SupraFaxModem, *See Modems*

Surround Sound, *See Spatial Enhancement*

Swap and Select

"Swap" and "Select" are two separate but connected programs from Human Software. Each addresses the color parameters of your selected graphic. Both Swap and Select require about 8MB of RAM on top of that required to run Photoshop. It's absolutely essential to any process that adjusts the color of an on-screen graphic that your monitor is color corrected to begin with. Kodak and other companies market various utilities that do this as part of the startup sequence. The older a monitor becomes, the more chance there is that its color display does not represent the true colors of an image for either video or print applications, no matter what color correction resides in the startup sequence. Keep this in mind when working with the following software, and any other software used to color adjust an image. Swap and Select looks as if it were designed for PAL screens, and its interface may not be totally visible on many RGB monitors. All that will be hidden, however, are non-essential parts of the interface.

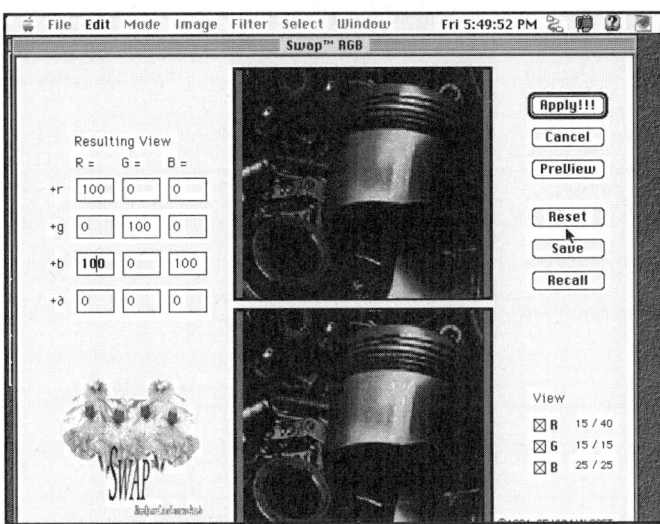

Swap Human Software's Swap is used to color correct either RGB or CMYK images in Photoshop or other software that accepts Photoshop plug-ins. When the initial Swap screen comes up, two choices are presented: Gradation and Swap. Gradation works only on CMYK (Cyan, Magenta, Yellow, and Black: associated with the four color printing process) palettes, while the Swap option works on RGB (Red, Blue, Green: associated with three color video signals) and

CMYK. The two choices have different interfaces. The Swap interface has what appears to be convolution controls (called "equations"), while the Gradation interface has four separate control splines for adjusting each of the CMYK gradation curves respectively.

Swap's Gradation choice works only with a CMYK picture, although you can translate RGB to CMYK, adjust the Swap gradation curves, and retranslate to RGB. RGB colorization methods are different from CMYK, however, and discrete changes may result. If you check all of the CMYK boxes next to the four CMYK curves, changes made on one curve will be applied to all others. All curves checked simultaneously will be altered exactly the same, giving you global as well as plate-by-plate control over adjustments. Adjusting the CMYK curves either singly or in groups changes the visual preview, allowing you to make exacting changes numerically and by eye. Numeric indicators next to each CMYK curve indicate the extent of the levels being changed. Image effects such as solarization and inverses can be created as well as color adjustments. Curve points are adjusted by clicking on them and moving them up or down with the mouse. Each curve, called a LUT spline, has five default points that can be manipulated. You can also add or delete points on the curve. Each plate can be turned off so that you can view singular plates or any desired mix.

The Swap option allows you to adjust the image color by applying a convolution equation, presented as a matrix of numbers that can be altered. As with Gradation, the preview shows the visual results of all manipulations. The best way to gain mastery over adjusting the convolution matrix is to see how it is configured when you use one of the preset library settings. These are available only for CMYK pictures, and include duotones, tritones, and other colorization effects. As you select each one, the matrix table changes accordingly and the preview

S

screen is updated. The Swap plug-in manual, although small, covers the technical applications possible with this software quite fully, although only experimentation and time will give you a real feel for what it can do.

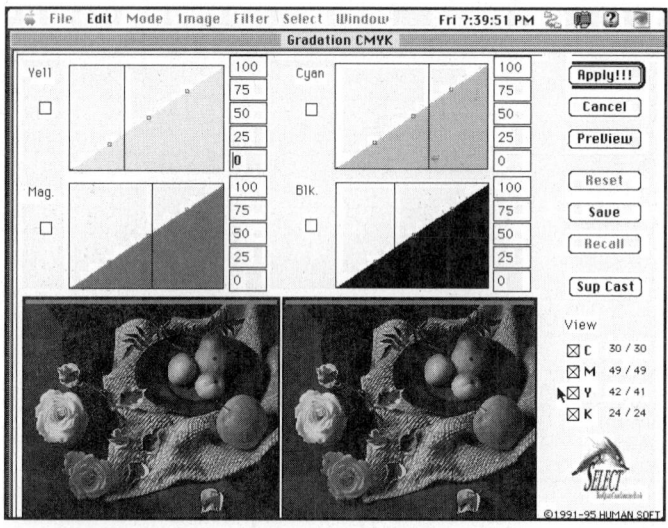

Select "Select" from Human Software is a high-end CMYK global and selective color correction plug-in for Photoshop and other Photoshop plug-in compatible software. It has both a Gradation and a Selective mode. The Gradation mode can be compared to Swap, except that selections of color can be taken from an eye-dropper tool so that targeted colors can be specified more exactly. RGB users know that colors meant for the video screen have much more tolerated variance than those targeted to print, hence software like "Select" is not as important for video use as for the delicate color balances DTP users need and demand.

Both Swap and Select enable you to save and recall each of the CMYK color curves in the Gradation mode (just check the square next to that curve's screen), so you can build up an effects library on your own and apply it to later projects. As in Swap's Gradation mode, Select's Gradation curves can have points added (Shift and click) and deleted (⌘-click). The Selective CMYK mode of Select gives you more precise control over each targeted color in the graphic, and allows you to choose that color with an eye-dropper tool right from

the visual display. Before and after images are shown, so that it's always possible to compare the alterations. A reset button brings all changes back to zero. Color boxes indicate the before and after colors, and the preview writes these alterations to the after image. A standard RGB color picker responds to mouse clicks in the before/after color boxes. There are six possible color changes that can be targeted at any one time. Blends are added to the color changes in either a cubic or a square choice. The cubic option applies the changes more globally across the image.

Because of its CMYK dedication, Human Software's Select is obviously geared more towards the DTP artist. It applies color changes so finely, however, that RGB artists (video output oriented) should also consider it as an essential tool. An RGB image can always be translated to CMYK and back again, and the color transformation capabilities of this software are of a very high quality.

Sweeping, *See Modeling*

Switches, *See Bridges*

SYLK, *See Import/Export, Spreadsheet*

SYM File, *See Debugging Tools*

Symantec AntiVirus for Macintosh (SAM)

SAM consists of an application and an INIT. The INIT sits on your Macintosh and scans inserted disks and monitors other activities that viruses use to infect files. When SAM encounters a known virus, it stops it and notifies the user with an alert box. In the case of an infected floppy disk, the user's only allowable response is to eject the disk.

When SAM is confronted by a suspicious activity of an unknown nature, an alert box is displayed and you can choose what action to take. Allowing the action lets it proceed just this once. Denying the action prevents it from completing. The Learn function adds this action to SAM's database of allowable activity so that it doesn't have to ask you again. Although monitoring the Mac's operation against known viruses is useful, showing a dialog every time some possibly legitimate but suspicious-looking activity occurs can be irritating to experienced users and cause unnecessary panic among novices.

Although all antivirus utilities can scan disks with driver-level compression, SAM also has the ability to scan compressed archives created with StuffIt and Compact Pro. Furthermore, SAM can detect viruses in HyperCard stacks. SAM supports the entry of code strings that allow it to detect (but not remove) new viruses.

Symbols

Many **fonts** include symbols such as bullets, foreign characters, mathematical symbols, and other nonstandard characters. There's also a font called Symbol, which contains the Greek alphabet in upper- and lowercase, as well as other common symbols. These can be combined with regular fonts when necessary to describe equations, or when a particular symbol is needed. *Dingbats* are a kind of symbol used by typographers to denote the end of a section or chapter.

Several other fonts, such as Zapf Dingbats and Cairo, provide other symbols, some of which can be used for fun.

Symantec C++

An **Integrated Development Environment** from Symantec.

The name Symantec C++ is a bit of a misnomer, as this development environment includes much more than just a **C++ compiler**. Symantec C++ is centered on the Symantec Project Manager (SPM), an IDE that includes several compilers and linkers, a source code **editor**, and a **browser** (see the following figure). This environment is the successor to the very popular THINK C product.

The Symantec Project Manager uses **Apple Events** to communicate with several other tools, including an **interface builder**, **Visual Architect**, and a high-level symbolic **debugger**. Visual Architect takes advantage of Symantec's C++ **framework**, the Think Class Library (or TCL).

Symantec C++ includes a multitude of tools other than the C++ compiler that gives it its name. Symantec **Caffeine**, a **Java** compiler, is the latest addition. Also, several third-party compilers have been written for the Symantec Project Manager.

Symantec's IDE has a number of very nice features. Project windows (at the upper right in the figure) are customizable and show a great deal of information about each file in the project. Projects also contain subprojects that are automatically brought up to date and built when the parent project is compiled. This enables the IDE to handle complex projects that traditionally have been very difficult to handle with an IDE.

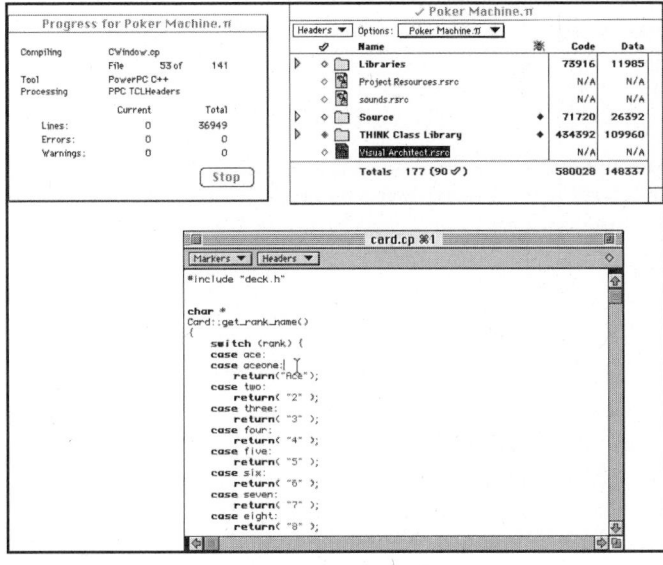

The Symantec Project Manager enables you to create option sets that you can save with your projects. If you find yourself toggling between two groups of preferences (for debugging and nondebugging version of an application, for example), this can be a real time-saver.

Symantec C++ is a subscription product distributed on CD-ROM. The CD-ROM includes an electronic **toolbox** reference, **THINK Reference**, and THINK Pascal, a 68K-only Pascal IDE no longer supported by Symantec.

> Symantec Corporation
> 10201 Torre Avenue, Cupertino, CA 95014-2132
> Fax: (408) 253-3968 Fax Marketing
> Phone :(408) 253-9600
> Email: **devtools@symantec.com**
> Web: **http://www.symantec.com/lit/dev/ dev.html**

See Also
C++; Integrated Development Environment

Symmetrical Compressors

Compressors can be divided into two broad categories of performance: symmetrical and **asymmetrical**.

Symmetrical compressors take approximately the same amount of time to compress and decompress a video sequence. This means that they can be used to capture video in real time. The **Apple Video Compressor** is asymmetrical.

See Also
Apple Video Compressor; Asymmetrical Compressor; Compression

Synchronous Communication

Transmissions between computing devices can take place either synchronously or asynchronously. In a synchronous transmission, data transfer can take place at very high speeds through the use of electronic clock signals to break the transmission into strictly defined intervals. This type of transfer is not supported by

most modems, and is generally found in Macintosh environments only when connecting a high speed wide area networking device, such as an ISDN terminal adapter or a T-1 CSU/DSU to a network router. As ISDN modem lines become more readily available, we can expect to see more telecommunication software that supports this option.

See Also
Asynchronous Data Transfers; Asynchronous Communication

Synthetic Fonts

Why buy **fonts** when you can just mix up your own? Products like FontChameleon allow users to synthesize fonts based on a set of master outlines that can be stretched and otherwise altered to look like classic designs or like nothing in this world.

By saving the settings used to create fonts, users can recreate them at any time—there's no need to store them on your hard drive when you don't need them. This technology is particularly useful when sending electronic documents to other users, who don't have to have the fonts you used—only their descriptions so they can make their own versions. The description files are tiny (only a few kilobytes) and can be embedded in documents.

The quality of fonts created this way can't match that of true designed fonts, but the technology will certainly come in handy in these days of electronic distribution of documents.

See Also
Fonts

SyQuest Cartridges, *See Backing Up with Removable Cartridge Drives*

SyQuest Drive

SyQuest drives utilize cartridges that can contain up to 44MB of data. Disks are coated with a nickel-cadmium slurry, and spin over 4,000 rpm to get rid of dust before settling in at a 3,260 rpm operating speed. Although the drives are initially expensive, disks are fairly cheap, making this an economical way to add space to your hard disk. The following figure shows a SyQuest drive.

See Also

Disks and Drives; ZIP Drives

System 7.0

Apple's System 7 was a new release of the **System software** and the first major overhaul of the Mac's operating system since System 6 was introduced in 1988. System 7 was a giant step forward for the Macintosh operating system, and it included a variety of important technologies and features, including:

- A redesigned **System Folder** that included system subfolders to help organize the system. In System 6, all items in the System Folder floated freely. In System 7, they are segregated into separate folders to make working with the System much easier. In System 7, control panels are stored in the **Control Panels folder**, extensions are stored in the **Extensions folder**, Preferences are stored in the **Preferences folder**, and so on.

- In System 6, **fonts** and **desk accessories** (DAs) were manually loaded into the System file using the **Font/DA Mover** utility. System 7.0 makes the Font/DA Mover virtually obsolete because you can store fonts in the System folder, and DAs (which appear on the **Apple menu**) can be installed by dragging the DA (or almost any application) into the **Apple Menu Items folder**.

- System 7 also introduced **aliases**: a copy of an icon that looks and works like the real

document or application but is actually a pointer to the real application. The advantage is you can have these alias pointers anywhere you want and as many as you want because they take up so little room. You can put aliases of applications in your Apple menu, out on your **desktop**; virtually anywhere you'd like.

- System 7 introduced an enhanced look for **icons** and enabled full color icons for documents and applications, and most notably it enabled you to **copy** and **paste** icons between the Get Info boxes of files and folders without the use of Apple's **ResEdit** resource editing utility. Other Finder enhancements enable you to choose the font you want your names displayed in and to have your fonts snap to a staggered grid.

- Some of the Apple Menu Items were updated, including the **Scrapbook**, the **Chooser**, and a more advanced **Find File** function was added that can be accessed through a standard key command (⌘-F).

- **File sharing** and networking capabilities were added as standard features in System 7.

- A **label menu** was added enabling you to color-code items for visual organization. The folder icons are now a solid color and are easily colorized using this feature. You can use the standard colors or create custom label colors, and you can give the labels a name. The new Find Function of System 7 is capable of finding similarly labeled items.

- System 7 introduced **Balloon Help**, an interactive type of help feature designed for beginners that enables you to point at an object and have a cartoon-like balloon appear with simple explanation of what the selected item does. Balloon Help is accessed from the **Help menu** in the **menu bar**.

- In System 7 you have the ability to see icons in **list views**, and determine in which of the

S

three available sizes you want to view these icons. You can also jump to any file in a list view (or icon view, for that matter) by pressing the first letter of the filename. If, for example, you're looking at a window with files named after the calendar months, the name at the top of the list would be April. To jump to September, you press the letter S, and the window jumps to the first alphabetical file that starts with S.

- In System 6, you could have only one application open at a time. If you wanted multiple applications open, you had to turn on MultiFinder. System 7 made the MultiFinder environment permanent, enabling you to have multiple applications open and be able to return to the Finder at any time without quitting an application.

- In System 7, Apple added the capability to use Apple's new font technology called **TrueType**, which enables you to resize fonts to any size on-screen and to printers that supported True Type with smooth clean output. TrueType fonts include both the printer font and the screen font in one suitcase.

- A new printing architecture was introduced with System 7 that enabled faster printing and printing of documents in the background while you worked. This **print spooling** was already available through third-party utilities, but Apple built it in as part of System 7.

- System 7 introduced **Publish and Subscribe**, which enables you to link certain items in documents together, so if you updated the information in one document, the other document would be updated for you. If, for example, you create a graphic and place it in 15 other documents using Publish and Subscribe, any edits or changes to the graphic would also be made in the 15 documents in which the graphic was placed.

- System 7 added **32-bit addressing**, which enables you to use more than the 8MB limit for system RAM imposed by System 6. System 7 also introduced **virtual memory**, which enables you to use the available hard disk as if it were RAM.

- There are dozens of other small enhancements (such as a new gray trash can icon) and other speed and productivity features, plus updated control panels, extensions, and system add-ons that make up System 7.

See Also

32-Bit Addressing; Apple Menu; Apple Menu Items; Balloon Help; Chooser; Control Panels; Desk Accessories; Desktop; Extensions Folder; File Sharing; Find File; Font/DA Mover; Help Menu; Icons; Label Menu; List Views; Menu Bar; Publish and Subscribe; ResEdit; System Folder; TrueType

System 7.0.1P

System 7.0.1P is the **Performa** model version of System 7.0.1. The System 7.0.1 update was introduced to support the **Quadras**, **PowerBooks**, and **Mac Classic II** models. There were Performa versions of the Quadras and the Mac Classic II that needed this update that included a minor enhancement for Macs with a **floating point coprocessor** (FPU).

Apple added the letter P to the System update's name to denote it was for Performa models. The two systems are identical, with the exception being that the Performa models have certain features, which Apple added for the home market, that didn't appear in non-Performa versions of the software. These Performa-specific features include:

- A Documents folder and an Applications folder where the computer defaults to when users use an **Open** or **Save dialog box**. If, for example, the users create a new document and want to save it, when they choose **Save** or

Save As from the **File menu**, the documents folder opens by default. If the users go to the **Open menu** to open a new application, the Applications folder opens by default. The Documents folder is where the documents new users create on a Performa are stored. Apple marketed Performas to the first-time home computer users and feared the new users would lose their files or not be able to find the applications, so they encouraged the users to save all documents they created into one folder by making it the default.

- A built-in **Launcher** palette makes frequently used applications and documents available by **clicking** the large tile's icons. Apple was concerned that first-time computer users would not be able to find their documents or applications, so they made the Launcher a standard feature of the Performa System to keep users from digging through folders on their **hard disk**.

- Apple set the monitor depth settings default to 256 colors, whereas in other Mac systems, the default was Black and White, and users have to find the Monitors extension and change the monitor depth setting and choose a bit depth to color to see color on the screen.

- Application hiding, which hides all other applications if the user chooses a different application. It is a fool-proof way of invoking the Hide Application command any time the users choose an application.

- A file **backup** application with the Performa System called Apple Backup that offers only two choices: to back up the System Folder (because Apple didn't send out system disks with Performa models) and back up the entire disk. This enhancement is not packed with features, but it is very easy to use. If a Performa users need to retrieve files from a backup disk, they can use Apple Restore to get the files back.

- A simplified version of the **General Controls control panel** was added to the Performa System to enable easier selection of **desktop background patterns** for Performa users.

- Apple thought children would be big users of these at home Performas, so they included an extension called **At Ease** that put a new interface over the standard one. This interface, which consists of a giant file folder with square tiles, gives one-click access to specified applications and documents, making it easy for children to use the computer. This also prevents children from accessing important items such as the **System Folder** or Application folders where they might accidentally delete files, application, support files, or move important system files out of the System Folder. At Ease is a kind of buffer zone that lets anyone turn on the computer and use the programs without having to learn the interface or worry about damaging the system.

System 7 also comes with a separate Apple utility called the Compatibility Checker, which searches your installed system and hard disk (on System 6) and gives you a list of which applications and extensions are compatible with System 7 before you installed the system update.

See Also

At Ease; Control Panels; Desktop Patterns; File Menu; General Controls Control Panel; Hard Disks; Launcher; Open Command; Open Dialog Box; PowerBook; Save As Command; Save Command; System Folder

System 7.1

System 7.1 was a significant update to **System 7** that included new features, bug fixes, and enhancements to existing features, including:

- An enhanced version of Apple's **QuickTime** extension (version 1.5).

- The addition of WorldScript, which enables the Mac interface to be customized for foreign languages.

- The addition of a separate **Fonts folder** where fonts are installed by dragging them into the folder itself, or by dragging the fonts onto the icon of the **System Folder**. The system places the fonts in the font folder for you, and enables you to install fonts while other applications are running.

- An updated **PowerBook Control Panel** that includes a slider to control how long a period of inactivity will be before the PowerBook goes to **sleep**.

- Memory-handling enhancements, including the addition of a third memory control in the **Get Info box** of an application. This box states the minimum amount of memory, as determined by the software developer, that this program can operate with. In systems prior to 7.1, there were only two boxes: suggested size and preferred size.

- System Enablers, which are of no use to users but are critical to Apple because this is how Apple updates the system each time a new model is introduced without designing an entirely new system to work on that particular model. In the past, Apple had to issue updates to make certain systems work on certain models, but by using these enablers, existing systems can be patched into other models by creating a small enabler file for each model. Your computer cannot run System 7.1 without an enabler for your particular machine.

TIP System enablers are of great use to systems administrators, who are responsible for maintaining multiple Macs that otherwise would have different versions of the OS running on them.

See Also

Get Info Box; PowerBook Control Panel; QuickTime; System 7; System Folder

System 7.1.1

System 7.1.1 is an update of the **System software 7.1** known as Macintosh Hardware System Update 1.0. This update came in the form of an **extension** that addressed a number of areas including:

- The ejection of **disks** at **shutdown**.

- Fixed a bug that hampered high-speed modem transmissions.

- Enhanced performance in low memory situations.

- Fixed a bug in the system's internal clock to make it more accurate.

See Also

Disks and Drives; Extensions Folder; Shutdown Command; System 7.1

System 7.1.2

System 7.1.2 came in as another hardware system update (HSU) and addressed bugs, compatibility problems, and high-speed modem transmission problems in certain models. This update also included:

- A newly updated version of **Disk First Aid** (version 7.2).

- The **AutoRemounter** extension that reconnects you to a **network** if you have a **PowerBook** that goes to **sleep**.

- An update to the **Sound Manager**.

See Also

AutoRemounter Control Panel; Disk First Aid; Networking; PowerBook; Sleep Mode; Sound Manager

System 7.1.3

System 7.1.3 came into being as System Update 3.0. This update was a hardware bug fix and enhancement package released by Apple for **Systems 7.1**, **7.1.1**, and **7.1.2**. In addition to addressing a number of bugs, 7.1.3 included an update of all the **system enablers**, as well as:

- The capability to see small versions of the real **icons** of the files in **Open and Save dialog boxes.**

- A new version of Apple's bare bones text editor **TeachText** called **SimpleText**.

- A new version of **Apple HD SC Setup** (for formatting Apple **hard disks**).

- A number of updated **control panels** for both desktop Macs and **PowerBooks**.

- The updates and bug fixes found in Apple's System hardware updates 1.0, 2.0, and 2.1.

See Also

Apple HD SC Setup; Control Panels; Hard Disks; Icons; Open Dialog Box; PowerBook; SimpleText; System 7.1; TeachText

System 7.1P

This is the **Performa** version of the **System 7.1** operating system except that it contains a number of Performa-only features designed for the at-home, first-time computer user, including:

- Apple's **At Ease** interface, an interface offering one-click access to documents and applications through a series of large tiles. It also limits access to the Finder, which protects the **System Folder** and applications from being accidentally deleted.

- Apple's **Launcher** control panel, which works similarly to At Ease, but the Finder is active and the launcher floats above the **desktop**.

- A **General Controls control panel** with an easy to use desktop patterns picker.

- A Documents folder and an Applications folder that appear as the default in **Open and Save dialog boxes** so new users can more easily find the documents they create and find applications to launch without digging through folders.

- The **Monitors control panel** default setting is color/256 colors, rather than black-and-white on standard systems.

- A backup program for **backing up** the System Folder or all files on the disk.

- **Application hiding** so when a user switches applications, the other application is hidden from view.

See Also

At Ease; Desktop Pattern; File Menu; General Controls Control Panel; Hard Disks; Launcher; Open Dialog Box; Open Command; Save Command; Save As Command; System Folder

System 7.1P2

This **Performa** version of hardware system update (HSU) 2.0 for the System 7.1P and 7.1.P1 operating system is identical to the standard System 7.1.1, except that it contains a number of Performa-only features designed for the at-home first time computer user.

See Also

Consumer Models, Macintosh Family; System 7.1P

System 7.1P3

This Performa version of the **hardware system update** (HSU) **3.0** for the **System 7.1P**, 7.1.P1, and 7.1P2 operating systems is identical to the standard System 7.1, 7.1.1, and 7.1.2, except that it contains a number of Performa-only features designed for the at-home, first-time computer user.

S

See Also
System 7.1P

System 7.5

System 7.5 is an update to the Macintosh operating system that introduces a range of enhancements and new technologies, along with the usual bug fixes and performance tweaks. The new features of System 7.5 included:

- A built-in hierarchical submenu for the **Apple menu** activated through the **Apple Menu Options control panel**, which enables you to toggle the submenu feature on or off. It also adds up to three folders to the Apple menu that contain **aliases** of the most recently used documents, applications, and servers, so you can relaunch a document, application, or remount a **server** without searching for the files themselves.

- An electronic version of post-it notes called **Stickies**, which enables you to have on-screen notes in your choice of size and color.

- Macintosh's **Drag-and-Drop** technology, enabling you to drag and drop items between applications, including the Finder.

- A new version of the **NotePad DA** that adds a host of new features and functionality, including drag and drop, the capability to create longer notes, and print notes.

- The capability to use **AppleScript** to automate certain tasks of the Finder.

- A total re-work of the online help system called **AppleGuide**, which offers interactive on-screen help and walks you through features and functions.

- A greatly improved **Find function**, with more flexibility and a new interface.

- A **menu bar clock** that incorporates into the new **Date & Time control panel**. The menu bar clock is a reworking of the widely popular

shareware menu bar clock extension SuperClock that was a staple on many users' machines.

- A larger collection of **desktop patterns** utilized through a new utility/application called Desktop Patterns.

- A larger and updated **Jigsaw Puzzle DA** that enables you to copy and paste your own **PICT** graphic into the DA to use as a puzzle.

- An alias of the **Control Panels folder** that appears on the Apple menu itself and enables you to have instant access to individual control panels when the Apple menu submenus are activated.

- A new **PowerBook** feature called the **Control Strip**; a thin, floating palette that enables one-click access to a range of commonly used PowerBook features.

- An updated **Scrapbook DA** that accepts sound and video clips. The Scrapbook also gives you on-screen info on the items it contains (such as dimensions of the file, size of the file, format of the file, and so on).

- A **Numbers control panel** to enhance the Mac's use in foreign countries. This control panel enables you to configure the Mac to display numbers and currency in popular foreign formats. There's also a **Text control panel** enabling you to choose from different text formats for languages that write from right to left, top to bottom, and so on.

- The **WindowShade** feature that started life as a popular shareware utility. WindowShade enables you to roll-up a window so only its title bar is showing, much like you would roll up a traditional window shade, by double-clicking the window's title bar, even within applications. WindowShade's options are accessed through the WindowShade Control Panel.

- An enhanced ability to make multiple selections with a marquee (**clicking and dragging** with the **arrow pointer** cursor produces a rectangular marquee around objects in active windows). Now you can use the marquee to select items in a **list view**, rather than just the icon view, as in previous versions of the system.

- A freeware extension called the **Extensions Manager**, which was created by an Apple employee but not officially supported by Apple. This extension enables you to choose which extensions load into your system at **startup** and to create sets of extensions for different purposes or users.

- A new control panel called the **Auto On/Off control panel** that enables you to set a startup and **shutdown** time for your Macintosh, even if you're not there.

- The **QuickDraw GX** extension, which adds a wide array of printing, font management, typographic, and other features, including a new printing architecture that enables you to have printer drivers on your desktop where you can drag and drop items to be printed. QuickDraw GX incorporates a version of Adobe Type Manager (ATM) called ATM GX that is used for smooth display of fonts on-screen and for output. QuickDraw GX adds Apple's updated version of **ColorSync** (version 2.0), which is aimed at giving users a color matching system for achieving more predictable results when working in color. QuickDraw GX also opens the door for high-end typography with features such as use of ligatures, precise letter kerning, and a host of advanced typography features accessed by using specially designed GX enhanced fonts.

- The **MacTCP and TCP/IP** system extensions (which were sold separately) with System 7.5 for use with the **Internet**.

- An enhanced version of the **General Controls Control Panel** that enables you to protect the **System Folder** from being accessed or renamed. You can also protect your applications folders. This is particular useful if children are using the machine.

- Version 8.0 of the LaserWriter Driver (besides the GX version of the LaserWriter Extension), which offers enhanced printing and a new print spooling extension.

- The **PC Exchange** extension, which enables you to read, write, and format PC disks.

- An updated **Monitors control panel** so you can change monitor resolutions on-the-fly without having to restart your machine.

- **PowerTalk**, an electronic mail and messaging feature for use over networks.

Other enhancements in System 7.5 include faster copying of files, faster switching between applications, and faster displaying of menus.

See Also

Apple Menu; Apple Menu Items Folder; Arrow Pointer; AutoPower On/Off Control Panel; Click and Drag; ColorSync; Control Panels; Control Strip; Desktop; Extension Manager; Find File; General Controls Control Panel; Icon View; Jigsaw Puzzle; LaserWriter Driver; List View; Mac TCP; Monitors Control Panel; Note Pad; Numbers; PC Exchange; PowerBook; QuickDraw GX; Scrapbook; Shutdown; Stickies; Submenus; System Folder; WindowShade

System 7.5.1

This update of **System 7.5** includes bug fixes and a set of enhancements, including:

- **File sharing** performance boosted by as much as 400 percent by updated file sharing features.

- An updated LaserWriter driver (version 8.2) that includes enhanced PostScript fax capabilities.

- An improved version of the **Launcher** utility, now included with System 7.5, that enables you to add items to the Launcher by dragging and dropping them on tiles in the Launcher itself, rather than adding the items to the **Launcher Items folder** within the System Folder. You can also choose from three different-sized tiles in this enhanced version of the Launcher.

- A new **startup screen** that replaces the familiar "Welcome to Macintosh" startup screen and features Apple's new MacOS logo, which was introduced for use with Macintosh Clones. A status bar has been added to this startup screen to show the startup loading procedure.

- Improved performance from **Quick-Draw GX**.

- The capability to shutdown from the keyboard by pressing the PowerOn key while the computer is running. When the PowerOn key is pressed, a dialog box appears asking, "Are you sure you want to shut down your computer now?" The dialog box offers you the choice of shutting down or restarting.

See Also

File Sharing; LaserWriter Driver; Launcher Control Panel; PowerOn Key; QuickDraw GX; Restart; Shutdown Command; Startup Screen; System 7.5

System 7.5.2

This update to **System 7.5**, was introduced on the new **PCI-based Power Macintosh** line and the **Performa** 5200 and 6200 series. This update includes bug fixes and enhancements, including:

- A **native** PowerPC version of the **SCSI manager** for increased SCSI performance.

- The addition of the **Energy Saver control panel**.

- The **Control Strip**, formerly available only to **PowerBook** users, adds one-click access to a number of commonly used features.

- A new **Sound and Displays** control panel.

- OpenTransport was supported.

See Also

Control Strip; Energy Saver Control Panel; PowerBook; SCSI Manager 4.3 Extension; Sound Control Panel; System 7.5

System 7.5.3

This update of System 7.5, 7.5.1, and 7.5.2 offers significant performance and stability enhancements, including:

- The capability to create a universal **System Folder** that boots any model of Macintosh from the Mac Plus through the PCI-based Power Macs and PowerBook 5000 series.

- The addition of more PowerPC **native** components of the system that enhance overall system performance on PowerPC-based Macs.

- Comments in **Get Info** message boxes are no longer erased when **rebuilding the desktop file**.

- An update, version 1.1, of Apple's Open Transport networking and communication technology, which allows inclusion of Nubus-based networks and infrared and **PCMCIA-based** network connections on Mac models capable of supporting those features.

- An enhanced version of Apple's **QuickTime** that offers a variety of high-end video features including a 256-color format that has been added to Cinepak, enabling high-quality video playback without any color remapping.

This version also supports the Apple MPEG media system, providing expanded MPEG support.

- An updated version of **QuickDraw GX** that enables better printing from color inkjet printers and adds support for Apple's new Color StyleWriter Pro inkjet printer.
- An updated version of **QuickDraw 3D** that provides better memory management.
- A version of **AppleGuide** that adds the capability to print out AppleGuide help documents.

This version of the **system software** reportedly fixes nearly 2,000 bugs and incompatibility problems within the system, and Apple claims it is the most stable system yet. It updates all previous versions of System 7.5 including System 7.5, 7.5.1, and 7.5.2.

See Also
Apple Guide; Get Info; QuickDraw 3D; QuickTime; Rebuilding the Desktop; System 7.5; System Folder

System 7 Pack!

This is a set of System 7 **shareware** enhancement utilities for System 7.0, 7.0.1, or 7.1 created by Adam Stein of Insanely Great Software. System 7 Pack! adds a number of speed and customization enhancements including:

- The capability to change **command keys** and the names of certain menu items.
- A **Quit** menu item for the Finder so you can quit the Finder (although you can do a forced quit at the Finder without this utility by pressing Option-⌘-Esc).
- The removal of the animated zoom rectangles that appear when you open a window (by removing this animation, the window is more quickly opened).

- The capability to remove the word "**Alias**" from an alias icon's name.
- The capability to increase the speed at which you copy files in the Finder.

A shareware product called SpeedyFinder offers many of the same kind of enhancement features as the System 7 Pack! including: removing zoom rectangles, speeding copying of files, and a host of cosmetic updates.

See Also
Make Alias Command

System 7 Pro

System 7 Pro is a **System 7** update that includes a number of enhancements and updates that appear in the shipping version of System 7.5. This update was packaged separately by Apple and marketed as System 7 Pro because it contained some long-awaited enhancements for higher-end users such as updates for **QuickTime**, **PowerTalk**, and **AppleScript**. System 7 Pro also included the updates from the Apple Hardware System Update version 2.0.1.

See Also
AppleScript; PowerTalk; QuickTime; System 7

System 7 Tune-Up

The System 7 Tune-Up was introduced by Apple as a bug fix for **System 7** or **7.0.1** designed to fix a number of problems users were experiencing. The Tune-Up addressed four main areas:

- Faster and more reliable **printing** from within System 7 or 7.0.1, including new StyleWriter and LaserWriter drivers, plus a new version of the Chooser.
- Better memory management resulting in fewer out of memory messages.
- More memory available to applications when the computer is not connected to a network. A new version of the File Sharing extension is installed as well.

S

■ Fixed seldom seen bug that in some rare cases could cause files or entire folders to disappear.

System 7 Tune-Up also contains an extension called the System 7 Tuner.

This update is available for download from the Apple forum on America Online.

See Also

Networking; Printing; System 7; System 7.0.1

System 8 (Copland)

Scheduled for release early 1997, System 8 (code-named Copland, after the famous composer Aaron Copland) is Apple's next major rewrite of its **System software**. It will be the first complete overhaul since **System 7** was introduced. Apple has noted that Copland will be aimed at addressing two major areas: user efficiency and raw speed.

Although the features that will appear in the shipping version of System 8.0 are subject to change by Apple at any time, some of the features slated for Copland are as follows:

■ A major cosmetic facelift for the Macintosh interface will be included along with ability for different users to have different interfaces. You will also be able to have one interface for children, another interface for novices, and a separate interface for more advanced users, all on the same machine. Copland will also add themed interface looks that can be selected to suit a particular users tastes for their working environment.

The standard interface update reportedly includes new 3D files and folders, a re-designed desktop, more built-in user control of the look of the interface, new menus, and a new typeface to replace the current system fonts of Geneva, Chicago, and Monaco.

■ Reportedly 95 percent of Copland's code is to be PowerPC **native** code, which will mean dramatic increases in the speed of PowerPC-based computers.

■ Apple is incorporating limited forms of protected memory to enable better overall system reliability by protecting the memory one application uses so it doesn't interfere with another open application. Copland is also going to be Apple's first step into pre-emptive **multitasking**, in which you have different applications sharing different operations more efficiently than they currently can. These long-awaited features are limited versions of what will reportedly appear in **System 9** (code-named Gershwin, also named after a famous composer, George Gershwin).

■ Much of Copland is being written as a series of modules, which enables Copland to run on nearly any Macintosh, including Macs with only 8MB of RAM. However, as more RAM is added, Copland's overall performance will increase.

■ A number of system **extensions**, such as **QuickDraw GX**, **QuickDraw 3D**, **PlainTalk**, **QuickTime Conferencing**, and **QuickTime VR** will be built into Copland.

■ Copland will add the capability to automate routine tasks for users.

■ Copland will have improved and enhanced **windows**, **open/save dialog boxes**, and desktop management features that will enable even greater ease in managing your files.

■ **OpenDoc** technology will be included in Copland, which enables software developers to create components or modules that will add functionality to applications. If, for example, you have a word processor and wish it could create Postscript graphics, you could install a module that would add this feature to your Word Processor. This will enable you to customize applications to have only the features you actually need, enabling two users to use the same application but with different features.

■ Copland will have updated **networking** capabilities enabling it to plug-and-play into most existing networks, which offers significantly greater ease in setting up and administering networks.

See Also
Extensions Folder; Multitasking; Networks; OpenDoc; QuickDraw 3D; QuickDraw GX; System 7; System 9 (Gershwin)

System 9 (Gershwin)
System 9 (code-named Gershwin after the composer George Gershwin) is a major System Software revision slated to follow System 8 (**Copland**) that will introduce full preemptive **multitasking** on the Macintosh. Multitasking is the capability to have multiple applications processing simultaneously. You could be, for example, copying a group of files on to a disk, performing a Photoshop CMYK conversion, performing a large spreadsheet calculation, and printing several documents from different applications, all at the same time, while you work in yet another application. Although this is literally true in 7.5, it will occur much more cleanly and efficiently in System 9. System 9 is expected to be released sometime in 1998.

See Also
Multitasking; System 8

System and Desktop Management Utilities
There are a number of third-party system and desktop management utilities available that offer diagnostic, customization, and performance enhancements to the Macintosh. They include **compression** utilities, software and hardware diagnostic tools that diagnose and repair common **system** software problems, system add-ons that enable you to customize the functionality and look of your system, and many other attributes.

Some of these utilities are stand-alone applications, and others are extensions or control panels added to your system. Many of these are **shareware** or **freeware** products as well as commercial utilities.

See Also
Compression

System Disks
When you buy a Macintosh, the **System software** is pre-installed at the factory for you, and with the exception of some **Performa** Models and the PowerBook 145B, you receive a set of system disks that contain the Macintosh operating system. These system disks may be a set of **disks** (at last count it took 14 disks) or your system disks may be contained on one **CD-ROM disc**. Either way, the contents are the same, as they contain **Apple's installer** and the files necessary to do a complete system software install on most models of Macintosh. The installer looks at your model of Macintosh and installs the proper software for your particular model. If you have the CD-ROM version of the system disks, you see 14 folders on the CD-ROM named for each of the 14 system disks.

If your system disks come on floppy disks, you'll see a disk named "Install me first!" and then, depending on which version of the system software you're using, the disks will be named, Disk 2 of 14, Disk 3 of 14, and so on. These disks will appear on the CD-ROM version of the system software as folders.

Having this **backup** copy of the system software is important for a number of reasons: If for some reason your current system becomes damaged or corrupted, you can install a new system from the system disks. Also, if you want to make a different disk your **startup disk**, you can install a clean system from these disks. There are items on the system disks that do not get installed in every Macintosh, and sometimes the only way to access these files is to find them on the system disks. **QuickDraw GX** and **PowerTalk**, for example, require a separate installation.

If your model of Macintosh did not come with a set of system disks, all is not lost. You can download the current system from an **online service** (such as America Online), or you can download the system disks from Apple's Web site at **http://www.apple.com**.

See Also

CD-ROM; Disks and Drives; Online Services; PowerTalk; QuickDraw GX; Startup Disk

System Error, *See Error, System*

System Files

Files with code for the operating system of your Macintosh are called the System files. The two primary system files are the System file and the Finder file, and they reside within the **System Folder**. These two files work together and are necessary to start up and operate a Macintosh. The System file is the core of the Macintosh system and contains the basic programming instructions the computer needs to operate. The Finder file contains the interface code that creates the look and feel of your Mac (the **desktop**, **windows**, **icons**, the **trash can**, and so on) plus the programming instructions for tasks such as file management, creating folders, icons, initializing disks, and all the tasks handled at the Finder level.

Although most of the System file's instructions are locked within the System file, there are a few items the user can alter. If, for example, you are using **System 7** or higher, you can double-click your system file to see the sound files your system uses. You can **double-click** a sound to hear it, remove the sounds by dragging them out of the system (where the system can no longer access them), or add sounds to the system. You'll also see the keyboard layout for your particular Macintosh in the System file.

If you purchased your Macintosh in the United States, the standard U.S. keyboard layout is installed, but you can drag layouts for other countries into the system file. Before System 7, the System file was used to store your fonts, desk accessories (DAs), F Keys, and sounds. With the advent of System 7.1, these extra files are now separate folders within the System Folder. In System 7.5, the only files you're likely to see within the System file are the system sounds and the US keyboard layout.

Many people refer to any file that resides in the System Folder (such as control panels, extensions, printer files, preference files, and so on) as a system file.

See Also

Desktop; Icons; System 7; System 7.5; System 9 (Gershwin); System Folder; Trash Can; Window

System Folder

When you **start up** your Mac, it searches for a disk with a System Folder containing the **system software** the Mac needs to start up and operate. This disk is called a **startup disk**. The System Folder contains the System file, Finder file, and other system resources such as **Extensions**, **Control Panels**, **Preferences**, **Apple Menu Items**, and **Fonts**. If a System Folder has a working version of the system software inside it, a small icon of a Mac appears on the face of the folder.

The System Folder also enables you to add additional functionality to your system by adding **extensions**. These extensions can add a variety of features to your Macintosh and are available from commercial sources and as shareware and freeware extensions. Extensions can be used to customize the look of your Mac or to add certain features that are not available in the system. To add an extension to **System 7** or higher, drag the extension onto the System Folder icon and release the **mouse** button. A **dialog box** appears asking you if you want the system to place the file in the appropriate area. If you click OK, the file is placed where it will load into the system at the next startup, adding this new feature or functionality to your system.

In System 7 and higher, the System Folder has its own set of subfolders within the System Folder for keeping things organized. They are:

- **The Apple Menu Items folder**, which enables items in this folder to be accessed from the Apple menu.

- **The Preferences folder**, which stores the preferences for the Finder and most applications.
- **The Fonts folder**, which stores fonts that you want loaded into the system at startup.
- **The Startup folder**, which enables you to have certain programs open after startup.
- **The PrintMonitor Documents folder**, which temporarily stores files being printed in the background.
- **The Launcher folder**, which stores files, or aliases of files, appearing in the Launcher Control Panel.
- **The Extensions folder**, which stores extensions loaded into the system during startup.
- **The Control Panels folder**, which also stores extensions loaded into the system during startup, but has separate interfaces for controlling certain aspects, preferences, or options of extensions.
- **Other folders**: Some applications install their own folders into the System Folder that are necessary as support files to the application itself.

See Also

Control Panels Folder; Desktop; Extensions Folder; Fonts; Freeware; Icons; Mouse Button; Preferences Folder; Startup; Startup Disk; Trash; Window

System Heap

System heap is a term used to refer to the amount of memory set aside to operate the system. To find out how much memory is set aside as a system heap on your Mac, from the Finder choose **About This Macintosh** from the **Apple menu**. (It should be the top item on the menu.) You see a listing for **System Software** and the amount of memory set aside for the system heap, followed by a bar graph representing the system heap. The amount of the heap being used appears darkened in the bar graph.

If you want to set aside a larger amount of memory for the system heap than the system gives you by default, you can alter it by using a utility. (There are commercial and shareware versions of system heap utilities.) With the introduction of **System 7**, adjusting the heap manually became obsolete as the system heap adjusts itself to add more memory to the system heap anytime the system requires it.

See Also

About this Macintosh; Apple Menu; Desktop Level; System 7

System Software and Versions

The software that contains the code for starting up and operating your Macintosh is called the System Software. This software is developed by Apple Computer, and the System Software is stored in a folder on the Mac called the **System Folder**, which holds the two primary system files: the System File and the Finder File. The System File itself is the core of the Macintosh system and contains the basic programming instructions that the computer needs to operate. The Finder File contains the interface code, which creates the look and feel of your Mac **desktop**, plus the programming instructions for tasks like file management, creating folders, icons, initializing disks, and all of the tasks that are handled at the Finder level.

The System Software is constantly being updated and tweaked by Apple to add features, fix bugs and compatibility problems, and add additional functionality to the system. When Apple has a major system overhaul, they will jump to the next higher round number. For example, in 1988 when Apple introduced System 6, they soon released Maintenance bug fixes and minor updates called System 6.1, System 6.2, and so on all the way to System 6.8. When the overhauled the system completely, they jumped to **System 7**. Then the maintenance updates and minor enhancements came as System 7.0.1. When a more significant update came out, it jumped to System 7.1. Then minor updates at 7.1.1, 7.1.2, and finally 7.1.3, then a significant update came out that jumped to **System 7.5** and then the minor updates started all over again,

S

with System 7.5.1, System 7.5.2, 7.5.3, and 7.5.5. When Apple releases its next major overhaul in late 1996, the system will jump to System 8 (code-named **Copland**.)

Most minor bug fixes and small enhancements are offered for free by Apple through Apple Dealers, major online services, and from Apple's Web site on the Internet. Major updates are packaged and sold by Apple through commercial avenues.

See Also

Desktop; Icons; System 7; System 7.5; System 8 (Copland); System Folder; Trash; Window

System Switcher

Apple warns you not to have two System Folders on the same startup disk because the Mac won't know which system to start up from, and the ensuing confusion caused erratic behavior, a system error, or the inability to start up at all. But if you have a situation where you want two systems on the same disk for a legitimate reason, the **shareware** utility System Switcher enables you to have two **System Folders** on the same hard disk.

An example of users wanting two System Folders on the same disk occurred when Apple introduced **System 7**. Many users had applications that only worked with **System 6**, so they would want their Mac to start up with System 6 and other times with System 7. This was useful for evaluating and testing the new system before making a total commitment to update the system.

See Also

System 7; System Folder

System Update 3.0

System update 3.0 is a hardware bug fix and enhancement package released by Apple for **System 7.1**, **7.1.1**, and **7.1.2**. The bug fix addressed a number of bugs and updated all the system enablers, but it most notably added some enhancements to the system such as:

- The capability to see small versions of the real icons of files in **Open and Save Dialog Boxes**
- A version of Apple's bare bones text editor **TeachText** called **SimpleText**.
- A new version of **Apple HD SC Setup** (for formatting Apple hard disks).
- A number of updated control panels for both desktop Macs and PowerBooks.

Another benefit of this update is that it includes the updates and bug fixes found in Apple's system hardware updates 1.0, 2.0, and 2.1.

See Also

Apple HD SC Setup; Open Dialog Box; SimpleText; System 7.1; System Update 3.0

System Updates

System updates have been available for Mac computers since the introduction of System 7.0. Such updates are traditionally free and offer performance improvements, bug fixes, and new versions of System software components (such as printer drivers, QuickDraw GX, and PowerTalk). These updates are available on most online services and on Apple's ftp site at **ftp.info.apple.com**.

System Version, *See Macintosh, Listing System Version*

SysX, *See INIT 9403*

T

T4 Virus

This virus spreads to other applications and to the Finder. It attempts to change the System file. After being infected, an application cannot be repaired and should be removed and replaced by a fresh copy of the application.

Tab-Delimited File

Used in both databases and word processing, tab-delimited files or tab delimited text is simply text that's been separated into fields or columns by tabs. Comma-delimited text is separated by commas. Tab-delimited and comma-delimited files can be easily transferred between databases, PIMs, spreadsheets, and word processors. Most applications recognize both data formats, but generally you'll have to specify which way you want to import or export your data.

Tab Key

The Tab key is used to set tabs in word processing and page layout applications, but it is also used as a navigation device within dialog boxes and **databases**. You can use the Tab key to move down a list of files in an active window, and you can use it to jump from field to field in most dialog boxes. Each press of the Tab key moves the cursor to the next available field.

If you press Shift-Tab key, the cursor moves to the previous field, or in the list view of an active Window, Shift-Tab moves you back up the list of files.

See Also
Active Window; Database

Tables, Creating in Netscape

A feature that enables authors of **World Wide Web page**s to present text or other data in a table format, with rows, columns, and headings. In general, the information is contained in rectangular table cells. The borders of the cells can either be visible in the **Web browser** screen or be invisible, however, thus opening a variety of **Web page** design options.

Tables are a relatively recent feature of HyperText Markup Language **(HTML)** version 3.0. Because tables are new, not all Web browsers display to them. Web page authors should consider presenting a table document with a non-table alternative, such as the <PRE> preformatted text tag.

Tables are contained within the <BODY> section of an HTML document, as indicated:

```
<HTML>
<HEAD>
<TITLE> </TITLE>
<BODY>
<TABLE>
</TABLE>
</BODY>
</HTML>
```

In order to create a table, an author needs to be familiar with three or four basic **HTML tags**: <TABLE>, <CAPTION>, <TR>, <TH>, and <TD>.

The following table lists the tags and attributes needed to create tables.

Tables: The Basic HTML Tags

HTML Tag	Description
<TABLE> </TABLE>	These tags contain the entire table. The tags are contained within the BODY section of the document.
<CAPTION> </CAPTION>	Specifies the name of a table; optional.
<TR> </TR>	Designates the contents of a table row—a horizontal set of cells.
<TH> </TH>	Used to mark table headings that describe the contents of a table row or column. Presented with emphasis, such as boldface.
<TD> </TD>	Used to designate table data, the contents of individual table cells.
<TABLE BORDER>	Specifies that the table will have a visible border.
<TABLE BORDER=n>	n describes the width of the table border
<TD or TR ALIGN=left|right|center VALIGN=top|middle|bottom>	Determines whether contents of table data cells is left-aligned, right-aligned, or center. VALIGN controls vertical alignment of table contents.
<TD NOWRAP>	Prevents table data from wrapping at ends of lines.
<TD or TH COLSPAN=n>	Enables data cell or heading cell to span more than one column, specified by n.
<TD or TH ROWSPAN=n>	Enables data cell or heading cell to span more than one column, specified by n.

Tables can bring several benefits to a Web page or **Web site**:

- They allow the presentation of material in columns.
- Unlike <PRE>, text in tables appears a variable width rather than monospaced font.
- Tables help to break up Web page content and add graphic interest to a document.

Before creating a table, an author should consider drawing the contents out by hand on paper to keep rows and columns straight. A very simple example of a table follows:

```
<TABLE BORDER>
<CAPTION><H1>Clothing Catalog</H1></CAPTION>
<TR>
        <TH>Shirts</TH>
        <TH>Slacks</TH>
        <TH>Socks</TH>
        <TH>Ties</TH>
</TR>
<TR>
        <TD>$24.99</TD>
        <TD>$29.99</TD>
        <TD>$8.99</TD>
        <TD>$12.99</TD>
</TR>
</TABLE>
```

The output is shown in the following figure.

Tables, Using to Format Text Some of the most innovative page design on the World Wide Web uses tables to arrange text and provide white space. Table borders are invisible, so text appears in columns, or more often, in a single column with "columns" of white space on either side.

Blank columns can be specified by enclosing a line break tag within table data tags:

```
<td width=90><br></td>
```

The column of text in the middle could be specified with a wider measure, for example:

```
<td valign=top align=left width=230>
```

Authors should consider providing an alternative to such layout for users with browsers that do not support tables.

See Also

HTML Tags; Hypertext Link; HyperText Markup Language; Netscape; Netscape Navigator; Web Browser; World Wide Web

Table of Contents

The table of contents appears at the front of a document to help you find the locations of chapters or **sections** within it. It's more general than an **index** and is usually compiled according to the order within the document of items included, rather than alphabetized by subject. It is created much in the same way an index is created, by marking the items to be included and then collating them. In some applications, including **Microsoft Word**, clicking a page number in the table of contents takes you to that page in the document.

See Also

Index

Table Editors

For desktop publishers, creating tables is nothing less than a chore. Setting up tab stops, rules, and shading manually can be done, and might be practical for those who set very few tables. But for those who need to streamline the process, table editors are a lifesaver.

Table editors work rather like spreadsheets, with rows, columns, and cells that expand as text is added. Along with the basics like font, size, and leading, they allow users to define ruling, shading, and more. Although users create default settings for each table, most table editors enable custom formatting for individual cells. The better ones handle multi-page tables, adding "continued" lines automatically and repeating column heads.

One of **FrameMaker's** strengths is its built-in table editor, which can convert text to tables or create empty tables to be filled in later. Tables are anchored in text and can appear where they're anchored or "float" to the top of the next page if there's not enough room on the present page. Multi-page tables are supported, with customizable "continued" lines, and columns can be automatically sized to fit the page in several different ways (proportionally, equal widths, and so on). FrameMaker enables the creation of table formats—style sheets that can be applied to any table to change its attributes.

Three QuarkXTensions enables users to create tables within **QuarkXPress**: TableMaker, Tableworks, and XTable. All three use standard XPress elements—tabs, rules, and boxes—but automate their creation, placement, and modification.

TableMaker is the simplest, with no custom formatting for individual cells; it creates tabs, lays down rules, and creates a style sheet containing the tab settings it builds. XTable's feature set is more extensive, including the ability to control column and gutter widths, set straddle heads, align type on special points within each of the columns, and change the positioning in the column of any data in the table.

T

Of the three XTensions, Tableworks supports the most complex styles. It can rotate text in table cells, automatically align columns on decimal points, automatically justify horizontal space between columns, and even apply a color blend as a table background. Perhaps most impressive, it can import text from database and spreadsheet files, enabling users to specify links between any database field and any column in the table. Like FrameMaker, Tableworks supports multi-page tables.

PageMaker users already have Adobe Table, which ships with Adobe PageMaker. This program has one big advantage over other table editors—it can export tables as graphics in PICT or EPS format. That means tables created with Adobe Table can be used with any other application, not just PageMaker.

See Also
FrameMaker; PageMaker; QuarkXPress; XTensions

Tabs, *See Margins and Tabs*

Tags in HTML, <IMG> and <FIG>

<IMG> and <FIG> are two tags used to insert **inline** or **external images** in HyperText Markup Language (**HTML**) documents. <IMG> and <FIG> control both the images themselves and the way the images interact with the surrounding contents on a **World Wide Web** page.

<IMG> was the image tag specified by all versions of HTML up to the 3.0 specification, but <IMG> has since been superceded by <FIG> as described in HTML 3.0. <FIG> is more powerful than <IMG>, particularly in relation to **client-side** or **server-side imagemaps.**

<IMG> and <FIG> are both empty HTML tags; that is, there is no </IMG> or </FIG>. Each tag has four attributes:

```
<SRC>, as in <IMG SRC>=" ">
<ALIGN>, as in <IMG ALIGN="  ">
<ALT>, as in <IMG ALT="  ">
<ISMAP>, as in <IMG ISMAP="  ">
```

<IMG SRC> is the basic tag for putting an image in a Web document, for example, <IMG SRC= "NAME.OF.IMAGE.GIF."> This HTML tag tells a **Web browser**: "I want to put an image (<IMG>) here. The source file (<SRC>) for the image can be found at the following **URL** (="NAME.OF.IMAGE.GIF").

<IMG ALIGN> enables the text that occurs before or after a graphic to be aligned at the top, bottom, or middle of the image.

<IMG ALT> is used to specify a text string that a nongraphical browser can display an as an alternative to an image. Its use is optional but recommended because many users connecting to the Internet with dial-up modems turn image display off for faster browsing.

<IMG ISMAP> tells a browser that the image is a clickable map or imagemap.

See Also
HTML; Imagemap; <TITLE> HTML Tag; Web Browser; World Wide Web

Take-A-Break! Crosswords, *See Traditional Games*

Talk:About

Talk:About is conversation software for the Macintosh that enables people who are nonspeaking to participate in communication. Unlike less sophisticated methods such as **Freedom**, it enables the user to maintain a real "give-and take" dialogue rather than just expressing prewritten phrases about wants and needs. It is an orthographic-based system (you can spell out the words) that provides point-and-click access to the various parts of a conversation through components such as Quick:Chat, Story:Talk and Story:Panel.

Talk:About is based on research conducted by the University of Dundee, Scotland, on pragmatic social interaction and the use of communication aids. Its studies find that conversations include specific components:

- Fast social interactions
- Beginning small talk
- Novel sentences
- Extended talk
- Wrap-ups
- Farewells

Talk:About combines all these components and includes them in one easily learned program, giving the user full participation in any conversation.

Quick:Chat buttons provide instant access to social interaction, helping the user to engage others in conversation. Phrases can be programmed with respect to specific people and/or time of day, so the user can speak appropriately to classmates, coworkers, or family and friends. Story:Talk files are stories, or bodies of conversation, written by the user, about events, experiences, opinions, and other things that come up in everyday conversation.

They might relate to a sports team, a movie, a favorite TV show, politics, or any of the thousands of things people talk about. Files can range in length from a sentence or two to several pages. Story:Talk uses artificial intelligence to link stories so that they are suggested appropriately, according to whom the user is talking with. Story:Panel is the toolbar across the top of Talk:About that is used to retrieve Story:Talk stories. The user selects his or her conversation partner. It might be a teacher, parent, or friend. The program will suggest an appropriate story for that partner, choosing from those the user has previously prepared.

The point-and-click interface makes for quick and easy chat. To start or carry on a conversation, the user selects an appropriate button, which brings up a menu of sentences. To say one, just choose it and click the speech button. When the listener responds, move on to the continuers, and so on.

Talk:About enables you to use text from almost any program or file on your computer.

If you have written letters, kept a journal or class notes, or sent or received email, all of these can be used as

Talk:About stories for conversations. Talk:About can also be used with the **Ke:nx** switch and **scanning software** by people who have difficulty using a keyboard as well as difficulty speaking. It's one more way that technology can improve the quality of life for everyone.

See Also
Co:Writer; Freedom; Ke:nx; Scanning Software

Tape Drives, *See DAT*

Targeted Window
A feature of the **World Wide Web** browser **Netscape Navigator** 2.0 that functions in response to a hyperlink click on a **Web page** that uses frames.

A targeted window is specified with <TARGET>, an attribute to the **<A>** anchor tag in an **HTML** document. (HTML stands for HyperText Markup Language, the language used to create World Wide Web documents.) Both the TARGET and FRAMES elements are Netscape extensions to "official" HTML and may not be displayed by all **Web browsers**.

The author of a **Web page** can use <TARGET> to get one frame to react to a click in another frame, or to open a new window in response to a click on an anchor (clickable text that leads to another location on the Internet).

An example is shown in the following figure. The source HTML for the document entitled "Printers' Row" contains several frames. The frame on the left side of the page contains a row of hypertext links to other documents.

In order to get the General Information link to open a new document in a targeted window, you can use the predesignated name "_blank" to open a document "info.html" linked to General Information in a new blank window. The HTML would be written as follows:

```
<p><A HREF="info.html"
TARGET="_blank">General Information</a></p>
```

The linked document "info.html" will open in a new window, as shown in the following figure.

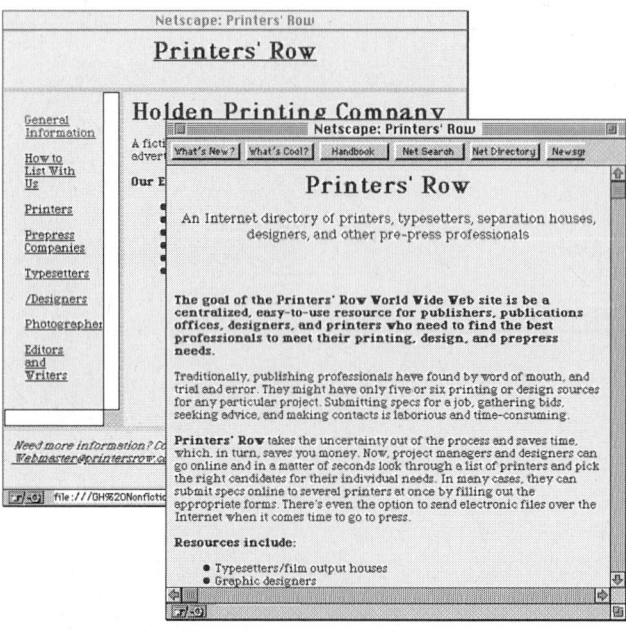

Other predesignated commands that can be used with TARGET can open a document:

- In the frame just clicked, for example:

    ```
    <p><A HREF='info.html
    Target="_self".>General
    Information</a></p>
    ```

- In a new separate ("parent") window over the main HTML page (the page that contains the frames):

    ```
    <p><A HREF='info.html
    Target="parent">General
    Information</a></p>
    ```

- At the top or "main" level of frames:

    ```
    <p><A HREF='info.html
    TARGET="_top">General Information</
    a></p>
    ```

See Also

<A> Anchor Tag; Frames, How to Create; HTML; HTML Markup Tags; Hypertext Link; Internet; World Wide Web

Tax Programs

Nobody likes paying taxes, but signing the check is often less painful than filling out all those forms. Can the Mac help? Definitely. There are programs like MacInTax to calculate your personal income tax. It does both Federal and State taxes (if you buy the supplement for your state) and can even print the necessary forms in a government-approved format.

Taxes for even the smallest of small businesses are a lot more complex. Federal and State Income tax returns for corporations really require the services of a good CPA or tax specialist. But there are also payroll taxes, FUTA, sales tax, and other forms that the business owner must file monthly, quarterly, or annually. Business accounting software, such as **Peachtree Accounting** and **MYOB,** will provide you with the necessary forms, with the numbers already in place. Tax tables within the program figure the taxes deducted from an employee's paycheck, based upon the employee's wages, residence, and work location. In addition to FICA-Social Security, FICA-Medicare and federal withholding taxes, MYOB Payroll calculates state withholding, State Unemployment and State Disability taxes for the 50 states, Puerto Rico, the Virgin Islands, and the District of Columbia. Local taxes are also calculated, if applicable. MYOB will even remind you when its time to file them. These programs can even handle non-cash wages, which are sums of money that must be included in an employee's gross pay for tax purposes, but which the employer doesn't actually pay the employee. Some examples of non-cash wages are excess life insurance, incentive travel costs, and other fringe benefits. In addition, there are two types of non-cash wages that are specific to the restaurant business—reported tips and allocated tips.

At the end of the year it takes only a mouse click to print the employees' W-2s. Another mouse click generates the quarterly reports for 940, 941, and FUTA taxes, as well as any state or local payroll taxes. Considering the penalties for improper or late filing of payroll taxes, this one function is reason enough to use the software.

See Also

Finance Programs; MYOB; Peachtree Accounting

Tcl, *See Alpha Editor*

TCP, *See MacTCP*

TCP/IP

A set of protocols designed to **host** and **client** computers to send and receive information across a network such as the **Internet**.

TCP (Transmission Control Protocol) and IP (Internet Protocol) are only two of several protocols in an "Internet protocol suite" that provides the foundation for information transport on the Internet. TCP/IP makes possible email, newsgroup, File Transport Protocol, Telnet, and other sorts of data transmission.

Originally developed by the Department of Defense's ARPA (Advanced Research Projects Agency), it deals with the physical layer of the OSI Model, whereas TCP resides in the transport layer. TCP/IP is designed to work across a wide range of computer types, all the way from the very biggest to the smallest.

TCP/IP is rapidly becoming part of every Mac's vocabulary, since it's included in System 7.5. Even if you're not tied into a local network with Sun workstations, IBM mainframes, and Cray supercomputers (all of which can talk to the Mac with TCP/IP); you're effectively tied into a Wide Area Network every time you sign on to your Internet Provider.

In very general terms, TCP is used to send messages from one location to another on a network, and IP is used to route those messages to the correct destinations (at the transport level).

For more information go to the World Wide Web site **http://www.netspace.org/netspace/tcpip/toc.html**.

See Also

Client; Host; Internet; IP; MacTCP; World Wide Web

TCP/IP for Systems Running Open Transport

This control panel enables your Mac to communicate and speak the same language of network services, such as the Internet, that use TCP/IP protocol. (Apple's language for networking is **AppleTalk**, but the **Internet** uses TCP/IP, which is the language of UNIX systems that are prevalent on the Internet.)

The **MacTCP** control panel is incompatible with Apple's Open Transport, so a new version called TCP/IP was introduced in System 7.5.2, and it enables you to specify TCP/IP settings for use with Apple's Open Transport networking.

There are two modes to this control panel: a Basic mode (the default), and an Advanced or administration mode (which can be entered through the Edit menu when the control panel is open).

See Also

AppleTalk; Internet; MacTCP

Teachers, Macintosh and

Today, the typical elementary school classroom is more likely to have a Macintosh than a pet hamster. Computers aren't a luxury. They're a necessity. As with anything else, there are good and bad points to this. It means that one more subject, computer education, has to be jammed into the already crowded school day. It means that teachers often have to go back to school themselves to learn how to use the computer, as well as how to teach with it. But it gives the teacher another tool to use, both in actual classroom teaching, and in handling all the paperwork that's required for grades, progress reports, IEP's, and anything else a school department requires.

T

Conversation with Bud Colligan

Bud Colligan helped launch the Mac in the higher education market, then took what he knew about the Mac over to Macromedia, the company that sells the Director Multimedia Studio, FreeHand, Graphics Studio, and Authorware Interactive Studio, plus Extreme 3D, SoundEdit 16, Fontographer, Xres (hi-res imaging), and Shockwave (for playing Macromedia files on the Web).

I tried everything I could to get a job at Apple...

Maclopedia: What was your first contact with Apple and the Mac?

Bud: Steve Jobs came to Stanford business school and showed us all the Lisa. I was blown away. I tried everything I could to get a job at Apple and ended up testing Lisa software for one week during spring break. I was able to get interviewed in the Mac group and finally got a job. On my first day (before the Mac was introduced in 1984), they showed me the Mac. It was so cool.

Maclopedia: What was the secret of the Mac's success in higher education?

Bud: Daniel Lewin started the Apple University Consortium. I was managing International Product Marketing in the Mac division in 1984 and kept seeing about one third of the sales going to U.S. universities. So I started the European University Consortium in 1985. After the big reorg in July 1985 when Steve left the company, I took over Higher Ed. We built programs for the universities, gave them excellent pricing, and let them tell us how to market to them. When we followed their advice, we were usually successful.

Maclopedia: What were Mac's strengths in higher education?

Bud: Graphic user interface, price, ease of use for students and faculty, lots of courseware, good programming tools for learning, like Mac Pascal, and other innovative tools, like our Videoshop (later Director), HyperCard, Authorware. Some of these areas have been eroded by Windows, but the Mac is still the easiest to use and has some of the best tools, particularly for publishing, curriculum, and multimedia.

Maclopedia: How do you see your work at Macromedia continuing what you started at Apple?

Bud: My Higher Ed group did all the first work with multimedia at Apple. We produced Apple's vision piece, "The Knowledge Navigator," and did all the marketing for HyperCard. We produced the first authoring tools guide. So in a way, the Higher Ed group was a precursor to all the work I have done since at Macromedia.

Maclopedia: How do your customers respond to the Mac these days?

Bud: We still have about 60 percent of our business on the Mac. It's a very loyal customer base among creative people. There are too many projects done to list them out loud, but if you are interested, go to **http://www.macromedia.com**.

Electronic grade books and test-making programs exist in both commercial and shareware forms. Chariot Software's *MicroGrade* and *MicroTest* are two commercial applications for the teacher. MicroGrade tracks up to 100 students in 16 subjects, grading as many as 128 separate assignments. Figure grades by weighted percent or total points, and mark absent, late, unexcused, and incomplete assignments. MicroTest provides preformatted screens to enter true/false, multiple choice, matching, fill in the blank, and essay questions. Exams are neat and professional-looking, tailored exactly to what you've taught. Shareware grading programs do much the same thing, for free or at a very low cost, but may not have as good documentation or as elegant an interface. One free and functional grading program is HyperGrade, available in the educational software area of America Online, or on the Internet at **http://www.tiac.net/users/jcrose/html**.

There are shareware exams and tests on virtually every topic from learning letters and numbers through college-level sciences and liberal arts. Check the educational libraries of **America Online** and **CompuServe**.

If the classroom computer is equipped with a modem and phone line, it can open doors to many educational experiences. Such programs as **MayaQuest**, linked to an actual expedition, give kids a chance to talk to scientists, archaeologists, and others who are actually doing the things they're reading about. Kids across America participate in the Iditarod Dog Sled Race every year, by way of America Online's Iditarod Trail updates. There are classroom activities linked to the race preparations. Students may "adopt" a team to follow during the race. They'll exchange **email** with the racers and read the daily accounts of training sessions, packing supplies, and other preparations. Many classes even make the protective booties the dogs wear, and ship dozens of sets to their favorite team.

Teachers can use the computer in dozens of other ways. In addition to assigning individuals or groups of students to work with the many excellent educational programs available, they can use desktop publishing programs to create a school newspaper or a literary magazine. Students can create and put a class home page on the **World Wide Web**. With it, they can solicit email penpals from similar classes in other parts of the country. They can use the resources of the Internet for research on any topic imaginable.

The computer can even help fulfill continuing education and professional development requirements. **America Online**'s Teacher Information Network offers all kinds of opportunities. There's an on-line connection to the American Federation of Teachers, the National Education Association, and to the Association for Curriculum and Development and the National Principals' Center. CNN in the Classroom, C-SPAN, and the Scholastic Network are also represented here. There are downloadable libraries of lesson plans, exams, and teaching aids. Most of these are completely free, some are low-cost shareware. All are placed there, by teachers, for teachers. **CompuServe** and **Prodigy** offer similar Education forums, also with libraries of software and places to go for more information.

See Also

Internet, Educational Resources; Software, Educational, Grades 7-12

TeachText

TeachText is a bare-bones text editor application that Apple included with every Macintosh **system** until it was replaced in **System 7** with **SimpleText**, which added more features. Although TeachText enables the creation of only the simplest type of text documents, it gained popularity with software developers as they started to include TeachText documents on the same disk with their shipping software. Anytime they needed to include a last minute user update and/or changes to the instruction manual, they'd just include a TeachText document on the same disk. They were pretty certain every Mac user would be able to open, read, and/or print the document. Even so, they'd often include a copy of TeachText on the same disk just in case.

TeachText is a small application, takes very little **memory**, and launches quickly, so it's perfect for jotting a quick note. TeachText also enables you to open a **PICT** document for viewing. You're limited to the default **font** and size, and you can only open one TeachText document at a time. For these and other reasons, SimpleText was introduced, which offers choices of font, size, integration of sound, and other features.

See Also

Font; Memory; PICT; System 7

Telecommunication Adapters,
See Modems

Telecommunication Programs

Like every other piece of hardware attached to your Macintosh, the modem needs software to tell the computer how to communicate with it, and to allow you to control it. The most basic software is known as a *terminal emulation* program, or a Dumb Terminal Program. More advanced software hides the details of operating the modem from you, letting you think about the task at hand, and enabling the computer and the modem to negotiate the proper commands without your direct input.

The most intelligent programs almost entirely insulate you from the technicalities of using a modem. They frequently ask you a few questions, such as your local area code, your modem type, and where the modem is connected, and from that point on require no further interaction. The only real disadvantage of this type of program is that they are very specific to the service they were designed for. The major online services, such as CompuServe, Prodigy, and America Online each have their own highly intelligent client software. In addition, many privately run or user group **Bulletin Board Systems** make use of this type of software as well, the most popular application being First Class. These programs are designed to be as "Mac-like" as possible, using icons and menus in a Graphical User Interface (GUI) rather than text commands like "goto catlover's forum."

Modem Software, Terminal Emulation Terminal emulation software makes your Mac act as if it is an old style teletype terminal. It connects the keyboard and monitor to the modem, giving very little computer interpretation to the input or output of the modem session. The software simply copies output from the modem to your screen and sends everything you type on the keyboard to the modem. Essentially, this type of software makes your computer an expensive display terminal, hence the name "dumb" terminal software. Software like this enables you to control your modem directly, using the **AT commands** that the modem understands. This is somewhat similar to using a PC-type computer through DOS using the "C:" interface. The most popular program of this type is Zterm, a shareware terminal emulator that is included with many Macintosh-specific modems, such as the Global Village brand. Many users find, however, that the combination of Zterm and a text-based service like Delphi or Bix lets them handle email, newsgroup retrieval, and forum messages far more efficiently than the more graphically oriented ones.

Commercial alternatives to Zterm include Microphone Pro, White Knight, and SITcomm. The commercial programs each provide a wealth of features for automation that sit them on the border line of more advanced dedicated terminal software. However, they still require a certain degree of direct modem interaction and are therefore more powerful but harder to use than the modem software included with standard online services.

Most service specific modem software, such as the packages included with America Online, configure the parameters of the modem communication for you. However, when working with a "dumb" terminal program you may need to configure the communication settings manually.

Although many options are provided, the following settings will almost always work: 1 stop bit, No Parity, full duplex. If a service requires something different, it'll usually tell you. If you're using a hardware flow control cable to connect to an external modem make sure you set Hardware Flow Control (also known as DTR/CTS or RTS/CTS) ON, and XON/XOFF (software flow control) OFF. If you're working with the internal modem in certain computers, such as the PowerBook Duo, you should turn both hardware and software handshaking off.

If you have a data compression modem (MNP 5 or v.42bis), your modem can probably accept data faster than the speed at which it's transmitting. One of the more misunderstood concepts with modems today is that of transmission speeds. In your side of the modem connection, there are two speeds of significance: the speed at which your modem is talking to the remote modem, and the speed at which your computer is talking to your modem. With today's advanced modems, these speeds don't necessarily need to, and probably shouldn't, be the same.

The modulation protocol will determine the speed at which your modem will connect to the remote modem. (14,400 or 28,800Bps, for example). However, because of data compression, the modem is occasionally able to reach a net rate of transfer to your computer of greater than this speed. Because of this, the modem has more data to transmit than is currently coming, the modem is willing to send data to the computer faster than it is receiving it remotely. To maximize your performance, you should use your communications software to set the speed your computer talks to the modem faster than the speed at which your modem talks to the remote computer.

Use the following table to pick your optimum computer speed.

Software vs. Modem Speeds

Modem Speed	Software Speed
28,800Bps	57,600Bps
14,400Bps	38,400Bps
9,600Bps	19,200Bps
2,400Bps	4,800Bps

As a general rule of thumb, you should set the speed of your software (both intelligent and dumb terminal packages) to a rate *above* that at which your modem is connected to the remote site. Generally, a computer serial port speed of 38,400 is fine for most situations. In the new PowerBook Duo 2300 computers, Apple has reported that using port speeds above 14,400 will actually slow down transmissions. Note that on older Macs, or when using the Printer Port, the Mac may not be able to keep up reliably with the fastest modems. If you have trouble, try slowing down the computer speed to closer to the modem speed.

TIP When using computer speed and modem speeds that don't match, it is once again absolutely critical that you make use of a hardware handshaking cable to provide for proper flow control between the two devices.

See Also

Modems

Telephony

The use of computers with analog or digital telephone lines for a variety of purposes, including data, fax, onscreen dialing, and the use of a computer for a voice phone. Sometimes telephony implies the mixture of voice with data and fax communications.

See Also

Modems

Telnet

Telnet is a means of using terminal emulation to connect to a computer somewhere else on the Internet and to do whatever that computer enables you to do. It can be likened to using a modem to connect to another computer.

Telnet is considered boring by a lot of Macintosh enthusiasts, especially when compared to the more exciting Web, news, and FTP clients. It involves 1980s rather than 1990s technology. But it is still useful and is the only way to access many Internet resources that are not held on an HTTP or FTP server, such as **BBSs** and libraries, as shown in the following figure.

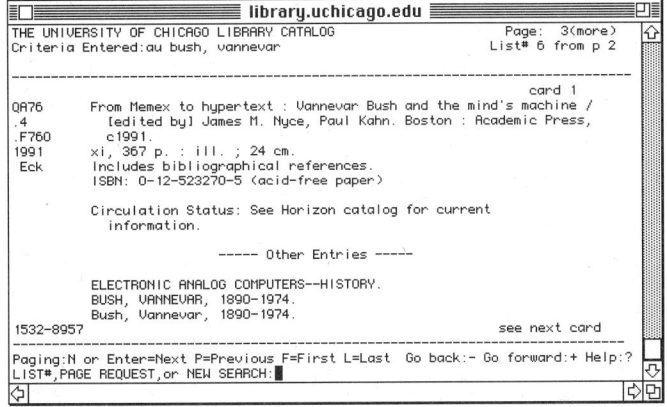

Telnet can provide a quick way to check whether your local library has the book you are looking for, before you go get it. When you Telnet to another machine, you use a UNIX-type command-line to reach the specific program that provides information you want. The information providers you connect to may have specific restrictions on the way you can use their site, and you should pay attention to these restrictions.

Features to look for in a Telnet program include the capability to save connection documents so you can automate the work of logging into a specific machine (but beware of security issues if they also store your password). You should also be able to copy and paste out of the Telnet program. Some programs, such as NCSA Telnet, also support drag-and-drop and Internet Config.

T

Some of the most common Telnet clients are Cornell University's Comet, the University of Illinois' NCSA **Telnet**, and Brown University's tn3270. They are all readily available from Info-Mac Archive sites. A database of Telnet sites, called Hytelnet, is also available. Some telecommunications programs, such as Software Ventures' MicroPhones, come with a Telnet Toolbox tool that enables them to serve as terminal emulators to Telnet.

See Also
BBS

Templates, *See Spreadsheet*

Temporal Compression

Temporal compression is a technique used to compress a sequence of images. In temporal compression, rather than simply compress the current frame in its entirety, you first subtract the current frame from the preceding frame. This results in only the differences between the two frames, which are often very similar in motion sequence frames. By saving only the differences, the amount of information that needs to be saved is reduced. Temporal compression also must use spatial compression techniques (first the differences between frames is determined, and then that resulting data is compressed).

See Also
Asymmetrical Compressors; Compression

THINK Reference

THINK Reference was the first hypertext online reference for the **Toolbox**. It includes all of the reference material in the six volumes of the original *Inside Macintosh* series, as well as a large number of programming tips and other tidbits.

Both Symantec C++ and CodeWarrior support THINK Reference. Using **AppleEvents**, either **IDE** can ask THINK Reference to look up and display

information, or return the prototype for any Toolbox function.

You can also interact directly with THINK Reference (see the following figure). Clicking any underlined text in the window links to that entry in the database. Code samples and function prototypes can be copied to the Clipboard from any page. Although THINK Reference predates the **World Wide Web**, anyone who has spent some time using a Web browser will find THINK Reference immediately familiar.

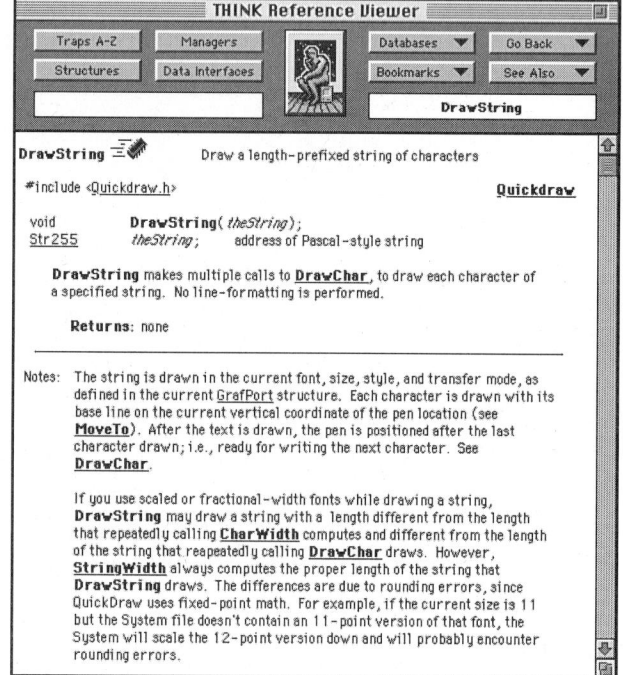

The THINK Reference databases have not been updated since the release of System 7.0. As a result, many **API**s introduced since then are absent, including **QuickDraw GX**, PowerTalk, Drag-and-Drop, and the Thread Manager. Also, THINK Reference does not include any documentation on the Power Mac, or the special programming considerations they entail. **Macintosh Programmer's Toolbox Assistant** is a similar reference from Apple that contains more up-to-date information.

Symantec recently sold the THINK Reference Viewer technology to Xplain Corporation, the publishers of *MacTech* magazine (**http://www.mactech.com/**).

MacTech has released a database of all past issues in THINK Reference format and is in the process of updating the viewer.

See Also

API; AppleEvents; IDE; Inside Macintosh; Macintosh Programmers Toolbox Assistant; QuickDraw GX; Toolbox; World Wide Web

Thread

Threads are subprocesses that run within a single program. In any **multitasking** system, each application is given a portion of the total processor time to do whatever it needs to do. Applications can further subdivide the time (and tasks) into individual threads of execution. Threads do not necessarily mean better performance (after all, the total amount of time the application uses is independent of whether it uses threads), but they can greatly simplify programming multiple simultaneous tasks.

A program that performs a very complex calculation, for example, normally pauses the calculation every so often to check and see if the user has canceled the operation, clicked a button, or chosen something from a menu. Using threads, the program could separate these user interface tasks from the calculation itself and run each in a separate thread, simplifying the programming complexity. The calculation thread could then be written without regard to the user interface, while the user interface thread could mostly ignore the calculation thread.

Programs written using threads make better use of multiple processors, as each thread can run on a separate processor. Although multiprocessor Macs have yet to appear, they are no doubt coming.

The Macintosh **Toolbox** provides a set of routines—known as the Thread Manager—to create and manage threads. The Thread Manager is built in to System 7.5 and is available as an Extension for earlier versions of System 7. Just as with multitasking as a whole, threads can be switched preemptively or co-

operatively. The current implementation of the Thread Manager supports both preemptive and cooperative threads on 68K Macs, but supports only cooperative threads on Power Macs.

See Also

Multitasking; Toolbox

Thread Manager, *See Thread*

Three by Five

An intuitive graphical **database** from MacToolkit.

Three by Five brings the ease of index cards to the Macintosh with the power of word processors, outliners, and databases, and the multimedia capabilities to bring your notes to life with movies and pictures.

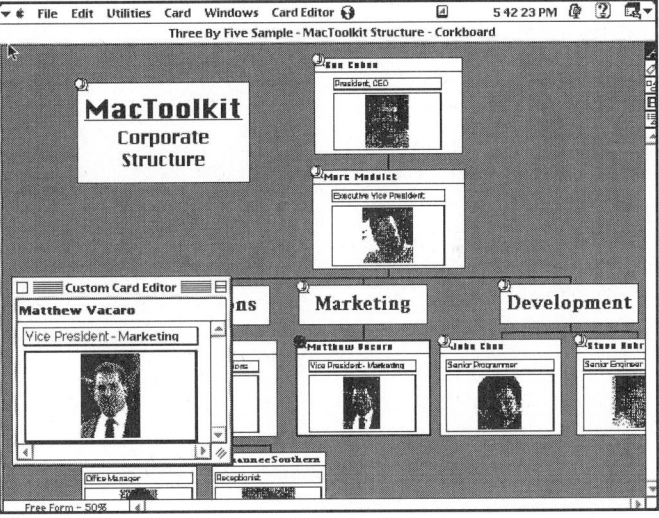

This figure, an outline of MacToolkit's corporate structure, shows the ease of using a graphical interface on an outline. By enabling users to view the links between sections, concepts and organizations can be quickly grasped.

MacToolkit is also able to do a text outline form, and switch between that and the graphical view with just a click of the mouse. The outline form has handy tools such as drag-and-drop editing, and single click expansion and compression of items, making outlining a quick and easy process.

T

In addition, Three by Five can be used to make and use flash cards and keep track of scores, print out research notes and index cards, create storyboards and presentations, and organize everything from business plans to recipe cards.

Three by Five has drag-and-drop capabilities, and has a built in spell checker and thesaurus to speed up work time. It can also import and export to other word processors, a handy feature for work on storyboards. In addition, Three by Five can categorize cards by style, font, size, and color, and can search and sort them in seconds.

Three by Five will run on everything from a Macintosh Plus to a Power Mac, and on System 6.0.5 or higher, making it perfect for use at work or home.

See Also

Database; Multimedia; Word Processors

Three-D, *See 3D; Macromind Three-D*

Terminal Software, *See Modems*

Terrazzo

Xaos Tools' Terrazzo is a **Photoshop** plug-in that creates symmetrically tiled graphics. Every alteration is accompanied by a real-time on-screen preview so that you know exactly what the render will look like. Terrazzo tiles can be used to create backgrounds or selected graphic fills. Tiled graphics can also serve as texture maps for 3D work, especially when mapped to a planar surface in 3D space. Terrazzo gives you a list of application options, from normal to light/dark, multiply, hue, saturation, color, luminosity and screen. The normal setting produces tiles, while the other settings create composited graphics that overlay the tiles in a transparent fashion on the original selection.

Symmetries Terrazzo uses symmetrical guides as a basis for the way the tiles are laid out. There are seventeen guides in the Terrazzo library: Gold Brick, Crab Claws, Pinwheel, Wings, Hither and Yon, Card Tricks, Honey Bees, Prickly Pear, Sunflower, Primrose Path, Spiderweb, Lightning, Storm at Sea, Winding Ways, Monkey Wrench, Whirlpool, and Turnstile. All of the symmetries work in conjunction with an opacity slider that determines the transparency of the tiles that are overlayed on the graphic, and a feathering slider that sets the sharpness of their edges (0 to 100). The feathering options can be seen on-screen with an expanding rectangular area that responds to the feathering setting. Tiles settings can be saved and applied to other images later. Images used as a basis for tiles can come from libraries or be based upon the current loaded image. This gives the digital artist an infinite number of compositing options above and beyond what the present image indicates.

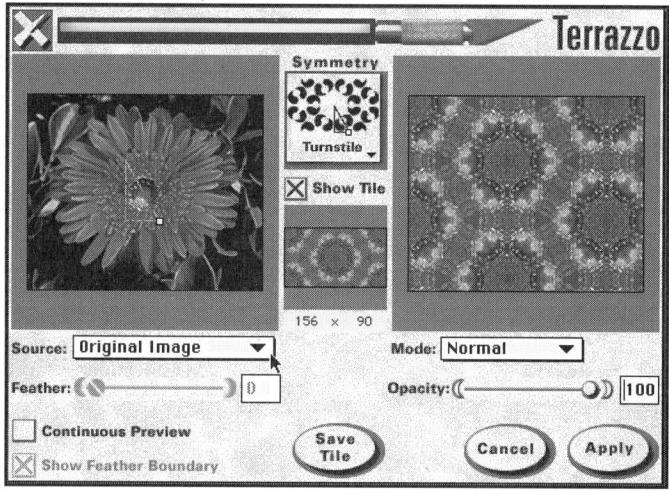

Tiles and Composites Terrazzo applies the tiled symmetries to the image in various modes. Normal mode applies the tile as an overlay, concentrating on the image selection alone. Other mode choices create more composited looks: light, dark, hue, saturation, color, luminosity, multiply, and screen. As a compositing tool, Terrazzo can be used in place of other dedicated compositing software, or even as a compositing utility to the compositing capabilities of Photoshop itself. As long as a graphic is a PICT file, it can be loaded in and composited over the existing on-screen image. Terrazzo does not work well in a multitasking environment, preferring to have its tasks completed before other programs are accessed.

Terrell, Paul, *See Byte Shop, The*

Tetris, *See Tetris Gold*

Tetris Gold

Tetris is considered by many to be the ultimate puzzle or brain game. This CD from Spectrum Holobyte contains the original Tetris, as well as five sequels. The original Tetris consists of different sets of four squares that drop from the top of the screen. You shift the set so that you get a straight line across the bottom of the screen. Each time a line is complete, it disappears. Each round goes faster. This may sound like a cakewalk, but Tetris is not easy. Welltris is a more difficult Tetris game in which you watch the sets drop down a two dimensional well.

Faces requires you to place faces together from different facial features and is a bit boring and Wordtris adds letters to the traditional blocks, which don't disappear unless you can spell a word. Super Tetris adds bombs to the mix, similar to the those in BreakThru. Not all the Tetris games are worth checking out and if you are a complete beginner, non-fanatic type, getting Super Tetris or the original on its own is probably your best bet. But for the price, this is a great way to try out a few brain games.

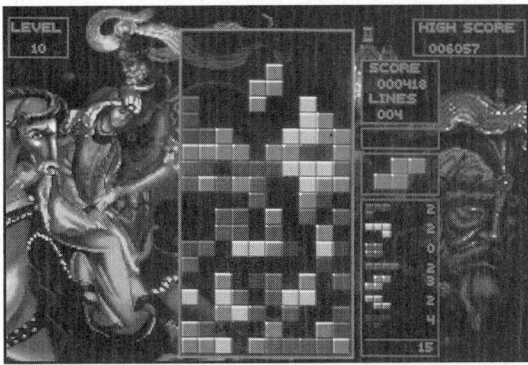

See Also

Breakout; Troubled Souls; Zoop

Text, Centering

Text may be automatically centered on the line by selecting center as an alignment option. This may be done from the toolbar in a word processor or desktop publishing program that uses one, or may be done from the Format menu, or from the Format paragraph dialog box, as shown in the figure. If you are centering text, be sure that it's not also indented. Indenting will throw the line off-center, as will extra spaces at the end of a line.

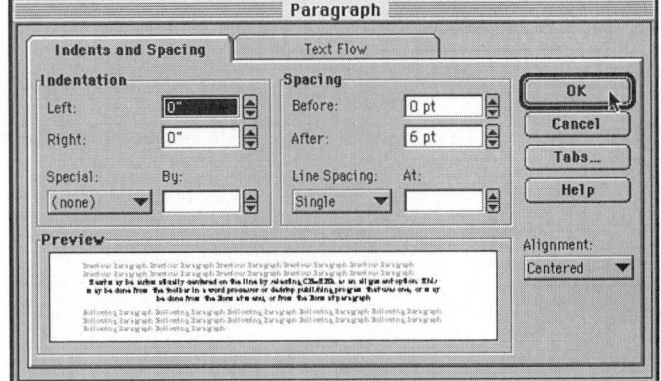

Centered text is good for headlines and posters, but not for business letters.

Text Control Panel

This **control panel** offers two choices: Script, which lets you write from left to right like English or right to left like a number of foreign languages, and Behavior, which lets you select a different character set for different countries. French, for example, would have a different character set than English.

To use the Text Control Panel, follow these steps:

1. Select Text from the Control Panels submenu in the Apple menu (or System folder).

2. Select the appropriate Script and Behavior for your language from the pull-down menus. Close the control panel when your selections are complete.

See Also
Control Panel

Text, Selecting

To select text for editing, move the **I-beam cursor** to either end of the word(s) you want to select, and drag the cursor over it while pressing the **mouse button**. Or, place the cursor within a single word and double-click to select that word. To select a graphic, click it. Some word processors have additional text-selection shortcuts. In Word 6, for example, clicking at the left margin of a line of type selects the whole line. You can also select an entire document in Word 6 by triple-clicking it.

See Also
Word Processing

Texture Mapping

Texture mapping is the application of a graphic, such as a **PICT** image, to the surface of a three-dimensional model to create a realistic appearance. Texture mapping is often used along with **bump mapping**, a technique that creates the illusion of raised details on the surface of an object.

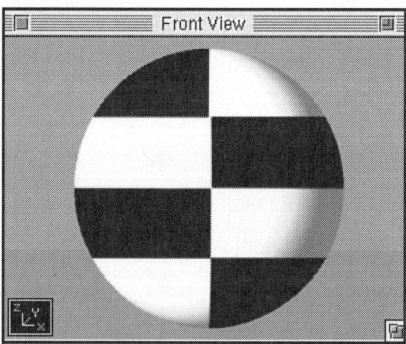

To create a realistic surface on a 3D model, you must take into account many different parameters. All 3D programs enable you to choose a solid color for the surface of an object. For more complicated objects, however, either texture mapping or shader algorithms are required.

The image used to create a texture map can be anything from a scanned picture of a wood plank to the logo of an airline. 3D programs usually provide controls over the type of mapping (how the surface is wrapped around the 3D object). Is it, for example, stretched to cover the shape, or copied multiple times over the surface of the object?

Texture mapping is not limited to simply applying a graphic to the surface. It is also important to be able to position the image on the object.

Bump mapping uses a graphic to create the illusion of a raised surface, usually with just a black-and-white image. The darker or the lighter areas of the graphic represent the higher and lower portions of the surface. While not useful for creating major modeling effects, bump mapping makes it possible to add little details that otherwise would be tedious to create with the modeler—for example, raised rivets on a spaceship.

Reflection defines the reflectivity of a surface, while transparency is used to define the transparency of an object. Some programs let you apply a reflection map—an image that appears reflected in the object. This can save modeling a background that you want reflected in a mirror or similar effect.

One significant advantage of texture mapping is that you are not limited by software. Using a scanner or a paint program, you can create custom surfaces for any object you imagine.

A feature offered by some programs is animated texture mapping. This applies a **QuickTime** movie or a sequence of still images to a surface as the object is rendered in an animated sequence. Use this to create effects, such as a television program on the screen of a 3D model of a TV set.

See Also
3D; Alias' Sketch; Shaders

TextureMaker

Adobe TextureMaker creates textures by combining layers of transparent pictures, procedural "materials," bump maps, overlayed texture, and lighting. Because of the way TextureMaker works, it can be used to generate composited graphics as well as textures. Each layer contains only one element, either lighting, an edge choice, a material, or a picture. The user can add more materials or pictures to the sandwich at any time. All of the layered elements are user configurable. There is also a separate control that enables you to set a definable edge around the finished rendered graphic, especially geared to those users who need to create buttons for Web pages or bevel-edged pictures for digital slide shows. As each parameter of TextureMaker is altered, a quick preview of the rendered results can be generated. The interface is designed with intuitive visual buttons and controls, greatly enhancing the learning process. Final rendered images can be saved out as PICT files or as movies.

Lighting TextureMaker enables you to set the parameters of up to three lights. Color, brightness, shininess, specularity, graininess, position, intensity of shadowing, and degree of reflectivity can be adjusted by sliders. Quick previews of the rendering let you adjust the lights to your needs.

Bevels The choices are none, very thin, thin, standard, large, and pyramid. Each (except for "none") adds an appropriate edge around the rendered image.

Overlaid Texture This acts like a "paper" texture applied in a paint program, in that it affects the apparent graininess of the image. The choices are no bumps, waves, ripples, wrinkles, bumps, dents, and bump map. The bump map choice enables you to add another picture (preferably a 256-grayscale image) as a texture. All of these choices have user configurable settings.

Materials Choices These include: solid color, clouds, marble, wood, checkers, spots, agate, granite, gradient, picture, and filter (lighten, darken, blur, add noise). If "picture" is chosen, you can add your own graphic from your personal library of images, but only if the image is in the PICT format.

Movies The software will generate a movie file from your finished image, but it can be configured only

according to a set list of possibilities. These include moving waves, push through, pan down, evolve, swaying lights, and rising bumps. Rendered previews of these animation effects are included. You can set the duration of the movie yourself.

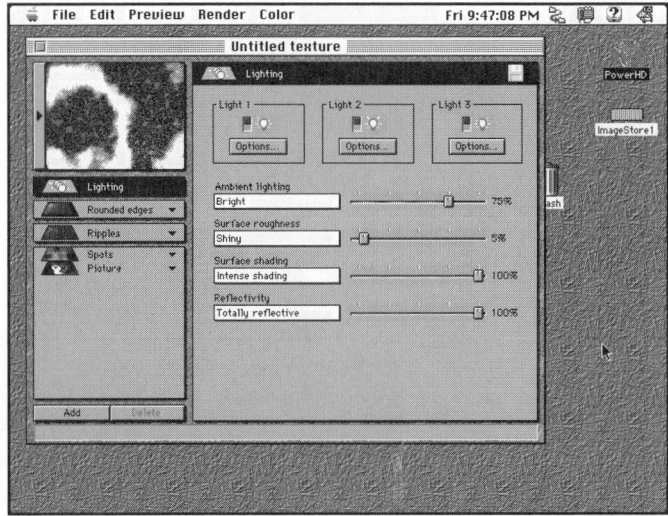

TextureScape 2.0

The version 2.0 edition of this software offers the user a number of advances over the first release. Major advances include the capability to utilize the full set of Bézier drawing tools now residing in TextureScape to create your own vector shape libraries. TextureScape has always been able to import shapes from programs like FreeHand and Illustrator, but with the release of 2.0 you can create shapes without leaving the program. TextureScape uses these vector drawings as a foundation from which textures are created. Version 2 also includes a full set of "combine" modes, so shapes can be added together, and now can also be subtracted, multiplied, and combined in several other ways. This results in even more shape variability in the final rendered textures.

A full-featured visual texture browser has been added, letting you see all of the rendered textures in a library. Any texture can be clicked while in TextureScape, and it will appear with all layers and data intact on the editing screen. This means that you can use any stored texture as a basis for creating limitless variations. To give your textures a reflective property, this version enables you to configure up to four colored lights, each of which can add a directional hi-light to the rendering. CMYK output is also supported for Desktop Publishing use.

The most novel addition in version 2.0 is the ability to drag and drop textures between any applications that support the drag-and-drop process. This is especially geared towards users who use 3D software, like Specular's flagship product, Infini-D. With both TextureScape and Infini-D open, you can take a rendered TextureScape texture and drag it onto a 3D object in Infini-D. Almost instantaneously, the 3D object is wrapped in the new texture. This process can save a 3D artist and animator a lot of time and expense. In essence, this makes TextureScape a texture library utility to all of the 3D software that supports drag-and-drop (Infini-D, RayDream Studio, and Strata Studio Pro to name a few).

TextureScape Tools and What They Do

The basic TextureScape process involves using a vector shape or drawing to generate a pixelated or raster image. Evenly tiled surfaces are created when the shape is simply repeated a number of times across the image, but very organic textures can be created when the shape is varied as it writes to the picture. TextureScape contains a good many tools used to vary the repetition of the original vector shape. Vector shapes are used as the basis for the texture because they are free of the dreaded "jaggies," as vector shapes are not really drawings at all, but directions to the computer that tell it what direction lines that make up the shape are headed in. **Pixelated** or **raster** images, on the other hand, are directions to the computer that tell it exactly what color each squarish pixel on the screen is to be. That's why raster images, if you zoom closely enough, evidence some degree of jagginess. No matter how large

or how small you make a vector shape, it never shows any jagged edges. That's why when a vector shape is used as the basis for constructing a raster or bitmapped shape, as is the case with TextureScape, the resulting bitmap image is as free of jaggedness as it can be. Considering that professional 3D animations often require a very close zooming in upon an object, the highest quality texture that can be wrapped on the object the better. TextureScape can generate textures to a maximum size of 4000×4000 pixels without any loss of resolution.

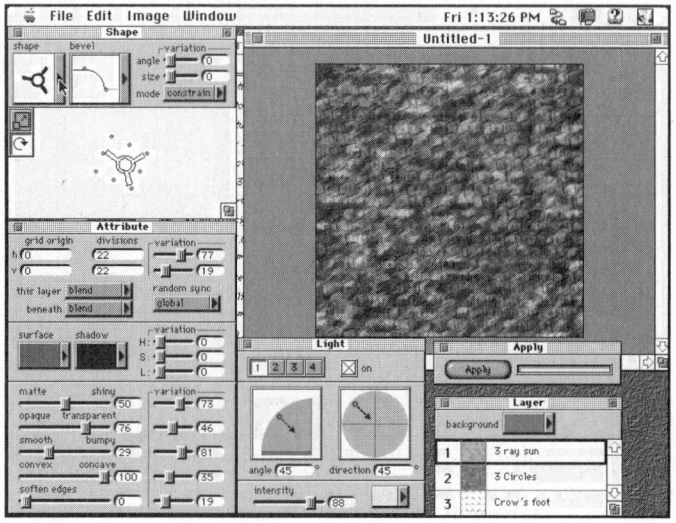

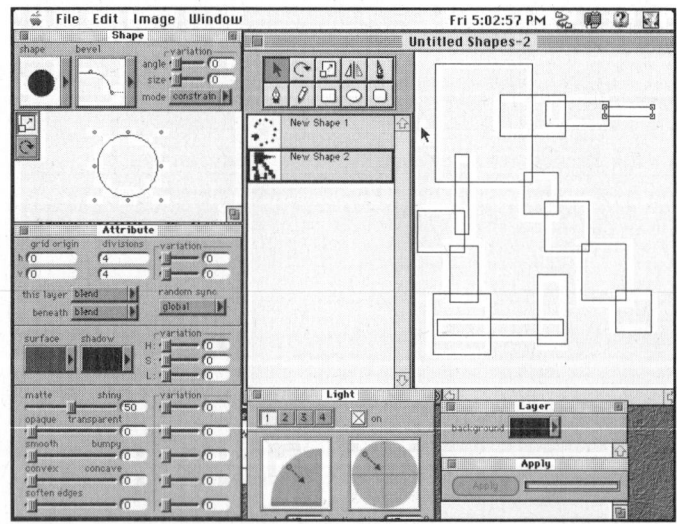

Shapes, Bevels, and Variations TextureScape Shapes are automatically filled in from vector drawing outlines. The outlined vectors are stored in libraries within TextureScape, and you can add shapes to these libraries by importing them from other drawing software (Illustrator, FreeHand, and others) or you can use the TextureScape drawing tools to create new shapes without ever leaving the program. Once a shape is accessed, it takes on 3D attributes. The major attribute is its bevel, or its depth outline. TextureScape enables you to edit this bevel in a visual window. The angle and size of this bevel may be varied over the rendering with each cloned shape from 0 to 100 percent. Non-varied shapes produce mechanical-like renderings, while varied shapes produce more organic and less repetitive renderings. Sliders set the variability for both size and degree of beveling. The shape itself appears in outline form in a separate window, and the mouse can be used to resize and rotate it.

Attributes Menu The attributes addressed to each repetition of the original includes the number of horizontal repetitions, vertical repetitions, color (hue, saturation, and luminance level), matte/shiny, opaque/transparent, smooth/bumpy, convex/concave, and the degree that the edges of a shape should be "softened" as it meets another repeated shape. Although each of these is determined by specific numeric or slider settings, it is in the variability settings that TextureScape's magic resides. Each of the mentioned attributes can be addressed by a slider with a range of 0 to 100 percent. A setting of 100 percent next to the hue control, for instance, results in the shape rendered with a randomized different hue. More variability equates to more organic looking textures.

Lights TextureScape includes an interactive menu for changing the XYZ direction and colorization of four lights. If the setting for "shininess" is turned up, each repeated shape will seem to reflect the lights.

Layers Users of Photoshop and other software that uses layers to composite images should be familiar with the way that TextureScape uses layers. Each layer in TextureScape represents a separate rendering, which can have different shapes and settings. The magic is in setting degrees of transparency for each layer, so that the renderings on the layers "below" the top layer shine through and influence the final texture.

Animated Textures TextureScape can generate animations that transform one texture into another. Many 3D programs allow animated sequences of images to be placed on 3D objects in a scene, useful in creating watery waves, moving sky phenomena and other special effects.

A TextureScape Walkthrough: How to Create a Basic Texture:

1. Choose "new image" from the file menu, use the default size and say OK.

2. Choose a shape from the shape library.

3. Adjust the beveling of the shape.

4. Set the size and color attributes that you desire, and adjust the variability sliders next to each attribute.

5. Adjust the light directions and colors.

6. Hit the "apply" button from the Apply menu.

7. Observe how your image renders to the screen for the preview.

8. Go to the final rendering menu, set the rendering parameters you desire, and render to a file.

9. Open up the rendered texture in Photoshop or any other 2D or 3D program of your choice.

Theorist

For those artists with a penchant for mathematics, Waterloo Maple's Theorist software may fill an important gap. With the capacity to translate complex numbers into 3D graphics, Theorist can serve as an investigative tool that builds bridges of understanding between the two seemingly different worlds of science and art. There are a number of artists who remain determined to use mathematics as the basis of visual design. For these and others seeking to comprehend the beauty of numbers in a new way, Theorist can act as a step in the right direction. Considering that the software that generates digital terrain is based upon a number of mathematical foundations, Theorist can also serve to at least enable the artist to appreciate the deep roots of the tools that are too many times taken for granted.

T

It's a bit challenging to pop Theorist out of the box and immediately generate interesting graphics based on manipulating equations. Most artists have either experienced a definite mental block concerning math or they are removed from their knowledge of it by intervening years. In either case, the Theorist manuals guide you back through the number maze step by step, reintroducing the algebraic necessities page by page. Without some comprehension of the mathematical equations that command Theorist graphics, there is no chance to explore the visual realms that Theorist can potentially open up.

After you get a grasp of the basics, the algorithms that function as graphics generators can be typed on the Theorist "Notebook" screen. There is an alternate way of entering the equations that might be more attractive to the math-challenged user because Theorist also contains a graphic interface that allows for point-click numeric entry. You first have to have (or recall) a basic knowledge of what the parameters are for entering the data, but this can be learned fairly quickly by studying the Theorist documentation. As you click on the targeted icon in Theorist's graphic menu, the appropriate symbol area is written on-screen, waiting for you to type a letter or number in place. The more comprehensive items like tangent, cosine, and other data chunks are also represented by buttons ready to click the formulas into place. Theorist comes in Mac, Notebook, and PowerMac native versions. After a 2D or 3D graphic is rendered in Theorist, it can be exported as a PICT or EPSF graphic for importation and more detailed rendering in either Bitmap or Vector graphics software.

Someone in the computer graphics chain, whether or not it's the artist who creates the final visuals, has to have a deep knowledge of mathematics and how computer graphics algorithms (mathematical strings that translate numbers to line and color) can be tamed and utilized. Usually, this is the programmer, an artist in her own right. Before graphics can be created on-screen, they must be wrestled with in the mind by those who invent the tools. The artist, however, can also gain a great deal by learning to create and manipulate visual algorithms at the root level. For those whose exposure to Theorist, or whose appetite for exploration in general, yearn for understanding deeper connections between math and graphics, Waterloo Maple presents its flagship software, Maple.

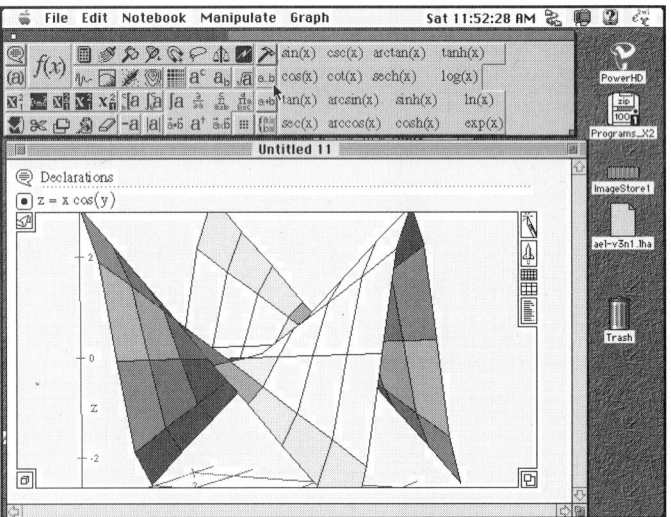

Maple is an explorative mathematical programming language that can help you understand and create very complex graphics. Because of Mandelbrot's discoveries of chaotic phenomena and fractal dimensions (which all scene-generating software incorporates), it has been difficult to tell where art ends and math begins. Waterloo Maple's extensive Maple software, although not as graphically interfaced as its Theorist package, gets to the root of algorithmic manipulation. Maple is probably more essential for the graphics programmer, but with a little time and effort, even the math-shy artist can begin to comprehend the tools that are at the root of computer graphics magic. Maple's documentation gently guides the novice and professional through these realms, while displaying some of the potential results in alluring full color.

Thermal Recalibration

A process performed by hard disk drive mechanisms to ensure that the disk drive head knows where the tracks on the disk are located. Changes in temperature can change the size of the disk drive platter enough to affect the accuracy of positioning of the **read/write head**.

For this reason, many hard drives routinely perform a recalibration routine to check for changes in the drive. These routines are performed automatically by the software in the drive, and may happen at the same time that you are attempting to read or write to the disk drive. While this process might take only fractions of a second, it can be an issue if you are performing a transfer-rate-critical process such as digitizing video or **burning** a **CD-ROM**.

Hard drive manufacturers have responded to this problem by releasing AV (audio-video) drives. These drives either don't need to perform recalibration or will postpone the recalibration if the user accesses the drive. Often, these drives cost more than a similarly sized non-AV drive. Whether you need to spend the extra money for an AV drive depends upon what your needs are. Newer drives are less likely to cause a problem, particularly if you aren't pumping large amounts of information into or out of the drive. For example, digitizing video for CD-ROM (which doesn't require a very high throughput) probably won't be a problem with newer drives, but if you are attempting to digitize full-screen video, you probably need to buy a **RAID** drive or certainly an AV one.

See Also
Hard Disk Drive

Thermal Wax Printing,
See Printing Technology, Color

Think C, See Symantec C++

Think Pascal, See Symantec C++

Thinkin' Things

EdMark's Thinkin' Things is a collection of logic puzzles and experiments for kids ages 7 to 13. As of this writing, there are three different sets, each with a half dozen different activities, and presumably there will be more to come. They help develop reasoning and analysis skills, memory and concentration, and listening skills. Each activity emphasizes a different kind of thinking. Kids learn Boolean logic as they fill orders at the Fripple shop, deductive reasoning as they match the Fripples with their houses, attributes and differences as they analyze a series of birds and attempt to assemble the next one in the series, and many other higher-level thinking skills with the other activities.

There's plenty of room for creativity, too. Many of the activities are "open-ended." They have no right or wrong answers, just tools to explore. Kids can construct moving art and three-dimensional illusions, program a marching band and cheerleaders through a halftime show, experiment with gravity, friction, and motion on a virtual ball field, and play with special effects and morphing on photos. Most of all, they'll be having so much fun they won't realize how much they're learning. Each activity has beginning and advanced levels and some require many steps to achieve a goal.

ThinNet (10Base-T),
See EtherNet

TIA

Stands for The **Internet** Adapter, an inexpensive commercial product offered by Cyberspace Development, Inc., for an Internet Service Provider's UNIX Web server that allows a user of that server to run a basic shell account as if it were a more powerful SLIP account. A user with a **MacTCP**-based connection who dials into the Net with an Internet Service Provider has to pay only for a simple UNIX-based shell account, which normally gives you the most basic Internet access, but enables you to use **Netscape**, **Fetch**, **Anarchie**, and other TCP/IP-based software.

To find out more about TIA, go to **http://marketplace.com/**.

See Also
Anarchie; Fetch; Internet Service Provider; MacTCP; Netscape; SLIP

TidBITS

A free weekly newsletter distributed solely over computer networks on the Internet. *TidBITS* focuses on the Macintosh and developments in the world of electronic communications. Edited by Adam C. Engst, author of *Internet Starter Kit*. Distributed by mailing list (**listserv@ricevm1.rice.edu**), and via a home page on the World Wide Web at **http://www.tidbits.com/**.

To subscribe to the TidBITS mailing list, send email to **listserv@ricevm1.rice.edu**. The contents of the message should assume a standard format that the **LISTSERV** will recognize:

```
SUBSCRIBE TIDBITS [your full name, at least
two words]
```

The LISTSERV will return an email message confirming your subscription and providing general information about the list you have joined (it's a good idea to save this list when it comes time to unsubscribe). After you have been on a list for some time, the LISTSERV may ask you to confirm your subscription.

See Also

Internet

Tilde Key

This key inserts a foreign language accent mark (´), or when pressed while holding the Shift key it inserts the foreign language tilde (~) mark. You can access letters with these foreign language accent marks already in place by using the Key Caps DA.

See Also

Shift Key; Special Characters

Time Base Corrector

Because **analog video** signals are often dependent upon mechanical devices (a VCR mechanism for example), the frames of the video aren't always displayed exactly on time. This creates timing errors (a jittery image), because the electron gun in the television tube continues scanning at the ideal rate even if the new image hasn't arrived. This becomes a real problem when mixing signals from two devices. A time base corrector, which is built into some VCRs and camcorders or can be purchased separately, acts as a frame buffer and ensures that a frame is delivered at the correct time. A frame buffer is simply memory that stores the current frame. If the next frame doesn't arrive on time, the last frame can be sent again by the Time Base Corrector. Although mostly used when editing video tape, these devices can help improve the quality of digitized sequences. For typically sized **QuickTime** movies (that is, smaller than quarter screen; 240×180 or 180×160 pixels in size), correctors are usually unnecessary.

See Also

Analog Video; Digital Video; QuickTime

Time Code

Time code provides an accurate method for finding a frame in a video sequence. Many semi-professional video decks and cameras support some (often proprietary) form of time code, although it might not always be recognized by other devices. The most recognized and standard form of time code is **SMPTE**.

Time code is sometimes seen burnt (or striped) into a dub of a video tape. This shows the time code numbers on-screen in the video, and enables a viewer to note sequences that are needed for editing. The time code then is used by editing equipment to specify the exact points at which an edit is to be made.

Time code is most useful when editing video or digital video sequences as a preview before editing the video tape. Time code makes it possible to find locations on a tape quickly and accurately.

If you plan to digitize and edit video on the computer and keep the material in a digital computer-based format, time code becomes less important. It's good to have a playback deck that has an accurate way of finding the segments you need to digitize, but after they are digitized, **QuickTime** adds its own timing mechanism.

Time code is required when using an **EDL** (Edit Decision List) to transfer editing information from one device to another.

See Also

EDL; SMPTE; Video Editing

Time-Saving Window Tips

There's much more than meets the eye when it come to working within windows in the **Finder**. Apple has added a host of shortcuts that make managing and working with windows much easier. Here are some of the most popular:

- To close any active window (not just in the Finder), press ⌘-W.

- To move an inactive window without making it the active window, hold the ⌘ key, and you can select and drag the window to a new location.

- If you're in the window of a **nested folder**, you can navigate your way backward to the folders your folder is nested in by holding the ⌘ key and clicking the window's name in the title bar. A pop-up menu appears listing any windows you can jump to from that folder. If, for example, you're in the Netscape Preferences folder in your Preferences folder, which is in your **System Folder**, which is in your Hard Disk folder, and you click the name of the Netscape Preferences folder in the window's title bar, a pop-up menu appears where you can choose to jump backwards to the Preferences folder, the System Folder, or the Hard Disk folder.

- To close all open windows, press and hold the Option key and click a window's close box, or press the keyboard shortcut ⌘-Option-W.

- To close a window and open a folder in that window at the same time, press the Option key while double-clicking the new folder and the previous window will automatically close as the new one opens.

- When viewing a window in a list view, you can change the method in which the items are sorted by clicking the name of the item in the list view. If you have a window whose contents are sorted by name, for example,

"Name" is underlined at the top of the window, indicating that the window is sorted by name. If you click "Size," the window resorts by size and "Size" becomes underlined. To sort by a different view, click the word at the top of the window.

You can also change the accent color of your window by choosing the Color Control Panel. At the top of this Color window you can select the color highlighted text items appear as, and at the bottom you can select the accent color for your window from a pop-up menu of colors. After you've made your selection, close the Color Control Panel, and your choice of window accent color takes effect.

See Also

Finder; System

TimeLapse: Ancient Civilizations

TimeLapse from GTE Interactive is slick. Like **Eastern Mind**, it presents a new twist on the **Myst**-like theme of roaming a foreign landscape, but the unique artwork is simply unbelievable. The development team for TimeLapse included a team of computer artists who used ancient artifacts as models for the 3D recreations of the lost and mythical civilizations you encounter in the game.

In TimeLapse, you play an inter-dimensional traveler who must unlock the secret connection between cities in different time periods. The civilizations you visit are based on cultures as varied as Ancient Egypt, Mayan culture, and the Anasazi civilization, (based in the southwestern United States from about 1300-1700). The best world you visit is the mythical Atlantis. Because there were no artifacts to copy or scrutinize, the artists had creative license in designing the background scenery and characters for the lost city. The images in TimeLapse are perfect right down to the computer generated shadows. Plus, game play is fun and the puzzles challenging. TimeLapse builds on the serene adventure-style of Myst and adds a new dimension in Mac gaming.

See Also

7th Guest, The; Daedalus Encounter, The; Eastern Mind; Full Throttle; Hell; Myst; Return to Zork; Riddle of Master Lu, The

Tint Screen, *See Halftones*

<TITLE> HTML Tag

Every **HTML** document on the **World Wide Web** requires a short, specific title displayed at the top of the **Web browser**'s window. The title should be placed within the <TITLE> start tag and </TITLE> end tag. For example:

```
<HTML>
<HEAD>
<TITLE>A Guide to Basic HTML</TITLE>
</HEAD>
<BODY>
...the rest of the document goes here...
</BODY>
</HTML>
```

Titles should be short enough to fit on a Web browser window, yet specific enough to give Web readers an idea of what the document is about.

See Also

HTML; Web Browser; Web Page; World Wide Web

TMON Professional

TMON Pro is a low-level **debugger** for the Macintosh that has a somewhat checkered past. Written in the early days of the Macintosh by Waldemar Horwat, TMON Pro rapidly gained an extensive following and was widely used among commercial developers. TMON was originally published by ICOM Simulations, Inc., a company best known for its multimedia titles. When ICOM was purchased by the media giant Viacom, TMON faded into the background. By the time the Power Macs were introduced, TMON had all but disappeared from the Mac development scene. Through a series of agreements and purchases, TMON ended up with MindVision Software, a company known for its custom development work and developer tools. TMON was reborn.

The new TMON has all the excellent features of the original, plus a slew of features designed for Power Macintosh debugging. TMON Pro can now debug PowerPC code, and it supports the new "modern" memory manager in the Power Macintosh, as well as the mixed mode Manager.

One of TMON's most unique features is its ability to modify both 68K and PowerPC code on-the-fly using an interactive assembler. This makes it easy to directly apply patches to code during debugging and testing. The interactive assembler enables programmers to enter assembly language instructions, convert them into machine language instructions, and patch them into the existing code on-the-fly.

TMON also provides formatting of memory locations into the high-level structures they hold and dynamic memory watching capabilities. Using this feature, you can watch memory locations change as the program runs. Any data displayed by TMON can also be edited in place.

TMON shares many features with **MacsBug,** including the capability to check any memory **heap** for validity and the ability to show the complete chain of subroutine calls that led the application being debugged to its current state.

TMON Pro is published by MindVision Software:

MindVision Software
840 South 30th St., Suite C
Lincoln, NE 68510
Email: **sales@mindvision.com**
Fax: (402) 477-1395
Phone: (402) 477-3269
Web: **http://www.mindvision.com/**

See Also

Debugger; Debugging Tools; MacsBug

TOC, *See Tables of Contents*

Tog, *See Tognazzini, Bruce*

Tognazzini, Bruce

Bruce "Tog" Tognazzini is a computer interface guru, now working for Sun Microsystems, who was Apple's human interface evangelist.

Tog developed and published Apple's first set of **human interface guidelines** that programmers use to keep their applications consistent and easy to use. Tog was involved in the interface design of a wide variety of Apple's computers, applications, and System software.

Tog is best known among programmers for the columns he wrote for *Apple Direct*, the predecessor to *Apple Directions*. Many of these columns are collected in his very popular book, *Tog on Interface*, in which he elucidates the Macintosh spirit and discusses the fundamental principles of the Macintosh human interface.

See Also

History and Culture of the Macintosh; Human Interface Guidelines

Toolbox

The Toolbox is a set of system routines available to programmers through the MacOS **Application Programming Interface** (API). The toolbox contains routines for virtually every aspect of Macintosh programming.

Related toolbox routines are categorized into *managers*. Each manager is responsible for one functionally related group of routines. Some of the most important managers are listed in the following table.

This table is just the tip of the iceberg. The Toolbox contains thousands of routines that do everything from drawing a simple line to playing a **QuickTime** movie. All but the very newest Toolbox routines are documented in the massive series of *Inside Macintosh* books. They also are documented in **THINK Reference** and the **Macintosh Programmer's Toolbox Assistant**, electronic references that enable you to search rapidly for any routine.

You don't need to know all of the Toolbox inside-out to program the Macintosh. In fact, you can become a competent Mac programmer knowing only a few dozen routines (provided you keep *Inside Macintosh* or one of the electronic references close at hand). There are very few programmers who know more than a couple hundred of the most common routines.

See Also

Application Programming Interface; Inside Macintosh; Macintosh Programmer's Toolbox Assistant; THINK Reference

A Few of the Toolbox Managers

Apple Event Manager	Code Fragment Manager	Control Manager
Window Manager	Dialog Manager	Menu Manager
Drag Manager	File Manager	Event Manager
Gestalt Manager	Mixed Mode Manager	TextEdit
Sound Manager	SCSI Manager	QuickDraw
Process Manager	Resource Manager	Printing Manager

Toolbox Assistant,

See Macintosh Programmers Toolbox Assistant

Top Cat Virus, *See MDEF Virus*

Touch Screens

Touch screens function the same as **graphics tablets**, except your finger is the pen. Touch screens are useful for self-running demos (especially **HyperCard**-based demos), and public information kiosks that permit people to operate the computer simply by tapping buttons on-screen. Touch screens replace keyboards and mice completely in these situations or can complement them in office and home use. Almost all are **Apple Desktop Bus devices** and are completely compatible with the Mac and its applications.

The attraction to touch screens is their directness and immediacy. In this respect, they surpass the mouse as a pointing device. The downside is that they require the user to be within arm's reach of the CRT screen to place a finger on the surface. The possible problems of radiation and electromagnetic fields become much greater the closer you are to the monitor or electromagnetic source. For casual, occasional use at a kiosk, this probably is not significant. For continual daily use at home or in the office, a touch screen might not be a good idea if the prospect of exposure to electromagnetic fields bothers you. Many researchers say its a non-issue. Others believe there may be cause for concern.

The following table provides an overview of the touch screen technology available for the Mac.

See Also

Apple Desktop Bus; Graphics Tablets; Keyboards; Mouse; Pen/Handwriting Devices; Trackballs; Touchpads

Touch Screens for the Mac

Manufacturer	*Model Name*	*Features*	*Street Price*
Edmark	Touch Window	ADB device.	$335
Elo TouchSystems, Inc.	Elographics Touchscreen	Clear glass panel with IntelliTouch surface acoustic wave sensing— greater than 900 touch points per square inch; ADB device.	$290
Elo TouchSystems, Inc.	TouchMonitors	Factory-installed touch screens. Available in 14-, 17-, and 19-inch sizes. Use Intellitouch (surface wave) or AccuTouch (resistive) technologies. Usable with a gloved or naked hand.	$970 to $2,800 plus controller
MicroTouch Systems, Inc.	Mac 'n' Touch	An overlay for monitors. Includes an ADB controller, ClearTek 1000 touch sensor, driver software.	N/A

Touchpads

The touchpad (or the trackpad, as it is sometimes called,) is a new and innovative pointing device. Touchpads are included in all PowerBooks after the 100 series, such as the 500 series, 5300, and 2600 duos which use this method of pointing and clicking in the place of the older trackball. The touchpad uses the principle of coupling capacitance to sense the presence of your finger. This is the same technology used in elevator buttons that you touch rather than push.

The touchpad uses capacitance sensing via a grid of conductive strips that underlie the pad. Controlling circuits emit high-frequency signals along the strips. The electrical field emanates through and above the surface of the pad. These circuits measure the change in capacitance (the electrical field produced between the strips and spaces) that is caused by running your finger over the pad. Your finger disrupts the electrical field for several of the conductive strips. A microprocessor in the touchpad calculates the center of the disturbance and tracks the movement and speed of your finger. The touchpad can detect 387 points per inch (generating measurements of very small movements). The touchpad, like the mouse, is a relative-motion device, calculating the relative location of the cursor rather than its exact location compared to the cursor on the screen. You click the screen to select by tapping on the pad's surface or by pressing buttons at the top, bottom, or side of the pad.

The touchpad provides significant advantages over the trackball:

- The touchpad has no moving parts that can break or get dirty.

- The touchpad uses less power than the trackball—a significant savings for PowerBook batteries.

- The touchpad is lighter and smaller than the trackball, leaving more internal space in PowerBooks for other internal components.

- The proportions of the touchpad matches that of the PowerBook screen, providing a more direct correlation between the movements of your finger and the corresponding movement of the cursor across the screen.

On the other hand, many users find touchpads difficult to use. You must touch the pad with your finger, and not your fingernail. If you have an adhesive bandage on your touchpad finger, the device will not respond.

Touchpads come with software that lets you program their buttons to perform keyboard shortcuts. Some touchpads let you set the button action, cursor acceleration, and touchpad response for specific applications.

The following table provides an overview of the touchpads available for use with desktop or portable Macs.

Touchpads for Your Mac

Manufacturer	Model Name	Features	Street Price
Hagiwara Sys-Com	Point Pad	A pressure-sensitive trackpad that uses a different technology than standard pads	$99
MicroQue	QuePoint II	Software loads that customize the pad for each application's requirements	$79.95
Alps Electric	GlidePoint	Three-button touchpad; software for adjusting finger-to-cursor tracking ratios; manufactures touchpads for PowerBook 520 and 540	$70
Touche Technologies	TouchPad	Color-coordinated touchpad for PowerBook users	$59.95
Cirque	GlidePoint	Four-button touchpad, programmable pad and buttons	$79.95

See Also

Absolute versus Relative Motion; Apple Desktop Bus; Graphics Tablets; Joysticks; Keyboards; Mouse; Pen/Handwriting Devices; PowerBooks; Touch Screens; Trackballs; Trackpad

Toyo

Similar in principle to the **FocolTone** and **Pantone** spot color systems, Toyo is used primarily in Japan. Offering both a printed swatchbooks and a digital one accessible through major graphics applications, the system enables designers to choose colors that can be reproduced by single inks (for best results) or converted to **CMYK** equivalents (usually imperfectly).

See Also

CMYK; Color Matching Systems; FocolTone; Pantone; Spot Color; TruMatch

Trackballs

If you do not have the desk space to move a mouse, then the trackball is the pointing device you should consider. The trackball is like an upside-down mouse. Trackballs don't require additional software to access the point-and-click functionality of a regular mouse. The trackball is a plastic ball that sits on rollers in a fixed location. You roll the ball with your fingers and press a button to select. Because of its smaller footprint, the trackball was the pointer of choice for the PowerBook 100 and 200 models. Some trackballs come with control panels and system extensions that offer programmability for the multiple buttons available on some models.

The benefit of a trackball, other than its smaller footprint, is that when using it, your hand stays in one position. If you experience shoulder pains from moving the mouse around, a trackball can provide welcome relief. On the other hand, that little bit of mouse movement exercises the arm and shoulder. Leaving the hand in one position on the trackball for extended periods of time (such as when you scroll through a series of database records during pruning and updating operations) can create ideal conditions for carpal tunnel syndrome. The best approach is to switch between mouse and trackball to provide physical relief and variety of movement. Trackballs are a convenience in many situations, particularly when you are working with graphics applications. In contrast to using a mouse, you do not run the risk of running out of mouse pad room when trying to draw lines, shapes, or edit pixels in a graphic image. Trackballs can also be programmed to select special key combinations.

In graphics applications, this can help automate magnifying an image or selecting a certain graphics tool before using the trackball.

Mice and Trackballs for Your Mac

Manufacturer	Model Name	Features	Street Price
Apple	ADB Mouse II	Opto-mechanical mouse with a round housing and large single button. Comes standard with current PowerMacs, LCs, and Performas.	$80
CH Products	Trackball Pro ADB	Simple trackball with limited programmability and functionality	$119.95
Kensington Microware	Thinking Mouse Macintosh ADB	Four programmable buttons to automate tasks and rubberized sides for easier grasping	$89.95
Kensington Microware	Mouse-in-a-Box	Single-button mouse	$39.95
Kensington Microware	Mouse	Dual-button mouse	$59.95

Manufacturer	Model Name	Features	Street Price
Kensington Microware	Turbo Mouse 5.0	Programmable buttons on the trackball for configuring keyboard commands. Versions prior to 4.0 can cause a Power Mac to crash.	$109.95
Logitech	MouseMan	Opto-mechanical mouse curved to fit the contours of the hand. Right- and left-hand versions.	$129
Logitech	TrackMan Marble	Optical mechanism, programmable buttons with trackball.	$89.95
MicroSpeed	Mouse Deluxe Mac	Multi-button, non-ergonomic mouse.	$49.95
MicroSpeed	MacTrac and HyperTrac	Three-button trackball with software that senses the program you are using and switches button shortcuts to accommodate.	N/A
Mouse Systems	A3 Mouse	Optical tracking, three-button mouse.	$64.95
Mouse Systems	A3 Trackball	Opto-mechanical device, Programmable trackball with three buttons.	$49.95
The Mace Group	MacAlly	ADB mouse.	$49
CoStar	Stingray	Ergonomically designed to fit the hand, two-button trackball.	$99.95

See Also

Absolute versus Relative Motion; Apple Desktop Bus; Graphics Tablets; Joysticks; Keyboards; Mouse; Pen/Handwriting Devices; PowerBook Trackballs and Trackpads; Touch Screens; Touchpads;

Tracking

Tracking adjusts the letter spacing of an entire line of type, as opposed to **kerning**, which adjusts individual pairs of letters. Tracking is sometimes called letter spacing or character spacing. Tracking can be set as loose, expanded, normal, tight, or condensed. The following figure shows the effects of different amounts of tracking.

This line is set with normal tracking.

This line is set with condensed tracking.

This line is set with expanded tracking.

This line is set with very condensed tracking.

This line is set with very expanded tracking.

Lines 2 and 3 were condensed and expanded by 1 point. Lines 4 and 5 used 1.5 point tracking. Any greater amount would have made the type unreadable.

See Also

Kerning; Leading

Trackpad

This **control panel** is used only by **PowerBooks** that have the Trackpad input device (rather than a mouse). The Trackpad was introduced with the 500 series of PowerBook Macintosh models and enables users to move the cursor by sliding their fingertip across a square flat pad. This pad appears on the PowerBook where the small trackball used to appear.

The Trackpad control panel enables PowerBook users to set preferences for the tracking of the Trackpad (how fast the Trackpad responds to their movement), and it enables the user to tell the PowerBook at which speed to interpret two clicks as a double-click. This control panel is almost identical, in features and layout, to the standard **Mouse control panel** found on desktop Macs.

See Also

Control Panel; Mouse Control Panel; PowerBook; Touchpads

Trade Shops, *See Service Bureaus, Trade Shops, and Desktop Publishing*

Trading Fonts

Fonts present a daily dilemma for desktop publishers. Designers' work doesn't stay where it's created—files usually have to be sent somewhere else for revisions or output. That means the fonts and graphics have to go along, too.

Or do they? The fact is, trading fonts is illegal. The software license supplied with most commercial fonts enables users to install the fonts on one or more work stations within their establishments, but not to send copies of the fonts along with jobs. Despite many people's impression that it's OK to trade screen fonts, or OK to trade printer fonts, but not both, the bottom line is that service bureaus are required to buy their own copies of any fonts they need to open a document.

There's no law against trading shareware fonts (in fact, that's how they're *supposed* to be distributed), but paying shareware fees is a moral obligation. When distributing a shareware product, always include all the files that came with it.

See Also

Fonts; Shareware

Traditional Games

You may feel like you are the only person in the world who doesn't want to parade around a medieval dungeon dressed up as an orc with a band of thieves looking for the Holy Grail while you dodge flying toilets, but chances are you are not. If you yearn for an old fashion board game, card game, or just a brain teaser without 3D paddles and sound effects, there are plenty of **traditional games** that have made it over to the computer.

Not all of us felt the immediate need to put all of our old board games into the furnace and load up **DOOM II** or **Myst**. We aren't all "fancy" gamers. Many companies have done a great job of switching favorite noncomputer games to the computer.

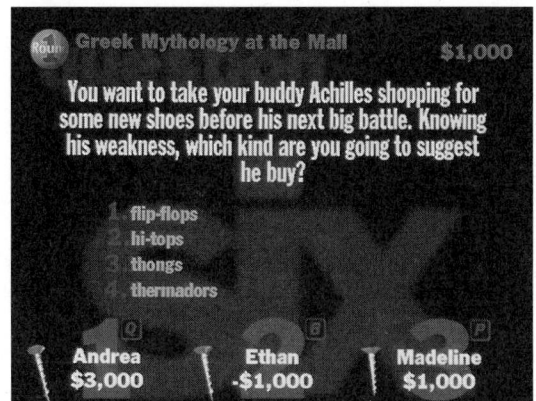

The main thing missing from most computer games (although it's changing with the onset of network gaming) is playing against a partner. Though **You Don't Know Jack** from Berkeley Systems brings a much more hip variation of the board game Trivial Pursuit to the screen and can handle multiple players smoothly, most computer games do not. Games like **Return to Zork** and **Rebel Assault** are great fun, but you can't sit around the screen with friends the way you do with Monopoly or Pictionary.

Consequently, a lot of attempts to bring board games to the screen don't really add up to much. Often the screen is small or the element of timing is skewed by having too many fingers at the keyboard.

TIP Many of the better "traditional games" are shareware. Look for variations of Yahtzee, Othello, VideoPoker, MilleBornes, Bridge, Gin Rummy, and the like in shareware collections or online game libraries.

Card games range in complexity from the standard solitaire game that probably shipped with your Mac, to the 3D complexity of the forthcoming Perfect Partner series from Canadian company Positronic. Most crossword and word-puzzle games add digital elements of help, online tips, freebies such as free words you can drop into a crossword, and the ability to make your own puzzles, but the overall game is the same as any newspaper puzzle. Crossword Wizard from Cogix and Take-A-Break! Crosswords from Dynamix are among the best of the bunch, but if you are into the idea of solving crosswords on your computer, even on a PowerBook, any of the titles available will most likely suit you.

See Also

Classic Collection; Chess; Sports Games; You Don't Know Jack

Training, *See Desktop Publishing Training*

Transferring Files on Internet, *See FTP*

Transition (Video Editing)

In video editing, a transition is an effect applied when jumping from one clip to another. Common effects are wipes and dissolves. During the transition, the second clip becomes visible through or over the first clip. This requires overlapping the end of the first clip and the beginning of the second clip to create the transition effect (see the following figure).

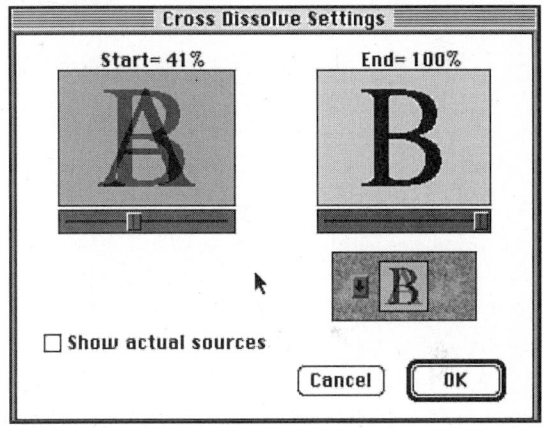

For example, if you have two clips that are four seconds long, and create a one-second transition, then the final movie will contain three seconds of video from the first clip, one second of transition (from both clips), and three seconds from the second clip. The resulting segment will be seven seconds long. If, however, a simple cut had been employed, the resulting segment would be eight seconds long.

Note that during the transition the audio also overlaps, and must either be merged or cut in some way.

See Also

Cut; Jump Cut; L-Cut; Premiere; VideoShop

T

Transitional Typefaces, *See Typeface Categories*

Translating Files, *See Converting and Translating Files*

Transmission Media

Transmission media is the physical cable that connects each workstation or computer to the others. The transmission media is responsible for distributing the messages between each computer on the network. It serves the same function in relation to the network that your spinal cord and nervous system does to get the signal from your brain to wiggle your toes. Unlike the human body, though, the network can run on several different kinds of cables. If you could replace a spinal cord with a piece of an artery, or a ligament, you'd have the same kind of interchangeability that network designers have in the choice of transmission media.

Note that these types of media are technically independent of the network protocols and data links in use. However in practical terms, the data link in use specifies the types of transmission media that are supported.

Twisted Pair Twisted pair wiring is an inexpensive and reliable means of connecting computers. Twisted pair is by far the most commonly used network transmission media. Ethernet, LocalTalk, and Token Ring all support the use of twisted pair cabling. However, each data link type requires slightly different wiring and different connectors.

The two major types of twisted pair wiring are shielded and unshielded. Shielded twisted pair cabling has a metal shield within the cable to protect the network signals from outside interference. The LocalTalk and Token Ring data link protocols support shielded twisted pair cabling.

LocalTalk over Shielded Twisted Pair Apple's original Locking LocalTalk connectors were designed to use shielded twisted pair cabling. However, due to the expense of purchasing and installing this type of wiring, it is fairly uncommon for LocalTalk networks.

(Even Apple headquarters has switched to the less expensive Farallon system described below.) The LocalTalk cabling system connected to the Mac's Printer (serial) port and to the appropriate LocalTalk port on other devices.

Token Ring over Shielded Twisted Pair Token ring connections are commonly used over shielded twisted pair as this is the "Type 1" cabling specified by IBM for use in most microcomputer networks.

Unshielded Twisted Pair Unshielded twisted pair (UTP) cabling makes use of regular twists within the cable to block outside interference. The frequency of the twists determines the level of interference that the cabling is protected from, and is rated accordingly as Category 1-5. UTP of category 3 through 5 are suitable for Ethernet, Token Ring, and LocalTalk.

The major drawback of unshielded twisted pair is that the signals are not well protected from electromagnetic interference or physical damage. Therefore, UTP serves well in an office environment, but may not be appropriate for industrial or long-distance outdoor applications. The shielded cable above is a better choice in an electrically noisy environment.

LocalTalk over Unshielded Twisted Pair This method of connecting Macs to LocalTalk was developed by Farallon and is called PhoneNet. Farallon's PhoneNet connectors use ordinary telephone cable and standard RJ-11 jacks and plugs. The incredible popularity of this type of networking stems from the relatively low cost and easy availability. The PhoneNet connection boxes can be had for as little as $10 each, and the wire, connectors, and the special crimping tool to apply them can all be purchased at Radio Shack or a well-equipped hardware store. Though it's quickly becoming replaced with UTP Ethernet, this type of network will be found *somewhere* at nearly all Mac network installations.

EtherNet over Unshielded Twisted Pair EtherNet is now very commonly run over unshielded twisted pair wiring. Ethernet requires slightly higher quality cabling than some telephone wire provides, so it's not always possible to use existing telephone wires. Ethernet running over UTP is referred to as 10Base-T. 10Base-T Transceivers make use of an RJ-45 Connector to attach the cable to the transceiver. It is critical to always use cabling of at least Category 3, or you will not get satisfactory results.

Thin Coaxial Thin coaxial cable is similar to the cabling used to connect cable television, but be careful! It's not quite the same… and the two types are not interchangeable! Token Ring and LocalTalk do not provide support for this type of connection, but it is supported and commonly used by Ethernet. A thin coaxial Ethernet network is generally referred to as Thin Ethernet or ThinNet. A ThinNet transceiver is required for each EtherNet node. They attach to the cable with BNC twist connectors.

Thick Coaxial Thick coaxial cable is not supported by LocalTalk or by Token Ring, but as with thin coaxial, only by Ethernet. Thick coaxial Ethernet is referred to as Thick Ethernet or ThickNet. It offers much better shielding from electronic interference, and can provide long distance connections. Unfortunately, it's also quite unwieldy and expensive to install. This type of cable is now used less frequently because fiber optic cabling can provide many of the same advantages at a lower cost. When used, it generally serves as the "backbone" for a network, and may also be used in applications that require the cable to go outdoors from one building to another or to stand up under other "tough use" conditions.

Fiber-Optic Fiber optic cabling sends its messages using pulses of light instead of by electromagnetic signals. Because of its form of transmission, fiber optic cabling is immune to electromagnetic interference and can be used over quite long distances, making it an ideal media for network connections between multiple buildings. Fiber optic cabling is also called FDDI, for Fiber Distributed Data Interface. These initials actually represent an ANSO/ISO standard for networks. FDDI has a bandwidth data throughput rate of 100MBps, 10 times faster than 10Base-T EtherNet, and equal to the new 100Base-T EtherNet networks recently introduced. Fiber optic Ethernet cabling is quickly becoming common on Macintosh networks, and is referred to as 10Base-F.

Fiber optic cabling is only now starting to become commonplace in microcomputer networking. With recent increases in the cost of high quality category 5 unshielded twisted pair cabling, Fiber Optic cabling no longer carries the huge price penalty it was once associated with, though it remains more difficult to install than UTP. However, FDDI requires plug-in cards, as EtherNet does, but the cost is higher, a bit over $1000 per card.

Transparent Images

Transparent images are graphics that have an invisible background and appear to be "floating" on a **World Wide Web page**.

Transparent images are a variant of the CompuServe **GIF** format that is recognized by virtually all Web browsers. This special type of GIF file, called GIF 89, allows one color in its palette (color number 89) to be rendered as "transparent."

A useful and popular freeware utility for converting GIF images to GIF89s is called Transparency, by Aaron Giles. Keep in mind that the best images to convert are icons or other line art because the images can be discerned clearly from the backgrounds. Also keep in mind that some **Web browsers** may not yet display transparent images.

To use Transparency, first set up your image in GIF format. Transparency doesn't allow you to retouch your image—you must remove the background or other area in an image-editing program, and replace the area in question with a solid color not used in the part of the image you wish to display. (In most cases the software you use to scan an image will allow you to edit it.)

Then:

1. Save your image as a GIF.

2. Open the image with Transparency by dragging the document's icon onto the Transparency icon. Your image will appear in transparency's window.

3. Click the color you wish to make transparent, and hold down the mouse button. A palette that contains all the colors in your GIF image appears under your cursor, and the color that you have clicked is selected. Release the mouse button.

4. Be sure to choose "Save as GIF 89…" from the "File" menu when you are through.

Transparency is available at **ftp://ftp.med.cornell.edu/ pub/aarong/transparency/**.

See Also

GIF89; Web Browser; World Wide Web Page

Transporting Files

Though it's a major concern for desktop publishers, anyone who trades files with other users who aren't on the same LAN needs to consider the best way to accomplish the transfer.

The most obvious way to get a file to another computer is to copy it to a floppy disk. Macs can read and write to PC-formatted disks, as well as to Mac-formatted ones, so for small files (1.2MB or less), this is the fastest solution. Larger files can be **compressed** and segmented into sections that will each fit on one floppy. When the file is decompressed, the pieces are rejoined.

The larger the files get, however, the less convenient floppy disks are. That's the time to turn to removable storage media like **SyQuest**, **Bernoulli**, magneto-optical, and other disk formats. While tape formats like DAT are useful for archiving, they're generally considered too slow to use for file transfer.

The first thing to consider in choosing a media format is compatibility. Which formats does the file's recipient use? It's no use sending a pile of Bernoullis if your service bureau only uses SyQuests. Make sure you inquire about disk capacity, too—some media come in more than one capacity, such as SyQuest disks, which are available in 44, 88, 200, 270, and 540MB sizes.

While service bureaus make it a point to accept as many formats as they can, SyQuest technology has been a standard with them for years. Newer formats will probably drive it out eventually, but it's still the best way to make sure almost anyone will be able to read your disk.

The next point to look at is reliability. This isn't nearly as much of a problem as it was just a few years ago, when removable drives often failed and had to be reformatted or thrown away. Newer technology has made all these formats much more reliable. To assess differences in this area, look at the manufacturers' data on mean time between failures.

Cost is another thing that's changed a lot in the last year or two. The cost of smaller-capacity media constantly falls as manufacturers come up with ways to make larger-capacity disks—44MB SyQuest disks cost half what they did just a few years ago. Disks for newer formats (SyQuest EZ135, Zip, Jaz, and others) are much cheaper than those for older formats (Bernoulli and SyQuest)—a 100MB Zip cartridge costs about $20, compared to $50 for a 44MB SyQuest cartridge.

If both parties have modems, a direct modem connection is another way to get files where they're going. It can certainly run up those phone bills, though, and "noise" on the phone lines can corrupt an entire file, so that it has to be resent.

The latest—and often quickest—way to transfer files is via the **Internet**, using **FTP** or **email**.

See Also

Compression Utilities; Email; FTP

Trapping

Trapping is the process of adjusting printed elements of different colors so they slightly overlap each other, preventing gaps caused by press misregistration. DTP programs such as **PageMaker** 6 and **QuarkXPress** will trap automatically.

See Also

Color Separations; Color Trapping; Printing Methods, Digital; Printing Methods, Traditional; Process Color; Register; Spot Color

Trash

When you want to permanently delete a file from your hard drive, drag it into the Trash. The Trash is an icon of a trash can on your desktop, as shown in the figure. When an item is placed in the Trash, the icon changes to a bulging trash can to let you know the Trash is not empty. The Trash acts as a holding area for items you want to delete. The items are not deleted until you go the **Special menu** and choose Empty Trash. Selecting Empty Trash deletes any items in the Trash, and returns the regular trash can icon, letting you know the Trash has been emptied.

If you place an item in the Trash and then decide you don't want to delete it, **double-click** the trash can to open the Trash. Drag the item out of the trash, or choose Put Away from the **File menu**, to return the item to its original location. This is possible only while the item is in the Trash. Once you choose Empty Trash, the item is deleted and cannot be retrieved.

An alert dialog box appears when you choose Empty Trash warning you that you are about to permanently delete files in the Trash. It also tells you how many items you're about to delete and their combined file size. If you click OK, the files are permanently deleted. If you do not want this alert dialog box to appear every time you empty the Trash, you can disable this alert by clicking the trash can and selecting Get Info from the File menu. When the Get Info window opens, click the "Warn before emptying" check box to deselect this option. Close the Get Info window.

To delete a file using the Trash, follow these steps:

1. Drag the file(s) you want to delete into the trash can on your desktop.

2. Choose Empty Trash from the Special menu.

3. When the alert box appears asking you whether you want to delete the items in the Trash, click OK.

See Also

Delete; Desktop; Dialog Box; Empty Trash; File Menu; Get Info; Hard Drive; Icon; Put Away; Special Menu

Trash Tips

If you choose **Empty Trash** (from the Special menu) to permanently delete files in the trash can and you get the alert box that says, "The **Trash** cannot be emptied because it contains items that are locked," you can still have those items removed. Before we look at getting around the locked item dilemma, it should be noted that files are locked to keep you from accidentally deleting them. Make sure you really want to delete a file before you work your way around this preventative measure.

The quickest way to delete a locked file is to hold the Option key and choose Empty Trash again. This deletes the file. The second method is slower, but by being slower, it gives you another chance to make certain that you really want to permanently delete the locked file. Double-click the trash can, select the locked file, and choose Get Info (⌘-I) from the File menu. This displays the Get Info window, and in the lower-left corner of this window is a checkbox marked "Locked." To unlock the file, click the checkbox. Close the Get Info box and choose Empty Trash to delete the file.

In System 7 and higher, a dialog box comes up each time you go to empty the trash telling you how many items are in the Trash, how much space they occupy, and asking you if you're sure you want to delete these items. This dialog box tends to get annoying after a while, and many users elect to have the dialog box disabled. You can do this by clicking the trash can and choosing Get Info (⌘-I) from the File menu. At the bottom of the Get Info window is a checkbox called "Warn before emptying." Uncheck this box to disable the warning dialog box.

Another popular tip that many System 7 users do is keep the Trash window open at all times and drag it across the bottom of the desktop to make it easier to put items in the Trash (as the Trash icon itself is rather small). This enables them to see what is in the Trash at any given time.

If you have an item in the Trash and decide you don't want to delete it, you can put the item back in its original location by selecting the file in the Trash you don't want to delete and choosing Put Away (⌘-Y) from the File menu. This returns your file to its original location.

You can also use the Trash for ejecting disks. If you have a disk mounted on the desktop and you want to eject it, drag the disk into the trash can and it is ejected. This dragging a disk to the trash can tip is a bit disconcerting to many new Mac users because the trash can is used for deleting files. It would only stand to reason that if you dragged a disk into the trash it would erase the files on the disk, right? Wrong. This only ejects the disk and leaves the contents of the disk as is. But if this method still makes you nervous, you can always select the disk and choose Put Away (⌘-I) from the File menu or Eject Disk (⌘-E) from the Special menu, and the disk ejects without you getting near the trash can.

Another popular trash can trick is to make aliases of the trash can and put them anywhere you want. You can put aliases in different locations on your desktop, in folders where you frequently delete a lot of files, even in your Apple menu. Although you can't put files into the Trash on the Apple menu, you can choose the Trash from the Apple menu to see the contents of the trash.

See Also
Empty Trash; Locked Files; Trash

Tree Professional

Even if you learn slowly, it will take you no more than half an hour to come close to mastering this software—a real tribute to its ease of use and clear interface design. Tree Professional is all that you ever wanted in a digital foliage generator. The CD-ROM that accompanies the software is loaded with libraries of American and Japanese tree parameters, ready to load into Tree Professional and open to infinite tweaking. The library of American trees is segmented into Broadleaves, Bushes, Conifers, Cute trees, and Palms. Each can be appreciated in the preview window before loading. Tree Professional saves out the parameters, PICT renderings, or DXF 3D object files. Be careful when it comes to DXFs, though. A standard tree with all of its leaves displayed can result in a DXF file of over ten megs quite easily. Make sure you have enough RAM to render larger DXF files. A helpful series of buttons in the Save dialog box has been added so that you can count the polygons in a specific DXF save, and see exactly how many megs the file will consume. You can also reduce the percentage of leaves (the main culprit) in the same Save dialog in an attempt to reduce the file size.

Tweaking Nature There are four icons representing Trunk and Boughs, Branches and Twigs, Trunk size and color, and broadleaves/conifers/palms. All have a list of items that are adjustable via on-screen sliders as follows:

> Trunk and Boughs: Random Seed, Trunk Height, Bottom Height, Crown Center, Bough Length Change, Bough Angle, Angle Change, Bough Curving, Bough Density, and Bough Twist.

> Branches and Twigs: Random Seed, Branch Length, Length Change, Branch Angle, Angle Change, Branch Curving, Branch Density, Twig Length, Twig Angle, Twig Curving, Twig Density, and Phyllotaxy. Phyllotaxy has to do with determining the group that various branches fall under, and like a biologist you can set various conditions to change the leaf shapes.

> Trunk Size and Color: Random Seed, Trunk and Branch Width, and Color.

> Broadleaves: Random Seed, Leaf Type, Leaf Density, Stem Length, Stem Angle, Stem Curving, Phyllotaxy, and Color.

> Conifers: Random Seed, Needle Length, Needle Angle, Needle Curving, Needle Density, and Color.

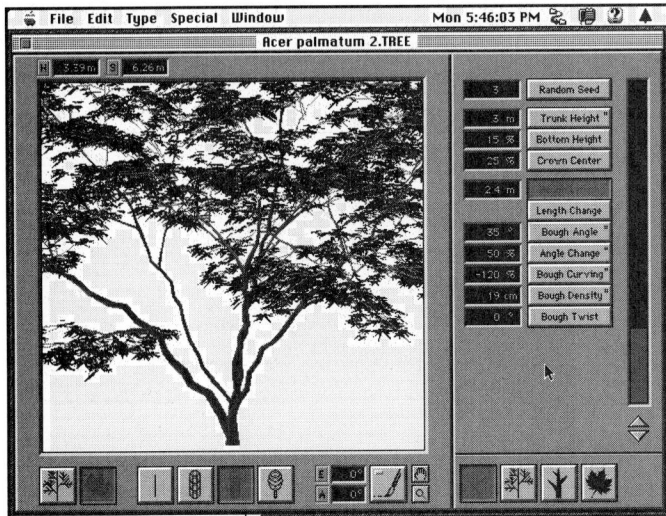

Plus, as the pipes gradually begin to incorporate different features, hands, skulls, eyeballs, and so on, you can only connect like to like pipes (hands to hands, eyes to eyes). A big bonus of Troubled Souls is the majestic background music. The eerie soundtrack provides a calming ambiance for playing the game, unlike most arcade and puzzle games where you end up switching the annoying music off.

See Also
Breakout; Tetris Gold; Zoop

Palms: Random Seed, Leaf Type, Leaf Length, Leaf Angle, Leaf Twist, Leaf Curving, Leaf Density, Petiole Length, Color.

Tree Professional is a superlative piece of digital bioengineering software, having uses for professional design and animation as well as dedicated classroom use. It's as easy to create fantasy flora as it is the real-world kind. Pink leaves? Why not…

Tristan, *See 3-D Ultra Pinball*

Trivia Games, *See You Don't Know Jack*

Trojan Horse, *See Virus*

Troubled Souls

Troubled Souls is a wonderful game. The premise, like all brain games, is simple, but puzzle games are never quite as easy as they sound. Various skeletal parts connected to pipes are dropped into a tube. Your job is to assemble them into whole shapes on-screen before the tube fills up to the top and you lose one of your three lives.

As the levels progress, the screen space you have to build your shapes becomes more and more limited.

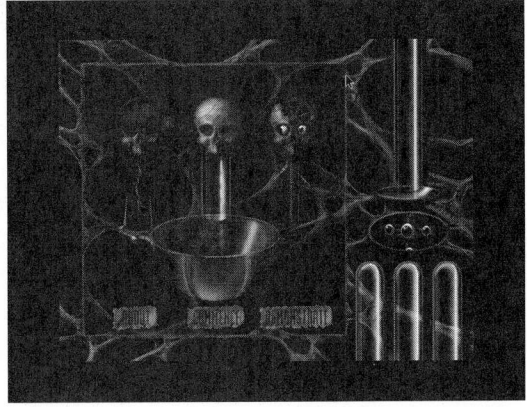

Troubleshooting the MacOS

Sometimes computers don't perform exactly as we'd like. Although it's easy to get frazzled when computers start to head off on their own track, through careful evaluation you can usually get your machine back on course fairly quickly. Your overall goal in troubleshooting is to find the difference between (a) what you want the computer to do, (b) what the computer thinks it's doing, and (c) what the computer is actually doing. To succeed in this task, you've got to think like a computer (Yes, it *does* think.).

Defining the Error Type Microcomputer troubleshooting can be as much art as science. Over time, you'll master the techniques presented here, and develop your own "sixth sense" of what's most likely to be causing the errors you run across. But no matter how experienced you become, you should always begin each troubleshooting session with a few basic questions.

1. When did you first notice the problem?

2. What exactly did you notice? Sound? Display abnormalities? Odors? Incorrect data?

3. Did this problem gradually begin to display itself, or did it suddenly appear?

4. Have you ever had this problem before? If so, how did you solve it?

5. Are you trying something new, or is this something *that used to work?* Is it possible that this has been broken all along and you just haven't used it till now?

These questions will give you a head start in determining the type of error you are dealing with.

User Errors Before assuming that your computer is misbehaving, you have to rule out a user error. This type of error occurs when the commands that you're using mean something different to the computer than they do to you. From the computer's point of view, nothing's wrong here—it did what you told it do, which it assumes is what you wanted it to do. Check for user errors first. They're usually the quickest to rule out.

Errors of this type are nobody's fault—they usually result from a difference in opinion in how a program should work. Unfortunately, it's quite possible that the steps to accomplish what you want don't make much sense! To get the computer to do your bidding, you have to think about your tasks the way the programmer did; the computer only has as much knowledge as the programmer gave it—it simply can't make the assumptions most people do.

If you think communication with the program may be the problem, take a moment to identify your assumptions. It may be logical, and "Mac-like" for a program to give more detail about something when you double-click it, but just because it doesn't, you can't assume that your mouse is broken!

Finally, look up the commands in question in the manual. See if the manual states that the commands you're using should give the results you want. If this doesn't help, check a few related topics in the manual's index to see if there's another way to accomplish what you want. Sometimes the manuals included with software aren't very helpful. If the manual doesn't answer your questions, check a local bookstore for a book on the subject.

Next, ask other users with a similar setup. Other users may have encountered the situation and found ways around the program's limitations and intricacies. If others have been successful with a similar setup to yours, try to identify what's different between your system and theirs, as this may be what's causing your problem.

A great source of this information is found online. If you have an account on an online service, such as **America Online** or **CompuServe**, try checking forums to see if other users have posted messages detailing similar problems. See if the vendor has a question and answer section or a tech support section in their forum. If you have access to the **World Wide Web**, check the vendor's web page (you can always try the address **http://www.companyname.com**) and see if they have a tech support area. You can also read Mac Usenet **newsgroups** to see what kind of help is offered there.

Finally, contact the manufacturer of the product—software authors use feedback from users to customize the interface and for ideas about new features. Before you call, check your manuals to see if the company charges for support. If they do, try the other methods again.

See Also

Repairing Your Mac

TrueType

Introduced by Apple in 1991, the TrueType format is an **outline font** format that competes with **PostScript Type 1**. Like PostScript fonts, TrueType fonts print accurately at any size; unlike PostScript fonts, you don't need **Adobe Type Manager** to make TrueType fonts look good on-screen.

TrueType fonts come in one piece, a suitcase file, so they're easier to install and keep track of than PostScript fonts. Macs running System 7 and above can use TrueType fonts; System 6.0.5 and above will recognize them with the addition of the TrueType extension.

TrueType is a popular font format among Mac home and business users, although desktop publishers generally prefer PostScript Type 1 fonts. TrueType fonts are very popular in the PC world. Most commercial fonts and many shareware ones are available in both PostScript and TrueType formats; Adobe's fonts are an exception, because Adobe created the PostScript technology.

See Also

Adobe Type Manager; Font Formats; Fonts; Outline Fonts; Type 1 Fonts

TruMatch

A color system similar to **Pantone**, **Toyo**, and **FocolTone**, TruMatch has one big difference—it's based on the four **process colors**, rather than on **spot color** inks.

Available as a printed swatchbook and in digital form supported by major graphics applications, TruMatch is useful for "spot" colors that will be printed using a four-color (**CMYK**) printing process. Rather than choosing colors based on, for example, the Pantone system, which will be imperfectly represented when printed using CMYK inks rather than Pantone inks, TruMatch allows designers to choose colors that can be perfectly reproduced by CMYK inks.

See Also

CMYK; Color Matching Systems; FocolTone; Pantone; Spot Color; Toyo

Tune Up Extension (System 7 Tuner)

The **System 7** Tune Up consists of a Tune-Up disk that is a bug-fixer and provides performance enhance-

ment for System 7 and **System 7.01** in a number of areas including: enhanced **printing** performance, faster copying of files at the **Finder** level, and **memory** management improvements.

See Also

Finder; Memory; Printing; System 7; System 7.0.1

Tuner Extension

The Tuner extension is part of Apple's free System tune-up for **System 7**. The Tuner extension was designed to improve the way System 7 was handling **memory**, in particular how it addressed a problem causing a significant number of **out-of-memory messages**.

See Also

Memory; Out-Of-Memory Message; System 7

Tunneling

A networking trick known as tunneling enables you to send a data packet in a particular networking protocol, such as **AppleTalk**, across a network that doesn't support it.

In effect, it hides the packet inside one of the "right" kind until it reaches a gateway where it can shed its disguise and go on its way. Here's how it works. Suppose you had to deliver a package to someone in the town of West Gerbilton. You live in East Gerbilton. The only way to get there is to travel through Center Gerbilton. But it is an unfriendly town to strangers. If they don't think you belong, they'll refuse to let you through, and throw your package away. So, you disguise yourself in a Center Gerbilton High jacket and cap, and tuck the package into the jacket. Then, you ride through town waving happily at everyone you see. Thinking they know you, they wave back and let you pass through. When you enter West Gerbilton, you take off the jacket and cap and deliver the package.

This scenario can be directly applied to networking as well. The process of placing one transport protocol inside another is called protocol encapsulation or tunneling. Tunneling AppleTalk inside another protocol,

T

such as **TCP/IP** or **DECnet**, might be necessary or desirable for several reasons.

One reason could be that an organization's wide-area network only supports a certain protocol. This has been fairly common in the past because a number of routers have only supported a single protocol. For example, many companies that have extensive wide-area DECnet networks interconnect them with DECnet-specific routers. For these companies to be able to offer AppleTalk services over the network, they would have to scrap all their existing DECnet routers and replace them with multiprotocol AppleTalk/DECnet routers.

Alternatively, they can tunnel AppleTalk protocols inside the DECnet protocol. In this case, an AppleTalk datagram (a packet of data plus its address) that is directed to a distant network is wrapped inside a DECnet packet by a special device and routed over the wide-area DECnet network to another special device, where the AppleTalk datagram is then extracted from its DECnet encapsulation and then passed along using AppleTalk protocols to its final destination.

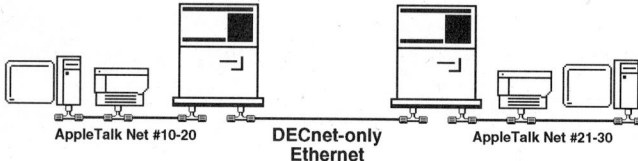

AppleTalk Net #10-20   DECnet-only   AppleTalk Net #21-30
                        Ethernet

In the case of AppleTalk/DECnet tunneling, the special device happens to be a DEC VAX that's running the AppleTalk for VMS and DECnet protocols simultaneously. The AppleTalk for VMS software establishes a connection with the DECnet software and performs the encapsulation and decapsulation of the AppleTalk datagrams.

TurboGopher

A client for navigating **Gopher servers** on the **Internet**. Like Gopher itself, TurboGopher was developed at the University of Minnesota.

Although most users access Gopherspace via a **World Wide Web** browser, TurboGopher still has some advantages, such as its speed (especially over slow modems using **PPP** or **SLIP**) and its multi-window format. TurboGopher's other features include:

- A bookmarks function.
- Support for the Gopher+ extensions (these permit alternative ways of viewing a Gopher object, among other things).
- Capability to download a file while you continue to browse.
- Capability to connect to **FTP** and **Archie** sites.

Follow these steps to download and begin using TurboGopher:

1. Download the software from `gopher://boombox.micro.umn.edu/11/gopher/Macintosh-TurboGopher`.

2. TurboGopher 2.0 requires the **Thread Manager** extension that comes with System 7.5. If you do not have System 7.5, copy the Thread Manager extension that comes with TurboGopher into your Extensions folder and restart your computer.

3. Double-click the TurboGopher icon to launch the program.

4. TurboGopher comes configured to connect to the Home Gopher Server at the University of Minnesota. You will see a window for the Home Gopher Server as well as a window for your Bookmark Worksheet and TurboGopher Help, as shown in the following figure.

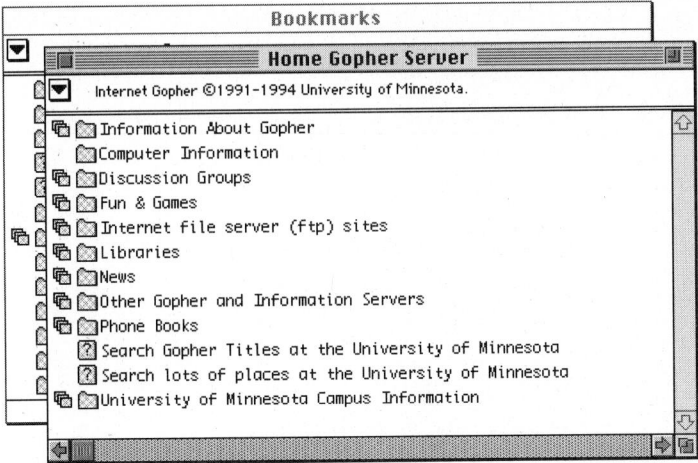

5. You can now begin to navigate by clicking folders in the active window.

As this was being written, a new version of the software, TurboGopherVR 2.1a1, was just released. TurboGopher VR is designed to combine a point-and-click browser interface to the Internet with a 3D virtual-reality interface. Find out more at **gopher:// boombox.micro.umn.edu/00/gopher/Macintosh-TurboGopher/TurboGopherVR/.**

See Also

Archie, FTP, Gopher, Internet, PPP, SLIP, Thread Manager, Veronica, Web Browser

Tweens, *See Inbetweening*

Type 1 Fonts

When Adobe introduced **PostScript fonts**, there were actually three types. Type 1 fonts are what most people think of as PostScript fonts today.

Adobe didn't release the specification for this format publicly until 1991, so other vendors before that time could only produce Type 3 fonts. This format didn't support **hinting**, so Type 3 characters didn't print clearly at laser printer resolutions. Type 2 was a format that Adobe never used commercially. Type 5 is the format of the fonts that are hard-coded into printer ROMs.

Some Type 3 fonts are still available, but if you're using them, be aware that **Adobe Type Manager** doesn't recognize them.

Today, Type 1 PostScript fonts are the standard for desktop publishing. They're composed of two parts: screen fonts, **bitmapped** representations of the letterforms that are used only for screen display, and printer fonts, the **outline** versions of the letterforms that are sent to an output device when the font is printed.

See Also

Adobe Type Manager; Bitmapped Fonts; Fonts; Outline Fonts; PostScript

Type 2 Fonts, *See Type 1 Fonts*

Type 3 Fonts, *See Type 1 Fonts*

Type 5 Fonts, *See Type 1 Fonts*

Type Code, *See Changing Type and Creator*

Type Foundries and Distributors

These companies range from huge corporations to one-person shops, with their font offerings varying just as much. From fine calligraphic fonts to foreign-language alphabets, it's all here—and this is just a taste of what's out there.

Adobe Systems, Inc.
Mountain View, CA
(415) 961-4400
800-521-1976
http://www.adobe.com

Agfa Division, Bayer Corp.
Wilmington, MA
(508) 658-5600
800-424-8973

T

Autologic, Inc.
Thousand Oaks, CA
(805) 498-9611
800-457-8973

Bitstream, Inc.
Cambridge, MA
(617) 497-6222
800-522-3668
sales@bitstream.com

Carter & Cone Type, Inc.
Cambridge, MA
(617) 576-0398
800-952-2129
Carter.Cone@applelink.com
70402.155@compuserve.com

Design Plus
New York, NY
(212) 477-8811
800-231-3461

Dubl-Click Software, Inc.
Bend, OR
(503) 317-0355
(503) 317-0430 (fax)

Educorp
San Diego, CA
(619) 536-9999
800-843-9497 (orders)
(619) 536-2345 (fax)

The Electric Typographer
Santa Barbara, CA
(805) 966-7563

Emigre, Inc.
Sacramento, CA
(916) 451-4344
800-944-9021
sales@emigre.com
http://www.emigre.com

The Font Bureau, Inc.
Boston, MA
(617) 423-8770
fontbureau@aol.com; prodigy, eWorld,
Microsoft Network

FontHaus, Inc.
Fairfield, CT
(203) 367-1993
800-942-9110

FontShop USA, Inc.
(312) 360-1990
800-897-3872
Fontshop.USA@applelink.com

Galapagos Design Group, Inc.
Littleton, MA
(508) 952-6200
islandtype@aol.com
galapagos@applelink.com
76501,147@compuserve.com

GarageFonts
Del Mar, CA
(619) 755-4761

The Hoefler Type Foundry, Inc.
New York, NY
(217) 777-6640

Image Club Graphics
Calgary, AB, Canada
(403) 262-8008
800-661-9410
http://www.adobe.com/imageclub

International Typeface Corp. (ITC)
New York, NY
(212) 371-0699
800-425-3882
typeface1@aol.com
typeface@applelink.apple.com
http://www.letraset.com/itc

Letraset USA
Paramus, NJ
(201) 845-6100
800-343-8973
http://www.esselte.com

Linotype-Hell Co.
Hauppauge, NY
(516) 434-2000
800-799-4922

Monotype Typography, Inc.
Chicago, IL
(312) 855-1440
800-666-6897
sales@monotypeusa.com

Precision Type, Inc.
Commack, NY
(516) 864-0167
800-248-3668

PrePress Solutions
East Hanover, NJ
(201) 887-8000
800-631-8134
info@prepress.pps.com
catalog@prepress.pps.com
http://www2.prepress.pps.com/

Stone Type Foundry, Inc.
Palo Alto, CA
(415) 324-1870
800-557-8663

T-26
Chicago, IL
(312) 787-8973
T26font@aol.com

Treacyfaces/Headliners
West Haven, CT
(203) 389-7037
74041,3336@compuserve.com
D3385@eworld.com

URW America
Nashua, NH
(603) 882-7445
800-229-8791
75054,574@compuserve.com

See Also
Fonts

Typeface, *See Typesetting Terms*

Typeface Categories

There are probably as many systems for classifying typefaces as there are people doing the job, but this listing will give an idea of the possibilities. These are the categories used by Precision Type, a New York-based font distributor whose Precision Type Guide contains samples of more than 13,000 fonts.

- The typefaces we now call *Oldstyle* were designed between about 1470 (Nicholas Jenson's faces) and 1700 (William Caslon, a Dutch designer). They're identified by a lack of contrast among stroke weights, and curves have a leftward stress. Oldstyle faces include Bembo, Caslon, Garamond, and Minion.

- *Transitional* typefaces include those designed during the 18th century, between the popularity of Oldstyle faces and Modern ones. There's greater stroke contrast than seen in Oldstyle faces, and serifs are sharper, while curved strokes have a vertical stress. Transitional faces include Baskerville, New Caledonia, Janson (don't confuse this one with Jenson!), Stone Serif, and Times.

- *Modern* faces like Bodoni were seen as quite radical in the late 17th and early 18th centuries. Their most obvious characteristic is an extreme contrast in stroke weight; in some, light strokes are almost hairlines, and heavy strokes are quite bold. They have a strong vertical stress. Melior is another well-known Modern face.

- *Slab serif* typefaces first appeared in the early 19th century, when they were called Antiques. Their serifs don't taper at all, and strokes tend to be of similar weights throughout, with vertical emphasis. They've also been called *Egyptian*—hence Memphis, which is a popular example of this type. Many of these faces look like typewriter letters, such as American Typewriter and Stymie.

- First introduced in 1916 by William Caslon and also known as *gothic* and grotesque, sans serif faces—obviously—don't have serifs. Their stroke weights have little contrast, and they generally don't have true italic versions; slanted sans serif fonts are called "oblique." Helvetica is the most commonly used sans serif, but most designers actually prefer faces like Frutiger, Gill Sans, and Stone Sans. Optima is a "humanistic" sans serif face, with more variation in stroke weight than is common.

- *Script, cursive,* and *brush* faces are based on handwriting. Some are connecting; others are not. Their only common characteristic is that they appear to have been written rather than printed or drawn. Zapf Chancery is a much-overused script face, while Mistral, Poetica, and Brush Script are other examples of this category.

- *Display* typefaces have nothing in common except that they're too ornate or unusual to be used for long stretches of text. So they're used for headlines and other short sections of text, at large sizes. They include such faces as Beesknees (a Roaring Twenties style), Castellar (an "inline" style that looks as though it's carved from stone), and Umbra (in which the black sections appear to be the sides, not the fronts, of three-dimensional letters).

- Historically, *blackletter* faces come first in type classications. They include German *fraktur* faces, *uncial* faces with crooked strokes, and others based on handwriting that predated movable type. Goudy Text, Fette Fraktur, and San Marco are blackletter faces.

- Precision uses the term *polyglot* to describe typefaces used in foreign-language typesetting. These include Cyrillic, Arabic, Hebrew, Greek, and Asian typefaces. Some are designed specifically for use in foreign-language typesetting, while others are variations on English typefaces, such as Minion Cyrillic and Times New Roman Greek.

- *Pi, symbol, logo, ornament,* and *picture* fonts are non-alphabetical fonts made up of symbols and pictures. They're used for special purposes like typesetting mathematical typesetting and mapmaking, and picture faces are often used by designers in place of **clip art.**

Oldstyle	Bembo
Transitional	Times
Modern	**Bodoni**
Slab serif	Memphis
Sans serif	Univers
Script	*Kaufmann Script*
Display	Dragonwick
Blackletter	Goudy Text
Polyglot	Пдфытщые (Cyrillic)
Logo	◑ ⅉ€ 𝓑𝓻𝓪𝓿𝓸 ¦ 𝗧𝗕𝗦 (Cable Dingbats)

See Also
Fonts; Typesetting Terms

Typesetting Terms

Ascender: Any part of a lowercase letter extending above the x-height, as in "b" or "h."

Baseline: The imaginary line on which the bases of letters sit.

Bold: Type with heavier strokes. Most typefaces have a bold face.

Black: Extra bold typefaces are often called "Black."

Cap height: The height of capital letters.

Condensed: Narrow, compressed letterforms.

Counter: The "hole" in a letter, such as the middle of "o."

Descender: Any part of a lower-case letter extending below the baseline, as in "y" and "j."

Expanded: Wide, extended letterforms.

Italic: Type with slanted strokes and an appearance closer to script than roman faces.

Ligature: Letters that are joined as a single unit, such as æ.

Oblique: Type slanted to the right.

Pi fonts: Special symbol characters, such as those used in mathematical equations and on maps.

Point: A unit of measure used in typesetting. There are 72 modern points in an inch, but traditionally points were smaller (72.27 to the inch). The change was made when PostScript was created, and it's generally accepted now.

Roman: Type with vertical stems, as opposed to italic or oblique type, which is angled.

Sans serif: A typeface that has no serifs.

Serif: A small cross-stroke at the end of the main stroke of a letter. Also used to refer to a typeface that has serifs.

Small caps: Capital letters that are the height of the lower-case letters in the typeface with which they're being used. Many page layout applications and word processors make small caps by scaling regular capital letters, but traditionally small caps are slightly different from capitals and were contained in a separate font.

Subscript: A small character set below the normal letters or figures.

Superscript: A small character set above the normal letters or figures.

Swash letters: Italic characters with extra flourishes.

Typeface: A collection of alphanumeric characters with a similar, distinctive design, intended to be used together. There are several categories of typeface: uncial, blackletter, serif, sans serif, script, and decorative. Within these categories, there are subcategories, such as old style, transitional, modern, and slab serif, which are subcategories of serif fonts.

X-height: The height of a letter excluding the ascenders and descenders.

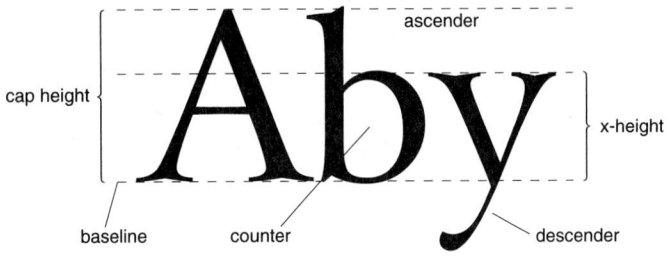

Typestry

Developed by **Pixar,** Typestry is a tool for creating animated 3D text and simple logos. The program creates extruded text using fonts available on the computer and from simple imported objects. It then renders the scene or creates a flying logo animation to export to a QuickTime movie. Because Typestry uses the **MacRenderMan** renderer, the quality of the output is very high, but you need a lot of memory to run the renderer successfully (one solution is to render parts of the scene and then glue the results together).

Pixar no longer supports any of its Macintosh products.

See Also

LogoMotion; MacRenderMan; Pixar; ShowPlace

TypeTamer

The most difficult part of having large numbers of **fonts** on your system is finding the one you want for a specific task. If the font's name starts with a letter at the end of the alphabet, you have to scroll down the whole list to find it. You also can't tell from a font's name if it's a **TrueType** or a **PostScript** font, and that may matter in certain applications. TypeTamer, from Impossible Software, is a help to everyone who uses fonts, from desktop publishing users to graphics artists, designers, and animators. TypeTamer reconfigures the Mac's font menu, enabling you to customize the contents.

TypeTamer provides a **hierarchical menu** structure when you access the styles comprising a type family. If the foundry name is available, it is included in brackets to the right of the font name. Most important, icons are included that tell you at a glance if the font is a TrueType, **bitmap**, or PostScript font. TopFonts, a TypeTamer utility, allows you to move your choice of fonts to the top of the font list, making long scrolling operations no longer necessary when looking for your most often accessed fonts. Holding the mouse cursor over the font's new TypeTamer icon will bring up an instantly visible display that shows the alphabet written in the chosen font (extremely helpful when a font's name indicates little about its visual character). Using special keystrokes (Shift and Option key augmented) while the font icon is visible, you can add special characters not normally associated with the selected font (trademarks, copyright, and other symbolic characters).

With a utility called SpeedFonts, TypeTamer allows you to seek out any font in a long list simply by entering the first few letters of its name. SpeedFonts fosters font categorization packets. A collection of your favorite fonts can be grouped together and saved. When the font menu is accessed in any software that uses the Mac font standard (which most graphics packages do), the separate SpeedFont category groups will be displayed as choices. Selecting a new font group will display only those fonts in the group, skipping over all of the extraneous fonts you may have in your font suitcase. Essentially, categorizing fonts in TypeTamer allows you to build any number of sub-suitcases, each of which may be devoted to separate job-related tasks, a great time and energy saver.

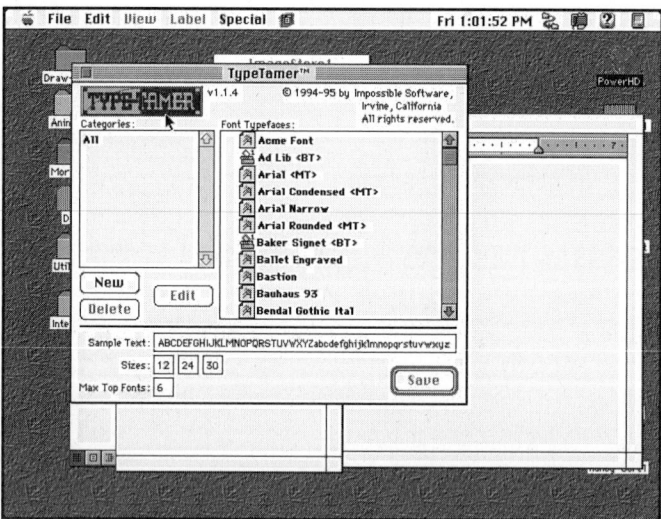

Type Twister

The real name of this software is "Simplicity" with a capital "S." With all of its text creation options represented by visual displays, Type Twister is one of the easiest ways to generate 3D text looks. It lacks the capacity to texturize type on the screen, but adds the ability to render hundreds of unique pseudo 3D displays for 2D color environments. Type Twister is not an animation program, and retrofitting it to accomplish animation tasks is daunting to say the least. Type Twister has no save options for writing to any file format. Instead, finished graphic compositions are saved to the Clipboard. To see them, you have to use Photoshop, Illustrator, or another graphics package that allows access to the clipboard. Create a new page and "paste" the graphic into the page.

Options Type Twister creates a 3D text block with several user selectable rendering options. The central shape of the text block takes your text input and configures according to a selection in the Type Twister shape library. This library contains several dozen choices, most of which involve adding color and drop shadow/cast shadow variables to your text block. That's only a start in most situations, because all of the default shape choices are open to further adjustment based upon layer/Depth extrusions, Font, Extruded Shapes and Color Sets. An on-screen adjustment box also provides user transformation of text block height/width and rotation. Since Type Twister is a 2D program, rotation of the graphic is allowed only in the XY plane. An automatic animated display of all of the shape choices (forward or backward) can be toggled on or off.

Type Twister is not limited to one-line text blocks, as some of its shapes require two or more user input text lines (most commonly, text around a circular space). Further options are provided in an Alignment menu, allowing you to align the text according to twelve possible options. The background color of the text block can be made visible, reversed, and lightened. Custom colors can be added to the background.

Custom Effects Type Twister invites the user to customize any of the defaulted shapes, and offers a dialog where shape colors and extruded elements may be adjusted to user specifications. Customized effects can be saved and are immediately added to the visual library display. Text blocks can be further stylized with Slant, Tilt, Disorder, Stagger, Cutout, Horizontal/Vertical Extension, Vertical Stretch, and Reversal (writes the text backwards). A "copy" command writes the finished work to the Clipboard.

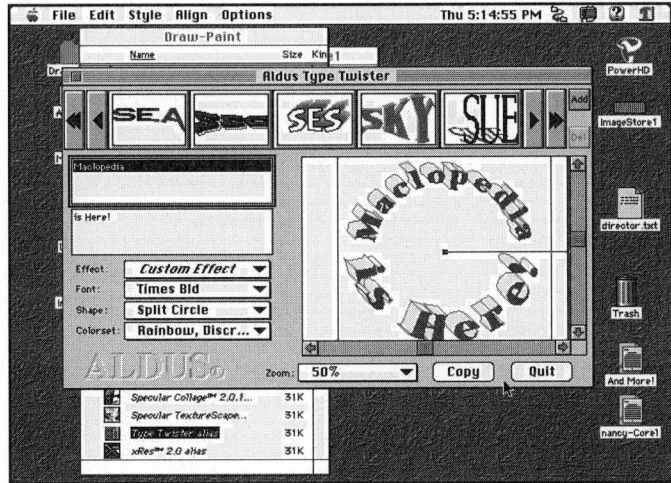

Typing Programs, *See Mavis Beacon Teaches Typing*

T

U

U-Boat, *See Sim Games*

UCR, *See Undercolor Removal*

Ultra Recorder

This utility can record, play, and convert among any of the following audio formats: **AIFF**, **SoundEdit**, **.WAV**, sound resource files, System 7 sound files, **CD Audio** tracks, **MOD** files, and audio tracks in **QuickTime** movies. Ultra Recorder also can play a folder of sounds.

Ultra Recorder can record sounds in the following formats: AIFF (directly to disk if your equipment is fast enough), SoundEdit, and System 7 sound files.

Ultra Recorder also can turn an AIFF file into a self-playing file (essentially, bundling the program code needed to play the file along with the sound file) or a startup AIFF sound, which is a sound packaged in an Extension file that plays at startup.

Available from many online services, the shareware fee is $10.

See Also

AIFF; AudioShop; MOD; Sample Editor; Sound Sculptor; SoundEdit 16; SoundEffects; SoundStudio Lite

Ultra SCSI, *See Ports, Future Trends*

Undefined Offending Command Message

This error message appears where you are having a problem printing a document. If you're working with large graphics documents, the document you're try-

ing to print might be too complex for your printer or the amount of RAM your printer has. It also might be that you're trying to print too many pages at once. Turning off the printer and "flushing" the printer's RAM may do the trick or printing the pages of a complex document one-by-one rather than sending a command to print 10 or 12 pages.

See Also

Memory; Printing

Undelete

Undelete (also called Trashback) is a data recovery program that helps you recover files you've deleted from your drive by emptying the **Trash**. Although this module is part of the repair/diagnostic and system enhancement package MacTools Pro, they've introduced a new module called TrashBack that is much more robust. Symantec recommends using Undelete only if you didn't install their TrashBack module.

> MacTools Pro Symantec
> 10201 Torre Ave,
> Cupertino, CA, 95104-2132
> Phone (800) 441-7234
> Web site at **http:// www.symantec.com**

See Also

MacTools Pro; Trash

Undercolor Removal

In the **process color** printing process, UCR removes **cyan**, **magenta**, and **yellow** ink from beneath areas in which solid black is printed. The technique is used to reduce ink **trapping** and the overall amount of ink needed for the printing run.

See Also

Color Printing; Gray Component Replacement; Process Color; Spot Color; Trapping

Undersea Adventure

Featuring some of the most spectacular movies and special effects seen on any CD-ROM, this is a terrific program for young scientists. The program opens with a vivid close up of a shark swimming toward you, and then veering off to attack underwater photographers who, even though they're inside a steel cage, are understandably nervous. And it gets even better. There are movies of fish, coral reefs, and marine mammals that take you right up close for a really good look.

Narrations provide interesting facts, and the music track adds to the experience. In the Seacology Lab, young marine biologists can watch simulated dissections of 12 different marine animals, learning about them literally from the inside out. The Undersea Encyclopedia contains over 200 photos, movies, animations, and articles.

There's a printing function to enable kids to use the information as research material for school reports. This program is rated for ages 5 to 10, but much of the content will interest older kids as well. The youngest users can follow along with the simple text in the Ocean Tour, while older students will get more out of the encyclopedia and movie sections. Everyone who sees this program is fascinated by the virtual reality 3-D underwater museum. Travel around in it with the mouse or arrow keys and learn about the exotic creatures on display.

Finally, play the games included. The best of these is the treasure hunt, which has you again swimming through the virtual museum, avoiding the predators as you head for the room with the treasure. You only have 60 seconds worth of air, so try to avoid bumping into the walls. It can be done, but younger children may find it frustrating. Still, this is a program they'll come back to again and again.

See Also

A.D.A.M., The Inside Story; Bumptz Science Carnival; MacFrog; What's the Secret; Widget Workshop

Undo/Redo Command

At the **desktop**, Undo enables you to undo changes in the name of a document while you're making the change. Within an application, Undo, if available, enables you to undo your last action.

At the desktop, you might use Undo if you were typing a new name for a document, and you suddenly realized you had a typo. You could select Undo (⌘-Z) from the **Edit menu** to undo your name change.

The Undo Command is also called the Redo Command, because if you select Undo to undo your last action, you can also select Undo to redo your change. An example would be: You have a folder named Applications. You decide to change the name of that folder to Apps, and while you're typing in the new name you decide it may have been better left named as Applications. You can select Undo and it undoes your name change. But if you then decided, "Aw, apps is really an OK name after all." Rather than retyping it, you can select Undo again (which does a redo at this point) and puts Apps back in as the name of your folder. You can continue this Undo and Redo scenario as many times as you like, as long as you don't make any other action. It toggles between your two choices until you take a different action. Undo is also available in most Macintosh programs to undo your last action.

There are a number of actions that Undo cannot undo. Undo does not physically move items at the desktop Level. If, for example, you move an item into the Trash and decide you want it out of the **Trash,** Undo does not move it back to your hard drive. You have to retrieve it yourself.

Many programs now are taking advantage of the capability to have multiple undos, and a number have as many as 99 undos. This gives you the opportunity to make changes as you like without the fear of them being permanent, because you can always go back a few steps, while that document is open, an undo any changes you didn't like. These programs, however, only remember these undo steps during the session that you're working on. If you close a document, the undos it was keeping in memory are deleted, so you cannot close a document, then later reopen it and use the undo feature to take you back to changes you made before you closed the document.

If an action cannot be undone (and many cannot), the Undo Command appears grayed out under the Edit menu. In some programs, if an action cannot be undone, it may read Can't Undo under the program's Edit menu in grayed out type.

To use the Undo Command to undo your last action, follow these steps:

1. Before you do anything else, and that includes clicking the mouse, select Undo from the Edit menu. (⌘-Z) If an Undo is available, Undo appears in black letters.

2. If Undo appears in gray letters, or the words Can't Undo appear, the Undo Command is not available for use.

See Also

Desktop; Edit Menu; Trash

Unexpected Quit Message

If you're running an application and it suddenly **quits** without warning, you may get a warning **message** stating, "The application unexpectedly quit." This occurs when a program needs more **memory** than is available and its only choice is to quit. In most cases, you get an **alert box** warning you that memory is low before the computer quits, and you are advised to close any open windows or documents to free some memory.

See Also

Alert Box; Memory; Message Box; Quit Command

Unicode

Unicode is a method of encoding characters that encompasses all of the characters in all of the world's alphabets.

For many years, the **ASCII** standard has been used to encode text for use with computers. Because of its widespread acceptance, ASCII has become the common language of computer communication. Unfor-

tunately, ASCII limits communication to the letters, numbers, and punctuation of the Roman alphabet. Very few languages can be written in their full richness using just the Roman alphabet. Even extended-ASCII, which includes many accented characters used in German, French, and Spanish, leaves out much of the world's languages.

A big part of the problem is that even extended-ASCII permits only one byte (or 8-bits) per character. That limits the total number of possible characters to 2^8 or 256. This is barely enough to contain the characters used in European languages, let alone the thousands of other characters used in languages such as Japanese and Arabic. Other encodings exist for these character sets, but they are not interchangeable, and using more than one at the same time (in a document written in Korean and Hebrew, for example) can be a real headache.

Unicode avoids the problem by using two bytes (16-bits) for each character, giving enough room in a single encoding system to include 2^{16} or 65,536 individual characters, or *glyphs*.

The first version of the Unicode standard includes encodings for the characters used by all of the world's major languages and many of its minor ones. Future versions of the standard will include many more languages and even "dead" or archaic ones.

See Also

ASCII

Universal Proc Pointer, *See* *Mixed Mode Manager*

Unlocking Files and Disks

Files are locked to prevent them from being accidentally **deleted**. You can unlock any document that has been locked by selecting the file and choosing **Get Info**(⌘-I) from the **File menu**. This opens the file's Get Info window. Located in the bottom left corner of this window is a **check box** marked **Locked**. To unlock the disk, click this check box to deselect the Locked feature. The file is now unlocked and can be deleted.

To unlock a locked file, follow these steps:

1. Click the file you want to unlock.

2. Choose Get Info (⌘-I) from the File menu.

3. In the Get Info window, click the Locked check box to deselect the Locked feature. The file is now unlocked.

TIP You also can delete locked files by holding down Option while choosing Empty Trash.

See Also

Checkbox; Click; Delete; File Menu; Get Info Command; Locked

Untitled

This is the **default** name given to any new document or **folder** to let you know it has not been named. When you create a new folder with ⌘-N, for example, its name is "untitled folder," and it is **highlighted** to let you enter a new name. If you choose not to name it, it retains the name "untitled folder." If you create another new folder, it is titled "untitled folder 2," followed by "untitled folder 3," and so on.

If you **launch** an application and create a new document, its default name is "Untitled1." If you create subsequent documents, they are titled "Untitled2," "Untitled3," and so on. This is the Macintosh computer's way of letting you know these documents have not yet been named or **saved**.

To name an untitled folder, follow these steps:

1. **Click** the name of the folder to highlight it. The **arrow pointer** converts to the **I-Beam** cursor.

2. Enter the folder's new name.

3. Click outside the folder to make the change complete.

To name an untitled document, follow these steps:

1. Choose Save or Save As from the application's File menu.

2. The standard Save dialog appears. You may enter a name for the file in this dialog box under, "Save this document as." Click OK to save the document with its new name.

See Also

Arrow Pointer; Click; Cursor; Default Settings; Highlighting; I-Beam Cursor; Save

Up Arrow Key

The Up Arrow key enables you to **select** items above a selected item in a list. If, for example, you're in a window displayed in a **list view**, you can **click** a **file** and then use the Up Arrow key to move up the list. Each time you press the Arrow key, the file above is selected (and the below file is deselected) until you reach the top of the list. The Up Arrow key also can be used in an application to navigate through an open document line by line without using the mouse.

There are a number of modifier keys you can use with the arrow keys. Here's a table of the most common keystrokes using the arrow keys.

Arrow Keystrokes

Sequence	Result
⌘-Left Arrow	Collapses Expanded Folder
⌘-Down Arrow	Open Folder/Open Next File
⌘-Right Arrow	Expand Folder
⌘-Up Arrow	Go to Previous Folder
⌘-Option-Up Arrow	Close to Previous Window
⌘-Shift-Up Arrow	In Open/Save Dialog it Selects Desktop
⌘-Option-Left Arrow	Collapses All Expanded Folders
⌘-Option-Right Arrow	Expands All Nested Folders
Shift-Right Arrow	Selects Character to the Right of Text Cursor

Sequence	Result
Shift-Left Arrow	Selects Character to the Left of Text Cursor
Shift-⌘-Right Arrow	Selects Word to the Right of Text Cursor
Shift-⌘-Left Arrow	Selects Word to the Left of Text Cursor

See Also
Arrow Keys; Click; List Views; Select; Window

upFront
An entry-level **3D** program originally developed by Alias. When Alias was purchased by Silicon Graphics, upFront was acquired by SketchTech. This program, which has an interface similar to Alias's other modeling package, **Sketch!**, sports a variety of modeling tools and exports to multiple file formats, including **Electric Image** or Pixar's **RenderMan**.

The unusual animation interface uses a tool that draws Spider Walls in the model to indicate camera direction and angle.

Like Sketch!, upFront can import a 2D image as a background and match the perspective of the model to the image. This enables you, for example, to match a 3D model of a table with a picture of an empty room.

Sketch! and upFront address slightly different markets: Sketch! lacks the animation features of upFront, but offers more modeling and texture and surface controls. The output quality of upFront, however, is lower than Sketch!

The combination of features upFront offers makes it best for architectural and other real-world simulation modeling tasks.

> SketchTech
> Price: $299
> Phone: (612) 379-1435
> Web: **http://www.diskovery.com/Diskovery/**
> **EPG/Indices/Software/ByPublisher**
> **/Sketchtech.html**

See Also
Modeling; Sketch!

Upgrade
You have performed an upgrade when you add or change something in your hardware or software setup so that you can achieve greater functionality, capacity, or speed. This function could be as complete as replacing your Macintosh SE with a new Power Mac, or as minor as adding a new hard disk to your SCSI chain on the hardware side. The most common forms of hardware upgrade are **CPU Upgrade**, **memory upgrade**, **logic board upgrade**, **hard disk upgrade**, **VRAM expansion**, and the addition of a **cache**.

A software upgrade means that you have purchased or received a new version of a program you already had or a new version of your operating system. When you replace a software program with one of its competitors, it is usually called a **sidegrade**. There is also a special term for certain software upgrades, a software **update**.

See Also
Cache Switch; CPU Upgrade; Hard Disk Upgrade; Logic Board Upgrade; Memory Upgrade; System Updates; VRAM Expansion

Upgrade Paths, PowerPC Options
PowerPC upgrades use two different designs: a full logic board upgrade that completely transforms the older Mac into a new PowerPC model, or a user-installed PPC upgrade card that plugs into the Mac's logic board and offers accelerated performance at a fraction of the price of a full upgrade or new Mac.

At the top of the heap are the full logic board upgrades for owners of the Mac IIvx, IIvi, Performa 600, Quadra/Centris 610 and 650, 660AV, 800, and 840AV.

Logic Board Upgrades Any Mac upgraded with a logic board is identical to its corresponding **Power Mac**. Keep in mind that **RAM** purchases are necessary for some owners of converted (upgraded) Mac systems. Apple continues to offer logic board upgrades to 6100, 7100, and 8100 models. Upgrades for the AV versions cost an additional $100-$400, depending on the model. PowerPC upgrade boards are still available from Apple for the Quadra/LC 605, 475, 575, 580, and 630 Mac and Performa models.

Upgrade Cards A PowerPC upgrade card is available for every 68040 Mac made. The PPC upgrade card is a PDS-based plug-in and works in every Quadra and Centris computer with a standard **PDS slot**. The PPC upgrade card has no SIMM socket for its own RAM. The Power Macintosh upgrade card (displayed in the following photograph) adds a PowerPC 601 processor that runs at twice the clock speed of the host system. Performance gained from the upgrade depends on the software and the types of tasks run on the system, but estimates are in the 200-300 percent range.

Two upgrade cards are available from DayStar Digital using Apple-licensed technology. The DayStar PowerPro 601 PowerPC upgrade card provides upgrades to 7100 and 8100 Power Mac levels at 100MHz and at 66MHz for Quadra or Centris Macs (see the following figure). The PowerPro can also be added as a coprocessor to the existing 68040 processor, because it is inserted into the **PDS slot** and the 68040 code runs without a performance degradation typical of emulated systems.

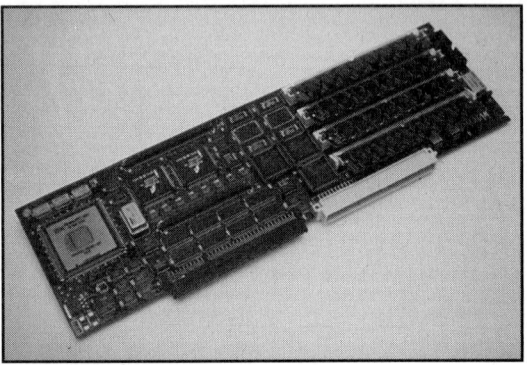

The following table provides an overview of upgrade options.

Upgrade Paths for Macs*

Model	Upgrade Type	Features	Price
Any compact Mac, Mac II, Iix, Iifx, MacTV, Performa 275, Performa 6100 series, Power Mac 6100	none	For extra speed on 68040 Macs, try Connectix Speed Doubler, or add more RAM. For Power Macs: add L-2 cache using a clock accelerator from Newer or Alacrity or a PowerPC 604-based Total Power application-accelerator card from Total Impact.	Speed Doubler $55; L-2 cache $125–260; Newer or Alacrity clock-chipper $100–300; Total Impact PPC total Power accelerator $1,500

Model	Upgrade Type	Features	Price
Mac IIcx, IIci, IIsi, IIvx, IIvi, Performa 600	DayStar 100MHz Turbo 601 PDS card or 66MHz Turbo 601 PDS card.	100- or 66MHz PPC 601 processor. Requires System 7.5 (not included with card). Includes 256K cache.	100MHz Turbo: $1,299, 66MHz Turbo: $899.
Mac IIvx, IIvi	Apple Power Mac 7100 motherboard	Requires an upgrade to a Mac IIci before upgrading further. **Motherboard** replacement. 80MHz PPC 601 processor. Requires dealer installation.	$1,599 plus $50 for dealer installation and L-2 cache at $125 to $260.
LC, LC II, LC III, LC 475, Performa 470 series, Quadra 605	Apple 50MHz Processor Upgrade; DayStar 100MHz PowerCard or 50MHz PowerCard 601	Requires upgrade to Performa or LC 475 before further upgrade. Processor replacement to 100 or 50MHz PPC 601 processor. Requires dealer installation for Apple processor, DayStar is do-it-yourself. Both include System 7.5 and ClarisWorks 3.0.	Apple Processor: $659 plus $50 dealer installation; DayStar 100MHz PowerCard: $999, 50MHz PowerCard: $649
LC 520, 550, 575, 580, 630, Performa 550, 560, 570 series, 630 series, Quadra 630	Apple 66MHz Processor Upgrade or DayStar 100MHz PowerCard 601 or 66MHz Power Card 601	Requires upgrade to Performa or LC 575 or better before further upgrade. Processor replacement to 100-or 66MHz PPC 601 processor. Requires dealer installation for Apple processor, DayStar is do-it-yourself. Both include System 7.5 and ClarisWorks 3.0.	Apple Processor: $659 plus $50 dealer installation; DayStar 100MHz PowerCard: $999, 66MHz PowerCard: $649
Centris/Quadra 610	DayStar 100MHz PowerPro 601 PDS card or 40/50MHz PowerPro 601 PDS card; Apple Power Mac 6100 motherboard	DayStar upgrade is PDS card with 100- or 40/50MHz PPC 601 processor; DayStar 100MHz PDS card works at 80MHz on Centris. DayStar cards require System 7.5 (not included). Apple upgrade is a motherboard replacement with a 66MHz PPC 601 processor that requires dealer installation.	DayStar 100MHz Power Procard: $1,299, NuBus card adapter: $79; PowerPro 40/50MHz card: $529, System 7.5: $98. Apple motherboard: $1,049 plus $50 for dealer installation

continues

U

Upgrade Paths for Macs* (continued)

Model	Upgrade Type	Features	Price
Centris/Quadra 650	Apple Power Mac 7100 motherboard or DayStar 100MHz PowerPro 601 PDS card	100- or 80MHz PPC 601 processor. DayStar PDS card is do-it-yourself. DayStar cards require System 7.5 (not included). The Apple motherboard must be installed by a dealer.	$1,599 plus $50 for dealer installation and L-2 cache at $125 to $260. DayStar 100 MHz PowerPro card: $1,299
Centris/Quadra 660AV	Apple Power Mac 6100 motherboard	Apple upgrade is a motherboard replacement with a 66MHz PPC 601 processor that requires dealer installation.	Apple motherboard: $1,049 plus $50 for dealer installation
Quadra 700, 900 series	DayStar 100MHz PowerPro 601 PDS card or 50/66MHz PowerPro 601 PDS card	DayStar upgrade is PDS card with 100- or 50/66MHz PPC 601 processor; DayStar cards require System 7.5 (not included).	DayStar 100MHz Power-Pro card: $1,299, Power-Pro 50/66MHz: $529, System 7.5: $98.
Quadra 800 series, Power Mac 8100 series	Apple Power Mac 8500 motherboard	120MHz PPC 604 processor in a motherboard replacement. Requires dealer installation. Quadra 800 owners can upgrade to Power Mac 8100 by installing 8100 motherboard with100MHz 601 processor.	Price for 8500 motherboard not determined. 8100 motherboard: $1,999.
Quadra 630, Performa 630 series, 5200 series, 6200 series, PowerMac 5200, 6200	Apple Power Mac 5300/6300 mother-board	100MHz PPC 603e processor motherboard replacement. Requires dealer installation. Performa and Quadra 630 owners require more RAM.	$699 – 799.
Power Mac 7200	Apple Power Mac 7500 motherboard	100MHz 601 processor on a daughterboard, making future upgrades easy. Requires dealer installation.	Price to be determined.
Power Mac 7500, 8500, 9500	none	Processors located on swappable daughterboards.	N/A

*Information taken from "Choosing the Right Mac: The Paths to Upgrades" by Roman Loyola, MacUser, December 1995.

Upgrade Card Limitations What advantages does a new Mac or a logic board upgrade have over the upgrade card? First, remember that Apple's upgrade card cannot be installed in every Mac. The logic board (motherboard) replacement is practically equivalent to a Power Mac; the only question is whether the internal hard drive, CD-ROM, and other hardware can handle this performance improvement. If not, consider a new Mac. A full motherboard upgrade adds extra features other than just speed—additional bit-depth, resolution support, and 16-bit sound might be important in your work.

Second, the performance of the upgrade card is limited because it relies on the old logic board and bus of the host Mac. Apple has tried to minimize this limitation by including 1MB of secondary RAM cache on the upgrade card. Regardless, the design of the logic board on a full-fledged Power Mac is better optimized for performance and yields better results than an accelerated Mac with a 601 chip.

See Also
Motherboard; PDS Slot; PowerPC Platform (PPCP)

Upgrade Paths, Types of
Upgrading your processor is the fastest and easiest way to accelerate your Mac. Apple's latest Macintosh computers provide upgrade slots on the **motherboard** that accept special processor daughterboards. Keep in mind that only some Mac computers can have the processor chip upgraded (PowerPC as well as 68040 models), and these may be limited to a specific type of accelerator.

Processor Upgrades to the Main Motherboard All Mac models prior to the PCI-based Power Macs (the 7500, 8500, and 9500) had processors soldered directly to the motherboard, eliminating the possibility of a processor upgrade. PowerBook processors are soldered onto the motherboard. Many of the 68040/68LC040-based Mac models have removable processor chips that support processor upgrades. The most common processor upgrades are the addition of a floating point unit (FPU) to a 68LC040-based LC Mac or a Performa model and the replacement of a 68040 chip with a 68LC040 processor (increases processor speed and adds a floating-point unit to the motherboard).

One thing you *cannot* do is add a PowerPC processor to a 68040 processor slot. The PowerPC chip won't fit into the 680x0 chip footprint, and the PowerPC processor was not created to be interchangeable with 680x0 chips. This is due to speed limitations of other chips on the motherboard and changes to the ROM, hard drive, and other hardware components.

Installing Accelerators Most accelerators require software and hardware components before they can be recognized by system software. Most 68K accelerators require the addition of dynamic RAM (DRAM) single inline memory modules (**SIMMs**) on the accelerator card before they are attached to the motherboard. PowerPC accelerators are designed to use the DRAM on the 68LC040 or 680409 motherboard; accelerator designs vary from vendor to vendor.

Apple is actively pursuing owners of traditional Mac systems that accept PowerPC upgrades and encouraging them to make the transition to the new architecture. A number of upgrade kits and upgrade cards are available that enable Mac owners to upgrade their systems to PowerPCs. In addition to Apple upgrades, third-party options are available that can be inexpensive routes to PowerPC computing.

Understanding Accelerator Cards PowerPC and 680x0 accelerators are a popular choice for increasing raw hardware speed on existing Mac models. **Accelerator card** upgrades, available for many years, can increase Mac performance without the need to buy a new computer.

Accelerator cards are the best choice for increasing performance if a lot of money has been invested in an existing Mac or exchanges are not possible. Users of older Mac models that have considerable money invested in (older) **RAM**, hard drives, or software that cannot be used with the PowerPC should purchase third-party accelerator boards. Fortunately, there is an accelerator for nearly every Mac and every Mac operation.

Accelerator boards (as opposed to CPU upgrades) only speed up certain information paths, such as the SCSI bus or QuickDraw graphic routines. Some cards are application-specific, such as Radius's PhotoEngine board, which speeds up Adobe Photoshop.

One argument against accelerators is that speeding up the clock and processor is only partially effective because the data bus through which data flows to the processor still runs at its original (slow) speed. This creates a bottleneck in the system that the processor cannot alleviate. To get around the data bus bottleneck, designers usually add high-speed static-RAM (SRAM) to the accelerator. SRAM acts as a cache between the main memory and the accelerator. In older compact Macs and some 020-based designs the main memory was added directly to the accelerator card to bypass the data bus. Some new PowerPC accelerators use a high-speed cache and RAM onboard the accelerator to optimize performance.

This configuration, although better from a performance standpoint, sometimes justifies the purchase of faster RAM memory. The use of slow SIMMs causes the accelerator to use more wait-states, slowing the system. Furthermore, the addition of SIMM sockets and memory management chips increases the cost of the board; vendors do not apply this design to low-cost or a wide range of products given the cost-sensitive nature of the current market. Macs have never been more inexpensive. Their low cost seriously affects the accelerator market, because the cost of an accelerator card is closer to the cost of an entire Mac system.

See Also
Motherboard; PDS Slot

Uploading Files
The opposite of downloading a file from an information service or a **network** such as the **Internet**. By uploading a file, you transfer data from your computer to a remote site. The remote site might be a **commercial online service,** a **bulletin board systems,** an **FTP site,** or other site on the **Internet.**

See Also
Asynchronous Transmissions; Bulletin Board Systems; Commercial Online Service; FTP; Internet; Network; World Wide Web

UPP, *See Mixed Mode Manager*

URL, See Internet

Usenet
Usenet newsgroups are a popular means of sharing information over the **Internet**. Usenet is a global computer network (originally called the User's Network) that is part of the Internet and that can be accessed either from within or outside the Internet (some **commercial online services** and **bulletin board services** (BBSs) allow connections to Usenet).

In many ways, Usenet is like a huge river of open email letters that circulates around the Internet. You can dip into the stream to see what's available and contribute to its flow. Usenet, however, is so extensive that it spreads even beyond the Internet to commercial carriers like Delphi and America Online and user group bulletin boards that have no other Internet connection.

Newsgroups resemble the conferences conducted on local computer bulletin boards or on commercial information services such as **America Online** or **CompuServe**. Users post messages, upload files, and read messages posted by others. Messages are sorted by topic, so you can read about subjects that interest you most. Thousands of topics are covered, including the Internet, political and social issues, popular culture, and the truly bizarre.

Newsgroups have what is referred to as a hierarchical structure. Most individual groups belong to one of about seven main categories, listed here.

Most Popular Newsgroup Categories

Abbreviation	Description
comp	computer issues
misc	miscellaneous issues
news	about Usenet itself

Abbreviation	Description
rec	recreational activities and popular culture
sci	science
soc	sociology and anthropology
talk	about many of the same subjects

Most news servers also subscribe to the *alt* category, which is described in the Usenet Frequently Asked Questions file as as "an anarchic collection of serious and silly subjects." Because some of the topics are trivial, and possibly offensive, they may not subscribe to all the *alt* subcatgories therein.

In addition, each news server probably carries a number of regional hierarchies pertaining to the city where the server is located or the company that operates it.

Every category has subcategories, and many subcategories contain subsubcategories. Newsgroup names are specified in a way that resembles **IP addresses**. Examples include:

> **alt.alien.visitors**
>
> **comp.publish.prepress**
>
> **rec.arts.music.bluenote**

Some newsgroups are moderated by an administrator who judges the appropriateness of an article before mailing it to a newsgroup. Most groups, though, are unmoderated: anyone who wants to can post anything.

Client Software Several shareware news browsers are available for the Mac. The excellent NewsWatcher, by John Norstad, is probably the one most commonly used.

Netscape Navigator 2.0 also has a newsgroup client. It has a number of features not offered by other news clients. One advantage is the ability to automate the proces of searching Usenet for information using **AppleScript**. Netscape 2.0 also offers the ability to display **inline graphics** inside the news window, when graphics are posted as attachments to articles. Netscape also provides clickable **hypertext link**s to all URLs mentioned in news articles.

News Servers To use Usenet, you must have access to a news server, also called an NNTP server. An NNTP server is a machine that collects postings, sorts them, and passes them along to other servers.

Your **Internet service provider** probably offers an NNTP server—just ask a technical support person for the IP address. If your Internet provider does not offer Usenet, you may still be able to gain acess to newsgroups via a public news server. Public news servers provide a free NNTP connection to a limited number of users on a first-come, first-served basis. Many of these servers are read-only, and do not allow posting.

Structure of Articles Most Usenet articles consist of several standard parts:

- Header
- Quoted material
- The message
- Signature files

The header contains basic information about the article. It contains the subject, the date the article was posted, the author of the article, the organization to which the poster belongs, and the groups to which the article has been posted. An article can be posted to more than one group *(cross-posted)*.

Often, a news article begins with quoted material from a previous posting. Usually, the quotes are marked with the > (right-angle bracket).

In contrast, the message itself or the actual content appears flush-left, unmarked by angle brackets. A signature file is a text file that appears at the bottom of your news posting. It can be as simple as your name and address but can also contain drawings made from alphanumeric characters.

After lurking (staying in the background, reading newsgroup exchanges) for a while, you might decide to talk back and post a news article of your own. You can also reply to a posted article. As an article makes its way around the news circuit, other readers of news often post replies to the article, which in turn evoke (or provoke) reactions from third parties and replies from the author. This series of follow-ups to an article is called a **thread**.

All exchanges on Usenet are governed by an informal set of conventions called "**Netiquette**" that cover what is acceptable and unacceptable to post on the Net. (These conventions originate with the users themselves rather than the government.)

See Also

America Online; AppleScript; Commercial Online Services; CompuServe; Hypertext; Internet; Internet Service Provider; IP Address; Netiquette; Netscape Navigator

Users and Groups

For Macintosh users on a **network**, this **control panel** enables you to allow access to individual users, or groups of users, that you create. These users, or groups of users, can access only the files and folders that you specifically designate they can access in the Sharing dialog box.

There are four types of users that can allow you access to your shared disk from this control panel: a registered user (a named individual network user), a guest (anyone signing on to the network), a group (a collection of individuals), and the owner (you).

When you open the Users and Groups control panel for the first time, you'll only see two icons (they look like cartoon faces): one representing you (the owner) and one representing a guest.

You create new users by choosing New User from the File menu when the Users and Groups control panel is open.(The Users and Groups control panel looks like a standard Finder window, but it is a control panel.) A new user icon is created that looks like a cartoon face, and you can name this icon to help you keep track of the user (generally, you would use the person's name for organizational purposes). Creating individual users limits access on a person by person or group by group basis. If you're going to enable all

users to have open access to your files, you don't have to create individual names for each user, just have all users sign on as guest.

Another feature is the ability to create groups. The benefit to using groups is that you can have separate groups of individuals and assign access privileges to an entire group at once, rather than assigning access privileges to each individual user. In a large company, there could be hundreds of users, and assigning individual access privileges could become very time consuming.

You create a New Group by choosing New Group from the File menu when the Users and Groups control panel is open. A cartoon icon with two faces (indicating it's a group) will appear as "untitled," and you can name the group (use a descriptive name if possible). You can add individual users to this group by dragging and dropping their individual user icons onto the group icon. (This will not delete their icon from the Users and Group control panel main window; it just adds a copy to the group.) This enables you to have one user assigned to many different groups.) To see which users are in a particular group, double-click the group icon. To remove a user from a group, simply drag the user's icon into the Trash. (Again, this will not delete their original icon from the Users and Groups control panel main window.)

See Also

Control Panels; Groups; Icons; Networking

UserTalk, *See Frontier*

Utility

A utility is a program designed to do maintenance, organization, and housekeeping-type duties on the Macintosh. For example, if you have a file that is too large to fit on a disk, you might want to use a **compression** utility to compress the file's size down to something more manageable. Or if you're having intermittent problems with your Mac, you can run a repair utility to diagnose your **System software** and repair any problems it might encounter. These utilities can come in a variety of sizes and formats and can

Utility	Developer	Purpose	Benefit
RAM Doubler	Connectix	Makes your Mac think it has more RAM	Enables you to open more applications
Now Utilities	Now Software	Repair, diagnose, and enhance your system	Adds system functionality and can repair common problems
QuicKeys	CE Software	Macro Program	Enables you to automate repetitive tasks
After Dark	Berkeley Systems	Screen Saver	Provides screen burn-in protection and entertainment
Conflict Catcher	Casady and Greene	Controls loading of extension	Helps you isolate system conflicts
Virex	Datawatch	Virus detection	Helps keep your computer free of viruses
SAM	Symantec	Virus Detection	Helps keep your computer free of viruses
Norton Utilities	Symantec	Hard disk maintenance	Repairs and optimizes hard disks
StuffIt	Aladdin	File Compression	Reduces size of files for backup or modem transfers
Disk First Aid	Apple	Repair Utility	Fixes some common software problems
DiskDoubler Pro	Symantec	File Compression	Reduces size of files for backup or modem transfers
Disk Express II	Alsoft	Disk Optimization	Speeds hard disk access by defragmenting files

be stand-alone applications or they can be in the form of **control panels** or **extensions** that are added to the system at **startup**. Apple has utilities of its own like **Disk Repair**, which is for repairing System software problems, and Apple's **HD SC Setup**, which is for formatting hard disks. Both of these are of the stand-alone variety.

The difference between utilities and regular applications is that utilities generally don't create documents, whereas most applications (besides games) are usually designed to create some sort of document—a letter, spreadsheet, graphic, or database.

See Also
Compression; Control Panels; Disk Express II; Disk First Aid; DiskDoubler Pro; Extensions Folder; HD SC Setup; Norton Utilities; Now Utilities; RAM Doubler; System Software; StuffIt; Virex

uuLite, *See Decoding/Decompressing Files*

uuUndo, *See Decoding/Decompressing Files*

V

V for Victory

V for Victory from Three Sixty is a CD-ROM release of four previously released war **strategy games**. Utah Beach, featuring the Battle of Normandy, Velikiye Luki, placing you on the Russian front, Market Garden, focusing on the air battle to secure Holland's bridges, and Gold-Juno-Sword are all groundbreaking games that drop you into the midst of World War II.

Although newer titles like U-Boat and Drumbeat are more visually appealing, the V for Victory titles are still worth checking out, especially if you are a World War II buff. These games are the most historically accurate of all. Other titles worth playing in this genre include the World at War series, developed by Atomic Games and distributed by Avalon Hill, and the spinoff war game, Onslaught from Frontal Assaultware, featuring one of the best interfaces in war strategy games and great graphics.

See Also

Allied General; Chaos Overlords; Pax Imperia; Sid Meier's Worlds; Spaceward Ho! 4.0; Strategy Games

V.22bis Standard, *See Data Communications Standards*

V.32bis Standard, *See Data Communications Standards*

V.32terbo Modem Protocol

V.32terbo is a modulation protocol used by modems to determine the speed and throughput of a connection. This protocol specifies a 19,200bps connection.

The v.32terbo protocol was developed unofficially by several manufacturers as an interim acceleration of the 14,400bps v.32bis protocol while they were awaiting the finalization of the 28,800bps v.34 protocol.

Global Village was the only major Macintosh modem manufacturer to use the v.32terbo standard in their modems. The product line that included this protocol was the "Mercury" series of products that included the PowerBook PowerPort Mercury and the external Teleport Mercury. Because few other modem manufacturers used the v.32 terbo standard, most connections made with "Mercury" modems were forced to revert to v.32bis 14,400bps speeds.

Upon the release of the v.34 standard, Global Village discontinued the Mercury series, and replaced them with the v.34 Teleport Platinum series, but provided no upgrade path.

Most other modem manufacturers skipped the v.32terbo modulation protocol, and instead opted for the speedier v.FAST 28,800bps protocol while awaiting finalization of v.34.

Currently, the only major modem to support the v.32terbo modulation protocol is the U.S. Robotics Courier "v.everything" modem, which—as its name suggests—covers all the bases.

See Also

Data Communications Standards; V.34 Modem Protocol; V.FAST Modem Protocol

V.34 Modem Protocol

The v.34 modulation protocol is the current "top of the line" modem speed protocol. It provides speeds of 28,800bps and above as well as advanced capabilities to sense and correct for changes in the quality of the telephone lines being used for data transmission.

The most interesting feature of v.34 is its line probing function. At the beginning of each call, the calling modem transmits a series of predefined signals which the answering modems analyzes to determine the exact characteristics of the telephone line currently in use. By understanding the various sensitivities and capability of the phone line, the modems are able to maximize throughput and reliability by choosing filters and power levels that are appropriate for the current call.

While the v.34 standard was being developed, two interim standards, v.32terbo (19,200bps) and v.FAST (28,800bps) were used. However, v.34 is a far superior protocol and should be used whenever possible. Because of its advanced capabilities as well as its high speeds, you should strongly consider a v.34 modem for all new modem purchases.

See Also

Data Communications Standards; V.32terbo Modem Protocol; V.FAST Modem Protocol

V.42 Standard, *See Data Communications Standards*

V.42bis Standard, *See Data Communications Standards*

V.FAST Modem Protocol

The V.FAST protocol, also known as V.FAST Class or v.FC, was developed by several modem manufactures who were anxious to provide the additional speed possible with the forthcoming v.34 protocol. This protocol was a "best guess" of what the final standard would be. Manufacturers such as Supra and U.S. Robotics produced products using the "V.FAST" protocol. It provides 28,800bps performance, but lacks the advanced error detection and correction capabilities of the final v.34 specification.

Unfortunately, because V.FAST is not an official standard, each vendor set his own exact specifications, which makes the V.FAST standard particularly unreliable when using between modems from different vendors.

Fortunately, once the v.34 standard was announced, manufacturers quickly added this protocol to their modem's feature sets, and provided low-cost upgrades to existing V.FAST units. Today V.FAST is no longer featured in modems, but is provided for backward compatibility with earlier models that were not upgraded to v.34.

See Also

Data Communications Standards; V.32 Modem Protocol; V.34 Modem Protocol

V.FC, V.FastClass, *See Modems Standards and Speeds*

Valis' Flo'

Valis Software's Flo' is a stand-alone program that also functions as a plug-in for Photoshop. For it to act like a plug-in, it must be running at the same time Photoshop is, so make sure you have enough memory if you make the plug-in choice. Valis is known for its high-end software, and Flo' adds to Valis' reputation in the field of image manipulation. Flo' accepts and can generate a number of graphics screen depths: Black and White, 4 grays, 16 Grays, 256 Grays, Thousands of Colors, and Millions of Colors.

Interface Design Flo' has an uncluttered interface with a large image area taking most of the screen and a narrow movable toolbox. Any operation that involves a Bézier curve shows that Flo' uses Béziers as an artist might, with an intuitive grasp for Bézier movements. Béziers in Flo' can be resized with the Control key, and repositioned with the Shift key. New points can be added simply by clicking on the Bézier perimeter. With a minimum of tools, Flo' is capable of a maximum amount of graphic manipulation.

How It Works Flo' works with a two-leveled system of closed Béziers, an internal Bézier whose alteration determines the extent of the warping, and an external Bézier perimeter that determines how far the warping effect will influence the rest of the picture. If the internal shape overlaps the external perimeter, the warping will still stop at the edge of the perimeter, although the effect will be very exaggerated (as if seen through a fish-eye lens). Small manipulations can build the final image over a long series of applications, and multiple undo levels guarantee that you can always step back to a previous unaltered condition. You can, in fact, step back and forward through a series of Undos and Redos. Alterations can be freeform, oval, and rectangular, and warping can be based upon size, alterations in shape, and both trapezoidal and slanted warping of selected areas. The only confusing part of its operation that takes a few minutes to get used to is that after a new editing screen is opened, the imported graphic has to be "placed."

Warping The end result of a Flo' session is a high-quality warping of the image to the artist's vision, with only those areas affected that were not protected by perimeter shapes. Because Undos are possible, several versions of the warped image can be saved, and even returned to after a save is initiated.

Morphing Flo' is not morphing software in that only one image is the target of its effects.

Animation Flo' has excellent animation possibilities based upon an easy-to-understand keyframe animation method. The Animations Settings control has two input areas: Frames per Second (defaulted at 30) and Fast Rendering (if checked, this will be of a somewhat lower quality than if left unchecked). Next, Start Keyframe is chosen, making the current frame the first keyframe. The graphic is manipulated, and Add Keyframe is selected. This allows you to set how many frames will be calculated from the last keyframe to this one. The same dialog has an Animate Settings dialog for setting the rendering size, frames per second, total number of frames, and other data. Close

loop completes the process, allowing the animation to run back and forth.

Save / Load Conventions Pictures can be saved as PICT or TIFF files at any point in the process. Animations can be saved as PICTs, numbered PICTs, or as QuickTime movies.

The documentation to Flo' is clear and direct, and tutorials are included to walk you through the processes involved. Flo' is an uncomplicated program that can be used to produce warped images and warping movies. You can learn to master it in hours if you have had any experience with computer graphics, and in days if you haven't.

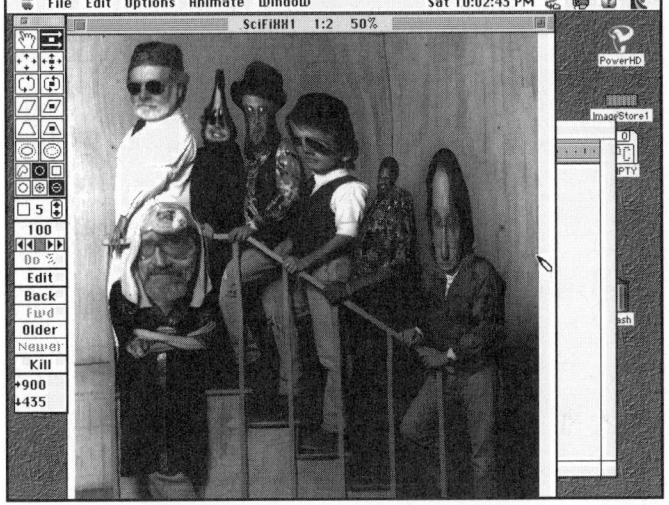

Variable

In programming, a variable is a symbolic representation of a piece of data relevant to a program. Programming variables are much like variables used in algebraic equations: They can represent any one of a range of values. Depending on the **programming language**, each variable may be assigned a variable *type* that indicates what range of values it can hold. A programmer, for example, may define an integer variable that can only hold integer numbers. Attempting to put a different kind of data (say, a string of characters) into that variable causes an error.

Typically, each variable used by a program represents a location in the computer's memory that contains the data. Although the variable name stays the same, the value of the variable (the actual data stored in memory) may change as the program executes.

See Also

Array; Constant; Programming; Programming Language

Vector Image

Vector Image describes a graphic created in a drawing software application characterized by distinct shapes and lines filled with colors or patterns. The printing resolution of a vector image is determined by the output device. Vector images are also known as object-oriented graphics.

See Also

Prepress; Printing

Veronica

A Veronica **server** provides a single interface that allows searching through large numbers of **Gopher** sites on the Internet so that users can locate specific files quickly and easily.

Veronica, which was developed at the University of Nevada, works by periodically searching the contents of Gopher sites around the world and recording the available data. It then puts these files' listings into a database and provides a simple way of searching them.

Only four to six Veronica sites exist around the world. The three in the U.S. are at NYSERNet, University of Texas, Dallas, and SCS Nevada.

You can usually find a Veronica menu within a Gopher directory entitled Other Gopher and Information Servers. When you perform a Veronica search, you either look for Gopher directories, which contain files, or you look for everything available via Gopher, which includes the files and information like **WAIS** sources as well.

See Also

Gopher; Internet Starter Kit; MacWAIS

VGA Monitors, Using

Just as multisync monitors have migrated from PC machines to Mac display capabilities, so have VGA and Super VGA (SVGA) monitors—once made exclusively for PC and workstation computers. Many Mac models can use VGA and SVGA monitors. This includes all Power Macintoshes (including the Performa Power Macs), Quadras and Centrises, the Performa 400 and 600 series, LCs, and PowerBook models with a monitor port.

If the VGA or SVGA monitor outputs the same picture resolution ratio that your Mac's on-board display circuitry or NuBus board is capable of generating, all you need is a simple cable adapter to use VGA and SVGA monitors on the Macintosh.

Because there many more PCs than Macs, VGA and SVGA vendors sell large quantities. You can often get good quality for less money by going to a PC vendor. However, you will also find cheap quality for less money. You'll find that the quality of cheaper PC monitors is not as high as with monitors from Apple, which usually meet high quality standards. Buying a monitor sight unseen is certainly a gamble, so it's a good idea to get a look at some of the monitors you're considering at computer stores.

You'll sometimes also find that tech support personnel at these PC companies will know little if anything about the Mac. *MacUser* magazine once reported that these companies often blame problems on the Apple video driver and the Mac adapter, which, in fact, are almost never the source of problems.

The best places to find VGA and SVGA monitors are PC magazines. The tabloid-sized *Computer Shopper* is as thick as a telephone book and can be found at most large newsstands. *Shopper* is filled with hundreds of dealers hawking PC peripherals. These dealers can tell you which cable-end adapter you need for their particular VGA/SVGA model so that you can run it from your Macintosh. Other good sources are *PC Computing*, *PC World*, and free regional publications such as *Computer Currents*.

See Also

Multisync Monitors

VHS

VHS is a videotape format that uses comparatively large, 1/2-inch, cassette tapes and provides comparatively low quality images—about 250 lines of resolution.

This format is very popular. The equipment is inexpensive, and for small sized digital video (less than 240×180 pixels), the resolution is acceptable. Because it uses a **composite signal**, the image quality (richness of color, clarity) is not as good as S-VHS and Hi-8 formats.

See Also

8mm; QuickTime; Video Digitizing

Video Digitizing

Turning a video image into a digital one can be surprisingly easy, provided you have the right equipment. This process is called digitizing because an analog signal is turned into a digital image. The most important piece of equipment you need to do this is video digitizing hardware. This equipment turns the NTSC analog signal into a sequence of digital pictures. Fortunately, many Macintosh models now come with that equipment built-in including the AV Macintosh models and the 7500, 7600, and 8500 model Power Macs.

With one of these computers, all you need is to connect a camcorder or VCR to the video and audio inputs, launch a video capture application, such as Adobe Photoshop, Strata's VideoShop, or Radius' QuickFLIX or VideoFusion, and record the video as a QuickTime movie.

Results are determined by several factors. Most importantly, realize that the compression of the images takes time; the larger the image the more time. Also, the faster the computer's processor, the larger the frame and the frame rate of the video you will be able to capture.

The 68K AV Macintosh can capture a 320 × 240 clip at a maximum of approximately 10 frames per second, whereas the NuBus Power Macintosh models can reach up to 20 frames per second. The fastest PCI Power Macs can reach 30 frames per second. None of these machines can capture 640 × 480 at 30 frames per second (the equivalent of NTSC video for those wanting to capture, edit, and then record to videotape) without some additional hardware compression acceleration, such as the Radius VideoVision Studio board, or the Truevision Targa 1000, or products from Data Translation or Avid.

Other factors that affect the performance you obtain during digitizing are

- The speed of the hard drive. A **RAID** drive provides the best performance, but at a price. An **AV** drive can eliminate **dropped frames** (missing a frame during the digitization process) caused by thermal calibration. Also, all drives should be optimized before recording.

- Optimize your system software. Turn off **Virtual Memory**, disable all unnecessary Extensions (don't turn off QuickTime!), and turn off the **AppleTalk** network. This software can cause interrupts in the system, which result in dropped frames. Note: Some QuickTime recording software will prompt you to turn the network off.

- Usually, the None compressor has the best results, but the Component Video (YUV) compressor can also produce good results.

- The capture bit depth must be at 16- or 24-bits when capturing video. If you must convert to a lower bit depth, capture at a higher setting and then perform the conversion during **recompression**.

- Set the black level (this is the point at which black appears to be black). It might seem odd, but if it's not done correctly, the video can appear murky because the blacks are actually dark gray. Also, adjusting the brightness and contrast may result in a better image. Although most software editing programs enable you to adjust brightness and contrast, you will get much better results if you do this when capturing the video.

- Use a frame rate that is evenly divisible into the frame rate of the original signal. NTSC has a frame rate of 30 frames per second, so use 30, 15, or 10 if possible.

- If you are recording from videotape, there will usually be a band across the bottom of the image; crop this during recording.

- The quality of the video itself plays a major factor in the quality of your final results. This may not be so obvious when capturing with the None compressor, but is the most evident when you recompress the video using one of the other video compressors.

- Better quality equipment (Hi8, SuperVHS) produces much better results than **8mm** and **VHS**. Using S-Video out (if your digitizer supports it) results in a better image. A well lit scene can make a dramatic difference, no matter what kind of equipment you use.

See Also
Compressing Files; QuickTime

Video Games, *See Entertainment*

Video on the Internet

Many sites on the Web serve video files. Most are in **QuickTime** format, which is native to the Mac, but you might also find files in MPEG format.

QuickTime movies can be played with the QuickTime extension and Movie Player applications included with System 7.1 and later operating systems. (Simple Player,

also by Apple and with controls identical to Movie Player's, has also been widely distributed.) A QuickTime plug-in for Netscape Navigator was still being eagerly awaited as this was written.

Apple's QuickTime VR Player is an exciting Internet application that plays both regular QuickTime movies and VR movies. VR moves are *visual representations* of scenes wherein you can pan around a full 360 degrees by clicking and dragging.

MPEG videos downloaded from the Web can be played with the application Sparkle, which also plays QuickTime clips.

See Also
Animation on the Internet; Audio on the Internet; Multimedia on the Internet

VideoFusion

QuickTime editing and effects software developed by VideoFusion Inc. and now published by Radius. Its collection of effects serves to complement the ones available in programs, such as Adobe's **Premiere** and Strata's **VideoShop**. In this respect, VideoFusion competes with Adobe's **After Effects**, which also provides a large number of effects (but at twice the price). After Effects offers high-end features, such as **SMPTE** support, and enables you to build effects using multiple layers of images and video. VideoFusion requires that you create an intermediate clip to apply an effect to separate clips.

VideoFusion uses a novel method for creating movies. First, QuickTime clips are pasted into the Storyboard Window. Then, when VideoFusion assembles the final movie, it starts at the top left clip in the Storyboard and adds each clip (left to right) across the Storyboard.

You can use the Storyboard to arbitrarily arrange clips; the first three clips could appear in row one, whereas the next two clips appear in row two. When it assembles the final movie, VideoFusion simply skips empty cells.

The Storyboard displays the first frame of a clip. If you double-click it, however, VideoFusion will play the whole clip. Also, a Time View window displays the individual frames of the movie clips.

Transitions are applied by selecting two adjacent clips in the Storyboard and then choosing Transition from the Effects menu. The length of the transition is adjusted using the time slider, and then previewed in a Preview window. This technique more closely resembles the editing technique used in VideoShop rather than Premiere. Your preferred editing method will most likely depend upon previous editing experience. Those who have used traditional video editing equipment will probably prefer Premiere's interface, whereas those with a graphics background might find VideoFusion or VideoShop easier to understand.

After you select two clips in the Storyboard, you can layer one clip on top of another using the Layer command. Note that one clip has to be made smaller than the other for you to see anything other than the clip on top!

VideoFusion can capture video if your computer supports video digitizing (such as an **AV Macintosh**, or has a **digitizing board** installed.) The program also support Avid's **Open Media Framework Standard** for transferring files between different computer platforms.

Effects include resize and crop, blend, Chroma key, composite, mix, replace, extract channels, threshold, posterize, mosaic, warp, morph, and over one hundred fades, wipes, and dissolves. Clip speed and direction also can be adjusted.

VideoFusion, Inc.

Original developer and publisher of the QuickTime editing programs VideoFusion and QuickFLIX!. This software is published by Radius.

See Also

VideoFusion; QuickFLIX!

VideoShop

VideoShop is a **QuickTime** movie editor designed for general purpose editing tasks. Originally developed by Diva, which was bought by Avid, the prod-

uct is now owned by Strata, developers of 3D software.

VideoShop, like its competitor Adobe **Premiere**, edits QuickTime movies. Like Premiere, VideoShop provides many transitions and effects, but the interface is very different. Whereas Premier provides an interface that should appeal to those with video editing background (complete with "A" and "B" tracks), VideoShop was designed for the new video editor. Clips can be edited together in a single track. Simply drag one clip and then another into the document. To add a transition, move the cursor over the joining point of the two clips. The cursor changes to indicate that a transition can be applied. Clicking and dragging in either direction causes VideoShop to highlight an equal amount of both clips (this is the region over which the transition will be applied). A transition effect is then chosen. VideoShop provides an easier to use and grasp interface for applying transitions, but it is more limited. You cannot create **L-Cuts** using this technique.

VideoShop enables you to add additional video tracks to a movie. Rather than use these to create transition effects, you can use them to overlay one movie on top of another. As long as the first track is smaller in frame size from the second, you can see the second track behind the first one. Click and drag to arrange the location of the first track in the preview window. This is much easier than in Premiere.

VideoShop has added **EDL** (Edit Decision List) support and other high-end features, but Adobe Premiere still beats VideoShop for sheer number of features. VideoShop, however, is priced lower than Premiere.

See Also

Premiere; QuickTime

VideoVision

A high-quality video digitizing and display board that adds video capabilities to non-AV Macintosh models. It can capture video to a **QuickTime** movie. The **VideoVision Studio** board adds a **JPEG** hardware compression expansion board that makes it possible to capture and play-back full-screen video.

Radius
Phone: (408) 541-6100
Web: **http://www.radius.com/**

See Also

QuickTime; Video Digitizing

VideoVision Studio

A high-quality video digitizing and display board that adds video capabilities to non-AV Macintosh models. It can be used to capture video to a **QuickTime** movie. The **VideoVision Studio** board is a bundle of the VideoVision board with a **JPEG** hardware compression expansion board, making it possible to capture and play-back full screen video (640×480 at 30 fps).

You must have the hardware compression board to view and play these movies at 30 frames per second, but Radius has released VideoVision SoftStudio, a software **compressor** that enables you to open and edit VideoVision movies on equipment that doesn't have the VideoVision board installed.

The VideoVision Studio is a step up from the built-in video digitizing hardware, because it adds the JPEG hardware compression, and can output **NTSC** video. The quality, however, does not quite match the more expensive boards, such as Data Translations Media 100 or Truevision Targa 2000, and audio is only 8-bit (unless you use the internal audio of an **AV Macintosh** or Power Macintosh).

Radius
Phone: (408) 541-6100
Web: **http://www.radius.com/**

See Also

QuickTime; Video Digitizing

View Commands

You can select a variety of options for displaying the contents of an **active window** by making a selection from the View menu at the **desktop**. The default view for windows is By Icon, which displays the files and folders by their icons at full size. Besides viewing a window's contents by Icon view, you can also view the contents by small icons, which is helpful when you have many items in one window and want to display as many items as possible. The View by Small Icons option displays a very small version of the file icon to the left of the filename. These drastically smaller icons give you more room in your window to display files.

You can also use the View command to view the contents of an active window in a list format, sorted by name, size, kind, label, or creation date. If you select Name as your view for a particular window, the contents of that window are displayed in an alphabetical list. If you choose to view a window by size, you'll see a list of the contents starting with the largest item in size first, listing down to the smallest item. If you select to show the window's contents by Kind, you'll see the contents listed by groups of similar kinds of files by label. For example, first all applications are listed in alphabetical order, followed by all documents in alphabetical order, and then all folders alphabetically, and so on.

If you choose to view a window by Date, you'll see a listing of the contents in a list starting with the most recently modified document, to the oldest modified document in that window. The View by Date option uses the modification date, not the creation date, to determine the order in which documents are displayed. Using the View by Date option is helpful when you're looking for your most recent files to **back up**.

If you're viewing a window in a list view (by date, name, size, or kind), you'll notice that the currently selected view option's name is underlined just below the title bar. You can use a shortcut to switch your view to a different list view by simply clicking the desired option's name. When you click one of those names, it then becomes underlined, telling you that the window is now sorted by that option.

When you're viewing a window in a list view, notice that folders appearing in this view have a small triangle to the left of their name in the window. This triangle enables you to view the contents of the folder by clicking the triangle. The triangle faces downward and a list of the folder's contents appears in the window, slightly indented from the rest of the list, to help you visually separate items in the window from items in a folder. This is called expanding the folder. If you no longer need to view the contents within the folder, you can "collapse" the folder by again clicking the triangle.

To use the View command to change how a window displays its contents, follow these steps:

1. Select a view option (by Small Icon, by Icon, Name, Size, Kind, or Date) from the View menu.

2. The currently active window changes to the appropriate icon or list view, based on your selection. The amount of information that appears in a list view is determined in the Views Control Panel (found under the Apple menu in the Control Panels folder). This lets you determine which information (size, date modified, label, and so on) is displayed, and you can also choose in which font and size the window's contents are displayed.

3. If you have selected a list view, you can switch to any other list view (Name, Size, Kind, or Date) by just clicking the name of the column header located just below the window's title bar. The currently active view option's name is underlined.

See Also
Active Window; Desktop; Views Control Panel

View Editor, *See Interface Builder*

View Menu
There are a number of ways to view the contents of an **active window** at the **desktop** on the View menu at the desktop. The default view for a window is by Icon, which displays the files and folders by their icons at full size. Besides viewing a windows contents by

Icon view, you can also View the contents by small icons, which is helpful when you have many items in one window and want to display as many items as possible. The View by Small Icons option displays a very small version of the file icon to the left of the file name. These drastically smaller icons give you much more room in your window to display files.

You can also view windows in one of four list views, which include: View by Name, Size, Kind, Date (modification date), Label, and Version.

To change how the contents of a window are viewed, follow these steps:

1. Open, or make active, the window whose view you want to change.

2. Choose the viewing option you'd like from the View menu at the desktop.

3. The window changes to the view you selected. You can adjust how much information a list view displays in the **Views control panel.**

See Also
Active Window; Desktop; Views Control Panel

View Windows By Option
You can view the contents of a window by:

- Icon
- Small Icon
- Name
- Size
- Kind
- Date
- Label
- Version

These options are selected in the **View menu:**

- View by **Icon** is the default view for a window and displays the contents of the windows using full-sized icons.

- View by Small Icon enables you to view a smaller version of the file's icon just to the right of the file's name. You choose this option if you want an icon view but have many files in the window. By making the icons smaller, you can fit more files in the window.

- View by Name is a list view, rather than an icon view, and it lists the contents of the window alphabetically by name.

- View by Size is a list view that displays the contents of the window from the largest file (measured in kilobytes) down to the smallest file.

- View by Kind groups the files by type and displays them in alphabetized groups. It will, for example, list all applications first, followed by documents, followed by folders.

- View by Date lists the contents of the window chronologically starting with the most recently modified or created document in the window and ending with the oldest.

- View by Label enables you to view files and folders by the labels you have marked them with from the Labels control panel.

To choose a View by option, follow these steps:

1. Open, or make active, the window whose view you want to change.

2. Choose the viewing option you want on the View menu at the desktop.

3. The window immediately changes to the view you have selected. You also can adjust how much information a list view is displayed in the **Views control panel.**

See Also
Active Window; Control Panels; Desktop; Icons; View Menu

Views Control Panel

The Views Control Panel enables you to customize how you view information appearing in a **list view** in an **active window,** and which font and size will be used to display filenames. You can set the mini-icon size for viewing items to small, medium, or large, and you can choose to view or not to view various attributes about a file such as:

- Size
- Kind
- Label
- Date
- Version
- Comments

There's even an option to have the Mac calculate the total size of each folder in a list view and display the size of that folder (see the following figure).

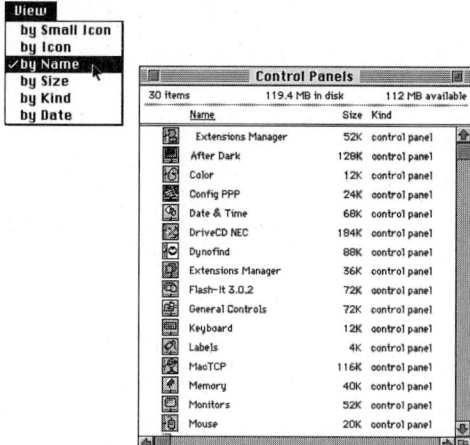

Other options in this control panel include:

- Setting the **default settings** and size for filenames.

- Setting file and folder icons to always snap to an invisible grid in any window with an icon view.

- Setting a staggered grid so that long filenames don't bump into each other in icon views.

To use the Views Control Panel, follow these steps:

1. Select Views from the Control Panels submenu on the Apple menu (or System Folder).

2. Select your default filename font and size from the pull-down menus.

3. Click Always Snap to Grid if you want files and folders to snap to an invisible alignment grid. If you select this option, choose straight or staggered grid.

4. Select the size of mini-icons that appear in a window when viewed in a list view, by clicking the appropriate icon. Use the check boxes to select what information you want calculated and displayed in a list view.

See Also
Apple Menu; Control Panels; Desktop

ViewSonic 17GA, *See Monitors, Common Models*

Vikings, *See Sid Meier's Worlds*

Violence in Games

Few games, aside from Night Trap by Digital Pictures, which was actually pulled from the shelves of many software stores a few years ago because of public condemnation of its violence and suggestive themes, have raised public warning flags like **First Person Perspective Shooters**. Instead of solving a puzzle or finding a door, to get to the next level in these games you usually have to kill every other living thing in sight. The games are full of violence and carnage. Some, like Hexen: Beyond Heretic, from GT Interactive and id, even add extra gore to the scene, mixing violence with humor. You can turn bad guys into pigs and then kill them (sure to raise an animal rights ruckus somewhere). However, there is no denying that these fast-paced games are fun, addictive, and are becoming even more popular.

Most of the violence in Shooter games for the Mac doesn't even comes close to the bloody wreckage of Mortal Kombat (MK III will soon be available for the Mac from GT, opening a whole new can of moral worms). If you'd prefer to avoid spilled blood and guts, and don't want your kids exposed to meaningless violence, steer clear of these titles.

See Also
Descent; DOOM II; First Person Perspective Shooters

Virex

Virex is a popular commercial **virus** detection and eradication program from DataWatch designed to catch viruses before they infect your computer. Virex can also perform a very thorough search of your **hard disk** and seek out any hidden viruses that may have infected your disks before you installed Virex.

Virex supports code strings that allow it to detect (but not remove) new viruses. Virex cannot scan compressed archives, but it can detect viruses in HyperCard stacks.

A nice feature of Virex is its capability to be updated on-the-fly as new viruses are detected, which enables enhanced protection without having to upgrade the entire program every time a new virus is discovered. DataWatch generally distributes these free **patches**, or updates to the program's virus database, online as soon as they're available.

DataWatch
234 Ballardvale St.
Wilmington, MA 01887
Phone (508) 988-9700
Street Price $69.95
Web: **http://www.datawatch.com**.

See Also

Anti-Virus; Hard Disks; SAM; Virus

Virtual Battlefield Environment in Flight Sims, *See A-10 Attack!*

Virtual FX Rack

A bundle of five **plug-ins** for Digidesign's audio products, Virtual FX includes a panning utility, reverberation, chorus, and other effects.

>   Steinberg North America
>   Price: $399
>   Phone: (818) 993-4091
>   Web: **http://www.midifarm.com/steinberg/ virtual.htm**

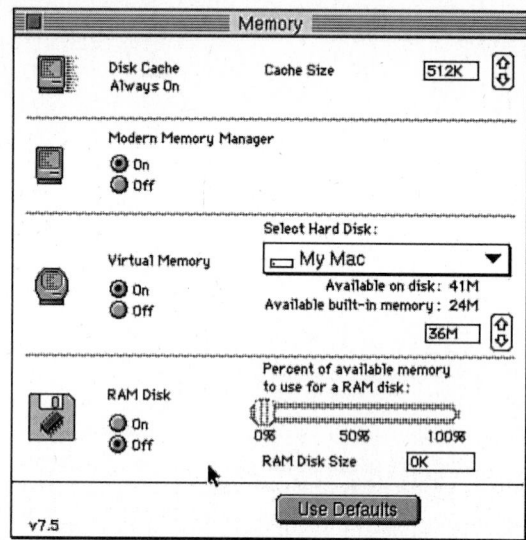

Virtual Memory

Introduced in **System 7**, virtual memory enables you to increase the computer's memory by using free space on your **hard disk** as RAM. This free space doesn't actually become RAM, but virtual memory makes the system think it is RAM, enabling the Mac to function as if it had more memory. You turn this on from the Memory control panel, as shown in the figure.

It sounds too good to be true, but there is a trade-off. First, performance with virtual memory RAM is slower than with installed RAM, and second, the space you allot for RAM is subtracted from the amount of space you have available on your hard disk, as virtual memory sets aside that amount. If, for example, you have a Mac with 8MB of RAM and a 240MB hard disk (100MB of which is still available), you can use virtual memory to add another 50MB of RAM the next time you **restart**. However, because virtual memory is substituting hard disk space for real RAM, it must set aside the combined amount of your internal built-in RAM plus 50MB of your 100MB of free hard disk space for use as virtual memory RAM. So, in this case, virtual memory would set aside 58MB of RAM.

Virtual memory is available only to users with a 68030 or higher processor (which includes SE/30s, Quadras, Power Macs, LC II, LC III, and Color Classics).

You can toggle virtual memory on or off in the **Memory control panel**. There's also a **pop-up menu** with a list of mounted disks for you to choose from as your virtual disk. You can choose how many MB of RAM you want to have (up to half the free hard disk space you have available) upon restart. And, yes, you have to restart to engage virtual memory. As a convenience, the amount of built-in RAM on your Mac and the amount of free hard drive space appears within the virtual memory portion of the Memory Control Panel just below the pop-up menu for choosing hard disks.

There is a limit to how much virtual memory RAM you can use. The limit on System 7.0 and 7.1 is 1,000MB, or one gigabyte (GB). Apple upped the limit on System 7.5, enabling you to use up to 2GB.

To turn on virtual memory, follow these steps:

1. Choose Memory from the Control Panels folder on the Apple menu.

2. Click the On radio button to toggle virtual memory on.

3. Select the hard disk that you want to be your virtual disk (the hard disk whose free space will be used as RAM).

4. Use the up/down arrows to determine how much RAM you want upon restart.

5. Close the Memory control panel and restart your machine to activate virtual memory.

See Also

Hard Disk; Memory Control Panel; Pop-Up Menu; Restart; System 7.0

Virtual Memory, in 680x0 Macs

System 7 introduced the concept of *virtual memory* (VM) to the Macintosh world. System 7 lets you designate a portion of your storage as memory. The term *virtual* is used to refer to this pseudo-memory. Macintoshes which use the 68040 and 68030 computer chips, and those 68020 systems with an additional board called a *Paged Memory Management Unit,* or PMMU, can use virtual memory to augment their actual RAM.

This means that all Macintosh models except the SE, LC, Plus, Classic, or Portable can allocate disk space as VM. If you have not turned on 32-bit addressing (a new System 7 feature which allocates a larger register space to memory, thus enabling you to access more disk space as VM), most Macintosh computers can only access up to 14MB of memory (6MB of VM and a maximum of 8MB of RAM). (Note that older Macintosh II models using NuBus cards can access 1MB less memory for each NuBus card they have installed.) With 32-bit addressing, Macintosh computers can access virtually unlimited memory—up to 1GB, if you have double that much free hard disk space.

Virtual memory subtracts storage availability from your hard disk in proportion to the amount of RAM you have installed. You need enough disk storage to fulfill your virtual memory and built-in RAM requirements together, because the way VM operates is to map the logical memory to the virtual memory so that there is a one-to-one correspondence between the two systems. The correct tracking and organization of sector numbers is very important to the continued health of the Virtual Storage area of the disk. Using this mapping scheme, the System can easily and rapidly locate pages to swap. Therefore, if you have 5MB of RAM, you can allocate up to an additional 5MB of virtual memory, but you must have 10MB of storage available.

The Macintosh considers disk space assigned to virtual memory to be no different than RAM. Virtual memory is actually slower than RAM, because it works by switching blocks of data called "pages" back and forth between the virtual memory area, called the VM Storage on the hard disk and RAM as they are required. When the application requires a new segment, the System swaps another least-used portion of the document out of RAM and replaces it with the required segment. VM can degrade the performance of your Macintosh because it actually resides on the hard disk and thus must pass the physical barrier of the disk drive to transfer data to RAM.

This takes a certain amount of time, and increases as you try to load additional large programs after the system has reserved its share of the RAM. The time it takes VM to swap in enough portions of the program to be workable is called *thrashing*. To avoid this problem, set VM no higher than double the amount of built-in RAM you have installed and do not use it to install many large programs at one time.

Another way to improve the performance of the system is to avoid any time where the system has to unnecessarily access the disk drive, such as when it refreshes the screen when running VM. To avoid unneeded refreshes, hide all windows except the currently open one. Hidden windows are not refreshed until you make them current:

To allocate virtual memory to your Macintosh, follow these steps:

1. Return to the Finder and select the Control Panels from the Apple menu.

2. When the Control Panel window opens, double-click the Memory panel.

3. When the dialog box is displayed, click the On radio button next to the Virtual Memory icon (a fat Mac).

4. From the resulting pull-down menu select the drive from which you want to take the memory.

5. Select the amount of memory you want to allocate scrolling up or down using the arrow keys or by typing a number in the box. Note that you cannot allocate more virtual memory than you have RAM. The number represents the resulting total amount of RAM (disk plus built-in RAM).

6. Close the dialog box and pull down the Restart command from the Special window to restart the Macintosh and activate the memory.

7. To check how VM affected your RAM use, select the About This Macintosh from the Apple menu.

How you use your built-in memory is important, because in today's Macintosh the performance of memory directly affects the performance of storage. If your memory is fragmented (lowering the processing power of your computer), or if you are using large amounts of VM to augment your memory (directly tying the performance of memory to that of storage), a disk crash is a major disaster. Understanding how memory works and is configured enables you to set up your Macintosh to make the most effective use of your resources.

See Also

Memory Control Panel; Virtual Memory in Power Macs

Virtual Memory, in Power Macs

The PowerPC processor works with RAM differently from the 68K processors. Rather than use a Paged-Memory-Management Unit (PMMU), the PowerPC logic board manages memory using a separate chip called the High-Speed Memory Controller. System

7.5.1 and later versions of the Mac operating system contains rewritten instructions to optimize memory management on the PowerPC. Suddenly, virtual memory is beneficial to the performance of the computer.

On the Power Mac, software is divided into chunks (called fragments) and loaded into memory. The Memory Manager runs more efficiently in native PPC programs. For example, when real RAM needs to be used for something else, virtual memory software does not swap the file currently in RAM out to the hard disk, but rather lets the RAM overwrite the data and remembers the location of the original code on the hard disk and retrieves it again from the original application file, when needed. When virtual memory is running, RAM requirements for programs are actually lower. As shown in the illustration, when you have VM running, the Get Info box displays an additional message giving a lower memory requirement.

A PPC-native program, such as Word 6.0.1, stores its executable code in the data fork of its application file. With virtual memory turned on, the Virtual Memory Manager in System 7.5.*x* on a Power Mac can reuse the data fork of the application as a paging file to help improve performance. Thus, only the needed portions of code get loaded into RAM, reducing the memory partition requirements of the application.

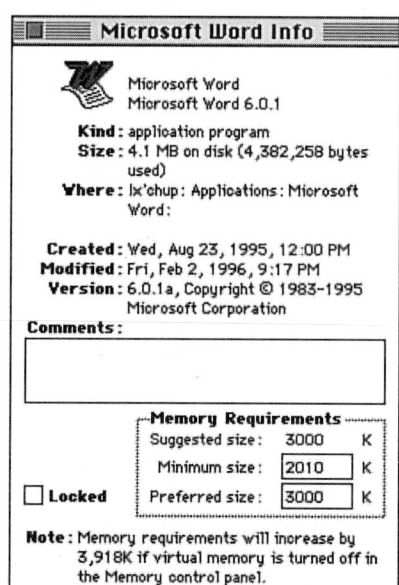

Turn on virtual memory when you are running native-mode applications. Set the virtual memory in the Memory control panel to 1MB above the amount of real RAM on your system. For example, as shown in the illustration, if you have 16MB of RAM, set the virtual memory to provide a total of 17MB.

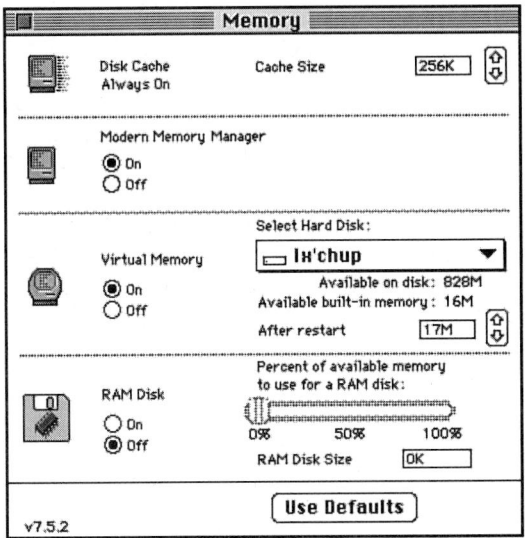

v7.5.2

See Also

Get Info Command; Memory Control Panel; PMMU; Virtual Memory

Virtus AlienSkin TextureShop,
See AlienSkin TextureShop

Virtus WalkThrough Pro

Virtus Corporation pioneered what Web surfers are beginning to take for granted, the capability to interact in real time with virtual 3D graphics worlds. Until you personally experience the thrill of moving in a 3D environment as easily as if you were taking a stroll around the block that you live on, and until you actually create an interactive 3D environment on your own, you are missing the point (and certainly the future) of computer graphics and animation. The future of 3D graphics is an interactive future, a non-linear environment very different from a videotape

or a QuickTime movie of a 3D scene that never varies in its playback. In an interactive 3D environment, you always have the choice of which way to turn and what to pay attention to, just as you do in the world outside of the computer.

Because of memory constraints (RAM), system speeds (MHz), storage issues (Terabyte drives) and other barriers that are being overcome slowly, the interactive virtual world we presently design and experience lacks the depth and variety to be totally believable. In twenty years, with the present rate of technological breakthroughs, that will not be the case. So appreciate the present when you look at a program like Virtus WalkThrough Pro, because the present will soon be the vintage history of the past. Explore like a pioneer on the edge of a whole new realm of interactive 3D design.

The Interface Virtus WalkThrough Pro has a two part interface. One side is devoted to object placement, manipulation, and the overall design of a 3D environment. The other side is the render screen, showing the 3D perspective of the design environment, including the assigned texture maps. What makes the 3D perspective part of the interface so interesting is that you can use the mouse to interactively move around inside your creation, in real time.

Modeling Tools Seven primitive polygonal structures are included in the toolbox. These can be placed anywhere on the edit screen, usually from the top view. A special set of alteration icons allows you to sculpt these further, and any of the control points of an object can be grabbed and moved to deform the object. Another set of transformation tools allows you to change an object's height or width, or to resize it globally. The object can be made opaque, transparent, or invisible by selecting the proper icon. By gluing primitives and altered primitives together, complex structures can be modeled.

Modeling can also take place on separate layers, which helps when it comes to tweaking an object's shape. It need not be nested on one layer, making it harder to select. In this way, Virtus WalkThrough reminds one of a high-end CAD program. DXF 2D files can be imported as a Trace layer, so that their designs can be traced into the environment. These traces cannot be made into 3D models however, and they will only show up in the view that was activated at their import time. Objects can also be sliced in the edit screen.

Texture Mapping The software comes with a library of textures (256 color is the format). You can import your own 256 color PICTs as textures and add them to the library selections. Placing a texture on an object is as easy as selecting it in the edit screen and double-clicking on the texture. Backgrounds can be added by mapping a 256 color PICT file to a suitable vertical plane in the background.

Lights Lights can be added or deleted from the scene at anytime. A 3D interactive Lights dialog allows you to spin the target plane of the lights and to adjust their color. Selecting "apply" from the menu shows the effects of the edited lights in the 3D perspective window.

Rendering Rendering as such doesn't apply in this software. Objects can be rendered as shaded or fully textured, but the scene is always rendered automatically in the 3D Perspective window. Separate snapshots can be saved out, as can sequenced frames, QuickTime movies, or VRML files.

Animation This is where Virtus WalkThrough Pro shines. Fully interactive animated walkthroughs of the scene are possible at anytime. By turning on a Record button, your mouse driven walkthrough is recorded. Selecting "Stop" and then play will play it back in the 3D window. This same animation is remembered for recording to a file as sequenced frames or as a movie.

Other Special Features This whole program and everything in it is special, from its modeling conventions to its animated walkthroughs of a scene.

File Load/Save Conventions Virtus WalkThrough Pro can import Trace Layers (PICT, DXF 2D, and TIFF), which are automatically converted to 256 colors. It can also export DXF 2D and 3D, Virtus Player, and VRML.

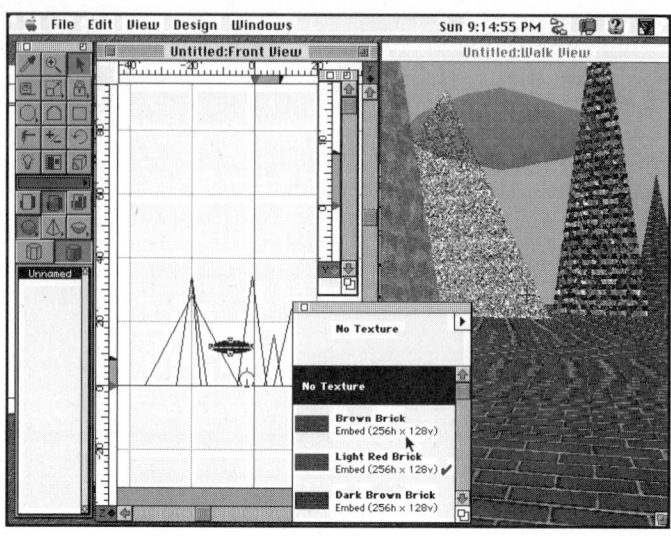

Virus

Computers follow the instructions provided by a program. A computer program that is written with the intent of causing harm is called a **virus**. The name is derived from the similarity between the way computer viruses and biological viruses infect a host system.

A computer virus comes in a variety of forms, but it is generally an application or hidden bits of code designed to damage the recipient's files or system in some way. It can be as harmless as a virus that displays a greeting or message on a certain predetermined day, or it can be as harmful as a virus that erases the contents of your hard disk or damages files.

One virus that spread throughout the Mac community was the WDEF virus, which infected a hard disk and then infected any disks that were mounted. This helped spread the virus as disks were exchanged between users. The WDEF virus attacked the desktop file, would sometimes crash certain models of Macintosh computers, and would set off your Mac's "alert" sound when a disk became infected.

Computer viruses are sometimes created when one modifies an existing computer virus. Computer users can protect their data by using virus detection and prevention utility software. The most popular titles include: SAM (Symantec Antivirus for the Macintosh), Disinfectant, Virex, CP Antivirus, and Gatekeeper.

The virus situation on the Macintosh is not serious, but it must be contained with a conscious effort on everyone's part to prevent the spread of infected files. Just a few minutes per week can keep your Macintosh, and possibly those computers you share files with, virus-free.

Why a person would create a virus and spread it throughout the computing world is a question that can be answered only by psychiatrists or therapists. Some people feel that viruses are created by disgruntled computer programmers. Other feel that the viruses are created by people who just want to see whether they can do it. It's probably a little of both. Recent studies show that approximately three new viruses are introduced each day to the computing world at large (Mac, PC, UNIX, and so on), and these studies reveal that most viruses are created by teenagers.

Viruses are designed to attached themselves to other documents or applications. After a virus starts to spread, and it can be spread over **online services**, the **Internet**, or even on disks, and the person who created the virus will never see the people it affects or gain any monetary value for creating this program designed to do nothing but harm. There have even been isolated cases of viruses being slipped into shipping versions of applications that come directly from the software manufacturer.

Computers can get viruses by disks, networks, and modems. The virus usually tries to copy itself to other disks, applications, and documents. Some computer viruses can lie dormant waiting for a specified time, date (such as Friday the 13th), or even an event before they begin to cause disruption.

Luckily for us, **anti-virus** utilities have become so prevalent that most users never come in contact with the effects of a real virus, and for that reason, some evil virus programmers try to devise new ways to create viruses that will slip past, undetected by anti-virus utilities. And then the anti-virus companies introduce a patch to the software that will stop the new virus in its tracks, and then the person who developed the virus comes out with another virus, and so on, and it continues in a vicious circle.

Because new viruses emerge periodically, you must be sure to use the most recent version of the anti-virus utility to scan and repair your disks. Rather than upgrading to an entirely new application, some of these programs allow you to upgrade by typing in codes that will detect newfound viruses. These codes are either sent to you in the mail (if you are a registered user) or posted to bulletin board systems, such as America Online and CompuServe.

For those periods of time between scanning for viruses, the anti-virus utilities also include a system extension that continually monitors your Macintosh for suspicious or virus-like activity. When a known virus is spotted, an alert message is displayed. At this point, the extension usually prompts you to run the application to remove the virus.

It is unlikely that any unknown viruses will find their way into your Macintosh computing environment. Changes in the way the operating system functions have reduced some of the risk of becoming infected with a virus, and the safety practice of using anti-virus utilities has become widespread. However, because the known viruses have had many years to make their way into Macs all over the world, there is still a small chance you may encounter one or more of these.

Even without virus detection software, you can employ a few techniques that decrease the likelihood of your Macintosh becoming infected by a virus:

- Keep your original software disks locked at all times and install only from these disks or a locked copy of these disks.

- Make routine backups of your hard drive and lock the backup disks. Check your disks with virus detection software before each backup.

- Run all new software (commercial, shareware, and freeware) with a virus detection utility before using it the first time.

- Look for strange activity on your computer (unusual messages, font display problems, increased disk activity) that might be the symptom of a virus.

Applications that intentionally do damage while masquerading as something entertaining or useful are called **trojan horses**. Trojan horses do not replicate. Viruses that do nothing other than replicate (into as many locations as possible) are called **worms**.

See Also

Aniti-Virus Utility; CDEF Virus; CODE 1 Virus; CODE 252 Virus; CP Anti-Virus; Disinfectant; Gatekeeper; MacMag Virus; MBDF Virus; MDEF Virus; nVIR Virus; SAM; Scores Virus; T4 Virus; Virex; WDEF Virus; ZUC Virus

Vision

Vision is a sophisticated **MIDI** sequencing program that also can record and edit audio tracks. Using Vision, a MIDI music track can be created and then a 16-bit digital audio file recorded in synchronization with the MIDI track. The program enables you to mix and edit the digital audio tracks, as well as the MIDI tracks. The program can, for example, record various keyboard and synthesizer tracks as MIDI files, while vocal track's and other acoustic instruments can be recorded as digital audio. The digital audio and MIDI tracks can be played back and adjusted until the desired effect is achieved (then the MIDI instruments can be digitized and a final recording mixed).

Vision is really a cross between a traditional sound editing application, which displays sound wave forms (such as SoundEdit), and a sequencing program. It supports **SMPTE** time code, markers, and punch-in and out points. A punch-in point is a point in an existing recording where a second recording or overdub starts. The audio editing and mixing effects are non-destructive (the original files are not altered).

Vision also supports Opcode's Open Music System, a cross-platform/software format for audio information, and comes with a synthesizer patch librarian, Gal-axy, which stores and retrieves patches (instrument programs) for synthesizer sounds.

> Opcode Systems
> Fax: (415) 856-3332
> Phone: (415) 856-3333
> Web: **http://www.opcode.com**

See Also

Deck II; MIDI; Sequencer; SoundEdit

Visual Architect

Visual Architect is an **interface builder** and code generator from Symantec. It can generate the graphical interface of applications written using the think class library (TCL) **framework**. Visual Architect is a part of the **Symantec C++** development environment.

Using Visual Architect, programmers can create the visual elements of a program, such as windows, dialog boxes, alerts, and menus, using graphical tools. Visual Architect goes a step further than many interface builders by generating **C++** code for the interface that takes direct advantage of the TCL framework. If, for example, a button created in Visual Architect is linked to an action, a skeleton of the code needed to perform the action is automatically generated. To get the button to work, the programmer need only fill in the skeleton with the details of that action.

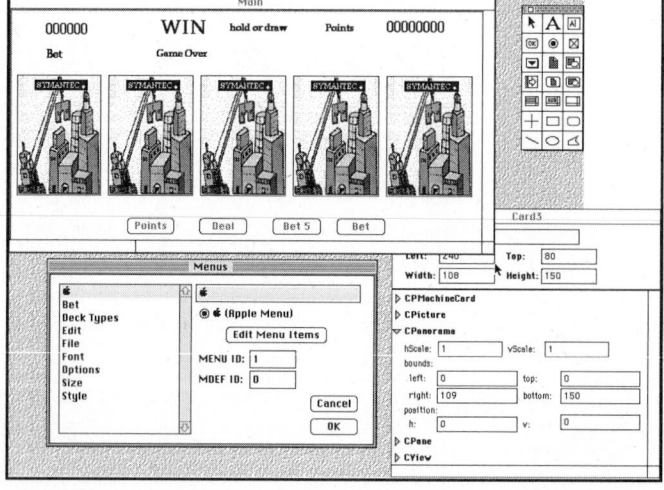

See Also

C++; Interface Builder; Symantec C++

Visual Arranger

Visual Arranger is a song-building program that makes use of **General MIDI**. You need a **MIDI keyboard** to use the software. Visual Arranger provides icons that represent different musical styles, and enables you to drag these icons together to assemble a song. To create more complicated structures, however, such as chords, you must use tools that are much more complicated to learn. This, along with limits in controls over dynamic expression (tempo, volume, and so on) makes the use of this software rather limited.

> Yamaha Corporation of America
> Price: $59.95
> Phone:(714) 522-9240
> Web: **http://www.midifarm.com/yamaha**

See Also

Entertainment; General MIDI; MIDI

Visual C++

A **C/C++** development environment from Microsoft, Visual C++ is unlike most of the programs in this book. Visual C++ doesn't run on the Macintosh. It runs only on PCs running Windows NT or Windows 95. It earns its place in a Mac book because it is capable of generating Mac applications. The *Visual C++ Cross-Development Edition for Macintosh* is a complete integrated development environment that can generate Windows or Macintosh executables.

Visual C++ enables you to develop Macintosh programs using Microsoft's **Win32 Application Program Interface** or using the Mac's own API, the **Toolbox**. Win32 programs running on the Mac use the Windows Portability Libraries (WPL) to translate Win32 calls into the corresponding Toolbox calls at a penalty of diminished speed.

A remote **debugger** is included with the Visual C++ Cross-Development Edition that enables you to debug a program running on a Macintosh from a networked Windows workstation.

Although Visual C++ is poorly suited to programmers setting out to write a Macintosh-only application, it's a quick and easy way for Windows programmers to port their applications to the Mac. Programs written to the Win32 API will run and behave much like their Windows counterparts. Unfortunately, this generally means that these programs do a poor job of adhering to the Macintosh **Human Interface Guidelines**.

On the other hand, programs that have been factored to separate user-interface code from other parts of the program can easily use the Toolbox on the Mac and the Win32 API on Windows. Using this approach, a programmer can take advantage of a single development environment without incurring the wrath of the interface police on either platform.

Visual C++ may be the best development environment for Windows programmers making their first forays into the Macintosh world. If you're in the opposite situation, Metrowerks **CodeWarrior** includes a similar option in reverse. The Gold and Academic version of CodeWarrior both include a compiler and remote debugger for Windows NT/Windows 95 applications that run on the Macintosh.

See Also

C; C++; CodeWarrior; Cross-Compiler; Microsoft Foundation Classes; Toolbox; Win32

Vocabulary Programs for Children, *See Mind Castle*

Voice Capability in Modems

Although not nearly as common as fax, a modem's capability to handle voice is an increasingly important feature in telecommunications. With voice capability, the modem can pass voice calls on to your Mac. With the proper software, you can use your Mac as a speakerphone, an answering machine or voice mail system, even a complex fax-back system. A voice/data/fax modem can make a one-room office seem like a major company to outside callers.

With a voice modem, you can run software that answers the telephone and gives the caller a voice message offering different options, much like office voice-mail systems costing tens of thousands of dollars. A caller can press buttons to be transferred to a particular extension, or can leave a message for a specific person. You can also use a voice/fax modem in combination with fax-back software, which lets you create an automated system for distributing faxes. Callers can choose among several options and get information faxed to them, all without even having to speak to you.

See Also
Fax Capability in Modems; Modems

Voice/Data/Fax Modems, *See Voice Capability in Modems*

Voyeur, *See Dungeon Master II: The Legends of Skullkeep*

Voyeur II, *See Hollywood Games Connection*

VRAM Expansion
VRAM expansion is the addition of memory to the video circuitry of your computer, enhancing the resolution and/or color support.

VRML
Acronym for Virtual Reality Modeling Language, a programming language for describing virtual reality environments on the **Internet's World Wide Web**.

Although **HTML** (Hypertext Markup Language) describes graphics and text in 2D representations, VRML allows Web authors to create 3D environments that can be displayed by VRML browser software.

Part of the promise of VRML is its potential for constructing 3D versions of buildings or sites. Businesses such as real estate developers can create models that visitors can virtually "tour" on the Web. Many computer games already use VRML.

Many firms are currently developing **plug-ins** for Web browsers that provide the capability to view and maneuver through 3D sites. For browsing VRML documents on the Macintosh, applications that use Apple's QuickDraw 3D programming interface work well, such as QuickTime VR.

VRML standards are currently being developed by the VRML Architecture Group (VAG) in San Francisco.

See Also
HTML; Internet; Web Browser; World Wide Web

Vult Virus, *See Scores Virus*

W

WAIS

WAIS stands for Wide Area Information Server. It is one of the Internet's primary means of free information and is used by many Internet search engines. WAIS was developed as a way of allowing big business to search for electronic information quickly and easily from a large number of sources by using English-language queries. In response to such a request, a WAIS server returns information using ranking and relevance feedback. The answers judged to be the most relevant to your query appear highest on the list. MacWAIS is the Mac-specific version. You can find a directory of WAIS servers by going to the W3 Search Engines page at **http://cuiwww.unige.ch/ meta-index.html**.

See Also

FTP; Gopher; Internet; World Wide Web, The

WAN, *See Wide Area Network*

War Games, *See Strategy Games*

Warcraft: Orcs and Humans

Warcraft builds on the premise of great **strategy games,** such as Empire Deluxe and Civilization, placing you in charge of a feudal village at war with mythical Orcs. Although it is mainly a war strategy game, Warcraft also incorporates the cause and effect play of games such as **SimCity 2000**. You start from scratch, building army barracks to train soldiers, lumber mills and blacksmiths to build houses and roads, and so on.

Your laborers are peons who, in addition to accomplishing menial tasks such as construction and mining, are also too stupid to fend for themselves against enemy soldiers and orcs and must be protected. As the game goes, you can see the complication in deciding which of your men will protect workers, how many you need to train, which can attack, and so on. Like **Spaceward Ho! 4.0** and **Chaos Overlords**, Warcraft supports network play so you can play against human opponents, as well as against the computer.

See Also

Allied General; Chaos Overlords; Pax Imperia; Sid Meier's Worlds; Spaceward Ho! 4.0; Strategy Games; V for Victory

Warping, *See Morphing*

Waterless Printing

In waterless printing, a silicone coating rather than water is used on the offset printing plate to repel ink. Waterless printing has several benefits over regular offset printing. It helps reduce **dot gain**, enabling finer **halftone** screens to be used; and seems to provide better ink coverage with faster makeready and less environmental impact.

See Also

Printing

Wave (.WAV)

The .WAV (pronounced WAVE) sound file format is native to the PC and cannot be played on a Macintosh without special software (QuickTime 2.2 may add support for WAV files). Some sound conversion software, such as Synclavier's S/Link, can convert a .WAV file. Use the **AIFF** file format instead.

See Also

AIFF; File Types, Internet; SND

Wayne, Ron

Ron Wayne is one of the three founders of Apple Computer. When **Steve Wozniak** and **Steve Jobs** formed their partnership on April Fools' Day 1976, Wayne was right there with them. Wayne worked with Jobs at Atari (as chief field service engineer), and Jobs convinced him to become a partner by offering him 10 percent of Apple's stock.

Wayne worked on the documentation for the original Apple I, and he designed the original **Apple logo**, a picture of Isaac Newton sitting under an apple tree. Apple did not use this logo for very long; Jobs had Rob Janov design the logo we know today.

After the first 50 Apple I computers were sold to **The Byte Shop** for a small profit, Jobs wanted to build more, which meant going into debt. Wayne worried about this and wanted out; he did not want responsibility for 10 percent of Apple's debt. He resigned and received $500 for his share of Apple. Later, he would receive just over $5000 when Apple incorporated and purchased the partnership to ensure that he would have no possible legal claim against Apple in the future.

See Also

Apple Computer, History; Apple logo; Byte Shop, The; Jobs, Steve; Wozniak, Steve

WDEF, *See Code Resource*

WDEF Virus

This virus infects only the invisible Desktop file used by the Finder. WDEF can spread just by mounting a disk on an infected Macintosh. The virus cannot affect System 7 disks. On other versions of System, WDEF causes system crashes and font problems.

See Also

ANTI Virus; CDEF Virus; CODE 1 Virus; CODE 252 Virus; Frankie Virus; INIT 17 Virus; INIT 29 Virus; INIT 1984 Virus; INIT 9403 Virus; INIT-M

Virus; MacMag Virus; MBDF Virus; MDEF Virus; nVIR Virus; Scores Virus; T4 Virus; ZUC Virus

Web Browser

Software that enables a user to *browse* (locate and examine) information on the Internet's **World Wide Web.**

A Web browser provides a *graphical user interface* to the **Internet** in general, and the World Wide Web in particular. A browser serves as a lens through which a user can see the information in cyberspace, whether that information consists of inline graphics, text formatted with **HTML**, sounds, video, or **Java** "live objects."

The following figure illustrates how browsers focus electronic information much like a lens. Browsers provide an interface to information.

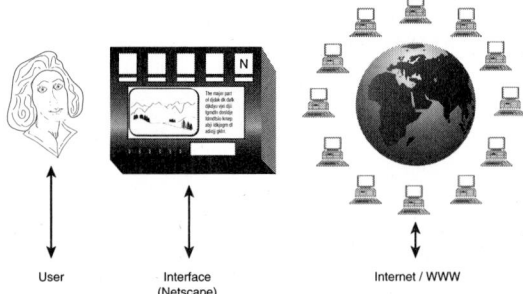

User   Interface   Internet / WWW
              (Netscape)

NCSA Mosaic, MacWeb, TCP/Connect, and **Netscape Navigator** are examples of popular browsers that access and process information on the Internet. All of these browsers can be downloaded as freeware from the Internet using an **FTP** client such as Fetch or **Anarchie.**

All browsers connect to remote host computers, request HTML or other files, display text and graphics, and permit the downloading of files. Browsers differ in speed with which they process data. Some programs not only download a Web page to a user's computer screen, but also store a copy of that page in disk **cache** for faster access should you decide to revisit that page.

Browsers also differ in the suite of tools they give the user. These tools include the buttons, menus, and text finders that track where you have been online, that find out where you want to go, and that provide you information such as the size of a file or progress reports on how quickly that file is being accessed.

A *browser*, like a newspaper, is an interface to information—but with one big difference. A newspaper takes a large amount of preselected content and arranges that content with page numbers and an index to help you select what you want to read. A browser is also a tool and a conduit for information.

The difference between a browser and a newspaper is that, although the Web and the Internet have a few good indexes (such as **Yahoo** and **Lycos**) and searching tools (such as **InfoSeek**), the selection is totally up to you. That's why having a good graphical interface to online information is so important.

See Also

Anarchie; Cache; FTP; HTML; Internet; InfoSeek; Java; MacWeb; NCSA Mosaic; Netscape Navigator; StuffIt Expander; Web Browser; World Wide Web

Web Page

The basic document available for viewing information on the **Internet**'s **World Wide Web**.

A Web page (also sometimes called a **home page**) consists of the following elements: text, graphics, **hypertext** links to other Web pages or files, and links to sounds or movies. Web pages are written using the **HTML** (HyperText Markup Language) programming language, which is essentially a set of instructions so the **browser** knows how to display the page (and its graphics and links) on-screen. An HTML file (which is text-only **ASCII**) consists of these instructions as well as the text that appears on-screen when that page is viewed (see the following figure).

Web pages are stored on Web **servers** that are constantly connected to the Internet. Each Web page has its own unique **URL** (Uniform Resource Locator) address, which looks something like this: **http:// www.mcp.com/hayden/index.html**. When a client machine requests a Web page from a server via that **URL**

or via a link on another Web page, the server sends out the **HTML** document as well as all the graphics that appear on that page. The user's browser then interprets the HTML and lays out the text and graphics on-screen.

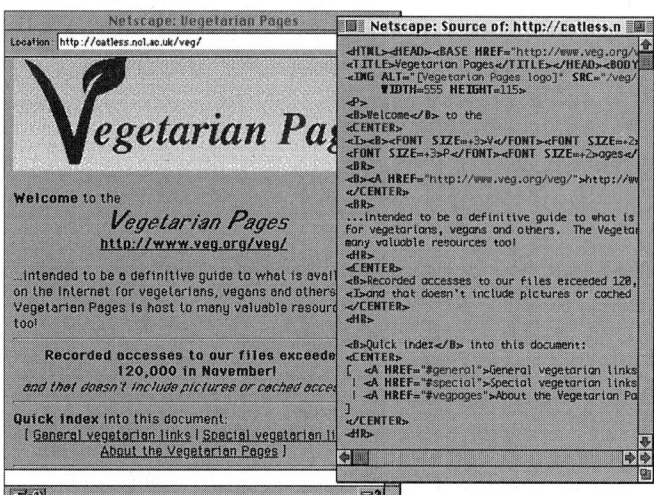

Web Page, Graphics and Multimedia Graphics on Web pages appear in two primary formats: **GIF** and **JPEG**. All images appear on-screen at the resolution of the monitor on which they're displayed, so high-resolution images are unnecessary. Graphics can be displayed inline, meaning that they appear right within a line of text, or they can be displayed on their own as graphics files connected to a Web page by a **link**.

Sound is possible via a Web page via linking, because no browser is currently capable of playing sounds directly. Linking on a sound file generally downloads the file to your hard drive, whereupon the browser usually calls up another application (such as **SoundMachine**) to play the sound. Audio files on the Internet come in two types: self-contained files or streamed files. Self-contained files must be downloaded completely before being played; these sounds generally appear in one of the following formats: **AIFF** (**.au**), **WAV** (**.wav**), and **MPEG** II (**.mpg2**). **RealAudio** is an example of a streamed file, which is played *while* downloading, not after.

Animation and video must be downloaded the same way sound is. Video file formats include MPEG I

(.mpg or .mpeg) or II (.mpg2), **QuickTime** (.mov), and **AVI** (.avi). There are also new streaming video formats now emerging.

Web Page, Interactivity As the Web evolves, Web pages are getting increasingly interactive. Forms enable users to fill out and send in forms electronically. CGI scripts (written in C, Perl, or AppleScript) running on Web servers enable the server to respond to those forms immediately. They also enable rudimentary animation directly on a Web page, customized Web page creation based on specific situations, and services such as online purchasing and voting.

Web Page, Text and Links Text on a Web page is quite limited in its formatting options. HTML provides little control over fonts and their presentation. For example, you can specify general headings, but not specific font size. Each browser interprets HTML a little differently, so Web pages will vary as seen on various computers.

Links are created using HTML, and certain words or graphics can be made to link to other Web pages, another location in the same Web page, Gopher or FTP sites, or individual files such as applications, documents, images, sounds, and movies. The following figure shows a Web page and the HTML that created it.

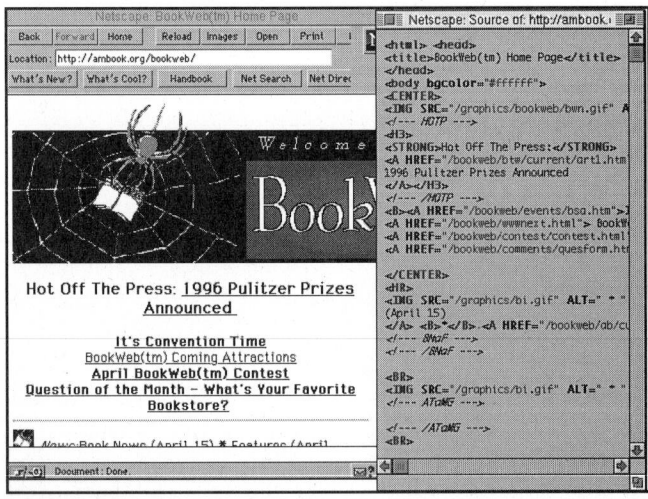

Web Page, How to Design The accessibility of HTML and the World Wide Web makes it possible for anyone to engage in page layout, no matter what their level of design experience. Although the idea of what constitutes "good design" varies widely, some general principles can be applied.

Two levels of page design are relevant to the Web:

- *Basic design,* which uses rudimentary HTML markup commands such as headings, paragraphs, lists, and inline images.

- *Advanced design,* which uses frames, tables, Java applets, imagemaps, and other advanced features.

Web page designers trying to achieve either level of design can benefit from applying the following principles:

- Less is more. Don't make a Web page too crowded. Don't try to fill every bit of available space. Use only one or two images and a simple **background**.

- Keep files small. Remember that much of your audience is connecting to the Web with a 14.4Kbps or 28.8Kbps **modem**. No matter how well a page is put together, if it takes too long to appear on-screen, the reader will move on to another site.

  - Tell your audience how big an image is before downloading it.

  - Provide a text-only alternative to your page and alt tags for graphics.

  - Conform to a page grid.

  - Put your personality into your page. The contents should convey something about the author's personality without making the layout hokey or overcrowded.

  - Avoid long rows of buttons. Instead, provide simple hypertext links that load on-screen more quickly.

  - Scan photos at 72 dots per inch and keep the file size as small as possible. Use the **RGB** color model when scanning.

Whatever approach is used, the design and content of a Web page should complement each other, and the design will lead the reader's eye to focus on the most important elements.

See Also

AIFF; AppleScript; .AU; Browser; C; CGI; Server Forms; FTP; GIF; Gopher; Home Page; HTML; Hypertext; Internet; Java; JPEG; MPEG; Multimedia on the Internet; QuickTime; RealAudio; Server; SoundMachine; .WAV; World Wide Web

Web Servers, *See Workgroup Servers, Macintosh Family*

Web Site, How to Organize

A Web site can either serve as an interface to a **server** that serves up documents on the **Internet**'s **World Wide Web** or can be a set of documents produced by a single publisher. Also referred to as an information "web" or a Web *presentation*.

Organizing a Web site is important because the clearer your information is organized, the more "hits" your Web site will receive, and the longer your visitors will stay.

The first step is to do some clear thinking and planning along the following topics:

1. Decide what you want to say. Analyze your content and distill your message or your goal into one or two sentences or main points.

2. Identify your goals. Decide whether you want more customers, more attention, or just want to speak out.

3. Assemble your contents. Make a list so you know how many documents you have and begin to organize them or get an idea what you want to do with them.

4. Decide on what type of site you want. Your site might fall into one of the following categories:

Types of Web sites

Type	Description
Personal	Who you are, what you do, why people might want to know about you.
Recreational	News about a club or group you belong to.
Institutional	An online "front door" or welcome page for a business or large corporation.
Educational	Teaching tools or information published by a school, university, or organization.
Informational	Writing, documentation, news, museum holdings.
Commercial	A shopping mall, a store, a service, merchandise, anything you have to sell.
Marketing	Surveys, polls, opinion seeking.
Creative	Short stories, poetry, art.
Societal	Political concerns, social causes, special interests.

5. Decide who will maintain your site. You can do the work yourself, or hire someone to handle the upkeep.

6. Set your budget.

7. Know where the page fits in your company or organization's communications program.

8. Divide your contents into five to seven main categories that you can present in your Web site's home page. Each category in the list can be a hypertext link leading to other documents on your site.

It's a good idea to provide consistent information on each page in a Web site that helps the reader navigate through topics and to the home page. Many readers will come to a document in your Web by chance and will want navigational links to get to your home page or to previous or next documents in a series.

Each page can also contain standard information indicating when a document was last updated, the email address of the **Webmaster** (the person who maintains the site), or the name of your company or organization.

Web site design should be simple. Too many links means readers have to click only once to get anywhere; but if, as a result, they end up with many possible places to go and no guidance, they will be confused (see the following figure).

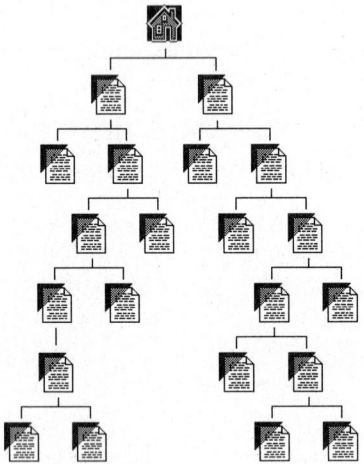

On the other hand, having only a few general categories in the beginning means that someone will have to make link after link before getting to a specific bit of information (as indicated in the following figure).

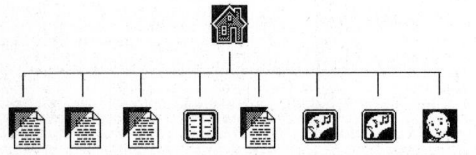

Readers should be able to get to the "bottom level" of a Web site in three to five clicks. Of course, that will vary depending on the amount of information your site contains (see the next figure).

Whenever possible, keep documents short (one or two computer screens' worth of information is sometimes suggested). It is preferable to link a series of short documents together rather than have long ones that are slow to load on a Web browser's screen.

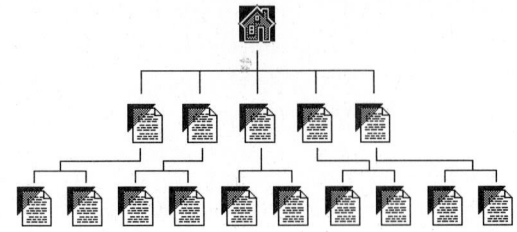

See Also

Home Page; HTML; Hypertext; Internet; Web Browser; Web Page; World Wide Web

WebCrawler

This Internet search engine was developed by Brian Pinkerton and originated as an experiment at the University of Washington in 1994. Today it is operated by **America Online**. It indexes the title of a document, as well as the full text. The results are arranged by their relevance to your original query. Because it returns only the title, it is important to make the search as specific as possible by including the most important keywords. WebCrawler also has a function that lets you randomly search the Internet and retrieve documents, as well as its own estimate of the number of Web servers in Cyberspace.

The WebCrawler home page is at **http:// www.webcrawler.com/**.

See Also

America Online; InfoSeek; Internet; Lycos

Webmaster

The Webmaster is the individual charged with setting up and/or maintaining a **server**, a computer set up to serve information on the **World Wide Web**.

A Webmaster might have a number of duties:

- Maintain and update **HTTP** server software on the server.
- Create the **HTML** documents to be served from the site.
- Organize and keep track of files on a site.

- Write Common Gateway Interface (CGI) scripts or other tools for processing **forms**, performing searches, **hit counters**, and other functions.

- Answer questions and process **email** from readers.

- Troubleshoot problems and questions.

- Update and maintain a **Web site**'s contents.

See Also

CGI; Email; HTML; HTTP; Internet; Web Site; World Wide Web

WebSTAR/MacHTTP

Two software packages, written by Chuck Shotton, that enable a Macintosh to function as a **World Wide Web server.**

MacHTTP was Shotton's original package for enabling a Macintosh to serve documents, graphics, and other data on the Web using HTTP (**HyperText Transfer Protocol**). StarNine Technologies bought the rights to MacHTTP and now offers it and a similar, more powerful commercial version called WebSTAR.

MacHTTP is regarded as an entry-level, easy-to-use way of turning a Macintosh into a Web server. WebSTAR is a more powerful application for experienced **Webmasters**. WebSTAR comes with a number of **CGI** plug-in modules to process **form** and **imagemap** data and perform other functions.

WebSTAR is PowerPC native, and requires a full **TCP/IP** connection to the **Internet**. The software also requires 8MB of RAM (optimal), and System 7.0.1 or greater.

See Also

Apple Internet Server Solution; Apple Network Server; CGI; Forms; HTTP; Imagemap; Internet; MacTCP; TCP/IP; Web Browser; Web Server; Web Site; Webmaster; World Wide Web

Welcome to the Future, *See Adventure Games*

What-If Calculations

A **spreadsheet** enables you to distill a screen full of numbers into a single profit figure, so it's fairly obvious that you can try changing some of the numbers to see what effect they have on the bottom line. This kind of business projection is hundreds of years old, but used to be too calculation-intensive to be used as a regular planning tool. Computers make the process so easy that solving What-if problems are one of the primary uses for a spreadsheet.

The simplest calculation can involve just two spreadsheet cells. If you enter a **formula** such as "=A1*.07" into cell B2 to figure a seven percent commission, you can then put various sales figures into A1 to see how persuasiveness can affect your lifestyle. Each time you enter a new number, B2 will change to show the commission. If you want to also try different commission rates, you can replace the ".07" with a reference to another cell.

The figure below shows a simple What-if mortgage calculator supplied as a **template** in **ClarisWorks**. Cells D2:D5 each contain **variables** that are referenced by a financial **function** in D9. This enables you to compare different rates and terms to see how they'll affect total cost. You can also try different loan amounts in D2, watching the monthly payment in D9 change, to find out how much house you can afford.

	A	B	C	D	
		D3	✕ ✓	0.095	
1					
2		Loan Amount		$360,000	
3		Annual Rate		9.50%	
4		Term (Years)		15	
5		Pmts/Year		12	
6		Start Date		3/1/97	
7					
8		# of Pmts		180	
9		Payment		$3,759.21	
10		Total Pmts		$676,657.59	
11					

Data Tables It's time-consuming to keep entering numbers while you watch a cell change, and it's difficult to show the range of results in printed form. So most spreadsheet programs let you automatically create a *data table* (sometimes called a *What-if table*) with variables spread across the top and side and solutions in the middle. The figure below shows such a table in **Excel**. Some programs can handle three variables at once, by displaying multiple tables next to each other.

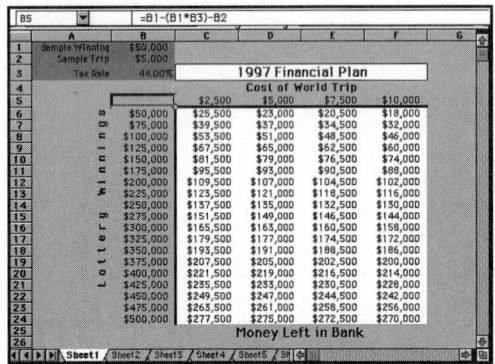

To create a data table in most programs, use the following steps:

1. Develop a formula in a single cell, making sure that there's enough room for the table below and to the right of it. It must refer to cells *outside* the table area. In our example, the formula in B5 refers to B1 through B3.

2. Enter a range of possible numbers for one variable along the top of the table area. In our example, C5 through F5 show some costs for a trip around the world.

3. Enter a similar range for the other variable, directly beneath the formula from step 1. In our example, B6 through B24 show possible lottery winnings.

4. Select the range of cells where you want the table, including the variables you entered in steps 2 and 3. In our example, it would be B5 through F24.

5. Choose the program's table command, usually from the Data menu.

6. A Dialog box will appear, asking for *input cells*. These are the original references from step 1, that you entered multiple examples of in steps 2 and 3. In our example, B1 and B2 are the input cells. You can enter them in the dialog box by typing their addresses, or you can click where the box asks for them and then click on the cells themselves.

7. When you're done, click OK. The table will fill in automatically.

See Also

Claris Works 4.0; Spreadsheet Notation

What's the Secret?

This science series from 3M Learning is based on the PBS television series *Newton's Apple*. It uses animation, **QuickTime** movies, sounds, and science experiments to explain how a roller coaster works, why glue sticks, what keeps a plane in the air, why bears hibernate, and much more. Take a field trip to the Arctic with explorer Will Steger and a team of sled dogs. Learn how mushers pack their sleds, how the dogs keep warm in snowstorms, and what it takes to survive at 50 degrees below zero. Spectacular photography sets this series apart.

Find out how your brain works, why you remember—or forget—things, how your heart pumps, and what's in blood. See what elephants pack in their trunks. Learn how bees make honey. Throughout the CD-ROMs in the series, there are puzzles to solve, experiments to do, video clips to watch, and suggestions for further reading. As you explore the contents of the CD, you'll pick up patches in your knapsack, which you can use as tokens to get additional puzzles and games. There's a great deal to do on these CDs and although they're rated for ages 7-13, kids of all ages will find something to intrigue them.

See Also

A.D.A.M., The Inside Story; Bumptz Science Carnival; MacFrog; Software, Educational, K-6; Software, Educational, Grades 7-12; Widget Workshop

Whois, *See Knowbots*

Whurlwind

A freeware **VRML** viewer that can be used as a Netscape Navigator **helper application**, Whurlwind requires a Power Macintosh (because it uses **QuickDraw 3D**) and System 7.5. Use this application to view virtual worlds created in VRML 1.0. An editor is required to create VRML files. Available from many online services.

See Also

Helper Applications, Web; Navigator; QuickDraw 3D; Virtus Walkthrough Pro; VRML

Wide Area Network (WAN)

A group of geographically separated computers connected thorugh dedicated lines or satellite links, a WAN is often created for large businesses by telecommunications companies. The **Internet** enables small organizations to simulate a wide area network without the cost of one.

A wide area network (WAN) is composed of multiple local area networks (LANs) that are spread over large geographic areas. The major difference between the two is that distances on a LAN are measured in feet, and those on a WAN frequently in miles. Through the use of dedicated hardware, a WAN enables users of different networks to function as if they were in the same physical location. Each member of the WAN can then make use of each network's shared resources, such as email, file servers, and databases.

Routers are most commonly used as the last link between each local area network and the WAN itself. After each computer has broken its communications down into **packets**, the routers serve as gateways, determining which packets are destined for the local network and which should be routed toward computers outside the local network. When they have determined that a packet is destined for a computer outside of the local office, they forward the information across a WAN link and on to the final destination. Currently ISDN, Frame Relay, and POTS (Plain old Telephone Service) are the most commonly used links between elements of a WAN.

See Also

Routers

WideTake, *See Kaidan*

Widget Workshop

This is a "hands-on" science kit for elementary school kids, which includes straws and thermometers and spinning tops and other odds and ends for non-computer experiments as well as software to invent and build widgets of all descriptions. It's a fascinating way for kids to experiment, solve puzzles, and try "what if" explorations. To build something, the user simply clicks the parts provided in the tool palette and drags them onto the workspace. Widget Workshop has sounds, switches, and gadgets.

There are timers, switches, counters, and all kinds of strange gadgets to build. Connect the pieces by dragging a wire between them. Most kids will jump right in and start creating, but there's a tutorial in the manual for parents or teachers who don't quite know how to get started. The workshop activities booklet has 30 different experiments kids can do with the materials provided. And there are 25 Widget puzzles to solve, with the combination of parts provided for each. Some are quite difficult, and will lead kids into working with logic gates, switch combinations, and some fairly sophisticated math and physics. Widget Workshop requires more thought than most software, but lets the user keep trying combinations of parts until something works. It's just right for kids who like to experiment and to build things.

See Also

Software, Educational, K-6

Widows and Orphans

In paragraphs, you occasionally will have a word (or two or three) left by itself on a line or moved into the next column or page where it sits alone and out of place. This sad bit of text is called a *widow*.

Similarly, a paragraph that starts at the bottom of a page or column sometimes has room only for its first

line. That lonely line at the bottom of the page is called an *orphan*. Generally speaking, you should adjust your paragraph spacing to keep widows and orphans from appearing. Sometimes, however, this is impossible if you need to print a specific number of lines per page or to fit as much text as possible on a page. Most word processors have widow/orphan controls that automatically paginate to avoid single lines at the beginning or end of a page or column. Page layout programs avoid widows and orphans by adjusting the spacing between paragraphs. Some word processors can do this, too.

Win32

Microsoft's 32-bit Windows **Application Programming Interface** (API) defines the set of system calls available to applications running under Windows 95 and Windows NT. Programmers can develop Macintosh applications using Win32 with Microsoft's **Visual C++** Cross-Compiler and the Windows Portability Library, a set of routines that translate Win32 calls into Macintosh **Toolbox** calls.

See Also

Application Programming Interface; Toolbox; Visual C++

Winchester Disk Drive

Winchester was the code-name used within IBM for the project that developed into what has become the modern hard disk drive.

The project team developed a fixed, magnetically sensitive disk made of aluminum coated with carbon/iron oxide on which data was recorded. A stack of these disks was mounted on a spindle and sealed within a chassis that also held the **read/write heads**, the access arms that moved the heads over the disk surface, and the stepper motor that controlled the access arms.

These read/write heads were significantly smaller and lighter than previous designs and moved over the face of the disks on a cushion of air only 18 millionths of an inch thick.

The code-name comes from the twin 30M disks used in the first drive built at IBM. It was dubbed the 30/

30, which led to its being named after the Winchester 30/30 rifle.

Although there have been significant improvements in materials used, increasing disk speeds, and decreasing latency periods, currently available fixed and removable hard drives still use Winchester technology.

See Also

Disks and Drives; Storage

Window

Anytime you have an **icon** of a document, **hard disk**, **disk**, **control panel**, and so on, and you open the item to view the contents, the contents are displayed in a window. If, for example, you see an icon of a disk on your **desktop** and want to see what's inside this disk, you open the disk by either clicking it and selecting the **Open command** from the **File menu**, or by **double-clicking** it, which is a shortcut for the Open command.

A window appears displaying the contents of the disk. If there are folders on the disk, you can view the contents of those folders in the same fashion. Every time you open a **folder**, a window appears displaying its contents. These windows are the cornerstone of working within the Macintosh environment.

At the top of every window is the title bar, which contains the name of the item you've opened. If you open your hard disk, the name of your hard disk is displayed in the title bar. The title bar is gray, and when active has small lines or stripes on either side of the item's name.

You can move a window around your desktop by clicking and holding the title bar, **dragging** the window to a new location, and releasing the **mouse** button. You can resize windows by clicking a tiny icon in the lower-right corner that looks like a small box on top of a larger box. This is the **size box**.

You can click and drag this size box to resize the window to any size you want. An outline of the window moves with you as you resize, enabling you to see the new size of the window as you're moving. When you've reached the desired size, release the mouse button, and the window resizes to your new choice. If you were to shrink the window and later decide you want the window open to its largest size (based on the size of your computer's monitor), click the **zoom box** in the upper-right corner of the title bar, and your window expands to its largest possible size.

If the number of items in a window becomes larger than the window can display at once, the window adds **scroll bars** on the right side and bottom of the window to enable you to scroll through the entire contents of the window, even if the contents are not visible on-screen. The following figure shows all the elements of a window.

To close a window, click the window's **Close Box** in the upper-left corner of the title bar, or choose Close from the File menu (⌘-W).

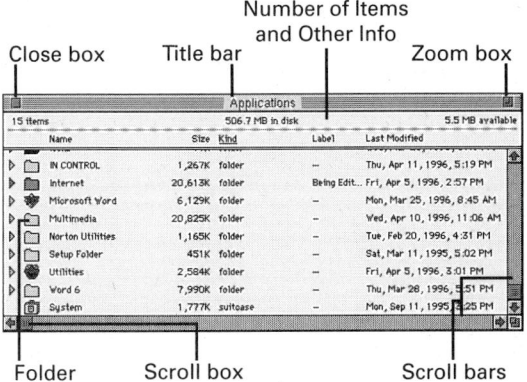

Close box   Title bar   Number of Items and Other Info   Zoom box

Folder   Scroll box   Scroll bars

See Also
Control Panel; Disk; Double-Clicking; File Menu; Hard Disk; Icons; Open Command; Scroll Bars; Size Box; Title Bar; Zoom Box

Windows and DOS Translation Utilities

The Macintosh now has a built-in DOS/Windows translation **utility** that enables you to mount DOS/Windows disks, read files and write to DOS/Windows disks, and even to format disks in a PC format. This is accomplished through a **control panel** called **PC Exchange.** Although PC Exchange comes built-in with System 7.5 and higher, there are also commercial PC translation utilities available including the very popular MacLink Plus from DataViz.

Besides the built-in capabilities of PC Exchange, this control panel also enables you to open PC files in Macintosh programs. It does this by using the three-letter DOS suffix used in PC file-naming conventions to enable you to designate an appropriate Macintosh application to open the PC document.

You can select which files that contain a particular three-letter DOS suffix will open which Macintosh application through the PC Exchange control panel. You type the three-letter suffix, and then choose which Mac application you want to open that file. When you double-click it, it will launch the designated application and open the file.

Conversation with James Plamondon

Once a Mac developer, cheerleader, and columnist, James Plamondon now works for Microsoft helping cross-platform developers create products for both the Mac and Windows. He stands in a unique position to analyze Apple, the Mac, and—do we dare say it?—Microsoft and Windows.

Maclopedia: What was your first personal experience with the Mac, and how did you react?

James: My parents had owned a TRS-80 and then an Apple II+, so getting a Mac was a natural evolution. They bought Mac #400 or thereabouts when they still had the Mac team's signatures inside the enclosure early in '84. I had already written some computer games for the Apple II, and was very interested in the Mac as a gaming platform, but Apple was actively discouraging the development of Mac games then (to avoid reinforcing the accusation that the Mac was a toy). There was a pretty active Mac developer group in Albuquerque, where I was getting my computer science degree at the time.

You were supposed to do all of your development on a Lisa, then dump it over to a Mac. I almost bought a Lisa for this purpose when they were dramatically discounted and called the "Mac XL," but fortunately I couldn't afford one, and loaned my girlfriend (now my wife) $3,000 to get a Fat Mac (512K RAM—Wow! What would I *do* with all of that memory?).

Maclopedia: What kind of development tools did you have in the early days?

continues

W

There were no decent tools at first. Mac ASM was it for a long time, then MacNosy. All we had was the phone book edition of Inside Mac. Soon, though, there came a flood of better tools—Consulair C, Manx Aztec C, Megamax C, Lightspeed Pascal—because everyone wanted to become one with this cool machine and needed tools to do it.

The Mac was a magical machine in those days. Too little RAM, tiny hard drives, carpal-tunnel-inducing disk-swapping, but that was not the point. The focus was not on the execution of the machine itself, but on the promise that it held: the Macintosh Dream. Compared to any other personal computer of its day, the Mac was a revelation. I and the other early Mac developers that I knew (and have come to know since) were captivated by the challenge of living up to the dream that the Macintosh held out to us—a dream of elegance, power, and harmony. We passed up jobs that would have paid far more so that we could concentrate on fulfilling the promise of the Macintosh Dream. We were going to change the world!

But Apple started letting us all down. First, they kept the price of the Mac high for far too long. The high price was justified at first—you always want to skim the cream—but keeping it high prevented the Mac from becoming the computer "for the rest of us;" it prevented the Macintosh Dream from becoming reality. They refused to license the MacOS to cloners because doing so would have exposed Apple's high prices to direct competition. And they rested on their laurels, failing to improve the basic OS memory management, file I/O, and so on while focusing solely on whiz-bang stuff such as QuickTime and QuickDraw 3D; Cool stuff, but kinda like adding another story on a house with a rotting foundation. All of these moves together gave Microsoft the opportunity to start catching up.

Maclopedia: When did you realize there was a problem?

I wasn't really aware of this at the time; as they say, hindsight is 20/20. Like most everyone else I knew, I was cocooned in "Biosphere Mac"—I hung out with Mac guys, read Mac magazines, went to Mac shows, and generally avoided contact with the distastefully ignorant DOS and UNIX folks (folks who just "didn't get it" about the Mac). I formed a local Bay Area chapter of the MacApp Developer's Association (MADA), I wrote technical articles for *Frameworks*, *MacTutor/MacTech*,

and *d e v e l o p*, and I gave presentations at developer conferences—all activities which thickened and hardened the walls of Biosphere Mac, keeping the rest of the world locked outside…or us locked in.

But then, Windows 3.0 shipped. The company I was working for at the time, PowerUp Software of San Mateo, California, most noted for their product Calendar Creator, reacted like a bomb had hit. They canceled all Mac development, and threw the DOS and Mac teams together to get a Windows version of Calendar Creator out the door *right now*, or else. I was amazed! Couldn't they see that Windows was a joke? That it was simply validating the Mac? That anyone who saw Windows would just turn to a Mac to get the "real thing?"

I was wrong, of course. Windows 3.0 sold like hotcakes. Software shops all over the Valley were responding to Windows just exactly as PowerUp had done. At a time when Apple was nickel-and-diming its developers to death, Windows development was wide-open. Windows' tools were laughable compared to ObjectMaster and Lightspeed Pascal, but they got better fast—much faster than the Mac tools were improving because there was so much more money in the Windows tools market to reinvest in R&D. I observed these developments and reported on them in a column in MADA's *Frameworks Magazine*: "A MacApp Programmer's Journey into WindowsLand." I sounded the alarm as best I could, but no one seemed to want to listen; the walls of Biosphere Mac, which I had helped thicken, had become impenetrable. Apple's response to Windows? Discarding all of the value that had built up in MacApp and promising the world with Bedrock, which I knew in my soul was doomed to failure (as proved, sadly, to be true).

My column eventually brought me to the attention of Microsoft, which hired me to work in the Bay Area helping Mac developers support Windows, too. It was a great job—I got to hang out with all of my Mac buddies, helping them wrestle with the cross-platform issues that they already knew that they had to face. Some said that I was giving them better support than they were getting from Apple. I tell you, I was the most conflicted guy at Microsoft. In many, many ways, I wished that I was working for Apple, helping them bring the poor, failing Windows developers to the booming world of Macintosh. But that world did not exist, and I could not feed my family with fantasies—not anymore, anyway. I had four kids by then.

Maclopedia: How do you see the historical relationship between Microsoft and Apple?

James: Microsoft was the earliest and strongest supporter of the Macintosh, and its support continued even when other vendors were dropping support for the Macintosh. Microsoft still ships more Mac titles than any other vendor and values its Mac business highly. Microsoft loves the Mac.

Microsoft's relationship with Apple has always been complicated, since both cooperate in some areas (such as Mac apps) and compete in others (such as operating systems). It is the most complex when Microsoft's Mac applications use technologies such as OLE that originated on the Windows side. But because Microsoft and Apple have so many users and developers in common, it behooves them to work together as much as possible. I am proud to have worked, over the last year or so, to help explore new areas of possible cooperation. It is too soon to know which, if any, will bear fruit, but I did my best to bring the two companies together and take considerable satisfaction in that.

Maclopedia: What's the situation like now? How are Apple's current troubles different from the crises of the past?

James: In the past, Apple had no credible competition—no other OS offered anything like the elegance, power, and simplicity of the Mac. That is no longer the case. Windows 95, and especially Windows NT 4.0, are very credible alternatives to the MacOS — very credible indeed. So Apple doesn't have the room to maneuver that it used to have neither in time-to-market, nor in margin, nor in technological advantage. Windows 95 especially has closed the gap between the Mac and Windows to the point that customers are no longer willing to pay a premium for the MacOS, especially at the cost of incompatibility with Windows—hence Apple's moves towards increased Windows compatibility.

The logical extension of these trends is for Apple to break into two units: 1) MacInc., which maintains, extends, and licenses the MacOS to all comers; and 2)

Apple Computer, Inc., which produces whatever hardware they can make money on; Macs, Wintel, you name it.

Apple was a great hardware company before the Mac; for ten years, they sold both the Mac and the Apple II line, making lots of money on both. There is no reason that Apple Computer, Inc. can't return to its roots and become once again the great hardware company that it once was: selling both Macs and the best, easiest-to-use Wintel boxes on the planet.

Maclopedia: One question for our readers in small business: What are the key issues when thinking about a fileserver for a mixed Mac and Windows environment?

But I would argue that Apple sold its developers down the river long before Windows came along by keeping its margins high and our markets small.

James: This is a no-brainer: If you've got a mixed environment of Macs and Windows machines, then Windows NT Server is the perfect server OS for you because it was designed with your needs in mind. No other server OS has so much support for both Mac and Windows so tightly integrated. And the soon-to-be-released (Summer '96) 4.0 version of Windows NT will add support for the Windows 95 user interface, making the power of NT easily accessible to people with a Mac-centered background.

And with the forthcoming PowerPC Platform-compliant computers from Apple, PowerComputing, and others, it is entirely possible that you can get one machine that can run both the MacOS and Windows NT Server to maximize the flexibility of your hardware usage.

Maclopedia: What happened to the Macintosh Dream?

Some would say that I sold out the Macintosh Dream. But I would argue that Apple sold its developers down the river long before Windows came along by keeping its margins high and our markets small. As soon as Windows offered serious competition to the MacOS, Apple's prices fell and margins collapsed, proving that they had been gouging all along. In pursuit of massive short-term profits, Apple sold its own long-term future short, and the futures of its independent developers as well.

continues

But one can still hold one's faith, even after one's local priest is found wanting. The Dream that I bought into, back in the mid-Eighties, was of elegance, power, and harmony. That Dream lives on. Andy Hertzfeld said, at a MacHack keynote address some years back, that most people now experienced the Macintosh Dream via Windows. I'm not sure that Windows is there yet, but it's getting better at a remarkable rate, and it is certainly bringing the Dream to a lot more of "the rest of us" than the Mac ever did.

It is with the deepest melancholy that I look back on the squandered promise of the Macintosh. But life, and technology, move on. I take the Dream with me. I do the best I can to carry the light of the Dream with me into new realms, and I hope that you will, too.

For example, if you encounter a PC document with a .txt file extension (which is a standard text file format on a PC), you can instruct PC Exchange to open that document in **Microsoft Word**. By making this designation, any time you launch a file with a .txt DOS suffix, Microsoft Word will try to open that document.

To open a PC file using a designated Macintosh application, follow these steps:

1. Choose PC Exchange from the Control Panels folder in the Apple menu.

2. Click the Add button and a dialog box will appear in which you can type the DOS suffix of the file you want to open. You can then select which application to open it with, and choose which type of document will be opened from a pop-up menu of PC file types.

3. When you've completed your selection, click OK, then close the PC Exchange control panel. When you double-click the PC file, it will now launch the application you designated to open the file.

See Also

Control Panel; Microsoft Word, Customizing; Mount; PC Exchange; Utility

Windows NT Server, *See Server*

WindowScript

WindowScript is an **XCMD** that can display true Macintosh windows. Use it from within applications, such as HyperCard, that support XCMDs. This tool is particularly useful with **Double-XX**, a small application that can run XCMDs.

Why use WindowScript with or in place of HyperCard? Primarily, because HyperCard provides only limited elements of the Macintosh interface. While you can create cards containing text fields and buttons, HyperCard does not support many standard Macintosh interface elements, such as modal dialog boxes and scrolling windows. You can use WindowScript to add these interface elements to HyperCard stacks.

WindowScript supports many interface elements, including all window styles (modeless, modal, palettes, moveable, modal and so on), scrolling windows, scrolling lists, color pictures, tear-off picture menus, standard menus, pop-up menus, and standard radio, checkbox, and round rect buttons.

Commercial products require a single $100 license fee. Public domain and shareware products do not require a fee, provided a standard splash screen is displayed.

Heizer Software
300 Cedar Lane
Largo, FL 34640
Price: $149
Fax: (813) 559-0614
Phone: (800) 888-7667 or (813) 559-6422
Web: **http://www.heizer.com**

See Also

Double-XX; HyperCard; SuperCard 2.5; XCMD and XFCNs

WindowShade

Included in **System 7.5** and higher, WindowShade enables you to roll your **active window** up like a window shade to just its title bar by double-clicking the title bar. The idea behind WindowShade (which started its life as a shareware extension) is to help reduce the clutter of multiple open **windows** and to enable you to access windows blocked by open applications or active windows. Applications often have a Window menu enabling you to switch between open windows, but this menu doesn't exist at the **desktop level**, and you often have to move one or more windows out of the way to reach the window you're looking for.

If, for example, you have a number of windows open on your desktop, the active window may block access to other open windows. To access a blocked window, you usually have to move the active window out of the way and then click the window that was behind it to make it active. With WindowShade, you can double-click the title bar to roll up your window, enabling you to see any open windows behind it. Even though this window is rolled up, it remains the active window until you click another one. To roll down the active window, double-click the title bar again. You can roll up as many windows as you want, as shown in the figure.

WindowShade also works within applications. If you're working in an application, chances are that your open document is covering up open documents in other applications as well as the desktop level behind it. Double-click your document's title bar and it rolls up, enabling you to see the next document's open application or the desktop.

You can set your preferences for how Window shade operates in the **WindowShade Control Panel**. Your options are how many clicks to hide or show the window or to turn WindowShade off. You can also choose to add modifier keys if you want. You can also choose to have the window shade sound effect enabled or disabled.

To use WindowShade to roll up a window, follow these steps:

1. Double-click the title bar of the active window.

2. The window rolls up, leaving just the title bar exposed.

3. To reveal the entire window again, double-click the title bar and the window unrolls.

To set your preferences for how WindowShade operates, follow these steps:

1. Select WindowShade from your Control Panels submenu on the **Apple Menu**.

2. Choose the number of clicks you want to hide or show a window by double- or triple-clicking a window's title bar.

3. If you want to add modifier keys, you can select them as well.

4. You also have a check mark to enable or disable the window shade sound effect, which simulates a window shade being rolled up and down.

See Also

Active Window; Apple Menu; Desktop Level; System 7.5; Windows; WindowShade Control Panel

WindowShade Control Panel

This controls the window shade feature that rolls windows up to their title bar to reduce **desktop** clutter. Your options are how many clicks to hide or show the window or to turn Window Shade off altogether. You can also choose to add modifier keys if you like. The last option lets you have the window shade sound effect enabled or disabled.

To use the WindowShade Control Panel, follow these steps:

1. Select WindowShade from the Control Panels submenu on the Apple menu (or System Folder).

2. Choose how many times you want the title bar clicked to hide or show a window. If you want to add modifier keys, you can select them as well.

3. Enable or disable the window shade sound effect.

See Also

Apple Menu; Control Panel; Desktop, The; Modifier Keys

Winer, Dave, *See Frontier*

Wing Commander III

Wing Commander III from Origin Systems takes you further into the conflict between the feline Kilrathi and the confederation of planets. As Chris Blair, you are a Confederation VIP who must ward off Kilrathi invasion.

Like **Rebel Assault II**, Wing Commander III merges live action with animated, outer-space backgrounds to give you the science-fiction feel you don't get from a regular flight sim. Because space sims are not based on actual planes, they tend to be less technical than straight flight sims and therefore less manual intensive. This makes them more palatable to inexperienced gamers who don't want to spend the time necessary to learn the controls of a technically accurate flight sim. The fast-paced action and complex controls of Wing Commander III are a challenge without alienating newcomers.

See Also
Absolute Zero; Rebel Assault II; Sim Games

Wireframe

Wireframe is a method of representing a **3D** object with lines that define the surfaces of the object. Wireframes are used frequently in 3D **modelers** for previewing scenes and models because of the speed with which they can be drawn.

See Also
3D; Modeling

Wireless Networks

As computers get smaller and smaller, the cabling systems used to connect them also tie them down to the desktop. The solution is to eliminate the cabling. Wireless networks are a recent development that does just that. There are several wireless technologies available for the Macintosh.

One option for a wireless network is to use Apple's Remote Access with a celluar phone/modem combination. This makes sense for wide-area network connections for a limited number of devices. It also lets you pursue the business executive's dream — running your office from the 12th hole at the country club, or checking your email while you're out sailing. More practically, paramedics are using this technology to check patient records while on the way into the ER. Repair people use it to log into the office computer and look up schematics or order needed parts, and to report their hours and costs when the job is done.

For LAN connectivity, wireless technology may be useful in locations where conventional wiring is difficult or impossible to run. Motorola, the leading manufacturer of cellular telephones, has a Macintosh product called EMBARC which provides a one-way wireless messaging service for remote Mac users. There are also options for LAN mediums such as LocalTalk and EtherNet. Photonics makes LocalTalk devices that use reflected infrared to link a number of nodes. The infrared devices focus their energy at a single point on the ceiling.

Motorola has developed a wireless version of EtherNet, the Altair II wireless network. These devices use low-power radio waves as a transmission medium. Altair's transmission rate of 5.7Mbps is somewhat less than EtherNet bandwidth, but adequate. Setup is easy. Each EtherNet device connects to a small desktop send/receive module. These desktop modules transmit radio waves to control modules that connect to walls or cubicle partitions. The send/receive modules support all kinds of EtherNet adapters and cost around $1,200. The control module can be used alone or connected to a conventional EtherNet cable. These devices can handle up to 50 wireless devices.

Compared to conventional wired networks, these new technologies are still somewhat expensive and are only cost-effective in those cases where wiring is difficult or where rewiring costs would exceed the cost of the wireless components. Expect wireless communications to continue to increase in popularity as Apple's Newton technology and other handheld computers become more popular.

See Also
Network Administration; Network Communication; Network Maintenance; Network Topology; Network Wiring Strategies; Networking, Why and How

Wireless Speakers, *See Speaker, Wireless*

Wirth, Niklaus, *See Pascal*

Wolfenstein 3-D, *See First Person Perspective Shooters; Violence in Games*

Word Processing

Word processing includes any operations that are performed on text. **Editing**, **copying**, **formatting**, **checking spelling** and grammar, and **printing** all happen within the word processing program. Because the Macintosh has a **consistent user interface**, these operations are done in the same way no matter what word processor you happen to be using.

There are, of course, minor differences in the way the various word processors function. Generally, though, the commands and operations you learn in any Macintosh program will work in any other program—even one of a different kind, such as a drawing program. **Cut**, for example is ⌘-X, whether you're cutting a word from a line of text in **WordPerfect**, a picture from **the scrapbook**, or a cloud from the sky in a **Photoshop** picture.

Undo always undoes the most recent thing you've done. However, if you "undo" repeatedly, you'll find that some programs will toggle between "undo" and "redo" with the ⌘-Z combination, whereas others support multiple levels of "undo," enabling you to retrace your steps backward. **MS Word 6.0** now also supports multiple levels of "redo," so you can change your mind about how much you want to undo.

Conversation with Jerzy Lewak

Experienced Mac developer, entrepreneur, and creator of a neat word processing program, Nisus Writer, Jerzy Lewak has watched the Mac grow and mutate since its birth.

Maclopedia: What was your first personal experience with the Mac and how did you react?"

Jerzy: My son, Stas, who in 1984 was an engineering student at the University of California at San Diego and part-time employed as a programmer, told me about the proposed release of this great new computer, and *made me* buy the first Mac, which appeared in the retail stores in San Diego...Here was a computer with the right kind of human interface. That is when I immediately became an Apple Developer.

Maclopedia: What's your perspective on the creation, development, and demise of MacWrite?

Jerzy: MacWrite, when it first came out with the first Mac, was an excellent, though limited, product. What is called "MacWrite" and "MacWrite Pro" is not even remotely related to the old MacWrite. So I am assuming you're referring to the old one. Can you believe that the first MacWrite had to work with the whole system in just 128K of memory? That was some feat! Of course that is why it would have been difficult to continue maintaining MacWrite; it was almost all assembly. I don't know the inside story on whether Apple had thoughts of maintaining and evolving it. All I know is that, except for some small enhancements, they did not. I would like to believe that there was a time when Apple wanted to give developers a chance, and so stayed out of competition with them. But I rather think their reason was more pragmatic: they were too busy developing the hardware and system.

Maclopedia: What's the Nisus way, and how do you position your products?

Jerzy: The philosophy behind the Nisus way is to empower the user and as much as possible remove limitations from features. The empowerment goal means that we make our products open to the creativity of the user: the more creative the user, the more he/she can get out of them. That is why Nisus Writer, from the first releases, included a macro language to enable you to create your own features. That is also why its search capability includes a very powerful text pattern description language (a superset of the UNIX GREP). The lack of limitations is reflected in such things as the fact that from the very beginning our Clipboard was fully editable, and, of course, for a long time we have had 10 clipboards; and the fact that you can draw and type without changing windows. That is a feature I have yet to see in any other word processor.

continues

Further, our WorldScript support has been there even before Apple had a "WorldScript." In our recent release of MailKeeper, our empowerment goal is exhibited in the new patented information access technology we have developed (Guided Information Access). By guiding the user in the process of describing the object of his search, it intelligently and instantly eliminates inappropriate possibilities. Even in its first version, MailKeeper can be used for many more purposes than archiving mail. It is also ideal for such diverse applications as collecting information before writing a book or article, or as a customer support or technical support database.

Nisus Writer is positioned as a very high-end word processor, particularly known for its support of the various language scripts of the world, such as Korean, Japanese, Chinese, Hebrew, and Arabic. The average user who uses his/her word processor for occasional memo and letter typing will not have time to even consider evaluating Nisus Writer; but the serious heavy user will, and should.

Here was a computer with the right kind of human interface. That is when I immediately became an Apple Developer.

Maclopedia: What's caused Apple's current troubles? (And are they significantly different from crises in the past?)

Jerzy: I agree with many press opinions on this question: Apple should have enabled cloning many years ago and should have assured greater affordability of the Mac. In other words, they should have played their cards such that everyone would have found it cheaper to buy a Mac than a PC. Currently we have examples of companies like Netscape offering a free product just to capture the market, even forgoing revenue! That is something many companies are trying with the Internet. It is too early to tell if it will work, but in the days of Macintosh beginnings, it would surely have worked to make the Mac pervasive in the market.

I have two more mistakes to point out to Apple. Instead of making sure that it would be profitable and easy for developers to develop for the Mac, they did the opposite. The Mac platform is, and always has been, the most difficult to develop for. Apple's feeble attempts at producing a development system have not worked. In addition and to compound the problem, Apple first started Claris, promising to sell it to the public and make it independent, then took it back and has since made it compete with other software developers. How can we compete when Claris is in bed with Apple? Why not make Claris the prime developer of cross-platform development tools? That would be both profitable in the short term and in the long term help keep Macintosh developers developing software.

Today, Macintosh development tools are way too far behind those for the PC. Apple's current problems are different than those in the past. They have to modernize their operating system, and come out with one quickly. If they do not then, they will wither and die. They also have to innovate. Open Doc could be it, if it's not too late. But a cross-platform development system, which would ease and speed the development of software, would be a winner. On the hardware side, I think Apple should look at a paradigm shift to make their computers plug and play instantly again. The hardware complexities (though considerably better than with Windows 95 machines) are daunting for the average user, and the startup process takes too long.

Maclopedia: So, what can Apple do better to help developers?

Jerzy: Get us a modern, cross-platform, Macintosh-based development system and phase out competing with us unfairly.

In the early days of Macintosh, the computer came with two programs installed. **MacWrite** was the first Mac word processor, and it set the standard for all the ones that followed. Functions such as spell checking and grammar checking weren't part of the original software, and the original MacWrite was quite limited in its ability to format pages and perform other functions we take for granted today. Nevertheless, it was a remarkable achievement. For the first time, you could actually see on-screen what your page would look like in print. The **WYSIWYG** interface enables you to set headlines in 24 point bold, body copy in 12 point italics, and see the difference—something **DOS**-based word processors couldn't possibly do.

As other companies developed competing word processors for the Mac, they kept the same consistent user interface, and it was very easy to switch from MacWrite to **Microsoft Word**, or **Nisus**, or **WriteNow**, or **WordPerfect.** Today's version of MacWrite, **Claris MacWrite Pro**, looks most like the original but, like the others, now has features that weren't even dreamed of ten years ago. Early versions of MacWrite could place a picture into the text, but today's word processors can also incorporate **QuickTime** movies, graphs and tables that will automatically update when they're changed in the application that created them, and even spoken messages within a document. Word processors also make it easy to create "form" letters, and to merge these with a mailing list and automatically type an envelope for each letter.

Most word processors support **outlining**, making it easy for you to organize your thoughts and then write your paper without switching programs. There are also separate "brainstorming" programs. Most also can generate an **index** and/or **table of contents** for your document. Word processors usually include a thesaurus, spelling and grammar checking software, or bundle it with the program (**WriteNow/Correct Grammar; WordPerfect/Grammatik**). The spelling and thesaurus components are helpful, the grammar less so.

When you choose a word processor, consider what kind of words you'll be processing. Writing books or technical documents is a different sort of word processing from writing short business letters, and the latter task might be easier on less "feature-heavy" software. Consider whether you'll need to work with graphics, tables, or equations within your documents. Consider whether you'll be using your word processor on a **PowerBook**, where smaller is an advantage, and whether you have the hard disk space and **RAM** to handle a "memory-hog" program such as Word 6. If your word processing needs are only part of your daily operations, consider a **Works** program with an integrated word processor, spreadsheets, and database. These can handle most ordinary tasks, up through simple desktop publishing.

Word Processors, Using Word processors and **laser printers** have changed the way certain things are done.

It used to be, when you typed a document on a typewriter, that you'd leave two spaces after a period. Typewriter type was **monospaced**, meaning that all the letters were the same width. The "l" took up the same amount of room on the line as the "w" did. The extra space was necessary to indicate the end of one sentence and the start of the next. However, computers use **fonts** that are proportionally spaced. Each letter takes up only as much space as it needs. Leaving two spaces after the period leaves an unnecessarily large gap in the line. So, typists switching from old fashioned typewriters to word processors had to learn not to use that second space. They also had to learn the difference between regular quotes and "**curly quotes.**" Typographers used pairs of left- and right-handed quotation marks to designate the beginning and end of a quotation, while typewriters compromised with only one of set **straight quotes** for both. The computer fonts usually include both straight and curly quotes, and word processors added a feature called "smart quotes," which enables you to type a straight quote and the program automatically converts it to the appropriate curly quote.

If you want to do this...	*Try this program...*
General writing	Claris MacWrite Pro, Microsoft Word, Nisus Writer, WordPerfect, WriteNow
Outline	Microsoft Word
Write on a PowerBook	WriteNow
Desktop publishing	Microsoft Word, Nisus Writer, WordPerfect, or a DTP program
Use foreign languages	Nisus Writer, WordPerfect

WordPerfect

Perfection is rarely achieved. Earlier Mac versions of this program came to be known by disgruntled users as WordImperfect. Written originally for DOS and adapted for the Mac, it originally retained too many DOS characteristics to satisfy users familiar with the easy and intuitive MacWrite. But it had potential. The current version, WordPerfect 3.5, fulfills that promise with a well-organized and intuitive interface, powerful AppleScript macros, and an excellent table generator.

There's no question about WordPerfect's cross-platform compatibility. It is available for DOS, Windows, UNIX, VAX, and NeXT systems, as well as for the Mac. Novell purchased WordPerfect's parent company about a year ago and recently re-sold it to Corel, a Canadian company known most for its Clip Art collections and for its drawing package, Corel Draw. Corel has said it will continue developing the Mac version of WordPerfect.

WordPerfect does everything well, but not spectacularly. Its strength is versatility. It has the most complete set of graphics tools of any of the word processors. In addition to the standard pen and fill tools, and the Bézier-curve drawing tools, WordPerfect's Graphics toolbar gives you the ability to freely rotate graphics. You can also place watermarks (ghosted images or designs imprinted behind text on a page) and overlays (graphics superimposed on the text) with a single button click. WordPerfect can save pages of mixed text and graphics in **HTML** for **World Wide Web** publishing. It can save documents in formats that are compatible with almost any other text handler on any platform. It can even password protect individual documents.

WordPerfect has a set of seven different toolbars as seen in the following figure:

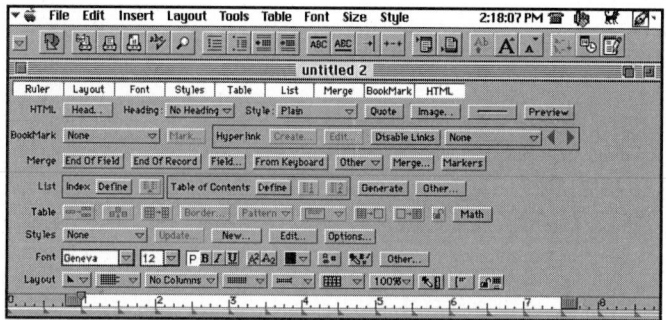

These enable you, via pop-up menus, to accomplish virtually anything in the way of text and graphic manipulation, from formatting text to generating a table of contents. With all of WordPerfect's toolbars enabled at once, the effect is somewhat overwhelming. Ordinarily, you'd only turn on the ones you needed to use. Otherwise, there's not much room left in the window for text.

WordPerfect has some excellent shortcut features, such as Make It Fit. This tool (see following figure) enables you to adjust the font, margins, and paragraph spacing of a formatted document that's a bit too long or too short for your needs, so that it fits the page layout or page count you had in mind.

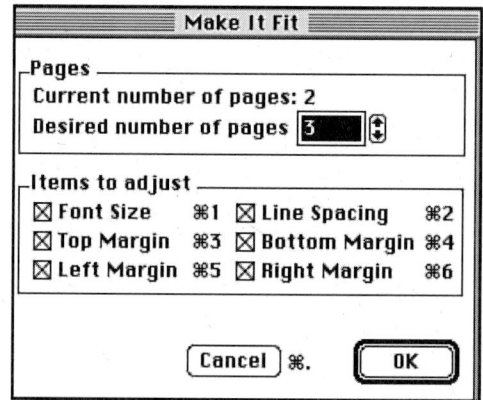

WordPerfect carries a low price tag compared to **Nisus** and **Microsoft Word**. The street price is under $200. If price is a consideration, check out the **Student Essentials** package from Corel. It includes WordPerfect 3.5, a dictionary, a thesaurus, an encyclopedia, and a term paper assistant called Bookends that organizes your bibliography and provides space to take notes on your reading. Printed manuals are not included, but all documentation is available on the product's two CD-ROMs. The cost, as of this writing, is $159.00.

See Also

MacWrite Pro; Nisus Writer; Word Processors; WriteNow 4 .0

Workgroup Servers, Macintosh Family

Apple Computer provides a suite of "jazzed-up" Power Macs designed to support small- to medium-sized workgroups. These Macintosh Computers are marketed as **Apple Workgroup Servers** and provide full-featured networking support via a selection of hardware and software. Workgroup Servers come in three sizes: "pizza box," "mini-tower," and tower.

There are two type of network configurations available to businesses: **distributed networks**, such as are supported by System 7.5's **File Sharing** software, where each Macintosh acts as a mini-server storing portions of a workgroup's data, which is shared between members of a network; or **dedicated servers** that serve as a central repository of workgroup data and runs specialized server software that manages how members of the network running related client software share this information. Apple Workgroup Servers are dedicated servers.

Workgroup servers (also sometimes called **Network Servers**) are basically computers that act as traffic cops to store data and manage its transfer among computers on a network. Because input and output performance is very critical to the mission of a server versus a stand-alone computer, these Power Macs have enhanced SCSI and networking hardware.

Networks are the physical wiring that connects computers together, the software that resides on each client computer that lets them share information, and the centralized computer with its server software that manages the flow of information. If you have small networks, such as those based on Apple's 32-node LocalTalk network, you can use any Mac workstation as your data repository or server. The more users accessing the computer, the more CPU it needs to dedicate to the task of serving, thus it is recommended that the Mac working as a server be solely dedicated to that task and not run any other software while it is serving.

Larger networks of computers require more performance from their servers, and thus use machines that have added input/output speed and more storage capacity than plain workstations. Other servers also act as gateways to large-scale networks, such as the Internet, that lie outside of the physical structure of the network. Networks of computers do not all have to be using the same operating systems, in fact most networks are composed of both Mac and PCs, as well as UNIX workstations. Apple provides server software called **AppleShare** (currently version 4.0). Each Mac also comes with AppleShare client software as part of the System 7.5 operating system.

Workgroup servers typically manage networks that contain more members than is supported by System 7.5 File Sharing (up to five), and who require faster access to data than can be supported by Apple's network protocol called **AppleTalk** and its attendant **LocalTalk** cabling system. Therefore, each Workgroup server supports the faster **EtherNet** cabling systems (whether coaxial or 10Base-T cabling) and the **EtherTalk protocol**, and uses AppleShare 4.1 that can support many more network members. There are currently three models of PowerPC-based Workgroup servers: Workgroup Server 6150/66, 8150/110, and 9150/120. Each server provides the following features:

- Compatibility with Windows-based PCs as well as Macintosh clients. The server comes pre-installed with AppleShare Client for Windows and also can have Apple Internet Server Solution for the World Wide Web software installed to create an Internet server.

- Large capacity hard disk drives and quadruple-speed, tray-loading CD-ROM drives for extensive storage capabilities.

- A **Digital Audio Tape (DAT)** drive and Retrospect Remote automatic server and client backup software provides data security via automatic backups of critical data.

- **Redundant Array of Inexpensive Disks (RAID)** software supporting disk mirroring and striping for system reliability.

- Network administration software such as server-based contact management and scheduling software, workgroup electronic publishing software, and network management software to ease the application, distribution, and updating of software on the

W

network. Bundled software often includes the following: Server Administrator and User Productivity Software such as Server Manager for AppleShare, FileWave, Viper Instant Access, Now Contact, Now Up-to-Date, Adobe Acrobat Reader, and AppleShare Client for Windows.

■ The Workgroup Server can be used as an Internet Server by installing the Apple Internet Server Solution for the World Wide Web. This software bundle includes: WebSTAR 1.0 server software, AppleSearch with CGI, BBEdit, HTML editors, Netscape WWW browser, WWW gateways with sample data and runtime un-modifiable versions of Butler SQL and FileMaker Pro, WWW gateway with sample data and full version of HyperCard, WWW gateways for clickable maps and electronic mail, and sample customizable WWW server pages.

The following table provides an overview of the components of each Workgroup Server.

See Also

Apple Internet Server Solution; AppleShare; CD-ROM; Desktop Models, Macintosh Family; DAT; Internet; RAID Array; World Wide Web

Works Programs

When we were kids, "Gimme the works" used to mean not just the hot fudge, but also the marshmallow, nuts, whipped cream, and the cherry on top of the sundae. Today, "the works" has a much less interesting connotation. A works program combines several different applications into one. The first of these was AppleWorks for the Apple II. It was an idea that caught on as the computer became more of a household appliance. You could write letters, balance your checkbook, and print a yard sale poster, all from the same program.

Apple Workgroup Servers

Model Number	Processor Type	Memory/Storage	Features
6150/66	PowerPC 601 at 66 MHz	16M DRAM, 256K level-2 cache/700M hard drive, 600i+ CD-ROM drive	AppleShare 4.1, RAID Software, and/or Apple Internet Server Solution for WWW, and built-in EtherNet. EtherNet transceivers, monitors, and keyboards sold separately.
8150/110	PowerPC 601 110 MHz	16M DRAM, 256K level-2 cache/1G hard drive, 600+ CD-ROM, Digital Audio Tape (DAT) drive	AppleShare 4.1, RAID Software, and/or Apple Internet Server Solution for WWW, and built-in EtherNet. EtherNet transceivers, monitors, and keyboards sold separately.
9150/120	PowerPC 601 at 120 MHz	16M DRAM, 1M level-2 cache, one or two 1 or 2G hard drives with slots for three more, 600i+ CD-ROM drive, DAT Drive	AppleShare 4.1, RAID Software, and/or Apple Internet Server Solution for WWW, and built-in EtherNet. EtherNet transceivers, monitors, and keyboards sold separately.

There used to be three or four different works programs for Macintosh users. Now the field has been reduced to just two: **ClarisWorks** and **Microsoft Works**. This might suggest that the notion isn't practical. Or, simply that these two programs are so superior to the others that there's no reason for any other publishers to try the concept. The truth is, the integrated works program *is* a practical idea, but only for users who need to do a little of everything, without needing a heavy-duty powerhouse program in one particular area. Works programs cover the basics, by providing modules that include word processing, drawing, database management, spreadsheets, and telecommunications. They do all this in a relatively small amount of space. ClarisWorks, for example, wants only 1.4MB RAM to run and less than 2MB of hard disk space. Microsoft Works occupies a little over 5MB of hard disk and about 2MB of RAM, which still is pretty good, especially if you consider that MSWord eats up nearly five times as much hard drive real estate. A Works program is a good choice for a PowerBook or Duo, because it packs so many functions into a small space. They'll also save you money. The current street price for ClarisWorks is $129. If you were to start adding up the cost of a stand-alone word processor, telecom program, spreadsheet, database, and drawing program, you'd come up with a figure that's close to five times as much. And you wouldn't have the seamless integration that a Works program gives you.

There's another kind of semi-integrated program called a **suite**. The one you're most likely to see on the shelf or in the catalog is **Microsoft Office**. Technically, it's not a works program, but rather a collection of stand-alone applications. In this case, you get Excel, Word, and PowerPoint, plus a launcher called Microsoft Office Manager, which gives you quick access to the three programs from the menu bar. The advantage is that you get three full-featured applications rather than scaled down "works" versions. The disadvantages are that the bundle is expensive, uses a lot of hard disk space, and, when you buy the Office package, you have to buy printed manuals separately. They're included as text files on the CD-ROM.

See Also
ClarisWorks 4.0; Microsoft Office; Microsoft Works

World at War, *See V for Victory*

World War II Games, *See Allied General, Strategy Games, V for Victory*

World Wide Web, The
A **hypertext**-based document retrieval system that enables people connected to the **Internet** to view text, graphics, sounds, and movies **online** and across different computer platforms.

People with a dedicated Internet connection or access to a computer set up as a **Web server** can go a step beyond information retrieval and publish a "home page" or series of interconnected pages on the Web containing words, images, audio, or other sorts of materials.

The World Wide Web (or WWW, or simply the Web) is the newest and most popular of the **Internet services**. Businesses, organizations, and individuals are rushing to the Web to create online presences via their own **Web sites**.

The Web was started in 1989 at CERN, a high-energy physics research center in Switzerland, as an academic project. It attempts to provide access to the widest range of information by linking not only documents made available via its native **HTTP** (HyperText Transfer Protocol), but also provides a simple interface to additional sources of information via **Usenet** news, **FTP**, **WAIS**, and **Gopher**.

No single person or group "runs" the Web, but the W3 Consortium is a group of organizations that fund the design and standards for its development, including the evolution of HyperText Markup Language (**HTML**) and security methods. Its director, **Tim Berners-Lee**, invented the Web while at CERN.

The amount of information available on the Web would be impossible to store on one computer. But the Internet makes possible information retrieval from interlinked systems distributed around the world, from personal computers to massive databases such as **software archives**. Servers and the information stored on them can be located by a system of addresses that includes Universal Resource Locators (**URLs**) and **domain names**.

The Web also enables the use of intelligent agents such as **search engines** that traverse the Web and locate information, which is especially important since the Web's contents are constantly changing and difficult to organize. Sites such as **Yahoo** perform the essential function of bringing order to a nonlinear, noncontrolled medium.

The most striking feature of the Web is the introduction of rich text (fonts, styles, sizes, and sophisticated formatting) and increasingly sophisticated **multimedia** elements in **Internet** documents.

World Wide Web, Using Authors of Web pages create HTML documents that contain special codes that tell a **Web browser** program to display the text in various fonts, styles, and sizes. **Web pages** can contain **inline graphics** that appear in the same content window as the text. **Hypertext links** take users to documents, software, objects, sounds, and video that are either displayed in the browser window or processed by **helper applications**. The HTML documents, **GIF** or **JPEG** graphics, and other materials are stored on computers set up to act as Web servers that have dedicated connections to the Internet so users can access their contents.

Browsers vary in speed, user configurability, and the variety of material they can handle. The most popular programs for "browsing" (the common term for exploring Web sites and their information and **links**) the Web are **Netscape Navigator**, Microsoft Internet Explorer, NCSA **Mosaic**, **MacWeb**, the **America Online** browser, and **Prodigy**'s browser.

World Wide Web, Hypertext Hypertext, the foundation of the Web, is a method for navigating through information in a nonlinear way. Information is joined by highlighted references known as links. Clicking a link with a mouse or selecting it from a keyboard allows a user to move from one place to another in a document, or from one document to another. Hypertext provides a single user interface between many different types of information—text, graphics, databases, and so on. The networking of this information joined by hypertextual links was a dubbed a "web" by the Web's creators.

World Wide Web, Interactivity The Web by its very nature is interactive because when users connect to a remote Web server they download a copy of a Web page and graphics onto their computer in order to view it. The Web introduced a more sophisticated type of two-way communciation to the Internet between information providers and consumers via the use of **forms**. Online forms consist of text-entry fields, buttons, and checkboxes that users can fill in with data that can then be submitted to a remote server. On the Internet, forms make possible all sorts of applications, ranging from surveys to online ordering to reservations to searching agents. Forms are increasingly used on the Web for marketing purposes—gathering information about how many and what sorts of people use the Internet.

World Wide Web, Security The very accessibility of material on the Web makes security measures difficult. The Web promises to become a hotbed of **electronic commerce** when the security of financial and other transactions can be assured. At the same time, as more and more businesses begin to establish a Web presence, more business transactions take place using the Web as a marketplace and more sentive information is transmitted over the Net using methods like **encryption**, **certificates**, **Secure HTTP**, and **Secure Sockets Layer**.

World Wide Web, Searching/Navigating A number of utilities can be used to search for specific data and navigate through the rich resources of information contained on the Internet.

Each of the **Internet services** organizes information differently; therefore, each has its own way of searching for information. The various **search engines** are described in detail elsewhere in *Maclopedia* (see entries in boldface). The following table summarizes the various search tools.

Internet Search Tools

Tool	How to Use it
FTP (File Transfer Protocol)	Users generally employ a *client program* (such as a **Fetch** or **Anarchie**) to gain access to an FTP server that holds a great deal of information they can download, such as **software archives** or **mailing lists.**
Anonymous FTP	Users can log in anonymously using a program like **Fetch**.
Archie	A directory of anonymous FTP sites around the world, accessible via **Telnet**, or **email**, Gopher, or **World Wide Web clients.**

Tool	How to Use it
Gopher	Users can run the client program **TurboGopher** to navigate Gopherspace, and conduct searches using **Veronica** or **Jughead**.
Telnet	**NCSA Telnet** is the most common Telnet application for the Macintosh.
Usenet	**NewsWatcher** is a popular client, as is **Netscape Navigator; DejaNews** and **InfoSeek** provide searches through newsgroup articles.
World Wide Web	Client software includes Netscape Navigator, Mosaic, **MacWeb, HotJava;** search engines include **InfoSeek, Lycos,** and **WebCrawler**.
WAIS	MacWAIS is a common client for WAIS servers.

See Also

Encryption; Forms in HTML, Creating; FTP; GIF; Gopher; Helper Applications; Home Page; HTML; HTTP; Hypertext; Internet; JPEG; MacWeb; Mosaic; Multimedia; Netscape Navigator; Search Engines; Secure HTTP; Secure Sockets Layer; Server; Usenet; WAIS; Web Page; Web site; Yahoo

Conversation with Sidnei Brandao

Sidnei Brandao is general manager for Apple Computer Brazil, a division of Apple selling to the Brazilian market.

Maclopedia: What was your first personal experience with the Macintosh like?

Sidnei: I have heard about the friendly features of the Mac for many years. It was a legend for me, even

continues

having had an Apple II as my first computer ever. My first impression was, "It's true; it's great!"

Maclopedia: In Brazil, what's the market like for personal computers at home, in school, and in business? And in that market, where does the Mac fit in?

Sidnei: Schools are just now turning to computers, so there is a good opportunity for the Mac; business is owned by the PC computer, but 50 percent still come from the black market.

Home is the market to own at this time in Brazil. It is Apple Brazil's main target at this time.

Maclopedia: Are there any aspects of the Mac that make it particularly appealing in Brazil?

Sidnei: Design, ease of use, and the Apple name carries a certain magic around it.

Maclopedia: When you localize, what are the most significant changes you need to make to ads, manuals, software, hardware, and marketing?

Sidnei: Localization is almost total for Brazil. We talk Portuguese, but it differs much too much from the language talked in Portugal.

Manuals need translation and adaptation for local laws. Software needs localization and adaptation in items referring to currency, plus the English language is more concise than Portuguese, so text in the manuals will be around 25 percent larger. Marketing has to be specific to Brazil. As a background it is important to have in mind that Brazil was the only Latin American country colonized by the Portuguese. As they came by sea, most large Brazilian towns were near the Atlantic. That puts the Amazon forest and thousands of kilometers of land between the Brazilian people and the other South American countries. This explains why we were culturally isolated and why advertising and marketing for the region will hardly ever work over here.

Worm, *See Virus*

Woz, *See Wozniak, Steve*

Wozniak, Steve

Steve "Woz" Wozniak was one of Apple Computer's founders. He grew up in Sunnyvale, California, in the heart of Silicon Valley. His father was an engineer who designed satellites for Lockheed.

In 1970, Wozniak met **Steve Jobs** through his neighbor, Bill Fernandez, a classmate of Jobs. Although Jobs and Woz had both attended Homestead High School, they never met there because Woz is five years older than Jobs. At the time, Steve Jobs was 15 years old and Wozniak was 20.

Woz attended the Colorado University but flunked out and returned to Sunnyvale. It was then that he began building his first computer. He was an electronics nut, as were many of his friends (including Jobs). Woz and Fernandez managed to build a computer using surplus parts gathered from local semiconductor companies such as Intel and Fairchild. Although the computer worked for a while, it eventually died in a puff of smoke.

Woz returned to school at U.C. Berkeley to study engineering. While there, he learned of a device called a "blue box" that could mimic the tones used for switching by long distance phone equipment and give its user free long distance service. Before he had a chance to see the plans for the blue box, he had designed one himself that was better, smaller, and cheaper than the original.

Following his junior year at Berkeley, Wozniak took a summer job at the Hewlett Packard Calculator division. He stayed on in the fall and did not return to finish his degree. He did, however, manage to realize his dream of building his own computer (that really worked). His design would become the Apple I and set in motion the founding of Apple Computer.

Wozniak went on to design the hugely successful Apple II and played an important role in many Apple technologies up to and including the Macintosh. Early in the Macintosh project, Woz was injured when he crashed his plane. As a result, he had little involvement in the later stages of the Macintosh.

From Apple's start, Wozniak was the technologist while Jobs was the marketer. He didn't mind staying in the background and allowing Jobs (or others) to stand in the spotlight. After all, it gave him the opportunity to do what he really loved: work with electronics.

Although Job's penchant for ruthlessness is well-known, that influence was balanced by Woz's sense of fairness and kind-heartedness. Woz, for example, felt it was unfair that many of Apple's earliest employees had been denied stock options. Shortly before Apple's stock went public, Woz helped some of these employees by offering the "WozPlan," an opportunity to buy up to 2,000 shares of his stock.

Although Woz never officially resigned from Apple, he ended his day-to-day involvement with the company in 1985, angry over the poor attention given to the Apple II division by Jobs and **John Sculley**. After leaving Apple, he decided to pursue his dream of becoming a teacher. To do so, he needed to finish his degree, so he returned to Berkeley under the pseudonym Rocky Raccoon Clark. He received his Bachelors degree in electrical engineering in June 1986. His involvement with Apple has varied since then, but he now spends most of his time teaching children how to use computers.

See Also

Apple Computer, History; Jobs, Steve; Sculley, John

Wristwatch, *See Beach Ball Cursor*

Write Out Loud

Write Out Loud is a talking word processor, from Don Johnston Inc. There are, according to educational psychologists, several different learning styles. Some people are visual learners; they see a word, and they learn it. Others have to hear it. For these auditory learners, and for anyone who's just learning to touch type or to write in English as a second language, it would be ideal to have a word processor that could read back what you'd typed.

Write Out Loud is the answer. It's a talking word processor that will read back each letter, or each word, or each sentence, or paragraph as you enter it. This program provides multisensory learning and positive reinforcement for writers of all ages.

It's also a big help for people with dyslexia, and for people with low vision. It's easy to use, and although not as versatile as a program such as WordPerfect, it's adequate for school work, letter writing, and similar projects. The program uses a talking toolbar. The simple toolbar gives access to program commands such as putting the cursor at the beginning or end of a file with one click, printing in one step, maneuvering through the text, and more.

Clicking the toolbar makes the program tell you what that tool does. There's even a talking spell checker, which reads the misspelled word in its sentence, isolates the word, and then spells it as it is written. A list of suggested words can be read and spelled aloud so that the user can benefit from auditory feedback. The user can even change the program's speaking voice by selecting a different one from the menu.

See Also

Co:Writer; Freedom; Ke:nx; Talk:About

Write-Protect Tab, *See Locking a Disk*

Writeable CD

A writeable CD is a **CD-ROM** on which data can be recorded (or written) using a special CD mechanism (called a burner or **CD-R drive**). While these discs are playable on most CD mechanisms, they are very different from pressed CDs, which are injection molded. It takes expensive equipment and more time to press a disc, but after that, they can be manufactured much faster and cheaper than burning discs.

Writeable CDs make it possible to have **multisession** discs, discs that have been updated (recorded) at different times. Writeable CDs should not be confused with rewriteable or erasable technologies. Writeable CDs cannot be changed after they are written—only additional information can be added to the end of the disc.

See Also

CD-ROM; Multisession CD

WriteNow 4.0

WriteNow has two really good features—speed and size. It's the fastest to open, fastest to change fonts, fastest to count words. Some of its speed comes from not needing to spend much time chewing through its own code. It's also compact. The entire program, including the dictionary and thesaurus, fits on two disks, and demands only 2.2MB of hard disk space and a scant 600K of RAM.

Despite its small size, it has most of the features you'd expect to see in a program costing three times as much and weighing even more. WriteNow gives you an easy-to-use style sheet with both paragraph- and character-based styles, tables, footnotes, spelling, Thesaurus, Print Preview, and **Balloon Help**. The only features it lacks are Autosave, small caps, and auto-hyphenation.

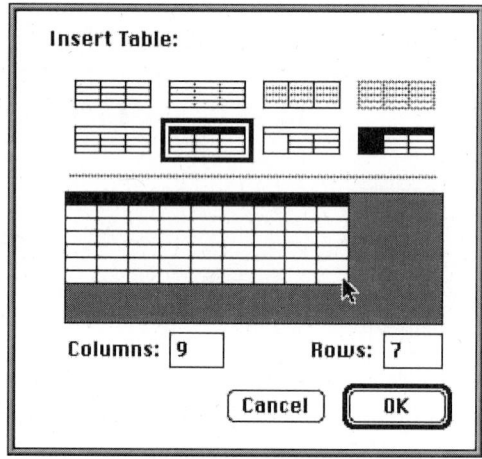

Working with tables is especially convenient in WriteNow. Tables are created graphically. To add a table, you select the format and size from the dialog box shown in the previous figure, and select the number of rows and columns. This is done either by entering numbers in the boxes or by clicking and dragging the table layout until it looks right. When the table appears on the screen, it comes with a handy tool palette. To add or remove rows or columns, just click the appropriate button. You can even add colors and patterns to your tables. This suggests that the table

might be adapted to some other purpose, and in fact, WriteNow's sample folder includes a colorful flyer that was produced as a table.

There's no built-in Help system in WriteNow, as there is in Word or MacWritePro. It does support Balloon Help, which isn't much help. The manual includes some very good tips on optimizing the program to run on a **PowerBook**. WriteNow has a very nice battery indicator, and a "fat" (wider) cursor to help overcome the problem of dim PowerBook screens. If you're considering a word processor for use on a PowerBook, or for ordinary business use (letters, memos, reports with tables and charts), WriteNow is ideal. The only question that remains is how long it will be around. WriteNow has gone through several publishers since its first release. As of this writing, it's handled by SoftKey, who took it over from WordStar, who took it over from somebody else. The problem is that it was written specifically for 680x0 machines. While it runs acceptably well on the Power Mac, it's not optimized to do so, and would have to be completely re-written. This is unlikely to happen, so chances are good that it will eventually fade away. Meanwhile, it's a good solid choice.

See Also

MacWrite Pro; Nisus Writer; WordPerfect; Word Processing

Writing Code

For most programmers, writing code is what programming is all about. They frequently jump right in and start coding on a new project before they nail down what the project is about. Before writing any code, a programming project should begin with thorough **problem analysis** and **program design** phases. These help clarify the purpose and design of a project before it's too late.

Once the problem is defined and the design of the program has been finalized, it's time to start writing code. Programmers use **editors** or **browsers** to create and edit code. An editor is a word processor specially optimized for writing code. The details of writing code vary depending on the **programming language** used, but some general guidelines apply no matter what language is used.

The most important guideline is to write clear, understandable code. There are two parts to this guideline: use plenty of comments, and write in a style that is clear and easy to read.

It is crucial that meaningful comments are included in the code. Although some source code is very easy to decipher without the advantage of comments, virtually any code can be made clear with good comments.

Comments should define each part of a program or section of a routine. It is generally not necessary to comment on every individual step in a program, but it is important to document the overall idea behind each piece of code, assumptions made in the code, and any interactions the code makes with other parts of the program. Even if you believe you are the only programmer who will see your code, comments can still be a lifesaver. Months (or years) after you've written a section of code, your original reasoning and logic is likely forgotten. If you can rely on your comments, you are able to understand your program for years to come.

Sometimes, even the best comments cannot make poorly written code easy to understand. You should strive to make the code itself easy to understand even without the comments. Avoid programming constructions that obscure the purpose of your code. Given the choice between code that is compact but difficult to understand and code that is more verbose but easy to understand, most programmers would choose the latter every time.

It is also important to follow established conventions for the style of your code. Many Macintosh C programmers, for example, begin their global variables with the letter "g" to make it clear which variables are global. Similarly, most **object-oriented** programming **frameworks** use a fixed style for naming classes and their member functions and data.

A complete discussion of methods used to ensure excellence in code is beyond the scope of this book. An excellent start is the book *Code Complete* by Steve McConnell. See the bibliography in the **programming** entry for information about this book.

See Also

Framework; Problem Analysis; Program Design; Programming; Programming Language

WYSIWYG

What you see is what you get (pronounced "wizzywig"). This term describes computer systems that display a page on-screen as it's created, as opposed to code-driven systems that only show what a page looks like when it's printed. The invention of WYSIWIG software was one of the driving forces behind the creation of desktop publishing.

X

X.500, *See Knowbots*

X-Height, *See Typesetting Terms*

Xanadu

Xanadu was a design for an interconnected network of computers serving HyperText documents. The creator of Xanadu, **Ted Nelson** (the creator of the word **HyperText**), spent many years promoting and developing the system. Although Xanadu never quite came to fruition, the **World Wide Web** effectively does much of what Xanadu promised.

Xanadu would have served up HyperText documents and enabled linking between documents by different authors, just like the Web. The single biggest difference between the design of Xanadu and the reality of the World Wide Web is that Xanadu included features to handle royalty payments, and enable one person to quote another's document without infringing on copyright. This was done through a system of payments where the author of the quoted passages would receive a percentage of the royalty paid to the author of the document containing the quote.

See Also

Hypertext; Internet

XCMDs and XFCNs

Although HyperCard provides a great deal of flexibility, there are some limitations in the scripting language because HyperTalk provides no calls to the **system toolbox**. HyperCard's functionality, however, *can* be extended using XCMDs (or eXternal commands, pronounced XCommands) and XFCNs (pronounced XFunctions). These are external programs called from within the HyperTalk language.

The routines are stored as **Resources**, and can be transported in a resource file or a HyperCard stack. They are then installed using a resource editor, such as **ResEdit**.

Xerox PARC

In 1970, Xerox established the Palo Alto Research Center near the campus of Stanford University. Xerox lured the best minds in computer science, physics, and electrical engineering to the lavish facility to create the next generation of information technology. The researchers were given big budgets and few restrictions. Unlike most corporate research centers, PARC was not expected to produce products, but rather ideas.

The first major project at PARC was a revolutionary computer called the Alto. Unlike most of the computers of its day, the Alto was designed to be *personal*—it was used interactively by a single person at a time. The Alto featured a high-resolution bitmapped display that could show text and graphics just as they would be printed. The Alto could print to a new high-resolution printer technology—the laser printer—and could be networked using EtherNet, another PARC innovation.

Alto could be programmed using yet another PARC invention, SmallTalk. This new **object-oriented** programming language enabled software to be written interactively and dynamically and provided a high degree of code reusability.

The Alto's interface included icons and direct selection using a new input device called the mouse. The mouse had been invented several years earlier by Douglas Englebart, a researcher at the Stanford Research Institute.

All in all, the Alto had all of the major features of a personal computer of the 1990s at a time when most computers were huge, unfriendly behemoths shared by many users. The personal computer industry was non-existent, and most electronics hobbyists could only dream of having their own computer.

The Alto was just a research project, however. Had it been commercialized, the price tag would have been close to $50,000. But the PARC researchers were proud of the Alto and used every opportunity to show it off to the rest of the computer community. One visitor who saw the Alto was **Jef Raskin**, a visiting scholar at the Stanford Artificial Intelligence Laboratory. Raskin would later begin the Macintosh project at Apple.

In 1979, during the **Lisa** project, Raskin and **Bill Atkinson** convinced **Steve Jobs** to make a visit to Xerox PARC to see the Alto. By that time, however, Xerox had tightened security at PARC. Xerox agreed to allow two Apple visits to PARC in exchange for the opportunity to invest in Apple. Xerox purchased 100,000 shares of Apple stock for $10 each.

Jobs was excited by what he saw at PARC and immediately began shifting the Lisa project toward the technologies he had seen. Eventually, the same ideas would make their way into the Macintosh as well.

Apple would later hire more than 15 PARC researchers to work on the Lisa and Macintosh projects. Among them were Larry Tesler, who demonstrated the Xerox technologies to the visitors from Apple, and Alan Kay, the visionary force behind the Alto.

Xerox did eventually make a half-hearted attempt to market the technologies embodied in the Alto. The Xerox Star was a bigger, better, faster Alto, but suffered from poor marketing and a very high price.

Xerox PARC continues to be a focal point for innovative research in information technology.

See Also
Atkinson, Bill; Jobs, Steve; Lisa; Programming; Raskin, Jef

XMODEM, *See File Transfer Protocols, Modem Transfer Protocols*

XMODEM-CRC, *See Modem Transfer Protocols*

XMODEM-IK, *See File Transfer Protocols*

XOFF, *See XOn/XOff*

XOn/XOff
XOn/Xoff is a term for "Software Flow Control." It functions by inserting characters into the stream of data being transmitted to indicate when to pause and resume. Flow control is important to any kind of data transmission, not just modem communications, although it's used there most often. Flow control is also a printer function, in that when your Mac is sending data to a printer, it may need to be told to pause and let the printer catch up.

When the modem or other receiving device wants the computer to stop transmitting (pause), it will send ASCII code 19 (Control-S, XOFF). When the modem is ready to resume transmission, it will transmit the XON character (ASCII 17, Control-Q) to inform the computer that it is ready to resume transmission. Users of "dumb terminal" programs can use the Control-S and Control-Q to interrupt the flow of data when scrolling through pages of text on a bulletin board or online service. (Some communication programs may use the ⌘ key rather than the Control key.)

Because modem speeds increased and modem users began transmitting binary files that actually contain the XON and XOFF characters as part of the files, this type of flow control has become less practical. High-speed modems have replaced it with hardware flow control, also called hardware handshaking, which sends a voltage to a signal pin instead of an ASCII character.

See Also

Flow Control

XPress Tags

Using XPress Tags, users can create plain text documents that, when imported into QuarkXPress, contain formatting and style sheets. This capability is particularly useful used in conjunction with text from a database, when it's desirable to automate formatting as much as possible.

XPress Tags files can be created from scratch or by exporting text from QuarkXPress using its XPress Tags filter. The tags are text codes that represent character attributes, paragraph formats, and style sheets; they toggle attributes on and off or specify information such as point size or font.

A code such as "@head1:" applies the "head1" style sheet to a paragraph, whereas character-based attributes are applied with codes such as "<B>" for bold and "<I>" for italic.

A third-party version of the XPress Tags filter called XTags offers all the functionality of XPress Tags, along with other features like the ability to create and fill text and graphics boxes, both anchored and freestanding; use a translation table so that other coding systems can be translated; and apply master pages.

See Also

QuarkXPress

xRes

Macromedia's xRes (version 2) for the Mac is a blend of the original xRes and one of the best painting programs originally written for Windows, Fauve Matisse. xRes is capable of assuming three personalities with ease, as an image editing program, a full-featured painting package, and an image compositor. It has the image editing power of Photoshop in numerous areas (and in some cases more), the task-oriented capacity to composit large images such as Live Picture, and can compete effectively in many ways with Fractal's Painter. A Swap Disk, an area on a targeted hard disk, is an essential part of the way that xRes works, so it is vital that you have enough space set aside for the Swap Disk (the documentation guides you through the process). There are multiple undo levels possible in xRes, but each undo level has an impact on the Swap Disk space that is necessary.

Image Editing xRes contains all of the standard image editing tools, and also a special menu dedicated to "objects" targeted as imported images. xRes Objects may be moved, rotated, resized, and repositioned according to the layer they rest on (front to back). xRes object tools are somewhat like vector drawing object tools, although xRes is strictly a bitmap program. An Object layer module in the Object/Channel/path dialog allows you to see the objects in an xRes document. Double-clicking their respective icons allows them to be renamed and numerically repositioned. Their icons contain a reduced visual image of the object's shape and color. A handy opacity slider at the top allows you to set the transparency of any targeted object in the stack. Moving members of the stack, either on-screen or in the dialog box, relocates them front to back. Any selected member may also be targeted for an applied effect. Any member can be cut, pasted, rotated, resized, skewed, and duplicated. The result of all of this can be a complex composite graphic accomplished in a short amount of time.

Internal Effects xRes has a list of its own effects, in addition to being open to all Photoshop plug-ins. Although many of its native filters are comparable to those offered as standard features in other image editing software, xRes adds the possibility of previewing either the whole selection or a movable screen's current resolution. Because xRes mode performs operations on the actual pixel data, it is not considered a proxy system.

xRes mode takes advantage of two of the addressed file formats, MMI and LRG. MMI files save all of the objects as separate reference data so that they can be manipulated after being reloaded. LRG files are xRes mode files that automatically put the program in xRes mode when loaded in. Maximum brush sizes in xRes mode are 100×the zoom level, so that at a zoom of 1/8, the maximum brush size will be 800×800 pixels! This accelerates image effects processing and painting. Files are automatically rendered as standard graphics when saved to non-LRG formats.

Features now available in xRes mode include the Magic Wand Tool, Bucket Tool, Drop Object and Drop Selection commands, and Indexed 256 Color mode.

Digital Painting xRes has painting tools far beyond those found in Photoshop, and rivaling many of the functions in Fractal's Painter software. It includes three sets of brushes (Media, Effects, and Styles) and an associated Shape Inspector dialog box that allows you to alter the brush parameters. The specific brushes include:

- Media Brushes

    Soft—Soft edged nib. Default variants include Semi-Opaque, Opaque, Precision, Fast Cover, Slick, Soft Square, and Large Semi-Opaque.

    Hard—Hard edged nib. Default variants include Anti-Aliased, Fast Cover, 1 Pixel, Semi-Opaque, Hard Square, Sharp Line, and Large Semi-Opaque.

    Airbrush—Digital Airbrush. Default variants include Basic, Light, Grainy, Textured, Flowing, Ink, Brush, and Dark Textured.

    Calligraphy—A thick and thin brush. Default variants include Shaded, Ribbon, Wet, Marker, Railroad, and Gift Wrap.

    Charcoal—Charcoal-like media. Default variants include Textured, Creamy, Grainy, Soft, Pastel, Chalk.

    Crayon—A brush that skips the surface a bit. Default variants include Wax, Wet, Chunky, and Monkey.

    Felt Tip—Like store-bought marker pens. Default variants include Basic Marker, Highlighter, and Thin.

    Japanese—Zen art brushes. Default variants include Bamboo, Sumi, and Rising Sun.

    Oil—Oil painting simulation. Default variants include Bristle, Rainbow, Strands, Fauve, Splatter, Textured Bristle, and Broad Splatter.

    Pencil—Drawing pencils. Default variants include Hard Edged, Number 2, Colored Pencil, and Chameleon.

    Quill—An old style Quill pen. Default variants include Feather, Dark, Splatter, and Watered Ink.

    Water—Artist's water media. Default variants include Watercolor, Thick, and Heavy.

- Effects Brushes

    Dodge—Lightens the image area. Default variants include Basic, Large, Strong, Weak, Large Weak, Precision, and Precision Weak.

    Burn—Darkens the image area. Default variants include Basic, Large, Strong, Weak, Large Weak, Precision, and Precision Weak.

    Sponge—Applied media with a sponge-like texture. Default variants include Saturate, Desaturate, Strong Saturate, Strong Desaturate, Weak Saturate, and Weak Desaturate.

    Tint—Adds a wash of the chosen color. Default variants include Basic, Strong, Weak, Very Strong, and Very Weak.

    Contrast—Applies a contrasted look. Default variants include Increase, Decrease, and Strong/Weak Increase/Decrease.

    Noise—Adds pixelated dirt. Default variants include Normal, Strong, Weak, Hue Protect, and Strong/Weak Hue Protect.

    Smear—Smears the underlying graphics (to smear floating objects, they have to be selected first). Default variants include Soft, Grainy, Heavy, and Sharp.

- Style Brushes

    These are brushes that emulate various artistic styles, and default variants include Pointillist, Cubist, Van Gogh, Rice, Spray, Nature, and Glass.

Any selected brush can also be cloned and saved under a new name and reconfigured to nib and other parameters (in the Shape Inspector dialog box), and then saved to take its place as a new option in the brush menu.

Texture Painting in xRes xRes features the most intuitive and easy-to-apply texture brush painting of any graphics software on the market. Any image area may be saved to the already full texture library.

xRes also lists some unique effects filters, among which are

- Luminosity can be targeted for sharpening, separated out from the other channels.

- Distort/Whirlpool, which adds more appeal to the standard twist option.

- Stylize/Glowing Edge, a new filter that adds stark glows to the selection.

xRes Image Compositing File Management

Macromedia's xRes uses its own method for working with large image files for compositing operations. xRes graphics can be worked on in Direct Mode (standard mode comparable to all other editing software) or in the proprietary xRes mode. xRes mode is much faster as far as all graphics operations are concerned, usually by 100 percent and more. xRes mode is made for working on image sizes 10MB and up, and those that may contain at least a dozen separate objects. Changes are applied only to the current image area visible on the screen, and not to the whole selection (unless you can see it), and only at the foreground/background colors). Very large textures can be created and saved. Airbrush and Charcoal brushes have options that apply the texture to the image area. Textures are tiled to repeat. Airbrushed applications are especially effective because you can manually control the fades.

File Load/Save Conventions Aside from the MMI and LRG formats already discussed, xRes allows you to save the following formats (xRes files are saved as MMI): Targa, TIFF, PICT, Photoshop 3, JPEG and JPEG Progressive, EPS, Scitex CT, BMP, GIF, and PMG (a favorite of Web page designers because of its small file size and lossless compression). It loads the same parameter files. File imports are treated as "Objects" and can be repositioned and manipulated as indicated previously.

LRG files are rendered on-screen if they need to be viewed in new resolutions. It can open (load) BMP, GIF, JPEG, LRG, MMI, PhotoCD, Photoshop 3, PICT, PNG, Scitex CT, Targa, and TIFF.

XTensions

QuarkXPress was the first page layout package to offer add-on software, XTensions, that could add features to the main program. Although its competitor PageMaker now supports plug-ins as well (previously called Additions), the library of XTensions is much bigger.

Ranging in price from a few dollars to hundreds, XTensions also range in functionality. PasteBoardXT has one simple function: It allows users to enlarge or shrink the size of the virtual pasteboard on which their pages sit in QuarkXPress. On the other end of the scale, AutoPage and Pianzhang automate many page-layout functions, such as picture placement and cross-aligning spreads.

XChange is a cooperative for XTension publishers: 1-800-788-7557 or **http://www.xpsi.com**.

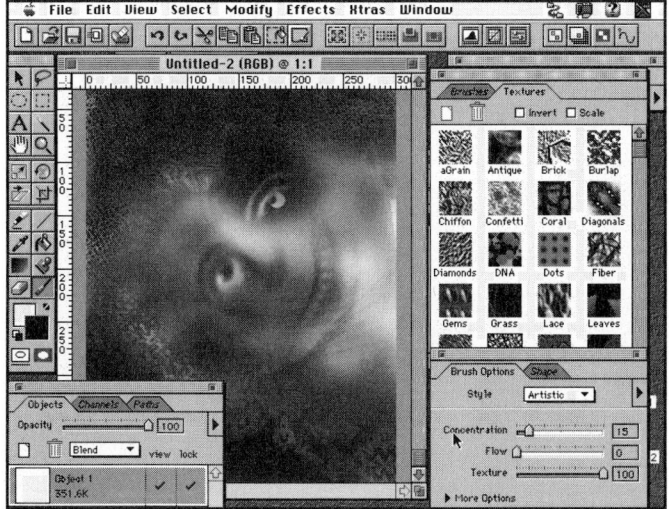

Y

Yahoo

Yahoo is a Web site that houses a topic-based database of the World Wide Web, enables users to perform keyword searches for Web sites.

David Filo and Jerry Yang, Ph.D. started Yahoo in April 1994 as a way to keep track of their personal interests on the Internet.

During 1994 they converted Yahoo! into a customized database designed to serve the needs of the thousands of users that began to use the service through the closely bound Internet community. They developed customized software to help them efficiently locate, identify, and edit material stored on the Internet.

The name Yahoo! is supposed to stand for "Yet Another Hierarchical Officious Oracle" but Filo and Yang insist they selected the name because they considered themselves yahoos. Yahoo! itself first resided on Yang's student workstation, "akebono" while the search engine was lodged on Filo's computer, "konishiki." (These machines were named after legendary Hawaiian sumo wrestlers.)

In early 1995, Marc Andreessen, co-founder of Netscape Communications in Mountain View, Ca. (and the developer of the two most popular Web-browsers), invited Filo and Yang to move their files over to larger computers housed at Netscape. As a result, Stanford's computer network returned to normal, and both parties benefited.

Home page: **http://www.yahoo.com/**.

See Also
Lycos; World Wide Web

Yellow Brick Road II

Both of Synergy's **Yellow Brick Road (YBR)** titles will be available together in the Emerald Collection Package by Christmas 1996. Together they offer an incredibly innovative alternative to most American games. Yellow Brick Road II, the double disc successor to the ground-breaking YBR I, is a much better game appealing to a much wider audience than the pre-teen targeted first title. Both titles bring you into a Japanese interpretation of the Oz novels by L. Frank Baum. YBR II brings you back to Oz after Glinda the Good has been incarcerated in a glass ball and the Gnomes seem to be intent on storming the Emerald City. Your androgynous character (you are never called "Dorothy" so you can be a boy or girl) travels the golden highway, encountering friends who join your troupe in the style of Adventure Games, and enemies, with whom you engage in battle a la Role Playing Games. The battles are non-violent and your foes simply run away when defeated, some of them may even join in on your journey when your fight is over. And, if you lose a battle, you aren't killed, you simply start the battle over.

Aside from the initiation to **adventure gaming**, puzzle solving, and strategy, Synergy's titles display some amazing 3D graphics. The scenery is rendered in 3D much the same way as the feature film *Toy Story*. Also, movement down the road is extremely fluid. When you switch directions, the scenery pans flawlessly instead of jumping quick to a new vantage point. Likewise, the creative, campy mix of humor and weird musical numbers (complete with singing radishes) make Yellow Brick Road II a sure-fire cult hit with more than just kids and their parents, almost like a Godzilla or Japanese animation midnight movie.

See Also
Are You Afraid of the Dark?; Family Entertainment; Masterpiece Mansion; Mortimer

YMODEM, *See File Transfer Protocols, Modem Transfer Protocols*

YMODEM-G, *See File Transfer Protocols, Modem Transfer Protocols*

You Don't Know Jack
Berkeley Systems' trivia game, You Don't Know Jack, is one of the best games available in any category. Jack takes its lead from board game Trivial Pursuit and schlock television game shows to bring a pop culture quiz show to the Mac. Amazingly, the game doesn't even use video or character animation to spice up the interface.

Instead, it focuses on great sound effects, hilarious background noise and comments, and a comedian/narrator. The game supports up to three players at a time, each assigned a key to use for buzzing in and answering trivia questions. You Don't Know Jack poses a wide variety of questions in all sorts of areas, wrapped in the guise of popular culture. For example, the answer to, "Which tasks would make the best use of the skills of Dr. Doolittle and *Love Boat's* Julie McCoy?" is not "running a Texas dude ranch," but "coordinating activities on Noah's Ark." Other questions get more in-depth with such scary topics as science, anatomy, and etymology. Berkeley Systems has also

released a new Jack X-tra Large pack with an added 400 new questions, which can also be purchased separately as the You Don't Know Jack Question Pack if you already own the first title.

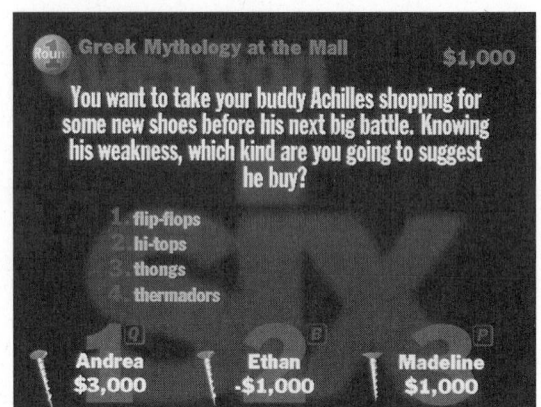

See Also
Card Games; Chess; Classic Collection; Traditional Games

YUV, *See Component Video*

Z

Zapf Dingbats, *See Ornament and Dingbat Fonts*

Zeddas: Servant of Sheol, *See Adventure Games*

Zimmerman, Scott "Zz," *See Dogcow*

Zip Drive

Iomega Corporation is a publicly held removable storage manufacturer based in Utah with offices in several European countries and distributors in Australia, Japan, and South-East Asia. It was formed in 1982 by 15 ex-IBM engineers who were the core of a project aimed to create a mass storage system that took advantage of the **Bernoulli Effect**. The project was canceled by IBM, a decision which led directly to the engineers leaving the computer giant to form Iomega.

In 1984, Iomega released a 5MB **Bernoulli** drive, which connected to the original Macintosh computer's serial port and has been a Macintosh storage vendor ever since.

However, even though Bernoulli drives were and are popular among PC-compatible users, Iomega never captured an equivalent share of the Macintosh market. Despite the apparent technical superiority of the Bernoulli cartridge, the emerging desktop publishing industry—and by extension the Macintosh industry—opted overwhelmingly for **SyQuest** drives and cartridges from SyQuest Corporation.

In March 1995, after ten years of playing second fiddle to SyQuest, Iomega released the Zip drive, a slow, 100MB removable drive that was cheap and very easy to use. It almost instantly transformed the company into the front runner in the Macintosh removable mass storage arena.

In December 1995, the first Jaz drives, another incompatible-with-the past drive system using 1GB cartridges, appeared in **RAID** arrays from **OEMs**. Stand-alone Jaz drives for both internal and external use appeared in the first months of 1996.

Iomega also produces a tape back-up system known as Ditto, which is only available for PC-compatible computers and used to manufacture **Floptical** drives.

These latter, despite being backwards compatible with the 1.44MB floppy disk, were an unsuccessful attempt to establish a new entry-level removable storage standard based around a hybrid of magnetic and optical technology.

See Also

Backing Up with Removable Cartridge Drives

ZMODEM, *See File Transfer Protocols, Modem Transfer Protocols*

ZoneRanger

A memory monitoring and debugging tool from Metrowerks, ZoneRanger enables you to view graphically the full contents of an application's memory **heap** (see following figure). Most low-level debuggers can display this information in a textual format, but the graphical view makes it much easier to see exactly what's going on in memory. Each block of memory in the heap is color-coded to identify whether it is a **handle**, a **pointer**, or free memory. It can further classify handles by whether they are locked, purgeable, or contain **resource** data.

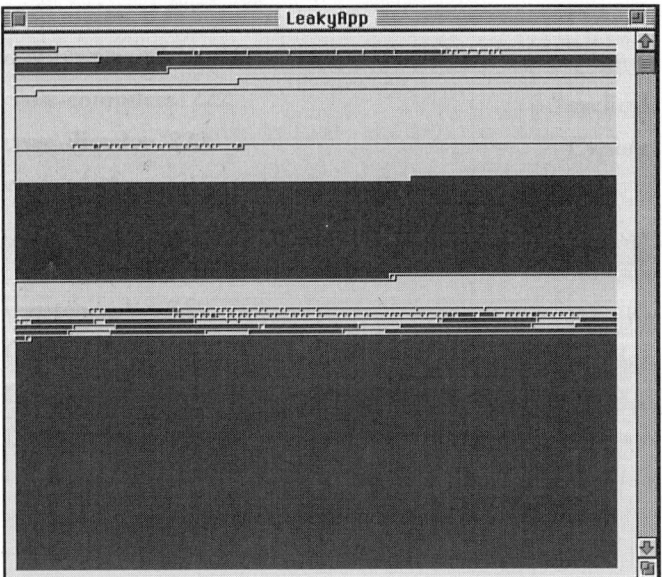

The graphical display of ZoneRanger also can show a summary of all blocks in the heap, including the total number and amount of memory occupied by each type of block. Both the graphical and summary displays are updated as your program runs.

The summary display can be augmented by ZoneRanger's **memory leak** detection feature. When this feature is activated, ZoneRanger keeps track of any blocks of memory that are allocated, but not released. These blocks might represent memory leaks in the application.

ZoneRanger also can display the actual contents of any block of memory (in **ASCII** and **hexadecimal** formats), as well as a number of other details about the block, such as its size, attributes, and, in the case of resources, resource type and ID.

ZoneRanger is distributed as a part of Metrowerks' **CodeWarrior**, but Metrowerks also has made it available for free.

See Also

ASCII; CodeWarrior; Handle; Heap; Hexadecimal; Memory Leak; Pointer; Resource

Zoom Box

Clicking a window's zoom box, (found in the **title bar** on the far right side, see the figure on the following page) resizes the box so that all the contents of the window can be seen at once (if possible, based on the size of your **monitor**). If the window is already zoomed out, the box will minimize the screen when clicked.

If you were to make a window very small, for example, by using the **size box** you could immediately zoom back to a size displaying as many items as possible by clicking the zoom box. Before **System 7**, clicking the zoom box merely opened the window as large as possible based on the size of your monitor. But in System 7 this feature is smarter and only opens enough to display as many items in the window as your monitor allows. If four items are in a window, it zooms open to display all four items.

To expand a window using the zoom box to see all items, follow these steps:

1. Open, or make active, the window you want to view.

2. Click the zoom box, located in the upper right corner of the title bar.

3. The window opens to display as much of the contents of the window as possible, based on the size of your monitor.

Zoom box

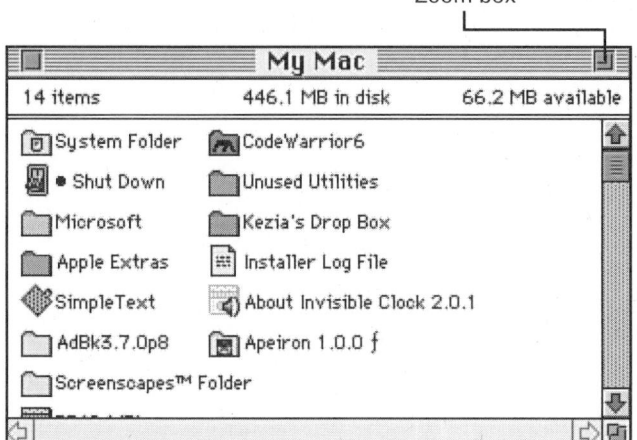

See Also

Active Window; Click; System 7; Window

Zoop

This **puzzle game** from Viacom New Media takes a different spin on **Tetris** and **BreakThru** to offer one of the best new brain teasers for the Macintosh. Players defend a center square from multicolored shapes that attack from all sides.

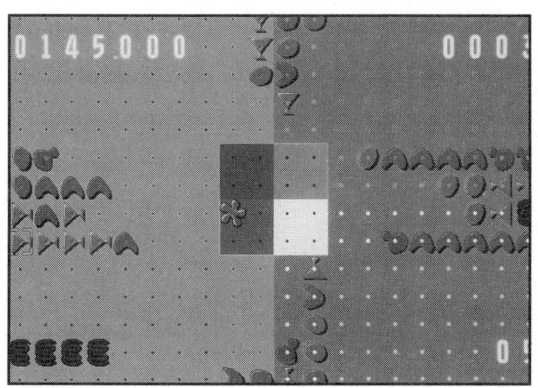

Your firing tool needs to be the same color as the shapes you shoot to make them disappear, much like in higher levels of Diamonds 3D from MacSoft. Zoop is just as addictive as the best of the puzzle games available and offers a refreshing twist to the colored blocks of the myriad Tetris clones. For beginners, levels are adjustable and enable you to choose which level of difficulty on which you want to start.

See Also

Tetris Gold; Troubled Souls

Zootopia

Interactive CD-ROM for kids aged eight and up, combining cartoons and **QuickTime** movies of some real animals, along with information about the animals' habits, diet, size, and so on. Throughout the zoo are information kiosks that give the details of a particular animal, sometimes including music videos, such as the poetry-quoting Raven who turns an old chestnut into the Nevermore Rap, and the trumpet-playing Trumpeter Swan with his back-up orchestra and night club act.

The music is catchy, and the song lyrics actually contain a few facts. Facts are somewhat sparse in this program, though. Travel between kiosks may require clicking several screens of scenery with no animals. The slow pace may frustrate some kids and adults. The animal I visited most was the tiger holding a sign that said, "Slow Down, Click Once." The opening sequence, which features a helicopter crashing, is unnecessarily scary and seems unrelated to the program. You can, and should, click past it.

See Also

CD-ROM; QuickTime

Zork, *See Return to Zork*

ZUC Virus

This virus infects only applications, and applications do not have to be run to become infected. On

March 2, 1990 or two weeks after an infected application is run, the cursor acts strangely when the mouse
button is held down.

See Also

ANTI Virus; CDEF Virus; CODE 1 Virus; CODE
252 Virus

Index

artifacts, 197
audio, IMA (Interactive Multimedia Association), 484
decompressing, 245, 437
files, 197
  decompression, 300
  extensions, 245
graphics, 437, 484-485
  Graphics Compressor, 434
JPEG (Joint Photographic Experts Group), 533-534
Now Compress utility, 732
recompression, 933
spatial compression, 199, 1023
temporal compression, 199, 1092
utilities, 198
video digitizing, 1147-1148
compressors, 199
Animation Compressor, 41
Apple's video compressor, 61
asymmetrical compressors, 79, 199
Cinepak, 153-154
CompactPro, 198
DiskDoubler, 198
limiter sound processors, 563
lossless compressors, 199
lossy compressors, 197
none compressors, 726
StuffIt Deluxe, 198
StuffIt Expander, 197
symmetrical compressors, 199, 1066
comps (comprehensive layouts), 276
Compton's Interactive (encyclopedia), 1054
CompuServe, 199-201, 749-750
dumb terminals, 200
Computer Aided Design, *see* **CAD**

Computer Aided Manufacturing (CAM), 437
computer icon (Finder), 382
Computer Ready Electronic Files (CREF), desktop publishing standards, 272
condensed text, 1124
Config PPP control panel, 601
configuring PowerBooks, 831-832
Conflict Catcher, 201-202, 1141
conflicts, numbering fonts, 391
Connectigon (IntelliDraw feature), 315
connections
I/O connections, 289-290
  AES/EBU, 27
Internet, 194
  error messages, 350-351
modems, 656-657
  analog telephone lines, 37-38
networks, foreign operating systems, 708-710
printers, non-Macintosh Laser printers, 860-861
connectivity, 450
Connectix, RAM Doubler, 1141
constants, 202
Constructor, 203-204
consumer models (Macintosh), 204-209
hardware, 451
context-switching multitasking, 689
continuous tone, 209
contrast
graphics, defined, 437
in printing, 874
Control key, 210
control panels, 210
AutoPower On/Off, 88
AutoRemounter, 88
Brightness, 120
Button Disabler, 130

F

G

J

K

L

Lewak, Jerry, Nisus Writer 1279

O

X

Y

WANT MORE INFORMATION?

Hayden
Books

CHECK OUT THESE RELATED TOPICS OR SEE YOUR LOCAL BOOKSTORE

Adobe Press

Published by Hayden Books, the Adobe Press Library reveals the art and technology of communication. Designed and written by designers for designers, best-selling titles include the Classroom in a Book (CIAB) series for both *Macintosh* and *Windows* (*Adobe Photoshop CIAB, Advanced Adobe Photoshop CIAB, Adobe PageMaker CIAB, Advanced Adobe PageMaker CIAB, Adobe Illustrator CIAB,* and *Adobe Premiere CIAB*), the Professional Studio Techniques series (*Production Essentials, Imaging Essentials, and Design Essentials, 2E*), and *Interactivity by Design*.

Design and Desktop Publishing

Hayden Books is expanding its reach to the design market by publishing its own mix of cutting-edge titles for designers, artists, and desktop publishers. With many more to come, these must-have books include *Designer's Guide to the Internet, Photoshop Type Magic, Adobe Illustrator Creative Techniques, Digital Type Design Guide,* and *The Complete Guide to Trapping, 2E*.

Internet and Communications

By answering the questions of what the Internet is, how you get connected, and how you can use it, *Internet Starter Kit for Macintosh* (now in 3rd ed.) and *Internet Starter Kit for Windows* (now in 2nd ed.) have proven to be Hayden's most successful titles ever, with over 500,000 Starter Kits in print. Hayden continues to be in the forefront by meeting your ever- popular demand for more Internet information with additional titles, including *Simply Amazing Internet for Macintosh, Create Your Own Home Page for Macintosh, Publishing on the World Wide Web, World Wide Web Design Guide, World Wide Web Starter Kit, net.speak: The Internet Dictionary,* and *Get on the Internet in 5 Minutes for Windows and Macintosh*.

Multimedia

As you embrace the new technologies shaping of multimedia, Hayden Books will be publishing titles that help you understand and create your own multimedia projects. Books written for a wide range of audience levels include *Multimedia Starter Kit for Macintosh, 3-D Starter Kit for Macintosh, QuickTime: The Official Guide for Macintosh Users, Virtual Playhouse, Macromedia Director Design Guide,* and *Macromedia Director Lingo Workshop*.

High-Tech

Hayden Books addresses your need for advanced technology tutorials and references by publishing the most comprehensive and dynamic titles possible, including *Programming Starter Kit for Macintosh, Tricks of the Mac Game Programming Gurus, Power Macintosh Programming Starter Kit, FoxPro Machete: Hacking FoxPro for Macintosh, 2E,* and *The Tao of AppleScript: BMUG's Guide to Macintosh Scripting, 2E*.

Orders/Customer Service   **800-763-7438**   Source Code   **HAYB**

Hayden Books   201 West 103rd Street ◆ Indianapolis, Indiana 46290 USA

Visit our Web page at http://www.mcp.com/hayden/

REGISTRATION CARD

Hayden
Books

Maclopedia

Name _____ Title _____

Company_____Type of business _____

Address _____

City/State/ZIP _____

Have you used these types of books before? ☐ yes ☐ no

If yes, which ones? _____

_____

How many computer books do you purchase each year? ☐ 1–5 ☐ 6 or more

How did you learn about this book?_____

☐ recommended by a friend ☐ received ad in mail

☐ recommended by store personnel ☐ read book review

☐ saw in catalog ☐ saw on bookshelf

Where did you purchase this book? _____

Which applications do you currently use? _____

Which computer magazines do you subscribe to? _____

What trade shows do you attend? _____

Please number the top three factors which most influenced your decision for this book purchase.

☐ cover ☐ price

☐ approach to content ☐ author's reputation

☐ logo ☐ publisher's reputation

☐ layout/design ☐ other _____

Would you like to be placed on our preferred mailing list? ☐ yes ☐ no e-mail address _____

☐ **I would like to see my name in print!** You may use my name and quote me in future Hayden products and promotions. My daytime phone number is: _____

Comments _____

_____

_____

Hayden Books Attn: Product Marketing ◆ 201 West 103rd Street ◆ Indianapolis, Indiana 46290 USA

Fax to **317-581-3576** Visit out Web Page **http://WWW.MCP.com/hayden/**

Fold Here

- -

BUSINESS REPLY MAIL
FIRST-CLASS MAIL PERMIT NO. 9918 INDIANAPOLIS IN

POSTAGE WILL BE PAID BY THE ADDRESSEE

HAYDEN BOOKS
Attn: Product Marketing
201 W 103RD ST
INDIANAPOLIS IN 46290-9058

![eye candy]

Eye Candy is a set of Photoshop-compatible filters from Alien Skin Software, makers of The Black Box. Eye Candy turns mundane images into dynamic explosions of light and color. A few of the filters in Eye Candy are shown above: Smoke, Polygon, and Water Drops. As a special promotion for owners of Maclopedia, you can get Eye Candy for just $99—less than half of the list price of $199. Just mention special offer **PEZ134** when you call.

ALIEN SKIN SOFTWARE *800 St. Mary's Street, Suite 100, Raleigh, NC 27605-1457 USA*
phone *(919) 832-4124* **fax** *(919) 832-4065* **email** *alien-skinfo@alienskin.com*
web site *http://www.alienskin.com/alienskin*

What's On the CD

On the CD, you will find the entire book, keyword searchable and alphabetically arranged, in Adobe Acrobat. You can use it to search for any term you need to find, as well as to link to the URLs listed, provided you have an Internet connection.

Just pop it in and click **Start Here** to begin.

The CD also contains many helpful utilities and demo versions of great software for you to try.

Commercial demos include:

- Black Box, Eye Candy (Alien Skin Software)
- AppMaker (Bowers)
- BBEdit 3.5 (Bare Bones)
- Illustrator, Photoshop, PageMaker (Adobe Systems)
- Intellibots
- QC 1.2 (Onyx)
- StuffIt products (Aladdin Systems)

Shareware programs include:

- AWOL Utilities (Ross Brown)
- Balloon Popper
- Chuck's Printer Driver 1.4.0
- Compact Pro (Bill Goodman)
- Data Converter 1.3
- Decor 3.0.1
- Dictionary Edit 1.3
- eDoc 1.1.1
- File Express 1.1
- Force Quit 1.0
- Gestalt Appl 2.6.6
- Godot's Faces 1.0.8
- Gopher Golf 3.0.6
- Hover Bar 1.2.8 (Guy Fullerton)
- I Ching Connexion 2.2
- Jade 1.0.2
- MacGzip 1.0
- Master FKEY 1.0
- Pandora's Box
- Phone Watcher 1.3.1
- PPPop 1.4
- Scrap It Pro 5.0.1

- Sleeper 2.0
- Style 1.4.1 (Marco Piovanelli)
- Yank 1.0 (Maui Software)
- Aaron 1.3.1
- Find Text 1.3.1
- Menu Bar Pattern 1.3
- Night Sky 2.2.1
- Pointing Device CDEV
- Suntar 2.0.5
- Super Save 1.1.3
- Symbionts 2.6.2
- Talk Show 1.0
- Tech Tool 1:0.9
- TGP II 1.4.1
- To Scrap 1.1
- Ultima III 1.3
- UnUU 2.1
- ValueFax 2.0.8
- Word Translator 1.3
- X-Timer 1.9.1
- ZipIt 1.3.5